The *American Heritage*®
College Writer's
Dictionary

Houghton Mifflin Harcourt
Boston | New York

EDITORIAL AND PRODUCTION STAFF

Senior Vice President, Publisher, General Interest Group
Bruce Nichols

Executive Editor
Steven R. Kleinedler

Senior Editor
Louise E. Robbins

Editor
Peter Chipman

Database Production Supervisor
Christopher J. Granniss

Proofreaders
Diane Fredrick
David R. Pritchard

Art and Production Supervisor
Margaret Anne Miles

Associate Production Editor
Sarah Iani

Text Design
Joyce C. Weston

Words are included in this dictionary on the basis of their usage. Words that are known to have current trademark registrations are shown with an initial capital and are also identified as trademarks. No investigation has been made of common-law trademark rights in any word, because such investigation is impracticable. The inclusion of any word in this dictionary is not, however, an expression of the publisher's opinion as to whether or not it is subject to proprietary rights. Indeed, no definition in this dictionary is to be regarded as affecting the validity of any trademark.

American Heritage and the eagle logo are registered trademarks of American Heritage Inc. Their use is pursuant to a license agreement with American Heritage Inc.

"Capitalization, Punctuation, and Style Guide" adapted from Grammar and Usage Guide in *Houghton Mifflin English, Grade 8*, by Shirley Haley-James et al. Copyright © 1988 by Houghton Mifflin Company. Reprinted by permission of Houghton Mifflin Harcourt Publishing Company.

Visit our websites: hmhbooks.com *and* ahdictionary.com

Library of Congress Cataloging-in-Publication Data
The American Heritage® College Writer's Dictionary.
    pages cm
ISBN 978-0-547-85785-5
1. English language — Dictionaries. 2. Americanisms — Dictionaries.
I. Houghton Mifflin Harcourt Publishing Company. II. Title: College Writer's Dictionary.
PE1628.A62278 2013
    423 — dc23

                    2012048168

Manufactured in the United States of America

1 2 3 4 5 6 7 8 9 10- DOC -18 17 16 15 14 13

Table of Contents

Guide to Using the Dictionary

This guide is designed to help you find and understand the information contained in this dictionary.

GUIDEWORDS

This dictionary has one main alphabetical list of entries, including single words, phrases, hyphenated compounds, abbreviations, proper names, prefixes, and suffixes. (A separate alphabetical gazetteer at the end of the dictionary lists geographical names, including continents, oceans and major seas, and countries, US states, and Canadian provinces along with their capital cities.) To help you find the word you want to look up, we have put a pair of boldface guidewords at the top of each page in this book:

chronic • chute

The guideword on the left represents the first boldface entry on that page. The guideword on the right represents the last boldface entry on that page. Thus, the entry words **chronic** and **chute** and all entries that fall between them are listed on the page that has these guidewords.

THE ENTRY WORD

The word or phrase you look up in the dictionary is called an *entry word* or an *entry*, or sometimes a *main entry*. The entry words are printed in boldface a little to the left of the rest of the column. They are listed in alphabetical order. Words that begin with the same letter are put into alphabetical order using their second letter, or, if the first two letters are the same, the third letter, and so on, as shown in the list below:

> roan
> roar
> roaring
> roast
> roaster
> rob

Some entries consist of more than one word. These may be written as phrases, such as *water buffalo* and *water mill*, or as hyphenated compounds, such as *heavy-duty* and *low-pressure*. Such phrases and compounds are listed in alphabetical order as if they were written as one word.

Superscript Numbers

Some words have identical spellings but different meanings and histories. These words, called homographs, are entered separately. Each has a superscript, or raised, number printed after the entry word:

sole¹ (sōl) *n.* **1.** The bottom surface of the foot. **2.** The bottom surface of a shoe or boot, often excluding the heel.
sole² (sōl) *adj.* **1.** Being the only one; single; only: *Her sole purpose in coming is to see you.* **2.** Belonging or relating exclusively to one person or group: *She took sole command of the ship.*
sole³ (sōl) *n., pl.* **sole** or **soles** Any of various flatfishes used as food.

VARIANTS

Some words have two or more different spellings. The variant spelling or spellings are shown in boldface after the entry word. The word *or* indicates that both spellings are used with equal frequency:

adviser or **advisor** (ăd-vī′zər) *n.*

The word *also* joining an entry word and variant form indicates that the variant form is used less frequently than the main entry word:

amoeba also **ameba** (ə-mē′bə) *n.*

Variants that fall more than two entries away from their main entry word in alphabetical order are entered at their own alphabetical places:

ameba (ə-mē′bə) *n.* Variant of **amoeba.** —a·me′bic (ə-mē′bĭk) *adj.*

A number of variants consist of spellings preferred in England and other parts of the United Kingdom. These variants, such as *defence* and *colour,* have the label *Chiefly British.* They are entered at their own alphabetical places but are not given as variants at the entries to which they refer:

defence (dĭ-fĕns′) *n. Chiefly British* Variant of **defense.**

PARTS OF SPEECH

The following italicized labels indicate the various parts of speech:

adj.	adjective
adv.	adverb
conj.	conjunction
def.art.	definite article
indef.art.	indefinite article

interj.	interjection
n.	noun
prep.	preposition
pron.	pronoun
v.	verb

Plurals are indicated by the label *pl.* The label *pl.n.* appears at entries for words, such as *clothes* and *cattle*, that are only used in the plural.

These italicized labels are used for the traditional classification of verbs:

tr.	transitive
intr.	intransitive
aux.	auxiliary

A transitive verb is a verb that takes a direct object that completes its meaning. *Enforce* and *foster* are examples of transitive verbs. An intransitive verb does not take an object; verbs such as *rejoice* and *tremble* are intransitive. Many verbs, of course, can be transitive or intransitive depending on how they are used. An auxiliary verb, such as *have* or *may*, is used with another verb to indicate tense, mood, or voice.

Certain entries do not carry part-of-speech labels. They include contractions (*I'll*), trademarks (*Band-Aid*), abbreviations (*Blvd.*), prefixes (*anti-*), and suffixes (*-ment*).

Parts of Speech in Combined Entries

Many words can be used as more than one part of speech. For example, *paint* can be both a verb (as in *to paint a wall*) and a noun (as in *a gallon of paint*). In such cases, the different parts of speech are defined in a single entry called a *combined entry*. In an entry of this kind, each part of speech receives its own part-of-speech label. Each part of speech that follows the first part of speech is preceded by the ❖ symbol.

If a piece of information, such as a pronunciation or a status label, appears before the first part of speech in an entry, that piece of information applies to all parts of speech in that entry. Labels and pronunciations appearing after a part of speech apply to that part of speech only:

> **rebel** (rĭ-bĕl′) *intr.v.* **rebelled, rebelling, rebels**
> **1.** To refuse loyalty to and oppose by force an established government or a ruling authority. **2.** To resist or defy an authority or a generally accepted convention: *rebelled against wearing a tie in summer.* ❖ *n.* (rĕb′əl) **1.** A person who rebels or is in rebellion.

INFLECTED FORMS

An inflected form of a word differs from the main entry form by the addition of a suffix or by a change in the normal spelling of the main entry. Thus, the verb *walk* forms its past tense

walked by the addition of the suffix *-ed*, and *swim* forms its past tense *swam* by changing its spelling.

In this dictionary, inflected forms are given in full. They appear in boldface and have pronunciations when necessary. An inflected form immediately follows the part-of-speech label or the number of the definition to which it applies.

Principal parts of verbs. The principal parts of verbs are entered in this order: *past tense, past participle, present participle,* and *third person singular present tense:*

> **fly¹** (flī) *v.* **flew** (flo͞o), **flown** (flōn), **flying, flies** (flīz)

When the past tense and the past participle are identical, one form represents both. For example, *walked* is the past tense and past participle of the verb *walk:*

> **walk** (wôk) *v.* **walked, walking, walks**

Comparison of adjectives and adverbs. Adjectives and adverbs that form the comparative and superlative degrees by adding *-er* and *-est* show these forms in full immediately after the part-of-speech label:

> **high** (hī) *adj.* **higher, highest 1a.** Being a relatively great distance above a certain level, as above sea level or the surface of the earth: *There's snow in the high mountains.* **b.** Extending a specified distance upward: *The fence is four feet high.* . . . ❖ *adv.* **higher, highest** At, in, or to a high position, level, or degree: *Hawks fly high in the sky. A general ranks high above a private.*

Irregular comparative and superlative forms are also given in full:

> **good** (go͝od) *adj.* **better** (bĕt′ər), **best** (bĕst)

Plural forms of nouns. Regular plurals formed by adding the suffixes *-s* or *-es* to a noun are not normally shown in this dictionary, but irregular plurals are always shown following the label *pl.:*

> **mouse** (mous) *n., pl.* **mice** (mīs)

When a noun has a regular and an irregular plural form, both forms appear, with the most common form shown first:

> **cerebrum** (sĕr′ə-brəm or sə-rē′brəm) *n., pl.* **cerebrums** or **cerebra** (sĕr′ə-brə or sə-rē′brə)

Regular plurals are also shown when spelling might be a problem:

> **potato** (pə-tā′tō) *n., pl.* **potatoes**

Sometimes inflected forms apply only to certain senses of a word. In such cases, the inflected form appears in boldface after the sense number or letter to which it applies:

fly[1] (flī) *v.* **flew** (flōō), **flown** (flōn), **flying, flies** (flīz) —*intr.* . . . . **7.** *past tense and past participle* **flied.** In baseball, to hit a fly ball.

From this example you can see that the verb *fly* usually has the past tense *flew* and the past participle *flown*, but when used in baseball, it has *flied* as its past tense and past participle.

Separate Entries for Inflected Forms

Irregular inflected forms involving a change in spelling of the main form of a word are entered separately when they fall more than two entries away from the main entry form. Thus, *flew*, the past tense of *fly*, and *men*, the plural of *man*, both have their own entries:

flew (flōō) *v.* Past tense of **fly**[1].
men (mĕn) *n.* Plural of **man**.

The dictionary does not normally give separate entries for inflected forms of words ending in *–y*, such as *berry, happy,* and *carry,* because forms such as *berries, happiest,* and *carried* entail a regular, easily recognized change in spelling. However, this dictionary does enter inflected forms of words having only one syllable ending in *–y*:

driest (drī′ĭst) *adj.* A superlative of **dry**.
spied (spīd) *v.* Past tense and past participle of **spy**.

LABELS

This dictionary uses labels to identify words and meanings whose use is limited in some way—to a particular style of expression, for example, or to a geographical region. When a label applies to all parts of an entry, it appears before the first part of speech:

snitch (snĭch) *Slang v.* **snitched, snitching, snitches** ❖ —*intr.* To tell on someone; turn informer: *snitched on his brother.* ❖ —*tr.* To steal (something of little value): *snitched candy from the store.* ❖ *n.* **1.** A thief. **2.** An informer.

Thus the positioning of the label *Slang* in the preceding example means that both the noun and verb senses of the word are slang.

A label may apply only to a single part of speech, in which case it follows the part-of-speech label. Sometimes a label applies only to a single definition or subdefinition, in which case it follows the sense number or letter to which it applies:

hot (hŏt) *adj.* **hotter, hottest** . . . **7.** *Informal* Most recent; new or fresh: *hot gossip.*

In this entry, the label *Informal* applies only to sense 7.

Status Labels

Status labels indicate that an entry word or a definition is limited to a particular level or style of usage. All words and definitions not restricted by such a label should be regarded as appropriate for use in all contexts.

Nonstandard. This, the most restrictive label in the dictionary, applies to forms and usages that educated speakers and writers consider unacceptable:

irregardless (ĭr′ĭ-gärd′lĭs) *adv. Nonstandard* Regardless.

Slang. This label indicates a style of language that uses extravagant, often humorous expressions as a means of making an effect. Some forms of slang occur in most educated speech but not in formal discourse. An example of a word labeled *Slang* follows:

rinky-dink (rĭng′kē-dĭngk′) *adj. Slang* **1.** Old-fashioned; worn-out. **2.** Unimportant. **3.** Of cheap or poor quality.

Informal. Words that people use commonly in conversation and in informal writing (such as an email to a friend) but not in formal writing (such as a job application or a research paper) are identified by the label *Informal*:

fishy (fĭsh′ē) *adj.* **fishier, fishiest 1.** Tasting, resembling, or smelling of fish. **2.** Cold or expressionless: *a fishy stare.* 3. *Informal* Inspiring doubt or suspicion: *something fishy about that excuse.* — **fish′i•ness** *n.*

Offensive. This label is reserved for words and expressions that are viewed as hurtful to the people they refer to.

Temporal Label

The temporal label *Archaic* signals words or senses that were once common but are now rare:

fain (fān) *Archaic adv.* Willingly or gladly. ❖ *adj.* Willing or glad.

English-Language Labels

These labels identify entries or senses whose use is restricted to specific areas of the English-speaking world:

bairn (bârn) *n. Scots* A child.
lorry (lôr′ē) *n., pl.* **lorries** *Chiefly British* A motor truck.
bonnet (bŏn′ĭt) *n.* . . . **3.** *Chiefly British* The hood of an automobile.

CROSS-REFERENCES

A cross-reference is a word referring you to another word. It signals that more information can be found at another entry. A cross-reference is helpful in avoiding the repetition of information at two entries, and it serves to indicate where further discussion of a word occurs.

The word referred to in a cross-reference appears in boldface and is preceded by a short phrase:

bade (băd or bād) *v.* A past tense of **bid**.

This cross-reference tells you that *bade* is a past tense of the word *bid*. This indicates that more information can be found at *bid*.

If a cross-reference refers to only one sense of a word that has more than one sense, then the cross-reference will show that sense number:

tzar (zär or tsär) *n.* Variant of **czar** (sense 1).

This cross-reference tells you that *tzar* is a variant spelling of *czar,* but that it refers only to the use that is defined at the first sense.

Some cross-references refer to tables. The word or words in boldface tell you at which entry word the table can be found:

kilogram (kĭl′ə-grăm′) *n.* **1.** *abbr.* **kg** The basic unit of mass or weight in the metric system, equal to 1,000 grams (about 2.2 pounds). See table at **measurement.**

Other cross-references refer you to a note that appears at another entry:

huge (hyo͞oj) *adj.* **huger, hugest** Of great size, extent, or quantity: *a huge tree; a huge difference.* See Synonyms at **large.**

proscribe (prō-skrīb′) *tr.v.* **proscribed, proscribing, proscribes 1.** To forbid; prohibit. **2.** To banish; outlaw: *The queen proscribed the rebels.* —SEE NOTE AT **prescribe.**

These cross-references tell you that there is more information about the word in a note at another entry.

ORDER OF SENSES

Entries having more than one sense are arranged with the central meanings first. The central meaning of a word will most often be the meaning you are seeking. In addition, senses and subsenses that are related in meaning are grouped together. For example, in the entry for *nice* shown below, the commonly sought meaning "Good; pleasant; agreeable" appears first, and the less common sense "Able to notice small differences" comes as sense 6b:

nice (nīs) *adj.* **nicer, nicest 1.** Good; pleasant; agreeable: *The seaside hotel was a nice place to stay.* **2.** Having a pleasant appearance; attractive: *a nice dress.* **3.** Courteous and polite; considerate: *It's nice of you to help.* **4.** Morally upright; respectable. **5.** Done with skill and delicacy: *a nice bit of work.* **6a.** Requiring the ability to notice small differences: *a nice distinction.* **b.** Able to notice small differences: *a nice ear for music.* **7.** Used as an intensive with *and: The weather at the beach was nice and warm.*

Division of senses. Letters that appear in boldface before senses indicate that two or more subsenses are closely related in meaning:

principal (prĭn′sə-pəl) *adj.* First or foremost in rank or importance; chief: *the principal character in the story.* ❖ *n.* **1.** A person who holds a leading position, especially the head of a school. **2.** A main participant, as in a business deal. **3a.** A sum of money originally invested, as opposed to the interest paid or accruing on it. **b.** A sum of money owed as a debt, on which interest is calculated.

When an entry has more than one part of speech, the definitions are numbered in separate sequence beginning with each new part of speech:

dream (drēm) *n.* **1.** A series of mental images, ideas, and emotions occurring during sleep. **2.** A daydream. **3.** A state of abstraction; a trance: *wandering about in a dream.* **4.** A hope or aspiration: *dreams of world peace.* **5.** Something especially gratifying, excellent, or useful: *The new car runs like a dream.* ❖ *v.* **dreamed** or **dreamt** (drĕmt), **dreaming, dreams** —*intr.* **1.** To have a dream while sleeping. **2.** To daydream: *dreaming of far-off places.* **3.** To consider as feasible or practical: *I wouldn't even dream of going.* —*tr.* **1.** To have a dream about (something) during sleep: *Did it storm last night, or did I dream it?* **2.** To conceive of; imagine: *We never dreamed it might snow so hard.* ◆ **dream up** To invent; concoct: *dreamed up a plan to get rich quick.*

Usage phrases. Some noun entries have added information that tells you whether the word takes a singular or plural verb or whether it can take either a singular or a plural verb. This information appears as a usage phrase in italics before the sense or part of speech that it applies to:

genetics (jə-nĕt′ĭks) *n.* **1.** *(used with a singular verb)* The branch of biology that deals with genes, especially their inheritance and expression and their distribution among different individuals and organisms. **2.** *(used with a plural verb)* The genetic makeup of an individual or group.

In the entry *genetics* above, the usage phrase tells you that sense 1 takes a singular verb only and sense 2 takes a plural verb only.

FORMS THAT APPLY TO SPECIFIC SENSES

Information such as an inflected form that applies only to a particular sense or subsense is shown after the number or letter of that sense or subsense:

> **brother** (brŭ*th***′**ər) *n.* **1a.** A boy or man having the same mother and father as someone else. **b.** A boy or man having one parent in common with someone else; a half brother. **c.** A stepbrother. **2a.** A boy or man who shares common ancestors, a common allegiance to a country, or a common purpose with another or others. **b.** A fellow male member of a group, such as a profession, fraternity, or labor union. **3.** *plural* **brothers** or **brethren** (brĕ*th***′**rən) **a.** A member of a men's Christian religious order who is not a priest. **b.** A fellow male member of a Christian church.

In this entry, the plural form *brethren* applies only to the third sense of brother. For all of the other senses, the only common plural is *brothers*.

Some nouns have senses in which they are usually used in the plural. In these cases, the boldface plural form of the noun appears just before the definition to show you that it is used in the plural:

> **jack** (jăk) *n.* . . . **5a. jacks** (*used with a singular or plural verb*) A game in which each player in turn bounces and catches a small ball while picking up small six-pointed metal pieces with the same hand.

In this entry, the sense of jack that refers to the game occurs only in the plural form *jacks*.

The same style is used for any change in the form of a word as it shifts from one sense to another:

> **Afghan** (ăf**′**găn**′**) *adj.* Relating to Afghanistan or the Afghans. ❖ *n.* **1.** A native or inhabitant of Afghanistan. **2. afghan** A colorful wool blanket or shawl knitted or crocheted in squares, circles, or other designs.

Here the boldface lowercase form of the word appears just before the definition it applies to, telling you that in this sense the word only occurs in the lowercase form *afghan.*

ILLUSTRATIVE EXAMPLES OF DEFINITIONS

In addition to giving clear definitions of words, this dictionary also gives you thousands of examples showing how a word is used in context. You will find that these examples are especially useful for illustrating figurative senses of a word, transitive and intransitive verbs, and multiple senses of very common words:

> **around** (ə-round**′**) *adv.* **1.** On all sides or in all directions: *We drove around looking for a park-*

ing place. **2.** In a circle or circular motion: *The skater spun around twice.* **3.** In or toward the opposite direction: *The horse turned around and ran toward the barn.* **4.** From one place to another; here and there: *wander around.* **5.** In or near one's current location: *He waited around all day.* **6.** To a specific place or area: *when you come around again.* **7.** Approximately; about: *Around 20 rafts floated down the Rio Grande.*

IDIOMS

An *idiom* is a group of words whose meaning as a group cannot be understood from the meanings of the individual words in the group. In this dictionary, idioms are defined at the entry for the first important word in the phrase. For example, *walk on air* is defined at *walk.*

In this dictionary, idioms appear at the very end of the definitions of an entry in alphabetical order, following the ◆ symbol. Each idiom is shown in boldface. Verbs form many idioms with adverbs or prepositions. Please refer to the entry at *take* for an example of an entry with many idioms.

This dictionary lists only nonliteral or unusual senses of idioms. Thus in the example below, *back out*, meaning "to retire or withdraw from something," is defined in that sense, but not in the sense "to leave a parking space in reverse." You should be able to figure out this latter meaning of the phrase by the meanings of the two words themselves, and therefore we do not define it:

> **back** (băk) . . . ◆ . . . **back out** To withdraw from something one has agreed to: *They accepted the invitation but backed out at the last minute.*

RUN-ON FORMS

This dictionary includes many additional words formed from an entry word by the addition of a suffix. These words are located at the end of an entry. They are obviously related to the main entry word and have the same essential meaning, but they have different endings and different parts of speech. Run-on entries appear in boldface followed by a part-of-speech label. Stress is indicated on run-on words that have more than one syllable, and pronunciations are given where needed:

> **regretful** (rĭ-grĕt**′**fəl) *adj.* Full of regret; sorrowful or sorry. —**re•gret′ful•ly** *adv.* —**re•gret′ful•ness** *n.*

When two or more run-on forms have the same part of speech, they are separated by a comma and have a single part-of-speech label:

rapid (răp′ĭd) *adj.* **rapider, rapidest** Fast; swift: *rapid progress; walking with rapid strides.* See Synonyms at **fast**[1]. ❖ *n.* often **rapids** An extremely fast-moving part of a river, caused by a steep descent in the riverbed: *went over the rapids in a kayak.* —**ra•pid′i•ty** (rə-pĭd′ĭ-tē), **rap′id•ness** *n.* —**rap′id•ly** *adv.*

SYNONYM LISTS

To help you build your vocabulary, this dictionary includes lists of synonyms at many entries, introduced by the heading *Synonyms.* Very few words have exactly the same meaning, so if you're unsure of the meaning of another word in the list, you can refer to that word's entry in the dictionary to see how it is used. For example, a list of synonyms is found at the end of the entry for the word *break*:

> ✦SYNONYMS **break, crack, fracture, shatter, splinter** *v.*

NOTES

This dictionary includes a variety of notes providing more information about individual words. These notes describe how words are and should be used, where words come from, and how their meanings can be deciphered from an understanding of their parts. These notes directly follow the entry they relate to.

Usage Notes. Some words are easily confused with others or present difficulties in how they should be used. These entries have Usage Notes that offer explanations and advice on how to avoid usage problems. A typical Usage Note can be found at the entry for *affect*[1].

When a word is discussed in a Usage Note at an entry elsewhere in the book, it has a cross-reference to that entry. Thus, at *effect* you are directed to the note at *affect*[1], where *effect* is also discussed.

Word History Notes. This dictionary provides informative notes that describe the history of certain words before Modern English. Some notes explain how a word has moved from one language to another before coming into English. Others discuss words that are spelled differently but have a common origin. Still others explain the processes by which words change or develop new meanings. Most entries that are homophones (such as *seal*[1] and *seal*[2]) have Word History Notes that explain how the two words, although spelled the same, developed from different sources. Examples of Word History Notes can be found at the entries for *seal*[2] and *pastry*.

Word Building Notes. Word Building Notes help you understand how word parts are joined together to make longer, more complex words. There are two kinds of Word Building Notes— notes that involve prefixes and suffixes and notes that involve word roots. Notes at prefixes and suffixes explain how these affixes are attached to words to make new words. For an example of this kind of Word Building Note, see the entry at *trans–*. Notes involving word roots describe how Greek and Latin roots form the heart of many words that have different but related meanings. For an example of this kind of Word Building Note, see the entry at *compose*.

Pronunciation Guide and Key

Pronunciations appear in parentheses after boldface entry words. If an entry word has a variant and they have the same pronunciation, the pronunciation follows the variant. If the variant does not have the same pronunciation, pronunciations follow the forms to which they apply. If a word has more than one pronunciation, the first pronunciation is usually more common than the other, but often they are equally common. Pronunciations are shown within an entry where necessary. An expanded version of the pronunciation key below appears on the last page of the dictionary.

Stress. Stress is the relative degree of emphasis with which a word's syllables are spoken. An unmarked syllable has the weakest stress in the word. The strongest, or primary, stress is indicated with a bold mark (**′**). A lighter mark (′) indicates a secondary level of stress:

dictionary (dĭk′shə-nĕr′ē)

Words of one syllable have no stress mark, because there is no other stress level to which the syllable is compared.

Pronunciation Symbols. The pronunciation symbols used in this dictionary are shown below. To the right of the symbols are words that show how the symbols are pronounced. The letters whose sound corresponds to the symbols are shown in boldface. The symbol (ə) is called *schwa*. It represents a vowel with the weakest level of stress in a word. The schwa sound varies slightly according to the vowel it represents or the sounds around it:

abundant (ə-bŭn′dənt)
moment (mō′mənt)
grateful (grāt′fəl)
civil (sĭv′əl)
propose (prə-pōz′)

In English, the consonants *l* and *n* can be complete syllables. Examples of words with syllabic *l* and *n* are **needle** (nēd′l) and **sudden** (sŭd′n).

Foreign Symbols. Some foreign words use sounds that are not found in English. The (œ) sound is made by rounding the lips as though you were going to make the (ō) sound, but instead you make an (ā) sound. The (ü) sound is made by rounding the lips as though you were going to make the (ōō) sound, but instead you make an (ē) sound. The (кн) sound is like a (k), but the air is forced through continuously, not stopped as with a (k). The N symbol shows that the vowel before it is nasalized—that is, air escapes through the nose (and the mouth) when you say it.

PRONUNCIATION KEY

ă	pat	îr	dear, deer, pier	ŏor	lure	w	with
ā	pay	j	judge	ōō	boot	y	yes
âr	care	k	kick, cat, school	ou	out	yōō	cure, pure
ä	father	kw	quick	p	pop	yōō	music, few
b	bib	l	lid, needle	r	roar	z	zebra, xylem
ch	church	m	mum	s	sauce	zh	vision, pleasure,
d	deed, mailed	n	no, sudden	sh	ship, dish		garage
ĕ	pet	ng	thing	t	tight, stopped	ə	ago, silent,
ē	bee	ŏ	dot	th	thin		pencil, lemon,
f	fife, phase, rough	ō	toe	th	this		circus
g	gag	ô	caught, paw	ŭ	cut	ər	butter
h	hat	ôr	core	ûr	urge, term, firm,		
ĭ	pit	oi	noise		word, heard		
ī	pie, by	ōō	took	v	valve		

Aa

a¹ or **A** (ā) *n., pl.* **a's** or **A's** or **As 1.** The first letter of the English alphabet: *There are three a's in "alfalfa."* **2. A** The best or highest grade: *get an A on a test; grade A eggs.* **3. A** In music, the sixth tone in the scale of C major. **4. A** One of the four blood types in the ABO system. ◆ **from A to Z** Completely; comprehensively: *This book covers everything about gardening from A to Z.*

a² (ə; ā *when stressed*) *indef.art.* **1.** One: *I didn't say a single word.* **2.** The same: *I can juggle three balls at a time.* **3.** Any: *A cat will always eat fish.* **4.** An example of a kind of: *Water is a liquid.*

a³ (ə) *prep.* In each; for each; per: *once a month; ten dollars a trip.*

A An abbreviation of: **1.** ampere. **2.** area.

a–¹ or **an–** A prefix that means without or not: *amoral; atypical.*

<hr>

WORD BUILDING The basic meaning of the prefix a– is "without." For example, *achromatic* means "without color." Before vowels and sometimes *h, a–* becomes *an–: anaerobic.* Many of the words beginning with this prefix are used in science or medicine, such as *aphasia, anoxia,* and *aseptic.*

<hr>

a–² A prefix that means: **1.** On or in: *abed; aboard.* **2.** In the direction of: *astern.* **3.** In a particular condition: *afire.*

aardvark (ärd′värk′) *n.* A burrowing mammal of sub-Saharan Africa having long claws and a long, sticky tongue used for feeding on ants and termites.

AAVE An abbreviation of African American Vernacular English.

AB (ā′bē′) *n.* One of the four blood types in the ABO system.

aback (ə-băk′) *adv.* By surprise: *I was taken aback by his angry words.*

abacus (ăb′ə-kəs) *n., pl.* **abacuses** or **abaci** (ăb′ə-sī′) A computing device consisting of a frame holding parallel rods with sliding beads.

abaft (ə-băft′) *prep.* Toward the stern from: *The cargo hatch is abaft the mainmast.* ❖ *adv.* Toward a ship's stern: *It was fast sailing with the wind abaft.*

abalone (ăb′ə-lō′nē) *n.* Any of various edible mollusks that have a large shallow shell lined with mother-of-pearl.

abandon (ə-băn′dən) *tr.v.* **abandoned, abandoning, abandons 1.** To withdraw one's support or help from: *abandon a friend in trouble.* **2.** To leave and not intend to return; desert: *abandon a sinking ship.* **3.** To give up completely; stop trying to accomplish: *They abandoned the attempt to climb the peak.* See Synonyms at **yield. 4.** To yield (oneself) to an impulse or emotion: *Don't abandon yourself to despair.* ❖ *n.* Great enthusiasm or lack of restraint: *skied down the hill with abandon.* —**a·ban′don·ment** *n.*

abandoned (ə-băn′dənd) *adj.* **1.** Deserted or given up; forsaken: *During the snowstorm the highway was littered with abandoned cars.* **2.** Recklessly unrestrained: *an abandoned life.*

abase (ə-bās′) *tr.v.* **abased, abasing, abases** To lower in rank, dignity, or reputation; humble or degrade: *abased himself by lying.* —**a·base′ment** *n.*

abash (ə-băsh′) *tr.v.* **abashed, abashing, abashes** To make ashamed or uneasy; embarrass: *I was abashed by my careless mistake.*

abate (ə-bāt′) *v.* **abated, abating, abates** —*tr.* To reduce in amount, degree, or intensity: *The horse galloped around the curve without abating its speed.* —*intr.* To become less in degree or intensity: *The storm abated.* —**a·bate′ment** *n.*

abattoir (ăb′ə-twär′) *n.* A slaughterhouse.

abaya (ə-bī′ə) *n.* A loose, usually black robe worn by Muslim women, especially in Arabic-speaking regions, covering the body from head to toe or the neck down and often worn with a headscarf and veil.

abbess (ăb′ĭs) *n.* A nun who is the head of a convent.

abbey (ăb′ē) *n., pl.* **abbeys 1.** A monastery or convent. **2.** A church that is or was once part of a monastery or convent.

abbot (ăb′ət) *n.* A monk who is the head of a monastery.

abbr. An abbreviation of abbreviation.

abbreviate (ə-brē′vē-āt′) *tr.v.* **abbreviated, abbreviating, abbreviates 1.** To reduce (a word or group of words) to a shorter form by leaving out some of the letters: *abbreviate "hour" to "hr."* **2.** To shorten: *abbreviate a long explanation.*

abbreviation (ə-brē′vē-ā′shən) *n.* **1.** The act or process of abbreviating; abridgement: *His abbreviation of the story left out many details.* **2.** A shortened form of a word or group of words, such as *Dr.* for *Doctor* or *USA* for *United States of America.*

ABCs also **ABC's** (ā′bē-sēz′) *pl.n.* **1.** The alphabet. **2.** The basic facts of a subject: *the ABCs of arithmetic.*

abdicate (ăb′dĭ-kāt′) *v.* **abdicated, abdicating, abdicates** —*tr.* To give up (power or responsibility): *abdicate the throne.* —*intr.* To give up power or responsibility formally: *The king abdicated to allow his son to take over.* —**ab·di·ca′tion** *n.* —**ab′di·ca′tor** *n.*

abdomen (ăb′də-mən) *n.* **1a.** In humans and other mammals, the front or lower part of the body from below the chest to about where the legs join, containing the stomach, intestines, and other organs. **b.** The corresponding part of other vertebrates. **2.** The last part of the body of an arthropod: *A bee's stinger is in its abdomen.*

abdominal (ăb-dŏm′ə-nəl) *adj.* Relating to or in the abdomen: *abdominal muscles.* ❖ *n.* An abdominal muscle: *exercises that strengthen the abdominals.* —**ab·dom′i·nal·ly** *adv.*

abduct (ăb-dŭkt′) *tr.v.* **abducted, abducting, abducts** To carry away by force; kidnap. —**ab·duct′ee** *n.* —**ab·duc′tor** *n.*

abeam (ə-bēm′) *adv.* At right angles to the keel of a ship.

abed (ə-bĕd′) *adv.* In bed: *She lay abed with a cold.*

Abenaki (ä′bə-nä′kē *or* ăb′ə-năk′ē) *n., pl.* **Abenaki** or

Abenakis 1. A member of any of various Native American peoples of the northeast United States and southeast Canada. **2.** Either of the Algonquian languages of the Abenaki.

aberrant (ăb'ər-ənt *or* ă-bĕr'ənt) *adj.* Differing from what is normal or typical: *aberrant behavior.*

aberration (ăb'ə-rā'shən) *n.* **1.** A departure or a differing from what is normal or typical: *Walking to work is an aberration for him.* **2.** A mental disorder or lapse. **3.** A deviation in the normal structure or number of chromosomes in an organism. **4.** The failure of a lens, mirror, or telescope to bring rays of light coming from a source, such as a star, to a single focus, causing a distorted or blurred image. **5.** The apparent change in the position of a celestial object caused by the motion of Earth during the time it takes for light from the object to reach an observer on Earth.

abet (ə-bĕt') *tr.v.* **abetted, abetting, abets** To encourage or help: *They have abetted our efforts to build a new gym.* —**a·bet'ment** *n.*

abettor or **abetter** (ə-bĕt'ər) *n.* A person who encourages or helps someone else.

abeyance (ə-bā'əns) *n.* A state or condition of being put off to a later time; a postponement or temporary suspension: *Let's hold the plan in abeyance until we know more about the details.*

abhor (ăb-hôr') *tr.v.* **abhorred, abhorring, abhors** To feel disgust or hatred for; regard with horror or loathing: *I abhor getting into needless arguments.* —**ab·hor'rer** *n.*

abhorrence (ăb-hôr'əns) *n.* **1.** A feeling of disgust or hatred: *an abhorrence of prejudice.* **2.** Something regarded with disgust or loathing: *Cruelty to animals is an abhorrence.*

abhorrent (ăb-hôr'ənt) *adj.* Causing disgust or loathing; hateful; horrible: *an abhorrent crime.*

abide (ə-bīd') *v.* **abode** (ə-bōd') or **abided, abiding, abides** — *tr.* To put up with; bear; tolerate: *Most gardeners can't abide weeds.* — *intr.* To continue in existence; endure: *Generations come and go, but the earth abides.* ◆ **abide by** To act in agreement with; comply with: *We abided by the terms of the agreement.* —**a·bid'er** *n.*

abiding (ə-bī'dĭng) *adj.* Continuing or lasting for a long time: *The doctor had an abiding faith in good nutrition.*

ability (ə-bĭl'ĭ-tē) *n., pl.* **abilities 1.** The power to do something: *Monkeys don't have the ability to speak.* **2.** Skill or talent: *a violinist of great musical ability.* **3.** The quality of being suited to a specified treatment: *a metal with the ability to be hammered into thin sheets.*

–ability or **–ibility** A suffix that means ability, preference, or appropriateness for some action or condition: *acceptability; accessibility.*

abiotic (ā'bī-ŏt'ĭk) *adj.* Nonliving: *The abiotic factors of the environment include light and temperature.*

abject (ăb'jĕkt') *adj.* **1.** Deserving contempt; base: *an abject coward.* **2.** Miserable; wretched: *Medieval serfs lived in abject poverty.* —**ab'ject·ly** *adv.* —**ab·ject'ness** *n.* —SEE NOTE AT **inject.**

abjure (ăb-jŏŏr') *tr.v.* **abjured, abjuring, abjures** To vow to give up; renounce; repudiate: *New citizens abjure allegiance to their former country.* —**ab'ju·ra'tion** *n.* —**ab·jur'er** *n.*

ablation (ă-blā'shən) *n.* **1.** The wearing away or destruction of the outer or forward surface of an object, such as a meteorite or spacecraft, as it moves very rapidly through the atmosphere. **2.** The process by which snow and ice are removed from a glacier or other mass of ice through melting or sublimation.

ablaze (ə-blāz') *adj.* **1.** On fire; in flames; blazing: *The barn was ablaze.* **2.** Brightly shining: *During the celebration the sky was ablaze with fireworks.* —**a·blaze'** *adv.*

able (ā'bəl) *adj.* **abler, ablest 1.** Having the power, ability, or means to do something: *We were not able to fix the leak. He is able to work part-time after school.* **2.** Having considerable skill or ability; capable or talented: *Most cats are very able hunters.* —**a'bly** *adv.*

–able or **–ible** A suffix that means: **1.** Capable of or likely to be affected by a certain action: *breakable; washable.* **2.** Worthy of a certain action: *honorable.* **3.** Inclined to a certain action: *variable.*

WORD BUILDING The suffix –able, which forms adjectives, comes from the Latin suffix –ābilis, meaning "capable or worthy of." Thus a *likable* person is one who is capable of or worthy of being liked. The suffix –ible is closely related to –able and has the same meaning, as in *flexible.* Since they sound exactly alike, it is important to consult your dictionary when spelling words that end in this suffix.

able-bodied (ā'bəl-bŏd'ēd) *adj.* Physically strong.

able seaman *n.* An experienced seaman certified to perform all routine duties at sea.

abloom (ə-blōōm') *adj.* In bloom; flowering.

ablution (ə-blōō'shən) *n.* A washing of the body, especially as part of a religious ceremony.

abnegate (ăb'nĭ-gāt') *tr.v.* **abnegated, abnegating, abnegates** To renounce or give up: *abnegated his citizenship.*

abnegation (ăb'nĭ-gā'shən) *n.* A giving up of one's rights, interests, or desires.

abnormal (ăb-nôr'məl) *adj.* Differing from what is normal, usual, or expected; not standard or ordinary: *flooding caused by an abnormal amount of rain.* —**ab·nor'mal·ly** *adv.*

abnormality (ăb'nôr-măl'ĭ-tē) *n., pl.* **abnormalities 1.** The condition of not being normal. **2.** Something that is not normal: *I wear glasses because of abnormalities in my eyes.*

aboard (ə-bôrd') *adv.* On, onto, or in a ship, train, or other passenger vehicle. ❖ *prep.* On, onto, or in: *life aboard ship.*

abode (ə-bōd') *v.* A past tense and a past participle of **abide.** ❖ *n.* The place where one lives; a home.

abolish (ə-bŏl'ĭsh) *tr.v.* **abolished, abolishing, abolishes** To put an end to; do away with: *Let's abolish the rule against eating in class.*

abolition (ăb'ə-lĭsh'ən) *n.* **1.** The act or state of abolishing: *Many people favor an abolition of smoking.* **2.** often **Abolition** The abolishing of slavery in the United States.

abolitionist (ăb'ə-lĭsh'ə-nĭst) *n.* **1.** A person who favors abolishing a custom, law, or practice. **2.** often **Abolitionist** A person favoring the abolition of slavery.

A-bomb (ā'bŏm') *n.* An atomic bomb.

abominable (ə-bŏm'ə-nə-bəl) *adj.* **1.** Causing disgust or hatred; detestable; horrible: *an abominable crime.* **2.** Thoroughly unpleasant or disagreeable: *We decided to postpone the picnic because the weather was abominable.* —**a·bom'i·na·bly** *adv.*

abominable snowman *n.* A hairy humanlike animal purported to inhabit the snows of the high Himalaya Mountains.

abominate (ə-bŏm′ə-nāt′) tr.v. **abominated, abominating, abominates** To detest; abhor: *He abominates most modern architecture.*

abomination (ə-bŏm′ə-nā′shən) n. **1.** A feeling of hatred or disgust: *an abomination of cruelty.* **2.** Something that causes hatred or disgust: *Many concrete buildings are abominations.*

aboriginal (ăb′ə-rĭj′ə-nəl) adj. **1.** Having existed in a region from the earliest times; native: *an aboriginal species.* **2a.** Relating to aborigines: *an aboriginal language.* **b.** often **Aboriginal** Relating to the peoples native to Australia.

aborigine (ăb′ə-rĭj′ə-nē) n. **1.** A member of a group of people who are the first known to have lived in a region. **2.** often **Aborigine** A member of any of the peoples native to Australia.

abort (ə-bôrt′) v. **aborted, aborting, aborts** —intr. **1.** To miscarry. **2.** To end something, such as a rocket launch, before it is completed. —tr. **1.** To cause the abortion of (an embryo or fetus). **2.** To end before completion: *Heavy fog forced the pilot to abort the landing.*

abortion (ə-bôr′shən) n. **1.** The termination of a pregnancy, either deliberately or spontaneously. **2.** The ending of something before it is completed: *A defective rocket engine forced the abortion of the launch.*

abortive (ə-bôr′tĭv) adj. **1.** Not successful; fruitless: *an abortive revolution.* **2.** Partially or imperfectly developed: *an abortive organ.* **3.** Causing or meant to cause abortion: *an abortive drug.* —**a·bor′tive·ly** adv.

ABO system (ā′bē-ō′) n. A system for classifying human blood that uses four groups, A, B, AB, and O, to determine compatibility for transfusion.

abound (ə-bound′) intr.v. **abounded, abounding, abounds 1.** To be present in large numbers; be plentiful: *Books abound on the library shelves.* **2.** To be full; teem: *The forest abounds in wildlife.*

about (ə-bout′) adv. **1.** Approximately; roughly: *The river is about 600 yards wide.* **2.** Almost; nearly: *The new highway is just about completed.* **3.** To or in a reverse direction: *Instantly the shark turned about.* **4.** In no particular direction: *We wandered about all afternoon.* **5.** To and fro: *Great waves tossed the ship about.* **6.** Everywhere; all around: *looking about for a hiding place.* **7.** In the area or vicinity; near: *people standing about, waiting for the store to open.* **8a.** On the point of. Followed by the infinitive with *to: We are just about to go.* **b.** *Informal* Anywhere near intending: *I'm not about to do anything he asks.* ❖ prep. **1a.** On all sides of; all around: *Thick fog is all about our boat.* **b.** Over different parts of; around: *a bear lumbering about the woods.* **2.** Near; close to: *The thief is still about the premises.* **3.** Concerning; having to do with; relating to: *stories about animals; the need to be careful about handling broken glass.* ❖ adj. Moving here and there; astir: *The patient is up and about.*

about-face (ə-bout′fās′) n. **1.** The act of turning the body to face in the opposite direction, especially in a military drill. **2.** A change to an opposite attitude or opinion: *The candidate's abrupt about-face on that issue startled everyone.* ❖ intr.v. **about-faced, about-facing, about-faces** To do an about-face.

above (ə-bŭv′) adv. **1.** In or to a higher place; overhead: *Clouds floated above.* **2.** In an earlier part of a book, article, or other written piece: *in remarks quoted above.* ❖ prep. **1.** Over or higher than: *seagulls hovering just above the waves; a tree that rises above the others.* **2a.** Higher in rank, degree, or number than: *The president is above*

all military officers. **b.** Too honorable to undertake: *He is above telling a lie.* **3.** Farther on than; beyond: *The road is closed above the bridge.* **4.** Beyond the level or reach of: *The noise was audible above the music.* **5.** North of: *Utah is above Arizona.* ❖ adj. Appearing or stated earlier: *the above figures.* ❖ n. **1.** An earlier part of a book, article, or other written piece. **2.** The people or things already referred to in a text: *All of the above are correct answers.* ◆ **above all** More than anything else: *truth above all.*

aboveboard (ə-bŭv′bôrd′) adv. & adj. Without deceit or trickery; open; honest: *All dealings of government should be aboveboard.*

abracadabra (ăb′rə-kə-dăb′rə) n. A word used as a magical incantation or charm.

abrade (ə-brād′) tr.v. **abraded, abrading, abrades** To wear down, rub away, or scrape by friction: *Flowing water abrades rocks in a stream.*

Abrahamic (ā′brə-hăm′ĭk) adj. Relating to any of the faiths traditionally held to descend from the biblical patriarch Abraham, especially Judaism, Christianity, and Islam.

abrasion (ə-brā′zhən) n. **1.** The act or process of scraping off or rubbing away by means of friction. **2.** A scraped area on the skin.

abrasive (ə-brā′sĭv or ə-brā′zĭv) adj. **1.** Causing a rubbing away or wearing off: *Sand is an abrasive substance.* **2.** Harsh and rough in manner: *an abrasive personality.* ❖ n. A substance used in rubbing, grinding, or polishing. —**a·bra′sive·ly** adv. —**a·bra′sive·ness** n.

abreast (ə-brĕst′) adv. **1.** Side by side in a line: *The band marched up the street four abreast.* **2.** Up to date: *keeping abreast of the latest news.*

abridge (ə-brĭj′) tr.v. **abridged, abridging, abridges 1.** To reduce the length of; condense: *abridge a long novel by leaving out some chapters.* **2.** To limit; curtail: *The law was ruled unconstitutional because it abridged the rights of citizens.*

abridgment also **abridgement** (ə-brĭj′mənt) n. **1.** The act of abridging or the condition of being abridged: *an abridgment of freedom.* **2.** An abridged version of something, such as a book or article.

abroad (ə-brôd′) adv. & adj. **1.** Out of one's country; in or to foreign places: *study abroad; traveling abroad.* **2.** Broadly or widely: *The wind scattered seeds abroad.* **3.** In circulation: *With rumors abroad, soon the whole town was in an uproar.*

abrogate (ăb′rə-gāt′) tr.v. **abrogated, abrogating, abrogates** To abolish (a law or privileges, for example); annul: *War abrogated the treaty between the neighboring countries.* —**ab′ro·ga′tion** n.

abrupt (ə-brŭpt′) adj. **1.** Unexpected; sudden: *an abrupt change in temperature.* **2.** Short and brief so as to suggest rudeness or displeasure; brusque: *an abrupt answer made in anger.* **3.** Very steep: *The path ends in an abrupt descent to the water.* —**a·brupt′ly** adv. —**a·brupt′ness** n.

abscess (ăb′sĕs′) n. A mass of pus formed at one place in the body and surrounded by inflamed tissue.

abscissa (ăb-sĭs′ə) n., pl. **abscissas** or **abscissae** (ăb-sĭs′ē) The distance of a point from the y-axis on a graph. It is measured parallel to the x-axis in the Cartesian coordinate system.

abscond (ăb-skŏnd′) intr.v. **absconded, absconding, absconds** To leave quickly and secretly and hide oneself, especially to avoid arrest: *The cashier absconded with the money.*

absence (ăb′səns) *n.* **1.** The state of being away: *Soccer practice was canceled because of the coach's absence.* **2.** The period during which one is away: *an absence of four days.* **3.** A lack: *Rumors spread in the absence of reliable information.*

absent (ăb′sənt) *adj.* **1.** Not present; not on hand: *Two students are absent today.* **2.** Lacking; missing: *Scales are absent in eels.* **3.** Not paying attention; absorbed in thought: *The dazed boy had an absent look on his face.* ❖ *tr.v.* (ăb-sĕnt′) **absented, absenting, absents** To keep (oneself) away: *I absented myself from work because of illness.*

absentee (ăb′sən-tē′) *n.* A person who is absent. ❖ *adj.* **1.** Absent. **2.** Living somewhere else: *an absentee landlord.*

absentee ballot *n.* A ballot that is submitted before an election by a voter who is unable to go to the polls.

absenteeism (ăb′sən-tē′ĭz′əm) *n.* Habitual failure to appear, especially for work or other regular duty.

absently (ăb′sənt-lē) *adv.* As if lost in thought: *stared absently out the window.*

absent-minded (ăb′sənt-mīn′dĭd) *adj.* Tending to be lost in thought and to forget what one is doing; forgetful or preoccupied. —**ab′sent-mind′ed·ly** *adv.* —**ab′sent-mind′ed·ness** *n.*

absent without leave *adj.* In the military, absent from one's post or duty without official permission.

absinthe (ăb′sĭnth) *n.* A strong green alcoholic liquor flavored with wormwood and anise.

absolute (ăb′sə-lo͞ot′ *or* ăb′sə-lo͞ot′) *adj.* **1.** Complete; total: *absolute silence.* **2.** Not limited in any way: *absolute monarchy; absolute freedom.* **3.** Being fully so; utter: *an absolute mess.* **4.** Not to be doubted; positive: *absolute proof.* **5.** Grammatically modifying a clause as a whole rather than a particular word or phrase in the clause. —**ab′so·lute′ness** *n.*

absolutely (ăb′sə-lo͞ot′lē *or* ăb′sə-lo͞ot′lē) *adv.* Completely; perfectly: *I am absolutely certain. Stand absolutely still.*

absolute pitch *n.* **1.** The precise pitch of a tone as established by its frequency. **2.** The ability to identify any pitch heard or produce any pitch referred to by name; perfect pitch.

absolute temperature *n.* Temperature measured relative to absolute zero.

absolute value *n.* The value of a number without regard to its sign. For example, +3 and −3 each have the absolute value of 3.

absolute zero *n.* The lowest possible temperature of matter, at which all molecules stop moving, and equal to −459.67°F or −273.15°C.

absolution (ăb′sə-lo͞o′shən) *n.* The formal forgiveness of a sin by a priest.

absolutism (ăb′sə-lo͞o′tĭz′əm) *n.* A form of government in which the ruler has unlimited power.

absolve (əb-zŏlv′ *or* əb-sŏlv′) *tr.v.* **absolved, absolving, absolves 1.** To clear of blame or guilt: *Evidence absolved the suspect of involvement in the crime.* **2.** To grant formal forgiveness to (someone) for sins committed. **3.** To release, as from a promise, duty, or obligation: *Paying off the loan absolved her of any obligation to the bank.* —**ab·solv′a·ble** *adj.*

absorb (əb-zôrb′) *tr.v.* **absorbed, absorbing, absorbs 1.** To take in; soak up: *A paper towel absorbed the water.* **2.** To take in and make a part of something: *Plants absorb en-*

ergy from the sun. *New York City has absorbed many immigrants.* **3.** To take in without transmitting or reflecting: *Thick curtains absorb sound.* **4.** To receive or withstand with little effect or reaction: *The car bumper absorbed the force of the collision.* **5.** To occupy the full attention of: *The video game completely absorbed her thoughts.* **6.** To learn; acquire: *They had trouble absorbing the new material in math.* **7.** To take up completely: *Planning and preparing for the party absorbed my entire weekend.* **8.** To assume the burden of: *Many businesses absorb the extra costs of mailing.* —**ab·sorb′er** *n.*

absorbent (ăd-zôr′bənt) *adj.* Capable of absorbing: *absorbent cotton.*

absorbing (əb-zôr′bĭng) *adj.* Extremely interesting: *an absorbing novel.*

absorption (əb-zôrp′shən) *n.* The act or process of absorbing or the condition of being absorbed: *absorption through the skin; absorption of new graduates in the job market.*

absorption spectrum *n.* A spectrum produced when light or other radiation passes through a gas or liquid that absorbs only certain wavelengths, resulting in a distinctive pattern of light and dark bands that indicates what chemical element or compound is present.

abstain (ăb-stān′) *intr.v.* **abstained, abstaining, abstains 1.** To keep from doing something by one's own choice; refrain: *He abstains from eating meat.* **2.** To refrain from voting: *Two councilors voted in favor of the measure and three councilors abstained.* —**ab·stain′er** *n.*

abstemious (ăb-stē′mē-əs) *adj.* Eating and drinking in moderation. —**ab·ste′mi·ous·ly** *adv.*

abstention (ăb-stĕn′shən) *n.* **1.** The practice of abstaining: *Abstention from candy helps prevent cavities.* **2.** A vote that is deliberately withheld, as in a meeting or legislature: *one vote for, two against, and four abstentions.*

abstinence (ăb′stə-nəns) *n.* The act or practice of refraining from indulging an appetite or desire. —**ab′sti·nent** *adj.*

abstract (ăb-străkt′ *or* ăb′străkt′) *adj.* **1.** Thought of apart from any particular object or thing. For example, *softness* is an abstract quality. **2.** Difficult to understand: *Your complicated explanation is too abstract for me.* **3.** In art, concerned with designs or shapes that do not realistically represent any person or thing: *an abstract painting full of strange shapes.* ❖ *n.* (ăb′străkt′) A brief summary of the main points of a text: *a short abstract of a speech.* ❖ *tr.v.* (ăb-străkt′) **abstracted, abstracting, abstracts 1.** To take away; remove. **2.** To consider (an idea, for example) as separate from particular examples or objects: *abstract a law of nature from a laboratory experiment.* **3.** To make a summary of: *It was not easy to abstract his article.* ◆ **in the abstract** In theory but not necessarily in practice: *In the abstract, canoeing is relaxing, but we found it to be hard work.* —**ab·stract′ly** *adv.* —**ab·stract′ness** *n.*

abstracted (ăb-străk′tĭd) *adj.* Lost or deep in thought; absent-minded. —**ab·stract′ed·ly** *adv.*

abstraction (ăb-străk′shən) *n.* **1.** The act or process of considering something, such as a quality, apart from particular instances or things. **2.** An idea or quality thought of apart from any particular instance or thing: *Truth and beauty are abstractions.* **3.** Absent-mindedness: *In his abstraction, he didn't say "hello."* **4.** An abstract work of art.

abstruse (ăb-stro͞os′) *adj.* Hard to understand: *abstruse theories of atomic interaction.* —**ab·struse′ly** *adv.* —**ab·struse′ness** *n.*

absurd (əb-sûrd′ *or* əb-zûrd′) *adj.* Plainly untrue or contrary to common sense; ridiculous: *It would be absurd to walk backward all the time.* —**ab·surd′ly** *adv.* —**ab·surd′ness** *n.*

absurdity (əb-sûr′dĭ-tē *or* əb-zûr′dĭ-tē) *n.* **1.** The state of being absurd; foolishness. **2.** An absurd action, thing, or idea.

abundance (ə-bŭn′dəns) *n.* **1.** A great amount or quantity; a plentiful supply: *This neighborhood has an abundance of good restaurants.* **2.** The condition of being in rich supply: *We found berries in abundance.*

abundant (ə-bŭn′dənt) *adj.* **1.** Existing in great supply; very plentiful: *Abundant rainfall swelled the rivers.* **2.** Rich; abounding: *a forest abundant in oak trees.* —**a·bun′dant·ly** *adv.*

abuse (ə-byoōz′) *tr.v.* **abused, abusing, abuses 1.** To use improperly; misuse: *abuse a special privilege.* **2.** To hurt or injure by treating badly; mistreat: *abused his eyesight by reading in poor light.* **3.** To subject to unwanted or improper sexual activity. **4.** To attack or injure with words; revile: *The candidates abused each other in sharp debate.* ❖ *n.* (ə-byoōs′) **1a.** Improper use; misuse: *drug abuse.* **b.** Rough treatment: *The truck received a lot of abuse when we moved the furniture.* **2a.** Treatment so harsh or severe as to cause injury to the body or mind: *physical abuse; psychological abuse.* **b.** Unwanted and inappropriate sexual activity, especially when forced on one person by another. **3.** A corrupt practice or evil custom: *Punishing his employees without reason was an abuse of power.* **4.** Insulting language: *Baseball umpires take a lot of abuse from the crowd.* —**a·bus′er** *n.*

abusive (ə-byoō′sĭv) *adj.* **1.** Using coarse and insulting language: *abusive remarks.* **2.** Causing physical or psychological harm to another person. —**a·bu′sive·ly** *adv.* —**a·bu′sive·ness** *n.*

abut (ə-bŭt′) *v.* **abutted, abutting, abuts** —*intr.* To touch at one end or side; lie adjacent: *Our fence abuts on our neighbor's property.* —*tr.* To border on; be next to: *The garage abuts the house.*

abutment (ə-bŭt′mənt) *n.* **1.** A support for the end of a bridge, arch, or beam. **2.** The point where a support joins the thing it is supporting.

abuzz (ə-bŭz′) *adj.* **1.** Filled with a buzzing sound. **2.** Filled with activity or talk.

abysmal (ə-bĭz′məl) *adj.* **1.** Too deep to be measured; bottomless: *abysmal despair; abysmal ignorance.* **2.** Very bad: *an abysmal performance.* —**a·bys′mal·ly** *adv.*

abyss (ə-bĭs′) *n.* A very deep and large hole; a seemingly bottomless space.

AC An abbreviation of: **1.** also **A/C** air conditioning. **2.** alternating current. **3.** area code.

acacia (ə-kā′shə) *n.* Any of various often spiny trees or shrubs of warm climates, having feathery leaves and clusters of small usually yellow flowers.

academia (ăk′ə-dē′mē-ə *or* ăk′ə-dā′mē-ə) *n.* The community of people engaged in study, learning, and teaching, especially at colleges and universities.

academic (ăk′ə-dĕm′ĭk) *adj.* **1.** Relating to a school or college: *an academic degree.* **2.** Relating to studies that involve reading and abstract thinking instead of practical or technical skills: *History and languages are academic studies.* **3.** Having no practical purpose or value: *Your point is purely academic and won't make any difference in the end.* —**ac′a·dem′i·cal·ly** *adv.*

academician (ăk′ə-də-mĭsh′ən *or* ə-kăd′ə-mĭsh′ən) *n.* A member of an academy or a society for promoting literature, art, science, and other studies.

academy (ə-kăd′ə-mē) *n., pl.* **academies 1.** A school for a special field of study: *a naval academy.* **2.** A private high school. **3.** A society of scholars, scientists, or artists.

Acadian (ə-kā′dē-ən) *adj.* Relating to the historic region of Acadia in eastern Canada and present-day Maine or to its people, language, or culture. ❖ *n.* **1.** One of the French settlers of Acadia. **2.** A descendant of these settlers.

acanthus (ə-kăn′thəs) *n., pl.* **acanthuses** or **acanthi** (ə-kăn′thī′) **1.** Any of various plants of the Mediterranean region with large spiny leaves and showy spikes of white or purplish flowers. **2.** A design in the form of acanthus leaves, such as the carving on the capital of a Corinthian column.

a cappella (ä′ kə-pĕl′ə) *adv.* In music, without instrumental accompaniment: *a duet sung a cappella.*

accede (ăk-sēd′) *intr.v.* **acceded, acceding, accedes 1.** To consent; agree; yield: *I acceded to her request and went in spite of my cold.* **2.** To come or succeed to a public office or position: *The young princess acceded to the throne.*

accelerando (ä-chĕl′ə-rän′dō) *adv. & adj.* In music, gradually becoming faster.

accelerant (ăk-sĕl′ər-ənt) *n.* A highly flammable substance, such as lighter fluid or gasoline, that is used to ignite other materials in starting a fire.

accelerate (ăk-sĕl′ə-rāt′) *v.* **accelerated, accelerating, accelerates** —*tr.* **1.** To cause to go faster; speed up: *accelerate one's pace to a run.* **2.** In physics, to change the speed or direction of (a moving body): *Gravity accelerates falling objects at 32 feet per second per second near the earth's surface.* **3.** To cause to happen earlier; hasten: *Eating a lot of candy may accelerate tooth decay.* —*intr.* To move, act, or occur at a faster pace: *The car accelerated on the downhill slope. Erosion of the soil accelerated after the brush fire.*

acceleration (ăk-sĕl′ə-rā′shən) *n.* **1.** The act or process of accelerating. **2.** The rate of change in the speed or direction of a moving body with respect to time.

accelerator (ăk-sĕl′ə-rā′tər) *n.* **1.** A device that controls the speed of a machine, especially the pedal that increases the flow of fuel to the motor of an automobile or truck. **2.** A substance that increases the rate of a chemical reaction. **3.** A particle accelerator.

accelerometer (ăk-sĕl′ə-rŏm′ĭ-tər) *n.* An instrument that measures acceleration, especially of an aircraft.

accent (ăk′sĕnt) *n.* **1.** The stress or force with which a speaker utters one or more syllables of a word compared with the other syllables of the word. In the word *butter,* the accent is on the first syllable. **2.** An accent mark. **3.** A style of speech or pronunciation that is typical of a certain region or country: *a French accent.* **4a.** Emphasis given to a musical note, as by making it louder or lengthening its duration. **b.** A mark in musical notation indicating such emphasis. **5.** Rhythmical stress given to a word or syllable in a line of poetry. **6.** A special feature or distinguishing quality; an emphasis: *a cooking show with an accent on hot spices.* ❖ *tr.v.* (ăk′sĕnt′ *or* ăk-sĕnt′) **accented, accenting, accents 1.** To stress in speech or in music: *accent the first syllable of a word; accent every third note.* **2.** To place an accent mark over. **3.** To give emphasis or prominence to; accentuate: *Her speech accented the accomplishments made over the last decade.*

accent mark *n.* **1.** A mark showing that a syllable in a word is accented or stressed when the word is pronounced. **2.** In certain foreign languages, and in English words bor-

rowed from such languages, a mark placed over a letter to indicate a certain feature of pronunciation. For example, in the word *exposé* the final *e* is pronounced like the *a* in *state*. **3.** A mark indicating rhythmical stress in a line of poetry.
accentuate (ăk-sĕn′chōō-āt′) *tr.v.* **accentuated, accentuating, accentuates 1.** To give prominence to; stress or emphasize: *A red background accentuates the letters of a stop sign.* **2.** To pronounce with a stress or accent. **3.** To mark with an accent mark. —**ac·cen′tu·a′tion** *n.*
accept (ăk-sĕpt′) *v.* **accepted, accepting, accepts** —*tr.* **1.** To receive (something offered), especially with approval: *accept a birthday gift.* **2.** To admit to a group: *They accepted me as a new member of the club.* **3.** To regard as proper or right: *Both sides accepted the judge's ruling.* **4.** To regard as correct or true; believe in: *We accept your explanation of what happened.* **5.** To put up with; endure: *You can accept the situation or do something to change it.* **6.** To say "yes" to; answer affirmatively: *I accept your invitation.* **7.** To take up; assume: *You must accept responsibility for your own actions.* —*intr.* To receive something offered.
acceptable (ăk-sĕp′tə-bəl) *adj.* **1.** Adequate to satisfy a need, requirement, or standard; satisfactory: *acceptable behavior.* **2.** Satisfactory but not superior: *Her work in chemistry is acceptable, but she could do better.* —**ac·cept′a·bil′i·ty** *n.* —**ac·cept′a·bly** *adv.*
acceptance (ăk-sĕp′təns) *n.* **1.** The act of taking something offered: *the acceptance of a new job.* **2.** The act of admitting to a group or organization: *acceptance of new members into the club.* **3.** A notification that someone or something has been accepted: *received an acceptance from her first-choice college.* **4.** Favorable reception; approval: *Public acceptance of seat belts has greatly reduced injuries in car accidents.* **5.** Belief in something as true; agreement: *Acceptance of the theory has been slow.*
accepted (ăk-sĕp′tĭd) *adj.* Widely used or recognized: *an accepted treatment for pneumonia.*
access (ăk′sĕs) *n.* **1.** The right to enter, reach, or use: *We have access to secret information.* **2.** A way of approaching or reaching: *The only access to the pond is by a dirt road.* ❖ *tr.v.* **accessed, accessing, accesses** To obtain access to: *accessed my bank account online.*
access card *n.* A plastic card that can be swiped or held near a sensor to make electronic transactions or to gain entry to a restricted area.
access code *n.* A code that allows a person access to something, such as a computer network.
accessible (ăk-sĕs′ə-bəl) *adj.* **1.** Easy to reach or approach: *The lake is accessible from the highway.* **2.** Easy to obtain: *The information is accessible on my smartphone.* **3.** Easy to understand or appreciate: *an accessible artwork.* —**ac·ces′si·bil′i·ty** *n.* —**ac·ces′si·bly** *adv.*
accession (ăk-sĕsh′ən) *n.* **1.** The act of coming to power or high office: *the king's accession to the throne.* **2.** An increase; an addition: *The museum has been improved by the accession of new fossils.* **3.** Something added: *The library's latest accession is a new encyclopedia.*
accessory (ăk-sĕs′ə-rē) *n., pl.* **accessories 1.** Something that is beyond what is needed but adds to the usefulness or appearance of something else: *a car full of accessories, including a DVD player; a red scarf worn as an accessory with a black coat.* **2.** A person who is not present at the time a crime is committed but who aids a criminal either

before or after a crime is committed. ❖ *adj.* Helping or adding to something more important: *The camera does not include accessory items like a flash.*
accident (ăk′sĭ-dənt) *n.* **1.** An unexpected and undesirable event, especially one resulting in damage or harm: *a car accident.* **2.** Something that happens without being planned or known in advance: *A series of happy accidents led to his promotion.* **3.** An instance of involuntary urination or defecation: *We stayed out too late, and the puppy had an accident.* **4.** Chance or coincidence: *She ran into an old friend by accident.*
accidental (ăk′sĭ-dĕn′tl) *adj.* Happening without being expected or intended: *the accidental discovery of gold in a river.* ❖ *n.* In music, a sharp, flat, or natural that is not in the key signature. —**ac′ci·den′tal·ly, ac′ci·dent′ly** *adv.*
accident-prone (ăk′sĭ-dənt-prōn′) *adj.* Tending to have accidents.
acclaim (ə-klām′) *tr.v.* **acclaimed, acclaiming, acclaims** To praise or approve publicly and enthusiastically: *The new movie has been acclaimed by all the critics.* ❖ *n.* Enthusiastic praise or approval.
acclamation (ăk′lə-mā′shən) *n.* **1.** Enthusiastic praise or applause; acclaim. **2.** An enthusiastic voice vote of approval taken without making an actual count.
acclimate (ăk′lə-māt′) *tr. & intr.v.* **acclimated, acclimating, acclimates** To adapt or become adapted to new environmental conditions or surroundings: *acclimating the fish to the tank; has acclimated to the new routine.*
acclimation (ăk′lə-mā′shən) *n.* The process of acclimating or the condition of being acclimated.
acclimatize (ə-klī′mə-tīz′) *tr. & intr.v.* **acclimatized, acclimatizing, acclimatizes** To acclimate. —**ac·cli′ma·ti·za′tion** (ə-klī′mə-tī-zā′shən) *n.*
accolade (ăk′ə-lād′ *or* ăk′ə-läd′) *n.* **1.** An expression of approval or praise: *That movie received an Academy Award and other accolades.* **2.** A ceremonial giving of knighthood, marked by a tap on the shoulder with the flat of a sword.
accommodate (ə-kŏm′ə-dāt′) *tr.v.* **accommodated, accommodating, accommodates 1.** To have enough space for: *an airport built to accommodate the largest planes.* **2.** To provide lodging or living space for: *accommodate guests at a hotel.* **3.** To take into consideration or make adjustments for; allow for: *a plan that accommodates the interests of teenagers.* **4.** To do (someone) a favor; oblige; help: *The clerk promised to accommodate us in our request.*
accommodating (ə-kŏm′ə-dā′tĭng) *adj.* Inclined or ready to give assistance; helpful and obliging: *a clerk with an agreeable and accommodating manner.* —**ac·com′mo·dat′ing·ly** *adv.*
accommodation (ə-kŏm′ə-dā′shən) *n.* **1.** The act of accommodating or the state of being accommodated; adjustment: *His accommodation to suburban life was a painful experience.* **2. accommodations** A furnished room or other space provided for lodging: *We found the accommodations a bit cramped.* **3.** Adjustment by the lens of the eye in focusing on objects at differing distances.
accompaniment (ə-kŭm′pə-nē-mənt *or* ə-kŭmp′nē-mənt) *n.* **1.** Something that goes along with or supplements something else: *Crackers are a good accompaniment to soup.* **2.** A musical part played as support or embellishment, especially for a soloist.
accompanist (ə-kŭm′pə-nĭst *or* ə-kŭmp′nĭst) *n.* A performer who plays or sings a musical accompaniment.

accompany (ə-kŭm**ʹ**pə-nē) *tr.v.* **accompanied, accompanying, accompanies 1.** To go along with: *The dog accompanied him through the woods.* **2.** To occur or happen in connection with: *Heat accompanies fire.* **3.** To provide with an addition; supplement: *The professor accompanied the lecture with diagrams.* **4.** To play a musical accompaniment for: *A guitarist accompanied the singer.*
✦ SYNONYMS accompany, chaperone, conduct, escort *v.*

accomplice (ə-kŏm**ʹ**plĭs) *n.* A person who helps another do something wrong or illegal.

accomplish (ə-kŏm**ʹ**plĭsh) *tr.v.* **accomplished, accomplishing, accomplishes** To carry out; achieve; complete: *We accomplished our goal of building a greenhouse.*

accomplished (ə-kŏm**ʹ**plĭsht) *adj.* Skilled because of practice or study; expert: *an accomplished musician.* See Synonyms at **proficient.**

accomplishment (ə-kŏm**ʹ**plĭsh-mənt) *n.* **1.** The act of carrying out; completion: *the accomplishment of a task.* **2.** Something accomplished; an achievement: *The first walk on the moon was a huge accomplishment in technology.* **3.** A skill acquired through training and practice: *Singing and painting are among her many accomplishments.*

accord (ə-kôrd**ʹ**) *v.* **accorded, according, accords** —*tr.* To give; grant: *Citizens are accorded certain rights by our Constitution.* —*intr.* To be in agreement or harmony: *Your ideas accord with mine.* ❖ *n.* **1.** Agreement; harmony: *His ideas are in accord with mine.* **2.** A formal act of agreement; settlement between conflicting parties: *The strikers and the employers reached an accord.* ◆ **of (one's) own accord** or **on (one's) own accord** By one's own choice or wish; voluntarily: *The children returned of their own accord.*

accordance (ə-kôr**ʹ**dns) *n.* Agreement; keeping: *Play the game in accordance with the rules.*

accordingly (ə-kôr**ʹ**dĭng-lē) *adv.* **1.** In keeping with what is known, stated, or expected: *Learn the rules and act accordingly.* **2.** Therefore; consequently: *The bus was late; accordingly, I was late for work.*

according to (ə-kôr**ʹ**dĭng) *prep.* **1.** As stated or indicated by; on the authority of: *According to the weather report, it will rain tomorrow.* **2.** In keeping with; in agreement with: *Proceed according to instructions.* **3.** As determined by: *a list arranged according to the first letter of each word.* **4.** In proportion to: *Salt is added according to the amount of water used.*

accordion (ə-kôr**ʹ**dē-ən) *n.* A portable wind instrument with a small keyboard and metal reeds that sound when air is forced past them by means of a pleated bellows. ❖ *adj.* Having folds like the bellows of an accordion: *a skirt with accordion pleats.*

accost (ə-kôst**ʹ**) *tr.v.* **accosted, accosting, accosts** To come up to and speak to, often in an aggressive or insistent way: *A stranger accosted me and asked me for money.*

account (ə-kount**ʹ**) *n.* **1.** A written or spoken description of events; a narrative: *The explorers gave an exciting account of their adventures.* **2a.** A reason given for an action or event: *Give an account for your strange behavior.* **b.** A basis or ground: *You do not have to worry on that account.* **3.** A record or written statement of business dealings or money received or spent: *A bookkeeper kept the company's accounts.* **4.** A business arrangement, as with a bank or store, in which money is kept, exchanged, or owed: *a savings account in the local bank.* **5.** A customer or client of a company or store: *an advertising agency with several accounts that are big manufacturing companies.* **6.** A for-

mal arrangement granting access to a computer system or online service, usually protected by a password. **7.** Importance; standing; worth: *Most gossip is of little account.* ❖ *tr.v.* **accounted, accounting, accounts** To believe to be; consider; regard: *The judge was accounted fair and wise.* ◆ **account for 1.** To give the reason for; explain: *How do you account for your absence from practice?* **2.** To be the reason for: *Bad weather accounted for the delay in their arrival.* **on account** On credit: *I bought this coat on account.* **on account of** Because of: *We were late on account of the traffic jam. Don't stay home on account of me.* **on no account** Under no circumstances: *On no account should you touch live wires.* **on (someone's) account** For someone's benefit: *Don't worry on my account.*

accountable (ə-koun**ʹ**tə-bəl) *adj.* Expected or required to answer for one's actions; responsible: *Senators are accountable to the people who elect them.* —**ac·count′-a·bil′i·ty** *n.*

accountant (ə-koun**ʹ**tənt) *n.* A person who keeps or inspects financial records, as of a business, government agency, or person.

accounting (ə-koun**ʹ**tĭng) *n.* The occupation or methods of keeping financial records, as of a business or government agency.

accoutre or **accouter** (ə-kōō**ʹ**tər) *tr.v.* **accoutred, accoutring, accoutres** or **accoutered, accoutering, accouters** To equip with clothing and equipment, especially for a particular purpose: *The explorers were accoutred for outdoor living.*

accoutrements or **accouterments** (ə-kōō**ʹ**tər-mənts or ə-kōō**ʹ**trə-mənts) *pl.n.* **1.** Articles of clothing or equipment: *boots, breeches, and other accoutrements of riding.* **2.** A soldier's equipment, including bedding and a backpack, but not including clothing and weapons.

accredit (ə-krĕd**ʹ**ĭt) *tr.v.* **accredited, accrediting, accredits 1.** To regard as the work of; ascribe or attribute: *The discovery of radium is accredited to Marie Curie.* **2.** To approve or record as having met certain standards: *This high school has been accredited by the state.* **3.** To give official standing to (an ambassador, envoy, or other representative).

accreditation (ə-krĕd′ĭ-tā**ʹ**shən) *n.* Official approval of a school, hospital, or agency for having met certain standards.

accretion (ə-krē**ʹ**shən) *n.* **1.** The process of increasing in size as a result of being added to or growing: *stalactites formed by the slow accretion of minerals.* **2.** Something added that produces such an increase: *thick accretions of rust on the pipes.*

accrual (ə-krōō**ʹ**əl) *n.* **1.** The process of accruing; increase: *Education leads to an accrual of knowledge.* **2.** Something that has accrued.

accrue (ə-krōō**ʹ**) *intr.v.* **accrued, accruing, accrues 1.** To come to someone as a gain or addition: *Interest accrues in my savings account.* **2.** To increase or come about as a result of growth: *Our knowledge of disease has accrued from scientific research.*

accumulate (ə-kyōōm**ʹ**yə-lāt′) *v.* **accumulated, accumulating, accumulates** —*tr.* To gather together; pile up; collect: *He accumulated a great number of old coins.* See Synonyms at **gather.** —*intr.* To become larger in amount or number: *Deep piles of snow accumulated on the sidewalk.*

accumulation (ə-kyōōm′yə-lā**ʹ**shən) *n.* **1.** The collection or amassing of something: *took steps to slow the accumulation of the national debt.* **2.** An accumulated amount or mass of something: *the weekly accumulation of rubbish.*

accuracy (ăk′yər-ə-sē) *n.* **1.** Freedom from error or mistake; correctness: *check the results for accuracy.* **2.** Exactness; precision: *a clock having great accuracy.*

accurate (ăk′yər-ĭt) *adj.* **1.** Free from errors or mistakes; correct: *accurate answers.* **2.** Exact; precise: *an accurate description; an accurate method of measurement.* **3.** Working carefully and making few or no mistakes; meticulous: *an accurate proofreader.* —**ac′cu·rate·ly** *adv.* —**ac′cu·rate·ness** *n.*

accursed (ə-kûr′sĭd *or* ə-kûrst′) also **accurst** (ə-kûrst′) *adj.* **1.** Under a curse; damned. **2.** Hateful or detestable: *the accursed trade in ivory.* —**ac·curs′ed·ly** *adv.* —**ac·curs′ed·ness** *n.*

accusation (ăk′yōō-zā′shən) *n.* **1.** A statement or formal declaration that a person is guilty of wrongdoing: *The accusations against the senator turned out to be false.* **2.** The act of accusing or the state of being accused of wrongdoing: *False accusation is a serious offense.*

accusative (ə-kyōō′zə-tĭv) *adj.* Relating to the grammatical case in languages like Latin that indicates the direct object of a verb or the object of certain prepositions. ❖ *n.* The accusative case.

accuse (ə-kyōōz′) *tr.v.* **accused, accusing, accuses 1.** To make a declaration charging (someone) with wrongdoing: *The lawyers accused them of polluting the river.* **2.** To find at fault; blame: *She accused her little brother of messing up her room.* —**ac·cus′er** *n.*

accused (ə-kyōōzd′) *n., pl.* **accused** The defendant in a criminal case: *The accused was put on trial for theft.*

accustom (ə-kŭs′təm) *tr.v.* **accustomed, accustoming, accustoms** To make familiar with; get (someone) used to: *Growing up in Florida had accustomed her to hot weather.*

accustomed (ə-kŭs′təmd) *adj.* Usual; habitual; familiar: *The researcher presented his discovery with his accustomed modesty.* ◆ **accustomed to** Used to; in the habit of: *Farmers are accustomed to working long days.*

ace (ās) *n.* **1.** A playing card with one figure of its suit in the center. **2.** A person who can do something very well or is an expert in some field: *the team's pitching ace.* **3.** In tennis, a point scored when one's opponent fails to return a serve. **4.** A fighter pilot who has destroyed a number of enemy planes. ❖ *tr.v.* **aced, acing, aces 1.** To serve an ace against (an opposing player) in tennis. **2.** *Slang* To perform extremely well on: *aced the interview.* ◆ **ace in the hole** A hidden advantage or resource kept in reserve until needed.

acellular (ā-sĕl′yə-lər) *adj.* Not made up of cells or not containing cells: *acellular vaccines.*

acerbic (ə-sûr′bĭk) *adj.* Sour or bitter, as in taste, character, or tone: *acerbic insults.* —**a·cer′bi·cal·ly** *adv.*

acetaminophen (ə-sē′tə-mĭn′ə-fən) *n.* An organic compound used in medicine to relieve pain and reduce fever.

acetate (ăs′ĭ-tāt′) *n.* **1.** A salt or ester of acetic acid: *lead acetate.* **2.** Cellulose acetate or a product derived from it, such as a fabric or fiber.

acetic acid (ə-sē′tĭk) *n.* A clear, pungent, colorless organic acid that occurs naturally in vinegar and is also produced commercially from ethyl alcohol and from wood. It is used as a solvent, in making rubber and plastics, and in photographic chemicals.

acetone (ăs′ĭ-tōn′) *n.* A colorless, strong-smelling liquid that vaporizes very easily, burns very readily, and is widely used as a solvent.

acetylcholine (ə-sēt′l-kō′lēn′) *n.* A chemical compound that acts as a neurotransmitter in the central and autonomic nervous systems and activates muscles in the peripheral nervous system.

acetylene (ə-sĕt′l-ēn′ *or* ə-sĕt′l-ən) *n.* A colorless, very flammable gas that is composed of carbon and hydrogen, is used in torches to cut through metal, and can be burned to produce light.

acetylsalicylic acid (ə-sēt′l-săl′ĭ-sĭl′ĭk) *n.* Aspirin.

ache (āk) *intr.v.* **ached, aching, aches 1.** To hurt with or feel a dull steady pain: *My tooth aches. I ache all over.* **2.** To feel sadness or sympathy: *My heart aches for the family whose house burned down.* **3.** To want very much; long; yearn: *I am aching to get home.* ❖ *n.* **1.** A dull, steady pain: *Growing pains often appear as aches in the legs.* **2.** A feeling of sadness or longing.

achieve (ə-chēv′) *tr.v.* **achieved, achieving, achieves 1.** To gain with effort or despite difficulty: *achieve fame as a singer.* See Synonyms at **reach. 2.** To succeed in accomplishing; bring about: *achieved a reduction in air pollution.* —**a·chiev′er** *n.*

achievement (ə-chēv′mənt) *n.* **1.** The act or process of attaining or accomplishing something: *The achievement of voting rights for women was the main focus of her life.* **2.** Something that has been achieved, especially as an outstanding accomplishment: *The development of the computer is a great achievement in technology.*

achievement test *n.* A test to measure how much a person has learned, especially at a particular grade level.

Achilles (ə-kĭl′ēz) *n.* In Greek mythology, a Greek hero of the Trojan War who was killed by an arrow shot into his heel, the only part of his body in which he could be wounded.

Achilles' heel (ə-kĭl′ēz) *n.* A point of weakness or a vulnerable place: *Poor defense is the Achilles' heel of their team.*

Achilles tendon *n.* A strong tendon at the back of the leg connecting the calf muscles with the bone of the heel.

achromatic (ăk′rə-măt′ĭk) *adj.* **1.** Refracting white light without breaking it up into the colors of the spectrum: *an achromatic telescope.* **2.** Lacking color; colorless.

achromatic lens *n.* A combination of lenses that forms an image in which the various colors of the spectrum that compose white light meet at a single focus.

achy (ā′kē) *adj.* **achier, achiest** Filled with aches; having an ache: *Flu is usually accompanied by an achy feeling.*

acid (ăs′ĭd) *n.* **1.** Any of a class of substances that release hydrogen ions when dissolved in water and can react with a base to form salts. Acids turn blue litmus paper red and have a pH of less than 7. **2.** *Slang* LSD. ❖ *adj.* **1.** Relating to or containing an acid: *an acid solution.* **2.** Having a sour taste: *the acid taste of lemons.* **3.** Sharp and biting; scornful or sarcastic: *an acid remark.* —**ac′id·ly** *adv.* —**ac′id·ness** *n.*

acidic (ə-sĭd′ĭk) *adj.* **1.** Relating to or containing an acid: *an acidic solution.* **2.** Tending to form an acid.

acidify (ə-sĭd′ə-fī′) *tr. & intr.v.* **acidified, acidifying, acidifies** To make or become acid.

acidity (ə-sĭd′ĭ-tē) *n.* The condition, quality, or degree of being acid: *The acidity of some soils is very high.*

acid rain *n.* Rain or other precipitation containing a high amount of acidity from polluting substances that form acid in water vapor. Acid rain is usually composed of a solution of sulfuric or nitric acid.

acid test *n.* A situation that provides a decisive test.

acknowledge (ăk-nŏl′ĭj) *tr.v.* **acknowledged, acknowledging, acknowledges 1.** To admit the existence or truth of: *acknowledge one's mistakes.* **2.** To recognize the standing or authority of: *My zoology professor is acknowledged as an authority on butterflies.* **3a.** To express thanks for: *acknowledge a favor.* **b.** To recognize and reply to: *acknowledge the cheers of the crowd.* **4.** To state that one has received: *The college acknowledged my application with a postcard.*

acknowledgment or **acknowledgement** (ăk-nŏl′ĭj-mənt) *n.* **1.** Something done or given in answer to or recognition of another's gift, favor, or message: *send an acknowledgment of an invitation.* **2.** The act of admitting the existence or truth of something; recognition: *His smile was acknowledgment that I had passed the test.*

ACL An abbreviation of anterior cruciate ligament.

acme (ăk′mē) *n.* The highest point, as of achievement or development: *the acme of perfection.*

acne (ăk′nē) *n.* A condition in which the oil glands of the skin become clogged and infected, often causing pimples to form, especially on the face.

acolyte (ăk′ə-līt′) *n.* **1.** A person who assists the priest in performing religious ceremonies. **2.** An assistant, attendant, or follower.

acorn (ā′kôrn′) *n.* The fruit of an oak, consisting of a thick-walled nut set in a woody base.

acorn squash *n.* A type of squash that is shaped somewhat like an acorn and has orange flesh and a hard, usually green rind.

acoustic (ə-kōō′stĭk) *adj.* **1.** also **acoustical** (ə-kōō′stĭ-kəl) **a.** Relating to sound, the sense of hearing, or the science of sound: *the acoustic quality of a concert hall.* **b.** Designed to absorb or direct sound: *an acoustic ceiling.* **2.** Relating to a musical instrument that does not have electronic components for producing or enhancing sound: *an acoustic guitar.* —**a·cous′ti·cal·ly** *adv.*

acoustics (ə-kōō′stĭks) *n.* **1.** *(used with a singular verb)* The scientific study of sound and its transmission. **2.** *(used with a plural verb)* The structural features of a room or building that determine how well sounds can be heard in it: *The acoustics of the concert hall were improved by lowering its ceiling.*

acquaint (ə-kwānt′) *tr.v.* **acquainted, acquainting, acquaints 1.** To inform: *Acquaint us with your plans as soon as possible.* **2.** To make familiar: *Let me acquaint myself with the facts of the case.*

acquaintance (ə-kwān′təns) *n.* **1.** Knowledge gained from experience; familiarity: *I have an acquaintance with Chinese painting.* **2.** A person whom one knows but who is not a close friend: *We have many acquaintances in town.* ◆ **make (someone's) acquaintance** To meet someone for the first time. —**ac·quain′tance·ship′** *n.*

acquainted (ə-kwān′tĭd) *adj.* **1.** Known to one or each other: *We've been acquainted for years.* **2.** Informed; familiar: *I am not acquainted with her novels.*

acquiesce (ăk′wē-ĕs′) *intr.v.* **acquiesced, acquiescing, acquiesces** To agree or yield without protest; consent quietly: *acquiesce to a demand; acquiesce in a decision.*

acquiescence (ăk′wē-ĕs′əns) *n.* Submission without protest; quiet agreement.

acquiescent (ăk′wē-ĕs′ənt) *adj.* Agreeing or submitting without protest. —**ac′qui·es′cent·ly** *adv.*

acquire (ə-kwīr′) *tr.v.* **acquired, acquiring, acquires 1.** To get as the result of planning or endeavor: *acquire a bicycle; acquire new skills.* **2.** To come to have: *acquired a*

dislike of cats after being bitten several times. —**ac·quir′a·ble** *adj.*

acquired immunity (ə-kwīrd′) *n.* Immunity to a disease that develops from the presence of antibodies in the blood, as after an attack of the disease or vaccination against it.

acquirement (ə-kwīr′mənt) *n.* **1.** The act or process of acquiring: *the acquirement of property by inheritance.* **2.** A skill or an ability gained by effort or experience; an attainment: *a talented student of many acquirements.*

acquisition (ăk′wī-zĭsh′ən) *n.* **1.** The act or process of acquiring: *The museum's acquisition of a large art collection took many years.* **2.** Something acquired, especially as an addition to a collection or one's possessions: *the museum's newest acquisitions to its art collection.*

acquisitive (ə-kwĭz′ĭ-tĭv) *adj.* **1.** Eager to acquire things, especially possessions: *an acquisitive collector of books.* **2.** Tending to acquire information: *the acquisitive mind of a scientist.* —**ac·quis′i·tive·ly** *adv.* —**ac·quis′i·tive·ness** *n.*

acquit (ə-kwĭt′) *tr.v.* **acquitted, acquitting, acquits 1.** To free or clear from a formal accusation of wrongdoing: *A jury acquitted the suspect of the crime.* **2.** To conduct (oneself); behave: *The firefighters acquitted themselves bravely.* —**ac·quit′ter** *n.*

acquittal (ə-kwĭt′l) *n.* The freeing of a person from an accusation of wrongdoing by the judgment of a court: *The jury's vote of not guilty resulted in the defendant's acquittal.*

acre (ā′kər) *n.* **1.** A unit of area used in measuring land, equal to 43,560 square feet or about 4,047 square meters. **2. acres** Property in the form of land.

acreage (ā′kər-ĭj *or* ā′krĭj) *n.* Land area measured in acres: *a national park of vast acreage.*

acre-foot (ā′kər-fŏot′) *n.* The volume of water that will cover an area of one acre to a depth of one foot; 43,560 cubic feet or about 1,235 cubic meters of water.

acrid (ăk′rĭd) *adj.* **1.** Harsh or bitter to the sense of taste or smell: *Acrid smoke from the blazing chemical plant filled the air.* **2.** Sharp or biting in tone or manner; nasty: *acrid comments of discontent.* —**ac′rid·ly** *adv.* —**ac′rid·ness** *n.*

acrimonious (ăk′rə-mō′nē-əs) *adj.* Bitter or stinging in language or tone: *acrimonious exchanges among the candidates.* —**ac′ri·mo′ni·ous·ly** *adv.* —**ac′ri·mo′ni·ous·ness** *n.*

acrimony (ăk′rə-mō′nē) *n.* Bitterness or ill-natured sharpness in manner or language: *sudden outbursts of acrimony between jealous partners.*

acrobat (ăk′rə-băt′) *n.* A person who performs athletic feats requiring great agility and balance, such as swinging on a trapeze or walking a tightrope.

acrobatic (ăk′rə-băt′ĭk) *adj.* Relating to or suggestive of an acrobat or acrobatics: *an acrobatic dive into the pool.* —**ac′ro·bat′i·cal·ly** *adv.*

acrobatics (ăk′rə-băt′ĭks) *n.* **1.** *(used with a singular or plural verb)* The art or performance of an acrobat. **2.** *(used with a plural verb)* A display of great skill and agility: *the singer's vocal acrobatics.*

acronym (ăk′rə-nĭm′) *n.* A word formed from the first letters or parts of a series of words, especially when pronounced as a word rather than as a series of letters. Examples of acronyms include *radar,* from *ra*dio *de*tection *a*nd *r*anging, and *OPEC,* from *O*rganization of *P*etroleum *E*xporting *C*ountries.

acrophobia (ăk′rə-fō′bē-ə) *n.* An abnormal fear of high places. —**ac′ro·phobe′** n. —**ac′ro·pho′bic** (ăk′rə-fō′-bĭk) adj. & n.

acropolis (ə-krŏp′ə-lĭs) n. **1.** The high, fortified part of an ancient Greek city. **2. Acropolis** The hill in Athens, Greece, on which the Parthenon stands.

across (ə-krôs′) prep. **1.** On, at, or from the other side of: a house across the road. **2.** From one side of to the other: a bridge across a river. **3.** So as to cross; over; through: draw lines across the paper. ❖ adv. **1.** From one side to the other: The bridge swayed as they drove across. **2.** On or to the opposite side: He sat across from me at the table. **3.** In a way that is understandable: put our ideas across to the listeners.

acrostic (ə-krô′stĭk) n. A poem or series of lines in which certain letters, usually the first in each line, spell out a name, phrase, or message.

acrylic (ə-krĭl′ĭk) n. **1.** An acrylic resin. **2.** A paint made with acrylic resin. **3.** Any of a number of artificial fibers derived from acrylic acid and used in making certain long-wearing fabrics.

acrylic acid n. A colorless strong-smelling liquid that is used to form acrylic resins and is soluble in alcohol and water.

acrylic resin n. Any of a number of tough, clear plastics derived from acrylic acid and used in making paints and automobile parts.

act (ăkt) n. **1.** The process of doing something: Police caught the robber in the act of stealing. **2.** Something done; a deed: an act of bravery. **3.** A law, especially one enacted by a legislative body: an act of Congress. **4a.** One of the main divisions of a play or other dramatic work: a play in three acts. **b.** A performance for an audience, often forming part of a longer show: a comedian's act. **5.** An insincere pretense; a false show: He sounded like he was sorry, but it was just an act. ❖ v. **acted, acting, acts** —intr. **1.** To behave; conduct oneself: She acts like a born leader. **2.** To perform in a dramatic presentation: act in a play. **3.** To put on a false show; pretend: He tried to look brave, but he was only acting. **4.** To appear or seem to be: The dog acted ferocious. **5.** To do something; perform an action: By acting quickly, we prevented the fire from spreading. **6.** To serve or function: I acted as an usher for the recital. The heart acts like a pump. —tr. **1.** To play the part of; perform as: She acted Juliet in the play. **2.** To behave like a fool. **3.** To behave as suitable for: Act your age. ◆ **act on** or **act upon** To do something as a result of: I acted on my doctor's advice and started exercising. **act out** To perform in or as if in a play; dramatize: act out a story. **act up 1.** To misbehave: The children were acting up all day, and their mother was upset. **2.** To work improperly: The car's motor was acting up. **3.** To become painful or troublesome again: His back is acting up.

ACTH (ā′sē′tē′āch′) n. A hormone secreted by a lobe of the pituitary gland. It stimulates the adrenal glands to produce cortisone and related hormones.

acting (ăk′tĭng) adj. Serving temporarily or in place of another person: the acting director. ❖ n. The occupation or performance of an actor or actress.

actinide (ăk′tə-nīd′) n. Any of a series of chemically similar, radioactive metallic elements with atomic numbers ranging from 89 to 103. See **Periodic Table.**

actinium (ăk-tĭn′ē-əm) n. Symbol **Ac** A highly radioactive metallic element somewhat like radium, found in

uranium ore and used as a source of alpha rays. Atomic number 89. See **Periodic Table.**

action (ăk′shən) n. **1.** The process or fact of doing something: firefighters springing into action; an emergency requiring immediate action. **2.** A thing done; a deed: take responsibility for one's actions. **3.** The series of events in a play or story: The action of the play takes place in a castle. **4.** A series of fast-moving, exciting, or dangerous events: a movie with lots of action. **5.** A physical change, as in position, mass, or energy, that an object or system undergoes: the action of a sail in the wind. **6a.** The way in which something works or acts, often upon a larger system: the action of the liver in digestion. **b.** The effect of this: the corrosive action of acid on metal. **7.** A lawsuit. **8.** Battle; combat: send the troops into action. **9.** The operating parts of a mechanism: the action of a piano.

action figure n. A small, usually plastic toy figure, often having movable joints and typically based on a character from a movie or comic book.

action verb n. A verb that describes an action or occurrence. Action verbs are either transitive, as activate (Electricity activates the fan's motor) or intransitive, as sleep (We all slept soundly).

activate (ăk′tə-vāt′) tr.v. **activated, activating, activates 1.** To make active; set in operation or motion: The motor is activated by a sensor. **2.** To start or accelerate a chemical reaction in, as by heating. **3.** To make (a substance) radioactive. —**ac′ti·va′tion** n.

active (ăk′tĭv) adj. **1.** Moving or tending to move about; engaging in physical action: Nurses are more active than office workers. **2.** Performing or capable of performing an action or process; functioning; working: an active volcano. **3a.** Taking part or involving participation in activities: had an active role in organizing the parade. **b.** Currently in use or effect: had an active membership in the club. **4.** Full of energy; busy: an active and useful life; an active mind. **5.** Causing an action or change; effective: active ingredients in the detergent. **6.** In grammar, relating to the active voice. ❖ n. The active voice in grammar. —**ac′tive·ly** adv. —**ac′tive·ness** n. —SEE NOTE AT **verb.**

active duty n. Military service with full pay and regular duty.

active transport n. The movement of ions or molecules across a cell membrane from an area of lower concentration to one of higher concentration using energy supplied by ATP. Active transport helps regulate a cell's metabolic activities, including food absorption and the secretion of hormones and enzymes.

active voice n. In grammar, a form of a verb that shows that the subject is performing or causing the action expressed by the verb. In the sentence John bought the book, bought is in the active voice because the buying is performed by the grammatical subject (John).

activism (ăk′tə-vĭz′əm) n. The use of direct action, as in a demonstration or strike, to support or oppose a cause. —**ac′tiv·ist** n.

activity (ăk-tĭv′ĭ-tē) n., pl. **activities 1.** The condition or process of being active: mental or physical activity. **2.** A particular kind of action or behavior: the nesting activities of birds. **3.** A planned or organized thing to do, as in a school subject or social group: hiking and other outdoor activities. **4.** Vigorous movement or action; liveliness: The department store was a scene of great activity.

actor (ăk′tər) n. **1.** A person who acts a part in a play, movie, or television program. **2.** A person or group that takes part in or accomplishes something: *England, France, and Spain were actors in the colonizing of North America.*

actress (ăk′trĭs) *n.* A woman who is an actor.

Acts of the Apostles (ăkts) *pl.n. (used with a singular verb)* A book of the New Testament giving a history of the early Christian Church.

actual (ăk′chōō-əl) *adj.* Existing or happening in fact; real: *Actual sales greatly exceeded our estimates.*

actuality (ăk′chōō-ăl′ĭ-tē) *n., pl.* **actualities** Real existence or circumstance; reality; fact: *In 1969, the human dream of walking on the moon became an actuality.*

actually (ăk′chōō-ə-lē) *adv.* In fact; really: *That tree is actually a fir, not a pine.*

actuary (ăk′chōō-ĕr′ē) *n., pl.* **actuaries** A person who estimates risks and calculates rates and premiums for an insurance company. —**ac′tu·ar′i·al** *adj.*

actuate (ăk′chōō-āt′) *tr.v.* **actuated, actuating, actuates** **1.** To put into action or motion: *Stepping on a pedal actuates the brake.* **2.** To move to action; motivate: *His remarks actuated a heated discussion.* —**ac′tu·a′tion** *n.* —**ac′tu·a′tor** *n.*

acuity (ə-kyōō′ĭ-tē) *n.* Keenness of mind or perception: *The doctor made the diagnosis with great acuity.*

acumen (ăk′yə-mən *or* ə-kyōō′mən) *n.* Quickness and wisdom in making judgments; keen insight: *The owner's business acumen permitted the store to grow rapidly.*

acupuncture (ăk′yōō-pŭngk′chər) *n.* A practice originating in traditional Chinese medicine, in which thin needles are inserted into the body at specific points in order to relieve pain, treat a disease, or anesthetize parts of the body during surgery.

acute (ə-kyōōt′) *adj.* **1.** Keen; perceptive: *an acute sense of hearing; an acute awareness of one's surroundings.* **2.** Sharp and intense: *A toothache can cause acute pain.* **3.** Developing suddenly and having a short but severe course: *acute appendicitis.* **4.** Very serious; critical: *an acute lack of funds.* **5.** Having an acute angle: *an acute triangle.* —**a·cute′ly** *adv.* —**a·cute′ness** *n.*

acute accent *n.* **1.** A mark (′) placed above a vowel to indicate that the vowel is pronounced differently than it would be without the mark, as in the word *cliché.* **2.** A similar mark (′) indicating metrical stress in poetry.

acute angle *n.* An angle whose measure is between 0° and 90°.

ad (ăd) *n.* An advertisement.

AD *or* **AD** An abbreviation of anno Domini (in the year of the Lord; that is, after the birth of Jesus). —SEE NOTE AT **Common Era.**

ad– A prefix that means toward or to: *adsorb.*

WORD BUILDING The prefix *ad–* comes from the Latin prefix *ad-,* meaning "to, toward, on top of." In Latin, when this prefix was followed by *c, f, g, l, n, p, r, s,* or *t,* it became *ac–, af–, ag–, al–, an–, ap–, ar–, as–,* or *at–,* respectively. Thus Latin *ad–* is easy to see in English words such as *adhere, admit,* and *adverse,* but it is not so obvious in words such as *affix, apply,* and *attend.*

adage (ăd′ĭj) *n.* A short proverb or saying generally considered to be wise and true; for example, "Haste makes waste" is an adage.

adagio (ə-dä′jō *or* ə-dä′jē-ō′) *adv. & adj.* In music, in a slow tempo. ❖ *n.* A slow musical passage, movement, or work.

adamant (ăd′ə-mənt) *adj.* Firm and unyielding; not giving in easily: *The referees were adamant and refused to reverse their decision.* —**ad′a·mant·ly** *adv.*

adamantine (ăd′ə-măn′tēn *or* ăd′ə-măn′tīn *or* ăd′-ə-măn′tĭn) *adj.* **1.** Having a hardness like that of a diamond: *an adamantine rock.* **2.** Unyielding; hard: *the tyrant's adamantine will.*

Adam's apple (ăd′əmz) *n.* The lump at the front of the throat where a part of the larynx projects forward, most noticeably in men.

adapt (ə-dăpt′) *v.* **adapted, adapting, adapts** —*tr.* **1.** To make fit or suitable for a new use or situation: *adapted the novel into a movie.* **2.** To cause to be able to survive and reproduce under certain conditions. Used in the passive: *a species that is adapted to a specific environment.* —*intr.* **1.** To change in order to meet the requirements of new circumstances or conditions: *The music business had to adapt to digital technology.* **2.** To become able to survive and reproduce under certain conditions: *Hawks have adapted to living in cities.*

✦ **SYNONYMS adapt, adjust, conform** *v.*

adaptable (ə-dăp′tə-bəl) *adj.* Able to change or be adjusted to fit in with new or different uses or situations: *an adaptable schedule that is easy to rearrange; an adaptable person.* —**a·dapt′a·bil′i·ty** *n.*

adaptation (ăd′ăp-tā′shən) *n.* **1.** The act or process of adapting; change or adjustment to meet new conditions: *Her adaptation to the new job was quick.* The builder has begun adaptation of the old warehouse.* **2.** Something that is produced by being adapted: *The movie was an adaptation of a story written by Charles Dickens.* **3a.** Change or adjustment in structure or habits by which a species becomes better able to function in its environment. Adaptation occurs during evolution through the action of natural selection. **b.** A structure or habit that results from this process: *The fur on the feet of polar bears is an adaptation to a cold climate.*

adapter *also* **adaptor** (ə-dăp′tər) *n.* **1.** A device for putting together different parts of an apparatus that otherwise would not fit together. **2.** A device for putting a machine or a piece of equipment to a different use.

adaptive (ə-dăp′tĭv) *adj.* **1.** Relating to or resulting from adaptation: *adaptive learning; large ears as an adaptive trait.* **2.** Tending to adapt easily: *an adaptive good nature.*

add (ăd) *v.* **added, adding, adds** —*tr.* **1.** To combine (two or more numbers) to form a sum: *If one adds 6 and 8, the total is 14.* **2.** To join or unite so as to increase, change, or improve something: *add a suffix to a word; add an annex to a building.* **3.** To say or write as something extra; say further: *She added a personal note to the invitation.* —*intr.* **1.** To find a sum in arithmetic: *I like to add in my head instead of using a calculator.* **2.** To cause an increase or addition: *He adds to his savings each week.* ✦ **add up** To be reasonable; make sense: *What she said did not add up.* **add up to** To amount to: *A group of friends and some music add up to a good time.*

ADD An abbreviation of attention deficit disorder.

addax (ăd′ăks′) *n.* A large grayish-white antelope of northern Africa, having long spirally twisted horns.

addend (ăd′ĕnd′ *or* ə-dĕnd′) *n.* A number or quantity to be added to another number. For example, in 9 + 2 = 11, the numbers 9 and 2 are addends.

addendum (ə-dĕn′dəm) *n., pl.* **addenda** (ə-dĕn′də) **1.** An appendix to a book or document. **2.** Something to be added; an addition.

adder (ăd′ər) *n.* **1.** Any of several venomous snakes, especially a viper of Eurasia or Africa. **2.** Any of several non-venomous snakes of North America, such as a hognose snake. —SEE NOTE AT **apron.**

addict (ăd′ĭkt) *n.* **1.** Someone who has a strong desire to keep taking a substance or doing an activity that is harmful. **2.** A person who is deeply involved in or very enthusiastic about something: *a baseball addict.*

addicted (ə-dĭk′tĭd) *adj.* **1.** Needing to take a habit-forming drug or other substance to avoid experiencing illness and other symptoms of withdrawal. **2.** Having a powerful psychological need to engage in some habitual behavior, such as gambling. **3.** Disposed or devoted, as by habit or interest: *addicted to playing soccer.*

addiction (ə-dĭk′shən) *n.* The condition of being addicted, especially dependence on harmful, habit-forming drugs.

addictive (ə-dĭk′tĭv) *adj.* Causing addiction; habit-forming: *Watching TV can become an addictive pastime.*

addition (ə-dĭsh′ən) *n.* **1.** The act, process, or operation of adding two or more numbers. **2.** The act or process of adding something extra to a thing: *the addition of seasoning to food.* **3.** An added thing, part, or person: *They are putting an addition on their house.* ◆ **in addition** Also; as well: *I bought an umbrella and some gloves in addition.* **in addition to** Along with; besides: *In addition to weeding, he also pruned some shrubs.* —SEE NOTE AT **together.**

additional (ə-dĭsh′ə-nəl) *adj.* Added; extra; more: *The instructions are incomplete; we need additional information to finish the project.* —**ad·di′tion·al·ly** *adv.*

additive (ăd′ĭ-tĭv) *n.* A substance added in small amounts to something in order to improve its performance or quality, preserve its usefulness, or make it more effective: *a food additive to prevent spoiling.* ◆ *adj.* **1.** Marked by or involving addition. **2.** Being any of the primary colors of light that can be mixed to produce light of any hue.

addle (ăd′l) *tr.v.* **addled, addling, addles** To confuse; befuddle: *Lack of sleep addled his mind.*

addlepated (ăd′l-pā′tĭd) *adj.* Confused or stupid; befuddled: *I won the debate only because my opponent was more addlepated than I was.*

add-on (ăd′ŏn′) *n.* **1.** One thing that is added to complete or improve another thing. **2.** An item of computer hardware or software that increases the capabilities of another item of hardware or software. **3.** An additional amount or charge: *the add-ons increased the price by $50.*

address (ə-drĕs′) *tr.v.* **addressed, addressing, addresses 1.** To speak to: *The police officer addressed the speeder in low tones.* **2.** To give a speech to: *The president will address the nation on TV.* **3.** To direct to a particular person, group, or place: *The valedictorian's remarks were addressed to her classmates.* **4.** To call (someone one is speaking to) by a particular name or term: *Address the judge as "Your Honor."* **5.** To put a destination on (a piece of mail) to show where it should go: *address an envelope.* **6.** To direct the efforts or attention of (oneself): *The committee addressed itself to plans for a new town hall.* **7.** To begin to deal with: *We must address this problem.* ◆ *n.* **1.** (*also* ăd′rĕs′) The place where a person lives or where a business is located: *your home address.* **2.** (*also* ăd′rĕs′) **a.** The information on a piece of mail, indicating where it is to be delivered. **b.** A name or a series of characters that designates an email account or a specific site on the Internet or another com-

puter network. **3.** A formal speech: *The president's inaugural address outlined plans for the economy.*

addressee (ăd′rĕ-sē′ *or* ə-drĕs′ē′) *n.* The person to whom a letter or package is addressed.

adduce (ə-dōōs′) *tr.v.* **adduced, adducing, adduces** To offer as a reason; give as an example or means of proof: *The defendant was unable to adduce evidence to support his innocence.*

adenine (ăd′n-ēn′ *or* ăd′n-ĭn) *n.* A base that is a component of DNA and RNA.

adenoidal (ăd′n-oid′l) *adj.* Relating to the adenoids.

adenoids (ăd′n-oidz) *pl.n.* A mass of tissue located at the back of the nose in the upper part of the throat in children. Adenoids are part of the immune system, but if they become infected and swollen they can obstruct normal breathing and make speech difficult.

adept (ə-dĕpt′) *adj.* Very skillful and effective; proficient: *Tailors are adept at sewing. The inventor was an adept mechanic.* See Synonyms at **proficient.** ◆ *n.* (ăd′ĕpt′) A highly skilled person; an expert. —**a·dept′ly** *adv.* —**a·dept′ness** *n.*

adequacy (ăd′ĭ-kwə-sē) *n.* The condition of being adequate; sufficiency.

adequate (ăd′ĭ-kwĭt) *adj.* Sufficient to satisfy a requirement or meet a need: *adequate supplies to meet our needs.* —**ad′e·quate·ly** *adv.* —**ad′e·quate·ness** *n.*

ADHD An abbreviation of attention deficit hyperactivity disorder.

adhere (ăd-hîr′) *intr.v.* **adhered, adhering, adheres 1.** To stick or hold fast: *The wallpaper adheres to the wall.* **2.** To remain devoted; support: *adhere to one's religious beliefs.* **3.** To carry out something without changes: *They adhered to the original plan.*

adherence (ăd-hîr′əns) *n.* **1.** The process or condition of adhering or sticking fast: *the adherence of the bandage.* **2.** Faithful attachment or support: *adherence to one's principles.*

adherent (ăd-hîr′ənt) *n.* A loyal supporter or faithful follower: *Adherents of conservatism oppose most increases in government spending.* ◆ *adj.* Sticking or holding fast; clinging.

adhesion (ăd-hē′zhən) *n.* The process or condition of sticking fast or adhering: *the adhesion of glue to wood.*

adhesive (ăd-hē′sĭv *or* ăd-hē′zĭv) *adj.* **1.** Tending to hold fast to another material; sticky. **2.** Coated with glue or another sticky substance: *an adhesive label.* ◆ *n.* An adhesive substance, such as paste or glue. —**ad·he′-sive·ness** *n.*

ad hoc (ăd hŏk′ *or* ăd hōk′) *adv. & adj.* For a specific and often unexpected purpose: *called an ad hoc meeting to deal with the emergency.*

ad hominem (ăd hŏm′ə-něm′) *adj.* **1.** Attacking a person's character or motivations rather than a position or argument: *Debaters should avoid ad hominem arguments that question their opponents' motives.* **2.** Appealing to the emotions rather than to logic or reason. —**ad hom′i·nem′** *adv.*

USAGE The phrase **ad hominem** originally meant "an argument designed to appeal to the listener's emotions rather than to reason," but it is now usually used to describe an argument based on one's opponent's personal failings rather than on the merits of the case.

adiabatic (ăd′ē-ə-băt′ĭk *or* ā′dī-ə-băt′ĭk) *adj.* Occurring without gain or loss of heat: *The passage of sound through air is generally adiabatic.* —**ad′i·a·bat′i·cal·ly** *adv.*

adieu (ə-dyōō′ or ə-dōō′) *interj.* An expression used to say goodbye; farewell. ❖ *n., pl.* **adieus** or **adieux** (ə-dyōōz′ or ə-dōōz′) A farewell: *say one's adieus upon leaving.*

ad infinitum (ăd ĭn′fə-nī′təm) *adv.* Without limit; forever; endlessly: *talk on ad infinitum.*

adios (ä′dē-ōs′) *interj.* An expression used to say goodbye; farewell.

adipose (ăd′ə-pōs′) *adj.* Relating to or consisting of animal fat: *adipose tissue.*

adj. An abbreviation of adjective.

adjacent (ə-jā′sənt) *adj.* **1.** Next to; adjoining: *I can hear all the noise from the room adjacent to mine.* **2.** Lying near or close; nearby; neighboring: *the city and adjacent farmlands.* —**ad·ja′cent·ly** *adv.*

adjacent angle *n.* Either of a pair of angles that have a vertex and a side in common.

adjectival (ăj′ĭk-tī′vəl) *adj.* Relating to or functioning as an adjective: *an adjectival phrase.* —**ad′jec·ti′val·ly** *adv.*

adjective (ăj′ĭk-tĭv) *n.* **1.** The part of speech that modifies a noun by describing it or adding to its meaning. **2.** A word belonging to this part of speech. For example, in the sentence *The young boy is very tall, young* and *tall* are adjectives.

adjoin (ə-join′) *v.* **adjoined, adjoining, adjoins** —*tr.* To be next to or connected with; share a boundary with: *The bath adjoins the bedroom.* —*intr.* To be side by side or connected: *These rooms adjoin.*

adjoining (ə-joi′nĭng) *adj.* Next to or connected with; alongside: *a bedroom and adjoining bath; a row of adjoining houses.*

adjourn (ə-jûrn′) *v.* **adjourned, adjourning, adjourns** —*tr.* To bring (a meeting or session) to a close, putting off further business until later: *The judge adjourned the trial for the holidays.* —*intr.* **1.** To stop proceedings until a later time; break up: *The court adjourned for the weekend.* **2.** To move to a less formal setting: *The dinner guests adjourned to the living room.*

adjournment (ə-jûrn′mənt) *n.* **1.** The act of adjourning or the state of being adjourned. **2.** The time during which a legislature or a court is not in session.

adjudge (ə-jŭj′) *tr.v.* **adjudged, adjudging, adjudges 1.** To determine, rule, or declare by law: *The accused thief was adjudged guilty.* **2.** To award by law: *The injured motorist was adjudged damages for medical costs.*

adjudicate (ə-jōō′dĭ-kāt′) *tr.v.* **adjudicated, adjudicating, adjudicates 1.** To hear and settle (a legal case). **2.** To study and settle (a dispute): *The mediator adjudicated the workers' complaints.* —**ad·ju′di·ca′tion** *n.*

adjunct (ăj′ŭngkt′) *n.* A separate, less important thing added to something: *The card shop is an adjunct of the bookstore.*

adjuration (ăj′ə-rā′shən) *n.* An earnest appeal: *a judge's adjuration to a witness to tell the whole truth.*

adjure (ə-jŏŏr′) *tr.v.* **adjured, adjuring, adjures 1.** To command solemnly. **2.** To ask or entreat earnestly: *I adjure you on your honor to keep my secret.*

adjust (ə-jŭst′) *v.* **adjusted, adjusting, adjusts** —*tr.* **1.** To bring the parts of (a mechanism, for example) into a more effective arrangement: *The mechanic adjusted the carburetor.* **2.** To change, set, or regulate in order to improve or make suitable: *She adjusted the seat to make it higher.* See Synonyms at **adapt. 3.** To decide how much is to be paid on (an insurance claim). —*intr.* To change oneself or one's behavior to suit new circumstances or conditions: *We can adjust to living in a smaller apartment.* —**ad·just′er** *n.*

adjustable (ə-jŭs′tə-bəl) *adj.* Capable of being adjusted: *an adjustable wrench; an adjustable lens of a telescope.*

adjustment (ə-jŭst′mənt) *n.* **1.** The act of adjusting or the state of being adjusted: *Winter weather requires an adjustment to colder temperatures.* **2.** The state of being adjusted: *valves in proper adjustment.* **3.** A means by which a device can be adjusted: *Our TV set has several adjustments to regulate the color of the picture.* **4.** A settlement of a claim or debt.

adjutant (ăj′ə-tənt) *n.* **1.** An army officer who acts as an assistant to a commanding officer. **2.** A helper or assistant.

ad-lib (ăd′lĭb′) *v.* **ad-libbed, ad-libbing, ad-libs** —*tr.* To make up (words, music, or actions) while performing: *ad-lib a joke.* —*intr.* To make up words, music, or actions while performing: *The actor forgot his lines and ad-libbed.* ❖ *n.* (ăd′lĭb′) A line, speech, action, or passage of music made up on the spot. ❖ *adj.* (ăd′lĭb′) Made up on the spot; improvised: *an ad-lib remark.*

administer (ăd-mĭn′ĭ-stər) *v.* **administered, administering, administers** —*tr.* **1.** To direct the affairs of; manage: *The mayor administers the city government.* **2.** To give formally or officially: *administer an oath of office.* **3.** To give as a remedy: *administer a sedative.* **4a.** To deal out; dispense: *A judge administers justice.* **b.** To give and supervise: *administer a test.* **5.** To manage (property), as under a will. —*intr.* To be helpful; contribute: *He administered to the needs of his elderly mother.*

administration (ăd-mĭn′ĭ-strā′shən) *n.* **1.** The act or process of administering: *the administration of justice; the administration of a vaccine.* **2.** The management of a government or large institution. **3.** The people who manage an institution or direct an organization: *The college administration is seeking to control cost increases.* **4.** often **Administration** The executive branch of a government. **5.** The time that a chief executive is in office or that a government is in power: *Many civil rights laws were enacted during the Johnson administration.*

administrative (ăd-mĭn′ĭ-strā′tĭv) *adj.* Relating to government or management: *a manager with administrative ability; the president and other administrative officers of the government.* —**ad·min′is·tra′tive·ly** *adv.*

administrator (ăd-mĭn′ĭ-strā′tər) *n.* **1.** A person in charge of directing or managing affairs; an executive. **2.** A person appointed by a court to manage the property left by a dead person.

admirable (ăd′mər-ə-bəl) *adj.* Worthy of admiration; excellent: *Honesty is an admirable quality.* —**ad′mi·ra·ble·ness** *n.* —**ad′mi·ra·bly** *adv.*

admiral (ăd′mər-əl) *n.* **1.** The commanding officer of a navy or fleet of ships. **2a.** A rank in the US Navy or Coast Guard that is above vice admiral and below Admiral of the Fleet. **b.** An officer in the US Navy or Coast Guard ranking above a captain, including admiral, vice admiral, and rear admiral. **3.** Any of various brightly colored butterflies.

Admiral of the Fleet *n.* The highest-ranking officer in the US Navy.

admiralty (ăd′mər-əl-tē) *n., pl.* **admiralties 1.** The body of law or the court that deals with matters involving ships and the sea. **2. Admiralty** The former department of the British government that was in charge of naval affairs.

admiration (ăd′mə-rā′shən) *n.* **1.** A feeling of pleasure, wonder, or approval: *We gazed at the sunset in admiration.* **2.** An object of great wonder or respect: *The bal-*

lerina was the admiration of younger dancers.
admire (ăd-mīr′) *tr.v.* **admired, admiring, admires 1.** To look at with wonder, pleasure, and delight: *admire a beautiful picture.* **2.** To have a high opinion of; feel great respect for: *People admire her ability as a musician.* —**ad·mir′ing·ly** *adv.*
admissible (ăd-mĭs′ə-bəl) *adj.* Accepted or permitted; allowable: *Admissible evidence in court must be based on fact.* —**ad·mis′si·bil′i·ty** *n.* —**ad·mis′si·bly** *adv.*
admission (ăd-mĭsh′ən) *n.* **1.** The act of accepting or allowing to enter: *Congress must approve the admission of new states to the Union.* **2.** The right to enter or be accepted: *Admission to public school is open to all children.* **3.** A price charged or paid to enter a place: *The spectators paid an admission of ten dollars each.* **4.** An acknowledgment of the truth; a confession: *an admission of guilt.*
admit (ăd-mĭt′) *v.* **admitted, admitting, admits** —*tr.* **1.** To acknowledge or confess to be true or real: *I must admit that you are right. Never admit defeat.* **2a.** To allow or permit to enter: *This pass will admit one person free.* **b.** To accept and take in as a new member, student, or patient: *The hospital admitted the accident victim.* **3.** To have room for: *The harbor is large enough to admit many ships at once.* —*intr.* **1.** To allow the possibility: *That problem admits of no solution.* **2.** To allow access: *The screen door admits to the porch.*
admittance (ăd-mĭt′ns) *n.* **1.** Permission or right to enter: *The sign said "no admittance."* **2.** The act of admitting: *gained admittance with a key.*
admittedly (ăd-mĭt′ĭd-lē) *adv.* By general admission; without denial: *Admittedly, I am an optimist, but I think things will get better.*
admixture (ăd-mĭks′chər) *n.* **1.** The act of mixing. **2.** Something formed by mixing; a combination, mixture, or blend: *An admixture of flour and water makes paste.* **3.** Something added in mixing.
admonish (ăd-mŏn′ĭsh) *tr.v.* **admonished, admonishing, admonishes 1.** To advise, warn, urge, or caution: *She admonished us to be careful on the ice.* **2.** To criticize for a fault in a kind but serious way: *The coach admonished the player for being careless.* —**ad·mon′ish·ment** *n.*
admonition (ăd′mə-nĭsh′ən) *n.* A gentle criticism or friendly warning: *Remember the doctor's admonition to keep the bandage dry.*
admonitory (ăd-mŏn′ĭ-tôr′ē) *adj.* Given or expressing a warning; urging caution: *an admonitory word of advice.*
ad nauseam (ăd nô′zē-əm) *adv.* To a disgusting or ridiculous degree; to the point of nausea.
ado (ə-do͞o′) *n.* Fuss; bother: *They said their goodbyes and set off quickly without further ado.*
adobe (ə-dō′bē) *n.* **1.** A building material consisting of clay mixed with straw or dung, fashioned into sun-dried bricks or used as mortar or plaster. **2.** Clay or soil from which such material is made. **3.** A building made with such material.
adolescence (ăd′l-ĕs′əns) *n.* **1.** The period of growth and physical development that leads from childhood to adulthood. **2.** A period of change and development to maturity: *the adolescence of the computer industry.*
adolescent (ăd′l-ĕs′ənt) *n.* A boy or girl, especially a teenager, in the stage of growth and development between childhood and adulthood. ❖ *adj.* Relating to or characteristic of adolescence: *an adolescent sense of humor.*

Adonis (ə-dŏn′ĭs) *n.* **1.** In Greek mythology, a young man loved by the goddess Aphrodite for his beauty. **2.** often **adonis** A very handsome and often vain young man.
adopt (ə-dŏpt′) *tr.v.* **adopted, adopting, adopts 1.** To take (a new member) into one's family through legal means and treat as one's own: *Our neighbors adopted a baby girl.* **2.** To take and make one's own: *Samuel Clemens adopted the name Mark Twain.* **3a.** To accept and use or follow: *adopt a suggestion; adopt new methods.* **b.** To pass by vote or approve officially: *The legislature adopted the proposed law.* **4.** To put on; assume: *Some people adopt a confident air to hide their uneasiness.* **5.** To take on; acquire: *English has adopted many foreign words.* —**a·dopt′a·ble** *adj.*

USAGE The words **adopted** and **adoptive** are similar in appearance, but they refer to different situations. Someone who is *adopted* has been taken into a family by legal means and raised as the child of that family. The word *adoptive* means "adopting" or "having adopted" and refers to the family who has adopted a child.

adoption (ə-dŏp′shən) *n.* **1.** The act of adopting: *the couple's adoption of a child; the city's adoption of a new zoning law.* **2.** The condition of being adopted: *the child's adoption by his stepfather; the new law's adoption by the city council.*
adoptive (ə-dŏp′tĭv) *adj.* Related by adoption: *the baby's adoptive mother.* —SEE NOTE AT **adopt.**
adorable (ə-dôr′ə-bəl) *adj.* **1.** Delightful; lovable; charming: *an adorable puppy.* **2.** Worthy of adoration. —**a·dor′a·ble·ness** *n.* —**a·dor′a·bly** *adv.*
adoration (ăd′ə-rā′shən) *n.* **1.** The act of worship. **2.** Great and devoted love: *Movie stars enjoy the adoration of millions of fans.*
adore (ə-dôr′) *tr.v.* **adored, adoring, adores 1.** To love deeply and devotedly; idolize: *The girl adored her mother.* **2.** To like very much: *Audiences everywhere adore the circus.* **3.** To worship as God or a god. —**a·dor′er** *n.* —**a·dor′ing·ly** *adv.*
adorn (ə-dôrn′) *tr.v.* **adorned, adorning, adorns** To decorate with something beautiful or ornamental: *The table was adorned with flowers.* —**a·dorn′er** *n.*
adornment (ə-dôrn′mənt) *n.* **1.** The act of adorning; decoration: *jewelry worn for personal adornment.* **2.** Something that adorns or beautifies; an ornament or a decoration: *They wore no jewels or other adornments.*
ADP (ā′dē′pē′) *n.* An organic compound, having the formula $C_{10}H_{15}N_5O_{10}P_2$, that is converted to ATP for the storage of energy during cell metabolism.
adrenal (ə-drē′nəl) *adj.* Relating to or derived from the adrenal glands: *adrenal disorders.* ❖ *n.* An adrenal gland.
adrenal gland *n.* Either of two endocrine glands, one located above each kidney, that produce epinephrine and certain other hormones.
adrenaline (ə-drĕn′ə-lĭn) *n.* Epinephrine.
adrift (ə-drĭft′) *adv. & adj.* **1.** Drifting or floating without direction: *The raft was adrift for weeks in the middle of the sea.* **2.** Without direction or purpose: *The editorial department was adrift until a new supervisor was hired.*
adroit (ə-droit′) *adj.* Skillful or clever at doing or handling something difficult: *The aide gave an adroit answer to a complicated question.* —**a·droit′ly** *adv.* —**a·droit′ness** *n.*
adsorb (ăd-zôrb′) *tr.v.* **adsorbed, adsorbing, adsorbs** To take up and hold (a gas, liquid, or dissolved substance) in a thin layer of molecules on the surface of a solid substance: *A dye is adsorbed in a tightly held layer on the*

surface of cloth fiber. **—ad·sorp′tion** (ăd-zôrp′shən) *n.*

adulate (ăj′ə-lāt′) *tr.v.* **adulated, adulating, adulates** To praise or admire too much.

adulation (ăj′ə-lā′shən) *n.* Excessive praise or admiration: *The leader sought respect, not adulation.*

adulatory (ăj′ə-lə-tôr′ē) *adj.* Praising or admiring too much: *an adulatory biography that avoided mention of the president's mistakes.*

adult (ə-dŭlt′ *or* ăd′ŭlt) *n.* **1.** A person of legal age, usually over 18 or 21 years old, typically having the right to vote, enter into legal contracts, and fulfill certain duties. **2.** An animal or plant that is fully grown and developed. ❖ *adj.* **1.** Fully developed; mature: *an adult cat and her kittens.* **2.** Intended or suitable for mature people: *adult education.*

adulterant (ə-dŭl′tər-ənt) *n.* A substance used to adulterate something.

adulterate (ə-dŭl′tə-rāt′) *tr.v.* **adulterated, adulterating, adulterates** To reduce the quality of (something) by adding impure, inferior, or improper substances: *adulterate milk with water.* **—a·dul′ter·a′tion** *n.*

adulterer (ə-dŭl′tər-ər) *n.* A person who commits adultery.

adulteress (ə-dŭl′trĭs *or* ə-dŭl′tər-ĭs) *n.* A woman who commits adultery.

adulterous (ə-dŭl′tər-əs) *adj.* Relating to or guilty of adultery. **—a·dul′ter·ous·ly** *adv.*

adultery (ə-dŭl′tə-rē *or* ə-dŭl′trē) *n.* Voluntary sexual intercourse between a married person and someone who is not the person's spouse.

adulthood (ə-dŭlt′hŏŏd′) *n.* The time or condition of being fully grown and developed; maturity.

adumbrate (ăd′əm-brāt′ *or* ə-dŭm′brāt′) *tr.v.* **adumbrated, adumbrating, adumbrates 1.** To give a sketchy outline of. **2.** To prefigure indistinctly; foreshadow. **3.** To disclose partially or guardedly. **4.** To overshadow; shadow or obscure. **—ad′um·bra′tion** *n.*

adv. An abbreviation of adverb.

advance (ăd-văns′) *v.* **advanced, advancing, advances** *—tr.* **1.** To move (something) forward, onward, or ahead: *In checkers, players advance their pieces one square at a time.* **2.** To put forward; propose or offer: *advance a theory.* **3.** To aid the growth or progress of; promote: *Scientific research advances knowledge.* **4.** To raise in rank or position: *advance a soldier from corporal to sergeant.* **5a.** To move ahead to a later time: *Advance your watch one hour in the spring.* **b.** To move from a later to an earlier time: *advance a deadline from June to May.* **6.** To lend or pay (money) ahead of time: *The company advanced him a week's pay. —intr.* **1.** To move forward, onward, or ahead: *A cat advanced toward the bird.* **2.** To make progress; improve or grow: *We are advancing in our studies.* **3.** To rise in rank or position: *The police officer advanced from sergeant to lieutenant.* ❖ *n.* **1.** Forward or onward movement: *the rapid advance of fire through the forest.* **2.** A forward step; an improvement or development: *recent advances in science.* **3.** A loan or payment made ahead of time. **4. advances** Approaches or efforts made to win someone's friendship or favor: *advances to make up after a quarrel.* ❖ *adj.* **1.** Made or given ahead of time: *advance warning.* **2.** Going before: *the advance guard.* ◆ **in advance** Ahead of time; beforehand: *Make your travel plans in advance.* **in advance of** In front of; ahead of: *She skied in advance of us, showing us the way.*

advanced (ăd-vănst′) *adj.* **1.** Highly developed or complex; beyond in progress: *an advanced technology.* **2.** At a

level higher than others: *an advanced student; advanced courses.* **3.** Far along in course or time: *illness in its advanced stages; advanced age.*

advanced degree *n.* A university degree, such as a master's or doctorate, that is completed after attaining a bachelor's.

advancement (ăd-văns′mənt) *n.* **1.** The act of advancing or the condition of being advanced. **2.** A forward step; an improvement or development: *new advancements in science.* **3.** A promotion: *an advancement to a managerial position.*

advantage (ăd-văn′tĭj) *n.* **1.** A beneficial factor or feature: *Museums and libraries are some of the advantages of city life.* **2.** Benefit or profit: *She learned from her mistake, turning it to her advantage.* **3.** A favorable or preferred position: *Their early start gave them the advantage.* ◆ **to advantage** To good effect; favorably: *The summer job let him display his talents to advantage.*

advantageous (ăd′vən-tā′jəs) *adj.* Providing an advantage: *an advantageous location.* **—ad′van·ta′geous·ly** *adv.* **—ad′van·ta′geous·ness** *n.*

advent (ăd′vĕnt′) *n.* **1.** The coming of a new person or thing: *before the advent of the airplane.* **2. Advent** In Christianity, the birth or coming of Jesus. **3. Advent** The period including the four Sundays before Christmas, observed by many Christians as a time of prayer and penitence.

Adventist (ăd′vĕn′tĭst *or* ăd-vĕn′tĭst) *n.* A member of a Christian denomination that believes Jesus's Second Coming and the end of the world are near. **—Ad′vent′-ism** *n.*

adventitious (ăd′vĕn-tĭsh′əs) *adj.* **1.** Acquired or happening by chance: *an adventitious occurrence.* **2.** In zoology and botany, appearing in an unusual place or in an irregular manner: *a plant with adventitious shoots.*

adventure (ăd-vĕn′chər) *n.* **1.** A bold, dangerous, or risky undertaking: *They set out on a daring adventure in the wilderness.* **2.** An unusual, exciting, or memorable experience: *Going to the art museum is always an adventure.* **3.** Excitement, danger, or discovery arising from bold action or new experience: *in search of adventure.* ❖ *v.* **adventured, adventuring, adventures** *—intr.* To go in search of new or exciting experiences. *—tr.* To venture; risk.

adventurer (ăd-vĕn′chər-ər) *n.* **1.** A person who seeks or has adventures. **2.** A person who seeks wealth in dangerous undertakings or by less than honest means: *The prospector was an old adventurer.*

adventuresome (ăd-vĕn′chər-səm) *adj.* Bold; daring; adventurous.

adventurous (ăd-vĕn′chər-əs) *adj.* **1.** Fond of adventure; seeking new experience; willing to take risks: *adventurous youths hiking in the wilderness.* **2.** Full of adventure or risk: *the pioneer's adventurous journey.* **—ad·ven′-tur·ous·ly** *adv.* **—ad·ven′tur·ous·ness** *n.*

adverb (ăd′vûrb) *n.* **1.** The part of speech that modifies a verb, adjective, or other adverb. **2.** A word belonging to this part of speech. For example, in the sentences *They left early, The peacock is very pretty,* and *The dog ran very fast,* the words *early, very,* and *fast* are adverbs.

adverbial (ăd-vûr′bē-əl) *adj.* Relating to or functioning as an adverb: *an adverbial phrase.* **—ad·ver′bi·al·ly** *adv.*

adversary (ăd′vər-sĕr′ē) *n., pl.* **adversaries** An opponent or enemy: *The lawyers for the two sides were adversaries.*

adverse (ăd-vûrs′ *or* ăd′vûrs′) *adj.* **1.** Not favorable; hostile: *adverse criticism; an adverse decision.* **2.** In an opposite direction: *Adverse currents pushed against the boat.* —ad·verse′ly *adv.* —ad·verse′ness *n.*

adversity (ăd-vûr′sĭ-tē) *n., pl.* **adversities** Great misfortune; hardship.

advertise (ăd′vər-tīz′) *v.* **advertised, advertising, advertises** —*tr.* **1.** To call public attention to (a product or business), especially in hopes of increasing sales: *Manufacturers advertise their products.* **2.** To make known; call attention to: *Mistakes in arithmetic advertised the student's carelessness.* —*intr.* To give public notice of something, as something wanted or offered for sale: *The building's owner advertised in the newspaper for a tenant.* —ad′ver·tis′er *n.*

advertisement (ăd′vər-tīz′mənt) *n.* A public notice, as in a newspaper or on television, designed to call attention to a product, meeting, or event.

advertising (ăd′vər-tī′zĭng) *n.* **1.** The activity of attracting public attention to a product or business. **2.** The business of preparing and distributing advertisements: *Many people are employed in advertising.* **3.** Advertisements considered as a group: *How much advertising does the magazine have?*

advice (ăd-vīs′) *n.* Guidance in solving a problem, especially by giving one's opinion: *I sought the advice of my mentor.*

Advil (ăd′vĭl) A trademark for the drug ibuprofen, used to treat pain, fever, or inflammation.

advisable (ăd-vī′zə-bəl) *adj.* Worth recommending or suggesting; wise; sensible: *Driving fast in the rain is not advisable.* —ad·vis′a·bil′i·ty *n.* —ad·vis′a·bly *adv.*

advise (ăd-vīz′) *tr.v.* **advised, advising, advises 1.** To give advice to: *The doctor advised the patient to get some rest.* **2.** To recommend: *Our mechanic advised a complete overhaul of the car's motor.* **3.** To inform; notify: *The radio advised us of the coming storm.*

advised (ăd-vīzd′) *adj.* **1.** Thought out; considered: *a poorly advised decision.* **2.** Informed; notified: *Police kept motorists advised of all new developments in road conditions.*

advisedly (ăd-vī′zĭd-lē) *adv.* With careful consideration; deliberately.

advisement (ăd-vīz′mənt) *n.* Careful consideration: *Your request will be taken under advisement.*

adviser or **advisor** (ăd-vī′zər) *n.* **1.** A person who offers advice, especially officially or professionally: *The local doctor served as the school's health adviser.* **2.** A teacher who advises students in selecting courses and planning careers.

advisory (ăd-vī′zə-rē) *adj.* **1.** Having the power to advise: *an advisory committee.* **2.** Relating to or containing advice: *an advisory report.* ❖ *n., pl.* **advisories** A report giving information and especially a warning: *a weather advisory.*

advocacy (ăd′və-kə-sē) *n.* Active support, as of an idea, cause, or policy.

advocate (ăd′və-kāt′) *tr.v.* **advocated, advocating, advocates** To be or speak in favor of; recommend; urge: *advocate changes in the law.* ❖ *n.* (ăd′və-kĭt) **1.** A person who supports or speaks in favor of a cause: *an advocate of animal rights.* **2.** A lawyer. —ad′vo·ca′tion *n.* —ad′vo·ca′tor *n.*

adze or **adz** (ădz) *n.* A tool used for shaping wood and resembling an axe but having a slightly curved blade that

is roughly parallel to the ground when the shaft is positioned vertically.

aegis (ē′jĭs) *n.* **1.** Protection or care: *an expanse of land under the aegis of the state.* **2.** Sponsorship or patronage: *a conference under the aegis of the United Nations.*

Aeneas (ĭ-nē′əs) *n.* In Greek and Roman mythology, the Trojan warrior and son of Aphrodite who escaped during the fall of Troy and wandered for seven years before settling in Italy.

Aeneid (ĭ-nē′ĭd) *n.* An ancient Latin epic poem written by Virgil, relating the adventures of Aeneas and his followers after the fall of Troy.

Aeolus (ē′ə-ləs) *n.* In Greek mythology, the god of the winds.

aeon (ē′ŏn′ *or* ē′ən) *n.* Variant of **eon.**

aer– Variant of **aero–.**

aerate (âr′āt) *tr.v.* **aerated, aerating, aerates 1.** To expose to the circulation of the air: *Open the windows and aerate the room.* **2.** To supply with oxygen: *The lungs aerate the blood.* **3.** To supply or charge (a liquid) with air or another gas, such as carbon dioxide. —aer·a′tion *n.* —aer′a′tor *n.*

aerial (âr′ē-əl) *adj.* **1.** In, relating to, or caused by air: *aerial currents.* **2.** For, by, or relating to aircraft: *aerial reconnaissance.* **3.** High; lofty. **4.** Growing in air without underground support: *aerial roots.* ❖ *n.* An antenna for receiving or transmitting radio or television signals. —aer′i·al·ly *adv.*

aerialist (âr′ē-ə-lĭst) *n.* An acrobat who performs in the air, as on a tightrope or trapeze.

aerie also **eyrie** (âr′ē *or* îr′ē) *n., pl.* **aeries** also **eyries 1.** The nest of an eagle or other bird of prey, built on a cliff or other high place. **2.** A house or stronghold built on a height.

aero– or **aer–** A prefix that means: **1.** Air or atmosphere: *aerodynamics; aeroplane.* **2.** Gas: *aerosol.* **3.** Aviation: *aeronautics.*

aerobatic (âr′ə-băt′ĭk) *adj.* Relating to spectacular maneuvers, such as rolls and loops, performed by an airplane or by groups of airplanes flying together.

aerobe (âr′ōb′) *n.* An organism that requires oxygen to live.

aerobic (â-rō′bĭk) *adj.* **1.** Needing or using oxygen to live: *aerobic bacteria.* **2.** Relating to exercise that is intended to improve the body's ability to use oxygen: *aerobic dancing.*

aerobics (â-rō′bĭks) *n. (used with a singular or plural verb)* Physical exercise intended to improve the body's use of oxygen. Aerobics often involves calisthenics, dance routines, and other activities that raise the heart rate.

aerodrome (âr′ə-drōm′) *n. Chiefly British* An airport or airfield.

aerodynamic (âr′ō-dī-năm′ĭk) *adj.* **1.** Relating to aerodynamics. **2.** Designed to reduce wind drag: *a car with an aerodynamic shape.* —aer′o·dy·nam′i·cal·ly *adv.*

aerodynamics (âr′ō-dī-năm′ĭks) *n. (used with a singular verb)* **1.** The scientific study of the motions of and forces associated with air and other gases, especially as they interact with objects moving through them. **2.** The interaction of a moving object with the atmosphere: *the aerodynamics of a new car design.*

aeronautic (âr′ə-nô′tĭk) also **aeronautical** (âr′ə-nô′tĭ-kəl) *adj.* Relating to aeronautics. —aer′o·nau′ti·cal·ly *adv.*

aeronautics (âr′ə-nô′tĭks) *n. (used with a singular verb)* **1.** The design and construction of aircraft. **2.** The theory and practice of flying aircraft.

aeroplane (âr′ə-plăn′) *n. Chiefly British* Variant of **airplane.**

aerosol (âr′ə-sôl′) *n.* **1.** A substance consisting of very fine particles of a liquid or solid suspended in a gas: *Mist and fog are aerosols.* **2.** A substance, such as paint, insecticide, or hair spray, packaged under pressure for use in this form. **3.** An aerosol can.

aerosol can *n.* A can containing a liquid, such as paint or a deodorant, packaged under pressure with a gas to be released as a spray.

aerospace (âr′ō-spās′) *adj.* **1.** Relating to Earth's atmosphere and the space beyond. **2.** Relating to the science and technology of flight.

Aesir (ā′sîr′ *or* ā′zîr′) *pl.n.* The gods of Norse mythology.

aesthetic (ĕs-thĕt′ĭk) *adj.* **1.** Relating to aesthetics. **2.** Relating to beauty or good taste: *a room with a strong aesthetic quality.* ❖ *n.* An underlying set of principles that influences style or taste: *the building's stark Modernist aesthetic.*

aestheticism (ĕs-thĕt′ĭ-sĭz′əm) *n.* **1.** often **Aestheticism** An artistic and intellectual movement originating in Britain in the late 1800s and promoting beauty as the basis of all other principles, especially moral ones. **2.** Devotion to and pursuit of the beautiful; sensitivity to artistic beauty and refined taste.

aesthetics (ĕs-thĕt′ĭks) *n.* (*used with a singular verb*) The study of the nature and forms of beauty, as in art.

AF An abbreviation of: **1.** air force. **2.** audio frequency.

afar (ə-fär′) *adv.* Far away; far off: *saw the bird far off.* ◆ **from afar** From a long distance: *a star shining afar.*

AFB An abbreviation of air force base.

affable (ăf′ə-bəl) *adj.* Easy to speak to; pleasant; friendly. —**af′fa·bil′i·ty** *n.* —**af′fa·bly** *adv.*

affair (ə-fâr′) *n.* **1.** An occurrence, action, event, or procedure: *Building a skyscraper is a costly affair.* **2.** A matter of concern: *Their argument was a private affair.* **3. affairs** Matters of business interest or public concern: *affairs of state.* **4.** A social gathering: *The ball was a glittering affair.* **5.** A brief romantic relationship between two people.

affect¹ (ə-fĕkt′) *tr.v.* **affected, affecting, affects 1.** To have an influence on; bring about a change in: *The drought has affected the fruit crop.* **2.** To touch or move the emotions of: *The movie affected us deeply.* **3.** To attack or infect: *Arthritis affects many older people.*

USAGE The words **affect** and **effect** look and sound similar. Their meanings, however, are very different. The verb *affect* means "to influence": *That decision will affect my whole life.* The verb *effect* means "to make happen": *We effected some helpful changes.* The noun *effect* can mean "a result" or "an influence," but only the verb *affect* means "to influence."

affect² (ə-fĕkt′) *tr.v.* **affected, affecting, affects** To put on a false show of; pretend to have: *He affected indifference, though he was hurt by the remark.*

WORD HISTORY Both **affect¹** and **affect²** come from Middle English *affecten,* from Old French *affecter,* both meaning the same thing as their respective senses in Modern English. *Affecter* came from Latin *affectāre* (meaning "to strive after, feign") which came from Latin *afficere,* meaning "to have an effect on." Although their development followed the same path, scholars believe the split in senses occurred during the Old French period.

affectation (ăf′ĕk-tā′shən) *n.* A way of behaving that is not natural but is adopted to impress others: *Everyone thought his British accent was an affectation.*

affected¹ (ə-fĕk′tĭd) *adj.* **1.** Acted upon, influenced, or changed: *a report on the affected businesses in this economy.* **2.** Acted upon in an injurious way, as by disease or malfunction: *rubbed ointment on the affected area.*

affected² (ə-fĕk′tĭd) *adj.* Speaking or behaving in an artificial way to make an impression: *an affected tone of voice.* —**af·fect′ed·ly** *adv.* —**af·fect′ed·ness** *n.*

affecting (ə-fĕk′tĭng) *adj.* Touching the emotions; moving: *an affecting tale of woe.*

affection (ə-fĕk′shən) *n.* A fond or tender feeling toward someone or something; fondness.

affectionate (ə-fĕk′shə-nĭt) *adj.* Having or showing affection; tender; loving. —**af·fec′tion·ate·ly** *adv.*

afferent (ăf′ər-ənt) *adj.* Directed or leading toward a central organ or part of an organism: *an afferent nerve.*

affiance (ə-fī′əns) *tr.v.* **affianced, affiancing, affiances** To promise to marry: *The lovers were affianced to each other.*

affidavit (ăf′ĭ-dā′vĭt) *n.* A written declaration made under oath before a notary public or other authorized officer.

affiliate (ə-fĭl′ē-āt′) *v.* **affiliated, affiliating, affiliates** —*tr.* To adopt or accept as a member, subordinate associate, or branch: *The local unit of the charity is affiliated with the national organization.* —*intr.* To become connected or associated: *The two unions voted to affiliate.* ❖ *n.* (ə-fĭl′ē-ĭt *or* ə-fĭl′ē-āt′) A person or organization associated or joined with a larger or more important body: *Our company has affiliates in Europe as well as the United States.*

affinity (ə-fĭn′ĭ-tē) *n., pl.* **affinities 1.** A natural attraction; a liking: *Our dog has an affinity for young children.* **2.** A similarity based on relationship: *The twins have a closer affinity than most members of their family.* **3.** An attraction or force between particles or chemicals that causes them to combine.

affirm (ə-fûrm′) *tr.v.* **affirmed, affirming, affirms 1.** To declare positively; say firmly: *She affirmed her intention to run for the Senate seat.* **2.** To give approval or validity to; confirm: *The appeals court affirmed the lower court's ruling.*

affirmation (ăf′ər-mā′shən) *n.* **1.** The act of affirming; assertion. **2.** Something declared to be true.

affirmative (ə-fûr′mə-tĭv) *adj.* **1.** Affirming that something is true, as with the answer "yes": *an affirmative response.* **2.** Giving assent or approval; confirming: *an affirmative vote.* **3.** Positive; optimistic: *an affirmative outlook.* ❖ *n.* **1.** A word or statement of agreement or assent. **2.** The side in a debate that supports the proposition in question. ◆ **in the affirmative** Expressing agreement; saying "yes." —**af·fir′ma·tive·ly** *adv.*

affirmative action *n.* A policy or program that actively attempts to correct past discrimination by improving the opportunities for members of underrepresented groups in employment and education.

affix (ə-fĭks′) *tr.v.* **affixed, affixing, affixes 1.** To fasten to something; attach: *affix a label to a package.* **2.** To add at the end; append: *I affixed my name to the letter.* ❖ *n.* (ăf′ĭks′) A word element, usually one or more syllables in length, that is added at the beginning or the end of a word or stem to make another word with a different but related meaning; a prefix or suffix.

afflict (ə-flĭkt′) *tr.v.* **afflicted, afflicting, afflicts** To cause distress to; cause to suffer: *Humans are afflicted with many diseases.*

affliction (ə-flĭk′shən) *n.* **1.** A condition of pain or distress. **2.** A cause of pain or suffering: *Scurvy used to be a common affliction among sailors.*

affluence (ăf′lōō-əns *or* ə-flōō′əns) *n.* A plentiful supply of goods or money; wealth.

affluent (ăf′lōō-ənt *or* ə-flōō′ənt) *adj.* Having plenty of money, property, or possessions; wealthy. —**af′flu·ent·ly** *adv.*

afford (ə-fôrd′) *tr.v.* **afforded, affording, affords 1.** To be able to pay for: *By saving we can afford a new computer.* **2.** To be able to give or spare: *I am too busy to afford the time just now.* **3.** To be able to do without harming oneself: *Anyone can afford to be kind.* **4.** To give or furnish; provide: *This window affords a view of the mountains.*

affray (ə-frā′) *n.* A noisy quarrel or brawl.

affright (ə-frīt′) *tr.v.* **affrighted, affrighting, affrights** To frighten; terrify.

affront (ə-frŭnt′) *tr.v.* **affronted, affronting, affronts** To insult intentionally or openly. ❖ *n.* An intentional insult or offense.

Afghan (ăf′găn′) *adj.* Relating to Afghanistan or the Afghans. ❖ *n.* **1.** A native or inhabitant of Afghanistan. **2.** **afghan** A colorful wool blanket or shawl knitted or crocheted in squares, circles, or other designs. **3.** A large, slender dog of a breed having long thick hair, a pointed snout, and drooping ears.

afghani (ăf-găn′ē *or* ăf-gä′nē) *n.* The basic monetary unit of Afghanistan.

Afghani *adj.* Relating to Afghanistan; Afghan. ❖ *n., pl.* **Afghanis** A native or inhabitant of Afghanistan; an Afghan.

aficionado (ə-fĭsh′ē-ə-nä′dō) *n., pl.* **aficionados** An enthusiastic admirer; a devotee.

afield (ə-fēld′) *adv.* **1a.** Away from one's usual environment; to or at a distance: *The children wandered far afield in search of butterflies.* **b.** Off or away from the subject: *The witness's remarks went farther afield.* **2.** In or on the field: *The geologist preferred working afield to reading papers in the office.*

afire (ə-fīr′) *adv. & adj.* On fire; burning: *The room was afire.*

aflame (ə-flām′) *adv. & adj.* **1.** In flames: *The house is aflame.* **2.** Intensely excited: *aflame with curiosity.*

AFL-CIO An abbreviation of American Federation of Labor and Congress of Industrial Organizations.

afloat (ə-flōt′) *adv. & adj.* **1.** In a floating condition: *The raft was afloat on the lake.* **2.** On a boat or ship; at sea. **3.** In circulation: *Talk of a change in managers is afloat.* **4.** Free of difficulty, especially financial difficulty: *couldn't keep the business afloat.*

aflutter (ə-flŭt′ər) *adj.* **1.** Fluttering: *The flags were aflutter.* **2.** Nervously excited.

afoot (ə-fŏŏt′) *adv. & adj.* **1.** On foot; walking: *They traveled afoot.* **2.** In the process of happening; astir: *Something strange is afoot.*

afore (ə-fôr′) *adv. & prep.* A dialectal variant of **before**.

aforementioned (ə-fôr′mĕn′shənd) *adj.* Mentioned before.

aforesaid (ə-fôr′sĕd′) *adj.* Spoken of earlier.

aforethought (ə-fôr′thôt′) *adj.* Planned beforehand; premeditated: *with malice aforethought.*

afoul of (ə-foul′) *prep.* **1.** In entanglement with: *The an-*

chor fell afoul of the fishing lines. **2.** In trouble with: *ran afoul of the law.*

afraid (ə-frād′) *adj.* **1.** Filled with fear; fearful: *afraid of the dark.* **2.** Reluctant; hesitant: *not afraid of work.* **3.** Feeling concern or regret: *I'm afraid you don't understand.*

A-frame (ā′frām′) *n.* A house built on a frame shaped like the letter A.

afresh (ə-frĕsh′) *adv.* Anew; again: *We must start afresh.*

African (ăf′rĭ-kən) *adj.* Relating to Africa or its peoples, languages, or cultures. ❖ *n.* **1.** A native or inhabitant of Africa. **2.** A person of African ancestry.

Africana (ăf′rĭ-kä′nə *or* ăf′rĭ-kä′nə) *n. (used with a plural verb)* Things that are examples of the history or culture of African peoples: *a collection of Africana.*

African American or **African-American** (ăf′rĭ-kən-ə-mĕr′ĭ-kən) *n.* A black American of African ancestry. —**Af′ri·can-A·mer′i·can** *adj.*

African American Vernacular English *n.* Any of the nonstandard varieties of English spoken by African Americans.

African elephant *n.* Either of two elephants native to sub-Saharan Africa, having larger ears than the Asian elephant. Both males and females usually have tusks.

African violet *n.* A popular houseplant, originally from Africa, with usually purplish flowers and velvety leaves.

Afrikaans (ăf′rĭ-käns′ *or* ăf′rĭ-känz′) *n.* A language that developed from 17th-century Dutch and is an official language of South Africa.

Afrikaner (ăf′rĭ-kä′nər) *n.* An Afrikaans-speaking South African of European and especially Dutch ancestry.

Afro (ăf′rō) *n., pl.* **Afros** A hairstyle in which the hair is rounded, thick, and tightly curled. ❖ *adj.* African in style or origin.

Afro-American (ăf′rō-ə-mĕr′ĭ-kən) *n.* An African American. —**Af′ro-A·mer′i·can** *adj.*

Afro-Asiatic (ăf′rō-ā′zhē-ăt′ĭk) *n.* A family of languages spoken in northern Africa and southwest Asia, including the Semitic and ancient Egyptian languages. —**Af′ro-A′si·at′ic** *adj.*

Afrocentric (ăf′rō-sĕn′trĭk) *adj.* Centered or focused on Africa or African peoples: *an Afrocentric history textbook.*

aft (ăft) *adv. & adj.* Toward or near the stern of a ship or aircraft: *going aft; the aft cabin.*

after (ăf′tər) *prep.* **1.** Behind in place or order: *Z comes after Y.* **2.** In pursuit of: *running after the fire engine.* **3.** About; concerning: *I asked after you.* **4.** At a later time than: *They arrived after dinner.* **5.** Past the hour of: *five minutes after three.* **6.** Suiting the nature or desires of: *a writer after my own heart.* **7.** With the same name as; in honor of: *named after his grandfather.* ❖ *adv.* **1.** At a later time: *We left shortly after.* **2.** Behind; in the rear: *First came the tractor and then the wagon came rumbling after.* ❖ *adj.* **1.** Later; following: *in after years.* **2.** Nearer a ship's stern: *the after quarter.* ❖ *conj.* Following the time that: *We can eat after we get home.* ◆ **after all** In spite of everything; nevertheless.

afterbirth (ăf′tər-bûrth′) *n.* The placenta and fetal membranes expelled from the uterus following birth.

afterburner (ăf′tər-bûr′nər) *n.* A device in a jet engine that increases its power by injecting extra fuel into the hot exhaust gases.

afterdeck (ăf′tər-dĕk′) *n.* The part of a ship's deck near or toward the stern.

aftereffect (ăf′tər-ĭ-fĕkt′) *n.* An effect that follows its cause after some delay, especially a delayed bodily or mental response to something: *The driver's nervousness was an aftereffect of the accident.*

afterglow (ăf′tər-glō′) *n.* **1.** Light that remains after its source has disappeared, as the atmospheric glow that remains for a short time after sunset. **2.** A comfortable feeling after a pleasant experience.

after-hours (ăf′tər-ourz′) *adj.* **1.** Occurring after closing time: *after-hours socializing.* **2.** Open after a legal or established closing time: *an after-hours club.*

afterimage (ăf′tər-ĭm′ĭj) *n.* An image that persists after the original source is no longer active: *the afterimage one sees after the flash of a camera.*

afterlife (ăf′tər-līf′) *n.* A life or existence believed to follow death.

aftermath (ăf′tər-măth′) *n.* **1.** A consequence or result, especially of a disaster or misfortune: *the aftermath of a hurricane.* **2.** A new growth or crop in the same season, especially of grass after mowing.

afternoon (ăf′tər-nōōn′) *n.* The part of day from noon until dinnertime or sunset.

afterschool (ăf′tər-skōōl′) *adj.* Relating to or being a program providing care for children following school classes.

after-shave (ăf′tər-shāv′) *n.* A usually fragrant lotion for use on the face after shaving.

aftershock (ăf′tər-shŏk′) *n.* A less powerful quake coming after an earthquake.

aftertaste (ăf′tər-tāst′) *n.* **1.** A taste that remains in the mouth after the substance that caused it is no longer there. **2.** A feeling that lingers after an event: *an experience that left an unpleasant aftertaste.*

afterthought (ăf′tər-thôt′) *n.* An idea that occurs to a person after something, such as an event or decision, has passed.

afterward (ăf′tər-wərd) also **afterwards** (ăf′tər-wərdz) *adv.* At a later time; subsequently.

again (ə-gĕn′) *adv.* **1.** Once more; anew: *If you don't win, try again.* **2.** To a previous place or position: *They left home but went back again.* **3.** As previously stated: *Again, I'm no expert.* **4.** On the other hand: *They might go, and again they might not.* **5.** In addition to a particular amount: *a new job paying half as much again as the old one.* ◆ **again and again** Often; repeatedly.

against (ə-gĕnst′) *prep.* **1.** In a direction or course opposite to: *sailing against the wind.* **2.** So as to come into contact with: *waves washing against the shore.* **3.** In hostile opposition or resistance to: *struggling against prejudice.* **4.** Contrary to: *against my better judgment.* **5.** In competition with: *raced against the record holder.* **6.** In contrast to: *dark colors against a light background.* **7.** As a defense or safeguard from: *wearing gloves against the cold.* **8.** To the account or debt of: *drew a check against my bank balance.*

agal (ə-gäl′) *n.* A band or series of cords used to hold a keffiyeh in place on the head.

Agamemnon (ăg′ə-mĕm′nŏn′) *n.* In Greek mythology, the king of Mycenae and leader of the Greeks in the Trojan War.

agape (ə-gāp′) *adv. & adj.* In a state of wonder or surprise: *The magician's dazzling tricks set the audience agape.*

agar (ä′gär′ *or* ä′gär′) also **agar-agar** (ä′gär-ä′gär′ *or* ä′-gär-ä′gär′) *n.* A gelatinous material obtained from certain algae, used as a base on which bacteria are grown and as a thickener and stabilizer in food products.

agate (ăg′ĭt) *n.* **1.** A type of quartz found in various col-

ors that are arranged in bands or in cloudy patterns. **2.** A marble used in games that is made of this quartz or of glass.

agave (ə-gä′vē) *n.* Any of numerous plants of hot dry regions of the Americas, having a tall flower stalk and tough, usually spiny leaves that were formerly an important source of fiber used for making rope or sacks.

age (āj) *n.* **1.** The length of time during which a person or thing has existed; a lifetime or lifespan: *Elephants are known for their great age.* **2.** One of the stages of life: *the age of adolescence.* **3.** The time in life when a person is allowed to assume adult rights and responsibilities, usually at 18 or 21 years: *Children are under age.* **4.** The state of being old; old age. **5.** often **Age** A distinctive period of history: *the Iron Age.* **6. ages** A long time: *It took ages to clean up after dinner.* ❖ *v.* **aged, aging, ages** —*tr.* **1.** To cause to grow old: *The crisis seemed to age the president.* **2.** To allow to mature or become flavorful: *They aged the wine in oak casks.* —*intr.* **1.** To become or look old: *The flimsy house aged poorly through the years.* **2.** To develop a certain quality of ripeness; become mature: *cheeses aging at room temperature.* ◆ **come of age** To reach maturity or adulthood.

-age a suffix that means: **1a.** Collection; mass: *leafage.* **b.** Amount: *mileage.* **2.** Condition; state: *patronage.* **3.** Charge or fee: *postage.* **4.** Residence or place: *orphanage.* **5.** Act or result: *breakage; spoilage.*

aged (ā′jĭd) *adj.* **1.** Old; elderly. **2.** (ājd) Having reached the age of: *a child aged five.* **3.** (ājd) Ripe; mature: *aged cheese.* ❖ *n.* Elderly people considered as a group: *Many of the aged continue to exercise.*

ageing (ā′jĭng) *n.* Chiefly British Variant of **aging.**

ageism (ā′jĭz′əm) *n.* Discrimination based on age, especially against elderly people, as in regard to employment and housing.

ageless (āj′lĭs) *adj.* **1.** Experienced or old and still active and vibrant: *an ageless movie star.* **2.** Existing forever or for a very long time: *ageless stories of daring and adventure.* —**age′less·ly** *adv.*

agency (ā′jən-sē) *n., pl.* **agencies 1.** The process of acting on behalf of someone else: *Through the producer's agency, another show was added to the schedule.* **2.** A business with agents who negotiate deals for clients: *a real estate agency.* **3.** A governmental department of administration or regulation: *an agency that runs the recycling program.*

agenda (ə-jĕn′də) *n., pl.* **agendas** A list of things to be considered or done, as a program of business at a meeting.

agent (ā′jənt) *n.* **1.** A person with the power or authority to act for another: *a ticket agent; a publicity agent.* **2.** A representative of a government or a governmental department: *an FBI agent.* **3a.** A substance that has a chemical or biological effect. **b.** An organism or other factor that causes disease, such as a bacterium or virus. **4.** A means by which something is done or caused: *Wind and rain are agents of erosion.* **5.** The one performing the action or process described by a verb. For example, in the sentence *The steeple was struck by lightning,* the word *lightning* is the agent because it is the one doing the striking.

age of consent *n.* The age at which a person is legally considered competent to give consent, as to sexual intercourse.

age-old (āj′ōld′) *adj.* Very old; ancient: *an age-old story.*

agglomerate (ə-glŏm′ə-rāt′) *tr. & intr.v.* **agglomerated,**

agglomerating, agglomerates To make or form into a rounded mass: *Heat and pressure have agglomerated much of the earth's rock.* ❖ *adj.* (ə-glŏm′ər-ĭt) Gathered and shaped into a rounded mass. ❖ *n.* (ə-glŏm′ər-ĭt) **1.** A jumbled mass of things heaped together. **2.** A volcanic rock consisting of rounded and angular fragments fused together.

agglomeration (ə-glŏm′ə-rā′shən) *n.* **1.** The act or process of massing things together: *the continual agglomeration of rocks at the foot of the cliff.* **2.** A jumbled mass; an agglomerate.

agglutinate (ə-glo͞ot′n-āt′) *v.* **agglutinated, agglutinating, agglutinates** —*tr.* To cause (red blood cells or bacteria) to clump together. —*intr.* To undergo agglutination.

agglutination (ə-glo͞ot′n-ā′shən) *n.* **1.** A process in which red blood cells or bacteria clump together into a mass. **2.** The mass formed in this way.

aggrandize (ə-grăn′dīz′ *or* ăg′rən-dīz′) *tr.v.* **aggrandized, aggrandizing, aggrandizes** To make greater, as in power or influence. —**ag·gran′dize·ment** (ə-grăn′dĭz-mənt) *n.* —**ag·gran′diz′er** *n.*

aggravate (ăg′rə-vāt′) *tr.v.* **aggravated, aggravating, aggravates 1.** To make worse: *aggravate an injury.* **2.** To annoy or provoke: *Our constant noise aggravated the neighbors.* —**ag′gra·vat′ing·ly** *adv.* —**ag′gra·va′tor** *n.*

aggravation (ăg′rə-vā′shən) *n.* **1.** The act or process of aggravating. **2.** Irritation; annoyance.

aggregate (ăg′rĭ-gĭt) *adj.* Gathered into or considered together as a whole; total. ❖ *n.* **1.** A total or whole; a gross amount. **2.** The mineral materials, such as sand and stone, used to make concrete. ❖ *tr.v.* (ăg′rĭ-gāt′) **aggregated, aggregating, aggregates 1.** To gather into a mass, sum, or whole. **2.** To amount to; total. ◆ **in the aggregate** Taken as a whole; considered collectively. —**ag′gre·gate·ly** *adv.* —**ag′gre·gate·ness** *n.*

aggregation (ăg′rĭ-gā′shən) *n.* **1.** The collecting of separate things into one mass or whole. **2.** The group or mass collected.

aggression (ə-grĕsh′ən) *n.* **1.** Hostile or violent action or behavior: *I was frightened by the dog's aggression and left the package outside the gate.* **2.** The practice of taking hostile actions or making military attacks. **3.** Behavior that is disagreeably assertive or overbearing: *The politician showed displeasure with the reporter's aggression.*

aggressive (ə-grĕs′ĭv) *adj.* **1.** Characterized by aggression: *aggressive behavior.* **2.** Given to aggression: *an aggressive person.* **3.** Vigorous; energetic: *an aggressive campaign to promote physical fitness.* —**ag·gres′sive·ly** *adv.* —**ag·gres′sive·ness** *n.*

aggressor (ə-grĕs′ər) *n.* **1.** A person or animal that behaves with aggression. **2.** A country that makes military attacks against another.

aggrieved (ə-grēvd′) *adj.* Feeling that one has been treated wrongly; offended: *The aggrieved workers went out on strike.*

aghast (ə-găst′) *adj.* Shocked or horrified, as by something terrible.

agile (ăj′əl *or* ăj′īl′) *adj.* **1.** Able to move quickly and easily; nimble: *an agile mountain climber.* **2.** Mentally quick or alert: *an agile mind.* —**ag′ile·ly** *adv.* —**ag′ile·ness** *n.*

agility (ə-jĭl′ĭ-tē) *n.* The quality or condition of being agile; nimbleness.

agitate (ăj′ĭ-tāt′) *v.* **agitated, agitating, agitates** —*tr.* **1.**

To shake or stir up violently: *The storm agitated the sea.* **2.** To disturb; upset: *Our quarrel agitated everyone present.* —*intr.* To stir up public interest in a cause: *agitate for civil rights.* —**ag′i·tat′ed·ly** *adv.*

agitation (ăj′ĭ-tā′shən) *n.* **1.** The act of agitating. **2.** Great emotional disturbance or excitement. **3.** Energetic action to arouse public interest in a cause.

agitator (ăj′ĭ-tā′tər) *n.* **1.** A person who is active in stirring up interest in a cause. **2.** A mechanism that stirs or shakes, as in a washing machine.

agleam (ə-glēm′) *adv. & adj.* Shining: *a lantern agleam in the window.*

aglitter (ə-glĭt′ər) *adv. & adj.* Glittering; sparkling: *eyes aglitter with excitement.*

aglow (ə-glō′) *adv. & adj.* Glowing: *a room aglow with lights.*

agnostic (ăg-nŏs′tĭk) *n.* One who believes that it is impossible to know whether there is a God. ❖ *adj.* Relating to or being an agnostic. —**ag·nos′ti·cal·ly** *adv.*

agnosticism (ăg-nŏs′tĭ-sĭz′əm) *n.* The belief that it is impossible to know whether or not a God exists.

Agnus Dei (ăg′nəs dē′ī′ *or* än′yo͞os dā′ē) *n.* **1.** In Christianity, the Lamb of God; Jesus. **2.** A Roman Catholic prayer to Jesus that is part of the Mass and begins with the words "Agnus Dei." **3.** A musical composition for this prayer.

ago (ə-gō′) *adv. & adj.* **1.** Gone by; past: *two years ago.* **2.** In the past: *They lived there long ago.*

agog (ə-gŏg′) *adv. & adj.* Full of eager anticipation; eagerly excited.

agonist (ăg′ə-nĭst) *n.* **1.** A drug or other chemical that can combine with a receptor on a cell to produce a physiologic reaction typical of a naturally occurring substance. **2.** A contracting muscle that is resisted or counteracted by another muscle, the antagonist. **3.** A person involved in a struggle or competition.

agonize (ăg′ə-nīz′) *intr.v.* **agonized, agonizing, agonizes** To suffer mental anguish or worry about something: *agonize over a decision.*

agonizing (ăg′ə-nī′zĭng) *adj.* Causing great pain or anguish: *an agonizing decision.* —**ag′o·niz′ing·ly** *adv.*

agony (ăg′ə-nē) *n., pl.* **agonies** Intense and prolonged pain or suffering.

agora (ăg′ər-ə) *n., pl.* **agorae** (ăg′ə-rē′) *or* **agoras** The marketplace of an ancient Greek city, used as a meeting place.

agoraphobia (ăg′ər-ə-fō′bē-ə *or* ə-gôr′ə-fō′bē-ə) *n.* Fear of public places or wide open spaces. —**ag′o·ra·phobe′** (ăg′ər-ə-fōb′ *or* ə-gôr′ə-fōb′) *n.* —**ag′o·ra·pho′bic** (ăg′-ər-ə-fō′bĭk *or* ə-gôr′ə-fō′bĭk) *adj. & n.*

agouti (ə-go͞o′tē) *n., pl.* **agoutis** Any of several brownish burrowing rodents of tropical America, which resemble a rabbit with short ears or a guinea pig with long legs.

agrarian (ə-grâr′ē-ən) *adj.* **1.** Relating to or concerning farmland or its ownership: *agrarian countries.* **2.** Relating to farming or farmers; agricultural.

agrarianism (ə-grâr′ē-ə-nĭz′əm) *n.* **1.** A movement promoting rural life and agriculture as the basis for society. **2.** A movement for equitable distribution of land and for agrarian reform.

agree (ə-grē′) *v.* **agreed, agreeing, agrees** —*intr.* **1.** To have or share the same opinion; concur: *I agree with you.* **2.** To consent: *A smart investor would never agree to such a crazy scheme.* **3.** To be in harmony or accord: *The two versions of the story do not agree.* **4.** To come to an understanding or settlement: *The jury could not agree on a verdict.* **5.** To be suitable, pleasing, or healthful: *Hot peppers do not agree with me.* **6.** In grammar, to correspond in number, gender, case, or person: *In this sentence the verb agrees with the subject.* —*tr.* To grant or concede: *My friend agreed that it was time to go.*

agreeable (ə-grē′ə-bəl) *adj.* **1.** Pleasing; pleasant: *an agreeable smell.* **2.** Willing to agree or consent: *My roommate was agreeable to my request.* —**a·gree′a·ble·ness** *n.* —**a·gree′a·bly** *adv.*

agreement (ə-grē′mənt) *n.* **1.** Harmony of opinion: *The neighboring countries were in agreement and signed a treaty.* **2.** An arrangement or understanding between two parties: *an agreement between states over water rights.* **3.** In grammar, agreement between words in gender, number, case, or person. An English verb should always agree with its subject in number and person. For example, as a subject, the first-person singular pronoun *I* should be paired with a first-person singular verb like *am* rather than with a plural form like *are* or a third-person form like *is.*

agribusiness (ăg′rə-bĭz′nĭs) *n.* The business of producing, processing, and distributing agricultural products in large quantities.

agricultural (ăg′rĭ-kŭl′chər-əl) *adj.* Relating to agriculture. —**ag′ri·cul′tur·al·ly** *adv.*

agriculture (ăg′rĭ-kŭl′chər) *n.* The science, art, and business of cultivating the soil, producing crops, and raising livestock; farming.

agronomy (ə-grŏn′ə-mē) *n.* The study of soil and the improvement of crop production; scientific farming. —**a·gron′o·mist** *n.*

aground (ə-ground′) *adv. & adj.* Stranded in shallow water or on a reef or shoal: *The ship ran aground.*

ague (ā′gyōō) *n.* A disease, such as malaria, characterized by periods of chills and fever.

ah (ä) *interj.* An expression used to show surprise, delight, pity, or other emotions.

aha (ä-hä′) *interj.* An expression used to show sudden, pleased recognition or understanding: *Aha! Just as I thought, the cat was hiding behind the couch!*

ahead (ə-hĕd′) *adv.* **1.** At or to the front: *Let's move ahead to the front of the bus.* **2.** In advance: *To get tickets, you have to phone ahead.* **3.** For the future: *plan ahead.* **4.** Forward or onward: *The train moved ahead.* **5.** In or into a more advantageous position: *wanted to get ahead in life.* ◆ **be ahead** To be winning or in a superior position: *Our team is ahead by two goals.*

ahead of *prep.* **1.** In front of: *the path ahead of us.* **2.** At an earlier time than: *She arrived ahead of us.* **3.** More successful than: *a factory that is ahead of others in energy efficiency.*

ahem (ə-hĕm′) *interj.* An expression used to attract attention or to express doubt or warning.

ahold (ə-hōld′) *n.* Hold; grip: *Grab ahold of the rope.*

ahoy (ə-hoi′) *interj.* An expression used to hail a ship or to attract someone's attention.

AI An abbreviation of artificial intelligence.

aid (ād) *v.* **aided, aiding, aids** —*tr.* To provide help or assistance to: *aid a friend in distress.* —*intr.* To provide help or assistance: *Many people aided in the effort to clean up the playground.* ◆ *n.* **1.** An act or thing that provides help or assistance: *The spy was caught giving aid to the enemy. The government sent aid to the flooded region.* **2.** An assistant or helper. **3.** A device that helps or is helpful: *a hearing*

aid; visual aids used in teaching. —**aid′er** *n.*

aide (ād) *n.* **1.** An assistant or helper: *a nurse's aide.* **2.** An aide-de-camp.

aide-de-camp (ād′dĭ-kămp′) *n., pl.* **aides-de-camp** A military officer acting as secretary and assistant to a general.

AIDS (ādz) *n.* A severe disease caused by HIV, in which the immune system is attacked and weakened, making the body susceptible to other infections and to certain kinds of cancer. AIDS is short for *acquired immune deficiency syndrome.*

aigrette or **aigret** (ā-grĕt′ *or* ā′grĕt′) *n.* **1.** A tuft of upright plumes or feathers, especially those from an egret's tail. **2.** An arrangement of jewels that resembles these feathers.

aikido (ī-kē′dō *or* ī′kē-dō′) *n.* A Japanese method of self-defense in which one uses sudden holds and twisting movements to throw one's opponent to the ground.

ail (āl) *v.* **ailed, ailing, ails** —*intr.* To be ill: *She has been ailing for months.* —*tr.* To cause pain; make ill: *A high temperature is a sign that something is ailing you.*

ailanthus (ā-lăn′thəs) *n.* The tree of heaven.

aileron (ā′lə-rŏn′) *n.* A small flap on the back edge of an airplane wing that can be moved up or down to control the plane's rolling and banking movements.

ailment (āl′mənt) *n.* A mild illness or disease: *a heart ailment.*

aim (ām) *v.* **aimed, aiming, aims** —*tr.* **1.** To cause (a weapon, a device, or stream of energy) to be turned toward someone or something; point: *aimed the telescope at the moon; aimed the flashlight down the stairs.* **2.** To propel toward a point: *aimed the snowball at the window.* **3.** To form or direct (something) with a particular goal or group in mind: *aimed her campaign speeches at improving health care; aimed his criticism at the movie's director.* —*intr.* **1.** To point an object such as a weapon: *She aimed carefully at the target.* **2.** To determine a course: *aim for a better education.* **3.** To propose; intend: *aim to solve a problem.* ◆ *n.* **1a.** The act of pointing something toward a target: *take careful aim.* **b.** The ability of a person to hit a target: *The hunter's aim was perfect.* **2.** Purpose; goal: *My aim is to be a writer.*

aimless (ām′lĭs) *adj.* Without direction or purpose: *We spent an aimless afternoon strolling in the park.* —**aim′less·ly** *adv.* —**aim′less·ness** *n.*

ain't (ānt) *Nonstandard* Contraction of am not, is not, are not, has not, or have not. —SEE NOTE AT **nonstandard.**

Ainu (ī′nōō) *n., pl.* **Ainu** or **Ainus** **1.** A member of a native people of Japan now living on its northernmost islands and on islands in the possession of Russia. **2.** The language of the Ainu.

air (âr) *n.* **1.** The colorless, odorless, tasteless mixture of gases that surrounds the earth. Air contains about 78 percent nitrogen and 21 percent oxygen, with the remaining part being made up of argon, carbon dioxide, neon, helium, and other gases. **2.** The sky: *a photograph taken from the air.* **3.** Transportation by aircraft: *travel by air; ship goods by air.* **4.** The appearance or manner of a person or thing: *The judge has a very dignified air.* **5.** **airs** An affected, unnatural way of acting, intended to impress people: *putting on airs by speaking with an accent.* **6.** A melody or tune. ◆ *v.* **aired, airing, airs** —*tr.* **1.** To expose to the air so as to dry, cool, or freshen: *air a blanket.* **2.** To express publicly: *air one's grievances.* **3.** To broadcast: *networks that aired the inauguration.* —*intr.* **1.** To become fresh or cool by exposure to the air: *give the room a chance to air out.* **2.** To be broadcast: *a show* *that airs during prime time.* ◆ **in the air** Noticeable; all about: *rumors in the air.* **off the air** Not being broadcast. **on the air** Being broadcast. **up in the air** Not yet decided; uncertain.

airbag (âr′băg′) *n.* A safety device in an automobile, consisting of a bag that inflates in a collision to prevent injury to the driver or passengers.

air base *n.* A base for military aircraft.

air bladder *n.* **1.** A swim bladder of a fish. **2.** An air-filled sac in certain aquatic organisms, such as kelp, that helps maintain buoyancy.

airborne (âr′bôrn′) *adj.* **1.** Carried or transported by air: *airborne troops.* **2.** In flight; flying: *Drinks are served shortly after the plane is airborne.*

air brake *n.* A type of brake, often used on large trucks or trains, that is operated by the power of compressed air.

airbrush (âr′brŭsh′) *n.* A small spray gun used to apply paints, inks, or dyes to a surface, as in painting or drawing. ❖ *tr.v.* **airbrushed, airbrushing, airbrushes 1.** To spray with an airbrush. **2.** To alter (an image or part of an image) in order to conceal an unwanted feature.

air-condition (âr′kən-dĭsh′ən) *tr.v.* **air-conditioned, air-conditioning, air-conditions 1.** To cool or ventilate (an enclosed space) by means of an air conditioner or air conditioners. **2.** To subject to or provide with air conditioning.

air-conditioned (âr′kən-dĭsh′ənd) *adj.* Having air conditioning: *an air-conditioned theater.*

air conditioner *n.* A device that uses refrigerating coils to cool the air and reduce the humidity in a room or other enclosed space.

air conditioning *n.* A system of one or more air conditioners.

air-cooled (âr′ko͞old′) *adj.* Cooled by having air blown on it: *an air-cooled engine.*

aircraft (âr′krăft′) *n., pl.* **aircraft** A machine or device, such as an airplane, helicopter, glider, or dirigible, that is capable of flying.

aircraft carrier *n.* A large naval vessel having a long flat deck acting as a runway on which airplanes can take off and land.

airdrop (âr′drŏp′) *n.* A delivery, as of supplies or troops, by parachute from aircraft in flight. ❖ *tr. & intr.v.* **airdropped, airdropping, airdrops** To drop or be dropped from an aircraft in flight.

Airedale (âr′dāl′) *n.* A large terrier of a breed developed in England, having a wiry tan and black coat.

airfare (âr′fâr′) *n.* Fare for travel by aircraft.

airfield (âr′fēld′) *n.* An area of fields and runways where aircraft take off and land.

airflow (âr′flō′) *n.* A flow of air, especially the air currents caused by the motion of an aircraft, automobile, or similar object.

airfoil (âr′foil′) *n.* A part, such as an airplane wing, propeller blade, or rudder, that interacts with a flow of air to provide stability, rotation, lift, or thrust.

air force or **Air Force** *n.* The branch of a country's armed forces in charge of fighting war by using aircraft.

airglow (âr′glō′) *n.* A faint glow visible in the night sky, caused by chemical reactions in the upper atmosphere.

air gun *n.* A gun that is discharged by compressed air.

airhead (âr′hĕd′) *n. Slang* A silly or unintelligent person.

air hole *n.* A hole that allows for the passage of air: *I put air holes in the box so the gerbil can breathe.*

airily (âr′ə-lē) *adv.* In a carefree, light-hearted, or unconcerned manner: *He airily told me that he didn't care what I thought.*

airiness (âr′ē-nĭs) *n.* The state or quality of being airy: *the airiness of the artist's studio.*

airing (âr′ĭng) *n.* **1.** Exposure to the air as for drying, cooling, or freshening. **2.** Public expression or discussion: *an airing of unpopular views.* **3.** A broadcast: *an airing of the presidential debate.*

airless (âr′lĭs) *adj.* **1.** Having no air: *The moon is airless.* **2.** Lacking fresh air; stuffy: *a cramped and airless room.*

airlift (âr′lĭft′) *n.* A system of transporting troops, civilian passengers, or supplies by aircraft, especially when surface routes are blocked. ❖ *tr.v.* **airlifted, airlifting, airlifts** To transport in an airlift.

airline (âr′līn′) *n.* A company that transports passengers and freight by air.

airliner (âr′lī′nər) *n.* A large commercial passenger plane.

airlock (âr′lŏk′) *n.* **1.** An airtight chamber in which air pressure can be regulated to allow passage between two areas of unequal pressure. **2.** A bubble or pocket of air in a pipe that stops the flow of fluid.

airmail (âr′māl′) *n.* **1.** The system of transporting mail by aircraft. **2.** Mail transported by aircraft. ❖ *tr.v.* **airmailed, airmailing, airmails** To send (a letter, for example) by aircraft: *airmailed a package to Japan.* ❖ *adj.* Relating to airmail: *an airmail letter.*

airman (âr′mən) *n.* **1.** A pilot or other crew member of an aircraft. **2.** An enlisted person of the lowest rank in the US Air Force.

air mass *n.* A large body of air that has approximately the same temperature and humidity throughout.

air mattress *n.* An inflatable mattress.

air mile *n.* A unit of distance in air navigation equivalent to a nautical mile, about 6,076 feet (1,852 meters).

air piracy *n.* The hijacking of aircraft in flight.

airplane (âr′plān′) *n.* Any of various aircraft, usually driven by jet engines or propellors, that are held aloft by the lift generated as air flows past their wings.

air plant *n.* An epiphyte.

airplay (âr′plā′) *n.* Broadcast time given to the playing of a song, movie, or other recording: *a song that gets regular airplay on the radio.*

air pocket *n.* **1.** An isolated space containing trapped air, as in bread dough or a collapsed mine shaft. **2.** A downward current of air that makes an aircraft lose altitude suddenly.

air pollution *n.* Contamination of the atmosphere, as by the discharge of harmful industrial gases, automobile exhaust, or smoke.

airport (âr′pôrt′) *n.* A level area for aircraft to take off and land, equipped with a control tower, hangars, refueling equipment, and accommodations for passengers and cargo.

airpower or **air power** (âr′pou′ər) *n.* The military power of a nation for carrying on war in the air.

air pressure *n.* The force that is exerted by air per unit of area of a surface.

air pump *n.* A pump for compressing, removing, or forcing a flow of air.

air raid *n.* An attack by military aircraft, usually armed with bombs or rockets.

air rifle *n.* A rifle that uses compressed air or gas to shoot pellets.

air rights *pl.n.* The rights to use airspace, especially above an existing structure, such as a building or road.

air sac *n.* An air-filled space in the body, especially an alveolus of a lung or one of the spaces in a bird's body connecting the lungs and bone cavities.

air shaft *n.* A passage for letting fresh air into a tunnel, building, or other structure.

airship (âr′shĭp′) *n.* A self-propelled aircraft that is lighter than air; a dirigible.

airsick (âr′sĭk′) *adj.* Having airsickness: *an airsick passenger.*

airsickness (âr′sĭk′nĭs) *n.* Nausea and discomfort caused by the motions of an aircraft during flight.

airspace or **air space** (âr′spās′) *n.* The space in the atmosphere above a particular section of the earth.

airspeed (âr′spēd′) *n.* The speed of an aircraft relative to the air it is traveling through.

airstrip (âr′strĭp′) *n.* An aircraft runway without airport facilities.

airtight (âr′tīt′) *adj.* **1.** Allowing no air or other gas to pass in or out: *an airtight seal.* **2.** Having no weak points; sound: *an airtight excuse.*

airtime (âr′tīm′) *n.* Time during a radio or television broadcast: *a news program giving more airtime to international events.*

air-to-air (âr′tə-âr′) *adj.* Passing between aircraft while flying: *air-to-air radio communications.*

airwaves (âr′wāvz′) *pl.n.* Radio waves as used for broadcasting radio or television signals.

airway (âr′wā′) *n.* **1.** A passage through which air circulates, as in ventilating a mine. **2.** The system of passages by which air enters and exits the lungs. **3.** often **airways** An airline.

airworthy (âr′wûr′thē) *adj.* **airworthier, airworthiest** In fit condition for flight: *an airworthy plane.* —**air′wor′- thi·ness** *n.*

airy (âr′ē) *adj.* **airier, airiest 1.** Allowing air in; open to the air: *an airy porch.* **2.** Extensive in area or height; spacious: *the mansion's airy entryway.* **3.** Light; delicate: *airy silk.* **4.** Impractical or unrealistic: *airy schemes.*

aisle (īl) *n.* **1.** A passageway between rows of seats, as in an airplane or a theater. **2.** A similar passageway, as between counters in a department store. **3.** A part of a church divided from the nave, transept, or choir by a row of columns.

ajar (ə-jär′) *adv. & adj.* Partially open: *Leave the door ajar.*

Ajax (ā′jăks′) *n.* In Greek mythology, a Greek hero of great strength and courage who fought against Troy.

akimbo (ə-kĭm′bō) *adv. & adj.* With the hands on the hips and the elbows bent outward: *stood akimbo before beginning the exercises.*

akin (ə-kĭn′) *adj.* **1.** Related by blood. **2.** Derived from the same origin: *The word "maternal" is akin to the word "mother."* **3.** Having a similar quality or character: *a feeling akin to sadness.*

–al[1] A suffix that means relating to or characterized by: *adjectival; postal.*

–al[2] A suffix that means action or process: *denial; arrival.*

alabaster (ăl′ə-băs′tər) *n.* Any of various smooth, translucent minerals that are white, tinted, or banded and consist mainly of salts of calcium.

à la carte also **a la carte** (ä′ lə kärt′ *or* ăl′ə kärt′) *adv. & adj.* With a separate price for each item on the menu: *Meals in many restaurants are à la carte.*

alack (ə-lăk′) *interj.* An expression used to show sorrow, regret, or alarm.

alacrity (ə-lăk′rĭ-tē) *n.* **1.** Speed or quickness: *The clerk was working with alacrity, so we got through the line fast.* **2.** Cheerful willingness; eagerness: *They approached the difficult assignment with alacrity.*

Aladdin (ə-lăd′n) *n.* In the *Arabian Nights*, a boy who acquires a magic lamp with which he can summon a genie to fulfill any desire.

alameda (ăl′ə-mē′də *or* ăl′ə-mā′də) *n.* A shaded public walk lined with trees.

à la mode (ä′ lə mōd′ *or* ăl′ə mōd′) *adj.* **1.** According to the prevailing style or fashion. **2.** Served with ice cream: *apple pie à la mode.*

alanine (ăl′ə-nēn′) *n.* A nonessential amino acid that is found in many proteins.

alarm (ə-lärm′) *n.* **1.** Sudden fear caused by a sense of danger: *There is no cause for alarm.* **2.** A warning of approaching danger: *Rumors that the boiler broke were only a false alarm.* **3.** A device sounded to warn people of danger: *a fire alarm; a burglar alarm.* **4.** An alarm clock. ❖ *tr.v.* **alarmed, alarming, alarms 1.** To fill with alarm; frighten: *The loud noise alarmed us.* See Synonyms at **frighten. 2.** To warn of approaching danger.

alarm clock *n.* A clock that can be set to wake someone up or alert attention at a particular time, as by sounding a bell or buzzer.

alarming (ə-lär′mĭng) *adj.* Causing great fear or anxiety: *The wind is increasing at an alarming rate.* —**a·larm′ing·ly** *adv.*

alarmist (ə-lär′mĭst) *n.* A person who frightens others needlessly or for little reason.

alarum (ə-lär′əm *or* ə-lăr′əm) *n.* A warning or alarm, especially a call to arms.

alas (ə-lăs′) *interj.* An expression used to show sorrow, regret, or grief.

Alaska Native *n.* A member of any of the peoples that are native to Alaska, including Native American, Eskimo, and Aleut peoples.

Alaskan malamute *n.* A malamute.

Alaska Standard Time *n.* Standard time in the ninth time zone west of Greenwich, England, used throughout most of Alaska.

alb (ălb) *n.* A long white linen robe worn by a priest or minister during church services.

albacore (ăl′bə-kôr′) *n., pl.* **albacore** or **albacores** A large tuna that is an important source of canned fish.

Albanian (ăl-bā′nē-ən) *adj.* Relating to Albania or its people, language, or culture. ❖ *n.* **1.** A native or inhabitant of Albania. **2.** The Indo-European language of Albania.

albatross (ăl′bə-trôs′) *n., pl.* **albatross** or **albatrosses 1.** Any of several large, web-footed seabirds with a hooked beak and very long wings. **2.** Something that prevents one from accomplishing something or is impossible to bring to completion: *the albatross of high debt.*

WORD HISTORY The word **albatross** sometimes means "something that is a sign of failure or is an obstacle to success," as in *The project started out well enough but has turned into an albatross.* How did this meaning get attached to the name of a seabird? By a poem! The poem is *The Rime of the Ancient Mariner,* by Samuel Taylor Coleridge. In the poem an old sailor tells the tale of how he shot an albatross with an arrow, and soon afterward the wind died and the ship he was on stalled out at sea. The crew members thought shooting the albatross had brought bad luck, and they blamed the ancient mariner, hanging the dead bird around his neck in punishment.

albedo (ăl-bē′dō) *n., pl.* **albedos** The fraction of light, expressed as a decimal, that is reflected by a surface such as a planet or a snow-covered area. An object with high albedo is bright; one with low albedo is dark.

albeit (ôl-bē′ĭt *or* ăl-bē′ĭt) *conj.* Even though; although: *They proposed an imaginative, albeit somewhat impractical, idea.*

albinism (ăl′bə-nĭz′əm) *n.* The condition of being an albino.

albino (ăl-bī′nō) *n., pl.* **albinos** A person or other animal born with little or no pigment in the skin, hair, and eyes, usually having light-colored skin and hair and problems with vision.

album (ăl′bəm) *n.* **1.** A book with blank pages on which to mount such things as photographs or stamps or to collect autographs. **2.** A collection of personal photographs or other images that are arranged for private viewing, as in book or on a computer. **3.** A set of musical recordings that are issued together, usually by a single artist.

albumen (ăl-byōō′mən) *n.* **1.** The white of an egg, consisting mostly of albumin dissolved in water. **2.** Albumin.

albumin (ăl-byōō′mĭn) *n.* Any of several simple proteins that dissolve in water, coagulate on being heated, and are found especially in egg white, blood, and milk.

alchemist (ăl′kə-mĭst) *n.* A person who practices alchemy.

alchemy (ăl′kə-mē) *n.* A medieval system of chemistry that had among its aims the changing of common metals into gold and the preparation of a potion that gives eternal youth. —SEE NOTE AT **alkali.**

alcohol (ăl′kə-hôl′) *n.* **1.** Any of a large number of flammable organic compounds that contain the hydroxyl group OH, especially ethanol, the form that occurs in wines and liquors. **2.** Alcoholic beverages in general.

alcoholic (ăl′kə-hô′lĭk) *adj.* **1.** Relating to or containing alcohol, especially ethanol: *an alcoholic beverage.* **2.** Having an addiction to alcoholic beverages. ❖ *n.* A person who has an addiction to alcoholic beverages.

alcoholism (ăl′kə-hô-lĭz′əm) *n.* Addiction to alcoholic beverages, which can lead to liver disease and other serious health problems.

alcove (ăl′kōv′) *n.* A small room opening on a larger one without being separated from it by a wall or door. —SEE NOTE AT **alkali.**

al dente (ăl dĕn′tē *or* äl dĕn′tā) *adj.* Cooked enough to be slightly softened but still firm to the bite: *pasta al dente.* —**al den′te** *adv.*

alder (ôl′dər) *n.* Any of various shrubs or small trees of cool damp places, having toothed leaves and woody, conelike catkins.

alderman (ôl′dər-mən) *n.* A member of the governing body of a city or town.

ale (āl) *n.* A traditional type of beer that is usually relatively dark and flavorful.

alee (ə-lē′) *adv.* Away from the wind; leeward.

alert (ə-lûrt′) *adj.* **1.** Watchful; attentive; vigilant: *A good driver must remain constantly alert.* **2.** Mentally quick; perceptive; intelligent: *an alert child.* ❖ *n.* **1.** A warning signal against danger or attack. **2.** The period during which one must obey this signal. ❖ *tr.v.* **alerted, alerting, alerts 1.** To warn of approaching danger. **2.** To make aware of: *alert the public to the need for pollution control.* ◆ **on the alert** Watchful and prepared: *The police are on*

the alert to prevent vandalism. —**a·lert′ly** *adv.* —**a·lert′ness** *n.*

Aleut (ə-lōōt′ *or* ăl′ē-ōōt′) *n., pl.* **Aleut** or **Aleuts 1.** A member of a Native American people inhabiting the Aleutian Islands of Alaska. **2.** Either of two languages, related to Eskimo, spoken by the Aleut. —**A·leu′tian** (ə-lōō′shən) *adj.*

alewife (āl′wīf′) *n., pl.* **alewives** (āl′wīvz′) A fish of North American Atlantic waters that swims up rivers to spawn.

Alexandrian (ăl′ĭg-zăn′drē-ən) *adj.* **1.** Relating to Alexandria, a city of northern Egypt on the Mediterranean Sea that was founded by Alexander the Great. **2.** Relating to Alexander the Great, ruler of the southeast European kingdom of Macedonia from 336 to 323 BC and conqueror of much of the Middle East.

alfalfa (ăl-făl′fə) *n.* A plant having compound leaves with three leaflets and clusters of purplish flowers, grown as feed for cattle and other livestock.

alfresco (ăl-frĕs′kō) *adv. & adj.* In the fresh air; outdoors: *dining alfresco.*

alga (ăl′gə) *n., pl.* **algae** (ăl′jē) Any of various green, red, or brown organisms that lack true roots, stems, and leaves, are usually found in water, and range from single cells to large spreading seaweeds. Algae make their own food through photosynthesis. —**al′gal** (ăl′gəl) *adj.*

algebra (ăl′jə-brə) *n.* A branch of mathematics that deals with the relations and properties of quantities by the use of letters and other symbols to represent unknown numbers, especially in equations, in order to solve problems. —**al′ge·bra′ic** (ăl′jə-brā′ĭk) *adj.* —SEE NOTE AT **alkali.**

Algonquian (ăl-gŏng′kwē-ən *or* ăl-gŏng′kē-ən) *n., pl.* **Algonquian** or **Algonquians 1.** A family of Native American languages spoken over a large area of North America, including Ojibwa, Cree, and Blackfoot. **2.** A member of a people traditionally speaking an Algonquian language. —**Al·gon′qui·an** *adj.*

Algonquin (ăl-gŏng′kwĭn *or* ăl-gŏng′kĭn) *n., pl.* **Algonquin** or **Algonquins 1a.** A member of a Native American people living along the Ottawa River in Canada. **b.** The Algonquian language of this people. **2a.** A member of an Algonquian people. **b.** An Algonquian language. —**Al·gon′quin** *adj.*

algorithm (ăl′gə-rĭth′əm) *n.* A mathematical rule or process for computing a desired result: *an algorithm used in a computer program.*

alias (ā′lē-əs) *n.* An assumed name used to conceal a person's real identity. ❖ *adv.* Otherwise named: *William Blake, alias James Flynn.*

Ali Baba (ä′lē bä′bə *or* ăl′ē bä′bə) *n.* In the *Arabian Nights,* a poor woodcutter who gains entrance to the treasure cave of the forty thieves by saying "Open Sesame!"

alibi (ăl′ə-bī′) *n., pl.* **alibis 1.** A claim that one was elsewhere when a crime or other wrongdoing was committed. **2.** Someone who can personally confirm such a claim. **3.** *Informal* An excuse: *No more of your alibis!*

alien (āl′yən, ā′lē-ən) *adj.* **1.** Belonging to or coming from another country; foreign: *alien residents.* **2.** Unfamiliar or strange: *Having lived in the city, he found the suburb an alien place.* **3.** Inconsistent or opposed; contradictory: *an idea wholly alien to my philosophy.* ❖ *n.* **1.** A person living in one country while remaining a citizen of another. **2.** A being from outer space: *In the movie, Earth is invaded by aliens.* **3.** A species that is living or growing in a region to which it is not native: *starlings and other aliens that were introduced to North America.*

alienate (āl′yə-nāt′) *tr.v.* **alienated, alienating, alienates** **1.** To lose the friendship or support of; estrange: *A barking dog tends to alienate the neighbors.* **2.** To cause to become emotionally withdrawn or isolated: *Treating people as if they were just numbers in a computer alienates them.* —**al′ien·a′tor** *n.*

alienation (āl′yə-nā′shən) *n.* The act of alienating or the condition of being alienated: *After two weeks of alienation, they made up and became friends again.*

alight[1] (ə-līt′) *intr.v.* **alighted** or **alit** (ə-līt′), **alighting, alights 1.** To come down and settle, as after flight: *A bird alighted on the branch.* **2.** To get off; dismount: *Passengers alighted from a train.*

alight[2] (ə-līt′) *adj.* **1.** On fire; burning: *The discarded match was still alight.* **2.** Lighted; lit up: *The sky was alight with millions of stars.*

WORD HISTORY Alight[1] and **alight**[2] ultimately come from two different Old English words spelled *līhtan*, one meaning "to make less heavy" and the other meaning "to shine."

align (ə-līn′) *v.* **aligned, aligning, aligns** —*tr.* **1.** To arrange in a straight line: *The chairs were aligned in two rows.* **2.** To ally (oneself) with one side, as of an argument or cause: *The allies usually align themselves behind the same position in foreign policy.* **3.** To adjust (a device, mechanism, or some of its parts) in order to produce a proper relationship or condition: *The mechanic aligned the wheels of my car.* —*intr.* To fall into line: *The soldiers aligned.*

alignment (ə-līn′mənt) *n.* **1.** Arrangement or position in a straight line: *perfect alignment of the teeth.* **2.** The process of aligning a device or the condition of being aligned: *A mechanic must perform a wheel alignment on the car. The wheels are out of alignment.* **3.** An arrangement or positioning of players on a sports team: *Once we got a lead, the coach used a new defensive alignment.* **4.** The act of allying or the state of being allied: *the administration's policy of alignment with other democratic nations.*

alike (ə-līk′) *adj.* **1.** Having close resemblance; similar: *Mother and daughter are very much alike.* **2.** Exactly or nearly exactly the same: *Parts for plumbing must be alike to fit.* ❖ *adv.* In the same way or manner or to the same degree: *We must try to treat everyone alike.*

alimentary (ăl′ə-měn′tə-rē *or* ăl′ə-měn′trē) *adj.* Relating to food, nutrition, or digestion.

alimentary canal *n.* The digestive tract.

alimony (ăl′ə-mō′nē) *n., pl.* **alimonies** An amount of money that a court orders a divorced person to pay as support to a former spouse.

aliphatic (ăl′ə-făt′ĭk) *adj.* Relating to organic chemical compounds in which the carbon atoms are linked together in straight chains rather than in rings.

alit (ə-līt′) *v.* A past tense and a past participle of **alight**[1].

alive (ə-līv′) *adj.* **1.** Having life; living: *The snake looked dead, but when it started to move we realized it was alive.* **2.** In existence or operation; active: *She kept her hopes alive despite the bad news.* **3.** Full of life; animated; alert: *The audience came alive when the band came onstage.* —**a·live′ness** *n.*

alkali (ăl′kə-lī′) *n., pl.* **alkalis** or **alkalies 1.** A strong base or hydroxide, such as ammonia or lye, that is soluble in water, neutralizes acids, and forms salts with them. Alkalis turn red litmus paper blue. **2.** A salt or mixture of salts that neutralizes acids and is found in arid soils.

WORD HISTORY Many English words that begin with *al*- are borrowed from Arabic, where *al*- means "the." Many of these words concern chemistry and mathematics, to which Arab scientists made important contributions in the early Middle Ages. Thus **alkali** is from *al-qily,* "the ashes, the lye." **Alchemy** is from *al-kīmiyā',* "the science of chemistry." **Algebra** is from *al-jabr,* "the setting of broken bones, the restoring"—that is, moving a term from one side of an equation to the other in order to put it in a form that is easier to solve. And **alcove** comes from *al-qubba,* "the vault."

alkali metal *n.* Any of a group of soft white metals that melt at low temperature, have a low density, and are highly reactive. They include lithium, sodium, potassium, rubidium, cesium, and francium. See **Periodic Table**.

alkaline (ăl′kə-lĭn *or* ăl′kə-līn′) *adj.* **1.** Relating to or containing an alkali. **2.** Having a pH greater than 7; basic.

alkaline-earth metal (ăl′kə-lĭn-ûrth′ *or* ăl′kə-līn′ûrth′) *n.* Any of a group of metallic elements that includes beryllium, magnesium, calcium, strontium, barium, and radium. See **Periodic Table**.

alkalinity (ăl′kə-lĭn′ĭ-tē) *n.* The alkali concentration or alkaline quality of a substance.

alkalize (ăl′kə-līz′) *tr. & intr.v.* **alkalized, alkalizing, alkalizes** To make or become alkaline or an alkali.

alkaloid (ăl′kə-loid′) *n.* Any of a class of alkaline organic compounds that contain nitrogen, including nicotine, quinine, and morphine. Many of these compounds are derived from plants.

all (ôl) *adj.* **1.** The total number of: *All cows eat grass. All the windows are open.* **2.** The whole of: *We spent all day in the museum.* **3.** The utmost possible: *In all seriousness, I think you should apply for the job.* **4.** Every: *He enjoys all manner of cooking.* **5.** Any: *proven beyond all doubt.* ❖ *n.* Everything one has: *The winning team gave their all.* ❖ *pron.* **1.** The whole amount: *All of the flowers grew.* **2.** Each and every one: *All aboard the ship were saved.* ❖ *adv.* **1.** Wholly; entirely: *The instructions are all wrong.* **2.** Each; apiece: *a score of five all.* ◆ **all along** From the beginning; throughout: *They saw through my disguise all along.* ◆ **all but** Nearly; almost: *The patient all but fainted.*

all in all Everything being taken into account: *All in all, she's a good athlete.* **all of** *Informal* Not more than: *I was gone for all of an hour.* **all that** *Informal* To the degree expected: *It's not all that hard.* **all the same** Nevertheless; anyway: *It was hard, but I managed all the same.* **at all 1.** In any way: *I couldn't sleep at all.* **2.** To any extent; whatever: *not at all sorry.* **in all** Altogether: *The two buses held 100 passengers in all.*

Allah (ä′lə) *n.* God, especially in Islam.

all-American (ôl′ə-měr′ĭ-kən) *adj.* **1.** Typical of the people of the United States or their ideals: *an all-American hero.* **2.** In sports, chosen as the best amateur in the United States at a particular position or event: *an all-American fullback.* **3.** Composed entirely of American elements or materials: *The band played an all-American program.* ❖ *n.* An all-American athlete.

allantois (ə-lăn′tō-ĭs) *n., pl.* **allantoides** (ăl′ən-tō′ĭ-dēz′) A membranous sac that develops from the lower end of the digestive tract in the embryos of mammals, birds, and reptiles. In most mammals it becomes part of the placenta and the umbilical cord.

all-around (ôl′ə-round′) also **all-round** (ôl′round′) *adj.*

1. Comprehensive in extent: *an all-around education.* **2.** Able to do many or all things well: *an all-around athlete.*

allay (ə-lā′) *tr.v.* **allayed, allaying, allays 1.** To set to rest; calm: *allay one's fears.* **2.** To lessen; reduce: *allay pain.* —**al·lay′er** *n.*

all clear *n.* A signal, usually by siren, that an air raid, threat of a tornado, or other danger is over.

allegation (ăl′ĭ-gā′shən) *n.* An assertion that someone has done something wrong, often made without proof.

allege (ə-lĕj′) *tr.v.* **alleged, alleging, alleges** To declare to be true, usually without offering proof: *The indictment alleges that the mayor took bribes.* —**al·lege′a·ble** *adj.* —**al·leg′er** *n.*

alleged (ə-lĕjd′ *or* ə-lĕj′ĭd) *adj.* Stated to be as described but without proof; supposed: *The alleged thief turned out to be innocent.* —**al·leg′ed·ly** (ə-lĕj′ĭd-lē) *adv.*

allegiance (ə-lē′jəns) *n.* Loyalty or devotion, as to one's country, a ruler, or a cause: *pledge allegiance to the United States.*

allegorical (ăl′ĭ-gôr′ĭ-kəl) *adj.* Relating to or containing allegory: *In the allegorical tale, the owl represents wisdom.* —**al′le·gor′i·cal·ly** *adv.*

allegory (ăl′ĭ-gôr′ē) *n., pl.* **allegories** A story, play, or picture in which characters or events stand for ideas or principles.

allegretto (ä′lĭ-grĕt′ō) *adv. & adj.* In music, in a manner slightly slower than allegro.

allegro (ə-lĕg′rō *or* ə-lā′grō) *adv. & adj.* In music, in a quick lively manner.

allele (ə-lēl′) *n.* Any of the versions in which a particular gene exists.

alleluia (ăl′ə-lōō′yə) *interj.* Hallelujah.

Allen wrench (ăl′ən) *n.* An L-shaped wrench with a six-sided end, used to turn screws that have a six-sided hole.

allergen (ăl′ər-jən) *n.* A substance, such as pollen, that causes an allergy.

allergenic (ăl′ər-jĕn′ĭk) *adj.* Causing an allergic reaction. —**al′ler·gen′i·cal·ly** *adv.*

allergic (ə-lûr′jĭk) *adj.* **1.** Relating to or caused by an allergy: *an allergic reaction.* **2.** Having an allergy: *allergic to fish.* **3.** *Informal* Having a dislike; averse: *allergic to hard work.*

allergist (ăl′ər-jĭst) *n.* A physician who specializes in the diagnosis and treatment of allergies.

allergy (ăl′ər-jē) *n., pl.* **allergies** A disorder in which exposure to a substance, such as pollen, cat dander, or certain foods, causes a reaction that may include difficulty in breathing, sneezing, watering of the eyes, and a skin rash.

alleviate (ə-lē′vē-āt′) *tr.v.* **alleviated, alleviating, alleviates** To make more bearable; relieve; lessen: *Medicine will alleviate the pain.* —**al·le′vi·a′tion** *n.* —**al·le′vi·a′-tor** *n.*

alley (ăl′ē) *n., pl.* **alleys 1.** A narrow street or passageway between or behind buildings. **2.** A path between flowerbeds or trees in a garden or park. **3.** A bowling alley. ◆ **up (one's) alley** *Informal* Suitable to one's interests or abilities.

alley cat *n.* A homeless or stray cat in an urban area.

alleyway (ăl′ē-wā′) *n.* A narrow passage between buildings.

All Fools′ Day *n.* April Fools′ Day.

Allhallows (ôl′hăl′ōz) *n.* All Saints′ Day.

alliance (ə-lī′əns) *n.* **1.** A formal agreement or union between nations, organizations, or individuals: *Britain and France sealed their alliance with a treaty.* **2.** A connection based on marriage, friendship, or common interest: *There is a strong alliance between cousins in that family.*

allied (ə-līd′ *or* ăl′īd′) *adj.* **1.** Joined together in an alliance: *the allied countries of Europe.* **2.** Similar; related: *Biology and medicine are allied sciences.* **3.** **Allied** Relating to allied countries, especially the countries that fought against Germany and its allies in World War I and World War II.

alligator (ăl′ĭ-gā′tər) *n.* **1.** Either of two large reptiles having tough skin, sharp teeth, and powerful jaws, and living in lakes, rivers, or other wet areas. An alligator's snout is broader and shorter than a crocodile's. **2.** Leather made from the hide of an alligator.

alligator pear *n.* An avocado.

all-important (ôl′ĭm-pôr′tnt) *adj.* Very important; vital; crucial: *all-important efforts to keep the peace.*

all-inclusive (ôl′ĭn-klōō′sĭv) *adj.* Including everything, especially for a single price: *an all-inclusive stay at a tropical resort hotel.* —**all′-in·clu′sive·ness** *n.*

alliteration (ə-lĭt′ə-rā′shən) *n.* The repetition of the same sounds, usually consonants, especially at the beginning of words, as in *large luscious lemons.*

alliterative (ə-lĭt′ə-rā′tĭv *or* ə-lĭt′ər-ə-tĭv) *adj.* Showing or characterized by alliteration: *an alliterative phrase.*

all-night (ôl′nīt′) *adj.* **1.** Continuing all night: *an all-night radio program.* **2.** Open all night: *an all-night diner.*

all nighter *or* **all-nighter** (ôl′nī′tər) *n. Informal* A project or event lasting all through the night, especially an intense period of study or work: *pulled an all nighter to finish the assignment on time.*

allocate (ăl′ə-kāt′) *tr.v.* **allocated, allocating, allocates** To set aside for a particular purpose: *allocated government funds for disaster relief.* —**al′lo·ca′tion** *n.*

allot (ə-lŏt′) *tr.v.* **allotted, allotting, allots 1.** To distribute or parcel out: *The profits of the business were allotted equally to each partner.* **2.** To assign a portion for a particular purpose; allocate: *We allotted 20 minutes for each speaker in the discussion.* —**al·lot′ter** *n.*

allotment (ə-lŏt′mənt) *n.* **1.** The act of allotting. **2.** Something allotted: *The soldiers′ allotment of coffee was reduced during the winter.*

allotrope (ăl′ə-trōp′) *n.* Any of the different structural forms that a chemical element may have. Charcoal, graphite, and diamond are allotropes of carbon.

allotropic (ăl′ə-trŏp′ĭk *or* ăl′ə-trō′pĭk) *adj.* Relating to or having allotropes.

allotropy (ə-lŏt′rə-pē) *n.* The existence of different forms of the same chemical element, each form having a different structure of atoms.

all out *adv.* With every possible effort; vigorously: *studied all out and got an A in the course.*

all-out (ôl′out′) *adj.* Using all available resources; vigorous: *an all-out effort.*

all over *adv.* **1.** Over the whole area or extent: *a cloth embroidered all over with roses.* **2.** Everywhere: *searched all over for the keys.* **3.** In every respect; utterly: *Carefree and fun-loving—that's him all over.*

allow (ə-lou′) *tr.v.* **allowed, allowing, allows 1.** To accept (an activity) as proper or right; not prevent or prohibit: *Is eating ever allowed in the library?* **2.** To accept the activity of (someone) as proper or right: *Please allow me to finish.* **3.** To let (someone) have (something): *We allowed* *ourselves a treat.* **4.** To accept the presence of; let in: *We do not allow the dog upstairs.* **5.** To make provision for; assign: *The schedule allows time for a break before the second speaker.* **6.** To admit; concede; grant: *I'll allow that some mistakes have been made.* **7.** To give as a discount or in exchange: *The store allowed me $20 on my old hockey equipment.* ◆ **allow for** To take into consideration and make a provision for: *Our plans allow for changes in the weather.*

allowable (ə-lou′ə-bəl) *adj.* Capable of being allowed; permissible. —**al·low′a·bly** *adv.*

allowance (ə-lou′əns) *n.* **1.** The act of allowing. **2.** An amount, as of money or food, given at regular intervals or for a specific purpose: *a weekly allowance of $10; a travel allowance.* **3.** A price reduction given in exchange for used merchandise: *an allowance of $500 on one's old car.*

alloy (ăl′oi′ *or* ə-loi′) *n.* **1.** A metal made by mixing and fusing two or more metals, or a metal and a nonmetal, to obtain desirable qualities such as hardness, lightness, and strength: *Pewter is an alloy of copper, antimony, and lead.* **2.** A combination or mixture: *an alloy of sadness and relief.* ◆ *tr.v.* (ə-loi′ *or* ăl′oi′) **alloyed, alloying, alloys** **1.** To combine (metals) to form an alloy. **2.** To combine; mix: *My excitement was alloyed with doubts.*

all-purpose (ôl′pûr′pəs) *adj.* Useful in many ways: *an all-purpose thread.*

all right *adj.* **1.** Satisfactory; in good condition: *The tires are old but all right.* **2.** Acceptable; allowable: *Going to the zoo is all right with me.* **3.** Correct: *These figures are perfectly all right.* **4.** Average; mediocre: *This work is all right, but it could be better.* **5.** Not injured; safe: *Are you all right?* ◆ *adv.* **1.** In a satisfactory way: *The motor was running all right.* **2.** Very well; yes: *All right, I'll go.* **3.** Without a doubt: *That's him, all right!*

all-round (ôl′round′) *adj.* Variant of **all-around.**

All Saints' Day *n.* November 1, observed by Christians as a feast in honor of all the saints.

All Souls' Day *n.* November 2, observed by Roman Catholics as a day of prayer for the souls in purgatory.

allspice (ôl′spīs′) *n.* **1.** The fragrant strong-flavored berries of a tropical American tree, dried and used as a spice. **2.** The tree that bears such berries.

all-star (ôl′stär′) *adj.* Made up entirely of star performers: *an all-star cast.* ◆ *n.* A person chosen for an all-star team, cast, or other group.

all-time (ôl′tīm′) *adj.* Unsurpassed until now; of all time: *set an all-time attendance record.*

allude (ə-lood′) *intr.v.* **alluded, alluding, alludes** To refer to something indirectly; mention something casually or in passing: *It is considered impolite to allude to how much money a person has.*

allure (ə-loor′) *tr.v.* **allured, alluring, allures** To attract; entice: *I was allured to the movie by the ads.* ◆ *n.* Strong attraction; fascination: *the allure of sailing.*

allusion (ə-loo′zhən) *n.* **1.** The act of alluding; indirect reference. **2.** An instance of indirect reference: *allusions to Greek mythology in the poems.*

allusive (ə-loo′sĭv) *adj.* Containing or making allusions; suggestive. —**al·lu′sive·ly** *adv.*

alluvial (ə-loo′vē-əl) *adj.* Relating to or found in alluvium: *rich alluvial deposits at the mouth of the river.*

alluvial fan *n.* A fan-shaped mass of alluvium deposited at the mouth of a ravine or where a tributary stream joins the main stream.

alluvium (ə-loo′vē-əm) *n., pl.* **alluviums** or **alluvia** (ə-loo′-vē-ə) Sand, silt, mud, or other matter deposited by flow-

ing water, as in a riverbed, river delta, or flood plain.

ally (ə-lī′ *or* ăl′ī) *tr.v.* **allied, allying, allies** To join or unite for a specific purpose: *The United States allied itself with the Soviet Union during World War II.* ◆ *n.* (ăl′ī *or* ə-lī′) *pl.* **allies** **1.** A person or country that is allied to another. **2. Allies a.** The nations, including Russia, France, Great Britain, and the United States, that were allied against the Central Powers during World War I. **b.** The nations, including Great Britain, the Soviet Union, and the United States, that were allied against the Axis during World War II.

alma mater *or* **Alma Mater** (äl′mə mä′tər *or* äl′mə mä′-tər) *n.* **1.** The school, college, or university that a person has attended. **2.** The song or anthem of a school, college, or university.

almanac (ôl′mə-năk′ *or* ăl′mə-năk′) *n.* **1.** A book published once a year containing calendars with weather forecasts, astronomical information, tide tables, and other related information. **2.** A book published once a year containing lists, charts, and other information, especially in many different fields.

almighty (ôl-mī′tē) *adj.* All-powerful; omnipotent: *almighty God.* ◆ *n.* **Almighty** God. —**al·might′i·ly** *adv.*

almond (ä′mənd *or* äl′mənd *or* ăm′ənd) *n.* **1.** An oval edible nut having a soft light-brown shell. **2.** The tree, native to the Mediterranean region, that bears such nuts.

almond milk *n.* A milky liquid made with ground almonds and water, used in foods or as a beverage.

almoner (äl′mə-nər *or* ä′mə-nər) *n.* A person who gives out alms, as for a king or monastery.

almost (ôl′mōst′ *or* ôl-mōst′) *adv.* Slightly short of; not quite: *was almost asleep when the doorbell rang.*

alms (ämz) *pl.n.* Money or goods given to the poor as charity.

almshouse (ämz′hous′) *n.* A home for the poor, especially one that is maintained by private charity.

alnico (ăl′nĭ-kō′) *n.* Any of several alloys of iron, aluminum, nickel, cobalt and sometimes copper, niobium, or tantalum, used to make strong permanent magnets.

aloe (ăl′ō) *n.* Any of various tropical plants, chiefly of Africa, having thick spiny-toothed leaves and red or yellow flowers.

aloe vera (vĕr′ə *or* vîr′ə) *n.* **1.** An aloe native to the Mediterranean region. **2.** The juice or gel obtained from the leaves of this plant, widely used in cosmetics and medicinal preparations, especially for use on the skin.

aloft (ə-lôft′) *adv.* **1.** In or into a high place; high or higher up: *Jet planes fly thousands of feet aloft.* **2.** In or toward a ship's upper rigging.

aloha (ə-lō′hə *or* ä-lō′hä′) *interj.* An expression used as a greeting or farewell. It is the Hawaiian word for "love." —SEE NOTE AT **ukulele.**

alone (ə-lōn′) *adj.* **1.** Apart from the company of anyone else: *Once her friends left and she was alone in the studio, she was able to practice without interruption.* **2.** Being without anyone or anything else; only: *The professor alone knows when the quiz will be given.* ◆ *adv.* **1.** Without others: *She likes to travel alone.* **2.** Without aid or help: *I can lift the rock alone.* ◆ **leave well enough alone** or **let well enough alone** To be satisfied with things as they are and not try to change them. —**a·lone′ness** *n.*

◆ **SYNONYMS** alone, lonely, lonesome, solitary *adj.*

along (ə-lông′) *prep.* **1.** Over the length of: *walked along the path.* **2.** On a line or course close to; beside: *trees growing along the river.* **3.** In accordance with: *Congress* *was split along party lines.* ❖ *adv.* **1.** Forward; onward: *The train moved along, crossing the plains.* **2.** As company: *Bring your friend along.* **3.** As an associate piece; together: *packed her binoculars along with her hiking boots.* **4.** On one's person; in hand: *He took a camera along.* —SEE NOTE AT **together.**

alongside (ə-lông′sīd′) *adv.* At or near the side; to the side: *stood with a bodyguard alongside; drove up alongside.* ❖ *prep.* By the side of; side by side with: *The boat is alongside the dock.*

aloof (ə-lōof′) *adj.* Distant, reserved, or indifferent in manner: *an aloof manner.* ❖ *adv.* At a distance but within view; apart; withdrawn: *The new student stood aloof from the others.* —a·loof′ly *adv.* —a·loof′ness *n.*

aloud (ə-loud′) *adv.* **1.** With the voice: *Read the story aloud.* **2.** In a loud tone; loudly: *If we speak aloud, it will awaken the baby.*

alp (ălp) *n.* A high mountain.

alpaca (ăl-păk′ə) *n., pl.* **alpaca** or **alpacas 1.** A South American mammal related to the llama, having long silky wool. **2.** Cloth made from the wool of this mammal. **3.** A fabric that is similar to alpaca.

alpenhorn (ăl′pən-hôrn′) *n.* A curved wooden horn traditionally used by herders in Switzerland and neighboring regions to call cows to pasture.

alpenstock (ăl′pən-stŏk′) *n.* A long staff with an iron point formerly used by mountain climbers.

alpha (ăl′fə) *n.* **1.** The first letter of the Greek alphabet, written A, α. In English it is represented as *A, a.* **2.** The first one; the beginning.

alpha and omega *n.* **1.** The first and the last. **2.** The most important part of something.

alphabet (ăl′fə-bĕt′) *n.* **1.** The letters of a language, arranged in the order fixed by custom. **2.** A system of characters or symbols representing sounds or things.

alphabetical (ăl′fə-bĕt′ĭ-kəl) also **alphabetic** (ăl′fə-bĕt′-ĭk) *adj.* **1.** Arranged in the order of the alphabet: *The dictionary lists words in alphabetical order.* **2.** Based on or using an alphabet: *an alphabetic writing system.* —al′pha·bet′i·cal·ly *adv.*

alphabetize (ăl′fə-bĭ-tīz′) *tr.v.* **alphabetized, alphabetizing, alphabetizes** To arrange in alphabetical order. —al′pha·bet′i·za′tion (ăl′fə-bĕt′ĭ-zā′shən) *n.*

alphanumeric (ăl′fə-nōō-mĕr′ĭk) *adj.* Consisting of or using letters, numbers, punctuation marks, and other conventional symbols: *an alphanumeric computer code.*

alpha particle *n.* A positively charged particle that consists of two protons and two neutrons bound together. It is identical with the nucleus of a helium atom.

alpha ray *n.* A narrow stream of alpha particles.

alpine (ăl′pīn′) *adj.* **1.** Relating to, living on, or growing in high mountains: *Edelweiss is an alpine plant.* **2. Alpine** Relating to the Alps, a mountain range of central and western Europe.

al-Qaeda (ăl-kī′də or ăl-kā′də) *n.* An international organization that tries to advance Islamic fundamentalism and disrupt the economies and influence of Western nations through attacks and bombings.

already (ôl-rĕd′ē) *adv.* **1.** By this time: *They are late and should be here already.* **2.** So soon: *Are you leaving already?*

alright (ôl-rīt′) *adv. Nonstandard* All right.

Alsatian (ăl-sā′shən) *adj.* Relating to the region of Alsace

in eastern France or to its inhabitants or culture. ❖ *n.* **1.** A native or inhabitant of Alsace. **2.** *Chiefly British* A German shepherd.

also (ôl′sō) *adv.* **1.** In addition; besides: *The label lists the ingredients and also gives nutritional information.* **2.** Likewise: *If you will stay, I will also.* ❖ *conj.* And in addition: *Many students studied French and math, also music and drawing.* —SEE NOTE AT **not.**

also-ran (ôl′sō-răn′) *n.* **1.** A horse that does not come in first, second, or third in a race. **2.** A person or thing that is defeated in a race, election, or other competition; a loser.

alt. An abbreviation of: **1.** alternate. **2.** altitude.

altar (ôl′tər) *n.* An elevated structure, often in the form of a table, before which religious ceremonies are conducted or upon which sacrifices are offered.

altar boy *n.* A boy who is an altar server.

altar girl *n.* A girl who is an altar server.

altarpiece (ôl′tər-pēs′) *n.* A painting, carving, or similar work of art behind and above an altar in a church.

altar server *n.* An attendant who helps a priest in performing a Christian religious service.

alter (ôl′tər) *v.* **altered, altering, alters** —*tr.* **1.** To change or make different; modify: *We altered our plans for the weekend.* **2.** To adjust (a garment) for a better fit: *You will have to have this jacket altered.* —*intr.* To change or become different: *Since their trip abroad, their whole outlook has altered.* —al′ter·a·ble *adj.* —al′ter·a·bly *adv.*

alteration (ôl′tə-rā′shən) *n.* **1.** The act or process of changing or altering: *Alteration of the school took several months.* **2.** A change: *many alterations to a suit.*

altercation (ôl′tər-kā′shən) *n.* A noisy angry quarrel.

alter ego *n.* **1.** Another side of oneself; a second personality. **2.** An intimate friend or constant companion.

alternate (ôl′tər-nāt′) *v.* **alternated, alternating, alternates** —*intr.* **1a.** To occur in a repeating pattern or succession: *Showers alternated with sunshine.* **b.** To act or proceed by turns: *We alternated at the computer.* **2.** To pass back and forth from one state, action, or place to another: *alternate between hope and despair.* **3.** To reverse direction of flow at regular intervals: *measured how frequently the current alternates.* —*tr.* To do, perform, or use in turns: *We alternated shoveling and raking the topsoil.* ❖ *adj.* (ôl′tər-nĭt) **1.** Occurring in turns; succeeding each other: *alternate periods of rain and drought.* **2.** Every other; every second: *She works on alternate days of the week.* **3.** In place of another: *an alternate route.* ❖ *n.* (ôl′tər-nĭt) A person acting in place of another.

alternate angles (ôl′tər-nĭt) *pl.n.* Two angles, both interior or both exterior but not adjacent, formed on opposite sides of a line that crosses two other lines. If the two lines are parallel, the alternate angles are equal.

alternately (ôl′tər-nĭt-lē) *adv.* In alternate order; in turn: *The crowd alternately booed and cheered.*

alternating current (ôl′tər-nā′tĭng) *n.* An electric current that reverses its direction of flow at regular intervals.

alternation (ôl′tər-nā′shən) *n.* Regular and repeated change between two or more things: *the alternation of the seasons.*

alternative (ôl-tûr′nə-tĭv) *n.* **1.** One of two or more possibilities from which to choose: *We had two alternatives: to continue driving or wait for the storm to pass.* **2.** A choice between two or more possibilities: *We face the alternative of raising more money or canceling the program.* See Synonyms at **choice.** **3.** A remaining choice: *I have no alternative but to go without you.* ❖ *adj.* **1.** Relating to or allowing a choice between two or more possibilities: *The highway is closed. Seek alternative routes.* **2.** Existing outside traditional or established institutions or systems: *sources of alternative energy.* —**al·ter′na·tive·ly** *adv.*

alternative medicine *n.* Any of various health care practices, such as homeopathy and acupuncture, that are generally not included in traditional Western medical teaching.

alternator (ôl′tər-nā′tər) *n.* An electric generator that makes alternating current, especially one powered by a car's engine and used to keep the battery charged.

although (ôl-*th*ō′) *conj.* **1.** Regardless of the fact that; even though: *Although the trunk is big, it won't hold all the luggage.* **2.** But; however: *He says he has a dog, although I've never seen it.*

altimeter (ăl-tĭm′ĭ-tər) *n.* An instrument that measures the height at which an object, such as an aircraft, is located.

altiplano (äl′tĭ-plä′nō) *n., pl.* **altiplanos** A high mountain plateau, as in certain parts of South America.

altitude (ăl′tĭ-tōōd′) *n.* **1.** The height of a thing above a reference level, usually above sea level or the earth's surface. **2.** In astronomy, the angle between a line aimed at the horizon and a line aimed at a celestial object: *a star at an altitude of 18°.* **3.** The perpendicular distance from the base of a geometric figure, such as a triangle, to the opposite vertex, side, or surface.

Alt key (ôlt) *n.* A key on a computer keyboard that is pressed along with another key to perform an alternate operation.

alto (ăl′tō) *n., pl.* **altos 1.** A low female singing voice; a contralto. **2.** A countertenor. **3.** The range between soprano and tenor. **4.** A singer whose voice lies within this range. **5.** An instrument whose sound falls within this range. **6.** A part written in this range.

altocumulus (ăl′tō-kyōō′myə-ləs) *n.* A round, fleecy white or gray cloud formation.

altogether (ôl′tə-gĕ*th*′ər) *adv.* **1.** Completely: *Soon the noise faded away altogether.* **2.** With all included or counted: *Altogether, there are 36 teachers in the school.* **3.** On the whole; with everything considered: *Altogether it was a successful field trip.*

USAGE The word **altogether** and the phrase **all together** sound alike, but their meanings differ. *Altogether* means "completely": *I was altogether amazed by her actions. All together* means "with everybody or everything together or acting at the same time": *My friends and I went all together. All together* can be used only if you can rephrase the sentence and separate *all* and *together* by other words: *The books lay all together in a heap. All the books lay together in a heap.*

altostratus (ăl′tō-strāt′əs *or* ăl′tō-strä′təs) *n.* A cloud formation that extends in bluish or gray sheets or layers.

altricial (ăl-trĭsh′əl) *adj.* Hatched or born with the eyes closed and requiring care from a parent or parents. The young of dogs, cats, and most birds are altricial.

altruism (ăl′trōō-ĭz′əm) *n.* Unselfish concern for the welfare of others. —**al′tru·ist** *n.*

altruistic (ăl′trōō-ĭs′tĭk) *adj.* Showing concern for the welfare of others: *After the earthquake some altruistic doctors treated patients for free.* —**al′tru·is′ti·cal·ly** *adv.*

alum (ăl′əm) *n.* Any of various crystalline salts in which a metal such as aluminum or chromium is combined with another metal such as potassium or sodium, used

in dyeing and sometimes in medicine to stop bleeding from a small cut.

alumina (ə-lōō′mə-nə) *n.* Any of several forms of aluminum oxide, Al_2O_3, such as bauxite or corundum, that occur naturally and are used in aluminum production and in ceramics and electrical insulation.

aluminium (ăl′yə-mĭn′ē-əm) *n. Chiefly British* Variant of **aluminum.**

aluminum (ə-lōō′mə-nəm) *n. Symbol* **Al** A lightweight, silvery-white metallic element that is easily shaped and conducts electricity well. It is used to make a wide variety of products from soda cans to airplane components. Atomic number 13. See **Periodic Table.**

alumna (ə-lŭm′nə) *n., pl.* **alumnae** (ə-lŭm′nē′) A woman who has graduated from a certain school, college, or university.

alumnus (ə-lŭm′nəs) *n., pl.* **alumni** (ə-lŭm′nī′) A man who has graduated from a certain school, college, or university.

alveolus (ăl-vē′ə-ləs) *n., pl.* **alveoli** (ăl-vē′ə-lī′) **1.** Any of numerous tiny air-filled sacs in the lungs where the exchange of oxygen and carbon dioxide takes place. Oxygen enters the blood and carbon dioxide leaves the blood through capillaries that surround the alveoli. **2.** A small bodily pit or cavity, such as a tooth socket in the jawbone. —**al·ve′o·lar** (ăl-vē′ə-lər) *adj.*

always (ôl′wāz *or* ôl′wĭz) *adv.* **1.** On every occasion; without exception: *I always leave at six o'clock.* **2.** For all time; forever: *They will always be friends.* **3.** At any time; in any event: *If the bus is late, we can always walk.*

Alzheimer's disease (älts′hī-mərz) *n.* A disease of the brain that primarily affects elderly people and is characterized by progressive loss of memory and other mental abilities. It is associated with the development of abnormal tissues and protein deposits in the cerebral cortex.

am (ăm) *v.* First person singular present tense of **be.**

AM An abbreviation of: **1.** amplitude modulation. **2.** *or* **AM** ante meridiem (before noon).

amalgam (ə-măl′gəm) *n.* **1.** An alloy of mercury with other metals: *The amalgam used in silvering mirrors contains mercury and tin.* **2.** A combination or mixture: *The play was an amalgam of satire and farce.*

amalgamate (ə-măl′gə-māt′) *v.* **amalgamated, amalgamating, amalgamates** —*tr.* **1.** To unite to make a unified whole; merge: *The company amalgamated several of its shops under one manager.* **2.** To alloy (a metal) with mercury. —*intr.* **1.** To be combined; consolidate: *Many different peoples amalgamated to form the United States.* **2.** To blend with another metal. —**a·mal′ga·ma′tor** *n.*

amalgamation (ə-măl′gə-mā′shən) *n.* **1.** The process of amalgamating. **2.** A consolidation or merger, as of businesses.

amanita (ăm′ə-nē′tə *or* ăm′ə-nī′tə) *n.* Any of various mushrooms with white spores and usually a ring around the stalk, many of which are very poisonous.

amanuensis (ə-măn′yōō-ĕn′sĭs) *n., pl.* **amanuenses** (ə-măn′yōō-ĕn′sēz) One who is employed as a literary assistant, especially to take dictation or to copy manuscript.

amaranth (ăm′ə-rănth′) *n.* Any of various annual plants having dense green or reddish clusters of tiny flowers and including weeds, garden plants, and species grown for their edible leaves and seeds.

amaryllis (ăm′ə-rĭl′ĭs) *n.* Any of several plants of tropical America having large, funnel-shaped flowers that are red, pink, or white.

amass (ə-măs′) *tr.v.* **amassed, amassing, amasses** To accumulate in large quantity: *amass wealth; amass knowledge.* —**a·mass′a·ble** *adj.*

amateur (ăm′ə-tûr′ *or* ăm′ə-chŏŏr′) *n.* **1.** A person who engages in art, science, or sport for enjoyment rather than as a profession or for money. **2.** A person who lacks the skill of a professional: *The fact that the window was not level showed that it was the work of an amateur.* ✦ *adj.* **1.** Relating to or done by an amateur: *an amateur gymnast.* **2.** Made up of amateurs: *an amateur orchestra.* **3.** Not skillful; amateurish: *an amateur performance.*

amateurish (ăm′ə-tûr′ĭsh *or* ăm′ə-chŏŏr′ĭsh) *adj.* Done or performed as one would expect of an amateur rather than a professional. —**am′a·teur′ish·ly** *adv.*

amatory (ăm′ə-tôr′ē) *adj.* Relating to or expressive of love: *an amatory look.*

amaze (ə-māz′) *tr.v.* **amazed, amazing, amazes** To fill with surprise or wonder; astonish: *The size of the skyscrapers amazed the tourists.* See Synonyms at **surprise.** —**a·maz′ed·ly** (ə-mā′zĭd-lē) *adv.*

amazement (ə-māz′mənt) *n.* Great surprise; astonishment.

amazing (ə-mā′zĭng) *adj.* Causing great surprise or amazement; astonishing: *The patient has made an amazing recovery.* —**a·maz′ing·ly** *adv.*

Amazon (ăm′ə-zŏn′ *or* ăm′ə-zən) *n.* A member of a legendary nation of women warriors believed in ancient times to have lived in Scythia near the Black Sea.

Amazonian (ăm′ə-zō′nē-ən) *adj.* **1.** Relating to the Amazon River of South America or the region it drains. **2a.** Relating to the Amazon warriors. **b.** *often* **amazonian** Resembling an Amazon; vigorous or aggressive.

ambassador (ăm-băs′ə-dər *or* ăm-băs′ə-dôr′) *n.* **1.** A diplomatic official of the highest rank who represents a government in another country. **2.** A messenger or representative: *a goodwill ambassador.*

amber (ăm′bər) *n.* A hard, translucent, usually brownish-yellow substance that is the fossilized resin of ancient trees and frequently contains fossil insects. Amber is often used to make jewelry. ✦ *adj.* Made of amber.

ambergris (ăm′bər-grĭs′ *or* ăm′bər-grēs′) *n.* A waxy substance formed in the intestines of sperm whales that was formerly used in making perfume.

ambiance *also* **ambience** (ăm′bē-əns) *n.* The special atmosphere or mood created by a particular environment: *a neighborhood restaurant with a casual ambiance.*

ambidextrous (ăm′bĭ-dĕk′strəs) *adj.* Able to use both hands equally well. —**am′bi·dex′trous·ly** *adv.*

ambient (ăm′bē-ənt) *adj.* Surrounding; encircling: *It was hard to hear each other in the restaurant because of all the ambient noise.*

ambiguity (ăm′bĭ-gyōō′ĭ-tē) *n., pl.* **ambiguities 1.** The condition of having two or more possible meanings. **2.** Something that is ambiguous: *There were several ambiguities in their conflicting statements.*

ambiguous (ăm-bĭg′yōō-əs) *adj.* Having more than one interpretation; unclear: *A number of ambiguous sentences made the report hard to understand.* —**am·big′u·ous·ly** *adv.*

✦ **SYNONYMS** ambiguous, equivocal, vague *adj.*

ambition (ăm-bĭsh′ən) *n.* **1.** A strong desire to achieve something: *The student's ambition was to become a great scientist.* **2.** Desire to achieve or do something, especially

something requiring work or energy: *With so little ambition, he was not likely to find a good job.*

ambitious (ăm-bĭsh′əs) *adj.* **1.** Full of ambition; eager to succeed: *The ambitious new worker learned very quickly.* **2.** Full of desire; eager: *The new doctor was ambitious for success.* **3.** Requiring great effort; challenging: *ambitious goals; an ambitious schedule.* —**am·bi′tious·ly** *adv.* —**am·bi′tious·ness** *n.*

ambivalence (ăm-bĭv′ə-ləns) *n.* The existence of two conflicting feelings at the same time: *His hesitation to join the band was evidence of his ambivalence.*

ambivalent (ăm-bĭv′ə-lənt) *adj.* Having or showing conflicting feelings about someone or something: *She was ambivalent about taking the job on the night shift.* —**am·biv′a·lent·ly** *adv.*

amble (ăm′bəl) *intr.v.* **ambled, ambling, ambles** To walk or move along at a slow leisurely pace: *We ambled aimlessly down the street.* ✦ *n.* A slow leisurely walk: *They took an amble through the park after dinner.* —**am′bler** *n.*

ambrosia (ăm-brō′zhə) *n.* **1.** In Greek mythology, the food of the gods, thought to give immortality. **2.** Something highly pleasing to one's taste or smell. **3.** A dessert containing primarily oranges and flaked coconut. —**am·bro′sial** *adj.*

ambulance (ăm′byə-ləns) *n.* A specially equipped vehicle used to transport sick and injured people.

ambulatory (ăm′byə-lə-tôr′ē) *adj.* **1.** Relating to walking or the ability to walk. **2.** Able to walk; not confined to one's bed: *an ambulatory patient.*

ambuscade (ăm′bə-skād′ *or* ăm′bə-skād′) *n.* An ambush. ✦ *tr.v.* **ambuscaded, ambuscading, ambuscades** To ambush. —**am′bus·cad′er** *n.*

ambush (ăm′bŏŏsh) *n.* **1.** A sudden attack made from a concealed position: *The soldiers at the rear of the column fell victim to an ambush.* **2.** The hiding place used for such an attack: *The tiger crouched in ambush.* ✦ *tr.v.* **ambushed, ambushing, ambushes** To attack from a concealed position: *The soldiers hid among the rocks to ambush the pursuing forces.*

ameba (ə-mē′bə) *n.* Variant of **amoeba.** —**a·me′bic** (ə-mē′bĭk) *adj.*

amebiasis *also* **amoebiasis** (ăm′ə-bī′ə-sĭs) *n.* Infection of the intestines with a certain kind of amoeba that is transmitted by contaminated food or water and causes diarrhea, cramps, and nausea.

amebic dysentery *n.* Amebiasis.

ameliorate (ə-mēl′yə-rāt′) *tr. & intr.v.* **ameliorated, ameliorating, ameliorates** To make or become better; improve: *Lower taxes will ameliorate the conditions for hiring new workers.* —**a·me′lio·ra′tion** *n.*

amen (ā-mĕn′ *or* ä-mĕn′) *interj.* An expression used at the end of a prayer or a statement to express approval.

Amen (ä′mən) *n.* Variant of **Amun.**

amenable (ə-mē′nə-bəl *or* ə-mĕn′ə-bəl) *adj.* **1.** Willing to consent: *I am amenable to your suggestion.* **2.** Responsible to an authority; accountable: *We are all amenable to the law.* **3.** Susceptible or open, as to testing or criticism: *a question that is amenable to scientific investigation.* —**a·me′na·bil′i·ty** *n.* —**a·me′na·bly** *adv.*

amend (ə-mĕnd′) *tr.v.* **amended, amending, amends 1.** To change for the better; improve: *I amended my earlier proposal to make it clearer.* **2.** To change or add to (a legislative motion, law, or constitution).

amendment (ə-mĕnd′mənt) *n.* **1.** The act of changing for the better; improvement: *Some treaties have provi-*

sions for amendment. **2.** A legally adopted change or addition to a law or body of laws: *Giving voting rights to women was accomplished in an amendment to the Constitution.*

amends (ə-mĕndz′) *pl.n. (used with a singular or plural verb)* Something given or done to make up for an injury or insult: *By offering to pay for the repairs, they hoped to make amends for the damage.*

amenity (ə-mĕn′ĭ-tē *or* ə-mē′nĭ-tē) *n., pl.* **amenities 1.** The quality of being pleasant and agreeable: *the amenity of vacationing in the countryside.* **2.** Something that provides or increases physical comfort; a convenience: *an apartment with all the amenities of modern living.* **3.** amenities Polite social behavior; social courtesies.

American (ə-mĕr′ĭ-kən) *adj.* **1.** Relating to the United States of America or its people, language, or culture: *American literature.* **2.** Relating to North or South America, the West Indies, or the Western Hemisphere: *American geology.* ❖ *n.* A native or inhabitant of the United States or of the Americas.

Americana (ə-mĕr′ə-kä′nə *or* ə-mĕr′ə-kăn′ə) *n. (used with a plural verb)* Things that are examples of American history, folklore, or geography.

American cheese *n.* A smooth mild white or yellow cheddar cheese.

American English *n.* English as used in the United States.

American Indian *n.* A member of any of the peoples native to the Americas except the Eskimo, Aleut, and Inuit. —**American Indian** *adj.* —SEE NOTE AT **Native American.**

Americanism (ə-mĕr′ĭ-kə-nĭz′əm) *n.* **1.** A word or phrase originating in or peculiar to American English. **2.** A custom, trait, or tradition originating in the United States. **3.** Allegiance to the United States and its customs and institutions.

Americanize (ə-mĕr′ĭ-kə-nīz′) *tr. & intr.v.* **Americanized, Americanizing, Americanizes** To make or become American in manner, customs, or speech. —**A·mer′i·can·i·za′-tion** (ə-mĕr′ĭ-kə-nĭ-zā′shən) *n.*

American Revolution *n.* The war between the American colonies and Great Britain (1775–1783), leading to the formation of the independent United States.

American Sign Language *n.* The sign language used predominantly by deaf and hearing-impaired people in the United States and Canada.

American Spanish *n.* The Spanish language as used in the Western Hemisphere.

americium (ăm′ə-rĭsh′ē-əm) *n. Symbol* **Am** A white, metallic, radioactive element that is artificially produced by scientists. Some of its isotopes are used as radiation sources in research, radiography, and smoke alarms. Atomic number 95. See **Periodic Table.**

Amerindian (ăm′ə-rĭn′dē-ən) also **Amerind** (ăm′ə-rĭnd′) *n.* An American Indian. —**Am′er·in′di·an** *adj.*

amethyst (ăm′ə-thĭst) *n.* **1.** A purple or violet form of transparent quartz used as a gemstone. **2.** A purple or violet color.

Amharic (ăm-hăr′ĭk *or* äm-hä′rĭk) *n.* A Semitic language that is the official language of Ethiopia.

amiable (ā′mē-ə-bəl) *adj.* Friendly; good-natured: *an amiable laugh.* —**a′mi·a·bil′i·ty, a′mi·a·ble·ness** *n.* —**a′-mi·a·bly** *adv.*

amicable (ăm′ĭ-kə-bəl) *adj.* Characterized by friendliness and goodwill: *an amicable discussion.* —**am′-i·ca·bil′i·ty** *n.* —**am′i·ca·bly** *adv.*

amid (ə-mĭd′) also **amidst** (ə-mĭdst′) *prep.* Surrounded by; in the middle of: *The swimmer's head appeared amid the waves.*

amidships (ə-mĭd′shĭps′) also **amidship** (ə-mĭd′shĭp′) *adv.* In or toward the middle part of a ship: *The cabin passengers lived amidships.*

amidst (ə-mĭdst′) *prep.* Variant of **amid.**

amigo (ə-mē′gō) *n., pl.* **amigos** A friend.

amine (ə-mēn′ *or* ăm′ēn) *n.* Any of a group of organic compounds formed from ammonia (NH_3) by substituting organic radicals for one or more of the ammonia's hydrogens.

amino acid (ə-mē′nō *or* ăm′ə-nō′) *n.* Any of a large number of organic compounds that contain carbon, oxygen, hydrogen, and nitrogen, 20 of which are the basic components that join together in different combinations to make proteins. Humans and other animals can make some amino acids but must obtain others from food.

amir (ə-mîr′ *or* ä-mîr′) *n.* Variant of **emir.**

Amish (ä′mĭsh *or* ăm′ĭsh) *n.* **1.** An Anabaptist sect whose followers practice simple living. Most of the Amish live in Ohio, Pennsylvania, and Indiana. **2.** The followers of this religion considered as a group. ❖ *adj.* Relating to this religion or its followers.

amiss (ə-mĭs′) *adj.* Faulty or incorrect: *Something is amiss when the train is this late.* ❖ *adv.* In an improper or defective way: *Your work is going amiss.*

amity (ăm′ĭ-tē) *n., pl.* **amities** A state of friendship, as between nations.

ammeter (ăm′mē′tər) *n.* An instrument that measures the amount of electric current in amperes.

ammonia (ə-mōn′yə) *n.* **1.** A colorless gas, with a strongly irritating odor, that is composed of nitrogen and hydrogen and has the formula NH_3. It is used to manufacture fertilizers, explosives, and plastics. **2.** A solution of ammonia in water; ammonium hydroxide.

ammonia water *n.* Ammonium hydroxide.

ammonite (ăm′ə-nīt′) *n.* A fossil shell of an extinct mollusk related to the octopuses and squids. Ammonite shells were coiled and had many internal chambers.

ammonium (ə-mō′nē-əm) *n.* An ion, with the formula NH_4, that consists of four hydrogen atoms bound to a single nitrogen atom and that has a single positive charge. Its compounds are similar to those of alkali metals.

ammonium chloride *n.* A white crystalline salt that consists of an ammonium ion and a chloride ion bound together. It is used in dry cells, in soldering, and in metal finishing.

ammonium hydroxide *n.* A solution of ammonia in water, often used as a general cleanser.

ammonium nitrate *n.* A colorless crystalline salt composed of ammonium ions and nitrate ions bound together. It is used in fertilizers and explosives.

ammunition (ăm′yə-nĭsh′ən) *n.* **1.** Projectiles, such as bullets, shells, and shot, that can be fired from guns. **2.** Explosive objects, such as bombs or rockets, that are used as weapons. **3.** Something that is used to attack or defend an argument or point of view: *The senator's improper conduct gave opponents ammunition during the election campaign.*

amnesia (ăm-nē′zhə) *n.* A partial or total loss of memory, usually caused by shock, brain injury, or illness.

amnesty (ăm′nĭ-stē) *n., pl.* **amnesties** A general pardon granted by a government: *The town government granted amnesty to people who failed to get licenses for their pets.*

amnion (ăm′nē-ən *or* ăm′nē-ŏn′) *n., pl.* **amnions** or **am-**

nia (ăm′nē-ə) A tough thin membrane forming a sac that contains a watery liquid in which the embryo or fetus of a reptile, bird, or mammal is suspended. —**am′ni·ot′ic** (ăm′nē-ŏt′ĭk) *adj.*

amoeba also **ameba** (ə-mē′bə) *n.* A one-celled organism that can change shape. Amoebas are protozoans, and some of them cause disease in humans. —**a·moe′bic, a·me′bic** (ə-mē′bĭk) *adj.*

amoebiasis (ăm′ə-bī′ə-sĭs) *n.* Variant of **amebiasis.**

amoebic dysentery *n.* Amebiasis.

amok (ə-mŏk′) also **amuck** (ə-mŭk′ *or* ə-mŏk′) *adv.* Into a state of uncontrolled or destructive activity: *Enraged by their team's loss, the fans ran amok.*

Amon (ä′mən) *n.* Variant of **Amun.**

among (ə-mŭng′) also **amongst** (ə-mŭngst′) *prep.* **1.** In the midst of; surrounded by: *an oak among the pines.* **2.** In the company of: *among friends.* **3.** In the number or class of: *I count myself among the lucky ones.* **4.** By many or all of: *a custom popular among the Greeks.* **5.** With portions to each of: *The soda was shared among them.* **6.** With or against one another: *The dogs were fighting among themselves.* —SEE NOTE AT **between.**

amoral (ā-môr′əl) *adj.* **1.** Not subject to moral distinctions or judgments; neither moral nor immoral: *Nature is amoral.* **2.** Not caring about right and wrong. —**a′mo·ral′i·ty** (ā′mô-răl′ĭ-tē) *n.* —**a·mor′al·ly** *adv.*

amorous (ăm′ər-əs) *adj.* **1.** Full of or strongly disposed to romantic love: *an amorous young knight.* **2.** Relating to or expressing romantic love or sexual desire: *an amorous look.* —**am′or·ous·ly** *adv.*

amorphous (ə-môr′fəs) *adj.* **1.** Lacking definite form or shape: *an amorphous mass of mud and rock.* **2.** Not made of crystals: *Glass is an amorphous substance.* —**a·mor′phous·ly** *adv.*

amortize (ăm′ər-tīz′ *or* ə-môr′tīz′) *tr.v.* **amortized, amortizing, amortizes** To pay back (a debt) in regular equal installments, often including both principal and interest. —**am′or·ti·za′tion** (ăm′ər-tĭ-zā′shən) *n.*

Amos (ā′məs) *n.* A book of the Bible in which the prophet Amos denounces greed and social injustice.

amount (ə-mount′) *n.* **1.** The total of two or more quantities: *The amount of your bill is $8.72.* **2.** A number; a sum. **3.** Quantity: *a meager amount of rainfall.* ❖ *intr.v.* **amounted, amounting, amounts 1.** To add up in number or quantity: *Total sales for the day amounted to $655.* **2.** To add up in significance or effect: *Our effort to convince them didn't amount to much.* **3.** To be equivalent: *In some cases, disobeying orders amounts to treason.*

amour (ə-mŏor′) *n.* A love affair, especially an illicit one.

amour-propre (ä-mŏor-prôp′rə) *n.* Respect for oneself; self-esteem.

amp (ămp) *n. Informal* **1.** An ampere. **2.** An amplifier, especially one used to amplify music.

amperage (ăm′pər-ĭj *or* ăm′pîr′ĭj) *n.* The strength of an electric current expressed in amperes.

ampere (ăm′pîr′) *n.* A unit used to measure the amount of an electric current, equal to a flow of one coulomb of charge passing a given point per second. See table at **measurement.**

ampersand (ăm′pər-sănd′) *n.* The character or symbol (&) representing *and.*

amphetamine (ăm-fĕt′ə-mēn′ *or* ăm-fĕt′ə-mĭn) *n.* Any of a group of drugs that stimulate the nervous system,

causing heightened alertness and a faster heartbeat and metabolism. Amphetamines are highly addictive.

amphibian (ăm-fĭb′ē-ən) *n.* **1.** Any of various cold-blooded vertebrate animals, including the frogs, salamanders, and caecilians, having skin that is usually smooth and moist. Most amphibians live in the water and breathe with gills in early life but develop lungs and breathe air as adults. **2.** An aircraft that is capable of taking off from and landing on either land or water. **3.** A vehicle capable of traveling both on land and in water.

amphibious (ăm-fĭb′ē-əs) *adj.* **1.** Able to live both on land and in water. **2.** Capable of traveling both on land and in water: *an amphibious vehicle.* **3.** Launched from the sea with navy, air, and land forces against an enemy on land: *an amphibious operation.* —**am·phib′i·ous·ly** *adv.* —**am·phib′i·ous·ness** *n.*

amphibole (ăm′fə-bōl′) *n.* Any of a large group of minerals composed of a silicate joined to various metals, such as calcium, magnesium, iron, or sodium.

amphitheater (ăm′fə-thē′ə-tər) *n.* **1.** An oval or round structure having tiers of seats rising gradually outward from a central open space or arena. **2.** A level area surrounded by ground that slopes upward.

amphora (ăm′fər-ə) *n., pl.* **amphorae** (ăm′fə-rē′) or **amphoras** A tall earthenware jar with two handles, used by the ancient Greeks and Romans to store wine or oil.

ample (ăm′pəl) *adj.* **ampler, amplest 1.** Of large or great size, amount, extent, or capacity: *a rich nation with ample food for all.* **2.** Fully sufficient to meet a need or purpose: *had ample time to prepare for the test.* —**am′ple·ness** *n.*

amplification (ăm′plə-fĭ-kā′shən) *n.* **1a.** The act or result of amplifying, enlarging, or extending. **b.** An increase in the magnitude or strength of an electric current, a force, or another physical quantity. **2.** An expansion of a statement or idea: *The report is an amplification of the committee's views.*

amplifier (ăm′plə-fī′ər) *n.* A device, especially an electronic device, that produces amplification of an electric signal.

amplify (ăm′plə-fī′) *tr.v.* **amplified, amplifying, amplifies 1.** To produce amplification of: *A public-address system amplifies a speaker's voice.* **2.** To add to (something spoken or written); expand; make complete: *amplify earlier remarks.*

amplitude (ăm′plĭ-tŏod′) *n.* **1.** Greatness of size; extent. **2.** Abundance; fullness. **3.** One half the full extent of a vibration, oscillation, or wave. For example, the distance between the position of rest and the highest swing of a pendulum is its amplitude; thus a pendulum swinging through an angle of 90 degrees has an amplitude of 45 degrees. **4.** The peak strength of an alternating electric current in a given cycle.

amplitude modulation *n.* A system of radio transmission in which the amplitude of the carrier wave is adjusted so that it is proportional to the sound or other information that is to be transmitted.

amply (ăm′plē) *adv.* More than sufficiently; generously, liberally: *The library was amply supplied with books, magazines, and computers.*

amputate (ăm′pyŏo-tāt′) *tr.v.* **amputated, amputating, amputates** To cut off (a projecting body part), especially by surgery. —**am′pu·ta′tion** *n.* —**am′pu·ta′tor** *n.*

amputee (ăm′pyŏo-tē′) *n.* A person who has had one or more limbs removed by amputation.

amt. An abbreviation of amount.

amuck (ə-mŭk′) *adv.* Variant of **amok.**

amulet (ăm′yə-lĭt) *n.* An object worn, especially around the neck, as a charm against evil or injury.

Amun also **Amen** or **Amon** (ä′mən) *n.* In Egyptian mythology, the god of life and reproduction, sometimes represented as a man with the head of a ram.

amuse (ə-myōōz′) *tr.v.* **amused, amusing, amuses 1.** To hold the attention of or occupy in an agreeable fashion: *The hosts let their guests amuse themselves however they wished.* **2.** To cause to laugh or smile by giving pleasure: *amused the crowd with jokes.* —**a·mus′a·ble** *adj.*

amusement (ə-myōōz′mənt) *n.* **1.** The state of being pleasantly entertained: *They were too overcome with amusement to say a word.* **2.** Something that amuses or entertains: *charades and similar amusements.*

amusement park *n.* A commercially operated park that offers rides, games, and other forms of entertainment.

amusing (ə-myōō′zĭng) *adj.* Pleasantly entertaining or comical: *an amusing trick.* —**a·mus′ing·ly** *adv.*

amygdala (ə-mĭg′də-lə) *n., pl.* **amygdalae** (ə-mĭg′də-lē) Either of two small, almond-shaped masses of gray matter, located in the temporal lobes of the brain, that are involved in the processing and display of emotion.

amylase (ăm′ə-lās′ *or* ăm′ə-lāz′) *n.* Any of various enzymes that are present in saliva, in pancreatic juice, and in plants and other organisms and that convert starches to sugars, as in digestion.

an (ən; ăn *when stressed*) *indef.art.* The form of *a* that is used before words beginning with a vowel sound: *an elephant; an hour; an umbrella.*

an– Variant of **a–**[1].

–an A suffix that means: **1.** Born in or being a citizen of: *American; Mexican.* **2.** Belonging to, associated with, or expert in: *Unitarian; librarian.* **3.** Relating to or resembling: *Herculean; Shakespearean.*

Anabaptist (ăn′ə-băp′tĭst) *n.* A member of a Protestant religious movement viewing baptism as an external sign of faith and advocating the separation of church and state. —**An′a·bap′tist** *adj.*

anabolic steroid *n.* Any of a group of steroid hormones that promote protein storage and tissue growth, sometimes used by athletes to increase muscle size and strength. Prolonged use of anabolic steroids can cause medical problems, and it is illegal to sell them without a prescription in the United States.

anabolism (ə-năb′ə-lĭz′əm) *n.* The phase of metabolism in which complex molecules, such as proteins and fats, are formed from simpler ones. —**an′a·bol′ic** (ăn′ə-bŏl′ĭk) *adj.*

anachronism (ə-năk′rə-nĭz′əm) *n.* **1.** The representation of something in a time other than its proper or historical time, as in a story. **2.** Something that is out of its proper time: *Cavalry is an anachronism in modern warfare.*

anachronistic (ə-năk′rə-nĭs′tĭk) *adj.* Out of proper time; misplaced chronologically: *One anachronistic detail in the play is having General Washington get a message by telegraph.* —**a·nach′ro·nis′ti·cal·ly** *adv.*

anaconda (ăn′ə-kŏn′də) *n.* Any of several large nonvenomous tropical American snakes that coil around and suffocate their prey.

anaerobe (ăn′ə-rōb′ *or* ăn-âr′ōb′) *n.* An organism that can live where there is no free oxygen.

anaerobic (ăn′ə-rō′bĭk) *adj.* Living or growing where there is no free oxygen: *anaerobic bacteria.*

anagram (ăn′ə-grăm′) *n.* **1.** A word or phrase formed by changing the order of the letters of another word or phrase. **2. anagrams** A game in which players form words from a group of randomly picked letters.

anal (ā′nəl) *adj.* **1.** Relating to or near the anus. **2.** Anal-retentive. —**a′nal·ly** *adv.*

analgesia (ăn′əl-jē′zē-ə) *n.* A condition of reduced sensitivity to pain, often produced by a drug, without loss of consciousness.

analgesic (ăn′əl-jē′zĭk *or* ăn′əl-jē′sĭk) *n.* A drug that produces analgesia; a painkiller: *Aspirin is a common analgesic.* ❖ *adj.* Relating to or causing analgesia.

analog also **analogue** (ăn′ə-lôg′) *n.* **1.** Something that bears an analogy to something else. **2.** An organ in a plant or animal that is similar in function to one in another kind of plant or animal. ❖ *adj.* **1.** Relating to analog computers. **2.** Relating to or using continuously varying physical quantities to encode a signal or represent changes in data. For example, the level of mercury in a thermometer is an analog representation of temperature.

analogous (ə-năl′ə-gəs) *adj.* Similar or parallel in certain ways: *The relation between addition and subtraction is analogous to that between multiplication and division.* —**a·nal′o·gous·ly** *adv.* —**a·nal′o·gous·ness** *n.*

analogy (ə-năl′ə-jē) *n., pl.* **analogies 1.** A similarity in some respects between things that are otherwise unlike: *sees an analogy between viral infection and the spread of ideas.* **2.** An explanation of something by comparing it with something similar: *The author uses the analogy of a beehive when describing the city.*

anal-retentive (ā′nəl-rĭ-tĕn′tĭv) *adj.* Indicating personality traits, such as extreme fastidiousness, stinginess, and obstinacy, supposed by psychoanalytic theory to originate from infantile pleasure in the retention of feces.

analysis (ə-năl′ĭ-sĭs) *n., pl.* **analyses** (ə-năl′ĭ-sēz′) **1.** The separation of something into its parts in order to determine its nature: *An analysis of the theory shows it is based on faulty evidence.* **2a.** The separation of a substance into its parts, usually by chemical means, for the study and identification of each component. **b.** A written report of the information obtained in this way. **3.** Psychoanalysis.

analyst (ăn′ə-lĭst) *n.* **1.** A person who performs an analysis. **2.** A psychoanalyst.

analytic (ăn′ə-lĭt′ĭk) or **analytical** (ăn′ə-lĭt′ĭ-kəl) *adj.* Relating to analysis: *analytical chemistry.* —**an′a·lyt′i·cal·ly** *adv.*

analytic geometry *n.* The use of algebra to solve problems in geometry. In analytic geometry, geometric figures are represented by algebraic equations and plotted using coordinates.

analyze (ăn′ə-līz′) *tr.v.* **analyzed, analyzing, analyzes 1.** To separate into parts in order to determine what something is or how it works: *They analyzed the ore and found gold in it.* **2.** To examine in detail: *analyze past expenses to make a budget for next year.* **3.** To psychoanalyze. —**an′a·lyz′a·ble** *adj.* —**an′a·ly·za′tion** (ăn′ə-lĭ-zā′shən) *n.* —**an′a·lyz′er** *n.*

anapest (ăn′ə-pĕst′) *n.* In poetry, a metrical foot consisting of two unstressed syllables followed by one stressed syllable, as in *seventeen.*

anaphase (ăn′ə-fāz′) *n.* The stage of mitosis and meiosis during which the chromosomes separate into two groups that move to opposite sides of the cell.

anaphylactic shock (ăn′ə-fə-lăk′tĭk) *n.* A sudden, severe allergic reaction that causes the body to go into shock, caused by exposure to a substance that one is sensitive to, such as a drug, a food, or venom from an insect.

anarchic (ăn-är′kĭk) or **anarchical** (ăn-är′kĭ-kəl) *adj.* **1.** Relating to or promoting anarchy. **2.** Lacking order or control; lawless: *the anarchic society of America's wild frontier.* —**an·ar′chi·cal·ly** *adv.*

anarchism (ăn′ər-kĭz′əm) *n.* **1.** The theory or doctrine that all forms of government are oppressive and undesirable and should be abolished. **2.** Rejection of all forms of coercive organization or authority.

anarchist (ăn′ər-kĭst) *n.* A person who advocates or supports anarchism.

anarchy (ăn′ər-kē) *n., pl.* **anarchies 1.** Absence of any governmental authority. **2.** Disorder and confusion resulting from lack of authority: *For several days after the hurricane the region was in a state of anarchy.*

Anasazi (ä′nə-sä′zē) *n., pl.* **Anasazi** or **Anasazis** A term sometimes used for the Native American people considered the ancestors of the Pueblo peoples. Their culture first developed around AD 100.

anathema (ə-năth′ə-mə) *n.* **1.** A person or thing that is intensely disliked: *The idea of giving up before the end of the race was anathema to her.* **2.** A strong denunciation or condemnation. **3.** A formal ban or excommunication imposed by a church.

anathematize (ə-năth′ə-mə-tīz′) *tr.v.* **anathematized, anathematizing, anathematizes** To proclaim an anathema on; denounce; curse. —**a·nath′e·ma·ti·za′tion** (ə-năth′ə-mə-tĭ-zā′shən) *n.*

anatomical (ăn′ə-tŏm′ĭ-kəl) also **anatomic** (ăn′ə-tŏm′ĭk) *adj.* **1.** Relating to anatomy or dissection: *anatomical illustrations.* **2.** Relating to the structure of an organism as opposed to its functioning: *an anatomical abnormality.* —**an′a·tom′i·cal·ly** *adv.*

anatomy (ə-năt′ə-mē) *n., pl.* **anatomies 1.** The structure of an organism or any of its parts: *Bones and muscles are part of the human anatomy.* **2.** The scientific study of the shape and structure of living things: *a professor of anatomy.* **3.** The human body: *the rugged anatomy of an athlete.*

–ance A suffix that means: **1.** State or condition: *resemblance.* **2.** Action: *compliance.*

ancestor (ăn′sĕs′tər) *n.* **1.** A person from whom one is descended, especially if of a generation earlier than a grandparent: *His ancestors came to America from China.* **2.** A forerunner; a predecessor: *The harpsichord is an ancestor of the piano.* **3.** An organism or a type of organism, either known or supposed to exist, from which later organisms evolved: *The ancestors of whales were mammals that lived on land millions of years ago.*

ancestral (ăn-sĕs′trəl) *adj.* Relating to or evolved from an ancestor or ancestors: *an ancestral trait.* —**an·ces′tral·ly** *adv.*

ancestry (ăn′sĕs′trē) *n., pl.* **ancestries 1.** A line of descent; lineage. **2.** Ancestors considered as a group: *descended from noble ancestry.*

anchor (ăng′kər) *n.* **1.** A heavy object attached to a boat or ship by a cable and dropped overboard to keep the vessel in place, either by its weight or by catching on the bottom. **2.** A rigid point of support, as for securing a rope or cable. **3.** Something that helps one feel secure: *Listening to music has been my anchor in tough times.* **4.** An anchorman or anchorwoman. ❖ *v.* **anchored, anchoring, anchors** —*tr.* **1.** To secure with a fastener or similar device. **2.** To act as an anchorman or anchorwoman on

(a news broadcast) or in (a relay race). —*intr.* To drop anchor or be held by an anchor: *The ship anchored off the coast.*

anchorage (ăng′kər-ĭj) *n.* **1.** A place where ships can anchor: *a safe anchorage in the harbor.* **2.** The action of anchoring or the condition of being held by an anchor.

anchorman (ăng′kər-măn′) *n.* **1.** A man who reads the news or introduces the reporters' stories on a newscast. **2.** A man who is the last member of a relay team in a race.

anchorperson (ăng′kər-pûr′sən) *n.* An anchorman or anchorwoman.

anchor store *n.* A large store in a shopping mall that draws customers who are then likely to go to the other, often smaller shops in the mall.

anchorwoman (ăng′kər-wŏom′ən) *n.* **1.** A woman who reads the news or introduces the reporters' stories on a newscast. **2.** A woman who is the last member of a relay team in a race.

anchovy (ăn′chō′vē or ăn-chō′vē) *n., pl.* **anchovy** or **anchovies** Any of various small ocean fishes that are often salted and preserved.

ancient (ān′shənt) *adj.* **1.** Very old; aged: *the ancient sequoias of the California forests.* **2.** Relating to times long past, especially the historical period before the fall of the Roman empire in AD 476. ❖ *n.* **1.** A very old person. **2.** **ancients** The Greeks or Romans of ancient times. —**an′cient·ly** *adv.*

ancillary (ăn′sə-lĕr′ē) *adj.* Serving as help or support but not of first importance: *an ancillary pump.*

–ancy A suffix that means condition or quality: *buoyancy.*

and (ənd *or* ən; *and when stressed*) *conj.* **1.** Together with or along with; as well as: *The weather is clear and crisp.* **2.** Added to; plus: *Two and two makes four.* **3.** As a result: *Go, and you will enjoy yourself.* **4.** *Informal* To: *Try and find it.* —SEE NOTE AT **both.**

andante (än-dän′tā) *adv. & adj.* In music, moderately slow.

andiron (ănd′ī′ərn) *n.* One of a pair of metal supports for holding up logs in a fireplace.

and/or (ănd′ôr′) *conj.* Used to indicate that either *and* or *or* may be used to connect words, phrases, or clauses, as in the sentence *Thin the paint with turpentine and/or linseed oil.*

Androcles (ăn′drə-klēz′) *n.* In Roman legend, a slave spared in the arena by a lion that remembered him as the man who had once pulled a thorn from its paw.

androgen (ăn′drə-jən) *n.* A hormone, such as testosterone, that controls the development and maintenance of physical characteristics in males. —**an′dro·gen′ic** (ăn′drə-jĕn′ĭk) *adj.*

androgynous (ăn-drŏj′ə-nəs) *adj.* **1.** Having both female and male characteristics; hermaphroditic. **2.** Seeming neither definitely masculine nor definitely feminine, as in dress, appearance, or behavior. —**an·drog′y·nous·ly** *adv.* —**an·drog′y·ny** (ăn-drŏj′ə-nē) *n.*

android (ăn′droid′) *n.* A robot or automaton that moves, especially one that resembles a human.

Andromache (ăn-drŏm′ə-kē) *n.* In Greek mythology, the brave and faithful wife of Hector, captured by the Greeks at the fall of Troy.

Andromeda (ăn-drŏm′ĭ-də) *n.* **1.** In Greek mythology, a princess who was offered as a sacrifice to a sea monster and married Perseus after he killed the monster. **2.** A constellation in the Northern Hemisphere, traditionally pictured as representing Andromeda.

anecdote (ănʹĭk-dōtʹ) *n.* A short account of an interesting or humorous event. —**anʹec·dotʹal** *adj.* —**anʹ-ec·dotʹal·ly** *adv.*

anemia (ə-nēʹmē-ə) *n.* A condition in which the blood cannot carry enough oxygen to the body tissues. It can be caused by lack of hemoglobin, too few red blood cells, or poorly formed red blood cells.

anemic (ə-nēʹmĭk) *adj.* **1.** Relating to or suffering from anemia. **2.** Lacking vitality; weak: *an anemic economic recovery.*

anemometer (ănʹə-mŏmʹĭ-tər) *n.* An instrument for measuring wind speed.

anemone (ə-nĕmʹə-nē) *n.* **1.** Any of various plants having lobed leaves and cup-shaped white, purple, or red flowers. **2.** A sea anemone.

anesthesia (ănʹĭs-thēʹzhə) *n.* **1.** Loss of sensation to pain or touch, usually produced by the administration of drugs, especially before surgery, or by an injury to a nerve. **2.** A drug that causes such loss of sensation.

anesthesiology (ănʹĭs-thēʹzē-ŏlʹə-jē) *n.* The medical study of anesthetics, their effects, and their use. —**anʹes·the·si·olʹo·gist** *n.*

anesthetic (ănʹĭs-thĕtʹĭk) *adj.* **1.** Relating to or causing anesthesia. **2.** Lacking sensation or feeling; insensitive. ❖ *n.* A drug that causes anesthesia.

anesthetist (ə-nĕsʹthĭ-tĭst) *n.* A person specially trained to administer anesthetics.

anesthetize (ə-nĕsʹthĭ-tīzʹ) *tr.v.* **anesthetized, anesthetizing, anesthetizes** To put into a condition of anesthesia, especially by means of a drug: *They anesthetized the injured dog in preparation for surgery.* —**a·nesʹthe·ti·zaʹ-tion** (ə-nĕsʹthĭ-tĭ-zāʹshən) *n.*

aneurysm (ănʹyə-rĭzʹəm) *n.* A swelling in a weakened part of a blood vessel or in the wall of the heart, caused by disease or injury.

anew (ə-nōōʹ) *adv.* Over again: *ready to start anew.*

angel (ānʹjəl) *n.* **1.** In Judaism, Christianity, and Islam, one of the immortal beings serving as attendants or messengers of God. **2.** A guardian spirit: *felt that an angel was with him during the ordeal.* **3.** A kind, lovable, or virtuous person.

Angeleno (ănʹjə-lēʹnō) *n., pl.* **Angelenos** A native or inhabitant of Los Angeles, California.

angelfish (ănʹjəl-fĭshʹ) *n.* Any of several brightly colored tropical fishes having a flattened body and often long extensions on the fins.

angel food cake *n.* A light sponge cake.

angel hair *n.* Pasta in long, extremely thin strands.

angelic (ăn-jĕlʹĭk) also **angelical** (ăn-jĕlʹĭ-kəl) *adj.* **1.** Relating to angels. **2.** Resembling an angel, as in goodness, kindness, or purity.

Angelus also **angelus** (ănʹjə-ləs) *n.* **1.** In some Christian churches, a devotional prayer at morning, noon, and sunset in celebration of the Annunciation. **2.** A bell rung as a call to recite this prayer.

anger (ăngʹgər) *n.* A feeling of great displeasure or hostility toward someone or something: *surprise and then anger at being cheated.* ❖ *tr.* & *intr.v.* **angered, angering, angers** To make or become angry: *I was angered by his rudeness. She angers slowly.*

✦ **SYNONYMS** anger, fury, indignation, rage *n.*

angina (ăn-jīʹnə *or* ănʹjə-nə) *n.* Angina pectoris.

angina pectoris (pĕkʹtər-ĭs) *n.* A severe tightening and pain in the chest, often extending into the left shoulder and arm. It generally results from an insufficient supply of blood to the heart muscle, usually because of coronary artery disease.

angiogenesis (ănʹjē-ō-jĕnʹĭ-sĭs) *n.* The formation of new blood vessels.

angiosperm (ănʹjē-ə-spûrmʹ) *n.* Any of a large group of plants that have flowers and produce seeds that are enclosed in an ovary; a flowering plant.

angle¹ (ăngʹgəl) *intr.v.* **angled, angling, angles 1.** To fish with a hook and line. **2.** To try to get something by using schemes or tricks: *By posing as a reporter, the tourist angled for a chance to meet the celebrity.*

angle² (ăngʹgəl) *n.* **1.** A geometric figure formed by two lines that begin at a common point or by two planes that begin at a common line. **2.** The distance between such lines or planes, often measured in degrees. **3.** A projecting corner, as of a building: *The angle of the building blocked our view.* **4.** The place, position, or direction from which an object is presented to view; point of view: *a building that looks impressive from any angle.* **5.** A particular part or phase, as of a problem; an aspect: *studying every angle of the question.* ❖ *v.* **angled, angling, angles** —*tr.* To move or hit at an angle: *angling the camera for a clearer view.* —*intr.* To turn or continue along at an angle: *The road angles sharply at the river.*

WORD HISTORY Angle¹ comes from Middle English *anglen* (meaning "to fish with a hook"), which comes from Middle English *angel*, meaning "fishhook." **Angle²** comes from Middle English *angle*, which comes from Latin *angulus*, both referring to the geometric figure.

Angle *n.* A member of a Germanic people who settled in England in the fifth century AD and together with the Jutes and Saxons formed the Anglo-Saxon peoples.

angle bracket *n.* **1.** Either of a pair of symbols, < >, used to enclose written or printed material. **2.** In mathematics, either of these symbols, used especially together to indicate quantities to be treated as a unit.

angle iron *n.* A length of iron or steel bent into a right angle to be used as a support.

angle of incidence *n.* The angle formed by a ray or wave, as of light or sound, striking a surface and a line perpendicular to the surface at the point of impact.

angle of reflection *n.* The angle formed by a ray or wave, as of light or sound, reflected from a surface and a line perpendicular to the surface at the point of reflection.

angle of refraction *n.* The angle formed by the path of a refracted ray or wave and a line drawn perpendicular to the refracting surface at the point where the refraction occurred.

angler (ăngʹglər) *n.* **1.** A person who fishes with a hook and line. **2.** An anglerfish.

anglerfish (ăngʹglər-fĭshʹ) *n.* Any of various ocean fishes having on the top of the head a slender projection with a fleshy tip that dangles in front of the large mouth and acts as a lure to attract smaller fish.

angleworm (ăngʹgəl-wûrmʹ) *n.* A worm, especially an earthworm, that is used as bait in fishing.

Anglican (ăngʹglĭ-kən) *adj.* Relating to the Anglican Church. ❖ *n.* A member of the Anglican Church.

Anglican Church *n.* The Church of England and those churches in other nations that are formally affiliated with it.

Anglicanism (ăngʹglĭ-kə-nĭzʹəm) *n.* The beliefs, practices, and form of organization of the Anglican Church.

Anglicize (ăngʹglĭ-sīzʹ) *tr.v.* **Anglicized, Anglicizing, An-**

glicizes 1. To adapt (a foreign word) to use in English, especially by changing its spelling or pronunciation: *The Greek name Odysseus, or Ulixes in Latin, was Anglicized as Ulysses.* **2.** To make English or similar to English in form, idiom, style, or character: *Some immigrants Anglicize their names when they move to the United States.*

angling (ăng′glĭng) *n.* The act or sport of fishing with a hook and line.

Anglo (ăng′glō) *n., pl.* **Anglos 1.** *Informal* An Anglo-American. **2.** An English-speaking person, especially a white North American who is not of Hispanic or French ancestry.

Anglo– A prefix that means English: *Anglo-American; Anglo-Saxon.*

Anglo-American (ăng′glō-ə-mĕr′ĭ-kən) *n.* An American, especially an inhabitant of the United States, who is of English ancestry. ❖ *adj.* **1.** Relating to or involving England and America, especially the United States. **2.** Relating to Anglo-Americans.

Anglocentric (ăng′glō-sĕn′trĭk) *adj.* Centered or focused on England or the English: *an Anglocentric view of history.*

Anglo-French (ăng′glō-frĕnch′) *adj.* Relating to or involving England and France, or their peoples. ❖ *n.* The dialect of Old French spoken by the Anglo-Normans or by English people after the Norman language fell out of use in England.

Anglo-Norman (ăng′glō-nôr′mən) *n.* **1.** One of the Normans who lived in England after the Norman Conquest of England in 1066 or a descendant of these settlers. **2.** The dialect of Old French, derived chiefly from Norman French, that was used by the Anglo-Normans. —**An′glo-Nor′man** *adj.*

Anglophile (ăng′glə-fīl′) *n.* One who admires England, its people, and its culture. —**An′glo·phile, An′glo·phil′ic** (ăng′glə-fīl′ĭk) *adj.* —**An′glo·phil′i·a** (ăng′glə-fīl′ē-ə) *n.*

Anglophone also **anglophone** (ăng′glə-fōn′) *n.* A person who speaks English, especially one in a country or region where at least one other language besides English is spoken. —**An′glo·phone′** *adj.*

Anglo-Saxon (ăng′glō-săk′sən) *n.* **1.** A member of one of the Germanic peoples, the Angles, the Saxons, and the Jutes, who settled in Britain in the fifth and sixth centuries. **2.** Any of the descendants of these people, who dominated England until the Norman Conquest in 1066. **3.** Old English. **4.** A person of English ancestry. —**An′glo-Sax′on** *adj.*

Angora (ăng-gôr′ə) *n.* **1.** An Angora cat, Angora goat, or Angora rabbit. **2. angora** Yarn or fabric made from the hair of an Angora goat or rabbit.

Angora cat *n.* A domestic cat having long silky hair.

Angora goat *n.* A domestic goat having long silky hair.

Angora rabbit *n.* A domestic rabbit having long, soft, usually white hair.

angry (ăng′grē) *adj.* **angrier, angriest 1.** Feeling or showing anger: *an angry customer; an angry expression.* **2.** Seeming to threaten: *angry dark storm clouds.* **3.** Inflamed: *an angry wound.* —**an′gri·ly** *adv.* —**an′gri·ness** *n.*

angst (ängkst) *n.* A feeling of anxiety or apprehension.

angstrom (ăng′strəm) *n.* A unit of length equal to one hundred-millionth (10^{-8}) of a centimeter. It is used mainly in measuring wavelengths of light and shorter electromagnetic radiation.

anguish (ăng′gwĭsh) *n.* Severe pain or suffering of mind or body; torment: *They were in anguish until their lost puppy was found.*

anguished (ăng′gwĭsht) *adj.* Feeling, expressing, or caused by anguish: *the anguished faces of people whose homes were destroyed by the hurricane.*

angular (ăng′gyə-lər) *adj.* **1.** Having, forming, or consisting of an angle or angles: *an angular point.* **2.** Measured by an angle: *angular distance.* **3.** Bony and lean: *an angular face.* **4.** Lacking grace or smoothness: *an angular gait.* —**an′gu·lar·ly** *adv.*

angularity (ăng′gyə-lăr′ĭ-tē) *n., pl.* **angularities** The condition or quality of being angular.

angular momentum *n.* A quantity that measures the motion of a body that is moving in a circle. The angular momentum depends on the mass and velocity of the body, and on the radius of the circle that it is moving along.

Angus (ăng′gəs) *n.* A breed of hornless beef cattle that originated in Scotland and are usually black but also occur in a red variety.

anhydride (ăn-hī′drīd′) *n.* A chemical compound formed from another by the removal of water.

anhydrous (ăn-hī′drəs) *adj.* Lacking water, especially water of crystallization: *Many crystals, like diamond and quartz, are anhydrous.*

aniline also **anilin** (ăn′ə-lĭn) *n.* A colorless, oily, poisonous liquid derived from benzene and used in making dyes, rubber, drugs, and varnishes. ❖ *adj.* Derived from aniline.

animadversion (ăn′ə-măd-vûr′zhən) *n.* Hostile criticism or a remark that directs criticism or blame.

animal (ăn′ə-məl) *n.* **1.** Any of a kingdom of many-celled organisms that cannot make their own food and are usually able to move around during at least part of their life cycle. Some animals, such as sponges, corals, and insects, do not have a backbone, and some, such as fishes, birds, amphibians, reptiles, and mammals, do have a backbone. **2.** An animal organism other than a human: *Some animals got into the tent and ate our food.* **3.** A person who behaves in a coarse or cruel way. ❖ *adj.* **1.** Relating to, characteristic of, or derived from an animal or animals, especially when not human: *animal behavior; animal fat.* **2.** Relating to the physical as distinct from the rational or spiritual nature of people: *following his animal instincts.*

animal cracker *n.* A small cookie in the shape of an animal.

animal husbandry *n.* The care and breeding of domestic animals such as cattle, sheep, and hogs.

animal rights *pl.n.* The idea that animals are entitled to some of the same legal protections given to people and should not be killed, hurt, or held captive by humans.

animate (ăn′ə-māt′) *tr.v.* **animated, animating, animates 1.** To give life to; cause to come alive: *the belief that the soul animates the body.* **2.** To give interest or vitality to; enliven: *The party was animated by the dance music.* **3.** To inspire or motivate: *an explorer who is animated by curiosity.* **4.** To make or depict using animation: *Many children's stories have been animated by movie companies.* ❖ *adj.* (ăn′ə-mĭt) **1.** Living: *Babies quickly learn the difference between animate and inanimate objects.* **2.** Belonging to the class of nouns that stand for living things: *The word "dog" is animate; the word "car" is inanimate.* —**an′i·ma·cy** (ăn′ə-mə-sē) *n.*

animated (ăn′ə-mā′tĭd) *adj.* **1.** Lively: *The band leader's personality was energetic and animated.* **2.** Made or depicted using animation: *an animated film.* —**an′i·mat′-ed·ly** *adv.*

animated cartoon *n.* A cartoon produced using the techniques of animation.

animation (ăn′ə-mā′shən) *n.* **1.** Liveliness; vitality. **2.** The art or process of making movies or videos that create the illusion of motion by rapidly displaying a series of drawings, objects, or computer graphics with slight changes from one to the next, rather than a series of photographs. **3.** A movie or video created through animation.

animato (ä′nē-mä′tō) *adv. & adj.* In music, in an animated or lively manner.

animator (ăn′ə-mā′tər) *n.* An artist or technician who works at making animation.

anime (ăn′ə-mā′) *n.* A style of animation originating in Japan.

animism (ăn′ə-mĭz′əm) *n.* The belief in individual spirits that exist in natural objects or forces, such as trees, waterfalls, stones, winds, and tides. —**an′i·mist′** *n.*

animosity (ăn′ə-mŏs′ĭ-tē) *n.* Hatred or hostility: *There was much animosity between the two nations even before war broke out.*

animus (ăn′ə-məs) *n.* **1.** A feeling of animosity; hatred: *animus among bitter rivals.* **2.** An intention or a purpose; a motive behind an action.

anion (ăn′ī′ən) *n.* An ion that has a negative charge and moves toward the positive electrode in electrolysis.

anise (ăn′ĭs) *n.* A plant related to parsley, having small licorice-flavored seeds used for flavoring.

anise seed or **aniseed** (ăn′ĭ-sēd′) *n.* The seed of the anise plant.

ankh (ängk) *n.* A cross shaped like a T with a loop at the top, used as a symbol of life in ancient Egypt.

ankle (ăng′kəl) *n.* **1.** The joint formed by the tibia and fibula of the lower leg and the talus of the foot. The ankle connects the foot with the leg. **2.** The slender part of the leg just above this joint.

anklebone (ăng′kəl-bōn′) *n.* The main bone of the ankle; the talus.

anklet (ăng′klĭt) *n.* **1.** A bracelet or chain worn around the ankle. **2.** A sock that reaches just above the ankle.

annals (ăn′əlz) *pl.n.* **1.** A record of events written in the order of their occurrence, year by year. **2.** A descriptive account or record; a history: *the annals of the American Revolution.*

anneal (ə-nēl′) *tr.v.* **annealed, annealing, anneals** To treat (glass or a metal) by heating and slow cooling in order to toughen and reduce brittleness.

annelid (ăn′ə-lĭd) *n.* Any of a group of worms and wormlike invertebrate animals, including the earthworms and leeches, having a long, soft, segmented body.

annex (ə-nĕks′ or ăn′ĕks′) *tr.v.* **annexed, annexing, annexes 1.** To add or join to, especially to a larger or more significant thing: *The new gym is to be annexed to the school.* **2.** To add (territory) to an existing country or other area: *The city is trying to annex two of the suburbs.* ❖ *n.* (ăn′ĕks′) An extra building that is added to another bigger building and used for some related purpose: *the library annex of the school.* —**an′nex·a′tion** (ăn′ĭk-sā′shən) *n.*

annihilate (ə-nī′ə-lāt′) *tr.v.* **annihilated, annihilating, annihilates 1.** To destroy completely; wipe out. **2.** To defeat decisively; vanquish: *annihilated the opposition in the tournament.* —**an·ni′hi·la′tion** *n.*

anniversary (ăn′ə-vûr′sə-rē) *n., pl.* **anniversaries 1.** The yearly returning of the date of an event that happened

in an earlier year: *a wedding anniversary.* **2.** A date that follows a certain event by a specified amount of time: *his six-month anniversary of becoming a vegetarian.*

anno Domini (ăn′ō dŏm′ə-nī′ *or* ăn′ō dŏm′ə-nē′) *adv.* In a specified year since the birth of Jesus, the founder of Christianity. Used chiefly in abbreviated form: AD 500.

annotate (ăn′ō-tāt′) *tr.v.* **annotated, annotating, annotates** To furnish (a written work) with explanatory notes: *Many textbooks are annotated with notes in the margin.* —**an′no·ta′tor** *n.*

annotation (ăn′ō-tā′shən) *n.* **1.** The act or process of annotating. **2.** An explanatory note: *an annotation in the margin.*

announce (ə-nouns′) *v.* **announced, announcing, announces** — *tr.* **1.** To bring to public notice; give formal notice of: *The transit system announced a change in bus schedules.* **2.** To make known the presence or arrival of: *The footman announced the guests.* **3.** To serve as an announcer of: *announced hockey games on television.* —*intr.* To serve as an announcer on radio or television.

announcement (ə-nouns′mənt) *n.* **1.** The act of announcing. **2.** A public declaration to make known something that has happened or that will happen; an official statement. **3.** A printed or published notice.

announcer (ə-noun′sər) *n.* A person who announces, especially a person who introduces a show, makes comments, or reads news on radio or television.

annoy (ə-noi′) *tr.v.* **annoyed, annoying, annoys** To cause (someone) to feel irritated or angry: *The children's screaming annoyed the neighbors.*

annoyance (ə-noi′əns) *n.* **1.** Irritation or displeasure: *Much to my annoyance, the bus was late.* **2.** Something causing trouble or irritation; a nuisance: *Heartburn is a relatively minor annoyance.*

annoying (ə-noi′ĭng) *adj.* Troublesome or irritating: *an annoying habit.* —**an·noy′ing·ly** *adv.* —**an·noy′ing·ness** *n.*

annual (ăn′yōō-əl) *adj.* **1.** Happening every year; yearly: *an annual medical examination.* **2.** Relating to or determined by a year's time: *What is the annual income of a nurse?* **3.** Living and growing only for one year or season: *annual plants.* ❖ *n.* **1.** A periodical published yearly; a yearbook. **2.** A plant that completes its entire life cycle in a single growing season. —**an′nu·al·ly** *adv.*

annual ring *n.* A growth ring in a woody plant that forms during a full year's growth.

annuity (ə-nōō′ĭ-tē) *n., pl.* **annuities 1a.** An amount of money paid at regular intervals. **b.** A sequence of such payments. **2.** A contract or agreement by which one receives fixed payments on an investment for a lifetime or for a specified number of years.

annul (ə-nŭl′) *tr.v.* **annulled, annulling, annuls** To make or declare void; nullify; cancel: *The court annulled their marriage.*

annular (ăn′yə-lər) *adj.* Forming or shaped like a ring. —**an′nu·lar′i·ty** (ăn′yə-lăr′ĭ-tē) *n.* —**an′nu·lar·ly** *adv.*

annular eclipse *n.* A solar eclipse in which the moon blocks all of the sun except for a bright ring around the edge of the sun.

annulment (ə-nŭl′mənt) *n.* **1.** The act of annulling. **2.** A legal declaration stating that a marriage was never valid.

annunciation (ə-nŭn′sē-ā′shən) *n.* **1.** The act of announcing: *The annunciation of the new policy stirred up controversy.* **2. Annunciation** In the New Testament, the angel Gabriel's announcement to Mary that she was to become the mother of Jesus. **3.** The Christian feast on March 25 celebrating this event.

anode (ăn′ōd′) *n.* **1.** The positively charged electrode of an electrolytic cell or electron tube. **2.** The negatively charged electrode of a voltaic cell, such as a battery.

anodyne (ăn′ə-dīn′) *adj.* **1.** Able to soothe or eliminate pain. **2.** Relaxing: *The anodyne effects of the drug cured his insomnia.* ❖ *n.* **1.** A medicine that relieves pain. **2.** Something that soothes or comforts.

anoint (ə-noint′) *tr.v.* **anointed, anointing, anoints 1.** To apply oil, ointment, or a similar substance to: *anoint the burn with salve.* **2.** To put oil on in a religious ceremony as a means of making pure or holy: *anoint a king.* —**a·noint′ment** *n.*

anomalous (ə-nŏm′ə-ləs) *adj.* Differing from what is normal or common; abnormal.

anomaly (ə-nŏm′ə-lē) *n., pl.* **anomalies** Something that is unusual, irregular, or abnormal: *Flooding is an anomaly in desert regions of Africa.*

anomie (ăn′ə-mē) *n.* **1.** Alienation and purposelessness experienced by a person or a class as a result of a lack of standards, values, or ideals: *a novel about a troubled teenager suffering from boredom and anomie.* **2.** Social instability caused by erosion of standards and values: *Rapid growth of the economy led to anomie.*

anon (ə-nŏn′) *adv.* **1.** At another time; later. **2.** In a short time; soon.

anon. An abbreviation of anonymous.

anonymity (ăn′ə-nĭm′ĭ-tē) *n., pl.* **anonymities** The condition of being anonymous: *The donor made a large contribution on the condition of anonymity.*

anonymous (ə-nŏn′ə-məs) *adj.* **1.** Nameless or unnamed: *The prize was awarded by a panel of anonymous judges.* **2.** Having an unknown source: *The anonymous letter was sent without a return address.* —**a·non′y·mous·ly** *adv.*

anorak (ăn′ə-răk′) *n.* A heavy jacket with a hood; a parka.

anorexia (ăn′ə-rĕk′sē-ə) *n.* **1.** Loss of appetite, especially as a result of illness. **2.** Anorexia nervosa.

anorexia nervosa (nûr-vō′sə) *n.* An eating disorder usually occurring in young women that is characterized by fear of gaining weight, revulsion toward food, and severe weight loss.

anorexic (ăn′ə-rĕk′sĭk) *adj.* Affected with anorexia nervosa.

another (ə-nŭth′ər) *adj.* **1.** Additional; one more: *another cup of coffee.* **2.** Different: *Let's try another route to the airport next time.* **3.** Some other: *We'll discuss this at another time.* ❖ *pron.* **1.** An additional one: *We ordered one pizza and then another.* **2.** Something or someone different: *A baby is one thing to take care of; a 6-year-old is another.* **3.** One of a group of things: *for one reason or another.*

anoxia (ăn-ŏk′sē-ə) *n.* A lack of oxygen in body tissue, caused by poor blood supply or insufficient levels of oxygen in the blood.

answer (ăn′sər) *n.* **1.** A series of words spoken or written in reaction to a question, request, or other prompting: *I wrote weeks ago but never got an answer.* **2.** An act that serves as a reply or response: *Their answer was to ignore me.* **3a.** A solution or result, as to a problem: *gave the wrong answer.* **b.** The correct solution or response: *guessed the answer to the riddle.* ❖ *v.* **answered, answering, answers** —*intr.* **1.** To speak or write as a reaction to a question or other prompting: *He couldn't take the call*

but answered with a text message. **2.** To act in reaction or as a response: *She answered with a wink.* **3.** To be liable or accountable: *You will have to answer for this mess.* **4.** To match or correspond: *a car answering to this description.* —*tr.* **1.** To produce an answer to: *answer a letter.* **2.** To respond correctly to: *I can't answer the question.* **3.** To fulfill the demands of: *A good rest answered the weary traveler's needs.* **4.** To match or correspond to: *That dog answers the description of the one you're looking for.*

✦ SYNONYMS answer, reply, respond, retort *v.*

answerable (ăn′sər-ə-bəl) *adj.* **1.** Responsible; accountable; liable: *You are answerable for the money in the account.* **2.** Capable of being answered or proved wrong: *scientific questions not wholly answerable.* —**an′swer·a·ble·ness** *n.*

answering machine (ăn′sər-ĭng) *n.* A device that answers a telephone and records messages from callers.

ant (ănt) *n.* Any of numerous insects that live in highly organized colonies and build nests underground or in trees. Most ants are wingless; only the males and fertile females have wings.

ant. An abbreviation of antonym.

ant– Variant of anti–.

–ant A suffix that means: **1.** Performing a certain action or being in a certain state: *defiant; flippant.* **2.** A person or thing that performs or causes a certain action: *coolant; deodorant.*

antacid (ănt-ăs′ĭd) *n.* A substance that neutralizes acids or counteracts acidity, especially one used to neutralize excess stomach acid.

antagonism (ăn-tăg′ə-nĭz′əm) *n.* **1.** Unfriendly feeling; hostility: *antagonism among rival factions.* **2.** Opposition, as between conflicting principles or forces.

antagonist (ăn-tăg′ə-nĭst) *n.* **1.** A person who opposes and actively competes with another; an adversary. **2.** Either of a pair of drugs or other substances that neutralize each other in the body: *An antitoxin is the antagonist of a toxin.* **3.** A muscle that counteracts the action of another muscle, the agonist.

antagonistic (ăn-tăg′ə-nĭs′tĭk) *adj.* **1.** Opposed; contending: *antagonistic points of view.* **2.** Unfriendly; hostile: *an antagonistic attitude.* —**an·tag′o·nis′ti·cal·ly** *adv.*

antagonize (ăn-tăg′ə-nīz′) *tr.v.* **antagonized, antagonizing, antagonizes** To cause (someone) to become angry or hostile; provoke bad feeling in: *They antagonized me by making fun of my suggestion.*

Antarctic (ănt-ärk′tĭk) *adj.* Relating to the regions surrounding the South Pole: *the Antarctic climate.* ❖ *n.* Antarctica and its surrounding waters.

ante (ăn′tē) *n.* In poker, a bet that each player must make to begin or stay in the game. ❖ *v.* **anted** or **anteed, anteing, antes** —*tr.* **1.** To put (one's stake) into the pool in poker. **2.** To pay (money or a fee): *After lunch we anted up the bill.* —*intr.* **1.** To put one's stake into the pool in poker: *The players anted before the cards were dealt.* **2.** To pay for something: *anted for the tickets.*

ante– A prefix that means: **1.** Prior to; earlier: *antedate; antediluvian.* **2.** In front of: *anteroom.*

anteater (ănt′ē′tər) *n.* **1.** Any of several tropical American mammals that lack teeth and feed on ants and termites. **2.** Any of several other animals that feed on ants, such as the aardvark.

antebellum (ăn′tē-bĕl′əm) *adj.* Belonging to the period prior to the Civil War: *an antebellum mansion.*

antecedent (ăn′tĭ-sēd′nt) *adj.* Going before; preceding; prior. ❖ *n.* **1.** A person or thing that precedes another. **2.**

An occurrence or event prior to another. **3. antecedents** A person's ancestors: *I do not know my antecedents beyond my grandparents.* **4.** The word, phrase, or clause to which a pronoun refers. In the sentence *I asked my sister how she was doing,* the phrase *my sister* is the antecedent of *she.* **—an′te·ce′dent·ly** *adv.*

antechamber (ăn′tē-chām′bər) *n.* A waiting room at the entrance to a larger room.

antedate (ăn′tĭ-dāt′) *tr.v.* **antedated, antedating, antedates 1.** To be of an earlier date than: *This novel antedates the writer's poetry.* **2.** To give (something) a date earlier than the actual date; date back: *Management antedated the union's contract to the first of the year.*

antediluvian (ăn′tĭ-də-lōo′vē-ən) *adj.* **1.** Believed to belong to the period before the flood described in Genesis. **2.** Very old; antiquated: *The horse and buggy is an antediluvian way of travel.*

antelope (ăn′tl-ōp′) *n., pl.* **antelope** or **antelopes 1.** Any of various swift-running mammals of Africa and Asia, having unbranched horns. **2.** The pronghorn of western North America.

ante meridiem (ăn′tē mə-rĭd′ē-əm) *adv. & adj.* Before noon. It is normally used in its abbreviated form to show time, as in 7:45 AM.

antenna (ăn-tĕn′ə) *n.* **1.** *pl.* **antennae** (ăn-tĕn′ē) One of a pair of long, slender, segmented structures on the head of an insect, a centipede, or a crustacean such as a lobster or shrimp. Most antennae are organs of touch, but some are sensitive to odors and other stimuli. **2.** *pl.* **antennas** A metallic device for sending and receiving electromagnetic waves, such as radio or television signals.

antepenult (ăn′tē-pē′nŭlt′ *or* ăn′tē-pĭ-nŭlt′) *n.* The third syllable from the end of a word, as *te* in *antepenult.*

antepenultimate (ăn′tē-pĭ-nŭl′tə-mĭt) *adj.* Coming third from the last in a series.

anterior (ăn-tîr′ē-ər) *adj.* **1.** Placed in front; located forward: *a small anterior room leading to the main hall.* **2a.** In, relating to, or near the side of the human body on which the abdomen is found. **b.** In, relating to, or near the head of a nonhuman animal. **3.** Prior in time; earlier.

anteroom (ăn′tē-rōom′ *or* ăn′tē-rōom′) *n.* An antechamber.

anthem (ăn′thəm) *n.* **1.** A song of praise or loyalty: *a national anthem.* **2.** A piece of music having words from a sacred text. **3.** A popular song, especially a rock song felt to sum up the attitudes or feelings associated with a period or social group.

anther (ăn′thər) *n.* The pollen-bearing part at the tip of the stamen of a flower.

anthill (ănt′hĭl′) *n.* A mound of earth or sand formed by ants in digging or building a nest.

anthology (ăn-thŏl′ə-jē) *n., pl.* **anthologies** A collection of writings, such as poems or stories, by various authors.

anthracite (ăn′thrə-sīt′) *n.* A hard shiny coal that has a high carbon content and burns with a clean flame.

anthrax (ăn′thrăks′) *n.* An infectious, usually fatal disease of mammals, especially cattle and sheep, caused by a bacterium. It can spread to people, causing symptoms ranging from blistering of the skin to potentially fatal infection of the lungs.

anthropocentric (ăn′thrə-pə-sĕn′trĭk) *adj.* **1.** Regarding humans as the most important element of the universe. **2.** Interpreting reality exclusively in terms of human values and experience. **—an′thro·po·cen′tri·cal·ly** *adv.* **—an′thro·po·cen′trism** *n.*

anthropoid (ăn′thrə-poid′) *adj.* **1.** Belonging to the group of primates that consists of the monkeys and the apes, including humans. **2.** Resembling a nonhuman ape; apelike: *We caught a glimpse of an anthropoid figure in the vegetation.* ❖ *n.* An ape or apelike animal.

anthropology (ăn′thrə-pŏl′ə-jē) *n.* The scientific study of the origin, the behavior, and the physical, social, and cultural development of humans. **—an′thro·po·log′i·cal** (ăn′thrə-pə-lŏj′ĭ-kəl) *adj.* **—an′thro·po·log′i·cal·ly** *adv.* **—an′thro·pol′o·gist** *n.*

anthropomorphism (ăn′thrə-pə-môr′fĭz′əm) *n.* Attribution of human motivation, characteristics, or behavior to inanimate objects, animals, or natural phenomena. **—an′thro·po·mor′phic** *adj.*

anthropomorphize (ăn′thrə-pə-môr′fīz′) *v.* **anthropomorphized, anthropomorphizing, anthropomorphizes** *—tr.* To ascribe human characteristics to. *—intr.* To ascribe human characteristics to things that are not human.

anti- or **ant-** A prefix that means: **1.** Opposite: *antihero.* **2.** Opposing: *anti-Semitism.* **3.** Counteracting or destroying: *antibiotic; antiaircraft.*

antiaircraft (ăn′tē-âr′krăft′) *adj.* Designed for defense, especially from a position on the ground, against attack by aircraft: *antiaircraft missiles.*

antiballistic missile (ăn′tĭ-bə-lĭs′tĭk) *n.* A missile designed to intercept and destroy a ballistic missile in flight.

antibiotic (ăn′tĭ-bī-ŏt′ĭk) *n.* A substance, such as penicillin, that is capable of destroying or weakening certain microorganisms, especially disease-causing bacteria. Most antibiotics are obtained from other bacteria or from fungi, but some are made synthetically. ❖ *adj.* Relating to antibiotics: *an antibiotic drug.*

antibody (ăn′tĭ-bŏd′ē) *n.* A protein produced in the blood or tissues in response to the presence of a specific antigen, such as a microorganism or a toxin. An antibody deactivates an antigen by binding with it.

antic (ăn′tĭk) *n.* A playful, foolish, or funny act: *The clown's antics amused us.*

antichrist (ăn′tĭ-krīst′) *n.* **1. Antichrist** In some branches of Christianity, the great enemy who is expected to set himself up against Christ in the last days before the end of the world. **2.** An enemy of Christ.

anticipate (ăn-tĭs′ə-pāt′) *tr.v.* **anticipated, anticipating, anticipates 1.** To consider as a probable occurrence; expect: *We hadn't anticipated such a crowd at the zoo.* **2.** To think of (a future event) with pleasure; look forward to: *We anticipated a pleasant vacation in Canada.* **3.** To deal with beforehand: *Store owners anticipated the storm by boarding up their windows.* **—an·tic′i·pa′tor** *n.*

anticipation (ăn-tĭs′ə-pā′shən) *n.* **1.** The act of expecting or foreseeing something, especially with eagerness or happiness: *She looked forward to vacation with great anticipation.* **2.** Action taken in order to prevent or counteract something: *The town's anticipation of big crowds made the street fair a success.*

anticlerical (ăn′tē-klĕr′ĭ-kəl) *adj.* Opposed to the influence of the church or the clergy in public life.

anticlimactic (ăn′tē-klī-măk′tĭk) *adj.* Relating to or being an anticlimax. **—an′ti·cli·mac′ti·cal·ly** *adv.*

anticlimax (ăn′tē-klī′măks′) *n.* **1.** A decline or letdown viewed as a disappointing contrast to what has gone before: *The rest of the story was an anticlimax to the scene in the courtroom.* **2.** A less important or trivial event that follows a series of significant ones: *Rain showers were an anticlimax after the full force of the hurricane.*

anticline (ăn′tĭ-klīn′) *n.* A fold of rock layers that slope downward on both sides from a crest. —**an′ti·cli′nal** (ăn′tĕ-klī′nəl) *adj.*

anticoagulant (ăn′tē-kō-ăg′yə-lənt) *n.* A substance that prevents or slows the clotting of blood.

anticyclone (ăn′tē-sī′klōn′) *n.* A system of winds that spiral outward around a region of high atmospheric pressure, circling clockwise in the Northern Hemisphere and counterclockwise in the Southern Hemisphere.

antidepressant (ăn′tē-dĭ-prĕs′ənt) *n.* A drug that is used to treat clinical depression. —**an′ti·de·pres′sant** *adj.*

antidote (ăn′tĭ-dōt′) *n.* **1.** A substance that counteracts the effects of poison. **2.** Something that relieves or counteracts something: *Volunteering can be an antidote to loneliness.*

antifreeze (ăn′tĭ-frēz′) *n.* A substance added to a liquid, such as water, to lower its freezing point.

antigen (ăn′tĭ-jən) *n.* A substance that stimulates the production of an antibody when introduced into the body. Antigens include toxins, bacterial cells, and foreign blood cells.

Antigone (ăn-tĭg′ə-nē) *n.* In Greek mythology, the daughter of Oedipus and Jocasta who performed funeral rites over her brother's body in defiance of her uncle, the king of Thebes.

antigravity (ăn′tē-grăv′ĭ-tē) *n.* A supposed physical force that would counteract gravity.

antihero (ăn′tē-hîr′ō) *n., pl.* **antiheroes** A main character in a novel, play, or other work who lacks traditional heroic qualities, such as courage.

antiheroine (ăn′tē-hĕr′ō-ĭn) *n.* An antihero who is a woman or girl.

antihistamine (ăn′tē-hĭs′tə-mēn′ *or* ăn′tē-hĭs′tə-mĭn) *n.* Any of various drugs that relieve symptoms of allergies or colds by interfering with the action of histamine in the body.

antilock brakes (ăn′tē-lŏk′ *or* ăn′tĭ-lŏk′) *pl.n.* A braking system in a motor vehicle in which electronic sensors detect when the wheels have suddenly slowed down and a computer chip repeatedly decreases and increases brake pressure in order to prevent the wheels from locking and the vehicle from skidding.

antilog (ăn′tĭ-lôg′) *n.* An antilogarithm.

antilogarithm (ăn′tē-lô′gə-rĭth′əm) *n.* The number whose logarithm is a given number. For example, the logarithm of 1,000 (or 10^3) is 3, so the antilogarithm of 3 is 1,000.

antimacassar (ăn′tĭ-mə-kăs′ər) *n.* A small cover placed on the back of a chair or sofa to keep it from getting dirty.

antimatter (ăn′tĭ-măt′ər) *n.* A form of matter having certain properties, including electric charge, that are opposite to or incompatible with the properties of regular matter. Antimatter is made of positrons, antiprotons, and antineutrons.

antimissile (ăn′tē-mĭs′əl) *adj.* Designed to intercept and destroy a missile in flight: *an antimissile system.*

antimony (ăn′tə-mō′nē) *n. Symbol* **Sb** A metallic element, the most common form of which is a hard, extremely brittle, blue-white crystal. It is used in a wide variety of alloys, especially with lead in car batteries. Atomic number 51. See **Periodic Table.**

antineutrino (ăn′tē-nōō-trē′nō) *n., pl.* **antineutrinos** The antiparticle of the neutrino.

antineutron (ăn′tē-nōō′trŏn′) *n.* The antiparticle of the neutron.

antinomian (ăn′tĭ-nō′mē-ən) *n.* **1.** *Christianity* One who holds that Christian believers are exempt from obedience to any law. **2.** One who denies the fixed meaning or universal applicability of moral law. —**an′ti·no′mi·an** *adj.*

antinuclear (ăn′tē-nōō′klē-ər) *adj.* Opposing the production or use of nuclear power or nuclear weaponry.

antioxidant (ăn′tē-ŏk′sĭ-dənt *or* ăn′tĭ-ŏk′sĭ-dənt) *n.* A chemical compound or substance that inhibits oxidation. Certain vitamins, such as vitamin E, are antioxidants and may protect body cells from damage due to oxidation.

antiparticle (ăn′tē-pär′tĭ-kəl) *n.* A particle of antimatter that corresponds to a particle of matter, such as an electron or proton, but has different electrical or magnetic properties. Positrons, antiprotons and antineutrons are examples of antiparticles.

antipasto (ăn′tē-päs′tō) *n., pl.* **antipastos** or **antipasti** (ăn′tē-päs′tē) An appetizer usually consisting of an assortment of foods, such as smoked meats, cheese, and vegetables.

antipathy (ăn-tĭp′ə-thē) *n., pl.* **antipathies 1.** A feeling of dislike or opposition: *Some people always express antipathy to new ideas.* **2.** Incompatibility: *the antipathy between emotion and logic.*

antiperspirant (ăn′tē-pûr′spər-ənt) *n.* A preparation applied to the skin to reduce or prevent perspiration.

antiphon (ăn′tə-fŏn′) *n.* A composition to be sung or chanted by two groups of singers in alternation, especially as part of a Christian liturgy.

antiphony (ăn-tĭf′ə-nē) *n., pl.* **antiphonies 1.** Singing by two singers or groups of singers in alternation. **2.** An antiphon. —**an·tiph′o·nal** (ăn-tĭf′ə-nəl) *adj.*

antipodal (ăn-tĭp′ə-dəl) *adj.* Relating to or situated on opposite sides of the earth.

antipodes (ăn-tĭp′ə-dēz′) *pl.n.* Two places on directly opposite sides of the earth: *The North Pole and the South Pole are antipodes.*

antiproton (ăn′tē-prō′tŏn′) *n.* The antiparticle of the proton.

antiquarian (ăn′tĭ-kwâr′ē-ən) *n.* A person who studies, collects, sells, or buys relics and ancient works of art. ❖ *adj.* Relating to antiquarians or the study of antiquities.

antiquary (ăn′tĭ-kwĕr′ē) *n., pl.* **antiquaries** An antiquarian.

antiquate (ăn′tĭ-kwāt′) *tr.v.* **antiquated, antiquating, antiquates** To make obsolete or old-fashioned.

antiquated (ăn′tĭ-kwā′tĭd) *adj.* Too old to be useful, suitable, or fashionable.

antique (ăn-tēk′) *adj.* **1.** Belonging to, made in, or typical of an earlier period: *antique furniture.* **2.** Relating to or belonging to ancient times, especially to ancient Greek or Roman civilization: *the antique legend of the founding of Rome.* **3.** Very old; old-fashioned: *an antique style of writing.* ❖ *n.* Something having special value because of its age, especially a work of art or handicraft that is over 100 years old. ❖ *tr.v.* **antiqued, antiquing, antiques** To give the appearance of an antique to: *That chair has been antiqued.*

antiquity (ăn-tĭk′wĭ-tē) *n., pl.* **antiquities 1.** Ancient times, especially the times before the Middle Ages: *The pyramids of ancient Egypt belong to antiquity.* **2.** The people of ancient times, especially the writers of those times:

an invention unknown to antiquity. **3.** The quality of being old: *a carving of great antiquity.* **4.** Something, such as a relic, that dates from ancient times: *That museum has a collection of many antiquities from ancient Greece.*

anti-Semitism (ăn′tē-sĕm′ĭ-tĭz′əm) *n.* Prejudice against or hostility toward Jews. —**an′ti-Se·mit′ic** (ăn′tē-sə-mĭt′ĭk) *adj.*

antiseptic (ăn′tĭ-sĕp′tĭk) *adj.* **1.** Preventing infection, fermentation, or rot by stopping the growth and activity of microorganisms. **2.** Free of microorganisms that cause infection; aseptic. ❖ *n.* An antiseptic substance or agent, such as alcohol or boric acid. —**an′ti·sep′ti·cal·ly** *adv.*

antislavery (ăn′tē-slā′və-rē) *adj.* Opposed to or against slavery.

antisocial (ăn′tē-sō′shəl) *adj.* **1.** Avoiding the society or company of others; not sociable: *an antisocial recluse.* **2.** Hostile to or violating accepted rules of behavior: *Criminal acts are examples of antisocial behavior.* —**an′ti·so′cial·ly** *adv.*

antiterrorist (ăn′tē-tĕr′ər-ĭst) *adj.* Designed to combat terrorists or terrorism: *antiterrorist experts.*

antithesis (ăn-tĭth′ĭ-sĭs) *n., pl.* **antitheses** (ăn-tĭth′ĭ-sēz′) **1.** Direct contrast; opposition: *Your behavior stands in antithesis to your beliefs.* **2.** The direct or exact opposite: *Hope is the antithesis of despair.* **3.** In speech or writing, the placing together of sharply opposed ideas.

antitoxin (ăn′tē-tŏk′sĭn) *n.* **1.** An antibody formed in response to and capable of acting against a biological toxin, such as one produced by bacteria. **2.** A serum containing antibodies, obtained from the blood of a human or other animal that has had a particular disease or was immunized against infection from the disease. The antitoxin is used to provide immunity against that disease.

antitrust (ăn′tē-trŭst′) *adj.* Opposing or regulating trusts or similar business monopolies, especially in order to promote competition: *antitrust laws that prevent unfair business practices.*

antivenin (ăn′tē-vĕn′ĭn) *n.* **1.** An antitoxin that counteracts the venom of a snake, scorpion, or other venomous animal. **2.** A human or animal serum containing such an antitoxin.

antiwar (ăn′tē-wôr′) *adj.* Opposing war: *an antiwar demonstration.*

antler (ănt′lər) *n.* One of a pair of bony growths on the head of a deer, moose, elk, or other related animal, usually having several branches. Antlers are shed and grown again every year and are usually found only on males.

ant lion *n.* Any of various insects whose larvae have large jaws and dig conical pits in the sand to trap ants and other insects for food.

antonym (ăn′tə-nĭm′) *n.* A word having a meaning opposite to that of another word; for example, *thick* is an antonym of *thin.*

antsy (ănt′sē) *adj.* **antsier, antsiest** *Slang* Uneasy; anxious; restless.

Anubis (ə-nōō′bĭs) *n.* In Egyptian mythology, a jackal-headed god who conducted the dead to the underworld.

anus (ā′nəs) *n., pl.* **anuses** The opening at the lower end of the digestive tract through which solid waste is excreted.

anvil (ăn′vĭl) *n.* **1.** A heavy block of iron or steel, with a smooth flat top on which metals are shaped by hammering. **2.** The incus.

anxiety (ăng-zī′ĭ-tē) *n., pl.* **anxieties** **1.** A feeling of uneasiness and distress, especially about something in the future; worry: *The settlers were filled with anxiety about*

food supplies in the coming winter. **2.** Eagerness or earnestness, often marked by uneasiness: *the pianist's anxiety to play well.*

anxious (ăngk′shəs *or* ăng′shəs) *adj.* **1.** Having a feeling of uneasiness; worried: *They were anxious about the upcoming exam.* **2.** Marked by uneasiness or worry: *anxious moments.* **3.** Eagerly desirous or earnest: *We were anxious for the bike race to begin.* —**anx′ious·ly** *adv.* —**anx′ious·ness** *n.*

any (ĕn′ē) *adj.* **1.** One or some; no matter which: *Take any book you want. Do you have any information on Chinese cooking?* **2.** No matter how many or how few; some: *Are there any oranges left?* **3.** Every: *Any dog likes meat.* ❖ *pron.* (*used with a singular or plural verb*) Any person or thing or any persons or things; anybody or anything: *We haven't any left. Any of the teachers can help you.* ❖ *adv.* At all: *The paint doesn't feel any better.*

anybody (ĕn′ē-bŏd′ē *or* ĕn′ē-bŭd′ē) *pron.* **1.** Any person; anyone. **2.** A person of importance: *Everybody who is anybody came to the party.*

anyhow (ĕn′ē-hou′) *adv.* **1.** Anyway: *The twins were sick, but they didn't want to go anyhow.* **2.** Nonetheless: *You may already know this, but I'll tell you anyhow.*

anymore (ĕn′ē-môr′) *adv.* **1.** Any longer; at the present: *Do they make this style anymore?* **2.** From now on: *The children promised not to yell anymore.*

anyone (ĕn′ē-wŭn′) *pron.* Any person; anybody.

anyplace (ĕn′ē-plās′) *adv.* Anywhere: *You can sit anyplace you like.*

anything (ĕn′ē-thĭng′) *pron.* Any object, occurrence, or matter whatever. ❖ *adv.* To any degree or extent; at all: *Is your bike anything like mine?* ◆ **anything but** By no means; not at all: *This room is anything but warm.*

anytime (ĕn′ē-tīm′) *adv.* At any time: *Anytime we come inside we should wipe our feet.*

anyway (ĕn′ē-wā′) *adv.* **1.** In any case; at least: *I don't know if the book is lost or stolen; anyway, it's gone.* **2.** In any manner whatever: *Get the job done anyway you can.* **3.** Just the same; nevertheless; anyhow: *The ball was slippery, but the fielder caught it anyway.*

anyways (ĕn′ē-wāz′) *adv.* Nonstandard In any case.

anywhere (ĕn′ē-wâr′) *adv.* **1.** To, in, or at any place: *They travel anywhere they want to.* **2.** At all: *We aren't anywhere near finished.* **3.** Used to indicate the limits of a range of values: *A wolf's color can be anywhere from white to black.*

ao dai (ou′ dī *or* ô′ dī) *n., pl.* **ao dais** A traditional garment worn by Vietnamese women, consisting of a sleeved blouse that extends to the knees and is slit on the sides up to the hips. It is worn over loose-fitting pants.

A-OK (ā′ō-kā′) *adj. Informal* Perfectly all right: *It's A-OK with me if you leave early.*

A-one (ā′wŭn′) *adj. Informal* First-class; excellent.

aorta (ā-ôr′tə) *n., pl.* **aortas** also **aortae** (ā-ôr′tē) The main artery of the body, starting at the left ventricle of the heart and extending into the abdomen, where it branches into smaller arteries that carry blood to all the organs of the body except the lungs.

apace (ə-pās′) *adv.* At a rapid pace; swiftly: *The building of the new hospital is proceeding apace.*

Apache (ə-păch′ē) *n., pl.* **Apache** or **Apaches** **1.** A member of a Native American people of the southwestern United States. **2.** Any of the Athabascan languages of the Apache.

apart (ə-pärt′) *adv.* **1.** Away from another in time or position: *two trees about ten feet apart.* **2.** In or into separate pieces; to pieces: *The wagon fell apart as it crashed into* *the rocks.* **3.** One from another: *Can you tell the puppies apart?* **4.** Aside or in reserve: *set money apart for a vacation.* **5.** Being excepted or excluded from consideration; aside: *Joking apart, I think you're crazy.* ❖ *adj.* Set apart; isolated: *Unusually strong winds made this storm one apart from the others.* —**a·part′ness** *n.*

apart from *prep.* Other than; not counting: *Apart from a few showers, we had fine weather on our vacation.*

apartheid (ə-pärt′hīt′ *or* ə-pärt′hāt′) *n.* An official policy of segregation formerly practiced in South Africa, involving legal and economic discrimination against nonwhites.

apartment (ə-pärt′mənt) *n.* A room or group of rooms to live in.

apartment building *n.* A building divided into apartments.

apartment house *n.* An apartment building.

apathetic (ăp′ə-thĕt′ĭk) *adj.* Feeling or showing little or no interest; uninterested; indifferent: *Adults who are apathetic about politics should not complain about poor government.* —**ap′a·thet′i·cal·ly** *adv.*

apathy (ăp′ə-thē) *n.* Lack of feeling or interest; indifference: *Apathy among our friends made it difficult to organize the skiing trip.*

apatosaurus (ə-păt′ə-sôr′əs) *n.* A very large plant-eating dinosaur of the Jurassic Period, having a long neck and tail and a relatively small head. —SEE NOTE AT **brontosaurus.**

ape (āp) *n.* Any of several large tailless primates. The apes include the gibbons, orangutans, gorillas, chimpanzees, bonobos, and humans. ❖ *tr.v.* **aped, aping, apes** To imitate the actions of; mimic: *Everyone laughed when Brian started aping his teacher.* —**ap′er** *n.*

apéritif (ä-pĕr′ĭ-tēf′) *n.* An alcoholic drink taken before a meal to stimulate the appetite.

aperture (ăp′ər-chər) *n.* **1.** A hole or an opening: *an aperture in the wall.* **2.** The diameter of the opening through which light can pass into a camera, telescope, or other optical instrument.

apex (ā′pĕks) *n., pl.* **apexes** or **apices** (ā′pĭ-sēz′ *or* ăp′ĭ-sēz′) **1.** The highest point of a geometric figure or of a structure: *the apex of a pyramid.* **2.** The highest level of a hierarchy: *working at the apex of a corporation.* **3.** The period of greatest achievement: *The runner won many victories at the apex of her great career.*

aphasia (ə-fā′zhə) *n.* The loss of some or all of the ability to speak, express ideas, or understand language, resulting from damage to the brain from injury or disease. —**a·pha′sic** (ə-fā′zĭk *or* ə-fā′sĭk) *adj. & n.*

aphelion (ə-fē′lē-ən) *n., pl.* **aphelia** (ə-fē′lē-ə) The point on the orbit of a celestial object that is farthest from the sun.

aphid (ā′fĭd *or* ăf′ĭd) *n.* Any of various small, soft-bodied insects that feed by sucking sap from plants.

aphorism (ăf′ə-rĭz′əm) *n.* A short saying expressing a general truth; for example, "The only way to have a friend is to be one" is an aphorism.

aphrodisiac (ăf′rə-dē′zē-ăk′ *or* ăf′rə-dĭz′ē-ăk′) *n.* A drug or food that stimulates sexual desire. ❖ *adj.* Sexually stimulating.

Aphrodite (ăf′rə-dī′tē) *n.* In Greek mythology, the goddess of love and beauty, identified with the Roman Venus.

API An abbreviation of Asian and Pacific Islander.

apiarist (ā′pē-ə-rĭst) *n.* A beekeeper.

apiary (ā′pē-ĕr′ē) *n., pl.* **apiaries** A place where bees and beehives are kept, especially a place where bees are raised for their honey.

apices (ā′pĭ-sēz′ *or* ăp′ĭ-sēz′) *n.* A plural of **apex.**

apiece (ə-pēs′) *adv.* To or for each one; each: *Give them an apple apiece.*

apish (ā′pĭsh) *adj.* **1.** Resembling an ape. **2.** Foolishly imitative. **3.** Silly, ridiculous: *an apish grin.* —**ap′ish·ly** *adv.*

aplenty (ə-plĕn′tē) *adj.* In abundance: *We'll have water aplenty when the floods come.*

aplomb (ə-plŏm′ *or* ə-plŭm′) *n.* Self-confidence; poise; assurance: *The waiter handled the situation with aplomb.*

apnea (ăp′nē-ə) *n.* Temporary absence of breathing.

APO An abbreviation of Army Post Office.

apocalypse (ə-pŏk′ə-lĭps′) *n.* **1. Apocalypse** The book of Revelation. **2.** The end of the world. **3.** A prophecy or revelation, especially about the end of the world.

apocalyptic (ə-pŏk′ə-lĭp′tĭk) *adj.* **1.** Relating to or predicting the end of the world, especially as described in the Bible or another religious text. **2.** Relating to or predicting widespread destruction or the collapse of civilization: *an apocalyptic novel.*

Apocrypha (ə-pŏk′rə-fə) *n.* (*used with a singular or plural verb*) **1.** Those books of the Old Testament that are accepted as canonical by Roman Catholic and Orthodox Christians but not by Protestants because they are not part of the Hebrew Scriptures. **2.** Various early Christian writings excluded from the New Testament.

apocryphal (ə-pŏk′rə-fəl) *adj.* **1.** Of doubtful origin; false: *Folk legend is full of apocryphal stories of animals coming to the aid of humans in distress.* **2.** Relating to the Apocrypha. —**a·poc′ry·phal·ly** *adv.*

apogee (ăp′ə-jē) *n.* **1.** The point in an orbit around Earth where a satellite is farthest from Earth. **2.** The highest point; apex.

Apollo (ə-pŏl′ō) *n.* In Greek and Roman mythology, the god of prophecy, music, medicine, and poetry, sometimes identified with the sun.

Apollonian (ăp′ə-lō′nē-ən) *adj.* **1.** In Greek and Roman mythology, relating to Apollo or the worship of Apollo. **2.** often **apollonian** Characterized by clarity, harmony, reason, and restraint.

apologetic (ə-pŏl′ə-jĕt′ĭk) *adj.* Expressing or making an apology: *an apologetic smile.* —**a·pol′o·get′i·cal·ly** *adv.*

apologetics (ə-pŏl′ə-jĕt′ĭks) *n.* (*used with a singular verb*) Formal argumentation in defense of something, such as a religion or a political system.

apologia (ăp′ə-lō′jē-ə) *n.* A formal defense or justification.

apologist (ə-pŏl′ə-jĭst) *n.* A person who argues in defense or justification of an idea or cause, especially one that is controversial: *an apologist for imperialism.*

apologize (ə-pŏl′ə-jīz′) *intr.v.* **apologized, apologizing, apologizes** To make an apology; say one is sorry: *Did he apologize for being late?*

apology (ə-pŏl′ə-jē) *n., pl.* **apologies 1.** A statement expressing regret for an offense or fault: *make an apology for being late.* **2.** A defense or justification, as of an idea or cause: *Her letter to the editor is an apology for animal rights.* **3.** An inferior substitute: *That short note was a poor apology for a letter.*

apoplectic (ăp′ə-plĕk′tĭk) *adj.* **1.** Extremely angry; furious. **2.** Relating to or resembling apoplexy. —**ap′o·plec′ti·cal·ly** *adv.*

apoplexy (ăp**ʹ**ə-plĕk**ʹ**sē) *n.* A condition in which a blood vessel in the brain breaks or becomes blocked, often resulting in paralysis, unconsciousness, or death; a stroke.

apostasy (ə-pŏs**ʹ**tə-sē) *n., pl.* **apostasies** A giving up of a particular religious faith, political party, or cause.

apostate (ə-pŏs**ʹ**tāt**ʹ** *or* ə-pŏs**ʹ**tĭt) *n.* A person who has abandoned a particular religious faith, political party, or cause.

apostle (ə-pŏs**ʹ**əl) *n.* **1.** often **Apostle** In Christianity, one of the twelve original disciples of Jesus. **2.** A missionary of the early Christian Church: *St. Patrick, the apostle of Ireland.* **3.** A person who leads or strongly supports a cause or movement: *an apostle of government reform.*

Apostles' Creed (ə-pŏs**ʹ**əlz) *n.* A Christian creed traditionally thought to have been written by the 12 Apostles.

apostolic (ăp**ʹ**ə-stŏl**ʹ**ĭk) *adj.* **1.** Relating to the 12 Apostles, their teaching, or their practices. **2.** In the Roman Catholic Church, relating to the pope as successor to Saint Peter: *apostolic authority.*

apostrophe (ə-pŏs**ʹ**trə-fē) *n.* A mark (') used to indicate the omission of a letter or letters from a word or phrase, as in *aren't,* or to show the possessive case, as in *Tom's hat,* or certain plurals, such as those of single letters, as in *A's.*

apothecaries' measure (ə-pŏth**ʹ**ĭ-kĕr**ʹ**ēz) *n.* A system of liquid volume measure used in pharmacy, now largely replaced by the metric system.

apothecaries' weight *n.* A system of weights used in pharmacy based on an ounce equal to 480 grains and a pound equal to 12 ounces, now largely replaced by the metric system.

apothecary (ə-pŏth**ʹ**ĭ-kĕr**ʹ**ē) *n., pl.* **apothecaries** A person who prepares or sells medicines; a pharmacist.

apothegm (ăp**ʹ**ə-thĕm**ʹ**) *n.* A short and witty instructive saying; a maxim.

apotheosis (ə-pŏth**ʹ**ē-ō**ʹ**sĭs) *n., pl.* **apotheoses** (ə-pŏth**ʹ**ē-ō**ʹ**sēz**ʹ**) **1.** The elevation to divine rank or status; deification: *the apotheosis of a Roman emperor.* **2.** A glorified ideal or example: *The dancer was considered the apotheosis of grace.*

app (ăp) *n.* A computer application.

appall (ə-pôl**ʹ**) *tr.v.* **appalled, appalling, appalls** To fill with horror and amazement; shock: *I was appalled at what my roommate had done to the bathroom.*

appalling (ə-pô**ʹ**lĭng) *adj.* Causing horrified disapproval or dismay: *the appalling working conditions of miners in the last century.* —**ap·pall**ʹ**ing·ly** *adv.*

Appaloosa (ăp**ʹ**ə-loo**ʹ**sə) *n.* Any of a breed of spotted horse originally bred in northwest North America.

apparatus (ăp**ʹ**ə-răt**ʹ**əs *or* ăp**ʹ**ə-rā**ʹ**təs) *n., pl.* **apparatus** or **apparatuses** **1.** A device, mechanism, or structure for a particular purpose: *an apparatus designed to measure radiation.* **2.** The means by which some function or task is performed: *Congress has a complicated apparatus for making laws.*

apparel (ə-păr**ʹ**əl) *n.* Clothing; attire: *a store that sells children's apparel.* ❖ *tr.v.* **appareled, appareling, apparels** or **apparelled, apparelling, apparels** To dress or clothe: *The queen was appareled in velvet robes.*

apparent (ə-pâr**ʹ**ənt) *adj.* **1.** Readily understood or seen; obvious: *for no apparent reason.* **2.** Appearing as such but not necessarily so; seeming: *an apparent advantage.* —**ap·par**ʹ**ent·ly** *adv.* —**ap·par**ʹ**ent·ness** *n.*

apparition (ăp**ʹ**ə-rĭsh**ʹ**ən) *n.* **1.** A ghost; a specter. **2.** An eerie sight.

appeal (ə-pēl**ʹ**) *n.* **1a.** An urgent or earnest request: *an appeal for help.* **b.** A request of a person to decide something in one's favor: *They made an appeal to the bus driver to stop at a restaurant.* **2.** The power of attracting or of arousing interest: *The waterfront has great appeal for tourists.* **3a.** A higher court's review of the correctness of a decision by a lower court. **b.** A case so reviewed: *The judge will hear the appeal on Friday.* **c.** A request for a new hearing: *grant an appeal.* ❖ *v.* **appealed, appealing, appeals** —*intr.* **1.** To make an urgent or earnest request: *I appeal to you to help us.* **2.** To be attractive or interesting: *Those shoes appeal to me.* **3.** To make or apply for a legal appeal: *If the judge decides against us, we will appeal.* —*tr.* To make or apply for a legal appeal of: *appealed the decision to a higher court.*

appealing (ə-pē**ʹ**lĭng) *adj.* Attractive or interesting: *appealing clothes.*

appear (ə-pîr**ʹ**) *intr.v.* **appeared, appearing, appears 1a.** To come into view: *A ship appeared on the horizon.* **b.** To be shown or included: *Their logo appears on all of their products.* **2.** To seem or look: *The child appears unhappy.* **3.** To present oneself formally before a court of law: *The criminal appeared before the judge.* **4.** To come before the public: *The violinist has appeared in two concerts.*

appearance (ə-pîr**ʹ**əns) *n.* **1.** The act of appearing; a coming into sight: *the sudden appearance of storm clouds on the horizon.* **2.** The act of coming into public view: *nine years since the pianist's last personal appearance.* **3.** The way something or someone looks or appears: *A neat appearance helps to make a good impression.* **4.** A semblance or false show: *The frightened soldier was only keeping up an appearance of bravery.* ◆ **by all appearances** or **to all appearances** From what one can tell from external circumstances: *By all appearances the car had been abandoned.*

appease (ə-pēz**ʹ**) *tr.v.* **appeased, appeasing, appeases 1a.** To calm the anger of (a person or group), especially by yielding to their demands: *The company's promise to raise wages appeased the striking miners.* **b.** To calm, soothe, or quiet (someone): *She appeased the baby with a pacifier.* **2.** To satisfy; relieve: *A tall glass of water appeased his thirst.* —**ap·peas**ʹ**er** *n.*

appeasement (ə-pēz**ʹ**mənt) *n.* **1.** An act of appeasing or a condition of being appeased. **2.** A policy of attempting to avoid war by meeting the demands of a threatening nation.

appellant (ə-pĕl**ʹ**ənt) *n.* A person who appeals a court decision.

appellate (ə-pĕl**ʹ**ĭt) *adj.* Having the legal power to hear appeals and to reverse previous court decisions: *an appellate court.*

appellation (ăp**ʹ**ə-lā**ʹ**shən) *n.* A name or title: *The telephone company was known by the appellation "Ma Bell."*

append (ə-pĕnd**ʹ**) *tr.v.* **appended, appending, appends** To attach; add: *appended a correction to the article.*

appendage (ə-pĕn**ʹ**dĭj) *n.* A part, such as an arm, leg, tail, or antenna, that hangs or projects from the body of an organism: *the feathery appendages of a barnacle.*

appendectomy (ăp**ʹ**ən-dĕk**ʹ**tə-mē) *n., pl.* **appendectomies** The removal of the appendix by surgery.

appendicitis (ə-pĕn**ʹ**dĭ-sī**ʹ**tĭs) *n.* Inflammation of the appendix.

appendix (ə-pĕn**ʹ**dĭks) *n., pl.* **appendixes** or **appendices** (ə-pĕn**ʹ**dĭ-sēz**ʹ**) **1.** A section at the end of a book containing additional material, tables, or other information relating to the subject of the book. **2.** The tubular projection attached to the large intestine near where it joins the small intestine.

appertain (ăp'ər-tān') *intr.v.* **appertained, appertaining, appertains** To belong as a function or part; have relation; pertain: *the policies of government that appertain to economic reform.*

appetite (ăp'ĭ-tīt') *n.* **1.** The desire for food or drink. **2.** A strong desire for something: *an appetite for learning.*

appetizer (ăp'ĭ-tī'zər) *n.* A food or drink taken before a meal to stimulate the appetite.

appetizing (ăp'ĭ-tī'zĭng) *adj.* Stimulating or appealing to the appetite; tasty: *an appetizing meal.* —**ap'pe·tiz'-ing·ly** *adv.*

applaud (ə-plôd') *v.* **applauded, applauding, applauds** —*intr.* To express approval, especially by clapping the hands: *The audience applauded for ten minutes.* —*tr.* **1.** To express approval of, especially by clapping: *applauded the actors.* **2.** To praise; approve: *I applaud your decision to study Chinese.* —**ap·plaud'a·ble** *adj.* —**ap·plaud'er** *n.* —SEE NOTE AT **explode.**

applause (ə-plôz') *n.* **1.** Praise or approval expressed by the clapping of hands: *The guitarist's performance was cheered with loud applause.* **2.** Public approval: *The vaccine for polio received applause from doctors everywhere.*

apple (ăp'əl) *n.* **1.** A firm, rounded, edible fruit having thin red, yellow, or green skin. **2.** The tree that bears such fruit. ◆ **apple of (one's) eye** A person or thing that is especially liked or loved: *Her grandson is the apple of her eye.*

apple butter *n.* A dark-brown spread made of stewed apples and spices.

applejack (ăp'əl-jăk') *n.* A strong alcoholic drink made by concentrating fermented cider.

applesauce (ăp'əl-sôs') *n.* Apples stewed to a pulp and sometimes sweetened and spiced.

appliance (ə-plī'əns) *n.* A device, especially an electrical one such as a toaster or washing machine, that performs a specific function for household use.

applicable (ăp'lĭ-kə-bəl *or* ə-plĭk'ə-bəl) *adj.* Capable of being applied; appropriate: *The new rule is not applicable in your case.* —**ap'pli·ca·bly** *adv.* —**ap'pli·ca·bil'i·ty** *n.*

applicant (ăp'lĭ-kənt) *n.* A person who applies for something: *an applicant for a job.*

application (ăp'lĭ-kā'shən) *n.* **1.** The act of applying: *Careless application of paint left streaks on the wall.* **2.** Something that is applied, such as a medicine or a cosmetic: *a thick application of salve on a burn.* **3.** A method of applying or using; a specific use: *the application of science to industry.* **4.** A computer program designed for a specific task. **5.** The capacity of being usable; relevance: *Geometry has practical application to flying an airplane.* **6.** Careful work and attention; diligence: *His boss commended him for his steady application to his work.* **7a.** A request, as for a job or admittance to a school. **b.** The form or document upon which such a request is made.

applicator (ăp'lĭ-kā'tər) *n.* An instrument for applying something, such as medicine or glue.

applied (ə-plīd') *adj.* Put into practice; used in a particular way: *applied physics.*

appliqué (ăp'lĭ-kā') *n.* A decoration, design, or trimming made by attaching pieces of one material to the surface of another. ❖ *tr.v.* **appliquéd, appliquéing, appliqués** To put on or apply as a decoration: *appliqué a monogram on a coat.*

apply (ə-plī') *v.* **applied, applying, applies** —*tr.* **1.** To put on: *apply a little bit of glue to the paper.* **2.** To put to or adapt for a special use: *The international charity applied all its money to medical supplies.* **3.** To put into action: *apply the brakes.* **4.** To use (a special word or phrase) in referring to someone or something: *Underground Railroad was the name applied to the system that helped fugitive slaves escape.* **5.** To direct the attention or energy of (oneself) to an activity or pursuit: *The students applied themselves to their homework.* —*intr.* **1.** To be pertinent or relevant: *This rule for quiet in the library does not apply during a fire drill.* **2.** To request employment, acceptance, or admission: *Several people applied for the same job. She is planning to apply to business school.* —**ap·pli'er** *n.*

appoint (ə-point') *tr.v.* **appointed, appointing, appoints** **1.** To select or designate for an office, position, or duty: *appoint a new police chief.* **2.** To decide on or set by authority: *appointed three o'clock for the next meeting.* **3.** To furnish; equip: *The playroom was appointed with sturdy furniture.* —**ap·point'er** *n.*

appointee (ə-poin'tē' *or* ăp'oin-tē') *n.* A person who is appointed to an office, position, or duty.

appointive (ə-poin'tĭv) *adj.* Relating to or filled by appointment: *an appointive office.*

appointment (ə-point'mənt) *n.* **1a.** The act of appointing someone to an office or position: *The appointment of a federal judge is an important decision.* **b.** The office or position to which a person has been appointed: *The professor accepted the appointment as dean of students.* **2.** An arrangement for a meeting at a particular time or place: *I called the dentist to change the time of my appointment.* **3.** **appointments** Furnishings, fittings, or equipment: *tables, chairs, lamps, and other appointments of the room.*

apportion (ə-pôr'shən) *tr.v.* **apportioned, apportioning, apportions** To divide and assign according to some plan or proportion; allot: *apportion money for several departments.*

apportionment (ə-pôr'shən-mənt) *n.* The act of apportioning or the condition of being apportioned: *the apportionment of taxes to pay for expenses of running the town government.*

apposite (ăp'ə-zĭt) *adj.* Appropriate or relevant.

apposition (ăp'ə-zĭsh'ən) *n.* **1a.** In grammar, a construction in which a noun or noun phrase is placed with another noun as a further explanation or description. **b.** The relationship between such nouns or noun phrases. For example, *Rufus* and *the scientist* are in apposition in the sentence *Rufus, the scientist, made another discovery.* **2.** The act of placing side by side or next to each other. —**ap'po·si'tion·al** *adj.* —**ap'po·si'tion·al·ly** *adv.*

appositive (ə-pŏz'ĭ-tĭv) *adj.* Relating to or being in apposition: *an appositive phrase.* ❖ *n.* A noun or phrase that follows and is in apposition with another noun. In the sentence *My friend the chemist works in a laboratory,* the appositive is *the chemist.*

appraisal (ə-prā'zəl) *n.* **1.** The act or an instance of appraising. **2.** An official or expert estimate of something, as for quality or worth.

appraise (ə-prāz') *tr.v.* **appraised, appraising, appraises** **1.** To estimate the price or value of: *The jeweler appraised the customer's ring at $500.* **2.** To make a careful judgment about; assess: *The captain appraised the condition of the scuba gear and found it was excellent.* —**ap·prais'er** *n.*

appreciable (ə-prē'shə-bəl) *adj.* Capable of being noticed or measured; noticeable: *an appreciable difference be-*

tween the two versions. —**ap·pre′cia·bly** *adv.*

appreciate (ə-prē′shē-āt′) *v.* **appreciated, appreciating, appreciates** —*tr.* **1.** To recognize the worth, quality, or importance of; value highly: *The citizens of the new democracy appreciate their freedoms.* **2.** To be aware of or sensitive to; realize: *I appreciate the difficulty of your situation.* **3.** To be thankful for: *The neighbors appreciated our help.* —*intr.* To rise in price or value: *The painting has appreciated greatly since the museum bought it.* —**ap·pre′ci·a′tor** *n.*

✦ **SYNONYMS appreciate, cherish, prize, treasure, value** *v.*

appreciation (ə-prē′shē-ā′shən) *n.* **1.** Recognition of the worth, quality, or importance of something: *Your appreciation of her accomplishments has meant a lot to her.* **2.** Gratitude; gratefulness: *They expressed their appreciation with a gift.* **3.** Awareness of artistic values; understanding and enjoyment: *showing a great appreciation of music and sculpture.* **4.** A rise in value or price: *Appreciation of land has made some farmers wealthy.*

appreciative (ə-prē′shə-tĭv *or* ə-prē′shē-ā′tĭv) *adj.* Showing or feeling appreciation: *applause of an appreciative audience.* —**ap·pre′cia·tive·ly** *adv.*

apprehend (ăp′rĭ-hĕnd′) *tr.v.* **apprehended, apprehending, apprehends** **1.** To take into custody; arrest: *Police officers apprehended the suspect.* **2.** To grasp mentally; understand: *Researchers finally apprehended the true nature of the phenomenon.* —**ap′pre·hend′er** *n.*

apprehension (ăp′rĭ-hĕn′shən) *n.* **1.** Fear or dread of what may happen; anxiety about the future: *The fall in prices caused apprehension among the investors.* **2.** The act of capturing; an arrest: *apprehension of a criminal.* **3.** The ability to understand; understanding.

apprehensive (ăp′rĭ-hĕn′sĭv) *adj.* Anxious or fearful; uneasy: *apprehensive about the future.* —**ap′pre·hen′sive·ly** *adv.*

apprentice (ə-prĕn′tĭs) *n.* A person who works for another without pay or at low wages in return for instruction in a craft or trade. ❖ *v.* **apprenticed, apprenticing, apprentices** —*tr.* To engage (someone) as an apprentice: *In earlier times many children were apprenticed to craftsmen.* —*intr.* To work as an apprentice: *She apprenticed at the ceramics studio.*

apprenticeship (ə-prĕn′tĭs-shĭp′) *n.* **1.** The condition of being an apprentice. **2.** The period during which one is an apprentice.

apprise (ə-prīz′) *tr.v.* **apprised, apprising, apprises** To cause to know; inform: *Please apprise me of any changes in the plan.*

approach (ə-prōch′) *v.* **approached, approaching, approaches** —*intr.* To come near or nearer in place or time: *As spring approached, our work neared completion.* —*tr.* **1.** To come near or nearer to (someone or something) in place or time: *The speaker approached the microphone. Our doctor is approaching retirement.* **2.** To come close to in quality, appearance, or other characteristics; approximate: *What could approach the beauty of this lake?* **3.** To begin to deal with or work on: *We approach the task with eagerness.* **4.** To make a proposal to; make overtures to: *I approached the owner for a job.* ❖ *n.* **1a.** The act of approaching: *The captain had to be cautious in his approach to the dock. Many birds fly south at the approach of winter.* **b.** The steps taken prior to a maneuver in a sport, such as the steps of a bowler before delivering the ball. **2.** A way or method of dealing or working with someone or something: *a new approach to the problem.* **3.** A way of reaching a place; an access: *the approach to the bridge.* —**ap·proach′er** *n.*

approachable (ə-prō′chə-bəl) *adj.* **1.** Capable of being reached; accessible: *a small town approachable only through a mountain pass.* **2.** Easy to talk to; friendly: *an approachable person.* —**ap·proach′a·bil′i·ty** *n.*

approbation (ăp′rə-bā′shən) *n.* **1.** The act of approving, especially officially; approval: *The bill to protect the marsh received the approbation of all.* **2.** Praise; commendation: *not a murmur of approbation or blame.*

appropriate (ə-prō′prē-ĭt) *adj.* Suitable for a particular person, condition, occasion, or place; proper: *What are the appropriate clothes for this occasion?* ❖ *tr.v.* (ə-prō′prē-āt′) **appropriated, appropriating, appropriates** **1.** To set apart for a particular use: *Congress appropriated money for education.* **2.** To take possession of exclusively for oneself, often without permission: *He appropriated the whole file cabinet for his own use.* —**ap·pro′pri·ate·ly** *adv.* —**ap·pro′pri·ate·ness** *n.* —**ap·pro′pri·a′tor** *n.*

appropriation (ə-prō′prē-ā′shən) *n.* **1.** The act of appropriating to oneself or to a specific use. **2.** Public funds set aside for a specific purpose: *Congressional appropriations for disaster relief.*

approval (ə-prōo′vəl) *n.* **1.** Favorable regard: *The voters expressed their approval by voting for our mayor again.* **2.** An official consent or sanction: *The article was published with the approval of the editors.* ✦ **on approval** For examination or trial by a customer without the obligation to buy: *We bought our new car on approval.*

approve (ə-prōov′) *v.* **approved, approving, approves** —*tr.* **1.** To confirm or consent to officially; sanction; ratify: *The Senate approved the treaty.* **2.** To regard favorably; consider right or good: *The country approved the president's decision to fund more medical research.* —*intr.* To feel, voice, or demonstrate approval: *The neighbors did not approve of our playing football in the street.*

approvingly (ə-prōo′vĭng-lē) *adv.* In a manner that expresses approval: *nodded approvingly.*

approx. An abbreviation of: **1.** approximate. **2.** approximately.

approximate (ə-prŏk′sə-mĭt) *adj.* Almost exact or accurate: *the approximate height of the building.* ❖ *v.* (ə-prŏk′sə-māt′) **approximated, approximating, approximates** —*tr.* To come close to; be nearly the same as: *The temperatures of the Mediterranean Sea approximate those of Caribbean waters.* —*intr.* To come near or close in degree, nature, or other characteristic. —**ap·prox′i·mate·ly** *adv.*

approximation (ə-prŏk′sə-mā′shən) *n.* Something that is almost but not quite exact, correct, or true: *This measurement is an approximation.*

appurtenance (ə-pûr′tn-əns) *n.* **1.** Something added to another, more important thing; an accessory: *The TV set is an appurtenance of modern living.* **2. appurtenances** Equipment, such as clothing or tools, used for a specific purpose; gear: *a tent, cooking utensils, and other appurtenances of camping.* **3.** In law, a right, privilege, or property that belongs with a principal property and goes along with it in case of sale or inheritance.

apricot (ăp′rĭ-kŏt′ *or* ā′prĭ-kŏt′) *n.* **1.** A yellow-orange fruit that is similar to a peach but smaller. Apricots are often eaten dried. **2.** The tree that bears such fruit.

April (ā′prəl) *n.* The fourth month of the year in the Gregorian calendar, having 30 days.

April Fools' Day *n.* April 1, traditionally celebrated as a day for playing practical jokes.

a priori (ä′ prē-ôr′ē *or* ä′ prī-ôr′ī) *adj.* **1.** Relating to the act of philosophical deduction without reference to particular facts or experience: *a priori reasoning about the nature of the universe.* **2.** Made before or without examination; not supported by factual study: *a priori assumptions about foreign cultures.* **—a′ pri·o′ri** *adv.*

apron (ā′prən) *n.* **1.** A garment, usually tied in the back, worn over the front of the body to protect the clothes. **2.** The paved strip in front of an airport hangar or terminal. **3.** The part of the stage in a theater in front of the curtain.

WORD HISTORY Sometimes the ear can play tricks on the speakers of a language. Things can be heard in more than one way, and misinterpreted, and the language can change as a result. This is what happened with the words **apron, adder,** and **umpire,** all of which once started with the letter *n.* Some people misheard "a napron" as if it were "an apron" and began writing it that way, moving the *n* to the article *a* as if the word began with a vowel. They did the same with the word *naeddre,* which meant "snake" and became our *adder.* The *nounpere* was literally a "nonequal," someone whose judgments were more important than the judgments of others. That *nounpere* is now calling balls and strikes behind home plate as an *umpire.*

apropos (ăp′rə-pō′) *adj.* Relevant or fitting: *A gift of flowers would be apropos to the occasion.* ❖ *adv.* At an appropriate time. ❖ *prep.* Concerning; regarding: *Apropos our appointment, I'm afraid I can't make it.*

apropos of *prep.* With regard to: *The candidate told a funny story apropos of the weather.*

apse (ăps) *n.* A semicircular, usually domed projection of a building, especially the end of a church in which the altar is located.

apt (ăpt) *adj.* **1.** Exactly suitable; appropriate: *She gave an apt reply to her critics.* **2.** Having a tendency; inclined: *Most people are apt to accept the advice of an expert.* **3.** Quick to learn: *an apt student with high grades.* **—apt′ly** *adv.* **—apt′ness** *n.*

apt. An abbreviation of apartment.

aptitude (ăp′tĭ-tōōd′) *n.* An inherent ability, as for learning; a talent: *a remarkable aptitude for mathematics.*

aptitude test *n.* A test used to measure a person's ability to learn some particular skill or acquire information.

aqua (ăk′wə *or* ä′kwə) *n., pl.* **aquae** (ăk′wē *or* ä′kwī′) *or* **aquas 1.** Water. **2.** A light bluish green.

aquaculture (ăk′wə-kŭl′chər *or* ä′kwə-kŭl′chər) *n.* The cultivation of marine or freshwater organisms, especially food fish or shellfish such as salmon or oysters, under controlled conditions.

aquamarine (ăk′wə-mə-rēn′ *or* ä′kwə-mə-rēn′) *n.* **1.** A transparent blue-green variety of beryl, used as a gemstone. **2.** A pale blue to light greenish blue.

aquaplane (ăk′wə-plān′ *or* ä′kwə-plān′) *n.* A board on which a person stands and rides while it is towed over the water by a motorboat. ❖ *tr.v.* **aquaplaned, aquaplaning, aquaplanes** To ride on an aquaplane. **—aq′ua·plan′er** *n.*

aqua regia (rē′jē-ə *or* rē′jə) *n.* A fuming corrosive mixture of nitric acid and hydrochloric acid, used for testing metals and dissolving gold and platinum.

aquarium (ə-kwâr′ē-əm) *n., pl.* **aquariums** *or* **aquaria** (ə-kwâr′ē-ə) **1.** A tank or other container, such as a glass bowl, filled with water for keeping and displaying fishes or other animals and plants. **2.** A place where fishes and other aquatic animals are displayed to the public.

Aquarius (ə-kwâr′ē-əs) *n.* **1.** A constellation in the Southern Hemisphere near Pisces, traditionally pictured as a man carrying a container of water. **2.** The eleventh sign of the zodiac in astrology.

aquatic (ə-kwăt′ĭk *or* ə-kwŏt′ĭk) *adj.* **1.** Consisting of, relating to, or being in water: *an aquatic environment.* **2.** Living or growing in or on the water: *aquatic insects; aquatic plants.* **3.** Taking place in or on the water: *diving and other aquatic sports.*

aqueduct (ăk′wĭ-dŭkt′) *n.* A large pipe or channel that carries water from a distant source. **2.** A structure that supports such a pipe or channel across low ground or a river.

aqueous (ā′kwē-əs *or* ăk′wē-əs) *adj.* Relating to, resembling, or containing water: *an aqueous solution of salt and water.*

aqueous humor *n.* A clear fluid that fills the space between the cornea and lens of the eye.

aquifer (ăk′wə-fər) *n.* An underground layer of sand, gravel, or porous rock that holds water.

aquiline (ăk′wə-lĭn′ *or* ăk′wə-lĭn) *adj.* **1.** Curved or hooked like an eagle's beak: *an aquiline nose.* **2.** Relating to or resembling an eagle.

–ar A suffix that means relating to or resembling: *angular; linear.*

Arab (ăr′əb) *n.* **1.** A member of a Semitic people inhabiting Arabia. **2.** A member of an Arabic-speaking people. **—Ar′ab** *adj.*

arabesque (ăr′ə-bĕsk′) *n.* **1.** A ballet position in which the dancer stands on one leg with the other leg extending straight back. **2.** An intricate or interwoven pattern or design: *walls adorned with an arabesque of flowers.*

Arabian (ə-rā′bē-ən) *adj.* Relating to Arabia or the Arabs. ❖ *n.* **1.** A native or inhabitant of Arabia. **2.** An Arabian horse.

Arabian horse *n.* Any of a breed of swift horse native to Arabia.

Arabian Nights *n.* A collection of ancient folktales derived partly from Persian and Indian sources, originally written in Arabic in the ninth century.

Arabic (ăr′ə-bĭk) *adj.* Relating to Arabia, the Arabs, or their language or culture. ❖ *n.* A Semitic language consisting of many dialects that is spoken in many countries in southwestern Asia and northern Africa.

Arabic numeral *n.* One of the numerical symbols 1, 2, 3, 4, 5, 6, 7, 8, 9, or 0. They originated in India but are called Arabic numerals because Europeans first learned about them from Arabic written sources.

arable (ăr′ə-bəl) *adj.* Fit for cultivation: *arable land.*

arachnid (ə-răk′nĭd) *n.* Any of a large group of invertebrate animals that resemble insects but have eight rather than six legs, no wings or antennae, and a body divided into two rather than three parts. Spiders, scorpions, ticks, and mites are arachnids.

Aramaic (ăr′ə-mā′ĭk) *n.* The Semitic language originally of the ancient Syrians, used in modern form in certain countries of southwest Asia.

Arapaho (ə-răp′ə-hō′) *n., pl.* **Arapaho** *or* **Arapahos 1.** A member of a Native American people living in Oklahoma and Wyoming. **2.** The Algonquian language of the Arapaho.

Araucanian (ăr′ô-kä′nē-ən) *n.* **1.** A family of languages spoken by native peoples of south-central Chile and western Argentina. **2.** A member of a people speaking an Araucanian language. —**Ar′au·ca′ni·an** *adj.*

Arawak (är′ə-wäk′) *n., pl.* **Arawak** or **Arawaks 1.** A member of an American Indian people formerly living in the West Indies and now living chiefly in northeast South America. **2.** The Arawakan language of the Arawak.

Arawakan (är′ə-wä′kən) *n., pl.* **Arawakan** or **Arawakans 1.** A member of a widespread group of native peoples living in northern South America and formerly in the islands of the northern Caribbean. **2.** A family of languages spoken by these peoples. —**Ar′a·wa′kan** *adj.*

arbiter (är′bĭ-tər) *n.* **1.** A person chosen to judge a dispute; an arbitrator. **2.** A person or thing having the power to ordain or judge at will: *Celebrities often act as unofficial arbiters of fashion.*

arbitrary (är′bĭ-trĕr′ē) *adj.* **1.** Based on a whim, impulse, or chance, not on reason or law: *Drawing numbers out of a hat was an arbitrary way to select the captain of the team.* **2.** Not limited by law; despotic: *The dictator's arbitrary government jailed many of his political opponents.* —**ar′bi·trar′i·ly** (är′bĭ-trâr′ə-lē) *adv.* —**ar′bi·trar′i·ness** *n.*

arbitrate (är′bĭ-trāt′) *v.* **arbitrated, arbitrating, arbitrates** —*tr.* **1.** To decide as an arbitrator: *arbitrate the boundary dispute between the two neighbors.* **2.** To submit to judgment by arbitration: *Management and labor agreed to arbitrate their differences.* —*intr.* To serve as an arbitrator: *Even strong nations must allow others to arbitrate between them.*

arbitration (är′bĭ-trā′shən) *n.* The process of referring the issues in a dispute to an impartial person or group for judgment or settlement: *Many disputes between labor and management are settled by arbitration.*

arbitrator (är′bĭ-trā′tər) *n.* **1.** A person chosen to settle a dispute or controversy. **2.** A person having the ability or power to make authoritative decisions; an arbiter.

arbor (är′bər) *n.* A shady resting place in a garden or park, often made of latticework on which vines or other climbing plants grow: *a grape arbor; a rose arbor.*

Arbor Day *n.* A day observed in many areas by planting trees, often occurring in the spring.

arboreal (är-bôr′ē-əl) *adj.* **1.** Living in trees: *arboreal marsupials.* **2.** Relating to or resembling a tree.

arboretum (är′bə-rē′təm) *n.* A place where trees and other plants are cultivated for scientific, educational, and ornamental purposes.

arborvitae (är′bər-vī′tē) *n.* Any of several evergreen trees or shrubs having scalelike leaves and small cones, often planted in hedges.

arbutus (är-byōō′təs) *n.* **1.** A low-growing eastern North American shrub having evergreen leaves and clusters of fragrant pink or white flowers. **2.** Any of various evergreen trees or shrubs of Europe and western North America, having flaky bark and small red fruit.

arc (ärk) *n.* **1.** Something shaped like a curve or arch: *the arc of a rainbow.* **2.** A segment of a circle. **3.** A stream of brilliant light or sparks produced when an electric current jumps across the gap between two electrodes separated by a gas. **4.** A progression of events in a story or narration, especially one that leads to a climax and settles in a conclusion. ❖ *intr.v.* **arced** (ärkt), **arcing** (är′kĭng), **arcs 1.** To form an arc. **2.** To take or follow a curved path: *The diver arced into the water.*

arcade (är-kād′) *n.* **1.** A series of arches supported by columns or pillars. **2.** A roofed passageway, especially one with shops on either side. **3.** A commercial establishment where customers pay to play mechanical or electronic games.

arcane (är-kān′) *adj.* Known or understood by only a few: *arcane economic theories.*

arcanum (är-kā′nəm) *n.* **1.** *pl.* **arcana** (är-kā′nəm) or **arcanums** A deep secret; a mystery. **2.** **arcana** Specialized knowledge or detail that is mysterious to the average person.

arch¹ (ärch) *n.* **1a.** A usually curved structure forming the upper edge of an open space and supporting the weight above it, as in a bridge or doorway. **b.** A structure, such as a monument, shaped like an upside-down U. **2.** A curved shape or object having the ends lower than the middle: *the arch of leaves overhanging the lane.* **3.** Any of various arch-shaped structures of the body: *the arch of the foot.* ❖ *v.* **arched, arching, arches** —*tr.* **1.** To cause to form an arch or a similar curve: *The cat arched its back.* **2.** To provide or build with an arch: *The entrance to the store was arched.* —*intr.* To extend in an arch: *The bridge arched across the river.*

arch² (ärch) *adj.* **1.** Chief; principal: *our arch rivals.* **2.** Teasing, ironic, or sardonic: *an arch reply.* —**arch′ly** *adv.* —**arch′ness** *n.*

WORD HISTORY Arch¹ comes from Latin *arcus,* meaning "part of a curve, curved structure." **Arch²** comes from the Modern English prefix *arch-,* which came from the Greek prefix *arkhi-,* both meaning "chief, primary."

arch– A prefix that means principal or chief: *archdiocese; archenemy.*

archaebacterium (är′kē-băk-tîr′ē-əm) *n., pl.* **archaebacteria** (är′kē-băk-tîr′ē-ə) An archaeon.

archaeology or **archeology** (är′kē-ŏl′ə-jē) *n.* The study of the remains of past human life and culture, such as graves, tools, and pottery. —**ar′chae·o·log′i·cal** (är′kē-ə-lŏj′ĭ-kəl) *adj.* —**ar′chae·o·log′i·cal·ly** *adv.* —**ar′chae·ol′o·gist** *n.*

archaeon (är′kē-ŏn′) *n., pl.* **archaea** (är′kē-ə) Any of a group of one-celled organisms that are similar to bacteria in some ways, as in lacking a nucleus, but different from them genetically and biochemically. Archaea usually live in extreme environments, such as hot springs.

archaeopteryx (är′kē-ŏp′tər-ĭks) *n.* A small extinct vertebrate having feathered wings with claws, a long snout with teeth, and a feathered bony tail. It is thought to have been one of the earliest birds.

archaic (är-kā′ĭk) *adj.* **1.** Not current; antiquated: *archaic laws to regulate horse-drawn traffic.* **2.** Relating to or characteristic of an early period of human culture or of evolutionary history: *archaic Greek art; archaic fishes from the Ordovician Period.* **3.** Relating to words that were once common but are now rare and used chiefly to suggest an earlier style: *Methinks is an archaic word meaning "It seems to me."* —**ar·cha′i·cal·ly** *adv.*

archaism (är′kē-ĭz′əm or är′kā-ĭz′əm) *n.* An archaic word or expression.

archangel (ärk′ān′jəl) *n.* An angel of high rank.

archbishop (ärch-bĭsh′əp) *n.* A bishop of the highest rank, heading an archdiocese or church province.

archdeacon (ärch-dē′kən) *n.* A church official, especially of the Anglican Church, in charge of business and other affairs in a diocese.

archdiocese (ärch-dī′ə-sĭs or ärch-dī′ə-sēs′) *n.* The area under an archbishop's jurisdiction.

archduchess (ärch-dŭch′ĭs) *n.* **1.** The wife or widow of an archduke. **2.** A princess of the former Austrian royal family.

archduke (ärch-dŏŏk′) *n.* A prince of the former Austrian royal family.

arched (ärcht) *adj.* **1.** Provided, made, or covered with an arch: *an arched bridge.* **2.** Forming a curve like that of an arch: *the arched dome of the night sky.*

archenemy (ärch-ĕn′ə-mē) *n.* A chief or most important enemy: *France was the archenemy of Britain in Colonial America.*

archeological (är′kē-ə-lŏj′ĭ-kəl) *adj.* Variant of **archaeological.**

archeologist (är′kē-ŏl′ə-jĭst) *n.* Variant of **archaeologist.**

archeology (är′kē-ŏl′ə-jē) *n.* Variant of **archaeology.**

archer (är′chər) *n.* A person who shoots with a bow and arrow.

archery (är′chə-rē) *n.* The sport or skill of shooting with a bow and arrow.

archetype (är′kĭ-tīp′) *n.* An original model or form after which other, similar things are patterned: *The Wright brothers' first plane served as the archetype for later airplanes.*

archipelago (är′kə-pĕl′ə-gō′) *n., pl.* **archipelagoes** or **archipelagos 1.** A large group of islands. **2.** A sea in which there is a large group of islands.

architect (är′kĭ-tĕkt′) *n.* **1.** A person who designs and directs the construction of buildings and other large structures. **2.** A person who plans, organizes, or designs something: *The delegates to the Constitutional Convention were the architects of the Constitution.*

architectural (är′kĭ-tĕk′chər-əl) *adj.* Relating to architecture. —**ar′chi·tec′tur·al·ly** *adv.*

architecture (är′kĭ-tĕk′chər) *n.* **1.** The art and occupation of designing and directing the construction of buildings and other large structures, such as bridges. **2.** A style of building: *Many government buildings in Washington, DC, are patterned on classical architecture.* **3.** Buildings and other large structures: *the stately architecture of the New York City skyline.* **4.** The orderly arrangement of parts; structure: *the architecture of a story.*

architrave (är′kĭ-trāv′) *n.* The bottom part of an entablature in classical architecture.

archive (är′kīv′) *n.* **1.** often **archives** A place or collection containing records and documents of historical interest: *a national archive; company archives.* **2.** A long-term storage area of computer memory for backup copies of computer files, or for inactive computer files. —**ar·chi′val** *adj.*

archway (ärch′wā′) *n.* **1.** A passageway under an arch. **2.** An arch that covers or encloses an entrance or passageway.

–archy A suffix that means a kind of rule or government: *oligarchy.*

arc lamp *n.* A lamp in which an electric current crosses between electrodes separated by a gas and generates an arc that produces light.

arctic (ärk′tĭk or är′tĭk) *adj.* Extremely cold; frigid: *arctic weather.*

Arcturus (ärk-tŏŏr′əs) *n.* The brightest star in the northern sky other than the sun. It is in the constellation Boötes.

ardent (är′dnt) *adj.* **1.** Expressing or full of warmth of passion, desire, or other emotion; passionate: *an ardent* *wish for his recovery.* **2.** Strongly enthusiastic; extremely devoted; eager: *an ardent defender of the free press.* —**ar′dent·ly** *adv.*

ardor (är′dər) *n.* Great warmth or intensity of passion, desire, or other emotion: *the driving ardor of a reformer.*

arduous (är′jŏŏ-əs) *adj.* Demanding great effort; difficult: *arduous training; an arduous task.* —**ar′du·ous·ly** *adv.* —**ar′du·ous·ness** *n.*

are (är) *v.* **1.** Second person singular present tense of **be. 2.** First, second, and third person plural present tense of **be.**

area (âr′ē-ə) *n.* **1a.** A section or region, as of a land: *an industrial area full of factories; the Los Angeles area including its suburbs.* **b.** A part or section, as of a building: *The cafeteria is an eating area for employees.* **2.** The extent of a surface or plane figure as measured in square units: *The area of a rectangle is the product of the length and the width.* **3.** A range, as of activity or study: *the area of medical research.* —**ar′e·al** *adj.*

area code *n.* A three-digit number used before a seven-digit telephone number. Area codes were originally assigned to specific geographical areas.

areaway (âr′ē-ə-wā′) *n.* **1.** A small sunken area allowing access or light and air to basement doors or windows. **2.** A passageway between buildings.

arena (ə-rē′nə) *n.* **1.** An enclosed area or building for presenting athletic contests and other events for large audiences. **2.** The space in the center of an ancient Roman amphitheater where athletic contests and other spectacles were held. **3.** An area of conflict or activity: *The new candidate stepped into the political arena.*

aren't (ärnt or är′ənt) **1.** Contraction of *are not: They aren't there.* **2.** Contraction of *am not.* Used in questions: *I'm on time, aren't I?*

areola (ə-rē′ə-lə or âr′ē-ō′lə) *n., pl.* **areolae** (ə-rē′ə-lē′ or âr′ē-ō′lē′) or **areolas** A small ring of color around a center portion, as about the nipple of the breast.

Ares (âr′ēz) *n.* In Greek mythology, the god of war, identified with the Roman Mars.

arginine (är′jə-nēn′) *n.* An essential amino acid that is found in plant and animal protein.

Argo (är′gō′) *n.* In Greek mythology, Jason's ship in his search for the Golden Fleece.

argon (är′gŏn′) *n. Symbol* **Ar** A colorless, odorless, chemically inert gaseous element that makes up about one percent of the atmosphere and is used in electric light bulbs and fluorescent tubes. Atomic number 18. See **Periodic Table.**

Argonaut (är′gə-nôt′) *n.* In Greek mythology, any of the men who sailed with Jason on the *Argo* in search of the Golden Fleece.

argosy (är′gə-sē) *n., pl.* **argosies 1.** A big sailing merchant ship. **2.** A fleet of such ships.

argot (är′gō or är′gət) *n.* The jargon or slang of a particular class or group of people, often used to conceal meaning from outsiders.

argue (är′gyōō) *v.* **argued, arguing, argues** —*tr.* **1.** To give reasons for or against (something, such as an opinion or proposal); debate: *The lawyer argued the case in court.* **2.** To prove or attempt to prove by reasoning; maintain: *I argued that the vacant lot should be turned into a park.* **3.** To give evidence of; indicate: *Her vocabulary argues that she has read a lot.* **4.** To persuade or influence, as by presenting reasons: *He would not let us argue him into leaving early.* —*intr.* **1.** To put forth reasons for or against something: *argue against building a new airport.* **2.** To engage in a quarrel; dispute: *The twins seldom argued with each other.* —**ar′gu·a·ble** *adj.* —**ar′gu·a·bly** *adv.* —**ar′gu·er** *n.*

argument (är′gyə-mənt) *n.* **1.** A quarrel or dispute: *an argument over who goes first.* **2.** A discussion of differing points of view; a debate: *a scientific argument.* **3.** A series of statements logically connected in support of a position: *tried to formulate an argument for tax reform.*

argumentative (är′gyə-mĕn′tə-tĭv) *adj.* **1.** Given to arguing: *an argumentative person.* **2.** Containing or full of arguments: *an argumentative paper.* —**ar′gu·men′-ta·tive·ly** *adv.*

Argus (är′gəs) *n.* In Greek mythology, a giant with one hundred eyes.

argyle also **argyll** (är′gīl′) *n.* **1.** A knitting pattern made up of diamond shapes in contrasting colors. **2.** A sock knit in such a pattern.

aria (ä′rē-ə) *n.* A melodic piece written for a solo singer accompanied by instruments, as in an opera, cantata, or oratorio.

Ariadne (är′ē-ăd′nē) *n.* In Greek mythology, the daughter of King Minos and Pasiphaë who helped Theseus escape from the Minotaur's labyrinth.

arid (är′ĭd) *adj.* **1.** Having little or no rainfall; dry: *an arid desert; an arid wasteland.* **2.** Lifeless; dull: *an arid lecture.* —**a·rid/i·ty** (ə-rĭd′ĭtē), **ar′id·ness** *n.* —**ar′id·ly** *adv.*

Aries (âr′ēz) *n.* **1.** A constellation in the Northern Hemisphere, traditionally pictured as a ram. **2.** The first sign of the zodiac in astrology.

aright (ə-rīt′) *adv.* Properly; correctly.

Arikara (ə-rĭk′ər-ə) *n., pl.* **Arikara** or **Arikaras 1.** A member of a Native American people of North Dakota. **2.** The Caddoan language of the Arikara.

arise (ə-rīz′) *intr.v.* **arose** (ə-rōz′), **arisen** (ə-rĭz′ən), **arising, arises 1.** To get up: *He arose from his chair to greet me.* **2.** To awaken and get up: *She arose at dawn.* **3.** To ascend; move upward: *Mist arose from the lake.* **4.** To come into being; appear: *Take advantage of opportunities as they arise.* **5.** To result; proceed: *The breakdown arose from some temporary defect.*

aristocracy (är′ĭ-stŏk′rə-sē) *n., pl.* **aristocracies 1a.** A social class based on inherited wealth, status, and sometimes titles. **b.** A government controlled by such a class. **2.** A group considered superior to others: *the aristocracy of local landowners.*

aristocrat (ə-rĭs′tə-krăt′ *or* ăr′ĭs-tə-krăt′) *n.* **1.** A member of a ruling class or of the nobility. **2.** A person who favors government by the aristocracy.

aristocratic (ə-rĭs′tə-krăt′ĭk *or* ăr′ĭs-tə-krăt′ĭk) *adj.* **1.** Relating to or characteristic of the aristocracy: *aristocratic manners.* **2.** Having an aristocracy as a form of government: *aristocratic city-states of ancient Greece.* —**a·ris′to·crat′i·cal·ly** *adv.*

Aristotelian (är′ĭ-stə-tē′lē-ən *or* ə-rĭs′tə-tē′lē-ən) *adj.* Relating to the ancient Greek philosopher Aristotle or his philosophy. ❖ *n.* **1.** A follower of Aristotle or his teachings. **2.** A person who is guided by experience or tends to be scientific in methods or thought. —**Ar′-is·to·te′li·an·ism** *n.*

arithmetic (ə-rĭth′mĭ-tĭk) *n.* **1.** The study of numbers and their properties under the operations of addition, subtraction, multiplication, and division. **2.** Calculation using these operations: *I added up the bill, but my arithmetic was wrong.* ❖ *adj.* (är′ĭth-mĕt′ĭk) **1.** Relating to arithmetic; according to the rules of arithmetic: *arith-*

metic computations. **2.** Changing according to an arithmetic progression. —**ar·ith·met·i·cal** (är′ĭth-mĕt′ĭ-kəl) *adj.* —**ar′ith·met′i·cal·ly** *adv.*

arithmetician (ə-rĭth′mə-tĭsh′ən) *n.* A person who specializes in the study of arithmetic.

arithmetic mean (är′ĭth-mĕt′ĭk) *n.* An average of a set of quantities obtained by adding all the quantities and dividing the result by the number of quantities in the set.

arithmetic progression (är′ĭth-mĕt′ĭk) *n.* A sequence of numbers such as 1, 3, 5, 7, 9 . . . or 14, 9, 4, –1 . . . in which the difference between any successive pair of numbers is the same.

ark (ärk) *n.* **1.** In the Bible, the ship built by Noah for survival during the Flood. **2.** The Ark of the Covenant. **3.** A cabinet in a synagogue in which the scrolls of the Torah are kept; the Holy Ark.

Ark of the Covenant *n.* In the Bible, the chest containing the Ten Commandments on stone tablets, carried by the Hebrews during their wanderings in the desert.

arm¹ (ärm) *n.* **1a.** Either of the upper limbs of the human body, connecting the hand and wrist to the shoulder. **b.** A part similar to a human arm, such as the forelimb of an animal or a long part projecting from a central support in a machine. **2.** A relatively narrow extension sticking out from a large mass: *an arm of the sea.* **3.** Something designed to cover or support a human arm: *the arm of a shirt; the arm of a chair.* **4.** A division or branch of an organization: *the investigative arm of the Justice Department.* **5.** The skill of throwing or pitching a ball well: *The shortstop has a good arm.* ◆ **an arm and a leg** An excessively high price: *charged me an arm and a leg for the antiques.* **at arm's length 1.** With the arm extended straight out from the body: *held the picture at arm's length.* **2.** At a distance; not on friendly or intimate terms: *keeps her coworkers at arm's length.* **with open arms** In a very friendly manner: *welcomed friends with open arms.*

arm² (ärm) *n.* **1.** A weapon, especially a firearm: *the troops stacked the arms and made camp.* **2. arms** Warfare or military power: *The besieged city could not be taken by force of arms.* **3. arms** A design or emblem used as an identifying mark, as by a family or nation. ❖ *v.* **armed, arming, arms** —*tr.* **1.** To equip with weapons or other means of defense: *armed the rebels with machine guns.* **2.** To equip or provide with something necessary or useful: *armed herself with the facts in preparation for the debate.* **3.** To make ready; prepare: *arm the mechanism of a trap.* —*intr.* To prepare for war, as by amassing weapons and training soldiers: *As the countries armed, the leaders reached a settlement.* ◆ **up in arms** Very upset; angry: *The whole neighborhood was up in arms when the mayor closed the fire station.*

WORD HISTORY Arm¹ comes from Old English *earm,* meaning "upper limb of the human body." **Arm²** comes from Middle English *armes,* which comes from Latin *arma,* both meaning "weapons."

armada (är-mä′də *or* är-mā′də) *n.* A big fleet of warships.

armadillo (är′mə-dĭl′ō) *n., pl.* **armadillos** Any of various burrowing mammals of southern North America and Central and South America, having an armorlike covering of jointed bony plates.

WORD HISTORY The Spanish word **armadillo** literally means "a little armored animal." It comes from the adjective *armado,* "armed, armored," and the suffix *–illo,* which forms *diminutives,* words that express youngness, smallness, or affection. English has a number of diminutive suffixes: *–let*, as in *booklet*, *–ette*, as in *kitchenette*, and *–ling*, as in *duckling* and *darling*. (The last of these comes from the adjective *dear* plus the suffix *–ling*.)

Armageddon (är′mə-gĕd′n) *n*. **1.** In the Bible, the prophesied place where armies will gather for battle at the end of the world. **2.** A decisive or catastrophic conflict.

armament (är′mə-mənt) *n*. **1.** The weapons and supplies of war with which a military unit is equipped. **2.** often **armaments** All the military forces and war equipment of a country. **3.** Preparation for war: *Armament is a function of national security in time of war.*

armature (är′mə-chər) *n*. **1a.** A rotating part of an electric motor or generator, consisting of wire wound around an iron core. **b.** A piece of soft iron connecting the poles of a magnet. **c.** The part of an electromagnetic device, such as a relay, buzzer, or loudspeaker, that moves or vibrates. **2.** A framework, especially one used as a support for clay sculpture. **3.** A part or organ on an animal or plant that helps to protect it from attack or injury. *A porcupine's quills are its armature.*

armband (ärm′bănd′) *n*. A piece of cloth worn around the upper arm, often as a sign of mourning or protest.

armchair (ärm′châr′) *n*. A chair with supports on the sides for one's arms. ❖ *adj*. Remote from the field of action: *an armchair detective.*

armed[1] (ärmd) *adj*. **1.** Having arms: *an armed chair.* **2.** Having arms of a certain number or kind: *an eight-armed squid.*

armed[2] (ärmd) *adj*. **1.** Furnished with a weapon or weapons: *an armed police escort.* **2.** Using a weapon or weapons: *an armed attack.*

armed forces *pl.n*. The organizations and people involved in waging wars and defending a country from physical attack, including the army, navy, and air force.

Armenian (är-mē′nē-ən) *adj*. Relating to Armenia or its people, language, or culture. ❖ *n*. **1.** A native or inhabitant of Armenia. **2.** The Indo-European language of the Armenians.

armful (ärm′fŏŏl′) *n*. As much as one or both arms can hold: *an armful of flowers.*

armhole (ärm′hōl′) *n*. An opening in a garment for an arm.

armistice (är′mĭ-stĭs) *n*. A temporary stop of fighting by mutual agreement; a truce.

Armistice Day *n*. Veterans Day as observed before 1954 to commemorate the the armistice that ended World War I in 1918.

armlet (ärm′lĭt) *n*. **1.** A band worn on the arm for ornament or identification. **2.** A small arm, as of the sea.

armload (ärm′lōd′) *n*. The amount that can be carried in one arm or both arms: *an armload of firewood.*

armlock (ärm′lŏk′) *n*. A hold in wrestling or martial arts in which the opponent's arm is held so that it cannot be moved.

armoire (ärm-wär′ *or* ärm′wär) *n*. A large, often highly decorated cabinet or wardrobe.

armor (är′mər) *n*. **1.** A covering worn to protect the body in battle. **2.** A protective covering, such as the bony plates covering an armadillo or the metal plates on tanks or warships. **3.** The armored vehicles of an army. ❖ *tr.v.* **armored, armoring, armors** To cover or protect with armor: *armor a warship.*

armored (är′mərd) *adj*. **1.** Covered with or having armor: *tanks and other armored vehicles.* **2.** Equipped with armored vehicles: *an armored division of the Marines.*

armorer (är′mər-ər) *n*. **1.** A person or business that makes or repairs weapons. **2.** An enlisted person in charge of maintenance and repair of the small arms of a military unit.

armor plate *n*. A specially made hard steel plate designed to withstand enemy fire and protect warships, military aircraft, and armored vehicles.

armory (är′mə-rē) *n., pl.* **armories 1.** A storehouse for weapons; an arsenal. **2.** A building that serves as the headquarters of a military reserve force. **3.** A weapons factory.

armour (är′mər) *n. & v. Chiefly British* Variant of **armor.**

armpit (ärm′pĭt′) *n*. The hollow place under the arm at the shoulder.

armrest (ärm′rĕst′) *n*. A support for the arm, as on a chair or couch.

army (är′mē) *n., pl.* **armies 1.** A large body of people organized and trained for warfare on land. **2.** often **Army a.** The entire military land forces of a country. **b.** The largest unit in a country's army, consisting of two or more corps: *the Ninth Army of the US Army.* **3.** A large group of people or things, especially when organized for a specific purpose: *an army of construction workers who built the bridge; a banquet with an army of waiters.*

arnica (är′nĭ-kə) *n*. **1.** Any of various plants having yellow flowers that resemble daisies. **2.** A medical preparation made from these flowers, used to treat sprains and bruises.

aroma (ə-rō′mə) *n., pl.* **aromas 1.** A quality that can be perceived by the sense of smell: *the aroma of fried onions.* See Synonyms at **smell. 2.** A pleasant characteristic smell, as of a plant or food: *the aroma of roses.*

aromatic (ăr′ə-măt′ĭk) *adj*. **1.** Having an aroma; fragrant: *the aromatic scent of roses.* **2.** Relating to organic chemical compounds containing at least one benzene ring or similar ring-shaped component. **—ar′o·mat′i·cal·ly** *adv.*

arose (ə-rōz′) *v*. Past tense of **arise.**

around (ə-round′) *adv*. **1.** On all sides or in all directions: *We drove around looking for a parking place.* **2.** In a circle or circular motion: *The skater spun around twice.* **3.** In or toward the opposite direction: *The horse turned around and ran toward the barn.* **4.** From one place to another; here and there: *wander around.* **5.** In or near one's current location: *He waited around all day.* **6.** To a specific place or area: *when you come around again.* **7.** Approximately; about: *Around 20 rafts floated down the Rio Grande.* ❖ *adj.* In circumference: *a pond two miles around.* ❖ *prep.* **1.** On all sides of: *There are trees around the field.* **2.** So as to encircle or enclose: *He wore a belt around his waist.* **3.** All about; throughout: *The reporter looked around the room.* **4.** On or to the farther side of: *the house around the corner.* **5.** Close by; near: *She lives right around here.* **6.** So as to pass or avoid: *How can we get around the problem?* **7.** Approximately at: *I woke up around seven.*

arousal (ə-rou′zəl) *n*. The act of arousing or the condition of being aroused.

arouse (ə-rouz′) *tr.v.* **aroused, arousing, arouses 1.** To give rise to (a feeling, for example); stir up: *a story that aroused our interest.* **2a.** To cause (someone) to be active, attentive, or excited: *a speech that aroused the crowd.* **b.** To stimulate sexual desire in. **3.** To awaken from sleep: *The baby's crying aroused me from my nap.* **—a·rous′a·ble** *adj.* **—a·rous′er** *n.*

arpeggio (är-pĕj′ē-ō *or* är-pĕj′ō) *n., pl.* **arpeggios 1.** The playing of the tones of a chord in succession rather than all at once. **2.** A chord played or sung in this way.

arquebus (är′kə-bəs *or* är′kwə-bəs) *n.* Variant of **harquebus.**

arraign (ə-rān′) *tr.v.* **arraigned, arraigning, arraigns** To summon before a court of law to answer a charge or indictment: *The suspect was arraigned on charges of fraud.* —**ar·raign′er** *n.* —**ar·raign′ment** *n.*

arrange (ə-rānj′) *v.* **arranged, arranging, arranges** —*tr.* **1.** To put in a specific order or relation: *Arrange these words alphabetically.* **2.** To plan or prepare for or bring about by planning: *How long did it take to arrange your trip?* **3.** To come to an agreement concerning; settle: *Have your friends arranged the date of the party?* **4.** To rework (a musical composition) for different voices or instruments or in a different style: *He arranged the piano piece for orchestra.* —*intr.* **1.** To cause something to happen by planning or to make plans for something to happen: *We arranged for a cab to pick us up at the airport.* **2.** To come to an agreement: *The company arranged with the union to grant more holidays.*

arrangement (ə-rānj′mənt) *n.* **1.** The act of arranging: *The arrangement of a time for the meeting was quite difficult.* **2.** The manner or style in which things are arranged: *The arrangement of ideas in the essay is clear and logical.* **3.** A collection or set of things that have been arranged: *a flower arrangement.* **4.** An agreement: *We have an arrangement about who cooks dinner and who washes the dishes.* **5.** often **arrangements** A plan or preparation: *arrangements for a vacation.* **6.** A version of a musical composition that differs from the original in style or use of instruments: *a jazz arrangement of a popular tune.*

arrant (ăr′ənt) *adj.* Thoroughgoing; out-and-out: *an arrant coward.* —**ar′rant·ly** *adv.*

array (ə-rā′) *tr.v.* **arrayed, arraying, arrays 1.** To put in an orderly arrangement, as troops. **2.** To dress, especially in fine clothes; adorn: *The dancers were arrayed in red velvet.* ❖ *n.* **1.** An orderly arrangement: *an array of data.* **2.** An impressively large number or group: *The cast for the play is a formidable array of talent.* **3.** Clothing or finery: *The princess was clad in rich array.* —**ar·ray′er** *n.*

arrears (ə-rîrz′) *pl.n.* **1.** An unpaid or overdue debt: *You have arrears of $23.00.* **2.** The state of being behind in fulfilling payments or an obligation: *After this is paid they will no longer be in arrears.*

arrest (ə-rĕst′) *tr.v.* **arrested, arresting, arrests 1.** To seize and hold under authority of law: *The police arrested the thief.* **2.** To stop the progress of; check: *The antibiotic arrested the spread of the infection.* **3.** To capture and hold; engage: *The exciting chapter arrested the reader's attention.* ❖ *n.* The act of arresting or the state of being arrested.

arresting (ə-rĕs′tĭng) *adj.* Capturing and holding the attention; striking: *the actor's arresting performance.* —**ar·rest′ing·ly** *adv.*

arrhythmia (ə-rĭth′mē-ə) *n.* Irregularity in the force or rhythm of the heartbeat.

arrival (ə-rī′vəl) *n.* **1.** The act of arriving: *the arrival of the passengers at the airport.* **2.** The attainment of a goal or objective: *The principal's arrival at a decision came after much thought.* **3.** A person or thing that has arrived: *the newest arrivals at the video store.*

arrive (ə-rīv′) *intr.v.* **arrived, arriving, arrives 1.** To reach a destination; come to a place: *They arrived in the city on*

time. **2.** To come; take place: *Spring arrived early this year.* **3.** To achieve success or fame: *She has finally arrived as an artist.* ✦ **arrive at** To reach through effort or a process: *The jury arrived at a decision.*

arrogance (ăr′ə-gəns) *n.* The quality or condition of being arrogant.

arrogant (ăr′ə-gənt) *adj.* **1.** Having or displaying excessive pride in oneself or an excessive sense of self-importance: *a conceited, arrogant person.* **2.** Marked by or arising from a feeling or assumption of one's superiority over others: *an arrogant refusal to listen to others.* —**ar′ro·gant·ly** *adv.*

✦ **SYNONYMS** arrogant, disdainful, haughty *adj.*

arrogate (ăr′ə-gāt′) *tr.v.* **arrogated, arrogating, arrogates** To take, claim, or assume for oneself without right: *The president cannot arrogate the power of Congress to declare war.* —**ar′ro·ga′tion** *n.*

arrow (ăr′ō) *n.* **1.** A straight thin shaft with a pointed head at one end and feathers at the other, meant to be shot from a bow. **2.** Something similar in shape, as a sign or mark used to indicate direction.

arrowhead (ăr′ō-hĕd′) *n.* The pointed tip of an arrow, typically a wedge-shaped stone or fitted metal cap.

arrowroot (ăr′ō-ro͞ot′ *or* ăr′ō-ro͝ot′) *n.* **1.** An edible, easily digested starch made from the rhizomes of a tropical American plant. **2.** The plant that has such rhizomes, having long leaves and small white flowers.

arroyo (ə-roi′ō) *n., pl.* **arroyos 1.** A small stream. **2.** A dry gulch in the southwest United States, formed by a stream.

arse (ärs) *n.* Chiefly British Slang Variant of **ass²**.

arsenal (är′sə-nəl) *n.* **1.** A building for the storage, manufacture, or repair of arms or ammunition. **2.** A stock of weapons.

arsenic (är′sə-nĭk) *n.* **1.** *Symbol* **As** A brittle, gray metallic element that occurs chiefly in combination with other elements. Arsenic forms poisonous compounds with oxygen and is used to make insecticides, weed killers, and various alloys. Atomic number 33. See **Periodic Table. 2.** A highly poisonous compound having the form of a white, odorless, tasteless powder, used to make insecticides, rat poisons, and weed killers.

arson (är′sən) *n.* The crime of intentionally setting fire to a building or other property. —**ar′son·ist** *n.*

art¹ (ärt) *n.* **1a.** The creation or production of something that is considered beautiful, as in painting, sculpture, poetry, or music. **b.** The study of these activities, especially the study of drawing, painting, and other visual arts: *I took art in school.* **c.** A work or works resulting from these activities, as a painting or a piece of sculpture: *an exhibit of modern art.* **2.** A practical skill: *the art of sewing; the art of negotiation.* **3.** **arts** The liberal arts; the humanities: *a college of arts and sciences.*

art² (ärt) *v.* Archaic Second person singular present tense of **be**.

art. An abbreviation of article.

art deco also **Art Deco** (dĕk′ō) *n.* A style of decoration that originated in the 1920s, using geometrical patterns, bold colors, and plastic and glass.

Artemis (är′tə-mĭs) *n.* In Greek mythology, the goddess of the moon and the hunt, identified with the Roman Diana.

arterial (är-tîr′ē-əl) *adj.* **1.** Relating to or contained in the arteries of the body: *arterial blood.* **2.** Serving as a main route of transportation: *This highway is the arterial route through town.* —**ar·te′ri·al·ly** *adv.*

arteriole (är-tîr′ē-ōl′) *n.* Any of the smaller branches of an artery, especially one that ends in capillaries.

arteriosclerosis (är-tîr′ē-ō-sklə-rō′sĭs) *n.* Hardening and thickening of the walls of the arteries, which can interfere with the circulation of the blood.

artery (är′tə-rē) *n., pl.* **arteries 1.** Any of a branching system of blood vessels that carry blood away from the heart to various parts of the body. **2.** A major route of transportation into which local routes flow.

artesian well (är-tē′zhən) *n.* A deep well that passes through hard impermeable rock and reaches water that is under enough pressure to rise to the surface without being pumped.

art film *n.* A film intended to be a serious artistic work, often experimental and not designed for commercial appeal.

art form *n.* A type of creative activity or created work that is regarded as art: *art forms such as painting, poetry, and ballet.*

artful (ärt′fəl) *adj.* **1.** Showing art or skill; skillful: *an artful cook.* **2.** Crafty; cunning: *an artful peddler.* **—art′ful·ly** *adv.* **—art′ful·ness** *n.*

arthritis (är-thrī′tĭs) *n.* Inflammation and stiffness of a joint or joints in the body.

arthropod (är′thrə-pŏd′) *n.* Any of numerous invertebrate animals having a segmented body, jointed legs or other appendages, and an external skeleton. Insects, crustaceans, spiders, and centipedes are all arthropods.

arthroscope (är′thrə-skōp′) *n.* An instrument that is used to examine the interior parts of a joint and is inserted through a small incision.

arthroscopy (är-thrŏs′kə-pē) *n., pl.* **arthroscopies** A surgical procedure that involves examination of the interior of a joint, such as the knee, with an arthroscope and often includes diagnosis and repair of joint problems. **—ar′-thro·scop′ic** (är′thrə-skŏp′ĭk) *adj.*

Arthur (är′thər) *n.* A legendary king of sixth-century Great Britain who gathered his knights at the Round Table and held court at Camelot. **—Ar·thu′ri·an** (är-thŏŏr′ē-ən) *adj.*

artichoke (är′tĭ-chōk′) *n.* **1.** The immature flower head of a plant related to the thistles, cooked and eaten as a vegetable. **2.** The plant that bears such a flower head.

article (är′tĭ-kəl) *n.* **1.** A written piece that forms an independent part of a publication; a report; an essay: *read an article about sports in the newspaper.* **2.** A section or item of a written document: *an article of the Constitution.* **3.** An individual thing; an item: *A bed is an article of furniture.* **4.** In grammar, the part of speech used to introduce nouns and to indicate whether the noun is definite and specific or indefinite and nonspecific. In English, the definite article is *the* and the indefinite articles are *a* and *an.*

articulate (är-tĭk′yə-lĭt) *adj.* **1.** Spoken clearly and distinctly: *a radio announcer's articulate speech.* **2.** Using or characterized by clear and effective language: *Teachers and lawyers must be articulate people.* **3.** Consisting of sections connected by joints: *The antennae of insects are articulate.* ❖ *v.* (är-tĭk′yə-lāt′) **articulated, articulating, articulates** *—tr.* **1.** To utter (a speech sound or sounds) distinctly; enunciate: *Children begin to articulate words around age two.* **2.** To put (a feeling, for example) into words, especially clearly and effectively; express: *Our leader articulated the sentiments of the group.* **3.** To con-

nect (body parts) by a joint or joints. *—intr.* **1.** To speak clearly and distinctly. **2.** To be jointed; form a joint: *the bones that articulate in the shoulder.* **—ar·tic′u·late·ly** *adv.* **—ar·tic′u·la′tor** *n.*

articulation (är-tĭk′yə-lā′shən) *n.* **1.** The act or process of speaking or expressing oneself, especially clearly and effectively: *Good articulation is essential for a radio broadcaster.* **2.** The manner in which things, such as the parts of a building, are joined together. **3.** A joint between rigid body segments, such as bones.

artifact (är′tə-făkt′) *n.* An object produced by human handiwork, especially one of archaeological or historical interest.

artifice (är′tə-fĭs) *n.* **1.** A clever device or stratagem; a ruse. **2.** Deception; trickery.

artificer (är-tĭf′ĭ-sər) *n.* A skilled worker; a person who practices a craft.

artificial (är′tə-fĭsh′əl) *adj.* **1.** Made by humans, especially in imitation of something natural: *an artificial sweetener; artificial flowers.* **2.** Not genuine or natural; affected: *an artificial display of tears and distress.* **—ar′ti·fi′ci·al·i·ty** (är′tə-fĭsh′ē-ăl′ĭ-tē) *n.* **—ar′ti·fi′cial·ly** *adv.*

artificial intelligence *n.* **1.** The ability of a computer or other machine to perform tasks normally thought to require intelligence, such as solving problems, recognizing specific human faces, or responding to spoken commands. **2.** The branch of computer science concerned with the development of machines having this ability.

artificial language *n.* An invented language developed for a specific purpose, such as computer programming.

artificial respiration *n.* Any of several methods for forcing air rhythmically in and out of the lungs, used to revive a living person who has stopped breathing.

artificial selection *n.* The process by which humans choose individual plants or animals with certain genetically based characteristics for breeding, so that those characteristics will become more common in future generations.

artillery (är-tĭl′ə-rē) *n., pl.* **artilleries 1.** Large mounted guns, such as cannons, that are operated by crews. **2.** The branch of an army that specializes in the use of such guns.

artilleryman (är-tĭl′ə-rē-mən) *n.* A soldier in the artillery.

artisan (är′tĭ-zən) *n.* A person who is skilled in making a product by hand.

artist (är′tĭst) *n.* **1.** A person who produces works of art, especially in the fine arts such as painting or sculpture. **2.** A person who works in one of the performing arts, such as dancing or acting. **3.** A person who shows skill and creativity in an occupation or pastime: *That surgeon is a real artist.*

artistic (är-tĭs′tĭk) *adj.* **1.** Relating to art or artists: *acclaimed by all artistic circles.* **2.** Sensitive to beauty: *an artistic temperament.* **3.** Showing imagination and skill: *an artistic flower arrangement.* **—ar·tis′ti·cal·ly** *adv.*

artistry (är′tĭ-strē) *n.* **1.** Artistic quality or workmanship: *the subtle artistry of a poem.* **2.** Artistic ability: *a painter of superb artistry.*

artless (ärt′lĭs) *adj.* **1.** Free from deceit; guileless: *an artless child.* **2.** Not artificial; natural: *the artless beauty of a sunset.* **—art′less·ly** *adv.* **—art′less·ness** *n.*

art nouveau often **Art Nouveau** (är′ nōō-vō′ *or* ärt′ nōō-vō′) *n.* A style of decoration and architecture that originated in the 1890s, using curved lines and flower shapes.

artwork (ärt′wûrk′) *n.* **1a.** A work of art. **b.** Works of art considered as a group: *The archaeologists saved the artwork on the walls of the cave.* **2.** The illustrations and decorative parts of a book or other publication as distinct from the text.

arty (är′tē) *adj.* **artier, artiest** *Informal* **1.** Artistic in an elaborate or showy manner: *an arty movie.* **2.** Relating to artists or the fine arts.

arugula (ə-rōō′gə-lə) *n.* A plant having pungent, edible leaves that are eaten raw in salads or cooked.

arum (âr′əm) *n.* Any of various plants having tiny flowers clustered on a fleshy spike and leaves that are often shaped like arrowheads.

–ary A suffix that means: **1.** Relating to: *legendary.* **2.** One that relates to or is connected with: *boundary.*

Aryan (âr′ē-ən) *n.* **1.** An Indo-Iranian. **2.** A member of a people speaking Proto-Indo-European or one of the Indo-European languages derived from it. In this sense, the word is not in technical use. **3.** In Nazi ideology, a non-Jewish Caucasian person, especially one of Nordic type. Nazis regarded Aryans as forming a master race. —**Ar′y·an** *adj.*

as (ăz; əz *when unstressed*) *adv.* Equally: *You won't easily find someone as nice.* ❖ *conj.* **1.** To the same degree or quantity that; equally with: *sweet as sugar.* **2.** In the same way that: *When in Rome, do as the Romans do.* **3.** At the same time that; while: *They smiled as their eyes met.* **4.** Since; because: *I wanted to stay home, as I was ill.* **5.** Though: *Nice as it is, I don't want it.* **6.** In accordance with which; a fact that: *The sun is hot, as everyone knows.* **7.** For instance: *large cats, as tigers and lions.* ❖ *pron.* That; who; which: *I got the same answer as you did. We brought such things as were necessary.* ❖ *prep.* **1.** The same as; like: *They treated the old car as an honored relic of the past.* **2.** In the role or function of: *The diplomat was acting as a peacemaker.* ◆ **as is** *Informal* Just the way it is; without changes: *I like your hair as is; don't cut it any shorter.* **as it were** In a manner of speaking; seemingly: *The optimistic words lifted him up, as it were, on wings of hope.* **as much** All that; the same: *I might have guessed as much.*

asafetida (ăs′ə-fĕt′ĭ-də) *n.* A brownish resin with a strong odor, obtained from various Asian plants and used in cooking and in medicinal preparations.

ASAP An abbreviation of as soon as possible.

asbestos (ăs-bĕs′təs *or* ăz-bĕs′təs) *n.* Any of several fibrous mineral forms of magnesium silicate that are resistant to heat, flames, and chemical action. Some forms have been shown to contribute to certain lung diseases. For this reason, asbestos is no longer used in making insulation, fireproofing material, and brake linings.

ascend (ə-sĕnd′) *v.* **ascended, ascending, ascends** —*intr.* **1.** To go or move upward; rise: *The balloon ascended rapidly.* **2.** To slope upward: *The trail ascends up the mountain.* **3.** To move to a higher rank or level: *The prince ascended to the throne and so became king.* —*tr.* **1.** To climb to or toward the top of: *The climbers ascended the mountain.* **2.** To slope upward toward or along: *The road ascends the ridge.* **3.** To come to occupy: *The queen ascended the throne upon the death of her father.*

ascendancy *also* **ascendency** (ə-sĕn′dən-sē) *n.* Dominance in position or power: *Britain lost ascendancy in the United States after the Revolution.*

ascendant *also* **ascendent** (ə-sĕn′dənt) *adj.* Coming into a position of power or influence: *Rome was the ascendant power in Europe before the Middle Ages.* ◆ **in the ascendant** Rising in power or influence.

ascending (ə-sĕn′dĭng) *adj.* Moving, going, or growing upward: *in ascending order of importance; a tree with ascending branches.*

ascension (ə-sĕn′shən) *n.* **1.** The act or process of ascending. **2. Ascension** In Christian belief, the rising of Jesus into heaven with 40 days after his resurrection.

Ascension Day *n.* The 40th day after Easter, on which the Christian feast of the Ascension of Jesus is observed.

ascent (ə-sĕnt′) *n.* **1.** The act or process of rising or going upward: *the rocket's ascent through the atmosphere.* **2.** The act or process of rising from a lower level, degree, or status; development: *the industrialist's ascent to the upper class.* **3.** An upward slope: *the steep ascent to the mountain pasture.*

ascertain (ăs′ər-tān′) *tr.v.* **ascertained, ascertaining, ascertains** To discover with certainty: *ascertain the truth.* —**as′cer·tain′a·ble** *adj.* —**as′cer·tain′a·bly** *adv.* —**as′cer·tain′ment** *n.*

ascetic (ə-sĕt′ĭk) *n.* A person who renounces comforts and pleasures in order to practice rigid self-denial, often as an act of religious devotion. ❖ *adj.* Relating to or characteristic of an ascetic; self-denying; austere: *Most hermits lead an ascetic life.* —**as·cet′i·cal·ly** *adv.*

asceticism (ə-sĕt′ĭ-sĭz′əm) *n.* Ascetic practice or discipline.

ASCII (ăs′kē) *n.* A standardized computer code for assigning binary numbers to letters, numbers, and symbols.

Asclepius (ə-sklē′pē-əs) *n.* In Greek mythology, the god of medicine.

ascorbic acid (ə-skôr′bĭk) *n.* Vitamin C.

ascot (ăs′kət *or* ăs′kŏt′) *n.* A broad neck scarf that is knotted so that one end lies flat on top of the other.

ascribe (ə-skrīb′) *tr.v.* **ascribed, ascribing, ascribes** To think of (something) as belonging to or coming from a specific cause, origin, or source; attribute: *The farmers ascribed their poor harvest to drought. Most scholars ascribe the poem to Chaucer.* —**as·crib′a·ble** *adj.*

ascription (ə-skrĭp′shən) *n.* The act of ascribing something: *the ascription of the poem to Shakespeare.*

aseptic (ə-sĕp′tĭk *or* ā-sĕp′tĭk) *adj.* Free from microorganisms that can cause infection: *aseptic surgical methods.* —**a·sep′ti·cal·ly** *adv.*

asexual (ā-sĕk′shōō-əl) *adj.* Not involving reproductive organs or the union of reproductive cells: *asexual reproduction.* —**a·sex′u·al·ly** *adv.*

as for *prep.* With regard to; concerning: *As for me, I'll stay.*

Asgard (ăs′gärd *or* ăz′gärd′) *n.* In Norse mythology, the heavenly dwelling place of the gods.

ash[1] (ăsh) *n.* **1.** The grayish-white powdery residue left when something is burned. **2.** The fine particles of solid matter thrown out of a volcano in an eruption. **3. ashes** The remains of a body after it has been cremated.

ash[2] (ăsh) *n.* **1.** Any of various trees having compound leaves, winged seeds, and strong tough wood. **2.** The wood of such a tree, used for making furniture, tool handles, and sporting goods such as baseball bats.

WORD HISTORY Ash[1] comes from Old English *æsce.* **Ash**[2] comes from Old English *æsc.* Both Old English forms meant the same as their Modern English counterparts.

ashamed (ə-shāmd′) *adj.* **1.** Feeling shame or guilt: *You should be ashamed for losing your temper.* **2.** Reluctant through fear of shame or embarrassment: *Don't be ashamed to ask for help.* —**a·sham′ed·ly** (ə-shā′mĭd-lē) *adv.*

Ashanti (ə-shǎn′tē *or* ə-shän′tē) *n., pl.* **Ashanti** or **Ashantis**
1. A member of a people of Ghana. **2.** The Twi language of this people.

ashen (ǎsh′ən) *adj.* **1.** Resembling ashes: *an ashen sky.* **2.** Whitish-gray in complexion: *knew something was wrong when she saw his ashen face.*

Ashkenazi (äsh′kə-nä′zē) *n., pl.* **Ashkenazim** (äsh′kə-näz′ĭm *or* äsh′kə-nä′zĭm) A member of the branch of European Jews, historically Yiddish-speaking, who settled in central and eastern Europe.

ashore (ə-shôr′) *adv.* **1.** To or onto the shore: *go ashore.* **2.** On land: *The sailors spent the day ashore.*

ashram (äsh′rəm) *n.* *Hinduism* A usually secluded residence of a religious community and its guru.

ashtray (ǎsh′trā′) *n.* A small receptacle for tobacco ashes.

Ash Wednesday *n.* The first day of Lent, when many Christians receive a mark of ashes on the forehead as a sign of penitence and mortality.

ashy (ǎsh′ē) *adj.* **ashier, ashiest 1.** Relating to, resembling, or containing ashes: *ashy soil where the fire pit had been.* **2.** Having the color of ashes: *a bird with ashy feathers.*

Asian (ā′zhən) *adj.* Relating to Asia or its peoples, languages, or cultures. ❖ *n.* **1.** A native or inhabitant of Asia. **2.** A person of Asian ancestry.

Asian American *n.* A US citizen or resident of Asian ancestry. **—A′sian-A·mer′i·can** *adj.*

Asian elephant *n.* An elephant native to southern and southeast Asia, having smaller ears than the African elephants. The females usually do not have tusks.

Asiatic (ā′zhē-ăt′ĭk) *adj.* Asian: *an Asiatic plant.*

aside (ə-sīd′) *adv.* **1.** To or toward one side: *step aside; draw the curtain aside.* **2.** Apart: *a day set aside for relaxation.* **3.** In reserve: *money put aside for a vacation.* **4.** Out of one's thoughts or mind: *put one's fears aside.* **5.** Being excepted or excluded from consideration: *Joking aside, can you swim 15 miles?* ❖ *n.* A remark spoken by a character in a play that the other actors on stage are not supposed to hear.

aside from *prep.* Apart from; except for: *Aside from a miracle, nothing can save their team from losing.*

as if *conj.* **1.** In the same way that it would be if: *She ran as if she would never tire.* **2.** That: *It seemed as if the day lasted forever.*

asinine (ăs′ə-nīn′) *adj.* Stupid or silly: *an asinine remark.*

ask (ăsk) *v.* **asked, asking, asks** —*tr.* **1.** To put a question to: *When we realized that we didn't know the answer, we asked the professor.* **2.** To seek an answer to: *asked a question.* **3.** To seek information about: *asked directions.* **4a.** To make a request of: *My sister asked me for help.* **b.** To make a request for. Often used with an infinitive or clause: *She asked to go along on the trip. He asked that he be allowed to stay out late.* **5.** To charge: *They are asking 20 dollars for this book.* **6.** To expect or demand: *Riding in a car all day is asking a great deal of a small child.* **7.** To invite: *Why don't we ask them to dinner?* —*intr.* **1.** To make inquiries: *We asked about the train schedule.* **2.** To make a request: *I asked for help.* —SEE NOTE AT **pretty.**

✦ SYNONYMS **ask, examine, inquire, question, quiz** *v.*

askance (ə-skăns′) *adv.* **1.** With a sidelong glance. **2.** With distrust or disapproval: *The reporter looked askance at such rumors.*

askew (ə-skyōō′) *adv. & adj.* Out of line; crooked; awry: *Wind knocked the sign askew.*

ASL An abbreviation of American Sign Language.

aslant (ə-slănt′) *adv. & adj.* At a slant: *trees standing aslant on the hill.*

asleep (ə-slēp′) *adj.* **1.** Sleeping: *You must have been asleep when the phone rang.* **2.** Numb: *My foot is asleep.* ❖ *adv.* Into a sleep: *The campers fell asleep quickly after their long hike.*

as long as *conj.* **1.** During the time that: *I'll stay as long as you need me.* **2.** Because of the fact that; since: *As long as you're offering, I accept.* **3.** On the condition that: *I'll go on the camping trip as long as you lend me a tent.*

asocial (ā-sō′shəl) *adj.* **1.** Avoiding the company of others; not sociable. **2.** Unable or unwilling to conform to normal standards of social behavior; antisocial.

as of *prep.* From or at the time of: *As of last week I have $800 in my savings account.*

asp (ăsp) *n.* Any of several venomous snakes of Africa and Eurasia, especially a small cobra of northern Africa and southwest Asia.

asparagine (ə-spär′ə-jēn′) *n.* A nonessential amino acid that is found in many proteins and some plants.

asparagus (ə-spär′ə-gəs) *n.* **1.** The young tender stalks of a plant with feathery leaves. The stalks are cooked and eaten as a vegetable. **2.** The plant that has such stalks.

aspartame (ăs′pər-tām′ *or* ə-spär′tăm′) *n.* An artificial sweetener, about 200 times as sweet as sugar, containing four calories per gram.

aspartic acid (ə-spär′tĭk) *n.* A nonessential amino acid that is found in certain plants.

ASPCA An abbreviation for American Society for the Prevention of Cruelty to Animals.

aspect (ăs′pĕkt) *n.* **1.** A way in which something can be considered: *From every aspect, the explorers were in a desperate situation.* **2.** A characteristic or feature of something: *This song has some interesting aspects.* **3.** The appearance or look of something: *the barren aspect of the desert.* **4.** A position facing or commanding a given direction; exposure: *a bright sunny room with a southern aspect.* **5.** A property of verbs that indicates whether the action or state described by the verb is completed, ongoing, or repeating at the time being spoken of.

aspen (ăs′pən) *n.* Any of various poplar trees having leaves that flutter readily in the wind because of their flattened leafstalks.

Asperger's syndrome (ăs′pər-gərz) *n.* A developmental disorder marked by difficulty in interacting with other people and often by the presence of repetitive behaviors.

asperity (ă-spĕr′ĭ-tē) *n.* Harshness of manner; irritability: *He responded with asperity.*

aspersion (ə-spûr′zhən *or* ə-spûr′shən) *n.* A damaging or slanderous report or remark: *The comment cast aspersions on my motives.*

asphalt (ăs′fôlt′) *n.* **1.** A thick, sticky, dark-brown material consisting of petroleum tars and used in paving, roofing, and waterproofing. Asphalt is obtained in the refining of petroleum or is found in natural deposits. **2.** This material mixed with crushed stone gravel or sand, used for paving or roofing. ❖ *tr.v.* **asphalted, asphalting, asphalts** To pave or coat with asphalt.

asphodel (ăs′fə-dĕl′) *n.* Any of several plants of the Mediterranean region having white or yellow flowers.

asphyxia (ăs-fĭk′sē-ə) *n.* Death or loss of consciousness caused by a lack of oxygen.

asphyxiate (ăs-fĭk′sē-āt′) *intr. & tr.v.* **asphyxiated, asphyxiating, asphyxiates** To undergo or cause to undergo asphyxia; suffocate: *Without air the bugs in the jar will asphyxiate. The thick smoke nearly asphyxiated us.* —as·phyx'i·a'tion *n.*

aspic (ăs'pĭk) *n.* A jelly made from gelatin and chilled meat juices or vegetable juices and served as a garnish or as a molded dish.

aspirant (ăs'pər-ənt *or* ə-spīr'ənt) *n.* A person who desires or strives for a particular position or honor: *an aspirant to high position and power.*

aspirate (ăs'pə-rāt') *tr.v.* **aspirated, aspirating, aspirates 1.** To remove (a liquid or gas) from a body cavity by suction: *aspirate fluid from the lungs.* **2.** To inhale (a foreign object): *aspirated a fish bone.* **3.** To pronounce (a vowel or word) with a puff of breath, as in *help.* ❖ *n.* (ăs'pər-ĭt) **1.** The sound of the letter *h* as in *help.* **2.** The puff of air accompanying or following certain speech sounds, as that accompanying *p* in *peach.*

aspiration (ăs'pə-rā'shən) *n.* **1a.** A strong desire, as for the realization of an ambition or ideal: *the student's aspiration to become a nurse.* **b.** An object of such desire; an ambitious goal: *To become an architect was my friend's aspiration.* **2.** The process of removing a liquid or gas from a body cavity by suction. **3.** The pronunciation of certain speech sounds with a puff of breath, especially at the beginning of a word, as *h* in *hurry.*

aspirator (ăs'pə-rā'tər) *n.* A suction pump, especially a small one used to draw fluids from body cavities.

aspire (ə-spīr') *intr.v.* **aspired, aspiring, aspires** To have a great ambition; desire strongly: *aspire to become a good musician; aspire to great knowledge.* —as·pir'er *n.*

aspirin (ăs'pər-ĭn *or* ăs'prĭn) *n.* **1.** A white crystalline compound derived from salicylic acid and used as a drug to relieve fever and pain; acetylsalicylic acid. **2.** A tablet of aspirin.

ass¹ (ăs) *n., pl.* **asses** (ăs'ĭz) **1.** Any of several hoofed mammals, such as the donkey, that resemble horses but have a smaller build and longer ears. **2.** A foolish or stupid person.

ass² (ăs) *n., pl.* **asses** (ăs'ĭz) *Vulgar Slang* The buttocks.

assail (ə-sāl') *tr.v.* **assailed, assailing, assails** To attack physically or with words: *The candidate for mayor assailed her opponents with strong criticism.* —as·sail'a·ble *adj.* —as·sail'er *n.*

assailant (ə-sā'lənt) *n.* A person who assails someone; an attacker.

assassin (ə-săs'ĭn) *n.* A person who kills someone by surprise attack, especially one who kills a public official or other prominent figure for political reasons.

assassinate (ə-săs'ə-nāt') *tr.v.* **assassinated, assassinating, assassinates** To murder (a public figure) by surprise attack, usually for political reasons. —as·sas'si·na'tion *n.* —as·sas'si·na'tor *n.*

assault (ə-sôlt') *n.* **1.** A violent physical or military attack: *The tanks made an assault upon the town.* **2.** An unlawful attempt or threat to injure another physically. **3.** A rigorous or energetic effort to accomplish something difficult: *an assault on poverty.* **4.** An act of expressing strong criticism; a denunciation: *a blogger's assaults on corrupt politicians.* ❖ *tr.v.* **assaulted, assaulting, assaults 1.** To attack violently: *The troops assaulted the fort.* **2.** To attack verbally; criticize or denounce. —as·sault'er *n.*

assault and battery *n.* A criminal act involving both a threat of violence and actual physical contact with the victim.

assault weapon *n.* A weapon, especially an automatic or

semiautomatic rifle, designed for use by infantry.

assay (ăs'ā' *or* ă-sā') *n.* **1.** A chemical analysis of something, especially an ore or drug. **2.** A specimen or sample subjected to an assay. ❖ *v.* (ă-sā' *or* ăs'ā') **assayed, assaying, assays** —*tr.* **1.** To analyze (an ore or alloy) to find out the quantity of gold, silver, or other metal in it. **2.** To test and evaluate; assess: *We assayed the chances of success and decided to make the film.* **3.** To attempt; try: *In spite of the dangers she still assayed the difficult journey.* —*intr.* To be shown by an assay to contain some ingredient: *The ore assayed at 1 percent uranium.* —as·say'er *n.*

assemblage (ə-sĕm'blĭj) *n.* **1.** A collection of people or things: *The mayor spoke before a large assemblage in the town square.* **2.** The act of gathering or fitting together.

assemble (ə-sĕm'bəl) *v.* **assembled, assembling, assembles** —*tr.* **1.** To bring together in one place or as a group: *The teachers assembled their classes in the auditorium. Assemble all the ingredients before you start cooking.* **2.** To perform the assembly of; put together: *The mechanic assembled the engine.* —*intr.* To come together; gather; congregate: *A group of friends assembled at the corner.* See Synonyms at **gather.** —as·sem'bler *n.*

assembly (ə-sĕm'blē) *n., pl.* **assemblies 1.** A group of people gathered together for a common purpose. **2. Assembly** The lower house of the legislature in certain US states. **3a.** The process of putting together a number of parts to make up a complete unit: *The assembly of a new car usually takes less than a day.* **b.** A set of parts that work together as a unit; an apparatus: *the steering assembly of a truck.*

assembly line *n.* An arrangement in which articles are assembled in successive stages, passing from worker to worker or machine to machine, often on some kind of conveyor.

assemblyman (ə-sĕm'blē-mən) *n.* A man who is a member of a legislative assembly.

assemblywoman (ə-sĕm'blē-wŏom'ən) *n.* A woman who is a member of a legislative assembly.

assent (ə-sĕnt') *intr.v.* **assented, assenting, assents** To express agreement: *All the students assented to putting off the final exam.* ❖ *n.* Agreement, as to a proposal, especially in a formal or impersonal manner: *The prime minister desired the king's assent.*

assert (ə-sûrt') *tr.v.* **asserted, asserting, asserts 1.** To state or declare positively; claim: *By opposing the bill, the senators asserted their independence from business leaders.* **2.** To insist upon recognition of; defend or maintain: *The lawyer asserted the defendant's right to a fair trial.* ◆ **assert (oneself)** To express oneself boldly or forcefully. —as·sert'er, as·ser'tor *n.*

assertion (ə-sûr'shən) *n.* **1.** The act of asserting. **2.** A statement or claim, especially one for which no proof is offered: *His assertions of innocence were later found to be true.*

assertive (ə-sûr'tĭv) *adj.* Self-confident, especially in putting forward one's opinions: *She was assertive in her request for a raise.* —as·ser'tive·ly *adv.* —as·ser'tive·ness *n.*

asses (ăs'ĭz) *n.* **1.** Plural of **ass¹.** **2.** *Vulgar Slang* Plural of **ass².**

assess (ə-sĕs') *tr.v.* **assessed, assessing, assesses 1.** To determine the value, significance, or extent of; estimate; evaluate: *conducted tests to assess the bridge's structural integrity.* **2.** To estimate the value of (property) for taxation: *The apartment building was assessed at several mil-*

lion dollars. **3a.** To set the amount of (a tax, fine, or other payment): *assess a tax for road repairs.* **b.** To charge (a person) with a tax, fine, or other special payment: *Each member of the team will be assessed five dollars for new equipment.* **4.** In sports, to charge a player, coach, or team with (a foul or penalty). —**as·sess′a·ble** *adj.*

assessment (ə-sĕs′mənt) *n.* **1.** The act of assessing. **2.** An amount assessed: *Property owners paid an assessment for street repairs.*

assessor (ə-sĕs′ər) *n.* An official whose job it is to assess the tax value of property.

asset (ăs′ĕt′) *n.* **1.** A valuable quality or possession: *An agreeable personality is a great asset.* **2. assets** All the property owned by a person or business that has monetary value and may be applied directly or indirectly to the payment of debts.

asseverate (ə-sĕv′ə-rāt′) *tr.v.* **asseverated, asseverating, asseverates** To declare seriously or positively; affirm.

assiduous (ə-sĭj′ōō-əs) *adj.* Diligent; industrious: *an assiduous worker.* —**as·sid′u·ous·ly** *adv.* —**as·sid′-u·ous·ness** *n.*

assign (ə-sīn′) *tr.v.* **assigned, assigning, assigns 1.** To select for a duty or office; appoint: *Which firefighters are assigned to the industrial area of the city?* **2.** To set apart for a purpose or place into a category; designate: *assign a day for the exam; assign rocks to mineral groups.* **3.** To give out as a task; allot: *The supervisor will assign duties to the staff.* **4.** To think of (something) as having a certain cause or origin; attribute: *The coach assigned blame for the loss to a lack of good defense.* —**as·sign′a·ble** *adj.* —**as·sign′-er** *n.* —SEE NOTE AT **sign.**

assignation (ăs′ĭg-nā′shən) *n.* **1a.** The act of assigning: *assignation of blame.* **b.** Something assigned, especially an allotment. **2a.** An appointment to meet in secret, especially between lovers. **b.** The meeting made by such an appointment.

assignment (ə-sīn′mənt) *n.* **1.** The act of assigning something: *The work was divided among us by assignment.* **2.** Something assigned, especially a task or job: *Your assignment is to find a location for the party.* See Synonyms at **task. 3.** A position or post of duty to which one is assigned: *The journalist will take an assignment outside the United States.*

assimilate (ə-sĭm′ə-lāt′) *v.* **assimilated, assimilating, assimilates** —*tr.* **1.** To take in and use (food or nutrients) in living tissue; absorb: *The body assimilates protein.* **2.** To make part of one's knowledge; incorporate into one's understanding: *heard the warning but failed to assimilate it.* **3.** To take into the cultural or social tradition of a group: *The United States has assimilated immigrants of many nationalities.* **4.** To alter (a speech sound) by assimilation. —*intr.* **1.** To be taken into the mind: *technological changes that are difficult to assimilate.* **2.** To be taken into a group: *immigrants assimilating into the broader culture.* —**as·sim′i·la′tor** *n.*

assimilation (ə-sĭm′ə-lā′shən) *n.* **1.** The act or process of assimilating: *the assimilation of new technology.* **2.** In biology, the process by which nutrients are taken in and converted into living tissue, as by absorption and digestion. **3.** In linguistics, the process by which a sound becomes similar or identical to a nearby sound. For example, the prefix *in-* becomes *im-* in *impossible* by assimilation.

Assiniboin (ə-sĭn′ə-boin′) *n., pl.* **Assiniboin** or **Assiniboins 1.** A member of a Native American people of northeast Montana, Alberta, and Saskatchewan. **2.** The Siouan language of the Assiniboin.

assist (ə-sĭst′) *v.* **assisted, assisting, assists** —*tr.* To give help or support to; aid: *Our friends assisted us in repairing the roof.* —*intr.* To give help or support: *We're having trouble with the computer. Could you assist?* ❖ *n.* **1.** An act of giving help; aid: *give someone a quick assist.* **2a.** In baseball, an act of fielding or throwing the ball that enables a teammate to put a runner out. **b.** A pass that enables a teammate to score, as in basketball or hockey. —**as·sist′er** *n.*

assistance (ə-sĭs′təns) *n.* Help; aid: *The government provided financial assistance to farmers.*

assistant (ə-sĭs′tənt) *n.* A person who assists; a helper: *the president's special assistant.* ❖ *adj.* Acting under the authority of another person: *an assistant curator.*

assisted living (ə-sĭs′tĭd) *n.* A living arrangement in which people with special needs reside in a facility that provides help with everyday tasks.

assizes (ə-sī′zĭz) *pl.n.* A court session formerly held periodically in each of the counties of England and Wales.

assn. An abbreviation of association.

assoc. An abbreviation of: **1.** associate. **2.** association.

associate (ə-sō′sē-āt′ *or* ə-sō′shē-āt′) *v.* **associated, associating, associates** —*tr.* **1.** To bring together in one's mind or imagination; connect: *We associate pumpkins with the harvest.* **2.** To connect or involve with a cause, group, or partner: *Which theater was Shakespeare associated with?* —*intr.* **1.** To keep company: *The neighbors like to associate with each other.* **2.** To join in or form a union or association: *the right for workers to associate in a union.* ❖ *n.* (ə-sō′sē-ĭt *or* ə-sō′shē-ĭt) **1.** A partner or colleague: *my business associate.* **2.** A companion; a comrade. **3.** A member who has only partial status: *an associate of the museum society.* ❖ *adj.* (ə-sō′sē-ĭt *or* ə-sō′-shē-ĭt) **1.** Joined with another and having equal or nearly equal status; sharing in responsibility or authority: *an associate judge.* **2.** Having only partial status: *an associate member of a club.* —**as·so′ci·a′tor** (ə-sō′sē-ā′tər *or* ə-sō′shē-ā′tər) *n.*

associate's degree (ə-sō′sē-ĭts′ *or* ə-sō′shē-ĭts′) *n.* A degree given by a college to a person who has completed a two-year program or its equivalent.

association (ə-sō′sē-ā′shən *or* ə-sō′-shē-ā′shən) *n.* **1.** A group of people joined together for a common purpose or interest: *a trade association; a teachers' association.* **2.** A partnership or friendship: *a close association with old schoolmates.* **3a.** An idea or thought triggered by another idea or thought or by a feeling or sensation: *What associations does the word* whale *bring to your mind?* **b.** A correlation or causal connection: *There is a clear association of exercise with improved health.* **4.** The act of associating: *The author made a striking new association of ideas.*

association football *n.* Chiefly British Soccer.

associative (ə-sō′shə-tĭv *or* ə-sō′sē-ā′tĭv *or* ə-sō′shē-ā′-tĭv) *adj.* **1.** Characterized by, resulting from, or causing association. **2.** In mathematics, of or relating to the associative property. —**as·so′ci·a′tive·ly** *adv.*

associative property *n.* In mathematics, a principle stating that different groupings of numbers being added or multiplied will not change their sum or product, as long as the order of the numbers remains the same. For example, $2 + (3 + 4)$ will give the same sum as

$(2 + 3) + 4$, and $(2 \times 3) \times 5$ will give the same product as $2 \times (3 \times 5)$.

assonance (ăs′ə-nəns) *n.* **1.** Similarity in sound, especially the repetition in poetry of the same vowel sounds. **2.** A partial rhyme in which the stressed vowel sounds are the same but the consonants are different, as in *tent* and *sense.*

assort (ə-sôrt′) *tr.v.* **assorted, assorting, assorts** To separate into groups according to kinds; classify: *assort books by author.* —**as·sort′er** *n.*

assorted (ə-sôr′tĭd) *adj.* Consisting of various kinds: *shirts of assorted sizes; assorted screws.*

assortment (ə-sôrt′mənt) *n.* A collection of various kinds; a variety: *people with an unusual assortment of skills; an assortment of vegetables.*

asst. An abbreviation of assistant.

assuage (ə-swāj′) *tr.v.* **assuaged, assuaging, assuages** **1.** To make less burdensome or painful: *Maybe your kind words will assuage their sorrow.* **2.** To satisfy; appease: *assuage one's thirst.* **3.** To pacify; calm: *Our apologies assuaged their anger.* —**as·suage′ment** *n.*

assume (ə-so͞om′) *tr.v.* **assumed, assuming, assumes** **1.** To take for granted; suppose: *Let's assume that our guests will come on time.* **2.** To take upon oneself; undertake: *He assumed responsibility for walking the dog.* **3.** To undertake the duties of: *The new governor assumes office in January.* **4.** To take over; seize: *She assumed control of the project during the crisis.* **5.** To take on; put on: *assume a disguise.* **6.** To feign; pretend: *always assuming an air of indifference.* —**as·sum′a·ble** *adj.* —**as·sum′a·bly** *adv.* —**as·sum′er** *n.*

assumed (ə-so͞omd′) *adj.* **1.** Fictitious; adopted: *an assumed name.* **2.** Taken for granted; supposed: *an assumed increase in funding.*

assuming (ə-so͞o′mĭng) *conj.* On the assumption that: *Assuming the snowboard is for sale, would you buy it?*

assumption (ə-sŭmp′shən) *n.* **1.** An idea or statement accepted as true without proof: *Let's start with the assumption that all people have equal rights under the law.* **2.** The act of taking on a task or responsibility: *the new governor's assumption of office.* **3. Assumption** August 15, observed as a holiday in some branches of Christianity to commemorate the taking up of the Virgin Mary into heaven after her death.

assurance (ə-sho͞or′əns) *n.* **1.** A statement or indication that inspires confidence; a guarantee or pledge: *The debtor gave the bank solemn assurance that the debt would be paid.* **2.** Confidence; certainty: *We had no assurance that the car was in good condition.* **3.** Self-confidence: *The veteran actor played the part with complete assurance.*

assure (ə-sho͞or′) *tr.v.* **assured, assuring, assures** **1.** To declare positively: *I can assure you that the train will be on time.* **2.** To cause to feel sure; convince: *She assured me of her good intentions.* **3.** To make certain; ensure: *The bank lent us the money to assure the success of the business.* **4.** To give confidence to; reassure: *The doctor assured me that I would recover quickly.*

USAGE The words **assure, ensure,** and **insure** all mean "to make secure or certain," but *assure* and *insure* have more specific meanings as well. Of the three, only *assure* means "to cause to feel sure," and it is the only one that can have a person for its direct object: *The duke assured the queen of his loyalty.* By contrast, *ensure* and *insure* never have a person for their direct object: *By changing his diet, he ensured* (or *insured*) *his good health.* Only *insure* can be

used to mean "to guarantee people or property against risk," as in *We insured the car.*

assured (ə-sho͞ord′) *adj.* **1.** Confident: *an assured manner.* **2.** Certain; guaranteed: *an assured success.* —**as·sur′ed·ly** (ə-sho͞or′ĭd-lē) *adv.*

AST An abbreviation of: **1.** Alaska Standard Time. **2.** Atlantic Standard Time.

Astarte (ə-stär′tē) *n.* In ancient Phoenician, Syrian, and Canaanite mythology, the goddess of love and war.

astatine (ăs′tə-tēn′ *or* ăs′tə-tĭn) *n. Symbol* **At** A highly unstable, radioactive nonmetallic element that is the heaviest element of the halogen group. The most stable of its many isotopes has a half-life of about eight hours. Atomic number 85. See **Periodic Table.**

aster (ăs′tər) *n.* Any of various plants having white, purplish, or pink flowers resembling daisies.

asterisk (ăs′tə-rĭsk′) *n.* A symbol (*) used in printed and written matter to indicate an omission or reference to a footnote, for example.

astern (ə-stûrn′) *adv. & adj.* **1.** Behind a ship or boat. **2.** At or toward the rear of a ship or boat. **3.** With the stern foremost; backward.

asteroid (ăs′tə-roid′) *n.* Any of numerous small, often irregularly shaped bodies that orbit the sun, chiefly in the region between Mars and Jupiter. They range from the size of a speck of dust to several hundred miles in diameter.

asteroid belt *n.* The region of the solar system between the orbits of Mars and Jupiter, where most of the asteroids are found.

asthma (ăz′mə *or* ăs′mə) *n.* A chronic disease that is often caused by an allergy and is marked by narrowing of the breathing passages. It results in attacks of wheezing, coughing, difficulty in breathing, and tightness of the chest.

asthmatic (ăz-măt′ĭk *or* ăs-măt′ĭk) *adj.* **1.** Relating to asthma. **2.** Having asthma: *an asthmatic child.* ❖ *n.* A person with asthma.

as though *conj.* As if: *They looked as though they were enjoying themselves.*

astigmatism (ə-stĭg′mə-tĭz′əm) *n.* A defect of the eye in which the curvature of the cornea or lens is uneven. This unevenness prevents rays of light from being focused at a single point on the retina, resulting in indistinct or imperfect images. —**as′tig·mat′ic** (ăs′tĭg-măt′ĭk) *adj.*

astir (ə-stûr′) *adj.* **1.** In motion; moving about: *The miners' camp was astir after the news of the gold discovery.* **2.** Having gotten out of bed; up.

as to *prep.* **1.** With regard to: *There is much controversy as to nuclear energy.* **2.** According to: *The fabrics were arranged as to color.*

astonish (ə-stŏn′ĭsh) *tr.v.* **astonished, astonishing, astonishes** To fill with wonder; amaze; surprise: *The results of the experiment astonished the researchers.* See Synonyms at **surprise.**

astonishing (ə-stŏn′ĭ-shĭng) *adj.* Greatly surprising; amazing: *an astonishing discovery.* —**a·ston′ish·ing·ly** *adv.*

astonishment (ə-stŏn′ĭsh-mənt) *n.* Great surprise; amazement: *our astonishment at seeing a shooting star.*

astound (ə-stound′) *tr.v.* **astounded, astounding, astounds** To astonish and bewilder: *The price of the fancy car astounded me.* See Synonyms at **surprise.**

astounding (ə-stoun′dĭng) *adj.* Surprising; amazing: *an astounding success.* —**a·stound′ing·ly** *adv.*

astraddle (ə-străd′l) *prep.* Astride; astride of: *astraddle a horse.*

astral (ăs′trəl) *adj.* Relating to, coming from, or resembling the stars.

astray (ə-strā′) *adv.* Away from the proper goal or path: *led astray by bad advice.*

astride (ə-strīd′) *adv.* **1.** With the legs on each side: *riding astride on a horse.* **2.** With the legs wide apart. ❖ *prep.* With a leg on each side of; bestriding: *The cowboy sat astride the horse's back.* ◆ **astride of** Astride: *She stood astride of the fallen tree.*

astringent (ə-strĭn′jənt) *adj.* Having the property of drawing together or contracting tissues. ❖ *n.* A substance that draws together or contracts body tissues. Astringents can be applied to the skin cosmetically or can be used medicinally to check the flow of blood or other secretions.

astro– A prefix that means: **1.** Star: *astrophysics.* **2.** Celestial object or objects: *astrometry.* **3.** Outer space: *astronaut.*

astrolabe (ăs′trə-lāb′) *n.* A medieval instrument formerly used to determine the altitude of the sun and other celestial objects.

astrology (ə-strŏl′ə-jē) *n.* The study of the positions of the stars and planets in the belief that they influence the course of human affairs and natural occurrences on earth. —**as·tro·log′i·cal** (ăs′trə-lŏj′ĭ-kəl) *adj.* —**as′tro·log′i·cal·ly** *adv.* —**as·trol′o·ger** *n.*

astrometry (ə-strŏm′ĭ-trē) *n.* The scientific measurement of the positions and motions of celestial objects.

astronaut (ăs′trə-nôt′) *n.* A person trained to serve as a member of the crew of a spacecraft.

astronautics (ăs′trə-nô′tĭks) *n.* *(used with a singular or plural verb)* The science and technology of space flight. —**as′tro·nau′tic, as′tro·nau′ti·cal** *adj.*

astronomer (ə-strŏn′ə-mər) *n.* A scientist who specializes in astronomy.

astronomical (ăs′trə-nŏm′ĭ-kəl) also **astronomic** (ăs′trə-nŏm′ĭk) *adj.* **1.** Relating to astronomy. **2.** Too large to be easily imagined; immense: *The budget for running the federal government is astronomical.* —**as′tro·nom′i·cal·ly** *adv.*

astronomical unit *n.* A unit of length equal to the mean distance from Earth to the sun, about 93 million miles (150 million kilometers), used to measure distances within the solar system.

astronomy (ə-strŏn′ə-mē) *n.* The science that deals with the study of the universe and the objects in it, including stars, planets, and nebulae. Astronomy studies the size, composition, and energy of the universe and the relative motion and positions of the objects in it.

astrophysics (ăs′trō-fĭz′ĭks) *n.* *(used with a singular verb)* The branch of astronomy that deals with the physical processes, such as energy generation and transmission, that occur in stars, galaxies, and interstellar space. —**as′tro·phys′i·cal** *adj.*

AstroTurf (ăs′trō-tûrf′) A trademark for an artificial ground covering that resembles grass.

astute (ə-stōōt′) *adj.* Having or showing keen judgment; shrewd: *The reporter was an astute observer. Before advising us the carpenter made an astute appraisal of the blueprints.* —**as·tute′ly** *adv.* —**as·tute′ness** *n.*

asunder (ə-sŭn′dər) *adv.* **1.** Into separate parts or groups:

A tornado tore the house asunder. **2.** Apart from each other in position or direction: *The curtains were drawn asunder.*

as well as *conj.* And in addition: *warm as well as sunny.* ❖ *prep.* In addition to: *The company's owner, as well as the board of directors, was present at the meeting.*

asylum (ə-sī′ləm) *n.* **1.** Protection and immunity from extradition granted to a political refugee from another country. **2.** Shelter or protection, especially from physical danger: *We sought asylum from the storm in an old shed.* **3.** An institution for the care of chronically ill patients, especially those with severe mental disorders.

asymmetric (ā′sĭ-mĕt′rĭk) also **asymmetrical** (ā′sĭ-mĕt′rĭkəl) *adj.* Not symmetrical; lacking symmetry. —**a′sym·met′ri·cal·ly** *adv.*

asymmetry (ā-sĭm′ĭ-trē) *n.* Lack of symmetry or balance.

asymptomatic (ā′sĭmp-tə-măt′ĭk) *adj.* Causing or showing no disease symptoms: *an asymptomatic infection.*

asymptote (ăs′ĭm-tōt′) *n.* A line whose distance to a given curve gets closer and closer to zero. The curve may come closer and closer without ever touching the asymptote, or it may cross back and forth over the asymptote like ripples that get smaller and smaller without completely flattening out.

at (ăt; ət *when unstressed*) *prep.* **1.** In or near the position or location of: *at home; at the center of the room.* **2.** To or toward the direction or goal of: *look at us; jump at the chance.* **3.** Present during; attending: *at the dance.* **4.** On, near, or by the time or age of: *at noon.* **5.** In the state or condition of: *He's at peace with himself.* **6.** In the activity or field of: *skilled at playing chess; good at math.* **7.** In the rate, extent, or amount of: *at 40 miles per hour; at two dollars a gallon.* **8.** Because of: *rejoice at victory.* **9a.** Dependent upon: *at your mercy.* **b.** According to: *at the judge's discretion.* **10.** Through; by way of: *Come in at the side entrance.*

atavism (ăt′ə-vĭz′əm) *n.* The reappearance of a characteristic in an organism after several generations of absence. —**at′a·vis′tic** *adj.*

ate (āt) *v.* Past tense of **eat.**

–ate[1] A suffix that means: **1.** Characterized by: *Latinate.* **2.** Resembling: *palmate.* **3.** One that is characterized by: *laminate.* **4.** Rank; office: *rabbinate.* **5.** To act upon in a specified manner: *insulate.*

–ate[2] A suffix that means a salt or an ester of a specified acid whose name ends in -ic: *acetate.*

atelier (ăt′l-yā′) *n.* A workshop or studio, especially for an artist or designer.

a tempo (ä tĕm′pō) *adv. & adj.* In music, returning to the original tempo.

Athabascan or **Athabaskan** (ăth′ə-băs′kən) *n.* A group of languages of Native American people of the western United States and Canada and parts of Alaska. Apache and Navajo are two important Athabascan languages. —**Ath′a·bas′can** *adj.*

atheism (ā′thē-ĭz′əm) *n.* Disbelief in or denial of the existence of God or gods. —**a′the·ist** *n.* —**a′the·is′tic** *adj.*

Athena (ə-thē′nə) *n.* In Greek mythology, the goddess of wisdom and the arts, identified with the Roman Minerva.

atherosclerosis (ăth′ə-rō-sklə-rō′sĭs) *n.* Hardening and thickening of the walls of the arteries caused by deposits of fatty material, especially cholesterol.

athlete (ăth′lēt′) *n.* A person who participates in physical exercise or sports, especially in competitive events.

athlete's foot (ăth′lēts) *n.* A contagious infection of the feet that usually affects the skin between the toes, causing it to itch, blister, and crack. It is caused by a fungus.

athletic (ăth-lĕt′ĭk) *adj.* **1.** Relating to athletics or athletes: *athletic ability; an athletic club.* **2.** Characterized by or involving physical activity or exertion: *an athletic workout.* **3.** Physically strong; muscular: *an athletic build.* See Synonyms at **muscular.** —**ath·let′i·cal·ly** *adv.*

athletics (ăth-lĕt′ĭks) *n. (used with a singular or plural verb)* Competitive sports or other recreational activities that involve physical exercise and typically require strength, speed, endurance, coordination, and agility.

athletic supporter *n.* An elastic support for the male genitals, often worn during athletic activities.

athwart (ə-thwôrt′) *prep.* Across: *threw the rope athwart the dock.* ❖ *adv.* From side to side; across.

–ation A suffix that means: **1.** Action or process: *strangulation.* **2.** The state, condition, or quality of: *starvation.* **3.** The result of an action or process: *discoloration.*

WORD BUILDING The very common suffix –*ation*, which comes from Latin, is used to change a verb to a noun. In English, –*ation* nouns were at first formed from verbs that ended in –*ate*, like the noun *creation* from the verb *create.* But –*ation* became so popular that it is now used to form nouns from verbs that do not end in –*ate*, such as *civilization* from the verb *civilize* and *starvation* from the verb *starve.*

–ative A suffix that means relating to or associated with: *talkative; authoritative.*

Atlantic Standard Time *n.* Standard time in the fourth time zone west of Greenwich, England, used, for example, in Puerto Rico and Nova Scotia.

Atlantis (ăt-lăn′tĭs) *n.* A fabled island or continent of ancient times, said to have sunk beneath the sea during an earthquake.

atlas (ăt′ləs) *n., pl.* **atlases** A book or bound collection of maps.

Atlas *n.* In Greek mythology, a Titan who supported the heavens on his shoulders as punishment for revolt against Zeus.

ATM (ā′tē′ĕm′) *n.* A computer terminal that allows a bank customer with an identification card to have access to his or her account, especially to withdraw or deposit money. ATM is short for *automatic* (or *automated*) *teller machine.*

atmosphere (ăt′mə-sfîr′) *n.* **1.** The mixture of gases that surrounds the earth or some other celestial object and is held by the force of gravity. The atmosphere of the earth is rich in nitrogen; that of Venus is mainly carbon dioxide. **2.** A unit of pressure equal to the pressure of the air at sea level, about 14.7 pounds per square inch or 1,013 millibars. **3.** The air or climate of a place: *the dry atmosphere of the desert.* **4.** A general feeling or mood: *the library's quiet atmosphere.*

atmospheric (ăt′mə-sfĕr′ĭk *or* ăt′mə-sfîr′ĭk) *adj.* **1.** Relating to, in, or from the atmosphere: *atmospheric disturbances; atmospheric flight.* **2.** Evoking some mood or aesthetic quality: *a restaurant with atmospheric lighting.* —**at′mos·pher′i·cal·ly** *adv.*

atmospheric pressure *n.* Pressure caused by the weight of the air. At sea level it has an average value of one atmosphere, but it diminishes with increasing altitude.

at. no. An abbreviation of atomic number.

atoll (ăt′ôl′ *or* ā′tôl′) *n.* An island or chain of islets connected by a coral reef that nearly or entirely encloses a lagoon.

atom (ăt′əm) *n.* The smallest unit of an element, consisting of protons and neutrons in a dense central nucleus orbited by a number of electrons. The number of protons in every atom of an element is different for each element; for example, every atom of helium has two protons, and every atom of carbon has six protons. In electrically neutral atoms, the number of electrons is the same as the number of protons. Atoms remain intact in chemical reactions, except for the removal, transfer, or exchange of certain electrons.

atom bomb *n.* An atomic bomb.

atomic (ə-tŏm′ĭk) *adj.* **1.** Relating to atoms. **2.** Using or produced by atomic energy; nuclear: *an atomic power plant.*

atomic age *n.* The present age considered as the time of the discovery and use of atomic energy; the nuclear age.

atomic bomb *n.* A very destructive bomb that gets its explosive power from the energy released by the fission of atomic nuclei, usually of plutonium or uranium, in an uncontrolled chain reaction.

atomic clock *n.* An extremely precise clock that is regulated by atomic vibrations.

atomic energy *n.* Nuclear energy.

atomic mass *n.* The mass of an atom, usually expressed in atomic mass units.

atomic mass unit *n.* A unit of mass equal to $\frac{1}{12}$ the mass of the most abundant kind of carbon atom, carbon-12; approximately 1.6604×10^{-24} gram.

atomic number *n.* The number of protons in the atomic nucleus of a chemical element.

atomic theory *n.* The physical theory of the structure, properties, and behavior of atoms.

atomic weight *n.* The average weight of an atom of an element, usually expressed relative to the most abundant isotope of carbon, which is assigned 12 atomic mass units.

atomize (ăt′ə-mīz′) *tr.v.* **atomized, atomizing, atomizes 1.** To break apart or separate into atoms. **2.** To reduce (a liquid) into a fine spray. —**at′om·i·za′tion** (ăt′ə-mī-zā′-shən) *n.*

atomizer (ăt′ə-mī′zər) *n.* A device for producing a fine spray, especially of a perfume or medicine.

atom smasher *n.* A particle accelerator.

atonal (ā-tō′nəl) *adj.* In music, having no key or tonality. —**a·ton′al·ly** *adv.*

atonality (ā′tō-năl′ĭ-tē) *n., pl.* **atonalities** The absence of a tonal center and of harmonies using a diatonic scale.

atone (ə-tōn′) *intr.v.* **atoned, atoning, atones** To make amends for a sin, fault, or other wrong: *atone for bad manners by apologizing.*

atonement (ə-tōn′mənt) *n.* **1.** The act of atoning; amends. **2. Atonement** In Christianity, the reconciliation between God and humans brought about by the life and death of Jesus.

atop (ə-tŏp′) *prep.* On top of: *The Supreme Court stands atop our judicial court system.*

ATP (ā′tē′pē′) *n.* An organic compound, having the formula $C_{10}H_{16}N_5O_{13}P_3$, that acts as an energy source in cell metabolism.

Atreus (ā′trōōs′ *or* ā′trē-əs) *n.* In Greek mythology, a king of Mycenae and the father of Agamemnon and Menelaus.

at-risk (ăt′rĭsk′) *adj.* **1.** In danger of suffering from mistreatment, injury, disease, or the effects of dysfunctional behavior: *after-school programs for at-risk youth; screening at-risk seniors for diabetes.* **2.** Likely to result in injury, disease, or other negative consequences: *at-risk occupations; at-risk behaviors.*

atrium (ā′trē-əm) *n., pl.* **atria** (ā′trē-ə) or **atriums 1a.** A central area in some modern buildings that often has skylights and contains plants. **b.** The open entrance court of an ancient Roman house. **2.** A cavity or chamber of the body, especially one of the chambers of the heart that receives blood from the veins and pumps it into a ventricle. —**a′tri·al** *adj.*

atrocious (ə-trō′shəs) *adj.* **1.** Extremely evil or cruel; wicked. **2.** Very bad; abominable: *atrocious weather.* —**a·tro′cious·ly** *adv.* —**a·tro′cious·ness** *n.*

atrocity (ə-trŏs′ĭ-tē) *n., pl.* **atrocities 1.** The condition of being atrocious. **2.** An act of extreme cruelty and violence.

atrophy (ăt′rə-fē) *n., pl.* **atrophies** The wasting away of a body part, most commonly caused by disease, injury, or lack of use. ❖ *tr. & intr.v.* **atrophied, atrophying, atrophies** To waste away or cause to waste away: *A month of inactivity had atrophied the patient's body.*

atropine (ăt′rə-pēn′ *or* ăt′rə-pĭn) *n.* A very poisonous bitter alkaloid that is obtained from belladonna and is used as a medicine to control muscle spasms and relax the pupils in examining the eye.

at sign *n.* The symbol (@) for the word *at.*

attach (ə-tăch′) *v.* **attached, attaching, attaches** —*tr.* **1.** To fasten or join; connect: *attached the wires to the post.* **2.** To add (something) at the end; append: *The lawyer had us attach our signatures to the document.* **3.** To add (a file) to an email message: *Please attach your resumé and cover letter.* **4.** To think of as belonging to something; ascribe: *I attach no importance to our different points of view.* **5.** To bind by ties of affection or loyalty: *The brother and sister are very attached to each other.* **6.** To assign (military personnel) to a unit on a temporary basis: *attach soldiers to an expeditionary force.* **7.** To take or seize (property) by court order: *The bank attached the debtor's salary.* —*intr.* **1.** To adhere or belong: *Acclaim attaches to the hero.* **2.** To be attached or attachable: *The helmet's chin strap attaches on the side just below the ear.* —**at·tach′a·ble** *adj.*

attaché (ăt′ə-shā′) *n.* A person assigned to the staff of a diplomatic mission to serve in some particular capacity: *a cultural attaché to the American Embassy.*

attaché case *n.* A briefcase resembling a small suitcase, with hinges and flat sides.

attachment (ə-tăch′mənt) *n.* **1.** The act of attaching or condition of being attached: *attachment of a horse to a wagon.* **2.** A supplementary part; an accessory: *This vacuum cleaner has several attachments.* **3.** A supplementary document attached to a main document. **4.** An electronic file attached to an email message. **5.** A bond of affection or loyalty: *a strong attachment to a friend.*

attack (ə-tăk′) *v.* **attacked, attacking, attacks** —*tr.* **1.** To set upon with violent force: *Even large animals will not attack elephants.* **2.** To criticize strongly or in a hostile manner: *The candidates attacked each other in their debate.* **3.** To cause harm to; affect harmfully: *a disease that attacks the nervous system.* **4.** To start work on with purpose and vigor: *attack the problem of costly health care.* —*intr.* To launch an assault: *The troops attacked at*

dawn. ❖ *n.* **1.** The act of violent attacking; an assault. **2.** An expression of strong criticism. **3.** An occurrence or onset of a disease, especially when sudden: *an attack of asthma.* **4.** The manner in which a musical tone, phrase, or passage is begun: *a hard, cutting attack.* **5.** In sports, offensive play: *Even the defenders got involved in the attack.* —**at·tack′er** *n.*

attain (ə-tān′) *tr.v.* **attained, attaining, attains 1.** To gain, accomplish, or achieve by effort: *attain a diploma by hard work.* See Synonyms at **reach. 2.** To arrive at or reach, as through time, growth, or movement: *Today many people attain the age of 80.* —**at·tain′a·bil′i·ty** *n.* —**at·tain′a·ble** *adj.*

attainment (ə-tān′mənt) *n.* **1.** The act of attaining: *My attainment of a college degree will make my family proud.* **2.** often **attainments** Something attained; an acquirement, as a skill or an ability: *Eleanor Roosevelt is noted for her attainments in diplomacy.*

attar (ăt′ər) *n.* A fragrant oil obtained from the petals of flowers, especially roses, and used in making perfume.

attempt (ə-tĕmpt′) *tr.v.* **attempted, attempting, attempts a.** To try (to do something): *He attempted to run a mile in under six minutes.* **b.** To try to perform, make, or achieve: *She attempted a difficult dive.* ❖ *n.* **1.** An effort or a try: *an attempt to solve the mystery.* **2.** An attack; an assault: *an attempt on the king's life.*

attend (ə-tĕnd′) *v.* **attended, attending, attends** —*tr.* **1.** To be present at; go to: *How many people attended the concert?* **2.** To follow as a result or occur as a circumstance of: *The speech was attended by wild applause.* **3.** To accompany and assist: *The squire attended the knight during the joust.* **4.** To take care of: *Two nurses attended the sick boy.* **5.** To pay attention to; heed: *I urge you to attend my words.* —*intr.* **1.** To be present at an event: *I wanted to go but was ill and could not attend.* **2.** To apply oneself; give care and thought: *Please attend to the matter at hand.* **3.** To pay attention; heed: *The audience attended to the lecture with great interest.*

attendance (ə-tĕn′dəns) *n.* **1.** The act or practice of being present: *The child's attendance at school has been perfect.* **2.** The people or number of people who are present: *an attendance of 50,000 at the football game.* **3.** The act or state of taking care of someone or something, as at a hospital: *a physician in attendance.*

attendant (ə-tĕn′dənt) *n.* A person who attends or waits on another: *a parking lot attendant.* ❖ *adj.* Accompanying or following as a result: *attendant circumstances.*

attention (ə-tĕn′shən) *n.* **1.** The act of close or careful observing or listening: *Read the article carefully and pay attention to the details.* **2.** Concentration of the mental powers upon something or someone: *The speaker held the listeners' attention for more than an hour.* **3.** Observant consideration; notice: *Your suggestion has come to our attention.* **4.** **attentions** Acts of courtesy or consideration, especially in trying to win a person's affection: *Do you think his attentions are sincere?* **5.** The posture taken by a soldier, with the body erect, eyes to the front, arms at the sides, and heels together: *Stand at attention.* ❖ *interj.* An expression used as a command to assume an erect military posture.

attention deficit disorder *n.* Attention deficit hyperactivity disorder.

attention deficit hyperactivity disorder *n.* A condition whose symptoms include impulsiveness, a short attention span, and often hyperactivity. It is usually diagnosed in childhood and can interfere with performance at school, in the workplace, and in social situations.

attention span *n.* The length of time during which a person can concentrate on a subject or idea.

attentive (ə-těn′tĭv) *adj.* **1.** Giving attention to something; alert: *Only the most attentive students understood the explanation.* **2.** Giving or marked by careful attention to the comfort of others; considerate: *an attentive host.* —**at·ten′tive·ly** *adv.* —**at·ten′tive·ness** *n.*

attenuate (ə-těn′yōō-āt′) *v.* **attenuated, attenuating, attenuates** —*tr.* **1.** To make slender or thin: *The drought attenuated the river to a narrow channel.* **2.** To reduce, as in strength, force, or power; weaken: *Medicine attenuated the effect of the fever.* —*intr.* To become thin or weak. —**at·ten′u·a′tion** *n.*

attest (ə-těst′) *v.* **attested, attesting, attests** —*tr.* **1.** To declare or state to be true, correct, or genuine, especially by signing one's name as a witness: *attest a will.* **2.** To give evidence or proof of; prove: *Their rounded shapes attest the great age of the mountains.* —*intr.* To bear witness: *I can attest to his presence at the concert.*

attested (ə-těs′tĭd) *adj.* Recorded in written form: *Use of the word* helicopter *is first attested in English in 1887.*

attic (ăt′ĭk) *n.* A story or room just below the roof of a building.

attire (ə-tīr′) *tr.v.* **attired, attiring, attires** To dress, especially in fine or formal clothing: *an emperor attired in ceremonial robes.* ❖ *n.* Clothing, costume, or apparel: *white tennis attire.*

attitude (ăt′ĭ-tōōd′) *n.* **1.** A state of mind with regard to someone or something: *She has a positive attitude about school.* **2.** A position of the body indicative of a mood or condition: *She sprawled on the couch in a relaxed attitude.* **3.** An arrogant or hostile state of mind or disposition: *We tried to help him, but so far he's given us nothing but attitude.* **4.** The position of an aircraft or spacecraft in relation to its direction of motion.

attorney (ə-tûr′nē) *n., pl.* **attorneys** A person who is legally qualified and licensed to represent a person in a legal matter, such as a transaction or lawsuit.

attorney-at-law (ə-tûr′nē-ət-lô′) *n., pl.* **attorneys-at-law** An attorney.

attorney general *n., pl.* **attorneys general** or **attorney generals** The chief law officer of a state or national government.

attract (ə-trăkt′) *v.* **attracted, attracting, attracts** —*tr.* To cause to draw near or adhere; direct to oneself or itself by some quality or action: *A magnet attracts nails by the physical force of magnetism. The fine beaches attract many tourists.* —*intr.* To have the power to draw to oneself or itself: *attract by magnetic force.* —**at·tract′er, at·trac′tor** *n.* —SEE NOTE AT **detract.**

attraction (ə-trăk′shən) *n.* **1.** The act or power of attracting: *the attraction of a magnet.* **2.** Something that attracts: *New York City's attractions include its many museums.* **3a.** The electric or magnetic force exerted by oppositely charged particles, as a proton and an electron, tending to draw them together. **b.** The gravitational force exerted by one body on another, as by Earth on the moon.

attractive (ə-trăk′tĭv) *adj.* **1.** Pleasing to the eye or mind; appealing: *an attractive young couple; an attractive offer that should be profitable.* **2.** Having the power to attract: *the attractive forces of magnetism and gravity.* —**at·trac′tive·ly** *adv.* —**at·trac′tive·ness** *n.*

attribute (ə-trĭb′yōōt) *tr.v.* **attributed, attributing, attri-** butes To consider (something) as belonging to or resulting from someone or something; ascribe: *We attribute much air pollution to trucks. This piece is attributed to Mozart.* ❖ *n.* (ăt′rə-byōōt′) A quality or characteristic belonging to a person or thing; a distinctive feature: *One of her best attributes is her quick wit.* See Synonyms at **quality.** —**at·trib′ut·a·ble** *adj.* —**at·trib′ut·er, at·trib′- u·tor** *n.* —**at′tri·bu′tion** (ăt′rə-byōō′shən) *n.*

attributive (ə-trĭb′yə-tĭv) *n.* In grammar, a word or phrase placed next to a noun to modify it. In the phrase *city streets,* the word *city* is an attributive modifying *streets.* ❖ *adj.* **1.** In grammar, relating to an attributive. **2.** Relating to an attribution or an attribute.

USAGE When nouns are used as **attributives,** they act much like adjectives. But unlike adjectives, nouns can't ordinarily be modified by adverbs or put into comparative or superlative form.

attrition (ə-trĭsh′ən) *n.* **1.** A wearing away or rubbing down by friction: *The rocks became sand by attrition.* **2.** A gradual loss of number or strength due to constant stress. **3.** A gradual natural reduction in membership or personnel, as through retirement, resignation, or death.

attune (ə-tōōn′) *tr.v.* **attuned, attuning, attunes** To bring into a harmonious relationship; adjust: *a person attuned to the times.* —**at·tune′ment** *n.*

Atty. An abbreviation of attorney.

at. wt. An abbreviation of atomic weight.

atypical (ā-tĭp′ĭ-kəl) *adj.* Not typical; abnormal: *atypical behavior.* —**a·typ′i·cal·ly** *adv.*

auburn (ô′bərn) *n.* A reddish brown. ❖ *adj.* Reddish brown: *auburn hair.*

au courant (ō′ kōō-rän′) *adj.* **1.** Informed on current affairs; up-to-date. **2.** Fully familiar; knowledgeable.

auction (ôk′shən) *n.* A public sale in which goods or property is sold to the highest bidder. ❖ *tr.v.* **auctioned, auctioning, auctions** To sell at an auction: *auction a diamond ring.*

auctioneer (ôk′shə-nîr′) *n.* A person who conducts an auction.

audacious (ô-dā′shəs) *adj.* **1.** Fearlessly daring: *an audacious explorer.* **2.** Arrogant; impudent: *a showoff's audacious behavior.* —**au·da′cious·ly** *adv.* —**au·da′cious·ness** *n.*

audacity (ô-dăs′ĭ-tē) *n., pl.* **audacities 1.** Courage and resolution; boldness. **2.** Insolence; impudence: *the customs official's audacity in demanding a bribe.*

audible (ô′də-bəl) *adj.* Loud enough to be heard: *Speak in an audible voice so that others may hear you.* —**au′di·bil′- i·ty, au′di·ble·ness** *n.* —**au′di·bly** *adv.*

audience (ô′dē-əns) *n.* **1.** The people gathered to see and hear a play, movie, concert, or other performance. **2.** The readers, hearers, or viewers reached by a book, radio broadcast, television program, or online source: *The audience for this TV series has been growing.* **3.** A formal hearing or conference: *an audience with the pope.* **4.** An opportunity to be heard; a hearing: *The planning committee gave the builders an audience before voting on the project.*

audio (ô′dē-ō′) *adj.* **1.** Relating to sound that is recorded, transmitted, or reproduced: *an MP3 player and other audio equipment.* **2.** Relating to sound that can be heard: *audio signals used in a hearing test.* ❖ *n., pl.* **audios 1.** Audible sound. **2.** Recorded or reproduced sound.

audio frequency *n.* A frequency corresponding to audible sound vibrations, usually between 20 hertz and 20,000 hertz for humans.

audiology (ô′dē-ŏl′ə-jē) *n.* The study of hearing, especially hearing defects and their treatment. —**au·di·ol′-o·gist** *n.*

audiometer (ô′dē-ŏm′ĭ-tər) *n.* An instrument used to measure how well a person can hear.

audiotape (ô′dē-ō-tāp′) *n.* A magnetic tape used to record sound for later playback. ❖ *tr.v.* **audiotaped, audiotaping, audiotapes** To record (sound) on magnetic tape: *audiotaped the lecture.*

audio-visual also **audiovisual** (ô′dē-ō-vĭzh′ōō-əl) *adj.* **1.** Relating to both hearing and sight. **2.** Conveying information through media, such as audio and video recordings, that are perceivable by both hearing and sight.

audit (ô′dĭt) *n.* **1.** An examination of financial records or accounts to check their accuracy. **2.** A thorough evaluation: *an audit of home energy use.* ❖ *tr.v.* **audited, auditing, audits** **1.** To examine and verify (financial records or accounts). **2.** To attend (a college course) without receiving academic credit.

audition (ô-dĭsh′ən) *n.* **1.** A trial performance, as by an actor, dancer, or musician, to demonstrate suitability or skill. **2.** The sense or power of hearing: *audition in bats.* ❖ *v.* **auditioned, auditioning, auditions** —*intr.* To perform in an audition: *Several musicians auditioned for a place in the orchestra.* —*tr.* To give (a performer) an audition: *The director of the movie auditioned many actors.*

auditor (ô′dĭ-tər) *n.* **1.** A person who audits financial records or accounts. **2.** A person who audits courses in college. **3.** A hearer or listener, especially of musical auditions.

auditorium (ô′dĭ-tôr′ē-əm) *n., pl.* **auditoriums** or **auditoria** (ô′dĭ-tôr′ē-ə) **1.** A room to seat a large audience in a building, such as a school. **2.** A large building used for public meetings or performances.

auditory (ô′dĭ-tôr′ē) *adj.* Relating to hearing or the organs of hearing: *the auditory canal of the ear.*

auditory nerve *n.* The nerve that carries impulses associated with hearing and balance from the inner ear to the brain.

auger (ô′gər) *n.* **1.** A tool for boring holes. **2.** A screwlike shaft that has a continuous, spiraling blade and is rotated to move material, such as snow in a snowblower. ❖ *tr.v.* **augered, augering, augers** To drill or bore a hole using an auger.

aught[1] also **ought** (ôt) *pron.* Anything at all: *He denied he felt aught but affection for his brother.*

aught[2] also **ought** (ôt) *n.* The digit zero.

WORD HISTORY Aught[1] comes from Old English *āuht.* **Aught**[2] comes from early Modern English *(an) aught,* an alteration of *(a) naught.*

augment (ôg-mĕnt′) *tr.v.* **augmented, augmenting, augments** To make larger; increase: *The library's collection has been augmented by 5,000 new books.* —**aug·ment′-a·ble** *adj.* —**aug′men·ta′tion** *n.*

au gratin (ō grät′n) *adj.* Topped with bread crumbs and often grated cheese and browned in an oven.

augur (ô′gər) *n.* An ancient Roman religious official who foretold events by omens from the entrails of birds, thunder, and other natural signs. ❖ *v.* **augured, auguring, augurs** —*tr.* **1.** To predict (something), especially from signs or omens. **2.** To be a sign of; give promise of: *Early returns augured victory for the young candidate.* —*intr.* **1.** To make predictions from signs or omens. **2.** To be a sign or omen: *A smooth dress rehearsal augured well for the play.*

augury (ô′gyə-rē) *n., pl.* **auguries** **1.** The art or practice of auguring. **2.** A sign or an omen.

august (ô-gŭst′) *adj.* Inspiring awe or reverence; majestic: *the august bearing of the king.* —**au·gust′ly** *adv.*

August (ô′gəst) *n.* The eighth month of the year in the Gregorian calendar, having 31 days.

au jus (ō zhōōs′ *or* ō zhü′) *adj.* Served with its own gravy or juice from cooking: *roast beef au jus.*

auk (ôk) *n.* Any of several black-and-white northern seabirds having a plump body and short wings.

auld (ôld) *adj. Scots* Old.

auld lang syne (ôld′ lăng zīn′) *n.* The times gone past; the good old days.

aunt (ănt *or* änt) *n.* **1.** The sister of one's father or mother. **2.** The wife of a sibling of one's mother or father.

au pair (ō pâr′) *n.* A young foreigner who provides child care or does domestic work for a family in exchange for room and board and a chance to learn the family's language.

aura (ôr′ə) *n., pl.* **auras** or **aurae** (ôr′ē) A distinctive air or quality that characterizes a person or thing: *an aura of mystery about the old house.*

aural (ôr′əl) *adj.* Relating to or perceived by the ear: *aural stimulation.* —**au′ral·ly** *adv.*

aureole (ôr′ē-ōl′) *n.* **1.** In art, an area of light around the head of a sacred figure; a halo. **2.** A glow that surrounds the sun or the moon, especially when seen through a fog or haze.

au revoir (ō′ rə-vwär′) *interj.* Used to express farewell.

auricle (ôr′ĭ-kəl) *n.* **1.** The external part of the ear. **2.** An atrium of the heart.

auricular (ô-rĭk′yə-lər) *adj.* **1.** Relating to hearing or the organs of hearing. **2.** Relating to an auricle of the heart.

aurochs (ou′rŏks′ *or* ôr′ŏks′) *n., pl.* **aurochs** A wild ox of Europe, northern Africa, and western Asia that became extinct in the 1600s and is believed to be the ancestor of domestic cattle.

aurora (ə-rôr′ə) *n.* A brilliant display of bands or streamers of light visible in the night sky, chiefly in the polar regions. It is thought to be caused by electrically charged particles from the sun that are drawn into the atmosphere by the earth's magnetic field.

Aurora *n.* In Roman mythology, the goddess of the dawn, identified with the Greek Eos.

aurora australis (ô-strā′lĭs) *n.* The aurora of the Southern Hemisphere; the southern lights.

aurora borealis (bôr′ē-ăl′ĭs) *n.* The aurora of the Northern Hemisphere; the northern lights.

auspices (ô′spĭ-sĭz *or* ô′spī-sēz′) *pl.n.* Protection and support; patronage: *The marathon was organized under the auspices of local athletic clubs.*

auspicious (ô-spĭsh′əs) *adj.* Showing signs of a successful outcome or result; favorable: *Their first large orders were an auspicious beginning for the new business.* —**aus·pi′-cious·ly** *adv.* —**aus·pi′cious·ness** *n.*

austere (ô-stîr′) *adj.* **austerer, austerest** **1.** Having a stern personality or appearance; somber: *an unsmiling, austere judge.* **2.** Living very simply, with few comforts: *a desert nomad's austere life.* **3.** Lacking decoration; plain or bare: *Their austere living quarters had no pictures on the walls.* —**aus·tere′ly** *adv.* —**aus·tere′ness** *n.*

austerity (ô-stĕr′ĭ-tē) *n., pl.* **austerities 1.** The condition of being austere. **2.** Lack of luxury; extreme restraint in spending: *wartime austerity.*

Australian (ô-strāl′yən) *adj.* Relating to Australia or its peoples, languages, or cultures. ❖ *n.* **1.** A native or inhabitant of Australia. **2.** A member of any of the Aboriginal peoples of Australia. **3.** Any of the languages of the Aboriginal peoples of Australia.

australopith (ô′strə-lə-pĭth′) *n.* Any of several extinct humanlike primates known from fossils dating from about four million to about one million years ago. Fossil remains of australopiths have been found in southern and eastern Africa.

auteur (ō-tûr′ *or* ō-tœr′) *n.* A filmmaker, usually a director, who exercises creative control over his or her works and has a strong personal style.

authentic (ô-thĕn′tĭk) *adj.* **1.** Being so in fact; not counterfeit or copied; genuine: *an authentic medieval sword.* **2.** In accord with fact and worthy of belief; true or credible: *an authentic account of the events.* —**au·then′-ti·cal·ly** *adv.*

✦ SYNONYMS authentic, genuine, real, true *adj.*

authenticate (ô-thĕn′tĭ-kāt′) *tr.v.* **authenticated, authenticating, authenticates 1.** To establish as being true; prove: *Witnesses will authenticate our account of the accident.* **2.** To establish (a painting, an antique, or another object) as being genuine: *Experts can authenticate the old violin.* —**au·then′ti·ca′tion** *n.* —**au·then′ti·ca′tor** *n.*

authenticity (ô′thĕn-tĭs′ĭ-tē) *n.* The condition or quality of being authentic: *The authenticity of our claim is established by these old records.*

author (ô′thər) *n.* **1.** A person who writes a book, story, article, or other written work. **2.** A person who writes or constructs an electronic document or system, such as a website. **3.** The creator or originator of something: *the author of an idea.* ❖ *tr.v.* **authored, authoring, authors** To be the author of: *He has authored several books. She authors the company's website.*

authoritarian (ə-thôr′ĭ-târ′ē-ən) *adj.* Characterized by, favoring, or demanding absolute obedience to authority: *the authoritarian government of a dictator.* ❖ *n.* A person who believes in or practices authoritarian behavior. —**au·thor′i·tar′i·an·ism** *n.*

authoritative (ə-thôr′ĭ-tā′tĭv) *adj.* **1.** Having or arising from proper authority; official: *an authoritative ruling.* **2.** Known to be accurate; reliable: *authoritative sources for the newspaper article.* —**au·thor′i·ta′tive·ly** *adv.* —**au·thor′i·ta′tive·ness** *n.*

authority (ə-thôr′ĭ-tē) *n., pl.* **authorities 1a.** The power to enforce laws, command obedience, determine, or judge: *The governor has the authority to call out the National Guard.* **b.** A person or organization having this power: *government authorities.* **2.** An accepted source of expert information, as a book or person: *an authority on history.* **3.** Power to influence or affect resulting from knowledge or experience: *She writes about science with authority.*

authorization (ô′thər-ĭ-zā′shən) *n.* **1.** The act of authorizing. **2.** An expression of authorized consent: *needed written authorization from his commanding officer.*

authorize (ô′thə-rīz′) *tr.v.* **authorized, authorizing, authorizes 1.** To grant authority or power to: *President Jefferson authorized Lewis and Clark to explore the lands beyond the Mississippi River.* **2.** To approve or give permission for: *The state legislature authorized a highway project.* —**au′thor·iz′er** *n.*

Authorized Version (ô′thə-rīzd′) *n.* The King James Bible.

authorship (ô′thər-shĭp′) *n.* The origin, as of a book: *a book of unknown authorship.*

autism (ô′tĭz′əm) *n.* A developmental disorder marked by difficulty in communicating and in relating to other people, and often by the presence of repetitive behaviors. —**au·tis′tic** (ô-tĭs′tĭk) *adj.*

auto (ô′tō) *n., pl.* **autos** An automobile.

auto– *or* **aut–** A prefix that means: **1.** Self; same: *autobiography.* **2.** Automatic: *autopilot.*

autobiography (ô′tō-bī-ŏg′rə-fē) *n., pl.* **autobiographies** The story of a person's life written by that person. —**au′-to·bi·og′ra·pher** *n.* —**au′to·bi′o·graph′i·cal** (ô′tō-bī′ə-grăf′ĭ-kəl) *adj.* —**au′to·bi′o·graph′i·cal·ly** *adv.*

autoclave (ô′tō-klāv′) *n.* A tank used especially for antiseptic sterilizing under high-pressure steam.

autocracy (ô-tŏk′rə-sē) *n., pl.* **autocracies 1.** Government by a person having absolute power. **2.** A country having this form of government.

autocrat (ô′tə-krăt′) *n.* **1.** A ruler having unlimited power. **2.** An arrogant person with unlimited power: *The boss is an autocrat.*

autocratic (ô′tə-krăt′ĭk) *adj.* **1.** Relating to autocracy: *an autocratic government.* **2.** Like an autocrat; arrogant: *The professor has a very autocratic manner.* —**au′to·crat′-i·cal·ly** *adv.*

autograph (ô′tə-grăf′) *n.* **1.** A signature, usually of a famous person and saved by an admirer or collector. **2.** A manuscript in the author's own handwriting. ❖ *tr.v.* **autographed, autographing, autographs** To write one's name or signature on. —**au′to·graph′ic, au′to·graph′-i·cal** *adj.*

Autoharp (ô′tō-härp′) A trademark for a musical instrument that is somewhat like a zither and that is equipped with a device that damps all of its strings except those that form a desired chord.

autoimmune (ô′tō-ĭ-myōōn′) *adj.* Relating to a reaction of the immune system in which antibodies are produced that attack the body's own cells and tissues, often causing illness: *an autoimmune disease.* —**au′to·im·mu′ni·ty** (ô′-tō-ĭ-myōō′nĭ-tē) *n.*

automaker (ô′tō-mā′kər) *n.* A manufacturer of automobiles.

automata (ô-tŏm′ə-tə) *n.* A plural of **automaton.**

automate (ô′tə-māt′) *v.* **automated, automating, automates** —*tr.* To operate (a process, factory, or machine) with automatic machinery or processes: *automate an assembly line with robots.* —*intr.* To make use of automatic machinery and processes: *Manufacturing costs fell as the industry automated.*

automated teller machine (ô′tə-mā′tĭd) *n.* An ATM.

automatic (ô′tə-măt′ĭk) *adj.* **1.** Acting or operating without the control of a human; self-operating or self-regulating: *an automatic elevator.* **2.** Done or produced by the body without conscious control or awareness; involuntary: *the automatic shrinking of the pupils in bright light.* **3.** Capable of firing continuously until ammunition is gone or the trigger is released: *an automatic rifle.* ❖ *n.* A device or machine, especially a firearm, that is completely or partially automatic. —**au′to·mat′i·cal·ly** *adv.*

automatic pilot *n.* A navigation device that automatically keeps to a preset course.

automation (ô′tə-mā′shən) *n.* **1.** The automatic operation or control of a process, machine, or system, often by electronic devices, such as computers or robots: *Automation has replaced many workers in manufacturing.* **2.** The engineering techniques and equipment needed to accomplish this.

automaton (ô-tŏm′ə-tŏn′ *or* ô-tŏm′ə-tən) *n., pl.* **automatons** or **automata** (ô-tŏm′ə-tə) **1.** An automatic machine, especially a robot. **2.** A person who behaves in a mechanical way.

automobile (ô′tə-mō-bēl′ *or* ô′tə-mō′bēl′) *n.* A passenger vehicle generally moving on four wheels and propelled by a gasoline engine on land.

automotive (ô′tə-mō′tĭv) *adj.* **1.** Relating to self-propelled vehicles, such as automobiles and trucks. **2.** Self-propelled or self-propelling.

autonomic nervous system (ô′tə-nŏm′ĭk) *n.* The part of the vertebrate nervous system that regulates involuntary actions, as in the heart, digestive system, and glands. It is divided into two parts, the sympathetic nervous system and the parasympathetic nervous system.

autonomous (ô-tŏn′ə-məs) *adj.* **1.** Acting independently: *an autonomous organization.* **2.** Self-governing with respect to local or internal affairs: *an autonomous region of a country.* —**au·ton′o·mous·ly** *adv.*

autonomy (ô-tŏn′ə-mē) *n., pl.* **autonomies** The ability or right to act independently.

autopilot (ô′tō-pī′lət) *n.* An automatic pilot.

autopsy (ô′tŏp′sē) *n., pl.* **autopsies** A medical examination of a dead human body to determine the cause of death. —SEE NOTE AT **triceratops.**

autotroph (ô′tə-trŏf′ *or* ô′tə-trōf′) *n.* An organism that manufactures its own food from inorganic substances, such as carbon dioxide and nitrogen, using light or chemical energy. Green plants, algae, and some bacteria are autotrophs. —**au′to·troph′ic** *adj.*

autumn (ô′təm) *n.* The season of the year occurring between summer and winter. In the Northern Hemisphere, it lasts from the autumnal equinox until the winter solstice, or in ordinary usage, from September until December. In the Southern Hemisphere, it lasts from March until June. ❖ *adj.* Occurring in or appropriate to the season of autumn: *autumn colors.*

autumnal (ô-tŭm′nəl) *adj.* Relating to, occurring in, or appropriate to the autumn. —**au·tum′nal·ly** *adv.*

autumnal equinox *n.* The equinox that occurs on September 22 or 23, when the sun crosses the celestial equator while moving in a southwesterly direction, marking the beginning of autumn in the Northern Hemisphere and spring in the Southern Hemisphere. —SEE NOTE AT **vernal equinox.**

auxiliary (ôg-zĭl′yə-rē *or* ôg-zĭl′ə-rē) *adj.* **1.** Giving assistance or support: *a sailboat with an auxiliary engine.* **2.** Additional, subsidiary, or supplementary: *auxiliary branches of the fire department in outlying areas.* ❖ *n., pl.* **auxiliaries 1.** A person or thing that helps; an assistant. **2.** An auxiliary verb. **3.** An organization that is subsidiary to a larger one: *Members of the hospital auxiliary visit patients and run errands.* **4.** A member of a body of foreign troops serving a country in war.

auxiliary verb *n.* A verb that comes first in a verb phrase and helps form the tense, mood, or voice of the main verb. *Have, may, can, must* and *will* can act as auxiliary verbs.

auxin (ôk′sĭn) *n.* Any of various plant hormones that regulate growth and development.

aux. v. An abbreviation of auxiliary verb.

AV An abbreviation of audio-visual.

av. An abbreviation of: **1.** average. **2.** avoirdupois.

Av. An abbreviation of avenue.

avail (ə-vāl′) *v.* **availed, availing, avails** —*tr.* To be of use or advantage to; help: *Nothing can avail us now.* —*intr.* To be of use or value; help: *A calculator avails little if you don't understand the problem.* ❖ *n.* Use, benefit, or advantage: *Since all the doors were locked, the burglar's efforts were to no avail.* ◆ **avail (oneself) of** To make use of; take advantage of: *While visiting Paris you must avail yourself of the museums.*

available (ə-vā′lə-bəl) *adj.* **1.** Capable of being obtained: *Tickets are available at the box office.* **2.** Close by and ready for use: *Keep a calculator available during the test.* **3.** Willing to serve: *All available volunteers were asked to help.* —**a·vail′a·bil′i·ty, a·vail′a·ble·ness** *n.* —**a·vail′a·bly** *adv.*

avalanche (ăv′ə-lănch′) *n.* **1.** The fall or slide of a large mass of material, as of snow or rock, down the side of a mountain. **2.** A massive or overwhelming amount: *an avalanche of mail.*

Avalon (ăv′ə-lŏn′) *n.* In legend, an island paradise in the western seas to which King Arthur was taken after he was mortally wounded in battle.

avant-garde (ä′vänt-gärd′) *n.* A group of people who are the leaders in promoting new or unconventional styles, ideas, or methods, especially in the arts. ❖ *adj.* Exhibiting new or unconventional styles, ideas, or methods: *an avant-garde magazine.*

avarice (ăv′ə-rĭs) *n.* Extreme desire for getting money or wealth; greed.

avaricious (ăv′ə-rĭsh′əs) *adj.* Extremely desirous of money or wealth; greedy. —**av′a·ri′cious·ly** *adv.* —**av′a·ri′cious·ness** *n.*

avast (ə-văst′) *interj.* An expression used as a command aboardship to stop an activity.

avatar (ăv′ə-tär′) *n.* **1.** The incarnation of a Hindu deity, especially Vishnu, in human or animal form. **2.** An embodiment or manifestation, as of a quality or concept. **3.** An image by which a person represents himself or herself on a communications network or in a virtual community, such as a chatroom or multiplayer game.

avaunt (ə-vônt′ *or* ə-vänt′) *interj.* Archaic An expression used as a command to get out or away.

Ave. An abbreviation of avenue.

Ave Maria (ä′vä mə-rē′ə) *n.* The Hail Mary prayer in Latin.

avenge (ə-vĕnj′) *tr.v.* **avenged, avenging, avenges 1.** To take revenge or satisfaction for: *The hockey team vowed to avenge the loss to their rivals.* **2.** To take revenge on behalf of: *avenge a betrayed friend.* —**a·veng′er** *n.*

avenue (ăv′ə-nōō′) *n.* **1.** A wide street or thoroughfare. **2.** A means of reaching or achieving something: *We must seek many avenues for peace.*

aver (ə-vûr′) *tr.v.* **averred, averring, avers** To state positively and firmly; assert; affirm.

average (ăv′ər-ĭj *or* ăv′rĭj) *n.* **1.** A number, especially the arithmetic mean, that is derived from and considered typical or representative of a set of numbers. **2.** A typical kind or usual level or degree: *That musician's abilities are above average.* ❖ *tr.v.* **averaged, averaging, averages 1.** To compute the average of (a set of numbers): *After the trip we averaged the number of miles we went each day.* **2.** To have or attain as an average: *The temperature averages* *about 75 degrees in the summer.* ❖ *adj.* **1.** Computed or determined as an average: *On our trip across the country our average speed was 50 miles per hour.* **2a.** Typical, usual, or ordinary: *an average American family.* **b.** Not exceptional; mediocre: *a bright boy who was only an average student in math.* ◆ **on the average** Using the average as a basis for judgment.

averse (ə-vûrs′) *adj.* Opposed; reluctant; unwilling: *Cats are extremely averse to getting wet.* —**a·verse′ly** *adv.* —**a·verse′ness** *n.*

aversion (ə-vûr′zhən *or* ə-vûr′shən) *n.* A strong dislike: *I have an aversion to crowds.*

avert (ə-vûrt′) *tr.v.* **averted, averting, averts 1.** To turn away or aside: *When we were stared at we averted our eyes.* **2.** To keep from happening; prevent: *She averted an accident by staying well behind the truck.* —**a·vert′a·ble, a·vert′i·ble** *adj.*

avg. An abbreviation of average.

avian (ā′vē-ən) *adj.* Relating to birds.

aviary (ā′vē-ĕr′ē) *n., pl.* **aviaries** A large cage or enclosure for birds, as in a zoo.

aviation (ā′vē-ā′shən) *n.* **1.** The art of operating and navigating aircraft. **2.** The design, development, and production of aircraft.

aviator (ā′vē-ā′tər) *n.* A person who flies an aircraft; a pilot.

avid (ăv′ĭd) *adj.* Having or marked by keen interest and enthusiasm: *an avid golfer; an avid interest in cooking.* —**av′id·ly** *adv.*

avidity (ə-vĭd′ĭ-tē) *n.* Eagerness or enthusiasm.

avionics (ā′vē-ŏn′ĭks) *n.* *(used with a singular verb)* The science and technology of electronics as applied to aircraft and spacecraft.

avocado (ăv′ə-kä′dō *or* ä′və-kä′dō) *n., pl.* **avocados 1.** An edible, tropical American fruit having leathery green or blackish skin, mild-tasting yellow-green flesh, and a single large seed. **2.** The tree that bears such fruit.

avocation (ăv′ō-kā′shən) *n.* An interest or activity that is done for enjoyment in addition to one's regular work.

Avogadro's number (ä′və-gä′drōz) *n.* The number of items in a mole of a given substance, approximately 6.0221×10^{23}.

avoid (ə-void′) *tr.v.* **avoided, avoiding, avoids 1.** To keep away from; stay clear of; shun: *avoid too many sweets; avoid the crowds at the mall.* **2.** To prevent; keep from happening: *avoid an accident.* —**a·void′a·ble** *adj.* —**a·void′a·bly** *adv.* —**a·void′ance** *n.*

avoirdupois weight (ăv′ər-də-poiz′) *n.* A system of weights based on a pound equal to 16 ounces, traditionally used in English-speaking countries to weigh everything except gems, precious metals, and drugs.

avow (ə-vou′) *tr.v.* **avowed, avowing, avows** To acknowledge openly; admit freely: *We avowed our support for the controversial law.* —**a·vow′a·ble** *adj.*

avowal (ə-vou′əl) *n.* An open admission or acknowledgment: *avowal of an unpopular opinion.*

avowed (ə-voud′) *adj.* Openly acknowledged: *Policies that are openly arrived at are the avowed platform of our democratic government.* —**a·vow′ed·ly** *adv.*

avuncular (ə-vŭng′kyə-lər) *adj.* **1.** Relating to an uncle. **2.** Resembling an uncle, especially in kindliness.

aw (ô) *interj.* An expression used to show sympathy, doubt, or disapproval.

await (ə-wāt′) *tr.v.* **awaited, awaiting, awaits 1.** To wait for: *We sat up awaiting news of the election results.* **2.** To

be in store for: *The health inspector's visit awaits us at the end of the week.*

awake (ə-wāk′) *v.* **awoke** (ə-wōk′) *or* **awaked, awaked** *or* **awoken** (ə-wō′kən), **awaking, awakes** —*tr.* **1.** To rouse from sleep; waken: *The alarm clock awoke me at seven.* **2.** To make (someone) aware of something: *The report awoke him to the possibilities of a compromise.* **3.** To stir up (memories, for example): *Seeing the old car awoke memories of my grandfather.* —*intr.* **1.** To wake up: *I awoke at dawn.* **2.** To become aware of something: *Americans are awaking to the need for recycling.* ❖ *adj.* **1.** Not asleep: *He was awake all night.* **2.** Alert, vigilant, or watchful: *awake to the dangers of an unhealthy diet.*

awaken (ə-wā′kən) *v.* **awakened, awakening, awakens** —*intr.* **1.** To wake up: *I awakened early because of the noise.* **2.** To become aware of something: *We finally awakened to the fact that our team needed more practice.* —*tr.* **1.** To cause to wake up: *A barking dog awakened me during the night.* **2.** To stir up or produce (a feeling or memory, for example): *Becoming an aunt awakened in her a sense of responsibility.* —**a·wak′en·er** *n.*

awakening (ə-wā′kə-nĭng) *n.* **1.** The act of waking up. **2.** The act or process of rousing from inactivity or indifference; a stirring up: *a great awakening of interest in our environment.*

award (ə-wôrd′) *tr.v.* **awarded, awarding, awards 1.** To give or bestow (a prize, medal, or other honor) for outstanding performance or quality: *The committee awarded a ribbon to the best dog in the show.* **2.** To give or grant by legal or governmental decision: *award damages to the injured driver; award a contract to the lowest bidder.* ❖ *n.* **1.** Something, such as a prize or medal, awarded for outstanding performance or quality: *an award for bravery.* **2.** Something judged as due by legal decision. —**a·ward′a·ble** *adj.* —**a·ward′er** *n.*

aware (ə-wâr′) *adj.* Mindful or conscious: *be aware of the abilities of each staff member.* —**a·ware′ness** *n.*

awash (ə-wŏsh′) *adv. & adj.* **1.** Level with or washed by waves: *The rocks were awash in the tide.* **2.** Floating on waves: *The wrecked ship's cargo was awash in the sea.*

away (ə-wā′) *adv.* **1.** From a particular thing or place: *They got in the car and drove away.* **2.** At or to a distance: *We live two miles away from the beach.* **3.** In a different direction: *Don't look away now.* **4.** Into an appropriate or secure place: *Please put your clothes away.* **5.** From one's presence or possession: *They gave away that old bicycle.* **6.** Out of existence: *The music faded away.* **7.** Continuously: *working away.* **8.** Freely; at will: *Fire away!* ❖ *adj.* **1.** Absent: *Who will take care of the cat while we're away?* **2.** Distant, as in space or time: *Those mountains are miles away. The game is a week away.* **3.** Played on the opposing team's home grounds: *home games and away games.* **4.** In baseball, out: *two away in the ninth.*

awe (ô) *n.* A feeling of wonder, fear, and respect inspired by something mighty or majestic: *gazing in awe at the mountains.* ❖ *tr.v.* **awed, awing, awes** To fill with awe: *The size of the huge plane awed everyone.*

aweigh (ə-wā′) *adj.* Hanging clear of the bottom: *With the anchor aweigh, the boat began to drift.*

awesome (ô′səm) *adj.* **1.** Inspiring awe: *an awesome sight.* **2.** Remarkable; outstanding: *an awesome party.* —**awe′some·ly** *adv.* —**awe′some·ness** *n.*

awestruck (ô′strŭk′) *also* **awestricken** (ô′strĭk′ən) *adj.* Full of awe: *awestruck by the beauty of the mountains.*

awful (ô′fəl) *adj.* **1.** Very bad or unpleasant; horrible:

awful weather; an awful book. **2.** Inspiring awe or fear; fearsome: *the awful stillness before the tornado.* **3.** Great; considerable: *an awful lot of work.* ❖ *adv. Informal* Very; extremely: *awful sick.* —**aw′ful·ness** *n.*

awfully (ô′fə-lē) *adv.* **1a.** In a manner that inspires awe; terribly: *The wind blew awfully.* **b.** *Informal* Very badly: *She behaved awfully.* **2.** *Informal* Very: *The tourists seemed awfully confused.*

awhile (ə-wīl′) *adv.* For a short time: *We waited awhile until they returned.*

awkward (ôk′wərd) *adj.* **1.** Not graceful; clumsy: *an awkward dancer.* **2.** Causing embarrassment; trying: *an awkward silence.* **3.** Difficult to handle or manage; cumbersome: *an awkward bundle to carry.* —**awk′ward·ly** *adv.* —**awk′ward·ness** *n.*

awl (ôl) *n.* A pointed tool for making holes, as in wood or leather.

awning (ô′nĭng) *n.* A protective structure set up over a window or door like a roof.

awoke (ə-wōk′) *v.* A past tense of **awake**.

awoken (ə-wō′kən) *v.* A past participle of **awake**.

AWOL or **awol** (ā′wôl′) *adj.* Absent without leave, as from an army base. ❖ *n.* A person who is absent without leave.

awry (ə-rī′) *adv.* **1.** Turned or twisted to one side or out of shape; askew: *The wind blew the curtains awry.* **2.** Wrong; amiss: *Our plans went awry.*

axe or **ax** (ăks) *n., pl.* **axes** (ăk′sĭz) A tool consisting of a head with a sharp blade on a long handle, used for cutting trees or chopping wood. ❖ *tr.v.* **axed, axing, axes** To cut or chop (something) with an axe. ◆ **axe to grind** A selfish or personal aim.

axel (ăk′səl) *n.* In figure skating, a jump in which the skater takes off while moving forward, makes one and one-half midair turns, and lands on one skate moving backward.

axes (ăk′sēz′) *n.* **1.** Plural of **axe**. **2.** Plural of **axis**.

axial (ăk′sē-əl) *adj.* On, around, forming, or relating to an axis: *A wheel turns by axial motion.*

axil (ăk′sĭl) *n.* The angle between the upper side of a leaf and the stem it is attached to. Each axil contains a bud.

axiom (ăk′sē-əm) *n.* **1.** A statement that is accepted as true or assumed to be true without proof; a postulate. **2.** An established rule, principle, or law: *One of the axioms of driving in the United States is to stay to the right.*

axiomatic (ăk′sē-ə-măt′ĭk) *adj.* Relating to or resembling an axiom; self-evident: *That all people are equal under the law is axiomatic.* —**ax′i·o·mat′i·cal·ly** *adv.*

axis (ăk′sĭs) *n., pl.* **axes** (ăk′sēz′) **1.** A straight line around which an object rotates or can be imagined to rotate: *The axis of the earth passes through both of its poles.* **2.** In ge-

ometry, a line, ray, or line segment with respect to which a figure or object is symmetrical: *the axis of a cone.* **3.** A reference line from which or along which distances or angles are measured in a system of coordinates: *the x-axis.* **4. Axis** The alliance of Germany, Italy, Japan, and other nations that opposed the Allies in World War II.

axle (ăk′səl) *n.* **1.** A shaft on which one or more wheels revolve. **2.** The spindle of an axletree.

axletree (ăk′səl-trē′) *n.* A crossbar or rod supporting a vehicle and having a spindle at each end on which a wheel turns.

axolotl (ăk′sə-lŏt′l) *n.* Any of several salamanders of Mexico and the western United States that unlike most amphibians do not go through metamorphosis. They continue to live in water and breathe with external gills when mature.

axon (ăk′sŏn′) *n.* The long extension of a nerve cell that carries impulses away from the body of the cell.

ayatollah (ī′yə-tō′lə) *n.* A high-ranking Shiite religious teacher of religious law and interpretation.

aye also **ay** (ī) *n.* **1.** A vote of yes. **2. ayes** Those who vote yes: *The ayes have it; the motion is approved.* ❖ *adv.* Yes; yea.

Aymara (ī′mä-rä′) *n., pl.* **Aymara** or **Aymaras 1.** A member of a South American Indian people inhabiting Bolivia and Peru. **2.** The language of this people. —**Ay′ma·ran′** *adj.*

Ayrshire (âr′shir *or* âr′shər) *n.* Any of a breed of reddish-brown and white dairy cattle originally raised in Scotland.

azalea (ə-zāl′yə) *n.* Any of various shrubs that are cultivated for their funnel-shaped, brightly colored flowers.

Azerbaijani (ăz′ər-bī-jä′nē *or* äz′ər-bī-jä′nē) *adj.* Relating to Azerbaijan or its people, language, or culture. ❖ *n., pl.* **Azerbaijanis 1.** A native or inhabitant of Azerbaijan. **2.** The Turkic language of Azerbaijan.

Azeri (ə-zĕr′ē) *adj.* Relating to Azerbaijan or its people, language, or culture. ❖ *n., pl.* **Azeris 1.** An Azerbaijani. **2.** The Azerbaijani language.

azimuth (ăz′ə-məth) *n.* An arc measured clockwise from a reference point, usually the northern point of the horizon, to the point where a vertical circle passing through a celestial object crosses the horizon.

Aztec (ăz′tĕk′) *n.* **1.** A member of an American Indian people of central Mexico whose civilization was at its height at the time of the Spanish conquest in the early 1500s. **2.** The Nahuatl language of the Aztecs. —**Az′tec′** *adj.*

azure (ăzh′ər) *n.* A bright blue, as of a clear sky.

Bb

b or **B** (bē) *n., pl.* **b's** or **B's** or **Bs 1.** The second letter of the English alphabet. **2. B** The second-best or second-highest grade: *get a B on a test.* **3. B** In music, the seventh tone in the scale of C major. **4. B** One of the four blood types in the ABO system.

BA An abbreviation of: **1.** Bachelor of Arts. **2.** batting average.

baa (bă *or* bä) *intr.v.* **baaed, baaing, baas** To bleat, as a sheep does. ❖ *n.* The bleating sound made by a sheep.

babble (băb′əl) *v.* **babbled, babbling, babbles** —*intr.* **1.** To utter indistinct or meaningless words or sounds: *Babies babble before they can talk.* **2.** To talk idly or foolishly; chatter: *babble on about neighborhood gossip.* **3.** To make a continuous low murmuring sound, as flowing water. —*tr.* To disclose without consideration; blurt out. ❖ *n.* **1.** Indistinct or meaningless words or sounds: *a babble of voices as we walked through the crowd.* **2.** Idle or foolish talk; chatter. **3.** A continuous low murmuring sound, as of flowing water. —**bab′bler** *n.*

babe (bāb) *n.* **1.** A baby; an infant. **2.** *Informal* Sweetheart; dear.

babel also **Babel** (băb′əl *or* bā′bəl) *n.* A confusion of sounds, voices, or languages: *a babel of voices in the street below.*

baboon (bă-bōōn′) *n.* Any of several large monkeys of Africa and Arabia that have a face with a projecting muzzle like that of a dog and spend most of their time on the ground rather than in trees.

babushka (bə-bōōsh′kə) *n.* A woman's headscarf, folded in a triangle and worn tied under the chin.

baby (bā′bē) *n., pl.* **babies 1.** A very young child; an infant: *Babies are not able to care for themselves.* **2.** A very young animal: *We went to the zoo to see the chimpanzee's new baby.* **3.** The youngest member of a family: *They moved to a smaller house once the baby of the family went off to college.* **4.** A person who behaves in an immature or selfish manner: *Don't be a baby and pout.* **5.** *Informal* A lover or sweetheart. ❖ *tr.v.* **babied, babying, babies** To treat like a baby; coddle: *baby a spoiled child.* See Synonyms at **pamper**.

baby boom *n.* A large increase in the number of babies born in a given population, especially the one in the United States from the later 1940s through the early 1960s.

baby boomer *n.* A person who is born during a baby boom, especially in the United States.

baby carriage *n.* A four-wheeled carriage, often with a hood that folds back, used for transporting an infant.

baby grand *n.* A small grand piano about 5 feet (1.5 meters) long.

babyhood (bā′bē-hōōd′) *n.* The time or condition of being a baby.

babyish (bā′bē-ĭsh) *adj.* **1.** Resembling a baby; childlike: *a babyish whimper.* **2.** Childish; immature: *a babyish attitude about sharing.*

Babylonian (băb′ə-lō′nē-ən) *adj.* Relating to the empire of Babylonia in ancient Iraq or to its people, language, or culture. ❖ *n.* **1.** A native or inhabitant of Babylonia. **2.** The Semitic language of the Babylonians.

babyproof (bā′bē-prōof′) *adj.* Made safe for babies or young children; childproof. ❖ *tr.v.* **babyproofed, babyproofing, babyproofs** To make safe for babies or young children; childproof: *babyproofed the room by placing plastic plugs in the electrical sockets.*

baby's breath (bā′bēz) *n.* Any of several plants having branching clusters of small white flowers.

babysit (bā′bē-sĭt′) *v.* **babysat** (bā′bē-săt′), **babysitting, babysits** —*intr.* To take care of a child or children in the absence of a parent or guardian: *babysit for the neighbors next door.* —*tr.* To take care of (a child): *He babysat his younger brother.*

babysitter (bā′bē-sĭt′ər) *n.* A person who babysits.

baby tooth *n.* Any of the temporary teeth that first grow in the mouth of a young mammal.

baccalaureate (băk′ə-lôr′ē-ĭt) *n.* **1.** A bachelor's degree. **2.** A farewell address delivered to a graduating class at a college or university.

bacchanal (băk′ə-năl′ *or* băk′ə-näl′) *n.* **1.** An ancient Roman festival in honor of the god Bacchus. **2.** A participant in this festival. **3.** A drunken or riotous celebration. **4.** A reveler.

Bacchus (băk′əs) *n.* Dionysus.

bachelor (băch′ə-lər *or* băch′lər) *n.* **1.** A man who has never been married. **2.** A person who has a bachelor's degree.

Bachelor of Arts *n.* A bachelor's degree in liberal arts.

Bachelor of Science *n.* A bachelor's degree in science or mathematics.

bachelor's button (băch′ə-lərz *or* băch′lərz) *n.* The cornflower.

bachelor's degree *n.* A degree given by a college or university to a person who has completed a four-year undergraduate program or its equivalent.

bacillus (bə-sĭl′əs) *n., pl.* **bacilli** (bə-sĭl′ī′) **1.** Any of various rod-shaped bacteria. **2.** A bacterium.

back (băk) *n.* **1.** The rear part of the human body between the neck and the pelvis. **2.** The part of another animal that corresponds to this part in humans: *a bird with a red head and black back.* **3.** The spine or backbone. **4.** The part or area farthest from the front: *the back of the theater.* **5.** The part or side that is not usually seen or used; the reverse side: *the back of a photograph.* **6.** A part that supports the back of a person: *the back of a chair.* **7.** In sports such as football and soccer, a player who is positioned behind the front line of other players. ❖ *v.* **backed, backing, backs** —*tr.* **1.** To cause to move backward or in a reverse direction: *backed the car out of the driveway.* **2.** To furnish or strengthen with a back or backing: *back a poster with cardboard.* **3a.** To support or aid: *We backed our team by going to all their games.* **b.** To be in favor of: *A* poll found that a majority of voters back the proposed tax. **4.** To provide with musical accompaniment: *The singer was backed up by a pianist.* —*intr.* To move backward: *The truck is backing out of the warehouse.* ❖ *adj.* **1.** Located at the back or rear: *the back porch.* **2.** Distant from a center of activity; remote: *a back road.* **3.** Overdue: *trying to pay the back rent.* **4.** Of a past date; not current: *a back issue of the magazine.* **5.** Being in a backward direction: *a back flip.* ❖ *adv.* **1.** At, to, or toward the rear: *Move back, please.* **2.** In, to, or toward a former place, time, or condition: *They went back to their old home.* **3.** In reserve or concealment: *It is dishonest to hold back the truth.* **4.** In reply or return: *Why didn't she call back?* **5.** In check: *The firefighter kept back the flames.* ◆ **back away** To withdraw from a position; retreat: *He backed slowly away from the skunk.* **back down** To withdraw from a stand that one has taken: *There was an argument because neither side was willing to back down.* **back off** To retreat or fall back, as from something dangerous or risky: *The senator backed off from his support of the unpopular bill.* **back out** To withdraw from something one has agreed to: *They accepted the invitation but backed out at the last minute.* **back to back** In a series, without interruption: *broadcast six episodes of the sitcom back to back.* **back up 1.** To make a copy of (a computer program or file). **2.** To accumulate: *Traffic backed up at the intersection.* **behind (one's) back** When one is not present: *Don't talk about me behind my back.*

backache (băk′āk′) *n.* An ache or pain in the region of the spine or back, especially the lower back.

back and forth *adv.* **1.** Backward and forward: *pushed the child back and forth in the swing.* **2.** From side to side or end to end: *paced back and forth in the waiting room.* **3.** From one to another and back again: *I emailed back and forth with my sister all summer.*

backbeat (băk′bēt′) *n.* A strong accent on the second and fourth beats of a measure with four beats, characteristic of rock music.

backbiting (băk′bī′tĭng) *n.* The saying of mean or spiteful things about an absent person. —**back′bit′er** *n.*

backboard (băk′bôrd′) *n.* **1.** In basketball, an elevated vertical sheet of wood or other material to which the basket is attached. **2a.** A board forming or placed at the back of something: *mounted the photos on a backboard.* **b.** A board used to support an injured person's back, especially when the person is being moved.

backbone (băk′bōn′) *n.* **1.** The system of bones that forms the main support of a vertebrate; the spinal column. **2.** A principal support; a mainstay: *Manufacturing is the backbone of the economy.* **3.** Strength of character; courage; fortitude: *It takes backbone to refuse to go along with the crowd.*

backbreaking (băk′brā′kĭng) *adj.* Requiring great physical exertion; exhausting: *backbreaking work.*

back-check (băk′chĕk′) *intr.v.* **back-checked, back-checking, back-checks** In ice hockey, to check or defend against an opponent while skating back toward one's own goal.

backcountry (băk′kŭn′trē) *n.* An uninhabited or sparsely inhabited region, especially one that is not accessible by road.

backcourt (băk′kôrt′) *n.* **1.** In tennis and similar net sports, the part of a court between the service line and the baseline. **2.** In basketball: **a.** The half of the court that

a team defends. **b.** The portion of the frontcourt farthest from the basket.

backdate (băk′dāt′) *tr.v.* **backdated, backdating, backdates** To supply with a date that is earlier than the actual date: *He backdated his rent check to the first of the month.*

back dive *n.* A dive in which the diver stands with the back to the water, leaps up, and rotates backward.

backdoor (băk′dôr′) *adj.* **1.** Secret or surreptitious; clandestine: *a backdoor romance.* **2.** Devious or underhanded: *a backdoor plan to win the election.* **3.** Relating to or directed toward a player who has slipped behind the opposing defense: *a backdoor pass.* ❖ *n.* **1.** An unofficial and often improper entrance or channel: *Most of the campaign money came through the backdoor.* **2.** A means by which unauthorized users can bypass the authentication procedures for a particular computer system. —**back′door′** *adv.*

backdrop (băk′drŏp′) *n.* **1.** A painted cloth hung at the back of a stage set. **2.** A background or setting: *The action of the novel takes place against the backdrop of the Civil War.*

backer (băk′ər) *n.* A person who supports or gives aid to a person, group, or enterprise.

backfield (băk′fēld′) *n.* **1.** In football, the players who are positioned some distance behind the line of scrimmage. **2.** The area in which these players are positioned.

backfire (băk′fīr′) *n.* **1.** In a gasoline engine, an explosion of fuel that ignites too soon or an explosion of unburned fuel in the exhaust system. **2.** A controlled fire started in the path of an oncoming uncontrolled fire in order to deprive it of fuel and thereby extinguish it. ❖ *intr.v.* **backfired, backfiring, backfires 1.** To explode in or make the sound of a backfire. **2.** To lead to a result opposite to that intended: *Their scheme to raise money backfired and everybody lost in the end.*

backflip (băk′flĭp′) *intr.v.* **backflipped, backflipping, backflips** To perform a backward somersault, especially in the air. ❖ *n.* A backward somersault.

back-formation (băk′fôr-mā′shən) *n.* **1.** A new word formed from an older word by dropping the ending or beginning of the older word, as the verb *burgle* formed from the noun *burglar* or the noun *flab* formed from the adjective *flabby.* **2.** The process of forming new words in this way. —SEE NOTE AT **enthuse.**

backgammon (băk′găm′ən) *n.* A game for two people played on a specially marked board with pieces whose moves are determined by throws of dice. The object is to move all of one's pieces to an end point where they are removed from the board.

background (băk′ground′) *n.* **1a.** The part of a picture, scene, or view that is or appears to be in the distance: *The painting was of a town with a line of mountains in the background.* **b.** The general scene or surface upon which designs, figures, or other forms are seen or represented: *The banner had a blue background covered with white stars.* **2.** An inconspicuous position: *The police remained in the background during the demonstration.* **3.** The circumstances or events surrounding or leading up to something: *The judge asked for more details on the background of the case.* **4.** A person's experience, training, and education: *had a perfect background for the job.* **5.** The social or cultural environment in which a person was brought up: *a class with students from many different backgrounds.*

background music *n.* Soft music played to accompany

an activity, such as shopping, or to enhance the mood or emotions in a play or movie.

background radiation *n.* A low level of naturally occurring radiation that is continuously present in the environment.

backhand (băk′hănd′) *n.* **1.** In sports, a stroke, as of a racket, made with the back of the hand facing forward. **2.** In hockey, a shot made with the back of the stick blade. **3.** In baseball, a catch made by reaching across the body with the palm turned toward the ball. **4.** Handwriting with letters that slant to the left. ❖ *adj.* Backhanded. ❖ *adv.* With a backhand stroke or motion: *hit the ball backhand.*

backhanded (băk′hăn′dĭd) *adj.* **1.** With the motion or direction of a backhand: *a backhanded stroke in tennis.* **2.** Indirect or insincere: *a backhanded compliment.* —**back′hand′ed·ly** *adv.* —**back′hand′ed·ness** *n.*

backhoe (băk′hō′) *n.* A machine used for digging, having a bucket attached to a hinged arm that is drawn back toward the operator when in use.

backing (băk′ĭng) *n.* **1.** Material that forms the back of something: *a mat with a felt backing.* **2a.** Support or aid: *financial backing for a new business.* **b.** Approval or endorsement: *received official backing from the mayor.*

backlash (băk′lăsh) *n.* **1.** A strong and hostile reaction to an earlier action or event: *There was an angry public backlash against the unpopular law.* **2.** A sudden or violent backward whipping motion.

backlight (băk′līt′) *n.* **1.** A type of spotlight, used in photography, that lights a subject from behind. **2.** A light that amplifies the brightness of an LCD screen by lighting it from behind. ❖ *tr.v.* **backlighted** or **backlit** (băk′lĭt′), **backlighting, backlights** To light from behind: *The photographer backlit the subject for a dramatic effect.*

backlog (băk′lôg′) *n.* An accumulation, especially of unfinished work: *a backlog of unfilled orders due to a shortage of parts.*

backpack (băk′păk′) *n.* **1.** A sturdy bag designed for carrying articles on a person's back, having shoulder straps and often mounted on a lightweight frame. **2.** A piece of equipment that may be used while being carried on the back: *a firefighter's backpack.* ❖ *intr.v.* **backpacked, backpacking, backpacks** To hike while carrying a backpack: *We backpacked to the lake.* —**back′pack′er** *n.*

backpedal (băk′pĕd′l) *intr.v.* **backpedaled, backpedaling, backpedaled** or **backpedalled, backpedalling, backpedals** **1.** To move the pedals of a bicycle or similar vehicle backward, especially to apply a brake. **2.** To retreat or withdraw from a previous stand: *The governor backpedaled after the proposals in his speech were criticized.*

backrest (băk′rĕst′) *n.* A rest or support for the back.

back-seat driver (băk′sēt′) *n.* **1.** A passenger in a car who frequently advises, corrects, or nags the driver. **2.** A person who persists in giving unwanted advice.

backside (băk′sīd′) *n. Informal* The buttocks.

backslash (băk′slăsh) *n.* A diagonal mark (\ ) used especially in computer commands.

backslide (băk′slīd′) *intr.v.* **backslid** (băk′slĭd′), **backsliding, backslides** To return to a bad habit or behavior after one had previously given it up. —**back′slid′er** *n.*

backspace (băk′spās′) *intr.v.* **backspaced, backspacing, backspaces** **1.** To move the cursor on a computer screen to the left by hitting the backspace key, usually deleting the character that is there. **2.** To move the carriage of a typewriter to the left one space by hitting the backspace key. ❖ *n.* A backspace key.

backspace key *n.* A computer or typewriter key used for backspacing.

backspin (băk′spĭn′) *n.* In sports, a spin on a ball that tends to slow or reverse its forward motion.

backsplash (băk′splăsh′) *n.* An upright surface or border, as of tile, that protects the wall behind a sink or stove.

backstabbing (băk′stăb′ing) *n.* The practice of saying critical or mean things about someone, especially when that person is not present. —**back′stab′** *v.* —**back′-stab′ber** *n.*

backstage (băk′stāj′) *adv.* **1.** In or toward the area of a theater that is behind the stage, especially the area where the dressing rooms are located. **2.** In or toward a place closed to public view: *backstage at a political convention.* ❖ *adj.* (băk′stāj′) **1.** Relating to or situated behind the stage: *a backstage orchestra.* **2.** Not open or known to the public: *backstage political dealings.*

backstop (băk′stŏp′) *n.* **1.** In baseball, a screen or fence used to prevent the ball from being thrown or hit far behind or to the sides of home plate. **2.** In baseball, a catcher.

backstory (băk′stôr′ē) *n.* The experiences of a character or the circumstances of an event that occur before the beginning of a literary, cinematic, or dramatic work: *At rehearsal, the actors developed backstories for their characters.* **2.** The set of background conditions and events leading to a real-life situation.

backstretch (băk′strĕch′) *n.* The part of an oval racecourse farthest from the spectators and opposite the homestretch.

backstroke (băk′strōk′) *n.* A swimming stroke made while lying on the back and moving the arms alternately upward and backward.

backswing (băk′swĭng′) *n.* The first part of a stroke, in which a person moves a tennis racket or golf club, for instance, to the position from which to start forward motion.

back talk or **backtalk** (băk′tôlk′) *n.* Rude and disrespectful remarks.

backtrack (băk′trăk′) *intr.v.* **backtracked, backtracking, backtracks** **1.** To return over the route by which one has come: *We backtracked to find the side trail we had missed.* **2.** To return to a previous point or subject, as in a lecture. **3.** To reverse one's position or policy: *The president backtracked on his pledge not to raise taxes.*

backup (băk′ŭp′) *n.* **1.** Something reserved for use in case of emergency or additional need: *If this generator fails, we have another one we can use as a backup.* **2.** People who act to help or support others: *Arriving on the scene of the trouble, the police officer called for backup.* **3.** A copy of a computer program or file that is stored separately from the original. **4.** An accumulation or overflow caused by the blockage or clogging of something: *a backup in the drain.* ❖ *adj.* Ready and available as a substitute or in an emergency; extra; standby: *a backup pilot.*

backward (băk′wərd) *adj.* **1.** Directed or moving toward the rear: *a backward glance; a backward tumble.* **2.** Done or arranged in a manner that is opposite to normal use or practice: *alphabetized the books in backward order, starting with Z.* **3.** Behind others, as in economic or social progress: *backward technology.* **4.** Unwilling to act; reluctant or shy. ❖ *adv.* or **backwards** (băk′wərdz) **1.** To or toward the back or rear. **2.** With the back or rear first: *With its hind legs a toad can dig its way into the ground backward.* **3.** In reverse order or direction: *count back-*

ward from 100; wore my T-shirt backward. **4.** Toward a worse condition: *During the Depression many people slipped backward.* **5.** To, toward, or into the past: *The study looks backward to discover the source of the problem.* **—back′ward·ly** *adv.*

backwash (băk′wŏsh′) *n.* **1.** The backward flow of water produced by the oars or propeller of a boat. **2.** The backward flow of air from a propeller of an aircraft.

backwater (băk′wŏ′tər) *n.* **1.** Water that is held back, as by a dam, or pushed upstream, as by a current. **2.** A place or situation regarded as stagnant or backward: *When the factory closed, people moved away and the town became a backwater.*

backwoods (băk′wŏŏdz′) *pl.n.* *(used with a singular or plural verb)* **1.** Heavily wooded, uncultivated, remote areas. **2.** An area that is far from population centers, often regarded as backward; a backwater.

backyard also **back yard** (băk′yärd′) *n.* A yard at the back of a house.

bacon (bā′kən) *n.* The salted and smoked meat from the back and sides of a pig.

bacteria (băk-tîr′ē-ə) *n.* Plural of **bacterium.**

bacterial (băk-tîr′ē-əl) *adj.* Relating to or caused by bacteria: *a bacterial enzyme; a bacterial disease.*

bacteriology (băk-tîr′ē-ŏl′ə-jē) *n.* The scientific study of bacteria. **—bac·te′ri·o·log′i·cal** (băk-tîr′ē-ə-lŏj′ĭ-kəl) *adj.* **—bac·te·ri·ol′o·gist** *n.*

bacterium (băk-tîr′ē-əm) *n., pl.* **bacteria** (băk-tîr′ē-ə) Any of a large group of very small one-celled organisms that lack a nucleus and reproduce by fission or by forming spores. Some kinds live in the digestive system or in soil or water, and some kinds can cause disease.

USAGE Bacteria is the plural of **bacterium** and is never singular. Saying *a bacteria* is incorrect. It is correct to say *The soil sample contains millions of bacteria,* and *Tetanus is caused by a bacterium.*

Bactrian camel (băk′trē-ən) *n.* A two-humped camel widely used to carry loads in desert regions of central and southwest Asia.

bad (băd) *adj.* **worse** (wûrs), **worst** (wûrst) **1.** Being below an acceptable standard; inferior; poor: *a bad book; a bad painter.* **2.** Evil or wicked; sinful. **3.** Disobedient; naughty: *bad behavior.* **4.** Vulgar or obscene: *bad language.* **5.** Unfavorable: *bad luck; bad weather.* **6.** Disagreeable, unpleasant, or disturbing: *a bad odor; bad news.* **7.** Faulty; incorrect; improper: *a bad choice of words.* **8.** Not working properly; defective: *a bad telephone connection.* **9.** Rotten; spoiled: *bad fish.* **10.** Harmful in effect; detrimental: *Candy is bad for your teeth.* **11.** Being in poor health or condition: *I feel bad today. The jogger has a bad knee.* **12.** Severe; violent; intense: *a bad cold; a bad snowstorm.* **13.** Sorry; regretful: *I feel very bad about what happened.* **14. badder, baddest** *Slang* Very good; great. ❖ *n.* Something bad: *You must learn to accept the bad with the good.* ◆ **my bad** *Slang* Used to admit that one is at fault. **not half bad** or **not so bad** *Informal* Reasonably good. **too bad** Regrettable; unfortunate: *It's too bad you can't come along.* **—bad′ness** *n.*

bad blood *n.* Bitterness or hostility between people or groups.

bad breath *n.* The condition of having breath that smells unpleasant.

bade (băd *or* bād) *v.* A past tense of **bid.**

badge (băj) *n.* **1.** An emblem worn to show rank, office, or membership. **2.** An emblem given as an award or honor.

badger (băj′ər) *n.* **1.** Any of several stocky burrowing mammals having short legs, long claws on the front feet, and thick grayish fur. Badgers feed mostly at night on worms, insects, and small animals. **2.** The fur of such a mammal. ❖ *tr.v.* **badgered, badgering, badgers** To bother with many questions or demands; pester: *The fans badgered the celebrity for her autograph.*

badlands (băd′lăndz′) *pl.n.* An area of barren land typically having rough, deeply eroded terrain.

badly (băd′lē) *adv.* **worse** (wûrs), **worst** (wûrst) **1.** In a bad manner; poorly: *a job badly done.* **2.** Very much; greatly: *He misses his brother badly.*

badminton (băd′mĭn′tən *or* băd′mĭt′n) *n.* A game in which players use a light long-handled racket to hit a shuttlecock back and forth over a high net.

badmouth (băd′mouth′ *or* băd′mouth′) *tr.v.* **badmouthed, badmouthing, badmouths** *Slang* To criticize or belittle, often unfairly or spitefully: *Why are you always badmouthing the coach behind her back?*

baffle (băf′əl) *tr.v.* **baffled, baffling, baffles 1.** To confuse (someone) in a way that frustrates or prevents further action from being taken; puzzle: *The patient's condition baffled the doctors.* **2.** To interfere with or impede the force or movement of (a gas, sound, or liquid). ❖ *n.* A partition or enclosure that stops or regulates the movement of a gas, sound, or liquid: *A baffle covering part of the opening prevents the air conditioner from blowing directly onto me.* **—baf′fle·ment** *n.* **—baf′fler** *n.*

bag (băg) *n.* **1.** A container made of flexible material, such as paper, cloth, or plastic, used for carrying various articles. **2a.** A bag with something in it: *buy a bag of onions.* **b.** The amount that a bag can hold: *ate a whole bag of peanuts.* **3.** A purse, handbag, or suitcase: *Many passengers carry their bags right onto the airplane.* **4.** The amount of game caught or killed in a hunting expedition. **5.** Something that is shaped like a bag or hangs loosely like a bag: *bags under one's eyes.* **6.** In baseball, a base. **7.** *Slang* An area of interest or skill: *Cooking is not my bag.* ❖ *v.* **bagged, bagging, bags** *—tr.* **1.** To put into a bag: *I bag groceries at the supermarket.* **2.** To capture and kill, as in hunting. **3.** *Slang* **a.** To fail to attend purposely; skip: *bagged class for the afternoon.* **b.** To stop doing or considering; abandon: *bagged their suggestion.* *—intr.* To hang loosely like a bag: *pants that bag at the knees.* ◆ **in the bag** Assured of a successful outcome; virtually accomplished or won.

bagatelle (băg′ə-tĕl′) *n.* An unimportant or insignificant thing; a trifle.

bagel (bā′gəl) *n.* A ring-shaped roll with a chewy texture.

baggage (băg′ĭj) *n.* **1.** The trunks, bags, suitcases, or boxes in which one carries one's belongings while traveling; luggage. **2.** The movable equipment and supplies of an army. **3.** Emotions or thoughts that stem from painful or unpleasant past experiences and that affect one's outlook or behavior.

baggy (băg′ē) *adj.* **baggier, baggiest** Bulging or hanging loosely; loose-fitting: *bought a pair of baggy pants.* **—bag′gi·ness** *n.*

bagpipe (băg′pīp′) *n.* often **bagpipes** A musical instrument that consists of a reed pipe for playing melodies and several other pipes that play continuous single tones, all being supplied with air from a large bag that is filled by the player's breath or by a bellows. —**bag′pip′er** *n.*

baguette (bă-gĕt′) *n.* A long narrow loaf of French bread.

bah (bä *or* bă) *interj.* An expression used to show contempt or disgust.

baht (bät) *n.* The basic monetary unit of Thailand.

bail¹ (bāl) *n.* **1.** Money supplied for the temporary release of an arrested person and guaranteeing a person's appearance for trial: *Friends posted bail of $500 for the accused thief.* **2.** The release so obtained: *The accused thief was out on bail until the trial.* **3.** A person who supplies the money for such a release. ❖ *tr.v.* **bailed, bailing, bails** **1.** To secure the release of (an arrested person) by providing bail. **2.** To release or deliver from a difficult situation: *The bank loan bailed out her business when sales dropped.*

bail² (bāl) *tr.v.* **bailed, bailing, bails 1.** To remove (water) from a boat by repeatedly filling a container and emptying it: *bail water with a coffee can.* **2.** To empty (a boat) of water by this means. ◆ **bail out 1.** To parachute from an aircraft; eject. **2.** To abandon a project or enterprise.

bail³ (bāl) *n.* **1.** The arched handle of a pail, kettle, or similar container. **2.** The pivoting U-shaped part of a fishing reel that guides the line during rewinding. **3.** A small, usually metal loop that is attached to a pendant to enable it to be strung on a necklace or bracelet.

WORD HISTORY Bail¹ comes from Middle English *bail* (meaning "custody"), which came from Middle French *baillier* (meaning "to take charge of"), which came from Latin *bāiulāre,* meaning "to carry a large load." **Bail²** comes from Middle English *baille* (meaning "a wooden bucket"), which also came from Latin *bāiulāre.* **Bail³** comes from Middle English *beil,* meaning "the arched handle of a pot."

---

bailiff (bā′lĭf) *n.* An official who guards prisoners and maintains order in a courtroom.

bailiwick (bā′lə-wĭk′) *n.* **1.** A person's specific area of interest, skill, or authority: *Responding to customer complaints is the supervisor's bailiwick.* **2.** The office or district of a bailiff.

bailout (bāl′out′) *n.* A rescue from financial difficulties: *The company, facing bankruptcy, turned to the government for a bailout.*

bairn (bârn) *n.* Scots A child.

bait (bāt) *n.* **1.** Food placed on a hook or in a trap to lure fish, birds, or other animals: *I always use worms for bait.* **2.** Something used to lure or entice: *A free book was the bait to get people to attend the book fair.* ❖ *tr.v.* **baited, baiting, baits 1.** To put bait on: *bait a fishhook.* **2.** To set dogs upon a (chained animal) for sport. **3.** To torment with repeated verbal attacks, insults, or ridicule.

baize (bāz) *n.* A thick, often green, woolen or cotton cloth that looks like felt, used chiefly on billiard tables.

bake (bāk) *v.* **baked, baking, bakes** —*tr.* **1.** To cook in an oven with dry heat: *We baked several loaves of bread.* **2.** To harden or dry by heating in or as if in an oven: *bake bricks in the sun.* —*intr.* **1.** To cook food by dry heat: *He loves to bake.* **2.** To become hardened or dry by or as if by baking: *The ground baked in the hot sun.*

baker (bā′kər) *n.* A person who bakes and sells bread, cakes, and pastries.

baker's dozen (bā′kərz) *n.* A group of thirteen; one dozen plus one.

bakery (bā′kə-rē) *n., pl.* **bakeries** A place where products such as bread, cake, and pastries are baked or sold.

baking powder (bā′kĭng) *n.* Any of several powdered mixtures of baking soda, starch, and a slightly acid compound such as cream of tartar, that are used to leaven biscuits and other baked goods.

baking soda *n.* A white crystalline compound having the formula $NaHCO_3$, used especially in beverages and as an ingredient in baking powder; sodium bicarbonate.

balaclava (băl′ə-klä′və) *n.* A knitted cap covering the head and neck with an opening for the eyes or face, used in cold weather especially by soldiers, mountain climbers, and skiers.

balalaika (băl′ə-lī′kə) *n.* A Russian musical instrument that is somewhat like a guitar but has a triangular body and three strings.

balance (băl′əns) *n.* **1.** A device in which the weight of an object is measured by putting it in a pan suspended from one end of a rod that swings on a pivot at its center and adding known weights to a pan suspended from the other end of the rod until the rod is level and motionless. **2.** A condition in which forces or influences are canceled or matched by opposite forces or influences: *She tried to maintain a balance between work and play.* **3a.** A state of bodily stability, as when standing erect: *I was thrown off balance by the gust of wind.* **b.** The ability to maintain bodily stability: *The gymnast has good balance.* **4.** Mental or emotional stability; sanity. **5.** A condition in which an equation represents a correct statement in mathematics or chemistry: *The balance in the equation is maintained as equal quantities are added to each side.* **6a.** An equality between the debit and credit sides of an account: *Our bookkeeper achieves a balance in books of account at the end of the month.* **b.** The difference between such sides: *There is a balance due of $50.* **7.** Something left over; a remainder: *After dinner the balance of the evening was spent playing cards.* **8.** A satisfying proportion or arrangement achieved between parts or elements; harmony: *The red curtains destroyed the balance of color in the room.* **9.** An action or influence that results in even, suitable, or fair distribution: *Part of the US system of checks and balances is the division of power between Congress and the president.* ❖ *v.* **balanced, balancing, balances** —*tr.* **1.** To bring into or keep in a condition of balance: *I balanced the book on my head.* **2.** To compare in the mind: *We tried to balance the pros and cons before deciding.* **3.** To act as an equalizing weight or factor to; offset: *Your skill in languages balances your lack of experience in foreign countries.* **4.** To equalize the sums of the debits and credits of (an account): *balance a checkbook.* **5.** In mathematics and chemistry, to bring (an equation) into balance. —*intr.* **1.** To be equal or equivalent, as in weight, force, or parts: *rewards that don't balance with the risks.* **2.** To be or come into a state of balance or stability: *He balanced on the top of the wall.* **3.** To be equal in accounts of debit and credit. ◆ **in the balance** In an undetermined and often critical position.

balance beam *n.* A horizontal raised beam on which competitors in gymnastics perform balancing feats.

balance of payments *n.* The amount of a nation's total payments to foreign countries after calculating the total receipts from abroad.

balance of power *n.* A distribution of power whereby no one nation is able to dominate or interfere with others.

balance of trade *n.* The difference in value between the total exports and the total imports of a nation.

balance sheet *n.* A statement that lists the assets and debts of a business or institution.

balance wheel *n.* A wheel that regulates the speed of a machine, as in a clock or watch.

balcony (băl′kə-nē) *n., pl.* **balconies 1.** A platform projecting from the wall of a building and surrounded by a railing. **2.** An upper section of seats in a theater or auditorium.

bald (bôld) *adj.* **balder, baldest 1.** Lacking hair on the head. **2.** Lacking a natural or usual covering: *a bald mountaintop without any vegetation.* **3.** Lacking treads: *replaced the bald tire.* **4.** Plain; blunt: *a bald statement of unpleasant facts.* —**bald′ness** *n.*

bald eagle *n.* A North American eagle having brownish-black feathers with a white head and tail.

balderdash (bôl′dər-dăsh′) *n.* Nonsense.

balding (bôl′dĭng) *adj.* Becoming bald.

baldric (bôl′drĭk) *n.* A belt worn over one shoulder and across the chest, used to support a sword or bugle.

bale (bāl) *n.* A large bound package or bundle of raw or finished material: *a bale of hay.* ✣ *tr.v.* **baled, baling, bales** To wrap in bales: *bale cotton.* —**bal′er** *n.*

baleen (bə-lēn′) *n.* Whalebone.

baleful (bāl′fəl) *adj.* **1.** Threatening; menacing: *a baleful look.* **2.** Producing evil or harm; harmful: *a baleful influence.* —**bale′ful·ly** *adv.* —**bale′ful·ness** *n.*

balk (bôk) *v.* **balked, balking, balks** —*intr.* **1.** To stop short and refuse to go on: *The horse balked and wouldn't jump the fence.* **2.** To refuse; recoil; shrink: *The workers balked at the low terms of the wage settlement.* **3.** In baseball, to make an illegal motion before pitching, allowing base runners to advance a base. —*tr.* To check or thwart: *The police balked the prisoners' plans to escape.* ✣ *n.* **1.** A hindrance, check, or defeat. **2.** In baseball, the act of balking.

Balkan (bôl′kən) *adj.* **1.** Relating to the Balkan Peninsula of southeast Europe. **2.** Relating to the countries of the Balkan Peninsula or to their inhabitants. ✣ *pl.n.*

Balkans (bôl′kənz) The countries of the Balkan Peninsula, including Albania, Bosnia and Herzegovina, Bulgaria, Croatia, continental Greece, Kosovo, Macedonia, Montenegro, southeast Romania, Serbia, and European Turkey.

Balkanize (bôl′kə-nīz′) *tr.v.* **Balkanized, Balkanizing, Balkanizes 1.** To divide (a region or territory) into small, often hostile units. **2.** To divide (an organization or system) into small, incompatible units: *changes that would Balkanize the corporation.* —**Bal′kan·i·za′tion** *n.*

balky (bô′kē) *adj.* **balkier, balkiest 1.** Given to stopping short and refusing to go on; stubborn: *a balky mule.* **2.** Difficult to start or operate: *She spent half an hour trying to start the balky engine.*

ball¹ (bôl) *n.* **1a.** Something that is spherical or nearly spherical; a round object: *The earth is a great round ball.* **b.** A round movable object used in various sports and games: *a tennis ball.* **c.** Such an object moving, thrown, hit, or kicked in a certain way: *a fly ball; a curve ball.* **2.** A game, especially baseball or basketball, played with such an object. **3.** In baseball, a pitch that does not pass through the strike zone and is not swung at by the batter. **4.** A rounded part of the body: *the ball of the foot.* **5.** A solid projectile or shot for a firearm: *a cannon ball.* ✣ *tr. & intr.v.* **balled, balling, balls** To form into a ball: *ball yarn for knitting.* ◆ **on the ball** *Informal* Alert, competent, or efficient.

ball² (bôl) *n.* **1.** A formal social dance. **2.** *Informal* A wonderful time: *had a ball at the beach.*

WORD HISTORY Ball¹ comes from Middle English *bal*, meaning "a round object." **Ball²** comes from French *bal* (meaning "a dance"), which comes from Greek *ballizein*, meaning "to dance."

ballad (băl′əd) *n.* **1.** A poem that tells a story in simple stanzas, often intended to be sung. **2.** The music for such a poem. **3.** A popular love song.

ball-and-socket joint (bôl′ən-sŏk′ĭt) *n.* **1.** A joint formed by a rounded part of one bone fitting into a hollow part of another bone, permitting rotary motion, as in the shoulder or hip joint. **2.** A similar joint in a mechanical device.

ballast (băl′əst) *n.* **1.** Heavy material carried especially in the hold of a ship or the gondola of a balloon to provide weight and steadiness: *Submarines use water as ballast in order to submerge.* **2.** Gravel or small stones used to form a foundation for a roadway or for railroad tracks. ✣ *tr.v.* **ballasted, ballasting, ballasts** To provide with or stabilize with ballast: *They used heavy stones to ballast the ship.*

ball bearing *n.* **1.** A bearing in which a ring-shaped track packed with small, freely revolving steel balls is used to reduce friction between a stationary part and a moving part, such as a rotating shaft or axle. **2.** A small steel ball used in such a bearing.

ballerina (băl′ə-rē′nə) *n.* A female dancer in a ballet company.

ballet (bă-lā′ *or* băl′ā′) *n.* **1.** An artistic form of dance characterized by precise, graceful movements based on established steps, poses, and gestures. **2.** A theatrical performance of dancing to music, usually in costume, to convey a story or theme. **3.** Music written or used for ballet.

ball game or **ballgame** (bôl′gām′) *n.* A game, especially baseball, that is played with a ball.

ballistic (bə-lĭs′tĭk) *adj.* Relating to ballistics or projectiles. ◆ **go ballistic** *Slang* To become very angry or irrational.

ballistic missile *n.* A missile that is guided by an internal system as it is propelled upward and then allowed to fall without further guidance or power toward its target.

ballistics (bə-lĭs′tĭks) *n.* (*used with a singular verb*) **1.** The scientific study of the characteristics of projectiles, such as bullets or missiles, and the way they move in flight. **2.** The study of firearms and ammunition.

ball joint *n.* A ball-and-socket joint in a mechanical device.

balloon (bə-lo͞on′) *n.* **1.** A large flexible bag filled with helium, hot air, or some other gas that is lighter than the surrounding air and designed to rise and float in the atmosphere. Balloons often carry a gondola or scientific instruments. **2.** A similar bag that is shaped like a figure or object when inflated; an inflatable. **3.** A small brightly colored rubber or plastic bag that is inflated and used for decoration or as a toy. ✣ *intr.v.* **ballooned, ballooning, balloons 1.** To swell out like a balloon: *The tire ballooned as it was inflated with air.* **2.** To increase or rise quickly: *John's debt ballooned while he was out of work.* **3.** To ride in a gondola suspended from a balloon: *We ballooned over the beautiful desert scenery.*

balloon mortgage *n.* A mortgage that is repaid in periodic installments until the completion of the term, when the balance is due all at once.

ballot (băl′ət) *n.* **1.** A piece of paper used to cast a vote, especially a secret vote. **2.** The act, process, or method of voting: *In a democracy, many decisions are made by the ballot.* **3.** A list of candidates running for office in an election. **4.** The total of all votes cast in an election: *The ballot is especially heavy in the year of a presidential election.* **5.** The right to vote; franchise: *Many countries do not have the ballot.* ❖ *intr.v.* **balloted, balloting, ballots** To cast a ballot or ballots; vote.

ballpark (bôl′pärk′) *n.* A stadium for playing baseball. ❖ *adj. Informal* Being approximately right or in the right range: *They gave us a ballpark estimate for what a new computer would cost.* ◆ **in the ballpark** *Informal* Approximately right or within the right range.

ballplayer (bôl′plā′ər) *n.* A baseball player.

ballpoint pen (bôl′point′) *n.* A pen having as its writing point a small ball bearing that transfers ink from a cartridge onto a writing surface.

ballroom (bôl′rōōm′ *or* bôl′rŏŏm′) *n.* A large room for dancing.

ballyhoo (băl′ē-hōō′) *n., pl.* **ballyhoos** Extravagant advertising or publicity. ❖ *tr.v.* **ballyhooed, ballyhooing, ballyhoos** To advertise or publicize in an extravagant manner.

balm (bäm) *n.* **1.** Any of several plants related to mint and having a pleasant scent. **2.** Any of various fragrant resins obtained from several trees and shrubs. **3.** A fragrant ointment or oil. **4.** Something that soothes or comforts: *Her apology was balm to his hurt feelings.*

balmy (bä′mē) *adj.* **balmier, balmiest** Mild and pleasant: *balmy subtropical climates.* —**balm′i·ly** *adv.* —**balm′i·ness** *n.*

baloney¹ (bə-lō′nē) *n., pl.* **baloneys** Variant of **bologna.**

baloney² (bə-lō′nē) *n. Slang* Nonsense. ❖ *interj.* An expression used to show disagreement or annoyance.

balsa (bôl′sə) *n.* **1.** A tropical American tree having wood that is unusually light in weight. **2.** The buoyant wood of this tree, used for rafts and floats and in making model airplanes.

balsam (bôl′səm) *n.* **1.** Any of several fragrant resins obtained from various trees and used in medicines and perfumes. **2.** A tree, especially the balsam fir, that yields such a resinous substance. **3.** A garden plant having colorful flowers.

balsam fir *n.* **1.** An evergreen cone-bearing tree of northern North America, widely used for pulpwood. Turpentine and varnish are made from its resin. **2.** The wood of such a tree.

balsamic vinegar (bôl-săm′ĭk) *n.* A dark, sweet vinegar that has been aged in wooden barrels.

Balt (bôlt) *n.* **1.** A member of a Baltic-speaking people. **2.** A native or inhabitant of Estonia, Latvia, or Lithuania.

Baltic (bôl′tĭk) *adj.* **1.** Relating to the Baltic Sea, a body of water lying between northern, eastern, and central Europe. **2.** Relating to the countries or regions adjoining the Baltic Sea. **3.** Relating to Baltic or a people that speaks Baltic. ❖ *n.* A group of Indo-European languages that includes Lithuanian and Latvian.

baluster (băl′ə-stər) *n.* One of the posts supporting a railing, as of a porch or banister.

balustrade (băl′ə-strād′) *n.* A handrail and the row of posts supporting it, as on a balcony or the edge of a staircase.

bambino (băm-bē′nō) *n., pl.* **bambinos** *or* **bambini** (băm-bē′nē) A baby or young child.

bamboo (băm-bōō′) *n., pl.* **bamboos 1.** Any of numerous grasses that often grow very tall and have jointed, hollow stems. **2.** The strong stems of these plants, used especially for construction and for making fabric. The young shoots of some types are used as food.

bamboozle (băm-bōō′zəl) *tr.v.* **bamboozled, bamboozling, bamboozles** *Informal* To deceive by elaborate trickery; hoodwink: *She bamboozled me into buying her worthless magazine collection.*

ban (băn) *tr.v.* **banned, banning, bans 1.** To prohibit (an action) or forbid the use of (something), especially by official decree: *The city council banned billboards on most streets.* **2.** To refuse to allow (someone) to do something, go somewhere, or be a participant; exclude: *The player was banned from the tournament for violating the rules.* ❖ *n.* A prohibition made by law or official decree: *a ban on cigarette smoking on airplanes.*

banal (bə-năl′ *or* bā′nəl *or* bə-näl′) *adj.* Commonplace; dull; trite: *Always remarking on the weather makes banal conversation.* —**ba·nal′ly** *adv.*

banality (bə-năl′ĭ-tē *or* bā-năl′ĭ-tē) *n., pl.* **banalities 1.** The quality or condition of being banal; triteness: *The banality of the speaker's remarks put the audience to sleep.* **2.** Something that is banal: *Television commercials are full of banalities.*

banana (bə-năn′ə) *n.* **1.** A crescent-shaped fruit having sweet soft flesh and yellow to reddish skin that peels off easily. **2.** Any of several tropical plants that bear such fruit.

bananas (bə-năn′əz) *adj. Slang* Crazy.

banana split *n.* A dessert consisting of ice cream and usually flavored syrups, nuts, and whipped cream served on a banana that has been split lengthwise.

band¹ (bănd) *n.* **1a.** A strip of metal, cloth, or other flexible material, used to bind, trim, support, or hold things together: *Metal bands hold the slats of the wooden barrel together.* **b.** A stripe, mark, or area suggestive of such a strip: *the band of colors forming the rainbow.* **c.** A simple ungrooved ring, especially a wedding ring. **2.** A specific range of wavelengths or frequencies in the electromagnetic spectrum, as those used in radio broadcasting: *the shortwave band.* ❖ *tr.v.* **banded, banding, bands 1.** To tie, bind, or encircle with a band: *band a skirt with a red ribbon.* **2.** To mark or identify with a band: *a program to band migrating birds.*

band² (bănd) *n.* **1.** A group of people or animals. **2.** A group of musicians who perform as an ensemble. **3.** A group of people or families who belong to a tribe but who live on their own for at least part of the year. ❖ *tr. & intr.v.* **banded, banding, bands** To form or gather in a group or association: *The homesteaders banded together for protection.*

WORD HISTORY Band¹ and **band**² both ultimately come from the same ancient Germanic root that meant "to bind," although their development followed separate paths.

bandage (băn′dĭj) *n.* A strip of cloth or other material to bind, cover, or protect a wound or other injury. ❖ *tr.v.* **bandaged, bandaging, bandages** To cover or bind with a bandage: *bandage a wound.*

Band-Aid (bănd′ād′) A trademark for an adhesive bandage with a gauze pad in the center.

bandanna *or* **bandana** (băn-dăn′ə) *n.* A large handkerchief usually patterned and brightly colored.

bandbox (bănd′bŏks′) *n.* A light round box used to hold small articles of apparel.

bandicoot (băn′dĭ-kōōt′) *n.* **1.** Any of several large rats of Asia and the Middle East that often destroy food crops. **2.** Any of several burrowing Australian marsupials that have a long tapering snout and feed on insects and plants.

bandit (băn′dĭt) *n.* A robber, often one who is a member of a gang of outlaws. ♦ **make out like a bandit** *Slang* To be highly successful in a given enterprise.

banditry (băn′dĭ-trē) *n.* The activity of a bandit.

bandleader (bănd′lē′dər) *n.* The conductor of a musical band.

bandoleer or **bandolier** (băn′də-lîr′) *n.* A military belt that has small pockets or loops for carrying cartridges and is worn over the shoulder and across the chest.

band saw *n.* A power saw consisting of a toothed metal band driven around two wheels in a loop.

bandstand (bănd′stănd′) *n.* An outdoor platform, usually with a roof, for a musical band to give concerts.

bandwagon (bănd′wăg′ən) *n.* **1.** A brightly decorated wagon for carrying musicians in a parade. **2.** *Informal* A popular cause, party, or trend: *Supermarkets began jumping on the organic foods bandwagon once they realized how many customers wanted to buy them.*

bandwidth (bănd′wĭdth′ or bănd′wĭth′) *n.* The amount of digital information that can be passed along a communications channel in a given period of time.

bandy (băn′dē) *tr.v.* **bandied, bandying, bandies** **1.** To toss, throw, or strike back and forth: *We bandied the ball over the net.* **2.** To give and take; exchange: *The opposing groups bandied insults at each other.* **3.** To say or discuss in a casual manner: *The movie star's name was bandied about in idle gossip.* ❖ *adj.* Bent or curved outward; bowed: *bandy legs.*

bandy-legged (băn′dē-lĕg′ĭd or băn′dē-lĕgd′) *adj.* Bowlegged.

bane (bān) *n.* A cause of great trouble or annoyance: *Fleas were the bane of the cat's existence.*

baneberry (bān′bĕr′ē) *n.* Any of several plants having clusters of white flowers and poisonous red, white, or blackish berries.

baneful (bān′fəl) *adj.* Causing harm, ruin, or death; harmful: *the baneful effect of pollution on the environment.*

bang¹ (băng) *n.* **1.** A loud, sharp, sudden noise: *The door slammed with a bang.* **2.** A sudden forceful blow; a thump: *a bang on the knee.* **3.** *Slang* A feeling of excitement; thrill: *Most kids get a real bang out of the circus.* ❖ *v.* **banged, banging, bangs** *—tr.* **1.** To strike or hit with a loud sharp noise: *The cook banged the pots and pans together.* **2.** To strike, hit, or move suddenly and with great force: *I banged my knee against the table.* **3.** To close suddenly and loudly; slam. *—intr.* **1.** To make a loud, sharp, sudden noise: *Firecrackers banged in the distance.* **2.** To crash noisily against or into something: *The toy car banged into the wall.* ❖ *adv.* **1.** Exactly; precisely: *The arrow hit bang on the target.* **2.** Suddenly; abruptly: *cut the conversation bang off.* **3.** To crash noisily against or into something: *The toy car banged into the wall.* ❖ *interj.* Used to indicate the sound of an explosion or collision. ♦ **bang up** To damage extensively.

bang² (băng) *n.* often **bangs** Hair cut straight across the forehead.

WORD HISTORY Bang¹ is probably related to Old Norse *bang*, meaning "a hammering." **Bang²** comes from the adverb sense of Modern English *bang¹*, meaning "abruptly."

bangle (băng′gəl) *n.* **1.** A rigid bracelet or anklet, especially one with no clasp. **2.** An ornament that hangs from a bracelet or necklace.

bang-up (băng′ŭp′) *adj.* *Slang* Very good; great: *a bang-up party.*

banish (băn′ĭsh) *tr.v.* **banished, banishing, banishes** **1.** To force to leave a country or place by official decree; exile: *The king banished the outlaw.* **2.** To drive away; cast out: *Banish all doubts from your mind.* **—ban′ish·ment** *n.*

banister also **bannister** (băn′ĭ-stər) *n.* **1.** A handrail, especially on a staircase. **2.** One of the posts supporting a handrail on a staircase.

banjo (băn′jō) *n., pl.* **banjos** or **banjoes** A musical instrument having a narrow neck, a hollow circular body with a covering of skin or plastic on one side, and four or sometimes five strings that are strummed or plucked.

bank¹ (băngk) *n.* **1.** A hillside or slope: *the steep bank leading down to the valley.* **2.** often **banks a.** The rising ground bordering a body of water, especially bordering a river. **b.** An elevated area of a sea floor. **3.** A mound, pile, or ridge of earth or other solid material: *a snow bank.* **4.** A pile or mass, as of clouds or fog. **5.** The sideways tilt of an aircraft in making a turn. ❖ *v.* **banked, banking, banks** *—tr.* **1.** To pile up (earth, snow, or other matter) in a ridge or sloping surface: *The plows banked snow along the edge of the road.* **2.** To pile ashes or fuel onto (a fire) to make it burn slowly: *bank a fire in the fireplace for the night.* **3.** To tilt (an aircraft) in making a turn. **4.** In sports, to propel (a ball or puck) in such a way as to make it bounce off a surface at an angle. *—intr.* To tilt an aircraft in making a turn: *The pilot banked to the left before descending.*

bank² (băngk) *n.* **1.** A place or organization in which money is kept for saving or business purposes or is invested, supplied for loans, or exchanged. **2.** The funds held by a dealer or banker in certain games, especially gambling games. **3.** A supply or stock for future use: *the blood bank of a hospital.* **4.** A place of safekeeping or storage: *a computer's memory bank.* ❖ *v.* **banked, banking, banks** *—tr.* **1.** To put (money) in a bank: *Many workers bank a part of their salary.* **2.** To store (something) for future use. *—intr.* To have an account or savings at a particular bank. ♦ **bank on** To rely on; count on: *I'm banking on you to get the job done.*

bank³ (băngk) *n.* **1.** A set or group arranged in a row: *a bank of elevators.* **2.** A row of keys on a keyboard instrument, especially on an organ. **3.** A row of oars in a galley.

WORD HISTORY Bank¹ comes from Middle English *bank* (meaning "ridge, slope") and is of Scandinavian origin. **Bank²** comes from Middle English *banke* (meaning "a financial organization") and is of Italian origin. **Bank³** comes from Middle English *bank* (meaning "bench") and is of Germanic origin.

bankbook (băngk′bŏŏk′) *n.* A book held by a depositor in which a bank enters the amounts added to or taken out of the depositor's account; a passbook.

bankcard (băngk′kärd′) *n.* A plastic card given by a bank to a customer for use at an ATM.

banker (băng′kər) *n.* A person who owns or is an executive of a bank.

banking (băng′kĭng) *n.* The business or occupation of running a bank.

banknote (băngk′nōt′) *n.* A piece of paper currency, such as a dollar bill, that is issued by a government's central bank.

bankroll (băngk′rōl′) *tr.v.* **bankrolled, bankrolling, bankrolls** To provide funds or financial support for: *The corporation agreed to help bankroll the new arts center.*

bankrupt (băngk′rŭpt′) *adj.* **1.** Legally declared unable to pay one's debts because of lack of money. The property of someone who is bankrupt is controlled by or divided among the people who are owed money. **2.** Completely without money; financially ruined: *a gambler who went bankrupt.* **3.** Lacking in or depleted of valuable qualities: *a book that is bankrupt of original ideas.* ❖ *n.* A person who is bankrupt. ❖ *tr.v.* **bankrupted, bankrupting, bankrupts** To cause to become bankrupt: *The stock market crash bankrupted him.*

bankruptcy (băngk′rəpt-sē *or* băngk′rəp-sē) *n.* The condition of being bankrupt.

bank shot *n.* **1.** A shot in billiards in which the player causes a ball to rebound off a cushion. **2.** A shot in basketball in which the ball bounces off the backboard at an angle of less than 90 degrees before reaching the basket.

banner (băn′ər) *n.* **1.** A flag or piece of cloth, often having words or a special design on it: *They marched in the parade with a banner for women's rights.* **2.** A headline spanning the width of a newspaper page. ❖ *adj.* Unusually good; outstanding: *a banner year for our team.*

bannister (băn′ĭ-stər) *n.* Variant of **banister.**

banns also **bans** (bănz) *pl.n.* An announcement in a church that a particular couple intends to be married.

banquet (băng′kwĭt) *n.* **1.** A large elaborate meal; a feast. **2.** A ceremonial dinner honoring a person or group: *All the nominees for prizes were invited to the awards banquet.* ❖ *tr. & intr.v.* **banqueted, banqueting, banquets** To honor (someone) at or eat a banquet.

banshee (băn′shē) *n.* In Gaelic folklore, a female spirit supposed to warn of a death in a family by wailing loudly.

bantam (băn′təm) *n.* **1.** A chicken of any of various small breeds. **2.** A small, aggressive person.

bantamweight (băn′təm-wāt′) *n.* A professional boxer weighing more than 112 and not more than 118 pounds (about 50–53 kilograms).

banter (băn′tər) *n.* Playful good-humored conversation. ❖ *intr.v.* **bantered, bantering, banters** To exchange joking or teasing remarks: *She bantered with her friends during lunch hour.* —**ban′ter·er** *n.*

Bantu (băn′tōō) *n., pl.* **Bantu** or **Bantus 1.** A member of a large group of peoples native to southern and central Africa. **2.** A family of languages spoken by these people, including Swahili and Zulu. —**Ban′tu** *adj.*

banyan (băn′yən) *n.* A tropical Indian fig tree having large oval leaves and spreading branches from which aerial roots grow to the ground to form new trunks.

banzai (bän-zī′) *n.* A Japanese battle cry or patriotic cheer.

baobab (bā′ō-băb′ *or* bä′ō-băb′) *n.* A tree of tropical Africa, having a very thick trunk and large, hard-shelled fruit with edible pulp.

baptism (băp′tĭz′əm) *n.* **1.** A Christian sacrament in which a person is sprinkled with or dipped in water as a sign of being cleansed of sin and admitted to membership in a Christian church. **2.** A first experience. —**bap·tis′mal** (băp-tĭz′məl) *adj.*

Baptist (băp′tĭst) *n.* A member of a Protestant church that believes in baptism only for people old enough to understand its meaning. Baptists are usually baptized by placing the whole body in water. —**Bap′tist** *adj.*

baptistery also **baptistry** (băp′tĭ-strē) *n., pl.* **baptisteries** also **baptistries** A part of a church or a separate building in which baptism is performed.

baptize (băp-tīz′ *or* băp′tīz′) *tr.v.* **baptized, baptizing, baptizes** To admit (a person) into Christianity or a particular Christian church by baptism.

bar¹ (bär) *n.* **1.** A narrow, straight, rigid piece of solid material, often used to close an opening or as part of a machine or other device: *That long iron bar serves as an axle for the wagon.* **2.** A solid oblong piece of a substance: *a chocolate bar; a bar of soap.* **3.** A narrow marking, such as a stripe or band: *a bird with bars of white on the tail.* **4a.** A horizontal rod that marks the height to be cleared in the high jump or pole vault. **b.** A standard, expectation, or degree of requirement: *His work raised the bar for other musicians.* **5.** Something that prevents entry or progress; a barrier; an obstacle: *Her lack of a college degree was a bar to her career advancement.* **6.** A ridge of sand or gravel on a shore or stream bed, formed by the action of tides or currents. **7a.** A high counter at which drinks, especially alcoholic drinks, and sometimes food, are served. **b.** A place having such a counter. **8a.** The railing in a courtroom separating the participants in a legal proceeding from the spectators. **b.** A court or courtroom: *a case argued at the bar.* **c.** The occupation of a lawyer; the legal profession: *She chose the bar for her career.* **d.** Lawyers considered as a group: *a meeting of the local bar.* **9.** Variant of **barre. 10a.** A vertical line dividing a musical staff into equal measures. **b.** A measure of music: *Let's practice the final bars of this march.* ❖ *tr.v.* **barred, barring, bars 1.** To close or fasten with a bar or bars: *barred the gate.* **2.** To block; close off; obstruct: *Fallen branches barred the way.* **3.** To keep out; exclude: *Hunters are barred from wildlife sanctuaries.* **4.** To prohibit (someone) from doing something: *Failing the eye test barred him from driving.* **5.** To rule out; except: *wrestling with no holds barred.* **6.** To mark with stripes or narrow bands. ◆ **bar none** With no exceptions: *This is the best pizza I've ever had, bar none.* **behind bars** In prison: *put the criminal behind bars.*

bar² (bär) *n.* A unit used to measure atmospheric pressure. It is equal to a force of 100,000 newtons per square meter of surface area, or 0.987 atmosphere.

WORD HISTORY Bar¹ comes from Middle English *barre,* meaning "barrier, obstruction." **Bar²** comes from Greek *baros,* meaning "weight."

barb (bärb) *n.* **1.** A sharp point projecting backward, as on a fishhook or arrow. **2.** One of the hairlike branches on the shaft of a feather. **3.** A cutting or biting remark: *The author saved her best barbs for her critics.*

barbarian (bär-bâr′ē-ən) *n.* **1.** A member of a people considered by those of another nation or group to be uncivilized or culturally inferior. **2.** A crude, uncivilized, or brutal person: *The pirates were barbarians.*

WORD HISTORY Our word **barbarian,** "a member of an uncivilized people," comes from the ancient Greek word for "foreigner," *barbaros.* Originally this word was probably an imitation of the unintelligible speech of non-Greeks ("bar-bar-bar"). It later came to mean "uncultured." The Romans borrowed the word from the Greeks and used it to mean "neither Greek nor Roman, outside the Roman Empire," and later "uncivilized."

barbaric (bär-băr′ĭk) *adj.* **1.** Relating to or characteristic of barbarians: *The native peoples considered the explorers barbaric.* **2.** Cruel or brutal: *a barbaric dictator; torture* *and other barbaric punishments.* **3.** Marked by crudeness or lack of restraint: *barbaric eating habits.*

barbarism (bär′bə-rĭz′əm) *n.* **1.** A barbarous uncivilized state. **2.** A barbarous act or custom: *Imprisoning debtors is now considered a barbarism.* **3.** A word or expression regarded as being incorrect and showing lack of education or refinement.

barbarity (bär-băr′ĭ-tē) *n., pl.* **barbarities 1.** Cruel or savage behavior: *a dictatorship known for its barbarity toward its people.* **2.** A cruel or savage act: *accused the army of committing barbarities against civilians during the war.*

barbarous (bär′bər-əs) *adj.* **1.** Primitive in culture and customs; uncivilized: *The barbarous invaders burned the library.* **2.** Brutal; cruel: *animals that were held in cramped, barbarous conditions.* **3.** Uncultured or unrefined, especially in language: *barbarous writing.* —**bar′-ba·rous·ly** *adv.* —**bar′ba·rous·ness** *n.*

barbecue (bär′bĭ-kyōō′) *n.* **1.** A grill, pit, or fireplace for roasting meat, often outdoors. **2.** A whole animal or a piece of it roasted over an open fire. **3.** A social gathering at which food is cooked over an open fire. ❖ *tr.v.* **barbecued, barbecuing, barbecues** To cook (food) over an open fire, often with a spicy sauce: *We barbecued ribs.*

barbed (bärbd) *adj.* **1.** Having barbs: *the barbed head of a harpoon.* **2.** Cutting; stinging: *barbed criticism.*

barbed wire *n.* Twisted strands of wire with barbs at regular intervals, used in making fences.

barbel (bär′bəl) *n.* A slender feeler extending from the head of certain fishes, such as a catfish.

barbell (bär′bĕl′) *n.* A bar with adjustable weights at each end, lifted for sport or exercise.

barber (bär′bər) *n.* A person whose work is cutting hair and shaving or trimming beards. ❖ *tr.v.* **barbered, barbering, barbers** To cut the hair of or shave or trim the beard of (someone).

barberry (bär′bĕr′ē) *n.* Any of various shrubs having small leaves, yellowish flowers, and small red, orange, or blackish berries.

barbershop (bär′bər-shŏp′) *n.* A barber's place of business. ❖ *adj. Informal* Relating to singing sentimental songs for unaccompanied, usually male voices in four-part harmony: *a barbershop quartet.*

barbican (bär′bĭ-kən) *n.* A tower at a gate or drawbridge at the entrance to a medieval castle or town.

barbiturate (bär-bĭch′ər-ĭt *or* bär-bĭch′ə-rāt′ *or* bär-bĭch′ə-wĭt) *n.* Any of a group of drugs that reduce the activity of the central nervous system and are used as sedatives. Barbiturates are highly addictive.

barbwire (bärb′wīr′) *n.* Barbed wire.

barcarole also **barcarolle** (bär′kə-rōl′) *n.* **1.** A song of a Venetian gondolier with a rhythm that suggests rowing. **2.** A musical composition imitating such a song.

barcode (bär′kōd′) *n.* A series of vertical bars of varying widths printed on a consumer product to allow a computer scanner to verify the product's price and to keep track of inventory.

bard (bärd) *n.* **1.** A poet of ancient times who composed and recited verses about heroes and heroic deeds. **2.** A poet.

bare (bâr) *adj.* **barer, barest 1.** Lacking clothing or covering; naked: *bare feet; a bare hillside.* **2.** Lacking the usual or expected furnishings, equipment, or supplies: *bare shelves; bare walls.* **3.** Having no addition or restric-

tion; simple or plain: *the bare facts.* **4.** Just sufficient or adequate; mere: *the bare necessities of life.* ❖ *tr.v.* **bared, baring, bares** To uncover; expose to view: *The dog bared its teeth and growled.* —**bare′ness** *n.*

bareback (bâr′băk′) *adv. & adj.* On a horse or other animal with no saddle: *riding bareback; a bareback rider.*

barefaced (bâr′fāst′) *adj.* Shameless; bold; brazen: *a barefaced lie.*

barefoot (bâr′fŏŏt′) also **barefooted** (bâr′fŏŏt′ĭd) *adv. & adj.* Without shoes or other covering on the feet: *running barefoot through the grass; a barefoot child.*

barehanded (bâr′hăn′dĭd) *adv. & adj.* With the hand or hands alone; without a glove, tool, weapon, or protection: *catching fish barehanded; a barehanded catch of a baseball.*

bareheaded (bâr′hĕd′ĭd) *adv. & adj.* Without a hat or other head covering: *walking bareheaded in the rain; bareheaded hikers.*

barelegged (bâr′lĕg′ĭd *or* bâr′lĕgd′) *adv. & adj.* With the legs uncovered: *ran barelegged through the surf; barelegged children at the beach.*

barely (bâr′lē) *adv.* **1.** By very little; hardly; just: *We could barely see the shore in the dark.* **2.** In a bare or scanty manner; sparsely: *a barely furnished room.*

bargain (bär′gĭn) *n.* **1.** An arrangement or agreement between two sides, often involving payment or trade; a deal: *We made a bargain that I would cut the grass for twenty dollars.* **2.** Something offered or bought at a low price: *The elegant dress that's now on sale is a bargain.* ❖ *intr.v.* **bargained, bargaining, bargains** To argue over or discuss the terms of an agreement, especially a price to be paid: *The hotel's cook bargained for vegetables in the market.* ◆ **bargain for** or **bargain on** To count on; expect: *That old car gave us more trouble than we bargained for.* **into the bargain** or **in the bargain** Over and above what is expected; in addition: *We bought the large-size bag of dog food and got a dog toy into the bargain.*

barge (bärj) *n.* **1.** A large flatbottom boat that is usually towed or pushed and is used to carry loads on rivers, canals, and coastal waters. **2.** A large open boat used for parties and ceremonies. ❖ *intr.v.* **barged, barging, barges 1.** To intrude or interrupt, especially rudely: *He barged into our conversation and told us what happened.* **2.** To move clumsily: *They barged through the crowded city square.*

bar graph *n.* A graph consisting of parallel bars or rectangles whose lengths are proportional to the value or frequency of each category.

barite (bâr′īt) *n.* A white or colorless crystalline mineral of barium sulfate that is the chief source of barium.

baritone (bär′ĭ-tōn′) *n.* **1.** A moderately low singing voice of a man, higher than a bass and lower than a tenor. **2.** A singer whose voice lies within this range. **3.** An instrument whose sound falls within this range, especially a valved brass instrument similar to but larger than the euphonium. **4.** A part written in this range.

barium (bâr′ē-əm) *n. Symbol* **Ba** A soft, silvery-white metallic element that occurs only in combination with other elements, especially in barite. Barium compounds are used in making fireworks and white pigments. Atomic number 56. See **Periodic Table.**

barium sulfate *n.* A compound of barium, sulfur, and oxygen that occurs as a fine white powder. It is used in taking x-rays of the digestive tract and in making textiles, rubber, and plastic.

bark¹ (bärk) *n.* **1.** The harsh sound made by a dog and certain other animals such as seals and coyotes. **2.** A sound similar to this, such as a cough or the firing of a gun. ❖ *v.* **barked, barking, barks** —*intr.* **1.** To make the sound of a bark: *The neighbor's dog barked all night.* **2.** To speak gruffly or sharply; snap: *The sergeant barked at the new recruits.* —*tr.* To say in a loud harsh voice: *The team captain barked commands.* ◆ **bark up the wrong tree** To misdirect one's energies or attention.

bark² (bärk) *n.* The protective outer covering of the trunk, branches, and roots of trees and other woody plants. ❖ *tr.v.* **barked, barking, barks** To bump or rub so as to scrape the skin from: *I barked my shin on the rocks.*

bark³ also **barque** (bärk) *n.* A sailing ship with three to five masts, all of them square-rigged except the after mast, which is fore-and-aft rigged.

WORD HISTORY Bark¹ comes from Middle English *berken*, which comes from Old English *beorcan,* both meaning "to make the harsh sound of a dog." **Bark²** comes from Middle English *bark,* which comes from Old Norse *börkr,* both meaning "protective outer covering of a woody plant." **Bark³** comes from Middle English *barke,* which comes from Latin *barca,* both meaning "boat."

barkeeper (bär′kē′pər) *n.* **1.** A person who owns or runs a bar for the sale of alcoholic beverages. **2.** A bartender.

barkentine (bär′kən-tēn′) *n.* A sailing ship with three to five masts, of which only the foremast is square-rigged, the other masts being fore-and-aft rigged.

barker (bär′kər) *n.* **1.** A person or animal that barks: *That dog is a loud barker.* **2.** A person who makes a loud entertaining sales pitch at the entrance to a show, carnival, or other attraction.

barley (bär′lē) *n.* **1.** The grain of a grass that grows in cool regions, used as food for humans and livestock and for making beer and whiskey. **2.** The plant that produces such grain.

barleycorn (bär′lē-kôrn′) *n.* A grain of barley.

barmaid (bär′mād′) *n.* A woman who serves drinks in a bar.

barman (bär′mən) *n.* A man who serves drinks in a bar.

bar mitzvah (bär mĭts′və) *n.* **1.** A ceremony in which a Jewish boy who is at least 13 years old is admitted as an adult into the religious community. **2.** The boy for whom this ceremony is held. ❖ *tr.v.* **bar mitzvahed, bar mitzvahing, bar mitzvahs** To recognize (a boy) in such a ceremony.

barn (bärn) *n.* **1.** A large farm building used for storing grain, hay, and other farm products and for sheltering livestock. **2.** A large shed for the housing of vehicles: *a bus barn.*

barnacle (bär′nə-kəl) *n.* Any of various small hard-shelled marine animals that have feathery structures used for filtering food particles from the water and that attach themselves to underwater objects such as rocks.

barn dance *n.* A social gathering, often held in a barn, with music and square dancing.

barnstorm (bärn′stôrm′) *tr. & intr.v.* **barnstormed, barnstorming, barnstorms** To travel about the countryside making political speeches or appearing in exhibits or sporting events. —**barn′storm′er** *n.*

barn swallow *n.* A widely distributed bird having a deeply forked tail, a dark-blue back, and a tan underside. Barn swallows often build their nests in the eaves of barns.

barnyard (bärn′yärd′) *n.* The yard or area of ground

around a barn. ❖ *adj.* Crude or indecent: *barnyard jokes.*

barograph (băr′ə-grăf′) *n.* A barometer that automatically records changes in air pressure.

barometer (bə-rŏm′ĭ-tər) *n.* **1.** An instrument for measuring atmospheric pressure, used to determine height above sea level and in weather forecasting. **2.** Something that shows shifts and changes like those of the weather; an indicator: *Opinion polls are used as a barometer of public mood.*

barometric (băr′ə-mĕt′rĭk) *adj.* Relating to or measured by a barometer: *take a barometric reading.*

barometric pressure *n.* Atmospheric pressure.

baron (băr′ən) *n.* **1a.** A British nobleman of the lowest rank. **b.** A nobleman of other parts of Europe, ranked differently in various countries. **2.** In feudal times, a man holding rights, lands, and a title directly from a king or another high-ranking nobleman. **3.** A businessman of great wealth and influence: *an oil baron.*

baroness (băr′ə-nĭs) *n.* **1.** The wife or widow of a baron. **2.** A woman holding the title to a barony.

baronet (băr′ə-nĭt *or* băr′ə-nĕt′) *n.* In Great Britain, a man holding a hereditary title of honor reserved for commoners, ranking just below the barons.

baronetess (băr′ə-nĭ-tĭs *or* băr′ə-nĕt′ĭs) *n.* In Great Britain, a woman holding a hereditary title of honor reserved for commoners, ranking just below the barons.

baronial (bə-rō′nē-əl) *adj.* **1.** Relating to a baron or a barony. **2.** Suitable for a baron; stately or splendid: *a large baronial home.*

barony (băr′ə-nē) *n., pl.* **baronies** The rank or domain of a baron.

baroque (bə-rōk′) *adj.* **1.** also **Baroque** Relating to or characteristic of a style of art and architecture developed in Europe from about 1600 to 1750, characterized by elaborate curving forms and intricate detail. **2.** also **Baroque** Relating to or characteristic of a style of musical composition that flourished in Europe from about 1600 to 1750 and was notable for its strict form and elaborate patterns. **3.** Elaborate and fantastic; outlandish: *a baroque plot with many twists and turns.* **4.** Irregular in shape: *a baroque pearl.* ❖ *n.* also **Baroque** The baroque style or period in art, architecture, or music.

barouche (bə-rōōsh′) *n.* A horse-drawn carriage with a folding top, two double passenger seats inside facing one another, and a driver's seat outside.

barque (bärk) *n.* Variant of **bark³.**

barrack (băr′ək) *n.* often **barracks** A building or group of buildings used to house soldiers, workers, or a large number of other people: *cleaned the barracks daily.*

barracuda (băr′ə-kōō′də) *n., pl.* **barracuda** or **barracudas** Any of various ocean fishes having a long narrow body and a projecting lower jaw with very sharp teeth, found mostly in tropical waters.

barrage (bə-räzh′) *n.* **1.** A concentrated firing of artillery, missiles, or other firearms directed at an enemy position. **2.** An overwhelming outpouring: *a barrage of customer complaints.* ❖ *tr.v.* **barraged, barraging, barrages** To direct a barrage at: *Gunboats barraged the fort. Reporters barraged the speaker with questions.*

barre also **bar** (bär) *n.* **1.** In ballet, a horizontal rail used as a support in exercises. **2.** A technique in which a finger is laid across the fingerboard of a stringed instrument to stop several strings at once.

barred (bärd) *adj.* **1.** Having been secured with bars: *barred windows.* **2.** Having stripes: *a bird with barred plumage.*

barrel (băr′əl) *n.* **1.** A large container of wood, metal, plastic, or cardboard with round flat ends of equal size. Wooden barrels usually have sides that bulge out slightly and are held together by hoops. **2.** The amount that a barrel can hold: *a barrel of sawdust.* **3.** Any of various measures of volume or capacity ranging from 31 to 42 gallons (117 to 159 liters). **4a.** The long tube of a gun, through which a bullet or shell travels. **b.** A cylindrical machine part. **5.** *Informal* A great amount: *a barrel of fun.* ❖ *v.* **barreled, barreling, barrels** or **barrelled, barrelling, barrels** —*tr.* To put or pack in a barrel: *barrel vinegar for shipping to market.* —*intr. Informal* To move at great speed: *The express train barreled along the tracks.* —**bar′rel·ful′** *n.*

barrel organ *n.* A portable musical instrument, similar to a small organ, in which air from a bellows is directed to the pipes by turning a barrel with a hand crank. Pins inside the barrel open the pipe valves in a particular sequence to play the notes of a tune.

barren (băr′ən) *adj.* **1.** Lacking plants or crops: *a barren desert; barren soil.* **2.** Unable to bear offspring or fruit: *barren trees.* **3.** Not useful or productive: *barren efforts.* **4.** Empty; bare: *barren of pleasure.* ❖ *n.* often **barrens** An area of barren or unproductive land. —**bar′ren·ness** *n.*

barrette (bə-rĕt′) *n.* A bar-shaped or oval clip used to hold the hair in place.

barricade (băr′ĭ-kād′ *or* băr′ĭ-kād′) *n.* **1.** A structure set up hastily to obstruct the passage of an enemy. **2.** A barrier or obstruction. ❖ *tr.v.* **barricaded, barricading, barricades** To close off, block, or protect with a barricade: *barricade streets to control the crowd at a parade.*

barrier (băr′ē-ər) *n.* **1.** A structure, such as a fence or wall, built to obstruct passage: *Police set up a barrier at each end of the street the night before the fair began.* **2.** Something that obstructs; an obstacle: *Lack of education can be a barrier to success.*

barrier island *n.* A long, narrow sand island that is parallel to the mainland and serves to protect the coast from erosion.

barrier reef *n.* A long narrow ridge of coral deposits parallel to the mainland and separated from it by a deep lagoon.

barring (băr′ĭng) *prep.* Apart from the occurrence of; excepting: *Barring a last-minute change, we'll be the first to arrive.*

barrio (bä′rē-ō′) *n., pl.* **barrios** **1.** A chiefly Spanish-speaking community or neighborhood in a US city. **2.** A village or district in a Spanish-speaking country.

barrister (băr′ĭ-stər) *n. Chiefly British* A lawyer who argues cases in a court of law.

barroom (băr′rōōm′ *or* băr′rōōm′) *n.* A room or building in which alcoholic beverages are sold at a counter or bar.

barrow¹ (băr′ō) *n.* **1.** A flat rectangular tray or cart with handles at each end, used for carrying loads. **2.** A wheelbarrow.

barrow² (băr′ō) *n.* A large mound of earth or stones placed over a grave in ancient times.

WORD HISTORY Barrow¹ comes from Middle English *barwe,* meaning "large tray." **Barrow²** comes from Old English *beorg,* meaning "hill."

bartender (băr′tĕn′dər) *n.* A person who mixes and serves alcoholic drinks at a bar. —**bar′tend′** *v.*

barter (băr′tər) *v.* **bartered, bartering, barters** —*intr.* To trade goods or services without using money. —*tr.* To trade (goods or services) without using money: *We bartered home-grown vegetables for firewood.* ❖ *n.* The act or practice of bartering. ❖ *adj.* Relating to or being something based on bartering: *a barter economy.*

basal (bā′səl *or* bā′zəl) *adj.* **1.** Located at, relating to, or forming a base: *a plant having a tuft of basal leaves.* **2.** Basic; fundamental; primary: *Most schools use basal readers in the early grades.*

basal metabolism *n.* The amount of energy used by an organism at complete rest.

basalt (bə-sôlt′ *or* bā′sôlt′) *n.* A dark, fine-grained igneous rock consisting mostly of feldspar, iron, and magnesium. Basalt makes up most of the ocean floor and commonly forms when volcanic lava becomes solid.

base¹ (bās) *n.* **1.** The lowest or bottom part: *the base of a cliff.* **2a.** A part or layer on which something rests or is placed for support; a foundation: *a skyscraper built on a base of solid rock.* **b.** A fundamental part: *The theory of evolution forms the base of modern biology.* **3.** A chief ingredient or element of something; a basis: *a paint with an oil base.* **4.** A starting point or central place; a headquarters: *The explorers established a base at the foot of the glacier.* **5.** A center of supplies or operations for a military force: *The army has many bases around the country.* **6a.** A starting point, safety area, or goal in certain games. **b.** In baseball, one of the four corners of the infield that must be touched by a runner to score a run. **7.** The side or face of a geometric figure to which an altitude can be drawn. **8a.** In a number system, the factor by which each place value of a number is multiplied to generate the next place value to the left. For example, 10 is the base of the decimal system and 100 represents $1 \times 10 \times 10$; 1000 represents $1 \times 10 \times 10 \times 10$. Two is the base of the binary system and 100 represents $1 \times 2 \times 2$; 1000 represents $1 \times 2 \times 2 \times 2$. **b.** A number that is raised to an exponent. For example, if $6^2 = 6 \times 6 = 36$, 6 is the base. **c.** The number to which the percent is applied in a percentage problem. In the example *20 percent of 40 is 8,* 40 is the base. **9.** A word or word part to which affixes or other word parts may be added. For example, in *filled, refill,* and *filling, fill* is the base. **10.** Any of a class of chemical compounds that are capable of neutralizing acids in solution and that react with acids and certain metals to form water and salts. Bases turn red litmus paper blue, have a bitter taste, and have a pH of greater than 7. **11.** One of the purines (adenine and guanine) or pyrimidines (cytosine, thymine, and uracil) that are found in DNA or RNA. ❖ *adj.* **1.** Forming or serving as a base: *a base layer of soil.* **2.** Situated at or near the bottom: *a base camp for the mountain climbers.* ❖ *tr.v.* **based, basing, bases** **1.** To find a basis for; establish: *base an opinion on facts.* **2.** To form or provide a base for: *The composer based this song on an old folk melody.* **3.** To locate; station: *The general based the troops in southern Europe.* ◆ **off base** Badly mistaken: *Your criticism of me is off base.*

base² (bās) *adj.* **baser, basest** **1.** Having or showing a lack of decency; mean; contemptible: *a base act.* **2.** Being a metal that is of little value. —**base′ly** *adv.* —**base′ness** *n.*

WORD HISTORY Base¹ comes from Middle English *bas,* which comes from Greek *basis,* both meaning "foundation." **Base²** comes from Middle English *bas,* which comes from Medieval Latin *bassus,* both meaning "low."

baseball (bās′bôl′) *n*. **1.** A game played with a bat and ball on a field with four bases laid out in a diamond pattern. Two teams of nine players take turns at bat and in the field, the members of the team at bat trying to score runs by touching all four bases. **2.** The ball used in this game.

baseboard (bās′bôrd′) *n*. A molding along the lower edge of a wall, where it meets the floor of a room.

base hit *n*. In baseball, a hit by which the batter reaches base safely without an error or a force play being made.

baseless (bās′lĭs) *adj*. Having no basis or foundation in fact; unfounded: *The manufacturers were forced to withdraw the baseless claims for their product.*

baseline or **base line** (bās′līn′) *n*. **1a.** A line serving as a base, as for measurement. **b.** A measurement, calculation, or location used as a basis for comparison: *The latest census figures will provide a baseline for measuring population growth in the next decade.* **2.** In baseball, an area within which a base runner must stay when running between bases. **3.** The boundary line at the back end of each side of a court, as in basketball or tennis.

baseman (bās′mən) *n*. In baseball, a player who plays at or near first, second, or third base.

basement (bās′mənt) *n*. The lowest story of a building, often below ground level.

base on balls *n., pl.* **bases on balls** In baseball, an advance to first base awarded to a batter who takes four pitches that are balls.

base runner *n*. A baseball player on the team at bat who has safely reached or is trying to reach a base.

bases (bā′sēz′) *n*. Plural of **basis**.

bash (băsh) *v*. **bashed, bashing, bashes** —*tr.* **1.** To strike or collide with (something) with a great force: *The car skidded off the road and bashed the fence.* **2.** *Informal* To criticize (a person or thing) harshly: *She's always bashing people who are different from her.* —*intr.* To strike or collide with something with great force: *The bus bashed into the railing.* ❖ *n*. **1.** *Informal* A forceful blow. **2.** *Slang* A party or celebration.

bashful (băsh′fəl) *adj*. Timid and embarrassed with other people; shy: *Some children are bashful around strangers.* —**bash′ful·ly** *adv.* —**bash′ful·ness** *n.*

basic (bā′sĭk) *adj*. **1.** Relating to or forming a base or basis; fundamental: *The basic idea of chess is to checkmate your opponent's king. Philosophy seeks to understand the basic truths of human experience.* **2.** Serving as a starting point; elementary: *a basic course in Chinese; a set of basic woodworking tools.* **3a.** Being or containing a chemical base. **b.** Alkaline. ❖ *n*. often **basics** Something basic or fundamental: *learn the basics of arithmetic before studying algebra.*

BASIC or **Basic** *n*. A simple computer programming language.

basically (bā′sĭ-klē) *adv*. In a basic way; fundamentally; essentially.

basil (băz′əl *or* bā′zəl) *n*. A fragrant plant related to mint, having leaves used as a seasoning.

basilica (bə-sĭl′ĭ-kə) *n*. **1.** A type of ancient Roman building having two rows of columns dividing the interior into a central hall with two side aisles, and an arched semicircular space at one end. **2.** A Christian church built in this design.

basilisk (băs′ə-lĭsk′ *or* băz′ə-lĭsk′) *n*. **1.** A legendary serpent or dragon that could kill with its breath and glance. **2.** Any of various tropical American lizards having a crest on the head and back.

basin (bā′sĭn) *n*. **1.** An open, shallow, usually round container used especially for holding liquids: *soaked our feet in a basin of hot water.* **2.** A sink, as in a bathroom: *Take the plug out of the basin.* **3.** An enclosed part of a river or harbor where the water remains relatively calm and level: *went swimming in the basin at the foot of the falls.* **4.** A geographical region drained by a river and the streams that flow into it: *the Amazon basin.*

basis (bā′sĭs) *n., pl.* **bases** (bā′sēz′) **1.** The foundation for something, such as a plan or idea: *On what basis did you make this decision?* **2.** The main part or basic ingredient: *The basis for most liquids is water.* **3a.** A pattern of behavior or action in time: *The teacher reviews student papers on a weekly basis.* **b.** A condition for relating or proceeding: *We are on a first-name basis.*

bask (băsk) *intr.v.* **basked, basking, basks** **1.** To expose oneself to or enjoy a pleasant warmth: *turtles basking in the sun.* **2.** To take pleasure; live happily: *We basked in the glory of our team's success.*

basket (băs′kĭt) *n*. **1.** A container made of interwoven strips, as of cane, wood, or other plant material. **2.** Something resembling such a container in shape or function: *a wastepaper basket.* **3.** The amount that a basket can hold: *a basket of peaches.* **4a.** A metal hoop from which an open net is hung, used as a goal in basketball. **b.** A score made by throwing the ball through this hoop.

basketball (băs′kĭt-bôl′) *n*. **1.** A game played by two teams of five players in which players try to throw a ball through an elevated basket on the opponent's end of a rectangular court. **2.** The ball used in this game.

basketful (băs′kĭt-fŏŏl′) *n*. The amount that a basket can hold.

basketry (băs′kĭ-trē) *n*. **1.** The craft or process of making baskets, especially by weaving. **2.** Baskets considered as a group.

basketweave or **basket weave** (băs′kĭt-wēv′) *n*. A pattern resembling that of a woven basket.

bas mitzvah (bäs mĭts′və) *n. & v.* Variant of **bat mitzvah**.

Basque (băsk) *n*. **1.** A member of a people who live in the mountains of southwest France and northeast Spain. **2.** The language of the Basques, unrelated to any other known language. —**Basque** *adj.*

bas-relief (bä′rĭ-lēf′) *n*. **1.** A sculptural technique in which figures or letters are raised slightly from a flat background: *The tombstone was carved in bas-relief.* **2.** A sculpture made using this technique.

bass¹ (băs) *n., pl.* **bass** or **basses** Any of several freshwater or saltwater fishes, often having spiny fins, caught for food or sport.

bass² (bās) *n*. **1.** A male singing voice in the lowest range. **2.** A singer who has such a voice. **3.** An instrument whose sound falls within this range. **4.** A part written in this range. **5.** A low-pitched sound or tone.

WORD HISTORY Bass¹ comes from Old English *bærs*, referring to the same kind of fish as in Modern English. **Bass²** comes from Middle English *bas*, meaning "low."

bass clef (bās) *n*. A symbol on a musical staff indicating that the note on the fourth line from the bottom of the staff is F below middle C.

bass drum (bās) *n*. A large cylindrical double-headed drum that makes a deep booming sound when struck.

basset hound (băs′ĭt) *n*. A dog of a breed originally bred for hunting, having a long body, short legs, and long drooping ears.

bassinet (băs′ə-nĕt′ *or* băs′ə-nĕt′) *n.* A bed for a small baby, resembling a basket and sometimes having a hood at one end.

basso (băs′ō *or* bä′sō) *n.*, *pl.* **bassos** or **bassi** (bä′sē) A bass singer, especially in opera.

bassoon (bə-soōn′) *n.* A low-pitched woodwind instrument having a long wooden body connected to a double reed by a U-shaped metal tube. —**bas·soon′ist** *n.*

bass viol (bās) *n.* A double bass.

basswood (băs′woŏd′) *n.* **1.** Any of several North American linden trees, having heart-shaped leaves and clusters of fragrant yellowish flowers. **2.** The soft light wood of such a tree.

bast (băst) *n.* A strong fiber found in the stalks of certain plants, such as flax and hemp, used for making rope, cord, and some textiles.

bastard (băs′tərd) *n.* Used as a disparaging term for a child born to parents who are not married to each other.

baste[1] (băst) *tr.v.* **basted, basting, bastes** To sew with long loose stitches meant to be taken out when the final sewing is done: *baste a hem.*

baste[2] (băst) *tr.v.* **basted, basting, bastes** To moisten (meat) with liquid such as melted fat while roasting.

WORD HISTORY Baste[1] and **baste**[2] come from different Middle English verbs, both spelled *basten* and both having the same meaning as their Modern English counterparts.

Bastille Day (bă-stēl′) *n.* July 14, celebrated as a holiday in France in memory of the invasion by French citizens of the Bastille, a fortress used as a prison, in 1789.

bastinado (băs′tə-nā′dō *or* băs′tə-nä′dō) *n.*, *pl.* **bastinadoes 1.** A beating with a stick or cudgel, especially on the soles of the feet. **2.** A stick or cudgel. ❖ *tr.v.* **bastinadoed, bastinadoing, bastinadoes** To subject to a beating; thrash.

bastion (băs′chən *or* băs′tē-ən) *n.* **1.** A projecting part of a fort or rampart that enables defenders to aim at attackers who have advanced to the foot of a wall. **2.** A strongly protected or well-defended position; a stronghold: *That magazine is a bastion of freedom of speech.*

bat[1] (băt) *n.* **1.** A wooden stick or club, especially one used for hitting a ball, as in baseball or cricket. **2.** A hard hit, such as one delivered with a stick. ❖ *v.* **batted, batting, bats** —*tr.* **1.** To hit, especially with a swinging motion or a bat: *The cat batted the toy mouse around the room.* **2.** In baseball, to have (a certain percentage) as a batting average: *He is batting .276 this season.* —*intr.* **1.** To use a bat: *She's batting well this season.* **2.** To be at bat: *Our team batted first.* ◆ **at bat** Taking one's turn to bat, as in baseball. **go to bat for** To give assistance to; defend: *She went to bat for her friend, who was wrongly accused.* **right off the bat** Without hesitation; immediately: *The children liked the new babysitter right off the bat.*

bat[2] (băt) *n.* Any of various nocturnal flying mammals having thin leathery wings that extend from the forelimbs to the hind legs and tail. Some kinds of bats eat fruit, while others eat insects.

bat[3] (băt) *tr.v.* **batted, batting, bats** To move with a flapping motion; blink: *bat one's eyelashes.* ◆ **not bat an eye** To show no change of expression: *They didn't bat an eye when the firecracker exploded.*

WORD HISTORY Bat[1] comes from Middle English *bat,* meaning "war club." **Bat**[2] comes from Middle English

bakke, referring to the same flying mammal as in Modern English, and is probably of Scandinavian origin. **Bat**[3] probably comes from Old French *batre,* meaning "to beat."

batboy (băt′boi′) *n.* A boy who takes care of a baseball team's bats and equipment.

batch (băch) *n.* **1.** An amount prepared at one time: *baked a batch of cookies; mixed a batch of cement.* **2.** A group or number of similar things: *recycle a batch of old newspapers.* **3.** In computer science, a set of data to be processed in a single run. ❖ *tr.v.* **batched, batching, batches** To assemble or process as a batch: *The author batched all the maps in a section at the back of the book.*

bate (băt) *tr.v.* **bated, bating, bates** To lessen the force or intensity of; moderate. ◆ **with bated breath** In a frightened or excited way, as if holding one's breath: *We waited with bated breath for the judge's decision.*

bateau (bă-tō′) *n.*, *pl.* **bateaux** (bă-tōz′) A light flatbottom boat or rowboat used on rivers and lakes, especially in Canada and Louisiana.

batgirl (băt′gûrl′) *n.* A girl who takes care of a baseball team's bats and equipment.

bath (băth) *n.*, *pl.* **baths** (băth*z* *or* băths) **1a.** The act of washing or soaking the body, as in water or steam: *give the baby a bath.* **b.** The water used for a bath: *run a hot bath.* **2.** A bathtub or bathroom: *an apartment with three rooms and a bath.* **3.** A building equipped for bathing. **4.** often **baths** A resort providing therapeutic baths; a spa. **5.** A liquid in which an object is dipped or soaked in order to process it in some way: *dipped the cloth in a bath of dye.*

bathe (băth) *v.* **bathed, bathing, bathes** —*intr.* **1.** To take a bath: *bathe before breakfast.* **2.** To go into the water for swimming or recreation: *bathe in the surf.* —*tr.* **1.** To wash in water; give a bath to: *bathe the baby.* **2.** To apply a liquid to, as for medicinal purposes: *bathed the wound in disinfectant.* **3.** To make wet; moisten: *Tears bathed the baby's cheeks.* **4.** To seem to wash or pour over; flood: *Moonlight bathed the side of the building.* —**bath′er** *n.*

bathetic (bə-thĕt′ĭk) *adj.* Marked by bathos: *a bathetic passage in a novel.*

bathhouse (băth′hous′) *n.* **1.** A building equipped for bathing. **2.** A building, as at a beach, used by swimmers for changing clothes.

bathing cap (bā′thĭng) *n.* A tight elastic cap worn to keep the hair dry or away from the face while swimming.

bathing suit *n.* A swimsuit.

bathmat (băth′măt′) *n.* A mat for use in a bathtub or on a bathroom floor to absorb water or prevent slipping.

batholith (băth′ə-lĭth′) *n.* A large mass of igneous rock that has melted and flowed into surrounding rock layers deep below the earth's surface.

bathos (bā′thŏs′) *n.* **1.** A sudden change from a dignified or serious style to one that is very commonplace, producing a ridiculous effect. **2a.** Insincere or grossly sentimental pathos. **b.** Banality; triteness.

bathrobe (băth′rōb′) *n.* A loose robe worn before and after bathing and for lounging.

bathroom (băth′roŏm′ *or* băth′roŏm′) *n.* **1.** A room equipped for taking a bath or shower and usually also containing a sink and toilet. **2.** A room containing a toilet and sink.

bathtub (băth′tŭb′) *n.* A tub for bathing, especially one installed in a bathroom.

bathyscaphe (băth′ĭ-skăf′ *or* băth′ĭ-skăf′) also **bathyscaph** (băth′ĭ-skăf′) *n.* A deep-sea research vessel having a large flotation hull and an observation capsule attached to its underside.

bathysphere (băth′ĭ-sfîr′) *n.* A strong spherical chamber in which a crew can be lowered by cable deep into the ocean to make underwater observations.

batik (bə-tēk′ *or* băt′ĭk) *n.* **1.** A method of dyeing a design on cloth by putting removable wax over the parts of the cloth not meant to be dyed. **2.** Cloth dyed by batik. —**ba·tik′** *v.*

batiste (bə-tēst′) *n.* A fine light fabric, usually of cotton or linen.

bat mitzvah (bät mĭts′və) *or* **bas mitzvah** (bäs mĭts′və) *n.* **1.** A ceremony in which a Jewish girl who is 12 or 13 years old is admitted as an adult into the religious community. **2.** A girl for whom such a ceremony is celebrated. ❖ *tr.v.* **bat mitzvahed, bat mitzvahing, bat mitzvahs** or **bas mitzvahed, bas mitzvahing, bas mitzvahs** To recognize (a girl) in such a ceremony.

baton (bə-tŏn′ *or* băt′n) *n.* **1.** A thin tapered stick often used by a conductor in leading a band, chorus, or orchestra. **2.** A stick or staff such as that twirled by a drum major, passed in a relay race, or carried as a symbol of office.

batsman (băts′mən) *n.* A batter in baseball or cricket.

battalion (bə-tăl′yən) *n.* **1.** A large group of soldiers organized as a unit, usually consisting of a headquarters and two or more companies of infantry or artillery. **2.** A large number: *a battalion of ants.*

batten[1] (băt′n) *intr.v.* **battened, battening, battens** **1.** To feed and grow fat. **2.** To thrive and prosper, often at another's expense: *politicians battening on a corrupt system.*

batten[2] (băt′n) *n.* A narrow strip of wood or plastic, such as one used on a boat or ship to fasten a covering over a hatch or to stiffen the edge of a sail. ❖ *tr.v.* **battened, battening, battens** To furnish, fasten, or secure with such strips: *batten down the hatch before the storm.* ◆ **batten down the hatches** To prepare for an approaching disaster or emergency.

WORD HISTORY Batten[1] comes from Old Norse *batna*, meaning "to improve." **Batten**[2] comes from Old French *batant*, meaning "wooden strip, clapper."

batter[1] (băt′ər) *v.* **battered, battering, batters** —*tr.* **1.** To strike or hit forcefully and repeatedly: *Heavy wind and rain battered the windows.* **2.** To injure or damage by rough treatment or hard wear: *The dented old car was badly battered.* **3.** To subject to repeated beatings or physical abuse. —*intr.* To hit forcefully and repeatedly; pound: *Waves battered against the pier.*

batter[2] (băt′ər) *n.* The player at bat in baseball or cricket.

batter[3] (băt′ər) *n.* A beaten mixture, as of flour, milk, and eggs, used in cooking: *a bowl of cake batter.* ❖ *tr.v.* **battered, battering, batters** To coat in batter: *battered the chicken before frying it.*

WORD HISTORY Batter[1] comes from Middle English *bateren*, meaning "to beat." **Batter**[2] comes from Modern English verb *bat* and the Modern English prefix *-er.* **Batter**[3] comes from Middle English *bature*, meaning "ingredients mixed together."

battering ram (băt′ər-ĭng) *n.* **1.** A heavy wooden beam used in ancient and medieval warfare to batter down walls and gates. **2.** A heavy metal bar used by firefighters and law enforcement officers to break down walls and doors.

battery (băt′ə-rē) *n., pl.* **batteries** **1a.** Two or more con- nected electric cells that supply a direct current by converting chemical energy to electrical energy. **b.** A small dry cell designed to power a flashlight or other portable electric device. **2a.** A group or set of large guns, as of artillery: *The fort had a battery of cannons.* **b.** A place where such guns are set up: *the old battery at the end of Manhattan Island.* **c.** A unit of soldiers in the artillery, corresponding to a company in the infantry. **3.** A group of things or people used or doing something together: *The celebrities faced a battery of cameras and reporters.* **4.** In baseball, the pitcher and catcher. **5.** The unlawful touching or beating of another person, with the intention of doing harm.

batting (băt′ĭng) *n.* Cotton or wool fibers wadded into rolls or sheets, used to stuff mattresses or furniture or to line quilts.

batting average *n.* A measure of a baseball batter's performance obtained by dividing the number of base hits by the number of times at bat, not including walks.

battle (băt′l) *n.* **1.** A fight between two armed forces, usually on a large scale. **2.** Armed fighting; combat: *wounded in battle.* **3.** A struggle or sharp conflict: *a political battle; a battle of wits.* ❖ *v.* **battled, battling, battles** —*intr.* To fight in or as if in battle; struggle: *The firefighters battled bravely against the flames.* —*tr.* To fight against: *The sailors battled the storm for hours.* —**bat′tler** *n.*

battle-axe *or* **battle-ax** (băt′l-ăks′) *n.* A heavy axe with a broad head, used formerly as a weapon.

battle cry *n.* **1.** A shout to spur on fighting, uttered by troops in battle. **2.** A slogan used by the supporters of a cause: *The campaign's battle cry was "Lower Taxes."*

battledore (băt′l-dôr′) *n.* **1.** An early form of badminton played with a flat wooden paddle and a shuttlecock. **2.** The paddle used in this game.

battlefield (băt′l-fēld′) *n.* A field or area where a battle is or was fought: *the Civil War battlefield at Gettysburg.*

battlefront (băt′l-frŭnt′) *n.* The line or area in which armed forces engage opponents in battle.

battleground (băt′l-ground′) *n.* A battlefield.

battlement (băt′l-mənt) *n.* A top part of a wall, especially on a castle or fortress, having notched openings through which soldiers defend the structure against attack.

battle royal *n., pl.* **battles royal** **1.** A battle in which many people take part. **2.** A bitter or intense quarrel: *a battle royal over spending for public works.*

battleship (băt′l-shĭp′) *n.* Any of a class of warships of largest size, having the heaviest guns and armor.

batty (băt′ē) *adj.* **battier, battiest** *Slang* Crazy or eccentric: *My uncle is kind of batty.*

bauble (bô′bəl) *n.* A showy ornament or trinket of little value.

baud (bôd) *n.* A unit of speed in data transmission equal to one change in a carrier signal per second.

Bauhaus (bou′hous′) *n.* A 20th-century school of design influenced by techniques and materials employed especially in industrial fabrication and manufacture.

bauxite (bôk′sīt′) *n.* A mixture of minerals, often resembling clay, that is the principal ore of aluminum.

bawdy (bô′dē) *adj.* **bawdier, bawdiest** Humorously coarse; ribald: *bawdy jokes.* —**bawd′i·ly** *adv.* —**bawd′-i·ness** *n.*

bawl (bôl) *v.* **bawled, bawling, bawls** —*intr.* **1.** To cry or weep loudly; wail: *The unhappy baby kicked and bawled.* **2.** To cry out loudly; shout: *I could hear the coach bawling from the sidelines.* —*tr.* To utter or call in a loud strong voice: *The sentry bawled an order to halt.* ◆ **bawl out** *Informal* To scold loudly or harshly.

bay¹ (bā) *n.* A body of water partially enclosed by land but having a wide outlet to the sea. A bay is usually smaller than a gulf and larger than a cove.

bay² (bā) *n.* **1.** A part of a building divided by vertical supports such as columns or pillars: *an arcade with ten bays.* **2.** A bay window. **3.** A section or compartment, as of a building or aircraft, set off for a specific purpose: *The cargo was stored in a loading bay.* **4.** A sickbay.

bay³ (bā) *adj.* Reddish-brown: *a bay horse.* ❖ *n.* **1.** A reddish brown. **2.** A reddish-brown horse with a black mane.

bay⁴ (bā) *n.* **1.** A deep, prolonged bark, such as the sound made by a hound. **2.** A position of or like that of an animal cornered and facing its pursuers: *The barking hounds kept the stag at bay. The policeman chased the dog and brought it to bay.* **3.** The position of being kept at a distance: *Lights around the factory kept intruders at bay.* ❖ *intr.v.* **bayed, baying, bays** To make deep, prolonged barks.

bay⁵ (bā) *n.* **1.** An evergreen tree of the Mediterranean region having glossy fragrant leaves that are used as a flavoring in cooking. **2.** Any of certain other trees or shrubs having fragrant leaves.

WORD HISTORY Bay¹ comes from Middle English *bai,* which comes from Old French *baie,* both meaning "a body of water partially enclosed by land." **Bay²** comes from Middle English *bai,* meaning "a compartment," which comes from Old French *baee,* meaning "an opening." **Bay³** comes from Middle English *bai,* which comes from Latin *badius,* both meaning "reddish-brown." **Bay⁴** comes from Middle English *abai,* meaning "cornering a hunted animal," which comes from Old French *abaiier,* meaning "to bark." **Bay⁵** comes from Middle English *bai,* which comes from Latin *bāca,* both meaning "berry."

bayberry (bā′běr′ē) *n.* **1.** The gray, waxy, aromatic berries of a North American shrub, used to make candles. **2.** The shrub that bears such berries.

bay leaf *n.* The dried leaf of the bay, used as a flavoring in cooking.

bayonet (bā′ə-nĕt′ *or* bā′ə-nĭt) *n.* A knife attached to the muzzle of a rifle for use in close combat. ❖ *tr.v.* **bayoneted, bayoneting, bayonets** *or* **bayonetted, bayonetting, bayonets** To stab or prod with a bayonet.

bayou (bī′ōō *or* bī′ō) *n.* A sluggish marshy stream connected with a river, lake, or gulf, common in the southern United States.

bay rum *n.* A fragrant lotion made from the leaves of a tropical American tree.

bay window *n.* A window or group of windows projecting from the outer wall of a building and forming an alcove within.

bazaar (bə-zär′) *n.* **1.** A market, usually consisting of a street lined with shops and stalls, especially in the Middle East. **2.** A store where various kinds of things are sold. **3.** A fair or sale, often to raise money for a charity: *a hospital bazaar.*

bazooka (bə-zōō′kə) *n.* A portable military weapon consisting of a tube from which antitank rockets are launched.

BB¹ (bē′bē) *n.* A metal pellet measuring ⁷⁄₄₀ of an inch (0.44 centimeter) in diameter, used in air rifles. BB is short for *ball bearing.*

BB² An abbreviation of base on balls.

BBC An abbreviation of British Broadcasting Corporation.

BB gun *n.* A small air rifle that shoots BBs.

BC An abbreviation of: **1.** *or* BC before Christ (in a specified year before the birth of Jesus). **2.** British Columbia.

BCE *or* BCE An abbreviation of before Common Era. —SEE NOTE AT **Common Era.**

B cell *n.* Any of the lymphocytes that mature in the bone marrow and are involved in the formation of antibodies.

B complex *n.* Vitamin B complex.

be (bē) *v. Present tense first person singular* **am** (ăm), *second person singular* **are** (är), *third person singular* **is** (ĭz), *plural* **are,** *present participle* **being** (bē′ĭng). *Past tense first and third person singular* **was** (wŭz *or* wŏz), *second person singular* **were** (wûr), *plural* **were,** *past participle* **been** (bĭn). —*intr.* **1.** To exist; have life or reality: *There are no longer any dinosaurs.* **2.** To occupy a position: *The food is on the table.* **3.** To take place; occur: *When is the party?* **4.** To come or go: *Have you ever been to Alaska?* **5a.** To equal to identity or meaning: *That experiment was a complete success.* **b.** To signify or stand for: *A is excellent; C is passing.* **c.** To belong to a specified class or group: *Snakes are reptiles.* **d.** To have or show a specified quality or characteristic: *Skyscrapers are tall.* **6.** To belong; befall: *Woe is me.* —*aux.* **1.** Used to form the passive voice in combination with the past participle of transitive verbs: *Elections are held once a year.* **2.** Used to express a continuing action in combination with the present participle of a verb: *We are working to improve housing conditions.* **3.** Used to indicate duty, possibility, or a future event with the infinitive of another verb: *I am to inform you that the package has arrived. How am I to know the answer? They are to be married Monday.*

be– A prefix that means: **1.** Completely; thoroughly: *bemoan.* **2.** On; around; over: *bespatter.* **3.** Make; cause to become: *becloud.* **4.** About; to: *bespeak.* **5.** Affect or provide with: *befriend.*

beach (bēch) *n.* The area of accumulated sand, stone, or gravel deposited above the water line at a shore by the action of waves. ❖ *tr.v.* **beached, beaching, beaches** To haul or run ashore: *We beached our canoes on a sandbar. The whale beached itself in shallow water.*

beach ball *n.* A large ball that can be inflated and used for games, especially at a beach or swimming pool.

beachcomber (bēch′kō′mər) *n.* **1.** A person who scavenges along beaches or in wharf areas. **2.** A seaside vacationer. —**beach′comb′** (bēch′kōm′) *v.*

beachfront (bēch′frŭnt′) *adj.* Located at or on a strip of land facing or running along a beach: *beachfront hotels.*

beachhead (bēch′hĕd′) *n.* A military position on an enemy shoreline captured by advance troops of an invading force.

beacon (bē′kən) *n.* **1.** A guiding or warning signal, such as a lighthouse located on a coast. **2.** A radio transmitter that sends a guidance signal for aircraft. **3.** A source of guidance or inspiration: *Her achievements were a beacon to others.*

bead (bēd) *n.* **1.** A small, often round piece of glass, wood, plastic, or other material that is pierced for placing on a string or wire. **2. beads** A necklace of beads on a string. **3. beads** A rosary. **4.** A small round object, such as a drop of moisture: *beads of sweat on one's forehead.* **5.** A small knob of metal located at the muzzle of a rifle or pistol and used in taking aim. ❖ *tr. & intr.v.* **beaded, beading,**

beads To furnish with or collect into beads: *bead the collar around a sweater; water beading on the soda can.*

beading (bē′dĭng) *n.* Ornamentation using beads; beadwork: *moccasins with colorful beading on top.*

beadle (bēd′l) *n.* A minor official in an English church, whose duties include keeping order and ushering during services.

beadwork (bēd′wûrk′) *n.* Decorative work in beads.

beady (bē′dē) *adj.* **beadier, beadiest** Small, round, and shining: *beady eyes.*

beagle (bē′gəl) *n.* A small hound of a breed having drooping ears and a smooth coat with white, black, and tan markings.

beak (bēk) *n.* **1.** A bird's bill, especially a strong curved one such as that of a hawk. **2.** A similar part in other animals, such as turtles and octopuses. **3.** A projecting part that resembles a bird's beak. —**beaked** (bēkt) *adj.*

beaker (bē′kər) *n.* **1.** A cylindrical glass container with a pouring lip, used especially in laboratories. **2.** A large drinking cup with a wide mouth.

beam (bēm) *n.* **1.** A long rigid piece of wood or metal used especially as a horizontal support in construction. **2.** One of the main horizontal supports of a building or ship. **3.** The width of a ship at its widest part. **4.** In a balance, the bar from which the weights are hung. **5.** A stream of particles or waves, as of light, sound, or other radiation: *the beam of a flashlight; a laser beam.* **6.** A radio beam used to help ships or aircraft navigate. ❖ *v.* **beamed, beaming, beams** —*intr.* **1.** To give off light; shine: *The sun is beaming in the sky.* **2.** To smile broadly: *His face beamed with delight.* —*tr.* To emit or transmit: *beam a TV program to Europe by satellite.*

beaming (bē′mĭng) *adj.* **1.** Shining; bright: *the beaming sun.* **2.** Smiling broadly; cheery; joyful: *a beaming face.*

bean (bēn) *n.* **1a.** Any of various plants related to the pea, having seeds in pods that are usually long and narrow. **b.** The edible seed or pod of such a plant. **2.** A seed or pod similar to a bean: *a coffee bean; a vanilla bean.* **3.** *Slang* A person's head: *got hit on the bean with a snowball.* ❖ *tr.v.* **beaned, beaning, beans** *Slang* To hit (a person) on the head with a thrown object, especially a pitched baseball. ◆ **full of beans** Energetic; lively: *The children were too full of beans to sit still.* **spill the beans** To disclose a secret.

beanbag (bēn′băg′) *n.* **1.** A small bag filled with pellets or dried beans and used as a toy for throwing in games. **2.** A large bag filled with pellets or dried beans and used as a chair or other piece of furniture.

bean ball *n.* In baseball, a pitch aimed at the batter's head.

bean curd *n.* Tofu.

beanie (bē′nē) *n.* A small brimless cap.

bean sprouts *pl.n.* The tender shoots of certain bean plants, used as food.

beanstalk (bēn′stôk′) *n.* The stem of a bean plant.

bear¹ (bâr) *v.* **bore** (bôr), **borne** (bôrn) or **born** (bôrn), **bearing, bears** —*tr.* **1.** To carry on one's person from one place to another: *He bore the heavy suitcase from the car into the house.* **2.** To move while containing or supporting (something); convey or transport: *a train bearing grain.* **3.** To have in the heart or mind: *bear a grudge.* **4.** To have as a visible characteristic; show: *buildings bearing the scars of time; twins bearing a strong resemblance to each other.* **5.** To carry (oneself) in a specified way: *Members of both teams bore themselves with pride.* **6.** To hold up; support: *a floor able to bear the weight of heavy machinery.* **7.** To be accountable for; assume: *We*

all shared in bearing the blame for our actions. **8.** To put up with; endure: *I can't bear his smug attitude.* **9.** To call for; warrant: *This case bears investigation.* **10.** To bring forth; produce: *Some trees bear fruit early in the spring. My savings account bears interest.* **11.** To give birth to: *The woman bore three children.* **12.** To give or offer; provide: *bear witness in a written statement.* —*intr.* **1.** To yield fruit; produce: *fruit trees that bear well.* **2.** To have influence or relevance; apply: *The police brought pressure to bear upon the accused. Your remark does not bear upon the problem.* **3.** To extend, turn, or be turned in a given direction: *After the bridge, the road bears to the left. At the corner, bear right. The cannons were brought to bear on the pirate ship.* ◆ **bear down 1.** To exert pressure; press down: *Concern about water bears down heavily in times of drought.* **2.** To exert oneself; make a special effort: *By bearing down, the staff was able to complete the job on time.* **bear down on 1.** To affect in a harmful way: *The large amount of work was bearing down on the entire staff.* **2.** To move toward or approach rapidly: *The runners bore down on the finish line.* **bear in mind** To hold in one's mind; remember: *Bear in mind that it might rain.* **bear out** To prove right; confirm: *The test results bear out our theory.* **bear up** To withstand difficulty or stress: *The patient bore up well during a long illness.* **bear with** To be patient or indulgent with: *Please bear with me while I find out where to go.*

bear² (bâr) *n.* **1.** Any of various large mammals having a shaggy coat, a very short tail, and a flat-footed walk. Bears usually eat both plants and animals, such as insects and small rodents. **2.** A large clumsy person. **3.** *Slang* Something that is difficult or unpleasant: *That exam was a bear!* **4.** A person who sells stocks or other securities expecting their price to fall. ❖ *adj.* Characterized by falling prices: *a bear market in stocks.*

WORD HISTORY Bear¹ comes from Old English *beran,* meaning "to carry." **Bear²** comes from Old English *bera,* referring to the same animal as in Modern English.

---

bearable (bâr′ə-bəl) *adj.* Capable of being borne; tolerable: *Resting from time to time made the long hike bearable.* —**bear′a·bly** *adv.*

beard (bîrd) *n.* **1.** A growth of hair on a man's chin, cheeks, and throat. **2.** A tuft or growth of hairs, bristles, or other hairlike threads on a plant or animal.

bearer (bâr′ər) *n.* **1.** A person who carries or supports something: *a stretcher bearer; a message bearer.* **2.** A person who holds or presents a check, money order, bond, or other note for payment: *Checks direct a bank to pay the bearer a certain sum of money.*

bearing (bâr′ĭng) *n.* **1.** The manner or way in which one carries oneself: *The judge has a dignified bearing.* **2.** Relevance or relationship: *That issue has no bearing on my situation.* **3.** A supporting part of a structure. **4.** A mechanical part that supports a moving part, especially a turning shaft, and allows it to move with little friction: *a wheel bearing.* **5.** Direction, especially angular direction as used in navigation: *The ship took a bearing on the lighthouse.* **6.** often **bearings** The knowledge of one's position in relation to one's surroundings: *The hikers lost their bearings in the dark.*

bearish (bâr′ĭsh) *adj.* **1.** Rough, clumsy, or rude. **2.** Expecting or characterized by falling prices: *a bearish outlook on the bond market.* —**bear′ish·ly** *adv.*

bearskin (bâr′skĭn′) *n.* **1.** The skin of a bear. **2.** A rug made from the skin of a bear. **3.** A tall military hat made of black fur.

beast (bēst) *n.* **1.** An animal other than a human, especially a large four-footed animal: *the beasts of the forest.* **2.** A cruel or brutal person.

beastly (bēst′lē) *adj.* **beastlier, beastliest 1.** Wicked or offensive: *beastly behavior.* **2.** Unpleasant; disagreeable: *a beastly drive through heavy rain.* ❖ *adv.* Chiefly British To an extreme degree; very: *a beastly hot day.* —**beast′·li·ness** *n.*

beast of burden *n., pl.* **beasts of burden** An animal, such as a horse, ox, or camel, used to carry loads or pull vehicles.

beat (bēt) *v.* **beat, beaten** (bēt′n) or **beat, beating, beats** —*tr.* **1.** To strike or hit repeatedly: *The baby beat the table with a spoon.* **2.** To punish or abuse by striking; batter. **3a.** To produce sound by striking, hitting, or tapping (something) repeatedly: *beat a drum.* **b.** To mark or count (a rhythm or pulse) by tapping, moving, or striking, as with a part of the body: *beat time with one's foot.* **4.** To shape or break by pounding: *Ancient artisans beat copper into spearheads.* **5.** To flap repeatedly: *Hummingbirds beat their wings very fast.* **6.** To mix rapidly with a utensil: *beat egg whites.* **7a.** To defeat or overcome, as in a contest or battle. **b.** To surpass or be superior to: *Riding a bike beats walking.* **c.** To force to retreat; drive away: *The soldiers beat back the enemy.* **8.** To act ahead of or arrive before: *We beat you to the restaurant.* **9.** To forge or make by treading over: *The children beat a path to the pond.* **10.** *Slang* To baffle or perplex: *How the magician did that trick beats me.* **11.** *Informal* To avoid or counter the effects of: *Let's leave early to beat the traffic.* —*intr.* **1.** To pound forcefully and repeatedly; dash: *Huge waves beat against the pier.* **2.** To fall in torrents: *The rain beat down on the field.* **3.** To shine or glare intensely: *The summer sun beat down on the thirsty bikers.* **4.** To make a sound when struck: *The drums beat loudly.* **5.** To throb; pulsate: *My heart beat faster with excitement.* **6.** To sail against the wind by tacking in a zigzag course. ❖ *n.* **1.** A stroke or blow, especially one that makes a sound: *the beat of the drums.* **2.** A pulsation or throb: *the beat of your heart.* **3a.** One of the succession of units that make up meter in music: *There are four beats in this measure.* **b.** A gesture with the hand, foot, or a baton that marks one of these units. **4.** An area regularly covered by a police officer, guard, or reporter: *The police officer patrolled her beat on a bicycle. The new reporter was given the arts beat.* ❖ *adj.* **1.** *Informal* Tired; worn-out: *I'm really beat after a full day's work.* **2.** Relating to the beatniks of the 1950s and 1960s. ◆ **beat around the bush** To avoid a subject; delay in coming to the point. **beat it** *Slang* To leave hurriedly.

beaten (bēt′n) *adj.* **1.** Thinned or formed by hammering: *a beaten copper bracelet.* **2.** Much traveled: *beaten paths.*

beater (bē′tər) *n.* **1.** A person or thing that beats, especially an instrument for beating: *Use an electric beater to mix bread dough.* **2.** A person who drives wild game from under cover in a hunt.

beatific (bē′ə-tĭf′ĭk) *adj.* Showing extreme happiness; joyful: *a beatific smile.* —**be′a·tif′i·cal·ly** *adv.*

beatify (bē-ăt′ə-fī′) *tr.v.* **beatified, beatifying, beatifies** In the Roman Catholic Church, to declare (a deceased person) to be blessed and worthy of public veneration.

beating (bē′tĭng) *n.* **1.** An act of repeated hitting or striking. **2.** An instance of rough or injurious treatment: *The car took a beating on the rough back roads.* **3.** A defeat: *The defending champions gave our team a beating.* **4.** A throbbing or pulsation, as of the heart.

beatitude (bē-ăt′ĭ-tōod′) *n.* **1.** Supreme blessedness. **2. Beatitude** In Christianity, any of the declarations made by Jesus in the Sermon on the Mount, beginning with the words "Blessed are."

beatnik (bēt′nĭk) *n.* A person who breaks convention in behavior, political opinions, and often style of dress, especially a member of a defiantly unconventional literary movement in the 1950s and early 1960s.

beat-up (bēt′ŭp′) *adj. Slang* In bad condition; rundown: *a beat-up old car.*

beau (bō) *n., pl.* **beaus** or **beaux** (bōz) **1.** The boyfriend of a woman or girl. **2.** A dandy; a fop.

Beaufort scale (bō′fərt) *n.* A scale of wind velocities ranging from 0 (calm) to 12 (hurricane).

beauteous (byōo′tē-əs) *adj.* Beautiful. —**beau′te·ous·ly** *adv.* —**beau′te·ous·ness** *n.*

beautician (byōo-tĭsh′ən) *n.* A person who is skilled in the cosmetic services offered by a beauty parlor.

beautiful (byōo′tə-fəl) *adj.* **1.** Showing or having beauty; pleasing to the senses or the mind: *beautiful scenery; beautiful music.* **2.** Excellent; wonderful: *made a beautiful jump shot to win the game.* —**beau′ti·ful·ly** *adv.* —**beau′ti·ful·ness** *n.*

beautify (byōo′tə-fī′) *tr.v.* **beautified, beautifying, beautifies** To make beautiful: *Green parks and wide boulevards help to beautify the city.* —**beau′ti·fi·ca′tion** (byōo′tə-fĭ-kā′shən) *n.* —**beau′ti·fi′er** *n.*

beauty (byōo′tē) *n., pl.* **beauties 1.** A pleasing quality, especially with regard to form, that delights the senses and appeals to the mind: *the beauty of the snowcapped mountains.* **2.** A person or thing that is beautiful: *Helen of Troy was a great beauty.* **3.** A feature that is most gratifying or effective: *The beauty of this scheme is that we come out ahead either way.*

beauty contest *n.* **1.** A contest in which a number of people, typically women, are judged with regard to their physical beauty and often their talents. **2.** A competition or comparison based mostly on superficial factors: *The election proved to be little more than a beauty contest.*

beauty parlor *n.* A beauty salon.

beauty salon *n.* A business offering hair styling, manicures, facial treatments, and other cosmetic services, especially for women.

beauty shop *n.* A beauty salon.

beaux (bōz) *n.* A plural of **beau.**

beaux arts (bō-zär′ or bō-zärt′) *pl.n.* The fine arts.

beaver¹ (bē′vər) *n.* **1a.** Either of two rodents of North America or Eurasia having thick fur, a flat broad tail, and large strong front teeth. Beavers live in and near lakes and streams and gnaw down trees to build dams and underwater lodges. **b.** The fur of a beaver. **2.** A hat made of beaver fur.

beaver² (bē′vər) *n.* **1.** A piece of armor attached to a helmet or breastplate to protect the throat or lower face. **2.** The visor on a helmet.

WORD HISTORY Beaver¹ comes from Middle English *bever,* which comes from Old English *beofor,* both referring to the same animal as in Modern English. **Beaver²** comes from Middle English *bavier* (referring to the same piece of armor as in Modern English), which comes from Old French *baviere,* meaning "child's bib."

beaverboard (bē′vər-bôrd′) *n.* A light building material of compressed wood pulp, used for walls, partitions, and bulletin boards.

bebop (bē′bŏp′) *n.* A style of jazz that developed in the 1940s and 1950s and is characterized by complex rhythms and harmonies and by improvised solo performances.

becalmed (bĭ-kämd′) *adj.* Motionless for lack of wind: *The becalmed sailboat waited for a breeze.*

became (bĭ-kām′) *v.* Past tense of **become.**

because (bĭ-kôz′ *or* bĭ-kŭz′) *conj.* For the reason that; since: *The room is uncomfortable because it is too hot.*

because of *prep.* On account of; by reason of: *I stayed home because of illness.*

beck (bĕk) *n.* A gesture of beckoning. ◆ **at (someone's) beck and call** Willingly obedient; ready to perform a service: *The staff of the hotel are generally at the beck and call of the guests.*

beckon (bĕk′ən) *v.* **beckoned, beckoning, beckons** —*tr.* **1.** To signal (a person) to come, as by nodding or waving: *The manager beckoned us to her office.* **2.** To attract because of an inviting appearance: *The lake beckoned me to dive in and cool off.* —*intr.* **1.** To signal to come: *The guide beckoned at the mouth of the cave.* **2.** To attract or entice: *Adventure beckoned down every road.*

becloud (bĭ-kloud′) *tr.v.* **beclouded, beclouding, beclouds** To darken with or as if with clouds; obscure: *The debate was beclouded by passionate emotions.*

become (bĭ-kŭm′) *v.* **became** (bĭ-kām′), **become, becoming, becomes** —*intr.* To grow or come to be: *As winter approaches the temperature becomes colder.* —*tr.* **1.** To be appropriate or suitable to: *It becomes a judge to act with dignity.* **2.** To look good with or cause to look good on: *The new coat becomes you.* ◆ **become of** To be the fate of; happen to: *What ever became of your friend that moved away?*

becoming (bĭ-kŭm′ĭng) *adj.* **1.** Pleasing or attractive to look at: *His suit is very becoming. That outfit is very becoming on you.* **2.** Appropriate; suitable: *"Please conduct yourselves in a manner becoming to your age," he said.* —**be·com′ing·ly** *adv.*

becquerel (bĕ-krĕl′ *or* bĕk′ə-rĕl′) *n.* A unit for measuring radioactivity, equal to the decay of one atomic nucleus per second.

bed (bĕd) *n.* **1a.** A piece of furniture for resting and sleeping, consisting usually of a flat rectangular frame and a mattress resting on springs. **b.** A mattress: *a feather bed.* **c.** A mattress and bedclothes: *make up a bed on the floor.* **2.** A place where one may sleep; lodging: *I have a bed for the night at the inn.* **3.** The time at which one goes to sleep: *I drank a glass of water before bed.* **4a.** A small plot for cultivating or growing things: *a bed of flowers.* **b.** A similar plot on the bottom of a body of water: *an oyster bed.* **5.** The bottom of a body of water: *a stream bed.* **6.** A supporting, underlying, or securing part: *Underneath the brick path is a bed of sand.* **7.** The part of a truck, trailer, or railroad car designed to carry loads. **8.** A layer of sediments or rock that extends under a large area and has other layers below: *a bed of coal.* ◆ *tr.v.* **bedded, bedding, beds 1.** To provide with a bed or sleeping quarters: *We bedded the guests in the living room.* **2.** To set or plant in a bed of soil: *bed tulip bulbs before the ground freezes.*

bed and breakfast *n.* A private residence that offers overnight lodging and breakfast as part of the charge.

bedaub (bĭ-dôb′) *tr.v.* **bedaubed, bedaubing, bedaubs** To smear; soil: *The chimney sweep was bedaubed with soot.*

bedazzle (bĭ-dăz′əl) *tr.v.* **bedazzled, bedazzling, bedazzles** To dazzle completely: *The magician bedazzled the audience with tricks.*

bedbug (bĕd′bŭg′) *n.* A small wingless insect with a flat reddish body that lives in dwellings and bedding and bites humans to feed on their blood.

bedchamber (bĕd′chăm′bər) *n.* A bedroom.

bedclothes (bĕd′klōz′ *or* bĕd′klōthz′) *pl.n.* Coverings, such as sheets and blankets, used on a bed.

bedding (bĕd′ĭng) *n.* **1.** Sheets, blankets, and mattresses for beds. **2.** Material, such as straw or hay, for animals to sleep on. **3.** A foundation or bottom layer: *a bedding of gravel supporting the road.* **4.** The way in which layers of sedimentary rock are arranged.

bedeck (bĭ-dĕk′) *tr.v.* **bedecked, bedecking, bedecks** To cover with decorations; adorn: *a hero bedecked with medals.*

bedevil (bĭ-dĕv′əl) *tr.v.* **bedeviled, bedeviling, bedevils** *or* **bedevilled, bedevilling, bedevils 1.** To plague; trouble; harass: *The project was bedeviled with accidents and injuries.* **2.** To possess with or as if with a devil; bewitch. —**be·dev′il·ment** *n.*

bedew (bĭ-dōō′) *tr.v.* **bedewed, bedewing, bedews** To wet with or as if with dew: *cheeks bedewed with tears.*

bedfellow (bĕd′fĕl′ō) *n.* **1.** A person with whom one shares a bed. **2.** An associate or ally: *The opponents made strange bedfellows in their efforts to secure the agreement.*

bedizen (bĭ-dī′zən *or* bĭ-dĭz′ən) *tr.v.* **bedizened, bedizening, bedizens** To ornament or dress in a showy or gaudy manner.

bedlam (bĕd′ləm) *n.* **1.** A place or situation of confusion, disorder, or noisy uproar: *the bedlam of a one-day sale in the department store.* **2.** *Archaic* A place where people with mental illness were once forced to stay.

Bedouin (bĕd′ōō-ĭn *or* bĕd′wĭn) *n., pl.* **Bedouin** *or* **Bedouins** An Arab belonging to any of the nomadic tribes of the Arabian, Syrian, or Sahara Deserts.

bedpan (bĕd′păn′) *n.* A container used as a toilet by a bedridden person.

bedpost (bĕd′pōst′) *n.* An upright post at the corner of a bed.

bedraggled (bĭ-drăg′əld) *adj.* **1.** Wet, drenched, or messy: *bedraggled clothes.* **2.** Run-down; deteriorated: *the bedraggled condition of the old buildings.*

bedridden (bĕd′rĭd′n) *adj.* Confined to bed because of sickness or weakness.

bedrock (bĕd′rŏk′) *n.* **1.** The solid rock that lies beneath the soil and other loose material on the surface of the earth. **2.** The basis or foundation: *A free press is the bedrock of democracy.*

bedroll (bĕd′rōl′) *n.* Blankets or a sleeping bag rolled up to be carried by a camper or a person who sleeps outdoors.

bedroom (bĕd′rōōm′ *or* bĕd′rŏŏm′) *n.* A room in which to sleep.

bedside (bĕd′sīd′) *n.* The side of a bed or the space alongside a bed: *The nurse stood at the patient's bedside.* ◆ *adj.* Near the side of a bed: *a bedside table; a bedside conversation.*

bedside manner *n.* The attitude and conduct of a physician in the presence of a patient.

bedsore (bĕd′sôr′) *n.* An ulcer of the skin caused by pressure, occurring in people who are bedridden for long periods.

bedspread (bĕd′sprĕd′) *n.* A covering for a bed.

bedspring (bĕd′sprĭng′) *n.* One of the springs supporting the mattress of a bed.

bedstead (bĕd′stĕd′) *n.* The frame supporting the springs and mattress of a bed.

bedtime (bĕd′tīm′) *n.* The time when a person usually goes to bed.

bee (bē) *n.* **1.** Any of numerous winged, often stinging insects that have a hairy body and gather pollen and nectar from flowers. Some bees, such as the honeybee, live in colonies. **2.** A gathering where people work together or compete against one another: *a quilting bee; a spelling bee.* ◆ **a bee in (one's) bonnet** An idea or plan that persistently occupies one's mind; a notion: *Once he has a bee in his bonnet about something, there's no stopping him.*

beech (bēch) *n.* **1.** Any of several trees having smooth gray bark, small edible nuts, and strong heavy wood. **2.** The wood of such a tree.

beechnut (bēch′nŭt′) *n.* The edible nut of a beech tree, encased in a prickly husk.

beef (bēf) *n., pl.* **beeves** (bēvz) or **beef 1a.** The flesh of a full-grown steer, bull, ox, or cow, used as meat. **b.** An animal raised to produce such meat. **2.** *Informal* Human muscle; brawn: *football players with plenty of beef.* **3.** *pl.* **beefs** *Slang* A complaint: *has a beef against the administration.* ❖ *intr.v.* **beefed, beefing, beefs** *Slang* To complain: *What are you beefing about now?* ◆ **beef up** *Informal* To make greater or stronger: *beef up efforts to combat crime.*

beefsteak (bēf′stāk′) *n.* A slice of beef suitable for broiling or frying.

beefy (bē′fē) *adj.* **beefier, beefiest** Heavy, strong, and muscular; brawny: *a beefy wrestler.* —**beef′i·ness** *n.*

beehive (bē′hīv′) *n.* **1.** A hive for bees. **2.** A very busy place: *The bus terminal is always a beehive of activity.* **3.** A woman's hairstyle in which the hair is arranged in a tall, rounded peak on top of the head.

beekeeper (bē′kē′pər) *n.* A person who cares for and raises bees for commercial or agricultural purposes.

beeline (bē′līn′) *n.* The fastest and most direct course, as one that might be taken by a bee going to its hive: *At noontime everybody made a beeline for the lunchroom.*

Beelzebub (bē-ĕl′zə-bŭb′) *n.* The Devil.

been (bĭn) *v.* Past participle of **be.**

beep (bēp) *n.* A short sound, as from an automobile's horn or a radio transmitter. ❖ *v.* **beeped, beeping, beeps** —*intr.* To make a beep: *The transmitter beeped steadily.* —*tr.* **1.** To cause to make a beep: *The drivers stuck in traffic beeped their horns.* **2.** To activate the beeper of (a person) by telephoning its number.

beeper (bē′pər) *n.* **1.** A person or thing that beeps. **2.** A small electronic device that beeps or vibrates to alert the person carrying it that someone is trying to contact him or her by telephone.

beer (bîr) *n.* **1.** A fermented alcoholic beverage brewed from malt and hops. **2.** A nonalcoholic drink flavored with extracts of roots or plants: *ginger beer.*

beer belly *n.* A protruding abdomen, especially as the result of habitual beer drinking.

beeswax (bēz′wăks′) *n.* **1.** The yellowish or brownish wax produced by honeybees for making their honeycombs. **2.** A processed and purified form of this wax used in making candles, crayons, and polishes.

beet (bēt) *n.* **1a.** A leafy plant having edible leaves and a rounded, usually red root eaten as a vegetable. **b.** A form of this plant having a large whitish root from which sugar is made; the sugar beet. **2.** The root of either of these plants.

beetle (bēt′l) *n.* Any of numerous insects that have biting or chewing mouthparts and hard front wings that fold over the delicate hind wings when at rest.

beetle-browed (bēt′l-broud′) *adj.* Having thick, prominent or projecting eyebrows.

WORD HISTORY Beetle-browed comes from the Middle English word *bitel-browed,* meaning "having grim brows, sullen." The exact origin is uncertain. One possibility is that *bitel* came from the Middle English word for *beetle* (which was spelled *bitil* or *betil*), referring to the resemblance of a pair of thick eyebrows to the tufted antennae of certain beetles. Another possibility is that it comes from the Middle English *bitel,* meaning "sharp."

beeves (bēvz) *n.* A plural of **beef.**

befall (bĭ-fôl′) *v.* **befell** (bĭ-fĕl′), **befallen** (bĭ-fô′lən), **befalling, befalls** —*intr.* To come to pass by chance; happen. —*tr.* To happen to: *Many serious mishaps befell the explorers.*

befit (bĭ-fĭt′) *tr.v.* **befitted, befitting, befits** To be suitable to or appropriate for: *He wore a tuxedo to befit the formal occasion.*

befog (bĭ-fôg′) *tr.v.* **befogged, befogging, befogs 1.** To cover or obscure with fog: *Clouds befogged the airport.* **2.** To cause confusion in; muddle: *His rambling explanation only befogged the issue.*

before (bĭ-fôr′) *adv.* **1.** Earlier in time: *I told you about this before.* **2.** In front; ahead: *The people who went before were turned away.* ❖ *prep.* **1.** Previous to; earlier than: *They got there before me.* **2.** In front of: *Eat what's set before you.* **3.** In store for; awaiting: *You've got a great future before you.* **4.** Into or in the presence of: *Each prisoner was brought before the judge.* **5.** Under the consideration of: *The case is now before the court.* **6.** In preference to or in higher esteem than: *I'd take a hamburger before a hot dog any day.* ❖ *conj.* **1.** In advance of the time when: *See me before you leave.* **2.** Sooner than; rather than: *I'd die before I'd give in.*

beforehand (bĭ-fôr′hănd′) *adv.* In advance; ahead of time: *The class starts at 9 o'clock, but I always get there beforehand.*

befoul (bĭ-foul′) *tr.v.* **befouled, befouling, befouls** To make dirty; soil: *smokestacks befouling the air.*

befriend (bĭ-frĕnd′) *tr.v.* **befriended, befriending, befriends** To act as a friend to; assist: *A perfect stranger befriended the lost tourists.*

befuddle (bĭ-fŭd′l) *tr.v.* **befuddled, befuddling, befuddles** To confuse; perplex: *The problem befuddled even the experts.* —**be·fud′dle·ment** *n.*

beg (bĕg) *v.* **begged, begging, begs** —*tr.* **1.** To ask (someone) for something in an urgent or humble manner: *We begged her for help.* **2.** To ask for (something) in an urgent or humble manner: *Could I beg a favor of you?* **3.** To ask for (food or money, for example) as a beggar. See Synonyms at **cadge.** —*intr.* To ask for something, especially money or food, in an urgent or humble manner. ◆ **beg off** To ask to be excused from something: *We had to beg off the invitation to the party.*

began (bĭ-găn′) *v.* Past tense of **begin.**

begat (bĭ-găt′) *v.* *Archaic* A past tense of **beget.**

beget (bĭ-gĕt′) *tr.v.* **begot** (bĭ-gŏt′), **begotten** (bĭ-gŏt′n) or **begot, begetting, begets 1.** To father; sire. **2.** To cause to exist; produce: *Violence often begets more violence.* **—be·get′ter** *n.*

beggar (bĕg′ər) *n.* **1.** A person who begs as a means of living. **2.** A person who is very poor; a pauper. ❖ *tr.v.* **beggared, beggaring, beggars 1.** To make very poor; ruin: *They feared that the stock market crash would beggar them.* **2.** To outdo; go beyond: *The beauty of the Grand Canyon beggars description.*

beggarly (bĕg′ər-lē) *adj.* **1.** Relating to or befitting a beggar; poor or meager: *a sweatshop that paid its workers beggarly wages.* **2.** Mean; contemptible: *a beggarly remark of envy.* **—beg′gar·li·ness** *n.*

beggary (bĕg′ə-rē) *n.* Extreme poverty.

begin (bĭ-gĭn′) *v.* **began** (bĭ-găn′), **begun** (bĭ-gŭn′), **beginning, begins** —*intr.* **1.** To do or undergo the first part of an action; start: *When I clean my room, I begin with my desk. The rain began around noon.* **2.** To come into being; originate: *Education begins at home.* **3.** To have as a first element or part: *The movie begins with a car chase.* **4.** To have as a first position, stage, or job: *The restaurant began as an ice-cream shop. The editor began as a proofreader.* —*tr.* **1.** To take the first step in doing (something); start: *She began the project last month. When did you begin taking photos? We began to eat lunch.* **2.** To say as the first in a series of remarks: *"I bought some plane tickets," he began.* **3.** To bring into being; originate: *The owner's grandfather began the newspaper many years ago.* **4.** To come first in: *The letter A begins the alphabet.*

✦ **SYNONYMS begin, commence, initiate, launch, start** *v.*

beginner (bĭ-gĭn′ər) *n.* A person who is just starting to learn or do something; a novice: *A beginner at the piano plays simple pieces.*

beginning (bĭ-gĭn′ĭng) *n.* **1.** The act or process of bringing or being brought into existence; a start: *The mayor took credit for the beginning of the recycling program.* **2.** The time or point when something begins or is begun: *was born at the beginning of the twenty-first century.* **3.** The place where something begins or is begun; an initial section, division, or part: *started rehearsing at the beginning of the play.* **4a.** A source or origin: *What was the beginning of the controversy?* **b.** often **beginnings** An early phase or rudimentary period: *the beginnings of life on the earth.*

begone (bĭ-gôn′) *v.* Used in the imperative to order someone to go away.

begonia (bĭ-gōn′yə) *n.* Any of various plants grown for their showy, colorful flowers.

begot (bĭ-gŏt′) *v.* Past tense and a past participle of **beget.**

begotten (bĭ-gŏt′n) *v.* A past participle of **beget.**

begrime (bĭ-grīm′) *tr.v.* **begrimed, begriming, begrimes** To soil with dirt or grime: *boots that were begrimed with mud.*

begrudge (bĭ-grŭj′) *tr.v.* **begrudged, begrudging, begrudges 1.** To envy (someone) for the possession or enjoyment of (something): *A generous person does not begrudge others their good fortune.* **2.** To give with reluctance: *He begrudged every penny spent on the repairs.* **—be·grudg′ing·ly** *adv.*

beguile (bĭ-gīl′) *tr.v.* **beguiled, beguiling, beguiles 1.** To deceive; trick: *The salesman beguiled me into buying more than I wanted.* **2.** To amuse; delight: *She beguiled us with song.* **3.** To pass pleasantly: *beguiled the time by sketching.* **—be·guile′ment** *n.* **—be·guil′er** *n.*

begun (bĭ-gŭn′) *v.* Past participle of **begin.**

behalf (bĭ-hăf′) *n.* Interest; benefit: *On whose behalf did*

they act? ◆ **on behalf of** or **in behalf of 1.** As the agent of; on the part of: *The lawyer spoke to the media on behalf of her client.* **2.** For the benefit of; in the interest of: *We're raising money in behalf of the hurricane victims.*

behave (bĭ-hāv′) *v.* **behaved, behaving, behaves** —*intr.* **1a.** To conduct oneself in a specified way: *behave badly.* **b.** To conduct oneself properly: *The babysitter told the child to behave.* **2.** To act, react, perform, or function in a certain way: *The car behaves well on rough roads.* —*tr.* **1.** To conduct (oneself) properly: *Please behave yourself at the party.* **2.** To conduct (oneself) in a specified way: *They behaved themselves with dignity at the funeral.*

behavior (bĭ-hāv′yər) *n.* **1.** The way in which a person behaves; conduct: *praised the children for their good behavior.* **2a.** The actions or reactions of people, animals, or things under specified circumstances: *the behavior of matter at very low temperatures.* **b.** One of these actions or reactions: *the nesting behaviors of birds.* **—be·hav′ior·al** (bĭ-hāv′yər-əl) *adj.* **—be·hav′ior·al·ly** *adv.*

behavioral science *n.* A branch of science that studies human behavior. Psychology is a behavioral science.

behaviour (bĭ-hāv′yər) *n.* Chiefly British Variant of **behavior.**

behead (bĭ-hĕd′) *tr.v.* **beheaded, beheading, beheads** To cut off the head of; decapitate.

beheld (bĭ-hĕld′) *v.* Past tense and past participle of **behold.**

behemoth (bĭ-hē′məth or bē′ə-məth) *n.* **1.** Something enormous in size or power. **2.** often **Behemoth** A huge animal, possibly the hippopotamus, mentioned in the Bible.

behest (bĭ-hĕst′) *n.* A command or urgent request: *At the behest of the fire marshal, no pyrotechnics will be allowed at the concert.*

behind (bĭ-hīnd′) *adv.* **1.** In, to, or toward the rear: *They did not see me because I was walking behind.* **2.** In a place or condition that has been passed or left: *I left my gloves behind.* **3.** In or into an inferior position; below the standard or acceptable level: *The sick student fell behind in the class.* **4.** Slow: *That clock is running behind.* ❖ *prep.* **1.** At the back or in the rear of: *the shed behind the barn.* **2.** On the farther side of or on the other side of: *The broom is behind the door.* **3.** In a place or time that has been passed or left by: *Their worries are behind them.* **4.** In a state less advanced than: *Many nations are behind the United States in space technology.* **5.** In the background or; underlying: *Behind the theory there is much research and observation.* **6.** In a position or attitude of support: *Most of the people are behind the president.* **7.** In pursuit of: *The fox raced for the woods with the dogs fast behind it.* ❖ *n.* Informal The buttocks or backside.

behindhand (bĭ-hīnd′hănd′) *adj.* Being late or slow in doing something: *That tenant is always behindhand with the rent.*

behold (bĭ-hōld′) *tr.v.* **beheld** (bĭ-hĕld′), **beholding, beholds** To gaze upon; look at; see: *In the tomb the treasure hunters beheld a rich store of gold and jewels.* **—be·hold′- er** *n.*

beholden (bĭ-hōl′dən) *adj.* Indebted: *We were beholden to our neighbors for shelter in the storm.*

behoove (bĭ-hōōv′) *tr.v.* **behooved, behooving, behooves** To be necessary or proper for: *It behooves you to study for the test.*

beige (bāzh) *n.* A light grayish or yellowish brown. ❖ *adj.* Light grayish or yellowish brown.

being (bēʹĭng) *n.* **1.** The state or quality of existing; existence: *Rock music came into being in the 1950s.* **2a.** A living organism, especially a person. **b.** An imaginary or supernatural creature: *extraterrestrial beings.* **3.** One's basic or essential nature: *an experience that became part of my very being.*

bejeweled (bĭ-jōōʹəld) *adj.* Decorated with jewels.

bel (bĕl) *n.* A unit for measuring the difference in intensity of sounds, equal to ten decibels.

belabor (bĭ-lāʹbər) *tr.v.* **belabored, belaboring, belabors** **1.** To go over repeatedly; harp on: *The audience got bored as the politician belabored the point.* **2.** To attack verbally; assail: *The candidate belabored her opponent on his weak record.* **3.** To attack with blows; beat.

belated (bĭ-lāʹtĭd) *adj.* Done or sent too late; tardy: *belated birthday wishes.* —**be·latʹed·ly** *adv.* —**be·latʹed·ness** *n.*

belay (bĭ-lāʹ) *v.* **belayed, belaying, belays** —*tr.* **1.** To secure (a rope) by winding it around a cleat or pin. **2.** To secure (a mountain climber) against a potential fall by using a rope that can be drawn in or let out in a controlled manner. —*intr.* Used in the imperative as an order to stop: *Belay there!*

belaying pin (bĭ-lāʹĭng) *n.* A pin on the rail of a ship used to secure ropes.

belch (bĕlch) *v.* **belched, belching, belches** —*intr.* **1.** To expel gas noisily from the stomach through the mouth; burp. **2.** To gush forth; pour out: *smoke belching from the truck's tailpipe.* —*tr.* To send out or eject (smoke or flames) violently: *The burning house belched smoke from its windows.* ❖ *n.* The act or an instance of belching: *The old car stopped with a belch of smoke.*

beleaguer (bĭ-lēʹgər) *tr.v.* **beleaguered, beleaguering, beleaguers** **1.** To persecute constantly, as by threats or demands; harass: *During the power outage the electric company was beleaguered by its customers.* **2.** To surround with troops; besiege: *The king's troops beleaguered the city until the rebels surrendered.*

belfry (bĕlʹfrē) *n., pl.* **belfries** A tower or steeple in which one or more bells are hung.

Belgian (bĕlʹjən) *adj.* Relating to Belgium or its people or culture. ❖ *n.* A native or inhabitant of Belgium.

Belial (bēʹlē-əl) *n.* In the Bible, the Devil.

belie (bĭ-līʹ) *tr.v.* **belied, belying, belies** **1.** To give a wrong or false idea of: *Her soft-spoken manner belied her strong feelings on the subject.* **2.** To be inconsistent with; contradict: *The rise in crime belied the city's reputation for being safe.*

belief (bĭ-lēfʹ) *n.* **1.** Mental acceptance or conviction of the truth or existence of something: *His belief in ghosts could not be shaken.* **2.** The mental act or condition of placing trust or confidence in a person: *My belief in you is as strong as ever.* **3.** Something believed or accepted as true, especially by a group of people: *We sometimes take our beliefs for granted until we meet someone who does not share them.*

believe (bĭ-lēvʹ) *v.* **believed, believing, believes** —*tr.* **1.** To accept (something) as true or real: *Do you believe his version of what happened?* **2.** To consider (someone) to be truthful or accurate in what they are saying: *I believe you when you say she is angry.* **3.** To expect or suppose; think: *I believe it will snow tomorrow. I believe the letters to be authentic.* —*intr.* **1.** To have religious faith: *believe*

in God. **2.** To have faith, trust, or confidence: *We believe in their ability to solve the problem.* **3.** To consider something to be important, worthwhile, or valuable: *I believe in free speech.* —**be·lievʹa·ble** *adj.* —**be·lievʹer** *n.*

belittle (bĭ-lĭtʹl) *tr.v.* **belittled, belittling, belittles** To represent or speak of as trivial or unimportant; disparage: *They belittled her accomplishments out of jealousy.*

bell (bĕl) *n.* **1.** A hollow metal musical instrument, usually cup-shaped with a flared opening, that makes a metallic tone when struck. **2.** Something having a flared opening like that of a bell: *the bell of a trumpet.* **3. bells** A musical instrument consisting of metal tubes that emit tones when struck. ❖ *tr.v.* **belled, belling, bells** To put a bell on: *bell a cat that lives outdoors.*

belladonna (bĕlʹə-dŏnʹə) *n.* **1.** A poisonous plant having purplish bell-shaped flowers and small black berries; deadly nightshade. **2.** A medicinal substance that contains the drug atropine and is derived from this plant.

bell-bottom (bĕlʹbŏtʹəm) *adj.* Having legs that flare out at the bottom: *bell-bottom pants.*

bell-bottoms (bĕlʹbŏtʹəmz) *pl.n.* Pants that flare out at the bottom.

bellboy (bĕlʹboiʹ) *n.* A male bellhop.

bell curve *n.* A bell-shaped curve representing the distribution and frequency of data in a set.

belle (bĕl) *n.* A popular, attractive girl or woman, especially the most attractive one of a group: *the belle of the ball.*

belles-lettres (bĕl-lĕtʹrə) *pl.n. (used with a singular verb)* Literature regarded for its artistic value rather than for its information or teaching content.

bellhop (bĕlʹhŏpʹ) *n.* A person employed by a hotel to carry luggage, run errands, and do other chores.

bellicose (bĕlʹĭ-kōsʹ) *adj.* Warlike in manner or disposition; belligerent: *the demands of a bellicose nation.* —**belʹli·cosʹi·ty** (bĕlʹĭ-kŏsʹĭ-tē) *n.*

belligerence (bə-lĭjʹər-əns) *n.* A warlike or hostile attitude, nature, or disposition.

belligerency (bə-lĭjʹər-ən-sē) *n.* **1.** The state of being at war or engaged in a conflict. **2.** Belligerence: *The lawyer was known for his belligerency toward witnesses during cross-examination.*

belligerent (bə-lĭjʹər-ənt) *adj.* **1.** Inclined to fight; hostile; aggressive: *a belligerent bully.* **2.** Relating to or engaged in warfare: *a belligerent nation.* ❖ *n.* A person, group, or nation engaged in war or a conflict. —**belʹlig·erʹent·ly** *adv.*

bell jar *n.* A large bell-shaped glass container with an open bottom, placed over delicate instruments to protect them and used in experiments to provide a space that is sealed off from the atmosphere.

bellow (bĕlʹō) *v.* **bellowed, bellowing, bellows** —*intr.* **1.** To roar as a bull does. **2.** To shout in a deep loud voice. —*tr.* To utter in a loud voice: *The crowd bellowed its disapproval of the umpire's call.* ❖ *n.* **1.** The loud roaring sound made by a bull or certain other large animals. **2.** A loud deep shout or cry.

bellows (bĕlʹōz) *pl.n. (used with a singular or plural verb)* A device for pumping air, consisting of a chamber with openings controlled by valves so that air enters at one opening and leaves at another as the chamber is forced to expand and contract.

bellwether (bĕlʹwĕthʹər) *n.* A person or thing that leads or begins something else: *a state that could be the bellwether for the country's economic recovery.*

belly (bĕlʹē) *n., pl.* **bellies 1.** In humans and other mammals, the front part of the body below the chest; the abdomen. **2.** The stomach: *I ate until my belly was full.* **3.** The underside of the body of certain vertebrates, such as snakes and fish. **4.** A part that bulges or protrudes: *the belly of a sail.* **5.** The hollow interior of something: *the belly of an airplane.* ❖ *intr. & tr.v.* **bellied, bellying, bellies** To swell; bulge: *The sails bellied in the breeze.*

bellyache (bĕl′ē-āk′) *n.* Pain in the stomach or abdomen. ❖ *intr.v.* **bellyached, bellyaching, bellyaches** *Slang* To grumble or complain, especially in a whining way. —**bel′ly·ach′er** *n.*

bellyband (bĕl′ē-bănd′) *n.* A band passed around the belly of an animal to secure something, such as a saddle.

bellybutton (bĕl′ē-bŭt′n) *n. Informal* The navel.

belly dance *n.* **1.** A dance probably of Middle Eastern origin, traditionally performed solo by a woman who makes wavelike movements with the hips, abdomen, and shoulders. **2.** A performance of this dance. —**bel′ly-dance′** *v.* —**belly dancer** *n.*

belly-land (bĕl′ē-lănd′) *intr.v.* **belly-landed, belly-landing, belly-lands** To crash-land an airplane without the aid of landing gear, so that the underside comes in direct contact with the land or water. —**belly landing** *n.*

belly laugh *n.* A deep laugh.

belong (bĭ-lông′) *intr.v.* **belonged, belonging, belongs 1.** To be owned by someone: *This watch belonged to my grandmother.* **2a.** To be a member of a group: *Many of the workers belong to a labor union.* **b.** To fit into a group naturally or comfortably: *I feel like I just don't belong at this school.* **3a.** To be proper or suitable: *Blue jeans don't belong at a formal dinner.* **b.** To be properly or suitably placed: *Ice cream belongs in the freezer.*

belongings (bĭ-lông′ĭngz) *pl.n.* The things that belong to someone; possessions: *We took all of our belongings when we moved out of state.*

beloved (bĭ-lŭv′ĭd *or* bĭ-lŭvd′) *adj.* Dearly loved: *my beloved grandparents; her beloved pets.* ❖ *n.* A person who is dearly loved.

below (bĭ-lō′) *adv.* **1.** In or to a lower place or level: *They paused on the bridge to admire the rapids below.* **2.** On or to a lower floor or deck: *The trunks were stowed in a compartment below.* **3.** Further down, as along a slope or stream: *There is a cabin in the valley below.* **4.** Following or farther down on a page: *A diagram is printed below with an explanation.* **5.** In a lower rank or class: *a decision of the courts below.* **6.** On the earth: *all creatures here below.* ❖ *prep.* **1.** Underneath; beneath: *We stood at the window watching the street below us.* **2.** Lower than, as in degree or rank: *temperatures below zero.* **3.** Unworthy of: *actions below contempt.* **4.** South of: *Arizona is below Utah.*

belowground (bĭ-lō′ground′) *adv. & adj.* Situated or occurring below the surface of the ground.

belt (bĕlt) *n.* **1.** A band of leather, cloth, or plastic worn around the waist to hold up pants, weapons, or tools, or to serve as decoration. **2.** A broad strip or band: *a belt of trees along the highway.* **3.** A seat belt or safety belt. **4.** A band that passes over two or more wheels or pulleys to transmit motion from one to another or to convey objects: *A belt connects the car motor to the fan.* **5.** A band of tough reinforcing material beneath the tread of a tire. **6.** A geographical region that is distinctive in some specific way: *the corn belt.* ❖ *tr.v.* **belted, belting, belts 1.** To support or attach with a belt: *The hikers belted canteens around their waists.* **2.** To strike; hit: *He belted three*

home runs in one game. **3.** *Informal* To sing loudly and forcefully: *The audience belted out the national anthem.* ◆ **below the belt** Not according to the rules; unfair or unfairly: *The candidate's false accusations were below the belt.* **tighten (one's) belt** To become thrifty and frugal: *We can save money if we tighten our belts.*

beltway (bĕlt′wā′) *n.* A high-speed highway that encircles or skirts an urban area.

beluga (bə-lōō′gə) *n.* **1.** A large white sturgeon of the Black and Caspian Seas, whose roe is used for caviar. **2.** A small white or grayish whale living in northern waters.

bemoan (bĭ-mōn′) *tr.v.* **bemoaned, bemoaning, bemoans** To mourn over; lament; grieve for: *bemoan one's fate.*

bemused (bĭ-myōōzd′) *adj.* **1.** Confused; bewildered: *bemused by all the conflicting opinions.* **2.** Lost in thought or showing that one is lost in thought: *She remembered her old neighborhood with a bemused smile.*

bench (bĕnch) *n.* **1.** A long seat, often without a back, for two or more people. **2.** A sturdy table on which a carpenter, shoemaker, or other skilled person works. **3a.** The seat for judges in a courtroom. **b.** The office or position of a judge: *appointed to the bench.* **c.** often **Bench** The judge or judges on a court. **4a.** The place where the members of an athletic team sit when they are not actively participating in a game. **b.** The reserve players on an athletic team. ❖ *tr.v.* **benched, benching, benches** To remove or keep (a player) from a game: *benched the goalie after she let in three quick goals.*

benchmark (bĕnch′märk′) *n.* **1.** A standard by which something can be measured or judged: *a hybrid car whose fuel economy is considered a benchmark for the automotive industry.* **2.** A surveyor's mark made on some stationary object, such as a boulder, used as a reference point in measuring elevation.

bench press *n.* In weightlifting, a lift done while lying face-up on a bench, in which a weight is pushed up from the chest to arm's length and then lowered back to the chest. —**bench′-press′** (bĕnch′prĕs′) *v.*

bend (bĕnd) *v.* **bent** (bĕnt), **bending, bends** —*tr.* **1.** To make curved or crooked: *Bend the wire around the post.* **2.** To cause to deviate from a straight line; deflect: *Light is bent as it passes through water.* **3.** To turn or direct: *bend one's steps toward home; bend their attention to the problem.* **4.** To force to yield; subdue: *He bent his employees to his will.* **5.** To change deceptively; distort: *You must not bend the facts to fit a conclusion.* **6.** To make an exception to: *bent the rules.* —*intr.* **1.** To deviate from a straight line or position: *The road bends to the right at the bridge.* **2.** To assume a curved, crooked, or angular form or direction: *The saplings bent in the wind.* **3.** To incline the body; stoop: *I bent over to pick up the ball.* **4.** To submit; yield: *bend to someone's wishes.* ❖ *n.* **1.** A turn, curve, or bent part: *a bend in the river.* **2. bends** *(used with a singular or plural verb)* Decompression sickness. Used with *the.* ◆ **bend over backward** To make an effort greater than is required: *They bent over backward to be fair.*

bender (bĕn′dər) *n.* **1.** One that bends: *a bender of iron bars.* **2.** *Slang* A spree, especially a drinking spree.

bend sinister *n.* In heraldry, a band passing from the upper right-hand corner of a coat of arms to the lower left-hand corner, from the point of view of the person looking at it, often taken to indicate birth out of wedlock.

beneath (bĭ-nēth′) *adv.* In a lower place; below: *From the top of the hill, we looked down at the valley beneath.* ❖ *prep.* **1a.** Lower than; below: *a drawer beneath the cabi-*

net. **b.** To or into a lower position than: *moved the picture beneath the light.* **2.** Covered or concealed by: *Most oil lies beneath the ground.* **3.** Under the force, control, or influence of: *The supervisor has six workers beneath her.* **4.** Unworthy of: *Lying is beneath me.*

Benedictine (běn′ĭ-dĭk′tĭn *or* běn′ĭ-dĭk′tēn′) *n.* A Roman Catholic monk or nun belonging to the order founded around 529 by Saint Benedict of Nursia (480?–547?). —**Ben′e·dic′tine** *adj.*

benediction (běn′ĭ-dĭk′shən) *n.* A blessing, especially one recited at the close of a religious service by a member of the clergy.

benefactor (běn′ə-făk′tər) *n.* A person who gives financial or other aid.

beneficence (bə-něf′ĭ-səns) *n.* **1.** The quality or condition of being kind or charitable. **2.** A charitable act or gift: *The contributor's beneficence was large enough to complete the church building.*

beneficent (bə-něf′ĭ-sənt) *adj.* Doing or bringing about good: *beneficent legislation that improved working conditions for low-paid laborers.* —**be·nef′i·cent·ly** *adv.*

beneficial (běn′ə-físh′əl) *adj.* Bringing benefit; advantageous: *Many bacteria are beneficial to human life.* —**ben′e·fi′cial·ly** *adv.*

beneficiary (běn′ə-físh′ē-ěr′ē *or* běn′ə-físh′ə-rē) *n., pl.* **beneficiaries 1.** A person who derives benefit from something: *We are all beneficiaries of the large new library.* **2.** A person who is designated to receive funds or property from an insurance policy or a will.

benefit (běn′ə-fĭt) *n.* **1.** Something that is of help; an advantage: *The field trip was of great benefit to the students.* **2.** A payment or favorable allowance made in accordance with a wage agreement, insurance policy, or public assistance program: *Her new job's benefits include three weeks of paid vacation.* **3.** A theatrical performance or social event held to raise money for a cause. ❖ *v.* **benefited, benefiting, benefits** also **benefitted, benefitting, benefits** —*tr.* To be helpful or beneficial to: *The clean-air program will benefit the environment.* —*intr.* To receive help; profit: *You might benefit from taking her advice.* ◆ **benefit of the doubt** A favorable judgment made in the absence of more complete information: *At first they didn't believe his excuse, but they decided to give him the benefit of the doubt.*

benevolence (bə-něv′ə-ləns) *n.* **1.** An inclination to do good; kindliness; good will. **2.** A kindly act.

benevolent (bə-něv′ə-lənt) *adj.* **1.** Characterized by doing good; kindly: *a benevolent king; a benevolent attitude.* **2.** Relating to or organized for charitable purposes: *a benevolent fund.* —**be·nev′o·lent·ly** *adv.*

Bengali (běn-gô′lē) *adj.* Relating to the region of Bengal in Bangladesh and eastern India or to its people, language, or culture. ❖ *n., pl.* **Bengali** or **Bengalis 1.** A native or inhabitant of Bengal. **2.** The Indic language of Bangladesh and western Bengal.

benighted (bĭ-nī′tĭd) *adj.* Resulting from or in a state of moral or intellectual backwardness; ignorant or unenlightened: *benighted prejudice; a benighted population whose rulers denied it access to basic education.*

benign (bĭ-nīn′) *adj.* **1a.** Causing little or no real harm; harmless: *a benign chemical.* **b.** Not likely to spread or get worse; not malignant: *a benign tumor.* **2a.** Kind; gentle: *a benign ruler.* **b.** Showing or expressing kindness or

gentleness: *a benign smile.* **3.** Mild; favorable: *a benign climate.*

benignity (bĭ-nĭg′nĭ-tē) *n.* The quality or condition of being benign: *a dynasty noted for the benignity of its rulers.*

benison (běn′ĭ-zən) *n.* A blessing; a benediction.

bent (běnt) *v.* Past tense and past participle of **bend.** ❖ *adj.* **1.** Curved or crooked: *a bent nail.* **2.** Resolved; determined: *a runner bent on becoming a champion.* ❖ *n.* A tendency or inclination: *a strong bent for studying science.*

benthic (běn′thĭk) *adj.* Relating to or inhabiting the bottom of a sea, lake, or river: *benthic invertebrates.*

benthos (běn′thŏs) *n.* **1.** The bottom of a sea, lake, or river. **2.** The organisms living on sea, lake, or river bottoms.

benumb (bĭ-nŭm′) *tr.v.* **benumbed, benumbing, benumbs** To make numb; deprive of feeling: *Cold benumbed our fingers.*

benzene (běn′zēn′ *or* běn-zēn′) *n.* A clear colorless liquid that burns easily and has the formula C_6H_6. It is derived from petroleum and used to make detergents, insect poisons, motor fuels, and other chemical products.

benzine (běn′zēn′ *or* běn-zēn′) *n.* Naphtha.

benzoate of soda (běn′zō-āt′) *n.* Sodium benzoate.

benzoic acid (běn-zō′ĭk) *n.* A white crystalline acid that is used as an antiseptic and a food preservative.

benzoin (běn′zō-ĭn *or* běn′zoin′) *n.* Any of various fragrant resins that are obtained from certain southeast Asian trees and contain benzoic acid. They are used in making incense, perfumes, ointments, and cough medicines.

Beowulf (bā′ə-woȯlf′) *n.* **1.** An Old English epic poem probably composed in the early 700s. **2.** The hero of this poem, who killed two water monsters and died in a fight with a dragon.

bequeath (bĭ-kwēth′ *or* bĭ-kwēth′) *tr.v.* **bequeathed, bequeathing, bequeaths 1.** To leave or give (personal property) by will. **2.** To pass on or hand down: *One generation bequeaths its knowledge to the next.*

bequest (bĭ-kwěst′) *n.* **1.** The act of bequeathing: *From her bequest, he inherited great wealth.* **2.** Something that is bequeathed in a will: *The will included a bequest of $1,000 to a local charity.*

berate (bĭ-rāt′) *tr.v.* **berated, berating, berates** To scold severely or angrily.

Berber (bûr′bər) *n.* **1.** A member of any of several Muslim peoples of northern Africa. **2.** Any of the Afro-Asiatic languages of the Berbers. —**Ber′ber** *adj.*

bereave (bĭ-rēv′) *tr.v.* **bereaved** or **bereft** (bĭ-rěft′), **bereaving, bereaves** To leave alone or desolate, especially by death: *She was bereaved by the death of her husband.* —**be·reave′ment** *n.*

bereft (bĭ-rěft′) *v.* A past tense and a past participle of **bereave.** ❖ *adj.* Deprived of something: *an act that left him bereft of dignity.*

beret (bə-rā′) *n.* A round, soft, brimless cap that fits snugly.

berg (bûrg) *n.* An iceberg.

beriberi (běr′ē-běr′ē) *n.* A disease caused by a lack of thiamine in the diet. It causes nerve damage, problems with the circulation, and loss of weight.

berkelium (bər-kē′lē-əm *or* bûrk′lē-əm) *n. Symbol* **Bk** A radioactive element that has been artificially produced by scientists. The half-life of its longest-lived isotope is about 1,380 years. Atomic number 97. See **Periodic Table.**

berm (bûrm) *n.* **1.** A raised bank or path, such as one along a canal. **2.** A bank of earth placed against the wall of a building to provide protection or insulation. **3.** The flat space between the edge of a moat and the wall of a castle or other fortification.

Bermuda shorts *pl.n.* Shorts that end slightly above the knees.

berry (bĕr′ē) *n., pl.* **berries 1.** A fruit having many seeds in fleshy pulp, such as a strawberry, blueberry, or raspberry. **2.** In botany, a fleshy fruit that develops from a single plant ovary, such as a tomato, avocado, or grape. **3.** A seed or dried kernel of certain grains or other plants, such as wheat or coffee. ❖ *intr.v.* **berried, berrying, berries** To hunt for or gather berries.

berserk (bər-sûrk′ or bər-zûrk′) *adv. & adj.* In or into a crazed or violent frenzy.

berth (bûrth) *n.* **1.** A built-in bed or bunk in a ship or train. **2.** A space at a wharf for a ship to dock or anchor. **3.** A job or position: *have a berth on the US Olympic Team.* ❖ *v.* **berthed, berthing, berths** —*tr.* **1.** To bring (a ship) to a berth. **2.** To provide with a berth. —*intr.* To come to a berth; dock: *berth at a pier along the river.*

beryl (bĕr′əl) *n.* A transparent to translucent mineral of varied colors that is a silicate of beryllium and aluminum. It is the chief source of beryllium. Transparent varieties, such as emeralds and aquamarines, are valued as gems.

beryllium (bə-rĭl′ē-əm) *n.* *Symbol* **Be** A grayish-white, hard, lightweight metallic element found in various minerals, especially beryl. Beryllium is used to make sturdy, lightweight alloys and to control the speed of neutrons in nuclear reactors. Atomic number 4. See **Periodic Table.**

beseech (bĭ-sēch′) *tr.v.* **besought** (bĭ-sôt′) or **beseeched, beseeching, beseeches** To ask earnestly; entreat; implore: *beseech the authorities for help.* —**be·seech′ing·ly** *adv.*

beseem (bĭ-sēm′) *tr.v.* **beseemed, beseeming, beseems** *Archaic* To be appropriate for; befit.

beset (bĭ-sĕt′) *tr.v.* **beset, besetting, besets 1.** To trouble persistently; harass: *I was beset by doubts about the right course to follow.* **2.** To attack from all sides: *Enemy troops beset the fort.* **3.** To hem in; surround: *Rising floodwaters beset the town.*

beshrew (bĭ-shrōō′) *tr.v.* **beshrewed, beshrewing, beshrews** *Archaic* To invoke evil upon; curse.

beside (bĭ-sīd′) *prep.* **1.** At the side of; next to: *The cat sat down beside the radiator.* **2.** In comparison with: *Your test score looks pretty good beside mine.* **3.** Not relevant to: *a remark that was beside the point.* **4.** In addition to; besides: *Three dogs beside my own started to bark.* ◆ **beside (oneself)** In a state of extreme excitement or emotion: *The winners were beside themselves with joy.*

besides (bĭ-sīdz′) *adv.* **1.** In addition; also: *We had dinner and a late-night snack besides.* **2.** Moreover; furthermore: *It was time to go; besides, I was getting bored.* ❖ *prep.* **1.** In addition to: *Dentists do other things besides drilling cavities.* **2.** Other than; except for: *There's nothing to eat here besides a little cheese.* —SEE NOTE AT **together.**

besiege (bĭ-sēj′) *tr.v.* **besieged, besieging, besieges 1.** To surround and blockade in order to capture; lay siege to: *The king's troops besieged the city until it surrendered.* **2.** To crowd around and hem in: *A crowd of fans besieged the movie star.* **3.** To harass, as with requests: *The reporters besieged the police for information.* —**be·sieg′er** *n.*

besmirch (bĭ-smûrch′) *tr.v.* **besmirched, besmirching, besmirches** To soil or tarnish; stain: *besmirch someone's good name by repeating slanderous remarks.*

besot (bĭ-sŏt′) *tr.v.* **besotted, besotting, besots** To muddle or stupefy, as with alcoholic liquor or infatuation.

besought (bĭ-sôt′) *v.* A past tense and a past participle of **beseech.**

bespatter (bĭ-spăt′ər) *tr.v.* **bespattered, bespattering, bespatters** To spatter: *The dripping paint bespattered the floor.*

bespeak (bĭ-spēk′) *tr.v.* **bespoke** (bĭ-spōk′), **bespoken** (bĭ-spō′kən) or **bespoke, bespeaking, bespeaks** To be or give a sign of; indicate: *a shake of the head that bespoke disbelief.*

bespectacled (bĭ-spĕk′tə-kəld) *adj.* Wearing eyeglasses.

besprinkle (bĭ-sprĭng′kəl) *tr.v.* **besprinkled, besprinkling, besprinkles** To sprinkle.

Bessemer process (bĕs′ə-mər) *n.* A method for making steel by forcing compressed air through molten iron to burn out excess carbon and impurities.

best (bĕst) *adj.* Superlative of **good. 1.** Surpassing all others in excellence, quality, or achievement: *the best singer in the choir.* **2.** Most satisfactory, suitable, or useful: *the best place to dig a well.* **3.** Largest or greatest: *We talked for the best part of the journey.* ❖ *adv.* Superlative of **well[2]. 1.** In the most excellent way; most properly or successfully: *Which of the three jackets fits best?* **2.** To the greatest degree or extent; most: *What do you like to eat best?* ❖ *n.* **1.** A person or thing that surpasses all others: *That skier is surely the best in the race.* **2.** The best part or value: *The best is yet to come.* **3.** One's best effort or appearance: *do your best; look your best.* **4.** One's nicest clothing: *She put on her best and went to the dance.* **5.** One's warmest wishes or regards: *Give them my best.* ❖ *tr.v.* **bested, besting, bests** To get the better of; defeat: *besting their rivals in every game.* ◆ **at best 1.** Viewed most favorably; at the most: *There were 20 people in the theater at best.* **2.** Under the most favorable conditions: *This car has a top speed of 40 miles per hour at best.* **for the best** With an ultimately positive or preferable result. **get the best of** or **have the best of** To outdo or outwit; defeat: *Nobody's ever gotten the best of me at checkers.*

bestial (bĕs′chəl or bēs′chəl) *adj.* **1.** Characteristic of a beast: *a bestial roar.* **2.** Brutal or cruel: *bestial crimes.* —**bes′tial·ly** *adv.*

bestiary (bĕs′chē-ĕr′ē or bēs′chē-ĕr′ē) *n., pl.* **bestiaries** A book consisting of a collection of descriptions of real and imaginary animals, often including a moral or allegorical interpretation of each animal's behavior.

bestir (bĭ-stûr′) *tr.v.* **bestirred, bestirring, bestirs** To stir to action; rouse: *He finally bestirred himself to look for a job.*

best man *n.* The chief attendant of the bridegroom at a wedding.

bestow (bĭ-stō′) *tr.v.* **bestowed, bestowing, bestows** To give or present, especially as a gift or honor; confer: *bestowed awards on the best actors and plays each season.* —**be·stow′al** *n.*

bestrew (bĭ-strōō′) *tr.v.* **bestrewed, bestrewed** or **bestrewn** (bĭ-strōōn′), **bestrewing, bestrews 1.** To scatter (a surface) with things so as to cover it: *The crowd bestrewed the street with confetti.* **2.** To lie or be scattered over: *Dead leaves bestrewed the yard.*

bestride (bĭ-strīd′) *tr.v.* **bestrode** (bĭ-strōd′), **bestridden** (bĭ-strĭd′n), **bestriding, bestrides** To sit or stand on with one leg on each side; straddle: *bestride a horse.*

bestseller (bĕst′sĕl′ər) *n.* A product, such as a book, that is among those sold in the largest numbers.

best-selling (bĕst′sĕl′ĭng) *adj.* Selling in the largest numbers at a given time: *a best-selling novel.*

bet (bĕt) *n.* **1.** An agreement, usually between two people or groups, that the one who has made an incorrect prediction about an event will give something, such as a sum of money, to the other: *We made a bet that I could beat him at checkers.* **2.** An object or amount of money risked in a wager; a stake: *People were placing bets of $10 on the outcome of the tournament.* **3.** A person, animal, or event on which a wager is or can be made: *That horse is a good bet to win the race.* **4.** A plan or option considered with regard to its likely outcome: *The short route is probably your best bet to get home on time.* ❖ *v.* **bet** or **betted, betting, bets** —*tr.* **1.** To risk (something) in a bet: *He bet $20 on the race.* **2.** To make a bet with (a person or group): *I bet my sister that she couldn't eat the hot pepper.* **3.** To state with confidence, as in a bet: *I bet you did well on the exam.* —*intr.* To make or place a bet. ◆ **you bet** *Informal* Of course; surely.

beta (bā′tə *or* bē′tə) *n.* **1.** The second letter of the Greek alphabet, written B, β. In English it is represented as *B, b.* **2.** The second item in a series. ❖ *adj.* Being the version of a software program used in a beta test.

beta carotene *n.* A form of carotene found in yellow fruits and vegetables and leafy green vegetables that is converted to vitamin A in the liver.

betake (bĭ-tāk′) *tr.v.* **betook** (bĭ-tŏŏk′), **betaken** (bĭ-tā′-kən), **betaking, betakes** To cause (oneself) to go or move: *They betook themselves to the distant kingdom.*

beta particle *n.* A high-speed electron or positron, especially one emitted by an atomic nucleus undergoing radioactive decay.

beta ray *n.* A stream of beta particles.

beta test *n.* The final stage in the testing of a new software or computer hardware product before its commercial release.

betatron (bā′tə-trŏn′ *or* bē′tə-trŏn′) *n.* A particle accelerator that uses a changing magnetic field to accelerate electrons to very high speeds.

beta version *n.* The version of software used in a beta test.

betel (bēt′l) *n.* An evergreen vine of southern and southeast Asia whose leaves are used to wrap betel nuts.

Betelgeuse (bēt′l-jŏŏz′) *n.* A bright-red star in the constellation Orion.

betel nut *n.* The seed of a tropical Asian palm, chewed with leaves from the betel plant as a mild stimulant.

bête noire (bĕt nwär′) *n.* A person or thing that is particularly disliked: *Speaking in public has long been my bête noire.*

betide (bĭ-tīd′) *tr.v.* **betided, betiding, betides** To happen to: *Woe betide anyone who is late for class.*

betimes (bĭ-tīmz′) *adv.* In good time; early: *I awoke betimes and got ready to go.*

betoken (bĭ-tō′kən) *tr.v.* **betokened, betokening, betokens** To be a sign of; point to: *Public concern betokens a new attitude about our environment.*

betook (bĭ-tŏŏk′) *v.* Past tense of **betake.**

betray (bĭ-trā′) *tr.v.* **betrayed, betraying, betrays** **1.** To give aid or information to an enemy of (a country, for example). **2.** To be disloyal to: *betray a friend; a corrupt politician betraying the confidence of the voters.* **3.** To make known in a breach of trust; divulge: *betray a secret.* **4.** To give evidence of; indicate: *The redness of her face betrayed embarrassment.* —**be·tray′er** *n.*

betrayal (bĭ-trā′əl) *n.* The act of betraying, especially through disloyalty and deception.

betrothal (bĭ-trō′thəl *or* bĭ-trô′thəl) *n.* A promise to marry; an engagement.

betrothed (bĭ-trōthd′ *or* bĭ-trôtht′) *adj.* Engaged to be married. ❖ *n.* A person to whom one is engaged to be married.

better (bĕt′ər) *adj.* Comparative of **good.** **1.** Greater in excellence or higher in quality than another of the same kind: *Which of the twins is the better skater?* **2.** More useful, suitable, or desirable: *I know a better way to go.* **3.** Larger; greater: *It took the better part of an hour to get there.* **4.** Healthier than before: *Many days passed before I began to feel better.* ❖ *adv.* Comparative of **well**². **1.** In a more excellent way: *He sings better than his father.* **2.** To a greater extent or larger degree: *I like fish better when it's broiled.* **3.** More: *The play was first performed better than 20 years ago.* ❖ *n.* The superior of two: *Both are good, but which is the better?* **2.** A superior: *I leave the major decisions to my betters.* ❖ *v.* **bettered, bettering, betters** —*tr.* **1.** To make better; improve: *The purpose of education is to better ourselves.* **2.** To surpass or exceed: *The old record stood until another athlete bettered it.* —*intr.* To become better: *Conditions bettered with time.* ◆ **better off** In a better condition: *People were better off after the war ended.* **for the better** Resulting in or aiming at an improvement. **had better** Ought to; must: *We had better leave before dark.*

USAGE In writing, the phrase *had better,* meaning "must, ought to," is correct only as long as the *had* or ('*d,* the contraction of *had*), is present. You should write *You had better do it* or *You'd better do it,* not *You better do it.*

betterment (bĕt′ər-mənt) *n.* An improvement: *work for the betterment of our children.*

bettor also **better** (bĕt′ər) *n.* A person who bets.

between (bĭ-twēn′) *prep.* **1a.** In or through the position or interval separating: *between the trees; between 11:00 and 12:00; waters flowing between the banks.* **b.** Intermediate to, as in amount or degree: *costs between $5 and $10.* **2.** Connecting over or through a space that is separating: *a long path between the cabin and the lake.* **3.** By the combined effect or effort of: *Between them, the friends finished the job.* **4.** In the combined ownership of: *We have $25 between us.* **5.** As measured against: *choose between milk and water; not much to choose between the two cars.* ❖ *adv.* In an intermediate space, position, or time: *The plane went from New York to Los Angeles, and several cities between.* ◆ **between you and me** In the strictest confidence: *We can surprise the others if we keep the plans between you and me.* **in between** In an intermediate situation: *There are two cities near each other, with a river running in between.* **in between times** During an intervening period; in the meantime.

USAGE When two people or objects are discussed, **between** is correct and **among** is wrong: *the friendship between Jill and Jane.* When more than two people or objects are involved, however, or when the number is unspecified, use *between* to suggest pairs of distinct individuals and *among* for a group or mass. *Friendship between team members* emphasizes that there are friendships between different pairs of teammates, but *friendship among team members* suggests that many or even all team members are friendly with each other.

betwixt (bĭ-twĭkst′) *adv. & prep.* Between. ◆ **betwixt and between** In an intermediate position; neither wholly one thing nor another.

BeV An abbreviation of billion electron volts.

bevel (bĕv′əl) *n.* **1.** A surface cut so that it is not at a right angle to another surface: *The edge of the counter has a bevel.* **2.** The angle at which such a surface is cut. **3.** A tool used to measure or mark such angles. ❖ *tr.v.* **beveled, beveling, bevels** or **bevelled, bevelling, bevels** To cut a bevel on (something): *bevel the edges of the picture frame.*

beverage (bĕv′ər-ĭj or bĕv′rĭj) *n.* A liquid for drinking, such as milk, tea, or juice.

bevy (bĕv′ē) *n., pl.* **bevies** A group of living things or objects that are all of the same kind: *a bevy of poets; a bevy of quail; a bevy of mistakes.*

bewail (bĭ-wāl′) *tr.v.* **bewailed, bewailing, bewails** To express sorrow or regret over; bemoan: *bewail one's fate.*

beware (bĭ-wâr′) *v.* **bewared, bewaring, bewares** —*tr.* To watch out for; be on guard against: *Beware the smooth talk of the salesman.* —*intr.* To be cautious: *Beware of the dog.*

bewilder (bĭ-wĭl′dər) *tr.v.* **bewildered, bewildering, bewilders** To confuse greatly; puzzle. —**be·wil′dered·ly** *adv.* —**be·wil′der·ment** *n.*

bewitch (bĭ-wĭch′) *tr.v.* **bewitched, bewitching, bewitches** **1.** To cast a spell over: *The prince was bewitched by a fairy.* **2.** To captivate completely; fascinate; charm: *Her piano solo bewitched the audience.*

bewitching (bĭ-wĭch′ĭng) *adj.* Fascinating; enchanting: *a bewitching smile.* —**be·witch′ing·ly** *adv.*

bey (bā) *n.* A governor of a province in the former Ottoman Empire.

beyond (bē-ŏnd′ or bĭ-yŏnd′) *prep.* **1.** On the far side of; past: *I planted carrots just beyond the fence.* **2.** To a degree or amount greater than: *rich beyond his wildest dreams.* **3.** Later than: *Don't stay up beyond midnight.* **4.** Past the reach, scope, or understanding of: *beyond hope; beyond recall.* ❖ *adv.* Farther along: *We walked under the trees into the bright sunlight beyond.*

Bhagavad-Gita (bä′gə-väd-gē′tə) *n.* A sacred Hindu text in the form of a philosophical dialogue in which Krishna instructs the prince Arjuna in ethical matters and the nature of God.

bi–[1] or **bin–** A prefix that means: **1.** Two: *bifocal.* **2.** Both sides, parts, or directions: *biconcave.* **3.** Occurring at intervals of two: *bicentennial.* **4.** Occurring twice during: *bimonthly.* —SEE NOTE AT **biweekly.**

bi–[2] Variant of **bio–.**

bialy (bē-ä′lē) *n., pl.* **bialys** A flat roll topped with onion flakes.

biannual (bī-ăn′yōō-əl) *adj.* **1.** Happening twice each year; semiannual. **2.** Occurring every two years; biennial. —**bi·an′nu·al·ly** *adv.* —SEE NOTE AT **biweekly.**

bias (bī′əs) *n.* **1.** The direction of a piece of fabric as it runs diagonal to the grain: *cut cloth on the bias.* **2.** A preference for or hostile feeling against a person or thing that interferes with impartial judgment; a prejudice. ❖ *tr.v.* **biased, biasing, biases** or **biassed, biassing, biasses** To cause to have a bias: *His stubbornness biased the employer against him.*

biased also **biassed** (bī′əst) *adj.* Marked by or showing bias; prejudiced.

biathlon (bī-ăth′lŏn′) *n.* **1.** A competition that combines events in cross-country skiing and rifle shooting. **2.** An athletic contest in which participants compete in two successive events, such as long-distance swimming and running.

bib (bĭb) *n.* **1.** A piece of cloth or plastic worn under the chin, especially by small children, to protect the clothes while eating. **2.** The part of an apron or a pair of overalls worn over the chest.

Bible (bī′bəl) *n.* **1.** The sacred book of Christianity, a collection of ancient writings including both the Old Testament and the New Testament. **2.** The Hebrew Scriptures, the sacred book of Judaism. **3.** often **bible** A book considered authoritative in its field: *the bible of French cooking.*

Bible Belt *n.* Those sections of the United States, especially in the South and Midwest, where Protestant fundamentalism is widely practiced.

biblical also **Biblical** (bĭb′lĭ-kəl) *adj.* **1.** Relating to or contained in the Bible. **2.** Very great in extent; enormous: *a disaster of biblical proportions.* —**bib′li·cal·ly** *adv.*

bibliographical (bĭb′lē-ə-grăf′ĭ-kəl) or **bibliographic** (bĭb′lē-ə-grăf′ĭk) *adj.* Relating to bibliography: *the vast bibliographical resources of a great library.*

bibliography (bĭb′lē-ŏg′rə-fē) *n., pl.* **bibliographies 1.** A list of the works of a specific author or publisher. **2.** A list of the writings on a specific subject: *a bibliography of Latin American history.*

bicameral (bī-kăm′ər-əl) *adj.* Composed of two chambers or branches, as a legislature: *The United States Congress is a bicameral legislature consisting of the Senate and the House of Representatives.*

bicarbonate (bī-kär′bə-nāt′ or bī-kär′bə-nĭt) *n.* The radical HCO_3 or a compound containing it, such as sodium bicarbonate.

bicarbonate of soda *n.* Sodium bicarbonate.

bicentennial (bī′sĕn-tĕn′ē-əl) *adj.* **1.** Relating to a 200th anniversary: *a bicentennial celebration.* **2.** Occurring once every 200 years. ❖ *n.* A 200th anniversary or its celebration.

biceps (bī′sĕps′) *n., pl.* **biceps** A muscle that has two points of origin, especially: **a.** The muscle at the front of the upper arm that bends the forearm. **b.** The muscle at the back of the thigh that bends the knee.

USAGE Each of our arms has a muscle called a **biceps.** The plural of *biceps* looks like the singular: *Since he started lifting weights, his biceps have become huge.* Some people say *bicep,* thinking that the *-s* on the end is like the *-s* in the plural word *weights,* and the singular is made by dropping the *-s.* But *bicep* is a mistake.

---

bicker (bĭk′ər) *intr.v.* **bickered, bickering, bickers** To argue or quarrel over an unimportant matter; squabble: *We bickered over whose turn it was to wash dishes.* ❖ *n.* A petty quarrel; a squabble. —**bick′er·er** *n.*

biconcave (bī′kŏn-kāv′ or bī-kŏn′kāv′) *adj.* Concave on both sides or surfaces: *a biconcave lens.*

biconvex (bī′kŏn-vĕks′ or bī-kŏn′vĕks′) *adj.* Convex on both sides or surfaces: *a biconvex lens.*

bicuspid (bī-kŭs′pĭd) *adj.* Having two points or cusps, as a crescent moon. ❖ *n.* A double-pointed premolar tooth that tears and grinds food. An adult human has eight bicuspids.

bicycle (bī′sĭk′əl or bī′sĭ-kəl) *n.* A vehicle consisting of a light metal frame mounted on two wheels one behind the other and having a seat for the rider, who steers the front wheel by handlebars and pushes pedals that drive the rear wheel. ❖ *intr.v.* **bicycled, bicycling, bicycles** To ride on a bicycle: *bicycle down to the store.* —**bi′cy·cler,** **bi′cy·clist** *n.*

bid (bĭd) *v.* **bade** (băd or bād) or **bid, bidden** (bĭd′n) or

bid, bidding, bids —*tr.* **1.** *past tense and past participle* **bid a.** To offer (an amount of money) as a price for something: *The collector bid $5,000 for the antique desk.* **b.** To state one's intention to take (a certain number of tricks) in card games, as in bridge. **2.** To say or express (a greeting, wish, or farewell): *He bade us good night.* **3.** To give a command to; direct: *The queen bid the courtiers rise.* **4.** To request to come; invite: *The host bid the guests come to dinner.* —*intr.* past tense and past participle **bid 1.** To make an offer to pay a certain price: *We bid on the old lamp.* **2.** To try to win or achieve something: *Both candidates bid for election to Congress.* ❖ *n.* **1a.** An offer to pay a certain amount of money for something: *The auctioneer called for bids on the antique desk.* **b.** An amount bid: *He made a bid of $5,000.* **2.** A declaration of the number of tricks one expects to win in certain card games such as bridge: *My bid is three hearts.* **3.** An effort to win or attain something: *Several candidates made a bid for the presidency.* ◆ **bid out** To offer (work) for bids from outside contractors.

bidder (bĭd′ər) *n.* A person who makes a bid at an auction, in seeking a contract, or in a card game.

bidding (bĭd′ĭng) *n.* **1.** An order or command: *Orchestras start to play at the conductor's bidding.* **2.** A request to appear; an invitation: *At my bidding, they accepted.* **3.** Bids considered as a group.

biddy (bĭd′ē) *n., pl.* **biddies** A hen; a fowl.

bide (bīd) *tr. & intr.v.* **bided** or **bode** (bōd), **bided, biding, bides** To wait or wait for. ◆ **bide (one's) time** To wait for further developments: *If you bide your time, you too shall have a chance.*

biennial (bī-ĕn′ē-əl) *adj.* **1.** Lasting or living for two years: *biennial plants.* **2.** Occurring every second year: *biennial elections to Congress.* ❖ *n.* A plant that grows and produces leaves in its first year and that flowers, produces seeds, and dies in its second year. Carrots are biennials. —**bi·en′ni·al·ly** *adv.*

bier (bîr) *n.* A stand on which a corpse or a coffin containing a corpse is placed before burial.

bifocal (bī-fō′kəl or bī′fō′kəl) *adj.* **1.** Focusing light rays at two different points: *a bifocal lens.* **2.** Having one section that corrects for distant vision and another that corrects for near vision: *bifocal eyeglasses.* ❖ *n.* **bifocals** (bī-fō′-kəlz or bī′fō′kəlz) A pair of eyeglasses having bifocal lenses to correct both near and distant vision.

bifurcate (bī′fər-kāt′ or bī-fûr′kāt′) *tr. & intr.v.* **bifurcated, bifurcating, bifurcates** To divide or be divided into two parts or branches. —**bi′fur·ca′tion** (bī′fər-kā′shən) *n.*

big (bĭg) *adj.* **bigger, biggest 1.** Of great size, number, quantity, or extent; large: *a big house; a big city; a big appetite.* See Synonyms at **large. 2a.** Mature or grown-up: *big enough to take the bus by herself.* **b.** Older or eldest. Used especially of a brother or sister: *She shares a room with her big sister.* **3.** Prominent; influential: *a big banker.* **4.** Of great significance; momentous: *a big day in my life; practice for the big game.* **5.** Loud; resounding: *a big voice.* **6.** Full of self-importance; boastful: *a big talker.* ❖ *adv.* **1.** With an air of self-importance; boastfully: *talked big about his career plans.* **2.** With considerable success: *made it big.* ◆ **big on** Enthusiastic about; partial to: *She's big on volleyball.* —**big′ness** *n.*

bigamist (bĭg′ə-mĭst) *n.* A person who practices bigamy.

bigamous (bĭg′ə-məs) *adj.* **1.** Relating to bigamy. **2.** Guilty of bigamy.

bigamy (bĭg′ə-mē) *n.* The crime of marrying one person while still being legally married to another.

Big Bang theory *n.* The scientific theory that the universe originated approximately 13.7 billion years ago in a violent expansion of a singular point of extremely high density and temperature.

big brother *n.* **1.** An older brother. **2.** A man who assumes the role of an older brother, as by providing guidance or protection. **3.** also **Big Brother** A state, organization, or leader regarded as exercising oppressive control over individual lives.

big business *n.* Large businesses and corporations considered as a group.

big cheese *n. Slang* The most important or powerful person in an enterprise or field.

Big Dipper *n.* A group of seven stars in the constellation Ursa Major, four forming the bowl and three the handle in the shape of a dipper.

Bigfoot (bĭg′fŏŏt′) *n.* A very large, hairy, humanlike creature purported to inhabit northwest North America.

bighearted (bĭg′härt′ĭd) *adj.* Generous; kind. —**big′-heart′ed·ly** *adv.* —**big′heart′ed·ness** *n.*

bighorn (bĭg′hôrn′) *n., pl.* **bighorn** or **bighorns** The bighorn sheep.

bighorn sheep *n.* A wild sheep of the mountains of western North America, the male of which has very large curved horns.

bight (bīt) *n.* **1a.** A loop in a rope. **b.** The middle or slack part of an extended rope. **2a.** A long curve, especially in a shoreline. **b.** A wide bay formed by such a curve.

big league *n.* **1.** A major league in a professional sport, especially in baseball. **2.** often **big leagues** *Informal* The highest level of accomplishment in a field: *Having an entourage is a sign that an actor has made it to the big leagues.* —**big′-league′** *adj.*

bigmouth (bĭg′mouth′) *n. Slang* A person who talks very loudly or who gossips a lot.

bigot (bĭg′ət) *n.* A person who is intolerant of people who are different, as in religion, race, or politics.

bigoted (bĭg′ə-tĭd) *adj.* Characteristic of a bigot; intolerant; prejudiced.

bigotry (bĭg′ə-trē) *n.* The attitude or behavior of a bigot; intolerance; prejudice.

big screen *n.* **1.** The large screen on which movies are displayed in movie theaters. **2.** The medium in which movies are shown: *a television star making her debut on the big screen.*

big-screen (bĭg′skrēn′) *adj.* **1.** Having a large screen: *a big-screen television.* **2.** Relating to movies shown in theaters: *a big-screen adaptation of a television sitcom.*

big shot *n. Slang* A very important person.

big sister *n.* **1.** An older sister. **2.** A woman who assumes the role of an older sister, as by providing guidance or protection.

bigtime or **big-time** (bĭg′tīm′) *Informal adj.* Significant or important; major. ❖ *adv.* To an extreme degree; very much: *Sales are expanding bigtime.*

big time *n. Informal* The highest level of attainment in a field, such as the arts, business, or sports.

big top *n.* **1.** The main tent of a circus. **2.** The circus: *worked as a clown in the big top for ten years.*

bigwig (bĭg′wĭg′) *n. Slang* An important person; a dignitary.

bijou (bē′zhōō′) *n., pl.* **bijoux** (bē′zhōō′ *or* bē′zhōōz′) A small, exquisitely wrought trinket.

bike (bīk) *n.* **1.** A bicycle. **2.** A motorbike or motorcycle. ❖ *intr.v.* **biked, biking, bikes** To ride a bike.

biker (bī′kər) *n.* A person who rides a bicycle, motorbike, or motorcycle.

bikeway (bīk′wā′) *n.* A lane or path for bicycles.

bikini (bĭ-kē′nē) *n.* **1a.** A very small two-piece bathing suit worn by women. **b.** A very small bathing suit worn by men. **2.** often **bikinis** Brief underpants that reach to the hips rather than to the waist.

bilateral (bī-lăt′ər-əl) *adj.* **1.** Having two sides; two-sided. **2.** Affecting or undertaken by two sides or parties: *bilateral negotiations.* **3.** Relating to both the right and left sides of the body or of a body structure: *bilateral brain damage.* —**bi·lat′er·al·ly** *adv.*

bilateral symmetry *n.* Symmetrical arrangement of right and left halves along a central axis, as in an organism or body part.

bile (bīl) *n.* **1.** A bitter, alkaline, greenish liquid that is produced by the liver and stored in the gallbladder. Bile aids digestion in the duodenum by neutralizing acids and emulsifying fats. **2.** Bitterness of temper; ill humor: *sarcastic remarks full of bile.*

bilge (bĭlj) *n.* **1.** The lowest inner part of a ship's hull. **2.** Bilge water.

bilge water *n.* **1.** Water that collects in the bilge of a ship. **2.** *Slang* Nonsense.

bilingual (bī-lĭng′gwəl) *adj.* **1.** Able to use two languages fluently: *Many diplomats are bilingual.* **2.** Relating to or expressed in two languages: *a bilingual dictionary.* —**bi·lin′gual·ly** *adv.*

bilious (bĭl′yəs) *adj.* **1.** Relating to or containing bile. **2.** Relating to or characterized by an excess of bile. **3.** Relating to or suggestive of bilious distress or disease: *a bilious complexion.* **4.** Having a peevish disposition; ill-humored: *Our bilious neighbor is always complaining about something.* —**bil′ious·ly** *adv.* —**bil′ious·ness** *n.*

bilk (bĭlk) *tr.v.* **bilked, bilking, bilks** To cheat, defraud, or swindle: *The art dealer bilked unsuspecting clients out of millions.*

bill¹ (bĭl) *n.* **1.** A statement of charges for goods supplied or work performed: *a telephone bill.* **2.** A piece of paper money worth a certain amount: *a ten-dollar bill.* **3.** The entertainment offered by a theater. **4.** An advertising poster: *Post no bills!* **5.** A draft of a law presented for approval to a legislature: *a conservation bill.* ❖ *tr.v.* **billed, billing, bills 1a.** To give or send a statement of charges to: *Bill me for the amount due.* **b.** To enter on a statement of charges; prepare a bill of: *Please bill these purchases to our account.* **2.** To advertise or schedule by public notice or as part of a program: *I see that the play is billed as a comedy.*

bill² (bĭl) *n.* **1.** The horny, projecting structure that extends forward from the head of a bird and has an upper and a lower part. Birds that eat different kinds of food have bills of different sizes and shapes. **2.** The visor of a cap.

WORD HISTORY Bill¹ comes from Middle English *bille,* meaning "formal document," which comes from Medieval Latin *bulla,* meaning "seal on a document." **Bill²** comes from Old English *bile,* meaning "beak."

billboard (bĭl′bôrd′) *n.* A large upright board for the display of advertisements in public places or alongside highways.

billet (bĭl′ĭt) *n.* Lodging for soldiers in a civilian building

such as a private house or hotel. ❖ *v.* **billeted, billeting, billets** —*tr.* To house (soldiers), especially in civilian buildings: *The army billeted the soldiers in the village.* —*intr.* To be housed; lodge: *The soldiers billeted in an old farmhouse.*

billet-doux (bĭl′ā-dōō′) *n., pl.* **billets-doux** (bĭl′ā-dōōz′) A love letter.

billfold (bĭl′fōld′) *n.* A small case that folds flat, used for carrying paper money and personal documents, as in a pocket or handbag.

billiard (bĭl′yərd) *n.* A shot in billiards in which the cue ball strikes two balls; a carom. ❖ *adj.* Relating to or used in billiards: *a billiard table; a billiard cue.*

billiards (bĭl′yərdz) *pl.n. (used with a singular verb)* **1.** A game played on a rectangular cloth-covered table with raised cushioned edges, in which a cue is used to hit three balls against one another or the side cushions of the table. **2.** One of several similar games, such as pool.

billing (bĭl′ĭng) *n.* **1.** Relative prominence in publicity, as in the order in which the names of performers are listed: *The two actors share top billing in the new play.* **2.** Advertising; promotion: *The movie did not live up to its advance billing.*

billingsgate (bĭl′ĭngz-gāt′ *or* bĭl′ĭngz-gĭt) *n.* Foul, abusive language.

billion (bĭl′yən) *n.* **1.** The number, written as 10^9 or 1 followed by nine zeros, that is equal to one thousand times one million. **2.** *Chiefly British* The number, written as 10^{12} or 1 followed by 12 zeros, that is equal to one million times one million. —**bil′lionth** *n.*

billionaire (bĭl′yə-nâr′) *n.* A person whose wealth amounts to at least a billion dollars, pounds, or similar units in another currency.

bill of exchange *n., pl.* **bills of exchange** A written order directing that a specified sum of money be paid to a particular person.

bill of fare *n., pl.* **bills of fare** A menu.

bill of health *n., pl.* **bills of health** A certificate stating whether it is infectious disease aboard a ship or in a port of departure, given to the ship's master for presentation at the next port of arrival. ◆ **clean bill of health** *Informal* A good report based on a past record or condition.

bill of lading *n., pl.* **bills of lading** A document listing and acknowledging receipt of goods for shipment.

bill of rights *n., pl.* **bills of rights 1.** A formal statement of those rights and liberties considered essential to a people or group of people: *a consumer bill of rights.* **2. Bill of Rights** The first ten amendments to the Constitution of the United States, guaranteeing certain rights and privileges to citizens, such as freedom of speech.

bill of sale *n., pl.* **bills of sale** A document that transfers ownership of something to a new owner.

billow (bĭl′ō) *n.* **1.** A great wave or surge of water. **2.** A great swell or mass of something: *billows of smoke.* ❖ *v.* **billowed, billowing, billows** —*intr.* **1.** To rise or surge in or as if in billows: *Smoke billowed through the whole building.* **2.** To swell out; bulge: *At the open window there were curtains billowing in the wind.* —*tr.* To cause to swell out: *The wind billowed the ship's sails.* —**bil′low·y** *adj.*

billy club (bĭl′ē) *n.* A short stick or club, especially a police officer's club.

billy goat *n. Informal* A male goat.

bimbo (bĭm′bō) *n., pl.* **bimbos** *Slang* A person, especially a

woman, who is regarded as being sexy but vacuous.
bimonthly (bī-mŭnth′lē) *adj.* **1.** Occurring once every two months: *There are six bimonthly meetings of the club each year.* **2.** Occurring twice a month. ❖ *adv.* **1.** Once every two months. **2.** Twice a month: *Many businesses pay bimonthly, on the first and the fifteenth.* ❖ *n., pl.* **bimonthlies** A publication issued bimonthly. —SEE NOTE AT **biweekly.**

bin (bĭn) *n.* A container or enclosed space for holding or storing something: *a coal bin; a recycle bin.*

bin– Variant of **bi–**[1].

binary (bī′nə-rē) *adj.* **1.** Relating to or based on the number 2 or the binary number system: *a binary numeral.* **2.** Relating to a system of encoding data using only 0's and 1's. **3.** Consisting of or involving two different parts, kinds, or things: *a binary chemical compound.*

binary digit *n.* Either of the digits 0 or 1, used in the binary number system.

binary fission *n.* A form of asexual reproduction in bacteria and other one-celled organisms that involves the dividing of a cell into two cells of approximately the same size.

binary number system *n.* A method of representing numbers as sums of powers of 2 in which all numbers can be written using just the digits 0 and 1.

binary star *n.* A pair of stars revolving around a common center of gravity, often appearing to observers as a single star.

binaural (bī-nôr′əl *or* bĭn-ôr′əl) *adj.* **1.** Having or hearing with two ears. **2.** Relating to sound coming from two sources in a way that causes a stereophonic effect.

bind (bīnd) *v.* **bound** (bound), **binding, binds** —*tr.* **1a.** To fasten, tie, or secure by tying, as with a rope or cord: *bind a package with string; bind a prisoner in chains.* **b.** To hold or restrain with or as if with bonds: *traditions that bind people to a way of life.* **2.** To bandage: *bound their wounds.* **3a.** To compel, obligate, or unite: *Duty binds me to remain at my post.* **b.** To place under legal obligation: *The terms of the contract bind the author and the publisher.* **c.** To hold or employ as an apprentice or servant; indenture: *The young man was bound out as a servant.* **4.** To form a chemical bond with. **5.** To cause to stick together in a mass: *Cement binds gravel to make concrete for paving roads.* **6.** To enclose and fasten between covers: *bind a book.* **7.** To cover with a border or edging for added protection or decoration: *bind a seam with tape.* —*intr.* **1.** To tie up or fasten something. **2.** To stick or become stuck: *Will that glue bind to glass?* **3.** To be tight and uncomfortable: *Once a sweater shrinks it binds.* **4.** To become compact or solid; stick together: *Cement will not bind without water.* **5.** To be compelling or unifying: *We have family ties that bind.* **6.** To combine chemically or form a chemical bond: *Hydrogen binds with oxygen to form water.* ❖ *n.* *Informal* A difficult or confining situation: *He was in a bind when his car broke down.*

binder (bīn′dər) *n.* **1.** A person who binds books. **2.** A notebook cover with rings or clamps for holding sheets of paper. **3.** Something used to tie or fasten, such as cord or rope. **4.** A material added to something to make it hold together: *Water is a binder in bread dough.* **5.** A farm machine that reaps and ties grain in bundles. **6.** A payment or written statement making an agreement legally binding until the completion of a contract, especially an insurance contract.

bindery (bīn′də-rē) *n., pl.* **binderies** A place where books are bound.

binding (bīn′dĭng) *n.* **1.** The cover that holds together the pages of a book: *an expensive book with leather binding.* **2.** A strip of tape or fabric sewn over an edge or seam to protect or decorate it. **3.** A fastening on a ski for securing the boot, especially when designed to release the boot in case of a fall. ❖ *adj.* Imposing a firm obligation; obligatory: *a binding agreement.*

binding energy *n.* The net energy necessary to break a molecule, atom, or nucleus into its smaller component parts.

bindweed (bīnd′wēd′) *n.* Any of various twining plants having pink or white trumpet-shaped flowers.

binge (bĭnj) *n.* A period of excessive or unrestrained activity, especially of eating or drinking. ❖ *intr.v.* **binged, bingeing** *or* **binging, binges** To indulge in some activity, especially eating, excessively or immoderately: *I felt a little sick after bingeing on chocolate.*

bingo (bĭng′gō) *n.* A game of chance played by covering numbers on a printed card as they are called out. The winner is the player who covers the first five numbers in a row in any direction.

binnacle (bĭn′ə-kəl) *n.* The case that supports a ship's compass, usually located near the helm.

binocular (bə-nŏk′yə-lər *or* bī-nŏk′yə-lər) *adj.* Relating to or involving both eyes at once: *binocular vision.*

binoculars (bə-nŏk′yə-lərz *or* bī-nŏk′yə-lərz) *pl.n.* A distance-viewing device consisting of two small telescopes mounted next to each other, designed for use by both eyes at the same time.

binomial (bī-nō′mē-əl) *adj.* Consisting of or relating to two names or terms: *a binomial expression in math.* ❖ *n.* A polynomial that is composed of two terms, such as $3a + 2b$.

bio– *or* **bi–** A prefix that means: **1.** Life or living organism: *biome.* **2.** Biology or biological: *biophysics.*

WORD BUILDING The prefix **bio–** comes from the Greek word *bios,* meaning "life." When used to form words in English, *bio–* generally refers to living organisms or to biology, the science of living organisms. Many of the words that begin with *bio–* only came into being in the 1900s, such as *bioethics* and *biotechnology.* Sometimes before an *o, bio–* becomes *bi–: biopsy.*

biochemical (bī′ō-kĕm′ĭ-kəl) *adj.* Relating to biochemistry. —**bi′o·chem′i·cal·ly** *adv.*

biochemist (bī′ō-kĕm′ĭst) *n.* A scientist who specializes in biochemistry.

biochemistry (bī′ō-kĕm′ĭ-strē) *n.* The study of the chemical composition of substances that form living matter and of chemical processes that go on in living organisms.

biodegradable (bī′ō-dĭ-grā′də-bəl) *adj.* Capable of being decomposed by biological agents, especially bacteria: *a biodegradable detergent.*

biodiesel (bī′ō-dē′zəl *or* bī′ō-dē′səl) *n.* A biofuel made by processing vegetable oils and other fats for use in a diesel engine, either in pure form or as an additive to conventional diesel fuel.

biodiversity (bī′ō-dī-vûr′sĭ-tē) *n.* The number and variety of species found within a particular geographic region.

bioethics (bī′ō-ĕth′ĭks) *n.* *(used with a singular verb)* The study of the ethical and moral questions raised by new biological and medical research, as in the fields of genetic engineering and cloning.

biofeedback (bī′ō-fēd′băk′) *n.* The use of monitoring devices in an attempt to gain some voluntary control over involuntary bodily functions, such as the heartbeat or blood pressure.

biofuel (bī′ō-fyōō′əl) *n.* Fuel that is produced from renewable resources, especially plants or treated municipal and industrial wastes.

biographer (bī-ŏg′rə-fər) *n.* A person who writes a biography.

biographical (bī′ə-grăf′ĭ-kəl) also **biographic** (bī′ə-grăf′-ĭk) *adj.* **1.** Relating to or based on a person's life: *The interviewer asked the singer for some biographical information.* **2.** Relating to biography: *She's written and produced several biographical films.*

biography (bī-ŏg′rə-fē) *n., pl.* **biographies** An account of a person's life written by someone else.

biohazard (bī′ō-hăz′ərd) *n.* A substance that can cause harm to humans because it contains infectious organisms such as bacteria or viruses. Medical waste, for example, often contains biohazards.

biological (bī′ə-lŏj′ĭ-kəl) *adj.* **1.** Relating to or affecting living organisms: *biological processes such as growth and digestion.* **2.** Relating to biology: *the biological sciences.* **3.** Related because of sharing genes transmitted by a parent or other ancestor: *He has one biological sister and one adoptive sister.* —**bi′o·log′i·cal·ly** *adv.*

biological clock *n.* **1.** An internal mechanism in organisms that controls the cycle of various functions, such as sleep cycles in mammals and photosynthesis in plants. **2.** The time period during which a person who desires to have a biological child, especially a woman approaching the decline of reproductive capability, is still able to do so.

biological warfare *n.* The use of disease-producing microorganisms or biological toxins as a weapon of war.

biology (bī-ŏl′ə-jē) *n.* The scientific study of life and of living organisms, including growth, structure, reproduction, and evolution. Botany, zoology, and bacteriology are all branches of biology. —**bi·ol′o·gist** *n.*

bioluminescence (bī′ō-lōō′mə-nĕs′əns) *n.* Emission of light by living organisms, such as fireflies, certain fungi, and many marine invertebrate animals. —**bi′o·lu′-mi·nes′cent** *adj.*

biomass (bī′ō-măs′) *n.* **1.** The total amount of living material in a given area. **2.** Crops, algae, agricultural waste, or other organic materials used as a fuel or energy source.

biome (bī′ōm′) *n.* A large community of organisms occupying a distinct region, such as a grassland or desert, that is defined chiefly by its climate and vegetation.

biomechanics (bī′ō-mĭ-kăn′ĭks) *n.* (*used with a singular verb*) The scientific study of the mechanics of motion in humans and other animals. —**bi′o·me·chan′i·cal** *adj.*

biometrics (bī′ō-mĕt′rĭks) *n.* (*used with a singular verb*) The statistical study of biological phenomena.

bionic (bī-ŏn′ĭk) *adj.* **1.** Relating to a body part that has been wholly or partly replaced by electronic or mechanical devices. **2.** Relating to bionics.

bionics (bī-ŏn′ĭks) *n.* (*used with a singular verb*) The use of a system or design found in nature, such as the ability of plants to store solar energy, as a model for designing artificial systems, especially mechanical or electronic systems.

biophysics (bī′ō-fĭz′ĭks) *n.* (*used with a singular verb*) The scientific study of biological systems and processes using the methods of physics.

biopsy (bī′ŏp′sē) *n., pl.* **biopsies 1.** The surgical removal of a sample of tissue from a living body for examination and diagnosis. **2.** A tissue sample obtained by surgery.

bioremediation (bī′ō-rĭ-mē′dē-ā′shən) *n.* The use of biological materials, such as bacteria or plants, to reduce the amount of contamination in polluted soil or water.

bioreserve (bī′ō-rĭ-zûrv′) *n.* An area set up as a wildlife preserve in which only limited visits by the public are allowed.

biosphere (bī′ə-sfîr′) *n.* The part of the earth and its atmosphere in which living organisms exist, along with all those organisms.

biotechnology (bī′ō-tĕk-nŏl′ə-jē) *n.* **1.** The use of living organisms or biological substances to perform certain industrial or manufacturing processes. **2.** The engineering and biological study of relationships between humans and machines. —**bi′o·tech′no·log′i·cal** (bī′ō-tĕk′nə-lŏj′ĭ-kəl) *adj.*

bioterrorism (bī′ō-tĕr′ə-rĭz′əm) *n.* The use of biological substances that cause disease for the purposes of terrorism.

biotic (bī-ŏt′ĭk) *adj.* Relating to living organisms: *the biotic components of an ecosystem.*

biotin (bī′ə-tĭn) *n.* A vitamin belonging to the vitamin B complex and important in the metabolism of carbohydrates and fats. It is found in liver, egg yolks, milk, yeast, and some vegetables.

bipartisan (bī-pär′tĭ-zən *or* bī-pär′tĭ-sən) *adj.* Composed of or supported by two political parties, especially the Republican and Democratic parties: *a bipartisan bill to fight crime.*

bipartite (bī-pär′tīt′) *adj.* **1.** Having or consisting of two parts. **2.** Drawn up in two corresponding parts, one for each party: *a bipartite treaty.*

biped (bī′pĕd′) *n.* An animal having two feet, such as a bird or human. —**bi·ped′al** *adj.*

biplane (bī′plān′) *n.* An airplane having two sets of wings, one above the other.

bipolar disorder (bī-pō′lər) *n.* A mental disorder characterized by periods of depression alternating with mania.

biracial (bī-rā′shəl) *adj.* **1.** For, consisting of, or relating to members of two racial groups: *a biracial committee for cooperation between black and white residents.* **2.** Having parents of two different races.

birch (bûrch) *n.* **1.** Any of various trees of the Northern Hemisphere having toothed leaves and papery bark that peels easily. **2.** The hard wood of such a tree.

bird (bûrd) *n.* **1.** Any of numerous warm-blooded, egg-laying vertebrate animals that have wings, a body covered with feathers, and a bill used for gathering food. **2.** A shuttlecock. **3.** *Slang* A person, especially one who is odd or unusual: *a strange bird.* ❖ *intr.v.* **birded, birding, birds** To observe and identify birds in their natural surroundings. ◆ **birds of a feather** People who are similar, as in character, personality, or tastes. **for the birds** Worthless or objectionable. —SEE NOTE AT **pretty.**

birdbath (bûrd′băth′) *n.* A basin filled with water for birds to drink or bathe in.

birdcage (bûrd′kāj′) *n.* A cage for birds.

birdcall (bûrd′kôl′) *n.* **1.** The song or cry of a bird. **2a.** An imitation of the song or cry of a bird. **b.** A small device for producing this sound.

bird dog *n.* A dog trained to hunt game birds.

birder (bûr′dər) *n.* A bird watcher.

birdhouse (bûrd′hous′) *n.* A box, often shaped like a house, that is provided as a nesting place for birds.

birdie (bûr′dē) *n.* **1.** *Informal* A small bird. **2.** In golf, a score of one stroke under par for a hole.

birdlime (bûrd′līm′) *n.* A sticky substance smeared on twigs to catch small birds.

bird of paradise *n.*, *pl.* **birds of paradise 1.** Any of various birds of New Guinea and Australia, usually having brightly colored, showy feathers in the male. **2.** Any of several African plants grown for their showy orange and blue flowers that emerge from a beak-shaped structure.

bird of prey *n.*, *pl.* **birds of prey** Any of various birds, such as a hawk, eagle, owl, or vulture, that hunt and kill other animals for food or feed on dead animals.

birdseed (bûrd′sēd′) *n.* Seed that is provided as food for caged or wild birds.

bird's-eye (bûrdz′ī′) *adj.* Seen from high above: *a bird's-eye view of the countryside.*

bird watcher *n.* A person who observes and identifies birds in their natural surroundings. —**bird watching** *n.*

biretta (bə-rĕt′ə) *n.* A stiff square cap worn by members of the Roman Catholic clergy. Birettas are black for priests, purple for bishops, and red for cardinals.

birth (bûrth) *n.* **1.** The emergence and separation of offspring from the body of the mother: *At birth she weighed seven pounds.* **2.** The act or process of bearing young: *A second birth is usually easier than the first.* **3.** A beginning or origin: *the birth of an idea.* **4.** Family background; ancestry: *an heir of noble birth.* ❖ *tr.v.* **birthed, birthing, births** To deliver (a baby).

birth certificate *n.* An official record of the date and place of a person's birth, usually including the names of the parents.

birth control *n.* **1.** Control of the number of children conceived or born, especially by the use of contraception. **2.** A contraceptive device or technique.

birthday (bûrth′dā′) *n.* **1.** The day of a person's birth. **2.** The anniversary of that day.

birth defect *n.* A physical defect or abnormality of the body that is present at the time of birth. Birth defects can be caused by heredity or by the injury or faulty development of the fetus before or during birth.

birthmark (bûrth′märk′) *n.* A mark or blemish present on the body from birth.

birth name *n.* **1.** The name given to a person at birth, especially that of an adopted child before he or she is renamed. **2.** A maiden name.

birthplace (bûrth′plās′) *n.* The place where someone is born or where something originates.

birthrate (bûrth′rāt′) *n.* The ratio of total live births to total population in a specified area or community over a particular period of time, usually one year.

birthright (bûrth′rīt′) *n.* A right to which a person is entitled because of birth or origin: *Freedom of speech is an American birthright.*

birthstone (bûrth′stōn′) *n.* A jewel associated with the specific month of a person's birth.

biscotti (bĭ-skŏt′ē) *pl.n.* Italian cookies traditionally baked in hard oblong slices and often containing almonds or other nuts.

biscuit (bĭs′kĭt) *n.*, *pl.* **biscuits 1.** A small flaky cake of bread leavened with baking powder or soda. **2.** *Chiefly British* **a.** A cracker. **b.** A cookie.

bisect (bī′sĕkt′ *or* bī-sĕkt′) *tr.v.* **bisected, bisecting, bi-**

sects To cut or divide into two equal parts: *bisect a triangle.* —**bi·sec′tion** *n.* —SEE NOTE AT **segment.**

bisector (bī′sĕk′tər *or* bī-sĕk′tər) *n.* A straight line that bisects an angle or line segment.

bisexual (bī-sĕk′shōō-əl) *adj.* **1.** Having a sexual orientation toward people of both sexes. **2.** Having male and female reproductive organs in a single individual; hermaphroditic: *Earthworms are bisexual.* ❖ *n.* A bisexual person. —**bi′sex·u·al′i·ty** (bī′sĕk-shōō-ăl′ĭ-tē) *n.*

bishop (bĭsh′əp) *n.* **1.** A high-ranking Christian cleric, in modern churches usually in charge of a diocese. **2.** A chess piece that can move diagonally across any number of unoccupied spaces of the same color.

bishopric (bĭsh′ə-prĭk) *n.* The office, rank, or diocese of a bishop.

bismuth (bĭz′məth) *n. Symbol* **Bi** A brittle, pinkish-white metallic element that occurs in nature as a free metal and in various ores. It is used in making low-melting alloys for fire-safety devices. Atomic number 83. See **Periodic Table.**

bison (bī′sən *or* bī′zən) *n.*, *pl.* **bison 1.** A large mammal of western North America that has a massive head, a shaggy mane, and short curved horns; a buffalo. **2.** A similar but smaller European animal. —SEE NOTE AT **buffalo.**

bisphenol A (bĭs′fē′nôl′) *n.* A chemical used in making polycarbonate and epoxy resins and other plastics. It is suspected of causing health problems by interfering with the body's hormones.

bisque (bĭsk) *n.* A thick cream soup: *lobster bisque.*

bistro (bē′strō *or* bĭs′trō) *n.*, *pl.* **bistros** A small restaurant, bar, or nightclub.

bit[1] (bĭt) *n.* **1.** A small piece or amount: *a bit of lint; a bit of luck.* **2.** A brief amount of time; a moment: *Wait a bit.* **3.** An entertainment routine given regularly by a performer; an act. **4.** *Informal* An amount equal to one eighth of a dollar: *two bits.* ◆ **a bit** To a small degree; somewhat: *The soup is a bit hot.* **bit by bit** Little by little; gradually: *My piano playing improved bit by bit.*

bit[2] (bĭt) *n.* **1.** A pointed tool for drilling that fits into a brace or electric drill. **2.** The sharp part of a tool, such as the cutting edge of a knife. **3.** The metal mouthpiece of a bridle, used to control the horse. **4.** The part of a key that enters the lock and works the mechanism.

bit[3] (bĭt) *n.* The smallest unit of computer memory. A bit holds one of two possible values, either of the binary digits 0 or 1.

WORD HISTORY Bit[1] comes from Old English *bita*, meaning "morsel, small amount of food." **Bit**[2] comes from Old English *bite*, meaning "act of biting." **Bit**[3] comes from the phrase *b(inary) (dig)it.*

bit[4] (bĭt) *v.* Past tense and a past participle of **bite.**

bitch (bĭch) *n.* A female dog or related animal, such as a coyote.

bite (bīt) *v.* **bit** (bĭt), **bitten** (bĭt′n) *or* **bit, biting, bites** —*tr.* **1.** To use the teeth to cut, tear, or hold: *He bit the bread and tore off a piece.* **2a.** To pierce the skin of (a person or animal) with the teeth, fangs, or mouthparts: *Did the snake bite you?* **b.** To sting with a stinger: *I got bitten by a wasp.* **3.** To tear or cut into. Used especially of implements: *The axe bit the tree trunk.* **4.** To seize (bait or a lure) with the mouth: *The fish just won't bite this lure.* **5.** To gain traction on or apply pressure on in order to prevent slipping; grip: *I couldn't get the wrench to bite the pipe.* **6.** To cause sharp pain to: *The cold wind was biting* *my face.* —*intr.* **1.** To use the teeth to tear or cut something: *I bit into the pizza.* **2.** To cut or tear something: *The chainsaw bit into the log.* **3.** To grip a surface: *The tires can't bite when the road is icy.* **4.** To seize bait or a lure with the mouth: *Fish seem to bite more just before it starts to rain.* **5.** To be deceived by a trick or scheme: *She tried to pass off the old car as a bargain, but no one would bite.* ❖ *n.* **1.** The act of biting: *The dog's bark is worse than his bite.* **2.** A wound or injury resulting from biting: *a mosquito bite.* **3.** An amount of food taken into the mouth at one time; a mouthful: *Let me have a bite of your sandwich.* **4.** *Informal* A light meal or snack: *We stopped at the coffee shop for a bite.* **5.** A secure grip or hold, as by a tool: *The pliers had a good bite on the nut.* **6.** The angle at which the upper and lower teeth meet: *He wore braces to correct his bite.* ◆ **bite off more than (one) can chew** To decide or agree to do more than one can accomplish. **bite the dust** *Slang* **1.** To fall dead. **2.** To come to an end. **bite the hand that feeds (one)** To repay generosity or kindness with ingratitude and injury. —**bit′er** *n.*

biting (bī′tĭng) *adj.* **1.** Causing a stinging sensation: *a biting wind blew across the field.* **2.** Injuring or capable of injuring the feelings: *biting criticism.* **3.** Capable of wounding with the teeth, fangs, or mouthparts: *biting flies.* —**bit′ing·ly** *adv.*

bitmap (bĭt′măp′) *n.* A set of bits forming a graphic image generated by a computer. Each bit or group of bits corresponds to a pixel in the image. —**bit′mapped′** (bĭt′-măpt′) *adj.*

bit part *n.* A small or insignificant role, as in a play or movie, usually with very few spoken lines.

bitten (bĭt′n) *v.* A past participle of **bite.**

bitter (bĭt′ər) *adj.* **bitterer, bitterest 1.** Having or being a taste that is sharp or unpleasant: *a bitter drink.* **2.** Causing sharp pain to the body; harsh: *a bitter wind.* **3.** Hard to accept, admit, or bear: *the bitter truth.* **4.** Showing or proceeding from strong dislike or animosity: *bitter foes; a bitter fight.* **5.** Resulting from severe grief, anguish, or disappointment: *cry bitter tears.* **6.** Having or showing a resentful feeling: *bitter about being cheated.* ❖ *n.* **1. bitters** A bitter, usually alcoholic liquid used in cocktails and as a tonic. **2.** *Chiefly British* A sharp-tasting beer made with hops. —**bit′ter·ly** *adv.* —**bit′ter·ness** *n.*

bitter end *n.* A final, painful, or disastrous extremity.

bittern (bĭt′ərn) *n.* Any of several long-necked wading birds having mottled brownish feathers and a deep booming cry.

bitterroot (bĭt′ər-rōot′ *or* bĭt′ər-rŏot′) *n.* A plant of western North America having showy pink or white flowers and a bitter but edible root.

bittersweet (bĭt′ər-swēt′) *n.* **1.** Any of several woody vines having yellow-orange fruits that split open and expose seeds with red coverings. **2.** A kind of nightshade plant that has violet flowers and poisonous red berries. ❖ *adj.* **1.** Bitter and sweet at the same time: *bittersweet chocolate.* **2.** Pleasant and unpleasant at the same time: *bittersweet memories.*

bitty (bĭt′ē) *adj.* **bittier, bittiest** *Informal* Tiny.

bitumen (bĭ-tōō′mən) *n.* Any of various flammable mixtures of hydrocarbons and other substances found in asphalt and tar. They occur naturally or are produced from petroleum and coal.

bituminous (bĭ-tōō′mə-nəs) *adj.* **1.** Resembling or containing bitumen. **2.** Relating to bituminous coal.

bituminous coal *n.* A grade of coal that contains a high percentage of bitumen and burns with much smoke and a yellow flame; soft coal.

bivalve (bī′vălv′) *n.* Any of numerous mollusks, such as a clam, oyster, or scallop, having a shell that consists of two parts hinged together. ❖ *adj.* Having a hinged shell.

bivouac (bĭv′ōō-ăk′ *or* bĭv′wăk′) *n.* A temporary camp made by soldiers in the field. ❖ *intr.v.* **bivouacked, bivouacking, bivouacs** also **bivouacs** To camp in a bivouac.

biweekly (bī-wēk′lē) *adj.* **1.** Occurring every two weeks. **2.** Occurring twice a week: *biweekly meetings on Tuesday and Thursday.* ❖ *n., pl.* **biweeklies** A publication issued every two weeks. ❖ *adv.* **1.** Once every two weeks: *The company gives out paychecks biweekly.* **2.** Twice a week.

USAGE Properly speaking, the word **biweekly** means "once every two weeks" and **bimonthly** means "once every two months." **Semiweekly** means "twice a week" and **semimonthly** means "twice a month." Because many people mix up these *bi-* and *semi-* words, it is safest to use phrases like *every two weeks* or *twice a month.* A publication that comes out every two weeks, however, is always called a *biweekly.* One appearing every two months is a *bimonthly.*

bizarre (bĭ-zär′) *adj.* Very strange or odd: *a bizarre hat; a bizarre idea.*

blab (blăb) *v.* **blabbed, blabbing, blabs** —*tr.* To tell (a secret), especially through careless talk. —*intr.* **1.** To reveal secret matters: *The secret was out when I blabbed without thinking.* **2.** To chatter indiscreetly.

blabber (blăb′ər) *intr.v.* **blabbered, blabbering, blabbers** To chatter. ❖ *n.* **1.** Idle chatter. **2.** A person who blabs.

blabbermouth (blăb′ər-mouth′) *n.* *Informal* A person who talks carelessly and at length.

black (blăk) *adj.* **blacker, blackest 1.** Being of the color black, producing or reflecting comparatively little light and having no predominant hue. **2.** Without light: *a black moonless night.* **3.** also **Black a.** Relating to or belonging to a racial group having dark skin, especially a group of African origin. **b.** Relating to or belonging to an American group of people descended from African peoples having dark skin; African-American. **4.** Evil; wicked: *black deeds.* **5.** Gloomy; depressing: *a black day; black thoughts.* **6.** Angry; sullen: *He gave me a black look.* **7.** Portraying tragic or unhappy events in a satirical or humorous way: *a black comedy about war.* **8.** Marked by disaster: *The stock market crashed on Black Friday.* **9.** Deserving of or indicating censure or dishonor: *the industry's blackest record as a polluter of the rivers.* **10.** Served without cream or milk: *black coffee.* ❖ *n.* **1a.** The darkest extreme of the series of colors that runs through all the shades of gray to white, being the opposite of white. **b.** A black paint, dye, or pigment. **2.** Clothing of this color, especially clothing worn for mourning: *At the funeral everyone was dressed in black.* **3.** also **Black a.** A member of a racial group having dark skin, especially one of African origin. **b.** An American descended from peoples of African origin having dark skin; an African American. ❖ *tr.v.* **blacked, blacking, blacks** To make black: *blacked the pair of scuffed shoes.* ◆ **black out 1.** To lose consciousness or memory temporarily: *He felt lightheaded and then blacked out.* **2.** To prevent the transmission of (a television program). **3.** To cover or make illegible with black marking: *The names in the report had been blacked out.* **4.** To turn off or conceal all lights in (a building or area) in order to make it difficult for enemy aircraft to find a target during an air raid. **5.** To cause a failure of electrical power in: *The storm blacked out the street lights.* **in the black** Making a profit; prosperous. —**black′ly** *adv.* —**black′ness** *n.*

black-and-blue (blăk′ən-blōō′) *adj.* Discolored from broken blood vessels and clotted blood under the skin; bruised.

black and white *n.* **1.** Writing or printing: *She did not believe it until she read it in black and white.* **2.** Photography or printmaking that uses only black and white, or black, white, and values of gray: *a movie shot in black and white.*

black-and-white (blăk′ən-wīt′) *adj.* **1.** Being done, drawn, or photographed in shades of black and white: *a black-and-white picture.* **2.** Partly black and partly white: *a black-and-white cow.* **3.** Making judgments based on two rigid categories, such as right and wrong: *black-and-white opinions.*

black art *n.* Black magic.

blackball (blăk′bôl′) *n.* A negative vote. ❖ *tr.v.* **blackballed, blackballing, blackballs 1.** To vote against and prevent (someone) from being admitted to an organization, as by placing a black ball in a ballot box. **2.** To shut out from participation: *actors who were blackballed for their political views.*

black bean *n.* A type of bean that has small, blackish seeds.

black bear *n.* **1.** A North American bear that lives in forests and has thick black or dark-brown fur. **2.** An Asian bear having a pointed snout and black or dark-brown fur with a white V-shaped mark on the chest.

black belt *n.* The rank of expert in a system of self-defense, such as judo or karate.

blackberry (blăk′běr′ē) *n.* **1.** A blackish, glossy, many-seeded fruit of any of various plants with long prickly stems. **2.** A shrub that bears such berries.

blackbird (blăk′bûrd′) *n.* Any of various birds having black or mostly black feathers.

blackboard (blăk′bôrd′) *n.* A hard, smooth, dark-colored panel for writing on with chalk; a chalkboard.

blackbody (blăk′bŏd′ē) *n., pl.* **blackbodies** A theoretical object that completely absorbs any radiation that strikes it.

black box *n.* A flight recorder.

blackdamp (blăk′dămp′) *n.* A suffocating gas, mostly a mixture of carbon dioxide and nitrogen, found in mines after fires and explosions.

Black Death *n.* A widespread outbreak of bubonic plague that killed large numbers of people throughout Europe and much of Asia in the 1300s.

blacken (blăk′ən) *v.* **blackened, blackening, blackens** —*tr.* **1.** To make black: *Smoke blackened the sky.* **2.** To speak evil of; defame: *The scandal blackened the athlete's reputation.* **3.** To sear (meat or fish that has been coated with pepper and other spices) in a very hot skillet: *blackened the salmon and served it with rice.* —*intr.* To become dark or black: *The sky blackened before the storm.*

Black English *n.* **1.** African American Vernacular English. **2.** Any of the nonstandard varieties of English spoken by black people throughout the world.

black eye *n.* **1.** A bruised discoloration of the skin around the eye, resulting from a blow. **2.** A bad name; a dishonored reputation: *Involvement in the scandal gave the politician a black eye.*

black-eyed pea (blăk′īd′) *n.* The cowpea.

black-eyed Susan (sōō′zən) *n.* Any of several North American plants having hairy stems and leaves and showy flowers with orange-yellow rays surrounding a dark-brown center.

blackface (blăk′fās′) *n.* Black makeup for the face, especially when worn by a performer in a minstrel show.

Blackfoot (blăk′fŏŏt′) *n., pl.* **Blackfoot** or **Blackfeet** (blăk′fēt′) **1.** A member of a Native American people of Montana, Alberta, and Saskatchewan. **2.** The Algonquian language of the Blackfoot.

blackguard (blăg′ərd *or* blăg′ärd′) *n.* A low unprincipled person; a scoundrel.

blackhead (blăk′hĕd′) *n.* A mass of fatty material and dirt that collects in and blocks one of the pores of the skin.

black hole *n.* An extremely dense celestial object that has a gravitational field so strong that nothing can escape, not even light. A black hole is formed by the collapse of a massive star's core in a supernova.

black ice *n.* A thin, nearly invisible coating of ice that forms on paved surfaces.

blacking (blăk′ĭng) *n.* A black paste or liquid used as a polish, as for shoes or stoves.

blackish (blăk′ĭsh) *adj.* Somewhat black in color.

blackjack (blăk′jăk′) *n.* **1.** A small leather-covered club with a flexible handle. **2.** A card game in which the object is to hold cards with a higher count than that of the dealer but not exceeding 21. ❖ *tr.v.* **blackjacked, blackjacking, blackjacks** To strike or threaten with a blackjack.

black-legged tick (blăk′lĕgd′) *n.* A deer tick.

black light *n.* Invisible ultraviolet or infrared light. Black light causes fluorescent materials to emit visible light.

blacklist (blăk′lĭst′) *n.* A list of people or organizations to be disapproved, boycotted, or penalized. ❖ *tr.v.* **blacklisted, blacklisting, blacklists** To place (a name) on a blacklist: *The government blacklisted the political dissidents.*

black lung *n.* A disease of the lungs caused by inhaling coal dust over a long period of time.

black magic *n.* Magic practiced for evil purposes, especially when invoking the help of evil spirits.

blackmail (blăk′māl′) *n.* **1.** The extortion of money or something of value from a person by the threat of exposing something criminal or discreditable about the person. **2.** Money or something of value paid or demanded as blackmail: *The official refused to pay blackmail.* ❖ *tr.v.* **blackmailed, blackmailing, blackmails** To subject (someone) to blackmail. —**black′mail′er** *n.*

black market *n.* **1.** The illegal business of buying or selling goods that are banned or restricted by a government. **2.** A place where this illegal business is carried on.

Black Muslim *n.* A member of a black American group, the Nation of Islam, that professes Islamic beliefs.

blackout (blăk′out′) *n.* **1.** A cutoff of electric power, especially as a result of a shortage, a mechanical failure, or overuse by consumers. **2.** The act of putting out or concealing all lights that might be visible to enemy aircraft during a night raid. **3.** A temporary loss of consciousness or memory: *The driver's blackout caused the crash.* **4.** A suppression by censorship: *a news blackout.* **5.** The suppression of a television broadcast, as of a popular sports event, in a particular area, often to support ticket sales within that area.

Black Power *n.* A movement among black Americans emphasizing racial pride and social equality.

black sheep *n.* **1.** A sheep with black fleece. **2.** An undesirable or disgraceful member of a family or group.

blacksmith (blăk′smĭth′) *n.* A person who forges and shapes iron into horseshoes and other objects of metal.

WORD HISTORY Originally, a *smith* was a skilled worker in metal, wood, or cloth, but the meaning of *smith* has narrowed to "a worker in metal." A **blacksmith** is "a smith who works with iron," the black metal, especially with forging iron, which is at the beginning of the metalworking process. A **whitesmith**, by contrast, is a person who works with white metal (any of various light-colored alloys usually containing tin or lead) or who polishes or otherwise finishes metal products.

blacksnake (blăk′snāk′) *n.* Any of various dark-colored, chiefly nonvenomous snakes of eastern North America.

blackthorn (blăk′thôrn′) *n.* A thorny shrub of Eurasia having white flowers and small bluish-black fruit.

black tie *n.* **1.** A black bow tie worn with a tuxedo or dinner jacket. **2.** A style of evening dress that includes a black bow tie with a tuxedo or dinner jacket for men and an evening gown or other formal dress for women. —**black′-tie′** *adj.*

blacktop (blăk′tŏp′) *n.* A bituminous material, such as asphalt, used to pave roads. ❖ *tr.v.* **blacktopped, blacktopping, blacktops** To pave with blacktop.

black widow *n.* Any of several spiders with a black shiny body, the female of which is venomous and often has red markings in the shape of an hourglass on the underside.

bladder (blăd′ər) *n.* **1.** A sac with an elastic membrane that stores urine secreted by the kidneys and is found in most vertebrates except birds. **2.** Any of other similar sacs in animals, such as a swim bladder. **3.** A hollow structure or sac in a plant, such as an air bladder in certain seaweeds. **4.** Something that is hollow and inflatable: *the bladder of a football.*

blade (blād) *n.* **1.** The flat sharp-edged part of a cutting tool or weapon. **2.** A sword. **3a.** The thin flat part of something: *the blade of an oar.* **b.** A long, thin, often curved piece, as of metal or rubber, used for plowing, clearing, or wiping. **4.** The broad flattened part of a leaf, extending from the stalk. **5.** The metal part of an ice skate that makes contact with the ice. **6.** A dashing young man.

blah (blä) *Informal n.* **1. blahs** A general feeling of dissatisfaction or depression: *She's had the blahs all week.* **2.** Meaningless or uninteresting remarks; blah-blah. ❖ *adj.* **1.** Dull and uninteresting: *The party turned out to be very blah.* **2.** Low in spirits or health: *I'm feeling blah.*

blah-blah (blä′blä′) *Informal n.* Meaningless or uninteresting remarks: *The opening presentation was nothing but a lot of blah-blah.*

blame (blām) *tr.v.* **blamed, blaming, blames 1.** To hold (a person or thing) responsible or at fault: *The driver blamed the icy road for the accident.* **2.** To find fault with; censure: *I can't blame you for wanting your fair share.* **3.** To place responsibility for (something) on a cause: *The article blamed the crisis on poor planning.* ❖ *n.* The state of being responsible for a fault or error: *I had to accept the blame for my mistake.* ◆ **to blame 1.** Deserving censure; at fault: *Who is to blame for this mess?* **2.** Being the cause or source of something: *The snowstorm was to blame for the cancellation of the flight.* —**blam′a·ble** *adj.*

blameless (blām′lĭs) *adj.* Free from blame or guilt; innocent: *Neither side is blameless in the dispute.* —**blame′less·ly** *adv.* —**blame′less·ness** *n.*

blameworthy (blām′wûr′thē) *adj.* **blameworthier, blame-**

worthiest Deserving blame: *All of us were blameworthy for leaving such a mess in the kitchen.* —**blame′wor′thi·ness** *n.*

blanch (blănch) *v.* **blanched, blanching, blanches** —*tr.* **1.** To make lighter in color; bleach or whiten. **2.** To place (almonds or tomatoes, for example) briefly in boiling water in order to remove the skins more easily. **3.** To scald (vegetables) by plunging into boiling water, as before freezing. **4.** To cause to become pale: *Fear blanched the startled child's face.* —*intr.* To turn pale: *They blanched at the awful news.*

bland (blănd) *adj.* **blander, blandest 1.** Pleasant or soothing in manner; gentle: *a bland smile.* **2.** Having a moderate, soft, or soothing quality; not irritating or stimulating: *a bland diet.* **3.** Having little or no distinctive flavor: *bland cooking.* **4.** Lacking distinctive character; dull; flat: *a bland speech.* —**bland′ly** *adv.* —**bland′ness** *n.*

blandish (blăn′dĭsh) *tr.v.* **blandished, blandishing, blandishes** To coax by flattery or wheedling; cajole.

blandishment (blăn′dĭsh-mənt) *n.* often **blandishments** A word or act meant to coax or flatter: *The diplomat used a variety of blandishments to bring the two sides together.*

blank (blăngk) *adj.* **blanker, blankest 1.** Free of marks or writing: *a blank wall; a blank piece of paper.* **2.** Containing no information: *a blank tape.* See Synonyms at **empty.** **3.** Having empty spaces to be filled in: *Fill in this blank application.* **4.** Showing no expression or interest: *a blank stare.* **5.** Lacking thought or attention: *a blank mind.* ❖ *n.* **1a.** An empty space on a document to be filled in with an answer or comment. **b.** A document or form with empty spaces to be filled in: *a pad of order blanks.* **2.** An empty space or place; a void: *My mind was a complete blank on the subject.* **3.** A gun cartridge having a charge of powder but no bullet. ❖ *v.* **blanked, blanking, blanks** —*tr.* To prevent (an opponent) from scoring in a game: *Our team blanked theirs 4–0.* —*intr.* To fail to find or remember something: *I blanked when I tried to remember her name.* —**blank′ly** *adv.* —**blank′ness** *n.*

blanket (blăng′kĭt) *n.* **1.** A large piece of cloth or other woven material used as a covering for warmth. **2.** A layer that covers: *a blanket of snow.* ❖ *adj.* Covering a wide range of topics, conditions, or requirements: *They gave the proposals a blanket approval.* ❖ *tr.v.* **blanketed, blanketing, blankets** To cover with or as if with a blanket: *Snow blanketed the countryside.*

blank verse *n.* Verse written in unrhymed lines, usually of iambic pentameter.

blare (blâr) *v.* **blared, blaring, blares** —*intr.* To sound loudly and stridently: *horns blaring in the traffic jam.* —*tr.* To cause to sound loudly and stridently: *A brass band blared the national anthem.* ❖ *n.* A loud strident noise: *the blare of a radio from the open window.*

blarney (blär′nē) *n.* Smooth flattering talk.

blasé (blä-zā′) *adj.* Uninterested or unexcited because of constant exposure or indulgence: *People who live on the coast tend to be blasé about the ocean.*

blaspheme (blăs-fēm′ *or* blăs′fēm′) *v.* **blasphemed, blaspheming, blasphemes** —*tr.* To speak of (God or something sacred) in a disrespectful way. —*intr.* To speak blasphemy. —**blas·phem′er** *n.*

blasphemous (blăs′fə-məs) *adj.* Committing or containing blasphemy: *a blasphemous critic; a blasphemous speech.* —**blas′phe·mous·ly** *adv.*

blasphemy (blăs′fə-mē) *n., pl.* **blasphemies** The act of saying or doing something that is disrespectful of God or of something considered sacred.

blast (blăst) *n.* **1a.** An explosion: *a blast of dynamite.* **b.** The force of an explosion: *The blast of the explosion blew out the windows.* **2.** A strong gust of wind or air. **3.** A strong stream of air, gas, or steam from an opening. **4.** A loud sudden sound, especially one produced by forced air: *the blast of the steam whistle.* **5.** *Slang* A very exciting or pleasurable experience or event: *We had a blast at the dance. The trip was a blast.* ❖ *v.* **blasted, blasting, blasts** —*tr.* **1a.** To knock down or tear apart with an explosive: *blasting rocks in a quarry.* **b.** To make or open by an explosion: *blast a road through the mountain.* **2.** To destroy or shatter: *Defeat blasted our hopes.* **3.** To cause to shrivel or wither before flowering or bearing fruit or seeds: *A severe drought blasted the crops.* **4.** To cause to sound loudly; blare: *Buglers blasted their horns. The radio blasted music out the window.* **5.** To criticize severely: *The reviewer blasted the movie.* —*intr.* **1.** To emit a loud unpleasant sound: *Car horns blasted from the street below.* **2.** To criticize or attack: *The paper blasted away at the corrupt city government.* ◆ **blast off** To take off, as a rocket. **full blast** At full speed, volume, or capacity: *turned the radio up full blast.*

blast furnace *n.* A furnace in which combustion is made more intense by a forced stream of air.

blastoff also **blast-off** (blăst′ôf′) *n.* The launching of a rocket or spacecraft.

blastula (blăs′chə-lə) *n., pl.* **blastulas** or **blastulae** (blăs′chə-lē′) An embryo at the stage immediately following the division of the fertilized egg cell, consisting of a ball-shaped layer of cells around a fluid-filled cavity.

blatant (blāt′nt) *adj.* Done with no attempt to disguise or hide wrongdoing; so obvious or shameless as to be offensive: *a blatant lie; a blatant attempt to rig the election.* —**bla′tan·cy** (blāt′n-sē) *n.* —**bla′tant·ly** *adv.*

blather (blăth′ər) *intr.v.* **blathered, blathering, blathers** To talk too much in a boring or nonsensical manner; babble. ❖ *n.* Nonsense; drivel.

blaze¹ (blāz) *n.* **1a.** A brightly burning fire: *make a blaze out of a pile of twigs.* **b.** A destructive fire: *A blaze destroyed the building.* **2.** A bright or steady glare: *the blaze of the sun.* **3.** A brilliant or striking display: *The flowers were a blaze of color.* **4.** A sudden outburst, as of activity or emotion: *in a blaze of speed; a blaze of anger.* ❖ *intr.v.* **blazed, blazing, blazes** **1.** To burn brightly: *a fire blazing in the fireplace.* **2.** To shine brightly: *The hot noonday sun blazed down on the beach.* **3.** To be resplendent: *The garden blazed with colorful flowers.* **4.** To flare up suddenly: *My temper blazed at the insulting remark.*

blaze² (blāz) *n.* **1.** A white or light-colored spot on the face of an animal, such as a horse. **2.** A mark to indicate a trail, usually painted on or cut into a tree. ❖ *tr.v.* **blazed, blazing, blazes** **1.** To indicate (a trail) by marking trees. **2.** To prepare or lead (the way in an endeavor): *blazed the way in space exploration.*

WORD HISTORY Blaze¹ comes from Old English *blæse,* meaning "torch." Although **blaze²** did not exist in Middle English and its origin is unknown, it is related to similar words in other archaic and modern Germanic languages. Both words ultimately come from an Indo-European root that refers to brightness or the color white.

blazer (blā′zər) *n.* A lightweight sports coat having pockets and a notched lapel.

blazing (blā′zĭng) *adj.* **1.** Flaming: *a blazing fire.* **2.** Shining; glaring: *the blazing sun.*

blazon (blā′zən) *tr.v.* **blazoned, blazoning, blazons** **1.** To decorate (a flag, for example) with a coat of arms. **2.** To decorate brightly; emblazon: *Stars blazoned the night sky.* **3.** To announce; proclaim: *Demonstrators marched with signs blazoning their protest.* ❖ *n.* A coat of arms.

bldg. An abbreviation of building.

bleach (blēch) *v.* **bleached, bleaching, bleaches** —*tr.* **1.** To remove the color from (fibers or fabrics, for example) by means of sunlight or chemicals; whiten: *bleach a shirt in the wash; old jeans bleached by the sun.* **2.** To lighten the color of (hair). —*intr.* To turn white or lose color: *boards bleaching in the desert sun.* ❖ *n.* A chemical agent used for bleaching.

bleachers (blē′chərz) *pl.n.* Tiers of wooden planks or pieces of flat metal used as seating by spectators at a public event, especially a sports contest.

bleaching powder (blē′chĭng) *n.* A white powder made by treating slaked lime with chlorine and used as a bleach and disinfectant.

bleak (blēk) *adj.* **bleaker, bleakest** **1.** Gloomy; dreary; depressing: *The prospects for success are bleak.* **2.** Cold and harsh: *a damp bleak wind.* **3.** Exposed to the elements; barren and windswept: *bleak treeless moors.* —**bleak′ly** *adv.* —**bleak′ness** *n.*

blear (blîr) *tr.v.* **bleared, blearing, blears** **1.** To blur or redden (the eyes), as with tears. **2.** To blur; dim: *Mist rising from the lake bleared our vision.*

bleary (blîr′ē) *adj.* **blearier, bleariest** **1.** Blurred by or as if by tears: *bleary eyes.* **2.** Vague or indistinct; blurred: *a bleary photograph.* —**blear′i·ness** *n.*

bleat (blēt) *n.* The characteristic cry of a goat or sheep. ❖ *intr.v.* **bleated, bleating, bleats** To utter the cry of a goat or sheep.

bleed (blēd) *v.* **bled** (blĕd), **bleeding, bleeds** —*intr.* **1.** To lose blood: *My finger bled when I cut it on the glass.* **2.** To feel sympathetic grief: *My heart bleeds for you in your sorrow.* **3.** To lose sap or other fluid, as a plant does that has been cut. **4.** To be lost or depleted gradually: *Their savings were bleeding away during the recession.* **5.** To become mixed and run, as dye in wet cloth. **6.** To show through a layer of paint as a stain in wood. —*tr.* **1a.** To take or remove blood from: *Long ago, doctors bled patients as a cure.* **b.** To remove sap or juice from (a plant). **2a.** To draw off (a liquid or gas) from a container or pipe: *bleed air from overinflated tires.* **b.** To draw liquid or gas from; drain: *bleed radiators to stop them from knocking.* **3.** To drain of a valuable resource: *Runaway inflation is bleeding the economy.*

bleeding heart (blē′dĭng) *n.* Any of various garden plants having nodding pink, red, or white heart-shaped flowers.

bleep (blēp) *n.* A brief high-pitched sound, as from an electronic device. ❖ *v.* —*intr.* **bleeped, bleeping, bleeps** To make a bleep. —*tr.* To remove (spoken material) from a broadcast or recording, especially by replacing with a bleep: *The vulgar words were bleeped out of the recording.*

blemish (blĕm′ĭsh) *tr.v.* **blemished, blemishing, blemishes** To impair or mar by a flaw; disfigure: *Scratches blemished the table.* ❖ *n.* Something that impairs or mars; a flaw: *skin blemishes; a blemish on one's reputation.*

blench (blĕnch) *intr.v.* **blenched, blenching, blenches** To draw back or shy away, as from fear; flinch.

blend (blĕnd) *v.* **blended, blending, blends** —*tr.* **1.** To combine so that the parts are not distinct; mix thoroughly:

The cook blended milk and flour. **2.** To combine (varieties or grades of something) to make a mixture with unique qualities: *We blended the two coffees.* **3.** To combine (different elements) into a single entity: *a college program that blends economics and liberal arts.* —*intr.* **1.** To form a mixture; be combined: *Oil does not blend with water.* **2.** To become merged into one; unite: *The blue blends into the green in this painting.* **3.** To be in harmony; go together: *Your tie blends with your jacket.* ❖ *n.* **1.** Something blended; a harmonious mixture or combination: *a blend of colors; a blend of teas.* **2.** A word produced by combining parts of other words, as *smog* from *smoke* and *fog.*

blender (blĕn′dər) *n.* An electrical appliance with whirling blades, used to blend or purée foods.

bless (blĕs) *tr.v.* **blessed** or **blest** (blĕst), **blessing, blesses 1.** To make holy; consecrate: *The minister blessed the water for baptism.* **2.** To call divine favor upon. **3.** To make the sign of the cross over: *The priest blessed the congregation.* **4.** To praise as holy; glorify: *Bless the Lord.* **5.** To endow, favor, or enrich: *The artist was blessed with unusual talent.*

blessed (blĕs′ĭd) also **blest** (blĕst) *adj.* **1.** Worthy of worship; holy. **2.** Enjoying happiness; very fortunate: *I feel blessed.* **3.** Bringing happiness; pleasurable: *A new baby in a family is a blessed event.* —**bless′ed·ly** *adv.* —**bless′ed·ness** *n.*

blessing (blĕs′ĭng) *n.* **1.** A prayer calling for divine favor. **2.** A short prayer given at mealtime; grace. **3.** often **blessings** Something that brings happiness or well-being: *the blessings of liberty.* **4.** Approval; sanction: *The expedition to explore the Northwest had the government's blessing.*

blest (blĕst) *v.* A past tense and a past participle of **bless.** ❖ *adj.* Variant of **blessed.**

blew (blōō) *v.* Past tense of **blow**[1].

blight (blīt) *n.* **1.** Any of numerous plant diseases that cause leaves, stems, or fruits to wither and die. **2.** The organism, such as a bacterium, fungus, water mold, or virus, that causes such a disease. **3.** Something that is harmful, destructive, or unattractive: *That abandoned house is a blight on the neighborhood.* ❖ *tr.v.* **blighted, blighting, blights** To ruin, damage, or destroy: *Several losses blighted the team's hopes of becoming county champions.*

blimp (blĭmp) *n.* An airship that does not have a rigid framework.

blind (blīnd) *adj.* **blinder, blindest 1a.** Lacking the sense of sight; sightless. **b.** Having a visual acuity of one-tenth normal vision or less while wearing corrective lenses. **2.** Performed by instruments and without the use of sight: *blind navigation.* **3.** Unwilling or unable to perceive or understand: *Many people are blind to their own faults.* **4.** Not based on reason or evidence: *blind faith.* **5.** Immoderate or unrestrained: *blind rage.* **6.** Performed without access to information that might prejudice the results: *a blind taste test in which participants were not told which brands they were sampling.* **7.** Performed without preparation or knowledge: *a blind attempt to fix the washing machine.* **8.** Hidden or screened from sight: *a blind driveway.* **9.** Closed at one end: *a blind alley.* ❖ *n.* **1.** (*used with a plural verb*) People who are sightless or have very little ability to see: *an organization that makes recorded books for the blind.* **2.** Something that shuts out light or hinders vision: *We pull the blinds over the windows at night.* **3.** A shelter for concealing hunters, photographers, or observers of wildlife. **4.** Something that conceals the true

nature of an activity, especially of an illegal or improper one; a subterfuge: *The spies used the restaurant as a blind for their operations.* ❖ *adv.* Without being able to see: *The pilot had to fly blind in the fog.* ❖ *tr.v.* **blinded, blinding, blinds 1.** To deprive of sight: *Lights from the oncoming cars blinded me.* **2.** To deprive (a person) of judgment or reason: *Prejudice blinds them to the advantages of the plan.* —**blind′ly** *adv.* —**blind′ness** *n.*

blind date *n.* A date between two people who have not previously met.

blinders (blīn′dərz) *pl.n.* A pair of leather flaps attached to a horse's bridle to prevent it from seeing things on either side.

blindfold (blīnd′fōld′) *tr.v.* **blindfolded, blindfolding, blindfolds** To cover the eyes of with a strip of cloth or other material: *blindfold a prisoner.* ❖ *n.* A strip of cloth put over the eyes and tied around the head to keep someone from seeing. —**blind′fold′ed** *adj.*

blindman's bluff or **blindman's buff** (blīnd′mănz′) *n.* A game in which a blindfolded person tries to catch and identify one of the other players.

blindside (blīnd′sīd′) *tr.v.* **blindsided, blindsiding, blindsides 1.** To hit or attack from a side in which one's vision is limited or away from which one's attention is directed. **2.** To catch or take unawares, especially with harmful or detrimental results: *The news blindsided us.*

blind spot *n.* **1.** The point on the retina, not sensitive to light, where the optic nerve leaves the eyeball. **2.** An area that one cannot see because of an obstruction or because of insufficient range of view: *the blind spot along the side of the car, which does not appear in the driver's mirror.* **3.** An area where radio or television reception is poor. **4.** An area about which a person is noticeably unaware or prejudiced: *He has a blind spot where his children are concerned—he thinks they can do no wrong.*

blink (blĭngk) *v.* **blinked, blinking, blinks** —*intr.* **1.** To close and open the eye or eyes rapidly: *blink at the bright light.* **2.** To flash off and on: *holiday lights blinking in the window.* —*tr.* **1.** To close and open (the eye or eyes) rapidly; wink: *The cat blinked its eyes in the bright light.* **2.** To make flash off and on: *blink the lights of a car.* ❖ *n.* A very quick closing and opening of the eye or eyes. ◆ **on the blink** Out of working order.

blinker (blĭng′kər) *n.* **1.** A light that blinks as a means of sending a message or warning. **2. blinkers** Blinders.

blintz (blĭnts) *n.* A thin rolled pancake with a filling such as cream cheese or fruit.

blip (blĭp) *n.* **1.** A spot of light on a radar or sonar screen indicating the position of a detected object, such as an aircraft. **2.** A high-pitched electronic sound; a bleep. **3.** A temporary, sharp increase or decrease: *a blip in stock prices.*

bliss (blĭs) *n.* Extreme happiness; joy.

blissful (blĭs′fəl) *adj.* Full of or causing bliss: *a blissful afternoon at the beach; blissful ignorance of the problem.* —**bliss′ful·ly** *adv.* —**bliss′ful·ness** *n.*

blister (blĭs′tər) *n.* **1.** A thin fluid-filled sac that forms on the skin as a result of a burn or irritation. **2.** A raised bubble, as on a painted surface. ❖ *intr. & tr.v.* **blistered, blistering, blisters** To form or cause to form blisters: *Her skin blistered from poison ivy. Tight shoes blistered the hiker's feet.* —**blis′ter·y** *adj.*

blistering (blĭs′tər-ĭng) *adj.* **1.** Extremely hot: *a blistering summer sun.* **2.** Very strong; intense: *blistering criticism.* **3.** Extremely rapid: *a blistering pace.*

blithe (blīth *or* blĭth) *adj.* **blither, blithest 1.** Carefree and lighthearted: *the blithe atmosphere of the birthday party.* **2.** Showing a lack of concern: *a blithe disregard of danger.* —**blithe′ly** *adv.* —**blithe′ness** *n.*

blithesome (blīth′səm *or* blĭth′səm) *adj.* Cheerful; merry; lighthearted. —**blithe′some·ly** *adv.* —**blithe′some·ness** *n.*

blitz (blĭts) *n.* **1.** A blitzkrieg. **2.** An intense campaign: *an advertising blitz.* **3.** In football, a charge upon the quarterback by one or more of the linebackers or defensive backs after the ball is snapped. ❖ *v.* **blitzed, blitzing, blitzes** —*tr.* **1.** To subject to a blitz. **2.** In football, to run toward (the quarterback) in a blitz. —*intr.* In football, to carry out a blitz.

blitzkrieg (blĭts′krēg′) *n.* A swift, sudden military attack, usually by air and land forces.

blizzard (blĭz′ərd) *n.* **1.** A very heavy snowstorm with strong winds. **2.** A great number or an unusually heavy flow: *a blizzard of phone calls congratulating the winning candidate.*

bloat (blōt) *intr. & tr.v.* **bloated, bloating, bloats** To swell or cause to swell or puff up, as with liquid or gas: *a stomach bloated by overeating.*

blob (blŏb) *n.* A soft formless mass: *a blob of wax.*

bloc (blŏk) *n.* A group of nations, parties, or people united by common interests or political aims: *representatives forming the farm bloc in Congress.*

block (blŏk) *n.* **1.** A solid piece of wood or another hard substance having one or more flat sides: *Blocks of marble form the front of that building.* **2.** One of a set of small wooden or plastic pieces, such as a cube or bar, used as a building toy. **3.** Such a piece on which chopping or cutting is done: *a butcher's block.* **4.** A stand from which articles are displayed at an auction. **5.** A mold or form upon which something is shaped or displayed: *a hat block.* **6.** A pulley or set of pulleys set in a casing. **7.** The metal casing that contains the cylinders of an engine. **8.** A set of like items sold or handled as a unit: *a block of tickets in the balcony.* **9a.** An obstacle or hindrance: *Road work caused a block in traffic.* **b.** In medicine, an obstruction of a bodily function: *an intestinal block.* **10a.** A usually rectangular section of a city or town enclosed by connecting streets: *Walk the dog around the block.* **b.** The part of a street that lies between two successive cross streets: *Our home is in the middle of the block.* **11.** A large building divided into separate units, such as apartments. **12.** In sports, an act of obstructing an opponent, especially in football a legal act of using one's body to obstruct an opponent and thus protect the teammate who has the ball. ❖ *v.* **blocked, blocking, blocks** —*tr.* **1a.** To stop the movement or progress of: *Road work was blocking traffic. The opposing members blocked every attempt at reform.* **b.** To stop movement through: *The stalled car blocked the intersection.* **2.** To be in the way of; obstruct visually: *You're blocking my view.* **3.** In medicine, to obstruct the functioning of (a nerve, for example). **4.** To shape or form with or on a block: *block a sweater after washing it.* **5.** In sports, to stop or hinder the movement of (an opponent or the ball) by physical interference. **6.** To indicate in a general way; sketch: *block out a plan of action.* —*intr.* In sports, to interfere with the movement of an opponent.

blockade (blŏ-kād′) *n.* **1.** The closing off of a city, harbor, or country by troops or warships in order to prevent peo-

ple and supplies from going in and out. **2.** The forces used in a blockade. **3.** Something that closes off or obstructs; an obstacle. ❖ *tr.v.* **blockaded, blockading, blockades** To set up a blockade against. —**block·ad′er** *n.*

blockade-runner (blŏ-kād′rŭn′ər) *n.* A ship or person that attempts to go through or past an enemy blockade.

blockage (blŏk′ĭj) *n.* **1.** The act of obstructing. **2.** An obstruction: *an intestinal blockage.*

block and tackle *n.* An arrangement of pulleys and ropes used for lifting heavy objects.

blockbuster (blŏk′bŭs′tər) *n.* **1.** Something, such as a movie or book, that is very popular or sells in large numbers. **2.** A large bomb capable of great destruction.

blockhead (blŏk′hĕd′) *n.* A stupid person; a dolt.

blockhouse (blŏk′hous′) *n.* **1.** A fort made of heavy timbers, with a projecting upper story and loopholes for firing. **2.** A fortification made of concrete with slits for firing or observation. **3.** A heavily reinforced building from which the launching of rockets or space vehicles is observed and controlled.

blog (blŏg) *n.* A website that displays postings by one or more individuals in the order they were written and usually has links to comments on specific postings. ❖ *intr.v.* **blogged, blogging, blogs** To write entries in, add material to, or maintain a blog. —**blog′ger** *n.*

bloke (blōk) *n. Chiefly British Slang* A fellow; a man.

blond also **blonde** (blŏnd) *adj.* **blonder, blondest 1.** Having fair hair and skin: *a blond baby.* **2.** Having a pale yellow or golden color: *blond hair.* **3.** Light-colored: *blond furniture.* ❖ *n.* A blond person. —**blond′ness** *n.*

blood (blŭd) *n.* **1a.** The red fluid that is circulated through the body of vertebrate animals by the action of the heart, distributing oxygen, nutrients, and hormones to the tissues and carrying away wastes. **b.** A similar fluid in invertebrate animals. **2.** Temperament or disposition: *a person of hot blood and a fiery temper.* **3.** Descent from a particular ancestor or ancestors; parental lineage: *Does the prince's wife have any royal blood?* ♦ **in cold blood** Deliberately, coldly, and dispassionately: *The judge was murdered in cold blood.*

blood bank *n.* **1.** A place where blood or blood plasma is classified according to blood type for use in transfusions. **2.** Blood or blood plasma stored in such a place.

bloodbath (blŭd′băth′) *n.* Savage and widespread killing; a massacre.

blood cell *n.* Any of the cells contained in blood; a red blood cell or white blood cell.

blood clot *n.* A mass of coagulated blood that consists of red blood cells, white blood cells, platelets, and fibrin. —**blood clotting** *n.*

blood count *n.* A count of the number of red and white blood cells and platelets in a sample of a person's blood.

bloodcurdling (blŭd′kûrd′lĭng) *adj.* Causing great horror; terrifying.

blooded (blŭd′ĭd) *adj.* **1.** Having blood or a temperament of a specified kind: *a cold-blooded reptile; a hot-blooded delinquent.* **2.** Thoroughbred: *blooded racehorses.*

blood group *n.* A blood type.

bloodhound (blŭd′hound′) *n.* A hound of a breed having a smooth coat, drooping ears, loose folds of skin around the face, and a keen sense of smell.

bloodless (blŭd′lĭs) *adj.* **1.** Having no blood. **2.** Pale and anemic in color: *cold and bloodless hands.* **3.** Accomplished without killing: *a bloodless revolution.* **4.** Lacking spirit: *a dull bloodless tale.*

bloodline (blŭd′līn′) *n.* A direct line of descent.

bloodmobile (blŭd′mə-bēl′) *n.* A motor vehicle equipped for collecting blood from donors.

blood orange *n.* A sweet orange having pulp that is red or streaked with red.

blood plasma *n.* The yellowish, liquid part of the blood, composed mainly of water and proteins, in which the blood cells are suspended.

blood poisoning *n.* A disease caused by microorganisms or their toxins in the blood; septicemia.

blood pressure *n.* The pressure that the blood exerts on the walls of the arteries or other blood vessels. Blood pressure varies with the strength of the heartbeat, the volume of the blood, the elasticity of the arteries, and the person's health, age, and physical condition.

bloodroot (blŭd′rōōt′ *or* blŭd′rŏŏt′) *n.* A woodland plant of eastern North America having a fleshy root with poisonous red sap, a lobed leaf, and a white flower.

blood sausage *n.* A sausage made of pig's blood, diced pork fat, and other ingredients.

bloodshed (blŭd′shĕd′) *n.* The shedding of blood, especially the injuring or killing of people.

bloodshot (blŭd′shŏt′) *adj.* Inflamed and overfilled with blood, often with the small blood vessels enlarged: *bloodshot eyes.*

bloodstained (blŭd′stānd′) *adj.* Stained or spotted with blood: *a bloodstained handkerchief.*

bloodstone (blŭd′stōn′) *n.* A deep-green, cloudy form of quartz that is flecked with red. It is used as a gem.

bloodstream (blŭd′strēm′) *n.* The blood as it flows through the circulatory system.

bloodsucker (blŭd′sŭk′ər) *n.* An animal, such as a leech, that sucks blood.

blood test *n.* An examination of a sample of blood to determine its contents, as for ascertaining the blood group or diagnosing illness.

bloodthirsty (blŭd′thûr′stē) *adj.* Eager to cause or see the shedding of blood; cruel. —**blood′thirst′i·ly** *adv.* —**blood′thirst′i·ness** *n.*

blood type *n.* Any of the four main types, A, B, AB, and O, into which human blood is divided on the basis of the presence or absence of certain proteins and antibodies; blood group.

blood vessel *n.* An elastic tubular structure in the body through which blood circulates; an artery, vein, or capillary.

bloody (blŭd′ē) *adj.* **bloodier, bloodiest 1.** Bleeding: *a bloody nose.* **2.** Stained with blood: *bloody bandages.* **3.** Causing or marked by bloodshed: *a bloody fight.* **4.** Bloodthirsty; cruel. ❖ *adv. Chiefly British Slang* Used as an intensive: *You're bloody right.* ❖ *tr.v.* **bloodied, bloodying, bloodies** To make bloody: *My elbow was bloodied in the fall.* —**blood′i·ly** *adv.* —**blood′i·ness** *n.*

bloom (blōōm) *n.* **1.** The flower or blossom of a plant. **2.** The condition or time of flowering: *a rosebush in bloom.* **3.** A condition or time of great development, vigor, or beauty: *a boy in the full bloom of youth.* **4.** A fresh rosy complexion: *a fine bloom to the cheeks.* **5.** A waxy or powdery coating sometimes occurring on fruits, leaves, or stems: *the bloom on a plum.* ❖ *intr.v.* **bloomed, blooming, blooms 1.** To bear flowers; blossom: *Tulips bloom in the spring.* **2.** To grow or flourish: *Volunteer groups to teach reading are blooming.* **3.** To show in a healthy or vigorous way; glow: *Joy bloomed in her face.*

bloomers (blōō′mərz) *pl.n.* **1.** Baggy pants gathered at the knee, once worn by women and girls for sports, such as riding bicycles. **2.** Similar pants worn as underwear.

blooming (blōō′mĭng) *adv. & adj. Chiefly British Slang* Used as an intensive: *a blooming hot day; a blooming idiot.*

blooper (blōō′pər) *n.* **1.** A clumsy mistake, especially one made in public. **2.** In baseball, a weakly hit ball that carries just past the infield.

blossom (blŏs′əm) *n.* **1.** A flower or cluster of flowers: *apple blossoms.* **2.** The condition or time of flowering: *spring flowers in blossom.* ❖ *intr.v.* **blossomed, blossoming, blossoms 1.** To come into flower; bloom. **2.** To develop and do well; flourish: *The public's interest in science blossomed with space flight.*

blot (blŏt) *n.* **1.** A stain or spot: *an ink blot.* **2.** A stain on one's character or reputation; a disgrace. ❖ *v.* **blotted, blotting, blots** —*tr.* **1.** To spot or stain: *Greasy fingerprints blotted the page.* **2.** To dry or soak up with absorbent material: *blot a spill with paper towels.* —*intr.* **1.** To spill or spread in a spot or stain. **2.** To become blotted or absorbed: *Watercolors blot easily.* ◆ **blot out 1.** To hide from view; obscure: *Storm clouds blotted out the sun.* **2.** To destroy completely; annihilate: *The frost blotted out the tomatoes.*

blotch (blŏch) *n.* **1.** A spot or blot; a splotch. **2.** A discoloration on the skin; a blemish. ❖ *tr. & intr.v.* **blotched, blotching, blotches** To mark or become marked with blotches. —**blotch′y** *adj.*

blotter (blŏt′ər) *n.* **1.** A piece or pad of thick absorbent paper used to soak up excess ink from a surface that has been written on. **2.** A book containing daily records of occurrences or transactions: *A blotter kept at a police station records the arrests made.*

blouse (blous *or* blouz) *n.* **1.** A woman's or child's loosely fitting shirt that extends to the waist. **2.** A loose garment resembling a smock, worn by some workmen and peasants in Europe. **3.** The jacket of a military uniform.

bloviate (blō′vē-āt′) *intr.v.* **bloviated, bloviating, bloviates** *Slang* To discourse at length in a pompous or boastful manner. —**blo′vi·a′tion** *n.*

blow¹ (blō) *v.* **blew** (blōō), **blown** (blōn), **blowing, blows** —*intr.* **1.** To be in motion. Used of the air or of wind: *The wind blew hard all night.* **2.** To be moved by a current of air: *My hat blew off.* **3.** To send out a current of air: *Blow on your soup to cool it.* **4.** To spout water and air from the blowhole, as a whale does. **5.** To sound: *The whistle blows at noon.* **6.** To burst suddenly: *The tire blew when we hit a rock.* **7a.** To fail or break down: *The furnace blew.* **b.** To burn out or melt: *The fuse blew.* **8.** *Informal* To move very fast in relation to something: *She blew by me on the final lap of the race.* —*tr.* **1.** To cause to move by a current of air: *The gale blew a tree across the power lines.* **2.** To expel (air) from the mouth. **3a.** To cause (a wind instrument) to sound by forcing breath through it: *blow a trumpet.* **b.** To sound (a melody): *a bugle blowing taps.* **4.** To cause to explode: *To build the tunnel they blew rock out of the way with dynamite.* **5.** To have or cause air or gas to be expelled suddenly from: *We blew a tire when we hit the curb.* **6.** To clear by forcing air through: *blowing his nose noisily.* **7.** To shape (a pliable material, such as molten glass) by forcing air into it. **8a.** To cause to fail or break down. **b.** To cause (an electrical fuse) to melt and open a circuit. **9.** *Slang* **a.** To spend (money) freely or foolishly: *He blew all his savings on a video game.* **b.** To spoil or lose by inept performance: *We blew a two-goal lead in the* *third period.* ❖ *n.* **1.** A blast of air or wind. **2.** A storm. **3.** The act or an instance of blowing. ◆ **blow away** *Slang* **1.** To kill by shooting, especially with a firearm. **2.** To defeat decisively. **3.** To affect intensely; overwhelm: *That concert blew me away.* **blow in** *Slang* To arrive, especially when unexpected. **blow off 1.** To relieve or release (pressure); let off. **2.** *Slang* To choose not to attend or accompany: *They blew off the meeting and went for a walk.* **blow off steam** To express pent-up emotion. **blow (one's) top** or **blow (one's) stack** To lose one's temper. **blow out 1.** To extinguish or be extinguished by a gust of air: *blow out the candles.* **2.** To fail, as an electrical apparatus: *The fuse blew out.* **blow over** To subside or pass over with little lasting effect: *The storm will blow over soon.* **blow up 1.** To come into being: *A storm blew up.* **2.** To fill with air; inflate: *blowing up balloons.* **3.** To enlarge (a photograph). **4.** To explode: *The gas tank blew up.* **5.** To lose one's temper.

blow² (blō) *n.* **1.** A sudden hard stroke or hit, as with the fist or a weapon. **2.** A sudden unexpected shock or great misfortune: *The criticism was a blow to her pride.* **3.** A sudden unexpected attack; an assault.

WORD HISTORY Blow¹ comes from Old English *blāwan,* meaning "to move as an air current." **Blow²** comes from Middle English *blou,* meaning "a blast of wind, a hit with a fist."

blow-dry (blō′drī′) *tr.v.* **blow-dried, blow-drying, blow-dries** To dry and often style (hair) with a blow dryer.

blow dryer *n.* A handheld electric blower for drying and styling hair.

blower (blō′ər) *n.* A device that produces a flow of air or other gas through a duct or an enclosed space.

blowfly (blō′flī′) *n.* Any of several flies that deposit their eggs in the bodies of dead animals or in wounds.

blowgun (blō′gŭn′) *n.* A long narrow pipe through which pellets or poison darts can be blown; a blowpipe.

blowhard (blō′härd′) *n. Informal* A boaster or braggart.

blowhole (blō′hōl′) *n.* **1.** An opening or one of a pair of openings for breathing in the top of the head of a whale, porpoise, or dolphin. **2.** A hole in the ice to which sea mammals such as seals and whales come to breathe.

blown (blōn) *v.* Past participle of **blow¹**.

blowout (blō′out′) *n.* **1.** A sudden and violent loss of air pressure, as from an automobile tire. **2.** A sudden escape of a confined gas or liquid, as from an oil well. **3.** A lop-sided victory: *The score was 45 to 0—a real blowout!*

blowpipe (blō′pīp′) *n.* **1.** A narrow tube for blowing air or gas into a flame to increase its heat, used especially in the identification of minerals. **2.** A long narrow iron pipe used to gather, work, and blow molten glass. **3.** A blowgun.

blowtorch (blō′tôrch′) *n.* A torch in which a pressurized mix of air and gas produces a very hot flame, used for soldering, welding, and glass blowing.

blowup (blō′ŭp′) *n.* **1.** An explosion. **2.** A photographic enlargement. **3.** An outburst of temper: *The coach had a blowup over the referee's call.* **4.** An angry argument or confrontation: *There was a blowup between the teachers and the administration.*

blowzy also **blowsy** (blou′zē) *adj.* **blowzier, blowziest** also **blowsier, blowsiest** Not tidy; disheveled; messy: *blowzy hair.*

BLT (bē′ĕl-tē′) *n.* A bacon, lettuce, and tomato sandwich.

blubber (blŭb′ər) *v.* **blubbered, blubbering, blubbers** —*intr.* To cry or sob in a noisy manner. See Synonyms at **cry.** —*tr.* To say while crying and sobbing: *The boy blubbered his name.* ❖ *n.* The fat of whales and some other marine mammals, lying under the skin and over the muscles, from which oil is obtained. Blubber insulates the animal from heat loss and serves as a food reserve. —**blub′ber·er** *n.*

bludgeon (blŭj′ən) *n.* A short heavy club with one end heavier or thicker than the other. ❖ *tr.v.* **bludgeoned, bludgeoning, bludgeons** To beat or strike with or as if with a bludgeon.

blue (blōō) *n.* **1.** The color of the sky on a clear day. In the spectrum it is between green and indigo. **2.** often **Blue a.** A Union soldier in the US Civil War. **b.** The Union Army. **3a.** The sea. **b.** The sky. ❖ *adj.* **bluer, bluest 1.** Of the color blue. **2.** Having a gray or purplish color, as from cold or a bruise: *lips blue from the chill.* **3.** Gloomy; depressed: *a sailor far from home, lonely and blue.* ❖ *tr. & intr.v.* **blued, bluing, blues** To make or become blue. ◆ **out of the blue 1.** From an unexpected or unforeseen source: *a problem that came out of the blue.* **2.** At a completely unexpected time: *My friend showed up out of the blue last night.* —**blue′ly** *adv.* —**blue′ness** *n.*

blue baby *n.* A newborn baby having a bluish tint to its skin because of a heart or lung defect, resulting in too little oxygen in its blood.

bluebeard (blōō′bîrd′) *n.* A man who first marries and then murders one wife after another.

bluebell (blōō′bĕl′) also **bluebells** (blōō′bĕlz′) *n.* Any of several plants having bell-shaped, usually blue flowers.

blueberry (blōō′bĕr′ē) *n.* **1.** A round, juicy, edible blue or blue-black berry. **2.** Any of various plants that bear such berries.

bluebird (blōō′bûrd′) *n.* Any of several North American songbirds having blue feathers and usually a rust-colored breast in the male.

blue blood *n.* **1.** Noble or aristocratic descent. **2.** A member of the aristocracy or other high social group.

bluebonnet (blōō′bŏn′ĭt) *n.* Any of several North American plants that have clusters of blue flowers.

bluebottle (blōō′bŏt′l) *n.* Any of several large blowflies having a bright metallic-blue body.

blue cheese *n.* A tangy semisoft cheese with greenish-blue mold.

blue-collar (blōō′kŏl′ər) *adj.* Relating to wage earners whose jobs are performed in work clothes and often involve manual labor.

bluefish (blōō′fĭsh′) *n.* A silvery bluish or greenish ocean fish caught for food or sport.

bluegill (blōō′gĭl′) *n., pl.* **bluegill** or **bluegills** A sunfish of North American lakes and streams, eaten as food.

bluegrass (blōō′grăs′) *n.* **1.** Any of various lawn and pasture grasses often having bluish leaves or flower heads. **2.** A type of country music that originated in the southern United States, typically played on stringed instruments such as banjos and guitars.

blue-green alga (blōō′grēn′) *n.* A cyanobacterium.

blueing (blōō′ĭng) *n.* Variant of **bluing**.

blueish (blōō′ĭsh) *adj.* Variant of **bluish**.

blue jay *n.* A North American bird having a crested head, blue feathers with white and black markings, and a harsh noisy cry.

blue jeans *pl.n.* Pants of blue denim or similar cloth.

blue law *n.* **1.** A law restricting certain activities, especially shopping, on Sunday. **2.** A law passed in colonial America to govern personal behavior and particularly to prohibit certain forms of recreation on Sunday.

blueline or **blue line** (bloo′līn′) *n.* Either of two blue lines running across an ice-hockey rink, dividing the rink into defensive, neutral, and offensive zones.

bluenose (bloo′nōz′) *n.* **1.** A puritanical person. **2.** often **Bluenose** *Canadian* A native or inhabitant of Nova Scotia. —**blue′nosed′** *adj.*

blueprint (bloo′prĭnt′) *n.* **1.** A photographic copy of architectural plans or technical drawings, typically appearing as white lines on a blue background. **2.** A carefully worked-out plan: *a blueprint for success.*

blue ribbon *n.* An award made from a blue ribbon, given to a competitor who finishes in first place.

blues (blooz) *pl.n.* (*used with a singular or plural verb*) **1.** A type of popular music that developed from southern African-American songs and usually has a slow tempo, a strong 4/4 rhythm, and flatted third and seventh tones in its scale. **2.** Lowness of spirit; melancholy: *The rainy weather is giving people the blues.*

blue state *n.* A US state in which a majority has voted for the Democratic candidate in a statewide election.

bluestocking (bloo′stŏk′ĭng) *n.* *Archaic* A woman with strong scholarly or literary interests.

bluets (bloo′ĭts) *pl.n.* (*used with a singular or plural verb*) Any of several low-growing plants of North America having small light-blue flowers with a yellow center.

blue whale *n.* A very large whale having a bluish-gray back and grooves on the throat. It is thought to be the largest animal ever to have lived on earth, reaching a length of up to 100 feet (30.5 meters).

bluff¹ (blŭf) *v.* **bluffed, bluffing, bluffs** —*intr.* **1.** To engage in a false display of confidence or aggression in order to deceive or intimidate someone: *The reporter was bluffing when she said she knew the movie star.* **2.** To make a display of aggression, as by charging or baring the teeth, as a means of intimidating another animal. **3.** To try to mislead opponents in a card game by betting a lot on a poor hand or by little or no betting on a good hand. —*tr.* To deceive or mislead by a false display of confidence or aggression: *He bluffed the guard into thinking he worked for the bank.* ❖ *n.* The act or an example of bluffing. ◆ **call (someone's) bluff** To force someone to reveal that he or she is bluffing. —**bluff′er** *n.*

bluff² (blŭf) *n.* A steep headland, cliff, or riverbank. ❖ *adj.* **bluffer, bluffest 1.** Gruff or blunt in manner but not unkind: *bluff speech.* **2.** Having a broad steep front: *bluff cliffs along the river.* —**bluff′ly** *adv.* —**bluff′ness** *n.*

WORD HISTORY The origin of **bluff¹** is uncertain. **Bluff²** probably comes from obsolete Dutch *blaf* or Middle Low German *blaff,* both meaning "broad."

bluing also **blueing** (bloo′ĭng) *n.* A blue powder or liquid added to rinse water to prevent white fabrics from turning yellow during laundering.

bluish also **blueish** (bloo′ĭsh) *adj.* Somewhat blue.

blunder (blŭn′dər) *n.* A foolish or careless mistake: *Using the wrong wax was a serious blunder.* ❖ *intr.v.* **blundered, blundering, blunders 1.** To make a foolish mistake: *We blundered in estimating the cost of the curtains.* **2.** To move clumsily or blindly; stumble: *blunder through the bushes into a stream.*

blunderbuss (blŭn′dər-bŭs′) *n.* A short musket with a wide muzzle for scattering shot at close range.

blunt (blŭnt) *adj.* **blunter, bluntest 1.** Having a thick dull edge or end; not sharp. **2.** Abrupt and frank in manner: *a blunt reprimand.* ❖ *tr. & intr.v.* **blunted, blunting, blunts** To make or become less sharp or keen; dull: *The knife was blunted from so much use.* —**blunt′ly** *adv.* —**blunt′ness** *n.*

blur (blûr) *v.* **blurred, blurring, blurs** —*tr.* **1.** To make indistinct or hazy in outline; obscure: *Clouds blurred the mountain peak.* **2.** To make dim or unclear; cloud: *Tears blurred my vision.* **3.** To make less distinct to the mind: *a book that blurs the line between fiction and nonfiction.* —*intr.* **1.** To become indistinct, vague, or hazy: *The streetlights blurred in the snowstorm. My memories of childhood have blurred with time.* **2.** To become unclear or clouded: *As he got sleepy his vision began to blur.* ❖ *n.* Something that is indistinct and hazy: *The crowd was a blur of colors in the distance.*

blurb (blûrb) *n.* A brief favorable publicity notice, as on the jacket of a book.

blurry (blûr′ē) *adj.* **blurrier, blurriest 1.** Unclear or out of focus: *a blurry picture.* **2.** Not clearly distinguished; indistinct: *a blurry line between categories.*

blurt (blûrt) *tr.v.* **blurted, blurting, blurts** To say suddenly and without thought: *She blurted out the secret.*

blush (blŭsh) *intr.v.* **blushed, blushing, blushes 1.** To become suddenly red in the face from modesty, embarrassment, or shame. **2.** To feel ashamed: *I blushed to think how rude I must have seemed to them.* ❖ *n.* **1.** A sudden reddening of the face caused by modesty, embarrassment, or shame. **2.** A reddish or rosy color: *the blush of dawn.* **3.** A blusher.

blusher (blŭsh′ər) *n.* A cosmetic used to give the cheeks a rosy tint.

bluster (blŭs′tər) *intr.v.* **blustered, blustering, blusters 1.** To blow in loud violent gusts: *Winds blustered on the mountaintop.* **2.** To utter noisy boasts or threats: *The angry customer blustered at the clerk.* ❖ *n.* **1.** A violent gusty wind: *the bluster of a March storm.* **2.** Loud boastful or aggressive talk, often full of empty threats: *The candidate's speech was full of bluster, but no one took it seriously.* —**blus′ter·er** *n.* —**blus′ter·ous** *adj.* —**blus′ter·y** *adj.*

Blvd. An abbreviation of boulevard.

boa (bō′ə) *n.* **1.** Any of various large nonvenomous snakes of tropical regions, including the anacondas and the boa constrictor, that coil around and suffocate their prey. **2.** A long fluffy scarf made of soft material, such as fur or feathers.

boa constrictor *n.* A large boa of tropical America that has dark brown markings on a lighter background.

boar (bôr) *n.* **1.** A male pig. **2.** A wild pig native to Eurasia and northern Africa, having dark bristles and short tusks.

board (bôrd) *n.* **1.** A flat thin length of sawed lumber; a plank: *The side of the hut was finished with old boards.* **2a.** A flat piece of wood or similar material adapted for some special use: *a bulletin board; a chess board.* **b.** A blackboard or similar upright flat surface used for writing. **c.** A flat piece of material designed to be ridden as a sport, such as a snowboard or skateboard. **d.** A diving board. **3.** Food served daily to paying guests: *room and board.* **4.** A group of people organized to transact or administer some particular business: *the board of trustees.* **5.** A backboard in basketball. **6. boards** The wooden structure enclosing a skating rink or similar playing area. **7.** A circuit board. ❖ *v.* **boarded, boarding, boards** —*tr.* **1.** To close with boards: *boarding up the windows.* **2.** To provide (someone) with food and lodging for a charge. **3.** To go aboard (a ship, train, or plane). —*intr.* To live as a paying guest: *board at the local hotel.*

boarder (bôr′dər) *n.* **1.** A person who pays for and receives both meals and lodging at another person's home. **2.** A person who rides a board, such as a snowboard or surfboard, as a sport.

board foot *n., pl.* **board feet** A unit of measure for lumber, equal to the volume of an unplaned board one foot long, one foot wide, and one inch thick; 144 cubic inches of wood.

board game *n.* A game of strategy, such as chess or backgammon, played by moving pieces on a board.

boarding house (bôr′dĭng) *n.* A private home that provides meals and lodging for paying guests.

boarding school *n.* A school where pupils are provided with meals and lodging.

board shorts also **boardshorts** (bôrd′shôrts′) *pl.n.* Shorts, usually knee-length but sometimes shorter, that are worn for surfing or other water sports.

boardwalk (bôrd′wôk′) *n.* A public walk or promenade along a beach, usually made of wooden planks.

boast (bōst) *v.* **boasted, boasting, boasts** —*intr.* To speak about oneself in a proud or self-admiring way; brag. —*tr.* **1.** To say (something about oneself) in a proud or self-admiring way: *The doctors boasted that their discovery would lead to a cure for cancer.* **2.** To have as a desirable feature: *The mall boasted 70 stores and an arcade with games and rides.* ❖ *n.* A bragging or boastful statement: *a boast not supported by fact.* —**boast′er** *n.*

boat (bōt) *n.* **1.** A small open craft for traveling on water. **2.** A large seagoing vessel; a ship or submarine. **3.** A dish shaped like a boat: *a gravy boat.* ❖ *intr. & tr.v.* **boated, boating, boats** To travel by boat; row or sail: *boat across the lake.* ◆ **in the same boat** In the same situation as someone else.

boastful (bōst′fəl) *adj.* Tending to boast or brag. —**boast′ful·ly** *adv.*

boathouse (bōt′hous′) *n.* A house in which boats are kept, often near the water's edge.

boatlift (bōt′lĭft′) *n.* An unofficial effort to transport large numbers of people, especially refugees, from one country to another by boats. —**boat′lift′** *v.*

boatload (bōt′lōd′) *n.* The number of passengers or the amount of cargo that a boat can hold.

boatman (bōt′mən) *n.* A person who works on, deals with, or operates boats.

boat people *pl.n.* Refugees who attempt to flee their country by boat and seek asylum in another country.

boatswain also **bo's'n** or **bosun** (bō′sən) *n.* A warrant officer or petty officer in charge of a ship's deck crew, rigging, and anchors.

bob¹ (bŏb) *v.* **bobbed, bobbing, bobs** —*intr.* **1.** To move up and down: *a cork bobbing on the water.* **2.** To grab at floating or hanging objects with the teeth: *bob for apples.* **3.** To fish with a bobber. —*tr.* To cause to move up and down: *bobbed their heads.* ❖ *n.* **1.** A quick jerking movement of the head or body. **2.** A bobber used in fishing. ◆ **bob up** To appear or arise unexpectedly or suddenly.

bob² (bŏb) *n.* **1.** A small hanging weight, such as a plumb bob. **2.** A small lock or curl of hair. **3.** A short haircut on a woman or child. ❖ *tr.v.* **bobbed, bobbing, bobs** To cut

short or reshape: *bobbed her hair; had his nose bobbed.*

bob³ (bŏb) *n., pl.* **bob** *Chiefly British* A shilling.

WORD HISTORY Bob¹ comes from Middle English *bobben,* meaning "to move up and down." **Bob²** comes from Middle English *bobbe,* meaning "cluster of fruit." The origin of **bob³** is unknown.

bobber¹ (bŏb′ər) *n.* **1.** A buoyant object used to suspend a fishing line. **2.** A person who fishes with such an object.

bobber² (bŏb′ər) *n.* A person who reshapes or trims something, especially hair.

bobbin (bŏb′ĭn) *n.* A spool or reel that holds something, such as thread or yarn, for spinning, weaving, knitting, sewing, or making lace.

bobble (bŏb′əl) *v.* **bobbled, bobbling, bobbles** —*intr.* To bob up and down. —*tr.* To lose one's grip on (a ball) momentarily. ❖ *n.* A mistake or blunder.

bobby (bŏb′ē) *n., pl.* **bobbies** *Chiefly British* A policeman.

bobby pin *n.* A small metal hairpin having springy ends pressed tightly together to hold the hair in place.

bobby socks also **bobby sox** *pl.n. Informal* Short thick socks worn by girls or women.

bobcat (bŏb′kăt′) *n.* A North American wildcat having spotted reddish-brown fur, tufted ears, and a short tail.

bobolink (bŏb′ə-lĭngk′) *n.* A songbird of the Americas that has black, white, and yellowish feathers in the male and is usually found in fields and grasslands.

bobsled (bŏb′slĕd′) *n.* **1.** A long racing sled with a steering device that controls the front runners. **2a.** A long sled made of two shorter sleds joined one behind the other. **b.** Either of these two smaller sleds. ❖ *intr.v.* **bobsledded, bobsledding, bobsleds** To ride or race in a bobsled. —**bob′sled·der** *n.*

bobtail (bŏb′tāl′) *n.* **1.** A short tail or a tail that has been cut short. **2.** An animal, especially a horse, having such a tail.

bobwhite (bŏb-wīt′) *n.* A brown and white North American quail having a call that sounds like its name.

bode¹ (bōd) *tr.v.* **boded, boding, bodes** To be a sign or omen of (something to come): *A heavy sea boded trouble for the passengers on board.* ◆ **bode ill** To be a bad sign: *The coming hurricane bodes ill for many store owners along the beach.* **bode well** To be a good sign: *A clear sky boded well for our trip to the mountains.*

bode² (bōd) *v.* A past tense of **bide.**

bodega (bō-dā′gə) *n.* A small grocery store that specializes in Caribbean and Latin American products. —SEE NOTE AT **boutique.**

bodhisattva (bō′dĭ-sŭt′və) *n. Buddhism* An enlightened being who, out of compassion, forgoes nirvana in order to save others.

bodice (bŏd′ĭs) *n.* **1.** The fitted upper part of a dress. **2.** A woman's vest that laces in front, worn over a blouse.

bodiless (bŏd′ē-lĭs) *adj.* Having no body, form, or substance: *a bodiless spirit.*

bodily (bŏd′l-ē) *adj.* Relating or belonging to the body: *bodily ailments; food and other bodily needs.* ❖ *adv.* **1.** In the flesh; in person: *a sleepy student who was present bodily but not mentally.* **2.** As a complete body; as a whole: *carried the child bodily up the stairs.*

bodkin (bŏd′kĭn) *n.* **1.** A small pointed instrument for punching holes in cloth or leather. **2.** A blunt needle for pulling tape or ribbon through loops or a hem. **3.** A small dagger. **4.** A long ornamental hairpin.

body (bŏd′ē) *n., pl.* **bodies** **1a.** The entire physical structure and substance of a living thing, especially of a human or other animal. **b.** A corpse or carcass: *The body of the drowned sailor was never found.* **2.** The main part of a person or other animal excluding the head and limbs; the trunk or torso: *After a feint to the head, the boxer landed a punch on his opponent's body.* **3.** A mass or collection of matter that is distinct from other masses: *a celestial body; a body of water.* **4.** A number of people or things considered as a group: *the student body; a body of information.* **5.** The main or central part of something: *the body of a ship.* **6.** A collection or quantity, as of material or information: *The investigators examined the body of evidence.*

bodyboard (bŏd′ē-bôrd′) *n.* A very short surfboard with one straight end, usually ridden by lying on one's chest. —**bod′y·board′** *v.*

bodybuilding (bŏd′ē-bĭl′dĭng) *n.* The process of building one's muscles through diet and exercise, such as weight-lifting. —**bod′y·build′er** *n.*

bodyguard (bŏd′ē-gärd′) *n.* A person or group of people responsible for the safety of someone else.

body language *n.* Gestures, facial expressions, and postures of the body by which a person communicates nonverbally or manifests various physical, mental, or emotional states.

body politic *n.* The whole people of a nation or state, regarded as a political unit.

body shop *n.* A shop or garage where the bodies of automotive vehicles are repaired.

bodysurf (bŏd′ē-sûrf′) *intr.v.* **bodysurfed, bodysurfing, bodysurfs** To ride a wave to shore without a surfboard.

Boer (bôr *or* bō′ər) *n.* A Dutch colonist or a descendant of a Dutch colonist in South Africa. —**Boer** *adj.*

bog (bŏg) *n.* An area of wet spongy ground that usually consists of a thick mat of decaying moss. ❖ *intr.v.* **bogged, bogging, bogs** To be hindered or slowed: *The plan to restore the building bogged down in government red tape.*

bogey also **bogy** or **bogie** (bō′gē) *n., pl.* **bogeys** also **bogies 1.** (*also* boōg′ē *or* boō′gē) An evil or mischievous spirit; a hobgoblin. **2.** In golf, a score of one stroke over par on a hole.

bogeyman (boōg′ē-măn′) *n.* Variant of **boogeyman.**

boggle (bŏg′əl) *v.* **boggled, boggling, boggles** —*intr.* To be staggered or overwhelmed, as with astonishment or dismay: *My mind boggles at the amount of studying I still have to do.* —*tr.* To stagger or overwhelm, as with astonishment or dismay: *The vast number of stars in our galaxy boggles the mind.*

bogie (bō′gē *or* boōg′ē) *n.* A variant of **bogey.**

bogus (bō′gəs) *adj.* **1.** Counterfeit; fake: *It is a crime to pass bogus money.* **2.** *Slang* Highly objectionable; senseless; pointless: *assigned us a task that was totally bogus.*

bogy (bō′gē *or* boōg′ē) *n.* A variant of **bogey.**

bohemian (bō-hē′mē-ən) *n.* A person, especially an artist, who does not follow conventional standards of behavior.

bohrium (bôr′ē-əm) *n. Symbol* **Bh** A radioactive element that has been artificially produced by agencies. The longest confirmed half-life of any of its isotopes is about 1.3 seconds. Atomic number 107. See **Periodic Table.**

boil¹ (boil) *v.* **boiled, boiling, boils** —*intr.* **1.** To change from a liquid state to a gaseous state by being heated to the boiling point: *Water boils at 212°F.* **2.** To be cooked by boiling or putting into boiling water: *I set the table while the potatoes were boiling.* **3.** To have the contents at a boil: *The kettle is boiling on the stove.* **4.** To be stirred up

or greatly excited, especially in anger: *boil with anger at the insult.* **5.** To rush or churn: *The water boiled through the rapids.* —*tr.* **1.** To heat (a liquid) to a temperature at which it turns into a gaseous state, with bubbles breaking though the liquid's surface. **2.** To cook by boiling: *boil an egg; boil syrup.* ❖ *n.* The condition or act of being boiled: *brought the soup to a rapid boil.* ◆ **boil down 1.** To reduce in volume or amount by boiling: *boil down maple sap into maple syrup.* **2.** To reduce or be reduced to a simpler form: *Let's boil the problem down to its basic elements. The problem boils down to a lack of money.* **boil over 1.** To overflow while boiling. **2.** To explode in rage; lose one's temper.

boil² (boil) *n.* A painful pus-filled swelling of the skin and the tissue beneath it, caused by a local bacterial infection.

WORD HISTORY Boil¹ comes from Middle English *boil-len,* which comes from Latin *bullīre,* both meaning "to change from liquid to gas with heat." **Boil²** comes from Old English *bȳle,* meaning "pus-filled swelling."

boiler (boi′lər) *n.* **1.** A vessel in which a liquid, usually water, is heated and often vaporized for use in an engine, turbine, or heating system. **2.** A container, such as a kettle, for boiling liquids. **3.** A storage tank for hot water.

boilerplate (boi′lər-plāt′) *n.* **1.** Steel in the form of flat plates used in making steam boilers. **2.** Journalistic material, such as syndicated features, made available by agencies in a form that is already typeset, originally in plate form, for easy incorporation into publications such as newspapers. **3.** Hackneyed or conventional language, usually expressing a generally accepted viewpoint. **4.** Standardized or set language that is meant to be used repeatedly, often in organizational publications or legal documents.

boiling point (boi′lĭng) *n.* The temperature at which a liquid boils, especially as measured at sea level.

boisterous (boi′stər-əs *or* boi′strəs) *adj.* Noisy and unruly or unrestrained: *a playground full of boisterous children; the boisterous cheers of an excited crowd.* —**bois′-ter·ous·ly** *adv.* —**bois′ter·ous·ness** *n.*

bola (bō′lə) also **bolas** (bō′ləs) *n.* A rope with weights attached, used in South America to catch cattle or game by entangling their legs.

bold (bōld) *adj.* **bolder, boldest 1a.** Having little fear; brave; courageous: *bold explorers.* **b.** Showing or requiring courage; daring; audacious: *a bold voyage to unknown lands.* See Synonyms at **brave. 2.** Lacking respectful restraint in behavior; arrogant or overbearing: *a bold, sassy child.* **3.** Strikingly different or unconventional; arresting or provocative: *a bold new way to tackle the problem of homelessness.* **4.** Clear and distinct to the eye; vivid; clear: *bold colors; a bold pattern.* **5.** Being in boldface: *bold type.* —**bold′ly** *adv.* —**bold′ness** *n.*

boldface (bōld′fās′) *n.* Type that has thick heavy lines: *Entry words in this dictionary are in boldface.* —**bold′-face′** *adj.*

bold-faced (bōld′fāst′) *adj.* **1.** Shamelessly bold and disrespectful; brazen: *a bold-faced lie.* **2.** Printed in boldface.

bole (bōl) *n.* The trunk of a tree.

bolero (bō-lâr′ō) *n., pl.* **boleros 1.** A very short jacket of Spanish origin, worn open in the front. **2a.** A lively Spanish dance or the music for this dance, in triple meter. **b.** A slow Latin American dance or the music for this dance, in triple meter.

boll (bōl) *n.* The rounded seed-bearing capsule of certain plants, especially cotton and flax.

boll weevil *n.* A long-snouted beetle that causes damage to the buds and bolls of cotton plants.

bologna also **baloney** (bə-lō'nē) *n.* A large sausage of finely ground pork or other meat, usually served as cold cuts.

Bolognese (bō'lə-nēz' *or* bō'lə-nēs') *adj.* 1. Relating to or characteristic of Bologna, Italy. 2. Being or served with a sauce containing meat, tomatoes and other vegetables, and often wine and cream: *spaghetti Bolognese.* ❖ *n.* 1. A native or inhabitant of Bologna, Italy. 2. Bolognese sauce.

Bolshevik (bōl'shə-vĭk') *n.* 1. A member of the Russian Social Democratic Workers' Party that adopted Lenin's ideas and seized control of the Russian government in November 1917. 2. A Communist.

Bolshevism also **bolshevism** (bōl'shə-vĭz'əm) *n.* The theories and practices developed by the Bolsheviks between 1903 and 1917 with a view to seizing governmental power and establishing the world's first Communist state.

Bolshevist also **bolshevist** (bōl'shə-vĭst) *n.* A Bolshevik. —**Bol'she·vist'** *adj.*

bolster (bōl'stər) *n.* A long narrow pillow or cushion. ❖ *tr.v.* **bolstered, bolstering, bolsters** To support or reinforce: *Visitors bolstered the patient's morale.*

bolt (bōlt) *n.* 1. A rod or pin with a head at one end and threads onto which a nut is screwed at the other end, used to hold two parts together. 2. A sliding bar of wood or metal for fastening a door or gate. 3. A metal bar or rod in a lock that is pushed out or withdrawn at a turn of the key. 4. A sliding bar that positions the cartridge in a rifle and closes the breech. 5. A large roll of cloth, especially as it comes from the loom. 6. A short heavy arrow used with a crossbow. 7. A flash of lightning; a thunderbolt. 8. A sudden movement toward or away from something: *Our cat made a bolt for the open door.* ❖ *v.* **bolted, bolting, bolts** —*tr.* 1. To attach or fasten with a bolt or bolts: *bolted the rack to the wall.* 2. To lock with a bolt: *Bolt the door.* 3. To eat hurriedly and with little chewing; gulp. 4. To break away from (a political party). —*intr.* 1. To move or spring suddenly: *bolting from the room.* 2. To break from a rider's control and run away: *a horse that shied and bolted.* 3. To break away from an affiliation, as from a political party. ◆ **bolt from the blue** A sudden, usually shocking surprise: *The news came as a bolt from the blue.*

bolt upright Stiff and straight: *Realizing he was late, he sat bolt upright in bed.*

bolus (bō'ləs) *n., pl.* **boluses** 1. A round mass. 2a. A single, relatively large quantity of a substance, such as a dose of a drug, intended for therapeutic use and taken orally. b. A concentrated mass of a substance administered intravenously for diagnostic or therapeutic purposes. 3. A soft mass of chewed food within the mouth or digestive tract.

bomb (bŏm) *n.* 1. An explosive weapon constructed to go off by striking something, by a timing mechanism, or by some other means. 2. A weapon exploded to release gas or other destructive materials: *a smoke bomb.* 3. In football, a long forward pass. 4. A container for holding a substance under pressure, as a preparation for killing insects, that can be released as a spray or gas. 5. *Slang* A dismal failure: *That new movie is a bomb.* 6. *Slang* One that is excellent or superior. Used with *the: That new movie is the bomb.* ❖ *v.* **bombed, bombing, bombs** —*tr.* To attack, damage, or destroy with a bomb or bombs: *bomb a bridge.* —*intr. Slang* To fail miserably: *That new*

movie bombed and closed after one week in the theaters.

bombard (bŏm-bärd' *or* bəm-bärd') *tr.v.* **bombarded, bombarding, bombards** 1. To attack with bombs, shells, or missiles: *bombard an enemy position.* 2. To barrage or shower, as with words: *Reporters bombarded the police with questions.* 3. To strike (the nucleus of an atom) with a stream of subatomic particles in order to study the structure of the nucleus. —**bom·bard'ment** *n.*

bombardier (bŏm'bər-dîr') *n.* The member of a bomber crew who works the bombsight and releases the bombs.

bombast (bŏm'băst') *n.* Extravagant or pompous speech or writing: *a politician full of bombast and bluster.*

bombastic (bŏm-băs'tĭk) *adj.* Having an extravagant pompous style: *a bombastic speech denouncing the government's policies.* —**bom·bas'ti·cal·ly** *adv.*

bomb bay *n.* The compartment in a bomber from which bombs are dropped.

bomber (bŏm'ər) *n.* 1. A military airplane that carries and drops bombs. 2. A person who makes and sets off bombs.

bombproof (bŏm'prōōf') *adj.* Designed to resist destruction by a bomb: *a bombproof bunker.*

bombshell (bŏm'shĕl') *n.* 1. A bomb. 2. Something that is shocking, surprising, or amazing: *The news of the senator's resignation came as a bombshell.*

bombsight (bŏm'sīt') *n.* A device in a military aircraft for aiming bombs.

bona fide (bō'nə fīd' *or* bŏn'ə fīd') *adj.* 1. Done or made in good faith; sincere: *a bona fide offer to buy.* 2. Genuine; authentic: *a bona fide painting by Rembrandt.*

bonanza (bə-năn'zə) *n.* 1. A rich mine or vein of ore. 2. A source of great wealth: *The rise in stock prices was a bonanza to shareholders.*

bonbon (bŏn'bŏn') *n.* A piece of candy, often with a creamy center and a chocolate coating.

bond (bŏnd) *n.* 1. Something, such as a cord or band, that binds or holds things together: *They tied bonds around the prisoner's wrists.* 2. A force that unites; a tie: *a bond of affection between the two brothers.* 3. A force of attraction that holds atoms or groups of atoms together in a molecule, produced in general by a transfer or sharing of one or more electrons. 4. A union of objects or parts created by an adhesive substance: *The glue formed a tight bond between the two surfaces.* 5. A binding agreement; a covenant: *My word is my bond.* 6. Money paid as bail: *The bond for the prisoner's release was set at $100,000.* 7. A certificate of debt issued by a government or corporation that guarantees repayment of the original investment with interest by a specified date. 8. An insurance contract that guarantees payment to an employer in the event of financial loss caused by the actions of an employee. ❖ *v.* **bonded, bonding, bonds** —*tr.* 1. To join securely, as with glue: *bonded the poster to the wall with paste.* 2. To connect by strong emotional or social ties: *The adventures we shared bonded us for life.* 3. To place (an employee) under bond so as to insure his or her employer against loss. —*intr.* To be joined together with a bond: *Oxygen bonds to hydrogen to form water.*

bondage (bŏn'dĭj) *n.* The condition of being bound as a slave or serf; slavery or servitude.

bondholder (bŏnd'hōl'dər) *n.* The owner of a government or corporate bond.

bondman (bŏnd'mən) *n.* A male bondservant.

bondservant (bŏnd'sûr'vənt) *n.* A person who is obligated to work for another without wages; a slave or serf.

bondsman (bŏndz′mən) *n.* **1.** A male bondservant. **2.** A person who provides bail for another.

bondwoman (bŏnd′wŏŏm′ən) *n.* A female bondservant.

bone (bōn) *n.* **1a.** The hard, dense, calcified tissue that forms the skeleton of most vertebrate animals. **b.** One of the many distinct structures making up such a skeleton: *the bones of the foot.* **2. bones a.** A corpse or skeleton: *Placed his bones in the coffin.* **b.** The body: *Sit down and rest your bones.* ❖ *tr.v.* **boned, boning, bones** In cooking, to remove the bones from: *bone fish.* ◆ **bone of contention** The subject of a dispute: *Who goes first is often a bone of contention.* **bone to pick** A reason for a complaint or dispute. **bone up** *Informal* To study a subject intensively, especially to prepare for something: *boned up for the final exam.* **in (one's) bones** In one's innermost feelings: *I knew in my bones that I was wrong.*

bone-dry (bōn′drī′) *adj.* Without a trace of moisture.

bonehead (bōn′hĕd′) *n. Informal* A stupid person.

bone marrow *n.* The soft material that fills the cavities inside most bones. It is the source of red blood cells and many white blood cells.

bone meal *n.* Bones crushed and ground to a coarse powder, used as fertilizer and animal feed.

bonfire (bŏn′fīr′) *n.* A large fire built outdoors.

bongos (bŏng′gōz) *pl.n.* A pair of small drums, usually tuned to different pitches, that are played by beating with the hands.

bonhomie (bŏn′ə-mē′) *n.* A pleasant and affable disposition; geniality. —**bon′ho·mous** (bŏn′ə-məs) *adj.*

bonito (bə-nē′tō) *n., pl.* **bonito** or **bonitos** Any of several ocean fishes that resemble a small tuna and are caught for food and sport.

bon mot (bŏN mō′) *n., pl.* **bons mots** (bŏN mō′ or bŏN mōz′) A clever saying; a witticism.

bonnet (bŏn′ĭt) *n.* **1.** A hat tied with ribbons under the chin and worn by a woman or child. **2.** A cap without a brim, worn by men or boys in Scotland. **3.** *Chiefly British* The hood of an automobile.

bonny also **bonnie** (bŏn′ē) *adj.* **bonnier, bonniest** *Scots* Pleasing to the eye; pretty: *a bonny lass.*

bonobo (bə-nō′bō) *n., pl.* **bonobos** A dark-haired African ape that is closely related to and resembles the chimpanzee but has a more slender build. Bonobos are found only in the Democratic Republic of the Congo, south of the Congo River.

bonsai (bŏn-sī′ or bŏn′sī′) *n., pl.* **bonsai 1.** The art of growing miniature trees in small pots or dishes. **2.** A tree grown in this way.

bonus (bō′nəs) *n., pl.* **bonuses** Something given or paid in addition to what is usual or expected: *Each worker got a bonus of three extra days off for the holidays.*

bon vivant (bŏN′ vē-väN′) *n., pl.* **bons vivants** (bŏN′ vē-väN′) A person with refined taste, especially one who enjoys superb food and drink.

bon voyage (bŏn′ voi-äzh′) *interj.* An expression used to wish a departing traveler a pleasant journey.

bony or **boney** (bō′nē) *adj.* **bonier, boniest** or **boneyer, boneyest 1.** Relating to, resembling, or consisting of bone. **2.** Full of bones: *a bony piece of fish.* **3.** Having bones that stick out or show through; thin; gaunt: *bony arms.* —**bon′i·ness** *n.*

bony fish *n.* Any of numerous fishes that have a bony skeleton, in contrast to the cartilaginous fishes, such as sharks.

boo (bōō) *n., pl.* **boos** A sound uttered to show dislike or disapproval: *There was a mix of cheers and boos when the speaker was finished.* ❖ *interj.* An expression used to show dislike or disapproval or to frighten or surprise. ❖ *v.* **booed, booing, boos** —*intr.* To utter a boo: *The fans booed angrily.* —*tr.* To say "boo" to; jeer: *The spectators booed the umpire's decision.*

boob (bōōb) *n. Slang* A stupid or foolish person; a dunce.

boo-boo also **booboo** (bōō′bōō) *n., pl.* **boo-boos** also **boo-boos** *Informal* **1.** A foolish or thoughtless mistake. **2.** A slight physical injury, such as a scratch.

booby (bōō′bē) *n., pl.* **boobies** Any of several large usually tropical seabirds having long pointed wings and a long bill.

booby prize *n.* An award given to the person who performs worst in a game or contest.

booby trap *n.* **1.** A device, often containing an explosive, designed to injure or kill an unsuspecting person who moves a seemingly harmless object. **2.** A situation for catching a person off-guard; a trap.

boogeyman or **bogeyman** (bōōg′ē-măn′) *n.* A terrifying spirit; a hobgoblin.

boogie-woogie (bōōg′ē-wōōg′ē or bōō′gē-wōō′gē) *n.* A style of blues piano playing characterized by a quick tempo, a repeated bass line, and a series of improvised variations in the treble.

book (bōōk) *n.* **1a.** A set of printed, written, or blank pages fastened together along one edge and enclosed between covers. **b.** An e-book or other electronic source of information structured like a book. **2a.** A printed or written literary work: *a book about Mexico.* **b.** A main division of a larger written or printed work: *a book of the Bible.* **3. Book a.** The Bible. **b.** The Koran. **4a.** A volume for recording financial transactions: *an account book.* **b. books** Financial records in which an accounting is kept of money received, owed, and paid: *A bookkeeper keeps books.* **5.** A set of established rules: *She runs the company by the book.* **6.** A small packet of similar things bound together: *a book of matches.* **7.** The words or script of a play, musical, or opera. ❖ *tr.v.* **booked, booking, books 1.** To arrange for in advance; reserve or schedule: *We booked tickets to the show.* **2.** To write down charges against (a person) in a police record: *book a suspect.* ◆ **in (one's) book** In one's opinion: *In my book she was one of the all-time greats.* **like a book** Thoroughly; completely: *I know the town like a book.* **throw the book at 1.** To make all possible charges against (an offender). **2.** To scold or punish severely.

bookbag (bōōk′băg′) *n.* A small backpack or bag used to carry books and papers.

bookbinder (bōōk′bīn′dər) *n.* A person whose business is binding books.

bookcase (bōōk′kās′) *n.* A piece of furniture with shelves for holding books.

book club *n.* **1.** A business organization that sells books to its members at a discount from a selected list. **2.** A group of readers who meet periodically to discuss assigned books.

bookend (bōōk′ĕnd′) *n.* A prop placed at the end of a row of books to keep them upright.

bookie (bōōk′ē) *n.* A person who accepts and pays off bets; a bookmaker.

bookish (bōōk′ĭsh) *adj.* **1.** Fond of books and study; studious: *a bookish scholar.* **2.** Depending too much on books rather than experience: *a bookish notion of the world.* **3.** Scholarly or formal in a dull, dry way: *bookish writing.*

bookkeeping (bōōk′kē′pĭng) *n.* The work or skill of

keeping records of money received, owed, or paid by a business. —**book′keep′er** n.

booklet (book′lĭt) n. A small book or pamphlet, usually with paper covers.

bookmaker (book′mā′kər) n. **1.** A person or business that edits, prints, or publishes books. **2.** A person who accepts and pays off bets, especially on sporting events such as horse races. —**book′mak′ing** n.

bookmark (book′märk′) n. **1.** An object, such as a ribbon or a strip of leather, placed between the pages of a book to mark the reader's place. **2.** A link in a web browser that allows a user to easily return to a webpage.

bookmobile (book′mō-bēl′) n. A truck or van with shelves of books in it, used as a traveling library.

Book of Common Prayer n. The book of services and prayers used in the Anglican Church.

Book of Mormon n. A sacred book of the Mormon Church, published in 1830 and believed by Mormons to be a sacred history of the Americas revealed by the prophet Mormon to Joseph Smith.

bookplate (book′plāt′) n. A label pasted inside a book and bearing the owner's name.

bookseller (book′sĕl′ər) n. A person or business that sells books.

bookshelf (book′shĕlf′) n., pl. **bookshelves** A shelf or set of shelves for holding books.

bookshop (book′shŏp′) n. A bookstore.

bookstand (book′stănd′) n. **1.** A small counter where books are sold. **2.** A frame for holding an open book.

bookstore (book′stôr′) n. A store where books are sold.

bookworm (book′wûrm′) n. A person who spends much time reading or studying.

Boolean algebra (boo′lē-ən) n. A form of algebra in which variables may have one of two values and the operations defined on them are logical OR, a type of addition, and logical AND, a type of multiplication. Boolean algebra is fundamental to computer programming.

boom¹ (boom) v. **boomed, booming, booms** —intr. **1.** To make a deep resonant sound: *The cannon boomed across the valley.* **2.** To grow, develop, or progress rapidly; thrive; flourish: *Business is booming.* —tr. To say or give forth with such a sound: *Rescuers boomed a message over their loudspeaker.* ✤ n. **1.** A deep hollow sound, as from an explosion. **2.** A sudden increase, as in growth or production: *a boom in farm production filled the markets.* **3.** A time of economic prosperity: *California had a boom after gold was discovered.*

boom² (boom) n. **1.** A long pole extending from the mast of a boat to hold or stretch out the bottom of a sail. **2a.** A long pole or similar structure that extends upward and outward from the mast of a derrick and supports the object being lifted. **b.** A similar support that holds a microphone. **3.** A chain, cable, or line of timbers that keeps logs from floating away. **4.** A floating barrier used to contain an oil spill.

WORD HISTORY Boom¹ comes from Middle English *bomben*, meaning "to make a buzzing sound." **Boom²** comes from Dutch *boom*, meaning "tree, pole."

boomer (boo′mər) n. *Informal* A baby boomer.

boomerang (boo′mə-răng′) n. **1.** A flat curved piece of wood that can be thrown so that it returns to the thrower. **2.** Something that comes back to harm or surprise the

originator. ✤ intr.v. **boomeranged, boomeranging, boomerangs** To have the opposite effect of that intended; backfire: *The advertising campaign boomeranged when people found out that the claims weren't entirely true.*

boomtown (boom′toun′) n. A town that experiences sudden growth and prosperity, as after a discovery of gold, silver, or oil.

boon¹ (boon) n. Something that provides a benefit or advantage: *Delay would be a blow to us and a boon to our competitors.*

boon² (boon) adj. Friendly and jolly; sociable: *a boon companion.*

WORD HISTORY Boon¹ comes from the Middle English noun *bon*, which comes from Old Norse *bōn*, both meaning "prayer." **Boon²** comes from the Middle English adjective *bon*, which comes from Latin *bonus*, both meaning "good."

boondocks (boon′dŏks′) pl.n. *Slang* **1.** Rough uncleared country. **2.** Rural country; the backwoods.

boondoggle (boon′dŏ′gəl) *Informal* n. **1.** An unnecessary or wasteful project or activity. **2a.** A braided leather cord worn as a decoration especially by Boy Scouts. **b.** A cord of braided leather, fabric, or plastic strips made by a child as a project to keep busy.

boor (boor) n. A crude person with rude or clumsy manners.

boorish (boor′ĭsh) adj. Crude, rude, and offensive: *loud boorish behavior.* —**boor′ish·ly** adv. —**boor′ish·ness** n.

boost (boost) tr.v. **boosted, boosting, boosts 1.** To lift by pushing up from below: *She boosted her friend into the tree.* **2.** To increase; raise: *Advertising often boosts sales.* **3.** To increase the strength of (an electric current or signal). **4.** To stir up enthusiasm for; promote: *She writes articles that boost her hometown.* ✤ n. **1.** A push upward or ahead: *Give me a boost up the pole.* **2.** An encouraging act or comment. **3.** An increase: *A boost in salary.*

booster (boo′stər) n. **1.** Something that increases the power or effectiveness of a system or device: *a battery booster.* **2.** An amplifier for radio or television signals: *a television booster.* **3.** A rocket used to launch a missile or space vehicle. **4.** A booster shot. **5.** A person or thing that boosts: *The holiday was a morale booster.*

booster shot n. An additional dose of a vaccine or serum given in order to sustain the immunity provided by an earlier dose of the same vaccine or serum.

boot¹ (boot) n. **1.** A kind of shoe that covers the foot and ankle and usually part of the lower calf, often made of leather or rubber. **2.** Something shaped like a boot, as a peninsula: *the boot of Italy.* **3.** A kick: *give a ball a good boot.* **4.** *Slang* The state of being fired from a job: *Half the staff was given the boot.* **5.** *Chiefly British* The trunk of an automobile. **6.** The process of starting or restarting a computer. ✤ tr.v. **booted, booting, boots 1.** To kick: *The soccer player booted the ball down the field.* **2.** To put boots on: *The soldiers carrying flags were booted.* **3.** To start (a computer) by loading the operating system. **4.** In baseball, to misplay (a ground ball).

boot² (boot) intr.v. **booted, booting, boots** *Archaic* To benefit, help, or avail. ◆ **to boot** In addition; besides: *He got a T-shirt and a baseball cap to boot.*

WORD HISTORY Boot¹ comes from Middle English *bote*, referring to the item of footwear. **Boot²** comes from Old English *bōt* meaning "good, advantage."

bootblack (bŏŏt′blăk′) *n.* A person who cleans and polishes shoes for a living.

boot camp *n.* **1.** A training camp for soldiers or sailors who have just joined the armed services. **2.** A facility, similar to a military boot camp, where convicted criminals undergo intense physical workouts as part of a program to teach self-discipline and respect for the law.

bootee also **bootie** (bŏŏ′tē) *n.* A soft, usually knitted baby shoe.

Boötes (bō-ō′tēz) *n.* A constellation in the Northern Hemisphere near the handle of the Big Dipper, traditionally pictured as a herdsman.

booth (bŏŏth) *n.*, *pl.* **booths** (bŏŏthz or bŏŏths) **1.** A small enclosed or partially enclosed compartment, usually for a single person: *a telephone booth; a voting booth.* **2.** A small enclosed compartment with a window, at which a service is provided: *a ticket booth; an information booth.* **3.** A small stall where merchandise is sold: *a booth at the market selling gourmet foods.* **4.** A seating compartment consisting of a table enclosed by two facing benches with high backs: *We ate in a booth at the restaurant.*

bootjack (bŏŏt′jăk′) *n.* A forked device that holds a boot while the foot is pulled out of it.

bootleg (bŏŏt′lĕg′) *v.* **bootlegged, bootlegging, bootlegs** —*tr.* To make, sell, or transport (a product, especially alcoholic liquor) illegally. —*intr.* To engage in bootlegging a product, especially alcoholic liquor. ❖ *n.* A product that is illegally made, sold, or transported. ❖ *adj.* Made, sold, or transported illegally: *bootleg music tapes.* —**boot′leg′ger** *n.*

bootless (bŏŏt′lĭs) *adj.* Without advantage or benefit; useless; fruitless: *a bootless effort.*

booty (bŏŏ′tē) *n.*, *pl.* **booties 1.** Plunder taken from an enemy in war: *Soldiers often carry off the booty of war.* **2.** Seized or stolen goods: *pirates' booty.* **3.** A valuable prize; a treasure: *Divers brought up booty from a sunken ship.*

booze (bŏŏz) *Slang n.* Alcoholic drink. ❖ *intr.v.* **boozed, boozing, boozes** To drink alcoholic beverages to excess. —**booz′er** *n.*

bop¹ (bŏp) *Informal tr.v.* **bopped, bopping, bops** To hit or strike. ❖ *n.* A blow or punch.

bop² (bŏp) *n.* Bebop.

WORD HISTORY Bop¹ is imitative in origin. **Bop²** is short for *bebop*, which is imitative of a two-note phrase in this kind of music.

borate (bôr′āt′) *n.* A salt or ester of boric acid.

borax (bôr′ăks′) *n.* A white crystalline powder and mineral, used as an antiseptic, as a cleansing agent, in fusing metals, and in making heat-resistant glass. The mineral is an ore of boron.

Bordeaux (bôr-dō′) *n.*, *pl.* **Bordeaux** (bôr-dō′ or bôr-dōz′) A red or white wine made in the region around Bordeaux, France.

bordello (bôr-dĕl′ō) *n.*, *pl.* **bordellos** A house of prostitution.

border (bôr′dər) *n.* **1.** The line where one country, state, or region ends and another begins; a boundary: *the border between the United States and Canada.* **2.** A margin or edge: *They picnicked on the border of the pond.* **3.** A strip put on or around an edge, as for ornament: *a border of lace around the tablecloth.* ❖ *tr.v.* **bordered, bordering, borders 1.** To lie along or next to: *Canada and Mexico border the United States.* **2.** To put a border or an edging on: *border a collar with lace.* ◆ **border on** or **border**

upon 1. To be next to; touch: *France borders on Germany.* **2.** To come close to; approach: *This weather borders on the ideal.*

✦ **SYNONYMS** border, brink, edge, margin, rim *n.*

border collie *n.* A dog of a medium-sized, agile breed developed on the border between England and Scotland for herding sheep, often having a wavy black coat with white markings.

borderland (bôr′dər-lănd′) *n.* **1.** Land on or near a border or frontier. **2.** An indefinite area or condition in which two different things seem to overlap: *the borderland between dreams and reality.*

borderline (bôr′dər-līn′) *n.* **1.** A dividing line; a border or boundary. **2.** An indefinite line between two different conditions: *on the borderline between good and excellent.* ❖ *adj.* **1.** Relating to an indefinite or uncertain area between two different conditions: *a borderline medical diagnosis.* **2.** Barely acceptable; nearly unacceptable or abnormal: *borderline behavior.*

bore¹ (bôr) *v.* **bored, boring, bores** —*tr.* **1.** To make (a hole, tunnel, or well) by drilling or digging: *bore a tunnel through a mountain.* **2.** To make a hole in or through (something), as with a drill or auger: *bore a mountain to make a tunnel.* —*intr.* To make a hole by drilling or digging: *The miners bored through the rock to get at the coal.* ❖ *n.* **1.** The inside diameter of a hole, tube, cylinder, or other hollow object: *a pipe with a bore of three inches.* **2.** A bored hole, as in a pipe or the barrel of a firearm.

bore² (bôr) *tr.v.* **bored, boring, bores** To make weary by being dull or repetitive: *The speaker bored the audience by talking too long.* ❖ *n.* An uninteresting person or thing.

bore³ (bôr) *n.* A sudden high tidal wave that rushes upstream, with great force, at the mouth of a river.

WORD HISTORY Bore¹ comes from Old English *borian*, meaning "to make a hole." The origin of **bore²** is unknown. **Bore³** comes from Middle English *bare*, which comes from Old Norse *bāra*, both meaning "wave."

bore⁴ (bôr) *v.* Past tense of **bear¹**.

boreal (bôr′ē-əl) *adj.* **1.** Relating to the north; northern. **2.** Relating to or concerning the north wind. **3.** Relating to the forest areas of the northern hemisphere that are dominated by coniferous trees such as spruces, firs, and pines.

boredom (bôr′dəm) *n.* The condition of being bored; weariness of mind.

borer (bôr′ər) *n.* **1.** A tool used for boring or drilling. **2.** Any of various insects or insect larvae that bore into the stems or trunks of plants. **3.** Any of various mollusks that bore into soft rock or wood.

boric acid (bôr′ĭk) *n.* A white or colorless crystalline compound occurring in nature or made from borax and composed of hydrogen, boron, and oxygen. It is used as an antiseptic, as a preservative, and in cements and enamels.

boring (bôr′ĭng) *adj.* Uninteresting; dull: *a long boring speech.* —**bor′ing-ly** *adv.*

✦ **SYNONYMS** boring, dull, tedious, tiresome *adj.*

born (bôrn) *v.* A past participle of **bear¹**. ❖ *adj.* **1.** Brought into life or existence: *a political movement born in the last century.* **2.** Having a natural talent from birth: *a born artist.* **3.** Destined from birth: *She was born to sing.* **4.** Coming or resulting: *wisdom born of experience.*

born-again (bôrn′ə-gĕn′) *adj.* **1.** Having discovered or renewed a commitment to Evangelical Christianity: *a*

born-again Christian. 2. Marked by renewed activity or revived interest or enthusiasm: *a born-again supporter of free speech.*

borne (bôrn) *v.* A past participle of **bear**[1].

boron (bôr′ŏn′) *n. Symbol* **B** A nonmetallic element extracted chiefly from borax and occurring as a brown powder or black crystalline solid. It is used in flares, in nuclear reactors to control the speed of neutrons, in abrasives, and in hard metallic alloys. Atomic number 5. See **Periodic Table.**

borough (bûr′ō) *n.* **1.** A self-governing incorporated town, as in certain states of the United States. **2.** One of the five administrative units of New York City. **3.** A governmental district in Alaska, corresponding to a county. **4.** A town in Great Britain that sends one or more representatives to Parliament.

borrow (bŏr′ō) *v.* **borrowed, borrowing, borrows** —*tr.* **1.** To obtain (something) with the promise of returning or replacing it later: *borrow a library book; borrow money.* **2.** To take (a word, idea, or method) from another source and use it as one's own: *We borrowed the word "kindergarten" from German in the 1800s.* **3.** In mathematics, to subtract (one) from a digit in a number in order to add ten to the value of the digit to the right. When subtracting 6 from 93, you borrow 1 from 9 to make 3 into 13, and then subtract 6, leaving 87. —*intr.* To obtain or receive something, especially money on loan: *I borrowed from the bank to buy a new car.* —**bor′row·er** *n.*

USAGE The word **borrow** means "to take (something) temporarily with the promise of returning it"; **lend** means "to give (something) temporarily on condition of having it returned." A library *lends* books; readers *borrow* them. Another verb very similar to "lend" is **loan**, meaning "to lend money or an object." A neighbor *loans* you a shovel. You *borrow* a shovel from your neighbor.

borrowing (bŏr′ō-ĭng) *n.* Something that is borrowed, especially a word or phrase borrowed from another language: *The English word "plateau" is a borrowing from French.*

borscht (bôrsht) also **borsch** (bôrsh) *n.* A beet soup served hot or cold, often with sour cream.

borzoi (bôr′zoi′) *n., pl.* **borzois** A large slender dog of a breed developed in Russia to hunt wolves, having a narrow pointed head and silky coat.

bosky (bŏs′kē) *adj.* **boskier, boskiest** Having many bushes and trees: *a bosky stretch of land along the river.*

bo's'n (bō′sən) *n.* Variant of **boatswain.**

bosom (bŏoz′əm *or* bŏō′zəm) *n.* **1a.** The chest: *He held the sleepy child to his bosom.* **b.** A woman's breasts. **2.** The part of a garment that covers the chest: *the starched bosom of a shirt.* **3.** The chest considered as the source of emotion: *empty one's bosom of sorrow.* **4.** Emotional closeness and comfort: *We welcomed her into the bosom of our family.* ❖ *adj.* Close; intimate: *bosom friends.*

boss[1] (bôs) *n.* **1.** A person who employs or directs workers. **2.** A person who is in charge or makes decisions: *Who is boss around here?* **3.** A powerful person who controls a political party or organization. ❖ *tr.v.* **bossed, bossing, bosses** To give orders to; order around: *The supervisor always bosses the cashiers around.*

boss[2] (bôs) *n.* A raised ornament projecting from a flat

surface. ❖ *tr.v.* **bossed, bossing, bosses** To decorate with bosses; emboss.

WORD HISTORY **Boss**[1] comes from Dutch *baas,* meaning "master." **Boss**[2] comes from Middle English *boce,* which comes from Old French *boce,* both meaning "raised ornament."

bossism (bô′sĭz′əm) *n.* The control of a political party or organization by a boss.

bossy (bô′sē) *adj.* **bossier, bossiest** Inclined to order others around; domineering.

Boston terrier (bô′stən) *n.* A small dog of a breed developed in New England, having a short muzzle and a black or brindled coat with white markings.

bosun (bō′sən) *n.* Variant of **boatswain.**

bot (bŏt) *n.* A software program that imitates human behavior, as by responding to questions and comments in chatrooms.

botanical (bə-tăn′ĭ-kəl) *adj.* Relating to plants or botany. —**bo·tan′i·cal·ly** *adv.*

botanical garden *n.* A place for the study, cultivation, and exhibition of plants.

botanist (bŏt′n-ĭst) *n.* A scientist who specializes in botany.

botany (bŏt′n-ē) *n., pl.* **botanies 1.** The branch of biology that deals with plants. **2.** The plant life of a particular area: *the botany of Arizona.*

botch (bŏch) *tr.v.* **botched, botching, botches** To spoil by careless or clumsy work; bungle: *botch a repair job.* ❖ *n.* A bad job or poor piece of work; a mess: *made a botch of the paint job.*

both (bōth) *adj.* One as well as the other; relating to or being two: *Both sides of the board are painted.* ❖ *pron.* The one as well as the other: *Both of them skate well.* ❖ *conj.* As well; equally: *The baby both walks and talks.*

USAGE The word **both** means "each of two, taken individually." *Both books weigh more than five pounds* means that each book weighs more than five pounds by itself, not that the two books weighed together come to more than five pounds. When *both* is used with *and* to link two words or phrases in a sentence, these words or phrases should be grammatically parallel. The phrases *in both India and China* and *both in India and in China* are parallel. The phrase *both in India and China* is not.

bother (bŏth′ər) *v.* **bothered, bothering, bothers** —*tr.* **1.** To disturb or anger; annoy: *Mosquitoes were bothering us.* **2.** To make nervous or upset: *Being in high places bothers some people.* **3.** To take the trouble (to do something): *She didn't bother to tell us she would be late.* —*intr.* To take the trouble; concern oneself: *He was in too much of a hurry to bother with the formalities.* ❖ *n.* An annoying thing; a nuisance: *Having to wait so long was a bother.*

bothersome (bŏth′ər-səm) *adj.* Causing trouble; troublesome: *He raised several bothersome questions about the details of the plan.*

Botox (bō′tŏks′) A trademark for a preparation of a bacterial toxin that is used to treat muscle spasms and certain other medical conditions and to smooth facial wrinkles.

bottle (bŏt′l) *n.* **1.** A container, usually made of glass or plastic, having a narrow neck and a mouth that can be corked or capped. **2a.** A bottle with something in it: *buy a bottle of ketchup.* **b.** The amount that a bottle holds: *A whole bottle of perfume spilled on the table.* **3.** A bottle filled with milk or formula with a nipple for feeding a baby. ❖ *tr.v.* **bottled, bottling, bottles** To put in a bottle or bottles: *a machine that bottles water.* ◆ **bottle up** To hold in or back; restrain: *bottle up one's anger; bottle up traffic for hours.* —**bot′tler** *n.*

bottleneck (bŏt′l-nĕk′) *n.* **1.** A narrow route or passage where movement is slowed down: *Highway construction caused a one-lane bottleneck that slowed traffic to a crawl.* **2.** A condition that slows or hinders progress: *The shortage of skilled welders created a bottleneck on the assembly line.*

bottom (bŏt′əm) *n.* **1.** The lowest or deepest part of something: *the bottom of a page; the bottom of the hill.* **2.** The underside of something: *the bottom of a boot.* **3.** The solid surface under a body of water: *The diver went to the bottom of the lake.* **4.** The underlying truth or cause; the basis or heart: *get to the bottom of the mystery.* **5.** often **bottoms** The low land that adjoins a river. **6.** The seat of a chair: *a cane bottom.* **7.** The part of a ship's hull below the water line: *barnacles growing on the bottom of a boat.* **8.** The second half of an inning in baseball. **9.** *Informal* The buttocks. ❖ *adj.* **1.** Situated at the bottom: *the bottom shelf.* **2.** Of the lowest degree, quality, rank, or amount: *the bottom team in the league.* ❖ *intr.v.* **bottomed, bottoming, bottoms** To have or strike the underside against something: *The car bottomed on the gravel.* ◆ **at bottom** Basically: *Though gruff, at bottom my coach was a kindly person.* **bottom out** To reach the lowest point possible, after which only a rise may occur: *Sales of personal computers have bottomed out.*

bottomland (bŏt′əm-lănd′) *n.* often **bottomlands** Low-lying land along a river: *Mississippi River bottomlands.*

bottomless (bŏt′əm-lĭs) *adj.* **1.** Having no bottom: *a bottomless container that rests on the ground.* **2.** Too deep to be measured: *a bottomless lake.* **3.** Having no limitations: *bottomless sympathy; a bottomless supply of money.*

bottom line *n.* **1.** The last line in a financial statement that shows the amount of profit or loss for a business. **2.** The final result or statement; the upshot: *The bottom line was that the play was a success.* **3.** The main or essential point: *The bottom line is that he forgives you.*

bottom-line (bŏt′əm-lĭn′) *adj.* **1.** Concerned mainly with costs and profits: *bottom-line business decisions.* **2.** Essential; crucial: *Plenty of exercise is a bottom-line requirement for good health.*

botulism (bŏch′ə-lĭz′əm) *n.* A serious, often fatal form of food poisoning caused by eating food contaminated with bacteria that produce a toxin that acts on the nervous system. The bacteria are usually found in improperly preserved foods.

boudoir (bōō′dwär′ *or* bōō′dwôr′) *n.* A woman's private sitting room, dressing room, or bedroom.

bouffant (bōō-fänt′) *adj.* Full and puffed-out, as a hairdo, skirt, or sleeve.

bough (bou) *n.* A large or main branch of a tree.

bought (bôt) *v.* Past tense and past participle of **buy.**

bouillabaisse (bōō′yə-bās′ *or* bōōl′yə-bās′) *n.* A highly seasoned thick soup made with several kinds of fish and shellfish.

bouillon (bōōl′yŏn′ *or* bōōl′yən) *n.* A clear thin broth usually made by simmering meat in water with seasonings: *beef bouillon.*

boulder (bōl′dər) *n.* A large rounded mass of rock lying on the ground or imbedded in the soil.

boulevard (bōōl′ə-värd′) *n.* A broad city street, often lined with trees.

bounce (bouns) *v.* **bounced, bouncing, bounces** —*intr.* **1.** To hit a surface and spring back from it; rebound: *The ball bounced off the wall.* **2.** To move with a bobbing, jolting, or vibrating motion: *Cars bounced down the dirt road.* **3.** To jump, spring, or bound: *The excited children bounced out of the room.* **4.** To be reflected: *Sunlight bounced off the water into my eyes.* **5.** To be left unpaid because of insufficient money in an account: *The check bounced because of insufficient funds.* —*tr.* **1.** To cause to bounce: *Bounce the ball to me.* **2.** To present or propose for comment or approval: *bounced an idea off my roommates.* **3.** *Slang* To throw (someone) out forcefully: *The rowdy group was bounced from the movie theater.* ❖ *n.* **1.** An act of bouncing or a bouncing movement; a bound or rebound: *catch a ball off the first bounce.* **2.** Capacity to bounce; springiness: *a rubber ball with plenty of bounce.* ◆ **bounce back** To return to a normal condition; recover or begin anew: *bounce back after a serious illness.*

bouncer (boun′sər) *n.* *Slang* A person employed to remove disorderly people from a nightclub, bar, or similar place of entertainment.

bouncing (boun′sĭng) *adj.* Big and strong; healthy; thriving: *a happy bouncing baby.*

bouncy (boun′sē) *adj.* **bouncier, bounciest 1.** Tending to bounce: *a bouncy ball.* **2.** Springy; elastic: *bouncy hair.* **3.** Lively; energetic: *bouncy tunes.* —**bounc′i·ly** *adv.*

bound¹ (bound) *intr.v.* **bounded, bounding, bounds 1.** To leap, jump, or spring: *The dog bounded over the gate.* **2.** To move forward by leaps or springs: *The deer bounded into the woods.* ❖ *n.* **1.** A leap or jump: *The deer was away in a single bound.* **2.** A rebound; a bounce.

bound² (bound) *n.* **1.** often **bounds** A limit; a boundary: *Their enthusiasm knew no bounds.* **2. bounds** The territory on, within, or near limiting lines: *the bounds of the kingdom.* ❖ *tr.v.* **bounded, bounding, bounds** To enclose or be the boundary of: *Water bounds the city on three sides.* ◆ **in bounds** In sports, within the area marked as the playing surface. **out of bounds 1.** In sports, outside the area marked as the playing surface. **2.** In a way that is unacceptable: *behavior that was out of bounds.*

bound³ (bound) *v.* Past tense and past participle of **bind.** ❖ *adj.* **1.** Being under obligation; obliged: *bound by a promise.* **2.** Certain: *If we leave after dark, we're bound to be late for dinner.* **3.** Confined by bonds; tied: *the bound hands of the prisoner.* **4.** Enclosed in a cover or binding: *a bound book.* ◆ **bound up with** Closely associated or connected with: *The migration of birds is bound up with change in the seasons.*

bound⁴ (bound) *adj.* Headed or intending to go in a certain direction: *We are bound for Quebec.*

WORD HISTORY Bound¹ comes from French *bondir,* meaning "to bounce." **Bound²** comes from Middle English *bound,* which comes from Medieval Latin *bodina,* both meaning "marker indicating a boundary." **Bound³** is the irregular past tense form of **bind. Bound⁴** comes from Middle English *boun* (meaning "ready"), which comes from Old Norse *būinn,* the past participle of *būa,* meaning "to get ready."

boundary (boun′də-rē *or* boun′drē) *n., pl.* **boundaries** A border or limit: *the southern boundary of Montana; the boundary between right and wrong.*

bounden (boun′dən) *adj.* Being an obligation; required: *a soldier's bounden duty.*

boundless (bound′lĭs) *adj.* **1.** Without any known limits;

infinite: *the boundless reaches of outer space.* **2.** Very great; enormous: *her boundless energy.* **—bound′less·ness** *n.*

bounteous (boun′tē-əs) *adj.* Existing in or producing great abundance: *a bounteous feast; a bounteous harvest.* **—boun′te·ous·ly** *adv.* **—boun′te·ous·ness** *n.*

bountiful (boun′tə-fəl) *adj.* **1.** Plentiful; abundant: *bountiful crops.* **2.** Giving generously and kindly: *a bountiful donor.* **—boun′ti·ful·ly** *n.* **—boun′ti·ful·ness** *n.*

bounty (boun′tē) *n., pl.* **bounties 1.** Generosity in giving: *an artist dependent on the bounty of patrons.* **2.** Plentiful gifts or provisions: *the bounty of the earth in a rich harvest.* **3.** A reward for performing a service for the government, as for capturing an outlaw or killing a destructive animal.

bouquet (bō-kā′ *or* bōo-kā′) *n.* **1.** A cluster or arrangement of flowers. **2.** A pleasant odor, especially of a wine.

bourbon (bûr′bən) *n.* A whiskey distilled mainly from fermented corn mash.

bourgeois (bōor-zhwä′ *or* bōor′zhwä′) *n., pl.* **bourgeois** A member of the middle class or bourgeoisie. ❖ *adj.* **1.** Relating to or typical of the middle class: *bourgeois merchants and shopkeepers.* **2.** Caring too much about respectability and possessions: *bourgeois attitudes about social standing.*

bourgeoisie (bōor′zhwä-zē′) *n.* **1.** The middle class in a society. **2.** In the political theory of the German philosopher Karl Marx (1818–1883), the social group opposed to the lower classes, consisting of landowners and other capitalists.

bourn also **bourne** (bôrn *or* bōorn) *n. Archaic* **1.** A boundary or limit. **2.** A goal or destination.

bourrée (bōo-rā′ *or* bōo-rā′) *n.* **1.** A lively French dance of the 1600s, resembling the gavotte. **2.** Music written for this dance.

bout (bout) *n.* **1.** A contest, such as a boxing match. **2.** A period or spell: *a severe bout of the flu.*

boutique (bōo-tēk′) *n.* A small retail shop that sells gifts, fashionable clothes, or other specialized merchandise.

WORD HISTORY Boutique, "a small, specialized retail shop," comes from French, as its spelling and pronunciation suggest. The French word *boutique* comes from Latin *apothēca,* "storehouse, warehouse." The same Latin word became *bodega* in Spanish, meaning "wine cellar, pantry, storeroom." In the United States, *bodega* refers to a grocery store in a Spanish-speaking neighborhood.

boutonniere (bōo′tə-nîr′) *n.* A flower worn in a buttonhole, usually on the lapel of a man's jacket.

bovine (bō′vīn) *adj.* **1.** Relating to or resembling a cow or a cowlike mammal, such as a yak. **2.** Dull and placid: *He sat in front of the TV with a bovine stare on his face.* ❖ *n.* A cow or a cowlike mammal.

bow¹ (bou) *n.* **1.** The front section of a ship or boat. **2.** Either of the sides of this front section: *the starboard bow.*

bow² (bou) *v.* **bowed, bowing, bows** —*intr.* **1.** To bend the body, head, or knee, as in greeting or agreement: *bow politely from the waist.* **2.** To bend downward; stoop: *The mover bowed beneath the heavy load.* **3.** To give in; yield: *They refused to bow to pressure.* —*tr.* **1.** To bend (the body, head, or knee), as in greeting, agreement, or respect: *bow the head in prayer.* **2.** To express by bowing: *They bowed their agreement.* ❖ *n.* A bending of the body or head, as when showing respect or accepting applause. ◆ **bow out**

To remove oneself; withdraw: *The candidate bowed out of the race for mayor.* **take a bow** To acknowledge or accept applause, as by standing up or coming out on stage: *The cast took a bow before the audience.*

bow³ (bō) *n.* **1.** A weapon used to shoot arrows, consisting of a flexible curved strip of wood or another material, with a string stretched tightly from end to end. **2.** A slender rod having horsehair stretched between two raised ends, used in playing the violin, viola, and other stringed instruments. **3.** A knot usually having two loops and two ends: *tie shoes with a bow.* **4.** A curve or arch, as of lips or eyebrows. **5.** A rainbow. ❖ *v.* **bowed, bowing, bows** —*tr.* **1.** To play with a bow: *bow a fiddle.* **2.** To bend into a curved shape: *The heavy snow bowed the branches until they broke.* —*intr.* **1.** To play a stringed instrument with a bow. **2.** To bend into a curved shape: *The branches bowed and snapped in the high wind.*

WORD HISTORY Bow¹ is ultimately related to the Old English word *bōg,* meaning "shoulder." In this sense, the bow of a ship is likened to the shoulders of a ship. **Bow²** comes from Old English *būgan,* meaning "to bend." **Bow³** comes from Old English *boga,* meaning "a thing that is bent."

bowdlerize (bōd′lə-rīz′ *or* boud′lə-rīz′) *tr.v.* **bowdlerized, bowdlerizing, bowdlerizes** To remove material that is considered offensive or objectionable from (a book, for example); expurgate. **—bowd′ler·i·za′tion** (bōd′lə-rĭ-zā′shən *or* boud′lə-rĭ-zā′shən) *n.*

bowel (bou′əl) *n.* **1.** often **bowels** The intestine, especially of a human. **2.** A part of the intestine: *the large bowel.* **3. bowels** The interior part of something: *the bowels of a ship.*

bower (bou′ər) *n.* A leafy shaded nook or shelter; an arbor.

bowie knife (bō′ē *or* bōo′ē) *n.* A long heavy knife with a single-edged blade, carried in a sheath and used for hunting.

bowl¹ (bōl) *n.* **1.** A rounded hollow container or dish that can hold liquid or food: *a soup bowl; a mixing bowl.* **2.** The amount that a bowl holds: *Eat a bowl of cereal.* **3.** Something shaped like a bowl, such as the hollow part of a spoon or a valley. **4a.** A stadium·or outdoor theater shaped like a bowl. **b.** One of several special football games played after the regular season ends.

bowl² (bōl) *n.* **1.** A wooden or plastic ball shaped to roll in a curving line, used in the game of lawn bowling. **2.** A throwing or rolling of the ball in various bowling games. ❖ *v.* **bowled, bowling, bowls** —*intr.* **1.** To play the game of bowling: *Do you like to bowl?* **2.** To roll or throw a ball in bowling: *You bowl first.* **3.** To move smoothly and rapidly: *Huge trucks bowled along the superhighway.* —*tr.* **1.** To play (a game) of bowling. **2.** To make (a score) in bowling: *The champion bowled a high score.* **3.** To knock down with or as if with a rolling ball: *The swimmer was bowled by the wave.* ◆ **bowl over** To take by surprise or overwhelm: *The unexpected announcement bowled them over.*

WORD HISTORY Bowl¹ comes from Old English *bolla,* meaning "round container." **Bowl²** comes Middle English *boule,* meaning "ball," which comes from Latin *bulla,* meaning "round object, bubble."

bowlegged (bō′lĕg′ĭd *or* bō′lĕgd′) *adj.* Having legs that curve outward near the knee: *a bowlegged horseman.*
bowler¹ (bō′lər) *n.* A person who bowls.

bowler² (bō′lər) *n.* A derby hat.

bowline (bō′lĭn *or* bō′lĭn′) *n.* A knot forming a loop that does not slip.

bowling (bō′lĭng) *n.* **1.** A game played by rolling a ball down a bowling alley to knock down ten wooden pins at the opposite end; tenpins. **2.** A similar game, such as ninepins or skittles. **3.** Lawn bowling.

bowling alley *n.* **1.** A smooth level wooden lane used in bowling. **2.** A building or room containing lanes for bowling.

bowling green *n.* A smooth grassy area on which the game of lawn bowling is played.

bowman (bō′mən) *n.* A person who shoots with a bow and arrow; an archer.

bowsprit (bou′sprĭt′ *or* bō′sprĭt′) *n.* A long pole sticking out of the front of a sailing ship, to which lines are attached for fastening sails.

bowstring (bō′strĭng′) *n.* The string of a bow that is pulled back to shoot an arrow.

bow tie (bō) *n.* A small necktie tied in a bow.

box¹ (bŏks) *n.* **1a.** A stiff container having four sides, a bottom, and often a top or lid. **b.** The amount that a box can hold: *eat a box of crackers.* **2.** A rectangle or square: *Draw a box around the right answer.* **3a.** A separated compartment holding seats in a theater or stadium. **b.** A small building serving as a shelter: *a sentry box.* **4.** A signaling device enclosed in a casing: *a fire-alarm box.* **5a.** A post office box. **b.** An inbox or outbox. **6.** An area on a baseball field marked by lines to show where the batter, catcher, or coach may stand. **7.** The driver's seat on a carriage, coach, or other horse-drawn vehicle. ❖ *tr.v.* **boxed, boxing, boxes 1.** To put or pack in a box: *box fruit before shipping.* **2.** To enclose in something shaped like a box: *box the title of the story.* **3.** To hinder or impede, as by blocking or restricting: *The bus was boxed in by the traffic jam.* ◆ **outside the box** In a very unconventional or original way: *Solving this puzzle requires thinking outside the box.*

box² (bŏks) *n.* A hit or slap with the hand: *a box on the ear.* ❖ *v.* **boxed, boxing, boxes** —*tr.* **1.** To take part in a boxing match with (an opponent). **2.** To hit or slap with the hand. —*intr.* To fight with the fists in a boxing match.

box³ (bŏks) *n., pl.* **box** *or* **boxes 1.** Any of several shrubs or trees having small evergreen leaves and hard yellowish wood, used for hedges and ornamental borders. **2.** The wood of such a shrub.

WORD HISTORY Box¹ comes from Old English *box,* which either referred to the shrub or tree sense of *box³* or else was an alteration of Latin *buxum,* meaning "an object made of boxwood." **Box²** comes from Middle English *box,* meaning "a hit or slap" and is of unknown origin. **Box³** comes from Old English *box,* which comes from Latin *buxus,* which comes from Greek *puxos,* all referring to the evergreen plant.

---

boxcar (bŏks′kär′) *n.* An enclosed railroad car used to carry freight that is loaded through a sliding door on each side.

box cutter *n.* A utility knife.

box elder *n.* A small maple tree of North America having compound leaves with toothed or lobed leaflets.

boxer¹ (bŏk′sər) *n.* A person who fights with the fists as a sport.

boxer² (bŏk′sər) *n.* A medium-sized dog having a short, smooth, brownish coat and a square-jawed face.

boxers (bŏk′sərz) *pl.n.* Boxer shorts.

boxer shorts *pl.n.* Loose-fitting shorts worn especially as underwear or for sport.

boxing (bŏk′sĭng) *n.* The sport of fighting with the fists, especially when boxing gloves are worn and blows must be landed on the front or sides and above the waist of the opponent.

boxing glove *n.* One of a pair of heavily padded leather mittens worn for boxing.

box office *n.* A booth where tickets are sold in a theater, auditorium, or stadium.

box score *n.* In sports, a printed summary of a game in the form of a table recording each player's performance.

box seat *n.* A seat in a box at a theater or stadium.

box spring *n.* A cloth-covered frame containing rows of coiled springs, placed under a mattress for support.

box turtle *n.* **1.** Any of several North American land turtles, having a high-domed shell into which they can withdraw entirely. **2.** Any of several similar land or water turtles of Asia.

boxwood (bŏks′wood′) *n.* The box plant or its wood.

boxy (bŏk′sē) *adj.* **boxier, boxiest** Resembling a box, as in shape: *The square rear end gave the car a boxy look.*

boy (boi) *n.* **1.** A male child. **2a.** A son: *her youngest boy.* **b.** *Informal* A fellow; a guy: *a night out with the boys.* **3.** *Offensive* A male servant. ❖ *interj.* An expression used to show astonishment, elation, or disgust: *Boy! What a great car!*

boycott (boi′kŏt′) *tr.v.* **boycotted, boycotting, boycotts** To act together in refusing to use, buy from, or deal with, especially as an expression of protest: *boycott a store; boycott a meeting.* ❖ *n.* The act or an instance of boycotting.

boyfriend (boi′frĕnd′) *n. Informal* **1.** A male sweetheart or favored companion. **2.** A male friend.

boyhood (boi′hood′) *n.* The time of being a boy: *spent his boyhood on a farm.*

boyish (boi′ĭsh) *adj.* Characteristic of or suitable for a boy: *a boyish sense of humor; boyish colors.* —**boy′ish·ly** *adv.*

Boyle's law (boilz) *n.* The physical principle that at a constant temperature the volume of a confined gas decreases as its pressure increases and increases as its pressure decreases.

Boy Scout *n.* A member of an organization for boys, having the goals of developing self-reliance, good citizenship, and outdoor skills.

boysenberry (boi′zən-bĕr′ē) *n.* **1.** A large dark-red to nearly black fruit that is similar to a blackberry. **2.** The plant that bears such fruit.

BPA An abbreviation of bisphenol A.

bra (brä) *n.* A brassiere.

brace (brās) *n.* **1.** A device that holds parts together or in place; a clamp. **2.** A supporting beam in a building or a connecting wire that holds something steady. **3.** An orthopedic device used to support or align a body part in the correct position. **4.** A handle that holds a drill or bit and is turned to bore holes. **5.** Either of the symbols, { or }, used in printing and writing to connect several lines of text or staves of music and in mathematics to enclose members of a set. **6. braces** Wires and bands attached to the teeth to straighten them. **7. braces** *Chiefly British* Suspenders. **8.** A pair; a couple: *a brace of dogs.* ❖ *tr.v.* **braced, bracing, braces 1.** To give support to; make firm; strengthen: *brace a tent with poles.* **2.** To prepare for a shock or difficulty: *The candidates braced themselves for the coming election.*

bracelet (brăs′lĭt) *n.* A band or chain worn around the wrist or arm as an ornament.

brachiopod (brā′kē-ə-pŏd′ *or* brăk′ē-ə-pŏd′) *n.* Any of various marine invertebrate animals having paired shells attached to a stalk and a ring of tentacles that sweep food into the mouth. Most brachiopods are extinct, but they are often found as fossils.

brachiosaurus (brā′kē-ə-sôr′əs *or* brăk′ē-ə-sôr′əs) *n.* A very large plant-eating dinosaur of the Jurassic Period, having forelegs longer than the hind legs.

bracing (brā′sĭng) *adj.* Giving strength and energy; refreshing: *a bracing wind.*

bracken (brăk′ən) *n.* **1.** A fern having large fronds divided into three parts. **2.** An area with dense thickets of this fern.

bracket (brăk′ĭt) *n.* **1.** A support or fixture fastened to a wall and sticking out to hold something, such as a shelf. **2.** A shelf supported by brackets. **3.** Either of the pair of symbols, [or], used to enclose printed or written material or to enclose a set of mathematical symbols that are to be considered a single expression. **4.** A group, class, or range within a numbered or graded series: *the 9-to-12 age bracket.* ❖ *tr.v.* **bracketed, bracketing, brackets 1.** To support with a bracket or brackets: *bracket shelves to strengthen them.* **2.** To place within brackets: *bracket words inserted in a quotation.* **3.** To classify or group together: *The law bracketed taxpayers according to their earnings.*

brackish (brăk′ĭsh) *adj.* Slightly salty; briny: *brackish marsh waters near the ocean.*

bract (brăkt) *n.* A small plant part resembling a leaf and growing at the base of a flower or a flower cluster. Most bracts are small and inconspicuous, but some, as in the poinsettia, are showy or brightly colored and resemble petals.

brad (brăd) *n.* A thin nail with a small head. ❖ *tr.v.* **bradded, bradding, brads** To fasten with brads.

brae (brā) *n. Scots* A hillside; a slope.

brag (brăg) *v.* **bragged, bragging, brags** —*intr.* To talk boastfully; boast: *brag about one's accomplishments.* —*tr.* To boast about; say boastfully: *He bragged that he could outrun all of us.* ❖ *n.* A boast. —**brag′ger** *n.*

braggadocio (brăg′ə-dō′shē-ō′) *n., pl.* **braggadocios a.** Empty or pretentious bragging. **b.** A swaggering, cocky manner.

braggart (brăg′ərt) *n.* A person who brags a lot.

Brahma (brä′mə) *n.* **1a.** One of the principal Hindu gods, worshipped as the creator of worlds. **b.** Variant of **Brahman** (sense 1). **2.** Variant of **Brahman** (sense 3).

Brahman (brä′mən) *n.* **1.** also **Brahma** (brä′mə) **a.** In Hinduism, the holy or sacred power that created and sustains the universe. **b.** In Hinduism, the single absolute being that is found throughout the universe and within the individual. **2.** also **Brahmin** (brä′mĭn) A member of the highest class in traditional Indian society, responsible for officiating at religious rites. **3.** also **Brahma** (brä′mə) or **Brahmin** (brä′mĭn) Any of a breed of beef cattle developed in the southern United States from cattle imported from India, having a hump between the shoulders and a fold of loose skin hanging below the neck.

Brahmanism (brä′mə-nĭz′əm) *n.* **1.** The religion of ancient India. **2.** The religious and social system of the Brahmans of India.

Brahmin (brä′mĭn) *n.* **1.** Variant of **Brahman** (sense 2). **2.** A member of the upper social class, especially a member of one of the old New England families: *a Boston Brahmin.* **3.** Variant of **Brahman** (sense 3).

braid (brād) *tr.v.* **braided, braiding, braids 1.** To weave or twist together three or more strands of (hair, fiber, or fabric); plait: *She braided her long hair.* **2.** To make by weaving strands together: *braid a straw rug.* **3.** To decorate or edge with an ornamental trim. ❖ *n.* **1.** A segment of braided hair, fabric, or other material. **2.** Ornamental cord or ribbon, used especially for trimming clothes. —**braid′er** *n.*

Braille or **braille** (brāl) *n.* A system of writing and printing for visually impaired or blind people in which raised dots representing letters, numbers, and punctuation are read by touching them.

brain (brān) *n.* **1.** The large mass of gray and white nerve tissue enclosed in the skull of humans and other vertebrates. It interprets impulses from sense organs, coordinates and controls bodily activities and functions, and is the center of memory, thought, and feeling. **2.** A similar part of an invertebrate animal. **3.** The mind: *The plan took shape in his brain.* **4.** often **brains** Intellectual power; intelligence: *It takes brains to be an economist.* **5.** *Informal* **a.** A highly intelligent person: *That new student is a brain.* **b.** often **brains** The main director or planner, as of an organization: *She is the brains of the business.* **6.** An electronic device, especially a computer, that is used to control a machine or vehicle, such as a ship. ❖ *tr.v.* **brained, braining, brains** *Informal* To hit (someone) on the head. ◆ **rack (one's) brain** *Informal* To think long and hard.

brainchild (brān′chīld′) *n. Informal* The product of a person's mind; an original plan, idea, or invention: *The telephone was Bell's brainchild.*

brain death *n.* Complete and irreversible loss of brain function. —**brain′-dead′** (brān′dĕd′) *adj.*

brainless (brān′lĭs) *adj.* Without thought; stupid; foolish: *I regretted my brainless reply.* —**brain′less·ly** *adv.* —**brain′less·ness** *n.*

brain stem or **brainstem** (brān′stĕm′) *n.* The part of the brain connecting the spinal cord to the forebrain.

brainstorm (brān′stôrm′) *n.* A sudden inspiration or clever idea. ❖ *v.* **brainstormed, brainstorming, brainstorms** —*intr.* To propose and discuss, usually in an informal group setting, a variety of ideas for accomplishing something or solving a problem. —*tr.* To consider or produce (an idea, for example) by brainstorming.

brainteaser (brān′tē′zər) *n.* A puzzle or problem that is very difficult to solve.

brainwash (brān′wŏsh′) *tr.v.* **brainwashed, brainwashing, brainwashes 1.** To indoctrinate (a person) forcibly so that his or her basic convictions are replaced with a different set of beliefs: *The prisoner was brainwashed into rejecting his country's ideals.* **2.** To persuade (a person) by intense means, such as repeated suggestions, to adopt a belief or behave in a certain way: *TV commercials brainwashed them into buying junk food.*

brainwashing (brān′wŏsh′ĭng) *n.* The act or process by which someone is brainwashed.

brain wave *n.* A rhythmic electric fluctuation arising from the brain and capable of being measured between points on the scalp. Brain waves are recorded by an electroencephalograph and are used to detect abnormalities in the brain.

brainy (brā′nē) *adj.* **brainier, brainiest** *Informal* Intelligent; smart.

braise (brāz) *tr.v.* **braised, braising, braises** To brown (meat or vegetables) in fat and then simmer in a small amount of liquid in a covered container.

brake¹ (brāk) *n.* **1.** A device for slowing or stopping motion, as of a vehicle or machine: *The brakes failed and the car ran off the road.* **2.** Something that slows or stops an action or process: *A bout of flu put a brake on my sightseeing.* ❖ *v.* **braked, braking, brakes** —*tr.* To slow or stop with a brake or brakes: *brake a train.* —*intr.* To operate or apply a brake or brakes: *Slow down and brake before turning.*

brake² (brāk) *n.* An area overgrown with dense bushes or briers; a thicket.

WORD HISTORY The origin of **brake¹** is uncertain. **Brake²** comes from Middle Low German *brake*, meaning "branch, stump."

brake light *n.* A light on the rear of a vehicle that goes on when the brakes are applied.

brakeman (brāk′mən) *n.* A member of a train crew who assists the conductor, as by uncoupling freight cars and checking on the operation of the train's brakes.

bramble (brăm′bəl) *n.* A prickly vine or shrub, such as a blackberry or raspberry. —**bram′bly** *adv.*

bran (brăn) *n.* The outer husks of wheat, rye, and other grains, sifted out from the flour after milling. Bran is used in animal feed and in some cereals and bread as a source of dietary fiber.

branch (brănch) *n.* **1a.** A woody stem or limb growing from the trunk or main stem of a tree or shrub or from another limb. **b.** A smaller part that extends from or connects to a main part: *the west branch of the river; the branches of an artery.* **2.** A part or division of a larger whole: *Botany and zoology are branches of biology. Congress is the legislative branch of the US government.* **3.** A subdivision of a family of languages. **4.** A local unit or office: *a bank branch.* ❖ *intr.v.* **branched, branching, branches 1.** To put forth branches. **2.** To develop as a branch or division; diverge: *A small road branches to the left at the bottom of the hill.* **3.** To expand one's interests, business, or activities: *The newspaper publisher branched out into television.*

brand (brănd) *n.* **1a.** A trademark or distinctive name that identifies a product, service, or organization: *This company owns several brands of breakfast cereal.* **b.** A particular kind or make of product, especially as shown by a trademark: *a popular brand of soap; a good brand of coffee.* **2.** A distinctive category or kind: *That comedian is known for a rough brand of slapstick humor.* **3a.** A mark indicating ownership burned into the hide of cattle with a hot iron. **b.** An iron used to make such a mark. **4.** A mark formerly burned into the flesh of criminals. **5.** A mark of disgrace; a stigma: *That store owner bears the brand of having defrauded customers.* **6.** A piece of burning or charred wood. ❖ *tr.v.* **branded, branding, brands 1.** To mark with a hot iron: *Cowhands branded the calves.* **2.** To mark with a label of disgrace; stigmatize: *The court branded the spies as traitors.* **3.** To provide with or publicize using a brand name or other readily recognized identifier: *branded the video game after a popular adventure story.* —**brand′er** *n.*

brandish (brăn′dĭsh) *tr.v.* **brandished, brandishing, brandishes** To wave or exhibit in a dramatic or threatening way: *brandish one's fist in defiance.*

brand-new (brănd′noo′) *adj.* Completely new; not used.

brandy (brăn′dē) *n., pl.* **brandies** An alcoholic liquor distilled from wine or fermented fruit juice. ❖ *tr.v.* **brandied, brandying, brandies** To mix, flavor, or preserve with brandy.

brant (brănt) *n., pl.* **brant** or **brants** A small wild goose that breeds in Arctic regions and has a black head and neck.

brash (brăsh) *adj.* **brasher, brashest 1.** Lacking respectful restraint in behavior; arrogant or overbearing: *disliked the brash newcomer on the team.* **2.** Hasty and unthinking; rash: *a brash move.* —**brash′ly** *adv.* —**brash′ness** *n.*

brass (brăs) *n.* **1.** A yellow alloy of copper and zinc. **2.** Ornaments, objects, or utensils made of such metal: *polishing the brass.* **3.** often **brasses** Wind instruments made of brass or some other metal, including the French horn, trumpet, trombone, and tuba. **4.** *Informal* Lack of respectful restraint in behavior; impudence or nerve: *She had the brass to ask for more money right after she got a raise.* **5.** *Slang* Military officers or civilian officials of high rank.

brass hat *n.* *Slang* **1.** A high-ranking military officer. **2.** A high-ranking civilian official.

brassiere (brə-zîr′) *n.* A woman's undergarment worn to support the breasts.

brass instrument *n.* A wind instrument, such as the trumpet or trombone, made of brass or other metal. Sound is produced through vibration of the lips and is modified by means of valves or a slide.

brass tacks *pl.n.* *Informal* Essential facts; basics: *Let's get down to brass tacks.*

brassy (brăs′ē) *adj.* **brassier, brassiest 1.** Made of, decorated with, or having the color of brass. **2.** Resembling or featuring the sound of brass instruments: *a brassy voice.* **3.** *Informal* Lacking respectful restraint in behavior; impudent: *the brassy behavior of a showoff.* —**brass′i·ly** *adv.* —**brass′i·ness** *n.*

brat (brăt) *n.* **1.** An ill-mannered or spoiled child. **2.** A child of a career military person.

bratwurst (brăt′wûrst′) *n.* A sausage made of seasoned pork.

bravado (brə-vä′dō) *n., pl.* **bravados** or **bravadoes** A show of pretended or defiant courage; false bravery: *Their noisy threats were nothing but bravado.*

brave (brāv) *adj.* **braver, bravest** Having or showing courage: *a brave defiance of danger.* ❖ *n.* A Native American warrior. ❖ *tr.v.* **braved, braving, braves** To undergo or face with courage: *Firefighters brave many dangers in the line of duty.* —**brave′ly** *adv.* —**brave′ness** *n.*

✦ SYNONYMS brave, bold, courageous, fearless, valiant *adj.*

bravery (brā′və-rē or brāv′rē) *n.* The quality or condition of being brave; courage.

bravo (brä′vō or brä-vō′) *interj.* An expression used to show approval, as for a musical performance. ❖ *n., pl.* **bravos** A shout or cry of "bravo."

bravura (brə-voor′ə) *n.* **1.** Excellent technique or style in a musical performance. **2.** A showy display: *Special effects gave the movie a visual bravura that critics raved about.*

brawl (brôl) *n.* A noisy quarrel or fight. ❖ *intr.v.* **brawled, brawling, brawls** To quarrel or fight noisily.

brawn (brôn) *n.* Muscular strength and power.

brawny (brô′nē) *adj.* **brawnier, brawniest** Strong and muscular. See Synonyms at **muscular**. —**brawn′i·ness** *n.*

bray (brā) *intr.v.* **brayed, braying, brays** To utter the loud harsh cry of a donkey. ❖ *n.* The loud harsh cry of a donkey.

braze (brāz) *tr.v.* **brazed, brazing, brazes** To join (pieces of metal) together using a hard solder with a high melting point.

brazen (brā′zən) *adj.* **1.** Rudely bold; impudent; insolent: *a brazen remark.* **2.** Having a loud harsh sound: *the sound of a brazen bell.* **3.** Made of or resembling brass: *the brazen sky at sunset.* ❖ *tr.v.* **brazened, brazening, brazens** To face or undergo with bold self-assurance: *The sailors brazened out the storm.* —**bra′zen·ly** *adv.* —**bra′zen·ness** *n.*

brazier (brā′zhər) *n.* A metal pan for holding burning coals or charcoal.

Brazil nut *n.* The edible oily seed of a tropical South American tree, having a hard, three-sided, dark-brown shell.

breach (brēch) *n.* **1.** A gap or hole, especially in a solid structure: *The crowd poured through a breach in the barrier.* **2.** A violation or infraction, as of a contract, law, legal obligation, or promise. **3.** A disruption of friendly relations; an estrangement: *An argument caused a breach between the friends.* ❖ *tr.v.* **breached, breaching, breaches** **1.** To make a hole or gap in; break through: *Floodwaters breached the dike.* **2.** To break or violate (an agreement, for example).

bread (brĕd) *n.* **1.** A food made from flour or meal mixed with water and other ingredients, usually combined with a leavening agent, and kneaded and baked in a loaf. **2.** Food in general, regarded as necessary to sustain life: *A farm family works long hours for its daily bread.* **3.** The necessities of life; livelihood: *earn one's bread as a writer.* **4.** *Slang* Money. ❖ *tr.v.* **breaded, breading, breads** To coat (food) with bread crumbs before cooking.

bread-and-butter (brĕd′n-bŭt′ər) *adj.* Reliable, as in producing a desired outcome: *a bread-and-butter product that sells well throughout the year.*

breadbasket (brĕd′băs′kĭt) *n.* **1.** A basket for serving bread. **2.** A region serving as a principal source of grain supply: *Iowa, Nebraska, and Kansas are part of America's breadbasket.* **3.** *Slang* The stomach.

breadbox (brĕd′bŏks′) *n.* A container for storing baked goods to maintain their freshness.

breadfruit (brĕd′frōot′) *n.* **1.** A large, round, edible fruit that has a rough skin and starchy flesh resembling bread when roasted. **2.** The tropical tree that bears such fruit.

breadline (brĕd′līn′) *n.* A line of people waiting to receive a free meal given out by a charitable organization or the government.

breadstuff (brĕd′stŭf′) *n.* **1.** Bread. **2.** Flour, meal, or grain used in the baking of bread.

breadth (brĕdth) *n.* **1a.** The distance from side to side of something; width: *The wall has a breadth of 20 feet and a height of 10 feet.* **b.** A piece of something having a regular width: *a breadth of cloth.* **2.** Freedom from narrowness, as of interests or attitudes: *a judge's great breadth and wisdom.* **3.** Wide extent or scope: *Her breadth of knowledge is impressive.*

breadwinner (brĕd′wĭn′ər) *n.* A person who earns money to support a household.

break (brāk) *v.* **broke** (brōk), **broken** (brō′kən), **breaking, breaks** —*tr.* **1.** To cause to separate into two or more pieces as the result of force: *broke the vase.* **2.** To snap off or detach: *break a twig from a branch.* **3.** To fracture a bone of: *break an arm.* **4.** To separate into components or parts: *broke the assignment into smaller tasks.* **5a.** To destroy the regularity, order, or completeness of: *hills that break the plain; a collector willing to break a set of books.* **b.** To exchange for smaller monetary units: *broke a dollar for change to pay the bus fare.* **6.** To create a gap across which electricity cannot pass: *break a circuit.* **7a.** To force a way through; puncture or penetrate: *The blade broke the skin.* **b.** To part or pierce the surface of: *break ground for a new building; fish breaking the water.* **8.** To produce (a sweat) copiously on the skin, as from exercise. **9.** To make or bring about by cutting or forcing: *break a trail through the brush.* **10.** To find the solution or key to: *break a code.* **11.** To make known, as news: *broke the sad news gently.* **12.** To surpass or outdo: *broke the league's home-run record.* **13.** To put an end to, as by force, opposition, or change: *One vote broke the tie.* **14.** To make unusable; ruin: *I accidentally broke the radio by dropping it.* **15.** To lessen or diminish in force or effect: *A big bush broke my fall.* **16.** To weaken or destroy; overwhelm: *Defeat broke the champion's spirit.* **17.** To call off; cancel: *break a date.* **18.** To violate by failing to follow, conform, or observe; fail to keep: *break a law; break a promise.* **19.** To give up (a habit). **20.** To reduce in rank; demote: *break a sergeant to a private.* **21.** To cause to be without money; bankrupt: *Big bills and few customers broke the new business.* **22.** To train to obey; tame: *The horse was difficult to break.* —*intr.* **1.** To become separated into pieces or fragments: *Glass breaks easily. The string broke with a snap.* **2.** To become unusable: *The radio broke.* **3.** To give way; collapse: *The bridge broke under the weight of the truck.* **4.** To burst: *The blister broke.* **5.** To scatter or disperse: *The clouds broke after the storm.* **6.** To move or escape suddenly: *The cattle broke out of their pen.* **7.** To change direction suddenly: *The fullback broke to the right.* **8.** To come into being or appear suddenly: *Crocuses broke from the soil.* **9.** To become known or noticed: *The story broke in the afternoon news.* **10.** To interrupt or cease an activity or association: *Let's break for five minutes.* **11.** To decrease rapidly: *Hot summer temperatures often break after a rainstorm.* **12.** To come to an end: *The cold spell finally broke.* **13.** To collapse or crash into surf or spray: *waves breaking on the beach.* **14.** To change suddenly in musical tone or pitch: *Her voice broke with emotion.* **15.** In baseball, to curve suddenly at or near home plate: *The pitch broke sharply.* ❖ *n.* **1.** A result of breaking; a fracture or crack: *a break in a bone.* **2a.** A gap or opening: *a break in the clouds.* **b.** The beginning or start: *the break of day.* **3.** An interruption or disruption of regularity or continuity: *a break in the conversation; a break in an electrical circuit.* **4.** A pause or interval, as from work: *Take a break for a few minutes.* **5.** A sudden run; a dash: *The rabbit made a break for cover.* **6.** An attempt to escape: *a jail break.* **7.** A sudden change: *a break in the weather.* **8.** A severing of ties: *a break between families.* **9.** An unexpected occurrence or chance: *a lucky break.* ◆ **break down 1.** To cause to collapse; destroy: *break down a wall.* **2.** To fail to function: *The truck broke down on the highway.* **3a.** To decompose chemically: *Plastic takes years to break down.* **b.** To analyze or consider in parts: *Break the exercise down into several steps.* **4.** To become distressed or upset: *They broke down and cried when they got lost.* **break even** To gain an amount equal to that invested, as in a business. **break in 1.** To enter a building or property forcibly or illegally: *The burglars broke in but could not find the jewels.* **2.** To interrupt a conversation: *The waiter broke in to take our order.* **3.** To train or instruct for some purpose: *break in a new worker.* **4.** To soften with use: *break in new shoes.*

break into 1. To enter forcibly: *The bear broke into the cabin.* **2.** To begin suddenly: *He broke into song.* **3.** To interrupt: *She broke into our discussion to tell us it was time to go.* **break off 1.** To stop suddenly, as in speaking: *break off in the middle of a sentence.* **2.** To stop being friendly: *When he moved, he broke off with his old friends.* **break out 1.** To be affected with a skin irritation, such as a rash: *An allergy to wool makes me break out.* **2.** To begin or develop suddenly: *Fire broke out during the night.* **3.** To ready for action or use: *Firefighters broke out the hoses.* **4.** To emerge or escape: *The horses broke out of the corral.* **break (someone's) heart** To disappoint or dispirit someone severely. **break up 1a.** To scatter; disperse: *The clouds are breaking up.* **b.** To separate into smaller parts: *break up a word into syllables.* **2.** To bring or come to an end: *The police broke up a fight. Their partnership broke up.* **3.** To interrupt: *broke up the long day by going swimming.* **break wind** To expel intestinal gas.

✦ **SYNONYMS break, crack, fracture, shatter, splinter** *v.*

breakable (brā′kə-bəl) *adj.* Capable of being broken; fragile.

breakage (brā′kĭj) *n.* **1.** The act of breaking something, or the fact of being broken: *They had to pay for the breakage of the window.* **2.** A quantity broken: *Breakage during shipping was extensive.*

breakdown (brāk′doun′) *n.* **1.** The act or process of failing to function properly: *The communications satellite suffered a total breakdown when it collided with a piece of debris.* **2.** The condition resulting from this process: *There was a breakdown in communication when the satellite stopped working.* **3.** A collapse of physical or mental health: *Not getting enough sleep will eventually cause a breakdown in health.* **4.** Decomposition or disintegration into parts or elements: *Bacteria are used in the breakdown of sewage.* **5.** An analysis or summary consisting of itemized data: *The sticker on the car window shows a breakdown of accessories.*

breaker (brā′kər) *n.* **1.** A person or thing that breaks: *a breaker of promises.* **2.** A circuit breaker. **3.** A wave that turns into foam when it crests.

breakfast (brĕk′fəst) *n.* The first meal of the day. ❖ *intr.v.* **breakfasted, breakfasting, breakfasts** To eat breakfast.

break-in (brāk′ĭn′) *n.* The act of entering a room or building by force for an illegal purpose: *The alarm went off because of a break-in.*

breaking and entering (brā′kĭng) *n.* The illegal act of forcibly going into someone else's house or building without permission.

breakneck (brāk′nĕk′) *adj.* Dangerously fast: *The ambulance drove at breakneck speed.*

breakout (brāk′out′) *n.* **1.** A forceful exit from a condition or situation that restricts or confines: *The prisoners were caught shortly after their breakout.* **2.** A sudden appearance or increase, as of a disease or condition; an outbreak: *a breakout of acne.*

breakthrough (brāk′thrōō′) *n.* A major achievement or success that permits further progress, as in technology: *Development of the transistor was a breakthrough in electronics.*

breakup (brāk′ŭp′) *n.* **1.** The act or an instance of breaking up; a separation or dispersal: *the breakup of an iceberg; the breakup of a large corporation.* **2.** The ending of a relationship, as of a marriage or friendship.

breakwater (brāk′wô′tər) *n.* A barrier that protects a harbor or shore from the full impact of waves.

bream (brēm *or* brĭm) *n., pl.* **bream** or **breams 1.** Any of several European freshwater fishes having a flattened body and silvery scales. **2.** Any of various freshwater sunfishes.

breast (brĕst) *n.* **1.** In human females, one of a pair of mammary glands that produce milk used to feed an infant. **2.** A corresponding but undeveloped gland in a human male. **3a.** The upper part of the front surface of the human body, extending from the neck to the abdomen. **b.** A corresponding part in other animals. **4.** The seat of affection or emotion: *Deep in his breast he felt an abiding sorrow.*

breastbone (brĕst′bōn′) *n.* The sternum.

breastfeed (brĕst′fēd′) *tr.v.* **breastfed** (brĕst′fĕd′), **breastfeeding, breastfeeds** To feed (a baby) mother's milk from the breast; nurse.

breastplate (brĕst′plāt′) *n.* A piece of metal armor worn over the chest.

breaststroke (brĕst′strōk′) *n.* A swimming stroke in which a person lies face down and extends the arms in front of the head, then sweeps them back to the sides under the surface of the water while performing a frog kick.

breastwork (brĕst′wûrk′) *n.* A temporary, hastily constructed fortification, usually breast-high.

breath (brĕth) *n.* **1.** A single act of breathing, especially an inhalation: *Take a deep breath.* **2.** The air inhaled into and exhaled from the lungs: *let out the breath in his lungs.* **3.** The ability to breathe, especially with ease: *I got short of breath as I ran up the hill.* **4.** Exhaled air, as shown by vapor, odor, or heat: *You can see your breath in the cold winter air.* **5.** A slight breeze: *Not a breath of air stirred the leaves.* **6.** A trace or suggestion: *the first breath of spring.* ✦ **out of breath** Breathing with difficulty, as from exertion; gasping: *I was out of breath when I got to the top of the hill.* **under (one's) breath** In a muted voice or whisper.

breathe (brēth) *v.* **breathed, breathing, breathes** —*intr.* **1.** To inhale and exhale air: *As we climbed higher, it got harder to breathe.* **2.** To exhale air: *Breathe on the window and see if it fogs up.* **3.** To exchange gases as part of respiration or photosynthesis: *Fish breathe with their gills. Stomata allow leaves to breathe.* **4.** To be alive; live: *As long as the dog breathed, it was loyal to its master.* **5.** To pause to rest or to regain breath, as after action: *Give me a moment to breathe.* —*tr.* **1.** To inhale and exhale (air, for example). **2.** To exhale; emit: *breathe a sigh of relief after the danger passed.* **3.** To impart (a quality) as if by breathing: *The artist breathed life into the painting of the children.* **4.** To utter, especially quietly; whisper: *Don't breathe a word of this.* **5.** To allow (a person or animal) to rest: *breathe a horse after a race.* ✦ **breathe down (someone's) neck** To watch or monitor closely, often annoyingly. **breathe (one's) last** To die.

breather (brē′thər) *n. Informal* A short rest period.

breathless (brĕth′lĭs) *adj.* **1.** Breathing with difficulty; gasping: *The runners were breathless after the race.* **2.** Holding the breath from excitement or suspense: *The audience was breathless as the acrobats performed.* **3.** Inspiring or marked by excitement that makes one hold the breath: *the breathless beauty of the mountains.* —**breath′less·ly** *adv.* —**breath′less·ness** *n.*

breathtaking (brĕth′tā′kĭng) *adj.* **1.** Inspiring awe; very exciting: *The fireworks are always a breathtaking spectacle.* **2.** Astonishing; astounding: *breathtaking stupidity.*

bred (brĕd) *v.* Past tense and past participle of **breed.** ❖ *adj.* Raised or brought-up: *a country-bred politician.*

breech (brēch) *n.* **1.** The lower rear part of the human trunk; the buttocks. **2.** The part of a firearm behind the barrel.

breechcloth (brĕch′klôth′) *n.* A cloth worn to cover the loins; a loincloth.

breeches (brĭch′ĭz *or* brē′chĭz) *pl.n.* **1.** Pants extending to or just below the knees. **2.** *Informal* Pants of any kind.

breeches buoy *n.* A device used for rescue at sea, made up of pants attached to a life preserver that is suspended from a line strung from ship to ship or ship to shore. A person sits in the pants and is transported to safety along the line by means of a pulley.

breed (brēd) *v.* **bred** (brĕd), **breeding, breeds** —*tr.* **1.** To produce (offspring): *Mice breed large litters.* **2a.** To arrange the mating of (animals) so as to produce offspring: *We hope to breed the dogs and sell the puppies.* **b.** To produce new varieties of (organisms) especially by selecting individuals with desired traits to mate with each other: *Scientists are hoping to breed disease-resistant crops.* **3.** To bring about; give rise to: *Poverty breeds crime.* **4.** To produce (fissionable material) in a breeder reactor. —*intr.* **1.** To produce offspring: *Mosquitoes breed rapidly.* **2.** To originate and grow: *Discontent breeds under a repressive government.* ❖ *n.* **1.** A group of organisms having common ancestors and certain characteristics, often produced by mating selected parents: *a hardy breed of cattle; a breed of hybrid corn.* **2.** A type or kind: *a new breed of politician.* —**breed′er** *n.*

breeder reactor *n.* A nuclear reactor that produces more fissionable material than it consumes.

breeding (brē′dĭng) *n.* **1.** Upbringing or education, especially in proper social behavior: *Good manners are evidence of good breeding.* **2.** The producing of offspring or young: *measures to control the breeding of mosquitoes.* **3.** The intentional propagation of a type of organism, especially to produce new or improved varieties: *the breeding of laboratory mice for experiments.*

breeze (brēz) *n.* **1.** A light current of air; a gentle wind. **2.** *Informal* Something that is easy to do. ❖ *intr.v.* **breezed, breezing, breezes** *Informal* To make rapid progress without effort: *He breezed through the crossword puzzle.*

breezeway (brēz′wā′) *n.* A roofed, open-sided passageway connecting two buildings, such as a house and a garage.

breezy (brē′zē) *adj.* **breezier, breeziest** **1.** Characterized by or full of breezes: *a warm breezy day.* **2.** Exposed to breezes; windy: *a breezy point along the shore.* **3.** Lively; sprightly: *a writer's breezy style.* —**breez′i·ly** *adv.* —**breez′i·ness** *n.*

brethren (brĕth′rən) *n.* A plural of **brother** (sense 3).

Breton (brĕt′n) *adj.* Relating to the region of Brittany in northwest France or to its people, language, or culture. ❖ *n.* **1.** A native or inhabitant of Brittany. **2.** The Celtic language of Brittany.

breve (brēv *or* brĕv) *n.* **1.** A mark (˘) placed over a vowel to show that it has a short sound, as in ă, the vowel sound in *bat.* **2.** A similar mark used to indicate that a syllable is unstressed in a foot of verse.

breviary (brē′vē-ĕr′ē *or* brĕv′ē-ĕr′ē) *n., pl.* **breviaries** In the Roman Catholic and Anglican churches, a book containing the daily prayers, hymns, and other readings for priests and members of certain religious orders.

brevity (brĕv′ĭ-tē) *n.* Briefness, as of expression; shortness: *The brevity of the speaker's remarks prevented boredom.*

brew (broo) *v.* **brewed, brewing, brews** —*tr.* **1.** To make (beer or ale) from malt and hops. **2.** To make (a beverage) by boiling, steeping, or mixing ingredients: *brew tea.* **3.** To devise or plan; concoct: *Members of the opposing party brewed a plot to disgrace the president.* —*intr.* **1.** To be brewed: *The tea brewed quickly.* **2.** To be imminent; threaten to occur: *A storm brewed on the horizon.* ❖ *n.* **1.** A beverage made by brewing. **2.** A serving of such a beverage. —**brew′er** *n.*

brewery (broo′ə-rē *or* broor′ē) *n., pl.* **breweries** A place where malt liquors, such as beer and ale, are made.

brewing (broo′ĭng) *n.* The act, process, or business of making malt liquors, such as beer and ale.

briar also **brier** (brī′ər) *n.* **1.** A Mediterranean shrub or small tree having a hard woody root used to make tobacco pipes. **2.** A pipe made from the root of this shrub. **3.** Variant of **brier.**

bribe (brīb) *n.* **1.** Something, such as money, property, or position, offered or given to someone in order to influence that person to act dishonestly: *Corrupt officials were dismissed for accepting bribes.* **2.** Something offered or serving to influence or persuade: *He used dessert as a bribe to get the child to behave.* ❖ *tr.v.* **bribed, bribing, bribes** To give or offer a bribe to: *It is a criminal act to bribe a judge.*

bribery (brī′bə-rē) *n., pl.* **briberies** The act of giving, offering, or taking a bribe.

bric-a-brac (brĭk′ə-brăk′) *n.* Small objects displayed in a room as ornaments.

brick (brĭk) *n.* **1.** A rectangular block of clay, baked by the sun or in a kiln until hard and used as a building and paving material. **2.** Such blocks of clay used as a building material: *a house made of brick.* **3.** An object shaped like such a block: *a brick of cheese.* ❖ *tr.v.* **bricked, bricking, bricks** **1.** To build, line, or pave with bricks. **2.** To close, wall, or fill with bricks: *The mason bricked up the window opening.*

brick-and-mortar (brĭk′ənd-môr′tər) *adj.* Existing or operating in a building, rather than as an online Internet service: *a brick-and-mortar pet store.*

brickbat (brĭk′băt′) *n.* **1.** A piece of brick thrown as a weapon. **2.** An unfavorable remark; a criticism: *The candidates exchanged brickbats during the debate.*

bricklayer (brĭk′lā′ər) *n.* A person who builds walls or other structures with bricks. —**brick′lay′ing** *n.*

brickwork (brĭk′wûrk′) *n.* **1.** The technique or work of constructing with bricks and mortar. **2.** A structure made of bricks.

brickyard (brĭk′yärd′) *n.* A place where bricks are made or sold.

bricolage (brē′kō-läzh′ *or* brĭk′ō-läzh′) *n.* Something made or put together using whatever materials happen to be available.

bridal (brīd′l) *adj.* Relating to a bride or a marriage ceremony: *a bridal veil; the bridal party.*

bride (brīd) *n.* A woman who is about to be married or has recently been married.

bridegroom (brīd′groom′ *or* brīd′groom′) *n.* A man who is about to be married or has recently been married.

bridesmaid (brīdz′mād′) *n.* A woman who attends the bride at a wedding.

bridge¹ (brĭj) *n.* **1.** A structure providing a way across a gap or obstacle, such as a river, railroad, or gorge. **2a.** The upper bony ridge of the human nose. **b.** The part of a pair of eyeglasses that rests against this ridge. **3.** A thin piece of wood that supports the strings above the sounding board in a violin, cello, and some other stringed instruments. **4.** A structure that replaces one or more missing teeth, usually anchored to teeth at both ends. **5.** A platform or enclosed area above the main deck of a ship from which the ship is controlled. **6.** A musical passage that connects two sections of a song or composition. **7.** A long stick with a notched plate at one end, used to steady the cue stick in billiards. ❖ *tr.v.* **bridged, bridging, bridges 1.** To build a bridge over: *bridge a river.* **2.** To cross by or as if by a bridge: *His career bridged two generations of technology.*

bridge² (brĭj) *n.* Any of several card games usually for four players, derived from whist.

WORD HISTORY Bridge¹ comes from Old English *brycg,* meaning "a structure over a gap." **Bridge²** comes from Russian *birich,* meaning "a call."

---

bridgehead (brĭj′hĕd′) *n.* A military position seized by advancing troops in enemy territory as a place for launching further attacks.

bridgework (brĭj′wûrk′) *n.* One or more dental bridges used to replace missing teeth.

bridle (brīd′l) *n.* **1.** A harness, consisting of straps, a bit, and reins, fitted about a horse's head and used to control the animal. **2.** A restraint or control: *The committee called for a bridle on new government spending.* ❖ *v.* **bridled, bridling, bridles** —*tr.* **1.** To put a bridle on: *bridle a horse.* **2.** To control with or as if with a bridle: *Bridle your temper!* —*intr.* To show anger; take offense: *The author bridled at the criticism.*

bridle path *n.* A trail for horseback riding.

Brie (brē) *n.* A mold-ripened, whole-milk cheese with a whitish rind and a soft, light yellow center.

brief (brēf) *adj.* **briefer, briefest 1.** Short in time or duration: *a brief nap.* **2.** Short in length or extent: *a brief report.* **3.** Covering only a small part of the body: *a brief undergarment.* ❖ *n.* **1.** A short statement or summary, especially a lawyer's summary of the facts relating to a case or argument. **2. briefs** Short, tight-fitting underpants. ❖ *tr.v.* **briefed, briefing, briefs** To give instructions, information, or advice to: *The pilot was briefed on weather conditions before takeoff.* —**brief′ly** *adv.* —**brief′ness** *n.*

briefcase (brēf′kās′) *n.* A flat rectangular case for carrying books or papers.

briefing (brē′fĭng) *n.* **1a.** The act or procedure of giving instructions or information: *Staff members gave the president a briefing before his news conference.* **b.** A meeting at which instructions or information are given: *There were 20 reporters at the briefing.* **2.** The instructions or information given during a briefing: *The briefing included a number of classified secrets.*

brier also **briar** (brī′ər) *n.* **1.** Any of various prickly vines or shrubs. **2.** Variant of **briar.**

brig (brĭg) *n.* **1.** A two-masted sailing vessel having one or more square sails on each mast and a fore-and-aft sail attached by a gaff to the aft mast. **2.** A ship's prison. **3.** A guardhouse or jail on a military base.

brigade (brĭ-gād′) *n.* **1.** A large army unit, especially such a unit composed of two or more battalions or regiments. **2.** A group organized for a specific purpose: *a fire brigade.*

brigadier (brĭg′ə-dîr′) *n.* A brigadier general.

brigadier general *n.* An officer ranking above a colonel

and below a major general in the US Army, Air Force, or Marine Corps.

brigand (brĭg′ənd) *n.* A member of a roving band of robbers.

brigantine (brĭg′ən-tēn′) *n.* A two-masted sailing vessel having a square-rigged foremast and a fore-and-aft-rigged mainsail.

bright (brīt) *adj.* **brighter, brightest 1.** Emitting or reflecting light readily or in large amounts; shining: *the bright sun shining in a cloudless sky; a cat's bright glistening eyes.* **2.** Containing little or no black, white, or gray; vivid or intense: *bright green.* **3.** Full of light: *a bright day.* **4.** Quick to learn or understand; smart: *a bright attractive little child; a bright idea.* See Synonyms at **intelligent. 5.** Happy; cheerful: *a bright face.* **6.** Full of promise and hope: *a bright future.* ❖ *adv.* In a bright manner: *The moon shines bright on a clear night.* —**bright′ly** *adv.*

brighten (brīt′n) *tr. & intr.v.* **brightened, brightening, brightens 1.** To make or become bright or brighter: *Sunlight brightened the room. Stars brighten as the sun goes down.* **2.** To make or become happy or more cheerful: *Their faces brightened at the clown's approach.*

brightness (brīt′nĭs) *n.* **1.** The quality or condition of being bright: *Brightness in the sky announced the dawn.* **2.** The amount of light that appears to come from an object or color: *an instrument that measures the brightness of a star.*

brilliance (brĭl′yəns) *n.* **1.** Extreme brightness: *the brilliance of the noonday sun.* **2.** Sharpness and clarity of musical tone: *Trumpets are noted for their brilliance.* **3.** Splendor; magnificence: *the brilliance of the palace.* **4.** Exceptional intelligence or inventiveness: *a discovery of great brilliance.*

brilliant (brĭl′yənt) *adj.* **1.** Full of light; shining brightly: *A brilliant sun blazed in the sky.* **2.** Very vivid in color: *The sky was a brilliant blue.* **3.** Clear and penetrating, as a musical sound: *The trumpet has a firm brilliant tone.* **4.** Splendid; magnificent: *the brilliant court life of the kings of France.* **5.** Excellent; wonderful: *The musicians gave a brilliant performance.* **6.** Having or showing unusual and impressive intelligence: *a brilliant mind; a brilliant solution to the problem.* See Synonyms at **intelligent.** ❖ *n.* A precious gem, especially a diamond, cut so that it catches the light and sparkles. —**bril′liant·ly** *adv.*

brim (brĭm) *n.* **1.** The uppermost edge of a hollow container or natural basin: *The pail was filled to the brim. He peered over the brim of the canyon.* **2.** A projecting rim on a hat. **3.** Full capacity: *a room full to the brim with people.* ❖ *intr.v.* **brimmed, brimming, brims 1.** To be full to the brim, often to overflowing. **2.** To be abundantly filled or supplied: *workers who brimmed with pride.*

brimful (brĭm′fo͝ol′) *adj.* Full to the brim; completely full: *a glass brimful of milk.*

brimstone (brĭm′stōn′) *n.* Sulfur, especially when associated with the torments of hell in Christianity.

brindle (brĭn′dl) *n.* A brindled color.

brindled (brĭn′dld) *adj.* Tan or gray with streaks or spots of a darker color.

brine (brīn) *n.* **1.** Water that contains a large amount of dissolved salt, especially sodium chloride. **2.** The water of a sea or ocean. **3.** Salt water used for preserving or pickling foods.

bring (brĭng) *tr.v.* **brought** (brôt), **bringing, brings 1.** To carry, convey, lead, or cause to go along to another place: *I brought the books upstairs.* **2.** To cause to occur as a result: *The flood brought much property damage.* **3.** To persuade; convince: *People were having such a good time they could not bring themselves to leave.* **4.** To cause to come; attract: *Smoke from the barn brought the neighbors.* **5.** To call to mind; recall: *This song brings back memories.* **6.** To put or force into a particular situation, location, or condition: *His refusal brought the project to a halt. Bring the potatoes to a boil.* **7.** To put forward (a legal action or charge) against someone in court: *bring suit.* **8.** To sell for: *Diamonds always bring high prices.* ◆ **bring about** To cause to happen: *Hard work brought about the success of the play.* **bring around 1.** To cause to adopt an opinion or take a certain course of action: *We tried to bring him around, but he did what he wanted anyway.* **2.** To cause to recover consciousness. **bring down 1.** To cause to fall or collapse: *The revolution brought down the king.* **2.** To kill. **3.** To disappoint; let down. **bring forth 1.** To give rise to; produce: *The bulbs brought forth flowers in the spring.* **2.** To give birth to (young). **bring forward** To present; produce: *bring forward proof.* **bring in 1.** To give or submit (a verdict) to a court. **2.** To produce, yield, or earn (profits or income). **bring off** To accomplish: *We brought off a successful play.* **bring on** To cause to appear: *Working in the rain brought on a cold.* **bring out 1.** To reveal or expose: *The article in the newspaper brought out the seriousness of the problem.* **2.** To produce or publish: *The company is bringing out a new book.* **3.** To nurture and develop (a quality, for example) to best advantage: *She brings out the best in us.* **bring to** To cause to recover consciousness: *The patient was brought to after surgery.* **bring up 1.** To take care of and educate (a child); rear. **2.** To introduce into discussion; mention: *I was surprised when they brought up the subject of my painting.*

USAGE The verbs **bring** and **take** are very close in meaning, but they can reflect different points of view. *Bring* suggests that the motion is *toward* the place of speaking: *Bring the book over here. Take* suggests that the motion is *away* from the place of speaking: *Take the book to the library.*

brink (brĭngk) *n.* **1.** The upper edge of a steep or vertical slope: *He stood at the brink of the crater.* See Synonyms at **border. 2.** The point at which something is likely to begin; the verge: *on the brink of extinction; at the brink of success.*
brinkmanship (brĭngk′mən-shĭp′) also **brinksmanship** (brĭngks′mən-shĭp′) *n.* The practice, especially in international politics, of seeking advantage by creating the impression that one is willing and able to push a highly dangerous situation to the limit rather than concede.
briny (brī′nē) *adj.* **brinier, briniest** Relating to or resembling brine; salty.
brio (brē′ō) *n.* Vigor; vivacity: *carried on the conversation with great brio.*
briquette also **briquet** (brĭ-kĕt′) *n.* A block of compressed coal dust, charcoal, or sawdust, used for fuel.
bris (brĭs) *n., pl.* **brises** The rite of male circumcision in Judaism.
brisk (brĭsk) *adj.* **brisker, briskest 1.** Moving or acting quickly; lively; energetic: *a brisk walk.* **2.** Very active; not sluggish: *Business is brisk when the store has a sale.* **3.** Fresh and invigorating: *a brisk fall morning.* **4.** Sharp in speech or manner: *He gave us a friendly but brisk reply.* —**brisk′ly** *adv.* —**brisk′ness** *n.*

brisket (brĭs′kĭt) *n.* **1.** The chest of an animal. **2.** Meat from the chest of an animal: *a brisket of beef.*
brisling (brĭz′lĭng *or* brĭs′lĭng) *n.* The sprat.
bristle (brĭs′əl) *n.* **1.** A short stiff hair. **2.** A short, stiff structure resembling a hair: *the plastic bristles of a hairbrush.* ❖ *intr.v.* **bristled, bristling, bristles 1.** To raise the bristles, as in anger or fright: *The dog bristled and showed his teeth.* **2.** To stand out stiffly like bristles: *The hair on the dog's neck bristled.* **3.** To show sudden anger or annoyance: *He bristled at the criticism.* **4.** To be thick with bristles or similar structures: *The path bristled with thorns.*
bristly (brĭs′lē) *adj.* **bristlier, bristliest 1.** Consisting of or similar to bristles: *a dog with a short bristly coat.* **2.** Easily angered or irritated: *gets bristly when interrupted.*
Britannia (brĭ-tăn′yə) *n.* A female personification of Great Britain.
britches (brĭch′ĭz) *pl.n. Informal* Breeches. ◆ **too big for (one's) britches** Overconfident; cocky.
Briticism (brĭt′ĭ-sĭz′əm) *n.* A word, phrase, or idiom characteristic of or peculiar to English as used in Great Britain.
British (brĭt′ĭsh) *adj.* Relating to Great Britain or its people, language, or culture. ❖ *n.* **1.** *(used with a plural verb)* The people of Great Britain. **2.** British English. **3.** The Celtic language of the ancient Britons.
British English *n.* The English language as used in Great Britain.
Britisher (brĭt′ĭ-shər) *n. Informal* A native or inhabitant of Great Britain.
British thermal unit *n.* The amount of heat that is needed to raise the temperature of one pound of water by one degree Fahrenheit. This unit is used mainly to measure heat, but it can be applied to other forms of energy.
Briton (brĭt′n) *n.* **1.** A native or inhabitant of Great Britain. **2.** A member of the Celtic people of ancient Great Britain.
brittle (brĭt′l) *adj.* **brittler, brittlest 1.** Likely to break or snap: *a brittle porcelain plate.* **2.** Easily ruined or disrupted: *a brittle peace; a brittle friendship.* —**brit′tle·ness** *n.*
Bro. An abbreviation of brother (religious title).
broach (brōch) *tr.v.* **broached, broaching, broaches 1.** To talk or write about for the first time; begin to discuss: *broach a subject tactfully.* **2.** To pierce in order to draw off liquid: *broach a keg of cider.* ❖ *n.* A pointed tool used to shape or enlarge a hole.
broad (brôd) *adj.* **broader, broadest 1.** Wide from side to side: *a broad river.* **2.** Large in expanse; spacious: *broad fields of wheat.* **3.** Clear; bright: *broad daylight.* **4.** Covering a wide scope; general: *a broad rule; a broad topic.* **5.** Main or essential: *the broad sense of a word.* **6.** Plain and obvious: *a broad hint.* **7.** Liberal; tolerant: *a broad point of view.* —**broad′ly** *adv.* —**broad′ness** *n.*
broadaxe or **broadax** (brôd′ăks′) *n.* An axe with a wide flat head and a short handle; a battle-axe.
broadband (brôd′bănd′) *adj.* **1.** Relating to high-bandwidth data transmission. **2.** Relating to data transmission that uses multiple channels so that multiple pieces of data can be transmitted simultaneously. —**broad′band′** *n.*
broadcast (brôd′kăst′) *v.* **broadcast** or **broadcasted, broadcasting, broadcasts** —*tr.* **1.** To transmit (a television program, for example) to many recipients at the same time over a communications network: *The news station will broadcast the president's speech.* **2.** To make known over a wide area: *Rumors were broadcast all over*

town. **3.** To sow (seed) over a wide area; scatter. —*intr.* To transmit a signal to many recipients at the same time over a communications network: *Many stations broadcast from tall buildings.* ❖ *n.* A signal, message, or audio or video program that is broadcast over a communications network: *We watched a live broadcast of the playoffs.* ❖ *adj.* Relating to the broadcasting of audio or video content over networks, as in television or radio: *Broadcast time for commercials is expensive.* —**broad′cast′er** *n.*

broadcloth (brôd′klôth′) *n.* **1.** A fine woolen cloth with a smooth glossy texture, used especially in making suits. **2.** A closely woven silk, cotton, or synthetic cloth with a narrow rib, used especially in making shirts.

broaden (brôd′n) *tr. & intr.v.* **broadened, broadening, broadens** To make or become broad or broader: *a trip that broadened our view of the world; a river that broadens as it nears the sea.*

broad jump *n.* The long jump.

broadloom (brôd′lōōm′) *adj.* Woven on a wide loom. ❖ *n.* A carpet woven on a wide loom.

broad-minded (brôd′mīn′dĭd) *adj.* Having liberal and tolerant views and opinions: *I try to keep a broad-minded attitude toward other people's beliefs.* —**broad′mind′ed·ly** *adv.* —**broad′mind′ed·ness** *n.*

broadside (brôd′sīd′) *n.* **1.** A ship's side above the water line. **2.** A firing of all the guns on one side of a warship. **3.** A forceful written or verbal attack, as in an editorial or speech. ❖ *adv.* With the side turned to a given point or object: *The wave caught them broadside and filled the canoe.*

broadsword (brôd′sôrd′) *n.* A sword with a broad blade for cutting rather than thrusting.

Brobdingnagian (brŏb′dĭng-năg′ē-ən) *adj.* Immense; enormous.

brocade (brō-kād′) *n.* A heavy cloth with a rich raised design. ❖ *tr.v.* **brocaded, brocading, brocades** To weave with a raised design.

broccoli (brŏk′ə-lē) *n.* A plant having dense clusters of green flower buds that are eaten as a vegetable.

brochure (brō-shŏŏr′) *n.* A small pamphlet or booklet: *a travel brochure.*

brogan (brō′gən) *n.* A heavy work shoe extending to the ankle.

brogue (brōg) *n.* **1.** A heavy oxford shoe decorated with rows of tiny holes on top. **2.** A heavy shoe of untanned leather, formerly worn in Scotland and Ireland. **3.** A strong dialectal accent, especially an Irish or Scottish accent when speaking English.

broil (broil) *v.* **broiled, broiling, broils** —*tr.* **1.** To cook close to a flame or other direct source of heat: *broiled the fish on the grill.* **2.** To expose to great heat: *The desert sun broiled the hikers.* —*intr.* **1.** To be cooked by direct heat: *The fish broiled for ten minutes.* **2.** To be exposed to great heat: *The tourists broiled under the tropical sun.*

broiler (broi′lər) *n.* **1.** A grill or a part of an oven used for broiling. **2.** A young chicken suitable for broiling.

broiling (broi′lĭng) *adj.* Burning; very hot: *The broiling sun withered the plants.*

broke (brōk) *v.* **1.** Past tense of **break. 2.** *Nonstandard* A past participle of **break.** ❖ *adj. Informal* **1.** Bankrupt: *They were completely broke after they lost their money in the stock market crash.* **2.** Lacking money: *Can you pay for lunch? I'm broke.*

broken (brō′kən) *v.* Past participle of **break.** ❖ *adj.* **1.** Separated into pieces by force; fractured: *broken pieces*

of glass; a broken leg. **2.** Out of order; not functioning: *a broken watch.* **3.** Not kept; violated: *a broken promise.* **4.** Spoken with gaps and errors: *broken English.* **5.** Overwhelmed, as by sadness or hardship: *a broken heart.* **6.** In a weakened condition: *broken health.* **7.** Stopping and starting at intervals having gaps; not continuous: *a broken line on a highway.* **8.** Rough; uneven: *patches of broken ground.* —**bro′ken·ly** *adv.*

broken-down (brō′kən-doun′) *adj.* **1.** Not in working order: *a broken-down car.* **2.** In poor condition, as from old age: *a broken-down cart horse.*

brokenhearted (brō′kən-här′tĭd) *adj.* Overwhelmed with sadness; very sad. —**bro′ken·heart′ed·ly** *adv.*

broken home *n.* A home in which the parents have separated or divorced.

broker (brō′kər) *n.* A person who acts as an agent for others by negotiating contracts, purchases, or sales in return for a fee or commission: *a commodities broker.*

brokerage (brō′kər-ĭj) *n.* **1.** The business of a broker. **2.** A fee or commission paid to a broker.

bromeliad (brō-mē′lē-ăd′) *n.* Any of various mostly epiphytic tropical American plants, usually having long stiff leaves, colorful flowers, and showy bracts.

bromide (brō′mīd′) *n.* **1.** A compound containing bromine and at least one other element, especially potassium, that is used as a sedative drug. **2.** A commonplace remark or notion; a platitude: *an editorial filled with the usual bromides about the importance of team spirit.*

bromine (brō′mēn) *n. Symbol* **Br** A reddish-brown nonmetallic liquid element that gives off a highly irritating vapor. It is used to make dyes, water purification compounds, and photographic chemicals. Atomic number 35. See **Periodic Table.**

bronchi (brŏng′kī′) *n.* Plural of **bronchus.**

bronchial (brŏng′kē-əl) *adj.* Relating to the bronchi or the bronchioles.

bronchial tube *n.* A bronchus or any of the tubes branching from a bronchus.

bronchiole (brŏng′kē-ōl′) *n.* Any of the fine thin-walled tubes that extend from a bronchus.

bronchitis (brŏn-kī′tĭs *or* brŏng-kī′tĭs) *n.* Inflammation of the mucous membrane of the bronchial tubes. —**bron·chit′ic** (brŏng-kĭt′ĭk) *adj.*

bronchoscope (brŏng′kə-skōp′) *n.* A slender tube with a small light on the end, used to examine the inside of the bronchi.

bronchus (brŏng′kəs) *n., pl.* **bronchi** (brŏng′kī′) Either of the two large tubes branching from the trachea and leading to the lungs, where they divide into smaller branches.

bronco (brŏng′kō) *n., pl.* **broncos** An untrained horse or pony of western North America that bucks when someone tries to ride it.

brontosaurus (brŏn′tə-sôr′əs) *n.* An earlier name for the apatosaurus.

WORD HISTORY Brontosaurus, or "thunder lizard," seems like a perfectly good name for a 70-foot-long, 30-ton vegetarian giant. Why do scientists claim that this name is invalid, and the dinosaur should be called **apatosaurus,** or "deceptive lizard"? The story begins in 1877, when the American paleontologist O. C. Marsh described the bones of a large dinosaur discovered in the western United States and named it *Apatosaurus.* Two years later, he described a more complete skeleton of a larger animal, which he named *Brontosaurus.* The brontosaurus skeleton was displayed in public and became widely known.

In 1903, however, another scientist determined that the two sets of bones belonged to the same type of dinosaur. Since it is a rule in taxonomy that the first name given to a newly discovered organism is the one that must be used, scientists have had to use the name *Apatosaurus*. But "thunder lizard" had popular appeal, and many people still prefer to call the beast a brontosaurus.

bronze (brŏnz) *n.* **1a.** An alloy of copper and tin, sometimes with traces of other metals. **b.** An alloy of copper and certain metals other than tin, such as aluminum. **2.** A work of art made of bronze: *The sculptor was known for his miniature bronzes of horses and riders.* **3.** A medal made of bronze, awarded for third place in a competition. **4.** A yellowish or olive brown. ❖ *adj.* **1.** Yellowish or olive brown. **2.** Made of or containing bronze: *bronze tools; a bronze statue.* ❖ *tr.v.* **bronzed, bronzing, bronzes** To give the appearance of bronze to: *The sun had bronzed the faces of the lifeguards.* —**bronz′y** *adj.*

Bronze Age *n.* The period of human culture between the Stone Age and the Iron Age, characterized by the use of bronze implements and weapons. In Europe, it began around 3500 BC.

brooch (brōch *or* brōōch) *n.* A large pin worn as an ornament, fastened to the clothing with a clasp.

brood (brōōd) *n.* **1.** The young of certain animals, especially a group of young birds hatched at one time and cared for together. **2.** The children in one family: *The little house was too small for the Bensons' brood.* ❖ *v.* **brooded, brooding, broods** —*intr.* **1.** To think at length and unhappily about something; worry: *It seems pointless to brood about the past.* **2a.** To sit on or protect eggs until they hatch or develop into larvae. **b.** To protect young. —*tr.* **1.** To sit on or protect (eggs) until they hatch or develop into larvae. **2.** To protect (young).

brooder (brōō′dər) *n.* **1.** A person or animal that broods. **2.** A heated enclosure in which young chickens or other young birds or livestock are raised.

broody (brōō′dē) *adj.* **broodier, broodiest 1.** Disposed to sit on eggs to hatch them: *a broody hen.* **2.** Meditative; contemplative: *became broody and withdrawn.* —**brood′i·ness** *n.*

brook¹ (brŏok) *n.* A small natural stream of fresh water; a creek.

brook² (brŏok) *tr.v.* **brooked, brooking, brooks** To put up with; tolerate: *We were late and not in the mood to brook further delay.*

WORD HISTORY Brook¹ comes from Old English *brōc*, meaning "small stream." **Brook²** comes from Old English *brūcan*, meaning "to use, enjoy."

brooklet (brŏok′lĭt) *n.* A small brook.

brook trout *n.* A speckled freshwater food fish that is native to eastern North America.

broom (brōōm *or* brŏom) *n.* **1.** An implement for sweeping, usually consisting of strands of straw or plastic bound together and attached to a long stick. **2.** Any of various European shrubs having yellow flowers, small leaves, and many slender, flexible branches formerly used for sweeping.

broomcorn (brōōm′kôrn′ *or* brŏom′kôrn′) *n.* A variety of sorghum having a flower cluster with many stiff branches, which are used to make brooms and brushes.

broomstick (brōōm′stĭk′ *or* brŏom′stĭk′) *n.* The long handle of a broom.

bros. An abbreviation of brothers.

broth (brôth) *n., pl.* **broths** (brôths *or* brôthz) A clear soup made from the water in which meat, fish, or vegetables have been boiled.

brothel (brŏth′əl) *n.* A house of prostitution.

brother (brŭth′ər) *n.* **1a.** A boy or man having the same mother and father as someone else. **b.** A boy or man having one parent in common with someone else; a half brother. **c.** A stepbrother. **2a.** A boy or man who shares common ancestors, a common allegiance to a country, or a common purpose with another or others. **b.** A fellow male member of a group, such as a profession, fraternity, or labor union. **3.** *plural* **brothers** or **brethren** (brĕth′rən) **a.** A member of a men's Christian religious order who is not a priest. **b.** A fellow male member of a Christian church.

brotherhood (brŭth′ər-hŏod′) *n.* **1.** The relationship of being a brother or brothers. **2.** Brotherly feelings or friendship toward other humans; fellowship. **3.** A group of people united for a common purpose, such as those belonging to a fraternity, labor union, or a profession.

brother-in-law (brŭth′ər-ĭn-lô′) *n., pl.* **brothers-in-law 1.** The brother of one's spouse. **2.** The husband of one's sibling. **3.** The husband of the sibling of one's spouse.

brotherly (brŭth′ər-lē) *adj.* Characteristic of or appropriate to brothers; affectionate: *a warm brotherly greeting.* —**broth′er·li·ness** *n.*

brougham (brōōm *or* brōō′əm) *n.* **1.** A four-wheeled carriage with a closed compartment for passengers and an open driver's seat. **2.** An automobile with an open driver's seat.

brought (brôt) *v.* Past tense and past participle of **bring.**

brow (brou) *n.* **1.** The forehead. **2.** An eyebrow. **3.** The upper edge of a steep place: *We stood on the brow of a hill overlooking the valley.*

browbeat (brou′bēt′) *tr.v.* **browbeat, browbeaten** (brou′-bēt′n), **browbeating, browbeats** To bully or intimidate, as with frightening looks or harsh words.

brown (broun) *n.* The color of chocolate or coffee. ❖ *adj.* **browner, brownest 1.** Of the color brown. **2.** Suntanned. ❖ *tr. & intr.v.* **browned, browning, browns 1.** To make or become brown: *Silt browned the stream after the heavy rains.* **2.** To cook until brown on the outside: *The chef browned the meat.* —**brown′ness** *n.*

brown bear *n.* A large bear of western North America and northern Eurasia, having dark brown to yellowish fur. There are several types of brown bear, including the grizzly bear.

brown Betty (bĕt′ē) *n.* A baked pudding of apples, bread crumbs, brown sugar, butter, and spices.

brown coal *n.* Lignite.

brown dwarf *n.* A starlike celestial object that does not emit light because it does not have enough mass for nuclear fusion to occur.

brownfield (broun′fēld′) *n.* An abandoned commercial property that is usually polluted but can be reclaimed and developed for new uses.

brownie (brou′nē) *n.* **1.** A bar of moist chocolate cake with nuts. **2.** **Brownie** A member of the Girl Scouts between six and eight years old. **3.** In folklore, a small elf said to do helpful work such as household chores while people are asleep.

brownish (brou′nĭsh) *adj.* Somewhat brown.

brownnose (broun′nōz′) *tr.v.* **brownnosed, brownnosing, brownnoses** *Informal* To curry favor with in an obsequious manner; fawn on. —**brown′nos′er** *n.*

brownout (broun′out′) *n.* A dimming or partial loss of electric lights and power, especially as the result of a shortage, a mechanical failure, or overuse by consumers.

brown rice *n.* Rice that still has the outer layer of bran on the grain.

brown sauce *n.* A sauce made from butter and flour that have been browned together and mixed with stock.

brownstone (broun′stōn′) *n.* **1.** A brownish-red sandstone used as a building material. **2.** A house built or faced with such stone.

brown sugar *n.* **1.** Unrefined or partially refined sugar that retains some molasses, giving it a brownish color. **2.** Refined white sugar with molasses added to it, sold as a commercial product.

browse (brouz) *v.* **browsed, browsing, browses** —*intr.* **1.** To look at in a leisurely and casual way: *browse through a book; browse through a department store.* **2.** To look for information on the Internet. **3.** To feed on leaves, young shoots, twigs, and other vegetation: *The deer have been browsing on the shrubs.* —*tr.* **1.** To look through (something) casually: *browse the newspaper.* **2.** To read (websites) casually on the Internet. **3.** To nibble at; graze on: *Cattle browsed the pasture.* ❖ *n.* Vegetation, such as leaves, young shoots, and twigs, eaten by animals: *Very little browse is available after a heavy snowfall.*

browser (brou′zər) *n.* **1.** A person or thing that browses. **2.** A computer program that accesses and displays files and other data available on the Internet and other networks.

bruin (brōō′ĭn) *n.* A bear.

bruise (brōōz) *v.* **bruised, bruising, bruises** —*tr.* **1.** To injure (a part of the body) without breaking the skin, as by a blow: *bruised my knee.* **2.** To hurt one's feelings; offend: *bruised his pride.* —*intr.* To become bruised: *skin that bruises easily.* ❖ *n.* **1.** An injury in which small blood vessels in the skin are broken by pressure or a blow, producing discoloration but leaving the skin itself unbroken: *get a bruise from a fall.* **2.** A similar injury to a fruit or vegetable.

bruiser (brōō′zər) *n. Informal* A large powerfully built man.

bruit (brōōt) *tr.v.* **bruited, bruiting, bruits** To spread news of; repeat: *The rumor was bruited about all over town.*

brunch (brŭnch) *n.* A meal eaten in the late morning or early afternoon that combines breakfast and lunch.

brunette also **brunet** (brōō-nĕt′) *adj.* Having dark or brown hair. ❖ *n.* A woman or girl with dark or brown hair.

brunt (brŭnt) *n.* The main impact, force, or burden: *Towns along the shore bore the brunt of the hurricane.*

brush (brŭsh) *n.* **1.** An implement consisting of bristles, hairs, or wire fastened to a handle, used especially for scrubbing, applying paint, or grooming the hair. **2.** An application of a brush: *give one's hair a good brush.* **3.** A sweeping movement or light touch: *the brush of a branch against my coat.* **4.** A brief encounter with something undesirable or dangerous: *a brush with the law.* **5.** Dense vegetation consisting of shrubs or small trees: *The explorers hacked a trail through the brush.* **6.** Broken or cut branches; brushwood: *Pile the brush at the curb.* **7.** A sliding connection completing a circuit between a fixed and a moving conductor, as in a motor or generator. ❖

v. **brushed, brushing, brushes** —*tr.* **1.** To clean, polish, or groom with a brush: *brush shoes until they shine.* **2.** To apply with a brush: *brush paint on evenly.* **3.** To remove with a brush or with sweeping strokes: *brush dirt off one's jacket.* **4.** To treat as unimportant; dismiss: *He brushed aside her objections and carried on.* **5.** To touch lightly in passing: *Her arm brushed mine in the crowded hall.* —*intr.* To touch something lightly in moving past it: *The wet paint got on my clothes when I brushed against it.* ◆ **brush up** To refresh one's memory or renew one's skill regarding something: *I'll have to brush up on my Spanish before going to Mexico.* —**brush′y** *adj.*

brushfire also **brush fire** (brŭsh′fīr′) *n.* A fire in an area of small trees, bushes, or other low-growing vegetation.

brushoff also **brush-off** (brŭsh′ôf′) *n.* An abrupt dismissal; a snub: *She gave him the brushoff.*

brushwood (brŭsh′wŏŏd′) *n.* **1.** Cut or broken branches. **2.** Dense, low-growing vegetation; brush.

brushwork (brŭsh′wûrk′) *n.* The way in which a painter applies paint with a brush: *a painter known for his detailed brushwork.*

brusque (brŭsk) *adj.* Rudely abrupt in manner or speech; curt; blunt: *The speaker gave a brusque reply to the heckler.* —**brusque′ly** *adv.* —**brusque′ness** *n.*

Brussels sprouts *pl.n. (used with a singular or plural verb)* **1.** Buds that resemble small cabbages growing on a long thick stem, eaten as a vegetable. **2.** The plant that bears such buds.

brutal (brōōt′l) *adj.* **1.** Cruel; ruthless: *a brutal attack.* **2.** Harsh; severe: *a brutal Arctic winter.* **3.** Unpleasantly direct or plain: *He is known for his brutal honesty.* —**bru′tal·ly** *adv.*

brutality (brōō-tăl′ĭ-tē) *n., pl.* **brutalities 1.** The quality or condition of being brutal: *The brutality of boxing offends many people.* **2.** A ruthless, cruel, or harsh act.

brutalize (brōōt′l-īz′) *tr.v.* **brutalized, brutalizing, brutalizes 1.** To make brutal. **2.** To treat cruelly or harshly: *The animal trainer was accused of brutalizing the dogs by locking them in narrow cages.*

brute (brōōt) *n.* **1.** An animal other than a human; a beast: *debates about whether brutes have souls.* **2.** A brutal person. ❖ *adj.* **1.** Having to do with animals other than humans. **2.** Lacking reason or intelligence: *a brute craving.* **3.** Entirely physical: *the brute force of the storm.*

brutish (brōō′tĭsh) *adj.* Resembling a brute; coarse, stupid, or cruel: *the brutish behavior of a gangster.* —**brut′ish·ly** *adv.*

bryophyte (brī′ə-fīt′) *n.* Any of numerous nonvascular plants that reproduce by spores, such as the mosses and liverworts.

BS An abbreviation of Bachelor of Science.

BSA An abbreviation of Boys Scouts of America.

Btu An abbreviation of British thermal unit.

bubble (bŭb′əl) *n.* **1.** A rounded thin film of liquid enclosing an amount of air or other gas: *soap bubbles.* **2.** A small rounded amount of gas that rises to the surface of a liquid or remains trapped in a solid or plastic material: *bubbles of air in ice cubes.* **3.** A glass or plastic dome: *a package of batteries enclosed under a plastic bubble.* **4.** A rounded or irregularly shaped outline containing the words that a character in a cartoon is represented to be saying. **5.** An increase in the price of something, such as housing, resulting from purchases by people expecting that the price will increase further. ❖ *intr.v.* **bubbled, bubbling, bubbles 1.** To form or give off bubbles: *Steam rose as wa-*

ter *bubbled in the vat.* **2.** To move or flow with a gurgling sound: *a brook bubbling over the rocks.* **3.** To show lively activity or emotion: *As they entered the theater, the little kids were bubbling with excitement.*

bubble chamber *n.* A device for detecting the paths of charged atomic particles by observation of the trails of gas bubbles that the particles leave in a superheated liquid.

bubblegum also **bubble gum** (bŭb′əl-gŭm′) *n.* Chewing gum that can be blown into bubbles.

bubbly (bŭb′lē) *adj.* **1.** Full of or producing bubbles. **2.** Resembling bubbles. **3.** Full of high spirits; animated and lively: *a bubbly personality.*

bubonic plague (boo-bŏn′ĭk) *n.* An often fatal disease caused by bacteria transmitted to humans by fleas from infected rats or other rodents. Its symptoms include fever, vomiting, diarrhea, and enlarged lymph nodes.

buccaneer (bŭk′ə-nîr′) *n.* A pirate.

buck¹ (bŭk) *n.* **1.** The adult male of certain animals, such as deer, antelopes, and rabbits. **2.** A sudden leap forward and upward, as by a horse or mule. ❖ *v.* **bucked, bucking, bucks** —*intr.* **1.** To leap upward while arching the back: *The bronco bucked and kicked.* **2.** To resist or defy a rule or expectation, for example: *bucking against the trend in fashion.* —*tr.* **1.** To throw off (a rider) by bucking. **2.** To struggle against; resist or defy: *a rebel who often bucks the rules.* ◆ **buck up** To summon one's courage or spirits; hearten: *urged the runner to buck up and keep going.*

buck² (bŭk) *n. Informal* A dollar.

WORD HISTORY Buck¹ comes from Old English *buc,* meaning "male deer" and Old English *bucca,* meaning "male goat." **Buck²** is short for *buckskin,* from its use in trade.

buckaroo (bŭk′ə-roo′) *n., pl.* **buckaroos** A cowboy.

buckboard (bŭk′bôrd′) *n.* An open four-wheeled carriage with the seat attached to a flexible board running between the front and rear axles.

bucket (bŭk′ĭt) *n.* **1.** A round open container with a curved handle, used for carrying liquids or solids; a pail. **2a.** The amount that a bucket holds: *pour a bucket of sand on an icy sidewalk.* **b.** An unexpectedly great amount or quantity: *The rain came down in buckets.* **3.** Something resembling a bucket, such as the scoop on a steam shovel. ◆ **a drop in the bucket** An insufficient or trifling amount in comparison with what is needed.

bucketful (bŭk′ĭt-fool′) *n.* The amount that a bucket can hold.

bucket seat *n.* A single, usually low seat with a rounded padded back, as in certain automobiles.

buckeye (bŭk′ī′) *n.* **1.** Any of various North American trees or shrubs having large divided leaves, reddish or white flower clusters, and a leathery capsule containing one or more large seeds. All parts of the plant are poisonous. **2.** The glossy brown seed of such a tree.

buckle (bŭk′əl) *n.* **1.** A clasp used to fasten one end of a strap or belt to the other: *the buckle on the strap of a watch.* **2.** An ornament that looks like such a clasp, as one on top of a shoe. **3.** A bend, bulge, warp, or other distortion: *A buckle in the dike showed it was soon going to break.* ❖ *v.* **buckled, buckling, buckles** —*tr.* **1.** To fasten with a buckle: *Buckle your seat belt before the car starts.* **2.** To cause to bend, warp, or crumple, as by pres-

sure or heat: *Too much pressure buckled the sides of the box.* —*intr.* To sag, bend, or collapse: *Walls buckled in the heat of the fire.* ◆ **buckle down** To apply oneself with determination.

buckler (bŭk′lər) *n.* A small round shield that is either carried or worn on the arm.

buckminsterfullerene (bŭk′mĭn-stər-fool′ə-rēn′) *n.* An extremely stable, ball-shaped carbon molecule that is shaped like a geodesic dome, and believed to occur naturally in soot. It was the first fullerene to be discovered.

buckram (bŭk′rəm) *n.* A coarse cotton cloth stiffened with glue, used especially for binding books.

bucksaw (bŭk′sô′) *n.* A saw usually set in an H-shaped frame, used for cutting wood.

buckshot (bŭk′shŏt′) *n.* The large lead shot used in shotgun shells, especially for hunting large game.

buckskin (bŭk′skĭn′) *n.* **1.** A soft, grayish-yellow leather, made from the skins of deer or sheep. **2. buckskins** Breeches or shoes made of this leather.

bucktooth (bŭk′tooth′) *n.* A prominent projecting upper front tooth. —**buck′toothed′** *adj.*

buckwheat (bŭk′wēt′) *n.* **1.** The small, starchy, triangular seeds of an annual plant native to Asia. The seeds are often ground into flour or used as livestock feed. **2.** The plant that bears such seeds.

buckyball (bŭk′ē-bôl′) *n.* A buckminsterfullerene.

bucolic (byoo-kŏl′ĭk) *adj.* **1.** Relating to or characteristic of shepherds; pastoral: *bucolic poetry.* **2.** Relating to or characteristic of country life; rustic: *a bucolic scene.*

bud (bŭd) *n.* **1.** A small swelling or structure on a branch or stem containing an undeveloped flower, shoot, or leaf. **2.** A small outgrowth on a simple organism, such as a yeast or hydra, that grows into a complete new organism of the same species. **3.** A small part or organ, such as a taste bud, that is shaped somewhat like a bud. **4.** An earbud. **5.** A stage of early or incomplete development: *the bud of a new idea.* ❖ *intr.v.* **budded, budding, buds 1.** To form or produce a bud or buds: *Tulips bud in the very early spring.* **2.** To be in an early stage; begin to develop: *Businesses using new research are budding near the university.*

Buddha (boo′də or bood′ə) *n.* **1.** The Indian mystic Siddhartha Gautama (563?–483? BC), who founded Buddhism. **2.** In Buddhism, a person who has achieved perfect spiritual enlightenment, thereby attaining Nirvana. **3.** A representation or likeness of a Buddha.

Buddhism (boo′dĭz′əm or bood′ĭz′əm) *n.* The religion, based on the teachings of the Buddha, that holds that suffering is unavoidable in life and that freeing oneself from desire and delusion leads to a state of enlightenment called Nirvana. —**Bud′dhist** *n. & adj.*

buddy (bŭd′ē) *n., pl.* **buddies** *Informal* A close friend; a comrade.

buddy system *n.* An arrangement in which people pair up, as during a hike, swim, or similar activity, to look out for each other's safety.

budge (bŭj) *intr. & tr.v.* **budged, budging, budges 1.** To move or cause to move slightly: *The boulder did not budge. We cannot budge the boulder.* **2.** To alter or cause to alter a position or attitude: *They won't budge once they have reached a decision. After the prime minister had made up her mind, no one could budge her.*

budgerigar (bŭj′ə-rē-gär′) *n.* A small green, blue, or yellow parakeet often kept as a pet.

budget (bŭj′ĭt) *n.* **1.** A plan or estimate of the amount of money that will be spent and received in a given period: *Congress must approve the federal budget each year.* **2.** The amount of money included in a budget: *a project with an annual budget of two million dollars.* ❖ *tr.v.* **budgeted, budgeting, budgets 1.** To plan in advance how to spend: *budget an allowance; did not budget my time wisely.* **2.** To enter or plan for in a budget: *We need to budget repairs into the estimated car expenses.* ❖ *adj.* **1.** Relating to a budget: *Were these budget items approved by Congress?* **2.** Appropriate to a restricted budget; inexpensive: *a budget car; budget meals.* —**bud′get·ar′y** (bŭj′ĭ-tĕr′ē) *adj.*

budgie (bŭj′ē) *n. Informal* A budgerigar.

buff¹ (bŭf) *n.* **1.** A soft, thick, yellowish leather made from the skins of oxen or related animals. **2.** The color of this leather; a yellowish tan. **3.** A piece of soft material used for polishing. ❖ *tr.v.* **buffed, buffing, buffs** To polish or shine with leather, cotton, or other soft material: *waxed and buffed the car.* ❖ *adj.* **1.** Made of buff. **2.** Of the color buff. **3. buffer, buffest** Physically fit and trim. ◆ **in the buff** Naked.

buff² (bŭf) *n. Informal* A person who has great interest in, and some knowledge of, a subject; an enthusiast: *a train buff.*

WORD HISTORY Buff¹ comes from French *buffle,* which comes from Latin *būfalus,* meaning "buffalo." **Buff²** comes from the buff-colored uniform once worn by New York City volunteer firemen, originally applied to an enthusiast of fires and firefighting.

buffalo (bŭf′ə-lō′) *n., pl.* **buffalo** or **buffaloes** or **buffalos 1.** The North American bison. **2.** Any of several large African or Asian mammals having large curving horns, such as the water buffalo.

WORD HISTORY Many of the English names of North American animals, like *moose* and *skunk,* come from Native American languages, but the term **buffalo** is not one of these. It can be traced back through Latin to the Greek word *boubalos,* meaning "an antelope or buffalo." The buffalo referred to by the Greek or Latin word was not of course the North American one, but an Asian or African animal such as the water buffalo. Scientists prefer to use the word **bison** for the North American animal, but the word *buffalo* is so much a part of the history of the Wild West that the name lives on in everyday speech.

Buffalo wing *n.* A fried chicken wing served with a spicy sauce and blue cheese dressing.

buffer¹ (bŭf′ər) *n.* A soft pad or a tool having such a pad, used to polish or shine objects.

buffer² (bŭf′ər) *n.* **1.** Something that reduces or absorbs the shock of a blow or collision: *hung tires along the dock as a buffer to protect boats when docking.* **2.** A substance that minimizes change in the acidity of a solution when an acid or a base is added to the solution. **3.** Something that separates two potential rivals and reduces the danger of conflict: *The railroad tracks served as a buffer between the two hostile neighborhoods.* **4.** A device or area of a computer that is used to store data temporarily. ❖ *tr.v.* **buffered, buffering, buffers** To treat (a solution) with a buffer.

WORD HISTORY Buffer¹ is derived from *buff¹.* **Buffer²** probably comes from obsolete English *buff,* meaning "to make a sound like a soft body being hit."

buffet¹ (bə-fā′) *n.* **1.** A large piece of furniture with drawers and cupboards for storing china, silverware, and table linens. **2.** A meal at which guests serve themselves from dishes arranged on a table or counter. **3.** A counter from which food is served. ❖ *adj.* Being a meal where diners serve themselves: *a buffet lunch.*

buffet² (bŭf′ĭt) *n.* A hit or blow, especially one made with the hand. ❖ *tr.v.* **buffeted, buffeting, buffets** To hit or strike against forcefully; batter: *The rough sea buffeted the small boat.*

WORD HISTORY Buffet¹ comes the French word *buffet,* referring to the same type of furniture as *buffet* does in English. **Buffet²** comes from Middle English *buffet,* which comes from Old French *buffet,* which is the diminutive of Old French *buffe,* meaning "a blow."

buffoon (bə-fōōn′) *n.* **1.** A clown or jester. **2.** A person given to making jokes. **3.** A bumbling or ridiculous person; a fool. —**buf·foon′er·y** *n.*

bug (bŭg) *n.* **1.** An insect having mouthparts used for piercing and sucking, such as an aphid, a bedbug, or a cicada. **2.** An insect of any kind, such as a cockroach or a ladybug, or another small invertebrate that looks like an insect, such as a spider or a centipede: *Let's go inside; there are too many bugs out here.* **3a.** A microorganism or virus that causes disease; a germ: *The bug that causes cholera.* **b.** A disease caused by such a microorganism or virus: *She's had that bug for a week.* **4a.** A fault or defect in a system or device: *work the bugs out of a plan.* **b.** An error or defect in a computer program. **5.** A hidden electronic device that allows private conversations to be overheard. **6.** *Slang* An enthusiast; a buff: *a model train bug.* ❖ *v.* **bugged, bugging, bugs** —*intr.* To grow large; bulge: *Their eyes bugged out with surprise.* —*tr. Slang* **1.** To annoy, pester, or trouble: *Stop bugging her to do the dishes.* **2.** To equip (a room or telephone circuit, for example) with a concealed electronic listening device. ◆ **bug off** *Slang* To leave someone alone; go away.

bugaboo (bŭg′ə-bōō′) *n., pl.* **bugaboos** An imaginary or real object of fear: *raised the bugaboo of inflation.*

bugbear (bŭg′bâr′) *n.* **1.** A recurring or persistent problem: *Spelling was my bugbear in school.* **2.** A bugaboo.

buggy (bŭg′ē) *n., pl.* **buggies 1.** A small light carriage with a single seat and four wheels, drawn by a horse. **2.** A baby carriage. **3.** A motor vehicle, usually with oversized tires, designed for off-road use.

bugle (byōō′gəl) *n.* A brass wind instrument similar to a trumpet but lacking valves. It is often used to sound signals in the military, such as reveille. ❖ *intr.v.* **bugled, bugling, bugles** To play a bugle. —**bu′gler** *n.*

build (bĭld) *v.* **built** (bĭlt), **building, builds** —*tr.* **1.** To make or form by fitting together materials or parts; construct: *It takes a long time to build a skyscraper. The body needs iron in the diet to build hemoglobin.* **2.** To develop according to a plan or process; create: *people working together to build a better society.* **3.** To increase or strengthen by adding gradually to: *Reading helps build a rich vocabulary.* —*intr.* To progress toward a climax; grow steadily; develop: *A good mystery builds from the first chapters to its climax. Scientific discoveries build on the work of others.* ❖ *n.* The physical make-up of a person or thing: *a muscular athletic build.* ◆ **build in** or **build into** To construct as a permanent part of: *build in kitchen cabinets.* **build on** or **build onto** To use as a basis or foundation: *We must build on our success.* **build up 1.** To cause to develop in stages or by degrees: *build up a business; build up a strong vo-*

cabulary. **2.** To cover with buildings: *The downtown area is getting built up.* **3.** To accumulate gradually: *sediments building up on the ocean floor.*

builder (bĭl′dər) *n.* **1.** A person or animal that builds: *Beavers are great dam builders.* **2.** A person who constructs new buildings or develops land: *the architects and builders of a great city.*

building (bĭl′dĭng) *n.* **1.** Something that is built; a structure. **2.** The act, process, or occupation of constructing.

buildup also **build-up** (bĭld′ŭp′) *n.* **1.** The act or process of building up or accumulating: *the buildup of ashes in a fireplace.* **2.** Widely favorable publicity; high praise: *The newspaper gave the fund-raising committee a nice buildup.*

built (bĭlt) *v.* Past tense and past participle of **build.**

built-in (bĭlt′ĭn′) *adj.* Constructed as a permanent part of a larger unit: *a built-in cupboard.*

built-up (bĭlt′ŭp′) *adj.* **1.** Made by fastening layers or sections one on top of the other: *a built-up roof.* **2.** Filled with buildings; developed: *a built-up neighborhood.*

bulb (bŭlb) *n.* **1.** A rounded underground stem surrounded by fleshy modified leaves, from which a shoot emerges that will grow into a new plant. Tulips and onions grow from bulbs. **2.** A similar underground structure, such as a corm, rhizome, or tuber. **3.** A rounded part of something: *the bulb of a thermometer.* **4.** A light bulb. **5.** Any of various rounded structures in the body of an animal.

bulbous (bŭl′bəs) *adj.* **1.** Growing from or producing a bulb: *The tulip is a bulbous plant.* **2.** Bulb-shaped: *a bulbous nose.*

Bulgarian (bŭl-gâr′ē-ən *or* bо̄о̆l-gâr′ē-ən) *adj.* Relating to Bulgaria or its people, language, or culture. ❖ *n.* **1.** A native or inhabitant of Bulgaria. **2.** The Slavic language of the Bulgarians.

bulge (bŭlj) *n.* A protruding part; an outward curve or a swelling: *A blister causes a bulge in the skin.* ❖ *intr. & tr.v.* **bulged, bulging, bulges** To swell or cause to swell beyond the usual size: *eyes bulging with surprise; groceries bulging a bag.* —**bulg′y** *adj.*

bulgur also **bulghur** (bŭl′gər *or* bо̄о̆l-gо̄о̆r′) *n.* Cracked wheat grains, often used in Middle Eastern dishes.

bulimia (bо̄о̆-lē′mē-ə) *n.* An eating disorder in which the eating of large amounts of food is followed by vomiting or other measures to prevent gaining weight.

bulk (bŭlk) *n.* **1.** Great size, mass, or volume: *the whale's enormous bulk.* **2.** The major portion of something; greater part: *The bulk of the evidence is negative.* ◆ **in bulk 1.** Unpackaged; loose: *That store sells apples in bulk.* **2.** In large numbers, amounts, or volume: *Flour mills buy wheat in bulk.*

bulkhead (bŭlk′hĕd′) *n.* **1.** One of the vertical walls that divide the inside of a ship or aircraft into compartments. **2.** A wall or embankment, as in a mine or along a waterfront, built to protect against earth slides, fire, water, or gas.

bulky (bŭl′kē) *adj.* **bulkier, bulkiest 1.** Extremely large; massive: *Elephants and whales are bulky animals.* **2.** Taking up much space; clumsy; unwieldy: *The new lamp came in a bulky package.* —**bulk′i·ly** *adv.* —**bulk′i·ness** *n.*

bull¹ (bо̄о̆l) *n.* **1a.** The uncastrated adult male of domestic cattle. **b.** The adult male of bovine mammals, such as bison or yaks, or of certain other large animals, such as alligators, elephants, moose, or whales. **2.** A person who buys stock or other securities expecting their price to

rise. ❖ *adj.* **1.** Male: *a bull seal.* **2.** Characterized by rising prices, especially in the stock market: *a bull market.*

bull² (bо̄о̆l) *n.* An official document issued by the pope.

WORD HISTORY Bull¹ comes from Old English *bula,* which refers to the same animal. **Bull²** comes from Middle English *bulle,* which comes from Medieval Latin *bulla,* meaning "blister, seal on a papal decree."

bulldog (bо̄о̆l′dôg′) *n.* A stocky short-haired dog of a breed originally developed in England, having a large head with strong, square jaws.

bulldoze (bо̄о̆l′dōz′) *tr.v.* **bulldozed, bulldozing, bulldozes 1.** To clear, dig up, or move with a bulldozer: *bulldoze land for a new development.* **2.** To bully, intimidate, or coerce: *bulldoze a committee into action.*

bulldozer (bо̄о̆l′dō′zər) *n.* A large powerful tractor equipped with treads and a metal blade in front for moving earth and grading land.

bullet (bо̄о̆l′ĭt) *n.* **1.** A small, rounded, usually pointed piece of metal to be fired from a firearm such as a rifle or pistol. **2.** A heavy dot (•) used to highlight printed information.

bulletin (bо̄о̆l′ĭ-tn) *n.* **1.** A statement on a matter of public interest, as on radio, television, or a website: *a weather bulletin.* **2.** A newsletter, pamphlet, or other publication produced regularly by an organization, such as a society or club.

bulletin board *n.* **1.** A board on which notices are posted. **2.** A service for computer users that enables participants to send or read messages or files that are of general public interest.

bulletproof (bо̄о̆l′ĭt-prо̄о̆f′) *adj.* Designed to stop or repel bullets: *bulletproof glass.*

bullet train *n.* A high-speed passenger train.

bullfight (bо̄о̆l′fīt′) *n.* A spectacle, especially in Spain, Portugal, and Mexico, in which a matador typically engages a bull in traditional maneuvers with a cape and kills it with a sword. —**bull′fight′er** *n.* —**bull′fight′ing** *n.*

bullfinch (bо̄о̆l′fĭnch′) *n.* A European songbird having a short thick bill and in the male a red breast.

bullfrog (bо̄о̆l′frôg′) *n.* Any of several large frogs native to eastern North America, having a deep hollow croak.

bullhead (bо̄о̆l′hĕd′) *n.* **1.** Any of several North American freshwater catfishes having a large head. **2.** Any of several other large-headed fishes.

bullheaded (bо̄о̆l′hĕd′ĭd) *adj.* Very stubborn; headstrong. —**bull′head′ed·ness** *n.*

bullhorn (bо̄о̆l′hôrn′) *n.* A portable electric device resembling a megaphone and used to make the voice louder.

bullion (bо̄о̆l′yən) *n.* Gold or silver in the form of bars or ingots.

bullish (bо̄о̆l′ĭsh) *adj.* **1.** Aggressive or bullheaded. **2a.** Causing, expecting, or characterized by rising stock market prices. **b.** Optimistic or confident: *bullish on the prospects for a negotiated settlement.* —**bull′ish·ly** *adv.* —**bull′ish·ness** *n.*

bullock (bо̄о̆l′ək) *n.* **1.** A castrated bull; a steer. **2.** A young ox or bull.

bullpen (bо̄о̆l′pĕn′) *n.* **1.** An area in a baseball park where relief pitchers warm up during a game. **2.** The relief pitchers of a baseball team considered as a group: *a team with an excellent bullpen.*

bullring (bо̄о̆l′rĭng′) *n.* A circular arena for bullfighting.

bull's-eye or **bull's eye** (boŏolz′ī′) *n.* **1a.** The small central circle on a target, as in archery or small arms practice. **b.** A shot that hits this circle. **2.** A direct hit: *scored a bull's-eye on the window with a snowball.*

bull terrier *n.* A dog of a breed developed in England from a cross between a bulldog and a terrier, having a short coat and a flat head with a tapering muzzle.

bully (boŏol′ē) *n., pl.* **bullies** A person who is habitually cruel or aggressive toward smaller, weaker, or less popular people. ❖ *tr.v.* **bullied, bullying, bullies** To hurt or intimidate (someone) as a bully does.

bulrush (boŏol′rŭsh′) *n.* Any of several tall plants that resemble grasses and grow in wet places.

bulwark (boŏol′wərk or boŏl′wôrk′) *n.* **1.** A wall or barrier serving as a fortification: *An extensive bulwark protected the city from attack.* **2.** Something that serves as a defense: *Freedom of speech is the citizen's bulwark against the power of government.* **3.** A breakwater. **4.** often **bulwarks** The part of a ship's side that is above the upper deck.

bum (bŭm) *n.* **1.** A tramp; a vagrant. **2.** A person who avoids work; a loafer or beggar. ❖ *v.* **bummed, bumming, bums** —*intr.* **1.** To wander about or pass the time idly: *spent the summer bumming around with friends.* **2.** To live by begging or scavenging. —*tr.* To obtain by begging; mooch: *bum a ride to the next town.* See Synonyms at **cadge.** ❖ *adj.* **bummer, bummest 1.** Worthless: *bum directions.* **2.** Disabled: *a bum knee.* **3.** Unfavorable or unfair: *Breaking your leg before vacation was a bum deal.* ◆ **bum out** *Slang* To depress, dishearten, or dismay: *Not winning the game bummed me out.*

bumblebee (bŭm′bəl-bē′) *n.* Any of various large hairy bees that fly with a humming sound and nest in underground colonies.

bummer (bŭm′ər) *n. Slang* An unpleasant or disappointing experience or situation: *Missing the bus home late at night was a real bummer.*

bump (bŭmp) *v.* **bumped, bumping, bumps** —*tr.* **1.** To come up or knock against (a person or thing) forcefully: *They bumped heads as they both stooped to pick up the dime.* **2.** To cause (something) to knock against an obstacle: *I bumped the vacuum cleaner against the table.* **3.** To cause to move or shift by knocking or colliding: *bumped the box out of the way with my knee.* **4.** To deprive (a passenger) of a reserved seat due to overbooking, usually offering a seat on another conveyance: *The airlines bumped us to a later flight.* —*intr.* **1.** To hit or knock against something forcefully: *My knee bumped against the wall.* **2.** To proceed with jerks and jolts: *The car bumped slowly over the rutted road.* ❖ *n.* **1.** A light blow, collision, or jolt: *fall and get a bump on the chin.* **2.** A small swelling, as from a blow or an insect sting. **3.** A small place that rises above the level of the surface surrounding it: *a bump in the road.* ◆ **bump into** To meet by chance: *We bumped into each other at the store.*

bumper¹ (bŭm′pər) *n.* A horizontal metal or rubber bar attached to the front or rear of an automobile to absorb the impact of a collision.

bumper² (bŭm′pər) *n.* A drinking vessel filled to the top. ❖ *adj.* Abundant: *a bumper crop.*

bumper sticker *n.* A sticker with a printed message to display on the bumper of a car or truck.

bumpkin (bŭmp′kĭn or bŭm′kĭn) *n.* An awkward or unsophisticated person: *a country bumpkin.*

bumpy (bŭm′pē) *adj.* **bumpier, bumpiest 1.** Full of bumps: *a bumpy road.* **2.** Marked by or causing jerks and jolts: *a*

bumpy ride. —**bump′i·ly** *adv.* —**bump′i·ness** *n.*

bun (bŭn) *n.* **1.** A small bread roll: *a hamburger bun; a cinnamon bun.* **2.** A roll or coil of hair worn at the back of the head.

bunch (bŭnch) *n.* **1.** A group of similar things that are growing, fastened, or placed together: *a bunch of fresh grapes; a bunch of keys.* **2.** *Informal* A group of people having a common interest or association: *claimed that the mayor and his bunch were all corrupt.* **3.** *Informal* A considerable number or amount: *a whole bunch of work.* ❖ *v.* **bunched, bunching, bunches** —*tr.* To gather into a bunch: *bunch flowers into a bouquet.* —*intr.* To form a cluster or group: *The cold hikers bunched around the campfire.*

bundle (bŭn′dl) *n.* **1.** A number of objects bound, tied, or wrapped together: *a bundle of sticks.* **2.** Something tied up for carrying; a package. ❖ *v.* **bundled, bundling, bundles** —*tr.* **1.** To tie, wrap, or bind securely together: *bundle newspapers for recycling.* **2.** To send quickly; hustle: *bundle the children off to school.* **3.** To dress (a person) warmly: *She bundled up the baby and went outside.* —*intr.* To go hastily: *The children came bundling in from the yard.*

bundt cake (bŭnt or boŏont) *n.* A ring-shaped cake with grooved sides, baked in a mold.

bung (bŭng) *n.* **1.** A stopper for the hole in a cask. **2.** A bunghole.

bungalow (bŭng′gə-lō′) *n.* A small one-story house or cottage.

bungee cord (bŭn′jē′) *n.* An elasticized rubber cord used to secure things and to engage in bungee jumping.

bungee jumping *n.* The sport of jumping from a great height while attached to a bungee cord.

bunghole (bŭng′hōl′) *n.* The hole in a cask through which liquid is poured or drained out.

bungle (bŭng′gəl) *tr.v.* **bungled, bungling, bungles** To do or manage (an action or task) poorly; botch: *He bungled the mixing of the ingredients, and his pancakes were terrible.* —**bun′gler** *n.*

bunion (bŭn′yən) *n.* A painful inflamed swelling in the joint at the base of the big toe.

bunk¹ (bŭngk) *n.* **1.** A narrow bed built like a shelf against a wall. **2.** A bunk bed. ❖ *intr.v.* **bunked, bunking, bunks 1.** To sleep, especially in a makeshift bed: *had to bunk on the sofa last night.* **2.** To stay the night as a guest: *bunk over at a friend's house.*

bunk² (bŭngk) *n.* Empty talk; nonsense.

WORD HISTORY Bunk¹ is probably a shortening of *bunker.* **Bunk²** is a shortening of *bunkum,* which comes from *Buncombe* County, North Carolina, from a remark made around 1820 by its congressman, who felt obligated to give a dull speech "for Buncombe."

bunk bed *n.* Either of a pair of narrow beds stacked one on top of the other.

bunker (bŭng′kər) *n.* **1.** An underground room or shelter, often having a fortified structure above ground for positioning guns. **2.** A bin or tank for storing fuel, especially on a ship. **3.** An obstacle on a golf course consisting of a depression filled with sand.

bunkhouse (bŭngk′hous′) *n.* A building having bunks or beds, used as sleeping quarters on a ranch or in a camp.

bunkum (bŭng′kəm) *n.* Empty talk; nonsense.

bunny (bŭn′ē) *n., pl.* **bunnies** A rabbit, especially a young one.

Bunsen burner (bŭn′sən) *n.* A gas burner used in laboratories. It consists of a vertical tube with adjustable holes at its base that allow air to mix with the gas in order to make a very hot flame.

bunt (bŭnt) *v.* **bunted, bunting, bunts** —*tr.* **1.** In baseball, to bat or tap (a pitched ball) lightly so that the ball rolls in the infield. **2.** To push or strike with the horns or head; butt. —*intr.* In baseball, to bat a pitched ball by tapping it lightly. ❖ *n.* **1.** An act of bunting. **2.** A ball that is bunted. —**bunt′er** *n.*

bunting[1] (bŭn′tĭng) *n.* **1.** A light cotton or woolen cloth used for making flags. **2.** Flags considered as a group. **3.** Long strips of cloth with stripes or colors, used for decoration.

bunting[2] (bŭn′tĭng) *n.* Any of various birds having a short cone-shaped bill. Some kinds of buntings have brightly colored feathers.

bunting[3] (bŭn′tĭng) *n.* A hooded sleeping bag for an infant, usually made of heavy cloth.

WORD HISTORY Bunting[1] may be from German *bunt*, meaning "colored." **Bunting**[2] comes from Middle English *bunting*, referring to the same type of bird as in Modern English. **Bunting**[3] may be from Scots *buntin*, meaning "plump, short."

buoy (boo′ē *or* boi) *n.* **1.** A float, often with a bell or light, used to warn ships of danger, such as a reef or bar, or to mark a channel or safe passage. ❖ *tr.v.* **buoyed, buoying, buoys 1.** To keep afloat or aloft: *The kite was buoyed by a strong breeze.* **2.** To cheer; hearten: *The good news buoyed our spirits.*

buoyancy (boi′ən-sē *or* boo′yən-sē) *n.* **1.** The tendency or capacity to float in a liquid or to rise in air or other gas: *the buoyancy of wood in water.* **2.** The upward force that a fluid exerts on an object less dense than itself: *the buoyancy of salt water.* **3.** Lightness of spirit; cheerfulness: *The nurse's buoyancy cheered up the patient.*

buoyant (boi′ənt *or* boo′yənt) *adj.* **1.** Having buoyancy; floating or tending to float: *a buoyant cork.* **2.** Lighthearted; cheerful: *a buoyant mood.* —**buoy′ant·ly** *adv.*

bur[1] also **burr** (bûr) *n.* **1.** A rough prickly covering enclosing a seed or fruit, as that of a chestnut or burdock. **2.** A plant that bears burs.

bur[2] (bûr) *n.* Variant of **burr**[2].

burble (bûr′bəl) *intr.v.* **burbled, burbling, burbles** To bubble; gurgle: *The stream burbled over the mossy rocks.*

burden[1] (bûr′dn) *n.* **1.** Something that is carried; a load: *mules carrying their heavy burden uphill.* **2.** Something that is endured or assumed, especially as a difficult duty or responsibility: *Citizens carry the burden of taxation. Having a sister who is so popular has been a burden to her.* ❖ *tr.v.* **burdened, burdening, burdens 1.** To load or overload: *heavy snow burdening the tree branches.* **2.** To cause difficulty or distress to: *burdened him with cares.*

burden[2] (bûr′dn) *n.* **1.** A main idea or recurring theme: *the burden of the argument rests on this central point.* **2.** *Archaic* **a.** The chorus or refrain of a song. **b.** A bass accompaniment for a song.

WORD HISTORY Burden[1] comes from Old English *byrthen*, meaning "something that is carried." **Burden**[2] comes from Middle English, where it was spelled both *burden*

and *bourdon*, meaning "bass pipe of a bagpipe tuned to produce a single tone."

burden of proof *n.* In a legal case, the responsibility for providing evidence in proof of a charge or allegation.

burdensome (bûr′dn-səm) *adj.* Imposing a burden; hard to bear; heavy; arduous: *a burdensome task of cleaning out the basement.*

burdock (bûr′dŏk′) *n.* Any of several plants having large leaves and pink or purplish flower heads surrounded by prickly bracts that form burs.

bureau (byoor′ō) *n., pl.* **bureaus** or **bureaux** (byoor′ōz) **1.** A chest of drawers, especially for holding clothes. **2.** An office for a specific kind of business: *a travel bureau; a news bureau of a television station.* **3.** A department of a government: *the Federal Bureau of Investigation.*

bureaucracy (byoo-rŏk′rə-sē) *n., pl.* **bureaucracies 1a.** The administration of a government or other organization through a hierarchy of departments with appointed officials instead of elected representatives. **b.** The officials of such a government or organization considered as a group: *promised to reorganize the federal bureaucracy.* **2.** Administration, as of a government or other organization, in which the need to follow rules and regulations slows or prevents effective action: *It took weeks to get a refund because of the accounting department's bureaucracy.*

bureaucrat (byoor′ə-krăt′) *n.* **1.** An official of a bureaucracy. **2.** An official who insists on rigid adherence to rules and routines. —**bu′reau·crat′ic** *adj.* —**bu′reau·crat′i·cal·ly** *adv.*

burg (bûrg) *n. Informal* A city or town.

burgeon (bûr′jən) *intr.v.* **burgeoned, burgeoning, burgeons 1.** To put forth new buds, leaves, or shoots; begin to sprout or grow. **2.** To develop as if by sprouting or growing; flourish: *New ideas burgeon when people are allowed to talk freely.*

burger (bûr′gər) *n.* **1.** A hamburger or cheeseburger. **2.** A similar sandwich with a nonbeef filling: *a turkey burger; a tofu burger.*

burgess (bûr′jĭs) *n.* A member of the lower house of colonial legislature of Virginia or Maryland.

burgher (bûr′gər) *n.* A citizen of a town, especially a merchant or trader in a medieval town.

burglar (bûr′glər) *n.* A person who commits burglary; a housebreaker.

burglarize (bûr′glə-rīz′) *tr.v.* **burglarized, burglarizing, burglarizes** To enter and steal from (a building or home, for example).

burglary (bûr′glə-rē) *n., pl.* **burglaries** The crime of breaking into a building, home, or some other place with the intention of stealing.

burgle (bûr′gəl) *tr.v.* **burgled, burgling, burgles** To burglarize.

burgomaster (bûr′gə-măs′tər) *n.* The mayor of a town in Austria, Flemish-speaking parts of Belgium, the Netherlands, or Germany.

Burgundy (bûr′gən-dē) *n., pl.* **Burgundies 1.** A red or white wine made in Burgundy, France. **2.** A similar wine made in another place.

burial (bĕr′ē-əl) *n.* The act of placing a dead body in a grave, a tomb, or the sea.

burka (boor′kə) *n.* Variant of **burqa**.

burl (bûrl) *n.* **1.** A large rounded outgrowth on a tree trunk or branch. **2.** Wood from such a growth, usually with a marked grain.

burlap (bûr′lăp′) *n.* A coarse cloth made of hemp, jute, or flax, used to make bags, sacks, curtains, and coverings.

burlesque (bər-lĕsk′) *n.* **1.** An imitation of something, especially in a play, story, or song, that makes it seem ridiculous by treating it too seriously or too frivolously. **2.** A variety show with singing, dancing, and ribald comedy. ❖ *tr.v.* **burlesqued, burlesquing, burlesques** To imitate mockingly: *Many comedies burlesque traditional stories of success.*

burly (bûr′lē) *adj.* **burlier, burliest** Heavy and strong; muscular: *burly football players.* See Synonyms at **muscular.** —**bur′li·ness** *n.*

Burmese (bər-mēz′ *or* bər-mēs′) *adj.* Relating to Myanmar (Burma) or its people, language, or culture. ❖ *n., pl.* **Burmese 1.** A native or inhabitant of Myanmar. **2.** The Sino-Tibetan language of Myanmar.

burn (bûrn) *v.* **burned** *or* **burnt** (bûrnt), **burning, burns** —*intr.* **1.** To undergo combustion or be consumed as fuel: *Wood and paper burn easily.* **2.** To be damaged, injured, or destroyed by fire, heat, a chemical, or radiation: *The house burned to the ground. The eggs burned in the pan.* **3.** To produce light and heat by fire or energy: *The sun burned bright in the sky.* **4.** To feel or look hot: *burning with fever.* **5.** To be irritated or painful, as by inflammation: *My eyes are burning from the smoke.* **6.** To become sunburned or windburned: *Fair skin burns easily.* **7.** To be full of strong emotion: *burn with anger; burning with a desire to win.* —*tr.* **1.** To cause to undergo combustion: *We burned the logs in the fireplace.* **2.** To damage, injure, or destroy with fire, heat, a chemical, or radiation: *Our town burns trash to generate electricity. The acid burned my fingers.* **3.** To use as fuel: *This furnace burns oil.* **4.** To produce by fire, heat, a chemical, or radiation: *The sparks burned holes in the rug.* **5.** To use up or process for energy: *In running a marathon you burn a lot of calories.* **6a.** To give a feeling of heat to: *Some highly seasoned food burns my mouth.* **b.** To make angry: *Their nasty remarks burned me up.* **7.** To affect with a sunburn or windburn: *My face got burned while I was skiing.* **8.** To swindle or deceive; cheat: *investors who were burned in a stock fraud.* **9.** To record data on (a compact disc). ❖ *n.* **1.** An injury produced by fire, heat, a chemical, or radiation: *I got a blister from the burn.* **2.** A burned place or area: *a burn in the tablecloth.* **3.** In aerospace, a firing of a rocket: *The rocket made a good burn.* **4.** A sunburn or windburn. ◆ **burn out 1.** To stop burning from lack of fuel: *A campfire burns out if you don't keep putting wood on it.* **2.** To wear out or fail, especially because of heat: *The fan motor burned out from the short.* **3.** To make or become exhausted, especially as a result of long-term stress: *Working overtime finally burned her out. She burned out from years of overwork.* **burn up** To consume or be consumed by fire: *The books burned up in the fire.* —**burn′a·ble** *adj.*

burner (bûr′nər) *n.* **1.** A furnace or other device in which something is burned: *An oil burner heats the house.* **2.** The part of a stove, furnace, or lamp in which a flame or heat is produced.

burning (bûr′nĭng) *adj.* **1.** On fire; flaming; hot: *a burning candle.* **2.** Inflamed with strong emotion; heated: *a burning desire; a burning issue.*

burning bush (bûr′nĭng-bŏosh′) *n.* **1.** In the Bible, a miraculous flaming bush through which God spoke to the Hebrew prophet Moses on Mount Sinai. **2.** Any of several shrubs or shrubby plants having foliage that turns bright red in autumn.

burnish (bûr′nĭsh) *tr.v.* **burnished, burnishing, burnishes** To make smooth and glossy by or as if by rubbing; polish: *burnish a brass plate.* ❖ *n.* A smooth glossy finish or appearance; luster.

burnous also **burnoose** (bər-nōōs′) *n.* A long cloak with a hood, worn especially by Arabs and Berbers.

burnout (bûrn′out′) *n.* **1.** A failure of a device because of burning, heat, or friction. **2.** The end of a burn in a rocket engine, especially when the fuel has been exhausted or shut off. **3.** Exhaustion of physical or emotional strength: *Working long hours at a stressful job can result in burnout.*

burnt (bûrnt) *v.* A past tense and a past participle of **burn.**

burp (bûrp) *n.* A belch. ❖ *intr. & tr.v.* **burped, burping, burps** To belch or cause to belch: *Chris burped and said "Excuse me." Pat burped the baby after her feeding.*

burqa or **burka** (bŏor′kə) *n.* A loose, usually black or light blue outer garment worn by Muslim women that covers the head and face and sometimes the entire body.

burr¹ (bûr) *n.* **1.** A rough edge or spot left on metal or other material after it has been cast, cut, or drilled. **2.** Variant of **bur¹.**

burr² also **bur** (bûr) *n.* **1.** The trilled "r" of Scottish pronunciation. **2.** A whirring sound.

burrito (bŏo-rē′tō) *n., pl.* **burritos** A dish consisting of a flour tortilla wrapped around a filling, as of beef, beans, or cheese.

burro (bûr′ō *or* bŏor′ō) *n., pl.* **burros** A small donkey, usually used for carrying loads.

burrow (bûr′ō) *n.* A hole or tunnel dug in the ground by a small animal, such as a rabbit or mole. ❖ *v.* **burrowed, burrowing, burrows** —*intr.* **1.** To make a tunnel, hole, or shelter by digging or tunneling: *gophers burrowing in the fields.* **2.** To move as if making a burrow: *burrowed under the covers.* —*tr.* To press or push (something) as though making a burrow: *She burrowed her toes into the sand.* —**bur′row·er** *n.*

bursa (bûr′sə) *n., pl.* **bursae** (bûr′sē) *or* **bursas** A body cavity resembling a sac, especially one containing a lubricating fluid that reduces friction between a muscle and a bone.

bursar (bûr′sər *or* bûr′sär′) *n.* A treasurer, as at a college or university.

bursitis (bər-sī′tĭs) *n.* Inflammation of a bursa, especially in the shoulder, elbow, or knee.

burst (bûrst) *v.* **burst, bursting, bursts** —*intr.* **1.** To break open suddenly and violently: *The balloon may burst.* **2.** To come forth, emerge, or arrive suddenly and in full force: *The police burst into the room.* **3.** To be or seem to be full to the point of breaking open; swell: *He's bursting with pride.* **4.** To give sudden utterance or expression: *burst out laughing; burst into tears.* —*tr.* To cause to break open suddenly and violently: *The heat of the lamp burst the balloon.* ❖ *n.* **1.** A sudden outbreak or outburst; an explosion: *a burst of laughter.* **2.** A firing of bullets from an automatic weapon. **3.** A sudden and intense increase; a rush: *a burst of speed.* **4.** A period of intense activity: *worked on the project in short bursts.*

bury (bĕr′ē) *tr.v.* **buried, burying, buries 1.** To place in the ground: *The dog buried a bone.* **2.** To place (a dead body) in a grave, a tomb, or the sea. **3.** To conceal; hide: *She buried her face in the pillow.* **4.** To occupy (oneself) with deep concentration; absorb: *I buried myself in my studies.* **5.** To put an end to; abandon: *Let's shake hands and bury our quarrel.*

bus (bŭs) *n., pl.* **buses** *or* **busses 1.** A long motor vehicle with rows of seats for carrying passengers. **2.** A circuit that connects the major components of a computer, allowing the transfer of electric impulses from one component to another. ❖ *v.* **bused, busing, buses** or **bussed, bussing, busses** —*tr.* **1.** To carry or transport in a bus: *The club bused us to the beach.* **2.** To transport (students) by bus to schools outside their neighborhoods, especially to achieve racial integration. **3.** To clear dishes from (a table). —*intr.* To travel in a bus: *Many people bus to work and school.*

busboy also **bus boy** (bŭs′boi′) *n.* A waiter's helper who sets and clears the table in a restaurant.

bush (bŏŏsh) *n.* **1.** A shrub, especially one having many separate branches starting from or near the ground. **2.** Vegetation consisting of a thick growth of shrubs: *We walked in a single file through the thick bush.* **3.** Land that is remote from human settlement: *a journey through the Australian bush.*

bushed (bŏŏsht) *adj. Informal* Extremely tired.

bushel (bŏŏsh′əl) *n.* **1.** A unit of volume or capacity, used in dry measure in the United States and equal to 4 pecks (about 35.24 liters or 2,150 cubic inches). **2.** A container that holds this amount.

bushing (bŏŏsh′ĭng) *n.* A metal tube that serves as a guide for or reduces wear on a moving part, as in machinery.

bush league *n. Sports* A minor league. —**bush leaguer** *n.*

Bushman (bŏŏsh′mən) *n.* A member of the San people.

bushmaster (bŏŏsh′măs′tər) *n.* A large venomous snake of Central and South America having brown and gray markings.

bush pilot *n.* A pilot who flies a small airplane to and from remote areas where larger planes cannot land.

bushwhack (bŏŏsh′wăk′) *v.* **bushwhacked, bushwhacking, bushwhacks** —*tr.* To attack suddenly from a place of hiding; ambush. —*intr.* To force one's way through an overgrown area where no path exists.

bushy (bŏŏsh′ē) *adj.* **bushier, bushiest 1.** Consisting of or covered with bushes: *bushy plants; a bushy area.* **2.** Thick and shaggy: *bushy eyebrows.* —**bush′i·ness** *n.*

busily (bĭz′ə-lē) *adv.* In a busy manner.

business (bĭz′nĭs) *n.* **1.** The occupation, trade, or work that provides a person with a means of living: *a group of salespeople in the automobile business.* **2.** Commercial, industrial, and professional dealings considered as a group: *Computers are used throughout business and industry.* **3.** A commercial establishment, such as a store or factory: *Will you go into the family business?* **4.** The volume or amount of trade: *Business falls off when summer begins.* **5.** One's rightful or proper concern: *What he does with his money is none of our business.* **6.** An affair; a matter: *The committee dealt with the business at hand.* **7.** Serious work: *Let's get down to business.*

business card *n.* A small card printed with a person's name and business affiliation, usually including the person's title, address, and telephone number.

businesslike (bĭz′nĭs-līk′) *adj.* Systematic; efficient; orderly: *a friendly but businesslike manner.*

businessman (bĭz′nĭs-măn′) *n.* A man engaged in business.

businessperson (bĭz′nĭs-pûr′sən) *n.* A businessman or businesswoman.

businesswoman (bĭz′nĭs-wŏŏm′ən) *n.* A woman engaged in business.

busk (bŭsk) *intr.v.* **busked, busking, busks** To play music or perform entertainment in a public place, usually while soliciting money. —**busk′er** *n.*

busload (bŭs′lōd′) *n.* The number of passengers or the quantity of cargo that a bus can carry.

buss (bŭs) *tr. & intr.v.* **bussed, bussing, busses** To kiss. ❖ *n.* A kiss.

busses (bŭs′ĭz) *n.* A plural of **bus.**

bust[1] (bŭst) *n.* **1.** A sculpture of a person's head, shoulders, and upper chest: *marble busts in the art museum.* **2.** A woman's breasts.

bust[2] (bŭst) *v.* **busted, busting, busts** —*tr.* **1.** *Slang* To smash or break: *I busted the ice with a hatchet.* **2.** *Slang* To make unusable; break: *He busted the vending machine by putting in foreign coins.* **3.** To break or tame (a horse). **4.** To cause to become bankrupt or short of money: *The long drought busted many farmers.* **5.** *Slang* To reduce the rank of; demote: *bust a sergeant to corporal.* **6.** To hit; punch. **7.** *Slang* To place under arrest: *The cops busted the thief.* —*intr.* **1.** *Slang* To become broken or unusable; break: *The bicycle chain busted as I went up the hill.* **2.** To become bankrupt or short of money. ❖ *n.* **1.** A failure; a flop: *That movie is a real bust.* **2.** A financial depression: *times of boom and bust.* **3.** A punch or blow. **4.** *Slang* An arrest: *a drug bust.*

WORD HISTORY Bust[1] is from French *buste*, which is from Italian *busto*, meaning "upper part of the body." **Bust**[2] is a variant of Modern English *burst.*

bustard (bŭs′tərd) *n.* Any of various large brownish or grayish birds of Africa, Asia, and Australia that have a long neck and legs and live in dry grassy plains.

busted (bŭs′tĭd) *adj. Slang* **1a.** Broken or fractured: *a busted window.* **b.** Not working; inoperable: *a busted car.* **2.** Bankrupt or out of funds. **3.** Captured or held by law enforcement; arrested: *a busted thief.*

bustle[1] (bŭs′əl) *intr.v.* **bustled, bustling, bustles** To move busily and energetically: *The mechanics bustled about the airplane.* ❖ *n.* Excited activity; commotion: *the hustle and bustle of city streets.*

bustle[2] (bŭs′əl) *n.* A pad or frame worn by women in earlier times to puff out the back of a long skirt.

busy (bĭz′ē) *adj.* **busier, busiest 1.** Occupied with work; active: *The doctor was busy with a patient.* **2.** Crowded with activity: *the doctor's busy morning.* **3.** In use, as a telephone line: *The doctor's phone is busy.* ❖ *tr.v.* **busied, busying, busies** To make (oneself) busy; occupy (oneself): *I busied myself with my chores.* —**bus′y·ness** *n.*

busybody (bĭz′ē-bŏd′ē) *n., pl.* **busybodies** A nosy or meddling person interested in the affairs of others.

busywork (bĭz′ē-wûrk′) *n.* An activity that takes up time but does not necessarily produce anything: *the busywork of sorting old newspapers.*

but (bŭt; bət *when unstressed*) *conj.* **1a.** On the contrary: *My bike is old, but yours is new. They have not two dogs but three.* **b.** Nevertheless; yet: *The plan may not work, but we must try. She was tired but happy.* **2.** That. Used in negative statements: *There is no doubt but right will win out.* **3.** With the exception that; except that: *I would have stayed longer but I was getting sleepy.* **4.** Without the result that: *It never rains but it pours.* ❖ *prep.* Other than; except: *No one went but me.* ❖ *adv.* Only; merely: *This is but one case in many.* ◆ **but for** Were it not for: *We would have gone but for the weather.* —SEE NOTE AT **not.**

butane (byŏŏ′tān′) *n.* A gaseous hydrocarbon having

the formula C_4H_{10}. It is produced from petroleum and is used as a fuel and in the making of synthetic rubber.

butch (bŏŏch) *Slang adj.* Exhibiting stereotypically masculine appearance or behavior. Used especially of lesbians and gay men. ❖ *n.* A haircut in which the hair is cropped close to the head.

butcher (bŏŏch′ər) *n.* **1.** A person who slaughters animals and prepares their meat for food. **2.** A person who sells meat: *buy a steak from the local butcher.* **3.** A person who kills cruelly or without reason. ❖ *tr.v.* **butchered, butchering, butchers 1.** To slaughter or prepare (animals) for market. **2.** To kill brutally and without reason. **3.** To botch up; bungle: *The actor butchered the part by forgetting many lines.*

butchery (bŏŏch′ə-rē) *n., pl.* **butcheries** Cruel or savage killing; slaughter.

butler (bŭt′lər) *n.* The chief male servant of a household.

butt[1] (bŭt) *tr.v.* **butted, butting, butts** To hit or push with the head or horns: *The goat butted the farmer.* ❖ *n.* A push or blow with the head or horns. ◆ **butt in** *Informal* To meddle; intrude: *Don't butt in on other people's conversations.*

butt[2] (bŭt) *n.* A person or thing that is an object of ridicule or scorn: *The clown was the butt of his own jokes.*

butt[3] (bŭt) *n.* **1.** The thicker end of something: *the butt of a rifle.* **2.** An unused or unburned end, especially of a cigarette. **3.** *Informal* The buttocks.

WORD HISTORY Butt[1] comes from Middle English *butten,* which comes from Old French *bouter,* both meaning "to strike." **Butt**[2] comes from Middle English *but* (meaning "target"), which comes from Old French *bout,* meaning "end, limit." **Butt**[3] comes from Middle English *butte* (meaning "end of a spear"), which is not related to Old French *bout.*

butte (byŏŏt) *n.* A steep-sided hill with a flat top, often standing alone.

butter (bŭt′ər) *n.* **1.** A soft, yellowish, fatty food churned from milk or cream. **2.** A similar substance, such as a fruit spread: *There are many fruit butters such as apple butter.* ❖ *tr.v.* **buttered, buttering, butters** To put butter in or on. ◆ **butter up** To flatter: *He's always buttering up the boss.*

butter bean *n.* A lima bean or a wax bean.

buttercup (bŭt′ər-kŭp′) *n.* **1.** Any of numerous plants having cup-shaped flowers that are usually yellow. **2.** A flower of this plant.

butterfat (bŭt′ər-făt′) *n.* The fat that is contained in milk and from which butter is made.

butterfingers (bŭt′ər-fĭng′gərz) *pl.n.* *(used with a singular verb)* A clumsy or awkward person who is apt to drop things.

butterfish (bŭt′ər-fĭsh′) *n.* Any of various fishes having oily flesh or slippery skin, especially a silvery edible ocean fish of the Atlantic coast of North America.

butterfly (bŭt′ər-flī′) *n.* **1.** Any of numerous insects having four broad, often colorful wings, a narrow body, and slender antennae with knobs at the tips. **2.** A swimming stroke in which the swimmer draws both arms upward out of the water and forward while kicking the legs up and down in unison.

buttermilk (bŭt′ər-mĭlk′) *n.* The thick sour liquid that remains after butter has been churned from milk.

butternut (bŭt′ər-nŭt′) *n.* **1.** The oily edible nut of a kind of walnut tree native to eastern North America. **2.** The tree that bears such nuts.

butterscotch (bŭt′ər-skŏch′) *n.* A syrup, sauce, candy, or flavoring made from brown sugar and butter.

buttery (bŭt′ə-rē) *adj.* **1.** Containing or spread with butter: *hot buttery muffins.* **2.** Resembling butter: *buttery soft leather.*

buttock (bŭt′ək) *n.* Either of the rounded fleshy parts of the human body situated between the lower back and the upper thighs.

button (bŭt′n) *n.* **1a.** A usually disk-shaped fastener used to join two parts of a garment by fitting through a buttonhole or loop. **b.** Such an object used on a garment for decoration. **2.** A part that is pushed to work a switch, as to ring a bell, turn on a light, or start a machine: *Push the button to get the elevator.* **3.** Something resembling a button, as a round flat pin with words or a design on it: *a candidate's campaign button.* **4.** A distinct area, such as a small box, on a computer screen that can be clicked to execute a command. ❖ *v.* **buttoned, buttoning, buttons** —*tr.* To fasten with a button or buttons: *button up a coat.* —*intr.* To become fastened with a button or buttons: *a coat that buttons down the front.* ◆ **on the button** Exactly; precisely: *We arrived at three o'clock on the button.*

buttonhole (bŭt′n-hōl′) *n.* A slit in a garment or in cloth used to fasten a button. ❖ *tr.v.* **buttonholed, buttonholing, buttonholes 1.** To make a buttonhole in. **2.** To make (a person) stop and listen, as if grabbing the buttonhole in a garment.

buttonwood (bŭt′n-wŏŏd′) *n.* **1.** The sycamore tree of North America. **2.** An evergreen shrub or tree of coastal tropical America and western Africa, having small buttonlike heads of greenish flowers.

buttress (bŭt′rĭs) *n.* **1.** A structure, often of brick or stone, built against a wall as a support. **2.** Something that serves to support or reinforce: *Testimony of witnesses was a strong buttress to our side of the story.* ❖ *tr.v.* **buttressed, buttressing, buttresses 1.** To brace or reinforce with a buttress: *buttress the roof of a tunnel with timbers.* **2.** To sustain or bolster: *buttress an argument with evidence.*

buxom (bŭk′səm) *adj.* Having large breasts. —**bux′om·ness** *n.*

buy (bī) *v.* **bought** (bôt), **buying, buys** —*tr.* **1.** To get in exchange for money or something of equal value: *go to the store to buy groceries; buy land through a bank.* **2.** To be capable of purchasing: *Money can buy comfort but not happiness.* **3.** To bribe (someone): *Money will not buy an honest judge.* **4.** *Informal* To accept as true; believe: *The coach didn't buy his excuse for missing practice.* —*intr.* To purchase goods: *Looked at the shoes but decided not to buy.* ❖ *n.* Something cheaper than usual; a bargain: *The coats on sale are a good buy.* ◆ **buy into 1.** To acquire a stake or interest in: *Investors are starting to buy into the new business.* **2.** To believe in, especially wholeheartedly or uncritically: *Everyone bought into the idea that a new highway would solve the town's economic problems.* **buy off** To bribe: *It is illegal to try to buy off a government official.* **buy out** To purchase the stock, rights, or interests of: *buy out a company.* **buy time** To increase the time available for a specific purpose: *We stayed with our friends so we could buy time in looking for a new apartment.* **buy up** To purchase all that is available: *Fans had bought up all the tickets.*

buyer (bī′ər) *n.* **1.** A person who buys goods; a customer. **2.** A person who buys merchandise for a retail store.

buyout (bī′out′) *n.* The purchase of a business by buying all of its stock.

buzz (bŭz) *v.* **buzzed, buzzing, buzzes** —*intr.* **1.** To make a low droning sound like that of a bee: *Flies buzzed near the cherries.* **2.** To talk in excited low tones: *The audience buzzed in anticipation of the show.* —*tr.* **1.** To signal, as with a buzzer: *The patient buzzed the nurse.* **2.** *Informal* To fly a plane low over: *The pilot buzzed the stadium.* ❖ *n.* **1.** A low droning sound, such as the one made by a bee: *the buzz of a fly.* **2.** A buzzcut. **3.** *Slang* Excited interest or attention: *There was a lot of buzz surrounding the new movie.* ◆ **buzz off** *Informal* To leave quickly; go away.

buzzard (bŭz′ərd) *n.* **1.** Any of various North American vultures. **2.** *Chiefly British* Any of various hawks having broad wings and a broad tail.

buzzcut (bŭz′kŭt′) *n.* A haircut in which the hair is cut very close to the scalp.

buzzer (bŭz′ər) *n.* An electrical device that makes a buzzing noise to give a signal or warning.

buzz saw *n.* A circular saw.

buzzword (bŭz′wûrd′) *n.* A stylish or trendy word or phrase, especially when occurring in a specialized field.

by (bī) *prep.* **1.** Close to; near: *the chair by the window; sitting by the wall.* **2.** Up to and beyond; past: *A car drove by us.* **3.** At or to: *came by the house; stopped by the bakery.* **4.** Through the agency or action of: *a building destroyed by fire; a novel by a young author.* **5.** With the help or use of; through: *come by the back road; crossing by ferry.* **6.** According to: *playing by the rules; by their own account.* **7.** With respect to: *related by blood.* **8.** In the course of; during: *sleeping by night and working by day.* **9.** In the amount of: *The president receives letters by the thousands.* **10.** Not later than: *finish by noon.* **11.** In the matter of; concerning: *They are storekeepers by trade.* **12.** After; following: *One by one they left.* **13.** Combined in multiplication, division, or measurement with: *Multiply 4 by 6. Divide 4 by 2. The room measures 12 by 20 feet.* **14.** With the difference of; to the extent of: *shorter by three inches.* ❖ *adv.* **1.** Close at hand; nearby: *We just stood by watching.* **2.** Aside; away: *putting some money by for later.* **3.** Up to and beyond; past: *The car raced by.* **4.** At or to one's home or location: *Stop by later on.* **5.** Into the past: *as time goes by.* ◆ **by and by** Before long; later: *The weather always changes by and by.* **by and large** On the whole; mostly: *By and large people are honest.* **by oneself 1.** Alone: *I walked by myself in the woods.* **2.** Without help: *I repaired the car by myself.* **by the way** Incidentally.

by– or **bye–** A prefix that means: **1.** Near; at hand: *by-*stander. **2.** Out of the way; aside: *bypass.* **3.** Secondary: *byproduct.* **4.** Past: *bygone.*

bye (bī) *interj.* An expression used to say goodbye.

bye-bye (bī′bī′ *or* bī-bī′) *interj.* An expression used to say goodbye.

bygone (bī′gôn′) *adj.* Gone by; past: *bygone days.* ❖ *n.* often **bygones** A past occurrence: *Let bygones be bygones.*

bylaw (bī′lô′) *n.* A law or rule made by a local government, corporation, club, or other organization governing its own affairs.

byline (bī′līn′) *n.* A printed line at the head of a newspaper or magazine article giving the writer's name.

bypass also **by-pass** (bī′păs′) *n.* **1.** A highway that passes around a city or other congested area. **2.** A path that leads around some component of a system, as in an electric circuit or a system of pipes. **3.** A surgical operation to make a new passage for blood around old vessels that are blocked: *a bypass around a blood vessel of the heart.* ❖ *tr.v.* **bypassed, bypassing, bypasses** To go or send around by or as if by means of a bypass: *We can bypass all the salespeople if we see the manager directly.*

by-path (bī′păth′) *n.* An indirect or little-used path.

byproduct or **by-product** (bī′prŏd′əkt) *n.* **1.** Something produced in the making of something else: *Asphalt and paraffin are byproducts of refining crude oil into gasoline.* **2.** A secondary result; a side effect: *Increased unemployment is a byproduct of the economic downturn.*

byroad (bī′rōd′) *n.* A side road; a back road.

bystander (bī′stăn′dər) *n.* A person who is present at an event but does not take part: *Bystanders crowded around the scene of the accident.*

byte (bīt) *n.* A sequence of adjacent bits operated on as a unit by a computer. A byte usually consists of eight bits.

byway (bī′wā′) *n.* A road not often used; a side road.

byword (bī′wûrd′) *n.* **1.** A well-known saying; a proverb. **2.** A person or thing thought of as representing a type, class, or quality: *That newspaper is the byword for honest reporting.*

Byzantine (bĭz′ən-tēn′ *or* bĭz′ən-tīn′ *or* bī-zăn′tĭn) *adj.* **1.** Relating to Byzantium, its inhabitants, or their culture. **2.** Relating to the Byzantine Empire. **3.** Relating to the style of architecture developed in Byzantium, characterized by round arches, massive domes, and the extensive use of mosaic designs. **4. byzantine** Highly complicated; intricate and involved. ❖ *n.* An inhabitant of Byzantium or the Byzantine Empire.

Cc

c or **C** (sē) *n., pl.* **c's** or **C's** or **Cs 1.** The third letter of the English alphabet: *There are two c's in the word "clock."* **2. C** The third best or third highest grade: *get a C on a test.* **3. C** In music, the first tone in the scale of C major.

WORD HISTORY Have you ever wondered why **c** is sometimes pronounced like a *k* and sometimes like an *s,* as in *candy* and *cereal*? Our letter *c* comes from the Roman alphabet, which was used to represent the sounds of Latin and was later adopted for English. In languages derived from Latin, such as Italian and French, the hard *c* sound (k) of Latin gradually changed before the vowels *e, i,* and *y* to (ch) or the soft *c* sound (s). When the Normans conquered England in 1066, they brought their French language and spelling with them. For this reason, scribes in England continued to write *c* for the soft sound before *e, i,* and *y* in words like *center* and *circle,* and they introduced *k* for the hard *c* sound in many words like *keep* and *king.* In Modern English, *c* is still usually soft before *e, i,* and *y* and hard before *a, o, u,* and consonants. (The letter *g* has a similar history to the letter *c,* which is why it is sometimes pronounced hard, as in *got,* and sometimes soft, as in *gene.*)

C¹ 1. also **c** The symbol for the Roman numeral one hundred. **2. c** The symbol for the speed of light in a vacuum.
C² ** An abbreviation of: **1. Celsius. **2.** centigrade. **3.** cold. **4.** consonant.
c. ** An abbreviation of: **1. cent. **2.** also **C.** century. **3.** circa (approximately). **4.** copyright.
**ca ** An abbreviation of circa (approximately).
cab (kăb) *n.* **1.** A taxicab. **2.** A one-horse carriage for public hire. **3.** A covered compartment for the operator or driver of a heavy vehicle or machine, such as a locomotive, truck, or crane.
cabal (kə-băl′ *or* kə-băl′) *n.* **1.** A small group of people organized to carry out a secret plot or conspiracy. **2.** A plot organized by such a group.
cabala (kăb′ə-lə *or* kə-bä′lə) *n.* Variant of **kabbalah**.
caballero (kăb′ə-lâr′ō *or* kä′bä-yĕ′rō) *n., pl.* **caballeros 1.** A Spanish gentleman; a cavalier. **2.** A skilled horseman.
cabana (kə-băn′ə) *n.* **1.** A shelter on a beach or at a swimming pool used as a bathhouse. **2.** A cabin or hut.
cabaret (kăb′ə-rā′) *n.* **1.** A restaurant or nightclub providing short programs of live entertainment. **2.** The entertainment presented in such a place.
cabbage (kăb′ĭj) *n.* Any of several plants having a large rounded head of tightly overlapping green or reddish leaves eaten as a vegetable.
cabby or **cabbie** (kăb′ē) *n., pl.* **cabbies** A cabdriver.
cabdriver (kăb′drī′vər) *n.* A driver of a taxicab.
cabin (kăb′ĭn) *n.* **1.** A small, simply built house; a cottage or hut. **2.** A room in a ship used as living quarters for a passenger or officer. **3.** An enclosed compartment in a boat that serves as a shelter or as living quarters. **4.** The

enclosed compartment in an airplane or spacecraft for passengers, crew, or cargo.
cabin boy *n.* A male servant who serves the officers and passengers on a ship.
cabin cruiser *n.* A large motorboat having a cabin equipped with living facilities.
cabinet (kăb′ə-nĭt) *n.* **1.** A case or cupboard with shelves, drawers, or compartments for storing or displaying objects: *a kitchen cabinet; a filing cabinet.* **2.** The box that houses the main parts of a computer. **3.** often **Cabinet** A group of people appointed by a head of state or prime minister to act as official advisers and to head the various departments of state.
cabinetmaker (kăb′ə-nĭt-mā′kər) *n.* A person who makes fine articles of wooden furniture.
cabinetwork (kăb′ə-nĭt-wûrk′) *n.* Fine woodwork made by a cabinetmaker.
cabin fever *n.* An uneasy feeling that results from a long stay in a remote area or in a small enclosed space.
cable (kā′bəl) *n.* **1.** A strong thick rope made of steel wires or fiber. **2.** A group of insulated electrical wires or optical fibers that are bound together. **3a.** Cable television. **b.** A similar service that provides Internet access. **4.** A cablegram. ❖ *adj.* Relating to a subscription television or Internet service that uses cables to carry signals between local distribution antennas and the subscriber's location. ❖ *tr.v.* **cabled, cabling, cables 1.** To send a cablegram to: *Several reporters cabled their newspapers about the earthquake.* **2.** To transmit (a message) by telegraph.
cable box *n.* An electronic device that allows channels transmitted by cable to be viewed on a television.
cable car *n.* A vehicle pulled by a cable that runs in an endless loop either overhead or beneath rails.
cablegram (kā′bəl-grăm′) *n.* A telegram sent by submarine cable.
cable television *n.* A subscription television service that uses cables to carry signals between local distribution antennas and the subscriber's location.
caboose (kə-bōōs′) *n.* The last car of a freight train, having living facilities for the train crew and used as a vantage point for spotting problems on the train. The introduction of electronic sensors has made the caboose unnecessary.
cabriolet (kăb′rē-ə-lā′) *n.* A two-wheeled carriage pulled by one horse, having two seats and a folding top.
cacao (kə-kä′ō *or* kə-kā′ō) *n., pl.* **cacaos 1.** The seeds from the pods of a tropical American evergreen tree, used to make chocolate, cocoa, and cocoa butter. **2.** The tree that bears such seeds.
cachalot (kăsh′ə-lŏt′ *or* kăsh′ə-lō′) *n.* The sperm whale.
cache (kăsh) *n.* **1.** A hiding place, as for a supply of provisions or weapons. **2.** A supply of something hidden in such a place: *a cache of food.* **3.** A fast storage buffer in the central processing unit of a computer. ❖ *tr.v.* **cached, caching, caches** To hide or store away in a cache: *squirrels caching nuts for winter.*

cachet (kă-shā′) *n.* **1a.** A mark or quality, as of distinction or individuality: *Doctors have a certain cachet in America.* **b.** Great prestige or appeal: *a designer label with cachet.* **2.** A seal on a letter or document.

cackle (kăk′əl) *v.* **cackled, cackling, cackles** —*intr.* **1.** To make the shrill cry of a hen that has just laid an egg. **2.** To laugh or speak in a shrill manner. —*tr.* To utter in cackles: *He cackled a sarcastic reply.* ❖ *n.* **1.** The act or sound of cackling. **2.** Shrill laughter or foolish chatter.

cacophonous (kə-kŏf′ə-nəs) *adj.* Harsh and unpleasant in sound; dissonant.

cacophony (kə-kŏf′ə-nē) *n., pl.* **cacophonies** Harsh unpleasant sound; dissonance: *a cacophony of car horns.*

cactus (kăk′təs) *n., pl.* **cacti** (kăk′tī′) *or* **cactuses** Any of various plants that have thick, leafless, usually spiny stems and that grow in hot dry places, chiefly in the Americas.

cad (kăd) *n.* A man whose behavior is unprincipled or dishonorable.

CAD An abbreviation of computer-aided design.

cadaver (kə-dăv′ər) *n.* A dead body, especially one that is to be dissected and studied.

cadaverous (kə-dăv′ər-əs) *adj.* Resembling a corpse; pale and gaunt.

caddie also **caddy** (kăd′ē) *n., pl.* **caddies** A person hired by a golfer to carry golf clubs. ❖ *intr.v.* **caddied, caddying, caddies** To serve as a caddie.

caddisfly or **caddis fly** (kăd′ĭs-flī′) *n.* Any of numerous flying insects that are usually found near lakes and streams. The larvae live in tubular cases covered with grains of sand or tiny pieces of wood or shell.

Caddo (kăd′ō) *n., pl.* **Caddo** or **Caddos 1.** A member of a group of Native American peoples living in central Oklahoma. **2.** Their Caddoan language.

Caddoan (kăd′ō-ən) *n.* A family of Native American languages spoken nowadays in North Dakota and Oklahoma.

caddy (kăd′ē) *n., pl.* **caddies 1.** A small container, such as a box, used especially for holding tea. **2.** Variant of **caddie.**

cadence (kăd′ns) *n.* **1.** Measured rhythmic flow, as of poetry or music: *poetry written in short quick cadences.* **2.** The measure or beat of movement, as in marching. **3.** A progression of chords that brings a phrase or other division of a musical composition to a close. **4.** The general rise and fall of the voice in speaking, as at the end of a question.

cadenza (kə-dĕn′zə) *n.* An elaborate section for the soloist, usually near the end of a concerto's movement.

cadet (kə-dĕt′) *n.* A student who is training to be an officer in the military or the police.

cadge (kăj) *intr. & tr.v.* **cadged, cadging, cadges** To beg or get by begging. —**cadg′er** *n.*

✦ **SYNONYMS cadge, beg, bum, mooch, scrounge** *v.*

cadmium (kăd′mē-əm) *n. Symbol* **Cd** A soft, bluish-white metallic element resembling tin that occurs only in combination with other elements. It is used in plating metals to prevent corrosion and in making alloys and storage batteries. Atomic number 48. See **Periodic Table.**

cadre (kä′drä *or* kăd′rē) *n.* A group of people trained to establish and teach new members in a larger organization.

caduceus (kə-dōō′sē-əs) *n., pl.* **caducei** (kə-dōō′sē-ī′) **1.** In Greek mythology, a winged staff with two serpents

coiled around it carried by Hermes. **2.** A similar staff used as a symbol of the medical profession.

caecilian (sə-sĭl′yən *or* sə-sēl′yən) *n.* Any of various legless, burrowing amphibians that have numerous grooved rings encircling the body and are found mostly in tropical regions.

caecum (sē′kəm) *n.* Variant of **cecum.**

caesar also **Caesar** (sē′zər) *n.* **1.** A title of Roman emperors after the reign of Augustus. **2.** A dictator or other ruler having absolute power.

caesarean (sĭ-zâr′ē-ən) *n. & adj.* Variant of **cesarean.**

caesar salad *n.* A tossed salad of greens, croutons, grated cheese, and sometimes anchovies, with a dressing of olive oil, lemon juice, garlic, and a raw or coddled egg.

caesura (sĭ-zhōōr′ə *or* sĭ-zōōr′ə) *n., pl.* **caesuras** or **caesurae** (sĭ-zhōōr′ē *or* sĭ-zōōr′ē) A short pause in a line of verse or in a melody.

café also **cafe** (kă-fā′) *n.* A restaurant where coffee and baked goods or light meals are served.

cafeteria (kăf′ĭ-tîr′ē-ə) *n.* **1.** A dining area, as at a school, where meals may be purchased or brought from home and eaten. **2.** A restaurant in which the customers are served at a counter and carry their meals on trays to tables.

caffeine also **caffein** (kă-fēn′ *or* kăf′ēn′) *n.* A bitter white alkaloid that acts as a stimulant and is found in coffee, tea, and cola beverages.

caffe latte (kăf′ā lä′tā) *n.* A strong espresso coffee topped with steamed frothed milk.

caftan or **kaftan** (kăf′tăn′ *or* kăf-tăn′) *n.* A full-length robe or tunic having long sleeves and worn mainly in eastern Mediterranean countries.

cage (kāj) *n.* **1.** An enclosure for confining birds or other animals, having a grating of wires or bars on at least one side to let in air or light. **2.** Something similar to a cage: *a ticket seller's cage at the stadium.* **3.** A wire backstop or enclosure placed around home plate, used to stop balls batted during practice. **4.** An enclosure to confine prisoners. ❖ *tr.v.* **caged, caging, cages** To put in a cage: *cage a wild animal.*

cagey also **cagy** (kā′jē) *adj.* **cagier, cagiest** Wary; shrewd; crafty: *a cagey lawyer with much experience.* —**cag′i·ly** *adv.* —**cag′i·ness** *n.*

cahoots (kə-hōōts′) *pl.n. Informal* Secret partnership: *a surprise party that she planned in cahoots with friends.*

caiman also **cayman** (kā′mən) *n., pl.* **caimans** also **caymans** Any of various large tropical American reptiles that resemble and are related to alligators and crocodiles and that live in rivers and wetlands.

cairn (kârn) *n.* A mound of stones built as a landmark or memorial.

caisson (kā′sŏn′ *or* kā′sən) *n.* **1.** A watertight structure inside of which construction work is done under water, as in the building of tunnels, bridges, or dams. **2.** A watertight container used to raise a sunken vessel by attaching it to the hull and filling it with air. **3.** A floating structure used to close the entrance of a dock or canal lock. **4.** A two-wheeled horse-drawn vehicle formerly used to carry military ammunition.

cajole (kə-jōl′) *tr.v.* **cajoled, cajoling, cajoles** To persuade by flattery or insincere talk; coax: *Immigrants were cajoled into going away by promises of great wealth and land.*

Cajun (kā′jən) *n.* A member of a group of people living in Louisiana and descended from French colonists exiled from Acadia in the 1700s. —**Ca′jun** *adj.*

cake (kāk) *n*. **1.** A sweet baked food made of flour, liquid, eggs, and other ingredients. **2.** A flat rounded mass of dough or batter that is baked or fried: *a wheat cake*. **3.** A flat rounded mass of chopped food that is baked or fried: *a fish cake*. **4.** A shaped or molded piece, as of soap. ❖ *v*. **caked, caking, cakes** —*tr*. To cover or fill with a thick layer; encrust: *My shoes are caked with mud*. —*intr*. To form into a compact mass: *The melted cheese caked on the counter as it cooled*.

cakewalk (kāk′wôk′) *n*. **1.** Something that is easily accomplished. **2.** A public entertainment among African Americans in the 1800s in which dancers performing the most accomplished or amusing steps won cakes as prizes. —**cake′walk′er** *n*.

cal or **Cal** An abbreviation of calorie.

calabash (kăl′ə-băsh′) *n*. **1a.** A large gourd having a hard rind. **b.** The vine that bears such gourds. **2a.** The similar fruit of a tropical American tree. **b.** The tree that bears such fruit. **3.** A bowl, ladle, or other article made from the hollowed-out shell of either of these fruits.

calaboose (kăl′ə-boōs′) *n*. A jail.

calamari (kä′lə-mä′rē or kăl′ə-mä′rē) *n*. Squid eaten as food.

calamata olive (kä′lə-mä′tə or kăl′ə-mä′tə) *n*. Variant of **kalamata olive.**

calamine (kăl′ə-mīn′ or kăl′ə-mĭn) *n*. A pink powder used in skin lotions and composed of zinc oxide mixed with a small amount of ferric oxide.

calamitous (kə-lăm′ĭ-təs) *adj*. Causing or resulting in a calamity; disastrous. —**ca·lam′i·tous·ly** *adv*.

calamity (kə-lăm′ĭ-tē) *n*., *pl*. **calamities 1.** An event that causes great distress and suffering; a disaster: *The long drought was a calamity for farmers*. **2.** Distress or misfortune: *the calamity of unemployment*.

calcareous (kăl-kâr′ē-əs) *adj*. Composed of or containing limestone, calcium, or calcium carbonate; chalky.

calcification (kăl′sə-fĭ-kā′shən) *n*. **1.** The process of calcifying: *Calcification of cartilage often causes stiffness in the joints of the body*. **2.** A calcified part, such as tissue or an organ.

calcify (kăl′sə-fī′) *tr*. & *intr.v*. **calcified, calcifying, calcifies** To make or become stony or chalky by the deposit of calcium salts.

calcimine (kăl′sə-mīn′) *n*. A white or tinted mixture of zinc oxide, water, and glue, formerly used to coat walls and ceilings.

calcine (kăl-sīn′ or kăl′sīn′) *tr.v*. **calcined, calcining, calcines** To dry, reduce, or oxidize (a substance) by heating it to a high temperature without causing it to melt: *a furnace to calcine limestone*. ❖ *n*. A substance produced by calcining. —**cal′ci·na′tion** (kăl′sə-nā′shən) *n*.

calcite (kăl′sīt′) *n*. A crystalline mineral that is the main component of chalk, limestone, and marble. It is a natural form of calcium carbonate.

calcium (kăl′sē-əm) *n*. *Symbol* **Ca** A silvery-white, moderately hard metallic element found in limestone, gypsum, milk, and bone. It is essential for the normal growth and development of most plants and animals, and is used in alloys, plaster, and cement. Atomic number 20. See **Periodic Table.**

calcium carbide *n*. A crystalline grayish-black compound of carbon and calcium that has the formula CaC_2 and reacts with water to form acetylene gas.

calcium carbonate *n*. A white or colorless crystalline compound of calcium, carbon, and oxygen that has the formula $CaCO_3$ and occurs naturally in chalk, limestone, and marble. It is used in the manufacture of toothpaste, white paint, and Portland cement.

calcium chloride *n*. A white crystalline salt composed of calcium and chlorine and having the formula $CaCl_2$. It attracts water very strongly and is used in refrigeration and on roads to settle dust or melt ice.

calcium hydroxide *n*. A soft white powder composed of calcium, hydrogen, and oxygen and having the formula $Ca(OH)_2$. It is made by adding water to lime and is used in making mortar and cement.

calcium oxide *n*. A white lumpy powder composed of calcium and oxygen and having the formula CaO; lime. It is obtained by heating limestone and used in making steel, glass, and insecticides and as an industrial alkali.

calculable (kăl′kyə-lə-bəl) *adj*. Capable of being calculated or estimated. —**cal′cu·la·bil′i·ty** *n*.

calculate (kăl′kyə-lāt′) *v*. **calculated, calculating, calculates** —*tr*. **1.** To find or determine (an answer or result) by using mathematics; reckon: *calculate the total cost of the trip*. **2.** To make an estimate of; evaluate: *calculate the possibilities of succeeding*. **3.** To make for a specific purpose; design: *His remarks were calculated to please the stockholders*. —*intr*. **1.** To perform a mathematical process, such as addition; figure. **2.** *Informal* To count, depend, or rely: *We are calculating on your help*.

calculated (kăl′kyə-lā′tĭd) *adj*. **1.** Carefully estimated in advance: *a calculated risk*. **2.** Made or planned to accomplish a specific purpose: *a smile calculated to win favor*. **3.** Determined by mathematical calculation.

calculating (kăl′kyə-lā′tĭng) *adj*. **1.** Used in or for performing calculation: *a calculating machine*. **2.** Shrewd; crafty: *the calculating defense of an experienced attorney*. **3.** Selfish; scheming: *a cold and calculating criminal*.

calculation (kăl′kyə-lā′shən) *n*. **1.** The act, process, or result of calculating: *It took a long time to do the calculations for the tax return*. **2.** Careful thinking or planning: *They won the game by clever calculation*.

calculator (kăl′kyə-lā′tər) *n*. **1.** A person who calculates. **2.** An electronic or mechanical device that performs mathematical calculations.

calculus (kăl′kyə-ləs) *n*., *pl*. **calculi** (kăl′kyə-lī′) or **calculuses 1.** An abnormal hard mass, usually of mineral salts, that forms in the body and is often found in the urinary bladder, gallbladder, or kidney. **2.** The branch of mathematics that extends the use of algebra to problems that involve rates of change in quantities.

caldera (kăl-dâr′ə or kăl-dâr′ə) *n*. A large crater formed by volcanic explosion or by collapse of a volcanic cone.

calendar (kăl′ən-dər) *n*. **1.** A chart showing the months, weeks, and days of a certain year. **2.** Any of various systems of reckoning time in which the beginning, length, and divisions of a year are defined, sometimes along with multiyear cycles: *the Aztec calendar*. **3.** A list of dates, as of events or things to be done, arranged in order of time of occurrence: *a court calendar*.

calf¹ (kăf) *n*., *pl*. **calves** (kăvz) **1.** A young cow or bull. **2.** One of the young of certain other mammals, such as a moose, elephant, or whale. **3.** A type of leather made from the hide of a calf; calfskin.

calf² (kăf) *n*., *pl*. **calves** (kăvz) The muscular back part of the human leg between the knee and ankle.

WORD HISTORY Calf¹ comes from Middle English *calf*, which comes from Old English *cælf, cealf*. **Calf²** comes from Middle English *calf*, which comes from Old Norse *kālfi.* The basic meaning of both forms of *calf* has remained unchanged through this development.

calfskin (kăf′skĭn′) *n.* The hide of a calf or leather made from it.

caliber (kăl′ə-bər) *n.* **1a.** The diameter of the inside of a tube. **b.** The inside diameter or bore of a firearm, usually expressed in decimal fractions. **2.** The diameter of a bullet or other projectile intended for a firearm: *a .45-caliber bullet.* **3.** Degree of worth; quality: *A judge should be a citizen of high caliber.*

calibrate (kăl′ə-brāt′) *tr.v.* **calibrated, calibrating, calibrates** **1.** To check, adjust, or standardize (a measuring instrument), usually by comparing with an accepted model: *calibrate an oven thermometer.* **2.** To determine the caliber of (a tube). —**cal′i·bra′tion** *n.*

calico (kăl′ĭ-kō′) *n., pl.* **calicoes** or **calicos** **1.** A cotton cloth with a brightly colored or closely printed pattern. **2.** An animal having a white coat with patches of different colors, often reddish-orange and black.

californium (kăl′ə-fôr′nē-əm) *n.* *Symbol* **Cf** A radioactive element that has been artificially produced by scientists. The half-lives of its isotopes range from 21 milliseconds to 898 years. Atomic number 98. See **Periodic Table.**

caliper (kăl′ə-pər) *n.* **1.** often **calipers** An instrument having two hinged legs that can be adjusted to measure diameter, thickness, or the distance between two points, as on a map or scale. **2.** The assembly housing or applying brake pads, as in a disc brake or on a bicycle.

caliph (kā′lĭf or kăl′ĭf) *n.* A leader of an Islamic nation, by tradition always male.

caliphate (kā′lĭ-fāt′ or kăl′ĭ-fāt′) *n.* The office or jurisdiction of a caliph.

calisthenics (kăl′ĭs-thĕn′ĭks) *n.* **1.** *(used with a plural verb)* Gymnastic exercises usually done without special equipment to develop muscular strength and general health. **2.** *(used with a singular verb)* The practice of such exercises. —**cal′is·then′ic** *adj.*

calk (kôk) *n.* A pointed piece of metal on the bottom of a horseshoe, designed to prevent slipping.

call (kôl) *v.* **called, calling, calls** —*tr.* **1.** To say in a loud voice; announce: *call the dog; call directions in a square dance.* **2.** To send for; summon: *call the fire department; call the guests in to dinner.* **3.** To summon to a particular career or pursuit: *felt he was called to the priesthood.* **4.** To order or invite to assemble; convoke: *call a meeting.* **5.** To bring into being, effect, or action, as by giving an order: *call an end to the trade agreements.* **6a.** To give a name to; name: *What did they call the baby?* **b.** To describe as; designate: *We call her the athlete of the family.* **7.** To estimate as being; regard as; consider: *I would call him a great writer.* **8a.** To speak with or attempt to speak with (someone) by telephone: *call a friend and chat.* **b.** To dial (a telephone number). **9.** To halt or postpone; suspend: *call a game on account of rain.* **10.** To predict accurately: *The reporter called the outcome of the election.* **11.** To demand payment of: *The bank called the loan.* **12.** In baseball, to indicate a decision in regard to (a pitch, ball, or player): *The umpire called him safe.* **13.** To choose or select (plays to be made), as in football. **14.** In poker, to equal the bet of (the preceding bettor). —*intr.* **1.** To attract attention by shouting: *call until help comes.* **2.** To utter a characteristic cry: *pheasants calling to each other.* **3.** To telephone someone: *You've already*

called several times. **4.** To pay a short visit: *We called to pay our respects.* **5.** In poker, to place a bet equal to the bet of the preceding bettor. ❖ *n.* **1.** A shout or loud cry: *A frightened call came from the woods.* **2a.** The typical cry of an animal, especially a bird: *the call of the blue jay.* **b.** An instrument or sound made to imitate such a cry, used as a lure: *a duck call used by hunters.* **c.** A word habitually used as a signal or direction: *Square dancing calls can be hard to follow.* **3.** A signal, such as one made by a horn or bell: *a bugle call to meals.* **4.** The act or an instance of communicating or trying to communicate by telephone: *gave his friend a call.* **5.** A short visit: *a friendly call on new neighbors.* **6a.** A strong urge or feeling: *felt she had a call to become a teacher.* **b.** Attraction or appeal; fascination: *the call of camping in the wilderness.* **7.** Need, reason, or cause: *There was no call to be unpleasant.* **8a.** Demand, as for a certain product: *There isn't much call for inkstands today.* **b.** A claim on one's time: *the call of duty.* **9.** In sports, a decision made by an official. ❖ **call back** **1.** To telephone in return. **2.** To summon (a person) to return: *The company called us back to work.* **call for** **1.** To go and get: *The taxi will call for you at eight.* **2.** To require; demand: *The recipe calls for half a cup of flour.* **call in** **1.** To summon for help or consultation: *call in a specialist.* **2.** To take out of circulation: *call in old dollar bills.* **call into question** To raise doubt about: *The whole story is called into question by the lack of evidence.* **call off** **1.** To cancel: *call off a game.* **2.** To restrain or recall: *Call off your dogs!* **call on** **1.** To ask or order (someone) to speak: *The professor called on the student in the back row.* **2.** To appeal to (someone) to do something: *The president called on each of us to contribute to the welfare of the country.* **call out** **1.** To say in a loud voice; yell: *The rescuers called out for more people to help.* **2.** To cause to assemble; summon: *The governor called out the National Guard after the earthquake struck.* **call to account** To demand an explanation from: *The employee was called to account for being late.* **call to mind** To cause one to think of (something), especially by being similar: *The movie calls to mind other adventure stories.* **call up** To summon into military service: *Reserve units are being called up for active duty.* **on call** Available when summoned; ready: *a nurse on call.*

calla lily (kăl′ə) *n.* Any of several southern African plants that are cultivated for their showy white, yellow, pink, or purple flowers.

call box *n.* A telephone by the side of a highway or road for the use of motorists to report an emergency.

caller (kô′lər) *n.* **1.** A person who calls, especially by paying a short visit or making a telephone call: *Several callers came by to see the new baby.* **2.** A person who calls out numbers or directions, as in bingo or square dancing.

caller ID *n.* A telephone service that displays an incoming caller's name and telephone number.

calligraphy (kə-lĭg′rə-fē) *n.* **1.** The art of fine handwriting. **2.** Handwriting. —**cal·lig′ra·pher** *n.*

calling (kô′lĭng) *n.* **1.** An inner urge or strong impulse, especially one that is believed to be divinely inspired: *felt a calling to become a priest.* **2.** An occupation, profession, or career: *Writing poetry is her calling.*

calling card *n.* **1.** A phone card. **2.** A small engraved card that has a person's full name printed on it.

calliope (kə-lī′ə-pē′ or kăl′ē-ōp′) *n.* A musical instrument having a keyboard that controls a set of steam whistles, used mostly at carnivals and circuses.

Calliope (kə-lī′ə-pē′) *n*. In Greek mythology, the Muse of epic poetry.

call letters *pl.n.* The letters that identify a radio or television station.

call number *n*. A number used in libraries to classify a book and indicate its location on the shelves.

callosity (kə-lŏs′ĭ-tē) *n., pl.* **callosities 1.** A hard growth or mass, such as a callus. **2.** Lack of feeling; hardheartedness.

callous (kăl′əs) *adj.* **1.** Having calluses: *the callous hands of a logger.* **2.** Unfeeling; unsympathetic. —**cal′lous·ly** *adv.*

callow (kăl′ō) *adj.* Not completely developed; immature; inexperienced: *a callow youngster.* —**cal′low·ly** *adv.* —**cal′low·ness** *n.*

call-up (kôl′ŭp′) *n*. An order to report for military service.

callus (kăl′əs) *n., pl.* **calluses** An area of the skin that has become hardened and thick, usually because of prolonged pressure or rubbing.

call waiting *n*. A telephone service that alerts someone using the phone that another call is incoming and allows switching between calls.

calm (käm) *adj.* **calmer, calmest 1.** Peacefully quiet; not excited; composed: *We remained calm throughout the storm.* **2.** Nearly motionless; undisturbed; still: *the calm lake waters.* ❖ *n.* **1.** A condition of being peaceful; tranquility; serenity: *Her calm was broken by the shouts in the street.* **2.** Lack of motion; stillness: *a calm in the air just before the storm hit.* ❖ *tr. & intr.v.* **calmed, calming, calms** To make or become calm or quiet: *calm a crying baby; calm down after an argument.* —**calm′ly** *adv.* —**calm′ness** *n.*

✦ **SYNONYMS calm, peaceful, placid, serene, tranquil** *adj.*

calomel (kăl′ə-mĕl′ *or* kăl′ə-məl) *n*. A white tasteless compound of mercury and chlorine, formerly used as a purgative and insecticide.

caloric (kə-lôr′ĭk) *adj.* Relating to heat or calories.

calorie (kăl′ə-rē) *n*. **1.** A unit of energy equal to the amount of heat needed to raise the temperature of one gram of water one degree Celsius. **2.** A unit that is used to measure the energy supplied by food, equal to the amount of heat needed to raise the temperature of 1,000 grams of water one degree Celsius; a kilocalorie.

calorific (kăl′ə-rĭf′ĭk) *adj.* Relating to or generating heat.

calorimeter (kăl′ə-rĭm′ĭ-tər) *n*. An apparatus for measuring the quantity of heat given off by or present in a body, such as the specific heat of different substances or the heat generated by a chemical reaction.

calumet (kăl′yə-mĕt′ *or* kăl′yə-mĕt′) *n*. A sacred or ceremonial pipe used by certain Native American peoples.

calumniate (kə-lŭm′nē-āt′) *tr.v.* **calumniated, calumniating, calumniates** To make false statements about; slander. —**ca·lum′ni·a′tion** *n.* —**ca·lum′ni·a′tor** *n.*

calumnious (kə-lŭm′nē-əs) *adj.* Containing or implying calumny; slanderous: *a calumnious attack.*

calumny (kăl′əm-nē) *n., pl.* **calumnies 1.** A false statement made to injure another person's reputation: *calumnies springing from jealousy.* **2.** The making of such statements; slander.

calve (kăv) *intr.v.* **calved, calving, calves 1.** To give birth to a calf. **2.** To break and drop off a large mass of ice: *Glaciers calving into the sea.*

calves (kăvz) *n*. **1.** Plural of **calf**[1]. **2.** Plural of **calf**[2].

Calvinism (kăl′vĭ-nĭz′əm) *n*. The Protestant doctrines

of John Calvin, a French-born Swiss theologian (1509–1564), emphasizing God's omnipotence and the predestination of souls to heaven and hell. —**Cal′vin·ist** *n. & adj.* —**Cal′vin·is′tic** *adj.*

Calypso or **calypso** (kə-lĭp′sō) *n*. A type of music that originated on the Caribbean island of Trinidad, characterized by improvised lyrics about humorous or timely subjects.

calyx (kā′lĭks *or* kăl′ĭks) *n., pl.* **calyxes** or **calyces** (kā′lĭ-sēz′ *or* kăl′ĭ-sēz′) The sepals of a flower considered as a group.

calzone (kăl-zō′nē *or* kăl-zōn′) *n*. A baked or fried turnover filled with vegetables, meat, or cheese.

cam (kăm) *n*. A wheel with a projecting part that is attached to a rotating shaft and changes a regular circular motion into a back-and-forth motion in a connected part.

camaraderie (kä′mə-rä′də-rē *or* kăm′rä′də-rē) *n*. Goodwill and warm feeling between or among friends; comradeship.

camber (kăm′bər) *n*. A slightly arched surface, as of a road or a ship's deck.

cambium (kăm′bē-əm) *n., pl.* **cambiums** or **cambia** (kăm′bē-ə) A tissue in the stems and roots of many seed-bearing plants that consists of cells that divide to form new layers of tissue toward the inside and toward the outside of the plant.

Cambrian (kăm′brē-ən *or* kām′brē-ən) *n*. The first period of the Paleozoic Era, from about 542 to 488 million years ago. During the Cambrian, there was a great increase in the numbers and kinds of invertebrate marine animals. —**Cam′bri·an** *adj.*

cambric (kăm′brĭk) *n*. A fine white linen or cotton cloth.

cambric tea *n*. A hot drink made from milk, sugar, water, and usually a small amount of tea.

camcorder (kăm′kôr′dər) *n*. A camera that records video on a storage device.

came (kām) *v*. Past tense of **come**.

camel (kăm′əl) *n*. Either of two cud-chewing mammals, the Bactrian camel or the dromedary, that have a humped back and long neck and are widely used in northern Africa, the Middle East, and Asia to carry loads and as a source of wool, milk, and meat.

camelhair (kăm′əl-hâr′) also **camel's hair** (kăm′əlz) *n*. **1.** The soft fine hair of a camel or a substitute for it. **2.** A soft, heavy, usually light tan cloth made chiefly of the hair of a camel.

camellia (kə-mēl′yə) *n*. **1.** Any of several shrubs or small trees having glossy evergreen leaves and red, pink, or white roselike flowers. **2.** The flower of such a plant.

Camelot (kăm′ə-lŏt′) *n*. In Arthurian legend, the site of King Arthur's court.

Camembert (kăm′əm-bâr′) *n*. A creamy rich cheese that softens on the inside as it matures.

cameo (kăm′ē-ō′) *n., pl.* **cameos 1.** A gem, shell, or medallion usually having a carved design that projects from a background of a different color. **2.** A brief appearance of a prominent actor, as in a movie.

camera (kăm′ər-ə *or* kăm′rə) *n*. A usually portable device containing a light-sensitive surface that records images through a lens.

cameraman (kăm′ər-ə-măn′ *or* kăm′rə-măn′) *n*. A man who operates a television or movie camera.

cameraperson (kăm′ər-ə-pûr′sən *or* kăm′rə-pûr′sən) *n*. A person who operates a television or movie camera.

camerawoman (kăm′ər-ə-wŏom′ən or kăm′rə-wŏom′-ən) *n.* A woman who operates a television or movie camera.

cami (kăm′ē) *n.*, *pl.* **camis** A camisole.

camisole (kăm′ĭ-sōl′) *n.* A woman's short, sleeveless undergarment, often having thin shoulder straps.

camouflage (kăm′ə-fläzh′ or kăm′ə-fläj′) *n.* **1.** A method of concealing military troops or equipment by making them appear to be part of the natural surroundings. **2.** A shape or coloring that conceals: *An alligator's camouflage makes it look like a log floating in the water.* **3a.** Cloth or other material used for camouflage: *planes covered with camouflage.* **b.** Fabric or clothing having a pattern often used for camouflage, usually with green, brown, and tan splotches: *hunters wearing camouflage.* ❖ *tr.v.* **camouflaged, camouflaging, camouflages** To conceal or hide by camouflage.

camp (kămp) *n.* **1.** A place where a group of people, such as vacationers, miners, or soldiers, live temporarily in tents, cabins, or other rough shelters. **2.** A cabin or shelter or group of such buildings: *They have a camp on a lake.* **3.** A place in the country that offers recreational activities or instruction, as for children on vacation. ❖ *intr.v.* **camped, camping, camps 1.** To make or set up a camp: *We camped next to the river.* **2.** To live in or as if in a camp: *Our friends camped for a month in the Rocky Mountains.*

campaign (kăm-pān′) *n.* **1.** A series of military operations undertaken to achieve an important objective during a war: *Grant's campaign secured the Mississippi River for the Union.* **2.** Organized activity to attain a political, social, or commercial goal: *an advertising campaign.* ❖ *intr.v.* **campaigned, campaigning, campaigns** To engage in a campaign: *The candidates campaigned on television.* —**cam·paign′er** *n.*

campanile (kăm′pə-nē′lē) *n.* A bell tower, especially one near but not attached to a church or other building.

camper (kăm′pər) *n.* **1.** A person who camps outdoors. **2.** A boy or girl who attends a summer camp. **3.** A motor vehicle having a space equipped as a dwelling place for camping on long trips.

campfire (kămp′fîr′) *n.* An outdoor fire in a camp, used for warmth or cooking.

campground (kămp′ground′) *n.* An area used for setting up a camp or holding a camp meeting.

camphor (kăm′fər) *n.* A white crystalline compound that is obtained from plants or made from turpentine and is used as an insect repellent, in making plastics, and as an external preparation to relieve mild pain and itching.

camp meeting *n.* An evangelistic gathering held in a tent or outdoors and often lasting a number of days.

campsite (kămp′sīt′) *n.* An area used for camping.

campus (kăm′pəs) *n.*, *pl.* **campuses** The grounds and buildings of a school, college, university, business, or hospital.

camshaft (kăm′shăft′) *n.* A shaft fitted with one or more cams, as in a gasoline engine.

can¹ (kăn; kən *when unstressed*) *aux.v.* Past tense **could** (kŏŏd) **1.** To know how to: *I can speak English, French, and Arabic.* **2.** To be able to: *I can skate backward.* **3.** To possess the right or power to: *The president can veto bills passed by Congress.* **4.** To have permission to; be allowed to: *You can borrow my car if you like.*

can² (kăn) *n.* **1a.** An airtight metal container in which

food and beverages are preserved: *Put the empty cans in the trash.* **b.** The contents of such a container: *This chili recipe calls for a can of pinto beans and a can of kidney beans.* **2.** A usually cylindrical metal container: *a garbage can.* ❖ *tr.v.* **canned, canning, cans** To preserve (food) in a sealed container: *spent the morning canning beans.*

WORD HISTORY Can¹ comes from Old English *cunnan,* meaning "to know, know how." **Can²** comes from Old English *canne,* meaning "container."

Canaanite (kā′nə-nīt′) *n.* **1.** A member of a group of Semitic peoples inhabiting the land of Canaan in southwest Asia from late prehistoric times, including the Israelites and Phoenicians. **2.** In the Bible, a member of any of these peoples other than the Israelites. —**Ca′naan·ite′** *adj.*

Canada Day *n.* July 1, observed in Canada to commemorate the formation of the Dominion of Canada in 1867.

Canada goose or **Canadian goose** *n.* A North American wild goose having gray, black, and white feathers and a white patch on the throat and the sides of the face.

Canadian bacon *n.* Cured, rolled, and very lean bacon from the loin of a pig.

Canadian French *n.* The French language as spoken in Canada.

canal (kə-năl′) *n.* **1.** An artificial waterway used for irrigation, drainage, or navigation. **2.** A tube or duct in the body of an organism, as for the passage of liquid, air, food, or other matter: *the alimentary canal; the ear canal.*

canapé (kăn′ə-pā′ or kăn′ə-pē) *n.* A cracker or piece of bread with meat, cheese, or other food spread on top, served as an appetizer.

canard (kə-närd′) *n.* An unfounded or false, deliberately misleading story.

canary (kə-nâr′ē) *n.*, *pl.* **canaries** A small greenish to yellow finch that is originally from the Canary Islands and is popular as a pet.

canasta (kə-năs′tə) *n.* A card game for two to six players that uses two decks and is related to rummy.

cancan (kăn′kăn′) *n.* An exuberant dance that originated in France, performed by women and marked by high kicking.

cancel (kăn′səl) *v.* **canceled, canceling, cancels** also **cancelled, cancelling, cancels** —*tr.* **1.** To cross out with lines or other markings: *cancel items on a shopping list.* **2a.** To decide or announce that (an event) will not take place as scheduled: *cancel an appointment; cancel the performance.* **b.** To make invalid: *cancel a credit card.* **3.** To mark or perforate (a postage stamp, for example) to indicate that it may not be used again. **4.** To make up for; offset; balance: *Two opposing votes cancel each other out.* **5a.** To remove (a common factor) from the numerator and denominator of a fraction. **b.** To remove (a common term or factor) from both sides of an equation. —*intr.* To balance or offset each other: *Spending and saving often cancel out.*

cancellation (kăn′sə-lā′shən) *n.* **1.** The act or process of canceling. **2.** A mark made, as on a stamp or check, to indicate that it has been canceled.

cancer (kăn′sər) *n.* **1.** A disease in which cells of a body part become abnormal and multiply without limit, sometimes spreading to and damaging other tissues of the body. **2.** A tumor, especially a malignant one. **3.** A destructive spreading evil: *Poverty is a fearful social cancer.* —**can′cer·ous** *adj.*

Cancer *n.* **1.** A constellation in the Northern Hemisphere, traditionally pictured as a crab. **2.** The fourth sign of the zodiac in astrology.

candela (kăn-dĕl′ə) *n.* A unit used to measure the brightness of a source of light. See table at **measurement**.

candelabra (kăn′dl-ä′brə *or* kăn′dl-äb′rə) *n.* A candelabrum.

candelabrum (kăn′dl-ä′brəm *or* kăn′dl-äb′rəm) *n., pl.* **candelabra** (kăn′dl-ä′-brə *or* kăn′dl-äb′rə) *or* **candelabrums** A large decorative candlestick with several arms or branches for holding candles.

candid (kăn′dĭd) *adj.* **1.** Direct and frank; straightforward: *a candid opinion.* **2.** Free from prejudice; impartial: *a candid judgment.* **3.** Not posed or rehearsed: *a candid photograph.* —**can′did·ly** *adv.* —**can′did·ness** *n.*

candidacy (kăn′dĭ-də-sē) *n., pl.* **candidacies** The fact or condition of being a candidate.

candidate (kăn′dĭ-dāt′ *or* kăn′dĭ-dĭt) *n.* **1.** A person who seeks or is nominated for an office, prize, or honor. **2.** A student who has nearly completed the requirements for a degree: *a master's degree candidate.*

candied (kăn′dēd) *adj.* Cooked in or coated with a glaze of sugar: *candied sweet potatoes; candied fruit.*

candle (kăn′dl) *n.* **1.** A solid stick of wax, tallow, or other fatty substance with a wick inside that is lit and burned to provide light. **2.** An obsolete unit of luminous intensity, replaced by the candela. ❖ *tr.v.* **candled, candling, candles** To examine (an egg) for freshness by holding it in front of a bright light.

candlelight (kăn′dl-līt′) *n.* **1.** The light given off by a candle. **2.** Dusk; twilight.

Candlemas (kăn′dl-məs) *n.* February 2, celebrated in some Christian churches to commemorate the presentation of the infant Jesus in the Temple and the ritual purification of his mother Mary.

candlepower (kăn′dl-pou′ər) *n.* The brightness or intensity of a source of light as expressed in candelas.

candlesnuffer (kăn′dl-snŭf′ər) *n.* An instrument with a small cup and often a long slender handle, used to extinguish the flame of a candle.

candlestick (kăn′dl-stĭk′) *n.* A usually tall holder with a cup or spike for a candle.

candlewick (kăn′dl-wĭk′) *n.* The wick of a candle.

can-do (kăn′dōō′) *adj.* Marked by willingness to tackle a job and confidence in the ability to finish it: *the can-do spirit of volunteers.*

candor (kăn′dər) *n.* **1.** The quality of saying freely what one thinks; openness; frankness: *criticize in all candor without regard to feelings.* **2.** Freedom from prejudice; fairness: *judge a matter in complete candor.*

candy (kăn′dē) *n., pl.* **candies** **1.** A sweet food made with sugar and often combined with fruit or nuts. **2.** A single piece of this food. ❖ *tr.v.* **candied, candying, candies** To cook, preserve, or coat with sugar or syrup: *candied the apples.*

candy cane *n.* A stick of peppermint candy, often white with red stripes, having a curved top like a walking cane.

candy striper (strī′pər) *n.* A volunteer worker in a hospital.

candytuft (kăn′dē-tŭft′) *n.* Any of several garden plants that have clusters of white, red, or light purple flowers.

cane (kān) *n.* **1.** A stick used as an aid in walking. **2a.** A thin hollow or woody plant stem that usually has joints and is easily bent. **b.** A plant, such as bamboo or sugar cane, having such stems. **c.** Strips of such stems woven together to make chair seats or other objects. **3.** A rod used in flogging. ❖ *tr.v.* **caned, caning, canes** **1.** To beat or flog with a cane. **2.** To make or repair (furniture, for example) with cane.

canebrake (kān′brāk′) *n.* A dense growth of cane plants.

cane sugar *n.* Sugar obtained from sugar cane.

canine (kā′nīn) *adj.* Relating to or resembling a dog or a doglike mammal, such as a wolf, fox, or coyote. ❖ *n.* **1.** A dog or a doglike mammal. **2.** One of the four pointed teeth next to the incisors; a cuspid.

canister (kăn′ĭ-stər) *n.* A usually cylindrical container used to hold dry foods such as flour and coffee or other materials, such as gas.

canker (kăng′kər) *n.* A sore similar to an ulcer on the lips or in the mouth.

cankerous (kăng′kər-əs) *adj.* **1.** Marked by or affected with a canker; ulcerous: *cankerous gums.* **2.** Tending to cause a canker: *a cankerous irritant.*

canker sore *n.* A canker.

cankerworm (kăng′kər-wûrm′) *n.* A moth caterpillar that damages trees by feeding on the leaves.

canna (kăn′ə) *n.* Any of various plants native to the tropics, having large leaves and showy red or yellow flowers.

cannabis (kăn′ə-bĭs) *n.* **1.** The hemp plant. **2.** The dried leaves or flowers of the hemp plant; marijuana.

canned (kănd) *adj.* **1.** Preserved and sealed in an airtight can or jar: *canned vegetables.* **2.** *Informal* Recorded or taped: *canned music.*

cannery (kăn′ə-rē) *n., pl.* **canneries** A factory where fish, fruit, vegetables, or other foods are canned.

cannibal (kăn′ə-bəl) *n.* **1.** A person who eats the flesh of other humans. **2.** An animal that feeds on others of its own kind.

cannibalism (kăn′ə-bə-lĭz′əm) *n.* The practices of a cannibal. —**can′ni·bal·is′tic** *adj.*

cannibalize (kăn′ə-bə-līz′) *tr.v.* **cannibalized, cannibalizing, cannibalizes** **1.** To remove useful parts from (a machine or equipment) to use in the repair of other equipment: *cannibalize an old truck for its motor.* **2.** To practice cannibalism on.

cannoli (kə-nō′lē) *n., pl.* **cannolis** A pastry roll with a creamy sweet filling.

cannon (kăn′ən) *n., pl.* **cannon** *or* **cannons** A large gun that is mounted on wheels or on a fixed base and fires heavy projectiles.

cannonade (kăn′ə-nād′) *tr. & intr.v.* **cannonaded, cannonading, cannonades** To assault or bombard with heavy artillery fire. ❖ *n.* A long heavy artillery assault or bombardment.

cannonball also **cannon ball** (kăn′ən-bôl′) *n.* **1.** An iron or steel ball fired from a cannon. **2.** A jump into water made with the arms grasping the knees, usually intended to make a big splash.

cannot (kăn′ŏt *or* kə-nŏt′ *or* kă-nŏt′) *aux.v.* The negative form of **can**[1].

canny (kăn′ē) *adj.* **cannier, canniest** Careful and shrewd in one's actions and dealings: *a canny investor.* —**can′ni·ly** *adv.* —**can′ni·ness** *n.*

canoe (kə-nōō′) *n.* A light, open, narrow boat that has pointed ends and is propelled by paddles. ❖ *intr.v.* **canoed, canoeing, canoes** To paddle or travel in a canoe. —**ca·noe′ist** *n.*

canola oil (kə-nō′lə) *n.* An oil made from the seeds of certain varieties of the rape plant, used in cooking and in industry as a lubricant.

canon¹ (kăn**′**ən) *n.* **1.** A law or code of laws enacted by a church. **2.** A principle or standard: *the canons of good behavior.* **3.** The books of the Bible accepted by a Christian church as authentic. **4.** A group of literary works generally accepted as important in a field: *the canon of Latin American literature.* **5.** A musical composition or passage in which a melody is repeated by different, overlapping voices.

canon² (kăn**′**ən) *n.* **1.** A cleric serving in a cathedral or collegiate church. **2.** A member of certain religious communities living according to established rules.

WORD HISTORY Although both **canon¹** and **canon²** both ultimately come from Greek *kanōn,* these two words came into Modern English along close but separate paths. In Middle English, they had the same meaning as in Modern English (although **canon²** was spelled *canoun*). **Canon¹** came to Middle English via Latin *canōn,* meaning "rule." **Canon²** came to Middle English via Late Latin *canōnicus,* meaning "one living under a rule."

canonical (kə-nŏn**′**ĭ-kəl) also **canonic** (kə-nŏn**′**ĭk) *adj.* **1.** Relating to or required by canon law. **2.** Relating to or appearing in the biblical canon. **3.** Relating to a literary canon: *canonical works of Romantic poetry.* **4.** Conforming to well-established rules or patterns.

canonize (kăn**′**ə-nīz′) *tr.v.* **canonized, canonizing, canonizes** To declare (a dead person) to be a saint. —**can′-on·i·za′tion** (kăn′ə-nĭ-zā′shən) *n.*

canon law *n.* The body of laws governing matters of faith and practice in a religious denomination, especially a Christian church.

canopy (kăn**′**ə-pē) *n., pl.* **canopies 1.** A covering, usually of cloth, hung above a bed or throne or supported by poles above important people or sacred objects. **2.** The uppermost layer in a forest, formed by the crowns of the trees. **3.** Any of various similar overarching coverings: *a canopy of roses; the canopy of a parachute.* ❖ *tr.v.* **canopied, canopying, canopies** To cover with a canopy.

canst (kănst) *aux.v. Archaic* A second person singular present tense of **can¹**.

cant¹ (kănt) *n.* **1.** A slant or slope: *The cant of the roof makes the rain run off.* **2a.** A push or motion that causes something to tilt to one side. **b.** The tilt resulting from such a push or motion. ❖ *v.* **canted, canting, cants** —*tr.* **1.** To give a slanted edge to; bevel. **2.** To cause to slant or tilt to one side: *A gust of wind canted the sailboat so that it capsized.* —*intr.* **1.** To tilt or slant to one side or turn over: *The sailboat's masts cant slightly as it sails.* **2.** To swing around: *The boat canted off toward the south.*

cant² (kănt) *n.* **1.** Insincere or trite talk, especially about moral or religious behavior: *hollow words that are mere cant.* **2.** The special vocabulary used by a certain group or class of people; jargon: *"Deadheading" is railroad cant for running without passengers or freight.*

WORD HISTORY Cant¹ comes from Middle English *cant,* meaning "side," which comes from Latin *canthus,* meaning "rim of a wheel, tire." **Cant²** comes Anglo-Norman *canter,* which comes from Latin *cantāre,* both of which mean "to sing."

can't (kănt) Contraction of *cannot.*

cantaloupe also **cantaloup** (kăn**′**tl-ōp′) *n.* A variety of melon having a rough rind and sweet orange flesh.

cantankerous (kăn-tăng**′**kər-əs) *adj.* Quarrelsome and ill-tempered; disagreeable: *a cantankerous manager who is difficult to work with.* —**can·tan′ker·ous·ness** *n.*

cantata (kən-tä**′**tə) *n.* A musical composition, often using a sacred text, containing recitatives, arias, and choruses.

canteen (kăn-tēn**′**) *n.* **1.** A container for carrying water or other liquid to drink. **2.** A store, restaurant, or recreational facility meant for the use of soldiers, especially on a military base. **3.** A place to get food or drinks in a school, factory, or camp.

canter (kăn**′**tər) *n.* A slow easy gallop. ❖ *intr. & tr.v.* **cantered, cantering, canters** To move or cause to move at a canter: *The horse and rider cantered down the road. She cantered her horse across the field.*

canticle (kăn**′**tĭ-kəl) *n.* A song or chant, especially a hymn whose words are taken from a biblical text other than the Book of Psalms.

cantilever (kăn**′**tl-ē′vər *or* kăn**′**tl-ĕv′ər) *n.* A projecting structure, such as a beam, that is supported only at one end and carries a load at the other end or along its length. ❖ *tr.v.* **cantilevered, cantilevering, cantilevers** To support by a cantilever.

cantilever bridge *n.* A bridge formed by two cantilevers each supported at one end by a pier and joined in the center by a connecting piece.

cantina (kăn-tē**′**nə) *n.* A bar serving primarily Mexican or Mexican-American food and drink.

cantle (kăn**′**tl) *n.* The raised part at the back of some saddles.

canto (kăn**′**tō) *n., pl.* **cantos** A principal division of a long poem.

canton (kăn**′**tən *or* kăn**′**tŏn′) *n.* A small division of a country, especially one of the states of Switzerland.

Cantonese (kăn**′**tə-nēz′ *or* kăn**′**tə-nēs′) *n., pl.* **Cantonese 1.** A native or inhabitant of Guangzhou (formerly Canton), China. **2.** The variety of Chinese spoken in and around Guangzhou. —**Can′ton·ese′** *adj.*

cantonment (kăn-tōn**′**mənt *or* kăn-tŏn**′**mənt) *n.* **1.** A group of structures for housing soldiers, often on a temporary basis. **2.** A military installation in India.

cantor (kăn**′**tər) *n.* **1.** The official who leads the congregation in the musical part of a Jewish religious service. **2.** The person who leads a church choir or congregation in singing.

canvas (kăn**′**vəs) *n.* **1.** A heavy coarse cloth of cotton, hemp, or flax, used for making tents and sails. **2a.** A piece of canvas used for painting. **b.** An oil painting on canvas: *That artist has several canvases hanging in this museum.*

canvasback (kăn**′**vəs-băk′) *n.* A North American duck having a reddish head and neck and a whitish back in the male.

canvass (kăn**′**vəs) *v.* **canvassed, canvassing, canvasses** —*tr.* **1.** To visit (a person or region) asking for votes, opinions, sales, or contributions. **2.** To examine or discuss thoroughly: *canvass the newspapers for a job; canvass ideas in a meeting.* —*intr.* To go about a region asking for votes, sales, opinions, or contributions: *canvassed for votes.* ❖ *n.* **1.** The act of canvassing. **2.** A thorough examination or discussion. —**can′vass·er** *n.*

canyon (kăn**′**yən) *n.* A deep narrow valley with steep cliff walls, cut into the earth by running water; a gorge.

caoutchouc (kou**′**chŏŏk′ *or* kou**′**chōŏk′) *n.* Crude natural rubber.

cap¹ (kăp) *n.* **1a.** A usually soft, close-fitting head covering, either having no brim or with a visor. **b.** A special covering for the head worn to show rank, occupation, or membership in a group: *a soldier's cap.* **2a.** The top or highest part: *the cap of the roof.* **b.** A layer or covering: *a mountain with a cap of snow.* **c.** A protective cover or seal: *a bottle cap; a cap on a tooth.* **d.** A limit or restraint: *a cap on government spending.* **3.** The feathers or fur on top of an animal's head, especially when of a distinctive color: *a bird with a black cap.* **4.** A truck cap. **5.** The umbrella-shaped or rounded cap of a mushroom, where the spores are produced. **6a.** A percussion cap. **b.** A small explosive charge enclosed in paper for use in a toy gun. ❖ *tr.v.* **capped, capping, caps 1.** To cover, protect, or seal with a cap: *cap a bottle; hills capped with snow.* **2.** To outdo; excel: *Each joke capped the one before.* ◆ **cap in hand** Humbly or submissively.

cap² (kăp) *n.* A capital letter.

cap. An abbreviation of: **1.** capacity. **2.** capital. **3.** capital letter.

capability (kā′pə-bĭl′ĭ-tē) *n., pl.* **capabilities 1.** The quality of being capable; ability: *prove one's capability for the job.* **2.** often **capabilities** Potential ability: *live up to one's capabilities.* **3.** The capacity to be used or developed for a specific purpose: *To become more energy-efficient we must make full use of our technological capability.*

capable (kā′pə-bəl) *adj.* **1.** Having capacity or ability; able; competent: *a capable teacher.* **2.** Having the tendency or disposition: *She's just not capable of saying such a thing.* **3.** Having qualities that permit an action to be performed: *a statement capable of several interpretations.* —**ca′pa·bly** *adv.*

capacious (kə-pā′shəs) *adj.* Capable of containing a large quantity; roomy: *a capacious dining room.* —**ca·pa′cious·ly** *adv.*

capacitance (kə-păs′ĭ-təns) *n.* The capacity of a device to collect and store electric charge. Capacitance is equal to the amount of stored charge divided by the electrical potential of the device.

capacitor (kə-păs′ĭ-tər) *n.* A device used in an electric circuit to store charge temporarily.

capacity (kə-păs′ĭ-tē) *n., pl.* **capacities 1.** The ability to hold, receive, or contain: *a can with a capacity of three quarts; a theater with a small seating capacity.* **2.** The maximum amount that can be contained: *a trunk filled to capacity.* **3.** The ability to perform or produce; capability: *a comedian's capacity to make people laugh.* **4.** The maximum amount that can be produced: *a machine operating at full capacity.* **5.** Mental ability: *a person's capacity for learning.* **6.** The position in which a person functions; a role: *in your capacity as sales manager.*

caparison (kə-păr′ĭ-sən) *n.* **1.** An ornamental covering for a horse or harness. **2.** Rich or fancy clothing; finery. ❖ *tr.v.* **caparisoned, caparisoning, caparisons 1.** To put a caparison on: *caparison a horse.* **2.** To dress in splendid clothes.

cape¹ (kāp) *n.* **1.** A sleeveless outer garment fastened at the throat and worn hanging loose over the shoulders. **2.** A brightly colored cloth used by a matador to maneuver the bull in a bullfight.

cape² (kāp) *n.* A point of land projecting into a body of water.

WORD HISTORY Cape¹ comes from Late Latin *cappa,* meaning "cloak." **Cape²** comes from Middle English *cap,* which comes from Latin *caput,* meaning "head."

caper¹ (kā′pər) *n.* **1.** A playful leap or hop: *the capers of*

a frisky pony. **2.** A prank: *Halloween capers.* **3.** *Slang* A criminal plot or act, especially one involving theft. ❖ *intr.v.* **capered, capering, capers** To jump about playfully; gambol: *The lambs capered about the meadow.*

caper² (kā′pər) *n.* **1.** A pickled flower bud of a spiny shrub of the Mediterranean region. Capers are used to flavor sauces and relishes. **2.** The shrub that bears such buds.

WORD HISTORY Caper¹ is an alteration of French *capriole,* meaning "a leap by a horse," which comes from Italian *capriola,* meaning "somersault," which comes from Latin *caper* meaning "goat." **Caper²** comes from Middle English *capar,* which comes from Greek *kapparis,* both referring to the same type of shrub as in Modern English.

capillarity (kăp′ə-lăr′ĭ-tē) *n.* Capillary action.

capillary (kăp′ə-lĕr′ē) *adj.* **1.** Relating to or resembling a hair; fine; slender. **2.** Having a very small inside diameter. **3.** Relating to the capillaries in the body. ❖ *n., pl.* **capillaries 1.** One of the tiny blood vessels that connect the smallest arteries to the smallest veins. **2.** A tube that has a very small inside diameter.

capillary action *n.* The tendency of the surface of a liquid to rise or fall where it is in contact with a solid, as in a capillary tube.

capillary attraction *n.* The force that causes a liquid to rise in a narrow tube or when in contact with a porous substance. It is the force that allows a paper towel to soak up a liquid or plants to draw up water from the ground.

capital¹ (kăp′ĭ-tl) *n.* **1.** A city that is the seat of a state or national government: *Every state has a capital.* **2.** Wealth in the form of money or property that has accumulated in a business and is often used to create more wealth. **3.** Assets or resources that can be used to accomplish something: *Does the president have the political capital to get the law passed?* **4.** A capital letter. ❖ *adj.* **1.** First and foremost; principal: *a decision of capital importance.* **2.** Excellent; first-rate: *a capital idea.* **3.** Punishable by or involving death: *a capital offense.* **4.** Relating to or involving wealth and its use in investment: *capital improvements in the plant site.* **5.** Relating to a seat of government: *a capital city.*

USAGE The word for a town or city that serves as a seat of government is **capital**: *Sacramento is the capital of California.* The term for the building in which a legislative assembly meets is **capitol**: *Daily tours of the capitol are offered.*

capital² (kăp′ĭ-tl) *n.* The top part of a pillar or column.

WORD HISTORY The spelling of both **capital¹** and **capital²** has not changed since Middle English, where the first meant "principal" and the second meant "the top of a pillar." Both forms ultimately come from Latin *caput,* meaning "head," but took slightly different paths from Latin to Modern English.

capital gain *n.* The profit made by selling an investment, such as a stock or piece of property.

capitalism (kăp′ĭ-tl-ĭz′əm) *n.* An economic system in which the means of production and distribution are privately owned by individuals or groups, and competition for business establishes the price of goods and services. The means of production include labor, land, factories, and services. The means of distribution include trains, trucks, and airlines.

capitalist (kăp′ĭ-tl-ĭst) *n.* **1a.** A person who invests capital in business, especially a large investor in an important business. **b.** A person of great wealth. **2.** A person who supports capitalism. ❖ *adj.* Relating to capitalism or capitalists: *a capitalist country.* —**cap′i·tal·is′tic** *adj.* —**cap′i·tal·is′ti·cal·ly** *adv.*

capitalize (kăp′ĭ-tl-īz′) *v.* **capitalized, capitalizing, capitalizes** —*tr.* **1.** To write or print with a capital letter or letters: *capitalize the title of a report.* **2.** To supply with capital or funds. —*intr.* To turn to advantage; profit by: *capitalize on an opponent's errors.* —**cap′i·tal·i·za′tion** (kăp′ĭ-tl-ĭ-zā′shən) *n.*

capital letter *n.* A letter, such as A or B, written or printed in a size larger than and often in a form differing from its corresponding lowercase letter.

capitally (kăp′ĭ-tl-ē) *adv.* In an excellent manner; admirably.

capital punishment *n.* The legal punishment of putting a person to death for certain crimes, such as murder or treason.

capital ship *n.* A warship of the largest class, such as a battleship or an aircraft carrier.

capital stock *n.* The total amount of stock issued by a corporation, including common and preferred stock.

capitol (kăp′ĭ-tl) *n.* **1. Capitol** The building in Washington, DC, where the Congress of the United States meets. **2.** A building in which a state legislature assembles.

capitulate (kə-pĭch′ə-lāt′) *intr.v.* **capitulated, capitulating, capitulates** To surrender under stated conditions; give in; yield: *The soldiers capitulated to the enemy after a long siege.*

capitulation (kə-pĭch′ə-lā′shən) *n.* **1.** The act of capitulating: *capitulation in the face of defeat.* **2.** A statement of the main points of a topic; an outline.

caplet (kăp′lĭt) *n.* A tablet of medicine coated to make it easy to swallow.

capon (kā′pŏn′ *or* kā′pən) *n.* A male chicken that has been castrated when young to improve the quality of its flesh for food.

cappuccino (kăp′ə-chē′nō) *n., pl.* **cappuccinos** A drink made with espresso coffee and steamed milk.

caprice (kə-prēs′) *n.* An impulsive change of mind; a whim: *the caprices of a vain and immature person.*

capricious (kə-prĭsh′əs *or* kə-prē′shəs) *adj.* Subject to sudden unpredictable changes: *a capricious child; capricious weather.* —**ca·pri′cious·ly** *adv.* —**ca·pri′cious·ness** *n.*

Capricorn (kăp′rĭ-kôrn′) *n.* **1.** A constellation in the Southern Hemisphere, traditionally pictured as a goat with the body of a fish. **2.** The tenth sign of the zodiac in astrology.

capri pants (kə-prē′) *pl.n.* Calf-length, usually tight-fitting pants, often having a slit on the outside of the leg bottoms.

capris (kə-prēz′) *pl.n.* Capri pants.

capsize (kăp′sīz′ *or* kăp-sīz′) *intr. & tr.v.* **capsized, capsizing, capsizes** To overturn or cause to overturn: *Our boat did not capsize in the storm. A huge wave capsized the ship.*

capstan (kăp′stən *or* kăp′stăn′) *n.* An apparatus used for lifting an anchor or other heavy weight, consisting of a vertical cylinder that is rotated manually or by machine and around which a cable is wound.

capstone (kăp′stōn′) *n.* **1.** The top stone of a structure or wall. **2.** A crowning achievement; a culmination: *The Pulitzer Prize was the capstone of her career.*

capsule (kăp′səl *or* kăp′sool) *n.* **1.** A small container, usu-

ally of gelatin or another soluble material, that contains a dose of a medicine to be taken by mouth. **2.** A covering, such as a membrane, that encloses an organ or another part of the body. **3.** An outer shell composed of carbohydrates that surrounds a microscopic organism, especially a bacterium. **4.** A seed case that opens when ripe. **5.** A space capsule. ❖ *adj.* Very brief; condensed: *a capsule description.* —**cap′su·lar** *adj.*

Capt. or **CAPT** An abbreviation of captain.

captain (kăp′tən) *n.* **1.** The leader of a group; chief: *the captain of the football team.* **2.** The person in command of a ship, aircraft, or spacecraft: *the captain of a tugboat; the captain of a 747 jet.* **3.** An officer in the US Army, Air Force, or Marine Corps ranking above a first lieutenant and below a major. **4.** An officer in the US Navy or Coast Guard ranking above a commander and below a rear admiral (lower half). **5.** An officer in a police or fire department ranking above a lieutenant. **6.** A person who is in the forefront of an enterprise; a leader: *a captain of industry.* ❖ *tr.v.* **captained, captaining, captains** To command or direct; lead: *captain a soccer team; captain a ship.*

captaincy (kăp′tən-sē) *n., pl.* **captaincies** The rank, authority, or skill of a captain.

captain's chair (kăp′tənz) *n.* A wooden chair having a low back with extensions that curve forward to provide armrests.

caption (kăp′shən) *n.* **1a.** A short explanation accompanying an illustration or photograph. **b.** Written dialogue placed at the bottom of television or movie frames. **2.** A heading, as of a legal document or a chapter of a book. ❖ *tr.v.* **captioned, captioning, captions** To furnish a caption for.

captious (kăp′shəs) *adj.* **1.** Inclined to criticize or find faults: *a captious movie critic.* **2.** Designed to confuse or ensnare, especially in an argument: *a captious question.* —**cap′tious·ly** *adv.* —**cap′tious·ness** *n.*

captivate (kăp′tə-vāt′) *tr.v.* **captivated, captivating, captivates** To fascinate or charm, as with wit, beauty, or intelligence: *The movie captivated audiences everywhere.* —**cap′ti·va′tion** *n.*

captive (kăp′tĭv) *n.* A person held under restraint or in bondage; a prisoner. ❖ *adj.* **1.** Held as a prisoner, as in war. **2.** Kept under restraint or control; confined: *saw captive tigers at the zoo.*

captivity (kăp-tĭv′ĭ-tē) *n., pl.* **captivities** The condition or period of being held captive: *Few wild animals thrive in captivity.*

captor (kăp′tər *or* kăp′tôr′) *n.* A person who takes or holds another as a captive.

capture (kăp′chər) *tr.v.* **captured, capturing, captures 1.** To get hold of, as by force or craft; seize: *Troops captured the rebel barricade.* **2.** To gain possession or control of: *The winner captured first prize.* **3.** To get or hold the interest of: *a mystery story that captures the imagination.* **4.** To hold or preserve in permanent form: *capture the sound of a howling wolf on tape.* ❖ *n.* **1.** The act of capturing or the process of being captured: *The capture of first prize was a triumph for our side.* **2.** Someone or something that has been captured: *The British warship was a great capture for the Colonial Navy.*

capuchin (kăp′yə-chĭn *or* kə-pyoo′chĭn) *n.* **1.** A member of an order of Franciscan friars that wear long pointed hoods. **2.** Any of several long-tailed monkeys of Central and South America that have a black or brown cap of hair on top of the head.

capybara (kăp′ə-bär′ə *or* kăp′ə-băr′ə) *n.* A short-tailed South American rodent that lives in or near water and may grow to a length of 4 feet (1.2 meters).

car (kär) *n.* **1.** An automobile. **2.** A vehicle, such as a railroad car, that moves on rails. **3.** The part of an elevator or hot-air balloon that holds passengers or cargo.

WORD HISTORY Our word **car** comes from the Latin word *carrus,* "heavy cart or wagon." Until the early 1800s, *car* meant "chariot" and was associated with dignity, solemnity, and splendor: *the sun rides in a celestial car in his orbit; the heroes of myth ride to battle in horse-drawn cars.* In about 1826 in the United States, *car* was used for a carriage pulled by a railway locomotive. *Motor car* first appears around 1895 for a horseless carriage. *Car* later came to mean any kind of wheeled vehicle and could be modified by words such as *passenger, freight,* and *street.*

---

carabao (kä′rə-bou′) *n., pl.* **carabaos** A water buffalo of the Philippine Islands.

carabiner (kăr′ə-bē′nər) *n.* An oblong metal ring with a hinged gate, used in activities such as mountaineering to secure ropes.

carafe (kə-răf′) *n.* **1.** A glass bottle for serving water or wine. **2.** A glass or metal container with a pouring spout, used in making or serving coffee.

caramel (kăr′ə-məl *or* kär′məl) *n.* **1.** A smooth chewy candy made with sugar, butter, and cream or milk. **2.** Sugar heated to a brown syrup and used for coloring and sweetening foods.

caramelize (kăr′ə-mə-līz′ *or* kär′mə-līz′) *v.* **caramelized, caramelizing, caramelizes** —*intr.* To be converted into a brown syrup: *Sugar caramelizes when heated.* —*tr.* To cook (food), often with sugar, until a brown syrup is formed: *caramelized the onions.* —**car′a·mel·i·za′tion** *n.*

carapace (kăr′ə-pās′) *n.* A shell or bony covering on the back part of an animal such as a turtle or a lobster.

carat (kăr′ət) *n.* **1.** A unit of weight for precious stones, equal to 200 milligrams or about ¹⁄₁₄₀ of an ounce. **2.** Variant of **karat.**

caravan (kăr′ə-văn′) *n.* **1.** A group of travelers journeying together for safety in hostile regions such as the desert. **2.** A group of vehicles or pack animals traveling together in single file: *a caravan of trucks.* **3.** *Chiefly British* A home on wheels, as a trailer or camper.

caravansary (kăr′ə-văn′sə-rē) also **caravanserai** (kăr′-ə-văn′sə-rī′) *n., pl.* **caravansaries** also **caravanserais** An inn with a large courtyard for the accommodation of caravans in central and western Asia.

caravel (kăr′ə-věl′) *n.* A small light sailing ship used by the Spanish and Portuguese in the 1400s and 1500s.

caraway (kăr′ə-wā′) *n.* A plant native to Eurasia, having strong-tasting crescent-shaped seeds used as a flavoring in baking and cooking.

carbide (kär′bīd′) *n.* A chemical compound, especially calcium carbide, consisting of carbon and a metal.

carbine (kär′bēn *or* kär′bīn′) *n.* A light rifle with a short barrel.

carbohydrate (kär′bō-hī′drāt′) *n.* Any of a large class of organic compounds consisting of only carbon, hydrogen, and oxygen and serving as a major source of energy for all living things. Carbohydrates are produced chiefly through the process of photosynthesis. Sugars, starches, and cellulose are carbohydrates.

carbolated (kär′bə-lā′tĭd) *adj.* Containing or treated with carbolic acid.

carbolic acid (kär-bŏl′ĭk) *n.* Phenol.

car bomb *n.* An explosive device that is placed in a motor vehicle and detonated in order to kill people or destroy nearby property, especially as an act of terrorism.

carbon (kär′bən) *n.* **1.** *Symbol* **C** A nonmetallic element that occurs in all organic compounds and many inorganic compounds, and can be found in all living things. Diamonds and graphite are pure carbon in the form of crystals; coal and charcoal are mostly carbon in uncrystallized form. Atomic number 6. See **Periodic Table. 2.** A gas containing carbon, such as carbon dioxide, or a collection of such gases, especially when considered as a contributor to the greenhouse effect: *equipment for measuring the carbon produced by power plants.* —**car′-bo·na′ceous** (kär′bə-nā′shəs), **car·bon′ic** (kär-bŏn′ĭk) *adj.*

carbon-12 (kär′bən-twĕlv′) *n.* The most common isotope of carbon, used as the standard for determining atomic weights.

carbon-14 (kär′bən-fôr-tēn′) *n.* A radioactive isotope of carbon that has an atomic mass of 14 and that occurs in all objects that contain carbon, notably animal and plant matter. Because the half-life of carbon-14 is 5,730 years, scientists can figure the age of archaeological materials and geologic formations that contain organic matter using radiocarbon dating.

carbonate (kär′bə-nāt′) *tr.v.* **carbonated, carbonating, carbonates** To add carbon dioxide gas to (a beverage) so that bubbles are produced upon release from a container: *This device carbonates tap water.* ❖ *n.* (kär′bə-nāt′ *or* kär′bə-nĭt) A salt or ester of carbonic acid. —**car′bon·a′-tion** *n.* —**car′bon·a′tor** *n.*

carbonated water (kär′bə-nā′tĭd) *n.* Water that has been charged with carbon dioxide under pressure, used in various drinks and refreshments.

carbon copy *n.* **1a.** A duplicate of something written or typed, made by using carbon paper or a photocopier. **b.** A copy of an electronic document sent to people in addition to the addressed recipient. **2.** A person or thing that closely resembles another. ❖ *tr.v.* **carbon copied, carbon copying, carbon copies 1a.** To reproduce something written or typed as a carbon copy. **b.** To send an electronic document as a carbon copy. **2.** To designate someone as the recipient of a carbon copy: *Carbon copy the lawyer on all correspondence regarding the contract.*

carbon cycle *n.* The circulation of carbon in nature through processes such as photosynthesis, respiration, decay, and combustion. For example, plants take in carbon dioxide from the atmosphere and convert it to carbohydrates through photosynthesis, and animals eat carbohydrates and release carbon dioxide through respiration.

carbon dating *n.* Radiocarbon dating.

carbon dioxide *n.* A colorless, odorless gas that does not burn, composed of carbon and oxygen in the proportion CO_2 and present in the atmosphere or formed when any fuel containing carbon is burned. It is exhaled from an animal's lungs during respiration and is used by plants in photosynthesis.

carbon footprint *n.* The amount of greenhouse gases containing carbon that are released into the environment by an activity, process, individual, or group, especially by the burning of fossil fuels.

carbonic acid *n.* A weak acid having the formula H_2CO_3. It exists only in solution and decomposes readily into carbon dioxide and water.

carboniferous (kär′bə-nĭf′ər-əs) *adj.* Producing or containing carbon or coal.

Carboniferous *n.* The fifth period of the Paleozoic Era, from about 359 to 299 million years ago, comprising the Mississippian (or Lower Carboniferous) and Pennsylvanian (or Upper Carboniferous) subdivisions. During the Carboniferous, widespread swamps formed in which plant remains accumulated and later hardened into coal. —**Carboniferous** *adj.*

carbonize (kär′bə-nīz′) *tr.v.* **carbonized, carbonizing, carbonizes 1.** To change an organic compound into carbon by heating. **2.** To treat, coat, or combine with carbon. —**car′bon·i·za′tion** (kär′bə-nĭ-zā′shən) *n.*

carbon monoxide *n.* A colorless odorless gas that is extremely poisonous and has the formula CO. Carbon monoxide is formed when carbon or a compound that contains carbon burns incompletely. It is present in the exhaust gases of automobile engines.

carbon-neutral (kär′bən-nōō′trəl) *adj.* Relating to a process or activity in which the total amount of carbon in carbon-containing gases released into the environment is offset by the amount of carbon in such gases removed from the environment.

carbon paper *n.* A lightweight paper coated on one side with a dark coloring matter, placed between two sheets of blank paper so that the bottom sheet will receive a copy of what is typed or written on the top sheet.

carbon tetrachloride (tĕt′rə-klôr′īd′) *n.* A colorless poisonous liquid of carbon and chlorine that does not burn, although it vaporizes easily. It is used in fire extinguishers and as a dry-cleaning fluid.

carbuncle (kär′bŭng′kəl) *n.* **1.** A painful inflammation in the tissue under the skin that is somewhat like a boil but releases pus from several openings. **2.** A red precious stone, especially a deep-red garnet.

carburetor (kär′bə-rā′tər *or* kär′byə-rā′tər) *n.* A device in a gasoline engine that vaporizes the gasoline with air to form an explosive mixture.

carcass (kär′kəs) *n.* **1.** The dead body of an animal. **2.** The body of a human. **3.** The remains of something: *the carcasses of old cars in a junkyard.*

carcinogen (kär-sĭn′ə-jən) *n.* A substance or agent that can cause cancer. Asbestos and tobacco products are examples of carcinogens. —**car′cin·o·gen′ic** (kär′sə-nə-jĕn′ĭk) *adj.*

carcinoma (kär′sə-nō′mə) *n., pl.* **carcinomas** *or* **carcinomata** (kär′sə-nō′mə-tə) A cancerous growth on the surface of the skin, blood vessels, or other organ or structure.

card¹ (kärd) *n.* **1a.** A decorative piece of folded, stiff paper used to send a note or greeting. **b.** A postcard. **c.** A stiff piece of paper bearing information, such as a person's name and email address or a book's title and author, and used for identification or classification. **2.** One of a set of 52 pieces of stiff heavy paper bearing numbers or figures and divided into four suits, used for various games and for telling fortunes; a playing card. **3. cards** *(used with a singular or plural verb)* **a.** A game played with one or more sets of 52 cards. **b.** The playing of such games. **4.** A stiff piece of paper bearing the image and often the statistics of a sports figure. **5.** A credit card or bankcard. **6.** A circuit board, especially for use in a computer. **7.** *Informal* An amusing or eccentric person: *My uncle is*

quite a card and entertains everyone with jokes. ◆ **in the cards** Likely; probable. **put (one's) cards on the table** or **lay (one's) cards on the table** To be frank and clear, as in one's intentions.

card² (kärd) *n.* A brush with teeth of wire, used to comb fibers of wool, flax, or cotton before spinning. ❖ *tr.v.* **carded, carding, cards** To comb with a card: *card wool.*

WORD HISTORY Card¹ comes from Middle English *carde* (meaning the same thing as in Modern English), which comes from Greek *khartēs,* meaning "paper made from papyrus." **Card²** comes from Middle English *card* (meaning the same thing as in Modern English), which comes from Latin *carduus,* meaning "thistle."

cardboard (kärd′bôrd′) *n.* A material similar to thick, stiff, heavy paper and made of pressed paper pulp or pasted sheets of paper.

card catalog *n.* An alphabetical listing, especially of books in a library, containing information about each item. A card catalog usually exists as separate cards kept in drawers or as a collection of electronic records.

cardholder (kärd′hōl′dər) *n.* A person who owns a card, especially a credit card.

cardiac (kär′dē-ăk′) *adj.* Relating to the heart: *a cardiac disorder.*

cardiac arrest *n.* Sudden stoppage of the heartbeat.

cardigan (kär′dĭ-gən) *n.* A knitted sweater or jacket that opens down the full length of the front.

cardinal (kär′dn-əl *or* kärd′nəl) *adj.* Of primary importance; chief; foremost: *A good design is the cardinal element of a successful building.* ❖ *n.* **1.** An official of the Roman Catholic Church who is appointed by a pope and whose rank is just below that of the pope. **2.** A North American bird having a crested head and bright red feathers in the male. **3.** A cardinal number.

cardinal flower *n.* A plant of eastern North America that bears a cluster of brilliant scarlet flowers.

cardinal number *n.* A number, such as 3 or 11 or 412, used in counting to indicate quantity but not order.

cardinal point *n.* One of the four principal directions on a compass; north, south, east, or west.

carding (kär′dĭng) *n.* The cleaning and combing of fibers, such as wool, cotton, or flax, to prepare them for spinning into yarn.

cardiogram (kär′dē-ə-grăm′) *n.* An electrocardiogram.

cardiologist (kär′dē-ŏl′ə-jĭst) *n.* A physician who specializes in cardiology.

cardiology (kär′dē-ŏl′ə-jē) *n.* The branch of medicine that deals with the diagnosis and treatment of disorders of the heart.

cardiopulmonary (kär′dē-ō-pool′mə-nĕr′ē *or* kär′dē-ō-pŭl′mə-nĕr′ē) *adj.* Relating to the heart and lungs.

cardiopulmonary resuscitation *n.* A procedure used to restore normal breathing and circulation after a person's heart has stopped beating. It employs mouth-to-mouth resuscitation, pushing on the chest to force blood from the heart, and sometimes drugs.

cardiovascular (kär′dē-ō-văs′kyə-lər) *adj.* Relating to or involving the heart and blood vessels: *cardiovascular disease.*

care (kâr) *n.* **1a.** A feeling of fear, doubt, or anxiety; worry: *on vacation and free from care.* **b.** An object or source of worry, attention, or concern: *The cares of running a business are many.* **2a.** Close attention, as in doing something well or avoiding harm: *addressed the invitations with*

care; handled the package with care. **b.** Upkeep; maintenance: *products for hair care.* **c.** Watchful oversight; charge or supervision: *The patient was left in the care of a nurse.* **3.** Attentive assistance or treatment to those in need: *a hospital that provides emergency care.* ❖ *v.* **cared, caring, cares** —*intr.* **1.** To be concerned or interested: *I don't care about going.* **2.** To provide protection or help: *Who will care for the dog while we are away?* **3.** To object or mind: *Would you care if I turned on the radio?* **4a.** To have a liking; like: *Do you really care for that person? Some people don't care for fish.* **b.** To have a wish; be inclined: *Would you care for another helping of peas?* —*tr.* **1.** To wish; desire: *Would you care to go for a walk?* **2.** To be concerned or interested in: *I don't care what they think.* ◆ **in care of** At the address of or in the name of: *Address all letters for the club in care of the secretary.*
✦ **SYNONYMS** care, charge, keeping, trust *n.*

careen (kə-rēn′) *v.* **careened, careening, careens** —*intr.* **1.** To lurch or swerve while in motion: *The car careened on the icy road.* **2.** To lean to one side, as a ship: *The ship careened wildly in the heavy winds.* —*tr.* **1.** To lean (a ship) onto its side for cleaning or repairing. **2.** To cause to lean to one side: *Strong winds will careen a small sailboat.*

career (kə-rîr′) *n.* **1.** A profession or occupation: *considering a career in medicine.* **2.** The general progress or course of one's life, especially in one's profession: *a police officer with a distinguished career.* ❖ *intr.v.* **careered, careering, careers** To move or run at full speed: *The startled horse went careering off through the meadow.*

carefree (kâr′frē′) *adj.* Free of worries or responsibilities: *a carefree vacation.*

careful (kâr′fəl) *adj.* **1.** Attentive to possible danger; cautious; prudent: *Be careful not to drive too fast.* **2.** Done with care; thorough; conscientious: *a careful job on the application.* **3.** Showing concern; mindful; solicitous: *being careful of other people's feelings.* —**care′ful·ly** *adv.* —**care′ful·ness** *n.*

caregiver (kâr′gĭv′ər) *n.* A person who cares for older people, children, or people who are ill.

careless (kâr′lĭs) *adj.* **1.** Taking insufficient care; negligent: *a careless worker; careless about one's appearance.* **2.** Done or made without care or attention: *a careless mistake.* **3.** Said or done without thought; inconsiderate: *a careless remark.* **4.** Free from cares; cheerful: *a careless smile.* —**care′less·ly** *adv.* —**care′less·ness** *n.*

caress (kə-rĕs′) *n.* A gentle touch or gesture of fondness, tenderness, or love: *The child's caresses reassured the frightened cat.* ❖ *tr.v.* **caressed, caressing, caresses** To touch or stroke affectionately.

caret (kăr′ĭt) *n.* A proofreading symbol (^) used to indicate where something is to be inserted in a line of printed or written material.

caretaker (kâr′tā′kər) *n.* A person employed to look after and take care of a thing, place, or person.

careworn (kâr′wôrn′) *adj.* Showing signs of worry or anxiety; haggard: *the parent's careworn face.*

carfare (kär′fâr′) *n.* The amount charged for a ride, as on a subway or bus.

cargo (kär′gō) *n., pl.* **cargoes** or **cargos** The freight carried by a ship, airplane, or other vehicle.

cargo pants *pl.n.* Loose-fitting, usually cotton pants having large exterior pockets partway down the sides.

carhop (kär′hŏp′) *n.* A person who waits on customers in their cars at a drive-in restaurant.

Carib (kăr′ĭb) *n., pl.* **Carib** or **Caribs** **1.** also **Cariban** (kăr′-ə-bən or kə-rē′bən) A member of a group of American Indian peoples of northern South America and the islands of the eastern Caribbean. **2.** Any of the languages of the Carib.

Cariban (kăr′ə-bən or kə-rē′bən) *n., pl.* **Cariban** or **Caribans** **1.** Variant of **Carib** (sense 1). **2.** A family of American Indian languages spoken by the Carib. —**Car′i·ban** *adj.*

Caribbean (kăr′ə-bē′ən or kə-rĭb′ē-ən) *adj.* **1.** Relating to the Caribbean Sea, its islands, or coastal lands. **2.** Relating to the peoples or cultures of this region. **3.** Relating to the Carib or their language or culture. ❖ *n.* **1.** A Carib. **2.** The Caribbean Sea.

caribou (kăr′ə-bōō′) *n., pl.* **caribou** or **caribous** A large deer of the Arctic tundra and northern forest regions of North America, having large spreading antlers in both the male and the female. Caribou and reindeer belong to the same species.

caricature (kăr′ĭ-kə-chŏŏr′ or kăr′ĭ-kə-chər) *n.* **1.** A picture or description of a person or thing in which certain distinctive features are greatly exaggerated or distorted to produce a comic effect. **2.** The art of creating such pictures or descriptions: *The cartoonist is a master of caricature.* ❖ *tr.v.* **caricatured, caricaturing, caricatures** To represent in caricature: *He caricatures political figures.* —**car′i·ca·tur′ist** *n.*

caries (kâr′ēz) *n., pl.* **caries** **1.** Decay of a bone or tooth. **2.** A cavity formed by decay in a tooth.

carillon (kăr′ə-lŏn′ or kăr′ə-lən) *n.* A set of bells hung in a tower, usually played from a keyboard.

caring (kâr′ĭng) *adj.* Feeling and showing concern and compassion for others: *caring volunteers who helped raise money for charity.*

carjack (kär′jăk′) *tr.v.* **carjacked, carjacking, carjacks** To seize or steal a (a motor vehicle) from its driver. —**car′jack′er** *n.*

carload (kär′lōd′) *n.* The number of passengers or the amount of cargo that a car can carry: *took a carload of children to the zoo.*

Carmelite (kär′mə-līt′) *n.* **1.** A monk or friar belonging to a Roman Catholic order founded in 1155. **2.** A member of a community of nuns in this order, founded in 1452. —**Car′mel·ite′** *adj.*

carmine (kär′mĭn or kär′mīn′) *n.* A deep or purplish red.

carnage (kär′nĭj) *n.* Great slaughter, especially in war: *the carnage of battle.*

carnal (kär′nəl) *adj.* **1.** Relating to bodily appetites; sensual. **2.** Worldly or earthly. **3.** Relating to the body: *carnal remains.* —**car′nal·ly** *adv.*

carnation (kär-nā′shən) *n.* **1.** Any of numerous forms of a garden plant cultivated for its fragrant many-petaled white, pink, or red flowers. **2.** A flower of this plant.

carnelian (kär-nēl′yən) *n.* A pale to deep red type of clear quartz used as a gem.

carnival (kär′nə-vəl) *n.* **1.** A traveling amusement show that offers rides, games, and sideshows. **2.** often **Carnival** A period of celebrating and feasting just before Lent. **3.** A time of merrymaking; a festival.

carnivore (kär′nə-vôr′) *n.* **1.** An animal that feeds on the flesh of other animals and generally has large sharp teeth. Dogs, cats, raccoons, and seals are carnivores. **2.** A plant that traps insects and absorbs nutrients from them.

carnivorous (kär-nĭv′ər-əs) *adj.* **1.** Feeding on the flesh of other animals: *Wolves are carnivorous.* **2.** Having leaves or other parts that trap insects and absorb nutrients from them: *carnivorous plants.* —**car·niv′o·rous·ly** *adv.*

carob (kăr′əb) *n.* An evergreen tree of the Mediterranean region that has compound leaves and bears long pods used as food.

carol (kăr′əl) *n.* A song of joy, especially for Christmas. ❖ *intr.v.* **caroled, caroling, carols** also **carolled, carolling, carols 1.** To sing joyously. **2.** To go from house to house singing Christmas carols. —**car′ol·er, car′ol·ler** *n.*

carom (kăr′əm) *n.* **1.** A collision followed by a rebound, as of a ball bouncing off a wall. **2.** A shot in billiards or similar games in which the cue ball successively strikes two other balls. ❖ *intr.v.* **caromed, caroming, caroms** To collide and rebound; make a carom: *The golf ball caromed off the tree.*

carotene (kăr′ə-tēn′) *n.* An organic compound that occurs as an orange-yellow to red pigment in many plants and in animal tissue. It is converted to vitamin A by the liver.

carotid (kə-rŏt′ĭd) *n.* Either of the two large arteries in the neck that carry blood to the head. ❖ *adj.* Relating to either of these arteries.

carouse (kə-rouz′) *intr.v.* **caroused, carousing, carouses** To have a noisy and enjoyable time with others, often while drinking alcohol. —**ca·rous′er** *n.*

carousel or **carrousel** (kăr′ə-sĕl′) *n.* **1.** A merry-go-round. **2.** A circular conveyor on which objects are displayed or presented: *the baggage carousel at the airport.*

carp¹ (kärp) *intr.v.* **carped, carping, carps** To find fault or complain in a petty or disagreeable way.

carp² (kärp) *n., pl.* **carp** or **carps 1.** A large freshwater fish of Eurasia, often bred in ponds and lakes and used as food. **2.** Any of various related fishes.

WORD HISTORY Carp¹ comes from Middle English *carpen,* meaning "to talk, chat," which comes from Old Norse *karpa,* meaning "to boast." **Carp²** comes from Middle English *carpe,* which comes from Medieval Latin *carpa,* which both referred to the same type of fish as in Modern English.

carpal (kär′pəl) *adj.* Relating to the carpus or wrist. ❖ *n.* A bone of the carpus.

carpal tunnel syndrome *n.* A condition marked by pain and numbness in the hand, caused by compression of a nerve in the wrist.

carpe diem (kär′pĕ dē′ĕm′) *interj.* Used as an admonition to seize the pleasures of the moment without concern for the future. ❖ *n.* Such an admonition.

carpel (kär′pəl) *n.* A part of the pistil of a flowering plant in which the seeds develop.

carpenter (kär′pən-tər) *n.* A person who builds or repairs wooden objects and structures such as cabinets, houses, and ships.

carpentry (kär′pən-trē) *n.* **1.** The work or trade of a carpenter. **2.** Woodwork done by a carpenter: *The palace is renowned for its intricate interior carpentry.*

carpet (kär′pĭt) *n.* **1.** A thick heavy covering for a floor, usually made of woven wool or synthetic fibers; a rug. **2.** The fabric used for floor covering: *a roll of carpet.* **3.** Something that covers a surface like a carpet: *a carpet of pine needles on the forest floor.* ❖ *tr.v.* **carpeted, carpeting, carpets** To cover with or as if with a carpet: *carpet the stairs.*

carpetbag (kär′pĭt-băg′) *n.* A traveling bag made of carpet fabric that was used chiefly in the United States during the 1800s.

carpetbagger (kär′pĭt-băg′ər) *n.* **1.** A Northerner who went to the South after the Civil War to make money by taking advantage of the unsettled conditions there. **2.** An outsider who aggressively seeks a position of advantage in a new place.

carpeting (kär′pĭ-tĭng) *n.* **1.** Material used for carpets: *pretty red carpeting.* **2.** A carpet or carpets: *a room with wall-to-wall carpeting.*

carpool also **car pool** (kär′pool′) *n.* **1.** An arrangement among a number of car owners who agree to take turns driving each other or their children to a regular destination, such as work or school. **2.** A group of people forming a car pool.

car-pool (kär′pool′) *v.* **car-pooled, car-pooling, car-pools** —*intr.* To travel in a car pool: *Four of us car-pool to work every day.* —*tr.* To transport by means of a car pool: *Several families car-pool their children to school.*

carport (kär′pôrt′) *n.* A shelter for a car, usually formed by a roof projecting from the side of a building.

carpus (kär′pəs) *n., pl.* **carpi** (kär′pī′) **1.** The group of eight bones forming the joint between the hand and the forearm in humans; the wrist. **2.** The corresponding joint in four-footed animals.

carrageenan also **carrageenin** (kăr′ə-gē′nən) *n.* Any of several substances derived from algae that are widely used as thickening, stabilizing, or emulsifying agents in foods, cosmetics, and industrial products.

carrel (kăr′əl) *n.* A small enclosed area with a desk for study in a library.

carriage (kăr′ĭj) *n.* **1.** A wheeled passenger vehicle, usually drawn by horses. **2.** A small vehicle for a baby or a doll that is pushed by someone walking behind it. **3.** A wheeled structure on which a heavy object, such as a cannon, is moved. **4.** A movable part of a machine that often holds or shifts another part: *Many typewriters have a carriage that holds the paper and moves it in front of the keys.* **5.** The manner in which one's head or body is held; posture. **6.** The act of transporting: *The explorers used porters for the carriage of supplies up the mountain.* **7.** The costs of transporting: *Carriage was added to the bill.*

carrier (kăr′ē-ər) *n.* **1.** A person or thing that transports or conveys: *a baggage carrier.* **2.** A person or business that deals in transporting passengers or goods: *Airlines, railroads, bus lines, and other carriers see an increase in business during holidays.* **3.** An aircraft carrier. **4.** A device or mechanism for moving or carrying something: *We attached our bikes to the carrier on top of the car.* **5a.** An organism that carries a disease agent in its body and is capable of transmitting it to others but usually shows no symptoms of disease. People who are carriers of typhoid, for example, can pass the bacteria on to others even though they do not feel sick. **b.** An organism that has one copy of a gene for a trait but shows no physical signs of the trait, usually because the gene is recessive. If two people who are carriers of a gene for cystic fibrosis have a child, for example, there is a chance that the child will inherit one copy of the gene from each parent and will develop the disease. **6.** A carrier wave. **7.** An organization that issues insurance policies or guarantees to pay off debts in case of a business failure. **8.** A telecommunications company.

carrier pigeon *n.* A homing pigeon.

carrier wave *n.* An electromagnetic wave whose amplitude or frequency is modulated to transmit speech, music, images, or other signals, as in radio broadcasting.

carrion (kăr′ē-ən) *n.* The decaying flesh of dead animals: *Vultures feed on carrion.*

carrot (kăr′ət) *n.* **1.** A plant having feathery leaves and a long, tapering, yellow-orange root. **2.** The root of this plant, eaten as a vegetable.

carrousel (kăr′ə-sĕl′) *n.* Variant of **carousel.**

carry (kăr′ē) *v.* **carried, carrying, carries** —*tr.* **1.** To hold or support while moving; bear: *carry the groceries into the house.* **2.** To take from one place to another; transport: *Airlines carry passengers and freight.* **3.** To serve as a means of conveying; transmit: *The pipes carry water from the reservoir.* **4.** To cause to move; propel: *The wind carried the ball over the fence.* **5.** To sustain the weight or responsibility of; bear: *She is carrying a heavy load of courses this semester.* **6.** To keep or have on one's person: *carry an umbrella.* **7.** To be pregnant with (a child). **8.** To hold and move (oneself, one's body or a part of it) in a certain way: *Dancers carry themselves very gracefully.* **9.** To have in stock; have for sale: *Drugstores carry many different health products.* **10.** To sing (a tune or melody) in key: *carry a tune.* **11.** To put (a digit) into the next column to the left, as in performing addition. **12.** To have as an attribute, consequence, or effect; involve: *The washing machine carries a guarantee for one year.* **13.** To express or contain: *The engineer's report carried a grim warning about unsafe bridges.* **14a.** To win a majority of the votes in: *The president carried almost all the states.* **b.** To win support or acceptance for: *The proposition is carried by a large majority of votes.* **15.** To prolong, extend, or continue: *carry a joke too far.* **16.** To print or broadcast: *All the papers carried the story.* **17.** To be propelled over (a distance) or advance beyond (a point or object), as in a golf stroke: *Did my shot carry the trees?* **18.** In sports, to control and advance (a ball or puck). **19.** In basketball, to palm (the ball) in violation of the rules. —*intr.* **1.** To act as a bearer: *The dog could fetch and carry.* **2.** To be transmitted or conveyed: *a voice that carries well.* **3.** To be approved or accepted: *The proposal carried by a wide margin.* ❖ *n., pl.* **carries 1.** The range of a gun or a projectile: *The first cannons had a short carry of only a few hundred feet.* **2.** The distance covered by a ball or projectile. **3.** An act of carrying something from one place to another: *A short overland carry was necessary to canoe down the whole length of the river.* **4.** In football, an act of running with the ball from the line of scrimmage: *The halfback averages four yards per carry.* ◆ **carry away** To arouse great emotion or excitement in: *I was carried away by the music.* **carry off 1.** To win: *He carried off first prize.* **2.** To handle successfully: *The debate was carried off without any difficulty.* **3.** To cause the death of; kill: *The epidemic carried off hundreds of sheep.* **carry on 1.** To engage in or conduct: *carry on a conversation; carry on a correspondence.* **2.** To continue despite difficulties; persevere: *carry on even with a bad cold.* **3.** To behave in an excited or improper manner: *What are they carrying on about?* **carry out 1.** To execute or accomplish: *carry out a plan.* **2.** To follow or obey: *carry out orders.*

carryall (kăr′ē-ôl′) *n.* A large bag, basket, or pocketbook.

carrying capacity (kăr′ē-ĭng) *n.* **1.** The maximum number of people or things that a vehicle or a receptacle can carry: *a van with a carrying capacity of 12.* **2.** The maximum number of individuals, as of humans or deer, that can be supported by the resources available in a given environment.

carry-on (kăr′ē-ŏn′) *adj.* Small or compact enough to be carried aboard an airplane, train, or bus by a passenger: *carry-on luggage.* ❖ *n.* A carry-on bag or piece of luggage.

carry-out (kăr′ē-out′) *adj.* Intended to be eaten off the premises; takeout: *carry-out pizza.*

car seat *n.* A small seat for securing and protecting young children that can be fastened to the seat of a vehicle and that contains a restraining device or harness.

carsick (kăr′sĭk′) *adj.* Nauseated by the motion of a car, bus, or other vehicle. —**car′sick′ness** *n.*

cart (kärt) *n.* **1.** A small wheeled vehicle pushed by hand: *a grocery cart.* **2.** A two-wheeled, usually wooden vehicle pulled by a draft animal or tractor and used to transport goods or people. **3.** The amount that a cart holds: *bought three carts of apples.* **4.** A light motorized vehicle: *a golf cart.* ❖ *tr.v.* **carted, carting, carts** To transport in or as if in a cart: *Trucks cart goods across the country.*

cartage (kär′tĭj) *n.* **1.** The act or process of transporting or carting: *Many movers offer cartage overseas.* **2.** The cost of transporting or carting: *overseas cartage in the amount of $2,000.*

carte blanche (kärt blänsh′ *or* kärt blänch′) *n., pl.* **cartes blanches** (kärt blänsh′ *or* kärts blänch′) Complete freedom of action: *The architect had carte blanche in designing the house.*

cartel (kär-tĕl′) *n.* An association of independent businesses, often from different countries, organized to control prices, production, and sales by its members.

Cartesian (kär-tē′zhən) *adj.* Relating to the philosophy or methods of the French mathematician and philosopher René Descartes (1596–1650).

Cartesian coordinate system *n.* A system in which a point's location is given by coordinates that represent its distances from perpendicular lines that intersect at a point called the origin. A Cartesian coordinate system in a plane has two perpendicular lines; in three-dimensional space, it has three.

cartilage (kär′tl-ĭj) *n.* A tough white connective tissue that in humans and most other vertebrates forms the major part of the skeleton of the embryo but changes largely to bone as the individual matures. It is more flexible than bone but not as hard.

cartilaginous (kär′tl-ăj′ə-nəs) *adj.* Relating to or consisting of cartilage.

cartilaginous fish *n.* Any of various fishes that have a skeleton consisting mainly of cartilage rather than bone. The sharks, skates, and rays are cartilaginous fishes.

cartography (kär-tŏg′rə-fē) *n.* The art of making maps or charts. —**car·tog′ra·pher** *n.*

carton (kär′tn) *n.* **1.** A cardboard or plastic box made in various sizes: *an egg carton.* **2.** The contents of a carton: *drink a carton of milk.*

cartoon (kär-tōōn′) *n.* **1.** A drawing, often accompanied by a caption, showing a humorous situation or illustrating an opinion on a public issue. **2a.** A usually short, animated movie or television program. **b.** An animated character in a movie or television program. **3.** A comic strip.

cartoonist (kär-tōōn′ist) *n.* A person who draws cartoons.

cartouche *or* **cartouch** (kär-tōōsh′) *n.* **1.** A figure, often in the shape of an oval shield or oblong scroll, used as an architectural or graphic ornament or to bear an inscription. **2.** An oval or oblong figure in ancient Egyptian hieroglyphics that encloses characters expressing a name, as of a pharaoh or a god.

cartridge (kär′trĭj) *n.* **1a.** A cylindrical casing of metal or cardboard that holds the powder to propel a bullet or shot. **b.** Such a casing fitted with a bullet or containing shot. **2.** A small unit designed to be inserted into a larger piece of equipment: *an ink cartridge.*

cartwheel (kärt′wēl′) *n.* **1.** The wheel of a cart. **2.** A handspring in which the body turns over sideways with the arms and legs spread like the spokes of a wheel.

carve (kärv) *v.* **carved, carving, carves** —*tr.* **1.** To make or form by cutting: *carved beams out of logs; carved our initials in the board.* **2.** To cut (a piece of material) in order to form or decorate something: *carve a block of marble into a statue.* **3.** To cut (meat or poultry) into pieces to be eaten: *carve a turkey.* —*intr.* To slice meat or poultry to eat: *My grandfather always carves at Thanksgiving dinner.* ◆ **carve out.** To make from something bigger: *a town that was carved out of the wilderness.* **2.** To make or accomplish by strenuous or persistent effort: *settlers carving out a living in the mountains.* —**carv′er** *n.*

carving (kär′vĭng) *n.* **1.** The act or process of carving, especially of cutting wood or stone to form an object or design. **2.** An object or design formed by cutting: *a wood carving.*

car wash *n.* A place or business equipped for washing cars or other vehicles.

casaba also **cassaba** (kə-sä′bə) *n.* A melon having a yellow rind and sweet whitish flesh.

Casanova (kăs′ə-nō′və) *n.* A man who habitually seduces or attempts to seduce women.

cascade (kăs-kād′) *n.* **1.** A waterfall or a series of small waterfalls that flows over steep rocks. **2.** Something resembling a cascade: *a cascade of sparks from a grinding wheel.* ❖ *intr.v.* **cascaded, cascading, cascades** To fall in or in the manner of a cascade: *The river cascades over a shelf of granite rock. The cards cascaded to the floor.*

case¹ (kās) *n.* **1.** An instance of something; an occurrence or example: *It was a case of mistaken identity.* **2.** A situation or state of affairs: *In that case there is nothing more we can do.* **3.** A situation that requires investigation: *the case of the missing diamonds.* **4.** An occurrence of a disease or disorder: *a case of chickenpox.* **5.** A person being assisted, treated, or studied, as by a doctor or social worker. **6a.** A legal action; a lawsuit: *The Supreme Court is the last court to consider a case.* **b.** A statement of facts by an attorney, for a court to consider: *The case was clearly presented by the defense.* **7.** A set of reasons or arguments offered in support of something: *There is a good case for changing the law.* **8.** In grammar, a distinct form of a noun, pronoun, or adjective that shows syntactic relationships among words in a sentence. English has three cases: nominative, objective, and genitive. ◆ **in any case** No matter what happens; in any event: *In any case, we will have to leave soon.* **in case 1.** As a precaution: *brought along an umbrella just in case.* **2.** If it happens that: *brought some water in case I got thirsty.* **in case of** If there should happen to be; in the event of: *In case of emergency, call the police.*

case² (kās) *n.* **1.** A container or protective cover: *a packing case; a case for eyeglasses.* **2.** A container and its contents: *We bought a case of soda.* **3.** The form of a written, printed, or keyed letter that distinguishes it as being lowercase or uppercase: *typed my password using the wrong case.* ❖ *tr.v.* **cased, casing, cases 1.** To put into or cover with

a case. **2.** *Slang* To examine carefully, as in planning a crime: *cased the bank before robbing it.*

WORD HISTORY Case¹ comes from Middle English *cas,* which comes from Latin *cāsus,* both meaning "an occurrence." **Case²** comes from Middle English *case,* which comes from Norman French *casse,* which comes from Latin *capsa,* all meaning "receptacle."

case history *n.* A detailed list of the facts affecting the condition of a person or group under treatment or study, especially in medicine or psychology.

casein (kā′sēn′ *or* kā′sē-ĭn) *n.* A white, tasteless, odorless protein derived from milk and cheese, used in making foods, plastics, adhesives, and paints.

caseload (kās′lōd′) *n.* The number of cases handled in a given period, as by a lawyer or a social services agency.

casement (kās′mənt) *n.* **1.** A window sash that opens outward on hinges. **2.** A window fitted with such sashes.

casework (kās′wûrk′) *n.* Social work devoted to individual people or cases. —**case′work′er** *n.*

cash (kăsh) *n.* **1.** Money in the form of bills and coins: *I have five dollars in cash in my pocket.* **2.** Payment in the form of currency or a check: *I paid in cash.* ❖ *tr.v.* **cashed, cashing, cashes** To exchange for or convert into money in the form of bills or coins: *cash a check.* ◆ **cash in on** *Informal* To take advantage of: *cash in on the sunshine and go to the beach.*

cash crop *n.* A crop that is grown for sale rather than for use by the producer.

cashew (kăsh′ōō *or* kə-shōō′) *n.* **1.** The kidney-shaped edible nut of a tropical American tree. **2.** The evergreen tree that bears such nuts.

cashier¹ (kă-shîr′) *n.* A person employed to receive and pay out money, as in a store, restaurant, hotel, or bank.

cashier² (kă-shîr′) *tr.v.* **cashiered, cashiering, cashiers** To dismiss in disgrace from a position of command or responsibility: *cashier a soldier for neglect of duty.*

WORD HISTORY Cashier¹ comes from French *caisse,* meaning "money box," which comes from Latin *capsa,* meaning "receptacle." **Cashier²** comes from Dutch *casseren,* meaning "to dismiss."

cashier's check (kă-shîrz′) *n.* A check drawn by a bank on its own funds and signed by the bank's cashier.

cash machine *n.* An ATM.

cashmere (kăzh′mîr′ *or* kăsh′mîr′) *n.* **1.** Fine soft wool growing beneath the outer hair of a goat native to the mountains of India and Tibet. **2.** Yarn or fabric made from this wool. —**cash′mere′** *adj.*

cash register *n.* A machine that records the amount of each sale and contains a drawer for holding money.

casing (kā′sĭng) *n.* **1.** A protective case or covering, as for an automobile tire or a rocket. **2.** A case usually made of animal intestines and used as a wrapping for sausage meat. **3.** The frame or framework for a door or window.

casino (kə-sē′nō) *n., pl.* **casinos 1.** A business providing gambling and other entertainment. **2.** A building or room where such gambling and entertainment takes place. **3.** A card game for two to four players in which cards on the table are matched with cards in the hand.

cask (kăsk) *n.* **1.** A barrel for holding liquids: *a cask of cider.* **2.** The amount that a cask can hold.

casket (kăs′kĭt) *n.* **1.** A coffin. **2.** A small case used to hold jewels or other valuables.

casque (kăsk) *n.* A helmet or other armor for the head.

Cassandra (kə-săn′drə) *n.* In Greek mythology, a daughter of Priam, endowed with the gift of prophecy but fated by Apollo never to be believed.

cassava (kə-sä′və) *n.* **1.** A tropical American plant having a large starchy root. **2.** The root of this plant, eaten as a staple food in the tropics after preparation to remove toxins. Cassava starch is also the source of tapioca.

casserole (kăs′ə-rōl′) *n.* **1.** A dish, usually of pottery or glass, in which food is both baked and served. **2.** Food baked in such a dish.

cassette (kə-sĕt′) *n.* A magnetic tape contained in a plastic case and used to make audio or video recordings and to store data in digital form.

Cassiopeia (kăs′ē-ə-pē′ə) *n.* A constellation in the Northern Hemisphere, traditionally pictured as a seated queen.

cassock (kăs′ək) *n.* A robe reaching to the feet, worn by the clergy and others assisting in church services.

cassowary (kăs′ə-wĕr′ē) *n., pl.* **cassowaries** Any of several large flightless birds of eastern Indonesia, Papua New Guinea, and Australia that resemble an ostrich and have a bony projection on the top of the head.

cast (kăst) *v.* **cast, casting, casts** —*tr.* **1.** To throw, fling, or hurl: *Tourists cast coins into the fountain.* **2.** To throw or force (a person) onto the ground, as in wrestling. **3.** To shed or molt: *The snake casts its skin as it grows.* **4a.** To cause to fall on something: *cast a shadow.* **b.** To cause to be associated with something: *cast doubt on the report.* **5.** To turn or direct: *cast a glance in the mirror.* **6.** To deposit or indicate (a ballot or vote). **7.** To assign a role to: *The director cast the actor as a judge.* **8a.** To form (an object) by pouring molten or soft material into a mold and allowing it to harden: *The artist cast the sculpture in bronze.* **b.** To pour (a liquid metal) in forming an object this way: *The factory casts molten iron into pipe.* —*intr.* **1.** To throw or force out something, especially a fishing line: *The fisherman cast in the river all morning.* **2.** To be shaped in a mold: *Some metals, such as lead, cast easily.* ❖ *n.* **1.** The act or an instance of throwing or casting: *a cast of the dice; a cast of the fishing line.* **2.** The distance thrown: *a winning cast of 40 meters.* **3.** The actors in a play or movie: *There were only four people in the cast.* **4.** A hard stiff bandage, usually of gauze and plaster, used to keep an injured bone or joint from moving. **5a.** An object cast in a mold: *a cast of a statue.* **b.** An impression formed in a mold: *a plaster cast of a face.* **6.** A hue or shade: *The cloth has a slightly reddish cast.* **7.** Outward form, quality, or appearance: *New facts put a different cast on the matter.* **8.** A slight squint or turning of the eye in a certain direction: *a cast in the left eye.* ◆ **cast about** To make a search; look around: *cast about for a way to escape.* **cast aside** To discard or abandon: *cast aside a suggestion.* **cast lots** To draw lots to determine something by chance. **cast off** To release a ship from being tied to a dock.

castanets (kăs′tə-nĕts′) *pl.n.* A rhythm instrument consisting of a pair of hollowed-out shells of wood or ivory, struck together with the fingers to make a sharp click.

castaway (kăst′ə-wā′) *adj.* **1.** Cast adrift or ashore; shipwrecked. **2.** Discarded; thrown away: *castaway clothes.* ❖ *n.* **1.** A shipwrecked person. **2.** A person or thing that has been discarded.

caste (kăst) *n.* **1.** In India, one of the hereditary social classes in Hindu society. **2.** A social class as distinguished by rank, profession, or wealth: *the priestly caste of Aztec civilization.* **3.** A social system based on caste.

castellated (kăs′tə-lā′tĭd) *adj.* Having turrets and battlements like a castle.

caster (kăs′tər) *n.* **1.** A person or thing that casts: *a caster of fishing nets.* **2.** also **castor** A small roller or wheel attached under a piece of furniture or other heavy object to make it easier to move. **3.** also **castor** A. A small bottle, pot, or shaker for holding vinegar, mustard, salt, or a similar seasoning. **b.** A stand for a set of these containers.

castigate (kăs′tĭ-gāt′) *tr.v.* **castigated, castigating, castigates** To criticize severely; rebuke; berate: *should be castigated for neglecting one's duty.* —**cas′ti·ga′tion** *n.* —**cas′ti·ga′tor** *n.*

Castile soap *n.* An odorless soap made with sodium hydroxide and a vegetable oil, usually olive oil.

Castilian (kă-stĭl′yən) *adj.* Relating to Castile, its people, language, or culture. ❖ *n.* **1a.** The Spanish dialect of Castile. **b.** The standard form of Spanish, based on this dialect. **2.** A native or inhabitant of Castile.

casting (kăs′tĭng) *n.* **1.** The act or process of making casts or molds. **2.** An object that has been formed in a mold. **3.** The selection of actors or performers, as for a play.

cast iron *n.* A hard brittle alloy of iron that contains carbon and small amounts of silicon, sulfur, manganese, and phosphorus.

cast-iron (kăst′ī′ərn) *adj.* **1.** Made of cast iron. **2.** Rigid or inflexible: *a cast-iron rule.* **3.** Hardy; strong: *With your cast-iron stomach you could eat anything!*

castle (kăs′əl) *n.* **1.** A large building or group of buildings with high thick walls, towers, and other defenses against attack, such as battlements or a moat. **2.** A building that resembles a castle in size or appearance. **3.** A rook in chess. ❖ *intr.v.* **castled, castling, castles** In chess, to move the king two squares toward a rook and place the rook on the square next past the king.

castoff (kăst′ôf′) *n.* A person or thing that has been discarded or thrown away. —**cast′-off′** *adj.*

castor (kăs′tər) *n.* Variant of **caster** (senses 2 and 3).

Castor *n.* In Greek mythology, one of the twin sons of Leda, who along with his brother Pollux was transformed by Zeus into the constellation Gemini.

castor oil *n.* An oil pressed from the seeds of a tropical plant, used as a light lubricant and in medicine as a laxative.

castrate (kăs′trāt′) *tr.v.* **castrated, castrating, castrates** To remove the testicles of; geld or emasculate. —**cas·tra′-tion** *n.*

casual (kăzh′ōō-əl) *adj.* **1.** Suited for everyday wear or use; informal: *casual dress.* **2.** Not serious or thorough; superficial: *a casual inspection.* **3a.** Showing little interest; unconcerned; nonchalant: *a breezy casual manner.* **b.** Not thought about beforehand; passing: *a casual remark about the weather.* **4.** Happening by chance; not planned; accidental: *a casual meeting of neighbors at the post office.* **5.** Not close or intimate: *a casual friendship.* —**cas′u·al·ly** *adv.* —**cas′u·al·ness** *n.*

casualty (kăzh′ōō-əl-tē) *n., pl.* **casualties 1a.** A person who is killed or injured in an accident. **b.** A person who is killed, wounded, captured, or missing during a military action. **2.** A serious accident, especially one in which someone is seriously injured or killed.

casuistry (kăzh′ōō-ĭ-strē) *n., pl.* **casuistries 1.** Specious or excessively subtle reasoning intended to rationalize or mislead. **2.** The determination of right and wrong in questions of conduct or conscience by analyzing cases that illustrate general ethical rules.

casus belli (kä′səs běl′ī *or* kä′səs běl′ē) *n., pl.* **casus belli** An act or event that provokes or is used to justify war.

cat (kăt) *n.* **1.** A small domesticated mammal having soft fur and sharp claws, kept as a pet or for catching mice and rats. **2.** Any of various related mammals, such as a lion, tiger, leopard, or lynx. ◆ **let the cat out of the bag** To give away a secret; let a secret be known.

catabolism (kə-tăb′ə-lĭz′əm) *n.* The phase of metabolism that yields energy by breaking down complex molecules, such as proteins and fats, into simpler ones. —**cat′a·bol′ic** (kăt′ə-bŏl′ĭk) *adj.*

cataclysm (kăt′ə-klĭz′əm) *n.* **1.** A sudden and violent change in the earth's crust, such as an earthquake or volcanic eruption. **2.** A great upheaval or disaster, such as a revolution or war. —**cat′a·clys′mic** (kăt′ə-klĭz′mĭk) *adj.*

catacombs (kăt′ə-kōmz′) *pl.n.* An underground cemetery consisting of chambers or tunnels with recesses used as graves.

catafalque (kăt′ə-fălk′) *n.* A decorated platform or framework on which a coffin rests in state during a funeral.

Catalan (kăt′l-ăn′ *or* kăt′l-än′) *adj.* Relating to the region of Catalonia in Spain or to its people, language, or culture. ◆ *n.* **1.** A native or inhabitant of Catalonia. **2.** The Romance language of Catalonia and the surrounding region.

catalepsy (kăt′l-ĕp′sē) *n., pl.* **catalepsies** A condition in which the muscles of the body become rigid and a person is unaware of his or her surroundings and does not respond to stimuli. Catalepsy has been associated with epilepsy, schizophrenia, and certain other mental disorders. —**cat′a·lep′tic** (kăt′l-ĕp′tĭk) *adj.*

catalog or **catalogue** (kăt′l-ôg′) *n.* **1.** A list of items, usually in alphabetical order, with a description of each item: *a library card catalog.* **2.** A book or pamphlet containing such a list: *a mail order catalog of merchandise.* ◆ *tr.v.* **cataloged, cataloging, catalogs** or **catalogued, cataloguing, catalogues** To list in a catalog; make a catalog of: *catalog the books in a library.* —**cat′a·log′er, cat′a·logu′er** *n.*

catalpa (kə-tăl′pə *or* kə-tôl′pə) *n.* Any of several trees of North America and Asia having large heart-shaped leaves, showy white flowers, and long slender pods.

catalysis (kə-tăl′ĭ-sĭs) *n.* The starting, speeding up, or changing of a chemical reaction by the action of a catalyst.

catalyst (kăt′l-ĭst) *n.* **1.** A substance that starts or speeds up a chemical reaction while undergoing no permanent change itself. The enzymes in saliva, for example, are catalysts in digestion. **2.** A person or thing that causes or speeds up a process or event. —**cat·a·lyt·ic** (kăt′l-ĭt′ĭk) *adj.*

catalytic converter *n.* A device that changes harmful exhaust gases of an automotive engine from hydrocarbons and carbon monoxide into carbon dioxide and water vapor.

catalyze (kăt′l-īz′) *tr.v.* **catalyzed, catalyzing, catalyzes** To change or bring about by catalysis: *The enzyme catalyzes the synthesis of a large molecule.*

catamaran (kăt′ə-mə-răn′) *n.* **1.** A boat with two parallel hulls. **2.** A long raft of logs tied together.

catamount (kăt′ə-mount′) *n.* A cougar.

catapult (kăt′ə-pŭlt′ *or* kăt′ə-pŏŏlt′) *n.* **1.** Any of various ancient military machines used to hurl stones, spears, ar-

rows, or other missiles at an enemy. **2.** A mechanism for launching aircraft from the deck of a ship. ◆ *v.* **catapulted, catapulting, catapults** —*tr.* To hurl or launch from or as if from a catapult: *The volcano catapulted large boulders high into the air.* —*intr.* **1.** To be catapulted or hurled: *The rider catapulted over the handlebars as her bike hit the curb.* **2.** To jump or spring: *When the firefighters heard the alarm, they catapulted out of bed.*

cataract (kăt′ə-răkt′) *n.* **1.** A large steep waterfall. **2.** A great downpour. **3.** A condition in which the lens of an eye or the membrane that covers it turns cloudy, causing total or partial blindness.

catarrh (kə-tär′) *n.* Abnormal discharge of mucus related to inflammation of mucous membranes, especially those of the nose and throat. —**ca·tarrh′al** *adj.*

catastrophe (kə-tăs′trə-fē) *n.* **1.** A great and sudden calamity, such as an earthquake or flood. **2.** A complete failure: *The dry and crumbly cake was a catastrophe.*

catastrophic (kăt′ə-strŏf′ĭk) *adj.* Relating to or resulting in a catastrophe: *a catastrophic fire.* —**cat′a·stroph′i·cal·ly** *adv.*

catatonia (kăt′ə-tō′nē-ə) *n.* A condition sometimes occurring in people with certain psychiatric disorders, variously characterized by stupor, mania, and either rigidity or extreme flexibility of the limbs. —**cat′a·ton′ic** (kăt′ə-tŏn′ĭk) *adj. & n.* —**cat′a·ton′i·cal·ly** *adv.*

Catawba (kə-tô′bə) *n., pl.* **Catawba** or **Catawbas 1.** A member of a Native American people of North and South Carolina. **2.** The Siouan language of the Catawba.

catbird (kăt′bûrd′) *n.* A dark-gray North American songbird having a call resembling the mewing of a cat.

catboat (kăt′bōt′) *n.* A small sailboat with a single sail on a mast set far forward in the bow.

cat burglar *n.* A stealthy burglar.

catcall (kăt′kôl′) *n.* A loud shrill call or whistle expressing disapproval or derision, usually directed from an audience toward a speaker or performer. ◆ *intr.v.* **catcalled, catcalling, catcalls** To make catcalls.

catch (kăch *or* kĕch) *v.* **caught** (kôt), **catching, catches** —*tr.* **1.** To get and hold (something that has been in motion), especially by using the hands or an implement: *catch a ball.* **2.** To capture or seize, especially after a chase: *The cat caught a mouse.* **3.** To discover or come upon suddenly: *We caught the puppy stealing the cat's food.* **4.** To reach in time to board: *Can we still catch the 3:00 train?* **5.** To become infected with; contract: *catch a cold.* **6.** To cause to be hooked, entangled, or fastened: *I caught my shirt on a nail.* **7.** To hit; strike: *The falling tree caught a corner of the porch.* **8.** To attract: *They tried to catch our attention by yelling and waving their arms.* **9.** To take in or get momentarily: *catch sight of a deer; catch what was said over the noise.* **10.** To go to see (a play, motion picture, or other entertainment). **11.** To stop or check (oneself) before or during an action: *I caught myself before laughing.* **12.** In baseball, to play (a game) as catcher. —*intr.* **1.** To become hooked, entangled, or fastened: *My coat caught in the car door.* **2.** To burn; ignite: *The fire caught quickly.* **3.** In baseball, to play as catcher. ◆ *n.* **1.** The act or an instance of catching: *The center fielder made a diving catch.* **2.** The amount of something caught, especially fish: *a huge catch of tuna.* **3.** A device, such as a hook or latch, for fastening or closing something: *a door catch.* **4.** A game in which two or more people throw a ball back and forth to each other: *They played catch until supper.* **5.** *Informal* A hidden or tricky condition; a pitfall: *The offer is generous but there must be a catch.* ◆ **catch fire 1.** To begin to burn. **2.** To become popular: *a hobby that has caught fire around the country.* **catch on 1.** *Informal* To understand; get the idea: *The dancers caught on to the new steps quickly.* **2.** To become fashionable or popular. **catch (one's) breath** To rest so as to be able to continue: *We caught our breath for a minute before climbing to the top of the mountain.* **catch up 1.** To move fast enough to reach another; draw even: *We've almost caught up with them.* **2.** To become up-to-date: *We have to catch up on the latest news.* **3.** To absorb completely; captivate: *The scientist was caught up in challenging research.*

Catch-22 also **catch-22** (kăch′twĕn-tē-to͞o′ *or* kĕch′twĕn-tē-to͞o′) *n.* A situation in which a desired outcome is impossible because the apparent ways of achieving the outcome are directly contradictory and end up causing failure for one another.

catchall (kăch′ôl′ *or* kĕch′ôl′) *n.* **1.** A place for keeping odds and ends, as a box, shelf, or closet. **2.** Something that covers many different situations, as a phrase, word, or law.

catcher (kăch′ər *or* kĕch′ər) *n.* A person or thing that catches, especially the baseball player stationed behind home plate who catches pitches.

catching (kăch′ĭng *or* kĕch′ĭng) *adj.* **1.** Easily transmitted; contagious: *Flu is catching.* **2.** Attractive; catchy: *a catching tune; a catching idea.*

catch phrase *n.* An often repeated word or slogan: *"No new taxes" is a catch phrase often heard at election time.*

catchword (kăch′wûrd′ *or* kĕch′wûrd′) *n.* A well-known word or phrase, especially one that sums up an idea or group.

catchy (kăch′ē *or* kĕch′ē) *adj.* **catchier, catchiest 1.** Attractive or appealing: *a catchy idea for a new book.* **2.** Easily remembered: *a catchy tune.* **3.** Tricky; deceptive: *a catchy question.*

catechism (kăt′ĭ-kĭz′əm) *n.* **1.** A series of questions along with the correct answers to them, used as a way of teaching the basic doctrines of a Christian denomination. **2.** A series of questions and answers used to examine something.

catechize (kăt′ĭ-kīz′) *tr.v.* **catechized, catechizing, catechizes 1.** To teach Christian doctrine to (a person) by means of questions and answers. **2.** To question closely: *The coach catechized the team on the new plays until everyone knew them perfectly.*

catechumen (kăt′ĭ-kyo͞o′mən) *n.* **1.** One who is being taught the principles of Christianity, especially by means of a catechism. **2.** One who is being instructed in a subject at an elementary level.

categorical (kăt′ĭ-gôr′ĭ-kəl) *adj.* Being without exception or qualification; absolute: *a categorical rejection of an offer.* —**cat′e·gor′i·cal·ly** *adv.*

categorize (kăt′ĭ-gə-rīz′) *tr.v.* **categorized, categorizing, categorizes** To put into a category; classify: *categorize news reports into those about domestic matters and those about international affairs.* —**cat′e·go·ri·za′tion** (kăt′-ĭ-gər-ĭ-zā′shən) *n.*

category (kăt′ĭ-gôr′ē) *n., pl.* **categories** A class or division in a system of classification.

cater (kā′tər) *v.* **catered, catering, caters** —*intr.* **1.** To provide and serve food and drinks: *His business caters for functions at the statehouse.* **2.** To try to satisfy or appeal to the wants and needs of someone: *The governor was ac-*

cused of catering to big business. —*tr.* To supply and serve food and drinks for: *cater a wedding.*

cater-cornered (kăt′ər-kôr′nərd) also **cater-corner** (kăt′-ər-kôr′nər) *or* **catty-cornered** (kăt′ē-kôr′nərd) *or* **catty-corner** (kăt′ē-kôr′nər) *or* **kitty-cornered** (kĭt′ē-kôr′-nərd) *or* **kitty-corner** (kĭt′ē-kôr′nər) *adj.* Diagonal. ❖ *adv.* In a diagonal position.

caterer (kā′tər-ər) *n.* A person or business that provides and serves food and drinks for weddings, banquets, meetings, and other occasions.

caterpillar (kăt′ər-pĭl′ər *or* kăt′ə-pĭl′ər) *n.* The wormlike larva of a butterfly or moth.

caterwaul (kăt′ər-wôl′) *intr.v.* **caterwauled, caterwauling, caterwauls** To utter a shrill cry or screech like that of a cat. ❖ *n.* A shrill or howling cry.

catfish (kăt′fĭsh′) *n.* Any of numerous scaleless, mostly freshwater fishes having feelers that resemble whiskers near the mouth.

catgut (kăt′gŭt′) *n.* A tough thin cord made from the dried intestines of certain animals, especially sheep, and used in making strings for musical instruments and tennis rackets and in sewing up surgical wounds.

cathartic (kə-thär′tĭk) *adj.* **1.** Tending to stimulate the intestines as a laxative. **2.** Purifying or cleansing the emotions: *a cathartic experience.* ❖ *n.* A cathartic drug or medicine.

cathedra (kə-thē′drə) *n., pl.* **cathedrae** (kə-thē′drē) A bishop's official chair or throne.

cathedral (kə-thē′drəl) *n.* **1.** The principal church of a bishop's diocese. **2.** A large or important church.

catheter (kăth′ĭ-tər) *n.* A thin, hollow, flexible tube inserted into a duct of the body to remove a blockage or drain fluid.

cathode (kăth′ōd′) *n.* **1.** A negative electrode. **2.** The positive terminal in a battery or other device that is supplying current.

cathode ray *n.* A beam of electrons from the cathode in a vacuum tube. When cathode rays strike a solid substance, they produce x-rays.

cathode-ray tube (kăth′ōd-rā′) *n.* A vacuum tube in which a beam of electrons is directed against a phosphorescent screen where, under the influence of electric or magnetic fields, it forms an image. Cathode-ray tubes were standard in TVs and computer screens before the introduction of flat-screen technology.

catholic (kăth′ə-lĭk *or* kăth′lĭk) *adj.* **1.** Broad in sympathies, interests, and understanding: *a person with catholic tastes.* **2. Catholic a.** Relating to the Roman Catholic Church. **b.** Relating to all Christians or the universal Christian church. ❖ *n.* **Catholic** A Roman Catholic.

Catholicism (kə-thŏl′ĭ-sĭz′əm) *n.* The faith, doctrine, practice, and organization of the Roman Catholic Church.

cation (kăt′ī′ən) *n.* A positively charged ion that moves toward the negative electrode in electrolysis.

catkin (kăt′kĭn) *n.* A dense, often drooping cluster of very small flowers without petals, found especially in willows, birches, and oaks.

catnap (kăt′năp′) *n.* A short nap. ❖ *intr.v.* **catnapped, catnapping, catnaps** To take a short nap.

catnip (kăt′nĭp′) *n.* A plant related to mint, having a strong smell that is very attractive to cats.

cat-o'-nine-tails (kăt′ə-nīn′tālz′) *n., pl.* **cat-o'-nine-tails** A whip consisting of nine knotted cords fastened to a handle, used for flogging.

CAT scan (kăt) *n.* A CT scan. —**CAT scanner** *n.*

cat's cradle (kăts) *n.* A children's game in which a loop of string is woven in patterns over the fingers of both hands and often transferred back and forth between the hands of two players.

cat's-paw also **catspaw** (kăts'pô') *n.* **1.** A person who is used by another to do something risky or illegal. **2.** A light breeze that ruffles small areas of water, as in a pool or pond.

catsup (kăt'səp *or* kăch'əp *or* kĕch'əp) *n.* Variant of **ketchup.**

cattail (kăt'tāl') *n.* Any of various tall marsh plants having long leaves and a dense cylindrical cluster of tiny brownish flowers.

cattle (kăt'l) *pl.n.* Large hoofed mammals that have been domesticated and are often raised for meat and dairy products. Cows, bulls, and oxen are cattle.

cattleman (kăt'l-mən) *n.* A man who tends or raises cattle.

catty (kăt'ē) *adj.* **cattier, cattiest 1.** Spiteful; mean; malicious: *catty gossip.* **2.** Like a cat; stealthy. —**cat'ti·ly** *adv.* —**cat'ti·ness** *n.*

catty-cornered (kăt'ē-kôr'nərd) *or* **catty-corner** (kăt'ē-kôr'nər) *adj. & adv.* Variants of **cater-cornered.**

catwalk (kăt'wôk') *n.* A narrow elevated platform or pathway, as on the sides of a bridge or above a stage.

Caucasian (kô-kā'zhən) *adj.* **1a.** Relating to a racial group having light skin; white. **b.** Relating to a human racial classification distinguished especially by light or brown skin color and straight, wavy, or curly hair. This classification, which includes peoples native to Europe, northern Africa, southwest Asia, and the Indian subcontinent, is no longer in scientific use. **2.** Relating to the Caucasus region or its peoples, languages, or cultures. ❖ *n.* **1a.** A white person. **b.** A person belonging to the Caucasian racial division. **2.** A native or inhabitant of the Caucasus.

caucus (kô'kəs) *n., pl.* **caucuses** *or* **caucusses** A meeting of members of a political party to decide on a question of policy or to choose a candidate for office. ❖ *intr.v.* **caucused, caucusing, caucuses** *or* **caucussed, caucussing, caucusses** To gather in or hold a caucus.

caudal (kôd'l) *adj.* **1.** At or near the tail or hind parts of an animal: *a fish's caudal fin.* **2.** Resembling a tail.

caudillo (kô-dēl'yō *or* kô-dē'yō) *n., pl.* **caudillos** A leader or chief, especially a military dictator.

caught (kôt) *v.* Past tense and past participle of **catch.**

caul (kôl) *n.* A portion of the amnion, especially when it covers the head of a fetus at birth.

cauldron (kôl'drən) *n.* **1.** A large kettle for boiling. **2.** A situation of turmoil or unrest: *a cauldron of political intrigue.*

cauliflower (kô'lĭ-flou'ər *or* kŏl'ĭ-flou'ər) *n.* A plant having a compact whitish head of undeveloped flowers that is eaten as a vegetable.

caulk (kôk) *n.* A material, such as a compound containing polyurethane, acrylic, or silicone, that is used to fill or seal narrow spaces, such as cracks around a window or the seams of a boat. ❖ *v.* **caulked, caulking, caulks** —*tr.* To make watertight or airtight by filling or sealing with caulking: *caulk the cracks around the door.* —*intr.* To apply caulking: *The plumber caulked around the bathtub to keep it from leaking.* —**caulk'er** *n.*

caulking (kô'kĭng) *n.* Caulk.

causal (kô'zəl) *adj.* Being or constituting a cause: *the causal connection between a scarcity of goods and higher prices.* —**caus'al·ly** *adv.*

cause (kôz) *n.* **1.** A person or thing that makes something happen: *Investigators finally found the cause of the fire.* **2.** A basis for a certain feeling, action, or decision; a reason: *There is no cause for alarm.* **3.** An idea or goal to which many people are dedicated: *the noble cause of peace.* ❖ *tr.v.* **caused, causing, causes** To be the cause of; make happen; bring about: *Many bacteria cause disease.*

causeway (kôz'wā') *n.* A raised roadway, as across marshland or water.

caustic (kô'stĭk) *adj.* **1.** Capable of burning, corroding, dissolving or destroying other substances, such as living tissue or metal. **2.** Sarcastic; biting; cutting: *caustic remarks.* ❖ *n.* A caustic material or substance. —**caus'ti·cal·ly** *adv.*

caustic soda *n.* Sodium hydroxide.

cauterize (kô'tə-rīz') *tr.v.* **cauterized, cauterizing, cauterizes** To burn or sear (a wound or dead tissue, for example), as with a caustic substance or a hot instrument, in order to stop bleeding or prevent infection. —**cau'ter·i·za'tion** (kô'tər-ĭ-zā'shən) *n.*

caution (kô'shən) *n.* **1.** Care to avoid danger or trouble: *climb icy steps with caution.* **2.** A warning: *My doctor ended his advice with a caution about not getting enough sleep.* ❖ *tr.v.* **cautioned, cautioning, cautions** To warn against possible trouble or danger: *The sign cautioned drivers to go slowly.*

cautious (kô'shəs) *adj.* Showing or having caution; careful: *a slow and cautious driver.* —**cau'tious·ly** *adv.* —**cau'tious·ness** *n.*

cavalcade (kăv'əl-kād *or* kăv'əl-kād') *n.* **1.** A ceremonial procession of people on horseback, in carriages, or in automobiles: *The president and his cavalcade drove through town.* **2.** A succession of notable people, scenes, or events: *The actress starred in a cavalcade of hit movies.*

cavalier (kăv'ə-lîr') *n.* **1.** An armed horseman; a knight. **2.** A gallant or chivalrous gentleman, especially one who escorts a lady. **3. Cavalier** A supporter of King Charles I during the English civil war (1642–1652). ❖ *adj.* Casual and indifferent, often in an arrogant manner: *The official gave a cavalier answer to our demands for more information.* —**cav'a·lier'ly** *adv.*

cavalry (kăv'əl-rē) *n., pl.* **cavalries 1.** A military unit using armored vehicles, such as tanks and helicopters. **2.** Troops trained to fight on horseback.

cave (kāv) *n.* A hollow or natural passage under the earth or in the side of a hill or mountain with an opening to the surface. ❖ *v.* **caved, caving, caves** —*tr.* To cause to collapse or fall: *A surge of water caved in the banks of the river.* —*intr.* **1.** To fall in; collapse: *The ground above the old mine caved in.* **2.** To give up all opposition: *caved in to our demands.* **3.** To explore caves.

caveat (kăv'ē-ät' *or* kăv'vē-ät') *n.* A warning or restriction: *The recommendation comes with several caveats.*

caveat emptor (ĕmp'tôr') *n.* Let the buyer beware; a warning to buyers to be sure of the quality of a product before purchasing it.

cave bear *n.* A large extinct bear of the Pleistocene Epoch. Most fossils have been found in caves in Europe.

cave dweller *n.* A person who lives in a cave, especially in prehistoric times.

cave-in (kāv'ĭn') *n.* **1.** A collapse, as of a tunnel or structure. **2.** A place where something has collapsed.

caveman also **cave man** (kăv′măn′) *n.* A prehistoric cave dweller.

caver (kā′vər) *n.* A person who explores or studies caves.

cavern (kăv′ərn) *n.* A very large cave.

cavernous (kăv′ər-nəs) *adj.* Resembling a cavern; huge, deep, and hollow: *the cavernous interior of a great cathedral.*

caviar (kăv′ē-är) *n.* The eggs of a sturgeon or other large fish, prepared with salt and eaten as a delicacy.

cavil (kăv′əl) *intr.v.* **caviled, caviling, cavils** also **cavilled, cavilling, cavils** To find fault unnecessarily; raise unimportant objections: *Let's not waste time caviling about the rules instead of getting on with the game.* ❖ *n.* A trivial objection.

cavitation (kăv′ĭ-tā′shən) *n.* The sudden formation and collapse of bubbles in a liquid caused by mechanical forces, such as the moving blades of a ship's propeller.

cavity (kăv′ĭ-tē) *n., pl.* **cavities** **1.** A hollow or hole. **2.** A hollow area within the body: *the abdominal cavity.* **3.** A pocket of decay in a tooth.

cavort (kə-vôrt′) *intr.v.* **cavorted, cavorting, cavorts** **1.** To leap about playfully; romp; frolic: *lambs cavorting in a pen.* **2.** To have lively or noisy fun: *The children cavorted in the pool.*

cavy (kā′vē) *n., pl.* **cavies** Any of various tailless South American rodents, such as the guinea pig.

caw (kô) *n.* The hoarse harsh sound made by a crow. ❖ *intr.v.* **cawed, cawing, caws** To make this sound.

cay (kē *or* kā) *n.* A small low island composed largely of coral or sand.

cayenne pepper (kī-ĕn′ *or* kā-ĕn′) *n.* A very strong sharp-tasting seasoning made from the ground pods of any of several red peppers.

cayman (kā′mən) *n.* Variant of **caiman.**

Cayuga (kā-yōō′gə *or* kī-yōō′gə) *n., pl.* **Cayuga** or **Cayugas** **1.** A member of a Native American people of western New York State. **2.** The Iroquoian language of the Cayuga.

cayuse (kī-yōōs′ *or* kī′yōōs′) *n.* A small sturdy horse, especially one of the western United States.

Cayuse *n., pl.* **Cayuse** or **Cayuses** **1.** A member of a Native American people of Oregon and Washington. **2.** The extinct language of the Cayuse.

CB An abbreviation of citizens band.

cc[1] (sē′sē′) *n.* A carbon copy of a document. ❖ *tr.v.* **cc′ed, cc′ing, cc′s** To send (someone) a carbon copy of a document.

cc[2] An abbreviation of cubic centimeter.

C clef *n.* A sign used to indicate which line of a musical staff represents middle C.

CD An abbreviation of: **1.** certificate of deposit. **2.** civil defense. **3.** compact disc.

CD-ROM (sē′dē′rŏm′) *n.* A compact disc whose data cannot be erased or changed.

CE or **CE** An abbreviation of Common Era. —SEE NOTE AT **Common Era.**

cease (sēs) *intr. & tr.v.* **ceased, ceasing, ceases** To come or bring to an end; stop: *The noise ceased. The factory ceased production.* See Synonyms at **stop.**

cease-fire or **ceasefire** (sēs′fīr′) *n.* A suspension of fighting in a war; a truce.

ceaseless (sēs′lĭs) *adj.* Having no pause; constant or continual. —**cease′less·ly** *adv.* —**cease′less·ness** *n.*

cecropia moth (sĭ-krō′pē-ə) *n.* A large North American moth having brownish wings with red and white markings.

cecum also **caecum** (sē′kəm) *n., pl.* **ceca** also **caeca** (sē′kə) A pouch that constitutes the beginning of the large intestine.

cedar (sē′dər) *n.* **1.** Any of various evergreen trees related to the pines and firs, having hard fragrant wood. **2.** The wood of such a tree, used to make furniture, shingles, chests, and pencils.

cedar waxwing *n.* A grayish-brown North American bird having a crested head, a yellow-tipped tail, and bright red tips on the wing feathers.

cede (sēd) *tr.v.* **ceded, ceding, cedes** To surrender possession of, especially by treaty; yield; give up: *France ceded Canada to Great Britain at the end of the French and Indian War.* See Synonyms at **yield.**

cedilla (sĭ-dĭl′ə) *n.* A mark (˛) placed beneath the letter *c* in French and Portuguese and in certain words in English, such as *façade,* indicating that the letter is to be pronounced like the *s* in *set.*

ceiling (sē′lĭng) *n.* **1.** The inside upper surface of a room: *lights hung from the ceiling.* **2.** The distance between the earth and the lowest clouds: *A ceiling of less than 500 feet gives poor visibility for an aircraft.* **3.** The maximum altitude at which an airplane can fly. **4.** A maximum limit: *a ceiling on gasoline prices; a ceiling on crop production; a debt ceiling.*

celebrant (sĕl′ə-brənt) *n.* **1.** A person who performs the official or religious duties of a ceremony or rite. **2.** The priest who conducts the celebration of the Mass. **3.** A participant in a celebration.

celebrate (sĕl′ə-brāt′) *v.* **celebrated, celebrating, celebrates** —*tr.* **1.** To have a party or engage in other festive activity in honor of (a special occasion): *celebrating her birthday.* **2.** To perform (a religious ceremony): *The priest celebrated Mass.* **3.** To praise publicly; honor; extol: *a poem that celebrates friendship.* —*intr.* To have a good time with others to mark a special occasion or an important event: *celebrate after hearing the good news.* —**cel′e·bra′tion** *n.* —**cel′e·bra·to′ry** (sĕl′ə-brə-tôr′ē *or* sə-lĕb′rə-tôr′ē) *adj.*

celebrated (sĕl′ə-brā′tĭd) *adj.* Known and praised by many people: *a celebrated musician.* See Synonyms at **famous.**

celebrity (sə-lĕb′rĭ-tē) *n., pl.* **celebrities** **1.** A famous person: *The singer is a celebrity wherever he goes.* **2.** Fame; renown: *She achieved celebrity as an architect.*

celerity (sə-lĕr′ĭ-tē) *n.* Quickness; speed: *move with celerity.*

celery (sĕl′ə-rē) *n.* **1.** The crisp, juicy, light-green stems of a plant related to parsley, eaten raw or cooked. **2.** The plant that bears such stems.

celesta (sə-lĕs′tə) also **celeste** (sə-lĕst′) *n.* A musical instrument with a keyboard and metal plates that are struck by hammers and produce bell-like tones.

celestial (sə-lĕs′chəl) *adj.* **1.** Relating to the sky or the astronomical universe: *Stars and planets are celestial objects.* **2.** Of heaven: *Angels are celestial beings.* —**ce·les′tial·ly** *adv.*

celestial equator *n.* A great circle on the celestial sphere in the plane of Earth's equator.

celestial longitude *n.* The angular distance eastward from the vernal equinox measured along the ecliptic to a great circle drawn through the pole of the ecliptic plane and a celestial object.

celestial pole *n.* Either of the points at which the imaginary extensions of Earth's axis intersect the celestial sphere.

celestial sphere *n.* An imaginary sphere, having Earth as its center, on which the sun, moon, and stars appear to be located.

celiac disease (sē′lē-ăk′) *n.* A long-lasting disease of the stomach and intestines that is characterized by sensitivity to gluten and poor absorption of nutrients.

celibacy (sĕl′ə-bə-sē) *n.* The condition of being unmarried or of abstaining from sexual intercourse, especially for religious reasons.

celibate (sĕl′ə-bĭt) *n.* A person who remains unmarried or abstains from sexual intercourse, especially for religious reasons. ❖ *adj.* Unmarried or abstaining from sexual intercourse, especially for religious reasons.

cell (sĕl) *n.* **1.** The basic unit of living matter in all organisms, consisting of cytoplasm and various organelles, all surrounded by a membrane. All cells except bacteria and archaea have a distinct nucleus that is also enclosed by a membrane. Some organisms consist of single cells, while others consist of vast numbers of cells. **2.** A single unit that is capable of changing some form of energy, such as chemical energy or radiant energy, into electricity. A flashlight battery is a single cell. **3.** A cell phone. **4.** A small confining room, as in a prison or convent. **5.** A small enclosed cavity or space, such as a compartment in a honeycomb.

cellar (sĕl′ər) *n.* **1.** A storage room beneath a house. **2.** A cool dark room for storing wines.

cellblock (sĕl′blŏk′) *n.* A group of cells that make up a section of a prison.

cell division *n.* The process by which a cell divides into two or more cells. Mitosis and meiosis are two types of cell division.

cellist (chĕl′ĭst) *n.* A person who plays the cello.

cell line *n.* A group of identical cells that come from a single cell or set of cells of the same type and are used for scientific and medical research. Under certain conditions, the cells can grow and divide for many years.

cell membrane *n.* The thin membrane that surrounds the cytoplasm of a cell and regulates the passage of materials in and out of the cell.

cello (chĕl′ō) *n., pl.* **cellos** A large musical instrument of the violin family, held upright between the knees and having four strings tuned an octave below those of a viola.

cellophane (sĕl′ə-fān′) *n.* **1.** A thin, flexible, transparent material made from cellulose that is obtained from wood pulp, used as a moistureproof wrapping. **2.** Plastic wrap.

cell phone or **cellphone** (sĕl′fōn′) *n.* A portable telephone that sends and receives calls through a network of short-range radio transmitters and relay stations that make connections to telephone lines.

cellular (sĕl′yə-lər) *adj.* **1.** Relating to or involving cells: *cellular division.* **2.** Made of or containing cells: *the cellular structure of the brain.* **3.** Relating to cell phones or to a cell phone network: *rates for cellular service.*

cellular respiration *n.* A process of cell metabolism that produces energy in the form of ATP, usually involving the use of oxygen to break down nutrients (such as glucose) and the release of carbon dioxide and water as byproducts.

cellular telephone *n.* A cell phone.

cellulite (sĕl′yə-līt′) *n.* A fatty deposit, as under the skin around the thighs.

celluloid (sĕl′yə-loid′) *n.* A colorless flammable material made from cellulose and formerly used in making photographic film.

cellulose (sĕl′yə-lōs′) *n.* A carbohydrate that is insoluble in water, forms the main component of the cell walls of plants, and is used in making products such as paper, insulation, cellophane, and textiles.

cellulose acetate *n.* Any of several durable materials made from cellulose and used in making magnetic tape, plastic film for wrapping and packaging, and textile fibers.

cell wall *n.* The rigid outer layer that surrounds the cell membrane in plants, fungi, and most algae and bacteria. In plants, it is composed mostly of cellulose.

Celsius (sĕl′sē-əs or sĕl′shəs) *adj.* Relating to a temperature scale on which the freezing point of water is 0° and the boiling point of water is 100° under normal atmospheric pressure. See table at **measurement.**

Celt (kĕlt or sĕlt) also **Kelt** (kĕlt) *n.* **1.** A member of an ancient Indo-European people inhabiting central and much of western Europe and the British Isles, especially a Briton or Gaul. **2.** A native speaker of a modern Celtic language or a descendant of such a speaker.

Celtic (kĕl′tĭk or sĕl′tĭk) also **Keltic** (kĕl′tĭk) *adj.* Relating to the Celts and their languages. ❖ *n.* A group of Indo-European languages including Welsh, Irish Gaelic, Scottish Gaelic, Breton, and the extinct languages Manx, Cornish, and Gaulish.

cement (sĭ-mĕnt′) *n.* **1.** A building material made by grinding heated limestone with clay to form a powder that can be mixed with water and poured to harden as a solid mass. **2.** Concrete. **3.** A substance that hardens to hold things together; glue: *use cement to mend a broken cup.* **4.** Something that unites or joins: *Respect for each other's opinions was the cement of their friendship.* ❖ *tr.v.* **cemented, cementing, cements 1.** To join or cover with cement: *cement bricks in a wall.* **2.** To make binding; establish or strengthen: *Signing the contract cemented the partners' agreement.*

cemetery (sĕm′ĭ-tĕr′ē) *n., pl.* **cemeteries** A place for burying the dead; a graveyard.

cenotaph (sĕn′ə-tăf′) *n.* A monument erected in honor of a dead person whose remains lie elsewhere. —**cen′o·taph′ic** *adj.*

Cenozoic (sĕn′ə-zō′ĭk or sē′nə-zō′ĭk) *n.* The most recent era of geologic time, from about 66 million years ago to the present. During the Cenozoic, birds and mammals diversified, and the continents developed into their present forms. —**Cen′o·zo′ic** *adj.*

censer (sĕn′sər) *n.* A container for burning incense, especially in a religious ceremony.

censor (sĕn′sər) *n.* **1.** A person who is authorized by a government or organization to examine books, movies, or other materials and to remove or prevent from becoming available anything that is considered improper or harmful. **2.** One of two ancient Roman officials responsible for taking the public census and supervising public behavior and morals. ❖ *tr.v.* **censored, censoring, censors** To remove material from or prevent the publication of: *censor classified information in a letter.*

censorious (sĕn-sôr′ē-əs) *adj.* Very critical: *The critic's censorious review seemed unfair.* —**cen·so′ri·ous·ly** *adv.* —**cen·so′ri·ous·ness** *n.*

censorship (sĕn′sər-shĭp′) *n.* **1.** The act or practice of censoring. **2.** The office or authority of a Roman censor.

censure (sĕn′shər) *n.* An expression of strong disapproval or harsh criticism. ❖ *tr.v.* **censured, censuring, censures** To express strong disapproval of; criticize: *The press censured the city government for corruption.* —**cen′sur·er** *n.*

census (sĕn′səs) *n.* An official counting of population, usually made at regular intervals and often including statistics on age, sex, occupation, and other information.

cent (sĕnt) *n.* **1.** A coin of the United States, Canada, Australia, New Zealand, and various other countries, that is ¹⁄₁₀₀ of a dollar. **2.** A coin of various other countries equal to ¹⁄₁₀₀ of the basic monetary unit. **3.** A small sum of money: *I haven't a cent to my name.*

cent. An abbreviation of: **1.** centigrade. **2.** central. **3.** century.

centaur (sĕn′tôr′) *n.* In Greek mythology, a creature having the head, arms, and trunk of a human and the body and legs of a horse.

centavo (sĕn-tä′vō) *n., pl.* **centavos** A unit of money equal to ¹⁄₁₀₀ of the basic monetary unit in many Spanish-speaking or Portuguese-speaking countries.

centenarian (sĕn′tə-nâr′ē-ən) *n.* A person who is one hundred years old or older.

centenary (sĕn-tĕn′ə-rē *or* sĕn′tə-nĕr′ē) *n., pl.* **centenaries** **1.** A period of 100 years. **2.** A centennial. ❖ *adj.* Centennial.

centennial (sĕn-tĕn′ē-əl) *n.* A 100th anniversary or a celebration of it. ❖ *adj.* **1.** Relating to a period of 100 years. **2.** Happening once every 100 years: *The United States has had two centennial celebrations of its founding.* —**cen·ten′ni·al·ly** *adv.*

center (sĕn′tər) *n.* **1a.** A point within a circle or sphere that is equally distant from all points on the circumference or surface. **b.** A point that is equally distant from each vertex of a regular polygon. **2.** The middle position, part, or place of something: *the center of a table; chocolates with soft centers.* **3.** A place of concentrated activity: *a shopping center; a port that is a trading center.* **4.** A person or thing that is the chief object of attention, interest, activity, or emotion: *Our guest was the center of the party.* **5.** often **Center** A political party or set of policies representing a moderate view between those of the right and left. **6.** A player on a team positioned in or near the middle of a playing area or forward line, as in football, basketball, and hockey. ❖ *v.* **centered, centering, centers** —*tr.* **1.** To place in or at the center: *center a picture on a page.* **2.** To consider, treat, or have as a main theme, interest, or concern: *The moderator centered the discussion on the most urgent problems.* —*intr.* **1.** To be concentrated: *Support for the political opposition centered in the cities.* **2.** To have something as a main theme, interest, or concern; focus: *The conversation centered on air pollution.*

centerboard (sĕn′tər-bôrd′) *n.* A flat board or metal plate that can be lowered through the bottom of a sailboat to prevent it from drifting.

center field *n.* **1.** In baseball, the middle part of the outfield, behind second base. **2.** The position played by the center fielder.

center fielder *n.* In baseball, the player who defends center field.

centerfold (sĕn′tər-fōld′) *n.* **1.** A magazine center spread, especially a foldout of an oversize photograph or feature. **2a.** The subject of a photograph used as a centerfold, often a nude model. **b.** A feature, such as an advertisement or calendar, inserted as a centerfold.

center of gravity *n., pl.* **centers of gravity** The point in a body around which its weight is evenly balanced.

center of mass *n., pl.* **centers of mass** The point in a body that moves as though the body's entire mass were concentrated in it. It is usually in the same place as the center of gravity.

centerpiece (sĕn′tər-pēs′) *n.* **1.** An ornamental object, such as a vase of flowers, placed at the center of a dining table. **2.** The central or most important feature: *the centerpiece of the president's speech.*

centi– A prefix that means one hundredth: *centigram.*

centigrade (sĕn′tĭ-grād′) *adj.* Celsius.

centigram (sĕn′tĭ-grăm′) *n.* A unit of mass or weight in the metric system equal to ¹⁄₁₀₀ gram.

centiliter (sĕn′tə-lē′tər) *n.* A metric unit of volume equal to ¹⁄₁₀₀ of a liter.

centimeter (sĕn′tə-mē′tər) *n.* A unit of length in the metric system equal to ¹⁄₁₀₀ meter. See table at **measurement**.

centipede (sĕn′tə-pēd′) *n.* Any of various small invertebrate animals having a body divided into many segments, each with a pair of legs. The front legs are used to inject venom into prey.

central (sĕn′trəl) *adj.* **1.** Situated at, near, or in the center: *a central position from which to view the game.* **2.** Forming the center: *the central part of the state.* **3a.** Having the dominant or controlling power: *the central office of the corporation.* **b.** Controlling all parts of a system from a particular place: *central air conditioning; central heating.* **4.** Essential or principal: *the central topic of a story.* **5.** Easily reached from many places: *a central location for the new grocery store.* —**cen′tral·ly** *adv.*

central angle *n.* An angle formed by two lines extending from the center of a circle.

central bank *n.* A nation's primary banking authority, which controls the amount of money circulating in the economy, especially by printing new bills and setting interest rates on borrowing.

Central Intelligence Agency *n.* An agency of the US government that gathers information on matters affecting national security.

centralize (sĕn′trə-līz′) *v.* **centralized, centralizing, centralizes** —*tr.* **1.** To draw into or toward a center; consolidate: *centralize records in one office.* **2.** To bring under a central controlling authority: *The Constitution centralizes political power in the federal government.* —*intr.* To come together at a center; concentrate: *Their attention centralized on the basic problem.* —**cen′tral·i·za′tion** (sĕn′trə-lĭ-zā′shən) *n.*

central nervous system *n.* The part of the vertebrate nervous system that consists of the brain and spinal cord.

Central Powers *n.* The alliance of Germany, Austria-Hungary, Bulgaria, and the Ottoman Empire that fought against the Allies in World War I.

central processing unit *n.* The part of a computer that interprets and carries out instructions.

Central Standard Time *n.* Standard time in the sixth time zone west of Greenwich, England, used in the central United States.

centre (sĕn′tər) *n. & v. Chiefly British* Variant of **center**.

centrifugal (sĕn-trĭf′yə-gəl *or* sĕn-trĭf′ə-gəl) *adj.* Moving or directed away from a center: *the centrifugal action of a spinning top.* —**cen·trif′u·gal·ly** *adv.*

centrifugal force *n.* The apparent force that seems to cause a body turning around a center to move away from the center. Centrifugal force is not a true force but is actually an example of inertia.

centrifuge (sĕn′trə-fyo͞oj′) *n.* A machine for separating substances of different densities, as cream from milk or bacteria from a fluid, by rotating them at very high speeds so that the denser substances move further outward. ❖ *tr.v.* **centrifuged, centrifuging, centrifuges** To rotate (something) in a centrifuge.

centriole (sĕn′trē-ōl′) *n.* Either of a pair of rod-shaped bodies within the centrosome of an animal cell. Centrioles organize other materials in the cell and help determine the arrangement of chromosomes during cell division.

centripetal (sĕn-trĭp′ĭ-tl) *adj.* Directed or moving toward a center or axis. —**cen·trip′e·tal·ly** *adv.*

centripetal force *n.* The force that pulls an object moving in a circle toward the center of the circle and causes the object to follow a curving path. Earth's gravity acts as a centripetal force on the moon.

centrist (sĕn′trĭst) *n.* A person who has moderate political views, such as views midway between liberal and conservative. ❖ *adj.* Marked by or holding moderate political views: *a centrist policy; a centrist representative.*

centromere (sĕn′trə-mîr′) *n.* A region near the center of a chromosome that plays an important role in the separation of chromosomes during cell division.

centrosome (sĕn′trə-sōm′) *n.* A region of the cytoplasm next to the nucleus of a cell that in animal cells contains the centrioles.

centurion (sĕn-to͝or′ē-ən) *n.* An officer commanding a unit of a hundred men in the army of the Roman empire.

century (sĕn′chə-rē) *n., pl.* **centuries 1.** A period of 100 years. **2.** Each of the 100-year periods counted forward or backward since the year 1 AD: *the 20th century.*

century plant *n.* Any of various tropical American agave plants having long thick stiff leaves and a tall flower stalk. Century plants live for 10 to 30 years and then die after flowering once.

CEO An abbreviation of chief executive officer.

cephalic (sə-făl′ĭk) *adj.* Relating to or located on, near, or in the head.

cephalopod (sĕf′ə-lə-pŏd′) *n.* Any of various ocean mollusks, such as a squid, octopus, or nautilus, having long arms or tentacles around the mouth, a large head, a pair of large eyes, and a sharp beak.

cephalothorax (sĕf′ə-lə-thôr′ăks′) *n.* The combined head and thorax of some animals, such as crabs and spiders.

Cepheid (sē′fē-ĭd *or* sĕf′ē-ĭd) *n.* A type of star whose brightness varies in a regular periodic way.

ceramic (sə-răm′ĭk) *n.* **1.** A hard brittle material that resists heat and corrosion and is made by treating clay or some other nonmetallic mineral with extreme heat. Ceramic is used in making pottery, electrical insulators, and other products. **2.** An object made of this material. **3.** **ceramics** (*used with a singular verb*) The art or technique of making things from this material: *She took a class in ceramics and made several vases.* —**ce·ram′ic** *adj.*

cereal (sîr′ē-əl) *n.* **1.** The seeds of certain grasses, such as wheat, oats, barley, rice, or corn, used as food. **2.** A grass bearing such seeds. **3.** A food, especially a breakfast food such as corn flakes or oatmeal, prepared from such seeds.

cerebellum (sĕr′ə-bĕl′əm) *n., pl.* **cerebellums** or **cerebella** (sĕr′ə-bĕl′ə) A part of the brain, located at the rear of the skull, that regulates balance and coordinates muscle activity.

cerebra (sĕr′ə-brə *or* sə-rē′brə) *n.* A plural of **cerebrum.**

cerebral (sĕr′ə-brəl *or* sə-rē′brəl) *adj.* **1.** Relating to the brain or cerebrum: *a cerebral blood vessel.* **2.** Concerned with the intellect rather than the emotions: *a cerebral kind of poetry that does not stir the heart.*

cerebral cortex *n.* The outer layer of gray tissue that covers the two parts of the cerebrum, responsible for most of the higher functions of the nervous system, such as learning and memory.

cerebral palsy *n.* A disorder caused by brain injury usually at or before birth, resulting in symptoms that affect a person's ability to move the muscles in a coordinated way and sometimes involving other forms of disability, such as problems with vision or hearing.

cerebrospinal (sĕr′ə-brō-spī′nəl *or* sə-rē′brō-spī′nəl) *adj.* Relating to the brain and spinal cord: *cerebrospinal fluid.*

cerebrum (sĕr′ə-brəm *or* sə-rē′brəm) *n., pl.* **cerebrums** or **cerebra** (sĕr′ə-brə *or* sə-rē′brə) The large rounded structure of the brain that fills most of the skull, divided by a deep groove into two parts that are joined at the bottom. It integrates information coming in from the senses and controls voluntary movements of the muscles and mental functions such as thought and emotion.

ceremonial (sĕr′ə-mō′nē-əl) *adj.* **1.** Relating to or appropriate to a ceremony: *ceremonial dances.* **2.** Characterized by or involved in ceremony: *ceremonial robes; ceremonial duties.* ❖ *n.* A set of ceremonies established for a specific occasion; a ritual.

ceremonious (sĕr′ə-mō′nē-əs) *adj.* **1.** In accordance with a set of customary forms or rites; formal: *Inauguration of the president is a ceremonious occasion.* **2.** Careful about ceremony and formality; formally polite: *a fancy restaurant with ceremonious waiters.* —**cer′e·mo′ni·ous·ly** *adv.* —**cer′e·mo′ni·ous·ness** *n.*

ceremony (sĕr′ə-mō′nē) *n., pl.* **ceremonies 1.** A formal act or set of acts performed in honor or celebration of an occasion, such as a wedding, funeral, or national event. **2.** Proper or polite behavior; formality: *the ceremony of shaking hands when introduced.*

Ceres (sîr′ēz) *n.* **1.** In Roman mythology, the goddess of agriculture, identified with the Greek Demeter. **2.** The closest dwarf planet to the sun. The orbit of Ceres is between Mars and Jupiter, and it was the first object in the asteroid belt to be discovered. —SEE NOTE AT **planet.**

cerium (sîr′ē-əm) *n. Symbol* **Ce** A grayish metallic element that occurs only in combination with other elements and is used in porcelain, glass, and alloys. Atomic number 58. See **Periodic Table.**

certain (sûr′tn) *adj.* **1.** Established or agreed upon; definite: *We save a certain amount each month.* **2.** Sure to come or happen; inevitable: *If the temperature keeps dropping, it is certain that the rain will turn to snow.* **3.** Established beyond doubt; indisputable: *It is certain that the planets revolve around the sun.* **4.** Reliable; dependable: *a certain remedy to the problem.* **5.** Confident; assured: *Are you certain that you left the book here?* **6.** Not named or specified but assumed to be known: *certain kinds of farm animals.* **7.** Named but not familiar or known: *a certain Mr. Smith.* **8.** Some but not much; limited: *The report is accurate to a certain degree.* ❖ *pron.* A certain number; some: *Certain of the watches are waterproof.* ◆ **for certain** Without doubt; definitely: *Winter will come for certain.*

certainly (sûr′tn-lē) *adv.* Surely; definitely: *I am certainly going to the movies if I get a chance.*

certainty (sûr′tn-tē) *n., pl.* **certainties 1.** The condition or quality of being certain; freedom from doubt; sureness: *There is no certainty that the package will arrive today.* **2.** A clearly established fact: *It is a certainty that the moon affects the tides.*

certificate (sər-tĭf′ĭ-kĭt) *n.* **1.** An official document that is proof of some fact, such as a date of birth. **2.** A document stating that a person has completed the requirements to practice a certain profession. **3.** A document that certifies ownership: *an automobile registration certificate; a stock certificate.*

certificate of deposit *n., pl.* **certificates of deposit** A certificate from a bank stating that a certain amount of money has been deposited at that bank by a particular person, usually paying a specified rate of interest over a stated period of time.

certification (sûr′tə-fĭ-kā′shən) *n.* **1.** The act of certifying or the condition of being certified: *All states require the certification of doctors.* **2.** A certified document or statement; a certificate: *Our doctor's certification hung in a frame on the wall.*

Certified Mail (sûr′tə-fīd′) A trademark used for a mail service that provides proof of delivery to the sender.

certify (sûr′tə-fī′) *tr.v.* **certified, certifying, certifies 1.** To guarantee to be true or valid by an official document: *Your license certifies that you know how to drive a car.* **2.** To guarantee the quality, value, or standard of: *The inspector certified the elevator as safe.* **3.** To issue a license or certificate to: *This document certifies that she can practice dentistry in this state.*

certitude (sûr′tĭ-tōōd′) *n.* The condition of being certain; confidence; complete assurance: *the doctor's certitude about my good health.*

cerulean (sə-rōō′lē-ən) *adj.* Sky-blue; azure.

cervical (sûr′vĭ-kəl) *adj.* Relating to the neck or to a cervix: *the cervical vertebrae of the upper backbone.*

cervix (sûr′vĭks) *n., pl.* **cervixes** or **cervices** (sûr′vĭ-sēz′) **1.** A neck-shaped part of the body, especially the narrow outer end of the uterus. **2.** The neck.

cesarean also **caesarean** (sĭ-zâr′ē-ən) *n.* A cesarean section. ❖ *adj.* Relating to a cesarean section.

cesarean section *n.* A surgical procedure in which an incision is made through the abdominal wall and uterus in order to deliver a baby.

cesium (sē′zē-əm) *n. Symbol* **Cs** A soft, silvery metallic element that becomes liquid just above room temperature and is used in photoelectric cells. The rate of vibration of cesium atoms is used as a standard for measuring time. Atomic number 55. See **Periodic Table.**

cessation (sĕ-sā′shən) *n.* The act of ceasing or stopping; a halt: *A computer failure caused a cessation of stock trading.*

cession (sĕsh′ən) *n.* A giving up or yielding to another: *the French cession of Quebec to Great Britain.*

cesspool (sĕs′pōōl′) *n.* A covered hole or pit in the ground for receiving drainage or sewage.

cetacean (sĭ-tā′shən) *n.* Any of various sea mammals having an almost hairless body resembling that of a fish, a flat notched tail, and forelimbs modified into broad flippers. Whales, dolphins, and porpoises are cetaceans. ❖ *adj.* Relating to or characteristic of cetaceans.

CF An abbreviation of: **1.** center field. **2.** cystic fibrosis.

cf. An abbreviation of compare.

CFC An abbreviation of chlorofluorocarbon.

CFO An abbreviation of chief financial officer.

cg An abbreviation of centigram.

CG An abbreviation of: **1.** coast guard. **2.** commanding general. **3.** consul general.

CGI An abbreviation of computer-generated imagery.

cgm. An abbreviation of centigram.

ch. An abbreviation of chapter.

Ch. An abbreviation of: **1.** chaplain. **2.** church.

chad (chăd) *n.* **1.** Scraps or bits of paper, such as the tiny rectangles punched out from cards once commonly used to enter data into computers. **2.** One of these scraps or bits of paper.

chador (chä-dôr′) *n.* A long, loose cloak worn over other garments by Muslim women, especially in Iran and southern Asia.

chafe (chāf) *v.* **chafed, chafing, chafes** —*tr.* **1.** To cause irritation by friction or rubbing: *The starched collar chafed his neck.* **2.** To annoy; vex: *The fans' taunts chafed the pitcher.* **3.** To warm by rubbing: *The skaters chafed their cold hands.* —*intr.* **1.** To become irritated or sore from rubbing: *My hands chafed from washing them with harsh soap.* **2.** To feel irritation or impatience: *chafe at the delay.*

chaff[1] (chăf) *n.* **1.** The husks of grain separated from the seeds by threshing. **2.** Finely cut straw or hay used as fodder. **3.** Trivial or worthless matter: *The exhibit had a few good paintings, but most were chaff.*

chaff[2] (chăf) *tr.v.* **chaffed, chaffing, chaffs** To make good-natured fun of; tease: *My friends chaffed me about my fear of spiders.*

chaffinch (chăf′ĭnch) *n.* A small European songbird often kept as a pet, the male of which has reddish-brown feathers and a blue-gray cap.

chafing dish (chā′fĭng) *n.* A pan set above a heating device, used to cook food or keep it warm at the table.

chagrin (shə-grĭn′) *n.* A strong feeling of unease or annoyance caused by disappointment, embarrassment, or humiliation, especially at a mistake or failure. ❖ *tr.v.* **chagrined, chagrining, chagrins** To cause to feel chagrin; annoy greatly: *I was chagrined at being corrected in front of my friends.*

chai (chī) *n.* A beverage made from spiced black tea, milk, and honey or sugar.

chain (chān) *n.* **1.** A series of connected links, usually of metal, used especially to bind or hold something or to transmit mechanical power. **2.** A set of such links used as an ornament. **3.** A series of connected or related things: *a chain of events; a chain of mountains.* **4.** A number of stores, restaurants, theaters, or other establishments under common ownership or management: *a chain of supermarkets around the state.* **5. chains** Something that restrains or confines: *They threw off the chains of slavery.* **6.** A unit of length used in land surveying, equal to 66 feet (20.1 meters). ❖ *tr.v.* **chained, chaining, chains** To bind or confine with or as with a chain or chains: *chain an elephant to a stake; be chained to one's job.*

chain gang *n.* A group of convicts chained together when doing heavy labor outside their prison.

chain letter *n.* A letter, email, or other message sent to a certain number of people, asking each of them to copy and send it to the same number of people.

chainlink fence (chān′lĭngk′) *n.* A fence made of thick steel wire woven together in a diamond pattern.

chain mail *n.* Flexible armor made of metal rings that are connected like links in a chain.

chain-react (chān′rē-ăkt′) *intr.v.* **chain-reacted, chain-reacting, chain-reacts** To undergo a chain reaction.

chain reaction *n.* **1.** A series of events each of which causes or influences the next: *The car crash caused a chain reaction on the highway that involved a number of other cars in accidents.* **2.** A continuous series of nuclear fissions in which neutrons released from the splitting of one atomic nucleus collide with nearby nuclei, which in turn release more neutrons to collide with more nuclei, thus keeping the reaction going.

chainsaw (chān′sô′) *n.* A power saw with teeth set on a circular chain.

chain-smoke (chān′smōk′) *v.* **chain-smoked, chain-smoking, chain-smokes** —*intr.* To smoke continually, as by lighting the next cigarette from the previous one. —*tr.* To smoke (cigarettes, for example) in continuing succession. —**chain smoker** *n.*

chain store *n.* One store of a number of retail stores under the same ownership or management.

chair (châr) *n.* **1.** A piece of furniture on which one may sit, usually consisting of a seat, back, legs, and sometimes arms at the sides. **2.** A position of authority, as that of a professor: *The head of the department has the chair of ancient history.* **3.** A chairperson: *address questions to the chair.* ❖ *tr.v.* **chaired, chairing, chairs** To preside over: *chair a meeting; chair a committee.*

chairlift (châr′lĭft′) *n.* A series of chairs or bars suspended from an endless cable and used to carry skiers and others up or down a slope.

chairman (châr′mən) *n.* **1.** A man who is a chairperson. **2.** A chairperson.

chairmanship (châr′mən-shĭp′) *n.* The office of a chairperson or the period during which a chairperson is in office.

chairperson (châr′pûr′sən) *n.* A person who is in charge of a meeting or is the head of a committee, board, or college department.

chairwoman (châr′wŏm′ən) *n.* A woman who is a chairperson.

chaise (shāz) *n.* **1.** A light, usually two-wheeled carriage with a folding top, drawn by one horse. **2.** A chaise longue.

chaise longue (shāz lông′) *n., pl.* **chaise longues** or **chaises longues** (shāz lông′) A chair having a long seat on which one can sit and stretch out one's legs.

chalcedony (kăl-sĕd′n-ē) *n., pl.* **chalcedonies** A type of quartz that has a waxy luster and varies from transparent to translucent. It is used as a gemstone. Agate and onyx are forms of chalcedony.

chalet (shă-lā′ or shăl′ā) *n.* **1.** A wooden house with a gently sloping roof and overhanging eaves. **2.** The hut of a herder in the mountains of Switzerland.

chalice (chăl′ĭs) *n.* **1.** A cup or goblet. **2.** A cup for the consecrated wine of the Eucharist.

chalk (chôk) *n.* **1.** A soft white, gray, or yellow limestone formed chiefly from fossil seashells. **2.** A piece of this material or a similar substance, used especially for making marks on a chalkboard or other surface: *make a picture using colored chalk.* ❖ *tr.v.* **chalked, chalking, chalks 1.** To mark, draw, or write with chalk: *chalk math problems on the blackboard.* **2.** To treat or cover with chalk: *chalk a field in order to neutralize its acid soil.* ◆ **chalk up 1.** To earn or score: *The team chalked up one victory after another.* **2.** To credit: *chalk up a success to pure luck.*

chalkboard (chôk′bôrd′) *n.* A smooth hard surface, usu-

ally green or black, for writing on with chalk.

chalky (chô′kē) *adj.* **chalkier, chalkiest 1.** Containing chalk: *chalky water from washing the blackboards.* **2.** Resembling chalk: *chalky bits of dried paint.* —**chalk′-i·ness** *n.*

challah (кнä′lə or hä′lə) *n.* A bread made with eggs, usually baked in the shape of a braid and traditionally eaten by Jews on the Sabbath.

challenge (chăl′ənj) *n.* **1.** A call to take part in a contest or fight: *a challenge to a duel.* **2.** Something that tests a person's skills, efforts, or resources: *the challenge of studying advanced mathematics.* **3.** A calling into question; a demand for an explanation: *The new scientific evidence poses a challenge to their theory.* **4.** A sentry's call for identification: *"Who goes there?" was the challenge of the soldier.* **5.** A formal objection, especially to the qualifications of a juror or to certain evidence or rulings in a trial. ❖ *tr.v.* **challenged, challenging, challenges 1.** To call to engage in a contest or fight: *I challenge you to a game of chess.* **2.** To question or dispute the truth or rightness of: *The reviewer challenged the author's conclusion.* **3.** To order to halt and be identified: *The sentries challenged every person who walked by.* **4.** To summon to action, effort, or use; stimulate: *a problem that challenges the imagination.* **5.** To make a formal objection to (a person being considered as a juror). —**chal′leng·er** *n.*

challenging (chăl′ən-jĭng) *adj.* Requiring the full use of one's abilities, skills, or attention: *a challenging job; a challenging homework assignment.*

challis (shăl′ē) *n.* A lightweight fabric of wool, cotton, or rayon, usually having a printed pattern.

chamber (chām′bər) *n.* **1.** A private room, especially a bedroom. **2.** A room in which a person of high rank receives visitors: *the pope's audience chamber.* **3. chambers** A judge's office in a courthouse: *Before the trial the lawyers met in the judge's chambers.* **4a.** The hall used by a group of lawmakers or judges: *Inside the Capitol are the two chambers where the laws are made, the Senate and the House of Representatives.* **b.** A legislative or judicial body: *The Senate is called the upper chamber of the legislature.* **5a.** An enclosed space or compartment in a machine or other device: *a bullet in the chamber of a rifle.* **b.** An enclosed space in the body of an organism, as in the brain or heart. ❖ *tr.v.* **chambered, chambering, chambers** To put into a chamber, as in a firearm: *chambered a bullet.*

chamberlain (chām′bər-lĭn) *n.* **1.** An official who manages the household of a monarch or noble. **2.** A treasurer.

chambermaid (chām′bər-mād′) *n.* A woman who is employed to clean and take care of bedrooms, as in a hotel.

chamber music *n.* Music written for a small group of instruments and suitable for performance in a private home or small concert hall.

chamber of commerce *n., pl.* **chambers of commerce** An association of businesspersons and merchants for the promotion of business interests in the community.

chamber pot *n.* A portable container used as a toilet, especially in a bedroom.

chambray (shăm′brā′) *n.* A fine, lightweight fabric woven with white threads crossing colored ones.

chameleon (kə-mēl′yən) *n.* **1.** Any of various tropical lizards chiefly of Africa and Madagascar, having a grasping tail, eyes that can move independently, and the ability to change color. **2.** Any of several other lizards that can change color.

chamois (shăm′ē) *n., pl.* **chamois** (shăm′ēz) **1.** Either of two animals of mountainous regions of Europe and western Asia that are similar to goats and antelopes. **2.** Soft yellowish material originally made from the skin of this animal, used as a drying or polishing cloth.

chamomile (kăm′ə-mīl′ *or* kăm′ə-mēl′) *n.* A strong-smelling plant having flowers similar to daisies and feathery leaves. The dried flowers can be steeped in hot water to make chamomile tea.

champ¹ (chămp) *tr. & intr.v.* **champed, champing, champs** To chew or bite upon noisily: *a horse champing its oats; heard the horses champing.* ◆ **champ at the bit** To be impatient at being held back or delayed: *He was champing at the bit to get back into the game.*

champ² (chămp) *n. Informal* A champion.

WORD HISTORY Champ¹ is probably of imitative origin. **Champ²** is a shortening of *champion.*

---

champagne (shăm-pān′) *n.* **1.** A sparkling white wine produced in Champagne, a region of France. **2.** A similar wine made in another area.

champion (chăm′pē-ən) *n.* **1.** A person or thing that holds first place or wins first prize in a contest, especially in sports. **2.** A person who fights for or defends something, such as a cause or movement: *a champion of human rights.* ❖ *tr.v.* **championed, championing, champions** To fight for or defend; support actively: *champion the rights of poor people.* ❖ *adj.* Holding first place or prize: *the champion team.*

championship (chăm′pē-ən-shǐp′) *n.* **1a.** The position or title of a champion: *hold the championship.* **b.** A contest held to determine a champion: *attend the championship.* **2.** Defense or support: *the championship of civil rights.*

chance (chăns) *n.* **1.** The unknown or uncertain course of events that has no apparent cause: *Most card games are games of chance. By chance did you find your glasses?* **2.** often **chances** The likelihood that something will happen; possibility or probability: *Chances are good that it will rain tonight. Is there any chance of snow?* **3.** An opportunity: *We never miss a chance to go dancing.* **4.** A risk or gamble: *You're taking a chance that the store will still be open.* ❖ *adj.* Caused by chance; not planned: *a chance meeting.* ❖ *v.* **chanced, chancing, chances** — *intr.* To do or experience something by accident: *I chanced to find a quarter on the sidewalk.* — *tr.* To take a chance with; risk: *They chanced crossing the river in a canoe.* ◆ **chance on** or **chance upon** To find or meet accidentally; happen upon: *I chanced on an old friend yesterday.*

chancel (chăn′səl) *n.* The space around the altar of a church for the clergy and choir, often set apart by a railing, lattice, or screen.

chancellery or **chancellory** (chăn′sə-lə-rē *or* chăn′slə-rē) *n., pl.* **chancelleries** or **chancellories 1.** The rank or position of a chancellor. **2.** The office or building in which a chancellor is located. **3.** The office of an embassy or consulate.

chancellor (chăn′sə-lər *or* chăn′slər) *n.* **1a.** The chief minister of state in some European countries. **b.** In the British government, any of various high officials, such as the Chancellor of the Exchequer. **2.** The president of certain American universities. **3.** The presiding judge of a court of equity in some states of the United States and in Great Britain.

Chancellor of the Exchequer *n.* The highest minister of finance in the British government and a member of the prime minister's cabinet.

chancellorship (chăn′sə-lər-shǐp′ *or* chăn′slər-shǐp′) *n.* The position or term of office of a chancellor.

chancery (chăn′sə-rē) *n., pl.* **chanceries 1.** A court dealing with cases that are not covered by common law and that have to be tried according to a special body of laws. **2.** An office for the collection and safekeeping of official documents. **3.** A chancellery, especially a country's embassy or consulate.

chancre (shăng′kər) *n.* A sore or ulcer that forms on the skin and often indicates a diseased condition.

chancy (chăn′sē) *adj.* **chancier, chanciest** Uncertain as to outcome; risky: *a chancy undertaking.*

chandelier (shăn′də-lîr′) *n.* A lighting fixture that holds a number of bulbs or candles on branches and is suspended from a ceiling.

chandler (chănd′lər) *n.* **1.** A person who makes or sells candles. **2.** A person who sells goods or equipment for use on a ship.

change (chānj) *v.* **changed, changing, changes** — *tr.* **1.** To cause to be different; alter: *change the rules; change the color of a room.* **2.** To take, put, or use (something) in place of another, usually of the same kind: *The company changed its name.* **3a.** To give and receive (one thing for another); exchange; switch: *The twins changed places to fool everybody.* **b.** To exchange (a unit of money) for smaller units or for a different currency: *The machine changes a dollar bill into coins.* **4.** To transfer from (one vehicle) to another: *change planes in Denver.* **5.** To put fresh clothes or coverings on: *change the baby; change the bed.* — *intr.* **1.** To become different or altered: *The town grew and changed over the years.* **2.** To make an exchange; switch: *If you would rather sit in this seat, I'll change with you.* **3.** To put on other clothing: *They changed into work clothes.* **4.** To transfer from one vehicle to another: *We changed in Chicago on our way to the coast.* **5.** To become deeper in tone: *His voice began to change.* ❖ *n.* **1.** The act, process, or result of changing: *a change in the schedule.* **2a.** Money of smaller denomination exchanged for a unit of higher denomination: *Will you give me change of four quarters for a dollar?* **b.** The money returned when the amount given in paying for something is more than what is due: *The change was only a dime.* **c.** A number of coins: *a purse full of change.* **3.** Something different; a break in one's routine: *We finished dinner early for a change.* **4.** A fresh article or set of clothing: *a change of shirts.* ◆ **change hands** To pass from one owner to another: *The store changed hands this year.* **change (one's) mind** To alter a decision or opinion. —**chang′er** *n.*

changeable (chānj′ə-bəl) *adj.* **1.** Likely to change; capricious: *changeable moods.* **2.** Capable of being altered: *changeable habits.* **3.** Changing color or appearance when seen from different angles: *the hummingbird's changeable, vivid plumage.* —**change′a·bil′i·ty, change′a·ble·ness** *n.* —**change′a·bly** *adv.*

changeful (chānj′fəl) *adj.* Having the tendency or ability to change; variable: *a changeful sky at sunset.* —**change′-ful·ly** *adv.* —**change′ful·ness** *n.*

changeless (chānj′lĭs) *adj.* Never changing; constant: *He was changeless in his opposition to our proposal.* —**change′less·ly** *adv.* —**change′less·ness** *n.*

changeling (chānj′lĭng) *n.* **1.** In folklore, a child of the fairies secretly exchanged for a human child. **2.** A human child secretly exchanged for another.

changeover (chānj′ō′vər) *n.* A change from one way of

doing something to another: *a changeover from typewriters to computers.*

changeup (chānj′ŭp′) *n.* In baseball, a pitch that is thrown with the same motion as a fastball but actually moves more slowly, causing the batter to swing too early.

channel (chăn′əl) *n.* **1.** The bed or deepest part of a stream or river. **2.** A part of a river or harbor deep enough to form a passage for ships and often maintained by dredging. **3.** A broad strait: *a channel between islands.* **4.** A passage or conduit for liquids: *Each side of the road had a channel for water to run off.* **5.** A course or way through which something, such as news, messages, or ideas, may be transmitted: *opening new channels of information; a channel of thought.* **6a.** A band of frequencies reserved for broadcasting or communication: *a television channel.* **b.** A station that distributes audio or video content on television, radio, or the Internet: *a sports channel.* **7.** A site on a computer network where people hold online conversations in real time. **8. channels** Official routes of communication: *go through channels to get permission to enter the secluded forest.* **9.** The sound recorded by a separate microphone and played back through a single loudspeaker in a stereo system. ❖ *tr.v.* **channeled, channeling, channels** *also* **channelled, channelling, channels 1.** To form a channel in or through: *The stream channeled the limestone.* **2.** To direct or guide along a desired route: *channel her thoughts towards making a movie.*

channel-surf (chăn′əl-sûrf′) *intr.v.* **channel-surfed, channel-surfing, channel-surfs** To watch different television channels in rapid succession.

chant (chănt) *n.* **1.** A simple melody in which many words or syllables are sung on the same note or a limited range of notes. **2.** A religious text sung to such a melody. **3.** A sustained rhythmic call or shout: *the chant of the crowd at a football game.* ❖ *v.* **chanted, chanting, chants** *—tr.* **1.** To sing to a chant: *The monks chanted psalms.* **2.** To call out in a sustained rhythmic way: *chant a slogan at a rally.* *—intr.* **1.** To call in a chant: *The crowd chanted for the president.* **2.** To sing a chant: *The monks chanted during the service.* *—***chant′er** *n.*

chanteuse (shän-tœz′) *n.* A woman singer, especially in a nightclub singer.

chantey (shăn′tē *or* chăn′tē) *n., pl.* **chanteys** *also* **chanties** A work song sung by sailors in earlier times to the rhythm of their work.

chanticleer (chăn′tĭ-klîr′ *or* shăn′tĭ-klîr′) *n.* A rooster.

Chanukah (КHÄ′nə-kə *or* hä′nə-kə) *n.* Variant of **Hanukkah.**

chaos (kā′ŏs′) *n.* **1.** Great disorder or confusion: *The street was in chaos after the car accident.* **2.** *often* **Chaos** The shapeless and disordered state of unformed matter and infinite space supposed to have existed before the creation of the universe.

chaotic (kā-ŏt′ĭk) *adj.* In a state of chaos; in great disorder or confusion. *—***cha·ot′i·cal·ly** *adv.*

chap¹ (chăp) *tr. & intr.v.* **chapped, chapping, chaps** To make or become dry, scaly, and cracked: *Harsh soaps will chap your hands. My lips chap easily in the cold weather.* ❖ *n.* A roughness and soreness of the skin, caused especially by cold.

chap² (chăp) *n.* Chiefly British A man or boy; a fellow.

WORD HISTORY Chap¹ comes from Middle English *chappen,* meaning "to become dry and cracked." **Chap²** is a

For pronunciation symbols, see the chart on the last page.

shortening of obsolete English *chapman* (meaning "peddler"), which comes from the Old English words *cēap* (meaning "trade") and *man* (meaning "man").

chap. An abbreviation of chapter.

chaparral (shăp′ə-răl′) *n.* An area covered by a dense growth of mostly small-leaved evergreen shrubs, especially in central and southern California.

chapbook (chăp′bŏok′) *n.* A small book or pamphlet containing poems, ballads, stories, or religious tracts.

chapeau (shă-pō′) *n., pl.* **chapeaus** *or* **chapeaux** (shă-pōz′) A hat.

chapel (chăp′əl) *n.* **1a.** A small church: *a little chapel in the hills.* **b.** A small place within a church with its own altar, reserved for special services: *The cathedral had a chapel dedicated to soldiers and sailors.* **2.** A place for religious services, as in a school, hospital, or military base. **3.** Religious services held at a chapel: *Students attended chapel before the holidays.*

chaperone *or* **chaperon** (shăp′ə-rōn′) *n.* **1.** An older person who attends and supervises a social gathering for young people. **2.** A person, especially an older or married woman, who accompanies a young unmarried woman in public. ❖ *tr.v.* **chaperoned, chaperoning, chaperones** To act as a chaperone for: *chaperone a party.* See Synonyms at **accompany.**

chapfallen (chăp′fô′lən) *adj.* Being in low spirits; dejected and disheartened.

chaplain (chăp′lĭn) *n.* **1.** A member of the clergy who conducts religious services and provides counseling for an institution, such as a prison or hospital. **2.** A lay person who provides counseling on spiritual matters to members of an organization or institution, such as a college.

chaplet (chăp′lĭt) *n.* **1.** A wreath for the head. **2.** A short rosary. **3.** A string of beads.

chaps (chăps) *pl.n.* Heavy leather coverings worn over pants by cowhands to protect their legs. Chaps buckle around the waist and have no seat.

chapter (chăp′tər) *n.* **1.** A main division of a book. **2.** A series of related events or a part of a person's life: *That was an exciting chapter in my life.* **3.** A local branch of a club, fraternity, or other organization.

char (chär) *v.* **charred, charring, chars** *—tr.* To burn the surface or edge of; burn partially: *The fire charred the papers.* *—intr.* To become burned on the surface or edge: *The edge of the paper charred when it was held next to a burning match.*

character (kăr′ək-tər) *n.* **1.** The combination of qualities or features that makes one person, group, or thing different from another: *The character of the town is calm and peaceful.* **2.** One's moral nature: *an honest and upstanding student of fine character.* **3.** Moral strength; integrity: *a respected citizen of character.* **4.** A person portrayed in a work of art, such as a novel, play, or movie: *The hero is the chief character in the play.* **5.** Informal An odd or eccentric person. **6a.** A letter in a writing system. **b.** A symbol, letter, or number used in a computer code. **7.** A physical feature of an organism. ❖ **in character** Consistent with someone's general character or usual behavior. **out of character** Not consistent with one's general character or usual behavior: *Being late is quite out of character for him.*

characteristic (kăr′ək-tə-rĭs′tĭk) *adj.* Being a feature or quality that distinguishes a person or thing; typical: *the zebra's characteristic stripes; my friend's characteristic laugh.* ❖ *n.* **1.** Something that distinguishes a person or thing; a typical feature or quality: *A curved bill is a* *characteristic of parrots.* See Synonyms at **quality. 2.** The whole number in a logarithm. For example, if 2.713 is a logarithm, 2 is the characteristic. —**char′ac·ter·is′-ti·cal·ly** *adv.*

characterization (kăr′ək-tər-ĭ-zā′shən) *n.* **1.** The act or an instance of characterizing. **2.** A description of qualities: *This book has characterizations of all the restaurants in town.* **3.** Representation of a character or characters in literature or drama: *The author uses very realistic characterization in the novel.*

characterize (kăr′ək-tə-rīz′) *tr.v.* **characterized, characterizing, characterizes 1.** To describe the character or qualities of; portray: *The supervisor's report characterized the nurse as very efficient.* **2.** To be a characteristic or quality of: *Spruce forests characterize that region.*

charade (shə-rād′) *n. (used with a singular or plural verb)* **1. charades** A game in which words or phrases are acted out in pantomime, often syllable by syllable, until guessed by the other players. **2.** Something done as a deception; a pretense: *Laughter is often a charade to cover up nervousness.*

charbroil (chär′broil′) *tr.v.* **charbroiled, charbroiling, charbroils** To broil (food) over charcoal or another heat source: *charbroiled some steaks.*

charcoal (chär′kōl′) *n.* **1.** A black porous material composed chiefly of carbon, produced by heating wood or sometimes bone until the lighter materials in it are burned away. It is used as a fuel, a filtering material, and for drawing. **2a.** A stick of this material, used for drawing. **b.** A drawing made with charcoal.

chard (chärd) *n.* A variety of beet having large succulent leaves that are eaten as a vegetable; Swiss chard.

charge (chärj) *v.* **charged, charging, charges** —*tr.* **1a.** To ask as a price: *The barber charges $20 for a haircut.* **b.** To demand payment from: *The store will charge you for wrapping the gift.* **2.** To postpone payment on (a purchase) by recording the amount owed: *We charged the groceries because we didn't have enough cash.* **3.** To rush toward or attack (someone or something): *The soldiers charged the hill.* **4.** In sports, to bump, check, or rush into (an opposing player) illegally. **5.** To accuse; blame: *The police charged the driver with reckless driving.* **6.** To command; order: *The judge charged the jury to consider all the evidence.* **7.** To entrust with a duty, task, or responsibility: *The reporter was charged with the task of discovering what really happened.* **8.** To load or fill: *They charged the furnace with coal.* **9.** To be present in every part of; fill: *The last scene of the movie was charged with excitement.* **10.** To fill with an amount of electrical energy; energize: *We can charge the car battery at the gas station.* —*intr.* **1.** To demand or ask payment: *They didn't charge for the repair.* **2a.** To rush forward in an attack: *The dog charged toward the stranger.* **b.** To move quickly or abruptly forward: *The children charged out of the room.* **3.** To postpone payment for a purchase. **4.** To become energized: *Don't unplug the battery while it's charging.* ❖ *n.* **1.** An amount asked or made as payment: *There is no charge for this delivery.* **2.** Care; supervision; control: *the scientist in charge of the laboratory.* See Synonyms at **care. 3.** A person or thing for which one is responsible: *The camp counselors took their charges to the amusement park.* **4.** A duty or task; a responsibility: *The commission's charge is to find out what happened.* **5.** An order or command: *received a written charge to attend the hearing.* **6.** An accusation, especially one made formally, as in a legal case: *The charge against*

the defendant was dismissed. **7.** A rushing forceful attack: *the charge of a bull elephant.* **8.** The amount of electrical energy contained in an object, particle, or region of space. A charge is positive if the object or space contains fewer electrons than protons. A charge is negative if the object or space contains more electrons than protons. **9.** The quantity that an apparatus or container can hold: *They gave the battery a full charge.* **10.** An amount of explosive to be set off at one time: *a box of dynamite charges.* **11.** *Informal* A feeling of excitement; a thrill: *They got a real charge from seeing the Grand Canyon.* ◆ **in charge** In a position of authority or management; in command: *The manager of the store is in charge.* **in charge of** Having control over or responsibility for: *The recreation department is in charge of the annual fireworks display.*

chargé d'affaires (shär-zhā′ dä-fâr′) *n., pl.* **chargés d'affaires** (shär-zhā′ dä-fâr′ *or* shär-zhāz′ dä-fâr′) **1.** A government official who temporarily takes over the duties of an absent ambassador or minister. **2.** A diplomat of the lowest rank.

charger (chär′jər) *n.* **1.** A device used to charge electric storage batteries. **2.** A horse ridden in battle.

chariot (chăr′ē-ət) *n.* A horse-drawn two-wheeled vehicle used in ancient times in battles, races, and processions.

charioteer (chăr′ē-ə-tîr′) *n.* A person who drives a chariot.

charisma (kə-rĭz′mə) *n., pl.* **charismata** (kə-rĭz′mə-tə) A special quality of individuals who show an exceptional ability to lead and win the devotion of large numbers of people.

charismatic (kăr′ĭz-măt′ĭk) *adj.* Having or showing charisma: *a charismatic leader.*

charitable (chăr′ĭ-tə-bəl) *adj.* **1.** Concerned with helping the needy: *a charitable organization.* **2.** Showing love or goodwill; full of kindness: *a warm charitable spirit.* **3.** Generous in giving money or help to the needy. **4.** Tolerant or lenient in judging others or their work: *a charitable review of the movie.* —**char′i·ta·ble·ness** *n.* —**char′-i·ta·bly** *adv.*

charity (chăr′ĭ-tē) *n., pl.* **charities 1.** Help or relief to the needy: *raising money for charity.* **2.** An institution or fund established to help the needy: *a ten-dollar donation to a charity.* **3.** Goodwill or kind feelings toward others: *known for her charity and generosity of spirit.* **4.** Tolerance and leniency in judging others: *Lincoln urged charity for all after the Civil War.*

charlatan (shär′lə-tən) *n.* A person who deceives others by falsely claiming to have expert knowledge or skill; a quack.

Charleston (chärl′stən) *n.* A quick lively dance popular in the 1920s.

charley horse (chär′lē) *Informal* A muscle cramp or stiffness, especially in the leg.

charm (chärm) *n.* **1.** The power or ability to please or delight; appeal: *The old house had a lot of charm.* **2.** A quality or manner that pleases or attracts: *Her wit is one of her many charms.* **3.** A saying, action, or thing supposed to have magical power, as in warding off evil. **4.** A trinket or small ornament worn hanging on a bracelet or chain. ❖ *tr.v.* **charmed, charming, charms 1.** To please greatly; delight: *The audience was charmed by the young pianist.* **2.** To attract and delight (someone) or cause (someone to do something) by being attractive or pleasant: *The children's laughter charmed us into playing the game again.*

3. To cast a magical spell on; bewitch. ◆ **like a charm** Exceedingly well. —**charm′er** *n.*

charming (chär′mĭng) *adj.* Delightful; attractive; very pleasing: *a charming person; charming manners.* —**charm′ing·ly** *adv.*

charnel house (chär′nəl) *n.* A building, room, or vault in which the bodies or bones of the dead are placed.

Charon (kâr′ən) *n.* In Greek mythology, the ferryman who carried the dead over the river Styx to Hades.

chart (chärt) *n.* **1.** Something written or drawn, as a table or graph, that presents information in an organized, easily viewed form: *a chart showing rainfall for the last ten years.* **2.** A map showing coastlines, water depths, or other information of use to navigators. **3.** often **charts** A list of best-selling recorded music: *The song reached the top of the charts only a few weeks after it was released.* ❖ *tr.v.* **charted, charting, charts 1.** To show or record on a chart; make a chart of: *chart the daily changes in temperature.* **2.** To plan in detail: *I hope to chart a course for success.*

charter (chär′tər) *n.* **1.** A written grant or document from a ruler, government, or other group, giving certain rights to a person, corporation, or entire people: *The Magna Carta is a famous charter granted by King John of England in 1215 to his nobles.* **2.** A document, such as a constitution, stating the principles, function, and form of a governing body or organization: *The United Nations is governed by a charter.* **3.** The hiring or renting of a bus, aircraft, boat, or other vehicle for a special use. ❖ *tr.v.* **chartered, chartering, charters 1.** To grant a charter to; establish by charter: *Congress chartered the bank for twenty years.* **2.** To hire or rent for private use: *The travel club chartered a plane.* —**char′ter·er** *n.*

charter school *n.* An independent public school, often with a distinct curriculum and educational philosophy.

chartreuse (shär-trōōz′ *or* shär-trōōs′) *n.* A light yellowish green.

charwoman (chär′wŏŏm′ən) *n.* A woman hired to do cleaning, usually in an office or a large building.

chary (châr′ē) *adj.* **charier, chariest 1.** Cautious; wary: *chary of walking on thin ice.* **2.** Not giving freely; sparing: *chary of compliments.* —**char′i·ly** *adv.* —**char′i·ness** *n.*

Charybdis (kə-rĭb′dĭs) *n.* In Greek mythology, a whirlpool opposite the cave of Scylla near the Italian island of Sicily, personified as a monster because of its ability to destroy ships.

chase (chās) *v.* **chased, chasing, chases** —*tr.* **1.** To follow quickly and try to catch or overtake; pursue: *Our dog chased the cat.* **2.** To drive away: *chased the rabbits from the garden.* —*intr.* **1.** To go or follow in pursuit: *chase after a loose dog.* **2.** *Informal* To hurry; rush: *chasing about town doing last-minute errands.* ❖ *n.* **1.** The act of chasing; rapid pursuit: *The police arrested the driver after a wild chase.* **2a.** The hunting of wild animals. **b.** Something that is hunted; quarry: *The hunters drove their chase into the open.*

chaser (chā′sər) *n.* **1.** A person or thing that chases or pursues. **2.** *Informal* A drink of water, beer, or other liquid taken after a drink of hard liquor.

chasm (kăz′əm) *n.* **1.** A deep crack or opening in the surface of the earth; a gorge. **2.** A gap, such as that caused by a difference of opinion or attitude: *a chasm in communication.*

chassis (chăs′ē) *n., pl.* **chassis** (chăs′ēz) **1.** The frame of an automotive vehicle that supports the body and includes the motor, gears, axles, and wheels. **2.** The landing gear of an aircraft. **3.** The structure that holds and supports the parts of a radio, television, or other piece of electronic equipment.

chaste (chāst) *adj.* **chaster, chastest 1a.** Having never experienced sexual intercourse; virginal. **b.** Abstaining from sexual intercourse; celibate. **2.** Not involving or suggestive of sexual desire or indecency: *a chaste conversation.* **3.** Not ornate or extreme; pure in style or simple in design. —**chaste′ly** *adv.* —**chaste′ness** *n.*

chasten (chā′sən) *tr.v.* **chastened, chastening, chastens 1.** To discipline or correct (someone) by punishment. **2.** To cause to become subdued or meek; restrain: *a spirit chastened by hard experience.* —**chas′ten·er** *n.*

chastise (chăs-tīz′ *or* chăs′tīz′) *tr.v.* **chastised, chastising, chastises** To punish or criticize severely for misbehavior or wrongdoing. —**chas·tise′ment** *n.* —**chas·tis′er** *n.*

chastity (chăs′tĭ-tē) *n.* The condition or quality of being chaste or pure.

chat (chăt) *intr.v.* **chatted, chatting, chats 1.** To converse in a relaxed, friendly, informal manner: *chat with friends.* **2.** To participate in an exchange of remarks over a computer network in real time. ❖ *n.* **1.** A relaxed, friendly, informal conversation. **2.** An exchange of remarks that takes place on a computer network and happens in real time. **3.** Any of several songbirds having a chattering call.

chateau also **château** (shă-tō′) *n., pl.* **chateaus** or **chateaux** (shă-tōz′) **1.** A French castle or manor house. **2.** A large country house.

chatelaine (shăt′l-ān′) *n.* **1.** The woman who is in charge of a castle or large house. **2.** A clasp or chain worn at the waist for holding keys, a watch, or a purse.

chatroom (chăt′rōōm′ *or* chăt′rŏŏm′) *n.* A site on a computer network where online conversations are held in real time.

chattel (chăt′l) *n.* **1.** An article of personal property that can be moved from place to place, as a piece of furniture or an animal. **2.** A slave.

chatter (chăt′ər) *v.* **chattered, chattering, chatters** —*intr.* **1.** To make short rapid sounds that resemble speech, as some animals and birds do: *Monkeys chattered in the trees.* **2.** To talk rapidly and at length about something unimportant; jabber. **3.** To make a rapid series of rattling or clicking noises: *My teeth chattered with cold.* —*tr.* To utter in a rapid and thoughtless way: *chatter nonsense.* ❖ *n.* **1.** Idle talk about unimportant matters: *All of that gossip is just neighborhood chatter.* **2.** The sharp rapid sounds made by some birds and animals. **3.** A series of quick rattling or clicking sounds: *the chatter of a typewriter.*

chatterbox (chăt′ər-bŏks′) *n.* A person who seems to talk all the time.

chatty (chăt′ē) *adj.* **chattier, chattiest 1.** Known for chatting, especially about unimportant things: *a chatty person full of gossip.* **2.** Having the tone or style of informal conversation: *a chatty website about current celebrities.* —**chat′ti·ly** *adv.* —**chat′ti·ness** *n.*

chauffeur (shō′fər *or* shō-fûr′) *n.* A person who is hired to drive an automobile. ❖ *tr.v.* **chauffeured, chauffeuring, chauffeurs** To serve as a driver for: *chauffeuring visiting relatives to see the local sights.*

chauvinism (shō′və-nĭz′əm) *n.* **1.** Extreme devotion to one's country or a cause; fanatical patriotism. **2.** Unwarranted belief in the superiority of one's own group; prejudice. —**chau′vin·ist** *n.* —**chau′vin·is′tic** *adj.*

cheap (chēp) *adj.* **cheaper, cheapest 1.** Low in price; inexpensive or comparatively inexpensive: *Tomatoes are cheap and plentiful in the summer months.* **2.** Charging low prices: *a cheap restaurant.* **3.** Requiring little effort; easily gotten: *a cheap victory.* **4.** Of little value or poor quality; inferior: *cheap shoes that wear out quickly.* **5.** Worthy of no respect; contemptible: *cheap humor.* **6.** Not spending or giving money generously; stingy: *a miser's cheap ways.* ❖ *adv.* **cheaper, cheapest** At a low price: *an old car that we bought cheap.* —**cheap′ly** *adv.* —**cheap′ness** *n.*

cheapen (chē′pən) *tr. & intr.v.* **cheapened, cheapening, cheapens** To make or become cheap or cheaper: *Rude behavior tends to cheapen one's reputation.*

cheap shot *n.* An unfair statement directed especially at a vulnerable person or group.

cheapskate (chēp′skāt′) *n. Slang* A stingy person; a miser.

cheat (chēt) *v.* **cheated, cheating, cheats** —*tr.* **1.** To deceive by trickery: *The grocer cheated customers by selling stale bread at full price.* **2.** To deprive of something dishonestly or unfairly; swindle: *The grain dealer cheated farmers out of their profits.* **3.** To elude or escape as if by trickery or deception: *The daring mountain climbers cheated death.* —*intr.* To act dishonestly: *cheat to pass a test; cheat at cards.* ❖ *n.* **1.** A person who cheats; a swindler. **2.** An act of cheating; a fraud or swindle: *a scheme that was nothing but a big cheat.* —**cheat′er** *n.*

Chechen (chěch′ən) *n.* **1a.** A native or inhabitant of the region of Chechnya in southern Russia. **b.** A member of the predominant, traditionally Muslim ethnic group of Chechnya. **2.** The language of this people. —**Chech′en** *adj.*

check (chěk) *v.* **checked, checking, checks** —*tr.* **1.** To test, examine, or make sure of: *checked her answers on the test; check the address before going.* **2.** To mark with a check: *check each name as it is called out.* **3.** To cause to stop suddenly; halt: *check erosion by building terraces.* **4.** To restrain or control: *check an urge to yell.* **5.** In sports such as hockey, to block or hinder (an opposing player with the puck) by using one's body or one's stick. **6.** In chess, to move a piece so as to place (an opponent's king) under direct attack. **7.** To place for temporary safekeeping or shipping: *checked their baggage at the airport.* **8.** To mark with a pattern of checks: *A pattern of blue and white squares checked the floor.* —*intr.* **1.** To make an examination or investigation; inquire: *check on departure times; check with the boss before leaving.* **2.** To correspond item for item; agree: *Our two lists checked exactly.* ❖ *n.* **1.** A careful examination or investigation to see that something is being done or working properly: *A check of the paper revealed several misspellings.* **2.** Something that stops motion or expression; a restraint: *The snowstorm was a check on all our travel.* **3.** The condition of being stopped or held back: *The dry weather kept the mosquitoes in check.* **4.** A mark made to show that something has been noted, selected, or is accurate. **5.** A ticket or slip for identifying and claiming something: *a baggage check.* **6.** A written order to a bank to pay a certain amount from funds on deposit in an account: *write a check to pay a bill.* **7.** A bill at a restaurant: *The waiter gave us our check at the end of the meal.* **8.** In chess, the situation of the king when under direct attack by an opponent's piece. **9.** In hockey, the action of checking an opposing player. **10a.** A pattern of squares resembling a checkerboard. **b.** A single square

in such a pattern: *a floor made of black and white checks.* **c.** A fabric printed or woven with such a pattern. ◆ **check in** To register or sign in, as at a hotel: *check in before the flight.* **check out 1.** To leave, as after paying a hotel bill. **2a.** To take after having paid the amount owed: *check out groceries at a supermarket.* **b.** To take after having recorded what is being taken: *check out books from the library.* **3.** To be confirmed as true: *The suspect's story checks out.*

checkbook (chěk′bŏŏk′) *n.* A book containing blank checks, given by a bank to a depositor who has a checking account.

check card *n.* A debit card that enables the user to withdraw money from a checking account.

checked (chěkt) *adj.* Having a pattern of squares; checkered: *a checked shirt.*

checker (chěk′ər) *n.* **1.** A person or thing that checks, as for accuracy: *Our word processor has a checker for spelling.* **2.** A person who receives items for safekeeping or shipping: *a baggage checker.* **3.** A cashier in a supermarket. **4.** One of the pieces used in the game of checkers. **5a.** A pattern of many squares. **b.** One of the squares in such a pattern. ❖ *tr.v.* **checkered, checkering, checkers** To mark with a pattern of squares.

checkerboard (chěk′ər-bôrd′) *n.* A game board divided into 64 squares of alternating colors, on which games of checkers are played.

checkered (chěk′ərd) *adj.* **1.** Marked with or divided into squares: *a checkered floor.* **2.** Varied in experiences, including some suspicious or immoral incidents: *a checkered career.*

checkers (chěk′ərz) *pl.n. (used with a singular verb)* A game played on a checkerboard by two players, each using 12 round, flat pieces. Each player tries to capture all of the opponent's pieces.

checking account (chěk′ĭng) *n.* A bank account from which payments may be made by writing checks against the amount on deposit.

checklist (chěk′lĭst′) *n.* A list of items to be checked, noted, or remembered.

check mark *n.* A mark placed next to an item to show that it has been noted, verified, approved, or otherwise dealt with.

checkmate (chěk′māt′) *tr.v.* **checkmated, checkmating, checkmates 1.** In chess, to move so as to place (an opponent's king) under threat of being taken on the next move with no chance of escape or defense, thus ending the game. **2.** To defeat completely. ❖ *n.* **1.** In chess, a move or situation that checkmates an opponent's king. **2.** A situation in which one is completely defeated.

checkout (chěk′out′) *n.* **1.** The act or process of checking out, as at a supermarket, library, or hotel. **2.** A test or inspection, as of a machine, for working condition or accuracy.

checkpoint (chěk′point′) *n.* A place where pedestrians or vehicles are stopped for inspection.

checkroom (chěk′rŏŏm′ *or* chěk′rŏŏm′) *n.* A room where coats, packages, or baggage may be left temporarily.

checkup (chěk′ŭp′) *n.* A thorough examination or inspection, as for health or general working condition: *regular medical checkups; an engine checkup.*

Cheddar *also* **cheddar** (chěd′ər) *n.* A firm, smooth, usually yellowish cheese first made in Cheddar, a village of southwest England.

cheek (chēk) *n.* **1.** The part of either side of the face below the eye and between the nose and ear. **2.** Rudely assertive behavior; disrespectful boldness: *have the cheek to tell one's elders what to do.* **3.** *Informal* A buttock.

cheekbone (chēk′bōn′) *n.* A small bone on the side of the face just below the eye, forming the outermost point of the cheek.

cheek pouch *n.* A pocketlike fold of skin in the cheeks of various animals in which food can be carried.

cheeky (chē′kē) *adj.* **cheekier, cheekiest** Impudent; impertinent: *a cheeky smart aleck.* —**cheek′i·ly** *adv.* —**cheek′i·ness** *n.*

cheep (chēp) *n.* A high-pitched chirp, like that of a young bird. ❖ *intr.v.* **cheeped, cheeping, cheeps** To make such a sound.

cheer (chîr) *n.* **1.** A shout of happiness, approval, encouragement, or enthusiasm: *The crowd gave a loud cheer for the winning team.* **2.** A slogan or chant shouted in encouragement or approval, as for a school's team at a game. **3.** Happiness; good spirits: *My grandparents are always full of cheer.* **4.** Something that gives joy or happiness: *Friends sent words of cheer and encouragement.* **5.** Food and drink: *came over for some holiday cheer.* ❖ *v.* **cheered, cheering, cheers** —*intr.* **1.** To shout in happiness, approval, encouragement, or enthusiasm: *The audience cheered and clapped.* **2.** To become cheerful: *In spite of my disappointment, I soon cheered up.* —*tr.* **1.** To praise, encourage, or urge by shouting: *The fans cheered the runner on.* **2.** To make happier or more cheerful: *A warm fire soon cheered us up.*

cheerful (chîr′fəl) *adj.* **1.** In good spirits; good-humored or happy: *Everyone was cheerful at breakfast.* See Synonyms at **glad. 2.** Producing a feeling of cheer: *a cheerful hello; a cozy, cheerful room.* —**cheer′ful·ly** *adv.* —**cheer′ful·ness** *n.*

cheerleader (chîr′lē′dər) *n.* **1.** A person who leads the cheering of spectators, as at a football game. **2.** A member of a group that performs coordinated routines combining gymnastic and dance moves, often in competition with similar groups. —**cheer′lead′** *v.*

cheerless (chîr′lĭs) *adj.* Lacking cheer; gloomy and depressing: *a cheerless rainy day.* —**cheer′less·ly** *adv.* —**cheer′less·ness** *n.*

cheery (chîr′ē) *adj.* **cheerier, cheeriest** Bright and cheerful: *a cheery smile; a cheery fire.* —**cheer′i·ly** *adv.* —**cheer′i·ness** *n.*

cheese (chēz) *n.* A food made from pressed curds of milk, often seasoned and aged.

cheeseburger (chēz′bûr′gər) *n.* A hamburger topped with melted cheese.

cheesecake (chēz′kāk′) *n.* A cake made with sweetened cream cheese or cottage cheese and often with various flavorings.

cheesecloth (chēz′klôth′) *n.* A thin, loosely woven cotton cloth resembling gauze, originally used for wrapping cheese.

cheesy (chē′zē) *adj.* **cheesier, cheesiest 1.** Containing or resembling cheese. **2.** *Informal* **a.** Of poor quality; shoddy: *a cheap room with cheesy furniture.* **b.** Lacking in refinement or subtlety: *a cheesy movie.* —**chees′i·ly** *adv.* —**chees′i·ness** *n.*

cheetah (chē′tə) *n.* A long-legged, swift-running wild cat of Africa and southwest Asia that has tawny fur with black spots.

chef (shĕf) *n.* A cook, especially the chief cook of a large kitchen staff, as in a restaurant.

chef-d'oeuvre (shā-dœ′vrə *or* shā-dûrv′) *n., pl.* **chefs-d'oeuvre** (shā-dœ′vrə *or* shā-dûrv′) A masterpiece, especially in literature or art.

chela (kē′lə) *n., pl.* **chelae** (kē′lē) A pincerlike claw of a scorpion or a crustacean such as a lobster or crab.

chelicera (kĭ-lĭs′ər-ə) *n., pl.* **chelicerae** (kĭ-lĭs′ə-rē′) Either of the first pair of fanglike appendages near the mouth of an arachnid, such as a spider, or a horseshoe crab, used for grasping, piercing, or injecting venom.

chemical (kĕm′ĭ-kəl) *adj.* **1.** Relating to chemistry: *a chemical discovery.* **2.** Used in or produced by means of chemistry: *a chemical symbol; a chemical change.* ❖ *n.* A substance obtained by or used in a chemical process. —**chem′i·cal·ly** *adv.*

chemical engineering *n.* The branch of engineering that deals with the industrial production of chemicals and chemical products. —**chemical engineer** *n.*

chemical weapon *n.* A poisonous chemical agent, usually a gas or aerosol, that has been prepared for release on the battlefield or within a civilian population in order to cause widespread illness or death.

chemise (shə-mēz′) *n.* **1.** A woman's undergarment that resembles a short, loose slip. **2.** A loosely fitting dress that hangs straight from the shoulders.

chemist (kĕm′ĭst) *n.* **1.** A scientist who specializes in chemistry. **2.** *Chiefly British* A pharmacist.

chemistry (kĕm′ĭ-strē) *n., pl.* **chemistries 1.** The science that deals with the structure, properties, and reactions of the elements and the compounds they form. **2.** The chemical properties of a substance or a system of substances: *the chemistry of the blood.* **3.** Mutual trust or understanding: *The two partners started a business, but there was no chemistry between them.*

chemosynthesis (kē′mō-sĭn′thĭ-sĭs) *n.* The formation of carbohydrates from carbon dioxide and water using energy obtained from chemical reactions rather than from light, as in photosynthesis. Certain bacteria, especially those that live deep in the ocean, use chemosynthesis for making their own food. —**che′mo·syn·thet′ic** (kē′mō-sĭn-thĕt′ĭk) *adj.*

chemotherapy (kē′mō-thĕr′ə-pē) *n.* The treatment of disease with chemicals that have a specific poisonous effect on the disease-causing organisms or cells. Chemotherapy is used especially to stop the spread or growth of certain cancers. —**che′mo·ther′a·peu′tic** *adj.*

chenille (shə-nēl′) *n.* **1.** Cord or yarn of silk, cotton, wool, or rayon with a fuzzy velvety pile, used for making fringes, tassels, or embroidery. **2.** Fabric made with this cord, used for bedspreads, rugs, and curtains.

cheque (chĕk) *n. Chiefly British* Variant of **check** (sense 6).

cherish (chĕr′ĭsh) *tr.v.* **cherished, cherishing, cherishes 1.** To treat with affection and tenderness; hold dear: *The children cherished the little kittens.* **2.** To keep fondly in mind; treasure: *She cherished the memories from her childhood.* See Synonyms at **appreciate.**

Cherokee (chĕr′ə-kē′ *or* chĕr′ə-kē′) *n., pl.* **Cherokee** or **Cherokees 1.** A member of a Native American people formerly living in the Appalachian Mountains of the western Carolinas, northern Georgia, and eastern Tennessee, now living mainly in Oklahoma and western North Carolina. **2.** The Iroquoian language of the Cherokee.

cherry (chĕr′ē) *n., pl.* **cherries 1.** Any of various small, round, fleshy fruits having smooth skin and a hard pit. Cherries range in color from yellow to bright red to dark purple and can be sour or sweet. **2.** A tree that bears such fruit. **3.** The wood of such a tree. **4.** A deep or bright red. —SEE NOTE AT **kudos.**

cherry bomb *n.* A round, red firecracker that explodes with a loud bang.

cherry tomato *n.* A small variety of tomato.

cherub (chĕr′əb) *n., pl.* **cherubim** (chĕr′ə-bĭm) **1.** An angel of high rank. **2.** *pl.* **cherubs a.** An angel, usually shown in pictures as a beautiful winged child with a chubby face. **b.** A sweet, pretty, or innocent-looking child. —**che·ru′-bic** (chə-rōō′bĭk) *adj.*

chess (chĕs) *n.* A game played on a chessboard by two players, each starting with 16 pieces that are moved in various ways. The object of the game is to checkmate the opponent's king.

chessboard (chĕs′bôrd′) *n.* A game board with 64 squares in alternating colors, used in playing chess.

chessman (chĕs′măn′) *n.* One of the pieces used in the game of chess; a king, queen, bishop, knight, rook, or pawn.

chest (chĕst) *n.* **1a.** The part of the body between the neck and the abdomen, enclosed by the ribs and breastbone. **b.** The front portion of this part of the body: *a man with a tattoo on his chest.* **2.** A sturdy box with a lid, used especially for holding or storing things: *a tool chest.* **3.** A small cabinet with shelves used to store things: *Bandages are kept in the medicine chest above the sink.* **4.** A chest of drawers.

chesterfield (chĕs′tər-fēld′) *n.* **1.** An overcoat, usually with a velvet collar. **2.** A large sofa with rounded armrests.

chestnut (chĕs′nŭt′) *n.* **1.** A smooth, reddish-brown, edible nut of any of several trees of northern regions that is enclosed in a prickly husk. **2.** A tree that bears such nuts. **3.** The wood of such a tree. **4.** A reddish brown. **5.** A reddish-brown horse. **6.** Something lacking freshness or originality, such as an old stale joke or story. ❖ *adj.* Reddish-brown.

chest of drawers *n., pl.* **chests of drawers** A piece of furniture with several drawers, used chiefly for keeping clothes; a bureau or dresser.

chevalier (shĕv′ə-lir′) *n.* **1.** A knight or nobleman. **2.** A member of certain male honorary groups or orders.

chevron (shĕv′rən) *n.* A badge of stripes meeting at an angle, worn on the sleeve, as of a military or police uniform, to show rank, merit, or length of service.

chew (chōō) *v.* **chewed, chewing, chews** —*tr.* To bite and grind with the teeth: *chew food thoroughly.* —*intr.* To make crushing or grinding motions with the teeth. ❖ *n.* **1.** The act of chewing: *puppies having a good chew on a bone.* **2.** Something held in the mouth and chewed. —**chew′a·ble** *adj.* —**chew′er** *n.*

chewing gum (chōō′ĭng) *n.* A sweet flavored gum for chewing, formerly made of chicle, but now made of synthetic substances.

chewy (chōō′ē) *adj.* **chewier, chewiest** Needing much chewing in order to swallow: *tough chewy steak.* —**chew′i·ness** *n.*

Cheyenne (shī-ĕn′ *or* shī-ăn′) *n., pl.* **Cheyenne** *or* **Cheyennes 1.** A member of a Native American people formerly living in parts of the eastern Rocky Mountains and the western Great Plains, now living mainly in Oklahoma and Montana. **2.** The Algonquian language of the Cheyenne. —**Chey·enne′** *adj.*

chez (shā) *prep.* At the home of; at or by.

chi¹ (kī *or* kē) *n.* The 22nd letter of the Greek alphabet, written X, χ. In English, it is represented as *Kh, kh* or *Ch, ch.*

chi² (chē) *n.* The vital force believed in Taoism and other Chinese philosophy to exist as part of all things.

WORD HISTORY Chi¹ is from Greek *khī,* referring to the Greek letter X. **Chi²** comes from the Mandarin word *qì,* meaning "air, spirit, energy of life."

chiaroscuro (kē-är′ə-skōōr′ō) *n., pl.* **chiaroscuros 1.** The technique of using light and shade in pictorial representation. **2.** The arrangement of light and dark elements in a pictorial work of art.

chiasmus (kī-ăz′məs) *n., pl.* **chiasmi** (kī-ăz′mī′) A figure of speech in which the second of two parallel structures is inverted, as in *"fresh woods, and pastures new,"* from John Milton's poem "Lycidas."

chic (shēk) *adj.* **chicer, chicest** Attractive and stylish; fashionable: *a chic gown; a chic crowd.* ❖ *n.* Style and elegance in dress or manner.

Chicana (chĭ-kä′nə *or* shĭ-kä′nə) *n.* A Mexican-American woman or girl. —**Chi·ca′na** *adj.*

chicanery (shĭ-kā′nə-rē *or* chĭ-kā′nə-rē) *n., pl.* **chicaneries** Deception by trickery.

Chicano (chĭ-kä′nō *or* shĭ-kä′nō) *n., pl.* **Chicanos** A Mexican American, especially a man or boy. —**Chi·ca′no** *adj.*

chick (chĭk) *n.* A young bird, especially a young chicken.

chickadee (chĭk′ə-dē′) *n.* Any of several small plump birds that are mostly gray with a darker marking on the head.

Chickasaw (chĭk′ə-sô′) *n., pl.* **Chickasaw** *or* **Chickasaws 1.** A member of a Native American people formerly living in Mississippi and Alabama and now living in Oklahoma. **2.** The Muskogean language of the Chickasaw.

chicken (chĭk′ən) *n.* **1.** The common domesticated fowl raised for eggs or food. **2.** The meat of this fowl. **3.** Any of various similar birds. **4.** *Slang* A person who is afraid or acts in a cowardly manner. ❖ *adj. Slang* Afraid; cowardly. ❖ *intr.v.* **chickened, chickening, chickens** *Slang* To lose one's nerve; act in a cowardly manner: *chicken out at the last moment.*

chicken-hearted (chĭk′ən-här′tĭd) *adj.* Cowardly; timid.

chickenpox *or* **chicken pox** (chĭk′ən-pŏks′) *n.* A contagious viral disease, mainly of young children, in which the skin breaks out in a rash and mild fever occurs.

chicken wire *n.* A hexagonal wire mesh used as light fencing.

chickpea (chĭk′pē′) *n.* **1.** The round edible seed of a bushy plant related to the pea; the garbanzo. **2.** The plant that bears such seeds.

chickweed (chĭk′wēd′) *n.* Any of various low-growing weeds having small white flowers.

chicle (chĭk′əl *or* chĭk′lē) *n.* The thickened milky sap of a tropical evergreen American tree, formerly used as the main ingredient of chewing gum.

chicory (chĭk′ə-rē) *n., pl.* **chicories 1.** A plant having blue flowers that resemble daisies. Some varieties are grown for their leaves, which are used as salad greens. **2.** The root of this plant, dried, roasted, and ground and added to or used as a substitute for coffee.

chide (chīd) *tr.v.* **chided, chiding, chides** To scold or reproach; reprove: *chided us for being late.*

chief (chēf) *n.* A person with the highest rank or authority; a leader: *the chief of a Scottish clan; the chief of the fire*

department. ❖ *adj.* **1.** Highest in rank or authority: *The chief engineer is in charge of the power station.* **2.** Most important; main; principal: *What is the country's chief crop?*
◆ **in chief** With the highest rank or greatest authority: *Our editor-in-chief determines this newspaper's policies.*
Chief Executive *n.* The President of the United States.
chief justice also **Chief Justice** *n.* A judge who presides over a court having several judges, especially the United States Supreme Court.
chiefly (chēf′lē) *adv.* **1.** Above all; especially: *They went home early, chiefly to avoid the storm.* **2.** For the most part; mostly; mainly: *grassy land used chiefly for grazing.*
chief of staff *n., pl.* **chiefs of staff 1.** The highest ranking officer of the US Army or Air Force, responsible to the secretary of his or her branch of service and to the president. **2.** The senior military officer on the staff of a general or admiral. **3.** The senior staff member at an organization or institution: *the president's chief of staff.*
chief of state *n., pl.* **chiefs of state** A person who is the formal head of a nation, but is not the head of the government: *In Great Britain the monarch is the chief of state.*
chieftain (chēf′tən) *n.* The leader or head of a group, especially of a clan or tribe.
chiffon (shǐ-fŏn′ *or* shǐf′ŏn′) *n.* A soft, sheer, light fabric of silk, cotton, or rayon, used for scarves, veils, dresses, and blouses. ❖ *adj.* **1.** Relating to or resembling chiffon. **2.** Made light and fluffy by the addition of beaten egg whites or gelatin: *lemon chiffon pie.*
chiffonier (shǐf′ə-nîr′) *n.* A narrow high chest of drawers, often with a mirror attached.
chigger (chǐg′ər) *n.* **1.** Any of various tiny mite larvae that parasitize humans and other vertebrates and whose bite causes intense itching. **2.** The chigoe.
chignon (shēn-yŏn′ *or* shēn′yŏn′) *n.* A roll or knot of hair worn at the back of the head or nape of the neck.
chigoe (chǐg′ō *or* chē′gō) *n.* **1.** A small tropical flea, the female of which burrows under the skin of humans and other mammals, causing intense itching and sores. **2.** Any of various mite larvae that cause itching; a chigger.
Chihuahua (chǐ-wä′wä) *n.* A very small dog of a breed developed in Mexico, having a smooth, usually tan or black coat and pointed ears.
chilblain (chǐl′blān′) *n.* An itchy redness and soreness of the hands, feet, or ears, caused by exposure to damp cold.
child (chīld) *n., pl.* **children** (chǐl′drən) **1.** A person between birth and physical maturity. **2a.** A son or daughter; an offspring: *There are several children in that big family.* **b.** An infant; a baby: *a newborn child.* **c.** An unborn baby; a fetus: *She is carrying a child in her womb.* **3.** An older person who behaves like a child; an immature person: *Most adults act the child now and then.* **4.** A descendant: *children of Abraham.* **5.** A person or thing considered as the product or result of something: *a child of the 20th century.* ◆ **with child** Pregnant.
childbearing (chīld′bâr′ǐng) *n.* Pregnancy and childbirth. ❖ *adj.* Relating to childbearing, especially with regard to the ability to become pregnant: *women of childbearing age.*
childbirth (chīld′bûrth′) *n.* The act or process of giving birth to a child.
childhood (chīld′hŏŏd′) *n.* The time or condition of being a child: *Friends are easily made during childhood.*
childish (chīl′dǐsh) *adj.* **1.** Relating to or suitable for a

child: *a high childish voice; childish games.* **2.** Immature; foolish or silly: *childish behavior.* —**child′ish·ly** *adv.* —**child′ish·ness** *n.*
childlike (chīld′līk′) *adj.* Similar to or suitable for a child; innocent and simple: *childlike faith in others.*
childproof (chīld′prŏŏf′) *adj.* **1.** Designed to resist tampering by young children: *a childproof medicine bottle.* **2.** Made safe for young children: *Is the living room childproof?* ❖ *tr.v.* **childproofed, childproofing, childproofs** To make safe for young children: *childproofed the kitchen by placing all the cleaning products on high shelves.*
children (chǐl′drən) *n.* Plural of **child.**
child's play (chīldz) *n.* Something very easy to do: *These problems of addition are mere child's play.*
chili (chǐl′ē) *n., pl.* **chilies 1.** The fresh or dried fruit of any of several red or green peppers, used especially as a flavoring in cooking; chili pepper. **2.** A stew made of meat or beans (or both) and usually tomatoes, spiced with chili peppers or chili powder.
chili con carne (kŏn kär′nē) *n.* Chili made with meat, usually beef.
chili powder *n.* A seasoning consisting of chilies that are ground and mixed with other spices, such as cumin and oregano.
chill (chǐl) *n.* **1.** A moderate but penetrating coldness: *a chill in the fall air.* **2.** A feeling of coldness: *Chills and sneezing are signs of a cold.* **3.** A discouraging of enthusiasm or depressing of spirit: *The bad news put a chill on the celebration.* **4.** A feeling of fear: *We all felt a chill when the lights went out.* ❖ *adj.* **1.** Moderately cold; chilly: *a chill north wind.* **2.** Not warm and friendly: *a chill greeting.* **3.** Discouraging: *My suggestions met with a chill response.* ❖ *v.* **chilled, chilling, chills** —*tr.* **1.** To make cold: *The icy wind chilled our faces.* **2.** To produce a feeling of cold, fear, or dismay in: *The eerie story chilled all who heard it.* **3.** To discourage; dampen: *Bad luck has chilled their enthusiasm.* —*intr.* **1.** To become cold: *Put the dessert in the refrigerator to chill.* **2.** To feel cold or be affected by a cold feeling: *The skaters chilled quickly in harsh wind.* **3.** *Slang* **a.** To calm down or relax: *needed to chill after a long day at school.* **b.** To pass time idly; loiter. —**chill′er** *n.*
chilly (chǐl′ē) *adj.* **chillier, chilliest 1.** Cold enough to cause or feel discomfort: *Damp chilly weather is common along the seacoast.* See Synonyms at **cold. 2.** Feeling cold; shivering. **3.** Not enthusiastic: *a chilly reaction to the new plan.* **4.** Unfriendly: *a chilly greeting.* —**chill′i·ness** *n.*
chime (chīm) *n.* **1.** often **chimes** A set of bells tuned to different pitches and rung to make musical sounds. **2.** often **chimes** An orchestral instrument consisting of a set of metal tubes tuned to a musical scale and struck to make bell-like sounds. **3.** A single bell: *The chime in that clock strikes on the hour.* **4.** A musical sound produced by or as if by bells or chimes: *hear the chime of the church clock.* ❖ *v.* **chimed, chiming, chimes** —*intr.* To ring, as a bell or set of chimes. —*tr.* **1.** To strike (a bell) to produce music: *chime the church bells in celebration of peace.* **2.** To announce (the time of day) by ringing bells: *The clock chimed three o'clock.* ◆ **chime in** To join in, as in song or conversation: *The audience chimed in on the chorus.*
chimera also **chimaera** (kī-mîr′ə *or* kǐ-mîr′ə) *n.* **1a.** An organism, organ, or part consisting of two or more tissues of different genetic composition, produced as a result of organ transplant, grafting, or genetic engineering. **b.** A substance, such as an antibody, created from the proteins or genes of two different species. **2.** An individual who has

received a transplant of genetically and immunologically different tissue. **3.** A fanciful mental illusion or fabrication: *The whole scheme turned out to be just a chimera.*

Chimera also **Chimaera** *n.* **1.** In Greek mythology, a fire-breathing female monster usually represented as being part lion, part goat, and part snake or dragon. **2.** A grotesque monster made up of dissimilar parts.

chimerical (kĭ-mĕr′ĭ-kəl *or* kī-mĕr′ĭ-kəl) *adj.* Imaginary; fantastic: *chimerical notions with little basis in reality.*

chimney (chĭm′nē) *n., pl.* **chimneys 1.** A hollow, usually vertical structure for the passage of smoke and gases rising from a fireplace, stove, or furnace. **2.** The part of such a structure that rises above a roof. **3.** The glass tube, often wide at the center and narrow at the top, placed around the flame of a lamp. **4.** Something resembling a chimney, as a narrow cleft in a cliff.

chimney sweep or **chimney sweeper** *n.* A person employed to clean soot from chimneys.

chimney swift *n.* A small dark bird of North America, somewhat resembling a swallow, that often nests in unused chimneys.

chimp (chĭmp) *n. Informal* A chimpanzee.

chimpanzee (chĭm′păn-zē′ *or* chĭm-păn′zē) *n.* A dark-haired ape that is smaller than a gorilla and is found in central and western Africa north of the Congo River.

chin (chĭn) *n.* The front part of the face below the lips formed by the lower jaw and extending to the neck. ❖ *tr.v.* **chinned, chinning, chins** To grasp an overhead horizontal bar and pull (oneself) up with the arms until the chin clears the bar.

china (chī′nə) *n.* **1.** A fine hard porcelain, originally made in China from a type of white clay, baked at high temperatures and often decorated with colored designs. **2.** Articles made from this porcelain or a similar material, especially dishes used at the table.

chinaberry (chī′nə-bĕr′ē) *n.* A spreading tree of Asia that has been widely planted in warm climates for its shade and attractive purplish flowers.

Chinatown (chī′nə-toun′) *n.* A part of a city that is inhabited chiefly by Chinese people.

chinaware (chī′nə-wâr′) *n.* Dishes and other articles made of china or similar pottery.

chinch (chĭnch) *n.* A bedbug.

chinch bug *n.* A small black-and-white insect that feeds on and damages wheat and other grains and grasses in dry weather.

chinchilla (chĭn-chĭl′ə) *n.* **1.** Either of two rodents native to the mountains of South America, resembling a squirrel and having soft pale-gray fur. **2.** The fur of either of these animals.

Chinese (chī-nēz′ *or* chī-nēs′) *adj.* Relating to China or to its people, languages, or culture. ❖ *n., pl.* **Chinese 1.** A native or inhabitant of China. **2a.** A group of Sino-Tibetan languages and dialects spoken by the Chinese people, including Mandarin and Cantonese. **b.** The official national language of China; Mandarin.

Chinese checkers *pl.n. (used with a singular or plural verb)* A game for two to six players in which marbles are moved from holes of one point of the star-shaped board to a set of holes on the opposite side.

Chinese lantern *n.* A decorative lantern of thin brightly colored paper that is made in such a way that it can be collapsed.

Chinese puzzle *n.* A very complicated puzzle or difficult problem.

chink[1] (chĭngk) *n.* A narrow crack or opening. ❖ *tr.v.* **chinked, chinking, chinks** To seal or close narrow cracks or openings by filling: *They chinked the spaces between the logs of the cabin wall with mud.*

chink[2] (chĭngk) *n.* A short clinking sound, as of metal striking together: *the chink of coins.* ❖ *intr. & tr.v.* **chinked, chinking, chinks** To make or cause to make such a sound: *Coins chinked in my pocket. I chinked the coins in my pocket.*

chino (chē′nō) *n., pl.* **chinos 1.** A strong cotton cloth used chiefly for uniforms and work clothes. **2. chinos** Pants made of this material.

chinook (shĭ-nŏok′ *or* chĭ-nŏok′) *n.* **1.** A moist warm wind that blows from the ocean in the northwest United States and southwest Canada. **2.** A warm dry wind that comes down from the eastern slopes of the Rocky Mountains in west-central North America.

Chinook *n., pl.* **Chinook** or **Chinooks 1.** A member of a Native American people living in the state of Washington. **2.** The language of this people.

Chinook Jargon *n.* A blend of English, French, Chinook, and other Native American languages, formerly used by traders in the Pacific Northwest.

chintz (chĭnts) *n.* A printed, usually brightly colored cotton fabric.

chintzy (chĭnt′sē) *adj.* **chintzier, chintziest 1.** Relating to or decorated with chintz. **2.** Gaudy; cheap: *chintzy trinkets.*

chin-up (chĭn′ŭp′) *n.* The act or exercise of chinning oneself on an overhead bar.

chip (chĭp) *n.* **1.** A small broken or cut-off piece; a fragment: *a chip of wood.* **2.** A dent or mark left when a small piece is broken off: *a chip in the marble.* **3a.** A thin slice of food: *a potato chip.* **b. chips** French fries: *fish and chips.* **4.** An integrated circuit. **5.** A small disk that is used in poker and other games to represent money. **6.** A chip shot in golf. ❖ *v.* **chipped, chipping, chips** —*tr.* **1.** To break off a small piece from (something), as by hitting, jarring, or scraping: *chip the edge of the glass.* **2.** To shape or carve by cutting or chopping: *chipped my name in stone.* —*intr.* **1.** To become broken off: *These dishes chip if you are not careful.* **2.** To make a chip shot in golf. ❖ **a chip off the old block** A child that closely resembles one parent or the other. **chip in** To contribute money or labor: *How many people chipped in for the present?* **chip on (one's) shoulder** An aggressive or hostile attitude: *My cousin has had a chip on his shoulder ever since our argument.*

Chipewyan (chĭp′ə-wī′ən) *n., pl.* **Chipewyan** or **Chipewyans 1.** A member of a Native American people living in north-central Canada. **2.** The Athabascan language of the Chipewyan.

chipmunk (chĭp′mŭngk′) *n.* Any of several burrowing rodents of North America that resemble a small squirrel and have a striped back.

chipotle (chə-pōt′lā) *n.* A ripe jalapeño pepper that has been dried and smoked for use in cooking.

chipped beef (chĭpt) *n.* Dried beef, smoked and thinly sliced.

chipper (chĭp′ər) *adj.* Active; cheerful; sprightly.

Chippewa (chĭp′ə-wô′ *or* chĭp′ə-wä′) *n., pl.* **Chippewa** or **Chippewas 1.** An Ojibwa. **2.** The Ojibwa language.

chip shot *n.* A short lofted golf stroke, used in approaching the green.

Chiron (kī′rŏn′) *n.* In Greek mythology, the wise centaur who tutored Achilles, Hercules, and Asclepius.

chiropody (kĭ-rŏp′ə-dē) *n.* Podiatry. —**chi·rop′o·dist** *n.*

chiropractic (kī′rə-prăk′tĭk) *n.* A method of treating diseases by manipulating the spine and certain other structures of the body, usually without the use of drugs or surgery.

chiropractor (kī′rə-prăk′tər) *n.* A person who practices chiropractic.

chirp (chûrp) *n.* A short high-pitched sound, such as the one made by a small bird or a cricket. ❖ *intr.v.* **chirped, chirping, chirps** To make such a sound.

chirrup (chûr′əp *or* chĭr′əp) *n.* The sound of repeated chirping, clicking, or clucking; a series of chirps, clicks, or clucks. ❖ *intr.v.* **chirruped, chirruping, chirrups** To make or utter such a sound.

chisel (chĭz′əl) *n.* A metal tool with a sharp beveled edge across the end of a thick blade, used to cut and shape stone, wood, or metal. ❖ *v.* **chiseled, chiseling, chisels** *or* **chiselled, chiselling, chisels** — *tr.* **1.** To cut into or shape with a chisel: *The sculptor chiseled the statue out of stone.* **2.** *Informal* To cheat or obtain by deception. — *intr.* To use a chisel. —**chis′el·er** *n.*

chitchat (chĭt′chăt′) *n.* **1.** Casual conversation; small talk. **2.** Gossip: *neighborhood chitchat.* ❖ *intr.v.* **chitchatted, chitchatting, chitchats** To engage in chitchat.

chitin (kīt′n) *n.* A tough substance that is the main component of the external skeletons of crustaceans, insects, and spiders. —**chi′tin·ous** *adj.*

chiton (kīt′n *or* kī′tŏn′) *n.* A loosely draped gown or tunic worn by men and women in ancient Greece.

chitterlings *also* **chitlins** *or* **chitlings** (chĭt′lĭnz) *pl.n.* The small intestine of a pig, fried as food.

chivalrous (shĭv′əl-rəs) *adj.* **1.** Relating to the age of chivalry: *the chivalrous adventures of King Arthur's knights.* **2.** Having or showing the qualities of the ideal knight; brave, honorable, and courteous: *a chivalrous act of self-sacrifice.* —**chiv′al·rous·ness** *n.*

chivalry (shĭv′əl-rē) *n., pl.* **chivalries 1.** The medieval institution of knighthood and its customs: *the code of chivalry.* **2.** The qualities of the ideal knight, such as bravery, courtesy, honor, and gallantry towards women: *the victorious general's chivalry toward the welfare of defeated enemy troops.* **3.** A group of knights or gallant gentlemen.

chive (chīv) *n.* **1.** A plant related to the onion, having long narrow leaves. **2. chives** The onion-flavored leaves of this plant, used as a seasoning.

chlamydia (klə-mĭd′ē-ə) *n.* A sexually transmitted disease caused by a bacterium, often resulting in inflammation of the reproductive organs. If untreated, it can lead to infertility in women.

chloral hydrate (klôr′əl) *n.* A colorless crystalline compound that is used as a sedative.

chloride (klôr′īd′) *n.* A chemical compound of chlorine and another element or radical.

chlorinate (klôr′ə-nāt′) *tr.v.* **chlorinated, chlorinating, chlorinates** To treat or combine with chlorine or one of its compounds, especially in order to kill bacteria in water. —**chlo′ri·na′tion** *n.*

chlorine (klôr′ēn′ *or* klôr′ĭn) *n. Symbol* **Cl** A greenish-yellow gaseous element found chiefly in combination with sodium as common salt. It is very poisonous and is used in water purification, sewage treatment, and the manufacture of bleach. Atomic number 17. See **Periodic Table.**

chlorofluorocarbon (klôr′ō-flŏŏr′ō-kär′bən *or* klôr′ō-

flôr′ō-kär′bən) *n.* Any of various compounds consisting of carbon, hydrogen, chlorine, and fluorine, formerly used as aerosol propellants and refrigerants. Chlorofluorocarbons are believed to cause depletion of the atmospheric ozone layer.

chloroform (klôr′ə-fôrm′) *n.* A clear, colorless, heavy liquid having the formula CHCl₃. It is used in refrigeration, in industrial chemicals, and sometimes as an anesthetic. ❖ *tr.v.* **chloroformed, chloroforming, chloroforms** To make unconscious or kill with chloroform.

chlorophyll (klôr′ə-fĭl) *n.* Any of several green pigments that are found in green plants, algae, and certain bacteria and that capture light energy which is used in photosynthesis to convert carbon dioxide and water into food molecules. Chlorophyll molecules are composed of carbon, hydrogen, magnesium, nitrogen, and oxygen.

chloroplast (klôr′ə-plăst′) *n.* A structure in the cells of green plants and algae that contains chlorophyll and is the site where photosynthesis takes place.

chock (chŏk) *n.* A block or wedge placed under something, such as a boat, barrel, or wheel, to keep it from moving. ❖ *tr.v.* **chocked, chocking, chocks** To hold in place with a chock or chocks: *chock the wheels of a truck parked on a hill.*

chock-full (chŏk′fŏŏl′) *adj.* Completely filled; stuffed: *a bus chock-full of people at rush hour.*

chocolate (chô′kə-lĭt *or* chôk′lĭt) *n.* **1.** A food made from cacao seeds that have been roasted and ground and often mixed with sweeteners and flavoring. Chocolate for cooking is sold in powdered or block form. **2.** A candy made from or covered with this substance, often with a soft filling. ❖ *adj.* Made of or flavored with chocolate: *a chocolate cake.*

Choctaw (chŏk′tô) *n., pl.* **Choctaw** *or* **Choctaws 1.** A member of a Native American people formerly living in parts of Mississippi and Alabama, now living mainly in Oklahoma, Mississippi, and Alabama. **2.** The Muskogean language of the Choctaw.

choice (chois) *n.* **1.** The act of choosing; selection: *Did price influence your choice?* **2.** The power, right, or possibility to choose; option: *You leave me no choice in this matter.* **3.** Someone or something chosen: *The customer's choices were roast beef, mashed potatoes, and peas.* **4.** A variety from which to choose: *The cafeteria has a wide choice of sandwiches.* **5.** An alternative: *There is no choice but to obey the rules.* ❖ *adj.* **choicer, choicest 1.** Of fine quality; very good; select: *choice tidbits; choice vegetables.* **2.** Selected with care: *reply in a few choice words.* —**choice′ly** *adv.*

✦ **SYNONYMS** choice, alternative, option, preference, selection *n.*

choir (kwīr) *n.* **1.** An organized group of singers, especially one that performs regularly in a church: *a children's choir; a cathedral choir.* **2.** The part of a church especially for the use of such singers.

WORD HISTORY Why don't we spell the word **choir** as *quire?* In fact, English did once spell it this way. Its spelling was changed because in the 1600s, a group of scholars in England decided that many words should be respelled to make them look more like Latin or Greek. Latin and Greek were the languages of classical learning, and their spelling was thought to be "proper." Since our word comes from Latin *chorus,* "dance, musical composition, band of singers or dancers," *quire* was respelled as *choir* to make it look more like *chorus.*

choirboy (kwīr′boi′) *n.* A boy who is a member of a choir.

choirgirl (kwīr′gûrl′) *n.* A girl who is a member of a choir.

choirmaster (kwīr′măs′tər) *n.* The director of a choir.

choke (chōk) *v.* **choked, choking, chokes** —*tr.* **1.** To interfere with the breathing of (a person or animal) by squeezing or blocking the windpipe. **2.** To reduce the amount of air supplied to (a gasoline engine) so that it will start and warm up more easily. **3.** To check or slow down the movement, growth, or action of: *Weeds are choking the garden.* **4.** To stop or suppress by or as if by strangling: *Sobs choked her words.* **5.** To clog up; congest: *Traffic choked the highway.* —*intr.* **1.** To be unable to breathe, swallow, or speak normally, as when the throat is blocked: *choke on a piece of bread.* **2.** To be blocked up or obstructed: *The drain choked up with kitchen scraps.* **3.** To fail to perform effectively, especially in a game or contest: *He choked when he missed a two-foot putt to win the match.* ❖ *n.* **1.** The act or sound of choking. **2.** A device that controls the amount of air taken in by a gasoline engine. ◆ **choke back** To hold back; control; suppress: *choke back tears.* **choke off** To put an end to; stop: *Closing the train station would choke off business in the area.* **choke up 1.** To be unable to speak because of strong emotion. **2.** To shorten one's grip on the handle, as of a baseball bat.

chokecherry (chōk′chĕr′ē) *n.* **1.** A shrub or small tree having narrow clusters of small white flowers and bitter-tasting dark-red or black fruit. **2.** The fruit of this plant.

choker (chō′kər) *n.* **1.** A person or thing that chokes: *Many dogs are trained on restraining collars that are chokers.* **2.** A short necklace that fits closely around the throat.

choler (kŏl′ər) *n.* Anger; irritability.

cholera (kŏl′ər-ə) *n.* An infectious, often fatal disease of the intestines that is caused by bacteria and is often epidemic. It is caught from contaminated water and food and causes severe diarrhea, vomiting, and dehydration.

choleric (kŏl′ə-rĭk *or* kə-lĕr′ĭk) *adj.* Easily made angry; bad-tempered. —SEE NOTE AT **humor.**

cholesterol (kə-lĕs′tə-rôl′) *n.* A white fatty substance that is found chiefly in animals and is important in metabolism and hormone production. It is manufactured by the body and taken in by eating foods such as meat, cheese, and eggs. High levels of certain kinds of cholesterol are thought to be a factor in developing heart disease.

chomp (chŏmp) *v.* **chomped, chomping, chomps** —*tr.* To chew or bite on noisily: *a horse chomping oats.* —*intr.* To chew or bite on something: *chomping on a carrot.*

choose (chōōz) *v.* **chose** (chōz), **chosen** (chō′zən), **choosing, chooses** —*tr.* **1.** To decide on and pick out from a greater number of people or things; select: *I chose a book in the library.* **2.** To decide: *We chose to walk to work.* —*intr.* To make a choice; select: *They had to choose for themselves.* —**choos′er** *n.*

choosy *also* **choosey** (chōō′zē) *adj.* **choosier, choosiest** Very careful in choosing: *She's very choosy about the clothes that she wears.*

chop¹ (chŏp) *v.* **chopped, chopping, chops** —*tr.* **1.** To cut by striking with a heavy sharp tool, such as an axe: *chop wood.* **2.** To make by cutting in this way: *chop a path through the woods.* **3.** To cut up into small pieces; mince: *chop onions.* **4.** To cut short; reduce: *chop a report that is too long.* **5.** In sports, to hit or hit at with a short swift downward stroke: *The batter chopped a grounder through the infield.* —*intr.* To make heavy cutting strokes: *chop away at a block of ice.* ❖ *n.* **1.** A quick short cutting stroke or blow: *A chop of the axe split the log.* **2.** A small cut of

meat that usually contains a bone: *lamb chops.* **3.** A short irregular movement of waves.

chop² (chŏp) *intr.v.* **chopped, chopping, chops** To change direction suddenly, as a ship in the wind.

WORD HISTORY Chop¹ comes Middle English *choppen,* which is probably a variant of *chappen,* meaning "to split." **Chop**² comes from an obsolete English sense of *chop* meaning "to exchange," which comes from the Middle English *choppen,* meaning "to barter."

chopper (chŏp′ər) *n.* **1.** *Informal* A helicopter. **2.** A person or thing that chops: *a food chopper.*

choppers (chŏp′ərz) *pl.n. Slang* Teeth, especially a set of false teeth.

chopping block (chŏp′ĭng) *n.* A wooden block on which food or wood is chopped.

choppy¹ (chŏp′ē) *adj.* **choppier, choppiest** Having many short irregular waves: *choppy seas.* —**chop′pi·ness** *n.*

choppy² (chŏp′ē) *adj.* **choppier, choppiest** **1.** Shifting quickly; variable: *choppy winds.* **2.** Not smooth; jerky: *choppy prose.*

chops (chŏps) *pl.n.* The jaws, cheeks, or jowls.

chopsticks (chŏp′stĭks′) *pl.n.* A pair of slender sticks usually made of wood or plastic and held between the fingers, used as an eating utensil in eastern Asia.

chop suey (sōō′ē) *n.* A Chinese-American dish made with bits of meat, bean sprouts, and other vegetables and served with rice.

choral (kôr′əl) *adj.* Relating to, intended for, or sung by a chorus or choir: *a choral society; a choral passage.*

chorale *also* **choral** (kə-răl′) *n.* **1.** A harmonized arrangement of a hymn melody, especially one forming part of a larger work. **2.** A chorus or choir.

chord¹ (kôrd) *n.* A combination of three or more musical pitches sounded at the same time. —**chord′al** *adj.*

chord² (kôrd) *n.* A line segment whose end points lie on a curve or on the circumference of a circle.

WORD HISTORY Chord¹ comes from Old French *acorde,* meaning "agreement, harmony." **Chord**² is an altered form of Modern English *cord,* meaning "string."

chordate (kôr′dāt *or* kôr′dĭt) *n.* Any of a large group of animals having at some stage of development a spinal column or a strip of cartilage along the back and openings to allow water to pass over the gills. Chordates include all vertebrates and certain other marine animals, such as the lancelets and the tunicates.

chore (chôr) *n.* **1.** A routine or minor task: *Feeding the cat is a daily chore.* See Synonyms at **task. 2.** An unpleasant task: *Taking out the garbage is a chore I'd like to forget.*

chorea (kô-rē′ə) *n.* Any of various disorders of the nervous system that cause the arms, legs, and face to twitch and move uncontrollably.

choreograph (kôr′ē-ə-grăf′) *v.* **choreographed, choreographing, choreographs** —*tr.* To create the choreography of (a ballet or other stage work). —*intr.* To engage in choreography.

choreographer (kôr′ē-ŏg′rə-fər) *n.* Someone who creates, arranges, and directs ballets or dances.

choreography (kôr′ē-ŏg′rə-fē) *n., pl.* **choreographies** The art of creating and arranging ballets or dances.

chorion (kôr′ē-ŏn′) *n.* The outer membrane that encloses the embryo or fetus of a reptile, bird, or mammal. In placental mammals it contributes to the development of the placenta. —**cho′ri·on′ic** (kôr′ē-ŏn′ĭk) *adj.*

chorister (kôr′ĭ-stər) *n.* **1.** A person who sings in a choir. **2.** A choir leader.

choroid (kôr′oid′) *n.* A delicate membrane between the sclera and the retina of the eyeball.

chortle (chôr′tl) *n.* A snorting chuckle. ❖ *intr.v.* **chortled, chortling, chortles** To laugh in a snorting joyful manner.

chorus (kôr′əs) *n., pl.* **choruses 1.** An organized group of singers who perform together. **2.** A musical composition or a part of a musical composition written for such a group. **3.** A group of people who speak or sing a part in a play all at the same time. **4.** A group of singers and dancers who play a supporting role in an opera, musical comedy, or other stage production. **5.** A section of music that is repeated after each verse of a song; a refrain. **6.** Something uttered by many people at one time: *a chorus of laughter.* ❖ *tr.v.* **chorused, chorusing, choruses** or **chorussed, chorussing, chorusses** To sing or utter at the same time. ◆ **in chorus** All together: *The group responded to the suggestion in chorus.*

chose (chōz) *v.* Past tense of **choose.**

chosen (chō′zən) *v.* Past participle of **choose.** ❖ *adj.* **1.** Selected from or preferred above others: *the chosen few.* **2.** Selected by God; elect: *the chosen people.*

chow¹ (chou) *n.* A dog of a breed developed in China, having a large head, a thick reddish-brown or black coat, and a blackish tongue.

chow² (chou) *n. Slang* Food.

WORD HISTORY Chow¹ may come from English *chow-chow,* meaning "miscellaneous knick-knacks exported from China." **Chow²** may come from Cantonese *zaap,* meaning "food, miscellany."

chow chow *n.* A chow dog.

chowder (chou′dər) *n.* **1.** A thick soup or stew containing fish or shellfish, especially clams, and vegetables in a milk base. **2.** A thin soup of seafood with tomatoes in a meat broth. **3.** A soup similar to either of these soups, made with a vegetable, such as corn, as the main ingredient.

chow mein (chou′ mān′) *n.* A Chinese-American dish of bits of meat and cooked vegetables served over fried noodles.

chrism (krĭz′əm) *n.* A consecrated mixture of oil and balsam, used for anointing in Christian sacraments such as baptism and confirmation.

Christ (krīst) *n.* **1.** The Messiah, as foretold by the prophets of the Bible. **2.** Jesus as considered in Christianity to be the Messiah.

christen (krĭs′ən) *tr.v.* **christened, christening, christens 1.** To baptize into a Christian church. **2.** To give a name to at baptism: *They christened him Joseph.* **3.** To name, especially at a ceremony: *christen a ship.* **4.** *Informal* To use for the first time: *christen a new car with a ride around the block.*

Christendom (krĭs′ən-dəm) *n.* **1.** Christians considered as a group. **2.** The countries of the world where Christianity is the principal religion.

christening (krĭs′ə-nĭng) *n.* **1.** The Christian ceremony of baptizing and naming a child. **2.** A ceremony at which something is named and declared ready for use, especially a ship.

Christian (krĭs′chən) *adj.* **1.** Believing in or associated with Christianity: *a Christian congregation; a Christian holiday.* **2.** Showing qualities, such as gentleness or hu-

mility, considered as advocated in Christianity: *a Christian act of forgiveness.* ❖ *n.* A person who believes in or practices Christianity.

Christianity (krĭs′chē-ăn′ĭ-tē *or* krĭs′tē-ăn′ĭ-tē) *n.* **1.** A religion based on the life and teachings of Jesus, a first-century Jewish religious leader who was crucified by the Roman authorities in Palestine. In Christianity, Jesus is worshiped as the living Messiah and the Son of God. **2.** Christians considered as a group; Christendom: *Christianity celebrates Christmas.* **3.** The condition or fact of being a Christian.

Christianize (krĭs′chə-nīz′) *tr.v.* **Christianized, Christianizing, Christianizes** To convert (another) to Christianity: *Missionaries tried to Christianize the native peoples of North America.* —**Chris′tian·i·za′tion** (krĭs′chə-nĭ-zā′-shən) *n.* —**Chris′tian·iz′er** *n.*

Christian name *n.* **1.** A name that is given at baptism. **2.** A name that precedes a person's family name, especially a first name.

Christian Science *n.* The church and religious system founded by the American religious leader Mary Baker Eddy (1821–1910) that emphasizes healing through spiritual means. —**Christian Scientist** *n.*

Christmas (krĭs′məs) *n.* **1.** A festival celebrated by Christians in commemoration of the birth of Jesus. **2.** December 25, the day on which this festival is observed as a public holiday in many countries. **3.** The period around Christmas, traditionally the period from December 24 (Christmas Eve) to January 5 (the eve of Epiphany).

Christmas Eve *n.* The day or evening before Christmas.

Christmas tree *n.* An evergreen or artificial tree decorated with ornaments and lights during the Christmas season.

chromatic (krō-măt′ĭk) *adj.* **1.** Relating to color or colors. **2.** Relating to or based on the chromatic scale, as a melody or chord. —**chro·mat′i·cal·ly** *adv.*

chromatic scale *n.* A musical scale consisting of twelve notes, each separated from the next by a semitone.

chromatid (krō′mə-tĭd) *n.* Either of the two strands formed when a chromosome duplicates itself during cell division.

chromatin (krō′mə-tĭn) *n.* A substance in the nucleus of a cell that consists of DNA and proteins. During cell division the chromatin becomes dense and compact, forming individual chromosomes.

chromatography (krō′mə-tŏg′rə-fē) *n.* A technique that separates the components of a chemical mixture by moving the mixture along a stationary material such as gelatin. The components are taken up and held in the material at different rates, thus forming isolated bands that scientists can further separate and analyze.

chrome (krōm) *n.* **1.** Chromium. **2.** A material plated with chromium or one of its alloys.

chromic (krō′mĭk) *adj.* Relating to or containing chromium.

chromium (krō′mē-əm) *n. Symbol* **Cr** A grayish, hard, brittle metallic element that does not rust or become dull easily. Chromium is used in plating other metals, in making stainless steel and other alloys, and in making dyes and paints. Atomic number 24. See **Periodic Table.**

chromosome (krō′mə-sōm′) *n.* A cellular structure that is composed mainly of DNA and includes the genes that determine heredity. In plants, animals, and other eukaryotic organisms, the chromosomes are located in the nucleus. —**chro′mo·so′mal** (krō′mə-sō′məl) *adj.*

chromosphere (krō′mə-sfîr′) *n.* **1.** A glowing transparent layer of gas surrounding the photosphere of the sun. It is several thousand miles thick and is rich in hydrogen, helium, and calcium. **2.** A similar layer around a star.

chronic (krŏn′ĭk) *adj.* **1.** Lasting for a long time or recurring frequently: *chronic bronchitis.* **2.** Subject to a habit for a long time: *a chronic complainer.* —**chron′i·cal·ly** *adv.*

chronic fatigue syndrome *n.* A syndrome characterized by debilitating fatigue and a combination of flulike symptoms such as sore throat, swollen lymph glands, headaches, and muscle pain or weakness.

chronicle (krŏn′ĭ-kəl) *n.* **1.** A record of historical events arranged in order of occurrence. **2. Chronicles** *(used with a singular verb)* Either of two books of the Bible that tell the history of the Israelite kings. ❖ *tr.v.* **chronicled, chronicling, chronicles** To record, as in a chronicle: *Medieval monks chronicled the events of each year.* —**chron′i·cler** *n.*

chronological (krŏn′ə-lŏj′ĭ-kəl) *adj.* Arranged in order of time in which the events took place: *keep all historical facts in chronological order.* —**chron′o·log′i·cal·ly** *adv.*

chronology (krə-nŏl′ə-jē) *n., pl.* **chronologies 1.** The science that deals with determining the dates and order of events. **2.** A chronological list or table: *a detailed chronology of modern history.* **3.** The arrangement of events in time.

chronometer (krə-nŏm′ĭ-tər) *n.* A very accurate clock or other timepiece, especially as used in scientific experiments, navigation, or astronomical observations.

chrysalis (krĭs′ə-lĭs) *n., pl.* **chrysalises** or **chrysalides** (krĭ-săl′ĭ-dēz′) A pupa of a butterfly, consisting of a tough case enclosing the insect as it undergoes metamorphosis and eventually emerges as a fully developed adult.

chrysanthemum (krĭ-săn′thə-məm) *n.* **1.** Any of various plants having many cultivated forms with showy, round, variously colored flowers. **2.** The flower of such a plant.

chub (chŭb) *n., pl.* **chub** or **chubs 1.** Any of various freshwater fishes of Europe and North America that are related to the carps and minnows. **2.** Any of various other freshwater fishes of North America.

chubby (chŭb′ē) *adj.* **chubbier, chubbiest** Round and plump: *a chubby face.* —**chub′bi·ness** *n.*

chuck¹ (chŭk) *tr.v.* **chucked, chucking, chucks 1.** To pat affectionately, especially under the chin. **2a.** To throw or toss: *chuck a stone in the pond.* **b.** *Informal* To throw out; discard: *chuck an old shoe; chuck a poor plan.* ❖ *n.* **1.** An affectionate pat, especially under the chin. **2.** A toss or throw.

chuck² (chŭk) *n.* **1.** A cut of beef extending from the neck to the ribs. **2.** In a machine such as a drill or lathe, a rotating clamp that holds either a tool or the work.

WORD HISTORY Chuck¹ may come from French *choc,* meaning "knock, blow." **Chuck²** may come from English *chock,* meaning "wedge."

chuckle (chŭk′əl) *intr.v.* **chuckled, chuckling, chuckles** To laugh quietly or to oneself. ❖ *n.* A quiet laugh of amusement or satisfaction.

chuck wagon *n.* A wagon with food and cooking utensils for a group of workers, especially those moving from place to place, as on a cattle drive.

chuckwalla (chŭk′wŏl′ə) *n.* Any of several large plant-eating lizards of the southwest United States and Mexico.

chug (chŭg) *n.* A dull explosive sound, especially a sound made by an engine working hard. ❖ *intr.v.* **chugged, chugging, chugs 1.** To make such sounds: *The old truck's*

motor chugged under the hood. **2.** To move while making such sounds: *The little train chugged up the mountain.*

chum¹ (chŭm) *n.* A close friend or companion; a pal. ❖ *intr.v.* **chummed, chumming, chums** To spend time together as friends; keep company: *After work, I chummed around with my coworkers.*

chum² (chŭm) *n.* Bait consisting of cut-up fish scattered on the water. ❖ *intr.v.* **chummed, chumming, chums** To fish with chum.

chummy (chŭm′ē) *adj.* **chummier, chummiest** Friendly; intimate: *a chummy bunch.*

chump (chŭmp) *n. Informal* A foolish or stupid person.

chunk (chŭngk) *n.* **1.** A thick piece of something: *a chunk of ice.* **2.** A large portion or amount: *They spent a chunk of their free time making music.*

chunky (chŭng′kē) *adj.* **chunkier, chunkiest 1.** Short, strong, and somewhat fat; stocky: *a chunky horse.* **2.** Containing small thick pieces: *chunky soup.* —**chunk′i·ness** *n.*

Chunnel (chŭn′əl) *n.* A railroad tunnel under the English Channel that connects Great Britain and France.

church (chûrch) *n.* **1.** A building for public worship, especially Christian worship. **2.** A Christian congregation: *Her church holds a children's fair each spring.* **3.** Religious service in a church: *They go to church every week.* **4.** often **Church** A specified Christian denomination: *the Baptist Church.* **5.** often **Church** All Christians regarded as a single spiritual body: *the Church and its beliefs.* **6.** The clerical profession; clergy. **7.** Ecclesiastical power as distinguished from secular power: *The separation of church and state is firmly established by the First Amendment to the Constitution.* ❖ *adj.* Relating to the church: *church music.*

churchgoer (chûrch′gō′ər) *n.* A person who attends church services regularly.

churchman (chûrch′mən) *n.* **1.** A man who is a cleric. **2.** A man who is a member of a church.

Church of Christ, Scientist *n.* Christian Science.

Church of England *n.* The national Christian church of England, which split off from the Roman Catholic Church in 1534 under the leadership of the English king Henry VIII.

Church of Jesus Christ of Latter-day Saints *n.* The Mormon Church.

churchwarden (chûrch′wôr′dn) *n.* A lay officer in an Anglican or Episcopal Church who helps manage parish business or legal affairs.

churchwoman (chûrch′wŏŏm′ən) *n.* **1.** A woman who is a cleric. **2.** A woman who is a member of a church.

churchyard (chûrch′yärd′) *n.* A yard adjacent to a church, often used as a cemetery.

churl (chûrl) *n.* **1.** A rude surly person; a boor. **2.** A medieval English peasant.

churlish (chûr′lĭsh) *adj.* Rude; surly; boorish: *The criminal's churlish answer offended the judge.* —**churl′ish·ly** *adv.* —**churl′ish·ness** *n.*

churn (chûrn) *n.* A container in which milk or cream is stirred or beaten vigorously in order to make butter. ❖ *v.* **churned, churning, churns** —*tr.* **1.** To stir or beat (milk or cream) in a churn to make butter. **2.** To move or swirl about violently: *Wind churned the leaves into piles.* —*intr.* **1.** To make butter in a churn. **2.** To stir or move violently: *waves churning in a storm.*

chute (shōōt) *n.* **1.** A vertical or inclined trough or passage down which things can be dropped or slid: *a laun-*

dry chute; a chute for toboggans. **2.** A waterfall or rapid. **3.** A parachute.

chutney (chŭt′nē) *n.* A spicy relish made of fruits and herbs.

chutzpah (кнŏŏt′spə *or* hŏŏt′spə) *n.* Shameless boldness; impudence; gall.

chyme (kīm) *n.* The thick soft mass of partly digested food that is passed from the stomach to the small intestine.

CIA An abbreviation of Central Intelligence Agency.

ciabatta (chə-bä′tə) *n.* A porous bread with a crispy crust, baked in a flattish, usually oblong loaf.

ciao (chou) *interj.* Used to express greeting or farewell.

WORD HISTORY The Italian salutation **ciao**, which is now popular in many parts of the world outside Italy, originated in the dialects of northern Italy. In the dialect of Venice, *ciau* literally means "servant, slave," and is also used as a casual greeting, "I am your servant." Dialectal *ciau* corresponds to standard Italian *schiavo*, "slave," and both words come from Medieval Latin *sclāvus*. Declaring yourself someone's slave might seem like an extravagant gesture today, but expressions such as *Your obedient servant* or *Your servant, madam* were once commonplace in English. Similarly, the Classical Latin word *servus*, meaning "slave," is still used as an informal greeting in southern Germany and in Austria, the Czech Republic, Slovakia, Hungary, Poland, Romania, Ukraine, and other parts of central Europe that were formerly part of the Austro-Hungarian Empire. At the opposite end of the world, in southeast and eastern Asia, one even finds words that originally meant "slave" or "your slave" but have developed into pronouns of the first person through their use in showing respect and humility. In Japanese, for example, the word *boku* is used to mean "I, me," especially by boys and young men, and it comes from a Middle Chinese word meaning "slave" or "servant" and now pronounced *pú* in Mandarin.

cicada (sĭ-kā′də) *n., pl.* **cicadas** or **cicadae** (sĭ-kā′dē′) Any of various insects having a broad head and transparent wings, the males of which produce a high-pitched droning sound from specialized organs. Some kinds of cicadas live underground as nymphs and emerge after 13 or 17 years.

cicerone (sĭs′ə-rō′nē) *n.* A guide for sightseers.

–cide A suffix that means: **1.** A killer of: *insecticide.* **2.** An act of killing: *suicide.*

cider (sī′dər) *n.* The juice pressed from apples, used as a beverage or to produce vinegar.

cigar (sĭ-gär′) *n.* A tight roll of tobacco leaves prepared for smoking.

cigarette (sĭg′ə-rĕt′ *or* sĭg′ə-rĕt′) *n.* A small roll of finely cut tobacco enclosed in a wrapper of thin paper for smoking.

cilantro (sĭ-län′trō *or* sĭ-län′trō) *n.* The stems and leaves of the coriander plant, used as a flavoring and garnish.

ciliary body (sĭl′ē-ĕr′ē) *n.* A ring-shaped structure inside the eye that adjusts the shape of the lens and produces the fluid of the aqueous humor.

ciliate (sĭl′ē-ĭt *or* sĭl′ē-āt′) *adj.* Having cilia. ❖ *n.* A microorganism, such as a paramecium, having cilia.

cilium (sĭl′ē-əm) *n., pl.* **cilia** (sĭl′ē-ə) One of usually many hairlike projections found on the outside of certain cells and capable of a whipping motion. Some microorgan-

isms use cilia to move themselves. The respiratory tract in humans is lined with cilia that remove foreign matter from air before it reaches the lungs.

cinch (sĭnch) *n.* **1.** A strap that encircles a horse's body and is used for holding a saddle or pack. **2.** Something easy to accomplish: *Riding a bike is a cinch once you know how.*

cinchona (sĭng-kō′nə *or* sĭn-chō′nə) *n.* Any of several evergreen trees and shrubs of South America whose bark is the source of quinine.

Cinco de Mayo (sēng′kō də mä′yō) *n.* May 5, observed by Mexican communities in the Americas in celebration of the 1862 defeat of French troops at the Battle of Puebla.

cincture (sĭngk′chər) *n.* A belt or sash worn around the waist.

cinder (sĭn′dər) *n.* **1a.** A burned or partly burned material, such as coal or wood, that cannot be burned further. **b.** A partly charred material that can burn further but without flame. **2. cinders** Ashes.

cinder block or **cinderblock** (sĭn′dər-blŏk′) *n.* A hollow concrete block made with coal cinders and used in building.

cinema (sĭn′ə-mə) *n.* **1a.** A film or movie. **b.** A movie theater: *the local cinema.* **2a.** The movie industry: *looking for a job in cinema.* **b.** The art of making movies or films: *studied cinema in college.* —**cin′e·mat′ic** (sĭn′ə-mät′ĭk) *adj.*

cinematographer (sĭn′ə-mə-tŏg′rə-fər) *n.* A movie photographer, especially one who is in charge of shooting a movie.

cinematography (sĭn′ə-mə-tŏg′rə-fē) *n.* The art or technique of movie photography.

cinnabar (sĭn′ə-bär′) *n.* **1.** A red or brown mineral that is the chief source of mercury. **2.** Red mercuric sulfide used as a pigment.

cinnamon (sĭn′ə-mən) *n.* **1.** A reddish-brown spice made from the dried and ground inner bark of certain tropical Asian trees. **2.** A tree from which this bark is obtained. ❖ *adj.* Having the flavor of cinnamon.

cipher also **cypher** (sī′fər) *n.* **1.** The numerical symbol 0 representing zero. **2.** A person or thing without influence or value. **3a.** A system of writing in which letters are changed or substituted for other letters according to a code. **b.** A message in secret code. ❖ *v.* **ciphered, ciphering, ciphers** also **cyphered, cyphering, cyphers** —*tr.* To put (a message) into a cipher. —*intr.* To do arithmetic: *a one-room school where pupils learned to read and cipher.*

circa (sûr′kə) *prep.* About: *a little-known painter who was born circa 1790.*

circadian (sər-kā′dē-ən) *adj.* Functioning or recurring in cycles of 24 hours: *Jet lag results from a disruption in a person's circadian rhythm.*

Circe (sûr′sē) *n.* In Greek mythology, a goddess who detained Odysseus on an island for a year and turned his men into swine.

circle (sûr′kəl) *n.* **1.** A closed curve that has all of its points at the same distance from a fixed point called the center. **2.** A flat surface or area bounded by such a closed curve: *colored the circles blue and yellow.* **3.** Something having the shape of a circle: *sit in a circle around a campfire.* **4.** A group of people sharing common interests or activities: *an astronomer well known in scientific circles.* ❖ *v.* **circled, circling, circles** —*tr.* **1.** To draw or form a circle around: *Circle the right answer.* **2.** To move or travel in a circle around: *A helicopter circled the city. Magellan's expedition circled the globe.* —*intr.* To move in a circle: *A hawk circled overhead.*

circle graph *n.* A pie chart.

circlet (sûr′klĭt) *n.* A small circle, especially a circular band worn on the head as an ornament.

circuit (sûr′kĭt) *n.* **1a.** A circular or elliptical line or route, especially a path that forms a circle around something: *the moon's elliptical circuit around Earth.* **b.** The act of following or completing such a route: *It takes a full year for Earth to make a circuit around the sun.* **2.** A closed path through which an electric current flows or may flow: *Using too many appliances at once blew the circuit to the kitchen.* **3.** A system of electrically connected parts or devices: *A microchip contains all the circuits for this computer.* **4a.** A regular route followed from place to place: *a salesperson on the West Coast circuit.* **b.** The district or area covered by such a route, especially the area under the jurisdiction of a judge who tries cases in various places. **5.** An association of theaters in which plays, shows, or films move from theater to theater for presentation: *The summer circuit brought good plays to many small towns.* **6.** A series of athletic competitions held in different places: *the professional tennis circuit.*

circuit board *n.* An insulated board on which circuits and electronic components are mounted.

circuit breaker *n.* A safety device that automatically switches off the flow of electricity in a circuit if the current becomes too strong.

circuit court *n.* In some states, a court holding sessions in various places in the area over which it has jurisdiction.

circuitous (sər-kyōō′ĭ-təs) *adj.* Not direct; roundabout: *take a circuitous route to the store; a confusing and circuitous argument.* —**cir·cu′i·tous·ly** *adv.* —**cir·cu′i·tous·ness** *n.*

circuitry (sûr′kĭ-trē) *n., pl.* **circuitries 1.** The plan for an electric or electronic circuit. **2.** Electric circuits considered as a group: *The circuitry of computers is very complex.*

circular (sûr′kyə-lər) *adj.* **1.** Relating to or shaped like a circle: *Most coins are circular pieces of metal.* **2.** Forming or moving in a circle: *circular motion.* **3.** Using a premise to prove a conclusion that in turn is used to prove the premise: *a circular argument.* ❖ *n.* A printed advertisement, notice, or other statement intended for public distribution. —**cir′cu·lar·ly** *adv.*

circular saw *n.* A power saw whose blade is a toothed metal disk that cuts as the blade rotates at a high speed.

circulate (sûr′kyə-lāt′) *v.* **circulated, circulating, circulates** — *intr.* **1.** To move or flow in a closed path: *Blood circulates through the body.* **2.** To move or flow freely: *The fan helps the air circulate.* **3.** To spread widely among people or places: *Rumors tend to circulate quickly.* —*tr.* **1.** To cause to move or flow: *The heart circulates blood throughout the body.* **2.** To spread or distribute among: *A topic that has been widely circulated in public discussion.*

circulation (sûr′kyə-lā′shən) *n.* **1a.** The act or process of circulating: *Opening the window will help the circulation of air.* **b.** The passage of something, such as money or news, from person to person or from place to place: *There aren't many two-dollar bills in circulation.* **2.** The flow of the blood from the heart through the arteries and veins back to the heart: *a person with poor circulation.* **3a.** The distribution of printed matter, such as newspapers and magazines: *This popular magazine has a wide circulation.* **b.** The number of copies of a newspaper, magazine, book, or other printed matter, sold or distributed to the public: *a newspaper with a daily circulation of 400,000.*

circulatory (sûr′kyə-lə-tôr′ē) *adj.* **1.** Relating to or involving circulation. **2.** Relating to the circulatory system: *Hardening of the arteries is a circulatory disease.*

circulatory system *n.* The system consisting of the heart and blood vessels that circulates blood throughout the body.

circum– A prefix that means around or about: *circumnavigate.*

circumambulate (sûr′kəm-ăm′byə-lāt′) *tr.v.* **circumambulated, circumambulating, circumambulates** To walk around (something), especially as part of a ritual. —**cir′-cum·am′bu·la′tion** *n.*

circumcise (sûr′kəm-sīz′) *tr.v.* **circumcised, circumcising, circumcises** To remove the foreskin of (a male).

circumcision (sûr′kəm-sĭzh′ən) *n.* The act or process of circumcising.

circumference (sər-kŭm′fər-əns) *n.* **1.** The boundary of a circle. **2.** The boundary line of an area or object: *walked around the circumference of the island.* **3.** The length of such a boundary: *The circumference of the moon is about 6,800 miles.*

circumflex (sûr′kəm-flĕks′) *n.* A mark (^) used over a vowel in certain languages or in a pronunciation key to indicate that the vowel is pronounced differently from the ordinary way.

circumlocution (sûr′kəm-lō-kyōō′shən) *n.* **1.** The use of wordy and indirect language: *The politician was a master of circumlocution.* **2.** A wordy or roundabout expression; for example, *the husband of my mother's sister* is a circumlocution for *my uncle.*

circumnavigate (sûr′kəm-năv′ĭ-gāt′) *tr.v.* **circumnavigated, circumnavigating, circumnavigates** To go completely around; circle: *an attempt to circumnavigate the earth in a balloon.* —**cir′cum·nav′i·ga′tion** *n.*

circumscribe (sûr′kəm-skrīb′) *tr.v.* **circumscribed, circumscribing, circumscribes 1a.** To draw (a figure) around another figure so as to touch as many points as possible: *A circle that is circumscribed around a triangle touches it at three points called the vertices of the triangle.* **b.** To enclose within a line or surface: *A circle will circumscribe a square but not a trapezoid.* **2.** To confine within or as if within bounds; limit: *Their plans for the future were circumscribed by their lack of money.*

circumspect (sûr′kəm-spĕkt′) *adj.* Careful of circumstances or consequences; cautious; prudent: *The president must be circumspect about statements made to reporters.* —**cir′cum·spec′tion** *n.* —**cir′cum·spect′ly** *adv.*

circumstance (sûr′kəm-stăns′) *n.* **1.** A condition, fact, or event connected with and usually affecting another event: *I'm not familiar with the circumstances of the case. We were delayed by weather and other circumstances.* **2.** A set of determining factors that are beyond one's control: *She tried hard, but in the end she was a victim of circumstance.* **3. circumstances** Financial condition: *a wealthy family in comfortable circumstances.* **4.** Formal display; ceremony: *the pomp and circumstance of graduation.* ◆ **under no circumstances** In no case; never: *Under no circumstances should you touch these two wires together.* **under the circumstances** or **in the circumstances** Given these conditions; such being the case: *A storm was brewing, and under the circumstances we left for home.*

circumstantial (sûr′kəm-stăn′shəl) *adj.* **1.** Relating to or dependent on circumstances: *the flexibility to react to any circumstantial developments.* **2.** Not of primary importance; incidental: *circumstantial matters having little* *bearing on the main plan.* **3.** Full of detail; complete: *a circumstantial account of what happened last night.*

circumstantial evidence *n.* Evidence not directly relevant to the facts in a legal case but describing known circumstances from which one might draw a conclusion about the facts in a case.

circumvent (sûr′kəm-věnt′) *tr.v.* **circumvented, circumventing, circumvents 1.** To avoid or get around by cleverness or ingenuity: *They tried to circumvent the building code when remodeling the garage.* **2.** To avoid by or as if by going around: *take side roads to circumvent construction.* —**cir′cum·ven′tion** *n.*

circus (sûr′kəs) *n.* **1a.** A public entertainment featuring acrobats, clowns, and trained animals. **b.** The traveling company of performers, animals, and workers that puts on the circus: *ran away to join the circus.* **2.** A roofless arena used by the ancient Romans for athletic contests and public spectacles. **3.** *Informal* Something suggestive of a circus, as in activity or disorder: *Holidays are a regular circus in our house.*

cirrhosis (sĭ-rō′sĭs) *n.* A chronic disease of the liver, in which normal tissue is gradually replaced by scar tissue so that its function is destroyed and the entire organ shrinks and hardens in the process.

cirri (sĭr′ī′) *n.* Plural of **cirrus.**

cirrocumulus (sĭr′ō-kyōōm′yə-ləs) *n.* A high-altitude cloud formation made up of many small puffy clouds, typically in the form of ripples or closely spaced patches.

cirrostratus (sĭr′ō-străt′əs *or* sĭr′ō-strā′təs) *n.* A thin hazy cloud formation made up of high-altitude ice crystals, often covering the sky and producing a halo effect.

cirrus (sĭr′əs) *n., pl.* **cirri** (sĭr′ī′) A high-altitude cloud formation made up of feathery white patches, bands, or streamers of ice crystals.

cistern (sĭs′tərn) *n.* A large tank or reservoir for holding liquid, especially for the collection and storage of rainwater.

citadel (sĭt′ə-dəl) *n.* **1.** A fortress overlooking a city. **2.** A stronghold or safe place: *The United States is often referred to as a citadel of democracy.*

citation (sī-tā′shən) *n.* **1.** A reference or quotation: *a report full of citations from books and scholarly articles.* **2.** A summons to appear in court: *The police officer issued a citation to the speeding driver.* **3.** An official recommendation for bravery. **4.** The act of citing: *Citation of diaries and official documents made the book seem authoritative.*

cite (sīt) *tr.v.* **cited, citing, cites 1a.** To quote as an authority or example. **b.** To mention or bring forward as support, illustration, or proof: *Let me cite two cases of what I have in mind.* **2.** To summon (someone) to appear in a court of law: *The police officer cited the juveniles for defacing public property.* **3.** To mention and commend for meritorious action: *The firefighter was cited for bravery beyond the call of duty.* —SEE NOTE AT **quote.**

citizen (sĭt′ĭ-zən) *n.* **1.** A person owing loyalty to and entitled to the protection of a given country. **2.** A resident of a city or town, especially one entitled to vote and enjoy other privileges there.

citizenry (sĭt′ĭ-zən-rē) *n., pl.* **citizenries** Citizens considered as a group.

citizens band (sĭt′ĭ-zənz) *n.* A radio frequency band available for private use, as by truck drivers or motorists.

citizenship (sĭt′ĭ-zən-shĭp′) *n.* The status of a citizen with its duties, rights, and privileges.

citrate (sĭt′rāt′) *n.* A salt or ester of citric acid.

citric acid (sĭt′rĭk) *n.* A white odorless acid with a sour taste, found in oranges, grapefruit, lemons, and other fruit. It is used in medicine and as a flavoring.

citron (sĭt′rən) *n.* **1a.** A yellowish thick-skinned fruit similar to a lemon. **b.** A tree that bears such fruit. **c.** The candied rind of this fruit, used especially in fruitcake, plum pudding, and other baked goods. **2.** A melon having white flesh and a thick hard rind. The rind and sometimes the flesh are pickled or preserved.

citronella (sĭt′rə-něl′ə) *n.* **1.** A pale yellow aromatic oil obtained from the leaves of a tropical Asian grass and used in insect repellents and perfumes. **2.** The plant from which this oil is obtained.

citrus (sĭt′rəs) *n., pl.* **citrus** *or* **citruses 1.** The fruit of any of various related evergreen trees or shrubs, having juicy flesh and a thick rind, such as an orange, lemon, lime, or grapefruit. **2.** A tree or shrub that bears such fruit. —**cit′rus** *adj.*

city (sĭt′ē) *n., pl.* **cities 1.** A center of population, commerce, and culture; a large and important town: *Many people go into the city to work each day.* **2.** In the United States, a division of local government with stated boundaries of jurisdiction set forth in a charter granted by the state: *Our city is governed by the mayor and his council.* **3.** The people living in a city considered as a group: *The city will vote in a special election next week.*

city hall *n.* **1.** The building in which the offices of a city government are located. **2.** A city government, especially its officials considered as a group: *City hall released a statement about the new budget.*

city manager *n.* An administrator appointed by a city council to manage the affairs of city government.

cityscape (sĭt′ē-skāp′) *n.* **1.** A part of a city that can be seen from one place. **2.** A painting or a picture that shows such a view.

city-state (sĭt′ē-stāt′) *n.* An independent state consisting of a city and its surrounding territory: *Sparta was a city-state of ancient Greece.*

citywide (sĭt′ē-wĭd′) *adj.* Including or occurring in all parts of a city: *citywide busing; a citywide strike.*

civet (sĭv′ĭt) *n.* **1.** Any of various often spotted mammals of Africa and Asia that resemble a cat and have scent glands that produce a fluid with a strong musky odor. **2.** This yellowish fluid, used in making perfumes.

civic (sĭv′ĭk) *adj.* **1.** Relating to or belonging to a city: *The town's Fourth of July parade is our chief civic event.* **2.** Relating to or belonging to a citizen or citizenship: *It is a civic duty to vote in elections.* —**civ′i·cal·ly** *adv.*

civics (sĭv′ĭks) *n.* (*used with a singular verb*) The study of the purpose and function of local and national government and of the rights and duties of citizens.

civil (sĭv′əl) *adj.* **1.** Relating to a citizen or citizens: *voting and other civil responsibilities.* **2.** Relating to citizens and their relations to the government: *Most departments of the government are concerned with civil affairs.* **3.** Relating to the general public rather than to military or religious matters: *a couple married in a civil ceremony at city hall.* **4.** Following accepted social usage or manners, often just barely; polite enough: *a civil reply.* See Synonyms at **polite.** **5.** Relating to the rights of private individuals and legal proceedings concerning these rights, especially as distinguished from criminal proceedings. —**civ′il·ly** *adv.*

civil defense *n.* The emergency measures to be taken for the protection of civilian life and property in the case of a natural disaster or enemy attack.

civil disobedience *n.* Nonviolent refusal by members of the public to obey laws, done in an effort to cause change in government policy or legislation.

civil engineer *n.* An engineer trained in the design and construction of projects such as bridges, roads, and dams. —**civil engineering** *n.*

civilian (sĭ-vĭl′yən) *n.* A person not serving in the armed forces or the police. ❖ *adj.* Relating to civilians: *civilian clothes; a civilian career.*

civility (sĭ-vĭl′ĭ-tē) *n., pl.* **civilities 1.** Courteous behavior; politeness: *Civility in daily affairs creates a harmonious atmosphere.* **2.** An act or expression of courtesy: *Saying "Good morning" is a pleasant civility.*

civilization (sĭv′ə-lĭ-zā′shən) *n.* **1.** A condition of human society in which there is a high level of development in political and social organizations and in the arts and sciences. **2.** The kind of culture and society developed by a particular people or nation in some period of history: *Mayan civilization.* **3.** *Informal* Modern society with its conveniences: *returned to civilization after two weeks of camping.*

civilize (sĭv′ə-līz′) *tr.v.* **civilized, civilizing, civilizes 1.** To bring to a higher level of development in the arts, sciences, culture, and political organization. **2.** To refine by education and training: *civilize young minds.*

civilized (sĭv′ə-līzd′) *adj.* **1.** Having or indicating a highly developed society and culture; not primitive: *civilized life.* **2.** Polite or cultured; refined: *a civilized person.*

civil law *n.* The body of law dealing with the rights of private citizens, as distinguished from military law and criminal law.

civil libertarian *n.* A person who is actively concerned with protecting civil liberties.

civil liberties *pl.n.* Fundamental individual rights, such as freedom of speech and religion, especially as guaranteed to citizens by a constitution.

civil rights *pl.n.* The rights belonging to an individual as a citizen, especially of the United States, including civil liberties and freedom from discrimination.

civil servant *n.* A person employed in the civil service.

civil service *n.* **1.** All branches of government service that are not legislative, judicial, or military. **2.** Those people employed by the civil branches of the government: *Most of the civil service in the US government is appointed after competitive examination.*

civil union *n.* A legally sanctioned relationship between two people, especially of the same sex, having many of the rights and responsibilities of marriage.

civil war *n.* **1.** A war between opposing groups of the same country. **2. Civil War a.** The war in the United States between the Union and the Confederacy from 1861 to 1865. **b.** The war in England between the supporters of Parliament and the supporters of the king, lasting from 1642 to 1648.

clabber (klăb′ər) *n.* Sour curdled milk. ❖ *tr. & intr.v.* **clabbered, clabbering, clabbers** To curdle.

clack (klăk) *intr. & tr.v.* **clacked, clacking, clacks** To make or cause to make a sudden sharp sound, as that of objects struck together. ❖ *n.* A sudden sharp sound: *the clack of wooden clogs on a tile floor.*

clad (klăd) *v.* A past tense and a past participle of **clothe.**

clade (klād) *n.* A grouping of organisms made on the ba-

sis of their presumed evolutionary history, consisting of a common ancestor and all of its descendants.

cladistics (klə-dĭs′tĭks) *n. (used with a singular verb)* A system of classification based on the presumed evolutionary relationships among groups of organisms, such as species, genera, or families. —**cla·dis′tic, cla·dis′ti·cal** *adj.* —**cla·dis′ti·cal·ly** *adv.*

claim (klām) *tr.v.* **claimed, claiming, claims 1.** To demand, ask for, or take (something) as one's own; assert one's right to: *claim luggage; claim a reward.* **2.** To declare to be true; assert: *claimed that they saw the accident.* **3.** To deserve or call for; require: *a difficult task that claimed all his attention.* ❖ *n.* **1.** A demand for something as one's rightful due: *file an insurance claim for losses from the fire.* **2.** A statement of something as fact; an assertion: *an advertisement that makes false claims concerning certain products.* **3.** A basis for demanding something; a right: *a sailor whose claim to fame was being the youngest to sail solo around the world.* **4.** Something claimed, especially a tract of land claimed by a miner or homesteader. ◆ **lay claim to** To assert one's right to or ownership of: *laid claim to the land along the river.*

claimant (klā′mənt) *n.* A person making a claim.

clairvoyance (klâr-voi′əns) *n.* The supposed power to see objects or events that cannot be perceived by the senses.

clairvoyant (klâr-voi′ənt) *n.* A person said to have power of clairvoyance. ❖ *adj.* Relating to or having the power of clairvoyance.

clam (klăm) *n.* Any of various freshwater or saltwater mollusks that have a hinged shell and burrow into sand or mud. Many kinds of clams are used as food. ❖ *intr.v.* **clammed, clamming, clams** To dig or hunt for clams: *clamming along the seashore at low tide.* ◆ **clam up** *Informal* To refuse to talk; stop talking: *The suspect clammed up when the police started asking questions.*

clambake (klăm′bāk′) *n.* A picnic at which clams and other kinds of seafood are served.

clamber (klăm′bər or klăm′ər) *intr.v.* **clambered, clambering, clambers** To climb with difficulty, especially on all fours: *clamber up a rocky slope.*

clammy (klăm′ē) *adj.* **clammier, clammiest** Unpleasantly damp, sticky, and usually cold: *clammy basement walls; clammy feet in wet boots.* —**clam′mi·ness** *n.*

clamor (klăm′ər) *n.* **1.** A loud, continuous, and usually confused noise: *the clamor of fans at a football game.* **2.** A strong or loud demand; an outcry: *a public clamor for clean air.* ❖ *intr.v.* **clamored, clamoring, clamors** To make a clamor: *The excited crowd clamored for an encore.*

clamorous (klăm′ər-əs) *adj.* **1.** Loud and noisy: *a clamorous birthday party.* **2.** Making or full of strong or loud demands: *a clamorous crowd of protesters.* —**clam′or·ous·ly** *adv.* —**clam′or·ous·ness** *n.*

clamp (klămp) *n.* A device for gripping or fastening things together, consisting of two parts that can be tightened together by pressure of a spring or by turning a screw. ❖ *tr.v.* **clamped, clamping, clamps** To grip or fasten with or as if with a clamp: *glue and clamp two boards together; clamped her fingers tightly around the rope.* ◆ **clamp down** To become more strict or repressive: *The government clamped down on dissent by closing several newspapers.*

clamshell (klăm′shĕl′) *n.* **1.** The shell of a clam. **2.** Any of various devices that have two hinged jaws and are used for dredging or digging.

clan (klăn) *n.* **1.** A group of families, as in the Scottish

Highlands, claiming a common ancestor: *the MacIntyre clan.* **2.** A division of a tribe often claiming descent from a common ancestor. **3.** A group of relatives, friends, or others having a common background or interest: *a clan of local politicians.*

clandestine (klăn-děs′tĭn) *adj.* Done secretly or kept secret, often for some unlawful purpose: *a clandestine meeting of conspirators.* —**clan·des′tine·ly** *adv.*

clang (klăng) *tr. & intr.v.* **clanged, clanging, clangs** To make or cause to make a loud metallic ringing sound: *Bells clanged to announce the new year.* ❖ *n.* A clanging sound: *the clang of an alarm.*

clangor (klăng′ər *or* klăng′gər) *n.* A loud repeated clanging or banging; a din: *the incessant clangor of the assembly line.* —**clan′gor·ous** *adj.* —**clan′gor·ous·ly** *adv.*

clank (klăngk) *n.* A loud, metallic ringing sound: *The gate closed with a clank.* ❖ *intr.v.* **clanked, clanking, clanks** To make a clank: *The old car clanked and sputtered down the road.*

clannish (klăn′ĭsh) *adj.* **1.** Relating to or characteristic of a clan. **2.** Inclined to cling together as a group and exclude outsiders. —**clan′nish·ly** *adv.*

clansman (klănz′mən) *n.* A man belonging to a clan.

clanswoman (klănz′wŏom′ən) *n.* A woman belonging to a clan.

clap (klăp) *v.* **clapped, clapping, claps** —*intr.* **1.** To strike the hands together with a sudden loud sound: *The audience clapped at the end of the play.* **2.** To make a sudden sharp sound: *The door clapped shut.* —*tr.* **1.** To strike (the hands) together with an abrupt loud sound: *We clapped our hands in rhythm to the music.* **2.** To make (something) come together suddenly with a sharp noise: *The baby clapped the spoon on the table.* **3.** To tap with the open hand, as in hearty greeting: *clap a friend on the shoulder.* **4.** To put or place suddenly: *I clapped the lid on the box before the cricket could jump out.* ❖ *n.* **1.** The act or sound of clapping the hands. **2.** A loud, sharp, or explosive noise: *a clap of thunder.* **3.** A slap: *a friendly clap on the back.*

clapboard (klăb′ərd *or* klăp′bôrd′) *n.* A long narrow board with one edge thicker than the other, overlapped to cover the outside walls of a building. ❖ *tr.v.* **clapboarded, clapboarding, clapboards** To cover with clapboards.

clapper (klăp′ər) *n.* **1.** The tongue of a bell. **2.** A person or thing that claps. **3. clappers** Two flat pieces of wood that are held between the fingers and struck together as a percussion instrument.

claptrap (klăp′trăp′) *n.* Insincere, empty speech or writing.

claque (klăk) *n.* **1.** A group of people hired to applaud at a performance. **2.** A group of fawning admirers.

claret (klăr′ĭt) *n.* **1.** A dry red wine. **2.** A dark purplish red.

clarify (klăr′ə-fī′) *v.* **clarified, clarifying, clarifies** —*tr.* **1.** To make clear or easier to understand: *gave a detailed explanation to clarify the instructions.* **2.** To make (a liquid, butter, or other substance) clear or pure by removing unwanted solid matter: *clarify butter by heating it; clarify vinegar by straining it.* —*intr.* To become clear. —**clar′·i·fi·ca′tion** (klăr′ə-fĭ-kā′shən) *n.*

clarinet (klăr′ə-nĕt′) *n.* A woodwind instrument having a cylindrical body, a flaring bell, and a mouthpiece with a single reed. It is played by covering holes in its body and pressing keys with the fingers. —**clar′i·net′ist** *n.*

clarion (klăr′ē-ən) *adj.* Shrill and clear: *the clarion call of a trumpet.* ❖ *n.* **1.** A medieval trumpet with a clear shrill tone. **2.** The sound made by this trumpet or a similar sound.

clarity (klăr′ĭ-tē) *n.* The condition or quality of being clear: *clarity of speech; complex ideas presented with great clarity.*

clash (klăsh) *v.* **clashed, clashing, clashes** —*intr.* **1.** To strike or collide with a loud harsh sound: *The cymbals clashed loudly.* **2.** To meet in violent conflict: *The armies clashed repeatedly with no clear victor.* **3.** To be in sharp disagreement: *The researcher's data clashed with previously published results.* **4.** To create an unpleasant or jarring effect: *That striped shirt clashes with your plaid pants.* —*tr.* To strike together or collide with a loud harsh noise: *At the end of the march I clashed the cymbals together.* ❖ *n.* **1.** A conflict, opposition, or disagreement: *a clash between political parties.* **2.** A loud, harsh, metallic sound: *a clash of cymbals.*

clasp (klăsp) *n.* **1.** A fastener, such as a hook or buckle, used to hold two objects or parts together. **2.** A firm grasp or embrace: *took my hand with a firm clasp.* ❖ *tr.v.* **clasped, clasping, clasps 1.** To fasten with a clasp: *clasp a necklace.* **2.** To grasp or embrace tightly: *clasped each other after their long separation.*

class (klăs) *n.* **1.** A group of people or things that are generally alike in some way; a kind or category: *the class of odd numbers; a class of ships.* **2.** A group of people having approximately the same economic and social standing: *the working class.* **3.** A taxonomic category of organisms that share certain characteristics, ranking above an order and below a phylum: *All mammals belong to the same class of animals.* **4a.** A group of people who graduated in the same year: *a reunion of the class of 1990.* **b.** A group of students who meet regularly to study the same subject: *Our biology class has 20 students.* **c.** The period during which such a group meets: *eat lunch before class; meet after class.* **d.** A course of instruction: *wants to take a ballet class next year.* **5a.** A grade of mail: *A letter is sent first class and a magazine third class.* **b.** The quality of accommodations on a public vehicle: *They flew by business class to Tokyo.* **6.** *Informal* Great style or quality: *This restaurant has a lot of class.* ❖ *tr.v.* **classed, classing, classes** To assign to a class; classify: *class a novel as a murder mystery.*

classic (klăs′ĭk) *adj.* **1.** Long regarded as a model; serving as an outstanding example of its kind: *a classic example of abstract art; a classic horror film.* **2.** Well-known and typical: *A runny nose and a cough are classic signs of a cold.* **3.** Simple and refined in form or in style: *the classic lines of a luxury automobile.* **4.** Relating to ancient Greek or Roman literature or art; classical: *a film based on a classic Greek tragedy.* ❖ *n.* **1.** A work of literature, music, or art generally considered to be of the highest rank: *Many early rock 'n' roll recordings are now classics.* **2. classics** Ancient Greek and Roman literature. **3.** A traditional event held annually, as in sports: *The World Series is baseball's fall classic.*

classical (klăs′ĭ-kəl) *adj.* **1.** Relating to ancient Greek and Roman art, architecture, literature, and culture: *classical architecture of the Roman forum; a classical scholar.* **2a.** Relating to a style of European music during the second half of the 1700s and early 1800s. **b.** Relating to music in the educated European tradition, such as symphony, concerto, and opera, as opposed to popular or folk music. **3.** Standard or traditional rather than new or experimental; established: *classical ballet.* **4.** Well-known; typical; classic: *Blue jeans, bandannas, and cowboy boots are classical items of Western clothing.* —**clas′si·cal·ly** *adv.*

classicism (klăs′ĭ-sĭz′əm) *n.* **1.** The rules and ideals that form the basis of ancient Greek and Roman art, architecture, and literature. They include the use of regular order in design, simplicity in style, and restraint or proportion in form. **2.** The use of such rules or principles in artistic creation. **3.** The scholarly study of ancient Greek and Roman art, literature, and culture.

classicist (klăs′ĭ-sĭst) *n.* A student of or an authority on ancient Greek and Roman art, architecture, literature, and culture.

classification (klăs′ə-fĭ-kā′shən) *n.* **1.** The act or process of classifying; grouping by categories: *The classification of books according to subject is the work of a librarian.* **2a.** The result of classifying, as by category, name, or rating; a systematic arrangement: *chemical elements arranged in a classification by atomic weight.* **b.** In biology, the systematic grouping of organisms by similarity of characteristics, often thought to reflect evolutionary relationships.

classified (klăs′ə-fīd′) *adj.* **1.** Arranged in separate classes or categories; categorized: *We searched the online classified ads for a used car.* **2.** Available only to authorized people; secret: *classified information.*

classified advertisement *n.* An advertisement, usually brief and in small type, printed in a newspaper along with others of the same category.

classify (klăs′ə-fī′) *tr.v.* **classified, classifying, classifies** **1.** To arrange in classes or assign to a class; sort; categorize: *A librarian classifies books according to subject matter.* **2.** To designate (information) as available only to authorized people. —**clas′si·fi′a·ble** *adj.* —**clas′si·fi′er** *n.*

classism (klăs′ĭz′əm) *n.* Bias based on social or economic class. —**class′ist** *adj. & n.*

classmate (klăs′māt′) *n.* A member of the same class in a school or college.

classroom (klăs′rōōm′ *or* klăs′rŏŏm′) *n.* A room in which classes are held in a school or college.

classy (klăs′ē) *adj.* **classier, classiest** *Informal* Stylish; elegant: *a classy suit; classy manners.*

clatter (klăt′ər) *v.* **clattered, clattering, clatters** —*intr.* **1.** To make a rattling sound: *The shutters clattered in the wind.* **2.** To move with a rattling sound: *A rickety old truck clattered down the road.* —*tr.* To cause to make a rattling sound: *The cook clattered pots and pans in the kitchen.* ❖ *n.* A rattling sound: *the clatter of dishes falling to the floor.*

clause (klôz) *n.* **1.** In grammar, a group of words containing a subject and a finite verb. In the complex sentence *The dog ran off before we caught it,* the words *The dog ran off* constitute an independent clause and the words *before we caught it* constitute a subordinate clause. **2.** A separate part of a document containing some distinct provision: *The contract had several clauses, each outlining the duties of the partners.*

claustrophobia (klô′strə-fō′bē-ə) *n.* An abnormal fear of being in small or confined spaces.

claustrophobic (klô′strə-fō′bĭk) *adj.* **1.** Relating to or suffering from claustrophobia: *He never takes elevators because he's claustrophobic.* **2.** Tending to induce claustrophobia; uncomfortably confined or crowded: *The meeting was in a claustrophobic little room.* —**claus′-tro·pho′bi·cal·ly** *adv.*

clavichord (klăv′ĭ-kôrd′) *n.* A keyboard musical instrument with a soft sound made by small metal hammers

that strike the strings as keys are pushed. The modern piano was developed from it.

clavicle (klăv′ĭ-kəl) *n.* The collarbone.

clavier (klə-vîr′ *or* klā′vē-ər *or* klăv′ē-ər) *n.* **1.** The keyboard of a musical instrument, such as a piano or organ. **2.** A stringed keyboard instrument, such as a harpsichord.

claw (klô) *n.* **1.** A sharp, curved, hard structure on the end of the toe of a vertebrate animal. **2a.** A pincer, as of a lobster or crab, used for grasping. **b.** A small curved structure at the tip of an appendage of an insect or other invertebrate animal. **3.** Something resembling a claw: *I pulled out the bent nail with the claw of the hammer.* ❖ *tr. & intr.v.* **clawed, clawing, claws** To scratch, dig, tear, or pull with the claws or fingernails: *The cat clawed the chair. She clawed at the package to open it.*

clay (klā) *n.* An earthy material that is soft and sticky when wet but that hardens when heated, consisting mainly of various silicates of aluminum. It is widely used in making bricks, pottery, and tiles.

clay pigeon *n.* A clay disk hurled as a flying target in skeet and trapshooting.

clean (klēn) *adj.* **cleaner, cleanest** **1.** Free from dirt, stain, or impurities; unsoiled: *clean clothing; drinking from a clean glass.* **2a.** Free from pollution or contamination: *clean drinking water.* **b.** Producing little pollution: *The new law calls for clean fuels in all cars.* **3.** Having a smooth edge or surface; even; regular: *A clean break in the bone heals quickly.* **4.** Entire; thorough; complete: *They made a clean escape, leaving no clues as to where they went.* **5.** Free from wrongdoing; honorable: *a clean life of hard work; a clean record.* **6.** Free from clumsiness; skillful; adroit: *a clean hit to center field.* **7.** Fit for all readers, listeners, or audiences; not ribald or obscene: *a clean joke.* **8.** Blank: *a clean page.* ❖ *adv.* **cleaner, cleanest** **1a.** So as to be unsoiled: *We washed the wall clean.* **b.** In a fair manner: *They played the game clean.* **2.** *Informal* Entirely; completely: *I clean forgot about the test.* ❖ *v.* **cleaned, cleaning, cleans** —*tr.* **1.** To rid of dirt, stain, or disorder: *clean a room.* **2.** To get rid of (dirt, for example); remove: *Let's clean the dirt from the floor.* **3.** To prepare (fowl or other food) for cooking, as by removing entrails: *clean a fish.* **4.** To remove the contents from; empty: *I cleaned my plate.* —*intr.* To undergo or perform cleaning: *A wool rug cleans easily. A damp rag cleans well.* ◆ **clean house** *Slang* To get rid of what is unwanted: *The new boss cleaned house and fired the unproductive workers.* **clean out 1.** To rid of dirt, trash, or disorder: *clean out the garage.* **2.** To empty of contents: *cleaned out the refrigerator to make sandwiches.* **3.** *Slang* To deprive completely, as of money; remove everything from: *Shopping cleaned out my savings.* **clean up 1.** To rid of dirt or disorder: *clean up one's room; clean up the city government.* **2.** *Slang* To make a large sum of money in a short period of time: *We cleaned up on the spring sale.* —**clean′ness** *n.*

clean and jerk *n.* A lift in weightlifting in which a weight is raised to shoulder height, held there briefly, and then pushed overhead in a rapid motion.

clean-cut (klēn′kŭt′) *adj.* **1.** Having a distinct sharp outline: *a racing car with clean-cut lines.* **2.** Neat and trim in appearance: *a clean-cut soldier.*

cleaner (klē′nər) *n.* **1.** A person whose work is cleaning: *a rug cleaner.* **2.** often **cleaners** A business that cleans clothes, often by dry cleaning: *took the shirts to the cleaners.* **3.** A machine or substance used in cleaning: *Ammonia is a common household cleaner.*

cleanliness (klĕn′lē-nĭs) *n.* The state of being clean: *Personal cleanliness is important for good health.*

cleanly (klēn′lē) *adv.* In a clean manner: *The fruit stems had been severed cleanly by a knife.* ❖ *adj.* (klĕn′lē) **cleanlier, cleanliest** Habitually and carefully neat and clean: *Cats are thought of as cleanly animals.*

clean room *n.* A room that is kept free of dust, bacteria, or other contaminants.

cleanse (klĕnz) *tr.v.* **cleansed, cleansing, cleanses** To free from dirt or guilt; clean or purge: *cleanse a wound.*

cleanser (klĕn′zər) *n.* A substance used for cleaning.

cleanup (klēn′ŭp′) *n.* **1.** The act or process of cleaning up: *a trash cleanup.* **2.** The fourth position in a baseball batting order. —**clean′up′** *adj.*

clear (klîr) *adj.* **clearer, clearest 1.** Free from clouds, mist, or haze: *a clear sky.* **2.** Free from anything that dims, darkens, or obscures; transparent: *a glass of cool clear water.* **3.** Free from obstruction or hindrance; open: *We had a clear view of the valley from the mountains. The road was clear of snow.* **4a.** Easily perceived by the eye or ear; dis-' tinct: *a clear picture on the TV; the clear sound of church bells; a crisp clear voice.* **b.** Free or evident to the mind; easily understood: *a clear explanation; clear directions.* **5.** Obvious; unmistakable: *a clear case of the flu.* **6.** Free from doubt or confusion; certain: *Are you clear about what has to be done?* **7.** Free from guilt; untroubled: *a clear conscience.* **8.** Free from flaw or blemish: *clear skin.* **9.** Free from charges or deductions; net: *earned a small but clear profit after paying for expenses.* ❖ *adv.* **1.** Out of the way: *The deer jumped clear of the oncoming car.* **2.** Distinctly; clearly: *spoke loud and clear before the audience.* **3.** *Informal* All the way; entirely: *The baby cried clear through the night.* ❖ *v.* **cleared, clearing, clears** —*tr.* **1.** To make clear, light, or bright: *The fan cleared the room of smoke.* **2a.** To make free of objects or obstructions: *clear the table after dinner; clear the road of snow.* **b.** To remove (objects or obstructions): *clear the dishes from the table; clear snow from the sidewalk.* **3.** To pass by, under, or over without contact: *The runner cleared every hurdle.* **4.** To free from a legal charge; acquit: *The jury cleared the accused of all charges.* **5.** To rid of confusion or doubt: *cleared up the questions surrounding the lost book.* **6.** To win the approval of: *The bill cleared the Senate.* **7.** To pass (a check or bill of exchange) through a clearing-house: *Banks clear checks every day.* **8.** To earn (an amount of money) as net profit or earnings: *cleared $45 selling pies.* —*intr.* **1.** To become clear, light, or bright: *The sky cleared in the afternoon.* **2.** To go away; disappear: *The fog cleared.* **3.** To pass through a clearing-house: *My check to pay the rent cleared today.* ◆ **clear out** *Informal* To leave a place, often quickly: *The raccoons cleared out before the campers returned.* **clear the air** To dispel emotional tensions or differences: *A joke cleared the air.* **in the clear** Free from burdens, dangers, guilt, or responsibility: *Once the facts were known, the suspect was in the clear.* —**clear′ly** *adv.* —**clear′ness** *n.*

clearance (klîr′əns) *n.* **1.** The act of clearing: *The city has begun land clearance where the abandoned buildings are.* **2.** A sale to dispose of old merchandise at reduced prices: *Department stores often have a clearance after the holidays.* **3.** The height or width of a passage: *This underpass has a clearance that is too low for many trucks.* **4.** Permission for an airplane, ship, or other vehicle to proceed: *The*

control tower gave us clearance to take off.* **5.** Official certification of blamelessness, trustworthiness, or suitability: *You need clearance to handle classified material.*

clear-cut (klîr′kŭt′) *adj.* Not vague or confused; obvious: *a clear-cut case of fraud.* ❖ *tr.v.* **clear-cut, clear-cutting, clear-cuts** To remove all of the trees in (a wooded area) at one time.

clearing (klîr′ĭng) *n.* An open space in a wooded or overgrown area: *a clearing in the forest where the trees were cut down.*

clearing-house or **clearinghouse** (klîr′ĭng-hous′) *n.* An office where banks exchange checks, drafts, and other notes and settle accounts.

cleat (klēt) *n.* **1a.** A projecting piece of iron, rubber, or leather attached to the sole of a shoe to keep it from slipping. **b.** **cleats** A pair of shoes having such projecting pieces. **2.** A piece of metal or wood with projecting arms or ends on which a rope can be wound.

cleavage (klē′vĭj) *n.* **1.** The act of splitting or state of being split: *Earthquakes are often accompanied by cleavage of the ground.* **2.** The breaking of certain minerals along specific planes, making smooth surfaces. **3a.** The series of cell divisions by which a fertilized egg becomes a blastula. **b.** A stage in this series of divisions. **4.** *Informal* The hollow between a woman's breasts, especially as revealed by a low neckline.

cleave[1] (klēv) *tr.v.* **cleft** (klĕft) or **cleaved** or **clove** (klōv), **cleft** or **cleaved** or **cloven** (klō′vən), **cleaving, cleaves 1.** To split, as by a sudden blow: *The axe cleft the piece of wood.* **2.** To make or proceed through as if by cutting: *a ship cleaving its way through the ice.*

cleave[2] (klēv) *intr.v.* **cleaved, cleaving, cleaves 1.** To cling; adhere; stick fast: *Barnacles cleave to a hull.* **2.** To remain faithful: *cleave to old beliefs.*

WORD HISTORY Cleave[1] comes from Old English *clēofan,* meaning "to split." **Cleave**[2] comes from Old English *cleofian,* meaning "to cling."

cleaver (klē′vər) *n.* A tool with a broad heavy blade and a short handle, used especially by butchers for cutting meat.

clef (klĕf) *n.* A symbol on a musical staff indicating the pitch of one of the lines in relation to middle C. The pitch of the other lines and spaces on the staff can be determined accordingly.

cleft (klĕft) *v.* A past tense and a past participle of **cleave**[1]. ❖ *adj.* Divided; split: *a cleft chin.* ❖ *n.* A crack or split: *My canteen fell into a cleft in the rock.*

cleft lip *n.* A split or cleft in the upper lip that sometimes occurs together with a cleft palate.

cleft palate *n.* A split in the roof of the mouth, occurring when the two parts of the developing palate do not close before birth.

clematis (klĕm′ə-tĭs *or* klĭ-măt′ĭs) *n.* Any of various climbing plants having white, pink, or purplish flowers and feathery seeds.

clemency (klĕm′ən-sē) *n., pl.* **clemencies 1.** Mercy, as toward an offender or enemy; leniency: *The judge showed clemency in sentencing the defendant.* **2.** Mildness, especially of weather.

clement (klĕm′ənt) *adj.* **1.** Inclined to be lenient or merciful: *a clement ruler.* **2.** Pleasant; mild: *clement spring weather.* —**clem′ent-ly** *adv.*

clementine (klĕm′ən-tēn′) *n.* A deep red-orange, often seedless mandarin orange.

clench (klĕnch) *tr.v.* **clenched, clenching, clenches 1.** To close (a hand or the teeth) tightly: *I clenched my fists in anger.* **2.** To grasp or grip tightly: *clenched the keys.*

clerestory also **clearstory** (klîr′stôr′ē) *n., pl.* **clerestories** also **clearstories 1.** The upper part of the nave, transepts, and choir of a church, containing windows. **2.** An upper portion of a wall containing windows for supplying natural light to a building.

clergy (klûr′jē) *n., pl.* **clergies** The group of people ordained or recognized by a religious community as spiritual leaders, as ministers, mullahs, or rabbis. —SEE NOTE AT **collective noun.**

clergyman (klûr′jē-mən) *n.* A man who is a member of the clergy.

clergywoman (klûr′jē-wŏŏm′ən) *n.* A woman who is a member of the clergy.

cleric (klĕr′ĭk) *n.* A member of the clergy.

clerical (klĕr′ĭ-kəl) *adj.* **1.** Relating to clerks or office workers: *typing and other clerical work.* **2.** Relating to the clergy: *dressed in clerical garb.* —**cler′i·cal·ly** *adv.*

clerk (klûrk) *n.* **1.** A person who works in an office doing such jobs as keeping records, filing, and typing. **2.** A person who keeps the records and performs the regular business of a court, legislative body, or municipal district. **3.** A person who sells merchandise in a store or works at a service desk, as in a hotel. ❖ *intr.v.* **clerked, clerking, clerks** To work or serve as a clerk: *My sister clerked in a supermarket as a summer job.*

clever (klĕv′ər) *adj.* **cleverer, cleverest 1.** Having the capacity to learn and think quickly; bright; quick-witted: *a clever student.* **2.** Showing wit or ingenuity: *a clever plan; a clever trick.* **3.** Skilled at doing something, especially with the hands: *a clever magician.* —**clev′er·ly** *adv.* —**clev′er·ness** *n.*

clew (klōō) *Chiefly British* & *v.* Variant of **clue.**

cliché (klē-shā′) *n.* An overused expression or idea that has lost its original quality or effect: *The expression "as sharp as a tack" is a cliché.*

click (klĭk) *n.* A short sharp sound: *the click of train wheels over the tracks.* ❖ *v.* **clicked, clicking, clicks** —*intr.* **1.** To produce a click or a series of clicks: *The wheels of the train clicked over the rails.* **2.** To press down and release a button on a computer mouse or other pointing device, as to activate a program or highlight text: *clicked on the icon.* **3.** *Slang* To be a success: *The new comedian clicked with the audience.* **4.** *Slang* To work well together or be in harmony: *We clicked as soon as we met.* **5.** *Slang* To become understandable; make sense: *The name clicked when I saw the actor's picture.* —*tr.* **1.** To cause to make such a sound: *clicked his ballpoint pen and started to write.* **2.** To press down and release (a button on a pointing device): *Click the left button to open the file.*

clicker (klĭk′ər) *n.* A thing that clicks or can be clicked, as a remote control for a television.

clickstream (klĭk′strēm′) *n.* The sequence of links that a user clicks on while browsing a website or series of websites.

client (klī′ənt) *n.* **1.** A person who uses the services of a professional person: *The lawyer defended his client in court.* **2.** A customer or patron: *That jewelry store has several wealthy clients.* **3.** A computer or program that can download files from a file server.

clientele (klī′ən-tĕl′) *n.* The group of regular clients or customers, as of a store.

cliff (klĭf) *n.* A high, steep, or overhanging face of rock

or earth: *stand on the cliffs overlooking the sea far below.*

cliff dweller *n.* A member of certain prehistoric peoples of the southwest United States who built rock or adobe dwellings on sheltered ledges in the sides of cliffs. The Pueblo peoples are their descendants.

cliffhanger (klĭf′hăng′ər) *n.* **1.** A melodrama presented in serial episodes, with each episode ending in high suspense. **2.** A suspenseful situation at the end of a chapter, scene, or episode. **3.** A contest whose outcome is uncertain until the end: *The game was a cliffhanger—tied until the last minute.*

climactic (klī-măk′tĭk) *adj.* Relating to or forming a climax: *climactic events leading to the end of the mystery story.*

climate (klī′mĭt) *n.* **1.** The general or average weather conditions of a certain region, including temperature, rainfall, and wind: *the climate of Southern California.* **2.** A region having certain weather conditions: *a tropical climate.* **3.** A general condition or attitude: *a climate of uncertainty.*

climatic (klī-măt′ĭk) *adj.* Relating to climate: *climatic changes; distinct climatic regions.* —**cli·mat′i·cal·ly** *adv.*

climatology (klī′mə-tŏl′ə-jē) *n.* The scientific study of climates.

climax (klī′măks′) *n.* **1.** The point in a series of events that is of greatest intensity or effect, usually occurring near the end: *Winning the presidency was the climax of a long political career.* **2.** The turning point in a plot or dramatic action: *The climax of the novel occurs when the main character meets his father for the first time.* **3.** An orgasm.

climax community *n.* An ecological community in which there is little change in the kinds and numbers of organisms present until a disturbance such as a fire occurs.

climb (klīm) *v.* **climbed, climbing, climbs** —*intr.* **1a.** To move upward, especially by using the hands and feet; ascend: *The hikers climbed all day to reach the summit.* **b.** To move in a stated direction, especially by means of the hands and feet: *The firefighter climbed across the roof and down the ladder.* **2.** To go higher; rise: *The morning sun climbed in the sky. The patient's fever began to climb.* **3.** To slant or slope upward: *The trail climbs to the top of the cliff.* **4.** To grow upward by clinging to or twining around something: *The vine climbs around the tree.* —*tr.* **1.** To go up, over, or through (something), especially by using the hands and feet; ascend: *Leopards can climb trees. The hikers climbed the mountain.* **2.** To grow up on (something): *Roses climbed the trellis.* ❖ *n.* **1.** The act of climbing: *a hard climb up the mountain; an executive's climb to power.* **2.** A place to be climbed: *That hill was a steep climb.* —**climb′a·ble** *adj.*

climber (klī′mər) *n.* **1.** A person or thing that climbs: *a mountain climber.* **2.** A plant, such as a vine, that climbs.

clime (klīm) *n.* Climate: *moved to a sunny clime.*

clinch (klĭnch) *v.* **clinched, clinching, clinches** —*tr.* **1.** To fix or secure (a nail or bolt) by bending down or flattening the end that sticks out. **2.** To fasten securely, as with a nail or bolt: *clinch rafters in place.* **3.** To settle definitely; confirm or complete: *clinch a deal.* **4.** To secure (a divisional championship, for example) before the end of regular season play by having an unbeatable lead. —*intr.* In boxing, to hold the opponent's body with one or both arms. ❖ *n.* In boxing, the act or an instance of clinching: *The boxers went into a clinch at the end of the second round.*

clincher (klĭn′chər) *n.* **1.** Something that clinches, especially a nail or bolt. **2.** A final and decisive point, fact, or remark, as in an argument.

cling (klĭng) *intr.v.* **clung, clinging, clings 1.** To hold tight to something: *clung to the rope to keep from falling.* **2.** To stick or adhere to something: *fabrics that cling to the body.* **3.** To stay near; remain close: *We clung together during the storm.* **4.** To remain attached emotionally; hold on: *cling to old beliefs; cling to a hope.*

clingstone (klĭng′stōn′) *n.* A fruit, such as a peach or apricot, having flesh that adheres to the pit.

clinic (klĭn′ĭk) *n.* **1.** A medical facility that provides diagnosis and treatment to patients who do not stay overnight. **2.** A place where medical specialists work together in research and treatment of particular illnesses: *an eye and ear clinic for the treatment of children.* **3.** A group offering special counseling or training: *an acting clinic; a tennis clinic.* **4.** A training session for medical students in which they observe while patients are examined and treated.

clinical (klĭn′ĭ-kəl) *adj.* **1.** Relating to or connected with a clinic: *a doctor on the clinical staff.* **2.** Involving or based on direct examination and treatment of patients: *a clinical diagnosis of disease.* **3.** Very objective; not emotional; analytical: *a clinical account of the state's economic problems.* —**clin′i·cal·ly** *adv.*

clinical depression *n.* A psychiatric disorder characterized by extreme and persistent sadness, and often feelings of guilt or helplessness, difficulty concentrating, changes in appetite and sleep patterns, and the inability to experience pleasure.

clink[1] (klĭngk) *tr. & intr.v.* **clinked, clinking, clinks** To make or cause to make a light, sharp, ringing sound: *They clinked glasses after the toast. The ice clinked in the glass.* ❖ *n.* A light, sharp, ringing sound: *the clink of glasses on a tray.*

clink[2] (klĭngk) *n.* Slang A prison or prison cell.

WORD HISTORY Clink[1] comes from Middle English *clinken,* which comes from Middle Dutch *klinken,* both meaning the same as the Modern English word. **Clink**[2] comes from *Clink,* a district of London, England, that is famous for its prison.

clinker (klĭng′kər) *n.* **1.** A lump of incombustible matter left over after coal has burned. **2.** Slang A mistake; a blunder.

Clio (klī′ō) *n.* In Greek mythology, the Muse of history.

clip[1] (klĭp) *v.* **clipped, clipping, clips** —*tr.* **1.** To cut, cut off, or cut out with scissors or shears: *clip a picture out of the newspaper.* **2.** To shorten by cutting; trim: *clip a hedge; clip a fingernail.* **3.** To shorten (a word or words) by leaving out letters or syllables: *clip one's words when speaking excitedly.* **4.** *Informal* To hit or strike with a quick sharp blow: *Their car clipped ours in the front fender.* **5.** In football, to block (an opposing player) illegally from behind. —*intr.* **1.** To cut or trim something. **2.** *Informal* To move rapidly: *The sailboat clipped along in the strong wind.* ❖ *n.* **1.** The act of clipping: *Just a few clips of the scissors will even your bangs.* **2.** The wool clipped from sheep at one shearing. **3.** Something clipped off, as a sequence clipped from a movie film. **4.** *Informal* A quick sharp blow: *a clip on the chin.* **5.** *Informal* A brisk pace: *The train sped along at a good clip.* **6.** In football, an act of clipping.

clip[2] (klĭp) *n.* **1.** A device, such as a paper clip, for gripping

or holding things together. **2.** A holder for cartridges to be loaded into an automatic rifle or pistol. **3.** A piece of jewelry, such as a pin, that fastens with a clasp or clip. ❖ *tr.v.* **clipped, clipping, clips** To fasten with a clip: *clip the papers together.*

WORD HISTORY Clip[1] comes from Middle English *clippen,* meaning "to cut off." **Clip**[2] comes from Middle English *clip* (meaning "hook"), which comes from a different Middle English verb, also spelled *clippen,* meaning "to embrace, grasp."

clip art *n.* Ready-made computerized graphic art used in decorating documents.

clipboard (klĭp′bôrd′) *n.* **1.** A small writing board with a spring-loaded clip at the top for holding papers or a writing pad. **2.** A computer file or an area in computer memory where the user can store text or graphics before inserting them into another document or file.

clipper (klĭp′ər) *n.* **1.** A person who clips, cuts, or shears. **2. clippers** A tool for clipping, cutting, or shearing: *nail clippers; a barber's clippers.* **3.** A sailing vessel built for great speed, having tall masts and sharp lines.

clipping (klĭp′ĭng) *n.* **1.** Something cut or trimmed off, especially an article or photograph clipped from a newspaper or magazine. **2.** A word formed by dropping one or more syllables from a longer word, such as *app,* a clipping formed from *application.*

clique (klēk *or* klĭk) *n.* A small group of people who stick together and remain aloof from others.

cliquish (klē′kĭsh *or* klĭk′ĭsh) *adj.* Relating to or characteristic of a clique. —**cliqu′ish·ly** *adv.* —**cliqu′ish·ness** *n.*

clitoris (klĭt′ər-ĭs *or* klī′tər-ĭs) *n.* A sex organ that is composed of erectile tissue and forms part of the external reproductive system in female mammals and some other animals.

cloaca (klō-ā′kə) *n.* The common cavity that serves as the opening for the intestinal, genital, and urinary tracts in many vertebrates, including amphibians, reptiles, birds, and some fishes.

cloak (klōk) *n.* **1.** A loose outer garment or wrap, usually having no sleeves. **2.** Something that covers or conceals: *A cloak of mystery surrounds their disappearance.* ❖ *tr.v.* **cloaked, cloaking, cloaks** To cover with or as if with a cloak: *A dense fog cloaked the city. The situation was cloaked in mystery.*

cloak-and-dagger (klōk′ən-dăg′ər) *adj.* Marked by melodramatic intrigue and often by espionage.

cloakroom (klōk′rōōm′ *or* klōk′rŏŏm′) *n.* A room where coats and other outdoor clothing may be left temporarily.

clobber (klŏb′ər) *tr.v.* **clobbered, clobbering, clobbers** Slang **1.** To hit or pound with great force: *The batter clobbered the ball for a triple.* **2.** To defeat completely: *Our team was clobbered by theirs.*

clock (klŏk) *n.* **1.** An instrument other than a watch for measuring and indicating time, often having a digital display or a numbered dial with moving hands that point to the numbers. **2.** A time clock. ❖ *tr.v.* **clocked, clocking, clocks** To record the time or speed of: *The bicyclist was clocked at 30 miles per hour.* ◆ **around the clock** Continuously: *Some convenience stores are open around the clock.*

clock radio *n.* A radio with a built-in clock that can be set to turn the radio on automatically.

clockwise (klŏk′wīz′) *adv. & adj.* In the same direction as the rotating hands of a clock: *turn clockwise; a clockwise movement.*

clockwork (klŏk′wûrk′) *n.* A mechanism of gears driven by a spring, as in a mechanical clock. ◆ **like clockwork** With perfect regularity and precision: *The assembly line in the factory operates like clockwork.*

clod (klŏd) *n.* **1.** A lump of earth or clay. **2.** A dull or stupid person; a dolt.

clodhopper (klŏd′hŏp′ər) *n.* **1.** A clumsy country fellow; a bumpkin. **2. clodhoppers** Big heavy shoes.

clog (klŏg) *n.* **1.** Something that obstructs or hinders: *a clog in the drain; a clog in the flow of traffic.* **2.** A heavy shoe, usually having a wooden sole. ❖ *v.* **clogged, clogging, clogs** —*tr.* To cause to become obstructed or blocked up: *Heavy traffic clogged the highway all the way to the airport.* —*intr.* To become obstructed or blocked up: *The drain clogs easily.*

cloister (kloi′stər) *n.* **1.** A covered walk along the side of a building, such as a convent or church, with open arches facing into a courtyard. **2.** A place of religious seclusion, as a monastery or convent. **3.** A quiet secluded place. ❖ *tr.v.* **cloistered, cloistering, cloisters** To shut away or confine in or as if in a cloister; seclude: *The author was cloistered in the library all morning.*

clomp (klŏmp) *intr.v.* **clomped, clomping, clomps** To walk heavily and noisily.

clone (klōn) *n.* **1.** An organism or a group of organisms produced asexually from a single ancestor and genetically identical to it. Cloning can occur naturally, as by fission in one-celled organisms, or can be performed artificially, as by taking the nucleus from the cell of an adult organism and placing it into an egg cell so that it grows into an adult with the same genes as the original organism. **2.** A person or thing that is copied from or closely resembles another: *The new governor is a clone of the previous one.* ❖ *tr.v.* **cloned, cloning, clones 1.** To produce a clone of (an organism, cell, or DNA sequence). **2.** To produce a copy of (a person or thing): *The criminals had cloned several cell phones.*

clop (klŏp) *n.* A sharp hollow sound, as of a horse's hoof striking the pavement. ❖ *intr.v.* **clopped, clopping, clops** To move with such a sound: *The team of horses clopped steadily along.*

close (klōs) *adj.* **closer, closest 1.** Near in space or time: *The airport is close to town.* **2.** Near in relationship: *They are close relatives.* **3.** Bound by loyalties or affection; intimate: *close friends.* **4.** Having little space in between: *chairs arranged in close rows.* **5.** Very short or near to the surface: *a close haircut; a close shave.* **6.** Fitting tightly: *a jacket with a close fit.* **7.** Very much like another or the original: *a close copy of an ancient statue.* **8.** Attentive or rigorous: *During the drought, rangers kept a close watch for forest fires.* **9.** Confining; narrow; crowded: *The little cabin was close quarters for the three of us.* **10.** Lacking fresh air; stuffy: *It's very close in this room with the windows shut.* **11.** Almost even, as in a contest: *a close race; a close election.* ❖ *v.* (klōz) **closed, closing, closes** —*tr.* **1.** To move (a door, for example) so that an opening or a passage is blocked; shut. **2.** To prevent passage through; obstruct: *closed the bridge for repairs.* **3.** To stop the operations of: *Most shopkeepers close their stores around six o'clock.* **4.** To fill up or stop up: *Close the cracks in the wall with plaster.* **5.** To bring to an end; conclude: *close a letter; close a meeting.* See Synonyms at **complete. 6.** To draw together the edges of: *It took eight stitches to close the wound.* —*intr.* **1.** To become shut: *The window closed with a bang.* **2.** To come to an end: *The book closes with a*

reunion of friends. **3.** To cease or suspend operation: *The museum closes on Wednesdays.* **4.** To draw near: *Our boat was closing fast on the one in front.* **5.** To come together: *The child's arms closed around the stuffed animal.* **6.** To be priced at a specified amount when trading ends: *Stocks closed higher today.* ❖ *n.* (klōz) A conclusion; an end: *Sunset marks the close of day. The meeting came to a quick close.* ❖ *adv.* (klōs) **closer, closest** In a close position or manner: *Let's stick close together.* ◆ **close down** To stop operating: *The old factory finally closed down.* **close in** To surround and advance upon: *The fog was quickly closing in on us.* **close out** To sell at a reduced price in order to dispose of quickly: *The store closed out all winter clothes in March.* **close to** On the brink of: *He was close to tears.* —**close′ly** *adv.* —**close′ness** *n.*

close call (klōs) *n. Informal* A narrow escape.

closed (klōzd) *adj.* **1.** Blocked to passage or entry: *a closed door; a tunnel closed off for repairs.* **2.** Not open for business or visitation: *The museum is closed on Mondays.* **3.** Not open to the public; conducted in secrecy: *a closed meeting of Congress.* **4.** Not open to new ideas; prejudiced: *a closed mind.* **5.** Relating to a curve, such as a circle, having no endpoints. **6.** Producing only elements of the same set in a given mathematical operation. The set of whole numbers is closed under addition because adding whole numbers to each other only produces other whole numbers. The set of whole numbers is not closed under division, since dividing whole numbers by each other can produce fractions. **7.** Allowing electricity to flow or pass: *a closed switch.*

closed-captioned (klōzd′kăp′shənd) *adj.* Having titles or captions that explain action or give dialogue on a television program but that can be seen only on a specially equipped receiver.

closed circuit *n.* **1.** An electric circuit through which current can flow in an uninterrupted path. **2.** A television system in which the signal is usually sent by cable to a limited number of receivers.

closed shop *n.* A company or business in which only union members or people who agree to join the union within a certain time may be hired.

close-fisted (klōs′fĭs′tĭd) *adj.* Stingy: *a close-fisted business manager.*

close-knit (klōs′nĭt′) *adj.* Closely joined by a common bond, as a relationship or interest: *They are a close-knit family.*

close-mouthed (klōs′mouthd′ *or* klōs′mουtht′) *adj.* Not talking much; giving away little information: *He was close-mouthed about his whereabouts last week.*

closeout (klōz′out′) *n.* A sale in which goods are offered at greatly reduced prices in order to dispose of them.

closer (klō′zər) *n.* **1.** A person or thing that closes something: *an automatic door closer.* **2.** In baseball, a relief pitcher who tries to protect a lead late in a game.

closet (klŏz′ĭt *or* klô′zĭt) *n.* **1.** A small room or cabinet for hanging clothes, storing linens or supplies, or keeping food: *a clothes closet; a broom closet.* **2.** A small private room for study or prayer. ❖ *tr.v.* **closeted, closeting, closets** To enclose in a private room, as for discussion: *The lawyers closeted themselves in conference for hours.* ❖ *adj.* Keeping something secret to avoid embarrassment or being accused of acting inconsistently with one's beliefs or positions: *a closet smoker.*

closeted (klŏz′ĭ-tĭd *or* klô′zĭ-tĭd) *adj.* Being in a state of secrecy or cautious privacy.

close-up (klōs′ŭp′) *n.* **1.** A photograph or a view in a movie in which the subject is shown at close range: *The portrait was a close-up of the president.* **2.** A close or intimate look or view: *The article presented a close-up of the daily life of a street vendor.*

closing (klō′zĭng) *n.* **1.** A concluding part: *In the closing of his letter, he thanks us.* **2.** A meeting for concluding something, especially a real estate transaction: *The buyers brought their lawyer to the closing.*

closure (klō′zhər) *n.* **1.** The act of closing: *Closure of the incision ended the operation.* **2.** Something that closes or shuts something: *a plastic bag with a resealable closure.* **3.** In mathematics, the property of being closed.

clot (klŏt) *n.* A thickened or solid mass formed from a liquid, such as a blood clot. ❖ *intr. & tr.v.* **clotted, clotting, clots** To form or cause to form into clots: *Blood clots when exposed to air.*

cloth (klôth) *n., pl.* **cloths** (klôths or klô*th*z) **1.** Fabric or material made by weaving, knitting, or matting fibers together. **2.** A piece of cloth used for a special purpose, as for a tablecloth. **3.** The clergy: *a man of the cloth.*

clothe (klō*th*) *tr.v.* **clothed** or **clad** (klăd), **clothing, clothes 1.** To put clothes on or provide clothes for; dress: *feed and clothe a family.* **2.** To cover, as if with clothing: *trees clothed in their fall colors.*

clothes (klōz or klō*th*z) *pl.n.* **1.** Coverings worn on the body; garments, such as shirts, pants, dresses, and coats. **2.** Bedclothes.

clotheshorse (klōz′hôrs′ or klō*th*z′hôrs′) *n.* **1.** A frame on which clothes are hung to dry or air. **2.** A person who has an excessive interest in clothes and frequently wears new outfits.

clothesline (klōz′līn′ or klō*th*z′līn′) *n.* A rope or wire on which clothes are hung to dry.

clothes moth *n.* Any of several small moths whose larvae feed on wool and fur.

clothespin (klōz′pĭn′ or klō*th*z′pĭn′) *n.* A clip of wood or plastic used to fasten clothes on a clothesline.

clothier (klō*th*′yər or klō′*th*ē-ər) *n.* A person who makes or sells clothing or cloth.

clothing (klō′*th*ĭng) *n.* Clothes or garments considered as a group: *wore warm clothing for the hike.*

cloture (klō′chər) *n.* A parliamentary procedure by which debate is ended and an immediate vote is taken on the matter under discussion.

cloud (kloud) *n.* **1a.** A visible mass of very fine water droplets or ice particles floating in the air at heights ranging up to several miles above sea level. **b.** A similar mass formed of suspended particles or droplets, as of dust, steam, or smoke. **2.** A collection of things on the ground, in the water, or in the air that is so large and dense that it appears to resemble a cloud: *A cloud of locusts swarmed above the field. A cloud of silt made it impossible to see the river bottom.* **3.** A state or cause of sadness or worry: *The bad news cast a cloud over the celebration.* **4.** A state or cause of suspicion or disgrace: *A cloud of mistrust hung over the stockbroker until he resigned.* **5.** The collection of data and services available through the Internet: *storing data in the cloud.* ❖ *v.* **clouded, clouding, clouds** —*tr.* **1.** To cover with clouds: *Heavy mist clouded the hills.* **2.** To make less clear or transparent; darken or obscure: *Steam clouded the bathroom mirror.* **3.** To make gloomy or confused: *Superstition clouded their thinking.* **4.** To taint;

tarnish; sully: *A charge of corruption clouded the mayor's reputation.* —*intr.* **1.** To become covered with clouds: *The sky clouded over.* **2.** To become dark, obscure, or less transparent: *The water in the bowl clouded up.*

cloudburst (kloud′bûrst′) *n.* A sudden heavy rainstorm; a downpour.

cloud chamber *n.* A device in which the paths of charged subatomic particles are made visible as trails of droplets. It contains a supersaturated vapor that condenses on the ions that are formed along the path of the charged particle.

cloud nine *n. Informal* A state of elation or great happiness: *was on cloud nine after winning the marathon.*

cloud seeding *n.* A method of making a cloud give up its moisture as rain, especially by releasing particles of dry ice or silver iodide into the cloud.

cloudy (klou′dē) *adj.* **cloudier, cloudiest 1.** Full of or covered with clouds; overcast: *a cloudy sky.* **2.** Not clear; murky: *cloudy water.* **3.** Confused, gloomy, or uncertain: *cloudy thinking; a project with a cloudy future.* —**cloud′i·ly** *adv.* —**cloud′i·ness** *n.*

clout (klout) *n.* **1.** A heavy blow, as with the fist: *a clout on the chin.* **2.** Power, prestige, or influence: *The president has great political clout.* ❖ *tr.v.* **clouted, clouting, clouts** To hit hard: *The batter clouted the ball over the fence.*

clove¹ (klōv) *n.* **1.** The dried aromatic flower bud of a tropical southeast Asian tree, used whole or ground as a spice. **2.** The plant that bears such flower buds.

clove² (klōv) *n.* One of the sections of a garlic bulb or a similar plant bulb.

WORD HISTORY Clove¹ comes the Middle English phrase *clow de gilofre,* which comes from the Old French phrase *clou de girofle,* both meaning "nail of the clove tree." Old French *clou* comes from Latin *clāvus,* meaning "nail." **Clove²** comes from Old English *clufu,* where it meant the same thing as the Modern English word.

clove³ (klōv) *v.* **1.** A past tense of **cleave¹**. **2.** *Archaic* A past participle of **cleave¹**.

clove hitch *n.* A knot, often used to tie a rope to a post, consisting of two half hitches.

cloven (klō′vən) *v.* A past participle of **cleave¹**. ❖ *adj.* Split or divided into two parts: *the cloven hooves of deer or cattle.*

clover (klō′vər) *n.* Any of various plants having leaves divided into three leaflets and tightly clustered heads of small, often fragrant flowers. Many kinds of clover are grown to feed cattle and horses.

cloverleaf (klō′vər-lēf′) *n.* A highway interchange whose exit and entrance ramps resemble a four-leaf clover and enable vehicles to go from one highway to the other in either direction.

clown (kloun) *n.* **1.** A performer, as in a circus or carnival, who jokes and does tricks or humorous stunts. **2.** A person who is always making jokes or acting foolishly: *the office clown.* ❖ *intr.v.* **clowned, clowning, clowns 1.** To perform as a clown in a circus or other show. **2.** To behave like a clown; act foolishly: *Practical jokers are always clowning around.*

clownish (klou′nĭsh) *adj.* Resembling or characteristic of a clown: *We laughed at the baby's clownish antics.* —**clown′ish·ly** *adv.*

cloying (kloi′ĭng) *adj.* Unpleasant because of an excess of a quality, such as sweetness, that in itself is pleasant.

club (klŭb) *n.* **1.** A heavy stick, usually thicker at one end than at the other, used as a weapon. **2.** A stick designed to drive a ball in certain games, especially golf. **3a.** A black figure, shaped like a trefoil or the leaf of a clover, on a playing card. **b.** A card bearing this figure. **c. clubs** The suit in a deck of cards having this figure as its symbol. **4a.** A group of people organized for a common purpose: *a chess club.* **b.** The room, building, or other facility used by such a group. ❖ *v.* **clubbed, clubbing, clubs** —*tr.* To strike or beat with or as if with a club. —*intr.* To join together for a common purpose: *All the tenants clubbed together to clean up the apartment building.*

clubfoot (klŭb′fŏot′) *n.* **1.** A deformity of the foot, usually marked by a curled or twisted shape, that arises as a birth defect. **2.** A foot that has such a deformity. —**club′foot′ed** *adj.*

clubhouse (klŭb′hous′) *n.* **1.** A building occupied by a club. **2.** A locker room used by an athletic team.

club moss *n.* Any of various low-growing evergreen plants that have small leaves resembling needles and do not have flowers or seeds.

club sandwich *n.* A sandwich made of two or three slices of bread with a filling of meat, tomato, lettuce, and mayonnaise.

club soda *n.* Carbonated water.

cluck (klŭk) *n.* The low short sound made by a hen sitting on eggs or calling for its chicks. ❖ *intr.v.* **clucked, clucking, clucks** To make this sound or a similar sound.

clue (klōō) *n.* A fact or object that helps to solve a problem or mystery: *Today's powerful telescopes can give us clues about the origin of the universe.* ❖ *tr.v.* **clued, clueing** or **cluing, clues** To give (someone) information: *Clue me in on what's happening.*

clueless (klōō′lĭs) *adj.* Lacking understanding or knowledge.

clump (klŭmp) *n.* **1.** A thick group or cluster, as of trees or bushes. **2.** A thick mass, as of dirt or sod. **3.** A heavy dull sound, as of footsteps. ❖ *v.* **clumped, clumping, clumps** —*intr.* **1.** To walk with a heavy dull sound. **2.** To form clumps: *Blood clumps as it forms a scab.* —*tr.* To gather into or form clumps of: *clumped all the boots by the door.* —**clump′y** *adj.*

clumsy (klŭm′zē) *adj.* **clumsier, clumsiest 1.** Lacking grace or deftness; awkward: *a clumsy walk; clumsy newborn puppies.* **2.** Difficult to handle or maneuver: *thick clumsy gloves; a big clumsy package.* **3.** Done without skill; inept: *a clumsy drawing of a horse.* —**clum′si·ly** *adv.* —**clum′si·ness** *n.*

clung (klŭng) *v.* Past tense and past participle of **cling.**

clunker (klŭng′kər) *n. Informal* **1.** A decrepit machine, especially an old car; a rattletrap. **2.** A failure; a flop.

clunky (klŭng′kē) *adj.* **clunkier, clunkiest** Clumsy in form or manner; awkward: *clunky hiking boots.*

cluster (klŭs′tər) *n.* **1.** A group of similar things growing, grouped, or occurring close together: *a cluster of flowers; a cluster of break-ins in the neighborhood.* **2.** Two or more consonants in a row, as *str* and *ct* in the word *strict.* ❖ *intr.v.* **clustered, clustering, clusters** To gather, grow, or occur in clusters: *Everyone clustered around the fire.*

clutch[1] (klŭch) *v.* **clutched, clutching, clutches** —*tr.* To hold or grasp tightly: *I clutched the railing as I started down the stairs.* —*intr.* To try to grasp or seize something: *I clutched at the chair as I started to fall.* ❖ *n.* **1.** A tight hold or grip. **2.** often **clutches** Control or power; possession: *fall into the clutches of the enemy.* **3a.** A device used to connect and disconnect a driveshaft in a transmission

system. **b.** The lever, pedal, or other control that operates such a device, as in an automobile or truck. **4.** A critical situation: *our best hitter in the clutch.*

clutch[2] (klŭch) *n.* **1.** The eggs produced at a single laying by a bird, turtle, or other animal. **2.** A brood of chicks hatched from such eggs.

WORD HISTORY Clutch[1] comes from Middle English *clicchen,* which comes from Old English *clyccan,* both meaning "to form a fist." **Clutch**[2] comes from Middle English *clekken,* which comes from Old Norse *klekja,* both meaning "to hatch."

clutter (klŭt′ər) *n.* A collection of things scattered about in a disorderly fashion; a jumble: *She stumbled over the clutter on the floor.* ❖ *tr.v.* **cluttered, cluttering, clutters** To fill in such a way as to block movement or action or to create disorder: *On Sundays our living room floor is cluttered up with newspapers.*

Clydesdale (klīdz′dāl′) *n.* A large powerful draft horse of a breed developed in the Clyde River valley of Scotland, having long white hair on the lower legs.

Clytemnestra (klī′təm-nĕs′trə) *n.* In Greek mythology, the wife of Agamemnon, who murdered him on his return from the Trojan War and was later murdered by her son, Orestes.

cm An abbreviation of centimeter.

cnidarian (nī-dâr′ē-ən) *n.* Any of various ocean-dwelling invertebrate animals that have a body with radial symmetry, tentacles, and a sac-like internal cavity. They include the jellyfishes, corals, and sea anemones.

Co. An abbreviation of: **1.** company. **2.** county.

c/o An abbreviation of care of.

co– A prefix that means: **1.** Together; jointly: *coexist.* **2.** Partner or associate: *coauthor.* **3.** To the same extent or degree: *coextensive.*

WORD BUILDING The prefixes **co–** and **com–** are similar in meaning, and both go back to Latin prefixes that meant "with." In English, *co–* means "together, joint, jointly." It can be used to form nouns like *costar* or *coworker,* and it can also be used to form verbs like *cosign* or *coedit.* If you find a noun or a verb beginning with *co–* that you've never seen before, you can probably guess its meaning correctly.

coach (kōch) *n.* **1.** A large closed carriage on four wheels, pulled by horses. **2.** A railroad passenger car. **3.** A bus, especially one designed for long-distance passenger service. **4.** A low-priced class of passenger accommodations on a train, airplane, or bus. **5.** A person who trains or instructs athletes or athletic teams. **6.** A person who gives private instruction, as in singing, test-taking, or job skills. ❖ *v.* **coached, coaching, coaches** —*tr.* To train or teach: *coach a lacrosse team.* —*intr.* To act as a coach.

coachman (kōch′mən) *n.* A man who drives a coach.

coagulant (kō-ăg′yə-lənt) *n.* A substance that causes coagulation.

coagulate (kō-ăg′yə-lāt′) *v.* **coagulated, coagulating, coagulates** —*intr.* To become solid or nearly solid: *Blood coagulates when exposed to air.* —*tr.* To change (a liquid) into a solid or nearly solid mass: *Cooking an egg coagulates both the yolk and the white.*

coagulation (kō-ăg′yə-lā′shən) *n.* **1.** The act or process of coagulating. **2.** A mass or clot that results from coagulation.

coal (kōl) *n.* **1a.** A natural, dark-brown to black, solid substance formed from fossilized plants under conditions of great pressure, high humidity, and lack of air. Coal consists mainly of carbon and is widely used as a fuel and raw material. **b.** A piece of this substance: *There were only a few coals left in the bin.* **2.** A glowing or charred piece of wood, coal, or other solid fuel; an ember: *Coals continue to give off heat long after the flame is out.* ❖ *tr. & intr.v.* **coaled, coaling, coals** To supply with or take on a supply of coal: *coal a ship.*

coalesce (kō′ə-lĕs′) *intr.v.* **coalesced, coalescing, coalesces 1.** To come or grow together into a single mass: *materials that coalesced to form stars.* **2.** To come together so as to form one whole; unite: *local groups that coalesced into a powerful national organization.* —**co′a·les′cence** *n.*

coal gas *n.* **1.** The mixture of gases given off when bituminous coal is heated without air, used as a fuel. **2.** The mixture of gases released when coal burns.

coalition (kō′ə-lĭsh′ən) *n.* An alliance of people, parties, or nations for some special purpose: *a coalition of small business owners to defeat a sales tax.*

coal tar *n.* A thick sticky black liquid obtained by heating coal in the absence of air. It is used as a raw material for many dyes, drugs, and paints.

coarse (kôrs) *adj.* **coarser, coarsest 1.** Not smooth; rough: *coarse skin; coarse material.* **2.** Consisting of large particles: *coarse sand.* **3.** Not refined; crude; rude: *coarse and vulgar language.* **4.** Of low, common, or inferior quality: *coarse lumber fit only for planking.* —**coarse′ly** *adv.* —**coarse′ness** *n.*

coarsen (kôr′sən) *tr. & intr.v.* **coarsened, coarsening, coarsens** To make or become coarse: *Hard work coarsened the laborer's hands. Wool fabric often coarsens with long use.*

coast (kōst) *n.* **1.** The land next to the sea; the seashore. **2.** The water near this land: *fishes of the Pacific coast.* ❖ *intr.v.* **coasted, coasting, coasts 1.** To slide or move without the use of power: *The car coasted to a stop.* See Synonyms at **slide. 2.** To move ahead or through with little effort: *Some students coast through math class.*

coastal (kō′stəl) *adj.* Relating to or being on or near a coast: *a coastal town; shallow coastal waters.*

coaster (kō′stər) *n.* **1.** A small flat object, such as a disk or plate, placed under a bottle or glass to protect a surface, especially of a table. **2.** A ship engaged in coastal trade. **3.** A roller coaster.

coast guard *also* **Coast Guard** *n.* A military organization whose job is to patrol the coast of a nation, carry out rescue operations of ships in trouble, and enforce immigration, navigation, and customs laws.

coastline (kōst′līn′) *n.* The shape, outline, or boundary of a coast.

coast-to-coast (kōst′tə-kōst′) *adj.* Reaching, airing, or traveling from one coast to another: *a coast-to-coast broadcast of the president's speech.*

coastward (kōst′wərd) *adj.* Directed toward a coast: *a coastward current.* ❖ *adv.* also **coastwards** (kōst′wərdz) Toward a coast: *The boat sailed coastward.*

coat (kōt) *n.* **1a.** An outer garment with sleeves, usually worn for warmth or protection. **b.** A jacket usually forming the top part of a suit. **2.** The hair or fur of an animal: *a dog with a short coat.* **3a.** The outer covering of a biological structure or organ: *a seed coat.* **b.** The outer covering of a virus. **4.** A layer of something spread over a surface: *a*

coat of paint. ❖ *tr.v.* **coated, coating, coats** To cover with a layer: *Dust coated the table.*

coati (kō-ä′tē) *n., pl.* **coati** *or* **coatis** Any of several mammals of South and Central America and the southwest United States that have a long flexible snout and a ringed tail.

coatimundi (kō-ä′tē-mŭn′dē) *n., pl.* **coatimundi** *or* **coatimundis** A coati.

coating (kō′tĭng) *n.* A layer of a substance spread over a surface, as for protection or decoration: *a sticky coating of varnish; a thin coating of ice on the streets.*

coat of arms *n., pl.* **coats of arms 1.** An emblem on a shield that serves as the insignia of a nation, family, institution, or group. **2.** A shield or drawing that represents such an emblem.

coat of mail *n., pl.* **coats of mail** A coat made of chain mail or overlapping metal plates, worn as armor during the Middle Ages.

coatroom (kōt′rōōm′ *or* kōt′rŏŏm′) *n.* A cloakroom.

coattail (kōt′tāl′) *n.* The loose rear flap of a coat that hangs below the waist. ◆ **on (someone's) coattails** As a result of the success of another: *When the governor won the election in a landslide, several local candidates from the same party were elected on her coattails.*

coauthor (kō-ô′thər) *n.* One of two or more people who work together in writing a book, story, report, or other piece of writing. ❖ *tr.v.* **coauthored, coauthoring, coauthors** To be the coauthor of.

coax (kōks) *tr.v.* **coaxed, coaxing, coaxes 1.** To persuade or try to persuade by gently urging: *The trainer coaxed the lion into the cage.* **2.** To obtain by gentle persuasion: *I couldn't coax the secret out of him.* **3.** To move gently or gradually toward a desired end; nudge: *coaxed the heavy girder into place.* —**coax′er** *n.*

coaxial cable (kō-ăk′sē-əl) *n.* A cable made of a conducting outer metal tube insulated from an inner conducting core. Coaxial cables are used to carry telephone, telegraph, and television signals.

cob (kŏb) *n.* **1.** The long hard central part of an ear of corn; a corncob. **2.** A male swan. **3.** A stocky short-legged horse.

cobalt (kō′bôlt′) *n. Symbol* **Co** A hard, silver-white metallic element that occurs widely in ores containing other metals. Cobalt is used in making alloys and pigments. Atomic number 27. See **Periodic Table.**

cobalt-60 *n.* A radioactive isotope of cobalt having a mass number of 60. It is an intense source of gamma rays and is used in the treatment of cancer.

cobalt blue *n.* **1.** A blue to green pigment consisting of a mixture of cobalt oxide and aluminum oxide. **2.** A deep vivid blue.

cobble¹ (kŏb′əl) *n.* A cobblestone. ❖ *tr.v.* **cobbled, cobbling, cobbles** To pave with cobblestones.

cobble² (kŏb′əl) *tr.v.* **cobbled, cobbling, cobbles** To make or mend (boots or shoes).

WORD HISTORY Cobble¹ is probably related to Middle English *cob,* meaning "round object." **Cobble²** is probably a back-formation from *cobbler* ("shoemaker").

---

cobbler¹ (kŏb′lər) *n.* A shoemaker.

cobbler² (kŏb′lər) *n.* A fruit pie topped with a biscuit crust and baked in a deep dish.

WORD HISTORY Cobbler¹ comes from Middle English *cobeler,* meaning "shoemaker." The origin of **cobbler²** is unknown.

cobblestone (kŏb′əl-stōn′) *n.* A naturally rounded stone formerly used for paving streets.

cobra (kō′brə) *n.* Any of several venomous Asian or African snakes capable of spreading out the skin of the neck to form a flattened hood.

cobweb (kŏb′wĕb′) *n.* A spider web, especially an old one that is covered in dust.

coca (kō′kə) *n.* Any of certain trees or shrubs native to South America whose leaves are chewed as a stimulant or processed for cocaine.

cocaine (kō-kān′ *or* kō′kān′) *n.* A drug obtained from coca leaves that stimulates the nervous system and is highly addictive. It is sometimes used in medicine as a local anesthetic.

coccus (kŏk′əs) *n., pl.* **cocci** (kŏk′sī *or* kŏk′ī) Any of various bacteria that are shaped like a sphere and are usually grouped together in chains or clusters.

coccyx (kŏk′sĭks) *n., pl.* **coccyges** (kŏk-sī′jēz *or* kŏk′sĭ-jēz′) or **coccyxes** A small triangular bone found at the base of the spinal column in humans and other apes.

cochineal (kŏch′ə-nēl′ *or* kŏch′ə-nēl′) *n.* A bright-red dye made from the dried bodies of a tropical American insect.

cochlea (kŏk′lē-ə) *n., pl.* **cochleae** (kŏk′lē-ē′) also **cochleas** A spiral tube of the inner ear that resembles a snail shell and contains the nerve endings necessary for hearing. —**coch′le′ar** *adj.*

cochlear implant (kŏk′lē-ər) *n.* An electronic device that is implanted in the inner ear and allows people with severe hearing loss to recognize some sounds, especially speech.

cock¹ (kŏk) *n.* **1.** An adult male chicken; a rooster. **2.** An adult male of various other birds. **3.** A faucet or valve for regulating the flow of a liquid or gas. **4.** The hammer of a gun. **5.** A tilting or jaunty turning upward: *the cock of a sailor's cap.* ❖ *tr.v.* **cocked, cocking, cocks 1.** To set the hammer of (a gun) in position to fire. **2.** To tilt or turn up to one side: *He cocked his head and thought about the question.*

cock² (kŏk) *n.* A cone-shaped pile of straw or hay. ❖ *tr.v.* **cocked, cocking, cocks** To arrange (straw or hay) in such piles.

WORD HISTORY Cock¹ comes Middle English *cok,* which comes from Old English *cocc,* both referring to the same animal as in Modern English. **Cock²** comes from a different Middle English word also spelled *cok,* having the same meaning as the Modern English word.

cockade (kŏ-kād′) *n.* An ornament, such as a rosette or knot of ribbon, usually worn on the hat as a badge. —**cock·ad′ed** *adj.*

cockamamie (kŏk′ə-mā′mē) *adj. Slang* Ludicrous; nonsensical: *gave me a cockamamie reason for not going.*

cockatoo (kŏk′ə-tōo′) *n., pl.* **cockatoos** Any of various large parrots of Australia and adjacent areas, having feathers on the head that can be raised in a crest.

cocked hat (kŏkt) *n.* A hat with the brim turned up in two or three places.

cockerel (kŏk′ər-əl) *n.* A young rooster.

cocker spaniel (kŏk′ər) *n.* A dog of an American or an English breed having long drooping ears and a silky coat.

cockeyed (kŏk′īd′) *adj. Informal* **1.** Tilted or crooked; askew: *The picture hung at a cockeyed angle on the wall.* **2.** Ridiculous; absurd: *cockeyed schemes that are sure to fail.*

cockfight (kŏk′fīt′) *n.* A fight between two gamecocks with metal spurs attached to their legs.

cockhorse (kŏk′hôrs′) *n.* A rocking horse or hobbyhorse.

cockle (kŏk′əl) *n.* **1.** Any of various mollusks having a pair of heart-shaped shells with narrow ribbed markings. **2.** A cockleshell. ❖ **cockles of one's heart** One's innermost feelings: *Their thoughtfulness warmed the cockles of my heart.*

cocklebur (kŏk′əl-bûr′) *n.* **1.** Any of several large weedy plants that have prickly burs. **2.** The bur of such a plant.

cockleshell (kŏk′əl-shĕl′) *n.* **1.** A shell of a cockle. **2.** A small light boat used in shallow waters.

Cockney (kŏk′nē) *n., pl.* **Cockneys 1.** A native of the eastern section of London, England. **2.** The distinctive dialect or accent of the Cockneys. —**Cock′ney** *adj.*

cockpit (kŏk′pĭt′) *n.* **1.** The space in an airplane that has seats for the pilot and copilot and sometimes passengers. **2.** The space in a small boat from which the boat is steered. **3.** An area used for cockfights.

cockroach (kŏk′rōch′) *n.* Any of numerous usually dark-colored insects that have a flat oval body and lay their eggs in hardened cases. Several kinds of cockroaches are common household pests.

cockscomb (kŏks′kōm′) *n.* **1.** The fleshy red comb on the head of a rooster. **2.** A jester's cap, topped with a strip of red cloth notched like the comb of a rooster. **3.** A garden plant having dense fan-shaped clusters of red, purple, or yellow flowers.

cocksure (kŏk′shŏŏr′) *adj.* Completely sure, especially too sure of oneself: *a cocksure young upstart.* —**cock′sure′ness** *n.*

cocktail (kŏk′tāl′) *n.* **1.** An alcoholic drink consisting of a liquor mixed with fruit juice, soda, or another liquor. **2.** An appetizer such as seafood, juice, or fruit: *a shrimp cocktail.*

cocky (kŏk′ē) *adj.* **cockier, cockiest** Too sure of oneself; arrogant; conceited: *a cocky showoff.* —**cock′i·ly** *adv.* —**cock′i·ness** *n.*

cocoa (kō′kō) *n.* **1.** A powder made of roasted ground cacao seeds from which much of the fat has been removed. **2.** A drink made by mixing this powder with sugar and hot milk or water.

cocoa butter *n.* A yellowish waxy solid obtained from cacao seeds and used in making soap, cosmetics, and confections.

coconut (kō′kə-nŭt′) *n.* **1.** The large hard-shelled nut of the coconut palm, having white meat and a hollow center filled with liquid. **2.** The edible white meat of this nut, often shredded and used as food and in confections. **3.** The coconut palm.

coconut milk *n.* A milky liquid extracted from the meat of a coconut.

coconut oil *n.* A semisolid or liquid oil obtained from coconut meat and used in foods, soaps, and cosmetics.

coconut palm *n.* A palm tree of tropical regions that bears coconuts as fruits.

coconut water *n.* The watery fluid inside a young coconut, used chiefly as a beverage.

cocoon (kə-kōōn′) *n.* **1.** A protective case of silky strands spun by the larva of a moth or other insect as a cover for the pupa. **2.** A similar protective covering or structure: *wrapped in a cocoon of blankets.*

cod (kŏd) *n., pl.* **cod** or **cods** Any of various large food fishes of the northern Atlantic and Pacific Oceans; a codfish.

COD An abbreviation of cash on delivery.

coda (kō′də) *n.* A passage that ends a musical movement or composition.

coddle (kŏd′l) *tr.v.* **coddled, coddling, coddles 1.** To cook in water just below the boiling point: *coddle eggs.* **2.** To treat indulgently; baby. See Synonyms at **pamper.**

code (kōd) *n.* **1.** A system of signals used to represent the letters and numerals in a message that is to be transmitted: *a telegraphic code.* **2.** A system of words, symbols, or letters given arbitrary meanings, usually used to keep messages secret. **3.** A system of symbols and rules used to represent instructions to a computer; a computer program. **4.** A special command, such as a sequence of keystrokes, that allows a user to activate a hidden or accidental feature in a computer program or video game. **5.** A system or collection of laws or rules and regulations: *a building code; an honor code.* ❖ *tr.v.* **coded, coding, codes** To put (a text, numbers, or information) into a code: *code information to store in a computer.*

code blue *n.* **1.** A medical emergency in which medical personnel work to revive a person whose heart has stopped. **2.** An order given to start such work: *called a code blue.*

codeine (kō′dēn′) *n.* A drug obtained from opium or morphine and used especially to relieve coughing or pain.

code name *n.* A name assigned to conceal the identity or existence of something or someone.

code word *n.* A secret word or phrase used as a code name or password.

codex (kō′dĕks′) *n., pl.* **codices** (kō′dĭ-sēz′ or kŏd′ĭ-sēz′) A manuscript volume, especially of a classic work or of the Scriptures.

codfish (kŏd′fĭsh′) *n.* **1.** A cod. **2.** The flesh of a cod, used as food.

codger (kŏj′ər) *n. Informal* An odd or somewhat eccentric old man.

codicil (kŏd′ə-sĭl) *n.* A supplement or appendix, especially to a will.

codify (kŏd′ĭ-fī′ or kō′də-fī′) *tr.v.* **codified, codifying, codifies** To arrange (laws, for example) in a systematic way. —**cod′i·fi·ca′tion** (kŏd′ĭ-fĭ-kā′shən) *n.* —**cod′·i·fi′er** *n.*

codling moth (kŏd′lĭng) *n.* A small moth whose caterpillars feed on and damage apples and other fruits.

cod-liver oil (kŏd′lĭv′ər) *n.* An oil rich in vitamins A and D, obtained from the livers of cod and related fishes.

codpiece (kŏd′pēs′) *n.* A pouch or flap hiding an opening in the front of the tight breeches worn by men in the 1400s and 1500s.

coed or **co-ed** (kō′ĕd′) *Informal n.* A woman who attends a coeducational college or university. ❖ *adj.* Relating to coeducation: *a coed school.*

coeducation (kō-ĕj′ə-kā′shən) *n.* The system of education in which both male and female students take classes together at a school or college. —**co′ed·u·ca′tion·al** *adj.*

coefficient (kō′ə-fĭsh′ənt) *n.* A number or symbol multiplying a variable or an unknown quantity in an algebraic term. In the term $4x$, 4 is the coefficient. In $x(a + b)$, x is the coefficient.

coelacanth (sē′lə-kănth′) *n.* Any of various fishes having lobed fleshy fins and several characteristics not found in other vertebrate animals. They were known only from fossil remains until a living specimen was caught off the coast of southern Africa in 1938. A second species was discovered in 1999 in Indonesia.

coelenterate (sĭ-lĕn′tə-rāt′ or sĭ-lĕn′tər-ĭt) *n.* A cnidarian.

coelom (sē′ləm) *n.* The fluid-filled cavity within the body of most multicellular animals, except some invertebrates such as flatworms, that lies between the body wall and the digestive tract and contains the internal organs.

coerce (kō-ûrs′) *tr.v.* **coerced, coercing, coerces** To force or compel (someone) to do something by pressure, threats, or intimidation: *The suspect claimed that the police coerced her to confess by intimidating her.* —**co·erc′er** *n.* —**co·er′cion** (kō-ûr′zhən) *n.*

coercive (kō-ûr′sĭv) *adj.* Tending to coerce: *Public opinion has a coercive effect on elected officials.* —**co·er′cive·ly** *adv.*

coevolution (kō′ĕv-ə-lōō′shən or kō′ē-və-lōō′shən) *n.* The process by which two or more interacting species evolve together, each changing as a result of changes in the other or others. It occurs, for example, between predators and prey and between insects and the flowers that they pollinate. —**co′e·volve′** (kō′ĭ-vŏlv′) *v.*

coexist (kō′ĭg-zĭst′) *intr.v.* **coexisted, coexisting, coexists** To live or exist together, at the same time, or in the same place: *Bears and wolves coexist in the Alaskan wilderness. Many nations coexist on the European continent.* —**co′ex·is′tence** *n.* —**co′ex·is′tent** *adj.*

coextensive (kō′ĭk-stĕn′sĭv) *adj.* Occupying the same space; having the same limits or boundaries: *The habitat of certain mammals is coextensive with the Great Plains.*

coffee (kô′fē) *n.* **1.** A brown drink prepared from the ground seeds of any of various tropical plants native to Africa. **2.** The dried whole or ground seeds of any of these plants. **3.** Any of various trees or shrubs that bear such seeds and are widely cultivated in the tropics.

coffeecake (kô′fē-kāk′) *n.* A cake made of sweetened dough with yeast, often containing nuts and raisins and covered with sugar or icing.

coffeehouse (kô′fē-hous′) *n.* A restaurant where coffee and other refreshments are served.

coffeepot (kô′fē-pŏt′) *n.* A covered pot with a handle and spout, for making and pouring coffee.

coffee shop *n.* A small restaurant in which coffee and light meals are served.

coffee table *n.* A low table, often placed in front of a sofa.

coffer (kô′fər) *n.* **1.** A strongbox for holding money or other valuables. **2. coffers** A treasury, as of a nation; financial resources: *The state coffers were opened to aid the flood victims.*

coffin (kô′fĭn) *n.* A box in which a dead person is buried.

cog (kŏg) *n.* **1.** One of a series of teeth on the rim of a wheel that fit between the teeth on another wheel so that one wheel can move the other. **2.** A cogwheel.

cogent (kō′jənt) *adj.* Forceful and convincing: *a cogent argument based on facts.* —**co′gen·cy** (kō′jən-sē) *n.* —**co′gent·ly** *adv.*

cogitate (kŏj′ĭ-tāt′) *intr.v.* **cogitated, cogitating, cogitates** To think carefully; ponder. —**cog′i·ta′tion** *n.*

cognac (kōn′yăk′) *n.* A brandy made from white wine near Cognac, a town in western France.

cognate (kŏg′nāt′) *adj.* **1.** Related in origin: *French and Spanish are cognate languages.* **2.** Related by blood; having a common ancestor: *cognate branches of the same family.* ❖ *n.* A word related to one in another language. For example, the Dutch word *kopje*, the English word *cup*, and the Italian word *coppa* are cognates derived from the Late Latin word *cuppa*.

cognition (kŏg-nĭsh′ən) *n.* The mental process of gaining knowledge, including the ability to perceive, reason, and be aware.

cognitive (kŏg′nĭ-tĭv) *adj.* Relating to cognition: *the cognitive development of young children.*

cognizance (kŏg′nĭ-zəns) *n.* **1.** Observation; notice: *The government was slow to take cognizance of the growing unrest.* **2.** Ability to understand: *The origins of life are still beyond the cognizance of modern science.*

cognizant (kŏg′nĭ-zənt) *adj.* Aware; conscious: *We were not cognizant of the risks involved.*

cognomen (kŏg-nō′mən) *n., pl.* **cognomens** or **cognomina** (kŏg-nŏm′ə-nə) **1a.** A family name; a surname. **b.** The third and usually last name of a citizen in the ancient Roman republic or empire, as *Caesar* in *Gaius Julius Caesar.* **2.** A nickname or epithet acquired through usage over a period of time. —**cog·nom′i·nal** (kŏg-nŏm′ə-nəl) *adj.*

cogwheel (kŏg′wēl′) *n.* A wheel with cogs on its rim that mesh with those of another wheel so that one wheel can move the other.

cohabit (kō-hăb′ĭt) *intr.v.* **cohabited, cohabiting, cohabits** To live together in a sexual relationship, especially when not legally married. —**co·hab′i·ta′tion** *n.*

cohere (kō-hîr′) *intr.v.* **cohered, cohering, coheres 1.** To stick together in a mass, as dough or wet clay does. **2.** To be logically connected: *The plot elements of that movie just don't cohere.*

coherence (kō-hîr′əns *or* kō-hĕr′əns) *n.* The quality or state of being coherent. —**co·her′en·cy** (kō-hîr′ən-sē *or* kō-hĕr′ən-sē) *n.*

coherent (kō-hîr′ənt *or* kō-hĕr′ənt) *adj.* **1.** Sticking together: *A snowball is a coherent mass of soft wet snow.* **2.** Logically connected; easy to understand: *a coherent argument.* **3.** Composed of waves that oscillate together and travel in the same direction: *the coherent red light of a laser.* —**co·her′ent·ly** *adv.*

cohesion (kō-hē′zhən) *n.* **1.** The attraction between molecules of the same kind: *The cohesion of molecules of H_2O produces drops of water.* **2.** The condition of cohering; a tendency to stick together; unity: *The cohesion of so many different groups is the result of common beliefs.*

cohesive (kō-hē′sĭv) *adj.* **1.** Tending to cohere; sticking together: *the cohesive nature of water molecules.* **2.** Producing cohesion: *the cohesive force of glue.* —**co·he′sive·ly** *adv.* —**co·he′sive·ness** *n.*

cohort (kō′hôrt′) *n.* **1.** A companion or associate: *My cohorts on the newspaper staff agreed to publish the article.* **2.** A group or band: *A cohort of protesters assembled in front of city hall.* **3.** One of the divisions of a legion in the army of the ancient Roman empire.

coif (koif) *n.* **1.** A tight-fitting cap worn under a veil, as by nuns. **2.** A skullcap, such as one worn under a knight's helmet or an English lawyer's wig. **3.** (*also* kwäf) A coiffure. ❖ *tr.v.* **coifed, coifing, coifs** (*also* kwäf) To arrange or dress (the hair): *hair coifed in an elaborate style.*

coiffure (kwä-fyŏŏr′) *n.* A way of arranging the hair; a hairstyle.

coil (koil) *n.* **1.** A series of connected spirals or gathered loops: *a coil of rope.* **2.** A spiral or loop in such a series. **3.** An electrical device consisting of a number of turns of insulated wire, used as an electromagnet or to store energy in the form of a magnetic field. **4.** A winding pipe or series of pipes through which a fluid is circulated for heating or cooling, as in a radiator or refrigerator. ❖ *v.* **coiled, coiling, coils** —*tr.* To wind into a series of spirals

or loops: *The snake coiled itself around a branch.* —*intr.* **1.** To form spirals or loops: *The hose that I was using coiled and knotted.* **2.** To move in a spiral course: *The smoke coiled up into the sky.*

coin (koin) *n.* **1.** A piece of metal, usually flat and round, issued by a government for use as money. **2.** Pieces of metal money considered as a group: *Only the government can issue coin.* ❖ *tr.v.* **coined, coining, coins 1.** To make (coins) from metal; mint: *The government coins dimes and quarters.* **2.** To make coins from (metal): *coin copper into pennies.* **3.** To invent (a word or phrase): *The computer industry has had to coin many new terms.*

coinage (koi′nĭj) *n.* **1.** The process of making coins: *the coinage of silver.* **2.** Coins considered as a group. **3a.** A new word or phrase. **b.** The invention of new words: *words of recent coinage.*

coincide (kō′ĭn-sīd′) *intr.v.* **coincided, coinciding, coincides 1.** To occur at the same time or during the same period of time: *The date of your party coincides with my birthday.* **2.** To agree; be identical: *Our opinions of the movie coincided.* **3.** To be in the same position or occupy the same space: *The park coincides with the site of an old settlement.*

coincidence (kō-ĭn′sĭ-dəns) *n.* **1.** A combination of events or circumstances that is accidental but seems to have been planned or arranged: *By a strange coincidence, John Adams and Thomas Jefferson both died on the 50th anniversary of the signing of the Declaration of Independence.* **2.** The state or fact of coinciding: *A curious coincidence of events brought the two nations together in agreement.*

coincident (kō-ĭn′sĭ-dənt) *adj.* **1.** Happening at the same time: *coincident elections in three different countries.* **2.** Very similar; agreeing: *coincident opinions.* **3.** Matching point for point; coinciding: *coincident circles.* —**co·in′ci·dent·ly** *adv.*

coincidental (kō-ĭn′sĭ-dĕn′tl) *adj.* Occurring as or resulting from coincidence: *a coincidental meeting of old friends.* —**co·in′ci·den·tal·ly, co·in′ci·dent′ly** *adv.*

coitus (kō′ĭ-təs *or* kō-ē′təs) *n.* Sexual union between a female and a male in which the penis enters the vagina.

coke (kōk) *n.* The solid material, chiefly carbon, that remains after the coal gas and coal tar have been removed from bituminous coal by heat. It is used as a fuel and in making steel.

col. An abbreviation of column.

Col. also **COL** An abbreviation of colonel.

col– Variant of **com–**.

cola[1] (kō′lə) *n.* A carbonated drink made with an extract from cola nuts or similar flavorings.

cola[2] also **kola** (kō′lə) *n.* Any of several tropical African evergreen trees having reddish fragrant nutlike seeds that are chewed as a stimulant and that yield an extract used in beverages and medicines.

colander (kŏl′ən-dər *or* kŭl′ən-dər) *n.* A bowl-shaped kitchen utensil with holes in the bottom, used for rinsing and draining off liquids from foods.

cold (kōld) *adj.* **colder, coldest 1a.** Having a low temperature: *cold water; a cold day.* **b.** Having a temperature lower than normal or desirable: *cold hands and feet; cold oatmeal.* **2.** Feeling no warmth; chilled: *I am cold without a jacket.* **3a.** Not friendly; aloof: *a cold and businesslike manner.* **b.** Showing no enthusiasm or interest: *a cold audience.* **4.** Having lost freshness; faint; weak: *The bear's trail was cold.* **5.** Characterized by repeated failure, as in a sport: *He has been cold shooting from the three-point*

line. ❖ *adv.* **1.** Completely; thoroughly; absolutely: *The player was stopped cold on the 40-yard line.* **2.** Without preparation or prior notice: *She took the test cold.* ❖ *n.* **1.** Relative lack of warmth: *Cold slows down chemical reactions.* **2.** The feeling resulting from lack of warmth; chill. **3.** Cold weather: *We were out in the cold all day.* **4.** A viral infection that causes a runny or stuffy nose, coughing, sneezing, and fever. ◆ **catch cold** or **take cold** To become sick with a cold. **out in the cold** Lacking benefits given to others; neglected: *Because she had just been hired, she was left out in the cold when raises were given.* —**cold′ly** *adv.* —**cold′ness** *n.*
◆ SYNONYMS **cold, chilly, frigid, frosty, icy** *adj.*

cold-blooded (kōld′blŭd′ĭd) *adj.* **1.** Having a body temperature that is maintained by external rather than internal sources of heat. Most fishes, amphibians, and reptiles are cold-blooded. **2a.** Having no feeling or emotion; cruel. **b.** Done without feeling or emotion: *a cold-blooded dismissal of an employee.* —**cold′-blood′ed·ly** *adv.* —**cold′-blood′ed·ness** *n.*

cold call *n.* A telephone call or visit made to someone who is not known or not expecting contact, often in order to sell something. —**cold-call, cold call** *v.*

cold cream *n.* A creamy cosmetic for cleansing and softening the skin.

cold cuts *pl.n.* Slices of cold cooked or cured meat.

cold feet *pl.n. Slang* The condition of being fearful or timid, resulting in the inability to complete a course of action: *He got cold feet before the talent show and refused to go onto the stage.*

cold front *n.* The forward edge of a mass of cold air in the atmosphere that replaces a mass of warm air, often accompanied by heavy showers.

cold-hearted (kōld′här′tĭd) *adj.* Lacking sympathy or feeling; callous: *made the cold-hearted decision to evict the tenants.* —**cold′-heart′ed·ly** *adv.* —**cold′-heart′ed·ness** *n.*

cold shoulder *n. Informal* Deliberate coldness or disregard; a snub: *He gave me the cold shoulder after our quarrel.*

cold sore *n.* A small sore on the lips that often accompanies a fever or cold; a fever blister.

cold storage *n.* The storage of food, furs, or other perishable things in a refrigerated place.

cold sweat *n.* Perspiration and cold moist skin resulting from pain, shock, or fear: *broke out into a cold sweat upon hearing the strange cry.*

cold turkey *Slang n.* Immediate, complete withdrawal from something on which one has become dependent, such as an addictive drug. ❖ *adv.* **1.** Immediately and without gradual reduction of use: *My roommate quit smoking cold turkey.* **2.** Frankly or directly; without mincing words: *spoke to her staff cold turkey about the likelihood of layoffs.*

cold war or **Cold War** *n.* A state of political tension and military rivalry that stops short of full-scale war, especially that which existed between the capitalist and Communist blocs from the end of World War II until the dissolution of the Soviet government in 1991.

coleslaw (kōl′slô′) *n.* A salad of shredded raw cabbage with mayonnaise or a vinaigrette; a slaw.

coleus (kō′lē-əs) *n.* Any of various plants grown for their colorful leaves, which are often marked with red, purple, or yellow.

colic (kŏl′ĭk) *n.* Severe pain or cramping in the abdomen. —**col′ick·y** *adj.*

coliseum also **colosseum** (kŏl′ĭ-sē′əm) *n.* A large stadium or hall for sports events, exhibitions, or other public entertainment.

colitis (kə-lī′tĭs) *n.* Inflammation of the colon.

coll. An abbreviation of: **1.** college. **2.** colloquial.

collaborate (kə-lăb′ə-rāt′) *intr.v.* **collaborated, collaborating, collaborates 1.** To work together on a project: *Scientists from several countries collaborated on the study.* **2.** To cooperate with an enemy that has invaded one's country: *Some Southerners collaborated with the Union during the Civil War.* —**col·lab′o·ra′tion** *n.* —**col·lab′o·ra′tor** *n.*

collage (kə-läzh′) *n.* A work of art made by pasting materials or objects, such as pieces of cloth, metal, colored paper, string, and pictures, onto a surface.

collagen (kŏl′ə-jən) *n.* The tough fibrous protein found in bone, cartilage, and connective tissue.

collapse (kə-lăps′) *v.* **collapsed, collapsing, collapses** —*intr.* **1.** To fall down or inward suddenly; cave in: *Part of the roof collapsed after the fire.* **2.** To break down or fail suddenly and completely: *collapse from overwork and fatigue; negotiations collapsing in disagreement.* **3.** To fold together compactly: *This folding chair collapses very easily.* —*tr.* To cause to collapse: *The weight of the books collapsed the flimsy shelf.* ❖ *n.* **1.** The act or an example of collapsing: *the collapse of the decrepit building; the collapse of a business deal.* **2.** A sudden and complete loss of strength or stamina; a breakdown: *suffered a collapse and was rushed to the hospital.*

collapsible (kə-lăp′sə-bəl) *adj.* Capable of being collapsed or folded compactly: *a collapsible tent.*

collar (kŏl′ər) *n.* **1.** The part of a shirt, coat, or dress that encircles the neck. **2.** A separate band for the neck, as one of lace, linen, or jewels. **3.** A leather, metal, or plastic band put around the neck of an animal, such as a dog. **4.** The cushioned part of a harness that presses against the shoulders of a draft animal, such as a horse. **5.** A band or marking, as around the neck of an animal, resembling a collar: *The buzzard has a collar of white feathers.* **6.** A device shaped like a ring and used to guide or secure a machine part. ❖ *tr.v.* **collared, collaring, collars 1.** To put a collar on: *collar a sheep to attach a bell.* **2.** *Slang* To seize, capture, or arrest: *The police collared the thief.*

collarbone (kŏl′ər-bōn′) *n.* A bone that connects the breastbone and the shoulder blade; the clavicle.

collard (kŏl′ərd) *n.* **1.** A plant having large, smooth, spreading leaves. **2. collards** The leaves of this plant, eaten as a vegetable.

collate (kō′lāt′ or kŏl′āt′) *tr.v.* **collated, collating, collates 1.** To examine and compare carefully (copies of texts or books, for example) in order to discover differences between them: *The scholar collated the early copies of the manuscript to determine which was the oldest.* **2.** To arrange in proper sequence: *a photocopier that collates pages as it prints them.*

collateral (kə-lăt′ər-əl) *adj.* **1.** Additional; supporting: *Further experiments provided collateral evidence for the theory.* **2.** Of a secondary nature, especially occurring as an unintended consequence: *The missile destroyed its target but caused collateral damage to nearby buildings.* **3.** Guaranteed by something that has been pledged as security: *a collateral loan.* **4.** Situated or running side by side; parallel: *the collateral lines of a parallelogram.* ❖ *n.*

Property, such as jewelry or bonds, pledged as security for a loan. —**col·lat′er·al·ly** *adv.*

collation (kə-lā′shən) *n.* **1.** The act or process of collating. **2.** A light meal.

colleague (kŏl′ēg) *n.* A fellow member of a profession, staff, or organization; an associate.

collect (kə-lĕkt′) *v.* **collected, collecting, collects** —*tr.* **1.** To bring together in a group; gather; assemble: *We collected firewood.* See Synonyms at **gather. 2.** To pick up and take away: *collect garbage.* **3.** To accumulate as a hobby or for study: *collect stamps; collect specimens of rare beetles.* **4.** To obtain payment of: *We collected a dollar from each student for the gift.* **5.** To recover control of; pull together: *They finally collected themselves after the accident.* —*intr.* **1.** To come together; congregate: *A group of bystanders collected on the sidewalk.* **2.** To build up; accumulate: *A pile of snow collected by the door.* **3.** To take in payments or donations: *volunteers collecting for cancer research.* ❖ *adv. & adj.* With payment to be made by the receiver: *call home collect; a collect call.* —**col·lect′a·ble, col·lect′i·ble** *adj.*

collected (kə-lĕk′tĭd) *adj.* **1.** In full control of oneself; composed; calm: *He did his best to remain cool and collected when speaking to a crowd.* **2.** Gathered together: *the collected works of Shakespeare.* —**col·lect′ed·ly** *adv.* —**col·lect′ed·ness** *n.*

collection (kə-lĕk′shən) *n.* **1.** The act or process of collecting: *Trash collection is on Tuesday.* **2.** A group of things brought or kept together for study or use or as a hobby: *a collection of folk songs; a coin collection.* **3.** An accumulation; a deposit: *the collection of dust on the piano.* **4a.** The act of seeking and obtaining money, as during a church service. **b.** The amount of money so obtained.

collective (kə-lĕk′tĭv) *adj.* **1.** Assembled into or viewed as a whole: *the collective accomplishments of the past.* **2.** Relating to a number of people or nations acting as a group: *the collective opinion of the committee; our collective security.* **3.** Owned, managed, or operated by a group: *collective farming in China.* ❖ *n.* A business or undertaking owned and controlled by its workers, usually under the supervision of a government. —**col·lec′tive·ly** *adv.*

collective bargaining *n.* Negotiation between the representatives of organized workers and their employer or employers to determine wages and working conditions.

collective farm *n.* A farm or a group of farms managed and worked by a group of laborers, usually under the supervision of a communist government.

collective noun *n.* A noun that refers to a collection of people or things regarded as a unit.

USAGE When referring to a collection as a whole, a **collective noun** takes a singular verb: *The family was united on this question.* A collective noun takes a plural verb when it refers to the members of the group as individuals, as in *My family are all good skiers.* Among the common collective nouns are *clergy, committee, company, enemy, family, flock, group, public,* and *team.*

---

collectivism (kə-lĕk′tə-vĭz′əm) *n.* The theory or system in which the means of producing and distributing goods are owned and managed by the people as a group, especially under the control of a government. —**col·lec′tiv·ist** *adj. & n.*

collectivize (kə-lĕk′tə-vīz′) *tr.v.* **collectivized, collectivizing, collectivizes** To organize (an economy, industry, or business) on the basis of collectivism. —**col·lec′tiv·i·za′tion** (kə-lĕk′tə-vĭ-zā′shən) *n.*

collector (kə-lĕk′tər) *n.* **1.** A person or thing that collects: *a garbage collector; a solar collector.* **2.** A person assigned to collect money: *a tax collector.* **3.** A person who assembles a collection: *a collector of autographs.*

colleen (kŏ-lēn′ *or* kŏl′ēn′) *n.* An Irish girl.

college (kŏl′ĭj) *n.* **1.** A school of higher learning, entered after high school, that grants a bachelor's degree. **2.** An undergraduate division within a university. **3.** A school for special study, often connected with a university: *a teachers' college.* **4.** A body of people having a common purpose or shared duties: *a college of surgeons.*

collegial (kə-lē′jə-əl) *adj.* **1.** Full of or conducive to good will among colleagues; friendly and respectful: *an office with a collegial atmosphere.* **2.** Characterized by or having power and authority vested equally among colleagues. —**col·le′gi·al·ly** *adv.*

collegian (kə-lē′jən *or* kə-lē′jē-ən) *n.* A college student.

collegiate (kə-lē′jĭt *or* kə-lē′jē-ĭt) *adj.* Relating to or typical of a college or college students: *collegiate activities.*

collide (kə-līd′) *intr.v.* **collided, colliding, collides 1.** To strike or bump together with violent direct impact: *The car was badly damaged when it collided with the tree.* **2.** To meet in opposition or conflict; clash: *The interests of the two nations collided over fishing rights in coastal waters.*

collie (kŏl′ē) *n.* A medium-sized to large dog of a breed originally developed in Scotland to herd sheep, having long white and tan hair and a narrow snout.

collier (kŏl′yər) *n.* **1.** A coal miner. **2.** A ship for carrying coal.

collinear (kə-lĭn′ē-ər) *adj.* **1.** Lying on the same straight line, as a set of points. **2.** Sharing a common line, as two intersecting planes.

collision (kə-lĭzh′ən) *n.* The act or process of colliding; a crash or conflict.

colloid (kŏl′oid′) *n.* A mixture in which very small particles of one substance are distributed evenly throughout another substance. Paints, milk, and fog are colloids. ❖ *adj.* Colloidal.

colloidal (kə-loid′l) *adj.* Relating to or containing a colloid: *Foam rubber is a colloidal suspension of air in a rubber mixture.*

colloquial (kə-lō′kwē-əl) *adj.* Characteristic of or suitable to spoken language or to writing that resembles speech; informal. —**col·lo′qui·al·ly** *adv.* —**col·lo′qui·al·ness** *n.*

colloquialism (kə-lō′kwē-ə-lĭz′əm) *n.* **1.** Colloquial style or quality: *That writer uses colloquialism to make her characters sound more natural.* **2.** A colloquial expression: *"Up a tree" is a colloquialism meaning "in a difficult situation."*

colloquium (kə-lō′kwē-əm) *n., pl.* **colloquiums** or **colloquia** (kə-lō′kwē-ə) **1.** An informal meeting for the exchange of views. **2.** An academic seminar on a broad field of study, usually led by a different lecturer at each meeting.

colloquy (kŏl′ə-kwē) *n., pl.* **colloquies** A conversation or conference, especially a formal one.

collude (kə-lōōd′) *intr.v.* **colluded, colluding, colludes** To act together, often in secret, to achieve an illegal or improper purpose. —**col·lud′er** *n.*

collusion (kə-lōō′zhən) *n.* The act of colluding. —**col·lu′sive** (kə-lōō′sĭv) *adj.*

cologne (kə-lōn′) *n.* A scented liquid made of alcohol and fragrant oils, used as light perfume.

colon¹ (kō′lən) *n.* **1.** A punctuation mark (:) used after a word introducing a quotation, explanation, example, or series. **2.** The sign (:) used between numbers or groups of numbers in expressions of time (2:30 AM, read as "two thirty AM") and ratios (1:2, read as "one to two").

colon² (kō′lən) *n.* The section of the large intestine, extending from the cecum to the rectum, in which solid waste is accumulated and prepared for excretion.

WORD HISTORY Colon¹ comes from Latin *cōlon,* referring to part of a verse, which comes from Greek *kōlon,* meaning "limb, metrical unit." **Colon²** comes from Middle English *colon,* which comes from Latin *colon,* which comes from Greek *kolon,* all meaning "large intestine."

---

colonel (kûr′nəl) *n.* An officer in the US Army, Air Force, or Marine Corps ranking below a brigadier general and above a lieutenant colonel.

colonial (kə-lō′nē-əl) *adj.* **1.** Relating to, forming, or possessing a colony or colonies: *France and England were colonial powers in Africa and Asia. Most corals are colonial animals.* **2.** often **Colonial** Relating to the 13 British colonies that became the United States of America: *the Colonial period of British rule before the Revolutionary War.* **3.** often **Colonial** Relating to the style of architecture and furniture often found in the British colonies in America. ❖ *n.* A person who lives in a colony: *French colonials in Vietnam.* —**co·lo′ni·al·ly** *adv.*

colonialism (kə-lō′nē-ə-lĭz′əm) *n.* A governmental policy of acquiring or maintaining foreign territory as colonies.

colonist (kŏl′ə-nĭst) *n.* **1.** An original settler or founder of a colony. **2.** A person who lives in a colony.

colonize (kŏl′ə-nīz′) *tr.v.* **colonized, colonizing, colonizes** **1.** To establish or settle a colony in: *Norwegian Vikings originally colonized Iceland.* **2.** To spread or proliferate in: *the birds that colonized Madagascar; beetles that colonize dead trees.* —**col′o·ni·za′tion** (kŏl′ə-nĭ-zā′shən) *n.* —**col′o·niz′er** *n.*

colonnade (kŏl′ə-nād′) *n.* A series of columns placed at regular intervals to support a roof or other structure of a building.

colony (kŏl′ə-nē) *n., pl.* **colonies 1.** A group of people who settle in a distant land but remain subject to their native country: *The English Pilgrims founded a colony at Plymouth.* **2.** A territory ruled by a distant power: *The government built railroads in each of its colonies.* **3. Colonies** The Thirteen Colonies. **4.** A group of people of the same nationality, religion, or interests, living together in one area: *the American colony in Paris; an artists' colony.* **5.** A group of the same kind of organisms living or growing together: *a colony of ants; a colony of bacteria.*

color (kŭl′ər) *n.* **1.** The property by which objects reflect, transmit, or emit particular wavelengths of light. Colors can be described in terms of their hue, their saturation, and their lightness or brightness. **2.** The distinct sensation produced when light of a particular wavelength or combination of wavelengths strikes the retina of the eye. **3.** A color other than black, white, or gray. **4.** A dye, pigment, paint, or other coloring substance. **5.** The general appearance of the skin, especially an appearance indicating good health: *The patient regained her color after a few days' rest.* **6a.** Skin pigmentation considered as a racial characteristic: *people of all colors; laws against dis-*

crimination based on color. **b.** Racial identity other than white: *Blacks, Asians, and other people of color.* **7. colors a.** A flag or banner, as of a country or military unit: *At the beginning of the ceremony, they raised the colors.* **b.** A distinguishing symbol, badge, ribbon, color, or mark of something: *a tie with the college's colors on it.* **8.** Vivid and interesting detail, as of a scene or of an event in writing: *The author's description of the political campaign had a great deal of color.* **9.** Traits of personality or behavior that are appealing. ❖ *v.* **colored, coloring, colors** —*tr.* **1.** To give color to or change the color of: *color a picture with crayons.* **2.** To give a distinctive character or quality to: *A sense of humor colored the author's writing.* **3.** To influence, especially by distortion or misrepresentation: *Anger colored the witness's account of the accident.* —*intr.* **1.** To take on or change color. **2.** To blush. —**col′or·er** *n.*

coloration (kŭl′ə-rā′shən) *n.* Arrangement of colors: *Protective coloration helps some animals to hide from their enemies.*

coloratura (kŭl′ər-ə-toŏr′ə) *n. Music* **1.** The ornamentation of music written for the voice with florid passages, especially trills and runs. **2.** Vocal music characterized by such ornamentation. **3.** A singer, especially a soprano, specializing in such ornamentation.

colorblind or **color-blind** (kŭl′ər-blīnd′) *adj.* Partly or totally unable to distinguish certain colors, such as red and green. —**col′or·blind′ness** *n.*

color-code (kŭl′ər-kōd′) *tr.v.* **color-coded, color-coding, color-codes** To color according to a code for easy identification: *color-code the sections of a telephone directory.*

colorectal (kō′lə-rĕk′təl) *adj.* Relating to or involving the colon and the rectum: *colorectal cancer.*

colored (kŭl′ərd) *adj.* **1.** Having color. **2.** often **Colored** *Offensive* Relating to or belonging to a racial or ethnic group having dark skin or descended from people with dark skin. **3.** Distorted by prejudice or biased by self-interest: *The drivers each gave a very colored version of the accident.*

colorfast (kŭl′ər-făst′) *adj.* Having color that will not run or fade with washing or wear: *a colorfast fabric.*

colorful (kŭl′ər-fəl) *adj.* **1.** Full of color or colors: *Many butterflies have colorful wings.* **2.** Rich in variety; vivid; distinctive: *a colorful description of life in a medieval castle.* —**col′or·ful·ly** *adv.* —**col′or·ful·ness** *n.*

coloring (kŭl′ər-ĭng) *n.* **1.** The manner or process of applying color: *The government regulates the artificial coloring of packaged foods.* **2.** A substance used to color something: *I'm thinking of using a hair coloring.* **3.** Appearance with regard to color: *Some animals are protected by their coloring.*

colorize (kŭl′ə-rīz′) *tr.v.* **colorized, colorizing, colorizes** To color (a black and white film) by means of a computer process. —**col′or·i·za′tion** (kŭl′ər-ĭ-zā′shən) *n.*

colorless (kŭl′ər-lĭs) *adj.* **1.** Lacking color: *Air is colorless.* **2.** Weak in color; pallid: *the colorless face of the sick boy.* **3.** Lacking in variety, interest, or distinction; dull: *a colorless account of the event.* —**col′or·less·ly** *adv.* —**col′or·less·ness** *n.*

colossal (kə-lŏs′əl) *adj.* Very great in size, extent, or degree; enormous; gigantic: *a city full of colossal buildings; a daring venture requiring colossal self-confidence.* —**co·los′sal·ly** *adv.*

colosseum (kŏl′ĭ-sē′əm) *n.* Variant of **coliseum.**

Colossians (kə-lŏsh′ənz) *pl.n. (used with a singular verb)* A book of the New Testament, traditionally attributed to the Apostle Paul and consisting of a letter to fellow Christians.

colossus (kə-lŏs′əs) *n.*, *pl.* **colossi** (kə-lŏs′ī′) or **colossuses** **1.** A huge statue. **2.** Something of enormous size or importance: *a colossus among software companies.*

colostomy (kə-lŏs′tə-mē) *n.*, *pl.* **colostomies 1.** Surgical construction of an artificial excretory opening from the colon. **2.** The opening created by such a surgical procedure.

colostrum (kə-lŏs′trəm) *n.* Thin yellowish milk that is secreted by the mammary glands for several days after birth and is rich in antibodies and minerals. —**co·los′-tral** (kə-lŏs′trəl) *adj.*

colour (kŭl′ər) *n. & v. Chiefly British* Variant of **color.**

colt (kōlt) *n.* A young male horse.

coltish (kōl′tĭsh) *adj.* **1.** Relating to a colt: *coltish behavior.* **2.** Resembling a colt; lively; playful: *the coltish antics of the children at the playground.*

columbine (kŏl′əm-bīn′) *n.* Any of various garden plants that have colorful flowers with five narrow projecting parts.

Columbus Day *n.* October 12, celebrated officially on the second Monday in October in honor of the Italian explorer Christopher Columbus (1451–1506).

column (kŏl′əm) *n.* **1.** A pillar, usually shaped like a cylinder, used in a building as a support or as a decoration. **2.** Something that resembles a pillar in shape or use: *a column of mercury in a thermometer.* **3.** One of two or more vertical sections of a page, lying side by side but separated from each other, in which lines of print are arranged: *Newspapers are often printed in six columns across the page.* **4.** A feature article that appears regularly in a newspaper or magazine: *a sports column; an advice column.* **5.** A formation, as of soldiers or trucks, in which members or rows follow one behind the other.

columnar (kə-lŭm′nər) *adj.* Having the shape of a column: *the columnar trunks of the redwoods.*

columnist (kŏl′əm-nĭst or kŏl′ə-mĭst) *n.* A person who writes a column for a newspaper or magazine.

Com. An abbreviation of: **1.** commissioner. **2.** commonwealth.

com– or **col–** or **con–** or **cor–** A prefix that means together or with: *commingle.*

WORD BUILDING The basic meaning of the prefix **com–** is "together, with." It comes from the Latin prefix *com–.* Before the consonants *l* and *r,* Latin *com–* became *col–* and *cor–,* respectively, as we see in our words *collaborate* and *correspond.* Before all other consonants except *p, b,* or *m, com–* became *con–,* as in *confirm, constitution,* and *contribute.* For more information, see Note at **co–.**

---

coma[1] (kō′mə) *n., pl.* **comas** A state of deep unconsciousness resulting from disease, injury, or poisoning.

coma[2] (kō′mə) *n., pl.* **comae** (kō′mē) A luminous gaseous cloud around the nucleus of a comet.

WORD HISTORY Coma[1] comes from Greek *kōma,* meaning "deep sleep." **Coma**[2] comes from Greek *komē,* meaning "hair."

Comanche (kə-măn′chē) *n., pl.* **Comanche** or **Comanches 1.** A member of a Native American people formerly of the south-central United States and now living in Oklahoma. **2.** The Uto-Aztecan language of the Comanche. —**Co·man′che** *adj.*

comatose (kō′mə-tōs′) *adj.* **1.** Being in a coma; deeply unconscious. **2.** Asleep, inactive, or not responding: *My friends sat comatose in front of the TV.*

comb (kōm) *n.* **1.** A thin toothed strip used to smooth, arrange, or fasten the hair. **2.** Something resembling a comb in shape or use, as a card for arranging and cleaning wool. **3.** The brightly colored ridge of flesh on the top of the head of a rooster, hen, or certain other birds. **4.** A honeycomb. ❖ *v.* **combed, combing, combs** —*tr.* **1.** To move a comb through (the hair) so as to arrange or groom. **2.** To search thoroughly: *combed many books for information.* —*intr.* To make a thorough search: *combed through the documents.*

combat (kəm-băt′ or kŏm′băt′) *tr.v.* **combated, combating, combats** or **combatted, combatting, combats 1.** To oppose in battle; fight against. **2.** To act or work in order to eliminate, curtail, or stop: *new drugs that combat infection.* See Synonyms at **oppose.** ❖ *n.* (kŏm′băt′) Fighting, especially with weapons: *naval combat.*

combatant (kəm-băt′nt or kŏm′bə-tnt) *n.* A person engaged in fighting or combat.

combat boot *n.* A boot that laces up the front and has a thick rubber outer sole, worn especially by soldiers.

combative (kəm-băt′ĭv) *adj.* Ready or disposed to fight; belligerent: *the lawyer's combative disposition.* —**com·bat′ive·ness** *n.*

comber (kō′mər) *n.* **1.** A person or thing that combs something, such as wool. **2.** A long wave that has reached its peak or broken into foam; a breaker.

combination (kŏm′bə-nā′shən) *n.* **1.** The act of combining or the condition of being combined: *The combination of fresh air and sunshine produced a beautiful day.* **2.** Something that results from combining two or more things: *An alloy is a combination of metals.* **3.** The series of numbers or letters used to open a combination lock. **4.** In mathematics, any of the possible arrangements of numbers or letters in a set.

combination lock *n.* A lock that can be opened only by turning its dial through a particular sequence of numbers or letters.

combine (kəm-bīn′) *v.* **combined, combining, combines** —*tr.* **1.** To bring together; make united; join: *a movie that combines an interesting story and a moral.* See Synonyms at **join. 2.** To join (two or more substances) to make a single substance; blend; mix: *combine water, gravel, and cement to make concrete.* —*intr.* **1.** To become united; come together: *Friends combined to help the family after the fire.* **2.** To form a compound: *Two atoms of hydrogen combine with one of oxygen to form water.* ❖ *n.* (kŏm′bīn′) **1.** A power-operated machine that cuts, threshes, and cleans grain. **2.** A group of people or companies acting together in a business transaction.

combining form (kəm-bī′nĭng) *n.* A form of a word that combines with other word forms to create new words, as *electro–* (from *electric*) in *electromagnet.*

combo (kŏm′bō) *n., pl.* **combos 1.** A small group of musicians: *a jazz combo.* **2.** *Informal* A combination.

combust (kəm-bŭst′) *intr.v.* **combusted, combusting, combusts** To catch fire or burn: *The oily rags suddenly combusted.*

combustible (kəm-bŭs′tə-bəl) *adj.* Capable of catching fire and burning. ❖ *n.* A substance that catches fire and burns quickly. —**com·bus′ti·bil′i·ty** *n.* —**com·bus′ti·bly** *adv.*

combustion (kəm-bŭs′chən) *n.* **1.** The process of burning: *the combustion of oil in the furnace.* **2.** A chemical reaction, especially a rapid combination with oxygen, accompanied by heat and light.

Comdr. An abbreviation of commander.

Comdt. An abbreviation of commandant.

come (kŭm) *intr.v.* **came** (kām), **come, coming, comes** **1.** To advance toward the speaker or toward a specified place; approach: *Come over here.* **2.** To arrive at a particular result or end: *The rivals came to an agreement. Their arrangements finally came to nothing.* **3.** To move toward or arrive at a particular condition: *The new garden is coming along well.* **4.** To move or be brought to a particular position: *The bus came to a stop.* **5.** To extend; reach: *The snow came up to the window ledge.* **6a.** To exist at a particular point or place: *The date of birth comes after the name in this listing.* **b.** To rank; have priority: *Work comes first. A comes before B.* **7a.** To happen: *How did they come to be invited?* **b.** To happen as a result: *Difficulty often comes from stubbornness.* **8.** To occur in the mind: *Sounds of the city come back to me.* **9.** To issue forth: *The giggle came from the back of the class.* **10.** To arise; originate: *Oaks come from acorns.* **11.** To be a native or resident of a particular place: *Her family comes from Chicago.* **12.** To become: *The knot came loose.* **13.** To be available or obtainable: *Shoes come in many styles.* **14.** To prove or turn out to be: *The dream came true.* ◆ **come about 1.** To occur; take place; happen: *It came about that we could go.* **2.** In sailing, to change tack or direction. **come across** To meet or find by chance: *We came across some letters in the attic.* **come around 1.** To recover; revive: *He fainted but came around quickly.* **2.** To change one's opinion or position: *The coach came around after hearing the whole story.* **come back 1.** To remember; recall: *The author's name came back to me.* **2.** To return to past success after a period of misfortune: *The town came back after the flood.* **come by** To acquire; get: *How did you come by that chair?* **come down 1.** To lose wealth or position. **2.** To be handed down by tradition: *a custom that comes down from Colonial times.* **come down with** To become sick with (an illness): *came down with a cold.* **come in for** *Informal* To receive; get: *The reporter's work came in for criticism.* **come off** To happen; occur: *The celebration came off on schedule.* **come out 1.** To become known: *The whole story came out in the trial.* **2.** To be issued or brought out: *The author's new book just came out.* **3.** To declare oneself publicly: *The president has come out for the tax proposal.* **4.** To result; end up; turn out: *Everything came out fine.* **5.** To make a formal social debut. **come through** To do what is required or expected: *I asked for their help, and they came through.* **come to 1.** To regain consciousness. **2.** To amount to: *The bill came to $15.* **come up 1.** To show up; arise: *The question didn't come up at the meeting.* **2.** To rise: *The sun came up.* **come up against** To encounter or confront: *We came up against many problems.* **come upon** To discover or meet by accident. **come up with** *Informal* To propose; produce: *The committee came up with some interesting new ideas.* **how come?** *Informal* Why: *How come they left early?*

comeback (kŭm′băk′) *n.* **1.** A return to prosperity, popularity, or high rank: *The struggling tennis star made a comeback by winning the latest tournament.* **2.** A reply, especially a quick witty one; a retort.

comedian (kə-mē′dē-ən) *n.* **1.** A professional entertainer who tells jokes or does other things intended to make audiences laugh. **2.** A person who amuses or tries to be amusing; a clown: *the office comedian.* **3.** An actor in comedy.

comedienne (kə-mē′dē-ĕn′) *n.* A woman professional entertainer who tells jokes or does other things intended to make audiences laugh.

comedown (kŭm′doun′) *n.* A decline or drop in status or position: *Losing so badly was quite a comedown for the former champion.*

comedy (kŏm′ĭ-dē) *n., pl.* **comedies 1.** A play, movie, operetta, or other work that has a funny story with humorous characters and usually a happy ending. **2.** The branch of drama made up of such plays or other dramatic works: *The actor found comedy more difficult than tragedy.* **3.** Popular entertainment consisting of jokes, satire, and other things meant to be humorous. **4.** A funny incident. —**co·me′dic** (kə-mē′dĭk) *adj.*

comely (kŭm′lē) *adj.* **comelier, comeliest** Having a pleasing appearance; attractive: *a comely face.* —**come′li·ness** *n.*

come-on (kŭm′ŏn′) *n.* Something offered to allure or attract; an inducement: *The come-on for renting cars was a free tank of gas.*

comer (kŭm′ər) *n.* **1.** A person or thing that arrives or comes: *All comers were welcome at the free soccer clinic.* **2.** A person or thing that shows promise of reaching success: *That young pitcher is a real comer.*

comestible (kə-mĕs′tə-bəl) *adj.* Fit to be eaten; edible. ❖ *n.* Something that can be eaten as food: *meat, cheese, and other comestibles.*

comet (kŏm′ĭt) *n.* An object in the solar system consisting of a dense nucleus of frozen gases and dust, which develops a luminous halo and tail when near the sun. Comets travel around the sun in an immense elongated orbit.

comeuppance (kŭm′ŭp′əns) *n.* Punishment or retribution that one deserves: *The bully finally got his comeuppance.*

comfort (kŭm′fərt) *tr.v.* **comforted, comforting, comforts** **1.** To soothe in time of grief or fear; console: *comfort a lost child.* **2.** To help relieve the pain and suffering of: *A nurse comforted the patient by putting a pillow behind her back.* ❖ *n.* **1.** A condition of ease or well-being: *Pillows are available for the comfort of the passengers.* **2.** Relief in time of pain, grief, or fear: *The frightened children ran to their mother for comfort.* **3.** A person or thing that provides relief, ease, or well-being: *His friends were a comfort to him during his long illness.* **4.** The capacity or ability to give ease or a sense of well-being: *Curtains and soft chairs added to the comfort of the room.*

comfortable (kŭm′fər-tə-bəl or kŭmf′tə-bəl or kŭmf′-tər-bəl) *adj.* **1.** Providing physical comfort: *a comfortable chair.* **2.** Free from worry or anxiety; at ease: *I felt very comfortable on stage.* **3.** Enough to meet a need; sufficient: *a comfortable income for a small family.* —**com′fort·a·ble·ness** *n.* —**com′fort·a·bly** *adv.*

comforter (kŭm′fər-tər) *n.* **1.** A person or thing that comforts: *a comforter of the sick.* **2.** A thick warm quilt used as a bed cover.

comfort food *n.* Food that is simply prepared and associated with a sense of home or contentment.

comfy (kŭm′fē) *adj.* **comfier, comfiest** *Informal* Comfortable.

comic (kŏm′ĭk) *adj.* **1.** Relating to comedy: *comic writing.* **2.** Humorous; amusing: *a comic situation.* ❖ *n.* **1.** A person who is funny or amusing, especially a comedian:

a nightclub where comics tell jokes before an audience. **2. comics** *Informal* Comic strips.

comical (kŏm′ĭ-kəl) *adj.* Causing amusement or laughter; funny: *The dog looked comical wearing a bow tie.* —**com′- i·cal·ly** *adv.* —**com′i·cal·ness** *n.*

comic book *n.* A book of comic strips or cartoons, usually telling a story.

comic strip *n.* A series of cartoons that tells a joke or a story, usually printed in a newspaper.

coming (kŭm′ĭng) *adj.* **1.** Approaching; next: *the coming storm.* **2.** Showing promise of fame or success: *a young and coming political leader.* ❖ *n.* Arrival: *the coming of spring.*

coming-out (kŭm′ĭng-out′) also **coming out** *n.* **1.** A social debut. **2.** A revelation or acknowledgment that one is a gay man, a lesbian, or a bisexual.

comma (kŏm′ə) *n.* A punctuation mark (,) used to indicate a separation of grammatical elements within a sentence or to separate other elements such as surnames and first names in a directory (for example, "Sanchez, Will") or groupings of digits in large numbers (for example, 12,350,000).

comma fault *n.* A comma splice.

command (kə-mănd′) *v.* **commanded, commanding, commands** —*tr.* **1.** To direct with authority; give orders to: *The control tower commanded the pilot to land elsewhere.* **2.** To have control or authority over; rule: *The general commands thousands of troops.* **3.** To receive as something that has been earned: *His bravery commands respect.* **4.** To occupy a dominant or strategic position over: *The fort commands the approach to the harbor.* —*intr.* **1.** To give orders: *The coach commanded loudly from the sideline.* **2.** To exercise authority as a commander; be in control: *The general commanded through a staff of junior officers.* ❖ *n.* **1.** An order or direction: *Dogs can be trained to follow commands.* **2.** The possession or exercise of authority to command: *The admiral was in command of the navy.* **3.** Ability to control or use; mastery: *She has a command of Arabic and French.* **4a.** The extent or range of a commander: *He has command over three battalions.* **b.** A military unit or area under the control of one officer. ❖ *adj.* **1.** Relating to or being a command: *a command decision.* **2.** Done in response to a command: *a command performance.*

commandant (kŏm′ən-dănt′ or kŏm′ən-dänt′) *n.* A commanding officer of a military organization.

commandeer (kŏm′ən-dîr′) *tr.v.* **commandeered, commandeering, commandeers** To seize (property) for public use, especially for military use: *The soldiers commandeered a heavy truck when their own vehicle broke down.*

commander (kə-măn′dər) *n.* **1.** A person who commands, especially a commanding military officer. **2.** An officer in the US Navy or Coast Guard ranking below a captain and above a lieutenant commander.

commander in chief *n., pl.* **commanders in chief 1.** The commander of all the armed forces of a nation: *The president is commander in chief of the armed forces of the United States.* **2.** The officer commanding a major armed force: *the commander in chief of Pacific forces.*

commanding (kə-măn′dĭng) *adj.* **1.** Having command; in charge: *The captain is the commanding member of a ship's crew.* **2.** Dominating, as by reason of position or size: *a commanding lead over an opponent.*

commanding officer *n.* A military officer in charge of a unit, post, camp, base, or station.

commandment (kə-mănd′mənt) *n.* **1. Commandment** One of the Ten Commandments in the Bible. **2.** A command; an order.

commando (kə-măn′dō) *n., pl.* **commandos** or **commandoes** A member of a small fighting force trained for making quick raids into enemy territory.

comma splice *n.* The improper use of a comma to join two independent clauses. For example, the sentence *We ran hard, we missed the bus anyway* has a comma splice that could be fixed by adding the conjunction *but* after the comma.

commemorate (kə-měm′ə-rāt′) *tr.v.* **commemorated, commemorating, commemorates 1.** To honor the memory of (someone or something), especially with a ceremony: *The crowd gathered in the park to commemorate the firefighters' sacrifice.* **2.** To be a memorial to, as a holiday, ceremony, or statue: *Independence Day commemorates the adoption of the Declaration of Independence.* —**com·mem′o·ra′tion** *n.*

commemorative (kə-měm′ər-ə-tĭv or kə-měm′ə-rā′tĭv) *adj.* Serving to commemorate: *a commemorative plaque; a commemorative service.*

commence (kə-měns′) *intr. & tr.v.* **commenced, commencing, commences** To begin; start: *The festivities commenced with the singing of the national anthem. Has the senate commenced the investigation?* See Synonyms at **begin.**

commencement (kə-měns′mənt) *n.* **1.** A beginning; a start: *The commencement of the Olympic Games is marked by a parade.* **2.** A graduation ceremony in which students receive their diplomas.

commend (kə-měnd′) *tr.v.* **commended, commending, commends 1.** To speak highly of; praise: *The professor commended me for my extensive vocabulary.* **2.** To recommend: *I commend the book without hesitation.* **3.** To put in the care of someone: *The sick patient was commended to the care of the doctor.*

commendable (kə-měn′də-bəl) *adj.* Praiseworthy: *a commendable performance of a difficult play.* —**com·mend′- a·bly** *adv.*

commendation (kŏm′ən-dā′shən) *n.* **1.** Praise: *a performance worthy of commendation.* **2.** An official award or citation: *a commendation from the mayor.* —**com·men′- da·to′ry** (kə-měn′də-tôr′ē) *adj.*

commensal (kə-měn′səl) *adj.* Relating to or characterized by commensalism. ❖ *n.* An organism living in a commensal relationship with another.

commensalism (kə-měn′sə-lĭz′əm) *n.* A relationship between two organisms of different species in which one benefits while the other is unaffected, as when an orchid uses a tree branch for support.

commensurable (kə-měn′sər-ə-bəl or kə-měn′shər-ə- bəl) *adj.* Properly proportioned; fitting; suitable: *The judge handed down a heavy sentence commensurable to the seriousness of the crime.* —**com·men′su·ra·bly** *adv.*

commensurate (kə-měn′sər-ĭt or kə-měn′shər-ĭt) *adj.* **1.** Of the same size, extent, or length of time as that of another: *Men and women should receive commensurate pay for the same job.* **2.** Corresponding in size or degree; proportionate: *I want a salary commensurate with my performance.* —**com·men′su·rate·ly** *adv.*

comment (kŏm′ĕnt) *n.* **1.** A written note or a remark that explains, interprets, or gives an opinion on something: *a critic's comment on a play; the newspaper's comments on the governor's speech.* **2.** Talk; gossip: *Their squabbling caused much comment among their friends.* ❖ *intr.v.* **com-**

mented, commenting, comments To make a comment; remark: *He commented on my new red coat.*

commentary (kŏm′ən-tĕr′ē) *n., pl.* **commentaries 1.** A series of explanations or interpretations: *a copy of the Bible that contained a commentary.* **2.** An ongoing series of spoken remarks, especially during a television or radio broadcast of an event: *A retired quarterback does the commentary on the games.* **3.** An illustrating comment: *The scandal is a sad commentary on the state of our city government.*

commentator (kŏm′ən-tā′tər) *n.* **1.** A person who makes commentaries: *Many social commentators criticize the state of our cities.* **2.** A writer or broadcaster who explains or gives opinions of events: *The commentators gave opposing views at the end of the newscast.*

commerce (kŏm′ərs) *n.* The buying and selling of goods, especially on a large scale; trade.

commercial (kə-mûr′shəl) *adj.* **1.** Relating to commerce: *a commercial loan from the bank.* **2.** Done primarily to make a profit: *The professor writes scholarly books, not commercial ones.* **3.** Sponsored by an advertiser or supported by advertising: *a commercial television station.* ❖ *n.* A paid advertisement on television or radio. —**com·mer′cial·ly** *adv.*

commercialism (kə-mûr′shə-lĭz′əm) *n.* The practices of commerce or business, especially those that give chief importance to the making of profit. —**com·mer′cial·is′tic** *adj.*

commercialize (kə-mûr′shə-līz′) *tr.v.* **commercialized, commercializing, commercializes 1.** To apply business methods to (something) in order to make a profit: *commercialize agriculture on a large scale.* **2.** To do, make, or exploit mainly for profit: *The town commercialized its beach by putting in a snack shop and video arcade.* —**com·mer′cial·i·za′tion** (kə-mûr′shə-lĭ-zā′shən) *n.*

commingle (kə-mĭng′gəl) *tr. & intr.v.* **commingled, commingling, commingles** To blend or mix together; combine: *a story that commingles comedy with tragedy; cities where people of many nationalities commingle.*

commiserate (kə-mĭz′ə-rāt′) *intr.v.* **commiserated, commiserating, commiserates** To feel or express sorrow or sympathy: *I commiserated with my friend over losing the competition.*

commiseration (kə-mĭz′ə-rā′shən) *n.* A feeling or expression of sorrow or sympathy for the misfortune of another.

commissar (kŏm′ĭ-sär′) *n.* The head of a Soviet commissariat.

commissariat (kŏm′ĭ-sâr′ē-ĭt) *n.* **1.** A department of an army in charge of providing food and other supplies for the troops. **2.** A department of the Soviet government before 1946.

commissary (kŏm′ĭ-sĕr′ē) *n., pl.* **commissaries 1.** A store maintained by a company or an army post for the sale of food and supplies to its employees or personnel. **2.** A lunchroom or cafeteria that serves the employees of a company or the personnel of an institution, such as a university. **3.** A person to whom a special duty is given by a superior; a deputy.

commission (kə-mĭsh′ən) *n.* **1.** The act of committing or doing something: *the commission of a crime.* **2.** A group of people who have been given authority by law to perform certain duties: *The president set up a commission to*

improve education. **3a.** The act of granting authority to someone to carry out a certain job or duty: *The commission of ambassadors is one of the president's duties.* **b.** The authority given by such a grant: *The secretary of state's commission is to direct US foreign policy.* **4a.** Appointment to the rank of a commissioned officer in the armed forces: *The pilot received a commission in the air force.* **b.** An official document issued by a government conferring such a rank. **5.** Money in the form of a fee or a percentage of a price paid to a salesperson or agent for services: *The dealer's commission on the $500 sale was $50.* ❖ *tr.v.* **commissioned, commissioning, commissions 1.** To grant a commission to: *The monarchs commissioned Columbus to find a western route to India. The Coast Guard commissioned new officers at graduation.* **2.** To place an order for: *The mayor commissioned a new sculpture for City Hall.* **3.** To put (a ship) into active service. ◆ **in commission 1.** In active service. Used of a ship. **2.** In use or in usable condition: *Only two computers are in commission.* **out of commission 1.** Not in active service. Used of a ship. **2.** Not in working condition: *Three machines are out of commission and awaiting repair.*

commissioned officer (kə-mĭsh′ənd) *n.* An officer who holds by a commission the rank of a second lieutenant or above in the US Army, Air Force, or Marine Corps or the rank of an ensign or above in the US Navy or Coast Guard.

commissioner (kə-mĭsh′ə-nər) *n.* **1.** A member of a commission. **2.** An official in charge of a governmental department: *a police commissioner.* **3.** An official chosen by an athletic association or league as administrative head of an organized professional sport: *a baseball commissioner.*

commit (kə-mĭt′) *tr.v.* **committed, committing, commits 1.** To do, perform, or be guilty of: *commit a crime; commit a serious blunder.* **2.** To place in the charge or keeping of another; entrust: *commit oneself to the care of a doctor; commit responsibilities to an assistant.* **3.** To place in confinement or custody, as by an official act: *The judge committed the criminal to prison for two years.* **4.** To give over, as for future use or for preservation; consign: *commit funds to a project; commit a text to memory.* **5.** To bind or obligate, as by a pledge: *The heirs were committed to follow the terms of the will. New citizens commit themselves to obey the laws of the United States.* **6.** To dedicate (oneself) to someone or something: *The doctor was committed to providing medical services to the poor.* —**com·mit′ta·ble** *adj.*

commitment (kə-mĭt′mənt) *n.* **1.** The act of committing something: *the commitment of a crime; the commitment of funds to a project.* **2.** A pledge or obligation, as to follow a certain course of action: *The president takes an oath that is a binding commitment to uphold the Constitution.* **3.** Dedication or devotion to another person or to a course of action: *We have a deep commitment to help clean up the environment.*

committee (kə-mĭt′ē) *n.* A group of people chosen to do a particular job or to fulfill specified duties: *appointed a committee to investigate the cause of the accident.* —SEE NOTE AT **collective noun.**

committeeman (kə-mĭt′ē-mən) *n.* A man who is a member of a committee.

committeewoman (kə-mĭt′ē-wŏom′ən) *n.* A woman who is a member of a committee.

commode (kə-mōd′) *n.* **1.** A low cabinet or chest of

drawers. **2.** A movable stand containing a washbowl or a chamber pot.

commodify (kə-mŏd′ə-fī′) *tr.v.* **commodified, commodifying, commodifies** To turn into or treat as a commodity; make commercial. —**com·mod′i·fi′a·ble** *adj.* —**com·mod′i·fi·ca′tion** (kə-mŏd′ə-fĭ-kā′shən) *n.*

commodious (kə-mō′dē-əs) *adj.* Having plenty of room; spacious: *a room with a commodious closet.* —**com·mo′di·ous·ly** *adv.* —**com·mo′di·ous·ness** *n.*

commodity (kə-mŏd′ĭ-tē) *n., pl.* **commodities 1.** A product, such as a raw material or an agricultural product, that can be bought and resold, especially in large quantities. Commodities usually do not have brand names or packaging. **2.** Something useful that can be turned to profit or advantage: *Time is a valuable commodity.*

commodore (kŏm′ə-dôr′) *n.* **1.** A commissioned rank formerly used in the US Navy that was above captain and below rear admiral. **2.** The presiding officer of a yacht club.

common (kŏm′ən) *adj.* **commoner, commonest 1a.** Belonging to or shared equally by two or more: *common interests of the United States and Canada.* **b.** Relating to the community as a whole; public: *health regulations enforced for the common good.* **2a.** Found or occurring often and in many places; widespread: *Cell phones have become common in many parts of the world.* **b.** Usual or expected: *The common reply to "Thank you" is "You're welcome."* **3.** Most widely known of its kind: *the common crow.* **4a.** Having no special rank or status; ordinary: *the common people.* **b.** Of no special quality; standard or regular: *Common sneakers cost less than running shoes.* **5.** Unrefined or coarse in manner; vulgar: *thought her behavior was common.* ❖ *n.* **1.** A tract of land belonging to or used by a community as a whole: *The early New England town had a common for citizens to graze their sheep.* **2. commons** The common people. **3. commons** *(used with a singular or plural verb)* A place for dining, especially at a college or university. **4. Commons** *(used with a singular or plural verb)* The House of Commons. ◆ **in common** Equally with another or others; jointly: *The partners have interests in common.* —**com′mon·ness** *n.*

common cold *n.* A viral infection marked by discharge of mucus, sneezing, and watering of the eyes; a cold.

common denominator *n.* A number that is a multiple of the denominators of a group of fractions. For example, since ¼ = ²⁵⁄₁₀₀, ¹⁄₂₅ = ⁴⁄₁₀₀, ³⁄₁₀ = ³⁰⁄₁₀₀, and ⅘ = ⁸⁰⁄₁₀₀, the fractions ¼, ¹⁄₂₅, ³⁄₁₀, and ⅘ can be expressed with the common denominator 100. By finding a common denominator it is possible to add and subtract fractions.

common divisor *n.* A number that will divide each of a group of numbers without a remainder. For example, 3 is a common divisor of 6, 9, 15, and 24.

commoner (kŏm′ə-nər) *n.* A person without noble rank or title.

Common Era *n.* The period of time that coincides with the period beginning with the birth of Jesus, the founder of Christianity. Year 1 CE is the same as year 1 AD.

USAGE The traditional system of dating in Europe and the Americas has for its focal point the date (or what was once thought to be the correct date) of the birth of Jesus, the founder of Christianity. Dates for events in the ancient world are thus followed by the abbreviations BC (before Christ) and AD (anno Domini, "in the year of the Lord"). But in the late 1900s many scholars and scientists switched to a dating system that is convenient and familiar but avoids the religious associations of the BC and AD designations. They adopted the term **Common Era.** It is abbreviated CE, with the date 1 CE being the same year as 1 AD. Dates before the Common Era are abbreviated BCE, with 1 BCE being the same year as 1 BC.

---

common factor *n.* A common divisor.

common fraction *n.* A fraction whose numerator and denominator are both whole numbers. For example, ¼, ⁴⁄₅, and ⅞ are common fractions.

common ground *n.* A shared set of beliefs, values, or views that can form the basis for mutual understanding.

common law *n.* The system of law based on court decisions and on customs and usages rather than on an organized body of written laws or statutes. —**com′mon-law′** (kŏm′ən-lô′) *adj.*

common-law marriage *n.* A form of marriage recognized in some jurisdictions, based on meeting certain legal requirements such as cohabitation and expression of intent to be regarded as married, rather than as a result of obtaining an official license.

common logarithm *n.* A logarithm for which the number ten is used as the base.

commonly (kŏm′ən-lē) *adv.* Generally; ordinarily: *Archaic words, such as "methinks," are not commonly used today.*

common multiple *n.* A number divisible by two or more numbers with remainder of zero. For example, 12 is a common multiple of 2, 3, 4, and 6.

common name *n.* An ordinary, everyday name as distinguished from a scientific name, as *sugar maple* for the tree *Acer saccharum.*

common noun *n.* A noun that is the name of a class or group of things or people. Common nouns refer to one or all members, as *aunt, car,* and *crowd,* and are different from proper nouns that name a specific person, place, or thing, as *Iowa, Mozart,* and *Brooklyn Bridge.* —SEE NOTE AT **noun.**

commonplace (kŏm′ən-plās′) *adj.* Ordinary; common; uninteresting: *a commonplace plot of good guys against bad guys.* ❖ *n.* A statement or remark that is dull or worn out through use.

common sense *n.* Good judgment gained from everyday experience.

common stock *n.* Stock shares in a corporation that entitle the owner to be paid dividends and often assets after payments are made to owners of preferred stock.

common time *n.* In music, a meter in which each measure contains four quarter notes.

commonweal (kŏm′ən-wēl′) *n.* **1.** The public good or welfare. **2.** *Archaic* A commonwealth.

commonwealth (kŏm′ən-wĕlth′) *n.* **1.** A nation or state that is governed by the people; a republic. **2. Commonwealth a.** The official title of some US states, specifically Kentucky, Maryland, Massachusetts, Pennsylvania, and Virginia. **b.** The official title of Puerto Rico. **c.** The official title of some democratic countries, such as Australia.

commotion (kə-mō′shən) *n.* **1.** A confused and noisy situation; a disturbance: *The argument created a commotion in the hall.* **2.** A condition of turbulent motion: *commotion of the water behind the propeller.*

communal (kə-myo͞o′nəl) *adj.* **1.** Relating to a community or to the common people; public: *our town's communal spirit.* **2.** Shared, owned, or used jointly by the members of a group or community: *communal grazing lands; a communal dining room.* —**com·mu′nal·ly** *adv.*

commune¹ (kə-myōōn′) *intr.v.* **communed, communing, communes** **1.** To feel a sense of closeness or intimacy: *a hiker communing with nature.* **2.** To receive the Eucharist.
commune² (kŏm′yōōn′ *or* kə-myōōn′) *n.* **1.** A small community whose members have common interests and in which property is often shared or owned jointly. **2.** In some European countries, such as France and Italy, the smallest division of local government.

WORD HISTORY Commune¹ comes from Middle English *communen* (meaning "to have common dealings with, converse"), which comes from Old French *communer*, meaning "to communicate, share." **Commune²** comes from French *commune*, which comes from Medieval Latin *commūnia*, meaning "community."

communicable (kə-myōō′nĭ-kə-bəl) *adj.* Capable of being communicated or transmitted from person to person: *Chickenpox and measles are communicable diseases.* **—com·mu′ni·ca·ble·ness** *n.* **—com·mu′ni·ca·bly** *adv.*
communicant (kə-myōō′nĭ-kənt) *n.* **1.** A person who receives or is entitled to receive the Eucharist. **2.** A person who communicates something.
communicate (kə-myōō′nĭ-kāt′) *v.* **communicated, communicating, communicates** *—tr.* **1.** To make known; impart: *A good speaker communicates thoughts and ideas clearly.* **2.** To transmit (a disease, for example); pass on. *—intr.* **1.** To have an exchange, as of ideas or information: *The telephone makes it possible to communicate over long distances.* **2.** To express oneself effectively, so as to be readily and clearly understood: *The ability to communicate is a valuable job skill.* **—com·mu′ni·ca′tor** *n.*
communication (kə-myōō′nĭ-kā′shən) *n.* **1.** The act of communicating; transmission: *Unsanitary conditions contribute to the communication of disease.* **2.** The exchange of thoughts, information, or messages, as by speech, signals, or writing: *Communication between people of different cultures is often difficult.* **3.** Something communicated; a message. **4. communications a.** A system for sending and receiving messages, as by mail, telephone, or radio: *The earthquake disrupted communications between towns.* **b.** The field of study concerned with the transmission of information by various means, such as print or broadcasting.
communications satellite *n.* An artificial space satellite used to aid communications, as by reflecting or relaying a television or radio signal from one ground station to another.
communicative (kə-myōō′nĭ-kā′tĭv *or* kə-myōō′-nĭ-kə-tĭv) *adj.* Communicating thoughts or information readily; not secretive: *The frightened child was not very communicative.* **—com·mu′ni·ca′tive·ly** *adv.* **—com·mu′ni·ca′tive·ness** *n.*
communion (kə-myōōn′yən) *n.* **1.** The act or an instance of sharing, as of thoughts, feelings, or interests: *We felt a communion with the others who had been through the same ordeal.* **2.** A body of Christians with the same religious faith; a denomination. **3. Communion a.** The Christian sacrament of the Eucharist received by a congregation. **b.** The part of the Mass in which the Eucharist is received.
communiqué (kə-myōō′nĭ-kā′ *or* kə-myōō′nĭ-kā′) *n.* An official announcement, such as one issued to the press after a meeting of world leaders.

communism or **Communism** (kŏm′yə-nĭz′əm) *n.* **1.** A theoretical economic system based on the writings of the nineteenth-century German philosophers Karl Marx and Friedrich Engels and characterized by common ownership of property and by the organization of labor for the benefit of society as a whole. **2a.** A system of government in which the state plans and controls the economy and a single party holds power, claiming to make progress toward a society in which all goods are shared equally by the people. **b.** The version of communist theory advanced by Vladimir Lenin, leader of the Russian Revolution (1917) and first Soviet premier (1922–1924). This theory advocates the violent overthrow of capitalism by the proletariat.
communist or **Communist** (kŏm′yə-nĭst) *n.* A person who believes in or advocates communism, especially a member of a political party that advocates communism. ❖ *adj.* Relating to, characteristic of, or resembling communism or communists.
communistic (kŏm′yə-nĭs′tĭk) *adj.* Based on or favoring the principles of communism. **—com′mu·nis′ti·cal·ly** *adv.*
community (kə-myōō′nĭ-tē) *n., pl.* **communities** **1a.** A group of people living in the same area: *Our community organized a parade.* **b.** The district or locality in which such a group lives: *a small community of only a few square miles.* **2.** A group of people who have close ties, as through common nationality or interests: *an area of controversy within the scientific community.* **3.** Sharing, participation, and fellowship: *Working together to clean up the park showed our sense of community.* **4.** A group of organisms interacting with one another and with the environment in a specific region.
community chest *n.* A fund raised by contributions from residents and businesses of an area and used for charity.
community college *n.* A junior college that does not have residential facilities and is often funded by the government.
community service *n.* Service that is done without pay to benefit a community or its institutions: *In order to graduate, each student had to perform 20 hours of community service.*
commutation (kŏm′yə-tā′shən) *n.* **1.** The act of lessening something or of making something less severe, as a prison sentence: *a commutation of a jail sentence to community service.* **2.** The travel of a commuter, especially to and from work.
commutative (kŏm′yə-tā′tĭv *or* kə-myōō′tə-tĭv) *adj.* Relating to the commutative property.
commutative property *n.* The property of addition and multiplication which states that the order in which numbers are added or multiplied will not change the result of the operation. For example, $2 + 3$ gives the same sum as $3 + 2$, and 2×3 gives the same product as 3×2.
commutator (kŏm′yə-tā′tər) *n.* A switching device in electric motors and generators that causes a current to reverse direction.
commute (kə-myōōt′) *v.* **commuted, commuting, commutes** *—intr.* To travel as a commuter: *commute to work.* *—tr.* To reduce (a legal sentence) to a less severe one: *commute a sentence of imprisonment to home confinement.* ❖ *n.* A trip made by a commuter: *a commute of 15 miles to work.*
commuter (kə-myōō′tər) *n.* **1.** A person who travels regularly between a home in one community and work

or school in another. **2.** A commercial airplane or airline that carries passengers short distances.

compact¹ (kəm-păkt′ *or* kŏm′păkt′) *adj.* **1.** Closely and firmly united or packed together; solid; dense: *flowers growing in tight compact clusters.* **2.** Occupying little space in comparison with others of the same kind: *a compact camera.* **3.** Brief and to the point; concise: *a compact news summary.* ❖ *tr.v.* (kəm-păkt′) **compacted, compacting, compacts** To press or join firmly together; pack together: *The dirt was compacted by the heavy trucks running over it.* ❖ *n.* (kŏm′păkt′) **1.** A small case containing face powder and sometimes blusher. **2.** An automobile that is smaller than a standard model. —**com·pact′ly** *adv.* —**com·pact′ness** *n.*

compact² (kŏm′păkt′) *n.* An agreement or covenant: *a compact between nations to reduce tariffs.*

WORD HISTORY Both **compact¹** and **compact²** come from Latin words, respectively *compingere* ("to put together") and *compacīscī* ("to make an agreement"). The *com-* prefix means "together." The Latin root of the first form is *pangere*, meaning "to fasten." The Latin root of the second form is *pacīscī*, meaning "to agree."

---

compact disc or **compact disk** (kŏm′păkt′) *n.* A small optical disc containing data, such as music, text, or graphic images, in digital form.

compactor or **compacter** (kəm-păk′tər *or* kŏm′păk′tər) *n.* A machine that compresses trash into small packs for easy disposal.

compadre (kəm-pä′drä) *n. Informal* A close friend; companion.

companion (kəm-păn′yən) *n.* **1.** A person who accompanies or associates with another; a comrade. **2.** A person hired to assist, live with, or travel with another: *working as a companion to an elderly couple.* **3.** One of a pair or set of things; a mate: *I lost the companion to this sneaker.*

companionable (kəm-păn′yə-nə-bəl) *adj.* Suited to be a good companion; friendly: *Most dogs are companionable pets.* —**com·pan′ion·a·bil′i·ty** *n.* —**com·pan′ion·a·bly** *adv.*

companionate (kəm-păn′yə-nĭt) *adj.* Characteristic of or behaving as a companion.

companionship (kəm-păn′yən-shĭp′) *n.* The relationship of companions; fellowship.

companionway (kəm-păn′yən-wā′) *n.* A staircase leading from a ship's deck to the area below.

company (kŭm′pə-nē) *n., pl.* **companies 1.** A group of people; a gathering: *A large company of tourists waited outside the White House.* **2.** A guest or guests: *We're having company for dinner.* **3a.** A companion or companions: *I find them very interesting company.* **b.** Companionship: *She went shopping with him, and he was grateful for the company.* **4.** A business enterprise; a firm: *That company makes many useful products.* **5.** A group of performers organized to present stage works, such as plays, operas, and ballets, or to produce motion pictures. **6.** A military unit consisting of two or more platoons. **7.** The officers and crew of a ship: *The ship's company went ashore.* **8.** A unit of firefighters. —SEE NOTE AT **collective noun.**

comparable (kŏm′pər-ə-bəl) *adj.* **1.** Capable of being compared: *The creation of the Internet is comparable to the invention of the printing press.* **2.** Worthy of being compared; similar: *Some photographs are comparable in quality to fine paintings.* —**com′pa·ra·bly** *adv.*

comparative (kəm-păr′ə-tĭv) *adj.* **1.** Relating to, based on, or involving a comparison: *the comparative study of related languages.* **2.** Estimated or considered in comparison to something else; relative: *He is a comparative beginner in computer skills.* **3.** Relating to or being the intermediate degree of comparison of adjectives or adverbs: *"Bigger" is the comparative form of "big."* ❖ *n.* **1.** In grammar, the comparative degree of an adjective or adverb. **2.** An adjective or adverb expressing the comparative degree. —**com·par′a·tive·ly** *adv.*

USAGE While most short adjectives can be put into comparative form by adding just *-er,* most adverbs and most longer adjectives are made **comparative** by being paired with the word *more,* as in *won more easily* or *a more unusual solution.* Likewise, **superlative** forms for most adverbs and longer adjectives are formed by adding the word *most.*

compare (kəm-pâr′) *v.* **compared, comparing, compares** —*tr.* **1.** To represent as similar; liken: *Shakespeare compared the world to a stage.* **2.** To examine so as to note the similarities and differences of: *Let's compare cooking over heat with cooking in a microwave oven.* —*intr.* To be worthy of comparison: *His photographs do not compare with yours.* ❖ *n.* Comparison: *Her singing ability is beyond compare.*

comparison (kəm-păr′ĭ-sən) *n.* **1.** The act of comparing: *A comparison of prices shows that you can save money if you shop online.* **2.** The quality of being similar; likeness: *There is no comparison between homemade bread and sliced bread bought in a supermarket.*

compartment (kəm-pärt′mənt) *n.* **1.** One of the parts or spaces into which something is subdivided: *A cash register drawer is divided into compartments for paper bills and coins.* **2.** A separate room, section, or chamber: *a built-in storage compartment under the stairs.*

compass (kŭm′pəs *or* kŏm′pəs) *n.* **1a.** A device used to determine geographical direction, usually consisting of a magnetic needle mounted so that it points to magnetic north. **b.** Any of several other devices, especially a gyrocompass or a radio compass, used to determine geographical direction. **2.** A device used for drawing circles and arcs and for measuring distances, consisting of two legs hinged together at one end. **3.** Range or scope; extent: *That decision is not within the compass of your authority.* **4.** An enclosing line or boundary; a circumference: *within the compass of the garden.* ❖ *tr.v.* **compassed, compassing, compasses 1.** To go around; make a circuit of: *an explorer who compassed the entire continent.* **2.** To surround or encircle; encompass: *a valley compassed by mountains.* **3.** To understand or comprehend: *phenomena too strange to be compassed.*

compassion (kəm-păsh′ən) *n.* The deep awareness of the suffering of another, together with a desire to relieve it.

compassionate (kəm-păsh′ə-nĭt) *adj.* Feeling or showing compassion; sympathetic: *a compassionate caregiver; compassionate acts.* —**com·pas′sion·ate·ly** *adv.*

compatible (kəm-păt′ə-bəl) *adj.* **1.** Capable of living or existing together in agreement or harmony: *They are very compatible with their cousins and enjoyed the trip together.* **2.** Capable of working together in the same system: *Is the printer compatible with the computer?* **3.** Capable of being grafted, transfused, or transplanted from one indivual to another without rejection: *Some blood types are not compatible with each other.* —**com·pat′i·bil′i·ty** *n.* —**com·pat′i·bly** *adv.*

compatriot (kəm-pā′trē-ət) *n.* A person from one's own country.

compel (kəm-pĕl′) *tr.v.* **compelled, compelling, compels** **1.** To make (a person) do something, as by force, necessity, or powerful influence: *Airlines compel all passengers to pass through a security check.* **2.** To make necessary; require or demand: *The teacher compelled obedience from the class. Social change often compels a new way of thinking.* **3.** To exert an irresistible influence on; command: *The book compelled my interest from the very first page.*

compelling (kəm-pĕl′ĭng) *adj.* Having a very strong influence or effect; powerful; forceful: *a compelling argument.* —**com·pel′ling·ly** *adv.*

compendious (kəm-pĕn′dē-əs) *adj.* Giving facts or information about a subject in brief but complete form: *News broadcasts are supposed to be compendious reviews of the events of the day.*

compendium (kəm-pĕn′dē-əm) *n., pl.* **compendiums** or **compendia** (kəm-pĕn′dē-ə) **1.** A short but complete summary of something: *a compendium of the committee's views.* **2.** A collection of various items: *a compendium of English poetry.*

compensate (kŏm′pən-sāt′) *v.* **compensated, compensating, compensates** —*tr.* To make satisfactory payment to; pay or reimburse: *The store compensates its clerks for extra time worked during the holiday season.* —*intr.* To act as or provide a balancing effect; make up: *We worked extra hard to compensate for the hour lost. In baseball speedy running can compensate for weak hitting.* —**com′pen·sa′tor** *n.* —**com·pen′sa·to′ry** (kəm-pĕn′sə-tôr′ē) *adj.*

compensation (kŏm′pən-sā′shən) *n.* **1.** Something given or received as payment or as a balance for a loss: *The family received little compensation for the loss of their belongings in the fire.* **2.** The act of compensating or the state of being compensated: *The payroll department handles the compensation of workers. We got a free night in a hotel in compensation for our flight that was canceled.*

compete (kəm-pēt′) *intr.v.* **competed, competing, competes** **1.** To strive against another or others to attain a goal: *compete in a race; compete for someone's business.* **2.** To attempt to use the same resource, such as food, living space, or light, as other organisms: *bacteria competing for nutrients.*

competence (kŏm′pĭ-təns) *n.* **1.** The ability to do what is required; adequate skill or knowledge: *She has great competence as a tennis player.* **2.** A range of ability, skill, or knowledge: *Is this task within his competence?* **3.** The condition of being legally qualified to perform an act.

competency (kŏm′pĭ-tən-sē) *n., pl.* **competencies** Competence.

competent (kŏm′pĭ-tənt) *adj.* **1.** Able to do something with adequate skill; capable: *a competent worker.* **2.** Legally qualified to perform an act, especially by mental fitness: *The judge ruled that the defendant was competent to stand trial.* —**com′pe·tent·ly** *adv.*

competition (kŏm′pĭ-tĭsh′ən) *n.* **1.** The act of competing, as for a prize; rivalry: *won the race in competition with ten contestants.* **2.** A test of skill or ability; a contest: *a skating competition.* **3.** A competitor: *Is the competition as good as our team?* **4.** Rivalry between businesses for the same customers: *trying to get clients away from the competition.* **5.** The simultaneous demand by two or more organisms

for resources such as nutrients, living space, and light: *competition between two predators for food.*

competitive (kəm-pĕt′ĭ-tĭv) *adj.* **1.** Involving or decided by competition: *competitive games.* **2.** Liking competition or inclined to compete: *Most athletes are competitive people.* —**com·pet′i·tive·ly** *adv.* —**com·pet′i·tive·ness** *n.*

competitor (kəm-pĕt′ĭ-tər) *n.* A person, team, business organization, or other group that competes with another or others; an opponent or rival.

compilation (kŏm′pə-lā′shən) *n.* **1.** The act of compiling: *Computers are useful in the compilation of facts and figures.* **2.** Something that has been compiled, such as a collection of written works or a report.

compile (kəm-pīl′) *tr.v.* **compiled, compiling, compiles** **1.** To put together (facts, information, or other matter from several sources) into a single collection, set, or record. **2.** To write or compose (a book) using material gathered from various sources: *compile a dictionary.* —**com·pil′-er** *n.*

complacence (kəm-plā′səns) *n.* Complacency.

complacency (kəm-plā′sən-sē) *n.* Contentment or self-satisfaction, especially when combined with a lack of readiness to respond to difficulty or controversy.

complacent (kəm-plā′sənt) *adj.* Full of complacency or self-satisfaction: *The team had won so often that they began to feel complacent.* —**com·pla′cent·ly** *adv.*

complain (kəm-plān′) *intr.v.* **complained, complaining, complains** **1.** To express feelings of pain, dissatisfaction, or resentment: *They worked hard all day and never complained.* **2.** To make an accusation about something that one considers wrong or troublesome: *complain to the telephone company about a mistake in one's bill.*

complainant (kəm-plā′nənt) *n.* A person who makes a formal complaint, as in a court of law.

complaint (kəm-plānt′) *n.* **1.** An expression of pain, dissatisfaction, or resentment: *There have been many complaints about the cafeteria food.* **2.** A cause or reason for complaining; a grievance: *The tenants sent a list of their complaints to the landlord.* **3.** A formal charge of the commission of a crime: *The storekeeper signed a complaint accusing the suspect of robbery.* **4.** Something, such as a minor ailment, that causes pain or discomfort: *We all had stomach complaints after eating too much.*

complaisance (kəm-plā′səns *or* kəm-plā′zəns) *n.* The desire to please or oblige others.

complaisant (kəm-plā′sənt *or* kəm-plā′zənt) *adj.* Showing a desire or willingness to please; cheerfully obliging: *The complaisant host was always asking if we needed anything.* —**com·plai′sant·ly** *adv.*

complement (kŏm′plə-mənt) *n.* **1.** Something that causes something else to be made into a whole or brought to a level of excellence: *Attractive shrubs are a complement to a fine building.* **2.** The number or amount needed to make something complete: *library shelves with a full complement of books.* **3.** In grammar, a word or group of words that follows a transitive or linking verb and completes a predicate. For example, *worm* in *The robin ate the worm,* and *cold* in *The water feels cold* are complements. **4.** An angle related to another so that their sum is 90°. If an angle measures 30°, its complement is 60°. **5.** A system of proteins found in the serum of the blood that helps antibodies destroy disease-causing bacteria or other foreign substances. **6.** Either of two complementary colors. ❖ *tr.v.* (kŏm′plə-mĕnt′) **complemented, complementing, complements** To make complete; be a complement to:

That easy chair complements the furnishings of the room.

USAGE The word **complement** means "something that completes or brings to perfection": *The flowers were a perfect complement to the beautifully set table.* **Compliment** means "an expression of courtesy or praise": *They gave us a compliment on our beautiful table.*

complementary (kŏm′plə-měn′tə-rē *or* kŏm′plə-měn′trē) *adj.* Serving as a complement; supplying what is lacking or needed: *The flowers on the dinner table provided a complementary touch.*

complementary angles *pl.n.* Two angles whose sum is 90 degrees.

complementary color *n.* One of two colors, such as red and green, that produce white (in the case of light) or gray (in the case of pigment) when mixed in the proper proportions.

complete (kəm-plēt′) *adj.* **completer, completest 1.** Having all necessary or normal parts; entire: *a complete set of dishes.* **2.** Having come to an end; finished: *The renovation of the kitchen is complete.* **3.** Absolute; total: *complete control of the situation.* **4.** In football, caught in bounds by a receiver: *a complete pass.* ❖ *tr.v.* **completed, completing, completes 1.** To bring to an end; finish: *The farmers completed the spring planting.* **2.** To add what is missing; make whole: *Fill in the blanks to complete the form.* **3.** In football, to throw (a forward pass) so as to be caught in bounds by a receiver. **—com·plete′ly** *adv.* **—com·plete′ness** *n.* —SEE NOTE AT **replete.**

✦ **SYNONYMS complete, close, conclude, end, finish** *v.*

completion (kəm-plē′shən) *n.* **1.** The act of completing something or the state of being completed: *Completion of the building took only three weeks.* **2.** In football, a forward pass that is caught in bounds by a receiver.

complex (kəm-plěks′ *or* kŏm′plěks′) *adj.* **1.** Consisting of many connected or interrelated parts: *the complex wiring of a computer.* **2.** Difficult to understand for being intricate or involved; complicated: *a mystery with a complex plot.* ❖ *n.* (kŏm′plěks′) **1.** A building or group of buildings used for a single purpose: *a sports complex.* **2.** A group of related ideas and emotions that influence a person's behavior and personality. **—com·plex′ly** *adv.*

complex fraction *n.* A fraction having a fraction in the numerator, denominator, or both.

complexion (kəm-plěk′shən) *n.* **1.** The color, texture, and appearance of the skin, especially of the face: *The skier had a ruddy complexion from being outside.* **2.** General character, aspect, or nature: *The whole complexion of the situation brightened with the good news.*

complexity (kəm-plěk′sĭ-tē) *n., pl.* **complexities 1.** The condition of being complex: *the complexity of modern civilization.* **2.** One of the components in something complicated: *the complexities of the immune system.*

complex number *n.* A number that can be expressed as *a + bi,* where *a* and *b* are real numbers and *i* is an imaginary number whose square equals −1.

complex sentence *n.* A sentence containing an independent clause and one or more subordinate clauses, for example, *When the rain ends, we will go home.*

compliance (kəm-plī′əns) *n.* **1.** The act of complying: *Compliance with a country's laws is expected of all citizens.* **2.** A tendency to yield to others.

compliancy (kəm-plī′ən-sē) *n.* Compliance.

compliant (kəm-plī′ənt) *adj.* **1.** Inclined or willing to yield to the wishes or requests of others. **2.** In compli-ance, as with a standard or regulation: *a refrigerator that is compliant with federal energy-saving regulations.* **—com·pli′ant·ly** *adv.*

complicate (kŏm′plĭ-kāt′) *tr.v.* **complicated, complicating, complicates** To make more complex or confusing: *The new development only complicates an already serious problem.*

complicated (kŏm′plĭ-kā′tĭd) *adj.* **1.** Not easy to understand or deal with; complex or confusing: *a complicated problem with her insurance claim.* **2.** Containing intricately combined or involved parts: *a complicated computer program.*

complication (kŏm′plĭ-kā′shən) *n.* **1.** Something that complicates something else: *Running out of milk was one more complication in trying to get dinner ready on time.* **2.** The state of being complicated or confused: *There is so much complication in these instructions that nobody can understand them.* **3.** A secondary medical condition that occurs during an illness and usually makes it worse.

complicit (kəm-plĭs′ĭt) *adj.* Associated with or participating in a questionable act or a crime; having complicity.

complicity (kəm-plĭs′ĭ-tē) *n., pl.* **complicities** Involvement as an accomplice in a crime or wrongdoing: *Complicity in the scheme cost the accountants their reputations.*

compliment (kŏm′plə-mənt) *n.* **1.** An expression of praise, admiration, or congratulation: *The author received many compliments on the new book.* **2.** An act showing honor or courtesy: *The neighbors paid us the compliment of an invitation to dinner.* **3. compliments** Good wishes; regards: *Please extend my compliments to your parents.* ❖ *tr.v.* **complimented, complimenting, compliments** To pay a compliment to: *The critic complimented both artists on their work.* —SEE NOTE AT **complement.**

complimentary (kŏm′plə-měn′tə-rē *or* kŏm′plə-měn′trē) *adj.* **1.** Expressing, using, or resembling a compliment: *The reviewer was not very complimentary about the movie.* **2.** Given free out of courtesy: *a complimentary copy of a new book.*

comply (kəm-plī′) *intr.v.* **complied, complying, complies** To act in accordance with a request, rule, or order: *The singer complied by giving several encores. Sick people should comply with their doctor's orders.*

component (kəm-pō′nənt) *n.* One of the parts that make up a whole: *Components such as batteries and resistors make up an electric circuit.* ❖ *adj.* Being or functioning as a part or ingredient: *The loudspeakers and amplifiers are component parts of our stereo system.*

comport (kəm-pôrt′) *v.* **comported, comporting, comports** *—tr.* To conduct or behave (oneself) in a certain way: *The students comported themselves very well in the teacher's absence.* *—intr.* To agree, correspond, or suit: *actions that comport with the dignity of a judge.*

comportment (kəm-pôrt′mənt) *n.* A manner of behaving; conduct; bearing: *the solemn comportment of the orchestra's conductor.*

compose (kəm-pōz′) *v.* **composed, composing, composes** *—tr.* **1.** To make up the parts of; form: *The heart, veins, arteries, and capillaries compose the circulatory system.* **2.** To make or create by putting parts or elements together: *She composed the speech from entries in her journal.* **3.** To create (a musical or literary work): *compose a symphony.* **4.** To make calm, controlled, or orderly: *compose oneself before making a speech.* **5.** To settle or adjust: *The two nations composed their differences and agreed to share the fishing grounds.* **6.** To arrange or set (type or matter to be printed): *compose type; compose a page.* —*intr.* To create literary or musical pieces: *Chopin composed mostly for the piano.*

WORD BUILDING The word root *pos-* in English comes from the French verb *poser,* "to put." **Compose** therefore literally means "to put together" (using the prefix *com-,* "with, together"); **expose** means "to put out" (*ex-,* "out, out of"); **propose** is literally "to put forward" (*prō,* "forward, in front"); **oppose** is literally "to put against" (*op-,* a form of *ob-,* "toward, against"). The French verb *poser* comes ultimately from the Latin verb *pōnere,* whose present participle was *pōnēns* or *pōnent-.* This is where the English nouns that contain *-ponent* and correspond to verbs containing *-pose* come from: **component, exponent, proponent,** and **opponent.**

composed (kəm-pōzd′) *adj.* Being in control of one's emotions; calm; serene. —**com·pos′ed·ly** (kəm-pō′zĭd-lē) *adv.*

composer (kəm-pō′zər) *n.* A person who composes, especially a creator of musical works.

composite (kəm-pŏz′ĭt) *adj.* **1.** Made up of distinctly different parts: *The photograph was a composite picture of several snapshots of family members.* **2.** Relating to or belonging to a plant family having flower heads made up of many small densely clustered flowers that give the impression of a single bloom. ❖ *n.* **1.** Something made by combining different parts: *An almanac is a composite of many facts and tables from different sources.* **2.** A composite plant, such as a daisy or dandelion.

composite number *n.* A whole number that is divisible without a remainder by at least one whole number other than itself and 1.

composition (kŏm′pə-zĭsh′ən) *n.* **1.** The act or process of putting together parts or elements to form a whole: *the composition of a piano concerto.* **2.** A work created by such a process, as a musical work or a short essay: *wrote a composition for English class.* **3.** The parts or constituents forming a whole; makeup: *the chemical composition of a mineral.* **4.** The arrangement of parts or elements forming a whole, as in an artistic work: *the orderly and colorful composition of a painting.* **5.** A mixture of substances: *Concrete is a composition of gravel and cement.* **6.** The setting of type for printing.

compositor (kəm-pŏz′ĭ-tər) *n.* A person who arranges or sets type for printing; a typesetter.

compos mentis (kŏm′pəs mĕn′tĭs) *adj.* Of sound mind; sane.

compost (kŏm′pōst′) *n.* A mixture of decayed organic matter, such as leaves, food waste, or manure, used to enrich the soil.

composting toilet (kŏm′pō′stĭng) *n.* A toilet that uses little or no water and is connected to a tank where aerobic bacteria decompose the waste material.

composure (kəm-pō′zhər) *n.* Control over one's emotions; calmness: *Don't lose your composure over a mistake.*

compote (kŏm′pōt) *n.* **1.** Sweetened stewed fruit, served as a dessert. **2.** A long-stemmed dish for holding fruit, candy, or nuts.

compound[1] (kəm-pound′ *or* kŏm′pound′) *tr.v.* **compounded, compounding, compounds 1.** To put together to form a whole; combine: *compounded pigments with an oil base to make paint.* **2.** To produce or create by combining parts or ingredients: *The pharmacist compounded the medicine our doctor ordered.* **3.** To compute (interest) on the principal and accumulated interest of a sum of money, as in a savings account. **4.** To add to; increase: *We had compounded our difficulties by making so many mistakes.* ❖ *adj.* (kŏm′pound′ *or* kəm-pound′) Consisting of two or more parts, ingredients, elements, or substances. ❖ *n.* (kŏm′pound′) **1.** Something consisting of a combination of two or more parts or ingredients: *Cough syrup is usually a compound of alcohol, sweet flavoring, and some medicine.* **2.** A word consisting of a combination of two or more other words and forming a single unit with its own meaning. *Loudspeaker, deep-fry,* and *cell division* are compounds. **3.** A substance formed by chemical combination of two or more elements in definite proportions by weight: *Water is a compound of hydrogen and oxygen.* —**com·pound′er** *n.*

compound[2] (kŏm′pound′) *n.* A group of houses or other buildings, enclosed by a wall, fence, or other barrier.

WORD HISTORY Compound[1] comes from Middle English *compounen,* which comes from Latin *compōnere,* both meaning "to put together." **Compound**[2] comes from Malay *kampong,* meaning "village."

compound-complex sentence (kŏm′pound-kŏm′plĕks) *n.* A sentence consisting of at least two independent clauses and one or more subordinate clauses.

compound eye *n.* An eye, as of an insect or crustacean, consisting of many small light-sensitive units, each of which forms part of an image.

compound fraction *n.* A complex fraction.

compound fracture *n.* A bone fracture in which a sharp piece of bone cuts through nearby soft tissue and makes an open wound.

compound interest *n.* Interest computed on an amount of money constituting the principal plus all the unpaid interest already earned.

compound leaf *n.* A leaf, as of clover, whose blade is divided into two or more distinct leaflets.

compound lens *n.* A combination of two or more simple lenses, sometimes with other optical devices such as prisms, used to form an image as in a camera or telescope.

compound sentence *n.* A sentence of two or more independent clauses, usually joined by a conjunction such as *and, but,* or *or.* For example, *The problem was difficult, but I finally found the answer* is a compound sentence.

comprehend (kŏm′prĭ-hĕnd′) *tr.v.* **comprehended, comprehending, comprehends 1.** To grasp mentally; understand: *Many people do not comprehend the theory of relativity.* **2.** To take in as a part; include: *The metropolitan area of a city comprehends the surrounding suburbs.*

comprehensible (kŏm′prĭ-hĕn′sə-bəl) *adj.* Readily understood; understandable: *I was able to make the menu comprehensible to our visitor from Japan.* —**com′pre·hen′si·bil′i·ty** *n.* —**com′pre·hen′si·bly** *adv.*

comprehension (kŏm′prĭ-hĕn′shən) *n.* **1.** The act or fact of understanding something: *Comprehension of basic chemistry is not as difficult as you think.* **2.** The capacity to understand something: *Calculus is well within your comprehension.*

comprehensive (kŏm′prĭ-hĕn′sĭv) *adj.* **1.** Including much; broad in scope; thorough: *The last chapter is a comprehensive review of the book's contents.* **2.** Marked by or showing extensive understanding: *comprehensive knowledge.* —**com′pre·hen′sive·ly** *adv.*

compress (kəm-prĕs′) *tr.v.* **compressed, compressing, compresses 1.** To squeeze or press together: *He compressed his lips into a thin line.* **2.** To make more compact by or as if by squeezing or pressing: *compress one's thoughts into a short statement.* **3.** To transform (data) in order to minimize the space needed to store or transmit it. ❖ *n.* (kŏm′prĕs′) A soft pad of gauze, cotton, or other material, often moistened or medicated, applied to some part of the body, especially to a wound or injury. —SEE NOTE AT **pressure.**

compressed (kəm-prĕst′) *adj.* Pressed together; made smaller by pressure: *The tank contains compressed gas.*

compressed air *n.* Air that has been put under pressure greater than the pressure of the atmosphere, as in a storage tank. When released, its force is often used to operate a mechanism, such as air brakes.

compressible (kəm-prĕs′ə-bəl) *adj.* Capable of being compressed. —**com·press′i·bil′i·ty** *n.*

compression (kəm-prĕsh′ən) *n.* **1.** The act or process of compressing. **2.** The condition of being compressed.

compressor (kəm-prĕs′ər) *n.* Something that compresses, especially a machine used to compress a gas, as in a refrigerator.

comprise (kəm-prīz′) *tr.v.* **comprised, comprising, comprises 1.** To consist of; be composed of; include: *The United Nations comprises more than 130 countries.* **2.** To make up; form; constitute: *Milk, butter, and cheese comprise the bulk of dairy products.*

compromise (kŏm′prə-mīz′) *n.* **1.** A settlement of differences between opposing sides in which each side gives up some claims and agrees to some demands of the other: *By agreeing to share the cost, our neighbors reached a compromise over rebuilding the fence.* **2.** Something that combines qualities or elements of different, often conflicting things: *The design of the car is a compromise between style and safety.* ❖ *v.* **compromised, compromising, compromises** —*tr.* **1.** To reduce in quality or value; weaken or lower: *He felt he compromised his standards in rushing through the job.* **2.** To expose to danger or risk: *The secret mission was compromised when news of it was leaked to the press.* **3.** To impair, as by disease or injury: *The patient's immune system was compromised by a viral infection.* —*intr.* To settle a difference by making a compromise: *We compromised and divided our time between the museum and the shopping district.*

comptroller (kən-trō′lər *or* kŏmp-trō′lər) *n.* also **controller** (kən-trō′lər) An officer who supervises the financial affairs of a business or a governmental body.

compulsion (kəm-pŭl′shən) *n.* **1.** The act of compelling or the state of being compelled: *the compulsion of prisoners to work on a chain gang; residents who were under compulsion to evacuate their homes due to flooding.* **2.** An irresistible urge or impulse: *a compulsion to stay up late.*

compulsive (kəm-pŭl′sĭv) *adj.* Relating to, having, or resulting from a strong irresistible impulse: *Some people have a compulsive desire to talk.* —**com·pul′sive·ly** *adv.* —**com·pul′sive·ness** *n.*

compulsory (kəm-pŭl′sə-rē) *adj.* **1.** Required by law, regulations, or duty: *Education is compulsory for children in most countries.* **2.** Using or involving compulsion: *compulsory powers of the law.*

compunction (kəm-pŭngk′shən) *n.* An uneasy feeling that one has done something wrong; remorse: *The children showed no compunction about eating all the cookies.*

computation (kŏm′pyoo-tā′shən) *n.* The act, process,

method, or result of computing; mathematical calculation.

compute (kəm-pyoot′) *tr.v.* **computed, computing, computes 1.** To work out (a result, answer, or solution) by mathematics; calculate: *The bank computes the interest on savings accounts.* **2.** To determine by use of a computer: *compute the most efficient design of a rocket.*

computer (kəm-pyoo′tər) *n.* A device that computes, especially a programmable electronic machine that performs high-speed mathematical or logical operations or that assembles, stores, correlates, or otherwise processes information.

computer graphics *n.* (*used with a singular or plural verb*) Graphic artwork, such as maps, diagrams, or pictures, produced with a computer.

computerize (kəm-pyoo′tə-rīz′) *tr.v.* **computerized, computerizing, computerizes 1.** To process or store (information) in an electronic computer: *computerize office files.* **2.** To furnish with a computer or a system of computers: *computerize an office.*

computer language *n.* A programming language.

computer literacy *n.* The ability to operate a computer and to understand how a computer works.

computer science *n.* The study of the design and operation of computers, including their software and hardware.

comrade (kŏm′răd) *n.* **1.** A friend or companion, especially a person who shares one's activities. **2.** often **Comrade** A fellow member of a group, especially a fellow member of the Communist Party.

comradeship (kŏm′răd-shĭp′) *n.* Association as comrades; companionship: *the comradeship of old friends.*

con¹ (kŏn) *n.* An argument or consideration against something: *discussing the pros and cons of the subject.* ❖ *adv.* In opposition or disagreement; against: *arguing a question pro and con.* ❖ *adj.* Opposing: *the arguments pro and con.*

con² (kŏn) *tr.v.* **conned, conning, cons** To direct the course of (a ship, for instance). ❖ *n.* **1.** The position from which a vessel's course is directed. **2.** The authority to direct a vessel's course.

con³ (kŏn) *tr.v.* **conned, conning, cons** *Slang* To trick or coax (someone) into doing something by first winning the person's confidence: *con someone into buying a junky old car.* ❖ *n.* A swindle.

con⁴ (kŏn) *n.* *Slang* A convict.

WORD HISTORY Con¹ comes from Latin *contrā*, meaning "against." **Con²** comes from Middle English *conduen* (meaning "to lead"), which comes from Latin *condūcere*, meaning "to draw together." **Con³** is short for *confidence.* **Con⁴** is short for *convict.*

con– Variant of **com–.**

concatenate (kŏn-kăt′n-āt′) *tr.v.* **concatenated, concatenating, concatenates** To connect or link in a series or chain. —**con·cat′e·na′tion** *n.*

concave (kŏn-kāv′ *or* kŏn′kāv′) *adj.* Curved inward like the inside of a circle or sphere: *Many birds build concave nests to hold their eggs.*

concavity (kŏn-kăv′ĭ-tē) *n., pl.* **concavities 1.** The condition of being concave: *The concavity of the mirror allows it to focus the rays of the sun into a beam.* **2.** A concave surface, line, or body.

conceal (kən-sēl′) *tr.v.* **concealed, concealing, conceals 1.** To keep from being seen; put out of sight: *A bank of* clouds *concealed the setting sun.* See Synonyms at **hide¹**. **2.** To keep secret: *conceal hurt feelings.* —**con·ceal'a·ble** *adj.* —**con·ceal'er** *n.* —**con·ceal'ment** *n.*

concede (kən-sēd′) *v.* **conceded, conceding, concedes** —*tr.* **1.** To admit as being true or real, often unwillingly; acknowledge: *The losing candidate finally conceded defeat the morning after election day.* **2.** To give, yield, or grant: *After the uprising, the government conceded the right to vote to all citizens.* —*intr.* To make a concession; yield.

conceit (kən-sēt′) *n.* **1.** An overly high opinion of one's abilities or worth; vanity: *The famous author's conceit was unpleasant.* **2.** A witty expression or fanciful idea.

conceited (kən-sē′tĭd) *adj.* Holding or showing an overly high opinion of oneself: *a conceited braggart.* —**con·ceit'ed·ly** *adv.* —**con·ceit'ed·ness** *n.*

conceivable (kən-sē′və-bəl) *adj.* Capable of being thought of; imaginable: *It is conceivable that life exists on other planets.*

conceive (kən-sēv′) *v.* **conceived, conceiving, conceives** —*tr.* **1.** To form or develop in the mind: *Albert Einstein conceived the theory of relativity.* **2.** To imagine or think of; consider: *We could not conceive that such a strange place existed.* **3.** To become pregnant with: *conceive a child.* —*intr.* **1.** To have an idea or concept; think: *People in ancient times conceived of the earth as flat.* **2.** To become pregnant. —**con·ceiv'er** *n.*

concentrate (kŏn′sən-trāt′) *v.* **concentrated, concentrating, concentrates** —*intr.* **1.** To keep or direct one's thoughts, attention, or efforts: *It's hard to concentrate on my reading with the TV on.* **2.** To come toward or meet in a common center: *The migrating geese concentrate at ponds and streams.* **3.** To have something as a main point of interest or concern; focus: *The first chapter concentrates on positioning of the hands on the keyboard.* —*tr.* **1.** To draw or gather toward one place or point; focus: *Europe's population is concentrated in large cities.* **2.** To make (a solution or mixture) stronger. ❖ *n.* Something that has been concentrated: *orange juice concentrate.*

concentration (kŏn′sən-trā′shən) *n.* **1.** The act or process of concentrating, especially the directing of close undivided attention: *The secret of doing your work in less time is complete concentration.* **2.** A close gathering or dense grouping: *Lights shone brightly from the concentration of houses in the new development.* **3.** The amount of a particular substance in a given amount of a solution or mixture: *the concentration of salt in sea water.*

concentration camp *n.* An area or camp where people are confined, often under harsh conditions, usually for belonging to a group that a government considers dangerous or undesirable.

concentric (kən-sĕn′trĭk) *adj.* Having the same center: *a set of concentric circles.* —**con·cen'tri·cal·ly** *adv.*

concept (kŏn′sĕpt′) *n.* **1.** A general idea or understanding, especially one based on known facts or observation: *the concept that all people have a right to equal treatment under the law.* See Synonyms at **idea**. **2.** A scheme; a plan: *a concept for a new mall.*

conception (kən-sĕp′shən) *n.* **1.** A general idea or understanding; a concept: *gained a clearer conception of the age of the universe.* See Synonyms at **idea**. **2.** A beginning or formation of an idea: *a history of the computer from its earliest conception.* **3.** The formation of a cell that is ca-

pable of developing into a new organism by the union of a sperm and egg cell; fertilization.

conceptual (kən-sĕp′chōō-əl) *adj.* Consisting of or based on a concept or mental conception: *the conceptual difference between a robot and a human being.* —**con·cep'tu·al·ly** *adv.*

conceptualize (kən-sĕp′chōō-ə-līz′) *tr. & intr.v.* **conceptualized, conceptualizing, conceptualizes** To form a general idea or a concept about: *It is difficult to conceptualize what the world will be like in the next century.*

concern (kən-sûrn′) *tr.v.* **concerned, concerning, concerns** **1.** To have to do with; relate to: *The new book concerns urban sprawl.* **2.** To be of importance or interest to; involve: *Cleaning up the environment concerns all of us.* **3.** To fill with care or anxiety; worry; trouble: *The lack of rain deeply concerned the farmers.* ❖ *n.* **1.** Something of interest or importance: *The author's chief concern is to write the history of the plastics industry.* **2.** Worry; anxiety: *the parents' concern for their sick child.* **3.** A business establishment; a firm: *Repair shops and banks are concerns that provide services rather than goods.*

concerned (kən-sûrnd′) *adj.* **1.** Interested or affected; involved: *Most concerned citizens recycle trash.* **2.** Worried; anxious; troubled: *a concerned expression on his face.*

concerning (kən-sûr′nĭng) *prep.* In reference to; about: *science-fiction stories concerning visitors from outer space.*

concert (kŏn′sərt) *n.* A musical performance given in front of an audience. ◆ **in concert** As a single unit or group; together: *Several nearby towns are working in concert to ease rush-hour traffic.*

concerted (kən-sûr′tĭd) *adj.* Planned or accomplished together with others; combined: *a concerted fundraising drive.*

concertina (kŏn′sər-tē′nə) *n.* A small accordion in the shape of a hexagon.

concerto (kən-chĕr′tō) *n., pl.* **concertos** or **concerti** (kən-chĕr′tē) A musical composition written for one or more solo instruments and an orchestra: *a piano concerto; a concerto for violin and orchestra.*

concession (kən-sĕsh′ən) *n.* **1.** An act of yielding or conceding: *settle a dispute by mutual concession.* **2.** Something yielded or conceded: *The workers demanded more time off and other concessions.* **3a.** A right to operate a business in a certain place: *The US government gave land concessions to the railroads to encourage their development.* **b.** A business that has such a right: *We got hot dogs at the food concession in the ballpark.*

concessionaire (kən-sĕsh′ə-nâr′) *n.* A person who holds or operates a business concession.

conch (kŏngk *or* kŏnch) *n., pl.* **conchs** (kŏngks) or **conches** (kŏn′chĭz) **1.** Any of various tropical marine snails having edible flesh and a large spiral shell. **2.** The shell of such an animal.

concierge (kŏn-syârzh′) *n.* **1.** A staff member of a hotel or apartment complex who assists guests or residents, as by storing luggage, taking messages, or making reservations for tours. **2.** A person, especially in France, who lives in an apartment house, attends the entrance, and serves as a janitor.

conciliate (kən-sĭl′ē-āt′) *tr.v.* **conciliated, conciliating, conciliates** **1.** To overcome the anger or distrust of; win over: *The babysitter tried to conciliate the angry child by reading a story.* **2.** To make harmonious; reconcile: *made an attempt to conciliate the conflicting theories.* —**con·cil'i·a'tion** *n.* —**con·cil'i·a'tor** *n.*

conciliatory (kən-sĭl′ē-ə-tôr′ē) *adj.* Intending to conciliate or having the effect of conciliating: *a conciliatory attitude.*

concise (kən-sīs′) *adj.* Expressing much in a few words; brief and clear: *a concise summary of the main points of the meeting.* —**con·cise′ly** *adv.* —**con·cise′ness** *n.*

conclave (kŏn′klāv′) *n.* A private or secret meeting.

conclude (kən-klōōd′) *v.* **concluded, concluding, concludes** —*tr.* **1.** To bring to an end; close: *concluded the rally with the school's alma mater.* See Synonyms at **complete. 2.** To arrange or settle finally: *conclude an agreement on trade between two countries.* **3.** To arrive at (a conclusion, judgment, or opinion) by the process of reasoning: *The scientist concluded that the bones were those of a dinosaur.* —*intr.* To come to an end; close: *The conference concluded with a call for action.* —**con·clud′er** *n.*

conclusion (kən-klōō′zhən) *n.* **1.** The closing or last part of something; the end: *the exciting conclusion of a story.* **2.** A judgment or decision reached by reasoning: *Scientists check their observations thoroughly to arrive at accurate conclusions.* **3.** A final arrangement or settlement, as of a treaty. ◆ **in conclusion** As a last statement; finally.

conclusive (kən-klōō′sĭv) *adj.* Putting an end to doubt, question, or uncertainty; decisive: *The new piece of evidence was conclusive and proved that he was guilty.* —**con·clu′sive·ly** *adv.*

concoct (kən-kŏkt′) *tr.v.* **concocted, concocting, concocts 1.** To make by mixing or combining ingredients or parts: *concoct a stew from leftover meat and vegetables.* **2.** To make up; invent: *concoct an excuse to avoid going to the concert.*

concoction (kən-kŏk′shən) *n.* Something concocted, especially a mixture of ingredients: *a concoction of orange juice and soda.*

concomitant (kən-kŏm′ĭ-tənt) *adj.* Happening or existing along with something else; accompanying: *A fever and rash are concomitant symptoms of chickenpox.* ❖ *n.* Something that happens or is found along with something else: *Poor health is often a concomitant of unsanitary living conditions.* —**con·com′i·tant·ly** *adv.*

concord (kŏn′kôrd′ *or* kŏng′kôrd′) *n.* **1.** A friendly or harmonious relationship: *The neighboring nations lived in peace and concord.* **2.** An agreement establishing such a relationship. **3.** The relationship between musical tones that produce a pleasing effect when they are sounded together.

concordance (kən-kôr′dns) *n.* **1.** A state of agreement or harmony; concord. **2.** An alphabetical index of the words in a written work or collection of works, showing where they occur: *a concordance to the Bible.*

concordat (kən-kôr′dăt′) *n.* **1.** A formal agreement; a compact. **2.** An agreement between the pope and a government concerning the legal status of the Roman Catholic Church within that government's territory.

concourse (kŏn′kôrs′) *n.* **1.** A large open space in which crowds gather or pass through, as in an airport. **2.** A wide road or avenue. **3.** A large crowd. **4.** The act of coming, moving, or flowing together: *Pittsburgh lies at the concourse of two rivers.*

concrete (kŏn′krēt′ *or* kŏn-krēt′) *n.* A building or paving material made of sand and pebbles or crushed stone, held together by cement. ❖ *adj.* (kŏn-krēt′ *or* kŏn′krēt′) **1.** Made of concrete: *a concrete sidewalk.* **2.** Existing in reality as something that can be perceived by the senses: *concrete objects such as rocks and trees.* **3.** Specific or

particular: *concrete evidence that led to a conviction.* —**con·crete′ly** *adv.* —**con·crete′ness** *n.*

concubine (kŏng′kyə-bīn′) *n.* In certain societies, a woman who cohabits with a man in a relationship similar to marriage but who does not have the full legal status of a wife.

concupiscence (kŏn-kyōō′pĭ-səns) *n.* A strong desire, especially sexual desire; lust. —**con·cu′pis·cent** *adj.*

concur (kən-kûr′) *intr.v.* **concurred, concurring, concurs 1.** To have the same opinion; agree: *Most people concur on the need to stop pollution.* **2.** To occur at the same time: *When rain concurs with melting snow, flooding often develops.* —SEE NOTE AT **cursive.**

concurrence (kən-kûr′əns) *n.* **1.** Agreement of opinion: *Concurrence among all of the partners led to a satisfactory business arrangement.* **2.** An occurrence, as of events, actions, or efforts, at the same time: *The concurrence of high tide and strong winds caused damage along the coast.*

concurrent (kən-kûr′ənt) *adj.* **1.** Happening at the same time: *concurrent events.* **2.** Being in accordance; harmonious: *concurrent opinions.* **3.** Meeting or tending to meet at the same point: *concurrent lines.* —**con·cur′rent·ly** *adv.*

concussion (kən-kŭsh′ən) *n.* **1.** A violent jarring; a shock: *A strong concussion from the blast shattered many windows.* **2.** An injury to the brain usually resulting from a violent blow to the head and causing a temporary disruption in the brain's ability to function normally.

condemn (kən-dĕm′) *tr.v.* **condemned, condemning, condemns 1.** To express strong disapproval of; denounce: *The governor condemned the waste of taxpayers' money.* **2a.** To judge to be guilty: *The suspect was condemned by the jury.* **b.** To sentence to a particular punishment: *He was condemned to 15 years in prison.* **3.** To declare unfit for use: *The city condemned the old warehouse after the fire.* **4.** To take over (private property) for public use: *The state condemned farms in the path of the new expressway.*

condemnation (kŏn′dĕm-nā′shən) *n.* The act of condemning or state of being condemned: *The angry speech drew strong condemnation from his colleagues. The building was torn down after condemnation.*

condensate (kŏn′dən-sāt′ *or* kən-dĕn′sāt′) *n.* The liquid produced by the condensation of a gas.

condensation (kŏn′dən-sā′shən) *n.* **1.** The change of a gas or vapor to a liquid, either by cooling or by being subjected to increased pressure: *Cooling causes the condensation of steam to water.* **2.** A liquid, especially water, formed by this process: *Breathing on a mirror often causes condensation to form.* **3a.** The act or process of condensing something: *The author spent several months in the condensation of his novel.* **b.** A shortened version of something; an abridgment: *The newspaper printed a condensation of the president's speech.*

condense (kən-dĕns′) *v.* **condensed, condensing, condenses** —*tr.* **1.** To cause (a gas or vapor) to change to a liquid form: *Cool temperatures at night condense water vapor in the air into dew.* **2.** To make more concentrated or dense: *We boiled the soup to condense it.* **3.** To make shorter or more concise: *The author condensed the book for use in a magazine.* —*intr.* **1.** To become denser or more compact: *Stars may condense from matter scattered in space.* **2.** To change from a gas to a liquid: *Water vapor condensed on the bathroom mirror.* —**con·dens′a·ble** *adj.*

condensed milk (kən-dĕnst′) *n.* Sweetened cow's milk that has been made very thick by evaporation before canning.

condenser (kən-dĕn′sər) *n*. **1.** A person or thing that condenses. **2.** An apparatus used to condense a gas or vapor. **3.** A capacitor.

condescend (kŏn′dĭ-sĕnd′) *intr.v.* **condescended, condescending, condescends 1.** To agree to do something willingly that is regarded as beneath one's social rank or dignity: *The princess graciously condescended to help at the charity auction.* **2.** To act in a manner that shows one considers oneself superior to others: *The snobbish family in the big house condescends to all their neighbors.*

condescending (kŏn′dĭ-sĕn′dĭng) *adj.* Showing that one considers oneself superior to others; patronizing: *a condescending manner.* —**con′de·scend′ing·ly** *adv.*

condescension (kŏn′dĭ-sĕn′shən) *n.* **1.** The act of condescending. **2.** An attitude or behavior that shows one considers oneself superior to others; haughtiness.

condign (kən-dīn′) *adj.* Deserved; adequate: *a condign punishment for the crime in question.* —**con·dign′ly** *adv.*

condiment (kŏn′də-mənt) *n.* A substance, such as a relish, vinegar, or spice, used to flavor or complement food.

condition (kən-dĭsh′ən) *n.* **1.** A state of being or existence: *They worked hard to restore the old house to its original condition.* **2. conditions** The existing circumstances: *Economic conditions have improved. What are the latest weather conditions?* **3a.** A state of health or fitness: *Have you exercised enough to get back into condition?* **b.** Readiness for use; working order: *A few repairs will put the car in condition.* **4.** A disease or physical ailment: *a heart condition.* **5.** Something that is necessary to the occurrence of something else: *I'll only go with you on this condition: that you let my sister come too.* ❖ *tr.v.* **conditioned, conditioning, conditions 1.** To put into good or proper condition; make fit: *Running five miles a day will condition the track team.* **2.** To adapt; accustom to: *The visitors from Sweden were not conditioned to the hot weather here.* **3.** To train (a person or other animal) to behave or react in a certain way: *The researchers conditioned the chicken to go outside when a light was turned on.* ◆ **on condition that** Provided that: *She gave us permission to use the computer on condition that we report any problems with it.*

conditional (kən-dĭsh′ə-nəl) *adj.* **1.** Depending on a condition or conditions: *While awaiting the court ruling, the committee gave conditional approval to the plan.* **2.** In grammar, expressing a condition on which an outcome or possibility depends. For example, *if it's sunny tomorrow* is a conditional clause in the sentence *We'll go swimming if it's sunny tomorrow.*

conditioned (kən-dĭsh′ənd) *adj.* **1.** Dependent on a condition or conditions; conditional: *gave the project her conditioned approval.* **2.** Physically fit. **3a.** Determined or established by means of conditioning: *a conditioned reflex.* **b.** Trained by means of conditioning.

conditioner (kən-dĭsh′ə-nər) *n.* A device or substance used to improve something in some way: *a leather conditioner; a bottle of hair conditioner.*

conditioning (kən-dĭsh′ə-nĭng) *n.* A process of behavior modification by which an experimental subject comes to associate a desired behavior with a previously unrelated stimulus.

condo (kŏn′dō′) *n., pl.* **condos** *Informal* A condominium.

condole (kən-dōl′) *intr.v.* **condoled, condoling, condoles** To express sympathy or sorrow: *She condoled with the family over their loss.*

condolence (kən-dō′ləns) *n.* Sympathy or an expression of sympathy for a person who has experienced sorrow or misfortune.

condom (kŏn′dəm) *n.* A flexible cover for the penis to be worn during sexual intercourse to prevent pregnancy and sexually transmitted diseases. Condoms are usually made of thin rubber or latex.

condominium (kŏn′də-mĭn′ē-əm) *n.* **1.** A building in which units of property, such as apartments, are owned by individuals. **2.** A unit in such a building.

condone (kən-dōn′) *tr.v.* **condoned, condoning, condones** To forgive, overlook, or ignore: *The school will not condone bullying in any form.* See Synonyms at **forgive**.

condor (kŏn′dôr′ or kŏn′dər) *n.* Either of two very large vultures, one living in the mountains of California and the other in the Andes, having a bare head and a ruff of feathers at the base of the neck.

conducive (kən-dōō′sĭv) *adj.* Tending to cause, promote, or help bring about a specific result: *The noise in the hospital was not conducive to sleeping.*

conduct (kən-dŭkt′) *tr.v.* **conducted, conducting, conducts 1.** To direct the course of; manage: *conduct an experiment; conduct negotiations.* **2.** To lead; guide: *The guide conducted us through the art museum.* See Synonyms at **accompany**. **3.** To direct the performance of (musicians or a musical work): *conduct an orchestra; conduct one of Mozart's symphonies.* **4.** To serve as a medium for conveying; transmit: *Most metals conduct electricity well.* ❖ *n.* (kŏn′dŭkt′) **1.** The way a person acts; behavior: *rude and disorderly conduct.* **2.** The act of directing or controlling; management: *The president is responsible for the conduct of foreign affairs.* ◆ **conduct (oneself)** To behave in a certain way: *They conducted themselves with dignity during the ceremony.* —**con·duct′i-bil′i·ty** *n.* —**con·duct′i·ble** *adj.*

conductance (kən-dŭk′təns) *n.* A measure of the ability of a material to conduct electric charge.

conduction (kən-dŭk′shən) *n.* The transmission or passage of something through a medium or along a path, especially the transmission of heat or electric charge through a substance.

conductive (kən-dŭk′tĭv) *adj.* Relating to or showing conductivity: *a highly conductive material.*

conductivity (kŏn′dŭk-tĭv′ĭ-tē) *n.* The ability or power to conduct heat, electricity, or sound.

conductor (kən-dŭk′tər) *n.* **1.** The person who conducts an orchestra or other group of musical performers. **2.** The person in charge of a train, bus, or streetcar, especially one who collects fares or checks tickets. **3.** A material or object that conducts heat, electricity, light, or sound: *Copper is a good conductor of heat and electricity.*

conduit (kŏn′dōō-ĭt or kŏn′dĭt) *n.* **1.** A channel or pipe for carrying fluids, such as water or natural gas. **2.** A tube or pipe through which electric wires or cables pass. **3.** A means by which something is transmitted: *The spy served as a conduit for secret information.*

cone (kōn) *n.* **1.** A solid made by extending line segments from a point to the perimeter of a circle at the base. **2.** Something having the shape of such a figure: *an ice-cream cone.* **3.** One of a group of cells in the retina of the eye that are shaped like such a figure and are sensitive to bright light and color. **4.** A rounded or long reproductive structure of certain seed plants, having scales that bear either pollen-containing structures or ovules and seeds. Pines, spruces, cedars, and related plants bear cones.

Conestoga wagon (kŏn′ĭ-stō′gə) *n.* A heavy covered wagon first built at Conestoga, Pennsylvania, used especially by American pioneers in their westward travel.

coney also **cony** (kō′nē *or* kŭn′ē) *n., pl.* **coneys** also **conies** **1.** A rabbit, especially the common European rabbit. **2.** The fur of a rabbit.

confabulate (kən-făb′yə-lāt′) *intr.v.* **confabulated, confabulating, confabulates 1.** To talk casually; chat. **2.** In psychology, to fill in gaps in one's memory with fabrications that one believes to be facts. —**con·fab′u·la′tion** *n.* —**con·fab′u·la′tor** *n.* —**con·fab′u·la·to′ry** (kən-făb′-yə-lə-tôr′ē) *adj.*

confection (kən-fĕk′shən) *n.* A sweet food or preparation, such as candy.

confectioner (kən-fĕk′shə-nər) *n.* A person who makes or sells candy and other confections.

confectioners′ sugar (kən-fĕk′shə-nərz) *n.* A fine powdery sugar used especially in frostings and as a topping on desserts.

confectionery (kən-fĕk′shə-nĕr′ē) *n., pl.* **confectioneries** A confectioner's shop.

confederacy (kən-fĕd′ər-ə-sē) *n., pl.* **confederacies 1.** A political union of peoples or states: *the confederacy of Native American peoples called the Iroquois Nation.* **2. Confederacy** The Confederate States of America. **3.** A group of people united for unlawful practices; a conspiracy: *A confederacy of dissidents plotted the overthrow of the government.*

confederate (kən-fĕd′ər-ĭt) *n.* **1.** An associate in a plot or crime; an accomplice. **2.** A member of a confederacy. **3. Confederate** A supporter of the Confederate States of America. ❖ *adj.* **1.** Belonging to a confederacy. **2. Confederate** Relating to the Confederate States of America. ❖ *tr. & intr.v.* (kən-fĕd′ə-rāt′) **confederated, confederating, confederates** To form into or become part of a confederacy.

confederation (kən-fĕd′ə-rā′shən) *n.* **1.** A group of people united for a common purpose; a league: *The teachers formed a national confederation to protect their interests.* **2.** A group of states, provinces, or territories united under a single government. **3.** The act of confederating or the state of being confederated.

confer (kən-fûr′) *v.* **conferred, conferring, confers** —*intr.* To meet in order to discuss something or compare opinions; consult: *The president conferred with cabinet advisers.* —*tr.* To bestow or award: *The mayor conferred a medal on the two heroic firefighters.* —SEE NOTE AT **transfer.**

conference (kŏn′fər-əns *or* kŏn′frəns) *n.* **1.** A meeting to discuss a subject or a number of subjects: *a peace conference.* **2.** A regional association of churches, athletic teams, or other groups. **3.** The act of conferring: *The attorneys were in conference for hours.*

conference call *n.* A conference by telephone in which three or more people participate.

confess (kən-fĕs′) *v.* **confessed, confessing, confesses** —*tr.* **1.** To state openly or admit (something wrong or bad that one has done): *The children confessed that they had been playing with matches.* **2a.** To make known (one's sins) to a priest or to God. **b.** To hear the confession of (a person). —*intr.* **1.** To admit or acknowledge something wrong or bad that one has done: *The driver confessed to driving too fast.* **2.** To tell one's sins to a priest.

confession (kən-fĕsh′ən) *n.* **1.** The act of confessing or admitting; acknowledgment: *The suspect's full confession of guilt cleared up the case.* **2.** The act of telling one's sins

to a priest or to God. **3.** Something confessed: *Did the prisoner sign her confession?*

confessional (kən-fĕsh′ə-nəl) *n.* A small booth in which a priest hears confessions.

confessor (kən-fĕs′ər) *n.* **1.** A priest who hears confession and gives absolution of sins. **2.** A person who accepts intimate confidences and consoles: *The counselor acted as confessor to the whole group.* **3.** A person who confesses.

confetti (kən-fĕt′ē) *pl.n. (used with a singular verb)* Small pieces of colored paper that are scattered about on festive occasions.

confidant (kŏn′fĭ-dănt′ *or* kŏn′fĭ-dänt′) *n.* A person to whom another person confides personal matters or secrets.

confide (kən-fīd′) *v.* **confided, confiding, confides** —*tr.* **1.** To tell (something) in confidence: *confide a secret to a friend.* **2.** To put into another's care; entrust: *Before going on vacation, he confided the task of mowing the lawn to his neighbor.* —*intr.* To tell or share one's secrets with: *Can I confide in you?* —**con·fid′er** *n.*

confidence (kŏn′fĭ-dəns) *n.* **1.** Belief in the effectiveness of one's own abilities or in one's favorable acceptance by others; self-confidence: *She finally developed the confidence to sing in public.* **2.** Trust or faith: *We are placing our confidence in you to solve the problem.* **3.** A trusting relationship: *I have decided to take you into my confidence.* **4.** A feeling of assurance that someone will keep a secret: *I am telling you this in strict confidence.* **5.** Something confided; a secret: *the many confidences of close friends.*

confident (kŏn′fĭ-dənt) *adj.* Feeling or showing confidence, especially in being sure of oneself; certain: *The lawyer is confident of winning the case. The surgeon approached the operation with a confident air.* —**con′-fi·dent·ly** *adv.*

confidential (kŏn′fĭ-dĕn′shəl) *adj.* **1.** Told in confidence; secret: *A person's medical history is confidential information shared only with a doctor.* **2.** Entrusted with the confidence of someone else: *a confidential secretary.* **3.** Showing confidence or intimacy: *a confidential tone of voice.* —**con′fi·den′tial·ly** *adv.*

confiding (kən-fī′dĭng) *adj.* Having a tendency to confide; trusting: *a confiding nature.*

configuration (kən-fĭg′yə-rā′shən) *n.* The form or arrangement of the parts of something: *a configuration of dots that form a picture when connected; the configuration of a computer system.*

confine (kən-fīn′) *tr.v.* **confined, confining, confines 1.** To keep within bounds; restrict; limit: *Firefighters confined the fire to the roof.* **2.** To shut or keep inside, as in prison: *The dogs were confined to a kennel.*

confinement (kən-fīn′mənt) *n.* **1.** The act of confining or condition of being confined: *The prisoner was held in solitary confinement.* **2.** The period of childbirth.

confines (kŏn′fīnz′) *pl.n.* The limits of a space or area; the borders: *The dog wandered beyond the confines of the yard.*

confirm (kən-fûrm′) *tr.v.* **confirmed, confirming, confirms 1.** To support or establish the certainty or validity of: *The results of the experiment confirmed the theory.* **2.** To make firmer; strengthen: *Reading about famous scientists confirmed her intention to study chemistry.* **3.** To make valid or binding by a formal or legal act; ratify: *The judge's appointment to the Supreme Court was confirmed by the Senate.* **4.** To admit to full membership in a church or synagogue by the rite of confirmation.

confirmation (kŏn′fər-mā′shən) *n.* **1.** The act of confirming: *The president needs the Senate's confirmation to appoint an ambassador.* **2.** Something that confirms; proof: *The license was confirmation of the doctor's qualification to practice medicine.* **3.** A Christian ceremony in which a baptized person is made a full member of a church. **4.** A Jewish ceremony marking the completion of a young person's religious training.

confirmed (kən-fûrmd′) *adj.* **1.** Firmly established; proved: *a confirmed theory.* **2.** Settled in a habit or condition: *a confirmed gossip.* —**con·firm′ed·ly** (kən-fûr′mĭd-lē) *adv.*

confiscate (kŏn′fĭ-skāt′) *tr.v.* **confiscated, confiscating, confiscates 1.** To seize (private property) from someone for the public treasury: *The government confiscated the boat and its illegal goods.* **2.** To seize by authority; take away: *The teacher confiscated the child's pack of chewing gum.* —**con′fis·ca′tion** *n.*

conflagration (kŏn′flə-grā′shən) *n.* A large fire.

conflate (kən-flāt′) *tr.v.* **conflated, conflating, conflates 1.** To treat or present (two or more distinct things) as the same thing: *a speech that conflated patriotism and support for the government.* **2.** To combine (two variant texts, for example) into one whole. —**con·fla′tion** *n.*

conflict (kŏn′flĭkt′) *n.* **1.** A state of fighting; a battle or war. **2.** A state of disagreement, as between people, ideas, or interests: *a conflict between two sets of instructions.* ❖ *intr.v.* (kən-flĭkt′) **conflicted, conflicting, conflicts** To be in opposition; differ; clash: *The meeting conflicts with my dental appointment.*

conflict of interest *n., pl.* **conflicts of interest** A conflict between a person's private interests and public obligations: *To avoid a conflict of interest, the judge refused to hear a trial involving a company owned by her brother.*

confluence (kŏn′flōō-əns) *n.* **1.** The point at which two or more rivers or streams come together: *The city is located at the confluence of two important rivers.* **2.** A gathering, flowing, or joining together of people, causes, or events: *A confluence of factors led to the financial collapse.*

confluent (kŏn′flōō-ənt) *adj.* Flowing or running together; blending into one: *confluent rivers.*

conform (kən-fôrm′) *intr.v.* **conformed, conforming, conforms 1.** To be or act in agreement with established customs, expectations, or rules: *Many young people do not like to conform to the way older people dress.* See Synonyms at **adapt. 2.** To be similar in form or pattern: *a tarp that conforms to the shape of the boat.* —**con·form′er** *n.*

conformation (kŏn′fər-mā′shən) *n.* **1.** The way something is formed; shape or structure: *The conformation of a snake's skeleton is elongated.* **2.** The act of conforming or the state of being conformed.

conformist (kən-fôr′mĭst) *n.* A person who conforms to current customs, rules, or styles.

conformity (kən-fôr′mĭ-tē) *n., pl.* **conformities 1.** Agreement; harmony: *practices that are in conformity with standards set by the industry.* **2.** Action or behavior that is in agreement with current customs, rules, or styles: *a policy that encouraged originality among employees rather than blind conformity.*

confound (kən-found′ or kŏn-found′) *tr.v.* **confounded, confounding, confounds 1.** To bewilder, puzzle, or perplex: *The dog's strange behavior confounded its master.* **2.** To mistake (one thing) for another; mix up: *The confused witness confounded fiction and fact.*

confront (kən-frŭnt′) *tr.v.* **confronted, confronting, confronts 1.** To come face to face with, especially in opposition: *She finally confronted her rival on the tennis court.* **2.** To bring face to face with; cause to encounter: *The defendant was confronted with all the evidence and confessed.* **3.** To come up against; encounter: *The scientists confronting many difficulties in creating the new vaccine.*

confrontation (kŏn′frŭn-tā′shən) *n.* **1.** The act of confronting or the state of being confronted: *The lawyer's confrontation of the witnesses proved their testimony was unreliable.* **2.** A direct encounter, especially a conflict or a clash, as of opponents: *The hikers hoped to avoid any confrontations with wild animals.*

Confucian (kən-fyōō′shən) *adj.* Relating to a set of principles of conduct that are based on the teaching of the ancient Chinese philosopher Confucius and that stress social harmony, justice, and devotion to family ancestors. —**Con·fu′cian·ism** *n.*

confuse (kən-fyōōz′) *tr.v.* **confused, confusing, confuses 1.** To cause to be unable to understand or think clearly; perplex or bewilder: *The audience was confused by the poorly organized presentation.* **2.** To mistake (a person or thing) for someone or something else; fail to identify correctly: *People often confuse me with my brother.* —**con·fus′ing·ly** *adv.*

confused (kən-fyōōzd′) *adj.* **1.** Bewildered; perplexed: *a confused look.* **2.** Mixed up; disordered: *a confused situation; a confused story.* —**con·fus′ed·ly** (kən-fyōō′zĭd-lē) *adv.*

confusion (kən-fyōō′zhən) *n.* **1.** The act of confusing: *The confusion of the addresses meant the package was not delivered to the right place.* **2.** The state of being confused: *The unexpected news threw us all into confusion.*

confute (kən-fyōōt′) *tr.v.* **confuted, confuting, confutes** To prove to be wrong or false; refute: *The facts confuted his testimony. An expert confuted the speaker.* —**con′fu·ta′tion** (kŏn′fyōō-tā′shən) *n.*

congeal (kən-jēl′) *v.* **congealed, congealing, congeals** —*intr.* **1.** To become thicker or turn into a solid: *Fat congealed in globs on the surface of the soup.* **2.** To come together and form a whole or produce a result: *Popular discontent finally congealed into political opposition.* —*tr.* To cause to congeal: *The cool air congealed the fat.* —**con·geal′ment** *n.*

congenial (kən-jēn′yəl) *adj.* **1.** Having similar tastes, habits, or dispositions: *two congenial people.* **2.** Of a pleasant disposition; friendly; amiable: *a congenial host.* **3.** Suited to one's nature; pleasant; agreeable: *The bright, airy room provided congenial surroundings.* —**con·ge′ni·al′i·ty** (kən-jē′nē-ăl′ĭ-tē) *n.* —**con·gen′ial·ly** *adv.*

congenital (kən-jĕn′ĭ-tl) *adj.* Existing at or before birth: *Many congenital defects can now be corrected by surgery.* —**con·gen′i·tal·ly** *adv.*

conger (kŏng′gər) *n.* Any of various large ocean eels, often caught for food in Europe.

congeries (kən-jîr′ēz′ or kŏn′jə-rēz′) *n.* (used with a singular verb) A collection; an aggregation: *a congeries of hangers-on.*

congest (kən-jĕst′) *v.* **congested, congesting, congests** —*tr.* **1.** To overfill; overcrowd: *Heavy traffic congested the highway.* **2.** To cause an abnormally large amount of fluid to collect in (a vessel or organ of the body). —*intr.* To become congested: *Pneumonia causes the lungs to congest with fluid.* —**con·ges′tive** *adj.*

congestion (kən-jĕs′chən) *n.* **1.** A condition of overcrowding: *traffic congestion during rush hour.* **2.** A condition in which fluid collects in an organ or tissue of the body: *Colds often produce bronchial congestion.*

congestive heart failure (kən-jĕs′tĭv) *n.* A medical condition characterized usually by shortness of breath, congestion in the lungs, fatigue, and fluid buildup resulting from the inability of a damaged heart to adequately pump blood to body tissues.

conglomerate (kən-glŏm′ə-rāt′) *intr. & tr.v.* **conglomerated, conglomerating, conglomerates** To form or cause to form into a mass; cluster. ❖ *n.* (kən-glŏm′ər-ĭt) **1.** A business corporation made up of a number of different companies that operate in widely diversified fields. **2.** A mass of material that clings together. **3.** A sedimentary rock that consists of pebbles, gravel, or seashells cemented together by hardened clay or a similar material. ❖ *adj.* (kən-glŏm′ər-ĭt) **1.** Formed together into a mass: *conglomerate rock formed of sand and pebbles.* **2.** Made up of many parts: *The reformers were a conglomerate group from several political parties.*

conglomeration (kən-glŏm′ə-rā′shən) *n.* A collection or accumulation of many different things or people.

Congolese (kŏng′gō-lēz′ *or* kŏng′gō-lēs′) *adj.* Relating to the Democratic Republic of the Congo or the Republic of the Congo. ❖ *n., pl.* **Congolese** A native or inhabitant of either of these countries.

congratulate (kən-grăch′ə-lāt′ *or* kən-grăj′ə-lāt′) *tr.v.* **congratulated, congratulating, congratulates** To express joy or good wishes to (someone) for an achievement or good fortune: *The crowd congratulated the newly elected mayor.*

congratulation (kən-grăch′ə-lā′shən *or* kən-grăj′ə-lā′shən) *n.* often **congratulations** An expression of joy or acknowledgement: *I shook the winner's hand in congratulation. We sent a card with our congratulations to the new parents.* ❖ *interj.* **congratulations** An expression used to show joy or acknowledgement: *You won first prize. Congratulations!*

congratulatory (kən-grăch′ə-lə-tôr′ē *or* kən-grăj′ə-lə-tôr′ē) *adj.* Expressing congratulations: *a congratulatory message.*

congregate (kŏng′grĭ-gāt′) *intr.v.* **congregated, congregating, congregates** To come together in a crowd or mass; assemble: *Salmon congregate at the falls in large numbers.* —**con′gre·ga′tor** *n.*

congregation (kŏng′grĭ-gā′shən) *n.* **1a.** A group of people gathered for religious worship: *The congregation bowed their heads in prayer.* **b.** The members of a specific religious group who regularly worship at a church or synagogue. **2.** A gathering of people or things: *The congregation of tourists crowded around the exhibit.* **3.** The act of assembling: *the congregation of birds on their nesting grounds.*

congregational (kŏng′grĭ-gā′shə-nəl) *adj.* **1.** Relating to a congregation: *congregational worship.* **2. Congregational** Relating to Congregationalism or Congregationalists.

congregationalism (kŏng′grĭ-gā′shə-nə-lĭz′əm) *n.* **1.** Church government in which each local congregation governs itself. **2. Congregationalism** The system of government and religious beliefs of a Protestant denomination in which each member church is self-governing. —**con′gre·ga′tion·al·ist, Con′gre·ga′tion·al·ist** *adj. & n.*

congress (kŏng′grĭs) *n.* **1.** A formal meeting of people representing various nations, organizations, or professions to discuss problems: *a medical congress of heart*

specialists. **2.** The lawmaking body of a republic. **3. Congress** The national legislative body of the United States, consisting of the Senate and the House of Representatives. —**con·gres′sion·al** (kən-grĕsh′ə-nəl *or* kəng-grĕsh′ə-nəl) *adj.*

congressman (kŏng′grĭs-mən) *n.* A man who is a member of the United States Congress, especially of the House of Representatives.

congresswoman (kŏng′grĭs-wŏŏm′ən) *n.* A woman who is a member of the United States Congress, especially of the House of Representatives.

congruence (kŏng′grōō-əns *or* kən-grōō′əns) *n.* The condition of being congruent.

congruency (kŏng′grōō-ən-sē *or* kən-grōō′ən-sē) *n., pl.* **congruencies** Congruence.

congruent (kŏng′grōō-ənt *or* kən-grōō′ənt) *adj.* **1.** In geometry, matching exactly; having the same size and shape: *congruent triangles.* **2.** Corresponding or agreeing; harmonious: *congruent objectives of policy.* —**con′gru·ent·ly** *adv.*

congruity (kən-grōō′ĭ-tē) *n., pl.* **congruities 1.** Agreement; harmony: *The two leaders worked in congruity to achieve peace in the region.* **2.** The state or fact of being congruent: *the congruity of superimposed triangles.*

conic (kŏn′ĭk) *adj.* Conical.

conical (kŏn′ĭ-kəl) *adj.* Relating to or shaped like a cone. —**con′i·cal·ly** *adv.*

conic section *n.* A curve, such as a circle, ellipse, hyperbola, or parabola, formed by the intersection of a plane with a cone.

conifer (kŏn′ə-fər *or* kō′nə-fər) *n.* Any of various trees or shrubs that bear cones. Conifers are usually evergreen and include the pines, firs, spruces, hemlocks, and yews.

coniferous (kō-nĭf′ər-əs *or* kə-nĭf′ər-əs) *adj.* **1.** Bearing cones: *coniferous trees such as pines and hemlocks.* **2.** Relating to conifers: *a coniferous forest.*

conj. An abbreviation of conjunction.

conjectural (kən-jĕk′chər-əl) *adj.* Based on or inclined to conjecture: *a conjectural forecast of economic improvement.*

conjecture (kən-jĕk′chər) *n.* **1.** The formation of an opinion or conclusion from incomplete or insufficient evidence; guesswork: *The origin of language is a matter of conjecture.* **2.** A statement, opinion, or conclusion based on guesswork; a guess: *make a conjecture about the election's outcome.* ❖ *intr.v.* **conjectured, conjecturing, conjectures** To make a conjecture; guess: *The radio commentator conjectured on who would be the new mayor.*

conjoin (kən-join′) *tr. & intr.v.* **conjoined, conjoining, conjoins** To join or become joined; connect; unite: *A strip of sand conjoined the two islands at low tide. The two parties conjoined into one.* —**con·join′er** *n.*

conjoined twin (kən-joind′) *n.* One of a pair of identical twins born with parts of their bodies joined together. Conjoined twins develop when an early embryo divides incompletely into two parts.

conjoint (kən-joint′) *adj.* Joined together; combined: *a conjoint military action involving air and naval forces.*

conjugal (kŏn′jə-gəl) *adj.* Relating to marriage or the relationship of spouses: *conjugal happiness.* —**con′ju·gal·ly** *adv.*

conjugate (kŏn′jə-gāt′) *v.* **conjugated, conjugating, conjugates** — *tr.* To list the inflected forms of a verb, usually in a set order. For example, in the simple present tense, indicative mood, and active voice, the verb "to have" is conjugated *I have, you have, she has, we have, you have, they have.* —*intr.* In biology, to unite or fuse in conjugation. ❖ *adj.* (kŏn′jə-gĭt *or* kŏn′jə-gāt′) Joined together, especially in pairs; coupled.

conjugation (kŏn′jə-gā′shən) *n.* **1a.** The inflection of a particular verb. **b.** A presentation of the complete set of inflected forms of a verb. **c.** A class of verbs having similar inflected forms. **2a.** A type of sexual reproduction in which single-celled organisms of the same species join together and exchange nuclear material before each organism undergoes cell division. **b.** The union of reproductive cells to form a fertilized cell.

conjunction (kən-jŭngk′shən) *n.* **1.** The act of joining or state of being joined; combination: *A happy conjunction of circumstances strengthened the economy.* **2a.** A part of speech that connects words, phrases, clauses, or sentences. **b.** A word belonging to this part of speech. *And, but, or,* and *yet* are examples of conjunctions in English. **3.** The position of two celestial objects when they have the same celestial longitude.

conjunctiva (kŏn′jŭngk-tī′və) *n., pl.* **conjunctivas** or **conjunctivae** (kŏn′jŭngk-tī′vē) The mucous membrane that lines the inside of the eyelid and covers the surface of the eyeball.

conjunctive (kən-jŭngk′tĭv) *adj.* **1.** Joined or serving to join together. **2.** In grammar, connecting or serving as a conjunction. Conjunctive adverbs, such as *however* and *therefore,* are used to connect sentences. —**con·junc′- tive·ly** *adv.*

USAGE Unlike a coordinating conjunction, a conjunctive adverb is not ordinarily used following a comma to connect clauses within a sentence. A conjunctive adverb can be used parenthetically, as in *The jar, however, was empty,* or it can follow a semicolon, helping to indicate the relationship between clauses, as in *We expected rain; however, the day was sunny.*

conjunctivitis (kən-jŭngk′tə-vī′tĭs) *n.* Inflammation of the conjunctiva, often in the form of pinkeye.

conjure (kŏn′jər *or* kən-jŏŏr′) *v.* **conjured, conjuring, conjures** —*tr.* **1.** To summon (a devil or spirit) by a magic or supernatural power. **2.** To influence or bring about as if by magic: *In saving the patient our doctor conjured a miracle.* **3.** To call to mind: *The mention of Kansas conjures up images of fields of grain.* —*intr.* To practice magic; perform magic tricks.

conjurer also **conjuror** (kŏn′jər-ər *or* kŭn′jər-ər) *n.* A magician or sorcerer.

conk (kŏngk) *Informal n.* A blow, especially on the head. ❖ *tr.v.* **conked, conking, conks** To hit, especially on the head. ◆ **conk out 1.** To fail suddenly; break down: *The engine conked out.* **2.** To fall asleep, especially suddenly: *He conked out while watching television.*

connect (kə-nĕkt′) *v.* **connected, connecting, connects** —*tr.* **1.** To join or fasten together; link: *A new road connects the two towns.* See Synonyms at **join. 2.** To consider as related; associate in the mind: *We connect summer with picnics and swimming.* **3.** To plug in (an electrical cord or device) to an outlet: *connect a TV set.* **4.** To link by telephone or other communications circuit: *The operator connected me with the order department. Her computer is connected to the Internet.* —*intr.* **1.** To be or become joined: *The two streams connected to form a river.* **2.** To

be scheduled so that passengers can transfer from one bus, train, or airplane to another: *The bus connected with the train at the station.* —**con·nect′er, con·nec′tor** *n.* —**con·nect′i·ble** *adj.*

connection (kə-nĕk′shən) *n.* **1.** The act of connecting or the condition of being connected: *Connection of the telephone cables took several hours. That doctor's connection to the hospital has benefited many patients.* **2.** Something that connects or joins; a link: *a telephone connection; rail connections between the two cities.* **3.** An association or relationship: *There is a connection between good health and eating well.* **4.** A person with whom one is associated, as by kinship, common interests, or marriage: *I heard about the job through family connections.* **5.** A usually influential or important person with whom one is associated: *used my connections to get a job in the newsroom.* **6.** A means of continuing transportation: *I missed my connection in Chicago.*

connective (kə-nĕk′tĭv) *adj.* Connecting or serving to connect. ❖ *n.* **1.** Something that connects. **2.** In grammar, a word such as a conjunction that connects words, phrases, clauses, or sentences.

connective tissue *n.* Tissue that forms the framework and supporting structures of the body, including bone, cartilage, mucous membrane, and fat.

connectivity (kŏn′ĕk-tĭv′ĭ-tē) *n., pl.* **connectivities 1.** The quality or condition of being connected or connective. **2.** The ability to make and maintain a connection between two or more points in a telecommunications system: *a phone company that offers excellent Internet connectivity.*

conning tower (kŏn′ĭng) *n.* **1.** A raised, enclosed structure on the deck of a submarine, used for observation and as an entrance or exit. **2.** The armored pilothouse of a warship.

conniption (kə-nĭp′shən) *n. Informal* A fit of violent emotion, such as anger or panic.

connive (kə-nīv′) *intr.v.* **connived, conniving, connives 1.** To cooperate secretly in an illegal or wrongful action: *The traitor connived with the enemy.* **2.** To pretend not to notice or fail to deal with something that should be reported or condemned: *The mayor connived at the bribery of city officials.* —**con·niv′ance** (kə-nī′vəns) *n.*

connoisseur (kŏn′ə-sûr′ *or* kŏn′ə-sŏŏr′) *n.* A person who has expert knowledge or excellent judgment of something, such as art or fine food.

connotation (kŏn′ə-tā′shən) *n.* A meaning suggested by a certain word in addition to its literal or most exact meaning: *The word "lamb" has connotations of simplicity and innocence.*

connote (kə-nōt′) *tr.v.* **connoted, connoting, connotes** To suggest or imply in addition to literal or exact meaning: *In a political leader, hesitation is apt to connote weakness.*

connubial (kə-nōō′bē-əl) *adj.* Relating to marriage or the relationship between spouses; conjugal: *connubial bliss.*

conquer (kŏng′kər) *tr.v.* **conquered, conquering, conquers 1.** To get control of or subdue by military force: *In 1066 the Normans conquered England.* **2.** To eliminate or overcome: *Scientists are trying to conquer cancer. I conquered my fear about speaking in public.* —**con′quer·or, con′- quer·er** *n.*

conquest (kŏn′kwĕst′ *or* kŏng′kwĕst′) *n.* **1.** An act of conquering: *the Spanish conquest of lands in the New World.* **2.** Something conquered: *one of the empire's conquests.*

conquistador (kŏn-kwĭs′tə-dôr′ *or* kŏng-kē′stə-dôr′) *n., pl.* **conquistadors** or **conquistadores** (kŏng-kē′stə-dôr′-

ās) One of the Spanish conquerors of Mexico, Central America, and Peru in the 1500s.

consanguinity (kŏn′săn-gwĭn′ĭ-tē) *n., pl.* **consanguinities** **1.** Relationship by blood or by a common ancestor. **2.** A close affinity or connection.

conscience (kŏn′shəns) *n.* A sense of right and wrong that urges one to act morally: *Listen to your conscience and you'll be glad in the long run.*

conscientious (kŏn′shē-ĕn′shəs) *adj.* **1.** Guided by or done with a sense of what is right or proper: *a conscientious decision.* **2.** Careful and thorough: *a conscientious worker.* —**con′sci·en′tious·ly** *adv.* —**con′sci·en′-tious·ness** *n.*

conscientious objector *n.* A person who on the basis of religious belief or moral principle refuses to serve in the armed forces or take up arms.

conscious (kŏn′shəs) *adj.* **1.** Able to perceive what is happening around oneself; awake: *The patient was fully conscious throughout the operation.* **2a.** Having an awareness of one's own existence, sensations, thoughts, and surroundings: *People are not always conscious of their talents.* **b.** Known to oneself or felt by oneself: *filled with conscious remorse.* **3.** Intentionally done; deliberate: *make a conscious effort to speak more distinctly.* —**con′-scious·ly** *adv.*

consciousness (kŏn′shəs-nĭs) *n.* **1.** The condition of being conscious: *The doctor asked if the patient had lost consciousness.* **2.** The sense of identity, especially the ideas, opinions, and feelings, held by a person or shared by a group: *Love of freedom runs deep in the national consciousness.*

conscript (kŏn′skrĭpt′) *n.* A person who is drafted, especially into the armed forces. ❖ *tr.v.* (kən-skrĭpt′) **conscripted, conscripting, conscripts** To enroll by force into service in the armed forces; draft: *Some volunteered for the army, while others were conscripted.* —**con·scrip′tion** (kən-skrĭp′shən) *n.*

consecrate (kŏn′sĭ-krāt′) *tr.v.* **consecrated, consecrating, consecrates** **1.** To declare or set apart as sacred: *consecrate a new church.* **2.** To dedicate to a worthy purpose: *The nurse's life was consecrated to caring for the ill.* —**con′se·cra′tion** *n.* —**con′se·cra′tor** *n.*

consecutive (kən-sĕk′yə-tĭv) *adj.* Following in order, without a break or interruption; successive: *It rained this week for five consecutive days.* —**con·sec′u·tive·ly** *adv.*

consensual (kən-sĕn′shōō-əl) *adj.* **1.** Relating to or expressing a consensus: *a consensual decision by the committee.* **2a.** Involving informal but legally binding mutual consent: *a consensual marriage; a consensual contract.* **b.** Involving the willing participation of both or all parties: *consensual sexual activity.* —**con·sen′su·al·ly** *adv.*

consensus (kən-sĕn′səs) *n.* An opinion reached by a group as a whole; general agreement: *The consensus among voters is for building the new school.* —SEE NOTE AT **consent.**

consent (kən-sĕnt′) *intr.v.* **consented, consenting, consents** To give permission; agree: *I will never consent to such a foolish plan.* ❖ *n.* Agreement and acceptance; permission: *The patient gave her consent to the experimental treatment.*

WORD BUILDING The word roots *sent-* and *sens-* in English words come from the Latin verb *sentīre,* "to feel, sense, judge," which has the past participle *sēnsus.* **Consent** therefore means "to feel with, agree" (using the prefix *con-,* a form of *com-,* "with, together"). **Dissent** is literally "to judge differently" (*dis-,* "apart"). A **consensus** is "a feeling all together, universal agreement"; **dissension** is the exact opposite—general disagreement.

consequence (kŏn′sĭ-kwĕns′) *n.* **1.** Something that follows from an action or condition; an effect: *Having a large vocabulary was a consequence of so much reading.* **2.** Importance; significance: *a minor matter of no consequence.*

consequent (kŏn′sĭ-kwĕnt′) *adj.* Following as an effect or result: *heavy rains and the consequent flooding of the farmlands.*

consequential (kŏn′sĭ-kwĕn′shəl) *adj.* **1.** Important; significant: *a consequential decision that affected us all.* **2.** Distinguished; influential: *She is the most consequential film critic writing today.* **3.** Consequent: *a downturn in the markets with a consequential rise in unemployment.* —**con′se·quen′tial·ly** *adv.*

consequently (kŏn′sĭ-kwĕnt′lē) *adv.* As a result; therefore: *I forgot my key and consequently was locked out of the house.*

conservation (kŏn′sûr-vā′shən) *n.* **1.** The act or process of conserving. **2.** Preservation from loss or damage, especially the protection, management, or restoration of wildlife and of natural resources, such as forests, soil, and water. **3.** The continuance of a physical quantity, such as mass, in the same amount during a physical or chemical change.

conservationist (kŏn′sûr-vā′shə-nĭst) *n.* A person who advocates or practices conservation, especially of natural resources.

conservation of energy *n.* A principle of physics stating that the total energy in any closed system does not vary, although energy can be changed from one form into another.

conservation of mass *n.* A principle of physics stating that the total mass of a closed system remains constant regardless of reactions within the system. In a chemical reaction, matter is thought to be neither created nor destroyed but changed from one substance to another.

conservation of mass-energy *n.* Mass-energy equivalence.

conservatism (kən-sûr′və-tĭz′əm) *n.* **1.** Conservative political views and policies. **2.** Caution or moderation, as in behavior or outlook: *an investor who practiced conservatism in managing her money.*

conservative (kən-sûr′və-tĭv) *adj.* **1.** Favoring things as they are; opposing change: *a conservative attitude toward manners.* **2.** Traditional in style; not showy: *a conservative dark suit.* **3.** Moderate; cautious; restrained: *a conservative estimate of expenses.* **4.** often **Conservative** Relating to or belonging to a political party or group that emphasizes respect for traditional institutions and that generally opposes the attempt to bring about social change through legislation or government programs. **5. Conservative** Relating to or belonging to Conservative Judaism. ❖ *n.* **1.** A person who is conservative. **2.** often **Conservative** A member of a conservative party. —**con·serv′a·tive·ly** *adv.*

Conservative Judaism *n.* The branch of Judaism that allows for changes in Jewish law that are authorized by rabbis.

conservatory (kən-sûr′və-tôr′ē) *n., pl.* **conservatories 1.** A greenhouse in which plants are arranged for display. **2.** A school of music, theater, or dance.

conserve (kən-sûrv′) *tr.v.* **conserved, conserving, con-**

serves 1. To protect from loss or harm; preserve: *conserve one's energy; conserve forests and other natural resources.* **2.** To use carefully; avoid wasting: *We turned down the thermostat to conserve energy.* **3.** To preserve (fruits) by cooking with sugar. **4.** To keep (a physical quantity, such as mass) in the same amount during a physical or chemical change. ❖ *n.* (kŏn′sûrv′) A jam made of fruits stewed in sugar.

consider (kən-sĭd′ər) *v.* **considered, considering, considers** —*tr.* **1.** To think about (something) carefully, especially before making a decision: *I will consider what you said and respond later.* **2.** To regard as; believe to be: *She considers this the most beautiful park in town.* **3.** To take into account; keep in mind: *He sings well if you consider the fact that he never had lessons.* **4.** To be thoughtful of; show consideration for: *Consider the feelings of other people.* —*intr.* To think carefully; reflect: *Give me time to consider.*

considerable (kən-sĭd′ər-ə-bəl) *adj.* **1.** Large or great in amount, extent, or degree: *They gave considerable thought to the matter.* **2.** Worth considering; important; significant: *a considerable issue.* —*con·sid′er·a·bly adv.*

considerate (kən-sĭd′ər-ĭt) *adj.* Taking into account other people's feelings; thoughtful: *quiet and considerate neighbors.* —*con·sid′er·ate·ly adv.* —*con·sid′er·ate·ness n.*

consideration (kən-sĭd′ə-rā′shən) *n.* **1.** Careful thought; deliberation: *The matter is complicated and needs consideration.* **2.** A factor to be considered in making a judgment or decision: *The health of the public is an important consideration when allocating tax dollars.* **3.** Thoughtful concern: *consideration for people's feelings.* **4.** A payment for a service rendered; a fee: *I agreed to take care of their dog for a small consideration.* ♦ **in consideration of 1.** In view of; on account of: *a medal awarded in consideration of bravery.* **2.** In return for: *payment in consideration of extra work.*

considered (kən-sĭd′ərd) *adj.* Reached after careful thought: *my considered opinion.*

considering (kən-sĭd′ər-ĭng) *prep.* In view of; taking into consideration: *Considering the mistakes that were made, it is amazing that the job was completed.*

consign (kən-sīn′) *tr.v.* **consigned, consigning, consigns 1.** To give or hand over, especially to the care of another: *The criminals have been consigned to prison.* **2.** To deliver (merchandise) for sale: *The manufacturer consigned the cars to the dealer.* —*con·sign′a·ble adj.*

consignment (kən-sīn′mənt) *n.* **1.** The delivery of something, as for sale or safekeeping: *The consignment of food for the earthquake victims was a top priority.* **2.** Something that is consigned, as for sale: *The store received a consignment of umbrellas.* ♦ **on consignment** With the agreement that payment is expected only after sales have been made and that unsold items may be returned: *The store owner accepted the shipment on consignment.*

consist (kən-sĭst′) *intr.v.* **consisted, consisting, consists 1.** To be made up or composed: *The United States consists of 50 states.* **2.** To have a basis; lie: *The beauty of the author's style consists in its simplicity.*

consistency (kən-sĭs′tən-sē) *n., pl.* **consistencies 1.** Agreement or harmony among things or parts: *A polite greeting is in consistency with good manners.* **2.** Adherence to or agreement with the same principles or course of action: *The game was confusing because the rules lacked*

consistency. **3.** The degree of firmness, density, or thickness: *mix water and clay to the consistency of thick cream.*

consistent (kən-sĭs′tənt) *adj.* **1.** In agreement; compatible: *The experimental results were consistent with theory.* **2.** Continually adhering to the same principles or course of action: *a consistent supporter of women's rights.* —*con·sis′tent·ly adv.*

consistory (kən-sĭs′tə-rē) *n., pl.* **consistories 1.** A council of the cardinals of the Roman Catholic Church, presided over by the pope. **2.** The governing assembly of certain Protestant churches.

consolation (kŏn′sə-lā′shən) *n.* **1.** The act or an instance of consoling or comforting. **2.** Something that consoles: *The one consolation in having my wisdom teeth out is that I'll get lots of ice cream.*

consolation prize *n.* A prize given to someone who participates in but does not win a contest.

console¹ (kən-sōl′) *tr.v.* **consoled, consoling, consoles** To comfort in time of disappointment or sorrow: *Friends consoled the widow at the funeral.*

console² (kŏn′sōl′) *n.* **1.** A cabinet for a radio, television set, or stereo system, designed to stand on the floor. **2.** A small storage compartment mounted between bucket seats in an automobile. **3.** A panel housing the controls for a system of electronic or mechanical equipment. **4.** A computer system designed to play a specific format of video game using special controllers. **5.** The part of an organ facing the player, containing the keyboard, stops, and pedals. **6.** A decorative bracket for supporting a cornice or shelf.

WORD HISTORY Console¹ comes from Latin *cōnsōlārī*, meaning "to comfort." **Console²** comes from French *console*, which is probably short for *consolider*, which comes from Latin *cōnsolidāre*, meaning "to strengthen."

consolidate (kən-sŏl′ĭ-dāt′) *v.* **consolidated, consolidating, consolidates** —*tr.* **1.** To combine into one; unite: *The ranch was formed when four small farms were consolidated.* **2.** To make secure and strong: *She consolidated her power during her first year in office.* —*intr.* To be united or combined: *The two businesses consolidated into one large firm.* —*con·sol′i·da′tion n.*

consommé (kŏn′sə-mā′ or kŏn′sə-mā′) *n.* A clear soup made of meat or vegetable broth.

WORD HISTORY The rich, thick, heavy broth we call **consommé** is soup that is all used up. *Consommé* in French means "finished, used up, completed," because the meat in the soup is slowly boiled to get all the nourishment out of it. *Consommé* is the past participle of the French verb *consommer*, "to finish, complete, end," and comes from the Latin word *cōnsummāre*, "to finish up, finish off." From *cōnsummāre* we also get the verb *consummate*, the adjective *consummate*, and the noun *consummation*.

consonance (kŏn′sə-nəns) *n.* **1.** Agreement; harmony; accord. **2.** A combination of musical tones that are regarded as pleasing.

consonant (kŏn′sə-nənt) *n.* **1.** A speech sound made by partially or completely blocking the flow of air through one's mouth. **2.** A letter of the alphabet representing such a sound, as *b, m, s,* or *t.* ❖ *adj.* **1.** Consonantal: *a consonant sound.* **2.** Being in agreement or accord: *Her remarks were consonant with her stated principles.* **3.** Musically harmonious.

consonantal (kŏn′sə-năn′tl) *adj.* Relating to or containing a consonant or consonants.

consort (kŏn′sôrt′) *n.* A husband or wife, especially of a monarch. ❖ *intr.v.* (kən-sôrt′) **consorted, consorting, consorts** To keep company; associate: *a musician who consorts with movie stars.*

consortium (kən-sôr′tē-əm *or* kən-sôr′shē-əm) *n., pl.* **consortia** (kən-sôr′tē-ə *or* kən-sôr′shē-ə) **1a.** An association or a combination, as of businesses, financial institutions, or investors, in order to engage in a joint venture. **b.** A cooperative arrangement among groups or institutions: *a library consortium.* **2.** An association or society.

conspicuous (kən-spĭk′yōō-əs) *adj.* **1.** Easily seen; obvious: *a conspicuous spot on the front of my shirt.* **2.** Attracting attention; striking; remarkable: *a conspicuous achievement.* —**con·spic′u·ous·ly** *adv.*

conspiracy (kən-spĭr′ə-sē) *n., pl.* **conspiracies 1.** The act of secretly planning with others to do something unlawful: *The prisoner was charged with conspiracy and treason.* **2.** A secret plan to commit an unlawful act; a plot: *A conspiracy to overthrow the government was uncovered.* **3.** A group planning such a secret act: *He was thought to be the leader of the conspiracy.*

conspirator (kən-spĭr′ə-tər) *n.* A person who takes part in a conspiracy; a plotter.

conspire (kən-spīr′) *intr.v.* **conspired, conspiring, conspires 1.** To plan together secretly to commit an illegal or wrongful act: *Traitors conspired to assassinate the military leader.* **2.** To work together; combine: *Good weather and a reliable car conspired to make the trip a happy one.* —**con·spir′er** *n.*

constable (kŏn′stə-bəl *or* kŭn′stə-bəl) *n.* **1.** A public officer in a town or village having somewhat less authority than a sheriff. **2.** *Chiefly British* A police officer.

constabulary (kən-stăb′yə-lĕr′ē) *n., pl.* **constabularies 1a.** The body of constables of a certain district. **b.** The district under the jurisdiction of a constable. **2.** An armed police force organized like a military unit.

constancy (kŏn′stən-sē) *n.* **1.** The quality of remaining constant; changelessness: *the constancy of the stars.* **2.** Faithfulness; steadfastness: *constancy in friendship.*

constant (kŏn′stənt) *adj.* **1.** Not changing or varying; continuous: *a constant gentle rain; drove at a constant speed.* **2.** Happening regularly or repeatedly; continual: *the constant barking of the dog next door; constant interruptions.* **3.** Steadfast in loyalty or affection; faithful: *a constant friend.* ❖ *n.* **1.** Something that never changes. **2a.** A quantity or factor that has a fixed value in a specific situation: *an experiment in which the temperature changed while pressure remained constant.* **b.** A number that never varies: *The ratio of the circumference to the diameter of a circle is π, a constant.* —**con′stant·ly** *adv.*

constellation (kŏn′stə-lā′shən) *n.* **1.** A group of stars, especially one perceived as a design or mythological figure: *Orion and Cassiopeia are two well-known constellations.* **2.** A group or gathering of distinguished people or things: *The Nobel Prize ceremony is usually attended by a constellation of scientists and scholars.*

consternation (kŏn′stər-nā′shən) *n.* Great fear or dismay: *To our consternation the dog darted out into the road.*

constipate (kŏn′stə-pāt′) *tr.v.* **constipated, constipating, constipates** To cause constipation in.

constipation (kŏn′stə-pā′shən) *n.* Difficult or infrequent movement of the bowels.

constituency (kən-stĭch′ōō-ən-sē) *n., pl.* **constituencies** A body of voters in a district represented by an elected representative or official: *The constituency repeatedly returned the senator to office.*

constituent (kən-stĭch′ōō-ənt) *adj.* **1.** Making up part of a whole: *An atom is a constituent element of a molecule.* **2.** Authorized to draw up or change a constitution: *a constituent assembly.* ❖ *n.* **1.** A constituent part; a component: *Flour is the main constituent of bread.* **2.** A person represented by an elected official: *The congresswoman met with her constituents.*

constitute (kŏn′stĭ-tōōt′) *tr.v.* **constituted, constituting, constitutes 1.** To be the elements or parts of; compose: *Four quarters constitute a dollar.* **2.** To set up; establish: *Police departments are constituted to maintain law and order.* **3.** To appoint, elect, or designate: *The assembly was constituted to write a new city charter.*

constitution (kŏn′stĭ-tōō′shən) *n.* **1.** The system of fundamental laws or principles by which a nation, government, or group is organized. **2.** A document in which such a system is written. **3. Constitution** The fundamental law of the United States, framed in 1787, ratified in 1789, and variously amended since. **4.** The way in which something or someone is made up, especially the physical makeup of a person or organization; nature: *a healthy person with a strong constitution.* **5.** The act of setting up: *the constitution of a new legal society.*

constitutional (kŏn′stĭ-tōō′shə-nəl) *adj.* **1.** Relating to a constitution: *a constitutional amendment.* **2.** Consistent with or permissible according to a constitution: *The proposed law is not constitutional.* **3.** Established by or operating under a constitution: *a constitutional government.* **4.** Basic or inherent in one's makeup: *a constitutional weakness in his health.* ❖ *n.* A walk taken regularly for one's health. —**con′sti·tu′tion·al·ly** *adv.*

constitutionality (kŏn′stĭ-tōō′shə-năl′ĭ-tē) *n.* Accordance with a constitution: *The Supreme Court will decide on the constitutionality of the new law.*

constrain (kən-strān′) *tr.v.* **constrained, constraining, constrains 1.** To keep (something) within certain limits; confine or limit: *We must constrain our spending.* **2.** To compel by physical force or moral obligation: *I felt constrained to ask why the park was closed down.* —**con·strain′ed·ly** (kən-strā′nĭd-lē) *adv.* —**con·strain′er** *n.*

constraint (kən-strānt′) *n.* **1.** Something that restricts, limits, or regulates: *Without moral constraints we would live in social chaos.* **2.** The holding back of one's natural feelings or behavior: *The new mayor showed constraint in the presence of television cameras.*

constrict (kən-strĭkt′) *tr. & intr.v.* **constricted, constricting, constricts 1.** To make or become smaller or narrower, as by contracting; compress: *This drug constricts blood vessels. I could feel the muscles in my body constrict with fright.* **2.** To limit or restrict: *Their lives were constricted by lack of education.* —**con·stric′tive** *adj.*

constriction (kən-strĭk′shən) *n.* **1.** The act or process of constricting. **2.** A feeling of pressure or tightness: *a constriction in one's throat.* **3.** Something that constricts: *The oppressive law was a constriction on their freedom.*

constrictor (kən-strĭk′tər) *n.* **1.** A muscle that contracts or compresses a part or organ of the body. **2.** Any of various snakes, such as a boa or python, that kill their prey by coiling around it and squeezing.

construct (kən-strŭkt′) *tr.v.* **constructed, constructing, constructs** To build or put together; erect or compose: *construct new houses; construct an argument.* —**con·struc′tor** *n.*

construction (kən-strŭk′shən) *n.* **1.** The act or process of constructing: *Two new hotels are under construction.* **2.** A thing that is put together; a structure: *The treehouse we built was an odd-looking construction.* **3.** The way in which something is put together; a design: *The shed is a building of simple construction.* **4.** An interpretation or explanation given to a certain statement: *I put a favorable construction on his reply.* **5a.** The arrangement of words to form a phrase, clause, or sentence. **b.** A group of words arranged in a meaningful way. —**con·struc′tion·al** *adj.* —**con·struc′tion·al·ly** *adv.*

constructionist (kən-strŭk′shə-nĭst) *n.* A person who construes a legal text or document in a specified way: *a strict constructionist.*

construction paper *n.* A heavy paper used in artwork, especially for designs that are folded and cut out.

constructive (kən-strŭk′tĭv) *adj.* Serving a useful purpose or helping to improve something: *She gave me constructive suggestions on my work.* —**con·struc′tive·ly** *adv.* —**con·struc′tive·ness** *n.*

construe (kən-strōō′) *tr.v.* **construed, construing, construes** To determine or explain the meaning of; interpret: *construed her smile as approval.*

consuetude (kŏn′swĭ-tōōd′) *n.* Custom; usage.

consul (kŏn′səl) *n.* **1.** An official appointed by a government to live in a foreign city, look after the government's interest, and give assistance to its citizens who live or travel there. **2.** Either of the two chief magistrates of the ancient Roman republic, elected for a term of one year. —**con′su·lar** (kŏn′sə-lər) *adj.*

consulate (kŏn′sə-lĭt) *n.* The building or offices occupied by a consul.

consult (kən-sŭlt′) *v.* **consulted, consulting, consults** —*tr.* **1.** To seek information or advice from: *Consult your doctor.* **2.** To refer to: *We consulted the dictionary to settle the question.* **3.** To have regard for; consider: *Consult the feelings of others before going ahead.* —*intr.* To exchange views; confer: *The United States consulted with the Canadian government.*

consultant (kən-sŭl′tənt) *n.* **1.** A person who gives expert or professional advice: *A lawyer is a consultant in legal matters.* **2.** A person who consults someone else.

consultation (kŏn′səl-tā′shən) *n.* **1.** An act of consulting: *Close consultation between the nurses and the doctor saved the patient.* **2.** A conference at which advice is given or views are exchanged: *Lawyers for the plaintiff and the defendant held a heated consultation.*

consultative (kən-sŭl′tə-tĭv) *adj.* For the purpose of consultation; advisory: *a consultative council.*

consume (kən-sōōm′) *v.* **consumed, consuming, consumes** —*tr.* **1.** To take in as food; eat or drink up: *The guests consumed all the ice cream.* **2.** To use up; expend: *The experiment consumed her entire summer.* **3.** To purchase (goods or services) for personal use or ownership. **4.** To destroy totally, as by fire: *Flames consumed the factory.* **5.** To occupy the attention of; engross: *The book consumed me for hours.* —*intr.* To purchase goods or services: *People often consume less during an economic downturn.* —**con·sum′a·ble** (kən-sōō′mə-bəl) *adj.*

consumer (kən-sōō′mər) *n.* **1.** A person or thing that consumes, especially a person who buys and uses goods and services: *The manufacturers passed on the price increase to consumers.* **2.** An organism that feeds on other organisms or particles of organic matter.

consumerism (kən-sōō′mə-rĭz′əm) *n.* **1.** A movement seeking to protect consumers by requiring honest advertising and packaging, fair prices, and improved safety standards of products. **2.** Attachment to materialistic values or possessions: *The social critic spoke out against the rampant consumerism gripping the nation.*

consummate (kŏn′sə-māt′) *tr.v.* **consummated, consummating, consummates** To bring to completion; conclude: *consummate a business deal.* ❖ *adj.* (kən-sŭm′ĭt *or* kŏn′sə-mət) **1.** Highly skilled; polished: *a consummate musician.* **2.** Complete or perfect in every respect: *consummate happiness.* —**con·sum′mate·ly** *adv.* —**con′-sum·ma′tion** *n.* —SEE NOTE AT **consommé.**

consumption (kən-sŭmp′shən) *n.* **1.** The act or process of consuming: *Much manufacturing is based on the consumption of oil.* **2.** A quantity consumed: *The consumption of wood used for paper can be reduced by recycling.* **3.** Tuberculosis of the lungs, especially the wasting of the body caused by this disease. This term is no longer used in medicine.

consumptive (kən-sŭmp′tĭv) *adj.* **1.** Tending to consume or use up, especially at an excessive or wasteful rate: *the consumptive use of natural resources.* **2.** Relating to tuberculosis of the lungs. This term is no longer used in medicine. ❖ *n.* A person with tuberculosis of the lungs. This term is no longer used in medicine.

cont. An abbreviation of continued.

contact (kŏn′tăkt′) *n.* **1a.** The touching or coming together of people or things: *Avoid any contact with the wet paint.* **b.** The state or condition of touching: *I have a rash where my skin came in contact with the poison ivy.* **2.** The condition of being in communication: *We lost contact with our former neighbors after they moved away.* **3.** *Informal* A person who is in a position to be of help; a connection: *His aunt has many contacts in politics.* **4a.** A connection between two conductors that allows an electric current to flow. **b.** A part or device that makes or breaks a connection in an electrical circuit: *the contacts of a switch.* **5.** A contact lens. ❖ *v.* (kŏn′tăkt′ *or* kən-tăkt′) **contacted, contacting, contacts** —*tr.* **1.** To bring or put into contact with; touch: *If water contacts the paper, it will leave a mark.* **2.** To get in touch with; communicate with: *I contacted my grandmother by email.* —*intr.* To be or come into contact: *Bare wires that contact will cause a short circuit.*

contact lens *n.* A thin plastic or glass lens designed to correct a defect in vision, worn directly on the cornea of the eye.

contagion (kən-tā′jən) *n.* **1.** The transmission of disease by direct or indirect contact between individuals: *Lack of sanitary conditions may lead to widespread contagion.* **2.** A disease that is or can be transmitted in this way: *The flu is a common contagion of the winter months.* **3.** Something, such as a virus, that causes a contagious disease. **4.** The tendency to spread, as of an influence or emotional state: *the contagion of panic.*

contagious (kən-tā′jəs) *adj.* **1.** Capable of being transmitted by direct or indirect contact: *Chickenpox is a highly contagious disease.* **2.** Capable of carrying disease: *He stayed home until he was no longer contagious.* **3.** Tending to spread from person to person: *contagious laughter.* —**con·ta′gious·ly** *adv.*

contain (kən-tān′) *tr.v.* **contained, containing, contains 1.** To have within; hold: *This bottle contains drinking water. The document contains important information.* **2.** To consist of; comprise; include: *A gallon contains four* quarts. **3.** To hold back; restrain: *I could scarcely contain my laughter.* **4.** To halt the spread or development of: *a method of containing disease.* —con·tain′a·ble *adj.* —SEE NOTE AT **tenacious.**

container (kən-tā′nər) *n.* Something, such as a box, can, jar, or barrel, used to hold something; a receptacle.

containment (kən-tān′mənt) *n.* **1.** The act or fact of containing something: *underground storage facilities for the containment of radioactive waste.* **2.** The policy of attempting to prevent the expansion of an hostile country or ideology.

contaminant (kən-tăm′ə-nənt) *n.* Something that contaminates: *Contaminants polluted the nearby stream.*

contaminate (kən-tăm′ə-nāt′) *tr.v.* **contaminated, contaminating, contaminates 1.** To make impure or unclean by mixture or contact; pollute; foul: *The waters were contaminated with oil from a leaking tanker.* **2.** To expose to or permeate with radioactivity: *A leak from the damaged reactor contaminated the air for miles around.* —con·tam′i·na′tor *n.*

contamination (kən-tăm′ə-nā′shən) *n.* **1.** The act of contaminating or the condition of being contaminated: *Dumping chemicals nearby caused contamination of the lake.* **2.** Something that contaminates; an impurity.

contd. An abbreviation of continued.

contemplate (kŏn′təm-plāt′) *v.* **contemplated, contemplating, contemplates** —*tr.* **1.** To think about (something) carefully; ponder: *I contemplated the offer of a job.* **2.** To think about doing (something); consider, intend, or expect: *We contemplated a trip to Africa.* **3.** To look at carefully and thoughtfully: *contemplate the stars in wonder.* —*intr.* To ponder; meditate: *He sat in the garden contemplating.*

contemplation (kŏn′təm-plā′shən) *n.* **1.** The act of looking at or thinking about something thoughtfully. **2.** Meditation on spiritual or religious matters.

contemplative (kən-těm′plə-tĭv *or* kŏn′təm-plā′tĭv) *adj.* Characterized by or given to contemplation: *the contemplative life of a monk.* —con·tem′pla·tive·ly *adv.* —con·tem′pla·tive·ness *n.*

contemporaneous (kən-těm′pə-rā′nē-əs) *adj.* Originating, existing, or occurring at the same time as something else.

contemporary (kən-těm′pə-rěr′ē) *adj.* **1.** Living or occurring during the same period of time: *contemporary figures in ancient Greek history.* **2.** Current; modern: *a trendy new store selling contemporary clothing.* ❖ *n., pl.* **contemporaries 1.** A person living at the same time as another: *Emily Dickinson and Walt Whitman were contemporaries.* **2.** A person of the present age.

contempt (kən-těmpt′) *n.* **1a.** A feeling that a person or thing is inferior, base, or worthless; scorn: *She has contempt for hypocrites.* **b.** The condition of being despised or dishonored: *a traitor who was held in contempt by his compatriots.* **2.** Open disobedience or disrespect to a court of law or to a legislative body: *Failure to appear before the judge put the witness in contempt.*

contemptible (kən-těmp′tə-bəl) *adj.* Deserving contempt; despicable: *a contemptible tyrant.* —con·tempt′i·ble·ness *n.* —con·tempt′i·bly *adv.*

contemptuous (kən-těmp′chōō-əs) *adj.* Feeling or showing contempt: *a haughty and contemptuous refusal.* —con·temp′tu·ous·ly *adv.* —con·temp′tu·ous·ness *n.*

contend (kən-těnd′) *v.* **contended, contending, contends** —*intr.* **1.** To struggle against difficulties: *Doctors contend*

with disease. Holiday shoppers had to contend with long lines at the checkout counters. **2.** To compete; vie: *The two teams contended for the championship.* —*tr.* To claim or maintain: *The lawyer contended that the evidence was inadmissible in court.* —con·tend′er *n.*

content¹ (kŏn′těnt′) *n.* **1.** often **contents** Something that is contained in a receptacle: *empty a jar of its contents.* **2.** often **contents** The subject matter of a written work, as a document or book: *The contents of the report were not revealed.* **3.** The substantive or meaningful part: *The content of the paper is fine, but the style needs work.* **4.** The amount of a substance contained in something: *the fat content of milk.*

content² (kən-těnt′) *adj.* Desiring no more than what one has; satisfied: *He was content to live in the small apartment.* ❖ *n.* A feeling of satisfied ease; contentment; satisfaction. ❖ *tr.v.* **contented, contenting, contents** To make content or satisfied: *I contented myself with a cup of tea and a book.*

WORD HISTORY Both content¹ and content² were also spelled *content* in Middle English. In fact, they come from the same Latin word, *continēre,* meaning "to contain, restrain." These two forms developed from different past participle forms of the Latin word.

---

contented (kən-těn′tĭd) *adj.* Satisfied with things as they are; content: *The baby looked perfectly contented after his meal.* —con·tent′ed·ly *adv.* —con·tent′ed·ness *n.*

contention (kən-těn′shən) *n.* **1.** A striving to win in competition; rivalry: *Several teams are in contention for first place.* **2.** A statement put forward in an argument: *The lawyer's contention was that the evidence was misleading.*

contentious (kən-těn′shəs) *adj.* Inclined to argue; quarrelsome: *a contentious troublemaker.* —con·ten′tious·ly *adv.* —con·ten′tious·ness *n.*

contentment (kən-těnt′mənt) *n.* The condition of being contented; satisfaction.

contest (kŏn′těst′) *n.* **1.** A struggle for victory or superiority between rivals: *The struggle for American independence was a long contest.* **2.** A competition, usually between entrants who perform separately and are rated by judges: *an essay contest; a skating contest.* ❖ *v.* (kən-těst′ *or* kŏn′těst′) **contested, contesting, contests** —*tr.* **1.** To compete or strive for: *a strategic waterway that was contested by several different countries.* **2.** To dispute; challenge: *contest a parking ticket; contest a will.* —*intr.* To struggle or compete: *rival teams contesting for first place.* —con·test′a·ble *adj.*

contestant (kən-těs′tənt *or* kŏn′těs′tənt) *n.* A person who takes part in a contest.

context (kŏn′těkst′) *n.* **1.** The part of a statement or text that surrounds a particular word or passage and makes clear its meaning: *In some contexts "mad" means "crazy"; in other contexts it means "angry."* **2.** A general setting or set of circumstances in which a particular event occurs; a situation: *Horses are out of place in the context of modern city life.*

contextual (kən-těks′chōō-əl) *adj.* Relating to or depending on context. —con·tex′tu·al·ly *adv.*

contiguous (kən-tĭg′yōō-əs) *adj.* **1.** Having a common boundary; adjoining: *Arizona is contiguous with New Mexico.* **2a.** Connected without a break: *the 48 contiguous states.* **b.** Connected in time; uninterrupted: *served three contiguous terms.* —con·tig′u·ous·ly *adv.* —con·tig′u·ous·ness *n.*

continent¹ (kŏn′tə-nənt) *n.* **1.** One of the seven great land masses of the earth, including Africa, Antarctica, Asia, Australia, Europe, North America, and South America. **2. Continent** The mainland of Europe: *left England by boat for the Continent.*

continent² (kŏn′tə-nənt) *adj.* **1.** Self-restrained in behavior. **2.** Able to keep normal control of urination or defecation. **—con′ti·nence** *n.*

WORD HISTORY Continent¹ comes from the Latin phrase *terra continēns,* meaning "continuous land." **Continent²** comes from the Latin word *continēns* as well. *Continēns* is the present participle of *continēre,* meaning "to contain; restrain."

continental (kŏn′tə-nĕn′tl) *adj.* **1.** Relating to or characteristic of a continent: *continental weather patterns; the continental United States.* **2.** often **Continental** Relating to the mainland of Europe. **3. Continental** Relating to the American colonies during and just after the Revolutionary War: *the Continental Army.* ❖ *n.* **1.** often **Continental** An inhabitant of the mainland of Europe. **2. Continental** A soldier in the Continental Army during the Revolutionary War. **3.** A piece of paper money issued by the Continental Congress during the Revolutionary War.

continental breakfast *n.* A light breakfast consisting usually of coffee or tea and a roll, pastry, or other baked good.

Continental Congress *n.* Either of two legislative assemblies of the Thirteen Colonies and then of the United States. The first met in 1774; the second was the legislative and executive body of the federal government from 1775 until the Constitution took effect in 1789.

continental divide *n.* A region of high ground from each side of which the river systems of a continent flow in opposite directions.

continental drift *n.* The gradual movement of the earth's continents toward or away from each other.

continental shelf *n.* The part of the edge of a continent covered by shallow ocean waters and extending to the steep slopes that descend into the deep part of the ocean.

contingency (kən-tĭn′jən-sē) *n., pl.* **contingencies 1.** An event that may occur but is not likely or intended; a possibility: *People who work in emergency medical service must be prepared for any contingency.* **2.** The condition of being contingent: *Whether we will be able to drive through the mountain pass is a matter of contingency.*

contingent (kən-tĭn′jənt) *adj.* **1.** Possible but not certain to occur; uncertain: *a contingent move of company offices.* **2.** Dependent on circumstances not yet known; conditional: *Our picnic's success is contingent on the weather.* **3.** Happening by chance; accidental; unexpected: *a quick contingent meeting in the hall.* ❖ *n.* **1.** A representative group forming part of a gathering; a delegation: *the Maine contingent at the Democratic National Convention.* **2.** A share, as of troops, contributed to a general effort: *The medical team at the earthquake site included a contingent of American doctors.* **—con·tin′gent·ly** *adv.*

continual (kən-tĭn′yōo-əl) *adj.* **1.** Repeated regularly and frequently: *the continual banging of the shutters in the wind.* **2.** Not broken or stopping; continuing over a long period of time; steady: *continual noise; made continual progress up the river.* **—con·tin′u·al·ly** *adv.*

USAGE Continual and **continuous** are sometimes confused because their meanings overlap. Both words can be used to mean "continuing without interruption": *living in a continual state of fear; enjoying a continuous state of peace.* But *continual* usually refers to something that recurs or is interrupted periodically: *a speech interrupted by continual outbursts of applause.* By contrast, *continuous* is used only when there are no breaks or interruptions: *the continuous whirring of the fan in the window.*

continuance (kən-tĭn′yōo-əns) *n.* **1.** The act, fact, or duration of continuing; continuation: *a continuance of good relations between the two countries.* **2.** Adjournment of legal proceedings to a future date: *The judge gave the defense a continuance until witnesses could be found.*

continuation (kən-tĭn′yōo-ā′shən) *n.* **1a.** The act or fact of going on or persisting: *The continuation of the heavy rain will cause flooding.* **b.** The act or fact of beginning again after stopping; resumption: *a continuation of the game after a rain delay.* **2.** Something by which another thing is continued; an extension to a further point; an added part: *There is a continuation of the story in the author's next book.*

continue (kən-tĭn′yōo) *v.* **continued, continuing, continues** —*intr.* **1.** To keep on or persist in doing something: *We continue in our efforts to improve the quality of our products.* **2.** To go on after stopping; resume: *Our program continues after these commercials.* **3.** To remain in the same condition, place, or direction: *The rainy weather continued for weeks.* —*tr.* **1.** To carry on or persist in: *The police continued their investigation.* **2.** To begin with again after stopping; resume: *We will continue our discussion tomorrow.* **3.** To cause to remain or last; retain; maintain: *continue a family business.*

continuing education (kən-tĭn′yōo-ĭng) *n.* **1.** An instructional program that brings participants up to date in a particular area of knowledge or skills. **2.** Instructional courses designed especially for part-time adult students.

continuity (kŏn′tə-nōō′ĭ-tē) *n., pl.* **continuities 1.** An uninterrupted succession: *A telephone call broke the continuity of my thoughts.* **2.** The condition of being continuous: *His erratic thoughts lacked continuity.*

continuous (kən-tĭn′yōo-əs) *adj.* Continuing without interruption; unbroken: *the continuous line of the horizon; a continuous supply of oxygen to the blood.* **—con·tin′-u·ous·ly** *adv.* **—con·tin′u·ous·ness** *n.* —SEE NOTE AT **continual.**

continuous spectrum *n.* A spectrum that covers a range of wavelengths without breaks or gaps.

continuum (kən-tĭn′yōo-əm) *n., pl.* **continua** (kən-tĭn′-yōo-ə) or **continuums** Something that continues or extends without interruption but can be divided into arbitrary units for analysis: *The past is a continuum that we divide into periods for historical study.*

contort (kən-tôrt′) *tr.v.* **contorted, contorting, contorts** To twist or bend severely out of shape; wrench: *The pain of a toothache contorted his face.*

contortion (kən-tôr′shən) *n.* A twist, turn, or distortion in the shape of something.

contortionist (kən-tôr′shə-nĭst) *n.* An acrobat or entertainer who twists into contorted positions.

contour (kŏn′tŏor′) *n.* **1.** The outline of a figure, body, or mass: *the twisted contour of the coastline.* See Synonyms at **outline. 2.** A contour line. ❖ *adj.* **1.** Following the contour lines of uneven terrain to limit erosion of topsoil: *contour plowing.* **2.** Shaped to fit the outline or form of something: *contour sheets on a bed.* ❖ *tr.v.* **contoured, contouring, contours 1.** To make or shape so as to fit

something else: *The seats are contoured to fit your body.*
2. To build (a road, for example) to follow the contour of the land.

contour line *n.* A line on a map joining points of the same elevation.

contour map *n.* A map that shows elevations above sea level and surface features of the land by means of contour lines.

contra– A prefix that means against or opposite: *contradistinction.*

contraband (kŏn′trə-bănd′) *n.* **1.** Goods that are prohibited by law from being imported or exported. **2.** Smuggling: *The suspect was arrested for contraband and forgery.* ❖ *adj.* Prohibited from being imported or exported: *a contraband shipment.*

contrabass (kŏn′trə-bās′) *n.* A double bass. ❖ *adj.* Pitched an octave below the normal bass range.

contrabassoon (kŏn′trə-bə-sōōn′) *n.* A large bassoon pitched about an octave below an ordinary bassoon.

contraception (kŏn′trə-sĕp′shən) *n.* The intentional prevention of conception and pregnancy, as by the use of drugs or a device such as a condom.

contraceptive (kŏn′trə-sĕp′tĭv) *adj.* Capable of preventing conception. ❖ *n.* A contraceptive substance or device.

contract (kŏn′trăkt′) *n.* **1.** An agreement between two or more people or groups, especially one that is written and enforceable by law: *The athlete negotiated a two-year contract with her new team.* **2.** A document stating the terms of such an agreement: *Both sides signed the new labor contract.* ❖ *v.* (kən-trăkt′ *or* kŏn′trăkt′) **contracted, contracting, contracts** —*tr.* **1.** To make smaller by drawing together: *Hot water contracted the wool fibers in my sweater, and it shrank.* **2.** To arrange or settle by a formal agreement: *contract a business deal.* **3.** To get; acquire: *contract the mumps; contract a debt.* **4.** To shorten (a word or words) by omitting or combining some of the letters or sounds: *Most people contract "I am" to "I'm" when they speak.* —*intr.* **1.** To draw together; become smaller: *The pupils of the cat's eyes contracted in the light.* **2.** To arrange by a formal agreement: *The developers contracted for construction of several new houses.*

contractile (kən-trăk′təl *or* kən-trăk′tīl′) *adj.* Capable of contracting or causing contraction: *contractile muscle fibers; contractile forces of cooling.*

contractile vacuole *n.* A vacuole in one-celled organisms that discharges a fluid by contracting.

contraction (kən-trăk′shən) *n.* **1.** The act of contracting or the condition of being contracted: *The pupil of the eye usually undergoes contraction in strong light.* **2.** A condensed word or phrase, formed by omitting or combining some of the letters or sounds. For example, *isn't* is a contraction of *is not.* **3.** The shortening and thickening of a muscle in action.

contractor (kŏn′trăk′tər *or* kən-trăk′tər) *n.* A person who contracts to do something, especially to provide materials and labor for a construction job.

contractual (kən-trăk′chōō-əl) *adj.* Relating to a contract: *a contractual arrangement between a worker and an employer.* —**con·trac′tu·al·ly** *adv.*

contradict (kŏn′trə-dĭkt′) *tr.v.* **contradicted, contradicting, contradicts 1.** To assert or express the opposite of (a statement): *The witness gave information that contradicted previous testimony.* **2.** To deny the statement of: *The two experts contradicted each other.* **3.** To be contrary to

or inconsistent with: *The results of the experiments contradicted his predictions.* —SEE NOTE AT **predict.**

contradiction (kŏn′trə-dĭk′shən) *n.* **1.** The act of contradicting or the condition of being contradicted: *His persistent contradiction of the lecturer embarrassed us.* **2.** An inconsistency; a discrepancy: *There's a contradiction between what you say and what your report states.* **3.** A statement that contradicts something: *The politician issued a contradiction of the allegations reported in the press.*

contradictory (kŏn′trə-dĭk′tə-rē) *adj.* **1.** Involving or having the nature of a contradiction; opposing; contrary: *Contradictory reports about the vaccine's effectiveness perplexed the doctors.* **2.** Given to contradicting: *a quarrelsome and contradictory nature.* —**con′tra·dic′to·ri·ly** *adv.* —**con′tra·dic′tor·i·ness** *n.*

contradistinction (kŏn′trə-dĭ-stĭngk′shən) *n.* Distinction by contrasting or by opposing qualities: *The critic called the new composition mere noise in contradistinction to music.*

contraindicate (kŏn′trə-ĭn′dĭ-kāt′) *tr.v.* **contraindicated, contraindicating, contraindicates** To indicate the inadvisability of (a medical treatment, for example): *This vaccine is contraindicated in individuals who are allergic to eggs.*

contralto (kən-trăl′tō) *n., pl.* **contraltos 1.** The lowest female singing voice or voice part, lower than soprano and higher than tenor. **2.** A woman having such a voice.

contraption (kən-trăp′shən) *n.* A mechanical device; a gadget.

contrarian (kən-trâr′ē-ən) *n.* One who takes a contrary view or action, especially an investor who makes decisions that contradict prevailing wisdom, as in buying securities that are unpopular at the time. —**contrarian** *adj.*

contrariwise (kŏn′trĕr′ē-wīz′ *or* kən-trâr′ē-wīz′) *adv.* **1.** In an opposite way or reverse order. **2.** On the contrary.

contrary (kŏn′trĕr′ē) *adj.* **1.** Completely different; opposed: *The debaters held contrary points of view.* **2.** Adverse; unfavorable: *Contrary economic conditions caused the business to go bankrupt.* **3.** (*also* kən-trâr′ē) Stubbornly opposed to others; willful: *Little children often become contrary when they need a nap.* ❖ *n., pl.* **contraries** Something that is opposite: *Their theory made sense at first, but experimentation proved the contrary to be true.* ◆ **on the contrary** In opposition to the previous statement; conversely: *I'm not sick; on the contrary, I'm feeling quite healthy.* —**con′trar′i·ly** *adv.* —**con′trar′i·ness** *n.*

contrast (kən-trăst′ *or* kŏn′trăst′) *v.* **contrasted, contrasting, contrasts** —*tr.* To compare in order to reveal differences: *The essay contrasts city and country life.* —*intr.* To show differences when compared: *light colors that contrast with a dark background.* ❖ *n.* (kŏn′trăst′) **1.** Comparison, especially in order to reveal differences: *the author's contrast of rural and urban America.* **2.** The state of being different when viewed in comparison: *Let's consider pioneer life in contrast to modern life.* **3.** Something that is strikingly different from something else: *Driving a truck is quite a contrast to driving a compact car.* **4.** The difference in brightness between the light and dark areas of a picture, such as a photograph.

contravene (kŏn′trə-vēn′) *tr.v.* **contravened, contravening, contravenes 1.** To act or be in violation of (a law, directive, or principle, for example); violate: *a sailor who contravened a direct order; a regulation that contravened the new tax policy.* **2.** To be inconsistent with; be contrary to: *a discovery that contravenes earlier assumptions about* *the structure of the atom.* —**con′tra·ven′er** *n.*

contretemps (kŏn′trə-tän′) *n., pl.* **contretemps** (kŏn′-trə-tän′ *or* kŏn′trə-tänz′) **1.** An unforeseen event that disrupts the normal course of things; an inopportune occurrence. **2.** An argument or dispute.

contribute (kən-trĭb′yo͞ot) *v.* **contributed, contributing, contributes** —*tr.* **1.** To give or supply in common with others: *contribute money to a charity; contributed a lot of my time to the project.* **2.** To submit (something written) for publication: *contributed an article to the magazine.* —*intr.* **1.** To give or supply something along with others: *contributes to several charities.* **2.** To help in bringing about a result: *Exercise contributes to better health.* **3.** To submit material for publication. —**con·trib′u·tor** *n.*

contribution (kŏn′trĭ-byo͞o′shən) *n.* **1.** The act of contributing: *A good discussion requires the contribution of several people.* **2.** Something contributed: *We made a contribution of food to the poor.*

contributory (kən-trĭb′yə-tôr′ē) *adj.* Contributing toward a result; helping to bring about a result: *Carelessness was a contributory factor in the accident.*

contrite (kən-trīt′ *or* kŏn′trīt′) *adj.* **1.** Feeling deep regret and sorrow for one's wrongdoing: *a contrite sinner.* **2.** Arising from or showing deep regret or sorrow: *contrite tears.* —**con·trite′ly** *adv.* —**con·trite′ness** *n.*

contrition (kən-trĭsh′ən) *n.* Sincere remorse for wrongdoing; repentance.

contrivance (kən-trī′vəns) *n.* **1.** The act of contriving: *the contrivance of friends to give a surprise party.* **2.** Something that is contrived, as a mechanical device or a clever plan: *The uproar was a contrivance to divert attention.*

contrive (kən-trīv′) *tr.v.* **contrived, contriving, contrives** **1.** To plan or devise cleverly: *contrive an excuse for being late.* **2.** To bring about, especially by scheming: *contrive a victory by surprise attack.* —**con·triv′er** *n.*

contrived (kən-trīvd′) *adj.* Obviously planned or calculated; unnatural: *a movie with a contrived plot.*

control (kən-trōl′) *tr.v.* **controlled, controlling, controls** **1.** To exercise authority or influence over; direct: *The mayor controls the city government.* **2.** To adjust or regulate: *This valve controls the flow of water.* **3.** To hold in check; restrain: *control one's anger.* **4.** To reduce or prevent the spread of: *controlled the fire.* ❖ *n.* **1.** Authority or power to regulate, direct, or dominate: *the coach's control over the team.* **2.** A restraining device, measure, or limit; a curb: *The government put a control on prices.* **3.** A standard of comparison for testing the results of a scientific experiment. **4.** often **controls** A device or set of devices used to operate, regulate, or guide a machine or vehicle: *The pilot was sitting at the controls of the airplane.* —**con·trol′la·ble** *adj.*

control key *n.* A key on a computer keyboard that is pressed in combination with other keys to perform a command.

controller (kən-trō′lər) *n.* **1.** A person who controls or regulates something, such as air traffic. **2.** A mechanism or device that regulates or operates something: *a video game controller.* **3.** Variant of **comptroller.**

control tower *n.* An observation tower at an airport from which the landing and takeoff of aircraft are controlled by radio and radar.

controversial (kŏn′trə-vûr′shəl *or* kŏn′trə-vûr′sē-əl) *adj.* Relating to, producing, or marked by argument or

sharp disagreement: *controversial writing; a controversial issue.* —**con′tro·ver′sial·ly** *adv.*

controversy (kŏn′trə-vûr′sē) *n., pl.* **controversies 1.** A dispute, especially a public one between sides holding sharply opposing views: *A controversy arose over the size of the school budget.* **2.** The act of engaging in such disputes: *Their lawyers are skilled at controversy.*

controvert (kŏn′trə-vûrt′ *or* kŏn′trə-vûrt′) *tr.v.* **controverted, controverting, controverts** To raise arguments against; dispute: *The prosecutor controverted the defendant's testimony.* —**con′tro·vert′i·ble** *adj.*

contusion (kən-to͞o′zhən) *n.* A bruise.

conundrum (kə-nŭn′drəm) *n.* A baffling or insoluble problem.

conurbation (kŏn′ər-bā′shən) *n.* A predominantly urban region including adjacent towns and suburbs; a metropolitan area.

convalesce (kŏn′və-lĕs′) *intr.v.* **convalesced, convalescing, convalesces** To regain health and strength after illness or injury; recuperate.

convalescence (kŏn′və-lĕs′əns) *n.* **1.** Gradual return to health after illness or injury. **2.** The time needed for this: *a short convalescence in bed.* —**con′va·les′cent** *adj.*

convection (kən-vĕk′shən) *n.* The transfer of heat from one place to another by the circulation of currents within a gas or liquid.

convene (kən-vēn′) *intr. & tr.v.* **convened, convening, convenes** To assemble or cause to assemble: *Members of the committee convene monthly to decide on club business. The governor convened the legislature.* —SEE NOTE AT **intervene.**

convenience (kən-vēn′yəns) *n.* **1.** The quality of being convenient; suitability: *the convenience of shopping at a supermarket.* **2.** Personal comfort or advantage: *Each hotel room has a telephone for the guests' convenience.* **3.** Something that provides comfort or saves effort, as a device or service: *A microwave oven is a modern convenience.* **4.** A suitable or agreeable time: *Please respond at your convenience.*

convenience store *n.* A small retail store that is open long hours and that typically sells snacks and basic groceries.

convenient (kən-vēn′yənt) *adj.* **1.** Suited or favorable to one's comfort, needs, or purpose: *a convenient kitchen appliance.* **2.** Easy to reach or close by: *convenient locations.* —**con·ven′ient·ly** *adv.*

convent (kŏn′vənt) *n.* **1.** A community of nuns. **2.** The building or buildings occupied by nuns; a nunnery.

convention (kən-vĕn′shən) *n.* **1a.** A formal meeting of a group for a particular purpose: *a political convention for nominating candidates.* **b.** The group of people attending such an assembly: *The convention will nominate its candidate tonight.* **2a.** General agreement on or acceptance of certain practices or attitudes: *Convention formerly required some judges to wear white wigs.* **b.** A widely accepted practice; a custom: *the convention of shaking hands.* **3.** A formal agreement or compact, as between nations. —SEE NOTE AT **intervene.**

conventional (kən-vĕn′shə-nəl) *adj.* **1a.** Based on or approved by general usage; customary: *Saying "Hello" is a conventional way of answering the telephone.* **b.** Following accepted practice, customs, or taste: *a conventional white wedding dress.* **2.** Following accepted practice so closely as to be dull or unimaginative: *a boring movie with a conventional love story.* **3.** Using means other than nuclear weapons or energy: *conventional warfare; conventional* power plants. —**con·ven'tion·al'i·ty** (kən-věn'shə-năl'ĭ-tē) n. —**con·ven'tion·al·ly** adv.

converge (kən-vûrj') v. **converged, converging, converges** —intr. **1.** To come together in one place; meet: *The three roads converge in the center of town.* **2.** To tend or move toward each other or toward the same conclusion or result: *Their minds converged on the same point.* —tr. To cause to converge: *A magnifying glass converges rays of light.*

convergence (kən-vûr'jəns) n. **1.** The act or process of converging; tendency to meet in one point. **2.** The point of converging; a meeting place: *Pittsburgh was built at the convergence of three rivers.* —**con·ver'gent** adj.

conversant (kən-vûr'sənt or kŏn'vər-sənt) adj. Familiar, as by study or experience: *She is conversant with medieval history.* —**con·ver'sant·ly** adv.

conversation (kŏn'vər-sā'shən) n. A spoken exchange of thoughts and feelings; a talk.

conversational (kŏn'vər-sā'shə-nəl) adj. **1.** Relating to conversation: *in a normal conversational tone.* **2.** Adept at or given to conversation: *Outgoing people are generally more conversational than others.* —**con'ver·sa'tion·al·ly** adv.

conversationalist (kŏn'vər-sā'shə-nə-lĭst) n. A person who is fond of or skilled at conversation.

converse¹ (kən-vûrs') intr.v. **conversed, conversing, converses** To talk informally with others: *converse about family matters.*

converse² (kən-vûrs' or kŏn'vûrs') adj. Reversed, as in order; contrary: *She read the names in converse order.* ❖ n. (kŏn'vûrs') Something that has been reversed; an opposite: *Dark is the converse of light.* —**con·verse'ly** adv.

WORD HISTORY Converse¹ comes from Middle English *conversen* (meaning "to associate with"), which comes from Latin *conversārī,* meaning "to occupy oneself with." **Converse²** comes from Latin *conversus,* the past participle of *convertere,* meaning "to turn around."

conversion (kən-vûr'zhən or kən-vûr'shən) n. **1.** The act or process of changing one thing, use, or purpose into another: *A generator is used for the conversion of water power into electricity.* **2.** A change in which a person adopts a new belief, opinion, or religion. **3.** The expression of a quantity in alternative units, as of length or weight: *conversion of miles to kilometers.*

convert (kən-vûrt') v. **converted, converting, converts** —tr. **1.** To change into another form, substance, or condition: *convert water into ice by freezing; a solar cell that converts sunlight into electricity.* **2.** To change from one use to another; adapt to a new purpose: *convert a bedroom into a study.* **3.** To persuade (a person) to adopt a particular religion or belief: *Missionaries tried to convert the native peoples to Christianity.* **4a.** To exchange for something of equal value: *Since we are going to France, we need to convert our dollars into euros.* **b.** To express (a quantity) in alternative units: *convert 100 yards into meters.* —intr. **1.** To undergo a change; be converted: *This sofa converts easily into a bed.* **2.** To adopt a particular religion or belief: *Many pagans converted to Christianity in the Middle Ages.* ❖ n. (kŏn'vûrt') A person who has adopted a new religion or belief.

converter (kən-vûr'tər) n. **1.** A machine that changes alternating current to direct current or direct current to alternating current. **2.** An electronic device that changes the frequency of a radio or other electromagnetic signal. **3.** A furnace in which pig iron is changed into steel by the Bessemer process.

convertible (kən-vûr'tə-bəl) adj. **1.** Capable of being converted: *The convertible couch is also a bed.* **2.** Having a top that can be folded back or removed: *a convertible sports car.* ❖ n. **1.** An automobile whose top can be folded back or removed. **2.** Something, such as a piece of furniture, that can be converted. —**con·vert'i·bil'i·ty** n. —**con·vert'i·bly** adv.

convex (kŏn'věks' or kən-věks') adj. Curving outward like the outside of a circle or sphere: *Rain rolled off the convex surface of the dome.*

convexity (kŏn-věk'sĭ-tē) n., pl. **convexities 1.** The condition of being convex. **2.** A convex surface, line, or body.

convey (kən-vā') tr.v. **conveyed, conveying, conveys 1.** To take or carry from one place to another; transport: *A helicopter conveyed the skiers to the top of the glacier.* **2.** To serve as a means of transmission for; transmit: *Cables convey electrical power.* **3.** To make known; communicate: *His smile conveyed his pleasure.* **4.** To transfer ownership of: *The deed conveyed the land to a close relative.*

conveyance (kən-vā'əns) n. **1.** The act of conveying: *Airlines now serve as the chief means of conveyance for transatlantic passengers.* **2.** Something used to convey, especially a vehicle such as an automobile or a bus. **3a.** The transfer of ownership from one person to another. **b.** A legal document that brings about such a transfer.

conveyor also **conveyer** (kən-vā'ər) n. **1.** A person or thing that conveys: *a conveyor of good news.* **2.** A mechanical device, such as a continuous moving belt, that carries things from one place to another: *put the groceries on the conveyor.*

convict (kən-vĭkt') tr.v. **convicted, convicting, convicts** To find or prove guilty of an offense, especially in a court of law: *The judge convicted the polluter of endangering public health.* ❖ n. (kŏn'vĭkt') **1.** A person who has been found guilty of a crime. **2.** A person who has been sentenced to prison.

conviction (kən-vĭk'shən) n. **1.** The judgment of a judge or jury that a person is guilty of a crime. **2.** The state of being found or proven guilty: *a trial ending in the swindler's conviction.* **3.** A strong opinion or belief: *act according to one's true convictions.*

convince (kən-vĭns') tr.v. **convinced, convincing, convinces** To cause (someone) to believe or feel certain; persuade: *More clues convinced us we were on the right track.*

convincing (kən-vĭn'sĭng) adj. Serving to convince; persuasive: *a convincing argument.* —**con·vinc'ing·ly** adv.

convivial (kən-vĭv'ē-əl) adj. **1.** Fond of food, drink, and good company; sociable. **2.** Festive: *a convivial reunion of old friends.* —**con·viv'i·al'i·ty** (kən-vĭv'ē-ăl'ĭ-tē) n. —**con·viv'i·al·ly** adv.

convocation (kŏn'və-kā'shən) n. **1.** The act of convoking: *the convocation of church leaders to enact new policy.* **2.** A summoned assembly, as of members of a college community.

convoke (kən-vōk') tr.v. **convoked, convoking, convokes** To call together; cause to assemble: *the president convoked the new Congress.*

convoluted (kŏn'və-lōō'tĭd) adj. **1.** Having many twists or coils: *a convoluted path winding around streams and boulders.* **2.** Complicated; intricate: *a convoluted argument that is difficult to understand.*

convolution (kŏn'və-lōō'shən) n. **1.** A part or development in something complicated, such as a story or explanation; a twist: *I couldn't follow the convolutions of the movie's plot.* **2.** A fold or coil: *the convolutions of a coiled* *snake.* **3.** One of the folds on the surface of the brain.

convoy (kŏn′voi′) *n.* **1.** A group, as of ships or motor vehicles, traveling with a protective military force or for safety or convenience. **2.** An accompanying and protecting force: *a convoy of warships protecting the supply ships.*

convulse (kən-vŭls′) *v.* **convulsed, convulsing, convulses** —*tr.* **1.** To cause (a human or other animal) to have violent involuntary muscle contractions: *The patient was convulsed by high fever.* **2.** To cause to laugh uproariously: *Her impersonations convulsed the audience.* **3.** To disturb violently; rock: *An earthquake convulsed the area.* —*intr.* To become affected by or as if by convulsions; shake: *The audience convulsed with laughter.*

convulsion (kən-vŭl′shən) *n.* **1.** A violent involuntary muscular contraction: *convulsions resulting from high fever.* **2.** An uncontrolled fit of laughter: *The audience went into convulsions watching the clown's antics.* **3.** A violent upheaval: *convulsions of the earth's crust.*

convulsive (kən-vŭl′sĭv) *adj.* **1.** Marked by or resembling convulsions: *convulsive movements.* **2.** Having or causing convulsions: *a convulsive disorder.*

cony (kō′nē *or* kŭn′ē) *n.* Variant of **coney.**

coo (kōō) *intr.v.* **cooed, cooing, coos 1.** To make the murmuring sound of a pigeon or dove or a sound similar to it: *The baby laughed and cooed.* **2.** To speak softly, with affection or approval: *Everyone cooed over her new dress.*

COO An abbreviation of chief operating officer.

cook (kŏok) *v.* **cooked, cooking, cooks** —*tr.* To prepare (food) for eating by using heat. —*intr.* **1.** To undergo cooking: *Fish cooks quickly.* **2.** To prepare food for eating by using heat: *A short-order chef must cook quickly.* ❖ *n.* A person who prepares food for eating. ◆ **cook up** *Informal* To concoct; invent: *cook up an excuse.*

cookbook (kŏok′bŏok′) *n.* A book containing recipes and other information about cooking.

cooker (kŏok′ər) *n.* An appliance used for cooking.

cookery (kŏok′ə-rē) *n.* The art or practice of preparing food.

cookie *also* **cooky** (kŏok′ē) *n., pl.* **cookies 1.** A small, usually flat and crisp cake made from sweetened dough. **2.** A collection of information about a person using the Internet that is stored on the user's computer and used by a website to identify the user on subsequent visits.

cookout (kŏok′out′) *n.* A meal cooked and eaten outdoors.

cool (kōol) *adj.* **cooler, coolest 1.** Moderately cold; neither warm nor very cold: *cool fall weather.* **2.** Giving or allowing relief from heat: *a cool summer breeze; a cool light blouse.* **3.** Calm; unexcited: *a cool head in a crisis.* **4.** Indifferent or disdainful; unenthusiastic: *They were cool to the idea of hosting the party.* **5.** *Slang* **a.** Excellent; first-rate: *saw a really cool movie.* **b.** Acceptable; satisfactory: *It's cool with me if you want to go to the mall.* **6.** *Slang* Entire; full: *a deal worth a cool million in profit.* ❖ *tr. & intr.v.* **cooled, cooling, cools 1.** To make or become less warm: *cool a room by opening a window; let the pie cool.* **2.** To make or become less intense: *Having to wait cooled their enthusiasm. My anger cooled as time went by.* ❖ *n.* **1.** A cool place, part, or time: *the cool of the evening.* **2.** *Slang* Calmness of mind; composure: *When told there were no tickets left, several people lost their cool.* ◆ **cool it** *Slang* To calm down; relax. **cool (one's) heels** *Informal* To wait or be kept waiting. —**cool′ly** *adv.* —**cool′ness** *n.*

coolant (kōo′lənt) *n.* Something that cools, especially a fluid that circulates through a machine or over some of its parts in order to draw off heat.

cooler (kōo′lər) *n.* A device or container for cooling something: *a water cooler.*

cool-headed (kōol′hĕd′ĭd) *adj.* Not easily excited or flustered; calm. —**cool′-head′ed·ly** *adv.* —**cool′-head′-ed·ness** *n.*

coon (kōon) *n. Informal* A raccoon.

coonskin (kōon′skĭn′) *n.* The pelt of a raccoon.

coop (kōop) *n.* An enclosure or cage for poultry. ❖ *tr.v.* **cooped, cooping, coops** To confine; shut in: *We cooped up inside all day because of the bad weather.*

co-op (kō′ŏp′ *or* kō-ŏp′) *n.* A cooperative.

cooper (kōo′pər) *n.* A person who makes or repairs wooden barrels, casks, and tubs.

cooperate (kō-ŏp′ə-rāt′) *intr.v.* **cooperated, cooperating, cooperates 1.** To work or act with another or others for a common purpose: *Everyone cooperated in raising the frame for the barn.* **2.** To agree or yield willingly; go along: *The children cooperated and went to bed.*

cooperation (kō-ŏp′ə-rā′shən) *n.* The act of working together toward a common end or purpose: *international cooperation to reduce air pollution.*

cooperative (kō-ŏp′ər-ə-tĭv *or* kō-ŏp′ə-rā′tĭv *or* kō-ŏp′-rə-tĭv) *adj.* **1.** Done in cooperation with others: *a cooperative effort.* **2.** Willing to help or cooperate: *a cooperative and helpful assistant.* **3.** Relating to a cooperative: *a cooperative apartment.* ❖ *n.* **1.** A business, farm, store, or residence owned jointly by those who use its facilities or services: *That apartment house is a cooperative in which the residents share the costs of operating the building.* **2.** An apartment in a building jointly owned by the residents: *a three-room cooperative on the first floor.* —**co·op′er·a·tive·ly** *adv.* —**co·op′er·a·tive·ness** *n.*

co-opt (kō-ŏpt′ *or* kō′ŏpt′) *tr.v.* **co-opted, co-opting, co-opts 1.** To cause (someone) to stop criticizing or opposing a person, group, or institution, especially by offering a job or some advantage through association: *By promising pay raises, the company co-opted many strikers.* **2.** To adopt or make use of (something such as an idea or practice) for one's own purposes, especially when originally used by an opposing person or group.

coordinate (kō-ôr′dn-ĭt *or* kō-ôr′dn-āt′) *n.* In mathematics, one of a set of numbers that determines the position of a point. If the point is on a line, only one coordinate is needed; if the point is in a plane, two are needed; and if the point is in space, three are required. ❖ *adj.* **1.** Of equal importance, rank, or degree: *A compound sentence has two or more coordinate clauses.* **2.** Relating to or involving coordinates: *a coordinate system.* ❖ *v.* (kō-ôr′dn-āt′) **coordinated, coordinating, coordinates** —*tr.* To arrange or cause to work efficiently in a common cause or effort: *the agency that is coordinating the relief efforts in the flood zone.* —*intr.* **1.** To work efficiently with others in a common cause or effort: *If we can coordinate with the bands at your school, we can hold a joint concert.* **2.** To be in a harmonious arrangement; harmonize: *Do the curtains coordinate with the rest of room?* —**co·or′di·nate·ly** *adv.*

coordinated universal time (kō-ôr′dn-ā′tĭd) *n.* An international time standard calculated by atomic clock and serving as the basis for standard time around the world.

coordinating conjunction (kō-ôr′dn-ā′tĭng) *n.* A conjunction that connects two grammatical elements that have the same syntactic role, for example, *or* in *books or* *pencils,* or *and* in *out of sight and out of mind.*

coordination (kō-ôr′dn-ā′shən) *n.* **1.** An act of coordinating or a condition or being coordinated: *Coordination among the rescue workers saved many of the earthquake victims.* **2.** The organized action of muscles or groups of muscles in the performance of complicated movements or tasks: *Gymnastics requires a great deal of coordination.*

coordinator (kō-ôr′dn-ā′tər) *n.* A person or thing that coordinates: *The mayor served as coordinator of the relief efforts.*

coot (kōōt) *n.* **1.** Any of several waterbirds of North America and Europe having dark-gray feathers and a short often white bill. **2.** *Informal* An eccentric or ornery person, especially an eccentric old man.

cootie (kōō′tē) *n. Slang* A body louse.

cop (kŏp) *n. Informal* A police officer.

copacetic or **copasetic** (kō′pə-sĕt′ĭk) *adj. Informal* Very satisfactory or acceptable; fine.

copay (kō′pā′) *n.* A copayment.

copayment (kō′pā′mənt) *n.* A specified sum of money that patients covered by a health insurance plan pay for a given type of service, usually at the time the service is rendered.

cope¹ (kōp) *intr.v.* **coped, coping, copes** To contend or deal, especially successfully: *Computers help us cope with vast amounts of information.*

cope² (kōp) *n.* A long cloak worn by priests or bishops during special ceremonies or processions.

WORD HISTORY Cope¹ comes from Middle English *copen* (meaning "to strike, fight against"), which comes from Late Latin *colpus,* which comes from Greek *kolaphos,* both meaning "a hit; a blow." **Cope²** comes from Middle English *cope,* which comes from Late Latin *cappa,* meaning "cloak."

---

copepod (kō′pə-pŏd′) *n.* Any of numerous very small animals that live in fresh water or salt water and are often parasitic on other organisms. Copepods are crustaceans.

copernicium (kō′pər-nē′sē-əm or kō′pər-nē′shē-əm) *n. Symbol* **Cn** A radioactive element that has been artificially produced by scientists. The half-life of its most stable isotope is about 34 seconds. Atomic number 112. See **Periodic Table.**

copier (kŏp′ē-ər) *n.* **1.** A machine that makes photocopies; a photocopier. **2.** A person who makes written copies; a copyist.

copilot (kō′pī′lət) *n.* The second or relief pilot of an aircraft.

coping (kō′pĭng) *n.* The top layer of a stone or brick wall, usually slanted so as to shed rainwater or snow.

coping saw *n.* A saw with a narrow short blade stretched across a U-shaped frame, used for cutting designs in wood.

copious (kō′pē-əs) *adj.* Large in quantity; abundant: *Rainfall is copious in the tropics.* —**co′pi·ous·ly** *adv.*

coplanar (kō-plā′nər) *adj.* Lying in the same plane: *coplanar points.*

cop-out (kŏp′out′) *n. Slang* An excuse for avoiding a commitment or responsibility: *It's a total cop-out to blame her for your failure.*

copper (kŏp′ər) *n.* **1.** *Symbol* **Cu** A reddish-brown metallic element that is an excellent conductor of heat and electricity. It is widely used for electrical wiring, water piping, and rust-resistant parts, either in pure form or in alloys such as brass and bronze. Atomic number 29. See **Periodic Table. 2.** A small coin made of copper or an alloy of copper. **3.** A reddish brown. ❖ *tr.v.* **coppered, coppering, coppers** To coat or finish with a layer of copper. —**cop′per·y** *adj.*

copperhead (kŏp′ər-hĕd′) *n.* **1.** A venomous snake of the eastern and central United States, having a tan body with reddish-brown markings. **2. Copperhead** A Northerner who sympathized with the South during the Civil War.

copperplate (kŏp′ər-plāt′) *n.* **1.** A copper printing plate engraved or etched with a pattern of the picture or other design to be printed. **2.** A print or engraving made with a copperplate.

coppersmith (kŏp′ər-smĭth′) *n.* A worker or manufacturer of objects in copper.

coppice (kŏp′ĭs) *n.* A copse.

copra (kō′prə or kŏp′rə) *n.* Dried coconut meat from which coconut oil is extracted.

copse (kŏps) *n.* A thicket of small tress or bushes.

Copt (kŏpt) *n.* **1.** A member of a historically Christian people of Egypt. **2.** A member of the Coptic Church.

copter (kŏp′tər) *n. Informal* A helicopter.

Coptic (kŏp′tĭk) *n.* The language of the Copts, related to the Semitic languages and now used only in the Coptic Church. ❖ *adj.* Relating to the Copts, the Coptic Church, or the Coptic language.

Coptic Church *n.* The Christian church of Egypt that believes that Jesus had a single nature that was simultaneously divine and human.

copula (kŏp′yə-lə) *n.* A linking verb.

copulate (kŏp′yə-lāt′) *intr.v.* **copulated, copulating, copulates 1.** To engage in sexual intercourse. **2.** To transfer male reproductive cells from one individual to another, usually into an internal organ or cavity, as in birds. —**cop′u·la′tion** *n.*

copy (kŏp′ē) *n., pl.* **copies 1.** An imitation or reproduction of something original; a duplicate. **2.** One specimen or example of a printed text or picture: *a copy of the June issue of the magazine.* **3.** Written material to be set in type and printed: *The reporter submitted her copy for the newspaper article.* **4.** The words that are to be printed or spoken in an advertisement. ❖ *v.* **copied, copying, copies** —*tr.* **1.** To make a reproduction of an original: *Medieval monks copied manuscripts by hand.* **2.** To follow as a model or pattern; imitate: *The builder copied the house next door.* See Synonyms at **imitate.** —*intr.* To make a copy or copies: *Good authors don't copy from others.*

copycat (kŏp′ē-kăt′) *n.* A person who mimics or imitates others, as in speech, dress, or action.

copyedit (kŏp′ē-ĕd′ĭt) *tr.v.* **copyedited, copyediting, copyedits** To correct and prepare (a manuscript, for example) for publication. —**cop′y·ed′i·tor** *n.*

copyist (kŏp′ē-ĭst) *n.* A person who makes written copies, as of a manuscript.

copyright (kŏp′ē-rīt′) *n.* The legal right to be the only one to publish, produce, sell, or distribute a literary, musical, dramatic, or artistic work. ❖ *tr.v.* **copyrighted, copyrighting, copyrights** To secure a copyright for: *She copyrighted her novel.*

copywriter (kŏp′ē-rī′tər) *n.* A person who writes advertising copy.

coquetry (kō′kĭ-trē or kō-kĕt′rē) *n., pl.* **coquetries** The behavior of a coquette; flirtation.

coquette (kō-kĕt′) *n.* A woman who flirts. —**co·quet′tish** *adj.* —**co·quet′tish·ly** *adv.*

coquina (kō-kē′nə) *n.* **1.** Any of various small clams having brightly colored shells. **2.** A soft porous limestone containing shells and coral, used for building.

cor– Variant of **com–**.

coracle (kôr′ə-kəl) *n.* A small rounded boat made of hide or other waterproof material stretched over a wicker or wooden frame.

coral (kôr′əl) *n.* **1.** A hard stony substance formed by the skeletons of tiny, usually tropical marine invertebrate animals that live together in large colonies. It is often white, pink, or reddish, and some kinds are used for making jewelry. **2.** Any of the various animals that form this substance.

coral reef *n.* A reef consisting mainly of coral that has been compacted together with algae and minerals such as calcium carbonate.

coral snake *n.* Any of various venomous American snakes marked with bright red, black, and yellow bands.

cord (kôrd) *n.* **1.** A string or small rope of twisted strands. **2.** An insulated flexible electric wire fitted with a plug or plugs. **3.** A structure of the body, such as a nerve or tendon, that resembles a cord. **4.** A unit of measure for cut firewood, equal to a stack that measures 4 feet by 4 feet by 8 feet or 128 cubic feet (3.6 cubic meters). **5a.** A raised ridge or rib on the surface of cloth. **b.** Cloth, such as corduroy, having raised ridges or ribs. **6. cords** *Informal* Pants made of corduroy. ❖ *tr.v.* **corded, cording, cords 1.** To fasten or bind with a cord: *Please cord the newspapers into bundles.* **2.** To cut and stack (firewood) in cords.

cordage (kôr′dĭj) *n.* **1.** Cords or ropes, especially the ropes in a ship's rigging. **2.** An amount of wood measured in cords.

corded (kôr′dĭd) *adj.* **1.** Tied or bound with cords: *a corded bundle.* **2.** Ribbed or twilled, as corduroy. **3.** Stacked in cords, as firewood.

cordial (kôr′jəl) *adj.* Warm and sincere; hearty: *cordial relations with the neighbors.* ❖ *n.* A liqueur. —**cor·dial′i·ty** *n.* —**cor′dial·ly** *adv.*

cordillera (kôr′dl-yâr′ə) *n.* An extensive chain of mountains, especially the main mountain range of a large land mass.

cordless (kôrd′lĭs) *adj.* Having no cord, usually using batteries as a source of power: *a cordless telephone.*

cordon (kôr′dn) *n.* **1.** A line of military posts, people, or ships stationed around an area to enclose or guard it. **2.** A rope or tape stretched around an area, usually by the police, in order to restrict access. ❖ *tr.v.* **cordoned, cordoning, cordons** To form a cordon around: *The firefighters had cordoned off the burned-out building.*

cordovan (kôr′də-vən) *n.* **1.** A soft fine leather used for shoes and other leather goods. **2.** A shoe made from this leather.

corduroy (kôr′də-roi′) *n.* **1.** A heavy cotton fabric with raised ribs or ridges. **2. corduroys** Pants made of this fabric.

cordwood (kôrd′wŏŏd′) *n.* **1.** Wood cut and piled in cords. **2.** Wood sold by the cord.

core (kôr) *n.* **1.** The innermost part of something: *the hard elastic core of a baseball.* **2.** The basic or most important part of something; the essence: *The core of the problem was a lack of funds.* **3.** The hard or stringy central part of certain fruits, such as an apple or pear, containing the seeds. **4.** A set of subjects or courses that make up a required portion of a curriculum. **5.** The central or innermost portion of the earth below the mantle, probably consisting of iron and nickel. **6.** A piece of magnetic material, such as a rod of soft iron, placed inside an electrical coil or transformer to intensify and provide a path for the magnetic field produced by the windings. **7.** A long, cylindrical sample of soil, rock, or ice, collected with a drill to study the layers of material that are not visible from the surface. **8.** The central part of a nuclear reactor, where atomic fission occurs. **9.** A computer memory or one of the magnetic devices in a computer memory. **10.** The muscles in the trunk of the human body, including those of the abdomen and chest, that stabilize the spine, pelvis, and shoulders. ❖ *tr.v.* **cored, coring, cores** To remove the core of: *core apples.* —**cor′er** *n.*

corgi (kôr′gē) *n., pl.* **corgis** A Welsh corgi.

coriander (kôr′ē-ăn′dər) *n.* **1.** A plant related to and resembling parsley, having aromatic seedlike fruits. **2.** The dried fruits of this plant, used whole or ground as a seasoning. **3.** The leaves of this plant, often known as cilantro, used as a flavoring and garnish.

Corinthian (kə-rĭn′thē-ən) *adj.* **1.** Relating to ancient Corinth or its people, language, or culture. **2.** Relating to an order of ancient Greek and Roman architecture characterized by a slender column with an ornate bell-shaped top decorated with a design of acanthus leaves. ❖ *n.* **1.** A native or inhabitant of ancient Corinth. **2.**

Corinthians Either of two books of the New Testament, containing letters from the Apostle Paul to the Christians in Corinth.

Coriolis effect (kôr′ē-ō′lĭs) *n.* The apparent deflection of a freely moving object as viewed from a rotating frame of reference. For example, to an observer on the earth's surface, an object moving due north from the equator would appear to curve toward the east. This effect explains why hurricanes rotate clockwise in the Southern Hemisphere and counterclockwise in the Northern Hemisphere.

cork (kôrk) *n.* **1.** The light spongy outer bark of the cork oak, used for bottle stoppers and in insulation, life rafts, and flooring. **2a.** Something made of cork, especially a bottle stopper. **b.** A bottle stopper made of other material, such as plastic. **3.** A protective tissue of dead cells that forms the outermost layer of the bark of woody plants. ❖ *tr.v.* **corked, corking, corks** To close up or stop with a cork: *cork a bottle.*

corker (kôr′kər) *n. Slang* A remarkable or astounding person or thing.

cork oak *n.* An evergreen oak tree of the Mediterranean region, having thick bark that is the source of cork.

corkscrew (kôrk′skrōō′) *n.* A device for drawing corks from bottles, consisting of a pointed metal spiral attached to a handle. ❖ *adj.* Spiral in shape; twisted: *the corkscrew motion of a slowly spinning top.*

corm (kôrm) *n.* A short, thick underground stem in which food is stored in the form of starch, as in a crocus.

cormorant (kôr′mər-ənt) *n.* Any of several large black waterbirds having webbed feet and a slender hooked bill.

corn¹ (kôrn) *n.* **1a.** The ears or grains, called kernels, of any of several varieties of a tall grass first cultivated in Mexico and used as food for humans and livestock and as a source of edible oil or starch. **b.** The plant that bears such ears or kernels, called maize in much of the world. **2.** *Chiefly British* Any of various cereal plants or grains, such as wheat or rye. **3.** *Slang* Something considered trite, outdated, or too melodramatic or sentimental. ❖

tr.v. **corned, corning, corns** To preserve and season with salt or in brine: *corn beef.*

WORD HISTORY Throughout the English-speaking world, people eat **corn**, but they don't all eat the same thing. In Old English *corn* meant "any small, hard particle or grain, as of sand or salt, or of a cereal or a seed." The cereal grains include wheat, oats, barley, maize, and so forth, and *corn* is used for the cereal grain most commonly grown in a given place. In most of England that crop is *wheat*, so *corn* usually means "wheat." In Ireland and Scotland that crop is *oats*, and *corn* means "oats" there. In North America *maize* was grown by many of the native peoples and soon also became the chief crop of the English settlers, who called it *Indian corn* at first and eventually just *corn*. *Corn* in the sense of "grain of salt" appears in *corned beef*; in the sense of "seed", it appears in *peppercorn*.

corn² (kôrn) *n.* A horny thickening of the skin, usually on or near a toe, resulting from pressure or rubbing.

WORD HISTORY Corn¹ comes from Old English *corn*, meaning "grain." (See the Word History note at **corn¹**.) **Corn²** comes from Middle English *corne* (meaning "horny thickening of the skin on the feet"), which comes from Latin *cornū* (meaning "horn").

corn bread or **cornbread** (kôrn′brĕd′) *n.* Bread made from cornmeal.

corncob (kôrn′kŏb′) *n.* The long hard central part of an ear of corn, bearing the kernels.

corncrib (kôrn′krĭb′) *n.* A bin or building for storing and drying ears of corn.

corn dog *n.* A baked or fried frankfurter encased in corn bread.

cornea (kôr′nē-ə) *n.* The tough transparent membrane of the outer coat of the eyeball that covers the iris and the pupil.

corned (kôrnd) *adj.* Preserved in strong salty water or with dry salt: *corned beef.*

corner (kôr′nər) *n.* **1a.** The point at which two lines, edges, or surfaces meet: *the upper left-hand corner of the page; the corner of a table.* **b.** The area enclosed by the intersection of two lines, edges, or surfaces: *I sat in the corner.* **2.** The place where two roads or streets meet: *Meet me at the corner of Oak and Pine.* **3.** A remote or secluded place: *Americans have come from all corners of the world.* **4.** A threatening or difficult position: *I got myself in a corner by boasting I could outrun everybody.* **5.** A monopoly, as of a stock or commodity, that enables the supplier to control the price: *tried to get a corner on the wheat market.* ❖ *tr.v.* **cornered, cornering, corners 1.** To force or drive into a corner: *The dog cornered the cat in a closet.* **2.** To gain a monopoly over: *He attempted to corner the market in silver.* ❖ *adj.* **1.** Located at a street corner: *the corner convenience store.* **2.** Designed for or used in a corner: *a corner cupboard for dishes.*

corner kick *n.* In soccer, a free kick from a corner of the field given to the offense when the defense has driven the ball out of bounds beyond the goal line.

cornerstone (kôr′nər-stōn′) *n.* **1.** A stone at one of the corners of a building's foundation, often inscribed and set in place with a special ceremony. **2.** The basis or foundation of something: *Good nutrition is the cornerstone of a healthy life.*

cornet (kôr-nĕt′) *n.* A brass instrument that is similar to the trumpet but has a mellower tone.

cornetist also **cornettist** (kôr-nĕt′ĭst) *n.* A person who plays a cornet.

corn flakes *pl.n.* A crisp, flaky, cold cereal prepared from coarse cornmeal and other ingredients.

cornflower (kôrn′flou′ər) *n.* An annual plant of gardens and fields, having flowers that are usually deep blue, but sometimes white or pink.

cornhusk (kôrn′hŭsk′) *n.* The leafy covering surrounding an ear of corn.

cornice (kôr′nĭs) *n.* **1.** The uppermost projection of stone or molding at the top of a wall or column. **2.** The molding at the top of the walls of a room, just below the ceiling. **3.** A horizontal frame used to conceal curtain rods.

Cornish (kôr′nĭsh) *adj.* Relating to the peninsula of Cornwall in southwest Great Britain. ❖ *n.* A Celtic language spoken in Cornwall until about 1800.

cornmeal also **corn meal** (kôrn′mēl′) *n.* Coarse meal made from ground corn kernels.

cornpone or **corn pone** (kôrn′pōn′) *n.* Corn bread that is made without milk or eggs, baked in rounded patties.

cornstarch (kôrn′stärch′) *n.* A starchy flour made from corn, used as a thickener in cooking.

corn syrup *n.* A thick sweet syrup that is made from corn starch and consists chiefly of glucose. It is often processed into high-fructose corn syrup for use in commercial foods and beverages.

cornucopia (kôr′nə-kō′pē-ə) *n.* **1.** A cone-shaped container overflowing with fruit, vegetables, and flowers, symbolizing prosperity; a horn of plenty. **2.** A cone-shaped ornament or container. **3.** An overflowing supply; an abundance: *a cornucopia of new ideas.*

corny (kôr′nē) *adj.* **cornier, corniest** *Slang* Trite, melodramatic, or sentimental: *a corny love scene.*

corolla (kə-rŏl′ə *or* kə-rōl′ə) *n.* The petals of a flower considered as a group.

corollary (kôr′ə-lĕr′ē) *n., pl.* **corollaries 1.** A statement that follows with little or no proof required from an already proven statement: *If we know A equals B, then the corollary is that B equals A.* **2.** A natural consequence or effect; a result: *Disease is a corollary of unsanitary living conditions.*

corona (kə-rō′nə) *n., pl.* **coronas** or **coronae** (kə-rō′nē) **1.** The extremely hot outer atmosphere of the sun, visible as a halo of light during a solar eclipse. **2.** A faintly colored shining ring seen around a celestial object, especially the moon or sun, when seen through a thin cloud or haze. **3.** A crown-shaped appendage on the inner side of the corolla in some flowers, such as the daffodil.

coronary (kôr′ə-nĕr′ē) *adj.* **1.** Relating to the coronary arteries. **2.** Relating to the heart: *coronary care unit.* ❖ *n., pl.* **coronaries** A coronary thrombosis or heart attack.

coronary artery *n.* Either of the two arteries that supply blood directly to the heart.

coronary thrombosis *n.* The blockage of a coronary artery by a blood clot.

coronation (kôr′ə-nā′shən) *n.* The act or ceremony of crowning a sovereign, such as a king or queen.

coroner (kôr′ə-nər) *n.* A public official who investigates any death not clearly due to natural causes.

coronet (kôr′ə-nĕt′) *n.* **1.** A small crown worn by princes, princesses, and other nobles. **2.** A band for the head, decorated with gold or jewels.

corp. An abbreviation of corporation.

corpora (kôr′pər-ə) *n.* Plural of **corpus.**

corporal¹ (kôr′pər-əl *or* kôr′prəl) *adj.* Relating to the body.

corporal² (kôr′pər-əl *or* kôr′prəl) *n.* A noncommissioned officer in the US Army or Marine Corps ranking below a sergeant.

WORD HISTORY Corporal¹ comes from Middle English *corporal*, which comes from Latin *corporālis* (both meaning "relating to the body"), which comes from Latin *corpus*, meaning "body." **Corporal²** comes from Old Italian *caporale* (referring to an army rank), which comes from Italian *capo*, which comes from Latin *caput*, both meaning "head."

corporate (kôr′pər-ĭt *or* kôr′prĭt) *adj.* **1.** Formed into a corporation; incorporated: *the corporate companies of industrial America.* **2.** Relating to a corporation: *The government taxes corporate profits.* **3.** United or combined; collective: *The team made a corporate effort to finish the project on time.* —**cor′po·rate·ly** *adv.*

corporation (kôr′pə-rā′shən) *n.* A group of people or an organization that has a charter recognizing it as a separate legal unit with rights, privileges, and liabilities that are separate from those of its individual members. Corporations act under the law as if they were a single person, as in entering into contracts or buying and selling property.

corporeal (kôr-pôr′ē-əl) *adj.* **1.** Relating to the body: *corporeal needs of food and water.* **2.** Of a material nature; tangible: *buildings, land, and other corporeal property.* —**cor·po′re·al·ly** *adv.*

corps (kôr) *n., pl.* **corps** (kôrz) **1.** A section or branch of the armed forces having a special function: *The Medical Corps is trained to take care of the wounded.* **2.** A large military unit composed of two or more divisions along with supporting units and commanded by a lieutenant general. **3.** A group of people acting together: *the press corps.*

corps de ballet (kôr′ də bă-lā′) *n.* The dancers in a ballet troupe who perform as a group with no solo parts.

corpse (kôrps) *n.* A dead body, especially that of a human.

corpsman (kôr′mən *or* kôrz′mən) *n.* An enlisted person in the US Navy or Marines who is trained as a medical assistant.

corpulent (kôr′pyə-lənt) *adj.* Having an abundance of fat or flesh; heavy or overweight. —**cor′pu·lence** *n.*

corpus (kôr′pəs) *n., pl.* **corpora** (kôr′pər-ə) A large collection of writings of a specific kind or on a specific subject: *a corpus of legal documents.*

corpuscle (kôr′pŭs′əl) *n.* **1.** A cell, such as a blood cell, that circulates freely in the body. **2.** A very small particle.

corpus delicti (dĭ-lĭk′tī′) *n.* The corroborating evidence that shows that a crime has been committed, other than a confession or an alleged accomplice's statement.

corral (kə-răl′) *n.* **1.** An enclosed area for keeping cattle, horses, or sheep. **2.** An enclosed area formed by a circle of wagons for defense against attack. ❖ *tr.v.* **corralled, corralling, corrals 1.** To drive into and hold in a corral: *corral cattle for shipment to market.* **2.** To arrange (wagons) in a corral. **3.** To surround or seize: *The soldiers corralled the revolutionaries.*

correct (kə-rĕkt′) *tr.v.* **corrected, correcting, corrects 1a.** To remove the mistakes from: *The author corrected her manuscript before it was printed.* **b.** To indicate or mark the errors in: *The teacher corrected our tests.* **2.** To change or adjust so as to bring improvement or meet a

standard: *Glasses will correct your vision.* **3.** To rebuke or punish for the purpose of improving: *Corporal punishment should never be used to correct a child.* ❖ *adj.* **1.** Free from error; accurate: *Your answers are absolutely correct.* **2.** Conforming to approved standards; proper: *the correct way to give artificial respiration.* —**cor·rect′ly** *adv.* —**cor·rect′ness** *n.*

correction (kə-rĕk′shən) *n.* **1.** The act or process of correcting: *Correction of all my spelling mistakes did not take long.* **2.** Something that is offered or substituted for a mistake or fault; an improvement: *Several corrections are written in the margin.* **3a.** Punishment intended to rehabilitate or improve a wrongdoer. **b.** often **corrections** A system for restoring legal offenders to a law-abiding and productive life, involving imprisonment, rehabilitation, parole, and probation. **4.** A brief or small decline in stock-market activity or prices following a period of increases. —**cor·rec′tion·al** *adj.*

corrective (kə-rĕk′tĭv) *adj.* Intended or tending to correct: *corrective lenses.* —**cor·rec′tive·ly** *adv.*

correlate (kôr′ə-lāt′) *v.* **correlated, correlating, correlates** —*tr.* To put or bring into a systematic relation: *We correlated the new data with the old and revised our theory.* —*intr.* To have systematic connection; be related: *The new data correlates perfectly with earlier studies.*

correlation (kôr′ə-lā′shən) *n.* **1.** A relation or connection: *a proven correlation between smoking and lung disease.* **2.** An act of correlating or a condition of being correlated: *The navigator's correlation of speed and position kept the ship on course.*

correlative (kə-rĕl′ə-tĭv) *adj.* **1.** Related; corresponding: *Reading and writing are correlative language skills.* **2.** In grammar, indicating a relation and usually used in pairs. In the sentence *Neither Jim nor Joe went along, neither* and *nor* are correlative conjunctions. —**cor·rel′a·tive·ly** *adv.*

correlative conjunction *n.* A conjunction that regularly occurs as part of a pair of conjunctions and that indicates a relation, such as *both* and *and* (as in *feeling both tired and discouraged*) or *either* and *or* (as in *either laughing or crying.*)

correspond (kôr′ĭ-spŏnd′) *intr.v.* **corresponded, corresponding, corresponds 1.** To be in agreement; match or compare closely: *The hotel room did not correspond with the pictures on the website.* **2.** To be very similar or equivalent: *A camera's shutter corresponds to an eyelid.* **3.** To communicate by writing, usually over a period of time: *They corresponded with each other over the summer.*

correspondence (kôr′ĭ-spŏn′dəns) *n.* **1.** Agreement; conformity: *Correspondence in the wording of the documents shows one is a copy of the other.* **2.** Resemblance, as in function or structure; similarity: *There is a close correspondence between the human arm and a seal's flipper.* **3a.** Communication by the exchange of letters or emails. **b.** The letters or emails exchanged: *filed the correspondence.*

correspondent (kôr′ĭ-spŏn′dənt) *n.* **1.** A person who communicates with another by letter or email, often on a regular basis. **2.** A person hired by a newspaper or radio or television station to report on news from a particular place. ❖ *adj.* Corresponding.

corresponding (kôr′ĭ-spŏn′dĭng) *adj.* Matching closely; similar: *the corresponding function of feathers and fur.* —**cor′re·spond′ing·ly** *adv.*

corridor (kôr′ĭ-dər) *n.* **1.** A hall or passageway, often with rooms opening onto it. **2.** A tract of land forming a passageway: *a corridor for trains through the city.*

corrigendum (kôr′ə-jĕn′dəm) *n., pl.* **corrigenda** (kôr′ə-jĕn′də) **1.** An error to be corrected, especially a printer's error. **2. corrigenda** A list of errors in a book along with their corrections.

corroborate (kə-rŏb′ə-rāt′) *tr.v.* **corroborated, corroborating, corroborates** To support or confirm by new or additional evidence; make certain: *Similar results of several experiments corroborated the new scientific theory.* —**cor·rob′o·ra′tion** *n.* —**cor·rob′o·ra′tive** *adj.*

corrode (kə-rōd′) *v.* **corroded, corroding, corrodes** —*tr.* To dissolve or wear away (a metal or alloy), especially by chemical action. —*intr.* To be dissolved or worn away: *Most metals corrode in a solution of salt.*

corrosion (kə-rō′zhən) *n.* **1.** The process of corroding metal: *Corrosion caused the pipe to leak.* **2.** The product or result of such a process: *corrosion on the car door.*

corrosive (kə-rō′sĭv) *adj.* Capable of producing or tending to produce corrosion: *The salt used to melt snow and ice on the highways is corrosive to the metal rods in the concrete.* ❖ *n.* A corrosive substance.

corrugated (kôr′ə-gā′tĭd) *adj.* Having parallel ridges and grooves: *a roof of corrugated tin.*

corrugation (kôr′ə-gā′shən) *n.* A groove or ridge in a corrugated surface.

corrupt (kə-rŭpt′) *adj.* **1.** Immoral; wicked; depraved: *the corrupt life of a swindler.* **2.** Willing to accept bribes; dishonest: *a corrupt government.* **3.** Containing errors or changes, as in a text: *A corrupt translation of the poem made it incomprehensible.* ❖ *v.* **corrupted, corrupting, corrupts** —*tr.* **1.** To ruin morally; cause to behave wickedly: *Greed corrupts some people.* **2.** To destroy the honesty or integrity of, as by bribing: *They corrupted the senator with offers of shares in their company.* **3.** To taint; infect; spoil: *Several chemical spills corrupted the water supply.* **4.** To change the original form of (a text, word, or language): *Careless copying corrupted later versions of the poem.* **5.** To damage (data) in a computer file or on a disk. —*intr.* To become corrupt: *Absolute power corrupts absolutely.* —**cor·rupt′er** *n.* —**cor·rupt′ly** *adv.*

corruptible (kə-rŭp′tə-bəl) *adj.* Capable of being corrupted, as by bribery. —**cor·rupt′i·bil′i·ty** *n.* —**cor·rupt′i·bly** *adv.*

corruption (kə-rŭp′shən) *n.* **1.** The act or process of corrupting by making wicked or dishonest: *money's corruption of a powerful official.* **2.** Dishonesty or improper behavior, as by a person in a position of authority: *The town government was riddled with corruption.* **3.** Decay; rot.

corsage (kôr-säzh′ *or* kôr-säj′) *n.* A small bouquet of flowers worn at the shoulder or waist or on the wrist, especially by women.

corsair (kôr′sâr′) *n.* **1.** A pirate, especially along the coast of northern Africa. **2.** A pirate ship, often acting with the approval of a government.

corselet (kôr′slĭt) *n.* Metal armor worn to protect the body, especially the upper body.

corset (kôr′sĭt) *n.* A close-fitting undergarment, worn by women to support or shape the waist and hips.

cortege (kôr-tĕzh′) *n.* **1.** A ceremonial procession, especially a funeral procession. **2.** A procession of attendants; a retinue.

cortex (kôr′tĕks′) *n., pl.* **cortices** (kôr′tĭ-sēz′) *or* **cortexes** **1.** The outer layer of an organ or part of the body, as of the adrenal glands. **2.** The cerebral cortex. **3.** A layer of tissue underneath the outermost part of plant stems and roots.

cortical (kôr′tĭ-kəl) *adj.* **1.** Relating to or consisting of a cortex: *the rind and other cortical tissue of an orange.* **2.** Relating to, associated with, or depending on the cerebral cortex: *the cortical functions of the brain.* —**cor′ti·cal·ly** *adv.*

cortisone (kôr′tĭ-sōn′ *or* kôr′tĭ-zōn′) *n.* A hormone produced by the adrenal gland or produced synthetically, used in treating arthritis, allergies, and gout.

corundum (kə-rŭn′dəm) *n.* An extremely hard mineral composed mainly of aluminum oxide. It occurs in gem varieties such as ruby and sapphire and in a dark-colored variety that is used for polishing and scraping.

corvette (kôr-vĕt′) *n.* **1.** A fast gunboat often used to protect convoys from submarines. **2.** A small sailing warship armed with one tier of guns.

cos An abbreviation of cosine.

cosecant (kō-sē′kănt′) *n.* In a right triangle, the ratio of the length of the hypotenuse to the length of the side opposite an acute angle.

cosign (kō-sīn′) *tr.v.* **cosigned, cosigning, cosigns** To sign (a legal document, such as a contract) with another or others.

cosine (kō′sīn′) *n.* In a right triangle, a function of an acute angle equal to the length of the side adjacent to the angle divided by the length of the hypotenuse.

cosmetic (kŏz-mĕt′ĭk) *n.* A preparation, such as face powder or skin cream, designed to beautify the body. ❖ *adj.* Done or used to improve the outward appearance, as of a person or building: *cosmetic surgery to remove a scar; a little paint and some other cosmetic repairs on a porch.*

cosmic (kŏz′mĭk) *adj.* **1.** Relating to the universe: *telescopes that reveal the cosmic past.* **2.** Infinitely extended; vast: *Overpopulation of the planet is an issue of cosmic importance.* —**cos′mi·cal·ly** *adv.*

cosmic dust *n.* Clouds of fine solid particles of matter in outer space.

cosmic ray *n.* A very rapidly moving particle, especially a proton or alpha particle, that enters the atmosphere from outer space.

cosmogony (kŏz-mŏg′ə-nē) *n., pl.* **cosmogonies 1a.** The astrophysical study of the origin and evolution of the universe. **b.** A specific theory or model of the origin and evolution of the universe. **2.** A philosophical, religious, or mythical explanation of the origin of the universe. —**cos′mo·gon′ic** (kŏz-mə-gŏn′ĭk), **cos′mo·gon′i·cal** *adj.* —**cos′mo·gon′i·cal·ly** *adv.* —**cos·mog′o·nist** *n.*

cosmology (kŏz-mŏl′ə-jē) *n., pl.* **cosmologies 1a.** The astrophysical study of the history, structure, and dynamics of the universe. **b.** A specific theory or model of this structure and these dynamics. **2.** A philosophical, religious, or mythical explanation of the nature and structure of the universe. —**cos′mo·log′ic** (kŏz-mə-lŏj′ĭk), **cos′mo·log′i·cal** *adj.* —**cos′mo·log′i·cal·ly** *adv.* —**cos·mol′o·gist** *n.*

cosmonaut (kŏz′mə-nôt′) *n.* A Russian or Soviet astronaut.

cosmopolitan (kŏz′mə-pŏl′ĭ-tn) *adj.* **1.** Composed of people or elements from many different parts of the world: *Montreal is a cosmopolitan city.* **2.** Having broad interests or wide experience of the world; sophisticated: *A cosmopolitan guest made the party interesting.* ❖ *n.* A cosmopolitan person.

cosmos (kŏz′məs *or* kŏz′mōs′) *n.* **1.** The universe regarded as an orderly and harmonious whole. **2.** Any of various tall garden plants having pink, white, or red flowers that resemble daisies.

Cossack (kŏs′ăk) *n.* A member of a people of southern Russia, whose men often served in the cavalry during the rule of the czars. —**Cos′sack**′ *adj.*

cost (kôst) *n.* **1.** An amount paid or charged for a purchase; a price: *The cost of a fishing license is going up.* **2.** The loss or sacrifice necessary to attain a goal: *He worked day and night at the cost of his health.* **3. costs** The expenses of a lawsuit. ❖ *tr.v.* **cost, costing, costs 1.** To have or require as a price: *A subscription to the magazine costs $35.* **2.** To cause to lose or sacrifice: *Years of drought cost them their farm.*

costal (kŏs′təl) *adj.* Relating to or near the ribs.

costar also **co-star** (kō′stär′) *n.* A starring actor given equal status with another or others in a play or film. —**co′star**′ *v.*

cost-effective (kôst′ĭ-fĕk′tĭv) *adj.* Economical in terms of the goods or services received for the money spent. —**cost**′-**ef·fec′tive·ly** *adv.*

costly (kôst′lē) *adj.* **costlier, costliest 1.** High-priced; expensive: *costly jewelry.* **2.** Involving great loss or sacrifice: *Going west was a costly decision for many pioneer families.* —**cost′li·ness** *n.*

cost of living *n.* The average cost of basic necessities, such as food, clothing, and shelter.

costume (kŏs′tōōm′) *n.* **1.** An outfit or disguise worn on special occasions such as Halloween. **2.** The style of clothing and hair typical of a certain time, place, or people: *The costume of the ancient Romans included togas and sandals.* **3.** A set of clothes suitable for a certain occasion or season: *a skating costume.* ❖ *tr.v.* (kŏ-stōōm′) **costumed, costuming, costumes** To dress in a costume: *Everyone was costumed for our Halloween party.*

costume jewelry *n.* Jewelry made from inexpensive metals and imitation gems or semiprecious stones.

costumer (kŏs′tōō′mər) *n.* A person who makes or supplies costumes, as for plays.

cot[1] (kŏt) *n.* A narrow bed usually made of canvas stretched over a folding frame.

cot[2] An abbreviation of cotangent.

cotangent (kō-tăn′jənt) *n.* In a right triangle, a function of an acute angle equal to the length of the side adjacent to the angle divided by the length of the opposite side.

cote (kōt) *n.* A small shed or coop for sheep or birds.

coterie (kō′tə-rē *or* kō′tə-rē′) *n.* A group of people who share interests and associate frequently.

cotillion (kō-tĭl′yən) *n.* A formal ball, especially one at which young women are presented to society.

cottage (kŏt′ĭj) *n.* **1.** A small house, usually in the country. **2.** A small house for vacation use.

cottage cheese *n.* A soft white cheese made of curds of sour skim milk.

cottage industry *n.* **1.** A usually small-scale industry carried on at home by family members using their own equipment. **2.** An informal, loosely organized, yet flourishing complex of activity or industry.

cottager (kŏt′ĭ-jər) *n.* A person who lives in a cottage.

cotter pin (kŏt′ər) *n.* A split pin that fits through a hole in order to fasten parts together and is secured by bending back the ends.

cotton (kŏt′n) *n.* **1.** Any of various shrubby plants grown in warm regions for the downy white fibers that surround their oil-rich seeds. **2.** The soft fine fibers of any of these plants, used in making textiles and other prod-

ucts. **3.** Thread or cloth made of cotton fibers. ❖ *intr.v.* **cottoned, cottoning, cottons** *Informal* To take a liking; become friendly: *Our dog doesn't cotton to strangers.*

cotton candy *n.* A candy made of sugar spun into thin fibers that form a fluffy mass.

cotton gin *n.* A machine that separates the seeds, hulls, and other small objects from cotton fibers.

cottonmouth (kŏt′n-mouth′) *n.* The water moccasin.

cottonseed (kŏt′n-sēd′) *n.* The seed of the cotton plant, the source of cottonseed oil.

cottonseed oil *n.* An oil obtained by pressing cottonseed, used in food products, paints, and soaps.

cottontail (kŏt′n-tāl′) *n.* Any of several rabbits of the Americas, having grayish or brownish fur and a short fluffy white tail.

cottonwood (kŏt′n-wŏŏd′) *n.* Any of several American poplar trees having triangular leaves and seeds with cottony tufts.

cottony (kŏt′n-ē) *adj.* Resembling cotton; fluffy or downy: *cottony clouds.*

cotyledon (kŏt′l-ēd′n) *n.* A leaf of the embryo of a seed-bearing plant. A cotyledon contains stored food and is the first leaf or the first of a pair of leaves in a newly developing plant.

couch (kouch) *n.* A sofa. ❖ *tr.v.* **couched, couching, couches** To word in a certain manner; phrase: *The negotiators couched their demands in tactful language.*

couch potato *n.* *Slang* A person who spends much time sitting or lying down, usually watching television.

cougar (kōō′gər) *n.* A large wild cat chiefly of mountainous regions of the Americas, having a long tail and a tawny coat; a mountain lion.

cough (kôf) *v.* **coughed, coughing, coughs** —*intr.* **1.** To force air from the lungs suddenly and noisily, usually to clear mucus or other matter from the throat or lungs: *cough from breathing smoke.* **2.** To make a noise similar to coughing: *The engine coughed and died.* —*tr.* To clear from the respiratory tract by coughing: *cough up mucus.* ❖ *n.* **1.** The act of coughing: *The student's cough disturbed the class.* **2.** An illness marked by coughing: *A bad cough kept me home from work.*

could (kŏŏd) *aux.v.* Past tense of **can**[1]. **1.** Used to indicate ability in the past: *I could run faster back then.* **2.** Used to indicate permission in the past: *Only friends of the musicians could go backstage after the concert.* **3.** Used to indicate possibility: *It could rain tomorrow.* **4.** Used to indicate politeness: *Could you help me?* —SEE NOTE AT **should**.

couldn't (kŏŏd′nt) Contraction of *could not.*

couldst (kŏŏdst) *aux.v. Archaic* A second person singular past tense of **can**[1].

coulee (kōō′lē) *n.* A deep gulch or ravine in the western United States, often dry in summer.

coulomb (kōō′lŏm′ *or* kōō′lŏm′) *n.* A unit used to measure electric charge. One coulomb is equal to the quantity of charge that passes a point in an electric circuit in one second when a current of one ampere is flowing through the circuit.

coulter (kōl′tər) *n.* A blade or wheel attached to a plow to cut the soil in front of the plowshare.

council (koun′səl) *n.* **1.** A gathering of people called together to discuss a problem or give advice. **2.** A body of people elected or appointed to make laws, policies, or decisions: *The president has a council of economic advisers.*

USAGE The word **council** refers to a decision-making assembly, as in *city council* or *student council*; its members are known as *councilors.* The word **counsel**, on the other hand, means "advice and guidance"; a person who provides such counsel, as at a summer camp or in a legal dispute, is a *counselor.*

councilman (koun′səl-mən) *n.* A member of a council, especially of the group that makes the laws of a city.

councilor also **councillor** (koun′sə-lər *or* koun′slər) *n.* A member of a council. —SEE NOTE AT **council.**

councilwoman (koun′səl-wŏŏm′ən) *n.* A woman who is a member of a council, especially of the group that makes the laws of a city.

counsel (koun′səl) *n.* **1.** The act of exchanging opinions and ideas; consultation: *Frequent counsel among the members kept the committee informed.* **2.** Advice; guidance: *I will not make a decision without your counsel.* **3.** A lawyer or group of lawyers giving legal advice. ❖ *tr.v.* **counseled, counseling, counsels** *or* **counselled, counselling, counsels 1.** To give (a person) advice; advise: *The school counseled parents to keep children at home during the storm.* **2.** To recommend: *counsel swift action.* —SEE NOTE AT **council.**

counselor also **counsellor** (koun′sə-lər *or* koun′slər) *n.* **1.** A person who advises or guides; an adviser: *a high-school counselor.* **2.** A lawyer. **3.** A person who supervises children at a summer camp. —SEE NOTE AT **council.**

count¹ (kount) *v.* **counted, counting, counts** —*tr.* **1.** To find the total of; add up: *Count your change before leaving the store. Count the books before you return them to the library.* **2.** To name the numbers in order up to and including (a particular number): *Count three and jump.* **3.** To take account of; include: *There are seven in my family, counting me.* **4.** To regard; consider: *Count yourself lucky that you didn't get sick.* —*intr.* **1.** To name numbers in order or list items: *count from 1 to 10.* **2.** To have importance or value: *It's the thought that counts.* **3.** To keep time in music by counting beats. ❖ *n.* **1.** The act of counting or calculating: *A count showed that two members were absent.* **2.** A number reached by counting: *The count of nesting birds was lower than last year.* **3.** In law, any of the separate charges listed in an indictment: *The thief was tried on five counts of robbery.* ◆ **count in** To include: *If you are going camping, count me in.* **count off** To separate into groups by counting: *count off by twos.* **count on 1.** To rely on: *You can count on me to help.* **2.** To be confident of; anticipate: *I am counting on an A in history.* **count out** To exclude: *If there's going to be any roughness, you can count me out.*

count² (kount) *n.* A nobleman in some European countries, corresponding to an English earl.

WORD HISTORY Count¹ comes from Middle English *counten,* which comes from Latin *computāre,* meaning "to calculate." **Count²** comes from Middle English *counte,* which comes from Late Latin *comes* (referring to an occupant of a state office), which comes from Latin *comes,* meaning "companion."

countdown (kount′doun′) *n.* **1.** The counting backward from a starting number to indicate the time remaining before a scheduled event, such as the launching of a rocket. **2.** The checks and preparations carried out during this process.

countenance (koun′tə-nəns) *n.* The face or the expression on the face: *The question left him with a puzzled countenance.* ❖ *tr.v.* **countenanced, countenancing, countenances** To accept or give support to; tolerate or

approve: *The school will not countenance cheating.*

counter¹ (koun′tər) *adj.* Contrary; opposing: *views counter to public opinion.* ❖ *n.* **1.** A person or thing that counters; an opposite. **2.** A blow given in return, as in boxing. **3.** A stiff piece of leather around the heel of a shoe. ❖ *v.* **countered, countering, counters** —*tr.* **1.** To move or act in opposition to; oppose: *They countered our plan with one of their own.* **2.** To return (a blow) with another blow. **3.** To offer or say in response: *She countered that she was too busy to write a long paper.* —*intr.* **1.** To move, act, or respond in opposition: *They countered with a weak argument.* **2.** To give a blow in return, as in boxing. ❖ *adv.* In a contrary manner or direction: *a new method that runs counter to the regular way.*

counter² (koun′tər) *n.* **1.** A flat surface on which goods are sold, money is counted, or food is prepared or served. **2.** A small object, such as a stone or bead, used for counting, as on an abacus, or for marking a place in a game. ◆ **over the counter** Without a doctor's prescription being legally required: *aspirin is usually sold over the counter.*

counter³ (koun′tər) *n.* A person or thing that counts, especially a mechanical or electronic device that automatically counts.

WORD HISTORY Counter¹ comes from Middle English *countre,* which comes from Latin *contrā,* both meaning "against." **Counter²** comes from Middle English *countour* (meaning both "table for counting money" and "counting house"), which comes from Medieval Latin *computātōrium,* which comes from Latin *computāre,* meaning "to calculate." **Counter³** is the Modern English verb *count* suffixed with Modern English *-er.*

counter– A prefix that means: **1.** Contrary or opposite: *counteract; counterclockwise.* **2.** In return or opposing: *counterattack.* **3.** Complementary; corresponding: *countersign.*

counteract (koun′tər-ăkt′) *tr.v.* **counteracted, counteracting, counteracts** To oppose and lessen the effects of by contrary action; check: *Aspirin often counteracts a fever.*

counterattack (koun′tər-ə-tăk′) *n.* An attack made in return for another attack. ❖ *intr. & tr.v.* (koun′tər-ə-tăk′) **counterattacked, counterattacking, counterattacks** To attack in return.

counterbalance (koun′tər-băl′əns) *n.* **1.** A force or an influence that counteracts another. **2.** A weight that balances another. ❖ *tr.v.* (koun′tər-băl′əns) **counterbalanced, counterbalancing, counterbalances** To act as a counterbalance to.

counterclaim (koun′tər-klām′) *n.* A claim made in opposition to another claim.

counterclockwise (koun′tər-klŏk′wīz′) *adv. & adj.* In a direction opposite to that of the movement of the hands of a clock: *move counterclockwise; counterclockwise motion.*

counterculture (koun′tər-kŭl′chər) *n.* A culture, especially of young people, with values or lifestyles in opposition to those of the established culture. —**coun′ter·cul′tur·al** *adj.*

counterfeit (koun′tər-fĭt′) *v.* **counterfeited, counterfeiting, counterfeits** —*tr.* **1.** To make a copy of (something) in order to deceive: *The defendant was found guilty of counterfeiting money.* **2.** To pretend; fake: *We counterfeited surprise to please the host.* —*intr.* **1.** To carry on a deception; pretend. **2.** To make fraudulent copies, especially of money. ❖ *adj.* **1.** Made in imitation of what is genuine in order to deceive: *a counterfeit dollar bill.* **2.** Pretended; simulated: *counterfeit friendliness.* ❖ *n.* Something counterfeited: *That $20 bill is a counterfeit.* —**coun'ter·feit'er** *n.*

counterinsurgency (koun'tər-ĭn-sûr'jən-sē) *n.* Actions taken by a government to oppose or suppress an insurgency.

counterintelligence (koun'tər-ĭn-tĕl'ə-jəns) *n.* Actions taken by a government to deceive enemy agents or prevent them from gathering political or military secrets.

counterintuitive (koun'tər-ĭn-too'ĭ-tĭv) *adj.* Contrary to what intuition or common sense would indicate: *found a counterintuitive solution to the problem.* —**coun'ter·in·tu'i·tive·ly** *adv.*

countermand (koun'tər-mănd' *or* koun'tər-mănd') *tr.v.* **countermanded, countermanding, countermands** To cancel or reverse (a command or order).

countermeasure (koun'tər-mĕzh'ər) *n.* A measure or action taken to oppose or offset another.

countermove (koun'tər-moov') *n.* A move in opposition to another move: *countermoves in chess.*

counteroffensive (koun'tər-ə-fĕn'sĭv) *n.* A large-scale attack by an army, intended to stop the offensive of an enemy force.

counteroffer (koun'tər-ô'fər) *n.* An offer made in return by a person who rejects an unsatisfactory offer.

counterpane (koun'tər-pān') *n.* A bedspread or quilt.

counterpart (koun'tər-pärt') *n.* **1.** A person or thing that corresponds to another, as in function, relation, or position: *The ancient counterpart to the car was the chariot.* **2.** A person or thing that is a natural complement to another: *He has one sock but lost its counterpart.*

counterpoint (koun'tər-point') *n.* **1.** A musical technique in which two or more distinct melodies are combined in harmony while at the same time keeping their distinctness. **2.** A secondary melody designed to go along with a principal melody.

counterpoise (koun'tər-poiz') *n.* **1.** A counterbalancing weight. **2.** A force or influence that balances or equally counteracts another. **3.** The state of being in equilibrium. ❖ *tr.v.* **counterpoised, counterpoising, counterpoises 1.** To oppose with an equal weight; counterbalance. **2.** To act against with an equal force or power; offset.

counterproductive (koun'tər-prə-dŭk'tĭv) *adj.* Tending to hinder rather than help one's purpose.

counterrevolution (koun'tər-rĕv'ə-loo'shən) *n.* A movement arising in opposition to a revolution and aiming to restore the conditions before the revolution.

counterrevolutionary (koun'tər-rĕv'ə-loo'shə-nĕr'ē) *adj.* Relating to or tending to promote counterrevolution. ❖ *n.* A person who is engaged in or supports counterrevolution.

countersign (koun'tər-sīn') *tr.v.* **countersigned, countersigning, countersigns** To sign (a document previously signed by another), as to guarantee authenticity: *The property deed was signed by the new owner and countersigned by a notary public.* ❖ *n.* **1.** A second or confirming signature. **2a.** A sign or signal to be given to a sentry in order to pass; a password. **b.** A secret sign or signal given in answer to another.

countersink (koun'tər-sĭngk') *n.* **1.** A hole with the top part enlarged so that the head of a screw or bolt will lie flush with or below the surface. **2.** A tool for mak-

ing such a hole. ❖ *tr.v.* **countersunk** (koun'tər-sŭngk'), **countersinking, countersinks 1.** To enlarge the top part of (a hole) so that the head of a screw or bolt will lie flush with or below the surface. **2.** To drive (a screw or bolt) into a hole so that the screw or bolt sits flush with or below the surface.

counterspy (koun'tər-spī') *n., pl.* **counterspies** A spy working to uncover or oppose enemy espionage.

countertenor (koun'tər-tĕn'ər) *n.* **1.** A man's singing voice with a range above that of tenor. **2.** A singer having such a voice.

counterterrorism (koun'tər-tĕr'ə-rĭz'əm) *n.* Actions taken by a government to prevent terrorist attacks or to defeat terrorists.

countervail (koun'tər-vāl') *v.* **countervailed, countervailing, countervails** —*tr.* **1.** To act against with equal force; counteract. **2.** To compensate for; offset. —*intr.* To act against an often detrimental influence or power.

counterweight (koun'tər-wāt') *n.* **1.** A weight used as a counterbalance. **2.** A force or influence that counteracts another: *The new conservative judge will provide a counterweight to the court's most liberal members.*

countess (koun'tĭs) *n.* **1.** A woman holding the title of count or earl. **2.** The wife or widow of a count or earl.

counting number (koun'tĭng) *n.* A number used to count objects; a whole number greater than zero. The numbers 1, 5, and 29 are counting numbers, but ¼ and −7 are not.

countless (kount'lĭs) *adj.* Too many to be counted; innumerable: *the countless stars.*

count noun *n.* A noun, such as *chair* or *pen*, that refers to a single object and can form a plural or occur with the article *a* or *an.*

countrified (kŭn'trĭ-fīd') *adj.* **1.** Resembling or having the characteristics of country life; rural; rustic: *The wide-brimmed hat gave the actor a countrified look.* **2.** Lacking in sophistication: *simple, countrified manners.*

country (kŭn'trē) *n., pl.* **countries 1a.** A nation or state: *Mexico and Canada are two countries in the Western Hemisphere.* **b.** The land of a nation or state: *Switzerland is a mostly mountainous country.* **2.** The land of one's birth or citizenship: *The sailors returned to their country at the end of the voyage.* **3.** The people of a nation or state: *The country will benefit from his invention.* **4.** A large area of land distinguished by certain physical, geographic, or cultural features: *hill country.* **5.** The region outside of cities or heavily populated districts; a rural area: *go to the country for a vacation.* **6.** Country music: *The new album is a mix of pop and country.* ❖ *adj.* **1.** Relating to or typical of the country: *country life.* **2.** Relating to country music.

country and western *n.* Country music.

country club *n.* A suburban club with facilities for social and sports activities, usually having a golf course.

countryman (kŭn'trē-mən) *n.* **1.** A person from one's own country; a compatriot. **2.** A native or inhabitant of a particular country. **3.** A man who lives in the country.

country music *n.* Popular music based on the folk style of the southern rural United States or on the music of cowboys in the American West.

countryside (kŭn'trē-sīd') *n.* **1.** A rural region. **2.** The inhabitants of the countryside: *The whole countryside resisted building the highway.*

countrywoman (kŭn'trē-woom'ən) *n.* **1.** A woman from one's own country; a compatriot. **2.** A woman who was born in or lives in a particular country. **3.** A woman who lives in the country.

county (koun′tē) *n., pl.* **counties 1.** The largest administrative division of most states in the United States. **2.** A major territorial division in Great Britain and Ireland. **3.** The people living in a county: *The county will vote on the school proposal.*

county seat *n.* A town or city that is the center of government in its county.

coup (kōō) *n., pl.* **coups** (kōōz) **1.** A brilliantly executed move or action that achieves the desired results: *Quickly restoring peace between the enemy nations was a real coup for the ambassador.* **2.** A coup d'état. **3.** Among certain Native American peoples, a feat of bravery performed in battle, especially the touching of an enemy's body without causing injury.

coup de grâce (kōō′ də gräs′) *n., pl.* **coups de grâce** (kōō′ də gräs′) **1.** A deathblow delivered to end the misery of a mortally wounded victim. **2.** A finishing stroke or decisive event.

coup d'état (kōō′ dā-tä′) *n., pl.* **coups d'état** (kōō′ dā-tä′) or **coup d'états** (kōō′ dā-täz′) The sudden overthrow of a government, bringing a new group into power.

coupe (kōōp) *n.* **1.** A closed two-door automobile. **2.** A closed four-wheel carriage with two seats inside and one outside.

couple (kŭp′əl) *n.* **1.** Two things of the same kind; a pair: *a couple of shoes.* **2a.** Two people united, as by marriage: *a young couple just starting a family.* **b.** Two people together: *a dance couple.* **3.** *Informal* A few; several: *vacation for a couple of days; have only a couple of dollars.* ❖ *v.* **coupled, coupling, couples** —*tr.* To link together; attach; join: *couple the cars of a train.* —*intr.* To form pairs; join: *The dancers coupled up as the music began.*

coupler (kŭp′lər) *n.* A person or thing that couples, especially a device that holds two railroad cars together.

couplet (kŭp′lĭt) *n.* A unit of verse consisting of two successive lines that usually rhyme and have the same meter.

coupling (kŭp′lĭng) *n.* A device that links or connects.

coupon (kōō′pŏn′ or kyōō′pŏn′) *n.* **1a.** A detachable part of a ticket, card, or advertisement that entitles the person holding it to certain benefits, such as a cash refund or a gift. **b.** A printed form to be used to order something or to obtain a discount. **2.** One of a number of small certificates attached to a bond that represent sums of interest that can be collected at specified dates.

courage (kûr′ĭj) *n.* The quality of mind or spirit that enables one to face danger or hardship with confidence, resolution, and firm control of oneself; bravery: *It takes courage to defend people who hold unpopular beliefs.*

courageous (kə-rā′jəs) *adj.* Having or characterized by courage. See Synonyms at **brave.** —**cou·ra′geous·ly** *adv.* —**cou·ra′geous·ness** *n.*

courier (kōōr′ē-ər or kûr′ē-ər) *n.* A messenger, especially one on official diplomatic business: *Government requests for a truce were sent by courier.*

course (kôrs) *n.* **1a.** Development in a particular way: *the course of events.* **b.** Onward movement in time; duration: *in the course of a week.* **2.** The route or direction taken by something or someone: *the course of a stream; strike a course due south.* **3.** An area of land or water on which a race is held or a sport is played: *the course of a marathon; a golf course.* **4.** A way of behaving or acting: *Your best course is to wait.* **5.** A typical manner of proceeding; regular development: *The law took its steady course.* **6.** An orderly sequence: *a course of medical treatments.* **7a.** A complete body of studies in a subject in a school, college, or university: *a four-year course in engineering.* **b.** A unit of such studies: *an English course.* **8.** A part of a meal served as a unit at one time: *Soup was our first course.* ❖ *intr.v.* **coursed, coursing, courses** To flow or move swiftly: *Blood courses through the veins.* ◆ **in due course** At the proper or right time. **of course 1.** As is to be expected under the circumstances; naturally or obviously: *Of course the sun is hot.* **2.** Without any doubt; certainly: *Of course we'll come to your party.*

courser (kôr′sər) *n.* A swift horse.

courseware (kôrs′wâr′) *n.* Educational software designed especially for classroom use.

court (kôrt) *n.* **1.** An area of open ground partly or completely enclosed by walls or buildings; a courtyard. **2.** A short street, especially an alley enclosed by buildings on three sides. **3a.** A person or body of officials who hear and make decisions on legal cases. **b.** The room or building in which such cases are heard; a courthouse or courtroom. **c.** The regular session of a judicial assembly: *Court is not held on a holiday.* **4a.** A sovereign's governing body of ministers and state advisers: *The British monarchy is often called the Court of St. James.* **b.** An official meeting of this body, presided over by the sovereign: *hold court to try a traitor.* **5a.** The people who attend a monarch, including family, servants, advisers, and friends: *In medieval days the court moved several times a year.* **b.** A royal mansion or palace. **6.** An open level area marked with lines for games such as tennis, handball, or basketball. ❖ *v.* **courted, courting, courts** —*tr.* **1.** To seek the affection of, especially with hopes of marrying: *He courted her for a year before proposing.* **2.** To seek the support or favor of; try to please: *Columbus courted the queen and king of Spain to help pay for his expeditions.* **3.** To try to gain; seek, often foolishly or unwittingly: *court danger.* **4.** To behave in such a way as to attract (a mate): *Male birds often court females by singing.* —*intr.* To pay loving attention to one other: *They courted in secret for a year.*

courteous (kûr′tē-əs) *adj.* Considerate toward others; gracious; polite: *a courteous manner.* See Synonyms at **polite.** —**cour′te·ous·ly** *adv.*

courtesan (kôr′tĭ-zən) *n.* A woman who is a prostitute to men of high social standing, especially in a royal court.

courtesy (kûr′tĭ-sē) *n., pl.* **courtesies 1.** Polite behavior: *We try to treat all of our customers with courtesy.* **2.** An act or gesture showing politeness: *Our host's many courtesies made the stay very enjoyable.*

courthouse (kôrt′hous′) *n.* **1.** A building in which courts of law are held. **2.** A building that houses a county government.

courtier (kôr′tē-ər) *n.* **1.** An attendant at the court of a king or other ruler. **2.** A person who seeks favor, especially by flattery.

courtly (kôrt′lē) *adj.* **courtlier, courtliest** Suitable for a royal court; dignified and elegant: *courtly manners.* —**court′li·ness** *n.*

court-martial (kôrt′mär′shəl) *n., pl.* **courts-martial 1.** A military court of officers who are appointed to try people for offenses under military law. **2.** A trial by such a court. ❖ *tr.v.* **court-martialed, court-martialing, court-martials** or **court-martialled, court-martialling, court-martials** To try (someone) by court-martial.

court order *n.* An order issued by a court that requires a person to do or refrain from doing something.

court reporter *n.* A stenographer who transcribes court proceedings word for word.

courtroom (kôrt′rōōm′ *or* kôrt′rŏŏm′) *n.* A room in which the proceedings of a court of law are held.
courtship (kôrt′shĭp′) *n.* **1.** The act or period of courting. **2.** Specialized behavior in animals that leads to mating.
courtyard (kôrt′yärd′) *n.* An open space that is partly or completely surrounded by walls or buildings.
couscous (kōōs′kōōs′) *n.* A pasta of northern African origin made of granules of crushed wheat.
cousin (kŭz′ĭn) *n.* **1.** A child of one's aunt or uncle. **2.** A relative descended from a common ancestor, such as a grandparent, by two or more generations. **3.** A member of a country or group having similar origins or interests: *our Canadian cousins.* **4.** Something similar in quality or character: *Cricket is the British cousin of baseball.*
covalent bond (kō-vā′lənt) *n.* A chemical bond formed when electrons are shared between two atoms.
cove (kōv) *n.* **1.** A small sheltered bay or inlet. **2a.** A recess or a small valley in the side of a mountain. **b.** A cave or cavern.
coven (kŭv′ən) *n.* A gathering or meeting of witches.
covenant (kŭv′ə-nənt) *n.* A formal binding agreement made by two or more people or parties: *Marriage is a legal covenant between two people.*
cover (kŭv′ər) *v.* **covered, covering, covers** —*tr.* **1.** To place something upon or over, so as to protect or conceal: *cover a table with a tablecloth; covered her smile with her hand.* **2.** To spread over the surface of: *Dust covered the furniture.* **3.** To hide from view or knowledge: *He tried to cover up his mistakes.* **4.** To extend over; include: *a farm covering 100 acres.* **5.** To travel or journey over: *We covered 200 miles a day.* **6.** To have as a subject; deal with: *This course covers basic first aid.* **7.** To be responsible for reporting the details of (an event or situation), as for a newspaper: *The reporter covered the crisis in the Middle East.* **8.** To be enough for: *Will five dollars cover the cost of it?* **9.** To protect, as from loss: *We have fire insurance to cover our belongings.* **10a.** To aim a firearm at: *The police officer covered the suspect.* **b.** To protect by having within range or by firing a gun at an enemy: *The entrance to the harbor is covered by the guns of the fort.* **11.** In sports: **a.** To guard (an opponent playing offense). **b.** To defend (an area or position): *The pitcher covers first base when the first baseman fields a grounder.* —*intr.* **1.** *Informal* To act as a substitute for someone absent: *The stand-in covered for the ailing star of the play.* **2.** To hide something in order to save someone from punishment, embarrassment, or loss: *cover for a friend's mistake.* ❖ *n.* **1.** Something placed on or attached to something else, as for protection: *the covers on a bed; the cover of a book.* **2.** Vegetation covering an area: *The rabbits hid in the dense cover.* **3.** Shelter or protection: *seek cover in a cave during a storm.* **4.** Something that conceals or disguises: *The enemy retreated under the cover of darkness.* **5.** A recording of a song that was previously recorded or made popular by another singer or musician. ◆ **take cover** To seek a hiding place or protection, as from enemy fire. **under cover** Secretly: *Spies work under cover.*
coverage (kŭv′ər-ĭj) *n.* **1.** The extent to or way in which something is analyzed and reported: *television news coverage of local events.* **2.** The extent of protection given by an insurance policy: *We carry accident and theft coverage on our car.*
coveralls (kŭv′ər-ôlz′) *pl.n.* A one-piece garment of pants

and shirt, worn over other clothes to protect them.
cover crop *n.* A crop planted to prevent soil erosion in winter and to enrich the soil when plowed into the ground in the spring.
covered wagon (kŭv′ərd) *n.* A large wagon covered with an arched canvas top, used by American pioneers for travel across the prairie.
covering (kŭv′ər-ĭng) *n.* Something that covers, protects, or hides: *a covering for a bed.*
coverlet (kŭv′ər-lĭt) *n.* A bedspread.
cover slip *n.* A small thin piece of glass used to cover a specimen on a microscope slide.
covert (kŭv′ərt *or* kō′vərt) *adj.* Concealed; secret: *a covert mission behind enemy lines.* ❖ *n.* **1.** A covered or sheltered place; a hiding place. **2.** Thick underbrush that provides cover for game animals or birds. —**cov′ert·ly** *adv.* —**cov′ert·ness** *n.*
cover-up *or* **coverup** (kŭv′ər-ŭp′) *n.* An effort or strategy designed to conceal something, such as a crime or scandal, that could be harmful or embarrassing if revealed.
covet (kŭv′ĭt) *tr.v.* **coveted, coveting, covets 1.** To desire (something belonging to another). **2.** To wish for strongly; crave: *an ambitious person who coveted success.*
covetous (kŭv′ĭ-təs) *adj.* Very desirous of something belonging to another. —**cov′et·ous·ly** *adv.* —**cov′et·ous·ness** *n.*
covey (kŭv′ē) *n., pl.* **coveys** A small group of partridges, grouse, or similar birds.
cow[1] (kou) *n.* **1.** The mature female of domestic cattle or other bovine mammals. **2.** The mature female of certain other large mammals, such as elephants or moose. **3.** A domestic bovine mammal of any sex or age: *a farm with cows, sheep, and chickens.*
cow[2] (kou) *tr.v.* **cowed, cowing, cows** To frighten or subdue with threats or a show of force: *The approach of the troops cowed the rioting crowd.*

WORD HISTORY Cow[1] is from Old English *cū*, referring to the same animal as in Modern English. **Cow**[2] is probably of Scandinavian origin.

coward (kou′ərd) *n.* A person who lacks courage to face danger or pain, or shows fear in a shameful way.
cowardice (kou′ər-dĭs) *n.* Lack of courage or a shameful show of fear when facing danger or pain.
cowardly (kou′ərd-lē) *adj.* **1.** Lacking courage: *a cowardly liar.* **2.** Characteristic of a coward: *cowardly behavior.* ❖ *adv.* In the manner of a coward: *acted cowardly under pressure.* —**cow′ard·li·ness** *n.*
cowbell (kou′bĕl′) *n.* A bell hung from a collar around a cow's neck to help in finding it.
cowbird (kou′bûrd′) *n.* Any of various blackbirds that lay their eggs in the nests of other birds and are often found near herds of grazing cattle.
cowboy (kou′boi′) *n.* A hired man who tends cattle, especially in the western United States, performing many of his duties on horseback.
cowboy boot *n.* A high leather boot often having tooled designs or ornamental stitching.
cowboy hat *n.* A felt hat having a tall crown and a very wide brim.
cowcatcher (kou′kăch′ər *or* kou′kĕch′ər) *n.* An iron grille or heavy metal plate on the front of a locomotive to clear away obstacles from the track.
cower (kou′ər) *intr.v.* **cowered, cowering, cowers** To crouch or draw back, as from fear or pain; cringe: *The*

dog cowered under the table in the thunderstorm.

cowgirl (kou′gûrl′) *n.* A hired woman who tends cattle, especially in the western United States, performing many of her duties on horseback.

cowhand (kou′hănd′) *n.* A cowboy or cowgirl.

cowherd (kou′hûrd′) *n.* A person who herds or tends cattle.

cowhide (kou′hīd′) *n.* **1.** The skin or hide of a cow. **2.** Leather made from this hide.

cowl (koul) *n.* **1a.** The hood worn especially by a monk. **b.** A robe or cloak having such a hood. **2.** The part of the front of an automobile body that supports the windshield and dashboard. **3.** The cowling on an aircraft.

cowlick (kou′lĭk′) *n.* A tuft of hair that stands up from the head and will not lie flat.

cowling (kou′lĭng) *n.* A removable metal cover for an engine, especially an engine of an aircraft.

coworker (kō′wûr′kər) *n.* A person with whom one works; a fellow worker.

cowpoke (kou′pōk′) *n.* A cowboy or cowgirl.

cowpox (kou′pŏks′) *n.* A contagious skin disease of cattle that is caused by a virus. When cowpox is transmitted to humans it provides immunity to smallpox.

cowpuncher (kou′pŭn′chər) *n.* A cowboy or cowgirl.

cowrie or **cowry** (kou′rē) *n., pl.* **cowries** Any of various tropical marine mollusks having glossy, often brightly marked shells that were formerly used as money in some parts of Africa and Asia.

cowslip (kou′slĭp′) *n.* **1.** A primrose usually having fragrant yellow flowers and used in herbal medicine. **2.** A marsh marigold.

coxcomb (kŏks′kōm′) *n.* A vain and often foolish person; a conceited dandy; a fop.

coxswain (kŏk′sən or kŏk′swān′) *n.* A person who steers a boat or racing shell or has charge of its crew.

coy (koi) *adj.* **coyer, coyest 1.** Pretending to be shy or modest, especially in a flirtatious way. **2.** Unwilling to make a commitment or give information; evasive: *He was always coy when asked how old he was.* —**coy′ly** *adv.* —**coy′ness** *n.*

coyote (kī-ō′tē or kī′ōt′) *n.* A wolflike mammal having grayish-brown or yellowish fur, large erect ears, and a drooping bushy tail.

coypu (koi′pōō) *n., pl.* **coypus** The nutria.

cozen (kŭz′ən) *tr.v.* **cozened, cozening, cozens** To deceive by means of a petty trick. —**coz′en·er** *n.*

cozy (kō′zē) *adj.* **cozier, coziest 1.** Snug and comfortable: *a cozy spot by the fire.* **2.** Friendly; intimate: *a cozy circle of friends.* **3.** *Informal* Marked by close association for devious purposes: *a cozy deal between management and union leaders.* ❖ *n., pl.* **cozies** A padded or knitted covering placed over a teapot to keep the tea hot. —**co′zi·ly** *adv.* —**co′zi·ness** *n.*

cp. An abbreviation of compare.

CPA An abbreviation of certified public accountant.

CPL or **Cpl** or **Cpl.** An abbreviation of corporal.

CPR An abbreviation of cardiopulmonary resuscitation.

cps An abbreviation of: **1.** characters per second. **2.** cycles per second.

CPU An abbreviation of central processing unit.

crab[1] (krăb) *n.* **1.** Any of various primarily marine animals related to the lobsters and shrimps, having a broad flattened hard-shelled body and five pairs of legs, the front pair of which are claws. **2.** Any of various similar animals, such as a horseshoe crab or a hermit crab. **3.** A

crab louse. ❖ *intr.v.* **crabbed, crabbing, crabs** To hunt or catch crabs. —**crab′ber** *n.*

crab[2] (krăb) *n.* **1.** A crabapple tree or its fruit. **2.** *Informal* A bad-tempered complaining person; a grouch. ❖ *intr.v.* **crabbed, crabbing, crabs** *Informal* To complain irritably.

crabapple or **crab apple** (krăb′ăp′əl) *n.* **1.** Any of various small trees having clusters of white, pink, or reddish flowers. **2.** The small sour fruit of such a tree, sometimes used to make jelly and preserves.

crabbed (krăbd or krăb′ĭd) *adj.* **1.** Difficult to read; cramped: *crabbed handwriting.* **2.** Crabby; ill-tempered. —**crab′bed·ly** *adv.* —**crab′bed·ness** *n.*

crabby (krăb′ē) *adj.* **crabbier, crabbiest** *Informal* Irritable and difficult to please; grouchy. —**crab′bi·ly** *adv.* —**crab′bi·ness** *n.*

crabgrass or **crab grass** (krăb′grăs′) *n.* Any of various grasses that spread rapidly and grow as weeds in lawns and agricultural fields.

crab louse *n.* A louse that infests the pubic region and causes severe itching.

crabmeat (krăb′mēt′) *n.* The edible flesh of a crab.

crack (krăk) *v.* **cracked, cracking, cracks** —*intr.* **1a.** To break without dividing into parts: *The mirror cracked when I bumped it.* **b.** To break or snap apart: *The branch cracked off and fell.* **2.** To make a sharp snapping sound: *The pond ice cracked.* **3.** To have a mental or physical breakdown: *The young doctor cracked under the strain of long hours.* **4.** To change sharply in pitch or timbre; break: *The reporter's voice cracked with emotion.* —*tr.* **1a.** To cause to break without dividing into parts: *The pebble cracked the car's windshield.* See Synonyms at **break**. **b.** To break with a sharp sound: *We cracked walnuts.* **2a.** To strike with a sudden sharp sound: *I cracked my head on the cabinet door.* **b.** To cause to make a sharp snapping sound: *The coach driver cracked a whip.* **3.** To open to a slight extent: *cracked the window to air out the room.* **4.** To break open or into: *Thieves cracked the safe.* **5.** To solve: *We cracked the spies' code.* **6.** *Informal* To tell or say (a joke or something witty). **7.** To break down (a complex substance, especially petroleum) into simpler chemical compounds: *crack oil into gasoline.* ❖ *n.* **1a.** A partial split or break: *a crack in a plate.* **b.** A narrow space: *The door was opened just a crack.* **2.** A sharp snapping sound: *a loud crack of thunder.* **3.** A sharp blow: *a crack on the head.* **4.** A cracking tone or sound: *a crack in the singer's voice.* **5.** An attempt: *Take a crack at the job.* **6.** A witty or sarcastic remark. **7.** An instant; a moment: *the crack of dawn.* **8.** *Slang* Crack cocaine. ❖ *adj.* Excelling in skill; first-rate: *a crack shot.* ◆ **crack down** To become more severe or strict: *The university cracked down on plagiarism.* **crack up** *Informal* **1.** To damage or wreck: *cracked up the car.* **2.** To have a mental or physical breakdown: *started to crack up from overwork.* **3.** To experience or cause to experience a great deal of amusement: *I cracked up when I heard the funny joke.*

crack cocaine *n.* Purified cocaine in pellet form that is smoked through a pipe and is highly addictive.

crackdown (krăk′doun′) *n.* An action taken to stop an illegal or disapproved activity: *a crackdown on gambling.*

cracked (krăkt) *adj.* **1.** Having a crack or cracks: *a cracked dish.* **2.** Broken into pieces: *cracked ice.* **3.** Changing in pitch or timbre; uneven: *a cracked voice.* **4.** *Informal* Crazy or deranged.

cracker (krăk′ər) *n.* **1.** A thin crisp wafer or biscuit: *cheese and crackers.* **2.** A firecracker. **3.** A person who uses a computer without permission, especially in order to tamper with data or programs.

crackerjack (krăk′ər-jăk′) *Slang n.* A person or thing of excellent quality or ability. ❖ *adj.* Of the highest quality or ability: *a crackerjack pilot.*

cracking (krăk′ĭng) *n.* The process of breaking down a complex substance, especially petroleum, into simpler compounds by means of heat and often various catalysts.

crackle (krăk′əl) *intr.v.* **crackled, crackling, crackles** To make slight sharp snapping or rustling sounds: *The fire crackled in the fireplace. The cellophane crackled as I crushed it.* ❖ *n.* **1.** The act or sound of crackling: *the crackle of dry leaves underfoot.* **2.** A network of fine cracks on the surface of glazed pottery, china, or glassware.

crackling (krăk′lĭng) *n.* **1.** Sharp snapping sounds like those produced by a fire or by the crushing of paper. **2.** **cracklings** Crisp bits remaining after fat from meat has been melted down, as in making lard.

crackly (krăk′lē) *adj.* Making or likely to make a crackling sound: *a crackly fire.*

crackpot (krăk′pŏt′) *n.* A person with very strange ideas. ❖ *adj.* Foolish; harebrained: *a crackpot theory.*

–cracy A suffix that means government or rule: *meritocracy.*

cradle (krād′l) *n.* **1.** A small bed for a baby, usually mounted on rockers. **2.** A place of origin; a birthplace: *Boston was the cradle of the American Revolution.* **3.** Infancy: *The great pianist showed an interest in music almost from the cradle.* **4.** A framework of wood or metal used to support something, such as a ship, being built or repaired. **5.** The part of a telephone on which the handset rests when not in use. **6.** A box on rockers, used for washing dirt that might contain gold. ❖ *tr.v.* **cradled, cradling, cradles** **1.** To place or hold in or as if in a cradle: *cradle a baby in one's arms.* **2.** To hold or support in a construction cradle: *cradle a ship in drydock.* **3.** To wash (dirt believed to contain gold) in a cradle.

cradleboard (krād′l-bôrd′) *n.* A board or frame on which an infant can be secured, carried on the back by certain Native American peoples as a portable cradle.

craft (krăft) *n.* **1.** Special skill or ability: *a table made with craft; the craft of fine needlework.* **2.** Skill in deception or evasion; cunning: *With great craft the spy escaped capture.* **3a.** An occupation or trade requiring special skill: *learning his craft as a printer.* **b.** The members of an occupation or trade. **4.** *pl.* **craft** A boat, ship, aircraft, or spacecraft. **5.** **crafts** Items made by hand; handicrafts. ❖ *tr.v.* **crafted, crafting, crafts** **1.** To make by hand: *craft fine watches.* **2.** To make or devise with great care and skill: *craft an agreement between the warring nations.*

craftsman (krăfts′mən) *n.* A man who practices a craft with great skill. —**crafts′man·ship′** *n.*

craftswoman (krăfts′wŏŏm′ən) *n.* A woman who practices a craft with great skill.

crafty (krăf′tē) *adj.* **craftier, craftiest** Skilled in underhanded dealing and deceit; cunning. —**craft′i·ly** *adv.* —**craft′i·ness** *n.*

crag (krăg) *n.* A steep projection of rock forming part of a cliff or mountain.

craggy (krăg′ē) *adj.* **craggier, craggiest** **1.** Having crags; steep and rugged: *a craggy mountain.* **2.** Rugged and uneven: *a craggy face.* —**crag′gi·ness** *n.*

cram (krăm) *v.* **crammed, cramming, crams** —*tr.* **1.** To

force, press, or squeeze (people or things) into a small space: *I crammed my clothes into the suitcase.* **2.** To fill tightly; crowd: *Students crammed the halls between classes.* —*intr.* **1.** To study hastily for an examination. **2.** To move into and fully occupy a space: *Commuters crammed into the subway car.*

cramp¹ (krămp) *n.* **1.** A sudden painful contraction of a muscle, often resulting from strain or chill: *A leg cramp forced the sprinter to drop out of the race.* **2.** A temporary partial paralysis of muscles that are used too much: *My fingers had writer's cramp after the test.* **3.** **cramps** Sharp persistent pains in the abdomen: *An upset stomach and cramps made me feel sick.* ❖ *intr. & tr.v.* **cramped, cramping, cramps** To have or cause to have a cramp or cramps: *The runner's leg cramped in the cold. Swimming so many laps eventually cramped her legs.*

cramp² (krămp) *n.* **1.** An iron bar bent at both ends, used to hold together blocks of stone or timbers. **2.** A force or influence that restrains: *The rain put a cramp in our picnic plans.* ❖ *tr.v.* **cramped, cramping, cramps** **1.** To hold together with a cramp. **2.** To confine or restrain: *The riders were cramped together on the crowded bus.* **3.** To jam (the wheels of a car) hard to the right or left: *cramp the wheels into the curb when parking on a hill.*

cramped (krămpt) *adj.* **1.** Confined and limited in space: *a cramped little apartment.* **2.** Small and difficult to read: *cramped handwriting.*

crampon (krăm′pŏn′ *or* krăm′pən) *n.* A spiked iron or steel framework attached to the bottom of a shoe or boot to prevent slipping when climbing on ice and snow.

cranberry (krăn′bĕr′ē) *n.* **1.** The tart, shiny, red berry of an evergreen shrub that grows in damp places, used in making jellies, beverages, and baked goods. **2.** The plant that bears such berries.

crane (krān) *n.* **1.** Any of various large wading birds having a long neck, long legs, and a long bill. **2.** A machine for lifting heavy objects by means of cables attached to a movable boom. **3.** Any of various devices in which a swinging arm or rod is used to support a load: *Colonial fireplaces had a crane to swing heavy pots over the fire.* ❖ *tr.v.* **craned, craning, cranes** To strain and stretch (the neck) in order to get a better view of something.

cranial (krā′nē-əl) *adj.* Relating to the skull: *cranial nerves.*

cranial nerve *n.* Any of several paired nerves, 12 of which occur in mammals, that arise from the brain stem and exit through openings in the skull. These nerves are involved with sight, hearing, smell, and balance.

cranium (krā′nē-əm) *n., pl.* **craniums** *or* **crania** (krā′nē-ə) **1.** The skull. **2.** The part of the skull that encloses the brain.

crank (krăngk) *n.* **1.** A rod and handle that can be attached to a shaft and turned to start a machine or run some device. **2.** *Informal* **a.** An irritable person; a grouch. **b.** An eccentric person; a person with odd ideas. ❖ *tr.v.* **cranked, cranking, cranks** **1.** To start or operate (an engine or device) by means of a crank: *Electric starters replaced the need to crank early car motors.* **2.** To move or operate (a window, for example) by or as if by turning a handle. ❖ *adj.* Produced by an irritable or eccentric person: *a crank letter.* ◆ **crank out** To produce, especially mechanically and rapidly: *The printing press is cranking out copies of the pamphlet.*

crankcase (krăngk′kās′) *n.* The bottom part of a gasoline engine that covers the crankshaft and holds the oil to lubricate it.

crankshaft (krăngk′shăft′) *n.* A shaft that turns or is turned by a crank. In a gasoline engine it is connected to and rotated by the pistons.

cranky (krăng′kē) *adj.* **crankier, crankiest** Easily annoyed; irritable; peevish: *a cranky two-year-old.* —**crank′i·ly** *adv.* —**crank′i·ness** *n.*

cranny (krăn′ē) *n., pl.* **crannies** A small opening, as in a wall or rock face; a crevice.

crape (krāp) *n.* **1.** A light cloth with a crinkled surface; crepe. **2.** An armband of black crepe, worn as a sign of mourning.

crappie (krŏp′ē) *n., pl.* **crappies** Either of two edible North American freshwater fishes related to the sunfishes.

craps (krăps) *pl.n. (used with a singular or plural verb)* A gambling game played with a pair of dice.

crapshoot (krăp′shōōt′) *n.* Informal An enterprise whose outcome is determined by chance.

crash (krăsh) *v.* **crashed, crashing, crashes** —*intr.* **1.** To break violently and noisily: *The dishes crashed to pieces on the floor.* **2.** To be damaged or destroyed by a collision or violent impact: *The car crashed into the tree.* **3.** To move noisily or violently: *The elephants crashed through the trees.* **4.** To undergo a sudden severe decline or downturn: *The stock market crashed in 1929.* **5.** To fail suddenly: *The computer crashed in the middle of an operation.* **6.** To make a sudden loud noise: *The cymbals crashed.* —*tr.* **1.** To cause to fall, strike, or collide suddenly, violently, and noisily: *The boy crashed his bike into the garage door.* **2.** Informal To join or enter without being invited: *crash a party.* ❖ *n.* **1.** A loud noise, as of a sudden impact or collapse: *a crash of thunder.* **2.** A violent collision: *Their car was destroyed in a crash.* **3.** A sudden severe decline in business: *the crash of 1929.* **4.** The sudden failure of a computer or computer program. ❖ *adj.* Informal Marked by an intense effort to produce or accomplish something: *a crash diet to lose weight.*

crash dive *n.* A rapid dive by a submarine, especially in an emergency.

crash helmet *n.* A padded helmet, as one worn by a pilot or racecar driver, to protect the head.

crash-land (krăsh′lănd′) *tr. & intr.v.* **crash-landed, crash-landing, crash-lands** To land (an aircraft) under emergency conditions, often resulting in damage to it.

crass (krăs) *adj.* **crasser, crassest** Crude or unfeeling; coarse: *a crass remark.* —**crass′ly** *adv.* —**crass′ness** *n.*

–crat A suffix that means one who takes part in or supports a certain form of government: *bureaucrat.*

crate (krāt) *n.* **1.** A container, such as a case made of wooden slats, used for storing or shipping. **2.** A container, such as a metal or plastic cage, used to house or transport an animal. ❖ *tr.v.* **crated, crating, crates** To put into a crate.

crater (krā′tər) *n.* **1.** A bowl-shaped depression at the top of a volcano or at the mouth of a geyser. **2.** A shallow, bowl-shaped hole in a surface formed by an explosion or by the impact of a body, such as a meteorite.

cravat (krə-văt′) *n.* A scarf or band of fabric worn around the neck as a tie.

crave (krāv) *tr.v.* **craved, craving, craves** **1.** To have a very strong desire for; long for: *The thirsty runners craved water.* See Synonyms at **desire. 2.** To beg earnestly for; implore: *crave a favor of someone.*

craven (krā′vən) *adj.* Very cowardly: *the traitor's craven behavior.* ❖ *n.* A coward. —**cra′ven·ly** *adv.* —**cra′ven·ness** *n.*

craving (krā′vĭng) *n.* A very strong desire; a yearning.

craw (krô) *n.* The crop of a bird. ◆ **stick in (one's) craw** To be a continuing cause of discontent or resentment for someone: *The harsh insult stuck in his craw for years afterward.*

crawfish (krô′fĭsh′) *n.* Variant of **crayfish.**

crawl (krôl) *intr.v.* **crawled, crawling, crawls** **1.** To move slowly on the hands and knees or by dragging the body along the ground: *The baby crawled across the room.* **2.** To move or advance slowly or haltingly: *The bus crawled along in the heavy traffic.* **3a.** To be covered with or as if with crawling things: *The scene was crawling with police.* **b.** To feel as if covered with crawling things: *The story made my skin crawl.* ❖ *n.* **1.** A very slow pace: *Traffic moved at a crawl.* **2.** A rapid swimming stroke performed face down with alternating overarm strokes and a flutter kick. —**crawl′er** *n.*

crawlspace (krôl′spās) *n.* A low or narrow space, such as one beneath a floor, that gives workers access to plumbing or wiring equipment.

crayfish (krā′fĭsh′) also **crawfish** (krô′fĭsh′) *n.* Any of various freshwater animals that resemble a small lobster and are often used as food.

crayon (krā′ŏn′ or krā′ən) *n.* **1.** A stick of colored wax used for drawing. **2.** A drawing made with crayons. ❖ *tr.v.* **crayoned, crayoning, crayons** To draw, color, or decorate with crayons.

craze (krāz) *tr.v.* **crazed, crazing, crazes** To cause to be mentally or emotionally disturbed or distressed: *The lost explorer was crazed by a lack of contact with other people.* ❖ *n.* Something very popular for a brief time; a fad.

crazy (krā′zē) *adj.* **crazier, craziest 1.** Having a serious mental disorder, especially one that distorts the perception of reality. **2.** Mentally or emotionally agitated or distressed: *The noise of the jackhammer is driving us crazy.* **3.** Informal Foolish or impractical; senseless: *a crazy idea for making money fast.* **4.** Informal Full of enthusiasm or excitement: *The whole family is crazy about their new car.* ◆ **like crazy** Informal To an exceeding degree: *They were running around like crazy, preparing for the holidays.* —**cra′zi·ly** *adv.* —**cra′zi·ness** *n.*

crazy quilt *n.* A patchwork quilt made of pieces of cloth of various shapes, colors, and sizes, sewn together in an irregular pattern.

creak (krēk) *intr.v.* **creaked, creaking, creaks** To make or move with a grating or squeaking sound: *The rusty gate creaked as it swung open.* ❖ *n.* A grating or squeaking sound: *a stair that makes a creak when stepped on.*

creaky (krē′kē) *adj.* **creakier, creakiest 1.** Likely to creak or giving off creaks: *a door on creaky hinges.* **2.** Shaky or weak, as with old age: *creaky knee joints.* —**creak′i·ly** *adv.* —**creak′i·ness** *n.*

cream (krēm) *n.* **1.** The yellowish fatty part of milk that is not homogenized, used in cooking and making butter. **2.** Any of various substances containing or resembling cream: *a pudding of lemon cream; hand cream.* **3.** A yellowish white. **4.** The best part: *These juicy tomatoes are the cream of the crop.* ❖ *v.* **creamed, creaming, creams** —*intr.* To form cream or a layer of foam or froth on the top. —*tr.* **1.** To prepare (foods) in a cream sauce: *cream spinach.* **2.** To remove the cream from; skim: *creamed the milk before drinking it.* **3.** To take or remove (the best part): *creamed the best jobs for her cronies.* **4.** Slang To defeat overwhelmingly: *We creamed them at the last basketball game.*

cream cheese *n.* A soft white cheese made of cream and milk.

creamer (krē′mər) *n.* **1.** A small pitcher for cream. **2.** A powdered or liquid substitute for cream, used in coffee or tea.

creamery (krē′mə-rē) *n., pl.* **creameries** A place where dairy products are prepared or sold.

cream of tartar *n.* Potassium bitartrate.

creamy (krē′mē) *adj.* **creamier, creamiest 1.** Rich in cream: *a creamy filling.* **2.** Resembling cream, as in richness, texture, or color: *a creamy lotion; a creamy yellow.* —**cream′i·ly** *adv.* —**cream′i·ness** *n.*

crease (krēs) *n.* **1.** A line or mark made by pressing or folding: *a crease in his pants.* **2.** A wrinkle: *creases on the old man's face.* ❖ *tr. & intr.v.* **creased, creasing, creases** To make or become creased, folded, or wrinkled: *crease a piece of paper; a face creased with age.*

create (krē-āt′) *tr.v.* **created, creating, creates 1.** To bring into being; cause to exist: *create a new music school.* See Synonyms at **establish**. **2.** To give rise to; produce: *The rumor created a panic among stockholders.* **3.** To produce through artistic effort: *create a poem.*

creation (krē-ā′shən) *n.* **1.** The act or process of creating: *the creation of a canyon by erosion.* **2.** Something produced by invention and imagination: *The x-ray machine and the computer are creations of modern science.* **3. Creation** In various religions, the divine act by which the world was brought into existence. **4.** The world and all things in it.

creationism (krē-ā′shə-nĭz′əm) *n.* Belief in the literal interpretation of the account of the creation of the universe contained in the Bible.

creative (krē-ā′tĭv) *adj.* **1.** Having the ability or power to create things; original: *a creative writer.* **2.** Showing imagination or originality: *a creative design.* —**cre·a′tive·ly** *adv.* —**cre·a′tive·ness** *n.*

creativity (krē′ā-tĭv′ĭ-tē) *n.* The quality of being creative; originality and inventiveness.

creator (krē-ā′tər) *n.* **1.** A person who creates: *creators of sculpture.* **2. Creator** God.

creature (krē′chər) *n.* **1.** A living being, especially a non-human animal: *birds, rabbits, and other creatures of the woods.* **2.** A human; a person: *What a handsome creature he is in that tuxedo!* **3.** An imaginary or fantastical being: *a creature from outer space.*

crèche (krĕsh) *n.* A model of the Nativity with statues of the infant Jesus, his mother Mary, her husband Joseph, and others.

credence (krēd′ns) *n.* Acceptance of something as true; belief: *Don't put any credence in that rumor.*

credential (krĭ-dĕn′shəl) *n.* **1.** Something that entitles a person to confidence, credit, or authority: *An honest face was the borrower's only credential.* **2. credentials** Letters or other written evidence of a person's qualifications or status: *The new ambassador presented his credentials to the foreign government.*

credibility (krĕd′ə-bĭl′ĭ-tē) *n.* The condition, quality, or power of being credible: *The leader lost his credibility by failing to back up his threats with action.*

credible (krĕd′ə-bəl) *adj.* Worthy of confidence or belief; believable: *a credible news report; a credible witness.* —**cred′i·bly** *adv.*

credit (krĕd′ĭt) *n.* **1.** Belief or confidence; trust: *We place full credit in our employees.* **2.** Reputation or standing: *It is to their credit that they worked so hard without complaining.* **3.** A source of honor or distinction: *This exceptional athlete is a credit to our team.* **4.** Recognition or approval for an act, ability, or quality: *The two authors shared the credit for the book's success.* **5a.** Certification that a student has fulfilled a requirement by completing a course of study: *She received full credit for her studies at a previous school.* **b.** A unit of study certified as properly completed: *Advanced courses are worth four credits.* **6.** often **credits** An acknowledgment of work done, as in the production of a movie or play: *There was a long list of credits at the end of the movie.* **7.** Reputation for repaying debts and being financially honest that entitles a person to be trusted in buying and borrowing: *I have good credit at all the local stores.* **8a.** A system of buying goods or services by requiring payment at a later time: *buy a car on credit.* **b.** The terms governing such payments: *a store that offers easy credit.* **9.** The amount of money in the account of a person or group, as at a bank. **10.** In accounting: **a.** The amount paid on a debt. **b.** The right-hand side of an account, on which such payments are entered. ❖ *tr.v.* **credited, crediting, credits 1.** To believe in; trust: *They credited my explanation of what happened.* **2a.** To regard (a person) as having done something: *Two Canadian scientists are credited with the discovery of insulin.* **b.** To attribute (something) to a person: *Some credit the song to Haydn.* **3.** To give educational credits to (a student). **4.** In accounting: **a.** To give credit for (a payment) in an account: *The store credited $100 to my account.* **b.** To give credit to (a person's account).

creditable (krĕd′ĭ-tə-bəl) *adj.* Deserving praise or credit: *a creditable attempt to solve the problem.* —**cred′it·a·bil′-i·ty, cred′it·a·ble·ness** *n.* —**cred′it·a·bly** *adv.*

credit card *n.* A plastic card issued by a bank or business authorizing the holder to buy goods or services on credit.

creditor (krĕd′ĭ-tər) *n.* A person or business to whom money is owed.

credo (krē′dō *or* krä′dō) *n., pl.* **credos** A statement of belief; a creed: *The store owner's credo is "The customer always comes first."*

credulity (krĭ-dōo′lĭ-tē) *n.* The tendency to believe too readily; gullibility: *Her credulity led her to believe stories that weren't true.*

credulous (krĕj′ə-ləs) *adj.* Tending to believe too readily; gullible: *A credulous person is easily fooled.* —**cred′-u·lous·ly** *adv.* —**cred′u·lous·ness** *n.*

Cree (krē) *n., pl.* **Cree** *or* **Crees 1.** A member of a Native American people living across a large area of Canada. **2.** The Algonquian language of the Cree.

creed (krēd) *n.* **1.** A formal statement of religious belief. **2.** A system of belief or principles that guides a person's actions: *His creed is to help others as much as possible.*

creek (krēk *or* krĭk) *n.* A small stream, often a shallow tributary to a river.

Creek (krēk) *n., pl.* **Creek** *or* **Creeks 1.** A member of a Native American people formerly living in eastern Alabama, Georgia, and northern Florida and now located in Oklahoma and southern Alabama. **2.** The Muskogean language of these people. **3.** A member of a Native American confederacy made up of the Creek and various other southeast peoples.

creel (krēl) *n.* A wicker basket used for carrying fish.

creep (krēp) *intr.v.* **crept** (krĕpt), **creeping, creeps 1.** To move slowly or cautiously with the body close to the ground: *The cat crept toward the mouse.* **2.** To move in a timid, cautious, or stealthy way: *The embarrassed host* *crept out of the room.* **3.** To advance or spread slowly: *Traffic crept along the freeway at rush hour. The ivy crept up the wall of the mansion.* **4.** To have a tingling sensation, as if covered with crawling things: *Thinking of ghosts makes my flesh creep.* ❖ *n.* **1.** The act of creeping: *the silent creep of a tiger.* **2.** *Slang* An unpleasant or annoying person. **3. creeps** *Informal* A sensation of fear and repugnance, as if things were crawling on one's skin: *This old house gives me the creeps.*

creeper (krē′pər) *n.* **1.** A person or thing that creeps. **2.** A plant having stems that grow along the ground or cling to a surface for support.

creepy (krē′pē) *adj.* **creepier, creepiest** *Informal* Producing a tingling sensation of uneasiness or fear, as if things were creeping on one's skin. —**creep′i·ly** *adv.* —**creep′-i·ness** *n.*

cremate (krē′māt′ *or* krĭ-māt′) *tr.v.* **cremated, cremating, cremates** To burn (a corpse) to ashes. —**cre·ma′tion** *n.*

crematorium (krē′mə-tôr′ē-əm) *n., pl.* **crematoriums** or **crematoria** (krē′mə-tôr′ē-ə) A furnace or building with a furnace for burning corpses.

crematory (krē′mə-tôr′ē *or* krĕm′ə-tôr′ē) *n., pl.* **crematories** A crematorium.

crème de la crème (krĕm′ də lä krĕm′) *n.* A thing or group of things of the highest quality.

Creole (krē′ōl′) *n.* **1.** A person of European ancestry born in the Caribbean or Spanish-speaking parts of the Americas. **2a.** A descendant of the original French settlers of the southern United States, especially Louisiana. **b.** The French dialect spoken by these people. **3. creole** A language formed when two or more groups of people speaking different languages have prolonged contact with one another: *Haitian Creole is a mixture of French and various languages of western Africa.* **4.** A person of mixed African and European ancestry who speaks such a language, especially one based on French or Spanish. ❖ *adj.* **1.** Relating to the Creoles or their languages and cultures. **2. creole** Cooked with a spicy sauce containing tomatoes, green peppers, and onions: *shrimp creole.*

creosote (krē′ə-sōt′) *n.* A yellow to brown oily liquid obtained from coal tar and used as a wood preservative. ❖ *tr.v.* **creosoted, creosoting, creosotes** To treat with creosote.

crepe also **crêpe** (krāp) *n.* **1.** A light, soft, thin cloth with a crinkled surface, made of silk, cotton, or another fiber. **2.** A band of black crepe, worn or hung as a sign of mourning. **3.** (*also* krĕp) A very thin pancake, usually served folded with a filling.

crepe paper *n.* Paper with crinkles or puckers in it, used especially for decoration.

crept (krĕpt) *v.* Past tense and past participle of **creep.**

crepuscular (krĭ-pŭs′kyə-lər) *adj.* **1.** Relating to or like twilight; dim: *the castle's crepuscular halls.* **2a.** Active primarily at dawn or dusk or both. Used of animals: *crepuscular bees.* **b.** Occurring at dawn or dusk or both: *crepuscular foraging; a crepuscular stroll through the park.*

crescendo (krə-shĕn′dō) *n., pl.* **crescendos** or **crescendi** (krə-shĕn′dē) **1.** In music, a gradual increase in loudness. **2.** A musical passage performed with a gradual increase in loudness. **3.** A steady increase in force or intensity: *The new movie received a crescendo of publicity after it was nominated for three awards.* ❖ *adj. & adv.* Gradually increasing in loudness: *a crescendo passage; played the passage crescendo.*

crescent (krĕs′ənt) *n.* **1.** The figure of the moon as it ap-

pears in its first or last quarter, with concave and convex edges ending in points. **2.** Something shaped like a crescent: *The ancient Middle East is known as the Fertile Crescent.* ❖ *adj.* **1.** Shaped like a crescent. **2.** Increasing; waxing: *the crescent phase of the moon.*

cress (krĕs) *n.* Any of several plants, such as watercress, having strong-tasting leaves used in salads.

crest (krĕst) *n.* **1.** A projecting tuft or outgrowth on the head of a bird or other animal. **2a.** The top of something, such as a mountain or wave. **b.** The highest point, as of a process or action: *The crest of a flood; had reached the crest of her career.* **3.** A plume worn as a decoration on top of a helmet. **4.** A design placed above the shield on a coat of arms. ❖ *v.* **crested, cresting, crests** —*tr.* **1.** To reach the top of: *The climbers crested the mountain.* **2.** To decorate or furnish with a crest. —*intr.* **1.** To form into a crest: *Waves crested over the sea wall.* **2.** To reach a crest: *The river crested after the heavy rain.*

crestfallen (krĕst′fô′lən) *adj.* Dejected; depressed: *He was crestfallen over the failure of his business.*

Cretaceous (krĭ-tā′shəs) *n.* The third and last period of the Mesozoic Era, from about 146 to 66 million years ago. During the Cretaceous, flowering plants developed. The period ended with the sudden mass extinction of dinosaurs and many other forms of life. —**Cretaceous** *adj.*

Cretan (krēt′n) *adj.* Relating to the Greek island of Crete or its people or culture. ❖ *n.* A native or inhabitant of Crete.

crevasse (krĭ-văs′) *n.* **1.** A deep crack, as in a glacier; a chasm. **2.** A crack in a dike or levee.

crevice (krĕv′ĭs) *n.* A narrow crack or opening; a fissure or cleft: *Snow seeped through the crevice under the door.*

crew (krōō) *n.* (*used with a singular or plural verb*) **1.** A group of people who work together: *A stage crew is needed to put on the new play.* **2.** The people working together to operate a ship, aircraft, spacecraft, or train: *The ship's crew were very helpful on our cruise across the Atlantic Ocean.* **3a.** A team of rowers. **b.** The sport of rowing. ❖ *tr.v.* **crewed, crewing, crews** To provide (a boat, for example) with a crew.

crewcut or **crew cut** (krōō′kŭt′) *n.* A closely cropped haircut.

crewel (krōō′əl) *n.* A loosely twisted worsted yarn used for a kind of embroidery.

crewelwork (krōō′əl-wûrk′) *n.* Needlework made with crewel.

crew neck *n.* **1.** A round, close-fitting neckline. **2.** A garment, especially a sweater, with such a neckline.

crib (krĭb) *n.* **1.** A small bed with high sides for a baby or young child. **2.** A small building for storing grain. **3.** A rack or trough from which cattle or horses eat. **4.** A framework to support or strengthen a mine or mine shaft. **5.** *Informal* A list of answers or information consulted dishonestly during an examination. **6.** *Slang* One's home. ❖ *v.* **cribbed, cribbing, cribs** —*intr.* *Informal* To use a list of answers or information on an examination; cheat: *The students who cribbed on the test were given a failing grade as punishment.* —*tr.* To copy dishonestly; plagiarize: *cribbed the answers straight from the book.*

cribbage (krĭb′ĭj) *n.* A card game in which the score is kept by inserting small pegs into holes arranged in rows on a small board.

crick (krĭk) *n.* A painful cramp or muscular spasm, especially in the back or the neck. ❖ *tr.v.* **cricked, cricking,**

cricks To cause a crick in, as by turning or wrenching: *cricked my back getting out of the car.*

cricket¹ (krĭk′ĭt) *n.* Any of various small insects that have long antennae and long legs used for leaping. The male produces a chirping sound by rubbing the front wings together.

cricket² (krĭk′ĭt) *n.* **1.** A game played with bats, a ball, and wickets by two teams of 11 players each. **2.** *Informal* Good sporting behavior and fair conduct: *Cheating is simply not cricket.* —**crick′et·er** *n.*

WORD HISTORY Cricket¹ comes from Middle English *criket,* which comes from Old French *criquet* (both referring to the same animal as in Modern English), which comes from Old French *criquer,* meaning "to click." **Cricket²** comes from Old French *criquet,* meaning "stick for a bowling game."

cri de coeur (krē′ də kœr′) *n., pl.* **cris de coeur** (krē′ də kœr′) An impassioned outcry, as of entreaty or protest.

cried (krīd) *v.* Past tense and past participle of **cry.**

crier (krī′ər) *n.* A person who cries, especially: **a.** An official who announces the orders of a court of law. **b.** A town crier. **c.** A hawker.

cries (krīz) *v.* Third person singular present tense of **cry.** ❖ *n.* Plural of **cry.**

crime (krīm) *n.* **1.** A violation of the law in which a person either acts in a way the law forbids or fails to act as the law requires: *Armed robbery is a serious crime.* **2.** Unlawful activity: *There is too much crime in our society.* **3.** A shameful or senseless act: *It's a crime to waste good food.*

criminal (krĭm′ə-nəl) *adj.* **1.** Relating to or involving crime: *criminal behavior.* **2.** Relating to criminal law and the punishment of crime: *criminal court.* **3.** Guilty of crime: *a criminal offender.* **4.** *Informal* Shameful; disgraceful: *a criminal waste of energy.* ❖ *n.* A person who has committed or been convicted of a crime: *The judge sentenced the criminal to jail for burglary.* —**crim′i·nal·ly** *adv.*

criminal law *n.* Law involving crime and its punishment.

criminologist (krĭm′ə-nŏl′ə-jĭst) *n.* A person who specializes in criminology.

criminology (krĭm′ə-nŏl′ə-jē) *n.* The scientific study of crime and criminals.

crimp (krĭmp) *tr.v.* **crimped, crimping, crimps** To press or bend into small regular folds or ridges: *crimp a pie crust.* ❖ *n.* **1.** Something produced by crimping, as a fold or crease. **2.** Something that hinders or obstructs; a snag: *The bad weather put a crimp in our plans.*

crimson (krĭm′zən) *n.* A vivid purplish red. —**crim′son** *adj.*

cringe (krĭnj) *intr.v.* **cringed, cringing, cringes** **1.** To shrink back, as in fear; cower: *The puppy cringed when I tried to pet it.* **2.** To behave in a slavish manner; fawn: *The new secretary cringed before the boss.* ❖ *n.* An act or an instance of cringing. —**cring′er** *n.*

crinkle (krĭng′kəl) *v.* **crinkled, crinkling, crinkles** —*intr.* **1.** To form wrinkles or creases: *Her face crinkles when she smiles.* **2.** To make a crackling sound; rustle: *The foil crinkled as I wrapped the leftovers.* —*tr.* **1.** To cause to form wrinkles or creases: *I crinkled the wrapping paper when my hand slipped.* **2.** To cause to crackle. ❖ *n.* A wrinkle or crease: *Crinkles form around the eyes from laughter.* —**crin′kly** *adj.*

crinoid (krī′noid′) *n.* Any of various marine invertebrate animals having a cup-shaped body, feathery arms, and a stalk by which they can attach themselves to a surface.

crinoline (krĭn′ə-lĭn) *n.* **1.** A cloth used to stiffen collars, linings, hats, and petticoats. **2.** A stiff petticoat of this cloth, worn to make a skirt stand out. **3.** A hoop skirt.

cripple (krĭp′əl) *n.* **1.** *Offensive* A person who is partially disabled, especially one who is not able to walk easily. **2.** An animal that is unable to use a limb or limbs. ❖ *tr.v.* **crippled, crippling, cripples** **1.** To cause to lose the use of a limb or limbs. **2.** To damage or disable: *The storm crippled the ship.* —**crip′pler** *n.*

crisis (krī′sĭs) *n., pl.* **crises** (krī′sēz) **1.** A situation of great difficulty or danger: *The sudden resignation of the president created a political crisis. She faced a crisis when she lost her job.* **2.** A point of change in the course of something; a decisive or crucial time: *The turmoil in that country has finally reached a crisis.* **3.** A sudden change in the course of a serious illness: *Fever often marks the crisis of measles, mumps, and pneumonia.*

crisp (krĭsp) *adj.* **crisper, crispest** **1.** Firm but easily broken or crumbled: *crisp toast; crisp fried chicken.* **2.** Fresh and firm: *crisp lettuce.* **3.** Clean and new; not wrinkled: *a crisp dollar bill.* **4.** Refreshing; bracing: *a walk in the crisp autumn air.* **5.** Sharp, clear, and concise: *a crisp reply.* ❖ *tr. & intr.v.* **crisped, crisping, crisps** To make or become crisp, as by heating or cooking. —**crisp′ly** *adv.* —**crisp′ness** *n.*

crispy (krĭs′pē) *adj.* **crispier, crispiest** Firm but easily broken or crumbled; crisp. —**crisp′i·ness** *n.*

crisscross (krĭs′krôs′) *v.* **crisscrossed, crisscrossing, crisscrosses** —*tr.* **1.** To mark with a pattern of crossing lines: *Animal trails crisscross the woods.* **2.** To move back and forth over or through: *Ships crisscrossed the sea.* —*intr.* To move back and forth: *Our paths crisscrossed throughout the day.* ❖ *n.* A mark or pattern made of crossing lines. ❖ *adj.* Crossing one another: *crisscross lines.* ❖ *adv.* In crossing directions: *umbrellas leaning crisscross in the stand.*

criterion (krī-tîr′ē-ən) *n., pl.* **criteria** (krī-tîr′ē-ə) A rule or standard on which a judgment can be based: *What criteria did the judges use to rate the contestants?*

USAGE The word **criteria** is a plural form of **criterion.** It is correct to say *The scientists used several criteria for determining water quality.* It is incorrect to say *Only one criteria was used in the study.*

critic (krĭt′ĭk) *n.* **1.** A person who forms and expresses judgments about the qualities of something, especially in a report on an artistic work or performance: *a movie critic.* **2.** A person who tends to make harsh judgments; a faultfinder.

critical (krĭt′ĭ-kəl) *adj.* **1.** Inclined to judge severely; likely to find fault: *A critical person is seldom pleased with anything.* **2.** Marked by or exercising careful evaluation and judgment: *critical analysis of a poem.* **3.** Extremely important or decisive: *a critical point in the political campaign.* **4a.** Relating to or being the crisis stage of a disease: *High fever is the critical point of pneumonia.* **b.** Extremely serious or dangerous: *a critical injury.* **5.** Being in a state of crisis or emergency: *a critical shortage of food.* —**crit′i·cal·ly** *adv.*

critical mass *n.* **1.** The smallest mass of a fissionable material that will sustain a nuclear chain reaction at a constant level. **2.** An amount or level needed for a specific result or new action to occur: *Once the new technology reaches* *critical mass, it will continue to spread worldwide.*

criticism (krĭt′ĭ-sĭz′əm) *n.* **1.** Unfavorable judgment; faultfinding; disapproval: *constant criticism with no encouragement.* **2.** The art or profession of forming and expressing judgments, especially about literary or artistic works. **3.** A comment, article, or review that expresses judgments: *Several reporters wrote criticisms of the new movie.*

criticize (krĭt′ĭ-sīz′) *v.* **criticized, criticizing, criticizes** —*tr.* **1.** To judge the merits and faults of; evaluate: *The painter stepped back to criticize her last hour's work.* **2.** To judge severely; find fault with: *Newspapers criticized the library closing.* —*intr.* To express or utter criticism, especially negative criticism: *Those two are always criticizing while others do the work.* —**crit′i·ciz′er** *n.*

critique (krĭ-tēk′) *n.* A critical review or commentary, such as an evaluation of an artistic work.

critter (krĭt′ər) *n. Informal* A creature, especially an animal.

croak (krōk) *n.* A low hoarse sound, such as that made by a frog or crow. ❖ *intr.v.* **croaked, croaking, croaks** **1.** To make such a sound: *Bullfrogs croaked in the pond.* **2.** To speak with a low hoarse voice.

Croat (krō′ăt′ *or* krōt) *n.* **1.** A native or inhabitant of Croatia. **2.** The Croatian language. —**Croat** *adj.*

Croatian (krō-ā′shən) *adj.* Relating to Croatia or its people, language, or culture. ❖ *n.* **1.** A Croat. **2.** The Slavic language of Croatia, written in the Latin alphabet and closely related to Serbian.

crochet (krō-shā′) *v.* **crocheted** (krō-shād′), **crocheting** (krō-shā′ĭng), **crochets** (krō-shāz′) —*tr.* To make by looping thread or yarn into connected links with a hooked needle: *crochet a sweater.* —*intr.* To crochet a piece of needlework. ❖ *n.* Needlework made by crocheting.

crock (krŏk) *n.* A pot or jar of earthenware.

crockery (krŏk′ə-rē) *n.* Earthenware.

crocodile (krŏk′ə-dīl′) *n.* **1.** Any of various large reptiles having rough thick skin, sharp teeth, and powerful jaws, living in lakes, rivers, and coastal areas of tropical regions. A crocodile's snout is longer and thinner than an alligator's. **2.** Leather made from crocodile skin.

crocodile tears *pl.n.* A display of grief that is not sincere.

crocus (krō′kəs) *n., pl.* **crocuses** Any of various small garden plants having purple, yellow, or white flowers that bloom in early spring.

croft (krôft) *n. Chiefly British* **1.** A small enclosed field or pasture near a house. **2.** A small tenant farm.

crofter (krôf′tər) *n. Chiefly British* A person who rents and cultivates a croft.

croissant (krə-sänt′) *n.* A rich crescent-shaped roll.

Cro-Magnon (krō-măg′nən *or* krō-măn′yən) *n.* An early form of modern human that lived throughout Europe from about 35,000 to 10,000 years ago. The Cro-Magnons made tools of stone and bone and decorated cave walls with elaborate paintings. —**Cro-Mag′non** *adj.*

crone (krōn) *n.* **1.** An old woman considered to be ugly; a hag. **2.** A woman respected for her wisdom and experience.

Cronus (krō′nəs) *n.* In Greek mythology, a Titan who ruled the universe until he was overthrown by his son Zeus.

crony (krō′nē) *n., pl.* **cronies** A close friend or companion.

crook (krŏŏk) *n.* **1.** An implement or tool, such as a shepherd's staff, with a hook or hooked part. **2.** Something bent or curved: *a bag of groceries held in the crook of one's*

arm. **3.** A curve or bend; a turn: *a crook in the road.* **4.** *Informal* A person who makes a living dishonestly; a thief or swindler. ❖ *tr. & intr.v.* **crooked, crooking, crooks** To curve or become curved; bend: *crook one's arm around a package; a road that crooks sharply to the right.*

crooked (krŏŏk′ĭd) *adj.* **1.** Not straight; bent or curved: *a crooked street.* **2.** *Informal* Dishonest; underhanded: *a crooked merchant.* —**crook′ed·ly** *adv.* —**crook′ed·ness** *n.*

croon (krōōn) *v.* **crooned, crooning, croons** —*tr.* To sing or hum softly: *croon a lullaby to the baby.* —*intr.* **1.** To sing or hum a melody softly. **2.** To sing popular songs in a sentimental manner. ❖ *n.* A soft singing, humming, or murmuring. —**croon′er** *n.*

crop (krŏp) *n.* **1a.** A cultivated plant or plant product such as a grain, fruit, or vegetable: *Wheat and other crops are grown here.* **b.** The amount of such a product grown or gathered in a single season or place: *Our orchard produced a huge crop of cherries last year.* **2.** A group or quantity appearing at one time: *training the crop of new volunteers.* **3.** A short whip with a loop used in horseback riding. **4.** An enlargement near the beginning of a bird's or insect's digestive tract where food is stored before digestion. **5.** A short haircut. ❖ *tr.v.* **cropped, cropping, crops** **1.** To cut or bite off the tops or ends of: *Sheep cropped the grass very short.* **2.** To cut (hair, for example) short. **3.** To trim (a photograph, for example). ◆ **crop up** To appear unexpectedly: *We thought we had fixed everything, but then more problems cropped up.*

crop-dusting (krŏp′dŭs′tĭng) *n.* The practice of spraying crops with powdered insecticide and fungicide from an airplane.

cropland (krŏp′lănd′) *n.* Land for or suitable for growing crops.

cropper¹ (krŏp′ər) *n.* A sharecropper.

cropper² (krŏp′ər) *n.* **1.** A heavy fall: *As the horse reared, the rider took a cropper.* **2.** A disastrous failure. ◆ **come a cropper** To fail suddenly or disastrously; come to grief.

WORD HISTORY Cropper¹ is short for *sharecropper.* **Cropper²** may come from the archaic phrase *neck and crop,* meaning "completely."

crop rotation *n.* The practice of planting a sequence of different crops on the same land in order to prevent nutrients in the soil from being depleted and to control insects and disease.

croquet (krō-kā′) *n.* An outdoor game in which each player uses a mallet to hit a wooden ball through a course of wickets.

croquette (krō-kĕt′) *n.* A small cake of minced food, often coated with bread crumbs and fried in deep fat.

crosier (krō′zhər) *n.* A staff with a crook or cross at the end, carried as a symbol of office by or before an abbot, bishop, or archbishop.

cross (krôs) *n.* **1a.** An upright post with a piece across it near the top, on which condemned people were executed in ancient times. **b.** often **Cross** In Christianity, the cross upon which Jesus was crucified. **c.** A representation of this cross; a crucifix. **d.** Any of various medals or emblems in the shape of a cross. **2.** A mark or pattern formed by the intersection of two lines, especially such a mark (X) used as a signature by a person who cannot read or write. **3.** A trial or affliction: *Having a talented older sibling can be a heavy cross to bear.* **4a.** The process of crossbreeding. **b.** An animal or plant produced by crossbreeding; a hybrid: *A mule is a cross between a horse and a donkey.* **5.** A combination of two different things: *The novel is a cross between a romance and a satire.* **6.** In soccer, a pass made into the center of the field when attempting to score. ❖ *v.* **crossed, crossing, crosses** —*tr.* **1.** To go or extend across: *The chicken crossed the road. The bridge crosses the river.* **2.** To intersect: *at the corner where Elm crosses Main Street.* **3.** To place crosswise: *cross one's legs.* **4.** To thwart or betray; double-cross: *You will regret it if you cross me.* **5.** To crossbreed or cross-fertilize: *cross a horse with a donkey; cross two varieties of carnation.* **6.** To draw a line across: *Cross your t's.* **7.** To make the sign of the cross on or over: *They crossed themselves and entered the chapel.* **8.** To delete or eliminate by or as if by drawing a line through: *cross the names off the list.* **9.** To meet and pass: *We crossed each other on the way to the market.* **10.** To turn (the eyes) inward toward the nose. **11.** In soccer, to pass (the ball) in a cross. —*intr.* **1.** To extend across; intersect: *The stream crosses through our yard.* **2.** To move across something; make a crossing: *We crossed into Mexico.* **3.** To meet in or as if in passing: *Our letters crossed in the mail.* **4.** To crossbreed or cross-fertilize. ❖ *adj.* **1.** Lying crosswise; intersecting: *a cross street.* **2.** Showing anger or irritation; annoyed: *Teasing makes some people very cross.* **3.** Contrary or opposite: *opponents having cross interests.* —**cross′ly** *adv.* —**cross′ness** *n.*

crossbar (krôs′bär′) *n.* A horizontal bar, line, or stripe.

crossbeam (krôs′bēm′) *n.* A horizontal beam or girder that crosses another or goes from one wall to another.

crossbill (krôs′bĭl′) *n.* Any of various songbirds having a curved bill with narrow crossed tips.

crossbones (krôs′bōnz′) *pl.n.* A representation of two bones placed crosswise, usually under a skull, used as a symbol of death or a warning of danger.

crossbow (krôs′bō′) *n.* A weapon consisting of a bow fixed across a wooden stock, with grooves on the stock to direct an arrow or other projectile.

crossbreed (krôs′brēd′) *v.* **crossbred** (krôs′brĕd′), **crossbreeding, crossbreeds** —*tr.* To produce (an organism) by mating individuals of different breeds or varieties. —*intr.* To mate with an individual of a different breed or variety. ❖ *n.* An organism produced by crossbreeding; a hybrid or cross.

cross-country (krôs′kŭn′trē) *adj.* **1.** Moving or directed across open countryside rather than following roads or tracks: *a cross-country race.* **2.** Going from one side of a country to the other: *a cross-country trip.* —**cross′-coun′try** *adv.*

cross-country skiing *n.* The sport of skiing over the countryside rather than downhill.

crosscut (krôs′kŭt′) *tr.v.* **crosscut, crosscutting, crosscuts** **1.** To cut across (the grain of a piece of wood). **2.** To cut (a piece of wood) using a crosscut saw. ❖ *adj.* Used for cutting crosswise: *crosscut teeth on a saw.* ❖ *n.* **1.** A course or cut going crosswise. **2.** A shortcut.

crosscut saw *n.* A handsaw for cutting wood across the grain.

cross-dress (krôs′drĕs′) *intr.v.* **cross-dressed, cross-dressing, cross-dresses** To dress in clothing that is usually worn by the opposite sex. —**cross′-dress′er** *n.* —**cross′-dress′ing** *n.*

cross-examine (krôs′ĭg-zăm′ĭn) *tr.v.* **cross-examined, cross-examining, cross-examines** **1.** To question (a witness already examined by the opposing side) in court. **2.** To question (someone) very closely, especially in order to check the answers against other answers given previously. —**cross′-ex·am′i·na′tion** *n.* —**cross′-ex·am′in·er** *n.*

cross-eyed (krôs′īd′) *adj.* Having one or both of the eyes turned inward toward the nose.

cross-fertilization (krôs′fûr′tl-ĭ-zā′shən) *n.* Fertilization by the union of gametes from different individuals, sometimes of different varieties or species.

cross-fertilize (krôs′fûr′tl-īz′) *intr. & tr.v.* **cross-fertilized, cross-fertilizing, cross-fertilizes** To undergo or cause to undergo cross-fertilization.

crossfire (krôs′fīr′) *n.* **1.** Lines of fire from two or more positions, crossing each other at a single point: *soldiers caught in a crossfire.* **2.** A rapid, often heated discussion: *The meeting erupted into a crossfire of threats and accusations.*

cross-grained (krôs′grānd′) *adj.* Having an irregular, transverse, or diagonal grain: *cross-grained wood.*

crosshairs (krôs′hârz′) *pl.n.* The two fine strands of wire crossed at right angles in the focus of the eyepiece of an optical instrument, such as the periscope of a submarine.

crosshatch (krôs′hăch′) *tr.v.* **crosshatched, crosshatching, crosshatches** To mark or shade with two or more sets of intersecting parallel lines: *crosshatched the mountainous regions on the map.*

crossing (krô′sĭng) *n.* **1.** A place at which something, such as a street, railroad, or river, may be crossed: *a crossing for cattle along the highway.* **2.** A place where two or more things cross; an intersection: *a traffic light at the street crossing.* **3.** The act of crossing, especially a voyage or flight across an ocean.

cross-legged (krôs′lĕg′ĭd) *adv. & adj.* **1.** With legs or ankles crossed and knees spread wide, as when sitting on the ground: *sitting cross-legged around the fire.* **2.** With one leg lying across the other.

crossover (krôs′ō′vər) *n.* Something, such as a bridge over a highway or a short stretch of connecting railroad track, that makes a crossing. ❖ *adj.* Using or incorporating two or more styles, so as to appeal to a broader audience: *a crossover artist who blended country music with contemporary rock.*

crosspatch (krôs′păch′) *n.* A peevish, irascible person; a grouch.

crosspiece (krôs′pēs′) *n.* A crossing or horizontal piece, such as a crossbeam.

cross-pollination (krôs′pŏl′ə-nā′shən) *n.* The transfer of pollen from the anther of one flower to the stigma of another flower on a different plant of the same species. Insects and wind are agents of cross-pollination. —**cross-pol′li·nate′** *v.*

cross-purpose (krôs′pûr′pəs) *n.* A conflicting or contrary purpose. ❖ **at cross-purposes** Misinterpreting or failing to understand each other's purposes: *The two committees were at cross-purposes.*

cross-question (krôs′kwĕs′chən) *tr.v.* **cross-questioned, cross-questioning, cross-questions** To question closely; cross-examine. ❖ *n.* A question asked during cross-examination.

cross-reference (krôs′rĕf′ər-əns) *n.* A note directing the reader from one part of a book, catalogue, index, or file to another part containing related information.

crossroad (krôs′rōd′) *n.* **1.** A road that crosses another road. **2.** **crossroads** *(used with a singular or plural verb)*

a. A place, often in the countryside, where two or more roads meet: *The bus for the city stops at the crossroads near our farm.* **b.** A crucial point or place, especially one where different courses of action may be taken: *I'm at a crossroads in my career.*

cross section *n.* **1a.** A slice or section of an object made by cutting through it in a plane, usually at right angles to an axis: *The growth rings are visible in the cross section of a tree trunk.* **b.** A piece cut in this way or a picture or drawing of such a piece: *The picture is a cross section of the eye.* **2.** A sample of something meant to be representative of the whole: *A popular show usually appeals to a cross section of the people.*

cross-stitch (krôs′stĭch′) *n.* **1.** A stitch shaped like an X, used in sewing and embroidery. **2.** Needlework made with the cross-stitch. ❖ *tr. & intr.v.* **cross-stitched, cross-stitching, cross-stitches** To make or embroider with cross-stitches.

crosstown or **cross-town** (krôs′toun′) *adj.* Running, extending, or going across a city or town: *a crosstown bus.* ❖ *adv.* Across a city or town: *get snarled in traffic going crosstown.*

cross-train (krôs′trān′) *intr.v.* **cross-trained, cross-training, cross-trains** To train in different sports, by alternating workouts in different activities such as bicycling, running, and swimming.

cross-trainer also **cross trainer** (krôs′trā′nər) *n.* **1.** A person who cross-trains, especially in different sports. **2.** An athletic shoe designed for cross-training, as for running and court sports.

crosswalk (krôs′wôk′) *n.* A path marked off on a street to show where pedestrians should cross.

crosswise (krôs′wīz′) also **crossways** (krôs′wāz′) *adv.* So as to be or lie in a cross direction; across: *logs laid crosswise on the fire.*

crossword (krôs′wûrd′) *n.* A puzzle in which an arrangement of numbered squares running both across and down is to be filled with words in answer to clues that are numbered in the same sequence as the squares.

crotch (krŏch) *n.* **1.** The place where something, such as a tree trunk, divides into two or more parts or branches. **2a.** The part of the human body where the legs extend from the trunk. **b.** The part of a pair of pants that is between the legs.

crotchety (krŏch′ĭ-tē) *adj.* Irritable or temperamental: *The frustrations of the day left me feeling crotchety.* —**crotch′et·i·ness** *n.*

crouch (krouch) *intr.v.* **crouched, crouching, crouches** **1.** To lower the body by bending or squatting: *The tiger crouched in the grass waiting for its prey.* **2.** To bend down or squat in fear; cringe: *The cats crouched in the corner while the dog growled at them.* ❖ *n.* The act or posture of crouching: *skiing in a crouch.*

croup (krōōp) *n.* A diseased condition that affects the throat and windpipe, especially in children, producing difficult and noisy breathing and a hoarse cough. —**croup′y** *adj.*

crouton (krōō′tŏn′ or krōō-tŏn′) *n.* A small piece of toasted or fried bread, used as a garnish in soups and salads.

crow¹ (krō) *n.* Any of several large birds having glossy black feathers and a harsh hoarse call. ◆ **as the crow flies** In a straight line: *The store is two miles from here as the crow flies, but it's five miles by car because you have to go around the lake.*

crow² (krō) *intr.v.* **crowed, crowing, crows** **1.** To utter the loud shrill cry of a rooster: *A rooster crowed at dawn.* **2.** To make a loud sound of pleasure or delight: *The happy baby kicked and crowed.* **3.** To boast, especially about someone else's defeat: *The winners crowed over their victory.* ❖ *n.* **1.** The loud high-pitched cry of a rooster. **2.** A loud sound expressing pleasure or delight.

WORD HISTORY Crow¹ comes from Old English *crāwe*, referring to the same kind of bird as in Modern English. **Crow²** comes from the Old English word *crāwan*, meaning "to make the cry of a rooster."

Crow *n., pl.* **Crow** or **Crows** **1.** A member of a Native American people formerly living on the northern Great Plains and now settled in Montana. **2.** The Siouan language of the Crow.

crowbar (krō′bär′) *n.* A straight iron or steel bar, usually having one end bent or curved with a wedge-shaped edge, used as a lever for lifting or prying.

crowd (kroud) *n.* **1.** A large number of people gathered together; a throng. **2.** The common people; the masses: *Do what you want to do and don't follow the crowd.* **3.** A particular group of people: *the college crowd; fall in with a bad crowd.* ❖ *v.* **crowded, crowding, crowds** —*tr.* **1.** To fill to overflowing: *Shoppers crowded the store.* **2.** To press tightly or cram together: *He crowded his old magazines into a cabinet.* **3.** To press or shove: *subway riders crowding each other at rush hour.* —*intr.* **1.** To gather together in a limited space: *Fans crowded around the rock star.* **2.** To move forward by shoving: *Everybody crowded into the cafeteria.*

crown (kroun) *n.* **1.** A head covering, often made of gold set with jewels, worn by a sovereign as a symbol of ruling power. **2.** often **Crown a.** The authority, power, or position of a sovereign: *the heir to the Crown.* **b.** The sovereign of a country: *The crowns of Europe signed the peace treaty.* **3.** A wreath worn on the head: *a crown of laurel.* **4.** The top part of something, especially of the head. **5.** The head itself. **6.** The top part of a hat. **7.** The upper, spreading part of a tree or shrub. **8a.** The part of a tooth that projects beyond the gum. **b.** An artificial substitute for the natural crown of a tooth. **9.** A former British coin worth five shillings. **10.** A title, distinction, or reward: *win the heavyweight boxing crown.* ❖ *tr.v.* **crowned, crowning, crowns** **1.** To place a crown or wreath on the head of: *crown the victor of the marathon.* **2.** To give regal power to; enthrone: *The king was crowned at the age of 15.* **3.** To give honor or recognition to (someone), especially as the best in an endeavor: *The critics crowned her as the best pianist of all.* **4.** To cover or form the topmost part of: *Snow crowned the mountain peaks.* **5.** To hit (someone) on the head. **6.** To put a crown on (a tooth).

crown prince *n.* The male heir to a throne.

crown princess *n.* **1.** The female heir to a throne. **2.** The wife of a crown prince.

crow's-feet (krōz′fēt′) *pl.n.* Small wrinkles at the outer corner of the eye.

crow's-nest (krōz′nĕst′) *n.* A small lookout platform located near the top of a ship's mast.

cruces (krōō′sēz) *n.* A plural of **crux.**

crucial (krōō′shəl) *adj.* Of the utmost importance; decisive; critical: *The crucial moment in the trial came when the witness contradicted himself.* —**cru′cial·ly** *adv.*

cruciate (krōō′shē-āt′) *adj.* Shaped like a cross: *the cruciate ligaments of the knee.*

crucible (krōō′sə-bəl) *n.* **1.** A container that can withstand very high temperatures, used to melt ores, metals, and other materials. **2.** A severe test or trial: *His strength of character was shaped during the crucible of the war years.*

crucifix (krōō′sə-fĭks′) *n.* **1.** A Christian symbol consisting of an image or a figure of Jesus on the cross. **2.** A cross viewed as a Christian symbol.

crucifixion (krōō′sə-fĭk′shən) *n.* **1.** The act of executing a person on a cross. **2. Crucifixion a.** In Christianity, the execution of Jesus on the cross. **b.** A Christian symbol consisting of a representation of the crucified Jesus.

cruciform (krōō′sə-fôrm′) *adj.* Having the shape of a cross.

crucify (krōō′sə-fī′) *tr.v.* **crucified, crucifying, crucifies 1.** To put (a person) to death by nailing or binding to a cross. **2.** To persecute or torment, as by harsh criticism: *The press crucified the senator for his moral failings.* —**cru′ci·fi′er** *n.*

crude (krōōd) *adj.* **cruder, crudest 1.** Being in an unrefined or natural state; raw: *crude oil; crude cotton.* **2.** Lacking tact or refinement; coarse or offensive: *a crude person with no manners; a crude remark made with little feeling.* **3.** Not carefully or skillfully made; rough: *a crude sketch on a paper napkin.* —**crude′ly** *adv.* —**crude′ness** *n.*

crudity (krōō′dĭ-tē) *n.* The condition or quality of being crude; crudeness.

cruel (krōō′əl) *adj.* **crueler, cruelest** or **crueller, cruellest 1.** Given to causing pain or suffering: *the reign of a cruel dictator.* **2.** Causing suffering; painful or distressing: *a cruel act; cruel words.* —**cru′el·ly** *adv.* —**cru′el·ness** *n.*

cruelty (krōō′əl-tē) *n., pl.* **cruelties 1.** The condition or quality of being cruel: *cruelty to animals.* **2.** A cruel act or remark.

cruet (krōō′ĭt) *n.* **1.** A small glass bottle for holding a condiment, such as vinegar. **2.** A small vessel for water and wine used in the consecration of the Eucharist.

cruise (krōōz) *v.* **cruised, cruising, cruises** —*intr.* **1.** To sail or travel about in an unhurried way: *A patrol boat cruised along the coast.* **2.** To move or travel about with no special destination: *Taxis cruised through the business district looking for fares.* **3.** To travel at steady efficient speed: *After takeoff the plane cruised at a high altitude.* —*tr.* To travel about or journey over: *A police car cruised the streets of the town.* ❖ *n.* A sea voyage for pleasure: *We enjoyed our cruise to Bermuda.*

cruise control *n.* A system in a motor vehicle for maintaining a constant speed.

cruise missile *n.* A guided missile having short wings that allow it to fly at low altitude along a preset course to its target.

cruiser (krōō′zər) *n.* **1.** A medium-sized warship of high speed and a large cruising range, with less armor and firepower than a battleship. **2.** A cabin cruiser. **3.** A squad car.

cruiserweight (krōō′zər-wāt′) *n.* **1.** A boxer weighing more than 175 pounds and not more than 190 pounds (about 79–86 kilograms). **2.** A contestant in other sports in a similar weight class.

cruller (krŭl′ər) *n.* A small, usually ring-shaped or twisted cake of sweet dough fried in deep fat.

crumb (krŭm) *n.* **1.** A tiny piece or particle of food: *brushed crumbs of bread off the table.* **2.** A little bit; a fragment; a scrap: *not a crumb of sympathy.*

crumble (krŭm′bəl) *v.* **crumbled, crumbling, crumbles**

—*tr.* To break into small pieces or crumbs: *He always crumbles crackers into his soup.* —*intr.* **1.** To break up into small pieces: *The lump of dry dirt crumbled easily.* **2.** To fall apart; disintegrate: *The old barn finally crumbled in decay.*

crumbly (krŭm′blē) *adj.* **crumblier, crumbliest** Easily crumbled: *crumbly cake.* —**crum′bli·ness** *n.*

crummy (krŭm′ē) *adj.* **crummier, crummiest** *Slang* **1.** Of poor quality: *a crummy movie.* **2.** Miserable; wretched: *I felt crummy when I thought of the hurtful things I'd said.*

crumpet (krŭm′pĭt) *n.* A light soft bread similar to a muffin, baked on a griddle and often toasted.

crumple (krŭm′pəl) *v.* **crumpled, crumpling, crumples** —*tr.* To crush so as to form creases or wrinkles: *Don't crumple that freshly ironed shirt.* —*intr.* **1.** To become wrinkled or crushed: *Tissue paper crumples easily.* **2.** To collapse: *Stomach cramps caused the runner to crumple to the ground.*

crunch (krŭnch) *v.* **crunched, crunching, crunches** —*tr.* **1.** To chew with a noisy crackling sound: *crunch peanuts.* **2.** To crush, grind, or tread noisily: *crunch ice in a blender.* —*intr.* **1.** To chew noisily: *crunch on celery.* **2.** To move with a crushing or cracking sound: *We crunched through the snow.* **3.** To make a crushing or cracking sound: *The snow crunched under my boots.* ❖ *n.* **1.** The act of crunching. **2.** A crushing or cracking sound: *the crunch of gravel as the car drove up the driveway.* **3.** A critical situation, especially one resulting from a shortage of time, money, or resources: *A disruption in the supply of oil created an energy crunch.*

crunchy (krŭn′chē) *adj.* **crunchier, crunchiest** Crisp; brittle: *crunchy potato chips.* —**crunch′i·ness** *n.*

crusade (krōō-sād′) *n.* **1.** often **Crusade** Any of a series of military expeditions undertaken by European Christians in the 11th, 12th, and 13th centuries to recover the Holy Land from the Muslims. **2.** A campaign or movement for a reform, cause, or ideal: *a crusade for women's rights.* ❖ *intr.v.* **crusaded, crusading, crusades** To take part in a crusade: *The parents crusaded for better schools.* —**cru·sad′er** *n.*

crush (krŭsh) *v.* **crushed, crushing, crushes** —*tr.* **1.** To press or squeeze with enough force to break or injure: *The tree limb crushed the front of the car.* **2.** To break, grind, or pound into small pieces or powder: *crush rocks into gravel.* **3.** To crumple; wrinkle: *Packing the suitcase too tight will crush your clothes.* **4.** To shove, crowd, or press: *I was crushed against the wall of the crowded elevator.* **5a.** To put down; subdue: *crush a rebellion.* **b.** To overwhelm; oppress: *The failure of the experiment did not crush the spirit of the researchers.* —*intr.* **1.** To be or become crushed: *The ice crushed under my feet.* **2.** To proceed or move by crowding or pressing: *The commuters crushed into the train.* ❖ *n.* **1.** The act of crushing; extreme pressure: *The crush of the collision destroyed the car's engine.* **2.** A great crowd: *I was caught in the crush and couldn't get across the square.* **3.** A substance prepared by or as if by crushing: *orange crush.* **4.** *Informal* A strong, often foolish and brief liking for someone. —**crush′er** *n.*

crust (krŭst) *n.* **1a.** The hard outer layer of bread. **b.** A hard dry piece of bread: *had only a few crusts of bread for breakfast.* **2.** A pastry shell, as of a pie. **3.** A hard outer layer or covering: *a layer of snow with a firm crust.* **4.** The solid outer layer of the earth, lying above the mantle. ❖ *v.* **crusted, crusting, crusts** —*tr.* To cover with a crust; encrust: *Snow and ice crusted the mountain trail.* —*intr.*

To become covered with a crust: *The gravy cooled and crusted over.*

crustacean (krŭ-stā′shən) *n.* Any of a group of arthropods, including the lobsters, crabs, shrimps, and barnacles, that usually live in water and have a segmented body, a hard shell, paired jointed limbs, and two pairs of antennae.

crusty (krŭs′tē) *adj.* **crustier, crustiest 1.** Having a crust: *crusty bread.* **2.** Abrupt in speech or manner; gruff; harsh; curt: *The crusty old soldier was easy to provoke.* —**crust′·i·ly** *adv.* —**crust′i·ness** *n.*

crutch (krŭch) *n.* A support used usually as one of a pair by an injured or disabled person as an aid to walking, having a vertical shaft that is sometimes forked and a horizontal grip for the hand. Crutches normally have a crosspiece that is positioned under the armpit or a cuff that wraps around the forearm.

crux (krŭks *or* krŏŏks) *n., pl.* **cruxes** or **cruces** (krŏŏ′sēz) A basic or essential point: *Let's not lose sight of the crux of the problem.*

cry (krī) *v.* **cried** (krīd), **crying, cries** (krīz) —*intr.* **1.** To shed tears, especially as a result of strong emotion such as grief, sorrow, pain, or joy. **2.** To call loudly; shout: *We cried to our friends across the street.* **3.** To utter a characteristic sound or call: *The monkeys cried in the treetops.* —*tr.* **1.** To call out loudly; shout: *The umpire cried "Strike!"* **2.** To proclaim or announce in public: *The peddlers cry their wares in the streets.* **3.** To bring (oneself) into a particular condition by shedding tears: *She cried herself to sleep.* ❖ *n., pl.* **cries** (krīz) **1.** A loud call; a shout: *a cry of warning.* **2.** A loud sound expressive of fear, grief, distress, or pain. **3.** A fit of weeping: *After a short cry the baby was fast asleep.* **4.** The characteristic sound or call of an animal: *the cry of an eagle swooping down on its prey.* **5.** A public or general demand or complaint; an outcry: *a cry for reform in city politics.* **6.** A call to action; a slogan: *a cry to arms.* **7.** A shout or call for help: *A neighbor heard their cries and called the police.* ◆ **cry over spilled milk** To regret what cannot be undone or fixed. **cry wolf** To raise a false alarm.

✦ **SYNONYMS cry, blubber, sob, wail, weep** *v.*

crybaby (krī′bā′bē) *n., pl.* **crybabies** A person who cries, whines, or complains frequently with little cause.

crying (krī′ing) *adj.* **1.** Demanding immediate action or remedy: *a crying need for a new hospital.* **2.** Abominable; reprehensible: *a crying shame.*

cryogenics (krī′ə-jĕn′ĭks) *n. (used with a singular or plural verb)* The branch of physics dealing with the production of low temperatures or the study of matter at low temperatures.

crypt (krĭpt) *n.* An underground vault or chamber, especially one that is used as a tomb beneath a church. —SEE NOTE AT **grotto.**

cryptic (krĭp′tĭk) *adj.* Having a hidden meaning or secret nature; mysterious; puzzling: *a cryptic message.* —**cryp′·ti·cal·ly** *adv.*

cryptogram (krĭp′tə-grăm′) *n.* Something written in a secret code or cipher.

cryptograph (krĭp′tə-grăf′) *n.* **1.** A cryptogram. **2.** A system or device used to encode and decode messages and documents.

cryptographer (krĭp-tŏg′rə-fər) *n.* A person who specializes in cryptography.

cryptography (krĭp-tŏg′rə-fē) *n.* The study and use of secret codes and ciphers.

crystal (krĭs′təl) *n.* **1a.** A solid composed of atoms, molecules, or ions arranged in regular patterns that are repeated throughout the structure to form a characteristic network: *Sugar crystals and salt crystals can be distinguished by the differences in their structure.* **b.** A transparent mineral, especially a transparent form of pure quartz. **c.** A crystalline material that is a semiconductor or has piezoelectric properties. **2a.** A clear colorless glass of high quality. **b.** An object, such as a drinking glass or an ornament, made of this glass. **c.** Such objects considered as a group: *The table was set with fine china and crystal.* **3.** A transparent cover that protects the face of a watch or clock. ❖ *adj.* Clear; transparent: *I could see to the bottom in the crystal water of the lake.*

crystal ball *n.* A globe of crystal or glass in which images believed to predict the future are supposed to appear.

crystalline (krĭs′tə-lĭn *or* krĭs′tə-līn′) *adj.* **1.** Composed of crystals: *a crystalline semiconductor.* **2.** Made of crystals: *Snowflakes are crystalline.* **3.** Clear; transparent: *crystalline waters.*

crystalline lens *n.* The lens of an eye.

crystallize (krĭs′tə-līz′) *v.* **crystallized, crystallizing, crystallizes** —*tr.* **1.** To cause to form crystals or take on crystalline structure: *crystallize a protein to determine its structure.* **2.** To give a definite and permanent form to: *finally crystallized her plan for the project.* —*intr.* **1.** To take on crystalline form. **2.** To take on a definite and permanent form: *The idea suddenly crystallized in his mind.* —**crys′tal·li·za′tion** (krĭs′tə-lĭ-zā′shən) *n.*

crystallography (krĭs′tə-lŏg′rə-fē) *n.* The science that deals with the structure and properties of crystals.

CSA An abbreviation of Confederate States of America.

csc An abbreviation of cosecant.

CST An abbreviation of Central Standard Time.

ct. An abbreviation of cent.

Ct. An abbreviation of court.

ctrl An abbreviation of control key.

CT scan (sē′tē′) *n.* **1.** A three-dimensional image of a part of the body, made by a computer that assembles a series of two-dimensional x-ray images that are taken at angles around a single axis. CT is short for *computed tomography.* **2.** The act or process of producing such an image. —**CT scanner** *n.*

cu. An abbreviation of cubic.

cub (kŭb) *n.* **1.** One of the young of certain animals, such as bears, wolves, lions, and pandas. **2.** A beginner, especially in newspaper reporting.

cubbyhole (kŭb′ē-hōl′) *n.* A small and sometimes cramped space or room: *work in a cluttered cubbyhole of an office.*

cube (kyōōb) *n.* **1.** A solid having six equal square faces or sides. **2.** Something having this shape or almost this shape: *a bouillon cube.* **3.** A cubicle, used for work or study. **4.** The product that results when the same number is used three times as a factor. For example, the cube of 4, written 4^3, is equal to $4 \times 4 \times 4$. ❖ *tr.v.* **cubed, cubing, cubes 1.** To form the cube of (a number). **2.** To cut or form into a cube or cubes: *The cook cubed beets for a salad.*

cube root *n.* The number whose cube is equal to a given number. For example, the cube root of 125 is 5.

cubic (kyōō′bĭk) *adj.* **1.** Shaped like or nearly like a cube: *Dice have a cubic form.* **2.** Having three dimensions, especially having equal length, breadth, and thickness: *bought a cubic yard of mulch.* **3.** Relating to or involving a number or a variable that has been raised to the third power: *a cubic equation.*

cubical (kyōō′bĭ-kəl) *adj.* **1.** Cubic: *a room of cubical shape.* **2.** Relating to volume: *cubical dimensions.*

cubicle (kyōō′bĭ-kəl) *n.* A small compartment, as for work or study.

cubic measure *n.* A system for measuring volume using units, such as cubic inches or cubic centimeters, that are the cubes of linear units.

cubism also **Cubism** (kyōō′bĭz′əm) *n.* A style of painting and sculpture in the early 1900s that portrays the subject matter as fragmented geometric forms, especially flat, sharply angled planes. —**cub′ist** *adj. & n.*

cubit (kyōō′bĭt) *n.* An ancient unit of linear measure originally equal to the distance from the tip of the middle finger to the elbow, or about 17 to 22 inches (43 to 56 centimeters).

Cub Scout or **cub scout** *n.* A member of the junior division of the Boy Scouts, for boys of ages eight through ten.

cuckold (kŭk′əld *or* kōōk′əld) *n.* A man whose wife is unfaithful. ❖ *tr.v.* **cuckolded, cuckolding, cuckolds** To make a cuckold of.

cuckoo (kōō′kōō *or* kŏŏk′ōō) *n., pl.* **cuckoos 1.** A bird of Eurasia and Africa having grayish feathers and a call of two notes that sounds like its name. Cuckoos lay their eggs in the nests of birds of other species. **2.** Any of various related birds, including several North American species. ❖ *adj. Slang* Crazy; foolish.

cuckoo clock *n.* A wall clock that marks the time by sounding a mechanical whistle imitating the cuckoo's call while a toy bird emerges from a small door.

cucumber (kyōō′kŭm′bər) *n.* **1.** The long cylindrical fruit of a climbing plant, having a green rind and white watery flesh, eaten in salads and used for making pickles. **2.** The vine that bears such fruit.

cud (kŭd) *n.* Food that has been partly digested and brought up from the first stomach to the mouth again for further chewing by mammals such as cattle and sheep.

cuddle (kŭd′l) *v.* **cuddled, cuddling, cuddles** —*tr.* To hold fondly or hug tenderly: *cuddle a baby in one's arms.* —*intr.* To nestle; snuggle: *The two cats cuddled up near the fire.* ❖ *n.* A hug or embrace.

cuddly (kŭd′lē) *adj.* **1.** Fond of cuddling or of being cuddled: *The cuddly kitten curled up in my lap.* **2.** Pleasant to cuddle or snuggle with: *a big cuddly teddy bear.*

cudgel (kŭj′əl) *n.* A short, heavy club. ❖ *tr.v.* **cudgeled, cudgeling, cudgels** or **cudgelled, cudgelling, cudgels** To strike or beat with a cudgel.

cue¹ (kyōō) *n.* A long tapered stick used to strike the cue ball in billiards and pool.

cue² (kyōō) *n.* **1.** A word or signal prompting an actor or singer to speak, sing, or do something during a performance. **2.** A signal for action; a reminder. **3.** A hint or suggestion as to how to behave or what should be done: *Our host's yawn was a cue that it was time to go home.* ❖ *tr.v.* **cued, cuing, cues 1.** To give (a person) a cue: *cue me when it's my turn.* **2.** To position (an audio or video recording) in readiness for playing: *cued the DVD to the chase scene.*

WORD HISTORY Cue¹ comes from Latin *cauda,* meaning "tail." **Cue²** may come from an abbreviation of Latin *quandō,* meaning "when," used in actors' copies of plays.

cue ball *n.* The white ball used to strike other balls in billiards and pool.

cuff¹ (kŭf) *n.* **1.** A band or fold of cloth at the bottom of a sleeve, often having a button and buttonhole. **2.** The turned-up fold at the bottom of a trouser leg. **3.** A handcuff. ◆ **off the cuff** With little or no preparation; not rehearsed: *remarks made off the cuff.*

cuff² (kŭf) *tr.v.* **cuffed, cuffing, cuffs** To strike with or as if with the open hand; slap: *The bear cuffed her cubs.* ❖ *n.* A blow or slap made with or as if with the open hand.

cufflink or **cuff link** (kŭf′lĭngk′) *n.* One of a pair of fasteners for shirt cuffs having a chain or shank that passes through the buttonholes.

cuirass (kwĭ-răs′) *n.* **1.** A piece of armor consisting of a breastplate and a piece for the back that are buckled together. **2.** The breastplate alone.

cuisine (kwĭ-zēn′) *n.* **1.** A style of cooking or preparing food: *French cuisine.* **2.** Food; fare: *a restaurant with excellent cuisine.*

cul-de-sac (kŭl′dĭ-săk′) *n., pl.* **cul-de-sacs** or **culs-de-sac** (kŭlz′dĭ-săk′) A blind alley or dead-end street.

culinary (kyōō′lə-nĕr′ē *or* kŭl′ə-nĕr′ē) *adj.* Relating to a kitchen or cookery: *a chef of great culinary skill.*

cull (kŭl) *tr.v.* **culled, culling, culls 1.** To pick out from others; gather selectively: *cull the prettiest flowers in the garden.* **2.** To remove undesirable members or parts from: *cull a herd of wild deer to keep the population healthy.*

culm (kŭlm) *n.* The stem of a grass, sedge, or other similar plant.

culminate (kŭl′mə-nāt′) *v.* **culminated, culminating, culminates** —*intr.* To reach the highest point or degree, often just before ending; climax: *The celebration culminated in a huge display of fireworks.* —*tr.* To bring to the highest point or degree, often just before completion: *An appearance by the president culminated the political convention.* —**cul′mi·na′tion** *n.*

culottes (kōō′lŏts′) *pl.n.* Women's pants cut to resemble a skirt.

culpable (kŭl′pə-bəl) *adj.* Deserving blame; blameworthy: *Neglect of one's duty is culpable behavior.* —**cul′-pa·bil′i·ty** *n.* —**cul′pa·bly** *adv.*

culprit (kŭl′prĭt) *n.* **1.** A person or thing guilty of a fault or crime: *We never found the culprit who broke the window.* **2.** A person charged with a crime in a court of law.

cult (kŭlt) *n.* **1a.** A system of religious worship and ritual: *the ancient cults of nature worship.* **b.** A religion or religious sect whose followers live in an unconventional manner under the guidance of a leader who demands strict obedience. **2.** A great or excessive attachment or devotion to a person, principle, or thing: *A cult of physical fitness has created large numbers of joggers and bikers nationwide.* **3.** A group of people sharing a usually artistic or intellectual interest.

cultivar (kŭl′tə-vär′ *or* kŭl′tə-vâr′) *n.* A race or variety of a plant that has been created or selected intentionally and maintained through cultivation.

cultivate (kŭl′tə-vāt′) *tr.v.* **cultivated, cultivating, cultivates 1a.** To prepare and improve (land), as by plowing or fertilizing, for raising crops; till. **b.** To loosen or dig soil around (growing plants). **2.** To grow, tend, or raise (plants or certain animals, for example): *cultivate wheat; cultivate oysters.* **3.** To encourage or foster: *The coach cultivates an atmosphere of respect.* **4.** To seek the acquaintance or goodwill of (a person): *cultivate the new neighbors.*

cultivated (kŭl′tə-vā′tĭd) *adj.* **1.** Planted with crops or prepared for the planting of crops: *cultivated land.* **2.** Grown by cultivation; not wild: *Many roses are cultivated flowers.* **3.** Cultured; refined: *cultivated people with a love of opera.*

cultivation (kŭl′tə-vā′shən) *n.* **1.** The process of tilling soil and growing or raising crops: *the cultivation of fruits and vegetables.* **2.** The process of raising certain animals: *the commercial cultivation of sea urchins.* **3.** Encouragement, fostering, or development: *the cultivation of her talents; the cultivation of friendly relations.* **4.** Culture; refinement: *a person of great cultivation.*

cultivator (kŭl′tə-vā′tər) *n.* **1.** A person who cultivates. **2.** An implement or machine for loosening the earth and destroying weeds around growing plants: *A cultivator works faster than a hoe.*

cultural (kŭl′chər-əl) *adj.* Relating to culture: *Paris is the cultural center of France.* —**cul′tur·al·ly** *adv.*

culture (kŭl′chər) *n.* **1a.** The arts, beliefs, customs, institutions, and all other products of human work and thought at a particular time: *the culture of Renaissance Italy.* **b.** The main attitudes that characterize a group or organization: *Hollywood culture; corporate culture.* **2.** The qualities of mind and the tastes that result from appreciation of the arts and sciences: *a writer of great culture.* **3.** The breeding or cultivation of animals or plants for food or other purposes: *wheat culture in Nebraska; silkworm culture.* **4a.** The growing of microorganisms or tissues in a specially prepared nutrient substance for scientific study or medicinal use. **b.** Such a growth, as of bacteria or tissue: *a culture of penicillin-producing mold.* ❖ *tr.v.* **cultured, culturing, cultures** To grow (microorganisms, tissues, or other living matter) in a specially prepared substance for scientific study.

cultured (kŭl′chərd) *adj.* **1.** Well-educated; refined: *a cultured supporter of the arts.* **2.** Grown or produced under artificial and controlled conditions: *cultured pearls.*

culture shock *n.* A condition of confusion and anxiety that can affect an individual suddenly exposed to an unfamiliar culture or environment.

culvert (kŭl′vərt) *n.* A water drain crossing under a road or embankment.

cumber (kŭm′bər) *tr.v.* **cumbered, cumbering, cumbers** To burden or trouble: *cumber a person with worries.*

cumbersome (kŭm′bər-səm) *adj.* Difficult to carry or manage: *cumbersome baggage; a cumbersome application process.* —**cum′ber·some·ly** *adv.* —**cum′ber·some·ness** *n.*

cumin (kŭm′ĭn or kŏŏ′mĭn or kyŏŏ′mĭn) *n.* The aromatic seeds of a Mediterranean plant that is related to parsley, used whole or ground as a seasoning.

cum laude (kŏŏm lou′də) *adv. & adj.* With honor: *She graduated cum laude. He is a cum laude graduate.*

cummerbund (kŭm′ər-bŭnd′) *n.* A broad sash worn around the waist, especially as part of a tuxedo.

cumulative (kyŏŏm′yə-lā′tĭv or kyŏŏm′yə-lə-tĭv) *adj.* Increasing or growing by steady addition or in stages: *The cumulative efforts of many people helped control the epidemic.* —**cu′mu·la′tive·ly** *adv.*

cumulonimbus (kyŏŏm′yə-lō-nĭm′bəs) *n., pl.* **cumulonimbuses** or **cumulonimbi** (kyŏŏm′yə-lō-nĭm′bī) A very dense cloud with massive projections that billow upward to great heights, usually producing heavy rains, thunderstorms, or hailstorms.

cumulus (kyŏŏm′yə-ləs) *n., pl.* **cumuli** (kyŏŏm′yə-lī′) A dense, white, fluffy cloud that billows upward from a flat base.

cuneiform (kyŏŏ′nē-ə-fôrm′ or kyŏŏ-nē′ə-fôrm′) *adj.* Relating to or being a kind of writing made with wedge-shaped characters, used by the Babylonians, Assyrians, Persians, and other peoples of ancient southwest Asia: *a cuneiform text written on a clay tablet.* ❖ *n.* Cuneiform writing.

cunning (kŭn′ĭng) *adj.* Sly; crafty; clever: *a cunning scheme.* ❖ *n.* Skill in deception; guile: *It takes great cunning to be a spy.* —**cun′ning·ly** *adv.*

cup (kŭp) *n.* **1.** A small open container, usually having a handle, from which to drink liquids: *The baby can now drink from a cup.* **2.** The contents of such a container: *drink a cup of cocoa.* **3.** In cooking, a measure equal to ½ pint, 8 ounces, or 16 tablespoons (237 milliliters). **4.** Something similar in shape to a cup: *the cup of a flower.* **5.** A cup-shaped vessel awarded as a prize or trophy: *We won the soccer cup.* **6.** In golf, a hole or the metal container inside a hole. ❖ *tr.v.* **cupped, cupping, cups 1.** To form in such a way as to resemble a cup: *cup one's hands to get a drink.* **2.** To place in or as if in a cup: *I cupped my ear with my hand to show I couldn't hear her.*

cupboard (kŭb′ərd) *n.* A closet or cabinet, usually having shelves for storing food, dishes, or other small items: *a kitchen cupboard.*

cupcake (kŭp′kāk′) *n.* A small cake baked in a cup-shaped container.

cupful (kŭp′fŏŏl′) *n.* The amount that a cup can hold.

Cupid (kyŏŏ′pĭd) *n.* **1.** In Roman mythology, the god of love, identified with the Greek Eros. **2. cupid** A figure of a winged boy used as a symbol of love.

cupidity (kyŏŏ-pĭd′ĭ-tē) *n.* Extreme desire for something, especially wealth; greed.

cupola (kyŏŏ′pə-lə) *n.* **1.** A small domelike structure on top of a roof. **2.** A domed roof or ceiling.

cur (kûr) *n.* **1.** A mongrel dog. **2.** A despicable or cowardly person.

curable (kyŏŏr′ə-bəl) *adj.* Capable of being healed or cured: *a curable illness.* —**cur′a·bil′i·ty** *n.*

curate[1] (kyŏŏr′ĭt) *n.* A member of the clergy who has charge of a parish or who assists a rector or vicar.

curate[2] (kyŏŏr′āt′) *tr.v.* **curated, curating, curates** To act as curator of; organize and oversee.

WORD HISTORY Curate[1] comes from Middle English *curat*, which comes from Late Latin *cūra,* meaning "spiritual responsibility." **Curate**[2] is a back-formation from Modern English *curator.*

curative (kyŏŏr′ə-tĭv) *adj.* Serving or tending to cure: *curative medicine.* ❖ *n.* Something that cures; a remedy.

curator (kyŏŏ-rā′tər or kyŏŏr′ə-tər) *n.* A person who manages an exhibition or collection at a museum or library.

curb (kûrb) *n.* **1.** A concrete or stone border along the edge of a street: *Don't trip over the curb!* **2.** Something that checks or restrains: *a curb on spending.* **3.** A chain or strap used together with a bit to restrain a horse. ❖ *tr.v.* **curbed, curbing, curbs** To check, restrain, or control: *curb one's temper.*

curbing (kûr′bĭng) *n.* **1.** The material used to construct a curb. **2.** A curb.

curbside (kûrb′sīd′) *n.* The side of a pavement or street bordered by a curb. ❖ *adj.* Located or occurring at or along the sidewalk or curb: *curbside trash collection; curbside check-in of luggage at the airport.*

curbstone (kûrb′stōn′) *n.* A stone or row of stones used to make up a curb.

curd (kûrd) *n.* **1.** The thick part of milk that separates from the whey and is used to make cheese. **2.** A lumpy liquid that resembles curd.

curdle (kûr′dl) *v.* **curdled, curdling, curdles** —*intr.* **1.** To form into curd: *The milk curdled overnight.* **2.** To seem to thicken and stop running, as because of fear or shock: *My blood curdled at the scream in the night.* —*tr.* To cause to form into curd: *You can curdle milk by adding vinegar to it.*

cure (kyoor) *n.* **1.** Restoration of health; recovery from illness: *The patient returned to work soon after her cure.* **2.** A medical treatment or a series of such treatments used to restore health: *Penicillin is used as a cure for infections.* **3.** Something that restores health or improves a condition: *A trip was the perfect cure for overwork.* ❖ *v.* **cured, curing, cures** —*tr.* **1.** To restore to health: *Antibiotics cured the patient.* **2.** To bring about a recovery from: *cure an infection.* **3.** To remove (a harmful condition or influence): *cure a social problem.* **4.** To use a chemical, physical, or natural process in preparing, preserving, or finishing (a substance or material): *cure fish in a smokehouse; cure leather by tanning it.* —*intr.* **1.** To be or become restored to good health: *The patient cured quickly.* **2.** To be prepared, preserved, or finished by a chemical or physical process: *The fish cured in the sun.*

curé (kyoo-rā′ *or* kyoor′ā′) *n.* A parish priest.

cure-all (kyoor′ôl′) *n.* Something that cures all diseases or ills; a panacea.

curfew (kûr′fyoo) *n.* **1.** A regulation requiring certain people to be off the streets and indoors at a certain hour. **2.** The time at which such a regulation is in effect: *a 10 PM curfew.* **3.** The signal, such as the ringing of a bell, announcing the beginning of this regulation.

curia (koor′ē-ə) *n.*, *pl.* **curiae** (koor′ē-ē′) **1.** An assembly, council, or senate. **2.** often **Curia** The central administration governing the Roman Catholic Church. —**cu′ri·al** *adj.*

curie (kyoor′ē *or* kyoo-rē′) *n.* A unit for measuring the intensity of radioactivity. In 1975, the curie was replaced by the becquerel as the standard unit of radioactivity.

curio (kyoor′ē-ō′) *n.*, *pl.* **curios** A rare or unusual object: *a cupboard filled with miniature teapots and other curios.*

curiosity (kyoor′ē-ŏs′ĭ-tē) *n.*, *pl.* **curiosities 1.** A desire to know or learn: *She was full of curiosity over who had sent the letter.* **2.** Something unusual or extraordinary: *The explorer brought back many curiosities from his travels.*

curious (kyoor′ē-əs) *adj.* **1.** Eager to learn more: *curious detectives.* **2.** Arousing interest because of strangeness: *We found a curious shell at the beach.* —**cu′ri·ous·ly** *adv.* —**cu′ri·ous·ness** *n.*

curium (kyoor′ē-əm) *n. Symbol* **Cm** A radioactive element that has been artificially produced by scientists. The half-life of its most stable isotope is about 15.6 million years. Atomic number 96. See **Periodic Table.**

curl (kûrl) *v.* **curled, curling, curls** —*tr.* **1.** To twist or form into coils or ringlets: *curl one's hair.* **2.** To make curved or twisted: *I curled the string around a pencil.* —*intr.* **1.** To form ringlets or curls: *Her hair curls when it dries.* **2.** To move in a curve or spiral: *Smoke curled from the chimney.* ❖ *n.* **1.** A coil or ringlet of hair. **2.** Something with a spiral or coiled shape: *a curl of smoke.* **3.** A weightlifting exercise in which a barbell is raised to the chest or shoulder

and lowered without moving the upper arms, shoulders, or back. ❖ **curl up** To sit or lie down with the legs drawn up: *He curled up on the sofa to read.*

curler (kûr′lər) *n.* A pin or roller on which strands of hair are wound for curling.

curlew (kûr′lyoo *or* kûr′loo) *n.* Any of several shorebirds that have brownish feathers, long legs, and a long downward-curving bill.

curlicue (kûr′lĭ-kyoo′) *n.* A fancy twist or curl, such as a flourish in a signature.

curling (kûr′lĭng) *n.* A game played on ice in which two teams of four players slide heavy rounded stones toward a mark in the center of a circle.

curling iron *n.* A rod-shaped metal tool that is electrically heated in order to curl the hair.

curly (kûr′lē) *adj.* **curlier, curliest 1.** Having curls or tending to curl: *curly hair.* **2.** Having a wavy grain or markings: *curly maple wood.* —**curl′i·ness** *n.*

curmudgeon (kər-mŭj′ən) *n.* An ill-tempered person, especially one who is older. —**cur·mudg′eon·ly** *adj.*

currant (kûr′ənt) *n.* **1a.** The small, usually red or black fruit of any of various shrubs, used especially for making jelly. **b.** A shrub that bears such fruit. **2.** A seedless raisin, used chiefly in baking.

currency (kûr′ən-sē) *n.*, *pl.* **currencies 1.** Money in any form when in actual use in a country: *US currency is in dollars, and Japanese currency is in yen.* **2.** General acceptance or use: *Many slang words and expressions have currency for only a short time.* **3.** A passing from one person to another; circulation: *By spreading gossip, people give currency to rumors.* **4.** The state of being current; up-to-dateness: *Can you check the currency of this address?*

current (kûr′ənt) *adj.* **1.** Belonging to the present time; present-day: *current events; my current address.* **2.** Commonly accepted or used; prevalent: *holiday traditions that are still current.* ❖ *n.* **1.** A mass of liquid or gas that is in motion: *a current of cool air flowing through the room.* **2a.** A flow of electric charge. **b.** The amount of electric charge that passes a point in a unit of time, usually expressed in amperes. **3.** A general tendency or movement, as of events or opinions: *The current of voter opinion supports the president.*

currently (kûr′ənt-lē) *adv.* At the time now passing; at present: *a movie currently showing at the theater.*

curriculum (kə-rĭk′yə-ləm) *n.*, *pl.* **curricula** (kə-rĭk′yə-lə) or **curriculums** A set of courses of study offered at a particular educational institution or department: *The school has recently updated its science curriculum.* —**cur·ric′u·lar** *adj.*

curriculum vitae (vī′tē *or* vē′tī) *n.*, *pl.* **curricula vitae** A summary of one's education, professional history, and job qualifications, as for a prospective employer; a resumé.

curry¹ (kûr′ē) *tr.v.* **curried, currying, curries** To groom (a horse) with a currycomb. ❖ **curry favor** To seek or gain favor by flattery: *The new worker tried to curry favor with the boss.*

curry² (kûr′ē) *n.*, *pl.* **curries 1.** A dish or sauce seasoned with a mixture of spices, usually including cumin, coriander, and turmeric: *lamb curry.* **2.** Curry powder. ❖ *tr.v.* **curried, currying, curries** To season (food) with curry: *curried the cauliflower.*

WORD HISTORY Curry¹ comes from Middle English *curreien,* which comes from Anglo-Norman *curreier,* both

meaning "to clean and groom a horse." **Curry**[2] comes from Tamil *kaṟi*, meaning "sauce."

currycomb (kûr′ē-kōm′) *n.* A comb with plastic or metal teeth used for grooming horses. ❖ *tr.v.* **currycombed, currycombing, currycombs** To curry (a horse).

curry powder *n.* A pungent seasoning prepared from cumin, coriander, turmeric, and other spices.

curse (kûrs) *n.* **1.** A remark or prayer that expresses a wish for evil or harm to happen to a person or thing: *The sorcerer placed a curse on the royal family.* **2.** A coarse or profane utterance; a swearword. **3.** Something that causes great evil or harm; a scourge: *The royal family was destroyed by the curse of madness.* ❖ *v.* **cursed** or **curst** (kûrst), **cursing, curses** — *tr.* **1.** To wish evil or harm on (a person, for example) with a curse. **2.** To bring great harm to; afflict: *The farmers were cursed with bad weather at harvest time.* **3.** To swear at: *The driver cursed the traffic in front of him.* — *intr.* To utter swearwords: *In this movie, most of the characters curse a lot.*

cursive (kûr′sĭv) *adj.* Written or printed with connected letters; flowing: *cursive handwriting.* ❖ *n.* A cursive character or letter.

WORD BUILDING Words in English having the elements *cur-, curr-,* and *curs-* all go back to the Latin verb *currere* (past participle *cursus*), "to run." **Cursive** handwriting is therefore literally "running" script, as opposed to printed letters that do not run together in a continuous line. If two people **concur**, they "run together" or agree. An army that makes an **incursion** into a country is literally "running into" it, while a **precursor** is something that "runs before or ahead of" something else. The **currents** of a river or ocean are the parts of it that "run" in a particular direction, as are—figuratively speaking—the currents of the times or of politics.

cursor (kûr′sər) *n.* A movable indicator, such as a thin bar or small square, on a computer screen that marks the position where a character can be entered or deleted or where an option can be selected.

cursory (kûr′sə-rē) *adj.* Hasty and superficial; not thorough: *A cursory search of the file showed that many folders were out of order.* —**cur′so·ri·ly** *adv.*

curst (kûrst) *v.* A past tense and a past participle of **curse.**

curt (kûrt) *adj.* **curter, curtest** Rudely brief and abrupt in speech or manner; brusque: *My former friend gave me a curt nod as we passed.* —**curt′ly** *adv.* —**curt′ness** *n.*

curtail (kər-tāl′) *tr.v.* **curtailed, curtailing, curtails** To cut short; reduce: *We had to curtail our spending on the rest of the trip.* —**cur·tail′ment** *n.*

curtain (kûr′tn) *n.* **1.** Cloth or other material hanging in a window or door as a decoration, shade, or screen: *opened the curtains.* **2.** Something that acts as a screen or cover: *mountains hidden by a thick curtain of fog.* **3.** The movable cloth or screen in a theater that separates the stage from the audience. **4.** The time at which a theatrical performance begins or is scheduled to begin. ❖ *tr.v.* **curtained, curtaining, curtains** To provide or shut off with or as if with a curtain.

curtain call *n.* The appearance of performers or a performer at the end of a performance to receive applause from the audience.

curtsy or **curtsey** (kûrt′sē) *n., pl.* **curtsies** or **curtseys** A gesture of respect made chiefly by women by bending the knees with one foot forward and lowering the body. ❖ *intr.v.* **curtsied, curtsying, curtsies** or **curtseyed, curtsey-** **ing, curtseys** To make a curtsy: *The singer curtsied before the audience.*

curvature (kûr′və-chŏŏr′ *or* kûr′və-chər) *n.* **1a.** The act of curving or the condition of being curved: *the curvature of the moon's orbit.* **b.** The degree to which something is curved: *a slight curvature in several warped boards.* **2.** A curving or bending of a body part, especially when abnormal: *curvature of the spine.*

curve (kûrv) *n.* **1.** A line or surface that bends in a smooth continuous way without sharp angles. **2.** Something that has the shape of a curve: *a curve in the road.* **3.** In baseball, a curve ball. ❖ *v.* **curved, curving, curves** — *intr.* To move in or take the shape of a curve: *The ball curved to the right. The road curves sharply just ahead.* — *tr.* To cause to curve: *curve a metal band.*

curve ball or **curveball** (kûrv′bôl′) *n.* **1.** A pitched baseball that veers to one side as it nears the batter. **2.** Something that is unexpected or designed to trick or deceive: *The last question on the exam was a curve ball—only one student got it right.*

cushion (kŏŏsh′ən) *n.* **1.** A pad or pillow with a soft filling, used to sit, lie, or rest on. **2.** Something used as a rest, support, or shock absorber. **3.** Something shaped like or used as a cushion: *He slept on a cushion of spruce boughs.* **4.** Something used to lessen a bad effect: *We have a savings account as a cushion against hard times.* **5.** The raised rim that borders the playing surface of a billiard table. ❖ *tr.v.* **cushioned, cushioning, cushions 1.** To place or seat on a cushion: *The cat cushioned itself on our pillows.* **2.** To furnish with a cushion or cushions: *Soft pillows cushioned the chair.* **3.** To lessen or soften the impact of: *My thick coat cushioned the fall.*

cusp (kŭsp) *n.* A pointed end or rounded projection, as on the crescent moon or a tooth. ◆ **on the cusp** At the point where something is about to begin or change: *an actor on the cusp of a successful career.*

cuspid (kŭs′pĭd) *n.* A tooth having a single cusp; a canine.

cuspidor (kŭs′pĭ-dôr′) *n.* A spittoon.

cuss (kŭs) *Informal intr. & tr.v.* **cussed, cussing, cusses** To curse. ❖ *n.* **1.** An odd or perverse person: *an unpleasant cuss.* **2.** A curse.

custard (kŭs′tərd) *n.* A pudding of milk, sugar, eggs, and flavoring that is baked or boiled.

custodian (kŭ-stō′dē-ən) *n.* **1.** A person who has charge of something; a caretaker or guardian: *the custodian of a museum collection.* **2.** A person who takes care of a building; a janitor.

custody (kŭs′tə-dē) *n., pl.* **custodies 1.** Supervision; care: *The children were in the custody of their aunt and uncle while their parents were away.* **2.** The condition of being detained or held under guard, especially by the police: *The suspect was held in custody for questioning.*

custom (kŭs′təm) *n.* **1.** An accepted practice or usual way followed by people of a particular group or region: *Shaking hands when meeting someone is a traditional custom.* **2.** A usual practice of an individual; a habit: *Their custom is to go to bed early.* See Synonyms at **habit. 3. customs a.** Duties or taxes imposed on goods imported from another country: *There were no customs due on our purchases on this trip.* **b.** *(used with a singular verb)* The government agency that collects these duties and inspects imported goods. **c.** *(used with a singular verb)* The place where goods and baggage entering a country are inspected by this agency: *We got through customs quickly.* ❖ *adj.* **1.** Made to order: *custom suits made to the instruc-*

tions of the buyer. **2.** Making or selling things to order: *a custom tailor.*

customary (kŭs′tə-mĕr′ē) *adj.* Established by custom; usual; habitual: *The customary place for a judge to sit is at the head of a courtroom.* —**cus′tom·ar′i·ly** (kŭs′tə-mâr′-ə-lē) *adv.*

custom-built (kŭs′təm-bĭlt′) *adj.* Built according to the specifications of the buyer: *custom-built cabinets.*

customer (kŭs′tə-mər) *n.* **1.** A person who buys goods or services, especially on a regular basis. **2.** *Informal* A person with whom one must deal: *a tough customer.*

customhouse (kŭs′təm-hous′) also **customshouse** (kŭs′-təmz-hous′) *n.* A government building where customs duties are collected and ships are given permission to enter and leave a country.

customize (kŭs′tə-mīz′) *tr.v.* **customized, customizing, customizes** To make or alter to suit an individual.

custom-made (kŭs′təm-mād′) *adj.* Made according to the specifications of the buyer: *custom-made draperies.*

cut (kŭt) *v.* **cut, cutting, cuts** —*tr.* **1.** To make an opening in with a sharp edge or instrument: *I cut my finger on a piece of broken glass.* **2.** To separate or divide by using a sharp instrument: *cut paper with scissors.* **3.** To separate from the main body of something; detach: *cut a limb from a tree.* **4.** To pass through or across; cross: *The path cuts the neighbor's yard.* **5.** To shorten; trim: *cut hair; cut the lawn.* **6.** To make or shape by using a sharp instrument: *I cut a hole in the board. I cut a doll from the paper.* **7.** To reap; harvest: *cut wheat.* **8.** To cause to fall by sawing: *Each year loggers cut millions of trees.* **9.** To have (a new tooth) grow through the gums: *The baby cut two new teeth last week.* **10.** To interrupt or stop: *A bad storm cut our electric power for two hours.* **11.** To reduce the size or amount of: *The governor cut taxes.* **12.** To lessen the strength of; dilute: *The waiter cut the strong iced tea by adding water.* **13.** To eliminate; remove: *The director cut several scenes from the play.* **14.** To edit (film or audio tape).* **15.** To remove (a segment) from a computer document or graphics file for storage in a buffer. **16.** To hurt the feelings of: *Their unfriendly remarks cut me deeply.* **17.** *Informal* To fail to attend purposely: *I cut my rehearsal today.* **18.** To divide (a deck of cards) in two, as before dealing. —*intr.* **1.** To make an opening or separation: *The knife cut right through the rind. Swirling water cut under the rocks.* **2.** To allow an opening or severing: *Butter cuts easily.* **3.** To be like a sharp instrument: *The cold wind cut through my thin jacket.* **4a.** To go by a short or direct route: *cut across the park to get home quickly.* **b.** To go across; cross: *This road cuts through the mountains.* **5.** To change direction abruptly: *The driver suddenly cut to the right.* **6.** To divide a deck of cards into two: *The dealer cuts first.* ❖ *n.* **1.** The result of cutting; an opening or a wound. **2.** A blow or stroke, as with an axe: *The tree fell with a few cuts of the axe.* **3.** A part that has been cut from a main body or part: *an expensive cut of beef; a cut of cloth.* **4.** A passage made by excavating or drilling: *The highway runs through a cut in the mountain.* **5.** A removal of a part: *He made several cuts in the speech.* **6.** A reduction: *had to take a cut in pay.* **7.** The style in which a garment is cut: *The fine cut of my suit made it fit well.* **8.** *Informal* A share of profits or earnings: *The salesman got a 5 percent cut at the end of the year.* **9.** A wounding remark; an insult: *That was an unkind cut you directed at*

me. **10.** A transition from one scene to another in a film, video, or television program. **11a.** An engraved block or plate. **b.** A print made from such a block: *old cuts of life along the Mississippi River.* ◆ **cut back 1.** To shorten by cutting; prune: *cut back a tree limb.* **2.** To reduce or decrease: *cut back prices in a sale.* **cut down 1.** To kill or strike down: *The cannon fire cut down the charging troops.* **2.** To reduce or curtail: *cut down one's spending.* **cut in 1.** To move into a line of people or things out of turn: *cut in at the head of the line.* **2.** To interrupt: *cut in on our conversation.* **3.** To interrupt a dancing couple in order to dance with one of them. **cut it** *Informal* To be or perform up to expectations or a standard; be acceptable. **cut off 1.** To stop suddenly; shut off or discontinue: *cut off the electricity.* **2.** To disinherit: *The rich landowner cut off most of the family without a cent.* **3.** To separate or isolate: *We were cut off from the mainland during the storm.* **cut out 1.** To remove by cutting: *cut out a long sentence from the paragraph.* **2.** To form or shape by cutting: *cut out pieces for a coat.* **3.** To assign or determine as necessary: *I have my work cut out for me.* **4.** To be suited: *Many people are not cut out for city life.* **5.** To stop; cease: *Cut out the noise right now!* **6.** To deprive or disinherit: *cut a relative out of a will.* **cut up** *Informal* To behave in a playful or noisy way; clown.

cut-and-dried (kŭt′n-drīd′) also **cut-and-dry** (kŭt′n-drī′) *adj.* **1.** Prepared and arranged in advance: *There are no cut-and-dried rules for good writing.* **2.** Lacking freshness or imagination; ordinary: *His advice was full of cut-and-dried old phrases.*

cutaneous (kyōō-tā′nē-əs) *adj.* Relating to or affecting the skin: *cutaneous blood vessels.*

cutback (kŭt′băk′) *n.* A decrease; a curtailment: *a cutback in government spending.*

cute (kyōōt) *adj.* **cuter, cutest 1.** Delightfully pretty or dainty: *a cute puppy.* **2.** Attractive; good-looking: *a cute boyfriend.* **3.** Witty or clever, especially in a teasing or disrespectful way: *made a remark that was a little too cute.* —**cute′ly** *adv.* —**cute′ness** *n.*

cuticle (kyōō′tĭ-kəl) *n.* **1.** The waxy outer surface of a plant. **2.** The hard skin around the sides and base of a fingernail or toenail.

cutlass also **cutlas** (kŭt′ləs) *n.* A heavy sword with a curved single-edged blade.

cutlery (kŭt′lə-rē) *n.* **1.** Knives, forks, and spoons used as tableware. **2.** Cutting instruments and tools, such as knives and scissors.

cutlet (kŭt′lĭt) *n.* **1.** A thin slice of meat, as of veal, cut from the leg or ribs. **2.** A patty of chopped meat or fish.

cutoff (kŭt′ôf′) *n.* **1.** An indicated limit or stopping point: *Saturday is the cutoff for new job applications.* **2.** The act or an instance of cutting something off: *a cutoff of electricity.* **3.** A device used to stop a flow, as of a liquid or gas: *That valve is the cutoff for our water.* **4.** A shortcut or bypass: *use the cutoff through the park.* **5. cutoffs** Pants made into shorts by cutting off part of the legs. ❖ *adj.* Indicating a limit or deadline: *a cutoff date.*

cutout (kŭt′out′) *n.* **1.** Something cut out or intended to be cut out from something else: *cutouts of paper dolls.* **2.** A device that acts as a bypass or cutoff, especially in an electric circuit.

cut-rate (kŭt′rāt′) *adj.* Sold or on sale at a reduced price.

cutter (kŭt′ər) *n.* **1.** A worker whose job involves cutting some material, such as cloth, glass, or stone. **2.** A cutting device or machine: *a cookie cutter.* **3.** A small, lightly armed boat used by the Coast Guard. **4.** A ship's boat, powered by a motor or pulled with oars, used for transporting stores or passengers. **5.** A fast single-masted sailing vessel.

cutthroat (kŭt′thrōt′) *n.* A murderer, especially one who cuts throats. ❖ *adj.* **1.** Cruel; murderous: *a cutthroat band of thieves.* **2.** Ruthless or merciless in competition: *a cutthroat business.*

cutting (kŭt′ĭng) *adj.* **1.** Capable of or designed for cutting: *a cutting blade.* **2.** Injuring the feelings of others; insulting: *a cutting remark.* ❖ *n.* **1.** A part cut off from a main body: *cuttings and scrapings.* **2.** A stem, twig, or leaf removed from a plant and placed in soil, sand, or water to form roots and develop into a new plant.

cutting edge *n.* The position of greatest advancement or innovation; the forefront: *research on the cutting edge.*

cuttlebone (kŭt′l-bōn′) *n.* The chalky shell inside the body of a cuttlefish, used to supply calcium to caged birds or as a mold for metal casting.

cuttlefish (kŭt′l-fĭsh′) *n.* Any of various marine mollusks related to the squids and octopuses, having eight arms and two tentacles and a chalky internal shell.

cutup (kŭt′ŭp′) *n. Informal* A mischievous person.

cutworm (kŭt′wûrm′) *n.* Any of various moth caterpillars that damage crops, often by cutting through plant stems at the soil surface.

cwt An abbreviation of hundredweight.

–cy A suffix that means: **1.** State; condition; quality: *bankruptcy.* **2.** Rank; office: *captaincy.*

cyanide (sī′ə-nīd′) *n.* Any of a large group of salts and esters containing a chemical unit with carbon and nitrogen bonded to each other, especially the very poisonous salts sodium cyanide and potassium cyanide. Cyanides are used in making plastics and extracting and treating metals.

cyanobacterium (sī′ə-nō-băk-tîr′ē-əm) *n., pl.* **cyanobacteria** (sī′ə-nō-băk-tîr′ē-ə) Any of various bacteria that are blue-green in color and are capable of photosynthesis. Cyanobacteria are usually found in water.

cyber– A prefix that means computer or computer network: *cyberspace.*

cyberbully (sī′bər-bŏŏl′ē) *n., pl.* **cyberbullies** A person who engages in cyberbullying.

cyberbullying (sī′bər-bŏŏl′ē-ĭng) *n.* The use of computer networks and other forms of digital communication, such as text messages or social networks, to bully a person or people.

cybercafe (sī′bər-kă-fā′) *n.* **1.** A cafe from which customers can access the Internet. **2.** A chatroom.

cybercast (sī′bər-kăst′) *n.* A news or entertainment program transmitted over the Internet.

cybernetics (sī′bər-nĕt′ĭks) *n. (used with a singular verb)* The theoretical study of communication and control processes in biological, mechanical, and electronic systems.

cyberpunk (sī′bər-pŭnk′) *n.* Fast-paced science fiction involving futuristic computer-based societies.

cyberspace (sī′bər-spās′) *n.* The interconnected system of computer networks in which online communication takes place.

cyborg (sī′bôrg′) *n.* In science fiction, a person who has a built-in mechanical or electronic device that controls or enhances a part of the body, especially the brain.

cycad (sī′kăd′ *or* sī′kəd) *n.* Any of various tropical evergreen plants that bear cones and have large leaves that resemble those of a palm tree.

cyclamen (sī′klə-mən *or* sĭk′lə-mən) *n.* Any of various plants having heart-shaped leaves and showy pink, red, or white flowers with petals that are turned outward.

cycle (sī′kəl) *n.* **1a.** A series of events that is periodically repeated: *New moon and full moon are two phases of the moon's cycle.* **b.** The time during which such a series of events occurs: *The moon's appearance changes daily throughout its cycle of 29.5 days.* **2.** A set of poems or stories about a central theme or hero: *the Arthurian cycle.* **3.** A bicycle, motorcycle, or similar vehicle. ❖ *intr.v.* **cycled, cycling, cycles 1.** To occur in or pass through a cycle: *The earth cycles through the seasons every year.* **2.** To ride a bicycle, motorcycle, or similar vehicle.

cyclic (sĭk′lĭk *or* sī′klĭk) or **cyclical** (sĭk′lĭ-kəl *or* sī′klĭ-kəl) *adj.* **1.** Relating to or occurring in cycles: *the cyclic motion of the tides; a cyclical weather pattern.* **2.** Relating to or containing an arrangement of atoms in a ring or closed chain.

cycling (sī′klĭng) *n.* The act or sport of riding or racing on a bicycle, motorcycle, or similar vehicle.

cyclist (sī′klĭst) *n.* A person who rides a bicycle, motorcycle, or similar vehicle.

cyclone (sī′klōn′) *n.* **1.** A system of winds spiraling inward around a region of low atmospheric pressure, often producing storms. In the Southern Hemisphere the winds circle clockwise, while in the Northern Hemisphere they circle counterclockwise. **2.** A violent rotating windstorm, such as a hurricane or tornado. —**cy·clon′ic** (sī-klŏn′ĭk) *adj.*

Cyclops (sī′klŏps) *n., pl.* **Cyclopes** (sī-klō′pēz) In Greek mythology, any of a race of giants having one eye in the middle of the forehead.

cyclotron (sī′klə-trŏn′) *n.* A device that uses alternating electric and magnetic fields to accelerate charged subatomic particles, such as protons and electrons, in an outwardly spiraling path. Cyclotrons are used to bring about high-speed particle collisions in order to study subatomic structures.

cygnet (sĭg′nĭt) *n.* A young swan.

cylinder (sĭl′ən-dər) *n.* **1.** A solid figure bounded by a curved surface and two parallel circles of equal size at the ends. The curved surface is formed by all the line segments joining corresponding points of the two parallel circles. In a right circular cylinder the circles are perpendicular to the line segments; in an oblique circular cylinder they are not. **2.** An object or container, such as a can, having such a shape. **3.** The chamber in which a piston moves up and down, as in an engine or pump. **4.** The rotating chamber of a revolver that holds the cartridges.

cylindrical (sə-lĭn′drĭ-kəl) also **cylindric** (sə-lĭn′drĭk) *adj.* Relating to or having the shape of a cylinder. —**cy·lin′-dri·cal·ly** *adv.*

cymbal (sĭm′bəl) *n.* One or a pair of musical instruments made into the shape of a dish from coils of brass fused together. Cymbals are sounded either by striking two of them together or by hitting one with a drumstick or brush.

cyme (sīm) *n.* A flower cluster in which the main stem and each branch end in a flower that opens before the flowers below or to the side of it.

cynic (sĭn′ĭk) *n.* A person who is scornfully negative and believes that people act mostly out of selfishness. —**cyn′-i·cal** *adj.* —**cyn′i·cal·ly** *adv.*

cynicism (sĭn′ĭ-sĭz′əm) *n.* A scornful attitude that comes from a deep distrust of the honesty and motives of others:

Recent scandals have increased cynicism about politics.

cynosure (sī′nə-shŏŏr′ *or* sĭn′ə-shŏŏr′) *n.* A center of attention or interest: *The early astronauts were the cynosure of the nation.*

cypher (sī′fər) *n. & v.* Variant of **cipher.**

cypress (sī′prĭs) *n.* **1a.** Any of various evergreen trees chiefly of Eurasia and western North America, having small scalelike leaves and roundish cones. **b.** The hard wood of any of these trees, used in making shingles and doors. **2.** Any of several similar trees of the southern United States and Mexico that grow in wetlands and shed their needles each year.

Cypriot (sĭp′rē-ət) also **Cypriote** (sĭp′rē-ōt′) *adj.* Relating to the island of Cyprus in the eastern Mediterranean Sea or to its people, language, or culture. ❖ *n.* **1.** A native or inhabitant of Cyprus. **2.** The ancient Greek or modern Greek dialect of Cyprus.

Cyrillic alphabet (sə-rĭl′ĭk) *n.* An alphabet derived from the Greek alphabet and used in writing Russian, Bulgarian, and several other languages of eastern Europe and the former Soviet Union.

cyst (sĭst) *n.* **1.** An abnormal sac in the body, composed of a membrane surrounding a fluid or a soft solid material. **2.** A protective capsule in which certain organisms enclose themselves during inactive or reproductive periods.

cysteine (sĭs′tə-ēn′) *n.* A nonessential amino acid that is found in most proteins.

cystic (sĭs′tĭk) *adj.* **1.** Relating to or having the characteristics of a cyst: *a cystic growth.* **2.** Having, containing, or enclosed in a cyst: *a cystic stage of an organism's development.* **3.** Relating to or involving the gallbladder or urinary bladder.

cystic fibrosis (fī-brō′sĭs) *n.* A hereditary disease that causes thick mucus to build up in certain organs of the body, such as the lungs and pancreas. It results in frequent infections and problems with breathing and digestion.

cystitis (sĭ-stī′tĭs) *n.* Inflammation of the urinary bladder.

cytochrome (sī′tə-krōm′) *n.* Any of various proteins that are important in cell metabolism and respiration.

cytokinesis (sī′tō-kə-nē′sĭs) *n.* The division of the cytoplasm of a cell following the division of the nucleus.

cytology (sī-tŏl′ə-jē) *n.* The branch of biology that deals with the formation, structure, and function of cells. —**cy·tol′o·gist** *n.*

cytoplasm (sī′tə-plăz′əm) *n.* All the material enclosed by a cell membrane, excluding the nucleus. —**cy′to·plas′mic** *adj.*

cytosine (sī′tə-sēn′) *n.* A base that is a component of DNA and RNA.

czar (zär *or* tsär) *n.* **1.** also **tsar** or **tzar** Any of the emperors who ruled Russia until the revolution of 1917. **2.** A person who has great authority or power: *The mayor appointed an education czar to oversee the schools.*

czarina (zä-rē′nə *or* tsä-rē′nə) *n.* The wife of a Russian czar.

czarist (zär′ĭst) *adj.* Relating to or in the time of the czars: *czarist Russia.*

czaritza (zä-rĭt′sə *or* tsä-rēt′sə) *n.* Any of the empresses who ruled Russia until the revolution of 1917.

Czech (chĕk) *adj.* Relating to the Czech Republic or its people, language, or culture. ❖ *n.* **1.** A native or inhabitant of the Czech Republic. **2.** The Slavic language of the Czechs.

Dd

d or **D** (dē) *n., pl.* **d's** or **D's** or **Ds 1.** The fourth letter of the English alphabet. **2. D** The lowest passing grade in school. **3. D** In music, the second tone in the scale of C major.

D¹ also **d** The symbol for the Roman numeral 500.

D² An abbreviation of: **1.** day **2.** democrat.

d. An abbreviation of: **1.** date. **2.** daughter. **3.** died. **4.** *Chiefly British* penny (¹⁄₁₂ of a shilling).

DA An abbreviation of district attorney.

dab (dăb) *v.* **dabbed, dabbing, dabs** —*tr.* **1.** To apply with short light strokes: *dabbed some paint on the worn spots.* **2.** To pat quickly and lightly, especially in covering with a moist substance: *dabbed his nose with sunscreen.* —*intr.* To make light patting or stroking motions: *dabbed at her eyes with a tissue.* ❖ *n.* **1.** A small amount: *a dab of butter.* **2.** A light poking stroke or pat: *a kitten making dabs at a string.*

dabble (dăb'əl) *v.* **dabbled, dabbling, dabbles** —*tr.* To splash in and out of water: *The children dabbled their feet in the pool.* —*intr.* **1.** To splash or play in water: *The puppies dabbled in the stream.* **2.** To do or work on something casually or without serious intent: *I dabbled in photography for a time.* —**dab'bler** *n.*

dab hand *n.* A person skilled in a particular activity: *a dab hand at gardening.*

da capo (dä kä'pō) *adv.* In music, from the beginning. Used as a direction to repeat a section of a composition.

dace (dās) *n., pl.* **dace** or **daces** Any of various small freshwater fishes of Eurasia and North America, related to the minnows.

dachshund (däk'sənd *or* däk'sənt) *n.* A small dog of a breed developed in Germany for hunting badgers, having a long body, very short legs, and drooping ears.

dactyl (dăk'təl) *n.* In poetry, a metrical foot consisting of one accented syllable followed by two unaccented syllables, as in *flattery.*

dad (dăd) *n. Informal* Father.

Dada or **dada** (dä'dä) *n.* A European artistic and literary movement (1916–1923) that mocked conventional aesthetic and cultural values by producing works marked by nonsense, travesty, and incongruity. —**Da'da·ism** *n.* —**Da'da·ist** *adj. & n.*

daddy (dăd'ē) *n., pl.* **daddies** *Informal* Father.

daddy longlegs (lông'lĕgz') *n., pl.* **daddy longlegs** Any of various spiderlike arachnids having a small rounded body and long slender legs.

dado (dā'dō) *n., pl.* **dadoes 1.** The section of a pedestal between the base and the crown or cap. **2.** The lower part of the wall of a room decorated with wooden panels or other material that is different from the rest of the wall.

Daedalus (dĕd'l-əs) *n.* In Greek mythology, an artist and inventor who built the Labyrinth in Crete. He was imprisoned with his son Icarus and fashioned wings for them to escape by flying.

daffodil (dăf'ə-dĭl) *n.* A garden plant that grows from a bulb and has long slender leaves and showy, usually yellow flowers with a trumpet-shaped central part.

daffy (dăf'ē) *adj.* **daffier, daffiest** *Informal* Silly or crazy: *That's a daffy idea.* —**daf'fi·ly** *adv.* —**daf'fi·ness** *n.*

daft (dăft) *adj.* **dafter, daftest 1.** Foolish; stupid: *a daft reply.* **2.** Crazy: *He must be daft!*

dagger (dăg'ər) *n.* **1.** A short pointed weapon, used for stabbing. **2.** A dagger-shaped symbol (‡) often used as a reference to a footnote in a book or to some special category before a word in a list.

daguerreotype (də-gâr'ə-tīp') *n.* **1.** An early photographic process in which an image is formed on a silver-coated metal plate that is sensitive to light. **2.** A photograph made by this process.

dahlia (dăl'yə *or* däl'yə) *n.* Any of several garden plants having thick roots and showy flowers of various colors.

daily (dā'lē) *adj.* **1.** Done, happening, or appearing every day or weekday: *a daily walk.* **2.** For each day: *a daily record.* ❖ *adv.* Every day: *Exercise daily.* ❖ *n., pl.* **dailies** A newspaper published every day or every weekday.

dainty (dān'tē) *adj.* **daintier, daintiest 1.** Delicately beautiful and usually small: *dainty slippers.* **2.** Very careful in choosing; fussy; finicky: *The cat is a dainty eater.* **3.** Delicious or choice; tasty: *a dainty dish of fancy sandwiches.* ❖ *n., pl.* **dainties** A choice delicious food; a delicacy. —**dain'ti·ly** *adv.* —**dain'ti·ness** *n.*

dairy (dâr'ē) *n., pl.* **dairies 1.** A room or building where milk and cream are stored, prepared for use, and made into butter and cheese. **2.** A business or store that prepares or sells milk and milk products. **3.** A dairy farm. **4.** Food containing or based on milk: *How much dairy should you have in your diet?* ❖ *adj.* For or relating to milk or milk products.

dairy cattle *pl.n.* Cows bred and raised for milk rather than meat.

dairy farm *n.* A farm for producing milk and milk products.

dairying (dâr'ē-ĭng) *n.* The business of running a dairy or a dairy farm.

dairymaid (dâr'ē-mād') *n.* A woman or girl who works in a dairy.

dairyman (dâr'ē-mən) *n.* A man who owns, manages, or works in a dairy.

dairywoman (dâr'ē-wŏom'ən) *n.* A woman who owns, manages, or works in a dairy.

dais (dā'ĭs *or* dī'ĭs) *n.* A raised platform for a throne, a speaker, or a group of honored guests.

daishiki (dī-shē'kē) *n.* Variant of **dashiki.**

daisy (dā'zē) *n., pl.* **daisies** Any of several plants having flowers with many narrow, usually white rays surrounding a flat, usually yellow center.

Dakota (də-kō'tə) *n., pl.* **Dakota** or **Dakotas 1.** A member of any of the Sioux peoples, especially of the Santee branch. **2.** The Siouan language of the Dakota. —**Da·ko'tan** *adj. & n.*

Dalai Lama (dä'lī lä'mə) *n.* The traditional leader of the dominant sect of Buddhism in Tibet and Mongolia.

dale (dāl) *n.* A valley.

Dalit (dä′lĭt) *n.* A member of the lowest class in traditional Indian society. Dalits fall outside the Hindu caste categories and are subject to extensive social restrictions.

dalliance (dăl′ē-əns) *n.* **1.** Playful flirting. **2.** A brief romantic relationship. **3.** A brief involvement or interest in something: *a dalliance with radical ideas.*

dally (dăl′ē) *intr.v.* **dallied, dallying, dallies 1.** To spend time doing something in a careless or unserious fashion: *For a while she dallied with the notion of becoming a dancer.* **2.** To waste time; dawdle: *Don't dally or we'll miss the train.* **3.** To flirt playfully: *We saw the two friends dallying during lunch.*

Dalmatian (dăl-mā′shən) *n.* A dog of a large breed having a short smooth white coat with many small black spots.

dam¹ (dăm) *n.* A barrier across a waterway to control the flow or raise the level of the water. ❖ *tr.v.* **dammed, damming, dams 1.** To hold back by means of a dam: *Engineers dammed the river.* **2.** To hold back or restrain: *dam up emotions.*

dam² (dăm) *n.* The mother of an animal, especially a domesticated animal such as a horse.

WORD HISTORY Dam¹ comes from Middle English *dam,* meaning "barrier across a waterway." **Dam²** comes from Middle English *dame,* which comes from Latin *domina,* both meaning "lady."

---

damage (dăm′ĭj) *n.* **1.** Destruction or loss in value, usefulness, or ability resulting from an action or event: *damage done to a car in an accident.* **2. damages** In law, money to be paid to make up for an injury or wrong: *sue for damages.* ❖ *tr.v.* **damaged, damaging, damages** To harm, hurt, or injure: *Some insects damage plants.*

Damascus steel *n.* An early form of steel having fine wavy markings, developed in southwest Asia and used mainly for making sword blades.

damask (dăm′əsk) *n.* **1.** A rich glossy fabric woven with patterns that show on both sides, such as a silk used for draperies or a linen used for tablecloths. **2.** Damascus steel.

dame (dām) *n.* **1.** Used formerly as a title for a woman in authority or a mistress of a household. **2.** *Chiefly British* **a.** A woman holding a nonhereditary title given by the queen or king to honor personal merit or service to the country. **b.** The wife or widow of a knight.

damn (dăm) *v.* **damned, damning, damns** —*tr.* **1a.** To condemn to everlasting punishment in the afterlife. **b.** To cause (something) to fail; ruin: *Without money the project was damned.* **2.** To condemn (something) as being very bad: *Reviewers damned the new movie.* **3.** To swear at or curse at. —*intr.* To swear; curse. ❖ *interj.* An expression used to show anger, irritation, or disappointment. ❖ *adj. & adv. Informal* Very; damned: *a damn fool.* ❖ *n. Informal* The least bit; a jot: *not worth a damn.*

damnable (dăm′nə-bəl) *adj.* Deserving to be strongly condemned; hateful: *a damnable traitor.* —**dam′na·bly** *adv.*

damnation (dăm-nā′shən) *n.* The act of damning or the condition of being damned to everlasting punishment.

damned (dămd) *adj.* **damneder** (dăm′dər), **damnedest** (dăm′dĭst) **1.** In various religions, condemned to eternal punishment. **2.** Destined to an unhappy fate: *We're*

damned if we do, and damned if we don't. **3.** *Informal* Dreadful; awful: *this damned weather.* **4.** Used as an intensive: *a damned fool.* ❖ *adv. Informal* Very; damn: *a damned good idea.*

Damon (dā′mən) *n.* A legendary Greek man who pledged his life as a guarantee that his condemned friend Pythias would return from arranging his affairs to face execution. Both Damon and Pythias were later pardoned.

damp (dămp) *adj.* **damper, dampest** Slightly wet; moist; humid: *a damp towel; damp air.* See Synonyms at **wet.** ❖ *n.* **1.** Moisture in the air; humidity: *Don't go out in the damp.* **2.** A foul or poisonous gas that pollutes the air in a coal mine. ❖ *tr.v.* **damped, damping, damps 1.** To make damp; moisten. **2.** To extinguish (a fire, for example) by cutting off air. **3.** To restrain or check: *He tried to damp down his anger.* —**damp′ly** *adv.* —**damp′ness** *n.*

dampen (dăm′pən) *v.* **dampened, dampening, dampens** —*tr.* **1.** To moisten: *dampen a sponge.* **2.** To diminish or depress, as in strength or feeling: *The delay dampened their excitement.* —*intr.* To become damp. —**damp′en·er** *n.*

damper (dăm′pər) *n.* **1.** A movable plate in the flue of a furnace, stove, or fireplace for controlling the draft. **2.** A device for reducing or deadening vibrations, especially a pad that presses against the strings of a keyboard instrument. **3.** A depressing or restraining influence: *The rain put a damper on our vacation.*

damsel (dăm′zəl) *n.* A young woman or girl.

damselfly (dăm′zəl-flī′) *n.* Any of various often brightly colored insects related to the dragonflies, having a slender body and transparent wings that are folded together when at rest.

damson (dăm′zən *or* dăm′sən) *n.* **1.** A small, egg-shaped, dark-purple plum. **2.** A tree that bears such plums.

dance (dăns) *v.* **danced, dancing, dances** —*intr.* **1.** To move with rhythmic steps and motions, especially in time to music. **2.** To leap, skip, or prance about: *excited children dancing about the room.* **3.** To bob up and down: *Moonlight danced on the water.* —*tr.* **1.** To engage in or perform (a dance): *dance a waltz.* **2.** To cause to dance: *He danced her across the room.* ❖ *n.* **1.** A series of rhythmic steps and motions, usually performed to music. **2.** A social gathering at which people dance: *Are you going to the dance?* **3.** One round or turn of dancing: *May I have this dance?* **4.** The art of dancing: *study dance at a ballet school.* **5.** A piece of music composed as an accompaniment for dancing or in a dance rhythm.

dancer (dăn′sər) *n.* A person who dances, especially as a performer.

dandelion (dăn′dl-ī′ən) *n.* A common weedy plant having bright yellow flowers and long notched leaves that are sometimes eaten in salads. After the flowers have bloomed, the ripe seeds form a fluffy rounded mass.

dander¹ (dăn′dər) *n. Informal* Temper or anger: *What got their dander up?*

dander² (dăn′dər) *n.* Tiny particles from the coat or feathers of various animals, sometimes causing allergies in humans.

WORD HISTORY Dander¹ might be an alteration of obsolete English *dunder,* meaning "fermented cane juice used in rum-making." **Dander²** is an alteration of *dandruff.*

---

dandle (dăn′dl) *tr.v.* **dandled, dandling, dandles** To move (a small child) up and down on the knee or in the arms in a playful way.

dandruff (dăn′drəf) *n.* Small white scales of dead skin that are shed from the scalp.

dandy (dăn′dē) *n., pl.* **dandies 1.** A man who prides himself on his elegant clothes and fine appearance; a fop. **2.** Something very good of its kind: *This horse is a dandy.* ❖ *adj.* **dandier, dandiest** Very good; fine; first-rate: *That's a dandy idea!*

Dane (dān) *n.* A native or inhabitant of Denmark.

danger (dān′jər) *n.* **1.** The chance or risk of harm or destruction: *a house in danger of being swept into the sea.* **2.** A possible cause or chance of harm; a threat or hazard: *Fog is a danger to pilots.*

dangerous (dān′jər-əs) *adj.* **1.** Involving danger; hazardous: *Mining is a dangerous job.* **2.** Able or likely to cause harm: *The crocodile is a dangerous animal.* —**dan′-ger·ous·ly** *adv.* —**dan′ger·ous·ness** *n.*

dangle (dăng′gəl) *v.* **dangled, dangling, dangles** —*intr.* To hang loosely and swing or sway: *A key dangled from the chain.* —*tr.* To cause to swing loosely: *The children sat dangling their feet in the water.* —**dan′gler** *n.*

dangling participle (dăng′glĭng) *n.* A participle that is not clearly connected with the subject of the sentence that it is supposed to modify. For example, in the sentence *Sitting at my desk, a loud noise startled me,* the word *sitting* is a dangling participle. —SEE NOTE AT **participle.**

Daniel (dăn′yəl) *n.* A book of the Bible, traditionally believed to have been written by the prophet Daniel, which tells of Daniel's adventures and prophetic dreams.

Danish (dā′nĭsh) *adj.* Relating to Denmark or its people, language, or culture. ❖ *n.* **1.** The Germanic language of the Danes. **2.** A Danish pastry.

Danish pastry *n.* A sweet buttery pastry made with raised dough.

dank (dăngk) *adj.* **danker, dankest** Uncomfortably damp; chilly and wet: *a dank and musty cellar.* —**dank′ness** *n.*

Daphne (dăf′nē) *n.* In Greek mythology, a nymph who turned into a laurel tree in order to escape from Apollo.

dapper (dăp′ər) *adj.* **1.** Neatly dressed; trim; spruce: *dapper soldiers on parade.* **2.** Brisk and jaunty: *The horses trotted at a dapper pace.*

dapple (dăp′əl) *tr.v.* **dappled, dappling, dapples** To mark with spots, streaks, or patches of a different color or shade: *Sunlight filtering through the leaves dappled the ground.* ❖ *adj.* Dappled: *dapple horses.*

dappled (dăp′əld) *adj.* Marked with spots, streaks, or patches of a different color or shade: *a dappled fawn.*

dare (dâr) *v.* **dared, daring, dares** —*tr.* **1.** To have the courage necessary for; be bold enough to try: *She dared her most difficult dive. I didn't dare go into the cave.* **2.** To challenge (someone) to do something requiring courage: *They dared me to dive off the high board.* **3.** To confront boldly; brave: *The rescuers dared the freezing waters in their search.* —*intr.* To be courageous enough to do something. ❖ *n.* A challenge: *I took their dare and swam across the pond.*

daredevil (dâr′dĕv′əl) *n.* A person who takes risks with reckless boldness. ❖ *adj.* Recklessly bold; fearless: *daredevil acrobatic feats.*

daresay (dâr′sā′) *intr. & tr.v.* To think very likely or almost certain; suppose. Used only in the present tense with *I* or *we: I daresay you're right.*

daring (dâr′ĭng) *adj.* **1.** Willing to take risks; bold: *a daring test pilot.* **2.** Involving great risk or danger: *a daring rescue.* ❖ *n.* Fearless bravery; boldness; courage: *Climbing the mountain requires great daring.* —**dar′ing·ly** *adv.*

dark (därk) *adj.* **darker, darkest 1a.** Lacking light or having very little light: *a dark tunnel.* **b.** Reflecting only a small amount of light; tending toward black: *dark clothing.* **2a.** Gloomy; dismal: *a dark view of the future.* **b.** Portraying tragic or unhappy events in a satirical or humorous way: *dark comedy.* **3a.** Secret; mysterious: *Keep our plans dark.* **b.** Lacking knowledge, understanding, or culture: *a dark age in the history of medicine.* **4.** Evil or sinister: *a story full of dark deeds.* ❖ *n.* **1.** Absence of light; darkness: *groping around in the dark.* **2.** Night or nightfall: *Come home before dark.* **3.** A dark shade or color: *the darks and lights in a photograph.* ◆ **in the dark 1.** In secret: *The coach kept his game plan in the dark until yesterday.* **2.** In a state of ignorance; uninformed: *We were kept in the dark about the surprise.* —**dark′ly** *adv.* —**dark′ness** *n.*

✦ **SYNONYMS** dark, dim, dusky, murky, shadowy, shady *adj.*

Dark Ages *pl.n.* The early part of the Middle Ages from about AD 476 to about the year 1000, thought of as a time when learning was neglected in Europe.

darken (där′kən) *tr. & intr.v.* **darkened, darkening, darkens 1.** To make or become dark or darker: *Clouds darkened the sky. Twilight darkens into night.* **2.** To make or grow gloomy, sad, or somber: *News of the defeat darkened their faces.* —**dark′en·er** *n.*

dark horse *n.* **1.** A little-known, unexpectedly successful competitor, as in a horse race. **2.** A person who receives unexpected support and success as a political candidate, especially during a convention.

darkling (därk′lĭng) *adj.* Dim; obscure; in the dark: *a darkling sky.*

dark matter *n.* Physical objects, such as very dim stars, that emit no light or other radiation but are believed to exist based on their gravitational effects on visible objects, such as galaxies.

darkroom (därk′rōōm′ *or* därk′rŏŏm′) *n.* A room in which photographs are developed, either in total darkness or in colored light to which they are not sensitive.

darling (där′lĭng) *n.* **1.** A dearly loved person. **2.** A favorite: *That star was a darling of the theater for years.* ❖ *adj.* **1.** Dearest; beloved: *my darling child.* **2.** *Informal* Charming; adorable: *The little kittens are darling.*

darmstadtium (därm′shtăt′ē-əm) *n. Symbol* Ds A radioactive element that has been artificially produced by scientists. The half-life of its most stable isotope is about 10 seconds. Atomic number 110. See **Periodic Table.**

darn¹ (därn) *v.* **darned, darning, darns** —*tr.* To mend (cloth) by weaving new thread across a hole: *darn socks.* —*intr.* To repair a hole, as in a garment, by weaving thread across it. ❖ *n.* A place repaired by darning. —**darn′er** *n.*

darn² (därn) *interj.* An expression used to show displeasure or annoyance. ❖ *adv. & adj.* Damn. ❖ *tr. & intr.v.* **darned, darning, darns** To damn.

WORD HISTORY Darn¹ may come from Norman French *darne,* meaning "piece." **Darn²** is an alteration of *damn.*

darning needle (där′nĭng) *n.* A long, often blunt needle with a large eye, used in darning.

dart (därt) *n.* **1.** A thin object with a sharp point, thrown at a target by hand or shot from a blowgun, crossbow, or other device. **2. darts** *(used with a singular or plural verb)* A game in which darts are thrown at a board or other target. **3.** A quick rapid movement: *The cat made a sudden dart at the mouse.* **4.** A tapered tuck sewn to adjust the fit of a garment. ❖ *v.* **darted, darting, darts** —*intr.* To move suddenly and swiftly: *A squirrel darted across the path.* —*tr.* To shoot out or send forth with a swift sudden movement: *The bear darted a paw at the fish. They darted frightened glances behind them.*

dartboard (därt′bôrd′) *n.* A circular board, often made of cork, used as the target in a game of darts.

dash (dăsh) *v.* **dashed, dashing, dashes** —*intr.* **1.** To race or rush with sudden speed: *The children dashed down the stairs.* **2.** To strike, knock, or hurl with violent force: *Heavy rain dashed against the car windshield.* —*tr.* **1.** To break or smash by striking violently: *The ship was dashed upon the rocks.* **2.** To hurl, knock, or thrust with sudden force: *He dashed the cup against the wall.* **3.** To splash: *A car passing through a puddle dashed water all over my clothes.* **4.** To destroy; wreck: *Illness dashed their hopes for a vacation.* **5.** To write hastily: *I dashed off an email before leaving.* ❖ *n.* **1.** A swift forceful stroke: *She knocked the cup to the floor with a dash of her hand.* **2.** A sudden movement; a rush: *a dash for shelter from a cloudburst.* **3.** A short footrace: *the 100-yard dash.* **4.** A small amount; a bit: *a dash of salt.* **5.** Lively spirit or style: *entertainers full of dash.* **6.** A punctuation mark (—) used to show a pause, break, or omission or to set off part of a sentence from the rest. **7.** A long sound or signal used in Morse code in combination with the dot and silent intervals to represent letters, numbers, or punctuation. **8.** A dashboard.

dashboard (dăsh′bôrd′) *n.* The panel beneath the windshield in an automobile, containing instruments, dials, and controls.

dashiki (də-shē′kē) also **daishiki** (dī-shē′kē) *n., pl.* **dashikis** also **daishikis** A loose, brightly colored garment worn especially in western Africa.

dashing (dăsh′ing) *adj.* **1.** Brave, bold, and daring: *a dashing hero.* **2.** Showy or stylish: *The band wore dashing uniforms.*

dastardly (dăs′tərd-lē) *adj.* Cowardly, low, and mean: *dastardly deeds.* —**das′tard·li·ness** *n.*

data (dā′tə *or* dăt′ə) *pl.n.* (*used with a singular or plural verb*) **1.** Facts that can be analyzed or used in an effort to gain knowledge or make decisions; information. **2.** Statistics or other information represented in a form suitable for processing by computer.

database (dā′tə-bās′ *or* dăt′ə-bās′) *n.* A collection of data arranged for easy and speedy retrieval.

data mining *n.* The extraction of useful information from large databases or data sets.

data processing *n.* The storing or processing of data by a computer.

date¹ (dāt) *n.* **1a.** Time stated in terms of the day, month, and year: *What is the date of your birthday?* **b.** A specified day of the month: *Is today's date June 15 or 16?* **c.** A statement of calendar time: *There is no date stamped on this coin.* **2.** A point or period of time in history: *At that date radio was unknown.* **3a.** An agreement to meet someone or be somewhere at a particular time, especially as a social engagement: *We made a date to have lunch on Thursday.* **b.** The experience or socializing that occurs as a result of such an agreement: *What did you do on your date?* **c.** A person with whom one has a social engagement: *Who is her date to the prom?* ❖ *v.* **dated, dating, dates** —*tr.* **1.** To mark with a date: *He dated the letter May 1.* **2.** To determine the age, time, or origin of: *They dated*

the rock by studying the fossils in it. **3.** *Informal* To go on dates with: *She's been dating him for two months.* —*intr.* **1.** To come from a particular time in the past: *This statue dates from about 500 BC.* **2.** To go on dates: *They dated a lot during vacation.* ◆ **to date** Up to the present time: *a new theory based on our observations to date.*

date² (dāt) *n.* **1.** The sweet, one-seeded, oval or oblong fruit of the date palm. **2.** The date palm.

WORD HISTORY Both **date¹** and **date²** were spelled *date* in Middle English and had the same meaning as in Modern English. **Date¹** comes from the Latin phrase *data Romae,* meaning "issued at Rome (on a certain day)." **Date²** comes from Greek *daktulos* which meant both "finger" as well as the fruit, which was so called because a date is shaped like a finger.

dated (dā′tĭd) *adj.* **1.** Marked with a date: *a dated receipt.* **2.** Old fashioned: *a dated style.*

dateline (dāt′līn′) *n.* A phrase at the beginning of a news story or report that gives its date and place of origin.

date line *n.* The International Date Line.

date palm *n.* A very tall tropical palm having a crown of feathery leaves and bearing clusters of dates.

dative (dā′tĭv) *adj.* Relating to the grammatical case that indicates the recipient of the action of a verb, the indirect object of the verb, or the object of a preposition. The dative case is used in Latin, Russian, and various other languages, and corresponds to phrases in English beginning with *to* or *for.* ❖ *n.* **1.** The dative case. **2.** A word or form in the dative case.

datum (dā′təm *or* dăt′əm) *n.* The singular of **data.**

daub (dôb) *v.* **daubed, daubing, daubs** —*tr.* **1.** To cover or smear with a soft sticky substance such as clay, plaster, or mud: *daub the cracks in the wall with mortar.* **2.** To spread or smear (a soft sticky substance): *daub mortar in the cracks.* **3.** To paint (something) with crude or careless strokes. —*intr.* To paint in a crude or amateurish fashion. ❖ *n.* **1.** Something daubed on: *A daub of glue will mend the cup.* **2.** A spot or smear, as of paint. **3.** An amateurish painting.

daughter (dô′tər) *n.* **1.** A person's female child. **2.** A female descendant. **3.** A woman or girl regarded as if in a relationship of child to parent: *daughters of the revolution.*

daughter cell *n.* Either of two cells formed when a cell undergoes cell division.

daughter-in-law (dô′tər-ĭn-lô′) *n., pl.* **daughters-in-law** The wife of one's child.

daunt (dônt *or* dänt) *tr.v.* **daunted, daunting, daunts** To frighten, discourage, or dishearten: *The chance of failure did not daunt the inventor.*

dauntless (dônt′lĭs *or* dänt′lĭs) *adj.* Not easily frightened or discouraged; fearless: *a dauntless explorer.* —**daunt′less·ly** *adv.* —**daunt′less·ness** *n.*

dauphin (dô′fĭn) *n.* The eldest son of a king of France from 1349 to 1830.

davenport (dăv′ən-pôrt′) *n.* A large sofa, often convertible into a bed.

davit (dăv′ĭt *or* dā′vĭt) *n.* A small crane that projects over the side of a ship, used for lowering and hoisting boats.

Davy Jones's locker (dā′vē jōn′zĭz *or* dā′vē jōnz′) *n.* The bottom of the sea, regarded as the grave of people drowned or buried at sea.

dawdle (dôd′l) *v.* **dawdled, dawdling, dawdles** —*intr.* To take more time than necessary: *If you dawdle over your* *work, it will take you hours to finish.* —*tr.* To waste (time): *dawdle the day away.* —**daw′dler** *n.*

dawn (dôn) *n.* **1.** The time of the first appearance of daylight in the morning: *get up at dawn.* **2.** A first appearance of something; a beginning: *the dawn of recorded history.* ❖ *intr.v.* **dawned, dawning, dawns 1.** To begin to grow light in the morning: *We rose when the day dawned.* **2.** To come into existence; begin; start: *a new age dawned with the first flights into space.* **3.** To begin to be seen or understood; come as a realization: *As they stood there, it dawned on me they were waiting for an answer.*

day (dā) *n.* **1.** The period of light between sunrise and sunset: *a clear sunny day.* **2.** The 24-hour period during which the earth makes one complete rotation on its axis: *It rained for three days without stopping.* **3.** The part of the day devoted to work or study: *work a seven-hour day; the school day.* **4.** A period that is filled with a certain activity: *a day of fishing.* **5.** A particular period of time: *before the days of automobiles.* ◆ **day after day** For many days in succession: *Day after day they marched across the desert.*

day in, day out Every day without a break: *Feeding a pet must be done day in, day out.*

daybreak (dā′brāk′) *n.* The time each morning when light first appears; dawn: *Farmers often get up before daybreak.*

daycare or **day care** (dā′kâr′) *n.* Daytime care for infants, toddlers, and children of preschool age or for the elderly or the disabled.

daydream (dā′drēm′) *n.* The act of thinking in a dreamy way, often about things one wishes could come true. ❖ *intr.v.* **daydreamed** or **daydreamt** (dā′drĕmt′), **daydreaming, daydreams** To have daydreams: *daydreaming of faraway places.* —**day′dream′er** *n.*

Day-Glo (dā′glō′) A trademark for fluorescent coloring agents and materials.

daylight (dā′līt′) *n.* **1.** The light of day; sunlight. **2.** Dawn: *at work before daylight.* **3.** Daytime. **4.** Knowledge or understanding of something that was formerly unknown: *They began to see daylight concerning the cause of the epidemic.*

daylight-saving time (dā′līt-sā′vĭng) *n.* Time during which clocks are set one hour ahead of standard time to provide extra daylight at the end of the working day during spring, summer, and fall.

daylong (dā′lông′) *adj.* Lasting through the whole day: *a daylong seminar.* ❖ *adv.* Through the day; all day.

Day of Atonement *n.* Yom Kippur.

day one *n. Informal* The very beginning; the first day: *He's been an asset to the team from day one.*

days (dāz) *adv.* During the daytime on every day or most days: *works days as a bank teller.*

day school *n.* **1.** A private school for pupils living at home. **2.** A school that holds classes during the day.

daystar (dā′stär′) *n.* **1.** A planet, especially Venus, that is visible in the east just before daylight. **2.** The sun.

daytime (dā′tīm′) *n.* The time between sunrise and sunset. —**day′time′** *adj.*

day-to-day (dā′tə-dā′) *adj.* **1.** Happening every day; daily: *day-to-day routine.* **2.** Surviving one day at a time with little regard for the future: *The lost mountain climbers were existing on a day-to-day basis.*

day trader *n.* A speculator who buys and sells securities on the basis of small short-term price movements. —**day trading** *n.*

daze (dāz) *tr.v.* **dazed, dazing, dazes** To stun or confuse, as

with a blow, shock, or surprise: *The explosion dazed and deafened them.* ❖ *n.* A stunned or confused condition: *The news left us all in a daze.* —**daz′ed·ly** (dā′zĭd-lē) *adv.*

dazzle (dăz′əl) *tr.v.* **dazzled, dazzling, dazzles 1.** To make nearly or momentarily blind with too much bright light: *The ranger's searchlight dazzled the eyes of the campers.* **2.** To amaze, impress, or astonish with a spectacular display: *The pianist dazzled us with his superb technique.* ❖ *n.* Blinding brightness; glare: *the dazzle of sunlight on the water.*

dazzling (dăz′lĭng) *adj.* Brilliant or spectacular: *dazzling sunlight; a dazzling burst of speed.* —**daz′zling·ly** *adv.*

dB An abbreviation of decibel.

DC An abbreviation of: **1.** direct current. **2.** District of Columbia.

DDS An abbreviation of Doctor of Dental Surgery.

DDT (dē′dē-tē′) *n.* A powerful insecticide that is also poisonous to humans, birds, and other animals when swallowed or absorbed through the skin. It remains active in the environment for many years and has been banned in the United States for most uses since 1972.

de– A prefix that means: **1.** Reverse: *decode.* **2.** Remove: *defrost.* **3.** Reduce: *demote.* **4.** Out of: *deplane.* **5.** Down: *descend.*

WORD BUILDING The prefix **de–** can be traced back through Middle English and Old French to Latin *dē–*, meaning "from, off, apart, away, down, out." In English, *de–* usually indicates reversal, removal, or reduction. Thus *deactivate* means "to make inactive," *decontaminate* means "to remove the contamination from," and *decompress* means "to remove or reduce pressure."

---

deaccession (dē′ăk-sĕsh′ən) *tr.v.* **deaccessioned, deaccessioning, deaccessions** To remove (an object) from a collection, especially in order to sell it and purchase other objects. —**de′ac·ces′sion** *n.*

deacon (dē′kən) *n.* **1.** A layperson who assists a Protestant minister. **2.** In certain churches, a cleric ranking below a priest.

deaconess (dē′kə-nĭs) *n.* A laywoman who assists a Protestant minister.

deactivate (dē-ăk′tə-vāt′) *tr.v.* **deactivated, deactivating, deactivates 1.** To make inactive or ineffective: *deactivate a bomb.* **2.** To remove from active military duty: *deactivate soldiers in time of peace.*

dead (dĕd) *adj.* **deader, deadest 1.** No longer alive or living: *The dead tree is starting to decay.* **2.** Having no life or living things; lifeless: *a dead planet.* **3.** Lacking feeling; numb: *My cold toes felt dead.* **4.** Not moving or circulating; motionless: *the dead air in a closed room.* **5a.** No longer important or relevant: *a dead issue.* **b.** No longer learned as a first language: *Latin is a dead language.* **c.** No longer active: *a dead volcano.* **d.** Unexciting: *a dead party.* **6a.** No longer functioning or in operation: *The pump is dead.* **b.** Lacking electric power or charge: *a dead circuit; a dead battery.* **7.** Weary and worn-out; exhausted: *After finishing work I was dead on my feet.* **8.** Complete; absolute: *dead silence.* **9.** Sudden; abrupt: *a dead stop.* **10.** In sports, out of play: *When it crosses the sideline, the ball is dead.* **11.** Exact: *hit the dead center of the target.* ❖ *n.* **1.** Those who have died; dead people: *The soldiers buried the dead.* **2.** The darkest, quietest, or coldest part: *the dead of night; the dead of winter.* ❖ *adv.* **1.** Completely; absolutely: *You can be dead sure of that.* **2.** Straight; directly: *A huge boulder lay dead ahead.* **3.** Suddenly: *We stopped dead in our tracks.*

deadbeat (dĕd′bēt′) *n. Informal* **1.** A person who avoids paying debts. **2.** A lazy person; a loafer.

deadbolt (dĕd′bōlt′) *n.* A bolt on a lock that is moved by turning the key or knob without activating a spring.

deaden (dĕd′n) *tr.v.* **deadened, deadening, deadens 1.** To make less sensitive, intense, or strong: *Anesthetics deaden pain.* **2.** To make soundproof: *Rugs helped deaden the room.*

dead end *n.* **1.** A street, alley, or other passage that is closed or blocked off at one end. **2.** A situation or subject that allows for no development or progress: *We reached a dead end in our argument.*

dead heat *n.* A race in which two or more contestants finish at the same time; a tie.

dead language *n.* A language, such as Latin, that is no longer learned as a person's native language.

dead letter *n.* A letter that is not delivered or claimed, usually because the address is wrong or impossible to read.

deadline (dĕd′līn′) *n.* A set time by which something must be done, finished, or settled; a time limit: *No one could enter the contest after the deadline.*

deadlock (dĕd′lŏk′) *n.* **1.** A standstill that occurs when opposing forces are equally strong and neither will give way. **2.** A tie between opponents, especially in a sporting event. ❖ *tr. & intr.v.* **deadlocked, deadlocking, deadlocks** To bring or come to a deadlock: *The peace talks deadlocked over treaty terms.*

deadly (dĕd′lē) *adj.* **deadlier, deadliest 1.** Causing or capable of causing death: *a deadly weapon.* **2.** Unable to be appeased; unyielding: *deadly enemies.* **3.** Suggesting death: *a total and deadly silence.* **4.** Absolute; extreme; utter: *deadly earnestness.* **5.** Very accurate or effective: *The hunter is a deadly shot.* **6.** Very dull and boring: *a deadly play.* **7.** Causing or capable of causing spiritual death: *Envy is a deadly sin.* ❖ *adv.* **1.** Extremely; utterly: *I'm deadly serious.* **2.** So as to suggest death: *turned deadly pale at the scream.* —**dead′li·ness** *n.*

deadly nightshade *n.* Belladonna.

dead-man's float (dĕd′mănz′) *n.* A floating position in which a person lies face down and extends the arms forward.

dead-on (dĕd′ŏn′) *adj. Informal* Precisely accurate: *criticisms that were dead-on; a dead-on imitation of the boss.*

deadpan (dĕd′pǎn′) *adj.* Characterized by or showing no emotion or amusement: *a deadpan expression.*

dead reckoning *n.* A method of estimating the position of a ship or aircraft without astronomical observations, as by determination from its speed, time traveled, and winds and currents encountered.

Dead Sea Scrolls *pl.n.* A number of ancient parchment and papyrus scrolls containing passages from the Hebrew Scriptures and other writings, found in caves near the Dead Sea.

deadwood (dĕd′wŏŏd′) *n.* **1.** Dead wood, including fallen or standing trees, branches, and stumps. **2.** People or things that are burdensome and no longer useful: *getting rid of the deadwood in the company.*

deaf (dĕf) *adj.* **deafer, deafest 1.** Partially or completely lacking the ability to hear: *Many deaf people use sign language.* **2. Deaf** Relating to the Deaf or their culture. **3.** Unwilling to listen: *The umpire was deaf to our complaints.* ❖ *n. (used with a plural verb)* **1.** Deaf people considered as

a group. **2. Deaf** The community of deaf people who use American Sign Language as their main means of communication. —**deaf′ly** *adv.* —**deaf′ness** *n.*

deafen (dĕf′ən) *tr.v.* **deafened, deafening, deafens** To make deaf: *The explosion deafened us temporarily.*

deal (dēl) *v.* **dealt** (dĕlt), **dealing, deals** —*intr.* **1.** To be occupied or concerned: *This book deals with the architecture of Los Angeles.* **2.** To behave in a certain way toward another or others: *The landlord dealt fairly with the tenants.* **3.** To take action regarding something: *deal with an emergency.* **4.** *Informal* To cope or contend: *I don't deal well with stress.* **5.** To do business; trade: *a merchant who deals in diamonds.* **6.** To distribute playing cards: *It's your turn to deal.* —*tr.* **1.** To give out in shares or portions: *We dealt out cookies to the children.* See Synonyms at **distribute. 2.** To give or deliver: *The champion dealt the opponent a hard blow.* **3.** To hand out (cards) to players in a card game: *Deal the cards.* ❖ *n.* **1.** *Informal* **a.** An agreement, as in business or politics: *We made a deal with our neighbors to buy their car.* **b.** A favorable sale; a bargain: *I got a real deal on a TV at sale prices.* **2.** A corrupt or secret arrangement: *The inspector made a deal with the builder to pass inferior materials.* **3.** Treatment; conduct: *a fair deal from the judge.* **4a.** The distribution of playing cards. **b.** A player's turn to deal: *It's your deal.* ◆ **a good deal** or **a great deal 1.** A considerable amount; a lot: *We learned a great deal.* **2.** Much; considerably: *a good deal thinner.*

dealer (dē′lər) *n.* **1.** A person engaged in buying and selling: *a furniture dealer.* **2.** A person who distributes the playing cards in a game of cards.

dealing (dē′lĭng) *n.* **1. dealings** Agreements or relations with others, especially when involving money or trade: *business dealings.* **2.** A way of acting or doing business; conduct toward others: *That store is known for its fair dealing.*

dealt (dĕlt) *v.* Past tense and past participle of **deal.**

dean (dēn) *n.* **1.** An official of a college or university in charge of a certain school or faculty: *dean of the medical school.* **2.** An official of a college or high school who counsels students and enforces rules. **3.** The head clergyman in charge of a cathedral. **4.** The oldest or most respected member of a group or profession: *the dean of American tennis.*

dear (dîr) *adj.* **dearer, dearest 1.** Loved and cherished: *my dear friend.* **2.** Greatly valued; precious: *Her dearest possessions are in the cabinet.* **3.** Highly esteemed or regarded, as in speaking to or writing letters: *my dear fellow.* **4.** High in price; expensive. **5.** Heartfelt; sincere: *my dearest wish.* ❖ *adv.* **1.** At a high cost: *You will pay dear for that mistake.* **2.** Fondly or affectionately: *memories of old friends held dear to one's heart.* ❖ *n.* A dearly loved person or animal: *the poor dear.* ❖ *interj.* An expression used to show distress or surprise: *Oh dear!* —**dear′ly** *adv.* —**dear′ness** *n.*

dearth (dûrth) *n.* A lack or scarcity: *a dearth of knowledge about the ocean floor.*

death (dĕth) *n.* **1.** The fact or process of dying; the end of life: *remained busy and active until death.* **2.** The condition of being dead: *where the body lay in death.* **3.** A cause of dying: *Such a fall is certain death.* **4.** The ending, destruction, or extinction of something: *the death of Communism.* ◆ **put to death** To kill; execute. **to death** To an unbearable degree; extremely: *We were bored to death by the presentation.*

deathbed (dĕth′bĕd′) *n.* **1.** The bed on which a person dies. **2.** A person's last hours of life.

deathblow (dĕth′blō′) *n.* **1.** A fatal blow. **2.** A destructive event: *The scandal was the deathblow for the previous government.*

deathless (dĕth′lĭs) *adj.* Enduring forever; undying; immortal: *His fame is deathless.* —**death′less·ness** *n.*

deathly (dĕth′lē) *adj.* Resembling or characteristic of death: *a deathly pallor.* ❖ *adv.* **1.** So as to resemble death: *She was deathly pale.* **2.** Very; extremely: *deathly ill.*

death penalty *n.* A sentence of punishment by execution.

death rate *n.* The ratio of total deaths to total population in a given community over a specified period of time.

death row *n.* The part of a prison for housing inmates who have received the death penalty: *a murderer on death row.*

death's-head (dĕths′hĕd′) *n.* The human skull as a symbol of death.

debacle (dĭ-bä′kəl *or* dĕb′ə-kəl) *n.* **1.** A sudden disastrous collapse, downfall, or defeat; a rout: *The party in power suffered a complete debacle in the election.* **2.** A total, often ridiculous failure.

debar (dē-bär′) *tr.v.* **debarred, debarring, debars** To forbid, prohibit, exclude, or bar: *A person not born a US citizen is debarred from running for the presidency.*

debase (dĭ-bās′) *tr.v.* **debased, debasing, debases** To lower in character, quality, or worth: *Don't debase yourself by feeling envious.* —**de·base′ment** *n.*

debatable (dĭ-bā′tə-bəl) *adj.* Open to question, argument, or dispute: *an unproven and debatable theory.*

debate (dĭ-bāt′) *v.* **debated, debating, debates** —*intr.* **1.** To consider something; try to decide about something: *We debated about which trail to take.* **2.** To present or discuss arguments for and against something: *We debated about the merits of a low-fat diet.* —*tr.* **1.** To consider; try to decide: *I debated what to do next.* **2.** To discuss or argue about (something): *We debated whether the play was truly a tragedy.* ❖ *n.* **1.** A discussion or consideration of the arguments for and against something: *the debate about reforming the health care system.* **2.** A formal contest in which opponents argue for opposite sides of an issue: *Two local schools held a debate on whether to register bicycles.* —**de·bat′er** *n.*

debauch (dĭ-bôch′) *v.* **debauched, debauching, debauches** —*tr.* To lead away from good toward evil; corrupt morally. —*intr.* To indulge in too much eating, drinking, and other sensual pleasures. ❖ *n.* An act or a period of debauchery.

debauchery (dĭ-bô′chə-rē) *n., pl.* **debaucheries** Too much indulgence in eating, drinking, and other sensual pleasures.

debilitate (dĭ-bĭl′ĭ-tāt′) *tr.v.* **debilitated, debilitating, debilitates** To make feeble; weaken: *A long illness usually debilitates the body.* —**de·bil′i·ta′tion** *n.*

debility (dĭ-bĭl′ĭ-tē) *n., pl.* **debilities** The condition of abnormal bodily weakness; feebleness.

debit (dĕb′ĭt) *n.* **1.** A debt charged to and recorded in an account. **2.** An entry of a sum in the debit or left-hand side of an account. **3.** The sum of such entries. ❖ *tr.v.* **debited, debiting, debits** To charge with or as a debt: *The bank debited my account for the checks I wrote.*

debit card *n.* A bank card that allows a customer to make purchases or get cash by transferring funds electronically from an account.

debonair *also* **debonaire** (dĕb′ə-nâr′) *adj.* Gracious

and charming in a cheerful carefree way: *Adoring fans mobbed the debonair movie star.*

WORD HISTORY The word **debonair** comes ultimately from the Old French phrase *de bon aire,* meaning "of good lineage or disposition." The *aire* in the phrase is not the air we breathe. Rather, *aire* is French for "nest" or "family" and is related to the English word *aerie.*

debone (dē-bōn′) *tr.v.* **deboned, deboning, debones** To remove the bones from; to bone: *debone a chicken breast.*

debrief (dē-brēf′) *tr.v.* **debriefed, debriefing, debriefs** To question in order to obtain knowledge, especially knowledge gathered on a mission: *The astronauts were debriefed after returning from their mission.*

debris (də-brē′) *n.* The scattered remains of something broken, destroyed, or discarded: *Debris from the storm was spread all over the beach.*

debt (dĕt) *n.* **1.** Something, such as money, owed by one person to another: *I will pay my debts as soon as I get paid. We owe a debt of gratitude to those who have died defending our country.* **2.** The condition of owing; indebtedness: *They are in debt to the bank for their loan.*

debtor (dĕt′ər) *n.* A person who owes something to another.

debug (dē-bŭg′) *tr.v.* **debugged, debugging, debugs** To search for and fix errors in (a computer program).

debunk (dē-bŭngk′) *tr.v.* **debunked, debunking, debunks** To expose or ridicule the falseness or exaggerated claims of: *Scientists have debunked the theory that baking soda can cure cancer.*

debut *also* **début** (dā-byōō′ *or* də-byōō′) *n.* **1.** The first public appearance: *a new actor's stage debut; the debut of a new line of computers.* **2.** The formal presentation of a young woman into society.

debutante (dĕb′yōō-tänt′) *n.* A young woman making a formal debut into society.

deca– a prefix that means ten: *decaliter.*

decade (dĕk′ād′) *n.* A period of ten years.

decadence (dĕk′ə-dəns) *n.* A process, condition, or period of deterioration, decay, or decline, as in morals or art.

decadent (dĕk′ə-dənt) *adj.* Marked by or in a condition of deterioration or decline; decaying: *a decadent society.* ❖ *n.* A person who is in the process of mental or moral decay. —**dec′a·dent·ly** *adv.*

decaffeinated (dē-kăf′ə-nā′tĭd) *adj.* Having the caffeine removed: *decaffeinated coffee.*

decagon (dĕk′ə-gŏn′) *n.* A polygon with ten sides and ten angles. —**dec·ag′o·nal** (dĭ-kăg′ə-nəl) *adj.*

decahedron (dĕk′ə-hē′drən) *n., pl.* **decahedrons** *or* **decahedra** (dĕk′ə-hē′drə) A solid geometric figure having ten faces.

decal (dē′kăl′ *or* dĭ-kăl′) *n.* A picture or design printed on specially treated paper to be transferred to another surface such as glass, metal, or plastic.

decaliter (dĕk′ə-lē′tər) *n.* A metric unit of volume equal to 10 liters, 11 dry quarts, or 2.6 gallons.

Decalogue *or* **Decalog** (dĕk′ə-lôg′) *n.* The Ten Commandments.

decamp (dĭ-kămp′) *intr.v.* **decamped, decamping, decamps** **1.** To pack up and leave a camping ground; break camp: *The battalion decamped at dawn.* **2.** To leave secretly or suddenly; run away: *The thief decamped while it was still dark outside.* —**de·camp′ment** *n.*

decant (dĭ-kănt′) *tr.v.* **decanted, decanting, decants** **1.** To pour off (a liquid, especially wine) without disturbing the sediment at the bottom. **2.** To pour (a liquid) from one container into another.

decanter (dǐ-kǎn′tər) *n.* A decorative glass bottle with a stopper, used for holding liquids such as wine.

decapitate (dǐ-kǎp′ǐ-tāt′) *tr.v.* **decapitated, decapitating, decapitates** To cut off the head of a person or animal; behead. —**de·cap′i·ta′tion** *n.*

decapod (dĕk′ə-pŏd′) *n.* Any of various crustaceans that typically have five pairs of walking legs attached to the thorax. Crabs, lobsters, and shrimps are decapods.

decathlon (dǐ-kǎth′lŏn′) *n.* A track-and-field event usually for men that includes the 100-meter, 400-meter, and 1,500-meter runs; the 110-meter high hurdles; the discus and javelin throws; the shot put; the pole vault; the high jump; and the long jump.

decay (dǐ-kā′) *intr.v.* **decayed, decaying, decays 1.** To rot or become rotten; decompose: *Leaves fall to the forest floor and decay.* **2.** To undergo radioactive decay. **3.** To fall apart or deteriorate: *The bridge is decaying and will have to be rebuilt.* ❖ *n.* **1.** The act or process of rotting: *tooth decay; decay of a corpse.* **2.** The natural disintegration of a radioactive substance by the emission of particles and radiation from its nuclei. **3.** A gradual deterioration or decline: *the decay of traditional values.*

decease (dǐ-sēs′) *intr.v.* **deceased, deceasing, deceases** To die. ❖ *n.* The act or fact of dying; death.

deceased (dǐ-sēst′) *adj.* No longer living; dead: *my deceased grandparents.* ❖ *n., pl.* **deceased** A dead person or dead people: *members of the deceased's family.*

decedent (dǐ-sēd′nt) *n.* In law, the deceased.

deceit (dǐ-sēt′) *n.* **1.** The act or practice of deceiving; deception: *A successful spy is an expert in deceit.* **2.** A trick used to deceive someone else. **3.** The quality of being deceitful: *a swindler full of deceit.*

deceitful (dǐ-sēt′fəl) *adj.* **1.** Practicing deceit: *a deceitful person.* **2.** Deliberately misleading; deceptive: *a deceitful excuse to avoid punishment.* —**de·ceit′ful·ly** *adv.* —**de·ceit′ful·ness** *n.*

deceive (dǐ-sēv′) *v.* **deceived, deceiving, deceives** —*tr.* To make (a person) believe something that is not true; mislead; trick: *He deceived her into thinking he was innocent when in fact he was guilty.* —*intr.* **1.** To use deceit. **2.** To give a false impression: *appearances can deceive.* —**de·ceiv′er** *n.*

decelerate (dē-sĕl′ə-rāt′) *v.* **decelerated, decelerating, decelerates** —*tr.* To decrease the speed or rate of: *decelerated the car by jamming on the brakes.* —*intr.* To decrease in speed; slow down: *The spinning top decelerated slowly.* —**de·cel′er·a′tion** *n.* —**de·cel′er·a′tor** *n.*

December (dǐ-sĕm′bər) *n.* The 12th month of the year in the Gregorian calendar, having 31 days.

decency (dē′sən-sē) *n., pl.* **decencies 1.** The state or condition of being decent: *the decency to act in an honest and proper manner.* **2. decencies a.** Decent or proper acts; proper observances: *the social decencies such as courtesy and good manners.* **b.** The things needed for a respectable and proper way of living: *A refrigerator is one of the decencies of life in a developed nation.*

decent (dē′sənt) *adj.* **1.** Conforming to the standards of proper behavior or to the rules and conventions of society: *Decent people abide by the law.* **2.** Kind; considerate: *It was very decent of you to help in time of trouble.* **3.** Ad-

equate; passable: *a decent salary.* **4.** *Informal* Properly or modestly dressed. —**de′cent·ly** *adv.*

decentralize (dē-sĕn′trə-līz′) *tr.v.* **decentralized, decentralizing, decentralizes 1.** To distribute the functions or powers of (a government or central authority) among several local authorities. **2.** To reorganize into smaller units of operation: *decentralize a school system.* —**de·cen′tral·i·za′tion** (dē-sĕn′trə-lī-zā′shən) *n.*

deception (dǐ-sĕp′shən) *n.* **1.** The use of deceit: *fraudulent advertising and other forms of deception.* **2.** The condition of being deceived: *The magician achieved complete deception of the audience.* **3.** Something that deceives, as a trick or lie: *The scarecrow was a deception to frighten away the deer.*

deceptive (dǐ-sĕp′tǐv) *adj.* Deceiving or tending to deceive: *a deceptive advertisement.* —**de·cep′tive·ly** *adv.* —**de·cep′tive·ness** *n.*

deci– A prefix that means one tenth: *deciliter.*

decibel (dĕs′ə-bəl *or* dĕs′ə-bĕl′) *n.* A unit used in measuring the loudness of sounds: *The speaking voice of most people ranges from 45 to 75 decibels.*

decide (dǐ-sīd′) *v.* **decided, deciding, decides** —*tr.* **1a.** To reach a conclusion or form a judgment about (something) by reasoning or consideration: *decide what to do.* **b.** To bring to a conclusion by removing uncertainty or resolving a conflict: *The court decided the case.* **2.** To influence or determine the outcome of: *A single goal decided the game.* —*intr.* **1.** To give a judgment: *The judge decided against the defendant.* **2.** To reach a decision; make up one's mind: *What took you so long to decide?*

decided (dǐ-sī′dǐd) *adj.* **1.** Clear-cut; definite; undoubted: *a decided advantage.* **2.** Free from hesitation; resolute: *The general has a decided manner of talking.* —**de·cid′ed·ly** *adv.* —**de·cid′ed·ness** *n.*

deciduous (dǐ-sǐj′ōō-əs) *adj.* **1.** Shedding leaves at the end of the growing season: *deciduous trees.* **2.** Falling off at the end of a season or growing period: *deciduous antlers.*

deciliter (dĕs′ə-lē′tər) *n.* A metric unit of volume equal to one-tenth of a liter.

decimal (dĕs′ə-məl) *n.* **1.** A number containing a decimal fraction, such as 3.1415, 0.099, or −1.04. **2.** A decimal fraction. ❖ *adj.* Based on 10; proceeding by tens: *The system of decimal notation is an invention of mathematicians in India.*

decimal fraction *n.* A fraction in which the denominator is 10 or a power of 10. Expressed as decimal fractions, $29/100$ is 0.29, and $29/1000$ is 0.029.

decimal place *n.* The position of a digit in a decimal fraction. In .079, for example, 0 is in the first decimal place, 7 is in the second decimal place, and 9 is in the third decimal place.

decimal point *n.* A dot written in a decimal number, used to separate whole numbers from fractions. For example, 1.3 represents 1 plus $3/10$.

decimal system *n.* **1.** A number system based on units of 10. **2.** A system of measurement in which all derived units, such as the deciliter, are multiples of 10 of the fundamental units, such as the liter.

decimate (dĕs′ə-māt′) *tr.v.* **decimated, decimating, decimates** To destroy or kill a large part of: *The hurricane decimated the island's bird population.* —**dec′i·ma′tion** *n.*

decimeter (dĕs′ə-mē′tər) *n.* A unit of length equal to one-tenth of a meter.

decipher (dǐ-sī′fər) *tr.v.* **deciphered, deciphering, deciphers 1.** To read or interpret (something hard to under-

stand or illegible): *I can't decipher your handwriting.* **2.** To change (a message) from a code or cipher to ordinary language; decode: *They deciphered the spy's message.* —de·ci**′**pher·a·ble *adj.*

decision (dĭ-sĭzh**′**ən) *n.* **1.** A conclusion or judgment reached after consideration: *Our friends have not come to a decision about going on the trip with us.* **2.** The act of deciding or making up one's mind: *The judge's decision is taking a long time.* **3.** In boxing, a victory won on points awarded by judges when the loser has not been knocked out.

decisive (dĭ-sī**′**sĭv) *adj.* **1.** Settling a matter or conflict; conclusive: *a decisive argument.* **2.** Characterized by decision and firmness; resolute: *a decisive leader.* —de·ci**′**sive·ly *adv.* —de·ci**′**sive·ness *n.*

deck[1] (dĕk) *n.* **1.** A platform extending from one side of a ship to the other. **2a.** A platform resembling the deck of a ship: *a parking deck on the roof of the building.* **b.** A roofless, floored structure, typically with a railing, that adjoins a house. **3.** A pack of playing cards: *shuffle the deck and deal.* **4.** A tape deck. ❖ *tr.v.* **decked, decking, decks 1.** To provide with a deck: *deck a ship.* **2.** To knock down with force. ◆ **on deck 1.** On hand; present. **2.** Waiting to take one's turn, especially as a batter in baseball.

deck[2] (dĕk) *tr.v.* **decked, decking, decks 1.** To put fine clothes on: *She decked herself out for the party.* **2.** To decorate: *decked the halls for the holidays.*

WORD HISTORY Deck[1] comes from Middle English *dekke* (meaning "roof or covering of a boat or ship"), which comes from Middle Dutch *dec,* meaning "covering." **Deck**[2] comes from Dutch *dekken,* meaning "to cover."

---

deck hand *n.* A member of a ship's crew who performs manual labor.

declaim (dĭ-klām**′**) *v.* **declaimed, declaiming, declaims** —*intr.* **1.** To deliver a speech, especially in a formal way. **2.** To speak loudly, pompously, or in a theatrical manner: *Everyone declaims against inefficient government, but few will do anything about it.* —*tr.* To recite formally: *declaim a poem.* —de·claim**′**er *n.*

declamation (dĕk′lə-mā**′**shən) *n.* **1.** The act of declaiming: *a sincere declamation of patriotism.* **2.** Something declaimed.

declamatory (dĭ-klăm**′**ə-tôr′ē) *adj.* **1.** Suitable for declaiming: *a declamatory poem.* **2.** Pretentious and bombastic: *a long declamatory explanation.*

declaration (dĕk′lə-rā**′**shən) *n.* **1.** The act or process of declaring. **2.** A formal statement or announcement: *the declaration of one's candidacy for office.* **3.** A document listing goods that are taxable or subject to duty: *Travelers made out declarations before going through customs.*

Declaration of Independence *n.* A proclamation, adopted on July 4, 1776, by the Second Continental Congress, declaring the Thirteen Colonies independent of Great Britain.

declarative (dĭ-klăr**′**ə-tĭv) *adj.* Making a statement, as opposed to asking a question or giving an order: *a declarative sentence such as "I'm going home."*

declare (dĭ-klâr**′**) *v.* **declared, declaring, declares** —*tr.* **1.** To state with emphasis; affirm: *I declared that I would rather go hungry than eat liver.* **2.** To state officially or formally: *Congress has the power to declare new national holidays.* **3.** To make a full statement of (dutiable goods) when entering a country at customs. —*intr.* To announce one's choice or opinion: *The senator declared against raising taxes.*

déclassé (dā′klä-sā**′**) *adj.* **1.** Low or lowered in class, rank, or social position. **2.** Characteristic of the lower classes; of low social status.

declension (dĭ-klĕn**′**shən) *n.* **1.** In certain languages, the inflection of nouns, pronouns, and adjectives in accordance with their grammatical case, number, and gender. **2.** A class of words of one language with the same or a similar system of inflections, such as the first declension in Latin.

declination (dĕk′lə-nā**′**shən) *n.* **1.** The angle between magnetic north and true north at a given point. **2.** The angular distance of a star or planet from the celestial equator.

decline (dĭ-klīn**′**) *v.* **declined, declining, declines** —*intr.* **1.** To refuse politely to do or accept something: *I asked them home for a snack, but they declined.* **2.** To become less or decrease, as in strength, value, or importance: *Her health declined until she saw the doctor. Prices tend to decline when business is poor.* —*tr.* **1.** To refuse politely: *They declined my offer to help. I have to decline the kitten, because we can't have pets.* **2.** In certain languages, to give the inflected forms of (a noun, pronoun, or adjective). ❖ *n.* **1.** The process or result of declining, as in strength or importance; deterioration: *The country was in a period of decline.* **2.** A change to a lower level or state, as in value: *a decline in prices.* **3.** The period when something is coming to an end: *Frost and bare trees marked the decline of fall.* **4.** A downward slope.

declivity (dĭ-klĭv**′**ĭ-tē) *n., pl.* **declivities** A downward slope, as of a hill.

decode (dē-kōd**′**) *tr.v.* **decoded, decoding, decodes 1.** To change (information) from a form that is in code or in ordinary language; decipher: *decode Egyptian hieroglyphics.* **2.** To convert (a scrambled electronic signal) into one that can be understood. —de·cod**′**er *n.*

décolletage (dā′kŏl-täzh**′**) *n.* A low neckline on a woman's garment, especially a dress.

decompose (dē′kəm-pōz**′**) *v.* **decomposed, decomposing, decomposes** —*tr.* **1.** To separate (a substance) into simpler substances or basic elements: *Heat decomposes chalk into lime and carbon dioxide.* **2.** To cause to rot; decay: *Microbes decomposed the dead plants on the forest floor.* —*intr.* **1.** To separate into component parts: *Sunlight decomposes into the colors of the spectrum as it passes through a prism.* **2.** To decay; rot: *Paper decomposes more quickly than plastic.*

decomposer (dē′kəm-pō**′**zər) *n.* An organism, often a bacterium or fungus, that feeds on and breaks down dead organic matter.

decomposition (dē-kŏm′pə-zĭsh**′**ən) *n.* The act or process of decomposing: *Leaves undergo decomposition after they fall to the forest floor.*

decompress (dē′kəm-prĕs**′**) *tr.v.* **decompressed, decompressing, decompresses** To bring (a person exposed to increased pressure) gradually to normal atmospheric pressure.

decompression (dē′kəm-prĕsh**′**ən) *n.* The act or process of bringing a person exposed to increased pressure back to normal atmospheric pressure in gradual stages: *Divers and workers building deep tunnels must undergo decompression.*

decompression sickness *n.* A disorder, seen especially in deep-sea divers, caused by the formation of nitrogen bubbles in the blood following a rapid drop in pressure and characterized by severe pain in the joints and chest, cramps, and paralysis.

decongestant (dē′kən-jĕs′tənt) *n.* A medication or treatment that decreases congestion in the nose or bronchial passages.

deconstruct (dē′kən-strŭkt′) *tr.v.* **deconstructed, deconstructing, deconstructs 1.** To break down into components; dismantle: *a toxic substance that can be deconstructed into harmless chemicals.* **2.** To analyze (a literary text, for example) in such a way as to expose underlying assumptions or implicit ideological stances. **3.** To adapt (a genre, style, or form) in a way that isolates familiar elements from their usual context in order to imply an ironic comment on the unspoken values of the original. —**de′con·struc′tion** *n.*

decontaminate (dē′kən-tăm′ə-nāt′) *tr.v.* **decontaminated, decontaminating, decontaminates** To free of contamination, especially by removing harmful substances, such as bacteria, poisonous chemicals, or radioactive materials. —**de′con·tam′i·na′tion** *n.*

decontrol (dē′kən-trōl′) *tr.v.* **decontrolled, decontrolling, decontrols** To free from control, especially from government control: *The government decontrolled the airlines, letting them set their own ticket prices.*

decor (dā-kôr′) or **décor** (dā′kôr′) *n.* **1.** The decorative style of a room, home, restaurant, or other area. **2.** Scenery in a theatrical or television show.

decorate (dĕk′ə-rāt′) *tr.v.* **decorated, decorating, decorates 1.** To make (something) attractive or impressive by adding things to it or altering its appearance: *The students decorated the auditorium with flowers for graduation.* **2.** To give a medal or other honor to: *The chief decorated the firefighter for bravery.*

decoration (dĕk′ə-rā′shən) *n.* **1.** The act or process of decorating: *Decoration of the auditorium for graduation took most of the morning.* **2.** Something that adorns or beautifies; an ornament: *We put up wreaths, streamers, and other decorations.* **3.** A medal, badge, or ribbon awarded as an honor: *The police officer received a decoration for bravery.*

decorative (dĕk′ər-ə-tĭv or dĕk′ə-rā′tĭv) *adj.* Serving to decorate; ornamental: *a decorative design in the ceiling.* —**dec′o·ra·tive·ly** *adv.*

decorator (dĕk′ə-rā′tər) *n.* A person who decorates, especially an interior decorator.

decorous (dĕk′ər-əs or dĭ-kôr′əs) *adj.* Characterized by decorum; proper: *decorous behavior.* —**dec′o·rous·ness** *n.*

decorum (dĭ-kôr′əm) *n.* Proper behavior or conduct; propriety.

decoupage also **découpage** (dā′kōō-päzh′) *n.* **1.** The technique of decorating a surface with cutouts, as of paper. **2.** A creation produced by this technique.

decoy (dē′koi′ or dĭ-koi′) *n.* **1.** A model of a duck or other bird, used by hunters to attract wild birds or animals. **2.** A person or thing used to lead another into danger or a trap: *A false delivery of money was a decoy to catch the robbers.* ✦ *tr.v.* (dĭ-koi′) **decoyed, decoying, decoys 1.** To lure (wild animals such as birds) into a trap or position to be hunted: *decoy geese into a marsh.* **2.** To lure (a person) into danger or a trap by a trick or temptation.

decrease (dĭ-krēs′) *tr. & intr.v.* **decreased, decreasing, decreases** To become or cause to become gradually less or smaller; diminish: *Oil supplies decreased during the winter. We must decrease spending to conserve our mon-*

ey. ✦ *n.* (dē′krēs′) **1.** The act or process of decreasing; a decline: *A decrease in sales forced the owners to close the store.* **2.** The amount by which something becomes less or smaller: *a decrease in the price of gasoline of five cents a gallon.*
✦ **SYNONYMS** decrease, diminish, dwindle, lessen *v.*

decree (dĭ-krē′) *n.* An authoritative order; an edict: *The falsely accused prisoner was released by court decree.* ✦ *tr.v.* **decreed, decreeing, decrees** To order, establish, or decide by decree: *The governor decreed a state holiday.*

decrement (dĕk′rə-mənt) *n.* In mathematics, the amount by which the value of a variable decreases.

decrepit (dĭ-krĕp′ĭt) *adj.* Weakened, worn-out, or broken down because of old age or long use: *a decrepit old car.* —**de·crep′it·ly** *adv.*

decrepitude (dĭ-krĕp′ĭ-tōōd′) *n.* The condition of being decrepit; weakness: *The abandoned house was in a state of decrepitude.*

decrescendo (dā′krə-shĕn′dō or dē′krə-shĕn′dō) *adv. & adj.* In music, with gradually diminishing force or loudness. ✦ *n., pl.* **decrescendos 1.** A gradual decrease in musical force or loudness. **2.** A musical passage performed with a decrescendo.

decriminalize (dē-krĭm′ə-nə-līz′) *tr.v.* **decriminalized, decriminalizing, decriminalizes** To reduce or abolish the legal penalties for doing or possessing (something): *Betting was decriminalized in many states.*

decry (dĭ-krī′) *tr.v.* **decried, decrying, decries 1.** To condemn as being wrong or bad; disapprove of strongly: *The judge decried the criminal's behavior.* **2.** To cause to seem unimportant or inferior; belittle: *decry watching television as a waste of time.*

decrypt (dē-krĭpt′) *tr.v.* **decrypted, decrypting, decrypts 1.** To decipher. **2.** To decode. ✦ *n.* (dē′krĭpt′) A deciphered or decoded message. —**de·cryp′tion** *n.*

dedicate (dĕd′ĭ-kāt′) *tr.v.* **dedicated, dedicating, dedicates 1.** To keep for a special purpose or honor: *This chapel is dedicated to the memory of sailors lost at sea.* **2.** To give or apply (one's time or self, for example) to a particular activity, pursuit, cause, or person; devote: *Nurses dedicate their lives to the care of the sick.* **3.** To address or inscribe (a book, performance, or other creative work) to someone as a mark of respect or affection: *The composer dedicated the new symphony to a friend.*

dedication (dĕd′ĭ-kā′shən) *n.* **1.** The act of dedicating or the state of being dedicated: *her dedication to helping others.* **2.** A ceremony dedicating something: *We went to the dedication of the new library.* **3.** A note in a book, musical composition, or other creative work dedicating it to someone. —**ded′i·ca·to′ry** (dĕd′ĭ-kə-tôr′ē) *adj.*

deduce (dĭ-dōōs′) *tr.v.* **deduced, deducing, deduces** To reach (a conclusion) by reasoning, especially from a general principle: *The engineers deduced from the laws of physics that the new airplane would fly.* —SEE NOTE AT **produce.**

deduct (dĭ-dŭkt′) *tr.v.* **deducted, deducting, deducts** To take away (a quantity from another); subtract: *The dealer deducted the amount of our earlier deposit from the final payment for the car.*

deductible (dĭ-dŭk′tə-bəl) *adj.* Capable of being deducted, especially from inclusion in one's taxable income.

deduction (dĭ-dŭk′shən) *n.* **1.** The act of deducting; subtraction: *The salesman's deduction of the cost of installation persuaded us to buy the dishwasher.* **2.** An amount that is or may be deducted: *a deduction from one's taxable* *income for medical expenses.* **3a.** The process of reaching a conclusion by reasoning, especially from general principles. **b.** A conclusion reached by this process: *the judge's deduction that the law violated the Fourteenth Amendment.*

deductive (dĭ-dŭk′tĭv) *adj.* Involving logical deduction: *deductive reasoning.* —**de·duc′tive·ly** *adv.*

deed (dēd) *n.* **1.** An act or action: *Returning the lost money was a good deed.* **2.** A legal document showing ownership of property. ❖ *tr.v.* **deeded, deeding, deeds** To transfer or give (property) by means of a deed: *The government deeded land to the miners.*

deejay (dē′jā′) *Informal n.* A disc jockey.

deem (dēm) *tr.v.* **deemed, deeming, deems** To regard as, consider, or believe: *The doctor deemed it essential for me to get more exercise.*

deep (dēp) *adj.* **deeper, deepest 1.** Extending far down below a surface: *a deep hole in the river ice.* **2.** Extending from front to rear, or from the outside to the inside: *a deep closet.* **3.** Extending a specified distance in a given direction: *snow three feet deep.* **4.** Far distant down or back: *The hunters were deep in the woods.* **5.** Extreme; profound; intense: *a deep silence; a deep sleep.* **6.** Very much absorbed or involved: *She was deep in thought.* **7.** Showing much thought or feeling; strongly felt: *a deep understanding; a deep love of books.* **8.** Difficult to understand; mysterious: *a deep theory.* **9.** Rich and vivid in shade of color: *a deep red.* **10.** Low in pitch: *a deep voice.* ❖ *adv.* **deeper, deepest 1.** To a great depth: *dig deep into the earth.* **2.** Well along in time; late: *The researchers worked deep into the night.* ❖ *n.* **1.** A deep place, such as the ocean or a place in the ocean: *We know little of life in the deep.* **2.** The most intense or extreme part: *the deep of night.* —**deep′ly** *adv.* —**deep′ness** *n.*

deep-dish (dēp′dĭsh′) *adj.* Made or used in a deep baking dish.

deepen (dē′pən) *tr. & intr.v.* **deepened, deepening, deepens** To make or become deep or deeper: *More digging slowly deepened the hole. Floodwaters deepened as the rain continued.*

deep-fry (dēp′frī′) *tr.v.* **deep-fried, deep-frying, deep-fries** To fry by immersing in a deep container filled with oil or fat: *deep-fried the chicken wings.*

deep-rooted (dēp′rōo′tĭd or dēp′rōot′ĭd) *adj.* **1.** Firmly implanted under the surface: *a deep-rooted oak.* **2.** Firmly fixed; deep-seated: *deep-rooted beliefs.*

deep-sea (dēp′sē′) *adj.* Relating to deep parts of the sea: *a deep-sea diver.*

deep-seated (dēp′sē′tĭd) *adj.* **1.** Deeply implanted below the surface: *a deep-seated infection.* **2.** Firmly fixed; deeply rooted; strongly entrenched: *a deep-seated problem.*

deep-six (dēp′sĭks′) *tr.v.* **deep-sixed, deep-sixing, deep-sixes** *Slang* **1.** To toss out; get rid of: *deep-sixed the incriminating papers.* **2.** To toss overboard.

deep space *n.* **1.** The regions of space that are beyond the gravitational influence of Earth. **2.** The regions of space that are beyond our solar system.

deer (dîr) *n., pl.* **deer** Any of various hoofed mammals, such as the elk or white-tailed deer, that chew their cud and have antlers, usually only in the male.

deerskin (dîr′skĭn′) *n.* **1.** The skin of a deer. **2.** Leather made from this skin.

deer tick *n.* Either of two small North American ticks that are parasitic on deer and other animals and that transmit the bacteria that cause Lyme disease.

de-escalate (dē-ĕs′kə-lāt′) *tr.v.* **de-escalated, de-escalating, de-escalates** To reduce the scale, size, or intensity of: *Calm words de-escalated the crisis.* —**de-es′ca·la′tion** *n.*

deface (dĭ-fās′) *tr.v.* **defaced, defacing, defaces** To mar or spoil the surface or appearance of; disfigure: *deface a poster with a crayon.* —**de·face′ment** *n.*

de facto (dĭ făk′tō or dā făk′tō) *adj.* Existing in fact, especially when contrary to or not established by law: *housing practices that resulted in de facto segregation; a de facto government.*

defamation (dĕf′ə-mā′shən) *n.* The act of making a statement that will damage a person's reputation; slander or libel: *defamation of a person's character.* —**de·fam′a·to′ry** (dĭ-făm′ə-tôr′ē) *adj.*

defame (dĭ-fām′) *tr.v.* **defamed, defaming, defames** To attack or damage the reputation of by slander or libel: *He defamed her good name by spreading false rumors.*

default (dĭ-fôlt′) *n.* **1.** A failure to do what is required, especially a failure to pay a debt: *The bankrupt company is guilty of default on its loans.* **2.** The failure of one or more competitors or teams to participate in or complete a contest: *win a contest by default.* **3.** A setting, such as the typeface for text, used by a computer unless the operator chooses a different setting. ❖ *intr.v.* **defaulted, defaulting, defaults 1.** To fail to do what is required: *default on a business contract.* **2.** To fail to pay money when it is due: *default on a loan.* **3.** To lose a contest by failing to participate in or complete it: *Illness caused the tennis star to default in the match.* —**de·fault′er** *n.*

defeat (dĭ-fēt′) *tr.v.* **defeated, defeating, defeats 1.** To win victory over; beat: *The mayor defeated all opponents in the last election.* **2.** To prevent the success of; thwart: *A misunderstanding defeated our efforts at a compromise.* **3a.** To dishearten or discourage: *The last setback defeated her, and she gave up.* **b.** To be beyond the comprehension of; mystify: *How the children found their way back home defeats me.* ❖ *n.* **1.** The act of defeating or the state of being defeated: *The veto was a defeat of the new environmental measures.* **2.** Failure to win: *admit defeat.*

defeatism (dĭ-fē′tĭz′əm) *n.* Acceptance of or resignation to the prospect of defeat: *Defeatism can prevent success.* —**de·feat′ist** *n.*

defecate (dĕf′ĭ-kāt′) *intr.v.* **defecated, defecating, defecates** To empty the bowels of waste matter. —**def′e·ca′tion** *n.*

defect (dē′fĕkt′ or dĭ-fĕkt′) *n.* A lack of something necessary or desirable for completion or perfection; a deficiency: *A defect in the engine made it sputter and stall.* ❖ *intr.v.* (dĭ-fĕkt′) **defected, defecting, defects 1.** To disavow allegiance to one's country and take up residence in another: *a Chinese pilot who defected to Russia.* **2.** To abandon a position or association, often to join an opposing group: *The American general Benedict Arnold defected to the British side.* —**de·fec′tor** *n.*

defection (dĭ-fĕk′shən) *n.* The act of deserting one's country, party, or cause, especially to join or take up residence in another.

defective (dĭ-fĕk′tĭv) *adj.* Having a defect or flaw; faulty: *The defective clock never kept time well.* —**de·fec′tive·ly** *adv.*

defence (dĭ-fĕns′) *n. Chiefly British* Variant of **defense.**

defend (dĭ-fĕnd′) *v.* **defended, defending, defends** —*tr.* **1.** To make or keep safe from attack, harm, or danger; guard: *The ants defended their colony against the invading predators.* **2.** To support or maintain, as by argument;

justify: *The scientist defended the theory that germs cause disease.* **3.** To represent (a defendant) in a civil or criminal lawsuit: *People accused of a crime have the right to be defended by a lawyer.* **4.** In sports, to compete against a challenger in an attempt to retain (a championship). —*intr.* In sports, to play defense: *tried to defend against the fast break.* —**de·fend′er** *n.*

✦ SYNONYMS **defend, guard, preserve, protect, shield** *v.*

defendant (dĭ-fĕn′dənt) *n.* The person or party against which a legal action or claim is brought.

defenestration (dē-fĕn′ĭ-strā′shən) *n.* An act of throwing someone or something out of a window.

defense (dĭ-fĕns′) *n.* **1.** The act of defending against attack, harm, or danger: *The patriots fought in defense of their freedom.* **2a.** A means or method of defending or protecting: *A heavy coat is a good defense against the cold.* **b.** An argument in support or justification of something: *This newspaper editorial is a strong defense for freedom of the press.* **3a.** The act of defending a legal case. **b.** The defendant and his or her legal counsel: *Where does the defense sit in the courtroom?* **4.** (*often* dē′fĕns′) In sports: **a.** The means or tactics used in trying to keep the opposition from scoring. **b.** The players or the team trying to keep the opposition from scoring.

defenseless (dĭ-fĕns′lĭs) *adj.* Having no defense; unprotected: *a defenseless infant.*

defensible (dĭ-fĕn′sə-bəl) *adj.* Capable of being defended, protected, or justified: *Blaming others for one's mistakes is not a defensible position.*

defensive (dĭ-fĕn′sĭv) *adj.* **1.** Intended to or appropriate for defense: *a defensive moat surrounding the castle; a successful defensive move in chess.* **2a.** Intended to withstand or deter aggression or attack: *developed a defensive shield to protect against missiles.* **b.** Performed so as to avoid risk or danger: *took defensive measures to prevent exposure to mercury.* **3.** Constantly protecting oneself from criticism or other real or perceived threats: *It's hard to say anything to you because you always get so defensive.* ✦ **on the defensive** Prepared to withstand or counter aggression or attack. —**de·fen′sive·ly** *adv.* —**de·fen′sive·ness** *n.*

defer¹ (dĭ-fûr′) *tr.v.* **deferred, deferring, defers** To put off; postpone: *defer going until we know what the weather will be.* —**de·fer′ra·ble** *adj.* —SEE NOTE AT **transfer.**

defer² (dĭ-fûr′) *intr.v.* **deferred, deferring, defers** To submit to the wishes, opinion, or decision of another, as through recognition of authority or knowledge: *Let's defer to an expert on that matter.*

WORD HISTORY Defer¹ comes from Middle English *differen,* which comes from Latin *differre,* both meaning "to put off." *Differre* is composed of the Latin prefix *dis-* (meaning "off") and the word *ferre,* meaning "to carry, put." **Defer²** comes from Middle English *deferen,* which comes from Latin *dēferre,* both meaning "to refer to." *Dēferre* consists of the Latin prefix *dē-* (meaning "away") and *ferre.*

deference (dĕf′ər-əns *or* dĕf′rəns) *n.* **1.** Submission or courteous yielding to the opinion, wishes, or judgment of another. **2.** Courteous respect: *The guests showed deference to their host by standing until he was seated.*

deferential (dĕf′ə-rĕn′shəl) *adj.* Marked by or showing deference; respectful: *deferential behavior.* —**def′er·en′tial·ly** *adv.*

deferment (dĭ-fûr′mənt) *n.* The act or an example of delaying or putting off: *the deferment of payments on a loan.*

defiance (dĭ-fī′əns) *n.* Bold resistance to an opposing force or authority: *shook their fists in a gesture of defiance.*

✦ **in defiance of** In spite of; contrary to: *We went on the picnic in defiance of bad weather forecasts.*

defiant (dĭ-fī′ənt) *adj.* Acting with or marked by defiance; boldly resisting: *The rebels took a defiant stance.* —**de·fi′ant·ly** *adv.*

defibrillator (dē-fĭb′rə-lā′tər) *n.* A device that uses a brief electric shock to counteract rapid twitching of the heart muscle and restore a normal heartbeat.

deficiency (dĭ-fĭsh′ən-sē) *n., pl.* **deficiencies 1.** The quality or condition of being deficient. **2.** A lack or shortage, especially of something essential to health: *A vitamin deficiency made the patient weak.*

deficiency disease *n.* A disease, such as pellagra or rickets, that results from a diet lacking in one or more vitamins or from an inability of the body to absorb or use certain essential nutrients.

deficient (dĭ-fĭsh′ənt) *adj.* **1.** Lacking an essential quality or element: *a diet deficient in vitamin D.* **2.** Lacking in amount or degree; insufficient: *a deficient education.*

deficit (dĕf′ĭ-sĭt) *n.* **1.** Inadequacy or insufficiency: *a deficit in grain production.* **2.** The amount by which a sum of money falls short of the required or expected amount; a shortage: *The deficit in the government's budget can be eliminated by raising taxes or reducing spending.*

deficit spending *n.* The use of borrowed money by a government in order to spend more money than available revenue allows.

defile¹ (dĭ-fīl′) *tr.v.* **defiled, defiling, defiles 1.** To make filthy or dirty; pollute: *Sewage seeping into the lake defiled the water.* **2.** To spoil the sacredness or purity of: *defile a temple.* —**de·file′ment** *n.*

defile² (dĭ-fīl′) *intr.v.* **defiled, defiling, defiles** To march in single file or in columns. ✤ *n.* A narrow gorge or pass that requires a group, as of soldiers, to move in file.

WORD HISTORY Defile¹ comes from Middle English *defilen,* a variant of *defoulen* (meaning "to trample on, abuse, pollute"), which comes from Old French *defouler,* meaning "to beat, trample down." **Defile²** comes from French *défiler,* meaning "to march in rows."

define (dĭ-fīn′) *tr.v.* **defined, defining, defines 1.** To state the precise meaning of (a word or phrase, for example): *Dictionaries define words.* **2.** To describe; specify distinctly: *The Constitution defines the powers of the president. She defined the properties of the new drug.* **3.** To make distinct or clear in outline: *The hills were defined against the bright morning sky.*

definite (dĕf′ə-nĭt) *adj.* **1.** Clearly defined or firmly decided: *a definite plan; a definite time.* **2.** Direct and clear in expression; forthright: *The doctor was definite about getting more exercise.* **3.** Indisputable; certain: *We are at a definite disadvantage without our best player.* —**def′i·nite·ly** *adv.* —**def′i·nite·ness** *n.*

definite article *n.* A word used to introduce and refer to a particular noun or noun phrase, especially one that has already been mentioned or is assumed to be known. In English *the* is the definite article.

definition (dĕf′ə-nĭsh′ən) *n.* **1.** A statement that explains the meaning of something, such as a word or phrase, as in a dictionary entry. **2.** The act or process of stating a precise meaning or significance: *The textbook begins* *with the definition of key terms.* **3.** The level of detail in a recording, production, or digital encoding of an image or sound: *The mountains in the snapshots had poor definition.*

definitive (dǐ-fǐn′ǐ-tǐv) *adj.* **1.** Serving to define or identify something as distinct from others: *plot twists that are definitive of the genre of horror movies.* **2.** Serving to settle, decide, or put an end to; conclusive: *a definitive answer; a definitive victory.* **3.** Authoritative and complete: *a definitive biography.* **—de·fin′i·tive·ly** *adv.*

deflate (dǐ-flāt′) *v.* **deflated, deflating, deflates** *—tr.* **1.** To release contained air or gas from: *A pin deflated the balloon.* **2.** To reduce or lessen the size or importance of: *The crowd's jeers soon deflated the speaker's confidence.* **3.** To reduce the amount or availability of (currency or credit), causing a decline in prices. *—intr.* To be or become deflated: *As the tire deflated, we pulled off to the side of the road.*

deflation (dǐ-flā′shən) *n.* **1.** The act of deflating or the condition of being deflated: *Deflation made the balloon slowly sink toward the ground.* **2.** A persistent decrease in the level of consumer prices or a persistent increase in the purchasing power of money.

deflect (dǐ-flěkt′) *intr. & tr.v.* **deflected, deflecting, deflects** To turn aside or cause to turn aside; bend or deviate: *Constant interruptions deflected the speaker's thoughts from his main purpose.* **—de·flec′tor** *n.*

deflection (dǐ-flěk′shən) *n.* **1.** The act or process of deflecting or the condition of being deflected. **2a.** The movement of something from its normal or zero position. **b.** The amount of this movement.

deflower (dē-flou′ər) *tr.v.* **deflowered, deflowering, deflowers** To have sexual intercourse with (a woman who is a virgin). **—de·flow′er·er** *n.*

defoliant (dē-fō′lē-ənt) *n.* A chemical sprayed or dusted on plants to cause the leaves to fall off.

defoliate (dē-fō′lē-āt′) *tr.v.* **defoliated, defoliating, defoliates** To cause the leaves of (a plant or plants) to fall off, especially by the use of a chemical dust or spray. **—de·fo′li·a′tion** *n.*

deforest (dē-fôr′ĭst) *tr.v.* **deforested, deforesting, deforests** To cut down and clear away the trees or forests from. **—de·for′es·ta′tion** *n.*

deform (dǐ-fôrm′) *v.* **deformed, deforming, deforms** *—tr.* **1.** To alter from previous, proper, or natural form; misshape: *The heat of the fire deformed the candles.* **2.** To spoil the beauty or appearance of; disfigure. *—intr.* To become deformed.

deformation (dē′fôr-mā′shən *or* děf′ər-mā′shən) *n.* **1.** The act or process of deforming: *the deformation of plastic by heat.* **2.** The condition of being deformed. **3.** A change in form for the worse: *deformations in plants caused by poor growing weather.*

deformed (dǐ-fôrmd′) *adj.* Misshapen or distorted in form.

deformity (dǐ-fôr′mǐ-tē) *n., pl.* **deformities** **1.** The condition of being deformed: *discarded the plastic parts because of their deformity.* **2.** Something that is misshapen or deformed: *Fish that are exposed to pollution sometimes have deformities.*

defraud (dǐ-frôd′) *tr.v.* **defrauded, defrauding, defrauds** To take something from by fraud; swindle: *defrauded the prospectors by selling them worthless land claims.*

defray (dǐ-frā′) *tr.v.* **defrayed, defraying, defrays** To undertake the payment of (a cost or expense): *Contribu-*

tions will defray the cost of the political campaign.

defrock (dē-frŏk′) *tr.v.* **defrocked, defrocking, defrocks** **1.** To strip of priestly privileges and functions. **2.** To deprive of the right to practice a profession. **3.** To deprive of an honorary position.

defrost (dē-frôst′) *v.* **defrosted, defrosting, defrosts** *—tr.* **1.** To remove ice or frost from: *defrost a windshield.* **2.** To thaw (frozen food): *We need to defrost the frozen burgers.* *—intr.* **1.** To become free of ice or frost: *a refrigerator that defrosts quickly.* **2.** To become thawed: *Has the meat defrosted?*

defroster (dē-frô′stər) *n.* A heating device that removes frost or prevents its formation, as on a car windshield.

deft (děft) *adj.* **defter, deftest** Quick and skillful; adroit: *the deft hands of a magician.* **—deft′ly** *adv.* **—deft′ness** *n.*

defunct (dǐ-fŭngkt′) *adj.* No longer in existence or use; dead: *a defunct business that failed years ago.*

defuse (dē-fyo͞oz′) *tr.v.* **defused, defusing, defuses** **1.** To remove the fuse from (an explosive device): *defused the bomb.* **2.** To make less dangerous, tense, or hostile: *The mediator defused the hostage crisis.*

defy (dǐ-fī′) *tr.v.* **defied, defying, defies** **1.** To resist openly or refuse to comply with: *He defied the court order by leaving the country.* **2.** To be beyond the power of: *That story defies belief.* **3.** To challenge or dare (someone) to do something: *I defy you to find an error in this report.*

deg. An abbreviation of degree.

degeneracy (dǐ-jěn′ər-ə-sē) *n.* The process of degenerating or the state of being degenerate.

degenerate (dǐ-jěn′ər-ĭt) *adj.* **1.** Having declined, as in function or nature, from a former or original state: *a degenerate form of ancient tool-making.* **2.** Having fallen into an inferior or undesirable state, especially in mental or moral qualities. ❖ *n.* A corrupt or depraved person. ❖ *intr.v.* (dǐ-jěn′ə-rāt′) **degenerated, degenerating, degenerates** To deteriorate into an undesirable condition, especially functionally or morally: *The discussion degenerated into a nasty argument.* **—de·gen′er·ate·ly** *adv.* **—de·gen′er·a′tion** (dǐ-jěn′ə-rā′shən) *n.*

deglaciation (dē-glā′shē-ā′shən *or* dē-glā′sē-ā′shən) *n.* The uncovering of land because of the melting of a glacier.

degradable (dǐ-grā′də-bəl) *adj.* Capable of being degraded or decomposed by stages: *degradable plastic.*

degradation (děg′rə-dā′shən) *n.* **1.** The act or process of degrading: *The erosion of rich soil causes the degradation of farmlands.* **2.** The state of being degraded: *the degradation of imprisonment.* **3.** A decline to a lower quality, condition, or level: *Pollution has caused the degradation of our air.*

degrade (dǐ-grād′) *tr.v.* **degraded, degrading, degrades** **1.** To lower in quality or value; make worse or less valuable: *The virus quickly degraded the computer's performance.* **2.** To reduce in grade, rank, or status; demote: *The officer was degraded to private.* **3.** To lower in dignity; dishonor or disgrace: *I refuse to degrade myself by arguing over trivia.*

degree (dǐ-grē′) *n.* **1.** One of a series of steps in a process, course, or progression. **2.** Relative social position or official rank: *An ambassador is a person of high degree.* **3.** Relative amount or extent: *a high degree of accuracy; various degrees of skill in acting.* **4.** A unit of measurement on a temperature scale: *The temperature of water at freezing is 32 degrees Fahrenheit.* **5a.** A unit for measuring an angle or an arc of a circle. One degree is $\frac{1}{360}$ of the circumference of a circle. **b.** This unit used to measure latitude or longitude on the earth's surface. **6a.** In a single algebraic term, the sum of the exponents of all the variables. For example, a^2b is a term of the third degree. **b.** In a polynomial, the degree of the term of highest degree. For example, $x^3 + 2xy + x$ is of the third degree. **7a.** An academic title awarded by a college or university after completion of a required course of study: *a bachelor's degree in chemistry.* **b.** A similar title granted as an honorary distinction: *an honorary degree awarded to the senator.* **8.** In law, classification of a crime according to its seriousness: *Accidental murder is murder in the second degree.* **9.** One of the forms used in the comparison of an adjective or adverb. There are three degrees in English: positive (as in *new*), comparative (as in *newer*), and superlative (as in *newest*). ◆ **by degrees** Little by little; gradually: *improved on the fiddle by degrees.*

degree-day (dĭ-grē′dā′) *n.* A unit used in estimating the amount of fuel or power required for heating buildings. It is equal to the number of degrees by which the average temperature on a given day falls below some standard temperature, usually 65°F (18°C).

dehumanize (dē-hyōō′mə-nīz′) *tr.v.* **dehumanized, dehumanizing, dehumanizes** To deprive of human qualities such as individuality or compassion: *Do you think that computers dehumanize our lives?* —**de·hu′man·i·za′tion** (dē-hyōō′mə-nĭ-zā′shən) *n.*

dehumidify (dē′hyōō-mĭd′ə-fī′) *tr.v.* **dehumidified, dehumidifies** To decrease the humidity of: *An air conditioner dehumidifies the air.* —**de′hu·mid′i·fi′er** *n.*

dehydrate (dē-hī′drāt′) *v.* **dehydrated, dehydrating, dehydrates** —*tr.* **1.** To cause the loss of water or body fluids in: *The hot sun was dehydrating the plants.* **2.** To preserve by removing water from: *dehydrated the vegetables.* —*intr.* To lose water or body fluids: *I started dehydrating toward the end of the race.*

dehydration (dē′hī-drā′shən) *n.* **1.** The act or process of dehydrating. **2.** A condition in which an organism loses a large amount of water.

deice (dē-īs′) *tr.v.* **deiced, deicing, deices** To make or keep free of ice: *deice the wings of an airplane.* —**de·ic′er** *n.*

deification (dē′ə-fĭ-kā′shən *or* dā′ə-fĭ-kā′shən) *n.* **1.** The act or process of deifying: *Deification of a great leader was common in early societies.* **2.** The condition of being deified: *After deification, the queen became the center of the religion.*

deify (dē′ə-fī′ *or* dā′ə-fī′) *tr.v.* **deified, deifying, deifies 1.** To make a god of: *Some religions deify volcanoes and stars.* **2.** To worship or revere as a god: *deify a great leader.*

deign (dān) *v.* **deigned, deigning, deigns** —*intr.* To be willing to do something that one considers beneath one's dignity; condescend: *The speaker deigned to answer the hecklers' questions.* —*tr.* To condescend to give; vouchsafe: *They didn't deign so much as a nod in our direction.*

deism (dē′ĭz′əm *or* dā′ĭz′əm) *n.* A religious belief holding that God created the universe and established moral and natural laws but does not intervene supernaturally in human affairs. —**de′ist** *n.* —**de·is′tic** *adj.*

deity (dē′ĭ-tē *or* dā′ĭ-tē) *n., pl.* **deities 1.** A god or goddess. **2.** The condition or nature of being a god; divinity: *The ancient Romans believed in the deity of Ceres, goddess of the harvest.* **3. Deity** God.

déjà vu (dā′zhä vōō′) *n.* The illusion of having already experienced something that is actually being experienced for the first time.

dejected (dĭ-jĕk′tĭd) *adj.* Being low in spirits; depressed: *The students felt dejected when it was announced that the holiday was canceled.* —**de·ject′ed·ly** *adv.* —**de·ject′ed·ness** *n.* —SEE NOTE AT **inject.**

dejection (dĭ-jĕk′shən) *n.* The condition of being dejected; low spirits: *experienced dejection after hearing the bad news.*

de jure (dē jōōr′ē) *adv. & adj.* According to law; by right.

Delaware (dĕl′ə-wâr′) *n., pl.* **Delaware** or **Delawares 1.** A member of a Native American people formerly living in the Delaware and Hudson River valleys, now living in Oklahoma, Kansas, Wisconsin, and Ontario. **2.** Either of the two Algonquian languages of the Delaware. —**Del′a·war′e·an** *adj.*

delay (dĭ-lā′) *v.* **delayed, delaying, delays** —*tr.* **1.** To put off until a later time; postpone: *We will have to delay dinner an hour.* **2.** To cause to be late or slower than expected or desired: *A traffic jam delayed me in getting home.* —*intr.* To act or move slowly; put off an action or decision. ❖ *n.* **1.** The act of delaying or the condition of being delayed: *Your order will be filled without delay.* **2.** A period of time during which one is delayed: *a delay of 15 minutes waiting for the bus to arrive.* —**de·lay′er** *n.*

delectable (dĭ-lĕk′tə-bəl) *adj.* Greatly pleasing or delicious; enjoyable: *a delectable hot biscuit.*

delegate (dĕl′ĭ-gāt′ *or* dĕl′ĭ-gĭt) *n.* **1.** A person chosen to speak and act for another; a representative or agent: *Delegates to the convention were elected at the meeting.* **2.** A representative of a US territory in the House of Representatives who is entitled to speak but not vote. ❖ *tr.v.* (dĕl′ĭ-gāt′) **delegated, delegating, delegates 1.** To authorize and send (another person) as one's representative: *The director delegated three employees to serve on the committee.* **2.** To give or entrust to another: *delegate responsibility for feeding the animals.*

delegation (dĕl′ĭ-gā′shən) *n.* **1.** The act of delegating: *delegation of power to an attorney.* **2.** The condition of being delegated; appointment. **3.** A person or persons chosen to represent another or others: *Each state sends a delegation to the convention.*

delete (dĭ-lēt′) *tr.v.* **deleted, deleting, deletes 1.** To remove (something) from a document or record: *delete the last sentence of a paragraph.* **2.** To remove (a file, for example) from a hard drive or other storage medium.

deleterious (dĕl′ĭ-tîr′ē-əs) *adj.* Harmful; injurious: *the deleterious effects of smoking.* —**del′e·te′ri·ous·ly** *adv.* —**del′e·te′ri·ous·ness** *n.*

deletion (dĭ-lē′shən) *n.* **1.** The act of deleting. **2.** A part that has been deleted, such as a word or sentence.

delft (dĕlft) *n.* Glazed earthenware of a usually blue-and-white style originally made in the city of Delft in the Netherlands.

deli (dĕl′ē) *n., pl.* **delis** *Informal* A delicatessen.

deliberate (dĭ-lĭb′ər-ĭt) *adj.* **1.** Done or said on purpose; intentional: *a deliberate lie.* **2.** Arising from or marked by careful consideration: *a deliberate choice.* **3.** Slow and careful: *crossed the bridge with deliberate steps.* ❖ *v.* (dĭ-lĭb′ə-rāt′) **deliberated, deliberating, deliberates** —*intr.* **1.** To think carefully and often slowly; reflect: *He deliberated over buying a new car.* **2.** To talk with others in an attempt to reach a decision: *The Senate deliberated throughout the night.* —*tr.* To consider (something) carefully and often slowly: *He deliberated the consequences of his act.* —de·lib'er·ate·ly *adv.*

deliberation (dĭ-lĭb'ə-rā'shən) *n.* **1.** The act or process of deliberating. **2. deliberations** Formal discussion and consideration of all sides of an issue: *The deliberations of Congress are printed in the* Congressional Record. **3.** Thoughtfulness in decision or action: *The mountain climber took each step with deliberation.*

deliberative (dĭ-lĭb'ə-rā'tĭv *or* dĭ-lĭb'ər-ə-tĭv) *adj.* Assembled or organized for deliberation or debate: *A legislature is a deliberative body.*

delicacy (dĕl'ĭ-kə-sē) *n., pl.* **delicacies 1.** The quality of being delicate. **2.** A choice food: *Truffles are considered delicacies.* **3.** Fineness of quality, appearance, construction, or execution: *embroidery of great delicacy.* **4.** Frailty of body or health: *The delicacy of small children makes them subject to many diseases.* **5.** Sensitivity of perception, discrimination, or taste. **6.** Sensitivity to the feelings of others; tact: *phrased the apology with delicacy.* **7.** Sensitivity to or undue concern for what is offensive or improper.

delicate (dĕl'ĭ-kĭt) *adj.* **1.** Very fine in quality or appearance; dainty: *delicate lace.* **2.** Easily broken or damaged; fragile: *a delicate china figurine.* **3.** Frail in health: *The patient is delicate and must get plenty of rest.* **4.** Requiring careful or tactful treatment: *a delicate matter that could embarrass one's friends.* **5.** Fine or soft in touch or skill: *a delicate surgeon.* **6.** Very responsive or sensitive: *a delicate thermometer to measure small variations.* **7.** Pleasing to the senses, especially in a subtle way: *a delicate pink; a delicate flavor.* —del'i·cate·ly *adv.*

delicatessen (dĕl'ĭ-kə-tĕs'ən) *n.* A store that sells cooked or prepared foods ready for serving, such as cheeses, salads, and smoked meats.

delicious (dĭ-lĭsh'əs) *adj.* Very pleasing or agreeable, especially to the senses of taste or smell: *delicious fresh fruit; a delicious supper.* —de·li'cious·ly *adv.* —de·li'cious·ness *n.*

delight (dĭ-līt') *n.* **1.** Great pleasure; joy: *The clown's face beamed with delight.* **2.** Something that gives great pleasure or enjoyment: *The birthday party was a delight to the whole family.* ❖ *v.* **delighted, delighting, delights** —*intr.* To take great pleasure or joy: *Most people delight in going to the zoo.* —*tr.* To please greatly: *Paris cannot fail to delight the visitor.*

delighted (dĭ-lī'tĭd) *adj.* Filled with delight: *The delighted winner waved to the crowd.* —de·light'ed·ly *adv.*

delightful (dĭ-līt'fəl) *adj.* Greatly pleasing: *We had a delightful time at the party.* —de·light'ful·ly *adv.* —de·light'ful·ness *n.*

delimit (dĭ-lĭm'ĭt) *tr.v.* **delimited, delimiting, delimits** To establish the limits or boundaries of: *delimited the line between our property and theirs.*

delineate (dĭ-lĭn'ē-āt') *tr.v.* **delineated, delineating, delineates 1.** To draw or trace the outline of: *delineate the state of California on a map.* **2.** To represent in a picture; depict: *an artist who delineates sunsets in watercolors.* **3.** To state or describe in words or gestures: *The instructions delineate my duties.* **4.** To show the distinguishing characteristics of: *The audition is supposed to delineate the best dancers from the others.* —de·lin'e·a'tion *n.*

delinquency (dĭ-lĭng'kwən-sē) *n., pl.* **delinquencies 1.** Juvenile delinquency. **2.** Failure to do what law or duty requires. **3.** An offense or a misdeed.

delinquent (dĭ-lĭng'kwənt) *adj.* **1.** Failing to do what law or duty requires: *The delinquent owners let their dog run*

free. **2.** Overdue in payment: *a delinquent account.* ❖ *n.* **1.** A juvenile delinquent. **2.** A person who fails to do what law or duty requires. —de·lin'quent·ly *adv.*

delirious (dĭ-lîr'ē-əs) *adj.* **1.** Suffering from or characteristic of delirium: *a delirious patient with a high fever.* **2.** Marked by uncontrolled excitement; ecstatic: *delirious happiness.* —de·lir'i·ous·ly *adv.* —de·lir'i·ous·ness *n.*

delirium (dĭ-lîr'ē-əm) *n., pl.* **deliriums** or **deliria** (dĭ-lîr'ē-ə) **1.** A temporary state of mental confusion and fluctuating consciousness resulting from high fever, intoxication, shock, or other causes. It is characterized by anxiety, disorientation, hallucinations, delusions, and incoherent speech: *a malaria patient experiencing delirium.* **2.** A state of uncontrolled excitement or emotion: *remarked on the fans' delirium after their team won the championship.*

delirium tremens (dĭ-lîr'ē-əm trē'mənz) *n.* An acute, sometimes fatal episode of delirium usually caused by withdrawal or abstinence from alcohol following habitual excessive drinking. It may also occur during an episode of heavy alcohol consumption.

deliver (dĭ-lĭv'ər) *v.* **delivered, delivering, delivers** —*tr.* **1.** To take or carry (something) to the proper place or person: *deliver the mail; deliver a package.* **2.** To surrender (a person or thing); hand over: *deliver a criminal to the authorities.* **3.** To throw or hurl; pitch: *Our pitcher delivers a good fastball.* **4.** To strike (a blow): *The logger delivered a blow of the axe that split the log completely.* **5.** To provide or achieve (something desired or expected): *The senate leader delivered the votes necessary to pass the bill.* **6.** To express in words; utter: *deliver a speech to an audience.* **7a.** To give birth to: *She delivered a baby girl.* **b.** To assist in the birth of: *The midwife delivered the baby.* **8.** To set free, as from captivity, peril, or evil: *deliver a captive from slavery.* —*intr.* **1.** To make deliveries: *Few stores deliver nowadays.* **2.** To provide or achieve what is desired or expected: *The senator delivered on her pledge.* **3.** To give birth. —de·liv'er·er *n.*

deliverance (dĭ-lĭv'ər-əns *or* dĭ-lĭv'rəns) *n.* **1.** The act of delivering or the condition of being delivered. **2.** Rescue from danger or slavery.

delivery (dĭ-lĭv'ə-rē *or* dĭ-lĭv'rē) *n., pl.* **deliveries 1a.** The act of conveying or delivering: *The post office makes deliveries every day but Sunday.* **b.** Something that is delivered: *There is a delivery for you downstairs.* **2.** The act of giving up; surrender: *delivery of a ransom for the king.* **3.** The act or manner of throwing or discharging: *an overhand delivery.* **4.** The act of giving birth: *The woman had a natural delivery of a healthy baby.* **5.** The act or manner of speaking or singing: *The content of his speech was excellent, but his delivery was poor.* **6.** The act of releasing or rescuing: *delivery for all prisoners captured in war.*

dell (dĕl) *n.* A small secluded valley.

Delphic (dĕl'fĭk) *adj.* **1.** Relating to the ancient holy site of Delphi in Greece or to the oracle of Apollo at Delphi: *a Delphic prophecy.* **2.** Obscurely prophetic: *ambiguous Delphic words.*

delphinium (dĕl-fĭn'ē-əm) *n.* A tall garden plant having long clusters of flowers that are usually blue but are sometimes white, purple, or pink.

delta (dĕl'tə) *n.* **1.** The fourth letter of the Greek alphabet, written Δ, δ. In English it is represented as *D, d.* **2.** An object resembling a triangle in shape. **3.** A mass of sand, mud, and earth that accumulates at the mouth of a river, usually shaped like a triangle.

delta wing *n.* A single-wing configuration in the shape of an isosceles triangle used on certain aircraft.

deltoid (dĕl′toid′) *n.* A thick triangular muscle covering the shoulder joint, used to raise the arm from the side. ❖ *adj.* **1.** Triangular. **2.** Relating to the deltoid.

delude (dĭ-loōd′) *tr.v.* **deluded, deluding, deludes** To cause (someone) to hold a false belief; deceive thoroughly: *The fans were deluded into believing the team could win without its best pitcher.*

deluge (dĕl′yoōj *or* dā′loōj) *n.* **1.** A great flood or heavy downpour: *The deluge from spring rains flooded roads for miles around.* **2.** Something that overwhelms as if by a great flood: *a deluge of mail in response to the editorial.* **3. Deluge** In the Bible, the great flood that occurred in the time of Noah. ❖ *tr.v.* **deluged, deluging, deluges 1.** To flood with water. **2.** To inundate with an overwhelming number or amount: *deluged with messages of congratulation.*

delusion (dĭ-loō′zhən) *n.* **1.** The act or process of deluding or the state of being deluded: *the delusion of a swindler's victim.* **2.** A false belief or opinion: *under the delusion that might makes right.*

delusive (dĭ-loō′sĭv) *adj.* Tending to delude; deceptive: *delusive claims about easy cures.* —**de·lu′sive·ly** *adv.*

deluxe also **de luxe** (dĭ-lŭks′ *or* dĭ-loōks′) *adj.* Particularly elegant, luxurious, or elaborate for its kind; of superior quality: *stayed in a deluxe hotel as part of the grand prize; ordered a hamburger deluxe.*

delve (dĕlv) *intr.v.* **delved, delving, delves 1.** To search deeply and laboriously: *delved into the court records.* **2.** To research or make inquiries into something: *scientists delving into promising cancer treatments.* **3.** To enter or move into an area in which movement is difficult: *The explorers delved into the jungle.* —**delv′er** *n.*

Dem. An abbreviation of: **1.** Democrat. **2.** democratic.

demagnetize (dĕ-măg′nĭ-tīz′) *tr.v.* **demagnetized, demagnetizing, demagnetizes 1.** To remove magnetic properties from. **2.** To erase (a magnetic tape or disk).

demagogic (dĕm′ə-gŏj′ĭk) *adj.* Relating to or characteristic of a demagogue: *a demagogic leader.*

demagogue (dĕm′ə-gôg′) *n.* A leader who wins people's favor by appealing to their emotions and prejudices: *The demagogue's speech worked the crowd into a frenzy.*

demagoguery (dĕm′ə-gô′gə-rē) *n.* The practices or emotional style of speech of a demagogue.

demagogy (dĕm′ə-gôj′ē *or* dĕm′ə-gôg′ē) *n.* The character or practices of a demagogue.

demand (dĭ-mănd′) *tr.v.* **demanded, demanding, demands 1.** To ask for urgently or insistently: *She demanded that they leave immediately.* **2.** To claim as just or due: *demand repayment of a loan.* **3.** To require as useful, just, proper, or necessary: *A lawyer's work demands skill and concentration.* ❖ *n.* **1.** The act of demanding. **2.** Something demanded: *striking workers making new wage demands.* **3.** A requirement, need, or claim: *This project has made many demands on my time.* **4.** The state of being sought after: *Firewood is in great demand during winter months.* **5.** A desire or readiness to purchase a certain commodity or service: *a demand for heating oil in the winter.* ❖ **on demand** When needed or asked for: *fed the baby on demand.* —**de·mand′a·ble** *adj.*

demanding (dĭ-măn′dĭng) *adj.* **1.** Requiring much effort or attention: *a very demanding task.* **2.** Requiring others

to work hard or meet high expectations: *a demanding teacher.* —**de·mand′ing·ly** *adv.*

demarcate (dĭ-mär′kāt′ *or* dē′mär-kāt′) *tr.v.* **demarcated, demarcating, demarcates 1.** To set the boundaries of: *A river demarcates the border between the two states.* **2.** To separate clearly as if by boundaries; distinguish: *demarcate categories of art.*

demarcation (dē′mär-kā′shən) *n.* **1.** The setting or marking of boundaries or limits: *the demarcation of fishing rights.* **2.** A separation; a distinction: *There is a fine demarcation between daring and foolishness.*

demean[1] (dĭ-mēn′) *tr.v.* **demeaned, demeaning, demeans** To conduct or behave (oneself) in a particular manner: *The knights demeaned themselves well in battle.*

demean[2] (dĭ-mēn′) *tr.v.* **demeaned, demeaning, demeans** To lower in status or character; degrade or humble: *demean oneself by continually asking for favors.*

WORD HISTORY Demean[1] comes from Middle English *demeinen,* meaning "to behave in a certain way." **Demean**[2] is related to the Modern English word *mean,* in the sense of "inferior."

demeanor (dĭ-mē′nər) *n.* The way in which a person behaves; deportment: *As head librarian, she has a demeanor of quiet authority.*

demented (dĭ-mĕn′tĭd) *adj.* **1.** Having a serious mental disorder; insane. **2.** Suffering from dementia. —**de·ment′ed·ly** *adv.*

dementia (dĭ-mĕn′shə) *n.* A condition in which the ability to think, remember, and understand is impaired as a result of disease.

demerit (dĭ-mĕr′ĭt) *n.* **1.** A quality or characteristic deserving of blame; a fault: *work that has the demerits of sloppiness and inaccuracy.* **2.** A mark against one's record for a fault or misconduct.

Demeter (dĭ-mē′tər) *n.* In Greek mythology, the goddess of the harvest, identified with the Roman Ceres.

demi– A prefix that means partly: *demigod.* —SEE NOTE AT **semi–.**

demigod (dĕm′ē-gŏd′) *n.* A male divine being of lower power or standing than certain other gods, often the offspring of a god and a human.

demigoddess (dĕm′ē-gŏd′ĭs) *n.* A female divine being of lower power or standing than certain other gods, often the offspring of a god and a human.

demijohn (dĕm′ē-jŏn′) *n.* A large bottle with a narrow neck, usually encased in wicker.

demilitarize (dē-mĭl′ĭ-tə-rīz′) *tr.v.* **demilitarized, demilitarizing, demilitarizes** To remove or forbid military troops in (an area): *demilitarized the former war zone.* —**de·mil′i·ta·ri·za′tion** (dē-mĭl′ĭ-tər-ĭ-zā′shən) *n.*

demimonde (dĕm′ē-mŏnd′) *n.* **1a.** A class of women supported by wealthy lovers and considered to be promiscuous or otherwise unrespectable. **b.** Women prostitutes considered as a group. **2.** A group whose respectability is dubious: *the literary demimonde of ghostwriters, hacks, and publicists.*

demise (dĭ-mīz′) *n.* **1.** Death. **2.** The end of existence or activity; termination: *The invasion of the barbarians signaled the demise of the empire.*

demitasse (dĕm′ē-tăs′ *or* dĕm′ē-täs′) *n.* **1.** A small cup of strong black coffee. **2.** The small cup used to serve this drink.

demiurge (dĕm′ē-ûrj′) *n.* **1.** A powerful creative force or personality. **2. Demiurge** A deity in various philosophical and religious traditions such as Platonism and Gnosticism who orders or fashions the material world out of chaos. —**dem′i·ur′gic** (děm′ē-ûr′jĭk) adj.

demo (děm′ō) n., pl. **demos** Informal **1a.** A demonstration, as of a product or service. **b.** A recording that shows the abilities of a musician or other performer. **2.** A product used for demonstration and often sold later at a discount.

demobilize (dē-mō′bə-līz′) tr.v. **demobilized, demobilizing, demobilizes** To discharge from military service or use: *demobilize an artillery unit.* —**de·mo′bi·li·za′tion** (dē-mō′bə-lĭ-zā′shən) n.

democracy (dĭ-mŏk′rə-sē) n., pl. **democracies 1a.** Government by the people, exercised either directly or through representatives. **b.** A political or social unit that has such a government. **2.** The principles of social equality and respect for the individual in a community.

democrat (děm′ə-krăt′) n. **1.** A person who advocates democracy. **2. Democrat** A member of the Democratic Party.

democratic (děm′ə-krăt′ĭk) adj. **1.** Characteristic of or advocating democracy. **2.** Relating to or for the people in general; popular: *a democratic movement.* **3. Democratic** Relating to or characteristic of the Democratic Party. —**dem′o·crat′i·cal·ly** adv.

Democratic Party n. One of the two major political parties of the United States, dating from 1828.

Democratic-Republican Party n. A US political party founded by Thomas Jefferson in 1792 in opposition to the Federalist Party.

democratize (dĭ-mŏk′rə-tīz′) tr.v. **democratized, democratizing, democratizes** To make democratic. —**de·moc′-ra·ti·za′tion** (dĭ-mŏk′rə-tĭ-zā′shən) n.

demographics (děm′ə-grăf′ĭks) n. *(used with a plural verb)* The characteristics of human populations, especially when used to identify consumer markets. —**dem′-o·graph′ic** adj.

demography (dĭ-mŏg′rə-fē) n. The study of the characteristics of human populations, such as growth, density, distribution, and birth and death rates.

demolish (dĭ-mŏl′ĭsh) tr.v. **demolished, demolishing, demolishes 1.** To tear down or break apart the structure of; raze: *demolish an old building.* See Synonyms at **destroy**. **2.** To do away with completely; put an end to: *demolish an argument.*

demolition (děm′ə-lĭsh′ən or dē′mə-lĭsh′ən) n. The act or process of wrecking or destroying, especially by means of explosives.

demon (dē′mən) n. **1.** An evil supernatural being; a devil. **2.** A tormenting person, force, or passion: *He was never able to deal with his demons.* **3.** A person who is very energetic, skillful, or diligent: *was working like a demon.* —**de·mon′ic** (dĭ-mŏn′ĭk) adj.

demoniac (dĭ-mō′nē-ăk′) adj. **1.** Possessed, produced, or influenced by a demon. **2.** Resembling or suggestive of a demon. ❖ n. A person who is or seems to be possessed by a demon. —**de′mo·ni′a·cal·ly** (dē′mə-nī′ə-kə-lē) adv.

demonize (dē′mə-nīz′) tr.v. **demonized, demonizing, demonizes 1.** To represent as evil or diabolical: *wartime propaganda that demonizes the enemy.* **2.** To afflict with a demon. —**de′mon·i·za′tion** (dē′mə-nī-zā′shən) n.

demonstrable (dĭ-mŏn′strə-bəl) adj. Capable of being demonstrated or proved: *a demonstrable truth.*

demonstrate (děm′ən-strāt′) v. **demonstrated, demonstrating, demonstrates** —tr. **1.** To show clearly and delib-

erately; manifest: *She demonstrated her skill as a gymnast.* **2.** To show to be true; prove: *demonstrate one's ability to do the job.* **3a.** To describe or explain by experiment, practical application, or example: *demonstrate the effect of light on plants.* **b.** To show the use of (a product), as to a prospective buyer: *demonstrate a washing machine.* —intr. To take part in a public display of opinion: *demonstrated against the new highway.*

demonstration (děm′ən-strā′shən) n. **1.** The act of showing that something is true or evident: *a demonstration of the medicine's effectiveness.* **2.** An exemplification or explanation of something, carried out in practice: *a demonstration of ballroom dancing.* **3.** A display or outward show, as of one's feelings: *The frown was another demonstration of her displeasure.* **4.** A public display of group opinion, as by a rally or march.

demonstrative (dĭ-mŏn′strə-tĭv) adj. **1.** Serving to manifest or prove: *demonstrative evidence.* **2.** Openly expressing one's feelings, especially affection: *a demonstrative person who hugged everyone at the party.* **3.** In grammar, specifying or singling out the person or thing referred to; for example, the word *these* is a demonstrative pronoun in *These are my books* and a demonstrative adjective in *These books are mine.* ❖ n. A demonstrative pronoun or adjective. —**de·mon′stra·tive·ly** adv. —**de·mon′-stra·tive·ness** n.

demonstrator (děm′ən-strā′tər) n. **1.** A person who demonstrates, such as a participant in a public display of opinion. **2.** An article or product used in a demonstration.

demoralize (dĭ-môr′ə-līz′ or dĭ-mŏr′ə-līz′) tr.v. **demoralized, demoralizing, demoralizes 1.** To weaken the confidence or morale of; dishearten: *Reading the negative reviews of the movie demoralized its director.* **2.** To weaken the morals of; corrupt: *Offers of favors have demoralized many politicians.* —**de·mor′al·i·za′tion** (dĭ-môr′ə-lĭ-zā′shən or dĭ-mŏr′ə-lĭ-zā′shən) n.

demote (dĭ-mōt′) tr.v. **demoted, demoting, demotes** To reduce in rank, grade, or status: *demoted from captain to lieutenant.* —**de·mo′tion** n.

demotic (dĭ-mŏt′ĭk) adj. **1.** Relating to the common people; popular: *demotic speech; demotic entertainments.* **2.** Relating to or written in the simplified form of ancient Egyptian writing. **3. Demotic** Relating to a form of modern Greek based on colloquial use.

demur (dĭ-mûr′) intr.v. **demurred, demurring, demurs** To raise objections; object: *demur at working such late hours.* ❖ n. An objection; a demurral.

demure (dĭ-myŏŏr′) adj. **demurer, demurest** Reserved and modest, as in manner or behavior: *a pleasant and demure person.* —**de·mure′ly** adv. —**de·mure′ness** n.

demurral (dĭ-mûr′əl) n. The act of demurring, especially a mild or polite expression of opposition.

den (děn) n. **1.** The place where a wild animal lives; a lair: *The fox was safe in its den.* **2.** A hidden or secret place where people such as criminals gather: *a den of thieves.* **3.** A room used for relaxation or study.

denature (dē-nā′chər) tr.v. **denatured, denaturing, denatures 1.** To change (alcohol) so that it is unfit for drinking but is still useful for other purposes. **2.** To change the structure of (a protein) so that its biological properties are reduced or eliminated. —**de·na′tur·a′tion** n.

dendrite (děn′drīt′) n. **1.** A branching extension of a nerve cell that receives impulses from other cells and transmits them inward toward the body of the cell. **2.** A mineral that crystallizes in another mineral in the form of a branching pattern.

denial (dĭ-nī′əl) *n.* **1.** A refusal to comply with or satisfy a request. **2.** A refusal to grant the truth of an accusation or allegation: *The charges of corruption prompted an immediate denial from the mayor.* **3.** A rejection of a doctrine or belief: *denial of a new theory of the origin of the universe.*

denier (dĭ-nī′ər) *n.* A person who denies.

denigrate (dĕn′ĭ-grāt′) *tr.v.* **denigrated, denigrating, denigrates** To attack the reputation or character of; speak ill of; defame. —**den′i·gra′tion** *n.*

denim (dĕn′ĭm) *n.* **1.** A coarse, twilled cotton fabric, often blue, traditionally used for overalls and work clothes and now used for jeans and casual wear. **2. denims** Pants or another garment made of this fabric.

denizen (dĕn′ĭ-zən) *n.* A person or animal that lives in a particular place; an inhabitant: *Lions and jackals are denizens of the African plains.*

denominate (dĭ-nŏm′ə-nāt′) *tr.v.* **denominated, denominating, denominates** To give a name to; designate.

denominate number (dĭ-nŏm′ə-nĭt) *n.* A number used with a unit of measure. In the measures 12 lb., 14¢, and 3 feet, 12, 14, and 3 are denominate numbers.

denomination (dĭ-nŏm′ə-nā′shən) *n.* **1.** An organized group of religious congregations under a common faith and name: *People of several denominations met to worship together.* **2.** One of a series of kinds, values, or sizes, as in a system of currency: *bills of different denominations.* **3.** A name, especially for a group or class of things; a designation.

denominational (dĭ-nŏm′ə-nā′shə-nəl) *adj.* Related to or under the control of a religious denomination; sectarian.

denominator (dĭ-nŏm′ə-nā′tər) *n.* The number below the line in a fraction that indicates the number of equal parts into which one whole is divided. For example, in the fraction ⅖, 7 is the denominator.

denotation (dē′nō-tā′shən) *n.* **1.** The act of denoting. The most specific or direct meaning of a word, in contrast to its figurative or associated meanings.

denote (dĭ-nōt′) *tr.v.* **denoted, denoting, denotes 1.** To be a sign of; mark: *The blue areas on the map denote water.* **2.** To signify directly; refer to specifically.

denouement also **dénouement** (dā′nōō-mäN′) *n.* The outcome or resolution of the plot of a drama or novel.

denounce (dĭ-nouns′) *tr.v.* **denounced, denouncing, denounces 1.** To declare openly as being wrong or reprehensible: *The senator denounced the policy as wasteful and foolish.* **2.** To accuse formally; inform against: *denounced the swindler to the police.*

dense (dĕns) *adj.* **denser, densest 1.** Having relatively high density. **2.** Crowded closely together; compact: *a dense population in the city.* **3.** Difficult to penetrate; thick: *a dense forest; a dense fog.* **4.** Difficult to understand because of complexity or obscurity: *a dense novel.* **5.** Slow to comprehend; thickheaded. —**dense′ly** *adv.* —**dense′-ness** *n.*

density (dĕn′sĭ-tē) *n., pl.* **densities 1.** In physics, the mass per unit of volume of a substance: *Lead has a greater density than water.* **2.** The amount of something in a unit or measure of length, area, or volume: *The population density in New York City is greater than in many other cities.* **3.** Thickness of consistency; impenetrability: *The density of the grass made the tiger invisible.* **4.** Stupidity; dullness.

dent (dĕnt) *n.* **1.** A hollow place in a surface, usually caused by pressure or a blow: *a dent in a garbage can.* **2.** *Informal* Meaningful progress; headway: *If we work all day we will make a significant dent in this assignment.* ❖ *v.* **dented, denting, dents** —*tr.* To make a dent in: *When I bumped the guard rail, I dented the car's fender.* —*intr.* To become dented: *Aluminum cans dent easily.*

dental (dĕn′tl) *adj.* **1.** Relating to the teeth: *a dental drill.* **2.** Relating to dentistry: *a dental school.*

dental floss *n.* A thread used to remove food particles and plaque from the teeth.

dental hygienist *n.* A person trained to provide care for the teeth, gums, and mouth, usually working with a dentist.

dentifrice (dĕn′tə-frĭs′) *n.* A powder, paste, or liquid used for cleaning the teeth.

dentin (dĕn′tĭn) or **dentine** (dĕn′tēn′) *n.* The hard, bonelike material that forms most of a tooth and lies beneath the enamel.

dentist (dĕn′tĭst) *n.* A person who is trained and licensed to practice dentistry.

dentistry (dĕn′tĭ-strē) *n.* **1.** The scientific study and treatment of diseases and disorders of the mouth, gums, and teeth. **2.** The practice of this science as a profession.

dentition (dĕn-tĭsh′ən) *n.* The type, number, and arrangement of the teeth of a human or other vertebrate animal: *the different dentitions of cats and guinea pigs.*

denture (dĕn′chər) *n.* **1.** A partial or complete set of artificial teeth for either the upper or lower jaw. **2.** often **dentures** A complete set of removable artificial teeth for both jaws.

denude (dĭ-nōōd′) *tr.v.* **denuded, denuding, denudes** To remove the covering from; make bare: *Cutting down the trees denuded the landscape.*

denunciation (dĭ-nŭn′sē-ā′shən) *n.* **1.** The act or an instance of denouncing, especially a public condemnation: *the editorial's denunciation of government corruption.* **2.** The providing of secret or damaging information about someone to the authorities: *the denunciation of the spy.*

deny (dĭ-nī′) *tr.v.* **denied, denying, denies 1.** To declare to be untrue; contradict: *deny an accusation.* **2.** To refuse to believe; reject. **3.** To refuse to acknowledge; disavow: *deny a friendship.* **4.** To decline to grant or allow: *We could not deny seed to the hungry birds.* **5.** To restrain (oneself), especially from indulgence in pleasures: *I denied myself an extra scoop of ice cream.*

deodorant (dē-ō′dər-ənt) *n.* A preparation used to conceal or suppress odors: *a room deodorant.*

deodorize (dē-ō′də-rīz′) *tr.v.* **deodorized, deodorizing, deodorizes** To conceal or neutralize the odor of or in: *deodorized the carpet.* —**de·o′dor·i·za′tion** (dē-ō′dər-ĭ-zā′shən) *n.* —**de·o′dor·iz′er** *n.*

deoxidize (dē-ŏk′sĭ-dīz′) *tr.v.* **deoxidized, deoxidizing, deoxidizes** To remove oxygen from (a chemical compound). —**de·ox′i·di·za′tion** (dē-ŏk′sĭ-dĭ-zā′shən) *n.* —**de·ox′i·diz′er** *n.*

deoxyribonucleic acid (dē-ŏk′sē-rī′bō-nōō-klē′ĭk) *n.* DNA.

depart (dĭ-pärt′) *intr.v.* **departed, departing, departs 1.** To go away; leave: *departed for work before dawn.* **2.** To vary, as from a regular course; deviate: *depart from our custom of eating out on Saturdays.*

departed (dĭ-pär′tĭd) *adj.* **1.** Bygone or past: *the departed days of vacation.* **2.** Dead; deceased. ❖ *n.* **1.** A dead person. **2.** Dead people considered as a group; the dead.

department (dĭ-pärt′mənt) *n.* **1.** A distinct division of an organization, such as a government, company, or college: *the fire department; the personnel department; the English department.* **2.** A section of a department store selling a particular line of merchandise: *the shoe department.*

departmental (dē′pärt-mĕn′tl) *adj.* **1.** Relating to a department: *a departmental newsletter.* **2.** Separated into departments: *a departmental organization.*

department store *n.* A large store selling many kinds of goods and services and organized in separate departments.

departure (dĭ-pär′chər) *n.* **1.** The act of going away: *Our departure was delayed by a flat tire.* **2.** A deviation or divergence, as from an established rule, plan, or procedure: *Going to bed early was a departure from our usual habit.* **3.** A starting out, as on a trip or a new course of action.

depend (dĭ-pĕnd′) *intr.v.* **depended, depending, depends** **1.** To rely, especially for support or maintenance: *Many people depend on a pension when they retire.* **2.** To place trust or confidence: *You can depend on me to be on time.* **3.** To be determined or influenced: *Our plans depend on the weather.*

dependable (dĭ-pĕn′də-bəl) *adj.* Trustworthy: *a dependable employee who always finishes his work on time.* —de·pend′a·bil′i·ty *n.* —de·pend′a·bly *adv.*

dependence (dĭ-pĕn′dəns) *n.* **1.** The state of being determined, influenced, or controlled by something else: *the dependence of a storekeeper on suppliers.* **2.** The state of being dependent on another for financial support. **3.** The condition of being dependent on a substance such as a drug or a given behavior.

dependency (dĭ-pĕn′dən-sē) *n., pl.* **dependencies** **1.** Dependence. **2.** Something dependent or subordinate. **3.** A minor territory under the jurisdiction of a government.

dependent (dĭ-pĕn′dənt) *adj.* **1.** Determined or influenced by something else: *The outcome is dependent on the voters.* **2.** Subordinate: *a clause dependent on the main clause.* **3.** Relying on or needing the help of another for support: *Plants are dependent upon sunlight.* **4.** Engaging in a behavior, such as drug use or gambling, that one is unable to stop without suffering physical symptoms or psychological distress. ❖ *n.* A person who relies on another, especially for financial support: *My parents have three dependents including me.* —de·pend′ent·ly *adv.*

dependent clause *n.* A subordinate clause.

dependent variable *n.* A mathematical variable whose value is determined by one or more independent variables. For example, in $y = x^2 + 2x$, y is the dependent variable.

depict (dĭ-pĭkt′) *tr.v.* **depicted, depicting, depicts** To represent in words or pictures; describe or show: *a book depicting life in ancient Rome; a painting that depicts a historical event.* —de·pic′tion *n.*

depilatory (dĭ-pĭl′ə-tôr′ē) *adj.* Able to remove hair: *a depilatory lotion.* ❖ *n., pl.* **depilatories** A preparation in the form of a liquid or cream used to remove unwanted body hair.

deplane (dē-plān′) *intr.v.* **deplaned, deplaning, deplanes** To disembark from an airplane.

deplete (dĭ-plēt′) *tr.v.* **depleted, depleting, depletes** To consume or reduce to a very low amount: *This cold snap has depleted our oil supplies.* —de·ple′tion *n.*

deplorable (dĭ-plôr′ə-bəl) *adj.* **1.** Worthy of strong disapproval or reproach: *rude and deplorable behavior.* **2.** Lamentable; woeful: *The kitchen was in a deplorable state*

after we finished cooking. **3.** Wretched; bad: *deplorable run-down housing.* —de·plor′a·bly *adv.*

deplore (dĭ-plôr′) *tr.v.* **deplored, deploring, deplores** **1.** To feel or express strong disapproval of; condemn: *We deplore cruelty to animals.* **2.** To express sorrow or grief over: *The world deplored the loss of the great actor.*

deploy (dĭ-ploi′) *tr. & intr.v.* **deployed, deploying, deploys** **1.** To position or be in position in readiness for combat: *deploy troops for a battle.* **2.** To distribute or be distributed systematically or strategically: *The ships were deployed along the coast to intercept smugglers.* —de·ploy′ment *n.*

depopulate (dē-pŏp′yə-lāt′) *tr.v.* **depopulated, depopulating, depopulates** To sharply reduce the population of: *Severe flooding depopulated much of the lowland region.* —de·pop′u·la′tion *n.*

deport (dĭ-pôrt′) *tr.v.* **deported, deporting, deports** **1.** To expel from a country; banish: *Government authorities deported the spy.* **2.** To behave (oneself) in a certain manner: *Visitors usually deport themselves with quiet respect while in the cathedral.*

deportation (dē′pôr-tā′shən) *n.* The act or an instance of deporting someone.

deportment (dĭ-pôrt′mənt) *n.* A manner of personal conduct; behavior: *an ambassador with a very dignified deportment.*

depose (dĭ-pōz′) *tr.v.* **deposed, deposing, deposes** **1.** To remove from office or power: *The king was deposed because of his misconduct.* **2.** To take a deposition from: *Investigators will depose the witness behind closed doors.*

deposit (dĭ-pŏz′ĭt) *tr.v.* **deposited, depositing, deposits** **1.** To put or set down; place: *Please deposit books returned to the library at the front desk.* **2.** To lay down or leave behind by a natural process: *The flooding river deposited debris in the roads.* **3.** To put (money) in a bank or financial account. **4.** To give as partial payment or security: *The store will hold the computer if we deposit half the cost now.* ❖ *n.* **1.** Something, especially an amount of money, put in a place for safekeeping, such as a bank. **2a.** A partial or initial payment of a cost or debt: *left a deposit on the coat.* **b.** An amount of money given as security for an item acquired for temporary use: *a deposit on a rented lawn mower.* **3a.** A mass, layer, or collection of material left or laid down by a natural process: *Deposits of mud and sticks choked the stream.* **b.** A mass of naturally occurring mineral material: *deposits of coal.* ❖ **on deposit** Placed somewhere for safekeeping: *money on deposit in a bank account.* —de·pos′i·tor (dĭ-pŏz′ĭ-tər) *n.*

deposition (dĕp′ə-zĭsh′ən) *n.* **1.** The act of deposing, as from high office. **2.** The act of depositing, especially the laying down of matter by a natural process: *deposition of rock by a retreating glacier.* **3.** Something deposited; a deposit. **4.** Sworn testimony recorded for use in court at a later date: *The expert's deposition was read to the court.*

depository (dĭ-pŏz′ĭ-tôr′ē) *n., pl.* **depositories** A place where something is deposited, as for storage or safekeeping.

depot (dē′pō *or* dĕp′ō) *n.* **1.** A railroad or bus station. **2.** A warehouse or storehouse: *a trucking depot for freight.* **3.** A place where military equipment and supplies are stored: *an army depot.*

deprave (dĭ-prāv′) *tr.v.* **depraved, depraving, depraves** To make morally bad; corrupt.

depraved (dĭ-prāvd′) *adj.* Morally corrupt; perverted.

depravity (dĭ-prăv′ĭ-tē) *n., pl.* **depravities** **1.** Moral corruption; degradation: *The depravity of the criminals knew no limits.* **2.** A depraved act or condition.

deprecate (dĕp′rĭ-kāt′) *tr.v.* **deprecated, deprecating, deprecates 1.** To speak of as having little value; belittle: *He tends to deprecate his own work and praise the work of others.* **2.** To express disapproval of: *Some people deprecated the mayor's handling of the matter.* —**dep′re·ca′-tion** *n.*

depreciate (dĭ-prē′shē-āt′) *v.* **depreciated, depreciating, depreciates** —*intr.* To become less in price or value: *The longer you own that car the more it will depreciate.* —*tr.* **1.** To reduce the value of the expenditure for (something) in a business's records: *The company depreciates its equipment every year throughout its useful life.* **2.** To think or speak of as being of little worth; belittle. —**de·pre′ci·a′-tor** *n.* —**de·pre′ci·a·to′ry** (dĭ-prē′shə-tôr′ē) *adj.*

depreciation (dĭ-prē′shē-ā′shən) *n.* A decrease or loss in value, as because of wear, age, or market conditions.

depredation (dĕp′rĭ-dā′shən) *n.* **1.** A predatory attack; a raid: *a bear's depredation of our campsite.* **2.** Damage or loss; ravage.

depress (dĭ-prĕs′) *tr.v.* **depressed, depressing, depresses 1.** To lower in spirits; deject: *The sad news depressed everyone.* **2.** To press down: *depress the brake pedal to stop the car.* **3a.** To lessen the activity or force of; weaken: *Widespread layoffs have further depressed the economy.* **b.** To lower prices in (a financial market). —SEE NOTE AT **pressure.**

depressed (dĭ-prĕst′) *adj.* **1.** Low in spirits; sad and dejected: *The news of the accident left me feeling very depressed.* **2.** Suffering from clinical depression. **3.** Sunk below the surrounding region: *the depressed center of a crater.* **4.** Affected by social and economic hardship, as from poverty and unemployment: *a program of aid for depressed areas of the country.*

depressing (dĭ-prĕs′ĭng) *adj.* Causing one to feel sad or despondent: *depressing news.*

depression (dĭ-prĕsh′ən) *n.* **1a.** The condition of feeling sad and despondent: *the players' depression after losing in the playoffs.* **b.** A psychiatric disorder characterized by extreme and persistent sadness, and often feelings of guilt or helplessness, difficulty concentrating, changes in appetite and sleep patterns, and the inability to experience pleasure; clinical depression. **2.** The act of depressing or the state of being depressed: *the depression of typewriter keys.* **3.** An area that is sunk below its surroundings; a hollow: *Depressions in the sidewalk made it hard to walk on.* **4.** A lowering in amount, degree, or position: *a depression in the temperature.* **5a.** A period of drastic decline in an economy: *A depression brings unemployment and hardship to many people.* **b. Depression** The Great Depression.

deprivation (dĕp′rə-vā′shən) *n.* **1.** The act or an instance of depriving; loss. **2.** The condition of being deprived.

deprive (dĭ-prīv′) *tr.v.* **deprived, depriving, deprives 1.** To take something away from; divest: *Revolution deprived the government of its power.* **2.** To prevent from having or enjoying; deny: *Heavy snow deprived the deer of food.*

dept. An abbreviation of department.

depth (dĕpth) *n.* **1.** The quality or condition of being deep. **2.** The measure or distance downward, backward, or inward: *Each lot reaches to a depth of about 300 feet from the street.* **3.** often **depths** A deep part or place: *the ocean depths.* **4.** The severest or worst part: *in the depth*

of despair. **5.** Intellectual complexity or penetration; profundity: *He wrote poetry and plays of unusual depth.* **6.** Lowness of pitch, as of a voice or a musical tone. **7.** Complete detail; thoroughness: *an interview conducted in great depth.*

depth charge *n.* An explosive charge designed for use underwater, especially one launched from a ship's deck for use against submarines.

depth perception *n.* The ability to see spatial relationships, especially distances between objects, in three dimensions.

deputation (dĕp′yə-tā′shən) *n.* A person or group appointed to act for others; a delegation: *A deputation of staff members urged officials to improve conditions at the hospital.*

depute (dĭ-pyōot′) *tr.v.* **deputed, deputing, deputes** To appoint as an agent or representative: *The president deputes ambassadors to foreign countries.*

deputize (dĕp′yə-tīz′) *tr. & intr.v.* **deputized, deputizing, deputizes** To appoint or serve as a deputy.

deputy (dĕp′yə-tē) *n., pl.* **deputies** A person appointed or empowered to act in place of or for another: *The health officer has several deputies to help enforce environmental laws.*

derail (dē-rāl′) *intr. & tr.v.* **derailed, derailing, derails** To go off or cause to go off the tracks: *The train derailed near Buffalo. A fallen tree on the tracks derailed the express.* —**de·rail′ment** *n.*

derailleur (dĭ-rā′lər) *n.* A mechanism on a bicycle that moves the pedal chain from one gearwheel to another.

derange (dĭ-rānj′) *tr.v.* **deranged, deranging, deranges 1.** To cause (someone) to become mentally unbalanced or unsound. **2.** To upset the arrangement, functioning, or order of: *a chemical that deranges the functioning of the heart.* —**de·range′ment** *n.*

deranged (dĭ-rānjd′) *adj.* **1.** Mentally unbalanced or unsound. **2.** Not ordered or functioning properly.

derby (dûr′bē) *n., pl.* **derbies 1.** Any of various annual horse races usually restricted to three-year-old horses. **2.** A formal race usually allowing anyone to enter: *a motorcycle derby.* **3.** A stiff felt hat with a round crown and a narrow curved brim.

derelict (dĕr′ə-lĭkt′) *adj.* **1.** Neglectful; remiss: *derelict in one's duty.* **2.** Deserted by an owner; abandoned: *a derelict building crumbling with the years.* ❖ *n.* **1.** A homeless or jobless person. **2.** Abandoned property, especially a ship abandoned at sea.

dereliction (dĕr′ə-lĭk′shən) *n.* Willful neglect, as of duty or principle.

deride (dĭ-rīd′) *tr.v.* **derided, deriding, derides** To laugh at, speak of, or write about with contempt or scorn; scoff at or mock: *derided the idea as foolish.*

de rigueur (də rē-gœr′) *adj.* Required by fashion or custom; socially obligatory.

derision (dĭ-rĭzh′ən) *n.* The act of ridiculing or laughing at someone or something.

derisive (dĭ-rī′sĭv) *adj.* Expressing ridicule; mocking: *Talk of the plan was silenced by derisive laughter.* —**de·ri′-sive·ly** *adv.*

derivation (dĕr′ə-vā′shən) *n.* **1.** The act or process of deriving. **2.** Something that is derived; a derivative. **3.** The source from which something is derived; origin: *The polka is a dance of eastern European derivation.* **4.** The historical origin and development of a word; an etymology. **5.** The process by which words are formed from existing words or bases, chiefly by the addition of prefixes or suffixes or by changing the form of the word or base.

derivative (dĭ-rĭv′ə-tĭv) *adj.* Resulting from or using derivation: *English has many derivative words.* ❖ *n.* **1.** Something derived: *Gasoline is a derivative of oil.* **2.** A word formed from another by derivation, such as *electricity* from *electric.*

derive (dĭ-rīv′) *v.* **derived, deriving, derives** —*tr.* **1.** To obtain or receive from a source: *derive pleasure from music.* **2.** To demonstrate the origin or development of (a word). —*intr.* To issue from a source; originate: *Rock music derives in part from blues.*

dermal (dûr′məl) *adj.* Relating to the skin.

dermatitis (dûr′mə-tī′tĭs) *n.* Inflammation of the skin.

dermatology (dûr′mə-tŏl′ə-jē) *n.* The branch of medicine that deals with the diagnosis and treatment of diseases and disorders of the skin. —**der′ma·tol′o·gist** *n.*

dermis (dûr′mĭs) *n.* The layer of skin beneath the epidermis, containing nerve endings and blood vessels.

derogate (dĕr′ə-gāt′) *v.* **derogated, derogating, derogates** —*intr.* To detract; take away: *Cheating will derogate from one's reputation.* —*tr.* To belittle; disparage: *The critic derogated the book.* —**der′o·ga′tion** *n.*

derogatory (dĭ-rŏg′ə-tôr′ē) *adj.* Tending to detract or make seem inferior; disparaging: *a derogatory remark.* —**de·rog′a·to′ri·ly** *adv.*

derrick (dĕr′ĭk) *n.* **1.** A machine for lifting and moving heavy objects. It consists of a movable boom that is equipped with pulleys and cables and is connected to the base of a stationary vertical beam. **2.** A tall framework that supports the equipment used in drilling an oil well or a similar hole.

derrière also **derriere** (dĕr′ē-âr′) *n.* The buttocks; the rear.

derring-do (dĕr′ĭng-dōō′) *n.* Daring or reckless action: *an acrobat of derring-do.*

derringer (dĕr′ĭn-jər) *n.* A small pistol with a short barrel and a large bore.

dervish (dûr′vĭsh) *n.* A member of any of various Muslim religious orders that practice self-denial and poverty. Some engage in chanting and whirling dances as acts of ecstatic devotion.

desalination (dē-săl′ə-nā′shən) or **desalinazation** (dē-săl′ə-nĭ-zā′shən) *n.* The removal of salt from something, such as seawater or soil. —**de·sal′i·nate′** (dē-săl′ə-nāt′) *v.*

descant (dĕs′kănt) *n.* An ornamental melody played or sung above a theme. ❖ *intr.v.* (dĕs′kănt′ or dĕ-skănt′) **descanted, descanting, descants** To talk at length; discourse: *descant on modern science.*

descend (dĭ-sĕnd′) *v.* **descended, descending, descends** —*intr.* **1.** To move from a higher to a lower place; go or come down: *The airplane descended for a landing.* **2.** To slope or incline downward: *The path descended along the side of the cliff.* **3.** To come from an ancestor or ancestry: *Our neighbor descends from New England settlers.* **4.** To pass by inheritance: *The farm descended through several generations to its present owner.* **5.** To lower oneself; stoop: *Both candidates chose not to descend to the level of personal accusations.* **6.** To arrive or attack suddenly or with overwhelming effect: *Our relatives descended on us this weekend.* —*tr.* To move from a higher to a lower part of; go down: *We descended a fire escape.*

descendant (dĭ-sĕn′dənt) *n.* A person or animal descended from specified ancestors.

descent (dĭ-sĕnt′) *n.* **1.** The act or an instance of descend-

ing: *the descent from the mountain.* **2.** A downward incline or slope: *Rocks and mud slid down the steep descent.* **3.** Hereditary derivation; lineage: *Many Americans are of a mixed descent.* **4.** A sudden visit or attack; an onslaught: *The descent of the children on the candy store sent the cashier running.*

describe (dĭ-skrīb′) *tr.v.* **described, describing, describes** **1.** To give an account of in words; tell or write about: *a newspaper report describing the fire; an oral report describing one's experiences.* **2.** To convey an impression of; characterize: *described him as gentle and kind.* **3.** To trace or draw: *Describe a circle with your compass.* —**de·scrib′-a·ble** *adj.*

description (dĭ-skrĭp′shən) *n.* **1.** The act or process of describing: *The writer is so good at description that the characters seem real.* **2.** An account or a statement describing something: *The newspaper carried a description of the plane crash.* **3.** A kind or variety; a sort: *The zoo has animals of every description.*

descriptive (dĭ-skrĭp′tĭv) *adj.* Involving or characterized by description; serving to describe: *descriptive words; a descriptive passage in a guidebook.* —**de·scrip′tive·ly** *adv.* —**de·scrip′tive·ness** *n.*

descry (dĭ-skrī′) *tr.v.* **descried, descrying, descries** To catch sight of (something difficult to see): *descry a ship through the mist.*

desecrate (dĕs′ĭ-krāt′) *tr.v.* **desecrated, desecrating, desecrates** To violate the sacredness of; profane. —**des′-e·crat′er** *n.* —**des′e·cra′tion** *n.*

desegregate (dē-sĕg′rĭ-gāt′) *tr.v.* **desegregated, desegregating, desegregates** To abolish racial segregation in (a school or workplace, for example). —**de·seg′re·ga′-tion** *n.*

desert¹ (dĕz′ərt) *n.* **1.** A dry region that has little or no vegetation. Deserts occur in hot climates, as in western Australia, and also in cold climates, as in Antarctica. **2.** An empty or forsaken place; a wasteland: *a cultural desert.* ❖ *adj.* **1.** Relating to, characteristic of, or inhabiting a desert: *desert conditions; desert plants.* **2.** Uninhabited: *a desert island.*

desert² (dĭ-zûrt′) *n.* often **deserts** Something deserved or merited, especially a punishment: *After conviction the thieves received their just deserts.*

desert³ (dĭ-zûrt′) *v.* **deserted, deserting, deserts** —*tr.* **1.** To leave empty or alone; abandon: *Miners deserted the valley after the ore ran out.* **2.** To abandon (a military post, for example) in violation of orders or an oath: *The soldiers deserted their posts just before the attack.* —*intr.* To forsake one's duty or post, especially without intending to return. —**de·sert′er** *n.*

WORD HISTORY Desert¹ comes from Middle English *desert,* which comes from Latin *dēsertum* (both referring to the same geographical feature as in Modern English), which comes from Latin *dēserere,* meaning "to abandon." **Desert²** comes from Middle English *desert,* which comes from Old French *deserte* (meaning "something deserved"), which comes from Old French *deservir,* meaning "to deserve." **Desert³** comes from French *déserter,* which comes from Latin *dēserere,* both meaning "to abandon."

deserted (dĭ-zûr′tĭd) *adj.* **1.** No longer occupied or used; abandoned: *a deserted sentry post.* **2.** Uninhabited: *a deserted island.*

desertion (dĭ-zûr′shən) *n.* **1.** The act or an instance of deserting: *Desertion from the military is considered a serious offense.* **2.** The state of being deserted.

deserve (dĭ-zûrv′) *tr.v.* **deserved, deserving, deserves** To be worthy of; merit: *The rescuers deserved a reward for their courageous act.*

deserved (dĭ-zûrvd′) *adj.* Merited or earned: *a richly deserved reward.* —**de·serv′ed·ly** (dĭ-zûr′vĭd-lē) *adv.*

deserving (dĭ-zûr′vĭng) *adj.* Worthy, as of aid, reward, or praise: *Scholarships are available for deserving students.*

deshabille (dĕs′ə-bēl′ *or* dĕs′ə-bē′) *n.* Variant of **dishabille.**

desiccate (dĕs′ĭ-kāt′) *tr.v.* **desiccated, desiccating, desiccates** To dry out thoroughly: *A long period of drought desiccated most of the farmland.*

desideratum (dĭ-sĭd′ə-rä′təm *or* dĭ-sĭd′ə-rä′təm) *n., pl.* **desiderata** (dĭ-sĭd′ə-rä′tə *or* dĭ-sĭd′ə-rä′tə) Something considered necessary or highly desirable.

design (dĭ-zīn′) *tr.v.* **designed, designing, designs** **1.** To conceive in the mind or make a plan for: *designed an interesting plot for the novel.* **2.** To make a sketch or drawing for: *design a building; design dresses.* **3.** To create or intend for a specific purpose: *This room was designed as a workshop.* ❖ *n.* **1.** A plan, drawing, or sketch, especially a detailed plan showing how something is to be made: *She drew up designs for the new gym.* **2.** The art of creating designs by making patterns, drawings, or sketches: *Engineers and architects are students of design.* **3.** An ornamental pattern: *a design on wallpaper.* **4.** A purpose or intention: *We left early by design to meet the train.* **5.** often **designs** A secretive plan or scheme: *The movie's main character fears that the new student has designs on her boyfriend.*

designate (dĕz′ĭg-nāt′) *tr.v.* **designated, designating, designates** **1.** To indicate or specify; point out: *The fence designates the boundary of our property.* **2.** To give a name or title to; characterize: *a period of history designated as the Space Age.* **3.** To select and set aside for a duty, office, or purpose; appoint: *We designated two delegates to represent us at the meeting.*

designated driver (dĕz′ĭg-nā′tĭd) *n.* A person who agrees to remain sober, as at a party, in order to be able to drive others home safely.

designated hitter *n.* In baseball, a player designated at the start of a game to bat instead of the pitcher in the lineup.

designation (dĕz′ĭg-nā′shən) *n.* **1.** The act of designating; a marking or pointing out: *The designation of the trail is clearly shown on the map.* **2.** Appointment or selection, as for a duty or office. **3.** An identifying name or title: *The designation of the head of a fire department is "Chief."*

designer (dĭ-zī′nər) *n.* A person who produces designs: *a book designer; a dress designer.*

designing (dĭ-zī′nĭng) *adj.* **1.** Conniving; crafty: *fooled by a designing partner.* **2.** Showing or using forethought.

desirable (dĭ-zīr′ə-bəl) *adj.* Worth wanting, seeking, or doing; good: *a desirable neighborhood; desirable changes in the law.* —**de·sir′a·bil′i·ty, de·sir′a·ble·ness** *n.* —**de·sir′a·bly** *adv.*

desire (dĭ-zīr′) *tr.v.* **desired, desiring, desires** To wish or long for; want; crave: *The puppy seemed to desire only attention. After I graduate from college, I desire to go to medical school.* ❖ *n.* **1.** A wish or longing: *She had a lifelong desire to fly airplanes.* **2.** A request or petition: *The citizens made their desires known to the mayor.* **3.** The object of longing: *My desire is a trip to Mexico.*

✦ SYNONYMS desire, crave, want, wish *v.*

desirous (dĭ-zīr′əs) *adj.* Having or showing desire; desiring: *desirous of a vacation.*

desist (dĭ-sĭst′ *or* dĭ-zĭst′) *intr.v.* **desisted, desisting, desists** To cease doing something: *Please desist from interrupting others.*

desk (dĕsk) *n.* **1.** A piece of furniture usually having a flat top for writing and often drawers or compartments. **2.** A table, counter, or booth at which a service is offered: *an information desk; a reservation desk.* **3.** A department of an organization in charge of a specific operation: *The shipping desk keeps track of all mail.*

desktop (dĕsk′tŏp′) *n.* **1.** The top of a desk. **2.** The area of a computer screen where windows, icons, and other graphical items appear.

desktop publishing *n.* The design and production of publications, such as newsletters and brochures, using personal computers with graphics capability.

desolate (dĕs′ə-lĭt) *adj.* **1.** Having few or no people, and often causing sadness as a result; deserted: *walked on the desolate moor.* **2.** Feeling or showing sadness or loneliness: *He was desolate when his marriage fell apart.* ❖ *tr.v.* (dĕs′ə-lāt′) **desolated, desolating, desolates** **1.** To rid or deprive of people or other forms of life: *A fire desolated the forest.* **2.** To make lonely, forlorn, or wretched: *The loss of our old dog desolated us.* —**des′o·late·ly** *adv.*

desolation (dĕs′ə-lā′shən) *n.* **1.** The state of being without people or other forms of life: *The drought brought desolation to the region.* **2.** Loneliness or sadness: *the desolation of being all alone in a foreign land.*

despair (dĭ-spâr′) *intr.v.* **despaired, despairing, despairs** To lose all hope: *despaired of finding the train.* ❖ *n.* **1.** Utter lack of hope: *gave up in despair as their supplies began to run out.* **2.** A person or thing despaired of or causing despair: *The leaky boat was the despair of the crew.*

despairing (dĭ-spâr′ĭng) *adj.* Marked by or resulting from despair: *despairing glances.* —**de·spair′ing·ly** *adv.*

desperado (dĕs′pə-rä′dō) *n., pl.* **desperadoes** or **desperados** A desperate or bold outlaw.

desperate (dĕs′pər-ĭt) *adj.* **1.** Having lost all hope; despairing. **2.** Willing to do or try anything as the result of an utter lack of hope: *desperate owners looking for their dog.* **3.** Marked by, arising from, or showing despair: *a desperate look.* **4.** Undertaken as a last resort: *desperate measures to save the business from failure.* **5.** Nearly hopeless; critical: *a desperate illness.* **6.** Suffering or driven by a great need for something: *desperate for medical attention.* **7.** Extremely intense: *in desperate need.* —**des′per·ate·ly** *adv.*

desperation (dĕs′pə-rā′shən) *n.* **1.** The condition of being desperate. **2.** Recklessness resulting from despair.

despicable (dĭ-spĭk′ə-bəl *or* dĕs′pĭ-kə-bəl) *adj.* Deserving contempt or scorn; hateful. —**de·spic′a·ble·ness** *n.* —**de·spic′a·bly** *adv.*

despise (dĭ-spīz′) *tr.v.* **despised, despising, despises** **1.** To regard with contempt or scorn: *Everyone despises a traitor.* **2.** To dislike intensely; loathe.

despite (dĭ-spīt′) *prep.* In spite of; notwithstanding: *The movie did well despite the bad reviews.*

despoil (dĭ-spoil′) *tr.v.* **despoiled, despoiling, despoils** To deprive of something valuable, especially by force; rob: *The pirates despoiled the coastal town.* —**de·spoil′er** *n.* —**de·spo′li·a′tion** (dĭ-spō′lē-ā′shən) *n.*

despondent (dĭ-spŏn′dənt) *adj.* Feeling depression of spirits from loss of hope, confidence, or courage; dejected: *became despondent during his long absence from* *home.* **—de·spon′dence, de·spon′den·cy** *n.* **—de·spon′-dent·ly** *adv.*

despot (dĕs′pət) *n.* **1.** A ruler with absolute power. **2.** A person who wields power oppressively; a tyrant.

despotic (dĭ-spŏt′ĭk) *adj.* Ruling with absolute power; tyrannical: *a despotic government.* **—des·pot′i·cal·ly** *adv.*

despotism (dĕs′pə-tĭz′əm) *n.* **1.** Rule by a despot or by someone acting like a despot. **2.** The actions of a despot; tyranny: *the despotism of a dictator.* **3.** A government in which a ruler holds absolute power.

dessert (dĭ-zûrt′) *n.* The last course of a meal, usually consisting of a sweet dish such as fruit, ice cream, or pastry.

destabilize (dē-stā′bə-līz′) *tr.v.* **destabilized, destabilizing, destabilizes 1.** To upset the stability or smooth functioning of: *The rising temperature of the ocean currents has destabilized the region's weather.* **2.** To undermine the power of (a government or leader) by subversive or terrorist acts.

destination (dĕs′tə-nā′shən) *n.* The place to which a person or thing is going or is sent: *The destination of that package is written on the label.*

destine (dĕs′tĭn) *tr.v.* **destined, destining, destines 1.** To determine beforehand; preordain: *a movie destined to become a classic.* **2.** To set aside for a specific use or purpose: *land destined to be a park.*

destiny (dĕs′tə-nē) *n.,* *pl.* **destinies 1.** The fortune, fate, or lot of a particular person or thing, considered as something inevitable or necessary: *Her destiny was to become a playwright.* **2.** The power believed to determine events in advance: *events shaped by destiny.*

destitute (dĕs′tĭ-tōōt′) *adj.* **1.** Being without food, shelter, or other basic necessities; completely impoverished. **2.** Having none; void: *a barren land destitute of trees.*

destitution (dĕs′tĭ-tōō′shən) *n.* The state of not having basic necessities like food and shelter; extreme poverty.

destroy (dĭ-stroi′) *tr.v.* **destroyed, destroying, destroys 1.** To break apart or cause to become unusable, as from damage; ruin completely: *The explosion destroyed several homes.* **2.** To put an end to; eliminate: *Hostile action destroyed all hope of a peaceful settlement.* **3.** To put to death; kill: *The rabid raccoon had to be destroyed.* **4.** To cause emotional trauma to; devastate: *The setback destroyed him.*

✦ **SYNONYMS destroy, demolish, raze, ruin, wreck** *v.*

destroyer (dĭ-stroi′ər) *n.* **1.** A person or thing that destroys. **2.** A small, fast, highly maneuverable warship armed with missiles, guns, torpedoes, and depth charges.

destructible (dĭ-strŭk′tə-bəl) *adj.* Breakable or easily destroyed.

destruction (dĭ-strŭk′shən) *n.* **1.** The act of destroying: *Destruction of the old house was completed in two days.* **2.** The condition of having been destroyed; ruin: *The tornado caused great destruction.* **3.** The cause or means of destroying: *A bitter argument almost proved the destruction of the relationship.*

destructive (dĭ-strŭk′tĭv) *adj.* **1.** Causing destruction; ruinous: *The coastal residents sought shelter from the destructive storm.* **2.** Designed or intending to disprove or discredit: *Destructive criticism does not offer helpful recommendations.* **—de·struc′tive·ly** *adv.* **—de·struc′-tive·ness** *n.*

destructive distillation *n.* A process by which substances such as wood and coal are heated in the absence of air and broken down to produce useful products such as coke, charcoal, and gases.

desuetude (dĕs′wĭ-tōōd′) *n.* A state of disuse or inactivity.

desultory (dĕs′əl-tôr′ē *or* dĕz′əl-tôr′ē) *adj.* Moving or jumping from one thing to another; disconnected: *The speaker talked in a desultory manner, skipping from topic to topic.* **—des′ul·to′ri·ly** *adv.* **—des′ul·to′ri·ness** *n.*

detach (dĭ-tăch′) *tr.v.* **detached, detaching, detaches 1.** To separate or unfasten; disconnect: *detach the trailer from the car; detach a plug from a wall socket.* **2.** To send (troops or ships, for example) on a special mission; assign: *detach a ship to take up patrol.*

detachable (dĭ-tăch′ə-bəl) *adj.* Capable of being detached: *The raincoat has a detachable hood.*

detached (dĭ-tăcht′) *adj.* **1.** Standing apart; disconnected; separate: *a house with a detached garage.* **2.** Marked by an absence of emotional involvement; impartial: *a detached view of this problem.*

detachment (dĭ-tăch′mənt) *n.* **1.** The act or process of separating or disconnecting. **2.** Indifference to or remoteness from the concerns of others; aloofness: *attended to various duties with a bored detachment.* **3.** Absence of prejudice or bias: *A judge must consider legal matters with detachment.* **4.** The dispatch of a military unit for a special duty or mission.

detail (dĭ-tāl′ *or* dē′tāl′) *n.* **1.** An individual part or item; a particular: *The story has many details about life on a schooner.* **2.** Particulars considered individually and in relation to a whole: *Scientific investigation is concerned with detail.* **3.** A minor or unimportant item or aspect: *Several lawyers are studying the details of the case.* **4a.** A small group assigned to a special duty, usually a fatigue duty. **b.** The duty assigned: *We have cleanup detail all week.* ✦ *tr.v.* (dĭ-tāl′) **detailed, detailing, details 1.** To report or relate minutely or in particulars: *The chief detailed the fire to the reporters.* **2.** To assign to a special duty: *The highway department detailed extra plows to clear the snow.* ◆ **in detail** With attention to particulars; minutely: *The planning board examined the design of the new park in detail.*

detailed (dĭ-tāld′ *or* dē′tāld′) *adj.* Marked by abundant use of detail or thoroughness of treatment: *a detailed drawing; a detailed study of the legal evidence.*

detain (dĭ-tān′) *tr.v.* **detained, detaining, detains 1.** To keep from going on; delay: *Friends detained me awhile at lunch.* **2.** To keep in custody; confine temporarily: *Police detained several suspects overnight.* **—de·tain′ment** *n.*

detect (dĭ-tĕkt′) *tr.v.* **detected, detecting, detects** To discover or determine the existence, presence, or fact of: *detect the smell of smoke; detect errors in a report.* **—de·tect′a·ble, de·tect′i·ble** *adj.*

detection (dĭ-tĕk′shən) *n.* The act or process of detecting; discovery: *the detection of cracks in a vase.*

detective (dĭ-tĕk′tĭv) *n.* A police officer or private investigator who investigates crimes and obtains evidence or information. ✦ *adj.* **1.** Relating to detectives or their work: *a detective story.* **2.** Suited for or used in detection: *detective methods.*

detector (dĭ-tĕk′tər) *n.* A person or thing that detects, especially a mechanical, chemical, or electrical device that indicates the presence of a particular substance or agent: *a smoke detector.*

détente (dā-tänt′) *n.* A relaxation or lessening of tensions between nations: *A policy of détente has increased trade.*

detention (dĭ-tĕn′shən) *n.* **1.** The act of detaining someone: *detention of the suspect by the police at the station.* **2.**

The state or a period of being detained in custody while awaiting trial or for other reasons: *The accused thief was held in detention.* **3.** Punishment requiring a student to stay in school after regular hours.

deter (dĭ-tûr′) *tr.v.* **deterred, deterring, deters 1.** To prevent or discourage from doing something, as by means of fear: *The threat of rain deterred us from picnicking.* **2.** To make less likely or prevent from happening: *installed surveillance cameras to deter vandalism.* —**de·ter′ment** *n.*

detergent (dĭ-tûr′jənt) *n.* A cleaning agent that increases the ability of water to penetrate fabric and to break down oils and fats. ❖ *adj.* Having cleansing power: *a detergent soap.*

deteriorate (dĭ-tîr′ē-ə-rāt′) *intr.v.* **deteriorated, deteriorating, deteriorates** To become inferior in quality, character, or value; worsen: *The neglected buildings are deteriorating. The state's financial situation is deteriorating.* —**de·te′ri·o·ra′tion** *n.*

determinant (dĭ-tûr′mə-nənt) *adj.* Tending, able, or serving to determine: *a determinant factor in one's thinking.* ❖ *n.* An influencing or determining factor: *A vote is the basic determinant of a democratic government.*

determination (dĭ-tûr′mə-nā′shən) *n.* **1.** Firmness of purpose; resolve: *The determination of the team helped them to win.* **2.** The act of finding out the quality, quantity, position, or character of something: *the determination of the ship's longitude.* **3.** The act or process of making a decision: *After long determination, the judges chose a winner.* **4.** A decision reached: *My determination was to buy a new car.*

determine (dĭ-tûr′mĭn) *tr.v.* **determined, determining, determines 1.** To figure out or establish definitely, as after consideration or investigation: *We determined how much paint we needed for the bedroom.* **2.** To make decisions about; devise or control: *The school board determines athletic policy.* **3.** To be the cause of or be the key factor in: *Climate determines how people in different parts of the world live.*

determined (dĭ-tûr′mĭnd) *adj.* Marked by or showing determination: *a determined leader; a determined effort.* —**de·ter′mined·ly** *adv.*

determiner (dĭ-tûr′mə-nər) *n.* A word belonging to a class of noun modifiers that includes articles, demonstratives, possessive adjectives, and other words such as *any, both,* and *whose.*

determinism (dĭ-tûr′mə-nĭz′əm) *n.* The philosophical doctrine that every state of affairs, including every human event, act, and decision, is the inevitable consequence of past states of affairs. —**de·ter′min·ist** *n.* —**de·ter′min·is′tic** *adj.* —**de·ter′min·is′ti·cal·ly** *adv.*

deterrence (dĭ-tûr′əns) *n.* The act or a means of deterring: *The fence around the yard served as a deterrence to dogs.*

deterrent (dĭ-tûr′ənt) *adj.* Tending to deter. ❖ *n.* A person or thing that deters: *The supervisor's lack of interest was a deterrent to the rest of us to work hard.*

detest (dĭ-tĕst′) *tr.v.* **detested, detesting, detests** To dislike strongly; abhor: *Many people detest snakes.*

detestable (dĭ-tĕs′tə-bəl) *adj.* Inspiring or deserving hatred or scorn: *Lying is a detestable habit.* —**de·test′a·ble·ness** *n.* —**de·test′a·bly** *adv.*

detestation (dē′tĕ-stā′shən) *n.* Strong dislike or hatred: *detestation of prejudice.*

dethrone (dē-thrōn′) *tr.v.* **dethroned, dethroning, dethrones 1.** To remove from the throne; depose. **2.** To remove from a position of power or prominence. —**de·throne′ment** *n.*

detonate (dĕt′n-āt′) *intr. & tr.v.* **detonated, detonating, detonates** To explode or cause to explode: *The explosives detonated in sequence. The miners detonated a charge of explosives.*

detonation (dĕt′n-ā′shən) *n.* **1.** The act of exploding. **2.** An explosion.

detonator (dĕt′n-ā′tər) *n.* A device used to set off an explosive charge.

detour (dē′tŏor′ *or* dĭ-tŏor′) *n.* **1.** A road used temporarily instead of a main route. **2.** A roundabout way or course. ❖ *intr. & tr.v.* **detoured, detouring, detours** To go or cause to go by a roundabout way: *Police detoured traffic because of heavy flooding.*

detox (dē-tŏks′) *Informal tr.v.* **detoxed, detoxing, detoxes** To subject to detoxification. ❖ *n.* (dē′tŏks′) **1.** A section of a hospital or clinic in which patients are detoxified. **2.** A course of treatment involving detoxification.

detoxification (dē-tŏk′sə-fĭ-kā′shən) *n.* The act or process of counteracting or removing poison or other harmful substances: *Some dumps need detoxification.*

detoxify (dē-tŏk′sə-fī′) *tr.v.* **detoxified, detoxifying, detoxifies 1.** To counteract or destroy the toxic properties of. **2.** To remove poison or other harmful substances from.

detract (dĭ-trăkt′) *v.* **detracted, detracting, detracts** —*tr.* To draw or take away; divert: *The controversy over the candidates' personal remarks detracted attention from the serious issues.* —*intr.* To reduce the value, importance, or quality of something: *Drab curtains detract from the beauty of the room.* —**de·trac′tion** *n.* —**de·trac′tor** *n.*

WORD BUILDING The word root *tract*– in English words comes from the past participle *tractus* of the Latin verb *trahere,* "to pull, drag, draw." Thus **detract** literally means "to drag down" (using the prefix *dē*–, "down"); **extract** means "to pull out" (*ex*–, "out, out of"); **protract** means "to drag forward" (*prō*–, "forward, in front"); **attract** is literally "to draw toward" (*at*–, a form of *ad*–, "to, toward"); and **retract** means "to draw back" (*re*–, "back"). **Tractor** and **traction** come from Latin words meaning "puller" and "pulling."

detriment (dĕt′rə-mənt) *n.* **1.** Damage, harm, or loss: *contended that costs could be cut without detriment to patient care.* **2.** Something that causes damage, harm, or loss: *Oil spills are a serious detriment to coastal wildlife.*

detrimental (dĕt′rə-mĕn′tl) *adj.* Causing damage or harm; injurious: *Being overweight is detrimental to one's health.* —**det′ri·men′tal·ly** *adv.*

detritus (dĭ-trī′təs) *n.* Loose fragments, such as sand or gravel, that have been worn away from rock.

deuce[1] (dōos) *n.* **1.** A playing card or side of a die bearing two spots; a two. **2.** In tennis, a tied score when a game can be won by winning two successive points.

deuce[2] (dōos) *Informal n.* The devil.

WORD HISTORY Deuce[1] comes from Middle English *deus,* which comes from Latin *duōs,* both meaning "two." **Deuce**[2] probably comes from Low German *duus* (meaning "a throw of two in dice games, bad luck"), which also comes from Latin *duōs.*

deus ex machina (dā′əs ĕks mä′kə-nə) *n.* **1.** In Greek and Roman drama, a god lowered by stage machinery to resolve a plot or extricate the protagonist from a difficult situation. **2.** An unexpected or implausible character or event introduced into a work of fiction or drama to resolve a situation or untangle a plot. **3.** A person or event that provides a sudden and unexpected solution to a difficulty.

deuterium (dōō-tîr′ē-əm) *n.* An isotope of hydrogen having one proton and one neutron in each atom. Deuterium occurs in heavy water.

Deuteronomy (dōō′tə-rŏn′ə-mē) *n.* The fifth book of the Bible, which includes many Jewish laws.

deutsche mark (doich′ märk′) *n.* The former basic monetary unit of Germany.

devalue (dē-văl′yōō) *tr.v.* **devalued, devaluing, devalues 1.** To lessen or cancel the value of: *The scientist never devalued the contributions of her assistants.* **2.** To lower the exchange value of (a currency). —**de·val′u·a′tion** *n.*

devastate (dĕv′ə-stāt′) *tr.v.* **devastated, devastating, devastates 1.** To lay waste; destroy: *The storms devastated much of the countryside.* **2.** To overwhelm; confound: *Layoffs devastated the old mill towns.* —**dev′as·tat′ing·ly** *adv.* —**dev′as·ta′tor** *n.*

devastation (dĕv′ə-stā′shən) *n.* The act of devastating or the condition of being devastated; ruin; destruction: *Dikes saved the land from devastation by flooding.*

develop (dĭ-vĕl′əp) *v.* **developed, developing, develops** —*intr.* **1.** To grow by degrees into a more advanced or mature state: *His musical ability developed with practice. Caterpillars develop into butterflies.* **2.** To increase or expand: *The town developed into a city over the years.* **3.** To come gradually into existence or activity: *A friendship soon developed between the two.* **4.** To come gradually to light; be disclosed: *I'll give you the details as they develop.* —*tr.* **1.** To cause to grow by degrees into a more advanced or mature state: *I want to develop my computer skills so I can be a programmer.* **2a.** To cause to increase or expand; build up: *She developed the business from a small store into a retail empire.* **b.** To strengthen: *developed his muscles by lifting weights.* **3.** To cause to come into existence or activity: *a researcher who developed a new way to treat the disease.* **4.** To increase the intricacy, complexity, or quality of: *develop one's vocabulary by reading; develop a story.* **5a.** To come to have gradually: *develop a liking for spicy food.* **b.** To become affected with; contract: *develop a rash on the arm.* **6.** To cause (a tract of land or a building) to serve a particular purpose: *developed the site as a community of condominiums.* **7.** To process (photographic film) in order to produce a photographic image.

developer (dĭ-vĕl′ə-pər) *n.* **1.** A person or thing that develops, especially a person who develops real estate by preparing a site for residential or commercial use. **2.** A chemical used in developing a photographic film or similar material.

developing (dĭ-vĕl′ə-pĭng) *adj.* Having a relatively low level of economic and industrial development: *a developing nation.*

development (dĭ-vĕl′əp-mənt) *n.* **1.** The act of developing: *The development of a vaccine requires much research.* **2.** The state of being developed: *The plans for the project are in development.* **3.** The process of change in the structure of an organism, especially as it grows. **4.** A significant event, occurrence, or change: *The newspaper related the latest developments in the peace talks.* **5.** A group of dwellings built by the same contractor: *The development*

includes a shopping center. —**de·vel′op·men′tal** *adj.*

deviant (dē′vē-ənt) *adj.* Differing from a norm or from accepted social standards: *deviant behavior.* ❖ *n.* A person whose attitude, character, or behavior differ from accepted social standards.

deviate (dē′vē-āt′) *intr.v.* **deviated, deviating, deviates 1.** To turn aside from a course or way: *hikers who deviated from the main path.* **2.** To change or vary, as from a norm or purpose; depart: *Their plans deviated from our original agreement.*

deviation (dē′vē-ā′shən) *n.* **1.** The act of deviating or turning aside. **2.** An abnormality; a departure: *Staying up late is a deviation from our routine.*

device (dĭ-vīs′) *n.* **1.** A contrivance or invention designed or used for a particular purpose; a mechanism: *An egg beater is a handy device.* **2.** A plan, scheme, or trick: *used crying and other devices to get his way.* **3.** A decorative design, figure, or pattern, as one used in embroidery. ◆ **leave to (one's) own devices** To allow to do as one pleases: *left the child to her own devices for an hour.*

devil (dĕv′əl) *n.* **1.** often **Devil** In many religions, the personified spirit of evil who is often also the ruler of Hell and the enemy of God. **2.** An evil spirit; a demon. **3.** A wicked or bad-tempered person. **4.** A person who is daring, clever, or full of mischief. ❖ *tr.v.* **deviled, deviling, devils** or **devilled, devilling, devils** To season (food) heavily, as with mustard: *devil eggs.*

devilfish (dĕv′əl-fĭsh′) *n.* Any of various aquatic animals having horns or thought to have a sinister appearance, including the manta ray and certain octopuses and squids.

devilish (dĕv′ə-lĭsh) *adj.* **1.** Resembling or characteristic of a devil; evil. **2.** Mischievous, teasing, or annoying: *That devilish kitten unrolled a ball of string.* —**dev′il·ish·ly** *adv.* —**dev′il·ish·ness** *n.*

devil-may-care (dĕv′əl-mā-kâr′) *adj.* Very careless; reckless: *His devil-may-care attitude led him to make a lot of mistakes.*

devilment (dĕv′əl-mənt) *n.* Devilish behavior; mischief.

devilry (dĕv′əl-rē) *n.* Variant of **deviltry.**

devil's advocate (dĕv′əlz) *n.* A person who argues against a position simply for the sake of argument or to test the validity of the position.

devil's food cake *n.* A rich chocolate cake.

deviltry (dĕv′əl-trē) or **devilry** (dĕv′əl-rē) *n., pl.* **deviltries** or **devilries 1.** Reckless mischief: *dangerous deviltry.* **2.** Extreme cruelty; wickedness.

devious (dē′vē-əs) *adj.* **1.** Not straightforward; shifty: *a devious character.* **2.** Veering from the correct or accepted way: *They achieved success by devious means.* **3.** Away from the main or direct road or course: *We took a devious route to avoid the traffic.* —**de′vi·ous·ly** *adv.* —**de′vi·ous·ness** *n.*

devise (dĭ-vīz′) *tr.v.* **devised, devising, devises** To form or arrange in the mind; plan: *devise a way to keep the window open with a stick.* —**de·vis′er** *n.*

devoid (dĭ-void′) *adj.* Completely lacking; destitute or empty: *a person devoid of humor.*

devolution (dĕv′ə-lōō′shən or dē′və-lōō′shən) *n.* **1.** A passing down or descent through successive stages of time or a process. **2.** Delegation of authority or duties to a subordinate or substitute. **3.** A transfer of powers from a central government to local units.

devolve (dĭ-vŏlv′) *intr. & tr.v.* **devolved, devolving, devolves** To pass or be passed on to another who acts as a substitute or delegate; transfer: *During his illness various duties devolved upon me.*

Devonian (dĭ-vō′nē-ən) *n.* The fourth period of the Paleozoic Era, from about 416 to 359 million years ago. During the Devonian, forests, amphibians, and insects first appeared. —**De·vo′ni·an** *adj.*

devote (dĭ-vōt′) *tr.v.* **devoted, devoting, devotes** To give or apply (one's time, attention, or self) entirely to a specified activity, cause, or person: *a musician who devotes time to helping students.*

devoted (dĭ-vō′tĭd) *adj.* **1.** Feeling or expressing strong affection or attachment: *a devoted friend.* **2.** Dedicated: *a devoted scientist.* —**de·vot′ed·ly** *adv.* —**de·vot′ed·ness** *n.*

devotee (dĕv′ə-tē′) *n.* A person who is ardently devoted to something; a fan: *A devotee of fishing will be out in all kinds of weather.*

devotion (dĭ-vō′shən) *n.* **1.** Affection, concern, and dedication, as to a person or principle: *the devotion of a parent to a child.* **2a.** Religious observance or worship. **b.** often **devotions** An act of religious observance or prayer, especially when private. **3.** The act of devoting: *devotion of time to teaching English to immigrants.*

devotional (dĭ-vō′shə-nəl) *adj.* Relating to or used in devotion, especially religious devotion.

devour (dĭ-vour′) *tr.v.* **devoured, devouring, devours 1.** To eat up greedily: *The hungry campers devoured their dinner.* **2.** To destroy or consume: *Flames devoured the building.* **3.** To take in greedily: *devour an exciting mystery story.* —**de·vour′ing·ly** *adv.*

devout (dĭ-vout′) *adj.* **devouter, devoutest 1.** Devoted to religion or to religious obligations: *a devout monk.* **2.** Sincere; earnest: *a devout wish for peace.* —**de·vout′ly** *adv.* —**de·vout′ness** *n.*

dew (dōō) *n.* **1.** Water droplets condensed from the air, mostly at night, onto cool surfaces. **2.** Something moist, fresh, renewing, or pure. **3.** Moisture appearing in small drops, as tears or perspiration. ❖ *tr.v.* **dewed, dewing, dews** To wet with or as if with dew.

dewberry (dōō′bĕr′ē) *n.* **1.** A purple or black berry from any of several low-growing prickly shrubs related to the blackberry. **2.** A shrub that bears such fruit.

dewclaw (dōō′klô′) *n.* A short digit that does not reach the ground, found on the feet of dogs and certain other mammals.

dewdrop (dōō′drŏp′) *n.* A drop of dew.

Dewey decimal classification (dōō′ē) *n.* A system for classifying library books and magazines into subject categories corresponding to three-digit numerals. Each category is subdivided by the addition of decimals to the number.

dewlap (dōō′lăp′) *n.* A loose fold of skin hanging from the neck of certain animals, such as some dogs, cattle, and lizards. Lizards can extend their dewlaps.

dew point *n.* The temperature at which air becomes saturated with water vapor and dew forms.

dewy (dōō′ē) *adj.* **dewier, dewiest** Moist with dew: *dewy fields of early morning.*

dexterity (dĕk-stĕr′ĭ-tē) *n.* Skill or grace in using the hands, body, or mind.

dexterous (dĕk′stər-əs *or* dĕk′strəs) *also* **dextrous** (dĕk′strəs) *adj.* Skillful in the use of the hands or mind: *a dexterous carpenter.* —**dex′ter·ous·ly** *adv.* —**dex′ter·ous·ness** *n.*

dextrose (dĕk′strōs′) *n.* A sugar that is the most common form of glucose. It is found in the cells and tissues of living organisms and can be derived from starch.

di– A prefix that means two, twice, or double: *dicotyledon; dioxide.*

dia– *or* **di–** A prefix that means through or across: *diaphanous; diagonal.*

diabetes (dī′ə-bē′tĭs *or* dī′ə-bē′tēz) *n.* Any of several disorders marked by abnormally high levels of sugar in the blood, caused by the body's inability to produce or use insulin properly. One type of diabetes usually develops in children and is treated with insulin, and another type usually develops in adults and is often managed with changes in exercise and diet.

diabetic (dī′ə-bĕt′ĭk) *adj.* Relating to or having diabetes. ❖ *n.* A person having diabetes.

diabolical (dī′ə-bŏl′ĭ-kal) *also* **diabolic** (dī′ə-bŏl′ĭk) *adj.* Concerning or characteristic of the devil; satanic. —**di′-a·bol′i·cal·ly** *adv.* —**di′a·bol′i·cal·ness** *n.*

diachronic (dī′ə-krŏn′ĭk) *adj.* Relating to the study of phenomena or events as they change over time: *a diachronic analysis of water quality.* —**di′a·chron′i·cal·ly** *adv.*

diaconate (dī-ăk′ə-nĭt) *n.* **1.** The rank, office, or tenure of a deacon. **2.** Deacons considered as a group.

diacritic (dī′ə-krĭt′ĭk) *n.* A mark, such as a cedilla or acute accent, added to a letter to indicate a certain pronunciation or stress.

diacritical (dī′ə-krĭt′ĭ-kəl) *adj.* **1.** Marking a distinction; distinguishing. **2.** Able to discriminate or distinguish: *a mind of great diacritical power.* **3.** Serving as a diacritic. —**di′a·crit′i·cal·ly** *adv.*

diadem (dī′ə-dĕm′) *n.* A crown worn as a sign of royalty.

diaeresis (dī-ĕr′ĭ-sĭs) *n.* Variant of **dieresis**.

diagnose (dī′əg-nōs′ *or* dī′əg-nōz′) *tr.v.* **diagnosed, diagnosing, diagnoses** To make a careful examination of; identify and study: *Doctors diagnose disease, and mechanics diagnose car trouble.*

diagnosis (dī′əg-nō′sĭs) *n., pl.* **diagnoses** (dī′əg-nō′sēz) **1.** The identification by a doctor or other medical professional of a disease or injury, made by examining and taking the medical history of a patient: *She just received a diagnosis of diabetes.* **2a.** A close analysis of the nature of something: *The consultant was hired to make a diagnosis of the company's financial situation.* **b.** The conclusions reached by such an analysis: *When the computer broke down, the diagnosis was a short circuit.*

diagnostic (dī′əg-nŏs′tĭk) *adj.* Relating to or used in diagnosis: *X-ray machines and stethoscopes are diagnostic tools of medicine.* —**di′ag·nos′ti·cal·ly** *adv.*

diagnostician (dī′əg-nŏ-stĭsh′ən) *n.* A person, especially a physician, who specializes in making medical diagnoses.

diagonal (dī-ăg′ə-nəl) *adj.* **1a.** Connecting two nonadjacent corners in a polygon: *a diagonal line sloping down across a square.* **b.** Connecting two nonadjacent corners in a polyhedron that do not lie in the same face. **2.** Slanting or oblique: *the diagonal stripes on a tie.* ❖ *n.* **1.** A diagonal line segment. **2.** Something, such as a row, course, or part, that is arranged in a sloping or slanting direction. —**di·ag′o·nal·ly** *adv.*

diagram (dī′ə-grăm′) *n.* A plan, drawing, or sketch that shows how something works or indicates how parts are put together: *A diagram of the apartment shows where each room is.* ❖ *tr.v.* **diagrammed, diagramming, dia-**

grams or **diagramed, diagraming, diagrams** To show or represent by or as if by a diagram: *diagram a floor plan.*

diagrammatic (dī′ə-grə-măt′ĭk) *adj.* **1.** In the form of a diagram: *A diagrammatic plan of the tunnel explains how it will be built.* **2.** In outline form only; sketchy: *an essay in diagrammatic form.* —**di′a·gram·mat′i·cal·ly** *adv.*

dial (dī′əl) *n.* **1.** A graduated surface or face on which a measurement, such as speed, is indicated by a moving needle or pointer. **2.** The control that selects the station to which a radio or television is tuned. **3.** A movable disk on a telephone with numbers and letters, used to signal the number to which a call is made. ❖ *v.* **dialed, dialing, dials** or **dialled, dialling, dials** —*tr.* **1.** To operate by using a dial, as in a combination lock: *We dialed the combination and the lock opened.* **2.** To control or select by means of a dial. **3.** To call (a party) on a telephone: *dialed her friend.* **4.** To make a telephone call to (a specific number): *Dial 911 for emergencies.* —*intr.* To use a dial, as on a telephone: *dial until you get an answer.*

dialect (dī′ə-lĕkt′) *n.* A variety of a language that is spoken in a particular region or by a particular group of people. For example, people in different regions of the United States speak different dialects of American English.

dialectal (dī′ə-lĕk′təl) *adj.* Relating to a dialect: *dialectal speech.*

dialectic (dī′ə-lĕk′tĭk) *n.* **1.** The art or practice of arriving at the truth by the exchange of logical arguments. **2.** The process especially associated with the German philosopher G. W. F. Hegel of arriving at the truth by stating a thesis, developing a contradictory antithesis, and combining and resolving them into a coherent synthesis. **3.** often **dialectics** *(used with a singular or plural verb)* In Marxist theory, the process of change through the conflict of opposing forces, whereby a given contradiction is characterized by a primary and a secondary aspect, the secondary succumbing to the primary, which is then transformed into an aspect of a new contradiction. **4. dialectics** *(used with a singular verb)* A method of argument or exposition that systematically weighs contradictory facts or ideas with a view to the resolution of their real or apparent contradictions. **5.** The contradiction between two conflicting forces viewed as the determining factor in their continuing interaction. —**di′a·lec′ti·cal, di′-a·lec′tic** *adj.* —**di′a·lec′ti·cal·ly** *adv.*

dialog box *n.* A window that appears on a computer screen, presenting information or requesting input.

dialogue or **dialog** (dī′ə-lôg′) *n.* **1.** A conversation between two or more people: *a friendly dialogue.* **2.** A discussion of ideas or opinions, especially between groups to resolve a disagreement: *a dialogue on global warming.* **3.** The words spoken by the characters of a play or story: *The dialogue of the comedy was very witty.* **4.** A literary work written in the form of a conversation: *Many students of philosophy have read the dialogues of Plato.* ❖ *intr.v.* **dialogued, dialoguing, dialogues** or **dialoged, dialoging** or **dialogs** To engage in a dialogue: *Company executives dialogued with the union leaders.*

dial tone *n.* A low steady tone in a telephone receiver, telling the user that a number may be dialed.

dial-up (dī′əl-ŭp′ or dīl′ŭp′) *adj.* Relating to a network connection, usually to the Internet, made by dialing a phone number: *a dial-up modem.*

dialysis (dī-ăl′ĭ-sĭs) *n., pl.* **dialyses** (dī-ăl′ĭ-sēz′) **1.** The process of separating dissolved substances by diffusion through a membrane that blocks the passage of large molecules but allows smaller molecules to penetrate the membrane. **2.** The removal of wastes from the bloodstream by a machine that performs dialysis when the kidneys do not function properly.

diam. An abbreviation of diameter.

diameter (dī-ăm′ĭ-tər) *n.* **1.** A straight line segment that passes through the center of a circle or sphere from one side to the other. **2.** The length of such a line segment.

diametrical (dī′ə-mĕt′rĭ-kəl) also **diametric** (dī′ə-mĕt′-rĭk) *adj.* **1.** Relating to or along a diameter: *a diametrical measurement.* **2.** Exactly opposite; contrary: *debaters with diametrical points of view.* —**di·a·met′ri·cal·ly** *adv.*

diamond (dī′ə-mənd or dī′mənd) *n.* **1.** A form of pure carbon that occurs as a clear crystal and is the hardest of all known minerals. It is used as a gemstone in its finer varieties and as an abrasive and an edge on cutting tools. **2a.** A rhombus, particularly when oriented so that one of its diagonals would extend directly ahead of an observer or a point of reference and the other diagonal is perpendicular to it. **b.** A playing card bearing a red figure shaped like this. **c.** often **diamonds** The suit in a deck of cards having this figure as its symbol. **3a.** A baseball infield. **b.** The whole playing field in baseball.

diamondback rattlesnake (dī′ə-mənd-băk′ or dī′mənd-băk′) *n.* Either of two large rattlesnakes of the United States and Mexico, having diamond-shaped markings on the back.

diamondback terrapin *n.* A turtle of coastal regions of the eastern and southern United States, having edible flesh and an upper shell with diamond-shaped ridged or knobby markings.

Diana (dī-ăn′ə) *n.* In Roman mythology, the goddess of the moon and the hunt, identified with the Greek Artemis.

diaper (dī′ə-pər or dī′pər) *n.* A piece of absorbent material, such as paper or cloth, that is typically placed between the legs and fastened at the waist to contain excretions. ❖ *tr.v.* **diapered, diapering, diapers** To put a diaper on (a baby, for example).

diaphanous (dī-ăf′ə-nəs) *adj.* Of such fine texture as to allow light to show through: *a diaphanous curtain.* —**di·aph′a·nous·ly** *adv.*

diaphragm (dī′ə-frăm′) *n.* **1.** A membrane of muscle that separates the chest cavity from the abdominal cavity. As the diaphragm contracts and expands it forces air into and out of the lungs. **2.** A membrane that divides or separates, as in a pump or other type of machinery. **3.** A thin disk, especially in a microphone or telephone receiver, that vibrates in response to sound waves to produce electrical signals or vibrates in response to electrical signals to produce sound waves. **4.** A disk with an opening in the center to regulate the amount of light entering a camera or microscope. **5.** A thin flexible disk, usually made of rubber, that is designed to cover the cervix of the uterus to prevent the entry of sperm during sexual intercourse.

diarrhea (dī′ə-rē′ə) *n.* A condition in which bowel movements are frequent and watery.

diary (dī′ə-rē) *n., pl.* **diaries** **1.** A daily record, especially a personal record of experiences, observations, and events. **2.** A book of blank pages for keeping such a record.

Diaspora (dī-ăs′pər-ə) *n.* **1.** The dispersion of Jews outside of Israel beginning in the sixth century BC, when they were exiled to Babylonia in what is now Iraq. **2. diaspora** A dispersion of a people from their original homeland. **3. diaspora** A dispersion of an originally homogeneous entity, such as a language or culture. —**di·as′po·ric,** **di·as′po·ral** *adj.*

diastole (dī-ăs′tə-lē) *n.* The phase of a heartbeat in which the chambers of the heart, especially the ventricles, relax and fill with blood. —**di′a·stol′ic** (dī′ə-stŏl′ĭk) *adj.*

diatom (dī′ə-tŏm′) *n.* Any of numerous one-celled algae that live in water, make their own food by photosynthesis, and have hard shells containing silica. Diatoms are an important component of plankton.

diatomic (dī′ə-tŏm′ĭk) *adj.* Made up of two atoms: *a diatomic molecule.*

diatonic (dī′ə-tŏn′ĭk) *adj.* Relating to or based on a scale using only seven tones, of which five are separated by whole steps and two by half steps. The major and minor scales are diatonic scales.

diatribe (dī′ə-trīb′) *n.* A bitter and abusive denunciation: *attack one's enemy in a fierce diatribe.*

dibs (dĭbz) *pl.n. Slang* A claim; rights: *I have dibs on the last waffle.*

dice (dīs) *n.* Plural of **die²** (sense 2). ❖ *v.* **diced, dicing, dices** —*intr.* To play or gamble with dice. —*tr.* To cut (food) into small cubes: *dice vegetables for soup.*

dicey (dī′sē) *adj.* **dicier, diciest** Involving or fraught with danger or risk.

dichotomy (dī-kŏt′ə-mē) *n., pl.* **dichotomies** Division into two parts or things that usually contradict or contrast with each other: *She sees a dichotomy between faith and reason.* —**di·chot′o·mous** (dī-kŏt′ə-məs) *adj.*

dickens (dĭk′ənz) *n. Informal* **1.** A reprimand or an expression of anger: *gave me the dickens for being late.* **2.** Used as an intensive: *Where the dickens did you get that?*

dicker (dĭk′ər) *intr.v.* **dickered, dickering, dickers** To bargain; barter: *dickered over the price of the chair.* ❖ *n.* The act or process of bargaining.

dickey (dĭk′ē) *n., pl.* **dickeys 1.** A woman's blouse front worn under a suit jacket or sweater. **2.** A man's detachable shirt front.

dicot (dī′kŏt′) *n.* A dicotyledon.

dicotyledon (dī′kŏt′l-ēd′n) *n.* A flowering plant having two cotyledons and usually other characteristics such as leaf veins that are netlike rather than parallel, flower parts in multiples of four or five, and the capacity for woody growth. Beans, roses, maples, and oaks are dicotyledons. —**di′cot′y·le′don·ous** *adj.*

dicta (dĭk′tə) *n.* A plural of **dictum.**

dictate (dĭk′tāt′ *or* dĭk-tāt′) *v.* **dictated, dictating, dictates** —*tr.* **1.** To say or read aloud to be recorded or written by another: *dictate an order over the phone; dictate a letter.* **2.** To establish with authority; impose: *Hospital rules dictate visiting hours.* —*intr.* **1.** To say or read aloud material to be recorded or written by another: *The reporter dictated into the tape recorder.* **2.** To issue orders or commands. ❖ *n.* (dĭk′tāt′) An order; a command.

dictation (dĭk-tā′shən) *n.* **1a.** The act or process of dictating material to another to be written down or recorded: *dictation of a letter over the telephone.* **b.** The material so dictated. **2.** An authoritative command or order.

dictator (dĭk′tā′tər *or* dĭk-tā′tər) *n.* **1.** An absolute ruler. **2.** A tyrant; a despot.

dictatorial (dĭk′tə-tôr′ē-əl) *adj.* **1.** Tending to tell others what to do in a presumptuous manner: *the chef's dictatorial manner in the kitchen.* **2.** Relating to or characteristic

of a dictator or dictatorship: *dictatorial power of an occupying army.* —**dic′ta·to′ri·al·ly** *adv.*

dictatorship (dĭk-tā′tər-shĭp′ *or* dĭk′tā′tər-shĭp′) *n.* **1.** The office or tenure of a dictator. **2.** A state or government under the rule of a dictator. **3.** Absolute or despotic control or power.

diction (dĭk′shən) *n.* **1.** Choice and use of words in speaking or writing: *A mystery writer's diction must be convincing to be successful.* **2.** Degree of clearness and distinctness in pronouncing words; enunciation: *The singer had good diction and so we could enjoy both words and music.* —SEE NOTE AT **predict.**

dictionary (dĭk′shə-nĕr′ē) *n., pl.* **dictionaries 1.** A reference work containing an alphabetical list of words, with information given for each word, usually including meaning, pronunciation, and etymology. **2.** A reference work containing an alphabetical list of words in one language with their translations in another language: *a Russian-English dictionary.* **3.** A reference work containing an alphabetical list of words in a particular category or subject with specialized information about them: *a medical dictionary.*

dictum (dĭk′təm) *n., pl.* **dicta** (dĭk′tə) *or* **dictums** An authoritative, often formal pronouncement: *Nutrition experts issued a new dictum about junk food.*

did (dĭd) *v.* Past tense of **do¹.**

didactic (dī-dăk′tĭk) *adj.* **1.** Intended to instruct: *Many legends have a didactic purpose.* **2.** Inclined to teach or moralize too much. —**di·dac′ti·cal·ly** *adv.*

diddle (dĭd′l) *intr.v.* **diddled, diddling, diddles 1.** To toy or fiddle: *diddling with the controls.* **2.** To waste time: *diddled around all day.*

didgeridoo *or* **didjeridoo** (dĭj′ə-rē-dōō′) *n., pl.* **digjeridoos** *or* **didjeridoos** A musical instrument of certain aboriginal peoples of Australia, consisting of a long hollow branch or stick that makes a deep drone when blown into while vibrating the lips.

didn't (dĭd′nt) Contraction of *did not.*

Dido (dī′dō) *n.* In Roman mythology, the founder and queen of the city of Carthage in North Africa who fell in love with Aeneas and killed herself when he abandoned her.

didst (dĭdst) *v. Archaic* Second person singular past tense of **do¹.**

die¹ (dī) *intr.v.* **died, dying** (dī′ĭng), **dies 1.** To stop living; become dead: *The sunflowers died in the first frost.* **2.** To cease existing, often gradually: *the conversation died; the sunlight is dying.* **3.** To want something very much: *I'm dying to see that movie.* **4.** To stop working or operating: *The motor died when we ran out of gas.* ♦ **die down** To lose strength; subside: *The winds died down.* **die off** To undergo a sudden sharp decline in population: *Bats are dying off in some regions.* **die out** To cease living or existing completely; become extinct: *Why did the dinosaurs die out? Those customs have died out.*

die² (dī) *n.* **1.** *pl.* **dies** A tool or device that shapes materials by stamping, cutting, or punching: *Dies are used to make coins.* **2.** *pl.* **dice** (dīs) A small cube marked on each side with one to six dots and usually used in pairs in games.

WORD HISTORY Die¹ comes from Middle English *dien,* which probably comes from Old Norse *deyja,* both meaning "to die." **Die²** comes from Middle English *de* (meaning "gaming die"), which comes from Latin *datum* (meaning "given"), a past participle of Latin *dare,* meaning "to give."

die-hard also **diehard** (dī′härd′) adj. Stubbornly resisting change or clinging to a seemingly hopeless cause: *a die-hard supporter.* ❖ n. A person who stubbornly refuses to give up a cause or resists change.

dieresis or **diaeresis** (dī-ĕr′ĭ-sĭs) n., pl. **diereses** or **diaereses** (dī-ĕr′ĭ-sēz′) **1.** A mark (¨) placed over the second of two adjacent vowels to show that the second vowel is to be pronounced as a separate sound, as in *naïve.* **2.** A mark (¨) placed over a vowel, such as the final vowel in *Brontë,* to indicate that the vowel is not silent.

diesel (dē′zəl or dē′səl) n. **1.** A diesel engine. **2.** A vehicle powered by a diesel engine. **3.** A type of fuel designed to power a diesel engine.

diesel engine n. An internal-combustion engine in which the fuel oil is ignited by the heat of air that has been highly compressed in the cylinder.

diet[1] (dī′ĭt) n. **1.** The usual food and drink eaten by a person or animal. **2.** A regulated selection of foods, as for medical reasons or weight loss: *a diet that excludes milk products.* ❖ intr.v. **dieted, dieting, diets** To eat and drink according to a regulated system, especially so as to control a medical condition or lose weight. ❖ adj. Relating to foods having few or no calories: *diet soft drinks.* —**di′et·er** n.

diet[2] (dī′ĭt) n. A national or local legislative assembly in certain countries, such as Japan.

WORD HISTORY Both **diet**[1] and **diet**[2] were spelled *diete* in Middle English, and both ultimately come from Greek *diaitâsthai* (meaning "to live one's life"), from which the Latin word *diaeta* (meaning "way of living") was derived. After Latin, the two words took different paths to Middle English, the first passing through Old French, whereas the latter became Medieval Latin *diēta* (meaning "day's journey, meeting day"), a form that was also influenced by Latin *diēs,* meaning "day."

dietary (dī′ĭ-tĕr′ē) adj. Relating to diet: *a good dietary plan.*

dietetic (dī′ĭ-tĕt′ĭk) adj. **1.** Relating to diet or its regulation. **2.** Made or processed for restricted diets: *dietetic foods prepared with less salt and sugar.*

dietetics (dī′ĭ-tĕt′ĭks) n. *(used with a singular verb)* The study of nutrition as it relates to health.

dietitian or **dietician** (dī′ĭ-tĭsh′ən) n. A person who specializes in dietetics: *The hospital dietitian plans the meals for each patient.*

differ (dĭf′ər) intr.v. **differed, differing, differs 1.** To be unlike, as in nature or amount: *The weather often differs from one part of a state to another.* **2.** To be of a different opinion; disagree: *The experts differ on what should be done to fix the economy.*

difference (dĭf′ər-əns or dĭf′rəns) n. **1.** The quality or condition of being unlike or dissimilar: *the difference between summer and winter.* **2.** An instance of being unlike or different: *There is a big difference in sound between a clarinet and an oboe.* **3.** A noticeable change or effect: *Exercise has made a big difference in her health.* **4.** A disagreement or controversy: *We settled our differences amicably.* **5.** The amount by which one quantity is greater or less than another; what is left when one number is subtracted from another: *The difference between 10 and 4 is 6.*

different (dĭf′ər-ənt or dĭf′rənt) adj. **1.** Unlike in form, quality, amount, or nature: *The two breeds of dog are very different.* **2.** Distinct or separate: *We ran into each other*

on three different occasions today. —**dif′fer·ent·ly** adv.

USAGE When you are making a comparison between two people or things, **different** should be followed by *from* instead of *than:* My book *is different from* (not *than*) *yours.* When you are making a comparison that ends with a full clause, *different* should be followed by *than* instead of *from: The school is different than it was 20 years ago.* However, if the clause starts with a word like *how* or *what,* you should use *from* to make the comparison: *The school is different from what it was 20 years ago.*

differential (dĭf′ə-rĕn′shəl) adj. Relating to or showing a difference: *differential rates in air fares.* ❖ n. **1.** A differential gear. **2.** A difference in amount, especially in price: *There is a substantial differential between the cost of flying to Florida in the winter and in the summer.* —**dif′fer·en′tial·ly** adv.

differential gear n. An arrangement of gears used in an automobile or truck that permits the drive shaft to turn the two rear-wheel or front-wheel axle shafts at different speeds, so that the wheels can rotate at different speeds when the vehicle is turning.

differentiate (dĭf′ə-rĕn′shē-āt′) v. **differentiated, differentiating, differentiates** —tr. **1.** To be the difference between: *Red shirts and blue shirts differentiate the teams.* **2.** To understand or show the differences between: *differentiated the various wildflowers.* —intr. **1.** To become distinct or specialized, especially during the process of biological development: *cells that differentiate into neurons.* **2.** To make distinctions; discriminate: *A doctor can differentiate between a rash and chickenpox.* —**dif′fer·en′ti·a′tion** n.

difficult (dĭf′ĭ-kŭlt′) adj. **1.** Not easy to do or accomplish: *a difficult task.* **2.** Not easy to endure; full of hardship or trouble; trying: *living in difficult times.* **3.** Hard to understand or solve: *a difficult math problem.* **4.** Hard to please, satisfy, or manage: *A perfectionist can be difficult.*

difficulty (dĭf′ĭ-kŭl′tē) n., pl. **difficulties 1.** The quality or condition of being difficult: *The difficulty of the subject made the book on botany hard to understand.* **2.** Something that is hard to deal with, accomplish, comprehend, or solve: *Technical difficulties plagued the new website.* **3.** often **difficulties** A troublesome or embarrassing state of affairs, especially financial affairs.

diffidence (dĭf′ĭ-dəns) n. A quality or state of being timid or shy: *Diffidence held him back from calling out the answer.*

diffident (dĭf′ĭ-dənt) adj. Lacking or marked by a lack of self-confidence; timid and shy. —**dif′fi·dent·ly** adv.

diffract (dĭ-frăkt′) intr. & tr.v. **diffracted, diffracting, diffracts** To undergo or cause to undergo diffraction.

diffraction (dĭ-frăk′shən) n. **1.** The bending or turning of a wave, such as a light wave, when it encounters an obstacle, such as an edge or a hole, whose size is similar to the wavelength of the wave. The colors of the spectrum can be produced by the diffraction of light. **2.** A similar spreading and bending of sound or other kinds of waves.

diffuse (dĭ-fyōōz′) v. **diffused, diffusing, diffuses** —tr. **1.** To cause to spread out freely: *The lamp diffuses light over the table.* **2.** To scatter; disseminate: *diffuses ideas over the Internet; diffuse knowledge.* —intr. **1.** To become spread out or scattered: *A lighthouse beam diffuses far out over the ocean.* **2.** To undergo diffusion: *In the lungs, oxygen diffuses into the bloodstream.* ❖ adj. (dĭ-fyōōs′) **1.** Widely spread or scattered: *Diffuse light is often hard to read by.*

2. Wordy or unclear: *a diffuse description.* —SEE NOTE AT **transfusion.**

diffusion (dǐ-fyoo′zhən) *n.* **1.** The process of diffusing or the condition of being diffused: *the diffusion of knowledge.* **2.** The scattering of light or other radiation as it reflects off a rough surface or passes through a translucent material. **3.** The gradual mixing together of different gases or liquids as a result of the random motions of their atoms or molecules.

dig (dǐg) *v.* **dug** (dǔg), **digging, digs** —*tr.* **1.** To break, turn over, or remove (earth, for example), as with a shovel, a spade, or the hands: *The dog was digging the dirt to crawl under the fence.* **2.** To make or form by removing earth or other material: *A woodchuck dug a hole in the garden.* **3.** To get by digging or by an action similar to digging: *dig clams; dug a quarter out of my pocket.* **4.** To learn or discover by investigation or research: *dig up information in a library.* **5.** To poke, prod, or thrust: *The cat dug its claws into a tree.* **6.** *Slang* **a.** To understand fully: *Do you dig what I mean?* **b.** To like, enjoy, or appreciate: *I dig their music.* **c.** To take notice of: *Dig that fantastic car!* —*intr.* **1.** To loosen, turn over, or remove earth or other material: *I'm going out to the garden to dig.* **2.** To make one's way by or as if by pushing aside or removing material: *dig through the trash to find a lost earring.* **3.** *Slang* To understand something. ❖ *n.* **1.** A poke or thrust: *a dig in the ribs.* **2.** A sarcastic taunting remark: *a nasty dig about my accent.* **3.** An archaeological excavation. **4. digs** *Informal* Lodgings: *liked his new digs.* ◆ **dig in 1.** To dig trenches for protection: *The army dug in for battle.* **2.** To begin to eat heartily: *We were hungry and quickly dug in.* —**dig′ger** *n.*

digest (dī-jěst′ *or* dī-jěst′) *v.* **digested, digesting, digests** —*tr.* **1.** To change (food) chemically into materials that a cell or organism can assimilate, store, or use as nourishment: *As carbohydrates are digested, the body turns them into sugar and starch.* **2.** To absorb mentally; comprehend: *Reporters must digest facts quickly in order to write their stories.* —*intr.* To assimilate or be assimilated as food: *Some foods do not digest easily. The snake is digesting.* ❖ *n.* (dī′jěst′) A collection of previously published materials, such as essays or reports, usually in condensed form: *a website that posts digests of international news.*

digestible (dī-jěs′tə-bəl *or* dī-jěs′tə-bəl) *adj.* Capable of being digested easily or readily. —**di·gest′i·bil′i·ty** *n.*

digestion (dī-jěs′chən *or* dī-jěs′chən) *n.* **1a.** The process of digesting food. **b.** The ability to carry on this process: *poor digestion.* **2.** The decomposition of organic matter in sewage by bacteria.

digestive (dī-jěs′tǐv *or* dī-jěs′tǐv) *adj.* Relating to, aiding, or active in digestion: *digestive juices.*

digestive system *n.* The system of organs that breaks down and absorbs food as nourishment in the body of an animal. In humans, it consists of the digestive tract and the glands, such as the salivary glands, liver, and pancreas, that produce secretions necessary for digestion.

digestive tract *n.* The tube of the digestive system through which food passes, in which digestion takes place, and from which wastes are eliminated. In humans, it extends from the mouth to the anus and includes the pharynx, esophagus, stomach, and small and large intestines.

diggings (dǐg′ǐngz) *pl.n.* An excavation site, as for mining ore.

digit (dǐj′ǐt) *n.* **1.** A human finger or toe. **2.** A corresponding part in other vertebrate animals. **3.** One of the ten Arabic numerals, 0 through 9.

digital (dǐj′ǐ-tl) *adj.* **1.** Relating to the fingers or toes: *digital mobility.* **2.** Expressed in numerical form, especially for use by a computer: *digital information.* **3a.** Relating to or being a device that can read, write, or store information represented in numerical form. **b.** Relating to or being a service that provides information expressed in numerical form: *digital cable.* **4.** Relating to or using digital devices: *digital photography; a digital librarian.* **5.** Using or giving a reading in digits: *a digital clock; a digital speedometer.* —**dig′i·tal·ly** *adv.*

digitalis (dǐj′ǐ-tǎl′ǐs) *n.* A drug prepared from the dried leaves of a kind of foxglove, used as a powerful heart stimulant.

digitize (dǐj′ǐ-tīz′) *tr.v.* **digitized, digitizing, digitizes** To put (data, for example) into digital form. —**dig′i·ti·za′-tion** (dǐj′ǐ-tǐ-zā′shən) *n.*

dignified (dǐg′nə-fīd′) *adj.* Having or expressing dignity: *the careful and dignified manner of an ambassador.*

dignify (dǐg′nə-fī′) *tr.v.* **dignified, dignifying, dignifies** **1.** To give dignity or honor to: *The mayor's presence dignified the event.* **2.** To raise the status of (something unworthy and lowly): *I would not dignify the gossip by responding to it.*

dignitary (dǐg′nǐ-těr′ē) *n., pl.* **dignitaries** A person of high rank or position.

dignity (dǐg′nǐ-tē) *n., pl.* **dignities 1.** The quality or state of being worthy of esteem or respect. **2.** A stately or poised manner: *The judge maintained his dignity in the court at all times.* **3.** The respect and honor that go with an important position or station. **4.** A high office or rank.

digress (dī-grěs′ *or* dī-grěs′) *intr.v.* **digressed, digressing, digresses** To speak or write temporarily about something different from the main subject: *digressed from the sermon to tell a personal story.* —SEE NOTE AT **progress.**

digression (dī-grěsh′ən *or* dī-grěsh′ən) *n.* **1.** The act of digressing. **2.** An instance of digressing, especially in speech or writing: *tiresome digressions in an otherwise interesting article.*

dihedral angle (dī-hē′drəl) *n.* An angle formed by two geometric planes that intersect.

dike (dīk) *n.* **1.** A wall or embankment built to hold back water and prevent flooding, as by a river or the sea. **2.** A long mass of igneous rock that cuts across the structure of adjoining rock. ❖ *tr.v.* **diked, diking, dikes** To protect or provide with a dike.

dilapidated (dī-lǎp′ǐ-dā′tǐd) *adj.* In a condition of deterioration or disrepair, as through neglect: *The dilapidated building was beyond repair.*

dilapidation (dī-lǎp′ǐ-dā′shən) *n.* A condition of deterioration or disrepair: *The run-down house showed signs of dilapidation.*

dilate (dī-lāt′ *or* dī′lāt′) *tr. & intr.v.* **dilated, dilating, dilates** To make or become larger or wider; expand: *When the horse whinnied, its nostrils dilated.* —**di·la′tion** *n.*

dilatory (dǐl′ə-tôr′ē) *adj.* **1.** Causing or intending to cause delay: *hold up legislation with dilatory tactics such as the filibuster.* **2.** Characterized by or given to delay or slowness: *a dilatory student who always hands her papers in late.*

dilemma (dǐ-lěm′ə) *n.* A situation that requires a person to choose between options that are or seem equally unfavorable: *faced the dilemma of taking a cut in pay or losing her job.*

dilettante (dĭl′ĭ-tänt′ *or* dĭl′ĭ-tänt′) *n.* A person who dabbles in an art or a branch of knowledge.

diligence (dĭl′ə-jəns) *n.* Earnest and persistent application or effort: *It took a lot of diligence to stick with such an unrewarding project.*

diligent (dĭl′ə-jənt) *adj.* Marked by persevering painstaking effort: *A diligent search of the records revealed new evidence.* —**dil′i·gent·ly** *adv.*

dill (dĭl) *n.* A perennial plant related to parsley that has aromatic leaves and seeds that are used as seasonings.

dill pickle *n.* A pickled cucumber flavored with dill.

dilly (dĭl′ē) *n., pl.* **dillies** *Slang* One that is remarkable or extraordinary, as in size or quality: *had a dilly of a fight.*

dilly-dally (dĭl′ē-dăl′ē) *intr.v.* **dilly-dallied, dilly-dallying, dilly-dallies** To waste time, especially in indecision; dawdle.

dilute (dĭ-lo͞ot′ *or* dī-lo͞ot′) *tr.v.* **diluted, diluting, dilutes 1.** To make thinner or less concentrated by adding a liquid such as water: *dilute thick soup.* **2.** To weaken the force, intensity, purity, or condition of: *A lack of facts diluted the argument.* ❖ *adj.* Weakened; diluted: *a dilute solution of acid.*

dilution (dĭ-lo͞o′shən *or* dī-lo͞o′shən) *n.* **1.** The act of diluting or the condition of being diluted. **2.** A diluted substance: *a 50 percent dilution of a concentrated solution.*

dim (dĭm) *adj.* **dimmer, dimmest 1.** Lacking in brightness: *a dim corner of the big room.* See Synonyms at **dark. 2.** Giving off only a small amount of light: *a dim light bulb.* **3.** Lacking luster; dull and subdued: *dim colors faded by the sun.* **4.** Faintly or unclearly perceived; indistinct: *the dim shape of a ship in the mist.* **5.** Lacking sharpness or clearness; vague: *a dim recollection.* **6.** Negative, unfavorable, or disapproving: *took a dim view of my excuses.* **7.** *Slang* Dull or unintelligent. ❖ *tr. & intr.v.* **dimmed, dimming, dims** To make or become dim: *Drivers must dim their headlights in traffic. The lights dimmed as the play began.* —**dim′ly** *adv.* —**dim′ness** *n.*

dime (dīm) *n.* A coin of the United States or Canada worth ten cents. ◆ **a dime a dozen** Overly abundant; commonplace: *Cell phones are a dime a dozen these days.* **on a dime** At a precise point; within a narrowly defined area: *This car stops on a dime.*

dimension (dĭ-mĕn′shən *or* dī-mĕn′shən) *n.* **1.** A measurement of length, width, or thickness: *The dimensions of the window are 2 feet by 4 feet.* **2.** often **dimensions** Extent or magnitude; scope: *a problem of huge dimensions.* **3.** A physical quantity, such as mass, length, or time, on which other measurements are based.

dimensional (dĭ-mĕn′shə-nəl) *adj.* **1.** Relating to a dimension or dimensions. **2.** Having a specified number of dimensions: *a two-dimensional picture.*

diminish (dĭ-mĭn′ĭsh) *tr. & intr.v.* **diminished, diminishing, diminishes** To make or become smaller or less; reduce or decrease: *A drought diminished their water supply. Light diminished steadily as the sun went down.* See Synonyms at **decrease.** —**di·min′ish·ing** *adj.*

diminuendo (dĭ-mĭn′yo͞o-ĕn′dō) *n. & adj. & adv.* Decrescendo.

diminution (dĭm′ə-no͞o′shən) *n.* The act or process of diminishing; a lessening or reduction: *Lack of exercise contributes to the diminution of strength.*

diminutive (dĭ-mĭn′yə-tĭv) *adj.* **1.** Extremely or extraordinarily small: *diminutive figures in a collection of miniatures.* **2.** Relating to a suffix that expresses smallness, youth, familiarity, affection, or contempt, as *-let* in

booklet or *-ie* in *dearie.* ❖ *n.* A diminutive suffix, word, or name. For example, *droplet* is a diminutive of *drop.* —**di·min′u·tive·ly** *adv.* —**di·min′u·tive·ness** *n.*

dimmer (dĭm′ər) *n.* A device used to vary the brightness of an electric light.

dimorphism (dī-môr′fĭz′əm) *n.* **1.** The existence among animals of the same species of two distinct forms that differ in one or more characteristics, such as coloration, size, or shape. **2.** The occurrence of two distinct forms of the same parts in one plant, as in the juvenile and adult leaves of ivy. **3.** The occurrence of two distinct forms of crystals of the same chemical compound. —**di·mor′phic** (dī-môr′fĭk) *adj.*

dimple (dĭm′pəl) *n.* A small indentation in the flesh on a part of the human body, especially in the chin or on the cheek. ❖ *intr.v.* **dimpled, dimpling, dimples** To form dimples by smiling.

dim sum (dĭm′ so͞om′ *or* dĭm′ sŭm′) *n.* A traditional Chinese meal in which small portions of a variety of foods, such as dumplings, are served.

dimwit (dĭm′wĭt′) *n.* A stupid person. —**dim′wit′ted** *adj.* —**dim′wit′ted·ly** *adv.*

din (dĭn) *n.* A jumble of loud, usually discordant sounds: *We couldn't hear them over the din of the traffic.* See Synonyms at **noise.**

dinar (dĭ-när′ *or* dē′när′) *n.* The basic monetary unit of numerous countries, including Algeria, Iraq, Jordan, and Libya.

dine (dīn) *intr.v.* **dined, dining, dines** To have dinner: *We dined early.*

diner (dī′nər) *n.* **1.** A person who dines. **2.** A restaurant that has a long counter and booths, often housed in a building designed to resemble a railroad dining car.

dinette (dī-nĕt′) *n.* **1.** A small dining room or alcove for informal meals. **2.** The table and chairs used to furnish such an area.

ding (dĭng) *intr. & tr.v.* **dinged, dinging, dings** To ring or cause to ring with a clanging sound. ❖ *n.* A ringing sound.

ding-dong (dĭng′dông′) *n.* The peal of a bell.

dinghy (dĭng′ē) *n., pl.* **dinghies** A small open boat, especially a rowboat carried by a larger boat.

dingle (dĭng′gəl) *n.* A small wooded valley; a dell.

dingo (dĭng′gō) *n., pl.* **dingoes** A wild dog of Australia, having a yellowish-brown coat.

dingy (dĭn′jē) *adj.* **dingier, dingiest** Darkened with grime or soot; dirty or discolored: *a dark and dingy room in need of paint.* —**din′gi·ly** *adv.* —**din′gi·ness** *n.*

dining car (dī′nĭng) *n.* A railroad car in which meals are served.

dining room *n.* A room, as in a house or hotel, in which meals are eaten.

dinky (dĭng′kē) *adj.* **dinkier, dinkiest** *Informal* Of small size or consequence; insignificant: *a dinky shack in the woods.*

dinner (dĭn′ər) *n.* **1.** The main meal of the day, eaten at midday or in the evening. **2.** A banquet or formal meal in honor of a person or event: *held a dinner to celebrate Katie's birthday.*

dinner jacket *n.* A man's short jacket worn with a bow tie for social events in the evening.

dinnertime (dĭn′ər-tīm′) *n.* The time when dinner is usually eaten.

dinoflagellate (dī′nō-flăj′ə-lĭt *or* dī′nō-flăj′ə-lāt′) *n.* Any of numerous one-celled organisms found mostly in the ocean, usually having two flagella. Dinoflagellates are one of the main components of plankton.

dinosaur (dī′nə-sôr′) *n.* **1.** One of a group of extinct meat-eating or plant-eating reptiles that lived on land millions of years ago, during the Mesozoic Era. The smallest dinosaurs were the size of chickens, and the largest were the largest land animals that have ever lived. **2.** Any of various other large extinct reptiles, such as an ichthyosaur.

dint (dĭnt) *n.* Force or effort; power: *By dint of practice, she became an accomplished musician.*

diocese (dī′ə-sĭs *or* dī′ə-sēs′) *n.* The district or churches under the authority of a bishop.

diode (dī′ōd′) *n.* An electron tube or a semiconductor that allows current to flow in one direction only.

dioecious (dī-ē′shəs) *adj.* Having male flowers or cones and female flowers or cones on separate plants. Junipers, willows, and hollies are dioecious.

Dionysian (dī′ə-nĭsh′ən *or* dī′ə-nĭs′ē-ən) *adj.* **1.** In Greek and Roman mythology, relating to Dionysus or the worship of Dionysus. **2.** often **dionysian** Ecstatic, orgiastic, or irrational in nature; frenzied or undisciplined.

Dionysus (dī′ə-nī′səs *or* dī′ə-nē′səs) *n.* In Greek and Roman mythology, the god of wine and of the power and fertility of nature.

diorama (dī′ə-răm′ə) *n.* A miniature or life-size scene with lifelike figures and objects set against a painted background.

dioxide (dī-ŏk′sīd) *n.* A compound with two atoms of oxygen per molecule.

dioxin (dī-ŏk′sĭn) *n.* Any of several toxic chemicals that are produced chiefly as byproducts of industrial processes. Dioxins persist for a long time in the environment and can cause cancer and other health effects.

dip (dĭp) *v.* **dipped, dipping, dips** —*tr.* **1.** To plunge briefly in or into a liquid: *dip a cracker into soup.* **2.** To color or dye by putting into a liquid: *dip eggs in dye.* **3.** To immerse (a sheep or other animal) in a disinfecting bath. **4.** To make (a candle) by repeatedly immersing a wick in melted wax or tallow. **5.** To scoop up by plunging the hand or a receptacle below the surface, as of a liquid: *dip water from a stream to get a drink.* **6.** To lower and raise (a flag) in salute. —*intr.* **1.** To plunge briefly into water or other liquid: *The oars dipped in and out of the water.* **2.** To plunge the hand or a receptacle into liquid or a container, especially so as to take something out: *dip into a pickle jar.* **3.** To drop down or sink out of sight suddenly: *The temperature dipped below freezing.* **4.** To slope downward; decline: *The path dips to the river.* ❖ *n.* **1.** A brief plunge, especially a quick swim: *a dip in the pool.* **2.** A liquid into which something is dipped, as for dyeing or disinfecting: *a flea dip for dogs.* **3.** A creamy food mixture into which crackers or other foods may be dipped: *a vegetable dip.* **4.** An amount taken up by dipping; a scoop: *a double dip of ice cream.* **5.** A downward slope; a decline: *a dip in the road.*

diphtheria (dif-thîr′ē-ə *or* dĭp-thîr′ē-ə) *n.* A serious contagious disease caused by a bacterium that produces a damaging toxin. Symptoms include fever and the formation of a dark fiberlike covering in the throat that causes difficulty in breathing.

diphthong (dĭf′thông′ *or* dĭp′thông′) *n.* A speech sound blending two vowels in the same syllable. For example, the speech sounds represented by *oy* in *boy* and *i* in *nice* are diphthongs.

diplodocus (dĭ-plŏd′ə-kəs) *n.* A very large plant-eating dinosaur having a long, slender neck and tail and a small head. It is one of the longest dinosaurs known, reaching a length of nearly 90 feet (27 meters).

diploid (dĭp′loid′) *adj.* Being a cell or composed of cells in which there is a pair of each type of chromosome. In animals, all cells except reproductive cells are diploid. ❖ *n.* A diploid cell or organism.

diploma (dĭ-plō′mə) *n.* A document or certificate issued by an educational institution showing that a person has earned a degree or completed a course of study.

diplomacy (dĭ-plō′mə-sē) *n.* **1.** The art or practice of handling international relations. It includes negotiating alliances, treaties, and trade agreements. **2.** Skill in dealing with others; tact: *The lawyer was known for her diplomacy.*

diploma mill *n. Informal* An unaccredited college or technical school that grants degrees to people who have received little or no instruction, often for a high price.

diplomat (dĭp′lə-măt′) *n.* **1.** A person, such as an ambassador, who has been appointed to represent a government in its dealings with other governments. **2.** A person who uses tact and skill in dealing with others.

diplomatic (dĭp′lə-măt′ĭk) *adj.* **1.** Relating to or involving diplomacy or diplomats. **2.** Using or marked by skill and tact in dealing with others: *a diplomatic handling of unpleasant matters.* —**dip′lo·mat′i·cal·ly** *adv.*

dipole (dī′pōl′) *n.* A pair of separated electric charges or magnetic poles, equal in strength but opposite in sign or polarity.

dipper (dĭp′ər) *n.* **1.** A person or thing that dips. **2.** A container for scooping up liquids.

dipsomania (dĭp′sə-mā′nē-ə) *n.* An insatiable craving for alcoholic beverages. —**dip′so·ma′ni·ac** (dĭp′sə-mā′nē-ăk′) *adj. & n.* —**dip′so·ma·ni′a·cal** (dĭp′sə-mə-nī′ə-kəl) *adj.*

dipstick (dĭp′stĭk′) *n.* A graduated rod for measuring the depth or amount of liquid in a container, as of oil in a crankcase.

dire (dīr) *adj.* **direr, direst 1.** Warning of or having dreadful or terrible consequences; calamitous: *a dire accident.* **2.** Urgent; desperate: *in dire want.*

direct (dĭ-rĕkt′ *or* dī-rĕkt′) *v.* **directed, directing, directs** —*tr.* **1.** To manage or conduct the affairs of; regulate: *direct a business.* **2.** To instruct, order, or command: *The general directed the soldiers to free all prisoners.* **3.** To manage or supervise the performance of (a play, for example). **4.** To cause to move or be turned toward a goal or object; aim: *directed the light toward center stage.* **5.** To show or indicate the way for: *I directed them to the post office.* **6.** To make (remarks, for example) to someone in particular or to an audience: *The dean directed a few words of welcome to the new students.* —*intr.* **1.** To give commands or directions: *police officers directing at an intersection.* **2.** To conduct a performance or rehearsal: *The conductor is directing in front of the orchestra.* ❖ *adj.* **1.** Proceeding in a straight course or line; not roundabout: *The dancers moved in a direct line across the stage.* **2.** Straightforward and candid; frank: *They gave direct answers to my questions.* **3.** Having no intervening people, agencies, or conditions; immediate: *direct sunlight; a direct line to the president.* **4.** Effected by action of the voters rather than through representatives or delegates: *direct election.* **5.** Being of unbroken descent; lineal: *the direct descendant of early settlers.* **6.** Consisting of the exact words of a writer or speaker: *a direct quote from the article.* **7.** Absolute: *direct opposites.* **8.** Varying in the same manner as another quantity; increasing if another quantity increases or decreasing if it decreases. **9.** In soccer, relating to a free kick that can score a goal without the ball being touched by a second player. ❖ *adv.* Straight; directly: *We flew direct from California to New York.* —**di·rect′ness** *n.*

direct current *n.* An electric current flowing in one direction only, as that of a battery.

direct deposit *n.* The electronic transfer of money directly from the account of the payer to that of the party being paid: *Every two weeks my employer pays me by direct deposit, so I don't need to deposit paychecks at the bank.*

direction (dĭ-rĕk′shən *or* dī-rĕk′shən) *n.* **1.** The management, control, or guidance of an action or operation: *The fire department is under the direction of the chief.* **2.** An order or command: *The supervisor shouted directions to employees in the warehouse.* **3. directions** Instructions for doing or finding something: *I read the directions for starting the snowblower.* **4.** The line or course along which a person or thing moves or lies: *The ship headed in a northerly direction. The old farmhouse is in the direction of the peach orchard.* **5.** A course or area of development: *The orchestra took a different direction by performing contemporary compositions.*

directional (dĭ-rĕk′shə-nəl *or* dī-rĕk′shə-nəl) *adj.* **1.** Indicating direction: *a car's directional signals.* **2.** Capable of receiving or sending signals in one direction only: *installed a directional radar antenna.* —**di·rec′tion·al·ly** *adv.*

direction finder *n.* A device for finding the direction from which a radio signal is transmitted. It consists of a radio receiver and a compass attached to a coiled antenna that can turn in any direction.

directive (dĭ-rĕk′tĭv *or* dī-rĕk′tĭv) *n.* An order or instruction, especially one issued by someone in authority: *a directive from the coach about attendance at practice.*

directly (dĭ-rĕkt′lē *or* dī-rĕkt′lē) *adv.* **1.** In a direct line or manner; straight: *The cat headed directly for its food.* **2.** Without anything intervening: *The students spoke directly to the superintendent about the issue.* **3.** Exactly or totally: *His views on this issue are directly opposite to mine.* **4.** Without delay; at once: *I'll meet you there directly after work.*

direct mail *n.* Advertising or marketing announcements sent by mail without being requested to residences and workplaces.

direct object *n.* The word or words in a sentence referring to the person or thing receiving the action of a transitive verb. For example, in the sentence *I mailed the letter,* the direct object is *the letter.*

director (dĭ-rĕk′tər *or* dī-rĕk′tər) *n.* **1.** A person who supervises, controls, or manages: *The magazine has a new art director.* **2.** A member of a group of people chosen to control or govern the affairs of a company or institution: *a meeting of the board of directors.* **3.** A person who supervises and guides the performers and others involved in a dramatic production, film, or other performance.

directorate (dĭ-rĕk′tər-ĭt *or* dī-rĕk′tər-ĭt) *n.* **1.** The office or position of a director. **2.** A board of directors, as of a corporation.

directorial (dĭ-rĕk′tôr′ē-əl *or* dī-rĕk′tôr′ē-əl) *adj.* **1.** Relating to a director or directorate: *directorial responsibilities.* **2.** Serving to direct: *a directorial report.*

directory (dĭ-rĕk′tə-rē *or* dī-rĕk′tə-rē) *n., pl.* **directories 1.** A list of names, addresses, or other facts, such as telephone numbers, in alphabetical or other order: *a building directory to the offices of different companies.* **2.** A listing of the data files stored in a computer memory.

direful (dīr′fəl) *adj.* Inspiring dread; terrible: *a direful tale of misery and starvation.* —**dire′ful·ly** *adv.*

dirge (dûrj) *n.* A sad solemn piece of music, such as a funeral hymn or lament.

dirham (də-răm′) *n.* The basic monetary unit of Morocco and the United Arab Emirates.

dirigible (dĭr′ə-jə-bəl *or* də-rĭj′ə-bəl) *n.* An airship.

dirk (dûrk) *n.* A dagger.

dirndl (dûrn′dl) *n.* **1.** A dress with a full skirt and tight bodice, that is sleeveless or has short full sleeves. **2.** A full skirt with a gathered waistband.

dirt (dûrt) *n.* **1.** Earth or soil: *Rock and dirt came tumbling down the mountain.* **2.** A substance that soils, such as mud, dust, or grease: *A detergent removes dirt from clothes.* **3.** A person or thing that is mean or contemptible. **4.** Malicious or scandalous gossip: *This magazine publishes all the dirt about movie stars.*

dirt bike *n.* A lightweight motorcycle for use on rough surfaces, such as dirt roads or trails.

dirt-cheap (dûrt′chēp′) *adv. & adj.* Very cheap: *buy a truck dirt-cheap; a dirt-cheap hotel.*

dirty (dûr′tē) *adj.* **dirtier, dirtiest 1a.** Covered or marked with dirt or an unwanted substance; unclean: *dirty water; dirty clothes; a dirty floor.* **b.** Apt to soil with dirt or grime: *Planting a garden is a dirty job.* **c.** Producing radioactive fallout. Used of explosives. **2a.** Mean or contemptible: *a dirty trick.* **b.** Obscene or indecent: *a dirty joke.* **3.** Not playing fair: *a dirty card player.* **4.** Expressing disapproval or hostility: *a dirty look.* ❖ *tr. & intr.v.* **dirtied, dirtying, dirties** To make or become soiled: *I dirtied the tablecloth. White clothes dirty easily.*
✦ SYNONYMS dirty, filthy, foul, grimy *adj.*

dis *or* **diss** (dĭs) *tr.v.* **dissed, dissing, disses** *Informal* To show disrespect to, often by insult or criticism: *always dissing his neighbor.*

dis– *prefix* **1.** Not: *dissimilar.* **2.** Absence of: *disfavor.* **3.** Opposite of: *distrust.* **4.** Do the opposite of: *disapprove.* **5.** Deprive of: *disarm.*

WORD BUILDING The prefix **dis–** has several senses, but its basic meaning is "not, not any." Thus *disbelieve* means "to refuse to believe" and *discomfort* means "a lack of comfort." *Dis–* came into English from the Old French prefix *des–,* which in turn ultimately came from the Latin adverb *dis,* meaning "apart, asunder." *Dis–* is an important prefix that occurs very frequently in English in words such as *discredit, disrepair,* and *disrespect.*

disability (dĭs′ə-bĭl′ĭ-tē) *n., pl.* **disabilities 1.** The condition of being disabled. **2.** A disadvantage or deficiency, especially a physical or mental impairment that makes certain tasks difficult or impossible. **3.** Financial support provided to people with such impairment: *has been on disability for a month.*

disable (dĭs-ā′bəl) *tr.v.* **disabled, disabling, disables** To weaken or impair the capacity, abilities, or effectiveness of; incapacitate: *The storm disabled the steamer's engine.* —**dis·a′ble·ment** *n.*

disabled (dĭs-ā′bəld) *adj.* **1.** Not working or functioning: *a disabled car.* **2.** Impaired in physical or mental functioning: *a disabled veteran.* ❖ *n. (used with a plural verb)*

Physically or mentally impaired people: *The new building has access for the disabled.*

disabuse (dĭs′ə-byōōz′) *tr.v.* **disabused, disabusing, disabuses** To free from a falsehood or misconception: *disabuse someone of preconceived notions.*

disadvantage (dĭs′əd-văn′tĭj) *n.* **1.** An unfavorable condition or circumstance: *Some students are at a disadvantage because they don't own computers.* **2.** Something that places one in an unfavorable condition or position: *One disadvantage of river transportation is its slowness.* **3.** Harm or loss: *The road will be closed for six months, to the disadvantage of commuters.*

disadvantaged (dĭs′əd-văn′tĭjd) *adj.* Deprived of some of the basic necessities or advantages of life, such as housing, health care, or education.

disadvantageous (dĭs-ăd′vən-tā′jəs *or* dĭs′ăd-vən-tā′jəs) *adj.* Detrimental; unfavorable: *disadvantageous living conditions.* —**dis·ad′van·ta′geous·ly** *adv.*

disaffect (dĭs′ə-fĕkt′) *tr.v.* **disaffected, disaffecting, disaffects** To cause to lose affection or loyalty. —**dis′af·fec′tion** *n.*

disaffected (dĭs′ə-fĕk′tĭd) *adj.* Resentful and rebellious, especially against authority: *The disaffected workers voted to go on strike.*

disagree (dĭs′ə-grē′) *intr.v.* **disagreed, disagreeing, disagrees** **1.** To have a differing opinion: *Scientists disagree on why dinosaurs died out.* **2.** To dispute or quarrel: *Rival countries often disagree about trade regulations.* **3.** To fail to correspond; differ: *Your answer disagrees with mine.* **4.** To cause bad effects: *Fried food disagrees with me.*

disagreeable (dĭs′ə-grē′ə-bəl) *adj.* **1.** Not to one's liking; unpleasant or offensive: *a strong and disagreeable odor.* **2.** Having a quarrelsome bad-tempered manner: *Many people are disagreeable if they don't get enough sleep.* —**dis′a·gree′a·bly** *adv.*

disagreement (dĭs′ə-grē′mənt) *n.* **1.** A failure or refusal to agree. **2.** A conflict or difference of opinion: *Their disagreement ended in loud words.*

disallow (dĭs′ə-lou′) *tr.v.* **disallowed, disallowing, disallows** **1.** To refuse to allow: *disallow eating in one's room.* **2.** To reject as invalid, untrue, or improper: *disallow an unsigned will as evidence.*

disambiguate (dĭs′ăm-bĭg′yōō-āt′) *tr.v.* **disambiguated, disambiguating, disambiguates** To remove ambiguity so as to establish a single clear meaning for. —**dis′am·big′-u·a′tion** *n.*

disappear (dĭs′ə-pîr′) *intr.v.* **disappeared, disappearing, disappears** **1.** To pass out of sight; vanish: *The ship disappeared over the horizon.* **2.** To cease to be seen; be missing or unfound: *Her purse disappeared from her locker.* **3.** To cease to exist: *Warm weather disappears in the fall.*

✦ SYNONYMS disappear, evaporate, fade, vanish *v.*

disappearance (dĭs′ə-pîr′əns) *n.* The act or an example of disappearing: *Disappearance of the ship during the storm led most to believe it sank.*

disappoint (dĭs′ə-point′) *tr.v.* **disappointed, disappointing, disappoints** **1.** To fail to satisfy the hope, desire, or expectation of: *The ads were exciting, but the movie disappointed me.* **2.** To frustrate or thwart: *So far our efforts to get payment have been disappointed.*

disappointed (dĭs′ə-poin′tĭd) *adj.* Thwarted in hope, desire, or expectation.

disappointing (dĭs′ə-poin′tĭng) *adj.* Not up to expecta-

tions or hopes: *He finished the marathon in a disappointing 12th place.*

disappointment (dĭs′ə-point′mənt) *n.* **1.** The act of disappointing. **2.** The condition or feeling of being disappointed: *couldn't hide their disappointment.* **3.** A person or thing that disappoints: *The picnic was a disappointment.*

disapproval (dĭs′ə-prōō′vəl) *n.* The act of disapproving; censure or condemnation.

disapprove (dĭs′ə-prōōv′) *v.* **disapproved, disapproving, disapproves** —*tr.* **1.** To have an unfavorable opinion of; condemn. **2.** To refuse to approve: *The state disapproved the new zoning proposal.* —*intr.* To have an unfavorable opinion: *disapprove of shouting.*

disarm (dĭs-ärm′) *v.* **disarmed, disarming, disarms** —*tr.* **1.** To take a weapon or weapons from: *The police officer disarmed the robber.* **2.** To make harmless: *disarm a charge of dynamite.* **3.** To overcome the suspicion or unfriendliness of: *Her kind words disarmed us right away.* —*intr.* **1.** To lay down arms. **2.** To reduce or get rid of armed forces: *The countries voted to disarm.*

disarmament (dĭs-är′mə-mənt) *n.* The reduction or abolition of a country's armed forces or weapons of destruction.

disarming (dĭs-är′mĭng) *adj.* Serving to remove suspicion or unfriendliness; winning favor or confidence: *a disarming smile.* —**dis·arm′ing·ly** *adv.*

disarrange (dĭs′ə-rānj′) *tr.v.* **disarranged, disarranging, disarranges** To upset the proper order or arrangement of: *The wind disarranged my hair.* —**dis′ar·range′ment** *n.*

disarray (dĭs′ə-rā′) *n.* A state of disorder; confusion: *The mail lay in disarray on the desk.* ❖ *tr.v.* **disarrayed, disarraying, disarrays** To throw into confusion; upset.

disassemble (dĭs′ə-sĕm′bəl) *v.* **disassembled, disassembling, disassembles** —*tr.* To take apart: *We have to disassemble the engine to repair it.* —*intr.* To come apart: *This telephone disassembles easily.*

disaster (dĭ-zăs′tər) *n.* **1.** Something that causes widespread destruction and distress; a calamity: *Tornadoes, earthquakes, and floods are natural disasters.* **2.** *Informal* A total failure.

disaster area *n.* An area that qualifies for emergency aid from the government because of a catastrophe, such as an earthquake or flood.

disastrous (dĭ-zăs′trəs) *adj.* Accompanied by or causing disaster; calamitous: *a disastrous earthquake; a disastrous error in judgment.* —**dis·as′trous·ly** *adv.*

disavow (dĭs′ə-vou′) *tr.v.* **disavowed, disavowing, disavows** To disclaim knowledge of, responsibility for, or association with.

disavowal (dĭs′ə-vou′əl) *n.* The act or an example of disavowing; a denial or repudiation.

disband (dĭs-bănd′) *v.* **disbanded, disbanding, disbands** —*tr.* To cause (an organization or group) to break up: *disband an orchestra.* —*intr.* To stop functioning as an organization: *The glee club disbanded last year.*

disbar (dĭs-bär′) *tr.v.* **disbarred, disbarring, disbars** To expel (a lawyer) from the practice of law by official action or procedure. —**dis·bar′ment** *n.*

disbelief (dĭs′bĭ-lēf′) *n.* Refusal or reluctance to believe: *express disbelief at a fantastic story.*

disbelieve (dĭs′bĭ-lēv′) *tr.v.* **disbelieved, disbelieving, disbelieves** To refuse or be unable to believe (someone or something): *disbelieved the stories of their fabulous wealth.*

disburden (dĭs-bûr′dn) *tr.v.* **disburdened, disburdening, disburdens 1.** To relieve (a pack animal, for example) of a burden. **2.** To free of a trouble or worry: *He disburdened his mind by telling the truth.*

disburse (dĭs-bûrs′) *tr.v.* **disbursed, disbursing, disburses** To pay out, as from a fund; expend: *disburse large sums to advertise a product.*

disbursement (dĭs-bûrs′mənt) *n.* **1.** The act or process of disbursing. **2.** Money paid out; expenditure: *small disbursements.*

disc (dĭsk) *n.* Variant of **disk.**

discard (dĭ-skärd′) *v.* **discarded, discarding, discards** —*tr.* **1.** To throw away; reject: *discard old shoes; discard a childish habit.* **2.** In card games, to throw out (a playing card) from one's hand. —*intr.* To throw out a playing card. ❖ *n.* (dĭs′kärd′) **1.** The act of discarding in a card game. **2.** A discarded playing card. **3.** Something that is discarded: *Charities will usually accept discards.*

disc brake also **disk brake** *n.* A brake that works by pressing pads against each side of a disk attached to the wheel of a car or truck.

discern (dĭ-sûrn′ *or* dĭ-zûrn′) *tr.v.* **discerned, discerning, discerns 1.** To perceive with the eyes; detect: *discern a figure in the shadows.* **2.** To recognize or understand as being different: *Researchers finally discerned the purpose of the gene.*

discernible (dĭ-sûr′nə-bəl *or* dĭ-zûr′nə-bəl) *adj.* Perceptible, as by the faculty of vision or the intellect: *few discernible differences between the two theories.* —**dis·cern′-i·bly** *adv.*

discerning (dĭ-sûr′nĭng *or* dĭ-zûr′nĭng) *adj.* Showing keen observation and good judgment; perceptive: *a discerning mind.* —**dis·cern′ing·ly** *adv.*

discernment (dĭ-sûrn′mənt *or* dĭ-zûrn′mənt) *n.* **1.** The act or process of using or showing keen insight and good judgment. **2.** Keenness of insight or judgment: *having great discernment for new art.*

discharge (dĭs-chärj′) *v.* **discharged, discharging, discharges** —*tr.* **1.** To release, as from confinement, care, or duty: *discharge a patient from the hospital.* **2.** To remove from office or employment; dismiss: *The steel plant closed and discharged its workers.* **3.** To send or pour forth: *Pipes discharge water into the lake.* **4.** To shoot: *discharged a volley of arrows.* **5.** To perform the obligations or requirements of (an office, duty, or task): *discharge the duties of mayor.* **6.** To comply with the terms of (a debt or promise, for example): *discharged the loan by making regular payments.* **7.** To take an electric charge from: *We discharged the battery while trying to start the car.* **8.** To unload (cargo, for example) from a ship. —*intr.* **1.** To be fired. Used of a gun: *The musket discharged loudly.* **2.** To pour forth contents: *Several streams discharge into the river.* **3.** To give off or lose an electric charge: *Flashlight batteries discharge when the light is on.* ❖ *n.* (dĭs′chärj′ *or* dĭs-chärj′) **1.** The act of firing or shooting a gun or projectile: *We could hear the discharges of a distant cannon.* **2.** A pouring out or flowing forth; an emission: *a discharge of pus from an infection.* **3.** Something poured or flowing forth: *a gummy discharge from a tree trunk.* **4.** Fulfillment of the terms of something, such as a debt or promise: *the discharge of the loan.* **5.** Dismissal or release: *got his discharge from the army.* **6a.** A release of electric charge from a capacitor in a circuit or from a conducting body, such as a cloud in a thunderstorm. **b.** The conversion of chemical energy to electric energy in a battery. **c.**

The passage of an electric current through a gas. **7.** The act of removing a load from a ship: *a discharge of freight from the ship.*

disc harrow *n.* Variant of **disk harrow.**

disciple (dĭ-sī′pəl) *n.* **1.** A person who accepts and assists in spreading the teachings of a leader. **2.** often **Disciple** In the New Testament, one of the original followers of Jesus.

disciplinarian (dĭs′ə-plə-nâr′ē-ən) *n.* A person who enforces or believes in strict discipline.

disciplinary (dĭs′ə-plə-nĕr′ē) *adj.* Relating to or used for discipline: *disciplinary measures.*

discipline (dĭs′ə-plĭn) *n.* **1a.** Training expected to produce a specific skill, behavior, or character. **b.** Controlled behavior resulting from such training. **c.** A systematic method to regulate behavior: *military discipline.* **2.** Punishment intended to correct or train. **3.** A branch of knowledge or of teaching: *Mathematics and computer science are related disciplines.* ❖ *tr.v.* **disciplined, disciplining, disciplines 1.** To train by instruction and practice. **2.** To punish in order to gain control or enforce obedience: *discipline a dog with a quick swat.*

disc jockey also **disk jockey** *n.* An announcer who presents popular recorded music, especially on the radio.

disclaim (dĭs-klām′) *tr.v.* **disclaimed, disclaiming, disclaims 1.** To deny or repudiate: *He disclaimed any involvement with the criminal group.* **2.** To give up one's legal right or claim to: *disclaimed any part of the inheritance.*

disclaimer (dĭs-klā′mər) *n.* A repudiation or denial of a responsibility or connection: *issue a disclaimer of involvement in an investment scheme.*

disclose (dĭ-sklōz′) *tr.v.* **disclosed, disclosing, discloses 1.** To expose to view; uncover: *The excavation disclosed remains of an ancient city.* **2.** To make known (something previously kept secret).

disclosure (dĭ-sklō′zhər) *n.* **1.** The act or process of revealing or uncovering: *The company withheld disclosure of information about its new car.* **2.** Something uncovered; a revelation.

disco (dĭs′kō) *n., pl.* **discos 1.** A discotheque. **2.** Popular dance music, especially of the late 1970s, having strong repetitive bass rhythms.

discolor (dĭs-kŭl′ər) *tr. & intr.v.* **discolored, discoloring, discolors** To alter or become altered in color; stain: *Floodwaters discolored the painting. Metal discolors with rust.*

discoloration (dĭs-kŭl′ə-rā′shən) *n.* **1.** The act of discoloring or the condition of being discolored: *the discoloration of curtains washed in rusty water.* **2.** A stain: *Water damage left several large discolorations on the carpet.*

discombobulate (dĭs′kəm-bŏb′yə-lāt′) *tr.v.* **discombobulated, discombobulating, discombobulates** To throw into a state of confusion. —**dis′com·bob′u·la′tion** *n.*

discomfit (dĭs-kŭm′fĭt) *tr.v.* **discomfited, discomfiting, discomfits** To make uneasy or confused; embarrass: *Trying to speak a foreign language discomfits many people.*

discomfiture (dĭs-kŭm′fĭ-chŏŏr′) *n.* **1.** Frustration; disappointment: *quit a project in total discomfiture.* **2.** Discomfort; embarrassment: *the discomfiture of a public scolding.*

discomfort (dĭs-kŭm′fərt) *n.* **1.** A lack of comfort; uneasiness: *a patient in discomfort.* **2.** Something that disturbs a person's comfort: *A lumpy mattress is a discomfort when sleeping.*

discommode (dĭs′kə-mōd′) *tr.v.* **discommoded, discommoding, discommodes** To put to inconvenience; trouble.

discompose (dĭs′kəm-pōz′) *tr.v.* **discomposed, discom-**

posing, discomposes To disturb the composure or calm of; perturb: *The shouts of a few protesters discomposed the speaker.*

discomposure (dĭs′kəm-pō′zhər) *n.* The absence of composure; confusion or uneasiness: *The pianist's discomposure was evident from the mistakes she made.*

disconcert (dĭs′kən-sûrt′) *tr.v.* **disconcerted, disconcerting, disconcerts** To upset the self-possession of; embarrass or confuse: *All of the horns honking disconcerted the student driver.* —**dis′con·cert′ing·ly** *adv.*

disconnect (dĭs′kə-nĕkt′) *tr.v.* **disconnected, disconnecting, disconnects** To break or interrupt the connection of or between; separate: *Disconnect the TV before you move it. Our phone call was disconnected during the storm.* ❖ *n.* (dĭs′kə-nĕkt′) A lack of connection; a disparity: *a disconnect between how legislators view the recession and how voters do.* —**dis′con·nec′tion** *n.*

disconnected (dĭs′kə-nĕk′tĭd) *adj.* **1.** Not connected; separate: *disconnected buildings.* **2.** Not clear or logical; disorderly: *a disconnected account of the accident; disconnected bits.* —**dis′con·nect′ed·ly** *adv.*

disconsolate (dĭs-kŏn′sə-lĭt) *adj.* Not able to be consoled; very sad or dejected: *We were left disconsolate when our cat disappeared.* —**dis·con′so·late·ly** *adv.* —**dis·con′so·late·ness** *n.*

discontent (dĭs′kən-tĕnt′) *n.* Lack of contentment; dissatisfaction: *Not getting a raise caused discontent among the workers.* ❖ *tr.v.* **discontented, discontenting, discontents** To make discontented: *No electricity for three days discontented everyone.* —**dis′con·tent′ment** *n.*

discontented (dĭs′kən-tĕn′tĭd) *adj.* Not contented; unhappy: *Discontented tenants refused to pay rent until they got heat.* —**dis′con·tent′ed·ly** *adv.* —**dis′con·tent′ed·ness** *n.*

discontinuation (dĭs′kən-tĭn′yoo-ā′shən) *n.* A termination; an ending: *discontinuation of bus service during the storm.* —**dis′con·tin′u·ance** (dĭs′kən-tĭn′yoo-əns) *n.*

discontinue (dĭs′kən-tĭn′yoo) *tr.v.* **discontinued, discontinuing, discontinues 1.** To stop doing or providing (something): *discontinued bus service after midnight.* **2.** To cease making or manufacturing: *This type of computer monitor has been discontinued.*

discontinuous (dĭs′kən-tĭn′yoo-əs) *adj.* Not continuous; broken up; interrupted: *a discontinuous supply of natural gas.* —**dis′con·tin′u·ous·ly** *adv.*

discord (dĭs′kôrd′) *n.* **1.** Lack of agreement or harmony: *an angry meeting filled with discord.* **2.** A combination of musical tones that sounds harsh or unpleasant; a lack of harmony. **3.** A confused or harsh mingling of sounds: *the early morning discord of rush-hour traffic.*

discordant (dĭ-skôr′dnt) *adj.* **1.** Not in agreement; conflicting: *a discordant meeting.* **2.** Disagreeable in sound; harsh: *discordant sounds of the city streets.* —**dis·cor′dance** *n.* —**dis·cor′dant·ly** *adv.*

discotheque (dĭs′kə-tĕk′ *or* dĭs′kə-tĕk′) *n.* A nightclub that offers dancing to recorded music.

discount (dĭs′kount′ *or* dĭs-kount′) *tr.v.* **discounted, discounting, discounts 1.** To deduct or subtract (an amount or percentage) from a cost or price of an item, as in a sale: *The dealer discounted 25 percent off the original price of the rug.* **2.** To sell or offer for sale at a reduced price: *The store discounts its coats each spring.* **3.** To disregard or doubt (something) as an exaggeration or not trust-

worthy: *The scientist discounted the rumors of a new energy source.* ❖ *n.* (dĭs′kount′) A reduction from the full amount of a price or debt. ❖ *adj.* (dĭs′kount′) **1.** Offering products or services for sale at low or reduced prices: *a discount retailer; a discount airline.* **2.** Sold or offered for sale at low or reduced prices: *discount merchandise.*

discourage (dĭ-skûr′ĭj) *tr.v.* **discouraged, discouraging, discourages 1.** To make less hopeful or confident; dishearten: *The size of the job discouraged me.* **2.** To try to prevent by expressing disapproval or raising objections; dissuade: *Friends discouraged them from going.* **3.** To hinder or deter: *Severe penalties are supposed to discourage tax evasion.*

discouragement (dĭ-skûr′ĭj-mənt) *n.* **1.** A condition of being or feeling discouraged: *Discouragement and hardship destroyed the hopes of many pioneers.* **2.** Something that discourages: *Harsh winters are a discouragement to living in the far north.* **3.** The act of discouraging: *The discouragement of my family made me more determined to be an actor.*

discourse (dĭs′kôrs′) *n.* **1.** Discussion; conversation: *cheerful discourse among friends.* **2.** A series of connected remarks or statements about a subject: *The minister gave a long discourse on morality. The book is a discourse on politics.* ❖ *intr.v.* (dĭ-skôrs′) **discoursed, discoursing, discourses** To speak or write formally and often at length: *The mayor discoursed on the role of the government in improving city life.*

discourteous (dĭs-kûr′tē-əs) *adj.* Lacking courtesy; not polite; rude. —**dis·cour′te·ous·ly** *adv.* —**dis·cour′te·ous·ness** *n.*

discourtesy (dĭs-kûr′tĭ-sē) *n., pl.* **discourtesies 1.** Lack of courtesy; rudeness. **2.** A rude or impolite act: *the discourtesy of interrupting others.*

discover (dĭ-skŭv′ər) *tr.v.* **discovered, discovering, discovers 1.** To find or see for the first time: *Using the new telescope, astronomers discovered quasars at the edge of the universe.* **2.** To learn of; gain knowledge of: *discover errors by checking.* —**dis·cov′er·er** *n.*

discovery (dĭ-skŭv′ə-rē) *n., pl.* **discoveries 1.** The act of discovering: *The discovery of gold in California led many people to travel west.* **2.** Something discovered: *The archaeologist gave a talk on her discoveries.*

discredit (dĭs-krĕd′ĭt) *tr.v.* **discredited, discrediting, discredits 1.** To damage in reputation; disgrace: *The report of corruption discredits our politicians.* **2.** To cast doubt on; cause to be distrusted: *new scientific evidence that discredits earlier theories.* **3.** To refuse to believe in: *discredit a story as mere gossip.* ❖ *n.* **1.** Loss or damage to one's reputation: *Dishonest officials brought discredit to the city government.* **2.** Lack or loss of trust or belief; doubt: *An eyewitness account that brings earlier testimony into discredit.* **3.** Something that brings disgrace or distrust: *He is a discredit to his family.*

discreditable (dĭs-krĕd′ĭ-tə-bəl) *adj.* Deserving or bringing discredit; disgraceful: *Lying in court is a discreditable act.* —**dis·cred′it·a·bly** *adv.*

discreet (dĭ-skrēt′) *adj.* Having or showing caution or self-restraint in one's speech or behavior; prudent: *The supervisor was discreet in discussing the employee's mistake. Keep a discreet distance from any wild animal.* —**dis·creet′ly** *adv.* —**dis·creet′ness** *n.*

discrepancy (dĭ-skrĕp′ən-sē) *n., pl.* **discrepancies** Lack of agreement; inconsistency: *There was a large discrepancy between their statement and the facts.*

discrepant (dĭ-skrĕp′ənt) *adj.* Showing discrepancy; disagreeing.

discrete (dĭ-skrēt′) *adj.* Separate from others; distinct: *The police commissioner oversees several discrete departments. I have only a few discrete memories of my early childhood.* —**dis·crete′ly** *adv.*

discretion (dĭ-skrĕsh′ən) *n.* **1.** The quality of being discreet; prudence: *Diplomats must use great discretion in negotiating treaties.* **2.** Freedom of action or judgment: *Choosing numbers for their jerseys was left to the players' discretion.*

discretionary (dĭ-skrĕsh′ə-nĕr′ē) *adj.* Left to or determined by one's own discretion or judgment: *The governor has a discretionary fund for emergencies.*

discriminate (dĭ-skrĭm′ə-nāt′) *v.* **discriminated, discriminating, discriminates** —*intr.* **1.** To make a clear distinction; distinguish: *The art dealer could discriminate among many painters' styles.* **2.** To show preference or prejudice: *It is illegal to discriminate against employees on the basis of age.* —*tr.* To make or see a clear distinction between: *A critic discriminates good books from poor ones.* —**dis·crim′i·na′tor** *n.*

discriminating (dĭ-skrĭm′ə-nā′tĭng) *adj.* **1.** Showing careful judgment or fine taste: *a discriminating critic of modern music.* **2.** Serving to distinguish or set apart from others; distinctive: *a discriminating characteristic.* **3.** Marked by or showing bias; discriminatory.

discrimination (dĭ-skrĭm′ə-nā′shən) *n.* **1.** The ability to recognize or make fine distinctions: *clothes bought without care or discrimination; discrimination of color essential to the work of an artist.* **2.** Treatment of people based on their belonging to a class or category rather than on individual merit; partiality or prejudice: *The Constitution protects citizens from racial and religious discrimination.*

discriminatory (dĭ-skrĭm′ə-nə-tôr′ē) *adj.* Showing prejudice; biased. —**dis·crim′i·na·to′ri·ly** *adv.*

discursive (dĭ-skûr′sĭv) *adj.* **1.** Wandering from one subject to another; rambling: *discursive talk without much point to it.* **2.** Proceeding by means of a logically connected series of statements or ideas: *expressed his opinions in discursive paragraphs; a philosophy that is intuitive rather than discursive.* —**dis·cur′sive·ly** *adv.*

discus (dĭs′kəs) *n., pl.* **discuses** A disk, typically wooden, plastic, or rubber with a metal rim, that is thrown for distance in athletic contests.

discuss (dĭ-skŭs′) *tr.v.* **discussed, discussing, discusses 1.** To speak with another or others about; talk over: *We met to discuss the plan for the new park.* **2.** To speak or write about (a subject): *In her new book the author discusses recent events in Latin America.*

discussion (dĭ-skŭsh′ən) *n.* **1.** A conversation about a subject; an exchange of views: *We had a discussion about what would be fair under the circumstances.* **2.** A usually formal treatment of a subject, as in a speech or book: *Have you read that author's discussion of foreign policy?*

disdain (dĭs-dān′) *tr.v.* **disdained, disdaining, disdains** To consider or treat with contempt; despise: *The playwright disdained the judgments of critics in the press.* ❖ *n.* A show of contempt and aloofness; scorn: *She responded with disdain to his offers of a bribe.*

disdainful (dĭs-dān′fəl) *adj.* Feeling or showing disdain; scornful. See Synonyms at **arrogant.** —**dis·dain′ful·ly** *adv.*

disease (dĭ-zēz′) *n.* A condition of an organism or one of its parts that makes it unable to function in the normal or proper way; sickness. A disease is usually identified by certain signs or symptoms and can result from various causes, such as infection, environmental factors, or a genetic defect.

diseased (dĭ-zēzd′) *adj.* Affected with or suffering from disease: *a diseased liver.*

disembark (dĭs′ĕm-bärk′) *v.* **disembarked, disembarking, disembarks** —*intr.* To get off a ship or airplane: *After the flight attendant opens the door, you may disembark.* —*tr.* To unload from a ship or airplane: *The ship docked and disembarked the passengers.* —**dis·em′bar·ka′tion** *n.*

disembodied (dĭs′ĕm-bŏd′ēd) *adj.* Freed or separated from the body: *disembodied spirits; a disembodied voice coming from somewhere in the dark.*

disembowel (dĭs′ĕm-bou′əl) *tr.v.* **disemboweled, disemboweling, disembowels** or **disembowelled, disembowelling, disembowels** To remove the bowels from: *The elephant disemboweled the lion with its tusks.* —**dis′em·bow′el·ment** *n.*

disenchant (dĭs′ĕn-chănt′) *tr.v.* **disenchanted, disenchanting, disenchants** To free from enchantment or false belief; disillusion: *One look at the crumbling house was enough to disenchant any buyer.* —**dis′en·chant′ment** *n.*

disencumber (dĭs′ĕn-kŭm′bər) *tr.v.* **disencumbered, disencumbering, disencumbers** To free from something that burdens, hinders, or troubles: *disencumber oneself of worry.*

disenfranchise (dĭs′ĕn-frăn′chīz′) *tr.v.* **disenfranchised, disenfranchising, disenfranchises** To disfranchise. —**dis′en·fran′chise′ment** *n.*

disengage (dĭs′ĕn-gāj′) *v.* **disengaged, disengaging, disengages** —*tr.* **1.** To make free from something that holds fast, entangles, or connects: *disengage the car's clutch.* **2.** To free or release (oneself) from an engagement, promise, or obligation. —*intr.* To become free or detach oneself: *As the brakes disengaged, the car rolled backwards.* —**dis′en·gage′ment** *n.*

disentangle (dĭs′ĕn-tăng′gəl) *tr.v.* **disentangled, disentangling, disentangles** To free from tangles or confusion: *disentangle a knotted clothesline; disentangle fact from a web of accusations.* —**dis′en·tan′gle·ment** *n.*

disfavor (dĭs-fā′vər) *n.* **1.** Unfavorable regard; disapproval. **2.** The condition of being regarded with dislike or disapproval: *The governor was in disfavor with voters.* ❖ *tr.v.* **disfavored, disfavoring, disfavors** To view or treat with dislike or disapproval: *The company disfavored any expenditure to clean up the environment.*

disfigure (dĭs-fĭg′yər) *tr.v.* **disfigured, disfiguring, disfigures** To spoil the appearance of; mar the beauty of: *Vandals disfigured the statue with paint.*

disfranchise (dĭs-frăn′chīz′) *tr.v.* **disfranchised, disfranchising, disfranchises** To deprive of a privilege or a right, especially the right to vote: *The law disfranchises a person guilty of a felony.* —**dis′fran′chise′ment** *n.*

disgorge (dĭs-gôrj′) *tr.v.* **disgorged, disgorging, disgorges 1.** To bring up and discharge from the throat or stomach; vomit. **2.** To pour forth violently; spew: *The volcano disgorged lava into the ocean.* **3.** To give up (stolen goods, for example) unwillingly.

disgrace (dĭs-grās′) *n.* **1.** Loss of honor, respect, or reputation; shame: *The scandal brought disgrace on the politician's family.* **2.** The condition of being strongly disapproved: *in disgrace for telling a secret.* **3.** A person or thing that brings dishonor or disfavor: *The dirty streets are a disgrace to the city.* ❖ *tr.v.* **disgraced, disgracing, dis-**

graces **1.** To bring shame or dishonor upon: *The thief's conviction disgraced family and friends.* **2.** To view or treat (someone) with disapproval: *The mayor disgraced the aide for failing to investigate the problem.*

disgraceful (dĭs-grās′fəl) *adj.* Causing or deserving disgrace; shameful. —**dis·grace′ful·ly** *adv.*

disgruntle (dĭs-grŭn′tl) *tr.v.* **disgruntled, disgruntling, disgruntles** To make discontented; displease or disgust: *Loss of two vacation days disgruntled all the employees.* —**dis·grun′tle·ment** *n.*

disgruntled (dĭs-grŭn′tld) *adj.* Discontented, dissatisfied or disgusted; cross: *The disgruntled employee filed a complaint.*

disguise (dĭs-gīz′) *tr.v.* **disguised, disguising, disguises 1.** To hide the identity of (someone) by changing the appearance: *The princess disguised herself as a shepherd boy.* **2.** To hide or cause to appear different: *She disguised her embarrassment with a smile.* ❖ *n.* **1.** Clothes or accessories that are worn to conceal one's true identity: *The two spies wore the disguise of repairmen.* **2.** The condition of having concealed one's true identity: *The nurse turned out to be a comedian in disguise.*

disgust (dĭs-gŭst′) *tr.v.* **disgusted, disgusting, disgusts** To cause feelings of sickening dislike, distaste, or annoyance: *We are disgusted by your refusal to cooperate.* ❖ *n.* A feeling of extreme dislike, distaste, or annoyance: *The fans showed their disgust by booing the umpire.*

disgusted (dĭs-gŭs′tĭd) *adj.* Filled with disgust: *a disgusted look.* —**dis·gust′ed·ly** *adv.*

disgusting (dĭs-gŭs′tĭng) *adj.* Causing disgust: *disgusting food; a disgusting remark.* —**dis·gust′ing·ly** *adv.*

dish (dĭsh) *n.* **1a.** A shallow container for holding, cooking, or serving food. **b.** The amount that a dish can hold: *I ate two dishes of fruit.* **2.** A particular kind or preparation of food: *Sushi is a Japanese dish.* **3.** A radio, television, or radar antenna having the shape of a dish. ❖ *tr.v.* **dished, dishing, dishes** To serve (food) in a dish or dishes: *dish out the vegetables.*

dishabille (dĭs′ə-bēl′ *or* dĭs′ə-bē′) also **deshabille** (dĕs′ə-bēl′ *or* dĕs′ə-bē′) *n.* **1.** The state of being partially or very casually dressed. **2.** Casual or lounging attire.

dishdasha (dĭsh-däsh′ə) *n.* A loose, long-sleeved garment; a thobe.

dishearten (dĭs-här′tn) *tr.v.* **disheartened, disheartening, disheartens** To cause to lose courage and hope: *Lack of interest in their new battery disheartened the inventors.* —**dis·heart′en·ing·ly** *adv.*

disheveled or **dishevelled** (dĭ-shĕv′əld) *adj.* Untidy; disorderly: *disheveled clothes; a disheveled look.*

dishonest (dĭs-ŏn′ĭst) *adj.* **1.** Inclined to lie, cheat, or deceive: *a dishonest art dealer.* **2.** Showing or resulting from falseness or fraud: *a dishonest answer; dishonest dealings.* —**dis·hon′est·ly** *adv.*

dishonesty (dĭs-ŏn′ĭ-stē) *n., pl.* **dishonesties 1.** Lack of honesty or integrity. **2.** A dishonest act or statement.

dishonor (dĭs-ŏn′ər) *n.* **1.** Loss of honor, respect, or reputation; shame. **2.** A person or thing that causes loss of honor: *a dishonor to the whole team.* ❖ *tr.v.* **dishonored, dishonoring, dishonors** To bring shame or disgrace on: *His rude behavior dishonors the reputation of his company.*

dishonorable (dĭs-ŏn′ər-ə-bəl) *adj.* Characterized by or causing dishonor: *the dishonorable acts of a swindler.*

—**dis·hon′or·a·ble·ness** *n.* —**dis·hon′or·a·bly** *adv.*

dishtowel (dĭsh′tou′əl) *n.* A towel for drying dishes.

dishwasher (dĭsh′wŏsh′ər) *n.* **1.** A machine that washes dishes. **2.** A person who washes dishes, especially in a restaurant.

dishwater (dĭsh′wô′tər) *n.* Water in which dishes are or have been washed.

disillusion (dĭs′ĭ-lōō′zhən) *tr.v.* **disillusioned, disillusioning, disillusions** To free from a false idea or belief: *Many immigrants were disillusioned by the high cost of living.* —**dis′il·lu′sion·ment** *n.*

disinclination (dĭs-ĭn′klə-nā′shən) *n.* Unwillingness, reluctance, or aversion: *a disinclination to try new foods.*

disinclined (dĭs′ĭn-klīnd′) *adj.* Unwilling; reluctant: *I am disinclined to take a job with such long hours.*

disinfect (dĭs′ĭn-fĕkt′) *tr.v.* **disinfected, disinfecting, disinfects** To cleanse so as to destroy or prevent the growth of microorganisms that can cause disease: *disinfect a cut.* —**dis′in·fec′tion** *n.*

disinfectant (dĭs′ĭn-fĕk′tənt) *n.* A substance that kills or prevents the growth of microorganisms that cause disease: *wash a wound with disinfectant.* ❖ *adj.* Destroying or preventing the growth of microorganisms that cause disease: *disinfectant soap.*

disinformation (dĭs-ĭn′fər-mā′shən) *n.* Deliberately misleading information provided by a government, especially by an intelligence agency, to influence public opinion or another nation's government.

disingenuous (dĭs′ĭn-jĕn′yōō-əs) *adj.* **1.** Not straightforward or candid; insincere or calculating. **2.** Pretending to be unaware or unsophisticated. —**dis′in·gen′u·ous·ly** *adv.*

disinherit (dĭs′ĭn-hĕr′ĭt) *tr.v.* **disinherited, disinheriting, disinherits** To take from (a person) an inheritance or the right to inherit: *The eccentric millionaire disinherited his entire family.*

disintegrate (dĭs-ĭn′tĭ-grāt′) *v.* **disintegrated, disintegrating, disintegrates** —*intr.* **1.** To break into small pieces; separate into bits: *rock disintegrating into sand.* **2.** To lose cohesion or unity: *a family that disintegrated.* **3.** In nuclear physics, to undergo disintegration. —*tr.* To cause to break into separate pieces or bits: *Water disintegrated the cement to pebble-sized pieces.*

disintegration (dĭs-ĭn′tĭ-grā′shən) *n.* **1a.** The act or process of disintegrating: *Freezing and thawing caused disintegration of the concrete.* **b.** The condition of being disintegrated. **2.** In nuclear physics, the transformation of an atomic nucleus when it loses mass as it throws off particles or rays.

disinter (dĭs′ĭn-tûr′) *tr.v.* **disinterred, disinterring, disinters 1.** To dig up or remove (a body) from a grave. **2.** To make public; disclose: *disinter old documents from the library.* —**dis′in·ter′ment** *n.*

disinterested (dĭs-ĭn′trĭ-stĭd *or* dĭs-ĭn′tə-rĕs′tĭd) *adj.* **1.** Free of bias and self-interest; impartial: *the disinterested decision of an umpire.* **2.** Uninterested or unconcerned: *My friends are totally disinterested in the movie.* —**dis·in′ter·est·ed·ly** *adv.*

disjoint (dĭs-joint′) *tr.v.* **disjointed, disjointing, disjoints 1.** To take apart at the joints: *The butcher disjointed the chicken for frying.* **2.** To pull out of joint; dislocate: *That tackle disjointed the football player's shoulder.* **3.** To break up; put out of order: *The flooding disjointed the business section of town.* ❖ *adj.* In mathematics, having no common members. {0, 1, 2} and {3, 4, 5} are disjoint sets.

disjointed (dĭs-join′tĭd) *adj.* **1.** Separated at the joints: *a disjointed leg of lamb.* **2.** Lacking order or coherence; disconnected: *a disjointed paragraph.* —**dis·joint′ed·ly** *adv.*

disk also **disc** (dĭsk) *n.* **1.** A thin, flat, circular object, such as a plate or coin. **2.** Something that resembles such an object: *the moon's disk reflected in the pond.* **3a.** A round flat plate coated with a magnetic substance on which computer data is stored. **b.** The data stored on such a disk. **c.** An optical disc, especially a compact disc. **4.** A phonograph record. **5.** A round flattened structure in an animal, such as one made of cartilage and lying between adjacent bones of the spine.

disk brake *n.* Variant of **disc brake.**

disk drive *n.* A device in a computer that reads data stored on a disk and writes data onto the disk for storage.

disk harrow or **disc harrow** *n.* A harrow consisting of a series of sharp, rotating metal disks on one or more axles, used to break up soil for seeding or planting.

disk jockey *n.* Variant of **disc jockey.**

dislike (dĭs-līk′) *tr.v.* **disliked, disliking, dislikes** To regard (someone or something) with an unfavorable attitude; not like: *She dislikes lemonade. He dislikes working on Saturday.* ❖ *n.* An unfavorable attitude: *I have a strong dislike of board games.*

dislocate (dĭs′lō-kāt′ or dĭs-lō′kāt) *tr.v.* **dislocated, dislocating, dislocates** **1.** To put (a body part, especially a joint or bone) out of its normal position: *I dislocated my thumb catching the ball barehanded.* **2.** To throw into confusion or disorder; upset: *The drought dislocated the state's economy. The snowstorm dislocated rail and air traffic.* —**dis′lo·ca′tion** *n.*

dislodge (dĭs-lŏj′) *tr.v.* **dislodged, dislodging, dislodges** To move or force out of position: *Heavy rains dislodged boulders from the hillside.*

disloyal (dĭs-loi′əl) *adj.* Lacking loyalty; unfaithful. —**dis·loy′al·ly** *adv.*

disloyalty (dĭs-loi′əl-tē) *n., pl.* **disloyalties** **1.** Lack of loyalty; unfaithfulness. **2.** A disloyal act: *Taking all the credit for the discovery was a disloyalty to fellow researchers.*

dismal (dĭz′məl) *adj.* **1.** Causing gloom or depression; dreary: *a dismal fog.* **2.** Feeling gloomy; depressed; miserable: *feeling dismal from a bad cold.* —**dis′mal·ly** *adv.* —**dis′mal·ness** *n.*

WORD HISTORY The English word **dismal** comes from the medieval French phrase *dis mal,* literally "bad days." The *dis mal* were the two unlucky days of each month, and they also meant unlucky days in general. Those English who didn't understand French spoke of *dismal days,* not realizing that this literally meant "bad days days"; eventually *dismal* was felt to be an adjective meaning "bad, unlucky," and then, ultimately "causing gloom" or "feeling gloom."

dismantle (dĭs-măn′tl) *tr.v.* **dismantled, dismantling, dismantles** **1.** To pull down; take apart: *We dismantled the table to get it through the door.* **2.** To strip of furnishings or equipment: *Movers dismantled the apartment.* —**dis·man′tle·ment** *n.*

dismay (dĭs-mā′) *tr.v.* **dismayed, dismaying, dismays** To upset or distress: *They were dismayed by the flood damage.* ❖ *n.* A sudden loss of courage or confidence in the face of danger or trouble: *Being lost in the woods filled the hikers with dismay.*

dismember (dĭs-mĕm′bər) *tr.v.* **dismembered, dismembering, dismembers** **1.** To cut, tear, or pull off the limbs of: *The fox dismembered the chicken.* **2.** To divide into pieces: *The Roman Empire has been dismembered into numerous states.* —**dis·mem′ber·ment** *n.*

dismiss (dĭs-mĭs′) *tr.v.* **dismissed, dismissing, dismisses** **1.** To end the employment or service of; discharge: *Several workers were dismissed for loafing on the job.* **2.** To direct or allow to leave: *The students were dismissed for the holidays.* **3.** To put out of one's mind or consider as unimportant: *We dismissed the story as gossip.* **4.** To put (a claim or action) out of court without further hearing: *The judge dismissed the case due to lack of evidence.*

dismissal (dĭs-mĭs′əl) *n.* **1.** The act of dismissing someone: *The teacher's angry outburst led to his dismissal.* **2.** The act of considering something unimportant: *Her dismissal of my concerns annoyed me.* **3.** An order or a notice of discharge: *The laid-off workers received their dismissals by email.*

dismount (dĭs-mount′) *v.* **dismounted, dismounting, dismounts** —*intr.* **1.** To get off or down, as from a horse or bicycle; alight. **2.** To execute a dismount in gymnastics. —*tr.* **1.** To unseat from a horse: *The frightened horse dismounted its rider.* **2.** To remove (a thing) from its support or mounting: *dismounted the old cannon for storage.* **3.** To take apart (a mechanism). ❖ *n.* (dĭs′mount′) **1.** The act or manner of dismounting, especially from a horse. **2.** A move in gymnastics whereby the gymnast gets off an apparatus or completes a floor exercise, typically landing on both feet.

disobedience (dĭs′ə-bē′dē-əns) *n.* Refusal or failure to obey.

disobedient (dĭs′ə-bē′dē-ənt) *adj.* Refusing or failing to obey: *a disobedient child.* —**dis′o·be′di·ent·ly** *adv.*

disobey (dĭs′ə-bā′) *tr. & intr.v.* **disobeyed, disobeying, disobeys** To refuse or fail to obey: *Pedestrians sometimes disobey traffic signals. A trained horse seldom disobeys.*

disorder (dĭs-ôr′dər) *n.* **1.** Lack of order or regular arrangement; confusion: *Your desk is always in a state of disorder.* **2.** A public disturbance: *Police responded to a disorder in our neighborhood.* **3.** A sickness or disturbance of the body or mind: *a nervous disorder.* ❖ *tr.v.* **disordered, disordering, disorders** **1.** To throw into disorder; muddle: *Early arrival of our guests disordered all our arrangements.* **2.** To upset the mental or physical health of: *Rich foods thoroughly disorder my digestion.*

disorderly (dĭs-ôr′dər-lē) *adj.* **1.** Lacking regular or orderly arrangement; messy: *a disorderly room.* **2.** Lacking discipline; unruly: *a noisy disorderly crowd.* —**dis·or′der·li·ness** *n.*

disorganize (dĭs-ôr′gə-nīz′) *tr.v.* **disorganized, disorganizing, disorganizes** To destroy the organization or orderly arrangement of; throw into confusion or disorder: *The strike by airline pilots disorganized air schedules.* —**dis·or′gan·i·za′tion** (dĭs-ôr′gə-nĭ-zā′shən) *n.*

disorganized (dĭs-ôr′gə-nīzd′) *adj.* Not organized; without organization or order: *a disorganized person; a disorganized room.*

disorient (dĭs-ôr′ē-ĕnt′) *tr.v.* **disoriented, disorienting, disorients** To cause to lose one's sense of direction or bearings; confuse: *Walking around in an unfamiliar part of the city disoriented us.* —**dis·o′ri·en·ta′tion** *n.*

disown (dĭs-ōn′) *tr.v.* **disowned, disowning, disowns** To refuse to claim or accept as one's own; reject: *The father disowned his son for refusing to join the family business.*

disparage (dĭ-spăr′ĭj) *tr.v.* **disparaged, disparaging, disparages** **1.** To speak of in an insulting or disrespectful

way; belittle: *He disparages the accomplishments of others.*
2. To lower in regard or position; discredit: *The article disparages environmentalists as busybodies.* —**dis·par′-age·ment** *n.* —**dis·par′ag·ing·ly** *adv.*

disparate (dĭs′pər-ĭt *or* dĭ-spăr′ĭt) *adj.* **1.** Completely distinct or different in kind; entirely dissimilar. **2.** Having dissimilar or opposing elements: *a disparate group.* —**dis′pa·rate·ly** *adv.*

disparity (dĭ-spăr′ĭ-tē) *n., pl.* **disparities 1.** Inequality; difference: *the disparity in population between one city and another.* **2.** Lack of similarity; unlikeness: *a great disparity in the accounts of what happened.*

dispassionate (dĭs-păsh′ə-nĭt) *adj.* Not influenced by strong feelings or emotions: *the dispassionate ruling of a judge.* —**dis·pas′sion·ate·ly** *adv.*

dispatch (dĭ-spăch′) *tr.v.* **dispatched, dispatching, dispatches 1.** To send off to a specific destination or on specific business: *dispatch a letter; dispatch a police car to the scene of a disturbance.* **2.** To complete or dispose of promptly: *The police dispatched their duty and left.* **3.** To put to death quickly and without ceremony: *The ranger dispatched the injured deer.* ❖ *n.* **1.** The act of sending off: *the dispatch of a representative to the conference.* **2.** Quickness and efficiency in performance: *The owl killed its prey with dispatch.* **3.** (*also* dĭs′păch′) **a.** A written message, especially an official communication, sent with speed: *The messenger carried a dispatch from headquarters.* **b.** A news item sent to a news organization, as by a correspondent. —**dis·patch′er** *n.*

dispel (dĭ-spĕl′) *tr.v.* **dispelled, dispelling, dispels** To drive away, disperse, or cause to disappear: *Light dispelled the fog.*

dispensable (dĭ-spĕn′sə-bəl) *adj.* Not essential; unimportant: *To shorten the report, I removed all of the dispensable comments.* —**dis·pens′a·bil′i·ty** *n.*

dispensary (dĭ-spĕn′sə-rē) *n., pl.* **dispensaries 1.** An office in a hospital, school, or other institution where medicines and medical supplies are given out. **2.** A place where medicines and medical treatment are provided, usually at little or no cost.

dispensation (dĭs′pən-sā′shən) *n.* **1.** The act or process of dispensing or giving out; distribution: *dispensation of medicine by the local clinic.* **2.** Something given out or distributed: *There were no red pens in this month's dispensation of supplies.* **3.** Freedom or a release from an obligation or rule, granted in a particular case: *a dispensation allowing new businesses relief from taxes.*

dispense (dĭ-spĕns′) *tr.v.* **dispensed, dispensing, dispenses 1.** To deal out or distribute, especially in parts or portions: *The relief worker dispensed food to the refugees.* See Synonyms at **distribute**. **2.** To prepare and give out (medicines). **3.** To carry out; administer: *The judge dispensed justice fairly.* ◆ **dispense with** To manage without; forgo: *Let's dispense with the formalities and get down to business.*

dispenser (dĭ-spĕn′sər) *n.* A person or thing that dispenses: *a paper cup dispenser.*

dispersal (dĭ-spûr′səl) *n.* The act of dispersing or the condition of being dispersed: *the dispersal of a crowd; dispersal of aid among the needy.*

disperse (dĭ-spûrs′) *v.* **dispersed, dispersing, disperses** —*tr.* **1.** To drive off or scatter in different directions: *The rain dispersed the crowd.* **2.** To cause to vanish or disap-

pear; dispel: *Winds dispersed the clouds.* **3.** To separate (light or other radiation) into its different wavelengths. —*intr.* **1.** To separate and move in different directions; scatter: *The protesters dispersed when the police arrived.* **2.** To vanish or disappear: *The mist had dispersed by noon.*

dispersion (dĭ-spûr′zhən *or* dĭ-spûr′shən) *n.* **1.** The separation of light or other radiation into components, usually according to wavelength. **2.** The act of dispersing or the state of being dispersed: *Bright sunlight caused dispersion of the fog.*

dispirit (dĭ-spĭr′ĭt) *tr.v.* **dispirited, dispiriting, dispirits** To lower in spirit; discourage; dishearten.

dispirited (dĭ-spĭr′ĭ-tĭd) *adj.* Depressed; disheartened; discouraged: *feeling tired and dispirited.* —**dis·pir′-it·ed·ly** *adv.*

displace (dĭs-plās′) *tr.v.* **displaced, displacing, displaces 1.** To change the place or position of: *The goal was displaced by a skater before the puck went in.* **2.** To force to leave a place of residence: *The refugees were displaced by the war.* **3.** To take the place of; replace: *Many workers have been displaced in their jobs by robots.* **4.** To take the space of (a quantity of liquid or gas): *An equal amount of oxygen displaced the carbon dioxide.* **5.** To dismiss from an office or position: *In the election, the voters displaced their representative.*

displaced person (dĭs-plāst′) *n.* A person who has been driven from his or her home country by war or other calamity; a refugee or evacuee.

displacement (dĭs-plās′mənt) *n.* **1a.** The weight or volume of fluid displaced by a body floating in it. The weight of the body is equal to the weight of the fluid it displaces. **b.** The measure of the distance that a body has been moved from one point to another through space. **2.** The act of displacing or the condition of being displaced: *Flooding caused the displacement of many people.*

display (dĭ-splā′) *tr.v.* **displayed, displaying, displays 1.** To put in view; exhibit: *The library displays its new books in a case.* **2.** To make noticeable; show evidence of: *a decision that displays poor judgment.* **3.** To show off; flaunt: *proudly displayed his new hat.* ❖ *n.* **1.** The act of displaying: *a display of kindness.* **2.** A public exhibition: *a display of Native American pottery.* **3.** A show designed to impress or to attract attention: *The lavish party was just a display of wealth.* **4.** A specialized pattern of behavior used by an animal to communicate visually: *a male bird spreading its feathers as part of a courtship display.* **5.** A device, such as a computer screen, that gives information in visual form.

displease (dĭs-plēz′) *v.* **displeased, displeasing, displeases** —*tr.* To cause annoyance or irritation to: *Bad manners displease me.* —*intr.* To cause annoyance or irritation.

displeasure (dĭs-plĕzh′ər) *n.* The condition of being displeased; dissatisfaction: *The conductor showed great displeasure with the orchestra's performance.*

disport (dĭ-spôrt′) *v.* **disported, disporting, disports** —*intr.* To frolic; play. —*tr.* To entertain (oneself) by sport or play.

disposable (dĭ-spō′zə-bəl) *adj.* **1.** Designed to be thrown away after use: *disposable razors.* **2.** Remaining to a person after taxes have been deducted: *disposable income.*

disposal (dĭ-spō′zəl) *n.* **1.** The act of getting rid of something: *The disposal of garbage is a serious problem for cities.* **2.** The act of attending to or settling a matter: *The mayor's decision led to a prompt disposal of the problem.* **3.** The act of transferring something, as by giving or selling: *the disposal of property to his children.* ◆ **at (one's)**

disposal Available for one's use: *All of the library books are at the disposal of patrons.*

dispose (dĭ-spōz′) *tr.v.* **disposed, disposing, disposes 1.** To make willing or ready; incline: *Her remorse disposed me to forgive her mistake.* **2.** To place or set in a particular order; arrange: *The gardeners disposed the tulips in circles throughout the park.* ◆ **dispose of 1.** To get rid of: *We disposed of the leftovers in the garbage.* **2.** To sell or give away: *The dealer quickly disposed of the cars.* **3.** To settle or decide: *We disposed of the problem quickly.*

disposed (dĭ-spōzd′) *adj.* Willing or inclined: *Cats are disposed to nap during the day.*

disposition (dĭs′pə-zĭsh′ən) *n.* **1.** The usual mood or attitude of a person or animal; temperament; nature: *a young child's affectionate disposition.* **2.** A tendency or inclination: *We are familiar with her disposition to argue over minor points.* **3.** Arrangement or distribution: *the disposition of books by subject on library shelves.* **4.** An act of settling; settlement: *disposition of legal matters at the lawyer's office.* **5.** An act of transferring: *the disposition of her property to her heirs.*

dispossess (dĭs′pə-zĕs′) *tr.v.* **dispossessed, dispossessing, dispossesses** To deprive (a person) of the possession of something, such as land or a house: *The bank may dispossess a person of land for failure to make loan payments.* —**dis′pos·ses′sion** (dĭs′pə-zĕsh′ən) *n.*

disproof (dĭs-pro̅o̅f′) *n.* **1.** An act of disproving. **2.** Evidence that disproves.

disproportion (dĭs′prə-pôr′shən) *n.* A lack of proportion; imbalance: *the disproportion between the size of a piece of balsa wood and its very light weight.*

disproportionate (dĭs′prə-pôr′shə-nĭt) *adj.* Out of proportion to something else, as in size or shape; not suitably proportioned. —**dis′pro·por′tion·ate·ly** *adv.*

disprove (dĭs-pro̅o̅v′) *tr.v.* **disproved, disproving, disproves** To prove to be false or in error; refute: *Shadows of buildings in the photograph disprove the witness's testimony that it was a stormy day.*

disputable (dĭ-spyo̅o̅′tə-bəl *or* dĭs′pyə-tə-bəl) *adj.* Open to dispute; debatable: *Your interpretation of the facts is disputable.* —**dis·put′a·bil′i·ty** *n.*

disputant (dĭ-spyo̅o̅t′nt *or* dĭs′pyə-tənt) *n.* A person taking part in an argument, debate, or quarrel.

disputation (dĭs′pyə-tā′shən) *n.* The act of disputing; debate.

dispute (dĭ-spyo̅o̅t′) *v.* **disputed, disputing, disputes** —*tr.* **1.** To argue about; debate: *The editors disputed the literary merit of the manuscript.* **2.** To question the truth or validity of; doubt: *We disputed her account of what happened.* **3.** To quarrel or fight over: *The nations disputed the territory.* —*intr.* **1.** To engage in discussion; argue: *The candidates disputed over where city expenses should be cut.* **2.** To quarrel angrily. ◆ *n.* **1.** A debate; an argument: *Each scientist in the dispute had a different theory.* **2.** A quarrel.

disqualification (dĭs-kwŏl′ə-fĭ-kā′shən) *n.* **1.** The act of disqualifying or the condition of being disqualified. **2.** Something that disqualifies: *Very poor vision is a disqualification for getting a driver's license.*

disqualify (dĭs-kwŏl′ə-fī′) *tr.v.* **disqualified, disqualifying, disqualifies 1.** To make unqualified or unfit: *Poor eyesight disqualifies many people who wish to become pilots.* **2.** To declare to be unqualified or ineligible: *The judges disqualified the swimmer from the race.*

disquiet (dĭs-kwī′ĭt) *tr.v.* **disquieted, disquieting, disquiets** To make uneasy; trouble; worry: *Strange noises dis-*

quieted the guard. ◆ *n.* Worry, uneasiness, or anxiety: *Rumors of engine trouble caused disquiet among the airplane passengers.*

disquieting (dĭs-kwī′ĭ-tĭng) *adj.* Troubling; worrying; disturbing: *Everyone was upset by the disquieting news.*

disquietude (dĭs-kwī′ĭ-to̅o̅d′) *n.* Worry; uneasiness; anxiety.

disquisition (dĭs′kwĭ-zĭsh′ən) *n.* A formal discourse on a subject, often in writing.

disregard (dĭs′rĭ-gärd′) *tr.v.* **disregarded, disregarding, disregards** To pay little or no attention to; ignore: *They disregarded the warnings not to hike in stormy weather.* ◆ *n.* Lack of attention or regard: *a disregard for safety.*

disrepair (dĭs′rĭ-pâr′) *n.* The condition of being in need of repair: *an abandoned house in disrepair.*

disreputable (dĭs-rĕp′yə-tə-bəl) *adj.* Having a bad reputation; not respectable: *a disreputable building contractor.* —**dis·rep′u·ta·bly** *adv.*

disrepute (dĭs′rĭ-pyo̅o̅t′) *n.* Damage to or loss of reputation; disgrace.

disrespect (dĭs′rĭ-spĕkt′) *n.* Lack of respect or courtesy; rudeness: *His behavior showed disrespect for the law.*

disrespectful (dĭs′rĭ-spĕkt′fəl) *adj.* Having or showing a lack of respect; rude: *disrespectful behavior.* —**dis′re·spect′ful·ly** *adv.* —**dis′re·spect′ful·ness** *n.*

disrobe (dĭs-rōb′) *tr. & intr.v.* **disrobed, disrobing, disrobes** To undress: *disrobe a doll; disrobe for an x-ray.*

disrupt (dĭs-rŭpt′) *tr.v.* **disrupted, disrupting, disrupts** To interrupt or throw into confusion or disorder: *Protesters disrupted the senator's speech.* —**dis·rupt′er** *n.*

disruption (dĭs-rŭp′shən) *n.* The act of disrupting or the state of being disrupted: *the storm's disruption of electric power.*

disruptive (dĭs-rŭp′tĭv) *adj.* Causing disruption: *The street repairs were disruptive to city traffic.* —**dis·rup′tive·ly** *adv.*

diss (dĭs) *v.* Variant of **dis.**

dissatisfaction (dĭs-săt′ĭs-făk′shən) *n.* The feeling of being displeased or dissatisfied; discontent: *dissatisfaction among local residents over the closing of the library.*

dissatisfied (dĭs-săt′ĭs-fīd′) *adj.* Feeling or showing a lack of contentment or satisfaction: *The dissatisfied customer returned his purchase.*

dissatisfy (dĭs-săt′ĭs-fī′) *tr.v.* **dissatisfied, dissatisfying, dissatisfies** To fail to satisfy; displease: *Your careless work dissatisfies me.*

dissect (dĭ-sĕkt′ *or* dī-sĕkt′ *or* dī′sĕkt′) *tr.v.* **dissected, dissecting, dissects 1.** To cut apart or separate (tissue) for study or examination: *dissect an animal in a lab.* **2.** To examine, analyze, or criticize in detail: *We dissected the plan to see where it might go wrong.*

dissection (dĭ-sĕk′shən *or* dī-sĕk′shən) *n.* **1.** The act or process of dissecting: *the complicated dissection of a frog.* **2.** Something that has been dissected, as a tissue being studied. **3.** A thoroughly conducted examination or analysis: *the lawyer's dissection of the evidence.*

dissemble (dĭ-sĕm′bəl) *v.* **dissembled, dissembling, dissembles** —*intr.* To hide one's real character, feelings, or motives under a false appearance. —*tr.* To conceal or hide behind a false appearance or manner: *dissembled his fear by making a joke.* —**dis·sem′bler** *n.*

disseminate (dĭ-sĕm′ə-nāt′) *tr.v.* **disseminated, disseminating, disseminates** To make known widely; spread abroad: *Many political blogs disseminated the election news instantly.* —**dis·sem′i·na′tion** *n.*

dissension (dĭ-sĕn′shən) *n.* Difference of opinion; disagreement. —SEE NOTE AT **consent.**

dissent (dĭ-sĕnt′) *intr.v.* **dissented, dissenting, dissents** To think or feel differently; disagree: *Many angry citizens dissented from the government action of raising taxes.* ❖ *n.* **1.** Difference of opinion or feeling; disagreement: *dissent over the British right to tax the American colonists.* **2.** The refusal to conform to the authority or rules of a government or church: *The Puritans' dissent from the Church of England led to their migration to the New World.* —SEE NOTE AT **consent.**

dissenter (dĭ-sĕn′tər) *n.* **1.** A person who dissents. **2.** often **Dissenter** A person who refuses to accept the beliefs and practices of an established or national church, especially a Protestant who dissents from the Church of England.

dissertation (dĭs′ər-tā′shən) *n.* A lengthy and formal discussion of a subject, especially one written at a university by a candidate for a doctoral degree.

disservice (dĭs-sûr′vĭs) *n.* A harmful action, especially one that is undertaken with good intentions.

dissever (dĭ-sĕv′ər) *tr. & intr.v.* **dissevered, dissevering, dissevers** To separate or divide into parts.

dissidence (dĭs′ĭ-dəns) *n.* Disagreement as in opinion or belief; dissent.

dissident (dĭs′ĭ-dənt) *adj.* Disagreeing, as in opinion or belief; dissenting: *Dissident opinions were voiced before the final vote was taken.* ❖ *n.* A person who disagrees; a dissenter.

dissimilar (dĭ-sĭm′ə-lər) *adj.* Unlike; different: *We have dissimilar views.* —**dis·sim′i·lar·ly** *adv.*

dissimilarity (dĭ-sĭm′ə-lăr′ĭ-tē) *n., pl.* **dissimilarities** **1.** The quality or condition of being unlike; difference: *There is marked dissimilarity of climate between the wet coastal regions and the arid inland plains.* **2.** A point of distinction or difference: *Even identical twins have some dissimilarities.*

dissimulate (dĭ-sĭm′yə-lāt′) *v.* **dissimulated, dissimulating, dissimulates** —*tr.* To hide (one's true feelings or intentions) under a false appearance. —*intr.* To conceal one's true feelings or intentions. —**dis·sim′u·la′tion** *n.*

dissipate (dĭs′ə-pāt′) *v.* **dissipated, dissipating, dissipates** —*tr.* **1.** To drive away by or as if by dispersing; scatter: *A strong wind dissipated the clouds.* **2.** To use up unwisely; waste; squander: *They dissipated their wealth on needless luxuries.* —*intr.* **1.** To vanish by dispersion; disappear: *The fog dissipated shortly after sunrise.* **2.** To become dispelled; vanish: *His anger dissipated in time.*

dissipated (dĭs′ə-pā′tĭd) *adj.* **1.** Indulging in harmful or destructive pleasures; dissolute: *a dissipated life.* **2.** Wasted; squandered: *a dissipated fortune.*

dissipation (dĭs′ə-pā′shən) *n.* **1.** The act of scattering or the condition of being scattered; dispersion: *the dissipation of storm clouds.* **2.** Wasteful use or expenditure, as of money, energy, or time. **3.** Overindulgence in pleasure.

dissociate (dĭ-sō′shē-āt′ or dĭ-sō′sē-āt′) *tr.v.* **dissociated, dissociating, dissociates** To break association with; separate: *We dissociated ourselves from the committee because we disagree with its report.* —**dis·so′ci·a′tion** *n.*

dissoluble (dĭ-sŏl′yə-bəl) *adj.* Capable of being dissolved.

dissolute (dĭs′ə-lōōt′) *adj.* Lacking moral restraint; immoral. —**dis′so·lute′ly** *adv.*

dissolution (dĭs′ə-lōō′shən) *n.* **1a.** The act or process of breaking up into parts; disintegration: *Failure to take in*

new members caused the gradual dissolution of the garden club. **b.** The ending of a formal or legal bond; termination: *dissolution of a business partnership.* **2.** The act or process of changing from a solid to a liquid. **3.** Excessive indulgence in pleasures.

dissolve (dĭ-zŏlv′) *v.* **dissolved, dissolving, dissolves** —*tr.* **1.** To cause to pass into solution: *dissolve salt in water.* **2.** To change a (solid matter) to a liquid: *Warm weather dissolved the ice on the lake.* **3.** To bring to an end; terminate: *dissolve a partnership; dissolve a meeting.* **4.** To cause to disappear; dispel: *The funny remark dissolved the tension in the room.* —*intr.* **1.** To be taken up into solution: *Alcohol dissolves in water, but oil does not.* **2.** To change from a solid into a liquid: *The ice cubes dissolved in the warm tea.* **3.** To break up; disperse: *The mist dissolved in the wind.* **4.** To fade away; disappear: *The team's confidence dissolved quickly after the loss.* **5.** To be overcome emotionally: *The lost child dissolved into tears.* —**dis·solv′a·ble** *adj.*

dissonance (dĭs′ə-nəns) *n.* **1.** A harsh combination of sounds; discord: *the dissonance of horns in heavy traffic.* **2.** Lack of agreement or consistency; conflict: *Dissonance among committee members brought their plans to a halt.*

dissonant (dĭs′ə-nənt) *adj.* **1.** Being or having a harsh combination of sounds: *a dissonant passage in the symphony.* **2.** Lacking agreement: *a dissonant meeting.* —**dis′so·nant·ly** *adv.*

dissuade (dĭ-swād′) *tr.v.* **dissuaded, dissuading, dissuades** To discourage or keep (a person) from a purpose or course of action by persuasion or advice: *She dissuaded her brother from dropping out of school.* —**dis·sua′sion** (dĭ-swā′zhən) *n.*

dist. An abbreviation of: **1.** distance. **2.** district.

distaff (dĭs′tăf′) *n.* A stick holding flax or wool that is pulled off to be spun by hand into yarn or thread.

distaff side *n.* The female side or branch of a family.

distal (dĭs′təl) *adj.* Located far from a point of reference such as an origin, a point of attachment, or the midline of the body: *the distal portion of the esophagus.* —**dis′tal·ly** *adv.*

distance (dĭs′təns) *n.* **1.** The extent of space between two points or things: *The distance between my house and the mall is ten miles.* **2.** A stretch of space without definite limits: *The ice covered vast distances.* **3.** A point or area that is far away: *In the distance we could see the whales swimming.* **4.** The full period or length of a contest or game. ❖ *tr.v.* **distanced, distancing, distances** To place or keep at or as if at a distance: *decided to distance herself from the controversy.*

distance learning *n.* Education in which students access information and interact with the instructor and other students over a computer network rather than in a classroom.

distant (dĭs′tənt) *adj.* **1.** Far away; remote: *a distant peak on the horizon.* **2.** Separate or apart in space: *Our house is two miles distant from the station.* **3.** Far away or apart in time: *the distant past.* **4.** Far apart in relationship: *a distant cousin.* **5.** Unfriendly in manner; aloof: *The new neighbors appeared cold and distant until we got to know them.* —**dis′tant·ly** *adv.*

distaste (dĭs-tāst′) *n.* A dislike or strong objection: *a distaste for modern music.*

distasteful (dĭs-tāst′fəl) *adj.* Unpleasant; disagreeable; offensive: *Cleaning the basement is a distasteful job.* —**dis·taste′ful·ly** *adv.* —**dis·taste′ful·ness** *n.*

distemper (dĭs-tĕm′pər) *n.* **1.** An often fatal infection of dogs and certain other animals such as raccoons, caused by a virus and characterized by discharge from the eyes and nose, coughing, fever, and vomiting. **2.** An often fatal infection of cats and certain other animals, caused by a virus and characterized by fever, vomiting, and diarrhea.

distend (dĭ-stĕnd′) v. **distended, distending, distends** —*intr.* To swell or expand from or as if from internal pressure: *The puppies ate until their stomachs distended.* —*tr.* To cause to expand by or as if by internal pressure: *Fluid distends a blister.*

distill also **distil** (dĭ-stĭl′) v. **distilled, distilling, distills** also **distilled, distilling, distils** —*tr.* **1.** To treat (a substance) by the process of distillation. **2.** To separate (a substance) from a mixture by distillation. **3.** To separate or extract the core or essential part of: *distill the important points of a book in a report.* —*intr.* **1.** To undergo or be produced by distillation. **2.** To fall in drops or small quantities.

distillate (dĭs′tə-lāt′ *or* dĭ-stĭl′ĭt) n. A liquid condensed from vapor and collected in distillation.

distillation (dĭs′tə-lā′shən) n. **1.** The process of boiling a liquid and condensing and collecting the vapor. Distillation is used to purify liquids, such as sea water, or to separate liquid mixtures, such as petroleum. **2.** Something distilled from another substance or from a more complex form; a distillate.

distiller (dĭ-stĭl′ər) n. **1.** A person or thing that distills, especially a condenser. **2.** A person or company that produces alcoholic liquors.

distillery (dĭ-stĭl′ə-rē) n., pl. **distilleries** An establishment for distilling, especially for distilling alcoholic liquors.

distinct (dĭ-stĭngkt′) adj. **1.** Different from all others; separate: *We discussed the issue on two distinct occasions.* **2.** Easily perceived by the senses or mind; definite: *Onions have a distinct odor.* **3.** Clearly defined; unquestionable: *Doctors have distinct limitations on their time.* —**dis·tinct′ly** adv. —**dis·tinct′ness** n.

distinction (dĭ-stĭngk′shən) n. **1.** The act of distinguishing; discrimination: *Employers must hire without distinction of age or race.* **2.** The condition or fact of being distinct; difference: *a distinction between studying and casual reading.* **3.** Something that sets one apart; a distinguishing mark or characteristic: *the distinction of being the best singer in the choir.* **4.** Excellence, as of performance, character, or reputation: *a composer of great distinction.* **5.** Recognition of achievement or superiority; honor: *She graduated with distinction.*

distinctive (dĭ-stĭngk′tĭv) adj. Serving to identify, characterize, or set apart from others: *a distinctive logo.* —**dis·tinc′tive·ly** adv. —**dis·tinc′tive·ness** n.

distinguish (dĭ-stĭng′gwĭsh) v. **distinguished, distinguishing, distinguishes** —*tr.* **1.** To recognize as being different or distinct: *Counting the number of legs is one way to distinguish spiders from ants.* **2.** To see or hear clearly; make out; discern: *the ear's ability to distinguish musical notes.* **3.** To make noticeable or different; set apart: *The beaver is distinguished by its broad flat tail.* **4.** To cause (oneself) to gain fame, esteem, or honor: *Some artists distinguished themselves as great portrait painters.* —*intr.* To recognize differences; discriminate: *distinguish between right and wrong.* —**dis·tin′guish·a·ble** adj.

distinguished (dĭ-stĭng′gwĭsht) adj. **1.** Recognized as excellent; eminent; renowned: *a distinguished composer.* **2.** Dignified in conduct or appearance: *the distinguished air of a great dancer.*

distort (dĭ-stôrt′) tr.v. **distorted, distorting, distorts 1.** To

twist (something) out of the usual shape; contort: *a grin that distorted the clown's face.* **2.** To give a false account of; misrepresent: *distort the facts.* **3.** To change (an electronic signal) so as to result in poor quality reception or reproduction, as of radio or recorded music.

distortion (dĭ-stôr′shən) n. **1a.** The act of distorting: *Distortion of the facts gave a false impression of what actually happened.* **b.** The condition of being distorted: *Playing a record at the wrong speed results in distortion of the sound.* **2.** Something distorted: *Their vague idea of what happened was full of distortions.*

distract (dĭ-străkt′) tr.v. **distracted, distracting, distracts 1.** To cause (someone) to have difficulty paying attention to something: *The noise distracted the students in the library.* **2.** To cause (a person's attention) to be diverted from its original focus. **3.** To make (someone) feel uneasy; unsettle: *Worries about moving to a new city distracted the whole family.*

distraction (dĭ-străk′shən) n. **1.** Something that makes it difficult to pay attention or that draws attention away from familiar or everyday concerns: *This article has tips on how to avoid distractions at work.* **2.** The act of distracting someone: *The babysitter's distraction of the child must have worked, since the child stopped crying.* **3.** The condition of being distracted, especially from everyday concerns: *people who seek distraction in video games.* **4.** Great mental agitation: *Worry over paying the bills nearly drove the shopkeeper to distraction.*

distraught (dĭ-strôt′) adj. Very worried or upset: *He was distraught when he lost his wallet.*

distress (dĭ-strĕs′) tr.v. **distressed, distressing, distresses 1.** To cause (a person) to suffer in mind or body. **2.** To mar or treat (an object or fabric, for example) to give the appearance of an antique or heavy prior use. ❖ n. **1.** Sorrow or anguish: *her distress when her dog ran away.* **2.** Bodily pain or dysfunction: *The accident victim was in severe distress.* **3.** The condition of being in need of immediate assistance: *a motorist in distress.* **4.** Suffering caused by poverty: *government programs to help relieve distress.* **5.** Something that causes discomfort: *Seeing an animal suffering is a great distress to me.*

distressful (dĭ-strĕs′fəl) adj. Causing or experiencing distress; painful. —**dis·tress′ful·ly** adv.

distribute (dĭ-strĭb′yo͞ot) tr.v. **distributed, distributing, distributes 1.** To give out in portions or shares; parcel out: *The hikers distributed the gear evenly among themselves.* **2.** To supply or give out; deliver: *distribute magazines to local stores.* **3.** To spread, scatter, or divide into portions over an area: *The storm distributed snow over the region. The weight of the roof is distributed evenly along the walls.* **4.** To separate into categories; classify: *This census distributes the population into five income classes.*

✦ **SYNONYMS distribute, deal, dispense, ration** v.

distribution (dĭs′trə-byo͞o′shən) n. **1.** The act or process of distributing: *the distribution of gifts at the holidays.* **2.** The process of marketing and supplying goods, especially to retailers. **3.** The way in which something occurs or is distributed over an area: *the distribution of wolves in North America.* **4.** Something distributed; a portion: *My grandmother receives distributions from her retirement account.*

distributive (dĭ-strĭb′yə-tĭv) adj. **1.** Relating to or involving distribution: *the distributive function of the blood stream.* **2.** In mathematics, relating to a property stating that the product of a factor and a sum is equal to the sum of the products. For example, 5 × (6 + 7) = (5 × 6) + (5 × 7) and $a × (b + c) = (a × b) + (a × c)$. **3.** In grammar, referring to each part or member of a group separately. *Each* and *every* are distributive words. —**dis·trib′u·tive·ly** *adv.*

distributor (dĭ-strĭb′yə-tər) *n.* **1.** A person or thing that distributes, especially a device that applies electric current at the proper time to each spark plug in an engine. **2.** A person or company that markets or sells merchandise, especially a wholesaler.

district (dĭs′trĭkt) *n.* **1.** A part of an area marked out by law for a particular purpose: *our school district.* **2.** An area, especially one having a particular characteristic or function: *a shopping district.* ❖ *tr.v.* **districted, districting, districts** To mark off or divide into districts.

district attorney *n.* The attorney who conducts the government's side of a case in a judicial district, especially the attorney who prosecutes people accused of a crime.

distrust (dĭs-trŭst′) *n.* Lack of confidence or trust; suspicion. ❖ *tr.v.* **distrusted, distrusting, distrusts** To lack confidence or trust in; doubt; suspect: *I distrust commercials that sound too good.*

distrustful (dĭs-trŭst′fəl) *adj.* Feeling or showing doubt; suspicious. —**dis·trust′ful·ly** *adv.* —**dis·trust′ful·ness** *n.*

disturb (dĭ-stûrb′) *tr.v.* **disturbed, disturbing, disturbs 1.** To break up or destroy the peace, order, or settled state of: *a breeze that disturbed the papers on my desk.* **2.** To make uneasy or anxious; trouble; upset: *I was disturbed when I didn't know where you were.* **3.** To intrude upon; bother: *The visitors disturbed the musician's practice.*

disturbance (dĭ-stûr′bəns) *n.* **1.** The act of disturbing or the condition of being disturbed: *a disturbance in the cable signal.* **2.** Something that disturbs; an interruption or intrusion: *The coughing of a few was a disturbance to the rest of the audience.* **3.** A commotion or scuffle: *Angry fans created a disturbance at the game.*

disturbed (dĭ-stûrbd′) *adj.* Having or resulting from emotional problems or mental illness.

disulfide (dī-sŭl′fīd′) *n.* A chemical group that has two sulfur atoms, or a compound in which two sulfur atoms combine with other elements or groups.

disunion (dĭs-yōōn′yən) *n.* **1.** The condition of being divided or broken up into parts; separation. **2.** Lack of unity or agreement; discord.

disunite (dĭs′yōō-nīt′) *tr. & intr.v.* **disunited, disuniting, disunites** To make or become separate or divided: *differences of opinion that disunited our club.*

disunity (dĭs-yōō′nĭ-tē) *n., pl.* **disunities** Lack of unity or agreement; discord; dissension.

disuse (dĭs-yōōs′) *n.* The condition of not being used or of being no longer in use.

ditch (dĭch) *n.* A long narrow trench dug in the ground. ❖ *tr.v.* **ditched, ditching, ditches 1.** To dig or make ditches in or around: *ditch swampy land to drain it.* **2.** To drive (a vehicle) into a ditch. **3.** *Slang* **a.** To throw aside; get rid of: *Why not ditch that old bike and get a new one?* **b.** To get away from (a person in one's company). **c.** To skip (class or school). **4.** To bring (an aircraft) to a forced landing on water.

dither (dĭth′ər) *n.* A condition of nervous excitement or indecision: *in a dither about getting ready for the party.* ❖ *intr.v.* **dithered, dithering, dithers** To be nervously unable to make a decision or act on something.

ditto (dĭt′ō) *n., pl.* **dittos 1.** The same as stated above or

before. **2.** A duplicate or copy, especially a mimeograph. **3.** A pair of marks (″) used to indicate that the word, phrase, or figure given directly above it is to be repeated.

ditty (dĭt′ē) *n., pl.* **ditties** A short simple song.

diuretic (dī′ə-rĕt′ĭk) *n.* A substance or drug that tends to increase the discharge of urine. ❖ *adj.* Tending to increase the discharge of urine.

diurnal (dī-ûr′nəl) *adj.* **1.** Occurring in a 24-hour period; daily: *The diurnal rise of the sun.* **2.** Most active during the daytime rather than at night: *diurnal birds of prey.* —**di·ur′nal·ly** *adv.*

diva (dē′və) *n.* **1.** An operatic prima donna. **2.** A very successful singer of nonoperatic music: *a jazz diva.* **3.** *Slang* One who demands that attention be paid to his or her needs, especially without regard to anyone else's needs or feelings.

divalent (dī-vā′lənt) *adj.* In chemistry, having valence 2.

divan (dĭ-văn′ *or* dī-văn′) *n.* A long couch, usually without a back or arms.

dive (dīv) *v.* **dived** *or* **dove** (dōv), **dived, diving, dives** —*intr.* **1.** To plunge into water, especially headfirst. **2.** To go toward the bottom of a body of water; submerge: *The submarine dived.* **3.** To swim underwater, especially using scuba gear. **4.** To descend rapidly at a steep angle: *The airplane turned and dived.* **5.** To drop sharply and rapidly; plummet: *Stock prices dived over 100 points yesterday.* **6.** To rush headlong and vanish into: *dive into the crowd.* **7.** To engage in something vigorously: *She dove into the project with great enthusiasm.* —*tr.* To cause to dive: *dive a plane.* ❖ *n.* **1.** A plunge into water, especially headfirst. **2.** A sharp downward descent or plunge, as of an airplane or submarine. **3.** A rapid or abrupt decrease: *Stock prices took a dive.* **4.** *Informal* A run-down bar or nightclub.

diver (dī′vər) *n.* **1.** A person who dives into water: *a champion diver.* **2.** A person who swims underwater, especially using scuba gear. **3.** Any of several diving birds.

diverge (dĭ-vûrj′ *or* dī-vûrj′) *intr.v.* **diverged, diverging, diverges 1.** To go or extend in different directions from a common point; branch out: *a small dirt road that diverged into two tracks.* **2.** To depart from a set course, standard, or norm; deviate: *She diverged from her lecture notes to tell a joke.* **3.** To be different, as in opinion or manner: *The twins diverged in their interests as they grew older.*

divergence (dĭ-vûr′jəns *or* dī-vûr′jəns) *n.* **1.** The act or process of diverging: *Making a hologram begins with the divergence of a laser beam into two beams.* **2.** Departure from an established course, pattern, or standard: *divergence from the regular schedule.* **3.** Difference, as of opinion: *Divergence among members of the board prevented it from coming to a decision.*

divergent (dĭ-vûr′jənt *or* dī-vûr′jənt) *adj.* **1.** Moving or extending apart from a common point; diverging. **2.** Differing: *widely divergent views of the problem.* —**di·ver′gent·ly** *adv.*

diverse (dĭ-vûrs′ *or* dī-vûrs′ *or* dī′vûrs′) *adj.* **1.** Distinct in kind; different or varying: *Members of the same family can have very diverse personalities.* **2.** Relating to or containing people from different ethnicities and social backgrounds: *a diverse student body.* —**di·verse′ly** *adv.*

diversification (dĭ-vûr′sə-fĭ-kā′shən) *n.* The act of diversifying or the condition of being diversified: *Education usually leads to a diversification of interests.*

diversify (dĭ-vûr′sə-fī′ *or* dī-vûr′sə-fī′) *v.* **diversified, diversifying, diversifies** —*tr.* **1.** To give diversity or variety to; make diverse: *After becoming successful as a portrait photographer, she diversified the kinds of pictures she took.* **2.** To add or produce (new or different products, for example) in different areas: *The cosmetics company diversified its product line by adding allergy treatments.* —*intr.* To become diversified, especially by making or dealing in different products: *The soap company diversified into producing a line of perfumes.*

diversion (dĭ-vûr′zhən *or* dī-vûr′zhən) *n.* **1.** The act of diverting: *the diversion of a stream for irrigation.* **2.** Something that relaxes or entertains; recreation: *Playing music has been a wonderful diversion for me.* **3.** Something that draws the attention to a different course, direction, or action: *We started yelling to create a diversion from the game.*

diversity (dĭ-vûr′sĭ-tē *or* dī-vûr′sĭ-tē) *n., pl.* **diversities 1.** The condition of being diverse; variety: *There was a considerable diversity of opinion about the new store.* **2.** The condition of having or including people from different ethnicities and social backgrounds: *diversity on campus.*

divert (dĭ-vûrt′ *or* dī-vûrt′) *v.* **diverted, diverting, diverts** —*tr.* **1.** To turn aside from a course or direction; deflect: *divert traffic around a fallen tree on the road.* **2.** To draw (the mind or attention) to another direction: *A passing fire truck diverted our attention from the game.* **3.** To amuse or entertain: *divert little children by singing songs on a rainy afternoon.* —*intr.* To turn aside: *The pilot had to divert from the airport closed in by fog.*

WORD BUILDING The word root **vert-** in English words comes from the Latin verb *vertere,* "to turn." Thus **divert** is literally "to turn aside" (using the prefix *di-,* a form of *dis-,* "apart, aside"), and **revert** means "to turn back" (*re-,* "back"). The past participle of *vertere* was *versus,* from which we form the words **reverse,** "turned around or backwards"; **obverse,** "turned to the front" (*ob-,* "in front of, in the way of"); and **transverse,** "turned sideways" (*trans-,* "across").

---

divertimento (dĭ-vĕr′tə-mĕn′tō) *n., pl.* **divertimentos** or **divertimenti** (dĭ-vĕr′tə-mĕn′tē) A chamber music form, usually in several movements, commonly written during the 1700s.

divest (dĭ-vĕst′ *or* dī-vĕst′) *tr.v.* **divested, divesting, divests 1.** To deprive, as of rights or property: *A person convicted of a felony is divested of the right to vote.* **2.** To free of, as by selling: *He divested himself of several properties.* **3.** To strip, as of clothes: *They divested themselves of their heavy winter coats before sitting down by the fire.*

divide (dĭ-vīd′) *v.* **divided, dividing, divides** —*tr.* **1a.** To separate into parts, groups, or branches: *The participants were divided into two teams.* See Synonyms at **separate. b.** To form a border or barrier between: *A mountain chain divides France and Spain.* **c.** To separate and group according to kind; classify: *divide books into fiction and nonfiction.* **2.** To separate into opposing factions: *Different opinions divided Congress over the issue of air pollution.* **3.** To apportion or distribute among a number: *Volunteers divided the different jobs among themselves.* **4a.** To determine how many times (one number) contains another: *I divided 24 by 4 and got 6.* **b.** To be a divisor of: *3 divides 9 evenly.* **c.** To use (a number) as a divisor: *divide 5 into 35.* —*intr.* **1.** To become separated into parts, groups, or factions: *The country divided on the issue of how to improve the economy.* **2.** To perform the mathematical operation of division. ❖ *n.* A dividing point or line: *hills that form a divide between rivers flowing eastward and westward.*

dividend (dĭv′ĭ-dĕnd′) *n.* **1.** A number or quantity that is to be divided. **2.** A share of profits paid to a stockholder of a company. **3.** A benefit or advantage: *Cleaning up our environment will provide dividends for us all.*

divider (dĭ-vī′dər) *n.* **1.** A person or thing that divides, especially a screen or other partition: *a room divider.* **2.** A device that is like a compass, used for dividing lines and transferring measurements.

divination (dĭv′ə-nā′shən) *n.* **1.** The art of foretelling the future by interpreting omens or using magic powers. **2.** Something that has been predicted by this art: *There have been numerous divinations about the end of the world.* **3.** A clever guess.

divine (dĭ-vīn′) *adj.* **diviner, divinest 1.** Relating to God or a god: *divine wisdom.* **2.** Coming from or given by God or a god: *divine guidance.* **3.** Directed to God or a god; sacred: *divine worship.* ❖ *n.* **1.** A cleric. **2.** A person learned in theology. ❖ *tr.v.* **divined, divining, divines 1.** To foretell or prophesy by divination: *Ancient seers divined disasters from the flights of birds.* **2.** To guess: *The mechanic divined my car's problem after looking at the tires.* —**di·vine′ly** *adv.* —**di·vine′ness** *n.* —**di·vin′er** *n.*

diving bell (dī′vĭng) *n.* A large chamber for people working underwater that is raised and lowered by a cable and supplied with air under pressure to keep water from coming in its open bottom.

diving board *n.* A flexible board from which a person can dive, secured at one end and sticking out over the water at the other.

divining rod (dĭ-vī′nĭng) *n.* A forked stick in the hand and believed to indicate the presence of underground water or minerals by bending downward when over a source.

divinity (dĭ-vĭn′ĭ-tē) *n., pl.* **divinities 1.** The quality or condition of being divine. **2.** Divinity **a.** God. **b.** A god or goddess. **3.** The study of God and religion; theology: *Ministers study at a school of divinity.*

divisible (dĭ-vĭz′ə-bəl) *adj.* Capable of being divided, especially with no remainder. —**di·vis′i·bil′i·ty** *n.* —**di·vis′i·bly** *adv.*

division (dĭ-vĭzh′ən) *n.* **1.** The act of dividing or the condition of being divided; separation into parts: *the division of a book into chapters.* **2.** The operation of dividing one number or quantity by another; the process of finding out how many times one number or quantity is contained in the other. **3.** One of the parts or groups into which something is divided: *a division in a company.* **4.** Something, such as a partition or boundary, that divides or keeps separate. **5.** Disagreement; disunity: *The meeting was marked by deep division among delegates from different sections of the country.* **6.** An army unit that is smaller than a corps and is composed of several regiments. **7.** The highest taxonomic category within the plant kingdom, made up of one or more related classes and roughly corresponding to a phylum in animal classification.

division sign *n.* The symbol (÷) placed between two quantities to indicate that the first is to be divided by the second, as in 12 ÷ 6 = 2.

divisive (dĭ-vī′sĭv) *adj.* Creating or tending to create disagreement or disunity: *a divisive political issue.* —**di·vi′sive·ly** *adv.* —**di·vi′sive·ness** *n.*

divisor (dĭ-vī′zər) *n.* The number or quantity by which another is to be divided.

divorce (dǐ-vôrs′) *n.* **1.** The legal ending of a marriage. **2.** A complete separation: *His view of the economy is noteworthy chiefly for its divorce from reality.* ❖ *v.* **divorced, divorcing, divorces** —*tr.* **1.** To end the marriage of (people): *The judge divorced husband and wife.* **2.** To end marriage with (one's spouse) by legal divorce: *She divorced her husband.* **3.** To separate or remove: *We cannot divorce a good diet from fitness.* —*intr.* To obtain a divorce.

divorcé (dǐ-vôr-sā′) *n.* A man who is divorced.

divorcée (dǐ-vôr-sā′) *n.* A woman who is divorced.

divot (dǐv′ət) *n.* A piece of turf torn up, especially by a golf club when hitting the ball.

divulge (dǐ-vŭlj′) *tr.v.* **divulged, divulging, divulges** To make known; reveal; tell: *divulge a secret.* —**di·vulg′er** *n.*

divvy (dǐv′ē) *tr.v.* **divvied, divvying, divvies** To divide; share: *We divvied up the pizza so that each of us got a piece.*

Dixieland (dǐk′sē-lǎnd′) *n.* A style of jazz developed in New Orleans in the early 1900s, usually involving improvised passages by multiple musicians.

DIY An abbreviation of do-it-yourself.

dizzy (dǐz′ē) *adj.* **dizzier, dizziest 1.** Having a sensation of whirling or feeling a tendency to fall; giddy: *A ride on the roller coaster made me feel dizzy.* **2.** Producing or tending to produce giddiness: *a dizzy height.* **3.** Bewildered or confused: *dizzy with excitement.* ❖ *tr.v.* **dizzied, dizzying, dizzies** To make dizzy: *So many facts and figures dizzied my brain.* —**diz′zi·ly** *adv.* —**diz′zi·ness** *n.*

DJ (dē′jā′) *n.* A disc jockey. ❖ *v.* **DJ'ed, DJ'ing, DJ's** —*tr.* To act as a DJ at (a social gathering or radio station). —*intr.* To act as a DJ.

DMZ An abbreviation of demilitarized zone.

DNA (dē′ĕn-ā′) *n.* An acid found in all living cells and certain viruses, forming the main part of chromosomes and having a double helix structure that resembles a ladder twisted into a spiral. DNA contains genes that determine or influence many of an organism's traits and that are passed on to the organism's offspring. DNA is short for *deoxyribonucleic acid.*

DNA fingerprinting *n.* DNA profiling.

DNA profiling *n.* The determination of the structure of certain regions of a DNA molecule. DNA profiling can be used to help identify individuals, as by analyzing DNA-containing evidence (such as hair) left at a crime scene.

DNA virus *n.* Any of a group of viruses whose genetic material is composed of DNA, including the viruses that cause chickenpox and herpes.

DNR An abbreviation of: **1.** Department of Natural Resources. **2.** do not resuscitate.

do¹ (dōō) *v.* **did** (dǐd), **done** (dǔn), **doing, does** (dǔz) —*tr.* **1.** To perform, carry out, or accomplish: *Do a good job. Do your duty.* **2a.** To create, produce, or make: *do a painting; do a website.* **b.** To create or produce for an audience: *The actors did a new play.* **3.** To bring about; effect: *Crying won't do any good.* **4.** To put into action; exert: *I'll do everything in my power to help you.* **5.** To put into order or take care of: *do one's hair; do the dishes.* **6.** To render or give: *do a favor.* **7.** To work at for a living: *I do house painting in the summer.* **8.** To work out the details of (a problem); solve: *I did this equation.* **9.** Used as a substitute for a preceding verb or verb phrase: *I know it, and she does too.* **10a.** To travel (a specified distance): *do a mile*

in 7 minutes. **b.** To travel at a speed of: *He was only doing 50 on the highway.* **11.** To be sufficient or convenient for; suffice: *This room will do us very nicely.* **12.** *Informal* To serve (a prison term): *Both did time for theft.* —*intr.* **1.** To behave or conduct oneself; act: *You did well on the test.* **2.** To get along; manage; get on: *The new café is doing well.* **3.** To serve a purpose: *That old coat will do for now.* **4.** Used instead of a preceding verb: *She reads as much as I do.* —*aux.* **1.** Used to ask questions: *Do you want to go? Did you understand?* **2.** Used to make negative statements: *I did not sleep at all. We do not understand.* **3.** Used to form inverted phrases: *little did I suspect.* **4.** Used to emphasize or make stronger: *We do want to go. I do want to be sure.* ❖ *n., pl.* **dos** or **do's** A statement of what should be done: *a long list of dos and don'ts.* ❖ **do away with 1.** To get rid of; dispose of: *doing away with outmoded laws.* **2.** To kill or destroy: *do away with rats and other vermin.* **do in 1.** *Slang* To exhaust: *That hike really did me in.* **2.** To kill: *Nobody really knows who did him in.* **do over** *Informal* To redecorate: *Professionals are doing over the room.* **do up 1.** To dress lavishly: *all done up for the party.* **2.** To wrap and tie (a package). **do without** To manage despite the absence of (something): *We can do without that kind of help.*

do² (dō) *n.* In music, the first tone of a major scale.

WORD HISTORY Do¹ comes from Old English *dōn,* meaning "to do, perform." **Do²** comes from Italian *do,* referring to the same musical tone as in English.

DOA An abbreviation of dead on arrival.

DOB An abbreviation of date of birth.

dobbin (dŏb′ĭn) *n.* A horse, especially an old or plodding workhorse.

Doberman pinscher (dō′bər-mən pĭn′shər) *n.* A large dog of a breed originally developed in Germany, having a short, smooth, usually black coat.

doc (dŏk) *n. Informal* A doctor.

docent (dō′sənt) *n.* **1.** A lecturer or tour guide in a museum or cathedral. **2.** A teacher or lecturer at some universities who is not a regular faculty member.

docile (dŏs′əl *or* dŏs′īl′) *adj.* Easy to train or handle; tractable; submissive: *a docile horse.* —**doc′ile·ly** *adv.* —**do·cil′i·ty** (dō-sĭl′ĭ-tē *or* dō-sĭl′ĭ-tē) *n.*

dock¹ (dŏk) *n.* **1a.** A structure extending from a shore over water and supported by piles or pillars, used for loading and unloading ships. **b.** A loading platform for loading and unloading trucks or trains. **2.** *often* **docks** A group of piers that serve as the landing area of a harbor: *We went down to the docks to look at the ships.* **3.** The area of water between or alongside piers for ships. ❖ *v.* **docked, docking, docks** —*tr.* **1.** To maneuver into a dock: *dock a big liner.* **2.** To join together (two or more spacecraft) while in space. —*intr.* To come into dock: *The ferry docked in the evening.*

dock² (dŏk) *tr.v.* **docked, docking, docks 1.** To clip or cut off (an animal's tail, for example). **2a.** To withhold a part of (a salary): *The restaurant docked the waiter's pay to make up for broken dishes.* **b.** To penalize (a worker) by such deduction: *Printers are docked if they make too many mistakes.*

dock³ (dŏk) *n.* An enclosed place where the defendant stands or sits in a criminal court.

dock⁴ (dŏk) *n.* Sorrel.

WORD HISTORY Dock¹ was spelled *dokke* in Early Modern English, meaning "area of mud in which a ship can rest at low tide," and is related to Middle Dutch *docke,* "area of water between two piers" **Dock²** comes from Middle English *dokken*, meaning "to cut short." **Dock³** comes from obsolete Flemish *docke*, meaning "cage." **Dock⁴** comes from Old English *docce*, referring to the same kind of plant as in Modern English.

docket (dŏk′ĭt) *n.* **1.** A calendar or list of cases awaiting court action. **2.** A list of things to be done; an agenda: *several jobs on the docket for today.* **3.** A label or ticket attached to a package and listing its contents. ❖ *tr.v.* **docketed, docketing, dockets 1.** To enter in a docket; schedule. **2.** To label or ticket (a parcel).

dockyard (dŏk′yärd′) *n.* A shipyard.

doctor (dŏk′tər) *n.* **1.** A person who is trained and licensed to diagnose, treat, and prevent disorders and diseases. **2.** A person who holds the highest degree given by a college or university. ❖ *tr.v.* **doctored, doctoring, doctors 1.** *Informal* To give medical treatment to. **2.** To tamper with or falsify: *doctor the results of an experiment.*

doctoral (dŏk′tər-əl) *adj.* Relating to a doctor or doctorate: *a doctoral dissertation.*

doctorate (dŏk′tər-ĭt) *n.* The degree or status of a doctor as awarded by a university: *a doctorate in Russian literature.*

doctrinaire (dŏk′trə-nâr′) *adj.* Characterized by rigid adherence to a theory or belief without considering whether it is practical or applicable: *a doctrinaire approach to a problem.*

doctrine (dŏk′trĭn) *n.* **1.** A principle or set of principles held and put forward by a religious or philosophical group; dogma. **2.** A statement of government policy, especially in foreign affairs. —**doc′tri·nal** *adj.*

document (dŏk′yə-mənt) *n.* **1.** A written or printed paper that can be used to give evidence or information: *A birth certificate is usually one's first document.* **2.** A piece of work created with a word processor or other computer application. ❖ *tr.v.* (dŏk′yə-mĕnt′) **documented, documenting, documents** To prove or support with evidence: *document a report with photographs and letters.*

documentary (dŏk′yə-mĕn′tə-rē) *adj.* **1.** Consisting of, relating to, or based on documents: *documentary evidence.* **2.** Presenting the facts of real events without adding fictional material, as in a movie. ❖ *n., pl.* **documentaries** A movie giving a factual account of some subject and often showing actual events.

documentation (dŏk′yə-mĕn-tā′shən) *n.* **1.** The act of supplying documents or supporting references: *Documentation of the scandal took many months to complete.* **2.** The documents or references provided: *Documentation for the trial was stored in several large boxes.*

dodder (dŏd′ər) *intr.v.* **doddered, doddering, dodders** To tremble or move shakily, as from old age; totter. —**dod′der·ing** *adj.*

dodecagon (dō-dĕk′ə-gŏn′) *n.* A polygon with 12 sides and 12 angles. —**do′dec·ag′o·nal** (dō′dĕ-kăg′ə-nəl) *adj.*

dodecahedron (dō′dĕk-ə-hē′drən) *n., pl.* **dodecahedrons** or **dodecahedra** (dō′dĕk-ə-hē′drə) A solid geometric figure having 12 faces.

dodge (dŏj) *v.* **dodged, dodging, dodges** —*tr.* **1.** To avoid by moving quickly aside or out of the way: *The dog dodged the cars as it ran across the street.* **2.** To evade by cunning, trickery, or other means: *The candidate dodged the reporter's questions.* —*intr.* To move by jumping aside suddenly: *The boy dodged through the crowd.* ❖ *n.* **1.** The act of dodging. **2.** A trick to cheat or avoid: *the dodges of a spy.*

dodgy (dŏj′ē) *adj.* **dodgier, dodgiest** *Chiefly British* **1.** Evasive; shifty. **2.** Unsound, unstable, and unreliable.

dodo (dō′dō) *n., pl.* **dodoes** or **dodos 1.** A large flightless bird that formerly lived on the island of Mauritius in the Indian Ocean but became extinct in the late 1600s. It had a hooked beak and very short wings. **2.** *Informal* A stupid person; an idiot.

doe (dō) *n., pl.* **doe** or **does 1.** A female deer. **2.** The female of various other mammals, such as a kangaroo, mouse, or rabbit.

doer (dō͞o′ər) *n.* A person who does something, especially an active and energetic person: *She is a doer and does not hesitate to act.*

does (dŭz) *v.* Third person singular present tense of **do**¹.

doeskin (dō′skĭn′) *n.* **1.** The skin of a female deer or of a sheep or lamb. **2.** Soft leather made from such skin, used especially for gloves. **3.** A soft smooth woolen fabric with a nap on it.

doesn't (dŭz′ənt) Contraction of *does not.*

doff (dŏf) *tr.v.* **doffed, doffing, doffs** To take off; remove: *They doffed their hats in salute to the passing flag.*

dog (dôg) *n.* **1.** A domesticated mammal that is related to wolves and is kept as a pet or trained to hunt, herd, or guard. There are many different breeds of dog. **2.** The male of this animal or of a related animal, such as a coyote. **3.** *Informal* **a.** A person regarded as undeserving or contemptible: *I'll never listen to that lying dog again.* **b.** Something considered inferior or of low quality, such as an investment that doesn't return a profit. **4.** *Informal* A hot dog. ❖ *tr.v.* **dogged, dogging, dogs** To trail persistently: *The detective dogged the suspect's every move.*

dogcart (dôg′kärt′) *n.* **1.** A vehicle drawn by one horse and accommodating two people seated back to back. **2.** A small cart pulled by dogs.

dogcatcher (dôg′kăch′ər) *n.* A person hired to catch stray dogs.

dog days *pl.n.* The hot sultry period between mid-July and early September.

doge (dōj) *n.* The elected chief magistrate of the former republics of Venice and Genoa.

dog-ear (dôg′îr′) *n.* A turned-down corner of a page in a book. ❖ *tr.v.* **dog-eared, dog-earing, dog-ears** To turn down the corner of (a page in a book). —**dog′-eared** *adj.*

dogfight (dôg′fīt′) *n.* **1.** A violent fight between or as if between dogs. **2.** A battle between fighter planes.

dogfish (dôg′fĭsh′) *n.* Any of various small sharks having two spiny dorsal fins and often found in large schools.

dogged (dô′gĭd) *adj.* Not giving up easily; persevering; stubborn: *After years of dogged effort, he finally found a publisher for his book.* —**dog′ged·ly** *adv.* —**dog′ged·ness** *n.*

doggerel (dô′gər-əl) *n.* Simple, trite, or poorly written verse, often having an irregular rhythm.

doggy or **doggie** (dô′gē) *n., pl.* **doggies** A dog, especially a small or a young dog.

doggy bag *n.* A bag for leftover food taken home from a restaurant.

doghouse (dôg′hous′) *n.* A small house or shelter for a dog. ◆ **in the doghouse** *Slang* In disfavor; in trouble: *You'll be in the doghouse for forgetting his birthday.*

dogleg (dôg′lĕg′) *n.* **1a.** Something that has a sharp bend, especially a road or route that bends abruptly. **b.** A sharp bend or turn: *Make a dogleg at the fire station and continue south.* **2.** A golf hole in which the fairway is abruptly angled. ❖ *intr.v.* **doglegged, doglegging, doglegs** To make a sharp bend or turn: *The street doglegs to the left.*

dogma (dôg′mə) *n., pl.* **dogmas 1.** A doctrine or system of doctrines that form the basis of a religion. **2.** A belief, opinion, or idea considered to be true: *Political dogmas of the past often seem barbaric today.*

dogmatic (dôg-măt′ĭk) *adj.* **1.** Relating to dogma; doctrinal: *a dogmatic idea.* **2.** Asserting that certain ideas or opinions are true, especially in an overbearing or arrogant way: *a dogmatic person.* —**dog·mat′i·cal·ly** *adv.*

dogmatism (dôg′mə-tĭz′əm) *n.* The tendency to assert that one's opinions or beliefs are true in an overbearing or arrogant way.

do-gooder (do̅o̅′go͝od′ər) *n. Informal* A person who is eager to make reforms and help people.

dog paddle *n.* A swimming stroke in which a person lies chest down while keeping the head out of the water. The arms remain under the water and the swimmer pushes them forward and then pulls them back while kicking the legs.

dogsled (dôg′slĕd′) *n.* A sled pulled by one or more dogs.

Dog Star *n.* Sirius.

dog-tired (dôg′tīrd′) *adj.* Extremely tired: *was dog-tired after swimming practice.*

dogtooth violet (dôg′to̅o̅th′) *n.* Any of several North American plants having leaves with reddish blotches and nodding, solitary flowers.

dogtrot (dôg′trŏt′) *n.* A steady trot like that of a dog.

dogwatch (dôg′wŏch′) *n.* Either of two periods of watch aboard a ship, from 4 to 6 PM or from 6 to 8 PM.

dogwood (dôg′wo͝od′) *n.* A tree having small greenish flowers that are surrounded by showy white or pink bracts resembling petals.

doily (doi′lē) *n., pl.* **doilies** A small fancy mat, usually of lace, linen, or paper and often used to protect or decorate a table top.

doings (do̅o̅′ĭngz) *pl.n.* Activities, especially social activities: *doings at the club.*

do-it-yourself (do̅o̅′ĭt-yər-sĕlf′) *adj.* Relating to or designed to be done or assembled by an amateur or as a hobby: *do-it-yourself home repairs.*

doldrums (dōl′drəmz′ *or* dŏl′drəmz′) *pl.n. (used with a singular or plural verb)* **1.** A period or condition of depression or inactivity: *in the doldrums over some bad luck.* **2.** A region of the ocean near the equator where there is little or no wind: *Several sailing ships were delayed by being caught in the doldrums.*

dole (dōl) *n.* **1.** The distribution by the government of relief payments to people who are unemployed. **2.** A share of money, food, or clothing distributed as charity. ❖ *tr.v.* **doled, doling, doles** To give out, especially in portions or shares; allot or distribute: *The judges of the contest doled out prize money to the winning contestants.*

doleful (dōl′fəl) *adj.* Filled with or expressing grief; mournful: *the cat's doleful cry.* —**dole′ful·ly** *adv.*

doll (dŏl) *n.* **1.** A child's usually small toy having the likeness of a human. **2.** *Slang* A sweetheart or darling. ❖ **doll up** To dress up elegantly, as for a special occasion: *The guests were dolled up for the party.*

dollar (dŏl′ər) *n.* The basic monetary unit in the United States and many other countries, including Australia, Canada, Fiji, New Zealand, Taiwan, and Zimbabwe.

dollar store *n.* A retail store selling a wide variety of inexpensive articles.

dollop (dŏl′əp) *n.* A lump or mass of something: *a dollop of ice cream.*

dolly (dŏl′ē) *n., pl.* **dollies 1.** *Informal* A child's doll. **2.** A low mobile platform that rolls on small wheels, used for moving heavy loads.

dolmen (dōl′mən *or* dŏl′mən) *n.* A Neolithic tomb consisting of two or more upright stones with a capstone, believed to have been buried in earth except for a central opening.

dolomite (dō′lə-mīt′ *or* dŏl′ə-mīt′) *n.* **1.** A white or light-colored mineral consisting mainly of a carbonate of calcium and magnesium. **2.** A rock containing dolomite and resembling limestone, used as a building stone.

dolor (dō′lər) *n.* Sorrow; grief.

dolorous (dō′lər-əs *or* dŏl′ər-əs) *adj.* Marked by or showing sorrow, grief, or pain. —**do′lor·ous·ly** *adv.*

dolphin (dŏl′fĭn) *n.* **1.** Any of various marine mammals related to the whales but smaller and having a snout shaped like a beak. Dolphins are noted for their remarkable intelligence. **2.** Either of two edible marine fishes of warm waters, having iridescent coloring when removed from the water.

dolt (dōlt) *n.* A stupid person.

–dom A suffix that means: **1.** Condition; state: *stardom.* **2.** Position; rank: *dukedom.*

domain (dō-mān′) *n.* **1.** A territory or range of rule or control; a realm: *the duke's domain.* **2.** A sphere of knowledge or activity; a field: *Ethics is in the domain of philosophy.* **3.** In mathematics, the set of all values that an independent variable can have. **4.** A division of organisms that ranks above a kingdom in systems of classification that are based on similarities in DNA sequences. The three domains are the archaea, the bacteria, and the eukaryotes. **5.** A group of networked computers whose users have email addresses that are the same to the right of the at sign, such as *hmhpub.com* in the address *host@hmhpub.com.*

domain name *n.* A series of letters or numbers separated by periods, such as *www.hmhpub.com*, that is the address of a computer network connection and identifies the owner of the address.

dome (dōm) *n.* **1.** A rounded roof or vault built in the shape of a hemisphere. **2.** A structure or other object resembling such a roof or vault: *the dome of the sky.* ❖ *tr.v.* **domed, doming, domes 1.** To cover with a roof or vault in the shape of a hemisphere. **2.** To shape like such a roof or vault.

domestic (də-mĕs′tĭk) *adj.* **1.** Relating to the family or household: *domestic chores.* **2.** Enjoying or interested in home life and household affairs: *They are very domestic and don't go out much.* **3.** Tame or domesticated. Used of animals: *cats and other domestic animals.* **4.** Relating to a country's internal affairs: *The president has been focusing more on domestic than on international issues.* **5.** Produced in, occurring in, or native to a particular country: *domestic cars; domestic flights.* ❖ *n.* A household servant. —**do·mes′ti·cal·ly** *adv.*

domesticate (də-mĕs′tĭ-kāt′) *tr.v.* **domesticated, domesticating, domesticates** To train or adapt (an animal or plant) to live with or to be useful to humans: *Humans domesticated cattle long ago.* —**do·mes′ti·ca′tion** *n.*

domesticity (dō′mĕ-stĭs′ĭ-tē) *n., pl.* **domesticities 1.** The quality or condition of being domestic. **2.** Home life or

devotion to it: *the intimate domesticity of a small family.*
3. domesticities The affairs of a household.

domestic partner *n.* A person other than a spouse with whom one lives and is romantically involved.

domestic violence *n.* Physical or emotional abuse of a household member, especially one's spouse or domestic partner.

domicile (dŏm′ĭ-sīl′ *or* dō′mĭ-sīl′) *n.* **1.** A residence; a home. **2.** A person's legal residence. ❖ *tr.v.* **domiciled, domiciling, domiciles** To establish (oneself or another person) in a residence.

dominance (dŏm′ə-nəns) *n.* The condition or fact of being dominant.

dominant (dŏm′ə-nənt) *adj.* **1.** Having the most influence or control: *the dominant dog in a pack.* **2.** Most prominent, as in position: *The tallest buildings are dominant in a city's skyline.* **3.** Relating to a gene that produces its characteristic effect if it is present on either or both of a pair of chromosomes. **4.** Relating to the fifth tone of a musical scale. For example, in the key of C major, a G major chord is said to be dominant. ❖ *n.* **1.** The fifth tone of a musical scale, or a chord based on this tone. **2.** A dominant gene. **—dom′i·nant·ly** *adv.*

dominate (dŏm′ə-nāt′) *v.* **dominated, dominating, dominates** *—tr.* **1.** To rule, control, or govern by superior power or authority: *Great Britain dominated about one-fourth of the world in the 1800s.* **2.** To occupy a commanding controlling position in or over: *The mountain dominates the countryside for miles around.* *—intr.* **1.** To have or exert strong authority or influence. **2.** To have the most prominent or superior position: *Tall people dominate in a crowd.*

domination (dŏm′ə-nā′shən) *n.* Control or power over another or others: *British domination of its colonies.*

domineer (dŏm′ə-nîr′) *intr. & tr.v.* **domineered, domineering, domineers** To rule over or control arbitrarily or arrogantly; tyrannize.

domineering (dŏm′ə-nîr′ing) *adj.* Tending to domineer; overbearing: *His domineering manner offended many people.* **—dom′i·neer′ing·ly** *adv.*

Dominican[1] (də-mĭn′ĭ-kən) *adj.* Relating to the Dominican Republic or its people or culture. ❖ *n.* A native or inhabitant of the Dominican Republic.

Dominican[2] (də-mĭn′ĭ-kən) *n.* A member of a Roman Catholic order of preaching friars established in 1216 by Saint Dominic (1170?–1221).

dominion (də-mĭn′yən) *n.* **1.** Control or exercise of control; sovereignty. **2.** A territory or sphere of influence or control; a realm: *The dominion of the British monarchy once included part of France.* **3. Dominion** One of the self-governing nations under the nominal rule of the British Commonwealth.

domino[1] (dŏm′ə-nō′) *n., pl.* **dominoes** *or* **dominos 1.** A small rectangular block, the face of which is divided into halves. Each half is blank or marked by dots resembling those on dice. **2. dominoes** *(used with a singular or plural verb)* A game played with a set of these small blocks.

domino[2] (dŏm′ə-nō′) *n., pl.* **dominoes** *or* **dominos 1.** A masquerade costume made up of a hooded robe worn with an eye mask. **2.** The mask so worn.

WORD HISTORY Domino[1] probably comes from the phrase *domino mask,* perhaps because of the resemblance between the eyeholes and the spots on some of the tiles. **Domino**[2] probably comes from the Latin phrase *benedīcāmus dominō,* meaning "let us praise the Lord."

domino theory *n.* A theory that one event will set off a chain of similar events.

don[1] (dŏn) *n.* **1. Don** (*also* dōn) Used as a courtesy title before the name of a man in a Spanish-speaking area. **2.** *Chiefly British* A college or university professor.

don[2] (dŏn) *tr.v.* **donned, donning, dons** To put on (clothing): *don a coat.*

WORD HISTORY Don[1] comes from Latin *dominus,* meaning "lord." **Don**[2] comes from Middle English *don,* which is a contraction of *do on,* meaning "to put on."

Doña (dō′nyä) *n.* Used as a courtesy title before the name of a woman in a Spanish-speaking area.

donate (dō′nāt′ *or* dō-nāt′) *tr.v.* **donated, donating, donates 1.** To present as a gift to a fund or cause; contribute: *donate clothing to a charity.* **2.** To provide (a body organ or other tissue) for transplant. **3.** To provide (an electron, for example) for combination with an ion, atom, or molecule.

donation (dō-nā′shən) *n.* **1.** The act of giving to a fund or cause. **2.** Something that is donated: *made a small donation to charity; made a blood donation.*

done (dŭn) *v.* Past participle of **do**[1]. ❖ *adj.* **1.** Having been completely accomplished or finished: *a done deed.* **2.** Cooked adequately: *Is the fish done?* **3.** Socially acceptable: *Eating with the fingers is not done in certain cultures.* ◆ **done for** Doomed to death or destruction.

done in Worn out; exhausted: *After the long hike, we were all done in.*

dong (dông) *n.* The basic monetary unit of Vietnam.

donjon (dŏn′jən *or* dŭn′jən) *n.* The main tower of a castle; a keep.

Don Juan (dŏn wŏn) *n.* A man who seduces or attempts to seduce women as a matter of habit.

donkey (dŏng′kē) *n., pl.* **donkeys** A kind of ass that has been domesticated and is used to carry loads.

Donna (dŏn′ə *or* dōn′nä) *n.* Used as a courtesy title before the name of a woman in an Italian-speaking area.

donnish (dŏn′ĭsh) *adj.* Relating to or typical of a university don; bookish.

donnybrook (dŏn′ē-brŏŏk′) *n.* A brawl or an uproar.

donor (dō′nər) *n.* **1.** A person who contributes something, such as money, to a cause or fund. **2.** A human or other animal from whom blood, tissue, or an organ is taken for use in grafting or in a transfusion or transplant. **3.** An atom, molecule, or ion that provides a component, especially a pair of electrons, to another atom or molecule, in order to form a molecular bond.

do-nothing (dōō′nŭth′ing) *Informal adj.* Making no effort for change, especially in politics: *a do-nothing mayor.* ❖ *n.* An idle or lazy person.

Don Quixote (dŏn′ kē-hō′tē) *n.* An impractical idealist who tries to right wrongs.

don't (dōnt) Contraction of *do not.*

donut (dō′nŭt′ *or* dō′nət) *n.* Variant of **doughnut.**

doodle (dōōd′l) *v.* **doodled, doodling, doodles** *—intr.* To draw or sketch aimlessly: *doodle on a pad during a phone call. —tr.* To draw (a design or figure) aimlessly. ❖ *n.* A design or figure drawn aimlessly. **—doo′dler** *n.*

doodlebug (dōōd′l-bŭg′) *n.* Any of several insects, especially a pillbug or the larva of an ant lion.

doom (dōōm) *n.* A tragic or ruinous fate: *The events meant doom for the revolution.* ❖ *tr.v.* **doomed, doom-**

ing, dooms To cause to have an unhappy end: *The injury doomed the patient to a lifetime of hardship.*

doomsday (do͞omz′dā′) *n.* Judgment Day.

door (dôr) *n.* **1.** A movable structure used to close off an entrance, typically made of a panel that swings on hinges or slides on a track. **2.** A doorway: *The neighbors stood in the door and talked.* **3.** The room or building to which a door belongs: *The deli is several doors down the street.* **4.** A means of approach or access: *Education can be a door to success.*

doorbell (dôr′bĕl′) *n.* A buzzer or bell outside a door that is rung to announce the presence of a visitor.

do-or-die (do͞o′ər-dī′) *adj.* Requiring a great effort to avoid dire consequences: *a do-or-die situation.*

doorjamb (dôr′jăm′) *n.* Either of the two vertical pieces framing a doorway.

doorknob (dôr′nŏb′) *n.* A knob-shaped handle for opening and closing a door.

doorman (dôr′mən) *n.* A man employed to attend the entrance of a hotel, apartment house, or other building.

doormat (dôr′măt′) *n.* A mat placed before a doorway for wiping the shoes.

doornail (dôr′nāl′) *n.* A large-headed nail. ◆ **dead as a doornail** Undoubtedly dead.

doorsill (dôr′sĭl′) *n.* The threshold of a doorway.

doorstep (dôr′stĕp′) *n.* A step leading to a door.

doorstop (dôr′stŏp′) *n.* **1.** A wedge inserted beneath a door to hold it open at a desired position. **2.** A weight or spring that prevents a door from slamming. **3.** A rubber-tipped projection on a wall to protect it from the impact of an opening door.

doorway (dôr′wā′) *n.* The entrance to a room or building.

dooryard (dôr′yärd′) *n.* A yard in front of the door of a house.

doozy or **doozie** (do͞o′zē) *n., pl.* **doozies** *Slang* Something extraordinary, impressive, or unique: *a doozy of a hailstorm.*

dopamine (dō′pə-mēn′) *n.* A neurotransmitter that is found in the brain and is essential for normal brain function.

dopant (dō′pənt) *n.* A substance added in small amounts to a semiconductor material to change how it conducts electricity.

dope (dōp) *n.* **1.** *Informal* An illegal drug, especially marijuana or a performance-enhancing drug. **2.** *Informal* A stupid person. **3.** *Informal* Information, especially from a person: *He gave me the dope on places to eat in town.* **4.** A sticky paste applied to seal pipe joints. ❖ *tr.v.* **doped, doping, dopes 1.** *Informal* To give an illegal drug to: *convicted of doping a racehorse.* **2.** To treat (a semiconductor) with a dopant.

dopey (dō′pē) *adj.* **dopier, dopiest** *Slang* **1.** Dazed or sleepy. **2.** Stupid or foolish.

doping (dō′pĭng) *n.* The practice of taking a banned substance in an attempt to enhance one's performance as an athlete.

doppelgänger (dŏp′əl-gĕng′ər) or **doppelganger** (dŏp′-əl-găng′ər) *n.* A ghostly double of a living person, especially one encountered by its fleshly counterpart.

Doppler effect (dŏp′lər) *n.* The apparent change in the frequency of waves, as of sound or light, when the source of the waves is moving toward or away from an observer. For example, as the source of sound waves and an observer approach each other, the observer hears a rising pitch. As the source and an observer move apart, the observer hears a falling pitch.

Doric (dôr′ĭk) *adj.* In the style of an order of classical Greek architecture characterized by heavy fluted columns with plain saucer-shaped capitals: *a Doric column.*

dork (dôrk) *n. Slang* A foolish, inept, or clumsy person. —**dork′y** *adj.*

dorm (dôrm) *n. Informal* A dormitory.

dormancy (dôr′mən-sē) *n.* The condition of being dormant: *dormancy in bacteria.*

dormant (dôr′mənt) *adj.* **1.** In an inactive state in which growth and development stop, only to start again when conditions are favorable: *dormant seeds.* **2.** Not active but capable of renewed activity: *a dormant volcano.*

dormer (dôr′mər) *n.* **1.** A small roofed structure projecting outward on a larger, sloping roof. **2.** A window that is set in such a structure.

dormitory (dôr′mĭ-tôr′ē) *n., pl.* **dormitories 1.** A building for housing a number of people, especially students. **2.** A room providing sleeping quarters for a number of people.

dormouse (dôr′mous′) *n., pl.* **dormice** (dôr′mīs′) Any of various small rodents of Eurasia and northern Africa that have long furry tails. Dormice sleep most of the winter.

dorsal (dôr′səl) *adj.* Relating to or located on the back or upper side of the body of a human or another animal: *the dorsal fin of a fish.* —**dor′sal·ly** *adv.*

dory (dôr′ē) *n., pl.* **dories** A small flatbottom fishing boat with high flaring sides.

dosage (dō′sĭj) *n.* **1.** The administration or application of medicine or some treatment in regulated amounts: *the dosage of a drug three times a day.* **2.** The amount administered or applied at one time: *The doctor reduced my dosage of antihistamine.* **3.** An amount of radiation that a person is exposed to.

dose (dōs) *n.* **1.** The amount of medicine or other substance or treatment given or taken at one time: *a dose of medicine every four hours.* **2.** An amount, especially of something unpleasant, to which one is subjected: *a dose of hard luck.* ❖ *tr.v.* **dosed, dosing, doses** To give or prescribe (medicine) in specified amounts.

do-si-do (dō′sē-dō′) *n., pl.* **do-si-dos 1.** A movement in square dancing in which two dancers approach each other and circle back to back, then return to their original positions. **2.** The call given to signal such a movement.

dossier (dŏs′ē-ā′) *n.* A collection of papers giving detailed information about a particular person or subject: *Army records included a dossier on each soldier.*

dost (dŭst) *v. Archaic* A second person singular present tense of **do**[1].

dot (dŏt) *n.* **1.** A small round mark; a spot: *a dot over the small letter i.* **2a.** A decimal point. **b.** A symbol (·) indicating multiplication. **c.** A period used to separate strings of words, as in email addresses and URLs. **3.** The short sound or signal used in Morse code in combination with the dash and silent intervals to represent letters, numbers, or punctuation. ❖ *tr.v.* **dotted, dotting, dots 1.** To mark with dots. **2.** To cover with or as if with dots: *Dandelions dotted the green field.* ◆ **on the dot** Exactly at the appointed time; punctual or punctually: *I arrived at 9:00 on the dot.*

dotage (dō′tĭj) *n.* A loss of the ability to think clearly as a result of aging.

dotard (dō′tərd) *n.* A person who is in his or her dotage.

dot-com (dŏt′kŏm′) *n.* A business whose services are conducted or provided over the Internet.

dote (dōt) *intr.v.* **doted, doting, dotes** To show excessive love or fondness: *They doted on their only grandchild.*

doth (dŭth) *v. Archaic* A third person singular present tense of **do**[1].

dotty (dŏt′ē) *adj.* **dottier, dottiest 1.** Mentally unbalanced; crazy. **2.** Amusingly eccentric or unconventional.

double (dŭb′əl) *adj.* **1.** Twice as much in size, strength, number, or amount: *a double dose.* **2.** Composed of two like parts: *double doors.* **3.** Composed of two unlike parts; dual: *a double meaning.* **4.** Accommodating or designed for two people: *a double hotel room.* **5.** Having more than the usual number of petals, usually in a crowded or overlapping arrangement: *a double chrysanthemum.* ❖ *n.* **1.** An accommodation for two people, as a room in a hotel. **2.** A person or thing that closely resembles another; a duplicate: *She's her sister's double.* **3. doubles** A form of a game, such as tennis or handball, having two players on each side. **4.** In baseball, a hit that enables the batter to reach second base safely. ❖ *v.* **doubled, doubling, doubles** —*tr.* **1.** To make twice as great: *Double the amount of food if both of you go hiking.* **2.** To be twice as much as: *doubled the score of her opponent.* **3.** To fold in two: *double the blanket to get more warmth.* **4.** To clench (one's fist). **5.** To duplicate; repeat: *Double the "t" in "hit" when you spell "hitting."* **6.** To sail around: *double a cape.* —*intr.* **1.** To be increased twofold: *Our rent has doubled in 10 years' time.* **2.** To turn sharply backward; reverse: *The bear doubled back on its trail.* **3.** To serve in an additional capacity: *My bed doubles as a couch.* **4.** To be a substitute: *The assistant doubled for the coach today.* **5.** In baseball, to hit a double. ❖ *adv.* **1.** To twice the amount or extent; doubly: *paid double for the customized car.* **2.** Two together; in pairs: *ride double on a horse.* **3.** In two: *bent double with laughter.* ◆ **double up 1.** To bend suddenly, as in pain or laughter: *The joke made us double up.* **2.** To share accommodations meant for one person. **on the double** Immediately or quickly: *We need help on the double!*

double agent *n.* A person pretending to spy for one government while actually spying for another.

double bar *n.* A pair of vertical lines or a heavy black line drawn through a musical staff to indicate the end of a large section of a composition.

double-barreled (dŭb′əl-băr′əld) *adj.* **1.** Having two barrels mounted side by side: *a double-barreled shotgun.* **2.** Serving two purposes; twofold: *a double-barreled question.*

double bass (bās) *n.* The largest and lowest pitched of the stringed instruments that are normally played with a bow, related to the violin family but having four strings tuned in intervals of a fourth.

double bassoon *n.* A contrabassoon.

double boiler *n.* A cooking utensil consisting of an upper pot fitted into a lower pot. Water boiling in the lower pot allows the slow even cooking or heating of food in the upper pot.

double-breasted (dŭb′əl-brĕs′tĭd) *adj.* Having two rows of buttons and fastened by lapping one edge of the front of a garment well over the other: *a double-breasted jacket.*

double-check (dŭb′əl-chĕk′) *tr.v.* **double-checked, double-checking, double-checks** To inspect or examine again; verify: *double-check one's subtraction.*

double chin *n.* A fold of fatty flesh beneath the chin.

double-click (dŭb′əl-klĭk′) *v.* **double-clicked, double-**

clicking, double-clicks —*tr.* To press down and release a button on (a pointing device) twice in rapid succession to activate a command on a computer screen. —*intr.* To double-click a pointing device.

double-cross (dŭb′əl-krôs′) *tr.v.* **double-crossed, double-crossing, double-crosses** To betray by acting contrary to a prior agreement. ❖ *n.* often **double cross** An act of betrayal. —**dou′ble-cross′er** *n.*

double-dealer (dŭb′əl-dē′lər) *n.* A person who engages in deceitful or treacherous behavior; a double-crosser.

double-dealing (dŭb′əl-dē′lĭng) *adj.* Duplicitous or deceitful; treacherous. ❖ *n.* Duplicity or deceit; treachery.

double-decker (dŭb′əl-dĕk′ər) *n.* Something, such as a vehicle, structure, or sandwich, that has two decks, floors, or layers.

double digits *pl.n.* A number that is greater than 9 and less than 100: *Our team's center has been shooting in double digits all season.* —**doub′le-dig′it** *adj.*

double dribble *n.* In basketball, an illegal dribble in which a player uses both hands at the same time to dribble the ball or begins to dribble the ball a second time after a complete stop.

double-edged (dŭb′əl-ĕjd′) *adj.* **1.** Having two cutting edges: *a double-edged knife.* **2.** Effective or capable of being interpreted in two ways: *a double-edged compliment.*

double-entendre (dŭb′əl-än-tän′drə) *n.* A word or phrase having a double meaning, especially when the second meaning is indecent or improper.

doubleheader (dŭb′əl-hĕd′ər) *n.* Two games played one after the other on the same day, especially in baseball.

double helix *n.* A spiral structure that consists of two helixes coiled around each other, especially the two strands of nucleotides that make up a molecule of DNA.

double jeopardy *n.* The condition of being tried a second time for the same offense. It is prohibited by the US Constitution.

double-jointed (dŭb′əl-join′tĭd) *adj.* Having unusually flexible joints, especially of the limbs or fingers.

double knit *n.* A fabric somewhat like jersey, knitted so that a double thickness of fabric is produced in which the two sides of the fabric are interlocked. —**doub′le-knit′** *adj.*

double negative *n.* A construction in which two negatives are used, especially to express one negative thought.

USAGE **double negative** The use of a **double negative,** such as *I didn't say nothing,* to express a negative idea should be avoided in Standard English. Instead, use a single negative word, as in *I said nothing* or *I didn't say anything.* A double negative can be used to say something affirmative, as in *I cannot just do nothing,* but such expressions can be confusing.

double-park (dŭb′əl-pärk′) *tr. & intr.v.* **double-parked, double-parking, double-parks** To park alongside another vehicle already parked parallel to the curb.

double play *n.* In baseball, a play in which two players are put out.

double-quick (dŭb′əl-kwĭk′) *adj.* Very quick; rapid. ❖ *n.* A marching cadence; double time.

double reed *n.* A pair of joined reeds that vibrate together to produce sound in certain wind instruments such as the bassoon and oboe.

doublespeak (dŭb′əl-spēk′) *n.* Talk that is purposefully ambiguous or evasive.

double standard *n.* A set of standards that allows greater freedom to one group than to another, especially one granting more freedom to men than to women.

double star *n.* A binary star.

doublet (dŭb′lĭt) *n.* **1.** A close-fitting jacket, with or without sleeves, worn by European men from the late 1300s to around 1650. **2.** One of two words derived from the same source but not through the same route.

double take *n.* A delayed reaction to something unusual: *She did a double take when she saw his strange costume.*

double talk *n.* **1.** Meaningless speech that consists of nonsense syllables mixed with real words. **2.** Talk that is purposefully ambiguous or evasive: *campaign double talk.*

double time *n.* **1.** A rapid marching pace of 180 three-foot steps per minute. **2.** A rate of pay that is twice the regular rate: *was paid double time when working on Saturday.*

double-time (dŭb′əl-tīm′) *intr. & tr.v.* To move or cause to move in double time.

doubloon (dŭ-blōōn′) *n.* A gold coin formerly used in Spain and Spanish America.

doubly (dŭb′lē) *adv.* To a double degree; twice: *Make doubly sure the totals are right.*

doubt (dout) *tr.v.* **doubted, doubting, doubts 1.** To be uncertain about (something); not believe in the truth of: *At first many people doubted the rumor.* **2.** To disbelieve (someone): *I should never have doubted such a good friend.* **3.** To regard as unlikely: *I doubt that we'll arrive on time.* ❖ *n.* **1.** The state of being uncertain about the truth or reliability of something: *The reports were met with doubt.* **2.** often **doubts** A feeling of uncertainty or distrust: *She had doubts about the claims made in the article she read online.* **3.** The condition of being unsettled or unresolved: *The outcome of the ball game is still in doubt.* ◆ **beyond doubt** or **without doubt** Without question; certainly; definitely. **no doubt** Certainly or probably.

doubtful (dout′fəl) *adj.* **1.** Subject to or causing doubt: *a doubtful claim.* **2.** Having or showing doubt; questioning: *We were doubtful about the proposed plan.* **3.** Questionable; suspicious: *a shady person with a doubtful past.* —**doubt′ful·ly** *adv.*

doubtless (dout′lĭs) *adv.* **1.** Certainly; assuredly: *The bad weather was doubtless a factor in the delay.* **2.** Presumably; probably: *They will doubtless reject our proposal.* —**doubt′less·ly** *adv.*

douche (dōōsh) *n.* **1.** A stream of liquid or air applied to a part or cavity of the body in order to cleanse or apply medication. **2.** An instrument for applying a douche. ❖ *tr. & intr.v.* **douched, douching, douches** To cleanse or treat by means of a douche.

dough (dō) *n.* **1.** A soft thick mixture of dry ingredients, such as flour or meal, and liquid, such as water, that is kneaded, shaped, and baked, especially as bread or pastry. **2.** *Slang* Money.

doughnut also **donut** (dō′nŭt′ *or* dō′nət) *n.* A small ring-shaped cake made of rich dough that is fried in deep fat.

doughty (dou′tē) *adj.* **doughtier, doughtiest** Marked by stouthearted courage; very brave. —**dough′ti·ness** *n.*

doughy (dō′ē) *adj.* **doughier, doughiest** Having the appearance or consistency of dough: *a doughy face.* —**dough′i·ness** *n.*

Douglas fir *n.* A tall evergreen tree of western North America having short needles, drooping cones, and strong heavy wood valuable as lumber.

dour (dŏŏr *or* dour) *adj.* **dourer, dourest 1.** Marked by sternness or harshness; forbidding. **2.** Silently ill-humored; gloomy: *had a dour temperament that won him few friends.* —**dour′ly** *adv.* —**dour′ness** *n.*

douse (dous) *tr.v.* **doused, dousing, douses 1.** To wet thoroughly; drench. **2.** To put out (a light or fire); extinguish: *She doused the campfire with a bucket of water.*

dove¹ (dŭv) *n.* **1.** Any of various birds, including the pigeons, having a small head and a characteristic cooing call. **2.** A person who advocates peace or negotiation rather than armed conflict or confrontation: *The doves in Congress opposed military intervention.*

dove² (dōv) *v.* A past tense of **dive.**

dovecote (dŭv′kōt′ *or* dŭv′kŏt′) also **dovecot** (dŭv′kŏt′) *n.* A small structure, often raised on a pole, for housing domesticated pigeons.

dovetail (dŭv′tāl′) *n.* **1.** One of a series of pieces cut into the end of a board so as to fit into corresponding indentations cut into another board. Both boards together form an interlocking joint. **2.** A joint formed by interlocking such pieces. ❖ *v.* **dovetailed, dovetailing, dovetails** —*tr.* **1.** To connect, fit together, or combine harmoniously: *Let's try to dovetail our travel plans so we see each other.* —*intr.* **1.** To be joined or fitted together by means of dovetails. **2.** To be combined or fitted together harmoniously: *Our travel plans dovetail for one weekend.*

dowager (dou′ə-jər) *n.* **1.** A widow who holds a title or property derived from her dead husband: *a dowager princess.* **2.** An elderly woman of high social station.

dowdy (dou′dē) *adj.* **dowdier, dowdiest** Lacking stylishness or neatness; shabby: *dowdy old clothes.* —**dow′di·ly** *adv.* —**dow′di·ness** *n.*

dowel (dou′əl) *n.* **1.** A long thin cylindrical piece of hard material, usually wood. **2.** A round, usually wooden pin that fits into a corresponding hole to fasten or align two adjacent pieces.

dower (dou′ər) *n.* The part of a deceased man's real estate allotted by law to his widow for her lifetime.

down¹ (doun) *adv.* **1a.** From a higher to a lower place: *hiked down from the summit.* **b.** To, on, or toward the ground, floor, or bottom: *tripped and fell down.* **2.** In or to a sitting or reclining position: *sat down; lay down on the grass.* **3.** Toward or in the south: *going down to Florida.* **4.** Away from a central place: *down on the farm.* **5.** In or into one's stomach: *washed the bagel down with juice.* **6.** Toward or at a lower point on a scale: *body temperature coming down after a fever.* **7.** To or into an inferior condition: *The mayor went down in defeat.* **8.** From an earlier to a later time: *traditions handed down through the ages.* **9.** In partial payment at the time of purchase: *put $300 down on the TV set.* **10.** In writing: *The reporter took the statement down.* **11.** To the source: *tracking a rumor down.* **12.** Seriously, intensely, or diligently: *Let's get down to work.* **13.** Into a secure position: *nail down the boards.* ❖ *adj.* **1a.** Moving or directed downward: *a down elevator.* **b.** Low or lower: *The room is dark because the blinds are down.* **2.** Sick; not feeling well: *He is down with a bad cold.* **3.** In low spirits; depressed. **4.** Not functioning or operating, especially temporarily: *They can't issue report cards because the school's computers are down.* **5.** Completed; done: *As for the exams, there are two down, and two to go.* **6.** Trailing an opponent, as in a game: *We were down by two points with a minute left.* **7.** In football, having had one's forward progress in carrying the ball stopped, especially by being tackled. **8.** In baseball, retired or put out: *got up to bat with two down and a runner* on third base. ❖ *prep.* **1.** In a descending direction upon, along, through, or into: *ran down the stairs.* **2.** Along the course of: *walking down the road.* ❖ *n.* **1.** A downward movement; a descent. **2.** A misfortune or difficulty: *went through a lot of ups and downs before succeeding.* **3.** In football, any of a series of four plays during which a team must advance at least ten yards to retain possession of the ball. ❖ *tr.v.* **downed, downing, downs 1.** To bring, strike, or throw down. **2.** To swallow hastily; gulp: *downed a lot of water before the race.* **3.** In football: **a.** To put (the ball) out of play by throwing it to the ground or touching a knee to the ground. **b.** To stop the advancement of the ball by (a ball carrier), as by tackling. ◆ **down on** *Informal* Hostile or negative toward: *She was down on jogging after her injury.*

down² (doun) *n.* **1.** Soft, fluffy feathers forming the first plumage of a young bird and lying under the outer feathers in certain adult birds: *the down of a chick.* **2.** A covering of soft, short hairs, as on some leaves or fruit.

down³ (doun) *n.* often **downs** An expanse of rolling grassy treeless land used for grazing.

WORD HISTORY Down¹ comes from Old English *dūne* (meaning "from a higher to lower place"), which comes from Old English *dūn,* meaning "hill." **Down²** comes from Middle English *doun,* which comes from Old Norse *dūnn,* both referring to the soft fluffy feathers of a young bird. **Down³** comes from Old English *dūn,* meaning "hill."

---

downbeat (doun′bēt′) *n.* **1.** The downward stroke made by a conductor to indicate the first beat of a musical measure. **2.** The first beat of a measure. ❖ *adj.* Depressing or pessimistic: *The downbeat economic news sent stock prices lower.*

downcast (doun′kăst′) *adj.* **1.** Directed downward: *downcast eyes.* **2.** Low in spirits; depressed: *feeling downcast after repeated failure.*

downcourt (doun-kôrt′) *adv. & adj.* To, into, or in the far end of a basketball court.

downer (dou′nər) *n. Slang* A depressing experience, situation, or person: *Failing the test was a real downer.*

downfall (doun′fôl′) *n.* **1.** A sudden loss of wealth, reputation, happiness, or status; ruin: *An investigation resulted in the downfall of the corrupt banker.* **2.** A cause of sudden ruin: *Careless spending was the treasurer's downfall.* **3.** A fall of rain or snow, especially one that is heavy or unexpected.

downfield (doun′fēld′) *adv. & adj.* In sports, to, into, or in the defensive team's end of the field.

downgrade (doun′grād′) *tr.v.* **downgraded, downgrading, downgrades 1.** To lower the status or salary of: *downgrade an employee for constant carelessness.* **2.** To minimize the importance, value, or reputation of. ❖ *n.* A descending slope, as in a road; a downward course: *The truck sped up on the downgrade.*

downhearted (doun′här′tĭd) *adj.* Low in spirits; depressed. —**down′heart′ed·ly** *adv.*

downhill (doun′hĭl′) *adv.* **1.** Down the slope of a hill or mountain: *We raced downhill.* **2.** Toward a worsening condition: *After they lost that sale, the whole business started going downhill.* ❖ *adj.* (doun′hĭl′) **1.** Sloping downward; descending: *a downhill direction.* **2.** Relating to skiing down slopes rather than across the countryside. **3.** Worsening: *a career with a downhill trajectory.* **4.** Easier: *The hardest part of the project is over—it's all*

downhill from here.

download (doun′lōd′) *tr.v.* **downloaded, downloading, downloads** To transfer (data or a program) from a central computer or website to another computer or device: *downloaded software from the Internet.* ❖ *n.* **1.** A file that has been downloaded. **2.** An instance of downloading data or a program. —**down·load′a·ble** *adj.*

down payment *n.* A partial payment made at the time of purchase, with the balance to be paid later.

downplay (doun′plā′) *tr.v.* **downplayed, downplaying, downplays** To minimize the importance of: *downplayed the severity of the earthquake.*

downpour (doun′pôr′) *n.* A heavy fall of rain.

downright (doun′rīt′) *adj.* **1.** Thoroughgoing; unequivocal: *a downright scoundrel.* **2.** Straightforward; candid. ❖ *adv.* Thoroughly; absolutely: *They acted downright unpleasant.*

downshift (doun′shĭft′) *intr.v.* **downshifted, downshifting, downshifts 1.** To shift a motor vehicle into a lower gear. **2.** To reduce the speed, rate, or intensity of something: *The factory is downshifting as the old products are phased out.*

downside (doun′sīd′) *n.* **1.** The lower side or portion. **2.** A disadvantageous aspect: *weighed the downsides and the benefits before making a decision.*

downsize (doun′sīz′) *v.* **downsized, downsizing, downsizes** —*tr.* **1.** To reduce in number or size, especially by eliminating workers: *The department was downsized during a reorganization.* **2.** To make in a smaller size: *cars that were downsized during an era of high gasoline prices.* —*intr.* **1.** To become smaller in size by reductions in personnel or assets: *Corporations continued to downsize after the economy recovered.* **2.** To live in a simpler way, especially by moving into a smaller residence.

downslope (doun′slōp′) *n.* A downward slope. ❖ *adv. & adj.* At or in the direction of a lower point on a slope.

downspout (doun′spout′) *n.* A vertical pipe for carrying rainwater down from a roof gutter.

downstage (doun′stāj′) *adv.* Toward, at, or on the front part of a stage. ❖ *adj.* (doun′stāj′) Relating to the front part of a stage. ❖ *n.* (doun′stāj′) The front half of a stage.

downstairs (doun′stârz′) *adv.* **1.** Down the stairs: *I slipped going downstairs.* **2.** To or on a lower floor: *I ran downstairs to answer the telephone.* ❖ *adj.* (doun′stârz′) Located on a lower floor: *a downstairs bedroom.* ❖ *n.* (doun′stârz′) *(used with a singular verb)* The lower or main floor of a building: *The whole downstairs was a mess after the party.*

downstream (doun′strēm′) *adv.* In the direction of a stream's current: *floated downstream.*

Down syndrome or **Down's syndrome** *n.* A disorder present from birth, characterized by intellectual disabilities, short stature, and a flattened facial profile. It is caused by the presence of an extra chromosome.

downtime (doun′tīm′) *n.* **1.** The period of time when something, such as a factory or a piece of machinery, is not in operation. **2.** A period of time when a person is not working or doing a planned activity.

down-to-earth (doun′tə-ûrth′) *adj.* **1.** Realistic; sensible: *a down-to-earth solution to the problem.* **2.** Not pretentious: *an easygoing, down-to-earth manner.*

downtown (doun′toun′) *n.* The business center or the lower part of a city or town. ❖ *adv.* (doun′toun′) Toward or in the business center or lower part of a town or city: *Let's walk downtown.* ❖ *adj.* (doun′toun′) Being in or going toward the business center of a city or town: *a downtown restaurant; a downtown bus.*

downtrodden (doun′trŏd′n) *adj.* Harshly treated; oppressed.

downturn (doun′tûrn′) *n.* A tendency downward, especially in business or economic activity: *In a recession there is a marked downturn in business.*

downward (doun′wərd) *adv.* or **downwards** (doun′-wərdz) **1.** In, to, or toward a lower place, level, or position: *floating downward.* **2.** From a prior source or an earlier time: *traditions passed downward through the ages.* ❖ *adj.* Directed toward a lower place or position: *a downward trend.*

downwind (doun′wīnd′) *adv.* In the direction toward which the wind blows.

downy (dou′nē) *adj.* **downier, downiest 1.** Covered with or made of down: *a downy chick.* **2.** Resembling down: *downy white clouds.*

dowry (dou′rē) *n., pl.* **dowries** Money or property brought by a bride to her husband at marriage.

dowse (douz) *intr.v.* **dowsed, dowsing, dowses** To use a divining rod to search for underground water or minerals. —**dows′er** *n.*

doxology (dŏk-sŏl′ə-jē) *n., pl.* **doxologies** A hymn or verse in praise of God.

doyen (doi-ĕn′ *or* dwä-yăN′) *n.* A man who is the eldest or senior member of a group.

doyenne (doi-ĕn′ *or* dwä-yĕn′) *n.* A woman who is the eldest or senior member of a group.

doz. An abbreviation of dozen.

doze (dōz) *v.* **dozed, dozing, dozes** —*intr.* To sleep lightly; nap: *doze on the porch in the sun.* —*tr.* To spend (time) dozing or as if dozing: *doze the afternoon hours away.* ❖ *n.* A short light sleep; a nap. ◆ **doze off** To fall into a light sleep: *I dozed off during the play's first act.*

dozen (dŭz′ən) *n.* **1.** *pl.* **dozen** A set of 12: *Two dozen were at the party.* **2.** **dozens** A large undetermined number: *Dozens of salmon swam below.* ❖ *adj.* Twelve: *a dozen eggs.*

dozenth (dŭz′ənth) *adj.* Twelfth.

Dr. An abbreviation of: **1.** doctor. **2.** drive (street).

drab (drăb) *adj.* **drabber, drabbest 1.** Faded and dull in appearance. **2.** Dull or commonplace in character; dreary: *a drab cheerless house.* ❖ *n.* **1.** A dull grayish to yellowish or light olive brown. **2.** Cloth of this color or of an unbleached natural color. —**drab′ly** *adv.* —**drab′ness** *n.*

drachma (drăk′mə) *n., pl.* **drachmas** or **drachmae** (drăk′-mē) **1.** The former basic monetary unit of Greece. **2.** A silver coin of ancient Greece. **3.** One of several modern units of weight, especially the dram.

draconian (drə-kō′nē-ən) *adj.* Exceedingly harsh; very severe: *a draconian legal code; draconian budget cuts.*

draft (drăft) *n.* **1.** A current of air in an enclosed area: *feel a cold draft on one's feet.* **2.** A device that controls the flow or circulation of air. **3.** The act of pulling loads; traction: *large horses used for draft.* **4.** The depth of a vessel's keel below the water line. **5.** A document for directing the payment of money from an account or fund. **6a.** A gulp, swallow, or inhalation. **b.** The amount taken in by a single act of drinking or inhaling. **7a.** The drawing of a liquid, as from a cask or keg. **b.** An amount of liquid so drawn. **8a.** The process of selecting one or more individuals from a group, as for a service or duty. **b.** Compulsory enrollment

in the armed forces; conscription. **c.** A body of people selected or conscripted. **d.** In sports, a system in which the exclusive rights to new players are distributed among professional teams. **9a.** The act of drawing in a fishing net. **b.** The amount of fish caught. **10a.** A preliminary version of a plan, document, or picture. **b.** A representation of something to be constructed: *The architect showed us a draft of the building.* ❖ *tr.v.* **drafted, drafting, drafts 1a.** To select from a group for some usually compulsory service: *draft citizens for military service.* **b.** To select (a player) in a sports draft. **2.** To draw up a preliminary plan, sketch, or version of: *drafted several versions of a speech.* ❖ *adj.* Suited for or used for drawing heavy loads: *a team of draft horses.*

draftee (drăf-tē′) *n.* A person who is drafted, especially into the armed forces.

draftsman (drăfts′mən) *n.* A man who draws plans or designs, as of structures to be built. —**drafts′man·ship′** *n.*

draftsperson (drăfts′pûr′sən) *n.* A person who drafts plans or designs.

draftswoman (drăfts′wŏom′ən) *n.* A woman who draws plans or designs, as of structures to be built.

drafty (drăf′tē) *adj.* **draftier, draftiest** Having or exposed to drafts of air: *a drafty old house.* —**draft′i·ly** *adv.* —**draft′i·ness** *n.*

drag (drăg) *v.* **dragged, dragging, drags** —*tr.* **1.** To pull (something) along with difficulty or effort; haul: *dragged the heavy box out of the way.* See Synonyms at **pull.** **2.** To cause or allow (something) to trail along the ground: *Don't drag your coat in the mud.* **3.** To cause (oneself) to move in a slow or reluctant fashion: *I dragged myself to the meeting.* **4.** To take or escort (a person, for example), especially in overcoming resistance or reluctance: *dragged my cousin to the reception.* **5.** To move (an item) on a computer screen using a pointing device, such as a mouse: *dragged the document icon into a folder.* **6.** To search the bottom of (a body of water), as with a hook or net: *They dragged the river looking for the suitcase that was thrown from the bridge.* **7.** To prolong tediously: *They dragged the discussion out.* —*intr.* **1.** To trail along the ground: *The chain dragged along behind the tractor.* **2.** To move slowly or with difficulty: *The exhausted hikers dragged back to camp.* **3.** To pass or proceed slowly or tediously: *The long speech dragged on and on.* ❖ *n.* **1.** A person or thing that slows or stops motion or progress: *High interest rates can act as a drag on the economy.* **2.** The force produced by friction that hinders motion through a fluid, such as air or water: *redesigned the race car to reduce drag.* **3.** Something that is pulled along the ground, especially something for carrying loads: *The horse was harnessed to the drag.* **4.** A device for dragging under water, such as a grappling hook. **5.** *Slang* A person or thing that is obnoxiously tiresome. **6.** An act of inhaling something, especially smoke from a cigarette. ◆ **drag (one's) feet** To act or work with intentional slowness: *drag one's feet about completing a chore.*

draggle (drăg′əl) *tr. & intr.v.* **draggled, draggling, draggles** To make or become wet and muddy by dragging along the ground.

dragnet (drăg′nĕt′) *n.* **1.** A coordinated system of search used by the police to find criminal suspects. **2.** A net for trawling; a trawl.

dragon (drăg′ən) *n.* A mythical giant reptile often represented as a winged fire-breathing monster.

dragonfly (drăg′ən-flī′) *n.* Any of various flying insects having a long slender body and two pairs of clear wings with fine networks of veins.

dragoon (drə-gōon′) *n.* A heavily armed mounted soldier in some European armies of the 1600s and 1700s. ❖ *tr.v.* **dragooned, dragooning, dragoons** To compel or force by violent measures: *dragooned the townspeople into supplying the troops with food.*

drag queen *n. Slang* A man, especially a performer, who dresses as a woman.

drag race *n.* A short race between cars to determine which can accelerate faster from a standstill.

drain (drān) *v.* **drained, draining, drains** —*tr.* **1.** To draw off (a liquid) gradually: *drain water from a sink.* **2.** To make dry or empty by drawing off liquid: *drain the pond.* **3.** To drink all the contents of: *The child drained the cup.* **4.** To deplete gradually, especially to the point of complete exhaustion: *The performance drained the cast and crew.* —*intr.* **1.** To flow off or out: *Melted snow drained off the roof.* **2.** To become empty by the draining off of liquid: *The tub drained slowly.* **3.** To discharge surface or excess water: *Most large rivers drain into the sea.* ❖ *n.* **1.** A pipe or channel by which liquid is drained off: *clog up the drain.* **2.** Something that causes a gradual loss: *Building a new library is a drain on the resources for buying more books.* ◆ **down the drain** To or into the condition of being wasted or lost: *When our first plan went down the drain, we quickly came up with another.*

drainage (drā′nĭj) *n.* **1.** The action or a method of draining: *Drainage in swampland is very poor.* **2.** A natural or artificial system of drains. **3.** Material that is drained off: *Storm sewers carried the drainage away.*

drainpipe (drān′pīp′) *n.* A pipe for carrying off water or sewage.

drake (drāk) *n.* A male duck.

dram (drăm) *n.* **1.** A unit of weight equal to ¹⁄₁₆ of an ounce or 27.3 grains (about 1.8 grams). See table at **measurement. 2.** A unit of apothecary weight equal to ⅛ of an ounce or 60 grains (about 3.9 grams).

drama (drä′mə) *n.* **1.** A literary work that tells a story in prose or verse and is meant to be performed by actors. **2a.** Theatrical plays of a particular kind or period: *modern drama.* **b.** The art and practice of writing and producing works for the stage. **3.** A situation or a series of events in real life that resemble a play: *the day-by-day drama within Congress.* **4.** The quality or condition of being dramatic: *a confrontation between rivals that was full of drama.*

dramatic (drə-măt′ĭk) *adj.* **1.** Relating to drama or the theater: *dramatic performances.* **2.** Resembling a drama in action or emotion: *the dramatic events that led to Lincoln's election.* **3.** Arresting or forceful in appearance or effect: *a dramatic mountain range.* —**dra·mat′i·cal·ly** *adv.*

dramatics (drə-măt′ĭks) *n. (used with a singular or plural verb)* **1.** The art or practice of acting in or staging plays. **2.** Dramatic or exaggerated behavior: *cut the dramatics and get to the point.*

dramatis personae (drăm′ə-tĭs pər-sō′nē *or* drä′mə-tĭs pər-sō′nī′) *pl.n.* The characters in a play or story.

dramatist (drăm′ə-tĭst *or* drä′mə-tĭst) *n.* A person who writes plays; a playwright.

dramatize (drăm′ə-tīz′ *or* drä′mə-tīz′) *tr.v.* **dramatized, dramatizing, dramatizes 1.** To adapt (a literary work) into a play or screenplay. **2.** To present or view in a dramatic or melodramatic way: *The report dramatizes the plight of the*

flood victims. —**dram′a·ti·za′tion** (drăm′ə-tĭ-zā′shən *or* drä′mə-tĭ-zā′shən) *n.*

drank (drăngk) *v.* Past tense of **drink.**

drape (drāp) *v.* **draped, draping, drapes** —*tr.* **1.** To cover or hang with or as if with cloth in loose folds: *The artist draped the painting with a cloth.* **2.** To arrange or let fall in loose folds: *draped a long cape over one shoulder.* **3.** To hang or rest limply: *I draped my legs over the back of the chair.* —*intr.* To fall or hang in loose folds: *Silk drapes easily.* ❖ *n.* **1.** A drapery; a curtain: *pull the drapes over the window.* **2.** The way in which cloth falls or hangs: *the drape of fine suit material.*

draper (drā′pər) *n. Chiefly British* A dealer in cloth or dry goods.

drapery (drā′pə-rē) *n., pl.* **draperies 1.** A piece or pieces of heavy fabric hanging straight in loose folds, used as a curtain. **2.** Cloth or clothing arranged in loose folds.

drastic (drăs′tĭk) *adj.* Severe or radical in nature; extreme: *Calling out troops was a drastic measure to restore order.* —**dras′ti·cal·ly** *adv.*

drat (drăt) *interj.* An expression used to show annoyance.

draught (drăft) *n. & v. & adj. Chiefly British* Variant of **draft.**

draughts (drăfts *or* dräfts) *n. (used with a singular or plural verb) Chiefly British* The game of checkers.

Dravidian (drə-vĭd′ē-ən) *n.* **1.** A large family of languages spoken in southern India and northern Sri Lanka. **2.** A member of a people that speaks one of these languages. —**Dra·vid′i·an, Dra·vid′ic** (drə-vĭd′ĭk) *adj.*

draw (drô) *v.* **drew** (drōō), **drawn** (drôn), **drawing, draws** —*tr.* **1a.** To pull or move (something) after or toward one by applying force; drag: *a team of horses drawing a load.* See Synonyms at **pull. b.** To cause to move, as by leading: *She drew us into the room to show us her presents.* **c.** To cause to move in a given direction or to a given position: *drew the curtain.* **2.** To cause to flow forth: *a deep scratch that drew blood; draw water for a bath.* **3.** To suck or take in (air, for example): *The singer drew a deep breath.* **4.** To require (a specified depth of water) for floating: *A boat drawing 18 inches.* **5a.** To pull or take out: *draw a sword from a sheath.* **b.** To take (cards) from a dealer or central stack, as in poker. **c.** To extract or take for one's own use: *drew strength from her example.* **6.** To attract; entice: *Our beaches draw many tourists.* **7.** To get as a response; elicit: *The comic drew laughter from the audience.* **8.** To earn; gain: *draw interest on a savings account.* **9.** To withdraw (money) from an account. **10.** To take or receive by chance: *I drew the lucky number.* **11.** To stretch tight: *draw a string around the package.* **12a.** To inscribe (a line or lines) with a pencil or other marking implement. **b.** To make a picture of, using mostly lines; sketch: *drawing illustrations for a new book.* **c.** To represent in words: *The poet drew scenes of far-off places with words.* **13.** To deduce from evidence at hand; formulate: *We can draw a conclusion from the facts already gathered.* —*intr.* **1.** To proceed or move steadily: *The boat drew near shore.* **2.** To take in a draft of air: *The fireplace chimney doesn't draw well.* **3.** To contract or tighten: *The smile drew into a frown.* **4.** To tie in a contest: *The chess players drew after 32 moves.* **5.** To make a likeness with lines on a surface: *Several students draw especially well.* ❖ *n.* **1.** An act of drawing: *a lucky draw of an ace from the deck of cards.* **2.** Something that attracts interest, customers, or spectators: *The movie is sure to be a good draw at the box office.* **3.** A contest ending in a tie. **4.** A ravine or gully that water drains into. **5.** In football, a play in which the quarterback drops back as if to pass and then runs or hands off to a running back. ◆ **draw down 1.** To reduce or deplete by consuming or spending: *drew down our food reserves.* **2.** To reduce (military forces in a specific deployment). **draw out** To prolong; protract: *drew out the meeting until we were quite bored.* **draw the line** To set a limit, as on behavior. **draw up 1.** To write up in a set form; compose: *draw up a list; draw up an agreement.* **2.** To bring (oneself) into an erect posture. **3.** To bring (troops, for example) into order. **4.** To bring or come to a halt: *The truck drew up at the gate.*

drawback (drô′băk′) *n.* A disadvantage or inconvenience: *The pay was good but the long hours were a drawback.*

drawbridge (drô′brĭj′) *n.* A bridge that can be raised or drawn aside either to prevent access or to permit passage beneath it.

drawer (drô′ər) *n.* **1.** A person who draws. **2.** (*also* drôr) A boxlike compartment in a piece of furniture that can be pulled in and out. **3. drawers** (drôrz) Underpants.

drawing (drô′ĭng) *n.* **1.** The act or an instance of drawing. **2.** The art of representing forms and figures on a surface by means of lines. **3.** A work produced by this art: *There are several fine drawings of horses on the wall.*

drawing room *n.* A large room in which guests are entertained.

drawknife (drô′nīf′) *n.* A knife with a handle at each of the blade, used for shaving wood surfaces.

drawl (drôl) *intr. & tr.v.* **drawled, drawling, drawls** To speak or utter with lengthened or drawn-out vowels. ❖ *n.* The speech or manner of speaking of one who drawls: *spoke with a pronounced drawl.*

drawn (drôn) *v.* Past participle of **draw.** ❖ *adj.* Haggard, as from fatigue or ill health: *The survivors looked drawn after their rescue.*

drawstring (drô′strĭng′) *n.* A cord or ribbon run through a hem or casing and pulled to tighten or close an opening.

dray (drā) *n.* A low heavy cart without sides, used for hauling. ❖ *tr.v.* **drayed, draying, drays** To haul by means of a dray.

dread (drĕd) *tr.v.* **dreaded, dreading, dreads 1.** To fear intensely: *Many people dread snakes.* **2.** To anticipate with alarm, distaste, or reluctance: *We were dreading the long drive home.* ❖ *n.* **1.** Profound fear; terror. **2.** Fearful or distasteful anticipation: *the dread of saying something foolish.* ❖ *adj.* Causing fear or terror: *a dread disease.*

dreadful (drĕd′fəl) *adj.* **1.** Causing dread; terrifying: *a dreadful epidemic.* **2.** Extremely unpleasant; distasteful or shocking: *dreadful furniture; dreadful behavior.* —**dread′ful·ly** *adv.* —**dread′ful·ness** *n.*

dreadlocks (drĕd′lŏks′) *pl.n.* Long ropelike locks or thin braids of twisted or curled hair extending from the scalp.

dreadnought (drĕd′nôt′) *n.* A heavily armed battleship.

dream (drēm) *n.* **1.** A series of mental images, ideas, and emotions occurring during sleep. **2.** A daydream. **3.** A state of abstraction; a trance: *wandering about in a dream.* **4.** A hope or aspiration: *dreams of world peace.* **5.** Something especially gratifying, excellent, or useful: *The new car runs like a dream.* ❖ *v.* **dreamed** or **dreamt** (drĕmt), **dreaming, dreams** —*intr.* **1.** To have a dream while sleeping. **2.** To daydream: *dreaming of far-off plac-*

es. **3.** To consider as feasible or practical: *I wouldn't even dream of going.* —*tr.* **1.** To have a dream about (something) during sleep: *Did it storm last night, or did I dream it?* **2.** To conceive of; imagine: *We never dreamed it might snow so hard.* ◆ **dream up** To invent; concoct: *dreamed up a plan to get rich quick.* —**dream′er** *n.*

dreamland (drēm′lănd′) *n.* **1.** An ideal or imaginary place. **2.** A state of sleep.

dreamy (drē′mē) *adj.* **dreamier, dreamiest 1.** Preoccupied or unattentive; trancelike: *walked around in a dreamy state looking at the trees.* **2.** Having a tendency to daydream: *a dreamy person who seldom pays attention.* **3.** Soothing and serene: *soft dreamy music.* **4.** *Informal* Very pleasant or attractive: *That new movie star is really dreamy!* —**dream′i·ly** *adv.* —**dream′i·ness** *n.*

drear (drîr) *adj.* Dreary.

dreary (drîr′ē) *adj.* **drearier, dreariest 1.** Dismal; bleak: *a dreary January rain.* **2.** Boring; dull: *the dreary tasks of housekeeping.* —**drear′i·ly** *adv.* —**drear′i·ness** *n.*

dredge[1] (drĕj) *n.* **1.** A machine equipped with an underwater scooping or suction device, used especially to deepen a harbor or waterway. **2.** A ship or barge equipped with such a machine. ❖ *v.* **dredged, dredging, dredges** —*tr.* **1.** To clean, deepen, or widen with a dredge: *dredged the channel.* **2.** To bring up with a dredge: *dredge dirt and rock out of the river to make a channel.* **3.** To bring to public notice; uncover: *a reporter who dredges up the dirt on celebrities.* —*intr.* To use a dredge.

dredge[2] (drĕj) *tr.v.* **dredged, dredging, dredges** To sprinkle (food) with fine particles of something, such as flour or bread crumbs.

WORD HISTORY Dredge[1] comes from Early Modern English *dreg-bot* (meaning "a boat used for dredging"), which comes from Old English *dragan,* meaning "to draw." **Dredge**[2] comes from Middle English *dragge,* meaning "a sweet confection."

dregs (drĕgz) *pl.n.* **1.** The sediment in a liquid: *rinse the dregs out of the coffeepot.* **2.** The basest or least desirable portion.

dreidel also **dreidl** (drād′l) *n.* A four-sided top spun in games of chance played by children and adults at Hanukkah.

drench (drĕnch) *tr.v.* **drenched, drenching, drenches** To wet through and through; soak: *A thunderstorm drenched everyone outside.*

dress (drĕs) *v.* **dressed, dressing, dresses** —*tr.* **1.** To put clothes on: *Dress the baby warmly.* **2a.** To decorate or adorn: *dress a Christmas tree.* **b.** To arrange a display in: *dress a store window.* **3.** To apply medicine or bandages to (a wound): *After the operation the nurse dressed the incision.* **4.** To arrange or style (the hair). **5.** To groom (an animal); curry. **6.** To clean (fish or fowl) for cooking or sale: *dress a turkey.* **7.** To arrange (troops) in ranks; align: *dress soldiers for a parade.* —*intr.* **1.** To put on clothes: *I got up late and dressed in a hurry.* **2.** To wear clothes of a certain kind or style: *We are allowed to dress casually at the office.* ❖ *n.* **1.** Clothing; apparel: *wore formal dress to the reception.* **2.** A style of clothing: *Bankers often wear conservative dress.* **3.** A one-piece outer garment worn by women and girls. ❖ *adj.* **1.** Suitable for formal occasions: *wear a tie with a dress shirt.* **2.** Calling for formal clothes: *a dress reception.* ◆ **dress down** To scold; reprimand. **dress up** To wear formal or fancy clothes: *They dressed up for the party.*

dressage (drə-säzh′) *n.* The guiding of a horse through a series of complex maneuvers by a rider using very slight movements of the hands, legs, and weight.

dresser¹ (drĕs′ər) *n.* **1.** A person who dresses: *She is a very chic dresser.* **2.** A wardrobe assistant, as for an actor.

dresser² (drĕs′ər) *n.* **1.** A chest of drawers, often having a mirror above it and typically used for holding clothing and personal items. **2.** A cupboard or set of shelves for dishes or kitchen utensils.

WORD HISTORY Dresser¹ is derived from the verb *dress.* **Dresser²** comes from Middle English *dressour,* meaning "table for preparing food," which comes from Old French *drecier,* meaning "to set up, arrange."

---

dressing (drĕs′ĭng) *n.* **1.** A medicinal or protective material applied to a wound. **2.** A sauce for certain dishes, such as salads. **3.** A stuffing, as for poultry or fish.

dressing gown *n.* A robe worn for lounging or before dressing.

dressing room *n.* A room, as in a theater, for changing costumes or clothes and applying makeup.

dressing table *n.* A low table with a mirror at which one sits while applying makeup.

dressmaker (drĕs′mā′kər) *n.* A person who makes women's clothing, especially dresses.

dressmaking (drĕs′mā′kĭng) *n.* The act or occupation of making women's clothing, especially dresses.

dress rehearsal *n.* A complete, uninterrupted rehearsal of a play with costumes and stage props.

dressy (drĕs′ē) *adj.* **dressier, dressiest 1.** Requiring or characterized by formal dress: *a dressy party.* **2.** Formal or elegant in style: *dressy shoes.*

drew (drōo) *v.* Past tense of **draw.**

dribble (drĭb′əl) *v.* **dribbled, dribbling, dribbles** —*intr.* **1.** To flow or fall in drops or an unsteady stream; trickle: *Water dribbled out of the leaky faucet.* **2.** To let saliva drip from the mouth; drool: *Most babies dribble when they are teething.* **3.** To move a ball or puck with repeated light bounces or kicks: *The player dribbled around an opponent.* —*tr.* **1.** To let flow or fall in drops or an unsteady stream: *I dribbled gravy on the potatoes.* **2.** To move (a ball or puck) by repeated light bounces or kicks, as in basketball or soccer: *The forward dribbled the ball right past the defender.* ❖ *n.* **1.** A small quantity; a drop: *a dribble of milk.* **2.** The act of dribbling a ball: *a fast dribble across the court.* —**drib′bler** *n.*

driblet (drĭb′lĭt) *n.* A small amount or portion: *pay off a loan in driblets.*

dried (drīd) *v.* Past tense and past participle of **dry.**

drier¹ also **dryer** (drī′ər) *n.* **1.** A person or thing that dries: *We did the dishes, and I was the drier.* **2.** A substance added, as to paint, to speed drying.

drier² (drī′ər) *adj.* A comparative of **dry.**

dries (drīz) *v.* Third person singular present tense of **dry.**

driest (drī′ĭst) *adj.* A superlative of **dry.**

drift (drĭft) *v.* **drifted, drifting, drifts** —*intr.* **1.** To be carried along by a current of water or air: *The boat drifted toward shore.* **2a.** To proceed or move unhurriedly and smoothly: *I drifted among the guests at the party.* **b.** To live or behave without a clear purpose or goal: *He drifted through the summer before applying for jobs in the fall.* **3.** To wander from a course or point of attention; stray: *My attention drifted from the game.* **4.** To be piled up in banks or heaps by the force of a current: *Snow drifted against the wall.* —*tr.* **1.** To cause to be carried in a current: *Waves drifted debris all along the shore.* **2.** To pile up in heaps or

banks: *The winds drifted the snow.* ❖ *n.* **1.** The act or condition of drifting: *a continuous drift of sand.* **2.** Something moving along in a current of air or water. **3.** The mass of material, such as sand or snow, deposited by a current of air or water: *snow drifts six feet high.* **4.** Fragments of rock that are carried and deposited by a glacier: *These drifts appeared at the end of the Ice Age.* **5.** A general meaning or direction of thought: *The drift of the lecture was hard to follow.* **6.** A gradual deviation from an original course, model, method, or intention.

drifter (drĭf′tər) *n.* A person who moves aimlessly from place to place or from job to job.

driftwood (drĭft′wood′) *n.* Wood floating in or washed up by a body of water.

drill¹ (drĭl) *n.* **1.** A tool used to bore holes in materials, usually by a rotating action or by repeated blows. **2.** Disciplined repetitive exercise as a means of teaching and perfecting a skill or procedure. **3.** A task or exercise for teaching a skill or procedure by repetition: *a fire drill.* ❖ *v.* **drilled, drilling, drills** —*tr.* **1.** To make a hole with a drill in (a hard material): *drilling wood.* **2.** To make (a hole) with or as if with a drill. **3.** To teach or train by continuous repetition: *drill a company of soldiers.* —*intr.* **1.** To make a hole in or as if with a drill: *drill into a board.* **2.** To perform a training exercise: *The astronauts drill before attempting repairs in space.*

drink (drĭngk) *v.* **drank** (drăngk), **drunk** (drŭngk), **drinking, drinks** —*tr.* **1.** To take into the mouth and swallow (a liquid): *drink water every day.* **2.** To swallow the liquid contents of (a vessel): *I drank a mug of hot cocoa.* **3.** To take in or soak up; absorb: *The parched earth drank up the rain.* **4.** To take in eagerly through the senses or intellect: *The tourists drank in the grandeur of the mountains.* **5.** To give or make (a toast): *We drank a toast to happiness.* —*intr.* **1.** To swallow liquid: *The thirsty hikers drank from a clear stream.* **2.** To salute a person or occasion with a toast: *We'll drink to your health.* **3.** To drink alcoholic beverages. ❖ *n.* **1.** A liquid for drinking; a beverage: *Iced tea is a satisfying drink.* **2.** An amount of liquid swallowed: *took a drink of water.* **3.** An alcoholic beverage: *The lawyers went out for a drink after work.* —**drink′a·ble** *adj.* —**drink′er** *n.*

drip (drĭp) *intr. & tr.v.* **dripped, dripping, drips** To fall or let fall in drops: *Water dripped from the faucet. I dripped paint on the floor.* ❖ *n.* **1.** The process of forming and falling in drops: *the drip of water from leaky gutters.* **2.** Liquid or moisture that falls in drops: *Drips of paint spattered the floor.* **3.** The sound made by liquid falling in drops: *The constant drip of the faucet was annoying.*

drip-dry (drĭp′drī′) *adj.* Made of a fabric that will not wrinkle when hung dripping wet for drying: *a drip-dry suit.* ❖ *intr.v.* **drip-dried, drip-drying, drip-dries** To dry with no wrinkles when hung dripping wet: *let a shirt drip-dry.*

drippings (drĭp′ĭngz) *pl.n.* The fat and juices from roasting meat, often used in making gravy.

drive (drīv) *v.* **drove** (drōv), **driven** (drĭv′ən), **driving, drives** —*tr.* **1a.** To push, propel, or press onward forcibly: *drove the horses into the corral.* **b.** To cause to retreat; put to flight: *The dog drove off the raccoon.* **2a.** To guide, control, or direct (a vehicle): *They drive their car to work every day.* **b.** To convey or transport in a vehicle: *The neighbors drove me to the store.* **3a.** To supply the motive force or power to and cause to function: *Electricity drives many motors.* **b.** To cause or sustain, as if by supplying force or power:

an economy that is driven by exports. **c.** To compel or force to work, often excessively: *The need for recognition drives him to work long hours.* **d.** To force into or from a particular state or act: *Constant interruptions drove me to despair.* **4.** To force to penetrate: *drive a nail into wood.* **5.** To carry through vigorously to a conclusion: *drive home one's point in an argument.* **6.** To hit or propel (a ball, for example) so that it travels with great speed or distance: *The batter drove the ball over the fence in center field.* —*intr.* **1.** To move along or advance quickly as if pushed by a force: *The car drove into the ditch.* **2.** To guide or control a vehicle or animal: *Many people drive too fast on this road.* **3.** To go or be carried in a vehicle: *We drove to the supermarket.* **4.** To make an effort to reach or achieve an objective; aim: *The author drove hard to complete the book on time.* **5.** In basketball, to move directly toward the basket with the ball. ❖ *n.* **1.** A trip or journey in a vehicle: *go for a quiet drive in the country.* **2a.** A road for automobiles and other vehicles: *Cars may use the drive in the park.* **b.** A driveway. **3a.** The means for transmitting motion to a machine: *Lathes often have a belt drive between the motor and the part that holds the piece being shaped.* **b.** The position or operating condition of such a mechanism: *put the car in drive.* **c.** The means by which automotive power is applied to a roadway: *Vehicles used by forest rangers often have four-wheel drive.* **4.** A device in a computer system that reads data from and often writes data onto a storage medium, such as an optical disc. **5a.** An organized effort to accomplish something: *a charity drive.* **b.** A massive and sustained military offensive. **6a.** In basketball, the act of moving with the ball directly to the basket. **b.** In football, a series of downs in which the ball is advanced by the offensive team. **7a.** Energy, push, or aggressiveness: *People who have drive and ambition often achieve their goals.* **b.** A strong motivating instinct: *the basic drive to satisfy one's hunger and thirst.* **8a.** The act of hitting a ball very swiftly. **b.** A golf shot made from a tee with a driver. **9a.** The act of rounding up and driving cattle, as to new pastures. **b.** A gathering and driving of logs down a river. ◆ **drive in** In baseball, to cause (a run) to be scored when batting. **drive at** To mean to do or say: *I'm not sure what you are driving at.*

drive-in (drīv′ĭn′) *n.* A business, such as an outdoor movie theater, that allows customers to receive services or be entertained while in their vehicles.

drivel (drĭv′əl) *v.* **driveled, driveling, drivels** or **drivelled, drivelling, drivels** —*intr.* **1.** To slobber; drool. **2.** To talk stupidly or childishly: *drivel on about nothing.* —*tr.* To say (something) stupidly: *driveled their usual empty promises.* ❖ *n.* **1.** Saliva flowing from the mouth. **2.** Stupid or senseless talk. —**driv′el·er, driv′el·ler** *n.*

driven (drĭv′ən) *v.* Past participle of **drive.** ❖ *adj.* **1.** Piled up or carried along by a current: *driven snow.* **2.** Motivated by or having an irresistible inner drive or compulsion to do something: *driven to become the world's richest person.* **3.** Caused, sustained, or stimulated: *an export-driven economic recovery.*

driver (drī′vər) *n.* **1.** A person who drives a motor vehicle. **2.** A tool, such as a screwdriver or hammer, that is used to give forceful pressure to another object. **3.** A golf club with a wide head, used for making long shots from the tee. **4.** A machine part that transmits motion or power to something else.

drive shaft *n.* A rotating shaft that transmits mechanical

power from a motor or engine to the place where power is applied.

drive-through or **drive-thru** (drīv′thrōō′) *adj.* Relating to or conducting business with customers who drive up to a window: *drive-through banking.*

driveway (drīv′wā′) *n.* A private road connecting a house, garage, or other building with the street.

drizzle (drĭz′əl) *v.* **drizzled, drizzling, drizzles** —*intr.* To rain gently in a fine mist. —*tr.* **1.** To let fall in fine drops: *drizzled sauce onto the meat.* **2.** To moisten with fine drops: *drizzled the asparagus with melted butter.* ❖ *n.* A fine gentle misty rain. —**driz′zly** *adj.*

DRM An abbreviation of digital rights management.

droll (drōl) *adj.* **droller, drollest** Amusingly odd; comical. —**droll′ness** *n.*

dromedary (drŏm′ĭ-děr′ē or drŭm′ĭ-děr′ē) *n., pl.* **dromedaries** A one-humped camel, widely used for riding and carrying loads in desert regions from northern Africa to western Asia.

drone[1] (drōn) *n.* **1.** A male bee, especially a honeybee that fertilizes the queen. Drones have no stings, do no work, and do not produce honey. **2.** An idle person who lives off others; a loafer. **3.** A person who does tedious or menial work; a drudge. **4.** An aircraft that has no crew on board and is operated by remote control.

drone[2] (drōn) *v.* **droned, droning, drones** —*intr.* **1.** To make a continuous low dull humming sound: *An airplane droned far overhead.* **2.** To speak in a monotonous or boring tone: *He droned on about how great his kids were.* —*tr.* To utter in a dull monotone. ❖ *n.* **1.** A continuous low humming or buzzing sound: *the drone of the bumblebee.* **2a.** A bagpipe pipe that has no fingerholes and makes a single continuous tone. **b.** A long sustained tone.

drool (drōōl) *intr.v.* **drooled, drooling, drools** **1.** To let saliva dribble from the mouth; drivel. **2.** To show great appreciation or desire: *They drooled over the expensive bicycles in the window.* ❖ *n.* Saliva: *wipe the drool from the baby's chin.*

droop (drōōp) *v.* **drooped, drooping, droops** —*intr.* **1.** To bend or hang downward; sag: *The flowers are beginning to droop.* **2.** To sag in dejection or exhaustion: *The sightseers began to droop toward the end of the day.* —*tr.* To let bend or hang down: *The dog drooped its ears.* ❖ *n.* The act or condition of drooping.

droopy (drōō′pē) *adj.* **droopier, droopiest** Bending or hanging downward; sagging: *droopy eyelids.* —**droop′i·ly** *adv.* —**droop′i·ness** *n.*

drop (drŏp) *n.* **1.** A small mass of liquid in a rounded shape: *drops of paint.* **2. drops** Liquid medicine administered in drops: *eye drops.* **3.** A small quantity of a substance: *There isn't a drop of juice left.* **4.** A trace or hint: *not a drop of pity.* **5.** Something resembling a drop in shape or size, especially a small globular piece of candy: *a lemon drop.* **6.** The act of falling; descent. **7.** A sudden fall or decrease, as in quality, quantity, or intensity: *a drop in temperature; a drop in prices.* **8.** The vertical distance from a higher to a lower level: *a drop of 200 feet.* **9.** A sheer incline, such as the face of a cliff: *The hikers avoided the drop.* **10.** Something that is arranged to fall or be lowered, as a curtain on a stage. ❖ *v.* **dropped, dropping, drops** —*intr.* **1.** To fall in drops: *rain dropping from an umbrella.* **2.** To fall from a higher to a lower place or position: *The plate dropped onto the floor.* **3.** To become less, as in intensity or number; decrease: *The tempera-*

ture dropped as the sun went down. **4.** To descend from one level to another: *The sun dropped toward the western hills.* **5.** To fall or sink into a state of exhaustion or death: *drop from overexertion.* **6.** To pass or sink into a specified state or condition: *dropped into a doze.* —*tr.* **1.** To let fall by releasing hold of: *I dropped the hot frying pan.* **2.** To let fall in drops: *drop medicine in a baby's ear.* **3.** To say or offer casually: *drop a hint.* **4.** To write at one's leisure: *drop a postcard to a friend.* **5.** To cease consideration or treatment of: *Let's drop the matter.* **6.** To terminate an association or relationship with: *drop one's friends.* **7.** To leave out (a letter, for example) in speaking or writing. **8.** To set down at a particular place; deliver or unload: *drop passengers at their destination; dropped a package off.* **9.** *Informal* To spend, especially lavishly or rashly: *dropped $800 at the mall while shopping.* ◆ **drop behind** To be unable to stay at the same pace as another: *One runner dropped behind as they came around the bend.* **drop by** To stop in for a short visit. **drop off 1.** To fall asleep. **2.** To decrease: *Temperatures usually drop off in the evening.* **drop out** To withdraw from participation, as in a game, club, or school. **drop over** To stop in for a short visit.

drop cloth *n.* A large cloth or sheet of plastic used to cover and protect furniture and floors while a room is being painted.

drop kick *n.* A kick made by dropping a ball to the ground and kicking it just as it starts to rebound.

drop leaf *n.* A hinged wing on a table that can be folded down when not in use.

droplet (drŏp′lĭt) *n.* A tiny drop.

dropout (drŏp′out′) *n.* **1.** A person who quits school. **2.** A person who withdraws from a given social group.

dropper (drŏp′ər) *n.* A small tube with a suction bulb at one end for drawing in a liquid and releasing it in drops.

droppings (drŏp′ĭngz) *pl.n.* The excrement of animals.

dropsy (drŏp′sē) *n.* Edema. This term is no longer used in medicine.

drosophila (drə-sŏf′ə-lə) *n.* Any of various small fruit flies, especially a kind used extensively in genetic research.

dross (drŏs) *n.* **1.** The waste material that rises to the surface of a molten metal as it is being smelted or refined. **2.** Worthless, commonplace, or trivial matter.

drought (drout) *n.* A long period of little or no rainfall.

drove[1] (drōv) *v.* Past tense of **drive**.

drove[2] (drōv) *n.* **1.** A flock or herd being driven in a group. **2.** A large mass of people moving or acting as a body: *droves of visitors on their way to the White House.*

drover (drō′vər) *n.* A person who drives cattle or sheep.

drown (droun) *v.* **drowned, drowning, drowns** —*tr.* **1.** To kill by submerging and suffocating in water or another liquid. **2.** To drench thoroughly or cover with or as if with a liquid: *He drowned the mashed potatoes in gravy.* **3.** To deaden one's awareness of; blot out: *drown disappointment in the company of friends.* **4.** To muffle or mask (a sound) with a louder sound: *Their laughter drowned out the speaker's voice.* —*intr.* To die by suffocating in water or other liquid: *Many animals drowned when the river flooded.*

drowse (drouz) *intr.v.* **drowsed, drowsing, drowses** To be half-asleep: *The cat drowsed in the sun.*

drowsy (drou′zē) *adj.* **drowsier, drowsiest 1.** Dull with sleepiness; sluggish: *feeling drowsy after dinner.* **2.** Causing sleepiness: *a drowsy lullaby.* —**drows′i·ly** *adv.* —**drows′i·ness** *n.*

drub (drŭb) *tr.v.* **drubbed, drubbing, drubs 1.** To beat with a stick. **2.** To instill forcefully: *drubbed the lesson into my head.* **3.** To defeat thoroughly: *drub an opposing team.*

drudge (drŭj) *n.* A person who does tedious, unpleasant, or menial work. ❖ *intr.v.* **drudged, drudging, drudges** To do tedious, unpleasant, or menial work.

drudgery (drŭj′ə-rē) *n.* Tedious, unpleasant, or menial work: *Cleaning my room always seems like drudgery.*

drug (drŭg) *n.* **1.** A substance used in medicine especially to cure a disease or relieve its symptoms. **2.** A narcotic or other substance that affects the central nervous system, causing changes in mood and behavior. Narcotic drugs tend to be addictive. ❖ *tr.v.* **drugged, drugging, drugs 1.** To administer a drug to: *drug a patient with an anesthetic before an operation.* **2.** To mix a drug into (food or drink).

druggist (drŭg′ĭst) *n.* A pharmacist or person who sells drugs in a store.

drugstore (drŭg′stôr′) *n.* A store where prescriptions are filled and medical supplies and other items are sold.

druid also **Druid** (drōō′ĭd) *n.* A member of an order of pagan priests in ancient Britain and Gaul.

drum (drŭm) *n.* **1.** A musical instrument consisting of a hollow container shaped like a cylinder or bowl with a membrane stretched tightly over one or both ends, played by beating with the hands or sticks. **2.** A sound produced by this instrument or a similar sound. **3.** Something having a shape or structure like a drum: *an oil drum; a cable drum.* ❖ *v.* **drummed, drumming, drums** —*intr.* **1.** To play a drum or drums. **2.** To thump or tap rhythmically or continually: *I drummed on the table with my pencil.* —*tr.* **1.** To produce (a beat or rhythm) on a drum. **2.** To make known to or force upon (a person) by constant repetition: *I drummed the facts into my head to pass the test.* **3.** To expel or dismiss in disgrace: *drummed the private out of the corps.* ◆ **drum up** To bring about by continuous persistent effort: *Students drummed up support for their trip.*

drumbeat (drŭm′bēt′) *n.* The sound produced by beating a drum.

drumhead (drŭm′hĕd′) *n.* The material stretched over one or both ends of a drum.

drumlin (drŭm′lĭn) *n.* A ridge or elongated hill with a smooth summit, formed from glacial deposits.

drum major *n.* A person who leads a marching band or drum corps, often twirling a baton.

drum majorette *n.* A girl or woman who leads a marching band or drum corps, often twirling a baton.

drummer (drŭm′ər) *n.* A person who plays a drum, as in a band.

drumroll (drŭm′rōl′) *n.* A rapid series of short sounds made by beating a drum.

drumstick (drŭm′stĭk′) *n.* **1.** A stick for beating a drum. **2.** The lower part of the leg of a cooked chicken or turkey.

drunk (drŭngk) *v.* Past participle of **drink**. ❖ *adj.* **1.** Intoxicated with an alcoholic beverage. **2.** Overcome by strong feeling or emotion: *The dictator is drunk with power.* ❖ *n.* **1.** A drunkard. **2.** A drunken spree.

drunkard (drŭng′kərd) *n.* A person who is habitually drunk.

drunken (drŭng′kən) *adj.* **1.** Drunk; intoxicated. **2.** Relating to, involving, or occurring during intoxication: *a drunken brawl.* —**drunk′en·ly** *adv.* —**drunk′en·ness** *n.*

drupe (drōōp) *n.* A fleshy fruit, such as a cherry, plum, or peach, whose seed is contained in a hard pit or stone surrounded by soft pulpy flesh.

druthers (drŭ*th*ʹərz) *pl.n. Informal* A choice or preference.

dry (drī) *adj.* **drier** (drīʹər), **driest** (drīʹĭst) or **dryer, dryest 1.** Free from liquid or moisture: *dry clothes; dry air.* **2.** Having little or no rainfall; arid: *the dry season; a dry area.* **3.** Not under water: *We stepped ashore on dry land.* **4.** Having all or almost all of the liquid or water drained away or used up: *a dry stream; a dry well.* **5.** No longer yielding milk: *a dry cow.* **6.** Not shedding tears: *dry sobs.* **7.** Needing or desiring drink: *My throat is dry.* **8.** Not sweet. Used of wines. **9.** Eaten or served without butter or other spread: *dry toast.* **10.** Having no adornment; plain: *a dry speaker; dry facts.* **11.** Quietly humorous; ironic: *a dry wit.* **12.** Not permitting the sale or consumption of alcoholic beverages: *a dry county.* ❖ *v.* **dried** (drīd), **drying, dries** (drīz) —*tr.* To remove the moisture from; make dry: *We dried the dishes after supper.* —*intr.* To become dry: *The laundry dried quickly in the sun.* ◆ **dry up** To make or become unproductive, especially to do so gradually: *The stream dried up over the hot arid summer.* —**dryʹly** *adv.* —**dryʹness** *n.*

dryad (drīʹəd or drīʹădʹ) *n.* In Greek mythology, a wood nymph.

dry cell *n.* An electric cell in which the chemical producing the current is a moist paste rather than a liquid.

dry-clean (drīʹklēnʹ) *tr.v.* **dry-cleaned, dry-cleaning, dry-cleans** To clean (clothing or fabrics) with chemical solvents that have little or no water.

dry cleaner *n.* A person or business that dry-cleans clothes.

dry cleaning *n.* The cleaning of fabrics with chemical solvents.

dry dock *n.* A large dock in the form of a basin from which the water can be emptied, used for building or repairing a ship below its water line.

dry-dock (drīʹdŏkʹ) *tr. & intr.v.* **dry-docked, dry-docking, dry-docks** To place in or go into a dry dock.

dryer (drīʹər) *n.* **1.** A appliance that removes moisture by heating or another process: *a clothes dryer.* **2.** Variant of **drier¹.**

dry farming *n.* A type of farming practiced in arid regions without irrigation by maintaining a mulch on the surface that protects the natural moisture of the soil from evaporation.

dry goods *pl.n.* Cloth, clothing, and related articles of trade.

dry ice *n.* Carbon dioxide that is compressed and chilled into a solid. It is used as a cooling agent.

drying oil (drīʹĭng) *n.* An organic oil, such as linseed oil, used in paints and varnishes. It dries into a tough elastic layer when exposed to air.

dry measure *n.* A system of units for measuring dry commodities, such as grains, fruits, and vegetables.

dry rot *n.* A decaying of timber that is caused by a fungus and results in the wood becoming brittle and crumbling into powder.

dry run *n.* A trial exercise; a rehearsal.

drysuit (drīʹso̅o̅tʹ) *n.* A garment made of rubber or other impermeable material that is sealed to prevent leakage and worn to keep the body warm and dry in cold water, used especially in scuba diving.

drywall (drīʹwôlʹ) *n.* **1.** A material consisting of rectangular sheets of plaster bonded to layers of heavy paper, used

to cover walls or ceilings. **2.** A stone wall constructed without mortar.

DST An abbreviation of daylight-saving time.

dual (do̅o̅ʹəl) *adj.* **1.** Composed of two parts; double: *dual controls for pilot and copilot.* **2.** Having a double character or purpose. —**duʹal·ly** *adv.*

dualism (do̅o̅ʹə-lĭzʹəm) *n.* **1.** The condition of being double; duality. **2.** The philosophical view that the world consists of or is explicable as two fundamental entities, such as mind and matter. **3.** The view that mental and physical properties are fundamentally different and that neither can be explained fully in terms of the other. **4a.** The theological concept that the world is ruled by the antagonistic forces of good and evil. **b.** The theological concept that humans have two basic natures, the physical and the spiritual. —**duʹal·ist** *n.* —**duʹal·is·tic** *adj.* —**duʹal·is·ti·cal·ly** *adv.*

duality (do̅o̅-ălʹĭ-tē) *n.* The quality or condition of being twofold.

dub¹ (dŭb) *tr.v.* **dubbed, dubbing, dubs 1.** To confer knighthood on (a man) by tapping him on the shoulder with a sword. **2.** To give a nickname to: *The cat was named Cleo, but the children dubbed it "Mittens."*

dub² (dŭb) *tr.v.* **dubbed, dubbing, dubs 1.** To transfer (recorded material) onto a new recording medium. **2.** To provide (a film) with a new soundtrack, often with the dialogue in a different language: *The Russian film was dubbed in English for American audiences.*

WORD HISTORY Dub¹ comes from Old English *dubbian,* meaning "to confer knighthood on." **Dub²** is short for *double.*

dubious (do̅o̅ʹbē-əs) *adj.* **1.** Feeling or showing doubt or uncertainty; uncertain: *I am dubious of the outcome.* **2.** Causing or arousing doubt; doubtful: *an argument based on dubious reasoning.* **3.** Of uncertain morality; questionable or suspicious: *He associates with some very dubious characters.* —**duʹbi·ous·ly** *adv.*

dubnium (do̅o̅bʹnē-əm) *n. Symbol* **Db** A radioactive element that has been artificially produced by scientists. Atomic number 105. See **Periodic Table.**

ducal (do̅o̅ʹkəl) *adj.* Relating to a duke or duchy.

ducat (dŭkʹət) *n.* Any of various gold or silver coins formerly used in Europe.

duchess (dŭchʹĭs) *n.* **1.** The wife or widow of a duke. **2.** A woman holding a duchy.

duchy (dŭchʹē) *n., pl.* **duchies** The territory ruled by a duke or duchess.

duck¹ (dŭk) *n.* **1.** Any of various wild or domesticated waterbirds having a broad flat bill, a short neck, short legs, and webbed feet. **2.** A female duck, as distinguished from a drake. **3.** The meat of a duck used as food.

duck² (dŭk) *v.* **ducked, ducking, ducks** —*tr.* **1.** To lower (the head and body) quickly: *She ducked her head getting into the car.* **2.** To evade; dodge: *duck a responsibility.* **3.** To push suddenly under water: *duck someone in the pool.* —*intr.* **1.** To lower the head or body quickly: *The boy ducked under the table.* **2.** To push or dip suddenly under water. **3.** *Informal* To enter or leave quickly or temporarily: *duck out of a meeting.*

duck³ (dŭk) *n.* **1.** A strong cotton or linen cloth that is lighter than canvas. **2. ducks** Pants, especially white ones, made of this fabric.

WORD HISTORY Duck¹ comes from Old English *dūce,* referring to the same kind of animal as in Modern English.

Duck² comes from Middle English *douken,* meaning "to dive." **Duck³** comes from Dutch *doek,* meaning "cloth."

duck-billed dinosaur (dŭk′bĭld′) *n.* Any of various plant-eating dinosaurs that had webbed feet, a ducklike bill, and sometimes a crest on the head.

duck-billed platypus *n.* The platypus.

duckling (dŭk′lĭng) *n.* A young duck.

duckweed (dŭk′wēd′) *n.* Any of various small stemless water plants that form floating masses on the surface of ponds and other quiet waters.

duct (dŭkt) *n.* **1.** An enclosed passage used to conduct something, such as a gas or liquid: *installed ducts for the air-conditioning system.* **2.** A tube in the body for carrying a bodily fluid, especially a fluid secreted by a gland: *bile duct.* **3.** A tube or pipe that encloses electric cables or wires.

ductile (dŭk′təl *or* dŭk′tīl′) *adj.* **1.** Easily drawn out into wire or hammered thin: *Silver is a ductile metal.* **2.** Easily molded or shaped: *Plastic pipe is ductile if heated.* **3.** Readily persuaded or influenced; tractable. —**duc·til′i·ty** (dŭk-tĭl′ĭ-tē) *n.*

ductless gland (dŭkt′lĭs) *n.* An endocrine gland.

duct tape *n.* A strong, adhesive tape made of cloth mesh coated with a waterproof material, originally designed for sealing heating and air-conditioning ducts.

dud (dŭd) *n.* **1.** A bomb or shell that fails to explode. **2.** A person or thing that turns out to be ineffective or unsuccessful: *Our hasty plan was a real dud.*

dude (dood) *Informal n.* **1a.** A man; a fellow. **b.** A person of either sex. **2.** A city person who vacations on a ranch in the American West. ◆ **duded up** Dressed in formal or fancy clothes.

dude ranch *n.* A resort patterned after a Western ranch, featuring horseback riding and other outdoor activities.

dudgeon (dŭj′ən) *n.* A sullen, angry, or indignant state of mind: *The insulted customer walked out of the shop in high dudgeon.*

due (doo) *adj.* **1a.** Owed as a debt: *We must pay the amount still due.* **b.** Required to be submitted: *books due back to the library; bills due tomorrow.* **2.** Fitting or appropriate; suitable: *Every citizen is required to show due respect for the law.* **3.** As much as needed; sufficient; adequate: *We left early, taking due care to be on time.* **4a.** Expected or scheduled: *When is the train due to arrive?* **b.** Expected to give birth: *She's due any day now.* **5.** Expecting or ready for something, as part of a normal course or sequence: *We're due for some rain.* ❖ *n.* **1.** Something that is owed or deserved: *a dedicated scholar who finally got his due.* **2.** **dues** A charge or fee for membership, as in a club. ❖ *adv.* Straight; directly: *The settlers traveled due west.*

duel (doo′əl) *n.* **1.** A fight using weapons and arranged in advance between two people, usually to settle a matter concerning personal honor. **2.** A struggle between two opponents: *a war of wits between lawyers in the courtroom.* ❖ *tr. & intr.v.* **dueled, dueling, duels** *or* **duelled, duelling, duels** To fight in a duel. —**du′el·er, du′el·ler, du′el·ist, du′el·list** *n.*

due process *n.* An established course of proceeding in judicial or other governmental activity that is designed to protect the legal rights of the individual.

duet (doo-ĕt′) *n.* **1a.** A musical composition for two voices or two instruments. **b.** The two performers of such a composition. **2.** A pair.

due to *prep.* Because of: *The cancellation of the concert was due to bad weather.*

duffel or **duffle** (dŭf′əl) *n.* **1.** A coarse woolen cloth with a nap on both sides. **2.** Clothing and other personal gear carried when camping.

duffle bag or **duffel bag** *n.* A large cylindrical cloth bag of canvas or duck for carrying personal belongings.

dug (dŭg) *v.* Past tense and past participle of **dig.**

dugong (doo′gŏng′) *n.* A plant-eating tropical sea mammal having a broad snout, a pair of front flippers, and a flat broad tail.

dugout (dŭg′out′) *n.* **1.** A boat or canoe made by hollowing out a log. **2.** A rough shelter dug into the ground or on a hillside and used especially in battle for protection from artillery. **3.** Either of two low shelters at the side of a baseball field where the players stay while not on the field.

duh (dŭ) *interj.* An expression used to show scorn, especially for a remark that is considered to be obvious.

DUI An abbreviation of driving under the influence (of drugs or alcohol).

du jour (də zhoor′ *or* doo zhoor′) *adj.* Offered on a given day: *the soup du jour.*

duke (dook) *n.* **1.** A nobleman of the highest rank, especially a man of the highest level of the British peerage. **2.** A man who rules an independent duchy. **3.** **dukes** *Slang* The fists: *Put up your dukes and let's fight.*

dukedom (dook′dəm) *n.* **1.** A duchy. **2.** The rank, office, or title of a duke.

dulcet (dŭl′sĭt) *adj.* Soothing and agreeable, especially to the ear: *sweet dulcet tones.*

dulcimer (dŭl′sə-mər) *n.* **1.** A narrow, often hourglass-shaped stringed instrument having three or four strings and a fretted neck, typically held flat across the knees and played by plucking or strumming. **2.** A musical instrument with wire strings stretched across a four-sided sound box, played by striking with two padded hammers.

dull (dŭl) *adj.* **duller, dullest 1.** Not sharp or pointed; blunt: *a dull knife; a dull pencil.* **2.** Not interesting; boring: *a dull book; dull work.* See Synonyms at **boring.** **3.** Mentally weak; stupid. **4.** Not keenly or intensely felt: *a dull ache in my throat.* **5.** Not bright or vivid; dim: *a dull red.* **6.** Not loud or clear; muffled: *the dull rumble of distant thunder.* ❖ *tr. & intr.v.* **dulled, dulling, dulls** To make or become dull: *The saw blade dulled as it cut more wood.* —**dull′ness** *n.* —**dull′y** *adv.*

dullard (dŭl′ərd) *n.* A dull or stupid person.

duly (doo′lē) *adv.* **1.** In a proper manner; rightfully: *a duly elected candidate.* **2.** At the expected time; punctually: *The loan was duly repaid.*

dumb (dŭm) *adj.* **dumber, dumbest 1.** Lacking the human ability to use speech: *dumb animals.* **2.** *Offensive* Incapable of using speech. Used of humans. **3.** Unwilling to speak; silent: *The witness remained dumb under questioning.* **4.** Temporarily speechless, as with shock or fear: *I was dumb with disbelief.* **5.** Unintelligent; stupid. —**dumb′ly** *adv.* —**dumb′ness** *n.*

dumbbell (dŭm′bĕl′) *n.* **1.** A weight consisting of a short bar with a metal ball or disk at each end that is lifted to exercise and develop the muscles. **2.** *Slang* A stupid or ignorant person; a dolt.

dumbfound (dŭm′found′) *tr.v.* **dumbfounded, dumbfounding, dumbfounds** To make speechless with astonishment; amaze or bewilder: *The sophistication of the young man's answers dumbfounded the experts.*

dumbwaiter (dŭm′wā′tər) *n.* A small elevator used to

transport food, dishes, or other articles from one floor to another.

dummy (dŭm′ē) *n., pl.* **dummies 1.** A model of the human body, used as a substitute for a person: *A dummy was used to test the seat belt.* **2.** Something made to look like a real object; an imitation or counterfeit: *The drawer in the cabinet is a dummy.* **3.** A person who acts in business deals on behalf of another person whose identity is concealed. **4.** A stupid person; a dolt. **5.** The player in a card game whose hand is shown and played by a partner. ❖ *adj.* **1.** Made to work like or resemble a real object; imitation; fake: *Dummy cannons fooled the enemy.* **2.** Secretly in the service of another: *a dummy corporation covering up their criminal activities.*

dump (dŭmp) *tr.v.* **dumped, dumping, dumps 1.** To release or throw down in a mass: *The factory dumped waste into the river. Don't dump your books on the table.* **2.** To empty out (a container or vehicle): *dump a wastebasket.* **3.** To get rid of or reject: *The president dumped several controversial candidates for the position.* **4.** To sell (goods) in large quantities and at a low price: *The company dumped its old stock of air conditioners in several countries.* **5.** To print out or transfer (information stored in computer memory) without processing it. ❖ *n.* **1.** A place where garbage, trash, or other waste is discarded or kept: *The town dump is nearly full.* **2.** A military storage place: *an ammunition dump.* **3.** A messy or shabby place: *The old house is a dump.*

dumpling (dŭmp′lĭng) *n.* **1.** A piece of dough, sometimes filled, that is steamed, fried, or cooked in liquid such as water or soup. **2.** Sweetened dough wrapped around fruit, such as an apple, baked and served as dessert.

dumps (dŭmps) *pl.n.* Low gloomy spirits; depression: *down in the dumps.*

Dumpster (dŭmp′stər) A trademark used for containers designed for receiving, transporting, and dumping waste materials.

dump truck *n.* A heavy-duty truck having a bed that tilts backward to dump loose material.

dumpy (dŭm′pē) *adj.* **dumpier, dumpiest 1.** Messy or shabby: *a dumpy office.* **2.** Short and plump.

dun[1] (dŭn) *tr.v.* **dunned, dunning, duns** To make persistent demands of (someone), especially for payment of a debt.

dun[2] (dŭn) *n.* **1.** A dull grayish brown. **2.** A horse of this color.

WORD HISTORY The origin of **dun**[1] is unknown. **Dun**[2] comes from Old English *dunn*, referring to the same color as in Modern English *dun*, and may be of Celtic origin.

dunce (dŭns) *n.* A stupid person.

dune (dōōn) *n.* A hill or ridge of wind-blown sand.

dune buggy *n.* A light, recreational motor vehicle with oversize tires, designed for use on sand dunes or beaches.

dung (dŭng) *n.* The excrement of animals, especially when used as manure.

dungaree (dŭng′gə-rē′) *n.* **1.** A sturdy, often blue denim fabric. **2.** **dungarees** Overalls or pants made from this fabric.

dungeon (dŭn′jən) *n.* A dark, often underground chamber or cell used to confine prisoners.

dunk (dŭngk) *tr.v.* **dunked, dunking, dunks 1.** To dip or briefly submerge (something) in a liquid: *dunk a doughnut in tea.* **2.** To submerge (someone) playfully, as in a

swimming pool. **3.** In basketball, to slam (a ball) through the basket from above. ❖ *n.* In basketball, a shot made by jumping and slamming the ball down through the basket.

duo (dōō′ō) *n., pl.* **duos 1.** A duet, as of musical performers. **2.** Two people or two things that are closely associated.

duodecimal (dōō′ə-dĕs′ə-məl) *adj.* Relating to or based on twelfths or the number 12: *a duodecimal digit.*

duodecimal system *n.* A number system with a base of 12. It uses twelve digits instead of the more familiar ten digits of the decimal system.

duodenum (dōō′ə-dē′nəm *or* dōō-ŏd′n-əm) *n., pl.* **duodena** (dōō′ə-dē′nə *or* dōō-ŏd′n-ə) or **duodenums** The portion of the small intestine starting at the lower end of the stomach and extending to the jejunum. —**du′-o·de′nal** *adj.*

dupe (dōōp) *n.* A person who is used or taken advantage of through deception or trickery. ❖ *tr.v.* **duped, duping, dupes** To deceive; trick; fool: *The advertisement duped us into believing the bicycles were on sale.*

duple (dōō′pəl) *adj.* **1.** Consisting of two parts or units; double. **2.** Consisting of two beats or some multiple of two beats to a musical measure.

duplex (dōō′plĕks′) *adj.* **1.** Having two parts; twofold; double: *Both plugs will fit in a duplex electrical outlet.* **2.** Having two apartments, divisions, or floors. ❖ *n.* A house divided into two living units, usually with separate entrances.

WORD BUILDING The word root *plex–* in English words comes from Latin *–plex*, which meant "multiplied by a specific number." **Duplex** means "twofold, double" (using the word *duo*, "two"); **triplex** is literally "threefold" (*tri–*, "three"); and **multiplex** means "manifold, multiple" (*multi–*, "many"). The Latin *–plex* is related to the verb *plicāre*, "to fold," from whose past participle *plicātus* we form the verb **duplicate** and the noun **multiplication**.

duplicate (dōō′plĭ-kĭt) *adj.* Exactly the same as something else, especially because of having been copied from an original: *a duplicate key.* ❖ *n.* **1.** An exact copy; a double: *That letter is a duplicate of the original.* **2.** Something that corresponds exactly to another: *Your bike is a duplicate of mine.* ❖ *tr.v.* (dōō′plĭ-kāt′) **duplicated, duplicating, duplicates 1.** To make an exact copy of: *duplicate a key.* **2.** To do or perform again; repeat: *duplicate an experiment.* —SEE NOTE AT **duplex.**

duplication (dōō′plĭ-kā′shən) *n.* **1.** The act or condition of being duplicated: *Duplication of the experiment confirmed the original results.* **2.** A replica; a replica: *an exact duplication of the document.* **3.** The occurrence of a repeated section of genetic material in a chromosome.

duplicator (dōō′plĭ-kā′tər) *n.* A machine or device that makes copies of printed or digital material.

duplicity (dōō-plĭs′ĭ-tē) *n., pl.* **duplicities** Deliberate deceptiveness in behavior or speech; deceit.

durable (dōōr′ə-bəl) *adj.* **1.** Capable of withstanding wear and tear; sturdy: *Denim is a durable fabric used for work clothes.* **2.** Lasting or enduring; stable: *a durable friendship.* —**du′ra·bil′i·ty, du′ra·ble·ness** *n.* —**du′ra·bly** *adv.*

durable goods *pl.n.* Manufactured products that can be used for a long time. Furniture, refrigerators, and automobiles are durable goods.

dura mater (dōōr′ə mā′tər *or* dōōr′ə mä′tər) *n.* A tough fibrous membrane covering the brain and the spinal cord and lining the inner surface of the skull. It is the outermost of the three membranes that surround the brain.

durance (dŏŏr′əns) *n.* Confinement or restraint by force; imprisonment.

duration (dŏŏ-rā′shən) *n.* The period of time during which something exists or persists: *the duration of a storm.*

duress (dŏŏ-rĕs′) *n.* **1.** The use of force or threat to compel someone to do something: *The prisoner confessed under duress.* **2.** Constraint or difficulty caused by misfortune: *They went bankrupt and sold their house under duress.*

during (dŏŏr′ĭng) *prep.* **1.** Throughout the course or duration of: *We talked during the entire evening.* **2.** Within the time of; at some time in: *He was born during the last half of the 1800s.*

durst (dûrst) *v.* Archaic A past tense and a past participle of **dare.**

durum (dŏŏr′əm) *n.* A kind of wheat having hard grains, used chiefly in making pasta.

dusk (dŭsk) *n.* The time of evening just before darkness; the darker stage of twilight: *Only a few stars shine at dusk.*

dusky (dŭs′kē) *adj.* **duskier, duskiest 1.** Having little light; dim: *a dusky room.* See Synonyms at **dark. 2.** Rather dark in color: *dusky blue.* —**dusk′i·ly** *adv.*

dust (dŭst) *n.* **1.** Fine dry particles of matter: *clouds of dust raised by a herd of cattle; the dust gathering on old books.* **2.** Pieces of earth or dirt, especially when regarded as the remains of a decayed body. ❖ *v.* **dusted, dusting, dusts** —*tr.* **1.** To remove dust from by wiping or brushing: *We dusted the shelves.* **2.** To sprinkle with a powdery substance: *I dusted my feet with powder.* —*intr.* To clean by removing dust: *The cleaning staff dusts every day.* ◆ **dust off** To restore or revise for current use: *dust off an old essay for publication.* **in the dust** Far behind, as in a race or contest: *left her competitors in the dust.*

dust bowl *n.* **1.** A region in which dry weather and dust storms have produced conditions like those of a desert. **2. Dust Bowl** A region in the south-central United States that was stricken with drought and dust storms in the 1930s.

duster (dŭs′tər) *n.* **1.** A person or thing that dusts. **2.** A cloth or brush used to remove dust. **3.** A device for spreading powder on plants. **4.** A coat or smock worn to protect one's clothing from dust.

dust jacket *n.* **1.** A paper cover used to protect the outside of a book. **2.** A cardboard sleeve used to protect a phonograph record.

dustpan (dŭst′păn′) *n.* A short-handled pan, shaped like a shovel, into which dust is swept.

dust storm *n.* A windstorm that sweeps clouds of dust across a large area, especially in a dry region.

dusty (dŭs′tē) *adj.* **dustier, dustiest 1.** Covered or filled with dust: *a dusty road; a dusty room.* **2.** Consisting of or resembling dust; powdery: *dusty soil.* **3.** Tinged with gray: *a dusty beard.* —**dust′i·ness** *n.*

Dutch (dŭch) *adj.* Relating to the Netherlands or its people, language, or culture. ❖ *n.* **1.** (*used with a plural verb*) The people of the Netherlands. **2.** The Germanic language of the Netherlands. ◆ **go Dutch** To pay one's own expenses, as on a date.

Dutch door *n.* A door divided in two horizontally so that one part may be left open or closed.

Dutchman (dŭch′mən) *n.* A man who is a native or inhabitant of the Netherlands.

Dutch oven *n.* **1.** A large heavy pot or kettle with a tight lid,

used for slow cooking. **2.** An open metal box equipped with shelves and placed before a fire for baking or roasting food. **3.** A wall oven in which food is baked by means of preheated brick walls.

Dutch treat *n.* Informal An outing, as for dinner or a movie, for which each person pays his or her own expenses.

Dutchwoman (dŭch′wŏŏm′ən) *n.* A woman who is a native or inhabitant of the Netherlands.

duteous (dŏŏ′tē-əs) *adj.* Obedient; dutiful: *a duteous and attentive assistant.* —**du′te·ous·ly** *adv.*

dutiable (dŏŏ′tē-ə-bəl) *adj.* Subject to a tax when imported into a country: *dutiable goods.*

dutiful (dŏŏ′tĭ-fəl) *adj.* **1.** Careful to perform one's duty; obedient. **2.** Expressing or coming from a sense of duty: *dutiful words.* —**du′ti·ful·ly** *adv.*

duty (dŏŏ′tē) *n., pl.* **duties 1.** Something that a person ought to or must do; an obligation: *In a democracy one of the chief duties of a citizen is to vote.* **2.** Required action or service: *You must report for jury duty.* **3.** Moral obligation: *It is your duty to tell the truth.* **4.** A task, assignment, or function that is part of one's work: *household duties.* **5.** A tax charged by a government on imported or exported goods.

duvet (dŏŏ-vā′) *n.* A quilt, usually with a washable cover, that may be used in place of a bedspread and top sheet.

DVD (dē′vē-dē′) *n.* A high-density optical disc used especially for storing movies. DVD is short for *digital videodisc.*

DVR An abbreviation of digital video recorder.

dwarf (dwôrf) *n., pl.* **dwarfs** or **dwarves** (dwôrvz) **1a.** A person who is much smaller than normal and whose limbs and features are often atypically proportioned or formed. **b.** An atypically small plant or animal. **2.** In fairy tales and legends, a small creature resembling a human with magical powers. ❖ *tr.v.* **dwarfed, dwarfing, dwarfs 1.** To check the natural growth of; stunt: *Lack of water dwarfed the trees.* **2.** To make seem small by comparison: *The skyscraper dwarfed the old church.*

dwarf planet *n.* A celestial object that orbits around the sun, is not a satellite of a planet, and has insufficient gravitational force to pull objects crossing its orbit around the sun into an orbit around it. —SEE NOTE AT **planet.**

dwarf star *n.* A star of relatively small size and mass that emits an average or below average amount of light. The sun is a dwarf star.

dwell (dwĕl) *intr.v.* **dwelt** (dwĕlt) or **dwelled, dwelling, dwells 1.** To live as a resident; reside: *dwell in a city.* **2.** To speak or write about at length: *The article dwells on the need for better health care.* **3.** To focus one's attention on; brood about: *Don't dwell on past mistakes.* —**dwell′er** *n.*

dwelling (dwĕl′ĭng) *n.* A place to live in; a residence: *Our house is a two-story dwelling.*

DWI An abbreviation of driving while intoxicated.

dwindle (dwĭn′dl) *intr.v.* **dwindled, dwindling, dwindles** To become gradually less until little is left: *Their savings dwindled away to nothing over the year.* See Synonyms at **decrease.**

dye (dī) *n.* **1.** A substance used to color food, hair, cloth, or other materials. **2.** A color produced by dyeing: *The dye in the curtains faded in sunlight.* ❖ *v.* **dyed, dyeing, dyes** —*tr.* To color with a dye: *dye a fabric red.* —*intr.* To become colored by a dye: *Some fabrics dye more easily than others.* —**dy′er** *n.*

dyed-in-the-wool (dīd′ĭn-thə-wŏŏl′) *adj.* Thoroughgoing; outright: *a dyed-in-the-wool conservative.*

dyestuff (dī′stŭf′) *n.* A substance used as a dye: *Indigo is a deep blue dyestuff.*

dying (dī′ing) *v.* Present participle of **die**[1]. ❖ *adj.* **1.** About to die: *the shriveled leaves of the dying plant.* **2.** Drawing to an end: *a dying day.* **3.** Done or uttered just before death: *dying words.*

dynamic (dī-năm′ĭk) *adj.* **1.** Marked by intensity and vigor; forceful: *the dynamic personality of a political leader.* **2.** Changing; active: *a dynamic stock market.* **3.** Relating to energy or to objects in motion. **4.** Relating to the science of dynamics. —**dy·nam′i·cal·ly** *adv.*

dynamics (dī-năm′ĭks) *n.* **1.** *(used with a singular verb)* The branch of physics that deals with the effects of forces on the motions of bodies. **2.** *(used with a plural verb)* The forces that produce activity and change in a particular area: *the dynamics that have increased international trade.*

dynamism (dī′nə-mĭz′əm) *n.* Continuous change or activity; vigor; energy: *the dynamism of a new government administration.*

dynamite (dī′nə-mīt′) *n.* A powerful explosive made of nitroglycerin or ammonium nitrate that is combined with an absorbent material and calcium carbonate or another antacid. ❖ *tr.v.* **dynamited, dynamiting, dynamites** To blow up or destroy with dynamite: *The old office building was dynamited to make space for new construction.* —**dy′na·mit′er** *n.*

dynamo (dī′nə-mō′) *n., pl.* **dynamos 1.** An electric generator, especially one that produces direct current. **2.** *Informal* An extremely energetic and forceful person.

dynasty (dī′nə-stē) *n., pl.* **dynasties 1.** A succession of rulers from the same family: *the Habsburg dynasty.* **2.** A family or group that maintains great power, wealth, or success for a sustained period. —**dy·nas′tic** (dī-năs′tĭk) *adj.*

dyne (dīn) *n.* A unit of force equal to the amount of force required to give a mass of one gram an acceleration of one centimeter per second for each second the force is applied.

dysentery (dĭs′ən-tĕr′ē) *n.* Severe diarrhea often with the presence of blood and mucus, usually caused by infection of the intestines by bacteria or parasites.

dysfunction (dĭs-fŭngk′shən) *n.* **1.** Abnormal functioning of a system or an organ of the body. **2.** Failure to function in a manner that is considered appropriate or effective in social situations or relationships.

dyslexia (dĭs-lĕk′sē-ə) *n.* A learning disability that interferes with a person's ability to recognize and comprehend written words.

dyslexic (dĭs-lĕk′sĭk) *n.* A person who is affected by dyslexia. ❖ *adj.* Relating to or affected with dyslexia.

dyspepsia (dĭs-pĕp′shə *or* dĭs-pĕp′sē-ə) *n.* Poor digestion; indigestion.

dyspeptic (dĭs-pĕp′tĭk) *adj.* **1.** Relating to or suffering from dyspepsia. **2.** Disgruntled or gloomy: *a dyspeptic outlook on life.*

dysplasia (dĭs-plā′zhə) *n.* Abnormal development or growth of tissues, organs, or cells. —**dys·plas′tic** (dĭs-plăs′tĭk) *adj.*

dysprosium (dĭs-prō′zē-əm *or* dĭs-prō′zhē-əm) *n. Symbol* **Dy** A soft, silvery metallic element that has a high melting point and is used in nuclear reactor control rods and in making laser materials. Atomic number 66. See **Periodic Table.**

dystopia (dĭs-tō′pē-ə) *n.* An imaginary place or state in which the condition of life is extremely bad, as from deprivation, oppression, or terror. —**dys·to′pi·an** *adj.*

dz. An abbreviation of dozen.

Ee

e or **E** (ē) *n., pl.* **e's** or **E's** or **Es 1.** The fifth letter of the English alphabet. **2. E** A failing grade in school. **3. E** In music, the third tone in the scale of C major.

E An abbreviation of: **1.** east. **2.** eastern. **3.** energy. **4.** error.

e– A prefix that means computer or computer network: *e-commerce.*

ea. An abbreviation of each.

each (ēch) *adj.* Being one of two or more people or things considered individually; every: *The supervisor talked to each employee for ten minutes.* ❖ *pron.* Every one of a group of people, objects, or things: *Each of us took a turn looking in the telescope.* ❖ *adv.* For or to each one; apiece: *The apples cost 25 cents each.*

USAGE When the subject of a sentence begins with **each**, the verb and following pronouns must be singular: *Each of the hotel rooms has its own bath.* When *each* follows a plural subject, however, the verb and pronouns remain in the plural: *The hotel rooms each have their own baths.*

each other *pron.* Each the other. Used to show that each person or thing does the same as the other: *The girls greeted each other.*

eager (ē′gər) *adj.* **eagerer, eagerest** Having or showing keen interest or desire: *The eager sports fans cheered the team.* —**ea′ger·ly** *adv.* —**ea′ger·ness** *n.*

eagle (ē′gəl) *n.* **1.** Any of various large birds of prey having a hooked bill, keen vision, and broad wings. **2.** In golf, a score of two strokes under par on a hole.

eagle-eyed (ē′gəl-īd′) *adj.* Having very keen eyesight: *an eagle-eyed watchdog.*

eaglet (ē′glĭt) *n.* A young eagle.

ear¹ (îr) *n.* **1a.** The organ of hearing in humans and other animals. In mammals, the ear is divided into the inner ear, the middle ear, and the outer ear. **b.** The part of this organ that shows on the outside of the body: *Some dogs' ears stick up and some flop over.* **2.** The sense of hearing: *The sound of wind in the trees is pleasant to the ear.* **3.** The ability to distinguish tones or sounds very accurately or acutely: *the sensitive ear of a musician.* **4.** Attention; heed: *Give me your ear until I finish the explanation.* ◆ **all ears** Listening eagerly; paying careful attention: *Some people are all ears when they hear gossip.* **in one ear and out the other** Without any influence or effect: *I could tell that my directions went in one ear and out the other.* **play by ear 1.** To perform (music) solely from having heard it: *The concert pianist played the sonata by ear without having seen the sheet music.* **2.** To play music on (a musical instrument) solely from having heard the music: *can play the piano by ear.* **play it by ear** To act according to the circumstances; improvise.

ear² (îr) *n.* The part of a cereal plant, such as corn, oats, barley, or rye, that bears the grains.

WORD HISTORY Ear¹ comes from Old English *ēare.* **Ear²** comes from Old English *ēar.* Both Old English words referred to the same thing as the primary sense of their Modern English counterparts.

earache (îr′āk′) *n.* A pain in the ear.

earbud (îr′bŭd′) *n.* A small headphone that fits inside the ear.

ear canal *n.* The narrow, tubelike passage through which sound enters the ear.

eardrum (îr′drŭm′) *n.* The membrane that separates the middle ear from the outer ear and vibrates when sound waves strike it; the tympanic membrane.

eared (îrd) *adj.* **1.** Having an ear or ears: *an eared seal.* **2.** Having a certain kind or number of ears: *a long-eared puppy.*

earful (îr′fool′) *n.* **1.** A flow of gossip or information: *I got an earful about the scandal from a neighbor.* **2.** A scolding or strong criticism: *The gardener gave me an earful for walking across the newly seeded grass.*

earl (ûrl) *n.* A British nobleman holding a title and rank below that of a marquis and above that of a viscount.

earldom (ûrl′dəm) *n.* **1.** The rank of an earl. **2.** The territory of an earl.

earlobe (îr′lōb′) *n.* The soft fleshy part at the bottom of the outer ear of humans.

early (ûr′lē) *adj.* **earlier, earliest 1.** Relating to or happening near the beginning of a time period, series, or course of development: *the early morning; people in their early twenties; the early stages of an animal's growth.* **2.** Relating to or belonging to a previous or distant period of time: *Early humans made simple tools.* **3.** Appearing or happening before the usual or expected time: *an early dinner.* **4.** Happening in the near future: *Lawyers predict an early end to the trial.* ❖ *adv.* **earlier, earliest 1.** Near the beginning of a period of time or course of events: *The hikers set out early in the morning.* **2.** Before the usual or expected time: *Our guests arrived early.* **3.** Far back in time; long ago: *The Greek islands were settled as early as 5000 BC.* ◆ **early on** At an early stage or point: *Early on in the movie, the main character loses his job.* —**ear′li·ness** *n.*

early bird *n. Informal* A person who wakes up, arrives, or starts being active before most others.

Early Modern English *n.* English from around 1500 to around 1700.

earmark (îr′märk′) *n.* **1.** A notch or mark made on the ear of an animal to show that it belongs to a particular person: *The ranchers find their cattle by their earmarks.* **2.** A special quality or mark that sets a person or thing apart: *Careful observation is one of the earmarks of a good scientist.* **3.** An item in a legislative bill that allots money for a project or institution in a specific place, often the district of a legislator who is sponsoring the bill. ❖ *tr.v.* **earmarked, earmarking, earmarks 1.** To mark the ear of (an animal) for identification: *The ranchers earmarked their sheep.* **2.** To set aside for some purpose: *We ear-*

marked part of the prize money for a new car. **3.** To allocate (funds) to be spent in a legislative earmark.

earmuff (îr′mŭf′) *n.* One of a pair of coverings for the ears, often attached to an adjustable headband and typically worn to protect the ears against cold weather.

earn (ûrn) *tr.v.* **earned, earning, earns 1.** To get by working or by supplying a product or service: *earn money by mowing lawns.* **2.** To deserve or win by one's efforts or actions: *earn a reputation for being very thoughtful.* **3.** To produce as income or profit: *A savings account earns interest on your money.* —**earn′er** *n.*

earned run (ûrnd) *n.* In baseball, a run considered the fault of the pitcher, scored when the pitcher's team has made no errors allowing runners to get on base or to advance to home plate.

earned run average *n.* In baseball, a measure of a pitcher's performance determined by dividing the total of earned runs by the total of innings pitched and multiplying by nine.

earnest (ûr′nĭst) *adj.* Showing or expressing sincerity or seriousness: *an earnest offer to help.* ✦ **in earnest** With serious purpose or intent: *After a slow start, we began working on the project in earnest.* —**ear′nest·ly** *adv.*

earnest money *n.* Money paid as partial payment of a purchase price to establish a binding contract of sale.

earnings (ûr′nĭngz) *pl.n.* **1.** Money earned for work; wages. **2.** Profits, as from a business or investment.

earphone (îr′fōn′) *n.* A small speaker that is worn over or in the ear.

earplug (îr′plŭg′) *n.* An object made of a soft, pliable material and placed in the ear canal to block the entry of water or sound.

earring (îr′rĭng *or* îr′ĭng) *n.* A piece of jewelry worn on or hanging from the ear, especially the earlobe.

earshot (îr′shŏt′) *n.* The range or distance within which sound can be heard: *Their shouts were not within earshot and went unnoticed.*

earsplitting (îr′splĭt′ĭng) *adj.* Loud enough to hurt the ears; deafening.

earth (ûrth) *n.* **1.** often **Earth** The third planet from the sun and the fifth largest in the solar system. Earth is the only planet known to support life and the only planet on which water in liquid form exists, covering more than 70 percent of its surface. **2.** Dry land; the ground: *snowflakes falling to the earth.* **3.** Dirt; soil: *seeds sprouting in the moist earth.* **4.** The human inhabitants of the world: *The earth rejoiced at the news of peace.*

earthen (ûr′thən) *adj.* Made of earth or clay: *the earthen floor of a cabin; an earthen pot.*

earthenware (ûr′thən-wâr′) *n.* Pottery made from a porous clay that is fired at relatively low temperatures. Delft is an example of earthenware.

earthling (ûrth′lĭng) *n.* A person who lives on the earth; a human.

earthly (ûrth′lē) *adj.* **1.** Relating to the earth rather than heaven: *the everyday earthly business of earning a living.* **2.** Possible; imaginable: *a remark with no earthly meaning.* —**earth′li·ness** *n.*

earthquake (ûrth′kwāk′) *n.* A sudden movement of the earth's crust, followed by a series of shocks. Earthquakes are caused by volcanic action or by the release of built-up stress along geologic faults.

earth science *n.* Any of several sciences, such as geology

or meteorology, concerned with the origin, composition, and physical features of the earth.

earthward (ûrth′wərd) *adv. & adj.* To or toward the earth: *rain falling earthward.* —**earth′wards** *adv.*

earthwork (ûrth′wûrk′) *n.* An earthen bank or wall used as a fortification.

earthworm (ûrth′wûrm′) *n.* Any of various worms that have a segmented body and burrow in soil.

earthy (ûr′thē) *adj.* **earthier, earthiest 1.** Relating to or resembling earth or soil: *the earthy smell of the woods after rain.* **2.** Crude; indecent: *earthy humor.* **3.** Hearty; natural: *an earthy enjoyment of life.* —**earth′i·ness** *n.*

earwig (îr′wĭg′) *n.* Any of various insects having a pair of movable pincers protruding from the rear of the body.

ease (ēz) *n.* **1.** Freedom from difficulty, strain, or great effort: *I solved the problem with ease.* **2.** Freedom from pain or worry: *Her mind was at ease, knowing the children had returned safely.* **3.** Freedom from awkwardness or embarrassment; naturalness: *She spoke before the crowd with ease.* ✦ *v.* **eased, easing, eases** —*tr.* **1.** To free from pain, worry, or agitation: *Knowing she was not offended eased his conscience.* **2.** To make less troublesome or difficult: *The school eased its entrance requirements.* **3.** To lessen the discomfort or pain of; relieve: *The medicine eased the earache.* **4.** To cause to move slowly and carefully: *The captain eased the ship alongside the dock.* **5.** To reduce the pressure or strain of; loosen: *ease the dog's collar.* —*intr.* To relax; let up: *The tension eased when the angry customer left the store.*

easel (ē′zəl) *n.* An upright stand or rack used to display or support something, such as an artist's canvas.

easement (ēz′mənt) *n.* **1a.** The act of easing or the condition of being eased. **b.** Something that affords ease or comfort. **2.** A legal right to make limited use of another's land, such as a right of way.

easily (ē′zə-lē) *adv.* **1.** In an easy manner; with ease: *Libraries are arranged so that you can find books easily.* **2.** Without doubt; surely: *That is easily the best movie I've ever seen.* **3.** Very likely: *With the new players, the team could easily win the championship this year.* **4.** Very quickly or readily: *I am easily embarrassed.*

east (ēst) *n.* **1.** The direction from which the sun is seen to rise, directly opposite west. **2.** often **East** A region or part of a country lying in the east. **3.** often **East a.** The eastern part of the earth, especially eastern Asia. **b.** The part of the United States along the Atlantic coast, especially from Maine to Maryland. ✦ *adj.* **1.** To, toward, facing, or in the east: *the east bank of the river; the east road to town.* **2.** From the east: *An east wind is blowing.* ✦ *adv.* In, from, or toward the east: *a river flowing east.*

eastbound (ēst′bound′) *adj.* Going toward the east.

Easter (ē′stər) *n.* A Christian feast commemorating the Resurrection of Jesus. In the Western Church it is held each year on the first Sunday following the full moon that occurs on or after March 21.

Easter egg *n.* **1.** A dyed or painted egg traditionally given as a gift or hidden and hunted for by children on Easter. **2.** A hidden message or feature, as in a video game or DVD.

easterly (ē′stər-lē) *adj.* **1.** Situated toward the east: *an easterly direction.* **2.** Coming from the east: *easterly wind.* ✦ *n., pl.* **easterlies** A storm or wind from the east. —**east′er·ly** *adv.*

eastern (ē′stərn) *adj.* **1.** Situated in, toward, or facing the east: *eastern Europe; the eastern slope of a mountain.* **2.** From the east: *an eastern wind.* **3.** often **Eastern a.** Relating to eastern regions or the East. **b.** Relating to the part of the United States along the Atlantic coast: *a large Eastern vote for the president.*

Eastern Church *n.* The Eastern Orthodox Church.

Eastern equine encephalitis *n.* Encephalitis that is caused by a mosquito-borne virus and can occur in small epidemics. It affects humans, horses, and some bird species.

easterner also **Easterner** (ē′stər-nər) *n.* A person who lives in or comes from the east, especially the eastern United States.

easternmost (ē′stərn-mōst′) *adj.* Farthest east.

Eastern Orthodox Church *n.* A group of churches, including the Greek Orthodox and the Russian Orthodox, that trace their origin to the early Christian Church established during the Byzantine Empire.

Eastern Standard Time *n.* Standard time in the fifth time zone west of Greenwich, England, used, for example, in the eastern United States.

Eastertide (ē′stər-tīd′) *n.* The Easter season.

eastward (ēst′wərd) *adv. & adj.* Toward, to, or in the east: *the eastward flow of the current.* ❖ *n.* A direction or region to the east. **—east′wards** *adv.*

easy (ē′zē) *adj.* **easier, easiest 1a.** Requiring or done with little effort or difficulty: *an easy victory; an easy problem.* **b.** Likely to happen by accident or without intention: *It's easy to slip on the wet floor. It's easy to push the wrong button.* **2.** Free from worry, strain, or pain: *an easy life.* **3.** Relaxed in attitude or appearance: *a natural easy manner; an easy smile.* **4.** Not strict or demanding; lenient: *Most teachers are easy on new students.* **5.** Not forced, hurried, or strenuous: *within easy walking distance; an easy drive.* ❖ *adv.* **1.** Without haste or worry: *Take it easy and you'll do a better job.* **2.** With little effort; easily: *Playing the banjo came easy to her.* **3.** Without much hardship or cost: *He got off easy with only a small fine.* **—eas′i·ness** *n.*

✦ **SYNONYMS easy, effortless, simple** *adj.*

easy chair *n.* A large comfortable upholstered chair.

easygoing (ē′zē-gō′ing) *adj.* **1.** Relaxed; carefree: *an artist's easygoing life; an easygoing manner of speech.* **2.** Not hurried; leisurely: *an easygoing pace.*

eat (ēt) *v.* **ate** (āt), **eaten** (ēt′n), **eating, eats** *—tr.* **1a.** To take into the body through the mouth: *Owls eat mice.* **b.** To take in and absorb as food: *a plant that eats insects.* **2.** To wear away, corrode, or destroy by or as if by eating: *Rust has eaten away the iron pipes.* **3.** To make by eating: *Moths ate holes in the blanket.* *—intr.* **1.** To take food; have a meal: *They usually eat about seven o'clock.* **2.** To wear away; corrode: *Home improvements ate into their savings.* ✦ **eat (one's) words** To retract something that one has said. **eat up** *Slang* To enjoy greatly; be greedy for: *The actor eats up compliments.* **—eat′er** *n.*

eatable (ē′tə-bəl) *adj.* Fit for eating; edible.

eatery (ē′tə-rē) *n., pl.* **eateries** *Informal* A restaurant.

eating disorder (ē′tĭng) *n.* Any of several disorders, such as anorexia nervosa or bulimia, that are characterized by abnormal eating behaviors.

eau de cologne (ō′ də kə-lōn′) *n., pl.* **eaux de cologne** (ō′ də kə-lōn′) A lightly perfumed cologne.

eaves (ēvz) *pl.n.* The part of a roof that forms the lower edge and projects beyond the walls.

eavesdrop (ēvz′drŏp′) *intr.v.* **eavesdropped, eavesdropping, eavesdrops** To listen secretly to the private conversation of others: *hid behind the door to eavesdrop.* **—eaves′drop′per** *n.*

WORD HISTORY The edge of the roof that overhangs the side of the building is the *eaves,* and an **eavesdrop** is the space on the ground where the rainwater falls from the eaves. If you stood in the eavesdrop by a window on the side of a building to listen secretly to a conversation inside, you were said to be *eavesdropping.* The meaning of *eavesdrop* has broadened so that now you can *eavesdrop* anywhere.

ebb (ĕb) *n.* **1.** Ebb tide. **2.** A period of decline: *The king's fortunes were at their lowest ebb.* ❖ *intr.v.* **ebbed, ebbing, ebbs 1.** To flow back; recede: *The floodwaters began to ebb after the storm passed.* **2.** To fade or fall away; decline: *The hooked fish struggled less as its strength ebbed.*

ebb tide *n.* **1.** The tide flowing away from the shore. **2.** The period between high tide and low tide.

ebonite (ĕb′ə-nīt′) *n.* A hard black rubber made by heating rubber in the presence of large amounts of sulfur and used as an electrical insulator.

ebony (ĕb′ə-nē) *n., pl.* **ebonies 1.** The hard black or blackish wood of any of several tropical trees of southern Asia or Africa, used for piano keys and for decorative work. **2.** A tree that yields such wood. **3.** The color black. ❖ *adj.* **1.** Made of ebony: *an ebony cabinet.* **2.** Black: *ebony hair.*

e-book (ē′bŏŏk) *n.* A book whose contents are in an electronic format.

ebullient (ĭ-bŏŏl′yənt *or* ĭ-bŭl′yənt) *adj.* Full of excitement, enthusiasm, or high spirits: *the ebullient feeling of victory.* **—e·bul′lient·ly** *adv.*

eccentric (ĭk-sĕn′trĭk) *adj.* **1.** Odd or unusual in appearance, behavior, or manner; peculiar: *an eccentric hat; an eccentric person; an eccentric habit.* **2.** Not perfectly circular: *an eccentric orbit.* ❖ *n.* A person who is odd or unusual in behavior. **—ec·cen′tri·cal·ly** *adv.*

eccentricity (ĕk′sĕn-trĭs′ĭ-tē) *n., pl.* **eccentricities 1.** The quality or condition of being eccentric: *The eccentricity of the moon's orbit.* **2.** An act or habit that is odd or strange; a peculiarity. **3.** The amount or degree by which something is eccentric.

Ecclesiastes (ĭ-klē′zē-ăs′tēz′) *n.* (*used with a singular verb*) A book of the Bible that stresses the vanity of human wishes and achievements.

ecclesiastic (ĭ-klē′zē-ăs′tĭk) *adj.* Ecclesiastical. ❖ *n.* A member of the Christian clergy; a minister or priest.

ecclesiastical (ĭ-klē′zē-ăs′tĭ-kəl) *adj.* Relating to a church: *ecclesiastical robes.* **—ec·cle′si·as′ti·cal·ly** *adv.*

echelon (ĕsh′ə-lŏn′) *n.* **1.** A formation of military aircraft, naval vessels, or soldiers resembling a series of steps. **2.** A level of command or authority: *The president and cabinet officers are among the highest echelons of government.*

echidna (ĭ-kĭd′nə) *n.* Any of several burrowing, egg-laying mammals of Australia, Papua New Guinea, and eastern Indonesia, having a spiny coat, slender snout, and sticky tongue used for catching insects.

echinoderm (ĭ-kī′nə-dûrm′) *n.* Any of numerous marine invertebrate animals, including the starfishes and sea urchins, that have a hard internal skeleton and are often covered with spines.

echo (ĕk′ō) *n., pl.* **echoes 1.** A repeated sound that is caused by the reflection of sound waves from a surface. **2.** A repetition or imitation of something: *New fashions in dress usually have echoes of earlier styles.* **3.** A reflected radio wave. Echoes of radio waves are the basis for radar. ❖ *v.* **echoed, echoing, echoes** *—tr.* **1.** To repeat (a sound) by an echo: *The canyon echoed their shouts.* **2.** To repeat or imitate: *She echoed our feelings in her statement to the board.* —*intr.* **1.** To be repeated by an echo: *The shouts echoed from the mountainside.* **2.** To resound with an echo; reverberate: *The long hallway echoed with many footsteps.* —**e·cho′ic** (ĕ-kō′ĭk) *adj.*

Echo *n.* In Greek mythology, a nymph whose love for Narcissus was not returned by him, causing her to pine away until nothing but her voice remained.

echolocation (ĕk′ō-lō-kā′shən) *n.* A sensory system in certain animals, such as bats and dolphins, in which the animal sends out high-pitched sounds and uses the echoes to determine the position of objects.

éclair (ā-klâr′ *or* ā′klâr′) *n.* An elongated pastry filled with custard or whipped cream and usually iced with chocolate.

eclectic (ĭ-klĕk′tĭk) *adj.* Choosing or taking what appears to be the best from various sources: *an eclectic painter blending elements of realism and abstract art.* ❖ *n.* A person whose opinions and beliefs are drawn from several sources. —**e·clec′ti·cal·ly** *adv.*

eclipse (ĭ-klĭps′) *n.* **1.** The partial or total blocking of light from one celestial object as it passes behind or through the shadow of another celestial object. In a solar eclipse, the moon comes between the sun and the earth. In a lunar eclipse, the moon enters the earth's shadow. **2.** A decline in importance, use, or fame: *The author's popularity has suffered an eclipse in recent years.* ❖ *tr.v.* **eclipsed, eclipsing, eclipses** **1.** To cause an eclipse of: *When the moon eclipsed the sun, it caused partial darkness.* **2.** To obscure or overshadow in importance, fame, or reputation; surpass: *The war eclipsed all other news for a while.*

ecliptic (ĭ-klĭp′tĭk) *n.* The apparent path of the sun among the stars in one year. The ecliptic is the great circle of the celestial sphere which is cut by the plane containing the orbit of Earth.

E. coli (ē kō′lī) *n.* A bacterium that is normally found in the intestines of humans and other mammals and is widely used in biological research. Some strains can cause disease.

ecologist (ĭ-kŏl′ə-jĭst) *n.* A scientist who specializes in ecology.

ecology (ĭ-kŏl′ə-jē) *n.* **1.** The science of the relationships between living things and their environment: *studying ecology.* **2.** The relationship between certain organisms and their environment: *the ecology of reef fishes.* —**ec′-o·log′i·cal** (ĕk′ə-lŏj′ĭ-kəl *or* ē′kə-lŏj′ĭ-kəl) *adj.* —**ec′-o·log′i·cal·ly** *adv.*

e-commerce (ē′kŏm′ərs) *n.* Commerce that takes place electronically, as over the Internet.

economic (ĕk′ə-nŏm′ĭk *or* ē′kə-nŏm′ĭk) *adj.* **1.** Relating to the production, development, and management of wealth, as of a country, household, or business: *The state's economic activity increased last month.* **2.** Relating to the science of economics: *economic theories of how money works in society.* **3.** Efficient; economical: *an economic use of home heating oil.*

economical (ĕk′ə-nŏm′ĭ-kəl *or* ē′kə-nŏm′ĭ-kəl) *adj.* Not wasteful or extravagant; prudent and thrifty: *an economical use of time; an economical way to produce better crops.* —**ec′o·nom′i·cal·ly** *adv.*

economics (ĕk′ə-nŏm′ĭks *or* ē′kə-nŏm′ĭks) *n.* **1.** *(used with a singular verb)* The science that deals with the ways in which goods and services are produced, transported,

sold, and used. Economics also deals with the effects of taxes and the distribution of money within an economy. **2.** *(used with a singular or plural verb)* Economic matters, especially those relating to cost and profit: *the economics of running a store.*

economist (ĭ-kŏn′ə-mĭst) *n.* A person who specializes in economics.

economize (ĭ-kŏn′ə-mīz′) *v.* **economized, economizing, economizes** —*intr.* To be thrifty; reduce expenses or avoid waste: *economize by bringing your own lunch to work.* —*tr.* To use or manage with thrift: *economize your time to get more done.*

economy (ĭ-kŏn′ə-mē) *n., pl.* **economies** **1.** The careful use or management of resources, such as money, materials, or labor: *practice economy in running the household.* **2.** An example or result of this; a saving: *the economy of using public transportation.* **3.** The economic system of a country, region, or state: *The rise in housing prices boosted the city's economy.* **4.** A specific kind of economic system: *an industrial economy.* **5.** The least expensive class of accommodations on an airliner or other mode of commercial transportation: *purchased tickets in economy instead of first class.* ❖ *adj.* Economical or inexpensive to buy or use: *an economy car; an economy hotel.*

ecosystem (ē′kō-sĭs′təm *or* ĕk′ō-sĭs′təm) *n.* A biological community, including plants, animals, and microorganisms, considered together with its environment: *A pond is a complex ecosystem.*

ecotourism (ē′kō-tŏŏr′ĭz′əm) *n.* Tourism that involves visiting scenic or remote natural areas while attempting to minimize negative impacts on the environment and on the local inhabitants. —**e′co·tour′ist** *n.*

ecru (ĕk′rōō *or* ā′krōō) *n.* A pale yellowish-brown color.

ecstasy (ĕk′stə-sē) *n., pl.* **ecstasies** Intense joy or delight: *The runner was in ecstasy over winning an Olympic medal.*

ecstatic (ĕk-stăt′ĭk) *adj.* **1.** Marked by or expressing intense joy or delight: *the ecstatic final movement of the symphony.* **2.** In a state of ecstasy; overjoyed: *was ecstatic over the chance to go to Tibet.* —**ec·stat′i·cal·ly** *adv.*

ecto– A prefix that means outer or external: *ectoderm.*

ectoderm (ĕk′tə-dûrm′) *n.* The outer cell layer of an early embryo, developing into the nervous system and the epidermis, such as the skin, hair, and nails.

ectoplasm (ĕk′tə-plăz′əm) *n.* The outer portion of the cytoplasm of a cell.

ectotherm (ĕk′tə-thûrm′) *n.* A cold-blooded animal. —**ec′to·ther′mic** *adj.*

ecumenical (ĕk′yə-mĕn′ĭ-kəl) *adj.* **1.** Worldwide in range or relevance; universal: *an ecumenical view of environmental planning.* **2.** Relating to the worldwide Christian church: *an ecumenical council.* **3.** Concerned with promoting unity among churches or religions. —**ec′-u·men′i·cal·ly** *adv.*

eczema (ĕk′sə-mə *or* ĕg′zə-mə) *n.* An inflammation of the skin, marked by redness, itching, and the formation of sores that discharge fluid and become crusted and scaly.

ed (ĕd) *n. Informal* Education: *driver's ed; adult ed.*

ed. An abbreviation of: **1.** edition. **2.** editor.

–ed¹ A suffix that forms the past tense of regular verbs: *cared; carried.*

–ed² A suffix that forms the past participle of regular verbs: *ended; expected.*

–ed³ A suffix that means having, characterized by, or resembling: *hardhearted; wretched.*

edamame (ĕd′ə-mä′mä) *pl.n.* Fresh green soybeans, typically prepared by boiling in salted water.

eddy (ĕd′ē) *n., pl.* **eddies** A current, as of water or air, that moves opposite to the direction of a main current, especially in a circular motion. ❖ *intr.v.* **eddied, eddying, eddies** To move in or as if in an eddy: *wisps of mist eddying through the valley.*

edelweiss (ā′dəl-vīs′ *or* ā′dəl-wīs′) *n.* A small plant native to high mountain areas of Europe, having small yellow flowers surrounded by bracts that resemble petals. The leaves and flowers are covered with whitish down.

edema (ĭ-dē′mə) *n.* A condition in which an excess amount of fluid collects in a body part or tissue and causes swelling.

Eden (ĕd′n) *n.* **1.** In the Bible, the garden of God and the home of the first people, Adam and Eve. Adam and Eve were banished from Eden for disobeying God. **2.** A delightful place; a paradise.

edge (ĕj) *n.* **1a.** The thin sharpened side of a blade. **b.** A slight sharpness or harshness: *His voice had an edge to it.* **2a.** The area or part farthest from the middle: *went to the mall at the edge of town.* **b.** The line or point where two surfaces meet: *the edge of a table.* **c.** The point at which something is likely to begin: *on the edge of war.* **3.** A dividing line; a border: *The stone fence marks the edge of their property.* See Synonyms at **border. 4.** An advantage: *We had a slight edge over the other team.* ❖ *v.* **edged, edging, edges** —*tr.* **1.** To give an edge to; sharpen. **2.** To be the edge of: *Flowers edged the lawn.* **3.** To put a border or edge on: *edge a sleeve with lace.* **4.** To advance or move gradually; push: *The photographers edged their way through the crowd.* —*intr.* To move gradually: *The child edged slowly toward the door.* ◆ **edge out** To surpass or beat by a small margin. **on edge** Tense or nervous; irritable: *He was on edge from listening to the baby cry.*

edgewise (ĕj′wīz′) also **edgeways** (ĕj′wāz′) *adv.* **1.** With the edge forward: *Turn the table edgewise to get it through the door.* **2.** On, by, with, or toward the edge: *The cricket moved edgewise along the side of the box.* ◆ **get a word in edgewise** To manage to say something in a conversation dominated by another person: *The others talked so much I couldn't get a word in edgewise.*

edging (ĕj′ĭng) *n.* Something that forms an edge or border: *an edging of bricks along the path.*

edgy (ĕj′ē) *adj.* **edgier, edgiest 1.** Nervous or irritable: *We got edgy waiting for the concert to begin.* **2.** Daring, provocative, or trend-setting: *an exhibition of edgy paintings.* —**edg′i·ness** *n.*

edible (ĕd′ə-bəl) *adj.* Fit to be eaten: *The spoiled cheese was no longer edible.*

edict (ē′dĭkt′) *n.* An order or decree issued by a person in authority.

edification (ĕd′ə-fĭ-kā′shən) *n.* Intellectual, moral, or spiritual improvement; enlightenment: *She wrote the book for the edification of the people.*

edifice (ĕd′ə-fĭs) *n.* A building, especially one that is very imposing in size or appearance.

edify (ĕd′ə-fī′) *tr.v.* **edified, edifying, edifies** To instruct so as to encourage intellectual, moral, or spiritual improvement: *His poems are intended to edify young readers.*

edit (ĕd′ĭt) *tr.v.* **edited, editing, edits 1.** To make (written material) ready for publication by correcting, revising, or marking directions for a printer: *The staff edited reporters' stories for publication in the newspaper.* **2.** To supervise and be responsible for the publication of (a newspaper or

magazine, for example): *edited a literary magazine.* **3.** To put together or cut out parts of (a film or soundtrack, for example): *We edited our videotape of the wedding down to a 30-minute show.* ◆ **edit out** To delete during the course of editing: *A controversial scene was edited out of the film.*

edition (ĭ-dĭsh′ən) *n.* **1a.** The entire number of copies of a book or newspaper printed at one time and having the same content: *today's edition of the newspaper.* **b.** A single copy from such a number: *I bought this month's edition of the magazine.* **2.** Any of the various forms in which a publication is issued: *a paperback edition of a novel.* **3.** The entire number of like or identical items issued or made as a set: *a limited edition of early jazz recordings.*

editor (ĕd′ĭ-tər) *n.* **1.** A person who edits written material for publication. **2.** A person who prepares a recording for viewing or hearing by assembling and deleting various parts. **3.** A person who directs the writing and layout of a newspaper or magazine or supervises one of its departments. **4.** A computer program used to edit text or data files.

editorial (ĕd′ĭ-tôr′ē-əl) *n.* **1.** An article in a newspaper or magazine expressing the opinions of its editors or publisher. **2.** A commentary on television or radio expressing the opinion of the owners. ❖ *adj.* **1.** Relating to an editor or editing: *an editorial position in a publishing company.* **2.** Expressing opinion rather than reporting news: *the editorial page of the newspaper.* —**ed′i·to′ri·al·ly** *adv.*

editorialize (ĕd′ĭ-tôr′ē-ə-līz′) *intr.v.* **editorialized, editorializing, editorializes 1.** To express an opinion in or as if in an editorial: *Most newspapers editorialize in each issue.* **2.** To express an opinion or opinions in what is supposed to be a report of facts: *The author feels so strongly about the issue, he cannot keep himself from editorializing.*

editorship (ĕd′ĭ-tər-shĭp′) *n.* The position, duties, or guidance of an editor.

educable (ĕj′ə-kə-bəl) *adj.* Capable of being educated.

educate (ĕj′ə-kāt′) *v.* **educated, educating, educates** —*tr.* To provide with knowledge or training, especially through formal schooling; teach. See Synonyms at **teach.** —*intr.* To provide instructions and training: *Their purpose is to educate through the use of visual aids.*

educated (ĕj′ə-kā′tĭd) *adj.* **1.** Having an education, especially one above the average: *Librarians are educated people.* **2.** Showing evidence of schooling; cultured; refined: *an educated taste for books and learning.* **3.** Based on experience or factual knowledge: *an educated guess.*

education (ĕj′ə-kā′shən) *n.* **1a.** The process of imparting or obtaining knowledge or skill: *Many people want to continue their education after high school.* **b.** The knowledge or skill obtained by such a process; learning: *It takes a lot of education to be an engineer.* **2.** A program of instruction of a specified kind or level: *a college education.* **3.** The field of study that is concerned with teaching and learning: *a graduate degree in education.*

educational (ĕj′ə-kā′shə-nəl) *adj.* **1.** Relating to education: *educational standards.* **2.** Serving to give knowledge or skill; instructive: *educational television.* —**ed′u·ca′tion·al·ly** *adv.*

educator (ĕj′ə-kā′tər) *n.* **1.** A person who is trained in teaching; a teacher. **2.** A specialist in the theory and practice of education.

educe (ĭ-dōōs′) *tr.v.* **educed, educing, educes** To draw or bring out; elicit: *By clever questions the judge educed the facts of the case from the witnesses.* —**e·duc′i·ble** *adj.* —SEE NOTE AT **produce.**

–ee A suffix that means: **1.** A person who receives or benefits from an action: *appointee; trainee.* **2.** A person or animal that performs an action: *absentee; escapee.* **3.** A person who possesses something: *grantee.*

EEE An abbreviation of Eastern equine encephalitis.

EEG (ē'ē'jē') *n.* **1.** An electroencephalogram. **2.** An electroencephalograph.

eel (ēl) *n., pl.* **eel** or **eels** Any of various long slender fishes that lack scales and resemble snakes.

e'en[1] (ēn) *n.* Evening.

e'en[2] (ēn) *adv.* Even.

–eer A suffix that means a person who is associated with or involved in: *auctioneer; racketeer.*

e'er (âr) *adv.* Ever.

eerie or **eery** (îr'ē) *adj.* **eerier, eeriest** Inspiring fear without a clear reason; strange and frightening: *The eerie old house made us feel uneasy.* **—ee'ri·ly** *adv.* **—ee'ri·ness** *n.*

efface (ĭ-fās') *tr.v.* **effaced, effacing, effaces 1.** To remove, as by rubbing out; erase: *Time had effaced the name on the gravestone.* **2.** To conduct (oneself) inconspicuously. **—ef·face'ment** *n.*

effect (ĭ-fĕkt') *n.* **1.** Something brought about by a cause or agent; a result: *The effect of advertising should be an increase in sales.* **2.** The power to bring about a result; influence: *The tougher laws had no effect on the crime rate.* **3a.** An artistic technique that produces a specific impression: *Thunder and lightning and other special effects can be used in making a movie.* **b.** The impression produced by some artistic technique: *a musical passage that was meant to create the effect of spring.* **4. effects** Movable belongings; goods. ❖ *tr.v.* **effected, effecting, effects** To produce as a result; cause to occur: *New technologies have effected many changes in the way people live.* ◆ **in effect 1.** In essence; actually: *By turning off the lights they were in effect telling us to go home.* **2.** In active force: *The new law is now in effect.* —SEE NOTE AT **affect**[1].

effective (ĭ-fĕk'tĭv) *adj.* **1.** Having an intended or expected effect: *a vaccine that is effective against polio.* **2.** Operative; in effect: *The law will be effective as soon as the governor signs it.* **3.** Producing a strong impression or response: *The president made an effective speech that united the country behind him.* **—ef·fec'tive·ly** *adv.* **—ef·fec'tive·ness** *n.*

effectual (ĭ-fĕk'chōō-əl) *adj.* Producing or sufficient to produce a desired effect; fully adequate: *Practice is the only effectual method of learning to play the piano.* **—ef·fec'tu·al·ly** *adv.*

effectuate (ĭ-fĕk'chōō-āt') *tr.v.* **effectuated, effectuating, effectuates** To bring about; effect: *effectuate a change in the rule.*

effeminate (ĭ-fĕm'ə-nĭt) *adj.* Having qualities associated with women rather than men. **—ef·fem'i·na·cy** (ĭ-fĕm'ə-nə-sē) *n.* **—ef·fem'i·nate·ly** *adv.*

efferent (ĕf'ər-ənt) *adj.* Directed away from a central organ or point: *Efferent nerves carry impulses from the brain to the muscles.*

effervesce (ĕf'ər-vĕs') *intr.v.* **effervesced, effervescing, effervesces 1.** To give off bubbles of gas, as a carbonated liquid. **2.** To show high spirits; be lively.

effervescence (ĕf'ər-vĕs'əns) *n.* **1.** The process of giving off small bubbles of gas: *the effervescence of soda water.* **2.** Sparkling high spirits; vivacity. **—ef'fer·ves'cent** *adj.*

effete (ĭ-fēt') *adj.* **1a.** Characterized by extreme refinement or self-indulgence. **b.** Pretentious; snobby. **2.** Having lost vitality, strength, or effectiveness: *an effete period of a once great civilization.* **—ef·fete'ly** *adv.*

efficacious (ĕf'ĭ-kā'shəs) *adj.* Producing or capable of producing the desired effect; effective: *an efficacious treatment of a disease.* **—ef'fi·ca'cious·ly** *adv.*

efficacy (ĕf'ĭ-kə-sē) *n.* Power or capacity to produce a desired effect; effectiveness: *The efficacy of most medicines declines over time.*

efficiency (ĭ-fĭsh'ən-sē) *n., pl.* **efficiencies 1.** The condition or quality of being efficient: *Tired people can't work with efficiency.* **2.** The ratio of the useful work a machine does to the energy required to operate it.

efficiency apartment *n.* A small, usually furnished apartment with a private bathroom and small kitchen area.

efficient (ĭ-fĭsh'ənt) *adj.* Acting or producing effectively with a minimum of waste, expense, or unnecessary effort: *an efficient worker; an efficient motor.* **—ef·fi'cient·ly** *adv.*

effigy (ĕf'ə-jē) *n., pl.* **effigies 1.** A crude figure or dummy of a hated person. **2.** A likeness or sculpture of a person or animal: *a stone effigy on a tomb.* ◆ **in effigy** In the form of an effigy: *The colonists burned King George in effigy.*

efflorescence (ĕf'lə-rĕs'əns) *n.* **1.** A state or period of flowering: *the splendid efflorescence of the roses.* **2.** The highest point in a process of development: *the efflorescence of mercantilism.* **3.** A deposit of salt crystals or powder on a surface, caused by the evaporation of water from a solution containing dissolved salts. **—ef'flo·res'cent** *adj.*

effluent (ĕf'lōō-ənt) *adj.* Flowing out or forth. ❖ *n.* **1.** Something that flows out or forth, such as a stream that flows from a lake. **2.** The liquid waste or sewage that flows from a factory, water purification plant, or other system.

effluvium (ĭ-flōō'vē-əm) *n., pl.* **effluvia** (ĭ-flōō'vē-ə) or **effluviums 1.** A usually invisible emanation or exhalation, as of vapor or gas. **2a.** A byproduct or residue; waste. **b.** The odorous fumes given off by waste or decaying matter. **—ef·flu'vi·al** *adj.*

effort (ĕf'ərt) *n.* **1.** The use of physical or mental energy to do something; exertion: *It took a lot of effort to plant the tree.* **2.** An attempt, especially an earnest attempt: *We made an effort to arrive on time.* **3.** Something done or produced through exertion; an achievement: *This painting is the artist's best and latest effort.*

effortless (ĕf'ərt-lĭs) *adj.* Requiring or showing little or no effort: *Watching TV is an effortless activity. The skater glided in effortless turns around the ice.* See Synonyms at **easy.** **—ef'fort·less·ly** *adv.*

effrontery (ĭ-frŭn'tə-rē) *n., pl.* **effronteries** Shameless or insulting boldness; audacity: *In spite of making several rude remarks they had the effrontery to ask for our help.*

effulgent (ĭ-fōŏl'jənt or ĭ-fŭl'jənt) *adj.* **1.** Shining brilliantly; resplendent: *an effulgent tiara.* **2.** Showing or expressing vitality, love, or joy: *gazed at her with effulgent eyes.* **—ef·ful'gence** *n.* **—ef·ful'gent·ly** *adv.*

effusion (ĭ-fyōō'zhən) *n.* **1.** An outpouring, as of fluid: *The effusion of blood was stopped by a compress.* **2.** An unrestrained outpouring of feeling, as in speech or writing: *Such an effusion of praise embarrassed me.*

effusive (ĭ-fyōō'sĭv) *adj.* Unrestrained or excessive in emotional expression; gushy: *an effusive display of gratitude.* **—ef·fu'sive·ly** *adv.* **—ef·fu'sive·ness** *n.*

eft (ĕft) *n.* A newt in an immature stage that lives on land.

e.g. An abbreviation of exempli gratia (for example).

egalitarian (ĭ-găl′ĭ-târ′ē-ən) *adj.* Affirming, promoting, or characterized by belief in equal rights for all people. ❖ *n.* One who supports such equal rights. —**e·gal′i·tar′i·an·ism** *n.*

egg¹ (ĕg) *n.* **1.** A female reproductive cell of humans and other animals from which an embryo develops; an egg cell or ovum. In animals such as birds, turtles, frogs, fish, and insects, an egg contains nourishment for the developing embryo and may have a protective shell or covering. **2.** A female reproductive cell of plants and most algae; an egg cell. **3.** A hard-shelled egg, the contents of which are used for food, especially a chicken egg: *We had scrambled eggs for breakfast.* **4.** *Informal* A person: *What a good egg!*

egg² (ĕg) *tr.v.* **egged, egging, eggs** To encourage or urge. Used with *on*: *egged me on to try to ski down that hill.*

WORD HISTORY Egg¹ comes from Middle English *eg, egge,* which comes from Old Norse *egg,* both meaning "bird's egg." **Egg**² comes from Middle English *eggen,* which comes from Old Norse *eggja,* both meaning "to urge, provoke."

---

eggbeater (ĕg′bē′tər) *n.* A kitchen utensil with rotating blades for beating eggs, whipping cream, or mixing ingredients together.

egg cell *n.* **1.** A female reproductive cell in animals; an egg. **2.** A female reproductive cell in plants and most algae; an egg.

egghead (ĕg′hĕd′) *n. Informal* An intellectual.

eggnog (ĕg′nŏg′) *n.* A drink of milk or cream, sugar, and beaten eggs, often mixed with an alcoholic liquor such as rum or brandy.

eggplant (ĕg′plănt′) *n.* **1.** The glossy, often egg-shaped fruit of a bushy plant, cooked and eaten as a vegetable. Eggplants are usually purple but can also be white, yellow, or green. **2.** The plant that bears such fruit.

egg roll *n.* A casing of egg dough filled with minced vegetables, sometimes with seafood or meat, and fried.

eggshell (ĕg′shĕl′) *n.* The thin, often brittle outer covering of the egg of a bird or reptile.

eglantine (ĕg′lən-tīn′ *or* ĕg′lən-tēn′) *n.* The sweetbrier.

ego (ē′gō) *n., pl.* **egos 1.** The awareness of oneself as separate and different from other things; the self. **2.** In Freudian theory, the division of the psyche that is conscious, most immediately controls thought and behavior, and is most in touch with external reality. **3.** Egotism; conceit: *He is so full of ego that he never notices anyone around him.* **4.** Self-confidence; self-esteem: *A leader needs enough ego to take a lot of criticism.*

egocentric (ē′gō-sĕn′trĭk) *adj.* Concerned only with oneself; self-centered: *An egocentric person usually does not work well in a group.*

egoism (ē′gō-ĭz′əm) *n.* **1.** The tendency to think or act with only one's own interests in mind; selfishness. **2.** Conceit; egotism. —**e′go·ist** *n.*

egomania (ē′gō-mā′nē-ə) *n.* Obsessive preoccupation with the self. —**e′go·ma′ni·ac′** (ē′gō-mā′nē-ăk′) *n.* —**e′go·ma·ni′a·cal** (ē′gō-mə-nī′ə-kəl) *adj.*

egotism (ē′gə-tĭz′əm) *n.* **1.** The tendency to speak or write about oneself excessively or boastfully. **2.** An exaggerated sense of one's own importance; conceit.

egotist (ē′gə-tĭst) *n.* A conceited boastful person. **2.** A selfish self-centered person. —**e′go·tis′ti·cal** *adj.* —**e′go·tis′ti·cal·ly** *adv.*

ego trip *n. Slang* An action done to boost one's feeling of importance or to call attention to oneself: *The candidate expected to lose and ran only as an ego trip.*

egregious (ĭ-grē′jəs) *adj.* Conspicuously bad or offensive: *An egregious error in the computer program caused the spacecraft to fall out of orbit.* —**e·gre′gious·ly** *adv.*

egress (ē′grĕs′) *n.* **1.** A path or means of going out; an exit: *When fire blocked the doorway there was no egress from the building.* **2.** The right to leave or go out: *The guard denied them egress.* **3.** The act of going out. —SEE NOTE AT **progress.**

egret (ē′grĭt *or* ĕg′rĭt) *n.* Any of several wading birds having a long neck, a pointed bill, and usually white feathers. Many egrets have long drooping plumes during the breeding season.

Egyptian (ĭ-jĭp′shən) *adj.* **1.** Relating to Egypt, the Egyptians, or their culture. **2.** Relating to the language of the ancient Egyptians. ❖ *n.* **1.** A native or inhabitant of Egypt. **2.** The extinct Afro-Asiatic language of the ancient Egyptians.

eh (ā *or* ĕ) *interj.* An expression used in asking for agreement or confirmation: *That's not a bad looking car, eh?*

Eid al-Fitr (ēd əl-fĭt′ər) *n.* A festival that ends the fast of Ramadan.

eider (ī′dər) *n.* Any of several large ducks of northern regions of the Atlantic and Pacific Oceans, having a layer of very soft downy feathers under the outer feathers.

eiderdown (ī′dər-doun′) *n.* **1.** The soft light down of the eider, used for stuffing coats, quilts, pillows, and sleeping bags. **2.** A quilt stuffed with eiderdown.

eight (āt) *n.* **1.** The number, written 8, that is equal to 7 + 1. **2.** The eighth in a set or sequence.

eighteen (ā-tēn′) *n.* **1.** The number, written 18, that is equal to 17 + 1. **2.** The 18th in a set or sequence.

eighteenth (ā-tēnth′) *n.* **1.** The ordinal number matching the number 18 in a series. **2.** One of 18 equal parts.

eighth (ātth *or* āth) *n.* **1.** The ordinal number matching the number eight in a series. **2.** One of eight equal parts. —**eighth** *adv. & adj.*

eighth note *n.* A musical note having one eighth the time value of a whole note.

eightieth (ā′tē-ĭth) *n.* **1.** The ordinal number matching the number 80 in a series. **2.** One of 80 equal parts.

eighty (ā′tē) *n., pl.* **eighties** The number, written 80, that is equal to 8 × 10.

einsteinium (īn-stī′nē-əm) *n. Symbol* **Es** A radioactive element that is usually produced artificially by scientists. It was first discovered in the debris of a hydrogen bomb explosion. The half-life of its longest-lived isotope is about 472 days. Atomic number 99. See **Periodic Table.**

either (ē′thər *or* ī′thər) *pron.* One or the other of two: *It was a while before either of them spoke.* ❖ *conj.* Used before the first of two or more words or groups of words linked by *or: Either we go now or we forget about going.* ❖ *adj.* **1.** One or the other; any one of two: *Wear either coat.* **2.** One and the other; each of the two: *Candles stood on either end of the mantelpiece.* ❖ *adv.* Any more than the other; likewise; also: *I didn't finish the race, and my friend didn't either.*

USAGE When used as a pronoun, **either** is singular and takes a singular verb: *You can take French or Spanish; either is a good choice.* This rule holds even when *either* is followed by *of* and a plural noun: *Either of the two languages is a good one to study.* In an *either . . . or* construction, you use the singular when the words used as the subject of a sentence are singular: *Either Jennifer or June* *is coming to the party.* When the words are plural, the verb is plural: *Either the Montoyas or the Smiths throw a party every year.* It is best to avoid sentences in which *either* is followed by one singular and one plural.

ejaculate (ĭ-jăk′yə-lāt′) *v.* **ejaculated, ejaculating, ejaculates** —*tr.* **1.** To discharge (semen). **2.** To utter suddenly and passionately; exclaim. —*intr.* To eject a body fluid, especially semen.

ejaculation (ĭ-jăk′yə-lā′shən) *n.* **1.** The act or process of ejaculating. **2.** A sudden utterance; an exclamation.

eject (ĭ-jĕkt′) *tr.v.* **ejected, ejecting, ejects 1.** To throw out with force; expel: *Active volcanoes eject hot ash and lava.* **2.** To force (someone) to leave; drive out: *The noisy people were ejected from the theater.*

ejection (ĭ-jĕk′shən) *n.* **1.** The act of ejecting or the condition of being ejected: *The ejection of the pilot from the stalled plane saved her.* **2.** Something ejected: *Heavy metal nets were laid over the rock to catch ejections from blasting.*

ejector (ĭ-jĕk′tər) *n.* A person or thing that ejects.

eke (ēk) *tr.v.* **eked, eking, ekes** To get with great effort or strain. Used with *out: The farmers managed to eke out an existence during the drought.*

EKG An abbreviation of: **1.** electrocardiogram. **2.** electrocardiograph.

el. An abbreviation of elevation.

elaborate (ĭ-lăb′ər-ĭt) *adj.* Planned or made with great attention to numerous parts or details; intricate: *We made elaborate plans for the party.* ❖ *v.* (ĭ-lăb′ə-rāt′) **elaborated, elaborating, elaborates** —*tr.* To work out with care and detail; develop thoroughly: *It may take scientists years to elaborate a theory.* —*intr.* To express oneself at greater length or in greater detail; provide further information: *The author elaborated on the difficulty of writing the book.* —**e·lab′o·rate·ly** *adv.* —**e·lab′o·ra′tion** *n.*

élan (ā-län′ *or* ā-län′) *n.* **1.** Enthusiastic vigor and liveliness. **2.** Distinctive style or flair.

eland (ē′lənd) *n., pl.* **eland** also **elands** Either of two large African antelopes having long twisted horns.

elapse (ĭ-lăps′) *intr.v.* **elapsed, elapsing, elapses** To pass; go by: *Months elapsed before I heard from my friend again.*

elastic (ĭ-lăs′tĭk) *adj.* **1.** Easily returning to an original shape after being stretched, compressed, or otherwise deformed: *Rubber bands are very elastic.* **2.** Capable of adapting or being adapted to change or a variety of circumstances; flexible: *an elastic application of the rules.* ❖ *n.* **1.** A fabric woven with strands of rubber or a similar synthetic fiber to make it stretch. **2.** A rubber band. —**e·las′ti·cal·ly** *adv.*

elasticity (ĭ-lă-stĭs′ĭ-tē *or* ē′lă-stĭs′ĭ-tē) *n.* The condition or property of being elastic: *The rubber band broke when it lost its elasticity.*

elate (ĭ-lāt′) *tr.v.* **elated, elating, elates** To fill with great joy or happiness; delight: *The news of victory elated the candidate's supporters.*

elated (ĭ-lā′tĭd) *adj.* Joyful; happy; in high spirits: *the elated feeling of winning a race.* —**e·lat′ed·ly** *adv.*

elation (ĭ-lā′shən) *n.* An intense feeling of happiness or joy: *the elation of succeeding after much effort.*

elbow (ĕl′bō′) *n.* **1a.** The joint or bend between the human forearm and the upper arm. **b.** A corresponding joint in another vertebrate animal. **2.** Something having a bend or sharp angle, such as a length of pipe that has a

sharp bend in it. ❖ *tr.v.* **elbowed, elbowing, elbows 1.** To poke or push with the elbow: *She elbowed me in the side to get my attention.* **2.** To make (one's way) by pushing with the body, especially the elbows: *The detectives elbowed their way through the crowd.*

elbow grease *n. Informal* Strenuous physical effort: *Polishing a car requires elbow grease.*

elbowroom (ĕl′bō-ro͞om′ *or* ĕl′bō-ro͞om′) *n.* Room to move around or function in; ample space: *Their cramped cubicles didn't give the artists enough elbowroom to lay out their work.*

elder[1] (ĕl′dər) *adj.* Born before another; older; senior: *my elder sister; an elder statesman.* ❖ *n.* **1.** An older person: *relies on her elders for guidance and support.* **2.** An older influential person of a family, tribe, or community: *a council of elders.* **3.** One of the officers of certain churches.

elder[2] (ĕl′dər) *n.* The elderberry plant.

WORD HISTORY Elder[1] comes from Old English *eldra*, meaning "older." **Elder**[2] comes from Old English *ellen*, referring to the same plant as in Modern English.

elderberry (ĕl′dər-bĕr′ē) *n.* **1.** Any of various shrubs or small trees having clusters of small white flowers and small red or purplish-black berrylike fruit. **2.** The fruit of certain of these plants, used to make wine or preserves.

elderly (ĕl′dər-lē) *adj.* Approaching old age; rather old: *an elderly person.* ❖ *n.* (*used with a plural verb*) Older people considered as a group. —**eld′er·li·ness** *n.*

eldest (ĕl′dĭst) *adj.* Oldest: *The king's eldest child became the new ruler.*

elect (ĭ-lĕkt′) *tr.v.* **elected, electing, elects 1.** To choose by vote for an office or for membership: *The citizens of each state vote to elect two senators.* **2.** To select from a group of options; choose: *I elected an art course. I elected to take geology, too.* ❖ *adj.* Elected but not yet installed in office: *The governor-elect will take office in January.* ❖ *n.* (*used with a plural verb*) A chosen or privileged group: *one of the elect who have power in the state government.*

election (ĭ-lĕk′shən) *n.* **1.** The act or process of choosing by vote among candidates to fill an office or position: *The election of representatives takes place every two years.* **2.** Selection or choice: *his election of a course in sculpting.*

electioneer (ĭ-lĕk′shə-nîr′) *intr.v.* **electioneered, electioneering, electioneers** To work actively for a particular candidate or party in an election.

elective (ĭ-lĕk′tĭv) *adj.* **1.** Filled or obtained by election: *The presidency is an elective office.* **2.** Chosen by election: *The president is the highest elective official.* **3.** Permitting a choice; not required; optional: *Italian is an elective course in my school.* ❖ *n.* An optional course in school: *My electives are music and woodworking.*

elector (ĭ-lĕk′tər) *n.* **1.** A person who has the right to vote in an election. **2.** A member of the Electoral College of the United States.

electoral (ĭ-lĕk′tər-əl) *adj.* **1.** Relating to electors, especially the members of the Electoral College: *The president had a majority of the electoral vote.* **2.** Relating to election: *electoral reforms that will make it easier to vote.*

Electoral College *n.* A group of electors chosen by the voters to elect the president and vice president of the United States. The number of electors allotted to each state is based on population.

electorate (ĭ-lĕk′tər-ĭt) *n.* All those people qualified to vote in an election: *The United States has a huge electorate, but many people do not vote.*

Electra (ĭ-lĕk′trə) *n.* In Greek mythology, a daughter of Agamemnon and Clytemnestra, who, with her brother Orestes, avenged her father's murder by killing her mother and stepfather.

electric (ĭ-lĕk′trĭk) *adj.* **1.** also **electrical** (ĭ-lĕk′trĭ-kəl) Relating to, producing, or operated by electricity: *electric power; an electrical appliance.* **2.** Amplified by an electronic device: *an electric guitar.* **3.** Charged with emotion; exciting; thrilling: *the electric feeling of watching a very close race.* —**e·lec′tri·cal·ly** *adv.*

electrical engineering *n.* The branch of engineering that deals with the practical uses of electricity and their effects. —**electrical engineer** *n.*

electric blanket *n.* A blanket fitted with an electric heating element and a control for regulating its temperature.

electric chair *n.* **1.** A device used to electrocute a person sentenced to death by restraining that person in a chair and applying a deadly electrical current to the body. **2.** Execution by electrocution.

electric eel *n.* A South American freshwater fish that resembles an eel and can produce a powerful electric discharge, which it uses to stun prey and to defend itself.

electric eye *n.* An electrical device that detects variations in the intensity of a light source by means of a photoelectric cell. If something obscures or blocks the light, the electric eye can activate or turn off another device (such as an alarm or mechanical door).

electric field *n.* A region of space characterized by the existence of a force generated by electric charge.

electrician (ĭ-lĕk-trĭsh′ən *or* ē′lĕk-trĭsh′ən) *n.* A person who installs, maintains, repairs, or operates electric equipment and electrical circuits.

electricity (ĭ-lĕk-trĭs′ĭ-tē *or* ē′lĕk-trĭs′ĭ-tē) *n.* **1.** The collection of physical effects resulting from the behavior and interactions of electrons and protons. Particles with like charge repel each other. Particles with opposite charges attract each other. **2.** Electric current used as a source of power: *Electricity lights our homes.* **3.** Emotional excitement: *the electricity among the fans during the last period of the game.*

electrify (ĭ-lĕk′trə-fī′) *tr.v.* **electrified, electrifying, electrifies** **1.** To charge with electricity: *throw the switch to electrify a circuit.* **2a.** To wire or equip for the use of electric power: *electrify a building.* **b.** To supply with electric power: *The new power station made it possible to electrify the whole valley.* **3.** To thrill, startle, or shock: *The goalie's play electrified the audience.* —**e·lec′tri·fi·ca′tion** (ĭ-lĕk′-trə-fĭ-kā′shən) *n.*

electro– or **electr–** A prefix that means: **1.** Electric: *electromagnet.* **2.** Electric or electrically: *electrocute.*

electrocardiogram (ĭ-lĕk′trō-kär′dē-ə-grăm′) *n.* **1.** A record of the electrical activity of the heart made by an electrocardiograph, used especially in the diagnosis of disease. **2.** The procedure performed to produce such a record.

electrocardiograph (ĭ-lĕk′trō-kär′dē-ə-grăf′) *n.* An instrument that records the electrical activity of the heart, usually in the form of a curve traced on paper or on a computer monitor.

electrochemistry (ĭ-lĕk′trō-kĕm′ĭ-strē) *n.* The study of chemical reactions that involve electricity, especially reactions that occur when an electric current flows through a solution. —**e·lec′tro·chem′i·cal** *adj.*

electrocute (ĭ-lĕk′trə-kyōōt′) *tr.v.* **electrocuted, electrocuting, electrocutes** To kill or execute with electricity:

The workers shut off the power to avoid any danger of being electrocuted.

electrocution (ĭ-lĕk′trə-kyōō′shən) *n.* Death caused by an electric current.

electrode (ĭ-lĕk′trōd′) *n.* A conductor through which an electric current enters or exits a liquid or gas during electrolysis.

electroencephalogram (ĭ-lĕk′trō-ĕn-sĕf′ə-lə-grăm′) *n.* **1.** A record of the electrical activity of the brain made by an electroencephalograph, used especially in the diagnosis of disease. **2.** The procedure performed to produce such a record.

electroencephalograph (ĭ-lĕk′trō-ĕn-sĕf′ə-lə-grăf′) *n.* An instrument that records the electrical activity of the brain, usually in the form of curved lines on a paper chart or a computer monitor.

electrolysis (ĭ-lĕk-trŏl′ĭ-sĭs) *n.* **1.** Chemical change, especially decomposition, produced in a chemical compound that breaks apart into ions when an electric current is passed through it. **2.** Destruction of living tissue, such as the roots of hairs, by an electric current.

electrolyte (ĭ-lĕk′trə-līt′) *n.* **1.** A substance that when dissolved or melted becomes electrically conductive by breaking apart into ions. **2.** Any of various ions, such as sodium, potassium, or chloride, required by cells to regulate the electric charge and flow of water molecules across the cell membrane.

electrolytic (ĭ-lĕk′trə-lĭt′ĭk) *adj.* **1.** Relating to electrolysis. **2.** Relating to or using electrolytes.

electrolyze (ĭ-lĕk′trə-līz′) *tr.v.* **electrolyzed, electrolyzing, electrolyzes** To cause to decompose by electrolysis.

electromagnet (ĭ-lĕk′trō-măg′nĭt) *n.* A magnet that consists of a coil of insulated wire wrapped around an iron core that becomes magnetized only when an electric current flows through the wire.

electromagnetic (ĭ-lĕk′trō-măg-nĕt′ĭk) *adj.* Relating to electromagnetism.

electromagnetic radiation *n.* Energy that moves through space and matter both in the form of electromagnetic waves and in the form of a stream of particles called photons.

electromagnetic spectrum *n.* The entire range of electromagnetic radiation, consisting of radio waves (which have the longest wavelengths and lowest frequencies), microwaves, infrared waves, visible light, ultraviolet rays, x-rays, and gamma rays (which have the shortest wavelengths and highest frequencies).

electromagnetic wave *n.* A wave of energy consisting of electric and magnetic fields that regularly swing back and forth around a central point as they move in a given direction. Radio waves, light waves, and x-rays are electromagnetic waves.

electromagnetism (ĭ-lĕk′trō-măg′nĭ-tĭz′əm) *n.* **1.** Magnetism produced by electric charge in motion. **2.** The scientific study of electricity and magnetism and the relationships between them.

electromotive (ĭ-lĕk′trō-mō′tĭv) *adj.* Relating to or producing an electric current.

electromotive force *n.* The energy that is converted from chemical, mechanical, or other forms of energy into electrical energy in a battery or dynamo. Electromotive force is measured in volts.

electron (ĭ-lĕk′trŏn′) *n.* A stable subatomic particle with a negative electric charge equal in strength to the positive charge of a proton. All atoms have at least one electron orbiting the nucleus. Electrons can move freely through space and can flow through a conducting material in an electric current.

electronic (ĭ-lĕk-trŏn′ĭk or ē′lĕk-trŏn′ĭk) *adj.* **1.** Relating to or produced by means of electronics: *an electronic book.* **2.** Relating to, done with, or controlled by a computer or computer network. **3.** Relating to electrons. —**e·lec·tron′i·cal·ly** *adv.*

electronics (ĭ-lĕk′trŏn′ĭks or ē′lĕk-trŏn′ĭks) *n.* **1.** *(used with a singular verb)* The science and technology concerned with the study of electrons in motion and the development of devices operated by a controlled flow of electrons, especially by means of integrated circuits: *Electronics has made the computer possible.* **2.** *(used with a plural verb)* Electronic devices and systems: *Most aircraft have very sophisticated electronics.*

electron microscope *n.* A microscope that uses electrons instead of visible light to produce images of objects that are too small to be seen or studied with an ordinary microscope.

electron tube *n.* A sealed glass tube containing either a vacuum or a small amount of gas, in which electrons flow between two or more electrodes.

electron volt *n.* A unit used to measure the energy of subatomic particles. It is equal to the energy gained by an electron that is accelerated until its electric potential is one volt greater than it was before being accelerated.

electroplate (ĭ-lĕk′trə-plāt′) *tr.v.* **electroplated, electroplating, electroplates** To cover or coat with a thin layer of metal by means of electrolysis.

electroscope (ĭ-lĕk′trə-skōp′) *n.* An instrument used to detect electric charges and to determine whether they are positive or negative.

electrostatic (ĭ-lĕk′trō-stăt′ĭk) *adj.* Relating to, produced by, or caused by stationary electric charges.

electrostatic generator *n.* A machine that generates high voltages by accumulating large quantities of static electric charges.

electrothermal (ĭ-lĕk′trō-thûr′məl) *adj.* **1.** Relating to or involving both electricity and heat. **2.** Relating to the production of heat by electricity.

elegance (ĕl′ĭ-gəns) *n.* **1.** Refinement, grace, and beauty in appearance or behavior: *The old castle still had signs of past elegance in its great staircase.* **2.** Something that is elegant: *Expensive jewelry is an elegance few can afford.*

elegant (ĕl′ĭ-gənt) *adj.* Marked by or showing elegance: *an elegant restaurant.* —**el′e·gant·ly** *adv.*

elegiac (ĕl′ə-jī′ək) *adj.* Relating to or involving elegy.

elegize (ĕl′ə-jīz′) *v.* **elegized, elegizing, elegizes** —*intr.* To compose an elegy. —*tr.* To compose an elegy about.

elegy (ĕl′ə-jē) *n., pl.* **elegies** A poem or song that expresses sorrow, especially one composed to lament a person who has died.

element (ĕl′ə-mənt) *n.* **1.** A part of a whole, especially a fundamental or essential part: *The story contains elements of a detective novel and a romance.* **2. elements** The basic principles: *Composers must learn the elements of music.* **3.** A substance whose atoms always have the same number of protons in their nuclei. An element cannot be broken down into simpler substances by chemical means. See the **Periodic Table** of elements on pages 706–707. Elements 113, 115, 117, and 118 have been produced by scientists but have not yet been officially

named. **4.** In mathematics, a member of a set. **5. elements** The forces of the weather, especially the cold, wind, and rain: *The rescuers braved the elements to hunt for the lost children.* **6.** An environment to which a person or thing is suited or adapted: *The sea was as much the sailors' element as the land.*

elemental (ĕl′ə-mĕn′tl) *adj.* **1.** Relating to an element. **2.** Relating to or resembling a force of nature in power or effect: *the elemental fury of the hurricane.* **3.** Fundamental; basic: *Most students are familiar with the elemental concepts of physics.*

elementary (ĕl′ə-mĕn′tə-rē or ĕl′ə-mĕn′trē) *adj.* Relating to or involving the basic or simplest aspects of a subject: *an elementary math textbook.*

elementary particle *n.* Any of the smallest known units of matter, such as quarks and neutrinos. Elementary particles are smaller than atoms, are not made up of smaller units, and cannot be broken apart by collisions with other particles.

elementary school *n.* A school attended for the first four to eight years of a child's formal classroom instruction, often including kindergarten.

elephant (ĕl′ə-fənt) *n.* Any of several large mammals of Asia and Africa having thick, almost hairless skin, a long flexible trunk, and long tusks.

elephantine (ĕl′ə-făn′tēn or ĕl′ə-făn′tīn′) *adj.* Extremely large: *elephantine portions; an elephantine problem.*

elevate (ĕl′ə-vāt′) *tr.v.* **elevated, elevating, elevates 1.** To raise to a higher place or position; lift up: *A nurse elevated the head of the bed so the patient could sit up to read.* **2.** To promote to a higher rank: *The publisher elevated him to editor-in-chief.* **3.** To bring to a higher moral, cultural, or intellectual level: *By using its melody in a symphony the composer elevated the folk song to heights of great beauty.*

elevated (ĕl′ə-vā′tĭd) *adj.* **1.** Raised or placed above a given level: *the elevated speaker's platform.* **2.** Increased in amount or degree: *an elevated temperature.* **3.** Formal; lofty: *an elevated style of prose.* ❖ *n.* An elevated railway.

elevated railway *n.* A railway that operates on a track raised high enough so that vehicles and pedestrians can pass beneath.

elevation (ĕl′ə-vā′shən) *n.* **1.** An elevated place or position: *That hill is the highest elevation for miles around.* **2.** The height to which something is elevated, especially the height above sea level: *The ridge rises to an elevation of 3,300 feet.* **3.** The act of elevating or the condition of being elevated: *Elevation to a high position in government is a great honor.*

elevator (ĕl′ə-vā′tər) *n.* **1.** A car, platform, or cage raised or lowered in a vertical shaft to carry freight or people, as from floor to floor in a building. **2.** A grain elevator. **3.** A movable piece attached to a horizontal part of an airplane tail used to turn the nose of the craft upward or downward.

eleven (ĭ-lĕv′ən) *n.* **1.** The number, written 11, that is equal to 10 + 1. **2.** The 11th in a set or sequence.

eleventh (ĭ-lĕv′ənth) *n.* **1.** The ordinal number matching the number 11 in a series. **2.** One of 11 equal parts.

eleventh hour *n.* The latest possible time: *They waited until the eleventh hour to buy tickets for the concert.*

elf (ĕlf) *n., pl.* **elves** (ĕlvz) A tiny, often mischievous creature supposed to have magical powers.

elfin (ĕl′fĭn) *adj.* Relating to or suggestive of an elf or elves: *a mischievous, elfin smile.*

elfish (ĕl′fĭsh) or **elvish** (ĕl′vĭsh) *adj.* Elfin.

elicit (ĭ-lĭs′ĭt) *tr.v.* **elicited, eliciting, elicits** To bring out; draw forth; evoke: *By clever questioning the lawyer elicited the truth from the witness.*

elide (ĭ-līd′) *tr.v.* **elided, eliding, elides** **1a.** To omit or slur over (a syllable, for example) in pronunciation. **b.** To strike out (something written). **2a.** To eliminate or leave out of consideration. **b.** To cut short; abridge.

eligible (ĕl′ĭ-jə-bəl) *adj.* Fit or worthy to be chosen; qualified or suited: *Eligible voters may go to the polls to vote on election day.* —**el′i·gi·bil′i·ty** *n.*

eliminate (ĭ-lĭm′ə-nāt′) *tr.v.* **eliminated, eliminating, eliminates** **1.** To get rid of; remove: *The company saved money by eliminating several positions.* **2.** To leave out or omit from consideration; reject: *The police eliminated two of the four suspects in the case.* **3.** To rid the body of (waste products); excrete.

elimination (ĭ-lĭm′ə-nā′shən) *n.* The act of eliminating or the state of being eliminated: *elimination of language barriers; elimination from the contest.*

elite or **élite** (ĭ-lēt′ or ā-lēt′) *n. (used with a plural verb)* **1.** Those considered as the best, superior, or wealthiest members of a society or group: *the elite of the sports world.* **2.** A small and privileged group.

elitism or **élitism** (ĭ-lē′tĭz′əm or ā-lē′tĭz′əm) *n.* **1.** The belief that certain people in a group deserve special treatment because they are superior to others. **2.** Rule or domination by an elite. —**e·lit′ist** *adj. & n.*

elixir (ĭ-lĭk′sər) *n.* **1.** A sweetened and flavored solution of alcohol and water containing one or more medicinal substances. **2.** In medieval alchemy, a substance believed to have the power to change base metals into gold. **3.** A substance believed to maintain life indefinitely. **4.** A substance believed to have the power to cure all ills.

Elizabethan (ĭ-lĭz′ə-bē′thən or ĭ-lĭz′ə-bĕth′ən) *adj.* Relating to or characteristic of the reign of Queen Elizabeth I of England, from 1558 to 1603: *Elizabethan style of dress; Elizabethan drama.*

elk (ĕlk) *n., pl.* **elk** or **elks** A large reddish-brown or grayish deer of western North America, having long, branching antlers in the male.

ell[1] (ĕl) *n.* A wing of a building at right angles to the main structure.

ell[2] (ĕl) *n.* **1.** An English measure of length equal to 45 inches (114 centimeters). **2.** Any of several other similar historical units of measure.

WORD HISTORY Ell[1] either comes from its resemblance to the shape of the capital letter L or is short for *elbow.* **Ell**[2] comes from Old English *eln,* a unit of measurement equal to the length from the elbow to the tip of the middle finger.

---

ellipse (ĭ-lĭps′) *n.* A figure that forms a closed curve shaped like an oval with both ends alike. The sum of the distances of any point on an ellipse from two fixed points remains constant.

ellipsis (ĭ-lĭp′sĭs) *n., pl.* **ellipses** (ĭ-lĭp′sēz) **1.** The omission of a word or phrase needed to make a sentence grammatically complete but not necessary to understanding. **2.** A mark or series of marks (for example, . . .) used in writing or printing to show the omission of a word or phrase.

elliptical (ĭ-lĭp′tĭ-kəl) or **elliptic** (ĭ-lĭp′tĭk) *adj.* **1.** Relating to or shaped like an ellipse: *an elliptical window over a door.* **2.** Containing or characterized by ellipsis: *an elliptical sentence.* —**el·lip′ti·cal·ly** *adv.*

elm (ĕlm) *n.* **1.** Any of various tall trees having arching or

curving branches. **2.** The hard strong wood of such a tree.

El Niño (ĕl nēn′yō) *n.* A warming of the surface water of the eastern and central Pacific Ocean, occurring every two to seven years, killing fish and plankton and causing unusual weather patterns.

elocution (ĕl′ə-kyōō′shən) *n.* The art of public speaking that emphasizes gestures and vocal delivery.

elongate (ĭ-lông′gāt′) *tr. & intr.v.* **elongated, elongating, elongates** To make or grow longer; lengthen: *The artist often elongates faces and figures in cartoons.* ❖ *adj.* or **elongated** Long and thin; lengthened; extended.

elongation (ĭ-lông′gā′shən or ē′lông-gā′shən) *n.* Something that elongates; an extension.

elope (ĭ-lōp′) *intr.v.* **eloped, eloping, elopes** To run away with a lover, especially with the intention of getting married. —**e·lope′ment** *n.*

eloquence (ĕl′ə-kwəns) *n.* Persuasive, moving, or graceful speaking or writing: *His eloquence brought many to tears.*

eloquent (ĕl′ə-kwənt) *adj.* Capable of or characterized by eloquence: *an eloquent spokesperson for the cause; an eloquent appeal for justice.* —**el′o·quent·ly** *adv.*

else (ĕls) *adj.* **1.** Other; different: *Somebody else will see you today.* **2.** Additional; more: *Would you like something else to eat?* ❖ *adv.* **1.** Differently: *How else could it have been done?* **2.** If not; otherwise: *Run, or else you will be caught in the rain.* ◆ **or else 1.** Used to indicate an alternative: *We either need to eat leftovers or else buy more food.* **2.** Used to indicate negative consequences if something isn't done: *We need to pay the bill, or else the electricity will be shut off.* **3.** Used after a command or demand to make a threat: *Be there on time, or else!*

elsewhere (ĕls′wâr′) *adv.* In or to a different or another place: *We decided to go elsewhere.*

elucidate (ĭ-lōō′sĭ-dāt′) *tr.v.* **elucidated, elucidating, elucidates** To make clear or plain; explain: *elucidated the meaning of the poem.* —**e·lu′ci·da′tion** *n.*

elude (ĭ-lōōd′) *tr.v.* **eluded, eluding, eludes 1.** To avoid or escape from, as by skill, cunning, or daring: *The fox eluded the hunters.* **2.** To be not remembered or understood by: *Very small details often elude us.*

elusive (ĭ-lōō′sĭv) *adj.* **1.** Difficult to catch or seize: *an elusive butterfly.* **2.** Difficult or impossible to attain: *an elusive goal.* **3.** Difficult to remember or understand: *an elusive metaphor.* —**e·lu′sive·ly** *adv.*

elver (ĕl′vər) *n.* A young eel.

elves (ĕlvz) *n.* Plural of **elf.**

elvish (ĕl′vĭsh) *adj.* Variant of **elfish.**

Elysian Fields *pl.n.* In Greek mythology, the abode of the blessed after death.

elytron (ĕl′ĭ-trŏn′) *n., pl.* **elytra** (ĕl′ĭ-trə) Either of the thickened forewings of a beetle that protect the thin hind wings used in flight.

em– Variant of **en–.**

'em (əm) *pron. Informal* Them.

emaciated (ĭ-mā′shē-ā′tĭd) *adj.* Very thin, as from disease or starvation: *an emaciated stray dog.*

email or **e-mail** (ē′māl′) *n.* **1.** A system for sending and receiving messages electronically over a computer network: *sent the information by email.* **2.** A message or messages sent or received by such a system: *received a lot of email while on vacation.* ❖ *tr.v.* **emailed, emailing, emails** or **e-mailed, e-mailing, e-mails** To send (a message) by such a system.

emanate (ĕm′ə-nāt′) *intr. & tr.v.* **emanated, emanating,**

emanates To come or send forth, as from a source: *The sound of a piano emanated from the house. The stove emanated a steady heat.*

emanation (ĕm′ə-nā′shən) *n.* **1.** The act or an instance of emanating: *the emanation of heat from a fire.* **2.** Something that emanates from a source: *steamy emanations from a kettle of boiling water.*

emancipate (ĭ-măn′sə-pāt′) *tr.v.* **emancipated, emancipating, emancipates** **1.** To free (someone) from bondage, oppression, or restraint; liberate. **2.** To release (a child) from the legal control of parents or a guardian. —**e·man′ci·pa′tor** *n.*

emancipation (ĭ-măn′sə-pā′shən) *n.* The act or an instance of emancipating or the condition of being emancipated: *The emancipation of the slaves happened during the Civil War.*

Emancipation Proclamation *n.* A proclamation issued by President Abraham Lincoln on January 1, 1863, freeing slaves in those areas of the Confederacy still at war against the United States.

emasculate (ĭ-măs′kyə-lāt′) *tr.v.* **emasculated, emasculating, emasculates** **1.** To castrate. **2.** To deprive of strength; weaken. —**e·mas′cu·la′tion** *n.*

embalm (ĕm-bäm′) *tr.v.* **embalmed, embalming, embalms** To treat (a corpse) with substances that prevent or slow decay. —**em·balm′er** *n.*

embankment (ĕm-băngk′mənt) *n.* A mound of earth or stone built up to hold back water or to support a roadway.

embargo (ĕm-bär′gō) *n., pl.* **embargoes** **1.** An order by a government prohibiting merchant ships from entering or leaving its ports. **2.** A prohibition by a government on certain or all trade with a foreign nation. **3.** A prohibition; a ban. ❖ *tr.v.* **embargoed, embargoing, embargoes** To place an embargo on.

embark (ĕm-bärk′) *intr.v.* **embarked, embarking, embarks** **1.** To go aboard an aircraft or ship. **2.** To set out on a venture; begin: *embark on a campaign to clean up the environment.* —**em′bar·ka′tion** (ĕm′bär-kā′shən) *n.*

embarrass (ĕm-băr′əs) *tr.v.* **embarrassed, embarrassing, embarrasses** **1.** To cause to feel self-conscious or ill at ease; disconcert: *Forgetting her name embarrassed me.* **2.** To hinder with obstacles or difficulties.

embarrassing (ĕm-băr′ə-sĭng) *adj.* Causing embarrassment: *an embarrassing remark.*

embarrassment (ĕm-băr′əs-mənt) *n.* **1.** The condition of being embarrassed: *My face turned red with embarrassment.* **2.** Something that embarrasses: *Their argument in public was an embarrassment.*

embassy (ĕm′bə-sē) *n., pl.* **embassies** **1.** A building containing the offices of an ambassador and staff. **2.** The position, function, or assignment of an ambassador. **3.** A staff of diplomatic representatives headed by an ambassador.

embattled (ĕm-băt′ld) *adj.* **1.** Prepared or fortified for battle or engaged in battle: *the embattled countries of Europe during World War II.* **2.** Beset with attackers, criticism, or controversy: *an embattled candidate fighting to win election.*

embed (ĕm-bĕd′) *tr.v.* **embedded, embedding, embeds** **1.** To fix firmly in a surrounding mass: *The splinter was deeply embedded in my finger.* **2.** To cause to be an integral part of a surrounding whole: *a newcomer who embedded herself in her town's social life.* **3.** To assign (a journalist)

to travel with a military unit during an armed conflict.

embellish (ĕm-bĕl′ĭsh) *tr.v.* **embellished, embellishing, embellishes** **1.** To make beautiful, as by ornamentation; decorate: *embellish a tablecloth with fine embroidery.* **2.** To add fanciful or fictitious details to: *embellish a story with some invented characters.* —**em·bel′lish·ment** *n.*

ember (ĕm′bər) *n.* **1.** A piece of glowing coal or wood, as in a dying fire. **2. ember** The smoldering coal or ash of a dying fire: *Embers still glowed in the fireplace.*

embezzle (ĕm-bĕz′əl) *tr.v.* **embezzled, embezzling, embezzles** To take (money that does not belong to one but that one has been entrusted with) for one's own use: *The bank president was caught embezzling funds.* —**em·bez′zle·ment** *n.* —**em·bez′zler** *n.*

embitter (ĕm-bĭt′ər) *tr.v.* **embittered, embittering, embitters** To arouse bitter feelings in.

emblazon (ĕm-blā′zən) *tr.v.* **emblazoned, emblazoning, emblazons** **1.** To ornament (a surface) richly with prominent markings: *An embroidered coat of arms emblazoned the tapestry.* **2.** To make brilliant with colors: *Fireworks emblazoned the sky.* **3.** To celebrate; make illustrious.

emblem (ĕm′bləm) *n.* An object or representation that functions as a symbol: *The bald eagle is the emblem of the United States.*

emblematic (ĕm′blə-măt′ĭk) or **emblematical** (ĕm′blə-măt′ĭ-kəl) *adj.* Relating to or serving as an emblem; symbolic: *The dove is emblematic of peace.*

embody (ĕm-bŏd′ē) *tr.v.* **embodied, embodying, embodies** **1.** To give a bodily form to; personify: *A hero embodies our ideal of bravery.* **2.** To make part of a system or whole; incorporate: *The US Constitution embodies a plan for a democracy.* —**em·bod′i·ment** *n.*

embolden (ĕm-bōl′dən) *tr.v.* **emboldened, emboldening, emboldens** To foster boldness or courage in; encourage: *Our many supporters emboldened us to present a list of demands.*

embolism (ĕm′bə-lĭz′əm) *n.* The obstruction of a blood vessel by an embolus.

embolus (ĕm′bə-ləs) *n., pl.* **emboli** (ĕm′bə-lī′) A substance, such as an air bubble or blood clot, that is carried in the bloodstream and leads to blockage of a blood vessel.

emboss (ĕm-bôs′) *tr.v.* **embossed, embossing, embosses** **1.** To mold or carve in relief: *emboss a head and lettering on a coin.* **2.** To decorate with or as if with a raised design: *emboss a leather belt.*

embouchure (äm′bŏŏ-shŏŏr′) *n.* **1.** The mouthpiece of a woodwind or brass instrument. **2.** The manner in which the lips and tongue are applied to such a mouthpiece.

embrace (ĕm-brās′) *v.* **embraced, embracing, embraces** —*tr.* **1.** To clasp or hold close with the arms, usually as a sign of affection; hug: *embrace a child.* **2.** To enclose or surround: *The warm water of the pool embraced us.* **3.** To take up willingly; adopt eagerly: *embraced the hectic life of the big city.* **4.** To include as part of something broader: *Her education embraced all the sciences.* —*intr.* To join in an embrace: *The twins embraced at their reunion.* ❖ *n.* **1.** The act of holding close with the arms; a hug. **2.** Eager acceptance: *her embrace of college life.*

embrasure (ĕm-brā′zhər) *n.* **1.** An opening in a thick wall for a window or door. **2.** A flared opening for a gun in a wall or parapet.

embroider (ĕm-broi′dər) *v.* **embroidered, embroidering, embroiders** —*tr.* **1.** To ornament with needlework: *embroider a pillowcase.* **2.** To make by means of needlework:

embroider a design on a handkerchief. **3.** To add imaginary or fanciful details to: *The author embroidered the general's biography.* *—intr.* **1.** To make needlework. **2.** To add embellishments or fanciful details.

embroidery (ĕm-broi′də-rē) *n., pl.* **embroideries 1.** The act or art of embroidering. **2.** A piece of embroidered fabric.

embroil (ĕm-broil′) *tr.v.* **embroiled, embroiling, embroils 1.** To involve in argument or contention: *embroiled the candidate in a debate.* **2.** To throw into confusion or disorder; entangle.

embryo (ĕm′brē-ō′) *n., pl.* **embryos 1.** An animal in its earliest stages of development, especially before it has reached a distinctively recognizable form. **2.** A plant in its earliest stages of development, especially a partly developed plant within a seed. **3.** An early or beginning stage: *an idea that was the embryo of a short story.*

embryologist (ĕm′brē-ŏl′ə-jĭst) *n.* A scientist who specializes in embryology.

embryology (ĕm′brē-ŏl′ə-jē) *n.* The branch of biology that deals with embryos and their development. **—em′-bry·o·log′i·cal** (ĕm′brē-ə-lŏj′ĭ-kəl) *adj.*

embryonic (ĕm′brē-ŏn′ĭk) *adj.* **1.** Relating to an embryo: *embryonic membranes.* **2.** In an early stage of development: *an embryonic democracy.*

emcee (ĕm′sē′) *n.* A master of ceremonies. ❖ *tr. & intr.v.* **emceed, emceeing, emcees** To serve as master of ceremonies of: *That announcer emcees a quiz program.*

emend (ĭ-mĕnd′) *tr.v.* **emended, emending, emends** To make corrections or improvements to (a text): *emended the preface so that it reads more smoothly.*

emendation (ĭ-mĕn′dā′shən *or* ē′mĕn-dā′shən) *n.* **1.** The act of emending. **2.** A change made with the purpose of improving: *made emendations to the text.*

emerald (ĕm′ər-əld *or* ĕm′rəld) *n.* **1.** A brilliant green transparent form of beryl that is used as a gem. **2.** A strong yellowish-green color. ❖ *adj.* Of a strong yellowish-green color.

emerge (ĭ-mûrj′) *intr.v.* **emerged, emerging, emerges 1.** To move out or away from a surrounding fluid, covering, or shelter: *Sea mammals must emerge to breathe. The leopard emerged from the forest.* **2.** To come forth from obscurity: *The new nation soon emerged as an important power.* **3.** To become known or evident: *The truth emerged at the hearing.*

emergence (ĭ-mûr′jəns) *n.* The act or process of emerging: *the emergence of a butterfly from a chrysalis; emergence of the truth under questioning.*

emergency (ĭ-mûr′jən-sē) *n., pl.* **emergencies** A serious situation or occurrence that happens suddenly and calls for immediate action: *A fire extinguisher is kept in the hall for use in case of an emergency.*

emergency medical technician *n.* A person who is trained to provide medical care in emergency situations and during transportation of patients to a hospital.

emergency room *n.* The section of a hospital or clinic where sick or injured people who need immediate treatment are admitted and examined.

emergent (ĭ-mûr′jənt) *adj.* Coming into existence, view, or attention: *an emergent political leadership.*

emerita (ĭ-mĕr′ĭ-tə) *adj.* Retired but retaining an honorary title corresponding to that held immediately before retirement. Used of a woman: *a professor emerita.*

emeritus (ĭ-mĕr′ĭ-təs) *adj.* Retired but retaining an honorary title corresponding to that held immediately before retirement: *a professor emeritus.*

emery (ĕm′ə-rē *or* ĕm′rē) *n.* A dark mineral that is very hard and is used in a crushed or powdered form for grinding and polishing.

emetic (ĭ-mĕt′ĭk) *adj.* Causing vomiting. ❖ *n.* An emetic drug or medicine.

EMF An abbreviation of electromotive force.

emigrant (ĕm′ĭ-grənt) *n.* A person who emigrates: *Many emigrants from Europe traveled to North America by ship.*

emigrate (ĕm′ĭ-grāt′) *intr.v.* **emigrated, emigrating, emigrates** To leave one country or region to settle in another: *My ancestors emigrated from Italy in the early 1900s.* **—em′i·gra′tion** (ĕm′ĭ-grā′shən) *n.*

USAGE The words **emigrate** and **immigrate** are both used of people involved in a permanent move, generally across a political boundary. *Emigrate* refers to the point of departure: *He emigrated from Germany* (that is, left Germany). By contrast, *immigrate* refers to the new location: *The promise of prosperity in the United States encouraged many people to immigrate* (that is, move to the United States).

émigré (ĕm′ĭ-grā′) *n.* A person who has left a native country, especially for political reasons.

eminence (ĕm′ə-nəns) *n.* **1.** A position of great distinction or superiority: *She rose to eminence as a scientist.* **2.** A rise of ground; a hill. **3.** also **Eminence** A title and form of address for a cardinal in the Roman Catholic Church: *Your Eminence.*

eminent (ĕm′ə-nənt) *adj.* Well-known and respected, especially for achievement in a particular field: *an eminent surgeon.* See Synonyms at **famous. —em′i·nent·ly** *adv.*

eminent domain *n.* The power of a government to take private property for public use without the owner's consent, provided just compensation is given.

emir also **amir** (ĭ-mîr′ *or* ā-mîr′) *n.* A prince, chieftain, or governor, especially in the Middle East.

emirate (ĕm′-ər-ĭt *or* ĭ-mîr′ĭt) *n.* **1.** The office of an emir. **2.** The nation or territory ruled by an emir.

emissary (ĕm′ĭ-sĕr′ē) *n., pl.* **emissaries** A person sent on a mission as the representative of another: *sent an emissary to discuss the new trade agreement.*

emission (ĭ-mĭsh′ən) *n.* **1.** The act or process of emitting: *The factory worked to reduce the emission of dangerous fumes and smoke.* **2.** Something that is emitted: *harmful emissions from cars.*

emissive (ĭ-mĭs′ĭv) *adj.* Emitting or tending to emit; radiating: *radio signals from a highly emissive star.*

emit (ĭ-mĭt′) *tr.v.* **emitted, emitting, emits 1.** To release or send out (matter or energy): *Volcanoes emit lava and hot gases.* **2.** To utter; express: *The baby emitted a cry.* **—e·mit′ter** *n.*

emollient (ĭ-mŏl′yənt) *adj.* Softening and soothing, especially to the skin: *an emollient cream.* ❖ *n.* Something that softens and soothes the skin: *Various oils act as emollients.*

emolument (ĭ-mŏl′yə-mənt) *n.* Payment for an office or employment; compensation.

emoticon (ĭ-mō′tĭ-kŏn′) *n.* A series of characters and punctuation marks used to indicate an emotion or attitude, especially in online communication. For example, :-) is an emoticon indicating intended humor.

emotion (ĭ-mō′shən) *n.* **1.** A mental state arising on its own rather than through conscious effort; a feeling: *Envy is a powerful emotion.* See Synonyms at **feeling. 2.** Such mental states or the qualities associated with them, especially in contrast to reason: *a decision based on emotion rather than logic; a speech delivered with emotion.*

emotional (ĭ-mō′shə-nəl) *adj.* **1.** Relating to emotion: *an emotional conflict.* **2.** Easily affected with or stirred by emotion: *an emotional person who is easily upset.* **3.** Arousing or intended to arouse the emotions: *an emotional piece of music.* **4.** Marked by or showing emotion: *their emotional reaction.* —**e·mo′tion·al·ly** *adv.*

empathy (ĕm′pə-thē) *n.* The ability to understand and share the feelings of someone else: *empathy between parent and child.*

emperor (ĕm′pər-ər) *n.* A man who is the ruler of an empire.

emphasis (ĕm′fə-sĭs) *n., pl.* **emphases** (ĕm′fə-sēz′) **1.** Special forcefulness of expression that gives importance or significance: *a lecture on computers with an emphasis on the Internet.* **2.** Prominence given to a syllable, word, or phrase.

emphasize (ĕm′fə-sīz′) *tr.v.* **emphasized, emphasizing, emphasizes** To give emphasis to; stress: *emphasize an idea by repeating it in several different ways.*

emphatic (ĕm-făt′ĭk) *adj.* **1.** Expressed or performed with emphasis: *an emphatic shake of the head.* **2.** Forceful and definite in expression or action: *an emphatic person.* **3.** Standing out in a striking way: *The party was an emphatic success.* —**em·phat′i·cal·ly** *adv.*

emphysema (ĕm′fĭ-sē′mə *or* ĕm′fĭ-zē′mə) *n.* A condition in which the small air sacs of the lungs become stretched and lose their elasticity, so that one becomes out of breath quickly.

empire (ĕm′pīr′) *n.* **1.** A group of territories or nations headed by a single supreme authority: *the empire of Alexander the Great.* **2.** The territories included in such a group. **3.** Imperial or imperialistic power and authority. **4.** An extensive enterprise under a unified authority: *a publishing empire of newspapers and magazines.*

empirical (ĕm-pîr′ĭ-kəl) *adj.* Relying on or derived from observation or experiment rather than theory: *empirical results that support the hypothesis.* —**em·pir′i·cal·ly** *adv.*

empiricism (ĕm-pîr′ĭ-sĭz′əm) *n.* **1.** The view that experience, especially of the senses, is the only source of knowledge. **2.** The employment of methods based on experience, experiment, and observation. —**em·pir′i·cist** *n.*

emplacement (ĕm-plās′mənt) *n.* A prepared position for heavy guns, as a mounting or platform, for example.

employ (ĕm-ploi′) *tr.v.* **employed, employing, employs** **1.** To engage the services of; put to work: *The store employs many salespeople.* **2.** To put to use or service: *They employed all their skills to build the bridge.* **3.** To devote (time, for example) to an activity or purpose: *He employed his time collecting antiques* ❖ *n.* The condition of being employed: *in the employ of the government.* —**em·ploy′a·ble** *adj.*

employee (ĕm-ploi′ē *or* ĕm′ploi-ē′) *n.* A person who receives money or other compensation in exchange for work.

employer (ĕm-ploi′ər) *n.* A person or business that employs people for financial or other compensation.

employment (ĕm-ploi′mənt) *n.* **1.** The act of employing or the condition of being employed: *the employment of new technology in industry.* **2.** The work in which a person is engaged; an occupation: *employment as a carpenter.*

emporium (ĕm-pôr′ē-əm) *n., pl.* **emporiums** or **emporia**

(ĕm-pôr′ē-ə) **1.** A place where various goods are bought and sold; a marketplace. **2.** A large retail store or place of business.

empower (ĕm-pou′ər) *tr.v.* **empowered, empowering, empowers 1.** To invest with power, especially legal power or official authority: *The state legislature empowered the governor to levy new taxes.* **2.** To equip or supply with an ability; enable: *Getting an education empowered them in the selection of a career.*

empress (ĕm′prĭs) *n.* **1.** A woman who is the ruler of an empire. **2.** The wife or widow of an emperor.

empty (ĕmp′tē) *adj.* **emptier, emptiest 1.** Holding or containing nothing: *an empty box.* **2.** Having no occupants or inhabitants; not being used: *an empty house.* **3.** Lacking force or power: *an empty threat.* **4.** Lacking purpose or substance; meaningless: *Everything you said was empty talk.* **5.** Needing food; hungry: *an empty stomach.* ❖ *v.* **emptied, emptying, empties** —*tr.* **1.** To remove the contents of: *I emptied the dishwasher.* **2.** To transfer or pour off: *Please empty the garbage from the wastebasket.* —*intr.* **1.** To become empty: *The sink emptied when the plumber cleared the drain.* **2.** To discharge or flow out: *The river empties into a bay.* ❖ *n., pl.* **empties** *Informal* An empty container. —**emp′ti·ly** *adv.* —**emp′ti·ness** *n.*

✦ **SYNONYMS** empty, blank, vacant, void *adj.*

empty-handed (ĕmp′tē-hăn′dĭd) *adj.* **1.** Bearing nothing: *They arrived at the birthday party empty-handed.* **2.** Having received or gained nothing.

empty-headed (ĕmp′tē-hĕd′ĭd) *adj.* Lacking sense or discretion: *an empty-headed clerk who misfiled my paperwork.*

empyreal (ĕm′pī-rē′əl *or* ĕm-pîr′ē-əl) *adj.* Relating to the sky; celestial.

empyrean (ĕm′pī-rē′ən *or* ĕm-pîr′ē-ən) *n.* **1.** The highest reaches of heaven. **2.** The sky. ❖ *adj.* Heavenly; celestial.

EMT An abbreviation of emergency medical technician.

emu (ē′myōō) *n.* A large flightless Australian bird that has brown feathers and resembles an ostrich.

emulate (ĕm′yə-lāt′) *tr.v.* **emulated, emulating, emulates** To strive to equal or excel, especially through imitation: *an experienced pianist whose style I tried to emulate.*

emulation (ĕm′yə-lā′shən) *n.* **1.** Effort or ambition to equal or surpass another: *the young writer's emulation of the famous novelist.* **2.** Imitation of another.

emulsify (ĭ-mŭl′sə-fī′) *tr.v.* **emulsified, emulsifying, emulsifies** To make into an emulsion: *Soap emulsifies fats in warm water.* —**e·mul′si·fi·ca′tion** (ĭ-mŭl′sə-fĭ-kā′shən) *n.*

emulsion (ĭ-mŭl′shən) *n.* **1.** A suspension of small droplets of one liquid in a second liquid with which the first does not mix, as the suspension of cream in homogenized milk. **2.** The coating of a photographic film or paper that is sensitive to light.

en– or **em–** or **in–** A prefix that means: **1.** To put into or onto: *encapsulate.* **2.** To go into or onto: *entrain.* **3.** To cover or provide with: *encircle.* **4.** To cause to be: *endear.* **5.** Thoroughly: *entangle.* —SEE NOTE AT **in–²**.

–en¹ A suffix that means: **1.** To cause to be: *cheapen.* **2.** To become: *redden.* **3.** To cause to have: *hearten.* **4.** To come to have: *lengthen.*

–en² A suffix that means made of or resembling: *earthen; wooden.*

WORD BUILDING The basic meaning of the suffix –en¹ is "to cause to be" or "to become." When added to nouns and adjectives, –en¹ forms verbs: *lengthen, soften.* The suffix **–en²**, meaning "made of; resembling," is an adjective suffix; that is, it changes nouns into adjectives: *wooden, golden.* The suffix *–en¹* comes from Old English *–nian,* and *–en²* is unchanged from Old English *–en.*

enable (ĕ-nā′bəl) *tr.v.* **enabled, enabling, enables** To give the means, ability, or opportunity to do something: *The new computer system enables the store owners to keep close track of inventory.*

enact (ĕn-ăkt′) *tr.v.* **enacted, enacting, enacts 1.** To make into law: *The Senate enacted legislation to help schools throughout the country.* **2.** To act (something) out, as on a stage: *They enacted the final scene without any mistakes.*

enactment (ĕn-ăkt′mənt) *n.* **1.** The act of enacting or the state of being enacted: *the enactment of laws by Congress.* **2.** Something that has been enacted.

enamel (ĭ-năm′əl) *n.* **1.** A glassy coating baked onto the surface of metal, porcelain, or pottery for decoration or protection. **2.** A paint that dries to a hard glossy surface. **3.** The hard substance that covers the exposed part of a tooth. ❖ *tr.v.* **enameled, enameling, enamels** or **enamelled, enamelling, enamels** To coat, inlay, or decorate with enamel.

enamelware (ĭ-năm′əl-wâr′) *n.* Objects of metal, porcelain, or pottery that are coated or decorated with enamel.

enamor (ĭ-năm′ər) *tr.v.* **enamored, enamoring, enamors** To inspire with love; captivate: *We were enamored with the beautiful landscape.*

encamp (ĕn-kămp′) *v.* **encamped, encamping, encamps** —*intr.* To set up camp or live in a camp: *encamp in the woods.* —*tr.* To provide quarters for in a camp.

encampment (ĕn-kămp′mənt) *n.* **1.** The act of encamping. **2.** The state of being encamped. **3.** A camp or campsite: *The encampment is just down the road.*

encapsulate (ĕn-kăp′sə-lāt′) *tr.v.* **encapsulated, encapsulating, encapsulates 1.** To enclose in or as if in a capsule. **2.** To express in a brief summary: *The statement encapsulated the long committee report.* —**en·cap′su·la′tion** *n.*

encase (ĕn-kās′) *tr.v.* **encased, encasing, encases** To enclose in or as if in a case: *The skull encases the brain.*

–ence A suffix that means: **1.** State or condition: *dependence.* **2.** Action: *emergence.*

encephalitis (ĕn-sĕf′ə-lī′tĭs) *n.* Inflammation of the brain, usually caused by viral infection.

enchant (ĕn-chănt′) *tr.v.* **enchanted, enchanting, enchants 1.** To cast a spell; bewitch. **2.** To attract and delight; entrance: *The play enchanted everyone who saw it.* —**en·chant′er** *n.*

enchanting (ĕn-chăn′tĭng) *adj.* Having the power to enchant; charming: *an enchanting melody.*

enchantment (ĕn-chănt′mənt) *n.* **1.** The act of enchanting. **2.** The state of being enchanted. **3.** Something that enchants; a magic spell.

enchantress (ĕn-chăn′trĭs) *n.* **1.** A sorceress; a witch. **2.** A woman of great charm or attractiveness.

enchilada (ĕn′chə-lä′də) *n.* A tortilla rolled and stuffed usually with a mixture containing meat or cheese and served with a sauce spiced with chili peppers.

encircle (ĕn-sûr′kəl) *tr.v.* **encircled, encircling, encircles 1.** To form a circle around; surround: *Trees encircled the house.* **2.** To move or go around completely: *It takes Earth one year to encircle the sun.* —**en·cir′cle·ment** *n.*

enclave (ĕn′klāv′ or ŏn′klāv′) *n.* **1.** A country or part of a country that lies completely within the boundaries of another. **2.** A distinctly separated area enclosed within a larger unit: *immigrant enclaves in a large city.*

enclose (ĕn-klōz′) *tr.v.* **enclosed, enclosing, encloses 1.** To surround on all sides; close in: *A high fence encloses the yard.* **2.** To equip with a roof and walls: *enclosed the deck for use in the winter.* **3.** To insert in the same envelope or package: *I enclosed a check for $25 with the order.*

enclosure (ĕn-klō′zhər) *n.* **1.** The act of enclosing or the state of being enclosed: *enclosure of a payment.* **2.** Something enclosed: *a garden in the middle of the enclosure; a business letter with enclosures.* **3.** Something that encloses, as a wall or fence: *The zoo had a high enclosure to keep the antelopes in.*

encode (ĕn-kōd′) *tr.v.* **encoded, encoding, encodes** To put (a message, for example) into code: *encoded the note.* —**en·cod′er** *n.*

encomium (ĕn-kō′mē-əm) *n., pl.* **encomiums** or **encomia** (ĕn-kō′mē-ə) A formal expression of praise; a tribute.

encompass (ĕn-kŭm′pəs) *tr.v.* **encompassed, encompassing, encompasses 1.** To form a circle or ring about; surround. **2.** To constitute or include: *The report encompassed a number of subjects.*

encore (ŏn′kôr′) *n.* **1.** A demand by an audience for an additional performance, usually expressed by applause. **2.** An additional performance in response to such a demand: *Three short songs made the perfect encore.* ❖ *interj.* An expression used to demand an additional performance.

encounter (ĕn-koun′tər) *n.* **1.** A chance or unexpected meeting: *a frightening encounter with a bear.* **2.** A hostile or adversarial confrontation: *an encounter between British and Colonial troops.* ❖ *tr.v.* **encountered, encountering, encounters 1.** To experience unexpectedly or by chance: *encounter many problems.* **2.** To meet, especially unexpectedly: *encountered an old friend in the park.* **3.** To confront in battle or contention.

encourage (ĕn-kûr′ĭj) *tr.v.* **encouraged, encouraging, encourages 1.** To give hope, courage, or confidence to; hearten: *The favorable report encouraged me somewhat.* **2.** To give support to; foster. **3.** To stimulate; spur: *Fertilizer encourages the growth of plants.*

encouragement (ĕn-kûr′ĭj-mənt) *n.* **1.** The act of encouraging: *the encouragement of friends to enter a contest.* **2.** A person or thing that encourages: *Kind words are an encouragement.*

encouraging (ĕn-kûr′ə-jĭng) *adj.* Giving courage, hope, or confidence: *We were heartened to hear the encouraging news.*

encroach (ĕn-krōch′) *intr.v.* **encroached, encroaching, encroaches 1.** To take another's possessions or rights gradually or stealthily: *encroach on a neighbor's land.* **2.** To advance beyond proper or former limits: *the ocean encroaching on the shore.* —**en·croach′ment** *n.*

encrust (ĕn-krŭst′) *tr.v.* **encrusted, encrusting, encrusts** To cover with or as if with a crust or hard layer: *Ice encrusted the windowpanes. The crown was encrusted with jewels.* —**en′crus·ta′tion** *n.*

encrypt (ĕn-krĭpt′) *tr.v.* **encrypted, encrypting, encrypts** To put (a message or computer data, for example) into code; encode.

encumber (ĕn-kŭm′bər) *tr.v.* **encumbered, encumbering, encumbers 1.** To put a heavy load on; burden: *The heavy pack encumbered the hiker.* **2.** To hinder or impede the action or performance of: *restrictions that encumber police work.* **3.** To burden with legal or financial obligations.

encumbrance (ĕn-kŭm′brəns) *n.* A person or thing that encumbers; a burden or obstacle.

–ency A suffix that means quality or condition: *dependency; emergency.*

encyclical (ĕn-sĭk′lĭ-kəl) *n.* A letter from the pope addressed to the bishops of the Roman Catholic Church or to the hierarchy of a particular country.

encyclopedia (ĕn-sī′klə-pē′dē-ə) *n.* A large reference work containing articles, usually arranged in alphabetical order and covering one particular field or a wide variety of subjects.

encyclopedic (ĕn-sī′klə-pē′dĭk) *adj.* **1.** Relating to or characteristic of an encyclopedia. **2.** Having or covering many subjects; comprehensive: *a scholar with encyclopedic knowledge.*

end (ĕnd) *n.* **1a.** Either point where something that has length begins or stops: *They sat at opposite ends of the table.* **b.** The extreme edge or limit of a space or area; a boundary: *Buffalo lies at the eastern end of Lake Erie.* **2.** The point in time when an action, event, or phenomenon ceases or is completed: *Summer vacation is coming to an end. I'll get paid at the end of the month.* **3.** Something toward which one strives; a goal or result: *wanted to be a doctor and studied hard to achieve that end.* **4.** The termination of life or existence; death: *The explorer met his end in the desert.* **5.** The ultimate extent of something; the final limit: *at the end of one's savings; at the end of one's patience.* **6.** A share of a responsibility: *your end of the bargain; the financial end of a business.* **7.** In football, either of two players stationed at the outermost position of a team's line. ❖ *v.* **ended, ending, ends** —*tr.* **1.** To bring to a conclusion; finish: *a nice way to end a trip.* **2.** To form the last or concluding part of: *the song that ended the performance.* See Synonyms at **complete.** —*intr.* **1.** To come to a finish; cease: *The game ended in a tie.* **2.** To arrive at a place, situation, or condition as a result of a course of action: *His laziness ended up costing him his job. She ended up happier than before.* ◆ **in the end** Eventually; ultimately: *It all worked out well in the end.* **no end** A great deal: *We have no end of stories to tell.*

endanger (ĕn-dān′jər) *tr.v.* **endangered, endangering, endangers** **1.** To put in danger; imperil: *Forest fires endanger wildlife.* **2.** To cause to become nearly extinct: *hunting practices that endangered whales.*

endangered species (ĕn-dān′jərd) *n.* A species present in such small numbers that it is at risk of extinction.

endear (ĕn-dîr′) *tr.v.* **endeared, endearing, endears** To make beloved or very sympathetic: *The kitten quickly endeared itself to the whole family.* —**en·dear′ing·ly** *adv.*

endearment (ĕn-dîr′mənt) *n.* **1.** The act of endearing. **2.** An expression of affection.

endeavor (ĕn-dĕv′ər) *n.* An earnest effort toward an end; a serious attempt: *her endeavor to start her own business.* ❖ *tr.v.* **endeavored, endeavoring, endeavors** To make an effort (to do or accomplish something); try: *endeavored to improve their quality of life.*

endemic (ĕn-dĕm′ĭk) *adj.* **1.** Constantly present in a particular region or group of people. Used of a disease: *Lyme disease is endemic in parts of New England.* **2.** Native to a particular region: *the endemic birds of Hawaii.* **3.** Common in or characteristic of an enterprise or situation: *an endemic problem in the energy industry.* ❖ *n.* An endemic organism or disease.

endgame also **end game** (ĕnd′gām′) *n.* **1.** The final stage of a chess game after most of the pieces have been removed from the board. **2.** The final stage of an extended process or course of events: *the diplomatic endgame that led to the treaty.*

ending (ĕn′dĭng) *n.* **1.** The concluding part, especially of a book, play, or film: *The comedy has a happy ending.* **2.** A letter or letters added to the end of a word to change the meaning or show some relationship of grammar, as in adding *-ed* to *walk* to make the past tense *walked.*

endive (ĕn′dīv′ *or* ŏn′dēv′) *n.* **1.** A variety of chicory having a narrow pointed cluster of whitish leaves used in salads. **2.** A related plant having curled or ruffled leaves with a bitter flavor, used in salads.

endless (ĕnd′lĭs) *adj.* **1.** Being or seeming to be without an end; infinite: *endless stretches of sandy beaches.* **2.** Formed with the ends joined; continuous: *an endless chain.* —**end′less·ly** *adv.*

end line *n.* In sports, a line that is at right angles to the sidelines and that marks an end boundary of a playing field or court.

endmost (ĕnd′mōst′) *adj.* Being at or closest to the end; last: *the endmost rooms on a hall.*

endnote (ĕnd′nōt′) *n.* A note at the end of an article, chapter, or book that comments on or cites a reference for a designated part of the text.

endo– or **end–** A prefix that means inside or within: *endoderm; endosperm.*

endocardium (ĕn′dō-kär′dē-əm) *n., pl.* **endocardia** (ĕn′-dō-kär′dē-ə) The smooth membrane that lines the cavities of the heart.

endocrine (ĕn′də-krĭn *or* ĕn′də-krēn′) *adj.* **1.** Producing secretions, especially hormones, directly into the blood. **2.** Relating to endocrine glands or the hormones they secrete: *an endocrine disease.*

endocrine gland *n.* Any of various glands, such as the thyroid gland or the pituitary gland, that produce hormones that pass directly into the bloodstream.

endocrine system *n.* The system of endocrine glands in a vertebrate animal that produce hormones that regulate internal body activities and processes.

endocrinology (ĕn′də-krə-nŏl′ə-jē) *n.* The branch of medicine that deals with the diagnosis and treatment of diseases and disorders of the endocrine glands.

endoderm (ĕn′də-dûrm′) *n.* The innermost of the three layers of cells found in an early embryo, developing into the lining of the digestive system and lungs and certain organs such as the liver and pancreas.

endometrium (ĕn′dō-mē′trē-əm) *n., pl.* **endometria** (ĕn′dō-mē′trē-ə) The membrane that lines the uterus, to which a fertilized egg must attach itself in order to develop. —**en′do·me′tri·al** *adj.*

endoplasm (ĕn′də-plăz′əm) *n.* The central, most fluid portion of the cytoplasm of a cell.

endoplasmic reticulum (ĕn′də-plăz′mĭk rĭ-tĭk′yə-ləm) *n.* A network of membranes within the cytoplasm of many cells that is important in the production and transport of proteins and other large molecules.

endorphin (ĕn-dôr′fĭn) *n.* Any of a group of hormones present chiefly in the brain that are involved in regulating various physiological functions and that reduce feelings of pain.

endorse (ĕn-dôrs′) *tr.v.* **endorsed, endorsing, endorses** **1.** To give approval of; support: *Many have already endorsed the idea of national health care.* **2.** To recommend (a product), often for payment, as in an advertisement: *The athlete endorsed a new brand of shaving cream.* **3.** To write one's signature on the back of (a check, for example) as evidence of the legal transfer of its ownership: *endorse a check in order to receive payment.* **—en·dors′er** *n.*

endorsement (ĕn-dôrs′mənt) *n.* **1.** Something, such as a signature, that endorses or validates. **2.** Approval; support: *The plan has the endorsement of the mayor.*

endoscope (ĕn′də-skōp′) *n.* An instrument for viewing the inside of a body canal or a hollow organ such as the colon.

endoskeleton (ĕn′dō-skĕl′ĭ-tn) *n.* An internal supporting structure within an organism, such as the skeleton in humans and other vertebrates or the rigid framework in a starfish.

endosperm (ĕn′də-spûrm′) *n.* The part of a plant seed that contains stored food and supplies nourishment for the developing embryo.

endospore (ĕn′də-spôr′) *n.* A thick-walled spore that is formed by some bacteria and can resist harsh environmental conditions.

endotherm (ĕn′də-thûrm′) *n.* A warm-blooded animal.

endothermic (ĕn′dō-thûr′mĭk) *adj.* **1.** Causing or characterized by absorption of heat: *an endothermic chemical reaction.* **2.** Warm-blooded: *Mammals are endothermic.*

endow (ĕn-dou′) *tr.v.* **endowed, endowing, endows 1.** To provide with property, income, or a source of income: *endow a school.* **2.** To provide with a talent or quality: *Nature endowed you with a good singing voice.*

endowment (ĕn-dou′mənt) *n.* **1.** Money or property donated to an institution or person as a source of income: *An endowment pays for new library books.* **2.** A natural gift, ability, or quality.

endpoint or **end point** (ĕnd′point′) *n.* **1.** Either of two points that mark the ends of a line segment. **2.** A tip or point of termination.

end run *n.* **1.** In football, a play in which the ball carrier tries to run around one end of the defensive line. **2.** *Informal* An action undertaken to get around an obstacle or hindrance: *The manager did an end run around the ban on spending and was able to order additional supplies.*

end table *n.* A small table, usually placed beside a chair or couch.

endurable (ĕn-do͝or′ə-bəl) *adj.* Capable of being endured; tolerable: *an endurable pain.* **—en·dur′a·bly** *adv.*

endurance (ĕn-do͝or′əns) *n.* **1.** The act, quality, or power to withstand stress or hardship: *Climbing a high mountain is a test of endurance.* **2.** The state or fact of persevering. **3.** Continuing existence; duration.

endure (ĕn-do͝or′) *v.* **endured, enduring, endures** *—tr.* **1.** To carry on through, despite hardship: *The early settlers of America endured long cold winters.* **2.** To bear with tolerance; put up with: *I could no longer endure such rudeness.* *—intr.* **1.** To continue to exist; last: *a name that will endure forever.* **2.** To suffer patiently without yielding: *The prisoners endured in spite of terrible conditions.*

enduring (ĕn-do͝or′ĭng) *adj.* Lasting; durable: *the enduring friendship of the old schoolmates.*

end user *n.* The consumer of a product seen as the person for whom the product has been designed.

endwise (ĕnd′wīz′) also **endways** (ĕnd′wāz′) *adv.* **1.** On end; upright: *Stand the books endwise on the shelf.* **2.** With the end forward: *a bookcase standing endwise out into the room.* **3.** Lengthwise: *a couch placed endwise along a wall.* **4.** End to end: *Lay the bricks endwise to make the wall.*

end zone *n.* In football, the area between the goal line and the end line at each end of the playing field.

enema (ĕn′ə-mə) *n.* **1.** The injection of a liquid into the rectum through the anus for cleansing or for stimulating the emptying of the bowels. **2.** The liquid used in this way.

enemy (ĕn′ə-mē) *n., pl.* **enemies 1.** A person who feels hatred toward, intends injury to, or opposes the interests of another; a foe. **2a.** A hostile power or force, such as a nation: *During a war, neighboring nations may be enemies.* **b.** A unit or member of such a force: *The enemy sailed into battle with guns blazing.* **3.** Something harmful or destructive: *Disease is an enemy of plant and animal life.* ❖ *adj.* Relating to or being a hostile power or force: *enemy soldiers.* —SEE NOTE AT **collective noun.**

energetic (ĕn′ər-jĕt′ĭk) *adj.* Possessing, exerting, or displaying energy: *The energetic efforts of the crew helped us meet our building deadline.* **—en′er·get′i·cal·ly** *adv.*

energize (ĕn′ər-jīz′) *tr.v.* **energized, energizing, energizes** To give energy to; activate or invigorate: *This switch energizes the electric circuit.* **—en′er·giz′er** *n.*

energy (ĕn′ər-jē) *n., pl.* **energies 1.** The capacity for work or vigorous activity; vigor; power: *lacked the energy to finish the job.* **2.** Exertion of power or vigor: *Only with a lot of energy were we able to finish the project.* **3.** Usable heat or power: *The town will need more energy as it grows.* **4.** The capacity of a physical system, such as a machine, to do work, as in turning, pushing, or raising something. Energy can be electrical, mechanical, chemical, thermal, or nuclear. It is measured by the amount of work done.

enervate (ĕn′ər-vāt′) *tr.v.* **enervated, enervating, enervates** To weaken or destroy the strength or vitality of: *The prolonged hot weather enervated everyone.* **—en′-er·va′tion** *n.*

enfeeble (ĕn-fē′bəl) *tr.v.* **enfeebled, enfeebling, enfeebles** To deprive of strength; make feeble. **—en·fee′ble·ment** *n.*

enfold (ĕn-fōld′) *tr.v.* **enfolded, enfolding, enfolds 1.** To cover with or as if with folds; envelop: *enfold a baby in a blanket.* **2.** To embrace.

enforce (ĕn-fôrs′) *tr.v.* **enforced, enforcing, enforces 1.** To compel observance of or obedience to: *enforce parking regulations.* **2.** To require that people practice (a certain behavior, for example); impose: *Ushers enforced silence in the theater.* **—en·force′a·ble** *adj.* **—en·force′ment** *n.*

enfranchise (ĕn-frăn′chīz′) *tr.v.* **enfranchised, enfranchising, enfranchises** To endow with the rights of citizenship, especially the right to vote: *An amendment to the Constitution enfranchised women.* **—en·fran′chise·ment** *n.*

Eng. An abbreviation of: **1.** England. **2.** English.

engage (ĕn-gāj′) *v.* **engaged, engaging, engages** *—tr.* **1.** To cause (someone) to participate or be involved in something: *I wanted to engage him in conversation, but he left early.* **2.** To attract and hold (the attention): *The puzzle engaged our attention for an hour.* **3.** To obtain or contract for the services of; employ: *engage a carpenter to build a porch.* **4.** To pledge or promise, especially to marry: *My aunt is engaged to a musician.* **5.** To require the use of; occupy: *Studying engages much of my time.* **6.** To enter or bring into conflict with: *planes that engaged the enemy over the bay.* **7.** To put into working position: *A lever engages the gears.* *—intr.* **1.** To involve oneself or become occupied; participate: *They engaged in a lively conversation.* **2.** To assume an obligation; agree: *They engaged to finish the project on schedule.* **3.** To enter into conflict or battle: *The armies engaged at dawn.* **4.** To move or be put into working position: *The car's transmission engaged.*

engaged (ĕn-gājd′) *adj.* **1.** Employed, occupied, or busy. **2.** Pledged to marry; betrothed: *an engaged couple.* **3.** Being in working position.

engagement (ĕn-gāj′mənt) *n.* **1.** An act of engaging or the state of being engaged. **2a.** A promise between two people to get married. **b.** The period during which this promise is kept: *the couple's long engagement.* **3.** A promise to be at a particular place at a certain time: *a dinner engagement.* **4.** Employment, especially for a set length of time: *an actor's two-week engagement.* **5.** A battle; a military encounter.

engaging (ĕn-gā′jĭng) *adj.* Charming; attractive: *an engaging smile.* See Synonyms at **interesting.** —**en·gag′-ing·ly** *adv.*

en garde (äɴ gärd′) *interj.* Used to warn a fencer to assume the position preparatory to a match.

engender (ĕn-jĕn′dər) *tr.v.* **engendered, engendering, engenders** To give rise to; bring into existence: *A candid manner engenders trust.*

engine (ĕn′jĭn) *n.* **1.** A machine that turns energy into mechanical force or motion, especially one that gets its energy from a source of heat, such as the burning of a fuel. **2.** A mechanical appliance, instrument, or tool: *The battering ram is an ancient engine of warfare.* **3.** A railroad locomotive: *The freight train was drawn by a diesel engine.*

engineer (ĕn′jə-nîr′) *n.* **1.** A person who is specially trained or works in a branch of engineering. **2.** A person who operates an engine: *a locomotive engineer.* **3.** A person who skillfully or shrewdly manages a project: *The head of our advertising department was the engineer of this sales campaign.* ❖ *tr.v.* **engineered, engineering, engineers** **1.** To plan, construct, or manage as an engineer: *engineer a new bridge.* **2.** To plan, manage, and accomplish by skill or shrewdness; maneuver: *engineered the entire party.*

engineering (ĕn′jə-nîr′ĭng) *n.* The use of scientific and mathematical principles to design and build structures, machines, and systems. Bridges, cars, and electronic circuits are products of engineering.

English (ĭng′glĭsh) *adj.* Relating to England or its people, language, or culture. ❖ *n.* **1.** *(used with a plural verb)* The people of England. **2.** The West Germanic language of England, the United States, and other countries that are or have been under English influence or control. **3.** often **english** The spin given to a ball by striking it on one side or releasing it with a sharp twist.

English horn *n.* A woodwind instrument similar to but larger than the oboe and pitched below it.

Englishman (ĭng′glĭsh-mən) *n.* A man who is a native or inhabitant of England.

English muffin *n.* A flat round muffin made of yeast dough, usually split and served toasted.

English sparrow *n.* The house sparrow.

Englishwoman (ĭng′glĭsh-wŏŏm′ən) *n.* A woman who is a native or inhabitant of England.

engorge (ĕn-gôrj′) *tr.v.* **engorged, engorging, engorges** **1.** To devour greedily: *engorged a meal in just minutes.* **2.** To congest or overfill with blood or other fluid: *The tick was engorged with blood.* —**en·gorge′ment** *n.*

engraft (ĕn-grăft′) *v.* **engrafted, engrafting, engrafts** —*intr.* To become successfully grafted: *The transplanted bone marrow cells have engrafted.* —*tr.* To graft (a shoot) onto a plant.

engrave (ĕn-grāv′) *tr.v.* **engraved, engraving, engraves** **1.** To carve, cut, or etch into a material: *engrave a name on a plaque.* **2.** To carve, cut, or etch a design or letters into: *engrave a marble stone with a coat of arms.* **3a.** To carve, cut, or etch into a block or surface used for printing: *engrave a poem into a copper plate using fine tools.* **b.** To print from a block or plate made by such a process. **4.** To have a lasting effect on (a person or a person's mind) as if by carving or etching; impress deeply: *engrave rules of safety in a child's mind.* —**en·grav′er** *n.*

engraving (ĕn-grā′vĭng) *n.* **1.** The art or technique of one that engraves. **2.** A design or text engraved on a surface. **3.** An engraved surface for printing. **4.** A print made from an engraved plate or block.

engross (ĕn-grōs′) *tr.v.* **engrossed, engrossing, engrosses** To occupy the complete attention of; absorb: *The interesting new book engrossed him.*

engrossing (ĕn-grō′sĭng) *adj.* Occupying one's complete attention; extremely interesting: *an engrossing film.*

engulf (ĕn-gŭlf′) *tr.v.* **engulfed, engulfing, engulfs** To swallow up or overwhelm by or as if by overflowing and enclosing: *Floodwaters engulfed the land near the river.*

enhance (ĕn-hăns′) *tr.v.* **enhanced, enhancing, enhances** To make greater, as in value, beauty, or reputation: *The gardens enhanced the grounds.* —**en·hance′ment** *n.*

enigma (ĭ-nĭg′mə) *n.* A person or thing that is puzzling, ambiguous, or hard to explain: *The disappearance of the dinosaurs remains an enigma.*

enigmatic (ĕn′ĭg-măt′ĭk) *adj.* Resembling an enigma; puzzling: *the enigmatic behavior of an eccentric person.* —**en′ig·mat′i·cal·ly** *adv.*

enjambment or **enjambement** (ĕn-jăm′mənt *or* ĕn-jämb′mənt) *n.* The continuation of a syntactic unit from one line of a poem to the next with no pause.

enjoin (ĕn-join′) *tr.v.* **enjoined, enjoining, enjoins** **1.** To urge or order (someone to do something): *The doctor enjoined the patient to walk one mile each day.* **2.** To require or impose (an action or behavior, for example); prescribe. **3.** To prohibit or forbid (someone from doing something): *The court enjoined the company from merging with its competitor.*

enjoy (ĕn-joi′) *v.* **enjoyed, enjoying, enjoys** —*tr.* **1.** To receive pleasure or satisfaction from: *I enjoy living in the country.* **2.** To have the use or benefit of: *You seem to enjoy good health.* —*intr.* To have a pleasurable or satisfactory time. ❖ **enjoy (oneself)** To have a good time: *I enjoyed myself at the ball game.*

enjoyment (ĕn-joi′mənt) *n.* **1.** The act or state of enjoying. **2.** Use or possession of something beneficial or pleasurable: *the enjoyment of good health.* **3.** Something that gives pleasure: *My grandparents' garden is their chief enjoyment.*

enlarge (ĕn-lärj′) *v.* **enlarged, enlarging, enlarges** —*tr.* To make larger in size, scope, or effect: *enlarge a house; enlarge one's understanding.* —*intr.* To become larger; grow: *The town enlarged as new businesses moved in.* See Synonyms at **increase.** ❖ **enlarge on** or **enlarge upon** To speak or write about more thoroughly: *The second article enlarged on the subject of the first.* —**en·larg′er** *n.*

enlargement (ĕn-lärj′mənt) *n.* **1.** An act of enlarging or the state of being enlarged: *Enlargement of the theater will permit the school to put on musicals.* **2.** Something that has been enlarged, especially a copy that is larger than the original.

enlighten (ĕn-līt′n) *tr.v.* **enlightened, enlightening, en-**

lightens To give spiritual or intellectual insight to: *The movie enlightened us about the difficulty of improving health care in developing countries.*

enlightenment (ĕn-līt′n-mənt) *n.* **1.** The act or means of enlightening or the state of being enlightened. **2. Enlightenment** A movement of the 1700s that called for critical examination of previously unchallenged beliefs. **3.** In Buddhism and Hinduism, a state in which a person overcomes desire and suffering and attains Nirvana.

enlist (ĕn-lĭst′) *v.* **enlisted, enlisting, enlists** —*tr.* **1.** To engage (a person or persons) for service in the armed forces: *The army enlisted three people from the same neighborhood.* **2.** To engage the support or cooperation of: *The minister enlisted our help in giving food to the homeless.* —*intr.* **1.** To join one of the armed forces voluntarily: *enlisted in the army after high school.* **2.** To participate actively in a cause or enterprise: *Many volunteers enlisted as drivers.*

enlisted (ĕn-lĭs′tĭd) *adj.* Relating to or being a member of a military rank below a commissioned officer or warrant officer.

enliven (ĕn-lī′vən) *tr.v.* **enlivened, enlivening, enlivens** To make lively or spirited; animate: *Music enlivened the party.*

en masse (ŏn măs′) *adv.* In a group or body; all together: *Our guests arrived en masse by taxi.*

enmesh (ĕn-mĕsh′) *tr.v.* **enmeshed, enmeshing, enmeshes** To entangle or catch in or as if in a net: *enmeshed in local politics.*

enmity (ĕn′mĭ-tē) *n., pl.* **enmities** Deep-seated, often mutual hatred.

ennoble (ĕn-nō′bəl) *tr.v.* **ennobled, ennobling, ennobles** **1.** To make noble: *Working for a good cause ennobles a person's life.* **2.** To confer nobility upon: *ennoble a person for distinguished service.* —**en·no′ble·ment** *n.*

ennui (ŏn-wē′) *n.* Dissatisfaction resulting from lack of interest; boredom.

enormity (ĭ-nôr′mĭ-tē) *n., pl.* **enormities** The quality of passing all moral bounds; excessive wickedness or outrageousness.

enormous (ĭ-nôr′məs) *adj.* Very great in size, extent, number, or degree: *an enormous elephant; the enormous cost of building a sports arena.* See Synonyms at **large.** —**e·nor′mous·ly** *adv.* —**e·nor′mous·ness** *n.*

enough (ĭ-nŭf′) *adj.* Sufficient to meet a need or satisfy a desire: *There is enough food for everybody.* ❖ *pron.* An adequate amount or quantity: *The hungry hiker ate enough for two.* ❖ *adv.* **1.** To a satisfactory amount or degree; sufficiently: *Are you warm enough?* **2.** Very; fully; quite: *We were glad enough to leave after waiting so long.* **3.** Tolerably; rather: *The songs were good enough, but the show didn't draw a big audience.*

enquiry (ĕn-kwīr′ē or ĕn′kwə-rē) *n., pl.* **enquiries** *Chiefly British* Variant of **inquiry.**

enrage (ĕn-rāj′) *tr.v.* **enraged, enraging, enrages** To put into a rage; infuriate: *The plan to put a highway right through town enraged the residents.*

enrapture (ĕn-răp′chər) *tr.v.* **enraptured, enrapturing, enraptures** To fill with rapture or delight: *The music enraptured the audience.*

enrich (ĕn-rĭch′) *tr.v.* **enriched, enriching, enriches** **1.** To make rich or richer: *Foreign words have enriched the English language.* **2.** To add fertilizer to (soil). **3.** To add nutrients, such as vitamins and minerals, to (food). **4.** To increase the amount of a radioactive isotope in (a material): *enrich nuclear fuel.* —**en·rich′ment** *n.*

enroll also **enrol** (ĕn-rōl′) *v.* **enrolled, enrolling, enrolls** also **enrols** —*tr.* To enter or register in a list, record, or roll: *enrolled the child in kindergarten; enroll new students for an art class.* —*intr.* To place one's name on a roll or register: *enroll as a voter before the elections; enroll in the statistics class.*

enrollment also **enrolment** (ĕn-rōl′mənt) *n.* **1.** The act or process of enrolling. **2.** The number enrolled: *The school has an enrollment of 600.*

en route (ŏn rōōt′ or ĕn rōōt′) *adv. & adj.* On or along the way: *We'll pick you up en route to the theater.*

ensconce (ĕn-skŏns′) *tr.v.* **ensconced, ensconcing, ensconces** **1.** To settle (oneself) comfortably or snugly: *Our visitors ensconced themselves on the couch.* **2.** To put or hide in a safe place.

ensemble (ŏn-sŏm′bəl) *n.* **1.** A group of musicians, singers, dancers, or actors who perform together. **2.** A musical work for two or more vocalists or instrumentalists. **3.** A coordinated outfit or costume: *a colorful ensemble of dress, shoes, and bag.*

enshrine (ĕn-shrīn′) *tr.v.* **enshrined, enshrining, enshrines** **1.** To enclose in or as if in a shrine. **2.** To cherish as sacred. —**en·shrine′ment** *n.*

enshroud (ĕn-shroud′) *tr.v.* **enshrouded, enshrouding, enshrouds** To cover with or as if with a shroud: *Fog enshrouded the city.*

ensign (ĕn′sən or ĕn′sīn′) *n.* **1.** A national flag displayed on ships and aircraft: *the naval ensign of the United States.* **2.** A badge of office or power; a token. **3.** (ĕn′sən) An officer in the US Navy or Coast Guard ranking below lieutenant junior grade.

enslave (ĕn-slāv′) *tr.v.* **enslaved, enslaving, enslaves** **1.** To make into a slave. **2.** To prevent from acting freely: *addicts enslaved by dependency on drugs.* —**en·slave′ment** *n.*

ensnare (ĕn-snâr′) *tr.v.* **ensnared, ensnaring, ensnares** To catch in or as if in a trap or snare: *ensnare customers into buying something they don't need.*

ensnarl (ĕn-snärl′) *tr.v.* **ensnarled, ensnarling, ensnarls** To entangle in or as if in a snare: *The net ensnarled the ship's propeller.*

ensue (ĕn-sōō′) *intr.v.* **ensued, ensuing, ensues** **1.** To follow as a consequence or result: *After their angry words a real fight ensued.* **2.** To follow immediately afterward. See Synonyms at **follow.**

ensure (ĕn-shōōr′) *tr.v.* **ensured, ensuring, ensures** To make sure or certain; guarantee: *measures to ensure good health.* —SEE NOTE AT **assure.**

-ent A suffix that means: **1.** Performing, promoting, or causing a specified action: *absorbent.* **2.** Being in a specified state or condition: *independent.* **3.** A person or thing that performs, promotes, or causes a specified action: *superintendent; correspondent.*

entablature (ĕn-tăb′lə-chōōr′) *n.* The upper section of a classical structure, resting on the columns and made up of the architrave, frieze, and cornice.

entail (ĕn-tāl′) *tr.v.* **entailed, entailing, entails** To impose or require as a necessary accompaniment or consequence: *Building a new tunnel will entail great expense.*

entangle (ĕn-tăng′gəl) *tr.v.* **entangled, entangling, entangles** **1.** To cause to become twisted together or caught in a snarl or entwining mass: *The fishing line got entangled. My foot got entangled in the hose.* **2.** To involve in a complicated situation or in circumstances from which it is difficult to disengage: *I don't want to get entangled in their feud.* —**en·tan′gle·ment** *n.*

entente (ŏn-tŏnt′) *n.* **1.** An agreement between two or more governments or powers for cooperative action or policy. **2.** The parties to such an agreement.

enter (ĕn′tər) *v.* **entered, entering, enters** —*tr.* **1.** To come or go into: *The train entered the tunnel.* **2.** To become a part of or participant in: *enter a discussion; enter a contest.* **3.** To cause to become a participant, member, or part of; enroll: *enter a child in kindergarten; enter a collie in a dog show.* **4.** To take up; make a beginning in; start: *enter a business as a clerk; enter a medical profession.* **5a.** To write or put in: *enter names in a guest book; enter data into a computer.* **b.** To place formally upon the records; record: *enter a plea of not guilty.* —*intr.* To come or go in: *We entered at the side of the building. Trucks enter from both sides of the road.* ◆ **enter into 1.** To participate in: *enter into a conversation; enter into an agreement.* **2.** To be a factor in: *Many considerations entered into the decision to move.* **enter on** or **enter upon** To begin; start: *The doctor entered on a career after graduating from medical school.*

enteritis (ĕn′tə-rī′tĭs) *n.* Inflammation of the intestinal tract.

enterprise (ĕn′tər-prīz′) *n.* **1.** An undertaking, especially one of some importance, complication, and risk: *a new business enterprise.* **2.** Readiness to undertake new ventures; initiative.

enterprising (ĕn′tər-prī′zĭng) *adj.* Showing initiative and willingness to undertake new projects: *An inventor must be an enterprising person.* —**en′ter·pris′ing·ly** *adv.*

entertain (ĕn′tər-tān′) *v.* **entertained, entertaining, entertains** —*tr.* **1.** To hold the attention of with something amusing or diverting: *A country music band entertained us.* **2.** To extend hospitality toward: *entertain friends at dinner.* **3.** To consider or keep in mind: *We entertained the idea of holding a fair.* —*intr.* To show hospitality to guests: *They entertain frequently.*

entertainer (ĕn′tər-tā′nər) *n.* A person, such as a singer or comic, who performs for an audience.

entertaining (ĕn′tər-tā′nĭng) *adj.* Amusing; agreeably diverting: *The clown told many entertaining stories.* —**en′ter·tain′ing·ly** *adv.*

entertainment (ĕn′tər-tān′mənt) *n.* **1.** The act of entertaining: *After a while the expenses of entertainment add up.* **2.** Something intended to amuse or divert, especially a performance or show. **3.** The pleasure that comes from being entertained; amusement: *offered to play the piano for our entertainment.*

enthrall (ĕn-thrôl′) *tr.v.* **enthralled, enthralling, enthralls 1.** To hold spellbound; captivate: *The magic show enthralled everyone.* **2.** To enslave. —**en·thrall′ment** *n.*

enthrone (ĕn-thrōn′) *tr.v.* **enthroned, enthroning, enthrones 1.** To place on a throne. **2.** To invest with sovereign power or with the authority of high office. **3.** To raise to a lofty position; exalt. —**en·throne′ment** *n.*

enthuse (ĕn-thōōz′) *tr.* & *intr.v.* **enthused, enthusing, enthuses** To cause (someone) to become enthusiastic or to show enthusiasm.

WORD HISTORY English can form new verbs by dropping a suffix from another word (such as a noun) that already exists. The new verb is then called a *back-formation.* An example is the verb **enthuse,** which was formed from the noun **enthusiasm.** Many writers dislike back-formations at first, but over time they tend to become accepted as everyday words. While *enthuse* is not yet fully accepted by all writers, no one objects to the verbs *donate* and *diagnose,* even though they are back-formations too—from the nouns *donation* and *diagnosis.*

enthusiasm (ĕn-thōō′zē-ăz′əm) *n.* Great interest in or excitement for a subject or cause: *The audience applauded with enthusiasm.*

enthusiast (ĕn-thōō′zē-ăst′) *n.* A person who is ardently absorbed in an interest or pursuit: *a golf enthusiast.*

enthusiastic (ĕn-thōō′zē-ăs′tĭk) *adj.* Having or showing enthusiasm: *an enthusiastic welcome; enthusiastic support of a team.* —**en·thu′si·as′ti·cal·ly** *adv.*

entice (ĕn-tīs′) *tr.v.* **enticed, enticing, entices** To attract by arousing hope or desire; lure: *Advertising entices people to buy things.* —**en·tice′ment** *n.*

entire (ĕn-tīr′) *adj.* **1.** Having no part missing or excepted; whole: *the entire country; his entire savings.* **2.** Without reservation or limitation; complete: *The plan has my entire approval.*

entirely (ĕn-tīr′lē) *adv.* **1.** Wholly; completely: *an argument entirely forgotten.* **2.** Solely or exclusively: *He was entirely to blame.*

entirety (ĕn-tī′rĭ-tē or ĕn-tīr′tē) *n., pl.* **entireties 1.** The condition of being entire; completeness: *I'd like to see the plan in its entirety.* **2.** The entire amount or extent; the whole: *They spent the entirety of their evening playing video games.*

entitle (ĕn-tīt′l) *tr.v.* **entitled, entitling, entitles 1.** To give a name or title to. **2.** To give a right or privilege to something: *This coupon entitles you to a discount.*

entitlement (ĕn-tīt′l-mənt) *n.* **1.** The act or process of entitling. **2.** The condition of being entitled. **3.** A government program that guarantees and provides benefits to a particular group.

entity (ĕn′tĭ-tē) *n., pl.* **entities** Something that exists and may be distinguished from other things: *American English and British English are distinct entities.*

entomb (ĕn-tōōm′) *tr.v.* **entombed, entombing, entombs** To place in or as if in a tomb or grave; bury: *The eruption of the volcano entombed whole buildings.* —**en·tomb′ment** *n.*

entomologist (ĕn′tə-mŏl′ə-jĭst) *n.* A scientist who specializes in entomology.

entomology (ĕn′tə-mŏl′ə-jē) *n.* The branch of zoology that deals with insects.

entourage (ŏn′tōō-räzh′) *n.* A group of associates or attendants who accompany an important person: *arrived with an entourage of staff members.*

entrails (ĕn′trālz′ or ĕn′trəlz) *pl.n.* The internal organs of the body, especially the intestines.

entrain (ĕn-trān′) *intr.* & *tr.v.* **entrained, entraining, entrains** To go or put aboard a train.

entrance¹ (ĕn′trəns) *n.* **1.** The act or an instance of entering: *an actor's entrance onstage.* **2.** A means or point by which to enter: *Use the back entrance of the building for deliveries.* **3.** The permission or power to enter; admission: *Entrance to the meeting was free.*

entrance² (ĕn-trăns′) *tr.v.* **entranced, entrancing, entrances 1.** To put into a trance. **2.** To fill with delight, enchantment, or wonder; fascinate: *The exciting movie entranced us all.* —**en·tranc′ing** *adj.*

WORD HISTORY Entrance¹ comes from Middle English and Old French *entraunce,* meaning "right to enter," which comes from Old French *entrer,* meaning "to enter." **Entrance²** is derived from Modern English *trance.*

entrant (ĕn′trənt) *n.* A person or animal that enters a competition, such as a race or contest.

entrap (ĕn-trăp′) *tr.v.* **entrapped, entrapping, entraps 1.** To catch in a trap: *A net entrapped the fish.* **2.** To lure into danger or difficulty: *She felt entrapped by her conflicting social commitments.* **3.** To trick or manipulate (someone) into doing something illegal so that he or she can be prosecuted for breaking the law. —**en·trap′ment** *n.*

entreat (ĕn-trēt′) *tr.v.* **entreated, entreating, entreats** To ask earnestly; beg; implore.

entreaty (ĕn-trē′tē) *n., pl.* **entreaties** An earnest request; a plea.

entrée or **entree** (ŏn′trā *or* ŏn-trā′) *n.* **1.** The main course of a meal. **2.** The power, permission, or liberty to enter; admittance: *gained entrée to the meeting.*

entrench (ĕn-trĕnch′) *tr.v.* **entrenched, entrenching, entrenches 1.** To provide with a trench, especially to fortify or defend: *The general entrenched the forces and waited for an attack.* **2.** To fix firmly or securely: *Their opinions are so entrenched they cannot change.* —**en·trench′ment** *n.*

entrepreneur (ŏn′trə-prə-nûr′ *or* ŏn′trə-prə-noŏr′) *n.* A person who organizes and operates a business enterprise and assumes the risks involved.

entropy (ĕn′trə-pē) *n., pl.* **entropies 1.** A measure of the amount of disorder or randomness in a self-contained physical system. **2.** The tendency for all matter and energy in the universe to evolve toward a state of inert uniformity. **3.** The deterioration of a system or society, especially when it seems inevitable: *urban activists trying to fight entropy by organizing neighborhood groups.* —**en·tro′pic** (ĕn-trō′pĭk *or* ĕn-trŏp′ĭk) *adj.* —**en·tro′pi·cal·ly** *adv.*

entrust (ĕn-trŭst′) *tr.v.* **entrusted, entrusting, entrusts 1.** To turn over (something) to another for safekeeping, care, or action: *Our neighbors entrusted the care of their dog to me.* **2.** To give as a trust to (someone): *entrusted an aide with an important message.*

entry (ĕn′trē) *n., pl.* **entries 1.** The act or right of entering; entrance: *A visa is needed for entry into the country.* **2.** A means or place by which to enter: *The entry is a narrow hall.* **3.** An item written in a diary, register, list, or other record: *Each sale is an entry in this account book.* **4.** A word, phrase, or term entered and defined, as in a dictionary or encyclopedia. **5.** A person or thing entered in a contest: *That horse was a late entry in the race.*

entryway (ĕn′trē-wā′) *n.* A passage or opening by which to enter.

entry word *n.* A headword.

entwine (ĕn-twīn′) *tr.v.* **entwined, entwining, entwines** To twine around or together: *Ivy entwined the pillars of the porch.*

enumerate (ĭ-noō′mə-rāt′) *tr.v.* **enumerated, enumerating, enumerates 1.** To count off or name one by one; list: *My list of objectives is too long to enumerate.* **2.** To determine the number of; count. —**e·nu′mer·a′tion** *n.* —**e·nu′mer·a′tor** *n.*

enunciate (ĭ-nŭn′sē-āt′) *v.* **enunciated, enunciating, enunciates** —*tr.* **1.** To pronounce; articulate: *The speaker enunciated every word clearly.* **2.** To state or set forth precisely or systematically: *The speech enunciated a new program of education reforms.* —*intr.* To pronounce words; speak aloud: *The professor enunciated so poorly that we hardly understood the lecture.* —**e·nun′ci·a′tion** (ĭ-nŭn′sē-ā′shən) *n.* —**e·nun′ci·a′tor** *n.*

envelop (ĕn-vĕl′əp) *tr.v.* **enveloped, enveloping, envelops** To enclose or encase completely with or as if with a covering: *Fog enveloped the tallest buildings.* —**en·vel′op·ment** *n.*

envelope (ĕn′və-lōp′ *or* ŏn′və-lōp′) *n.* **1.** A flat paper container, especially for a letter. **2.** Something that envelops; a wrapping. **3.** The section of an airship or balloon that is filled with gas.

enviable (ĕn′vē-ə-bəl) *adj.* Admirable or desirable enough to be envied: *an enviable achievement.* —**en′vi·a·bly** *adv.*

envious (ĕn′vē-əs) *adj.* Feeling, expressing, or characterized by envy: *Other contestants were envious of the winner.* —**en′vi·ous·ly** *adv.* —**en′vi·ous·ness** *n.*

environment (ĕn-vī′rən-mənt *or* ĕn-vī′ərn-mənt) *n.* **1a.** The entire natural world, often excluding humans: *chemicals that pollute the environment.* **b.** A designated part of the natural world; an ecosystem: *the desert environment.* **2.** The combination of physical and biological conditions that affect the development and survival of an organism or group of organisms: *how whales respond to changes in their environment.* **3.** The social and cultural conditions affecting a person or community: *He grew up in an urban environment.* **4.** The general set of conditions in which an activity is carried out: *a good environment for business.*

environmental (ĕn-vī′rən-mĕn′tl *or* ĕn-vī′ərn-mĕn′tl) *adj.* **1.** Relating to or associated with the environment: *climate and other environmental factors.* **2.** Relating to or concerned with the impact of human activities on the natural environment: *the environmental movement.* **3.** Relating to potentially harmful factors originating in the environment: *environmental health.* **4.** —**en·vi′ron·men′tal·ly** *adv.*

environs (ĕn-vī′rənz *or* ĕn-vī′ərnz) *pl.n.* A surrounding area, especially of a city: *The historical environs of Boston include Lexington and Concord.*

envisage (ĕn-vĭz′ĭj) *tr.v.* **envisaged, envisaging, envisages** To form a picture of in the mind; conceive of: *envisage world peace.*

envision (ĕn-vĭzh′ən) *tr.v.* **envisioned, envisioning, envisions** To picture in the mind; imagine.

envoy (ĕn′voi′ *or* ŏn′voi′) *n.* **1.** A representative of a government who is sent on a special diplomatic mission. **2.** A diplomat who represents a government and ranks next below an ambassador. **3.** A messenger; an agent.

envy (ĕn′vē) *n., pl.* **envies 1.** A feeling of discontent and resentment caused by wanting something that is possessed by or is achieved by someone else: *felt envy for her friend's new car.* **2.** The object of such a feeling: *The racing bike was the envy of everyone who saw it.* ❖ *tr.v.* **envied, envying, envies 1.** To feel envy toward: *I envy you for the chance to travel to Mexico.* **2.** To regard with envy: *envy the talent of a great musician.*

enwrap (ĕn-răp′) *tr.v.* **enwrapped, enwrapping, enwraps** To wrap up or enclose: *The delicate vase was enwrapped in tissue paper.*

enzyme (ĕn′zīm) *n.* Any of numerous proteins produced in living cells and acting as catalysts in the chemical processes of living organisms. Digestive enzymes, for example, help break down large food molecules into smaller molecules that can be absorbed by the body.

Eocene (ē′ə-sēn′) *n.* The second epoch of the Tertiary Period, from about 56 to 34 million years ago. During the Eocene, climates were warm and most modern families of mammals arose. —**E′o·cene′** *adj.*

eohippus (ē′ō-hĭp′əs) *n.* The hyracotherium.

eon also **aeon** (ē′ŏn′ *or* ē′ən) *n.* **1.** An extremely long period of time; an age; eternity. **2.** A division of geologic time that contains two or more eras.

Eos (ē′ŏs′) *n.* In Greek mythology, the goddess of the dawn, identified with the Roman Aurora.

epaulet also **epaulette** (ĕp′ə-lĕt′ *or* ĕp′ə-lĕt′) *n.* An ornamental strap worn on the shoulder of an officer's uniform.

ephemeral (ĭ-fĕm′ər-əl) *adj.* **1.** Lasting only a brief time; short-lived: *For most people, fame is ephemeral, and their achievements are soon forgotten.* **2.** Living or growing for only a short time, as certain plants or insects do. —e·phem′er·al·ly *adv.*

Ephesian (ĭ-fē′zhən) *adj.* Relating to ancient Ephesus or its people, language, or culture. ❖ *n.* **1.** A native or inhabitant of ancient Ephesus. **2. Ephesians** *(used with a singular verb)* A book of the New Testament consisting of a letter from the Apostle Paul to the Christians of Ephesus.

epi– or **ep–** A prefix that means: **1.** On; upon: *epiphyte.* **2.** Over; above: *epicenter.*

epic (ĕp′ĭk) *n.* **1.** A long poem about the deeds of heroic characters. **2.** A literary or other artistic work that has the qualities of an epic. ❖ *adj.* **1.** Relating to or resembling an epic: *an epic film.* **2.** Resembling something described in an epic; grand; tremendous: *an epic achievement.* —ep′i·cal·ly *adv.*

epicenter (ĕp′ĭ-sĕn′tər) *n.* The point of the earth's surface directly above the focus of an earthquake.

epicure (ĕp′ĭ-kyŏŏr′) *n.* A person who knows much about and has excellent taste in good food and drink.

epicurean (ĕp′ĭ-kyŏŏ-rē′ən *or* ĕp′ĭ-kyŏŏr′ē-ən) *adj.* **1.** Devoted to the pursuit of pleasure, especially to the enjoyment of good food and comfort. **2.** Suited to the tastes of an epicure: *an epicurean meal of exotic foods.* ❖ *n.* An epicure.

epidemic (ĕp′ĭ-dĕm′ĭk) *n.* **1.** An outbreak of a disease, especially a contagious disease, in a region or among a group of people: *an epidemic of cholera after the earthquake.* **2.** A rapid spread or development: *an epidemic of homelessness.* ❖ *adj.* Spreading rapidly and widely among the inhabitants of an area: *conditions for an outbreak of epidemic typhus.*

epidemiology (ĕp′ĭ-dē′mē-ŏl′ə-jē) *n.* The branch of medicine that deals with the study of the causes, distribution, and control of disease in populations. —ep′i·de′mi·ol′o·gist *n.*

epidermis (ĕp′ĭ-dûr′mĭs) *n.* **1.** The outer protective layer of the skin of vertebrates. **2.** The outer protective layer of cells of the stems, roots, and leaves of plants.

epiglottis (ĕp′ĭ-glŏt′ĭs) *n.* A thin triangular flap of cartilage at the base of the tongue that covers the glottis during swallowing to keep food from entering the windpipe.

epigram (ĕp′ĭ-grăm′) *n.* **1.** A short witty poem expressing a single thought. **2.** A short witty saying.

epigrammatic (ĕp′ĭ-grə-măt′ĭk) *adj.* **1.** Resembling an epigram; terse; witty. **2.** Containing or inclined to use epigrams. —ep′i·gram·mat′i·cal·ly *adv.*

epigraph (ĕp′ĭ-grăf′) *n.* **1.** An inscription, as on a building or statue. **2.** A quotation at the beginning of a book or a chapter of a book that suggests its theme.

epilepsy (ĕp′ə-lĕp′sē) *n.* Any of various disorders of the nervous system characterized by recurring seizures, often resulting in convulsions or the loss of consciousness.

epileptic (ĕp′ə-lĕp′tĭk) *adj.* Relating to or affected with epilepsy: *an epileptic attack.* ❖ *n.* A person who has epilepsy.

epilogue also **epilog** (ĕp′ə-lôg′) *n.* **1.** A short section at the end of a literary work, often discussing what happens to the characters after the main story. **2.** A short poem or speech spoken to the audience at the end of a play.

epinephrine (ĕp′ə-nĕf′rĭn) *n.* A hormone secreted by the adrenal glands that quickens the heartbeat and raises blood pressure, thereby preparing the body for vigorous action, as in response to danger or other stress. It is also prepared synthetically and used to treat asthma.

epiphany (ĭ-pĭf′ə-nē) *n., pl.* **epiphanies 1. Epiphany** A Christian feast traditionally held on January 6 that in the Western Church celebrates the visit of the Magi to the infant Jesus and in the Eastern Church celebrates the baptism of Jesus. **2.** A revelatory manifestation of a divine being. **3.** A sudden understanding or perception by means of intuition.

epiphyte (ĕp′ə-fīt′) *n.* A plant growing on another plant that provides support but not nutrients. Spanish moss and many orchids are epiphytes. —ep′i·phyt′ic (ĕp′ə-fĭt′ĭk) *adj.*

episcopal (ĭ-pĭs′kə-pəl) *adj.* **1.** Relating to or governed by bishops. **2. Episcopal** Relating to the Episcopal Church.

Episcopal Church *n.* The church in the United States that agrees with the Church of England in doctrine and most practices.

Episcopalian (ĭ-pĭs′kə-pā′lē-ən) *adj.* Relating to the Episcopal Church. ❖ *n.* A member of the Episcopal Church.

episode (ĕp′ĭ-sōd′) *n.* **1a.** An event or incident in the course of a larger series: *Living in India was an exciting episode in her life.* **b.** An incident that forms a distinct part of a story. **2.** A part of a novel or radio or television program presented as a series: *The story was divided into six episodes for TV.* —ep·i·sod′ic (ĕp′ĭ-sŏd′ĭk) *adj.*

episodic (ĕp′ĭ-sŏd′ĭk) *adj.* **1.** Relating to or resembling an episode. **2.** Composed of a series of episodes: *an episodic novel.* **3.** Limited to the duration of an episode; temporary. —ep′i·sod′i·cal·ly *adv.*

epistemology (ĭ-pĭs′tə-mŏl′ə-jē) *n.* The branch of philosophy that examines the nature of knowledge, its presuppositions and foundations, and its extent and validity. —e·pis′te·mo·log′i·cal (ĭ-pĭs′tə-mə-lŏj′ĭ-kəl) *adj.*

epistle (ĭ-pĭs′əl) *n.* **1.** A letter, especially a formal one. **2. Epistle** One of the letters written by the early Christians and included as books in the New Testament.

epistolary (ĭ-pĭs′tə-lĕr′ē) *adj.* **1.** Relating to or associated with letters or the writing of letters. **2.** Being in the form of a letter or letters: *an epistolary novel.* **3.** Carried on by means of letters: *an epistolary friendship.*

epitaph (ĕp′ĭ-tăf′) *n.* An inscription on a tombstone or monument in memory of the person buried there.

epithelium (ĕp′ə-thē′lē-əm) *n., pl.* **epitheliums** or **epithelia** (ĕp′ə-thē′lē-ə) The thin tissue that covers most of the inner and outer surfaces of an animal body and lines the inside of certain organs. —ep′i·the′li·al *adj.*

epithet (ĕp′ə-thĕt′) *n.* A term used to describe the nature of a person or thing; for example, *The Big Apple* is an epithet for New York City.

epitome (ĭ-pĭt′ə-mē) *n.* **1.** A person or thing that is a typical example of an entire class or type: *Her remark was the epitome of good judgment.* **2.** A summary of a book, article, or other literary work; an abstract.

epitomize (ĭ-pĭt′ə-mīz′) *tr.v.* **epitomized, epitomizing, epitomizes** To be a typical example of: *Daniel Boone epitomizes the independent frontiersman.*

e pluribus unum (ē′ plŏŏr′ə-bəs yōō′nəm) Out of many, one (the official motto of the seal of the United States).

epoch (ĕp′ək *or* ē′pŏk′) *n.* **1.** A period, especially one in history marked by certain important events or developments; an era: *the epoch of space exploration.* **2.** A unit of time that is a division of a geologic period.

epochal (ĕp′ə-kəl) *adj.* **1.** Relating to or characteristic of an epoch. **2.** Highly important or significant; momentous: *epochal decisions made by Lincoln during the Civil War.*

eponymous (ĭ-pŏn′ə-məs) *adj.* Named after something else or deriving from an existing name or word.

epoxy (ĭ-pŏk′sē) *n., pl.* **epoxies** Any of various artificial resins that are tough, strongly adhesive, and resistant to chemicals, used in making protective coatings and glues.

epsilon (ĕp′sə-lŏn′) *n.* The fifth letter of the Greek alphabet, written E, ε. In English it is represented as *E, e.*

Epsom salts (ĕp′səm) *pl.n.* *(used with a singular verb)* A colorless crystalline compound of magnesium, sulfur, and oxygen, used in making textiles, in fertilizers, and for medical purposes.

eq. An abbreviation of: **1.** equal. **2.** equation. **3.** equivalent.

equable (ĕk′wə-bəl *or* ē′kwə-bəl) *adj.* **1.** Not varying; steady; even: *the equable climate of the Caribbean.* **2.** Even-tempered; not easily upset; serene: *Our teacher has an equable disposition.* —**eq′ua·bil′i·ty** *n.* —**eq′ua·bly** *adv.*

equal (ē′kwəl) *adj.* **1a.** Having the same quantity, measure, or extent as another: *equal strength; equal size.* **b.** Having the same value, as 3 + 2 and 6 − 1. **2.** Having the same privileges, status, or rights: *All citizens are equal before the law.* **3.** Being the same for all members of a group; even: *Every player had an equal chance to win.* ❖ *n.* A person or thing that is equal to another: *Most people want to be treated as equals.* ❖ *tr.v.* **equaled, equaling, equals** *or* **equalled, equalling, equals 1.** To be equal to: *Two pints equal a quart. My ability equals theirs.* **2.** To do, make, or produce something equal to: *The athlete equaled the world's record in the mile run.* —**e′qual·ly** *adv.*

equality (ĭ-kwŏl′ĭ-tē) *n., pl.* **equalities** The condition of being equal, especially the condition of enjoying equal rights: *equality under the law.*

equalize (ē′kwə-līz′) *tr.v.* **equalized, equalizing, equalizes 1.** To make equal: *Opening the bottle equalizes the pressure with the outside air.* **2.** To make uniform: *Move this box to equalize the weight on both sides of the car.* —**e′qual·i·za′tion** (ē′kwə-lĭ-zā′shən) *n.* —**e′qual·iz′er** *n.*

equal sign *n.* The symbol (=) used in mathematics to show that something is equal, as in $a = b$ and $2 + 2 = 4$.

equanimity (ē′kwə-nĭm′ĭ-tē *or* ĕk′wə-nĭm′ĭ-tē) *n.* The condition or quality of being calm and even-tempered; composure: *Judges are expected to show equanimity in court.*

equate (ĭ-kwāt′) *tr.v.* **equated, equating, equates** To make equal or consider as equal or equivalent: *Many people equate fame with success.*

equation (ĭ-kwā′zhən *or* ĭ-kwā′shən) *n.* **1.** A mathematical statement asserting that two expressions are equal. For example, $3 \times 2 = 6$, $y = 2 + 8$, and $x + y = 18$ are all equations. **2.** An expression using chemical formulas and symbols to show the quantities and substances in a chemical reaction. For example, two hydrogen molecules reacting with an oxygen molecule to form two molecules of water is expressed by the equation $2H_2 + O_2 = 2H_2O$.

equator (ĭ-kwā′tər) *n.* **1.** The imaginary line that circles the earth halfway between the North and South Poles. It divides the earth into the Northern Hemisphere and the Southern Hemisphere. **2.** A similar circle on any celestial object: *the sun's equator.* **3.** The celestial equator.

equatorial (ē′kwə-tôr′ē-əl *or* ĕk′wə-tôr′ē-əl) *adj.* **1.** Relating to or near the equator: *an equatorial region of Brazil.* **2.** Characteristic of conditions at the earth's equator: *equatorial heat.*

equerry (ĕk′wə-rē) *n., pl.* **equerries 1.** An officer in charge of the horses in a royal or noble household. **2.** In England, a personal attendant to a member of the royal family.

equestrian (ĭ-kwĕs′trē-ən) *adj.* **1.** Relating to horseback riders or horseback riding: *equestrian ability.* **2.** Mounted or represented as mounted on horseback: *an equestrian statue of the king.* ❖ *n.* A person who rides a horse or performs on horseback.

equestrienne (ĭ-kwĕs′trē-ĕn′) *n.* A woman who rides a horse or performs on horseback.

equi– A prefix that means equal or equally: *equidistant.*

WORD BUILDING The prefix **equi–** means "equal" or "equally." *Equi–* is from the Latin prefix *aequi–*, which came from the Latin word *aequus,* meaning "equal." Thus *equidistant* means "equally distant." *Equi–* often occurs in words with Latin elements. For example, *equinox* means "having the night equal (to the day)," from Latin *nox,* "night." *Equivalent* is from *valēre,* "to be worth, amount to," and so is literally "amounting to the same thing."

equiangular (ē′kwē-ăng′gyə-lər) *adj.* Having all angles equal: *Rectangles are equiangular.*

equidistant (ē′kwĭ-dĭs′tənt) *adj.* Equally distant. —**e′qui·dis′tant·ly** *adv.*

equilateral (ē′kwə-lăt′ər-əl) *adj.* Having all sides equal: *an equilateral triangle.* —**e′qui·lat′er·al·ly** *adv.*

equilibrium (ē′kwə-lĭb′rē-əm) *n.* **1.** A condition of balance or stability: *Ideally, the supply of a product should be in equilibrium with the demand for it.* **2.** Mental or emotional balance; poise: *The quarrel upset their equilibrium for the whole morning.*

equine (ē′kwīn *or* ĕk′wīn′) *adj.* Relating to or resembling a horse.

equinoctial (ē′kwə-nŏk′shəl *or* ĕk′wə-nŏk′shəl) *adj.* **1.** Relating to an equinox. **2.** Occurring at or near the time of an equinox: *an equinoctial storm.*

equinox (ē′kwə-nŏks′ *or* ĕk′wə-nŏks′) *n.* Either of the times of year when the sun crosses the celestial equator and day and night are about equal in length. In the Northern Hemisphere, the vernal equinox occurs around March 20 and the autumnal equinox occurs around September 22.

equip (ĭ-kwĭp′) *tr.v.* **equipped, equipping, equips** To supply with what is needed; provide: *The expedition was equipped with oxygen tanks for climbing at high altitudes.*

equipage (ĕk′wə-pĭj) *n.* **1.** Equipment, as of an army. **2.** An elegantly equipped horse-drawn carriage, usually attended by footmen.

equipment (ĭ-kwĭp′mənt) *n.* **1.** The things needed or used for a particular purpose: *camping equipment.* **2.** The act of equipping or state of being equipped: *The equipment of the expedition took months to complete.*

equipoise (ē′kwə-poiz′ *or* ĕk′wə-poiz′) *n.* **1.** Equality in distribution, as of weight or force; balance; equilibrium. **2.** A weight or force that balances another; a counterbalance.

equitable (ĕk′wĭ-tə-bəl) *adj.* Just and impartial: *Judges are expected to make equitable decisions.* —**eq′ui·ta·bly** *adv.*

equity (ĕk′wĭ-tē) *n., pl.* **equities 1.** Justice or fairness: *No one questioned the equity of the jury's verdict.* **2a.** The amount that a person's ownership in a business or property is worth after subtracting the debts that are owed by the business or on the property. **b. equities** Common or preferred stock: *How much of their life savings is in equities?*

equivalence (ĭ-kwĭv′ə-ləns) *n.* The condition or property of being equivalent.

equivalent (ĭ-kwĭv′ə-lənt) *adj.* **1.** Equal, as in value, meaning, or force: *The wish of the king is equivalent to a command.* **2.** Having a one-to-one correspondence, as between parts: *equivalent geometric figures.* ❖ *n.* Something that is equivalent: *A dime is the equivalent of two nickels.*

equivocal (ĭ-kwĭv′ə-kəl) *adj.* **1.** Open to two or more interpretations and often intended to conceal the truth: *The politician gave an equivocal answer to the reporter's question.* See Synonyms at **ambiguous. 2.** Characterized by a mixture of opposing elements and therefore questionable or uncertain: *The experiment gave equivocal results that we could not interpret with certainty.* —**e·quiv′o·cal·ly** *adv.*

equivocate (ĭ-kwĭv′ə-kāt′) *intr.v.* **equivocated, equivocating, equivocates** To use language that can be interpreted in more than one way, especially in order to mislead: *Stop equivocating and tell us what you really think.* —**e·quiv′o·ca′tor** *n.*

equivocation (ĭ-kwĭv′ə-kā′shən) *n.* **1.** The use of equivocal language. **2.** An equivocal statement: *The defense lawyer's remarks were full of equivocations.*

ER An abbreviation of emergency room.

–er[1] A suffix that means: **1.** A person or thing that does a specified action: *swimmer; blender.* **2.** A person who is born in or lives in a place: *islander; New Yorker.* **3.** A person or thing that is: *foreigner; six-footer.* **4.** A person or thing that is associated or involved with: *banker; gardener.*

–er[2] A suffix that forms the comparative degree of adjectives and adverbs: *neater; slower.*

era (îr′ə *or* ĕr′ə) *n.* **1.** A period of time as marked from a specific date or event: *The atomic era and the postwar era began in 1945.* **2.** A period of time characterized by particular circumstances, events, or people: *the Colonial era of American history.* **3.** A major division of geologic time, containing one or more periods.

eradicate (ĭ-răd′ĭ-kāt′) *tr.v.* **eradicated, eradicating, eradicates 1.** To get rid of; eliminate: *a campaign to eradicate smallpox.* **2.** To tear up by the roots. —**e·rad′i·ca′tion** *n.*

erase (ĭ-rās′) *tr.v.* **erased, erasing, erases 1.** To remove (something written or drawn) by rubbing, scraping, or wiping: *erase a mistake.* **2a.** To remove (recorded material) from a magnetic tape, computer disk, or other storage medium. **b.** To remove recorded material from (a magnetic tape, for example). **3.** To destroy or remove as if by wiping out: *Time will erase hurt feelings.* —**e·ras′a·ble** *adj.*

eraser (ĭ-rā′sər) *n.* An implement that erases marks made with pencil, ink, or chalk.

erasure (ĭ-rā′shər) *n.* **1.** The act of erasing. **2.** Something erased, as a word or number: *The paper had numerous erasures.*

Erato (ĕr′ə-tō′) *n.* In Greek mythology, the Muse of lyric poetry.

erbium (ûr′bē-əm) *n. Symbol* **Er** A soft, silvery metallic element used in nuclear research and in coloring glass and porcelain. Atomic number 68. See **Periodic Table.**

ere (âr) *prep.* Previous to; before. ❖ *conj.* Sooner than; rather than.

e-reader (ē′rē′dər) *n.* A device with a screen on which electronic texts may be read.

erect (ĭ-rĕkt′) *adj.* **1.** In a vertical or upright position: *a soldier's erect posture; an erect flower stalk.* **2.** Being enlarged and stiff as a result of sexual excitement. ❖ *tr.v.* **erected, erecting, erects 1.** To build; put up; construct: *erect a skyscraper.* **2.** To raise upright; set on end: *erect a new telephone pole.* **3.** To set up; establish: *The country erected a model legal system.* —**e·rect′ly** *adv.* —**e·rect′ness** *n.*

erectile (ĭ-rĕk′təl *or* ĭ-rĕk′tīl′) *adj.* **1.** Capable of being raised to an upright position: *a fish with erectile spines.* **2.** Relating to tissue that is capable of filling with blood and becoming rigid.

erection (ĭ-rĕk′shən) *n.* **1.** The act of erecting, building, or raising upright: *The erection of the new temple took nearly two years.* **2.** The stiffening of certain body parts, especially the penis or the clitoris, when the tissues within them fill with blood.

erg (ûrg) *n.* A unit used to measure energy or work, equal to the force of one dyne over a distance of one centimeter. This unit has been mostly replaced by the joule.

ergo (ûr′gō *or* âr′gō) *conj. & adv.* Consequently; therefore.

ergonomics (ûr′gə-nŏm′ĭks) *n.* **1.** *(used with a singular verb)* The applied science of designing objects such as tools or furniture with consideration for the user's comfort, health, and productivity. **2.** *(used with a plural verb)* The design factors with which this science is concerned: *The ergonomics of the new office were felt to be optimal.* —**er′go·nom′ic** *adj.* —**er′go·nom′i·cal·ly** *adv.*

ergot (ûr′gət *or* ûr′gŏt′) *n.* A fungus that infects rye, wheat, and other grain plants, forming black masses among the seeds. Grain infected with ergot is poisonous and can cause serious illness.

Erie (îr′ē) *n., pl.* **Erie** *or* **Eries 1.** A member of a Native American people formerly living in the region south of Lake Erie. **2.** The Iroquoian language of the Erie.

Erinyes (ĭ-rĭn′ē-ēz′) *pl.n.* In Greek mythology, the terrible winged goddesses who pursued and punished those who committed unavenged crimes, identified with the Roman Furies.

Eris (îr′ĭs *or* ĕr′ĭs) *n.* **1.** In Greek Mythology, the goddess of discord. **2.** A dwarf planet with a diameter of about 1,500 miles (2,400 kilometers). It is the largest known dwarf planet in our solar system and has a moon of its own. —SEE NOTE AT **planet.**

ermine (ûr′mĭn) *n.* **1.** A weasel of northern regions having brownish fur that turns white in winter. **2.** The valuable white fur of this animal.

erode (ĭ-rōd′) *v.* **eroded, eroding, erodes** —*tr.* **1.** To wear away by or as if by rubbing or scraping: *Wind eroded the hillside.* **2.** To eat into; corrode: *The acidity of the water* *eroded the pipes.* **3.** To form by wearing away: *The river eroded a deep gorge through the rock.* **4.** To cause to diminish or deteriorate: *The bookkeeper's mistakes eroded their trust in his work.* —*intr.* **1.** To become worn away gradually: *The cliffs along the seashore have eroded over the centuries.* **2.** To diminish or deteriorate: *Public confidence in the mayor eroded.*

Eros (ĕr′ŏs′ *or* îr′ŏs′) *n.* In Greek mythology, the god of love, identified with the Roman Cupid.

erosion (ĭ-rō′zhən) *n.* **1.** The action of eroding or the condition of being eroded: *soil erosion.* **2.** Diminishment or deterioration: *the erosion of public confidence.*

erosive (ĭ-rō′sĭv) *adj.* Causing erosion: *erosive winds.*

erotic (ĭ-rŏt′ĭk) *adj.* Relating to or arousing sexual desire. —**e·rot′i·cal·ly** *adv.*

err (ĕr *or* ûr) *intr.v.* **erred, erring, errs 1.** To make a mistake or error; be incorrect: *We erred in thinking the bus would be on time.* **2.** To commit an act that is wrong; do wrong.

errand (ĕr′ənd) *n.* **1.** A short trip taken to do something, usually for someone else: *Our neighbor asked me to run an errand to the store downtown.* **2.** The purpose or object of such a trip: *My errand was to mail a letter.*

errant (ĕr′ənt) *adj.* **1.** Roving or wandering: *knights errant seeking adventure.* **2.** Straying from the proper course or correct behavior: *an errant youth.*

erratic (ĭ-răt′ĭk) *adj.* **1.** Lacking a fixed course; wandering: *a moth's erratic flight.* **2.** Lacking consistency, regularity, or uniformity; irregular: *an erratic heartbeat.* **3.** Straying from the usual course in conduct or opinion; eccentric: *erratic behavior.* —**er·rat′i·cal·ly** *adv.*

erratum (ĭ-rä′təm) *n., pl.* **errata** (ĭ-rä′tə) An error in printing or writing, especially such an error noted in a list of corrections and bound into a book.

erroneous (ĭ-rō′nē-əs) *adj.* Containing or derived from error; mistaken: *an erroneous belief.* —**er·ro′ne·ous·ly** *adv.*

error (ĕr′ər) *n.* **1.** Something that is incorrect, wrong, or false: *The waiter made an error in adding up our bill.* **2.** The condition of being incorrect or wrong: *The statement is in error.* **3.** The difference between the measured value of a quantity and its exact or true value: *The error in the thermostat was 10 degrees.* **4.** In baseball, a fielding or throwing play in which a player misses the ball or throws it inaccurately, allowing a runner to reach first base or advance one or more bases.

ersatz (ĕr′zäts′) *adj.* Being a substitute or imitation; artificial: *ersatz leather.*

erstwhile (ûrst′wīl′) *adv.* In times past; formerly. ❖ *adj.* Former: *an erstwhile foe.*

erudite (ĕr′yə-dīt′ *or* ĕr′ə-dīt′) *adj.* Having or marked by great knowledge or learning; learned: *an erudite book; an erudite person.* —**er′u·dite′ly** *adv.*

erudition (ĕr′yə-dĭsh′ən *or* ĕr′ə-dĭsh′ən) *n.* Extensive learning.

erupt (ĭ-rŭpt′) *intr.v.* **erupted, erupting, erupts 1.** To throw or force out something violently, such as lava, ash, and gases: *The volcano erupted.* **2.** To be thrown or forced out: *Water erupted from the geyser.* **3.** To develop suddenly: *War erupted between the two nations.* **4.** To express oneself suddenly and loudly: *The audience erupted in laughter.* **5.** To break through the gums in developing. Used of teeth. **6.** To appear on the skin: *A rash erupted on the child's back.* —**e·rup′tive** *adj.*

eruption (ĭ-rŭp′shən) *n.* **1.** The act or an instance of erupting: *the eruption of a geyser.* **2.** A sudden, almost

violent outburst: *an eruption of anger.* **3.** A rash or blemish on the skin: *an eruption caused by a virus.*

–ery *or* **–ry** A suffix that means: **1.** A place for: *bakery.* **2.** A collection or class: *greenery.* **3.** A state or condition: *slavery.* **4.** Act or practice: *bribery.* **5.** Characteristics or qualities of: *snobbery*

erythrocyte (ĭ-rĭth′rə-sīt′) *n.* A red blood cell.

–es[1] Variant of **–s**[1].

–es[2] Variant of **–s**[2].

escalate (ĕs′kə-lāt′) *intr. & tr.v.* **escalated, escalating, escalates 1.** To increase or cause to increase: *Rents escalated during the 1990s. The cold weather escalated the number of flu cases.* **2.** To become or cause to become more intense: *Bad feeling between the countries escalated. The diplomatic blunder escalated the crisis.* —**es′ca·la′tion** *n.*

escalator (ĕs′kə-lā′tər) *n.* A moving stairway consisting of steps attached to a continuously circulating belt.

escapade (ĕs′kə-pād′) *n.* An adventurous, often reckless act or undertaking.

escape (ĭ-skāp′) *v.* **escaped, escaping, escapes** —*intr.* **1.** To break loose from confinement; get free: *The prisoners escaped by climbing the wall.* **2.** To avoid capture, danger, or harm: *The thieves escaped every time the police tried to catch them.* **3.** To leak or seep out: *All the air escaped from the balloon.* —*tr.* **1.** To get free of; break loose from: *A vacation will allow me to escape the noise of the city.* **2.** To succeed in avoiding (capture, danger, or harm): *I barely escaped injury when the ladder fell.* **3.** To fail to be noticed or remembered by: *The name of the new worker escapes me.* **4.** To come out of (someone or someone's lips) involuntarily: *A cry of delight escaped the child's lips.* ❖ *n.* **1.** The act or means of escaping: *prisoners planning an escape.* **2.** A means of escaping: *An open gate provided the dog's escape.* **3.** A means of obtaining temporary freedom from worry, care, or unpleasantness: *For her, running provides an escape from everyday problems.* **4.** A key on a computer keyboard pressed to interrupt a command or exit a program.

escapee (ĭ-skā′pē′) *n.* A person who has escaped, especially an escaped prisoner.

escapement (ĭ-skāp′mənt) *n.* A device in clocks and watches that controls the speed at which the movement runs. It consists of a gearwheel controlled by a ratchet having teeth that fit into the wheel as the ratchet swings, allowing the wheel to escape or move one tooth at a time.

escape velocity *n.* The minimum velocity that a body, such as a rocket, must achieve to overcome the gravitational pull of the earth or another celestial object.

escape wheel *n.* The rotating notched gearwheel in an escapement.

escapism (ĭ-skā′pĭz′əm) *n.* The tendency to escape from daily routine or responsibilities by engaging in daydreams, entertainment, or other forms of distraction. —**es·cap′ist** *adj. & n.*

escargot (ĕs′kär-gō′) *n., pl.* **escargots** (ĕs′kär-gō′) An edible snail.

escarpment (ĭ-skärp′mənt) *n.* **1.** A steep slope or long cliff formed by erosion or by vertical movement of the earth's crust along a fault. **2.** A steep slope or embankment in front of a fortification.

–escence A suffix that means the state or process: *convalescence; luminescence.*

–escent A suffix that means beginning to be or becoming: *convalescent; luminescent.*

eschatology (ĕs′kə-tŏl′ə-jē) *n.* **1.** The branch of theology that is concerned with the end of the world or of humankind. **2.** A belief or a doctrine concerning the ultimate or final things, such as death, the destiny of humanity, the Second Coming, or the Last Judgment. —**es·chat′·o·log′i·cal** (ĭ-skăt′l-ŏj′ĭ-kəl or ĕs′kə-tə-lŏj′ĭ-kəl) adj.

eschew (ĕs-chōō′) tr.v. **eschewed, eschewing, eschews** To take care to avoid; shun: eschew bad company.

escort (ĕs′kôrt′) n. **1.** One or more people accompanying another to give protection or guidance or to pay honor: The visiting foreign leader was given a police escort. **2.** One or more airplanes, warships, or other vehicles accompanying another or others to provide protection. **3.** A man who is the companion of a woman, especially on a social occasion. ❖ tr.v. (ĭ-skôrt′ or ĕs′kôrt′) **escorted, escorting, escorts** To accompany or guide, especially as an escort: An honor guard escorted the president during the parade. See Synonyms at **accompany.**

escrow (ĕs′krō or ĕ-skrō′) n. Money, property, a deed, or a bond put into the custody of a third party until certain conditions are fulfilled. ◆ **in escrow** In the care of another until various conditions are met: The bank is holding the savings account in escrow until the heirs reach their twenty-first birthday.

escudo (ĭ-skōō′dō) n., pl. **escudos** The former primary unit of currency in Portugal.

escutcheon (ĭ-skŭch′ən) n. A shield or emblem in the shape of a shield bearing a coat of arms.

–ese A suffix that means: **1.** Relating to or originating from a certain place: Japanese. **2.** Native or inhabitant of: Chinese. **3.** A language or dialect of: Portuguese.

esker (ĕs′kər) n. A ridge of coarse gravel deposited by a stream flowing in or under a sheet of glacial ice.

Eskimo (ĕs′kə-mō′) n., pl. **Eskimo** or **Eskimos 1.** A member of a group of peoples inhabiting the Arctic coastal regions of North America and parts of Greenland and northeast Siberia. **2.** Any of the languages of the Eskimo peoples. —**Es′ki·mo′** adj.

Eskimo dog n. **1.** A dog of a large breed developed in the Canadian Arctic to pull sleds, having a thick coat, erect ears, and a feathery tail. **2.** A dog of a small to medium-sized breed developed in the United States, having a thick white coat, erect ears, and a feathery tail, and formerly popular in circus acts.

ESL An abbreviation of English as a second language.

esophageal (ĭ-sŏf′ə-jē′əl) adj. Relating to the esophagus.

esophagus (ĭ-sŏf′ə-gəs) n., pl. **esophagi** (ĭ-sŏf′ə-jī′) The part of the digestive tract that consists of a muscular tube connecting the throat to the stomach.

esoteric (ĕs′ə-tĕr′ĭk) adj. **1.** Intended for or understood by only a small group: an esoteric book. **2.** Not publicly disclosed; confidential. —**es′o·ter′i·cal·ly** adv.

ESP (ē′ĕs-pē′) n. The supposed ability to perceive events and information by means other than the physical senses.

esp. An abbreviation of especially.

espadrille (ĕs′pə-drĭl′) n. A shoe having a rope sole and a canvas upper part.

especial (ĭ-spĕsh′əl) adj. Of special note; exceptional: a portrait painted with especial skill.

especially (ĭ-spĕsh′ə-lē) adv. To an extent or degree deserving of special emphasis; particularly: We came by especially to visit our friend.

Esperanto (ĕs′pə-răn′tō or ĕs′pə-rän′tō) n. An artificial language for international use, based on word roots common to many European languages.

espionage (ĕs′pē-ə-näzh′ or ĕs′pē-ə-nĭj) n. The practice of spying or of using spies to gain secret information about a government or business: Many countries engage in espionage in time of war.

esplanade (ĕs′plə-näd′ or ĕs′plə-näd′) n. A flat open stretch of pavement or grass used as a promenade, especially along a shore.

espousal (ĭ-spou′zəl or ĭ-spou′səl) n. **1.** Adoption of an idea or cause: espousal of equal rights. **2a.** A betrothal. **b.** A wedding ceremony.

espouse (ĭ-spouz′) tr.v. **espoused, espousing, espouses 1.** To give loyalty or support to (an idea or cause); adopt: Their government espouses free elections. **2.** To take in marriage; marry. **3.** To promise or present (a woman) in marriage.

espresso (ĕ-sprĕs′ō) n., pl. **espressos** A strong coffee brewed by forcing steam through long-roasted, powdered coffee beans.

esprit (ĕ-sprē′) n. Liveliness of mind and expression; wit.

esprit de corps (də kôr′) n. A spirit of devotion and enthusiasm among members of a group for one another, their group, and its cause.

espy (ĭ-spī′) tr.v. **espied, espying, espies** To catch sight of; glimpse: The lookout espied a sail on the horizon.

Esq. An abbreviation of Esquire.

–esque A suffix that means in the manner of or resembling: statuesque.

esquire (ĕs′kwīr′) n. **1.** In medieval times, a man or boy who wished to become a knight and served as a knight's attendant and shield bearer. **2.** A man belonging to the English gentry ranking just below a knight. **3. Esquire** In the United States, a title of courtesy used especially after the name of a lawyer: John Doe, Esq.

–ess A suffix that makes female: heiress; lioness.

essay (ĕs′ā′ or ĕ-sā′) n. **1.** A short literary composition on a single subject, usually presenting the personal views of the author. **2.** An attempt; a try: He made a brief essay at politics before settling on a teaching career. ❖ tr.v. (ĕ-sā′ or ĕs′ā′) **essayed, essaying, essays** To make an attempt at; try: The actor essayed a new role on television.

essayist (ĕs′ā′ĭst) n. A writer of essays.

essence (ĕs′əns) n. **1.** The quality or qualities of a thing that give it its identity or character: The essence of democracy is freedom to choose. **2.** The most important aspect of something: The essence of her argument is that the policy should be revised. **3.** A concentrated form or extract of a substance that keeps the basic or most desirable properties: Turpentine is an essence of pine tar. **4.** A perfume or scent.

essential (ĭ-sĕn′shəl) adj. **1.** Relating to or being the essence of something; basic or inherent: The essential difficulty is getting so many independent thinkers to cooperate. **2.** Of the greatest importance; indispensable; necessary: The essential requirements for combustion are heat, oxygen, and fuel. **3.** Relating to a substance that is necessary for normal functioning but cannot be made by the body and therefore must be included in the diet: an essential amino acid. ❖ n. Something fundamental, necessary, or indispensable: Take along only the essentials when traveling. —**es·sen′tial·ly** adv.

essentialism (ĭ-sĕn′shə-lĭz′əm) n. The philosophical tenet that objects and classes of objects have essential and not merely accidental characteristics. —**es·sen′tial·ist** adj.

essential oil *n.* An oil that evaporates quickly and usually has the odor or flavor of the plant from which it is obtained. Essential oils are used to make perfumes and flavorings.

EST An abbreviation of Eastern Standard Time.

–est¹ A suffix that forms the superlative degree of adjectives and adverbs: *greatest; earliest.*

–est² A suffix that forms the archaic second person singular of verbs: *wherever thou goest.*

establish (ĭ-stăb′lĭsh) *tr.v.* **established, establishing, establishes 1a.** To begin or set up; found: *Their ancestors established the company in 1789.* **b.** To bring about; generate or effect: *The dinner established goodwill between the diplomats.* **2.** To settle securely in a position or condition; install: *It took several years for the new family to establish itself in this town.* **3.** To cause to be recognized and accepted: *a discovery that established the researcher's reputation.* **4.** To show to be true; prove: *The defense attorneys established the innocence of the accused.*

✦ **SYNONYMS establish, create, found, institute** *v.*

establishment (ĭ-stăb′lĭsh-mənt) *n.* **1.** The act of establishing or the condition of being established: *The new government's first priority was the establishment of peace.* **2.** An organization or institution, such as a business, hospital, or school: *Most of the town's commercial establishments contributed to the fund for the new playground.* **3.** often **Establishment** A group of people holding most of the power and influence in a government, society, or field of endeavor.

estate (ĭ-stāt′) *n.* **1.** A large piece of land, usually with a large house. **2.** Everything one owns, especially all of the property and debts left by a deceased person: *When the shopkeeper died, the family inherited a small estate.* **3.** A class of citizens, such as the nobility, the commons, or the clergy, formerly possessing distinct political rights.

esteem (ĭ-stēm′) *tr.v.* **esteemed, esteeming, esteems 1.** To regard with respect; value: *Judges are esteemed for their fairness and honesty.* **2.** To judge to be; regard as; consider: *Improving public transportation was esteemed the best way to deal with the parking problem.* ✦ *n.* Favorable regard; respect: *The doctor is held in high esteem.*

ester (ĕs′tər) *n.* Any of a large group of organic chemical compounds formed when an acid and an alcohol interact. Animal and vegetable fats and oils are esters.

Esther (ĕs′tər) *n.* A book of the Bible that tells the story of Esther, a Jewish queen of Persia who saved her people from massacre.

estimable (ĕs′tə-mə-bəl) *adj.* Worthy of or deserving high regard; admirable: *Patience, honesty, and fairness are estimable characteristics.* —**es′ti·ma·bly** *adv.*

estimate (ĕs′tə-māt′) *tr.v.* **estimated, estimating, estimates** To make a judgment about the approximate cost, quantity, or extent of; calculate roughly: *I estimate that 25 people will come to the party.* ✦ *n.* (ĕs′tə-mĭt) **1.** A rough calculation: *Our estimate is that we will arrive in about an hour.* **2.** A preliminary calculation of the cost of work to be undertaken: *The plumber's estimate to fix the pipe was reasonable.*

estimation (ĕs′tə-mā′shən) *n.* **1.** The act or an instance of estimating: *Estimation of the storm damage took several weeks.* **2.** An opinion; a judgment: *In my estimation that is a good painting.*

estivate (ĕs′tə-vāt′) *intr.v.* **estivated, estivating, estivates** To be in a dormant or inactive state during a hot dry period, such as the summer months: *Some tortoises estivate*

in burrows. —**es′ti·va′tion** (ĕs′tə-vā′shən) *n.*

Estonian (ĕ-stō′nē-ən) *adj.* Relating to Estonia or its people, language, or culture. ✦ *n.* **1.** A native or inhabitant of Estonia. **2.** The language of Estonia, related to Finnish.

estrange (ĭ-strānj′) *tr.v.* **estranged, estranging, estranges** To cause (a person) to change from friendly or affectionate to unfriendly or indifferent: *The neighbors were estranged because of a property dispute.* —**es·trange′ment** *n.*

estrogen (ĕs′trə-jən) *n.* **1.** Any of several hormones produced primarily in the ovaries of mammals. They are responsible for the development of female secondary sex characteristics and are involved in the regulation of the female reproductive cycle. **2.** Any of several synthetic compounds that mimic the physiologic activity of estrogen, used primarily in oral contraceptives.

estrous (ĕs′trəs) *adj.* Relating to estrus.

estrous cycle *n.* The recurrent set of physiological and behavioral changes that take place in a female mammal from one period of estrus to another.

estrus (ĕs′trəs) *n.* A regularly recurring period during which female mammals, excluding humans and certain other primates, are ready to mate; heat.

estuary (ĕs′chōō-ĕr′ē) *n., pl.* **estuaries 1.** The wide lower course of a river where its current is met by the tides. **2.** An arm of the sea that extends inland to meet the mouth of a river.

–et A suffix that means small: *eaglet.*

eta (ā′tə *or* ē′tə) *n.* The seventh letter of the Greek alphabet, written H, η. In English it is represented as *Ē, ē.*

et al. An abbreviation of et alii (and others).

etc. An abbreviation of et cetera.

et cetera (ĕt sĕt′ər-ə *or* ĕt sĕt′rə) And other things of the same type; and so forth.

etch (ĕch) *v.* **etched, etching, etches** —*tr.* **1.** To cut into (metal, glass, or other material), especially by using acid. **2.** To make (a picture or pattern) by cutting into a material. **3.** To impress or imprint clearly: *The sight of that waterfall is etched in my memory.* —*intr.* To practice the art of etching.

etching (ĕch′ĭng) *n.* **1.** The art or technique of making etched metal plates and printing pictures and designs from them. **2.** A design or picture etched on such a plate: *The artist finished the etching.* **3.** A print made from such a plate: *Several etchings hung on the wall.*

eternal (ĭ-tûr′nəl) *adj.* **1.** Having no beginning or end; existing outside of time. **2.** Continuing without interruption: *For that favor you have my eternal gratitude.* ✦ *n.* **Eternal** God. —**e·ter′nal·ly** *adv.*

eternity (ĭ-tûr′nĭ-tē) *n., pl.* **eternities 1.** All of time without beginning or end; infinite time: *We cannot measure eternity.* **2a.** The timeless state following death. **b.** The afterlife; immortality. **3.** A very long or seemingly very long time: *It was an eternity before the bus arrived.*

–eth¹ *or* **–th** A suffix that forms the archaic third person singular of the present tense of verbs: *He leadeth.*

–eth² Variant of **–th.**

ethane (ĕth′ān′) *n.* A colorless odorless gas composed of carbon and hydrogen and having the formula C_2H_6. It occurs in natural gas and is used as a fuel and in refrigeration.

ethanol (ĕth′ə-nôl′) *n.* An alcohol obtained from the fermentation of sugars and starches and also made artificially. It is found in beer, wine, and liquor and is also used as a solvent.

ether (ē′thər) *n.* **1.** An organic compound in which two hydrocarbon groups are linked by an oxygen atom. **2.** A colorless flammable liquid that is formed from ethanol and used as a solvent and formerly as an anesthetic. **3.** The region of space beyond the earth's atmosphere; the heavens.

ethereal (ĭ-thîr′ē-əl) *adj.* **1.** Delicate; light and airy: *ethereal music.* **2.** Relating to heaven; heavenly: *Angels are ethereal beings.* —e·the′re·al·ly *adv.*

ethic (ĕth′ĭk) *n.* **1.** A set of principles of right conduct; a system of moral values. **2. ethics** *(used with a singular verb)* The branch of philosophy that deals with the general nature of morals and specific moral choices. **3. ethics** *(used with a singular or plural verb)* Standards of right behavior or conduct; moral principles: *The code of medical ethics keeps patient records confidential.*

ethical (ĕth′ĭ-kəl) *adj.* **1.** Conforming to accepted standards of right behavior or conduct: *It is not considered ethical for a lawyer to represent both sides in a dispute.* **2.** Relating to or dealing with ethics: *ethical standards of right and wrong.* —eth′i·cal·ly *adv.*

ethnic (ĕth′nĭk) *adj.* Relating to a group of people that have the same racial, national, religious, linguistic, or cultural background. ❖ *n.* A member of a particular ethnic group. —eth′ni·cal·ly *adv.*

ethnic cleansing *n.* The systematic elimination of an ethnic group or groups from a region or society, as by deportation, forced emigration, or genocide.

ethnicity (ĕth-nĭs′ĭ-tē) *n.* The condition of belonging to a particular ethnic group.

ethnocentrism (ĕth′nō-sĕn′trĭz′əm) *n.* Belief in the superiority of one's own ethnic group. —eth′no·cen′tric *adj.*

ethnography (ĕth-nŏg′rə-fē) *n.* **1.** The branch of anthropology that deals with the description of specific human cultures, using methods such as close observation and interviews. **2.** A text produced using such methods. —eth·nog′ra·pher *n.* —eth′no·graph′ic (ĕth′nə-grăf′ĭk) *adj.* —eth′no·graph′i·cal·ly *adv.*

ethnology (ĕth-nŏl′ə-jē) *n.* The branch of anthropology that studies human cultures, especially their social structure, language, religion, and technology. —eth′no·log′i·cal (ĕth′nə-lŏj′ĭ-kəl) *adj.*

ethyl (ĕth′əl) *adj.* Relating to or being a hydrocarbon unit, C_2H_5, that is present in many organic compounds, such as ethanol and ether.

ethyl alcohol *n.* Ethanol.

ethylene (ĕth′ə-lēn′) *n.* A colorless flammable gas having the formula C_2H_4. It is obtained from petroleum and natural gas and is used as a fuel, in ripening and coloring citrus fruits, and as an anesthetic.

ethylene glycol (glī′kôl′) *n.* A poisonous, syrupy, colorless alcohol composed of carbon, hydrogen, and oxygen. It is used as an antifreeze in heating and cooling systems that use water.

e-ticket (ē′tĭk′ĭt) *n.* A reservation, as for a seat on an airplane, that exists as an electronic record and that makes a printed ticket unnecessary.

etiology (ē′tē-ŏl′ə-jē) *n., pl.* **etiologies 1.** The branch of medicine that deals with the causes of diseases. **2.** The cause or origin of a disease.

etiquette (ĕt′ĭ-kĕt′ *or* ĕt′ĭ-kĭt) *n.* The forms and rules of proper behavior required by custom among people:

Good etiquette requires a person to thank another for a gift or favor.

Etruscan (ĭ-trŭs′kən) *n.* **1.** A member of an ancient people who lived in what is now west-central Italy. **2.** The extinct language of the Etruscans. —E·trus′can *adj.*

–ette A suffix that means: **1.** Small: *kitchenette.* **2.** Female: *majorette.* **3.** Imitation or substitute: *leatherette.*

etude (ā′to͞od′) *n.* A piece of music, usually written for a solo instrument, meant to develop some point of playing technique.

etymological (ĕt′ə-mə-lŏj′ĭ-kəl) *adj.* Relating to etymology. —et′y·mo·log′i·cal·ly *adv.*

etymologist (ĕt′ə-mŏl′ə-jĭst) *n.* A person who specializes in etymology.

etymology (ĕt′ə-mŏl′ə-jē) *n., pl.* **etymologies 1.** The origin and development of a word as shown by its earliest use and changes in form and meaning: *Many medical terms have etymologies that go back to ancient Greek.* **2.** The study of the origin and history of words: *Etymology requires a knowledge of many languages.*

EU An abbreviation of European Union.

eucalyptus (yo͞o′kə-lĭp′təs) *n.* Any of numerous Australian evergreen trees that have fragrant leaves and are valued as a source of oil, gum, and wood.

Eucharist (yo͞o′kər-ĭst) *n.* **1.** The Christian rite commemorating Jesus's Last Supper in which bread and wine are consecrated and consumed in remembrance of Jesus's death; Communion. **2.** The consecrated bread and wine used in this rite.

eugenics (yo͞o-jĕn′ĭks) *n. (used with a singular verb)* The study or practice of attempting to improve the genes of the human race as a whole by encouraging the reproduction of people considered to have desirable traits and discouraging or preventing the reproduction of people considered to have undesirable traits. —eu·gen′ic *adj.*

euglena (yo͞o-glē′nə) *n.* Any of various green one-celled water organisms that move by means of flagella and produce their own food through photosynthesis.

eukaryote (yo͞o-kăr′ē-ōt) *n.* Any of numerous organisms whose cells contain a nucleus surrounded by a membrane. All organisms except bacteria and archaea are eukaryotes. —eu·kar′y·ot′ic (yo͞o-kăr′ē-ŏt′ĭk) *adj.*

eulogize (yo͞o′lə-jīz′) *tr.v.* **eulogized, eulogizing, eulogizes** To praise highly in speech or writing, especially in a formal eulogy. —eu′lo·gist (yo͞o′lə-jĭst) *n.*

eulogy (yo͞o′lə-jē) *n., pl.* **eulogies** A speech or piece of writing praising a person or thing, especially a person who has just died.

eunuch (yo͞o′nək) *n.* A castrated man, especially one who was traditionally employed as a household attendant in certain Asian courts.

euphemism (yo͞o′fə-mĭz′əm) *n.* An inoffensive or indirect word or expression substituted for one considered harsh, blunt, or offensive; for example, *pass away* is a euphemism for *die.* —eu′phe·mis′tic (yo͞o′fə-mĭs′tĭk) *adj.*

euphonious (yo͞o-fō′nē-əs) *adj.* Pleasing in sound; agreeable to the ear. —eu·pho′ni·ous·ly *adv.*

euphonium (yo͞o-fō′nē-əm) *n.* A brass musical instrument that looks like a tuba but has a mellower and higher sound.

euphony (yo͞o′fə-nē) *n., pl.* **euphonies** Agreeable sound, especially in the use of words.

euphoria (yo͞o-fôr′ē-ə) *n.* A feeling of happiness and well-being: *After peace was declared, the whole country was in a state of euphoria.*

Eurasian (yŏō-rā′zhən) *adj.* **1.** Relating to Eurasia. **2.** Of mixed European and Asian ancestry. ❖ *n.* **1.** A native or inhabitant of Eurasia. **2.** A person of mixed European and Asian ancestry.

eureka (yŏō-rē′kə) *interj.* An expression used to express triumph upon discovering something or finding a solution to a problem.

euro or **Euro** (yŏōr′ō) *n., pl.* **euro** or **euros** The basic monetary unit of most of the members of the European Union and several nearby nonmember states.

Euro-American (yŏōr′ō-ə-měr′ĭ-kən) *n.* An American of European ancestry. **—Eu′ro-A·mer′i·can** *adj.*

Eurocentric (yŏōr′ō-sĕn′trĭk) *adj.* Centered or focused on Europe or European peoples.

European (yŏōr′ə-pē′ən) *n.* **1.** A native or inhabitant of Europe. **2.** A person of European descent. ❖ *adj.* Relating to Europe or its peoples, languages, or cultures.

European Union *n.* An economic and political union established in 1993 by most of the countries of western Europe and since expanded to include numerous central and eastern European nations. The nations of the European Union cooperate on matters pertaining to commerce and security and have mostly adopted a common currency, the euro.

europium (yŏō-rō′pē-əm) *n. Symbol* **Eu** A soft, silvery-white metallic element used in making color television tubes and lasers and in scientific research. Atomic number 63. See **Periodic Table.**

Eurydice (yŏō-rĭd′ĭ-sē) *n.* In Greek mythology, the wife of Orpheus, whom he almost rescued from the underworld.

eustachian tube or **Eustachian tube** (yŏō-stā′shən or yŏō-stā′shē-ən) *n.* The narrow tube that connects the middle ear and the pharynx and serves to equalize air pressure on the two sides of the eardrum.

Euterpe (yŏō-tûr′pē) *n.* In Greek mythology, the Muse of lyric poetry and music.

euthanasia (yŏō′thə-nā′zhə) *n.* The intentional ending of the life of a person or a domestic animal that is suffering from an incurable illness or has a medical condition that causes unbearable pain.

euthanize (yŏō′thə-nīz′) *tr.v.* **euthanized, euthanizing, euthanizes** To subject to euthanasia.

evacuate (ĭ-văk′yŏō-āt′) *v.* **evacuated, evacuating, evacuates** *—tr.* **1.** To send away or remove (people) from an area: *evacuate a neighborhood threatened by toxic fumes.* **2.** To withdraw or depart from; vacate: *The firefighters quickly evacuated the burning building.* **3.** To discharge waste matter from: *evacuated his bowels. —intr.* To withdraw or depart from a place or area, especially as a protective measure: *Residents were ordered to evacuate because of the flood.*

evacuation (ĭ-văk′yŏō-ā′shən) *n.* **1.** The act of evacuating or the condition of being evacuated: *The evacuation of children was begun at the first sign of danger.* **2.** Discharge of waste materials from the body, especially from the bowels.

evacuee (ĭ-văk′yŏō-ē′) *n.* A person who has been evacuated from a dangerous area.

evade (ĭ-vād′) *tr.v.* **evaded, evading, evades 1.** To escape or avoid, as by cleverness or deceit: *evade arrest.* **2.** To avoid the fulfillment or performance of: *evade responsibility; evade taxes.* **3.** To avoid giving a direct answer to: *evaded the question by talking about something else.*

evaluate (ĭ-văl′yŏō-āt′) *tr.v.* **evaluated, evaluating, evaluates 1.** To find out or estimate the value or worth of; examine and appraise: *evaluate a course of action; evaluate paintings for sale.* **2.** To find the numerical value of (an algebraic expression). **—e·val′u·a′tion** *n.*

evanesce (ĕv′ə-nĕs′) *intr.v.* **evanesced, evanescing, evanesces** To dissipate or disappear like vapor. **—ev′a·nes′-cence** *n.*

evanescent (ĕv′ə-nĕs′ənt) *adj.* Tending to vanish or last only a short time: *the rainbow's evanescent beauty.* **—ev′-a·nes′cence** *n.* **—ev′a·nes′cent·ly** *adv.*

evangelical (ē′văn-jĕl′ĭ-kəl) also **evangelic** (ē′văn-jĕl′ĭk) *adj.* **1.** Relating to or in accordance with the Christian gospel, especially the four Gospels of the New Testament. **2. Evangelical** Relating to or being a Protestant group that stresses belief solely in the authority of the Bible and salvation through faith in Jesus. **3.** Ardently advocating something: *an evangelical vegan.* ❖ *n.* **Evangelical** A member of an evangelical church. **—e′van·gel′-i·cal·ly** *adv.*

evangelism (ĭ-văn′jə-lĭz′əm) *n.* **1.** The practice of preaching and spreading the gospel, as through missionary work. **2.** Ardent advocacy of a cause. **—e·van′gel·is′tic** (ĭ-văn′jə-lĭs′tĭk) *adj.*

evangelist (ĭ-văn′jə-lĭst) *n.* **1.** often **Evangelist** Any of the authors of the New Testament Gospels: Matthew, Mark, Luke, or John. **2.** A person who practices evangelism, especially a Protestant preacher or missionary. **3.** One who promotes something enthusiastically.

evangelize (ĭ-văn′jə-līz′) *v.* **evangelized, evangelizing, evangelizes** *—tr.* **1.** To convert or try to convert (someone) to Christianity. **2.** To promote (a doctrine or idea, for example) enthusiastically. *—intr.* **1.** To preach the gospel. **2.** To promote something enthusiastically.

evaporate (ĭ-văp′ə-rāt′) *v.* **evaporated, evaporating, evaporates** *—tr.* **1.** To cause to change from a liquid into a vapor, especially without boiling: *The sun evaporates water from the ocean.* **2.** To extract water or other liquid from: *evaporate milk.* *—intr.* **1.** To change from a liquid into a vapor: *The dew evaporated as the sun came up.* **2.** To disappear; vanish; fade: *My fear evaporated as the airplane took off.* See Synonyms at **disappear. —e·vap′-o·ra′tion** *n.*

evaporated milk (ĭ-văp′ə-rā′tĭd) *n.* Unsweetened milk that has been slightly thickened by evaporation of some of the water in it.

evasion (ĭ-vā′zhən) *n.* **1.** The act or an instance of evading: *His evasion of paying taxes led to his imprisonment.* **2.** A means of evading; an excuse: *Every evasion we tried to avoid the test was unsuccessful.*

evasive (ĭ-vā′sĭv) *adj.* **1.** Tending or intended to evade: *The submarine took evasive action to elude its pursuers.* **2.** Intentionally misleading or ambiguous: *the candidate's evasive answers to her questions.* **—e·va′sive·ly** *adv.* **—e·va′sive·ness** *n.*

eve (ēv) *n.* **1.** The evening or day preceding a special day, such as a holiday. **2.** The period immediately preceding a certain event: *the eve of war.* **3.** Evening. Used chiefly in poetry.

even¹ (ē′vən) *adj.* **1a.** Having a horizontal surface; flat: *The even lawn is good for playing croquet.* **b.** Having no roughness, dents, or bumps; smooth: *an even board.* **c.** Being in the same plane or line; parallel: *Is your writing even with the top of the page?* **2.** Having no variation; uniform: *an even speed.* **3.** Calm; peaceful: *an even temper.* **4a.** Equally matched: *an even fight.* **b.** Equal in degree, extent or amount: *even portions of a meal.* **5.** Exactly divisible by 2: *6, 20, and −478 are even numbers.* **6.** Having equal probability: *Our team has an even chance of winning.* **7a.** Having an equal score: *The teams are even.* **b.** Being equal for each opponent: *an even score.* **8.** Having nothing due: *Pay me one dollar, and we are even.* **9.** Having an exact amount, extent, or number: *an even pound.* ❖ *adv.* **1.** To a higher or greater degree; yet; still: *an even better idea.* **2.** At the same time as; just: *Even as we watched, the tree fell.* **3.** Indeed; moreover: *She was relieved, even happy, to see us.* **4.** Used to emphasize something that is unexpected: *He refused even to consider our idea.* ❖ *tr.v.* **evened, evening, evens** To make even: *even out a garden with a rake.* ◆ **on an even keel** In a stable or unimpaired state: *The new contract put the relationship between the company and its workers on an even keel.* —**e′ven·ly** *adv.* —**e′ven·ness** *n.*

even² (ē′vən) *n. Archaic* Evening.

evenhanded (ē′vən-hăn′dĭd) *adj.* Dealing fairly with all; impartial.

evening (ēv′nĭng) *n.* **1.** The period of decreasing daylight between afternoon and night: *At evening the moon rose over the lake.* **2.** The period between sunset and bedtime: *We spent a quiet evening at home.* **3.** A later period or time: *in the evening of life.*

evening gown *n.* A woman's formal dress, usually reaching to the floor or close to it.

evening star *n.* A planet, especially Venus, that shines brightly in the western sky shortly after sunset.

evensong (ē′vən-sông′) *n.* **1.** A daily evening service in the Anglican Church. **2.** A song sung in the evening.

event (ĭ-vĕnt′) *n.* **1.** An occurrence, incident, or experience, especially one of significance: *A trip to Brazil was the great event of her adolescence.* **2.** A social gathering or activity: *a fundraising event.* **3.** An item in a program of sports: *track and field events.* ◆ **in any event** In any case; anyhow. **in the event** If it should happen; in case: *In the event of the president's death, the vice president takes over.* —SEE NOTE AT **intervene.**

eventful (ĭ-vĕnt′fəl) *adj.* **1.** Full of events: *an eventful afternoon.* **2.** Important; momentous: *an eventful decision to change jobs.* —**e·vent′ful·ly** *adv.*

eventide (ē′vən-tīd′) *n.* Evening. Used chiefly in poetry.

eventual (ĭ-vĕn′chōō-əl) *adj.* Occurring at an unspecified future time; ultimate: *We never lost hope of eventual victory.* —**e·ven′tu·al·ly** *adv.*

eventuality (ĭ-vĕn′chōō-ăl′ĭ-tē) *n., pl.* **eventualities** Something that may occur; a possibility: *One prepares for the worst eventuality and hopes for the best outcome.*

ever (ĕv′ər) *adv.* **1.** At all times; always: *They lived happily ever after.* **2.** At any time: *Have you ever visited Miami?* **3.** By any chance; in any possible case or way: *How could they ever have thought they would get away with that?* **4.** To a great extent or degree. Used for emphasis often with *so: She's ever so sorry.*

everglade (ĕv′ər-glād′) *n.* A large area of marshland, usually underwater with tall grass growing in places.

evergreen (ĕv′ər-grēn′) *adj.* Having leaves that remain green all year: *spruces and other evergreen trees.* ❖ *n.* An evergreen plant: *a nursery that sells evergreens.*

everlasting (ĕv′ər-lăs′tĭng) *adj.* **1.** Lasting forever; eternal. **2.** Continuing for a long time: *everlasting happiness.*

3. Lasting too long; wearisome: *everlasting work.* —**ev′er·last′ing·ly** *adv.*

evermore (ĕv′ər-môr′) *adv.* Forever; always.

every (ĕv′rē) *adj.* **1.** Each and all without exception: *searched every room in the house.* **2.** Each in a specified series or at specific intervals: *every third seat; every two hours.* **3.** Being the highest degree or expression of: *I have every confidence they will succeed.* ◆ **every bit** *Informal* In all ways; equally: *every bit as clever as we thought.* **every now and then** or **every now and again** From time to time; occasionally: *The whole family goes camping every now and then.* **every other** Each alternate: *every other seat.* **every so often** At intervals; occasionally: *We exchange letters every so often.*

everybody (ĕv′rē-bŏd′ē or ĕv′rē-bŭd′ē) *pron.* Every person; everyone.

everyday (ĕv′rē-dā′) *adj.* **1.** Suitable for ordinary days or occasions: *everyday clothes.* **2.** Ordinary; usual: *an everyday event.*

everyone (ĕv′rē-wŭn′) *pron.* Every person; everybody: *Everyone has bought a ticket.*

everything (ĕv′rē-thĭng′) *pron.* **1.** All things or all of a group of things: *Everything in this room must be packed.* **2.** The most important fact or consideration: *When telling a joke, timing is everything.*

everywhere (ĕv′rē-wâr′) *adv.* In any or every place; in all places: *People were celebrating the news everywhere in town.*

evict (ĭ-vĭkt′) *tr.v.* **evicted, evicting, evicts** To put out (a tenant) by legal process; expel: *The landlord evicted the tenants for failure to pay rent.* —**e·vic′tion** *n.*

evidence (ĕv′ĭ-dəns) *n.* **1.** A thing or things helpful in making a judgment or coming to a conclusion: *The fossils of seashells were evidence that the region had once been covered by water.* **2.** The statements, objects, and facts accepted for consideration in a court of law: *The evidence was not clear enough to convince the jury that the defendant was guilty.* **3.** Something that indicates; a sign: *Constant laughter was evidence that the show was very funny.* ❖ *tr.v.* **evidenced, evidencing, evidences** To indicate clearly; prove: *Cheers and applause evidenced the audience's approval.* ◆ **in evidence** Plainly visible; to be seen: *The welcome signs were much in evidence among the crowd at the airport.*

evident (ĕv′ĭ-dənt) *adj.* Easily seen or understood; clear; plain: *From the warm temperature and abundant flowers, it is evident that spring is here.*

evidently (ĕv′ĭ-dənt-lē or ĕv′ĭ-dĕnt′lē) *adv.* Plainly; clearly: *They evidently did not practice enough and played poorly.*

evil (ē′vəl) *adj.* **eviler, evilest** **1.** Morally bad or wrong; wicked: *evil deeds.* **2.** Causing pain or injury; harmful: *an evil temper; an evil tongue.* **3.** Indicating misfortune: *evil signs.* ❖ *n.* **1.** The quality of being morally bad or wrong; wickedness: *a story about good and evil.* **2.** Something that causes harm: *the social evil of poverty.* —**e′vil·ly** *adv.* —**e′vil·ness** *n.*

evildoer (ē′vəl-dōō′ər) *n.* A person who does evil things.

evil eye *n.* A gaze or stare believed to cause injury or misfortune.

evince (ĭ-vĭns′) *tr.v.* **evinced, evincing, evinces** To show or demonstrate clearly; exhibit: *The lawyer evinced surprise at the witness's statement.*

eviscerate (ĭ-vĭs′ə-rāt′) *tr.v.* **eviscerated, eviscerating, eviscerates** **1.** To remove the intestines or other internal organs of. **2.** To take away a vital or essential part of: *Leaving out the facts and figures eviscerated the report.* —e·vis′cer·a′tion *n.*

evocation (ĕv′ə-kā′shən *or* ē′və-kā′shən) *n.* The act of calling forth: *the evocation of a pleasant memory.*

evocative (ĭ-vŏk′ə-tĭv) *adj.* Tending to evoke: *The walk in the woods was evocative of the hikes I took in my childhood.*

evoke (ĭ-vŏk′) *tr.v.* **evoked, evoking, evokes 1.** To summon or call forth; inspire: *The question evoked a complicated reply.* **2.** To call to mind by naming or suggesting: *a song that evokes memories.*

evolution (ĕv′ə-loo′shən) *n.* **1.** A gradual process by which something changes into a different form: *the evolution of jazz from ragtime to bop.* **2.** Change in the genes of a group of organisms over many generations, so that descendants are different from their ancestors and may develop into a new species. Evolution is caused by natural selection and certain other factors, such as mutation. **3.** The historical development of a related group of organisms: *the evolution of horses.* —ev′o·lu′tion·ar′y (ĕv′ə-loo′shə-nĕr′ē) *adj.*

evolve (ĭ-vŏlv′) *v.* **evolved, evolving, evolves** —*tr.* **1.** To develop or achieve gradually: *The committee evolved a plan for a new civic center.* **2.** To develop (a characteristic) by biological evolution: *Many bacteria have evolved resistance to antibiotics.* —*intr.* **1.** To undergo biological evolution: *Biologists believe that whales evolved from mammals that lived on land.* **2.** To undergo change or development: *a small company that has evolved into a huge corporation; a bud evolving into a flower.*

ewe (yoo) *n.* A full-grown female sheep.

ewer (yoo′ər) *n.* A large, wide-mouthed pitcher or jug.

ex. An abbreviation of example.

ex– A prefix that means former: *ex-president.*

WORD BUILDING In cases where the prefix **ex–** doesn't mean "former," it is usually part of a word of Latin origin and has the meaning "out of, from." Thus combining *ex–* with the Latin verb *tendere,* "to stretch," gives us *extend,* "to stretch out." Similarly, in *express,* it combines with the root *press–,* which comes from the Latin verb *premere,* "to squeeze." Words that use the Latin *ex–* this way usually drop the *x* if the root begins with *b, d, f, g, j, l, m, n,* or *r,* as in *educate, eject, emit,* and *erode.*

exacerbate (ĭg-zăs′ər-bāt′) *tr.v.* **exacerbated, exacerbating, exacerbates** To make worse or more severe; aggravate: *The rumor exacerbated tensions between groups.* —ex·ac′er·ba′tion *n.*

exact (ĭg-zăkt′) *adj.* **1.** Fully in agreement with fact or an original: *a person's exact words; an exact duplicate.* **2.** Characterized by accurate measurement: *An exact reading of these instruments is necessary in this experiment.* ❖ *tr.v.* **exacted, exacting, exacts 1.** To force the payment of: *The king exacted new taxes from the people.* **2.** To require or demand, especially by force or authority: *The chef exacts strict discipline in the kitchen.* **3.** To inflict (vengeance or punishment, for example). —ex·act′ness *n.* —SEE NOTE AT **react.**

exacting (ĭg-zăk′tĭng) *adj.* **1.** Making great demands: *I learn the most from an exacting teacher.* **2.** Requiring great effort, attention, or care: *A medical operation is an exacting procedure.* —ex·act′ing·ly *adv.*

exaction (ĭg-zăk′shən) *n.* **1.** The act of exacting or demanding. **2.** Something exacted or demanded, as a tax considered to be excessive.

exactitude (ĭg-zăk′tĭ-tood) *n.* The quality or condition of being exact; exactness.

exactly (ĭg-zăkt′lē) *adv.* **1.** In an exact manner; precisely: *The cake did not rise because I failed to follow the recipe exactly.* **2.** In all respects; just: *Do exactly as you see fit.* **3.** As you say. Used to indicate agreement: *"Exactly," he replied. "I feel the same way."*

exaggerate (ĭg-zăj′ə-rāt′) *v.* **exaggerated, exaggerating, exaggerates** —*tr.* To consider, represent, or cause to appear as larger, more important, or more extreme than is actually the case; overstate: *exaggerated his own role in the incident; exaggerated the size of the enemy force; exaggerated how difficult the project would be.* —*intr.* To make overstatements: *It's important not to exaggerate when writing stories for a newspaper.* —ex·ag′ger·a′tion *n.*

exalt (ĭg-zôlt′) *tr.v.* **exalted, exalting, exalts 1.** To raise in position, status, rank, or regard; elevate: *The emperor exalted the faithful servant to a place among his most trusted advisors.* **2.** To praise; honor; glorify. —ex′al·ta′tion (ĕg′zôl-tā′shən) *n.*

exalted (ĭg-zôl′tĭd) *adj.* **1.** Having high rank or status; dignified: *The emperor is an exalted personage.* **2.** Elevated as in style or condition; lofty; noble: *the exalted style of epic poetry.*

exam (ĭg-zăm′) *n.* An examination; a test.

examination (ĭg-zăm′ə-nā′shən) *n.* **1.** The act of examining or the state of being examined: *Close examination of the diamond showed it was a fake.* **2.** A set of questions or exercises testing knowledge or skill; a test. **3.** A formal interrogation: *the lawyer's examination of the witness in a trial.*

examine (ĭg-zăm′ĭn) *tr.v.* **examined, examining, examines 1.** To observe carefully; inspect or study: *examined the plant cells under a microscope.* **2.** To test or check the condition or health of: *examined the patient.* **3.** To determine the qualifications, aptitude, or skills of (someone) by means of questions or exercises: *examined the job candidates in interviews.* See Synonyms at **ask. 4.** To interrogate or question formally to obtain information or facts: *The prosecutor examined the witness.* —ex·am′in·er *n.*

example (ĭg-zăm′pəl) *n.* **1.** A person or thing that is typical of a whole class or group; a sample or specimen: *The Empire State Building is an example of a graceful skyscraper.* **2.** A person or thing that is worthy of imitation; a model: *This article is an example of good writing.* **3.** A person or thing that is intended to serve as a warning to others: *The court made an example of the fraudulent dealer by imposing heavy fines on him.* **4.** A problem or exercise worked out to illustrate a principle or method: *an example of multiplication; an example of the form of a composition.* ◆ **for example** As an illustration; for instance: *We have several team sports, for example, baseball and soccer.*

exasperate (ĭg-zăs′pə-rāt′) *tr.v.* **exasperated, exasperating, exasperates** To make angry or impatient; irritate greatly: *The dog's constant barking exasperated the neighbors.* —ex·as′per·a′tion (ĭg-zăs′pə-rā′shən) *n.*

Excalibur (ĕk-skăl′ə-bər) *n.* In Arthurian legend, the sword of King Arthur.

excavate (ĕk′skə-vāt′) *tr.v.* **excavated, excavating, excavates 1.** To make a hole in; hollow out: *excavate a hillside to build a tunnel.* **2.** To form by digging out: *excavate the foundation for a house.* **3.** To remove by digging or scooping out: *The bulldozer excavated ten truckloads of earth.* **4.**

To expose or uncover by or as if by digging: *excavated the remains of an ancient settlement.*

excavation (ĕk′skə-vā′shən) *n.* **1.** The act or process of excavating: *Excavation of the basement is to begin soon.* **2.** A hole formed by excavation: *a deep excavation for the new skyscraper.*

excavator (ĕk′skə-vā′tər) *n.* A person or thing that excavates, especially a backhoe.

exceed (ĭk-sēd′) *tr.v.* **exceeded, exceeding, exceeds 1.** To be greater than; surpass: *The results exceeded everyone's hopes.* **2.** To go beyond the limits of: *Do not exceed the speed limit.*

exceeding (ĭk-sē′dĭng) *adj.* Extreme; extraordinary: *a night of exceeding darkness.*

exceedingly (ĭk-sē′dĭng-lē) *adv.* To an advanced or unusual degree; extremely: *exceedingly hot weather; exceedingly delicate work.*

excel (ĭk-sĕl′) *v.* **excelled, excelling, excels** —*tr.* To do or be better than; surpass: *Their performance excelled all the others.* —*intr.* To be better than others: *Few people excel at every sport.*

excellence (ĕk′sə-ləns) *n.* The condition or quality of excelling; superiority: *artistic excellence; a prize given for excellence in writing.*

Excellency (ĕk′sə-lən-sē) *n., pl.* **Excellencies** Used as a title and form of address for certain high officials, such as ambassadors, viceroys, or bishops: *Your Excellency.*

excellent (ĕk′sə-lənt) *adj.* Of the highest or finest quality; superb: *an excellent performance.* —**ex′cel·lent·ly** *adv.*

except (ĭk-sĕpt′) *prep.* With the exclusion of; but: *All the apartments except one have been rented. Everybody went to the movies except for Gary.* ❖ *conj.* **1.** If it were not for the fact that; only: *We would go swimming except that the waves are too big.* **2.** Otherwise than: *He would not open his mouth except to argue.* ❖ *tr.v.* **excepted, excepting, excepts** To leave out; exclude: *No one is excepted from following the rules.* ◆ **except for** Were it not for: *I would have finished except for the interruption.*

excepting (ĭk-sĕp′tĭng) *prep.* With the exception of: *No one excepting Charlie wanted to go fishing in the rain.*

exception (ĭk-sĕp′shən) *n.* **1.** The act of excepting or the condition of being excepted: *All our guests have arrived with the exception of two.* **2.** A person or thing that is excepted: *I like all my classes with one exception. Certain exceptions to the rule will be considered.* **3.** An objection or criticism: *opinions that are open to exception.*

exceptionable (ĭk-sĕp′shə-nə-bəl) *adj.* Open or liable to objection or disapproval: *an exceptionable description of their opponents.*

exceptional (ĭk-sĕp′shə-nəl) *adj.* **1.** Being an exception; uncommon: *The speaker discussed the topic with exceptional frankness.* **2.** Well above average; extraordinary: *an exceptional memory.* —**ex·cep′tion·al·ly** *adv.*

excerpt (ĕk′sûrpt′) *n.* A passage or scene selected from a longer work, such as a book, film, or piece of music. ❖ *tr.v.* (ĭk-sûrpt′) **excerpted, excerpting, excerpts** To select or use (a passage or segment from a longer work): *The author excerpted parts of several famous speeches.*

excess (ĭk-sĕs′ or ĕk′sĕs′) *n.* **1.** The state of exceeding what is normal or sufficient: *filled my glass to excess.* **2.** An amount or quantity beyond what is normal or sufficient; a surplus. **3.** The amount or degree by which one quantity exceeds another: *an excess of four pounds.* ❖ *adj.* Being

more than what is usual, permitted, or required: *Skim off the excess fat.* ◆ **in excess of** Greater than; more than: *a package weighing in excess of 40 pounds.*

excessive (ĭk-sĕs′ĭv) *adj.* Exceeding a normal, usual, reasonable, or proper limit: *Excessive rains cause flooding.* —**ex·ces′sive·ly** *adv.* —**ex·ces′sive·ness** *n.*

exchange (ĭks-chānj′) *tr.v.* **exchanged, exchanging, exchanges 1.** To give in return for something received: *I exchanged my pesos for dollars. He exchanged labor for a room to sleep in.* **2.** To give and receive mutually; interchange: *exchange gifts; exchange ideas.* **3.** To give up for a substitute: *She exchanged her job as a professor for a position in the government.* **4.** To turn in for replacement: *exchanged the tie for a belt at the store.* ❖ *n.* **1.** An act or an instance of exchanging: *an exchange of gifts; an exchange of ideas.* **2.** A person or thing that is exchanged: *The watch seemed a fair exchange for the compass.* **3.** A place where things, especially stocks or commodities, are exchanged or traded: *a commodities exchange.* —**ex·change′a·ble** *adj.* —**ex·chang′er** *n.*

exchange rate *n.* A rate of exchange.

exchange student *n.* A high school or college student taking part in a program of arranged exchanges between a local and a foreign institution or group.

exchequer (ĕks′chĕk′ər or ĭks-chĕk′ər) *n.* **1. Exchequer** The department of the British government in charge of the national revenue. **2.** A treasury, as of a nation or organization.

excise¹ (ĕk′sīz′) *n.* An excise tax.

excise² (ĭk-sīz′) *tr.v.* **excised, excising, excises** To remove by or as if by cutting: *excised two scenes from the movie.* —**ex·ci′sion** (ĭk-sĭzh′ən) *n.*

WORD HISTORY Excise¹ comes from Middle Dutch *accijs*, which may come from Latin *cēnsus*, both meaning "tax." **Excise²** comes from Latin *excīdere*, which means "to cut out" and comes from the Latin prefix *ex-* (meaning "out") and the Latin word *cadere*, which means "to cut."

excise tax (ĕk′sīz′) *n.* A tax on production, sale, or use of certain items or services within a country.

excitable (ĭk-sī′tə-bəl) *adj.* Easily excited: *a jumpy and excitable cat.* —**ex·cit′a·bil′i·ty, ex·cit′a·ble·ness** *n.* —**ex·cit′a·bly** *adv.*

excitation (ĕk′sī-tā′shən) *n.* The act of exciting or the condition of being excited.

excite (ĭk-sīt′) *tr.v.* **excited, exciting, excites 1.** To arouse strong feeling in: *The charismatic speaker excited the audience.* **2.** To call forth (a reaction or emotion, for example); elicit: *The news report excited our curiosity.* **3.** To cause to become more active: *Lowering interest rates should excite the market for housing.* **4.** To produce increased activity or response in (an organ or other body part): *The vaccine excites the immune system to produce antibodies against the disease.* **5.** To increase the energy of (an electron, atom, or molecule).

excited (ĭk-sī′tĭd) *adj.* Emotionally aroused; stirred: *The astronomers were very excited about their discovery of a new star.* —**ex·cit′ed·ly** *adv.*

excitement (ĭk-sīt′mənt) *n.* The act or an instance of exciting or the state of being excited: *In all of the excitement of the party, I couldn't hear the phone ring.*

exciting (ĭk-sī′tĭng) *adj.* Creating or producing excitement: *an exciting rafting trip down the river.* —**ex·cit′ing·ly** *adv.*

exclaim (ĭk-sklām′) *v.* **exclaimed, exclaiming, exclaims**

—*tr.* To say or express (something) by crying out suddenly, as from surprise: *"How nice of you to stop by!" he exclaimed.* —*intr.* To cry out suddenly, as from surprise: *She exclaimed with pleasure when she saw the new car.*

exclamation (ĕk'sklə-mā'shən) *n.* **1.** Something said suddenly or forcefully: *exclamations of surprise.* **2.** An outcry, as of protest.

exclamation mark *n.* An exclamation point.

exclamation point *n.* A punctuation mark (!) used after an exclamation.

exclamatory (ĭk-sklăm'ə-tôr'ē) *adj.* Containing, using, or being an exclamation: *a sudden exclamatory remark; an exclamatory sentence.*

exclude (ĭk-sklōōd') *tr.v.* **excluded, excluding, excludes 1.** To prevent from entering; keep out: *a rule that excludes young children from the big swimming pool.* **2.** To prevent from being included, considered, or accepted: *Let's not exclude the possibility of rain in making our plans.*

exclusion (ĭk-sklōō'zhən) *n.* **1.** The act or practice of excluding: *The exclusion of large trucks from some streets eases traffic congestion.* **2.** The condition or fact of being excluded.

exclusive (ĭk-sklōō'sĭv) *adj.* **1.** Not divided or shared with others: *the exclusive owner of the estate.* **2.** Undivided; complete: *The spectators gave the diver their exclusive attention.* **3.** Not including the specified endpoints but only the area between them. For example, "20–25, exclusive" refers to 21, 22, 23, and 24. **4.** Excluding some or most, as from membership or participation; restricted: *an exclusive school.* —**ex·clu'sive·ly** *adv.* —**ex·clu'sive·ness** *n.*

exclusive of *prep.* Not including; besides: *Exclusive of last-minute changes, this report is finished.*

excommunicate (ĕks'kə-myōō'nĭ-kāt') *tr.v.* **excommunicated, excommunicating, excommunicates** To deprive of the right of church membership by official authority: *In 1533, the pope excommunicated Henry VIII.*

excommunication (ĕks'kə-myōō'nĭ-kā'shən) *n.* **1.** The act of excommunicating. **2.** The state of being excommunicated.

excoriate (ĭk-skôr'ē-āt') *tr.v.* **excoriated, excoriating, excoriates 1.** To criticize or denounce harshly. **2.** To tear or scrape off (the skin). —**ex·co'ri·a'tion** *n.*

excrement (ĕk'skrə-mənt) *n.* Waste matter that is passed from the body after digestion.

excrescence (ĭk-skrĕs'əns) *n.* An abnormal growth, such as a wart, on a surface.

excrete (ĭk-skrēt') *tr.v.* **excreted, excreting, excretes** To eliminate (waste matter) from a living organism, organ, or tissue: *Kidneys excrete urea and other waste products.*

excretion (ĭk-skrē'shən) *n.* **1.** The act or process of excreting. **2.** The waste matter, such as urine or sweat, that is excreted.

excretory (ĕk'skrĭ-tôr'ē) *adj.* Involving or used in excretion: *excretory organs.*

excruciating (ĭk-skrōō'shē-ā'tĭng) *adj.* Intensely painful; agonizing: *the excruciating pain of a toothache.* —**ex·cru'ci·at'ing·ly** *adv.*

excursion (ĭk-skûr'zhən) *n.* **1.** A usually short journey made for pleasure; an outing: *an excursion to the park.* **2.** A roundtrip on a passenger vehicle at a special reduced fare: *Excursions are a cheap way to travel abroad.*

excuse (ĭk-skyōōz') *tr.v.* **excused, excusing, excuses 1.** To seek to remove the blame from: *She excused herself for being late.* **2.** To pardon; forgive: *Excuse me for taking your chair.* See Synonyms at **forgive. 3.** To serve as an apology for; justify: *Nothing excuses such rudeness.* **4.** To free or release, as from a duty, activity, or obligation: *All seniors will be excused from school early today.* ❖ *n.* (ĭk-skyōōs') **1.** An explanation offered to justify a fault or offense: *What is your excuse for being late?* **2.** *Informal* An inferior example: *Their old station wagon is a poor excuse for a car.*

◆ **excuse me 1.** Used to acknowledge and ask forgiveness for an action that could cause offense. **2.** Used to request that a statement be repeated. —**ex·cus'a·ble** *adj.* —**ex·cus'a·bly** *adv.* —**ex·cus'er** *n.*

execration (ĕk'sĭ-krā'shən) *n.* **1.** The act of cursing. **2.** A curse.

execute (ĕk'sĭ-kyōōt') *tr.v.* **executed, executing, executes 1.** To put into effect; carry out: *The government must execute the law fairly.* **2.** To perform; do: *execute a U-turn.* **3.** To create (a work of art, for example) according to a design. **4.** To make valid, as by signing: *execute a deed.* **5.** To put to death, especially by carrying out a legal sentence: *execute a convicted criminal.* **6.** To run or carry out (a computer program or instruction).

execution (ĕk'sĭ-kyōō'shən) *n.* **1.** The act of executing something: *administrators responsible for the execution of a new school policy; the execution of a will.* **2.** The manner, style, or result of executing something: *the flawless execution of a plan.* **3a.** The act of putting a person to death, especially as a lawful penalty. **b.** An instance of a person being put to death, especially as a lawful penalty.

executioner (ĕk'sĭ-kyōō'shə-nər) *n.* A person who puts someone to death, especially someone convicted of a capital crime.

executive (ĭg-zĕk'yə-tĭv) *n.* **1.** A person or group that manages the affairs of an organization, especially a corporation: *the executive who heads the company.* **2.** The chief officer of a government, state, or political division. **3.** The branch of government responsible for putting laws into effect or managing the affairs of a country. ❖ *adj.* **1.** Relating to or capable of carrying out plans, duties, or other tasks: *a committee having executive powers.* **2.** Having, marked by, or relating to administrative or managerial authority. **3.** Relating to the branch of government concerned with putting laws into effect or managing the affairs of a country: *an executive department.*

executor (ĭg-zĕk'yə-tər *or* ĕk'sĭ-kyōō'tər) *n.* A person who is responsible for carrying out the terms of a will.

exegesis (ĕk'sə-jē'sĭs) *n., pl.* **exegeses** (ĕk'sə-jē'sēz) Critical explanation or analysis, especially of a text. —**ex'e·get'ic** (ĕk'sə-jĕt'ĭk), **ex'e·get'i·cal** *adj.*

exemplar (ĭg-zĕm'plär') *n.* **1.** One that is worthy of imitation; a perfect example or model. **2.** One that is typical or representative; an example: *an exemplar of poor research.*

exemplary (ĭg-zĕm'plə-rē) *adj.* **1.** Worthy of imitation; commendable: *exemplary behavior.* **2.** Serving as an illustration; typical: *an exemplary Supreme Court case.* **3.** Serving as a warning: *an exemplary glance.*

exemplify (ĭg-zĕm'plə-fī') *tr.v.* **exemplified, exemplifying, exemplifies** To serve as an example of; illustrate: *a movie that exemplifies a director's style.* —**ex·em'pli·fi·ca'tion** (ĭg-zĕm'plə-fĭ-kā'shən) *n.*

exempt (ĭg-zĕmpt') *tr.v.* **exempted, exempting, exempts** To free from a duty or obligation; excuse: *Regulations exempt certain people from serving on juries.* ❖ *adj.* Freed from a duty or obligation required of others; excused: *Church property is exempt from taxes.* —**ex·empt'i·ble** *adj.*

exemption (ĭg-zĕmp'shən) *n.* The act of exempting or the condition of being exempt: *the exemption of food from the sales tax.*

exercise (ĕk′sər-sīz′) *n.* **1a.** Activity that requires physical exertion, especially when performed to develop or maintain fitness: *He swims for exercise.* **b.** A specific activity performed to develop or maintain fitness or a skill: *situps and other exercises; a piano exercise.* **2.** The active use or performance of something: *the exercise of good judgment; the exercise of official duties.* **3.** An activity having a specified aspect: *Trying to get him to clean his room is an exercise in futility.* **4.** A military maneuver or training activity. **5. exercises** A program that includes speeches and other ceremonial activities performed before an audience: *high school graduation exercises.* ❖ *v.* **exercised, exercising, exercises** —*tr.* **1.** To subject to practice or exertion in order to train, strengthen, or develop: *exercise a horse; exercise your abdominal muscles.* **2.** To make active use of; employ: *By voting we exercise our rights as citizens.* —*intr.* To take exercise: *I exercise every day.*

exert (ĭg-zûrt′) *tr.v.* **exerted, exerting, exerts 1.** To put to use or effect; put forth: *exerted all my strength to move the box.* **2.** To put (oneself) to strenuous effort: *The hikers exerted themselves to climb the mountain by noon.*

exertion (ĭg-zûr′shən) *n.* The act or an instance of exerting, especially a strenuous effort: *the tremendous exertion of running a marathon.*

exeunt (ĕk′sē-ənt) Used as a stage direction to indicate that two or more performers leave the stage.

exfoliate (ĕks-fō′lē-āt′) *v.* **exfoliated, exfoliating, exfoliates** —*tr.* **1.** To remove (a layer of bark or skin, for example) in flakes or scales; peel. **2.** To cast off in scales, flakes, or splinters. —*intr.* To come off or separate into flakes, scales, or layers. —**ex·fo′li·a′tion** *n.* —**ex·fo′li·a′-tive** *adj.* —**ex·fo′li·a′tor** *n.*

exhalation (ĕks′hə-lā′shən *or* ĕks′sə-lā′shən) *n.* **1.** The act or process of exhaling: *exhalation of air from the lungs.* **2.** Something, such as air or vapor, that is exhaled.

exhale (ĕks-hāl′ *or* ĕk-sāl′) *v.* **exhaled, exhaling, exhales** —*intr.* To breathe out. —*tr.* To breathe (something) out or blow (something) forth: *The dragon exhaled fire and smoke. The spring flowers exhaled a delicate perfume.*

exhaust (ĭg-zôst′) *tr.v.* **exhausted, exhausting, exhausts 1.** To wear out completely; tire: *Moving the heavy furniture exhausted us.* **2.** To use up completely: *Tickets and snacks exhausted our money.* **3.** To drain the contents of; empty: *exhaust the fuel tank.* **4.** To let out or draw off: *exhaust wastes through a pipe.* **5.** To treat completely; cover thoroughly: *exhaust a topic of conversation.* ❖ *n.* **1.** The escape or release of waste gases or vapors, as from an engine: *The fan is too small to ensure quick exhaust of the fumes.* **2.** The vapors or gases so released: *a cloud of exhaust.* **3.** A device or system that allows vapors or gases to escape: *replaced the exhaust on the truck.*

exhausted (ĭg-zô′stĭd) *adj.* **1.** Used up; consumed: *The oil reserves are nearly exhausted.* **2.** Worn out completely; very tired: *an exhausted swimmer.* —**ex·haust′ed·ly** *adv.*

exhaustion (ĭg-zôs′chən) *n.* **1.** An act or an instance of exhausting: *exhaustion of the water supply.* **2.** The state of being exhausted; extreme fatigue: *The runner collapsed from exhaustion.*

exhaustive (ĭg-zô′stĭv) *adj.* Complete; thorough: *an exhaustive search for a solution.* —**ex·haus′tive·ly** *adv.* —**ex·haus′tive·ness** *n.*

exhibit (ĭg-zĭb′ĭt) *tr.v.* **exhibited, exhibiting, exhibits 1.** To present for the public to view; display: *exhibit new artworks at a gallery.* **2.** To give evidence of; show; demonstrate: *The dentist exhibited great skill in repairing the tooth.* ❖ *n.* **1.** Something exhibited; a display: *She studied the museum's fossil exhibits.* **2.** A public showing; an exhibition: *The art exhibit will open next month.* **3.** Something formally introduced as evidence in a court of law. —**ex·hib′i·tor, ex·hib′it·er** *n.*

exhibition (ĕk′sə-bĭsh′ən) *n.* **1.** The act or an instance of exhibiting. **2.** Something exhibited; an exhibit. **3.** A large-scale public showing: *an exhibition of boating equipment.*

exhibitionism (ĕk′sə-bĭsh′ə-nĭz′əm) *n.* The act or practice of deliberately behaving so as to attract attention. —**ex′hi·bi′tion·ist** *n.*

exhilarate (ĭg-zĭl′ə-rāt′) *tr.v.* **exhilarated, exhilarating, exhilarates 1.** To cause to feel happy; elate: *The victory exhilarated the whole school.* **2.** To invigorate; stimulate: *A walk in the cold will exhilarate us.* —**ex·hil′a·ra′tion** *n.*

exhort (ĭg-zôrt′) *tr.v.* **exhorted, exhorting, exhorts** To urge by strong argument or earnest appeal: *The candidate exhorted the crowd to vote.*

exhortation (ĕg′zôr-tā′shən *or* ĕk′sôr-tā′shən) *n.* **1.** The act or an instance of exhorting: *No amount of exhortation could persuade them to give up.* **2.** A speech intended to advise or encourage: *delivered a fiery exhortation to her team.*

exhume (ĭg-zōōm′) *tr.v.* **exhumed, exhuming, exhumes 1.** To dig up or remove from a grave: *an order to exhume the body.* **2.** To bring to light; uncover.

exigency (ĕk′sə-jən-sē) *n., pl.* **exigencies 1.** A pressing or urgent situation. **2.** An urgent requirement; a pressing need: *The exigencies of the schedule meant no holiday.*

exigent (ĕk′sə-jənt) *adj.* Requiring immediate action or remedy; urgent.

exile (ĕg′zīl′ *or* ĕk′sīl′) *n.* **1a.** The condition or period of being forced to live away from one's native country or home: *Exile was the punishment for opposing political activities.* **b.** The period or condition of self-imposed absence from one's country or home: *The author chose exile over living in a country he found oppressive.* **2.** A person who lives away from his or her native country. ❖ *tr.v.* **exiled, exiling, exiles** To send into exile; banish: *The dictator exiled members of the opposition party.*

exist (ĭg-zĭst′) *intr.v.* **existed, existing, exists 1.** To have actual being; be real: *How many chemical elements have been shown to exist?* **2a.** To have life; live: *Dinosaurs existed millions of years ago.* **b.** To live at a minimal level; subsist: *Animals cannot exist without food and water.* **3.** To continue to be; persist: *old traditions that still exist in parts of the country.* **4.** To be present; occur: *A new spirit of cooperation existed on both sides.*

existence (ĭg-zĭs′təns) *n.* **1.** The fact or condition of existing; being. **2.** The fact or condition of continued being; life: *our existence on the earth.* **3.** A manner of existing: *lived an ordinary existence.* **4.** Occurrence; presence: *the existence of oil deposits in the rocks.*

existent (ĭg-zĭs′tənt) *adj.* **1.** Having life or being; existing: *existent creatures.* **2.** Occurring or present at the moment; current: *existent customs.*

existential (ĕg′zĭ-stĕn′shəl *or* ĕk′sĭ-stĕn′shəl) *adj.* **1.** Relating to existence: *existential questions such as "Why am I here?"* **2.** Affecting or potentially affecting one's existence: *an existential threat to human civilization.* **3.** Relating to existentialism or existentialists: *an existential writer.* —**ex′is·ten′tial·ly** *adv.*

existentialism (ĕg′zĭ-stĕn′shə-lĭz′əm or ĕk′sĭ-stĕn′shə-lĭz′əm) *n*. A philosophy that emphasizes the isolation of the individual in a hostile or indifferent universe, regards human existence as unexplainable, and stresses freedom of choice and responsibility for one's own actions. —**ex′is·ten′tial·ist** *adj. & n*.

exit (ĕg′zĭt or ĕk′sĭt) *n*. **1**. The act of going away or out: *I made a hasty exit from the snake house at the zoo*. **2**. A passage or way out: *Exits must be clearly marked*. **3**. A performer's departure from the stage. ❖ *v*. **exited, exiting, exits** —*intr*. To make one's exit; depart: *Please exit to the left*. —*tr*. **1**. To go out of; leave: *exited the plane through a rear door*. **2**. To stop the execution of and close down (a computer application).

exit poll *n*. A poll of voters taken as they leave a polling place.

exo– A prefix that means outside or external: *exoskeleton*.

exocrine gland (ĕk′sə-krĭn or ĕk′sə-krēn) *n*. Any of various glands, such as a sweat gland or mammary gland, that discharge their product through a duct that opens onto an external or internal surface rather than directly into the bloodstream.

exodus (ĕk′sə-dəs) *n*. **1**. A departure of a large number of people: *an exodus from the cities to the suburbs*. **2. Exodus a**. In the Bible, the departure of the Israelites from Egypt. **b**. The book of the Bible that tells of this departure and of God's giving of the Ten Commandments to the Hebrew prophet Moses.

ex officio (ĕks′ ə-fĭsh′ē-ō′) *adv. & adj*. By virtue of the office or position one holds: *The mayor is ex officio a member of the city council*.

exonerate (ĭg-zŏn′ə-rāt′) *tr.v*. **exonerated, exonerating, exonerates** To free from blame: *The jury's decision exonerated the defendant*. —**ex·on′er·a′tion** *n*.

exoplanet (ĕk′sō-plăn′ĭt) *n*. An extrasolar planet.

exorbitant (ĭg-zôr′bĭ-tənt) *adj*. Exceeding what is reasonable or customary, especially in cost: *an exorbitant price on an imported car*. —**ex·or′bi·tance** *n*. —**ex·or′bi·tant·ly** *adv*.

exorcise (ĕk′sôr-sīz′) *tr.v*. **exorcised, exorcising, exorcises 1**. To drive away (an evil spirit), often by incantation, prayer, or command. **2**. To eliminate or suppress (a negative feeling, for example). **3**. To free from evil spirits: *the exorcising of an old house*. —**ex′or·cis′er** *n*.

exorcism (ĕk′sôr-sĭz′əm) *n*. **1**. The act or practice of exorcising. **2**. A formula used in exorcising. —**ex′or·cist** *n*.

exoskeleton (ĕk′sō-skĕl′ĭ-tn) *n*. A hard outer covering, such as the shell of a grasshopper or a crab, that provides protection and support.

exosphere (ĕk′sō-sfĭr′) *n*. The transitional zone between the thermosphere (the outermost layer of the earth's atmosphere) and outer space. —**ex′o·spher′ic** (ĕk′sō-sfĭr′ĭk or ĕk′sō-sfĕr′ĭk) *adj*.

exothermic (ĕk′sō-thûr′mĭk) also **exothermal** (ĕk′sō-thûr′məl) *adj*. Releasing or giving off heat: *an exothermic chemical reaction*.

exotic (ĭg-zŏt′ĭk) *adj*. **1**. From another part of the world; foreign: *exotic imported birds*. **2**. Strikingly unfamiliar or unusual; excitingly strange: *the exotic beauty of a distant nebula*. —**ex·ot′i·cal·ly** *adv*. —**ex·ot′ic·ness** *n*.

exp. An abbreviation for: **1**. exponent. **2**. express.

expand (ĭk-spănd′) *v*. **expanded, expanding, expands** —*tr*. **1**. To increase the size, number, volume, or scope of; enlarge: *expand a balloon with air; expanded the business into new areas*. **2**. To express at length or in detail; enlarge upon: *She promised to expand her ideas in her next presentation*. **3**. To open (something) up or out: *The owl expanded its wings and flew away. The article expanded the author's ideas*. **4**. To express or write (a number or mathematical expression) in an extended form: *We expand 452 by writing it as 400 + 50 + 2*. —*intr*. **1**. To become greater in size, volume, quantity, or scope: *Gases expand when heated*. See Synonyms at **increase**. **2**. To open up or out; unfold: *The sofa expands into a bed*. **3**. To speak or write at length or in detail: *expanded on the issues at the meeting*. —**ex·pand′a·ble** *adj*.

expanse (ĭk-spăns′) *n*. A wide and open extent, as of surface, land, or sky: *a vast expanse of desert*.

expansion (ĭk-spăn′shən) *n*. **1**. The act or process of expanding: *the growth and expansion of industry*. **2**. Something formed or produced by expansion: *These suburbs are an expansion of the city*. **3**. The extent or amount by which something has expanded: *a 40 percent expansion in sales*. **4**. A number or other mathematical expression written in an extended form; for example, $a^2 + 2ab + b^2$ is the expansion of $(a + b)^2$.

expansionism (ĭk-spăn′shə-nĭz′əm) *n*. A nation's practice or policy of territorial or economic expansion. —**ex·pan′sion·ist** *adj. & n*.

expansive (ĭk-spăn′sĭv) *adj*. **1**. Capable of expanding or tending to expand: *Balloons are made of expansive material*. **2**. Broad in size or extent; comprehensive: *an expansive view of world affairs*. **3**. Disposed to be open, communicative, and generous. **4**. Grand in scale: *the calm expansive lake*. —**ex·pan′sive·ly** *adv*. —**ex·pan′sive·ness** *n*.

expatiate (ĭk-spā′shē-āt′) *intr.v*. **expatiated, expatiating, expatiates** To speak or write at length; elaborate: *Our guide expatiated on the history and wildlife of the area*. —**ex·pa′ti·a′tion** *n*.

expatriate (ĕk-spā′trē-āt′) *tr.v*. **expatriated, expatriating, expatriates 1**. To send into exile. **2**. To remove (oneself) from residence in one's native land: *Many writers expatriated themselves to France in the 1920s*. ❖ *n*. (ĕk-spā′trē-ĭt) A person who has taken up residence in a foreign country. —**ex·pa′tri·a′tion** *n*.

expect (ĭk-spĕkt′) *tr.v*. **expected, expecting, expects 1**. To look forward to the probable occurrence or appearance of: *expecting a telephone call*. **2**. To consider reasonable or due: *The host will expect an apology for breaking the dish*. **3**. *Informal* To presume; suppose: *I expect you're right*.

expectancy (ĭk-spĕk′tən-sē) *n., pl*. **expectancies 1**. The act or state of expecting; anticipation: *I was filled with expectancy as I waited for my flight*. **2**. Something that is expected.

expectant (ĭk-spĕk′tənt) *adj*. **1**. Having or marked by expectation: *an expectant audience; an expectant look*. **2**. Awaiting the birth of a child: *expectant parents*. —**ex·pec′tant·ly** *adv*.

expectation (ĕk′spĕk-tā′shən) *n*. **1**. The act of expecting. **2**. Anticipation: *eyes shining with expectation*. **3**. **expectations** Prospects, especially of success or gain.

expectorant (ĭk-spĕk′tər-ənt) *adj*. Helping to discharge phlegm or mucus from the respiratory tract. ❖ *n*. An expectorant medicine or drug.

expectorate (ĭk-spĕk′tə-rāt′) *v*. **expectorated, expectorating, expectorates** —*tr*. To force from the mouth; spit. **2**. To cough up and spit (phlegm, for example). —*intr*. To spit. —**ex·pec′to·ra′tion** *n*.

expedience (ĭk-spē′dē-əns) *n*. Expediency.

expediency (ĭk-spē′dē-ən-sē) *n., pl.* **expediencies 1.** Appropriateness to the purpose at hand; fitness. **2.** Adherence to self-serving means: *Their plans seem to be nothing but expediency.* **3.** A means; an expedient.

expedient (ĭk-spē′dē-ənt) *adj.* **1.** Suitable or efficient for accomplishing a purpose: *Email is an expedient way to communicate.* **2.** Convenient but based on a concern for self-interest rather than principle: *She changed her position when it was politically expedient.* ❖ *n.* Something that is a means to an end, especially when based on self-interest: *He compromised his integrity as an expedient to boost his career.* —**ex·pe′di·ent·ly** *adv.*

expedite (ĕk′spĭ-dīt′) *tr.v.* **expedited, expediting, expedites** To speed up the progress of or execute quickly: *expedite a loan application.*

expedition (ĕk′spĭ-dĭsh′ən) *n.* **1.** A trip made by a group of people with a definite purpose: *a geological expedition through the canyon.* **2.** The group making such a trip: *The expedition set off at dawn.* **3.** Speed in performance; promptness: *The cleanup was done with expedition.*

expeditionary (ĕk′spĭ-dĭsh′ə-nĕr′ē) *adj.* Relating to or being an expedition.

expeditious (ĕk′spĭ-dĭsh′əs) *adj.* Acting or done with speed and efficiency: *The most expeditious transportation over long distances is by airplane.* See Synonyms at **fast**[1]. —**ex′pe·di′tious·ly** *adv.* —**ex′pe·di′tious·ness** *n.*

expel (ĭk-spĕl′) *tr.v.* **expelled, expelling, expels 1.** To force or drive out; eject forcefully: *expel air from the lungs.* **2.** To deprive (someone) of membership or rights in an organization; force to leave: *The bridge club expelled several members for cheating.*

expend (ĭk-spĕnd′) *tr.v.* **expended, expending, expends 1.** To lay out; spend: *expend tax money on health care.* **2.** To use up; consume: *expend energy.*

expendable (ĭk-spĕn′də-bəl) *adj.* **1.** Subject to being used up or consumed: *an expendable source of energy that is not renewable.* **2.** Not worth salvaging or reusing: *expendable rocket boosters.* **3.** Not strictly necessary; dispensable: *an expendable budget item.*

expenditure (ĭk-spĕn′dĭ-chər) *n.* **1.** The act or process of expending; outlay: *the expenditure of city funds for a recycling plant.* **2.** An amount expended.

expense (ĭk-spĕns′) *n.* **1.** Something spent to attain a goal or achieve a purpose: *an expense of time and effort on the project.* **2.** A loss for the sake of something gained; a sacrifice: *outlaw demonstrations at the expense of free speech.* **3.** An expenditure of money; a cost: *With so many visitors, food is our biggest expense.* **4. expenses** Charges brought about by an employee in doing a job or in carrying out an assignment: *My expenses include food and lodging.* **5.** Something requiring the expenditure of money: *Owning a car can be a big expense.*

expensive (ĭk-spĕn′sĭv) *adj.* **1.** Requiring a large expenditure; costly: *an expensive limousine.* **2.** Marked by high prices: *an expensive store.* —**ex·pen′sive·ly** *adv.* —**ex·pen′sive·ness** *n.*

experience (ĭk-spîr′ē-əns) *n.* **1a.** Active participation in events or activities, leading to the accumulation of knowledge or skill: *learned more from experience than from reading books.* **b.** The knowledge or skill so derived: *a carpenter with a lot of experience.* **2.** An event or series of events participated in or lived through: *the experience of traveling in space.* ❖ *tr.v.* **experienced, experiencing,**

experiences To participate in personally; undergo: *experience a great adventure; experience fear.*

experienced (ĭk-spîr′ē-ənst) *adj.* Skilled or knowledgeable through active participation or practice: *an experienced teacher.*

experiment (ĭk-spĕr′ə-mənt) *n.* A test or procedure that is designed to determine the validity of a hypothesis or the effects of something and is carried out under conditions that are carefully controlled: *an experiment to test a theory about plant hormones; conducted an experiment to evaluate a new drug.* ❖ *intr.v.* (ĭk-spĕr′ə-mĕnt′) **experimented, experimenting, experiments 1.** To conduct an experiment; make tests or trials. **2.** To try something new, especially in order to gain experience: *They experimented with new ways of growing corn.* —**ex·per′i·ment′er** *n.*

experimental (ĭk-spĕr′ə-mĕn′tl) *adj.* **1.** Relating to or based on experiments: *an experimental approach to psychology.* **2.** Not yet proven to work; still being tested: *an experimental drug for diabetes.* —**ex·per′i·men′tal·ly** *adv.*

experimentation (ĭk-spĕr′ə-mĕn-tā′shən) *n.* The act, process, or practice of experimenting: *I discovered how to make good biscuits after much experimentation.*

expert (ĕk′spûrt′) *n.* A person with great knowledge of or skill in a particular field: *Doctors are experts in medicine.* ❖ *adj.* Having or showing great knowledge or skill as the result of experience or training: *The forest ranger was an expert guide.* See Synonyms at **proficient**. —**ex′pert′ly** *adv.*

expertise (ĕk′spûr-tēz′) *n.* Skill or knowledge in a particular area: *a researcher with expertise in infectious diseases.*

expiate (ĕk′spē-āt′) *tr.v.* **expiated, expiating, expiates** To atone or make amends for: *expiate sins by acts of penance.* —**ex′pi·a′tion** *n.*

expiration (ĕk′spə-rā′shən) *n.* **1.** The act of coming to a close; termination: *the expiration of a contract.* **2.** The act or process of breathing out; exhalation.

expire (ĭk-spîr′) *intr.v.* **expired, expiring, expires 1.** To come to an end; terminate: *When our dog's license expires, we have to renew it.* **2.** To die: *The injured bird expired before we could get help for it.* **3.** To breathe out; exhale.

explain (ĭk-splān′) *v.* **explained, explaining, explains** —*tr.* **1.** To make plain or comprehensible: *explain the rules of a game; explain a job to a substitute.* **2.** To define or interpret: *The professor explained the meaning of the poem.* **3.** To offer reasons for or a cause of; justify: *The student was asked to explain her absence.* —*intr.* To make something plain or comprehensible. ❖ **explain away** To dismiss or minimize the significance of (something) by means of an explanation or excuse: *There is no way to explain away my carelessness.* —**ex·plain′a·ble** *adj.* —**ex·plain′er** *n.*

explanation (ĕk′splə-nā′shən) *n.* **1.** The act or process of explaining. **2.** Something that explains: *Give a simple explanation of how to make a kite. The police looked for an explanation for the crime.*

explanatory (ĭk-splăn′ə-tôr′ē) *adj.* Serving or intended to explain: *The math book has explanatory notes to go along with some problems.*

expletive (ĕk′splĭ-tĭv) *n.* **1.** An exclamation or oath, especially one that is profane, vulgar, or obscene. **2.** A word or phrase that does not communicate meaning but is included for the sake of the syntax of a sentence (such as *it* in *It's raining*) or for poetic meter or rhyme (such as *do* in the first line of William Shakespeare's sonnet beginning *Rough winds do shake the darling buds of May*).

explicable (ĭk-splĭk′ə-bəl or ĕk′splĭ-kə-bəl) *adj.* Possible to explain: *explicable phenomena.* —**ex·plic′a·bly** *adv.*

explicate (ĕk′splĭ-kāt′) *tr.v.* **explicated, explicating, explicates** To make clear the meaning of; explain: *explicate a scientific theory.* —**ex′pli·ca′tion** *n.*

explicit (ĭk-splĭs′ĭt) *adj.* **1.** Fully and clearly expressed or defined; having nothing left out: *an explicit statement of their plans for a new school.* **2.** Clear and outspoken: *We were explicit in demanding that the marsh should be preserved.* —**ex·plic′it·ly** *adv.* —**ex·plic′it·ness** *n.*

explode (ĭk-splōd′) *v.* **exploded, exploding, explodes** —*intr.* **1.** To release energy in an explosion; blow up: *Fireworks exploded all around.* **2.** To burst violently as a result of internal pressure: *Suddenly the bottle of soda water exploded.* **3.** To make an emotional outburst: *exploded with anger at the trespassers.* **4.** To increase suddenly and sharply: *The population has exploded in the past decade.* —*tr.* **1.** To cause to undergo an explosion; detonate: *The engineers exploded the dynamite to open a passage through the rock.* **2.** To show to be false or unreliable: *explode a hypothesis.* —**ex·plod′er** *n.*

WORD HISTORY The word **explode** has not always had the same meaning as it does today. It comes from the Latin verb *explōdere*, "to drive away by clapping." The modern meaning ultimately comes from the bursting sound made by clapping. The Latin verb is composed of the prefix *ex–*, "out, away," and the verb *plaudere*, "to clap." This verb shows up also in English *applaud*, where the sense of "clapping" is more immediately apparent. **Applaud** comes from Latin *applaudere*, "to clap at" (*ad–*, "to, toward"). We also get the word **plausible** from the same source; it once meant "likely to be applauded or received favorably," and later, "believable."

---

exploit (ĕk′sploit′) *n.* An act or deed, especially a brilliant or heroic one: *the exploits of legendary figures such as Robin Hood.* ❖ *tr.v.* (ĭk-sploit′) **exploited, exploiting, exploits 1.** To use to the greatest possible advantage: *exploit an idea to make a profit.* **2.** To make use of selfishly or unethically: *exploit unskilled workers.* —**ex·ploit′a·ble** *adj.* —**ex·ploit′er** *n.*

exploitation (ĕk′sploi-tā′shən) *n.* **1.** The act of using to the greatest possible advantage: *the exploitation of oil fields.* **2.** The use of a person or group for selfish purposes: *the exploitation of immigrant labor.*

exploration (ĕk′splə-rā′shən) *n.* The act or an instance of exploring: *Arctic exploration; an exploration of new medical treatments.* —**ex·plor′a·to′ry** (ĭk-splôr′ə-tôr′ē) *adj.*

explore (ĭk-splôr′) *v.* **explored, exploring, explores** —*tr.* **1.** To investigate systematically; examine: *explored the possibilities of a new trade agreement.* **2.** To travel in or search into for the purpose of discovery: *explore a vast region of rainforest.* —*intr.* To make a careful examination or search: *Geologists were hired to explore for oil.*

explorer (ĭk-splôr′ər) *n.* A person or thing that explores, especially a person who explores a geographic area.

explosion (ĭk-splō′zhən) *n.* **1.** The act of bursting apart or blowing up with a sudden violent release of energy: *an explosion of fireworks.* **2.** The loud sharp sound made by bursting apart or blowing up: *an explosion heard for miles.* **3.** A sudden, often vehement outbreak: *an explosion of laughter.* **4.** A sudden great increase: *a population explosion.*

explosive (ĭk-splō′sĭv) *adj.* **1.** Having the nature of an explosion: *an explosive laugh; an explosive fit of tem-*

per. **2.** Tending to explode: *an explosive powder.* ❖ *n.* A substance that tends to explode or is capable of exploding: *Explosives were used to make the tunnel through the mountain.* —**ex·plo′sive·ly** *adv.* —**ex·plo′sive·ness** *n.*

expo (ĕk′spō) *n., pl.* **expos** *Informal* An exposition.

exponent (ĭk-spō′nənt or ĕk′spō′nənt) *n.* **1.** A person who is an enthusiastic supporter of or advocates something: *exponents of free trade.* **2.** A number or symbol, placed to the right of and above the expression to which it applies, that indicates the number of times a mathematical expression is used as a factor. For example, the exponent 3 in 5^3 indicates $5 \times 5 \times 5$; the exponent 2 in $(x + y)^2$ indicates $(x + y) \times (x + y)$.

exponential (ĕk′spə-nĕn′shəl) *adj.* Containing or involving one or more exponents in a mathematical expression: *an exponential increase.*

export (ĭk-spôrt′ or ĕk′spôrt′) *tr.v.* **exported, exporting, exports 1.** To send or transport (goods or products) to another country, especially for trade or sale: *export fruit to England.* **2.** To cause the spread of (an idea, for example) in another part of the world; transmit. ❖ *n.* (ĕk′spôrt′) Exportation. —**ex·port′a·ble** *adj.* —**ex·port′er** *n.*

exportation (ĕk′spôr-tā′shən) *n.* The act or an instance of exporting: *The exportation of automobiles is an important element of the Japanese economy.*

expose (ĭk-spōz′) *tr.v.* **exposed, exposing, exposes 1.** To lay open or subject to an action or an influence: *expose young children to literature; expose a visitor to a cold.* **2.** To subject (a photographic film, for example) to the action of light. **3.** To make visible; reveal: *Paint remover exposed the old wood underneath.* **4.** To make known (something discreditable) or reveal the guilt of: *exposed the criminal activity; expose a dishonest official.* —**ex·pos′er** *n.* —SEE NOTE AT **compose.**

exposé (ĕk′spō-zā′) *n.* An exposure or revelation of something discreditable: *a magazine exposé of corruption in government.*

exposition (ĕk′spə-zĭsh′ən) *n.* **1.** An exact and detailed explanation of difficult material: *The astronomer gave a long exposition on the nature of the eclipse.* **2.** The first part of a musical composition in sonata form that introduces the themes. **3.** A large public exhibition or fair: *an international computer exposition.* —**ex·pos′i·to′ry** (ĭk-spŏz′ĭ-tôr′ē) *adj.* —**ex·pos′i·tor** *n.*

ex post facto (ĕks′ pōst făk′tō) *adj.* Enacted after an event but applying to it nonetheless. Used especially of a law.

expostulate (ĭk-spŏs′chə-lāt′) *intr.v.* **expostulated, expostulating, expostulates** To reason earnestly with someone, explaining in an effort to dissuade or correct: *The parent expostulated with the committee on the need for new computers in school.* —**ex·pos′tu·la′tion** *n.*

exposure (ĭk-spō′zhər) *n.* **1.** The act or an instance of exposing, as: **a.** An act or instance of subjecting or being subjected to an action or influence: *a child's exposure to measles; her exposure to city living.* **b.** Appearance in public or in the mass media. **c.** Revelation, especially of crime or guilt. **2.** A position in relation to climatic or weather conditions or points of the compass: *Our house has a southern exposure.* **3a.** The act of exposing a photographic film or plate. **b.** The amount of light needed to expose a photographic film: *This exposure will not produce a clear image.* **c.** An exposed section of a roll of film: *We took several exposures.*

expound (ĭk-spound′) *v.* **expounded, expounding, ex-**

pounds —*tr.* To set forth or give a detailed statement of: *Debaters must always expound their views clearly.* —*intr.* To make a detailed statement: *The candidate expounded on the need for good government.* —**ex·pound′er** *n.*

express (ĭk-sprĕs′) *tr.v.* **expressed, expressing, expresses 1a.** To state or communicate in words: *Residents expressed their opinions at the town meeting.* **b.** To manifest or communicate without using words; show: *The winner's face expressed great joy. He expressed his displeasure by walking out of the room.* **c.** To make known the opinions or feelings of (oneself): *She expressed herself in a letter to the editor.* **2.** To represent by a sign, symbol, number, or formula: *A fraction can be expressed as a decimal.* **3.** To squeeze or press out, as juice from an orange: *a machine that expresses juice from fruits.* **4.** To manifest a trait encoded by (a gene): *a gene that is expressed during development.* ❖ *adj.* **1.** Clearly stated; explicit: *my express wish to go home.* **2.** Particular; specific: *The express object of the exercise was to teach cooperation.* **3a.** Direct, rapid, and usually making few or no stops: *an express train.* **b.** Relating to or sent by rapid transportation: *an express package; an express service.* ❖ *adv.* By express transport or delivery: *send a package express.* ❖ *n.* A means of transportation, such as a train, that travels rapidly and makes few or no stops before its destination: *take an express to the airport.* —**ex·press′i·ble** *adj.* —SEE NOTE AT **pressure.**

expression (ĭk-sprĕsh′ən) *n.* **1.** The act of expressing something, as in words, art, action, or movement: *the expression of one's opinion by voting.* **2a.** Something that expresses or communicates: *These flowers are an expression of my gratitude.* **b.** A facial aspect or look that indicates a certain mood or feeling: *an expression of joy in his eyes.* **3.** A symbol or arrangement of symbols that indicates a mathematical quantity or relationship between quantities. For example, $x + y$ is an algebraic expression. **4.** A manner of speaking, depicting, or performing that expresses particular feeling or meaning: *The poet read several poems with great expression.* **5.** A particular word or phrase: *Burnt to a crisp is a familiar expression.* **6.** The act or process of expressing a gene.

expressionism or **Expressionism** (ĭk-sprĕsh′ə-nĭz′əm) *n.* A movement in the fine arts during the early 1900s that emphasized the expression of artists' feelings and experiences.

expressionless (ĭk-sprĕsh′ən-lĭs) *adj.* Lacking expression: *a dull expressionless voice.*

expressive (ĭk-sprĕs′ĭv) *adj.* **1.** Serving to express or indicate: *The kitten's crying was expressive of its hunger.* **2.** Full of meaning; significant: *an expressive smile.* —**ex·pres′sive·ly** *adv.* —**ex·pres′sive·ness** *n.*

expressly (ĭk-sprĕs′lē) *adv.* **1.** In an express or a definite manner; explicitly: *The rules expressly say that only four can play at a time.* **2.** For a specific purpose; particularly: *scissors made expressly for left-handed people.*

expressway (ĭk-sprĕs′wā′) *n.* A major divided highway designed for high-speed travel, having few or no intersections.

expropriate (ĕk-sprō′prē-āt′) *tr.v.* **expropriated, expropriating, expropriates** To take (a property) for public use: *The government expropriated the farmers' lands to create the national park.* —**ex·pro′pri·a′tion** *n.*

expulsion (ĭk-spŭl′shən) *n.* The act of expelling or the

state of being expelled: *the expulsion of gases from a jet engine; expulsion from the team.*

expunge (ĭk-spŭnj′) *tr.v.* **expunged, expunging, expunges** To remove completely; delete; erase: *expunge a statement from the records of a trial.*

expurgate (ĕk′spər-gāt′) *tr.v.* **expurgated, expurgating, expurgates** To remove objectionable passages from (a book, for example) before publication: *References to several living people were expurgated from the play.* —**ex′pur·ga′tion** *n.*

exquisite (ĕk′skwĭ-zĭt or ĭk-skwĭz′ĭt) *adj.* **1.** Characterized by intricate and beautiful design or execution: *an exquisite vase.* **2.** Showing careful judgment or fine taste: *exquisite taste in art.* **3.** Intense; keen: *took exquisite pleasure in their children's success.* —**ex′qui·site·ly** *adv.*

ext. An abbreviation of extension.

extant (ĕk′stənt or ĕk-stănt′) *adj.* Still in existence; not destroyed, lost, or extinct: *extant diaries of early settlers.*

extemporaneous (ĭk-stĕm′pə-rā′nē-əs) *adj.* Done or made with little or no preparation; impromptu: *The scientist stood up and made extemporaneous comments on the situation.* —**ex·tem′po·ra′ne·ous·ly** *adv.* —**ex·tem′po·ra′ne·ous·ness** *n.*

extempore (ĭk-stĕm′pə-rē) *adj.* Spoken, carried out, or composed with little or no preparation or forethought: *an extempore speech.* ❖ *adv.* In an extemporaneous manner.

extend (ĭk-stĕnd′) *v.* **extended, extending, extends** —*tr.* **1.** To cause (something) to be longer, wider, or cover more area: *extended the dock to accommodate larger boats.* See Synonyms at **increase. 2.** To increase the scope or effect of: *research that extended our knowledge of the universe.* **3.** To cause (something) to last longer: *extended our visit by a day.* **4.** To open or straighten (something) out: *Extend your left arm.* **5.** To offer or provide: *extend congratulations to the graduates; extend aid to a developing nation.* **6.** To prolong the time allowed for payment of: *The bank extended our loan for another month.* —*intr.* To be or become long, large, or comprehensive: *The beach extends for miles. Her influence extends beyond the world of jazz.*

extended (ĭk-stĕn′dĭd) *adj.* **1.** Stretched or pulled out: *extended arms.* **2.** Continued for a long period of time; prolonged: *an extended vacation in the Caribbean.* **3.** Enlarged or broad in meaning, scope, or influence: *extended television coverage of the Congressional hearings.*

extended family *n.* A family that includes parents, children, and other relatives, often living with or near to each other.

extension (ĭk-stĕn′shən) *n.* **1.** The act of extending or the condition of being extended: *extension of the highway farther up the coast.* **2.** The amount, degree, or range to which something extends or can extend: *The wire has an extension of 50 feet.* **3a.** The act of straightening or extending a part of the body by a muscle: *extension of the leg to relieve muscle cramps.* **b.** The position assumed by an extended limb. **4.** Something that extends from a main part; an addition: *An extension was added to the back of the building.* **5.** An additional telephone connected to a main line. **6.** A string of letters or numbers following the name of a computer file that identify the kind of file: *The extension .txt indicates that a file is a text file.*

extension cord *n.* An insulated electric wire fitted with a plug and one or more sockets, used to plug in devices whose cords are not long enough to reach a wall outlet.

extensive (ĭk-stĕn′sĭv) *adj.* Large in extent, range, or amount: *An extensive park runs along the ocean. We made extensive renovations to the old building.* ❖ **—ex·ten′sive·ly** *adv.* **—ex·ten′sive·ness** *n.*

extensor (ĭk-stĕn′sər) *n.* A muscle that extends or stretches a limb of the body.

extent (ĭk-stĕnt′) *n.* **1.** The area, magnitude, or distance over which something extends; size: *increased the extent of their lands; underestimated the extent of the damage.* **2.** The degree to which something extends: *prosecuted to the fullest extent of the law.* **3.** An extensive space or area: *an extent of pine forest.*

extenuate (ĭk-stĕn′yoō-āt′) *tr.v.* **extenuated, extenuating, extenuates** To lessen or appear to lessen the seriousness or extent of, especially by providing partial excuses: *Lack of experience extenuated the fault of the goalie in the team's loss.*

extenuation (ĭk-stĕn′yoō-ā′shən) *n.* The act of extenuating or the condition of being extenuated; partial justification.

exterior (ĭk-stîr′ē-ər) *adj.* **1.** Outer; external: *the exterior walls of a castle.* **2.** Originating or acting from the outside: *exterior pressures.* **3.** Suitable for use outside: *an exterior paint able to withstand sun and rain.* ❖ *n.* **1.** A part or surface that is outside: *the exterior of the house.* **2.** An outward appearance: *The town had a cheerful exterior.*

exterior angle *n.* The angle formed between a side of a polygon and an extended adjacent side.

exterminate (ĭk-stûr′mə-nāt′) *tr.v.* **exterminated, exterminating, exterminates** To get rid of by destroying completely; wipe out: *exterminate a colony of termites.* **—ex·ter′mi·na′tion** *n.*

exterminator (ĭk-stûr′mə-nā′tər) *n.* A person whose occupation is exterminating insects, rodents, or other pests.

external (ĭk-stûr′nəl) *adj.* **1.** Relating to, existing on, or connected with the outside or an outer part; exterior: *external repairs on a house.* **2.** Suitable for application to an outer surface: *a salve for external use only.* **3.** Acting or coming from the outside: *an external force.* **4.** Relating chiefly to outward appearance; superficial: *an external display of pleasure.* **5.** Relating to foreign affairs or foreign countries. **—ex·ter′nal·ly** *adv.*

external ear *n.* The outer ear.

extinct (ĭk-stĭngkt′) *adj.* **1.** No longer existing or living: *an extinct species.* **2.** No longer in use: *extinct languages.* **3.** No longer burning or erupting; no longer active: *an extinct volcano.*

extinction (ĭk-stĭngk′shən) *n.* **1.** The fact of being extinct or the process of becoming extinct: *Colonization by humans has led to the extinction of many plant and animal species on the Hawaiian Islands.* **2.** The act of extinguishing: *Extinction of the fire took many hours.*

extinguish (ĭk-stĭng′gwĭsh) *tr.v.* **extinguished, extinguishing, extinguishes 1.** To put out (a fire, for example); quench: *extinguish a candle; extinguish the lights.* **2.** To put an end to (hopes, for example); destroy: *Missing the bus extinguished our hope of arriving on time.* **—ex·tin′guish·a·ble** *adj.*

extinguisher (ĭk-stĭng′gwĭ-shər) *n.* A portable device for spraying and extinguishing a fire with chemicals.

extirpate (ĕk′stər-pāt′) *tr.v.* **extirpated, extirpating, extirpates** To destroy totally; exterminate: *extirpate the evils of prejudice.* **—ex′tir·pa′tion** *n.*

extol also **extoll** (ĭk-stōl′) *tr.v.* **extolled, extolling, extols** or **extolls** To praise highly; laud: *extol the achievements of a great humanitarian.* **—ex·tol′ler** *n.*

extort (ĭk-stôrt′) *tr.v.* **extorted, extorting, extorts** To obtain by coercion, intimidation, or psychological pressure: *The blackmailer extorted money from a man who had lied about his past.* **—ex·tort′er** *n.*

extortion (ĭk-stôr′shən) *n.* The act or practice of obtaining something by coercion, intimidation, or psychological pressure, especially in violation of the law. **—ex·tor′tion·ist** *n.*

extortionate (ĭk-stôr′shə-nĭt) *adj.* **1.** Characterized by extortion: *the extortionate demands of the rebel forces.* **2.** Exorbitant; immoderate: *extortionate prices for gasoline.* **—ex·tor′tion·ate·ly** *adv.*

extra (ĕk′strə) *adj.* More than what is usual, normal, expected, or necessary; additional: *earn extra money by working part-time.* ❖ *n.* **1.** Something additional, for which one pays an added charge: *We bought a new car with all the extras such as a stereo.* **2.** A special edition of a newspaper: *The extra gave the latest news of the crisis.* **3.** A performer hired to play a minor part, as in a crowd scene in a film. ❖ *adv.* To an exceptional extent or degree; unusually: *The audience was extra quiet during the vocalist's solo.*

extra– or **extro–** A prefix that means outside or beyond: *extracurricular.*

extra-base hit (ĕk′strə-bās′) *n.* In baseball, a double, triple, or home run.

extract (ĭk-străkt′) *tr.v.* **extracted, extracting, extracts 1.** To draw or pull out, often with great force or effort: *extract a tooth; extract ore from a mine.* **2.** To obtain despite resistance: *extract a confession.* **3.** To obtain from a substance by a chemical or physical process: *extract aluminum from bauxite; extract the juice of berries.* **4.** To remove for separate consideration or publication; excerpt. **5.** To derive or gain from an experience or source: *extract pleasure from listening to music.* ❖ *n.* (ĕk′străkt′) **1.** A passage from a literary work; an excerpt: *The book is made up of extracts from other works.* **2.** A concentrated substance from a food or flavoring: *vanilla extract; an extract of coffee.* **—ex·trac′tor** *n.* —SEE NOTE AT **detract.**

extraction (ĭk-străk′shən) *n.* **1.** The act of extracting or the condition of being extracted: *The extraction of impacted wisdom teeth is quite common.* **2.** Something obtained by extraction; an extract. **3.** Descent; origin: *of French-Canadian extraction.*

extracurricular (ĕk′strə-kə-rĭk′yə-lər) *adj.* Being outside the regular course of study of a school or college: *Debating is an extracurricular activity.*

extradite (ĕk′strə-dīt′) *tr.v.* **extradited, extraditing, extradites** To give up or deliver (a prisoner or fugitive, for example) to the jurisdiction of another government or authority.

extradition (ĕk′strə-dĭsh′ən) *n.* The surrender of an individual by one nation or state to another nation or state where that individual is wanted for trial or punishment for the commission of a crime.

extramarital (ĕk′strə-măr′ĭ-tl) *adj.* **1.** Being in violation of marriage vows; adulterous: *an extramarital affair.* **2.** Having to do with a person other than one's spouse: *an extramarital friendship.*

extraneous (ĭk-strā′nē-əs) *adj.* **1.** Not essential; irrelevant: *These minor points are extraneous to my report.* **2.** Coming from the outside; foreign. **—ex·tra′ne·ous·ly** *adv.* **—ex·tra′ne·ous·ness** *n.*

extraordinaire (ĕk′strə-ôr′dn-âr′) *adj.* Extraordinary: *a jazz singer extraordinaire.*

extraordinary (ĭk-strôr′dn-ĕr′ē or ĕk′strə-ôr′dn-ĕr′ē) *adj.* Very unusual; exceptional; remarkable: *Landing on the moon was an extraordinary accomplishment. Great intelligence is an extraordinary gift.* —**ex·traor′di·nar′i·ly** (ĭk-strôr′dn-âr′ə-lē or ĕk′strə-ôr′dn-âr′ə-lē) *adv.*

extrapolate (ĭk-străp′ə-lāt′) *v.* **extrapolated, extrapolating, extrapolates** —*tr.* **1.** To infer or estimate (something unknown) on the basis of known information: *We extrapolated next year's expenses from a review of this year's bills.* **2.** In mathematics, to estimate the value of a quantity that falls outside the range in which its values are known. —*intr.* To make an estimate or prediction of something not known on the basis of known information. —**ex·trap′o·la′tion** *n.*

extrasensory (ĕk′strə-sĕn′sə-rē) *adj.* Outside the normal range of the physical senses: *Extrasensory powers are said to enable some people to predict the future.*

extrasensory perception *n.* ESP.

extrasolar (ĕk′strə-sō′lər) *adj.* Existing or originating outside the solar system: *an extrasolar planet.*

extraterrestrial (ĕk′strə-tə-rĕs′trē-əl) *adj.* Beyond the earth or outside its atmosphere: *extraterrestrial bodies such as stars and comets.* ❖ *n.* An extraterrestrial being or life form.

extraterritoriality (ĕk′strə-tĕr′ĭ-tôr′ē-ăl′ĭ-tē) *n.* **1.** The operation of the law of a state or country outside of its physical boundaries. **2.** Exemption from local legal jurisdiction, such as that granted to foreign diplomats.

extravagance (ĭk-străv′ə-gəns) *n.* **1.** The quality of being extravagant: *the extravagance of the party decorations.* **2.** Immoderate spending: *Such extravagance can lead to debt.* **3.** Something that is excessively costly: *Their latest extravagance is an expensive car.*

extravagant (ĭk-străv′ə-gənt) *adj.* **1.** Excessive or unreasonable: *extravagant fees for the service.* **2.** Given to lavish or imprudent spending: *an extravagant executive.* —**ex·trav′a·gant·ly** *adv.*

extravaganza (ĭk-străv′ə-găn′zə) *n.* An elaborate spectacular display or entertainment: *The circus is one huge extravaganza.*

extreme (ĭk-strēm′) *adj.* **1.** The farthest possible; outermost: *the extreme end of the room.* **2.** Very great or intense: *exercise extreme caution; suffer from the extreme cold.* **3.** Extending far beyond the norm: *hold extreme opinions in politics.* **4.** Drastic; severe: *The doctors took extreme measures to control the baby's temperature.* **5a.** Relating to environmental conditions that normally do not support living organisms. **b.** Adapted to life under such conditions: *extreme microorganisms.* **6a.** Very dangerous or difficult: *extreme sports.* **b.** Participating in a very dangerous or difficult sport: *an extreme skier.* ❖ *n.* **1.** The greatest or utmost degree or point: *eager to the extreme.* **2.** Either of two things set at opposite ends of a range: *the extremes of boiling and freezing.* **3.** A drastic measure: *resort to extremes in an emergency.* **4.** In mathematics, the first or last term of a proportion. —**ex·treme′ly** *adv.* —**ex·treme′ness** *n.*

extremely high frequency *n.* A radio frequency between 30,000 and 300,000 megahertz.

extremely low frequency *n.* A radio frequency below 300 hertz.

extremist (ĭk-strē′mĭst) *n.* A person with views extending far beyond the norm, especially in politics. —**ex·trem′ism** *n.*

extremity (ĭk-strĕm′ĭ-tē) *n., pl.* **extremities 1.** The outermost or farthest point: *Patagonia is at the southern extremity of South America.* **2.** The greatest or utmost degree or condition: *the extremity of the recent weather.* **3.** An extreme or severe measure: *resort to extremities in a crisis.* **4. extremities** Limbs or appendages, especially the hands and feet: *Boots and gloves protect the extremities from cold.*

extremophile (ĭk-strē′mə-fīl′) *n.* Any of various organisms that thrive only in extreme conditions, such as very hot or very salty environments. Many archaea are extremophiles.

extricate (ĕk′strĭ-kāt′) *tr.v.* **extricated, extricating, extricates** To set free from an entanglement or difficulty; disengage: *extricate oneself from an embarrassing situation.* —**ex′tri·ca′tion** *n.*

extrinsic (ĭk-strĭn′sĭk or ĭk-strĭn′zĭk) *adj.* **1.** Not essential or basic; extraneous: *Your arguments are extrinsic to the discussion.* **2.** Originating from the outside; external: *extrinsic forces on the environment.* —**ex·trin′si·cal·ly** *adv.*

extrovert (ĕk′strə-vûrt′) *n.* A person who is sociable and outgoing and who is more interested in external circumstances than in his or her personal thoughts or feelings. —**ex′tro·vert′ed** *adj.*

extrude (ĭk-strōōd′) *v.* **extruded, extruding, extrudes** —*tr.* **1.** To push or thrust out. **2.** To shape (plastic, for example) by forcing it through a die. —*intr.* To protrude or project: *Lava extruded from a crack in the mountainside.*

extrusion (ĭk-strōō′zhən) *n.* **1.** The act or process of extruding: *Pieces for plastic furniture are often made by extrusion.* **2.** Something that has been extruded.

exuberance (ĭg-zōō′bər-əns) *n.* The condition or quality of being exuberant: *The crowd cheered in wild exuberance.*

exuberant (ĭg-zōō′bər-ənt) *adj.* **1.** Full of unrestrained enthusiasm or joy: *exuberant sports fans; exuberant smiles.* **2.** Lavish or extravagant; overflowing: *exuberant praise of the hero.* —**ex·u′ber·ant·ly** *adv.*

exudation (ĕks′yōō-dā′shən) *n.* **1.** The act or an instance of oozing forth: *a slight exudation of blood from a cut.* **2.** Something that has oozed forth.

exude (ĭg-zōōd′ or ĭk-sōōd′) *tr. & intr.v.* **exuded, exuding, exudes** To give or come forth by or as if by oozing: *The body exudes sweat through the pores. Sap exuded from the cuts in the plant's stem. Confidence exuded in their cocky manner.*

exult (ĭg-zŭlt′) *intr.v.* **exulted, exulting, exults** To rejoice greatly; be jubilant or triumphant: *The entire town exulted in the team's victory.*

exultant (ĭg-zŭl′tənt) *adj.* Marked by great joy or jubilation: *an exultant victor.* —**ex·ult′ant·ly** *adv.*

exultation (ĕk′səl-tā′shən or ĕg′zəl-tā′shən) *n.* The act or condition of rejoicing greatly.

exurb (ĕk′sûrb′) *n.* A community lying just beyond the suburbs of a larger city. —**ex·ur′ban** *adj.* —**ex·ur′ban·ite′** *n.*

–ey Variant of –y[1].

eye (ī) *n.* **1a.** An organ by means of which an animal is able to see or sense light. In vertebrates the eye consists of a hollow structure containing a lens that focuses incoming light on a photosensitive retina. **b.** The outer visible part of this organ, especially the colored iris: *Tina has brown eyes.* **c.** The area and the structures around the eye, including the eyelids, eyelashes, and eyebrows: *She put her hands over her eyes.* **2.** A light-sensitive organ of an invertebrate animal. **3.** The ability to observe carefully: *A lifeguard must have a sharp eye.* **4.** The ability to estimate, judge, or note: *The coach had an eye for new talent.* **5.** A way of regarding something; a point of view or an opinion: *saw the world with a critical eye.* **6.** Something that resembles an eye, as a bud on a potato or a spot on a peacock's tail feather. **7.** The hole in a needle that the thread goes through. **8.** A loop, as of metal, rope, or thread. **9.** The relatively calm area at the center of a hurricane or similar storm. ❖ *tr.v.* **eyed, eyeing** or **eying** (ī′ĭng), **eyes** To look at; watch; regard: *The child eyed the big dog suspiciously.* ◆ **an eye for an eye** Punishment in which an offender suffers what the victim has suffered: *Execution of the murderer was defended as an eye for an eye.* **have (one's) eye on** To look at, especially attentively or continuously: *He's got his eye on that piece of cake.* **lay (one's) eyes on** or **set (one's) eyes on** To see: *the cutest dog I've ever laid eyes on.* **eye to eye** In agreement: *see eye to eye on most issues.* **in the public eye** Frequently seen in public or in the media: *celebrities who are constantly in the public eye.* **with an eye to** With a view to: *We left early with an eye to getting home before dark.*

eyeball (ī′bôl′) *n.* The ball-shaped part of the eye of a vertebrate animal, enclosed by the socket and covered by the eyelids. It is connected at the rear to the optic nerve.

eyebrow (ī′brou′) *n.* **1.** The bony ridge of the skull that extends over the eye. **2.** The line of short hairs covering this ridge.

eyecup (ī′kŭp′) *n.* A small cup with a rim shaped to fit over the eye, used for washing the eye or applying liquid medicine to it.

eyedropper (ī′drŏp′ər) *n.* A dropper for applying liquid medicine to the eye.

eyeful (ī′fŏŏl′) *n.* **1.** An amount of something that gets into the eye: *The wind was blowing and I got an eyeful of dust.* **2.** A complete view; a good look: *We got a real eyeful during the tour of the auto plant.*

eyeglasses (ī′glăs′ĭz) *pl.n.* A pair of lenses worn in front of the eyes to correct vision; glasses.

eyelash (ī′lăsh′) *n.* **1.** A row of hairs that forms a fringe on the edge of the eyelid. **2.** One of the hairs in this row.

eyelet (ī′lĭt) *n.* **1a.** A small hole for a lace, cord, or hook to fit through: *Shoelaces are threaded through eyelets.* **b.** A metal ring used as a rim to strengthen such a hole: *The*

eyelets on the flag protected it from tearing. **2.** A small hole edged with embroidered stitches as part of a design.

eyelid (ī′lĭd′) *n.* Either one of a pair of folds of skin and muscle that can be brought together to cover the eyeball.

eyeliner (ī′lī′nər) *n.* Makeup used to outline the eyes.

eye opener *n. Informal* A startling or shocking revelation: *The article about the water shortage was a real eye opener.*

eyepiece (ī′pēs′) *n.* The lens or group of lenses closest to the eye in a telescope, microscope, or similar optical instrument.

eye shadow *n.* A cosmetic applied to the eyelids to enhance the eyes.

eyesight (ī′sīt′) *n.* **1.** The ability to see; vision; sight: *People wear glasses to correct poor eyesight.* **2.** Range of vision; view: *a stream within eyesight of the house.*

eye socket *n.* The bony cavity in the skull that holds the eyeball.

eyesore (ī′sôr′) *n.* An ugly or unpleasant sight: *That junkyard is an eyesore.*

eyespot (ī′spŏt′) *n.* **1.** An area that is sensitive to light and functions somewhat like an eye, found in certain one-celled organisms and many invertebrate animals. **2.** A round marking resembling an eye, as on a butterfly's wing.

eyestalk (ī′stôk′) *n.* A movable structure having an eye on its tip, found on crabs, lobsters, and certain other crustaceans.

eyestrain (ī′strān′) *n.* Pain and fatigue of the eyes, often resulting from prolonged use of the eyes or uncorrected defects of vision.

eyetooth (ī′tōōth′) *n.* Either of the two canine teeth of the upper jaw.

eyewash (ī′wŏsh′) *n.* **1.** A solution used to wash or medicate the eyes. **2.** *Informal* Actions or remarks intended to conceal the facts of a situation.

eyewitness (ī′wĭt′nĭs) *n.* A person who has seen something or someone and can bear witness to the fact.

eyrie (âr′ē *or* îr′ē) *n.* Variant of **aerie.**

Ezekiel (ĭ-zē′kē-əl) *n.* A book of the Bible containing the prophet Ezekiel's prophecies on the destruction and restoration of Israel.

Ezra (ĕz′rə) *n.* A book of the Bible describing the return of the Hebrew exiles from Babylon and their efforts to build a temple in Jerusalem.

Ff

f or **F** (ĕf) *n.*, *pl.* **f's** or **F's** or **Fs 1.** The sixth letter of the English alphabet: *There are two f's in off.* **2. F** A failing grade in school. **3.** In music, the fourth tone in the scale of C major.

F An abbreviation of: **1.** Fahrenheit. **2.** fail. **3.** female.

fa (fä) *n.* In music, the fourth tone of a major scale.

fable (fā′bəl) *n.* **1.** A usually short tale or story that teaches a useful lesson about human nature, often with animal characters that speak and act like humans. **2.** A legend or myth. **3.** A falsehood; a lie.

fabled (fā′bəld) *adj.* **1.** Made known or famous by fables; legendary: *the fabled city of El Dorado.* **2.** Existing only in fables; fictitious.

fabric (făb′rĭk) *n.* **1.** A cloth produced usually by knitting, weaving, or pressing fibers together: *Lace, felt, and jersey are different types of fabric.* **2.** An underlying structure or framework: *the fabric of American society.*

fabricate (făb′rĭ-kāt′) *tr.v.* **fabricated, fabricating, fabricates 1.** To make, build, or manufacture, especially by assembling parts: *fabricate refrigerators on an assembly line.* **2.** To make up; invent: *fabricate an excuse for being late.* —**fab′ri·ca′tion** *n.*

fabulist (făb′yə-lĭst) *n.* A person who composes fables.

fabulous (făb′yə-ləs) *adj.* **1.** Extremely pleasing or successful; wonderful: *a fabulous vacation.* **2.** Astonishing or remarkable: *a fabulous rise to fame.* **3.** Legendary or mythical: *the fabulous phoenix who rises from its ashes every 500 years.* —**fab′u·lous·ly** *adv.*

façade also **facade** (fə-säd′) *n.* **1.** The face or front of a building: *the decorated façade of a great cathedral.* **2.** An artificial or false front: *The salesman's friendly manner was only a façade to gain our confidence.*

face (fās) *n.* **1.** The front of the head: *had a mask over her face.* **2a.** The expression of the face; countenance: *a friendly face.* **b.** A twisted facial expression: *The baby learned to make faces.* **3.** The surface presented to view; the front: *the face of a building.* **4.** An outer surface: *the face of the earth.* **5.** The upper or marked side: *the face of a playing card.* **6.** A plane surface that bounds a geometric solid: *the face of a cube.* **7.** The outward appearance; look: *With so many new buildings, the face of the city has changed.* **8.** Value or standing in the eyes of others; dignity; prestige: *They saved face by saying they were misled.* ❖ *v.* **faced, facing, faces** —*tr.* **1.** To have or turn the face toward: *The actor faced the audience.* **2.** To have the front toward; look out on: *The cathedral faces the square.* **3.** To meet or confront with self-assurance: *How can I face my friends when I know that I've let them down?* **4.** To acknowledge and accept or deal with: *You've got to face the facts. We must be willing to face our problems.* **5.** To cover a surface with a different material: *face the front of the fireplace with marble.* **6.** To line or trim the edge of: *face a cloth collar with satin.* —*intr.* **1.** To be turned or placed with the front in a certain direction: *The house faces toward the west.* **2.** To turn the face in a certain direction: *I faced into the wind.* ◆ **face off** To start play in ice hockey, lacrosse, and other games by releasing the puck or ball between two opposing players. **face up** To confront an unpleasant situation boldly: *finally faced up to the problem.* **in the face of** In spite of; despite: *The team won in the face of strong competition.*

face card *n.* A king, queen, or jack in a deck of playing cards.

faceless (fās′lĭs) *adj.* **1.** Having no face. **2.** Without identity; anonymous; impersonal: *a huge faceless corporation.*

face-lift also **facelift** (fās′lĭft′) *n.* **1.** An operation to tighten wrinkles or sagging skin of the face. **2.** A change or renovation to improve the appearance: *a plan to give the old building a face-lift.*

facemask (fās′măsk′) *n.* **1.** A covering for the face or head that is worn for protection or as a disguise: *Hockey players in our league must wear a helmet with a facemask.* **2.** A transparent, watertight covering for the face used in seeing underwater: *wore a facemask while scuba diving.*

face-off (fās′ôf′) *n.* **1.** A method of starting play in ice hockey, lacrosse, and other games in which an official drops the puck or ball between two opposing players who then try to gain possession of it. **2.** A confrontation.

facet (fās′ĭt) *n.* **1.** One of the flat polished surfaces cut on a gem or occurring naturally on a crystal. **2.** One of the ways of considering something; an aspect: *a complex problem with many facets to consider.* **3.** One of the individual outer visual units or lenses of a compound eye.

facetious (fə-sē′shəs) *adj.* Trying or meant to be funny; joking or humorous: *a facetious remark.* —**fa·ce′tious·ly** *adv.* —**fa·ce′tious·ness** *n.*

face value *n.* **1.** The value indicated on postage stamps, money, checks, bonds, or other paper securities: *an old coin worth 10 times its face value.* **2.** The apparent value or meaning: *Take such compliments at face value.*

facial (fā′shəl) *adj.* Relating to the face: *a comic with amusing facial expressions.* ❖ *n.* A treatment for the face, usually including a massage.

facile (făs′əl) *adj.* **1.** Done with little effort or difficulty; easy: *a facile task.* **2.** Working, acting, or speaking effortlessly or quickly: *a facile speaker; a facile writer.* **3.** Arrived at or presented without proper care or effort; superficial: *We don't need another facile solution to the problem.*

facilitate (fə-sĭl′ĭ-tāt′) *tr.v.* **facilitated, facilitating, facilitates 1.** To make easier; assist: *The bank loans will facilitate the building of a new sports arena.* **2.** To lead (a discussion). —**fa·cil′i·ta′tion** *n.* —**fa·cil′i·ta′tor** *n.*

facility (fə-sĭl′ĭ-tē) *n.*, *pl.* **facilities 1.** Ease in moving, acting, or doing; aptitude: *She has a real facility for learning foreign languages.* **2.** often **facilities** Something built or designed to provide a service or convenience: *The building has ample storage facilities.*

facing (fā′sĭng) *n.* **1.** A piece of material sewn to the edge of a garment as a lining or decoration. **2.** An outer covering of different material applied to a surface for decoration or protection: *a wood house with a stone facing.*

facsimile (făk-sĭm′ə-lē) *n.* **1.** An exact copy or reproduction: *The exhibit contained facsimiles of medieval manuscripts.* **2a.** A fax machine. **b.** A page received or sent by a fax machine.

fact (făkt) *n.* **1.** Knowledge or information based on real occurrences: *The account is based on fact. The movie is a mixture of fact and fiction.* **2.** Something whose reality, existence, or occurrence is known: *Genetic engineering is now a fact. That the Civil War happened is a fact. We are unsure of the facts in the case.* **3.** A thing that has been done, especially a crime: *an accessory after the fact.* ◆ **in fact** In reality; in truth.

faction (făk′shən) *n.* **1.** A group of people who have certain interests that are not shared with others in a larger group: *Factions form in organizations when members feel discontented with things as they are.* **2.** Internal discord; conflict within a nation, an organization, or another group: *The town government was torn by faction.*

factional (făk′shə-nəl) *adj.* **1.** Relating to factions: *factional disputes.* **2.** Causing conflict or discord: *factional questions arose during the conference.*

factionalism (făk′shə-nə-lĭz′əm) *n.* A condition of discord or conflict; a tendency toward the creation of factions: *Factionalism within the group caused the organization to break up.*

factious (făk′shəs) *adj.* Tending to cause conflict or discord; divisive: *factious members of a group.* —**fac′tious·ly** *adv.* —**fac′tious·ness** *n.*

factoid (făk′toid) *n.* **1.** A brief, somewhat interesting fact. **2.** A piece of information that is not true or cannot be verified but which is accepted as true because of frequent repetition.

factor (făk′tər) *n.* **1.** Something that helps bring about a certain result; an element or ingredient: *Many factors contributed to the success of the celebration.* **2.** One of two or more numbers or expressions that are multiplied to obtain a given product. For example, 2 and 3 are factors of 6, and $a + b$ and $a − b$ are factors of $a^2 − b^2$. **3.** A substance found in the body, such as a protein, that is essential to a biological process: *Growth factors are needed for proper cell development.* ❖ *tr.v.* **factored, factoring, factors** To find the factors of (a number or expression). ◆ **factor in** To figure in: *We factored in traffic when we determined when to start the meeting.* —**fac′tor·a·ble** *adj.*

factorial (făk-tôr′ē-əl) *n.* The product of all of the positive integers from 1 to a given positive integer. For example, the factorial of 4, written 4!, is $1 × 2 × 3 × 4 = 24.$ ❖ *adj.* Relating to a factorial: *a factorial symbol.*

factory (făk′tə-rē) *n., pl.* **factories** A building or group of buildings in which goods are manufactured; a plant: *The new automobile factory is filled with automated machines.*

factory farm *n.* A large-scale farming operation designed for efficient production, especially a large complex where animals are kept in small cages. —**factory farming** *n.*

factual (făk′chōō-əl) *adj.* Based on or containing facts: *a factual account of what happened.* —**fac′tu·al·ly** *adv.*

faculty (făk′əl-tē) *n., pl.* **faculties** **1.** One of the powers of the mind or body: *the faculty of speech.* **2.** A special ability or skill: *He has a faculty for doing impersonations.* **3.** The teaching staff of a school, college, or university.

fad (făd) *n.* Something that is done or adopted with great enthusiasm by many people for a brief period of time; a craze.

fade (fād) *v.* **faded, fading, fades** —*intr.* **1.** To lose brightness or loudness gradually: *The colors faded in the wash. The bird's call faded as we left the forest.* **2.** To lose freshness; wither: *The flowers are beginning to fade.* **3.** To pass out of existence slowly; disappear gradually: *Our chances of winning faded when they scored late in the game.* See Synonyms at **disappear. 4.** In football, to move back from the scrimmage line. Used of a quarterback. —*tr.* To cause to lose brightness: *The sun faded the colors in the quilt.*

fade-in or **fadein** (fād′ĭn′) *n.* A gradual appearance of an image, light, or sound, especially as a transition in a film, performance, or audio recording.

fade-out or **fadeout** (fād′out′) *n.* A gradual decrease in intensity of an image, light, or sound, especially as a transition in a film, performance, or audio recording.

faerie also **faery** (fā′ə-rē or fâr′ē) *n., pl.* **faeries** A fairy.

fagot (făg′ət) *n.* A bundle of twigs, sticks, or branches bound together, especially for firewood.

Fahrenheit (făr′ən-hīt′) *adj.* Relating to or based on a temperature scale that indicates the freezing point of water as 32° and the boiling point of water as 212° under standard atmospheric pressure.

fail (fāl) *v.* **failed, failing, fails** —*intr.* **1.** To be unsuccessful in attempting to do something, especially something wanted or expected: *Their first attempt at climbing the mountain failed.* **2.** To be lacking or not enough; fall short: *After months of drought the water supply failed.* **3.** To receive a grade that is less than acceptable in school. **4.** To stop functioning correctly; break down: *The brakes on the car failed.* **5.** To decline, as in strength or effectiveness: *The light began to fail.* **6.** To become bankrupt: *A number of downtown stores failed in the recession.* —*tr.* **1.** To leave (something) undone; neglect: *The defendant failed to appear in court.* **2.** To disappoint or prove undependable to: *I won't fail you this time.* **3.** To abandon; forsake: *His strength failed him on the homestretch.* **4a.** To receive an academic grade that is below the acceptable minimum in (a course, for example): *Did any students fail geometry?* **b.** To give an academic grade indicating unacceptability to: *The professor failed several students in the class.* ◆ **without fail** Definitely; certainly: *The job will be finished tomorrow without fail.*

failing (fā′lĭng) *n.* **1.** A fault or weakness; a shortcoming: *One of my failings is impatience.* **2.** The act of a person or thing that fails; a failure: *a failing of the water supply.* ❖ *prep.* In the absence of; without: *Failing directions, we will have to find the office on our own.*

fail-safe or **failsafe** (fāl′sāf′) *adj.* **1.** Capable of stopping or making safe the operation of a mechanism in case of a failure or malfunction: *Fail-safe switches on machinery can save workers' lives.* **2.** Guaranteed not to fail: *a fail-safe plan.*

failure (fāl′yər) *n.* **1.** The condition of not achieving something desired; lack of success: *Early airplane experiments ended in failure.* **2.** The neglect or inability to do something: *My failure to return library books meant a large fine.* **3.** The condition of being insufficient or falling short: *a crop failure during a drought.* **4.** A stopping of function or performance: *an electric power failure.* **5.** Bankruptcy: *The failure of the shop put several people out of work.* **6.** A person or thing that has failed: *I'm a failure as a trombone player.*

fain (fān) *Archaic adv.* Willingly or gladly. ❖ *adj.* Willing or glad.

faint (fānt) *adj.* **fainter, faintest 1.** So weak as to be difficult to perceive: *a faint light; a faint odor.* **2.** Small in degree or amount; meager: *a faint hope of getting the part.* **3.** Lacking in strength, energy, or interest: *only a faint attempt to understand their concerns.* **4.** Likely to fall unconscious; dizzy and weak: *Hunger made the hiker feel faint.* ❖ *n.* A sudden, usually short loss of consciousness, often caused by too little blood flowing to the brain. ❖ *intr.v.* **fainted, fainting, faints** To lose consciousness for a short time; swoon: *The dancer fainted in the heat.* ◆ **faint at heart** Lacking boldness or courage; faint-hearted. —**faint′ly** *adv.* —**faint′ness** *n.*

faint-hearted (fānt′här′tĭd) *adj.* Lacking courage; cowardly; timid. —**faint′-heart′ed·ly** *adv.*

fair¹ (fâr) *adj.* **fairer, fairest 1.** Free of favoritism; impartial or just: *a fair price; a fair trial.* **2.** Conforming to the rules or moral standards: *fair play.* **3.** Pleasing to look at; beautiful; lovely: *a fair face.* **4.** Light in color or complexion: *fair hair; fair skin.* **5.** Clear and sunny; free of clouds or storms: *fair weather.* **6.** Somewhat good; acceptable: *The movie was only fair.* **7.** In baseball, lying or falling within the foul lines: *a fair ball.* ❖ *adv.* In a fair manner; properly: *I believe in playing fair.* ◆ **fair and square** Just and honest. **no fair** Something contrary to the rules. —**fair′ness** *n.*

fair² (fâr) *n.* **1.** A gathering for the buying and selling of goods, often held at a particular time and place; a market: *We went to the annual book fair.* **2.** An exhibition of home or farm products and skills, usually with competitions and entertainment: *Her pumpkin won first prize at the county fair.* **3.** An exhibition intended to inform people about products or opportunities: *a technology fair; a jobs fair.* **4.** A social event held for charity and usually including the sale of articles; a bazaar: *the hospital fair.*

WORD HISTORY Fair¹ comes from Old English *fæger,* meaning "lovely, pleasant, agreeable, beautiful," and the original meanings survive in expressions like "fair weather" and "fair price." *Fair* in the sense "neither very bad nor very good" probably came from people using the word *fair* to avoid hurting other people's feelings about something that was not very well done. **Fair²** comes from Middle English *feire,* which comes from Late Latin *fēria,* both meaning "holiday."

fair catch *n.* In football, a catch of a kicked ball by a receiving player who has signaled the intention not to run with the ball. The receiving player may not be if no attempt is made to advance the ball after catching it.

fair game *n.* **1.** Animals that can be legally hunted: *Deer are fair game in many states in the fall.* **2.** A person or thing that seems suitable for pursuit or attack: *Politicians are fair game for reporters, especially during a campaign.*

fairground (fâr′ground′) *n.* An outdoor space where fairs, exhibitions, or other public events are held.

fair-haired (fâr′hârd′) *adj.* **1.** Having blond hair. **2.** Favorite: *the fair-haired member of the family.*

fairly (fâr′lē) *adv.* **1.** In a fair or just manner: *treating everyone fairly.* **2.** Moderately; rather: *felt fairly sick.* **3.** Actually; positively: *The walls fairly shook from the wind.*

fair-minded (fâr′mīn′dĭd) *adj.* Just and impartial; not prejudiced: *a fair-minded judge.*

fairway (fâr′wā′) *n.* The part of a golf course covered with short grass and extending from the tee to the putting green.

fairy (fâr′ē) *n., pl.* **fairies** An imaginary being in human form, supposed to have magical powers.

fairyland (fâr′ē-lănd′) *n.* **1.** An imaginary place where fairies are supposed to live. **2.** An enchanting place; a wonderland: *Snow turned the woods into a fairyland.*

fairy tale *n.* **1.** A story about fairies, magical creatures, or legendary deeds, usually intended for children. **2.** An explanation that is not true; a very fanciful story.

fait accompli (fā′tä-kôn-plē′) *n., pl.* **faits accomplis** (fā′-tä-kôn-plē′ *or* fā′tä-kôn-plēz′) An accomplished fact; something done that cannot be undone.

faith (fāth) *n.* **1.** Belief in God or in the teachings of a religion: *a person of great faith.* **2.** The set of teachings of a religion: *the Muslim faith.* **3.** Confidence or trust in a person or thing: *You must have faith in yourself.* **4.** Loyalty to a person or thing: *The senator vowed to keep faith with his supporters.* ◆ **on faith** With trust; confidently: *You'll have to accept my promise on faith.*

faithful (fāth′fəl) *adj.* **1.** Loyal and dutiful; trustworthy: *a faithful friend; faithful performance of duty.* **2.** Keeping trust in a marriage or relationship by having sexual relations solely with one's spouse or romantic partner. **3.** Having or full of faith: *the faithful children in the procession.* **4.** Accurate; exact: *a faithful copy of the manuscript.* ❖ *n.* (used with a plural verb) **1.** The practicing members of a religion considered as a group. **2.** Loyal followers or supporters considered as a group: *The faithful journeyed to the huge rock concert in the park.* —**faith′-ful·ly** *adv.* —**faith′ful·ness** *n.*

faithless (fāth′lĭs) *adj.* **1.** Not trustworthy; disloyal: *The candidate was betrayed by a faithless friend.* **2.** Having no religious faith. —**faith′less·ly** *adv.* —**faith′less·ness** *n.*

fajita (fə-hē′tə) *n.* A dish consisting of strips of marinated meat or vegetables grilled over an open fire and wrapped in a tortilla.

fake (fāk) *adj.* Not genuine or real; counterfeit or false: *a fake document; a fake diamond.* ❖ *n.* **1.** A person who deceives others by pretending and making false claims: *The doctor turned out to be a fake.* **2.** Something that looks authentic but is not; a forgery: *Experts discovered a fake in the museum's art collection.* **3.** In sports, a brief action, such as a change of direction, that is intended to mislead an opponent. ❖ *tr.v.* **faked, faking, fakes 1.** To pretend or feign: *fake illness.* **2.** To make in order to deceive; counterfeit: *fake an identification card.* **3.** In sports, to mislead (an opponent) with a fake. —**fak′er** *n.*

fakery (fā′kə-rē) *n.* **1.** The act or process of faking: *An artist was responsible for the fakery of many famous paintings.* **2.** Something faked: *The Roman statue proved to be a complete fakery.*

fakir (fə-kîr′ *or* fā-kîr′) *n.* A Muslim or Hindu holy person who lives by begging, especially a Hindu one who performs unusual feats of endurance or magic.

falafel (fə-lä′fəl) *n.* A mixture of ground chickpeas and spices that is shaped into balls and fried.

falcon (făl′kən *or* fôl′kən *or* fô′kən) *n.* Any of various swift, small to medium-sized birds of prey having a short curved beak, sharp claws, and long pointed wings. Certain falcons can be trained to hunt small animals and birds for sport.

falconer (făl′kə-nər *or* fôl′kə-nər *or* fô′kə-nər) *n.* A person who raises, trains, or hunts with falcons.

falconry (făl′kən-rē *or* fôl′kən-rē *or* fô′kən-rē) *n.* **1.** The sport of hunting with falcons. **2.** The art of training falcons for hunting.

fall (fôl) *intr.v.* **fell** (fĕl), **fallen** (fô′lən), **falling, falls 1.** To drop or come down without restraint: *The snow fell silently to the ground.* **2a.** To drop oneself to a lower or less upright position: *She fell into a chair.* **b.** To come down from an upright position suddenly: *Several people slipped on the ice and fell.* **c.** To be wounded or killed, especially in battle. **3.** To hang down: *The horse's mane fell smoothly on its neck.* **4.** To be directed toward or come into contact; rest: *Her gaze fell on the letter. Light fell on the book.* **5.** To come into existence or occur as if by falling: *Darkness fell and all was silent. A hush fell over the crowd.* **6.** To occur at a specific time or place: *The holiday falls on a Thursday. The accent of "control" falls on the last syllable.* **7.** To be uttered; come out: *Angry words fell from my lips.* **8.** To assume a downcast look: *The child's face fell upon seeing the injured puppy.* **9.** To suffer defeat, destruction, capture, or overthrow: *The monarchy fell in the revolution.* **10.** To slope downward: *The fields fall steeply toward the river.* **11.** To become lower or less, as in value, intensity, or amount: *The temperature fell below freezing.* **12.** To decline, as in moral standing; err or sin. **13.** To pass from one state or condition into another: *fall asleep; fall ill.* **14.** To come by chance: *The papers fell into the enemy's hands.* **15.** To be given by assignment or distribution: *The task of cleaning the room fell to us.* **16.** To be divided or put into categories: *The books fall into three categories: novels, biographies, and scholarly works.* ❖ *n.* **1.** A dropping or coming down from a higher place without restraint: *the fall of leaves from trees; a heavy fall of snow.* **2.** A sudden drop from an upright position: *a bad fall on the ice.* **3.** The distance that something falls: *a fall of ten feet.* **4.** An amount of something that has fallen: *We expect a fall of two inches of snow.* **5.** The season of the year occurring between summer and winter; autumn. **6.** A specific place or position: *the fall of an accent on the last syllable.* **7. falls** *(used with a singular or plural verb)* A waterfall; a cascade. **8.** A downward movement or slope: *the gentle fall of fields toward the river.* **9.** A capture, overthrow, or collapse: *the fall of a corrupt government.* **10.** A reduction in amount, intensity, or value: *a fall in water pressure.* **11.** A decline in standing, rank, or importance: *a story of one family's fall from wealth to poverty.* **12.** A moral decline; a lapse. **13. Fall** In the Bible, the loss of humanity's original innocence and happiness resulting from Adam and Eve's eating of the forbidden fruit in the Garden of Eden. **14.** In wrestling, the act of pinning one's opponent to the ground. ❖ *adj.* Occurring in or appropriate to the season of fall: *fall fashions.* ◆ **fall back** To give ground; retreat. **fall back on** To rely on or resort to: *fall back on savings.* **fall behind** To fail to keep up with: *We fell behind the group we were traveling with. They fell behind in paying their bills.* **fall flat** To produce no result; fail: *Their hasty plans fell flat.* **fall for 1.** To become infatuated with; fall in love with. **2.** To be taken in by: *They fell for the swindler's scheme.* **fall in** To take one's place in a military formation. **fall in with 1.** To associate or begin to associate with: *She fell in with a new crowd at school.* **2.** To agree to: *They immediately fell in with my suggestions.* **fall off** To become smaller or fewer; decline: *Attendance fell off in the spring.* **fall on** or **fall upon 1.** To attack suddenly: *The cat fell on the mice.* **2.** To find; come across: *They fell upon the ruins of an ancient city in the desert.* **fall out 1.** To quarrel; become estranged: *The cousins fell out over an inheritance.* **2.** To leave one's place in a military formation. **3.** To be readily explainable; follow logically or naturally: *These facts fall out nicely from the new theory.* **fall short 1.** To fail to reach a specified amount or degree: *Our donations fell short of expectations.* **2.** To be inadequate: *Food supplies fell short.* **fall through** To fail; collapse: *Their plans for a vacation fell through.* **fall to** To begin an activity; start: *The shoppers fell to as soon as the doors were opened.* **fall under** To come under the influence of: *The student fell under the spell of his teacher and became a great cellist.*

fallacious (fə-lā′shəs) *adj.* **1.** Based on a fallacy: *fallacious arguments based on a misunderstanding of the facts.* **2.** Tending to mislead; deceptive: *made fallacious claims about the car's gas mileage.* —**fal·la′cious·ly** *adv.*

fallacy (făl′ə-sē) *n., pl.* **fallacies 1.** A false notion or mistaken belief: *It is a fallacy that money can buy happiness.* **2.** False reasoning, belief, or argument.

fallen (fô′lən) *v.* Past participle of **fall.**

fallible (făl′ə-bəl) *adj.* Capable of making mistakes; tending to err: *Every human is fallible.* —**fal′li·bil′i·ty** *n.* —**fal′li·bly** *adv.*

falling-out (fô′lĭng-out′) *n., pl.* **fallings-out** or **fallingouts** A disagreement; a quarrel.

falling star (fô′lĭng) *n.* A meteor.

fall line *n.* **1.** The steepest possible line of descent from a given point on a slope. **2.** A line connecting the waterfalls of upland rivers before they reach a common coastal plain.

fallopian tube also **Fallopian tube** (fə-lō′pē-ən) *n.* Either of a pair of tubes found in female mammals that carry egg cells from the ovaries to the uterus.

fallout (fôl′out′) *n.* **1.** The tiny particles of debris discharged into the atmosphere by an explosion, especially radioactive debris from a nuclear explosion. **2.** The fall of such particles back to the earth.

fallow (făl′ō) *adj.* Plowed and tilled but left unseeded during a growing season: *The soil in a fallow field will be more fertile when next planted.*

false (fôls) *adj.* **falser, falsest 1.** Not true; incorrect: *The information she gave you is false.* **2.** Deliberately untrue: *false testimony.* **3.** Meant to mislead; deceitful: *false promises.* **4.** Based on mistaken ideas or information: *The early news report raised false hopes.* **5.** Unfaithful; disloyal: *a false friend.* **6.** Not natural or genuine; not real: *a false signature.* **7.** In music, of a pitch that is not correct or within a specific range: *False notes spoiled the singer's performance.* —**false′ly** *adv.* —**false′ness** *n.*

falsehood (fôls′hŏŏd′) *n.* **1.** An untrue statement; a lie or an inaccuracy: *a report filled with falsehoods.* **2.** The quality of being false; untruthfulness: *the falsehood of the accusation.* **3.** The practice of making false statements; lying.

falsetto (fôl-sĕt′ō) *n., pl.* **falsettos** A person's voice in a range that is higher than the person's usual range.

falsify (fôl′sə-fī′) *v.* **falsified, falsifying, falsifies** —*tr.* **1.** To state untruthfully; misrepresent: *It is a crime to falsify the facts when testifying under oath.* **2.** To change a document, for example) in order to deceive; counterfeit: *falsify a driver's license.* —*intr.* To make an untrue statement; lie. —**fal′si·fi·ca′tion** (fôl′sə-fĭ-kā′shən) *n.* —**fal′si·fi′er** *n.*

falsity (fôl′sĭ-tē) *n., pl.* **falsities 1.** The condition of being false; falseness: *Experiment proved the falsity of that theory.* **2.** Something false; a lie.

falter (fôl′tər) *intr.v.* **faltered, faltering, falters 1.** To lose confidence or purpose; hesitate or waver: *He never faltered in his efforts to help us.* **2.** To speak hesitatingly;

stammer: *Several times the speaker faltered from embarrassment.* **3.** To move haltingly; stumble: *We faltered along the slippery path.* **4.** To continue in an unsteady or weakening manner: *Business was strong during the holidays but faltered afterward.* —**fal′ter·er** *n.* —**fal′ter·ing·ly** *adv.*

fame (fām) *n.* The state of being widely known, widely recognized, or of great popular interest; renown.

famed (fāmd) *adj.* Widely known; renowned.

familial (fə-mĭl′yəl) *adj.* **1.** Relating to family. **2.** Occurring among the members of a family, usually by heredity: *the familial tendency for diabetes.*

familiar (fə-mĭl′yər) *adj.* **1.** Well-known; often encountered; common: *a familiar sight.* **2.** Having some knowledge; acquainted: *I am familiar with those streets in your neighborhood.* **3.** Of established friendship; close: *We are on familiar terms with the neighbors.* **4.** Unduly forward; presumptuous: *It is a mistake to be too familiar with one's boss.* —**fa·mil′iar·ly** *adv.*

familiarity (fə-mĭl′yăr′ĭ-tē *or* fə-mĭl′ē-ăr′ĭ-tē) *n., pl.* **familiarities 1.** Acquaintance with or knowledge of something: *Familiarity with the city's streets is a necessity for a cab driver.* **2.** Friendship or informality: *the familiarity of close associates.* **3.** Improper friendliness; forwardness: *I was offended by the salesperson's familiarity.*

familiarize (fə-mĭl′yə-rīz′) *tr.v.* **familiarized, familiarizing, familiarizes 1.** To make acquainted with: *They familiarized themselves with the new library.* **2.** To make (something) known or recognized: *TV familiarized the special vocabulary of the space program.*

family (făm′ə-lē *or* făm′lē) *n., pl.* **families 1.** A social group typically consisting of one or two parents and their children: *She lived with her family until she left home at 21.* **2.** All the members of a household living under one roof: *His family includes his grandmother and his uncle, who live on the first floor.* **3.** The children of the same parents: *They raised a large family.* **4.** A group of people sharing common ancestors; relatives: *Each year our whole family gets together.* **5.** Line of descent; ancestry: *I come from an old Virginia family.* **6.** A group of things that are alike; a class: *The family of brass instruments includes the trumpet and trombone.* **7.** A taxonomic category of organisms that share certain characteristics, ranking above a genus and below an order: *Dogs, wolves, coyotes, and foxes belong to the same family.* **8.** A group of languages derived from the same parent language: *French, Spanish, and Italian are of the same family.* —SEE NOTE AT **collective noun.**

family leave *n.* A period during which a person is allowed time off of work to take care of a family member, such as a new baby.

family name *n.* A surname.

family planning *n.* The planned timing of children born into a family through the use of birth control.

family tree *n.* A diagram showing the relationships among the ancestors of a family.

famine (făm′ĭn) *n.* A drastic, widespread shortage of food: *Famine may strike after a prolonged drought.*

famished (făm′ĭsht) *adj.* Extremely hungry; starving.

famous (fā′məs) *adj.* Widely known; famed; renowned: *a famous singer; a country famous for its beaches.*

✦ **SYNONYMS famous, celebrated, eminent, illustrious, noted, renowned** *adj.*

fan¹ (făn) *n.* **1.** A collapsible flat implement, usually shaped like a half-circle, waved in the hand to create a cooling breeze. **2.** Something that resembles an open fan: *The turkey's tail feathers spread into a fan.* **3.** An electrical device that moves air, especially for cooling, by means of rotating metal or plastic blades. ❖ *v.* **fanned, fanning, fans** —*tr.* **1.** To direct a current of air to blow upon (a person or thing), especially in order to cool: *We sat fanning ourselves under a tree.* **2.** To move or create a current of (air) with or as if with a fan. **3.** To stir up by or as if by fanning: *Rumors fanned smoldering anger in the crowd.* **4.** To open (something) out into the shape of a fan: *The peacock fanned its tail.* **5.** In baseball, to strike out (a batter): *The pitcher fanned three batters in succession.* —*intr.* **1.** To spread like a fan: *The search parties fanned out in different directions.* **2.** In baseball, to strike out.

fan² (făn) *n.* An enthusiastic devotee or admirer: *a baseball fan.*

WORD HISTORY Fan¹ comes from Old English *fann*, which comes from Latin *vannus*, both of which referred to a kind of winnowing device. **Fan²** is short for *fanatic*.

fanatic (fə-năt′ĭk) *n.* A person who is excessively or unreasonably devoted to a cause or belief. ❖ *adj.* Fanatical.

fanatical (fə-năt′ĭ-kəl) *adj.* Unreasonably enthusiastic or zealous. —**fa·nat′i·cal·ly** *adv.*

fanaticism (fə-năt′ĭ-sĭz′əm) *n.* Unreasonable or excessive enthusiasm, especially in politics or religion.

fancied (făn′sēd) *adj.* Imaginary; invented: *the fancied monsters of dreams.*

fancier (făn′sē-ər) *n.* A person with a special interest in something: *a cat fancier.*

fanciful (făn′sĭ-fəl) *adj.* **1.** Created in the mind; imaginary; unreal: *fanciful tales.* **2.** Using or tending to use the imagination: *a fanciful mind.* **3.** Original in design; imaginative: *fanciful figures made with odds and ends of cloth.* —**fan′ci·ful·ly** *adv.* —**fan′ci·ful·ness** *n.*

fancy (făn′sē) *adj.* **fancier, fanciest 1.** Highly decorated; elaborate: *fancy carvings around the door.* **2.** Requiring or done with great skill; complex; intricate: *a tap dancer's fancy footwork.* **3.** Elegantly fashionable or sophisticated: *a fancy restaurant.* **4.** Of superior grade; fine: *fancy fruits and vegetables.* **5.** Exorbitant; excessive: *That store charges very fancy prices.* ❖ *n., pl.* **fancies 1.** Imagination, especially of a playful or whimsical sort: *The characters are all creations of the author's fancy.* **2.** An impulsive idea or thought; a whim: *We had a sudden fancy to go to the diner.* **3.** A liking, fondness, or inclination: *The stray dog took a fancy to our family.* ❖ *tr.v.* **fancied, fancying, fancies 1.** To picture in the mind; imagine: *I tried to fancy myself as an actor.* **2.** To have a liking for; enjoy: *Would you fancy a movie tonight?* **3.** To suppose; guess; surmise: *I fancy the meeting will end soon.* —**fan′ci·ly** *adv.* —**fan′ci·ness** *n.*

fancy-free (făn′sē-frē′) *adj.* Having no commitments or restrictions; carefree.

fanfare (făn′fâr′) *n.* **1.** A short melody played by one or more brass instruments; a flourish. **2.** A spectacular public display or ceremony: *The soldiers were welcomed home with great fanfare.*

fang (făng) *n.* **1.** A long pointed tooth, such as one used by a venomous snake to inject venom into its prey. **2.** Something thin and tapering that is shaped like a fang.

fanny (făn′ē) *n., pl.* **fannies** *Slang* The buttocks.

fantail (făn′tāl′) *n.* **1.** A pigeon, goldfish, or other animal having a fan-shaped tail. **2.** A tail or end resembling a fan. **3.** The stern overhang of a ship.

fantasize (făn′tə-sīz′) *v.* **fantasized, fantasizing, fantasizes** —*intr.* To indulge in fantasies: *fantasized about traveling to the moon.* —*tr.* To portray in the mind; imagine: *fantasized a world without war.*

fantastic (făn-tăs′tĭk) *adj.* **1.** Based on or existing only in fantasy; unreal: *a fantastic story of life in another galaxy.* **2.** Weird; bizarre: *dancers dressed in fantastic costumes.* **3.** Remarkable; outstanding; superb: *You did a fantastic job of renovating the kitchen.* —**fan·tas′ti·cal·ly** *adv.*

fantasy (făn′tə-sē) *n., pl.* **fantasies 1.** The creative imagination: *Her fantasy is vigorously at work in her latest science fiction novel.* **2.** Something that is a creation of the imagination, such as a fanciful work of fiction. **3.** An imagined event or situation, especially one that fulfills a wish: *He has this fantasy about becoming a movie star.*

FAQ (făk) *n.* A list of frequently asked questions along with their answers about a given topic.

far (fär) *adv.* **farther** (fär′thər), **farthest** (fär′thĭst) or **further** (fûr′thər), **furthest** (fûr′thĭst) **1.** To, from, or at a great distance in space or time: *My home is situated far from town. The movie takes place far in the future.* **2.** To a great degree; much: *I feel far better today than I did yesterday.* ❖ *adj.* **farther, farthest** or **further, furthest 1.** Being at great distance in space or time: *a far country halfway around the world; the far past.* **2.** More distant than another; opposite: *the far side of the mountain.* **3.** Extensive or long: *a far trek into the desert.* **4.** Politically extreme: *the far right.* ◆ **as far as** To the distance, extent, or degree that: *As far as I know they left an hour ago.* **by far** To a great degree: *Her room is messier than mine by far.* **far and away** By a wide margin: *This is far and away the best movie we've seen.* **far and wide** Everywhere. **far from** Not at all; anything but: *You are far from a failure.* **so far 1.** Up to the present moment: *We haven't heard from anyone so far.* **2.** To a limited extent: *You can only go so far on $10.*

farad (făr′əd or făr′ăd′) *n.* A unit used to measure electric capacitance. A capacitor in which a charge of one coulomb can produce a change of one volt between its two storage plates has a capacitance of one farad.

faraday (făr′ə-dā′) *n.* A unit of electric charge, equal to about 96,494 coulombs, or the electric charge carried by one mole of electrons. It is used frequently to measure charge in electrolysis.

faraway (făr′ə-wā′) *adj.* **1.** Very distant; remote: *The explorer spent years traveling in faraway places.* **2.** Dreamy; preoccupied: *a faraway look in his eyes.*

farce (färs) *n.* **1.** A comic play with an unlikely story and characters exaggerated for humorous effect. **2.** Something ridiculous or laughable; a mockery: *Baseball practice turned into a farce after the coach left.*

farcical (fär′sĭ-kəl) *adj.* Relating to or resembling a farce; absurd; foolish: *farcical errors.* —**far′ci·cal·ly** *adv.*

fare (fâr) *intr.v.* **fared, faring, fares 1.** To get along; progress: *How are you faring with your project?* **2.** To travel; go. ❖ *n.* **1.** The money charged for transportation from one place to another: *The subway fare has gone up.* **2.** A passenger who pays a fare: *The taxi stopped to pick up a fare.* **3.** Food and drink: *The fare at this inn is superb.*

farewell (fâr-wĕl′) *interj.* An expression used to say goodbye. ❖ *n.* **1.** The act of saying goodbye, usually with good wishes: *a nod of farewell.* **2.** An expression used at parting; goodbye: *It was hard to say our farewells.*

far-fetched (fär′fĕcht′) *adj.* Hard to believe; strained and improbable: *a far-fetched story.*

far-flung (fär′flŭng′) *adj.* Extending over a large area: *the far-flung operations of an international airline.*

farina (fə-rē′nə) *n.* A fine meal used as a cooked cereal or in puddings.

farm (färm) *n.* **1.** An area of land on which crops or domestic animals are raised. **2.** An area of water devoted to raising aquatic animals: *a trout farm.* **3.** A facility for the generation of energy by converting it from a particular source: *a wind farm.* ❖ *v.* **farmed, farming, farms** —*tr.* **1.** To cultivate or produce a crop on: *We farm 1,000 acres.* **2.** To cultivate, breed, or raise (plants or animals): *companies that farm salmon.* —*intr.* To engage in farming; grow crops or raise livestock. ◆ **farm out** To send (work) out to be done by another business: *All the sewing done by hand is farmed out by the manufacturer.*

farmer (fär′mər) *n.* A person who owns or operates a farm.

farmers' market (fär′mərz) *n.* A market at which farmers sell their produce directly to customers.

farm hand *n.* A person who works on a farm.

farmhouse (färm′hous′) *n.* A house on a farm.

farmland (färm′lănd′) *n.* Land suitable or used for farming.

farmstead (färm′stĕd′) *n.* A farm, including its land and buildings.

farm team *n.* In baseball, a minor-league team that trains young players and supplies players as needed to an affiliated major-league team.

farmyard (färm′yärd′) *n.* An area surrounded by or next to farm buildings: *Chickens and geese wandered freely in the farmyard.*

far-off (fär′ôf′) *adj.* Faraway; distant: *Home seemed very far-off.*

far-out (fär′out′) *adj.* *Slang* Extremely unconventional; very unusual: *a far-out movie.*

far-reaching (fär′rē′chĭng) *adj.* Having a wide influence or effect: *a tax with far-reaching effects on the economy.*

farrier (făr′ē-ər) *n.* A person who shoes horses; a blacksmith.

farrow (făr′ō) *n.* A litter of pigs. ❖ *intr.v.* **farrowed, farrowing, farrows** To give birth to a litter of pigs.

farseeing (fär′sē′ĭng) *adj.* **1.** Able to see far; keen-sighted. **2.** Planning wisely for the future; foresighted.

Farsi (fär′sē) *n.* The modern form of the Persian language, especially the western dialect of Persian that is the national language of Iran.

farsighted or **far-sighted** (fär′sī′tĭd) *adj.* **1.** Able to see distant objects better than objects at close range: *I am farsighted and wear glasses to read.* **2.** Planning wisely for the future; foresighted. —**far′sight′ed·ly** *adv.*

farther (fär′thər) *adv.* A comparative of **far.** **1.** To or at a greater distance: *We walked farther than we had expected.* **2.** To a greater extent or degree: *I've read farther in the book and I like it now.* ❖ *adj.* A comparative of **far.** More distant; remoter: *at the farther end of the street.*

USAGE The word **farther** tends to be used in reference to physical distance, while the word **further** tends to be used in reference to nonphysical advancement: *If you are planning to drive any farther, you'd better stop at a gas station. We won't be able to answer these questions until we are further along in our research.*

farthermost (fär′thər-mōst′) *adj.* Farthest; most remote:

explore the farthermost corners of the earth.

farthest (fär′thĭst) *adj.* A superlative of **far.** Most remote or distant: *the farthest regions of the Arctic.* ❖ *adv.* A superlative of **far. 1.** To or at the greatest distance in space or time: *The tallest people in the photograph stood farthest in the back.* **2.** By the greatest extent or degree; most: *Their research had progressed farthest of all.*

farthing (fär′thĭng) *n.* **1.** A coin formerly used in Great Britain worth one-fourth of a penny. **2.** Something of very little value.

farthingale (fär′thĭn-gāl′ *or* fär′thĭng-gāl′) *n.* A framework worn under a skirt or petticoat to make it stand out around the waist, worn by European women in the 1500s and 1600s.

fascinate (făs′ə-nāt′) *tr.v.* **fascinated, fascinating, fascinates** To capture and hold the interest and attention of; captivate: *This book fascinates me so much I cannot put it down.*

fascinating (făs′ə-nā′tĭng) *adj.* Arousing great interest and attention: *a fascinating story.* See Synonyms at **interesting. —fas′ci·nat′ing·ly** *adv.*

fascination (făs′ə-nā′shən) *n.* **1.** The condition of being fascinated: *Everyone watched in fascination as the rocket took off.* **2.** The power of fascinating; charm; attraction: *All the stories are about the fascination of the sea.*

fascism or **Fascism** (făsh′ĭz′əm) *n.* **1.** A system of government marked by dictatorship, government control of the economy, violent suppression of dissent, and belligerent nationalism. **2.** A political movement advocating such a system of government.

fascist or **Fascist** (făsh′ĭst) *n.* A person who advocates or believes in fascism. ❖ *adj.* Relating to fascism or fascists: *a fascist regime.*

fashion (făsh′ən) *n.* **1.** The current style or custom, as in dress or behavior: *an idea now in fashion.* **2.** Something, such as a garment, that is in the current style: *a store carrying the latest fashions.* **3.** A manner of doing something; a way: *She works in an organized fashion.* ❖ *tr.v.* **fashioned, fashioning, fashions** To shape or form into: *fashion figures from clay.*

fashionable (făsh′ə-nə-bəl) *adj.* **1.** Conforming to the current styles or trends; stylish: *a fashionable wardrobe.* **2.** Adopting or setting current styles or trends: *a fashionable artist.* **3.** Associated with or used by stylish people: *a fashionable hotel.* **—fash′ion·a·bly** *adv.*

fast¹ (făst) *adj.* **faster, fastest 1.** Moving, acting, or capable of moving or acting quickly; swift: *a fast train; a fast computer.* **2.** Accomplished in very little time: *We ate a fast lunch.* **3.** Suitable or made for rapid movement: *a fast racetrack.* **4.** Quick to understand or learn: *a class for the faster students.* **5.** Ahead of the correct time: *My watch is fast.* **6.** Firmly fixed or fastened: *Keep a fast grip on the rope.* **7.** Permanent; not likely to fade: *Fast colors will not run in the wash.* **8.** Loyal; firm: *fast friends.* **9a.** Disposed to dissipation; wild: *He hangs out with a fast crowd.* **b.** Sexually promiscuous. ❖ *adv.* **faster, fastest 1.** Quickly; rapidly: *You are driving too fast.* **2.** Firmly; securely: *Hold fast to the railing.* **3.** Deeply; soundly: *The child is fast asleep.* **4.** So as to run ahead of the correct time: *My watch runs fast.*

✦ SYNONYMS fast, expeditious, quick, rapid, swift *adj.*

fast² (făst) *intr.v.* **fasted, fasting, fasts** To eat little or no food or only certain foods, especially for religious rea-

sons or as a form of protest. ❖ *n.* The act or a period of fasting.

WORD HISTORY Fast¹ comes from Old English *fæst,* meaning "firm, fixed." **Fast²** comes from Old English *fæstan,* meaning "to eat little or no food."

fastball (făst′bôl′) *n.* In baseball, a pitch that is thrown at maximum speed.

fast break *n.* In sports, a rush by the offense toward the goal before the defense is ready.

fasten (făs′ən) *v.* **fastened, fastening, fastens** *—tr.* **1.** To attach firmly to; join; connect: *fasten a button to a shirt; unable to fasten blame on anyone.* **2.** To make fast or secure: *Fasten your seat belts.* **3.** To fix or direct steadily: *She fastened her gaze on the stranger. —intr.* **1.** To become attached, fixed, or joined: *The helmet fastens under your chin.* **2.** To fix or focus steadily: *My eyes fastened on the approaching plane.*

fastener (făs′ə-nər) *n.* A person or thing that fastens or holds separate things together, such as a zipper, snap, hook, or button.

fastening (făs′ə-nĭng) *n.* Something, such as a hook, used to fasten things together.

fast food *n.* Inexpensive food, such as hamburgers, prepared and served quickly. **—fast′-food′** *adj.*

fast-forward or **fast forward** (făst-fôr′wərd) *intr.v.* **fast-forwarded, fast-forwarding, fast-forwards** To advance an audio or video recording rapidly. ❖ *n.* A control mechanism for fast-forwarding an audio or video recording.

fastidious (fă-stĭd′ē-əs *or* fə-stĭd′ē-əs) *adj.* **1.** Showing or acting with careful attention to detail: *Reporters must be fastidious in recording the facts.* **2.** Difficult to please; choosy or finicky: *a fastidious eater.* **3.** Excessively scrupulous or sensitive, as in taste, propriety, or neatness: *a fastidious hotel clerk.* **—fas·tid′i·ous·ly** *adv.*

fastness (făst′nĭs) *n.* **1.** A remote or secure place, as a stronghold or fortress: *a mountain fastness.* **2.** The condition or quality of being secure or firmly fixed: *Check the locks for fastness.* **3.** Rapidity; swiftness: *Sport cars are known for their elegance and fastness.*

fat (făt) *n.* **1.** Any of a large class of oily organic compounds that are widely found in animal tissues and in nuts, seeds, and some fruits. Fats serve mainly as a reserve source of energy. **2.** Animal tissue containing such compounds: *cut the fat off the steak.* **3.** A substance of this kind prepared for use in cooking: *potatoes cooked in fat.* **4.** Something that is unnecessary or excessive: *cut the fat from the budget.* ❖ *adj.* **fatter, fattest 1.** Having much body fat: *The cat is too fat, so we are giving her less food.* **2.** Full of fat or oil; greasy: *a menu full of fat foods.* **3.** Big; ample; generous: *a fat paycheck.* **4.** Thick; large. *a fat book.* ◆ **fat chance** *Slang* Very little or no chance. **—fat′ness** *n.*

fatal (fāt′l) *adj.* **1.** Causing or capable of causing death: *a fatal disease.* **2.** Causing ruin or destruction; disastrous: *The investment was a blunder that proved fatal to the business.* **3.** Most decisive; fateful: *the fatal moment of going onstage to perform.* **—fa′tal·ly** *adv.*

fatalism (fāt′l-ĭz′əm) *n.* **1.** The belief that all events are determined in advance by fate and cannot be altered. **2.** Acceptance of this belief; submission to fate: *His fatalism prevented him from acting to improve the situation.* **—fa′tal·ist** *n.* **—fa′tal·is′tic** *adj.*

fatality (fā-tăl′ĭ-tē *or* fə-tăl′ĭ-tē) *n., pl.* **fatalities 1.** A death resulting from an accident or disaster: *Three fatalities oc-*

curred in the fire. **2.** The ability to cause death: *a disease known for its fatality.*

fatback (făt′băk′) *n.* Salt-cured fat from the upper part of a side of pork.

fate (fāt) *n.* **1.** A force or power that is supposed to determine the course of events. **2.** Something supposed to be caused by fate, especially an unfavorable destiny: *It was his fate never to defeat his rival.* **3.** A final result; an outcome: *The fate of the plane remains unknown.* **4. Fates** In Greek and Roman mythology, the three goddesses who governed human destiny.

fateful (fāt′fəl) *adj.* **1.** Decisively important; momentous: *the colonists' fateful decision to go to war against Great Britain.* **2.** Indicating approaching trouble or disaster; unfavorably prophetic: *The fever was a fateful sign that the patient was getting worse.* **3.** Bringing death or disaster; fatal: *a fateful battle in which thousands died.* **4.** Controlled by or as if by fate: *a fateful journey.* —**fate′ful·ly** *adv.* —**fate′ful·ness** *n.*

father (fä′thər) *n.* **1.** A male parent or guardian of a child. **2.** A male parent of an animal. **3.** A male ancestor; a forefather: *the land of our fathers.* **4.** A male leader or official: *the city fathers.* **5.** A man who creates, starts, or founds something: *Chaucer is considered the father of English poetry.* **6. Father** In Christianity, another name for God. **7. Father** Used as a title and form of address for a Christian priest or other clergyman. ❖ *tr.v.* **fathered, fathering, fathers 1.** To be the male parent of; beget: *father two children.* **2.** To act or serve as a father to: *He willingly undertook the duties of fathering his new stepchildren.*

fatherhood (fä′thər-hŏod′) *n.* The condition of being a father.

father-in-law (fä′thər-ĭn-lô′) *n., pl.* **fathers-in-law** The father of one's husband or wife.

fatherland (fä′thər-lănd′) *n.* **1.** A person's native land; the country of one's birth. **2.** The land of one's ancestors.

fatherless (fä′thər-lĭs) *adj.* Having no living or known father.

fatherly (fä′thər-lē) *adj.* Relating to, like, or appropriate to a father: *fatherly affection.* —**fa′ther·li·ness** *n.*

Father's Day (fä′thərz) *n.* The third Sunday in June, observed in the United States in honor of fathers.

fathom (făth′əm) *n., pl.* **fathom** or **fathoms** A unit of length equal to six feet (1.8 meters), used for measurements of the depth of water. ❖ *tr.v.* **fathomed, fathoming, fathoms 1.** To measure the depth of; sound: *fathom a channel in a river.* **2.** To understand; comprehend: *Motives are often hard to fathom.* —**fath′om·a·ble** *adj.*

fathomless (făth′əm-lĭs) *adj.* **1.** Too deep to be measured: *the fathomless oceans.* **2.** Impossible to understand.

fatigue (fə-tēg′) *n.* **1.** Weariness or exhaustion resulting from hard work or great effort. **2.** Manual nonmilitary work, such as barracks cleaning, assigned to soldiers. **3. fatigues** Clothing worn by soldiers for heavy work or field duty. ❖ *tr.v.* **fatigued, fatiguing, fatigues** To tire out; exhaust: *The long hike fatigued us.*

fatten (făt′n) *intr.* & *tr.v.* **fattened, fattening, fattens** To make or become fat: *fatten cattle; fatten on a rich diet; fatten one's bank account.*

fatty (făt′ē) *adj.* **fattier, fattiest 1.** Composed of or containing fat: *fatty food.* **2.** Characteristic of fat; greasy. —**fat′ti·ness** *n.*

fatty acid *n.* Any of a large group of organic acids, especially those found in animal and vegetable fats and oils.

fatuous (făch′ōō-əs) *adj.* Foolish and self-satisfied; silly:

a fatuous smile. —**fat′u·ous·ly** *adv.* —**fat′u·ous·ness** *n.*

fatwa (fät′wä′) *n.* A ruling issued by an Islamic scholar.

faucet (fô′sĭt) *n.* A device with an adjustable valve that regulates the flow of liquid from a pipe; a tap.

fault (fôlt) *n.* **1.** A defect or shortcoming: *A fault in the book is its small type. Laziness is one of my few faults.* **2.** A mistake; an error: *a fault in addition.* **3.** Responsibility for a mistake or error: *The mix-up was all my fault.* **4.** A crack in a rock mass along which there has been movement caused by a shifting of the earth's crust. **5.** In tennis and other racquet games, a serve that falls outside a boundary. ❖ *tr.v.* **faulted, faulting, faults** To find fault in; criticize: *No one can fault such a fine performance.* ◆ **at fault** Deserving of blame; guilty: *He admitted to being at fault.* **to a fault** To the highest possible or an excessive degree: *He is polite to a fault.*

faultfinder (fôlt′fīn′dər) *n.* A person who habitually finds fault with and freely criticizes others. —**fault′find′ing** *n. & adj.*

faultless (fôlt′lĭs) *adj.* Being without fault or flaw: *The lifeguard was faultless in her handling of the emergency.* See Synonyms at **perfect.** —**fault′less·ly** *adv.*

faulty (fôl′tē) *adj.* **faultier, faultiest** Having a fault or faults; imperfect or defective: *faulty electric wiring; a faulty argument.* —**fault′i·ly** *adv.* —**fault′i·ness** *n.*

faun (fôn) *n.* In Roman mythology, one of numerous minor gods dwelling in woods and fields and depicted as having the body of a man and the ears, horns, tail, and sometimes the legs of a goat.

fauna (fô′nə) *n. (used with a singular or plural verb)* The animals of a particular region or time period considered as a group: *tropical fauna; prehistoric fauna.*

Faust (foust) also **Faustus** (fou′stəs *or* fô′stəs) *n.* A magician in German legend who sold his soul to the devil in exchange for power and knowledge.

faux (fō) *adj.* Artificial; fake: *faux pearls.*

faux pas (fō pä′) *n., pl.* **faux pas** (fō päz′) A social blunder: *Wiping your mouth on the tablecloth is a major faux pas.*

fave (fāv) *Informal n.* Someone or something that is preferred above others or likely to win; a favorite. ❖ *adj.* Favorite.

favicon (făv′ĭ-kŏn′ *or* făv′ī-kŏn′) *n.* A symbol or graphic associated with a website.

favor (fā′vər) *n.* **1.** A kind or helpful act: *My neighbor shoveled my walk as a favor.* **2.** Approval or support; liking: *The plan is fast gaining favor.* **3.** A small gift given to each guest at a party. **4.** Friendly regard; partiality: *A judge cannot show favor in the court.* **5.** Behalf; interest: *The cashier made an error in our favor.* ❖ *tr.v.* **favored, favoring, favors 1.** To perform a kindness or service for; oblige: *The singer favored us with two more songs.* **2.** To approve or support: *I favor longer vacations.* **3.** To be partial to; indulge: *a father who favored his youngest child.* **4.** To make easier or more likely; aid; promote: *The climate there favors fruit farming.* **5.** To be gentle with; treat with care: *The lineman favored his left leg while walking off the field.* **6.** To resemble; look like: *She favors her father.* ◆ **in favor of 1.** In support of: *All those in favor of the motion say "aye."* **2.** To the advantage of: *The judge decided in favor of the defendant.*

favorable (fā′vər-ə-bəl *or* fāv′rə-bəl) *adj.* **1.** Helpful; advantageous: *The boat sailed swiftly before favorable winds.* **2.** Pleasing or promising: *The new student made a favorable impression on us.* **3.** Approving or praising: *favorable movie reviews.* **4.** Granting what has been desired or requested: *a favorable reply.* —**fa′vor·a·bly** *adv.*

favorite (fā′vər-ĭt *or* fāv′rĭt) *n.* **1.** A person or thing viewed or treated with special regard, especially one preferred to all others: *That song is my favorite.* **2.** A contestant believed most likely to win: *Our team is the favorite in today's game.* ❖ *adj.* Liked or preferred above all others: *Green is my favorite color.*

favoritism (fā′vər-ĭ-tĭz′əm *or* fāv′rĭ-tĭz′əm) *n.* Better treatment given to one person or group over another: *gain promotion by favoritism rather than by skill.*

fawn[1] (fôn) *intr.v.* **fawned, fawning, fawns** **1.** To show affection or attempt to please, as a dog does by crawling or whining. **2.** To try to gain favor by flattery or acting submissively: *The clerk fawned on the customer hoping to make a sale.*

fawn[2] (fôn) *n.* A young deer, especially one less than a year old.

WORD HISTORY **Fawn**[1] comes from Old English *fagnian,* meaning "to rejoice." **Fawn**[2] comes from Middle English *foun* (meaning "young deer"), which comes from Old French *faon* (meaning "young animal"), which comes from Latin *fētus,* meaning "offspring."

fax (făks) *n.* **1.** A fax machine. **2.** A document sent or received by a fax machine: *a fax of a birth certificate.* ❖ *tr.v.* **faxed, faxing, faxes** To send by a fax machine: *I faxed the contract to my lawyer.*

fax machine *n.* A device that sends and receives exact copies of documents over telephone lines.

fay (fā) *n.* A fairy or elf.

faze (fāz) *tr.v.* **fazed, fazing, fazes** To upset; bother: *Even though a cell phone rang in the audience, it didn't faze the actors.*

FBI An abbreviation of Federal Bureau of Investigation.

F clef *n.* In music, a bass clef.

FDA An abbreviation of Food and Drug Administration.

fealty (fē′əl-tē) *n., pl.* **fealties** **1.** In feudal times, the loyalty owed by a vassal to his lord. **2.** Loyalty; faithfulness: *the fealty of friends.*

fear (fîr) *n.* **1.** A feeling of alarm or fright caused by the expectation of danger. **2.** A state or condition marked by this feeling: *The citizens of the besieged town lived in fear.* **3.** An anxious feeling; concern: *a fear of looking foolish.* **4.** A cause for fear; dread: *My greatest fear is having to finish the job by myself.* ❖ *v.* **feared, fearing, fears** —*tr.* **1.** To be afraid of; be frightened of: *The boy does not fear spiders.* **2.** To feel anxious or concerned about; worry about: *We fear mistakes will show up.* —*intr.* **1.** To be afraid; feel fear. **2.** To feel anxious or worried: *The captain feared for the ship near the rocks.*

fearful (fîr′fəl) *adj.* **1.** Feeling fear; afraid: *I was fearful of losing my way in the forest.* **2.** Causing fear; terrible: *We heard a fearful explosion.* **3.** Feeling or showing anxiety, fear, or terror: *a fearful driver; a fearful glance.* **4.** Very bad; dreadful: *a fearful blunder.* —**fear′ful·ly** *adv.*

fearless (fîr′lĭs) *adj.* Having no fear; brave: *a fearless explorer.* See Synonyms at **brave.** —**fear′less·ly** *adv.*

fearsome (fîr′səm) *adj.* **1.** Causing or capable of causing fear; frightening; awesome: *A tornado is a fearsome sight.* **2.** Fearful; afraid. —**fear′some·ly** *adv.*

feasible (fē′zə-bəl) *adj.* **1.** Capable of being done or carried out; possible: *Development of rockets made space exploration feasible.* **2.** Likely; logical: *That answer seems feasible enough.* —**fea′si·bil′i·ty** *n.* —**fea′si·bly** *adv.*

feast (fēst) *n.* **1.** A large elaborate meal, especially one prepared for a special occasion; a banquet. **2.** A religious festival. ❖ *v.* **feasted, feasting, feasts** —*tr.* **1.** To give a feast for; entertain lavishly: *feasted all their friends with an elaborate dinner party.* **2.** To give pleasure to; delight: *feast one's eyes on the beautiful landscape.* —*intr.* To eat heartily: *feast on the first corn of summer.*

Feast of Lights *n.* Hanukkah.

feat (fēt) *n.* An outstanding deed or accomplishment; an exploit that requires much skill or daring: *The dam is a remarkable feat of engineering.*

feather (fĕth′ər) *n.* **1.** One of the light flat structures that cover the skin of birds. A feather is formed of numerous slender, closely arranged parallel barbs forming a vane on either side of a hollow shaft. **2.** A fringe or tuft of long hair, as on the legs or tail of some dogs. ❖ *tr.v.* **feathered, feathering, feathers** **1.** To cover or fit with a feather or feathers: *feather an arrow.* **2.** To turn (an oar) so that its blade is parallel to the surface of the water between strokes. ◆ **a feather in (one's) cap** Something to be proud of; a great achievement. **feather (one's) nest** To get rich by taking advantage of circumstances.

feather bed *n.* A soft mattress or quilt stuffed with feathers or down.

feathered (fĕth′ərd) *adj.* Covered or trimmed with feathers: *a feathered headdress.*

featherweight (fĕth′ər-wāt′) *n.* **1.** A boxer weighing more than 118 and not more than 126 pounds (about 53–57 kilograms). **2.** *Informal* A very small or unimportant person or thing.

feathery (fĕth′ə-rē) *adj.* **1.** Made of or covered with feathers. **2.** Resembling or suggestive of a feather or feathers, as in form or lightness: *the feathery leaves of the hemlock.*

feature (fē′chər) *n.* **1.** A prominent part, quality, or characteristic: *Dust and craters are features of the moon's surface. Several features of the plan caught our attention.* See Synonyms at **quality.** **2.** Any of the distinct parts of the face: *couldn't make out his features from a distance.* **3.** The main film presentation at a theater. **4.** A special article or column in a newspaper or magazine. ❖ *tr.v.* **featured, featuring, features** **1.** To display or offer prominently: *an exhibit that features Native American pottery.* **2.** To have or include as a prominent part or characteristic: *The play featured a famous actor.*

February (fĕb′rōō-ĕr′ē *or* fĕb′yōō-ĕr′ē) *n., pl.* **Februaries** The second month of the year in the Gregorian calendar, having 28 days, or in leap years, 29 days.

fecal (fē′kəl) *adj.* Relating to feces.

feces (fē′sēz) *n. (used with a singular or plural verb)* Waste matter excreted from the intestine.

feckless (fĕk′lĭs) *adj.* **1.** Lacking purpose or vitality; weak or ineffective. **2.** Careless and irresponsible: *an idle feckless youth.* —**feck′less·ness** *n.*

fecund (fē′kənd *or* fĕk′ənd) *adj.* Productive; fertile; fruitful: *the artist's fecund imagination.*

fecundity (fĭ-kŭn′dĭ-tē) *n.* **1.** The ability to produce offspring or seeds, especially in abundance. **2.** Productive or creative power.

fed (fĕd) *v.* Past tense and past participle of **feed.**

Fed *n. Informal* **1.** The Federal Reserve. **2.** often **fed** A federal agent or official.

federal (fĕd′ər-əl *or* fĕd′rəl) *adj.* **1a.** Relating to or being a form of government in which separate states retain control over local affairs but are united under a central government that manages affairs of common concern to all the states. **b.** Relating to the central government of such a union rather than to the governments of its member states: *federal courts; federal laws applying to all the states.* **2a.** often **Federal** Relating to the central government of the United States: *the Federal Court of Appeals.* **b. Federal** Relating to or supporting the Union during the American Civil War: *a Federal soldier.* **c. Federal** Relating to Federalism or the Federalist Party. ❖ *n.* **Federal** A supporter of the Union during the American Civil War. —**fed′er·al·ly** *adv.*

Federal Bureau of Investigation *n.* An agency of the US Department of Justice responsible for investigating violations of federal law.

federalism (fĕd′ər-ə-lĭz′əm *or* fĕd′rə-lĭz′əm) *n.* **1.** A system of government in which power is divided between a central government and member states. **2.** Advocacy of or belief in such a system of government. **3. Federalism** The principles of the Federalist Party.

federalist (fĕd′ər-ə-lĭst *or* fĕd′rə-lĭst) *n.* **1.** A person who supports federalism. **2. Federalist** A supporter or member of the Federalist Party.

Federalist Party *n.* A US political party that flourished in the 1790s under the leadership of Alexander Hamilton (1755?–1804) and advocated a strong central government.

federalize (fĕd′ər-ə-līz′ *or* fĕd′rə-līz′) *tr.v.* **federalized, federalizing, federalizes 1.** To unite in a federal union. **2.** To subject to the authority of a federal government: *federalized the local transportation departments.*

Federal Reserve or **Federal Reserve System** *n.* The US central bank, a system consisting of 12 Federal Reserve banks, each of which serves the banks located within its own district. The system has broad powers over US monetary policy and regulation of the banking industry.

federate (fĕd′ə-rāt′) *tr. & intr.v.* **federated, federating, federates** To bring or join together in a league, federal union, or other association: *The unions voted to federate under one national organization.*

federation (fĕd′ə-rā′shən) *n.* **1.** The act of joining together in a league, federal union, or other association. **2.** A league or association formed by federating: *a federation of independent store owners.*

fedora (fĭ-dôr′ə) *n.* A soft felt hat with a crown creased lengthwise and a brim that can be turned up or down.

fed up *adj.* Unable or unwilling to put up with something any longer: *I'm fed up with your excuses for being late.*

fee (fē) *n.* **1.** A charge or payment for a service or privilege: *an admission fee to the movies; fees for advice from our lawyer; a tuition fee for school.* **2.** In feudal times, an estate of land granted by a lord to a vassal; a fief.

feeble (fē′bəl) *adj.* **feebler, feeblest 1.** Lacking strength; weak: *a very old and feeble person recovering from surgery.* **2.** Without adequate force, power, or intensity; inadequate: *a feeble attempt; a feeble voice.* —**fee′ble·ness** *n.* —**fee′bly** *adv.*

feeble-minded (fē′bəl-mīn′dĭd) *adj.* **1.** Lacking intelligence or foresight: *a feeble-minded plan to build housing in the park.* **2.** A term formerly used for people with impaired mental development. —**fee′ble-mind′ed·ly** *adv.*

feed (fēd) *v.* **fed** (fĕd), **feeding, feeds** —*tr.* **1.** To give food to; supply with nourishment: *People feed the birds in the park.* **2.** To provide as food or nourishment: *We fed the fish to the cat when we got home.* **3a.** To serve as food for: *a turkey large enough to feed a dozen.* **b.** To produce food for: *This valley feeds an entire country.* **4.** To provide

(something) for growth, maintenance, or operation: *We fed more wood to the fire. Scientists fed data into a computer.* —*intr.* To eat or ingest something as food: *Young turtles feed on insects.* ❖ *n.* **1.** Food for animals, especially livestock. **2.** *Informal* A meal, especially a large one.

feedback (fēd′băk′) *n.* **1.** The return of a part of the output of a system or process to the input, especially when used to regulate an electrical system or an electronic process. Computers use feedback to regulate their operations. **2.** A response or reaction: *We asked the employees for feedback on the new cafeteria.*

feeder (fē′dər) *n.* **1.** A person or thing that supplies feed: *a bird feeder on a window ledge.* **2.** A person or animal that feeds on something. **3.** Something that feeds materials into a machine to be processed. **4.** A branch or tributary, as of a river, railroad, or corporation.

feel (fēl) *v.* **felt** (fĕlt), **feeling, feels** —*tr.* **1.** To be aware of through the sense of touch: *feel the softness of velvet.* **2.** To be aware of as a physical sensation: *feel a sharp pain; feel the cold.* **3.** To touch or examine by touching in order to find something out: *The nurse felt the patient's forehead for fever.* **4.** To find (one's way) by touching; grope: *In the dark we felt our way up the steps.* **5.** To sense or experience: *They felt my annoyance over their loud music.* **6.** To be affected by: *She still feels the loss of her cat.* **7.** To believe; consider: *We feel the idea is worth trying.* —*intr.* **1.** To experience sensations of touch: *The doctor poked my finger to see if it could feel.* **2.** To produce a particular sensation or feeling: *The sheets felt cool and smooth. It feels good to be home.* **3.** To be aware of a quality or emotional state: *We all felt satisfied with the results of our work.* **4.** To try to find something by touching: *We felt around for the light switch.* **5.** To have compassion or sympathy: *I feel for him.* ❖ *n.* **1.** Awareness or sensation caused by physical touch: *the feel of raindrops.* **2.** A quality that can be sensed by touching: *the smooth and slippery feel of satin.* ◆ **feel in (one's) bones** To have an intuition about: *I feel in my bones that this project will succeed.* **feel like** *Informal* To be in the mood for: *I did not feel like going for a walk.* **feel like (oneself)** To be aware of oneself as being in the usual state of health or spirits: *I don't feel quite myself this morning.* **feel out** To try cautiously to find out the viewpoint of (a person): *We felt them out about playing a football game.*

feeler (fē′lər) *n.* **1.** A slender body part, such as the antenna of an insect, used for touching or feeling. **2.** A remark, question, or suggestion used to find out the attitude or intention of others: *The letter was a feeler sent to see if there was any interest in our project.*

feeling (fē′lĭng) *n.* **1.** The sense of touch: *I had no feeling in my cut finger.* **2.** A physical sensation, especially one produced by touch: *the feeling of ice.* **3.** An emotion, such as joy or sorrow: *a feeling of excitement.* **4.** Strong emotion or emotional quality: *She plays the violin with real feeling.* **5.** An awareness; an impression: *a feeling of danger nearby.* **6. feelings** The sensitive nature of one's emotions: *His lack of concern hurt my feelings.* **7.** An opinion based strongly on emotion; a sentiment: *What are your feelings about the proposed tax increase?*

◆ **SYNONYMS feeling, emotion, sentiment** *n.*

feet (fēt) *n.* Plural of **foot.**

feign (fān) *v.* **feigned, feigning, feigns** —*tr.* To give a false appearance of; pretend: *feign illness.* —*intr.* To make a false appearance; pretend: *The opossum isn't really dead; it's only feigning to fool the dog.*

feint (fānt) *n.* **1.** A movement or attack that is meant to deceive by diverting attention from the real target or objective: *With a feint to the left, she fooled the goalie and scored.* **2.** An action meant to mislead: *The robbers made a feint of repairing the window they were going to break into.* ❖ *intr.v.* **feinted, feinting, feints** To make a feint: *My opponent feinted as if to take a shot at the basket.*

feisty (fī′stē) *adj.* **feistier, feistiest 1.** Full of spirit or determination. **2.** Quarrelsome or aggressive.

feldspar (fĕld′spär′ *or* fĕl′spär′) *also* **felspar** (fĕl′spär′) *n.* Any of a group of crystalline minerals that occur widely in various rocks and are composed largely of silicates combined with sodium and either potassium or calcium. Feldspars are used in the manufacture of glass.

felicitate (fĭ-lĭs′ĭ-tāt′) *tr.v.* **felicitated, felicitating, felicitates** To wish happiness to; congratulate: *Guests felicitated the newlyweds.*

felicitations (fĭ-lĭs′ĭ-tā′shənz) *pl.n.* Expressions of joy or acknowledgment: *Family and friends offered their felicitations to the graduating senior.*

felicitous (fĭ-lĭs′ĭ-təs) *adj.* **1.** Well-chosen; apt; appropriate: *a felicitous choice of words.* **2.** Having an agreeable manner or style: *a felicitous greeting.* —**fe·lic′i·tous·ly** *adv.*

felicity (fĭ-lĭs′ĭ-tē) *n., pl.* **felicities 1.** Great happiness; bliss: *the felicity of the moment of victory.* **2.** A source of great happiness: *the felicity of a generous heart.* **3.** An appropriate and pleasing manner or style: *She writes with felicity of expression.* **4.** A pleasing and appropriate expression; a well-chosen phrase: *The felicities of their greeting touched everyone.*

feline (fē′līn′) *adj.* **1.** Relating to the family of carnivorous mammals that includes the cats, lions, tigers, and leopards. **2.** Suggestive of a cat: *walking with feline grace.* ❖ *n.* An animal belonging to the feline family.

fell¹ (fĕl) *tr.v.* **felled, felling, fells** To cause to fall; cut or knock down: *They felled trees to build a cabin.*

fell² (fĕl) *adj.* **1.** Of a cruel nature; fierce and ruthless: *a fell crew of pirates.* **2.** Capable of destroying; lethal: *a fell potion.* ♦ **at one fell swoop** or **in one fell swoop** All at once.

WORD HISTORY Fell¹ comes from Old English *fellan,* meaning "to cause to fall." **Fell²** comes from Middle English *fel,* which comes from Old French *fel* (both meaning "cruel, ruthless"), which comes from Old French *felon,* meaning "evil."

fell³ (fĕl) *v.* Past tense of **fall.**

fellow (fĕl′ō) *n.* **1.** A man or boy: *Where are those fellows going?* **2.** A comrade or associate: *Robin Hood and his fellows hid in the forest.* **3.** A member of a learned society or professional organization. **4.** A graduate student who receives a grant of money for further study. **5.** A physician who enters a training program in a medical specialty after completing a residency. **6.** One of a matched pair; a counterpart: *Here's the fellow of your sneaker.* ❖ *adj.* Being of the same kind, group, or class; sharing certain characteristics or interests: *our fellow workers.*

fellowship (fĕl′ō-shĭp′) *n.* **1.** Friendly association of people; companionship: *We enjoyed the fellowship of our neighbors.* **2.** A group of people sharing common interests. **3.** A grant of money awarded a graduate student in a college or university.

felon (fĕl′ən) *n.* A person who has committed a felony.

felonious (fə-lō′nē-əs) *adj.* Having the nature of a felony: *carrying a gun with felonious intent.*

felony (fĕl′ə-nē) *n., pl.* **felonies** A serious crime, such as murder, rape, or robbery, for which the punishment is more severe than for a misdemeanor.

felt¹ (fĕlt) *n.* A smooth firm cloth made by pressing and matting wool, fur, or other fibers together instead of weaving them. ❖ *adj.* Made of or resembling felt.

felt² (fĕlt) *v.* Past tense and past participle of **feel.**

fem. An abbreviation of: **1.** female. **2.** feminine.

female (fē′māl′) *adj.* **1a.** Relating to or characteristic of the sex that produces eggs or gives birth to offspring. **b.** Relating to or being a reproductive organ that produces female gametes: *female flower parts.* **c.** Relating to or being the gamete that is larger and less motile than the other corresponding gamete: *female reproductive cells.* **2.** Composed of women or girls: *a female choir.* **3.** Having a part into which a corresponding male part fits: *a female plug.* ❖ *n.* **1.** A female organism. **2.** A woman or girl.

feminine (fĕm′ə-nĭn) *adj.* **1.** Relating to women or girls. **2.** Marked by or possessing qualities traditionally attributed to a woman: *The lace curtains gave the house a feminine feeling.* **3.** In grammar, relating to or belonging to the gender of nouns that refer to females or to things classified as female: *In German, the word for "world" is feminine.* —**fem′i·nine·ly** *adv.*

femininity (fĕm′ə-nĭn′ĭ-tē) *n.* The quality or condition of being feminine.

feminism (fĕm′ə-nĭz′əm) *n.* **1.** Belief in or support for the idea that women and men have the same social, political, and economic rights. **2.** The movement organized around this belief. —**fem′i·nist** *n. & adj.*

femoral (fĕm′ər-əl) *adj.* Relating to or located in the thigh or femur: *femoral arteries and veins.*

femur (fē′mər) *n., pl.* **femurs** or **femora** (fĕm′ər-ə) **1.** The long bone of the leg between the knee and pelvis in humans; the thighbone. **2.** A corresponding bone in other vertebrate animals.

fen (fĕn) *n.* An area of low wet ground that is usually less acidic than a bog.

fence (fĕns) *n.* **1.** A structure usually made of posts or stakes joined together by wire, boards, or rails, that serves as an enclosure, boundary, or barrier. **2.** A person who receives and sells stolen goods. ❖ *v.* **fenced, fencing, fences** —*tr.* To surround or separate with a fence: *fence a pasture to keep cows in; fence in the dog for the night.* —*intr.* To practice the sport of fencing: *The actor fenced with skill.* ♦ **on the fence** *Informal* Undecided as to which of two sides to support. —**fenc′er** *n.*

fencing (fĕn′sĭng) *n.* **1.** The art or sport of using a sword, especially a foil, in attack and defense. **2.** Material, such as wire, stakes, and rails, used in building fences: *That lumber yard sells fencing.* **3.** A barrier or enclosure of fences: *Low stone fencing surrounds the park.*

fend (fĕnd) *v.* **fended, fending, fends** —*tr.* To ward off: *fend off an attack.* —*intr.* To attempt to manage without assistance: *The climbers decided to fend for themselves rather than hiring a guide.*

fender (fĕn′dər) *n.* **1.** A guard over each wheel of an automobile or other vehicle that is shaped and positioned so as to keep mud or water from splashing up. **2.** A device at the front end of a locomotive or streetcar designed to push aside obstructions. **3.** A cushion made of fiber, rubber, or wood and hung over the side of a dock or vessel to absorb friction or impact. **4.** A screen or metal frame placed in front of a fireplace to keep hot coals and debris from falling out.

fender-bender or **fender bender** (fĕn′dər-bĕn′dər) *n. Informal* A collision between two or more automobiles that results in only minor damage.

fennel (fĕn′əl) *n.* An edible perennial plant that has feathery leaves and tastes like licorice. The seeds are used as a flavoring, and the bulbous stalks are eaten as a vegetable.

feral (fîr′əl *or* fĕr′əl) *adj.* **1.** Existing in a wild or untamed state, especially after having been domesticated: *feral cats living in the park.* **2.** Relating to or suggestive of a wild animal; savage: *a feral grin.*

fer-de-lance (fĕr′dl-äns′ *or* fĕr′dl-äns′) *n., pl.* **fer-de-lance** Any of several large venomous snakes of tropical America, having brown and grayish markings.

ferment (fər-mĕnt′) *v.* **fermented, fermenting, ferments** —*intr.* **1.** To undergo fermentation: *The apple cider had fermented overnight.* **2.** To develop actively or rapidly: *an idea that was fermenting in his mind for months.* —*tr.* To cause to undergo fermentation: *Yeasts ferment sugars.* ❖ *n.* (fûr′mĕnt′) A state of agitation, unrest, or rapid development: *It was a time of great intellectual ferment.*

fermentation (fûr′mĕn-tā′shən) *n.* A chemical reaction in which enzymes break down complex organic compounds into simpler compounds. Yeasts obtain energy by using fermentation to convert sugar into alcohol and carbon dioxide without the use of oxygen.

fermium (fûr′mē-əm) *n. Symbol* **Fm** A radioactive element that has been artificially produced by scientists. The half-life of its longest-lived isotope is about 100 days. Atomic number 100. See **Periodic Table.**

fern (fûrn) *n.* Any of numerous plants having feathery fronds usually divided into many leaflets. Ferns do not have flowers or seeds but reproduce by means of spores.

ferocious (fə-rō′shəs) *adj.* **1.** Extremely aggressive or violent: *the tiger's ferocious attack.* **2.** Extreme powerful or destructive: *ferocious heat.* —**fe·ro′cious·ly** *adv.*

ferocity (fə-rŏs′ĭ-tē) *n.* The state or quality of being ferocious; fierceness.

ferret (fĕr′ĭt) *n.* **1.** A small domesticated mammal with a long slender body, short legs, and brown, black, or whitish fur, often kept as a pet and formerly trained to hunt rats or rabbits. **2.** A North American mammal with a long slender body, short legs, yellowish-brown fur and black feet. ❖ *v.* **ferreted, ferreting, ferrets** —*tr.* **1.** To bring to light by searching; uncover: *ferreted out the solution to the mystery.* **2.** To hunt (rabbits, for example) with ferrets. —*intr.* **1.** To search intensively: *ferreting among old records.* **2.** To engage in hunting with ferrets.

ferric (fĕr′ĭk) *adj.* Relating to or containing iron, especially iron with a valence of 3.

ferric oxide *n.* A reddish-brown to black, iron-containing compound that is often used as a pigment.

Ferris wheel (fĕr′ĭs) *n.* An amusement ride consisting of an upright wheel having seats suspended from its rim that remain horizontal as the wheel revolves.

ferromagnetic (fĕr′ō-măg-nĕt′ĭk) *adj.* Relating to substances that become magnetic when subjected to a magnetic field under certain conditions. Ferromagnetic substances, such as iron and cobalt, retain the magnetism for some time even after the magnetic field has been removed.

ferrous (fĕr′əs) *adj.* Relating to or containing iron, especially iron with a valence of 2.

ferry (fĕr′ē) *v.* **ferried, ferrying, ferries** —*tr.* **1.** To trans-port (people, vehicles, or goods) by boat across a body of water. **2.** To cross (a body of water) by a ferry: *We ferried the river before a bridge was built.* **3.** To deliver (a vehicle) under its own power to its eventual user. **4.** To transport (people or things) by vehicle: *Volunteers ferried everyone from the disaster area to the hospital.* —*intr.* To cross a body of water on or as if on a ferry: *We ferried across the bay.* ❖ *n., pl.* **ferries 1.** A boat used to transport passengers, vehicles, or goods across a body of water; a ferryboat. **2.** A place where passengers or goods are transported across a body of water by a ferry.

ferryboat (fĕr′ē-bōt′) *n.* A boat used to transport passengers, vehicles, or goods across a body of water.

fertile (fûr′tl) *adj.* **1.** Capable of producing offspring; able to reproduce: *a fertile cow.* **2.** Capable of developing into a complete organism; fertilized: *A fertile egg from a hen will produce a chick.* **3.** Capable of supporting plant life; favorable to the growth of crops or other plants: *fertile soil; a fertile valley.* **4.** Highly productive or active; inventive: *the writer's fertile imagination.*

fertility (fər-tĭl′ĭ-tē) *n.* The quality or condition of being fertile: *the fertility of good soil; factors influencing the fertility of cows.*

fertilization (fûr′tl-ĭ-zā′shən) *n.* **1.** The act or process of fertilizing. **2.** The union of a male reproductive cell and a female reproductive cell to form a cell that is capable of developing into a new organism.

fertilize (fûr′tl-īz′) *tr.v.* **fertilized, fertilizing, fertilizes 1.** To cause (a female reproductive cell) to become able to develop into a new organism, especially by union with a male reproductive cell such as a sperm cell. **2.** To make (soil, for example) fertile: *Manure from grazing animals fertilizes the grasslands.* **3.** To spread fertilizer on: *fertilize the garden.*

fertilizer (fûr′tl-ī′zər) *n.* A material, such as manure, compost, or a chemical compound, added to soil to increase its productivity or fertility.

ferule (fĕr′əl) *n.* A cane or flat stick formerly used in punishing children.

fervency (fûr′vən-sē) *n., pl.* **fervencies** The quality or condition of being fervent.

fervent (fûr′vənt) *adj.* Having or showing great emotion or zeal; ardent: *the fervent leaders of the reform movement; a fervent plea for help.* —**fer′vent·ly** *adv.*

fervid (fûr′vĭd) *adj.* Marked by great passion or zeal: *a fervid desire to play baseball.* —**fer′vid·ly** *adv.*

fervor (fûr′vər) *n.* Intensity of emotion; ardor.

festal (fĕs′təl) *adj.* Related to a feast or festival; festive: *Flags gave a festal appearance to the village.*

fester (fĕs′tər) *intr.v.* **festered, festering, festers 1.** To form pus as an infected wound does: *An unclean cut will fester and become painful.* **2.** To be or become a source of irritation; rankle: *bitterness that festered and grew.*

festival (fĕs′tə-vəl) *n.* **1.** An occasion for feasting or celebration, especially a day or time of religious significance. **2.** An often regularly recurring series of cultural performances, exhibitions, or competitions: *a film festival.*

festive (fĕs′tĭv) *adj.* **1.** Relating to a feast or festival. **2.** Merry; joyous: *a festive party; festive decorations.* —**fes′tive·ly** *adv.* —**fes′tive·ness** *n.*

festivity (fĕ-stĭv′ĭ-tē) *n., pl.* **festivities 1.** The fun and excitement of a celebration or festival: *a holiday full of festivity.* **2. festivities** The activities or events of a festival: *Mardi Gras festivities include parades and banquets.*

festoon (fĕ-stōōn′) *n.* **1.** A string or garland, as of leaves or flowers, suspended in a curve between two points. **2.** A representation of such a string or garland, as in painting or sculpture. ❖ *tr.v.* **festooned, festooning, festoons 1.** To decorate with or as if with festoons. **2.** To form or make into festoons.

feta (fĕt′ə *or* fā′tə) *n.* A white moderately soft cheese usually made of goat's or sheep's milk and often preserved in brine.

fetal (fēt′l) *adj.* Relating to or characteristic of a fetus: *a fetal heartbeat.*

fetal position *n.* A position of the body at rest in which the spine is curved, the head is bent forward, and the arms and legs are drawn in toward the chest.

fetch (fĕch) *v.* **fetched, fetching, fetches** — *tr.* **1.** To go after and bring or take back; get: *Could you fetch my bags?* **2.** To cause to come; succeed in bringing: *My phone call fetched them home quickly.* **3.** To bring in as a price: *The painting fetched $200 at the auction.* — *intr.* To go after something and return with it: *If you throw the ball, the dog will fetch.*

fetching (fĕch′ĭng) *adj.* Very attractive; charming: *a fetching smile.* — **fetch′ing·ly** *adv.*

fete *also* **fête** (fāt *or* fĕt) *n.* **1.** A festival or feast. **2.** An elaborate party. ❖ *tr.v.* **feted, feting, fetes** *also* **fêted, fêting, fêtes** To honor with a festival, feast, or elaborate entertainment: *They feted the veterans on Memorial Day.*

fetid (fĕt′ĭd *or* fē′tĭd) *adj.* Having an offensive odor. — **fet′id·ly** *adv.* — **fet′id·ness** *n.*

fetish (fĕt′ĭsh) *n.* **1.** An object that is believed to have magical or spiritual powers. **2.** An object of too much attention or reverence.

fetishism (fĕt′ĭ-shĭz′əm) *n.* **1.** Worship of or belief in magical fetishes. **2.** Too much attention to or attachment for something. — **fet′ish·ist** *n.*

fetlock (fĕt′lŏk′) *n.* **1.** A joint that forms a projection on the back of the leg of a horse or related animal, just above the hoof. **2.** A tuft of hair on this projection.

fetter (fĕt′ər) *n.* **1.** A device, usually one of a pair of rings connected to a chain, that is attached to a person's ankles or feet to restrict movement. **2.** often **fetters** Something that restricts or restrains: *the fetters of rigid traditions.* ❖ *tr.v.* **fettered, fettering, fetters 1.** To put fetters on; shackle. **2.** To restrict or restrain: *attempts to fetter free speech.*

fettle (fĕt′l) *n.* Proper or sound mental or physical condition or state: *The horse is in fine fettle for today's race.*

fettuccine (fĕt′ə-chē′nē) *n.* **1.** Pasta in narrow flat strips. **2.** A dish made with such strips of pasta.

fetus (fē′təs) *n., pl.* **fetuses** The unborn young of a mammal at the later stages of its development, especially a human embryo from its eighth week of development to its birth.

feud (fyōod) *n.* A bitter quarrel or state of enmity between two people, families, or groups, often continuing for generations: *An ancient feud came between the two families.* ❖ *intr.v.* **feuded, feuding, feuds** To carry on a bitter quarrel or state of enmity.

feudal (fyōod′l) *adj.* Relating to or characteristic of feudalism.

feudalism (fyōod′l-ĭz′əm) *n.* A political and economic system in Europe during the Middle Ages, in which a landowner granted the use of land to a vassal in exchange for military service and various other duties. — **feu′-dal·is′tic** *adj.*

fever (fē′vər) *n.* **1.** A body temperature higher than normal. **2.** A disease in which a high body temperature is one

of the main symptoms. **3.** A condition of great activity or excitement: *a fever of enthusiasm during the game.*

fever blister *n.* A cold sore.

feverish (fē′vər-ĭsh) *adj.* **1a.** Relating to or resembling a fever. **b.** Having a fever or symptoms characteristic of a fever: *The sick child was feverish.* **c.** Causing or tending to cause fever. **2.** Marked by intense agitation, emotion, or activity: *a feverish worker.* **3.** Intensely excited or active: *a feverish desire to win.* — **fe′ver·ish·ly** *adv.*

few (fyōo) *adj.* **fewer, fewest** Amounting to a small number; not many: *Few people like to swim in cold water.* ❖ *n. (used with a plural verb)* A small number of people or things: *I invited only a few to my party.* ❖ *pron. (used with a plural verb)* A small number of people or things: *Many felt it was an interesting idea, but few seemed willing to do anything about it.*

fez (fĕz) *n., pl.* **fezzes** A man's brimless felt cap in the shape of a flat-topped cone, usually red with a black tassel, worn chiefly in the eastern Mediterranean region.

fiancé (fē′än-sā′ *or* fē-än′sā′) *n.* A man to whom one is engaged to be married.

fiancée (fē′än-sā′ *or* fē-än′sā′) *n.* A woman to whom one is engaged to be married.

fiasco (fē-ăs′kō) *n., pl.* **fiascoes** *or* **fiascos** A complete failure: *Without enough rehearsal, the play was a fiasco.*

fiat (fē′ăt′ *or* fē′ät′) *n.* An arbitrary order or decree: *The dictator raised taxes by fiat.*

fib (fĭb) *n.* A lie about something unimportant or small: *She told a fib about why she was late.* ❖ *intr.v.* **fibbed, fibbing, fibs** To tell a fib. — **fib′ber** *n.*

fiber (fī′bər) *n.* **1a.** A slender strand; a thread: *wool fibers spun into yarn.* **b.** Material made of such strands: *organic cotton fiber.* **2.** Any of various elongated cells in the body, especially those of muscle or nerve tissue. **3.** Any of the elongated, thick-walled cells that give strength and support to plant tissue. **4a.** The essential character or nature of a person: *She's a person of strong moral fiber.* **b.** An element of a person's character or nature: *He missed her with every fiber of his being.* **5.** The part of vegetable foods such as grains, fruits, and vegetables that contains cellulose and other substances that are not digested in the human intestinal tract. Eating foods with fiber helps stool move through the intestines and is thought to have other health benefits.

fiberboard (fī′bər-bôrd′) *n.* A building material made from wood chips or plant fibers bonded together and compressed into rigid sheets.

fiberglass (fī′bər-glăs′) *n.* A material made up of very fine glass fibers, used in making various products, such as building insulation and boat hulls.

fiber optics *n. (used with a singular verb)* The technology of transmitting light through very thin glass or plastic fibers that can be curved. Fiber optics is used for medical imaging instruments and long-distance telephone and computer lines. — **fi′ber-op′tic** (fī′bər-ŏp′tĭk) *adj.*

fibre (fī′bər) *n. Chiefly British* Variant of **fiber.**

fibrillation (fĭb′rə-lā′shən *or* fī′brə-lā′shən) *n.* A rapid twitching of muscle fibers, especially of the heart.

fibrin (fī′brĭn) *n.* A fibrous, elastic, and insoluble protein that is formed when blood clots.

fibrinogen (fī-brĭn′ə-jən) *n.* A soluble protein that is normally present in the plasma of the blood and forms fibrin.

fibroid (fī′broid′) *adj.* Made up of or resembling fibers or fibrous tissue: *a fibroid tumor.*

fibromyalgia (fī′brō-mī-ăl′jə) *n.* A syndrome marked by chronic, widespread pain in the muscles and often other symptoms, such as fatigue, anxiety, and digestive problems.

fibrous (fī′brəs) *adj.* Made up of, resembling, or having fibers: *fibrous tissue.*

fibula (fĭb′yə-lə) *n., pl.* **fibulae** (fĭb′yə-lē′) *or* **fibulas 1.** The outer and smaller of the two bones of the leg in humans. It extends from the knee to the ankle. **2.** A similar bone in the hind leg of other vertebrate animals.

–fic A suffix that means making or causing: *soporific.*

fickle (fĭk′əl) *adj.* Changeable; not stable or constant, especially with regard to affections: *a fickle friend.* —**fick′-le·ness** *n.*

fiction (fĭk′shən) *n.* **1.** The category of literature, drama, or film whose content is imagined and is not necessarily based on fact. **2.** Works, especially novels, in this category: *the fiction of Virginia Woolf.* **3.** Explanation or belief that is not true: *The notion that he was at the scene of the crime is pure fiction.* **4.** An explanation or belief that is not true: *Your explanation for why this keeps happening is a fiction.* —**fic′tion·al** *adj.*

fictionalize (fĭk′shə-nə-līz′) *tr.v.* **fictionalized, fictionalizing, fictionalizes** To treat as fiction or make into fiction: *A writer may fictionalize real-life stories.*

fictitious (fĭk-tĭsh′əs) *adj.* **1.** Made up, especially in order to mislead: *The criminal used a fictitious name.* **2.** Relating to the characters, settings, or plots created for a work of fiction: *The novel takes place in a fictitious country.* —**fic·ti′tious·ly** *adv.* —**fic·ti′tious·ness** *n.*

fiddle (fĭd′l) *n.* A violin, especially one used to play folk or country music. ❖ *v.* **fiddled, fiddling, fiddles** —*intr.* **1.** To play the fiddle. **2.** To touch or handle something in a nervous way: *She fiddled with her bracelet while she waited.* **3.** To tinker with something in an attempt to fix or adjust it: *Don't fiddle with the television!* —*tr.* To play (a tune) on a fiddle: *The musicians fiddled a reel.* ◆ **fiddle around** To act foolishly, playfully, or without purpose: *Stop fiddling around and get to work.* **fiddle away** To waste or squander: *We fiddled away the last week of summer vacation.* —**fid′dler** *n.*

fiddlehead (fĭd′l-hĕd′) *n.* A young, coiled, edible frond of any of various ferns.

fiddler crab (fĭd′lər) *n.* Any of various burrowing crabs of warm coastal areas, the male of which has one front claw much larger than the other.

fiddlesticks (fĭd′l-stĭks′) *interj.* An expression used to show mild annoyance or impatience.

fidelity (fĭ-dĕl′ĭ-tē *or* fī-dĕl′ĭ-tē) *n., pl.* **fidelities 1.** Faithfulness to obligations, duties, or observances: *the soldier's fidelity to duty.* **2.** Exact correspondence with the facts; accuracy: *the fidelity of the witness's account of the accident.* **3.** The degree to which an electronic system, such as a tape recorder or compact disc player, reproduces sound without distortion.

fidget (fĭj′ĭt) *intr.v.* **fidgeted, fidgeting, fidgets** To behave or move nervously or restlessly: *The children fidgeted in their seats.* —**fidg′et·y** *adj.*

fidgets (fĭj′ĭts) *pl.n.* Nervousness or restlessness: *had a case of the fidgets while waiting to speak before the class.*

fiduciary (fĭ-do͞o′shē-ĕr′ē *or* fĭ-do͞o′shə-rē) *adj.* Relating to a duty of acting in good faith with regard to another's interests: *a company's fiduciary responsibility to investors.* ❖ *n., pl.* **fiduciaries** One, such as a company director, who has a duty to act in good faith with regard to another's interests.

fie (fī) *interj.* An expression used to show distaste or shock.

fief (fēf) *n.* **1.** In feudal times, an estate of land granted by a lord to a vassal. **2.** A group or part of an organization over which one has influence or control.

fiefdom (fēf′dəm) *n.* A fief.

field (fēld) *n.* **1.** A broad, level, open expanse of land. An area of land that is cultivated or used for grazing: *cotton fields; cows in the field.* **3.** A portion of land or a geologic formation containing a natural resource: *oil fields; a gold field.* **4.** A wide unbroken expanse, as of ice. **5.** A battleground. **6.** A background area, as on a flag or painting: *white stars on a field of blue.* **7a.** The area in which a game in a team sport such as soccer or football takes place. **b.** The area inside or near to a running track, where events such as the long jump and shot put are held. **8.** All the contestants or participants in an event: *a large field of horses in the race; the field of candidates running for office.* **9.** An area of human activity, interest, or knowledge: *the field of botany.* **10.** An area or setting of practical work or observation outside an office, school, factory, or laboratory: *experiments done in the field.* **11.** A region of space throughout which a physical force operates: *An electric field surrounds a charged body. The moon is within Earth's gravitational field.* **12.** The area in which an image is visible to the eye or an optical instrument: *the field of a microscope; the field of vision.* **13.** An element in a computer database record in which one item of information is stored: *typed "May 5" in the date field.* ❖ *adj.* **1.** Growing, living, or cultivated in fields or open land: *field poppies.* **2.** Made, used, or done in the field: *field operations.* ❖ *v.* **fielded, fielding, fields** —*tr.* **1.** In sports, especially baseball, to stop or catch (a ball): *fielded several fly balls.* **2.** In sports, to place in the field to play: *field a team.* **3.** To respond to: *fielded questions from the reporters.* —*intr.* To play as a fielder: *The team fielded well.*

field day *n.* **1.** A day set aside for sports or athletic competition. **2.** A time of great activity, pleasure, or opportunity: *The children had a field day in the toy store.*

fielder (fēl′dər) *n.* In baseball, a player stationed in the field who attempts to put out the team at bat.

fielder's choice (fēl′dərz) *n.* In baseball, a play made on a ground ball in which the fielder chooses to put out an advancing base runner while the batter reaches first base safely.

field event *n.* A throwing or jumping event of a track-and-field meet.

field glasses *pl.n.* Portable binoculars used especially outdoors for viewing distant objects.

field goal *n.* **1.** In football, a score worth three points made on an ordinary down by place-kicking the ball over the crossbar and between the goalposts. **2.** In basketball, a basket made in regulation play, normally worth two points, but worth three points if attempted from beyond a specified distance.

field hockey *n.* A game played on a field in which two teams of players using curved sticks try to drive a ball into each other's goal.

field house *n.* A building at an athletic field having storage and training facilities and locker rooms.

field magnet *n.* A magnet used to produce a magnetic field for the operation of an electrical device such as a motor or generator.

field marshal *n.* An officer in some European armies, usually ranking just below the commander in chief.

field test *n.* A test of a new product under actual operating conditions.

field-test (fēld′tĕst′) *tr.v.* **field-tested, field-testing, field-tests** To test (a technique or product) under conditions of actual operation or use: *field-test a new kind of lawn-mower.*

field trip *n.* A group excursion for the purpose of firsthand observation, as to a museum, the woods, or a historic place.

fieldwork (fēld′wûrk′) *n.* **1.** The collection of biological, anthropological, or sociological data through firsthand observation outside a laboratory, school, or other controlled environment. **2.** A temporary military fortification built at or near a battleground. **—field′work′er** *n.*

fiend (fēnd) *n.* **1.** An evil spirit; a demon. **2.** An evil or wicked person. **3.** *Informal* A person absorbed in or obsessed with a certain thing: *a baseball fiend.*

fiendish (fēn′dĭsh) *adj.* **1.** Relating to or suggestive of a fiend; evil, wicked, or cruel: *a fiendish weapon; a fiendish tyrant.* **2.** Extremely bad, disagreeable, or difficult: *a fiendish problem.* **—fiend′ish·ly** *adv.*

fierce (fîrs) *adj.* **fiercer, fiercest** **1.** Having a violent and aggressive nature; ferocious: *a fierce beast.* **2.** Very severe or violent; terrible: *a fierce storm.* **3.** Very intense or ardent: *fierce loyalty.* **—fierce′ly** *adv.* **—fierce′ness** *n.*

fiery (fîr′ē or fī′ə-rē) *adj.* **fierier, fieriest** **1.** Consisting of or containing fire: *the fiery crater of the volcano.* **2.** Having the color of fire: *a fiery sunset.* **3.** Very hot: *the fiery pavements of the city in summer.* **4.** Burning or glowing: *fiery coals.* **5.** Easily excited or provoked; tempestuous: *a fiery temper.* **6.** Charged with emotion; high-spirited: *The candidate delivered a fiery speech.* **—fier′i·ly** *adv.*

fiesta (fē-ĕs′tə) *n.* **1.** A festival or religious holiday, especially a saint's day celebrated in Spanish-speaking countries. **2.** A celebration or party.

FIFA An abbreviation of Fédération Internationale de Football Association (International Federation of Association Football).

fife (fīf) *n.* A small high-pitched musical instrument similar to a flute, often used with drums to accompany military music.

fifteen (fĭf-tēn′) *n.* **1.** The number, written 15, that is equal to 14 + 1. **2.** The 15th in a set or sequence.

fifteenth (fĭf-tēnth′) *n.* **1.** The ordinal number matching the number 15 in a series. **2.** One of 15 equal parts.

fifth (fĭfth) *n.* **1.** The ordinal number matching the number five in a series. **2.** One of five equal parts. **3.** One fifth of a gallon or four fifths of a quart of liquor. **4a.** The interval covering five tones in a musical scale, as C, D, E, F, and G. **b.** The fifth tone of a musical scale; the dominant. **5.** The transmission gear used to produce speeds

next higher than those of fourth in a motor vehicle. **6. Fifth** The Fifth Amendment: *The defendant pled the Fifth.* **—fifth** *adv. & adj.*

Fifth Amendment *n.* An amendment to the Constitution of the United States, ratified in 1791, that deals with the rights of accused criminals by providing for due process of law, forbidding double jeopardy, and stating that no person may be forced to testify as a witness against himself or herself. It also prohibits the government from confiscating private property for public use without fairly compensating the property owner.

fifth column *n.* A secret organization working within a country to further the political and military aims of that country's enemies.

fiftieth (fĭf′tē-ĭth) *n.* **1.** The ordinal number matching the number 50 in a series. **2.** One of 50 equal parts.

fifty (fĭf′tē) *n.* **1.** The number, written 50, that is equal to 5 × 10. **2.** A fifty-dollar bill.

fifty-fifty (fĭf′tē-fĭf′tē) *adj.* **1.** Divided or shared in two equal portions: *The partners agreed on a fifty-fifty split of the money.* **2.** Being equally likely or unlikely: *I had a fifty-fifty chance of winning the coin toss.* **—fif′ty-fif′ty** *adv.*

fig (fĭg) *n.* **1.** A sweet pear-shaped fruit of any of various trees or shrubs that grow in warm regions. Figs have many seeds and may be eaten fresh or dried. **2.** A tree or shrub that bears such fruit. **3.** A very small or trivial amount: *not worth a fig.*

fig. An abbreviation of figure.

fight (fīt) *v.* **fought** (fôt), **fighting, fights** *—intr.* **1.** To attempt to harm or gain power over an adversary by blows or with weapons: *fought bravely against the invaders.* **2.** To participate in boxing or wrestling: *They fought for the gold medal.* **3.** To engage in a quarrel; argue: *The neighbors fought for years over the boundary.* **4.** To strive vigorously and resolutely: *fought for their rights in court.* See Synonyms at **oppose.** *—tr.* **1.** To contend physically or in battle: *The Union troops fought the Confederates at Gettysburg.* **2.** To carry on or engage in (a battle). **3.** To box or wrestle against in a ring: *fight a contender in the Olympics.* **4a.** To contend with or struggle against: *fight illiteracy; fight rising floodwaters.* **b.** To try to extinguish (an uncontrolled fire). **5.** To make (one's way) by struggle or striving: *We fought our way through the dense undergrowth.* ❖ *n.* **1a.** A physical conflict between two or more individuals. **b.** A quarrel or conflict: *a fight over who would empty the trash.* **2.** A battle waged between opposing forces. **3.** A boxing or wrestling match. **4.** A struggle to achieve a goal: *the fight for freedom.* **5.** The power or will to battle or struggle: *Is there any fight left in him?* ◆ **fight fire with fire** To combat one evil or one set of negative circumstances by reacting in kind. **fight off** To defend against or drive back (a hostile force, for example): *A fever is one way in which the body fights off germs.*

fighter (fī′tər) *n.* **1.** A person who fights, such as a soldier or boxer. **2.** A fast maneuverable airplane used in combat. **3.** A person who is unyielding or determined.

figment (fĭg′mənt) *n.* Something invented, made up, or imagined: *a mere figment of the imagination.*

figurative (fĭg′yər-ə-tĭv) *adj.* **1.** Based on or using figures of speech; metaphorical: *figurative language.* **2.** Containing many figures of speech; ornate. **3.** Represented by a likeness or figure; emblematic: *A light bulb is a figurative representation of an idea.* **—fig′ur·a·tive·ly** *adv.*

figure (fĭg′yər) *n.* **1.** A written or printed symbol, especially a numeral, representing something that is not a letter. **2. figures** Mathematical calculations: *Accountants need to have a good head for figures.* **3.** An amount represented in numbers: *priced at a high figure.* **4.** In geometry, any combination of points, lines, or surfaces: *Circles and triangles are plane figures.* **5.** The shape or form of a human body: *People buy clothes to suit their figures.* **6.** An indistinct object or shape: *I turned and saw a tall figure standing in the doorway.* **7.** A person, especially a well-known one: *The president is an important public figure.* **8.** Impression or appearance made: *cuts an impressive figure in uniform.* **9.** A pictorial or sculptural representation, especially of the human body: *The museum featured many lifelike figures in wax.* **10a.** A diagram: *On that page, the figure shows a bird in flight.* **b.** A design or pattern, as on cloth: *silk with a paisley figure.* **11.** A group of movements in dancing or ice skating: *the lovely figures of the minuet.* **12.** A brief or melodic harmonic unit, often the basis of a larger musical phrase or structure; a motif: *the opening figure of a symphony.* ❖ *v.* **figured, figuring, figures** —*tr.* **1.** To calculate with numbers: *She figured the cost of renovating the bathroom.* **2.** *Informal* To conclude, believe, or predict: *I figured that you'd want to go swimming.* —*intr.* **1.** To calculate; compute: *Most store clerks can figure quickly and accurately.* **2.** To be or seem important: *The opening of the store figured in the local news.* **3.** To seem reasonable or expected: *It figures that they decided to work as a team because they work well together.* ◆ **figure on** *Informal* To depend on: *You can always figure on some guests to be late.* **figure out** To solve, decipher, or discover: *figure out a puzzle.*

figure eight *n.* A form or representation, such as a knot or an ice-skating maneuver, that has the shape of the numeral 8.

figurehead (fĭg′yər-hĕd′) *n.* **1.** A carved figure on the prow of a ship. **2.** A person who is given a position of leadership in name only and who has no actual authority.

figure of speech *n., pl.* **figures of speech** An expression in which words are used in unusual or nonliteral ways to create vivid or dramatic effects. Metaphor, simile, hyperbole, and personification are figures of speech.

figure skating *n.* Ice-skating consisting of sequences of required and optional spins, jumps, and dancelike maneuvers. —**figure skater** *n.*

figurine (fĭg′yə-rēn′) *n.* A small molded or sculpted figure; a statuette.

filament (fĭl′ə-mənt) *n.* **1.** A fine or slender thread, wire, or fiber. **2.** The slender stalk that bears the anther in the stamen of a flower. **3.** A fine wire that is enclosed in an incandescent light bulb and gives off light when it is heated by the passage of an electric current.

filbert (fĭl′bərt) *n.* A hazelnut.

filch (fĭlch) *tr.v.* **filched, filching, filches** To steal (something, especially something of little value) in a sly manner; pilfer. —**filch′er** *n.*

file¹ (fīl) *n.* **1.** A container, such as a cabinet or folder, for keeping papers in order: *drawings stored in large files.* **2.** A collection of papers or published materials kept or arranged in convenient order. **3.** A collection of related computer data stored as a unit with a single name. **4.** A row or single line of people or things arranged one behind the other: *The ducks waddled across the road in a file.* ❖ *v.* **filed, filing, files** —*tr.* **1.** To put or keep (papers, for example) in useful order for storage or reference. **2.** To submit or send (copy) to a newspaper: *Reporters file stories daily.* **3.** To enter (a legal document) on public of-

ficial record: *file a claim in court for payment of damages.* —*intr.* **1.** To march or walk in a line: *The nine justices solemnly filed in.* **2.** To submit an application; apply: *Candidates for election must file with the county clerk.* —**fil′er** *n.*

file² (fīl) *n.* Any of several steel tools having a series of sharp ridges, used in smoothing, shaping, or grinding down. ❖ *tr.v.* **filed, filing, files** To smooth, reduce, or remove with or as if with a file: *filed the edge of the blade so it cut better.*

WORD HISTORY File¹ comes from Middle English *filen* (meaning "to put documents on file"), which comes from Late Latin *filāre* (meaning "to spin, draw out in a long line"), which comes from Latin *filum,* meaning "thread." **File²** comes from Old English *fīl,* meaning "metal tool for smoothing or abrading a surface."

---

filename (fīl′nām′) *n.* The name of a computer file, often containing an extension that shows what kind of file it is.

file server *n.* A computer connected to a network on which users of the networks can store files.

filet¹ (fĭ-lā′ or fĭl′ā′) *n.* A net or lace with a simple pattern of squares.

filet² (fĭ-lā′ or fĭl′ā′) also **fillet** (fĭl′ĭt) *n.* A boneless piece of meat or fish, especially the beef tenderloin. ❖ *v.* **fileted, fileting, filets** also **filleted, filleting, fillets** To slice, bone, or make into filets: *I watched the fisherman filet a trout.*

filet mignon (fĭ-lā′ mēn-yôṉ′) *n., pl.* **filets mignons** (fĭ-lā′ mēn-yôṉ′) A round, choice cut of beef from the loin.

filial (fĭl′ē-əl or fē′lē-əl) *adj.* Relating to or befitting a son or daughter: *filial duty; filial love.* —**fil′i·al·ly** *adv.*

filibuster (fĭl′ə-bŭs′tər) *n.* **1.** The delaying or obstructing of action in a legislature, especially by making long speeches. **2.** An instance of this. ❖ *v.* **filibustered, filibustering, filibusters** —*intr.* To delay or obstruct the passage of a legislative bill by filibuster. —*tr.* To use a filibuster against (a legislative bill, for example). —**fil′i·bus′ter·er** *n.*

filigree (fĭl′ĭ-grē′) *n.* **1.** Delicate and intricate ornamental work of twisted gold or silver wire. **2.** A lacy delicate design or pattern. ❖ *tr.v.* **filigreed, filigreeing, filigrees** To decorate with or as if with filigree: *Frost filigreed the windowpanes.*

filing (fī′lĭng) *n.* A particle or shaving removed by a file: *metal filings.*

Filipina (fĭl′ə-pē′nə) *n.* A Filipino woman or girl.

Filipino (fĭl′ə-pē′nō) *adj.* Relating to the Philippines or its peoples, languages, or cultures. ❖ *n., pl.* **Filipinos 1.** A native or inhabitant of the Philippines. **2.** The official language of the Philippines, based mostly on Tagalog.

fill (fĭl) *v.* **filled, filling, fills** —*tr.* **1a.** To put as much into (a container, for example) as can be held: *fill a glass with milk.* **b.** To supply or provide to the fullest extent: *filled the mall with new stores.* **2a.** To stop or plug up (an opening, for example). **b.** To repair a cavity in (a tooth). **3.** To satisfy or meet; fulfill: *fill the requirements for a job.* **4.** To supply as required: *fill a prescription; fill an order for 20 books.* **5.** To place a person in: *We filled the job with an experienced worker.* **6.** To take up the whole of; occupy: *Music filled the room. A dense fog filled the valley.* **7.** To engage or occupy completely: *Memories of the summer filled my mind.* —*intr.* To become full: *The boat quickly filled with water.* ❖ *n.* **1.** An amount that is needed to make full, complete, or satisfied: *We ate our fill of the blueberries.* **2.** Earth, gravel, or other material used to build up or fill in land. ◆ **fill in 1.** To provide with information that is essential or newly acquired: *We filled in the police chief on the details of the theft.* **2.** To act as a substitute; stand in: *an understudy who filled in at the last minute.* **fill out 1.** To complete (a form, for example) by providing required information: *Did you fill out the job application?* **2.** To become or make more fleshy: *The pup filled out to become a full-grown dog.* **fill (someone's) shoes** To take someone's position or duties: *It will be hard to fill the manager's shoes.*

filler (fĭl′ər) *n.* Something added to increase weight or size or to fill space: *The radio program ended early, so some patriotic music was played as filler.*

fillet (fĭl′ĭt) *n.* **1.** A narrow band or ribbon, often worn as a headband. **2.** Variant of **filet**². ❖ *tr.v.* Variant of **filet**².

fill-in (fĭl′ĭn′) *n. Informal* A person or thing that serves as a substitute: *The understudy was a fill-in for the star.*

filling (fĭl′ĭng) *n.* **1.** Something used to fill a space, cavity, or container: *a gold filling in a tooth.* **2.** A mixture used to fill pastries, sandwiches, or cakes: *a pie with a cherry filling.*

filling station *n.* A gas station.

fillip (fĭl′əp) *n.* **1.** Something that mildly excites or leads one to take action. **2.** A snap made by pressing a finger against the thumb and suddenly releasing it.

filly (fĭl′ē) *n., pl.* **fillies** A young female horse.

film (fĭlm) *n.* **1.** A thin coating, layer, skin, or sheet: *a film of oil over the puddle; a film of dust on a tabletop.* **2.** A thin, flexible, transparent sheet, as of plastic, used in wrapping or packaging. **3.** A thin flexible roll or sheet of material coated with a substance that is sensitive to light, used to make photographs. **4.** A movie, especially one that is recorded on film. ❖ *v.* **filmed, filming, films** —*tr.* **1.** To cover with or as if with a film. **2.** To record on film or video using a movie camera: *film a rocket launch; film a scene from a ballet.* —*intr.* **1.** To become coated or obscured with or as if with a film: *My glasses filmed over when I came in from the cold.* **2.** To make or shoot scenes for a movie.

filmmaker (fĭlm′mā′kər) *n.* A person who directs or produces movies.

filmstrip (fĭlm′strĭp′) *n.* A length of film containing a series of still images prepared for projecting onto a screen or blank wall.

filmy (fĭl′mē) *adj.* **filmier, filmiest 1.** Resembling film in thinness or translucence; gauzy: *filmy curtains.* **2.** Covered with a film: *filmy eyes.* —**film′i·ly** *adv.* —**film′i·ness** *n.*

filo (fē′lō *or* fī′lō) *n.* Variant of **phyllo**.

filter (fĭl′tər) *n.* **1.** A device that strains solid particles from a liquid or gas passing through it. **2.** Paper, sand, screening, charcoal, felt, or other porous material used in such a device. **3.** A device that allows certain frequencies of waves to pass and blocks the passage of others. For example, filters on photographic lenses allow only certain colors of light to enter the camera. **4.** A computer program that blocks access to certain kinds of information: *The filter blocks access to websites that use obscenities.* ❖ *v.* **filtered, filtering, filters** —*tr.* **1.** To pass (a liquid or gas) through a filter: *filter water for drinking.* **2.** To remove by passing through a filter: *The screen filters leaves from the water.* **3.** To use a data filter to block access to: *a program that filters spam.* —*intr.* **1.** To flow through or as if through a filter: *Light filtered through the blinds.* **2.** To come or go gradually and in small groups: *The audience*

filtered out after the movie. The students filtered in to the gymnasium.

filth (fĭlth) *n.* **1.** Foul or dirty matter or refuse. **2.** Something, such as language, considered obscene or immoral.

filthy (fĭl′thē) *adj.* **filthier, filthiest 1.** Covered or smeared with filth; disgustingly dirty: *filthy streets strewn with litter.* See Synonyms at **dirty.** **2.** Obscene or offensive: *filthy language.* —**filth′i·ly** *adv.* —**filth′i·ness** *n.*

filtrate (fĭl′trāt′) *tr. & intr.v.* **filtrated, filtrating, filtrates** To put or go through a filter. ❖ *n.* A liquid or another material that has passed through a filter.

filtration (fĭl-trā′shən) *n.* The act or process of filtering.

fin (fĭn) *n.* **1.** One of the movable parts that extends from the body of a fish or other aquatic animal and is used for propelling, steering, and balancing the body in water. **2.** Something shaped or used like a fin, as the tail of an aircraft that keeps it stable in flight. **3.** A rubber or plastic covering for the foot having a flat flexible extension, used in swimming and certain other water sports.

finagle (fə-nā′gəl) *v.* **finagled, finagling, finagles** *Informal* —*tr.* **1.** To get or achieve by indirect, usually deceitful methods: *finagle free tickets to the museum.* **2.** To cheat or swindle: *The dishonest stockbrokers finagled their clients out of millions.* —*intr.* To use crafty or deceitful methods. —**fi·na′gler** *n.*

final (fī′nəl) *adj.* **1.** Forming or occurring at the end; last: *final preparations before leaving on a trip; the exciting final moments of a game.* **2.** Not to be reconsidered or changed; conclusive: *The judge's decision is final.* ❖ *n.* **1.** The last or one of the last in a series of contests: *the finals of a spelling bee.* **2.** The last examination of an academic course: *Our final covered a whole year's work.*

finale (fə-nǎl′ē *or* fə-nä′lē) *n.* The concluding part, especially of a musical composition.

finalist (fī′nə-lĭst) *n.* A contestant in the final session of a competition.

finality (fī-nǎl′ĭ-tē *or* fə-nǎl′ĭ-tē) *n., pl.* **finalities** The fact or condition of being final: *a decision given with finality; the finality of leaving.*

finalize (fī′nə-līz′) *tr.v.* **finalized, finalizing, finalizes** To put into final form; complete or conclude: *finalize travel plans; finalize an agreement.* —**fi′nal·i·za′tion** (fī′-nə-lĭ-zā′shən) *n.* —**fi′nal·iz′er** *n.*

finally (fī′nə-lē) *adv.* **1.** At last; at the end: *After much delay, the taxi finally arrived.* **2.** Decisively; with finality: *That problem has been disposed of finally.*

finance (fə-nǎns′ *or* fī′nǎns′) *n.* **1.** The management of money, banking, investments, and credit: *A banker is a specialist in matters of finance.* **2.** **finances** Monetary resources; funds: *My finances were getting low.* ❖ *tr.v.* **financed, financing, finances** To provide or raise funds or capital for: *We financed our new car with a bank loan.*

financial (fə-nǎn′shəl *or* fī-nǎn′shəl) *adj.* Relating to or involving finance, finances, or financiers: *The treasurer is responsible for the financial affairs of our club.* —**fi·nan′cial·ly** *adv.*

financier (fĭn′ən-sîr′ *or* fə-nǎn′sîr′) *n.* A person who engages in investing or in raising large amounts of money.

finch (fĭnch) *n.* Any of various songbirds having a short thick bill used for cracking seeds.

find (fīnd) *tr.v.* **found** (found), **finding, finds 1.** To come upon, often by accident: *I found a quarter on the sidewalk.* **2a.** To come upon or discover by searching or making an effort: *At last I found my glasses. The plumber found the leak in the pipe.* **b.** To discover or ascertain through observation, experience, or study: *Can you find the solution to these problems?* **3.** To perceive to be after observation or experience: *found the book entertaining.* **4.** To recover the use of; regain: *I found my voice and shouted for help.* **5.** To succeed in reaching; arrive at: *The arrow found its mark.* **6.** To obtain or acquire by effort: *find the money to make the trip.* **7.** To decide on and make a declaration about: *The jury found the accused innocent of all charges.* **8.** To furnish; supply: *We can find a bed for you in the house tonight.* **9.** To perceive (oneself) to be in a specific location or condition: *The lost hikers found themselves in difficulty.* ❖ *n.* Something that is found, especially an unexpectedly valuable discovery: *news of oil finds in Alaska.* ◆ **find out 1.** To discover (something), as through examination or inquiry: *I found out when she's arriving.* **2.** To detect the true nature or character of: *The imposter was soon found out.*

finder (fīn′dər) *n.* **1.** A person who finds something. **2.** A device, usually an extra lens or telescope, used to help locate an object or area for a camera or large telescope.

fin-de-siècle (făn′də-sē-ĕk′lə) *adj.* Relating to or characteristic of the last part of the 1800s, especially with reference to its artistic climate of decadence and sophistication.

WORD HISTORY Fin-de-siècle comes from a French phrase meaning "end of the century."

finding (fīn′dĭng) *n.* **1.** Something that has been found: *The tomb was a great finding for the archaeologist.* **2.** A conclusion reached after an examination or investigation: *one of the findings in the report about the accident.*

fine¹ (fīn) *adj.* **finer, finest 1.** Of superior quality, skill, or appearance: *a fine day; a fine performance.* **2.** Very small in size, weight, or thickness: *fine paper.* **3.** Free from impurities: *a fine metal.* **4.** Very sharp; keen: *a fine point on a pencil.* **5.** Very thin; slender: *fine hair.* **6.** Showing delicate and careful artistry: *a fine painting; fine china.* **7.** Consisting of small particles; not coarse: *fine dust; the fine spray of a garden hose.* **8.** Subtle or precise: *the fine differences between a rabbit and a hare.* **9.** Characterized by refinement or elegance: *fine manners.* **10.** Being in a state of good health; quite well; *I'm fine, thank you.* **11.** Satisfactory; acceptable: *It's fine if you want to do it that way instead.* ❖ *adv.* **finer, finest** *Informal* **1.** In small pieces or parts: *Chop the onions fine.* **2.** Very well; splendidly: *The two dogs are getting along fine.* —**fine′ness** *n.*

fine² (fīn) *n.* A sum of money imposed as a penalty for an offense: *a $40 fine for parking too close to an intersection.* ❖ *tr.v.* **fined, fining, fines** To impose a fine on: *fine a borrower who doesn't return library books.*

WORD HISTORY Both **fine¹** and **fine²** were spelled *fin* in Middle English and ultimately come from Latin *finis,* meaning "end." **Fine²** included developments in Old French where the meaning "end of a legal case, settlement" arose.

fine art *n.* often **fine arts** Any of the art forms, such as painting, sculpture, and music, that are used to create works intended for beauty rather than utility.

fine-drawn (fīn′drôn′) *adj.* **1.** Drawn out to a slender threadlike state: *fine-drawn wire.* **2.** Subtly or precisely fashioned: *a fine-drawn analysis.*

fine-grained (fīn′grānd′) *adj.* **1.** Having a fine, smooth, even grain: *a bookshelf made from fine-grained wood.* **2.** Slightly or subtly different: *a fine-grained distinction.*

finely (fīn′lē) *adv.* **1.** In a fine manner; splendidly: *a finely groomed horse.* **2.** To a small point; discriminatingly. **3.** In small pieces or parts: *finely chopped nuts.*

fine print *n.* The part of a document, especially a contract, containing qualifications or restrictions in small type or obscure language.

finery (fī′nə-rē) *n., pl.* **fineries** Elaborate adornment, especially fine clothing and accessories: *a portrait of the captain in naval finery.*

finesse (fə-nĕs′) *n.* **1.** Refinement and delicacy of performance, execution, or artisanship: *the finesse of an experienced glassblower.* **2.** Subtle handling of a situation; tact and skill: *the lawyer's finesse in forging an agreement between the partners.* ❖ *tr.v.* **finessed, finessing, finesses** To accomplish or handle with finesse.

finger (fĭng′gər) *n.* **1.** One of the five parts that extend outward from the palm of the hand, especially one other than the thumb. **2.** The part of a glove that covers a finger. **3.** Something, such as an oblong peninsula, that resembles a finger: *a finger of land extending into the ocean.* **4.** The length or width of a finger: *Add about two fingers of juice.* ❖ *tr.v.* **fingered, fingering, fingers 1.** To handle or feel with the fingers; touch: *stooped to finger the dry soil.* **2.** To play (a musical instrument) by using the fingers in a particular way. **3.** *Informal* To inform on; point out as responsible: *finger a thief for the police.* ◆ **keep (one's) fingers crossed** To hope for a successful or advantageous outcome: *I'm keeping my fingers crossed until our team has won the game.* **put (one's) finger on** To remember; recall: *I couldn't put my finger on his name.*

fingerboard (fĭng′gər-bôrd′) *n.* A strip of wood on the neck of a stringed instrument against which the strings are pressed in playing.

finger hole *n.* **1.** Any of the holes on a wind instrument that cause a change in pitch when covered by a finger. **2.** A hole or opening for a finger, as on a bowling ball.

fingering (fĭng′gər-ĭng) *n.* **1.** The technique used in playing a musical instrument with the fingers: *The fingering for the flute is different from that for the clarinet.* **2.** The symbols on a musical score that show which fingers are to be used in playing.

fingerling (fĭng′gər-lĭng) *n.* **1.** A young fish, especially one less than a year old and about the size of a human finger. **2.** A long, thin potato shaped like a finger.

fingernail (fĭng′gər-nāl′) *n.* The thin layer of horny transparent material that covers the back of the tip of each finger.

finger painting *n.* **1.** The technique of painting by applying color to paper with the fingers. **2.** A painting made with this technique.

fingerprint (fĭng′gər-prĭnt′) *n.* **1.** A mark left on a surface by a person's fingertip: *Why are there dirty fingerprints all over this towel?* **2.** An image of the ridges on a person's fingertip made by putting ink on the fingertip and pressing it against a surface or by using a digital scanning device: *The police obtained the suspect's fingerprints.* ❖ *tr.v.* **fingerprinted, fingerprinting, fingerprints** To take the fingerprints of (a person).

fingertip (fĭng′gər-tĭp′) *n.* The extreme tip or end of a finger. ◆ **at (one's) fingertips** Ready or instantly available: *The Internet puts a vast amount of information at your fingertips.*

finicky (fĭn′ĭ-kē) *adj.* Very fussy; fastidious: *finicky about certain food.*

finis (fĭn′ĭs *or* fē-nē′) *n.* The end; the conclusion.

finish (fĭn′ĭsh) *v.* **finished, finishing, finishes** —*tr.* **1a.** To stop (doing an activity or task) after reaching the point at which there is nothing left to do: *Once we finish raking the leaves, we can play soccer.* **b.** To bring to a desired or required state: *took a year off to finish my novel.* See Synonyms at **complete. 2.** To arrive at or attain the end of: *finish a race.* **3.** To consume all of; use up: *finish a bottle of ketchup.* **4.** To give (a surface) a desired texture: *finish a floor with clear varnish.* —*intr.* **1.** To come to an end; stop: *Call me when the washing machine finishes.* **2.** To reach the end of a task, course, or relationship: *The runner finished well ahead of the pack.* ❖ *n.* **1.** The conclusion of something; the end: *The finish of the play was exciting.* **2a.** The surface or texture produced by preparing or coating something: *a shiny finish to the waxed floor.* **b.** The material used in surfacing or finishing something: *Paint is a good finish for wood.* **3.** Completeness, refinement, or smoothness of execution; polish: *The musicians lacked finish.* —**fin′ish·er** *n.*

finished (fĭn′ĭsht) *adj.* **1.** Brought to a state of completion: *a finished painting.* **2.** In a state of having completed something: *I'm finished with the chores.* **3.** Highly skilled or accomplished: *a finished actor.* **4.** Having no more use, value, or potential; washed-up: *Because of her injury, she is finished as a figure skater.*

finite (fī′nīt′) *adj.* **1.** Having bounds; limited: *a finite list of choices.* **2a.** That can be reached by counting: *The number of whole numbers between 1 and 100 is finite.* **b.** Neither infinite nor infinitesimal: *a finite sum; a finite line segment.* **3.** Relating to any of the forms of a verb that distinguish categories such as person, number, and tense, as the verb *sees* in *She sees the sign.* Every complete clause contains at least one finite verb. —**fi′nite·ly** *adv.*

Finn (fĭn) *n.* A native or inhabitant of Finland.

finnan haddie (fĭn′ən hăd′ē) *n.* Smoked haddock.

finned (fĭnd) *adj.* Having a fin or fins: *a finned whale.*

Finnish (fĭn′ĭsh) *adj.* Relating to Finland or its people, language, or culture. ❖ *n.* The language of the Finns.

fiord (fyôrd) *n.* Variant of **fjord.**

fir (fûr) *n.* **1.** Any of various evergreen trees having flat needles and bearing cones. **2.** The wood of such a tree.

fire (fīr) *n.* **1.** The flame, light, and heat given off when something is burning: *The fire was bright enough to read by.* **2.** Something that is burning, especially a pile of burning fuel, such as wood: *We started a fire in the fireplace.* **3.** Burning intensity of feeling; ardor: *The veterans played with the fire of rookies.* **4.** The discharge of firearms: *heard the fire of cannon.* ❖ *v.* **fired, firing, fires** —*tr.* **1.** To cause to burn; ignite: *A match fired this pile of leaves.* **2.** To maintain or fuel a fire in: *fire a furnace with oil.* **3.** To bake in a kiln: *fire clay pots to harden them.* **4a.** To arouse or excite (an emotion, for example): *The book fired my interest in science.* **b.** To make (someone) enthusiastic or excited: *The players were all fired up before the big game.* **5.** To discharge (a firearm) or launch (a missile): *fire a cannon; fire a rocket.* **6.** *Informal* To hurl with force and speed: *fire a fast ball across the plate.* **7.** *Informal* To discharge from a job; dismiss: *The company fired several workers today.* —*intr.* **1.** To shoot a weapon: *The soldiers fired into the air as a warning.* **2.** To ignite fuel, as in an engine: *The car motor will not fire properly when it's wet.* ◆ **fire up** To start up (an engine, for example). **on fire 1.** Burning; ablaze. **2.** Filled with enthusiasm or excitement: *The team was on*

fire after tying the game. **under fire** Under attack: *The new regulation came under fire.*

fire alarm *n.* **1.** The signal, especially a loud noise, that warns of fire. **2.** A device, such as a siren, that sets off such a warning.

fire ant *n.* Any of various ants that build large mounds and can inflict a painful burning sting, especially a species that is native to South America and is now present in the southern United States.

firearm (fīr′ärm′) *n.* A weapon, especially a pistol or rifle, that uses an explosive charge to propel a projectile.

fireball (fīr′bôl′) *n.* **1.** Something that resembles a burning ball, such as a ball of lightning. **2.** The hot, brightly glowing cloud of dust and gases formed by a nuclear explosion. **3.** A very bright meteor.

fireboat (fīr′bōt′) *n.* A boat equipped to put out fires in harbors and on ships.

firebomb (fīr′bŏm′) *n.* A bomb used to start a fire. ❖ *tr.v.* **firebombed, firebombing, firebombs** To attack (a target) with a firebomb: *firebombed the palace.* —**fire′bomb′er** *n.*

firebrand (fīr′brănd′) *n.* **1.** A person who stirs up trouble or kindles a revolt. **2.** A piece of burning wood.

firebreak (fīr′brāk′) *n.* A strip of land that has been cleared, plowed, or planted with vegetation that is resistant to fire in order to prevent a fire from spreading.

firebug (fīr′bŭg′) *n.* *Informal* A person who commits arson; an arsonist.

firecracker (fīr′krăk′ər) *n.* A small explosive charge and a fuse in a heavy paper casing, exploded to make noise, as at celebrations.

firedamp (fīr′dămp′) *n.* A gas that occurs naturally in coal mines and forms a dangerously explosive mixture with air.

fire drill *n.* An exercise in the use of firefighting equipment or the evacuation of a building in case of a fire.

fire engine *n.* Any of various large motor vehicles that carry firefighters and equipment to a fire.

fire escape *n.* A metal stairway or ladder attached to the outside of a building and used as an emergency exit in case of a fire.

fire extinguisher *n.* A portable container filled with chemicals to spray on a small fire to put it out.

firefight (fīr′fīt′) *n.* An exchange of gunfire, as between infantry units.

firefighter also **fire fighter** (fīr′fī′tər) *n.* A member of a fire department who fights fires. —**fire′fight′ing** *n.*

firefly (fīr′flī′) *n.* Any of various beetles that fly at night and give off a flashing light from the tip of the abdomen; a lightning bug.

firehouse (fīr′hous′) *n.* A fire station.

fire hydrant *n.* A large upright pipe with a nozzle for drawing water from a water main.

firelight (fīr′līt′) *n.* The light from a fire, as in a fireplace.

fireman (fīr′mən) *n.* **1.** A firefighter. **2.** A man who tends fires, as in a steam engine; a stoker. **3.** An enlisted man in the US Navy engaged in the operation of engineering machinery.

fireplace (fīr′plās′) *n.* **1.** An open recess in a room for holding a fire at the base of a chimney; a hearth. **2.** A structure, usually of stone or brick, for holding a fire outdoors.

fireplug (fīr′plŭg′) *n.* A fire hydrant.

firepower (fīr′pou′ər) *n.* **1.** The capacity, as of a weapon, military unit, or position, for delivering fire. **2.** The ability to deliver fire against an enemy in combat.

fireproof (fîr′proof′) *adj.* Made of material that is impervious or resistant to fire: *Many fireproof buildings are made of concrete.* ❖ *tr.v.* **fireproofed, fireproofing, fireproofs** To make fireproof.

fireside (fîr′sîd′) *n.* **1.** The area surrounding a fireplace or hearth: *We sat about the fireside and chatted.* **2.** A home.

fire station *n.* A building for firefighters and firefighting equipment.

firestorm (fîr′stôrm′) *n.* **1.** A fire of great size and intensity that generates and is fed by strong winds coming in from all sides: *the firestorm that follows an atomic blast.* **2.** An intense or violent response: *a firestorm of criticism.*

fire tower *n.* A tower from which a lookout watches for fires, especially forest fires.

firetrap (fîr′trăp′) *n.* A building that can catch fire easily or is difficult to escape from in the event of fire.

fire truck *n.* A fire engine.

firewall (fîr′wôl′) *n.* **1.** A fireproof wall used as a barrier to prevent the spread of fire. **2.** A software program or hardware device that restricts communication between a private network or computer system and outside networks.

firewood (fîr′wŏod′) *n.* Wood used as fuel.

firework (fîr′wûrk′) *n.* **1.** An explosive device, often attached to a small rocket, set off to create bright lights and loud noises for amusement. **2. fireworks** A display of such devices.

firing line (fîr′ĭng) *n.* **1.** The line of positions from which gunfire is directed against a target. **2.** The foremost position in a pursuit or activity.

firing pin *n.* The part of the bolt of a firearm that strikes the primer and causes the charge of a projectile to explode.

firing squad *n.* **1.** A group of people designated to shoot a person condemned to death. **2.** A detachment of soldiers chosen to fire a salute at a military funeral.

firm¹ (fûrm) *adj.* **firmer, firmest 1.** Resistant to externally applied pressure: *a firm mattress; an athlete's firm muscles.* **2.** Securely fixed in place; not easily moved: *a firm fence post set in concrete.* **3.** Showing or having resolution or determination: *a firm voice; a firm belief.* **4.** Constant; steadfast: *a firm friendship.* **5.** Not subject to change; fixed and definite: *a firm price on the car.* **6.** Strong and sure: *a firm grip on the handlebars.* ❖ *tr. & intr.v.* **firmed, firming, firms** To make or become firm: *One must firm the dirt around newly potted plants. The gelatin firmed quickly.* ❖ *adv.* **firmer, firmest** Without wavering; resolutely: *stood firm.* —**firm′ly** *adv.* —**firm′ness** *n.*

firm² (fûrm) *n.* A business partnership of two or more people.

WORD HISTORY Firm¹ comes from Middle English *ferm,* which comes from Latin *firmus,* both meaning "strong, steady." Although **firm²** also ultimately comes from the same Latin word, it entered English from the Italian noun *firma* (meaning "business partnership") from the Italian verb *firmare,* meaning "to ratify by signature."

firmament (fûr′mə-mənt) *n.* The heavens; the sky.

first (fûrst) *n.* **1.** The ordinal number matching the number one in a series. **2.** A person or thing coming, occurring, or ranking before or above all others. **3.** The beginning; the outset: *At first he was afraid of the water, but now he enjoys swimming.* **4.** The transmission gear used to produce the lowest range of speeds in a motor vehicle. ❖ *adj.* **1.** Corresponding in order to the number one. **2.**

Coming before all others in order or location: *January is the first month of the year.* **3.** Ranking above all others, as in importance or quality: *first in her class.* **4.** Being highest in pitch or carrying the principal part: *first soprano; first trumpet.* **5.** Relating to the transmission gear used to produce the lowest range of speeds in a motor vehicle. **6.** Relating to or being a member of the US president's household: *first daughter Sasha Obama.* ❖ *adv.* **1.** Before or above all others: *Who will speak first?* **2.** For the first time: *When did you first meet the new neighbors?* **3.** Rather; preferably: *The musicians said they would quit first and not accept lower pay.* ◆ **first off** From the start; immediately: *First off, let me introduce myself.*

first aid *n.* Emergency care given to an injured or sick person before professional medical care is available. —**first′-aid′** *adj.*

first base *n.* **1.** In baseball, the base that must be touched first by a batter who has hit a fair ball, located to the right as one looks toward the pitcher from home plate. **2.** The position played by a first baseman. **3.** *Slang* The first step or stage toward completion or success: *The reform bill never got to first base.*

first baseman *n.* The baseball player defending the area near first base.

firstborn (fûrst′bôrn′) *adj.* First in order of birth; born first. ❖ *n.* The child in a family who is born first.

first class *n.* **1.** The first, highest, or best group in a system of classification. **2.** The best and most expensive class of accommodations on a train, ship, or airplane. ❖ *adv.* By means of first-class travel accommodations.

first-class (fûrst′klăs′) *adj.* **1.** Relating to the first, highest, or best group in a system of classification: *first-class mail; a first-class hotel.* **2.** Relating to the foremost excellence or highest quality; first-rate: *a first-class poet.*

first-degree burn (fûrst′dĭ-grē′) *n.* A mild burn that produces redness of the skin.

first down *n.* In football: **a.** The first in the series of four downs in which an offensive team must advance ten yards to retain possession of the ball. **b.** A gain of ten or more yards entitling the offensive team to a new series of downs.

first-generation (fûrst′jĕn′ə-rā′shən) *adj.* **1.** Relating to an immigrant or a child of an immigrant. **2.** Relating to a member of the first generation of a family to do something or achieve something: *scholarships for first-generation college students; a first-generation millionaire.* **3.** Relating to or being the first form or version of a product or technology: *first-generation computer software; first-generation antidepressants.*

firsthand (fûrst′hănd′) *adj.* Received from the original source: *firsthand information.* —**first′hand′** *adv.*

first lady *n.* **1.** often **First Lady** The wife or hostess of the chief executive of a country, state, or city. **2.** The foremost woman of a specified group or profession: *the first lady of modern dance.*

first lieutenant *n.* An officer in the US Army, Air Force, or Marine Corps ranking above a second lieutenant and below a captain.

firstly (fûrst′lē) *adv.* In the first place; to begin with.

First Nation *n.* An organized American Indian group or community in Canada, especially any of the bands officially recognized by the Canadian government.

first person *n.* **1.** A group of words or word forms, such as verbs and pronouns, that designate a speaker or writer referring to himself or herself, either alone or along with other people. *I* and *we* are pronouns in the first person. **2.** The style of writing in which forms in the first person are used: *a novel written in the first person.*

first-rate (fûrst′rāt′) *adj.* Foremost in quality, rank, or importance: *a first-rate hotel; a first-rate mechanic.*

first responder *n.* A police officer, firefighter, or other person trained in emergency medical procedures and prepared to move quickly to an accident or disaster to provide help.

first string *n.* A group of players that play regularly or start games for a sports team. —**first′-string′** *adj.*

First World War *n.* World War I.

firth (fûrth) *n.* A long narrow inlet of the sea.

fiscal (fĭs′kəl) *adj.* **1.** Relating to the treasury or finances of a government: *senators debating fiscal policies.* **2.** Relating to finance or finances: *The accountant is our fiscal agent.* —**fis′cal·ly** *adv.*

fiscal year *n.* A twelve-month period for which an organization plans the use of its funds.

fish (fĭsh) *n.*, *pl.* **fish** or **fishes** **1.** Any of numerous cold-blooded vertebrate animals that live in water, obtain oxygen through gills, and have fins. Most fish are covered with scales. **2.** The flesh of a fish used as food. ❖ *v.* **fished, fishing, fishes** —*intr.* **1.** To catch or try to catch fish. **2.** To try to find something by using the hands or fingers; grope: *I fished in my pocket for a quarter.* **3.** To try to get someone to say something one wants to hear by being indirect or sly: *He was only fishing for compliments when he mentioned his new skateboard.* —*tr.* **1a.** To catch or try to catch (fish): *to fish salmon.* **b.** To catch or try to catch fish in: *We fished the lake for several hours.* **2.** To remove or pull (something) from water or a container: *fish the keys out of the drawer.* ◆ **like a fish out of water** Completely unfamiliar with one's surroundings or activity.

fish and chips *pl.n.* Fried fillets of fish and French fries.

fisher (fĭsh′ər) *n.* **1.** A person who fishes. **2a.** A North American meat-eating mammal related to the mink and weasel, having thick dark-brown fur. **b.** The fur of this mammal.

fisherman (fĭsh′ər-mən) *n.* A man who fishes as an occupation or for sport.

fisherwoman (fĭsh′ər-wŏm′ən) *n.* A woman who fishes as an occupation or for sport.

fishery (fĭsh′ə-rē) *n.*, *pl.* **fisheries** **1.** The industry or occupation of catching, processing, and selling fish or other aquatic animals. **2.** A place where fish or other aquatic animals are caught: *the cod fisheries of the northwest Atlantic.* **3.** A hatchery for fish.

fish farm *n.* A commercial facility having tanks or ponds where fish are raised for food.

fish hawk *n.* The osprey.

fishhook (fĭsh′hŏok′) *n.* A barbed hook for catching fish.

fishing (fĭsh′ĭng) *n.* The act, occupation, or sport of catching fish.

fishing rod *n.* A rod of wood, steel, or fiberglass used with a line for catching fish.

fishmonger (fĭsh′mŏng′gər or fĭsh′mŭng′gər) *n.* Chiefly British A person who sells fish.

fishnet (fĭsh′nĕt′) *n.* **1.** Netting used to catch fish. **2.** **fishnets** Stockings made from a mesh fabric resembling a netting.

fishpond (fĭsh′pŏnd′) *n.* A pond containing or stocked with fish.

fish stick *n.* An oblong piece of breaded fish fillet.

fishtail (fĭsh′tāl′) *intr.v.* **fishtailed, fishtailing, fishtails** To swerve out of control from side to side. Used of the back end of a vehicle that is moving forward.

fishwife (fĭsh′wīf′) *n.*, *pl.* **fishwives** (fĭsh′wīvz′) **1.** A woman who sells fish. **2.** A woman regarded as coarse or abusive.

fishy (fĭsh′ē) *adj.* **fishier, fishiest 1.** Tasting, resembling, or smelling of fish. **2.** Cold or expressionless: *a fishy stare.* **3.** *Informal* Inspiring doubt or suspicion: *something fishy about that excuse.* —**fish′i·ness** *n.*

fission (fĭsh′ən) *n.* **1.** The act or process of splitting into parts. **2.** The splitting of the nucleus of an atom into two or more nuclei either spontaneously or because the nucleus has collided with a free-moving neutron. The splitting of a nucleus releases one or more neutrons and energy in the form of radiation. **3.** A reproductive process in which a single cell splits to form two independent cells that later grow to full size.

fissionable (fĭsh′ə-nə-bəl) *adj.* Capable of undergoing fission: *Uranium and plutonium are fissionable elements.*

fissure (fĭsh′ər) *n.* **1.** A long narrow crack or opening, as in the face of a rock. **2.** A groove or furrow that divides an organ, such as the brain, into lobes or parts.

fist (fĭst) *n.* The hand closed tightly with the fingers bent against the palm.

fistfight (fĭst′fīt′) *n.* A fight with the bare fists.

fistful (fĭst′fŏol′) *n.*, *pl.* **fistfuls** The amount a fist can hold.

fisticuffs (fĭs′tĭ-kŭfs′) *pl.n.* **1.** A fistfight. **2.** The activity of fighting with the fists.

fistula (fĭs′chə-lə) *n.*, *pl.* **fistulas** or **fistulae** (fĭs′chə-lē′) An abnormal passageway that connects a hollow structure of the body to another hollow structure or to the surface, caused by a disease or wound.

fit¹ (fĭt) *v.* **fitted** or **fit, fitted, fitting, fits** —*tr.* **1.** To be the proper size and shape for: *These shoes fit me.* **2.** To cause to be the proper size and shape: *The tailor fitted the new pants perfectly.* **3.** To be appropriate for or suitable to: *listened to music that fit her mood.* **4.** To equip or provide: *She fitted the car with new tires.* **5.** To provide a place or time for: *He fit all of his books in one bag.* —*intr.* **1.** To be the proper size and shape: *If the key fits, open the door.* **2.** To be suited; agree; belong: *Their happy mood fit in with the joyous occasion.* ❖ *adj.* **fitter, fittest 1.** Suited, adapted, or acceptable for a given purpose or circumstance: *The spoiled food was not fit to eat.* **2.** Appropriate; proper: *Do as you see fit.* **3.** Physically sound; healthy: *Fresh air and exercise help keep people fit.* ❖ *n.* The state, quality, or way of being fitted: *a perfect fit.* **2.** The way something fits: *The fit of the sweater was too tight.*

fit² (fĭt) *n.* **1.** A seizure or convulsion, especially one caused by epilepsy. **2.** A sudden appearance of coughing, sneezing, laughing, or a similar physical outburst: *I had a fit of coughing from the smoke.* **3.** A sudden outbreak of emotion or activity: *a fit of jealousy; a fit of organizing.* ◆ **by fits and starts** or **in fits and starts** With irregular intervals of action and inaction; intermittently: *slept in fits and starts.*

WORD HISTORY Fit¹ comes from Middle English *fitten*, meaning "to be proper or fitting." **Fit²** comes from Middle English *fit* (meaning "hardship"), which probably comes from Old English *fitt*, meaning "struggle."

fitful (fĭt′fəl) *adj.* Occurring in or marked by intermittent bursts, as of activity; irregular: *fitful coughing; fitful sleep.* —**fit′ful·ly** *adv.* —**fit′ful·ness** *n.*

fitness (fĭt′nĭs) *n*. The state or condition of being physically fit, especially as the result of exercise and proper nutrition.

fitting (fĭt′ĭng) *adj*. Being in keeping with a situation; appropriate: *a fitting remark*. ❖ *n*. **1.** The act of trying on clothes whose fit is being adjusted. **2.** A small part for a machine or mechanical device: *a box of nuts, washers, and other fittings*.

five (fīv) *n*. **1.** The number, written 5, that is equal to 4 + 1. **2.** The fifth in a set or sequence. **3.** A five-dollar bill.

five-and-ten (fīv′ən-tĕn′) *n*. A store selling a wide variety of inexpensive articles.

Five Nations *pl.n*. The Iroquois confederacy as it originally existed, consisting of the Cayuga, Mohawk, Oneida, Onondaga, and Seneca peoples.

fix (fĭks) *tr.v*. **fixed, fixing, fixes 1a.** To correct or set right: *fixed the mistakes in the manuscript*. **b.** To restore to proper condition or working order; repair: *fixed a flat tire*. **2.** To make ready; prepare: *Who's fixing dinner tonight?* **3.** To place securely; make stable or firm: *fix a post in the ground*. **4.** To direct steadily: *We fixed our eyes on the screen*. **5.** To establish definitely; specify: *fix a time for the meeting; fix a price on a house*. **6.** To attribute; assign: *A witness fixed the blame on the careless driver*. **7.** To convert (nitrogen or carbon) into compounds that can be used by an organism: *bacteria that fix atmospheric nitrogen*. **8.** To treat (a photographic image) with a chemical that prevents it from fading or changing color. **9.** *Informal* To take revenge upon (someone); get even with. **10.** *Informal* To influence the outcome of by unlawful means: *fix a horse race*. ❖ *n*. **1.** The act of adjusting, correcting, or repairing: *His fix of the computer problem took an hour*. **2.** The position, as of a ship or aircraft, determined by visual observations or by radio signals: *get a fix on a disabled ship*. **3.** A difficult or embarrassing situation; a predicament: *We lost our oars and were in a fix out in the middle of the lake*. **4.** *Slang* An amount of something that is craved, especially an intravenous injection of a narcotic. ◆ **fix up 1.** To improve the appearance or condition of: *They fixed up the old house with a fresh coat of paint*. **2.** To supply; provide: *We fixed up a bed for our guests*. —**fix′a·ble** *adj*. —**fix·er** *n*.

USAGE The phrase *fixing to* is used in the South to mean "on the verge of or in preparation for (doing a given thing)." The phrase can refer only to events that immediately follow the point in time that the speaker is referring to. You cannot say *I'm fixing to go to college in a few years*, but you would say *I'm fixing to leave in a few minutes*.

fixate (fĭk′sāt′) *v*. **fixated, fixating, fixates** — *tr*. **1.** To cause (a person or animal) to look at or pay attention to something steadily: *The cat was fixated on the bird outside the window*. **2.** To command the attention of exclusively or repeatedly; preoccupy obsessively: *The reporters were fixated by the scandal*. — *intr*. To focus the eyes or attention: *He always fixates on problems instead of solutions*.

fixation (fĭk-sā′shən) *n*. **1.** The act or process of fixing something chemically: *the fixation of nitrogen by bacteria*. **2.** An obsessive preoccupation or emotional attachment: *The child had a fixation on a particular blanket*.

fixative (fĭk′sə-tĭv) *n*. A substance used to treat something and make it permanent or resistant to change: *Fixative keeps chalk drawings from smudging*.

fixed (fĭkst) *adj*. **1.** Firmly in position; stationary: *a row of fixed desks*. **2.** Not subject to change or variation; con-

stant: *living on a fixed income*. **3.** Firmly held; steady: *a fixed stare; old and fixed ideas*. **4.** Illegally prearranged as to outcome: *a fixed election*.

fixed star *n*. A star that appears to remain in the same position in relation to other celestial objects, in contrast to the planets and celestial objects whose changes in position are readily observable by telescope or by the unaided eye. All stars except the sun are considered fixed stars.

fixer-upper (fĭk′sər-ŭp′ər) *n*. A house or other dwelling that is badly in need of repair, usually for sale at a low price.

fixings (fĭk′sĭngz) *pl.n*. *Informal* Side dishes and condiments accompanying the main dish at a meal; trimmings: *a Thanksgiving dinner with all the fixings*.

fixture (fĭks′chər) *n*. **1.** Something that is installed in a permanent location: *a plumbing fixture*. **2.** A person or thing that stays or seems to stay in one place: *After 30 years of teaching, he seems like a fixture at the high school*.

fizz (fĭz) *intr.v*. **fizzed, fizzing, fizzes** To make a hissing or bubbling sound: *Baking soda will fizz if you pour water on it*. ❖ *n*. **1.** A hissing or bubbling sound: *the fizz of soda*. **2.** Effervescence. —**fizz′y** *adj*.

fizzle (fĭz′əl) *intr.v*. **fizzled, fizzling, fizzles 1.** To make a hissing or sputtering sound: *The hot coals of our campfire fizzled in the rain*. **2.** *Informal* To fail or end weakly, especially after a hopeful beginning. ❖ *n*. *Informal* A failure.

fjord or **fiord** (fyôrd) *n*. A long narrow inlet from the sea between steep slopes.

fl. An abbreviation of: **1.** fluid. **2.** flourished.

flab (flăb) *n*. Soft fatty body tissue.

flabbergast (flăb′ər-găst′) *tr.v*. **flabbergasted, flabbergasting, flabbergasts** To cause to be overcome with astonishment; astound: *The news flabbergasted us*.

flabby (flăb′ē) *adj*. **flabbier, flabbiest 1.** Soft and hanging loosely in folds: *a flabby belly*. **2.** Fleshy and soft, as though slightly overweight: *flabby around the waist*. —**flab′bi·ness** *n*.

flaccid (flăs′ĭd *or* flăk′sĭd) *adj*. **1.** Lacking firmness; hanging limply: *flaccid muscles*. **2.** Lacking force or vigor: *a flaccid acting performance*. —**flac·cid′i·ty** *n*. —**flac′cid·ly** *adv*.

flag¹ (flăg) *n*. **1.** A piece of cloth of a particular color or design, used as a symbol for a nation, an emblem for a monarch or organization, or a signal: *flags of member nations flying at the United Nations*. **2.** A marking device attached to an object to make it more noticeable: *placed a flag on each page that had a revision*. ❖ *tr.v*. **flagged, flagging, flags 1.** To signal with or as if with a flag: *flagged a motorist to get help*. **2.** To signal to stop: *flag down a passing car*.

flag² (flăg) *intr.v*. **flagged, flagging, flags** To lose vigor or strength; weaken: *Our spirits flagged when we saw how much we had to do*.

WORD HISTORY The origin of **flag¹** is unknown. **Flag²** may be of Scandinavian origin.

Flag Day *n*. June 14, observed in commemoration of the adoption in 1777 of the official US flag.

flagellate (flăj′ə-lāt′) *tr.v*. **flagellated, flagellating, flagellates** To whip or flog. ❖ *adj*. (flăj′ə-lĭt *or* flăj′ə-lāt′) **1.** Having a flagellum, as certain one-celled organisms. **2.** Resembling a flagellum. ❖ *n*. (flăj′ə-lĭt *or* flăj′ə-lāt′) A one-celled organism, such as a euglena, having one or more flagella used for moving through the water and for obtaining food. —**flag′el·la′tion** *n*.

flagellum (flə-jĕl′əm) *n*., *pl*. **flagella** (flə-jĕl′ə) A slender part extending from certain cells or single-celled organisms that moves rapidly back and forth to produce movement.

flagger (flăg′ər) *n.* A person who holds a sign or a flag to direct traffic, especially around a construction project.

flagman (flăg′mən) *n.* A man employed as a flagger.

flagon (flăg′ən) *n.* **1.** A large container for liquids, usually of metal or pottery, having a handle, a spout, and often a lid. **2.** The amount of liquid that such a container can hold.

flagpole (flăg′pōl′) *n.* A pole on which a flag is raised.

flagrant (flā′grənt) *adj.* Conspicuously offensive; notorious or scandalous: *a flagrant misuse of public funds.* —**fla′grant·ly** *adv.*

flagship (flăg′shĭp′) *n.* A ship that carries a fleet or squadron commander and bears the commander's flag.

flagstaff (flăg′stăf′) *n.* A flagpole.

flagstone (flăg′stōn′) *n.* A flat stone slab used as a paving material.

flail (flāl) *n.* A tool for threshing grain by hand, having a long wooden handle and a shorter and heavier free-swinging stick attached to its end. ❖ *v.* **flailed, flailing, flails** —*tr.* **1.** To beat or strike vigorously: *He flailed the horse with the reins.* **2.** To wave or swing vigorously: *I flailed my arms to get their attention.* —*intr.* **1.** To move vigorously or erratically; thrash about: *The swimmer flailed about until the lifeguard arrived.* **2.** To hit about or lash out violently: *a boxer flailing away in the center of the ring.* **3.** To make a vigorous but unproductive effort: *flailed about in search of a better solution.*

flair (flâr) *n.* A natural talent or aptitude; a knack: *a flair for imitating voices.*

flak (flăk) *n.* **1a.** Antiaircraft artillery. **b.** The bursting shells fired from such artillery: *many planes hit by flak.* **2.** *Informal* Criticism; opposition: *Our plan got a lot of flak.*

flake (flāk) *n.* **1.** A flat thin piece or layer; a chip: *Large flakes of paint had fallen on the floor.* **2.** A snowflake. **3.** *Slang* A person who is somewhat eccentric. ❖ *intr.v.* **flaked, flaking, flakes** To come off in flakes: *The paint is flaking off the fence.*

flaky (flā′kē) *adj.* **flakier, flakiest** **1.** Forming or tending to form flakes or thin crisp fragments: *flaky crackers.* **2.** *Slang* Eccentric; odd. —**flak′i·ly** *adv.* —**flak′i·ness** *n.*

flamboyant (flăm-boi′ənt) *adj.* **1.** Exaggerated or showy in style or manner: *the wild gestures of the flamboyant performer.* **2.** Brilliant; vivid: *flamboyant colors.* —**flam·boy′ance, flam·boy′an·cy** *n.* —**flam·boy′ant·ly** *adv.*

flame (flām) *n.* **1.** The hot, glowing mixture of burning gases and tiny particles that arises from combustion. **2.** The condition of active blazing combustion: *burst into flame.* **3.** A burning or intense feeling; a passion: *a flame of enthusiasm.* **4.** *Informal* A sweetheart. ❖ *intr.v.* **flamed, flaming, flames** **1.** To burn brightly; blaze: *The logs flamed as I fanned them.* **2.** To flush; acquire color: *My cheeks flamed with embarrassment.* ◆ **flame out** To fail: *The business flamed out shortly after it opened.*

flamenco (flə-mĕng′kō) *n., pl.* **flamencos** **1.** A dance style of the Romani of Andalusia, characterized by forceful rhythms and the clicking of castanets. **2.** The guitar music for this dance style.

flamethrower (flăm′thrō′ər) *n.* A weapon that shoots out a steady stream of burning fuel.

flaming (flā′mĭng) *adj.* **1.** On fire; blazing: *flaming logs.* **2.** Resembling a flame in brilliance, color, or form: *flaming red and yellow autumn leaves.*

flamingo (flə-mĭng′gō) *n., pl.* **flamingos** or **flamingoes** Any of several long-legged, long-necked tropical wading birds having reddish or pinkish feathers and a large bill that curves downward.

flammable (flăm′ə-bəl) *adj.* Easily ignited and capable of burning rapidly: *Kerosene is flammable.*

flan (flăn *or* flän) *n.* **1.** A custard that is baked in a caramel-lined mold and served chilled with the caramel side up. **2.** A tart with a filling of custard, fruit, or cheese.

flange (flănj) *n.* A projecting rim or edge, as on a wheel or a pipe, used to strengthen an object, hold it in place, or attach it to something.

flank (flăngk) *n.* **1a.** The side of the body between the ribs and the hip. **b.** A cut of meat from this part of an animal. **2.** A side part: *The flank of the mountain rose steeply from the valley.* **3.** The right or left side of a military formation or a fort. ❖ *tr.v.* **flanked, flanking, flanks** **1.** To protect or guard the flank of. **2.** To attack or maneuver around the flank of: *flank an opposing force.* **3.** To occupy a place at the side of: *Two chairs flanked the fireplace.*

flanker (flăng′kər) *n.* **1.** A person or thing that protects a flank. **2.** In football, a halfback stationed to the side of the linemen, used chiefly as a pass receiver.

flannel (flăn′əl) *n.* **1.** A soft woven cloth of wool or a blend of wool and cotton or synthetic material. **2. flannels** Pants and other clothes made out of flannel. **3.** Flannelette.

flannelette (flăn′ə-lĕt′) *n.* Soft cotton flannel.

flap (flăp) *n.* **1.** A flat piece attached along one side of something: *the flap of an envelope.* **2.** A section of the rear edge of an aircraft wing that moves up and down in order to control the lift and drag. **3.** The sound or action of waving or fluttering: *the flap of a bird's wings.* **4.** *Informal* A state of disturbance or nervous excitement: *We all got into a flap when no one could find the car keys.* ❖ *v.* **flapped, flapping, flaps** —*tr.* **1.** To move (the wings or arms) up and down; beat. **2.** To cause to move with a waving or fluttering motion: *A brisk wind flapped the clothes on the line.* —*intr.* **1.** To wave the arms or wings up and down. **2.** To wave about while attached to something stationary; flutter: *A flag flapped softly in the breeze.*

flapjack (flăp′jăk′) *n.* A pancake.

flapper (flăp′ər) *n.* **1.** A broad part that flaps: *the flapper on an exhaust pipe.* **2.** A young woman of the 1920s who rebelled against conventional ideas of ladylike behavior and dress.

flare (flâr) *intr.v.* **flared, flaring, flares** **1.** To burn with a sudden or unsteady flame: *The candle flared briefly and went out.* **2.** To burst out or erupt: *Tempers flared during the tense meeting.* **3.** To spread outward in shape: *A horn flares at the end.* ❖ *n.* **1.** A brief wavering blaze of light. **2.** A device that produces a bright light for signaling or lighting. **3.** An outbreak, as of emotion or activity: *a flare of anger.* **4.** A shape or form that spreads out: *the flare of a trumpet.* **5.** In football, a quick pass to a running back heading toward the sideline.

flare-up (flâr′ŭp′) *n.* **1.** A sudden outbreak of flame or light. **2.** An outburst or eruption: *a flare-up of anger.* **3.** A recurrence of a disease or condition: *a flare-up of acne.*

flash (flăsh) *v.* **flashed, flashing, flashes** —*intr.* **1.** To give off a sudden bright light: *Bursts of fireworks flashed in the sky.* **2.** To be lighted on and off: *A lighthouse flashed in the distance.* **3.** To appear or occur suddenly: *an idea* *for a story flashed through my mind.* **4.** To move rapidly: *A shooting star flashed across the sky.* **5.** *Slang* To expose oneself in an indecent manner. —*tr.* **1.** To send forth suddenly or for an instant: *flash a light into a cave.* **2.** To make known or signal by flashing lights: *The yellow light flashed its warning.* **3.** To send (a message) at great speed: *flash a news bulletin to the world capitals.* **4.** To exhibit briefly: *flashed his badge.* **5.** To display ostentatiously; flaunt: *flashed her ring.* ❖ *n.* **1.** A short sudden display of light: *a flash of lightning.* **2.** A sudden brief burst: *a flash of insight.* **3.** A split second; an instant: *The twig burned up in a flash.* **4.** A brief important item of very current news: *The political website published news flashes about the election all day.* ◆ **flash in the pan** A person or thing that promises great success but fails. —**flash′er** *n.*

flashback (flăsh′băk′) *n.* **1.** The insertion of an earlier event into a story, play, or movie. **2.** A scene or an episode showing an earlier event that is inserted in a story, play, or movie. **3.** A recurring, vivid mental image of a past experience.

flashbulb (flăsh′bŭlb′) *n.* An electric bulb that produces a flash of light for taking photographs.

flash card *n.* One of a set of cards marked with words, numbers, or other symbols to be learned through drill.

flash drive *n.* A portable, thumb-sized data storage device that can be plugged into a computer component and uses flash memory.

flash flood *n.* A sudden violent flood after a heavy rain.

flashlight (flăsh′līt′) *n.* A portable electric light that is powered by batteries.

flash memory *n.* A type of computer memory that can be erased and rewritten and is smaller and lighter than a hard drive.

flash point *n.* **1.** The lowest temperature at which the vapor of a flammable liquid can be made to catch fire in air. **2.** The point at which something, such as a disagreement or quarrel, becomes an open conflict.

flashy (flăsh′ē) *adj.* **flashier, flashiest 1.** Creating a brief impression of brilliance; eye-catching: *the acrobat's flashy performance.* **2.** Cheap and showy; gaudy: *a flashy tie.* —**flash′i·ly** *adv.* —**flash′i·ness** *n.*

flask (flăsk) *n.* **1.** A small bottle with a flattened shape, made to fit in one's pocket. **2.** A rounded container with a long neck, used in laboratories.

flat¹ (flăt) *adj.* **flatter, flattest 1.** Having a smooth even surface; level: *flat land.* **2.** Having a broad surface and little thickness or depth: *a flat dish.* **3.** Extending or lying full length; horizontal: *flat on my back in bed.* **4.** Having lost air; deflated: *a flat tire.* **5.** Lacking interest or excitement; dull: *a flat performance.* **6.** Having lost effervescence or sparkle: *flat soda.* **7.** Complete; absolute: *a flat refusal to help.* **8.** Not changing; fixed: *The taxi charges a flat rate.* **9.** Not glossy; dull: *finished with a flat paint.* **10a.** Lower in musical pitch than is correct. **b.** Lower in pitch by a half step than a corresponding natural tone or key: *D flat.* ❖ *adv.* **1.** On or against a flat surface: *press dough flat.* **2.** Exactly: *He ran the race in 50 seconds flat.* **3.** Completely: *I bought a new cell phone, and now I'm flat broke.* **4.** Below the correct pitch: *Don't sing flat.* ❖ *n.* **1.** A flat surface or part: *the flat of my hand.* **2.** often **flats** An area of level low-lying ground: *dig clams in the mud flats.* **3.** A deflated tire: *The car has a flat.* **4.** A shoe with a flat heel. **5.** A shallow box or frame for growing seeds. **6a.** A musical note or tone that is a half step lower than a corresponding natural tone or key. **b.** A sign (♭) used to

indicate that a note is to be lowered by a half step. ❖ *tr. & intr.v.* **flatted, flatting, flats** To sing or play flat. —**flat′ly** *adv.* —**flat′ness** *n.*

flat² (flăt) *n.* An apartment usually on one floor of a building.

WORD HISTORY Flat¹ comes from Middle English *flat,* which comes from Old Norse *flatr,* both meaning "level, flat, even." **Flat²** comes from Old English *flet,* meaning "floor, dwelling."

flatbed (flăt′bĕd′) *n.* **1.** An open truck bed or trailer with no sides, used to carry large objects. **2.** A railroad flatcar. **3.** A wide, flat surface onto which documents or other materials are placed for printing or scanning.

flatboat (flăt′bōt′) *n.* A flatbottom barge for transporting freight in shallow rivers or canals.

flatbottom (flăt′bŏt′əm) or **flatbottomed** (flăt′bŏt′əmd) *adj.* Having a flat bottom: *a flatbottom boat.*

flatbread (flăt′brĕd′) *n.* Any of various breads that are made from usually unleavened dough and are baked in loaves that are flat and often round.

flatcar (flăt′kär′) *n.* A railroad car without sides or a roof, used for carrying bulky freight.

flatfish (flăt′fĭsh′) *n.* Any of numerous fishes, such as the flounder, halibut, or sole, that have a flattened body and both eyes on one side.

flat-footed (flăt′fŏŏt′ĭd) *adj.* **1.** Having a condition in which the arch of the foot is very low and most or all of the sole touches the ground. **2.** Unable to react quickly; unprepared: *The question caught me flat-footed.* —**flat′-foot′ed·ness** *n.*

Flathead (flăt′hĕd′) *n., pl.* **Flathead** or **Flatheads 1.** A member of a Native American people living in western Montana and northern Idaho. **2.** The Salishan language of the Flathead.

flatiron (flăt′ī′ərn) *n.* An iron for pressing clothes.

flatland (flăt′lănd′) *n.* **1.** Land that has almost no hills or valleys. **2.** **flatlands** A geographic area made up chiefly of flatland.

flatline (flăt′līn′) *intr.v.* **flatlined, flatlining, flatlines 1.** To show a horizontal line on a monitor that indicates electrical activity of the heart or the brain. **2.** *Informal* To die. **3.** To be in an unchanging condition: *Participation in civic activities has flatlined in recent years.*

flat-screen (flăt′skrēn′) *adj.* Relating to or being a thin computer monitor or television, such as a liquid-crystal display.

flatten (flăt′n) *v.* **flattened, flattening, flattens** —*tr.* **1.** To make flat or flatter: *A rolling pin flattens dough.* **2.** To knock down; lay low: *The wind flattened the old shed.* —*intr.* To become flat or flatter: *All the wrinkles flattened out when the shirt was ironed.* —**flat′ten·er** *n.*

flatter (flăt′ər) *v.* **flattered, flattering, flatters** —*tr.* **1.** To compliment too much or praise insincerely, especially in order to win favor. **2.** To please or gratify: *The award flattered me.* **3.** To portray or show favorably: *This photograph flatters her.* —*intr.* To use flattery. —**flat′ter·er** *n.*

flattery (flăt′ə-rē) *n., pl.* **flatteries** Excessive or insincere praise.

flattop (flăt′tŏp′) *n. Informal* **1.** An aircraft carrier. **2.** A short haircut in which the hair is brushed straight up and cut flat across the top of the head.

flatulent (flăch′ə-lənt) *adj.* Having excessive gas in the digestive tract. —**flat′u·lence** *n.*

flatware (flăt′wâr′) *n.* **1.** Tableware that is fairly flat, as plates. **2.** Table utensils such as knives, forks, and spoons.

flatworm (flăt′wûrm′) *n.* Any of various worms, such as a tapeworm or planarian, having a flattened body and living in water or as a parasite in a human or other animal.

flaunt (flônt) *tr.v.* **flaunted, flaunting, flaunts** To display (something) in order to impress others: *flaunt one's knowledge.* —**flaunt′ing·ly** *adv.*

USAGE The verbs **flaunt** and **flout** sound similar but have different meanings. *Flaunt* means "to display in a proud or showy manner": *They flaunted their wealth by driving an expensive car. Flout* means "to show contempt for": *an artist who flouted conventional styles.*

flautist (flô′tĭst *or* flou′tĭst) *n.* A flutist.

flavor (flā′vər) *n.* **1.** Distinctive taste of something; savor: *the spicy flavor of applesauce.* **2.** A seasoning or flavoring: *Vanilla is a common flavor.* **3.** A quality felt to be characteristic of a thing: *a story full of the flavor of India.* ❖ *tr.v.* **flavored, flavoring, flavors** To give flavor to: *Vinegar flavored the salad.* —**fla′vor·ful, fla′vor·some** *adj.*

flavoring (flā′vər-ĭng) *n.* A substance, such as an extract or a spice, used to flavor food: *raspberry flavoring.*

flaw (flô) *n.* A defect, shortcoming, or imperfection: *The flaws in the bridge's design led to its collapse.* ❖ *tr.v.* **flawed, flawing, flaws** To make defective: *The report was flawed with several errors.*

flawless (flô′lĭs) *adj.* Without a flaw; perfect: *The singer gave a flawless performance.* See Synonyms at **perfect.** —**flaw′less·ly** *adv.*

flax (flăks) *n.* **1.** The light-colored fibers from which linen is made. **2.** The plant from which such fibers are obtained, having blue flowers and seeds that yield linseed oil.

flaxen (flăk′sən) *adj.* Made of flax: *flaxen thread.* **2.** Having the pale-yellow color of flax fiber: *flaxen hair.*

flaxseed (flăks′sēd′) *n.* The seed of the flax plant, used to obtain linseed oil and as a dietary supplement.

flay (flā) *tr.v.* **flayed, flaying, flays 1.** To strip off the skin of: *flay a deer.* **2.** To criticize or scold harshly.

flea (flē) *n.* Any of various small, wingless, jumping insects that live on the bodies of humans and other animals and suck their blood.

flea collar *n.* A collar, especially for a cat or dog, that contains a substance for killing fleas.

flea market *n.* A market, usually held outdoors, where antiques, used household goods, and collectibles are sold.

fleck (flĕk) *n.* **1.** A small mark or spot: *flecks of gray paint on the floor.* **2.** A small bit or flake: *a fleck of paper.* ❖ *tr.v.* **flecked, flecking, flecks** To mark with flecks; spot: *Spots of paint flecked the floor.*

fled (flĕd) *v.* Past tense and past participle of **flee.**

fledge (flĕj) *v.* **fledged, fledging, fledges** —*intr.* To develop feathers and leave the nest: *Robins fledge in just a few weeks.* —*tr.* **1.** To take care of (a young bird) until it is ready to fly: *The pair of birds fledged two chicks.* **2.** To provide or cover with feathers: *fledge an arrow.*

fledgling (flĕj′lĭng) *n.* **1.** A young bird that has just left the nest. **2.** A young or inexperienced person. ❖ *adj.* New and inexperienced: *a fledgling skier.*

flee (flē) *v.* **fled** (flĕd), **fleeing, flees** —*intr.* **1.** To run away, as from trouble or danger: *The thieves fled when they heard the police siren.* **2.** To pass swiftly away; vanish: *The night fled and the sky brightened.* —*tr.* To run away from; escape from: *flee the burning house.*

fleece (flēs) *n.* **1.** The coat of wool of a sheep or similar animal. **2.** The amount of wool sheared from a sheep or similar animal at one time. **3a.** A soft, warm, lightweight, usually synthetic fabric with a deep pile, often used for lining coats, boots, and other outer clothing. **b.** A garment, especially a shirt or jacket, made of such fabric. ❖ *tr.v.* **fleeced, fleecing, fleeces 1.** To shear the fleece from. **2.** To swindle or cheat (a person) of money or belongings: *A dishonest dealer fleeced the car buyer.*

fleecy (flē′sē) *adj.* **fleecier, fleeciest** Relating to or resembling fleece: *fleecy blankets; fleecy clouds.* —**fleec′i·ness** *n.*

fleet¹ (flēt) *n.* **1.** A group of warships under one commander. **2.** A number of boats or vehicles owned or operated as a group: *a fishing fleet; a fleet of taxis.*

fleet² (flēt) *adj.* **fleeter, fleetest** Moving swiftly; nimble: *fleet as a deer.* ❖ *intr.v.* **fleeted, fleeting, fleets** To move or pass swiftly: *clouds fleeting across the sky.* —**fleet′ly** *adv.* —**fleet′ness** *n.*

WORD HISTORY Fleet¹ comes from Old English *flēot* (meaning "a group of ships"), which comes from Old English *flēotan,* meaning "to float." **Fleet²** probably comes from Old Norse *fljótr,* meaning "moving quickly."

Fleet Admiral *n.* Admiral of the Fleet.

fleeting (flē′tĭng) *adj.* Passing quickly; very brief: *a fleeting glimpse of the eclipse.* —**fleet′ing·ly** *adv.*

Fleming (flĕm′ĭng) *n.* **1.** A native or inhabitant of the region of Flanders in northern Belgium. **2.** A Belgian who is a native speaker of Flemish.

Flemish (flĕm′ĭsh) *adj.* Relating to Flanders, the Flemings, or their language or culture. ❖ *n.* **1.** (*used with a plural verb*) The people of Flanders; the Flemings. **2.** A group of Dutch dialects spoken in the southwestern Netherlands, northwest Belgium, and parts of northern France.

flense (flĕns) *tr.v.* **flensed, flensing, flenses** To strip the blubber or skin from: *flense a whale.*

flerovium (flə-rō′vē-əm) *n. Symbol* **Fl** A radioactive element that has been artificially produced by scientists. The half-life of its most stable isotope is about 2.7 seconds. Atomic number 114. See **Periodic Table.**

flesh (flĕsh) *n.* **1.** The soft tissue of the body of a vertebrate animal, composed mostly of muscles and fat and covering the bones. **2.** Such tissue used as food: *fish with white flesh.* **3.** The pulpy part of a fruit or vegetable used as food: *the sweet flesh of a ripe melon.* **4.** The body as distinguished from the mind or soul: *The spirit is willing, but the flesh is weak.* ◆ **flesh and blood** A blood relative or relatives; kin. **in the flesh** In person; actually present: *I have never seen the president in the flesh, only on TV.*

fleshly (flĕsh′lē) *adj.* **fleshlier, fleshliest 1.** Relating to the body; physical: *fleshly need of nourishment.* **2.** Not spiritual; sensual or worldly: *fleshly pleasures.*

fleshy (flĕsh′ē) *adj.* **fleshier, fleshiest 1.** Relating to, consisting of, or having flesh. **2.** Having much flesh; plump: *fleshy cheeks.*

fleur-de-lis *or* **fleur-de-lys** (flûr′də-lē′) *n., pl.* **fleurs-de-lis** *or* **fleurs-de-lys** (flûr′də-lēz′) **1a.** A design in heraldry that has a three-petaled iris flower, used to symbolize the royal family of France. **b.** A similar design used as a decorative motif. **2.** An iris.

flew (floo) *v.* Past tense of **fly¹.**

flex (flĕks) *tr.v.* **flexed, flexing, flexes 1.** To bend: *Flex your elbow.* **2.** To cause (a muscle) to contract. **3.** To exhibit or use (power): *The dean flexed her authority.*

flexible (flĕk′sə-bəl) *adj.* **1.** Capable of bending or being bent; supple; pliable: *a flexible hose.* **2.** Capable of or responsive to change; adaptable: *Our plans are flexible.* —**flex′i·bil′i·ty** *n.* —**flex′i·bly** *adv.*

flexion (flĕk′shən) *n.* **1.** The act of bending a part of the body by a muscle: *flexion of the leg.* **2.** The position assumed by a flexed limb.

flexor (flĕk′sər) *n.* A muscle that bends a joint in the body.

flick¹ (flĭk) *n.* **1.** A light quick motion in striking or touching something: *turn on a light with a flick of the finger.* **2.** The sound made by such a motion: *We heard the flick of the switch.* ❖ *tr.v.* **flicked, flicking, flicks** **1.** To touch or hit with a light quick motion: *The horse flicked flies with its tail.* **2.** To cause to move with a light quick motion: *flick a switch.* **3.** To remove with a light quick motion: *flick a bug off the table.*

flick² (flĭk) *n. Slang* A movie.

flicker¹ (flĭk′ər) *intr.v.* **flickered, flickering, flickers** **1.** To burn or shine waveringly: *The candles flickered in the breeze.* **2.** To move unevenly; flutter: *Shadows flickered on the wall.* ❖ *n.* **1.** An uneven or wavering light: *The flicker of a candle lit our way.* **2.** A brief or slight indication or sensation: *a flicker of anger.* **3.** A short quick movement; a tremor: *the flicker of a butterfly's wings.*

flicker² (flĭk′ər) *n.* Any of various large woodpeckers of the Americas that have a spotted breast and often forage on the ground.

flied (flīd) *intr.v.* Past tense and past participle of **fly¹** (sense 7).

flier also **flyer** (flī′ər) *n.* **1.** A person or thing that flies, especially: **a.** A pilot or aviator. **b.** A passenger on an aircraft. **2.** *Informal* A pamphlet or circular; a handbill: *We distributed fliers for the candidate.*

flies (flīz) *v.* Third person singular present tense of **fly¹**. ❖ *n.* Plural of **fly¹** and **fly²**.

flight (flīt) *n.* **1.** The act or process of flying: *a bird's flight.* **2.** A scheduled airline trip: *My flight to Boston is on Friday.* **3.** The distance covered in such a trip: *The flight was 900 miles.* **4.** A group, especially of birds or aircraft, flying together. **5.** An effort that soars above the ordinary: *a brilliant flight of the imagination.* **6.** A series of stairs, as between floors: *We climbed four flights to the roof.* **7.** An act of running away; an escape: *the convict's flight from prison.*

flight attendant *n.* A person who assists passengers in an aircraft.

flightless (flīt′lĭs) *adj.* Incapable of flying: *Ostriches and penguins are flightless birds.*

flight recorder *n.* An electronic device that records information about the operation of each flight of an aircraft and is kept in a sealed box for recovery after a crash.

flighty (flī′tē) *adj.* **flightier, flightiest.** **1.** Exhibiting unsteady or fickle behavior. **2.** Irresponsible, especially in a silly way. —**flight′i·ness** *n.*

flimsy (flĭm′zē) *adj.* **flimsier, flimsiest.** **1.** Thin or light: *flimsy cloth.* **2.** Not solid or strong; likely to fall apart: *a flimsy table.* **3.** Not believable; unconvincing: *a flimsy excuse.* —**flim′si·ly** *adv.* —**flim′si·ness** *n.*

flinch (flĭnch) *intr.v.* **flinched, flinching, flinches** To shrink or wince, as from pain or fear; draw back: *I flinched when the nurse put iodine on my injury.*

fling (flĭng) *tr.v.* **flung** (flŭng), **flinging, flings** **1.** To throw with violence or force: *flung the dishes against the wall.* See Synonyms at **throw.** **2.** To put or send suddenly or unexpectedly: *fling troops into battle.* ❖ *n.* **1.** The act of

flinging; a throw. **2.** The Highland fling. **3.** A brief period of doing whatever one wants; a spree or binge. **4.** A brief romantic relationship.

flint (flĭnt) *n.* **1.** A very hard, gray to black form of quartz found in sedimentary rocks that makes sparks when it is struck with steel. **2.** A piece of flint used to produce sparks, as in a musket.

flintlock (flĭnt′lŏk′) *n.* A musket in which the powder charge is ignited when a flint strikes a metal plate, producing a spark.

flinty (flĭn′tē) *adj.* **flintier, flintiest** **1.** Composed of or containing flint: *gray flinty hills.* **2.** Unyielding; stony: *a cold flinty look.* —**flint′i·ness** *n.*

flip (flĭp) *v.* **flipped, flipping, flips** —*tr.* **1.** To toss with a light quick motion, especially with a spin or turn: *flip a coin.* **2.** To turn over with a light quick motion: *flip the pages of a magazine.* **3.** To buy and sell (a house, for example) in a short period of time for profit. —*intr.* **1.** To turn over: *The canoe flipped in the rapids.* **2.** To move in twists and turns: *The fish flipped in the net.* **3.** To turn a somersault, especially in the air: *This dog flips for treats.* ❖ *n.* **1.** An act of flipping, especially a quick turning movement: *give the pancake a flip.* **2.** A somersault. ❖ *adj.* **flipper, flippest** *Informal* Flippant: *a flip attitude.*

flip-flop (flĭp′flŏp′) *n.* **1.** The movement or sound of repeated flapping: *the flip-flop of a shade against a window.* **2.** A reversal of opinion or direction: *did a flip-flop on the parking ban.* **3.** A backward somersault or handspring. **4.** A backless, often foam rubber sandal held to the foot at the big toe by means of a thong. ❖ *intr.v.* **flip-flopped, flip-flopping, flip-flops** **1.** To reverse a stand or position: *The mayor flip-flopped on raising taxes.* **2.** To move back and forth between two conditions: *The weather flip-flopped between snow and rain.*

flippant (flĭp′ənt) *adj.* Casually or humorously disrespectful: *He took offense because he thought she was being flippant.* —**flip′pan·cy** *n.* —**flip′pant·ly** *adv.*

flipper (flĭp′ər) *n.* **1.** A wide flat limb, as of a seal, walrus, or sea turtle, used for swimming. **2.** A fin worn for swimming, snorkeling, or certain other water sports.

flirt (flûrt) *intr.v.* **flirted, flirting, flirts** **1.** To act as if one is sexually attracted to another person, usually in a playful manner. **2.** To deal with (something) in a playful way as being of little importance; trifle: *a daredevil who flirts with danger.* ❖ *n.* A person given to romantic flirting.

flirtation (flûr-tā′shən) *n.* **1.** The act or practice of flirting. **2.** A casual or brief romance.

flirtatious (flûr-tā′shəs) *adj.* **1.** Given to flirting: *a flirtatious person.* **2.** Indicating that one is sexually attracted to someone, especially in a playful way: *a flirtatious look.* —**flir·ta′tious·ly** *adv.*

flit (flĭt) *intr.v.* **flitted, flitting, flits** **1.** To move quickly and nimbly: *Birds flitted about in the thicket.* **2.** To pass quickly: *A smile flitted across his face.*

flitter (flĭt′ər) *intr.v.* **flittered, flittering, flitters** To flutter.

float (flōt) *v.* **floated, floating, floats** —*intr.* **1.** To rest within or on the surface of a fluid without sinking: *The raft floated down the river. The balloon floated in the sky.* **2.** To move or drift through space as if supported by a fluid: *The spacecraft floated toward the distant planet.* —*tr.* **1.** To cause to float or move on the surface of a fluid: *float logs down the river.* **2.** To offer for sale: *float a new company.* **3.** To arrange for (a loan). **4.** To offer for consideration; suggest: *floated an idea about a camping trip.* ❖ *n.* **1.** An object designed to float, especially: **a.** A buoy or raft fixed in place. **b.** A cork or ball on a fishing line that keeps the line up in the water and bobs when a fish bites. **c.** A hollow ball attached to a lever to regulate the water level in a tank, as in a toilet tank. **2.** An air-filled sac that keeps an aquatic organism afloat. **3.** A decorated exhibit displayed on a large flat vehicle in a parade. **4.** A soft drink with ice cream in it. —**float′er** *n.*

floating rib (flō′tĭng) *n.* A rib that has one end not connected to cartilage or bone. The lowest two pairs of human ribs are floating ribs.

flock (flŏk) *n.* **1.** A group of animals, such as birds or sheep, that live, travel, or feed together. **2.** The members of a church. **3.** A large crowd or number: *A flock of weekend visitors crowded into the museum.* ❖ *intr.v.* **flocked, flocking, flocks** To gather or travel in a flock or crowd: *People flocked to the cities for jobs.* —SEE NOTE AT **collective noun.**

floe (flō) *n.* A mass or sheet of floating ice.

flog (flŏg) *tr.v.* **flogged, flogging, flogs** To beat harshly with a whip or rod. —**flog′ger** *n.*

flood (flŭd) *n.* **1a.** An overflowing of water onto land that is normally dry. **b. Flood** In the Bible, the covering of the earth with water in the time of Noah. **2.** A large amount or number: *a flood of job applications.* ❖ *v.* **flooded, flooding, floods** —*tr.* **1.** To cover or submerge with water: *The heavy rain flooded the cellar.* **2.** To fill or overwhelm with too much of something: *Phone calls flooded the electric company during the outage.* **3.** To put too much fuel into the carburetor of (an engine), with the result that the engine will not start. —*intr.* **1.** To become covered or submerged with water: *That field floods every spring.* **2.** To overflow; pour forth: *The stream floods after a heavy rain.*

floodgate (flŭd′gāt′) *n.* A gate used to control the flow of water, as from a lake or a river.

floodlight (flŭd′līt′) *n.* **1.** An electric lamp that produces a broad, intensely bright beam of light. **2.** The beam of light produced by such a lamp: *The fountain sparkled in the floodlight.* ❖ *tr.v.* **floodlighted** or **floodlit** (flŭd′līt′), **floodlighting, floodlights** To light with a floodlight.

floodplain (flŭd′plān′) *n.* A plain that borders a river and is subject to flooding.

flood tide *n.* The incoming or rising tide.

floodwater (flŭd′wô′tər) *n.* often **floodwaters** The water of a flood.

floor (flôr) *n.* **1.** The surface of a room on which one stands. **2.** The ground or bottom surface, as of a forest or ocean. **3.** A story or level of a building: *Our apartment is on the fifth floor.* **4.** The part of a building where the members of a legislature meet and carry on their business. **5.** The right to address an assembly: *The representative from Hawaii has the floor.* ❖ *tr.v.* **floored, flooring, floors** **1.** To provide with a floor: *floor a deck with planks.* **2.** To knock down: *The boxer was floored twice.* **3.** To stun; overwhelm: *The thrilling news floored me.*

floorboard (flôr′bôrd′) *n.* **1.** A board in a floor. **2.** The floor of a motor vehicle.

floor exercise *n.* An event in competitive gymnastics that consists of various tumbling maneuvers on a mat.

flooring (flôr′ĭng) *n.* **1.** A floor: *My house has wood flooring.* **2.** Material, such as lumber, used to make floors.

floor plan *n.* A diagram of a room or building drawn as if seen from above.

floorshow (flôr′shō′) *n.* A series of entertainments, such as singing or comedy acts, presented in a nightclub.

flop (flŏp) *v.* **flopped, flopping, flops** —*intr.* **1.** To fall or lie down heavily and noisily; plop: *I flopped on my bed.* **2.** To move about loosely or limply: *The dog's ears flopped as it ran along.* **3.** *Informal* To fail: *The musical comedy totally flopped in New York.* —*tr.* To drop or lay (something) down heavily or drop noisily: *I flopped the heavy package on the table.* ❖ *n.* **1.** The action or sound of flopping. **2.** *Informal* A failure: *The play was a complete flop.*

floppy (flŏp′ē) *adj.* **floppier, floppiest** Tending to flop: *floppy ears; big floppy sleeves.* —**flop′pi·ness** *n.*

floppy disk *n.* A flexible plastic disk coated with magnetic material and covered by a protective jacket, formerly used to store computer data.

flora (flôr′ə) *n.* *(used with a singular or plural verb)* **1.** The plants of a particular region or time period considered as a group: *desert flora.* **2.** The bacteria and other microorganisms that normally inhabit a bodily organ or part: *intestinal flora.*

floral (flôr′əl) *adj.* Relating to or suggestive of flowers: *a floral arrangement; floral perfume.*

floret (flôr′ĭt or flôr′ĕt) *n.* **1.** A small or reduced flower, especially one in the flower cluster of a grass or sedge or in the flower head of a composite plant such as a daisy or dandelion. **2.** One of the clusters of flower buds that together form a head of cauliflower or broccoli.

florid (flôr′ĭd) *adj.* **1.** Flushed with rosy color: *a florid complexion.* **2.** Elaborate; flowery: *a florid writing style.*

florin (flôr′ĭn) *n.* **1.** A guilder. **2.** Any of several former European gold or silver coins.

florist (flôr′ĭst) *n.* A person who raises or sells ornamental plants and flowers.

floss (flôs) *n.* **1.** Dental floss. **2.** Soft, loosely twisted silk or cotton thread used in embroidery. ❖ *v.* **flossed, flossing, flosses** —*tr.* To clean with dental floss: *flossed my teeth.* —*intr.* To clean the teeth with dental floss. —**floss′y** *adj.*

flotilla (flō-tĭl′ə) *n.* A fleet of boats or ships.

flotsam (flŏt′səm) *n.* Floating wreckage or cargo from a shipwreck.

flounce[1] (flouns) *n.* A strip of decorative cloth gathered or pleated along one edge and sewn to a curtain or clothing as a trimming. ❖ *tr.v.* **flounced, flouncing, flounces** To trim with a flounce or flounces.

flounce[2] (flouns) *intr.v.* **flounced, flouncing, flounces 1.** To move in a lively or bouncy manner: *The children flounced about the room.* **2.** To move with exaggerated or affected motions: *flounce out of the room in a huff.*

WORD HISTORY Flounce[1] comes from Middle English *frounce,* meaning "pleat." **Flounce**[2] may be of Scandinavian origin.

flounder[1] (floun′dər) *intr.v.* **floundered, floundering, flounders 1.** To move clumsily or with difficulty: *The children floundered through deep snow.* **2.** To act or function with confusion or without direction: *flounder through a speech.* —SEE NOTE AT **founder**[1].

flounder[2] (floun′dər) *n., pl.* **flounder** or **flounders** Any of various flatfishes used as food.

WORD HISTORY Flounder[1] is probably an alteration of *founder,* meaning "to sink." **Flounder**[2] is from Middle English *flounder* and Anglo-Norman *floundre,* both referring to the same kind of fish as in Modern English.

flour (flou′ər or flour) *n.* **1.** A fine powdery foodstuff made by grinding and sifting the meal of a grain, especially wheat. **2.** Any of various similar powdery foods, as that made from cassavas or potatoes. ❖ *tr.v.* **floured, flouring, flours** To cover or coat with flour: *flour chicken before frying.*

flourish (flûr′ĭsh) *v.* **flourished, flourishing, flourishes** —*intr.* **1.** To grow or develop well or luxuriantly; thrive: *Most flowers flourish in sunlight.* **2.** To do well; prosper: *The lawyer's practice flourished.* **3.** To be actively working, especially in a period of great accomplishment: *a writer who flourished in the 1920s.* —*tr.* To wave vigorously or dramatically: *Marchers flourished their hats in front of the crowd.* ❖ *n.* **1.** A dramatic action or gesture: *the flourish of a sword.* **2.** An added decorative touch; an embellishment: *handwriting with many flourishes.* **3.** In music, a showy passage or a fanfare: *Trumpets played a flourish.*

flout (flout) *tr.v.* **flouted, flouting, flouts** To ignore or disregard (a rule or convention, for example) in an open or defiant way: *a rebel who flouted convention.* —**flout′er** *n.* —SEE NOTE AT **flaunt.**

flow (flō) *intr.v.* **flowed, flowing, flows 1.** To move or run smoothly in a stream: *Oil flowed from the well. Blood flows through the arteries and veins of the body. Traffic flowed through the tunnel.* **2.** To proceed steadily and easily: *The preparations for the party flowed smoothly.* **3.** To be plentiful: *a river flowing with fish.* **4.** To be full or overflow: *Their hearts flowed with warm feelings.* **5.** To hang loosely and gracefully: *The judges' robes flowed behind them.* **6.** To rise. Used of the tide. ❖ *n.* **1.** A stream or current: *a lava flow.* **2.** A continuous movement: *the flow of traffic.* **3.** The act of flowing: *Downstream the flow is much slower.* **4.** The rising of the tide: *the ocean's flow towards shore.* **5.** A general movement or tendency: *policies that followed the flow of general opinion.*

flow chart also **flowchart** (flō′chärt′) *n.* A diagram that shows the order of operations or sequence of tasks for solving a problem or managing a complex project.

flower (flou′ər) *n.* **1.** The reproductive part of a large group of plants (the angiosperms), having female or male reproductive structures or both and in its complete form including a pistil and stamens, sepals, and petals. **2.** A plant that is grown mainly for its flowers: *planted irises and other flowers in the garden.* **3.** The best example or representative of something. ❖ *intr.v.* **flowered, flowering, flowers 1.** To produce flowers; bloom: *Some maple trees flower early in the spring.* **2.** To develop fully; reach a peak: *His artistic talents flowered late in life.*

flowering plant (flou′ər-ĭng) *n.* A plant that produces flowers and fruit; an angiosperm.

flowery (flou′ə-rē) *adj.* **flowerier, floweriest 1.** Full of or suggestive of flowers: *flowery meadows; a flowery fragrance.* **2.** Full of fancy words or expressions: *a flowery speech.* —**flow′er·i·ness** *n.*

flown (flōn) *v.* Past participle of **fly**[1].

fl. oz. An abbreviation of fluid ounce.

flu (flōō) *n.* Influenza.

flub (flŭb) *tr.v.* **flubbed, flubbing, flubs** To botch; bungle: *I flubbed the test and failed.* ❖ *n.* A blunder; an error.

fluctuate (flŭk′chōō-āt′) *intr.v.* **fluctuated, fluctuating, fluctuates** To change or vary irregularly; waver: *In summer the temperature fluctuates a great deal.* —**fluc′tu·a′tion** *n.* —SEE NOTE AT **fluent.**

flue (flōō) *n.* A pipe, tube, or other channel for carrying smoke, steam, or waste gases, as from a fireplace to a chimney.

fluency (flōō′ən-sē) *n.* Smoothness and ease, especially in speaking or writing.

fluent (flōō′ənt) *adj.* **1.** Capable of expressing oneself smoothly and effortlessly: *a fluent speaker; fluent in German and French.* **2.** Flowing effortlessly; polished: *speaks fluent Russian.* —**flu′ent·ly** *adv.*

WORD BUILDING The word roots *flu-, flux-,* and *fluc-* in English words come from the Latin verb *fluere,* "to flow." The Latin present participle of *fluere* has the form *fluent-* and meant "flowing." It is the source of the English word **fluent,** "flowing, graceful, smooth." The Latin noun *influentia,* meaning "an inflow" (using the prefix *in-²,* "in, into") is the source of our word **influence.** The past participle of *fluere* was *flūxus,* from which we form the word **influx,** "an inflow." Latin also had a noun *flūctus* meaning "wave," from which the verb *flūctuāre* was made, meaning "to make waves"; this is the source of the word **fluctuate.**

fluff (flŭf) *n.* **1.** Light down or fuzz: *the fluff from a woolen sweater.* **2.** Something having a very light or downy appearance: *The ducklings were little balls of fluff.* **3.** Something having very little substance, meaning, or importance: *The report was mostly fluff, with very little new information.* **4.** *Informal* An error; a flub. ❖ *tr.v.* **fluffed, fluffing, fluffs 1.** To make light and puffy by patting or shaking: *fluff a pillow.* **2.** *Informal* To ruin or spoil by making a mistake: *fluff an exam; fluff a speech.*

fluffy (flŭf′ē) *adj.* **fluffier, fluffiest 1.** Relating to, resembling, or covered with fluff or down: *a fluffy blanket.* **2.** Light and airy; soft: *fluffy whipped potatoes; fluffy curls.* —**fluff′i·ness** *n.*

fluid (flōō′ĭd) *n.* A substance, such as air or water, that flows easily and takes on the shape of its container. All liquids and gases are fluids. ❖ *adj.* **1.** Capable of flowing; liquid or gaseous: *The waters of this lake remain fluid all winter.* **2.** Smooth and flowing; graceful: *the fluid motion of a ballet dancer.* **3.** Easily changed or tending to change: *My vacation plans are fluid.* —**flu·id′i·ty** *n.*

fluid ounce *n.* A liquid measure equal to ¹⁄₁₆ of a pint (29.57 milliliters).

fluke[1] (flōōk) *n.* **1.** Any of numerous parasitic flatworms, especially a trematode. **2.** Any of various flatfishes, especially a flounder.

fluke[2] (flōōk) *n.* **1.** The triangular blade at the end of either arm of an anchor, designed to dig into the ocean bottom to hold the anchor in place. **2.** The barbed head of a harpoon, lance, or arrow. **3.** Either of the two flattened fins of a whale's tail.

fluke[3] (flōōk) *n.* Something happening by chance, especially a stroke of good luck: *It was a fluke that we all arrived at the same time.*

WORD HISTORY Fluke[1] comes from Old English *flōc,* meaning "flounder, flatfish." **Fluke**[2] possibly comes from the "flounder" sense of *fluke¹.* The origin of **fluke**[3] is unknown.

flume (flōōm) *n.* **1.** A narrow gorge with a stream flowing through it. **2.** An artificial channel or chute for flowing water, as for floating logs or furnishing waterpower.

flummox (flŭm′əks) *tr.v.* **flummoxed, flummoxing, flummoxes** *Informal* To confuse; perplex: *I was flummoxed by a question I could not answer.*

flung (flŭng) *v.* Past tense and past participle of **fling.**

flunk (flŭngk) *Informal v.* **flunked, flunking, flunks** —*intr.* To fail, especially in an examination or a course. —*tr.* **1.** To fail (a test or subject in school). **2.** To give (a person) a failing grade.

flunky also **flunkey** (flŭng′kē) n., pl. **flunkies** also **flunkeys** **1.** A person who submissively obeys and fawns on someone in order to win that person's favor. **2.** A person who does menial or trivial work. **3.** A servant in uniform.

fluoresce (floॅo-rĕs′ or flô-rĕs′) intr.v. **fluoresced, fluorescing, fluoresces** To produce or show fluorescence.

fluorescence (floॅo-rĕs′əns or flô-rĕs′əns) n. **1.** The giving off of electromagnetic radiation, especially visible light, by a substance when it is exposed to electromagnetic radiation having shorter wavelengths, such as ultraviolet rays. Light is emitted only as long as the exposure continues. **2.** The light produced in this way.

fluorescent (floॅo-rĕs′ənt or flô-rĕs′ənt) adj. Relating to, showing, or produced by fluorescence: *fluorescent light.*

fluorescent light n. A device that produces visible light by fluorescence, especially a glass tube coated on the inside with a fluorescent material and filled with an ionized gas that emits ultraviolet rays.

fluoridate (floॅor′ĭ-dāt′ or flôr′ĭ-dāt′) tr.v. **fluoridated, fluoridating, fluoridates** To add a compound of fluorine to (drinking water) in order to prevent tooth decay. —**fluor′i·da′tion** n.

fluoride (floॅor′īd′ or flôr′īd′) n. A chemical compound of fluorine and another element or radical. It is added to the water supply to prevent tooth decay.

fluorine (floॅor′ēn′ or flôr′ēn′) n. Symbol **F** A pale-yellow, poisonous, gaseous element that is highly corrosive. Atomic number 9. See **Periodic Table.**

fluoroscopy (floॅo-rŏs′kə-pē) n. A technique used in medicine that involves passing x-rays through the body to create an image on a fluorescent surface. It is used to view internal parts of the body, especially during movement or during medical procedures. —**fluor′o·scop′ic** (floॅor′ə-skŏp′ĭk or flôr′ə-skŏp′ĭk) adj.

flurry (flûr′ē) n., pl. **flurries 1.** A brief light fall of snow. **2.** A sudden gust of wind. **3.** A sudden burst of confusion, excitement, or activity; a stir: *a flurry of interest in the new product.* ❖ tr.v. **flurried, flurrying, flurries** To confuse, excite, or agitate; fluster: *Unexpected questions flurried the speaker.*

flush¹ (flŭsh) v. **flushed, flushing, flushes** —intr. **1.** To turn red in the face: *Her face flushed with anger.* **2.** To be emptied or cleaned by a rapid gush of water. —tr. **1.** To cause to redden or glow: *The disappointed customer was flushed with annoyance.* **2.** To excite or elate, as with a feeling of pride or accomplishment: *The winning team was flushed with victory.* **3.** To wash, empty, or purify with a sudden rapid flow of water: *We flushed the pipe of debris with a hose.* **4.** To drive away with a rapid flow of a liquid: *We flushed the debris from the pipe.* ❖ n. **1.** A flow or rush of water. **2.** A blush or rosy glow. **3.** A rush of strong feeling or excitement; exhilaration: *a flush of enthusiasm.* **4.** A state of freshness or vigor: *the first flush of youth.* ❖ adj. **flusher, flushest 1.** Having an abundant supply of money: *The company was flush with cash from sales of its latest product.* **2.** Marked by abundance; plentiful: *rivers flush with spring rains.* **3.** Having surfaces that are even, level, or close together: *sections of the sidewalk that are flush.* **4.** Aligned evenly with a margin, as along the left or right edge of a document; not indented. ❖ adv. So as to be even or aligned: *The figures are written flush down the column.*

flush² (flŭsh) n. In card games, a hand in which all of the cards are of the same suit.

flush³ (flŭsh) v. **flushed, flushing, flushes** —tr. **1.** To cause (an animal, especially one that is being hunted) to run or fly up from a hiding place: *The dog flushed several ducks from the tall grass.* **2.** To drive or force into the open: *The police threw tear gas in the building to flush out the criminals.* —intr. To run out or fly up from a hiding place: *The dog barked and the geese flushed from the thicket.*

WORD HISTORY Flush¹ is closely related to *flush³*, but may have also been influenced by the similarity to the word *flash.* **Flush²** comes from Latin *flūxus,* meaning "flux." **Flush³** comes from Middle English *flusshen,* meaning "to cause an animal to leave a hiding place."

fluster (flŭs′tər) tr.v. **flustered, flustering, flusters** To make nervous, excited, or confused: *Shouts from the protesters flustered the speaker.* ❖ n. A state of excitement, confusion, or agitation.

flute (floॅot) n. **1.** A woodwind instrument consisting of a tube with finger holes and keys on the side, sounded by blowing across a hole near one end. **2.** A rounded groove, especially one carved on the shaft of a column. **3.** A groove in cloth, as in a pleated ruffle. ❖ tr.v. **fluted, fluting, flutes** To make grooves in: *A carpenter fluted the tops of the new columns.*

fluting (floॅo′tĭng) n. A series of rounded grooves, as on a column of a building.

flutist (floॅo′tĭst) n. A person who plays the flute.

flutter (flŭt′ər) v. **fluttered, fluttering, flutters** —intr. **1.** To wave or flap rapidly with an irregular motion: *curtains fluttered in the breeze.* **2a.** To fly with a quick light flapping of the wings. **b.** To flap the wings while making short hops: *The chicken fluttered across the yard.* **3.** To vibrate or beat rapidly or irregularly: *When I was scared, my heart fluttered wildly.* **4.** To move quickly in a nervous, restless, or excited fashion; flit: *Clerks fluttered about trying to look busy.* —tr. To cause to flutter: *A light breeze fluttered the curtain.* ❖ n. **1.** An act of fluttering: *the flutter of a butterfly.* **2.** A condition of nervous excitement or agitation: *We were in a flutter getting ready for the party.*

flutter kick n. A swimming kick used in crawl and backstroke in which the legs are extended straight back and alternately moved up and down.

fluvial (floॅo′vē-əl) adj. **1.** Relating to or inhabiting a river or stream: *fluvial ecosystems.* **2.** Produced by the action of a river or stream: *fluvial sediments.*

flux (flŭks) n. **1.** Continual change: *The price of gold is in flux.* **2.** A flow or flowing of a fluid: *the flux of the outgoing tide.* **3.** A substance applied to a metal surface that is to be soldered or welded. Flux cleans the surface, improves the flow of solder, and prevents the formation of oxides that would weaken the joint. **4.** A substance used in a smelting furnace to make metals melt more easily. **5a.** The rate of flow of fluids, particles, or energy across a given surface or area. **b.** Magnetic flux. **6.** A heavy discharge of fluid from the body, especially the discharge of watery waste material from the intestines.

fly¹ (flī) v. **flew** (floॅo), **flown** (flōn), **flying, flies** (flīz) —intr. **1.** To move through the air by means of wings: *Birds fly south in winter.* **2a.** To move or travel by air: *We flew to Seattle for vacation.* **b.** To pilot an aircraft or spacecraft: *The crew flew from New York to Tokyo.* **3a.** To rise or be carried through the air by the wind: *Dust and pollen flew through the air.* **b.** To float or flutter in the air: *pennants flying from buildings.* **4.** To be sent or driven through the air with great speed or force: *The plate flew from my hands* *when I tripped.* **5.** To move with great speed; rush; flee: *flew down the hall; fly from danger.* **6.** To pass by swiftly: *a vacation flying by.* **7.** *past tense and past participle* **flied** In baseball, to hit a fly ball. **8.** To react explosively; burst: *fly into a rage.* —*tr.* **1.** To cause to float or flutter in the air: *fly a kite.* **2a.** To pilot (an aircraft or spacecraft). **b.** To carry or transport in an aircraft or spacecraft: *fly supplies to a remote area.* **c.** To pass over in flight: *fly the ocean.* **3.** To flee from: *Many people flew the country.* ❖ *n., pl.* **flies** **1.** A fly ball in baseball. **2.** A cloth flap covering a zipper or set of buttons, especially one on the front of pants. **3.** A piece of protective fabric secured over a tent and often extended over the entrance. **4. flies** The area directly over a theater's stage where lights and curtains are hung and equipment for raising and lowering sets is located. ◆ **fly at** To attack fiercely; assault. **let fly 1.** To shoot, hurl, or release (a weapon). **2.** To lash out; criticize harshly: *The mayor let fly with an attack on her critics.* **on the fly 1.** On the run; in a hurry: *I got a sandwich on the fly.* **2.** While in the air; in flight: *The bird was singing on the fly.*

fly² (flī) *n., pl.* **flies 1a.** Any of numerous two-winged insects, especially a housefly. Fruit flies and mosquitoes are also flies. **b.** Any of various other flying insects, such as a mayfly or a caddisfly. **2.** A fishhook made to look like such an insect, as by attaching bits of feathers.

WORD HISTORY Fly¹ comes from Old English *flēogan,* meaning "to move through the air by means of wings." **Fly²** comes from Old English *flēoge, flȳge,* referring to various two-winged insects, as in Modern English.

---

fly ball *n.* In baseball, a ball that is batted high in the air, usually to the outfield.

fly-by-night (flī′bī-nīt′) *Informal adj.* **1.** Unreliable or unscrupulous, especially with regard to business dealings. **2.** Of an impermanent or insubstantial nature: *fly-by-night fashions in clothing.*

flycatcher (flī′kăch′ər *or* flī′kĕch′ər) *n.* Any of various birds that catch insects while flying, such as the phoebe.

flyer (flī′ər) *n.* Variant of **flier.**

fly-fishing (flī′fĭsh′ĭng) *n.* The art or sport of fishing using artificial flies for bait.

flying (flī′ĭng) *adj.* **1.** Relating to aviation: *flying lessons.* **2.** Capable of or engaged in flight: *a flying insect.* **3.** Swiftly moving: *the pianist's flying fingers.* **4.** Brief; hurried: *a flying visit.* ❖ *n.* **1.** Flight, as in an aircraft: *Flying is an exciting way to travel.* **2.** The operation of an aircraft: *A pilot is an expert in flying.*

flying buttress *n.* An arched masonry support that leans against the outside of a building to counteract forces, such as the weight of a vaulted ceiling, that tend to push the wall outwards.

flying fish *n.* Any of various ocean fishes having large side fins that spread out like wings as they leap from the water and make brief gliding flights.

flying jib *n.* A light triangular sail that extends beyond the jib.

flying saucer *n.* An unidentified flying object, usually described as a glowing disk and thought to be from another planet.

flying squirrel *n.* Any of various squirrels that make long gliding leaps between trees with the aid of broad folds of skin that stretch along each side of the body between the front and hind legs.

flyleaf (flī′lēf′) *n.* A blank or specially printed page at the beginning or end of a book.

flypaper (flī′pā′pər) *n.* Paper coated with a sticky, sometimes poisonous substance, used to catch flies.

fly swatter *n.* An implement used to kill flies or other insects, usually consisting of a piece of plastic or wire mesh attached to a long handle.

flyway (flī′wā′) *n.* A route followed by migrating birds.

flyweight (flī′wāt′) *n.* **1.** A boxer of the lightest weight class, weighing not more than 112 pounds (about 50 kilograms). **2.** *Informal* A very small or unimportant person or thing: *The new product proved to be a flyweight in the market and was soon discontinued.*

flywheel (flī′wēl′) *n.* **1.** A wheel with a heavy rim, attached to a shaft of a machine to keep it turning at a steady speed. **2.** A similar device used to regulate the speed of the mechanisms inside a clock.

FM An abbreviation of frequency modulation.

foal (fōl) *n.* The young offspring of a horse, zebra, or similar animal, especially one less than a year old. ❖ *intr.v.* **foaled, foaling, foals** To give birth to a foal: *a mare ready to foal.*

foam (fōm) *n.* **1.** A mass of bubbles formed in a liquid, as in surf or liquid soap, from shaking, boiling, or fermenting; froth. **2.** Frothy saliva or sweat: *wiped the froth from the horse's back.* **3.** A light, porous, flexible or spongy material full of small holes, used as a building material, for insulation, or to absorb shock in packaging. ❖ *intr.v.* **foamed, foaming, foams** To form foam or come forth in foam; froth: *The milk foamed and boiled over.*

foam rubber *n.* A light spongy rubber used for cushioning, packaging, and insulation.

foamy (fō′mē) *adj.* **foamier, foamiest** Relating to, full of, covered with, or resembling foam: *foamy suds.* —**foam′-i·ly** *adv.* —**foam′i·ness** *n.*

fob¹ (fŏb) *n.* **1.** A small pocket in a man's pants or a vest, used to hold a watch, change, or other small items. **2.** A short chain or ribbon attached to a watch carried in a pocket. **3.** An ornament attached to a chain or ribbon. **4.** A key fob.

fob² (fŏb) *tr.v.* **fobbed, fobbing, fobs** *Archaic* To cheat someone. ◆ **fob off 1.** To get rid of by some trick or dishonest scheme: *fob off a copy as an original.* **2.** To put (a person) off by trickery: *He fobbed off the bill collector with a phony excuse.*

WORD HISTORY Fob¹ is probably of Germanic origin. **Fob²** comes from Middle English *fobben,* meaning "to cheat, trick."

---

focaccia (fə-kä′chē-ə *or* fə-kä′chə) *n.* A flat Italian bread flavored with olive oil and often topped with onions, herbs, or other items.

focal (fō′kəl) *adj.* Relating to a focus: *The focal point of the discussion was education.* —**fo′cal·ly** *adv.*

focal length *n.* The distance from the surface of a mirror or lens to its point of focus.

fo'c's'le (fōk′səl) *n.* Variant of **forecastle.**

focus (fō′kəs) *n., pl.* **focuses** *or* **foci** (fō′sī′ *or* fō′kī′) **1a.** A point at which rays of light come together or from which they appear to spread apart, as after passing through a lens. **b.** Focal length. **2a.** The degree of clarity with which an eye or optical instrument produces an image: *a telescope with excellent focus.* **b.** The condition or adjustment in which an eye or optical instrument gives its best image: *The camera is out of focus.* **3.** A center of interest, attention, or activity: *The senator was the focus of attention at the assembly.* **4.** Concentration or emphasis: *The* narrator's focus is on the characters in the story rather than the action. **5.** A central point or region, such as the point at which an earthquake starts or a region of the body in which an infection is largely confined. **6.** A fixed point or one of a pair of fixed points used in constructing a curve such as an ellipse, a parabola, or a hyperbola. ❖ *v.* **focused, focusing, focuses** or **focussed, focussing, focusses** —*tr.* **1a.** To bring (an object or image) into focus by adjusting the eyes or an optical instrument. **b.** To adjust (the eyes or an optical instrument) to produce a clear image: *Focus the telescope on the moon.* **2.** To concentrate or center: *Focus your attention on the bass guitar part in the song.* —*intr.* **1.** To adjust one's eyes or an optical instrument to produce a clear image. **2.** To concentrate attention or energy: *Let's focus on the problem at hand.*

fodder (fŏd′ər) *n.* **1.** Food, such as chopped corn stalks or hay, for livestock. **2.** Raw material: *The scandal provided fodder for his political enemies.*

foe (fō) *n.* An enemy, opponent, or adversary: *Foes of the new city dump met to fight the plan.*

fog (fŏg) *n.* **1.** Condensed water vapor in cloudy masses lying close to the surface of the ground or water. It is difficult to see very far in fog. **2.** A cloud of material, such as dust or smoke, that floats in the air: *a fog of insect spray.* **3.** A confused or unthinking condition: *I was so sleepy I was walking around in a fog.* ❖ *v.* **fogged, fogging, fogs** —*tr.* **1.** To cover with fog or a similar substance: *Steam fogged the bathroom mirror.* **2.** To make uncertain or unclear; confuse: *The strong medicine fogged the patient's mind.* —*intr.* To become covered with fog or a similar substance: *The car windows fogged up in the rain.*

foggy (fŏg′gē) *adj.* **foggier, foggiest 1.** Full of or surrounded by fog: *a foggy valley.* **2.** Confused or vague; clouded: *I have only a foggy memory of what happened.* —**fog′gi·ly** *adv.* —**fog′gi·ness** *n.*

foghorn (fŏg′hôrn′) *n.* A horn, usually having a deep tone, blown to warn ships of danger in foggy weather.

fogy also **fogey** (fō′gē) *n., pl.* **fogies** also **fogeys** A person with old-fashioned or conventional habits or attitudes.

foible (foi′bəl) *n.* A minor personal fault or failing: *Laughing too loudly is an annoying foible.*

foil¹ (foil) *tr.v.* **foiled, foiling, foils** To prevent from being successful; thwart: *an alarm system to foil thieves.*

foil² (foil) *n.* **1.** A thin flexible sheet of metal: *aluminum foil.* **2.** A person or thing that makes another stand out by contrast: *The serious official was a perfect foil for the comedian.* ❖ *tr.v.* **foiled, foiling, foils** To wrap (strands of hair) in pieces of foil to isolate them after applying bleach or color.

foil³ (foil) *n.* A long thin sword used in fencing, having a blunt point to prevent injury.

WORD HISTORY Foil¹ comes from Middle English *foilen,* meaning "to trample, defile." **Foil²** comes from Middle English *foil,* which comes from Latin *folium,* both meaning "leaf." The origin of **foil³** is unknown.

foist (foist) *tr.v.* **foisted, foisting, foists** To pass off as genuine, valuable, or worthy; palm off: *The dishonest merchant tried to foist damaged goods on his customers.*

fold¹ (fōld) *v.* **folded, folding, folds** —*tr.* **1.** To bend over or double up so that one part lies over another: *Fold your paper in half.* **2.** To close or flatten by bending, pressing, or doubling jointed or connected parts: *The bird folded*

its wings. *The sunbathers folded their chairs and left.* **3a.** To clasp or embrace: *I folded the infant in my arms.* **b.** To enclose or wrap: *fold the garbage in a newspaper.* **4.** To blend (an ingredient) into a mixture by gently turning one part over another: *Fold the beaten egg whites into the batter.* **5.** To withdraw (one's hand) in defeat, as by laying cards face down on the table: *folded her hand instead of calling the bet.* —*intr.* **1.** To be folded or be capable of being folded: *My wallet folds in the middle.* **2.** *Informal* To fail and close: *The business folded during the recession.* **3.** To withdraw one's hand of cards in defeat: *The first player next to the dealer folded.* ❖ *n.* **1.** A line or crease formed by folding: *Tear the paper along the fold.* **2.** A folded edge or part: *the folds of the curtain.* **3.** A bend in a layer or in several layers of rock. Folds occur in rocks when they are compressed by plate-tectonic forces. ◆ **fold out** To put in an extended position; unfold: *fold out a map.*

fold² (fōld) *n.* **1.** A fenced area for livestock, especially sheep. **2.** An established group, such as a church or political party, whose members share the same beliefs, aims, or interests.

WORD HISTORY Fold¹ comes from Old English *fealdan,* meaning "to bend so that one part lies over another." **Fold²** comes from Old English *fald,* meaning "enclosure for animals, pen."

–fold A suffix that means: **1.** Divided into a specified number of parts: *a threefold problem.* **2.** Multiplied by a specified number: *a fivefold increase in sales.*

folder (fōl′dər) *n.* **1.** A folded sheet of cardboard or heavy paper used as a holder for loose papers: *a file folder.* **2.** An organizational unit for computer files kept on a storage device. **3.** A person or machine that folds things.

foliage (fō′lē-ĭj *or* fō′lĭj) *n.* Plant leaves considered as a group: *colorful fall foliage.*

folic acid (fō′lĭk *or* fŏl′ĭk) *n.* A vitamin belonging to the vitamin B complex that is important in cell growth and metabolism and in the formation of red blood cells. It is found especially in leafy green vegetables and fresh fruit.

folio (fō′lē-ō′) *n., pl.* **folios 1a.** A large sheet of paper folded once, making two leaves or four pages of a book. **b.** A book of the largest common size, consisting of such folded sheets, usually about 15 inches (38 centimeters) high. **2.** A page number in a book.

folk (fōk) *n., pl.* **folk** or **folks 1.** The common people of a nation or region, considered as representing a distinctive culture and preserving traditional customs, beliefs, and arts. **2.** People: *city folk; honest folk.* **3. folks** *Informal* **a.** People considered as a group: *The warning sign scared folks away.* **b.** One's family or relatives, especially one's parents: *My folks are coming to visit.* ❖ *adj.* Relating to, occurring in, or coming from the common people or their culture: *a folk hero; a folk tune.*

folk dance or **folkdance** (fōk′dăns′) *n.* **1a.** A traditional dance originating among the common people of a nation or region. **b.** The music for such a dance. **2.** A social gathering at which folk dances are performed. —**folk′-dance′** *adj.* —**folk dancer** *n.* —**folk dancing** *n.*

folk etymology *n.* Change in the form of a word in order to make part of it sound like another word that it is associated with or mistakenly thought to contain. For example, some varieties of English have changed the word *asparagus* by folk etymology to *sparrow-grass,* because it was thought to contain the word *sparrow* and to be a type of grass.

folklore (fōk′lôr′) *n.* The traditional beliefs, legends, and customs, handed down by a people from generation to generation.

folk music *n.* Traditional music of the people of a country or region, usually passed down from generation to generation.

folk-rock (fōk′rŏk′) *n.* A variety of popular music that combines elements of rock music and folk music.

folksinger (fōk′sĭng′ər) *n.* A singer of folk songs. —**folk singing** *n.*

folk song or **folksong** (fōk′sông′) *n.* **1.** A song that is part of the folk music of a people. **2.** A song composed in the style of such a song.

folksy (fōk′sē) *adj.* **folksier, folksiest** *Informal* Simple and informal: *folksy people.*

folktale (fōk′tāl′) *n.* A traditional story or legend handed down by the people of a country or region from one generation to the next.

follicle (fŏl′ĭ-kəl) *n.* **1.** A small cavity, sac, or gland in the body. Hairs grow from follicles. **2.** A dry one-celled fruit that splits open along one seam only, such as the fruit of a milkweed.

follow (fŏl′ō) *v.* **followed, following, follows** —*tr.* **1.** To go or come after (a person, for example): *Follow the usher to your seats.* **2.** To go behind (a person or thing) while watching closely and often while trying not to be noticed: *The detectives followed the suspect at a distance.* **3.** To move along the same course as: *We followed a path to the beach.* **4.** To come after (something) in order, time, or position: *Night follows day.* **5.** To occur as a result of: *General agreement followed the discussion.* **6a.** To act in agreement with; obey: *follow the rules of the game.* **b.** To use as a guide or model: *Follow my example. Follow the recipe carefully.* **7.** To accept, believe in, or support: *follow a religion.* **8.** To work at (a trade or occupation): *follow a trade such as carpentry.* **9.** To listen to or watch closely: *I followed the progress of the storm on the radar screen.* **10.** To keep up with; stay informed about: *Scientists follow new developments in genetics.* **11.** To grasp the meaning of; understand: *Do you follow what I'm saying?* —*intr.* **1.** To come, move, or take place after another person or thing in order or time: *A picnic followed after the baseball game.* **2.** To occur as a result: *Success will follow if you keep practicing.* ◆ **follow through 1.** To carry something to completion: *She followed through on her promise.* **2.** In sports, to continue a stroke beyond the point of hitting the ball: *The batter followed through with a full swing.* **follow up 1.** To make a (previous action) more effective by doing something else: *He followed up his interview with a thank-you letter.* **2.** To carry to completion: *We followed up their recommendation with a plan.*

◆ SYNONYMS **follow, ensue, result, succeed** *v.*

follower (fŏl′ō-ər) *n.* **1.** A person or thing that follows. **2.** A person who follows the beliefs or ideas of another. **3.** A person who has a strong interest or pays close attention to something; a fan.

following (fŏl′ō-ĭng) *adj.* **1.** Coming next in order or time: *the following afternoon.* **2.** Now to be listed: *Please submit the following documents.* ❖ *n.* **1.** A group of admirers, supporters, or disciples: *a popular politician with a large following.* **2.** The item or items to be mentioned next: *Please buy the following: milk, bread, and eggs.* ❖ *prep.* After: *Following dinner, we watched a movie.*

follow-up or **followup** (fŏl′ō-ŭp′) *n.* Something that reinforces or enhances a previous action or event: *The*

software was a successful follow-up to the original product.

folly (fŏl′ē) *n., pl.* **follies 1.** Lack of good sense or judgment; foolishness. **2.** A foolish act or idea. **3. follies** *(used with a singular or plural verb)* An elaborate theatrical revue with music, dance, and skits. **4.** A pavilion or other structure that is chiefly decorative rather than practical.

foment (fō-mĕnt′) *tr.v.* **fomented, fomenting, foments** To stir up; arouse; provoke: *The protesters were charged with fomenting a riot.*

fond (fŏnd) *adj.* **fonder, fondest 1.** Having a strong liking: *Are you fond of gardening?* **2.** Loving or affectionate: *a fond embrace.* **3.** Strongly or foolishly held dear: *my fondest hopes.* —**fond′ly** *adv.*

fondle (fŏn′dl) *tr. & intr.v.* **fondled, fondling, fondles** To touch or stroke lovingly; caress.

fondness (fŏnd′nĭs) *n.* **1.** Liking or inclination: *a fondness for the outdoors.* **2.** Warm affection.

fondue (fŏn-do͞o′) *n.* A dish consisting of a hot sauce, such as melted cheese or chocolate, or hot oil in which pieces of food are dipped and then eaten.

font¹ (fŏnt) *n.* **1.** A basin that holds holy water or water used in baptism. **2.** A source or origin: *The professor is a font of knowledge.*

font² (fŏnt) *n.* A complete set of printing type of one size and style.

WORD HISTORY Font¹ comes from Old English *font,* which comes from Latin *fōns,* both meaning "fountain." **Font²** comes from French *fonte* (meaning "casting"), which comes from Latin *fundere,* meaning ("to pour forth").

---

food (fo͞od) *n.* **1.** Material, especially carbohydrates, fats, and proteins, that an organism uses for energy, growth, and maintaining the processes of life. Plants, algae, and some bacteria make their own food through photosynthesis, while animals and most other organisms obtain food by eating other organisms. **2.** A supply of things to eat: *Is there any food in the house?* **3.** A particular kind of nourishment: *plant food; dog food.* **4.** Something that stimulates or encourages some activity or growth: *The movie gave them food for thought.*

food bank *n.* An organization that collects and distributes donated food for free or at low cost to organizations that serve people in need.

food chain *n.* A succession of organisms in an ecological community that are linked to each other through the transfer of energy and nutrients, beginning with an organism, such as a plant, that makes its own food and continuing with each organism being eaten by one higher in the chain.

food court *n.* An area within a mall or other public space where prepared food is sold from counters or booths clustered around a common eating area.

foodie (fo͞o′dē) *n. Informal* A person who has a passionate or refined interest in food; a gourmet.

food pantry *n.* **1.** An organization or group that sorts and packages donated foodstuffs for distribution directly to people in need. **2.** The building or location where such distribution takes place.

food poisoning *n.* Illness that results from eating food that has become contaminated with bacteria or viruses.

food processor *n.* An appliance with interchangeable blades that processes food, as by slicing or shredding, at high speeds.

food stamp *n.* A coupon that is worth a certain amount

of money or a debit card that gives access to a certain amount of money in an account, issued by a government to people with low incomes so that they can buy food at stores.

foodstuff (fo͞od′stŭf′) *n.* A substance that can be used or prepared for use as food.

food web *n.* A group of interrelated food chains in a particular ecological community.

fool (fo͞ol) *n.* **1.** A person who lacks judgment or good sense. **2.** A member of a royal or noble household who provided entertainment, as by telling jokes and clowning; a jester. ❖ *v.* **fooled, fooling, fools** —*tr.* **1.** To deceive or trick; mislead: *They fooled me into thinking they had left.* **2.** To surprise (someone) or prove (someone) wrong: *We were sure their plan would fail, but they fooled us.* —*intr.* **1.** To act or speak in jest; joke: *I'm not really mad—I was just fooling.* **2.** To play or meddle foolishly: *Don't fool with the knobs on the oven.* ◆ **fool around 1.** To act frivolously or idly; waste time: *fooling around with friends on a summer afternoon.* **2.** To engage in casual sexual activity.

foolhardy (fo͞ol′här′dē) *adj.* **foolhardier, foolhardiest** Unwisely bold or daring; rash: *a foolhardy beginner trying to ski down the steepest slopes.* —**fool′har′di·ness** *n.*

foolish (fo͞o′lish) *adj.* **1.** Lacking in good sense or judgment; unwise: *a foolish choice.* **2.** Absurd; ridiculous: *I looked foolish dressed as a clown.* —**fool′ish·ly** *adv.* —**fool′ish·ness** *n.*

foolproof (fo͞ol′pro͞of′) *adj.* So safe, simple, and reliable that error or misuse is impossible: *a foolproof plan.*

foolscap (fo͞olz′kăp′) *n.* Writing paper in large sheets about 13 inches (33 centimeters) wide and 16 inches (41 centimeters) long.

fool's gold (fo͞olz) *n.* Any of several minerals, especially pyrite, sometimes mistaken for gold.

foosball (fo͞os′bôl′) *n.* A table game in which players turn rods mounted with plastic figures in order to strike a small ball to score a goal on a miniature soccer field.

foot (fo͞ot) *n., pl.* **feet** (fēt) **1.** The part of the leg of a vertebrate animal that rests on or touches the ground or floor in standing or walking. **2.** A similar part used for moving or attachment in an invertebrate animal, such as the muscular organ extending from the shell of a snail or clam. **3.** A part or base resembling a foot, as the end of a table leg. **4.** The lowest part of something high or long; the bottom: *the foot of the stairs; the foot of the page.* **5.** The end opposite the head in position or rank: *the foot of the bed; the foot of the class.* **6.** The part of a boot or stocking that covers the foot. **7.** A unit of length equal to ⅓ of a yard or 12 inches (about 30.48 centimeters). See table at **measurement. 8.** A unit of poetry, such as an iamb or dactyl, consisting of a combination of stressed and unstressed syllables. ❖ *tr.v.* **footed, footing, foots** To pay: *I'll foot the bill.* ◆ **on foot** or **by foot** Walking or running: *We're going to the restaurant on foot.*

footage (fo͞ot′ij) *n.* **1.** Length, extent, or amount of something as measured in feet: *estimated the square footage of the apartment.* **2.** Recorded film or video, especially of a specific kind or topic: *footage of the royal wedding.*

foot-and-mouth disease (fo͞ot′n-mouth′) *n.* A highly contagious disease of cattle and other hoofed animals, marked by fever and blisters around the mouth and hooves.

football (fo͞ot′bôl′) *n.* **1a.** A game played with an oval ball by two teams of 11 players each on a rectangular field with goals at either end. The object is to carry the ball across the opponent's goal line or to kick it between the opponent's goalposts. **b.** The inflated oval ball used in this game. **2.** *Chiefly British* **a.** Soccer or rugby. **b.** The ball used in soccer or rugby.

footboard (fo͞ot′bôrd′) *n.* **1.** An upright board across the foot of a bedstead. **2.** A board or small platform on which to support or rest the feet.

footbridge (fo͞ot′brĭj′) *n.* A bridge used only by people on foot.

foot-candle (fo͞ot′kăn′dl) *n.* A unit of light intensity equal to one lumen per square foot. Originally, this unit was defined with respect to a standardized candle burning a foot away from the illuminated surface.

footed (fo͞ot′ĭd) *adj.* Having a foot or feet: *a footed sofa; a four-footed animal.*

footer (fo͞ot′ər) *n.* **1.** A person or thing that is a certain number of feet in length or height: *a six-footer.* **2.** Printed information at a page's bottom margin, usually repeated throughout a document.

footfall (fo͞ot′fôl′) *n.* The sound made by a footstep.

foothill (fo͞ot′hĭl′) *n.* A low hill located near the base of a mountain or mountain range.

foothold (fo͞ot′hōld′) *n.* **1.** A place to put the foot so that it won't slip, especially when climbing. **2.** A firm secure position from which it is possible to advance: *He got a foothold in business by first working as an assistant.*

footing (fo͞ot′ĭng) *n.* **1.** A firm placing of the feet allowing one to stand or move without falling: *lose one's footing.* **2.** A secure place to put the foot; a foothold. **3.** The condition of a surface for walking or running: *The road was icy and the footing treacherous.* **4.** A basis or standing: *You'll be on an equal footing with the others.*

footlights (fo͞ot′līts′) *pl.n.* Lights placed in a row along the front of a stage floor.

footlocker (fo͞ot′lŏk′ər) *n.* A trunk for storing personal belongings, especially one kept at the foot of a bed, as in a barracks.

footloose (fo͞ot′lo͞os′) *adj.* Having no attachments or responsibilities; free to do as one pleases.

footman (fo͞ot′mən) *n.* A man employed as a servant to open doors, run errands, or serve food and drinks, as in a palace.

footnote (fo͞ot′nōt′) *n.* A note at the bottom of a page explaining something in the text or giving the source of a quotation, fact, or idea.

footpath (fo͞ot′păth′) *n.* A narrow path for people to walk on.

foot-pound (fo͞ot′pound′) *n.* A unit of work equal to the work or energy needed to lift a one-pound weight a distance of one foot against the force of the earth's gravity.

footprint (fo͞ot′prĭnt′) *n.* **1.** A mark left by a foot or shoe, as in sand or snow. **2.** The surface space occupied by a building. **3.** The area affected or covered by a device or phenomenon: *the footprint of a communications satellite.*

footrace (fo͞ot′rās′) *n.* A race run by people on foot.

footrest (fo͞ot′rĕst′) *n.* A low stool, metal bar, or other support on which to rest the feet.

footsie (fo͞ot′sē) *n. Informal* The act of flirting in which one secretly touches the feet of another with one's own, as under a table. ◆ **play footsie** To flirt with someone by secretly touching feet with one's own.

foot soldier *n.* A soldier in the infantry.

footsore (fŏŏt'sôr') *adj.* Having sore or tired feet from much walking.

footstep (fŏŏt'stĕp') *n.* **1.** A step with the foot. **2.** The sound of a foot stepping: *I heard their footsteps on the stairs.* **3.** A footprint. ◆ **follow in (someone's) footsteps** To carry on the behavior, work, or tradition of.

footstool (fŏŏt'stōol') *n.* A low stool on which to rest the feet while sitting.

footwear (fŏŏt'wâr') *n.* Coverings for the feet, such as shoes or boots.

footwork (fŏŏt'wûrk') *n.* The movement of the feet, as in boxing or dancing.

fop (fŏp) *n.* A man who is vain about his clothes and manners; a dandy. **—fop'pish** *adj.* **—fop'pish·ly** *adv.*

foppery (fŏp'ə-rē) *n., pl.* **fopperies** The dress or manner of a fop.

for (fôr; fər *when unstressed*) *prep.* **1a.** With the purpose, goal, or object of: *swimming for exercise; studying for the exam; eager for fame.* **b.** In order to go toward or arrive at: *Let's head for home.* **2.** On behalf of: *She spoke for all of us.* **3.** In favor or support of: *Are you for the idea or not?* **4.** In place of: *She used her coat for a blanket.* **5.** In the amount of; at the price of: *a bill for $50; a camera bought for $150.* **6.** To the extent of or through the duration of: *We drove for miles. We talked for an hour.* **7.** At the stated time of: *I have an appointment for 2:00.* **8.** With the indicated number of attempts: *shot three for four from the foul line.* **9.** As a result of: *They were rewarded for their hard work.* **10a.** As regards; concerning: *He's a stickler for neatness.* **b.** Considering the usual character of: *It's a warm day for October.* **c.** In honor of: *She was named for her aunt.* **11.** Suitable to: *It's really for her to decide.* **12.** In spite of: *For all his complaining, he seems to like his job.* ◆ *conj.* Because; since: *We must be careful measuring the windows, for it's easy to make mistakes.*

forage (fôr'ĭj) *n.* Plant material that livestock graze or that is cut and fed to them. ◆ *v.* **foraged, foraging, forages** *—intr.* To search for something, especially food: *She foraged in the woods for mushrooms. I foraged for clean socks.* *—tr.* **1.** To get by searching about: *We foraged cookies from the pantry.* **2.** To obtain food, supplies, or other goods from, often by force; plunder: *Pirates foraged the coastal towns.* **—for'ag·er** *n.*

forasmuch as (fôr'əz-mŭch') *conj.* Inasmuch as; since.

foray (fôr'ā') *n.* **1.** A sudden raid or military expedition. **2.** A venture or the beginning of an attempt, especially outside one's usual area: *the actor's foray into politics.* ◆ *intr.v.* **forayed, foraying, forays** To make a raid: *foray into enemy territory.*

forbad (fôr-băd') *v.* A past tense of **forbid.**

forbade (fôr-băd' *or* fôr-băd') *v.* A past tense of **forbid.**

forbear¹ (fôr-bâr') *v.* **forbore** (fôr-bôr'), **forborne** (fôr-bôrn'), **forbearing, forbears** *—intr.* **1.** To keep oneself from doing something; hold back; refrain: *forbear from replying.* **2.** To be patient or tolerant: *Forbear with my misunderstanding.* *—tr.* To keep from; refrain from; resist: *I could not forbear telling him the truth.*

forbear² (fôr'bâr') *n.* Variant of **forebear.**

forbearance (fôr-bâr'əns) *n.* **1.** Patience, tolerance, or restraint: *He showed forbearance in disciplining the unruly children.* **2.** The act of giving one who has a debt that is due more time to pay rather than enforcing immediate repayment.

forbid (fôr-bĭd') *tr.v.* **forbade** (fôr-băd' *or* fôr-băd') *or* **forbad** (fôr-băd'), **forbidden** (fôr-bĭd'n) *or* **forbid, for-**

bidding, forbids 1. To order (a person) not to do something: *I forbid you to go.* **2.** To refuse to allow; prohibit or deny: *The law forbids robbery.*

forbidding (fôr-bĭd'ĭng) *adj.* Looking threatening, dangerous, or unfriendly: *a forbidding desert.*

forbore (fôr-bôr') *v.* Past tense of **forbear¹.**

forborne (fôr-bôrn') *v.* Past participle of **forbear¹.**

force (fôrs) *n.* **1.** The capacity to do work or cause physical change; energy, strength, or active power: *the force of an explosion.* See Synonyms at **strength.** **2.** Power, pressure, or violence used on a person or thing that resists: *a promise obtained by force.* **3.** Something that causes a body to move, changes its speed or direction, or distorts its shape. One force may be counteracted by another, so that there is no change or distortion. **4a.** A group of people organized or available for a certain purpose: *a large labor force; a police force.* **b. forces** Military units, as of an army: *Napoleon's forces.* **5.** A strong influence acting as an urge or a restraint: *forces affecting modern life.* **6.** The power to influence or persuade; verbal effectiveness: *We felt his argument had considerable force.* ◆ *tr.v.* **forced, forcing, forces 1.** To cause (a person) to do something, as through pressure or necessity: *The storm forced us to postpone our meeting.* **2.** To get by the use of force: *I forced the ball from his hand.* **3.** To impose or inflict: *The invaders forced their laws on the peoples they conquered.* **4.** To move, push, or drive by pressure: *The pump forces water through the pipe.* **5.** To bring on or bring about through effort or pressure: *I forced a smile on my face.* **6.** To make (one's way) by pushing, thrusting, or breaking: *They forced their way through the thorn hedge.* **7.** To break open or pry open by using violence: *force the door; force a lock.* **8.** To cause to grow or bloom rapidly by artificial means: *force flowers in a greenhouse.* ◆ **in force 1.** In effect; in operation; valid: *a rule no longer in force.* **2.** In full strength: *The protesters turned out in force.* **—forc'er** *n.*

forced (fôrst) *adj.* **1.** Done under force, not by free choice; compulsory: *forced labor.* **2.** Not natural; strained: *forced laughter.*

forceful (fôrs'fəl) *adj.* Full of force; effective: *The winning candidate is a forceful speaker.* **—force'ful·ly** *adv.* **—force'ful·ness** *n.*

force play *n.* In baseball, a play in which a runner is put out when forced by the batter to move to the next base.

forceps (fôr'səps) *n., pl.* **forceps** A pair of special pincers or tongs used especially by surgeons or dentists for grasping, holding, or pulling.

forcible (fôr'sə-bəl) *adj.* **1.** Accomplished through the use of force: *The firefighters broke in by forcible entry.* **2.** Having force; forceful: *a forcible personality.* **—for'ci·bly** *adv.*

ford (fôrd) *n.* A shallow place in a stream or river where one can walk, ride, or drive across. ◆ *tr.v.* **forded, fording, fords** To cross (a stream or river) by wading, riding, or driving through a ford. **—ford'a·ble** *adj.*

fore (fôr) *adj.* In, at, or toward the front; forward: *The fore part of the new building faces the avenue.* ◆ *n.* **1.** Something that is located at or toward the front. **2.** The front part: *checked the ropes at the fore.* ◆ *adv.* At, toward, or near the front; forward: *ran fore to check the damage.* ◆ *interj.* An expression used by golfers to warn others on the course that a ball is headed in their direction. ◆ **to the fore** In, into, or toward a position of prominence: *New issues bring new leaders to the fore.*

fore– A prefix that means: **1.** Before; earlier: *foresight; forefather.* **2.** Front; in front of: *forepaw; foremast.*

WORD BUILDING The prefix **fore–** means "before, in front." A *forerunner* is "one that goes before," and a *foreleg* is "a front leg of an animal." It is important not to confuse *fore–* with the prefix *for–*, which appears in many English words but is no longer used to form new words. *For-* bears the meaning of exclusion or rejection, and survives in words like *forbid* and *forget*.

---

fore and aft *adv.* **1.** From the bow of a ship to the stern; lengthwise: *sails rigged fore and aft.* **2.** In, at, or toward both ends of a ship.

fore-and-aft (fôr′ən-ăft′) *adj.* Extending lengthwise along a structure, such as a ship; from bow to stern.

forearm¹ (fôr-ärm′) *tr.v.* **forearmed, forearming, forearms** To arm or prepare in advance of a conflict.

forearm² (fôr′ärm′) *n.* The part of the arm between the wrist and elbow.

forebear also **forbear** (fôr′bâr′) *n.* An ancestor.

forebode (fôr-bōd′) *tr.v.* **foreboded, foreboding, forebodes** **1.** To indicate the likelihood of; portend: *A dark sky sometimes forebodes a storm.* **2.** To have a sense or feeling of (something bad to come): *The scowls on their faces foreboded a fight.* —**fore·bod′er** *n.*

foreboding (fôr-bō′dĭng) *n.* A sense of impending evil or misfortune.

forebrain (fôr′brān′) *n.* The part of the brain that includes the cerebrum, the thalamus, and the hypothalamus.

forecast (fôr′kăst′) *tr.v.* **forecast** or **forecasted, forecasting, forecasts** To tell in advance what might or will happen, especially to predict weather conditions: *forecast snow for the weekend.* ❖ *n.* A prediction, as of coming events or conditions: *the weather forecast.* —**fore′cast′er** *n.*

forecastle (fōk′səl or fôr′kăs′əl) also **fo′c′s′le** (fōk′səl) *n.* **1.** The section of a ship's upper deck located forward of the foremast. **2.** The crew's quarters at the bow of a merchant ship.

foreclose (fôr-klōz′) *v.* **foreclosed, foreclosing, forecloses** —*tr.* **1.** To take away the right to pay off (a mortgage), as when payments have not been made: *The bank foreclosed the mortgage and took away the property.* **2.** To shut out or rule out; bar. —*intr.* To bar a right to redeem a mortgage: *The bank foreclosed on the property.*

foreclosure (fôr-klō′zhər) *n.* The act of foreclosing, especially a legal proceeding by which a mortgage is foreclosed.

foredoom (fôr-dōōm′) *tr.v.* **foredoomed, foredooming, foredooms** To doom or condemn beforehand.

forefather (fôr′fä′thər) *n.* **1.** An ancestor, especially a male ancestor. **2.** A person, especially a man, from an earlier time who has originated or contributed to a common tradition shared by a particular group.

forefend (fôr′fĕnd′) *v.* Variant of **forfend.**

forefinger (fôr′fĭng′gər) *n.* The finger next to the thumb; the index finger.

forefoot (fôr′fŏŏt′) *n.* One of the front feet of a four-legged animal.

forefront (fôr′frŭnt′) *n.* **1.** The part or area at the very front. **2.** The most important or most advanced position: *at the forefront in the fight against crime.*

foregather (fôr-găth′ər) *v.* Variant of **forgather.**

forego¹ (fôr-gō′) *tr.v.* **forewent** (fôr-wĕnt′), **foregone** (fôr-gôn′), **foregoing, foregoes** (fôr-gōz′) To precede, as in time or place.

forego² (fôr-gō′) *v.* Variant of **forgo.**

foregoing (fôr-gō′ĭng or fôr′gō′ĭng) *adj.* Said, written, or encountered just before; previous: *Refer to the foregoing figures.*

foregone *v.* (fôr-gôn′) Past participle of **forego¹.** ❖ *adj.* (fôr′gôn′) Having gone before; previous.

foreground (fôr′ground′) *n.* The part of a scene or picture that is nearest to and in front of the viewer.

forehand (fôr′hănd′) *n.* In sports, a stroke, as of a racket, made or done with the palm of the hand turned forward. —**fore′hand′** *adj.*

forehead (fôr′hĕd′ or fôr′ĭd′) *n.* The part of the face above the eyebrows.

foreign (fôr′ĭn) *adj.* **1.** Located away from one's own country: *a foreign country.* **2.** Relating to or from another country or place: *a foreign language; foreign customs.* **3.** Conducted or involved with other nations or governments: *foreign trade.* **4.** Not naturally or normally belonging; alien: *Jealousy is foreign to my nature.*

foreigner (fôr′ə-nər) *n.* **1.** A person from a foreign country or place: *Millions of foreigners have immigrated to the United States.* **2.** An outsider.

foreknow (fôr-nō′) *tr.v.* **foreknew** (fôr-nōō′), **foreknown** (fôr-nōn′), **foreknowing, foreknows** To have knowledge of something before its existence or occurrence.

foreknowledge (fôr-nŏl′ĭj or fôr′nŏl′ĭj) *n.* Knowledge of something before its occurrence or existence.

foreleg (fôr′lĕg′) *n.* One of the front legs of a four-legged animal.

forelimb (fôr′lĭm′) *n.* A front limb such as an arm, wing, foreleg, or flipper.

forelock (fôr′lŏk′) *n.* A lock of hair that grows from or falls on the forehead.

foreman (fôr′mən) *n.* **1.** A man who has charge of a group of workers, as in a factory. **2.** A man who chairs and speaks for a jury.

foremast (fôr′məst or fôr′măst′) *n.* The forward mast on a sailing ship.

foremost (fôr′mōst′) *adj.* First in time, place, rank, or position; most important: *the world's foremost authority on bees.* ❖ *adv.* In the first or front position.

foremother (fôr′mŭth′ər) *n.* **1.** A female ancestor. **2.** A woman from an earlier time who has originated or contributed to a common tradition shared by a particular group.

forenoon (fôr′nōōn′ or fôr-nōōn′) *n.* The period of time between sunrise and noon; morning.

forensic (fə-rĕn′sĭk or fə-rĕn′zĭk) *adj.* **1.** Relating to, used in, or appropriate for courts of law or for public discussion. **2.** Relating to the techniques used in investigating facts or acquiring evidence, as in a criminal case: *a forensic laboratory.*

foreordain (fôr′ôr-dān′) *tr.v.* **foreordained, foreordaining, foreordains** To determine or appoint beforehand; predestine: *They believed their fate was foreordained.*

forepart (fôr′pärt′) *n.* The first, early, or front part.

forepaw (fôr′pô′) *n.* The paw of an animal's foreleg.

foreplay (fôr′plā′) *n.* Sexual activity preceding intercourse.

forequarter (fôr′kwôr′tər) *n.* The front part of a side of beef, lamb, or other animal carcass.

forerunner (fôr′rŭn′ər) *n.* **1.** A person or thing that precedes, as in time; a predecessor: *Roller skates were the forerunners of skateboards.* **2.** A person who announces the coming of another; a herald. **3.** A warning sign or symptom: *A sore throat is often the forerunner of a cold.*

foresail (fôr'səl or fôr'sāl') *n.* **1.** The principal sail on the foremast of a square-rigged ship. **2.** The principal fore-and-aft sail on the foremast of a fore-and-aft rigged vessel.

foresee (fôr-sē') *tr.v.* **foresaw** (fôr-sô'), **foreseen** (fôr-sēn'), **foreseeing, foresees** To see or know beforehand: *As the mountain got steeper, the hikers foresaw a difficult climb.* —**fore·see'a·ble** *adj.* —**fore·se'er** *n.*

foreshadow (fôr-shăd'ō) *tr.v.* **foreshadowed, foreshadowing, foreshadows** To present an indication or suggestion of beforehand: *Everyone hoped that the border dispute did not foreshadow a wider war.*

foreshorten (fôr-shôr'tn) *tr.v.* **foreshortened, foreshortening, foreshortens** To shorten the lines of (an object) in a drawing or painting so as to give the illusion of depth or distance.

foresight (fôr'sīt') *n.* **1.** Perception of the importance and nature of events before they occur. **2.** Care in providing for the future: *Spending all of your money at once shows little foresight.* —**fore'sight'ed** *adj.*

foreskin (fôr'skĭn) *n.* The loose fold of skin that covers the end of the penis; the prepuce.

forest (fôr'ĭst) *n.* **1.** A growth of trees and other plants covering a large area. **2.** A large number of objects bearing a similarity to such a growth, especially a dense collection of tall objects: *a forest of skyscrapers.* —**for'es·ta'tion** *n.*

forestall (fôr-stôl') *tr.v.* **forestalled, forestalling, forestalls** **1.** To prevent, delay, or hinder by acting in advance: *ended the news conference to forestall any more questions.* **2.** To deal with or think of beforehand; anticipate. —**fore·stall'er** *n.*

forester (fôr'ĭ-stər) *n.* A person trained in forestry.

forestry (fôr'ĭ-strē) *n.* The science or work of cultivating, developing, and maintaining forests.

foretaste (fôr'tāst') *n.* A slight taste or sample of something to come: *Her first published story was a foretaste of later successful novels.*

foretell (fôr-tĕl') *tr.v.* **foretold** (fôr-tōld'), **foretelling, foretells** To tell or indicate beforehand; predict: *Can you foretell what will happen?*

forethought (fôr'thôt') *n.* Thought, planning, or consideration for the future; foresight.

forever (fər-ĕv'ər) *adv.* **1.** For everlasting time; eternally: *No one can live forever.* **2.** At all times; incessantly: *The baby is forever fussing.* ❖ *n.* A seemingly very long time: *The bus is taking forever to come.*

forevermore (fər-ĕv'ər-môr') *adv.* Forever.

forewarn (fôr-wôrn') *tr.v.* **forewarned, forewarning, forewarns** To warn in advance.

forewent (fôr-wĕnt') *v.* Past tense of **forego**[1].

forewing (fôr'wĭng') *n.* Either of a pair of front wings of a four-winged insect, such as a butterfly, dragonfly, or beetle.

forewoman (fôr'wŏom'ən) *n.* **1.** A woman who has charge of a group of workers, as in a factory. **2.** The woman who chairs and speaks for a jury.

foreword (fôr'wərd) *n.* A preface or an introductory note, as for a book.

forfeit (fôr'fĭt) *tr.v.* **forfeited, forfeiting, forfeits** To surrender or give up the right to (something) as a penalty or punishment for a crime, error, or offense: *By failing to appear, the opposing team forfeited the game.* ❖ *n.* **1.** Something surrendered or paid as a punishment or penalty.

2. The act of forfeiting: *The team lost the game by forfeit.*

forfeiture (fôr'fĭ-chōor' or fôr'fĭ-chər) *n.* **1.** The act of surrendering something as a forfeit. **2.** Something that is forfeited; a penalty.

forfend also **forefend** (fôr-fĕnd') *tr.v.* **forfended, forfending, forfends** also **forefended, forefending, forefends 1.** To keep or ward off; avert. **2.** *Archaic* To forbid.

forgather also **foregather** (fôr-găth'ər) *intr.v.* **forgathered, forgathering, forgathers** To gather together; assemble.

forgave (fər-gāv' or fôr-gāv') *v.* Past tense of **forgive**.

forge[1] (fôrj) *n.* A furnace or hearth where metal is heated so that it can be hammered into shape; a smithy. ❖ *tr.v.* **forged, forging, forges 1.** To form (metal, for example) by heating in a forge and hammering into shape. **2.** To give form or shape to, especially by means of careful effort: *The coach forged a close relationship with her players.* **3.** To reproduce or copy for fraudulent purposes; counterfeit: *forge a signature.* —**forg'er** *n.*

forge[2] (fôrj) *intr.v.* **forged, forging, forges 1.** To move forward gradually but steadily: *The explorers forged through the swamp.* **2.** To advance with an abrupt increase in speed: *forged into first place.*

WORD HISTORY Forge[1] comes from Middle English *forge*, which comes from Latin *fabrica*, both meaning "workshop of a metalsmith." The origin of **forge**[2] is uncertain.

forgery (fôr'jə-rē) *n., pl.* **forgeries 1.** The act of forging, especially the illegal production of something counterfeit: *the forgery of a painting.* **2.** Something counterfeit, forged, or fraudulent.

forget (fər-gĕt' or fôr-gĕt') *tr.v.* **forgot** (fər-gŏt' or fôr-gŏt'), **forgotten** (fər-gŏt'n or fôr-gŏt'n) or **forgot, forgetting, forgets 1.** To be unable to remember (something): *I forgot her email address. He completely forgot his lines in the play.* **2.** To fail to remember (to do something): *I forgot to give you the message.* **3.** To leave behind unintentionally: *I forgot my toothbrush.* ❖ **forget oneself** To lose one's reserve, temper, or self-restraint: *The bystanders forgot themselves and ran to ask the celebrity for an autograph.* —**for·get'ta·ble** *adj.* —**for·get'ter** *n.*

forgetful (fər-gĕt'fəl or fôr-gĕt'fəl) *adj.* **1.** Tending or likely to forget: *When I am sleepy I can be forgetful.* **2.** Neglectful; thoughtless: *forgetful of one's responsibilities.* —**for·get'ful·ly** *adv.* —**for·get'ful·ness** *n.*

forget-me-not (fər-gĕt'mē-nŏt' or fôr-gĕt'mē-nŏt') *n.* Any of various low-growing garden plants having clusters of small blue flowers.

forgive (fər-gĭv' or fôr-gĭv') *v.* **forgave** (fər-gāv' or fôr-gāv'), **forgiven** (fər-gĭv'ən or fôr-gĭv'ən), **forgiving, forgives** —*tr.* **1.** To excuse for a fault or offense; pardon: *Our friends forgave us for making them late.* **2.** To absolve from payment of (a debt, for example). —*intr.* To grant forgiveness: *A parent usually forgives easily.* —**for·giv'a·ble** *adj.* —**for·giv'er** *n.*

✦ **SYNONYMS forgive, condone, excuse, pardon** *v.*

forgiveness (fər-gĭv'nĭs or fôr-gĭv'nĭs) *n.* The act of forgiving; pardon.

forgiving (fər-gĭv'ĭng or fôr-gĭv'ĭng) *adj.* Inclined or able to forgive: *a kind, forgiving person.*

forgo also **forego** (fôr-gō') *tr.v.* **forwent** (fôr-wĕnt'), **forgone** (fôr-gŏn' or fôr-gŏn'), **forgoing, forgoes** To give up; do without: *I will forgo the day at the beach and finish my work instead.*

forgot (fər-gŏt' or fôr-gŏt') v. Past tense and a past participle of **forget.**

forgotten (fər-gŏt'n or fôr-gŏt'n) v. A past participle of **forget.**

forint (fôr'ĭnt') n., pl. **forint** The basic monetary unit of Hungary.

fork (fôrk) n. 1. A utensil with two or more prongs, used to serve or eat food. 2. A large farm tool of similar shape, used to pick up hay or turn up ground. 3a. The place where something, such as a stream or road, divides into two or more branches: *stood at the fork in the road.* b. One of the branches beginning at such a place: *the right fork of the road.* ❖ v. **forked, forking, forks** —tr. 1. To raise, carry, pitch, or pierce with a fork. 2. *Informal* To pay: *forked over the money for the bill.* —intr. To divide into two or more branches: *The road forks beyond the hill.*

forked (fôrkt or fôr'kĭd) adj. Having a fork or forks; divided: *a forked river; a snake's forked tongue.*

forklift (fôrk'lĭft') n. A small, power-operated, wheeled device having two flat prongs that can be slid under a load to be lifted and moved.

forlorn (fər-lôrn' or fôr-lôrn') adj. 1. Appearing sad or lonely because deserted or abandoned: *a forlorn puppy.* 2. Wretched or pitiful in appearance or condition: *a forlorn shack.* —**for·lorn'ly** adv.

form (fôrm) n. 1. The shape and structure of an object: *the form of a snowflake.* 2. The body or outward appearance of a person or animal; figure: *In the fog we could see two forms standing on the bridge.* 3. The manner in which a thing exists, acts, or manifests itself: *an element usually found in the form of a gas.* 4. A kind or sort: *What form of dessert did you make?* 5. The manner in which an artistic, musical, or literary work is arranged or put together: *in sonata form; arranged my ideas in outline form.* 6. A document with blanks that are to be filled in: *The patient's condition is recorded on a medical form.* 7. Fitness or good condition of mind or body: *The athlete is in top form this season.* 8. A mold for the setting of concrete. 9. A grade in a British school or in some American private schools. 10. One of the ways a word may be spelled or pronounced: *"Feet" is the plural form of "foot."* ❖ v. **formed, forming, forms** —tr. 1. To give form to; shape: *form clay into figures.* 2. To develop in the mind; conceive: *form an opinion.* 3. To organize or arrange: *form a students' committee.* 4. To come to have; develop or acquire: *form a bad habit.* 5a. To produce (a tense, for example) by adding certain elements: *form a plural by adding an "s" to the singular.* b. To make (a word) by combining different word elements: *form a word by adding "-tion" to the root.* —intr. To come into being by taking form; arise: *Buds form in the spring.*

formal (fôr'məl) adj. 1. Relating to outward form rather than structure. 2. Structured according to forms or conventions: *a formal meeting.* 3. Executed, carried out, or done in proper or regular form: *a formal document.* 4. Stiffly ceremonious: *a formal manner.* ❖ n. Something, such as a gown or a social affair, that is formal in nature. —**for'mal·ly** adv.

formaldehyde (fôr-mǎl'də-hīd') n. A colorless gas with the formula CH_2O. It is used in making plastics, fertilizers, and building materials, and is mixed with water to form a solution for preserving biological specimens.

formalism (fôr'mə-lĭz'əm) n. Strict observance of accepted or recognized forms, as in religion or art.

formality (fôr-mǎl'ĭ-tē) n., pl. **formalities 1.** Strict observance of accepted rules, forms, or customs: *There was no formality at our dinner table.* 2. An established rule, form, or custom, especially one followed merely for the sake of procedure: *the legal formalities of a trial.*

formalize (fôr'mə-līz') tr.v. **formalized, formalizing, formalizes 1.** To give a definite form or shape to: *formalize the contents of a lab report.* 2. To make formal or official: *They formalized the treaty by signing it.* —**for'mal·iz'er** n.

format (fôr'mǎt') n. 1. A plan for the organization or arrangement of something: *The format of the new television program was a series of interviews.* 2. The form or layout of a publication: *the format of a newspaper.* 3. The arrangement of computer data for storage or display. ❖ tr.v. **formatted, formatting, formats 1.** To plan or arrange in a specified form: *format a conference; formatted the document to have large margins.* 2. To divide (a computer disk) into sectors so that it may store data.

formation (fôr-mā'shən) n. 1. The act or process of forming something or of taking form: *the formation of political parties.* 2a. Something formed: *a cloud formation.* b. A layer of sediments or rocks that look alike and were formed at the same time. 3. A specified arrangement: *The geese flew overhead in a V formation.*

formative (fôr'mə-tĭv) adj. 1. Forming or capable of forming: *Childhood experiences often have a formative influence on writers.* 2. Relating to growth or development: *The growth of industry marked a formative period in the history of the United States.*

former (fôr'mər) adj. 1. Relating to or taking place in the past: *the tools of former civilizations; our former president.* 2. Being the first of two mentioned.

formerly (fôr'mər-lē) adv. At an earlier time; once: *Machines do work formerly done by people.*

Formica (fôr-mī'kə) A trademark for several types of plastic sheets that are used especially as surfaces for tables and counters.

formidable (fôr'mĭ-də-bəl or fôr-mĭd'ə-bəl) adj. 1. Frightening or difficult to undertake or deal with: *a formidable challenge; a formidable opponent.* 2. Admirable; awe-inspiring: *a formidable musical talent.* —**for'mi·da·bil'i·ty** n. —**for'mi·da·bly** adv.

formless (fôrm'lĭs) adj. 1. Having no definite form; shapeless: *a formless mist.* 2. Having no material existence: *a formless void.* —**form'less·ly** adv.

formula (fôr'myə-lə) n., pl. **formulas** or **formulae** (fôr'myə-lē') 1. An established set of words or symbols used in a ceremony or procedure. 2. A set of symbols showing the composition of a chemical compound; for example, H_2O is the formula for water. 3. A set of symbols in mathematics that expresses a rule or principle; for example, the formula for the area of a rectangle is $a = lw$, where a is the area, l the length, and w the width. 4. A list of the ingredients and processes used in making something; a recipe: *the formula for making toothpaste.* 5. A liquid food for infants, containing many of the nutrients in human milk. —**for'mu·la'ic** (fôr'myə-lā'ĭk) adj.

formulate (fôr'myə-lāt') tr.v. **formulated, formulating, formulates** To express in or as if in a formula; plan in an orderly way: *formulate a process; formulate an idea.* —**for'mu·la'tion** n.

fornicate (fôr'nĭ-kāt') intr.v. **fornicated, fornicating, fornicates** To have sexual intercourse with someone to whom one is not married. —**for'ni·ca'tor** n. —**for'ni·ca'tion** (fôr'nĭ-kā'shən) n.

forsake (fôr-sāk′) *tr.v.* **forsook** (fôr-sŏŏk′), **forsaken** (fôr-sā′kən), **forsaking, forsakes 1.** To give up (something formerly held dear); renounce. **2.** To leave altogether; abandon: *Do not forsake us when we need help.*

forsooth (fôr-sŏŏth′ *or* fər-sŏŏth′) *adv.* In truth; indeed.

forswear (fôr-swâr′) *tr.v.* **forswore** (fôr-swôr′), **forsworn** (fôr-swôrn′), **forswearing, forswears 1.** To decide or state that one will not or will no longer engage in (an activity or habit, for example): *forswore violence.* **2.** To decide or state that one will not or no longer use or be associated with (something): *forswore junk food.* ◆ **be forsworn** To lie under oath; commit perjury. **forswear (oneself)** To lie under oath; commit perjury.

forsythia (fôr-sĭth′ē-ə *or* fər-sĭth′ē-ə) *n.* Any of several shrubs having yellow flowers that bloom in early spring.

fort (fôrt) *n.* A fortified place or position stationed with troops; a fortification.

forte[1] (fôr′tā′ *or* fôrt) *n.* Something in which a person excels; a strong point: *The trumpet player's forte was jazz.*

forte[2] (fôr′tā′) *adv. & adj.* In music, in a loud forceful manner.

WORD HISTORY Both forms of **forte** come from Latin *fortis.* **Forte**[1] entered English by way of French *fort.* **Forte**[2] entered English by way of Italian *forte.* Latin *fortis,* French *fort,* and Italian *forte* all mean "strong."

---

forth (fôrth) *adv.* **1.** Forward in time, place, or order: *from this time forth.* **2.** Out into view: *After the movie, the audience poured forth from the theater.*

forthcoming (fôrth-kŭm′ĭng) *adj.* **1.** About to appear or take place; approaching: *The authors gave an interview about their forthcoming book.* **2.** Available when required or as promised: *More funds were not forthcoming.*

forthright (fôrth′rīt′) *adj.* Direct and without evasion; straightforward: *gave a forthright answer to my question.*

forthwith (fôrth-wĭth′ *or* fôrth-wĭth′) *adv.* At once; immediately.

fortieth (fôr′tē-ĭth) *n.* **1.** The ordinal number matching the number 40 in a series. **2.** One of 40 equal parts.

fortification (fôr′tə-fĭ-kā′shən) *n.* **1.** The act or process of fortifying: *the fortification of the city against enemy invaders.* **2.** Something that fortifies or defends, especially military works erected to fortify a position or place.

fortify (fôr′tə-fī′) *tr.v.* **fortified, fortifying, fortifies 1.** To strengthen and secure (a position) with fortifications: *They fortified the castle with a moat.* **2.** To strengthen physically; invigorate: *The hikers fortified themselves with granola.* **3.** To strengthen or improve (food, for example), as by adding vitamins; enrich. **—for′ti·fi·er** *n.*

fortissimo (fôr-tĭs′ə-mō′) *adv. & adj.* In music, in a very loud manner.

fortitude (fôr′tĭ-tōōd′) *n.* Strength of mind that allows one to deal with pain or adversity with courage.

fortnight (fôrt′nīt′) *n.* A period of two weeks.

fortnightly (fôrt′nīt′lē) *adj.* Appearing or happening once in or every two weeks. ◆ *adv.* Once every two weeks.

fortress (fôr′trĭs) *n.* A fortified place, especially a large military stronghold.

fortuitous (fôr-tōō′ĭ-təs) *adj.* **1.** Happening by accident or chance; unplanned. **2.** Lucky; fortunate: *A fortuitous change in the weather made the picnic possible.* **—for·tu′i·tous·ly** *adv.*

fortunate (fôr′chə-nĭt) *adj.* **1.** Bringing something good and unforeseen. **2.** Having good fortune; lucky: *I am for-*

tunate in having good friends. **—for′tu·nate·ly** *adv.*

fortune (fôr′chən) *n.* **1.** The chance happening of fortunate or adverse events; chance: *I had the good fortune to meet interesting people during my visit.* **2.** Extensive amounts of material possessions or wealth; riches. **3.** Destiny; fate: *told fortunes at the fair.*

fortune cookie *n.* A cookie made from a thin layer of dough that is folded and baked around a slip of paper bearing a prediction of fortune or a maxim.

fortuneteller (fôr′chən-tĕl′ər) *n.* A person who claims to predict future events. **—for′tune·tell′ing** *n.*

forty (fôr′tē) *n., pl.* **forties** The number, written 40, that is equal to 4×10.

forty-niner (fôr′tē-nī′nər) *n.* A person who took part in the California gold rush of 1849.

forum (fôr′əm) *n., pl.* **forums 1.** The public square of an ancient Roman city, especially the public square of ancient Rome, Italy. **2.** A public meeting or presentation involving a discussion usually among experts and often including audience participation. **3.** A public medium for the discussion of ideas, such as a newspaper, radio program, or website.

forward (fôr′wərd) *adj.* **1.** At, near, or belonging to the front of something: *the forward section of an airplane.* **2.** Going or moving toward the front: *a bad forward fall.* **3a.** Enthusiastically inclined; eager: *a forward student wanting to answer every question.* **b.** Lacking restraint or modesty; pushy or presumptuous: *I resented the clerk's forward manner in suggesting a choice.* **4.** Being ahead of current economic, political, or technological trends; progressive: *forward ideas about recycling.* ◆ *adv.* or **forwards** (fôr′wərdz) **1.** Toward or tending to the front; frontward: *All volunteers please step forward.* **2.** In or toward the future: *I look forward to my vacation.* **3.** In the direction or sequence for normal use: *clicked forward through the slide show.* ◆ *n.* A player in certain sports, such as basketball or soccer, who is part of the front line of offense. ◆ *tr.v.* **forwarded, forwarding, forwards 1.** To send on to a further destination or address: *forward letters to a new address.* **2.** To promote or advance: *forward one's own interests.* **—for′ward·ly** *adv.* **—for′ward·ness** *n.*

forward dive *n.* A dive in which the diver leaves the board facing the open water and rotates the body forward.

forwent (fôr-wĕnt′) *v.* Past tense of **forgo.**

fossil (fŏs′əl) *n.* **1.** The hardened remains or imprint of an organism that lived long ago. Fossils are often found in layers of sedimentary rock and along the beds of rivers that flow through them. **2.** A person or thing that is regarded as old-fashioned or outdated.

fossil fuel *n.* A fuel that comes from the remains of organisms that lived millions of years ago and were buried in the earth. Petroleum, coal, and natural gas are examples of fossil fuels.

fossilize (fŏs′ə-līz′) *tr. & intr.v.* **fossilized, fossilizing, fossilizes** To change into or become a fossil: *The shells of many prehistoric invertebrates have fossilized in layers of rock.* **—fos′sil·i·za′tion** (fŏs′ə-lĭ-zā′shən) *n.*

fossorial (fŏ-sôr′ē-əl) *adj.* **1.** Burrowing or living underground: *fossorial lizards.* **2.** Used for burrowing or digging: *fossorial feet.*

foster (fô′stər) *tr.v.* **fostered, fostering, fosters 1.** To bring up; nurture: *foster a child.* **2.** To promote the development or growth of; cultivate: *A cultural climate that fosters innovation.* ◆ *adj.* Giving or receiving parental care or nurture to or from those not legally related: *a foster child; a foster parent.*

fought (fôt) *v.* Past tense and past participle of **fight.**

foul (foul) *adj.* **fouler, foulest 1.** Offensive or unpleasant to the taste or smell: *the foul flavor of spoiled food; a foul smell of automobile exhaust.* **2.** Full of dirt or mud; dirty: *the foul fur of the stray dog.* See Synonyms at **dirty. 3.** Morally offensive; wicked: *foul rumors.* **4.** Bad or unfavorable: *foul weather.* **5.** Of a vulgar or obscene nature: *foul language.* **6.** In sports, contrary to the rules of a game: *A foul blow in boxing is one below the waist.* **7.** In baseball, outside the foul lines: *a foul fly ball.* ❖ *n.* **1.** In sports, a violation of the rules of play: *a foul in a game of basketball.* **2.** In baseball, a foul ball. ❖ *adv.* In a foul manner. ❖ *v.* **fouled, fouling, fouls** —*tr.* **1.** To make dirty or foul: *Factory smoke fouls the air.* **2.** To clog or obstruct: *Leaves fouled the drainpipe.* **3.** To entangle or catch (a rope, for example): *The dog fouled its leash in trying to get at the cat.* **4.** In sports, to commit a foul against (a player). **5.** In baseball, to hit (a ball) outside the foul lines. —*intr.* To become entangled or twisted: *The anchor line fouled on a rock.* ◆ **foul out 1.** In sports such as basketball, to be put out of a game for exceeding the number of permissible fouls. **2.** In baseball, to be put out by hitting a fly ball that is caught outside the foul lines. **foul up** To blunder or cause to blunder because of mistakes or poor judgment; botch: *I fouled up the recipe by adding too much milk.*

foul ball *n.* In baseball, a batted ball that touches the ground outside of fair territory.

foul line *n.* **1.** In baseball, one of two lines extending from home plate to the outfield barriers to indicate the area in which a fair ball can be hit. **2.** In basketball, a line 15 feet in front of the backboard from which a fouled player shoots a free throw. **3.** In sports, a boundary limiting the playing area, as in tennis or soccer.

foul play *n.* Unfair or treacherous action, especially when involving violence.

foul shot *n.* In basketball, an unobstructed shot from the foul line that is awarded to a player who has been fouled. It is scored as one point if successful.

foul-up (foul′ŭp′) *n.* **1.** A condition of confusion caused by mistakes or poor judgment. **2.** A mechanical failure.

found¹ (found) *tr.v.* **founded, founding, founds 1.** To originate or establish (something); create; set up: *founded the college in 1871.* See Synonyms at **establish. 2.** To establish the foundation or basis of: *founded the report on facts.*

found² (found) *tr.v.* **founded, founding, founds 1.** To melt (metal) and pour into a mold. **2.** To make (objects) by pouring molten material into a mold; cast.

WORD HISTORY Found¹ and **found²** come from two distinct Middle English words, both spelled *founden.* **Found¹** ultimately comes from Latin *fundāre* (meaning "to establish"), while **found²** ultimately comes from Latin *fundere,* meaning "to pour out; shed."

found³ (found) *v.* Past tense and past participle of **find.**

foundation (foun-dā′shən) *n.* **1.** The act of founding or establishing. **2.** The basis on which something stands, is founded, or is supported: *the foundations of modern science; the foundation of a building.* **3.** Funds for the support of an institution; an endowment. **4.** An institution that is founded and supported by an endowment. **5.** A cosmetic used as a base for facial makeup.

founder¹ (foun′dər) *intr.v.* **foundered, foundering, founders 1.** To sink below the water: *The ship foundered in the gale.* **2.** To fail: *Their business foundered.* **3.** To stumble, especially to stumble and go lame: *The horse foundered on the muddy ground.*

USAGE Because they have similar meanings, the verbs **founder¹** and **flounder¹** are often confused. *Founder* means "to come to ruin, fail utterly." It is used of plans and enterprises, such as businesses: *The effort to build a new ballpark has foundered. Flounder* means "to struggle or proceed with difficulty." It is usually used of people: *I'm floundering in algebra, so I asked for help.*

founder² (foun′dər) *n.* A person who founds or establishes something: *the founders of the school.*

Founding Father (foun′dĭng) *n.* **1.** A member of the convention that drafted the US Constitution in 1787. **2. founding father** A man who founds or establishes something.

foundling (found′lĭng) *n.* A deserted or abandoned child of unknown parentage.

foundry (foun′drē) *n., pl.* **foundries** A place where metals are cast and molded.

fount (fount) *n.* **1.** A fountain. **2.** A person or thing that initiates or dispenses; a source.

fountain (foun′tən) *n.* **1a.** An artificially created jet or stream of water. **b.** A structure, often decorative, from which such a jet or stream rises and flows: *the beautiful fountains of Rome; a drinking fountain.* **2.** A spring, especially the source of a stream. **3.** A device equipped with a nozzle that provides a stream of drinking water for public use. **4.** A point of origin; a source: *The zookeeper was a fountain of knowledge about animals.*

fountainhead (foun′tən-hĕd′) *n.* **1.** A spring that is the source of a stream. **2.** A chief source or an originator: *The old philosopher was a fountainhead of wisdom.*

fountain pen *n.* A pen having a refillable or replaceable ink reservoir that feeds ink to the writing point.

four (fôr) *n.* **1.** The number, written 4, that is equal to 3 + 1. **2.** The fourth in a set or sequence. **3.** Something having four parts or units, such as a musical quartet. ◆ **all fours** All four limbs of an animal or person: *Babies crawl around on all fours.*

4-H Club (fôr′āch′) *n.* A group for young people that offers instruction in agriculture and home economics.

four-leaf clover (fôr′lēf′) *n.* A clover leaf that has four leaflets instead of the usual three, considered a sign of good luck.

four-o′clock (fôr′ə-klŏk′) *n.* Any of several garden plants having variously colored flowers that have a funnel shape and open in the late afternoon.

401(k) (fôr′ō-wŭn-kā′) *n.* A retirement plan in which a person invests a part of his or her wages in an account that is not taxed until he or she retires and takes money from it.

four-poster (fôr′pō′stər) *n.* A bed with tall corner posts originally intended to support curtains or a canopy.

fourscore (fôr′skôr′) *n.* Four times twenty; eighty.

foursome (fôr′səm) *n.* **1.** A group of four people or things, especially two couples. **2.** An activity involving four people, such as a golf match.

foursquare (fôr′skwâr′) *adj.* **1.** Having four equal sides and four right angles; square. **2.** Firm and unwavering; forthright: *a foursquare refusal to yield.* ❖ *adv.* In a forthright manner; squarely. ❖ *n.* A game in which each of four players stands in one of four boxes drawn on the ground in a two-by-two grid and must bounce a ball into another player's box without holding the ball or stepping out of bounds.

fourteen (fôr-tēn′) *n.* **1.** The number, written 14, that is equal to 13 + 1. **2.** The 14th in a set or sequence.

fourteenth (fôr-tēnth′) *n.* **1.** The ordinal number matching the number 14 in a series. **2.** One of 14 equal parts.

fourth (fôrth) *n.* **1.** The ordinal number matching the number four in a series. **2.** One of four equal parts. **3a.** The interval covering four tones in a musical scale, as C, D, E, and F. **b.** The fourth tone in a musical scale; the subdominant. **4.** The transmission gear used to produce speeds next higher than those of third in a motor vehicle. **5. Fourth** The Fourth of July; Independence Day. **—fourth** *adv. & adj.*

fourth dimension *n.* In physics, time regarded as a dimension along with the three spatial dimensions of length, width, and height.

fourth estate *n.* Journalists considered as a group.

Fourth of July *n.* Independence Day.

four-wheel drive (fôr′wēl′) *n.* An automotive drive system in which mechanical power is transmitted from the drive shaft to all four wheels.

fowl (foul) *n., pl.* **fowl** or **fowls 1a.** A chicken or related bird, such as a duck or turkey. **b.** The meat of any of these birds used as food. **2.** A bird of any kind: *a diet of fish and fowl.*

fox (fŏks) *n.* **1.** *pl.* **foxes** also **fox** Any of various meat-eating mammals related to the dogs and wolves, having a pointed snout, upright ears, and a long bushy tail. **2.** The fur of any of these mammals. **3.** A crafty, clever, or sly person: *The old fox outwitted everyone.*   •

Fox *n.* **1.** A member of a Native American people formerly inhabiting parts of Michigan, Wisconsin, Illinois, and Iowa, now living in Iowa and Oklahoma. **2.** The Algonquian language of the Fox.

foxglove (fŏks′glŭv′) *n.* Any of several plants having a long cluster of tubular purplish, yellow, or white flowers, used as a source of digitalis.

foxhole (fŏks′hōl′) *n.* A shallow pit dug by a soldier for protection in combat.

foxhound (fŏks′hound′) *n.* Any of various short-haired dogs originally developed for fox hunting.

fox terrier *n.* Any of various small terriers having a smooth or wiry white coat with black and tan markings, originally used to drive foxes from their burrows.

foxtrot (fŏks′trŏt′) *intr.v.* **foxtrotted, foxtrotting, foxtrots** To dance the fox trot.

fox trot *n.* **1.** A ballroom dance in 4/4 time, consisting of a combination of fast and slow steps. **2.** The music for this dance.

foxy (fŏk′sē) *adj.* **foxier, foxiest** Slyly clever; crafty: *a foxy scheme.* **—fox′i·ly** *adv.* **—fox′i·ness** *n.*

foyer (foi′ər *or* foi′ā′) *n.* **1.** A lobby or anteroom, as of a theater or hotel. **2.** An entrance hall, as of a private house or apartment.

fpm An abbreviation of feet per minute.

fps An abbreviation of: **1.** feet per second. **2.** frames per second.

fr. An abbreviation of from.

Fr. An abbreviation of father (religious title).

fracas (frā′kəs *or* frăk′əs) *n.* A noisy, disorderly fight or quarrel.

fracking (frăk′ĭng) *n.* Hydraulic fracturing.

fractal (frăk′təl) *n.* A geometric pattern repeated at ever smaller scales and used especially in computer modeling of irregular patterns and structures in nature.

fraction (frăk′shən) *n.* **1.** A number that is written in the form ⅗, where *a* and *b* are whole numbers and *b* is not zero. Fractions are used to compare parts to a whole, as in *Joe ate ¼ of the cake.* **2.** A small part or bit of something: *a fraction of the original price.* —SEE NOTE AT **fragile.**

fractional (frăk′shə-nəl) *adj.* **1.** Relating to or composed of a fraction or fractions. **2.** Very small; insignificant: *a fractional share of the popular vote.* **—frac′tion·al·ly** *adv.*

fractious (frăk′shəs) *adj.* **1.** Likely to make trouble; unruly. **2.** Cross; peevish; cranky. **—frac′tious·ly** *adv.*

fracture (frăk′chər) *n.* **1.** The act or process of breaking: *enough pressure to cause the fracture of solid rock.* **2.** A break, rupture, or crack, as in bone. ❖ *tr. & intr.v.* **fractured, fracturing, fractures** To break or cause to break: *I fractured my arm in the fall. The foundation of the building fractured in the earthquake.* See Synonyms at **break.** —SEE NOTE AT **fragile.**

fragile (frăj′əl *or* frăj′īl′) *adj.* **1.** Easily damaged or broken; frail: *a fragile glass vase.* **2.** Lacking physical or emotional strength; delicate. **3.** Lacking substance; flimsy: *a fragile claim.* **—frag′ile·ly** *adv.* **—fra·gil′i·ty** (frə-jĭl′ĭ-tē) *n.*

WORD BUILDING The word root *frag–* in English words comes from a form of the Latin verb *frangere,* "to break." That verb gave rise to the Latin adjective *fragilis,* "breakable," the source of our **fragile.** The same Latin adjective became *frele* in Old French, from which we get the word **frail.** The past participle of *frangere* was *frāctus,* from which the Latin nouns *frāctiō,* "a breaking," and *frāctūra,* "a break," were formed. From these words we get **fraction** and **fracture.**

fragment (frăg′mənt) *n.* **1.** A small part that is broken off or detached from a whole: *a fragment of a shattered china plate.* **2.** An incomplete or isolated portion; a bit: *We could overhear fragments of their conversation.* **3.** A sentence fragment. ❖ *tr. & intr.v.* (frăg′mĕnt′) **fragmented, fragmenting, fragments** To break or become broken into fragments: *An explosion had fragmented the sinking ship. After the election, the committee fragmented.*

fragmentary (frăg′mən-tĕr′ē) *adj.* Consisting of small disconnected parts: *Only fragmentary sentences of the damaged document were legible.*

fragmentation (frăg′mən-tā′shən) *n.* The act or process of fragmenting or breaking into pieces.

fragrance (frā′grəns) *n.* **1.** A sweet or pleasant odor; a scent: *the fresh fragrance of pine.* **2.** A substance, such as a perfume, designed to give off a pleasant odor.

fragrant (frā′grənt) *adj.* Having a pleasant odor; sweet-smelling: *a fragrant flower garden.* **—fra′grant·ly** *adv.*

frail (frāl) *adj.* **frailer, frailest 1.** Physically weak; not robust. **2.** Easily broken or destroyed; fragile: *a flower with a frail stem.* **3.** Easily led astray; morally weak. **—frail′-ness** *n.* —SEE NOTE AT **fragile.**

frailty (frāl′tē) *n., pl.* **frailties 1.** The quality or condition of being frail; weakness. **2.** A fault arising from human weakness; a failing: *Greed is a common human frailty.*

frame (frām) *n.* **1a.** A structure that shapes or supports: *the frame of a car.* **b.** An open structure or rim used to encase, hold, or border: *a door frame; a picture frame.* **c.** The structure of a human or animal body: *a lanky frame.* **2.** A general structure or system: *the frame of government.* **3.** A round of play in some games, such as bowling. **4a.** One of the set of still images that makes up a film or video. **b.** An individual drawing within a comic strip or graphic novel. **5.** A rectangular area in which text or graphics can be shown, especially one of several rectangular areas on a web page displaying different documents simultaneously. ❖ *tr.v.* **framed, framing, frames 1.** To build by putting together the structural parts of: *frame an agreement; frame a house.* **2.** To enclose in a frame: *frame a picture.* **3.** To put into words, especially in a way that does not acknowledge another point of view: *The questionnaire framed the question to get a favorable response.* **4.** *Informal* To make up evidence so as to incriminate (someone) falsely: *The witness was paid to frame an innocent bystander.* —**fram′a·ble, frame′a·ble** *adj.* —**fram′er** *n.*

frame-up (frām′ŭp′) *n. Informal* A plot to incriminate an innocent person.

framework (frām′wûrk′) *n.* **1.** A structure that shapes or supports; a frame: *The building was constructed on a framework of steel girders.* **2.** A fundamental structure, as for a written work or a system of ideas: *Education is the framework on which to build a productive life.* **3.** A set of assumptions, concepts, values, and practices that constitutes a way of viewing or thinking about something.

franc (frăngk) *n.* **1.** The former basic monetary unit of Belgium, France, and Luxembourg. **2.** The basic monetary unit of Liechtenstein, Switzerland, and many African countries that were formerly colonies of France.

franchise (frăn′chīz′) *n.* **1.** The right to vote; suffrage: *In earlier times only landowners had the franchise.* **2a.** Authorization that is granted to someone to sell or distribute a company's goods or services in a certain area: *The franchise for collecting trash in the town was awarded to a private company.* **b.** A business or group of businesses established or operated under such authorization. **c.** A professional sports team: *a baseball franchise.*

Franciscan (frăn-sĭs′kən) *n.* A member of a Roman Catholic order established in 1209 by Saint Francis of Assisi (1182?–1226) and dedicated to the virtues of humility and poverty.

francium (frăn′sē-əm) *n. Symbol* **Fr** A radioactive element that has been artificially produced by scientists. The half-life of its longest-lived isotope is about 22 minutes. Atomic number 87. See **Periodic Table.**

Francophone also **francophone** (frăng′kə-fōn′) *n.* A person who speaks French, especially in a country or region where at least one other language besides French is spoken. —**Fran′co·phone′** *adj.*

frank¹ (frăngk) *adj.* **franker, frankest** Open and sincere in expression; straightforward: *made several frank remarks about the quality of their work.* ❖ *tr.v.* **franked, franking, franks 1.** To put an official mark on (mail) so that it can be sent free of charge. **2.** To send (mail) free of charge. ❖ *n.* **1.** A mark placed on a piece of mail to indicate the right to send it free of charge. **2.** The right to send mail free of charge. —**frank′ness** *n.*

frank² (frăngk) *n. Informal* A frankfurter.

WORD HISTORY Frank¹ is from Middle English *frank,* meaning "free, open." **Frank²** is short for *frankfurter.*

Frank (frăngk) *n.* A member of a Germanic tribe that conquered Gaul around AD 500 and established a large empire.

frankfurter (frăngk′fər-tər) *n.* A sausage usually made of beef or beef and pork.

frankincense (frăng′kĭn-sĕns′) *n.* A fragrant gum resin obtained from certain African and Asian trees, used as incense and in perfumes.

Frankish (frăng′kĭsh) *adj.* Relating to the Franks or their language. ❖ *n.* The West Germanic language of the Franks.

frankly (frăngk′lē) *adv.* **1.** In a frank manner; candidly: *Speaking frankly, the lawyer warned us our case was very weak.* **2.** Honestly; in truth: *Frankly, I don't know.*

frantic (frăn′tĭk) *adj.* Very excited with fear or anxiety; desperate; frenzied: *frantic with worry.* —**fran′ti·cal·ly** *adv.* —**fran′tic·ness** *n.*

frappe (frăp) *n.* A milkshake.

frappé (fră-pā′) *n.* A fruit drink served almost frozen or poured over crushed ice.

frat (frăt) *n. Informal* A college fraternity.

fraternal (frə-tûr′nəl) *adj.* **1a.** Relating to brothers: *a close fraternal tie.* **b.** Showing comradeship: *a fraternal greeting.* **2.** Relating to or consisting of a fraternity: *The Masons are a fraternal society.* **3.** Relating to twins that develop from egg cells that have been fertilized by two different sperm. Fraternal twins, in contrast to identical twins, can be of different sexes and do not share all of the same genes. —**fra·ter′nal·ly** *adv.*

fraternity (frə-tûr′nĭ-tē) *n., pl.* **fraternities 1.** A group of people associated or linked by similar interests, backgrounds, or occupations: *the local business fraternity; the medical fraternity.* **2.** A social organization at a college or university, traditionally consisting of male students. **3.** The quality or condition of being brothers.

fraternize (frăt′ər-nīz′) *intr.v.* **fraternized, fraternizing, fraternizes 1.** To associate with others in a brotherly or friendly way: *Teachers and students fraternize in the cafeteria.* **2.** To associate on friendly terms with the people of an enemy or opposing group. —**frat′er·ni·za′tion** (frăt′ər-nĭ-zā′shən) *n.*

fratricide (frăt′rĭ-sīd′) *n.* **1.** The killing of one's brother or sister. **2.** Someone who kills his or her brother or sister. —**frat′ri·cid′al** *adj.*

Frau (frou) *n., pl.* **Frauen** (frou′ən) Used as a title in a German-speaking area before the surname or professional title of a woman.

fraud (frôd) *n.* **1.** Deception carried out in order to get something, usually money or property, from someone: *a government agency with the purpose of protecting consumers against fraud in advertising.* **2.** A person who tries to deceive others, especially by claiming to have abilities that he or she does not possess.

fraudulent (frô′jə-lənt) *adj.* Relating to, gained by, or engaging in fraud: *a fraudulent scheme; a fraudulent merchant.* —**fraud′u·lence** *n.* —**fraud′u·lent·ly** *adv.*

fraught (frôt) *adj.* Filled with something specified; charged: *an incident fraught with danger.*

Fräulein (froi′līn′ *or* frou′līn′) *n., pl.* **Fräulein** Used as a title for an unmarried woman or a girl in a German-speaking area.

fray¹ (frā) *n.* A scuffle; a brawl: *Several bystanders were caught up in the fray.*

fray² (frā) *v.* **frayed, fraying, frays** —*tr.* **1.** To wear away (the edges of fabric, for example) by rubbing. **2.** To strain; chafe: *Traffic frayed the driver's nerves.* —*intr.* To become worn away or tattered along the edges.

WORD HISTORY Fray¹ comes from Middle English *frai*, meaning "brawl, attack," which comes from Old French *esfraier*, meaning "to disturb." **Fray²** comes from Middle English *fraien* (meaning "to wear away, bruise"), which comes from Latin *fricāre*, meaning "to rub."

frazzle (frăz′əl) *Informal v.* **frazzled, frazzling, frazzles** —*tr.* **1.** To wear away along the edges; fray. **2.** To exhaust physically or emotionally: *frazzled by hard work and pressure.* —*intr.* To become frazzled. ❖ *n.* A frayed, tattered, or exhausted condition.

freak (frēk) *n.* **1.** A thing or occurrence that is markedly unusual or irregular: *The summer snowstorm was a freak of nature.* **2.** *Slang* An enthusiast: *a movie freak; a running freak.* ❖ *adj.* Highly unusual or irregular: *a freak accident.*

freakish (frē′kĭsh) *adj.* Markedly abnormal or unusual; strange: *freakish warm weather in winter.* —**freak′ish·ly** *adv.*

freckle (frĕk′əl) *n.* Any of the small brownish spots on the skin that often turn darker or increase in number when the skin is exposed to the sun. ❖ *tr. & intr.v.* **freckled, freckling, freckles** To mark or become marked with freckles or spots of color.

free (frē) *adj.* **freer, freest 1.** Not imprisoned or confined; at liberty. **2.** Not controlled or enslaved by another person: *You're free to go.* **3a.** Having political independence: *a free country.* **b.** Not subject to arbitrary interference by a government: *a free press.* **4a.** Not affected by a given condition or circumstance: *free of germs; free from worry.* **b.** Not subject to taxes or other charges; exempt: *Medicine is free of sales tax.* **5.** Not literal or exact: *a free translation.* **6.** Costing nothing; gratuitous: *a free meal.* **7.** Unobstructed; clear: *a free lane.* **8a.** Not occupied or used: *free space.* **b.** Not taken up by scheduled activities: *a free hour at lunchtime.* **9.** Unguarded in expression or manner; frank. **10.** Liberal or lavish: *very free with the inherited money.* **11.** In chemistry, not combined with something else: *Oxygen exists free in air.* ❖ *adv.* **1.** In a free manner; without restraint: *The rope swung free.* **2.** Without charge: *We were admitted free.* ❖ *tr.v.* **freed, freeing, frees 1.** To make free, as from confinement or oppression: *The convict was freed from prison.* **2.** To relieve of a burden, obligation, or restraint: *Vacation frees us from daily jobs for a short time.* **3.** To unfasten or untangle; detach: *We freed the rope caught on a nail.* ◆ **for free** *Informal* Without charge: *I used a coupon to get tickets for free.* —**free′ly** *adv.* —**free′ness** *n.*

freebooter (frē′bōō′tər) *n.* A person who plunders, especially a pirate.

freedman (frĕd′mən) *n.* A man who has been freed from slavery.

freedom (frē′dəm) *n.* **1.** The condition of not being in captivity: *After ten years in prison, he regained his freedom.* **2.** The condition of being free from restraints; the power to act without restraint: *freedom of assembly.* **3.** The ability of a country or group to govern itself; political independence. **4.** The capacity to exercise choice; free will: *the freedom to do what we want.* **5.** Frankness or boldness; lack of reserve: *a casual freedom in their manner.* **6.** Ease or facility of movement: *The paved paths gave us the freedom to skateboard throughout the park.* **7.** The use of or access to something: *Investigators were given the freedom of the files.*

freedom of speech *n.* The right to express any opinion in public without censorship or restraint by the govern-ment. The freedom of speech is protected in the United States as a right under the First Amendment to the US Constitution.

freedom rider *n.* One of a group of civil rights activists in the early 1960s who rode buses through parts of the southern United States for the purpose of challenging racial segregation.

freedwoman (frĕd′wōōm′ən) *n.* A woman who has been freed from slavery.

free enterprise *n.* The freedom of private businesses to operate competitively for profit with minimal government regulation.

free fall *n.* **1.** The fall of a body toward the earth without any force restraining it other than the drag produced by the atmosphere. **2.** Rapid, uncontrolled decline: *the news sent the company's stock price into a free fall.*

free-for-all (frē′fər-ôl′) *n.* A disorderly fight, argument, or competition in which everyone present participates.

freehand (frē′hănd′) *adj.* Drawn by hand without the aid of tracing or drafting tools. —**free′hand′** *adv.*

free kick *n.* In soccer and rugby, a kick of a stationary ball that a referee grants to one team after the other team has committed a foul or violated a rule.

freelance (frē′lăns′) *intr.v.* **freelanced, freelancing, freelances** To work as a freelancer: *a journalist who freelances.* —**free′lance** *adv. & adj.*

freelancer (frē′lăn′sər) *n.* A person who sells his or her services to employers without a long-term commitment.

freeman (frē′mən) *n.* **1.** A person not in slavery or serfdom. **2.** A person who possesses the rights and privileges of a citizen.

Freemason (frē′mā′sən) *n.* A member of the Free and Accepted Masons, an international fraternal and charitable organization.

Freemasonry (frē′mā′sən-rē) *n.* The institutions, precepts, and rites of the Freemasons.

free-range (frē′rānj′) *adj.* Relating to or produced by animals, especially poultry, that range freely for food rather than being confined: *free-range eggs.*

free-soil (frē′soil′) *adj.* **1.** Prohibiting slavery: *free-soil states.* **2. Free-Soil** Relating to or being a US political party founded in 1848 to oppose the spread of slavery into US Territories and the admission of slave states into the Union.

free speech *n.* **1.** Freedom of speech. **2.** Speech protected by the law from being restrained or curtailed by the government.

freestanding (frē′stăn′dĭng) *adj.* Standing without support or attachment: *a freestanding garage.*

Free State *n.* Any state of the Union in which slavery was illegal before the Civil War.

freestone (frē′stōn′) *n.* A fruit, such as a peach or apricot, having flesh that separates easily from the pit.

freestyle (frē′stīl′) *n.* **1.** A rapid swimming stroke performed face down with alternating overarm strokes and a flutter kick; the crawl. **2.** A competitive sports event in which any style, maneuver, or movement may be used by the competitor. —**free′style′** *adv. & adj.*

freethinker (frē′thĭng′kər) *n.* A person who forms opinions independently and does not follow traditional dogma, especially in matters of religion. —**free′think′ing** *adj. & n.*

free throw *n.* A foul shot in basketball.

free verse *n.* Poetry that does not have a regular meter or rhyme scheme.

freeware (frē'wâr') *n.* Free software, usually available over the Internet.

freeway (frē'wā') *n.* A highway for high-speed travel, having several lanes.

freewheeling (frē'wē'lĭng) *adj.* Free of restraints or limits; acting freely: *freewheeling advertising campaigns.*

freewill (frē'wĭl') *adj.* Done of one's own accord; voluntary.

free will *n.* The power to make free choices that are not limited by people or things beyond one's control.

freeze (frēz) *v.* **froze** (frōz), **frozen** (frō'zən), **freezing**, **freezes** —*intr.* **1.** To change from a liquid to a solid by loss of heat: *Pure water freezes at a higher temperature than salt water.* **2.** To have ice form in or on: *The pond freezes early in winter. The pipes froze.* **3.** To be harmed or killed by cold or frost: *Many fruits freeze in very cold weather.* **4.** To be or feel very cold: *We froze without sweaters.* **5.** To stop functioning, usually temporarily: *The computer screen froze when I opened the infected program.* **6.** To become motionless or unable to move: *The climber froze with fear on the slippery rocks.* —*tr.* **1.** To convert (a liquid substance) into ice. **2.** To cause ice to form upon: *The cold snap froze the river.* **3.** To preserve (food, for example) by subjecting to a freezing temperature: *freeze vegetables.* **4.** To harm or kill by cold: *The deep cold froze the oranges.* **5.** To make very cold: *The winter wind froze my fingers.* **6.** To make motionless or unable to move: *Fear froze the deer in the beam of our lights.* **7.** To keep (prices or wages) from changing: *The company froze wages at last year's levels.* ❖ *n.* **1a.** The act of freezing: *a freeze on hiring.* **b.** The state of being frozen: *a price freeze.* **2.** A period of cold weather; a frost: *crops ruined by the early freeze.* ◆ **freeze out** To shut out or exclude, as by cold or unfriendly treatment: *large chain stores that freeze out small merchants.*

freeze-dry (frēz'drī') *tr.v.* **freeze-dried, freeze-drying, freeze-dries** To preserve (food, for example) by rapid freezing and drying in a vacuum.

freezer (frē'zər) *n.* A refrigerated compartment that is kept at a very low temperature for freezing and storing items that spoil easily, especially food.

freezing point (frē'zĭng) *n.* The temperature at which a liquid freezes.

freight (frāt) *n.* **1.** Goods carried as cargo by truck, train, ship, or aircraft. **2a.** Commercial transportation of goods. **b.** The charge for transporting goods. **3.** A railway train carrying goods only. ❖ *tr.v.* **freighted, freighting, freights** **1.** To transport commercially as cargo. **2.** To load or fill with cargo: *ships waiting to be freighted.*

freight car *n.* A railroad car designed to carry freight.

freighter (frā'tər) *n.* A vehicle, especially a ship, for carrying freight. **2.** A shipper of cargo.

freight train *n.* A railroad train made up of an engine and freight cars.

French (frĕnch) *adj.* Relating to France or its people, language, or culture. ❖ *n.* **1.** *(used with a plural verb)* The people of France. **2.** The Romance language of France and parts of Switzerland, Belgium, Canada, and certain other countries.

French and Indian War *n.* A war (1756–1763) fought in North America between England and France and involving some Native Americans as allies of the French.

French braid *n.* A hairstyle in which the hair is gathered in increasingly greater amounts into one braid that begins at the crown and extends down the back of the head.

French bread *n.* Bread made with water, flour, and yeast and baked in long crusty loaves.

French Canadian *n.* A Canadian of French ancestry. —**French'-Ca·na'di·an** *adj.*

French curve *n.* A flat drafting instrument with curved edges and scroll-shaped cutouts, used as a guide in drawing curves.

French door *n.* A door, usually one of a pair, with glass panes extending for most of its length.

French dressing *n.* **1.** A salad dressing of oil, vinegar, and seasonings. **2.** A commercially prepared creamy salad dressing that is usually pinkish in color and often sweet.

french fry or **French fry** *n.* A thin strip of potato fried in deep fat: *squirted ketchup onto my french fries.*

french-fry (frĕnch'frī') *tr.v.* **french-fried, french-frying, french-fries** To fry (potato strips, for example) in deep fat.

French horn *n.* A brass musical instrument that has valves and a long, coiled tube ending in a wide bell.

Frenchman (frĕnch'mən) *n.* A man who is a native or inhabitant of France.

French toast *n.* Sliced bread soaked in a batter of milk and egg and lightly fried.

Frenchwoman (frĕnch'wŏŏm'ən) *n.* A woman who is a native or inhabitant of France.

frenetic (frə-nĕt'ĭk) *adj.* Wildly active or excited; frantic; frenzied: *worked at a frenetic pace to get the project done.* —**fre·net'i·cal·ly** *adv.*

frenzied (frĕn'zēd) *adj.* Affected with or marked by frenzy; frantic: *There was a frenzied rush for the nearest exit.* —**fren'zied·ly** *adv.*

frenzy (frĕn'zē) *n., pl.* **frenzies** A state of violent agitation or wild excitement: *The frightened horses dashed about in a frenzy.*

frequency (frē'kwən-sē) *n., pl.* **frequencies** **1.** The condition of occurring repeatedly at short intervals: *annoyed at the frequency of the telemarketers' calls.* **2.** The number of times some event occurs within a given period; rate of occurrence. **3.** The number of complete cycles of a wave, such as a radio wave, that occur per second. **4.** The ratio of the number of occurrences of some event to the number of opportunities for its occurrence.

frequency modulation *n.* A method of broadcasting in which the frequency of the carrier wave is varied according to the signal being transmitted. Frequency modulation reduces static in radio transmission.

frequent (frē'kwənt) *adj.* Occurring or appearing quite often or at close intervals: *frequent visits to the doctor; a frequent visitor.* ❖ *tr.v.* (*also* frē-kwĕnt') **frequented, frequenting, frequents** To pay frequent visits to; be in or at often: *They frequented the museum on weekends.* —**fre'quent·ly** *adv.*

fresco (frĕs'kō) *n., pl.* **frescoes** or **frescos** **1.** The art of painting on fresh moist plaster. **2.** A painting done in this manner.

fresh (frĕsh) *adj.* **fresher, freshest** **1.** New to one's experience; not known before: *fresh reports from the scene of the earthquake.* **2.** Being unusual or different; novel: *a fresh approach to old problems.* **3.** Recently made, produced, or gathered; not stale or spoiled: *fresh bread; fresh fruit.* **4.** Not preserved, as by canning, smoking, or freezing: *fresh vegetables.* **5.** Not saline or salty: *fresh water.* **6.** Not yet used or soiled; clean: *fresh paper towels.* **7.** Free from impurity or pollution; pure: *fresh air.* **8.** Bright and clear;

not dull or faded: *recent experiences that are fresh in one's memory.* **9.** Fairly strong; brisk: *a fresh morning breeze.* **10.** New or additional; further: *a fresh coat of paint.* **11.** Not tired; refreshed; rested: *felt fresh after a short nap.* **12.** Having the glowing unspoiled appearance of youth: *a bright fresh face.* **13.** *Informal* Lacking respect or restraint in behavior; impudent. **—fresh′ly** *adv.* **—fresh′ness** *n.*

freshen (frĕsh′ən) *v.* **freshened, freshening, freshens** *—intr.* To become fresh, as in vigor or appearance. *—tr.* To make fresh: *Rain freshened the air.*

freshet (frĕsh′ĭt) *n.* **1.** A sudden overflow of a stream as a result of a heavy rain or a thaw. **2.** A stream of fresh water that runs into a body of salt water.

freshman (frĕsh′mən) *n.* A student in the first-year class of a high school, college, or university.

freshwater (frĕsh′wô′tər) *adj.* Relating to, living in, or consisting of water that is not salty: *freshwater fish; a freshwater pond.*

fret¹ (frĕt) *v.* **fretted, fretting, frets** *—intr.* To be uneasy, troubled, or worried: *fretted over each detail.* *—tr.* To cause to be uneasy; vex: *I tried not to fret my parents.*

fret² (frĕt) *n.* One of several ridges set across the fingerboard of certain stringed instruments, such as guitars. **—fret′ted** *adj.*

fret³ (frĕt) *n.* An ornamental design within a band or border, consisting of repeated and symmetrical designs. ❖ *tr.v.* **fretted, fretting, frets** To provide with such a design.

WORD HISTORY Fret¹ comes from Old English *fretan,* meaning "to eat up." The origin of **fret²** is unknown. **Fret³** comes from Middle English *fret,* which comes from Old French *frete,* both meaning "interlaced work."

fretful (frĕt′fəl) *adj.* Feeling or showing worry and distress; troubled. **—fret′ful·ly** *adv.* **—fret′ful-ness** *n.*

fret saw *n.* A saw with a narrow, fine-toothed blade, used for cutting thin wood or metal.

fretwork (frĕt′wûrk′) *n.* Ornamental work consisting of three-dimensional frets; geometric openwork.

Freudian (froi′dē-ən) *adj.* Relating to the psychoanalytic theories of Sigmund Freud (1856–1939), an Austrian physician. ❖ *n.* A person who accepts the basic tenets of the psychoanalytic theories of Sigmund Freud, especially a psychiatrist or psychologist who applies Freudian theory and method in conducting psychotherapy.

Freudian slip *n.* A verbal mistake that is thought to reveal a repressed belief, thought, or emotion.

friable (frī′ə-bəl) *adj.* Easily crumbled; brittle: *friable stone.* **—fri′a·bil′i·ty, fri′a·ble·ness** *n.*

friar (frī′ər) *n.* A man who is a member of certain Roman Catholic orders.

fricassee (frĭk′ə-sē′ *or* frĭk′ə-sē′) *n.* Poultry or meat cut up and stewed in a thick gravy. ❖ *tr.v.* **fricasseed, fricasseeing, fricassees** To prepare as a fricassee.

friction (frĭk′shən) *n.* **1.** The rubbing of one object or surface against another: *Friction of flint and steel can produce sparks.* **2.** The force that resists motion between two objects in contact: *By oiling the wheels, we reduced the friction.* **3.** The conflict or irritation that occurs between people who have different opinions or beliefs: *The debate caused friction between the two senators.* **—fric′tion·al** *adj.* **—fric′tion·al·ly** *adv.*

Friday (frī′dē *or* frī′dā′) *n.* The day of the week that comes after Thursday and before Saturday. **—Fri′days** *adv.* —SEE NOTE AT **friend.**

fridge (frĭj) *n. Informal* A refrigerator.

fried (frīd) *v.* Past tense and past participle of **fry¹.**

friend (frĕnd) *n.* **1.** A person who is known and liked by another: *My friends took me out for dinner on my birthday.* **2.** A person who supports a group, cause, or movement; a person on the same side: *Their support of conservation made them friends of the environmental group.* **3. Friend** A member of the Society of Friends; a Quaker. ❖ *tr.v.* **friended, friending, friends** *Informal* To add (someone) as a friend on a social networking website.

WORD HISTORY Friend originally meant "loving, one who loves another." It comes from a word in Old English, the language spoken in England over 1,000 years ago. This word can be traced back to the present participle of an old verb meaning "to love." Though that verb no longer exists, it has a hidden relative in the name of the last day of the week, **Friday.** This day was named for Frigg, the goddess of love in the mythology of the Germanic peoples of northern Europe. The name of our day *Friday* or "Frigg's day" came about as a translation of the Latin name for the same day, *Veneris diēs,* "day of Venus," after Venus, the Roman goddess of love.

friendly (frĕnd′lē) *adj.* **friendlier, friendliest 1.** Characteristic or behaving as a friend: *a friendly greeting.* **2.** Outgoing and pleasant: *a friendly clerk.* **3.** Not feeling or showing enmity or hostility: *a government friendly to our interests.* **4.** Welcoming to or accommodating a particular sort of user: *a vegan-friendly restaurant; a child-friendly hotel.* **—friend′li·ness** *n.*

friendship (frĕnd′shĭp′) *n.* **1.** The condition or fact of being friends: *a friendship from childhood.* **2.** A feeling of warmth toward another; friendliness: *friendship between people who like the same things.*

frier (frī′ər) *n.* Variant of **fryer.**

fries (frīz) *v.* Third person singular present tense of **fry¹.** ❖ *n.* Plural of **fry¹.**

frieze (frēz) *n.* **1.** In classical architecture, a plain or decorated horizontal band that is above the columns and below the roof. **2.** A decorative horizontal band, as along the upper part of a wall in a room.

frigate (frĭg′ĭt) *n.* **1.** A warship used as an escort and to destroy submarines. **2.** A fast square-rigged warship of the 1600s, 1700s, and 1800s.

frigatebird (frĭg′ĭt-bûrd′) *n.* Any of various tropical seabirds having long powerful wings, dark feathers, and a forked tail. Frigatebirds snatch food from other birds in flight.

Frigg (frĭg) also **Frigga** (frĭg′ə) *n.* In Norse mythology, the goddess of the heavens and the wife of Odin.

fright (frīt) *n.* **1.** Sudden intense fear, as of something immediately threatening; alarm: *Fright caused the flock of birds to take flight.* **2.** *Informal* Something very unsightly or alarming: *Their dirty wind-blown hair looked a fright.*

frighten (frīt′n) *v.* **frightened, frightening, frightens** *—tr.* **1.** To fill with fear; alarm or startle: *A loud noise frightened me.* **2.** To drive or force by arousing fear: *frightened him into making a confession.* *—intr.* To become afraid: *Our dog frightens easily.*

✦ SYNONYMS frighten, alarm, panic, scare, terrify *v.*

frightening (frīt′n-ĭng) *adj.* Causing fright or sudden alarm: *a frightening thunderstorm.* **—fright′en·ing·ly** *adv.*

frightful (frīt′fəl) *adj.* **1.** Causing disgust or shock; horrifying: *The number of hungry refugees is frightful.* **2.** Causing fright; terrifying: *frightful Halloween masks.* **3.**

Informal Extreme; excessive: *frightful traffic at rush hour.*
—**fright′ful·ly** *adv.*

frigid (frĭj′ĭd) *adj.* **1.** Extremely cold: *a frigid room.* See Synonyms at **cold. 2.** Lacking warmth of feeling or enthusiasm: *His suggestion received a frigid reception.* —**fri·gid′i·ty** (frĭ-jĭd′ĭ-tē), **frig′id·ness** *n.* —**frig′id·ly** *adv.*

frijoles (frē-hō′lĕs or frē-hō′lāz) *pl.n.* Beans cultivated and used for food, especially in Latin American cooking.

frill (frĭl) *n.* **1.** A ruffled, gathered, or pleated piece of fancy trimming, as on a fabric edge: *frills on a doll's dress.* **2.** *Informal* Something desirable but unnecessary added on as an extra: *a straightforward speech without any frills.* ❖ *tr.v.* **frilled, frilling, frills** To put a ruffle or frill on: *frill a skirt.* —**frill′y** *adj.*

fringe (frĭnj) *n.* **1.** A decorative border or edging of hanging threads or cords, often attached to a separate band. **2.** Something that resembles such a border or edging: *a fringe of eyelashes.* **3.** An outer part; a margin; an edge: *stand on the fringe of the crowd.* ❖ *tr.v.* **fringed, fringing, fringes 1.** To decorate with or as if with a fringe: *fringe curtains.* **2.** To form a fringe along the edge of: *Sunlight fringed the horizon.*

fringe benefit *n.* An employment benefit, such as medical care, given in addition to wages or salary.

frippery (frĭp′ə-rē) *n., pl.* **fripperies 1.** Pretentious showy finery. **2.** Pretentious elegance; ostentation.

Frisbee (frĭz′bē) A trademark used for a plastic disk-shaped toy that players throw and catch.

Frisian (frĭzh′ən or frē′zhən) *n.* **1.** A native or inhabitant of the coast and islands of the North Sea between the northern Netherlands and southern Denmark. **2.** The West Germanic language of the Frisians. —**Fri′sian** *adj.*

frisk (frĭsk) *v.* **frisked, frisking, frisks** —*tr.* To search (a person) for something concealed, especially a weapon. —*intr.* To move about briskly and playfully; frolic: *Squirrels frisked in the trees.*

frisky (frĭs′kē) *adj.* **friskier, friskiest** Energetic, lively, and playful: *a frisky kitten.* —**frisk′i·ly** *adv.* —**frisk′i·ness** *n.*

frisson (frē-sôN′) *n., pl.* **frissons** (frē-sôNz′ or frē-sôN′) A moment of intense excitement; a shudder: *The story's ending arouses a frisson of terror.*

frittata (frĭ-tä′tə) *n.* An omelet that is not folded over on itself, made with ingredients, such as cheese or vegetables, mixed into the eggs rather than used as a filling.

fritter¹ (frĭt′ər) *tr.v.* **frittered, frittering, fritters** To reduce or squander little by little; waste: *frittered the day away watching TV.* —**frit′ter·er** *n.*

fritter² (frĭt′ər) *n.* A small fried cake of batter that often contains fruit, vegetables, or seafood.

WORD HISTORY Fritter¹ probably comes from an obsolete English word *fitters,* meaning "fragments." **Fritter²** comes from Middle English *friture* (meaning "a small fried cake of batter"), which comes from Latin *frīctus,* meaning "roasted, fried."

frivolity (frĭ-vŏl′ĭ-tē) *n., pl.* **frivolities 1.** The quality or condition of being frivolous. **2.** A frivolous act or thing.

frivolous (frĭv′ə-ləs) *adj.* **1.** Not worthy of serious attention; trivial: *wasting time on frivolous ideas.* **2.** Inappropriately silly: *a frivolous purchase.* —**friv′o·lous·ly** *adv.*

frizz (frĭz) *tr. & intr.v.* **frizzed, frizzing, frizzes** To form or be formed into small tight tufts or curls. ❖ *n.* A small tight curl or tuft.

frizzle (frĭz′əl) *tr. & intr.v.* **frizzled, frizzling, frizzles** To form or cause to be formed into small tight curls. ❖ *n.* A small tight curl.

frizzly (frĭz′lē) *adj.* **frizzlier, frizzliest** Frizzy.

frizzy (frĭz′ē) *adj.* **frizzier, frizziest** Tightly curled: *frizzy hair.*

fro (frō) *adv.* Away; back: *A pendulum swings to and fro.*

frock (frŏk) *n.* **1.** A woman's dress. **2.** A long loose outer garment, such as a priest's robe or an artist's smock.

frock coat *n.* A man's dress coat or suit coat that extends to the knees.

frog (frôg) *n.* **1.** Any of numerous tailless amphibians that have a short body, large head, and long legs used for leaping. Most frogs live chiefly in and around water. **2.** An ornamental fastener made of braid or cord with a looped piece that fits around a button. **3.** *Informal* Hoarseness in the throat.

frog kick *n.* A swimming kick in which the legs are drawn up close to the hips and then thrust outward and drawn together when straightened.

frogman (frôg′măn′) *n.* A swimmer provided with breathing apparatus and other equipment to perform underwater maneuvers, especially military maneuvers.

frolic (frŏl′ĭk) *n.* Playful behavior or merriment. ❖ *intr.v.* **frolicked, frolicking, frolics** To move about or behave playfully: *The puppies frolicked on the lawn.*

frolicsome (frŏl′ĭk-səm) *adj.* Full of fun; frisky and playful: *a frolicsome puppy.*

from (frŭm or frŏm; frəm *when unstressed*) *prep.* **1.** Used to indicate a specified place or time as a starting point: *walked home from the station; from midnight until dawn.* **2.** Used to indicate a source, agent, or instrument: *a gift from a friend; a message from my uncle.* **3.** Used to indicate a cause: *faint from hunger.* **4.** Out of or off of: *taking a book from the shelf.* **5.** Out of the control or possession of: *They took the ball from us.* **6.** So as not to be engaged in: *kept from playing.* **7.** In contrast to: *knowing right from wrong.*

frond (frŏnd) *n.* **1.** The leaf of a fern or a palm tree, usually divided into smaller leaflets. **2.** A plant part that resembles a leaf, as of seaweed.

front (frŭnt) *n.* **1.** The forward part or surface, as of a building: *a shirt with buttons down the front; a desk at the front of the room.* **2.** The area, location, or position directly before or ahead: *A crowd gathered in front of the building.* **3.** A person's outward manner, behavior, or appearance: *keeping up a brave front despite misfortune.* **4.** Land bordering a lake, river, or street: *a lake front.* **5.** In warfare, an area where a battle is taking place. **6.** The boundary between two air masses having different temperatures: *a cold front.* **7.** A field of activity: *Conditions on the economic front are poor.* **8.** A group or movement uniting persons or organizations that seek a common goal; a coalition: *Unions and workers formed a labor front.* **9.** An outwardly respectable person or business that serves as a cover for secret or illegal activity. ❖ *adj.* Relating to, aimed at, or located in the front: *the front door; the front pages; the front view.* ❖ *v.* **fronted, fronting, fronts** —*tr.* To face or look out upon: *The building fronts the main street.* **2.** To meet in opposition; directly confront. —*intr.* To have a front; face onto something else: *The motel fronts on the highway.*

frontage (frŭn′tĭj) *n.* **1.** The front part of a piece of property. **2.** The land between a building and the street. **3.** The land adjacent to something, such as a building, street, or body of water.

frontal (frŭn′tl) *adj.* **1.** Relating to, at, or concerning the front: *a frontal assault.* **2.** Relating to the forehead. **3.** Relating to a weather front. —**fron′tal·ly** *adv.*

frontal bone *n.* A bone of the skull, consisting of a part that corresponds to the forehead and a part that forms the roof of the eye sockets and cavities of the nose.

frontal lobe *n.* The largest and most anterior part of each cerebral hemisphere.

frontcourt (frŭnt′kôrt′) *n.* In basketball, the half of the court in which the team on offense tries to make baskets.

frontier (frŭn-tîr′ or frŭn′tîr′) *n.* **1.** A boundary between countries or the land along such a boundary; a border. **2.** A region just beyond or at the edge of a settled area. **3.** An undeveloped area or field of research or interest: *exploring new frontiers in space.*

frontiersman (frŭn-tîrz′mən) *n.* A man who lives on the frontier.

frontierswoman (frŭn-tîrz′wŏŏm′ən) *n.* A woman who lives on the frontier.

frontispiece (frŭn′tĭ-spēs′) *n.* An illustration that faces or comes just before the title page of a book.

frontline (frŭnt′līn′) *n.* A front or boundary, especially one between political or military positions. ❖ *adj.* **1.** Located or used at a military front. **2.** Relating to the most advanced position in a field or an undertaking: *frontline research.* **3.** Performing the most basic tasks or interacting directly with customers, patients, or clients: *frontline caregivers.*

front-runner also **frontrunner** (frŭnt′rŭn′ər) *n.* A person who leads in a race or other competition.

frost (frôst) *n.* **1.** A deposit of small ice crystals, formed from frozen water vapor, covering a surface: *I scraped the frost from the car windshield.* **2.** A period of weather when such deposits form. ❖ *v.* **frosted, frosting, frosts** —*tr.* **1.** To cover with frost: *frosted the glasses by putting them in the freezer.* **2.** To damage or kill (plants) by frost. **3.** To cover or decorate (a cake, cupcake, or other baked goods) with icing. —*intr.* To become covered with frost: *The windows frosted up.*

frostbite (frôst′bīt′) *n.* Injury to a part of the body as a result of exposure to freezing temperatures. ❖ *tr.v.* **frostbit** (frôst′bĭt′), **frostbitten** (frôst′bĭt′n), **frostbiting, frostbites** To injure (a part of the body) by freezing.

frosting (frô′stĭng) *n.* **1.** A sweet mixture of sugar and other ingredients, used to cover and decorate cakes or cookies; icing. **2.** A roughened or speckled surface on glass or metal.

frosty (frô′stē) *adj.* **frostier, frostiest 1.** Producing or characterized by frost: *A sudden chill made the night frosty and cold.* See Synonyms at **cold. 2.** Covered with frost or having a surface resembling frost: *the frosty bedroom window; a frosty texture.* **3.** Cold in manner; unfriendly: *The hostility between the neighbors was noticeable in their frosty greeting.* —**frost′i·ly** *adv.* —**frost′i·ness** *n.*

froth (frôth) *n.* **1.** A mass of bubbles in or on a liquid; foam. **2.** Something lacking in substance or depth: *Most gossip is mere froth.* ❖ *v.* (also frôth) **frothed, frothing, froths** —*intr.* To give off or form foam: *The sick dog frothed at the mouth.* —*tr.* **1.** To cover with foam. **2.** To cause to foam. —**froth′i·ly** *adv.* —**froth′i·ness** *n.* —**froth′y** *adj.*

froward (frō′wərd or frō′ərd) *adj.* Stubbornly contrary and disobedient; obstinate. —**fro′ward·ly** *adv.* —**fro′ward·ness** *n.*

frown (froun) *intr.v.* **frowned, frowning, frowns 1.** To wrinkle the brow, as in thought or displeasure; scowl.

2. To regard something with disapproval or distaste: *frowned on the use of so much salt in the food.* ❖ *n.* An act of wrinkling the brow in thought or displeasure; a scowl.

frowzy (frou′zē) *adj.* **frowzier, frowziest 1.** Untidy; slovenly; unkempt: *frowzy wind-blown hair.* **2.** Having an unpleasant smell; musty: *frowzy odors from the old clothes.* —**frow′zi·ness** *n.*

froze (frōz) *v.* Past tense of **freeze.**

frozen (frō′zən) *v.* Past participle of **freeze.** ❖ *adj.* **1a.** Made into ice: *frozen orange juice.* **b.** Covered with or surrounded by ice: *a frozen pool.* **2.** Very cold: *the frozen North.* **3.** Preserved by freezing: *frozen strawberries.* **4.** Incapable of moving, as from fright: *frozen with fear.* **5.** Unfriendly; cold: *a frozen stare.*

fructose (frŭk′tōs′ or frŏŏk′tōs′) *n.* A simple sugar found in honey, many fruits, and some vegetables.

frugal (frŏŏ′gəl) *adj.* **1.** Careful in spending or in using resources; thrifty: *Frugal use of energy saves natural resources.* **2.** Costing little; inexpensive: *a frugal meal.* —**fru·gal′i·ty** (frŏŏ-găl′ĭ-tē) *n.* —**fru′gal·ly** *adv.*

frugivorous (frŏŏ-jĭv′ər-əs) *adj.* Feeding on fruit; fruit-eating: *frugivorous bats.*

fruit (frŏŏt) *n., pl.* **fruit** or **fruits 1a.** The ripened ovary or ovaries of a seed-bearing plant, occurring in many different forms. Acorns, berries, pods, and squashes are all fruits. **b.** A fleshy, usually sweet plant part of this kind that is eaten as food, such as an apple or a mango. **2.** A result of work or action: *the fruit of their labor.* ❖ *intr. & tr.v.* **fruited, fruiting, fruits** To produce or cause to produce fruit: *Apple trees fruit in the fall.*

fruitcake (frŏŏt′kāk′) *n.* A rich spiced cake containing various dried and preserved fruits and nuts.

fruit fly *n.* Any of various small flies whose larvae feed on ripening or decaying plant material, especially fruit.

fruitful (frŏŏt′fəl) *adj.* **1.** Producing or bearing fruit. **2.** Producing useful or desired results; productive: *a fruitful approach.* —**fruit′ful·ly** *adv.* —**fruit′ful·ness** *n.*

fruition (frŏŏ-ĭsh′ən) *n.* The achievement of something desired or worked for; accomplishment: *The plan came to fruition after many years of hard work.*

fruitless (frŏŏt′lĭs) *adj.* **1.** Having little or no result; unproductive: *Only after many fruitless attempts did explorers reach the South Pole.* **2.** Producing no fruit: *a fruitless variety of mulberry.* —**fruit′less·ly** *adv.* —**fruit′less·ness** *n.*

fruit sugar *n.* Fructose.

fruity (frŏŏ′tē) *adj.* **fruitier, fruitiest** Tasting or smelling of fruit: *the fruity smell of ripe peaches.* —**fruit′i·ness** *n.*

frump (frŭmp) *n.* **1.** A girl or woman regarded as dull, plain, or unfashionable. **2.** A person regarded as colorless and primly sedate. —**frump′i·ly** *adv.* —**frump′i·ness** *n.* —**frump′y** *adj.*

frustrate (frŭs′trāt′) *tr.v.* **frustrated, frustrating, frustrates 1.** To prevent (a plan, effort, or desire) from succeeding or being fulfilled: *Bad weather frustrated our plans to go fishing.* **2.** To prevent (someone) from accomplishing something; thwart: *A persistent wind frustrated me as I tried to rake the leaves.* **3.** To cause feelings of discouragement or bafflement in: *The scientists were frustrated by the negative results of the experiment.* —**frus·tra′tion** *n.*

frustum (frŭs′təm) *n., pl.* **frustums** or **frusta** (frŭs′tə) The part of a solid, such as a cone or pyramid, between the base and a plane that cuts through the solid and is parallel to the base.

fry¹ (frī) *v.* **fried** (frīd), **frying, fries** (frīz) ❖ *tr.v.* To cook (food) over direct heat in hot oil or fat: *We fried potatoes in a pan.* ❖ *intr.v.* To be cooked over direct heat in hot oil or fat: *Eggs fry quickly.* ❖ *n., pl.* **fries** (frīz) **1.** A french fry: *ordered a hamburger with fries.* **2.** An informal gathering where food is fried and eaten: *a fish fry.*

fry² (frī) *pl.n.* Small fish, especially young, recently hatched fish.

WORD HISTORY Fry¹ comes from Middle English *frien*, which comes from Latin *frīgere*, both meaning "to cook in hot oil." **Fry²** comes from Middle English *fri*, which probably comes from Anglo-Norman *frie* (both meaning "the young of fish"), which comes from Old French *frier*, meaning "to rub, spawn."

---

fryer also **frier** (frī′ər) *n.* **1.** A pot or pan having a basket for frying foods. **2.** A small young chicken suitable for frying.

frying pan (frī′ing) *n.* A shallow pan with a long handle, used for frying food.

ft. An abbreviation of foot.

Ft. An abbreviation of fort.

fuchsia (fyōō′shə) *n.* **1.** Any of various tropical plants grown for their drooping, often red, purple, or pink flowers. **2.** A bright purplish red.

fuddle (fŭd′l) *tr.v.* **fuddled, fuddling, fuddles 1.** To put into a state of confusion; muddle. **2.** To make drunk; intoxicate.

fudge (fŭj) *n.* A soft rich candy, often flavored with chocolate. ❖ *tr.v.* **fudged, fudging, fudges 1.** To fake or falsify: *The scientist fudged the results of the experiment to support his hypothesis.* **2.** To be evasive in expressing: *The politican fudged her response to the reporter because she didn't want to commit to a position.*

fuel (fyōō′əl) *n.* **1.** A substance, such as coal, wood, oil, or gas, that is burned to produce useful heat or energy. **2.** A substance that can be made to undergo a nuclear reaction and produce energy. **3.** Material that an organism breaks down to use for energy; food: *I needed fuel for the race, so I ate a big plate of pasta.* **4.** Something that feeds or encourages a feeling: *Being insulted added fuel to his anger.* ❖ *v.* **fueled, fueling, fuels** also **fuelled, fuelling, fuels** — *tr.* To provide with fuel: *She pulled into the gas station and fueled the car.* — *intr.* To take in fuel: *The freighter fueled at the nearest port.*

fuel cell *n.* A device that produces electricity by the chemical reaction between a fuel and an oxidizer.

fugitive (fyōō′jĭ-tĭv) *adj.* **1.** Running or having run away, as from law enforcement agents. **2.** Lasting only a short time; fleeting: *relaxing for a few fugitive hours.* ❖ *n.* A person who flees: *The escaped criminal was a fugitive from the law.*

fugue (fyōōg) *n.* A musical composition in which one or more themes are repeated by different voices or instruments with variations on the themes.

–ful A suffix that means: **1.** Full of: *eventful; playful.* **2.** Characterized by: *boastful.* **3.** Tending or able to: *helpful; useful.* **4.** A quantity that fills: *armful; cupful.*

WORD BUILDING The suffix **–ful** comes from the Old English adjective *full*, meaning "full." *Full* was commonly added to a noun in order to form adjectives meaning "full of, characterized by" whatever quality was denoted by the noun, as in the modern words *playful* and *careful*.

The use of *–ful* to form nouns meaning "a quantity that would fill" a particular receptacle (such as *cupful, mouthful*) also goes back to Old English. In modern usage the correct way to form the plural of these nouns is to add an *s* to the end of the suffix rather than the base noun: *cupfuls* (not *cupsful*).

---

fulcrum (fōōl′krəm or fŭl′krəm) *n.* The point or support on which a lever pivots.

fulfill also **fulfil** (fōōl-fĭl′) *tr.v.* **fulfilled, fulfilling, fulfills** also **fulfils 1.** To make real; cause to be come true: *After many years they fulfilled their lifelong dream.* **2.** To do, perform, or obey (a duty or order): *Citizens should fulfill their duty as voters.* **3.** To meet (a requirement or condition); satisfy: *fulfilling all requirements.* **—ful·fill′ment** *n.*

full (fōōl) *adj.* **fuller, fullest 1.** Containing all that is normal or possible; filled: *a full bucket.* **2.** Not deficient; complete: *I need your full attention.* **3.** Of highest degree or development: *at full speed; in full bloom.* **4.** Having a great many or a great deal of: *shelves full of books.* **5.** Rounded in shape; plump: *a full face and figure.* **6.** Having or made with a generous amount of fabric: *a full skirt.* **7.** Filled with food; abundantly fed: *The guests were full after the huge banquet.* **8.** Having depth and body; rich: *a full flavor.* **9.** Having both parents in common: *full sisters; a full brother.* ❖ *adv.* **1.** To a complete extent; entirely: *Fill the pitcher full.* **2.** Exactly; directly: *The tree fell full across the middle of the road.* ❖ **in full** To the maximum amount or degree that is necessary; completely: *a bill paid in full.* **—full′ness** *n.*

fullback (fōōl′băk′) *n.* **1.** In football, a running back usually positioned directly behind the quarterback when the ball is snapped. **2.** In certain sports such as soccer and field hockey, one of usually two defensive players other than the goalie positioned closest to the goal.

full-blooded (fōōl′blŭd′ĭd) or **fullblood** (fōōl′blŭd′) *adj.* Of unmixed ancestry; purebred: *a full-blooded Arabian horse.*

full-blown (fōōl′blōn′) *adj.* Fully developed: *a full-blown case of chickenpox.*

full dress *n.* Clothing appropriate or required for formal occasions or ceremonies.

fullerene (fōōl′ə-rēn′) *n.* Any of various molecules of carbon that always have an even number of carbon atoms, are often shaped like a sphere, and are made of groups of atoms arranged in hexagons and pentagons.

full-fledged (fōōl′flĕjd′) *adj.* **1.** Having reached full development: *a full-fledged hurricane.* **2.** Having full standing or rank: *a full-fledged lawyer.*

full house *n.* A poker hand containing three of a kind and a pair, ranked above a flush and below four of a kind.

full-length (fōōl′lĕngkth′ or fōōl′lĕngth′) *adj.* **1.** Covering the entire length of a person or thing: *a full-length mirror; a full-length coat.* **2.** Of normal or standard length: *a full-length movie.*

full moon *n.* The moon when the side that faces Earth is fully illuminated by the sun, halfway through a lunar month.

full-scale (fōōl′skāl′) *adj.* **1.** Of the actual or full size; not reduced: *The design for the new car was produced in a full-scale model.* **2.** Not limited; complete; all-out: *Everyone turned out for a full-scale demonstration against local water pollution.*

full-size (fōōl′sīz′) *adj.* Of the standard or normal size: *a full-size poodle; a full-size car.*

full-time (fōōl′tīm′) *adj.* Employed for or involving a standard number of hours of working time: *a full-time editor; a full-time job.* —**full′-time′** *adv.*

fully (fŏŏl′ē) *adv.* **1.** Totally or completely: *The deer was fully aware of our presence.* **2.** At least; no less than: *Fully half the students had to take the test over.*

fulminate (fŏŏl′mə-nāt′ or fŭl′mə-nāt′) *intr.v.* **fulminated, fulminating, fulminates 1.** To make a loud strong verbal attack or denunciation: *The speaker fulminated against the waste of resources.* **2.** To explode with sudden violence or force. ❖ *n.* Any of a number of salts that explode violently at the slightest shock and are used as detonators. —**ful′mi·na′tion** *n.*

fulsome (fŏŏl′səm) *adj.* **1a.** Excessively flattering: *received fulsome praise for her efforts.* **b.** Insincerely earnest. **2.** Disgusting or offensive: *a fulsome smell coming from the garbage bin.* —**ful′some·ly** *adv.* —**ful′some·ness** *n.*

fumble (fŭm′bəl) *v.* **fumbled, fumbling, fumbles** —*intr.* **1.** To touch or handle something nervously or idly: *The driver fumbled with the car keys.* **2.** To feel around awkwardly while searching; grope: *She fumbled for the light switch in the dark.* **3.** In sports, to mishandle or drop a ball. —*tr.* **1.** To handle clumsily or idly: *He fumbled the glass and it broke.* **2.** To make a botch of; bungle: *The bank robber fumbled the job.* **3.** In sports, to mishandle or drop (a ball). ❖ *n.* **1.** An act of fumbling. **2.** A ball that has been fumbled.

fume (fyōōm) *n.* Smoke, vapor, or gas, especially if irritating, harmful, or smelly: *the choking fumes from a smokestack.* ❖ *intr.v.* **fumed, fuming, fumes 1.** To produce or give off fumes. **2.** To feel or show anger or agitation; seethe: *After being put off for the third time, he was fuming.*

fumigant (fyōō′mĭ-gənt) *n.* A poisonous compound used in fumigating.

fumigate (fyōō′mĭ-gāt′) *tr.v.* **fumigated, fumigating, fumigates** To expose (a room or object) to fumes in order to kill insects, rats, or other pests. —**fu′mi·ga′tion** *n.* —**fu′mi·ga′tor** *n.*

fun (fŭn) *n.* **1.** Enjoyment; amusement: *We had fun at the picnic.* **2.** A source of enjoyment or amusement: *The trampoline was fun.* ❖ *adj. Informal* Enjoyable; amusing: *a fun party.* ◆ **for fun** or **in fun** As a joke; playfully.

function (fŭngk′shən) *n.* **1.** The normal or proper activity of a person or thing; a purpose: *The function of the heart is to pump blood.* **2.** An assigned duty or activity: *Creating a menu is part of her function as head chef.* **3a.** A quantity whose value depends on the value given to one or more related quantities: *The area of a square is a function of the length of its side.* **b.** A relationship between two sets that matches each member of the first set with a unique member of the second set. **4.** A formal social gathering or official ceremony. —*intr.* **functioned, functioning, functions** To have or perform a function; serve: *Posts function as a support for the deck.*

functional (fŭngk′shə-nəl) *adj.* **1.** Relating to a function or functions: *the functional responsibilities of a manager.* **2.** Having or carrying out a function; working: *Is this clock functional?* **3.** Designed for or adapted to a particular purpose or use: *The log cabin is an example of functional architecture.* —**func′tion·al·ly** *adv.*

functionality (fŭngk′shə-nǎl′ĭ-tē) *n.* **1.** The quality or capability of being functional. **2.** A useful function within a computer application or program.

functionary (fŭngk′shə-nĕr′ē) *n., pl.* **functionaries** A person who holds a position of authority or trust; an official:

The tax collector is a functionary in the local government.

function word *n.* A word, such as a preposition, auxiliary verb, or conjunction, that expresses relationships between words, clauses, and sentences. In the sentence *It rained and we did not go until later,* the words *and* and *until* are function words.

fund (fŭnd) *n.* **1.** A sum of money raised or set aside for a certain purpose: *Our library has a new book fund each year.* **2. funds** Available money; ready cash: *I'm a little short of funds.* **3.** A source of supply; a stock: *An encyclopedia is a fund of knowledge.* ❖ *tr.v.* **funded, funding, funds** To provide money for: *Several citizens of the town funded our sports program.*

fundamental (fŭn′də-mĕn′tl) *adj.* Relating to or forming a foundation; elemental or basic: *The students gained a fundamental understanding of algebra.* ❖ *n.* **1.** Something that is an elemental or basic part; an essential: *the fundamentals of good cooking.* **2.** The lowest frequency of a periodically varying quantity, such as a sound wave. —**fun′da·men′tal·ly** *adv.*

fundamentalism (fŭn′də-mĕn′tl-ĭz′əm) *n.* **1.** A religious movement or point of view characterized by strict following of fundamental principles and often by intolerance of other views. **2.** Belief that that the Bible is a completely accurate historical record and statement of prophecy. —**fun′da·men′tal·ist** *n. & adj.*

fundraiser (fŭnd′rā′zər) *n.* **1.** A person who raises funds. **2.** A social function or activity, such as a raffle or musical concert, held for raising funds.

funeral (fyōō′nər-əl) *n.* **1.** The ceremonies that accompany burial or cremation of a dead person. **2.** The procession accompanying a body to the grave.

funeral director *n.* A person whose business is to prepare the dead for burial or cremation and to assist at funerals.

funeral home *n.* A building in which the dead are prepared for burial and cremation, and in which wakes and funerals are held.

funereal (fyōō-nîr′ē-əl) *adj.* Relating to, suitable for, or suggestive of a funeral: *funereal gloom.* —**fu·ne′re·al·ly** *adv.*

fungal (fŭng′gəl) *adj.* Relating to or caused by a fungus or fungi: *fungal hyphae; a fungal disease.*

fungicide (fŭn′jĭ-sīd′ or fŭng′gĭ-sīd′) *n.* A substance that destroys or prevents the growth of fungi.

fungus (fŭng′gəs) *n., pl.* **fungi** (fŭn′jī or fŭng′gī) or **funguses** Any of a kingdom of organisms, including the mushrooms, molds, yeasts, and certain mildews, that reproduce by spores and obtain their nourishment from other organisms.

funk¹ (fŭngk) *n.* A strong, usually unpleasant smell.

funk² (fŭngk) *n.* A kind of popular music that has a lively beat and is a mixture of jazz, rock, blues, and often soul.

funk³ (fŭngk) *n.* **1.** A state of fear; panic. **2.** A state of depression: *They were in a funk because their trip was canceled.*

WORD HISTORY Funk¹ probably comes from *funquer,* a word in a French dialect of northern France that means "to produce smoke." **Funk²** is a back-formation from *funky.* **Funk³** probably comes from obsolete Flemish *fonck,* meaning "disturbance, agitation."

funky (fŭng′kē) *adj.* **1.** Relating to funk music. **2.** *Slang* Original; unconventional; offbeat: *a funky shirt.* **3.** Having a moldy or musty smell: *funky cheese.* —**funk′i·ness** *n.*

funnel (fŭn′əl) *n.* **1.** A conical utensil with a wide opening at one end and a narrow tube or small hole at the other, used to pour liquids or other substances into a container with a small mouth. **2.** Something shaped like a funnel: *the funnel of a tornado.* **3.** The smokestack of a ship or steam engine. ❖ *v.* **funneled, funneling, funnels** or **funnelled, funnelling, funnels** —*intr.* To move through or as if through a funnel: *Tourists funneled through the museum exhibit.* —*tr.* To cause to move through or as if through a funnel: *funnel juice into a pitcher.*

funnies (fŭn′ēz) *pl.n.* **1.** Comic strips. **2.** A newspaper section containing comic strips.

funny (fŭn′ē) *adj.* **funnier, funniest 1.** Causing laughter or amusement: *a funny cartoon.* **2.** Strange; odd; curious: *It's funny that I can't remember where I left my shoes.* —**fun′-ni·ly** *adv.* —**fun′ni·ness** *n.*

funny bone *n. Informal* A point near the elbow where a nerve can be pressed against the bone, producing a numb or tingling feeling in the arm.

fur (fûr) *n.* **1.** The thick soft hair covering the body of certain mammals, such as a rabbit, squirrel, or fox. **2.** The skin and hair of such a mammal, treated and used for clothing, trimming, or lining: *gloves lined with fur.* **3.** An item of clothing made of fur: *She gave away her furs.*

furbish (fûr′bĭsh) *tr.v.* **furbished, furbishing, furbishes 1.** To brighten by cleaning or rubbing; polish: *The jeweler furbished the old silver bracelet.* **2.** To restore to a usable condition; renovate. —**fur′bish·er** *n.*

furious (fyŏŏr′ē-əs) *adj.* **1.** Full of or marked by extreme anger; raging. **2.** Full of intensity; energetic or fierce: *the storm's furious winds; worked at a furious pace.* —**fu′-ri·ous·ly** *adv.* —**fu′ri·ous·ness** *n.*

furl (fûrl) *v.* **furled, furling, furls** —*tr.* To roll up and fasten (a flag or sail) to a pole, yard, or mast. —*intr.* To become rolled up: *The flag furled around the pole in the wind.* ❖ *n.* **1.** The act of furling. **2.** A rolled section of something furled.

furlong (fûr′lông′) *n.* A unit for measuring distance, equal to ⅛ mile or 220 yards (201 meters). See table at **measurement.**

furlough (fûr′lō) *n.* **1.** A vacation or leave of absence, especially one granted to a member of the armed forces. **2.** A usually temporary suspension of an employee from work. ❖ *tr.v.* **furloughed, furloughing, furloughs 1.** To grant a leave to (someone). **2.** To place (an employee) on a furlough.

furnace (fûr′nĭs) *n.* An enclosed chamber in which fuel is burned to produce heat. Furnaces are used to heat buildings and to manufacture metal and glass.

furnish (fûr′nĭsh) *tr.v.* **furnished, furnishing, furnishes 1.** To outfit with furniture and other necessities: *furnish each room of an apartment.* **2.** To supply; give: *The lamp furnished enough light to read.* —**fur′nish·er** *n.*

furnishing (fûr′nĭ-shĭng) *n.* **1.** A piece of equipment necessary or useful for comfort or convenience. **2. furnishings** The furniture, appliances, and other movable articles in a house or other building. **3. furnishings** Clothes and accessories: *This store specializes in children's furnishings.*

furniture (fûr′nĭ-chər) *n.* The movable articles, such as chairs, tables, or appliances, that make a room fit for living or an office suitable for working.

furor (fyŏŏr′ôr′ *or* fyŏŏr′ər) *n.* **1.** A noisy outburst; a commotion or uproar: *Rumors of the president's arrival caused a furor of excitement.* **2.** Violent anger; frenzy: *the furor of the mob.*

furrier (fûr′ē-ər) *n.* A person who deals in fur or makes and repairs fur garments.

furrow (fûr′ō) *n.* **1.** A long narrow groove made in the ground by a plow or other tool: *furrows cut in the field for planting.* **2.** A rut, groove, or narrow depression: *The car's tires made deep furrows in the dirt road.* ❖ *tr.v.* **furrowed, furrowing, furrows 1.** To make furrows in; plow: *furrowed the cornfield into neat rows.* **2.** To form deep wrinkles in: *Months of worry had furrowed the banker's brow.*

furry (fûr′ē) *adj.* **furrier, furriest 1.** Consisting of or resembling fur: *a furry coat.* **2.** Covered with fur: *a furry kitten.* —**fur′ri·ness** *n.*

fur seal *n.* Any of several seals having thick fur and external ears. Fur seals were heavily hunted for their pelts, but most species are now protected.

further (fûr′thər) *adj.* A comparative of **far. 1.** More distant in space, time, or degree: *You couldn't be further from the truth.* **2.** Additional; more: *Stay tuned for further bulletins.* ❖ *adv.* A comparative of **far. 1.** To a greater extent; more: *We will explore the matter further at a later time.* **2.** In addition; furthermore; also: *He stated further that he thought the mayor's remarks were unfair.* **3.** At or to a more distant or advanced point: *I read five pages further.* ❖ *tr.v.* **furthered, furthering, furthers** To help the progress of; forward; advance: *Learning a second language will help further your career.* —SEE NOTE AT **farther.**

furtherance (fûr′thər-əns) *n.* The act of advancing or helping forward; advancement.

furthermore (fûr′thər-môr′) *adv.* Moreover; in addition; besides.

furthermost (fûr′thər-mōst′) *adj.* Most distant or remote.

furthest (fûr′thĭst) *adj.* A superlative of **far.** Most distant in space, time, or degree: *Radio can transmit to the furthest corners of the earth.* ❖ *adv.* A superlative of **far. 1.** To the greatest extent or degree: *The scientist's explanation went furthest toward providing a solution.* **2.** At or to the most distant or advanced point: *The champion threw the javelin furthest.*

furtive (fûr′tĭv) *adj.* Done or acting in a stealthy manner: *He cast a furtive glance at the clock.* —**fur′tive·ly** *adv.*

fury (fyŏŏr′ē) *n., pl.* **furies 1.** Violent anger; rage. See Synonyms at **anger. 2.** Violent and uncontrolled action; turbulence; agitation: *the blizzard's fury.* **3. Furies** In Roman mythology, the terrible winged goddesses who pursued and punished those who committed unavenged crimes, identified with the Greek Erinyes.

furze (fûrz) *n.* A gorse plant.

fuse¹ also **fuze** (fyōōz) *n.* **1.** A cord of easily burned material that is lighted at one end to carry a flame that detonates an explosive charge at the other end. **2.** often **fuze** A mechanical or electronic device used to set off an explosive charge or device, such as a bomb or grenade.

fuse² (fyōōz) *v.* **fused, fusing, fuses** —*tr.* **1.** To join (different pieces or elements) together, especially by melting or heating: *fused the metal parts together with a torch.* **2.** To blend or combine: *The music fuses African and Caribbean rhythms.* —*intr.* **1.** To become joined together, especially by melting or heating. **2.** To become blended or combined: *The two cultures fused over the years to produce a new civilization.* ❖ *n.* A safety device that protects an electric circuit from carrying too much current, containing a length of metal that melts and breaks the circuit when the current reaches an unsafe level.

WORD HISTORY Fuse[1] comes from Italian *fuso*, meaning "spindle" (because fuses in early bombs were shaped like spindles). *Fuso* comes from Latin *fūsus*, also meaning "spindle." **Fuse**[2] comes from the past participle *fūsus* of the Latin verb *fundere*, meaning "to pour, melt, found."

fuselage (fyo͞o′sə-läzh′ *or* fyo͞o′zə-läzh′) *n.* The main body of an airplane that holds cargo, passengers, and crew.

fusible (fyo͞o′zə-bəl) *adj.* Capable of being fused or melted. —**fu′si·bil′i·ty** *n.*

fusillade (fyo͞o′sə-läd′ *or* fyo͞o′sə-läd′) *n.* **1.** The discharge of many guns at the same time or in rapid succession. **2.** A rapid outburst: *a fusillade of complaints.*

fusion (fyo͞o′zhən) *n.* **1.** The act or process of melting or mixing different things into one by heat: *the fusion of copper and zinc to produce brass.* **2.** A mixture or blend formed by fusing two or more things: *An alloy is a fusion of two or more metals.* **3.** A union formed by merging different things or groups: *The building is a fusion of different styles of architecture.* **4.** A nuclear reaction in which light nuclei combine to form heavier nuclei, releasing large amounts of energy. Fusion reactions power the sun and stars.

fuss (fŭs) *n.* **1.** Needlessly nervous or useless activity; commotion: *There was a lot of fuss in the confusion of moving to a new office.* **2.** A display of concern or worry, especially over an unimportant matter: *Why make a fuss about a harmless remark?* **3.** A protest; a complaint: *The cancellation of the party provoked a fuss from the workers.* ❖ *intr.v.* **fussed, fussing, fusses 1.** To be overly careful or concerned: *The caterer fussed over what to make for dinner.* **2.** To try to adjust or arrange something in a nervous or overly concerned way: *He was fussing with the collar of his shirt all night.* —**fuss′er** *n.*

fussbudget (fŭs′bŭj′ĭt) *n.* A person who fusses over unimportant things.

fussy (fŭs′ē) *adj.* **fussier, fussiest 1.** Easily upset; given to bouts of fussing: *a fussy baby.* **2.** Paying great or too much attention to small details: *She is very fussy about the arrangement of her room.* **3.** Requiring attention to small details: *Organizing a big wedding is a fussy job.* —**fuss′i·ly** *adv.* —**fuss′i·ness** *n.*

fusty (fŭs′tē) *adj.* **fustier, fustiest 1.** Smelling of mildew or decay; musty; moldy: *a fusty smell in the damp basement.* **2.** Old-fashioned or out-of-date. —**fus′ti·ly** *adv.*

futile (fyo͞ot′l *or* fyo͞o′tīl′) *adj.* Having no useful result; hopeless; vain: *It is futile to argue that the earth is flat.* —**fu′tile·ly** *adv.*

futility (fyo͞o-tĭl′ĭ-tē) *n., pl.* **futilities 1.** The condition or quality of being futile; uselessness; ineffectiveness: *The attempt to turn iron into gold was an exercise in futility.* **2.** Lack of importance or purpose.

futon (fo͞o′tŏn) *n.* A pad of cotton batting or similar material used on a floor or on a raised platform as a mattress or comforter.

future (fyo͞o′chər) *n.* **1.** The period of time yet to come: *Let's try to do better in the future.* **2.** Something that will happen in time to come: *The business's future is in the hands of new management.* **3.** Chance of success or advancement; outlook: *The young doctor faced a bright future.* **4.** The future tense. ❖ *adj.* That will be or occur in time to come: *Let's review our progress at some future date.*

future perfect *n.* A verb form combining future tense with perfect aspect. It is formed in English by combining *will have* with a past participle, as in the sentence *By noon tomorrow the train will have arrived there.*

future progressive *n.* A verb form combining future tense with progressive aspect to express action or a state considered as ongoing at a specified time in the future. It is formed in English by combining *will be* with a present participle, as in the sentence *By noon tomorrow I will be relaxing on the beach.*

future tense *n.* A verb tense used to express action or a state in the future. It is usually formed in English with the auxiliary verb *will* as in the sentence *They will leave in half an hour.*

futuristic (fyo͞o′chə-rĭs′tĭk) *adj.* **1.** Relating to the future. **2.** Characterized by or expressing a vision of the future: *a futuristic movie in which robots rule the world.* —**fu′tur·is′ti·cal·ly** *adv.*

futurity (fyo͞o-to͝or′ĭ-tē *or* fyo͞o-cho͝or′ĭ-tē) *n., pl.* **futurities 1.** The time yet to come; the future. **2.** The condition or quality of being in or of the future: *the futurity of experimental car design.* **3.** A future event or possibility.

fuze (fyo͞oz) *n.* Variant of **fuse**[1].

fuzz (fŭz) *n.* Soft short fibers or hairs; down: *the fuzz on a peach.*

fuzzy (fŭz′ē) *adj.* **fuzzier, fuzziest 1.** Covered with fuzz: *a fuzzy peach.* **2.** Relating to or resembling fuzz: *fuzzy hair of a little kitten.* **3.** Not clear; blurred: *a fuzzy memory.* —**fuzz′i·ly** *adv.* —**fuzz′i·ness** *n.*

–fy *or* **–ify** A suffix that means to make or cause to become: *beautify; solidify.*

WORD BUILDING The verb suffix **–fy**, which means "to make or cause to become," derives from Latin *–ficāre*, from the verb *facere*, "to do or make." Thus *purify* means "to make pure, cleanse" (coming from Latin *pūrificāre*, from *pūrus* "clean" + *–ficāre*). In English the suffix *–fy* now normally takes the form *–ify*: *acidify, humidify.* Verbs ending in *–fy* often have related nouns ending in *–fication* or *–faction*: *magnify, magnification; satisfy, satisfaction.*

FYI An abbreviation of *for your information.*

Gg

g¹ or **G** (jē) *n., pl.* **g's** or **G's** or **Gs 1.** The seventh letter of the English alphabet. **2.** In music, the fifth tone in the scale of C major. —SEE NOTE AT **c**.

g² An abbreviation of: **1a.** gravity. **b.** acceleration due to gravity. **2.** gram.

G¹ A trademark used for a movie rating that allows admission to people of all ages.

G² *n. Slang* One thousand dollars: *made 20 Gs on the deal.*

gab (găb) *Slang intr.v.* **gabbed, gabbing, gabs** To talk about unimportant matters; chatter: *The neighbors gabbed over the fence.* ❖ *n.* Idle talk.

gabardine also **gaberdine** (găb′ər-dēn′ or găb′ər-dēn′) *n.* A firm woven cloth of cotton, rayon, or wool, having a smooth surface and slanting ribs and used for coats or suits.

gabby (găb′ē) *adj.* **gabbier, gabbiest** *Slang* Tending to talk too much. —**gab′bi·ness** *n.*

gable (gā′bəl) *n.* **1.** The triangular section of wall between the two slopes of a pitched roof. **2.** The whole end wall of a building or wing having a pitched roof. —**ga′bled** *adj.*

gable roof *n.* A pitched roof.

Gabriel (gā′brē-əl) *n.* In the Bible, an angel who explained signs from God and announced the conception, birth, and mission of Jesus to Mary. In Islam, Gabriel is also revered as the angel who revealed the Koran to Muhammad.

gad (găd) *intr.v.* **gadded, gadding, gads** To roam about seeking amusement or social activity.

gadabout (găd′ə-bout′) *n.* A person who roams about seeking amusement or social activity.

gadfly (găd′flī′) *n.* **1.** A person who annoys, criticizes, or provokes others: *She is an outspoken gadfly who always raises objections at the meetings.* **2.** Any of various flies that bite and annoy cattle, horses, and other animals.

gadget (găj′ĭt) *n.* A small mechanical device; a contrivance: *can openers, whisks, and other kitchen gadgets.*

gadolinium (găd′l-ĭn′ē-əm) *n. Symbol* **Gd** A silvery-white metallic element used to improve the heat and corrosion resistance of iron, chromium, and several alloys. Atomic number 64. See **Periodic Table.**

Gaea (gā′ə) *n.* In Greek mythology, the goddess of the earth, who gave birth to and married Uranus and became the mother of the Titans.

Gael (gāl) *n.* **1.** A Gaelic-speaking Celt of Scotland, Ireland, or the Isle of Man, an island between Great Britain. **2.** A Scottish highlander.

Gaelic (gā′lĭk) *adj.* Relating to the Gaels or their culture or languages. ❖ *n.* Any of the Celtic languages of Ireland, Scotland, and the Isle of Man.

gaff (găf) *n.* **1.** An iron hook attached to a pole or handle and used to land large fish. **2.** A spar used to support the top edge of a fore-and-aft sail. ❖ *tr.v.* **gaffed, gaffing, gaffs** To hook or land (a fish) with a gaff.

gaffe (găf) *n.* **1.** A clumsy social error; a faux pas. **2.** A blatant mistake or misjudgment.

gaffer (găf′ər) *n.* **1.** An electrician in charge of the lighting on a movie or television set. **2.** *Chiefly British* An old man.

gag (găg) *n.* **1.** Something put into or over a person's mouth to prevent speaking or crying out. **2.** Something, such as a law or ruling, that limits or censors free speech: *The judge put a gag on press reporting during the trial.* **3a.** A humorous remark intended to make people laugh; a joke. **b.** A practical joke; a hoax. ❖ *v.* **gagged, gagging, gags** —*tr.* **1.** To prevent (someone) from speaking or crying out by using a gag. **2.** To prevent (someone) from exercising free speech. **3.** To cause to choke or retch: *The strong gas fumes gagged several passers-by.* —*intr.* To choke or retch: *I gagged on the bitter medicine.*

gaggle (găg′əl) *n.* **1.** A flock of geese. **2.** A cluster or group: *a gaggle of fans.*

gaiety (gā′ĭ-tē) *n., pl.* **gaieties 1.** The condition of being lively and joyful; cheerfulness: *the gaiety of the laughing children.* **2.** Lively and joyful celebration: *Mardi Gras is a season of gaiety.* **3.** Showiness or brightness in dress or appearance; finery: *The gaiety of the colorful flowers brightened the room.*

gaily also **gayly** (gā′lē) *adv.* **1.** In a joyful, cheerful, or happy manner; merrily. **2.** Brightly; colorfully; showily: *The room for the party was gaily decorated.*

gain (gān) *v.* **gained, gaining, gains** —*tr.* **1.** To obtain; acquire: *We gained experience by working during the summer.* **2.** To acquire in competition; win: *The general gained a decisive victory over the enemy.* **3a.** To get an increase of; build up: *gain speed; gain strength after an illness.* **b.** To increase by (a certain amount): *gained 10 pounds over the winter.* **4.** To come to; reach: *gained the top of the mountain.* See Synonyms at **reach.** —*intr.* **1.** To increase; grow: *Has your house gained in value?* **2.** To become better; improve: *The recovering patient is gaining in strength.* **3.** To come nearer; get closer: *The hounds gained on the fleeing fox.* ❖ *n.* **1a.** Something gained or acquired: *territorial gains.* **b.** Progress; advancement: *We have made great social gains since the early 1900s.* **2.** An increase in amount or degree: *a financial gain; a gain in popularity.*

gainer (gā′nər) *n.* **1.** A person or thing that gains. **2.** A reverse dive.

gainful (gān′fəl) *adj.* Providing an income or advantage; profitable: *gainful employment.* —**gain′ful·ly** *adv.*

gainsay (gān-sā′ or gān′sā′) *tr.v.* **gainsaid** (gān-sĕd′ or gān-sĕd′), **gainsaying, gainsays** (gān-sāz′ or gān-sĕz′) To declare to be false; deny or contradict: *She was the only witness, so there was no one to gainsay her account of the robbery.*

gait (gāt) *n.* **1.** A way of walking or running: *a shuffling gait.* **2.** The way in which a horse moves, as a walk, trot, or gallop.

gaiter (gā′tər) *n.* **1.** A covering for the lower leg or ankle, worn especially by skiers and hikers. **2.** A tubular collar fitting closely around the neck, often worn by skiers. **3.** An ankle-high shoe with elastic sides. **4.** An overshoe with a cloth top.

gal (găl) *n. Informal* A girl.

gal. An abbreviation of gallon.

gala (gā′lə *or* găl′ə *or* gä′lə) *n.* A festive occasion or celebration. ❖ *adj.* Festive: *The city greeted the home team's victory with a gala celebration.*

galactic (gə-lăk′tĭk) *adj.* Relating to a galaxy, especially the Milky Way.

Galahad (găl′ə-hăd′) *n.* In Arthurian legend, the most virtuous of King Arthur's knights, who found the Holy Grail.

Galatians (gə-lā′shəns) *pl.n. (used with a singular verb)* A book of the New Testament consisting of a letter by Saint Paul to Christians in Galatia, a country in Asia Minor.

galaxy (găl′ək-sē) *n., pl.* **galaxies 1a.** A vast grouping of stars, gas, and dust held together by the force of gravity. A galaxy has billions of stars. **b.** often **Galaxy** The galaxy that contains our solar system; the Milky Way. **2.** An assembly of brilliant, beautiful, or distinguished people or things: *a galaxy of movie stars.*

gale (gāl) *n.* **1.** A very strong wind. **2.** A storm at sea: *The ship was blown off course by the gale.* **3.** A noisy outburst: *gales of laughter.*

galena (gə-lē′nə) *n.* A gray mineral, composed of lead and sulfur, that is the main ore of lead.

gall[1] (gôl) *n.* **1.** Insulting boldness; impudence; nerve: *They had the gall to barge into the party uninvited.* **2.** Bitter feeling; spite: *The feuding neighbors were full of gall.* **3.** A bitter yellow or green liquid secreted by the liver to aid digestion; bile.

gall[2] (gôl) *n.* A sore on the skin caused by rubbing: *a saddle gall on a horse.* ❖ *v.* **galled, galling, galls** —*tr.* **1.** To irritate or exasperate: *It galls me to see people littering.* **2.** To make sore or chafed. —*intr.* To become sore by rubbing.

gall[3] (gôl) *n.* An abnormal swelling on a plant, usually caused by insects, bacteria, or mites.

WORD HISTORY All three forms of **gall** were spelled *galle* in Middle English. The first two can be traced to Old English *gealla,* meaning "bile," and the third can be traced to, and the second might be influenced by, Latin *galla,* referring to the swelling on a plant. The similarity in the spelling of these three words influenced the historical development of their meanings.

gallant (găl′ənt) *adj.* **1.** Stylish in appearance; dashing: *He was very gallant at the ball.* **2.** Brave and noble; courageous; valorous: *a gallant resistance to the invasion.* **3.** Stately or majestic; grand: *a gallant ship.* **4.** (gə-lănt′ *or* gə-länt′) Polite and attentive to women; chivalrous: *our host's gallant manner.* ❖ *n.* (gə-lănt′ *or* gə-länt′ *or* găl′ənt) **1.** A fashionable young man. **2.** A man who is polite and attentive to women. —**gal′lant·ly** *adv.*

gallantry (găl′ən-trē) *n., pl.* **gallantries 1.** Heroic courage or brave and noble conduct. **2.** Considerate attention to women; courtliness. **3.** A gallant act or action.

gallbladder also **gall bladder** (gôl′blăd′ər) *n.* A small, pear-shaped muscular sac, located near the right lobe of the liver, in which bile is stored.

galleon (găl′ē-ən *or* găl′yən) *n.* A large three-masted sailing ship of the 1400s, 1500s, and 1600s, used especially by the Spanish.

gallery (găl′ə-rē) *n., pl.* **galleries 1.** A long narrow walk or passage, often with a roof and windows along one side. **2.** An enclosed passageway, such as a hall or corridor: *a shooting gallery.* **3.** A narrow balcony, usually with railing, along the outside of a building. **4a.** The balcony in a theater or church: *The gallery in the concert hall has the cheapest seats.* **b.** The seats in such a balcony. **c.** The people occupying these seats: *The gallery applauded and whistled.* **5.** A large audience, as at a sports event: *The golfer tipped his hat toward the gallery.* **6.** A building or hall for displaying works of art. **7.** An underground tunnel or other passageway, as in a mine.

galley (găl′ē) *n., pl.* **galleys 1.** A long narrow ship driven by sails and oars and used primarily in the Mediterranean until the 1600s. **2.** The kitchen on a ship, airliner, or camper. **3.** A trial sheet of printed material; a proof.

gallfly (gôl′flī′) *n.* Any of various small insects that deposit their eggs on plant stems or in the bark of trees, causing galls to form.

Gallic (găl′ĭk) *adj.* Relating to France, to the French, or to the ancient Gauls.

galling (gô′lĭng) *adj.* Very irritating or exasperating: *A mechanical problem caused another galling delay in our flight.* —**gall′ing·ly** *adv.*

gallium (găl′ē-əm) *n. Symbol* **Ga** A rare, silvery metallic element that is liquid near room temperature and is used in thermometers, semiconductors, and transistors. Atomic number 31. See **Periodic Table.**

gallivant (găl′ə-vănt′) *intr.v.* **gallivanted, gallivanting, gallivants** To travel or roam about in search of pleasure or amusement.

gallon (găl′ən) *n.* **1.** A unit of volume or capacity used for measuring liquids, equal to 4 quarts (3.8 liters). See table at **measurement. 2a.** A container having a capacity of one gallon. **b.** The amount that can be held in such a container: *a gallon of milk.*

gallop (găl′əp) *n.* **1.** A fast gait of a horse or other four-footed animal, in which all four feet are off the ground at the same time during each stride. **2.** A ride on a horse going at a gallop. ❖ *v.* **galloped, galloping, gallops** —*tr.* To cause to gallop: *The rider galloped the horse around the track.* —*intr.* **1.** To ride at a gallop: *gallop around the field.* **2.** To move or progress swiftly: *Summer is galloping by.* —**gal′lop·er** *n.*

gallows (găl′ōz) *n., pl.* **gallows** or **gallowses 1.** An upright framework from which a noose is suspended, used for execution by hanging. **2.** Execution on a gallows or by hanging: *was sentenced to the gallows.*

gallstone (gôl′stōn′) *n.* A small hard mass that forms in the gallbladder or in a bile duct.

galore (gə-lôr′) *adj.* In great numbers; in abundance: *The streets were filled with shoppers galore during the holiday season.*

galosh (gə-lŏsh′) *n.* A waterproof overshoe.

galvanic (găl-văn′ĭk) *adj.* **1.** Relating to electricity that is produced by chemical action. **2.** Producing electricity by chemical action: *a galvanic cell.*

galvanism (găl′və-nĭz′əm) *n.* Direct-current electricity produced by chemical action.

galvanize (găl′və-nīz′) *tr.v.* **galvanized, galvanizing, galvanizes 1.** To coat (iron or steel) with zinc as protection against rust. **2.** To stir to action or awareness; spur: *Destruction of important habitats in our state galvanized us to support the conservation law.* —**gal′va·ni·za′tion** (găl′və-nĭ-zā′shən) *n.*

galvanometer (găl′və-nŏm′ĭ-tər) *n.* An instrument that detects, measures, and determines the direction of small electric currents.

gambit (găm′bĭt) *n.* **1.** An opening move in chess in which a pawn or piece is sacrificed in order to gain a favorable position. **2.** An action or remark designed to bring about a desired result.

gamble (găm′bəl) *v.* **gambled, gambling, gambles** —*intr.* **1.** To bet money on the outcome of a game, contest, or other event. **2.** To take a risk in the hope of gaining an advantage: *The builder is gambling on the need for more houses soon.* —*tr.* **1.** To risk (something) in gambling; wager. **2.** To expose to hazard; risk: *The daredevil gambled his life in his latest stunt.* ❖ *n.* **1.** A bet or wager. **2.** An act of undertaking something uncertain; a risk. —**gam′bler** *n.*

gambol (găm′bəl) *intr.v.* **gamboled, gamboling, gambols** or **gambolled, gambolling, gambols** To skip or run about playfully; frolic. ❖ *n.* The act of skipping or frolicking about.

gambrel roof (găm′brəl) *n.* A ridged roof that has two different slopes on each side, with the lower slope steeper than the upper slope.

game¹ (gām) *n.* **1.** An activity that provides entertainment or amusement: *The children made a game of counting cars that passed.* **2.** A sport or contest governed by specific rules: *Tennis is my favorite game.* **3.** A single contest between two opponents or teams: *The game was canceled due to rain.* **4.** The number of points needed to win a game. **5.** The equipment, such as a board and pieces, needed for playing certain games: *The game came with its own box.* **6.** A particular style or ability at a certain game: *A few of the golfers seemed off their game today.* **7a.** Wild animals hunted for food or sport. **b.** The flesh of these animals, used as food. **8.** *Informal* A plan or scheme: *Anyone can see through that old game.* **9.** *Informal* An occupation, profession, or activity: *the game of politics.* ❖ *tr. & intr.v.* **gamed, gaming, games** To gamble. ❖ *adj.* **gamer, gamest** **1.** Courageous; plucky: *They put up a game fight.* **2.** Ready and willing: *I'm game for climbing the mountain.* —**game′ly** *adv.* —**game′ness** *n.*

game² (gām) *adj.* **gamer, gamest** Lame or injured: *a game leg.*

WORD HISTORY Game¹ comes from Middle English *game,* which comes from Old English *gamen,* both meaning "amusement, fun, sport." The origin of **game²** is unknown.

game bird *n.* A bird, such as a pheasant or grouse, that is widely hunted for sport.

gamecock (gām′kŏk′) *n.* A rooster bred and trained for fighting.

gamekeeper (gām′kē′pər) *n.* A person employed to protect and maintain game birds and other wildlife, especially on an estate or preserve.

gamer (gā′mər) *n.* A person who plays a game, especially a role-playing or computer game.

game show *n.* A television show in which contestants compete for prizes by playing a game, such as a quiz.

gamester (gām′stər) *n.* A person who plays games, especially a gambler.

gamete (găm′ēt′) *n.* A cell that unites with another to form a fertilized cell that develops into a new organism; a reproductive cell.

gametophyte (gə-mē′tə-fīt′) *n.* In plants and most algae, the individual organism or generation of organisms that produces reproductive cells. The life cycle of such an organism involves an alternation between the gametophyte and the sporophyte.

game warden *n.* An official who enforces hunting and fishing regulations.

gaming (gā′mĭng) *n.* **1.** Gambling. **2.** The playing of games, especially computer or video games.

gamma (găm′ə) *n.* The third letter of the Greek alphabet, written Γ, γ. In English it is represented as *G, g,* except before *g, k,* or *kh,* when it is often represented as *N, n.*

gamma globulin *n.* A solution of antibodies derived from human blood plasma and used in the treatment of certain diseases.

gamma ray *n.* Electromagnetic radiation with wavelengths shorter than those of x-rays and having greater energy and penetrating power. Gamma rays are given off by unstable nuclei during radioactive decay.

gamut (găm′ət) *n.* **1.** The entire range of musical tones. **2.** The complete range of something: *the gamut of feelings from high hope to utter despair.*

gamy (gā′mē) *adj.* **gamier, gamiest** **1.** Having the flavor or odor of game, especially slightly spoiled game. **2.** Showing great spirit; plucky: *a gamy horse that loves to run.* —**gam′i·ly** *adv.* —**gam′i·ness** *n.*

gander (găn′dər) *n.* **1.** A male goose. **2.** *Informal* A look or glance: *Take a gander at this flat tire and see what you think.*

gang (găng) *n.* **1.** An organized group of criminals. **2.** A group of young people who band together, especially a group of delinquents. **3.** *Informal* A group of friends: *The whole gang went to see a movie.* **4.** A group of laborers who work together under a single supervisor: *a road gang filling potholes.* ❖ *intr.v.* **ganged, ganging, gangs** To band together in a group or gang: *The reporters ganged around the governor.* ◆ **gang up** **1.** To join together in criticism or attack: *The author felt that the critics were ganging up on her.* **2.** To act together as a group: *Researchers ganged up to fight the disease.*

gangbuster (găng′bŭs′tər) *n.* *Slang* A law enforcement officer who works to break up organized criminal groups. ◆ **like gangbusters** *Slang* With great impact, vigor, or zeal: *came on like gangbusters at the start of his campaign; a career that took off like gangbusters.*

ganglion (găng′glē-ən) *n., pl.* **ganglia** (găng′glē-ə) or **ganglions** A compact group of nerve cells forming a nerve center, especially one located outside the brain or spinal cord.

gangly (găng′glē) *adj.* **ganglier, gangliest** Tall and awkward; lanky.

gangplank (găng′plăngk′) *n.* A board or ramp used as a bridge between a ship and a pier.

gangrene (găng′grēn′ *or* găng-grēn′) *n.* Decay of tissue in a living body, caused by a stoppage of the blood supply from injury or disease. ❖ *tr. & intr.v.* **gangrened, gangrening, gangrenes** To affect or become affected with gangrene. —**gan′gre·nous** (găng′grə-nəs) *adj.*

gangster (găng′stər) *n.* A member of an organized group of criminals.

gangway (găng′wā′) *n.* **1a.** A gangplank. **b.** An opening in the side of a ship through which passengers may board. **2.** A passage along either side of a ship's upper deck.

gannet (găn′ĭt) *n.* Any of several large, mostly white seabirds that have long pointed wings and a long bill and that nest in large colonies on rocky coasts.

gantlet (gônt′lĭt or gănt′lĭt) *n.* Variant of **gauntlet**.

gantry (găn′trē) *n., pl.* **gantries 1a.** A large framework designed to carry a crane from one spot to another along a set of rails. **b.** A similar structure on which signals are mounted over railroad tracks. **2.** A large vertical structure somewhat like a scaffold, used in assembling or servicing a rocket, especially on a launching pad.

Ganymede (găn′ə-mēd′) *n.* In Greek mythology, a Trojan boy of great beauty whom Zeus carried away to be cupbearer to the gods.

gaol (jāl) *n. Chiefly British* Variant of **jail**.

gap (găp) *n.* **1.** An opening or break, as in a wall or fence. **2.** A break in something continuous: *There are many gaps in our knowledge of the universe.* **3.** A pass through mountains. **4.** A wide difference or imbalance: *There is a gap between what he says and what he does.*

gape (gāp or găp) *intr.v.* **gaped, gaping, gapes 1.** To open the mouth wide, as if to bite or swallow. **2.** To stare in amazement, often with the mouth open: *The fans gaped as the baseball went soaring out of the park.* **3.** To open wide; form a gap: *Cracks gaped in the ground after the earthquake.* ❖ *n.* The act or an instance of gaping: *the wide gape of a lion's yawn.*

gap year *n.* A year taken off from a person's education, especially between high school and college, often to travel or gain practical experience.

gar (gär) *n.* Any of several freshwater fishes of North and Central America having a long body and long narrow jaws with sharp teeth.

garage (gə-räzh′ or gə-räj′) *n.* **1.** A building or indoor space in which to park a motor vehicle. **2.** A business where cars are repaired, serviced, or parked. ❖ *tr.v.* **garaged, garaging, garages** To put or keep (a vehicle) in a garage.

garage sale *n.* A sale of used household items or clothing held at the home of the seller.

garb (gärb) *n.* A style or form of clothing: *folk dancers in traditional rural garb.* ❖ *tr.v.* **garbed, garbing, garbs** To clothe or dress: *The judge was garbed in a long black robe.*

garbage (gär′bĭj) *n.* **1.** Food wastes, as from a kitchen. **2.** Worthless or inferior material; trash: *That novel is nothing but garbage.*

garbanzo (gär-bän′zō) *n., pl.* **garbanzos** The chickpea.

garble (gär′bəl) *tr.v.* **garbled, garbling, garbles** To distort or mix up: *The report sounded great, but she garbled the facts.* ❖ *n.* The act or an instance of garbling: *a confused garble of voices.*

garden (gär′dn) *n.* **1.** A piece of land used for growing flowers, vegetables, herbs, or fruit. **2.** A park or other public place ornamented with flowers and other plants: *a botanical garden.* ❖ *intr.v.* **gardened, gardening, gardens** To plant or tend a garden.

gardener (gärd′nər or gär′dn-ər) *n.* A person who works in or takes care of a garden.

gardenia (gär-dēn′yə) *n.* Any of various shrubs having glossy evergreen leaves and large, fragrant, usually white flowers.

garden-variety (gär′dn-və-rī′ĭ-tē) *adj.* Common; unremarkable: *I'm getting bored with the same old garden-variety video games they're making now.*

garfish (gär′fĭsh′) *n.* A gar.

gargantuan (gär-găn′chŏŏ-ən) *adj.* Of immense size; huge: *a stadium of gargantuan proportions.*

gargle (gär′gəl) *v.* **gargled, gargling, gargles** —*intr.* To wash or rinse the mouth or throat by exhaling air through a liquid held there. —*tr.* To circulate (a liquid) in the mouth or throat by gargling. ❖ *n.* A liquid used for gargling.

gargoyle (gär′goil′) *n.* **1.** A drain spout in the form of a grotesque animal or person projecting from the gutter of a building. **2.** A grotesque, usually projecting ornamental figure.

garish (gâr′ĭsh) *adj.* Too bright or ornamented; gaudy: *The clown wore a suit of garish colors.* —**gar′ish·ly** *adv.*

garland (gär′lənd) *n.* A wreath or chain, as of flowers or leaves, worn as a crown or used for ornament. ❖ *tr.v.* **garlanded, garlanding, garlands** To decorate with a garland.

garlic (gär′lĭk) *n.* **1.** The bulb of a plant related to the onion, having a strong taste and odor and used as seasoning. The bulb can be divided into separate parts called cloves. **2.** The plant that bears such a bulb. —**gar′lick·y** *adj.*

garment (gär′mənt) *n.* An article of clothing.

garment bag *n.* A long zippered bag, usually capable of being folded in half, used to carry and protect clothes when traveling.

garner (gär′nər) *tr.v.* **garnered, garnering, garners** To receive or gather: *The band garnered much praise for their new album.*

garnet (gär′nĭt) *n.* **1.** A common crystalline silicate mineral of aluminum or calcium. It is usually red and is used as a gem and as an abrasive. **2.** A dark red color.

garnish (gär′nĭsh) *tr.v.* **garnished, garnishing, garnishes 1.** To decorate or embellish: *garnish iced tea with a slice of lemon; mashed potatoes garnished with parsley.* **2.** To take or keep (someone's pay or property) by a legal proceeding in order to use it to pay off a debt. ❖ *n.* A decoration, especially one added to a food or drink to give it extra color or flavor.

garret (gär′ĭt) *n.* A room on the top floor of a house, typically under a pitched roof; an attic.

garrison (găr′ĭ-sən) *n.* **1.** A military post. **2.** The troops stationed at such a post. ❖ *tr.v.* **garrisoned, garrisoning, garrisons 1.** To assign (troops) to a military post. **2.** To supply (a post or other place) with troops for defense.

garrulity (gə-rōō′lĭ-tē) *n.* The quality of being overly talkative.

garrulous (găr′ə-ləs or găr′yə-ləs) *adj.* Excessively talkative, especially about unimportant matters: *a garrulous neighbor.* —**gar′ru·lous·ness** *n.*

garter (gär′tər) *n.* An elastic band or strap worn on the leg to hold up a stocking or sock. ❖ *tr.v.* **gartered, gartering, garters** To fasten and hold with a garter.

garter snake *n.* Any of various small nonvenomous North and Central American snakes that usually have a dark body with three lighter-colored lengthwise stripes.

gas (găs) *n., pl.* **gases** or **gasses 1.** One of the three basic forms of matter, composed of molecules in constant random motion. Unlike a solid, a gas has no fixed shape and will take on the shape of the space available. Unlike a liquid, it has no fixed volume and will expand to fill the space available. **2.** A gas or mixture of gases burned as fuel for cooking or heating. **3.** Gasoline. **4.** A chemical gas that chokes, irritates, or poisons, used as a weapon. **5.** An anesthetic that is in the form of gas. **6.** *Slang* A highly exciting or entertaining person or thing: *That new ride is a gas.* ❖ *tr.v.* **gassed, gassing, gases** or **gasses 1.** To treat chemically with gas. **2.** To injure or poison with gas.

◆ **gas up** To supply a vehicle with gas or gasoline: *We gassed the car up before going on our trip.*

gaseous (găs′ē-əs *or* găsh′əs) *adj.* Relating to or existing as a gas: *Water in its gaseous state is called water vapor.*

gas giant *n.* A large planet that has a thick gaseous atmosphere and lacks a solid surface because it has relatively little rock or other solid material. Jupiter, Saturn, Uranus, and Neptune are gas giants.

gash (găsh) *tr.v.* **gashed, gashing, gashes** To make a long deep cut or wound in. ❖ *n.* A long deep cut or wound.

gasket (găs′kĭt) *n.* Any of a wide variety of seals or packings placed between machine parts or around pipe joints to prevent the escape of gas or fluid.

gaslight (găs′līt′) *n.* **1.** Light made by burning gas in a lamp. **2.** A lamp that uses gas as fuel.

gaslit (găs′lĭt′) *adj.* Lighted by gaslight: *a gaslit street in the old section of town.*

gas mask *n.* A mask that covers the face or the face and head and is equipped with an air filter as protection against poisonous gases.

gasohol (găs′ə-hôl′) *n.* A fuel for cars that is a blend of ethyl alcohol and unleaded gasoline.

gasoline (găs′ə-lēn′ *or* găs′ə-lēn′) *n.* A highly flammable mixture of liquid hydrocarbons that are derived from petroleum. Gasoline is used as a fuel for internal-combustion engines, as in automobiles, motorcycles, and small trucks.

gasp (găsp) *v.* **gasped, gasping, gasps** —*intr.* To inhale in a sudden, sharp, and usually fitful way, as from shock, surprise, or great exertion. —*tr.* To say in a breathless manner: *"Wait!," she gasped.* ❖ *n.* A sudden, violent, or fitful intake of the breath.

gas station *n.* A business at which motor vehicles are refueled.

gassy (găs′ē) *adj.* **gassier, gassiest** Resembling, containing, or filled with gas.

gastric (găs′trĭk) *adj.* Relating to the stomach: *a gastric ulcer.*

gastroenteritis (găs′trō-ĕn′tə-rī′tĭs) *n.* Inflammation of the mucous membrane of the stomach and intestines.

gastrointestinal (găs′trō-ĭn-tĕs′tə-nəl) *adj.* Relating to the stomach and intestines.

gastronomic (găs′trə-nŏm′ĭk) *also* **gastronomical** (găs′-trə-nŏm′ĭ-kəl) *adj.* Relating to gastronomy: *The chef brought out his latest gastronomic creation.* —**gas′-tro·nom′i·cal·ly** *adv.*

gastronomy (gă-strŏn′ə-mē) *n.* The art or science of good eating.

gastropod (găs′trə-pŏd′) *n.* Any of numerous mollusks, such as a snail, slug, cowrie, or limpet, having a distinct head with eyes and tentacles, usually a single coiled shell, and a muscular foot on the underside of the body.

gastrula (găs′trə-lə) *n., pl.* **gastrulas** *or* **gastrulae** (găs′-trə-lē′) An embryo at the stage following the blastula, in which the cells are distributed into layers that eventually develop into the different tissues and organs of the body.

gat (găt) *v. Archaic* A past tense of **get.**

gate (găt) *n.* **1a.** A hinged or sliding barrier that serves as a door in a wall or fence. **b.** An opening in a wall or fence; a gateway. **2.** A device for controlling the flow of water or gas through a pipe, dam, or similar system. **3.** A passageway in an airport through which passengers proceed when boarding or leaving an airplane. **4.** The number of

people attending an event or performance: *a gate of 500 people.* **5.** The total amount of money paid for people attending an event or performance: *The gate for the rock concert was $775,000.*

gatecrasher (găt′krăsh′ər) *n. Slang* A person who attends a gathering, performance, private party, or sports event without being invited or without paying.

gated community (gā′tĭd) *n.* A residential neighborhood that is closed off by a gate or other barrier, with entrance permitted only to residents and their guests.

gatehouse (găt′hous′) *n.* A house built over or near a gate, usually lived in by a gatekeeper.

gatekeeper (găt′kē′pər) *n.* A person in charge of the passage of people or vehicles through a gate, as on an estate or at a castle.

gatepost (găt′pōst′) *n.* An upright post on which a gate is hung or against which a gate closes.

gateway (găt′wā′) *n.* **1.** An opening, as in a wall or fence, that may be closed with a gate. **2.** Something that serves as a means of access or an entrance: *Denver is thought of as the gateway to the Rockies.*

gather (găth′ər) *v.* **gathered, gathering, gathers** —*tr.* **1.** To bring together in a group; convene; assemble: *The guide gathered the tourists around the museum exhibit.* **2.** To pick; collect: *Squirrels gather nuts.* **3.** To accumulate gradually: *The old bureau gathered dust in the attic.* **4.** To summon up; muster (mental or physical powers): *Give me a minute to gather my thoughts.* **5.** To gain or increase gradually: *The avalanche gathered speed.* **6.** To conclude; infer: *I gather that you didn't like the movie.* **7.** To draw (cloth) into small folds or pleats, as by sewing: *gather material at the waist of a full skirt.* **8.** To draw or bring closer: *gather a frightened kitten in one's arms.* —*intr.* **1.** To come together in a group; assemble: *We gathered on the porch for a group photo.* **2.** To grow or increase bit by bit; accumulate: *Dust gathered under the couch.* ❖ *n.* One of the small folds or pleats made in cloth by gathering it. —**gath′er·er** *n.*

✦ **SYNONYMS** gather, accumulate, assemble, collect *v.*

gathering (găth′ər-ĭng) *n.* **1.** An assembly of people; a meeting: *a family gathering.* **2.** The act of a person or thing that gathers.

Gatling gun (găt′lĭng) *n.* A machine gun having a cluster of barrels that are fired as the cluster is turned.

gator (gā′tər) *n. Informal* An alligator.

gauche (gōsh) *adj.* Lacking social grace; tactless; clumsy: *Talking with your mouth full is gauche.*

gaucho (gou′chō) *n., pl.* **gauchos** A cowhand of the South American pampas.

gaudy (gô′dē) *adj.* **gaudier, gaudiest** Too brightly colored and showy to be in good taste. —**gaud′i·ly** *adv.* —**gaud′-i·ness** *n.*

gauge (gāj) *n.* **1.** A standard dimension, quantity, or capacity, especially: **a.** The distance between the two rails of a railroad. **b.** The thickness or diameter of a material such as sheet metal or wire. **c.** The diameter of a shotgun barrel as determined by the number of lead balls of a size fitting the barrel that make one pound. **2.** An instrument for measuring or testing something: *We checked the air pressure in the tires with a gauge.* **3.** A means of estimating or evaluating; a test: *How a person handles a difficult situation is a good gauge of character.* ❖ *tr.v.* **gauged, gauging, gauges 1.** To measure precisely: *gauge the depth of the ocean.* **2.** To evaluate or judge: *gauge a person's ability.* —**gauge′a·ble** *adj.*

Gaul (gôl) *n.* **1.** A Celt of ancient Gaul, a region of Europe lying mostly in what is now France. **2.** A French person.

Gaulish (gô'lĭsh) *adj.* Relating to Gaul, the ancient Gauls, or their language or customs. ❖ *n.* The Celtic language of ancient Gaul.

gaunt (gônt) *adj.* **gaunter, gauntest 1.** Thin and bony; emaciated. **2.** Bleak and desolate; stark: *gaunt, forbidding mountains.* —**gaunt'ly** *adv.* —**gaunt'ness** *n.*

gauntlet[1] also **gantlet** (gônt'lĭt *or* gănt'lĭt) *n.* **1.** A heavy protective glove, especially a glove covered with chain mail and worn with medieval armor. **2.** A challenge: *The candidate threw down the gauntlet, daring his opponent to debate him face to face.*

gauntlet[2] also **gantlet** (gônt'lĭt *or* gănt'lĭt) *n.* **1.** A form of punishment in which a person is forced to run between two lines of people and is beaten with clubs, sticks, or other weapons. **2.** An attack from all sides. **3.** A severe trial; an ordeal. ◆ **run the gauntlet** To undergo an ordeal.

WORD HISTORY Gauntlet[1] comes from Middle English *gauntelet* (meaning "armored glove"), which comes from Old French *gauntelet*, the diminutive of *gant,* meaning "glove." **Gauntlet**[2] comes from Swedish *gatlopp* (*gata,* meaning "lane" + *lopp,* meaning "course, running").

---

gauze (gôz) *n.* A loosely woven, somewhat transparent cloth used especially for bandaging.

gauzy (gô'zē) *adj.* **gauzier, gauziest** Resembling gauze in thinness or transparency. —**gauz'i·ness** *n.*

gave (gāv) *v.* Past tense of **give.**

gavel (găv'əl) *n.* A small wooden mallet used by a presiding officer to signal for attention or order or by an auctioneer to mark the conclusion of a transaction.

gavotte (gə-vŏt') *n.* **1.** A French peasant dance in moderately quick duple meter. **2.** Music written for this dance.

Gawain (gə-wān' *or* gä'wän' *or* gou'ən) *n.* In Arthurian legend, a nephew of King Arthur and a Knight of the Round Table.

gawk (gôk) *intr.v.* **gawked, gawking, gawks** To stare stupidly; gape. —**gawk·er** *n.*

gawky (gô'kē) *adj.* **gawkier, gawkiest** Awkward; clumsy: *a gawky colt.* —**gawk'i·ly** *adv.* —**gawk'i·ness** *n.*

gay (gā) *adj.* **gayer, gayest 1.** Relating to or having a sexual orientation toward people of the same sex. **2.** Merry; light-hearted: *a gay mood; gay music.* **3.** Bright or lively, especially in color: *The package was tied with gay ribbons.* ❖ *n.* **1.** A person whose sexual orientation is toward people of the same sex. **2.** A man whose sexual orientation is toward men: *an alliance of gays and lesbians.*

USAGE Although **gay** can refer to either men or women, it is often used to refer solely to men, in contrast to **lesbian,** used for women. *Gay* is generally used not in the singular to refer to an individual person, but rather in the plural to refer collectively either to gay men or to gay men and lesbians.

---

gayly (gā'lē) *adv.* Variant of **gaily.**

gaze (gāz) *intr.v.* **gazed, gazing, gazes** To look intently, as with wonder or curiosity; stare: *We gazed in awe at the soaring eagle.* ❖ *n.* An intent steady look: *The crowd fixed their gaze on the speaker.*

gazebo (gə-zā'bō *or* gə-zē'bō) *n., pl.* **gazebos** or **gazeboes** A small roofed structure, usually having open sides, that provides a shady place to sit or rest.

gazelle (gə-zĕl') *n.* Any of various slender swift-running antelopes of Africa and Asia.

gazette (gə-zĕt') *n.* **1.** A newspaper. **2.** An official journal or periodical.

gazetteer (găz'ĭ-tîr') *n.* A dictionary, listing, or index of geographic terms.

gazpacho (gə-spä'chō) *n.* A chilled soup made with chopped tomatoes, cucumbers, onions, and peppers.

Gb An abbreviation of gigabit.

GB An abbreviation of gigabyte.

gcd An abbreviation of greatest common divisor.

G clef *n.* A treble clef.

GDP An abbreviation of gross domestic product.

gear (gîr) *n.* **1a.** A wheel with teeth around its rim that mesh with the teeth of another wheel to transmit motion. **b.** An arrangement of such interlocking wheels, as in an automobile or bicycle, that transmits motion in a particular way that balances speed and power. A low gear results in greater power but less speed, while a high gear results in greater speed but less power. **2.** Equipment used for a particular activity: *fishing gear.* **3.** Personal belongings, including clothing: *The campers stored their gear under their bunks.* ❖ *v.* **geared, gearing, gears** —*tr.* **1.** To provide with or connect by gears: *gear a motor to a propeller.* **2.** To adjust or adapt: *The scientists geared their remarks to a youthful audience.* —*intr.* To be or become in gear; mesh: *The cogs of an automobile transmission gear into each other.* ◆ **gear up** To get ready for a coming action or event: *We are geared up for our family's upcoming camping trip.*

gearbox (gîr'bŏks') *n.* The transmission in a motor vehicle.

gearshift (gîr'shĭft') *n.* A device for changing from one gear to another in a transmission, as in an automobile.

gearwheel also **gear wheel** (gîr'wēl') *n.* A wheel having teeth around its rim; a cogwheel.

gecko (gĕk'ō) *n., pl.* **geckos** or **geckoes** Any of various small insect-eating lizards of warm climates that have adhesive toe pads with which they cling to walls and other vertical surfaces.

gee[1] (jē) *interj.* An expression used to command an animal pulling a load to turn to the right or to go forward.

gee[2] (jē) *interj.* An expression used as a mild oath or as an exclamation of surprise.

geek (gēk) *n. Slang* **1a.** An inept or clumsy person. **b.** A person who is accomplished in scientific or technical pursuits but is socially awkward or inept. **2.** A person who performs bizarre acts in a carnival show. —**geek'y** *adj.*

geese (gēs) *n.* Plural of **goose.**

gefilte fish (gə-fĭl'tə) *n.* Seasoned chopped fish mixed with bread or cracker crumbs and eggs, formed into balls and cooked in a broth.

Geiger counter (gī'gər) *n.* An electronic instrument that detects and measures nuclear radiation, such as x-rays, gamma rays, or cosmic rays, by counting the ions produced as the radiation passes through a gas-filled tube.

geisha (gā'shə *or* gē'shə) *n., pl.* **geisha** or **geishas** A Japanese woman trained to entertain social or professional gatherings of men with singing, dancing, or amusing talk.

gel (jĕl) *n.* **1.** A semisolid mixture formed when particles suspended in a liquid become relatively large, as when boiled fruit juices thicken and cool to form a jelly or colloid. **2.** A jellylike substance used in styling hair. ❖ *intr.v.* **gelled, gelling, gels** To become a gel.

gelatin (jĕl'ə-tn) *n.* **1.** An odorless, colorless protein substance obtained by boiling a mixture of water and the skin, bones, and tendons of animals. The preparation forms a gel when allowed to cool and is used in foods, drugs, glue, and photographic film. **2.** A flavored jelly made with gelatin, often used as a dessert or in salads.

gelatinous (jə-lăt′n-əs) *adj.* **1.** Similar in texture to gelatin; thick and viscous: *the gelatinous body of a jellyfish.* **2.** Relating to or containing gelatin.

gelato (jə-lä′tō) *n., pl.* **gelati** (jə-lä′tē) An Italian ice cream or sorbet.

geld (gĕld) *tr.v.* **gelded, gelding, gelds** To remove the testicles of (a horse or another animal).

gelding (gĕl′dĭng) *n.* A gelded animal, especially a horse.

gem (jĕm) *n.* **1.** A precious or semiprecious stone cut and polished as a jewel. **2.** Something that is much admired or appreciated: *This painting is the gem of the museum's collection.* ❖ *tr.v.* **gemmed, gemming, gems** To set or adorn with gems: *The artisan gemmed a gold box with stones of different colors.*

Gemini (jĕm′ə-nī′ *or* jĕm′ə-nē′) *pl.n. (used with a singular verb)* **1.** A constellation in the Northern Hemisphere, traditionally pictured as the twins Castor and Pollux. **2.** The third sign of the zodiac in astrology.

gemstone (jĕm′stōn′) *n.* A precious or semiprecious stone used as a jewel when cut and polished.

gen. An abbreviation of: **1.** gender. **2.** genitive. **3.** general. **4.** genus.

Gen. An abbreviation of general.

gendarme (zhän′därm′) *n.* A police officer in France and other French-speaking countries.

gender (jĕn′dər) *n.* **1.** In some languages, a grammatical category, usually feminine, masculine, or neuter, used to classify nouns, pronouns, and adjectives. In Spanish, for example, *casa* (meaning "house") is feminine and *pan* (meaning "bread") is masculine. **2.** Either of the two divisions, designated female and male, by which most organisms are classified on the basis of their reproductive organs and functions; sex. **3.** A person's identity as either female or male or as neither entirely female nor entirely male.

gene (jēn) *n.* A segment of DNA, located at a particular point on a chromosome, that determines hereditary characteristics. Hair and eye color in humans are characteristics controlled by genes.

genealogist (jē′nē-ŏl′ə-jĭst *or* jē′nē-ăl′ə-jĭst) *n.* A person who studies and traces genealogies.

genealogy (jē′nē-ŏl′ə-jē *or* jē′nē-ăl′ə-jē) *n., pl.* **genealogies 1.** A record of the descent of a family or person from an ancestor or ancestors: *My grandparents gave us a copy of our family genealogy that goes back six generations.* **2.** Direct descent from an ancestor or ancestors; lineage: *There are many websites than can help in researching a family's genealogy.* **3.** The study of ancestry and family histories. —**ge′ne·a·log′i·cal** (jē′nē-ə-lŏj′ĭkəl) *adj.*

genera (jĕn′ər-ə) *n.* Plural of **genus.**

general (jĕn′ər-əl) *adj.* **1.** Concerned with, applying to, or affecting all members of a category: *An election is supposed to express the general will of the people.* **2.** Affecting a majority of those involved; prevalent; widespread: *general satisfaction.* **3.** Not limited in scope, area, or application: *as a general rule; general studies.* **4.** Involving only the main features of something rather than details or particulars: *The witness could only give a general account of what happened.* **5.** Highest or superior in rank: *the*

general manager. ❖ *n.* **1a.** An officer holding any of the ranks above colonel in the US Army, Air Force, or Marine Corps. **b.** An officer holding the rank above lieutenant general in the US Army, Air Force, or Marine Corps. **2.** A person who holds such a rank in another military organization. ◆ **in general** Generally; for the most part.

general assembly *n.* **1.** A legislative body, especially a US state legislature. **2. General Assembly** The main body of the United Nations, in which each member nation is represented and has one vote.

generalist (jĕn′ər-ə-lĭst) *n.* A person with general knowledge and skills in several fields.

generality (jĕn′ə-răl′ĭ-tē) *n., pl.* **generalities 1.** The state or quality of being general. **2.** A statement or principle that has general application: *As a generality, hard work is more important than talent in achieving success.* **3.** A statement or idea that is vague or imprecise: *a speech full of generalities and empty phrases.*

generalization (jĕn′ər-ə-lĭ-zā′shən) *n.* **1.** The act of generalizing: *The judge instructed the jury only to consider the facts of the case and not to engage in generalization.* **2.** A general statement or principle; a generality: *Do you agree with the generalization that money can't buy happiness?*

generalize (jĕn′ər-ə-līz′) *v.* **generalized, generalizing, generalizes** —*tr.* To consider or state in terms of a general form or principle: *The researchers generalized their observations in a report aimed at the average reader.* —*intr.* To draw a general conclusion from particular facts: *Scientists generalize about dinosaurs from their fossilized bones.*

generally (jĕn′ər-ə-lē) *adv.* **1.** Usually; as a rule: *I generally go for a walk before breakfast.* **2.** Widely; commonly: *The fact is not generally known.* **3.** In general terms: *Generally speaking, there are two ways to handle the problem.*

General of the Air Force *n.* An officer having the highest rank in the US Air Force.

General of the Army *n.* An officer having the highest rank in the US Army.

general practitioner *n.* A doctor who does not specialize in one field but treats a variety of medical problems.

generalship (jĕn′ər-əl-shĭp′) *n.* **1.** The rank of general. **2.** Leadership or skill in the command of an army. **3.** Skillful leadership or management.

generate (jĕn′ə-rāt′) *tr.v.* **generated, generating, generates** To bring into being; produce: *generate heat; generate interest among voters; generate a computer program.*

generation (jĕn′ə-rā′shən) *n.* **1.** A group of people who grow up at about the same time, often thought to have similar social and cultural attitudes: *the younger generation; the hippie generation.* **2.** The average length of time between the birth of parents and the birth of their offspring: *Many generations have passed since this land was cleared for a farm.* **3.** All of the offspring that are at the same stage of descent from a common ancestor: *My cousins are in the same generation as I am.* **4.** A class of things derived from an earlier class, usually by making improvements and refinements: *the new generation of computers.* **5.** The act or process of generating: *the generation of electric power; the generation of new ideas.*

generation gap *n.* A difference in values and attitudes between one generation and the next, especially between young people and their parents.

Generation X *n.* The generation following the American baby boom of the 1950s and 1960s, especially people born from the early 1960s to the late 1970s.

Generation Y *n.* The generation following Generation X, especially people born in the United States from the early 1980s to the late 1990s.

generative (jĕn′ər-ə-tĭv *or* jĕn′ə-rā′tĭv) *adj.* Having the ability to generate, produce, or reproduce: *a generative process; generative cells.*

generator (jĕn′ə-rā′tər) *n.* A person or thing that generates, especially a machine that converts mechanical energy into electrical energy.

generic (jə-nĕr′ĭk) *adj.* **1.** Relating to an entire group or class; general: *The guest speaker gave generic advice to the graduating seniors.* **2.** Relating to a genus: *Musca is the generic name of the housefly* Musca domestica. **3.** Not protected by a trademark and therefore applicable to an entire class of products: *"Aspirin" is the generic name for a painkiller sold under many different brand names.* —**ge·ner′i·cal·ly** *adv.*

WORD BUILDING The word root *gen–* in English words comes both from Latin and from Greek. In Latin the noun *genus* means "type, kind, class, origin, race." A form of the Latin noun *genus,* which occurs for example in the plural *genera,* gives us **general, generic,** and **generation.** From French, which is derived from Latin, we have **genre.** From the Greek noun *genos,* which has the same meanings as Latin *genus,* we have the word **gene.** The Greek adjective *genetikos,* "relating to the origin," is the source of our word **genetic.**

generosity (jĕn′ə-rŏs′ĭ-tē) *n., pl.* **generosities 1.** The quality or condition of being generous: *The charity sent out letters thanking donors for their generosity.* **2.** Nobility of thought or behavior: *The coach speaks of our rivals with generosity.* **3.** A generous act.

generous (jĕn′ər-əs) *adj.* **1.** Willing to give or share; unselfish: *a generous contributor to worthy causes.* **2.** Large; abundant; ample: *This restaurant serves very generous portions.* **3.** Having or showing high moral character; gracious; kind: *The critic gave a generous review of the inexperienced actor's performance.* —**gen′er·ous·ly** *adv.*

genesis (jĕn′ĭ-sĭs) *n., pl.* **geneses** (jĕn′ĭ-sēz′) **1.** The coming into being of something; the origin: *the genesis of an idea.* **2. Genesis** The first book of the Bible, describing the creation of the world, the banishment of Adam and Eve from the Garden of Eden, and the early history of the Jewish people.

gene splicing *n.* The process in which genetic material from one or more organisms is combined to form recombinant DNA.

genetic (jə-nĕt′ĭk) *adj.* **1.** Relating to genetics: *genetic research.* **2.** Involving or determined by the genes: *a genetic disorder; a genetic trait.* —**ge·net′i·cal·ly** *adv.* —SEE NOTE AT **generic.**

genetically modified organism *n.* An organism whose genetic characteristics have been altered by inserting a modified gene or a gene from another organism into its genome.

genetic code *n.* The sequence of chemical compounds in DNA or RNA that determines the order of amino acids when a protein is made. A group of three bases specifies a particular amino acid or designates the beginning or end of a protein.

genetic engineering *n.* The alteration of the genetic material of an organism, usually by inserting a gene from another organism, to produce a new trait, such as resistance to herbicides, or to make a biological substance, such as a protein or hormone.

geneticist (jə-nĕt′ĭ-sĭst) *n.* A scientist who specializes in genetics.

genetics (jə-nĕt′ĭks) *n.* **1.** *(used with a singular verb)* The branch of biology that deals with genes, especially their inheritance and expression and their distribution among different individuals and organisms. **2.** *(used with a plural verb)* The genetic makeup of an individual or group.

genial (jēn′yəl) *adj.* **1.** Having a pleasant or friendly manner: *an enthusiastic and genial personality.* **2.** Favorable to health or growth; warm and pleasant: *the genial sunshine of springtime.* —**ge′ni·al′i·ty** (jē′nē-ăl′ĭ-tē) *n.* —**gen′-ial·ly** *adv.*

genie (jē′nē) *n.* **1.** A spirit that appears in human form and fulfills wishes with magic powers. **2.** A jinni.

genii (jē′nē-ī′) *n.* Plural of **genius** (sense 6).

genital (jĕn′ĭ-tl) *adj.* **1.** Relating to biological reproduction: *the genital organs.* **2.** Relating to the genitals.

genitalia (jĕn′ĭ-tā′lē-ə *or* jĕn′ĭ-tāl′yə) *pl.n.* The genitals.

genitals (jĕn′ĭ-tlz) *pl.n.* The reproductive organs, especially the external reproductive organs and associated structures in humans and other mammals.

genitive (jĕn′ĭ-tĭv) *adj.* Relating to the grammatical case that expresses possession, source, or relationship. In the sentences *Bill's car was being repaired* and *Mary greeted her neighbor,* the words *Bill's* and *her* are in the genitive case. ❖ *n.* The genitive case.

genius (jēn′yəs) *n., pl.* **geniuses 1.** A person of extraordinary mental ability or creative power: *The great inventor was a genius.* **2.** Extraordinary mental ability or creative power: *Artists of genius are remembered centuries after their deaths.* **3.** A strong natural talent or ability: *She has a genius for leadership.* **4.** A person who has a natural talent or ability: *My cousin is a mechanical genius.* **5.** The special spirit or character of a person, place, time, or group: *the genius of ancient Rome.* **6.** *pl.* **genii** (jē′nē-ī′) In Roman mythology, the guardian spirit of a person or place.

genocide (jĕn′ə-sīd′) *n.* The systematic extermination or attempted extermination of a national, racial, religious, or ethnic group. —**gen′o·cid′al** (jĕn′ə-sīd′l) *adj.*

Genoese (jĕn′ō-ēz′ *or* jĕn′ō-ēs′) *adj.* Relating to the city of Genoa in Italy or to its people. ❖ *n.* A native or inhabitant of Genoa.

genome (jē′nōm) *n.* The total amount of genetic information in the chromosomes of an organism or in the DNA or RNA of viruses.

genomics (jə-nō′mĭks) *n.* *(used with a singular verb)* The scientific study of the entire genome of an organism.

genotype (jĕn′ə-tīp′ *or* jē′nə-tīp′) *n.* The genetic makeup of an organism, as distinguished from its physical characteristics or phenotype.

genre (zhän′rə) *n.* A particular type or class of literary, musical, or artistic composition: *Science fiction and mystery are different genres of literary fiction.* —SEE NOTE AT **generic.**

gent (jĕnt) *n. Informal* A man or gentleman.

genteel (jĕn-tēl′) *adj.* **1.** Refined or polite, often in an affected or pretentious way. See Synonyms at **polite. 2.** Elegantly stylish: *She had a genteel appearance.* —**gen·teel′-ly** *adv.*

gentian (jĕn′shən) *n.* Any of numerous plants usually having deep-blue trumpet-shaped flowers.

gentile (jĕn′tīl) *n.* **1.** often **Gentile** A person who is not a Jew. **2.** A person who is not a Mormon. ❖ *adj.* often **Gentile** Relating to a Gentile.

gentility (jĕn-tĭl′ĭ-tē) *n.* **1.** Good manners; politeness; refinement. **2.** The condition of coming from a family of high social standing. **3.** People of high social standing considered as a group.

gentle (jĕn′tl) *adj.* **gentler, gentlest 1.** Considerate or kindly in manner; thoughtful and tender: *a gentle nature.* **2.** Not harsh or severe; mild and soft: *a gentle breeze; a gentle tap on the shoulder.* **3.** Not steep or sudden; gradual: *a gentle slope.* **4.** Easily managed or handled; docile: *a gentle horse.* **5.** Of good family; wellborn: *a child of gentle birth.* —**gen′tle·ness** *n.* —**gen′tly** *adv.*

gentlefolk (jĕn′tl-fōk′) *pl.n.* People of good family and usually high social standing.

gentleman (jĕn′tl-mən) *n.* **1.** A man of high social standing. **2.** A man with good manners or polite behavior. **3.** A man, especially when spoken of in a polite way: *I believe this gentleman was here first.* **4. gentlemen** (jĕn′tl-mən) Used as a form of address for a group of men: *Good evening, ladies and gentlemen.*

gentleman's agreement or **gentlemen's agreement** (jĕn′tl-mənz) *n.* An informal agreement guaranteed only by the promise of the people involved to honor it.

gentlewoman (jĕn′tl-wŏŏm′ən) *n.* **1.** A woman of high social standing. **2.** A woman acting as a personal attendant to a noblewoman.

gentrification (jĕn′trə-fĭ-kā′shən) *n.* The restoration or upgrading of rundown urban property, especially by middle-class or wealthy people, often resulting in displacement of people with low incomes.

gentrify (jĕn′trə-fī′) *tr.v.* **gentrified, gentrifying, gentrifies** To restore (rundown urban property) by gentrification.

gentry (jĕn′trē) *n., pl.* **gentries 1.** People of good family and high social standing. **2.** In England, the class of landowners ranking next below the nobility.

genuflect (jĕn′yə-flĕkt′) *intr.v.* **genuflected, genuflecting, genuflects** To bend one knee to or toward the ground, as a gesture of respect and worship. —**gen′u·flec′tion** *n.*

genuine (jĕn′yōō-ĭn) *adj.* **1.** Being so in fact; not spurious or counterfeit: *genuine leather.* See Synonyms at **authentic. 2.** Free from hypocrisy or dishonesty; sincere: *genuine affection.* —**gen′u·ine·ly** *adv.*

genus (jē′nəs) *n., pl.* **genera** (jĕn′ər-ə) **1.** A taxonomic category of organisms that are closely related and share many characteristics, ranking below a family and above a species: *Dogs, wolves, and coyotes belong to the same genus.* **2.** A class, group, or kind with common characteristics: *the genus of boats known as pleasure crafts.*

geo- or **ge-** A prefix that means: **1.** Earth: *geocentric.* **2.** Geography: *geopolitical.*

WORD BUILDING The basic meaning of the prefix **geo-** is "earth." It comes from the Greek prefix *geō-*, from the Greek word *gē*, meaning "earth." Thus *geography* (from Greek *geō-* plus *–graphiā*, "writing") is "the study of the earth and its surface features." When used to form words in English, *geo-* can mean either "earth" or "geography." For example, *geomagnetism* refers to the magnetism of the earth, while *geopolitics* refers to the relationship between politics and geography.

geocentric (jē′ō-sĕn′trĭk) *adj.* **1.** Relating to or measured from the earth's center. **2.** Having the earth as the center: *an ancient representation of a geocentric universe.*

geochemistry (jē′ō-kĕm′ĭ-strē) *n.* The study of the chem-

istry of the earth, including its crust, waters, and atmosphere.

geode (jē′ōd′) *n.* A small, hollow, usually rounded rock lined on the inside with crystals.

geodesic (jē′ə-dĕs′ĭk *or* jē′ə-dē′sĭk) *adj.* **1.** Relating to geodesy. **2.** Relating to the branch of geometry that deals with finding the shortest line between two points on a curved surface.

geodesic dome *n.* A structure having the shape of a hemisphere, assembled of straight pieces that form triangles or polygons that fit rigidly together.

geodesy (jē-ŏd′ĭ-sē) *n.* The scientific study of the size and shape of the earth.

geodetic (jē′ə-dĕt′ĭk) *adj.* Geodesic.

geographer (jē-ŏg′rə-fər) *n.* A person who specializes in geography.

geographic (jē′ə-grăf′ĭk) also **geographical** (jē′ə-grăf′ĭkəl) *adj.* Relating to geography: *geographic boundaries; geographical names.* —**ge′o·graph′i·cal·ly** *adv.*

geographic mile *n.* A nautical mile.

geography (jē-ŏg′rə-fē) *n., pl.* **geographies 1.** The study of the earth's surface and its various climates, continents, countries, peoples, resources, industries, and products. **2.** The physical features of a region or place: *the rugged geography of the West.* **3.** A book on geography.

geologic (jē′ə-lŏj′ĭk) or **geological** (jē′ə-lŏj′ĭ-kəl) *adj.* Relating to geology: *the geologic force of uplift; a geological survey.* —**ge′o·log′i·cal·ly** *adv.*

geologic time *n.* The period of time covering the formation and development of the earth, from about 4.6 billion years ago to today.

geologist (jē-ŏl′ə-jĭst) *n.* A scientist who specializes in geology.

geology (jē-ŏl′ə-jē) *n., pl.* **geologies 1.** The science that studies the origin, history, and structure of the earth. **2.** The structure of a specific region, including its rocks, soils, mountains, and other features.

geomagnetism (jē′ō-măg′nĭ-tĭz′əm) *n.* The magnetic properties of the earth. —**ge′o·mag·net′ic** (jē′ō-măg-net′ĭk) *adj.*

geometric (jē′ə-mĕt′rĭk) also **geometrical** (jē′ə-mĕt′rĭ-kəl) *adj.* **1.** Relating to geometry and its methods and principles: *a geometric problem.* **2.** Increasing or decreasing in a geometric progression. **3.** Consisting of or using simple shapes formed from straight lines or curves: *geometric figures; a geometric design.* —**ge′o·met′ri·cal·ly** *adv.*

geometric progression *n.* A sequence of numbers in which each number is multiplied by the same factor to obtain the next number in the sequence. In the geometric progression 5, 25, 125, 625, each number is multiplied by the factor of 5 to obtain the following number.

geometry (jē-ŏm′ĭ-trē) *n., pl.* **geometries 1.** The mathematical study of the properties, measurement, and relationships of points, lines, planes, surfaces, angles, and solids. **2.** A shape or an arrangement of parts, as in a design: *the geometry of a building.*

geomorphology (jē′ō-môr-fŏl′ə-jē) *n.* The scientific study of the formation and alteration of landforms, such as mountains and valleys.

geophysics (jē′ō-fĭz′ĭks) *n.* *(used with a singular verb)* The application of physics to the study of the earth and its environment. —**ge′o·phys′i·cal** *adj.*

geopolitics (jē′ō-pŏl′ĭtĭks) *n.* *(Used with a singular verb)* The study of how a nation's foreign policy is affected by geography, demographics, and economics. —**ge′-o·po·lit′i·cal** (jē′ō-pə-lĭt′i-kəl) *adj.*

Georgian (jôr′jən) *adj.* **1.** Relating to the reigns of the four kings of England named George who ruled from 1714 to 1830: *Georgian architecture.* **2.** Relating to the US state of Georgia or its inhabitants. **3.** Relating to the country of Georgia or its people, language, or culture. ❖ *n.* **1.** A native or inhabitant of the US state of Georgia. **2a.** A native or inhabitant of the country of Georgia. **b.** The language of the Georgians.

geothermal (jē′ō-thûr′məl) *adj.* Relating to the internal heat of the earth: *geothermal energy.*

geotropism (jē-ŏt′rə-pĭz′əm) *n.* Gravitropism.

geranium (jə-rā′nē-əm) *n.* **1.** Any of various plants having rounded leaves and showy clusters of red, pink, or white flowers, often grown as potted plants. **2.** Any of various related plants having pink or purplish flowers with five equal petals.

gerbil (jûr′bəl) *n.* Any of various small rodents that have long hind legs and a long tail and are native to desert regions of Africa and Asia. One kind of gerbil is often kept as a pet.

geriatric (jĕr′ē-ăt′rĭk) *adj.* **1.** Relating to geriatrics or to the elderly: *geriatric psychiatry; geriatric hip fractures.* **2.** Elderly: *a geriatric crowd at the concert; my geriatric cat.*

geriatrics (jĕr′ē-ăt′rĭks) *n.* *(used with a singular verb)* The branch of medicine that deals with the diagnosis and treatment of diseases of old age.

germ (jûrm) *n.* **1.** A bacterium or virus, especially one that causes disease: *The nurse used a disinfectant to kill the germs.* **2.** The earliest form of a living thing; a seed, spore, or bud: *wheat germ.* **3.** Something that serves as the basis of further growth or development: *a germ of an idea.*

German (jûr′mən) *adj.* Relating to Germany or its people, language, or culture. ❖ *n.* **1.** A native or inhabitant of Germany. **2.** The Germanic language of Germany, Austria, and part of Switzerland.

germane (jər-mān′) *adj.* Closely or naturally related; appropriate; pertinent: *Their comments were not germane to the discussion.*

Germanic (jər-măn′ĭk) *adj.* **1.** Relating to Germany or its people, language, or culture. **2.** Relating to the branch of the Indo-European language family that includes English, German, Dutch, and the Scandinavian languages. **3.** Relating to the ancient Teutons; Teutonic. ❖ *n.* The Germanic branch of the Indo-European language family.

germanium (jər-mā′nē-əm) *n. Symbol* **Ge** A brittle grayish metallic element found in zinc ores, coal, and certain minerals. It is widely used as a semiconductor. Atomic number 32. See **Periodic Table.**

German measles *n.* *(used with a singular or plural verb)* Rubella.

German shepherd *n.* A large dog of a breed developed in Germany, having a thick black or brownish coat and often trained to help police officers.

germ cell *n.* A reproductive cell of a plant or animal, as an egg or sperm.

germicide (jûr′mĭ-sīd′) *n.* A substance that kills germs, especially those that cause disease; a disinfectant. —**ger′mi·cid′al** (jûr′mĭ-sīd′l) *adj.*

germinal (jûr′mə-nəl) *adj.* **1.** Relating to or having the nature of a germ cell. **2.** Relating to or occurring in an early stage of development: *a germinal sprout.*

germinate (jûr′mə-nāt′) *intr. & tr.v.* **germinated, germinating, germinates** To begin or cause to begin to grow;

sprout: *Seeds need water and warmth to germinate. We germinated the seeds indoors.* —**ger′mi·na′tion** *n.* —**ger′mi·na′tor** *n.*

germline (jûrm′līn′) *n.* **1.** The gamete-producing cells in a sexually reproducing organism, by means of which genetic material is passed on to subsequent generations. **2.** The collection or sequence of such cells in an individual and all its descendants.

germ warfare *n.* Biological warfare.

gerrymander (jĕr′ē-măn′dər) *tr.v.* **gerrymandered, gerrymandering, gerrymanders** To divide (voting districts of a state or county) in such a way as to give unfair advantage to one political party.

gerund (jĕr′ənd) *n.* A noun formed from a verb. In English the gerund ends in *-ing.* In the sentence *Hitting a ball hard requires strength,* the word *hitting* is a gerund. Like other nouns, a gerund may be the subject of a sentence, but like a verb it may have a direct object and be modified by an adverb.

gesso (jĕs′ō) *n., pl.* **gessoes** A preparation of plaster of Paris and glue used as a base for low relief or as a surface for painting.

gestalt or **Gestalt** (gə-shtält′) *n., pl.* **gestalt** or **gestalten** (gə-shtält′n) A configuration or pattern of elements that is so unified that its properties cannot be derived from a simple summation of its parts.

Gestapo (gə-stä′pō) *n.* The secret police force of Nazi Germany, known for its ruthlessness against people thought to be disloyal.

gestate (jĕs′tāt′) *v.* **gestated, gestating, gestates** —*tr.* **1.** To carry within the uterus from conception to delivery: *ewes that are gestating more than one lamb.* **2.** To conceive and develop in the mind: *plans that he had been gestating for years.* —*intr.* **1.** To gestate offspring: *a woman who is gestating.* **2.** To develop gradually: *a story that gestated in her imagination.*

gestation (jĕ-stā′shən) *n.* **1.** The carrying and development of young in the uterus from conception to birth; pregnancy. **2.** The period of gestation. **3.** The formation or development of a plan or idea.

gesticulate (jĕ-stĭk′yə-lāt′) *intr.v.* **gesticulated, gesticulating, gesticulates** To make gestures in order to emphasize meaning or express one's feelings: *The angry speaker gesticulated wildly by flailing his hands in the air.* —**ges·tic′u·la′tion** *n.*

gesture (jĕs′chər) *n.* **1.** A movement of the limbs, head, or body to help express meaning: *A mime must rely on gestures to tell a story.* **2.** Something done or said for its effect on the feelings or opinions of others: *Sending someone a birthday card is a thoughtful gesture.* ❖ *v.* **gestured, gesturing, gestures** —*intr.* To make a gesture or gestures: *The police officer gestured for the car to proceed.* —*tr.* To express or signal by gesture: *With a nod the judge gestured a willingness to listen.*

gesundheit (gə-zŏont′hīt′) *interj.* Used to wish good health to a person who has just sneezed.

get (gĕt) *v.* (gŏt), **gotten** (gŏt′n) or **got, getting, gets** —*tr.* **1.** To come to have or use; receive: *She got a new camera for her birthday.* **2.** To go after and obtain; acquire: *I got a new coat at the store.* **3.** To go after and bring; fetch: *Please get me a pencil.* **4.** To succeed in reaching or boarding: *Did you get the bus on time?* **5.** To earn: *She got an A in biochemistry.* **6a.** To become affected with; catch: *I've got the flu.* **b.** To be subjected to; experience: *He got a broken ankle.* **7.** To have; possess: *She's got a* *great singing voice.* **8.** To cause to be or become: *The long journey got us tired and cross.* **9.** To cause (someone to do something): *got the guide to give us the complete tour.* **10.** To be obligated; need. Used only with a form of *have*: *We have got to leave early.* **11.** To begin or start (doing something): *We had better get going or we'll be late.* **12.** To hit; strike: *The snowball got me on the arm.* **13.** To understand or comprehend: *I don't get the connection between those ideas.* **14.** To make contact with: *We got the manager on the telephone.* —*intr.* **1.** To reach; come to: *get to the airport; get to shore.* **2.** To be or become: *get well; get stuck in traffic.* **3.** To come or go: *finally got to Wichita; got up the icy steps.* **4.** To be allowed or permitted: *I never got to see the movie.* ◆ **get across** To make understandable or clear: *The candidate got her point across.* **get along 1.** To be or remain friendly with: *Although they were rivals, they got along well.* **2.** To manage with reasonable success: *We're not rich, but we're getting along.* **3.** To advance; make progress: *How's your project getting along?* **4.** To move on; leave: *I think I'll be getting along now.* **get around 1.** To evade; overcome: *Many lazy people try to get around rules.* **2.** To trick: *You can't get around me with that story.* **3.** To travel from place to place. **4.** To become widely known; spread: *The rumor got around quickly.* **get around to** To find the time or occasion for: *A week after we moved, we finally got around to unpacking everything.* **get at 1.** To reach: *The sponge fell behind the sink where I can't get at it.* **2.** To express or mean: *Do you understand what I am getting at?* **get away 1.** To go away: *We want to get away on a trip to the country.* **2.** To escape: *The lion got away from the zoo.* **get away with** To do something without being punished or found out: *get away with a crime.* **get back** To go back or return: *Let's get back to work.* **get back at** To take revenge on. **get by 1.** To manage; survive: *They were unprepared for rain but got by somehow.* **2.** To pass without being noticed: *The prisoners got by the guards.* **get even** To obtain revenge: *After I fell for his prank, I thought of a way to get even.* **get even with** To do something to (someone) in response to an act, as for revenge: *I restrained my urge to get even with him for his prank.* **get in 1.** To enter or be allowed to enter: *Can we get in without a ticket?* **2.** To arrive: *The plane gets in at midnight.* **3.** To put in: *I couldn't get in a word during the conversation.* **get it 1.** To understand; comprehend: *I just don't get it.* **2.** *Informal* To be punished or scolded: *You're really going to get it when your boss hears how you spend your time.* **get nowhere** To make no progress: *After three months, negotiations still had gotten nowhere.* **get off 1.** To get down from or out of: *get off the train.* **2.** To leave; depart: *Tomorrow we get off early in the morning.* **3.** To escape punishment or obligation: *The thief got off with a light sentence.* **get on 1.** To climb up onto or into; enter: *Get on the boat before it leaves.* **2.** To be on friendly terms: *The neighbors got on for years and then suddenly had a fight.* **3.** To advance in years: *The old dog is getting on in years.* **4.** To continue, proceed, or progress: *I got on with the work.* **get out 1.** To leave or escape: *Our canary got out.* **2.** To become known: *The secret finally got out.* **3.** To publish: *That author gets out a new book every year.* **get out of** To escape from or be released from: *The cows somehow got out of the pasture.* **get over** To recover from: *get over a cold.* **get through 1.** To finish; complete: *trying to get through a big job.* **2.** To succeed in making contact:

I telephoned twice, but couldn't get through. **get together 1.** To meet; assemble: *getting together for supper tonight.* **2.** To come to an agreement: *The feuding parties finally got together.* **get up 1.** To arise: *They got up early to see the sunrise.* **2.** To sit or stand up: *He got up out of the chair.*

USAGE The past participles **got** and **gotten** have some interesting differences in meaning. The phrase *have got* expresses need or obligation. The sentence *She has got to practice tonight* means that she needs to practice. But the sentence *She has gotten to practice tonight* means that she has been given the permission or opportunity to practice. Also, *got* often suggests that you have something in your possession right now (as in *I've got fifty dollars*), while *gotten* suggests that you've made an effort to obtain something or been paid for doing or selling something (as in *I've gotten fifty dollars for one of my paintings*).

getaway (gĕt′ə-wā′) *n.* **1.** The act of getting away; an escape: *The robbers made a quick getaway.* **2.** The start, as of a race.

get-go (gĕt′gō′) *n. Informal* The beginning; the outset: *had trouble from the get-go.*

get-together (gĕt′tə-gĕth′ər) *n.* A small party or gathering.

getup (gĕt′ŭp′) *n. Informal* An outfit or costume, especially one that is odd or different.

get-up-and-go (gĕt′ŭp′ən-gō′) *n. Informal* Ambition and energy.

gewgaw (gyoō′gô′ *or* goō′gô′) *n.* A showy trinket of little value; a bauble.

geyser (gī′zər) *n.* A natural hot spring that regularly ejects a spray of steam and boiling water into the air.

ghastly (găst′lē) *adj.* **ghastlier, ghastliest 1.** Terrifying; horrible: *a ghastly crime.* **2.** Resembling a ghost; pale: *The patient had a ghastly complexion.* **3.** Extremely unpleasant or bad: *His cooking is ghastly.* —**ghast′li·ness** *n.*

gherkin (gûr′kĭn) *n.* A small cucumber used for making pickles.

ghetto (gĕt′ō) *n., pl.* **ghettos** or **ghettoes 1.** A usually poor section of a city inhabited primarily by people of the same race, religion, or social background, often because of discrimination. **2.** A section or quarter in a European city where Jews were formerly restricted.

ghost (gōst) *n.* **1.** The spirit of a dead person, especially one that is believed to haunt or appear to living people. **2.** A slight trace; a bit: *a ghost of a smile; a ghost of a chance.*

ghostly (gōst′lē) *adj.* **ghostlier, ghostliest** Relating to or resembling a ghost: *Dressed all in white, she had a ghostly appearance in the moonlight.* —**ghost′li·ness** *n.*

ghost town *n.* A formerly thriving town, especially a boomtown in the American West, that has been completely abandoned.

ghostwrite (gōst′rīt′) *tr.v.* **ghostwrote** (gōst′rōt′), **ghostwritten** (gōst′rĭt′n), **ghostwriting, ghostwrites** To write (something, such as a speech or autobiography) for another person who is credited as the author. —**ghost′writ′er** *n.*

ghoul (goōl) *n.* **1.** In Islamic folklore, an evil spirit believed to plunder graves and feast on corpses. **2.** In popular folklore, an undead or subhuman being, especially one that eats human flesh. **3.** A person who robs graves. **4.** A person who delights in brutal or horrible things. —**ghoul′ish** *adj.* —**ghoul′ish·ly** *adv.*

GI¹ (jē′ī′) *n.* An enlisted person in or a veteran of any of the US armed forces. ❖ *adj.* Relating to or characteristic of a GI: *a GI uniform.*

GI² An abbreviation of: **1.** gastrointestinal. **2.** Government Issue.

giant (jī′ənt) *n.* **1.** A person or thing of great size, ability, or importance: *a musical giant.* **2.** A being of great size and strength having human form and found in myth or folklore. ❖ *adj.* Gigantic; huge: *a giant airport.*

giant star *n.* A very large, bright star of low density.

gibber (jĭb′ər) *intr.v.* **gibbered, gibbering, gibbers** To speak rapidly and in a nonsensical way; chatter. ❖ *n.* Gibberish.

gibberish (jĭb′ər-ĭsh) *n.* Meaningless or nonsensical talk or writing.

gibbet (jĭb′ĭt) *n.* **1.** A gallows. **2.** A wooden arm that projects from an upright post where the bodies of executed criminals were hung for public viewing. ❖ *tr.v.* **gibbeted, gibbeting, gibbets** or **gibbetted, gibbetting, gibbets 1.** To execute by hanging. **2.** To hang on a gibbet for public viewing.

gibbon (gĭb′ən) *n.* Any of several small tree-dwelling apes of southeast Asia, having a slender body, long arms, and no tail.

gibbous (gĭb′əs) *adj.* **1.** More than half but not fully illuminated: *a gibbous moon.* **2.** Curved out; convex.

gibe also **jibe** (jīb) *n.* A scornful remark; a jeer. ❖ *intr.v.* **gibed, gibing, gibes** also **jibed, jibing, jibes** To make scornful or jeering remarks: *They gibed at my first efforts to water-ski.*

giblets (jĭb′lĭts) *pl.n.* The edible heart, liver, and gizzard of a fowl.

giddy (gĭd′ē) *adj.* **giddier, giddiest 1a.** Having a whirling sensation in the head; dizzy: *The climber became giddy at the top of the mountain.* **b.** Causing or capable of causing dizziness: *The roller coaster moved at a giddy speed.* **2.** Frivolous; not serious: *The good news put everyone in a giddy mood.* —**gid′di·ly** *adv.* —**gid′di·ness** *n.*

gift (gĭft) *n.* **1.** Something given willingly with no payment in return; a present. **2.** A special talent, aptitude, or ability: *a gift for mathematics.* **3.** The act of giving: *Ownership of the car was transferred by gift.*

gifted (gĭf′tĭd) *adj.* Endowed with great natural ability, intelligence, or talent: *a gifted athlete.*

gift-wrap (gĭft′răp′) *tr.v.* **gift-wrapped, gift-wrapping, gift-wraps** To wrap (something intended as a gift) with fancy paper, ribbon, or other trimmings.

gig¹ (gĭg) *n.* **1.** A light two-wheeled carriage drawn by one horse. **2.** A long light ship's boat, usually used only by the ship's captain.

gig² (gĭg) *n.* **1.** A set of fishhooks usually dragged through a school of fish to hook them in their bodies. **2.** A pronged fishing spear. ❖ *tr. & intr.v.* **gigged, gigging, gigs** To fish with a gig.

gig³ (gĭg) *n. Slang* A job for a musician, especially at a club.

gig⁴ (gĭg or jĭg) *n. Informal* A gigabyte.

WORD HISTORY Gig¹ may be from obsolete English *gig*, meaning "spinning top." **Gig²** is short for English *fishgig*, which comes from Spanish *fisga*, meaning "harpoon." The origin of **gig³** is unknown. **Gig⁴** is short for *gigabyte*.

giga– A prefix that means: **1.** One billion (10^9): *gigahertz; gigabit.* **2.** 1,073,741,824 (2^{30}): *gigabyte.*

gigabit (gĭg′ə-bĭt′) *n.* One billion bits, used as a unit to measure the rate of the transmission of computer data.

gigabyte (gĭg′ə-bīt′) *n.* A unit of computer memory equal to 1,024 megabytes (2^{30} bytes).

gigahertz (gĭg′ə-hûrtz′) *n.* A unit of frequency equal to one billion hertz.

giganotosaurus (jĭg′ə-nŏt′ə-sôr′əs) *n.* A very large meat-eating dinosaur that lived during the Cretaceous Period and had a huge skull and large teeth.

gigantic (jī-găn′tĭk) *adj.* Huge; enormous: *a gigantic basketball player; a gigantic factory.* —**gi·gan′ti·cal·ly** *adv.*

giggle (gĭg′əl) *intr.v.* **giggled, giggling, giggles** To laugh in a silly or nervous way; titter. ❖ *n.* A short silly laugh. —**gig′gler** *n.* —**gig′gly** *adj.*

gigolo (jĭg′ə-lō′) *n., pl.* **gigolos** A man who engages in an ongoing sexual relationship with a client in exchange for financial support.

Gila monster (hē′lə) *n.* A large venomous lizard of the southwest United States and northern Mexico, having a thick body with black and orange, pink, or yellowish beadlike scales.

gild (gĭld) *tr.v.* **gilded** or **gilt** (gĭlt), **gilding, gilds 1.** To cover with a thin layer of gold: *gild the frame of a mirror.* **2.** To give a deceptively attractive or improved appearance to (something): *In gilding the facts the author made the commander seem less cruel.*

gill¹ (gĭl) *n.* **1.** The organ that enables fish and many other aquatic animals to take oxygen from the water. A gill consists of a series of thin membranes that are full of small blood vessels. As water flows across the membranes, oxygen passes into the blood vessels and carbon dioxide passes out of them. **2.** One of the thin plates on the underside of a mushroom cap. ◆ **to the gills** *Informal* As full as possible; completely.

gill² (jĭl) *n.* A unit of volume or capacity used mainly for liquids. It is equal to 4 ounces or 7.2 cubic inches (118 milliliters). See table at **measurement**.

WORD HISTORY Gill¹ comes from Middle English *gile* (meaning "the gill of a fish") and is of Scandinavian origin. **Gill²** comes from Middle English *gille*, which comes from Late Latin *gillō*, meaning "vessel for cooling liquids."

gill net (gĭl) *n.* A fishing net set vertically in the water so that fish swimming into it are caught by the gills.

gilt (gĭlt) *v.* A past tense and a past participle of **gild.** ❖ *n.* A thin layer of gold or something similar to gold, like gold-colored paint, applied to a surface. ❖ *adj.* Covered with gold or something resembling gold; gilded: *a picture in a gilt frame.*

gimcrack (jĭm′krăk′) *n.* A cheap and showy object of little or no use.

gimlet (gĭm′lĭt) *n.* A small hand tool with a screw tip, used to bore holes.

gimmick (gĭm′ĭk) *n.* **1.** A device or strategy employed to cheat, deceive, or trick: *accounting gimmicks.* **2.** A clever idea, scheme, or device, often used to promote something: *two-for-one coupons and other advertising gimmicks.* **3.** A hidden or tricky condition; a catch: *They said delivery and installation is free, but there's probably a gimmick.* **4.** A gadget.

gin¹ (jĭn) *n.* A strong alcoholic liquor distilled from grain and flavored with juniper berries.

gin² (jĭn) *n.* A cotton gin. ❖ *tr.v.* **ginned, ginning, gins** To remove the seeds from (cotton) with a gin. —**gin′ner** *n.*

gin³ (jĭn) *n.* Gin rummy.

WORD HISTORY Gin¹ comes from Dutch *jenever*, which comes from Latin *iūniperus*, both meaning "juniper." **Gin²** comes from Middle English *gin* (meaning "device"), which is from Old French *engin*, meaning "skill." **Gin³**

from the compound *gin rummy,* a compound formed from *gin¹*.

ginger (jĭn′jər) *n.* **1a.** A tropical plant having a root with a sharp spicy flavor. **b.** The root of this plant, often powdered and used for flavoring. **2.** *Informal* Liveliness; vigor: *a kitten full of ginger.*

ginger ale *n.* A soft drink flavored with ginger.

ginger beer *n.* A nonalcoholic or slightly alcoholic beverage strongly flavored with ginger.

gingerbread (jĭn′jər-brĕd′) *n.* **1.** A cake flavored with ginger and molasses. **2.** A ginger and molasses cookie cut in various shapes, often elaborately decorated with icing. **3.** Elaborate ornamentation, especially in architecture or furniture.

gingerly (jĭn′jər-lē) *adv.* Cautiously; carefully; warily: *The cat rubbed herself gingerly against the horse's legs.* ❖ *adj.* Cautious; careful: *It is best to offer advice in a gingerly fashion.*

gingersnap (jĭn′jər-snăp′) *n.* A flat crisp cookie made with molasses and ginger.

gingham (gĭng′əm) *n.* A light cotton cloth woven with colored thread in checks, stripes, plaids, or solid colors.

gingiva (jĭn′jə-və) *n.* The gums of the mouth.

gingivitis (jĭn′jə-vī′tĭs) *n.* Inflammation of the gums.

ginkgo also **gingko** (gĭng′kō) *n., pl.* **ginkgoes** also **gingkoes** A tree native to China that has fan-shaped leaves and is widely planted as an ornamental.

gin rummy *n.* A kind of rummy, usually for two players.

ginseng (jĭn′sĕng′) *n.* **1.** Any of several plants of Asia and North America having small greenish flowers and a forked root. **2.** The roots of these plants, used in herbal medicine.

Gipsy (jĭp′sē) *n.* Variant of **Gypsy.**

giraffe (jə-răf′) *n., pl.* **giraffes** or **giraffe** An African mammal having a very long neck and legs, a tan coat with brown patches, and short horns. It is the tallest living land animal.

gird (gûrd) *tr.v.* **girded** or **girt** (gûrt), **girding, girds 1.** To encircle or attach with a belt or band: *The monks girded their robes with a long cord.* **2.** To prepare (oneself) for action: *The employees girded themselves to ask for a raise in pay.* **3.** To encircle or surround: *Bushes and flowers girded the cottage.*

girder (gûr′dər) *n.* A beam, as of steel or wood, used as a main horizontal support in a building or bridge.

girdle (gûr′dl) *n.* **1.** An elastic undergarment worn over the waist and hips, especially by women, to give the body a more slender appearance. **2.** A belt, sash, or band worn around the waist. **3.** Something that surrounds like a belt: *a girdle of mountains around the valley.* ❖ *tr.v.* **girdled, girdling, girdles 1.** To encircle (the waist) with a belt or cord. **2.** To form a circle around: *The town was girdled by low hills.* **3.** To remove a strip of bark from around the trunk of (a tree), usually as a means of killing it.

girl (gûrl) *n.* **1.** A female child. **2.** A daughter: *our youngest girl.* **3.** *Informal* A woman: *an evening out with the girls.* **4.** *Informal* A female sweetheart; a girlfriend. **5.** *Offensive* A female servant, such as a maid.

girlfriend (gûrl′frĕnd′) *n.* **1.** A female sweetheart or favored companion. **2.** A female friend.

girlhood (gûrl′ho͝od′) *n.* The time of being a girl: *In her girlhood, she studied ballet.*

girlish (gûr′lĭsh) *adj.* Characteristic of or suitable for a

girl: *a girlish smile; girlish colors.* —**girl′ish·ly** *adv.*

Girl Scout *n.* A member of an organization for girls whose goals include helping girls develop self-reliance, good citizenship, and character.

girt (gûrt) *v.* A past tense and past participle of **gird.**

girth (gûrth) *n.* **1.** The distance around something; the circumference: *the girth of a tree trunk.* **2.** A strap encircling the body of a horse or pack animal in order to hold a load or saddle on its back.

gist (jĭst) *n.* The central idea; main point: *the gist of a message.*

give (gĭv) *v.* **gave** (gāv), **given** (gĭv′ən), **giving, gives** —*tr.* **1.** To make a present of: *I gave my mother a new sweater.* **2.** To place in the hands of; hand over; pass: *Please give me the salt.* **3.** To hand over or deliver in exchange or in payment; sell or pay: *We gave them the bike for $75. They gave us $75 for the bike.* **4a.** To bestow; confer; award: *They gave first prize to the best speller.* **b.** To administer: *The doctor gave the baby a vaccine.* **c.** To convey or deliver by physical action: *She gave me a hug.* **5.** To provide; furnish; supply: *Green vegetables give us vitamins and minerals.* **6.** To grant; let have: *The town gave them permission to build an addition.* **7.** To allot; assign: *My boss gave me the task of contacting the newspaper.* **8.** To direct or apply (one's attention or time, for example) to a pursuit or person: *She gave all of her free time to the charity.* **9a.** To offer or present: *Could you give us your ideas on the state of the economy?* **b.** To offer as entertainment: *We gave a party in his honor.* **10.** To emit or issue; put forth; utter: *She gave a sigh and shook her head.* **11.** To be a source of; afford: *Music gives me great pleasure.* **12.** To produce; yield: *Cows give milk.* **13.** To yield, as to pressure: *give ground to the enemy.* —*intr.* **1.** To make a gift or donation: *They give generously to local charities.* **2.** To yield to force or pressure: *The door gave when he kicked it.* ❖ *n.* Elasticity; flexibility: *The diving board has a lot of give.* ◆ **give away 1.** To make a gift of: *We gave away many of the vegetables from our garden.* **2.** To present (a bride) to the bridegroom at a wedding ceremony. **3.** To reveal or make known, often by accident: *I gave away the surprise party when I mentioned buying balloons and streamers.* **give back** To return: *Give me back my book.* **give birth to** To bear as offspring. **give in** To surrender; yield: *The babysitter gave in and let the children watch TV.* **give it to** *Informal* To punish or scold severely. **give off** To send forth; emit: *The moon gave off an eerie light.* **give or take** Plus or minus (a small specified amount): *The project should be finished on June 1, give or take a few days.* **give out 1.** To let (something) be known: *gave out the bad news.* **2.** To distribute: *give out paychecks to employees.* **3.** To stop working; fail: *The water pump gave out.* **4.** To become used up; run out: *The runner's energy gave out after five miles.* **give over 1.** To hand over. **2.** To make available for a purpose; devote: *The last part of the program is given over to questions from the audience.* **give rise to** To be the cause or origin of; bring about: *The new law gave rise to violent protests.* **give (someone) the axe** or **give (someone) the boot** To remove (someone) ruthlessly or suddenly: *The owner gave the research department the axe to save money.* **give up 1.** To surrender: *The thieves gave themselves up to the police.* **2.** To stop: *My uncle has given up smoking.* **3.** To admit defeat and stop trying: *They finally gave up and stopped looking for the ring.* **4.** To abandon hope for: *We gave the cat up as lost.* **give way 1.** To withdraw; retreat: *The animals gave way before the advancing fire.* **2.** To abandon oneself: *Don't* *give way to panic.* **3.** To collapse; break: *The old flooring might give way.* —**giv′er** *n.*

give-and-take also **give and take** (gĭv′ən-tāk′) *n.* **1.** The practice of making concessions in order to secure similar concessions from the other side during a negotiation; compromise: *the give-and-take necessary to reach an agreement.* **2.** A lively exchange of talk: *the give-and-take of a political debate.*

giveaway (gĭv′ə-wā′) *n.* **1.** *Informal* **a.** The act or an instance of giving something away for free or for very little in return: *the giveaway of free tickets to the concert.* **b.** An act of accidentally revealing something that is otherwise not known: *His refusal to answer the question was a giveaway that he knew more about what happened.* **2.** *Sports* The act of losing possession of the ball or puck to the opposing team.

given (gĭv′ən) *v.* Past participle of **give.** ❖ *adj.* **1.** Specified; stated: *obtain all the facts on one given country.* **2.** Assumed; acknowledged; granted: *Given the condition of the car, it's a wonder it runs at all.* **3.** Having a tendency; inclined: *given to talking too much.* ❖ *n.* Something that is assumed or taken for granted: *It's a given that the test will be hard.*

given name *n.* A name given to a person at birth or at baptism, as distinguished from a surname.

gizmo (gĭz′mō) *n., pl.* **gizmos** A gadget whose name is forgotten or not known.

gizzard (gĭz′ərd) *n.* A muscular pouch behind the stomach in birds. It often contains sand or gravel, which helps to grind up hard pieces of food.

glacial (glā′shəl) *adj.* **1.** Relating to or produced by a glacier: *glacial ice; a glacial lake.* **2.** Suggesting the extreme slowness of a glacier: *moved at a glacial pace.* **3.** Extremely cold; icy. **4.** Lacking warmth or friendliness: *a glacial stare.* —**gla′cial·ly** *adv.*

glacier (glā′shər) *n.* A large mass of ice slowly moving over a landmass or through a valley, formed over many years from packed snow in areas where snow accumulates faster than it melts.

glad (glăd) *adj.* **gladder, gladdest** **1.** Experiencing or showing joy and pleasure: *We were so glad to get your letter.* **2.** Providing joy and pleasure: *The wedding was a glad occasion.* **3.** Pleased; willing: *I would be glad to help.* —**glad′ly** *adv.* —**glad′ness** *n.*

✦ **SYNONYMS glad, cheerful, happy, joyful, lighthearted** *adj.*

gladden (glăd′n) *tr.v.* **gladdened, gladdening, gladdens** To make glad: *The good news gladdened our hearts.*

glade (glād) *n.* An open space in a forest.

gladiator (glăd′ē-ā′tər) *n.* In the ancient Roman empire, a person, especially a slave, captive, or criminal, who engaged in mortal combat in an arena to entertain the public.

gladiolus (glăd′ē-ō′ləs) also **gladiola** (glăd′ē-ō′lə) *n., pl.* **gladioli** (glăd′ē-ō′lī) or **gladioluses** also **gladiolas** Any of numerous plants having sword-shaped leaves and long spikes of showy, variously colored flowers.

gladsome (glăd′səm) *adj.* **1.** Glad; joyful. **2.** Causing gladness: *gladsome tidings.* —**glad′some·ly** *adv.*

glamor (glăm′ər) *n.* Variant of **glamour.**

glamorize also **glamourize** (glăm′ə-rīz′) *tr.v.* **glamorized, glamorizing, glamorizes** also **glamourized, glamourizing, glamourizes** To make glamorous: *Motion pictures have glamorized the life of gangsters.*

glamorous also **glamourous** (glăm′ər-əs) *adj.* Having or

showing glamour; charming; alluring: *a glamorous movie star; a glamorous life of wealth and adventure.* —**glam′or·ous·ly** *adv.*

glamour also **glamor** (glăm′ər) *n.* An air of romantic charm or excitement surrounding a person or thing; allure: *the glamour of being a famous actor.*

gland (glănd) *n.* **1.** An organ or group of cells in the body of an animal that produces and secretes a specific substance, such as a hormone or enzyme. The pancreas, pituitary, and thyroid are glands. **2.** A lymph node or other organ of the body that resembles a gland. **3.** An organ or structure in a plant that secretes a substance.

glance (glăns) *intr.v.* **glanced, glancing, glances 1.** To look briefly or hastily: *They didn't even glance at my new outfit.* **2.** To strike a surface at such an angle as to fly off to one side: *The axe glanced off the log and struck the ground.* ❖ *n.* **1.** A brief or hasty look: *a quick glance over the shoulder.* **2.** A glancing off; a deflection. ◆ **at first glance** On initial consideration: *At first glance it seemed impossible, but then I saw how we could make it work.*

glandular (glăn′jə-lər) *adj.* **1.** Relating to, affecting, or resembling a gland or its secretion. **2.** Functioning as a gland.

glare (glâr) *v.* **glared, glaring, glares** —*intr.* **1.** To stare fiercely or angrily: *The angry customer glared at the sales clerk.* **2.** To shine intensely; dazzle: *The sun glared off the windshield.* —*tr.* To express with a fierce or angry stare: *The prisoners glared defiance at their captors.* ❖ *n.* **1.** A fixed angry stare. **2.** A very strong and blinding light: *the sun's glare.*

glaring (glâr′ĭng) *adj.* **1.** Staring fiercely or angrily: *glaring eyes.* **2.** Shining intensely: *a glaring summer sun.* **3.** Too showy; gaudy: *The clown wore a suit of glaring colors.* **4.** Obvious; conspicuous: *a glaring error.* —**glar′ing·ly** *adv.*

glary (glâr′ē) *adj.* **glarier, glariest** Dazzlingly bright; glaring.

glass (glăs) *n.* **1.** A hard material made by melting sand with soda and lime. Glass is generally transparent or translucent and usually breaks or shatters easily. **2.** Something made of glass, as a mirror or a windowpane: *I hit the ball right through the glass.* **3.** A container used for drinking, especially one made of glass. **4.** The amount contained in a drinking container; a glassful: *spilled a whole glass of milk.* **5a. glasses** A pair of lenses mounted in a light frame, used to correct faulty vision or protect the eyes. **b.** A spyglass: *The captain spotted land through the glass.* ❖ *tr.v.* **glassed, glassing, glasses** To cover or enclose with glass: *We glassed in the breezeway.*

glass blowing *n.* The art or process of shaping an object from a mass of molten glass by blowing air into it through a tube. —**glass blower** *n.*

glassful (glăs′fool′) *n.* The quantity that a glass can hold.

glass lizard *n.* Any of several slender legless lizards having a tail that breaks off easily and later grows back. Glass lizards are sometimes called glass snakes.

glassware (glăs′wâr′) *n.* Objects, especially containers, made of glass.

glassy (glăs′ē) *adj.* **glassier, glassiest 1.** Resembling glass; smooth: *the glassy surface of a quiet pool.* **2.** Having no expression; lifeless; blank: *a glassy stare.* —**glass′i·ly** *adv.* —**glass′i·ness** *n.*

glaucoma (glou-kō′mə *or* glô-kō′mə) *n.* An eye disease in which the pressure of fluid inside the eyeball becomes abnormally high, often damaging the optic nerve and leading to loss of vision.

glaze (glāz) *n.* **1.** A thin, smooth, shiny coating: *A glaze of ice covered the roads.* **2.** A coating, as of colored material, applied to ceramics before firing in a kiln. ❖ *v.* **glazed, glazing, glazes** —*tr.* **1.** To fit or furnish with glass: *glaze a window.* **2.** To apply a glaze to: *The baker glazed the buns with egg white. The potter glazed the mugs and bowls.* —*intr.* To become glassy or blank: *His eyes glazed over from boredom.*

glazier (glā′zhər) *n.* A person who cuts and fits glass for windows, doors, and picture frames.

GLBT An abbreviation of gay, lesbian, bisexual, transgender.

gleam (glēm) *n.* **1.** A brief beam or flash of light: *occasional gleams of sunshine through the clouds.* **2.** A steady reflected shininess: *the gleam of polished silver.* **3.** A brief or faint indication; a trace: *a gleam of hope.* ❖ *intr.v.* **gleamed, gleaming, gleams 1.** To give off a gleam; shine: *The frost gleamed like diamonds.* **2.** To be reflected as a gleam: *The moon gleamed on the water.*

glean (glēn) *tr.v.* **gleaned, gleaning, gleans 1.** To gather (grain) left behind by reapers. **2.** To gather bit by bit: *After weeks of investigation, the reporter gleaned enough information for the article.* —**glean′er** *n.*

glee (glē) *n.* **1.** A feeling of delight; joy. **2.** A song for three or more usually male and unaccompanied voices, popular in the 1700s.

glee club *n.* A group of singers who perform usually short pieces of choral music.

gleeful (glē′fəl) *adj.* Full of glee; merry. —**glee′ful·ly** *adv.* —**glee′ful·ness** *n.*

glen (glĕn) *n.* A small, secluded valley.

glib (glĭb) *adj.* **glibber, glibbest** Speaking or writing smoothly but suggesting lack of thought or sincerity: *a glib reply to a serious question.* —**glib′ly** *adv.* —**glib′ness** *n.*

glide (glīd) *v.* **glided, gliding, glides** —*intr.* **1.** To move smoothly and with little effort: *The skaters glided over the ice.* See Synonyms at **slide.** **2.** To pass or occur without notice: *The weekend had glided by.* **3.** To fly without using propelling power. —*tr.* **1.** To cause to move smoothly and with little effort: *glided the paintbrush back and forth over the wall.* **2.** To operate or guide (an aircraft) without propelling power. ❖ *n.* **1.** The act or process of gliding. **2.** A smooth effortless movement.

glider (glī′dər) *n.* **1.** An aircraft that has no engine and is designed to glide after being towed aloft by an airplane or launched from a catapult. **2.** A long swinging seat that hangs in a vertical frame.

glimmer (glĭm′ər) *n.* **1.** A dim or unsteady light; a flicker: *the glimmer of candles in the breeze.* **2.** A faint indication; a trace: *a glimmer of understanding.* ❖ *intr.v.* **glimmered, glimmering, glimmers** To give off a dim or flickering light: *A single lamp glimmered in the window.*

glimpse (glĭmps) *n.* A brief incomplete view or look: *a glimpse of the sun on a cloudy day.* ❖ *tr.v.* **glimpsed, glimpsing, glimpses** To obtain a brief incomplete view of: *glimpsed a deer through the leaves.*

glint (glĭnt) *n.* **1.** A brief flash of light; a sparkle: *a glint of polished silver in the darkened room.* **2.** A faint indication; a trace: *a glint of suspicion in the guard's face.* ❖ *intr.v.* **glinted, glinting, glints** To gleam or flash; sparkle: *The creek glinted in the moonlight.*

glissando (glĭ-sän′dō) *n., pl.* **glissandi** (glĭ-sän′dē) or **glis-sandos** In music, a rapid glide from one tone to another.

glisten (glĭs′ən) *intr.v.* **glistened, glistening, glistens** To shine with a sparkling reflected light: *The snow glistened in the sunlight.* ❖ *n.* A shine or sparkle.

glitch (glĭch) *n.* A mishap, malfunction, or problem: *a glitch in the computer program.*

glitter (glĭt′ər) *n.* **1.** A sparkling light or brightness: *the glitter of a diamond necklace.* **2.** Brilliant, often superficial appeal; showiness: *the glitter of movie stardom.* **3.** Small pieces of shiny decorative material: *tossed handfuls of glitter in the air at the celebration.* ❖ *intr.v.* **glittered, glittering, glitters 1.** To sparkle brilliantly: *The stars glittered in the night sky.* **2.** To be brilliantly, often deceptively attractive: *The chance of making a fortune glittered in front of them.* —**glit′ter·y** *adj.*

glitz (glĭts) *Informal n.* Ostentatious showiness; flashiness: *the glitz of the show business industry.* —**glitz′i·ness** *n.* —**glitz′y** *adj.*

gloat (glōt) *intr.v.* **gloated, gloating, gloats** To feel or express great, often spiteful pleasure: *The rival team gloated over their victory.*

glob (glŏb) *n.* A soft rounded mass or lump: *a glob of mashed potatoes.*

global (glō′bəl) *adj.* **1.** Shaped like a globe; spherical. **2.** Of the entire earth; worldwide: *a global population figure.* **3.** Comprehensive; total: *a global approach to the problem.* —**glob′al·ly** *adv.*

Global Positioning System *n.* A system for determining one's exact position on the earth by comparing radio signals received from different satellites.

global warming *n.* An increase in the average temperature of the earth's atmosphere, especially one that is large enough to cause changes in the earth's overall climate.

globe (glōb) *n.* **1.** An object having the general shape of a ball or sphere, especially a representation of the earth or the celestial sphere. **2.** The earth: *The space station is designed to circle the globe constantly.* **3.** A spherical container, especially a glass sphere covering a light bulb.

globular (glŏb′yə-lər) *adj.* **1.** Having the shape of a globe or globule: *A cantaloupe is a globular fruit.* **2.** Made up of globules.

globule (glŏb′yōol) *n.* A very small rounded mass, especially a small drop of liquid.

globulin (glŏb′yə-lĭn) *n.* Any of a class of simple proteins found in blood, milk, muscle tissue, and plant seeds. Globulins are insoluble in water and coagulate when heated.

glockenspiel (glŏk′ən-spēl′ or glŏk′ən-shpēl′) *n.* A musical instrument consisting of a series of tuned metal bars and played with two light hammers.

gloom (glōōm) *n.* **1.** Partial or total darkness; dimness: *He peered into the gloom of the night.* **2.** Sadness; dejection: *I was full of gloom over the loss.*

gloomy (glōō′mē) *adj.* **gloomier, gloomiest 1.** Partially or totally dark; dismal: *a gloomy basement.* **2.** Showing or filled with gloom; sad: *His gloomy face indicated the news was bad.* **3.** Causing low spirits; depressing: *damp, gloomy weather.* —**gloom′i·ly** *adv.* —**gloom′i·ness** *n.*

glop (glŏp) *n. Slang* A soft soggy mixture, as of food: *All we can get at the cafeteria is tasteless glop.*

Gloria (glôr′ē-ə) *n.* **1.** A Christian hymn of praise to God, beginning with the Latin word *Gloria.* **2.** The music for one of these hymns.

glorify (glôr′ə-fī′) *tr.v.* **glorified, glorifying, glorifies 1.** To give glory or honor to, especially through worship; exalt:

a culture that glorifies its ancestors; prayers that glorify God. **2.** To make seem more glorious or excellent than is actually the case: *Their description glorified the old house as a mansion.* —**glo'ri·fi·ca'tion** (glôr'ə-fĭ-kā'shən) *n.*

glorious (glôr'ē-əs) *adj.* **1.** Having or deserving glory; famous: *the glorious achievements of the Renaissance.* **2.** Giving or bringing glory: *a glorious victory.* **3.** Having great beauty or splendor; magnificent: *a glorious sunset.* —**glo'ri·ous·ly** *adv.*

glory (glôr'ē) *n., pl.* **glories 1.** Great honor or praise given by others; fame; renown: *The swimmer won glory by breaking the world record.* **2.** Something that brings honor, praise, or renown: *a symphony that is one of the glories of music of the 1700s.* **3.** Adoration or praise offered in worship: *giving glory to God.* **4.** Great beauty: *The sun was setting in a blaze of glory.* **5.** A period of highest achievement or prosperity: *Rome in its greatest glory.* ❖ *intr.v.* **gloried, glorying, glories** To rejoice: *The team gloried in its victory.*

gloss¹ (glôs) *n.* **1.** A shine on a surface; a sheen: *the gloss of a polished table.* **2.** A cosmetic that adds shine or luster: *lip gloss.* **3.** A superficially attractive appearance intended to hide the real nature of something: *A few new buildings gave the town the gloss of prosperity, but economic problems persisted.* ❖ *tr.v.* **glossed, glossing, glosses 1.** To give a bright shine or luster to. **2.** To make attractive or acceptable by concealing or misrepresenting: *The committee glossed over serious problems in its report.*

gloss² (glôs) *n.* A brief note that explains or translates a difficult word, phrase, or section of a text or manuscript. ❖ *tr.v.* **glossed, glossing, glosses** To provide (a text) with glosses: *This science textbook glosses all technical terms.*

WORD HISTORY Gloss¹ may be of Scandinavian origin. **Gloss²** comes from Middle English *glose*, which comes from Late Lain *glōssa* (meaning "foreign word requiring explanation"), which comes from Greek *glōssa,* meaning "tongue, language."

glossary (glô'sə-rē) *n., pl.* **glossaries** A list of specialized words with their definitions: *a glossary of computer terms.*

glossy (glô'sē) *adj.* **glossier, glossiest** Smooth and shiny: *Satin is a glossy fabric.* —**gloss'i·ly** *adv.* —**gloss'i·ness** *n.*

glottal stop (glŏt'l) *n.* A speech sound produced by closing the glottis to hold one's breath momentarily and then releasing it suddenly, as in the middle of the interjection *uh-oh* or between the two *i*'s in some pronunciations of *Hawaii.*

glottis (glŏt'ĭs) *n., pl.* **glottises** or **glottides** (glŏt'ĭ-dēz') The space between the vocal cords at the upper part of the larynx. —**glot'tal** (glŏt'l) *adj.*

glove (glŭv) *n.* **1.** A covering for the hand, with a separate section for each finger and the thumb. **2a.** A protective covering for the hand, often made of padded leather, used in playing baseball, handball, or some other sport. **b.** A boxing glove. ❖ *tr.v.* **gloved, gloving, gloves 1.** To cover or provide with a glove. **2.** To catch in a baseball glove: *The outfielder gloved a long fly ball.*

glow (glō) *intr.v.* **glowed, glowing, glows 1.** To shine brightly and steadily with heat: *The embers glowed in the fireplace.* **2.** To have a bright warm color: *The skier's cheeks glowed in the cold.* **3.** To be radiant with emotion: *glow with happiness.* ❖ *n.* **1.** A light given off by something that is hot: *the glow of molten steel.* **2.** A brilliance or warmth of color: *the rosy glow of an adobe wall in the setting sun.* **3.**

A feeling of warmth, especially when caused by emotion: *the glow on a child's happy face.*

glower (glou'ər) *intr.v.* **glowered, glowering, glowers** To look or stare angrily: *The unfriendly neighbors glowered at us.* ❖ *n.* An angry or threatening stare.

glowing (glō'ĭng) *adj.* **1.** Giving or reflecting brilliant light: *glowing coals.* **2.** Having a rich warm color, as from health or strong emotion: *a glowing complexion.* **3.** Enthusiastic; highly favorable: *the glowing reports of their success.* —**glow'ing·ly** *adv.*

glowworm (glō'wûrm') *n.* Any of various beetle larvae or wingless female beetles that give off a glowing light, especially the larva or female of a firefly.

glucose (glōō'kōs') *n.* A sugar having the formula $C_6H_{12}O_6$, found in living organisms and created by plants during photosynthesis. It is essential to the animal diet and is the main source of energy for cellular processes.

glue (glōō) *n.* A thick sticky substance used to join things together. Glues were originally made from animal skin and bones or from plant resins, but now they are usually made from synthetic chemicals. ❖ *tr.v.* **glued, gluing, glues 1.** To stick or fasten together with glue: *glued the broken leg of a chair.* **2.** To fix or hold firmly as if with glue: *The dog glued its eyes on the stranger.*

glum (glŭm) *adj.* **glummer, glummest** Feeling or appearing sad or dejected; gloomy: *a glum expression.* —**glum'ly** *adv.* —**glum'ness** *n.*

glut (glŭt) *tr.v.* **glutted, glutting, gluts 1.** To fill beyond capacity, especially with food: *The lions slept after glutting themselves on their kill.* **2.** To provide (a market) with too many goods so that the supply is much greater than the demand. ❖ *n.* An excess amount; an oversupply: *A glut of gasoline caused lower prices.*

glutamic acid (glōō-tăm'ĭk) *n.* A nonessential amino acid that is found in plant and animal tissue.

glutamine (glōō'tə-mēn') *n.* A nonessential amino acid that is found in plant and animal tissue and produced in the laboratory for use in research.

gluten (glōōt'n) *n.* Any of various plant proteins found in cereal grains, especially certain ones in wheat, rye, and barley that can cause digestive disorders.

glutinous (glōōt'n-əs) *adj.* Resembling glue; thick and sticky: *a glutinous mixture of flour and water.*

glutton (glŭt'n) *n.* **1.** A person who eats to excess. **2.** A person with an unusually great capacity to receive or withstand something: *a glutton for work.* —**glut'ton·ous** *adj.* —**glut'ton·ous·ly** *adv.*

gluttony (glŭt'n-ē) *n., pl.* **gluttonies** Excess in eating.

glycerin also **glycerine** (glĭs'ər-ĭn) *n.* Glycerol.

glycerol (glĭs'ə-rôl' *or* glĭs'ə-rōl') *n.* A sweet syrupy liquid obtained from animal fats and oils. It is used as a solvent, sweetener, and antifreeze and in the manufacture of explosives and soaps.

glycine (glī'sēn') *n.* A nonessential amino acid that is found in most proteins.

glycogen (glī'kə-jən) *n.* A carbohydrate that is stored in the muscles and liver of animals and is converted to glucose for energy.

glyph (glĭf) *n.* **1.** A graphic symbol that provides information without using words. An emoticon, such as a smiley, and the arrow on a "ONE WAY" traffic sign are glyphs. **2.** A symbolic figure that is usually engraved or carved.

gm. An abbreviation of gram.

G-man (jē'măn') *n.* An agent of the Federal Bureau of Investigation.

GMO An abbreviation of genetically modified organism.

gnarl (närl) *n*. A knot in wood: *a smooth board without gnarls*. ❖ *tr.v.* **gnarled, gnarling, gnarls** To make knotted or deformed; twist: *Disease gnarled the patient's fingers.* —**gnarl′y** *adj*.

gnarled (närld) *adj*. Having gnarls; knotty and misshapen: *gnarled tree roots; gnarled fingers.*

gnash (năsh) *tr.v.* **gnashed, gnashing, gnashes** To grind (the teeth) together.

gnat (năt) *n*. Any of various tiny flies, especially those that form swarms.

gnaw (nô) *v*. **gnawed, gnawing, gnaws** —*tr*. **1.** To bite, chew, or erode with the teeth: *animals gnawing the bark of trees.* **2.** To produce by gnawing: *Rats gnawed a hole in the wall.* **3.** To reduce gradually as if by gnawing: *The waves gnawed at the base of the cliff.* **4.** To cause distress or pain to. —*intr*. **1.** To bite or chew on: *The dog gnawed on the rope.* **2.** To trouble or distress: *The lack of success gnawed at the scientist for weeks.*

gneiss (nīs) *n*. A type of metamorphic rock consisting of light-colored layers, usually of quartz and feldspar, alternating with dark-colored layers of other minerals.

gnocchi (nyō′kē *or* nyŏk′ē) *pl.n*. Dumplings made of flour or potatoes, boiled or baked and served with grated cheese or a sauce.

gnome (nōm) *n*. In folklore, a dwarf that dwells underground and guards treasure.

Gnosticism (nŏs′tĭ-sĭz′əm) *n*. Any of various religious sects especially of the ancient Middle East, teaching that the world is the flawed creation of a subordinate deity and that the soul can transcend material existence by means of hidden knowledge.

gnu (no͞o) *n*. Either of two large African antelopes having a drooping mane, a beard, a long tufted tail, and curved horns.

go (gō) *v*. **went** (wĕnt), **gone** (gôn), **going, goes** (gōz) —*intr*. **1.** To move along or forward; proceed: *The bus went along steadily in the rain.* **2.** To move or proceed to a specified place; advance: *I am going to New York.* **3.** To move from a place; depart: *We must go at once.* **4.** To function, operate, move, or work: *A battery makes the watch go.* **5.** To pursue a course of action: *go to a lot of trouble; go through college.* **6a.** To belong in a definite place or position: *This book goes on that shelf.* **b.** To be suitable as an accessory: *Does this tie go with my shirt?* **7.** To extend between two points or in a certain direction: *The windows go from the ceiling to the floor. The road goes north.* **8a.** To extend in time: *The house goes back to the 1800s.* **b.** To pass; elapse: *Time goes quickly when you're busy.* **9.** To be allotted or awarded: *First prize went to my friend. This money goes for food.* **10.** To proceed or end in a particular way; turn out: *How did your day go? How does the rest of the story go?* **11.** To be expressed or phrased: *How does that nursery rhyme go?* **12.** To be typically or in general: *well behaved, as dogs go.* **13a.** To become weak; fail: *My eyes are going.* **b.** To come apart; break up: *The pier looks about ready to go.* **14.** To cease living; die: *The old horse went peacefully last night.* **15.** To be sold or auctioned off: *Most of the old books went for high prices.* **16.** To come to be in a certain state or condition: *go mad; go to sleep; a tire going flat.* **17.** Used to indicate future intention or expectation: *I am going to climb that mountain.* **18.** *Informal* To urinate or defecate: *Let's*

pull off the highway at the next rest area; I really need to go. —*tr*. **1.** To proceed or move along: *We went separate ways.* **2.** To engage in: *We went swimming.* **3.** *Informal* To say, utter, or produce as sound: *The cow goes moo. Whenever I tell my friend a story, he goes "No way!"* ❖ *n., pl.* **goes 1.** An attempt; an effort: *Let's have a go at the puzzle.* **2.** Something successful; a success: *They tried to make a go of their store.* **3.** *Informal* Energy; vitality: *That athlete has got a lot of go and will be a winner.* **4.** A situation in which a plan is certain to be put into effect: *Our weekend at the lake is still a go.* ❖ *adj*. *Informal* Ready for action or working correctly: *Everything is go for the parade.* ◆ **go about** To set about to do; undertake: *How does one go about building a house?* **go along** To cooperate: *Why don't you stop criticizing the project and go along?* **go around 1.** To satisfy a demand or requirement: *We have enough food to go around.* **2.** To go here and there; move from place to place. **3.** To circulate: *rumors going around.* **go at 1.** To attack, especially with energy. **2.** To approach; undertake: *He went at the assignment diligently.* **go back on** To fail to honor or keep: *Don't go back on your word!* **go by 1.** To elapse; pass: *Time goes by fast sometimes.* **2.** To be called; be known as: *He goes by Billy.* **go down 1a.** To drop below the horizon; set: *The sun went down.* **b.** To fall to the ground. **c.** To sink. **2.** To be easy to swallow: *This cough syrup goes right down.* **3.** To come to be remembered in posterity: *He went down in history as a famous inventor.* **go for 1.** *Informal* To have a special liking for: *I really go for jazz.* **2.** To attack. **go in for 1.** To have interest in: *I go in for folk music.* **2.** To take part in: *She goes in for water skiing.* **go off 1.** To explode: *fireworks going off.* **2.** To make a noise; sound: *The alarm went off, but it was just a test.* **3.** To leave: *They went off for a hike.* **go on 1.** To take place; happen: *What's going on?* **2a.** To continue: *How long has this discussion been going on?* **b.** To keep on (doing something): *They went on talking.* **c.** To proceed: *She went on to be a famous scientist.* **3.** *Informal* To talk volubly: *He does go on.* **go out 1.** To become extinguished. **2a.** To go outdoors; leave one's residence. **b.** To take part in social life outside the home: *Let's go out for ice cream.* **c.** To be romantically involved: *Are they going out now?* **3.** To become unfashionable: *That dance went out years ago.* **go out of (one's) way** To inconvenience oneself in doing something beyond what is required. **go over 1.** To gain acceptance or approval: *My idea went over well.* **2.** To examine: *Did you go over my paper yet?* **go steady** To date someone exclusively. **go the distance** To carry a course of action through to completion: *He is pitching well, but can he go the distance?* **go through 1.** To examine carefully: *I've gone through your paper and it's great!* **2.** To experience or be subjected to: *We all go through some sad times. The house is going through a renovation.* **go under** To fail: *The business went under.* **go with** To date regularly. **go without saying** To be self-evident: *Some rules go without saying.* **on the go** Constantly busy or active. **to go 1.** To be taken out, as restaurant food or drink: *He ordered a pizza to go.* **2.** Still to be done or taken care of; remaining: *That's one exam down and one to go.*

goad (gōd) *n*. **1.** A long stick with a pointed end used for prodding animals, especially cattle. **2.** Something that prods or urges: *Competition is often a goad to hard work.* ❖ *tr.v.* **goaded, goading, goads** To stir to action; prod: *His criticism goaded me to do better.*

go-ahead (gō′ə-hĕd′) *n*. *Informal* Permission to go ahead or proceed.

goal (gōl) *n.* **1.** The purpose toward which one is working; an objective: *The student's goal was to become a doctor.* **2.** The finish of a race. **3a.** In certain sports, a structure or area into which players must propel the ball or puck in order to score. **b.** The score awarded for doing this.

goalie (gō′lē) *n.* A goalkeeper.

goalkeeper (gōl′kē′pər) *n.* The player who defends the goal in sports such as hockey and soccer.

goal kick *n.* A free kick in soccer awarded to a defensive team when the ball has been driven out of bounds over the goal line by an opponent.

goal line *n.* **1.** A line at either end of a playing area, as in soccer, on which a goal or goalpost is positioned. **2.** In football, a line crossing either end of the playing field over which the ball must be moved to score a touchdown.

goalpost or **goal post** (gōl′pōst′) *n.* **1.** One of a pair of posts usually joined with a crossbar and set at each end of a playing field to form a goal, as in ice hockey or soccer. **2.** A post or a pair of posts supporting a crossbar and either supporting or extending into the uprights of a goal, as in football.

goaltender (gōl′tĕn′dər) *n.* A goalkeeper.

goaltending (gōl′tĕn′dĭng) *n.* **1.** The act of protecting a goal, as in hockey. **2.** In basketball, an illegal play in which a player touches a ball that is on a downward path to the basket or that is on or within the rim of the basket, resulting in an automatic score when committed by the defense or not scoring the field goal when committed by the offense.

goat (gōt) *n.* **1.** A domesticated hoofed mammal having backward-curving horns and a beard, raised in many parts of the world for wool, milk, and meat. **2.** Any of various similar wild mammals.

goatee (gō-tē′) *n.* A small beard, especially one connected to a mustache or trimmed into a point.

goatskin (gōt′skĭn′) *n.* **1.** The skin of a goat. **2.** Leather made from the skin of a goat. **3.** A container, as for water, made out of this leather.

gob (gŏb) *n.* **1.** A small piece or lump: *a gob of wax.* **2.** often **gobs** *Informal* A large quantity: *a gob of money; gobs of time.*

gobble¹ (gŏb′əl) *tr.v.* **gobbled, gobbling, gobbles** To devour in big greedy gulps.

gobble² (gŏb′əl) *n.* The throaty chortling sound made by a male turkey. ❖ *intr.v.* **gobbled, gobbling, gobbles** To make this sound.

WORD HISTORY Gobble¹ comes from Middle English *gobben,* meaning "to drink greedily." **Gobble²** is of imitative origin.

gobbledygook also **gobbledegook** (gŏb′əl-dē-gook′) *n.* Unclear, often wordy speech or writing.

gobbler (gŏb′lər) *n.* A male turkey.

go-between (gō′bĭ-twēn′) *n.* A person who acts as an intermediary or messenger between two sides.

goblet (gŏb′lĭt) *n.* A drinking glass that has a stem and a base.

goblin (gŏb′lĭn) *n.* An ugly elfin creature of folklore, thought to cause mischief or evil.

god (gŏd) *n.* **1. God** A being regarded as the creator and ruler of the universe, forming the object of worship in monotheistic religions. **2.** A being of supernatural powers, worshiped by a people, especially a male being thought to control some part of nature: *the Egyptian sun god Ra; a rain god.* **3.** An image or idol of a god. **4.** Some-

thing considered to be of great value or high importance: *Absolute power was his god.*

godchild (gŏd′chīld′) *n.* A child for whom a person serves as sponsor at baptism.

goddaughter (gŏd′dô′tər) *n.* A female godchild.

goddess (gŏd′ĭs) *n.* **1.** A female being of supernatural powers, worshiped by a people: *Venus, the Roman goddess of love and beauty.* **2.** An image or idol of a goddess.

godfather (gŏd′fä′thər) *n.* A man who serves as sponsor at one's baptism.

godhead (gŏd′hĕd′) *n.* **1.** The essential and divine nature of God; divinity. **2. Godhead** God, especially the Christian Trinity.

godless (gŏd′lĭs) *adj.* **1.** Not believing in God or a god. **2.** Immoral; wicked. —**god′less·ly** *adv.* —**god′less·ness** *n.*

godlike (gŏd′līk′) *adj.* Resembling or of the nature of God or a god; divine.

godly (gŏd′lē) *adj.* **godlier, godliest** Having great reverence for God; pious. —**god′li·ness** *n.*

godmother (gŏd′mŭth′ər) *n.* A woman who serves as sponsor at one's baptism.

godparent (gŏd′pâr′ənt) *n.* A godfather or godmother.

godsend (gŏd′sĕnd′) *n.* Something wanted or needed that comes or happens unexpectedly: *The $500 holiday bonus was a godsend.*

godson (gŏd′sŭn′) *n.* A male godchild.

Godspeed (gŏd′spēd′) *n.* Success or good fortune: *With a wish of Godspeed they bid me farewell.*

gofer also **go-fer** (gō′fər) *n. Slang* An employee who runs errands in addition to performing regular duties.

go-getter (gō′gĕt′ər or gō′gĕt′ər) *n. Informal* An energetic person with much determination and ambition.

goggle (gŏg′əl) *intr.v.* **goggled, goggling, goggles** To stare with wide and bulging eyes.

goggle-eyed (gŏg′əl-īd′) *adj.* Having prominent or rolling eyes: *a goggle-eyed frog; tourists who were goggle-eyed with wonder at the Great Wall of China.*

goggles (gŏg′əlz) *pl.n.* Eyeglasses worn tight against the head to protect the eyes from hazards such as wind, glare, water, or flying debris.

going (gō′ing) *n.* **1.** The act of leaving or moving away; departure: *comings and goings of passengers in the terminal.* **2.** The condition of the ground or road as it affects how one walks or rides: *It was rough going over the icy roads, but we made it.* **3.** *Informal* Progress toward a goal: *Learning this new computer program has been easy going.* ❖ *adj.* **1.** Working; running: *The clock is in going order.* **2.** In full operation; flourishing: *Our business is at last a going operation.* **3.** Available or now in existence: *We make the best bikes going.* **4.** Current; prevailing: *The going rates for bank loans will soon increase.*

goiter (goi′tər) *n.* An enlargement of the thyroid gland, visible as a swelling at the front of the neck and often associated with a diet that contains too little iodine.

gold (gōld) *n.* **1.** *Symbol* **Au** A soft, shiny, yellow metallic element that resists corrosion and is a good conductor of heat and electricity. It is used in making jewelry and in plating electrical and mechanical components. Atomic number 79. See **Periodic Table. 2.** A deep, strong, or metallic yellow: *when fall leaves turn to red and gold.* **3.** Gold coins. **4.** Money; riches. **5.** A medal made of gold, awarded for first place in a competition. **6.** Something thought of as having great value or goodness: *a heart of gold.* ❖ *adj.* **1.** Relating to or containing gold: *a gold ring; a gold coin.* **2.** Having a deep, strong, or metallic yellow color.

goldbrick (gōld′brĭk′) *Slang n.* A person, especially a soldier, who avoids duties or work. ❖ *intr.v.* **goldbricked, goldbricking, goldbricks** To avoid one's duties or work. —**gold′brick′er** *n.*

golden (gōl′dən) *adj.* **1.** Relating to, made of, or containing gold: *golden earrings.* **2.** Having the color of gold or a yellow color suggestive of gold: *a golden wheat field.* **3a.** Of great value or importance; precious: *golden memories of a happy childhood.* **b.** Very favorable; excellent: *a golden opportunity.* **4.** Marked by peace, prosperity, and often creativeness: *a golden era in our past.*

golden age *n.* A period usually of peace and prosperity when a nation and its culture are at their height: *Spain's golden age of art and cultural influence was based on the riches of the New World.*

Golden Fleece *n.* In Greek mythology, the fleece of the golden ram, stolen by Jason and the Argonauts.

golden goal *n.* In soccer, a goal that is scored in overtime, resulting in the immediate end of the game.

golden mean *n.* The course between extremes; moderation.

goldenrod (gōl′dən-rŏd′) *n.* Any of numerous plants having tall stalks with clusters of small, usually yellow flowers that bloom in late summer or fall.

golden rule *n.* The rule of conduct that one should behave toward others as one would have others behave toward oneself.

gold-filled (gōld′fĭld′) *adj.* Made of inexpensive metal with an outer layer of gold: *gold-filled jewelry.*

goldfinch (gōld′fĭnch′) *n.* **1.** Any of several small North American finches, especially a common species in which the male has yellow feathers with a black forehead, wings, and tail. **2.** A European finch having black, yellow, and red markings.

goldfish (gōld′fĭsh′) *n.* A small freshwater fish, usually orange or reddish, often kept in outdoor ponds and home aquariums.

gold leaf *n.* Gold beaten into extremely thin sheets used for gilding.

gold rush *n.* A rush of miners or prospectors and other people to an area where gold has been discovered.

goldsmith (gōld′smĭth′) *n.* A person who makes, repairs, or deals in objects of gold.

gold standard *n.* A monetary system in which a country's currency is backed by and exchangeable for gold.

golf (gŏlf) *n.* A game played over a large outdoor course having a series of 9 or 18 holes spaced far apart. A player, using various clubs, tries to take as few strokes as possible in hitting a ball into one hole after another. ❖ *intr.v.* **golfed, golfing, golfs** To play golf. —**golf′er** *n.*

golf club *n.* **1.** One of a set of clubs, having a slender shaft and a head usually made of wood or iron, used in golf. **2.** An association of golfers.

golf course *n.* A large tract of land laid out for golf.

Golgi apparatus or **Golgi complex** (gōl′jē) *n.* A structure within many cells that is composed of a series of sacs and plays a role in the storage, modification, and transport of proteins and other large molecules.

–gon A suffix that means a figure having a specified number of angles: *octagon.*

gonad (gō′năd′) *n.* An organ, such as an ovary or testis, in which egg cells or sperm cells are produced.

gondola (gŏn′dl-ə *or* gŏn-dō′lə) *n.* **1.** A long narrow boat with a high pointed prow and stern, propelled from the stern by a single oar and used on the canals of Venice. **2.** An open railroad freight car with low sides. **3.** A basket or cabin attached to the underside of a balloon. **4.** An enclosed car suspended from a cable used for transporting passengers, as up and down a ski slope.

gondolier (gŏn′dl-îr′) *n.* The person who rows a gondola.

gone (gôn) *v.* Past participle of **go.** ❖ *adj.* **1.** Being away from a place; absent or departed: *I'll be gone for a few days.* **2.** Used up or consumed: *When natural resources are gone they cannot be replaced. Their strength was gone.* **3.** Dead.

goner (gô′nər) *n. Slang* A person or thing that is ruined or doomed: *A car with a bent frame is usually a goner.*

gong (gông) *n.* A saucer-shaped metal disk that produces a loud ringing tone when struck.

gonorrhea (gŏn′ə-rē′ə) *n.* A sexually transmitted bacterial disease that causes inflammation of the genitals and urinary tract.

goo (gōō) *n. Informal* A sticky wet substance.

goober (gōō′bər) *n. Informal* A peanut.

WORD HISTORY Most Southerners know that a **goober** is a peanut. The word *goober* is related to *n-guba*, "peanut," in a Bantu language of west-central Africa. *Goober* is one of a small group of words that came into American English from the languages spoken by the Africans who were enslaved and brought to the Americas between the 1600s and the 1800s. *Gumbo* is also of Bantu origin, and *okra* and *yam* are of western African origin.

good (gŏŏd) *adj.* **better** (bĕt′ər), **best** (bĕst) **1.** Having positive or desirable qualities; not bad or poor: *a good book; good food.* **2.** Providing a benefit; helpful: *Earthworms are good for our soil.* **3.** Serving the desired purpose; suitable: *Is this a good shirt to wear to the party?* **4.** Superior to average; skilled: *a good painter.* **5.** Not spoiled or ruined: *The milk is still good.* **6.** Genuine; real: *a good dollar bill.* **7.** Valid; true: *a good reason.* **8.** In effect; valid: *The warranty on that car is still good.* **9.** Providing pleasure; enjoyable: *a good time.* **10.** Attractive; handsome: *good looks.* **11a.** Doing or showing what is right; morally upright: *A good person is honest. It is always good to tell the truth.* **b.** Loyal; devoted: *a good friend.* **c.** Honorable: *a good name.* **12a.** Well-behaved; obedient: *a good dog.* **b.** Proper; correct: *good manners.* **13.** Judged as in play or scoring: *a good tennis return; a good field goal.* **14.** Substantial; ample: *a good income.* **15.** Not less than; full: *It is a good mile to the station.* **16.** Thorough; complete: *a good housecleaning.* **17.** More than a little likely: *Our team has a good chance of winning the competition.* ❖ *n.* **1.** Something good: *You must learn to accept the bad with the good.* **2.** Benefit; welfare: *for the good of the country.* **3.** Value; use: *What good is a bicycle without a chain?* **4. goods a.** Things that can be bought and sold; merchandise. **b.** Personal belongings: *They lost all their household goods in the fire.* **c.** *(used with a singular or plural verb)* Cloth; fabric. ◆ **as good as** Nearly; almost: *This car is as good as new.* **for good** Permanently; forever: *They left town for good.* **good and** *Informal* Very; entirely: *We are good and mad at them.* **no good** Useless; worthless: *It's no good arguing with them.* **to the good** Advantageous; in one's favor.

USAGE The adjective **good** is often used with linking verbs such as *be, seem,* or *appear: The future looks good. He seems very good as an actor. Good* should not be used as an adverb with other verbs: *The car runs well* (not *good*).

goodbye or **good-bye** (good-bī′) *n., pl.* **goodbyes** also **good-byes 1.** An acknowledgement at parting, especially by saying "goodbye": *I said my goodbye and left.* **2.** An act of parting: *There were many long goodbyes among the students at the end of year.* ❖ *interj.* An expression used to make such an acknowledgment.

good-for-nothing (good′fər-nŭth′ing) *n.* A person who is considered worthless or useless. ❖ *adj.* Having little worth; useless.

Good Friday *n.* The Friday before Easter, observed by Christians in commemoration of the crucifixion of Jesus.

goodhearted (good′här′tĭd) *adj.* Kind and generous: *a goodhearted person.* —**good′heart′ed·ly** *adv.*

good-humored (good′hyoo′mərd) *adj.* Cheerful; amiable: *He was good-humored about losing the card game.* —**good′-hu′mored·ly** *adv.*

good-looking (good′look′ing) *adj.* Having a pleasing appearance; attractive; handsome: *a good-looking actor; good-looking clothes.*

goodly (good′lē) *adj.* **goodlier, goodliest** Quite large; considerable: *a goodly number of people.*

good-natured (good′nā′chərd) *adj.* Having an easygoing, pleasant disposition; cheerful. —**good′-na′tured·ly** *adv.* —**good′-na′tured·ness** *n.*

goodness (good′nĭs) *n.* **1.** The quality or condition of being good; excellence. **2.** The best or nutritious part. ❖ *interj.* An expression used to show surprise.

Good Samaritan *n.* **1.** In one of Jesus's parables in the New Testament, the only passerby who helped a man who had been beaten and robbed. **2.** A person who unselfishly helps others; a good neighbor.

good-sized (good′sīzd′) *adj.* Of a fairly large size: *a good-sized swimming pool; a good-sized serving.*

goodwill also **good will** (good′wĭl′) *n.* **1.** An attitude of kindliness or friendliness: *Her goodwill made us feel welcome in the neighborhood.* **2.** Cheerful consent or willingness: *The lender accepted the risk with goodwill.* **3.** A good relationship of a nation with other nations or a business with its customers.

goody (good′ē) *Informal interj.* An expression used to show delight. ❖ *n.* also **goodie** *pl.* **goodies** Something attractive or delectable, especially something good to eat: *a plate of cupcakes and other goodies.*

gooey (goo′ē) *adj.* **gooier, gooiest** Thick and sticky: *gooey tar.*

goof (goof) *Slang n.* **1.** A careless mistake; a slip. **2.** An incompetent or stupid person. ❖ *v.* **goofed, goofing, goofs** —*intr.* **1.** To make a careless mistake; blunder. **2.** To waste or kill time: *We goofed off all afternoon.* —*tr.* To spoil, as through clumsiness; bungle: *He goofed up his lines in the play.*

goofy (goo′fē) *adj.* **goofier, goofiest** *Slang* Silly; ridiculous: *a goofy hat.* —**goof′i·ness** *n.*

googol (goo′gôl′) *n.* The number 10 raised to the 100th power, written as 10^{100} or as 1 followed by 100 zeros.

goon (goon) *n. Slang* **1.** A thug hired to intimidate or harm people, especially workers on strike. **2.** A stupid or oafish person.

goose (goos) *n., pl.* **geese** (gēs) **1a.** Any of various waterbirds that resemble ducks but are larger and have a longer neck and a shorter, more pointed bill. **b.** The female of such a bird: *The goose and the gander made a nest by the lake.* **c.** The meat of such a bird, used as food. **2.** *Informal* A silly person.

gooseberry (goos′běr′ē or goos′bə-rē) *n.* **1.** A juicy greenish berry that grows on a spiny shrub, used chiefly for making jam or pies. **2.** A shrub that bears such berries.

goose bumps *pl.n.* Small bumps that form around the hairs on the skin as a reaction to cold or fear: *The eerie sound gave me goose bumps.*

goose flesh *n.* Goose bumps.

gooseneck (goos′něk′) *n.* A slender curved object or part, such as the flexible shaft of a type of desk lamp.

goose step *n.* A marching step made by swinging the legs forward from the hips with the knees unbent.

GOP An abbreviation of Grand Old Party (the Republican Party).

gopher (gō′fər) *n.* **1.** Any of various burrowing North American rodents having large cheek pouches. **2.** A ground squirrel.

gore¹ (gôr) *tr.v.* **gored, goring, gores** To pierce or stab with a horn or tusk.

gore² (gôr) *n.* A triangular piece of cloth forming a part of something, as in a skirt or sail.

gore³ (gôr) *n.* Blood, especially dried blood from a wound.

WORD HISTORY Gore¹ comes from Middle English *goren* (meaning "to stab"), which probably comes from Middle English *gore*, meaning "spear." **Gore²** comes from Old English *gāra*, meaning "triangular piece of land." **Gore³** comes from Old English *gor*, meaning "filth."

gorge (gôrj) *n.* A deep narrow canyon with very steep sides: *The river grew swifter as it entered the gorge.* ❖ *v.* **gorged, gorging, gorges** —*tr.* **1.** To stuff with food; satiate: *gorged themselves with spaghetti.* **2.** To devour greedily: *gorged my dinner.* —*intr.* To eat greedily: *We gorged on the local seafood.*

gorgeous (gôr′jəs) *adj.* Dazzlingly beautiful or magnificent: *The snowcapped mountains were gorgeous in the sunset.* —**gor′geous·ly** *adv.* —**gor′geous·ness** *n.*

Gorgon (gôr′gən) *n.* In Greek mythology, one of three sisters whose hair was made of snakes and who would turn anyone who looked at them into stone.

Gorgonzola (gôr′gən-zō′lə) *n.* A strongly-flavored, blue-veined Italian cheese.

gorilla (gə-rĭl′ə) *n.* Either of two large apes of the central African forests and mountains, having a stocky body and dark hair.

gorse (gôrs) *n.* Any of several spiny shrubs having fragrant yellow flowers.

gory (gôr′ē) *adj.* **gorier, goriest 1.** Covered or stained with gore; bloody. **2.** Full of or marked by bloodshed and violence: *a gory movie.* —**gor′i·ly** *adv.* —**gor′i·ness** *n.*

gosh (gŏsh) *interj.* An expression used to show mild surprise or delight.

goshawk (gŏs′hôk′) *n.* Any of various powerful hawks having broad rounded wings and a long tail, especially one found in North America and Europe.

gosling (gŏz′lĭng) *n.* A young goose.

gospel (gŏs′pəl) *n.* **1.** often **Gospel** In Christianity, the teachings of Jesus and the Apostles. **2. Gospel a.** One of the first four books of the New Testament, describing the life and teachings of Jesus. **b.** A reading from any of the Gospels included as part of a religious service. **3.** Something, such as an idea or principle, believed to be unquestionably true: *They took her explanation as gospel.* **4.** Gospel music.

gospel music *n.* A style of Christian music performed

especially in African-American churches, marked by strong rhythms and combining elements of American folk music, blues, jazz, and spirituals.

gossamer (gŏs′ə-mər) *n.* **1.** A fine silky film of cobwebs often seen caught on bushes or grass. **2.** Something that is light, delicate, or sheer, such as fabric. ❖ *adj.* Light, sheer, or delicate.

gossip (gŏs′əp) *n.* **1.** Trivial talk, often involving rumors of people and their personal affairs. **2.** A person who habitually engages in such talk. ❖ *intr.v.* **gossiped, gossiping, gossips** To engage in or spread gossip: *gossip about one's neighbors.* —**gos′sip·er** *n.*

got (gŏt) *v.* Past tense and a past participle of **get**.

goth (gŏth) *n.* **1.** A style of rock music that usually has mournful dark lyrics, evokes a somber mood, and is often written in a minor key. **2.** A performer or follower of this style of music.

Goth *n.* A member of a Germanic people who invaded the Roman empire in the third, fourth, and fifth centuries AD.

Gothic (gŏth′ĭk) *adj.* **1.** Relating to the Goths or their language. **2.** Relating to a style of architecture used in western Europe from the 1100s through the 1400s and characterized by pointed arches, tall windows, and great height overall. **3.** Relating to a style of fiction that emphasizes the grotesque and mysterious: *a Gothic novel.* ❖ *n.* **1.** The extinct Germanic language of the Goths. **2.** Gothic art or architecture.

gotten (gŏt′n) *v.* A past participle of **get**.

gouache (gwäsh *or* gōō-äsh′) *n.* **1a.** A method of painting with opaque watercolors mixed with a preparation of gum. **b.** An opaque pigment used in this method of painting. **2.** A painting executed using this method.

Gouda (gōō′də *or* gou′də) *n.* A mild, pale-yellow cheese.

gouge (gouj) *n.* **1.** A chisel with a blade that has a rounded, angled, or troughlike indentation along its length. **2.** A groove or hole made with or as if with such a chisel: *Dragging the heavy couch across the room left a deep gouge in the floor.* ❖ *tr.v.* **gouged, gouging, gouges** **1.** To cut or scoop out: *gouge a decorative groove in the table leg; gouged out watermelon seeds with our fingers.* **2.** *Informal* To get (money) from someone by force; extort. —**goug′er** *n.*

goulash (gōō′läsh′) *n.* A meat and vegetable stew seasoned with paprika.

gourd (gôrd *or* gōōrd) *n.* **1.** The fruit of any of several vines related to the squashes, having a hard rind and sometimes an irregular shape. **2.** The dried shell of such a fruit, used as a decorative object or as a bowl or ladle. **3.** A vine that bears such fruit.

gourmand (gōōr-mänd′ *or* gōōr′mənd) *n.* **1.** A lover of good food; a gourmet. **2.** A person who often eats too much; a glutton.

gourmet (gōōr-mā′ *or* gōōr′mā′) *n.* A person who enjoys and is knowledgeable about fine food and drink.

gout (gout) *n.* A painful disease in which salts of uric acid are deposited in and near the joints, especially of the feet and hands. —**gout′i·ness** *n.* —**gout′y** *adj.*

Gov. An abbreviation of governor.

govern (gŭv′ərn) *v.* **governed, governing, governs** —*tr.* **1.** To make and administer the public policy and affairs of: *In elections the voters decide who will govern the country.* **2.** To exercise a determining influence on: *The weather governs the success or failure of crops.* **3.** To keep under

control; restrain: *a child who could not be governed.* —*intr.* To exercise political authority. —**gov′ern·a·ble** *adj.*

governess (gŭv′ər-nĭs) *n.* A woman employed to teach and train the children of a household.

government (gŭv′ərn-mənt) *n.* **1.** The act or process of governing, especially the control and administration of a political unit: *effective government.* **2.** A system by which a political unit is governed: *democratic government.* **3.** The people who make up a governing body: *The local government has decided to raise taxes.* —**gov′ern·men′tal** (gŭv′ərn-mĕn′tl) *adj.*

governor (gŭv′ər-nər) *n.* **1.** The chief executive of a state in the United States. **2.** An official appointed to govern a colony or territory. **3.** A person who directs the operation of a business or organization: *The corporation's board of governors meets every month.* **4.** A device that automatically regulates the speed, pressure, or temperature of a machine.

governorship (gŭv′ər-nər-shĭp′) *n.* The office or duties of a governor or the period during which a governor is in office.

govt. An abbreviation of government.

gown (goun) *n.* **1.** A long loose flowing garment, such as a nightgown. **2.** A woman's dress, especially a long formal one. **3.** A robe or smock worn in a hospital to guard against contamination: *a surgical gown.* **4.** An outer robe for official ceremonies, worn by scholars and clerics, for example.

goy (goi) *n., pl.* **goyim** (goi′ĭm) or **goys** *Often Offensive* A person who is not Jewish. —**goy′ish** *adj.*

GP An abbreviation of general practitioner.

GPA An abbreviation of grade point average.

GPS (jē′pē′ĕs′) *n.* A system of satellites, computers, and receivers that determine the position of a receiver on Earth by calculating the difference in time it takes for signals from different satellites to reach the receiver.

gr. An abbreviation of: **1.** grain (measurement). **2.** gram. **3.** gross.

grab (grăb) *v.* **grabbed, grabbing, grabs** —*tr.* **1.** To take suddenly; snatch: *The monkey grabbed the peanut out of my hand.* **2.** To obtain forcibly: *The dictator grabbed power.* **3.** *Slang* To capture the attention of: *a plot that grabs the reader.* —*intr.* To make a snatch: *She grabbed for the dog's leash.* ❖ *n.* The act of grabbing; a snatch: *I made a grab at the railing.*

grab bag *n.* A container filled with articles, such as party gifts, to be drawn out unseen.

grace (grās) *n.* **1.** Seemingly effortless beauty of movement, form, or manner: *the grace of a swan swimming across a lake.* **2.** A charming or pleasing quality or characteristic: *The prince had not yet mastered the social graces.* **3.** In Christianity, the state of being favored by God, as in being granted redemption from sin. **4.** A short prayer of blessing or thanks said before or after a meal. **5.** **Grace** A title and form of address for a duke, duchess, or archbishop: *Your Grace.* **6. Graces** In Greek mythology, three sister goddesses who dispensed charm and beauty. ❖ *tr.v.* **graced, gracing, graces** **1.** To give honor to (an event, for example) by one's presence: *The governor's presence graced the meeting.* **2.** To give beauty, elegance, or charm to: *A bouquet of flowers graced the mantelpiece.* ◆ **in the bad graces of** Out of favor with. **in the good graces of** In favor with.

graceful (grās′fəl) *adj.* Showing grace of movement,

form, or proportion: *a graceful dance; a graceful archway.*
—**grace′ful·ly** *adv.* —**grace′ful·ness** *n.*
graceless (grās′lĭs) *adj.* **1.** Lacking grace; clumsy: *a graceless fall on the ice.* **2.** Lacking charm; ungracious: *a graceless remark.* —**grace′less·ly** *adv.* —**grace′less·ness** *n.*
grace note *n.* A very short musical note added to a melody as an embellishment.
gracious (grā′shəs) *adj.* **1.** Characterized by kindness and courtesy: *a gracious host.* **2.** Characterized by tact and propriety: *responded to the insult with gracious good humor.* **3.** Of a merciful or sympathetic nature: *a gracious ruler.* ❖ *interj.* An expression used to show surprise or mild emotion: *Goodness gracious!* —**gra′cious·ly** *adv.*
grackle (grăk′əl) *n.* Any of several blackbirds of the Americas that have shiny blackish feathers and a harsh call.
grad (grăd) *n. Informal* A graduate of a school or college.
gradation (grā-dā′shən) *n.* **1.** A series of gradual successive stages or steps: *the gradation in shading from light to dark.* **2.** Any of the stages or steps in such a series.
grade (grād) *n.* **1a.** A position in a scale of size, quality, or intensity: *a poor grade of lumber.* **b.** A group of people or things within the same quality, rank, or value; a class: *several sheets of the finest grade sandpaper.* **2a.** A slope or incline, as of a road: *The truck couldn't stop on the grade.* **b.** The degree to which something, such as a road or railroad track, slopes: *the steep grade of a mountain road.* **3.** A division or section of the course of study in elementary and high school, usually determined as a year's work: *the ninth grade.* **4.** A number, letter, or symbol showing the quality of a student's work: *The test was so hard that no one got a grade above a C.* ❖ *v.* **graded, grading, grades** —*tr.* **1.** To arrange in a series or according to a scale: *the agency that grades meat.* **2.** To give a grade to (a student or assignment, for example): *grade book reports.* **3.** To level or smooth to a desired or horizontal gradient: *bulldozers grading a road.* —*intr.* To change or progress gradually: *The various piles of gravel grade from coarse to fine.*
grade crossing *n.* An intersection where roads, railroad tracks, or a combination of roads and railroad tracks cross each other at the same level.
grade point *n.* A number that corresponds to the letter grade made in a course or subject.
grade point average *n.* The average grade of a student, determined by dividing the grade points earned by the number of courses taken.
grader (grā′dər) *n.* **1.** A student in a specific grade at school: *a fifth grader; a tenth grader.* **2.** A person who grades students' work. **3.** A piece of heavy equipment used to level or smooth road surfaces.
grade school *n.* Elementary school.
gradient (grā′dē-ənt) *n.* **1.** The degree to which something inclines; a slope: *the steep gradient of the hillside.* **2.** A part that slopes upward or downward; an incline: *skidded on the icy gradient.* **3.** The rate at which a variable, such as temperature or pressure, changes over a distance.
gradual (grăj′ŏō-əl) *adj.* Occurring in small stages or degrees or by even, continuous change: *the gradual increase in prices.* —**grad′u·al·ly** *adv.*
graduate (grăj′ŏō-āt′) *v.* **graduated, graduating, graduates** —*intr.* To receive an academic degree or diploma: *graduate from high school.* —*tr.* **1.** To grant an academic degree or diploma to: *Our high school graduated 100 students.* **2.** *Informal* To graduate from: *She graduated law school in 2012.* **3.** To divide or mark into intervals

indicating measures, as of length or volume: *A thermometer is graduated into degrees.* ❖ *n.* (grăj′ŏō-ĭt) A person who has received an academic degree or diploma. ❖ *adj.* (grăj′ŏō-ĭt) **1.** Possessing an academic degree or diploma. **2.** Relating to studying beyond the bachelor's degree: *graduate courses.*
graduate school *n.* An institution of higher learning that grants master's degrees or doctorates or both.
graduation (grăj′ŏō-ā′shən) *n.* **1.** The conferral or receipt of an academic degree or diploma. **b.** A ceremony for giving out academic degrees or diplomas. **2.** Any of the marks made on a container or instrument to show amounts or measures: *The graduations on this thermometer are in red.*
graffiti (grə-fē′tē) *n.* Drawings or inscriptions made on a wall or other surface, usually so as to be seen by the public: *Graffiti is a problem in some cities.*
graft[1] (grăft) *tr.v.* **grafted, grafting, grafts** **1.** To join (a plant shoot or bud) to another living plant so that the two grow together as a single plant. **2.** To transplant (tissue or an organ) by means of surgery from one part of the body to another or from one person to another. ❖ *n.* **1.** A shoot or bud that has been grafted onto another plant. **2.** An organ or a piece of tissue transplanted by surgery.
graft[2] (grăft) *n.* **1.** The dishonest use of one's position to derive profit or advantage; extortion. **2.** Money or an advantage gained by such use.

WORD HISTORY Graft[1] comes from Middle English *graften* (meaning "to graft"), which comes from Old French *graffe,* which means "stylus" (because a graft on a plant can look like a stylus). The origin of **graft**[2] is unknown.

graham cracker (grăm or grā′əm) *n.* A slightly sweet, usually rectangular cracker made with whole-wheat flour.
graham flour *n.* Whole-wheat flour.
Grail (grāl) *n.* The Holy Grail.
grain (grān) *n.* **1a.** A small hard seed of a cereal plant such as wheat, corn, or rice: *picked up one grain of rice.* **b.** The seeds of such plants considered as a group: *buying and selling grain.* **2a.** A cereal grass: *Wheat and rye are grains.* **b.** Cereal plants considered as a group: *a field of grain.* **3a.** A small particle similar to a seed: *a grain of salt.* **b.** A small amount or the smallest possible amount: *There isn't a grain of truth in that statement.* **4.** A unit of weight equal to ⅟₅₀₀ of an ounce (0.07 gram). See table at **measurement.** **5a.** The markings, pattern, or texture in wood: *cherry wood has a fine grain.* **b.** The direction of such markings: *cut a board with the grain.* **6.** The direction or texture of fibers in a woven fabric. ❖ **with a grain of salt** With reservations; skeptically: *Take everything he says with a grain of salt.*
grain alcohol *n.* Ethanol.
grain elevator *n.* A tall hollow building for storing grain, equipped with machinery that lifts the grain so that it can be added from the top.
grainy (grā′nē) *adj.* **grainier, grainiest** **1.** Consisting of or resembling grains; granular: *grainy flour.* **2.** Resembling the grain of wood: *a grainy surface.* **3.** Having a granular appearance: *a grainy photograph.*
gram (grăm) *n.* A unit of mass or weight in the metric system, equal to about ⅟₂₈ of an ounce. See table at **measurement.**
-gram A suffix that means something written or drawn: *cardiogram; telegram.*
grammar (grăm′ər) *n.* **1.** The study of the structure of

words, the relationships between words, and the arrangement of words to make sentences. **2.** The system of rules that allow sentences to be made in a given language: *Latin grammar relies heavily on inflections.* **3.** The use of words with reference to an accepted standard among educated speakers of a language: *Students should try to write with good grammar.* **4.** A book containing the rules for making sentences in a given language: *The library has several grammars of French.*

grammarian (grə-mâr′ē-ən) *n.* A specialist in grammar.

grammar school *n.* **1.** An elementary school. **2.** *Chiefly British* A secondary or preparatory school.

grammatical (grə-măt′ĭ-kəl) *adj.* **1.** Relating to grammar: *grammatical principles.* **2.** Conforming to the rules of grammar: *a grammatical sentence.* —**gram·mat′i·cal·ly** *adv.*

gramme (grăm) *n. Chiefly British* Variant of **gram.**

gramophone (grăm′ə-fōn′) *n.* A record player; a phonograph.

granary (grăn′ə-rē *or* grā′nə-rē) *n., pl.* **granaries** A building for storing grain.

grand (grănd) *adj.* **grander, grandest 1.** Large and impressive in size, extent, or splendor; magnificent: *The grand entryway of the palace has two curved staircases.* **2.** Very pleasing or wonderful: *The children had a grand time playing in the barn.* **3a.** Having higher rank than others of the same category: *the grand admiral of the fleet.* **b.** Being the most important of a category; principal: *the grand prize.* **4.** Intended to fulfill noble or dignified wishes: *The United Nations has a grand purpose.* **5.** Including or covering all units or aspects: *the grand total.* ❖ *n.* **1.** A grand piano. **2.** *pl.* **grand** *Slang* A thousand dollars: *paid ten grand for the used car.* —**grand′ly** *adv.* —**grand′ness** *n.*

✦ SYNONYMS **grand, imposing, magnificent, majestic, stately** *adj.*

grandaunt (grănd′ănt′ *or* grănd′änt′) *n.* A great-aunt.

grandchild (grănd′chīld′ *or* grăn′chīld′) *n.* A child of one's daughter or son.

granddad (grăn′dăd′) *n. Informal* A grandfather.

granddaddy (grăn′dăd′ē) *n., pl.* **granddaddies** *Informal* A grandfather.

granddaughter (grăn′dô′tər) *n.* A daughter of one's daughter or son.

grandee (grăn-dē′) *n.* **1.** A nobleman of the highest rank in Spain or Portugal. **2.** A person of high rank or great importance.

grandeur (grăn′jər *or* grăn′jŏŏr′) *n.* The quality or condition of being grand; magnificence: *the grandeur of the pyramids in Egypt.*

grandfather (grănd′fä′thər *or* grăn′fä′thər) *n.* The father of one's mother or father.

grandfather clock *n.* A pendulum clock enclosed in a tall narrow cabinet.

grandfatherly (grănd′fä′thər-lē *or* grăn′fä′thər-lē) *adj.* Typical of or befitting a grandfather.

grandiloquent (grăn-dĭl′ə-kwənt) *adj.* Using lofty words or having a pompous style or manner. —**gran·dil′o·quence** *n.* —**gran·dil′o·quent·ly** *adv.*

grandiose (grăn′dē-ōs′ *or* grăn′dē-ōs′) *adj.* **1.** Characterized by greatness of scope or intent; grand: *The mayor unveiled a grandiose plan to develop the city's waterfront.* **2.** Characterized by excessive self-importance or affected

grandeur; pompous: *She was insulted by his grandiose apology.* —**gran′di·ose′ly** *adv.* —**gran′di·os′i·ty** (grăn′dē-ŏs′ĭ-tē), **gran′di·ose′ness** *n.*

grand jury *n.* A jury of 12 to 23 people that meets in private to evaluate accusations against a person charged with a crime and determines whether an indictment should be made.

grandma (grănd′mä′ *or* grän′mä′ *or* grăm′mä′) *n. Informal* A grandmother.

grandmother (grănd′mŭth′ər *or* grăn′mŭth′ər) *n.* The mother of one's father or mother.

grandmotherly (grănd′mŭth′ər-lē *or* grăn′mŭth′ər-lē) *adj.* Typical of or befitting a grandmother.

grandnephew (grănd′něf′yōō *or* grăn′něf′yōō) *n.* A son of one's nephew or niece.

grandniece (grănd′nēs′ *or* grăn′nēs′) *n.* A daughter of one's nephew or niece.

grandpa (grănd′pä′ *or* grän′pä′ *or* grăm′pä′) *n. Informal* A grandfather.

grandparent (grănd′pâr′ənt) *n.* A parent of one's mother or father.

grand piano *n.* A piano whose strings are mounted horizontally in a harp-shaped frame supported usually on three legs.

grand slam *n.* **1.** In baseball, a home run hit when three runners are on base. **2.** The set of major or most prestigious competitions in a sport, especially when won in a single season. **3.** In bridge, the winning of all the tricks in one hand.

grandson (grănd′sŭn′ *or* grăn′sŭn′) *n.* A son of one's daughter or son.

grandstand (grănd′stănd′ *or* grăn′stănd′) *n.* **1.** A roofed stand for spectators at a stadium or racetrack. **2.** The spectators or audience at an event. ❖ *intr.v.* **grandstand·ed, grandstanding, grandstands** To do something showily, especially in front of an audience.

granduncle (grănd′ŭng′kəl) *n.* A great-uncle.

Grange (grānj) *n.* An association of farmers founded in the United States in 1867.

granite (grăn′ĭt) *n.* A common, coarse-grained igneous rock composed mostly of quartz, feldspar, and mica, used in buildings and monuments.

granny *or* **grannie** (grăn′ē) *n., pl.* **grannies** *Informal* A grandmother.

granny knot *n.* A knot resembling a square knot but with the second tie crossed incorrectly.

granola (grə-nō′lə) *n.* Rolled oats mixed with various ingredients, such as dried fruit, brown sugar, and nuts, and used especially as a breakfast cereal.

grant (grănt) *tr.v.* **granted, granting, grants 1.** To give or allow (something asked for): *grant a request.* **2.** To confer or bestow as a favor, prerogative, or privilege: *The Constitution grants certain powers to the Supreme Court.* **3.** To concede; acknowledge: *I'll grant that it's not the best car, but it still is reliable.* ❖ *n.* **1.** The act of or an example of granting. **2.** Something granted: *The student received a grant of $10,000 for college tuition.*

grantee (grăn-tē′) *n.* A person to whom a grant is made.

grantor (grăn′tər *or* grăn′tôr′) *n.* A person or organization that makes a grant.

granular (grăn′yə-lər) *adj.* Made of or appearing to be made of grains or granules: *the granular surface of a rock; clouds with a granular texture.*

granulate (grăn′yə-lāt′) *v.* **granulated, granulating, granulates** —*tr.* **1.** To form into grains or granules. **2.** To roughen the surface of. —*intr.* To become granular or grainy. —**gran′u·la′tion** *n.*

granule (grăn′yōol) *n.* A small grain or pellet, as of sand, sugar, or ice.

grape (grāp) *n.* **1.** A small, rounded, juicy fruit having smooth purple, red, or green skin and growing in clusters on a vine. Grapes are eaten fresh, dried as raisins, or used for making wine, juice, and jelly or jam. **2.** A vine that bears such fruit.

grapefruit (grāp′frōot′) *n.* **1.** A large round fruit of an evergreen tree related to the orange, having a yellow skin and a somewhat sour taste. **2.** The tree that bears such fruit, found in warm climates.

grapeshot (grāp′shŏt′) *n.* A cluster of small iron balls fired as a single shot from a cannon.

grape sugar *n.* Dextrose obtained from grapes.

grapevine (grāp′vīn′) *n.* **1.** A vine on which grapes grow. **2.** The informal transmission of gossip, rumor, or information from person to person: *We heard through the grapevine that the coach had been fired.*

graph (grăf) *n.* **1.** A diagram showing the relationship of quantities, especially such a diagram in which lines, bars, or proportional areas represent how one quantity depends on or changes with another. **2.** A pictorial device, such as a pie chart, that illustrates quantitative relationships. **3.** A curve or line showing a mathematical function or equation. ❖ *tr.v.* **graphed, graphing, graphs** To make a graph of: *graphed seasonal rainfall over a ten-year period.*

–graph A suffix that means: **1.** Something that writes or records: *seismograph; telegraph.* **2.** Something written or drawn: *homograph.*

grapheme (grăf′ēm′) *n.* A letter of an alphabet or combination of letters that represents a phoneme. For example, *f* and *ph* are both graphemes for the phoneme *f* in *fun* and *phone.*

–grapher A suffix that means someone who writes or records: *stenographer.*

graphic (grăf′ĭk) *adj.* **1a.** Relating to written or drawn representations: *A pronunciation key is a graphic representation of speech sounds.* **b.** Relating to graphics. **c.** Relating to the graphic arts. **2.** Relating to or represented by a graph: *the graphic scale of a map.* **3.** Described or shown in vivid detail: *a witness's graphic description of the incident; graphic violence in a movie.* —**graph′i·cal·ly** *adv.*

graphic arts *pl.n.* **1.** The visual arts that involve the application of lines and strokes to a flat surface. **2.** The visual arts that involve producing images from blocks, plates, or type, as in engraving or lithography.

graphic novel *n.* A novel whose story is told through a combination of words and art, often having the form of a long comic book.

graphics (grăf′ĭks) *n.* **1.** (*used with a singular verb*) **a.** The making of drawings in accordance with the rules of mathematics, as in engineering and architecture. **b.** The process by which a computer produces and displays information as pictures, diagrams, and charts, rather than as text. **2.** (*used with a plural verb*) Graphic arts.

graphite (grăf′īt′) *n.* A crystalline form of carbon that is steel-gray to black in color and rather soft. It is used in making lubricants, paints, electrodes, and as the writing substance in pencils.

–graphy A suffix that means: **1.** Writing or representation produced in a certain way: *photography.* **2.** Writing about a specific subject: *oceanography.*

grapnel (grăp′nəl) *n.* **1.** A small anchor with three or more claws. **2.** A grappling iron.

grapple (grăp′əl) *n.* **1.** A grappling iron. **2.** A grapnel. **3.** The act of grappling. ❖ *v.* **grappled, grappling, grapples** —*tr.* To grasp and hold, as with a grappling iron. —*intr.* **1.** To hold tightly to something. **2.** To grasp someone closely, as in wrestling. **3.** To struggle: *grapple with a difficult problem.*

grappling iron (grăp′lĭng) *n.* An iron bar with claws at one end for grasping or holding something.

grasp (grăsp) *v.* **grasped, grasping, grasps** —*tr.* **1.** To seize and hold firmly with or as if with the hands: *grasped the rope and pulled; grasped the chance to play first base.* **2.** To get the full meaning of; understand: *You fail to grasp the problem.* —*intr.* **1.** To make a motion of seizing, snatching, or clutching: *grasped at the loose paddle.* **2.** To show eager acceptance: *grasped at the opportunity to go to college.* ❖ *n.* **1.** A firm hold or grip: *The puppy wriggled out of my grasp.* **2.** The ability to attain; reach: *Victory was within the team's grasp.* **3.** Understanding; comprehension: *A lecturer needs a thorough grasp of his or her subject.*

grasping (grăs′pĭng) *adj.* Eager for material gain; greedy. —**grasp′ing·ly** *adv.* —**grasp′ing·ness** *n.*

grass (grăs) *n.* **1a.** Any of numerous plants having narrow leaves, usually hollow stems, and long clusters of very small flowers. The grasses include wheat, corn, sugar cane, bamboo, and plants grown for pastures and lawns. **b.** These plants considered as a group: *planted grass in the yard.* **2.** A piece of land, such as a lawn, covered with grass: *kids playing on the grass.*

grasshopper (grăs′hŏp′ər) *n.* Any of numerous insects having two pairs of wings and long hind legs used for jumping. Grasshoppers feed on plants and sometimes destroy crops.

grassland (grăs′lănd′) *n.* An area, such as a prairie or meadow, covered with grass.

grassroots (grăs′rōots′ *or* grăs′rōots′) *pl.n.* (*used with a singular or plural verb*) Citizens at a local level rather than at the center of political activity: *The candidate received strong support from the grassroots.*

grassy (grăs′ē) *adj.* **grassier, grassiest** **1.** Covered with grass: *a grassy plain.* **2.** Resembling or suggestive of grass: *a grassy green; a grassy aroma.*

grate[1] (grāt) *v.* **grated, grating, grates** —*tr.* **1.** To reduce to fragments, shreds, or powder by rubbing against a rough surface: *grated the cabbage for coleslaw.* **2.** To cause to make a harsh grinding or rasping sound by rubbing: *She grated her teeth in anger.* —*intr.* **1.** To make a harsh grinding or rasping sound by rubbing: *The wagon grated on its rusty wheels.* **2.** To cause irritation or annoyance: *Your sarcasm grates on my nerves.*

grate[2] (grāt) *n.* **1.** A framework of parallel or interwoven bars for blocking an opening. **2.** A similar framework used to hold fuel or food in a stove, furnace, or fireplace.

WORD HISTORY Grate[1] comes from Middle English *graten* (meaning "to reduce to powder"), which comes from Old French *grater,* meaning "to scrape." **Grate**[2] comes from Middle English *grate* (meaning "framework"), which comes from Latin *crātis,* meaning "wickerwork."

---

grateful (grāt′fəl) *adj.* **1a.** Appreciative of benefits received: *I'm grateful for your help.* **b.** Expressing gratitude: *a grateful look.* **2.** Affording pleasure; agreeable: *grateful relief from the hot sun.* —**grate′ful·ly** *adv.* —**grate′ful·ness** *n.*

grater (grā'tər) *n.* A kitchen utensil with slits and perforations, used to grate food.

gratification (grăt'ə-fĭ-kā'shən) *n.* **1.** The act of gratifying or the condition of being gratified. **2.** An instance or a cause of being gratified: *Winning that prize was a great gratification to me.*

gratify (grăt'ə-fī') *tr.v.* **gratified, gratifying, gratifies 1.** To please or satisfy (someone): *I was gratified by his praise.* **2.** To give in to (a desire); indulge: *I gratified my curiosity by trying the hors d'oeuvres.* —**grat'i·fi'er** *n.* —**grat'i·fy'-ing** *adj.*

grating (grā'tĭng) *n.* A grill or network of bars set across an opening, such as a window or a street drain; a grate.

gratis (grăt'ĭs *or* grā'tĭs *or* grä'tĭs) *adv. & adj.* Without charge: *We went to the show gratis. The tickets are gratis.*

gratitude (grăt'ĭ-tōod') *n.* The state of being grateful; thankfulness: *The family was full of gratitude for their neighbor's help during the fire.*

gratuitous (grə-tōo'ĭ-təs) *adj.* **1.** Given without cost or obligation; free: *gratuitous help.* **2.** Unnecessary or unwarranted: *a gratuitous criticism.* —**gra·tu'i·tous·ly** *adv.*

gratuity (grə-tōo'ĭ-tē) *n., pl.* **gratuities** A favor or gift, usually of money, given in return for service; a tip.

grave¹ (grāv) *n.* **1.** A hole dug in the ground for the burial of a corpse. **2.** A place of burial: *The sea is the grave of many sailors.* **3.** Death or extinction.

grave² (grāv) *adj.* **graver, gravest 1.** Requiring serious thought; momentous: *a grave decision.* **2.** Fraught with danger or harm: *a grave illness.* **3.** Dignified and somber in conduct or character: *The judge looked grave.* —**grave'ly** *adv.* —**grave'ness** *n.*

grave³ (grāv) *tr.v.* **graved, graven** (grā'vən) *or* **graved, graving, graves** To sculpt or carve; engrave.

WORD HISTORY Grave¹ comes from Old English *græf,* meaning "place of burial." **Grave²** comes from Latin *gravis,* which means "heavy, important." **Grave³** comes from Old English *grafan,* which means "to dig, carve."

grave accent (grăv *or* grāv) *n.* **1.** A mark (`) indicating that an additional syllable is pronounced, as *burnèd.* **2.** A similar mark used in various languages, usually to show how a vowel is pronounced.

gravel (grăv'əl) *n.* A loose mixture of pebbles or small pieces of rock, often used for roads and walks. ❖ *tr.v.* **graveled, graveling, gravels** *or* **gravelled, gravelling, gravels** To cover with gravel: *gravel a driveway.*

gravelly (grăv'ə-lē) *adj.* **1.** Covered with or containing gravel: *gravelly soil.* **2.** Having a harsh rasping sound: *a low gravelly voice.*

graven (grā'vən) *v.* A past participle of **grave³.**

graven image *n.* An idol carved in wood or stone.

gravesite (grāv'sīt') *n.* The place where a grave is located.

gravestone (grāv'stōn') *n.* A stone placed over a grave as a marker; a tombstone.

graveyard (grāv'yärd') *n.* A cemetery.

gravid (grăv'ĭd) *adj.* Carrying developing young or eggs: *a gravid uterus; a gravid snake.* —**gra·vid'i·ty** (grə-vĭd'ĭ-tē) *n.*

gravitas (grăv'ĭ-täs') *n.* Seriousness or solemnity: *a candidate who lacks gravitas; an article with sufficient gravitas to be compelling.*

gravitate (grăv'ĭ-tāt') *intr.v.* **gravitated, gravitating, gravitates 1.** To move under the influence of gravity:

Clumps of mass gravitated together to form the galaxy. **2.** To moved toward or be attracted by something: *The grazing sheep gravitated toward the greener parts of the hillside.*

gravitation (grăv'ĭ-tā'shən) *n.* **1.** The force of attraction that tends to draw together any two objects in the universe. Gravitation increases as the mass of the objects increases and as their distance from each other decreases. **2.** The act or process of gravitating. **3.** A movement toward a source of attraction: *the gravitation of the middle class to the suburbs.* —**grav'i·ta'tion·al** *adj.* —**grav'i·ta'tion·al·ly** *adv.*

gravitropism (grə-vĭt'rə-pĭz'əm) *n.* The movement or growth of an organism in response to the earth's gravity. Examples of gravitropism include the downward growth of plant roots and the upward growth of new shoots on a plant. —**grav'i·tro'pic** (grăv'ĭ-trō'pĭk) *adj.*

gravity (grăv'ĭ-tē) *n.* **1a.** The natural force that causes objects to move or tend to move toward the center of the earth as a result of gravitation. **b.** The force of attraction that makes objects move or tend to move toward each other; gravitation. **2.** Grave consequence; seriousness or importance: *Everyone understood the gravity of the situation.*

gravy (grā'vē) *n., pl.* **gravies 1.** The juices that drip from cooking meat. **2.** A sauce made by thickening and seasoning these juices.

gray¹ also **grey** (grā) *n.* **1.** A color made by mixing black and white. **2.** often **Gray a.** A Confederate soldier in the US Civil War. **b.** The Confederate Army. ❖ *adj.* **grayer, grayest** also **greyer, greyest 1.** Having the color gray. **2.** Having gray hair. **3.** Lacking in cheer; gloomy: *a gray mood.* ❖ *tr. & intr.v.* **grayed, graying, grays** also **greyed, greying, greys** To make or become gray: *Age grays the hair. The driftwood grayed in the sun.* —**gray'ly** *adv.* —**gray'ness** *n.*

gray² (grā) *n.* A unit used to measure the energy absorbed from radiation, equal to one joule per kilogram, or to 100 rads.

WORD HISTORY Gray¹ comes from Middle English *grei,* which comes from Old English *græg,* both referring to the same color as in Modern English. **Gray²** is named after the British scientist Louis Harold *Gray* (1905–1965).

graybeard (grā'bîrd') *n.* An old man.

grayish (grā'ĭsh) *adj.* Somewhat gray.

gray matter *n.* **1.** The brownish-gray tissue of the brain and spinal cord, made up of nerve cells and fibers and some supporting tissue. **2.** *Informal* Brains; intellect: *Use your gray matter to figure out the answer.*

gray wolf *n.* A wolf of northern North America and Eurasia that ranges in color from whitish to gray to almost black.

graze¹ (grāz) *v.* **grazed, grazing, grazes** —*intr.* To feed on growing grasses and leafy plants: *Cattle grazed in the field.* —*tr.* **1.** To feed on the grass of (a piece of land): *The goats grazed the mountain pasture.* **2.** To put (livestock) out to feed: *grazed their cattle on the plains.*

graze² (grāz) *tr.v.* **grazed, grazing, grazes 1.** To touch (something) lightly in passing: *The suitcase just grazed my leg.* **2.** To scrape or scratch (something) slightly: *I fell off my bike and grazed my knees and elbows.*

WORD HISTORY Graze¹ comes from Old English *grasian,* meaning "to feed on grass." Scholars are not certain of the exact history of **graze²** but some think there is a connection between touching something lightly and grazing on grass close to the ground.

grease (grēs) *n.* **1.** Animal fat when melted or soft, often used in cooking. **2.** A thick sticky oil or similar material, used to lubricate moving parts, as of a machine. ❖ *tr.v.* (grēs *or* grēz) **greased, greasing, greases** To apply grease to: *grease the pan before cooking; grease the track of a sliding door.*

greasepaint also **grease paint** (grēs′pānt′) *n.* Makeup worn by actors, clowns, and other performers.

greasy (grē′sē *or* grē′zē) *adj.* **greasier, greasiest 1.** Coated or soiled with grease: *greasy pots and pans.* **2.** Containing grease; oily: *a greasy hamburger.* **3.** Slippery. —**greas′i·ly** *adv.* —**greas′i·ness** *n.*

great (grāt) *adj.* **greater, greatest 1.** Very large in size, number, amount, or extent: *a great pile of rubble; a great storm.* See Synonyms at **large**. **2.** Remarkable or outstanding in magnitude or degree: *a great crisis.* **3.** Important; significant: *The signing of the treaty was a great moment in history.* **4.** Prominent; distinguished: *a great athlete.* **5.** Being one generation removed from the relative specified: *a great-granddaughter.* **6.** *Informal* Enthusiastic: *a great tennis fan.* **7.** *Informal* **a.** Very good; first-rate: *a great party; a great time.* **b.** Very skillful: *great at algebra.* —**great′ness** *n.*

great-aunt or **great aunt** (grāt′ănt′ *or* grāt′änt′) *n.* A sister of one's grandparent.

great circle *n.* A circle on a sphere that has its plane passing through the center of the sphere, as the great circle of the earth's equator does.

greatcoat (grāt′kōt′) *n.* A heavy overcoat.

Great Dane *n.* A large dog of a breed developed in Europe to hunt boars, having a muscular body, a smooth short coat, and a narrow head.

Great Depression *n.* The worldwide economic depression from the late 1920s through the 1930s.

greatest common divisor (grā′tĭst) *n.* The largest number that divides evenly into each of a given set of numbers. For example, the greatest common divisor of 16, 20, and 32 is 4.

great-grandchild (grāt′grănd′chīld′ *or* grāt′grăn′chīld′) *n.* A child of one's grandchild.

great-grandparent (grāt′grănd′pâr′ənt) *n.* The parent of one's grandparent.

greathearted (grāt′här′tĭd) *adj.* **1.** Courageous or noble in spirit. **2.** Generous; magnanimous: *The great-hearted landowner donated land for a park.*

greatly (grāt′lē) *adv.* To a great degree; very much: *Families vary greatly in size.*

Great Spirit *n.* The principal god in the religion of many Native American peoples.

great-uncle or **great uncle** (grāt′ŭng′kəl) *n.* A brother of one's grandparent.

greave (grēv) *n.* A piece of armor worn below the knee to protect the front of the leg.

grebe (grēb) *n.* Any of various diving birds having a pointed bill and fleshy membranes along each toe that help them swim.

Grecian (grē′shən) *adj.* Greek. ❖ *n.* A native or inhabitant of Greece.

greed (grēd) *n.* A selfish desire for more than one needs or deserves.

greedy (grē′dē) *adj.* **greedier, greediest 1.** Filled with greed; wanting more than one needs or deserves: *The greedy prospector refused to share with his partners.* **2.**

Having or showing a desire to consume large amounts of food or drink. —**greed′i·ly** *adv.* —**greed′i·ness** *n.*

Greek (grēk) *adj.* Relating to Greece or its people, language, or culture. ❖ *n.* **1.** The Indo-European language of ancient or modern Greece. **2.** A native or inhabitant of Greece. **3.** Something that is unintelligible: *Robotics is Greek to me.*

Greek alphabet *n.* The alphabet of ancient and modern Greece, derived from the alphabet used by the Phoenicians.

Greek Orthodox Church *n.* Any of several branches of the Eastern Orthodox Church that use Greek liturgy, such as the state church of Greece.

green (grēn) *n.* **1.** The color of most plant leaves and growing grass. In the spectrum it is between yellow and blue. **2. greens a.** The branches and leaves of green plants used for decoration: *decorated the house with greens.* **b.** Leaves that are eaten as vegetables: *salad greens.* **3.** A grassy area located usually at the common of a town or city; a common: *the village green.* **4.** In golf, the area of short smooth grass that surrounds a hole. **5.** often **Green** A person or movement that supports environmental protection. ❖ *adj.* **greener, greenest 1.** Of the color green: *a green sweater.* **2.** Covered with growing plants, grass, or foliage: *green meadows.* **3.** Not mature or ripe: *a green banana.* **4.** Lacking training or experience: *green musicians.* **5.** Beneficial to the environment or supporting environmentalism: *green recycling laws; green voters.*

greenback (grēn′băk′) *n.* A piece of paper money of US currency.

green bean *n.* A string bean.

green card *n.* A card issued by the US government to citizens of foreign countries, allowing them to work legally in the United States.

greenery (grē′nə-rē) *n.* Green plants or leaves, especially when used for decoration.

greengrocer (grēn′grō′sər) *n. Chiefly British* A person who sells fresh fruit and vegetables.

greenhorn (grēn′hôrn′) *n.* An inexperienced or immature person, especially one who is easily fooled.

greenhouse (grēn′hous′) *n.* A room or building with the roof and sides made of glass or clear plastic, used for growing plants that need an even, usually warm temperature; a hothouse.

greenhouse effect *n.* The trapping of the sun's radiation in the earth's atmosphere. It is caused by the presence of carbon dioxide, water vapor, and other gases in the atmosphere, which allows incoming sunlight to pass through but retains heat radiated back from the earth's surface. Most scientists believe that the greenhouse effect has increased since the late 1800s because of the burning of fossil fuels.

greenhouse gas *n.* An atmospheric gas that contributes to the greenhouse effect.

greenish (grē′nĭsh) *adj.* Somewhat green.

green light *n.* **1.** A green light that signals traffic to proceed. **2.** Permission to proceed: *The city gave us the green light to start a community garden.*

green pepper *n.* The unripened green fruit of any of various varieties of the pepper plant.

greenskeeper (grēnz′kē′pər) *n.* A person who is responsible for maintaining a golf course.

greenstrip (grēn′strĭp′) *n.* A strip of land planted with vegetation that is resistant to fire in order to slow the spread of wildfires.

greensward (grēn′swôrd′) *n.* Ground that is green with grass.

green thumb *n.* An ability to make plants grow well.

Greenwich Mean Time *n.* Coordinated universal time, used as the standard time in the United Kingdom.

greet (grēt) *tr.v.* **greeted, greeting, greets 1.** To speak to (someone) in a friendly manner to acknowledge their presence or welcome them to a place or gathering: *The hosts greeted their guests.* **2.** To receive or acknowledge (information, for example) with a specified reaction: *Our parents greeted the news with great joy.* **3.** To be perceived by: *A cry of "Surprise!" greeted our ears.*

greeting (grē′tĭng) *n.* A gesture or word of welcome or salutation.

gregarious (grĭ-gâr′ē-əs) *adj.* **1.** Seeking out and enjoying the company of others; sociable: *a gregarious person.* **2.** Living in flocks, herds, colonies, or similar groups with others of the same kind: *Zebras are gregarious.* —**gre·gar′i·ous·ly** *adv.* —**gre·gar′i·ous·ness** *n.*

Gregorian calendar (grĭ-gôr′ē-ən) *n.* The calendar in use throughout most of the world, sponsored by Pope Gregory XIII (1502–1585) in 1582 as a corrected version of the Julian calendar.

Gregorian chant *n.* A liturgical chant that is sung without accompaniment.

gremlin (grĕm′lĭn) *n.* An imaginary creature whose mischief is said to cause mechanical failures.

grenade (grə-nād′) *n.* **1.** A small bomb detonated by a fuse and thrown by hand or fired from a launcher. **2.** A glass bottle filled with a chemical that is scattered when the bottle is thrown and smashed.

grenadier (grĕn′ə-dîr′) *n.* **1.** A soldier equipped with grenades. **2.** A member of the British Grenadier Guards, the first regiment of the royal household infantry.

grew (grōō) *v.* Past tense of **grow.**

grey (grā) *n. & adj. & v.* Variant of **gray**[1].

greyhound (grā′hound′) *n.* A dog of a tall slender breed having a narrow head and a smooth coat. It was originally bred to hunt fast prey and is often used for racing.

grid (grĭd) *n.* **1.** A pattern of regularly spaced horizontal and vertical lines forming squares of equal size, such as those used on a map or graph as a reference for locating points: *The map grid is labeled with letters for ease of reference.* **2.** A framework of parallel or crisscrossed bars; a grating. **3.** Something resembling such a framework, as in organization: *city streets arranged as a grid.* **4.** A network of power stations and wires for the distribution of electricity to buildings, street lights, and other facilities. **5.** A metal conducting plate in a storage battery.

griddle (grĭd′l) *n.* A heavy flat metal surface, such as a pan, that is used for cooking by dry heat.

griddlecake (grĭd′l-kāk′) *n.* A pancake.

gridiron (grĭd′ī′ərn) *n.* **1.** A flat framework of parallel metal bars used to broil meat or fish; a grill. **2.** A football field.

gridlock (grĭd′lŏk′) *n.* **1.** A complete halt in the movement of motor vehicle traffic, especially at an intersection of major streets. **2.** A complete halt in an activity, resulting in a backup: *Political gridlock between the president and Congress is preventing progress on this year's budget.*

grief (grēf) *n.* **1.** Deep anguish or sorrow, such as that caused by someone's death. **2.** Annoyance, frustration, or difficulty: *The new software has caused us nothing but*

grief. 3. *Informal* Criticism: *They gave him grief for being so late.*

grievance (grē′vəns) *n.* **1.** A real or imagined wrong regarded as just cause for complaint: *Lack of affordable housing is a legitimate grievance.* **2.** A complaint based on such a circumstance: *delivered a list of grievances to the mayor.*

grieve (grēv) *v.* **grieved, grieving, grieves** —*tr.* **1.** To cause to be sorrowful; distress: *The news grieved us deeply.* **2.** To mourn or sorrow for: *grieved the death of his favorite aunt.* —*intr.* To experience or express grief.

grievous (grē′vəs) *adj.* **1.** Causing grief, pain, or sorrow: *a grievous loss.* **2.** Serious or grave; dire: *a grievous crime.* —**griev′ous·ly** *adv.* —**griev′ous·ness** *n.*

griffin also **griffon** or **gryphon** (grĭf′ən) *n.* A fabled beast with the head and wings of an eagle and the body of a lion.

grill (grĭl) *tr.v.* **grilled, grilling, grills 1.** To cook on a grill: *grill fish in the backyard.* **2.** *Informal* To question closely and relentlessly; cross-examine: *The lawyer grilled a witness on the stand.* ❖ *n.* **1.** A cooking utensil of parallel metal bars; a gridiron. **2.** Food cooked by broiling or grilling. **3.** An informal restaurant where grilled foods are served. **4.** Variant of **grille.**

grille also **grill** (grĭl) *n.* A metal or wood grating, often of decorative design, that covers a door, window, or other opening or the front end of a motor vehicle.

grim (grĭm) *adj.* **grimmer, grimmest 1.** Discouraging or depressing: *The business news has been very grim lately.* **2.** Stern or unnerving in appearance or behavior; forbidding: *The judge was grim when sentencing the criminal.* **3.** Dismal; gloomy: *We started our trip on a grim, rainy morning.* **4.** Repellent or horrifying: *the grim task of searching for survivors of the crash.* **5.** Unrelenting; rigid: *worked with grim determination.* —**grim′ly** *adv.* —**grim′ness** *n.*

grimace (grĭm′ĭs) *n.* A sharp contortion of the face, expressing pain, disgust, or contempt: *His face contracted in a grimace.* ❖ *intr.v.* **grimaced, grimacing, grimaces** To make a sharp contortion of the face: *Most people grimace when tasting a lemon.*

grime (grīm) *n.* Black dirt or soot clinging to or ground into a surface.

Grim Reaper *n.* The personification of death as a cloaked man or skeleton carrying a scythe.

grimy (grī′mē) *adj.* **grimier, grimiest** Covered with grime: *The window was so grimy it was impossible to see through it.* See Synonyms at **dirty.** —**grim′i·ly** *adv.* —**grim′i·ness** *n.*

grin (grĭn) *v.* **grinned, grinning, grins** —*intr.* To smile broadly: *grin with delight.* —*tr.* To express with a grin: *Our host grinned a warm welcome.* ❖ *n.* A broad smile: *a happy grin.*

grind (grīnd) *v.* **ground** (ground), **grinding, grinds** —*tr.* **1.** To reduce to small bits or crush to a fine powder: *grind wheat into flour; grind coffee beans.* **2.** To shape, smooth, or sharpen by rubbing on something rough: *grind scissors to a fine edge; grind lenses for eyeglasses.* **3.** To rub or press (two surfaces) together harshly: *grind the teeth.* **4.** To bear down on harshly; crush: *The team's spirit was ground down by a string of losses.* **5.** To operate by turning a crank: *grind a hurdy-gurdy.* **6.** To produce mechanically or without inspiration: *grinding out cheap novels.* —*intr.* **1.** To become crushed, pulverized, or powdered by friction. **2.** To move noisily with great friction: *The train* *ground to a halt.* **3.** *Informal* To devote oneself to study or work: *grind away at a long report.* ❖ *n.* **1.** The action or sound of grinding: *the grind of the brakes.* **2a.** A specific grade or degree of pulverization: *a fine grind of coffee.* **b.** **grinds** Grounds, as of coffee. **3.** *Informal* A laborious task, routine, or study: *the daily grind of commuting.* **4.** *Informal* A student who works or studies all the time. —**grind′ing·ly** *adv.*

grinder (grīn′dər) *n.* **1.** A person who grinds, especially a person who sharpens scissors, knives, or other tools. **2.** A mechanical device for grinding: *a meat grinder.* **3.** One of the back teeth used for grinding food; a molar. **4.** A submarine sandwich.

grindstone (grīnd′stōn′) *n.* **1.** A revolving stone disk used for grinding, polishing, or sharpening tools. **2.** A mill-stone. ◆ **keep (one's) nose to the grindstone** To work hard and steadily.

gringa (grĭng′gə) *n. Often Offensive* A foreign woman in Spanish-speaking parts of North or South America, especially one who is American or English.

gringo (grĭng′gō) *n., pl.* **gringos** *Often Offensive* A foreign man in Spanish-speaking parts of North or South America, especially one who is American or English.

griot (grē-ō′ *or* grē′ōt) *n.* A storyteller in western Africa who perpetuates the oral tradition and history of a village or family.

grip (grĭp) *n.* **1.** A tight hold; a firm grasp: *a good grip on the rope.* **2.** A manner of grasping and holding: *The grip for holding a baseball bat is different from the grip for swinging a golf club.* **3.** A part designed to be grasped and held; a handle: *the grips on the handlebars of a bicycle.* **4.** Ability to function well or properly; competence: *have a good grip on the new technique.* **5.** Understanding; mastery: *He now has a good grip on Spanish.* **6.** A suitcase or valise. ❖ *tr.v.* **gripped, gripping, grips** **1.** To grasp and hold tightly; seize firmly: *The gymnast gripped the bar as she swung herself back and forth.* **2.** To gain traction on or apply pressure that does not slip to (a surface): *The new tires grip the road really well.* **3.** To hold the interest and attention of: *a real-life drama that gripped the nation.*

gripe (grĭp) *v.* **griped, griping, gripes** —*intr. Informal* To complain; grumble: *Everyone griped about the new regulations.* —*tr. Informal* To irritate; annoy: *The criticisms really griped me.* ❖ *n.* **1.** *Informal* A complaint: *Everyone has some gripe about winter weather.* **2.** **gripes** Sharp repeated pains in the bowels.

grippe (grĭp) *n.* Influenza.

grisly (grĭz′lē) *adj.* **grislier, grisliest** Inspiring repugnance; gruesome. —**gris′li·ness** *n.*

grist (grĭst) *n.* **1.** Grain or a quantity of grain for grinding. **2.** Grain that has been ground.

gristle (grĭs′əl) *n.* Tough tissue or cartilage, especially when found in meat.

gristly (grĭs′lē) *adj.* **gristlier, gristliest** Composed of, resembling, or containing gristle: *a gristly piece of steak.*

gristmill (grĭst′mĭl′) *n.* A mill for grinding grain.

grit (grĭt) *n.* **1.** Tiny rough particles, as of sand or stone: *Grit had collected on the chain of my bicycle.* **2.** A coarse sandstone used for grindstones and millstones. **3.** *Informal* Indomitable spirit; great courage and determination: *To be a good athlete one needs plenty of grit.* ❖ *v.* **gritted, gritting, grits** —*tr.* To clamp or grind (the teeth) together. —*intr.* To make a grinding noise: *Wagon wheels gritted over the lane.*

grits (grĭts) *pl.n.* (used with a singular or plural verb) **1.** Coarsely ground hominy or corn kernels cooked and served for breakfast or as a side dish. **2.** Coarsely ground grain, especially corn.

gritty (grĭt′ē) *adj.* **grittier, grittiest** **1.** Containing, covered with, or resembling grit. **2.** Showing determination and strength; plucky. —**grit′ti·ness** *n.*

grizzled (grĭz′əld) *adj.* **1.** Streaked with or partly gray: *a grizzled beard.* **2.** Having fur or hair streaked or tipped with gray.

grizzly (grĭz′lē) *adj.* **grizzlier, grizzliest** Grayish or flecked with gray. ❖ *n., pl.* **grizzlies** A grizzly bear.

grizzly bear *n.* A large brown bear of western North America having grizzled fur.

groan (grōn) *v.* **groaned, groaning, groans** —*intr.* **1.** To utter a deep and prolonged sound, as of pain, grief, or displeasure: *groan over a toothache.* **2.** To make a low creaking sound resembling this: *The floorboards groaned.* —*tr.* To utter or communicate by groaning: *The audience groaned their dissatisfaction.* ❖ *n.* The sound made in groaning. —**groan′er** *n.*

groats (grōts) *pl.n.* (used with a singular or plural verb) Grain or seeds, such as oats, barley, or buckwheat, from which the hulls have been removed.

grocer (grō′sər) *n.* A storekeeper who sells food and household supplies.

grocery (grō′sə-rē) *n., pl.* **groceries** **1.** A store selling food and household supplies. **2.** **groceries** The goods sold by a grocer.

grog (grŏg) *n.* Rum or another liquor diluted with water.

groggy (grŏg′ē) *adj.* **groggier, groggiest** Unsteady and dazed; shaky: *still groggy from a bout with the flu.* —**grog′gi·ly** *adv.* —**grog′gi·ness** *n.*

groin (groin) *n.* **1.** The area of the body where the thighs join the trunk of the body. **2.** In architecture, the curved line where two ceiling vaults come together.

grommet (grŏm′ĭt) *n.* **1.** A reinforced eyelet, as in cloth or leather. **2.** A small metal or plastic ring used to reinforce an eyelet.

groom (grōom *or* grŏŏm) *n.* **1.** A person employed to take care of horses. **2.** A man who is about to be married or has recently been married. ❖ *tr.v.* **groomed, grooming, grooms** **1.** To make neat and trim, especially in personal appearance: *groomed themselves in front of the mirror before going to the party.* **2.** To clean and brush (an animal). **3.** To remove dirt and parasites from the skin, fur, or feathers of: *The baboons groomed each other.* **4.** To train (a person), as for a certain job or position: *groom a successor to the manager.* **5.** To prepare (terrain) for use in a sport, as by packing down new snow and leveling bumps for skiers: *groom a ski slope; groom a trail for hiking.*

groomsman (grōomz′mən *or* grŏŏmz′mən) *n.* A man who accompanies and assists the bridegroom at a wedding.

groove (grōov) *n.* **1.** A long narrow furrow or channel: *The drawer moves in and out on grooves.* **2.** *Slang* A settled or comfortable routine: *We got out of the groove over vacation.* ❖ *tr.v.* **grooved, grooving, grooves** To cut a groove or grooves in: *groove the surface of a highway.* ◆ **in the groove** *Informal* **1.** In a condition where a person consistently performs a task well. **2.** In a condition where a person feels good or content.

groovy (grōo′vē) *adj.* **groovier, grooviest** *Slang* Very pleasing; wonderful: *a groovy song.* —**groov′i·ly** *adv.* —**groov′i·ness** *n.*

grope (grōp) *v.* **groped, groping, gropes** —*intr.* To reach about or search blindly or uncertainly: *grope for the light switch; grope for an answer.* —*tr.* To make (one's way) by reaching about uncertainly: *grope one's way down a long dark hall.* —**grop′ing·ly** *adv.*

grosbeak (grōs′bēk′) *n.* Any of various birds having a thick rounded bill and often colorful feathers.

grosgrain (grō′grān′) *n.* **1.** A heavy woven silk or rayon fabric having narrow horizontal ribs. **2.** A ribbon made of this fabric.

gross (grōs) *adj.* **grosser, grossest 1.** Very easy to see; obvious or glaring: *a gross error.* **2.** On a large scale; not fine or detailed: *gross anatomical similarities between the two species.* **3.** Having nothing subtracted; total: *gross pay of $9.50 an hour.* **4.** Vulgar; coarse: *a gross remark.* **5.** Offensive; disgusting: *They haven't done the dishes in days, and the kitchen is gross.* **6.** Overweight; fat. ❖ *n., pl.* **gross 1.** The entire body or amount, as of income, before the necessary deductions have been made: *The company's gross was impressive, but once expenses were figured in, it didn't seem so great.* **2.** A group of 144 items; 12 dozen: *This box holds a gross of oranges.* ❖ *tr.v.* **grossed, grossing, grosses** To earn as a total income or profit before deductions: *The business grosses about $10,000 each month.* ◆ **gross out** To fill with disgust; nauseate: *The violent scene in the movie grossed me out.* —**gross′ly** *adv.* —**gross′ness** *n.*

gross domestic product *n.* The total market value of all the goods and services that are produced inside a nation during a specified period.

gross national product *n.* The total market value of all goods and services produced by a nation during a specified period.

grotesque (grō-tĕsk′) *adj.* **1.** Distorted or unattractive in a repulsive or laughable way: *the grotesque features of a gargoyle.* **2.** Outlandish or bizarre, especially in a shocking way: *a grotesque story of a mistreated dog that takes revenge on humans.* —**gro·tesque′ly** *adv.* —**gro·tesque′ness** *n.*

grotto (grŏt′ō) *n., pl.* **grottoes** or **grottos 1.** A small cave or cavern. **2.** A structure or excavation built to look like a cave or cavern.

WORD HISTORY The word **grotto** comes from Italian, where its form is *grotta.* This in turn comes from an earlier word *grupta* or *crupta. Crupta* comes from the Latin word *crypta,* "an underground vault, chamber, or pit," the source of our word **crypt.**

grouch (grouch) *n.* **1.** A person who habitually complains or grumbles. **2.** A grumbling or sulky mood: *in a grouch for no good reason.* ❖ *intr.v.* **grouched, grouching, grouches** To complain; grumble: *Why grouch about the weather?*

grouchy (grou′chē) *adj.* **grouchier, grouchiest** Tending to complain or grumble; peevish: *Don't be so grouchy!* —**grouch′i·ly** *adv.* —**grouch′i·ness** *n.*

ground¹ (ground) *n.* **1.** The solid surface of the earth; land; soil: *The ground is still frozen.* **2.** often **grounds** An area or plot of land set aside for a special purpose: *parade grounds; a burial ground.* **b.** The land surrounding a house or other building: *the school grounds.* **3.** often **grounds** The basis or reason for a belief or action: *grounds for making an accusation.* **4.** An area of reference or discussion; a subject: *covered new ground in today's talk.* **5.** A surrounding area; a background: *The flag has white stars on a blue ground.* **6. grounds a.** The

sediment that settles at the bottom of a liquid, such as coffee. **b.** Particles of ground coffee beans for use in making coffee for drinking; grinds. **7.** A connection between an electrical conductor and the earth. ❖ *v.* **grounded, grounding, grounds** —*tr.* **1.** To place on or cause to touch the ground. **2.** To run (a vessel) aground: *We grounded our boat by accident.* **3.** To instruct in fundamentals or basics: *This class grounds students in basic economics.* **4.** To provide a basis for (a theory, for example); justify: *grounded his argument on facts.* **5.** To connect (an electric circuit or conductor) with the earth. **6.** To prevent (an aircraft or pilot) from flying: *Bad weather grounded all flights.* **7.** To restrict (someone) to a certain place as a punishment: *Her parents grounded her for a week because of her bad behavior.* **8.** In baseball, to hit (a ball) onto the ground. —*intr.* **1.** To touch or reach the ground. **2.** To run aground: *The ship grounded in the storm.* **3.** In baseball, to hit a ground ball. ◆ **ground out** In baseball, to be put out by hitting a ground ball that is fielded and thrown to first base.

ground² (ground) *v.* Past tense and past participle of **grind.**

ground ball *n.* In baseball, a batted ball that rolls or bounces along the ground.

groundbreaking (ground′brā′kĭng) *n.* The act or ceremony of turning up ground to start construction: *Groundbreaking for the new hospital is happening today.* ❖ *adj.* Characterized by originality and innovation: *groundbreaking technology.*

ground crew *n.* A team of mechanics and technicians that maintain and service aircraft on the ground.

grounder (groun′dər) *n.* A ground ball.

ground floor *n.* **1.** The floor of a building at or nearest ground level. **2.** *Informal* The start of something, as a project or business: *I started in this business on the ground floor as a messenger.*

groundhog (ground′hôg′) *n.* The woodchuck.

Groundhog Day *n.* February 2. According to popular legend, there will be an early spring if the groundhog does not see its shadow when coming out of its burrow on this day, or there will be six more weeks of winter weather if it does see its shadow.

groundless (ground′lĭs) *adj.* Having no ground or foundation; unsupported by the facts: *groundless worries.* —**ground′less·ly** *adv.* —**ground′less·ness** *n.*

groundnut (ground′nŭt′) *n.* **1.** Any of several plants having edible underground tubers that resemble nuts. **2.** Any of several plants, such as the peanut, having edible underground seeds. **3.** The seed or tuber of any of these plants.

ground pine *n.* Any of various low-growing club mosses that look like miniature evergreen trees.

ground rule *n.* often **ground rules** A basic rule: *ground rules for tennis; set ground rules for a club.*

ground squirrel *n.* Any of several small burrowing rodents that have large eyes and small ears and sometimes a spotted or striped back.

groundswell (ground′swĕl′) *n.* **1.** Deep rolling waves in the ocean, often the result of a distant storm or an earthquake. **2.** A sudden gathering of force, as of public opinion: *a groundswell of support for the proposed law.*

groundwater also **ground water** (ground′wô′tər) *n.* Water that flows or seeps beneath the surface of the earth, soaking soil or porous rock and supplying wells and springs.

groundwork (ground′wûrk′) *n.* Work that lays the basis for something; a foundation.

ground zero *n.* **1a.** The site of a terrorist bombing or other violent act of destruction. **b.** The site directly below, directly above, or at the point of detonation of a nuclear weapon. **2.** The center of rapid or intense development or change. **3.** The starting point or most basic level: *My client didn't like my preliminary designs, so I returned to ground zero.*

group (grōōp) *n.* **1.** A number of people or things gathered or located together: *a group of students in a museum; a group of islands off the coast of Alaska.* **2.** A number of people or things classed together because of similarities: *The idea has a small group of supporters across the country.* **3.** Two or more atoms bound together that act as a unit in a number of chemical compounds: *a hydroxyl group.* **4.** In the periodic table, a vertical column that contains elements having similar properties. ❖ *v.* **grouped, grouping, groups** —*tr.* To place or arrange in a group: *group books on the same topic together.* —*intr.* To belong to or form a group: *The class grouped on the steps to pose for a picture.*

USAGE The word **group** as a *collective noun* can be followed by a singular or plural verb. It takes a singular verb when those making up the group are considered as a body: *The group is all here for the party. Group* takes a plural verb when those making up the group are considered individually: *The group are arguing about where to go for pizza.*

grouper (grōō′pər) *n., pl.* **grouper** or **groupers** Any of various large tropical or subtropical ocean fishes, many of which are valued as food.

grouping (grōō′pǐng) *n.* **1.** The act or process of uniting in groups: *The grouping of the children into teams took several minutes.* **2.** A collection of things or people united in a group: *There is a large grouping of reference books in the library.*

grouse[1] (grous) *n., pl.* **grouse** or **grouses** Any of various plump, ground-dwelling birds having mottled brown or grayish feathers on the body and legs, often hunted as game.

grouse[2] (grous) *Informal intr.v.* **groused, grousing, grouses** To complain; grumble: *groused about the poor hotel service.*

WORD HISTORY The origin of **grouse**[1] is unknown. **Grouse**[2] may come from Old French *grouchier*, meaning "to complain."

grout (grout) *n.* **a.** A thin mortar used to fill cracks and crevices in masonry. **b.** A thin plaster for finishing walls and ceilings. ❖ *tr.v.* **grouted, grouting, grouts** To fill or finish with a thin mortar or plaster. —**grout′er** *n.*

grove (grōv) *n.* A group of trees with open ground between them, as in an orchard: *an orange grove.*

grovel (grŏv′əl *or* grŭv′əl) *intr.v.* **groveled, groveling, grovels** also **grovelled, grovelling, grovels** **1.** To behave in a servile or demeaning manner; cringe: *Be proud of yourself and do not grovel.* **2.** To lie flat or crawl on one's belly, as in humility or submission: *The dog began to grovel at its owner's feet.* —**grov′el·er, grov′el·ler** *n.*

grow (grō) *v.* **grew** (grōō), **grown** (grōn), **growing, grows** —*intr.* **1.** To become bigger by a natural process of development; mature: *The seedlings grew into plants.* **2.** To be capable of growth; thrive; flourish: *Banana trees grow well in tropical climates.* **3.** To increase or spread; expand: *The business grew rapidly.* **4.** To come to be by a gradual process or by degrees: *grow rich; grow dark outside.* —*tr.* **1.** To cause to grow; produce; cultivate: *grow vegetables in a garden.* **2.** To allow (something) to develop or increase by a natural process: *grow a beard.* ◆ **grow out of** To develop or come into existence from: *The book grew out of our scribbled notes.* **grow up** To become an adult. —**grow′er** *n.*

growl (groul) *n.* **1.** A low, throaty, menacing sound made by an animal: *the growl of a dog.* **2.** A gruff surly utterance: *answered me with a growl.* ❖ *v.* **growled, growling, growls** —*intr.* **1.** To make a low throaty sound or utterance. **2.** To speak in a surly or angry manner. —*tr.* To utter by growling: *The dog growled a warning.*

grown (grōn) *v.* Past participle of **grow.** ❖ *adj.* **1.** Having full growth; mature: *act like a grown person.* **2.** Produced or cultivated: *locally grown produce.*

grownup also **grown-up** (grōn′ŭp′) *n.* An adult.

grown-up (grōn′ŭp′) *adj.* **1.** Relating to or intended for adults: *a grown-up movie.* **2.** Having or showing maturity in outlook, attitude, or appearance: *Apologizing was a very grown-up thing to do.*

growth (grōth) *n.* **1.** The process of growing; development: *the growth of a child.* **2.** Something that grows or has grown: *A thick growth of weeds covered the yard.* **3.** An amount grown; an increase or expansion: *measure the growth of a country's population.* **4.** An abnormal mass of tissue growing in or on a living organism: *A wart is a growth on the body.*

growth ring *n.* A layer of wood formed in a plant during a single period of growth, appearing as a ring-shaped band when a tree or shrub is cut crosswise.

grub (grŭb) *v.* **grubbed, grubbing, grubs** —*tr.* **1.** To dig up by the roots: *grub turnips.* **2.** To clear of roots and stumps by digging: *grubbed a small plot.* —*intr.* **1.** To dig in the ground: *grub for potatoes.* **2.** To work hard, especially at menial tasks; drudge: *grub for a living.* ❖ *n.* **1.** The thick wormlike larva of certain beetles and other insects. **2.** *Slang* Food: *buy the grub for a camping trip.*

grubby (grŭb′ē) *adj.* **grubbier, grubbiest** Dirty; grimy: *grubby work clothes.* —**grub′bi·ly** *adv.* —**grub′bi·ness** *n.*

grubstake (grŭb′stāk′) *n.* Supplies or funds advanced to a mining prospector or a person starting a business in return for a promised share of the profits. ❖ *tr.v.* **grubstaked, grubstaking, grubstakes** To supply with a grubstake.

grudge (grŭj) *tr.v.* **grudged, grudging, grudges** To be reluctant to give or admit: *grudged me a small discount for paying in cash.* ❖ *n.* A deep-seated feeling of resentment: *holds a grudge about the accident.*

grudging (grŭj′ĭng) *adj.* Reluctant; unwilling: *grudging admiration for his opponent's success.* —**grudg′ing·ly** *adv.*

gruel (grōō′əl) *n.* A thin, watery porridge.

grueling (grōō′ə-lĭng *or* grōō′lĭng) *adj.* Physically or mentally exhausting: *Working in a coal mine is a grueling job.*

gruesome (grōō′səm) *adj.* Causing horror and shock; frightful: *a gruesome accident.* —**grue′some·ly** *adv.* —**grue′some·ness** *n.*

gruff (grŭf) *adj.* **gruffer, gruffest** **1.** Brusque or stern in manner or appearance: *a gruff reply.* **2.** Harsh-sounding; hoarse: *a gruff voice.* —**gruff′ly** *adv.* —**gruff′ness** *n.*

grumble (grŭm′bəl) *v.* **grumbled, grumbling, grumbles** —*intr.* **1.** To complain in a surly manner; mutter in discontent: *They grumbled about the store's prices.* **2.** To rumble or growl. —*tr.* To express in a grumbling or discontented manner: *grumbled a response.* ❖ *n.* **1.** A muttered complaint. **2.** A rumble; a growl: *the grumble of distant thunder.* —**grum′bler** *n.*

grumpy (grŭm′pē) *adj.* **grumpier, grumpiest** Surly and peevish; cranky: *a grumpy mood.* —**grump′i·ly** *adv.* —**grump′i·ness** *n.*

grunge (grŭnj) *n.* **1.** *Informal* Filth; dirt. **2.** Raucous rock music with lyrics that express dissatisfaction, despair, or apathy.

grungy (grŭn′jē) *adj.* **grungier, grungiest** *Informal* In a dirty, rundown, or inferior condition: *grungy socks.*

grunt (grŭnt) *v.* **grunted, grunting, grunts** —*intr.* **1.** To make a deep throaty sound, as a hog does. **2.** To make a sound similar to a grunt, as in disgust. —*tr.* To utter or express with a deep throaty sound: *The irritated clerk grunted a reply.* ❖ *n.* **1.** A deep throaty sound, as that made by a hog. **2.** Any of the various chiefly tropical ocean fishes that make grunting sounds. **3.** *Slang* A soldier in the infantry, especially during the Vietnam War. **4.** *Slang* A person who performs routine or mundane tasks.

Gruyère (grōō-yâr′) *n.* A nutty, pale yellow, firm cheese made from cow's milk.

gryphon (grĭf′ən) *n.* Variant of **griffin.**

guacamole (gwŏk′ə-mō′lē) *n.* A thick paste of mashed avocado, often combined with citrus juice, onion, and seasonings and usually served as a dip.

guanaco (gwə-nä′kō) *n., pl.* **guanacos** or **guanaco** A brownish South American mammal that resembles the llama and has fine, soft wool.

guanine (gwä′nēn′) *n.* A base that is a component of DNA and RNA.

guano (gwä′nō) *n.* The dung of certain seabirds or bats, used as fertilizer.

Guarani (gwä′rə-nē′) *n., pl.* **Guarani** or **Guaranis** **1.** A member of a South American Indian people of Paraguay, Argentina, and Brazil. **2.** The language of this people.

guarantee (găr′ən-tē′) *n.* **1.** Something that assures a particular condition or outcome: *Wealth is not a guarantee of happiness.* **2.** A promise or assurance that attests to the quality or durability of a product or service. **3.** A guaranty. ❖ *tr.v.* **guaranteed, guaranteeing, guarantees** **1.** To render certain; make sure: *The rains guarantee a good crop.* **2.** To undertake to accomplish (something) for another: *Jefferson wanted to guarantee freedom of speech for future generations.* **3.** To assume responsibility for the quality or performance of: *The manufacturer guarantees these microwave ovens for two years.* **4.** To provide security for: *Insurance guarantees a car owner against costs of injury or of repairs.*

guarantor (găr′ən-tôr′ *or* găr′ən-tər) *n.* A person or business that makes or gives a guarantee or guaranty.

guaranty (găr′ən-tē) *n., pl.* **guaranties** **1.** An agreement to assume the responsibility of payment or fulfillment of another's debts or obligations: *My cousin signed a guaranty for my bank loan.* **2.** Something given as security for the fulfillment of an obligation or the payment of a debt. **3.** A guarantee, as for a product or service. ❖ *tr.v.* **guarantied, guarantying, guaranties** **1.** To provide a guaranty for: *Employers sometimes guaranty loans for trusted employees.* **2.** To guarantee.

guard (gärd) *v.* **guarded, guarding, guards** —*tr.* **1a.** To watch over (a place or person, for example) in order to keep from being damaged, robbed, or injured: *guard a bank; guard a witness.* See Synonyms at **defend. b.** To supervise the entry and exit through; keep watch at: *guarded the door.* **c.** To watch over so as to prevent escape: *guard a prisoner.* **2.** To keep (an opposing player) from scoring or playing efficiently in certain sports, such as basketball and hockey. —*intr.* To take precautions: *guard against illness by getting exercise.* ❖ *n.* **1.** A person who keeps watch, protects, or acts as a sentinel: *a prison guard.* **2.** Protection or watch: *The sheepdog kept guard over the herd.* **3.** Something that gives protection; a safeguard: *a guard against tooth decay.* **4.** A device or attachment that protects or shields the user: *a helmet with a face guard.* **5.** In football, either of the two players on a team's offensive line on each side of the center. **6.** In basketball, either of two players who usually move the ball up the court and start offensive plays. ◆ **off guard** Unprepared; not alert: *The thunderclap caught me off guard, and I jumped.* **on guard** Alert and watchful; cautious: *Be on guard for patches of ice on the sidewalk.*

guard cell *n.* Either of a pair of crescent-shaped cells that control the opening and closing of one of the tiny pores on the surface of a leaf or stem.

guarded (gär′dĭd) *adj.* **1.** Defended; protected: *a heavily guarded border.* **2.** Cautious; restrained: *give a guarded answer.* —**guard′ed·ly** *adv.*

guardhouse (gärd′hous′) *n.* **1.** A building that accommodates soldiers on guard. **2.** A jail for military personnel guilty of minor offenses or awaiting court-martial.

guardian (gär′dē-ən) *n.* **1.** A person or thing that guards, protects, or watches over: *The courts act as a guardian of the law.* **2.** A person who is legally responsible for the care and management of the person or property of someone who cannot manage his or her own affairs.

guardrail (gärd′rāl′) *n.* A protective railing, as on a highway or staircase.

guardroom (gärd′rōōm′ *or* gärd′rōōm′) *n.* A room used by guards on duty.

guardsman (gärdz′mən) *n.* **1.** A person who acts as a guard. **2.** A member of the US National Guard.

guava (gwä′və) *n.* **1.** The fruit of a tropical American tree, having greenish skin and sweet pink or white flesh. Guavas are used especially to make jelly and preserves. **2.** The tree that bears such fruit.

gubernatorial (gōō′bər-nə-tôr′ē-əl) *adj.* Relating to a governor.

Guernsey (gûrn′zē) *n., pl.* **Guernseys** Any of a breed of brown and white cattle raised for milk.

gudgeon (gŭj′ən) *n.* A small freshwater fish of Eurasia that is often used for bait.

Guenevere (gwĕn′ə-vîr) *n.* Variant of **Guinevere.**

guerrilla or **guerilla** (gə-rĭl′ə) *n.* A member of a usually indigenous military force operating in small bands in occupied territory to harass the enemy, as by surprise raids.

guess (gĕs) *v.* **guessed, guessing, guesses** —*tr.* **1.** To assume or estimate (a fact or result) without sufficient information: *The reporter guessed that 6,000 people would be at the concert.* **2.** To form a correct statement or estimate regarding (something) without sufficient information or understanding: *I guessed the answer.* —*intr.* To make a guess or estimate: *We can only guess at their reason for staying home.* ❖ *n.* A statement, opinion, or conclusion based on insufficient evidence: *If you're not* *sure of the answer, at least make a guess.* —**guess′er** *n.*

guesstimate (gĕs′tə-mĭt) *n. Informal* An estimate based on conjecture.

guesswork (gĕs′wûrk′) *n.* **1.** The process of making guesses: *There is a lot of guesswork involved in predicting sales of a new product.* **2.** An estimate or judgment made by guessing.

guest (gĕst) *n.* **1a.** A person who is a recipient of hospitality at the home or table of another: *We invited several guests for dinner.* **b.** A person who is a recipient of hospitality or entertainment by a host or hostess, as at a party. **2.** A person who pays for meals or accommodations at a restaurant, hotel, or other establishment. **3.** A visiting performer, speaker, or contestant, as on a television program. —SEE NOTE AT **host³**.

guffaw (gə-fô′) *n.* A hearty, boisterous burst of laughter. ❖ *intr.v.* **guffawed, guffawing, guffaws** To laugh heartily and boisterously: *The audience guffawed at the jokes.*

guidance (gīd′ns) *n.* **1.** The act or process of guiding: *Success of the expedition depended on the guidance of their scouts.* **2.** Counseling, as to help someone make a decision or deal with a personal problem: *Her job is to provide guidance to high school students applying to college.*

guide (gīd) *n.* **1.** A person or thing that shows the way, directs, leads, or advises: *a tour guide; a guide to good manners.* **2.** A person employed to conduct others, as through a museum, and give information. **3.** A guidebook. **4.** A device, such as a ruler, tab, or bar, that acts to regulate operation or direct motion. ❖ *tr.v.* **guided, guiding, guides** **1.** To serve as a guide for; conduct: *The ranger guided the tourists through the park.* **2.** To direct the course of; steer: *guide a car down a narrow street.* **3.** To exert control or influence over: *Lincoln guided our nation through the Civil War.* —**guid′a·ble** *adj.* —**guid′er** *n.*

✦ **SYNONYMS** guide, lead, shepherd, steer, usher *v.*

guidebook (gīd′bŏŏk′) *n.* A handbook of directions and information, especially for travelers and tourists.

guided missile (gī′dĭd) *n.* A missile whose course can be controlled while it is in flight.

guide dog *n.* A dog trained to guide a visually impaired or blind person.

guideline (gīd′līn′) *n.* A statement or other indication of policy or procedure, intended to give practical guidance: *The president presented guidelines for economic development and aid to other countries.*

guidepost (gīd′pōst′) *n.* A signpost.

guideword (gīd′wûrd′) *n.* A word or term placed at the top of a column or page in a reference book to indicate the first or last entry on the page.

guild (gĭld) *n.* **1.** An association of people who share a trade or pursuit, formed to protect mutual interests and maintain standards. **2.** A similar association, as of merchants or artisans, in medieval times.

guilder (gĭl′dər) *n.* The former basic monetary unit of the Netherlands.

guildhall (gĭld′hôl′) *n.* **1.** The meeting hall of a guild. **2.** A town hall.

guile (gīl) *n.* Treacherous cunning; skillful deceit. —**guile′ful** *adj.*

guileless (gīl′lĭs) *adj.* Free of guile; artless.

guillotine (gĭl′ə-tēn′ *or* gē′ə-tēn′) *n.* A device consisting of a heavy blade held aloft between two upright guides and dropped to behead a person condemned to die. ❖ *tr.v.* **guillotined, guillotining, guillotines** To behead with a guillotine.

guilt (gĭlt) *n.* **1.** The fact of being responsible for committing an offense or error: *The investigation uncovered the suspect's guilt.* **2.** Remorseful awareness of having done something wrong: *Does he feel any guilt for forgetting my birthday?*

guiltless (gĭlt′lĭs) *adj.* Free of guilt; innocent.

guilty (gĭl′tē) *adj.* **guiltier, guiltiest** **1.** Having done wrong; deserving of blame; culpable: *The thief was found guilty.* **2.** Burdened with or prompted by a sense of guilt: *a guilty conscience.* —**guilt′i·ly** *adv.* —**guilt′i·ness** *n.*

guinea (gĭn′ē) *n.* **1.** A gold coin formerly used in England and worth one pound and one shilling. **2.** The sum of one pound and one shilling.

guinea fowl *n.* Any of several African birds that resemble the pheasants, especially one that has dark feathers with many small white spots and is raised for food.

guinea hen *n.* The guinea fowl, especially a female.

guinea pig *n.* **1.** Any of various small rodents that have short ears, short legs, and little or no tail. They are often kept as pets or used as laboratory animals. **2.** A person who is used as a subject for experimentation.

Guinevere (gwĭn′ə-vîr′) also **Guenevere** (gwĕn′ə-vîr′) *n.* In Arthurian legend, King Arthur's wife, who was loved by Lancelot.

guise (gīz) *n.* **1.** Outward appearance; aspect: *a shadowy figure that has the guise of a person.* **2.** False appearance; pretense: *gained my confidence under the guise of friendship.* **3.** Mode of dress; garb: *showed up for the interview in conservative guise.*

guitar (gĭ-tär′) *n.* A stringed musical instrument having a flat-backed, rounded body that narrows in the middle and a long, fretted neck. It is played by plucking or strumming.

guitarist (gĭ-tär′ĭst) *n.* A person who plays the guitar.

gulag also **Gulag** (gŏŏ′läg) *n.* A forced labor camp or prison for political dissidents.

gulch (gŭlch) *n.* A deep narrow ravine, especially one cut by the course of a stream or sudden water flow.

gulf (gŭlf) *n.* **1.** A large body of ocean or sea water that is partly surrounded by land. **2.** A deep wide chasm in the earth; an abyss: *Eruption of the volcano blew a gulf in the side of the mountain.* **3.** A wide gap, as in understanding: *the gulf between one generation and the next.*

Gulf Stream *n.* A warm ocean current of the northern Atlantic Ocean off eastern North America. It flows from the Gulf of Mexico up the eastern coast of the United States and then northeast toward Europe.

Gulf War *n.* A war fought in 1990 and 1991 in which a group of countries led by the United States drove the Iraqi army out of Kuwait and destroyed much of Iraq's military capability.

gull¹ (gŭl) *n.* Any of various chiefly coastal seabirds having a strong bill, webbed feet, long wings, and usually gray and white feathers.

gull² (gŭl) *n.* A person who is easily tricked or cheated; a dupe. ❖ *tr.v.* **gulled, gulling, gulls** To deceive or cheat.

WORD HISTORY Gull¹ comes from Middle English *gulle,* referring to the same kind of bird as in Modern English. **Gull²** comes from Middle English *golen,* meaning "to make swallowing motions."

Gullah (gŭl′ə) *n.* **1.** One of a group of people of African ancestry mostly inhabiting the coast and islands of South Carolina, Georgia, and northern Florida. **2.** The language of the Gullahs, based on English but including vocabulary elements and grammatical features from several African languages.

gullet (gŭl′ĭt) *n.* **1.** The tube that connects the throat and stomach; the esophagus. **2.** The throat.

gullible (gŭl′ə-bəl) *adj.* Easily deceived or duped: *He's so gullible that he'll believe anything you tell him.* **—gul′li·bil′i·ty** *n.*

gully (gŭl′ē) *n., pl.* **gullies** A ditch or channel cut in the earth by running water, especially after heavy rain.

gulp (gŭlp) *v.* **gulped, gulping, gulps** —*tr.* To swallow greedily or rapidly in large amounts: *We were late and had to gulp our lunch.* —*intr.* To choke, gasp, or swallow air: *She gulped a few times before starting her speech.* ❖ *n.* **1.** The act of gulping: *His bag of peanuts disappeared in just a few gulps.* **2.** An amount swallowed at one time: *a large gulp of water.*

gum¹ (gŭm) *n.* **1a.** Any of various thick sticky substances produced by certain plants that dry into brittle water-soluble solids. **b.** A tree that is a source of gum, such as a eucalyptus tree. **2.** Rubber made from a plant substance. **3.** A sticky or adhesive substance made from the natural gum of plants or from other substances. **4.** Chewing gum. ❖ *tr.v.* **gummed, gumming, gums** To cover, clog, seal, or fasten with gum: *gummed the seams of the canoe.* ◆ **gum up** To cause (something) to malfunction or work less efficiently: *A computer glitch is gumming up the processing of orders.*

gum² (gŭm) *n.* The firm connective tissue that surrounds and supports the bases of the teeth. ❖ *tr.v.* **gummed, gumming, gums** To chew (food) with toothless gums.

WORD HISTORY Gum¹ comes from Middle English *gomme*, which comes from Late Latin *gumma*, which comes from Greek *kommi*, all referring to a sticky substance produced by trees. **Gum²** comes from Old English *gōma*, meaning "palate, jaw."

---

gum arabic *n.* A gum produced by certain African acacia trees, used in making pills, cosmetics, various foods, and emulsions.

gumbo (gŭm′bō) *n., pl.* **gumbos 1.** The okra plant and its pods. **2.** A soup or stew thickened with okra pods. **3.** A fine soil that contains much clay and becomes sticky when wet. —SEE NOTE AT **goober.**

gumdrop (gŭm′drŏp′) *n.* A small sugar-coated candy made of sweetened gum gelatin or gelatin.

gummy (gŭm′ē) *adj.* **gummier, gummiest 1.** Consisting of, containing, or covered with gum. **2.** Thick and sticky: *gummy tar on my shoes.* **—gum′mi·ness** *n.*

gumption (gŭmp′shən) *n. Informal* Boldness, initiative, or spunk.

gum resin *n.* A mixture of gum and resin produced by various plants.

gumshoe (gŭm′shōō′) *n.* **1.** A sneaker or rubber overshoe. **2.** *Slang* An investigator, especially a detective. ❖ *intr.v.* **gumshoed, gumshoeing, gumshoes** *Slang* **1.** To work as a detective. **2.** To move about stealthily; sneak.

gun (gŭn) *n.* **1.** A weapon that shoots bullets, shells, or other projectiles through a heavy metal tube, usually by the explosion of gunpowder. Pistols, rifles, and cannons are guns. **2.** A device that resembles a gun, as in its ability to project something under pressure: *Painting with a spray gun is quick.* **3.** A discharge of a gun as a signal or salute. ❖ *tr.v.* **gunned, gunning, guns 1.** To shoot (a person).

2. To open the throttle of (an engine) so as to accelerate: *gunned the engine and sped away.* ◆ **gun for 1.** To plan or take action to harm or cause trouble for (someone). **2.** To try to obtain (something) with determination or energy: *gunning for a promotion.* **under the gun** Under great pressure to do something.

gunboat (gŭn′bōt′) *n.* A small armed vessel.

gun control *n.* Government regulation restricting or limiting the sale and possession of handguns and rifles in an effort to reduce violent crime and accidents.

gunfire (gŭn′fīr′) *n.* The firing of guns.

gung ho (gŭng′ hō′) *adj. Slang* Extremely dedicated or enthusiastic: *a gung ho baseball fan.*

gunlock (gŭn′lŏk′) *n.* The mechanism in a gun that explodes the charge of gunpowder.

gunman (gŭn′mən) *n.* A man armed with a gun, especially a killer or criminal.

gunner (gŭn′ər) *n.* **1.** A member of the armed forces who operates a gun. **2.** In the US Marine Corps, a warrant officer in charge of a ship's guns. **3.** A person who hunts with a gun.

gunnery (gŭn′ə-rē) *n.* **1.** The science that deals with the techniques and procedures of operating guns. **2.** The use of guns; shooting.

gunny (gŭn′ē) *n., pl.* **gunnies** A strong coarse cloth made of jute or hemp, used especially for sacks.

gunnysack (gŭn′ē-săk′) *n.* A bag or sack made of gunny.

gunpowder (gŭn′pou′dər) *n.* An explosive powder used in guns, fireworks, and blasting, especially a mixture of potassium nitrate, charcoal, and sulfur.

gunshot (gŭn′shŏt′) *n.* **1.** Shot fired from a gun. **2.** The range of a gun: *within gunshot.* **3.** The shooting of a gun.

gunsmith (gŭn′smĭth′) *n.* A person who makes or repairs firearms.

gunwale also **gunnel** (gŭn′əl) *n.* The upper edge of the side of a ship or boat.

guppy (gŭp′ē) *n., pl.* **guppies** A small tropical American freshwater fish that is bred in many colorful varieties and is often kept in home aquariums. The female does not lay eggs but bears live offspring.

gurgle (gûr′gəl) *v.* **gurgled, gurgling, gurgles** —*intr.* **1.** To flow while making a bubbling sound: *A stream gurgled over the rocks.* **2.** To make such a bubbling sound: *The baby gurgled with contentment.* —*tr.* To express with a bubbling sound: *The baby gurgled her delight.* ❖ *n.* A bubbling sound.

guru (gŏor′ōō) *n., pl.* **gurus 1.** A Hindu, Sikh, or Tibetan Buddhist spiritual teacher. **2.** A person who is followed as a leader or teacher.

gush (gŭsh) *v.* **gushed, gushing, gushes** —*intr.* **1.** To flow forth suddenly in great volume: *Water gushed from the broken pipe.* **2.** To make an excessive display of enthusiasm or sentiment: *Be sincere when thanking someone, but don't gush.* —*tr.* To emit abundantly; pour forth: *The new well gushed oil.* ❖ *n.* **1.** A sudden outpouring: *a gush of tears.* **2.** A display of too much enthusiasm or sentiment.

gusher (gŭsh′ər) *n.* An oil or gas well that pours out a steady flow without pumping.

gushy (gŭsh′ē) *adj.* **gushier, gushiest** Showing excessive enthusiasm or sentiment. **—gush′i·ly** *adv.* **—gush′i·ness** *n.*

gusset (gŭs′ĭt) *n.* A triangular insert, as in the seam of a garment, for added strength or expansion.

gussy (gŭs′ē) *tr.v.* **gussied, gussying, gussies** *Slang* To dress or decorate elaborately; adorn or embellish: *gussied herself up in sequins and feathers.*

gust (gŭst) *n.* **1.** A sudden strong rush of wind. **2.** A sudden burst, as of rain or smoke. **3.** An outburst of feeling: *a gust of anger.*

gustatory (gŭs′tə-tôr′ē) *adj.* Relating to the sense of taste.

gusto (gŭs′tō) *n.* Great enjoyment; zest: *We were hungry and ate lunch with gusto.* See Synonyms at **zest.**

gusty (gŭs′tē) *adj.* **gustier, gustiest** Blowing in or marked by gusts: *gusty March weather.* —**gust′i·ly** *adv.* —**gust′i·ness** *n.*

gut (gŭt) *n.* **1.** The digestive tract or any of its parts, especially the stomach or intestines. **2. guts** The intestines; bowels. **3.** Catgut. **4. guts** *Slang* Courage, fortitude, or nerve: *It took guts to stand up to such a powerful foe.* ❖ *tr.v.* **gutted, gutting, guts 1.** To remove the intestines of; eviscerate: *gutting a deer.* **2.** To destroy the contents or interior of: *The fire gutted their apartment.* ❖ *adj. Slang* Arousing or involving basic emotions: *The student's gut reaction was to protest.*

gutless (gŭt′lĭs) *adj. Slang* Lacking courage, drive, or fortitude. —**gut′less·ness** *n.*

gutter (gŭt′ər) *n.* **1a.** A channel near a curb for draining off water at the edge of a street. **b.** A trough fixed under or along the eaves for draining water off a roof. **2.** A groove or trough, as the one on either side of a bowling alley. ❖ *intr.v.* **guttered, guttering, gutters** To burn low and unsteadily; flicker: *The candle guttered and then went out.*

guttural (gŭt′ər-əl) *adj.* **1.** Relating to the throat. **2.** Having a harsh sound, as those produced in the back of the mouth: *a deep guttural voice.* **3.** Velar. —**gut′tur·al·ly** *adv.*

guy[1] (gī) *n.* A rope, cord, or cable used to steady, guide, or secure something.

guy[2] (gī) *n.* **1.** *Informal* A man or boy; a fellow. **2. guys** People of either sex.

WORD HISTORY Guy[1] comes from Middle English *gie* (meaning "guide, guy"), which comes from Old French *guier,* meaning "to guide." **Guy**[2] comes from the name of the English conspirator *Guy* Fawkes (1570–1606).

guzzle (gŭz′əl) *tr. & intr.v.* **guzzled, guzzling, guzzles** To drink greedily or habitually: *guzzle a can of soda.* —**guz′zler** *n.*

gym (jĭm) *n.* **1.** A gymnasium. **2.** A class in physical education: *I have gym at 10:15.*

gymnasium (jĭm-nā′zē-əm) *n., pl.* **gymnasiums** or **gymnasia** (jĭm-nā′zē-ə) **1.** A room or building equipped for indoor sports: *play basketball in the gymnasium.* **2.** (gĭm-nä′zē-ŏŏm′) A high school in some European countries, especially Germany.

gymnast (jĭm′năst′ *or* jĭm′nəst) *n.* A person who is skilled in gymnastics.

gymnastic (jĭm-năs′tĭk) *adj.* Relating to gymnastics: *gymnastic exercise.*

gymnastics (jĭm-năs′tĭks) *n.* Physical exercises designed to develop and display strength, balance, and agility, especially those performed on or with special apparatus.

gymnosperm (jĭm′nə-spûrm′) *n.* Any of a group of plants that produce seeds that are not enclosed in an ovary. Conifers and cycads are gymnosperms.

gynecologist (gī′nĭ-kŏl′ə-jĭst) *n.* A physician who specializes in gynecology.

gynecology (gī′nĭ-kŏl′ə-jē) *n.* The branch of medicine that deals with the diagnosis and treatment of disorders of the female reproductive system. —**gy′ne·co·log′i·cal** (gī′nĭ-kə-lŏj′ĭ-kəl) *adj.*

gyoza (gyō′zə) *n.* A pocket of dough that is stuffed with a filling and fried, steamed, or boiled.

gyp (jĭp) *Offensive Slang tr.v.* **gypped, gypping, gyps** To deprive (another person) of something by fraud; cheat or swindle. ❖ *n.* A fraud or swindle.

gypsum (jĭp′səm) *n.* A white mineral containing calcium, used in manufacturing plaster of Paris, drywall, and fertilizers.

Gypsy also **Gipsy** (jĭp′sē) *n., pl.* **Gypsies** also **Gipsies 1.** *Often Offensive* A Romani. **2.** One who lives a wandering lifestyle.

gypsy moth *n.* A small moth having hairy caterpillars that feed on leaves and do great damage to trees.

gyrate (jī′rāt′) *intr.v.* **gyrated, gyrating, gyrates 1.** To revolve around a fixed point or axis: *The earth gyrates about its axis.* **2.** To move in a spiral or spirallike path: *The dancers gyrated around the room.* —**gy·ra′tion** *n.*

gyrfalcon (jûr′făl′kən *or* jûr′fôl′kən *or* jûr′fô′kən) *n.* A large falcon of northern regions, usually having white and gray feathers.

gyro[1] (jī′rō) *n., pl.* **gyros** A gyroscope.

gyro[2] (jī′rō *or* yē′rō) *n., pl.* **gyros** A sandwich made usually of sliced roasted lamb, onion, and tomato on pita bread.

WORD HISTORY Gyro[1] is short for *gyroscope.* **Gyro**[2] comes from Greek *guros,* meaning "a turning," because the meat for a gyro is turned on a spit. Both **gyro**[1] and **gyro**[2] ultimately come from Greek *gûros,* meaning "circle."

gyrocompass (jī′rō-kŭm′pəs *or* jī′rō-kŏm′pəs) *n.* A compass using a gyroscope instead of a magnetic needle. It points to true north instead of magnetic north.

gyroscope (jī′rə-skōp′) *n.* An instrument consisting of a disk or wheel that spins rapidly about an axis like a top. The spinning motion keeps the axis fixed, though its base may be turned in any direction, making the gyroscope an accurate navigational instrument and an effective stabilizing device in ships and airplanes. —**gy′ro·scop′ic** (jī′rə-skŏp′ĭk) *adj.*

Hh

h¹ or **H** (āch) *n., pl.* **h's** or **H's** or **Hs** The eighth letter of the English alphabet.

h² An abbreviation of: **1.** height. **2.** hour.

H An abbreviation of: **1.** high. **2.** hit (in baseball). **3.** hot.

ha also **hah** (hä) *interj.* An expression used to show surprise, wonder, triumph, or puzzlement.

Habakkuk (hăb′ə-kook′ *or* hə-băk′ək) *n.* A book of the Bible in which the prophet Habakkuk foretells that God will punish oppressors and sustain the innocent.

habeas corpus (hā′bē-əs) *n.* **1.** A court order requiring that a person be brought before a court to determine whether he or she has been unlawfully imprisoned. **2.** The right of a citizen to obtain such an order.

haberdasher (hăb′ər-dăsh′ər) *n.* A dealer in articles of clothing for men.

haberdashery (hăb′ər-dăsh′ə-rē) *n., pl.* **haberdasheries 1.** A haberdasher's shop: *You can get a belt and cufflinks at the haberdashery.* **2.** The goods a haberdasher sells.

habiliment (hə-bĭl′ə-mənt) *n.* often **habiliments** Clothes or garb, especially that associated with an office or profession: *the habiliments of the theater.*

habit (hăb′ĭt) *n.* **1.** A recurrent pattern of behavior that is acquired through repetition and is often done without thinking. **2.** Customary practice or manner: *the habit of taking an early-morning walk.* **3.** An addiction. **4a.** The distinctive clothing or costume worn by members of a religious order: *a nun's habit.* **b.** A riding habit.

✦ SYNONYMS **habit, custom, practice** *n.*

habitable (hăb′ĭ-tə-bəl) *adj.* Suitable or fit to live in or on: *a habitable house; a habitable planet.* —**hab′it·a·bil′i·ty** *n.*

habitat (hăb′ĭ-tăt′) *n.* **1.** The natural environment in which a species or group of species lives: *managing wildlife habitat.* **2.** A particular kind of natural environment: *the birds found in a prairie habitat.*

habitation (hăb′ĭ-tā′shən) *n.* **1.** A place in which to live; a residence. **2.** The act of inhabiting or the condition of being inhabited: *The Antarctic climate is not suitable for human habitation.*

habit-forming (hăb′ĭt-fôr′mĭng) *adj.* Leading to or causing addiction: *a habit-forming drug.*

habitual (hə-bĭch′oo-əl) *adj.* **1a.** Being a habit: *habitual lateness.* **b.** Behaving in a certain manner by habit: *a habitual early riser.* **2.** Established by long use; usual: *her habitual route.* —**ha·bit′u·al·ly** *adv.*

habituate (hə-bĭch′oo-āt′) *tr.v.* **habituated, habituating, habituates** To familiarize by repetition or constant exposure; accustom: *He is habituated to commuting to work every day.* —**ha·bit′u·a′tion** *n.*

habitué (hə-bĭch′oo-ā′) *n.* One who frequents a particular place, especially a place offering a specific pleasurable activity.

hacienda (hä′sē-ĕn′də) *n.* **1.** A large estate or plantation in a Spanish-speaking region. **2.** The house of the owner of such an estate.

hack¹ (hăk) *v.* **hacked, hacking, hacks** —*tr.* **1.** To cut or chop with repeated and irregular blows: *hacked down the saplings.* **2.** To make or shape by such blows using a sharp implement: *hack a trail through the thickets.* **3.** *Informal* **a.** To modify (a computer program). **b.** To gain access to (a computer file or network) without authorization. **4.** *Slang* To cut or mutilate as if by hacking: *hacked a large amount off the budget.* **5.** *Slang* To cope with successfully; manage: *Do you think you can hack such responsibilities?* —*intr.* **1.** To chop or cut by hacking: *hack at a tree stump.* **2.** To work or perform as a hacker. **3.** To cough roughly or harshly: *hacking with a bad cold.* ✦ *n.* **1.** A rough irregular cut or notch made by hacking. **2.** A blow or swing made with a cutting implement. **3.** A rough dry cough.

hack² (hăk) *n.* **1.** A horse used for routine riding or driving; a hackney. **2.** A person, especially a writer, who does routine work for hire. **3.** A carriage or hackney for hire. **4.** *Informal* A taxicab.

WORD HISTORY Hack¹ comes from Middle English *hakken*, meaning "to chop by hacking." **Hack²** is short for *hackney.*

hacker (hăk′ər) *n. Informal* **1.** A person skilled in using or programming a computer; a computer buff. **2.** A person who illegally accesses a computer network, as to gain secret information.

hackle (hăk′əl) *n.* **1.** One of the long, slender, often glossy feathers on the neck of a bird, especially a rooster. **2.** **hackles** The hairs along the back of the neck of an animal, such as a dog, that can be raised upright: *The wolf raised its hackles and bared its teeth.*

hackney (hăk′nē) *n., pl.* **hackneys 1.** A horse suited for routine riding or driving. **2.** A coach or carriage for hire.

hackneyed (hăk′nēd) *adj.* Overfamiliar through overuse; trite: *writing full of hackneyed phrases.*

hacksaw (hăk′sô′) *n.* A saw with a tough, fine-toothed blade stretched taut in a frame, used especially for cutting metal.

had (hăd) *v.* Past tense and past participle of **have.**

haddock (hăd′ək) *n., pl.* **haddock** or **haddocks** A food fish of the northern Atlantic Ocean, related to and resembling the cod but having a dark spot on each side.

Hadean Time (hā-dē′ən) *n.* The period of time between 4.6 and 3.8 billion years ago. During Hadean Time, the solar system was forming and the earth was solidifying.

Hades (hā′dēz) *n.* **1.** In Greek mythology, the god of the underworld and the dispenser of earthly riches, identified with the Roman Pluto. **2.** In Greek mythology, the underworld kingdom. **3.** also **hades** Hell.

hadn't (hăd′nt) Contraction of *had not.*

hadrosaur (hăd′rə-sôr′) *n.* A duck-billed dinosaur.

hadst (hădst) *v. Archaic* A second person singular past tense of **have.**

hafnium (hăf′nē-əm) *n.* *Symbol* **Hf** A silvery metallic element that is found in zirconium ores and is used to control nuclear reactions. Atomic number 72. See **Periodic Table.**

haft (hăft) *n.* A handle or hilt, especially the handle of a tool or weapon.

hag (hăg) *n.* **1.** An old woman considered ugly or frightful. **2.** A witch; a sorceress.

hagfish (hăg′fĭsh′) *n.* Any of various long thin slimy ocean fishes that lack jaws and vertebrae and have a sucking mouth with sharp toothlike projections.

Haggai (hăg′ē-ī′ *or* hăg′ī′) *n.* A book of the Bible in which the prophet Haggai urges the rebuilding of the Temple of Jerusalem.

haggard (hăg′ərd) *adj.* Appearing worn and exhausted; gaunt: *a haggard face.* —**hag′gard·ly** *adv.* —**hag′gard·ness** *n.*

haggle (hăg′əl) *intr.v.* **haggled, haggling, haggles 1.** To bargain, as over the price of something: *a shopper haggling with a fruit seller.* **2.** To argue in an attempt to come to terms: *haggled over the contract.* —**hag′gler** *n.*

Hagiographa (hăg′ē-ŏg′rə-fə *or* hā′jē-ŏg′rə-fə) *n.* The third division of the Hebrew Scriptures; the Writings.

hah (hä) *interj.* Variant of **ha.**

Haida (hī′də) *n., pl.* **Haida** or **Haidas 1.** A member of a Native American people of several islands off the coasts of Alaska and British Columbia. **2.** Any of the languages of the Haida. —**Hai′dan** *adj.*

haiku (hī′kōō) *n., pl.* **haiku** also **haikus** A form of Japanese poetry consisting of three unrhymed lines of five, seven, and five syllables.

hail¹ (hāl) *n.* **1.** Precipitation in the form of rounded pellets of ice and hard snow that usually falls during thunderstorms. **2.** Something that falls with the force of a shower of hail: *a hail of pebbles; a hail of criticism.* ❖ *v.* **hailed, hailing, hails** —*intr.* To fall as hail: *It hailed this afternoon.* —*tr.* To pour (something) down or forth: *The two drivers hailed insults at each other.*

hail² (hāl) *tr.v.* **hailed, hailing, hails 1.** To salute or greet: *hail a friend across the street.* **2.** To call out or yell in order to catch the attention of: *hail a cab.* ❖ *interj.* An expression used to show a greeting or tribute. ◆ **hail from** To come or originate from: *They hail from Ohio.* —**hail′er** *n.*

WORD HISTORY Hail¹ comes from Old English *hægl*, referring to the same kind of precipitation as in Modern English. **Hail²** comes from Middle English *heilen*, meaning "to shout 'Hail!' as a greeting."

Hail Mary *n., pl.* **Hail Marys** A Roman Catholic prayer addressed to the Virgin Mary.

hailstone (hāl′stōn′) *n.* A pellet of hail.

hailstorm (hāl′stôrm′) *n.* A storm in which hail falls.

hair (hâr) *n.* **1.** One of the fine strands that grow from the skin of humans and other mammals: *She plucked some hairs from her eyebrows.* **2.** A slender growth resembling a mammalian hair, found on insects and other animals. **3.** A mass of such fine strands: *My cat has soft hair. This caterpillar is covered with hair.* **4.** A fine strand growing from the outer layer of a plant. **5.** A tiny distance or narrow margin: *We won by a hair.*

hairball (hâr′bôl′) *n.* A small mass of hair in an animal's stomach or intestine that forms as the animal swallows hair while licking its coat.

hairbreadth (hâr′brĕdth′) *adj. & n.* Variant of **hairsbreadth.**

hairbrush (hâr′brŭsh′) *n.* A brush for the hair.

haircloth (hâr′klôth′) *n.* A wiry fabric with horsehair or camelhair woven into it, used in upholstery or to stiffen clothing.

haircut (hâr′kŭt′) *n.* **1.** The act or an instance of cutting the hair: *You need a haircut.* **2.** A style in which hair is cut: *a short haircut.*

hairdo (hâr′dōō) *n., pl.* **hairdos** A hairstyle.

hairdresser (hâr′drĕs′ər) *n.* A person who cuts or styles hair.

hairless (hâr′lĭs) *adj.* Having little or no hair.

hairline (hâr′līn′) *n.* **1.** The edge of hair growing above the forehead or around the head. **2.** A very thin line.

hairnet (hâr′nĕt′) *n.* A mesh for holding the hair in place.

hairpiece (hâr′pēs′) *n.* A covering or bunch of human or artificial hair worn to cover a bald spot or as part of a hairdo.

hairpin (hâr′pĭn′) *n.* A fine metal pin, often bent into the shape of a U, used to secure a hairdo.

hair-raising (hâr′rā′zĭng) *adj.* Causing excitement, terror, or thrills: *a hair-raising ride on a roller coaster.*

hairsbreadth or **hair's-breadth** (hârz′brĕdth′) also **hairbreadth** (hâr′brĕdth′) *n.* A small space, distance, or margin: *win by a hairsbreadth.*

hairsplitting (hâr′splĭt′ĭng) *n.* The making of distinctions that are too fine to be important: *The hairsplitting between the lawyers annoyed the judge.* —**hair′split′ter** *n.*

hair spray *n.* A preparation sprayed on the hair to keep it in place.

hairspring (hâr′sprĭng′) *n.* A fine spring that regulates the movement of the balance wheel of a watch or clock.

hairstyle (hâr′stīl′) *n.* A style in which hair is cut and arranged.

hair trigger *n.* A gun trigger that responds to a very slight pressure.

hairy (hâr′ē) *adj.* **hairier, hairiest 1.** Covered with hair or projections resembling hair: *a hairy caterpillar.* **2.** Consisting of or resembling hair: *a hairy blanket.* **3.** *Slang* Fraught with difficulties: *a hairy escape.* —**hair′i·ness** *n.*

Haitian (hā′shən) *adj.* Relating to Haiti or its people or culture. ❖ *n.* **1.** A native or inhabitant of Haiti. **2.** Haitian Creole.

Haitian Creole *n.* A language spoken by the majority of Haitians, based on French and various African languages.

hajj or **haj** (hăj) *n., pl.* **hajjes** or **hajes** A pilgrimage to Mecca, Saudi Arabia, during the last month of the Islamic calendar. Every Muslim who is capable of it is expected to undertake the hajj at least once in his or her life.

hake (hāk) *n., pl.* **hake** or **hakes** Any of various ocean fishes that closely resemble the cod but are usually smaller.

halal (hə-läl′) *adj.* **1.** Relating to or being meat from animals slaughtered in the manner prescribed by Islamic law: *a halal butcher; a halal label.* **2.** In accordance with or permitted under Islamic law. ❖ *n.* Halal meat.

halberd (hăl′bərd *or* hôl′bərd) *n.* A weapon used in the 1400s and 1500s, having an axe blade and a spike mounted on a long pole.

halcyon (hăl′sē-ən) *adj.* Calm and peaceful; tranquil: *halcyon days.* ❖ *n.* A fabled bird identified with the kingfisher that is supposed to have the power to calm the wind and the waves while it nests on the sea during the winter solstice.

hale¹ (hāl) *adj.* **haler, halest** Free from infirmity or illness; healthy.

hale² (hāl) *tr.v.* **haled, haling, hales 1.** To force to go: *hale an offender into court.* **2.** *Archaic* To pull, drag, or hoist.

WORD HISTORY Hale¹ comes from Old English *hāl,* meaning "healthy." **Hale²** comes from Middle English *halen,* which comes from Old French *haler,* both meaning "to pull, drag."

half (hăf) *n., pl.* **halves** (hăvz) **1a.** One of two equal parts that together make up a whole: *Fifty cents is one half of a dollar.* **b.** One of two approximately equal parts: *the smaller half of a sandwich.* **2.** In football and other sports, either of the two equal time periods that make up a game. **3.** Half an hour: *at half past one.* ❖ *adj.* **1a.** Being one of two equal parts. **b.** Being approximately a half: *a half glass of milk.* **2.** Partial or incomplete: *a half truth.* ❖ *adv.* **1.** To the extent of exactly or nearly 50 percent: *a half empty tank.* **2.** Not completely; partly: *I was still half asleep.* ◆ **in half** Into halves. **not half** Not at all: *not half bad.*

USAGE The phrases *a half, half of,* and *half a* or *half an* are all correct. They may differ slightly in meaning. For example, we say *a half day* when *day* has the special sense "a working day," and the phrase then means "4 hours." *Half of a day* and *half a day* are not restricted in this way and can mean either 4 or 12 hours.

half-and-half (hăf′ənd-hăf′) *adj.* Being half one thing and half another: *a half-and-half mixture of linseed oil and turpentine.* ❖ *n.* A mixture of two things in equal portions, especially a mixture of equal parts of milk and cream.

halfback (hăf′băk′) *n.* **1.** In football, one of two running backs positioned to the sides behind the quarterback when the ball is snapped. **2.** In certain sports such as soccer and field hockey, one of several players positioned behind the forward line and in front of the fullbacks.

half-baked (hăf′bākt′) *adj.* **1.** Only partly baked. **2.** *Informal* Not fully thought out; poorly conceived: *a half-baked idea.*

half brother *n.* A brother who has only one biological parent in common with another sibling.

half-dollar (hăf′dŏl′ər) *n.* A US coin worth 50 cents.

half gainer *n.* A dive in which the diver leaves the board facing the water and rotates through half a backward somersault to enter the water headfirst.

halfhearted (hăf′här′tĭd) *adj.* Showing or feeling little enthusiasm, interest, or heart; uninspired: *With so much work left, I made only a halfhearted attempt to finish it.* —**half′heart′ed·ly** *adv.*

half hitch *n.* A knot made by looping a rope around an object and then back around itself, bringing the end of the rope through the loop.

half-hour (hăf′our′) *n.* **1.** A period of 30 minutes. **2.** The middle point of an hour: *News bulletins are broadcast on the half-hour.*

half-life (hăf′līf′) *n.* The time needed for half the nuclei in a sample of radioactive material to undergo decay.

half-mast (hăf′măst′) *n.* The position about halfway up a mast or pole at which a flag is flown as a symbol of mourning for the dead or as a signal of distress.

half-moon (hăf′mo͞on′) *n.* The moon when just half of its disk appears lighted, at the end of the first or third quarter.

half nelson *n.* A wrestling hold in which one arm is passed under an opponent's arm from behind to the back of the neck.

half note *n.* A musical note having one half the time value of a whole note.

halfpenny (hă′pə-nē *or* hāp′nē) *n., pl.* **halfpence** (hā′pəns) or **halfpennies** A former British coin worth one half of a penny.

half-pint (hăf′pīnt′) *Slang n.* A small person or animal.

halfpipe (hăf′pīp′) *n.* A structure that is shaped like a trough and used for stunts in sports such as in-line skating and snowboarding.

half rest *n.* A musical rest having one-half the time value of a whole rest.

half sister *n.* A sister who has only one biological parent in common with another sibling.

half-staff (hăf′stăf′) *n.* Half-mast.

half step *n.* A musical interval equal to one half the interval between full tones in a scale. Half steps separate C, C-sharp, and D.

halftime (hăf′tīm′) *n.* The intermission between halves in games of certain sports, such as basketball and football.

halftone (hăf′tōn′) *n.* **1.** A tone or color between very light and very dark. **2.** A picture in which the shades of light and dark are produced by tiny dots either closely or more widely spaced. **3.** A half step; a semitone.

half-track (hăf′trăk′) *n.* A lightly armored military vehicle that has caterpillar treads in the rear and conventional wheels in front.

halfway (hăf′wā′) *adj.* **1.** Midway between two points or conditions: *the halfway point on the trail to the summit.* **2.** Reaching or including only half or a portion; partial: *halfway measures to control pollution.* ❖ *adv.* **1.** To or at half the distance: *I'll meet you halfway between your house and mine.* **2.** Partially: *I halfway gave in to their demands.*

halfway house *n.* A building providing temporary housing for people who have been released from an institution, where they may receive special services, such as job training and counseling, before living independently.

halibut (hăl′ə-bət *or* hŏl′ə-bət) *n., pl.* **halibut** or **halibuts** Any of several large edible flatfishes of northern ocean waters.

halite (hăl′īt′ *or* hā′līt′) *n.* Rock salt.

halitosis (hăl′ĭ-tō′sĭs) *n.* Bad breath.

hall (hôl) *n.* **1.** A corridor or passageway in a building: *The hall had several classrooms off it.* **2.** An entrance room or vestibule in a building; a lobby: *We waited in the hall at the elevators.* **3.** A building where meetings, parties, concerts, or other gatherings are held: *a lecture hall.* **4.** A building used for the meetings, entertainments, or living quarters of a social or religious organization. **5.** A school, college, or university building: *Students live in three halls at the back of campus.* **6.** The main house of an English landowner.

hallelujah (hăl′ə-lo͞o′yə) *interj.* An expression used to show praise or joy. ❖ *n.* **1.** An exclamation of "hallelujah." **2.** A song or hymn of praise based on the word *hallelujah.*

Halley's comet (hăl′ēz *or* hā′lēz) *n.* A comet last observed from Earth in 1986, having a period of 76 years.

hallmark (hôl′märk′) *n.* **1.** A mark that indicates excellence or quality. **2.** A mark indicating a certain level of purity, stamped in England on articles made of gold and silver. **3.** A distinguishing characteristic, feature, or trait: *Good design and quality materials are hallmarks of fine automobiles.*

halloo (hə-lōō′) *interj.* **1.** An expression used to get someone's attention. **2.** An expression used to urge on hounds in a hunt. ❖ *n., pl.* **halloos** A shout or call of "halloo."

hallow (hăl′ō) *tr.v.* **hallowed, hallowing, hallows 1.** To make or set apart as holy: *An ancient burial mound hallows this ground.* **2.** To respect or honor greatly: *hallow the memory of one's ancestors.*

hallowed (hăl′ōd) *adj.* **1.** Sanctified; consecrated: *hallowed ground.* **2.** Honored; revered: *a hallowed name.*

Halloween also **Hallowe'en** (hăl′ə-wēn′ or hŏl′ə-wēn′) *n.* October 31, celebrated by children going door to door in costumes and begging treats and playing pranks.

hallucinate (hə-lōō′sə-nāt′) *intr.v.* **hallucinated, hallucinating, hallucinates** To have hallucinations.

hallucination (hə-lōō′sə-nā′shən) *n.* An image, sound, or other sensory perception that is experienced mentally but has no basis in reality: *People with high fevers may have hallucinations.*

hallucinatory (hə-lōō′sə-nə-tôr′ē) *adj.* **1.** Relating to or marked by hallucination: *a hallucinatory experience.* **2.** Hallucinogenic.

hallucinogen (hə-lōō′sə-nə-jən) *n.* A drug that produces or tends to produce hallucinations.

hallucinogenic (hə-lōō′sə-nə-jĕn′ĭk) *adj.* Producing or tending to produce hallucinations: *a hallucinogenic drug.*

hallway (hôl′wā′) *n.* **1.** A corridor in a building. **2.** An entrance hall: *The mail is left in the hallway of our apartment building.*

halo (hā′lō) *n., pl.* **halos** or **haloes 1.** A ring or disk of light surrounding the heads or bodies of sacred figures, such as saints in religious paintings. **2.** A circular band of light that surrounds the sun, the moon, a star, or another light source, resulting from effects such as reflection and refraction of light through ice crystals suspended in air.

halogen (hăl′ə-jən) *n.* A group of elements with similar properties, including fluorine, chlorine, bromine, iodine, and astatine. Halogens combine directly with most metals to form salts. ❖ *adj.* **1.** Relating to the group of elements that are halogens. **2.** Relating to a bright incandescent light bulb that contains a halogen gas that keeps the filament from falling apart at higher temperatures.

halt (hôlt) *n.* A temporary stop of movement or progress: *The car rolled to a halt when it stalled.* ❖ *intr. & tr.v.* **halted, halting, halts** To stop or cause to stop: *The hikers halted for lunch and some rest. The government hopes to halt air pollution.* See Synonyms at **stop.**

halter (hôl′tər) *n.* **1.** A device of rope or leather straps that fits around the head or neck of an animal and is used to lead or secure the animal. **2.** A rope with a noose used for execution by hanging. **3.** A woman's top that ties behind the neck, leaving the shoulders and back bare.

halting (hôl′tĭng) *adj.* Hesitant or wavering: *a low and halting voice.*

halve (hăv) *tr.v.* **halved, halving, halves 1.** To divide (something) into two equal portions or parts: *A friend and I halved the remaining apple.* **2.** To reduce or lessen by half: *The storekeeper halved the prices for the sale.*

halves (hăvz) *n.* Plural of **half.**

halyard (hăl′yərd) *n.* A rope that runs through a pulley on a mast or flagpole and is used to raise or lower a sail or a flag.

ham (hăm) *n.* **1.** The hind leg of certain animals, especially of a hog. **2.** A cut of meat from the thigh of a hog. **3. hams** The buttocks and backs of the thighs. **4.** A performer who overacts or exaggerates. **5.** A licensed amateur radio op-

erator. ❖ *intr.v.* **hammed, hamming, hams** To exaggerate or overdo a dramatic role, for example; overact.

hamburger (hăm′bûr′gər) *n.* **1.** Ground meat, usually beef. **2.** A patty of such meat. **3.** A sandwich made with a patty of ground meat usually in a roll or bun.

hamlet (hăm′lĭt) *n.* A small village.

hammer (hăm′ər) *n.* **1.** A hand tool consisting of a heavy, usually metal head attached at a right angle to a handle, used chiefly for driving in nails or for pounding and shaping metals. **2.** Something used or shaped like a hammer, such as one of the padded wooden pieces that strikes the strings of a piano, or the device used to strike a gong or bell, or the part of a gun that strikes the firing pin of a gun. **3.** A metal ball weighing 16 pounds and having a long wire or wooden handle by which athletes throw it for distance in track-and-field competitions. **4.** The largest of the three small bones in the middle ear that transmit vibrations to the inner ear; the malleus. **5.** A small mallet used by auctioneers. ❖ *v.* **hammered, hammering, hammers** —*tr.* **1.** To hit, especially repeatedly, with a hammer; pound: *hammer a nail.* **2.** To beat into shape with a hammer: *hammer iron into a horseshoe.* **3.** To accomplish or produce with difficulty or effort: *The two sides in the dispute hammered out an agreement.* **4.** To force upon by constant repetition: *hammered the safety guidelines into the students' heads.* **5.** To defeat soundly: *hammered the visiting team 49–0.* —*intr.* **1.** To hit something repeatedly and firmly, especially with a hammer: *hammer on a door.* **2.** *Informal* To keep doing or trying to do something: *The researchers hammered away at the problem.* —**ham′mer·er** *n.*

hammerhead (hăm′ər-hĕd′) *n.* Any of several predatory sharks having the sides of the head elongated into fleshy extensions with the eyes at the ends.

hammerlock (hăm′ər-lŏk′) *n.* A wrestling hold in which the opponent's arm is pulled behind the back and twisted upward.

hammock (hăm′ək) *n.* A hanging, easily swung length of canvas or heavy netting suspended between two trees or other supports and used as a seat or a bed.

hamper¹ (hăm′pər) *tr.v.* **hampered, hampering, hampers** To prevent the progress, free movement, or action of: *The snowstorm hampered our plane's flight.*

hamper² (hăm′pər) *n.* A large basket, usually with a cover.

WORD HISTORY Hamper¹ comes from Middle English *hamperen,* meaning "to pack together, enclose." **Hamper²** comes from Middle English *hamper* (meaning "receptacle, case, basket"), which comes from Old French *hanepier* (meaning "a case for holding goblets"), which comes from Old French *hanap,* meaning "goblet."

hamster (hăm′stər) *n.* Any of various small rodents native to Eurasia, having soft fur, large cheek pouches, and a short tail. Hamsters are often kept as pets or used as laboratory animals.

hamstring (hăm′strĭng) *n.* **1.** Either of two large tendons at the back of the human knee. **2.** Any of the three muscles at the back of the thigh that together act to bend the knee. **3.** A large tendon at the back of the hind leg of a horse or other four-footed animal. ❖ *tr.v.* **hamstrung** (hăm′strŭng′), **hamstringing, hamstrings 1.** To cripple (a person or animal) by cutting a hamstring. **2.** To destroy or hinder the efficiency of; frustrate: *A lack of resources hamstrung the company's growth.*

hand (hănd) *n.* **1a.** The part of the human arm that is below the wrist. It consists of a palm to which four fingers and a thumb are attached, and is used for holding or grasping. **b.** A similar part in other animals, such as monkeys and other primates. **2.** Something like a hand in shape or use, especially a pointer on a dial, as that of a clock or gauge. **3.** A person's handwriting or a style of handwriting: *The manuscript is written in the author's own hand.* **4.** Side or direction indicated according to the way in which one is facing: *At my right hand you see a box.* **5.** Assistance with a task: *Give me a hand with this heavy carton.* **6.** A person who does manual labor; a laborer: *The field hands picked cotton.* **7.** A member of a group or crew: *All hands on deck!* **8.** An aptitude or ability: *decided to try my hand at painting.* **9.** A manner or way of performing something: *The surgeon works with a delicate hand.* **10.** An influence or effect: *She had a hand in the decision.* **11.** A round of applause: *The audience gave us a tremendous hand.* **12.** A pledge of marriage or permission to marry: *ask for someone's hand.* **13a.** A player in card games: *We need four hands for bridge.* **b.** The cards dealt to and held by such a player: *Don't look at my hand.* **c.** One round of a card game: *I'll play one more hand.* **14.** often **hands** Possession, ownership, or keeping: *The books should be in your hands by noon.* **15.** A unit of length equal to four inches (10.2 centimeters), used especially to indicate the height of horses. ❖ *tr.v.* **handed, handing, hands 1.** To give or pass with or as if with the hands; transmit: *Hand the flashlight to me.* **2.** To lead or help with the hand: *The usher handed the guests to their seats.* ◆ **at hand 1.** Close by; near: *remain close at hand.* **2.** About to occur; imminent: *Spring is at hand.* **at the hand of** or **at the hands of** By the action of: *He died at the hands of an assassin.* **by hand** Performed manually: *These dresses have been sewn by hand.* **hand and foot** With concerted, never-ending effort: *We waited on them hand and foot.* **hand down 1.** To give or pass on, as an inheritance to one's heirs: *The family handed down the painting from generation to generation.* **2.** To make and pronounce an official decision, especially a court verdict. **hand in** To turn in; submit: *Hand in your term papers by May 1.* **hand in glove** In close association or on intimate terms. **hand in hand** In cooperation; jointly: *Economic growth and literacy go hand in hand.* **hand off** In football, to put the ball in a teammate's arms without throwing it. **hand out** To give out; distribute: *handed out leaflets to passers-by.* **hand over** To release or relinquish to another: *Hand over the goods.* **hand over fist** *Informal* At a tremendous rate: *making money hand over fist.* **hands down** With no trouble; easily: *win the award hands down.* **in hand 1.** Under control: *We succeeded in keeping the situation in hand.* **2.** Held in one's hand: *I arrived at the birthday party with my gift in hand.* **on the one hand** or **on one hand** From one standpoint. **on the other hand** From another standpoint. **out of hand** Out of control: *We can't let our expenses get out of hand.*

handbag (hănd′băg′) *n.* **1.** A woman's purse used to hold money, keys, or other personal items. **2.** A piece of small hand luggage.

handball (hănd′bôl′) *n.* **1.** A game in which two or more players hit a ball against a wall with the hand usually while wearing a special glove. **2.** The small rubber ball used in this game. **3.** often **hand ball** In soccer, a violation of the rules in which a player other than the goalie strikes or carries the ball with the hand or arm.

handbill (hănd′bĭl′) *n.* A printed sheet or pamphlet distributed by hand; a leaflet.

handbook (hănd′bŏŏk′) *n.* A small reference book or manual providing specific information on a certain subject.

handcart (hănd′kärt′) *n.* A small, usually two-wheeled cart pushed or pulled by hand.

handcraft (hănd′krăft′) *n.* Variant of **handicraft.** ❖ *tr.v.* (hănd-krăft′) **handcrafted, handcrafting, handcrafts** To fashion or make by hand: *handcraft wooden toys.*

handcuff (hănd′kŭf′) *n.* often **handcuffs** A restraining device consisting of a pair of strong, connected hoops that can be tightened and locked about the wrists. ❖ *tr.v.* **handcuffed, handcuffing, handcuffs** To restrain with or as if with handcuffs: *The sheriff handcuffed the prisoner. Critics warned that the new law would handcuff small businesses.*

handed (hăn′dĭd) *adj.* **1.** Relating to dexterity, preference, or size with respect to a hand or hands: *left-handed; large-handed.* **2.** Relating to a specified number of people: *a four-handed card game.*

handful (hănd′fŏŏl′) *n., pl.* **handfuls 1.** The amount that a hand can hold: *a handful of coins.* **2.** A small but unspecified quantity or number: *a handful of people.* **3.** A person or thing that is difficult to control or handle: *That toddler is a real handful.*

handgun (hănd′gŭn′) *n.* A firearm that can be used with one hand; a pistol.

handheld or **hand-held** (hănd′hĕld′) *adj.* Compact enough to be used while being held in the hand or hands: *a handheld video camera.*

handicap (hăn′dē-kăp′) *n.* **1.** A race or contest in which contestants are given advantages or compensations to equalize the chances of winning. **2.** Such an advantage or disadvantage. **3.** A physical or mental disability. **4.** A hindrance: *Disorganization is my chief handicap.* ❖ *tr.v.* **handicapped, handicapping, handicaps 1.** To cause to be at a disadvantage; impede: *A sore throat handicapped the singer.* **2.** To give a handicap or handicaps to (a contestant): *handicap a contestant in a golf match.*

handicapped (hăn′dē-kăpt′) *adj.* Physically or mentally disabled. ❖ *n.* (*used with a plural verb*) People with a physical or mental disability.

handicraft (hăn′dē-krăft′) also **handcraft** (hănd′krăft′) *n.* **1.** Skill and facility with the hands. **2.** A craft or occupation requiring skilled use of the hands, as weaving or basketry. **3.** An object produced by skilled hands: *The shop sells handicrafts from Bolivia.*

handily (hăn′dĭ-lē or hăn′dl-ē) *adv.* **1.** Easily: *The student answered the test questions handily.* **2.** In a convenient manner.

handiwork (hăn′dē-wûrk′) *n.* **1.** Work performed by hand: *Knitting is a handiwork that requires dexterity.* **2.** The product of a person's efforts and actions.

handkerchief (hăng′kər-chĭf or hăng′kər-chēf′) *n., pl.* **handkerchiefs** also **handkerchieves** (hăng′kər-chĭvz or hăng′kər-chēvz′) **1.** A small square of cloth used especially to wipe the nose and mouth. **2.** A kerchief or scarf.

handle (hăn′dl) *v.* **handled, handling, handles** *—tr.* **1.** To touch, hold, or lift with the hands: *Please do not handle the merchandise.* **2.** To operate with the hands; manipulate: *know how to handle chopsticks.* **3.** To deal with or treat in a specified way: *handles problems well.* **4.** To manage, direct, or train: *handle a tennis player.* **5.** To deal with, perform, or manage successfully: *I couldn't handle the difficult math* *test.* **6.** To deal in; buy and sell: *Drugstores handle a wide variety of goods.* —*intr.* To act or function in a given way while in operation: *This new car handles well on the highway.* ❖ *n.* **1.** A part that is designed to be held or operated with the hand: *carry a pail by its handle.* **2.** Understanding or control: *has a handle on the situation.*

handlebar (hăn′dl-bär′) *n.* often **handlebars** A cylindrical, straight or curved steering bar, as on a bicycle: *gripped the handlebars tightly.* ❖ *adj.* Shaped like a long and curved handlebar: *a handlebar mustache.*

handler (hănd′lər) *n.* **1.** A person who handles a person or thing: *handlers of food in a restaurant; the mayor's campaign handlers.* **2.** A person who trains an animal and exhibits it in shows: *a dog handler.* **3.** A person who acts as the trainer or second of a boxer.

handmade (hănd′mād′) *adj.* Made or prepared by hand rather than by machine: *a handmade quilt.*

handmaid (hănd′mād′) also **handmaiden** (hănd′mād′n) *n.* A woman attendant or servant.

hand-me-down (hănd′mē-doun′) *n.* Something, such as an article of clothing, passed on from one person to another: *The sweater is a hand-me-down from my sister.*

handoff (hănd′ôf′) *n.* **1.** In football, the act of handing the ball to a teammate during a play. **2.** In track and field, the act of handing a baton to a teammate during a relay race.

hand organ *n.* A barrel organ operated by turning a crank with the hand.

handout (hănd′out′) *n.* **1.** A gift to the needy, as of food, clothing, or money. **2.** A folder or leaflet given out free of charge. **3.** A sheet of paper with information that is given out, as at a lecture. **4.** A prepared news or publicity release.

handpick (hănd′pĭk′) *tr.v.* **handpicked, handpicking, handpicks** **1.** To gather or pick by hand. **2.** To select personally: *handpick members of a committee.*

handrail (hănd′rāl′) *n.* A narrow railing to be grasped with the hand for support.

handsaw (hănd′sô′) *n.* A saw operated with one hand.

handset (hănd′sĕt′) *n.* The part of a telephone containing the receiver and transmitter and often a dial or pushbuttons.

handshake (hănd′shāk′) *n.* The grasping of hands by two people, as in greeting or leave-taking or to express mutual agreement.

handsome (hăn′səm) *adj.* **handsomer, handsomest** **1.** Pleasing and dignified in form and appearance: *a handsome couple.* **2.** Generous or liberal: *a handsome reward.* —**hand′some·ly** *adv.* —**hand′some·ness** *n.*

hands-on (hăndz′ŏn′) *adj.* Involving active participation; applied, as opposed to theoretical: *This is a hands-on course, in which you will create your own website.*

handspike (hănd′spīk′) *n.* A bar used as a lever.

handspring (hănd′sprĭng′) *n.* A gymnastic feat in which the body is flipped completely forward or backward from an upright position, landing first on the hands and then on the feet.

handstand (hănd′stănd′) *n.* The act of balancing on one's hands with one's feet in the air.

hand-to-hand (hănd′tə-hănd′) *adj.* Being at close quarters: *hand-to-hand combat.* —**hand to hand** *adv.*

hand-to-mouth (hănd′tə-mouth′) *adj.* Having or providing only the bare essentials: *a hand-to-mouth existence.* —**hand to mouth** *adv.*

handwork (hănd′wûrk′) *n.* Work done by hand rather than by machine: *Sewing buttons on is handwork.*

handwoven (hănd′wō′vən) *adj.* **1.** Woven on a hand-operated loom. **2.** Woven by hand: *handwoven baskets.*

handwriting (hănd′rī′tĭng) *n.* **1.** Writing done with the hand. **2.** The writing characteristic of a particular person.

handy (hăn′dē) *adj.* **handier, handiest** **1.** Skillful in using one's hands: *A carpenter must be handy with tools.* **2.** Readily accessible: *a handy supply of wood for the fireplace.* **3.** Easily or effectively used; convenient or useful: *A can opener is a handy gadget.*

handyman also **handy man** (hăn′dē-măn′) *n.* A man hired to perform various odd jobs.

hang (hăng) *v.* **hung** (hŭng), **hanging, hangs** —*tr.* **1.** To fasten from above with no support from below; suspend: *hang a clothesline.* **2.** To fasten so as to allow free movement at or about the point of suspension: *hang a door.* **3.** *Past tense and past participle* **hanged** (hăngd) To execute by suspending by the neck. **4.** To hold or bend downward; let droop: *hang one's head in sorrow.* **5.** To attach to a wall: *hang wallpaper.* **6.** To furnish or decorate by suspending objects around or about: *We've decided to hang the walls with pictures.* **7.** To display by attaching to a wall or other structure: *The museum curator chose which paintings would be hung in the main hall.* **8.** To deadlock (a jury) by failing to come to a unanimous verdict. —*intr.* **1.** To be attached from above with no support from below: *A sign hung over the door.* **2.** To be fastened so as to allow free movement from a hinge or hook: *The gate hangs on its hinges.* **3.** To die as a result of hanging. **4.** To remain unresolved or uncertain: *His future hangs in the balance.* **5.** To be dependent; depend: *A great deal hangs on your decision.* **6.** To incline downward; droop: *The spectators hung over the rail.* **7.** To remain suspended over a place or an object; hover: *A rain cloud hangs over the field.* **8.** To be exhibited: *Many famous paintings hang in this museum.* **9.** To pay strict attention: *The audience hung on the speaker's every word.* ❖ *n.* **1.** The way in which something hangs. **2.** *Informal* The proper way of doing, handling, or using something: *I can't get the hang of this new camera.* ◆ **hang around** *Informal* To spend time idly; loiter: *hang around the beach all day.* **hang back** To be averse; hold back: *When the teacher asked a question, several students hung back.* **hang on to** To cling tightly to something: *Hang on to the rope and pull yourself up.* **2.** To wait for a short period of time. **3.** To continue persistently; persevere: *This fever keeps hanging on.* **hang out** *Slang* To spend one's free time in a certain place. **hang together** **1.** To stand united; stick together: *hang together as a group.* **2.** To make sense as a whole; be understandable: *The sentences hang together to form a good paragraph.* **hang up** **1.** To end a telephone conversation. **2.** To suspend on a hook or hanger: *He took his shirts out of the suitcase and hung them up.* **3.** To delay or impede; hinder.

USAGE *Hanged* is used as the past tense and past participle of **hang** in the sense of "to kill by suspending by the neck," as in *Frontier courts hanged many a prisoner after a summary trial.* In all other senses of the word, *hung* is the preferred form as past tense and past participle, as in *I hung my children's picture above my desk.* This also applies to the various phrasal verbs and idioms that are made with *hang: hang around, hang on, hang out,* and so on.

hangar (hăng′ər *or* hăng′gər) *n.* A building used for housing or repairing aircraft.

hangdog (hăng′dôg′) *adj.* Shamefaced or guilty: *a hangdog look on the criminal's face.*

hanged (hăngd) *v.* Past tense and past participle of **hang** (sense 3).

hanger (hăng′ər) *n.* **1.** A frame or hook on which an article of clothing can be hung. **2.** A person who hangs something: *a wallpaper hanger.*

hanger-on (hăng′ər-ŏn′) *n., pl.* **hangers-on** A person who cultivates the friendship of an influential person in the hope of achieving personal gain; a parasite.

hang-glide (hăng′glīd′) *intr.v.* **hang-glided, hang-gliding, hang-glides** To glide in the air by means of a hang glider.

hang glider *n.* A device resembling a kite from which a rider hangs in a harness while gliding from a height.

hang gliding *n.* The sport of riding a hang glider.

hanging (hăng′ĭng) *n.* **1.** Execution on a gallows: *death by hanging.* **2.** Something, such as a tapestry, that is hung: *a wall hanging.* ❖ *adj.* Projecting downward; overhanging: *a hanging lamp; hanging moss.*

hangman (hăng′mən) *n.* A man who is employed to execute convicted criminals by hanging.

hangnail (hăng′nāl′) *n.* A small flap of dead skin that hangs from the side or base of a fingernail.

hangout (hăng′out′) *n. Slang* A frequently visited place: *The mall is a favorite hangout of teenagers.*

hangover (hăng′ō′vər) *n.* **1.** A condition, often characterized by nausea and a headache, that results from drinking more alcohol than the body can tolerate. **2.** Something left from an earlier time; a holdover.

hang-up (hăng′ŭp′) *n. Informal* **1.** An inhibition or emotional difficulty with something. **2.** An obstacle or inconvenience.

hank (hăngk) *n.* **1.** A coil or loop: *a hank of rope.* **2.** A looped bundle, as of yarn.

hanker (hăng′kər) *intr.v.* **hankered, hankering, hankers** To have a strong, often restless desire: *hanker to travel abroad.*

Hansen's disease (hăn′sənz) *n.* Leprosy.

hansom (hăn′səm) *n.* A two-wheeled, covered carriage with the driver's seat above and behind the passenger compartment.

Hanukkah also **Chanukah** (кнä′nə-kə *or* hä′nə-kə) *n.* A Jewish festival lasting eight days and celebrating the victory in 165 BC of the Maccabees over the king of Syria and the rededication of the Temple at Jerusalem.

haphazard (hăp-hăz′ərd) *adj.* Dependent on or characterized by mere chance; random: *He had left the papers in a haphazard arrangement on the desk.* —**hap·haz′ard·ly** *adv.* —**hap·haz′ard·ness** *n.*

hapless (hăp′lĭs) *adj.* Unfortunate; unlucky: *a hapless business scheme.* —**hap′less·ly** *adv.*

haploid (hăp′loid′) *adj.* Being a cell or composed of cells in which there is only one of each type of chromosome. In animals, reproductive cells are haploid. ❖ *n.* A haploid cell or organism.

haply (hăp′lē) *adv.* By chance or accident.

happen (hăp′ən) *intr.v.* **happened, happening, happens** **1.** To occur or take place. **2.** To come upon something by chance: *I happened upon an interesting article in the newspaper last week.*

happening (hăp′ə-nĭng) *n.* Something that happens; an event or occurrence: *an interesting recent happening.*

happenstance (hăp′ən-stăns′) *n.* A chance circumstance: *By happenstance I met an old friend at the mall.*

happy (hăp′ē) *adj.* **happier, happiest** **1.** Having, showing, or marked by a feeling of joy or pleasure: *a happy child; the happiest day of my life.* See Synonyms at **glad.** **2.** Cheerful; willing: *We'll be happy to help.* **3.** Characterized by good luck; fortunate: *a happy sequence of events.* **4.** Being especially well adapted or suited: *Their greeting was a happy choice of words.* —**hap′pi·ly** (hăp′ə-lē) *adv.* —**hap′pi·ness** *n.*

happy-go-lucky (hăp′ē-gō-lŭk′ē) *adj.* Taking things easy; carefree: *a happy-go-lucky attitude.*

hara-kiri (här′ĭ-kîr′ē *or* hä′rē-kîr′ē) *n., pl.* **hara-kiris** Suicide by cutting open the abdomen with a dagger or knife, formerly practiced by Japanese samurai.

harangue (hə-răng′) *n.* A long loud speech, often one in which the speaker denounces a person, group, or thing: *The dictator delivered a harangue against enemies of the government.* ❖ *tr.v.* **harangued, haranguing, harangues** To deliver a harangue to: *harangue one's followers for their shortcomings.*

harass (hə-răs′ *or* här′əs) *tr.v.* **harassed, harassing, harasses** **1.** To subject to socially inappropriate remarks or actions: *a boss who was accused of harassing employees.* **2.** To irritate or torment persistently: *harass a speaker with whistles and shouts.* **3.** To carry out repeated attacks and raids against. —**ha·rass′ment** *n.*

harbinger (här′bĭn-jər) *n.* Something that indicates or foreshadows what is to come; a forerunner: *The robin is a harbinger of spring.*

harbor (här′bər) *n.* **1.** A sheltered part of a body of water deep enough for ships and boats to anchor. **2.** A place of shelter; a refuge: *Home is always a safe harbor.* ❖ *tr.v.* **harbored, harboring, harbors** **1.** To give shelter to: *harbor a fugitive.* **2.** To have (a specified thought or feeling): *harboring a grudge against an old enemy.*

hard (härd) *adj.* **harder, hardest** **1.** Resistant to pressure; not readily penetrated: *a hard surface; hard as a rock.* **2.** Difficult to accomplish or finish: *Was the test hard?* **3.** Difficult to understand, express, or convey: *a hard question; a hard concept to explain.* **4.** Performing or acting with great energy, persistence, or care: *a hard worker.* **5.** Forceful or intense: *a hard blow; a hard twist of the knob.* **6.** Difficult to endure; trying; harsh: *a hard life.* **7.** Bad; adverse: *hard luck.* **8.** Strict and demanding; stern: *My music teacher is a hard taskmaster.* **9.** Making few concessions: *The opposing lawyer drove a hard bargain.* **10.** Realistic or practical: *take a hard look at the facts.* **11.** Definite or real; true and unchangeable: *hard facts of the evidence.* **12.** Causing damage to; tending to wear down quickly: *Freezing weather is hard on a car.* **13.** Bitter; rancorous; resentful: *There is much hard feeling between those old enemies.* **14a.** Designating currency as opposed to checks or notes: *pay in hard cash.* **b.** Readily exchanged for gold or other currency: *hard currency.* **15.** Being the sound of *c* in *cat* or *g* in *go,* rather than in *certain* or *general.* **16a.** Having high alcoholic content; intoxicating: *hard liquor.* **b.** Rendered alcoholic by fermentation: *hard cider.* **17.** In printed rather than electronic form: *The typist made a hard copy of the manuscript.* **18.** Containing dissolved salts that interfere with the action of soap: *hard water of high mineral content.* ❖ *adv.* **harder, hardest** **1.** With much effort; intently; earnestly: *work hard.* **2.** With great force, vigor, or energy: *Press hard on the lever.* **3.** In such a way as to cause great damage or hardship: *A number of towns were hit hard by the storm.* **4.** With great distress, grief, pain, or resentment: *took the news hard.* **5.** Toward or into a solid condition: *The little pond is frozen hard all winter.* **6.** Near in space or time; close: *The trees stand hard by the edge of the road.* ◆ **hard and fast** Defined, fixed, and invariable: *a hard and fast rule.* **hard of hearing** Having a partial loss of hearing. **hard put** Undergoing great difficulty: *I'm hard put to explain what he meant.* **hard up** *Informal* In need; poor. —**hard′ness** *n.*

hardback (härd′băk′) *adj. & n.* Hardcover.

hardball (härd′bôl′) *n.* **1.** Baseball. **2.** *Informal* The use of tough and aggressive means to obtain an objective: *The negotiator played hardball to get the opposition to cave in.*

hard-bitten (härd′bĭt′n) *adj.* Made tough by experience: *a hard-bitten criminal lawyer.*

hard-boiled (härd′boild′) *adj.* **1.** Boiled in the shell to a solid consistency. Used of eggs. **2.** Unsentimental and practical; tough: *a hard-boiled journalist.*

hard coal *n.* Anthracite.

hardcore or **hard-core** (härd′kôr′) *adj.* **1.** Intensely loyal: *a hardcore golfer.* **2.** Resistant to improvement or change: *a hardcore criminal.*

hardcover (härd′kŭv′ər) *adj.* Bound in cloth, cardboard, or leather rather than paper. Used of books. ❖ *n.* A hardcover book.

hard disk *n.* A rigid magnetic disk fixed within a disk drive and used for storing computer data.

hard drive *n.* A disk drive that reads data stored on hard disks.

harden (här′dn) *v.* **hardened, hardening, hardens** —*tr.* **1.** To make hard or harder: *harden steel.* **2.** To toughen; make rugged: *harden young athletes by long periods of exercise.* **3.** To make unfeeling, unsympathetic, or callous: *Seeing so much poverty and disease hardened the young doctor's heart.* —*intr.* **1.** To become hard or harder: *Allow the mixture to cool until it hardens.* **2.** To rise and become stable. Used of prices.

hardhat or **hard-hat** (härd′hăt′) *n.* **1.** A lightweight protective helmet worn by workers in industrial settings. **2.** *Informal* A construction worker.

hardheaded (härd′hĕd′ĭd) *adj.* **1.** Stubborn; willful: *a hardheaded mule.* **2.** Pragmatic; realistic: *a hardheaded business manager.* —**hard′head′ed·ly** *adv.*

hardhearted (härd′här′tĭd) *adj.* Lacking in feeling or compassion; pitiless. —**hard′heart′ed·ly** *adv.*

hardihood (här′dē-hŏod′) *n.* Boldness and daring.

hard line *n.* A firm uncompromising policy, position, or stance: *a hard line on crime.* —**hard′-line′** *adj.*

hardly (härd′lē) *adv.* **1.** Barely; only just: *We hardly noticed it was getting late.* **2.** Probably or almost surely not: *I would hardly expect visitors on such a snowy day.* **3.** With severity; harshly.

USAGE The words **hardly, rarely,** and **scarcely** act as if they were negatives and so should not be used with other negatives. You should write *I could hardly believe it* rather than *I couldn't hardly believe it.*

---

hard palate *n.* The hard bony forward part of the roof of the mouth.

hardpan (härd′păn′) *n.* **1.** A layer of hard, often clayey subsoil. Plant roots do not usually grow through hardpan. **2.** Hard unbroken ground.

hard-pressed (härd′prĕst′) *adj.* Undergoing a difficult time: *was hard-pressed to think of an answer right away.*

hardscrabble (härd′skrăb′əl) *adj.* Earning a bare subsistence, as on the land; marginal: *the sharecropper's hardscrabble life.* ❖ *n.* Barren or marginal farmland.

hardship (härd′shĭp′) *n.* A cause of suffering or difficulty: *The settlers suffered great hardships.*

hardtack (härd′tăk′) *n.* A hard biscuit or bread made of flour and water.

hardware (härd′wâr′) *n.* **1.** Articles made of metal, as tools, locks, and cutlery. **2.** A computer and its equipment, such as the keyboard, monitor, hard drive, and printer. **3.** Machinery used in industry and by the military.

hardwood (härd′wŏod′) *n.* **1.** Any of various trees that usually have broad leaves, in contrast to the conifers. Oaks, maples, and mahoganies are hardwoods. **2.** The wood of such a tree, which is usually harder than that of a softwood.

hardy (här′dē) *adj.* **hardier, hardiest** Capable of withstanding harsh or difficult conditions, such as cold weather or poor food: *hardy plants; hardy explorers.*

hare (hâr) *n.* Any of various mammals that are similar to rabbits but have longer ears and give birth to active, furred young.

harebell (hâr′bĕl′) *n.* A plant having slender stems, narrow leaves, and blue flowers shaped like bells.

harebrained (hâr′brānd′) *adj.* Foolish; flighty: *a harebrained idea.*

harelip (hâr′lĭp′) *n.* A cleft lip. This term is no longer used in medicine.

harem (hâr′əm) *n.* **1.** A house or a section of a house reserved for women members of a Muslim household. **2.** The women who live in a Muslim household. **3.** A group of female animals that breed exclusively with a single male.

hark (härk) *intr.v.* **harked, harking, harks** To listen carefully. ◆ **hark back** To recall or be reminiscent of a past event or condition.

harken (här′kən) *v.* Variant of **hearken.**

harlequin (här′lĭ-kwĭn or här′lĭ-kĭn) *n.* **1. Harlequin** A comic pantomime character, usually appearing in a mask and a costume of many colors. **2.** A clown; a buffoon.

harlot (här′lət) *n.* A woman who is a prostitute.

harm (härm) *n.* **1.** Injury or damage: *Locusts often cause great harm to crops.* **2.** Wrong; evil: *There was no harm meant in their careless mistake.* ❖ *tr.v.* **harmed, harming, harms** To do harm to.

harmful (härm′fəl) *adj.* Causing or capable of causing harm; injurious: *Insects can be harmful to plants.* —**harm′ful·ly** *adv.* —**harm′ful·ness** *n.*

harmless (härm′lĭs) *adj.* **1.** Incapable of causing harm: *a harmless kitten.* **2.** Not meant to harm or offend; inoffensive: *a harmless joke.* —**harm′less·ly** *adv.*

harmonic (här-mŏn′ĭk) *n.* **1.** Any of a series of tones whose frequency is a whole number multiple of that of a fundamental tone, often sounded as overtones of the fundamental. **2. harmonics** (*used with a singular verb*) The theory or study of the physical properties and characteristics of musical sound. ❖ *adj.* **1.** Relating to musical harmony. **2.** Relating to overtones produced when a lower tone occurs or is played. —**har·mon′i·cal·ly** *adv.*

harmonica (här-mŏn′ĭ-kə) *n.* A small, rectangular musical instrument consisting of a row of tuned metal reeds set back in air holes, played by exhaling or inhaling.

harmonious (här-mō′nē-əs) *adj.* **1.** Showing accord in feeling or action: *a harmonious neighborhood.* **2.** Having elements pleasingly or appropriately combined: *a harmonious arrangement of colors.* **3.** Characterized by harmony of sound: *the harmonious tones of a handbell choir.* —**har·mo'ni·ous·ly** *adv.*

harmonize (här'mə-nīz') *v.* **harmonized, harmonizing, harmonizes** —*tr.* **1.** To bring into agreement; make harmonious: *harmonize different ideas into a plan.* **2.** To provide harmony for (a melody). —*intr.* **1.** To be in agreement; be harmonious. **2.** To sing or play in harmony: *The choir harmonized in song.* —**har'mo·ni·za'tion** (här'mə-nĭ-zā'shən) *n.*

harmony (här'mə-nē) *n., pl.* **harmonies 1.** A pleasing combination of elements that form a whole: *the harmony of a flower arrangement.* **2.** Agreement in feeling or opinion; accord: *a family that lives in harmony.* **3a.** The combination of notes forming a chord: *The piano fills in the harmony for the voice part of the singer.* **b.** The study of the structure, succession, and relationships of chords. **c.** A combination of musical sounds considered to be pleasing.

harness (här'nĭs) *n.* **1.** A set of leather straps and metal pieces by which an animal is attached to and pulls a vehicle or plow. **2.** Something resembling a harness, as the arrangement of straps used to hold a parachute to the body. ❖ *tr.v.* **harnessed, harnessing, harnesses 1.** To put a harness on (a draft animal): *harness a horse to a wagon.* **2.** To bring under control and direct the force of: *Solar panels harness the sun's energy.* ◆ **in harness** At one's work; on duty: *get back in harness after a vacation.*

harp (härp) *n.* **1.** A musical instrument consisting of an upright triangular frame on which a series of strings are played by plucking with the fingers. **2.** *Informal* A harmonica. ❖ *intr.v.* **harped, harping, harps** To play a harp. ◆ **harp on** To write or talk about to an excessive or tedious degree: *harping on how expensive movie tickets are.*

harpist (här'pĭst) *n.* A person who plays the harp.

harpoon (här-pōon') *n.* A weapon like a spear with a barbed head that is used in hunting whales and large fish. ❖ *tr.v.* **harpooned, harpooning, harpoons** To strike, kill, or catch with a harpoon. —**har·poon'er** *n.*

harp seal *n.* A seal of the North Atlantic and Arctic Oceans whose young pups have a white coat.

harpsichord (härp'sĭ-kôrd') *n.* A keyboard instrument that resembles a piano, having strings that are plucked by means of quills or plectrums.

Harpy (här'pē) *n., pl.* **Harpies 1.** In Greek mythology, a hideous monster with the head and trunk of a woman and the tail, wings, and claws of a bird. **2. harpy** A predatory person.

harquebus (här'kə-bəs *or* här'kwə-bəs) also **arquebus** (är'kə-bəs *or* är'kwə-bəs) *n.* A heavy portable gun invented during the 1400s.

harridan (här'ĭ-dn) *n.* A woman regarded as critical and scolding.

harrier¹ (här'ē-ər) *n.* **1.** A person or thing that harries. **2.** Any of various slender hawks having narrow wings and preying on small animals.

harrier² (här'ē-ər) *n.* A small hound of a breed originally developed in England to hunt hares and rabbits.

WORD HISTORY The bird sense of **harrier¹** is an alteration (influenced by *harry*) of the obsolete English word *harrower*, meaning "plunderer." **Harrier²** comes from Middle English *hairer, eirer,* referring to the same animal as in Modern English. The Middle English form is possibly an alteration (influenced by Middle English *hair,* meaning "hare") of Old French *errier,* meaning "wanderer."

harrow (här'ō) *n.* A farm implement consisting of a heavy frame with sharp teeth or upright disks, pulled over plowed fields to break up and even the soil. ❖ *tr.v.* **harrowed, harrowing, harrows 1.** To break up and level (soil or land) with a harrow. **2.** To inflict great distress or torment on. —**har'row·er** *n.*

harrowing (här'ō-ĭng) *adj.* Extremely distressing; agonizing: *a harrowing experience.*

harry (här'ē) *tr.v.* **harried, harrying, harries 1.** To disturb or distress by or as if by repeated attacks; harass: *harried me with constant phone calls.* **2.** To raid, as in war; sack or pillage: *The invading army harried the countryside.*

harsh (härsh) *adj.* **harsher, harshest 1.** Unpleasantly coarse and rough to the touch: *harsh burlap.* **2.** Unpleasant to the sense of sound or sight: *a harsh angry voice; harsh lighting.* **3.** Unpleasant, uncomfortable, or hostile to survival: *a harsh winter.* **4.** Extremely severe or cruel; stern: *harsh punishment.* **5.** Expressing displeasure or disapproval: *a harsh look.* —**harsh'ly** *adv.* —**harsh'ness** *n.*

hart (härt) *n., pl.* **harts** or **hart** The adult male of various deer.

hartebeest (här'tə-bēst' *or* härt'bēst') *n., pl.* **hartebeests** or **hartebeest** Any of various African antelopes having a brownish coat, a long narrow head, and horns that curve outward in the middle.

harum-scarum (hâr'əm-skâr'əm) *adj.* Lacking a sense of responsibility; reckless. ❖ *adv.* With abandon; recklessly: *ran harum-scarum around the yard.*

harvest (här'vĭst) *n.* **1.** The act or process of gathering a crop. **2.** The crop that ripens or is gathered in a season: *a large corn harvest.* **3.** The time or season of such gathering: *Harvest lasts about six weeks.* **4.** The result or consequence of an action: *Our trip to the Grand Canyon yielded a rich harvest of memories.* ❖ *v.* **harvested, harvesting, harvests** —*tr.* **1.** To gather (a crop): *harvest wheat.* **2.** To gather a crop from: *harvest an apple orchard.* **3.** To take, catch, or remove for a specific purpose: *harvest fish; harvest trees.* **4.** To receive (the benefits or consequences of an action): *harvest the rewards of hard work.* —*intr.* To gather a crop.

harvester (här'vĭ-stər) *n.* **1.** A person who gathers a crop. **2.** A machine for harvesting crops; a reaper.

harvest moon *n.* The full moon that occurs nearest the beginning of autumn.

has (hăz) *v.* Third person singular present tense of **have.**

has-been (hăz'bĭn') *n., pl.* **has-beens** *Informal* A person whose fame, popularity, or success has passed: *The actor is a has-been.*

hash (hăsh) *n.* **1.** A dish of chopped meat, potatoes, and onions or other vegetables browned and cooked together. **2.** A jumble or hodgepodge: *a hash of disconnected sentences.* ❖ *tr.v.* **hashed, hashing, hashes 1.** To chop into pieces; mince: *hash potatoes.* **2.** *Informal* To discuss carefully; review: *hash over a problem.*

hash browns *pl.n.* Potatoes that are chopped, cooked, and fried until they are brown.

hashish (hăsh'ēsh' *or* hă-shēsh') *n.* A dry resinous extract prepared from the hemp plant, used as a narcotic or intoxicant.

Hasid or **Hassid** (кнä'sĭd *or* hä'sĭd) *n., pl.* **Hasidim** or **Hassidim** (кнä-sē'dĭm *or* hä-sē'dĭm) A member of a movement of Jewish mysticism founded in eastern Europe in the 1700s. —**Ha·sid'ic** *adj.*

hasn't (hăz'ənt) Contraction of *has not.*

hasp (hăsp) *n.* A metal fastener with a hinged slotted part that is passed over a staple and secured by a pin, bolt, or padlock.

hassium (hä'sē-əm) *n. Symbol* **Hs** A radioactive element that has been artificially produced by scientists. The half-life of its longest-lived isotope is about 16.5 minutes. Atomic number 108. See **Periodic Table.**

hassle (hăs'əl) *Informal n.* **1.** A cause of annoyance or difficulty: *Driving in the snow is a real hassle.* **2.** An argument or fight. ❖ *v.* **hassled, hassling, hassles** —*intr.* To argue or fight. —*tr.* To bother or harass: *Creditors were hassling him to pay his bills.*

hassock (hăs'ək) *n.* **1.** A thick cushion used as a footstool or for kneeling. **2.** A dense clump of grass.

hast (hăst) *v. Archaic* Second person singular present tense of **have.**

haste (hāst) *n.* **1.** Swiftness of motion or action; rapidity. **2.** Overeagerness to act: *In their haste they forgot to lock the front door.* ◆ **make haste** To move or act swiftly; hurry: *Make haste to get there on time.*

hasten (hā'sən) *v.* **hastened, hastening, hastens** —*intr.* To move or act swiftly; hurry: *I hastened to tell them the good news.* —*tr.* **1.** To cause to hurry: *When the rain started, the teacher hastened the children inside.* **2.** To cause (something) to happen faster or sooner: *The medicine hastened my recovery.*

hasty (hā'stē) *adj.* **hastier, hastiest** **1.** Acting with or marked by speed; swift; rapid: *a hasty departure.* **2.** Done or made too quickly to be accurate or wise; rash: *hasty judgments.* —**hast'i·ly** *adv.* —**hast'i·ness** *n.*

hasty pudding *n.* Cornmeal mush served with a sweetener such as maple syrup or brown sugar.

hat (hăt) *n.* A covering for the head, especially one with a crown and brim. ◆ **at the drop of a hat** At the slightest pretext or provocation. **pass the hat** To take up a collection of money: *passed the hat to collect donations.* **take off (one's) hat to** To respect, admire, or congratulate: *I take my hat off to anyone who can pass that test.*

hatband (hăt'bănd') *n.* A band of ribbon or cloth worn just above the brim on a hat.

hatbox (hăt'bŏks') *n.* A box or case for a hat.

hatch[1] (hăch) *n.* **1.** An opening, as in the deck of a ship, in the roof or floor of a building, or in an airplane. **2.** A trap door or cover for such an opening. **3.** A hatchback.

hatch[2] (hăch) *v.* **hatched, hatching, hatches** —*intr.* To come out of an egg: *The ducklings hatched today.* —*tr.* **1.** To cause to come out of an egg: *The hen hatched a brood of ten chicks.* **2.** To cause (an egg or eggs) to produce young: *We used an incubator to hatch the eggs.* **3.** To devise or plot, especially in secret: *hatching a plan of escape.*

WORD HISTORY Hatch[1] comes from Middle English *hatch,* which comes from Old English *hæc,* both meaning "small door." **Hatch**[2] comes from Middle English *hacchen,* meaning "to cause to come out of an egg."

hatchback (hăch'băk') *n.* **1.** A door that opens upward on the rear of certain automobiles. **2.** A compact automobile having such a door.

hatchery (hăch'ə-rē) *n., pl.* **hatcheries** A place where eggs, especially those of fish or poultry, are hatched.

hatchet (hăch'ĭt) *n.* A small axe with a short handle used with one hand.

hatchling (hăch'lĭng) *n.* A young animal that has just hatched from an egg.

hatchway (hăch'wā') *n.* A passage or opening leading to a hold, compartment, or cellar.

hate (hāt) *v.* **hated, hating, hates** —*tr.* **1.** To have a great dislike for; detest. **2.** To feel dislike or distaste for: *We hate washing dishes.* —*intr.* To feel hatred. ❖ *n.* Intense animosity or dislike; hatred. —**hat'er** *n.*

hate crime *n.* A crime motivated by prejudice against a social group.

hateful (hāt'fəl) *adj.* **1.** Arousing or deserving hatred. **2.** Feeling or showing hatred; full of hate: *They stared at me in a hateful manner.* —**hate'ful·ly** *adv.* —**hate'ful·ness** *n.*

hate speech *n.* Bigoted speech attacking or disparaging a social group or a member of such a group.

hath (hăth) *v. Archaic* Third person singular present tense of **have.**

hatpin (hăt'pĭn') *n.* A long straight pin used to fasten a hat to the hair.

hatred (hā'trĭd) *n.* Intense animosity or hostility.

hatter (hăt'ər) *n.* A person who makes, sells, or repairs hats.

hat trick *n.* Three goals scored by one player in one game, as in ice hockey.

hauberk (hô'bərk) *n.* A long tunic made of chain mail.

haughty (hô'tē) *adj.* **haughtier, haughtiest** Scornfully and condescendingly proud: *The haughty waiter offended many customers.* See Synonyms at **arrogant.** —**haugh'ti·ly** *adv.* —**haugh'ti·ness** *n.*

haul (hôl) *v.* **hauled, hauling, hauls** —*tr.* **1.** To pull or drag forcibly; tug: *We hauled the wood into the shed.* **2.** To transport, as with a truck or cart: *used trucks to haul away the dirt and debris.* —*intr.* To pull or tug. ❖ *n.* **1.** The act of pulling or dragging. **2.** A distance, especially the distance over which something is transported or pulled: *a long haul across country.* **3.** Everything collected or acquired by a single effort; a take: *a big haul of fish.* —**haul'er** *n.*

haunch (hônch) *n.* **1.** The hip, rump, and upper thigh of humans and certain other animals: *The dog settled back on its haunches.* **2.** The loin and leg of an animal, especially as used for food: *a haunch of beef.*

haunt (hônt) *tr.v.* **haunted, haunting, haunts** **1.** To visit, appear to, or inhabit in the form of a ghost or other supernatural being: *spirits haunting the woods.* **2.** To visit often; frequent: *haunts the local bookstores.* **3.** To come continually to the mind of; obsess: *That bad experience has haunted me ever since.* ❖ *n.* A place that is visited often: *This café is a favorite haunt of artists.*

haunting (hôn'tĭng) *adj.* Continually recurring to the mind; unforgettable: *a haunting melody.* —**haunt'ing·ly** *adv.*

Hausa (hou'sə *or* hou'zə) *n., pl.* **Hausa** or **Hausas** **1.** A member of a chiefly Muslim people living in Nigeria and Niger. **2.** The language of the Hausa.

hautboy (hō'boi' *or* ō'boi') *n., pl.* **hautboys** *Archaic* An oboe.

hauteur (hō-tûr') *n.* Haughtiness in bearing and attitude; arrogance: *Their hauteur made them unbearable.*

Havarti (hə-vär'tē) *n.* A mild, semisoft, pale yellow cheese of Danish origin.

have (hăv) *v.* **had** (hăd), **having, has** (hăz) —*tr.* **1.** To be in possession of; own: *I have two pairs of red shoes.* **2.** To display or be capable of displaying a particular characteristic: *That singer has a good voice.* **3.** To feature or contain as a part: *This pencil has an eraser.* **4.** To be in a certain relationship to: *I have a brother and a sister.* **5.** To be trained or experienced in: *This class has had no Spanish at all.* **6.** To hold in the mind: *I have many doubts about this trip. She has a good idea.* **7.** To receive or get: *I had a dozen cards on my birthday.* **8.** To accept; take: *Will you have an orange?* **9.** To go through; experience: *We had a good vacation.* **10a.** To cause (someone) to do something, especially by a request or command: *The coach had us do ten laps.* **b.** To cause (someone or something) to be in a specified place or state: *We had the neighbors over for coffee. In an hour we had the kitchen spotless.* **11.** To allow; permit: *My grandmother won't have rude behavior in her house.* **12.** To carry on; engage in: *We have arguments but are still good friends.* **13.** To be forced or obliged; must: *We have to leave now.* **14.** To give birth to; bear: *Our cat is having kittens soon.* **15.** To partake of: *I'd like to have a snack.* **16.** *Informal* To get the better of; cheat or deceive: *The travelers were had by the swindler.* — *aux.* Used with a past participle to form the perfect tenses indicating completed action: *They had already had their lunch. We will have finished lunch by the time they arrive.* ❖ *n.* A person or country enjoying material wealth: *the gap between the haves and the have-nots.* ◆ **have at** To attack: *We watched two birds have at each other over some seeds.* **have done with** To stop; cease: *Let's have done with this nonsense once and for all.* **have had it** To have endured all that one can: *I've had it with this traffic.* **have it in for (someone)** To intend to harm, especially because of a grudge. **have it out** To settle decisively, especially through discussion or argument: *We had it out and decided to share our chores.* **have on** To wear: *The band members have on their uniforms.* **have to do with** To be concerned or associated with: *The book has to do with World War I.*

haven (hā′vən) *n.* **1.** A harbor or anchorage; a port. **2.** A place of refuge or safety; a sanctuary: *The library is a haven from noise.*

have-not (hăv′nŏt′) *n.* A person or country enjoying little or no material wealth.

haven't (hăv′ənt) Contraction of *have not.*

haversack (hăv′ər-săk′) *n.* A bag worn over one shoulder to carry supplies, as on a hike.

havoc (hăv′ək) *n.* Very great destruction; devastation: *The hurricane created havoc throughout the coastal area.*

haw¹ (hô) *n.* A sound made by a speaker who is trying to think of what to say. ❖ *intr.v.* **hawed, hawing, haws** To make this sound during a pause in speaking: *The manager hawed before deciding to close early.*

haw² (hô) *n.* **1.** The fruit of a hawthorn. **2.** A hawthorn or similar tree or shrub.

haw³ (hô) *interj.* An expression used to command an animal pulling a load to turn to the left.

WORD HISTORY Haw¹ is imitative in origin. **Haw²** comes from Old English *haga,* referring to the same kind of fruit and plant as in Modern English. The origin of **haw³** is unknown.

Hawaiian or **Hawai'ian** (hə-wä′yən) *adj.* Relating to Hawaii or its people, language, or culture. ❖ *n.* **1.** A native or inhabitant of Hawaii. **2.** A Native Hawaiian. **3.** The Polynesian language of the Hawaiians.

Hawaiian shirt *n.* A loose-fitting, collared shirt made of a colorfully printed fabric and usually having short sleeves and buttons down the front.

hawk¹ (hôk) *n.* **1.** Any of various birds having a short hooked bill, keen eyesight, and strong claws with which they catch small birds and other animals for food. **2.** *Informal* A person who favors aggressive action or military intervention rather than negotiation: *The senator is a hawk on national defense.* ❖ *intr.v.* **hawked, hawking, hawks** To hunt with a trained hawk.

hawk² (hôk) *tr.v.* **hawked, hawking, hawks** To sell (goods) in the street by calling out; peddle.

hawk³ (hôk) *intr.v.* **hawked, hawking, hawks** To clear or try to clear the throat by coughing up phlegm.

WORD HISTORY Hawk¹ comes from Middle English *hauk,* which comes from Old English *hafoc,* both referring to the same kind of bird as in Modern English. **Hawk²** comes from Middle English *hauken* (meaning "to peddle"), which comes from Middle Low German *höker,* meaning "street peddler." The origin of **hawk³** is unknown.

hawker (hô′kər) *n.* A person who peddles goods in the street, especially by calling out.

hawk-eyed (hôk′īd′) *adj.* Having very sharp eyesight.

hawkmoth or **hawk moth** (hôk′môth′) *n.* Any of various moths that have a thick body and long front wings. Hawkmoths feed on the nectar of flowers while hovering.

hawkweed (hôk′wēd′) *n.* Any of numerous plants that resemble dandelions and have yellow or orange flowers and often hairy stems and leaves.

hawser (hô′zər) *n.* A heavy line or cable used to moor or tow a ship.

hawthorn (hô′thôrn′) *n.* Any of various usually thorny shrubs or trees having white, red, or pinkish flowers and small red fruits.

hay (hā) *n.* Grass, clover, alfalfa, and other plants cut and dried as food for horses, cattle, or other animals. ❖ *v.* **hayed, haying, hays** — *intr.* To cut and dry grass or other plants so as to make them into hay. — *tr.* To feed with hay.

haycock (hā′kŏk′) *n.* *Chiefly British* A cone-shaped mound of hay in a field.

hay fever *n.* A severe irritation of the eyes, nose, and breathing passages, caused by an allergy to various pollens that are blown about in the air.

hayfork (hā′fôrk′) *n.* **1.** A pitchfork. **2.** A machine for moving or loading hay.

hayloft (hā′lôft′) *n.* A loft in a barn or stable for storing hay.

haymow (hā′mou′) *n.* **1.** A hayloft. **2.** The hay stored in a hayloft.

hayrack (hā′răk′) *n.* **1.** A rack from which livestock feed. **2.** A rack mounted on a wagon for carrying hay. **3.** A wagon fitted with such a rack.

hayrick (hā′rĭk′) *n.* A haystack.

hayride (hā′rīd′) *n.* A ride taken for pleasure in a wagon piled with hay.

hayseed (hā′sēd′) *n.* **1.** Grass seed that is shaken out of hay. **2.** *Slang* A person from the country who is considered unsophisticated.

haystack (hā′stăk′) *n.* A large stack of hay, especially one that is left in a field.

haywire (hā′wīr′) *n.* Wire used for tying up bales of hay. ❖ *adj. Informal* **1.** Not functioning properly; broken: *The ship went haywire when the rudder broke.* **2.** Mentally confused; upset: *The writer went haywire when told he would have to revise the article again.*

hazard (hăz**′**ərd) *n.* **1a.** A chance of being injured or harmed; danger: *the hazards of sailing.* **b.** A possible source of danger: *The stacks of old newspapers were a fire hazard.* **2.** A sandtrap, pond, or other obstacle on a golf course. ❖ *tr.v.* **hazarded, hazarding, hazards 1.** To expose to danger; risk: *Firefighters hazard their lives for the safety of others.* **2.** To dare; venture: *hazard a guess.*

hazardous (hăz**′**ər-dəs) *adj.* Full of danger; risky; perilous: *a hazardous voyage.*

hazardous waste *n.* A material, such as nuclear or industrial waste products, that can damage the environment and harm the health of humans and other organisms.

haze¹ (hāz) *n.* **1.** Fine dust, smoke, or water vapor suspended in the air: *The skyscrapers were shrouded in haze.* **2.** A vague or confused state of mind: *Many people are in a haze just after waking up.*

haze² (hāz) *tr.v.* **hazed, hazing, hazes** To play rough or humiliating jokes on or force to perform humiliating or unpleasant tasks: *The fraternities at our school no longer haze new members.*

WORD HISTORY Haze¹ is probably a back-formation from *hazy.* **Haze²** may come from obsolete French *haser,* meaning "to annoy."

---

hazel (hā**′**zəl) *n.* **1.** Any of various shrubs or small trees having edible nuts enclosed in a leafy husk. **2.** A light yellowish brown.

hazelnut (hā**′**zəl-nŭt**′**) *n.* **1.** The edible nut of a hazel. **2.** A hazel.

hazy (hā**′**zē) *adj.* **hazier, haziest 1.** Marked by the presence of haze; misty: *a hazy sun.* **2.** Not clear; vague: *a hazy recollection of an incident long past.* —**haz′i·ly** *adv.* —**haz′i·ness** *n.*

H-bomb (āch**′**bŏm**′**) *n.* A hydrogen bomb.

HD An abbreviation of high definition.

he (hē) *pron.* **1.** The male person or animal previously mentioned: *My brother can't dance, but he can sing. Our dog's toenails click when he walks.* **2.** A person whose gender is not specified or known: *He who laughs last laughs best.* ❖ *n.* A male animal or person: *If the puppy is a he, we'll call him Spot.*

USAGE Many people do not like to use the pronoun **he** to stand for any person, since half of all people are female. This means that *he* and its other forms *him* and *his* should be avoided in sentences like *Any student who hands in his paper early will get extra credit.* The easiest way to avoid this problem is to write in the plural: *Students who hand in their papers early will get extra credit.* For more information, see Notes at **me** and **they.**

---

head (hĕd) *n.* **1.** The uppermost or forwardmost part of the body of a vertebrate animal, containing the brain and the eyes, ears, nose, mouth, and jaws. **2.** A similar part in other organisms: *the head of an ant.* **3.** One's mind: *I can do the addition in my head. These problems are all in your head.* **4.** A mental ability or aptitude: *She has a good head for mathematics.* **5.** A part of something that sticks out or widens at the end: *the head of a pin.* **6.** The part of a tool used to cut or strike: *the head of a hammer.* **7.** A rounded, tightly clustered mass of leaves, buds, or flowers growing from the main stem: *a head of cabbage.* **8.** A person who leads, rules, or is in charge of something: *the head of the corporation.* **9.** The most important part or leading position: *The girl marched at the head of the parade.* **10.** The uppermost part of something; the top: *Place the appro-*

priate name at the head of each column. **11.** A headline or heading. **12.** A point when something decisive happens; a turning point: *Continual smog over the city brought the matter of air pollution to a head.* **13a.** An individual; a person: *charged $40 a head for the buffet.* **b.** *pl.* **head** A single animal: *20 head of cattle.* **14.** often **heads** (*used with a singular verb*) The side of a coin having the principal design, often the profile of a political leader's head. **15.** The tip of a boil, pimple, or abscess, in which pus forms. **16.** Water that forms the source of a river or stream: *the little stream that forms the head of a great river.* **17.** The pressure exerted by a liquid or gas: *a head of steam.* **18.** The membrane or skin stretched across an instrument such as a drum or banjo. **19.** A device for recording, playing, or erasing a magnetic tape or electronic disk: *a tape recorder with three heads.* ❖ *adj.* **1.** Most important; ranking first; chief: *the head coach.* **2.** Placed on top or in the front: *the head name on a list; the head truck of a convoy.* ❖ *v.* **headed, heading, heads** —*tr.* **1.** To aim, point, or turn in a certain direction: *They headed the team of horses up the hill.* **2.** To be in charge of; lead: *The mayor headed the delegation.* **3.** To be in the first or foremost position of: *Collins heads the list of candidates for the job.* **4.** To place a heading on: *head each column with a number.* **5.** In soccer, to hit (a ball) in the air with one's head. —*intr.* To proceed or go in a certain direction: *head for home.* ◆ **head off** To block the progress or completion of; intercept: *They tried to head him off before he went home.* **head over heels 1.** Rolling, as in a somersault: *He tripped and fell head over heels.* **2.** Completely; hopelessly: *Those two are head over heels in love.* **over (one's) head 1.** Beyond one's understanding: *At first he thought physics was over his head.* **2.** Beyond one's financial means: *After buying a new house and a luxury car, they were over their heads in debt.*

headache (hĕd**′**āk**′**) *n.* **1.** A pain in the head. **2.** *Informal* Something that causes trouble: *Their continual interruptions are a real headache.*

headband (hĕd**′**bănd**′**) *n.* A band worn around the head, as to absorb sweat or hold hair in place.

headboard (hĕd**′**bôrd**′**) *n.* A board, frame, or panel that stands at the head of a bed.

head count or **headcount** (hĕd**′**kount**′**) *n.* **1.** The act of counting people in a group: *After the fire drill, the monitor conducted a head count to make sure everyone left the building.* **2.** The number of people counted in this way.

headdress (hĕd**′**drĕs**′**) *n.* An ornamental covering for the head.

headed (hĕd**′**ĭd) *adj.* **1.** Having a specified kind or number of heads: *a yellow-headed blackbird; a three-headed monster.* **2.** Having a specified kind of disposition: *a cool-headed surgeon.*

header (hĕd**′**ər) *n.* **1.** A beam that supports the ends of joists, studs, or rafters. **2.** A headlong jump or dive. **3.** A shot or pass made in soccer by heading the ball. **4.** Printed information at the top margin of a page.

headfirst (hĕd**′**fûrst**′**) *adv.* **1.** With the head leading; headlong: *dove headfirst into the water.* **2.** Hastily and with little thought; rashly: *rushing headfirst into a complicated project.*

headgear (hĕd**′**gîr**′**) *n.* **1.** A covering for the head, as a hat or helmet. **2.** A brace extending around the head from one side of the mouth to the other, used to reposition the teeth or to restrict the growth of the upper jaw. **3.** The part of a harness that fits about a horse's head.

heading (hĕd**′**ĭng) *n.* **1.** A title, subtitle, or topic put at the head of a page, chapter, or section of a printed or written work: *Each chapter has a heading on the first page.* **2.** The course or direction in which a ship or aircraft is moving: *The ship's heading was due south.*

headland (hĕd′lənd *or* hĕd′lănd′) *n.* A point of land, usually high and with a sheer drop, extending out into a body of water; a promontory.

headless (hĕd′lĭs) *adj.* **1.** Having no head. **2.** Lacking a leader or director.

headlight (hĕd′līt′) *n.* A bright light mounted on the front of an automobile, a train, or another vehicle.

headline (hĕd′līn′) *n.* The title of a newspaper article, usually printed in large type. ❖ *tr.v.* **headlined, headlining, headlines 1.** To give a headline to (a page or article). **2.** To perform as the main attraction at: *a singer headlining a hip-hop festival.*

headlock (hĕd′lŏk′) *n.* A wrestling hold in which the head of an opponent is encircled and held tightly between the arm and chest.

headlong (hĕd′lông′) *adv.* **1.** With the head leading; headfirst: *He slid headlong into third base.* **2.** At reckless speed or with uncontrolled force: *The wolf ran headlong in pursuit.* **3.** Hastily and without thinking; rashly. ❖ *adj.* (hĕd′lông′) **1.** Done with the head leading: *a headlong fall down the steps.* **2.** Recklessly fast or uncontrollably forceful: *a headlong race to the finish.* **3.** Done in a rush; caused by or characterized by little thought: *a headlong decision to go.*

head louse *n.* A small parasitic wingless insect that lives on the human scalp, where it bites the skin and feeds on blood, often causing itching.

headman (hĕd′mən *or* hĕd′măn′) *n.* The male leader or chief, especially of a small village or community.

headmaster (hĕd′măs′tər) *n.* A man who is a school principal, usually of a private school.

headmistress (hĕd′mĭs′trĭs) *n.* A woman who is a school principal, usually of a private school.

head-on (hĕd′ŏn′) *adj.* **1.** Having the front end receiving the impact: *a head-on crash of two cars.* **2.** Facing forward; direct: *the head-on fury of the storm.* ❖ *adv.* **1.** With the head or front first: *The truck ran head-on into the fence.* **2.** In open conflict; directly: *Their opponent attacked the idea head-on.*

headphone (hĕd′fōn′) *n.* A small speaker that is worn over or in the ear.

headpiece (hĕd′pēs′) *n.* A helmet or cap worn to protect the head.

headpin (hĕd′pĭn′) *n.* The front or central pin in a group of bowling pins.

headquarters (hĕd′kwôr′tərz) *pl.n. (used with a singular or plural verb)* **1.** The building or offices from which a commander, as of a military unit or police force, issues orders. **2.** A center of operations: *That company's headquarters are in Cleveland.*

headrest (hĕd′rĕst′) *n.* A support for the head, as at the back of a chair.

headroom (hĕd′rōōm′ *or* hĕd′rōōm′) *n.* Space above one's head, as in a vehicle or tunnel; clearance.

headscarf (hĕd′skärf′) *n., pl.* **headscarfs** or **headscarves** (hĕd′skärvz) **1.** A scarf worn over or around the head, often folded and tied. **2.** A hijab.

headset (hĕd′sĕt′) *n.* A pair of headphones, usually equipped with a microphone.

headstand (hĕd′stănd′) *n.* A position in which one balances oneself vertically on one's head, placing the hands on the floor for support.

head start *n.* **1.** A start before other competitors in a race. **2.** An early start that provides some advantage.

headstone (hĕd′stōn′) *n.* A memorial stone set at the head of a grave.

headstrong (hĕd′strông′) *adj.* **1.** Determined to have one's own way; stubbornly and often recklessly willful. See Synonyms at **obstinate. 2.** Resulting from willfulness or stubbornness: *a headstrong decision.*

heads up (hĕdz) *interj.* An expression used as a warning to watch out for a source of danger, as at a construction site.

headwaiter (hĕd′wā′tər) *n.* A waiter who is in charge of other waiters and is often responsible for taking reservations and seating guests.

headwaters (hĕd′wô′tərz) *pl.n.* The water that forms the source of a river.

headway (hĕd′wā′) *n.* **1.** Movement forward; an advance: *The canoe barely made headway against the strong current.* **2.** Progress toward a goal: *We made a great deal of headway in planning our experiment.* **3.** The distance that separates a bridge, archway, or other overhead structure from the surface beneath it; clearance.

headwind (hĕd′wĭnd′) *n.* A wind blowing in the direction directly opposite the course of a moving object, such as a ship, aircraft, or runner.

headword (hĕd′wûrd′) *n.* A word, phrase, or name usually set in bold type and serving as the heading of an entry in a dictionary, encyclopedia, or similar reference work.

heady (hĕd′ē) *adj.* **headier, headiest 1.** Tending to make one dizzy or foolish: *the heady effects of high altitude.* **2.** Characterized by hasty action or willfully rash behavior; headstrong: *a heady outburst of resentment.* —**head′i·ly** *adv.* —**head′i·ness** *n.*

heal (hēl) *v.* **healed, healing, heals** —*tr.* **1.** To make healthy and sound; cure: *heal the sick.* **2.** To set right; amend: *We need to heal the rift in our friendship.* —*intr.* To become healthy and sound: *The small cut healed quickly.* —**heal′er** *n.*

health (hĕlth) *n.* **1.** The overall condition of an organism or thing at a particular time: *How is your mother's health? Investors are worried about the health of the company.* **2.** Freedom from disease, injury, or defect; soundness of body and mind: *Smoking is bad for your health.*

health care also **healthcare** (hĕlth′kâr′) *n.* The treatment of illness and the preservation of health through the services of medical professionals. ❖ *adj.* also **health-care** Relating to health care: *the health care industry.*

health food *n.* Food considered to be especially beneficial to health and usually grown organically and free of chemical additives.

healthful (hĕlth′fəl) *adj.* **1.** Tending to promote good health; beneficial: *a healthful diet.* **2.** Healthy: *a healthful athlete.* —**health′ful·ly** *adv.* —**health′ful·ness** *n.*

health maintenance organization *n.* An HMO.

healthy (hĕl′thē) *adj.* **healthier, healthiest 1.** In a state of good health: *a healthy baby girl.* **2.** Promoting good health; healthful: *a healthy climate.* **3.** Indicating or characteristic of good health: *a healthy appearance.* **4.** Great or sizable: *a healthy portion of squash.* —**health′i·ly** *adv.* —**health′i·ness** *n.*

✦ **SYNONYMS healthy, robust, sound, well** *adj.*

heap (hēp) *n.* **1.** A group of things thrown together; a pile: *Why is there a heap of dirty rags thrown in the corner? Please dump these banana peels on the compost heap.* **2.** often **heaps** *Informal* A great amount; a lot: *I have heaps of emails to answer.* ❖ *tr.v.* **heaped, heaping, heaps 1.** To put or throw in a heap; pile up: *They heaped wood by the fireplace.* **2.** To fill to overflowing; pile high: *They heaped the cart with groceries.* **3.** To give or bestow in abundance: *The critics heaped compliments on the popular author.*
♦ **SYNONYMS heap, mound, pile, stack** *n.*

hear (hîr) *v.* **heard** (hûrd), **hearing, hears** —*tr.* **1.** To be aware of or receive (sound) by the ears: *Did you hear the knock at the door?* **2.** To learn by hearing; be told by others: *We heard the news from a friend.* **3.** To listen attentively: *They loved to hear their grandmother's stories.* **4.** To listen to officially or formally: *The judge will hear the case in court.* —*intr.* To be capable of perceiving or receiving by the ear: *I don't hear well.* ♦ **hear from** To get a letter, phone call, email, or other form of communication from: *I haven't heard from her in years.* —**hear′er** *n.*

heard (hûrd) *v.* Past tense and past participle of **hear.**

hearing (hîr′ĭng) *n.* **1.** The sense by which sound is perceived; the capacity to hear: *Dogs have excellent hearing.* **2.** The region within which sounds from a particular source can be heard; earshot: *They were talking within my hearing.* **3.** An opportunity to be heard: *The protesters deserve a hearing on their concerns.* **4.** A formal session for listening to testimony or arguments: *Congress holds hearings before passing new laws.* ❖ *adj.* Able to hear: *a deaf child born to hearing parents.*

hearing aid *n.* A small electronic device that amplifies sound and is worn in or behind the ear of a person whose hearing is impaired.

hearing-impaired (hîr′ĭng-ĭm-pârd′) *adj.* **1.** Having a weakened sense of hearing; hard of hearing. **2.** Completely unable to hear; deaf. ❖ *n. (used with a plural verb)* People who are hard of hearing or are deaf: *The movie was shown with captions to benefit the hearing-impaired.*

hearken or **harken** (här′kən) *intr.v.* **hearkened, hearkening, hearkens** or **harkened, harkening, harkens** *Archaic* To listen attentively; pay close attention.

hearsay (hîr′sā′) *n.* Information that is received from another person and for which the truth cannot be verified.

hearse (hûrs) *n.* A vehicle for carrying a dead person to a church or cemetery.

heart (härt) *n.* **1a.** The hollow muscular organ in vertebrate animals that pumps blood throughout the body by contracting and relaxing. **b.** A similar organ in invertebrate animals. **2.** The general area of the chest containing this organ; the breast. **3.** The vital center and source of one's being, emotions, and sensibilities: *I could feel joy welling up in my heart.* **4a.** Emotional state, disposition, or mood: *I walked to the park with a light heart.* **b.** Love; affection: *The children won their teacher's heart.* **c.** The capacity to feel sympathy, kindness, or concern; compassion: *Have you no heart for these people?* **5.** Courage; determination: *The captain's stirring talk gave the crew heart.* **6a.** The central part; the center: *the heart of the city.* **b.** The essential part; the basis: *the heart of the matter.* **7.** A two-lobed representation of the heart, often colored red or pink. **8a.** A red heart-shaped figure on certain playing cards. **b.** A playing card bearing this figure. **c. hearts** The suit of such playing cards. **9. hearts** A card game in which the object is to avoid hearts in taking tricks or to take all the hearts. ♦ **by heart** Learned by rote; memorized

word for word: *He knows that poem by heart.* **from the bottom of (one's) heart** With the deepest appreciation; most sincerely. **have (one's) heart in the right place** To be well-intentioned. **near (one's) heart** or **close to (one's) heart** Loved by or important to one. **take to heart** To take seriously and be affected or troubled by: *Don't take my criticism too much to heart.* **to (one's) heart's content** To one's entire satisfaction; without limitation. **with all (one's) heart** With the deepest feeling or devotion.

heartache (härt′āk′) *n.* Emotional anguish; deep sorrow.

heart attack *n.* A sudden interruption in the normal functioning of the heart that is often accompanied by severe pain and is caused by an insufficient supply of blood to the tissues of the heart.

heartbeat (härt′bēt′) *n.* **1.** A single cycle of contraction and relaxation of the heart. **2.** The general nature of the heart's contractions or the rate at which they occur: *a rapid heartbeat.* **3.** An instant: *ready in a heartbeat.*

heartbreak (härt′brāk′) *n.* Great sorrow, grief, or disappointment.

heartbreaker (härt′brā′kər) *n.* **1.** A person or thing that causes sorrow, grief, or disappointment. **2.** A narrow or last-minute defeat, as in a sporting event.

heartbreaking (härt′brā′kĭng) *adj.* Causing great sorrow, grief, or disappointment: *heartbreaking news.*

heartbroken (härt′brō′kən) *adj.* Suffering from great sorrow, grief, or disappointment; overcome by grief or despair. —**heart′bro′ken·ly** *adv.*

heartburn (härt′bûrn′) *n.* A burning feeling in the chest area, usually caused by excess acid in the stomach.

hearten (här′tn) *tr.v.* **heartened, heartening, heartens** To give strength or courage to; encourage: *The break in the clouds heartened the campers.*

heartfelt (härt′fĕlt′) *adj.* Deeply felt; sincere: *my heartfelt good wishes.*

hearth (härth) *n.* **1.** The floor of a fireplace, often extending into a room. **2.** Family life; the home: *The weary travelers longed for their own hearth.* **3.** The lower part of a blast furnace, from which the molten metal flows.

hearthstone (härth′stōn′) *n.* **1.** Stone used in the construction of a hearth. **2.** Family life; the home.

heartily (här′tl-ē) *adv.* **1.** In a warm and friendly manner; sincerely: *They welcomed their old friends heartily.* **2.** With vigor or enthusiasm: *Everyone plunged heartily into the game.* **3.** Thoroughly; completely: *The mayor heartily disapproved of the plan.* **4.** With much appetite or enjoyment: *After a long day the workers ate heartily.*

heartland (härt′lănd′) *n.* An important central geographical area considered vital to a nation, region, or culture.

heartless (härt′lĭs) *adj.* Lacking sympathy or compassion; pitiless. —**heart′less·ly** *adv.* —**heart′less·ness** *n.*

heart of palm *n., pl.* **hearts of palm** The tender edible portion of certain palms of Central and South America, consisting of a bud with small leaves around it or the soft center of a young stem.

heart-rending or **heartrending** (härt′rĕn′dĭng) *adj.* Causing grief, anguish, or suffering: *a heart-rending story of misfortune.*

heartsease also **heart's-ease** (härts′ēz′) *n.* Peace of mind.

heartsick (härt′sĭk′) *adj.* Profoundly disappointed; very unhappy.

heartstrings (härt′strĭngz′) *pl.n.* A person's deepest feelings: *The actor's lines of grief tugged at the audience's heartstrings.*

heart-to-heart (härt′tə-härt′) *adj.* Personal and sincere; frank: *a heart-to-heart talk.*

heartwarming (härt′wôr′mĭng) *adj.* Causing gladness and tender feelings: *a heartwarming poem.*

heartwood (härt′wŏŏd′) *n.* The older, nonliving central wood of a tree or shrub, usually darker and harder than the sapwood.

heartworm (härt′wûrm′) *n.* **1.** A parasitic nematode worm that infects the heart and the arteries of the lungs of dogs and related animals. It is transmitted by mosquitoes. **2.** The condition that results from infection with heartworms.

hearty (här′tē) *adj.* **heartier, heartiest 1.** Showing warm feelings; cheerful and friendly: *a hearty greeting.* **2.** Complete; thorough: *We gave the team our hearty support.* **3.** Vigorous; robust: *a hearty appearance of health.* **4a.** Giving much nourishment; substantial: *a hearty soup.* **b.** Enjoying or requiring much food: *a hearty appetite.* ❖ *n., pl.* **hearties** A good comrade, especially a sailor. —**heart′i·ness** *n.*

heat (hēt) *n.* **1.** A form of energy produced by the motion of molecules that make up a substance. Heat can be transferred from one substance to another through conduction, convection, or radiation. **2.** The condition of being hot; warmth: *feel the heat of the sun.* **3.** A period of hot weather: *We left for the mountains to escape the summer heat.* **4.** A furnace or other source of warmth: *Is the heat on?* **5.** *Informal* Pressure or stress, as from hostile criticism: *Unable to take the heat from the press, the candidate withdrew from the election.* **6.** The most intense or active stage: *In the heat of their debate both candidates were shouting.* **7.** A single contest in a competition, such as a race: *The competition was reduced to six runners after the first heat.* **8.** A regularly recurring period during which female mammals, excluding humans and certain other primates, are ready to mate; estrus. ❖ *tr. & intr.v.* **heated, heating, heats** To make or become warm or hot: *The sun heats the earth. The soup is heating.* ◆ **heat up** *Informal* To become acute or intense: *Their quarrel heated up rapidly.*

heated (hē′tĭd) *adj.* Excited or angry: *a heated debate.* —**heat′ed·ly** *adv.*

heater (hē′tər) *n.* An apparatus, such as a furnace or stove, that supplies heat.

heat exchanger *n.* A device, such as an automobile radiator, used to transfer heat from a fluid on one side of a barrier to a fluid on the other side without bringing the fluids into direct contact.

heat exhaustion *n.* A condition caused by exposure to heat, resulting in the loss of body fluids through excessive sweating and causing weakness, dizziness, and nausea.

heath (hēth) *n.* **1.** Any of various usually low-growing shrubs having small evergreen leaves and small, colorful, urn-shaped flowers. **2.** An open uncultivated stretch of land covered with low-growing plants; a moor.

heathen (hē′thən) *n., pl.* **heathens** or **heathen 1.** *Offensive* **a.** A person who does not believe in the God of Judaism, Christianity, or Islam. **b.** Such people considered as a group. **2.** A person regarded as uncivilized or uncultured.

heather (hĕth′ər) *n.* A low-growing shrub native to Eurasia, having small evergreen leaves and clusters of small, bell-shaped purple or pink flowers.

heat lightning *n.* Distant flashes of light seen near the horizon, especially on hot summer evenings.

heat shield *n.* A barrier that prevents the heating of an object, as a layer of tiles or other coating on a spacecraft to protect it against the tremendous heat of friction caused by reentry into Earth's atmosphere.

heat stroke *n.* A severe illness caused by prolonged exposure to heat and characterized by headache, fever, hot and dry skin, rapid heartbeat, and sometimes loss of consciousness.

heat wave *n.* A period of unusually hot weather.

heave (hēv) *v.* **heaved, heaving, heaves** —*tr.* **1a.** To raise or lift with effort or force; hoist: *heaved the pack onto the mule's back.* **b.** *Past tense and past participle* **hove** (hōv) To raise or haul by means of a rope, line, or cable: *They hove anchor and set sail.* **2.** To throw with force or effort; hurl: *heave rocks down the hill.* **3.** To utter painfully or with effort: *heaved a sigh of relief.* —*intr.* **1.** To pull with force or effort; haul: *We heaved on the rope to raise the flag.* **2.** To rise and fall repeatedly: *Seaweed heaved on the gentle waves.* **3.** To be forced upward; bulge: *Parts of the sidewalk heaved after the ground froze.* **4.** To vomit. **5.** *Past tense and past participle* **hove** To move to a specified position: *A tugboat hove alongside the huge tanker.* ❖ *n.* **1.** An act or effort of heaving; a throw: *Each heave on the line loosened the anchor a bit more.* **2.** **heaves** (used with a singular or plural verb) A disease of horses affecting the lungs and characterized by coughing and difficulty in breathing. ◆ **heave into sight** or **heave into view** To rise over the horizon into view, as land or a ship. **heave to** To bring a ship at sea to a standstill.

heave-ho (hēv′hō′) *n.* *Slang* Dismissal from one's job or from one's position: *gave him the old heave-ho last week.*

heaven (hĕv′ən) *n.* **1.** often **heavens** The sky or universe as seen from the earth: *a star shooting across the heavens.* **2a.** often **Heaven** In Christianity, the home of God, the angels, and the souls of those who are granted salvation. **b.** Any of the places in or beyond the sky thought of as homes of God or the gods in various religions. **3. Heaven** God: *Thank Heaven you're safe.* **4. heavens** Used in exclamations to express surprise: *Good heavens! Look at that crowd!* **5.** A place or condition of great happiness; bliss: *It'll be heaven to vacation in the quiet of the country.*

heavenly (hĕv′ən-lē) *adj.* **1.** Relating to the heavens; celestial: *the planets and other heavenly bodies.* **2.** Relating or belonging to the dwelling place of God; divine. **3.** Very pleasing; delightful; lovely: *a heavenly summer's day.* —**heav′en·li·ness** *n.*

heavenward (hĕv′ən-wərd) *adv. & adj.* Toward, to, or in heaven.

heavy (hĕv′ē) *adj.* **heavier, heaviest 1.** Having great or unusually great weight: *a heavy package; a heavy skillet.* **2.** Large in amount or intensity: *a heavy rain; heavy traffic.* **3.** Having great power or force; violent: *a heavy blow; heavy seas.* **4a.** Having considerable thickness, density, body, or strength: *a heavy winter coat; drew a heavy line.* **b.** Thick or dense; slow to disperse: *a heavy mist.* **5.** Weighed down, as from weight: *branches heavy with apples; eyelids heavy with sleep.* **6.** Gloomy or sad, as from grief or depression: *a heavy heart.* **7.** Deserving careful consideration; grave; serious: *a heavy issue.* **8a.** Requiring much effort to accomplish; arduous: *heavy reading.* **b.** Hard to endure; severe or burdensome: *a heavy penalty.* **9.** Not easily digested; too rich: *a heavy dessert.* **10.** Moving with or as if with difficulty: *the heavy* *steps of the movers.* **11.** Involving large-scale manufacturing of basic products, such as steel: *heavy industry.* **12.** Indulging or participating to a great degree: *a heavy eater; a heavy investor.* ❖ *adv.* **heavier, heaviest** Heavily: *These thoughts weigh heavy on his mind.* ❖ *n., pl.* **heavies 1.** A serious or tragic role in a play. **2.** A villain in a story or play. —**heav′i·ly** *adv.* —**heav′i·ness** *n.*

heavy-duty (hĕv′ē-doō′tē) *adj.* Made to withstand hard use or wear.

heavy-handed (hĕv′ē-hăn′dĭd) *adj.* **1.** Awkward or clumsy: *a heavy-handed performance on the piano.* **2.** Harsh in treating others; oppressive: *heavy-handed discipline.* —**heav′y-hand′ed·ness** *n.*

heavy-hearted (hĕv′ē-här′tĭd) *adj.* Melancholy; sad; depressed. —**heav′y-heart′ed·ness** *n.*

heavy hydrogen *n.* An isotope of hydrogen with a mass greater than that of ordinary hydrogen; deuterium or tritium.

heavy metal *n.* **1.** A metal that has a high specific gravity, especially one that is greater than 5. Heavy metals, such as lead and mercury, are often poisonous. **2.** Very loud, brash rock music, often having angry or aggressive lyrics.

heavyset (hĕv′ē-sĕt′) *adj.* Having a heavy build; stocky: *The wrestler was heavyset and muscular.*

heavy water *n.* Water formed of oxygen and deuterium. Heavy water is much like ordinary water, but has higher freezing and boiling points and is used in certain nuclear reactors for cooling.

heavyweight (hĕv′ē-wāt′) *n.* **1.** A person or thing of more than average weight. **2a.** A boxer in the heaviest weight class, usually weighing more than 200 pounds (about 90.7 kilograms). **b.** A contestant in the heaviest weight class in others sports, such as wrestling and weightlifting. **3.** *Informal* A person of great importance or influence: *a heavyweight on the national political scene.*

Hebraic (hĭ-brā′ĭk) *adj.* Relating to the Hebrews or their language or culture.

Hebrew (hē′brōo) *n.* **1a.** A member of an ancient Semitic people claiming descent from Abraham, Isaac, and Jacob; an Israelite. **b.** A modern descendant of this people; a Jew. **2a.** The Semitic language of the ancient Hebrews. **b.** The modern form of this language, used especially in Israel. **3. Hebrews** *(used with a singular verb)* A book of the New Testament consisting of an epistle from an unknown writer to a group of Hebrew Christians. —**He′brew** *adj.*

Hebrew Scriptures *pl.n.* The Jewish Bible, consisting of the Torah, the Prophets, and the Writings. The Hebrew Scriptures also form the Old Testament of the Christian Bible.

Hecate (hĕk′ə-tē *or* hĕk′ĭt) *n.* In Greek mythology, an ancient fertility goddess who later became identified with Persephone as queen of Hades and protector of witches.

heck (hĕk) *interj.* Used as a mild oath. ❖ *n. Slang* **1.** An outstanding or noteworthy example: *She has a heck of a lot of money.* **2.** Used as an intensive: *What the heck is going on?*

heckle (hĕk′əl) *tr.v.* **heckled, heckling, heckles** To harass or bother with questions, annoying remarks, or mocking yells: *The crowd heckled the speaker at the rally.* —**heck′ler** *n.*

hectare (hĕk′târ′) *n.* A unit of area in the metric system, equal to 2.471 acres.

hectic (hĕk′tĭk) *adj.* Marked by intense activity, confusion, or excitement: *Constantly changing plans resulted in a hectic departure.* —**hec′ti·cal·ly** *adv.*

hecto– *or* **hect–** A prefix that means hundred: *hectometer.*

hectometer (hĕk′tə-mē′tər *or* hĕk-tŏm′ĭ-tər) *n.* A unit of length in the metric system, equal to 100 meters.

hector (hĕk′tər) *n.* A bully. ❖ *tr.v.* **hectored, hectoring, hectors** To try to frighten or control by bullying.

Hector *n.* In Greek mythology, the bravest Trojan warrior and eldest son of Hecuba and Priam, killed by Achilles.

Hecuba (hĕk′yə-bə) *n.* In Greek mythology, the wife of Priam and mother of Cassandra, Hector, and Paris.

he'd (hēd) Contraction of *he had* or *he would.*

hedge (hĕj) *n.* **1.** A row of closely planted shrubs or small trees forming a fence or boundary. **2.** A means of protection or defense: *They put some of their savings in stocks as a hedge against inflation.* ❖ *v.* **hedged, hedging, hedges** —*tr.* **1.** To enclose or separate with a hedge or hedges: *hedge a yard.* **2.** To restrict or confine; hem in: *The flooded river hedged us in on one side.* **3.** To protect against possible losses on (a bet, investment, or other risk) by balancing one risk against another: *She hedged her investment in stocks by investing in bonds.* —*intr.* To avoid giving a clear or direct answer or statement.

hedgehog (hĕj′hôg′) *n.* Any of several small mammals of Eurasia and Africa that feed on insects and are covered with short stiff spines. Hedgehogs roll up into a ball for protection when frightened.

hedgerow (hĕj′rō′) *n.* A row of bushes or small trees forming a hedge.

heed (hēd) *v.* **heeded, heeding, heeds** —*tr.* To pay attention to; listen to and consider: *I did not heed his warning.* —*intr.* To pay attention. ❖ *n.* Close attention or consideration; notice: *They gave no heed to my greeting. Take heed while crossing the highway.*

heedful (hēd′fəl) *adj.* Paying close attention; mindful: *The builder was heedful of the architect's advice.*

heedless (hēd′lĭs) *adj.* Paying little or no attention; unmindful: *heedless of danger.* —**heed′less·ly** *adv.* —**heed′less·ness** *n.*

heehaw (hē′hô′) *n.* **1.** The loud harsh sound made by a braying donkey. **2.** *Informal* A noisy laugh; a guffaw. ❖ *intr.v.* **heehawed, heehawing, heehaws** To make such a sound.

heel¹ (hēl) *n.* **1a.** The rounded rear part of the human foot below the ankle. **b.** A similar part of the hind leg of some other vertebrates. **2.** The rounded fleshy base on the palm of the human hand. **3.** The part of a sock, shoe, or stocking that covers the heel of the foot. **4.** The part of a shoe or boot that supports the heel of the foot. **5.** A lower or back part, such as the crusty end of a loaf of bread or the end of a tool next to the handle. **6.** *Informal* A dishonest person; a cad. ❖ *v.* **heeled, heeling, heels** —*tr.* To put a heel or heels on: *The cobbler heeled the old shoes.* —*intr.* To follow at one's heels: *I taught the dog to heel.* ◆ **on the heels of** *or* **upon the heels of** Directly behind or immediately following: *The first spring birds come on the heels of winter.* **take to (one's) heels** To run away; flee.

heel² (hēl) *intr. & tr.v.* **heeled, heeling, heels** To tilt or cause to tilt to one side: *Gale winds dangerously heeled the ship. The cargo shifted, and the ship heeled over.*

WORD HISTORY Heel¹ comes from Old English *hēla,* meaning "the rear, rounded part of the foot." **Heel²** comes from Old English *hyldan,* meaning "to tilt to one side."

heft (hĕft) *n.* Weight; heaviness; bulk. ❖ *tr.v.* **hefted, hefting, hefts 1.** To lift or hoist up: *Hefting picks and axes, they went to work.* **2.** To lift (something) in order to estimate or test its weight: *I hefted the heavy package and decided I could carry it.*

hefty (hĕf′tē) *adj.* **heftier, heftiest 1.** Weighty; heavy: *a truck carrying a hefty load.* **2.** Big and strong; muscular: *a hefty sailor.* **3.** *Informal* Substantial or considerable: *The cowhand ate a hefty meal.*

hegemony (hĭ-jĕm′ə-nē *or* hĕj′ə-mō′nē) *n., pl.* **hegemonies** The predominance of one nation or social group over others.

hegira also **hejira** (hĭ-jī′rə *or* hĕj′ər-ə) *n.* **1.** also **Hegira** The flight of the Muslim prophet Muhammad from Mecca to Medina (both in present-day Saudi Arabia) in 622, marking the beginning of the Muslim era. **2.** A flight, as from danger or hardship.

heifer (hĕf′ər) *n.* A young cow that has not given birth to a calf.

heigh-ho (hī′hō′ *or* hā′hō′) *interj.* An expression used to show fatigue, boredom, or disappointment.

height (hīt) *n.* **1.** The distance from the top to the bottom of something: *The height of that tree is more than 60 feet.* **2.** Elevation above a given level; altitude: *What is the height of that mountain?* **3.** The condition of being relatively high or tall: *Height is an advantage in basketball.* **4.** often **heights** A high place, such as a hill or mountain. **5.** The highest point or most advanced degree: *the height of the tourist season; the height of an empire's power.*

heighten (hīt′n) *tr. & intr.v.* **heightened, heightening, heightens 1.** To increase or rise in degree or quantity; intensify: *His angry glare heightened the tension.* **2.** To make or become high or higher; raise or be raised: *The barber heightened the chair for the little boy.*

Heimlich maneuver (hīm′lĭk′) *n.* A method of discharging something lodged in the throat of a choking person. It consists of a firm upward thrust just below the rib cage to force air out of the windpipe.

heinous (hā′nəs) *adj.* Very wicked or evil; abominable: *a heinous crime.* **—hei′nous·ly** *adv.*

heir (âr) *n.* A person who inherits or is legally entitled to inherit the property or title of another.

heir apparent *n., pl.* **heirs apparent** A person who will inherit property or a title if the owner or ancestor dies first.

heiress (âr′ĭs) *n.* A woman who inherits or is legally entitled to inherit the property or title of another.

heirloom (âr′lōōm′) *n.* **1.** A possession passed down through succeeding generations of a family. **2.** A variety of fruit or vegetable that was developed in the past and is not widely grown commercially.

heir presumptive *n., pl.* **heirs presumptive** A person who will inherit property or a title unless a relative with a stronger legal claim to the inheritance is born.

heist (hīst) *Slang tr.v.* **heisted, heisting, heists 1.** To steal: *heisted the collection of jewels from the museum.* **2.** To hold up; rob. ❖ *n.* A robbery; a burglary.

hejira (hĭ-jī′rə *or* hĕj′ər-ə) *n.* Variant of **hegira**.

held (hĕld) *v.* Past tense and past participle of **hold¹**.

Helen (hĕl′ən) *n.* In Greek mythology, the wife of Menelaus. Her abduction by Paris caused the Trojan War.

helical (hĕl′ĭ-kəl *or* hē′lĭ-kəl) *adj.* Relating to or having the shape of a helix. **—hel′i·cal·ly** *adv.*

helices (hĕl′ĭ-sēz′ *or* hē′lĭ-sēz′) *n.* A plural of **helix**.

helicon (hĕl′ĭ-kŏn′ *or* hĕl′ĭ-kən) *n.* A large circular tuba that fits around the player's shoulder.

helicopter (hĕl′ĭ-kŏp′tər) *n.* A wingless aircraft that is

lifted by blades that rotate above the aircraft on a vertical shaft.

heliocentric (hē′lē-ō-sĕn′trĭk) *adj.* **1.** Relating to or measured from the center of the sun: *a spacecraft with a heliocentric orbit.* **2.** Having the sun as center: *Copernicus's heliocentric model of the solar system.*

Helios (hē′lē-ŏs′) *n.* In Greek mythology, the god of the sun, who drives his chariot across the sky from east to west each day.

heliotrope (hēl′lē-ə-trōp′) *n.* Any of several garden plants having clusters of small, fragrant, purplish flowers.

heliotropism (hē′lē-ŏt′rə-pĭz′əm) *n.* Growth or movement of an organism, especially a plant, toward or away from sunlight.

heliport (hĕl′ə-pôrt′) *n.* A place for helicopters to take off and land.

helium (hē′lē-əm) *n. Symbol* **He** A very lightweight, colorless, odorless gaseous element. It has the lowest boiling point of any substance and is the second most abundant element in the universe. Atomic number 2. See **Periodic Table**.

helix (hē′lĭks) *n., pl.* **helixes** or **helices** (hĕl′ĭ-sēz′ *or* hē′lĭ-sēz′) **1.** A three-dimensional curve that lies on a cone or cylinder in such a way that its angle to a plane perpendicular to the axis is constant. **2.** A spiral form or structure, such as the thread of a screw.

hell (hĕl) *n.* **1.** A place, such as Hades, where the spirits of the dead remain for eternity; the underworld. **2.** often **Hell** In certain religions, the place where the souls of the wicked reside in torment after death. **3a.** Misery, torment, or anguish: *the hell of battle.* **b.** A place of misery, torment, or anguish: *City streets are a real hell when choked with traffic.*

he'll (hĕl) Contraction of *he will*.

hellacious (hĕ-lā′shəs) *adj.* **1.** Distasteful and repellent: *hellacious smog.* **2.** *Slang* Extraordinary; remarkable: *a hellacious catch of fish.*

hellbender (hĕl′bĕn′dər) *n.* A large salamander of rivers and streams of the eastern United States, having a flattened brownish body.

hellebore (hĕl′ə-bôr′) *n.* **1.** Any of various plants of Eurasia having large showy flowers and thick roots formerly used in medicine. **2.** Any of various poisonous plants of North America and Eurasia having large leaves, greenish flowers, and thick roots formerly used in medicine.

Hellene (hĕl′ēn′) *n.* A Greek.

Hellenic (hĕ-lĕn′ĭk) *adj.* Relating to the ancient Greeks or their language or history. ❖ *n.* The Greek branch of the Indo-European family.

Hellenistic (hĕl′ə-nĭs′tĭk) *adj.* Relating to Greek history and culture from the death of Alexander the Great in 323 BC until the time that Augustus became the first Roman emperor in 27 BC.

hellion (hĕl′yən) *n.* A mischievous, troublesome, or unruly person.

hellish (hĕl′ĭsh) *adj.* Relating to, resembling, or worthy of hell; terrible: *hellish confusion and noise.* **—hell′ish·ly** *adv.* **—hell′ish·ness** *n.*

hello (hĕ-lō′ *or* hə-lō′) *interj.* An expression used to greet someone, answer the telephone, or express surprise. ❖ *n., pl.* **hellos** A call or greeting of "hello."

helm¹ (hĕlm) *n.* **1.** The steering apparatus of a ship, especially the wheel or tiller. **2.** A position of leadership or control: *a new president at the helm.*

helm² (hĕlm) *n. Archaic* A helmet.

WORD HISTORY Helm¹ comes from Old English *helma*, meaning "the tiller or wheel of a ship." **Helm²** comes from Old English *helm*, meaning "armored helmet."

helmet (hĕl′mĭt) *n.* A covering of metal, plastic, or other hard material worn to protect the head from injury, as in battle, work, or sports.

helmsman (hĕlmz′mən) *n.* A man who steers a ship.

helmsperson (hĕlmz′pûr′sən) *n.* A helmsman or helmswoman.

helmswoman (hĕlmz′wŏŏm′ən) *n.* A woman who steers a ship.

helo (hĕl′ō) *n., pl.* **helos** *Informal* A helicopter.

helot (hĕl′ət) *n.* **1. Helot** A member of a class of serfs in the city-state of Sparta in ancient Greece. **2.** A serf; a slave.

help (hĕlp) *v.* **helped, helping, helps** —*tr.* **1.** To give assistance or support to (someone); aid: *The salesperson helped the customer.* **2.** To make (something) better or more effective; improve or advance: *new ways to help the environment; a remark that didn't help the situation.* **3.** To have a positive effect on (an action or effort). Used with an infinitive: *Your wisecracks are not helping to improve the situation. This program helps create jobs.* **4.** To relieve; ease: *This medicine will help your cold.* **5.** To be able to prevent or change: *I cannot help it if the train is late.* **6.** To refrain from; avoid: *We couldn't help laughing.* —*intr.* To be of service; give assistance: *Do what you can to help.* ❖ *n.* **1.** The act of helping; assistance; aid: *With your help, we can unload these boxes in an hour.* **2.** A person or thing that helps: *A vacuum cleaner is a help in doing housework.* **3.** A person or a group of people hired to work as a helper or helpers: *The restaurant needs kitchen help.* ◆ **cannot help but** To be compelled to; be unable to avoid or resist: *I cannot help but admire their efforts to assist those in need.* **help (oneself) to** To take what one wants, sometimes without permission: *The guests were told to help themselves to the punch.* —**help′er** *n.*

helper T cell *n.* Any of various T cells that promote the activation and function of other cells in the immune system, especially B cells and killer T cells.

helpful (hĕlp′fəl) *adj.* Providing assistance; useful: *gave me some helpful advice.* —**help′ful·ly** *adv.* —**help′ful·ness** *n.*

helping (hĕl′pĭng) *n.* A portion of food for one person.

helping verb *n.* An auxiliary verb.

helpless (hĕlp′lĭs) *adj.* **1.** Unable to help oneself; powerless: *as helpless as a baby.* **2.** Lacking support or protection: *The townspeople were helpless in the violent storm.* —**help′less·ly** *adv.* —**help′less·ness** *n.*

helpmate (hĕlp′māt′) *n.* A helper or helpful companion, especially a husband or wife.

helpmeet (hĕlp′mēt′) *n.* A helpmate.

helter-skelter (hĕl′tər-skĕl′tər) *adv.* In disorderly haste: *The toys were strewn helter-skelter in the living room.* ❖ *adj.* Hurried and confused: *a helter-skelter retreat.*

helve (hĕlv) *n.* A handle of a tool, such as an axe or hammer.

hem¹ (hĕm) *n.* An edge or border of a garment or piece of cloth, made by folding the unfinished edge under and sewing it down. ❖ *tr.v.* **hemmed, hemming, hems 1.** To fold back and sew down the edge of: *The tailor hems skirts and pants.* **2.** To surround and shut in; enclose: *a valley hemmed in by mountains.*

hem² (hĕm) *n.* A short cough or clearing of the throat made especially to gain attention, hide embarrassment, or fill in a pause when speaking. ❖ *intr.v.* **hemmed, hemming, hems** To make this sound. ◆ **hem and haw** To be hesitant and indecisive: *I hemmed and hawed before making a decision.*

WORD HISTORY Hem¹ comes from Old English *hem*, meaning "sewn edge of a piece of cloth." **Hem²** comes from Middle English *heminge*, meaning "coughing."

hematite (hē′mə-tīt′) *n.* A mineral that is the most abundant iron ore. It is reddish-brown when crushed to powder.

hematoma (hē′mə-tō′mə) *n.* An abnormal buildup of blood in a body organ or tissue, caused by a break in a blood vessel.

hemi– A prefix that means half: *hemisphere.* —SEE NOTE AT **semi–**.

hemisphere (hĕm′ĭ-sfîr′) *n.* **1.** One half of a sphere formed by a plane that passes through the center of the sphere. **2.** One half of the earth's surface. The Northern and Southern Hemispheres are divided by the equator. The Eastern and Western Hemispheres are divided by a meridian. **3.** Either of the two sides of the brain of a vertebrate animal. —**hem′i·spher′ic, hem′i·spher′i·cal** *adj.*

hemlock (hĕm′lŏk′) *n.* **1a.** Any of various evergreen trees having short flat needles and small cones. **b.** The wood of any of these trees. **2a.** Any of several poisonous plants having feathery leaves and clusters of small white flowers. **b.** A poison made from any of these plants.

hemo– or **hema–** or **hem–** A prefix that means blood: *hemophilia.*

hemoglobin (hē′mə-glō′bĭn) *n.* The iron-containing protein that gives the red blood cells of vertebrate animals their characteristic color. Hemoglobin binds to oxygen and carries it through the bloodstream from the respiratory organs to the body tissues.

hemophilia (hē′mə-fĭl′ē-ə *or* hē′mə-fēl′yə) *n.* An inherited blood disease, principally affecting males, in which the blood does not clot properly, making it very difficult to stop bleeding.

hemophiliac (hē′mə-fĭl′ē-ăk′ *or* hē′mə-fē′lē-ăk′) *n.* A person who has hemophilia.

hemorrhage (hĕm′ər-ĭj) *n.* A great amount of bleeding. ❖ *intr.v.* **hemorrhaged, hemorrhaging, hemorrhages** To have a hemorrhage; bleed heavily.

hemorrhoids (hĕm′ə-roidz′) *pl.n.* Itching or painful swollen tissue and enlarged veins near the anus.

hemp (hĕmp) *n.* **1.** Tough fibers obtained from the stems of a tall plant and used for making rope, cord, and fabric. **2.** The plant that yields such fibers. Marijuana is made from the leaves and flowers of certain varieties of the hemp plant.

hempen (hĕm′pən) *adj.* Made of or resembling hemp.

hemstitch (hĕm′stĭch′) *n.* **1.** A fancy stitch that leaves an open design in cloth, made by pulling out several parallel threads and drawing the remaining threads together in even bunches. **2.** Decorative needlework made with hemstitching. ❖ *tr.v.* **hemstitched, hemstitching, hemstitches** To hem or decorate with this stitch.

hen (hĕn) *n.* **1.** A female bird, especially an adult female chicken. **2.** The female of certain aquatic animals, such as an octopus or lobster.

hence (hĕns) *adv.* **1.** For this reason; therefore: *These dolls are handmade and hence expensive.* **2.** From this time; from now: *30 years hence.* **3.** From this place; away from here: *Get thee hence!*

henceforth (hĕns′fôrth′) *adv.* From this time on; from now on.

henceforward (hĕns-fôr′wərd) *adv.* Henceforth.

henchman (hĕnch′mən) *n.* **1.** A loyal and trusted follower, as of a politician. **2.** A member of a criminal gang.

henley (hĕn′lē) *n., pl.* **henleys** A collarless knit shirt with long or short sleeves and buttons extending partway down the front.

henna (hĕn′ə) *n.* **1a.** A reddish-brown dye obtained from the leaves of a shrub of northern Africa and southwest Asia, used especially to color the hair or to make designs on the skin. **b.** The shrub that yields such dye. **2.** A reddish-brown color. ❖ *tr.v.* **hennaed, hennaing, hennas** To dye or color with henna.

henpeck (hĕn′pĕk′) *tr.v.* **henpecked, henpecking, henpecks** *Informal* To dominate or harass (someone, usually a man) with persistent nagging.

henry (hĕn′rē) *n., pl.* **henries** or **henrys** A unit used to measure electrical inductance. When a current varies at the rate of one ampere per second and induces an electromotive force of one volt, the circuit has an inductance of one henry.

hepatic (hĭ-păt′ĭk) *adj.* Relating to the liver.

hepatica (hĭ-păt′ĭ-kə) *n.* Any of several low woodland plants having lavender, white, or pink flowers and leaves with three lobes.

hepatitis (hĕp′ə-tī′tĭs) *n.* Inflammation of the liver, usually caused by a virus and characterized by jaundice and fever.

Hephaestus (hĭ-fĕs′təs) *n.* In Greek mythology, the god of fire and metalworking, identified with the Roman Vulcan.

hepta– or **hept–** A prefix that means seven: *heptagon.*

heptagon (hĕp′tə-gŏn′) *n.* A plane figure with seven sides and seven angles. —**hep·tag′o·nal** (hĕp-tăg′ə-nəl) *adj.*

heptahedron (hĕp′tə-hē′drən) *n., pl.* **heptahedrons** or **heptahedra** (hĕp′tə-hē′drə) A solid geometric figure having seven faces.

heptathlon (hĕp-tăth′lŏn′) *n.* A track-and-field event usually for women that includes the 200-meter and 800-meter runs, the 100-meter hurdles, the shot put, the javelin throw, the high jump, and the long jump.

her (hər; hûr *when stressed*) *adj.* The possessive form of **she.** Relating or belonging to her: *Her greatest pleasure is playing her guitar.* ❖ *pron.* The objective form of **she. 1.** Used as the direct object of a verb: *We brought her to the airport.* **2.** Used as the indirect object of a verb: *I wrote her a letter.* **3.** Used as the object of a preposition: *I gave all the popcorn to her.* —SEE NOTE AT **me.**

Hera (hîr′ə) *n.* In Greek mythology, the chief goddess and the wife and sister of Zeus, worshipped as the goddess of women, marriage, and childbirth. She came to be identified with the Roman Juno.

Heracles or **Herakles** (hĕr′ə-klēz′) *n.* Variants of **Hercules.**

herald (hĕr′əld) *n.* **1.** A person who carries messages or makes announcements. **2.** A person or thing that gives an indication of something to come; a harbinger: *The crocus is a herald of spring.* ❖ *tr.v.* **heralded, heralding, heralds** To indicate the coming of; foretell; announce: *The evening star heralds the arrival of nightfall.*

heraldic (hə-răl′dĭk) *adj.* Relating to heralds or heraldry.

heraldry (hĕr′əl-drē) *n., pl.* **heraldries** The study or art concerned with devising and interpreting coats of arms

and tracing the history of families, including the order of succession for aristocratic titles.

herb (ûrb *or* hûrb) *n.* **1.** Any of various usually aromatic plants, such as basil or ginseng, used as a seasoning or for medicinal purposes. **2.** A plant that does not produce a woody stem and often dies back at the end of each growing season.

herbaceous (hûr-bā′shəs *or* ûr-bā′shəs) *adj.* Relating to or characteristic of an herb, in contrast to a woody plant.

herbage (ûr′bĭj *or* hûr′bĭj) *n.* Grass or other leafy plants having soft stems, especially when grown to be eaten by grazing animals.

herbal (ûr′bəl *or* hûr′bəl) *adj.* Relating to or containing aromatic or medicinal herbs: *herbal tea; herbal remedies.* ❖ *n.* A book that describes the kinds and uses of aromatic or medicinal herbs.

herbal medicine *n.* **1.** The use of herbs to prevent or treat disease. **2.** A medicine made from herbs.

herbarium (hûr-bâr′ē-əm *or* ûr-bâr′ē-əm) *n., pl.* **herbariums** or **herbaria** (hûr-bâr′ē-ə *or* ûr-bâr′ē-ə) **1.** A collection of dried plants mounted and labeled for use in scientific study. **2.** A special place or building where such a collection is kept.

herbicide (hûr′bĭ-sīd′ *or* ûr′bĭ-sīd′) *n.* A chemical substance used to destroy or reduce the growth of plants.

herbivore (hûr′bə-vôr′ *or* ûr′bə-vôr′) *n.* An animal that feeds mainly on plants.

herbivorous (hûr-bĭv′ər-əs *or* ûr-bĭv′ər-əs) *adj.* Feeding mainly on plants: *Cattle, deer, and rabbits are herbivorous animals.*

Herculean (hûr′kyə-lē′ən *or* hûr-kyōō′lē-ən) *adj.* **1.** often **herculean** Demanding great strength or courage; tremendously difficult: *Moving the whole library was a herculean task.* **2.** Relating to or resembling Hercules: *It took Herculean strength to move the fallen tree trunk.*

Hercules (hûr′kyə-lēz′) also **Heracles** or **Herakles** (hĕr′-ə-klēz′) *n.* In Greek mythology, a mortal son of Zeus known for his great strength and courage.

herd (hûrd) *n.* **1a.** A group of large domestic animals such as cattle or sheep. **b.** A number of large plant-eating wild animals that stay together as a group: *a herd of elephants.* **2.** A large number of people; a crowd. ❖ *v.* **herded, herding, herds** —*tr.* **1.** To gather or keep (a herd) together: *Dogs herded the sheep into the pen.* **2.** To tend or watch over (a herd): *herding sheep in the mountains.* —*intr.* To come together in a herd: *Buffalo herded together on the plains.*

herder (hûr′dər) *n.* A person who takes care of or drives a herd, as of sheep or cattle.

herdsman (hûrdz′mən) *n.* A person who owns or breeds livestock.

here (hîr) *adv.* **1.** At or in this place: *Put the package here.* **2.** At this time; now: *Let's stop practicing here and break for lunch.* **3.** To this place; hither: *Come here and sit beside me.* ❖ *interj.* An expression used to answer to one's name in a roll call, to call to an animal, or to get someone's attention. ❖ *n.* **1.** This place: *I went from here to the store.* **2.** This life or this time: *We should think more about the here and now than about what might happen.* ◆ **neither here nor there** Not to the point; off the subject; unimportant: *Their vague remarks were neither here nor there.*

hereabouts (hîr′ə-bouts′) *adv.* In this general area; around here: *I dropped my keys somewhere hereabouts.*

hereafter (hîr-ăf′tər) *adv.* From now on; after this: *Hereafter, when you write use my full address.* ❖ *n.* Life after death.

hereby (hîr**′**bī**′**) *adv.* By virtue of this; by this means: *All drivers are hereby required to have an eye test.*

hereditary (hə-rĕd**′**ĭ-tĕr**′**ē) *adj.* **1.** Passed or capable of being passed from parent to offspring by means of genes: *a hereditary trait.* **2.** Passed down by inheritance to a legal heir: *a hereditary title.* **3.** Passed down from one generation to the next: *a hereditary prejudice.*

heredity (hə-rĕd**′**ĭ-tē) *n.* **1.** The passage of traits or characteristics from parents to offspring by biological inheritance through genes. **2.** The traits or characteristics passed to an offspring in this way.

Hereford (hûr**′**fərd *or* hĕr**′**ə-fərd) *n.* Any of a breed of cattle originally developed in England and having a reddish-brown coat with a white face, chest, and belly.

herein (hîr-ĭn**′**) *adv.* In this thing, matter, fact, or place: *She likes to read, and herein lies the source of her large vocabulary.*

hereof (hîr-ŭv**′** *or* hîr-ŏv**′**) *adv.* Of this: *We will speak no more hereof.*

hereon (hîr-ŏn**′**) *adv.* On this: *This is the Constitution, and our Bill of Rights was founded hereon.*

heresy (hĕr**′**ĭ-sē) *n., pl.* **heresies 1.** An opinion or belief that is different from the established beliefs of a religion. **2.** An opinion that is contrary to prevailing views, as in politics or science. **3.** The holding of such a belief or opinion.

heretic (hĕr**′**ĭ-tĭk) *n.* A person who holds beliefs or opinions that are different from accepted beliefs or opinions, as of a church or a political party.

heretical (hə-rĕt**′**ĭ-kəl) *adj.* Relating to, characterized by, or revealing heresy: *The speaker's heretical statements made the audience uneasy.*

hereto (hîr-tōō**′**) *adv.* To this document or matter: *Attached hereto is my signature.*

heretofore (hîr**′**tə-fôr**′**) *adv.* Before this; previously: *Such a huge ship had not been seen heretofore.*

hereunto (hîr-ŭn**′**tōō) *adv.* Hereto.

hereupon (hîr**′**ə-pŏn**′**) *adv.* **1.** Immediately after this: *A few bystanders shouted taunts and hereupon began an argument.* **2.** Upon this point; upon this: *We believe in free speech and hereupon the court has remained firm.*

herewith (hîr-wĭth**′** *or* hîr-wĭth**′**) *adv.* **1.** Along with this: *I am sending herewith a snapshot of the baby.* **2.** By means of this; hereby: *I herewith renounce all claim to the estate.*

heritable (hĕr**′**ĭ-tə-bəl) *adj.* Capable of being inherited: *heritable property; a heritable disease.* —**her′i·ta·bil′i·ty** *n.*

heritage (hĕr**′**ĭ-tĭj) *n.* **1.** Property that is or can be inherited. **2.** Something other than property passed down from preceding generations; a tradition: *Our country has a great heritage of folk music.*

hermaphrodite (hər-măf**′**rə-dīt**′**) *n.* **1.** An organism, such as an earthworm, that typically has both male and female reproductive organs in a single individual. **2.** A person who has both male and female reproductive organs and secondary sexual characteristics.

Hermes (hûr**′**mēz) *n.* In Greek mythology, the messenger of the gods and patron of travelers, thieves, and commerce, identified with the Roman Mercury.

hermetic (hər-mĕt**′**ĭk) also **hermetical** (hər-mĕt**′**ĭ-kəl) *adj.* Sealed so that air cannot enter or escape; airtight. —**her·met′i·cal·ly** *adv.*

hermit (hûr**′**mĭt) *n.* A person who has withdrawn from society and lives a solitary existence.

hermitage (hûr**′**mĭ-tĭj) *n.* The home of a hermit.

hermit crab *n.* Any of various crabs that use an empty snail shell or a similar shell to protect their soft bodies.

hernia (hûr**′**nē-ə) *n., pl.* **hernias** or **herniae** (hûr**′**nē-ē**′**) A condition in which an organ or other structure of the body protrudes through an abnormal opening in the wall that normally contains it; a rupture.

hero (hîr**′**ō) *n., pl.* **heroes 1.** In mythology and legend, a man of great courage and strength who is celebrated for his bold deeds. **2.** A person noted for courageous acts or significant achievements: *a sports hero.* **3.** The protagonist in a novel, poem, play, or movie. **4.** A submarine sandwich.

heroic (hĭ-rō**′**ĭk) also **heroical** (hĭ-rō**′**ĭ-kəl) *adj.* **1.** Having or showing the qualities of a hero; courageous; noble: *heroic deeds; the heroic voyage of Magellan's crew.* **2.** Relating to, or resembling the heroes of literature, legend, or myth. ❖ *n.* **heroics** Heroic behavior or action. —**he·ro′i·cal·ly** *adv.*

heroin (hĕr**′**ō-ĭn) *n.* A bitter white crystalline chemical compound derived from morphine. It is a powerful and highly addictive narcotic drug.

heroine (hĕr**′**ō-ĭn) *n.* **1.** A woman noted for courageous acts or significant achievements. **2.** The female protagonist in a novel, poem, play, or movie.

heroism (hĕr**′**ō-ĭz**′**əm) *n.* Heroic conduct or action; courage; bravery.

heron (hĕr**′**ən) *n.* Any of various wading birds having a long neck, long legs, and a long pointed bill.

herpes (hûr**′**pēz) *n.* Any of several diseases caused by viruses in which there is an eruption of blisters on the skin or mucous membranes.

herpetology (hûr**′**pĭ-tŏl**′**ə-jē) *n.* The branch of zoology that deals with reptiles and amphibians. —**her′pe·tol′o·gist** *n.*

herring (hĕr**′**ĭng) *n., pl.* **herring** or **herrings** Any of various slivery fishes of northern Atlantic and Pacific waters, caught in large numbers and used as fresh or preserved foods.

herringbone (hĕr**′**ĭng-bōn**′**) *n.* **1.** A zigzag pattern made up of short parallel lines arranged in rows that slant first one way, then another. **2.** Cloth woven in this pattern.

hers (hûrz) *pron.* (*used with a singular or plural verb*) The one or ones belonging to her: *If his desk is occupied, use hers.*

herself (hûr-sĕlf**′**) *pron.* **1.** That one that is the same as her: **a.** Used as the direct object or indirect object of a verb or as the object of a preposition to show that the action of the verb refers back to the subject: *She pulled herself up by the rope. She bought herself a new pen. She had a photograph of herself.* **b.** Used to give emphasis: *Carla herself is going. She herself saw it.* **2.** Her real, normal, or healthy self: *She has not been herself since her friend left town.*

hertz (hûrts) *n., pl.* **hertz** A unit used to measure the frequency of vibrations and waves, equal to one cycle per second.

he's (hēz) Contraction of *he is* or *he has.*

hesitancy (hĕz**′**ĭ-tən-sē) *n.* The condition or quality of being hesitant; a hesitancy in speaking one's mind.

hesitant (hĕz**′**ĭ-tənt) *adj.* Inclined or tending to hesitate; doubtful, uncertain, or reluctant: *We were hesitant to fly in such bad weather.* —**hes′i·tant·ly** *adv.*

hesitate (hĕz**′**ĭ-tāt**′**) *intr.v.* **hesitated, hesitating, hesitates 1a.** To be slow to act, speak, or decide: *We hesitated about whether to go over the rickety bridge.* **b.** To pause or wait in uncertainty: *I hesitated before answering since I was not* *sure how he would react.* **2.** To be reluctant or unwilling: *They hesitated to ask for help when they saw how busy I was.*

hesitation (hĕz′ĭ-tā′shən) *n.* The act or an instance of hesitating: *After a short hesitation, we decided to continue the game.*

Hessian (hĕsh′ən) *adj.* Relating to Hesse or its people. ❖ *n.* **1.** A native or inhabitant of Hesse. **2.** A German soldier hired to fight in the British army in America during the Revolutionary War.

hetero– or **heter–** A prefix that means other or different: *heterogeneous.*

heterodox (hĕt′ər-ə-dŏks′) *adj.* Not in agreement with generally accepted beliefs, especially in religion.

heterodoxy (hĕt′ər-ə-dŏk′sē) *n., pl.* **heterodoxies 1.** The condition of being heterodox. **2.** A heterodox belief.

heterogeneous (hĕt′ər-ə-jē′nē-əs *or* hĕt′ər-ə-jēn′yəs) *adj.* **1.** Consisting of parts that are not alike; having unlike elements: *the museum's vast heterogeneous collection of insects.* **2.** Different in kind; not alike: *the heterogeneous insects in the museum's collection.* —**het′er·o·ge′ne·ous·ly** *adv.* —**het′er·o·ge′ne·ous·ness** *n.*

heterosexual (hĕt′ə-rō-sĕk′shoo-əl) *adj.* Relating to or having a sexual orientation toward people of the opposite sex. ❖ *n.* A heterosexual person.

heterosexuality (hĕt′ə-rō-sĕk′shoo-ăl′ĭ-tē) *n.* Sexual orientation toward people of the opposite sex.

heterotroph (hĕt′ər-ə-trŏf′ *or* hĕt′ər-ə-trōf′) *n.* An organism that cannot manufacture its own food and instead obtains its food and energy by eating other organisms or by taking in parts or remains of other organisms. Animals, fungi, and most bacteria are heterotrophs. —**het′er·o·troph′ic** *adj.*

heterozygous (hĕt′ər-ə-zī′gəs) *adj.* Having two different forms of the same gene for a trait such as eye color (for example, brown and blue) at corresponding positions on a pair of chromosomes.

heuristic (hyoo-rĭs′tĭk) *adj.* **1.** Relating to the use of generally useful strategies that are likely to provide good if not optimal solutions to a specific problem. **2.** Relating to a problem-solving technique in which the most appropriate solution of several found by alternative methods is selected at successive stages of a computer program for use in the next step of the program. ❖ *n.* **1.** A heuristic method or process. **2. heuristics** *(used with a singular verb)* The study and application of heuristic methods and processes. —**heu·ris′ti·cal·ly** *adv.*

hew (hyoo) *v.* **hewed, hewn** (hyoon) or **hewed, hewing, hews** —*tr.* **1.** To cut with heavy chopping strokes: *hew a log into pieces.* **2.** To make with heavy chopping strokes: *We hewed a path through the jungle.* —*intr.* To adhere; keep; hold: *hew closely to the regulations.*

hex (hĕks) *n.* **1.** An evil spell; a curse. **2.** A person or thing that brings bad luck: *The new player seemed to be a hex on the team, for we lost four games in a row.* ❖ *tr.v.* **hexed, hexing, hexes 1.** To put a hex on. **2.** To bring bad luck to.

hexa– or **hex–** A prefix that means six: *hexagon.*

hexadecimal (hĕk′sə-dĕs′ə-məl) *adj.* Relating to or using 16 as the base of a number system.

hexagon (hĕk′sə-gŏn′) *n.* A polygon with six sides and six angles. —**hex·a·g′o·nal** (hĕk-săg′ə-nəl) *adj.*

hexahedron (hĕk′sə-hē′drən) *n., pl.* **hexahedrons** or **hexahedra** (hĕk′sə-hē′drə) A solid figure having six faces, as a cube.

hexameter (hĕk-săm′ĭ-tər) *n.* A line of verse made up of six metrical feet.

hey (hā) *interj.* **1.** An expression used to show surprise, appreciation, or wonder: *Hey, that's nice!* **2.** An expression used to attract attention: *Hey, you!* **3.** *Informal* An expression used as a greeting: *Hey, how's it going?*

heyday (hā′dā′) *n.* The period of greatest popularity, success, or power; prime: *The heyday of very large cars seems to have passed.*

hf. An abbreviation of half.

hi (hī) *interj. Informal* An expression used as a greeting.

hiatus (hī-ā′təs) *n., pl.* **hiatuses** or **hiatus** A gap or interruption in space, time, or continuity; a break: *She took a hiatus from work while on maternity leave.*

hibachi (hĭ-bä′chē) *n., pl.* **hibachis** A small, portable charcoal-burning stove used for cooking.

hibernate (hī′bər-nāt′) *intr.v.* **hibernated, hibernating, hibernates** To be in an inactive state during a cold period. In cold climates, many animals hibernate during the winter. —**hi′ber·na′tion** *n.*

hibiscus (hī-bĭs′kəs) *n.* Any of various tropical shrubs or trees having large trumpet-shaped red, white, or pink flowers.

hiccup also **hiccough** (hĭk′əp) *n.* **1.** A sudden and uncontrolled contraction of the muscles of the diaphragm and throat causing the breath to be quickly cut off with a short sharp sound. **2. hiccups** An attack in which spasms of this kind occur repeatedly. ❖ *intr.v.* **hiccupped, hiccupping, hiccups** also **hiccoughed, hiccoughing, hiccoughs 1.** To make the sound of a hiccup. **2.** To have the hiccups.

hick (hĭk) *Informal n.* A person regarded as unsophisticated from having lived in the country. ❖ *adj.* Considered rural and unsophisticated: *a hick town.*

hickory (hĭk′ə-rē) *n., pl.* **hickories 1.** Any of several mostly North American trees that have compound leaves and bear edible nuts. **2.** The tough, heavy wood of such a tree.

hide[1] (hīd) *v.* **hid** (hĭd), **hidden** (hĭd′n) or **hid, hiding, hides** —*tr.* **1.** To put or keep out of sight; conceal: *I hid his birthday present in my closet.* **2.** To prevent from being known; keep secret: *The disguise was a perfect way to hide her true identity.* **3.** To cut off from sight; cover up: *Clouds hid the stars.* —*intr.* To keep oneself out of sight: *The lion hid in the tall grass.* ◆ **hide out** To be in hiding, as from a pursuer: *The gangsters hid out in a remote cabin until it was safe to return to the city.*

✦ **SYNONYMS** hide, conceal, screen, secrete *v.*

hide[2] (hīd) *n.* The skin of an animal, especially the thick tough skin or pelt of a large animal.

WORD HISTORY Hide[1] comes from Old English *hȳdan,* meaning "to put out of sight." **Hide**[2] comes from Old English *hȳd,* meaning "animal skin."

hide-and-seek (hīd′n-sēk′) *n.* A children's game in which one player tries to find and catch the other players who are hiding.

hideaway (hīd′ə-wā′) *n.* **1.** A hideout. **2.** A secluded or isolated place: *Spend a vacation at a hideaway in the mountains.*

hidebound (hīd′bound′) *adj.* Displaying stubborn attachment to one's own opinions or prejudices; narrow-minded: *a hidebound refusal to change his ways.*

hideous (hĭd′ē-əs) *adj.* Repulsive, especially to the sight; revoltingly ugly: *a hideous monster; a hideous murder.* —**hid′e·ous·ly** *adv.* —**hid′e·ous·ness** *n.*

hideout (hīd′out′) *n.* A place of shelter or concealment.

hie (hī) *intr. & tr.v.* **hied, hieing** or **hying** (hī′ing), **hies** To hasten; hurry.

hierarchical (hī′ə-rär′kĭ-kəl *or* hī-rär′kĭ-kəl) *or* **hierarchic** (hī′ə-rär′kĭk *or* hī′rär′kĭk) *adj.* Relating to or organized in a hierarchy. —**hi′er·ar′chi·cal·ly** *adv.*

hierarchy (hī′ə-rär′kē *or* hī′rär′kē) *n., pl.* **hierarchies 1.** An arrangement or categorization of people or things according to rank or grade, with each level having less importance or authority than the one above: *We made a chart to show the hierarchy of positions in the corporation.* **2.** A group of people organized in such an arrangement or categorization.

hieroglyph (hī′ər-ə-glĭf′ *or* hī′rə-glĭf′) *n.* A picture or symbol used in hieroglyphic writing.

hieroglyphic (hī′ər-ə-glĭf′ĭk *or* hī′rə-glĭf′ĭk) *adj.* Related to a system of writing, such as that of ancient Egypt, in which pictures or symbols are used to represent words or sounds: *The ancient Egyptians used hieroglyphic writing.* ❖ *n.* **1.** A hieroglyph. **2. hieroglyphics** Hieroglyphic writing, especially that of the ancient Egyptians. —**hi′- er·o·glyph′i·cal·ly** *adv.*

hifalutin (hī′fə-lōōt′n) *adj. Informal* Variant of **highfalutin.**

hi-fi (hī′fī′) *n., pl.* **hi-fis** *Informal* **1.** High fidelity. **2.** An electronic system for reproducing high-fidelity sound from radio or recordings.

higgledy-piggledy (hĭg′əl-dē-pĭg′əl-dē) *adv.* In complete disorder or confusion. ❖ *adj.* Disordered; jumbled.

high (hī) *adj.* **higher, highest 1a.** Being a relatively great distance above a certain level, as above sea level or the surface of the earth: *There's snow in the high mountains.* **b.** Extending a specified distance upward: *The fence is four feet high.* **2.** Far or farther from a reference point: *too high in the offensive zone to take a shot.* **3.** Greater than usual in degree, amount, force, or intensity: *high temperature; a high standard of living; high winds.* **4.** Above the middle range of musical pitch; shrill; sharp: *the high tones of a flute; a high shriek.* **5.** Being at or near the peak: *Election to the presidency was the high point of a long career in politics.* **6.** Advanced in development or complexity: *higher forms of animal life.* **7.** Greater than others in rank, status, or importance: *a high official; a high priority.* **8.** Serious; grave: *Treason is a high crime.* **9.** Showing joy or excitement: *high spirits.* **10.** Favorable: *The students held their teacher in high regard.* **11.** Expensive; extravagant: *accustomed to high living.* **12.** Situated far from the equator: *high latitudes.* ❖ *adv.* **higher, highest** At, in, or to a high position, level, or degree: *Hawks fly high in the sky. A general ranks high above a private.* ❖ *n.* **1.** A high degree or level: *Gold prices reached a new high.* **2.** A mass of atmospheric air that exerts greater pressure than the air in the regions surrounding it: *This clear dry weather is the result of a high from the west.* **3.** *Informal* An elevated state of good feeling or well-being: *The runner was on a high after winning the race.* **4.** The gear in a transmission that produces the fastest speeds. ◆ **high and dry** Helpless and alone: *When our car broke down in the wilderness we were left high and dry.* **high and low** Everywhere: *I looked high and low for the keys.*

high blood pressure *n.* Hypertension.

highborn (hī′bôrn′) *adj.* Of noble birth.

highboy (hī′boi′) *n.* A tall chest of drawers divided into two sections and supported on four legs.

highbrow (hī′brou′) *adj.* Highly cultured or intellectual:

highbrow literature. ❖ *n.* A person who is or seems to have a high degree of culture or learning.

highchair (hī′châr′) *n.* A very young child's feeding chair that has long legs, a footrest, and usually a tray that can be detached.

high definition *n.* A format for recording and displaying video, having wider proportions and a higher resolution than older television formats. —**high′-def′i·ni′tion** *adj.*

high-end (hī′ĕnd′) *adj. Informal* Appealing to or designed for wealthy consumers: *a high-end department store; high-end video equipment.*

higher education (hī′ər) *n.* Education beyond the high-school level.

highfalutin or **hifalutin** (hī′fə-lōōt′n) *adj. Informal* Pompous or making a showy pretense: *highfalutin words.*

high fidelity *n.* The electronic reproduction of sounds, as on records or magnetic tape, with very little distortion.

high-five (hī′fīv′) *Slang n.* A gesture used for congratulating or greeting in which one person slaps a raised palm against another person's raised palm.

high-flown (hī′flōn′) *adj.* **1.** Lofty; exalted: *high-flown ideals.* **2.** Full of showy pretense; inflated: *high-flown language.*

high frequency *n.* A radio wave frequency in the range between 3 and 30 megahertz.

high-fructose corn syrup (hī′frŭk′tōs′ *or* hī′frōōk′tōs′) *n.* Corn syrup that has been processed to convert some of the glucose to fructose. It is used to sweeten many foods and beverages.

high-grade (hī′grād′) *adj.* Of superior quality.

highhanded (hī′hăn′dĭd) *adj.* Arrogant; overbearing: *The manager's highhanded rejection of my application annoyed me.* —**high′hand′ed·ly** *adv.* —**high′hand′ed·ness** *n.*

high-hat (hī′hăt′) *Informal tr.v.* **high-hatted, high-hatting, high-hats** To be condescending or snobbish toward. ❖ *adj.* Snobbish.

high heels *pl.n.* Women's shoes that have long, thin heels.

High Holy Days *pl.n.* The period from Rosh Hashanah until the end of Yom Kippur.

high jinks or **hijinks** (hī′jĭnks′) *pl.n.* Playful, often noisy and rowdy activity, usually involving mischievous pranks.

high jump *n.* A jump for height made over a raised horizontal bar in an athletic contest.

highland (hī′lənd) *n.* **1.** Elevated land. **2. highlands** A mountainous or hilly part of a country; a region at a high elevation. ❖ *adj.* Relating to a highland.

highlander (hī′lən-dər) *n.* A person who lives in the highlands.

Highland fling *n.* A lively folk dance of the highlands of Scotland.

highlight (hī′līt′) *n.* **1.** An area in a painting or photograph where light is represented as most intense. **2.** The most outstanding event or part: *The highlight of the trip was visiting the botanical gardens.* **3. highlights** Strands of hair that have been lightened, as by bleaching or coloring. ❖ *tr.v.* **highlighted, highlighting, highlights 1.** To cast light on or make brighter with the use of lighter colors: *The artist highlighted the woman's head.* **2.** To make prominent; emphasize: *The article highlighted the painstaking work of the detectives.* **3.** To mark important passages of (text), as with a colored marker, for later reference.

highlighter (hī′lī′tər) *n.* **1.** A usually fluorescent marker that is used for marking passages of text. **2.** A cosmetic for emphasizing areas of the face, such as the eyes or cheekbones.

highly (hī′lē) *adv.* **1.** To a great degree; extremely; very: *highly developed; highly amusing.* **2.** In a good or favorable way: *I think highly of the candidate.* **3.** In a high position or rank: *a highly placed official of our state.* **4.** At a high price, cost, or rate: *a highly paid executive.*

high-minded (hī′mīn′dĭd) *adj.* Having lofty ideals; noble: *a mayor with a high-minded approach to politics.*

highness (hī′nĭs) *n.* **1.** The quality or condition of being tall or high; height. **2. Highness** Used as a title and form of address for a prince or princess: *Her Royal Highness the Princess Margaret.*

high noon *n.* **1.** Exactly noon; the very middle of the day. **2.** The highest stage or most advanced period: *The judge was at the high noon of his career.*

high-pitched (hī′pĭcht′) *adj.* **1.** High in pitch; shrill: *a high-pitched flute.* **2.** Steeply sloped: *a high-pitched roof.*

high-pressure (hī′prĕsh′ər) *adj.* **1.** Having, using, or withstanding pressures higher than normal: *a high-pressure tire.* **2.** Having a high atmospheric pressure: *a high-pressure area moving across the Great Plains.* **3.** *Informal* Using vigorous and persistent methods of persuasion: *a high-pressure sales pitch.*

high-resolution (hī′rĕz′ə-lōō′shən) *adj.* **1.** Relating to an image that has fine detail. **2a.** Relating to a device that produces images that contain a large number of dots per unit of area and are therefore sharp and detailed: *a high-resolution printer; a high-resolution computer screen.* **b.** Relating to an image that contains a large number of pixels per unit of area: *a high-resolution digital photograph.*

high-rise (hī′rīz′) *adj.* Very tall and having many stories: *high-rise apartment building.* ❖ *n.* or **high rise** A high-rise building.

high road *n.* **1.** The easiest or surest path or course. **2.** The most positive or ethical path or course.

high school *n.* A secondary school that usually includes grades 9 or 10 through 12. —**high′-school′** *adj.*

high seas *pl.n.* The open waters of an ocean or sea beyond the limits of any nation's jurisdiction.

high-speed (hī′spēd′) *adj.* **1.** Designed for use at high speed: *a high-speed blender; a high-speed train.* **2.** Taking place at high speed: *a high-speed chase.*

high-spirited (hī′spīr′ī-tĭd) *adj.* **1.** Vivacious; lively: *the students' high-spirited antics.* **2.** Having a proud or unbroken spirit: *a high-spirited horse.*

high-sticking (hī′stĭk′ĭng) *n.* The act of carrying a hockey stick so that the blade rises above a specified height, as above an opponent's waist or shoulders, in violation of the rules.

high-strung (hī′strŭng′) *adj.* Very nervous and easily excited; tense.

hightail (hī′tāl′) *Slang intr.v.* **hightailed, hightailing, hightails** To go as fast as possible, especially in fleeing: *hightailed out of town.* ❖ **hightail it** To hurry or flee.

high-tech (hī′tĕk′) *adj. Informal* Relating to high technology: *high-tech electronic gadgets.*

high technology *n.* Technology involving highly advanced or innovative devices, systems, or materials. —**high′-tech·nol′o·gy** *adj.*

high-tension (hī′tĕn′shən) *adj.* Having a high voltage: *high-tension wires.*

high tide *n.* **1.** The tide when the water reaches its highest level. **2.** The time at which this occurs.

high time *n.* An appropriate time for doing something, especially something that should not be put off any longer: *If you want to catch the train, it's high time we left.*

high-top (hī′tŏps′) *adj.* Extending to or above the ankle: *high-top hiking boots.* ❖ *n.* A high-top shoe, especially a sneaker or athletic shoe that laces up to the ankle.

high-water mark (hī′wô′tər) *n.* **1.** A mark showing the highest level reached by a body of water. **2.** The highest point of something; the apex: *The band reached a high-water mark with its third album.*

highway (hī′wā′) *n.* A main public road: *A highway connects the cities.*

highwayman (hī′wā′mən) *n.* A man who robs travelers on a road.

high wire *n.* A tightrope on which acrobats perform, stretched tightly above the ground.

hijab (hĭ-jäb′) *n.* Any of several cloth head coverings worn by Muslim women.

hijack (hī′jăk′) *tr.v.* **hijacked, hijacking, hijacks 1.** To seize or take control of (a moving vehicle) by use of force, especially in order to reach a different destination. **2.** To stop and rob (a vehicle in transit). **3.** To steal (goods) from a vehicle in transit: *The rebels hijacked medical supplies.* **4.** To seize control of (something) and use it for one's own purposes: *spammers who hijacked a computer network.* —**hi′jack′er** *n.*

hike (hīk) *v.* **hiked, hiking, hikes** —*intr.* To go on an extended walk, especially for pleasure: *hike through the woods.* —*tr.* **1.** To pull or raise, especially with a sudden motion; hitch: *I hiked up my socks.* **2.** To increase or raise: *The new sales tax will hike up prices.* ❖ *n.* **1.** A long walk or trip on foot. **2.** A hitch or tug upward: *Give your socks a hike.* **3.** A rise; an increase: *a hike in gasoline prices.* —**hik′er** *n.*

hila (hī′lə) *n.* Plural of **hilum.**

hilarious (hĭ-lâr′ē-əs) *adj.* Very funny; provoking much laughter: *a hilarious story.* —**hi·lar′i·ous·ly** *adv.*

hilarity (hĭ-lăr′ĭ-tē) *n.* Great merriment or fun.

hill (hĭl) *n.* **1.** A landform that rises above its surroundings but is lower and usually less rugged than a mountain. **2.** A small heap, mound, or pile: *an ant hill.* **3.** A mound of earth that covers seeds or a plant: *hills of corn.* ❖ **over the hill** *Informal* Declining in ability because of age; past one's prime.

hillbilly (hĭl′bĭl′ē) *n., pl.* **hillbillies** *Often Offensive* A person who lives in the backwoods or a mountain area that is remote from settled communities.

hillock (hĭl′ək) *n.* A small hill.

hillside (hĭl′sīd′) *n.* The side of a hill.

hilltop (hĭl′tŏp′) *n.* The top or crest of a hill.

hilly (hĭl′ē) *adj.* **hillier, hilliest** Having many hills: *Northern Missouri is hilly.* —**hill′i·ness** *n.*

hilt (hĭlt) *n.* The handle of a sword or dagger. ❖ **to the hilt** To the limit; completely: *They played their roles to the hilt.*

hilum (hī′ləm) *n., pl.* **hila** (hī′lə) A mark or scar on a seed, such as a bean, showing the point of attachment to the plant.

him (hĭm) *pron.* The objective form of **he. 1.** Used as the direct object of a verb: *We helped him.* **2.** Used as the indirect object of a verb: *She gave him a ride.* **3.** Used as the object of a preposition: *This package is for him.* —SEE NOTES AT **he, me.**

himself (hĭm-sĕlf′) *pron.* **1.** That one that is the same as him: **a.** Used as the direct object or indirect object of a verb or as the object of a preposition to show that the action of the verb refers back to the subject: *He dressed himself. He gave himself plenty of time. He saved some popcorn for himself.* **b.** Used to give emphasis: *He took care of his problem himself.* **2.** His real, normal, or healthy self: *He looks more like himself after the vacation.*

hind¹ (hīnd) *adj.* Located at or forming the rear or back, especially of an animal: *a horse's hind legs.*

hind² (hīnd) *n.* The adult female of various deer.

WORD HISTORY Hind¹ comes from Middle English *hinde,* which is short for *behinde* and comes from Old English *bihindan,* which all mean "located behind." **Hind²** comes from Old English *hind,* which also means "an adult female deer."

hindbrain (hīnd′brān′) *n.* The rear part of the brain, consisting of the pons and the medulla oblongata.

hinder (hīn′dər) *tr.v.* **hindered, hindering, hinders** To prevent the action or progress of; hamper: *Heavy rains hindered traffic on the highway.*

Hindi (hĭn′dē) *n.* An Indic language widely spoken in northern India. —**Hin′di** *adj.*

Hindi-Urdu (hĭn′dē-ōōr′dōō or hĭn′dē-ûr′dōō) *n.* Hindi and Urdu, viewed as essentially the same language with respect to their grammar and basic vocabulary, though very different in their literary forms.

hindmost (hīnd′mōst′) *adj.* Farthest to the rear.

hindquarter (hīnd′kwôr′tər) *n.* **1. hindquarters** The rump or haunches of a four-footed animal. **2.** The rear part of a side of beef, lamb, or other animal carcass.

hindrance (hĭn′drəns) *n.* **1.** A person or thing that hinders; an obstacle: *The heavy backpack was a hindrance to the hiker.* **2.** The act of hindering or the condition of being hindered: *The senator's hindrance of debate effectively prevented the bill's passage.*

hindsight (hīnd′sīt′) *n.* Understanding of the significance of a past event: *In hindsight I know I should have ignored their rude remarks.*

Hindu (hĭn′dōō) *adj.* **1.** Relating to Hinduism. **2.** Relating to the Hindus or their culture. ❖ *n.* A believer in Hinduism.

Hinduism (hĭn′dōō-ĭz′əm) *n.* A diverse body of religion, philosophy, and culture native to India, marked especially by a belief in reincarnation and a supreme being who has many forms and natures.

Hindustani (hĭn′dōō-stä′nē or hĭn′dōō-stăn′ē) *adj.* Relating to northern India, its people, or their Indic dialects. ❖ *n.* Any of these dialects, especially the spoken form of Hindi-Urdu.

hinge (hĭnj) *n.* **1.** A joint on which a door, gate, lid, or cover turns or swings. **2.** A similar structure or part, such as one that enables the shell of a clam to open and close. ❖ *v.* **hinged, hinging, hinges** —*tr.* To attach by a hinge or hinges: *The carpenter hinged the door.* —*intr.* To depend: *This plan hinges on her approval.*

hinny (hĭn′ē) *n., pl.* **hinnies** The sterile hybrid offspring of a male horse and a female donkey.

hint (hĭnt) *n.* **1.** A slight indication or indirect suggestion; a clue: *Can't you give me a hint about the answer to this math problem?* **2.** A small amount; a trace: *There is just a hint of vanilla in these cookies.* ❖ *v.* **hinted, hinting, hints** —*tr.* To make known or indicate in an indirect manner: *Our host hinted that it was time to leave.* —*intr.* To give a hint: *She refused to hint at what really happened.* —**hint′er** *n.*

hinterland (hĭn′tər-lănd′) *n.* **1.** Land away from a seacoast; an inland area. **2.** An area far from cities or towns.

hip¹ (hĭp) *n.* **1.** The projecting part of the human body between the waist and thigh. **2.** A similar part in a four-footed animal, where the hind leg joins the body. **3.** The hipbone or the hip joint.

hip² (hĭp) *adj.* **hipper, hippest** *Slang* Knowledgeable about or aware of what is new.

hip³ (hĭp) *n.* A rose hip.

WORD HISTORY Hip¹ comes from Old English *hype,* referring to the same anatomical body part as in Modern English. The origin of **hip²** is unknown. **Hip³** comes from Old English *hēope,* referring to the same fruit as in Modern English.

hipbone (hĭp′bōn′) *n.* Either of the large, flat, irregularly shaped bones that with the lower backbone form the pelvis.

hip boot *n.* A very high boot that goes up to the hip.

hip-hop (hĭp′hŏp′) *n.* **1.** A style of music usually based on rap, often including elements of other styles such as funk or rhythm and blues. **2.** A popular urban youth culture, closely associated with hip-hop music and the style of African Americans living in major cities.

hip joint *n.* The ball-and-socket joint between the hipbone and the femur.

hippie (hĭp′ē) *n., pl.* **hippies** A member of a social movement originating in the 1960s, typically opposing war and favoring extreme personal freedom in dress and behavior.

hippo (hĭp′ō) *n., pl.* **hippos** A hippopotamus.

hippocampus (hĭp′ə-kăm′pəs) *n., pl.* **hippocampi** (hĭp′-ə-kăm′pī′) A ridge in the floor of each lateral ventricle of the brain that consists mainly of gray matter and has a central role in memory processes. —**hip′po·cam′pal** (hĭp′ə-kăm′pəl) *adj.*

Hippocratic oath (hĭp′ə-krăt′ĭk) *n.* A statement dating from ancient times that sets forth the duties and obligations of a physician. Today many physicians still swear to abide by its principles.

hippodrome (hĭp′ə-drōm′) *n.* **1.** A stadium with an oval racetrack, used for horse and chariot races in ancient Greece and the Roman empire. **2.** An arena used for horse shows.

Hippolyta (hĭ-pŏl′ĭ-tə) *n.* In Greek mythology, a queen of the Amazons.

hippopotamus (hĭp′ə-pŏt′ə-məs) *n., pl.* **hippopotamuses** or **hippopotami** (hĭp′ə-pŏt′ə-mī′) A large, heavy African mammal having dark, almost hairless thick skin, short legs, a broad snout, and a wide mouth. Hippopotamuses live in and near rivers and lakes, eating plants and staying under water for long periods of time.

hipster (hĭp′stər) *n. Informal* A young, usually urban bohemian who cultivates an ironic sensibility. —**hip′-ster·ism** (hĭp′stə-rĭz′əm) *n.*

hire (hīr) *tr.v.* **hired, hiring, hires 1.** To pay (a person) for working or performing a service; employ: *hire teachers for the new school.* **2.** To pay for the use of (something) for a limited time; rent: *hire a car.* ❖ *n.* **1.** A person who has recently become an employee: *The new hires attended a meeting in the human resources office.* **2.** Payment for doing work or for the use of something: *The day's hire for the car is ten dollars.*

hireling (hīr′lĭng) *n.* A person who works only for money, especially a person willing to do tedious or unpleasant tasks for a fee.

hirsute (hûr′sōōt′ *or* hir′sōōt′) *adj.* Hairy. —**hir′sute′- ness** *n.*

his (hĭz) *adj.* The possessive form of **he.** Belonging to or relating to him: *We were impressed by his dedication to his garden.* ❖ *pron.* (*used with a singular or plural verb*) The one or ones belonging to him: *If you can't find your hat, take his.* —SEE NOTE AT **he.**

Hispanic (hĭ-spăn′ĭk) *adj.* **1.** Relating to Spain or to the parts of Latin America where Spanish is spoken. **2.** Relating to a Spanish-speaking people or culture. ❖ *n.* A person of Spanish or Latin-American descent, especially one living in the United States.

hiss (hĭs) *n.* A sound like that made by pronouncing the letter *s: the hiss of air escaping from a tire.* ❖ *v.* **hissed, hiss- ing, hisses** —*intr.* **1.** To make a sound like that of the letter *s: A cat will hiss when frightened.* **2.** To express dislike or disapproval with such a sound: *The crowd hissed and booed at the referee's call.* —*tr.* To say or express by hiss- ing: *The audience hissed its displeasure with the comedian.*

histamine (hĭs′tə-mēn′ *or* hĭs′tə-mĭn′) *n.* A chemical compound found in fungi, plants, and animal tissue and released in allergic reactions in humans, causing expan- sion of blood vessels and tightening of the airways.

histidine (hĭs′tĭ-dēn′ *or* hĭs′tĭ-dĭn′) *n.* An essential amino acid that is important for the growth and repair of tis- sues.

histogram (hĭs′tə-grăm′) *n.* A bar graph in which the length of each bar represents the proportion of data points falling within a particular range of values in a set of data.

histology (hĭ-stŏl′ə-jē) *n., pl.* **histologies** The scientific study of the structure of plant and animal tissues.

historian (hĭ-stôr′ē-ən) *n.* A scholar or writer of history.

historic (hĭ-stôr′ĭk) *adj.* **1.** Important or famous in his- tory: *the historic city of Williamsburg.* **2.** Historical.

USAGE The word **historic** refers to what is important in history: *The Revolutionary War was a historic event.* **Historical** refers to whatever existed in the past, whether regarded as important or not: *The author used many historical characters in her novels.* There is overlap in the meanings of these two words, but if you use them as de- scribed here, your meaning will be clear.

historical (hĭ-stôr′ĭ-kəl) *adj.* **1.** Relating to history: *his- torical events.* **2.** Based on or concerned with events in history: *a historical novel.* **3.** Historic. —**his·tor′i·cal·ly** *adv.* —SEE NOTE AT **historic.**

history (hĭs′tə-rē) *n., pl.* **histories 1.** A written account or record of past events: *I read a history of early aviation.* **2.** The study of past events as a special field of knowledge: *History is her favorite subject.* **3.** The totality of past events in human culture: *printing and other important inven- tions in history.* **4.** A past that is known and sometimes recorded: *an old building with an interesting history.* **5.** An established pattern of behavior: *a person with a history of getting into trouble.*

histrionic (hĭs′trē-ŏn′ĭk) *adj.* **1.** Excessively dramatic or emotional. **2.** Relating to actors or acting.

histrionics (hĭs′trē-ŏn′ĭks) *n.* (*used with a singular or plu- ral verb*) Showy, exaggerated emotional behavior.

hit (hĭt) *v.* **hit, hitting, hits** —*tr.* **1.** To strike against with force; crash into: *The car hit the fence.* **2.** To cause an im- plement or missile to come forcefully into contact with:

I hit the tennis ball with the racket. **3.** To cause (some- thing) to come against a person or thing: *He hit his fist against the table.* **4a.** To get to; reach: *hit a high note; going smoothly until we hit a bumpy road.* **b.** To be affected by (a negative development): *His career hit a snag.* **5.** In base- ball, to make (a base hit): *The batter hit a home run.* **6.** To affect painfully or severely, as if by a blow: *A period of bad business hit the store hard.* —*intr.* **1.** To give or strike a blow: *The post went in deeper every time I hit.* **2.** To come against a person or thing; collide: *The two boats hit in the fog.* **3.** To happen or occur: *The blizzard hit during the night.* **4.** To make an attack: *The enemy hit at midnight.* **5.** To achieve or find something desired or sought: *We hit on the right answer.* ❖ *n.* **1.** A blow that strikes some- thing: *Two or three hits of the hammer will drive the nail in.* **2.** A person or thing that is a popular success: *The new musical is the hit of the season.* **3.** A base hit in baseball. **4a.** A match that is made when searching a collection of data for a particular sequence of characters: *I searched the Web for the phrase "poodle tricks" and got over 40,000 hits.* **b.** A connection made to a website: *My website has received over 1,000 hits since July.* ◆ **hit it off** To get along well together. **hit the nail on the head** To be absolutely right. —**hit′ter** *n.*

hit-and-run (hĭt′n-rŭn′) *adj.* Involving a driver of a ve- hicle who hits someone or damages something and flees to avoid responsibility.

hitch (hĭch) *v.* **hitched, hitching, hitches** —*tr.* **1.** To tie or fasten something with a rope, strap, or loop: *hitch a dog team to the sled.* **2.** To raise or pull with a tug or jerk: *hitch up one's pants.* **3.** *Informal* To get (a ride) by hitchhik- ing: *hitch a lift to the gas station.* **4.** *Slang* To marry: *get hitched.* —*intr.* **1.** To move slowly and in a jerky manner: *The weary climber hitched along the narrow rocky ledge.* **2.** *Informal* To hitchhike. ❖ *n.* **1.** Any of various knots used for temporary fastening, as the timber hitch. **2.** A device used to connect one thing to another; a fasten- ing. **3.** A short pull or jerk; a tug. **4.** A delay or difficulty; a snag: *a hitch in our plans.* **5.** A time period, especially of military service. **6.** *Informal* A ride obtained by hitch- hiking.

hitchhike (hĭch′hīk′) *intr.v.* **hitchhiked, hitchhiking, hitch- hikes** To travel by seeking free rides from drivers of pass- ing vehicles. —**hitch′hik′er** *n.*

hither (hĭth′ər) *adv.* To or toward this place: *Come hither.* ◆ **hither and thither** *or* **hither and yon** In or to many places; here and there: *running hither and thither all day.*

hitherto (hĭth′ər-tōō′) *adv.* Until this time; up to now: *hitherto unobserved stars.*

hit-or-miss (hĭt′ər-mĭs′) *adj.* Careless or unplanned; ran- dom.

Hittite (hĭt′īt′) *n.* **1.** A member of a people who lived in Turkey and northern Syria from 2000 to 1200 BC. **2.** The Indo-European language of this people. ❖ *adj.* Relating to the Hittites or their language or culture.

HIV (āch′ī-vē′) *n.* The virus that causes AIDS by infecting the body's immune system. HIV is transmitted through body fluids such as semen and blood. HIV is short for *human immunodeficiency virus.*

hive (hīv) *n.* **1a.** A structure for housing honeybees. **b.** A colony of honeybees living in such a structure. **2.** A place full of people doing things: *The bus station is a hive of activity around the holidays.* ❖ *tr.v.* **hived, hiving, hives** To gather (honeybees) in a hive.

hives (hīvz) *pl.n.* (*used with a singular or plural verb*) A skin rash characterized by itchy red welts and often resulting from an allergic reaction.

HMO (āch′ĕm-ō′) *n.* A health insurance organization that seeks to control health care costs by requiring people to use only those doctors and facilities on an approved list. HMO is short for *health maintenance organization.*

Hmong (hmŏng) *n.* **1.** A member of a group of peoples native to the mountains of southern China and nearby areas of Vietnam, Laos, and Thailand. **2.** The language of the Hmong. —**Hmong** *adj.*

HMS An abbreviation of Her (or His) Majesty's Ship.

ho (hō) *interj.* An expression used to show surprise or to attract attention: *Land ho!*

hoagie (hō′gē) *n.* A submarine sandwich.

hoar (hôr) *adj.* White or gray; hoary.

hoard (hôrd) *n.* A hidden supply that is stored for future use: *the squirrel's hoard of nuts for winter.* ❖ *tr.v.* **hoarded, hoarding, hoards** To save and store away; accumulate: *The squirrel hoarded nuts for winter.* —**hoard′er** *n.*

hoarfrost (hôr′frôst′) *n.* A white coating of ice crystals that forms when water vapor in the air freezes on an exposed object.

hoarse (hôrs) *adj.* **hoarser, hoarsest 1.** Low and gruff in sound; husky: *The cold reduced my voice to a hoarse whisper.* **2.** Having a low gruff voice: *The football fans were hoarse with shouting.* —**hoarse′ly** *adv.* —**hoarse′ness** *n.*

hoary (hôr′ē) *adj.* **hoarier, hoariest 1.** White or grayish: *a hoary beard.* **2.** Very old; aged: *hoary ruins of the ancient city.* —**hoar′i·ness** *n.*

hoax (hōks) *n.* A trick or act intended to deceive others, often in the form of a practical joke or false report: *The report that the store was going out of business proved to be a hoax.* ❖ *tr.v.* **hoaxed, hoaxing, hoaxes** To deceive or cheat by using a hoax. —**hoax′er** *n.*

hob (hŏb) *n.* A shelf at the back or side of a fireplace for keeping food warm.

hobble (hŏb′əl) *v.* **hobbled, hobbling, hobbles** —*intr.* To walk with difficulty; limp: *The patient hobbled along with one leg in a cast.* —*tr.* **1.** To put a device around the legs of (an animal) to hamper but not prevent movement. **2.** To impede or hinder: *Quarreling hobbled the efforts of the committee to reach a decision.* ❖ *n.* **1.** An awkward walk or a limp. **2.** A device used to hobble an animal.

hobby (hŏb′ē) *n., pl.* **hobbies** An activity, such as collecting stamps or gardening, that is outside one's regular occupation and is engaged in for pleasure. —**hob′by·ist** *n.*

hobbyhorse (hŏb′ē-hôrs′) *n.* **1.** A toy made of a stick with an imitation of a horse's head on one end. **2.** A rocking horse. **3.** A topic that one frequently brings up or dwells on; a fixation.

hobgoblin (hŏb′gŏb′lĭn) *n.* **1.** A mischievous or troublesome elf; a goblin. **2.** A source of fear or dread.

hobnail (hŏb′nāl′) *n.* A short nail with a thick head that is used to protect the soles of shoes or boots.

hobnob (hŏb′nŏb′) *intr.v.* **hobnobbed, hobnobbing, hobnobs** To meet, talk, or spend time together in a friendly familiar manner: *hobnobbing with celebrities at a party.*

hobo (hō′bō) *n., pl.* **hoboes** or **hobos** A person who wanders from place to place without a permanent home or regular way of making a living.

Ho-Chunk (hō′chŭngk′) *n., pl.* **Ho-Chunk** or **Ho-Chunks 1.** A member of a Native American people formerly inhabiting eastern Wisconsin, with present-day populations in Wisconsin and Nebraska. **2.** The Siouan language of the Ho-Chunk.

hock¹ (hŏk) *n.* **1.** The joint of the hind leg of certain four-footed animals, such as horses, dogs, and cats, corresponding to the human ankle. **2.** A small cut of meat, especially ham, from the front or hind leg directly above the foot.

hock² (hŏk) *tr.v.* **hocked, hocking, hocks** *Slang* To pawn: *I hocked my ring for some cash.*

WORD HISTORY Hock¹ comes from Middle English *hokke* (referring to the same joint as in Modern English), which comes from Old English *hōh,* meaning "heel." **Hock²** probably comes from Dutch *hok,* meaning "prison."

---

hockey (hŏk′ē) *n.* **1.** Ice hockey. **2.** Field hockey. **3.** Street hockey.

hocus-pocus (hō′kəs-pō′kəs) *n.* **1.** Meaningless syllables or words used in performing magic tricks. **2.** Meaningless speech or behavior used to deceive: *the hocus-pocus of a swindler.*

hod (hŏd) *n.* **1.** A trough fastened to a long handle and carried over the shoulder for moving bricks, cement, or mortar. **2.** A coal scuttle.

hodgepodge (hŏj′pŏj′) *n.* A mixture of various things; a jumble: *a hodgepodge of items in a desk drawer.*

hoe (hō) *n.* A tool with a flat blade on a long handle, used to loosen the soil and weed around plants. ❖ *v.* **hoed, hoeing, hoes** —*tr.* To weed or dig up with a hoe: *We hoed the garden.* —*intr.* To use a hoe: *We hoed for an hour.* —**ho′er** *n.*

hoecake (hō′kāk′) *n.* A flat baked or fried cake of cornmeal.

hoedown (hō′doun′) *n.* **1.** A square dance. **2.** The music for a square dance. **3.** A social gathering at which square dancing takes place.

hog (hôg) *n.* **1a.** Any of various hoofed mammals having short legs, bristly hair, and a blunt snout used for digging, including the domesticated pig and wild species such as the warthog. **b.** A full-grown pig raised for meat. **2.** A person regarded as greedy, selfish, or filthy. ❖ *tr.v.* **hogged, hogging, hogs** *Informal* To take more than one's share of: *Don't hog the sofa!*

hogan (hō′gän′ *or* hō′gən) *n.* A one-room Navajo dwelling traditionally built of logs and covered with earth.

hoggish (hô′gĭsh) *adj.* **1.** Very greedy or selfish. **2.** Very dirty; filthy. —**hog′gish·ly** *adv.* —**hog′gish·ness** *n.*

hognose snake (hôg′nōz′) *n.* Any of several nonvenomous North American snakes having a thick body and an upturned snout.

hogshead (hôgz′hĕd′) *n.* A large barrel or cask. In the United States, a hogshead usually holds 63 gallons (238 liters).

hogtie (hôg′tī′) *tr.v.* **hogtied, hogtieing** or **hogtying, hogties 1.** To tie together the legs or feet of: *Cowhands usually hogtie cattle to brand them.* **2.** To restrain in movement or disrupt in action; hamper: *The legislature was hogtied in lengthy debate.*

hogwash (hôg′wŏsh′) *n.* **1.** Worthless or ridiculous speech or writing; nonsense. **2.** Garbage fed to hogs.

ho-hum (hō′hŭm′) *adj. Informal* Boring and dull; routine: *The restaurant is elegant but has a ho-hum menu.*

hoi polloi (hoi′ pə-loi′) *n.* The common people; the masses.

hoist (hoist) *tr.v.* **hoisted, hoisting, hoists** To raise or haul up, usually with the help of a pulley or machinery: *A tall crane hoisted bricks to the top of the new building.* ❖ *n.* **1.** A device for hoisting, as a crane, winch, or rope and pulley. **2.** A pull or lift: *Let's give the log a hoist onto the wagon.*

hokey (hō′kē) *adj.* **hokier, hokiest** *Slang* **1.** Mawkishly sentimental; corny. **2.** Noticeably contrived; artificial. —**hok′i·ly** *adv.* —**hok′i·ness, hok′ey·ness** *n.*

hold¹ (hōld) *v.* **held** (hĕld), **holding, holds** —*tr.* **1.** To have and keep in one's grasp: *The baby can hold a rattle now.* **2.** To keep from moving or getting away: *He held the dog by a leash.* **3.** To restrain, stop, or control: *Hold your tongue!* **4.** To keep in prison or custody: *The suspect is being held in the county jail.* **5.** To occupy by force: *The army held the town for a month.* **6.** To have or take as contents; contain: *This box holds a dozen eggs.* **7.** To support; bear: *Will that bridge hold such a heavy load?* **8.** To have in one's possession: *That family holds hundreds of acres of land.* **9.** To have as a position or privilege: *Thomas Jefferson held the office of president for two terms.* **10.** To have as an achievement: *She holds the school record for goals scored.* **11.** To carry on; engage in: *Hold elections; hold a conversation.* **12.** To keep or capture the attention or interest of: *The speaker held the audience spellbound.* **13.** To regard in a certain way: *I hold my doctor in high regard.* **14.** To consider; judge: *That painting was held to be the best.* **15.** To state or affirm: *The court holds that the law is not constitutional.* —*intr.* **1.** To continue in a state or condition; last: *The good weather held for two weeks.* **2.** To remain firm or secure: *The knot held against the strain.* **3.** To continue in the same direction: *The ship held to a southerly course.* **4.** To be true or correct: *The theory holds in all cases.* ❖ *n.* **1.** The act or a means of grasping: *keep a firm hold on the handle.* **2.** Something that may be grasped or used for support: *The rocks had many holds for climbers.* **3.** A very strong influence or power: *England's hold over the American colonies ended with the Revolution.* **4.** In music, a symbol over a note or a rest to show that it should be held for a longer time. **5.** A telephone service that allows one to temporarily interrupt a call without severing the connection. ◆ **get hold of 1.** To get possession of; find: *Where can I get hold of that magazine?* **2.** To communicate with, especially by telephone: *I tried to get hold of you.* **3.** To gain control of: *Get hold of yourself.* **hold a candle to** To have the same stature or abilities as: *Though a good trumpeter, he doesn't hold a candle to Louis Armstrong.* **hold down** To work at and keep: *hold down a job.* **hold forth** To talk at great length; make a long speech. **hold off** To delay or wait: *I hope the rain holds off until after the picnic.* **hold on 1.** To keep a grip; cling. **2.** To continue to do something: *He held on arguing until we were angry.* **3.** To stop or wait for a person or thing: *Hold on a minute.* **hold (one's) own** To do well despite difficulty. **hold out 1.** To last: *How long will our water supply hold out?* **2.** To continue to resist: *The strikers held out against the management.* **hold over 1.** To delay or postpone. **2.** To keep for an additional period of time: *The play was held over for another week.* **hold the bag** To be forced into a state of total responsibility when it ought to have been shared: *She was left holding the bag when the project director quit.* **hold the fort** To assume responsibility, especially in someone's absence: *I'll hold the fort while you're on vacation.* **hold to** To remain loyal or faithful to: *Have you held to your resolutions?* **hold up 1.** To stop or delay. **2.** To remain in good condition; function well: *This car should hold up for many years.* **3.** To show as an example: *The essay was held up as an example of good writing.* **4.** To

rob by threatening with harm or force. **no holds barred** Without limits or restraints. **on hold 1.** Into or in a state of temporary interruption without total disconnection during a telephone call: *put someone on hold.* **2.** Into or in a state of delay for an unknown period of time: *The project is on hold until further notice.*

hold² (hōld) *n.* The lower inside part of a ship or aircraft, where cargo is stored.

WORD HISTORY Hold¹ comes from Old English *healdan,* meaning "to hold." **Hold²** comes from Middle English *hole,* which comes from Old English *hulu,* both meaning "husk, hull of a ship."

---

holder (hōl′dər) *n.* **1.** A person who holds, owns, or possesses something: *a ticket holder; a job holder.* **2.** A device for holding something: *a napkin holder.*

holding (hōl′dĭng) *n.* **1.** often **holdings** Legally owned property, such as land, stocks, or bonds: *has huge holdings in the oil industry.* **2.** In sports, an illegal hampering of an opponent's movements with the hands or arms.

holding company *n.* A company that is formed to own stocks and bonds in other companies, usually for the purpose of controlling them.

holdout (hōld′out′) *n.* A person or group who refuses to cooperate or agree: *Environmentalists are the last holdouts against building the highway.*

holdover (hōld′ō′vər) *n.* One that is held over from an earlier time: *a political adviser who was a holdover from the Reagan era; a family tradition that is a holdover from my grandparents' childhood.*

holdup (hōld′ŭp′) *n.* **1.** A stopping of progress or activity; a delay: *a holdup in production.* **2.** A robbery committed by an armed person.

hole (hōl) *n.* **1.** An opening or open place; a gap or space: *wear a hole in the elbow of a sweater; a hole in a fence; a hole in the clouds.* **2.** A hollowed place in something solid; a cavity or pit: *dug a hole to plant the tree.* **3.** *Informal* A shabby or dismal dwelling: *His apartment is a real hole.* **4.** A bad or troublesome situation; a difficulty: *help a friend out of a hole.* **5.** A fault or defect: *They found holes in her argument.* **6a.** In golf, one of the small cups into which the ball must be hit. **b.** One of the 9 or 18 divisions of a golf course. ❖ *tr.v.* **holed, holing, holes** To hit (a golf ball) into the hole. ◆ **hole up** To sleep, hide, or take shelter in a burrow or other shelter: *The bear has holed up for the winter. She was so angry that she holed herself up in her room all day.*

hole in one *n.* The driving of a golf ball from the tee into the hole in a single stroke.

holiday (hōl′ĭ-dā′) *n.* **1.** A day on which general business activity is stopped to commemorate or celebrate a particular event. **2.** *Chiefly British* A period of time for relaxing away from work; a vacation. **3.** A religious feast day; a holy day.

holiness (hō′lē-nĭs) *n.* **1.** The condition or quality of being holy. **2. Holiness** Used as a title for the head of certain religions, such as the pope or the Dalai Lama.

holism (hō′lĭz′əm) *n.* The theory that living matter or reality is made up of organic or unified wholes that are greater than the simple sum of their parts. —**ho′list** *n.*

holistic (hō-lĭs′tĭk) *adj.* **1.** Relating to holism. **2.** Concerned with systems or individuals as wholes rather than as combinations of separate, unrelated parts: *holistic medicine; a holistic approach to education.* —**ho·lis′-ti·cal·ly** *adv.*

holler (hŏl′ər) *tr. & intr.v.* **hollered, hollering, hollers** To yell or shout: *Don't holler at me. She hollered a greeting to friends across the street.* See Synonyms at **yell.** ❖ *n.* A shout or yell.

hollow (hŏl′ō) *adj.* **hollower, hollowest 1.** Having a space or opening inside: *a hollow log.* **2.** Shaped like a bowl or cup; concave or indented: *A puddle always forms in the hollow spot in the back yard.* **3.** Echoing as if coming from an empty place: *the hollow sound of far-off thunder.* **4.** Not true or sincere; empty: *a hollow promise.* ❖ *n.* **1.** An opening or space; a hole: *The rabbits made a hollow at the foot of the tree.* **2.** A small valley between hills or mountains. ❖ *tr.v.* **hollowed, hollowing, hollows 1.** To make hollow: *hollow out a pumpkin.* **2.** To scoop or form by making into the shape of a bowl or cup: *The turtle hollowed out a nest in the sand.* —**hol′low·ly** *adv.* —**hol′low·ness** *n.*

holly (hŏl′ē) *n., pl.* **hollies 1.** Any of numerous shrubs or trees often having evergreen leaves with prickly edges and bright red berries. **2.** Sprigs or branches of such a shrub or tree, traditionally used as Christmas decorations.

hollyhock (hŏl′ē-hŏk′) *n.* A tall garden plant having long spikes of showy, variously colored flowers.

holmium (hŏl′mē-əm) *n. Symbol* **Ho** A soft, silvery metallic element found in certain minerals and used mainly in scientific research. Atomic number 67. See **Periodic Table.**

holocaust (hŏl′ə-kôst′ *or* hō′lə-kôst′) *n.* **1.** Great or total destruction resulting in massive loss of life, especially by fire. **2. Holocaust** The mass killing of European Jews and other groups by the Nazis during World War II. **3.** Widespread destruction or slaughter. **4.** A sacrificial offering that is entirely consumed by flames.

Holocene (hŏl′ə-sēn′ *or* hō′lə-sēn′) *n.* The more recent of the two epochs of the Quaternary Period, beginning at the end of the last Ice Age, about 12,000 years ago. Human civilizations developed during the Holocene. —**Hol′o·cene′** *adj.*

hologram (hŏl′ə-grăm′ *or* hō′lə-grăm′) *n.* The photographic record of an image produced by holography.

holograph (hŏl′ə-grăf′ *or* hō′lə-grăf′) *n.* A document, such as a letter, will, or manuscript, written entirely in the handwriting of the person who signs it.

holography (hə-lŏg′rə-fē) *n.* A method of producing a three-dimensional image of an object by using a divided beam of light from a laser. The laser light is directed by mirrors so that one beam reflects off the object onto a photographic plate or film and the other beam illuminates the plate or film at the same time.

holster (hōl′stər) *n.* **1.** A case to hold a pistol, usually made of leather and attached to a belt, strap, or saddle. **2.** A belt with loops or slots for carrying small tools or other equipment.

holy (hō′lē) *adj.* **holier, holiest 1.** Belonging to, coming from, or associated with a divine power; sacred: *The Bible and the Koran are holy books.* **2.** Living according to highly moral or religious principles; saintly: *a holy person.* **3.** Regarded with special respect or awe; revered: *To music lovers this concert hall is a holy place.*

Holy Ark *n.* The cabinet in a synagogue in which the scrolls of the Torah are kept.

Holy Communion *n.* The Christian rite commemorating Jesus's last supper, in which bread and wine or juice are blessed and eaten in remembrance of Jesus's death.

holy day *n.* A day of a special religious observance.

Holy Ghost *n.* The Holy Spirit.

Holy Grail *n.* In medieval legend, the cup used by Jesus at the Last Supper and the object of many quests by Knights of the Round Table.

holy of holies *n.* **1.** The innermost sanctuary of the temple of Jerusalem in ancient Israel, where the Ark of the Covenant was kept. **2.** A sacred or revered place.

Holy See *n.* The official position, authority, or court of the pope.

Holy Spirit *n.* The third person of the Christian Trinity.

holy water *n.* Water blessed by a priest and used for baptism and in other religious services.

Holy Week *n.* The week before Easter.

Holy Writ *n.* The Bible.

Holstein (hōl′stīn′ *or* hōl′stēn′) *n.* Any of a breed of black and white dairy cattle.

homage (hŏm′ĭj *or* ŏm′ĭj) *n.* **1.** Special honor or respect; reverence: *The president paid homage to the poet by quoting her in his speech.* **2.** The acknowledgment of allegiance made by a vassal to a lord in a ceremony under feudal law.

hombre (ŏm′brā′) *n. Slang* A man; a fellow.

home (hōm) *n.* **1.** A place in which a person lives: *Our home is in that apartment building.* **2.** A group of people, especially a family, that lives together in a dwelling place; a household: *Those children come from a loving home.* **3.** The place in which one was born, grew up, or has lived a long time: *No matter where I live, I will always think of Montana as my home.* **4.** The region or place in which a living thing or an object is commonly found: *Coral reefs are home to many different kinds of fish. Where is the stapler's home?* **5.** A place where people are cared for: *a home for the elderly.* **6.** The place, such as a city or stadium, where a sports team originates or plays most of its games. **7.** In certain games, a goal or place of safety that the players try to reach. **8.** In baseball, home plate. ❖ *adj.* **1.** Relating to or taking place in a home: *home life; home cooking.* **2.** Played on the grounds where a team originates or plays most of its games: *a home game.* ❖ *adv.* **1.** At, to, or toward one's home: *The children raced home from school.* **2.** On or into the point or mark at which something is directed: *The arrow struck home.* **3.** To the center or heart of something; deeply: *Their arguments struck home.* ❖ *intr.v.* **homed, homing, homes** To move or advance toward a destination or target: *The missile homed in on the ship.* ◆ **at home 1.** In one's home or country: *While we were abroad, we read about problems at home.* **2.** Comfortable and relaxed; at ease: *felt at home with strangers.*

home free Out of danger; assured of success: *Our hardest exams are first; after they're done we should be home free.*

home base *n.* **1.** A goal toward which players of certain games try to make progress. **2.** Home plate. **3.** A center of operations; a headquarters.

homebody (hōm′bŏd′ē) *n.* A person whose interests and pleasures center on the home.

homecoming (hōm′kŭm′ing) *n.* **1.** A return to one's home: *The soldier's homecoming was a joyous occasion.* **2.** In some high schools and colleges, a yearly celebration held for returning graduates.

home economics *n.* (*used with a singular or plural verb*) The art and practice of managing a household. —**home economist** *n.*

home fries *pl.n.* Sliced or chopped potatoes that are fried in a pan until brown and crisp.

homegrown (hōm′grōn′) *adj.* **1.** Made or grown at home:

homegrown tomatoes from our garden. **2.** Coming from or characteristic of a particular place: *homegrown Appalachian music.*

homeland (hōm′lănd′) *n.* **1.** The country in which a person was born; a person's native land. **2.** A country, region, or territory that is identified with a particular people or ethnic group.

homeless (hōm′lĭs) *adj.* Having no home or haven. ❖ *n.* *(used with a plural verb)* People who have no home considered as a group. —**home′less·ness** *n.*

homely (hōm′lē) *adj.* **homelier, homeliest 1.** Not attractive or good-looking. **2.** Simple and plain: *a homely manner.* —**home′li·ness** *n.*

homemade (hōm′mād′) *adj.* **1.** Made at home: *delicious homemade bread.* **2.** Crudely or simply made, as if made at home: *rough homemade furniture.*

homemaker (hōm′mā′kər) *n.* A person who manages a household, especially as one's main daily activity. —**home′mak′ing** *n.*

homeopathy (hō′mē-ŏp′ə-thē) *n.* A system for treating disease in which patients are given tiny doses of a drug that, when given in large amounts to healthy people, produces symptoms like those of the disease itself. Homeopathy is a kind of alternative medicine. —**ho′me·o·path′ic** *adj.*

homeostasis (hō′mē-ō-stā′sĭs) *n.* The ability or tendency of an organism or cell to maintain stable internal conditions regardless of changing outside conditions. —**ho′me·o·stat′ic** (hō′mē-ō-stăt′ĭk) *adj.*

homepage (hōm′pāj′) *n.* The main page of a website, usually providing information about the site.

home plate *n.* In baseball, the base at which the batter stands when hitting and which a base runner must touch in order to score.

homer (hō′mər) *n.* A home run. ❖ *intr.v.* **homered, homering, homers** To hit a home run.

homeroom (hōm′rōom′ *or* hōm′rŏŏm′) *n.* A classroom in which a group of pupils are required to gather each day, as for attendance.

home run *n.* In baseball, a hit that allows the batter to touch all the bases and score a run.

homeschool (hōm′skōol′) *tr.v.* **homeschooled, homeschooling, homeschools** To educate (a pupil, for example) at home rather than in an established school. —**home′school′er** *n.*

homesick (hōm′sĭk′) *adj.* Longing for home. —**home′sick′ness** *n.*

homespun (hōm′spŭn′) *adj.* **1.** Spun or woven at home: *homespun cloth.* **2.** Made of homespun cloth: *a homespun shirt.* **3.** Plain and simple; folksy: *homespun humor.* ❖ *n.* A plain coarse cloth woven from homespun yarn, or a similar cloth made from yarn spun by machine.

homestead (hōm′stĕd′) *n.* **1.** A house, especially a farmhouse or similar dwelling, together with the land and buildings belonging to it. **2.** A piece of land given to a settler by the US government, usually with conditions such as clearing and working the land for five years. ❖ *intr.v.* **homesteaded, homesteading, homesteads** To settle on land claimed as a homestead. —**home′stead′er** *n.*

homestretch (hōm′strĕch′) *n.* **1.** The part of a racetrack from the last turn to the finish line. **2.** The last stage of something: *I am in the homestretch of writing this report.*

hometown (hōm′toun′) *n.* The town or city of one's birth, rearing, or main residence.

homeward (hōm′wərd) *adv. & adj.* Toward or at home: *They turned their canoe and paddled homeward; the homeward journey.* —**home′wards** *adv.*

homework (hōm′wûrk′) *n.* **1.** Work that is done at home. **2.** School assignments that are done at home or outside the classroom.

homey (hō′mē) *adj.* **homier, homiest** *Informal* Suggesting a home; pleasant, cheerful, and comfortable: *a restaurant with a homey atmosphere.*

homicide (hŏm′ĭ-sīd) *n.* **1.** The killing of one person by another. **2.** A person who kills another person. —**hom′i·cid′al** *adj.*

homily (hŏm′ə-lē) *n., pl.* **homilies 1.** A sermon, especially one explaining the practical and moral implications of a passage in scripture. **2.** A tiresome lecture or warning that urges virtuous behavior.

homing pigeon (hō′mĭng) *n.* A pigeon trained to fly back to its home roost.

hominid (hŏm′ə-nĭd) *n.* Any of various primates belonging to a family that includes orangutans, gorillas, chimpanzees, bonobos, humans, and their extinct relatives. Scientists formerly defined this scientific family as including only humans and their extinct ancestors, and the word *hominid* is still sometimes used in this way. —**hom′i·nid** *adj.*

hominin (hŏm′ĭ-nĭn′) *n.* Any of various primates belonging to a group that includes modern humans and their extinct relatives from the Pliocene and Pleistocene Epochs. The hominins were formerly classified as hominids. —**hom′i·nin′** *adj.*

hominy (hŏm′ə-nē) *n.* Hulled and dried kernels of corn.

homo– or **hom–** A prefix that means same or similar: *homogeneous.*

Homo erectus (hō′mō ĭ-rĕk′təs) *n.* An extinct species of humans known from fossil remains found in Africa and Eurasia and dating from about 1.9 million to less than 100,000 years ago. *Homo erectus* is widely regarded as an ancestor of modern humans.

homogeneity (hō′mə-jə-nē′ĭ-tē *or* hō′mə-jə-nā′ĭ-tē) *n., pl.* **homogeneities** The state or quality of being homogeneous.

homogeneous (hō′mə-jē′nē-əs *or* hō′mə-jēn′yəs) *adj.* **1.** Of the same or similar kind; uniform throughout: *a homogeneous class of students having the same abilities.* **2.** Made up of similar parts; having similar elements: *a housing development of homogeneous architecture.* —**ho′mo·ge′ne·ous·ly** *adv.* —**ho′mo·ge′ne·ous·ness** *n.*

homogenize (hə-mŏj′ə-nīz′) *tr.v.* **homogenized, homogenizing, homogenizes 1.** To make homogeneous or uniform throughout. **2.** To reduce to particles and disperse throughout a fluid: *homogenize paint.* **3.** To make (milk) uniform in consistency by reducing the fat to small globules so that the fat does not rise to the top as cream. —**ho·mog′e·ni·za′tion** (hə-mŏj′ə-nĭ-zā′shən) *n.*

homograph (hŏm′ə-grăf′ *or* hō′mə-grăf′) *n.* A word that has the same spelling as another word but differs in meaning, origin, and sometimes in pronunciation; for example, *ring* (circle) and *ring* (sound), and *bass* (fish) and *bass* (deep tone) are homographs.

Homo habilis (hō′mō hăb′ə-ləs) *n.* An extinct species of humans known from fossil remains found in Africa and dating from about 2 million to 1.6 million years ago.

homologous (hə-mŏl′ə-gəs) *adj.* **1.** Similar in structure and evolutionary origin, as the arm of a human and the flipper of a seal. **2.** Relating to or indicating either of a pair of chromosomes having the same structure, with genes for the same traits arranged in the same order.

homonym (hŏm**′**ə-nĭm**′** *or* hō**′**mə-nĭm**′**) *n.* A word that has the same sound and sometimes the same spelling as another word but a different meaning and origin; for example, *die* (stop living), *die* (marked cube used in board games), and *dye* (color) are all homonyms. —**ho·mon′-y·mous** (hō-mŏn**′**ə-məs *or* hə-mŏn**′**ə-məs) *adj.*

homophobia (hō**′**mə-fō**′**bē-ə) *n.* Fear, hatred, or mistrust of lesbians and gay men. —**ho′mo·phobe′** *n.* —**ho′-mo·pho′bic** (hō**′**mə-fō**′**bĭk) *adj.*

homophone (hŏm**′**ə-fōn**′** *or* hō**′**mə-fōn**′**) *n.* A word that has the same sound as another word but differs in spelling, meaning, and origin; for example, *for*, *fore*, and *four* are homophones. —**ho·moph′o·nous** (hō-mŏf**′**ə-nəs *or* hə-mŏf**′**ə-nəs) *adj.*

Homo sapiens (hō**′**mō sā**′**pē-ənz) *n.* The modern species of humans.

homosexual (hō**′**mə-sĕk**′**shoo-əl) *adj.* Relating to or having a sexual orientation toward people of the same sex. ❖ *n.* A homosexual person.

homosexuality (hō**′**mə-sĕk**′**shoo-ăl**′**ĭ-tē) *n.* Sexual orientation toward people of the same sex.

homozygous (hō**′**mō-zī**′**gəs) *adj.* Having two identical forms of the same gene for a trait such as eye color at corresponding positions on a pair of chromosomes.

Hon. An abbreviation of: **1.** honorable (title). **2.** honorary.

honcho (hŏn**′**chō) *n., pl.* **honchos** *Slang* A person who is in charge; a manager or leader: *the head honcho of the organization.*

hone (hōn) *tr.v.* **honed, honing, hones 1.** To sharpen (a knife or other sharp tool) on a fine-grained stone. **2.** To make more effective: *Authors must hone their skills by writing a great deal.* ❖ *n.* A fine-grained stone used to sharpen knives or other sharp tools.

honest (ŏn**′**ĭst) *adj.* **1.** Not lying, stealing, or cheating; trustworthy: *The bank teller is an honest worker.* **2.** Done or obtained without lying, cheating, or stealing: *an honest profit.* **3.** Not hiding anything; frank; straightforward; sincere: *an honest opinion.* **4.** Being just what it appears to be; not false; true; genuine: *a scale certified to give honest weight.*

WORD HISTORY Why do we pronounce *h* in *hostile* but not in *honest?* The letter *h* comes from the Roman, or Latin, alphabet, which later came to be used for English. The (h) sound was lost in late Latin and in the languages descended from it such as French, although it survived in the spellings of many words. In English, *h* is often silent in words borrowed from French, such as *honor, honest, hour,* and *heir.* In contrast, most words derived directly from Latin, such as *habitat, hibernate, hostile,* and *humus,* are pronounced in English with the (h) sound.

honestly (ŏn**′**ĭst-lē) *adv.* **1.** In an honest manner: *answered the question as honestly as I could.* **2.** Really; truly: *Do I honestly look that bad?*

honesty (ŏn**′**ĭ-stē) *n.* The quality of being honest; truthfulness, sincerity, or genuineness: *No one questioned the honesty of the judge's statement.*

honey (hŭn**′**ē) *n., pl.* **honeys 1.** A sweet, thick substance made by bees from the nectar of flowers and used as food. **2.** Any of various similar sweet substances. **3.** Sweetness; pleasantness: *Her words flowed with honey.* **4.** *Informal* Sweetheart; dear.

honeybee (hŭn**′**ē-bē**′**) *n.* Any of several bees that produce honey, especially a domesticated bee raised commercially for its honey and beeswax.

honeycomb (hŭn**′**ē-kōm**′**) *n.* **1.** A wax structure having many small six-sided compartments, used by honeybees to hold honey, pollen, and eggs. **2.** Something full of openings or spaces like those in a honeycomb: *The building was a honeycomb of small rooms and passages.* ❖ *tr.v.* **honeycombed, honeycombing, honeycombs** To fill with openings or spaces like those in a honeycomb: *Caves and tunnels honeycomb these cliffs.*

honeydew (hŭn**′**ē-doo**′**) *n.* **1.** A sweet sticky substance given off by aphids and certain other insects that feed on plant juices. **2.** A honeydew melon.

honeydew melon *n.* A melon having a smooth whitish rind and sweet green flesh.

honeyed (hŭn**′**ēd) *adj.* Intended to coax or please: *honeyed words.*

honeymoon (hŭn**′**ē-moon**′**) *n.* **1.** A trip or vacation taken by a newly married couple. **2.** A period of harmony early in a relationship: *the honeymoon between the new president and Congress.* ❖ *intr.v.* **honeymooned, honeymooning, honeymoons** To go on a honeymoon. —**hon′ey·moon′er** *n.*

honeysuckle (hŭn**′**ē-sŭk**′**əl) *n.* Any of various vines or shrubs having tubular, often fragrant yellowish, white, or pink flowers.

honk (hôngk) *n.* A loud harsh sound such as that made by a goose or an automobile horn. ❖ *intr. & tr.v.* **honked, honking, honks** To make or cause to make a honk: *A flock of geese honked overhead. The impatient driver honked the car horn.* —**honk′er** *n.*

honor (ŏn**′**ər) *n.* **1.** Special respect or high regard: *The award is given to show honor to great film directors.* **2.** A source of credit or mark of distinction: *a great writer who is an honor to the profession.* **3.** An act or token that shows respect or high regard: *a hero's funeral with full honors.* **4.** A sense of what is right; high principles; integrity: *A person of honor does not lie, cheat, or steal.* **5.** Good name or reputation: *I must defend my honor.* **6.** Great privilege: *It is an honor to meet you.* **7.** often **Honor** Used as a title and form of address for certain officials, such as judges and some mayors: *her Honor, Judge Jones.* **8. honors a.** Special recognition of a student for unusual achievement: *graduated from high school with honors.* **b.** A program of advanced study for exceptional students. ❖ *tr.v.* **honored, honoring, honors 1.** To show special respect or recognition to; treat with honor: *We honored the volunteers with a party.* **2.** To think highly of; esteem: *a doctor who was honored everywhere for achievements in medicine.* **3.** To accept as payment: *honor a check.* ❖ **on (one's) honor** Under a solemn pledge to be truthful and do what is right.

honorable (ŏn**′**ər-ə-bəl) *adj.* **1.** Deserving honor and respect: *Teaching is an honorable profession.* **2.** Bringing distinction or recognition: *honorable efforts to achieve peace.* **3.** Having or showing a sense of what is right or just: *an honorable person; an honorable solution to a difficult problem.* **4.** Done with or accompanied by marks of honor: *an honorable burial.* **5.** Distinguished; illustrious; great: *an honorable family.* **6.** often **Honorable** Used as a title for certain high officials or people of importance. —**hon′or·a·ble·ness** *n.* —**hon′or·a·bly** *adv.*

honorarium (ŏn**′**ə-râr**′**ē-əm) *n., pl.* **honorariums** or **honoraria** (ŏn**′**ə-râr**′**ē-ə) A payment made to a professional person for services, such as a lecture, for which a fee is not legally required.

honorary (ŏn′ə-rĕr′ē) *adj.* Given or held as an honor: *an honorary degree from a university.*

honor system *n.* A set of rules by which students are trusted to act properly or honestly without being closely supervised.

honour (ŏn′ər) *n. & v. Chiefly British* Variant of **honor.**

hood¹ (hŏŏd) *n.* **1.** A loose covering for the head and neck, often attached to a coat, cape, or robe: *The Inuit wear heavy parkas with hoods attached.* **2.** The hinged metal lid over the engine of an automobile. **3.** The raised metal cover of a ventilator over a stove. **4.** An expanded part or marking on or near an animal's head, as the flaring skin around a cobra's neck. ❖ *tr.v.* **hooded, hooding, hoods** To supply or cover with a hood.

hood² (hŏŏd) *n. Slang* A hoodlum.

***

WORD HISTORY Hood¹ comes from Middle English *hod,* which comes from Old English *hōd,* both meaning "head covering." **Hood²** is short for *hoodlum.*

***

–hood A suffix that means: **1.** Condition or quality: *manhood; falsehood.* **2.** A group sharing a certain condition or quality: *sisterhood; priesthood.*

hooded (hŏŏd′ĭd) *adj.* Covered with or having a hood: *a hooded rider; a hooded cape.*

hoodie (hŏŏd′ē) *n. Informal* A piece of clothing with a hood, especially a hooded sweatshirt.

hoodlum (hŏŏd′ləm *or* hŏŏd′ləm) *n.* **1.** A gangster or thug. **2.** A tough, often aggressive or violent youth.

hoodwink (hŏŏd′wĭngk′) *tr.v.* **hoodwinked, hoodwinking, hoodwinks** To deceive or mislead; trick.

hoof (hŏŏf *or* hŏŏf) *n., pl.* **hooves** (hŏŏvz *or* hŏŏvz) or **hoofs 1.** The tough horny covering on the lower part of the foot of certain mammals, such as horses, cattle, deer, and pigs. **2.** The whole foot of such an animal. ❖ *intr.v.* **hoofed, hoofing, hoofs** *Slang* **1.** To dance, especially to tap-dance. **2.** To go on foot; walk. ◆ **hoof it** To walk: *We hoofed it into town.*

hoofed (hŏŏft *or* hŏŏft) *adj.* Having hooves.

hook (hŏŏk) *n.* **1.** A curved or sharply bent piece of metal or other stiff material, used to catch, hold, fasten, or pull something: *Coats hung on hooks in the hall.* **2.** A fishhook. **3.** Something shaped or used like a hook. **4.** A sharp curve or bend, as in a river. **5.** A spit of land with a curved end. **6.** A means of catching or ensnaring; a trap. **7.** In sports, the flight of a ball that goes to the left when propelled by a right-handed player or to the right when propelled by a left-handed player. **8.** In boxing, a short swinging blow delivered with a crooked arm. ❖ *v.* **hooked, hooking, hooks** *—tr.* **1.** To catch, hang, or connect with a hook: *hook a tuna while fishing.* **2.** To fasten by means of a hook: *hook a picture on the wall.* **3.** To make (a rug, for example) by looping yarn through a loosely woven material with a hook. **4.** In sports, to hit or throw (a ball) with a hook: *hook a shot in golf; hook the ball into the basket.* **5.** To hit with a hook in boxing. *—intr.* **1.** To move, throw, or extend in a curve: *The road hooks toward the river.* **2.** To be fastened by means of a hook: *The gate hooks on the post.* ◆ **by hook or by crook** By whatever means possible, fair or unfair. **hook up 1.** To connect or make a connection between: *The electricity was hooked up to the house.* **2.** *Slang* To meet or associate: *hooked up with*

a group of artists. **3.** *Slang* To become sexually involved with someone, especially casually. **off the hook** *Informal* Free of blame or obligation: *My cousin's going to drive me to the airport, so you're off the hook now.*

hookah (hŏŏk′ə) *n.* A smoking pipe used chiefly in southwest Asia and northern Africa. It has a long tube attached to a container of water that cools the smoke as it is drawn through.

hook and eye *n.* **1.** A fastener for clothes consisting of a small hook and loop which can be linked together. **2.** A latch consisting of a hook that is inserted in a screw eye.

hooked (hŏŏkt) *adj.* **1.** Curved or bent like a hook: *the owl's hooked beak.* **2.** Having a hook or hooks: *a hooked spear.* **3.** Made by hooking: *a hooked rug.* **4.** *Slang* Addicted or devoted to something: *She's hooked on canoeing.*

hooker (hŏŏk′ər) *n.* **1.** One that hooks. **2.** *Slang* A prostitute.

hookup (hŏŏk′ŭp′) *n.* **1.** A system of electrical circuits or equipment designed to operate together: *a nationwide radio and television hookup.* **2.** A connection or arrangement: *a hookup between buyer and seller.* **3.** *Informal* An act of casual sex, especially between people who are not in a romantic relationship with each other.

hookworm (hŏŏk′wûrm′) *n.* Any of numerous parasitic worms that fasten themselves to the inside wall of the intestines of various animals, including humans.

hooky (hŏŏk′ē) *n. Informal* Absence without permission: *play hooky from school.*

hooligan (hŏŏ′lĭ-gən) *n. Informal* A tough and aggressive or violent youth.

hoop (hŏŏp *or* hŏŏp) *n.* **1.** A circular band or ring of wood, metal, bone, or plastic used to hold something together, as the staves of a barrel, or to spread something out, as a piece of embroidery or a fancy skirt. **2.** A large ring of wood, plastic, or metal used as a toy. **3a.** In basketball, the basket. **b.** often **hoops** *Informal* The game of basketball: *shoot some hoop; play some hoops.* ❖ *tr.v.* **hooped, hooping, hoops** To bind or fasten together with a hoop.

hoopla (hŏŏp′lä′ *or* hŏŏp′lä′) *n. Informal* **1.** Noisy or confusing commotion. **2.** Extravagant publicity: *The new book was published with great hoopla.*

hoop skirt *n.* A woman's long skirt worn over a framework of connected flexible hoops that keep it spread out.

hooray (hŏŏ-rā′ *or* hə-rā′) also **hurrah** (hŏŏ-rä′ *or* hə-rä′) also **hurray** (hŏŏ-rā′ *or* hə-rā′) *interj.* An expression used to show approval, pleasure, or victory. ❖ *n.* A shout of "hooray." ❖ *intr.v.* **hoorayed, hooraying, hoorays** also **hurrahed, hurrahing, hurrahs** also **hurrayed, hurraying, hurrays** To applaud or cheer with shouts of "hooray."

hoot (hŏŏt) *v.* **hooted, hooting, hoots** *—intr.* **1.** To make the cry of an owl. **2.** To make a shout or loud cry of contempt or disapproval: *Protesters hooted at the speaker.* *—tr.* **1.** To shout at or drive away with scornful cries or jeers: *The hecklers hooted the candidate off the platform.* **2.** To express by hooting: *The fans hooted their anger.* ❖ *n.* **1.** The cry of an owl. **2.** A sound similar to this, especially the sound of a horn. **3.** A shout of scorn or disapproval. **4.** *Informal* A person or thing that is hilariously funny: *My roommate cracks jokes all the time; she's a real hoot!* ◆ **not give a hoot** or **not care a hoot** To be completely indifferent to: *I don't give a hoot if it rains.*

hootenanny (hŏŏt′n-ăn′ē) *n., pl.* **hootenannies** An informal performance by folksingers, usually with the audience joining in.

hooves (hŏŏvz *or* hŏŏvz) *n.* A plural of **hoof.**

hop¹ (hŏp) v. **hopped, hopping, hops** —intr. **1.** To move with light springing leaps or skips: *The frightened rabbit hopped away.* **2.** To jump on one foot or with both feet at the same time. —tr. **1.** To jump over: *hopped the fence in a single bound.* **2.** *Informal* To jump aboard: *hop a freight train.* ❖ n. **1.** A hopping motion; a springy jump: *The squirrel crossed the lawn in short hops.* **2.** A trip, especially by air: *It is a short hop between Boston and New York.* **3.** A rebound; a bounce: *The ball took a bad hop.*

hop² (hŏp) n. **1.** A twining vine having green flower clusters that resemble small pine cones. **2. hops** The dried flowers of this plant, used in making beer.

WORD HISTORY Hop¹ comes from Middle English *hoppen,* which comes from Old English *hoppian,* both meaning "to hop." **Hop²** comes from Middle English *hoppe,* which comes from Middle Dutch *hoppe,* both referring to the same plant as in Modern English.

---

hope (hōp) v. **hoped, hoping, hopes** —intr. To desire or wish that something will happen: *We were hoping for better weather for the picnic.* —tr. **1.** To desire or wish (that something will happen): *I hope that the audience likes our play.* **2.** To expect (to do something) with a feeling of confidence: *I hope to be there by five o'clock.* ❖ n. **1.** The longing or desire for something accompanied by the belief that it is possible: *The young composer is full of hope for success.* **2.** An instance of such longing or desire: *His hopes of becoming a famous singer are not very realistic.* **3.** A reason for or cause of such longing or desire: *A home run is the team's only hope for victory.*

hopeful (hōp′fəl) adj. **1.** Feeling or showing hope; expectant: *The immigrants arrived hopeful of a better life.* **2.** Inspiring hope; encouraging: *We were gladdened by hopeful signs of peace.* ❖ n. A person who wishes to succeed or shows promise of succeeding in something: *Several hopefuls tried out for the lead in the play.* —**hope′ful·ness** n.

hopefully (hōp′fə-lē) adv. **1.** In a hopeful manner: *We began the new soccer season hopefully.* **2.** *Informal* It is to be hoped that: *Hopefully, there will be enough snow to go sledding.*

hopeless (hōp′lĭs) adj. **1.** Having no hope; despairing: *After hours of wandering in the forest the lost hikers felt hopeless.* **2.** Offering or causing no hope: *The search for my wallet proved hopeless.* **3.** Having no hope of improvement; incompetent: *I'm hopeless at crosswords.* —**hope′less·ly** adv. —**hope′less·ness** n.

Hopi (hō′pē) n., pl. **Hopi** or **Hopis 1.** A member of a Native American people of northeast Arizona. **2.** The Uto-Aztecan language of this people.

hopper (hŏp′ər) n. **1.** A person or thing that hops. **2.** A container having a wide open top and a narrow opening at the bottom through which the contents, such as coal or grain, can be emptied, as for feeding into a machine.

hopscotch (hŏp′skŏch′) n. A children's game in which players toss a small object into the numbered spaces of a pattern of rectangles marked on the ground or pavement and then hop through the spaces to pick up the object and return.

hora (hôr′ə) n. A traditional dance of Romania and Israel performed by dancers moving around in a circle.

horde (hôrd) n. **1.** A large group, crowd, or swarm: *hordes of people at the fair.* **2.** A wandering tribe or group of people: *In 1264 the Mongol hordes invaded China.*

horehound (hôr′hound′) n. An aromatic plant having woolly whitish leaves that yield a bitter substance used in cough medicine and in flavoring. **2.** An extract, medicine, or candy prepared using this plant.

horizon (hə-rī′zən) n. **1.** The line along which the earth and sky appear to meet. **2.** The limit of one's experience, knowledge, or interests: *Lack of education narrows a person's horizons.*

horizontal (hôr′ĭ-zŏn′tl) adj. **1.** Parallel to or in the plane of the horizon; level. **2.** Relating to or near the horizon. ❖ n. A horizontal line or plane. —**hor′i·zon′tal·ly** adv.

hormonal (hôr-mō′nəl) adj. Relating to or caused by a hormone or hormones: *a hormonal imbalance.*

hormone (hôr′mōn′) n. **1.** A substance produced by an endocrine gland in a vertebrate animal and usually carried in the bloodstream to another part of the body, where it acts to regulate, control, or stimulate a specific activity, such as growth or metabolism. **2.** A similar substance in an invertebrate animal or a plant. **3.** A synthetic compound that acts like a hormone in the body.

horn (hôrn) n. **1.** One of the hard bony growths on the heads of cattle, sheep, goats, and other hoofed mammals. **2.** A hard growth, such as an antler or a growth on the head of a giraffe, that resembles a horn. **3.** The hard durable substance that forms the outer covering of the horns of cattle and related animals: *old buttons made of horn.* **4.** A container made from an animal's horn: *a powder horn.* **5.** Something shaped like a horn, as either end of a new moon or the pommel of a saddle. **6.** Any of various instruments that are sounded by blowing and vibrating the lips and that usually flare at the end, especially a French horn. Horns can be made of animal horn, metal, wood, or plastic. **7.** A warning device that produces a loud sound: *a car horn.* ❖ intr.v. **horned, horning, horns** *Slang* To join in without being invited; intrude: *The older children horned in on the game of tag.*

hornbill (hôrn′bĭl′) n. Any of various large birds of Africa and tropical Asia that have a large curved bill, often with a horny lump on top.

hornblende (hôrn′blĕnd′) n. A common green to black mineral found in many metamorphic and igneous rocks. Iron, calcium, magnesium, and other metals occur in hornblende.

hornbook (hôrn′bŏok′) n. An early primer consisting of a single page, usually with the alphabet on it and protected by a transparent sheet of horn.

horned (hôrnd) adj. Having a horn, horns, or a hornlike growth: *a horned lark.*

horned lizard n. Any of several small lizards of western North America and Central America, having short horns on the head, a wide flattened spiny body, and a short tail.

horned toad n. A horned lizard.

hornet (hôr′nĭt) n. Any of various large stinging wasps that live in colonies and build large papery nests.

horn of plenty n., pl. **horns of plenty** A cornucopia.

hornpipe (hôrn′pīp′) n. **1.** A wind instrument with a single reed, finger holes, and a bell and mouthpiece made of horn. **2.** A lively dance, usually performed by one person and originally popular among sailors. **3.** Music for this dance.

hornwort (hôrn′wûrt′ or hôrn′wôrt′) n. Any of various small plants that are related to the mosses and have a thin, flat plant body from which tall hornlike spore-producing structures grow.

horny (hôr′nē) adj. **hornier, horniest 1.** Having horns or hornlike projections. **2.** Made of horn or a similar substance: *the horny shell of a lobster.* **3.** Tough and callous: *the horny hands of a mason.* **4.** *Slang* Eager for sexual activity.

horoscope (hôr′ə-skōp′) *n.* **1.** The relative position of the planets and stars at a given moment, such as at the hour of a person's birth. **2.** A prediction, especially of a person's future, based on the position of the planets and stars.

horrendous (hô-rĕn′dəs *or* hə-rĕn′dəs) *adj.* Terrible; dreadful. **—hor·ren′dous·ly** *adv.*

horrible (hôr′ə-bəl) *adj.* **1.** Causing horror; dreadful: *a horrible crime.* **2.** Extremely unpleasant: *a horrible noise.* **—hor′ri·ble·ness** *n.* **—hor′ri·bly** *adv.*

horrid (hôr′ĭd) *adj.* **1.** Causing horror; horrible. **2.** Extremely disagreeable; offensive. **—hor′rid·ly** *adv.* **—hor′rid·ness** *n.*

horrific (hô-rĭf′ĭk) *adj.* Causing horror; terrifying. **—hor·rif′i·cal·ly** *adv.*

horrify (hôr′ə-fī′) *tr.v.* **horrified, horrifying, horrifies 1.** To cause to feel horror: *The possibility of a violent earthquake horrified people.* **2.** To surprise unpleasantly; shock: *The cost of the new tires horrified us.*

horror (hôr′ər) *n.* **1.** A feeling of fear and disgust; terror. **2.** Something that causes horror: *the horrors of war.* **3.** Intense dislike; loathing: *Winston has a horror of rats.*

hors d'oeuvre (ôr dûrv′) *n., pl.* **hors d'oeuvres** (ôr dûrvz′) *or* **hors d'oeuvre** An appetizer served before a meal.

horse (hôrs) *n.* **1.** A large hoofed mammal having a short coat and a long mane and tail. Horses are used for riding, pulling vehicles, and carrying loads. **2.** An adult male horse. **3.** A frame consisting of a crossbar and four legs, used for supporting or holding. **4.** A pommel horse. ❖ *tr.v.* **horsed, horsing, horses** To provide with a horse: *After the knights were horsed, they rode off to battle.* ◆ **beat a dead horse 1.** To dwell tiresomely on a matter that has already been decided. **2.** To continue to pursue a cause that has no hope of success. **hold (one's) horses** To restrain oneself. **horse around** *Informal* To indulge in horseplay or frivolous activity. **on (one's) high horse** Self-righteous and disdainful. **the horse's mouth** A source of information regarded as original and beyond doubt: *I know it's true because I got it from the horse's mouth.*

horseback (hôrs′băk′) *n.* The back of a horse: *police officers on horseback.* ❖ *adv. & adj.* On the back of a horse: *ride horseback; horseback riding.*

horse chestnut *n.* **1.** Any of several large trees having upright clusters of white flowers and shiny brown seeds enclosed in a usually spiny capsule. **2.** The inedible nutlike seed of any of these trees.

horsefly (hôrs′flī′) *n.* Any of numerous large flies, the female of which bites and sucks blood from horses, cattle, and other animals.

horsehair (hôrs′hâr′) *n.* **1.** The coarse hair from a horse's mane or tail. **2.** Stiff cloth made of the hair of horses.

horse latitudes *pl.n.* Either of two regions notable for high barometric pressure and calm or light variable wind. They are found over the oceans at about 30 to 35 degrees north and south latitudes.

horseman (hôrs′mən) *n.* **1.** A man who rides a horse. **2.** A man skilled at riding horses.

horsemanship (hôrs′mən-shĭp′) *n.* The skill of riding horses: *Rodeo riders must have superior horsemanship.*

horseplay (hôrs′plā′) *n.* Rough or rowdy play.

horsepower (hôrs′pou′ər) *n.* A unit used to measure the power of engines and motors, equal to the power needed to lift 550 pounds one foot in one second.

horseradish (hôrs′răd′ĭsh) *n.* **1.** A tall plant having long leaves, white flowers, and a large whitish root with a sharp taste. **2.** A sharp condiment made from the roots of this plant.

horse sense *n. Informal* Common sense.

horseshoe (hôrs′shoō′ *or* hôrsh′shoō′) *n.* **1.** A flat U-shaped metal plate fitted and nailed to a horse's hoof for protection. **2.** Something shaped like a horseshoe. **3.** **horseshoes** *(used with a singular verb)* A game in which the players try to toss horseshoes around or near a stake.

horseshoe crab *n.* Any of various marine invertebrate animals that have a large oval shell and a stiff pointed tail. Horseshoe crabs, like insects and crustaceans, are arthropods.

horsetail (hôrs′tāl′) *n.* Any of various plants that have a jointed hollow stem and small scalelike leaves and do not have flowers or seeds.

horsewhip (hôrs′wĭp′) *n.* A whip used to drive or control a horse. ❖ *tr.v.* **horsewhipped, horsewhipping, horsewhips** To beat with a horsewhip.

horsewoman (hôrs′woōm′ən) *n.* **1.** A woman who rides a horse. **2.** A woman skilled at riding horses.

hortatory (hôr′tə-tôr′ē) *adj.* Marked by exhortation or strong urging: *a hortatory speech.*

horticulture (hôr′tĭ-kŭl′chər) *n.* **1.** The science or art of cultivating fruits, vegetables, flowers, or ornamental plants. **2.** The cultivation of a garden. **—hor′ti·cul′tur·al** *adj.*

horticulturist (hôr′tĭ-kŭl′chər-ĭst) *n.* A person who specializes in horticulture.

hosanna (hō-zăn′ə) *interj.* An expression used to show praise or adoration of God. ❖ *n.* A cry of "hosanna."

hose (hōz) *n.* **1.** *pl.* **hose** Stockings; socks. Used only in the plural. **2.** *pl.* **hose** Tights once worn by men as pants. Used only in the plural. **3.** *pl.* **hoses** A flexible tube for carrying liquids or gases under pressure: *use an air hose to fill the car tires.* ❖ *tr.v.* **hosed, hosing, hoses** To wash or spray with water from a hose: *hose down a car while washing it.*

Hosea (hō-zē′ə *or* hō-zā′ə) *n.* A book of the Bible in which the prophet Hosea rebukes the Israelites for unfaithfulness and urges repentance.

hosiery (hō′zhə-rē) *n.* Stockings and socks; hose.

hospice (hŏs′pĭs) *n.* **1.** A program providing care and support for people who are terminally ill. **2.** A shelter or lodging for travelers or those who are very poor, often maintained by a religious order.

hospitable (hŏs′pĭ-tə-bəl *or* hŏ-spĭt′ə-bəl) *adj.* **1.** Disposed to treat guests with warmth and generosity: *The hotel staff is extremely hospitable.* **2.** Having an open mind; receptive: *The new manager is hospitable to new ideas.* **—hos′pi·ta·bly** *adv.*

hospital (hŏs′pĭ-tl *or* hŏs′pĭt′l) *n.* **1.** An institution providing medical, surgical, or psychiatric care and treatment for sick or injured people. **2.** An institution providing veterinary care and treatment for sick or injured animals. **—SEE NOTE AT host³.**

hospitality (hŏs′pĭ-tăl′ĭ-tē) *n., pl.* **hospitalities** Welcoming or generous treatment of guests.

hospitalization (hŏs′pĭ-tl-ĭ-zā′shən) *n.* **1.** The act of placing a person in a hospital as a patient. **2.** The condition of being hospitalized: *Hospitalization may increase the* *chances of recovery from serious illness.* **3.** Insurance that fully or partially covers a patient's hospital expenses.

hospitalize (hŏsʹpĭt-l-īzʹ) *tr.v.* **hospitalized, hospitalizing, hospitalizes** To place in a hospital for treatment, care, or observation: *I was hospitalized for two days with appendicitis.*

host¹ (hōst) *n.* **1a.** A person who receives or entertains guests in a social or official capacity: *The new neighbors were our hosts for the evening.* **b.** The keeper of an inn or hotel. **c.** The emcee or interviewer on a radio or television program. **2a.** An organism on or in which a parasite lives and feeds. **b.** A cell that is infected by a virus. **3.** A computer containing data or programs that another computer can access by network or modem. ❖ *tr.v.* **hosted, hosting, hosts 1.** To serve as host to or at: *host a party; host an interview on TV.* **2.** To furnish facilities and resources for (a function or event): *Beijing hosted the Olympic Games in 2008.*

host² (hōst) *n.* **1.** An army. **2.** A great number; a multitude.

host³ also **Host** (hōst) *n.* The consecrated bread or wafer of the Eucharist.

WORD HISTORY Host¹ comes from Middle English *host,* meaning both "the giver of a party" and "guest." **Host²** comes from Middle English *host* (meaning "an army"), which comes from Latin *hostis,* meaning "enemy." Both **host¹** and **host²** ultimately come from an Indo-European root form that meant "stranger," "guest," and "host" (that is, "someone with whom one has reciprocal duties of hospitality"). Other Modern English words that come from this root include *guest, hospital, hostage, hostile,* and words that begin with the suffix *xeno-* (meaning "stranger, foreign") such as *xenophobia,* "fear or contempt of foreigners or of foreign culture." **Host³** comes from Middle English *host* (meaning "Eucharistic wafer"), which comes from Latin *hostia,* meaning "sacrifice."

hostage (hŏsʹtĭj) *n.* **1.** A person who is held by a group or another person in a conflict as security that a specified demand will be met. **2.** A person or thing that serves as security against an implied threat. —SEE NOTE AT **host³.**

hostel (hŏsʹtəl) *n.* An inexpensive lodging place for travelers, especially young travelers.

hostelry (hŏsʹtəl-rē) *n., pl.* **hostelries** An inn; a hotel.

hostess (hōʹstĭs) *n.* **1.** A woman who receives or entertains guests in a social or official capacity. **2.** A woman who is the keeper of an inn or hotel. **3.** A woman who is employed to greet and assist patrons, as at a restaurant.

hostile (hŏsʹtəl or hŏsʹtīlʹ) *adj.* **1.** Relating to or characteristic of an enemy: *hostile forces.* **2.** Feeling or showing enmity or ill will: *a hostile crowd.* **3.** Unfavorable to health or well-being: *a hostile climate.* —**hosʹtile·ly** *adv.* —SEE NOTE AT **host³.**

hostility (hŏ-stĭlʹĭ-tē) *n., pl.* **hostilities 1.** The state of being hostile; antagonism or enmity: *The hostility of the former enemies was felt by everyone.* **2. hostilities** Acts of war; open warfare: *Hostilities broke out between the two countries.*

hostler (hŏsʹlər or ŏsʹlər) also **ostler** (ŏsʹlər) *n.* **1.** A person who is employed to tend horses, especially at an inn. **2.** A person who maintains and repairs a large vehicle or engine, such as a locomotive.

hot (hŏt) *adj.* **hotter, hottest 1.** Having great heat; being at a high temperature; very warm: *a hot stove; a horse that was hot after working in the sun; a forehead hot with fever.* **2.** Charged with electricity: *a hot wire.* **3.** Radioac-

tive or designed to use radioactive materials. **4.** Causing a burning sensation, as in the mouth; spicy: *hot chili; hot mustard.* **5.** Marked by intense feeling; fiery: *a hot temper; a hot argument.* **6.** Very eager or enthusiastic: *We were hot to go to the beach.* **7.** *Informal* Most recent; new or fresh: *hot gossip.* **8.** *Informal* Currently very popular: *a hot destination.* **9.** *Slang* Sexually attractive. **10.** Close to a successful solution or conclusion: *hot on the trail of the robbers.* **11.** Having or characterized by repeated successes: *a hot goalie.* **12.** *Slang* Stolen: *a hot DVD player.* ❖ *adv.* In a hot manner; with much heat: *The engine runs hot. The sun shone hot on the pavement.* —**hotʹly** *adv.* —**hotʹness** *n.*

hot air *n. Slang* Empty, exaggerated talk.

hotbed (hŏtʹbĕdʹ) *n.* **1.** A place that fosters rapid and excessive growth or development, especially of something bad: *a hotbed of intrigue.* **2.** A bed of soil covered with glass or plastic and heated by decaying manure or electricity, used for growing seeds or protecting young plants.

hot-blooded (hŏtʹblŭdʹĭd) *adj.* Easily excited: *a hot-blooded youth.*

hotcake (hŏtʹkākʹ) *n.* A pancake. ◆ **go like hotcakes** or **sell like hotcakes** *Informal* To be disposed of quickly and in great amounts: *The raffle tickets are selling like hotcakes.*

hot chocolate *n.* A drink made by mixing powdered chocolate with a sweetener and hot milk or water; cocoa.

hot cross bun *n.* A sweet bun marked on top with a cross of frosting, traditionally eaten during Lent.

hot dog or **hotdog** (hŏtʹdôgʹ) *n.* A frankfurter, especially one served hot in a long roll.

hotel (hō-tĕlʹ) *n.* A house or other building that provides lodging and often meals and other services for paying guests.

hot flash *n.* A sudden brief sensation of heat, often over the entire body, caused by a short-term widening of the blood vessels of the skin and experienced by many women during menopause.

hotfoot (hŏtʹfo͝otʹ) *intr.v.* **hotfooted, hotfooting, hotfoots** *Informal* To go in great haste: *hotfoot it to the market before it closes.*

hotheaded (hŏtʹhĕdʹĭd) *adj.* **1.** Easily angered; quick-tempered: *a crowd of hotheaded protestors.* **2.** Impetuous; rash: *a hotheaded plan.* —**hotʹheadʹed·ly** *adv.* —**hotʹheadʹed·ness** *n.*

hothouse (hŏtʹhousʹ) *n.* A heated building with a glass roof and sides, used for growing plants; a greenhouse. ❖ *adj.* Grown in a hothouse: *hothouse tomatoes.*

hotline (hŏtʹlīnʹ) *n.* **1.** A direct and immediate communications link, usually a telephone line, as between heads of governments for use in a crisis. **2.** A telephone line that provides information or help: *the clinic's health hotline.*

hotly (hŏtʹlē) *adv.* In an intense or fiery manner: *a hotly debated subject.*

hot plate *n.* An electrically heated plate for cooking or warming food.

hot rod *n. Slang* An automobile rebuilt or modified for greater acceleration and speed.

hotshot (hŏtʹshŏtʹ) *n. Slang* A person with unusual skill and daring, especially one who is highly successful and self-assured.

hot spot *n.* **1.** A place of dangerous unrest or hostile action. **2.** *Slang* A lively and popular place, as a nightclub: *a downtown hot spot for food and dancing.* **3.** In geology, a source of great heat in the earth. **4.** A public place where high-speed access to the Internet is made available.

hot spring *n.* A natural spring of warm water, usually having a temperature greater than that of the human body.

hot toddy *n.* A drink made of whiskey or another liquor mixed with hot water, sugar, and spices.

hot water *n. Informal* A difficult or uncomfortable situation; trouble: *Neglecting to cite his sources got the student into hot water.*

hound (hound) *n.* **1.** A dog of any of various breeds originally bred and used for hunting, usually having short hair and drooping ears. **2.** A dog of any kind. **3.** A person who is very enthusiastic about something: *She's a serious art hound.* ❖ *tr.v.* **hounded, hounding, hounds** To pursue or harass: *Reporters hounded the mayor for a statement.*

hour (our) *n.* **1.** A unit of time equal to one of the 24 equal parts of a day; 60 minutes. **2.** One of these units of time as shown on a clock or watch or marked by a bell or other signal: *The hour is 3 PM. The church clock strikes on the hour.* **3.** The distance that can be traveled in an hour: *The airport is about an hour from our house by car.* **4.** A particular time of day: *At what hour does the store open?* **5.** A customary or fixed time: *the dinner hour.* **6. hours** A set period of time for a specified activity: *open hours from eight to three; keeps office hours.*

hourglass (our′glăs′) *n.* An instrument for measuring time, consisting of two glass chambers connected by a narrow neck and containing an amount of sand or another substance that passes from the top chamber to the bottom one in a fixed amount of time, often one hour.

hourly (our′lē) *adj.* **1.** Occurring every hour: *hourly temperature readings; hourly news reports during the hurricane.* **2.** By the hour as a unit: *an hourly wage.* **3.** Frequent; continual: *hourly changes in the weather.* ❖ *adv.* At or during every hour: *doses of medicine given hourly.*

house (hous) *n., pl.* **houses** (hou′zĭz or hou′sĭz) **1a.** A structure serving as a dwelling for one or more persons, especially for a family. **b.** A dwelling for a group of people, such as students, who live together as a unit: *a sorority house.* **2.** All of the people living in a house; a household. **3.** A building or other structure used for some special purpose: *a movie house; a house of worship.* **4.** The people in an audience: *a full house.* **5.** A noble family including its ancestors and descendants. **6.** A business firm: *a banking house; a publishing house.* **7a.** An assembly having the duty and power of making laws; a legislature. **b. House** The House of Representatives, especially of the US government. ❖ *tr.v.* (houz) **housed, housing, houses 1.** To provide living quarters for: *The apartment building houses ten families.* **2.** To keep or store in a house or other shelter or space: *We housed our car in the garage. The electrical controls are housed inside a metal box.* ◆ **on the house** Paid for by the establishment; free.

house arrest *n.* Confinement of a criminal to his or her residence, rather than prison, by court order.

houseboat (hous′bōt′) *n.* A barge designed and equipped for use as a floating dwelling.

housebreak (hous′brāk′) *tr.v.* **housebroke** (hous′brōk′), **housebroken** (hous′brō′kən), **housebreaking, housebreaks** To train (a pet) to have excretory habits that are appropriate for indoor living.

housebreaker (hous′brā′kər) *n.* A person who unlawful-

ly breaks into another's house in order to steal or commit some other crime.

housebreaking (hous′brā′kĭng) *n.* The act of unlawfully breaking into and entering another's house.

housebroke (hous′brōk′) *v.* Past tense of **housebreak**.

housebroken (hous′brō′kən) *v.* Past participle of **housebreak.** ❖ *adj.* Trained to have excretory habits that are appropriate for indoor living: *a housebroken dog.*

house call *n.* A professional visit made to a home, especially by a physician.

housecleaning (hous′klē′nĭng) *n.* The cleaning and tidying of a house and its contents.

housefly (hous′flī′) *n.* A common fly that is found in all parts of the world around human dwellings and farms. Houseflies breed in manure and garbage and can carry many diseases.

household (hous′hōld′) *n.* **1.** The members of a family and others living together as a domestic unit. **2.** The living spaces and possessions belonging to such a unit. ❖ *adj.* Relating to or used in a household: *household appliances; household expenses.*

householder (hous′hōl′dər) *n.* **1.** A person who occupies or owns a house. **2.** The head of a household.

househusband (hous′hŭz′bənd) *n.* A married man who manages the household as his main occupation.

housekeeper (hous′kē′pər) *n.* **1.** A person hired to perform or direct the domestic tasks of a household. **2.** An employee of an establishment, such as a hotel, who performs or coordinates housekeeping tasks.

housekeeping (hous′kē′pĭng) *n.* **1.** Performance or management of household tasks, such as cooking, cleaning, and shopping. **2.** The management of the property and equipment of a hospital, hotel, or similar institution.

housemaid (hous′mād′) *n.* A woman or girl employed to do housework.

House of Commons *n.* The lower house of Parliament in the United Kingdom and Canada.

house of correction *n., pl.* **houses of correction** An institution for confining people convicted of minor criminal offenses.

House of Lords *n.* The upper house of Parliament in the United Kingdom, made up of members of the nobility and high-ranking clergy.

House of Representatives *n.* The lower house of the US Congress and of most state legislatures.

houseplant (hous′plănt′) *n.* A plant grown indoors, often for decorative purposes.

house sparrow *n.* A small bird having brown and gray feathers and a distinctive black mark on the throat of the male. House sparrows are native to Eurasia but are now found worldwide, usually near human settlements.

housetop (hous′tŏp′) *n.* The roof of a house.

housewares (hous′wârz′) *pl.n.* Articles used especially in the kitchen, such as cooking utensils and dishes.

housewarming (hous′wôr′mĭng) *n.* A party to celebrate moving into a new home.

housewife (hous′wīf′) *n.* A married woman who manages the household as her main occupation.

housework (hous′wûrk′) *n.* The tasks performed in housekeeping, such as cleaning and cooking.

housing (hou′zĭng) *n.* **1.** Buildings or other shelters in which people live. **2.** Provision of lodging or shelter: *The employment agreement included housing.* **3.** Something that covers, contains, or protects a mechanical part.

housing project *n.* A group of publicly funded houses

or apartment buildings, usually for people with low incomes.

hove (hōv) *tr.v.* Past tense and past participle of **heave** (sense 1b). ❖ *intr.v.* Past tense and past participle of **heave** (sense 5).

hovel (hŭv′əl or hŏv′əl) *n.* A small shabby dwelling.

hover (hŭv′ər or hŏv′ər) *intr.v.* **hovered, hovering, hovers 1.** To stay floating, suspended, or fluttering in the air: *Hummingbirds hover over the flowers they feed on.* **2.** To remain close by: *The mother fox hovered around the den.* **3.** To be in a state of uncertainty; waver: *The patient hovered between recovery and relapse.*

hovercraft (hŭv′ər-krăft′ or hŏv′ər-krăft′) *n.* A vehicle that travels over land or water on a thin cushion of air created by fans blowing downward.

HOV lane (āch′ō-vē′) *n.* An expressway lane restricted to vehicles carrying more than one person, designed to encourage car-pooling and reduce traffic.

how (hou) *adv.* **1.** In what manner or way; by what means: *My father taught me how to use a chainsaw.* **2.** In what state or condition: *How do you feel today?* **3.** To what extent, amount, or degree: *How strong is the rope? How much do these gadgets cost?* **4.** For what reason; why: *How did you manage to miss the train?* **5.** With what meaning: *How should I take that remark?* ❖ *conj.* **1.** The manner or way in which: *I forgot how the song goes.* **2.** In whatever way or manner that: *Cook the beans how you like.* ❖ *n.* The way something is done: *I am more interested in the how than the why of a thing.* ◆ **how about** What is your thought, feeling, or desire regarding: *How about some ice cream?* **how come** *Informal* How is it that; why: *How come you're late?*

howdah (hou′də) *n.* A seat for riding on the back of an elephant or camel, usually fitted with a canopy and railing.

howdy (hou′dē) *interj.* An expression used to greet someone.

however (hou-ĕv′ər) *adv.* **1.** To whatever extent or degree: *However long the process, an education is absolutely necessary.* **2.** In whatever way or manner: *However you manage it, the job must be done.* **3.** Nevertheless; yet: *It was a difficult time; however, there were amusing moments.*

howitzer (hou′ĭt-sər) *n.* A short cannon that fires shells in a high curving path.

howl (houl) *v.* **howled, howling, howls** —*intr.* **1.** To utter or emit a long, mournful, plaintive sound: *The dogs howled at the loud siren.* **2.** To cry or wail loudly, as in pain, sorrow, or anger: *The patient howled when the dentist pulled the tooth.* **3.** *Slang* To laugh heartily: *The audience howled at the comedian's jokes.* —*tr.* To express or utter with a howl. See Synonyms at **yell.** ❖ *n.* A long wailing cry.

howsoever (hou′sō-ĕv′ər) *adv.* **1.** To whatever extent or degree. **2.** By whatever means.

hp An abbreviation of horsepower.

HPV An abbreviation of human papillomavirus.

HQ An abbreviation of headquarters.

HR An abbreviation of: **1.** home run. **2.** House of Representatives.

hr. An abbreviation of hour.

ht An abbreviation of height.

HTML (āch′tē-ĕm-ĕl′) *n.* A markup language used to structure documents and to set up hypertext links between documents, especially on the World Wide Web.

hub (hŭb) *n.* **1.** The center part of a wheel, fan, or propeller. **2.** A center of activity or interest; a focal point: *Nashville is the hub of country music.*

hubbub (hŭb′ŭb′) *n.* Noisy confusion; uproar: *the hubbub of traffic; the hubbub in a crowded room.*

hubby (hŭb′ē) *n., pl.* **hubbies** *Informal* A husband.

hubcap (hŭb′kăp′) *n.* A round covering over an automobile wheel.

hubris (hyōō′brĭs) *n.* Overbearing pride or presumption; arrogance. —**hu·bris′tic** (hyōō′brĭs′tĭk) *adj.*

huckleberry (hŭk′əl-bĕr′ē) *n.* **1.** The edible, usually bluish-black berry of any of various shrubs related to the blueberries. **2.** A shrub that bears such berries.

huckster (hŭk′stər) *n.* **1.** A person who sells goods in the street; a peddler. **2.** A person who used aggressive, sometimes devious methods to promote or sell a product. **3.** *Informal* A writer of advertising copy, especially for radio or television.

huddle (hŭd′l) *n.* **1.** A densely packed group or crowd, as of people or animals. **2.** In football, a grouping of a team's players behind the line of scrimmage to plan the next play. **3.** A small private conference or meeting: *The two lawyers went into a huddle.* ❖ *v.* **huddled, huddling, huddles** —*intr.* **1.** To crowd together, as from cold or fear: *They huddled around the fire to keep warm.* **2.** To draw one's limbs close to one's body: *When it started to rain, she huddled under her poncho.* **3.** In football, to gather in a huddle. **4.** *Informal* To confer; meet: *The two friends huddled and talked over the problem.* —*tr.* To cause to crowd together: *The dog huddled the sheep into a group.*

hue (hyōō) *n.* **1.** The property that distinguishes one color in the spectrum of visible light from another, as red from yellow or blue from green: *all the hues of the rainbow; the basic hues of red, blue, and yellow.* **2.** A shade or tint of color: *hues of blue from light to dark.*

hue and cry *n.* A public clamor, as of protest or demand.

huff (hŭf) *n.* A fit of anger or annoyance: *left the room in a huff.* ❖ *v.* **huffed, huffing, huffs** —*intr.* To puff; blow: *I huffed all the way up the hill.* —*tr.* To anger; annoy: *Their snooty attitude huffed me.*

huffy (hŭf′ē) *adj.* **huffier, huffiest 1.** Easily offended; touchy: *Why are you so huffy today?* **2.** Irritated or annoyed; indignant: *Their rude remarks made me huffy.* —**huff′i·ly** *adv.* —**huff′i·ness** *n.*

hug (hŭg) *v.* **hugged, hugging, hugs** —*tr.* **1.** To clasp or hold closely; embrace: *hug a child.* **2.** To keep or stay close to: *This car hugs the road well on corners.* **3.** To hold steadfastly to; cherish: *hugs his eccentric ideas.* —*intr.* To cling together closely; embrace: *We hugged and said goodbye.* ❖ *n.* An affectionate or tight embrace.

huge (hyōōj) *adj.* **huger, hugest** Of great size, extent, or quantity: *a huge tree; a huge difference.* See Synonyms at **large.** —**huge′ly** *adv.* —**huge′ness** *n.*

Huguenot (hyōō′gə-nŏt′) *n.* A French Protestant of the 1500s to 1700s.

huh (hŭ) *interj.* An expression used to ask a question or show surprise, contempt, or indifference.

hula (hōō′lə) *n.* A Polynesian dance characterized by swaying movements of the hips and miming movements of the arms and hands.

hulk (hŭlk) *n.* **1.** The hull of an old, unseaworthy, or wrecked ship. **2.** A heavy unwieldy ship. **3.** A large clumsy person or thing: *a hulk of a football player.* **4.** A wrecked or abandoned shell usually of a large object, such as a building.

hulking (hŭl′kĭng) *adj.* Unwieldy or bulky; massive: *a great hulking St. Bernard.*

hull (hŭl) *n.* **1.** The framework or body of a ship or airplane. **2.** The outer covering of certain seeds or fruits; a husk or pod. **3.** The cluster of green sepals at the stem end of certain fruits, such as the strawberry. ❖ *tr.v.* **hulled, hulling, hulls** To remove the hulls of (fruits or seeds): *hull berries.* —**hull′er** *n.*

hullabaloo (hŭl′ə-bə-lōō′) *n., pl.* **hullabaloos** A great noise or excitement; an uproar.

hullo (hə-lō′) *interj. & n.* Chiefly British Variant of **hello.**

hum (hŭm) *v.* **hummed, humming, hums** —*intr.* **1.** To make the continuous droning sound of a bee in flight; buzz: *Bees hummed around the flower. The TV set hums when we turn it on.* **2.** To make a continuous low droning sound like that of the speech sound *m* when prolonged. **3.** To sing without words, with the lips kept closed: *hum while working.* **4.** To be full of or alive with activity: *The street hums with traffic.* —*tr.* To sing (a tune) without opening the lips: *hum a melody.* ❖ *n.* **1.** The act of humming. **2.** The sound produced by humming.

human (hyōō′mən) *n.* **1.** A member of the species *Homo sapiens*; a person. **2.** Any of various extinct species that are closely related to modern humans. The first ancient humans are thought to have evolved over 2 million years ago. ❖ *adj.* **1.** Relating to or characteristic of humans: *the human body; the course of human events.* **2.** Relating to or having any of the qualities that are considered characteristic of humans: *human kindness; mistakes that show she's only human.* **3.** Made up of people: *The protesters linked their arms in a human chain.* —**hu′man·ness** *n.*

human being *n.* A human; a woman, man, or child.

humane (hyōō-mān′) *adj.* Marked by kindness, compassion, or mercy: *a humane judge; humane treatment of animals.* —**hu·mane′ly** *adv.* —**hu·mane′ness** *n.*

humanism (hyōō′mə-nĭz′əm) *n.* **1.** A system of thought centering on humans and their welfare, interests, and values. **2.** The study of the humanities; learning in the liberal arts. **3.** often **Humanism** The major intellectual movement of the European Renaissance, emphasizing secular concerns and critical ways of thinking as a result of a revival of interest in ancient Greek and Roman art, literature, and civilization.

humanist (hyōō′mə-nĭst) *n.* **1.** A believer in the principles of humanism. **2.** A student of the liberal arts. **3.** A person who is concerned with the interest, welfare, and values of humans.

humanitarian (hyōō-măn′ĭ-târ′ē-ən) *n.* A person who promotes human welfare and the advancement of social reforms; a philanthropist. ❖ *adj.* Relating to or characteristic of humanitarianism.

humanitarianism (hyōō-măn′ĭ-târ′ē-ə-nĭz′əm) *n.* The belief that humans have an obligation to work for the improvement of human welfare.

humanity (hyōō-măn′ĭ-tē) *n., pl.* **humanities 1.** Humans considered as a group; the human race: *The measles vaccine is of benefit to humanity.* **2.** The quality or fact of being human. **3.** The quality of being humane; kindness: *Taking in the war refugees was an act of great humanity.* **4.**

humanities The branches of knowledge, such as art, philosophy, and literature, that are concerned with human thought and culture.

humanize (hyōō′mə-nīz′) *tr.v.* **humanized, humanizing, humanizes 1.** To give human characteristics to; make human: *The writer humanizes animal characters by showing how they feel.* **2.** To make humane: *courteous acts that*

humanize life in the city. —**hu′man·i·za′tion** (hyōō′mə-nĭ-zā′shən) *n.*

humankind (hyōō′mən-kīnd′) *n.* The human race.

humanly (hyōō′mən-lē) *adv.* **1.** In a human way. **2.** Within the scope of human means, abilities, or powers: *as soon as is humanly possible.*

human nature *n.* The sum of qualities and traits shared by all humans.

humanoid (hyōō′mə-noid′) *adj.* Having human characteristics or form: *a humanoid robot.* ❖ *n.* A being, especially an android, that resembles a human.

human papillomavirus (păp′ə-lō′mə-vī′rəs) *n.* Any of various viruses that can cause genital warts and several types of cancer, especially cervical cancer.

human rights *pl.n.* The basic rights of all humans, often held to include the right to life and liberty, equality before the law, freedom from torture and slavery, and freedom of thought and expression.

humble (hŭm′bəl) *adj.* **humbler, humblest 1.** Marked by meekness or modesty in behavior, attitude, or spirit: *a humble manner; humble thanks.* **2.** Low in rank, quality, or station: *My career began as a humble clerk.* ❖ *tr.v.* **humbled, humbling, humbles** To cause to be meek or modest in spirit; humiliate: *Defeat humbled the proud general.* —**hum′ble·ness** *n.* —**hum′bly** *adv.*

humbug (hŭm′bŭg′) *n.* **1.** Nonsense; rubbish: *That argument is simply humbug.* **2.** Something meant to deceive; a hoax. **3.** A person who claims to be other than what he or she is; an impostor. ❖ *tr.v.* **humbugged, humbugging, humbugs** To deceive or trick; cheat: *The scheme humbugged many people.*

humdrum (hŭm′drŭm′) *adj.* Lacking variety or excitement; dull: *the humdrum work of filing papers.*

humerus (hyōō′mər-əs) *n., pl.* **humeri** (hyōō′mə-rī′) **1.** The long bone of the upper arm in humans, extending from the shoulder to the elbow. **2.** A corresponding bone in the forelimb of other vertebrate animals.

humid (hyōō′mĭd) *adj.* Having a large amount of water or water vapor; damp; moist: *humid air before a shower of rain.* See Synonyms at **wet.**

humidify (hyōō-mĭd′ə-fī′) *tr.v.* **humidified, humidifying, humidifies** To make moist or damp: *humidify the air in a greenhouse.* —**hu·mid′i·fi′er** *n.*

humidity (hyōō-mĭd′ĭ-tē) *n.* **1.** The condition of being humid; dampness: *The painting was ruined by the humidity of the warehouse.* **2.** Relative humidity.

humiliate (hyōō-mĭl′ē-āt′) *tr.v.* **humiliated, humiliating, humiliates** To lower the pride, dignity, or self-respect of: *The parents were humiliated by the rude behavior of their children.*

humiliation (hyōō-mĭl′ē-ā′shən) *n.* **1.** The act of humiliating; degradation: *the humiliation of an opponent.* **2.** The condition of being humiliated; disgrace: *They felt deep humiliation after losing so badly.*

humility (hyōō-mĭl′ĭ-tē) *n.* The quality or condition of being humble: *accept a prize with humility.*

hummingbird (hŭm′ĭng-bûrd′) *n.* Any of numerous very small birds of the Americas, having a long slender bill and usually brightly colored feathers. Hummingbirds move their wings so rapidly that they make a humming noise.

hummock (hŭm′ək) *n.* **1.** A low mound or ridge, as of earth or snow. **2.** A ridge or hill of ice in an ice field.

hummus (hŏŏm′əs or hŭm′əs) *n.* A smooth mixture of mashed chickpeas, tahini, garlic, and lemon juice, often eaten as a dip for pita.

humor (hyōō′mər) *n.* **1.** The quality of being funny or comical: *We laughed at the humor of the story.* **2.** The ability to see or express what is funny or comical: *A sense of humor can help a person in a bad situation.* **3.** An often temporary state of mind; a mood: *The beautiful day put me in good humor.* **4.** That which is intended to induce laughter or amusement: *a writer of humor; an actor known for humor.* **5.** In ancient and medieval medicine, one of the four fluids of the body—blood, phlegm, black bile, and yellow bile—thought to determine one's health and character. ❖ *tr.v.* **humored, humoring, humors** To go along with the wishes or ideas of; indulge: *The babysitter humored the child.*

WORD HISTORY Doctors in ancient times and in the Middle Ages thought the human body contained a mixture of four substances, called **humors**, that determined a person's health and character. The word *humor* comes from Latin and means "fluid"; the four fluids were blood, phlegm, black bile, and yellow bile. Illnesses and defects in personality were thought to be caused by too much of a particular humor. Too much black bile, for example, was thought to make one gloomy, and too much yellow bile was thought to make one short-tempered. Modern English has words referring to these moods that come from the Greek words for the relevant humors. We call a gloomy person **melancholic**, from the Greek term for "black bile," and we call a short-tempered person **choleric**, from the Greek word for "yellow bile." Our word **humorous**, in fact, originally meant "having changeable moods due to the influence of different humors."

humorist (hyōō′mər-ĭst) *n.* A person with a sharp sense of humor, especially a writer or performer of humorous material.

humorless (hyōō′mər-lĭs) *adj.* **1.** Lacking a sense of humor: *a dull, humorless person.* **2.** Said or done without humor: *humorless remarks.*

humorous (hyōō′mər-əs) *adj.* Characterized by or expressing humor; funny: *a humorous writer; a humorous story.* —**hu′mor·ous·ly** *adv.* —SEE NOTE AT **humor.**

humour (hyōō′mər) *n. & v. Chiefly British* Variant of **humor.**

hump (hŭmp) *n.* **1.** A rounded mass or lump, as on the back of a camel. **2.** A low mound; a bump: *a hump in the road.* ❖ *tr.v.* **humped, humping, humps** To bend or make into a hump; arch: *The kitten humped its back.* ◆ **over the hump** Past the worst or most difficult part or stage: *Once exams are finished, we'll be over the hump.*

humpback (hŭmp′băk′) *n.* A hunchback. —**hump′-backed′** *adj.*

humpback whale *n.* A large whale that arches its back when it dives, has long knobby flippers, and communicates with complex songs.

humph (hŭmf *or* həmf) *interj.* An expression used to show doubt, contempt, or displeasure.

humus (hyōō′məs) *n.* A dark brown or black substance made up of decayed leaves and other organic material that provides nutrients for plants and increases the ability of soil to retain water.

Hun (hŭn) *n.* A member of a group of nomadic central Asian peoples who invaded Europe in the fourth and fifth centuries AD.

hunch (hŭnch) *n.* **1.** A suspicion or intuition; a premonition: *I had a hunch it would get chilly, so I brought a sweater.* **2.** A hump. ❖ *v.* **hunched, hunching, hunches** —*tr.* To

draw up or bend into a hump: *I hunched my shoulders against the cold wind.* —*intr.* To go into a crouched or cramped posture: *The cat hunched in the corner.*

hunchback (hŭnch′băk′) *n.* **1.** A person whose upper back has a hump in it caused by an abnormally curved spine. **2.** A back having such a hump. —**hunch′backed′** *adj.*

hundred (hŭn′drĭd) *n., pl.* **hundred** or **hundreds 1.** The number, written as 100 or 10², that is equal to 10 × 10. **2.** A one-hundred-dollar bill.

hundredth (hŭn′drĭdth) *n.* **1.** The ordinal number matching the number 100 in a series. **2.** One of one hundred equal parts.

hundredweight (hŭn′drĭd-wāt′) *n., pl.* **hundredweight** or **hundredweights** A unit of weight equal to 100 pounds (45.36 kilograms) in the United States.

hung (hŭng) *v.* Past tense and a past participle of **hang.**

Hungarian (hŭng-gâr′ē-ən) *adj.* Relating to Hungary or its people, language, or culture. ❖ *n.* **1.** A native or inhabitant of Hungary. **2.** The language of Hungary, distantly related to Finnish.

hunger (hŭng′gər) *n.* **1.** A strong desire or need for food: *Hunger drove the wolves to hunt closer to the town.* **2.** The discomfort, pain, or weakness caused by a lack of food: *faint with hunger.* **3.** A strong desire or craving: *Scholars have a hunger for learning.* ❖ *intr.v.* **hungered, hungering, hungers 1.** To have a need or desire for food: *The hikers hungered for something hot and delicious.* **2.** To have a strong desire or craving: *Our team hungered for victory.*

hungry (hŭng′grē) *adj.* **hungrier, hungriest 1.** Experiencing a need or desire for food. **2.** Having a strong desire or craving: *The oppressed people were hungry for freedom.* **3.** Showing or feeling hunger or need: *shot a hungry glance at my sandwich.* —**hun′gri·ly** *adv.* —**hun′gri·ness** *n.*

hunk (hŭngk) *n. Informal* A large piece; a chunk: *I broke a hunk of freshly baked bread off the loaf.*

Hunkpapa (hŭngk′pä′pä) *n., pl.* **Hunkpapa** or **Hunkpapas** A member of a Native American people that is a subdivision of the Sioux, living in North and South Dakota.

hunt (hŭnt) *v.* **hunted, hunting, hunts** —*tr.* **1.** To attempt to catch or kill (wild animals) for food or sport: *Uncle Ted hunts wild turkeys.* **2.** To search for; seek out: *hunting bargains at the local stores.* **3.** To search (a place) thoroughly in pursuit of something: *The detective hunted the streets for the suspect.* —*intr.* **1.** To attempt to catch or kill wild animals for food or sport: *My uncle loves to hunt.* **2.** To search thoroughly; seek: *I hunted for shoes online.* ❖ *n.* **1.** A hunting expedition: *The town approved a deer hunt in the park.* **2.** A diligent search or pursuit: *She's on a hunt for her missing keys.*

hunter (hŭn′tər) *n.* **1.** A person who hunts. **2.** A dog or horse bred and trained for use in hunting.

hunting (hŭn′tĭng) *n.* The activity of pursuing wild animals for food or sport.

Huntington's disease (hŭn′tĭng-tənz) also **Huntington disease** (hŭn′tĭng-tənz) *n.* A rare inherited disease of the central nervous system characterized by progressive dementia, loss of motor skills, behavioral disturbances, and involuntary movements. The typical age of onset is between 30 and 50 years.

huntsman (hŭnts′mən) *n.* **1.** A man who hunts. **2.** A man who manages a pack of dogs in a hunt.

hurdle (hûr′dl) *n.* **1a.** A light portable barrier over which competitors must leap in certain races. **b. hurdles** *(used with a singular verb)* A race in which such barriers must be jumped, without the competitors' breaking their stride. **2.** An obstacle or problem to be overcome: *Getting the money was the chief hurdle I had in going to college.* ❖ *v.* **hurdled, hurdling, hurdles** — *tr.* **1.** To jump over (a hurdle or other barrier): *The dog hurdled the fence after the rabbit.* **2.** To overcome or deal with successfully: *hurdled all obstacles.* — *intr.* To jump over a hurdle or other barrier. —**hur′dler** *n.*

hurdy-gurdy (hûr′dē-gûr′dē) *n.*, *pl.* **hurdy-gurdies** A musical instrument played by turning a crank.

hurl (hûrl) *tr.v.* **hurled, hurling, hurls 1.** To throw with great force; fling: *The volcano hurled smoke and ash high into the air.* See Synonyms at **throw. 2.** To utter vehemently: *The children hurled insults at each other.* —**hurl′er** *n.*

hurly-burly (hûr′lē-bûr′lē) *n.*, *pl.* **hurly-burlies** Noisy confusion; uproar.

Huron (hyoor′ən *or* hyoor′ŏn′) *n.*, *pl.* **Huron** or **Hurons 1.** A member of a Native American confederacy formerly living in present-day southern Ontario, with small groups now living in Quebec and Oklahoma. **2.** The Iroquoian language of the Huron.

hurrah (hoo-rä′ *or* hə-rä′) also **hurray** (hoo-rä′ *or* hə-rā′) *interj. & n. & intr.v.* Variants of **hooray.**

hurricane (hûr′ĭ-kān′) *n.* A severe swirling tropical storm with heavy rains and winds exceeding 74 miles (119 kilometers) per hour. Hurricanes originate in the tropical parts of the Atlantic Ocean or the Caribbean Sea and move generally northward.

hurried (hûr′ēd) *adj.* Done very quickly or in haste; rushed: *Because we got up late, we ate a hurried breakfast.* —**hur′ried·ly** *adv.*

hurry (hûr′ē) *v.* **hurried, hurrying, hurries** — *intr.* To move or act very quickly or in haste: *The children hurried along in the rain.* — *tr.* **1.** To cause to move or act with speed or haste: *The pirates hurried their captives onto the ship.* **2.** To cause to move or act too quickly; rush: *hurried me into making a choice.* **3.** To speed the progress or completion of: *Using a computer hurried the job along.* ❖ *n.*, *pl.* **hurries 1.** The act or an instance of hurrying: *In my hurry to get to the bus, I forgot my umbrella.* **2.** The need or wish to hurry; a condition of urgency: *The police were in a hurry to get to the accident.*

hurt (hûrt) *v.* **hurt, hurting, hurts** — *tr.* **1.** To cause physical damage or pain to; injure: *The fall hurt my leg.* **2.** To cause mental or emotional suffering to; distress: *The criticism hurt my feelings.* **3.** To damage: *The dry summer hurt this year's crops.* **4.** To hinder or impair: *The penalties in the first half hurt our chances for victory.* — *intr.* **1.** To have or produce a feeling of physical pain or discomfort: *My feet hurt from walking all day.* **2.** To cause distress or damage: *It hurt not to be picked for the team.* **3.** To have a bad effect: *Their advice hurt more than it helped.* ❖ *n.* **1.** Something that hurts; an injury or wound. **2.** Mental suffering; anguish: *I still feel the hurt of being rejected.* **3.** A wrong; harm: *an incident that caused lasting hurt to the politician's reputation.*

hurtful (hûrt′fəl) *adj.* Causing injury or suffering; painful: *Air pollution is hurtful to the environment.* —**hurt′ful·ly** *adv.* —**hurt′ful·ness** *n.*

hurtle (hûr′tl) *intr. & tr.v.* **hurtled, hurtling, hurtles** To move or cause to move with great speed: *The speeding train hurtled through the tunnel. The gust of wind hurtled leaves into the air.*

husband (hŭz′bənd) *n.* A man joined to another person in marriage; a male spouse. ❖ *tr.v.* **husbanded, husbanding, husbands** To use sparingly or economically; conserve: *With so many debts, we had to husband our funds.*

WORD HISTORY The Vikings, besides doing a lot of raiding and plundering, also settled peacefully in many places, including England. Because of this, English borrowed many words from Old Norse, the Vikings' language. One of these words is **husband.** Yet the word *wife* is a native Anglo-Saxon (Old English) word. Why should *husband* be Old Norse and *wife* be native English? The reason is that when the Vikings settled in England, they generally took Anglo-Saxon women to be their wives. The men continued to be called by the Old Norse term (it literally means "one bound to a house"), and the women continued to be called by the Anglo-Saxon term (which used to mean just "woman" as well as "wife"). Thus the pairing of *husband* and *wife* shows how historical developments and different social groups can influence the words we use.

husbandry (hŭz′bən-drē) *n.* **1.** The work of raising crops and farm animals; farming. **2.** Good or careful management; thrift: *practice husbandry of scarce natural resources.*

hush (hŭsh) *v.* **hushed, hushing, hushes** — *tr.* **1.** To make silent or quiet: *The parents tried to hush the infant.* **2.** To keep from public knowledge; suppress: *The mayor tried to hush up news of the city scandal.* — *intr.* To be or become silent or still: *The audience hushed as the curtain went up.* ❖ *n.* A silence or stillness; quiet: *A hush fell over the courtroom when the verdict was announced.*

hush puppy or **hushpuppy** (hŭsh′pŭp′ē) *n.* A small, round or slightly oblong cake of cornmeal fried in deep fat.

husk (hŭsk) *n.* The dry outer covering of certain seeds or fruits, as of an ear of corn or a nut. ❖ *tr.v.* **husked, husking, husks** To remove the husk from: *husk ears of corn.* —**husk′er** *n.*

husky¹ (hŭs′kē) *adj.* **huskier, huskiest** Hoarse or rough in quality: *a husky voice.* —**husk′i·ly** *adv.* —**husk′i·ness** *n.*

husky² (hŭs′kē) *adj.* **huskier, huskiest** Strongly built; burly: *a husky football player.* —**husk′i·ness** *n.*

husky³ (hŭs′kē) *n.*, *pl.* **huskies** A strong, thick-coated dog of any of various Arctic breeds that were originally developed as sled dogs, especially the Siberian husky.

WORD HISTORY Husky¹ comes from *husk,* and **husky²** possibly does as well. **Husky³** is probably a shortening and alteration of *Eskimo.*

hussar (hə-zär′ *or* hə-sär′) *n.* A soldier of the light cavalry in some European armies.

hussy (hŭz′ē *or* hŭs′ē) *n.*, *pl.* **hussies** A woman considered to be brazen, impudent, or promiscuous.

hustle (hŭs′əl) *v.* **hustled, hustling, hustles** — *tr.* **1.** To push or convey in a hurried or rough manner: *The guards hustled the prisoner into a cell.* **2.** To cause to move hurriedly; rush: *They hustled the project to its completion.* — *intr.* **1.** To jostle and push: *We hustled through the busy crowds.* **2.** To work or move energetically and rapidly: *You need to hustle to get the job done.* **3.** *Slang* To obtain something by deceitful or illicit methods. ❖ *n.* **1.** The act or an instance of hustling: *It was a hustle to get to the airport on time.* **2.** Energetic activity; drive: *The new player shows lots of hustle.*

hut (hŭt) *n.* A small, crudely made house or shelter; a shack.

hutch (hŭch) *n.* **1.** A pen or coop for small animals, especially rabbits. **2.** A cupboard with drawers for storage and an upper part having open shelves. **3.** A chest or bin for storage.

Hutu (hōō′tōō′) *n., pl.* **Hutu** or **Hutus** A member of a Bantu people inhabiting Rwanda and Burundi.

hwy. An abbreviation of highway.

hyacinth (hī′ə-sĭnth) *n.* Any of various plants that grow from a bulb and have narrow leaves and a cluster of fragrant, variously colored flowers.

hybrid (hī′brĭd) *n.* **1.** An organism that is the result of the mating of individuals of different species or varieties: *A mule is a hybrid between a donkey and a horse.* **2.** Something that is made up of parts that are of two different types: *a movie that is a hybrid between a romance and a thriller; a car that is a hybrid, powered by both an electric motor and an internal combustion engine.*

hybridize (hī′brĭ-dīz′) *intr. & tr.v.* **hybridized, hybridizing, hybridizes** To produce or cause to produce hybrids; crossbreed: *Scientists hybridized different varieties of corn. These two oak species sometimes hybridize.* —**hy′brid·i·za′tion** (hī′brĭ-dĭ-zā′shən) *n.*

hydr– Variant of **hydro–**.

hydra (hī′drə) *n.* Any of several small freshwater animals having a tubular body and a mouth opening surrounded by stinging tentacles. Hydras are related to coral and jellyfish and when cut into pieces can form a new individual from each piece.

Hydra *n.* In Greek mythology, a monster that had many heads and grew back two more if one was cut off.

hydrangea (hī-drăn′jə *or* hī-drăn′jə) *n.* Any of various shrubs having large rounded clusters of white, pink, or blue flowers.

hydrant (hī′drənt) *n.* A fire hydrant.

hydrate (hī′drāt′) *n.* A solid compound produced when certain substances unite chemically with water in definite proportions. ❖ *v.* **hydrated, hydrating, hydrates** ❖ *tr.v.* **1.** To combine (a chemical compound) with water, especially to form a hydrate. **2.** To supply water to (a person, for example) in order to restore or maintain a balance of fluids in the body. ❖ *intr.v.* To combine with water to form a hydrate. —**hy·dra′tion** *n.*

hydraulic (hī-drô′lĭk) *adj.* **1.** Operated by the pressure of water or other fluids. Hydraulic systems transmit mechanical force by pumping the fluid through pipes or tubes: *a hydraulic brake; a hydraulic jack.* **2.** Relating to hydraulics. **3.** Capable of hardening under water: *hydraulic cement.* —**hy·drau′li·cal·ly** *adv.*

hydraulic fracturing *n.* The process of extracting oil or natural gas by injecting a mixture of water, sand or gravel, and certain chemicals under high pressure into well holes in dense rock to create fractures that the sand or gravel holds open, allowing the oil or gas to escape.

hydraulics (hī-drô′lĭks) *n. (used with a singular verb)* The science that deals with water and other liquids at rest or in motion, their uses in engineering, and the laws of their actions.

hydrazine (hī′drə-zēn′ *or* hī′drə-zĭn) *n.* A colorless liquid compound of nitrogen and hydrogen, used as a jet and rocket fuel.

hydride (hī′drīd′) *n.* A chemical compound of hydrogen with another element or radical.

hydro– or **hydr–** A prefix that means: **1.** Water: *hydroelectric.* **2.** Hydrogen: *hydrocarbon.*

WORD BUILDING The prefix **hydro–** is from the Greek prefix *hudro–* or *hudr–*, which comes from the noun *hudōr*, "water." The prefix is used frequently to coin technical words, such as *hydroelectric, hydroplane,* and *hydrosphere.* Before a vowel, *hydro–* sometimes becomes *hydr–*, as in *hydrate* and *hydraulic.*

hydrocarbon (hī′drə-kär′bən) *n.* An organic compound that contains only carbon and hydrogen. Hydrocarbons form a large class of chemical compounds and include gasoline, benzene, and butane.

hydrochloric acid (hī′drə-klôr′ĭk) *n.* A strong, poisonous, corrosive acid that is a solution of hydrogen chloride gas in water and has the formula HCl. It is used in food processing, metal cleaning, and dyeing.

hydrocyanic acid (hī′drō-sī-ăn′ĭk) *n.* A colorless poisonous liquid having an odor of bitter almonds and used in making plastics, pesticides, and dyes.

hydrodynamic (hī′drō-dī-năm′ĭk) *adj.* **1.** Relating to or operated by a moving liquid. **2.** Relating to hydrodynamics. —**hy′dro·dy·nam′i·cal·ly** *adv.*

hydrodynamics (hī′drō-dī-năm′ĭks) *n. (used with a singular verb)* The branch of science that deals with the forces exerted by fluids in motion.

hydroelectric (hī′drō-ĭ-lĕk′trĭk) *adj.* Generating electricity through the use of water power: *a hydroelectric power station.*

hydrofoil (hī′drə-foil′) *n.* **1.** A winglike structure on the bottom of a boat that lifts the hull partly or completely out of the water at high speeds, decreasing friction and allowing the boat to travel faster and use less fuel. **2.** A boat equipped with hydrofoils.

hydrogen (hī′drə-jən) *n. Symbol* **H** A colorless, odorless, highly flammable gaseous element that is the lightest and most abundant element in the universe. It occurs in water in combination with oxygen, in most organic compounds, and in small amounts in the atmosphere. Atomic number 1. See **Periodic Table.**

hydrogenate (hī′drə-jə-nāt′ *or* hī-drŏj′ə-nāt′) *tr.v.* **hydrogenated, hydrogenating, hydrogenates** To combine chemically with hydrogen. Liquid vegetable oils are often hydrogenated to convert them to a solid fat. —**hy′dro·gen·a′tion** *n.*

hydrogen bomb *n.* An extremely destructive bomb that gets its explosive power from the energy released when hydrogen atoms combine under extreme pressure to form helium atoms in the process called fusion.

hydrogen chloride *n.* A colorless, corrosive, suffocating gas, HCl, used in making plastics and in many industrial processes. When mixed with water, it forms hydrochloric acid.

hydrogen peroxide *n.* A colorless compound of hydrogen and oxygen having the formula H_2O_2. It is an unstable oxidizing agent, and is often used in water solution as an antiseptic and bleaching agent.

hydrogen sulfide *n.* A poisonous chemical compound containing hydrogen and sulfur and having the formula H_2S. It is a flammable gas having a characteristic odor of rotten eggs.

hydrology (hī-drŏl′ə-jē) *n.* The scientific study of the distribution and properties of water on and under the earth's surface and in the atmosphere. —**hy′dro·log′ic** (hī′-drə-lŏj′ĭk) *adj.*

hydrolysis (hī-drŏl′ĭ-sĭs) *n.* Decomposition of a chemical compound by reaction with water. Hydrolysis is an important process in the digestion of food.

hydrolyze (hī′drə-līz′) *tr. & intr.v.* **hydrolyzed, hydrolyzing, hydrolyzes** To separate or break down by hydrolysis.

hydrometer (hī-drŏm′ĭ-tər) *n.* An instrument used to measure the specific gravity of liquids.

hydrophobia (hī′drə-fō′bē-ə) *n.* **1.** Rabies. **2.** An abnormal fear of water.

hydroplane (hī′drə-plān′) *n.* **1.** A motorboat with a flattened bottom that skims the surface of the water, allowing it to travel very fast. **2.** A seaplane.

hydroponic (hī′drə-pŏn′ĭk) *adj.* Grown in water supplied with nutrients rather than in soil: *hydroponic tomatoes.* —**hy′dro·pon′ics** *n.*

hydrosphere (hī′drə-sfîr′) *n.* All the water of the earth, including surface water, groundwater, snow, ice, and the water vapor in the atmosphere.

hydrostatics (hī′drə-stăt′ĭks) *n.* *(used with a singular verb)* The branch of physics that deals with fluids at rest and under pressure. —**hy′dro·stat′ic** *adj.*

hydrotherapy (hī′drə-thĕr′ə-pē) *n., pl.* **hydrotherapies** The use of water to treat pain or the symptoms of disease, as with compresses, therapeutic baths, or whirlpool treatments.

hydrous (hī′drəs) *adj.* Containing water as a constituent: *hydrous salts.*

hydroxide (hī-drŏk′sīd′) *n.* A chemical compound consisting of an element or radical joined to one or more hydroxyl radicals. Metal hydroxides are bases and nonmetal hydroxides are acids.

hydroxyl (hī-drŏk′sĭl) *n.* The chemical group OH. It has a valence of 1 and is the characteristic group present in alcohols.

hydrozoan (hī′drə-zō′ən) *n.* Any of numerous aquatic invertebrate animals, such as the hydras and the Portuguese man-of-war, that are closely related to jellyfish and sea anemones.

hyena (hī-ē′nə) *n.* Any of several meat-eating mammals of Asia or Africa having coarse, sometimes spotted or striped hair. Hyenas have powerful jaws for stripping flesh from dead animals and a piercing cry resembling a laugh.

hygiene (hī′jēn′) *n.* **1.** Practices that promote good health and the prevention of disease. **2.** The study of methods that promote and maintain good health and the prevention of disease.

hygienic (hī-jĕn′ĭk *or* hī-jē′nĭk) *adj.* **1.** Relating to hygiene: *hygienic studies.* **2.** Tending to promote good health; clean; sanitary: *a hygienic kitchen; food preparation following hygienic practices.* —**hy′gien′i·cal·ly** *adv.*

hygienist (hī-jē′nĭst *or* hī-jĕn′ĭst) *n.* A specialist in hygiene, especially a person who is trained to clean and examine the teeth.

hygrometer (hī-grŏm′ĭ-tər) *n.* An instrument that measures the humidity of the air.

hygrometric (hī′grə-mĕt′rĭk) *adj.* Relating to the measurement of moisture in the air.

hygroscope (hī′grə-skōp′) *n.* An instrument that records changes in the amount of moisture in the air.

hygroscopic (hī′grə-skōp′ĭk) *adj.* Tending to absorb moisture from the air: *a hygroscopic salt.*

hying (hī′ĭng) *v.* A present participle of **hie.**

hymen (hī′mən) *n.* A membrane that partly closes the opening of the vagina.

hymn (hĭm) *n.* **1.** A song of praise to God or to another deity. **2.** A song of praise or joy.

hymnal (hĭm′nəl) *n.* A book or collection of church hymns.

hyper (hī′pər) *adj. Slang* Excitable; high-strung.

hyper– A prefix that means excessively: *hypercritical; hypersensitive.*

WORD BUILDING The basic meaning of the prefix **hyper–** is "excessive or excessively." For example, *hyperactive* means "highly or excessively active." *Hyper–* comes from the Greek prefix *huper-*, which comes from the preposition *huper,* "over, beyond." *Hyper–* has been used actively in English since the 1600s and is now frequently used to make up new words, such as *hypercritical* and *hypersensitive.* In fact, most of the words in our language beginning with *hyper–* are relatively recent. Only a few, such as *hyperbole,* were formed already in Greek.

hyperactive (hī′pər-ăk′tĭv) *adj.* **1.** Having or showing greater than normal activity; overactive: *a hyperactive gland; hyperactive children running around the playground.* **2.** Having attention deficit hyperactivity disorder. —**hy′per·ac·tiv′i·ty** (hī′pər-ăk-tĭv′ĭ-tē) *n.*

hyperbola (hī-pûr′bə-lə) *n.* A plane curve with two branches that is formed by the intersection of a plane with two similar cones.

hyperbole (hī-pûr′bə-lē) *n.* A figure of speech in which exaggeration is used for effect; for example, the sentence *It rained last night and our yard is a lake* makes use of hyperbole.

hyperbolic (hī′pər-bŏl′ĭk) *adj.* **1.** Relating to or using hyperbole; exaggerated. **2.** Relating to or shaped like a hyperbola: *a hyperbolic curve.*

hypercritical (hī′pər-krĭt′ĭ-kəl) *adj.* Too ready to find fault; overly critical. —**hy′per·crit′i·cal·ly** *adv.*

hyperlink (hī′pər-lĭngk′) *n.* A link in a webpage or other electronic document.

hyperopia (hī′pə-rō′pē-ə) *n.* A defect of the eye that makes near objects appear blurred because their images are focused behind the retina rather than on it; farsightedness. —**hy′per·o′pic** (hī′pər-ō′pĭk *or* hī′pər-ŏp′ĭk) *adj.*

hypersensitive (hī′pər-sĕn′sĭ-tĭv) *adj.* Unusually or overly sensitive: *skin that is hypersensitive to the sun.* —**hy′per·sen′si·tive·ness** *n.* —**hy′per·sen′si·tiv′i·ty** (hī′pər-sĕn′sĭ-tĭv′ĭ-tē) *n.*

hypersonic (hī′pər-sŏn′ĭk) *adj.* Moving or able to move at a speed at least five times the speed of sound.

hypertension (hī′pər-tĕn′shən) *n.* A condition in which the pressure of the blood, especially in the arteries, is abnormally high; high blood pressure.

hypertext (hī′pər-tĕkst′) *n.* Digital text that contains hyperlinks to other texts. Hypertext is sometimes used to give stories multiple plots.

hypertrophy (hī-pûr′trə-fē) *n., pl.* **hypertrophies** An increase in the size of an organ or tissue, resulting from disease or overuse.

hyperventilate (hī′pər-vĕn′tl-āt′) *intr.v.* **hyperventilated, hyperventilating, hyperventilates** **1.** To breathe abnormally fast or deeply, resulting in the loss of carbon dioxide from the blood and consequently a fall in blood pressure, tingling of the extremities, and sometimes fainting. **2.** To breathe in this manner as from excitement or anxiety: *News reporters were hyperventilating over the approaching storm.* —**hy′per·ven′ti·la′tion** *n.*

hypha (hī′fə) *n., pl.* **hyphae** (hī′fē) Any of the long slender filaments that form the structural parts of the body of a fungus. Masses of hyphae make up the mycelium.

hyphen (hī′fən) *n.* A punctuation mark (-) used between the parts of a compound word or between syllables of a word that is divided at the end of a line of text.

hyphenate (hī′fə-nāt′) *tr.v.* **hyphenated, hyphenating, hyphenates** To divide or connect (syllables, word elements, or names) with a hyphen. —**hy′phen·a′tion** *n.*

hypnosis (hĭp-nō′sĭs) *n., pl.* **hypnoses** (hĭp-nō′sēz) **1.** A condition resembling sleep in which a person becomes very responsive to suggestions from another. Hypnosis can be self-induced through concentration and relaxation. **2.** Hypnotism.

hypnotic (hĭp-nŏt′ĭk) *adj.* **1.** Relating to hypnosis. **2.** Relating to hypnotism. **3.** Causing sleep: *the hypnotic effect of television.* ❖ *n.* A drug or other agent that causes sleep. —**hyp·not′i·cal·ly** *adv.*

hypnotism (hĭp′nə-tĭz′əm) *n.* **1.** The theory, method, or process of putting a person into a state of hypnosis. **2.** The act of inducing hypnosis.

hypnotist (hĭp′nə-tĭst) *n.* A person who practices hypnotism.

hypnotize (hĭp′nə-tīz′) *tr.v.* **hypnotized, hypnotizing, hypnotizes 1.** To put (a person) into a state of hypnosis: *The patient was hypnotized to relieve pain.* **2.** To fascinate, as if by hypnosis: *The exciting movie hypnotized the audience.* —**hyp′no·tiz′er** *n.*

hypo– or **hyp–** A prefix that means: **1.** Beneath or below: *hypodermic.* **2.** Less than normal: *hypoglycemia.*

WORD BUILDING The prefix **hypo–** means "beneath, below, or under." It can be traced back to the Greek prefix *hupo–,* from the word *hupo,* "beneath, under." A few English words, such as *hypocrite* and *hypochondria,* come from Greek words; but most English words beginning with *hypo–* have been made up by scientists and physicians in recent times. In such words, *hypo–* either means "under," as in *hypodermic,* or "less than normal," as in *hypoglycemia.*

---

hypochondria (hī′pə-kŏn′drē-ə) *n.* A condition in which a person believes that he or she is ill or worries too much about becoming ill.

hypochondriac (hī′pə-kŏn′drē-ăk′) *n.* A person with hypochondria. ❖ *adj.* Relating to or exhibiting hypochondria.

hypocrisy (hĭ-pŏk′rĭ-sē) *n., pl.* **hypocrisies 1.** The practice of showing or expressing feelings, beliefs, or virtues that one does not actually hold or possess. **2.** The act or an instance of hypocrisy.

hypocrite (hĭp′ə-krĭt′) *n.* A person who practices hypocrisy.

hypocritical (hĭp′ə-krĭt′ĭ-kəl) *adj.* **1.** Characterized by hypocrisy: *hypocritical praise.* **2.** Being a hypocrite: *a hypocritical politician.* —**hyp′o·crit′i·cal·ly** *adv.*

hypodermic (hī′pə-dûr′mĭk) *adj.* **1.** Beneath the skin: *a hypodermic injection of penicillin.* **2.** Injected or used to inject beneath the skin: *a hypodermic needle.* ❖ *n.* **1.** An injection given under the skin. **2.** A hypodermic syringe.

hypodermic syringe *n.* A syringe that is fitted with a hollow needle and used especially to inject fluids under the skin.

hypoglycemia (hī′pō-glī-sē′mē-ə) *n.* An abnormally low level of sugar in the blood, often resulting from too much insulin and causing dizziness and weakness.

hypotenuse (hī-pŏt′n-ōōs′) *n.* The side of a right triangle opposite the right angle.

hypothalamus (hī′pō-thăl′ə-məs) *n.* The region of the brain under the thalamus, controlling temperature, hunger, and thirst, and producing hormones that influence the pituitary gland.

hypothermia (hī′pə-thûr′mē-ə) *n.* Abnormally low body temperature.

hypothesis (hī-pŏth′ĭ-sĭs) *n., pl.* **hypotheses** (hī-pŏth′ĭ-sēz′) A statement that appears to explain a set of facts and that can become the basis for a scientific experiment.

hypothesize (hī-pŏth′ĭ-sīz′) *intr.v.* **hypothesized, hypothesizing, hypothesizes** To make a hypothesis.

hypothetical (hī′pə-thĕt′ĭ-kəl) *adj.* **1.** Relating to or based on a hypothesis; theoretical. **2.** Supposed or made up: *The lawyer used a hypothetical case to prove a point.* ❖ *n.* A hypothetical situation or scenario: *Let's suppose they win this game, just as a hypothetical—what happens then?* —**hy′po·thet′i·cal·ly** *adv.*

hyracotherium (hī′rə-kō-thîr′ē-əm) *n.* A small extinct horselike mammal that lived about 50 million years ago. It had an arched back, a relatively short neck, four-toed front feet, and three-toed hind feet.

hyrax (hī′răks′) *n., pl.* **hyraxes** or **hyraces** (hī′rə-sēz′) Any of several mammals of Africa and Asia that resemble the woodchuck but are more closely related to the hoofed mammals.

hyssop (hĭs′əp) *n.* **1.** A fragrant plant having clusters of small blue flowers, used in perfumes, as a flavoring, and formerly as a medicine. **2.** In the Bible, a plant that was used in certain purification rituals.

hysterectomy (hĭs′tə-rĕk′tə-mē) *n., pl.* **hysterectomies** Surgical removal of part or all of the uterus. —**hys′-ter·ec′to·mize′** (hĭs′tə-rĕk′tə-mīz′) *v.*

hysteria (hĭ-stĕr′ē-ə *or* hĭ-stîr′ē-ə) *n.* **1.** Uncontrollable excitement or emotion. **2.** A group of feelings and behaviors, such as anxiety and fainting, that were once considered symptoms of a distinct psychiatric disorder. This term is no longer used in medicine.

hysteric (hĭ-stĕr′ĭk) *n.* **1. hysterics** *(used with a singular or plural verb)* A fit of uncontrollable laughing or crying: *The clown's antics sent all of the children into hysterics.* **2.** A person who suffers from hysteria. This term is no longer used in medicine.

hysterical (hĭ-stĕr′ĭ-kəl) *adj.* **1.** Laughing or crying for a prolonged period of time: *a screaming and hysterical child.* **2.** *Informal* Extremely funny: *told a hysterical story.* **3.** Relating to or resulting from hysteria. This term is no longer used in medicine. —**hys·ter′i·cal·ly** *adv.*

Hz An abbreviation of hertz.

Ii

i or **I** (ī) *n., pl.* **i's** or **I's** or **Is** The ninth letter of the English alphabet.

I¹ (ī) *pron.* The person who is speaking or writing. —SEE NOTE AT **me.**

I² also **i** The Roman numeral for 1.

I³ An abbreviation of: **1.** incomplete. **2.** interstate.

I. An abbreviation of: **1.** island. **2.** isle.

iamb (ī′ămb′ *or* ī′ăm′) *n., pl.* **iambs** In poetry, a metrical foot consisting of an unstressed syllable followed by a stressed syllable, as in *delay.* —**i·am′bic** *adj. & n.*

–ian A suffix that means: **1.** Relating to or resembling: *reptilian.* **2.** One relating to, belonging to, or resembling: *pediatrician.*

Iberian (ī-bîr′ē-ən) *adj.* **1.** Relating to the Iberian Peninsula, its peoples, languages, or cultures. **2.** Relating to the ancient peoples that inhabited the Iberian Peninsula or their languages or cultures.

ibex (ī′běks′) *n., pl.* **ibex** or **ibexes** Any of several wild goats of mountainous regions of Eurasia and Africa, having long, ridged, backward-curving horns.

ibidem (ĭb′ĭ-děm′ *or* ĭ-bī′dəm) *adv.* In the same place. Used in footnotes and bibliographies, often in its abbreviated form *ibid.*, to refer to something just cited.

ibis (ī′bĭs) *n., pl.* **ibis** or **ibises** Any of various large wading birds that have a long downward-curving bill.

–ible Variant of **–able.**

Ibo (ē′bō) *n.* Variant of **Igbo.**

ibuprofen (ī′byōō-prō′fən) *n.* A drug used to treat pain, fever, or inflammation.

–ic A suffix that means: **1.** Relating to or characterized by: *allergic; atomic.* **2.** Having a higher valence or oxidation state in a compound or ion of an element than indicated by the suffix *-ous: ferric; chloric.*

Icarus (ĭk′ər-əs) *n.* In Greek mythology, the son of Daedalus who, in escaping from Crete on wings made by his father, disobeyed his father by flying too close to the sun. As a result, the wax in his wings melted and he fell into the Aegean Sea.

ice (īs) *n.* **1.** Water frozen solid, normally at or below a temperature of 32 degrees Fahrenheit (0 degrees Celsius). **2.** A surface or mass of frozen water: *Before skating on the pond, test the ice.* **3.** Something resembling frozen water. **4.** A frozen dessert consisting of water, sugar, and a liquid flavoring. ❖ *v.* **iced, icing, ices** —*tr.* **1.** To coat or cover with ice: *Sleet iced the road.* **2.** To chill with ice: *After catching the fish, we iced them.* **3.** To decorate (a cake or cookies) with icing. **4.** In ice hockey, to shoot (the puck) from one's defensive half of the rink across the opponent's goal line outside of the goal. —*intr.* To turn into or become covered or blocked with ice; freeze: *The river iced over during the cold spell.*

ice age *n.* **1.** Any of several cold periods during which glaciers covered much of the earth. **2. Ice Age** The most recent glacial period, which occurred during the Pleistocene Epoch and ended about 10,000 years ago.

iceberg (īs′bûrg′) *n.* A massive body of floating ice that has broken away from a glacier.

iceberg lettuce *n.* A variety of lettuce with crisp, pale green leaves that form a compact, round head.

iceboat (īs′bōt′) *n.* **1.** A vehicle resembling a boat set on runners and having a sail that can propel it at great speed over ice. **2.** An icebreaker.

icebound (īs′bound′) *adj.* **1.** Locked in by surrounding ice: *a ship icebound in the frozen sea.* **2.** Obstructed or covered over by ice: *a harbor icebound during the winter.*

icebox (īs′bŏks′) *n.* **1.** An insulated box into which ice is put to cool and preserve food. **2.** A refrigerator.

icecap or **ice cap** (īs′kăp′) *n.* A year-round cover of ice and snow that spreads over a large area, especially of land or a polar region.

ice-cold (īs′kōld′) *adj.* Extremely cold: *The waiter served us ice-cold lemonade.*

ice cream *n.* A smooth sweet frozen food made of a mixture of milk products, sugar, and flavorings.

ice-cream cone (īs′krēm′) *n.* **1.** A cone-shaped wafer used to hold ice cream. **2.** One of these wafers with ice cream in it.

ice-cream soda *n.* A refreshment made of ice cream mixed with carbonated water and syrup.

iced (īst) *adj.* **1.** Covered over with ice: *an iced windshield.* **2.** Chilled with ice: *drank a glass of iced coffee.* **3.** Decorated or coated with icing: *a bakery that sells iced cakes.*

iced tea or **ice tea** *n.* A cold drink consisting of tea that has been chilled, often served with sugar or sweetener and flavorings such as lemon.

ice field *n.* A large expanse of ice and snow among the peaks of a mountainous region.

ice hockey *n.* A game played on ice in which two teams of skaters use sticks with blades to try to drive a puck into the goal of the opposing team.

Icelandic (īs-lăn′dĭk) *adj.* Relating to Iceland or its people, language, or culture. ❖ *n.* The Germanic language of Iceland.

icemaker (īs′mā′kər) *n.* A machine, often built into a refrigerator, that freezes water into ice cubes.

iceman (īs′măn) *n.* A man who delivers or sells ice.

ice pack *n.* **1.** A large mass of floating ice formed from small fragments that have pressed together and frozen solid. **2.** A bag or cloth filled with crushed ice and applied to a sore or swollen part of the body to reduce pain and inflammation.

ice pick *n.* A hand tool with a long sharp point, used for chipping or breaking ice.

ice skate *n.* A boot or shoe with a metal runner or blade attached to the sole, used for skating on ice.

ice-skate (īs′skāt′) *intr.v.* **ice-skated, ice-skating, ice-skates** To skate on ice with ice skates.

ice skater *n.* A person who ice-skates.

ice storm *n.* A storm in which snow or rain freezes on contact, forming a coat of ice on the surfaces it touches.

ichneumon (ĭk-nōō′mən) *n.* **1.** Any of numerous parasitic wasps whose larvae feed on the larvae of other insects. The females have very long ovipositors. **2.** A large gray mongoose of Africa and southern Europe.

ichthyology (ĭk′thē-ŏl′ə-jē) *n.* The branch of zoology that deals with fishes. —**ich′thy·ol′o·gist** *n.*

ichthyosaur (ĭk′thē-ə-sôr′) *n.* Any of various extinct sea reptiles having a long beak, four flippers, a tapering body, and a tail with a large fin.

icicle (ī′sĭ-kəl) *n.* A hanging spike of ice formed by the freezing of dripping or falling water.

icily (ī′sə-lē) *adv.* In an icy or chilling manner: *an icily cold wind; eye an opponent icily.*

iciness (ī′sē-nĭs) *n.* The condition or quality of being icy.

icing (ī′sĭng) *n.* **1.** A sweet glaze of sugar and egg whites or milk, used to decorate cakes or cookies. **2.** In ice hockey, a minor violation of the rules in which a player ices the puck when the opposing team is not on a power play.

icky (ĭk′ē) *adj.* **ickier, ickiest** *Informal* **1.** Offensive; distasteful: *icky sentimentality.* **2.** Disagreeably gooey or sticky: *an icky mess on the stove.*

icon (ī′kŏn′) *n.* **1.** An important and well-known symbol: *The covered wagon is an icon of the pioneer days.* **2.** A picture on a computer screen representing a specific file, directory, window, option, or program that can be opened or activated when the user clicks on it. **3.** A religious image or picture venerated in the Eastern Orthodox Church, especially one depicting Jesus, his mother Mary, or another holy figure. —**i·con′ic** *adj.*

iconoclast (ī-kŏn′ə-klăst′) *n.* **1.** A person who attacks and opposes popular or traditional ideas, beliefs, or practices. **2.** A person who destroys sacred religious images. —**i·con′o·clas′tic** *adj.*

iconography (ī′kə-nŏg′rə-fē) *n., pl.* **iconographies** The symbolic forms associated with the subject or theme of a work of art. —**i′co·nog′ra·pher** *n.* —**i·con′o·graph′ic** (ī-kŏn′ə-grăf′ĭk), **i·con′o·graph′i·cal** *adj.*

–ics A suffix that means: **1.** Science, art, study, or knowledge of, or skill in: *graphics; mathematics.* **2.** Activities, actions, or practices of: *athletics; ceramics.* —SEE NOTE AT **politics.**

icy (ī′sē) *adj.* **icier, iciest** **1.** Containing or covered with ice; frozen: *an icy sidewalk.* **2.** Very cold: *icy waters.* See Synonyms at **cold. 3.** Unfriendly or hostile: *an icy stare.*

id (ĭd) *n.* In Freudian theory, the division of the psyche that is totally unconscious and serves as the source of instinctual impulses and demands for immediate satisfaction of basic needs.

ID (ī′dē′) *Informal n.* A form of identification, especially an ID card. ❖ *tr.v.* **ID′ed, ID′ing, ID′s** To check the identification of, especially to verify legal age: *The bouncer ID'ed patrons as they entered the bar.*

I'd (īd) Contraction of *I had* or *I would.*

ID card *n.* A card that gives identifying information about a person, such as name, age, and date of birth, and often includes the person's photograph.

idea (ī-dē′ə) *n.* **1.** A product of mental activity, such as a thought, opinion, belief, or fancy: *She developed her idea for the project over several months.* **2.** A plan, scheme, or method: *My idea is to become a doctor.* **3.** The point or purpose of something: *The idea is to make people aware of the problem by putting up posters.*

✦ SYNONYMS **idea, concept, conception, notion, thought** *n.*

ideal (ī-dēl′) *n.* **1.** A conception of something in its perfection: *Equality and justice are some of our society's ideals.* **2.** A person or thing that is regarded as an example of excellence or perfection: *She remains the ideal among mathematics teachers.* **3.** An ultimate or worthy object of endeavor; a goal: *Their ideal is to own their own restaurant.* ❖ *adj.* **1.** Perfect or the best possible: *The hot summer sun made this an ideal day for swimming.* **2.** Existing only in the mind; imaginary: *A line without thickness is an ideal geometric object.*

idealism (ī-dē′ə-lĭz′əm) *n.* **1.** The tendency to think of ideas or people in terms of some standard of perfection. **2.** The practice of following one's personal ideals: *His idealism led him to work for world peace.* **3.** A philosophical belief that all things exist only as ideas in the mind, not as objects independent of the mind.

idealist (ī-dē′ə-lĭst) *n.* **1.** One who follows personal ideals, often with little regard for practical considerations. **2.** One who believes in philosophical idealism.

idealistic (ī-dē′ə-lĭs′tĭk) *adj.* Relating to idealism or idealists: *an idealistic belief; an idealistic philosopher.* —**i′de·al·is′ti·cal·ly** *adv.*

idealize (ī-dē′ə-līz′) *tr.v.* **idealized, idealizing, idealizes** To regard as ideal or perfect: *Often we idealize our friends so much that we do not see their faults.* —**i·de′al·i·za′tion** (ī-dē′ə-lĭ-zā′shən) *n.*

ideally (ī-dē′lē) *adv.* **1.** In agreement with an ideal; perfectly: *The two friends were ideally suited to each other.* **2.** In theory or imagination: *Ideally, the prison would house a maximum of 200 inmates.*

identical (ī-dĕn′tĭ-kəl) *adj.* **1.** Exactly equal and alike: *We're riding identical bicycles.* **2.** The very same: *The candidate used those identical words in his speech.* **3.** Relating to twins developed from the same fertilized egg. Identical twins are always the same sex and have the same genetic traits. —**i·den′ti·cal·ly** *adv.*

identification (ī-dĕn′tə-fĭ-kā′shən) *n.* **1.** The act of identifying or the condition of being identified. **2.** Evidence of a person's identity: *A driver's license is usually accepted as sufficient identification.*

identification card *n.* An ID card.

identify (ī-dĕn′tə-fī′) *v.* **identified, identifying, identifies** —*tr.* **1.** To establish or recognize as a certain person or thing: *We identified the bird as a thrush.* **2.** To consider as identical; equate: *The Greek god Ares is identified with the Roman god Mars.* **3.** To associate or connect closely: *That economist is identified with conservative political groups.* —*intr.* **1.** To be or feel closely associated with a person or thing: *He identifies strongly with his grandfather.* **2.** To self-identify. —**i·den′ti·fi′a·ble** *adj.*

identity (ī-dĕn′tĭ-tē) *n., pl.* **identities** **1.** The condition of being a certain person or thing; individuality: *The police tried to establish the suspect's identity.* **2.** The awareness that an individual or group has of being a distinct, persisting entity: *the main character's identity as an outsider.* **3.** Information, such as an identification number, used to allow a person to prove who he or she is. **4.** The condition of being identical: *The identity of the two signatures was established by a handwriting expert.*

ideogram (ĭd′ē-ə-grăm′ *or* ī′dē-ə-grăm′) *n.* A written character or symbol that represents an idea or thing rather than a particular word or phrase.

ideograph (ĭd′ē-ə-grăf′) *n.* An ideogram.

ideology (ī′dē-ŏl′ə-jē *or* ĭd′ē-ŏl′ə-jē) *n., pl.* **ideologies** A set of doctrines or beliefs that are shared by members of a group, such as a political party or social class. —i'-de·o·log'i·cal (i'dē-ə-lŏj'ĭ-kəl or ĭd'ē-ə-lŏj'ĭ-kəl) adj. —i'de·o·log'i·cal·ly adv.

ides (īdz) pl.n. (used with a singular or plural verb) In the ancient Roman calendar, the 15th day of March, May, July, or October or the 13th day of the other months.

idiocy (ĭd'ē-ə-sē) n., pl. idiocies 1. Great foolishness or stupidity. 2. A foolish or stupid action or remark.

idiom (ĭd'ē-əm) n. 1. A phrase or expression having a special meaning that cannot be understood from the individual meanings of its words; for example, fly off the handle is an idiom in English meaning lose one's temper. 2. The accepted way in which words are used in a language. 3. The language or dialect of a particular region or group of people: the idiom of Cajun French.

idiomatic (ĭd'ē-ə-măt'ĭk) adj. 1. Following the pattern of word usage particular to a given language: It takes many years of study to speak idiomatic Chinese. 2. Being or relating to an idiom or idioms: a dictionary of idiomatic expressions. —id'i·o·mat'i·cal·ly adv.

idiosyncrasy (ĭd'ē-ō-sĭng'krə-sē) n., pl. idiosyncrasies A trait or mannerism peculiar to an individual: One of my uncle's idiosyncrasies is putting lots of pepper on everything he eats. —id'i·o·syn·crat'ic (ĭd'ē-ō-sĭn-krăt'ĭk) adj. —id'i·o·syn·crat'i·cal·ly adv.

idiot (ĭd'ē-ət) n. A person who is considered stupid or foolish.

idiotic (ĭd'ē-ŏt'ĭk) adj. Showing stupidity or foolishness: an idiotic mistake. —id'i·ot'i·cal·ly adv.

idle (īd'l) adj. idler, idlest 1. Not employed or busy: idle employees; idle machines; idle time on the holiday. 2. Avoiding work; lazy; shiftless. 3. Not in use or operation: The presses are idle. 4. Lacking substance, value, or basis: idle talk. ❖ v. idled, idling, idles —intr. 1. To pass time without working or in avoiding work: The men idled on the park benches. 2. To run at a low speed or without transmitting power: The engine idled smoothly. —tr. 1. To pass (time) without working or in order to avoid work: They idled the afternoon away. 2. To cause to be unemployed or inactive: The drivers' strike idled every bus in the city. —i'dle·ness n. —i'dler (īd'lər) n. —i'dly adv.

idol (īd'l) n. 1. An image or object that is worshiped as a god. 2. A person or thing that is adored or admired, often to fanatical degree: a pop star who was an idol to her fans.

idolater or idolator (ī-dŏl'ə-tər) n. A person who worships idols.

idolatrous (ī-dŏl'ə-trəs) adj. 1. Relating to idolatry. 2. Given to idolatry.

idolatry (ī-dŏl'ə-trē) n., pl. idolatries 1. The worship of idols. 2. Fanatical adoration of someone or something: The fan's idolatry made him blind to the sports star's faults.

idolize (īd'l-īz') tr.v. idolized, idolizing, idolizes 1. To regard with fanatical adoration: Many fans idolize their favorite performers. 2. To worship or treat as an idol: Early Egyptians idolized cats.

idyll also idyl (īd'l) n. 1. A short poem or prose work describing a pleasant scene or event of country life. 2. A scene or event having a simple peaceful nature.

idyllic (ī-dĭl'ĭk) adj. 1. Simple and carefree: an idyllic childhood. 2. Charming and picturesque: an idyllic tropical beach. —i·dyl'li·cal·ly adv.

i.e. An abbreviation of id est (that is).

–ie Variant of –y³.

if (ĭf) conj. 1. In the event that; supposing that: If it rains, then we won't take a walk. 2. On condition that: I'll go only if you do. 3. Even though; although possibly: a handsome if useless gadget. 4. Whether: I asked if they were coming. 5. Indicating a strong wish: If they had only come sooner!

iff An abbreviation of if and only if.

iffy (ĭf'ē) adj. iffier, iffiest Informal Doubtful; uncertain: It's looking iffy for getting concert tickets.

–ify Variant of –fy.

Igbo (ĭg'bō) also Ibo (ē'bō) n., pl. Igbo or Igbos also Ibo or Ibos 1. A member of a people living in southeast Nigeria. 2. The language of the Igbo.

igloo (ĭg'lōō) n., pl. igloos A house made of blocks of snow, such as those built by the Inuit.

igneous (ĭg'nē-əs) adj. 1. Relating to fire. 2. Formed by the cooling and hardening of molten rock: Basalt is an igneous rock.

ignite (ĭg-nīt') v. ignited, igniting, ignites —tr. 1. To cause to start burning: A lightning bolt ignited the forest fire. 2. To bring about or provoke suddenly; stir up: His remarks ignited a controversy. —intr. To begin to burn; catch fire: Wet logs do not ignite easily.

ignition (ĭg-nĭsh'ən) n. 1. The act or process of igniting a substance. 2. An electrical system that provides the spark to ignite the fuel mixture of an internal-combustion engine. 3. A switch that activates this system: Pump the gas pedal and turn the ignition.

ignoble (ĭg-nō'bəl) adj. 1. Not noble, as in character or purpose; base; dishonorable: an ignoble act. 2. Not of high social rank; common: Royal princes do not usually marry someone of ignoble birth. —ig·no'bly adv.

ignominious (ĭg'nə-mĭn'ē-əs) adj. 1. Characterized by shame or disgrace; humiliating: an ignominious defeat at the polls. 2. Deserving disgrace or shame; despicable: an ignominious crime. —ig'no·min'i·ous·ly adv.

ignominy (ĭg'nə-mĭn'ē) n. Great personal dishonor or disgrace.

ignoramus (ĭg'nə-rā'məs) n., pl. ignoramuses An ignorant person.

ignorance (ĭg'nər-əns) n. The condition of being ignorant; lack of education or knowledge: The professor was surprised by the students' ignorance of history. Ignorance of the law is no excuse for committing a crime.

ignorant (ĭg'nər-ənt) adj. 1. Lacking education or knowledge. 2. Showing or arising from a lack of knowledge: an ignorant mistake. 3. Unaware or uninformed: Many pioneers were ignorant of the hardships they were to face. —ig'no·rant·ly adv.

ignore (ĭg-nôr') tr.v. ignored, ignoring, ignores To refuse to pay attention to; disregard: I ignored the sound of the television in the next room.

iguana (ĭ-gwä'nə) n. Any of various large plant-eating lizards that have a ridge of spines along the back and are found in the American tropics.

il– Variant of in–.

ileum (ĭl'ē-əm) n., pl. ilea (ĭl'ē-ə) The lowest section of the small intestine.

Iliad (ĭl'ē-əd) n. An ancient Greek epic poem attributed to Homer, recounting the siege of the city of Troy in western Turkey.

ilium (ĭl'ē-əm) n., pl. ilia (ĭl'ē-ə) The uppermost of the three bones that make up each of the hipbones.

ilk (ĭlk) n. Type or kind; sort; class: Flies, mosquitoes, and other insects of that ilk can be annoying.

ill (ĭl) adj. worse (wûrs), worst (wûrst) 1. Not healthy; sick:

went home feeling ill. **2.** Not normal; unsound: *ill health.* **3.** Resulting in suffering; harmful or distressing: *the ill effects of the storm.* **4.** Having evil intentions; hostile or unfriendly: *ill feeling between rivals.* **5.** Not favorable or promising: *an ill omen.* ❖ *adv.* **worse, worst 1.** In a sickly or unsound manner; unwell. **2.** Scarcely or with difficulty: *We can ill afford another mistake.* ❖ *n.* **1.** Evil; wrongdoing: *the choice between doing good or doing ill.* **2.** Harm; disaster: *The drought was a terrible ill for farmers.* **3.** A source of suffering; an affliction: *the ills of living in an overcrowded city.* **4.** Unfavorable or unkind words: *Do not speak ill of him.* ◆ **ill at ease** Anxious; uneasy.

ill. An abbreviation of: **1.** illustrated. **2.** illustration.

I'll (īl) Contraction of *I will.*

ill-advised (ĭl′əd-vīzd′) *adj.* Done with bad advice or with insufficient thinking: *an ill-advised scheme to build a pipeline through a region prone to earthquakes.*

ill-bred (ĭl′brĕd′) *adj.* Badly brought up; impolite.

illegal (ĭ-lē′gəl) *adj.* **1.** Against the law; not legal: *It's illegal to drive over the speed limit.* **2.** Against the official rules, as of a game: *Fouls are illegal acts in basketball.* —**il·le′gal·ly** *adv.*

illegality (ĭl′ē-găl′ĭ-tē) *n., pl.* **illegalities 1.** The condition of being illegal; unlawfulness. **2.** An illegal act: *The company was fined for illegalities in their hiring practices.*

illegible (ĭ-lĕj′ə-bəl) *adj.* Impossible or very hard to read: *a note written in an illegible scrawl.* —**il·leg′i·bil′i·ty** *n.* —**il·leg′i·bly** *adv.*

illegitimate (ĭl′ĭ-jĭt′ə-mĭt) *adj.* **1.** Against an established rule or law: *an illegitimate seizure of property.* **2.** *Offensive* Born to parents who are not married to each other. —**il′le·git′i·ma·cy** (ĭl′ĭ-jĭt′ə-mə-sē) *n.* —**il′le·git′i·mate·ly** *adv.*

ill-fated (ĭl′fā′tĭd) *adj.* **1.** Destined for misfortune; doomed: *The ill-fated ship never reached port.* **2.** Marked by or causing misfortune; unlucky: *an ill-fated decision.*

ill-gotten (ĭl′gŏt′n) *adj.* Obtained by evil or dishonest means: *ill-gotten wealth.*

ill-humored (ĭl′hyōō′mərd) *adj.* Irritable; surly.

illiberal (ĭ-lĭb′ər-əl) *adj.* Narrow-minded; intolerant. —**il·lib′er·al·ly** *adv.*

illicit (ĭ-lĭs′ĭt) *adj.* Not permitted by law; unlawful. —**il·lic′it·ly** *adv.* —**il·lic′it·ness** *n.*

illimitable (ĭ-lĭm′ĭ-tə-bəl) *adj.* Impossible to limit; limitless. —**il·lim′it·a·bly** *adv.*

Illinois (ĭl′ə-noi′) *n., pl.* **Illinois 1.** A member of a group of Native American peoples originally living in Illinois, Iowa, Wisconsin, and Missouri, with a present-day population in Oklahoma. **2.** The Algonquian language of the Illinois.

illiteracy (ĭ-lĭt′ər-ə-sē) *n., pl.* **illiteracies 1.** The condition of being unable to read and write. **2.** A lack of education or knowledge: *scientific illiteracy.*

illiterate (ĭ-lĭt′ər-ĭt) *adj.* **1.** Unable to read and write. **2.** Showing a lack of knowledge in a certain subject: *illiterate in history.* —**il·lit′er·ate·ly** *adv.*

ill-mannered (ĭl′măn′ərd) *adj.* Showing a lack of good manners; impolite; rude. —**ill′-man′nered·ly** *adv.*

ill-natured (ĭl′nā′chərd) *adj.* Disagreeable, cross, or mean. —**ill′-na′tured·ly** *adv.*

illness (ĭl′nĭs) *n.* **1.** An unhealthy condition; poor health: *often missing school because of illness.* **2.** A disease: *Diphtheria is a serious illness.*

illogical (ĭ-lŏj′ĭ-kəl) *adj.* **1.** Having or showing a lack of sound reasoning; not logical: *Your argument is illogical.*

2. Unreasonable; senseless: *an illogical fear of being hit by a meteor.* —**il·log′i·cal·ly** *adv.*

ill-starred (ĭl′stärd′) *adj.* Unlucky; ill-fated.

ill-tempered (ĭl′tĕm′pərd) *adj.* Having a bad temper; irritable. —**ill′-tem′pered·ly** *adv.*

ill-timed (ĭl′tīmd′) *adj.* Done or occurring at the wrong time; untimely: *I regretted my ill-timed remark.*

ill-treat (ĭl′trēt′) *tr.v.* **ill-treated, ill-treating, ill-treats** To treat badly or cruelly; abuse. —**ill′-treat′ment** *n.*

illuminate (ĭ-lōō′mə-nāt′) *tr.v.* **illuminated, illuminating, illuminates 1.** To provide with light: *A lamp illuminated the steps.* **2.** To make clear; explain: *The film illuminated the events leading up to the war.* **3.** To decorate with ornamental designs, pictures, or colors: *Medieval manuscripts were often illuminated by monks.*

illumination (ĭ-lōō′mə-nā′shən) *n.* **1.** The act of illuminating or the state of being illuminated: *the illumination of a dark corner.* **2.** An amount of light; brightness: *the soft illumination of a candle.* **3.** Decoration with lights: *festive outdoor illumination.* **4.** Decoration of a book, manuscript, or other writing. **5.** A design, picture, or other adornment in a book or manuscript.

illumine (ĭ-lōō′mĭn) *tr.v.* **illumined, illumining, illumines** To give light to; illuminate.

illus. An abbreviation of illustrated.

ill-use (ĭl′yōōz′) *tr.v.* **ill-used, ill-using, ill-uses** To treat badly or unjustly; mistreat. ❖ *n.* (ĭl′yōōs′) Poor or unjust treatment.

illusion (ĭ-lōō′zhən) *n.* **1.** An unreal or misleading appearance or image: *A three-dimensional movie creates an illusion of depth even though the screen is flat.* **2.** An idea or belief that is mistaken or false: *His illusion that he did not need to study for tests did not last long.*

illusory (ĭ-lōō′sə-rē or ĭ-lōō′zə-rē) *adj.* Produced by, based on, or having the nature of an illusion; deceptive: *The white sand had the illusory appearance of snow.*

illustrate (ĭl′ə-strāt′ or ĭ-lŭs′trāt′) *tr.v.* **illustrated, illustrating, illustrates 1.** To make clear or explain, as by using examples or comparisons: *The geologist illustrated how the rocks folded by pushing on the ends of a piece of paper.* **2.** To provide with pictures or diagrams that explain or adorn: *The artist illustrated the story.*

illustration (ĭl′ə-strā′shən) *n.* **1.** Something, such as a picture, diagram, or chart, that serves to make clear, explain, or decorate something else: *The illustrations improve the book.* **2.** Something serving as an example, comparison, or proof: *A ball falling to the ground is an illustration of gravity.* **3.** The act of illustrating or the state of being illustrated: *The illustration of the children's book took the artist several months.*

illustrative (ĭ-lŭs′trə-tĭv or ĭl′ə-strā′tĭv) *adj.* Serving to illustrate or explain: *a science book with many illustrative photos and diagrams.* —**il·lus′tra·tive·ly** *adv.*

illustrator (ĭl′ə-strā′tər) *n.* An artist who illustrates books, magazines, or other material.

illustrious (ĭ-lŭs′trē-əs) *adj.* Well-known and very distinguished; eminent: *an illustrious author; illustrious deeds.* See Synonyms at **famous.**

ill will *n.* Unfriendly feeling; hostility.

IM (ī′ĕm′) *Informal tr.v.* **IMed, IMing, IMs** or **IM'ed, IM'ing, IM's 1.** To send (someone) an instant message: *Matt IMed me to let me know that he would be late.* **2.** To express in an instant message: *Sharon IMed that she wanted to borrow my math textbook.* ❖ *n.* An instant message.

im– Variant of **in–.**

I'm (īm) Contraction of *I am.*

image (ĭm′ĭj) *n.* **1.** An artistic representation of a person or thing, especially a painting or statue. **2.** A visual presentation or reproduction of an object, especially by reflection in a mirror or refraction through a lens or lens system: *a microscopic image.* **3.** A mental picture of something not real or present: *Our image of the new apartment did not conform with reality.* **4.** A vivid description in words, especially a metaphor or simile: *The poem is full of images of country life.* **5.** The concept of a person or thing that is held by the public, especially as a result of advertising or publicity: *The toy company has a friendly image.* **6.** A person or thing that closely resembles another: *a child who is the image of a parent.* ❖ *tr.v.* **imaged, imaging, images** To produce, transmit, or display a visual representation of: *Astronomers set up the telescope to image Mars.*

imagery (ĭm′ĭj-rē) *n., pl.* **imageries 1.** The use of figures of speech or vivid descriptions in writing or speaking: *We discussed the poem's imagery.* **2.** Visual images considered as a group: *imagery of the planet's moons sent back by the probe.*

imaginable (ĭ-măj′ə-nə-bəl) *adj.* Capable of being imagined: *a book that has information on every imaginable topic.* —**i·mag′i·na·bly** *adv.*

imaginary (ĭ-măj′ə-nĕr′ē) *adj.* **1.** Existing only in the imagination; not real: *The book describes an imaginary world of talking animals.* **2.** Relating to an imaginary number.

imaginary number *n.* A number whose square is negative.

imagination (ĭ-măj′ə-nā′shən) *n.* **1.** The act or ability of forming mental images of something that is not real or present: *Characters for the story were born in the lively imagination of the writer.* **2.** The ability to use the mind effectively; resourcefulness: *The new mayor solved the city's budget problems with imagination.*

imaginative (ĭ-măj′ə-nə-tĭv *or* ĭ-măj′ə-nā′tĭv) *adj.* **1.** Having a strong imagination, especially creative imagination: *an imaginative artist.* **2.** Created by or marked by originality and creativity: *an imaginative solution to a problem.* —**i·mag′i·na·tive·ly** *adv.*

imagine (ĭ-măj′ĭn) *v.* **imagined, imagining, imagines** —*tr.* **1.** To form a mental picture of: *Can you imagine what weightlessness would feel like?* **2.** To make a guess; suppose: *I imagine this bad weather will make them late.* —*intr.* To use the imagination: *The mind is able to think, remember, and imagine.*

imago (ĭ-mā′gō *or* ĭ-mä′gō) *n., pl.* **imagoes** or **imagines** (ĭ-mā′gə-nēz′ *or* ĭ-mä′gə-nēz′) An insect in its fully developed adult stage.

imam *also* **Imam** (ĭ-mäm′) *n.* **1.** A male prayer leader in a mosque. **2.** A male Muslim leader regarded as a successor or descendant of the prophet Muhammad. **3.** Any of 12 descendants of Muhammad regarded by most Shiite Muslims as forming a divinely appointed succession of leaders.

imbalance (ĭm-băl′əns) *n.* A lack of balance, as between amounts or forces: *an imbalance between income and expenditures.*

imbecile (ĭm′bə-sĭl) *n.* A person who is considered stupid or foolish. —**im′be·cil′ic** *adj.*

imbibe (ĭm-bīb′) *v.* **imbibed, imbibing, imbibes** —*tr.* **1.** To drink. **2.** To absorb or take in as if by drinking: *Thirsty plants imbibe moisture through the roots.* **3.** To take or

absorb into the mind: *The painter went to Asia to imbibe new ideas.* —*intr.* To drink alcoholic beverages. —**im·bib′er** *n.*

imbroglio (ĭm-brōl′yō) *n., pl.* **imbroglios** A confused or difficult situation; a predicament.

imbue (ĭm-byōō′) *tr.v.* **imbued, imbuing, imbues** To fill thoroughly, as with a quality or emotion: *Reading the novel imbued them with a desire to travel to Africa.*

imitable (ĭm′ĭ-tə-bəl) *adj.* Capable or worthy of being imitated: *imitable behavior.*

imitate (ĭm′ĭ-tāt′) *tr.v.* **imitated, imitating, imitates 1.** To follow as a model or example: *Your little brother imitates you because he admires you.* **2.** To copy the speech or actions of; mimic: *The actor imitated the president perfectly.* **3.** To copy exactly; reproduce: *Few artists can imitate the paintings of Rembrandt.* **4.** To look like; resemble: *a fishing lure that imitates a minnow.* —**im′i·ta′tor** *n.*

✦ **SYNONYMS imitate, copy, mimic, simulate** *v.*

imitation (ĭm′ĭ-tā′shən) *n.* **1.** The act or an instance of imitating: *I learned the song through imitation.* **2.** Something made to look like something else; a likeness or copy: *This bell is an imitation of the Liberty Bell.* ❖ *adj.* Made to resemble another: *imitation leather.*

imitative (ĭm′ĭ-tā′tĭv) *adj.* **1.** Involving imitation: *The words woof and meow are imitative of animal sounds.* **2.** Tending to imitate or copy: *Parrots are imitative birds.* —**im′i·ta′tive·ly** *adv.*

immaculate (ĭ-măk′yə-lĭt) *adj.* **1.** Impeccably clean; spotless: *an immaculate tablecloth.* **2.** Free from sin. **3.** Free from fault or error; flawless: *an immaculate record on the job.* —**im·mac′u·late·ly** *adv.*

Immaculate Conception *n.* The doctrine of the Roman Catholic Church that the Virgin Mary was conceived free from original sin.

immanent (ĭm′ə-nənt) *adj.* Existing within; inherent: *They believed that goodness is immanent in all humans.*

immaterial (ĭm′ə-tîr′ē-əl) *adj.* **1.** Of no importance or consequence; unimportant: *The wedding will be indoors, so it is immaterial what the weather is like.* **2.** Having no physical body or form; spiritual: *ghosts and other immaterial beings.* —**im′ma·te′ri·al·ly** *adv.*

immature (ĭm′ə-tyŏŏr′ *or* ĭm′ə-chŏŏr′) *adj.* **1.** Not fully grown or developed: *immature corn.* **2.** Showing a lack of maturity; childish: *selfish, immature behavior.* See Synonyms at **young.** —**im′ma·ture′ly** *adv.* —**im′ma·tur′i·ty** *n.*

immeasurable (ĭ-mĕzh′ər-ə-bəl) *adj.* Impossible to measure: *the immeasurable number of stars in the heavens.* —**im·meas′ur·a·bly** *adv.*

immediate (ĭ-mē′dē-ĭt) *adj.* **1.** Taking place at once or very soon; happening without delay: *needing immediate medical care in an emergency room.* **2.** Relating to or near the present time: *the immediate future.* **3.** Close at hand: *our immediate surroundings.* **4.** Next in line or relation: *the king's immediate successor.* **5.** Occurring with nothing coming between or interfering; direct: *You should avoid any immediate contact of this glue with the skin.* —**im·me′di·a·cy** (ĭ-mē′dē-ə-sē) *adv.* —**im·me′di·ate·ly** *adv.*

immemorial (ĭm′ə-môr′ē-əl) *adj.* Reaching beyond the limits of memory or history: *Humans have created art since time immemorial.* —**im′me·mo′ri·al·ly** *adv.*

immense (ĭ-mĕns′) *adj.* Of great size, extent, or degree; huge: *immense rocks; an immense length of time.* —**im·mense′ly** *adv.* —**im·men′si·ty** *n.*

immerse (ĭ-mûrs′) *tr.v.* **immersed, immersing, immerses 1.** To cover completely with a liquid; submerge: *immersed the pans in soapy water.* **2.** To baptize by submerging in water. **3.** To involve deeply; absorb: *I immersed myself in the exciting story.* —**im·mers′i·ble** *adj.*

immersion (ĭ-mûr′zhən *or* ĭ-mûr′shən) *n.* **1.** An act of immersing or the condition of being immersed. **2.** Baptism performed by immersing a person in water.

immigrant (ĭm′ĭ-grənt) *n.* A person who immigrates.

immigrate (ĭm′ĭ-grāt′) *intr.v.* **immigrated, immigrating, immigrates** To come into a foreign country to live: *People from many parts of the world immigrate to Europe each year.* —**im′mi·gra′tion** *n.* —SEE NOTE AT **emigrate.**

imminent (ĭm′ə-nənt) *adj.* About to happen; looming; impending: *It is cold and windy, and snow seems imminent.* —**im′mi·nence** *n.* —**im′mi·nent·ly** *adv.*

immobile (ĭ-mō′bəl *or* ĭ-mō′bēl′ *or* ĭ-mō′bīl′) *adj.* **1.** Not able to move; fixed: *A broken axle made the car immobile.* **2.** Not moving; motionless: *The deer stood immobile in the field.* —**im′mo·bil′i·ty** (ĭm′ō-bĭl′ĭ-tē) *n.*

immobilize (ĭ-mō′bə-līz′) *tr.v.* **immobilized, immobilizing, immobilizes** To make immobile; render incapable of moving: *The doctor immobilized the broken finger with a splint.* —**im·mo′bi·li·za′tion** (ĭ-mō′bə-lĭ-zā′shən) *n.*

immoderate (ĭ-mŏd′ər-ĭt) *adj.* Going beyond what is normal or proper; extreme: *loud and immoderate laughter.* —**im·mod′er·ate·ly** *adv.*

immodest (ĭ-mŏd′ĭst) *adj.* **1.** Morally offensive or indecent: *Older people considered the new dance immodest.* **2.** Lacking modesty; arrogant or boastful: *She gave an immodest description of her role in the project.* —**im·mod′est·ly** *adv.* —**im·mod′es·ty** *n.*

immolate (ĭm′ə-lāt′) *tr.v.* **immolated, immolating, immolates 1.** To kill (an animal) as a religious sacrifice. **2.** To kill by burning. —**im′mo·la′tion** *n.*

immoral (ĭ-môr′əl) *adj.* Contrary to what is considered moral: *immoral behavior.* —**im·mor′al·ly** *adv.*

immorality (ĭm′ô-răl′ĭ-tē) *n., pl.* **immoralities 1.** The quality or condition of being immoral: *the immorality of war.* **2.** An immoral act or practice.

immortal (ĭ-môr′tl) *adj.* **1.** Never dying; living forever: *The Greek gods were believed to be immortal.* **2.** Having eternal fame: *the immortal words of Shakespeare.* ❖ *n.* **1.** An immortal being: *The ancient Greeks believed their gods were immortals.* **2.** A person with enduring fame: *Mozart and Beethoven are immortals in the field of music.* —**im·mor′tal·ly** *adv.*

immortality (ĭm′ôr-tăl′ĭ-tē) *n.* **1.** The condition of being immortal. **2.** Enduring fame: *the immortality of Michelangelo.*

immortalize (ĭ-môr′tl-īz′) *tr.v.* **immortalized, immortalizing, immortalizes** To make immortal; give enduring fame to: *Longfellow's poem immortalizes the midnight ride of Paul Revere.*

immovable (ĭ-mōō′və-bəl) *adj.* **1.** Not capable of moving or of being moved: *Mountains are immovable objects.* **2.** Unyielding; steadfast: *an immovable purpose.* ❖ *n.* **immovables** Property, such as real estate, that cannot be moved. —**im·mov′a·bly** *adv.*

immune (ĭ-myōōn′) *adj.* **1a.** Protected from disease naturally or by vaccination or inoculation: *I'm immune to chickenpox, since I had it when I was young.* **b.** Relating to or producing immunity: *Immune cells help the body resist infections.* **2.** Protected; guarded; safe: *No country is immune from economic problems.* **3.** Not affected by

something; unresponsive: *I am immune to your charms.*

immune response *n.* A response of the immune system to bacteria, viruses, or other substances that are foreign to the body. The immune response usually involves the formation of antibodies.

immune system *n.* The system in humans and other animals that enables the body to resist disease, especially by producing white blood cells and antibodies.

immunity (ĭ-myōō′nĭ-tē) *n., pl.* **immunities 1.** The ability of an organism to resist disease, especially through the production of antibodies. **2.** Freedom from certain duties, penalties, or restrictions: *Diplomatic immunity protects ambassadors from being prosecuted for most crimes.* **3.** A condition conferred upon a contestant that prevents him or her from being eliminated from a competition for a certain time period: *The winner of the challenge was given immunity for the following challenge.*

immunization (ĭm′yə-nĭ-zā′shən) *n.* **1.** A vaccination: *Have you received your immunization for measles?* **2.** The production of immunity: *rates of immunization in rural areas; undertook a program of immunization.*

immunize (ĭm′yə-nīz′) *tr.v.* **immunized, immunizing, immunizes** To produce immunity in, as by vaccination: *The pediatrician immunized the infant against measles.*

immunodeficiency (ĭm′yə-nō-dĭ-fĭsh′ən-sē *or* ĭ-myōō′-nō-dĭ-fĭsh′ən-sē) *n.* The inability to produce a normal immune response, usually as a result of a disease.

immunology (ĭm′yə-nŏl′ə-jē) *n.* The scientific study of the structure and function of the immune system.

immure (ĭ-myōōr′) *tr.v.* **immured, immuring, immures** To confine within walls; imprison.

immutable (ĭ-myōō′tə-bəl) *adj.* Not subject to change; unchangeable: *the immutable laws of nature.* —**im·mu′ta·bil′i·ty, im·mu′ta·ble·ness** *n.* —**im·mu′ta·bly** *adv.*

imp (ĭmp) *n.* **1.** A mischievous child. **2.** A small demon or devil.

imp. An abbreviation of: **1.** imperative. **2.** imperfect. **3.** imported.

impact (ĭm′păkt′) *n.* **1.** The action of one body striking against another; collision: *The impact of the meteorite left a large crater.* **2.** The effect or impression of something: *the impact of science on modern society; the emotional impact of a poem.* ❖ *tr.v.* **impacted, impacting, impacts 1.** To strike or collide with forcefully: *The meteorite impacted the earth's surface.* **2.** To have an effect or influence on: *The budget cuts will severely impact the public schools.*

impacted (ĭm-păk′tĭd) *adj.* Wedged into the gum or bone so as not to be able to emerge properly. Used of a tooth: *impacted wisdom teeth.*

impair (ĭm-pâr′) *tr.v.* **impaired, impairing, impairs** To diminish in strength, quantity, or quality; weaken: *An ear infection impaired my hearing for a week.* —**im·pair′ment** *n.*

impala (ĭm-pä′lə) *n.* An African antelope having a reddish-brown coat and long curved horns in the male, noted for its ability to leap high.

impale (ĭm-pāl′) *tr.v.* **impaled, impaling, impales 1.** To pierce with a sharp stake or point: *The salesclerk impaled the receipts on a spike.* **2.** To torture or kill by pushing onto a stake.

impalpable (ĭm-păl′pə-bəl) *adj.* **1.** Not perceptible to the touch; intangible: *impalpable shadows.* **2.** Difficult to define or pin down; vague: *There was an impalpable feeling of sadness in the music.* —**im·pal′pa·bil′i·ty** *n.* —**im·pal′pa·bly** *adv.*

impanel (ĭm-păn′əl) tr.v. **impaneled, impaneling, impanels** or **impanelled, impanelling, impanels 1.** To enroll or place on a panel or list. **2.** To choose (a jury) from a list or lottery. —**im·pan′el·ment** n.

impart (ĭm-pärt′) tr.v. **imparted, imparting, imparts 1.** To give; bestow: *Sunlight imparted a cheerful feeling to the room.* **2.** To make known; reveal: *impart a secret.*

impartial (ĭm-pär′shəl) adj. Not favoring either side; fair; unprejudiced: *Sports officials must be impartial in their judgments.* —**im′par·ti·al′i·ty** (ĭm′pär-shē-ăl′ĭ-tē) n. —**im·par′tial·ly** adv.

impassable (ĭm-păs′ə-bəl) adj. Impossible to travel across or over; not passable: *an impassable gorge.* —**im·pass′a·bil′i·ty** n. —**im·pass′a·bly** adv.

impasse (ĭm′păs′) n. **1.** A road or passage that has no exit. **2.** A difficult situation that has no practical solution: *When members could not agree, the committee reached an impasse.*

impassioned (ĭm-păsh′ənd) adj. Filled with intense feeling; ardent: *an impassioned plea for human rights.*

impassive (ĭm-păs′ĭv) adj. Feeling or showing no emotion; calm: *The judge was impassive through all the lawyer's dramatic arguments.* —**im·pas′sive·ly** adv.

impatience (ĭm-pā′shəns) n. The quality or condition of being impatient.

impatiens (ĭm-pā′shənz or ĭm-pā′shəns) n., pl. **impatiens** Any of various garden plants that have colorful flowers and attractive leaves.

impatient (ĭm-pā′shənt) adj. **1.** Unable to wait patiently or endure irritation: *I became impatient standing in line, so I left.* **2.** Expressing or produced by impatience: *an impatient answer.* **3.** Restlessly eager: *We were impatient to go home.* —**im·pa′tient·ly** adv.

impeach (ĭm-pēch′) tr.v. **impeached, impeaching, impeaches 1.** To charge (a public official) formally with misconduct in office: *The president of the United States can be impeached only before Congress.* **2.** To challenge or discredit; attack: *Scientists impeached the report's accuracy.* —**im·peach′ment** n.

impeccable (ĭm-pĕk′ə-bəl) adj. Having no flaws; faultless: *has impeccable table manners.* See Synonyms at **perfect.** —**im·pec′ca·bly** adv.

impecunious (ĭm′pĭ-kyōō′nē-əs) adj. Lacking money; penniless. —**im′pe·cu′ni·ous·ly** adv.

impede (ĭm-pēd′) tr.v. **impeded, impeding, impedes** To obstruct or slow down the movement or progress of; hinder: *Road repairs impeded traffic all summer. A lack of funds impeded the research.*

impediment (ĭm-pĕd′ə-mənt) n. **1.** Something that impedes or encumbers progress; a hindrance or obstruction: *Youth is no impediment to success in sports and music.* **2.** A physical defect that prevents clear speech.

impel (ĭm-pĕl′) tr.v. **impelled, impelling, impels 1.** To urge to action; drive; spur: *Their curiosity impelled them to investigate the noise.* **2.** To drive forward; propel: *A strong current impelled the little boat toward the rocks.*

impending (ĭm-pĕn′dĭng) adj. About to occur; imminent: *an impending appointment.*

impenetrable (ĭm-pĕn′ĭ-trə-bəl) adj. **1.** Impossible to penetrate or enter: *an impenetrable fortress.* **2.** Impossible to understand; incomprehensible: *an impenetrable mystery.* —**im·pen′e·tra·bly** adv.

impenitent (ĭm-pĕn′ĭ-tənt) adj. Showing no sorrow for having done something wrong; unrepentant. —**im·pen′i·tent·ly** adv.

imperative (ĭm-pĕr′ə-tĭv) adj. **1.** Necessary or urgent: *It is imperative that we arrive on time.* **2.** Relating to the mood of a verb that expresses a command, order, or request. For example, *do* in "Please do it!" and *go* in "Go at once!" are in the imperative mood. ❖ n. **1.** Something that is necessary or urgent: *Gaining control of the river was a military imperative.* **2a.** The imperative mood. **b.** A verb form in the imperative mood. —**im·per′a·tive·ly** adv.

imperceptible (ĭm′pər-sĕp′tə-bəl) adj. Impossible or difficult to perceive or feel: *an imperceptible difference; the imperceptible movement of the stars overhead.* —**im′per·cep′ti·bil′i·ty** n. —**im′per·cep′ti·bly** adv.

imperfect (ĭm-pûr′fĭkt) adj. **1.** Not perfect; having faults or defects. **2.** Relating to the imperfect tense. ❖ n. **1.** The imperfect tense. **2.** A verb in the imperfect tense. —**im·per′fect·ly** adv.

imperfection (ĭm′pər-fĕk′shən) n. **1.** The condition or quality of being imperfect: *human imperfection.* **2.** A defect; a fault or flaw: *scratches and other imperfections in the surface of the table.*

imperfect tense n. A verb tense, especially the past progressive tense, that expresses incomplete or continuous action.

imperial (ĭm-pîr′ē-əl) adj. Relating to an empire, emperor, or empress: *imperial Rome; the imperial court of Kublai Khan.* —**im·pe′ri·al·ly** adv.

imperialism (ĭm-pîr′ē-ə-lĭz′əm) n. **1.** The extension of a nation's authority by acquiring foreign territories or by establishing economic and political dominance over other nations. **2.** A political doctrine or system promoting dominance of one nation over others in this way.

imperialist (ĭm-pîr′ē-ə-lĭst) n. A person who believes in or practices imperialism. ❖ adj. Relating to or supporting imperialism.

imperialistic (ĭm-pîr′ē-ə-lĭs′tĭk) adj. Relating to imperialism or imperialists. —**im·pe′ri·al·is′ti·cal·ly** adv.

imperil (ĭm-pĕr′əl) tr.v. **imperiled, imperiling, imperils** or **imperilled, imperilling, imperils** To put into peril; endanger: *Pollution imperils the health of the shellfish in the bay.*

imperious (ĭm-pîr′ē-əs) adj. Arrogant; overbearing; domineering: *The boss's imperious treatment of the workers caused many to quit.* —**im·pe′ri·ous·ly** adv.

imperishable (ĭm-pĕr′ĭ-shə-bəl) adj. Not perishable: *imperishable food; imperishable hopes.*

impermanent (ĭm-pûr′mə-nənt) adj. Not lasting or durable.

impermeable (ĭm-pûr′mē-ə-bəl) adj. Impossible to permeate, as by a liquid or gas: *an impermeable raincoat; an impermeable cell wall.*

impersonal (ĭm-pûr′sə-nəl) adj. **1.** Not referring to or intended for any particular person: *The speaker's remarks were very general and impersonal.* **2.** Showing no emotion; impassive: *an aloof impersonal manner.* **3.** Not existing as a human personality: *A storm is an impersonal force and does not care where it goes.* **4.** Having no subject or having the indefinite *it* as subject. For example, *snow* in the construction *It is snowing* is an impersonal verb. —**im·per′son·al′i·ty** (ĭm-pûr′sə-năl′ĭ-tē) n. —**im·per′son·al·ly** adv.

impersonate (ĭm-pûr′sə-nāt′) tr.v. **impersonated, impersonating, impersonates 1.** To assume the character or appearance of: *He was arrested for impersonating a police officer.* **2.** To imitate the appearance, voice, and manner of:

an entertainer who impersonates Elvis Presley. —im·per'·son·a'tion *n.* —im·per'son·a'tor *n.*

impertinence (ĭm-pûr'tn-əns) *n.* **1.** Rudeness; insolence: *I find your impertinence very annoying.* **2.** An impertinent act or statement. **3.** Irrelevance.

impertinent (ĭm-pûr'tn-ənt) *adj.* **1.** Offensively disrespectful; rude: *The clerk's impertinent manner offended me.* **2.** Not pertinent; irrelevant: *The discussion was interrupted with many impertinent questions and remarks.* —im·per'ti·nent·ly *adv.*

imperturbable (ĭm'pər-tûr'bə-bəl) *adj.* Unshakably calm and collected: *The senator remained imperturbable even in the heat of the debate.* —im'per·turb'a·bil'i·ty *n.* —im'per·turb'a·bly *adv.*

impervious (ĭm-pûr'vē-əs) *adj.* **1.** Incapable of being penetrated: *A good raincoat should be impervious to water.* **2.** Incapable of being affected: *The racing driver seemed impervious to fear.* —im·per'vi·ous·ly *adv.*

impetigo (ĭm'pĭ-tī'gō) *n.* A contagious disease chiefly affecting children, characterized by the formation of pimples and thick yellow crusts on the skin.

impetuosity (ĭm-pĕch'ōō-ŏs'ĭ-tē) *n., pl.* **impetuosities 1.** The quality or condition of being impetuous. **2.** An impetuous act.

impetuous (ĭm-pĕch'ōō-əs) *adj.* **1.** Characterized by rash or hasty actions; impulsive: *This impetuous decision has brought disaster.* **2.** Marked by violent force or motion: *impetuous waves smashing against the pier.* —im·pet'·u·ous·ly *adv.*

impetus (ĭm'pĭ-təs) *n., pl.* **impetuses 1.** A driving force; a cause of action: *A sense of fairness is often the impetus for reform.* **2.** The force or energy exhibited by a moving body; momentum: *The impetus of the speeding train made it difficult to stop quickly.*

impiety (ĭm-pī'ĭ-tē) *n., pl.* **impieties 1.** Lack of piety or reverence. **2.** An impious act.

impinge (ĭm-pĭnj') *intr.v.* **impinged, impinging, impinges 1.** To encroach; infringe; trespass: *Censorship impinges on our right of free speech.* **2.** To have an effect or influence: *Have your allergies impinged on your singing ability?* **3.** To collide; strike: *Light rays impinge on the eye.* —im·pinge'ment *n.* —im·ping'er *n.*

impious (ĭm'pē-əs *or* ĭm-pī'əs) *adj.* Lacking reverence; not pious. —im'pi·ous·ly *adv.* —im'pi·ous·ness *n.*

impish (ĭm'pĭsh) *adj.* Relating to or befitting an imp; mischievous: *impish pranks.* —imp'ish·ly *adv.*

implacable (ĭm-plăk'ə-bəl *or* ĭm-plā'kə-bəl) *adj.* Impossible to placate or appease; unyielding: *an implacable enemy; an implacable demand for justice.* —im·plac'a·bil'i·ty *n.* —im·plac'a·bly *adv.*

implant (ĭm-plănt') *tr.v.* **implanted, implanting, implants 1.** To establish securely, as in the mind; instill: *The parents implanted a strong sense of values in their children.* **2.** To insert or set in firmly; fix: *implant fence posts in the ground.* **3.** To graft or set (a tissue or device) inside the body: *The doctors implanted a pacemaker in the patient's chest.* ❖ *n.* (ĭm'plănt') A tissue or device that has been surgically grafted or inserted within the body. —im'·plan·ta'tion (ĭm'plăn-tā'shən) *n.*

implausible (ĭm-plô'zə-bəl) *adj.* Difficult to believe; not plausible: *an implausible excuse.* —im·plau'si·bly *adv.*

implement (ĭm'plə-mənt) *n.* A tool or piece of equipment used in doing a task: *Rakes and hoes are gardening implements.* ❖ *tr.v.* (ĭm'plə-mĕnt') **implemented, implementing, implements** To put into effect; carry out: *We need a*

plan in order to implement your idea. —im'ple·men·ta'tion (ĭm'plə-mən-tā'shən) *n.*

implicate (ĭm'plĭ-kāt') *tr.v.* **implicated, implicating, implicates** To show to be involved or connected with an activity, especially a crime: *The witness's testimony implicated several people in the scandal.*

implication (ĭm'plĭ-kā'shən) *n.* **1.** Something implied; an indirect indication: *Although he did not say so directly, his implication was that he'd lost his job.* **2.** The act of implying or the condition of being implied: *The writer's thoughts were conveyed more by implication than by direct statement.* **3.** The act of implicating or the condition of being implicated: *The suspect denied any implication in the affair.*

implicit (ĭm-plĭs'ĭt) *adj.* **1.** Implied or understood without being directly expressed: *The threat of a lawsuit was implicit in the lawyer's letter.* **2.** Having no doubts; unquestioning: *We have implicit trust in your judgment.* —im·plic'it·ly *adv.* —im·plic'it·ness *n.*

implode (ĭm-plōd') *v.* **imploded, imploding, implodes** —*intr.* **1.** To collapse inward violently: *The submarine imploded from the deep water pressure.* **2.** To undergo a sudden catastrophic failure: *His political career imploded after the scandal.* —*tr.* To cause to implode: *demolished the old skyscraper by imploding it.* —im·plo'sion (ĭm-plō'zhən) *n.*

implore (ĭm-plôr') *tr.v.* **implored, imploring, implores 1.** To ask (a person) earnestly or anxiously; beseech: *implored my boss to give me a second chance.* **2.** To plead or beg for (something) earnestly: *The defendant implored the judge's mercy.*

imply (ĭm-plī') *tr.v.* **implied, implying, implies 1.** To say or convey indirectly; suggest without stating outright: *Our neighbor said something that implied he might be moving soon.* **2.** To involve as a necessary part or consequence: *Life implies growth and eventual death.* —SEE NOTE AT **infer.**

impolite (ĭm'pə-līt') *adj.* Not polite; discourteous: *an impolite remark.* —im'po·lite'ly *adv.*

impolitic (ĭm-pŏl'ĭ-tĭk) *adj.* Socially unwise or imprudent: *an impolitic approach to a sensitive issue.* —im·pol'i·tic·ly *adv.*

import (ĭm-pôrt' *or* ĭm'pôrt') *tr.v.* **imported, importing, imports 1.** To bring in (goods) from a foreign country for sale or use. **2.** To convey as a meaning; mean; signify: *The president's speech imported a major change in the country's foreign policy.* ❖ *n.* (ĭm'pôrt') **1.** Something imported for sale or use. **2.** The act of importing; importation: *The import of fruits and vegetables is strictly regulated.* **3.** Importance; significance: *an event of enormous import.* **4.** Meaning; significance: *Since they found its import unclear, I tried again to explain my letter.*

importance (ĭm-pôr'tns) *n.* The quality or condition of being important; significance: *The trainer stressed the importance of regular workouts.*

important (ĭm-pôr'tnt) *adj.* **1.** Marked by or having great value, significance, or influence: *Coffee is an important crop in South America.* **2.** Having high social rank or influence; prominent: *government leaders and other important people.* **3.** Believing or acting as if one has high social rank or influence: *Some guests strutted about the party in an important manner.* —im·por'tant·ly *adv.*

importation (ĭm'pôr-tā'shən) *n.* **1.** The act of importing, especially as a business: *importation of cars and TVs from*

Japan. **2.** Something imported; an import: *Many fine shoes are importations from Italy.*

importer (ĭm-pôr′tər) *n.* A person, company, or country that imports goods: *Japan is a large importer of North American timber.*

importunate (ĭm-pôr′chə-nĭt) *adj.* Annoyingly persistent in pressing a request or demand: *importunate letters and phone calls from fundraisers.* —**im·por′tu·nate·ly** *adv.* —**im·por′tu·nate·ness** *n.*

importune (ĭm′pôr-tōōn′ *or* ĭm-pôr′chən) *tr.v.* **importuned, importuning, importunes** To beset with frequent requests; ask insistently: *We importuned the management to locate the factory in our town.* —**im′por·tu′ni·ty** *n.*

impose (ĭm-pōz′) *v.* **imposed, imposing, imposes** —*tr.* **1.** To place (a burden or obligation) on a person: *impose a tax; impose a punishment.* **2.** To bring about by exercising authority; force to prevail: *The United Nations imposed peace on the warring countries.* **3.** To force (oneself) upon another or others: *Our visitors have imposed themselves on us for too long.* —*intr.* To force oneself upon another or others; take unfair advantage: *We don't mean to impose, but could we stay for dinner?* ♦ **impose on** or **impose upon** To take advantage of: *The guests imposed on the good nature of their host by asking to borrow the car.* —**im·pos′er** *n.* —SEE NOTE AT **compose.**

imposing (ĭm-pō′zĭng) *adj.* Impressive, as in size, power, or accomplishment: *an imposing statue.* See Synonyms at **grand.** —**im·pos′ing·ly** *adv.*

imposition (ĭm′pə-zĭsh′ən) *n.* **1.** The act of imposing: *the imposition of new taxes.* **2.** Something imposed, such as a tax, burden, or obligation: *The Colonists resented such impositions as the tax on imported tea.* **3.** An unfair demand upon someone's time, friendship, or hospitality: *These daily requests for help have become an imposition.*

impossibility (ĭm-pŏs′ə-bĭl′ĭ-tē) *n., pl.* **impossibilities 1.** The quality or condition of being impossible: *The impossibility of being in two places at once.* **2.** Something that is impossible: *I found being a member of the swimming team and singing in the glee club to be an impossibility.*

impossible (ĭm-pŏs′ə-bəl) *adj.* **1.** Not capable of happening or existing: *A square circle is impossible.* **2.** Not capable of being accomplished: *an impossible task.* **3.** Difficult to tolerate or deal with: *That dog is impossible!* —**im·pos′si·bly** *adv.*

impost (ĭm′pōst′) *n.* Something, such as a tax or duty, that is imposed or levied.

impostor or **imposter** (ĭm-pŏs′tər) *n.* A person who deceives others by pretending to be someone else.

imposture (ĭm-pŏs′chər) *n.* Deception or fraud by the assumption of a false identity.

impotence (ĭm′pə-təns) *n.* The quality or condition of being impotent.

impotent (ĭm′pə-tənt) *adj.* **1.** Lacking strength, power, or effectiveness: *Loss of popular support left the government impotent to deal with the crisis.* **2.** Incapable of sexual intercourse because of an inability to achieve or sustain an erection. —**im·po′tent·ly** *adv.*

impound (ĭm-pound′) *tr.v.* **impounded, impounding, impounds 1.** To seize and hold in legal custody: *A judge can impound all records in a trial.* **2.** To capture and confine in a pound: *The city impounds stray dogs.* **3.** To collect (water) in a natural or artificial lake.

impoverish (ĭm-pŏv′ər-ĭsh *or* ĭm-pŏv′rĭsh) *tr.v.* **impoverished, impoverishing, impoverishes 1.** To make very poor: *Bad harvests impoverished the family.* **2.** To use up the natural richness, strength, or resources of: *Erosion can impoverish the soil.* —**im·pov′er·ish·ment** *n.*

impoverished (ĭm-pŏv′ər-ĭsht *or* ĭm-pŏv′rĭsht) *adj.* Very poor: *hungry and impoverished citizens.*

impracticable (ĭm-prăk′tĭ-kə-bəl) *adj.* Impossible to do or carry out: *an impracticable scheme to grow crops in Antarctica.* —**im·prac′ti·ca·bly** *adv.*

impractical (ĭm-prăk′tĭ-kəl) *adj.* **1.** Unwise or foolish to do or carry out: *She suggested that we abandon our impractical plans.* **2.** Incapable of dealing well with practical matters: *an impractical dreamer.* —**im·prac′ti·cal′i·ty** (ĭm-prăk′tĭ-kăl′ĭ-tē) *n.*

imprecation (ĭm′prĭ-kā′shən) *n.* A curse.

imprecise (ĭm′prĭ-sīs′) *adj.* Not precise or clear: *an imprecise description.* —**im′pre·cise′ly** *adv.*

impregnable (ĭm-prĕg′nə-bəl) *adj.* **1.** Impossible to capture or enter by force: *an impregnable fort.* **2.** Impossible to refute; firm: *an impregnable argument.*

impregnate (ĭm-prĕg′nāt) *tr.v.* **impregnated, impregnating, impregnates 1.** To make pregnant. **2.** To fill completely; saturate: *impregnated the cotton ball with alcohol.* —**im′preg·na′tion** *n.*

impresario (ĭm′prĭ-sär′ē-ō′ *or* ĭm′prĭ-sär′ē-ō′) *n., pl.* **impresarios** A person who organizes, manages, or directs entertainment, such as operas, ballets, or concerts.

impress¹ (ĭm-prĕs′) *tr.v.* **impressed, impressing, impresses 1.** To have a strong, often favorable effect on the mind or feelings of: *The worker's performance impressed the manager.* **2.** To fix firmly in the mind, as by force or influence: *The coach impressed upon the team the importance of good defense.* **3.** To mark or stamp with pressure: *impress a design on soft clay.* ♦ *n.* (ĭm′prĕs′) **1.** The act of impressing. **2.** A mark or imprint made by pressure. —SEE NOTE AT **pressure.**

impress² (ĭm-prĕs′) *tr.v.* **impressed, impressing, impresses 1.** To force (a person) to serve in the military. **2.** To seize (property): *During the war, the government impressed all foreign funds.*

WORD HISTORY Impress¹ comes from Middle English *impressen,* meaning "to imprint," which comes from Latin *imprimere,* meaning "to press into." **Impress²** is related to obsolete English *imprest,* meaning "money paid for enlisting."

impression (ĭm-prĕsh′ən) *n.* **1.** A marked effect, image, or feeling that stays in the mind: *The new director made a good impression on everyone.* **2.** A vague notion, memory, or feeling: *I have the impression that we've met before.* **3.** A mark or imprint made on a surface by pressure: *There was an impression left on the cushion where the dog had slept.* **4.** A humorous imitation of a person's speech and manner: *He gave impressions of movie stars.*

impressionable (ĭm-prĕsh′ə-nə-bəl) *adj.* Easily influenced or affected; suggestible: *The impressionable students were excited by their first trip outside the country.*

impressionism (ĭm-prĕsh′ə-nĭz′əm) *n.* **1.** often **Impressionism** A style of painting developed in France in the late 1800s that uses small brush strokes to give the impression of the natural light of a scene or object. **2.** A musical style of the late 1800s and early 1900s that uses unconventional harmonies and tonal effects to create an often dreamy or mysterious mood.

impressionist (ĭm-prĕsh'ə-nĭst) *n.* An artist or musician who uses impressionism. ❖ *adj.* Impressionistic: *an impressionist painting.*

impressionistic (ĭm-prĕsh'ə-nĭs'tĭk) *adj.* Relating to impressionism or the impressionists.

impressive (ĭm-prĕs'ĭv) *adj.* Making a strong or vivid impression; commanding attention: *an impressive monument; an impressive science project.* —**im·pres'sive·ly** *adv.* —**im·pres'sive·ness** *n.*

imprimatur (ĭm'prə-mä'tŏŏr) *n.* **1.** Official approval or license to print or publish, especially as granted by a censor or an ecclesiastical authority. **2a.** Official approval; sanction: *Does their idea get your imprimatur?* **b.** A mark of official approval: *a directive bearing the imprimatur of high officials.*

imprint (ĭm-prĭnt') *tr.v.* **imprinted, imprinting, imprints 1.** To make (a mark or pattern) on a surface by pressing: *imprint a name with a rubber stamp.* **2.** To produce a mark on (a surface) by pressure. **3.** To establish firmly, as on the mind or memory: *Memories of childhood are often deeply imprinted on our minds.* ❖ *n.* (ĭm'prĭnt') **1.** A mark or pattern made by pressing something on a surface: *the imprints in the sand left by the feet of bathers.* **2.** A marked influence or effect; an impression: *Spanish culture has left its imprint on the Southwestern states.*

imprison (ĭm-prĭz'ən) *tr.v.* **imprisoned, imprisoning, imprisons** To put in or as if in prison; confine. —**im·pris'on·ment** *n.*

improbable (ĭm-prŏb'ə-bəl) *adj.* Not probable; unlikely: *an improbable tale; an improbable victory.* —**im·prob'a·bil'i·ty** *n.* —**im·prob'a·bly** *adv.*

impromptu (ĭm-prŏmp'tŏŏ) *adj.* Spoken or done with little or no preparation: *The mayor devised an impromptu reply to the unexpected question.* ❖ *adv.* With little or no preparation: *The president commented impromptu on the startling events.* ❖ *n.* Something made or done without rehearsal, as a musical composition or speech.

improper (ĭm-prŏp'ər) *adj.* **1.** Not conforming to accepted standards; incorrect: *an improper diet.* **2.** Not in keeping with circumstances or needs; unsuitable: *A swamp is an improper place to build a house.* **3.** Not conforming to standards of decency; unseemly: *It is improper to interrupt a speaker.* —**im·prop'er·ly** *adv.* —**im·prop'er·ness** *n.*

improper fraction *n.* A fraction in which the numerator is greater than or equal to the denominator. For example, ³⁄₂ and ⅔ are improper fractions.

impropriety (ĭm'prə-prī'ĭ-tē) *n., pl.* **improprieties 1.** The quality or condition of being improper: *the impropriety of playing a radio in the library.* **2.** An improper act or expression.

improv (ĭm'prŏv') *n. Informal* **1.** Improvisation: *practiced improv in acting class.* **2.** An improvised sketch or skit: *a funny improv about golf lessons.*

improve (ĭm-prŏŏv') *v.* **improved, improving, improves** —*tr.* To make better: *Taking lessons really improved my guitar skills.* —*intr.* To become or get better: *The patient improved after receiving treatment.*

improvement (ĭm-prŏŏv'mənt) *n.* **1.** A change or addition that improves something: *A new kitchen was one of our improvements to the house.* **2.** The act or process of improving: *The student's homework shows great improvement.* **3.** A person or thing that is better than another: *This toaster is an improvement over our old one.*

improvident (ĭm-prŏv'ĭ-dənt) *adj.* Not planning or providing for the future; careless of one's resources: *avoided making improvident expenditures.* —**im·prov'i·dence** *n.* —**im·prov'i·dent·ly** *adv.*

improvisation (ĭm-prŏv'ĭ-zā'shən *or* ĭm'prə-vĭ-zā'shən) *n.* **1.** The act or an instance of improvising: *a pianist famous for his brilliant improvisations.* **2.** Something improvised, such as a comedic skit.

improvise (ĭm'prə-vīz') *v.* **improvised, improvising, improvises** —*tr.* **1.** To invent, compose, or perform without preparation: *The actors improvised a set of scenes based on the audience's suggestions.* **2.** To make or provide on the spur of the moment from materials found nearby: *The hikers improvised a bridge out of fallen logs.* —*intr.* **1.** To invent, compose, or perform something on the spot: *The musicians finished by improvising on the main theme.* **2.** To make do with whatever materials are at hand: *If the tent pole breaks we'll have to improvise.* —**im'pro·vis'er** *n.*

imprudent (ĭm-prŏŏd'nt) *adj.* Not prudent; unwise. —**im·pru'dence** *n.* —**im·pru'dent·ly** *adv.*

impudence (ĭm'pyə-dəns) *n.* **1.** The quality of being impudent; insolence. **2.** An impudent act or behavior.

impudent (ĭm'pyə-dənt) *adj.* Rudely or arrogantly disrespectful; insolent: *The impudent student demanded to be assigned another instructor.* —**im'pu·dent·ly** *adv.*

impugn (ĭm-pyŏŏn') *tr.v.* **impugned, impugning, impugns** To challenge as false or questionable; cast doubt on: *How dare you impugn my honesty?*

impulse (ĭm'pŭls') *n.* **1.** A driving force: *Customer complaints provided the impulse for the company to improve its product.* **2.** A strong motivation; a drive or instinct: *Most animals have a natural impulse to care for their young.* **3.** A sudden wish or urge: *We had to control our impulse to giggle during the lecture. I try not to buy things on impulse.* **4.** A surge of electrical power in one direction. **5.** A nerve impulse.

impulsion (ĭm-pŭl'shən) *n.* **1.** The act of impelling or the condition of being impelled. **2.** An impelling force; a thrust. **3.** Motion produced by an impelling force; momentum. **4.** A sudden wish or urge; an impulse.

impulsive (ĭm-pŭl'sĭv) *adj.* **1.** Tending to act on impulse rather than careful thought: *An impulsive shopper usually doesn't find the best bargains.* **2.** Motivated or caused by impulse: *an impulsive act of generosity.* —**im·pul'sive·ly** *adv.* —**im·pul'sive·ness** *n.*

impunity (ĭm-pyŏŏ'nĭ-tē) *n.* Freedom from punishment, harm, or injury: *Did they really expect to break the law with impunity?*

impure (ĭm-pyŏŏr') *adj.* **impurer, impurest 1.** Not pure or clean; contaminated: *People were sickened from drinking the impure water.* **2.** Mixed with other substances often of lower value; adulterated: *impure gold.* **3.** Immoral or sinful: *confessed to impure thoughts.* —**im·pure'ly** *adv.*

impurity (ĭm-pyŏŏr'ĭ-tē) *n., pl.* **impurities 1.** The quality or condition of being impure. **2.** A substance that makes another substance impure: *The treatment plant filters all the impurities out of our water.*

impute (ĭm-pyŏŏt') *tr.v.* **imputed, imputing, imputes** To assign the blame or credit for (something); attribute: *I impute my mistakes to my own carelessness.* —**im'pu·ta'tion** (ĭm'pyŏŏ-tā'shən) *n.*

in¹ (ĭn) *prep.* **1a.** Within the confines or area of; inside: *The bird is in its cage.* **b.** From outside to a point within; into: *couldn't get in the house.* **2.** Within the time of; after: *I will finish in an hour.* **3.** To or at the condition or situation of: *in good health.* **4.** Wearing; clothed by: *in a* *bathing suit.* **5.** Having the activity or function of: *a career in politics.* **6.** With the purpose of; for: *follow in pursuit.* **7.** Made with or through the medium of: *a note written in Spanish.* **8.** With reference to; as to: *10 feet in length.* **9.** Among; out of: *One person in five can play a musical instrument.* ❖ *adv.* **1.** To or toward the inside: *coming in out of the rain.* **2.** To or toward a goal: *The researchers are closing in on a cure.* **3.** So as to score, as by crossing home plate in baseball: *runs driven in.* **4.** Within a place, as of business or residence: *Is the doctor in? The water is cold and the children won't be in long.* **5.** So as to be available or under one's control: *the evidence is now in.* **6.** So as to include: *Did you fold the egg whites in?* **7.** So as to occupy a position of success or favor: *was voted in.* ❖ *adj.* **1.** Located inside; inner. **2.** *Informal* Fashionable; popular; prestigious: *Short haircuts are in.* **3.** Having influence or power: *The in government was made up of a coalition of parties.* **4.** Incoming; inward: *the in bus.* ❖ *n.* **1.** *Informal* A means of access or influence: *the musician has an in with the conductor.* **2.** A person having power or influence: *The ins are always at an advantage over the outs.* ❖ **in for** About to get or have: *We're in for a cold winter.* **in on** Informed about; participating in: *was in on the scheme.* **ins and outs** The details of an activity or process: *had to learn the ins and outs of local politics.* **in that** For the reason that; since: *Their arguments are unconvincing in that their reasons are so weak.*

in² or **in.** An abbreviation of inch.

in–¹ or **il–** or **im–** or **ir–** A prefix that means not: *inaccurate; illegible; immoral; irresponsible.*

WORD BUILDING The basic meaning of the prefix **in–¹** is "not." Thus *inactive* means "not active." *In–¹* is related to and sometimes confused with the prefix *un–¹*, which also means "not." In fact, sometimes *in–¹* is used interchangeably with *un–¹*, as when *incommunicative* is used instead of *uncommunicative*. Before the consonants *l* and *r*, *in–¹* becomes *il–* and *ir–* respectively: *illogical, irregular.* Before the consonants *b, m,* and *p, in–¹* becomes *im–*: *imbalanced, immeasurable, impossible.* For more information, see Note at **in–².**

in–² or **il–** or **im–** or **ir–** A prefix that means: **1.** in, within, or into: *inbound; infield.* **2.** Variant of **en–¹.**

WORD BUILDING Although **in–¹** and **in–²** are both from Latin, they are not related to each other. The basic meaning of *in–²* is "in, within, or into." For example, *inlay* means "to set something in something else." *In–²* is also a form of the prefix *en–*. And in pairs such as *enclose/inclose, enquire/inquire, ensure/insure,* the two prefixes can be used somewhat interchangeably. As with the prefix *in–¹,* before the consonants *l* and *r, in–²* becomes *il–* and *ir–*. And before the consonants *b, m,* and *p, in–²* becomes *im–*.

inability (ĭn′ə-bĭl′ĭ-tē) *n.* Lack of ability or means: *inability to sleep; inability to pay the rent.*

in absentia (ĭn ăb-sĕn′shə) *adv.* While or although not present; in absence: *was tried and convicted in absentia.*

inaccessible (ĭn′ăk-sĕs′ə-bəl) *adj.* Not accessible; unapproachable: *an inaccessible cave high on the cliff.* —**in′-ac·ces′si·bly** *adv.*

inaccuracy (ĭn-ăk′yər-ə-sē) *n., pl.* **inaccuracies 1.** The quality or condition of being inaccurate: *The report was*

criticized for its inaccuracy. **2.** An error; a mistake: *many inaccuracies in their hasty observations.*

inaccurate (ĭn-ăk′yər-ĭt) *adj.* Mistaken or incorrect; not accurate: *an inaccurate answer; an inaccurate description.* —**in·ac′cu·rate·ly** *adv.*

inaction (ĭn-ăk′shən) *n.* Lack or absence of action.

inactivate (ĭn-ăk′tə-vāt′) *tr.v.* **inactivated, inactivating, inactivates** To render inactive. —**in·ac′ti·va′tion** *n.*

inactive (ĭn-ăk′tĭv) *adj.* Not active; not functioning; idle: *an inactive volcano; an inactive life.* —**in·ac′tive·ly** *adv.*

inadequacy (ĭn-ăd′ĭ-kwə-sē) *n., pl.* **inadequacies 1.** The quality or condition of being inadequate: *a feeling of inadequacy in math class.* **2.** A failing or lack: *my inadequacies as a musician.*

inadequate (ĭn-ăd′ĭ-kwĭt) *adj.* Not enough; insufficient: *We lost the gymnastics competition because of inadequate practice.* —**in·ad′e·quate·ly** *adv.*

inadmissible (ĭn′əd-mĭs′ə-bəl) *adj.* Not admissible: *Inadmissible evidence cannot be used in a trial.* —**in′ad·mis′-si·bil′i·ty** *n.*

inadvertent (ĭn′əd-vûr′tnt) *adj.* Not intended; unintentional: *an inadvertent error.* —**in′ad·ver′tence** *n.*

inadvisable (ĭn′əd-vī′zə-bəl) *adj.* Not recommended; unwise: *It is inadvisable to swim out past the reef.* —**in′-ad·vis′a·bil′i·ty** *n.*

inalienable (ĭn-āl′yə-nə-bəl *or* ĭn-ā′lē-ə-nə-bəl) *adj.* Impossible to give up or take away: *Life and liberty are two of the inalienable rights listed in the Declaration of Independence.* —**in·al′ien·a·bly** *adv.*

inane (ĭn-ān′) *adj.* **inaner, inanest** Lacking sense or substance: *an inane comment.* —**in·ane′ly** *adv.*

inanimate (ĭn-ăn′ə-mĭt) *adj.* **1.** Not living: *A stone is an inanimate object.* **2.** Belonging to the class of nouns that stand for nonliving things: *The word "car" is inanimate; the word "dog" is animate.*

inanity (ĭ-năn′ĭ-tē) *n., pl.* **inanities 1.** The quality or condition of being inane. **2.** Something inane, especially a meaningless statement.

inapplicable (ĭn-ăp′lĭ-kə-bəl *or* ĭn′ə-plĭk′ə-bəl) *adj.* Not applicable: *Speed limits are inapplicable to emergency vehicles.* —**in·ap′pli·ca·bil′i·ty** *n.*

inappreciable (ĭn′ə-prē′shə-bəl) *adj.* Too small to be noticed or to make a significant difference; negligible: *inappreciable changes in temperature.* —**in′ap·pre′cia·bly** *adv.*

inappropriate (ĭn′ə-prō′prē-ĭt) *adj.* Not appropriate; unsuitable or improper: *behavior that was inappropriate in a restaurant.* —**in′ap·pro′pri·ate·ly** *adv.* —**in′ap·pro′-pri·ate·ness** *n.*

inapt (ĭn-ăpt′) *adj.* **1.** Inappropriate: *an inapt remark.* **2.** Inept. —**in·apt′ly** *adv.* —**in·apt′ness** *n.*

inaptitude (ĭn-ăp′tĭ-tōōd′) *n.* **1.** Inappropriateness; unfitness. **2.** Lack of talent or skill; ineptitude.

inarticulate (ĭn′är-tĭk′yə-lĭt) *adj.* **1.** Uttered without the use of normal words or syllables: *an inarticulate cry.* **2.** Unable to speak; speechless: *I was inarticulate with astonishment.* **3.** Unable to speak clearly or effectively: *He's too inarticulate to be a successful politician.* **4.** Unexpressed: *inarticulate sorrow.* —**in′ar·tic′u·late·ly** *adv.*

inartistic (ĭn′är-tĭs′tĭk) *adj.* Lacking taste or interest in art. —**in′ar·tis′ti·cal·ly** *adv.*

inasmuch as (ĭn′əz-mŭch′) *conj.* Because of the fact that; since: *I decided to go swimming inasmuch as it was hot and sunny.*

inattention (ĭn′ə-tĕn′shən) *n.* Lack of attention, notice, or regard; heedlessness: *careless mistakes caused by inattention to details.*

inattentive (ĭn′ə-tĕn′tĭv) *adj.* Showing a lack of attention; negligent: *sleepy and inattentive.* —**in′at·ten′tive·ly** *adv.* —**in′at·ten′tive·ness** *n.*

inaudible (ĭn-ô′də-bəl) *adj.* Impossible to hear: *Dogs can hear sounds that are inaudible to most humans.* —**in·au′di·bly** *adv.*

inaugural (ĭn-ô′gyər-əl) *adj.* **1.** Relating to an inauguration: *the president's inaugural address.* **2.** First; initial: *an inaugural flight of a new airliner.* ❖ *n.* **1.** An inaugural speech, especially that of the president of the United States. **2.** An inaugural ceremony or activity.

inaugurate (ĭn-ô′gyə-rāt′) *tr.v.* **inaugurated, inaugurating, inaugurates 1.** To install in office by a formal ceremony: *inaugurate a president.* **2.** To open for use with a ceremony; dedicate: *inaugurate a new office building.* **3.** To begin or start officially: *The governor inaugurated a new policy to combat air pollution.*

inauguration (ĭn-ô′gyə-rā′shən) *n.* **1.** A formal ceremony installing a person in a position or office. **2.** A formal beginning or introduction.

inauspicious (ĭn′ô-spĭsh′əs) *adj.* Not auspicious; unfavorable: *Despite an inauspicious weather forecast, we went on the picnic.* —**in′aus·pi′cious·ly** *adv.*

in between *prep. & adv.* Between: *mortar in between the bricks; layers with a filling in between.*

inboard (ĭn′bôrd′) *adj.* **1.** In the hull or toward the center of a ship: *an inboard motor.* **2.** Close to the fuselage of an aircraft: *the left inboard engine.*

inborn (ĭn′bôrn′) *adj.* Existing naturally or by heredity rather than being learned through experience: *an inborn talent for music; the inborn ability of a dolphin to swim.*

inbound (ĭn′bound′) *adj.* Inward bound; coming in: *an inbound ship; inbound traffic.*

inbox (ĭn′bŏks) *n.* **1.** An electronic folder for incoming emails or text messages. **2.** A container for incoming documents, located in or near one's work area.

inbred (ĭn′brĕd′) *adj.* **1.** Produced by inbreeding: *an inbred dog.* **2.** Firmly fixed, as if by heredity; deep-seated: *a painter with an inbred sense of color.*

inbreed (ĭn′brēd′) *v.* **inbred** (ĭn′brĕd′), **inbreeding, inbreeds** —*tr.* To breed by mating closely related individuals in each succeeding generation: *farmers who began inbreeding corn.* —*intr.* To mate or breed with a closely related individual: *plants that often inbreed.*

inbreeding (ĭn′brē′dĭng) *n.* The mating of closely related individuals in each succeeding generation.

Inc. An abbreviation of incorporated.

Inca (ĭng′kə) *n., pl.* **Inca** or **Incas** A member of the group of Quechuan peoples of highland Peru who established an empire from northern Ecuador to central Chile before being conquered by Spain in the 1500s. —**In′can** *adj.*

incalculable (ĭn-kăl′kyə-lə-bəl) *adj.* **1.** Too great or too large to be calculated or described; enormous: *an incalculable number of ants; caused incalculable damage.* **2.** Impossible to foresee. —**in·cal′cu·la·bil′i·ty** *n.* —**in·cal′cu·la·bly** *adv.*

incandescent (ĭn′kən-dĕs′ənt) *adj.* **1.** Heated to such a high temperature that it gives off light; glowing with heat. **2.** Shining brilliantly; very bright. —**in′can·des′cence** *n.* —**in′can·des′cent·ly** *adv.*

incandescent light *n.* A device that produces light by the glow of a fine wire, or filament, heated by an electric current.

incantation (ĭn′kăn-tā′shən) *n.* **1.** A formula of words or sounds recited or chanted to cast a spell or perform magic. **2.** The act of reciting or chanting such a formula.

incapable (ĭn-kā′pə-bəl) *adj.* Lacking the necessary power or ability; not capable: *Humans are incapable of breathing on their own under water.* —**in·ca′pa·bil′i·ty** *n.*

incapacitate (ĭn′kə-păs′ĭ-tāt′) *tr.v.* **incapacitated, incapacitating, incapacitates** To deprive of power or ability; disable: *A knee injury incapacitated the wrestler.*

incapacity (ĭn′kə-păs′ĭ-tē) *n., pl.* **incapacities 1.** Inadequate strength or ability: *the incapacity of the small air conditioner to cool such a large space.* **2.** A disability or handicap.

incarcerate (ĭn-kär′sə-rāt′) *tr.v.* **incarcerated, incarcerating, incarcerates** To put in jail; imprison. —**in·car′cer·a′tion** *n.*

incarnate (ĭn-kär′nĭt) *adj.* Embodied in flesh, especially in human form; personified: *a villain who seemed evil incarnate.* ❖ *tr.v.* (ĭn-kär′nāt′) **incarnated, incarnating, incarnates** To be a perfect embodiment of; personify: *a successful leader who incarnated the ideals of her time.*

incarnation (ĭn′kär-nā′shən) *n.* **1.** The taking on of bodily form by a supernatural being: *the incarnation of the devil in the form of a serpent.* **2. Incarnation** The Christian doctrine that the Son of God was born to a human mother as Jesus and that Jesus is both true God and true man. **3.** A person or thing thought to be the perfect example of a quality or idea. **4.** A period of time passed in a given bodily form or condition: *hopes for a better life in another incarnation.*

incautious (ĭn-kô′shəs) *adj.* Not cautious; rash: *an incautious decision to go hiking alone.* —**in·cau′tious·ly** *adv.*

incendiary (ĭn-sĕn′dē-ĕr′ē) *adj.* **1.** Causing or designed to cause fires: *an incendiary bomb.* **2.** Arousing anger or conflict; inflammatory: *an incendiary speech that riled up the mob.* ❖ *n., pl.* **incendiaries** A bomb or explosive designed to cause fires.

incense[1] (ĭn-sĕns′) *tr.v.* **incensed, incensing, incenses** To make very angry; enrage: *The factual errors in the article incensed the editor.*

incense[2] (ĭn′sĕns′) *n.* **1.** A plant substance, such as a gum or resin, that is burned to produce a pleasant odor. **2.** The smoke or odor produced by the burning of such a substance. **3.** A pleasant smell: *the incense of flowers.*

WORD HISTORY Incense[1] comes from the Middle English verb *encensen,* which comes from the Latin past participle *incēnsus,* meaning "set on fire." **Incense**[2] comes from the Middle English noun *encens,* which comes from the Latin noun *incēnsum,* both meaning "the smoke or odor made by burning a resinous plant substance." Both *incēnsus* and *incēnsum* are derived from the Latin verb *incendere,* meaning "to set on fire."

incentive (ĭn-sĕn′tĭv) *n.* Something that prompts action or effort; a stimulus: *Seeing his name in print is incentive enough for him to keep writing.*

inception (ĭn-sĕp′shən) *n.* The beginning of something; a start: *The telephone has gone through many changes since its inception in 1876.*

incessant (ĭn-sĕs′ənt) *adj.* Continuing without interruption; constant: *The incessant sound of the traffic made it hard to concentrate.* —**in·ces′sant·ly** *adv.*

incest (ĭn′sĕst′) *n.* Sexual relations between people who are so closely related that they cannot be legally married.

incestuous (ĭn-sĕs′chōō-əs) *adj.* **1.** Relating to or involving incest. **2.** Having committed incest.

inch (ĭnch) *n.* **1.** A unit of length equal to ¹⁄₁₂ of a foot (2.54 centimeters). See table at **measurement. 2.** A very small degree or amount: *The union would not yield an inch in its demands.* ❖ *intr.v.* **inched, inching, inches** To move or proceed very slowly or by small degrees: *We are inching closer to an understanding of the origin of the universe.* ◆ **every inch** In every detail; entirely: *The actor looked every inch a pirate.* **inch by inch** Little by little; very gradually or slowly. **within an inch of** Almost to the point of; very near: *The team was within an inch of gaining the state championship.*

inchoate (ĭn-kō′ĭt *or* ĭn-kō′āt′) *adj.* **1.** Being in a beginning or early stage; incipient. **2.** Imperfectly formed or developed; disordered or incoherent. —**in·cho′ate·ly** *adv.* —**in·cho′ate·ness** *n.*

inchworm (ĭnch′wûrm′) *n.* A caterpillar that moves by drawing the rear of its body forward to form a loop and then stretching the front forward.

incidence (ĭn′sĭ-dəns) *n.* **1.** The rate or frequency with which something occurs: *The incidence of measles has fallen dramatically since vaccines became available.* **2.** The falling or striking of a ray or beam of light or other radiation upon a surface.

incident (ĭn′sĭ-dənt) *n.* **1.** A particular occurrence; an event, especially one of minor importance: *I cannot remember all the incidents that happened in my childhood.* **2.** A disturbance or mishap: *The damaged plane managed to land without incident.* ❖ *adj.* Tending to happen at the same time; accompanying or related to something else: *His ankle injuries are incident to a career in basketball.*

incidental (ĭn′sĭ-dĕn′tl) *adj.* **1.** Occurring or likely to occur as a minor consequence; attendant: *Besides the costs of food and lodging there were many incidental expenses.* **2.** Happening unexpectedly: *an incidental encounter with an old friend.* ❖ *n.* A minor item or expense: *Do not spend our entire budget on mere incidentals.*

incidentally (ĭn′sĭ-dĕn′tl-ē) *adv.* **1.** Apart from the main subject; by the way: *Incidentally, what time is it?* **2.** As a minor matter: *She is a stockbroker and incidentally a runner.*

incinerate (ĭn-sĭn′ə-rāt′) *tr.v.* **incinerated, incinerating, incinerates** To destroy by burning; burn to ashes. —**in·cin′er·a′tion** *n.*

incinerator (ĭn-sĭn′ə-rā′tər) *n.* A furnace or other device for burning rubbish.

incipient (ĭn-sĭp′ē-ənt) *adj.* Beginning to exist or appear: *The gathering clouds were the signs of an incipient storm.* —**in·cip′i·en·cy, in·cip′i·ence** *n.*

incise (ĭn-sīz′) *tr.v.* **incised, incising, incises 1.** To cut into: *incise wood with a chisel.* **2.** To engrave into a surface; carve: *incise a design into leather.*

incision (ĭn-sĭzh′ən) *n.* **1.** The act of incising: *the incision of a design.* **2.** A cut made into something, especially a surgical cut.

incisive (ĭn-sī′sĭv) *adj.* Sharp and clear; penetrating: *The incisive analysis was clear and to the point.* —**in·ci′sive·ly** *adv.* —**in·ci′sive·ness** *n.*

incisor (ĭn-sī′zər) *n.* A tooth having a sharp edge adapted for cutting, located in mammals in the front of the mouth between the canine teeth.

incite (ĭn-sīt′) *tr.v.* **incited, inciting, incites** To provoke; stir up; urge on: *The announcement of a cut in pay incited the workers to strike.* —**in·cite′ment** *n.*

incl. An abbreviation of: **1.** including. **2.** inclusive.

inclement (ĭn-klĕm′ənt) *adj.* **1.** Stormy; rough: *inclement weather.* **2.** Unmerciful; harsh: *the severe penalties of inclement justice.* —**in·clem′en·cy** *n.*

inclination (ĭn′klə-nā′shən) *n.* **1.** A natural tendency to be or act in a certain way: *Many people have an inclination to sleep late on weekends.* **2.** The act of inclining or the state of being inclined: *The inclination of the child's head suggested that she was tired.* **3.** A slant or slope: *the steep inclination of the roof.*

incline (ĭn-klīn′) *v.* **inclined, inclining, inclines** —*tr.* **1.** To cause (someone) to have a certain tendency or preference; dispose: *This book might incline you to change your mind on the issue. I am inclined to disagree with you.* **2.** To cause to lean, slant, or slope: *We inclined the boards against the side of the barn.* **3.** To cause to bend or bow: *The conductor inclined his head as a signal for us to get ready to play.* —*intr.* **1.** To slant or slope: *a road that inclines steeply.* **2.** To have a preference; tend: *I incline to a different view of the matter.* ❖ *n.* (ĭn′klīn′) A surface that slants; a slope: *The car skidded down the icy incline.*

inclined plane *n.* A plane surface, such as a ramp, set at an acute angle to a horizontal surface. It is a simple machine because it requires less force to slide or roll a load up the plane than to raise the load vertically.

include (ĭn-klōōd′) *tr.v.* **included, including, includes 1.** To have as a part or member; contain: *The museum's collection includes some masterpieces of modern art.* **2.** To put into a group, class, or total: *I included your whole family in my invitation.*

inclusion (ĭn-klōō′zhən) *n.* **1.** The act of including or the condition of being included: *the inclusion of a story in an anthology.* **2.** Something that is included: *a surprising inclusion in the list of Oscar nominees.*

inclusive (ĭn-klōō′sĭv) *adj.* **1.** Taking everything into account; comprehensive: *We assembled an inclusive list of the gear we needed for the trip.* **2.** Including the specified endpoints as well as what is between them. For example, "ages 10 to 14, inclusive" refers to ages 10, 11, 12, 13, and 14. —**in·clu′sive·ly** *adv.* —**in·clu′sive·ness** *n.*

incognito (ĭn′kŏg-nē′tō *or* ĭn-kŏg′nĭ-tō′) *adv. & adj.* With one's identity hidden or disguised: *The movie star stayed at the hotel incognito.*

incoherent (ĭn′kō-hîr′ənt) *adj.* **1.** Lacking order or logical connection; not coherent: *an incoherent jumble of confused thoughts.* **2.** Unable to think or express one's thoughts in a clear or orderly manner: *The delirious patient was incoherent and confused.* —**in′co·her′ence** *n.* —**in′co·her′ent·ly** *adv.*

incombustible (ĭn′kəm-bŭs′tə-bəl) *adj.* Incapable of burning. ❖ *n.* An incombustible material.

income (ĭn′kŭm′) *n.* The amount of money received for labor or services, from the sale of property or goods, or from financial investments: *One's monthly income is all the money one receives in a month.*

income tax *n.* A tax on the income of a person or business.

incoming (ĭn′kŭm′ĭng) *adj.* **1.** Coming in or about to come in: *incoming mail.* **2.** About to take an office or position: *the incoming president.*

incommensurate (ĭn′kə-mĕn′sər-ĭt *or* ĭn′kə-mĕn′-shər-ĭt) *adj.* **1.** Not corresponding in size or degree; inadequate: *The salary for the job is incommensurate with the responsibilities.* **2.** Impossible to measure. —**in′com·men′su·rate·ly** *adv.*

incommunicable (ĭn′kə-myōō′nĭ-kə-bəl) *adj.* Impossible

to communicate: *He found his feelings were so complex as to be incommunicable.*

incommunicado (ĭn′kə-myōō′nĭ-kä′dō) *adv. & adj.* Without the means or right of communicating with others: *The judge ordered the jurors to remain incommunicado until the trial was over.*

incomparable (ĭn-kŏm′pər-ə-bəl) *adj.* **1.** Above all comparison; unsurpassed: *the incomparable value of an education.* **2.** Impossible to compare: *two theories of the origin of the universe that are so different as to be incomparable with each other.* —**in·com′pa·ra·bly** *adv.*

incompatible (ĭn′kəm-păt′ə-bəl) *adj.* **1.** Not capable of existing in agreement or harmony with something else: *Speeding is incompatible with safe driving.* **2.** Not capable of living or working together happily or smoothly; antagonistic: *incompatible roommates.* —**in′com·pat′i·bil′i·ty** *n.* —**in′com·pat′i·bly** *adv.*

incompetent (ĭn-kŏm′pĭ-tənt) *adj.* **1.** Not having adequate abilities or qualifications; incapable: *an apprentice mechanic who was incompetent to do complicated repairs.* **2.** Not qualified under the law: *The judge ruled that the defendant was incompetent to stand trial.* ❖ *n.* An incompetent person. —**in·com′pe·tence** *n.* —**in·com′pe·tent·ly** *adv.*

incomplete (ĭn′kəm-plēt′) *adj.* **1.** Not complete; unfinished: *The composer's last symphony is incomplete.* **2.** In football, not caught in bounds or intercepted: *an incomplete pass.* —**in′com·plete′ly** *adv.*

incomprehensible (ĭn′kŏm-prĭ-hĕn′sə-bəl *or* ĭn-kŏm′-prĭ-hĕn′sə-bəl) *adj.* Difficult or impossible to understand: *an incomprehensible sentence.* —**in′com·pre·hen′-si·bil′i·ty** *n.* —**in′com·pre·hen′si·bly** *adv.*

inconceivable (ĭn′kən-sē′və-bəl) *adj.* Difficult or impossible to understand or imagine: *It was inconceivable for the expedition to turn back when their goal was so close.* —**in′con·ceiv′a·bly** *adv.*

inconclusive (ĭn′kən-klōō′sĭv) *adj.* Not conclusive: *The inconclusive election returns left neither candidate sure of victory.* —**in′con·clu′sive·ly** *adv.*

incongruity (ĭn′kŏn-grōō′ĭ-tē) *n., pl.* **incongruities 1.** The quality or condition of being incongruous. **2.** Something that is incongruous.

incongruous (ĭn-kŏng′grōō-əs) *adj.* **1.** Lacking in harmony; incompatible or inconsistent: *The senator's vote was incongruous with her stated beliefs.* **2.** Not in keeping with what is correct, proper, or logical; inappropriate: *incongruous behavior.* —**in·con′gru·ous·ly** *adv.*

inconsequential (ĭn-kŏn′sĭ-kwĕn′shəl) *adj.* Lacking importance; trivial: *an inconsequential and boring debate.* —**in·con′se·quen′tial·ly** *adv.*

inconsiderable (ĭn′kən-sĭd′ər-ə-bəl) *adj.* Too small or unimportant to be worth attention or consideration; trivial. —**in′con·sid′er·a·bly** *adv.*

inconsiderate (ĭn′kən-sĭd′ər-ĭt) *adj.* Not considerate; thoughtless: *It is inconsiderate to make noise while we're trying to read.* —**in′con·sid′er·ate·ly** *adv.* —**in′con·sid′-er·ate·ness** *n.*

inconsistency (ĭn′kən-sĭs′tən-sē) *n., pl.* **inconsistencies 1.** The quality or condition of being inconsistent. **2.** Something that is inconsistent: *inconsistencies in spelling.*

inconsistent (ĭn′kən-sĭs′tənt) *adj.* **1.** Not in agreement or harmony: *The witness's testimony was inconsistent with the facts.* **2.** Not steady or predictable; erratic: *a baseball team whose biggest problem was inconsistent pitching.* **3.** Lacking in logical relation; contradictory: *inconsistent principles.* —**in′con·sis′tent·ly** *adv.*

inconsolable (ĭn′kən-sō′lə-bəl) *adj.* Difficult or impossible to console: *The children were inconsolable at the loss of their pet.* —**in′con·sol′a·bly** *adv.*

inconspicuous (ĭn′kən-spĭk′yōō-əs) *adj.* Not readily noticeable; not obvious: *Fortunately the stain on my shirt was in an inconspicuous spot.* —**in′con·spic′u·ous·ly** *adv.* —**in′con·spic′u·ous·ness** *n.*

inconstant (ĭn-kŏn′stənt) *adj.* Not constant or steady; changeable or fickle: *inconstant loyalties.* —**in·con′-stan·cy** *n.* —**in·con′stant·ly** *adv.*

incontinent (ĭn-kŏn′tə-nənt) *adj.* **1.** Not restrained, as in behavior: *incontinent rage.* **2.** Unable to keep normal control of urination or defecation. —**in·con′ti·nence** *n.*

incontrovertible (ĭn-kŏn′trə-vûr′tə-bəl *or* ĭn′kŏn-trə-vûr′tə-bəl) *adj.* Impossible to dispute; unquestionable: *incontrovertible evidence pointing to the suspect's guilt.* —**in·con′tro·vert′i·bly** *adv.*

inconvenience (ĭn′kən-vēn′yəns) *n.* **1.** The quality or condition of being inconvenient. **2.** Something that causes difficulty, trouble, or discomfort: *Lack of central heating is an inconvenience.* ❖ *tr.v.* **inconvenienced, inconveniencing, inconveniences** To cause inconvenience to; trouble; bother: *Road construction inconvenienced many drivers.*

inconvenient (ĭn′kən-vēn′yənt) *adj.* Not convenient; causing difficulty: *It is inconvenient to have no cafeteria in this building.* —**in′con·ven′ient·ly** *adv.*

incorporate (ĭn-kôr′pə-rāt′) *tr.v.* **incorporated, incorporating, incorporates 1.** To include as a part in a whole; combine with something else: *a new car that incorporates features of earlier models.* **2.** To form into a legal corporation: *incorporate a business.*

incorporated (ĭn-kôr′pə-rā′tĭd) *adj.* Organized and maintained as a legal corporation: *an incorporated business.*

incorporeal (ĭn′kôr-pôr′ē-əl) *adj.* Lacking material form or substance: *Spirits are incorporeal beings.* —**in′cor·po′-re·al·ly** *adv.*

incorrect (ĭn′kə-rĕkt′) *adj.* **1.** Not correct; faulty; wrong: *The test had many incorrect answers.* **2.** Inappropriate or improper: *incorrect dress for the occasion.* —**in′cor·rect′-ly** *adv.* —**in′cor·rect′ness** *n.*

incorrigible (ĭn-kôr′ĭ-jə-bəl) *adj.* Incapable of being corrected or reformed: *an incorrigible habit.* ❖ *n.* A person who cannot be reformed. —**in·cor′ri·gi·bil′i·ty** *n.* —**in·cor′ri·gi·bly** *adv.*

incorruptible (ĭn′kə-rŭp′tə-bəl) *adj.* **1.** Incapable of being morally corrupted: *The honest judge is incorruptible.* **2.** Not subject to decay or rot: *Cedar is a nearly incorruptible wood.* —**in′cor·rupt′i·bil′i·ty** *n.* —**in′cor·rupt′i·bly** *adv.*

increase (ĭn-krēs′) *tr. & intr.v.* **increased, increasing, increases** To make or become greater or larger in size, number, or power: *Machines increase the rate at which goods are manufactured. The world's population increased rapidly over the last decade.* ❖ *n.* (ĭn′krēs′) **1.** The act of increasing; growth: *a steady increase in sales over the last two years.* **2.** The amount or rate by which something is increased: *a ten percent increase in tax rates.* ◆ **on the increase** Becoming greater or more frequent; increasing. —**in·creas′ing·ly** *adv.*

◆ **SYNONYMS** increase, enlarge, expand, extend *v.*

incredible (ĭn-krĕd′ə-bəl) *adj.* **1.** Astonishing; unbelievable: *The new plane flies at an incredible speed.* **2.** Hard to believe; implausible: *an incredible alibi.* —**in·cred′i·bly** *adv.*

incredulity (ĭn′krĭ-dōō′lĭ-tē) *n.* The state or quality of disbelief; doubt.

incredulous (ĭn-krĕj′ə-ləs) *adj.* **1.** Disbelieving or doubtful; skeptical: *We were incredulous of the stories about flying saucers.* **2.** Expressive of disbelief or astonishment: *There were incredulous gasps at the gymnast's performance.* —**in·cred′u·lous·ly** *adv.*

increment (ĭn′krə-mənt) *n.* **1.** An increase in number, size, amount, or extent: *The increment in sales made the company profitable.* **2.** An added amount, especially one of a series of regular additions: *The crowd grew by increments throughout the day.*

incriminate (ĭn-krĭm′ə-nāt′) *tr.v.* **incriminated, incriminating, incriminates** **1.** To accuse of a crime or other wrongful act: *The indictment incriminates six conspirators.* **2.** To cause to appear guilty of a crime or fault; implicate: *The new evidence incriminated other suspects in the robbery.* —**in·crim′i·na′tion** *n.* —**in·crim′i·na′tor** *n.*

incubate (ĭn′kyə-bāt′) *v.* **incubated, incubating, incubates** —*tr.* **1.** To sit on (eggs) to provide heat until hatching. **2.** To keep (eggs, organisms, or other living tissue) in conditions favorable for growth and development. **3.** To be infected with (a virus or bacterium) before showing signs or symptoms of disease: *a child who is incubating a cold.* **4.** To form or consider slowly: *She is incubating her outline for a book.* —*intr.* **1.** To sit on eggs; brood. **2.** To go through the process of incubation: *The bacterial cultures have been incubating for two days.*

incubation (ĭn′kyə-bā′shən) *n.* **1.** The act of incubating or the condition of being incubated. **2.** The development of a disease from the time of infection until the appearance of symptoms. **3.** The maintenance of an infant, especially a premature infant, in an environment of controlled temperature, humidity, and oxygen concentration.

incubator (ĭn′kyə-bā′tər) *n.* **1.** An apparatus in which conditions such as temperature and humidity can be controlled and maintained, used for hatching eggs or for growing cultures of microorganisms. **2.** A similar apparatus supplied with oxygen for the special care of very small or premature babies.

incudes (ĭng-kyōō′dēz) *n.* Plural of **incus.**

inculcate (ĭn-kŭl′kāt′ *or* ĭn′kŭl-kāt′) *tr.v.* **inculcated, inculcating, inculcates** To fix in the mind by frequent repetition; impress: *Our instructor inculcated the importance of being careful when working with chemicals.* —**in′cul·ca′tion** *n.*

incumbency (ĭn-kŭm′bən-sē) *n., pl.* **incumbencies** **1.** The quality or condition of being incumbent. **2.** The term of an incumbent.

incumbent (ĭn-kŭm′bənt) *adj.* **1.** Currently holding a specified office: *the incumbent mayor.* **2.** Imposed as an obligation or duty; required: *It is incumbent on all citizens to pay their taxes.* ❖ *n.* A person currently holding an office.

incur (ĭn-kûr′) *tr.v.* **incurred, incurring, incurs** **1.** To acquire or come into (something); sustain: *The investor incurred big losses during the stock market crash.* **2.** To become subject to as a result of one's actions; bring upon oneself: *She incurred her neighbors' anger by playing her music so loud.*

incurable (ĭn-kyŏŏr′ə-bəl) *adj.* Impossible to cure: *an incurable disease.* —**in·cur′a·bly** *adv.*

incursion (ĭn-kûr′zhən) *n.* A raid or invasion into a foreign territory: *The Vikings made many incursions along the European coast.* —SEE NOTE AT **cursive.**

incus (ĭng′kəs) *n., pl.* **incudes** (ĭng-kyōō′dēz) One of the three small bones in the middle ear; the anvil.

indebted (ĭn-dĕt′ĭd) *adj.* Owing another money or gratitude for a loan, gift, or useful service; beholden: *We are indebted to you for your hospitality.*

indebtedness (ĭn-dĕt′ĭd-nĭs) *n.* **1.** The state of being indebted. **2.** Something that is owed to another.

indecency (ĭn-dē′sən-sē) *n., pl.* **indecencies** **1.** The quality or condition of being indecent. **2.** Something that is indecent.

indecent (ĭn-dē′sənt) *adj.* **1.** Not in good taste; improper; unsuitable: *Our dinner guests left with indecent haste shortly after the meal.* **2.** Morally offensive; immodest or obscene: *indecent clothing; an indecent joke.* —**in·de′cent·ly** *adv.*

indecipherable (ĭn′dĭ-sī′fər-ə-bəl) *adj.* Impossible to decipher: *an indecipherable security code.*

indecision (ĭn′dĭ-sĭzh′ən) *n.* The condition of being unable to make up one's mind.

indecisive (ĭn′dĭ-sī′sĭv) *adj.* **1.** Unable to make up one's mind; wavering; vacillating: *The indecisive executive constantly put off important purchases.* **2.** Having no clear result; inconclusive: *an indecisive election in which no candidate received a clear majority.* —**in′de·ci′sive·ly** *adv.* —**in′de·ci′sive·ness** *n.*

indecorous (ĭn-dĕk′ər-əs) *adj.* Not in good taste; lacking propriety: *loud and indecorous behavior.* —**in·dec′o·rous·ly** *adv.*

indeed (ĭn-dēd′) *adv.* **1.** Without a doubt; certainly: *They were indeed happy.* **2.** In fact; in reality: *I said the car would break down, and indeed it did.* ❖ *interj.* An expression used to show surprise, irony, or disbelief.

indef. An abbreviation of indefinite.

indefatigable (ĭn′dĭ-făt′ĭ-gə-bəl) *adj.* Never giving up or becoming tired; tireless: *indefatigable rescuers who worked through the night searching the wreckage.* —**in′de·fat′i·ga·bly** *adv.*

indefensible (ĭn′dĭ-fĕn′sə-bəl) *adj.* **1.** Vulnerable to attack: *an indefensible town in the middle of a valley.* **2.** Incapable of being justified or excused; inexcusable: *rude and indefensible behavior.* —**in′de·fen′si·bly** *adv.*

indefinable (ĭn′dĭ-fī′nə-bəl) *adj.* Impossible to define, describe, or analyze: *a vague and indefinable feeling of suspicion.* —**in′de·fin′a·bly** *adv.*

indefinite (ĭn-dĕf′ə-nĭt) *adj.* **1.** Not fixed or limited: *an indefinite period of time.* **2.** Not clear or exact; vague: *indefinite outlines of people standing in the shadows.* **3.** Not decided; uncertain: *indefinite plans.* —**in·def′i·nite·ly** *adv.* —**in·def′i·nite·ness** *n.*

indefinite article *n.* An article, in English either *a* or *an,* that does not fix the identity of the noun modified.

indefinite pronoun *n.* A pronoun, such as *any* or *some,* that does not specify the identity of its object.

indelible (ĭn-dĕl′ə-bəl) *adj.* **1.** Impossible to remove, erase, or wash away; permanent: *an indelible stain.* **2.** Making an indelible mark: *an indelible pen.* **3.** Impossible to forget; memorable: *an indelible memory.* —**in·del′i·bil′i·ty, in·del′i·ble·ness** *n.* —**in·del′i·bly** *adv.*

indelicacy (ĭn-dĕl′ĭ-kə-sē) *n., pl.* **indelicacies** **1.** The quality or condition of being indelicate. **2.** Something that is indelicate.

indelicate (ĭn-dĕl′ĭ-kĭt) *adj.* Lacking good taste; crude or improper: *indelicate language.* —**in·del′i·cate·ly** *adv.*

indemnify (ĭn-dĕm′nə-fī′) *tr.v.* **indemnified, indemnifying, indemnifies** **1.** To protect against possible damage, injury, or loss; insure: *Motorists are indemnified by automobile insurance.* **2.** To make compensation to for damage, injury, or loss suffered: *The shipper indemnified the grower for the lost truckload of fruit.* —**in·dem′ni·fi·ca′-tion** (ĭn-dĕm′nə-fĭ-kā′shən) *n.*

indemnity (ĭn-dĕm′nĭ-tē) *n., pl.* **indemnities 1.** Insurance or other security against possible damage, loss, or injury. **2.** Payment or compensation for damage, loss, or injury.

indent¹ (ĭn-dĕnt′) *tr.v.* **indented, indenting, indents 1.** To set (the first line of a paragraph) in from the margin. **2.** To make notches in the edge of; make jagged: *He indented the board to make a secure joint.* ❖ *n.* (ĭn-dĕnt′ *or* ĭn′-dĕnt′) An indentation.

indent² (ĭn-dĕnt′) *tr.v.* **indented, indenting, indents** To make a dent, recess, or other impression in: *The coast is indented with coves.* ❖ *n.* (ĭn-dĕnt′ *or* ĭn′dĕnt′) An indentation.

WORD HISTORY Indent¹ comes from Middle English *endenten,* which comes from Medieval Latin *indentāre,* both meaning "to notch." The root of *indentāre* is Latin *dēns,* meaning "tooth." **Indent²** comes from Middle English *endenten* (meaning "to decorate, as with precious stones"), which comes from Middle English *denten,* meaning "to make a dent in."

---

indentation (ĭn′dĕn-tā′shən) *n.* **1.** The act of indenting or the condition of being indented. **2.** The blank space between a margin and the beginning of an indented line. **3.** A recess or notch, as in a border or coastline.

indenture (ĭn-dĕn′chər) *n.* A deed or contract between two or more parties, especially one binding a servant or apprentice to another person for a specified period of time. ❖ *tr.v.* **indentured, indenturing, indentures** To bind by an indenture: *Many European immigrants in the 1600s were indentured to American landowners.*

independence (ĭn′dĭ-pĕn′dəns) *n.* The quality or condition of being independent: *Many countries of colonial Africa won their independence from European nations in the 1950s and 1960s.*

Independence Day *n.* A national holiday celebrated on July 4 to commemorate the adoption of the Declaration of Independence in 1776.

independent (ĭn′dĭ-pĕn′dənt) *adj.* **1.** Not governed by a foreign country; ruling or governing itself: *The United States became an independent nation after the Revolution.* **2.** Not controlled or guided by others; self-reliant: *an independent mind.* **3.** Not dependent on or connected with a larger or controlling group; separate: *an independent drugstore.* **4.** Not committed to any one political party: *an independent voter.* **5.** Earning one's own living; self-supporting: *With this job I am independent of my parents.* **6.** Providing enough income to allow one to live without working: *a person of independent means.* ❖ *n.* One who is independent, especially a voter, candidate, or officeholder who is not committed to any one political party: *Independents turned out in large numbers during the election.* —**in′de·pen′dent·ly** *adv.*

independent clause *n.* A clause in a sentence that can stand alone as a complete sentence. For example, in the sentence *When the sun came out, we went for a walk,* the clause *we went for a walk* is an independent clause.

in-depth (ĭn′dĕpth′) *adj.* Detailed; thorough: *an in-depth interview of the candidate.*

indescribable (ĭn′dĭ-skrī′bə-bəl) *adj.* Impossible to describe adequately: *indescribable delight.* —**in′de·scrib′-a·bly** *adv.*

indestructible (ĭn′dĭ-strŭk′tə-bəl) *adj.* Impossible to destroy: *a pet toy made of indestructible plastic.* —**in′-de·struc′ti·bly** *adv.*

indeterminate (ĭn′dĭ-tûr′mə-nĭt) *adj.* Not precisely determined; not defined; vague: *a person of indeterminate age.* —**in′de·ter′mi·nate·ly** *adv.*

index (ĭn′dĕks′) *n., pl.* **indexes** *or* **indices** (ĭn′dĭ-sēz′) **1.** A list of names or subjects arranged in alphabetical order and presented at the end of a printed work, along with the page numbers on which each item is mentioned. **2.** Something that reveals or indicates; a sign: *The baby's face is an index to its feelings.* **3.** An indicator or pointer, as the arrow on a dial or other device. ❖ *tr.v.* **indexed, indexing, indexes 1.** To furnish with an index: *index a history textbook.* **2.** To enter (an item) in an index.

index finger *n.* The finger next to the thumb; the forefinger.

index of refraction *n.* The ratio of the speed of light in a vacuum to the speed of light in another medium, such as water or oil.

India ink *n.* Black ink or paint made from lampblack.

Indian (ĭn′dē-ən) *adj.* **1.** Relating to India or the East Indies or to their peoples, languages, or cultures. **2.** Relating to any of the American Indian peoples. ❖ *n.* **1.** A native or inhabitant of India or the East Indies. **2a.** An American Indian. **b.** Any of the languages of the American Indians. —SEE NOTE AT **Native American.**

Indian corn *n.* **1.** The corn plant that is native to the Americas, or its ears or kernels; maize. **2.** Dried ears of corn having colorful kernels, often hung in a cluster for decoration.

Indian paintbrush *n.* **1.** Any of various plants having spikes bearing small greenish flowers surrounded by bright red, yellow, or pink bracts that resemble petals. **2.** A hawkweed with red-orange flowers.

Indian pipe *n.* A waxy whitish woodland plant having a single nodding flower. Indian pipes are parasitic on fungi.

Indian summer *n.* A period of mild weather occurring in late autumn.

Indic (ĭn′dĭk) *adj.* **1.** Relating to India or its people or cultures. **2.** Relating to a branch of the Indo-European language family that includes Sanskrit and the languages descended from it, spoken on the Indian subcontinent and Sri Lanka. ❖ *n.* The Indic branch of Indo-European.

indicate (ĭn′dĭ-kāt′) *tr.v.* **indicated, indicating, indicates 1.** To show or point out: *indicate a route on a map.* **2.** To serve as a sign or symptom of: *Dark clouds indicate rain. Fever indicates illness.* **3.** To state or express: *Their faces indicated they did not like spinach at all.*

indication (ĭn′dĭ-kā′shən) *n.* **1.** The act of indicating: *His indication of refusal came in the form of a frown.* **2.** Something that indicates; a sign: *flowers, birds, and other indications of spring.*

indicative (ĭn-dĭk′ə-tĭv) *adj.* **1.** Serving to indicate: *A cough is often indicative of a cold.* **2.** Relating to the mood of a verb used in ordinary statements of fact or in factual questions. For example, in *We went* and *Who says so?,* the words *went* and *says* are in the indicative mood. ❖ *n.* **1.** The indicative mood. **2.** A verb form in this mood.

indicator (ĭn′dĭ-kā′tər) *n.* **1.** A person or thing that indicates, especially: **a.** A meter or gauge that tells about the operation of an engine or other machine or system. **b.**

The needle or dial of such a meter or gauge. **2.** A chemical compound that changes color under certain conditions, used in chemical tests. Litmus is an indicator that shows the amount of acid present in a solution by changes in color.

indicator species *n.* A species whose abundance in a given area is believed to be a sign of certain environmental or ecological conditions, such as the level of pollution.

indices (ĭn′dĭ-sēz′) *n.* A plural of **index.**

indict (ĭn-dīt′) *tr.v.* **indicted, indicting, indicts 1.** To accuse of wrongdoing or misconduct: *a protest song that indicts the country's leaders as warmongers.* **2.** To charge with a crime by means of an indictment: *The grand jury indicted the suspect on charges of assault.* —**in·dict′er, in·dic′tor** *n.*

indictment (ĭn-dīt′mənt) *n.* **1.** The act of indicting or the condition of being indicted: *under indictment for fraud.* **2.** A written statement issued by a grand jury that charges a person with the commission of a crime.

indie (ĭn′dē) *Informal adj.* **1.** Relating to a person or a company that is not affiliated with a larger, more commercial organization: *an indie film company.* **2.** Relating to an artistic work produced by such a person or company: *a radio station that plays indie rock.*

indifference (ĭn-dĭf′ər-əns *or* ĭn-dĭf′rəns) *n.* **1.** Lack of concern or interest: *The regime's indifference to the worsening economic conditions brought about its downfall.* **2.** Lack of importance; insignificance: *Their opinion is a matter of indifference to me.*

indifferent (ĭn-dĭf′ər-ənt *or* ĭn-dĭf′rənt) *adj.* **1.** Having or showing no interest; not caring one way or the other: *indifferent to the troubles of others.* **2.** Being neither good nor bad; mediocre: *The band gave an indifferent performance.* **3.** Showing no preference; impartial: *an indifferent judge.* —**in·dif′fer·ent·ly** *adv.*

indigence (ĭn′dĭ-jəns) *n.* The condition of being poor; poverty.

indigenous (ĭn-dĭj′ə-nəs) *adj.* **1.** Originally living or growing in a particular place or region; native: *The bald eagle is indigenous to North America.* **2.** Originally inhabiting a particular place or region: *the indigenous peoples of Taiwan.*

indigent (ĭn′dĭ-jənt) *adj.* Poor; needy.

indigestible (ĭn′dĭ-jĕs′tə-bəl *or* ĭn′dĭ-jĕs′tə-bəl) *adj.* Difficult or impossible to digest: *indigestible fatty foods.*

indigestion (ĭn′dĭ-jĕs′chən *or* ĭn′dĭ-jĕs′chən) *n.* Discomfort or illness resulting from difficulty in digesting food: *I got indigestion from eating too many hot dogs.*

indignant (ĭn-dĭg′nənt) *adj.* Feeling or expressing indignation: *I was indignant over their thoughtless remarks.* —**in·dig′nant·ly** *adv.*

indignation (ĭn′dĭg-nā′shən) *n.* Anger aroused by something perceived as unfair or wrongful: *The voters expressed their indignation over the government's continuing neglect of serious problems.* See Synonyms at **anger.**

indignity (ĭn-dĭg′nĭ-tē) *n., pl.* **indignities** Something that offends a person's pride and sense of dignity: *I felt it was an indignity to be asked to do such menial tasks.*

indigo (ĭn′dĭ-gō′) *n., pl.* **indigos** *or* **indigoes 1a.** Any of various plants that yield a dark violet-blue dye. **b.** A dark violet-blue dye obtained from these plants or an artificial dye of the same color. **2.** A dark violet blue.

indirect (ĭn′dĭ-rĕkt′ *or* ĭn′dī-rĕkt′) *adj.* **1.** Not following a direct course; roundabout: *an indirect route.* **2.** Not

straight to the point, as in talking: *an indirect answer.* **3.** Not directly connected or planned for; secondary: *The boom in bicycle sales was an indirect effect of the new gasoline tax.* **4.** In soccer, relating to a free kick that counts as a goal only if the ball has been touched by a second player. —**in′di·rect′ly** *adv.* —**in′di·rect′ness** *n.*

indirect object *n.* A word or phrase in a sentence referring to a person or thing that is indirectly affected by the action of a transitive verb. For example, in the sentences *Sing me a song* and *We fed the turtle lettuce,* the words *me* and *turtle* are both indirect objects.

indiscreet (ĭn′dĭ-skrēt′) *adj.* Lacking discretion; unwise or tactless: *an indiscreet remark.* —**in′dis·creet′ly** *adv.*

indiscretion (ĭn′dĭ-skrĕsh′ən) *n.* **1.** Lack of discretion. **2.** An indiscreet act or remark.

indiscriminate (ĭn′dĭ-skrĭm′ə-nĭt) *adj.* **1.** Careless in making choices or distinctions: *an indiscriminate shopper.* **2.** Random; haphazard: *indiscriminate violence; an indiscriminate assortment of used books for sale.* —**in′dis·crim′i·nate·ly** *adv.*

indispensable (ĭn′dĭ-spĕn′sə-bəl) *adj.* Absolutely necessary; essential: *A good education is indispensable to becoming a doctor.* —**in′dis·pens′a·bly** *adv.*

indisposed (ĭn′dĭ-spōzd′) *adj.* **1.** Mildly ill: *He was indisposed with a slight cold.* **2.** Unwilling; reluctant: *They were indisposed to help at all.*

indisposition (ĭn-dĭs′pə-zĭsh′ən) *n.* **1.** Unwillingness. **2.** A minor ailment.

indisputable (ĭn′dĭ-spyoo′tə-bəl) *adj.* Beyond doubt; unquestionable: *an indisputable fact.* —**in′dis·put′a·bly** *adv.*

indissoluble (ĭn′dĭ-sŏl′yə-bəl) *adj.* **1.** Not capable of being broken or undone; permanent: *an indissoluble bond between friends.* **2.** Impossible to dissolve or disintegrate. —**in′dis·sol′u·bly** *adv.*

indistinct (ĭn′dĭ-stĭngkt′) *adj.* Not clearly heard, seen, or understood: *an indistinct sound heard from far away; saw an indistinct figure in the distance.* —**in′dis·tinct′ly** *adv.* —**in′dis·tinct′ness** *n.*

indistinguishable (ĭn′dĭ-stĭng′gwĭ-shə-bəl) *adj.* Lacking clear differences; impossible to tell apart: *a shopping mall indistinguishable from all the others.*

indium (ĭn′dē-əm) *n. Symbol* **In** A soft, silvery metallic element found mainly in ores of zinc and lead. It is used in making semiconductors and mirrors. Atomic number 49. See **Periodic Table.**

individual (ĭn′də-vĭj′oo-əl) *adj.* **1.** Relating to a single organism, especially a human: *Each individual child will get a prize.* **2.** By or for one person: *an individual portion of food.* **3.** Existing as a separate unit; distinct: *individual drops of rain.* **4.** Having a special quality; unique; distinct: *Each variety of apple has its individual flavor.* ❖ *n.* A single organism, especially a human: *There were three individuals in the car. Among the redwoods in the grove, two individuals stood out for their great height.*

individualism (ĭn′də-vĭj′oo-ə-lĭz′əm) *n.* **1.** Belief in following one's own interests without concern for the opinions of others or the usual way of doing things. **2.** A way of living based on this belief; personal independence. **3.** The doctrine that the interests of an individual are more important than the interests of a group or state.

individualist (ĭn′də-vĭj′oo-ə-lĭst) *n.* **1.** A person who is independent in thought and action. **2.** A person who supports or believes in individualism. —**in′di·vid′u·al·is′tic** *adj.* —**in′di·vid′u·al·is′ti·cal·ly** *adv.*

individuality (ĭn′də-vĭj′o͞o-ăl′ĭ-tē) *n., pl.* **individualities 1.** The qualities that make a person or thing different from others; identity: *He expresses his individuality in the way he dresses.* **2.** The condition of being individual; distinctness: *At the rock concert, we felt like we had lost our individuality and become part of a larger experience.*

individualize (ĭn′də-vĭj′o͞o-ə-līz′) *tr.v.* **individualized, individualizing, individualizes 1.** To give individuality to: *The artist individualized his painting when he developed a unique style.* **2.** To change to fit or satisfy an individual: *individualize exercises according to each person's need.*

individually (ĭn′də-vĭj′o͞o-ə-lē) *adv.* As individuals; singly; separately: *The dean knows all the students individually.*

individual retirement account *n.* A personal investment account whose dividends and interest are not taxable until the person making the investment retires.

indivisible (ĭn′də-vĭz′ə-bəl) *adj.* **1.** Incapable of being divided or separated: *states bound together in an indivisible union; childhood friends who seemed indivisible.* **2.** Incapable of being divided without leaving a remainder; for example, 7 is indivisible by 3. —**in′di·vis′i·bil′i·ty** *n.* —**in′di·vis′i·bly** *adv.*

indoctrinate (ĭn-dŏk′trə-nāt′) *tr.v.* **indoctrinated, indoctrinating, indoctrinates** To instruct (a person) in the doctrines or beliefs of a particular group, especially a political or religious group. —**in·doc′tri·na′tion** *n.*

Indo-European (ĭn′dō-yŏor′ə-pē′ən) *n.* **1.** A family of languages that includes most of the languages of Europe, along with many languages of Iran, India, and some other parts of Asia. **2.** An unrecorded language that is the ancestor of these languages. **3.** A member of a people speaking an Indo-European language. —**In′do-Eu′ro·pe′an** *adj.*

Indo-Iranian (ĭn′dō-ĭ-rä′nē-ən) *n.* **1.** A branch of the Indo-European language family that includes many languages spoken in Iran and India, such as Hindi-Urdu and Persian. **2.** A member of any of the peoples speaking an Indo-Iranian language.

indolent (ĭn′də-lənt) *adj.* Preferring not to work or be active; habitually lazy. —**in′do·lence** *n.*

indomitable (ĭn-dŏm′ĭ-tə-bəl) *adj.* Incapable of being overcome or subdued; unconquerable: *an indomitable foe; a determined leader with an indomitable will.* —**in·dom′i·ta·bly** *adv.*

Indonesian (ĭn′də-nē′zhən) *adj.* Relating to Indonesia or its people, languages, or cultures. ❖ *n.* **1.** A native or inhabitant of Indonesia. **2.** A dialect of Malay that is the official language of the Republic of Indonesia.

indoor (ĭn′dôr′) *adj.* Situated in or done within a house or other building: *an indoor pool; an indoor party.*

indoors (ĭn-dôrz′) *adv.* In or into a house or building: *staying indoors because of a cold.*

indubitable (ĭn-do͞o′bĭ-tə-bəl) *adj.* Too obvious or apparent to be doubted; unquestionable: *the indubitable truth of the evidence.* —**in·du′bi·ta·bly** *adv.*

induce (ĭn-do͞os′) *tr.v.* **induced, inducing, induces 1.** To prompt or persuade (someone) to do something: *Nothing could induce me to stay in that awful job.* **2.** To cause to occur; bring about: *induce vomiting in a patient who has swallowed poison.* **3.** To arrive at (a conclusion or general principle) by a reasoned examination of particular facts. **4.** To produce (electricity or magnetism) by induction. —SEE NOTE AT **produce.**

inducement (ĭn-do͞os′mənt) *n.* **1.** The act or process of inducing: *the inducement of labor in a pregnant woman.* **2.** Something that helps bring about an action; an incentive: *Free samples are an inducement to try new products.*

induct (ĭn-dŭkt′) *tr.v.* **inducted, inducting, inducts 1.** To place formally in office; install: *inducted the officer as treasurer.* **2.** To call into military service; draft. **3.** To admit as a member; initiate: *The honor society inducts new students in the spring.*

inductance (ĭn-dŭk′təns) *n.* The property of an electric circuit that makes it possible for an electromotive force to be created in a nearby circuit by a change of current in either circuit.

inductee (ĭn′dŭk-tē′) *n.* A person inducted or about to be inducted into the armed forces.

induction (ĭn-dŭk′shən) *n.* **1.** The act of installing formally in office: *the induction of the new president.* **2.** The process of being enrolled in the armed forces. **3.** A method of reasoning in which a conclusion is reached or a general principle is discovered on the basis of particular facts. **4.** The process by which an object having electrical or magnetic properties produces similar properties in a nearby object without direct contact.

induction coil *n.* A type of transformer in which an interrupted direct current of low voltage is changed into a high-voltage alternating current.

inductive (ĭn-dŭk′tĭv) *adj.* **1.** Relating to or using logical induction: *inductive reasoning.* **2.** Relating to or caused by electric or magnetic induction. —**in·duc′tive·ly** *adv.*

inductor (ĭn-dŭk′tər) *n.* A part of an electric circuit, typically a coil of wire, that works by or produces inductance.

indulge (ĭn-dŭlj′) *v.* **indulged, indulging, indulges** —*tr.* **1.** To give in to or satisfy (a desire); gratify: *indulge a craving for rich desserts.* **2.** To yield to the desires or whims of (someone): *They always indulge their daughter on her birthday.* See Synonyms at **pamper.** —*intr.* To allow oneself some special pleasure; have or do what one wants: *indulge in a nap.*

indulgence (ĭn-dŭl′jəns) *n.* **1.** The act of indulging a desire or a person: *surrender to an occasional indulgence in junk food.* **2.** Something indulged in: *A long vacation is a worthwhile indulgence.* **3.** Liberal or lenient treatment; favor: *The child expects to be treated with indulgence.* **4.** In the Roman Catholic Church, the freeing from noneternal punishment due for a sin that has been pardoned in confession.

indulgent (ĭn-dŭl′jənt) *adj.* Inclined to pamper or indulge; lenient: *The indulgent owner spoiled the puppy with treats.* —**in·dul′gent·ly** *adv.*

industrial (ĭn-dŭs′trē-əl) *adj.* **1.** Relating to industry: *industrial products.* **2.** Having highly developed industries: *an industrial nation.* **3.** Used in industry: *industrial tools and equipment.* —**in·dus′tri·al·ly** *adv.*

industrialist (ĭ-dŭs′trē-ə-lĭst) *n.* A person who owns or runs an industrial enterprise.

industrialize (ĭn-dŭs′trē-ə-līz′) *v.* **industrialized, industrializing, industrializes** —*tr.* To develop industries in: *a government seeking to industrialize its economy.* —*intr.* To become industrial: *a country that has been slow to industrialize.* —**in·dus′tri·al·i·za′tion** (ĭn-dŭs′trē-ə-lĭ-zā′shən) *n.*

industrial park *n.* An area that is zoned for a group of industries and businesses, usually located on the outskirts of a city.

Industrial Revolution *n.* The gradual shift from hand tools and home manufacturing to power-driven tools and large-scale factory production that began in England in about 1760 and continued into the 1800s.

industrious (ĭn-dŭs′trē-əs) *adj.* Working hard as a steady habit; diligent: *The industrious worker got a raise.* —**in·dus′tri·ous·ly** *adv.* —**in·dus′tri·ous·ness** *n.*

industry (ĭn′də-strē) *n.*, *pl.* **industries 1a.** The manufacture or production of goods on a large scale: *Industry has expanded in many Asian nations.* **b.** A specific branch of such activity: *the computer hardware industry.* **2.** Hard work; steady effort: *Most people admire industry and thrift.*

inebriate (ĭn-ē′brē-āt′) *tr.v.* **inebriated, inebriating, inebriates** To intoxicate; make drunk. ❖ *n.* (ĭn-ē′brē-ĭt) An intoxicated person, especially a drunkard.

inedible (ĭn-ĕd′ə-bəl) *adj.* Unfit to be eaten; not edible: *The peel of a banana is inedible.*

ineffable (ĭn-ĕf′ə-bəl) *adj.* Impossible to express adequately; indescribable: *the ineffable majesty of a starlit sky.* —**in·ef′fa·bly** *adv.*

ineffective (ĭn′ĭ-fĕk′tĭv) *adj.* **1.** Not effective; not producing results: *Their attempt to patch the bicycle tire proved ineffective.* **2.** Not performing satisfactorily; incompetent: *The corrupt politician was an ineffective governor.* —**in′ef·fec′tive·ly** *adv.* —**in′ef·fec′tive·ness** *n.*

ineffectual (ĭn′ĭ-fĕk′chōō-əl) *adj.* **1.** Not having the desired effect; useless: *The pill was ineffectual in relieving my headache.* **2.** Lacking forcefulness or effectiveness; inadequate: *an ineffectual ruler.* —**in′ef·fec′tu·al·ly** *adv.*

inefficiency (ĭn′ĭ-fĭsh′ən-sē) *n.*, *pl.* **inefficiencies 1.** The condition, quality, or fact of being inefficient: *The clerk's inefficiency cost the company a great deal of money.* **2.** An inefficient act or procedure: *There are several inefficiencies in the new system for handling business orders.*

inefficient (ĭn′ĭ-fĭsh′ənt) *adj.* **1.** Wasteful of time, energy, or materials: *an inefficient gasoline engine.* **2.** Lacking in ability; incompetent: *an inefficient manager.* —**in′ef·fi′cient·ly** *adv.*

inelastic (ĭn′ĭ-lăs′tĭk) *adj.* Not capable of returning to its original shape or dimensions after being stretched or deformed; stiff or unyielding. —**in′e·las·tic′i·ty** (ĭn′ĭ-lă-stĭs′ĭ-tē) *n.*

inelegant (ĭn-ĕl′ĭ-gənt) *adj.* Not elegant; lacking grace or refinement: *inelegant manners.* —**in·el′e·gance** *n.* —**in·el′e·gant·ly** *adv.*

ineligible (ĭn-ĕl′ĭ-jə-bəl) *adj.* Not eligible; not qualified: *ineligible to vote; ineligible for citizenship.* —**in·el′i·gi·bil′i·ty** *n.* —**in·el′i·gi·bly** *adv.*

ineluctable (ĭn′ĭ-lŭk′tə-bəl) *adj.* Not to be avoided or escaped; inevitable. —**in′e·luc′ta·bil′i·ty** *n.* —**in′e·luc′ta·bly** *adv.*

inept (ĭn-ĕpt′) *adj.* Awkward or clumsy; lacking skill or competence: *an inept actor; an inept performance.* —**in·ept′ly** *adv.* —**in·ept′ness** *n.*

ineptitude (ĭn-ĕp′tĭ-tōōd′) *n.* **1.** Lack of skill or competence. **2.** An inept act or remark.

inequality (ĭn′ĭ-kwŏl′ĭ-tē) *n.*, *pl.* **inequalities 1.** The condition of being unequal, as in size, rank, or amount: *the growing inequality between rich and poor.* **2.** A mathematical statement that one number is greater than or less than another number.

inequitable (ĭn-ĕk′wĭ-tə-bəl) *adj.* Not equitable; unfair; unjust: *inequitable pay; an inequitable division of work.* —**in·eq′ui·ta·bly** *adv.*

inequity (ĭn-ĕk′wĭ-tē) *n.*, *pl.* **inequities** Lack of equity; injustice; unfairness.

inerrant (ĭn-ĕr′ənt) *adj.* **1.** Incapable of erring; infallible. **2.** Containing no errors.

inert (ĭn-ûrt′) *adj.* **1.** Unable to move or act: *Rock is composed of inert matter.* **2.** Slow to move, act, or respond; sluggish: *the inert forms of lizards sunning on a rock.* **3.** Incapable of reacting with other elements to form chemical compounds: *Helium is an inert gas.* —**in·ert′ly** *adv.*

inertia (ĭ-nûr′shə) *n.* **1.** The tendency of a body at rest to remain at rest, or of a body in motion to continue moving in a straight line at a constant speed unless a force is applied to it. **2.** Resistance to motion, action, or change: *the inertia of a large bureaucracy.*

inescapable (ĭn′ĭ-skā′pə-bəl) *adj.* Incapable of being escaped or avoided; inevitable: *The facts led to an inescapable conclusion.* —**in′es·cap′a·bly** *adv.*

inestimable (ĭn-ĕs′tə-mə-bəl) *adj.* **1.** Impossible to estimate: *inestimable damage.* **2.** Of immeasurable worth; invaluable: *General Washington performed an inestimable service for the new nation.* —**in·es′ti·ma·bly** *adv.*

inevitable (ĭn-ĕv′ĭ-tə-bəl) *adj.* Impossible to avoid or prevent; certain to happen: *Traffic is inevitable during rush hour.* —**in·ev′i·ta·bly** *adv.*

inexact (ĭn′ĭg-zăkt′) *adj.* Not exact; not quite accurate or precise: *Because of inexact measurements, I cut the boards too short.* —**in′ex·act′ly** *adv.*

inexcusable (ĭn′ĭk-skyōō′zə-bəl) *adj.* Impossible to excuse, pardon, or justify: *an inexcusable error.* —**in′ex·cus′a·bly** *adv.*

inexhaustible (ĭn′ĭg-zô′stə-bəl) *adj.* **1.** Not capable of being used up; unlimited: *an inexhaustible supply of food.* **2.** Tireless; indefatigable: *an inexhaustible rescue worker.* —**in′ex·haust′i·bly** *adv.*

inexorable (ĭn-ĕk′sər-ə-bəl) *adj.* **1.** Impossible to stop, alter, or resist; inevitable: *the inexorable passage of time.* **2.** Not capable of being persuaded or moderated by pleas: *an inexorable judge.* —**in·ex′o·ra·bly** *adv.*

inexpedient (ĭn′ĭk-spē′dē-ənt) *adj.* Not expedient; inadvisable. —**in′ex·pe′di·ent·ly** *adv.*

inexpensive (ĭn′ĭk-spĕn′sĭv) *adj.* Not high in price; cheap. —**in′ex·pen′sive·ly** *adv.*

inexperience (ĭn′ĭk-spîr′ē-əns) *n.* Lack of experience or of knowledge gained from experience: *mistakes due to inexperience.*

inexperienced (ĭn′ĭk-spîr′ē-ənst) *adj.* Lacking experience or the knowledge gained from experience: *an inexperienced driver.*

inexpert (ĭn-ĕk′spûrt′) *adj.* Not expert; unskilled. —**in·ex′pert·ly** *adv.* —**in·ex′pert·ness** *n.*

inexplicable (ĭn-ĕk′splĭ-kə-bəl *or* ĭn′ĭk-splĭk′ə-bəl) *adj.* Incapable of being explained or understood: *an inexplicable mystery.* —**in·ex′pli·ca·bly** *adv.*

inexpressible (ĭn′ĭk-sprĕs′ə-bəl) *adj.* Incapable of being expressed, especially in words; indescribable: *inexpressible joy.* —**in′ex·press′i·bly** *adv.*

inextinguishable (ĭn′ĭk-stĭng′gwĭ-shə-bəl) *adj.* Impossible to extinguish or put an end to: *an inextinguishable desire to become a musician.*

inextricable (ĭn-ĕk′strĭ-kə-bəl *or* ĭn′ĭk-strĭk′ə-bəl) *adj.* **1.** Impossible to escape from: *an inextricable maze.* **2.** Difficult or impossible to disentangle or untie: *an inextricable snarl in my fishing line.* **3.** Too complicated or involved to solve: *an inextricable problem.* —**in·ex′tri·ca·bly** *adv.*

infallible (ĭn-făl′ə-bəl) *adj.* **1.** Incapable of making a mistake: *We had an infallible guide on our journey.* **2.** Incapable of failing; sure: *an infallible cure.* —**in·fal′li·bil′i·ty** *n.* —**in·fal′li·bly** *adv.*

infamous (ĭn′fə-məs) *adj.* **1.** Having an exceedingly bad reputation; notorious: *an infamous traitor.* **2.** Deserving condemnation; shocking; outrageous: *infamous deeds.* —**in′fa·mous·ly** *adv.*

infamy (ĭn′fə-mē) *n.* **1.** The condition of being infamous: *a name that will live in infamy.* **2.** Evil reputation; disgrace: *The infamy of the dishonest politician was known far and wide.*

infancy (ĭn′fən-sē) *n., pl.* **infancies 1.** The earliest period of childhood, especially before the ability to walk has been acquired. **2.** The earliest stage of something: *Space exploration was in its infancy in the 1960s.*

infant (ĭn′fənt) *n.* **1.** A child in the earliest period of life, especially before being able to walk. **2.** In law, a person who has not yet reached the age of majority; a minor. ❖ *adj.* **1.** Relating to an infant: *infant years.* **2.** Intended for infants: *infant clothing.* **3.** Newly begun or formed: *an infant industry.*

infanticide (ĭn-făn′tĭ-sīd′) *n.* **1.** The act of killing an infant. **2.** The practice of killing newborn infants. **3.** One who kills an infant. —**in·fan′ti·cid′al** (ĭn-făn′tĭ-sīd′l) *adj.*

infantile (ĭn′fən-tīl′ *or* ĭn′fən-tĭl) *adj.* **1.** Relating to infants or infancy: *infantile stages of development.* **2.** Lacking in maturity; childish: *The two leaders showed an infantile reluctance to deal with each other.*

infantile paralysis *n.* Poliomyelitis.

infantry (ĭn′fən-trē) *n., pl.* **infantries 1.** Soldiers armed and trained to fight on foot: *The infantry encamped near the town.* **2.** The branch of an army made up of units trained to fight on foot.

infantryman (ĭn′fən-trē-mən) *n.* A soldier in the infantry.

infatuate (ĭn-făch′o͞o-āt′) *tr.v.* **infatuated, infatuating, infatuates** To fill with foolish love or attachment: *The stage assistant was infatuated with the famous actress.* —**in·fat′u·a′tion** *n.*

infect (ĭn-fĕkt′) *tr.v.* **infected, infecting, infects 1.** To enter and grow or multiply in, often resulting in disease. Used of bacteria, viruses, fungi, or other infectious agents: *Many people were infected with salmonella.* **2.** To transmit a disease or an infectious agent to: *The sick child infected the rest of the class.* **3.** To become transmitted to and copied on (a hard drive, for example). Used of a computer virus or other harmful software. **4.** To affect as if by a contagious disease: *Their enthusiasm for baseball infected all of us.*

infection (ĭn-fĕk′shən) *n.* **1a.** The invasion of bodily tissue by bacteria, viruses, fungi, or other agents that grow or multiply and often cause disease: *Sterile techniques reduce the chance of infection.* **b.** An instance of being infected: *I have an infection in my toe.* **2.** An instance of a virus or similar software program infecting a computer.

infectious (ĭn-fĕk′shəs) *adj.* **1.** Capable of being spread by infection: *an infectious disease.* **2.** Capable of causing infection: *infectious microorganisms.* **3.** Capable of transmitting a disease; contagious: *an infectious person.* **4.** Tending to spread easily or catch on: *infectious laughter.* —**in·fec′tious·ly** *adv.* —**in·fec′tious·ness** *n.*

infectious mononucleosis *n.* A contagious disease caused by a virus and characterized by fever, sore throat, swollen lymph nodes, and tiredness that may last for several weeks.

infelicitous (ĭn′fĭ-lĭs′ĭ-təs) *adj.* **1.** Inappropriate; ill-chosen: *an infelicitous remark.* **2.** Causing unhappiness; unfortunate. —**in′fe·lic′i·tous·ly** *adv.*

infer (ĭn-fûr′) *tr.v.* **inferred, inferring, infers** To decide or conclude by reasoning from evidence: *I inferred from their laughter that the children were having fun.*

USAGE When we say that a speaker or sentence **implies** something, we mean that it is indicated or suggested without being stated outright: *Even though you say you like sports, your lack of enthusiasm implies that you don't.* To **infer** something, on the other hand, is to draw conclusions that are not stated openly in what is said: *I infer from your lack of enthusiasm that you don't like sports.*

inference (ĭn′fər-əns) *n.* **1.** The act or process of inferring: *arrive at a conclusion by inference.* **2.** Something inferred; a conclusion: *The evidence is too scanty to draw any inferences from it.*

inferior (ĭn-fîr′ē-ər) *adj.* **1.** Low or lower in order, rank, or importance: *A lieutenant is inferior to a captain.* **2.** Low or lower in quality, value, or estimation: *That computer is an inferior brand.* ❖ *n.* A person lower in rank, status, or accomplishment than another: *She gave orders to her inferiors.*

inferiority (ĭn-fîr′ē-ôr′ĭ-tē) *n.* The fact or quality of being inferior.

inferiority complex *n.* An enduring feeling of being inferior to others, sometimes accompanied by overly aggressive behavior.

infernal (ĭn-fûr′nəl) *adj.* **1.** Relating to hell or a world of the dead: *infernal damnation.* **2.** Abominable; awful: *an infernal nuisance.* —**in·fer′nal·ly** *adv.*

inferno (ĭn-fûr′nō) *n., pl.* **infernos** A place or condition suggestive of hell, as in being chaotic, noisy, or intensely hot: *The fire flared out of control, becoming a raging inferno.*

infertile (ĭn-fûr′tl) *adj.* **1.** Not capable of producing offspring; unable to reproduce: *an infertile cow.* **2.** Not capable of developing into a complete organism; unfertilized: *an infertile egg.* **3.** Not capable of supporting plant life; unfavorable to the growth of crops or other plants: *infertile soil.* —**in′fer·til′i·ty** (ĭn′fər-tĭl′ĭ-tē) *n.*

infest (ĭn-fĕst′) *tr.v.* **infested, infesting, infests** To live in or overrun in large numbers so as to be harmful or unpleasant: *bedbugs infesting the apartment; a park that was infested with poison ivy.* —**in′fes·ta′tion** *n.*

infidel (ĭn′fĭ-dəl *or* ĭn′fĭ-dĕl′) *n.* **1.** *Often Offensive* A person who does not believe in a particular religion, especially Christianity or Islam. **2.** A person who has no religious beliefs.

infidelity (ĭn′fĭ-dĕl′ĭ-tē) *n., pl.* **infidelities 1.** Unfaithfulness to another person, especially by committing adultery. **2.** An unfaithful or adulterous act. **3.** Lack of religious belief.

infield (ĭn′fēld′) *n.* **1.** The area of a baseball field bounded by all four bases. **2.** The four infielders of a baseball team.

infielder (ĭn′fēl′dər) *n.* A baseball player whose defensive position is first base, second base, shortstop, or third base.

infighting (ĭn′fī′tĭng) *n.* **1.** Strife or competition among associates in a group or organization: *Infighting on the president's staff caused a delay in the policy announcement.* **2.** Fighting or boxing at close range.

infiltrate (ĭn-fĭl′trāt′ *or* ĭn′fĭl-trāt′) *tr.v.* **infiltrated, infiltrating, infiltrates 1a.** To pass (troops) secretly into enemy territory. **b.** To penetrate or slip through with hostile intentions: *Enemy troops infiltrated our border.* **2.** To enter without being noticed for purposes such as spying: *Government agents infiltrated the criminal operation.* **3.** To cause (a liquid or gas) to pass through the small spaces of a substance; filter. **4.** To fill or saturate (a substance) by filtering; permeate. —**in′fil·tra′tion** *n.*

infinite (ĭn′fə-nĭt) *adj.* **1.** Having no limit or bound; endless. **2a.** Greater in value than any countable number, however large: *an infinite number.* **b.** Having an infinite size or measure; unlimited: *an infinite plane; an infinite set of numbers.* **3.** Very great; immense; boundless: *His joy was infinite.* —**in′fi·nite·ly** *adv.* —**in′fi·nite·ness** *n.*

infinitesimal (ĭn′fĭn-ĭ-tĕs′ə-məl) *adj.* Immeasurably small; minute: *a high-grade steel with only infinitesimal amounts of impurities.* —**in′fin·i·tes′i·mal·ly** *adv.*

infinitive (ĭn-fĭn′ĭ-tĭv) *n.* A verb form that is not inflected to indicate person, number, or tense. In English, it is usually preceded by *to* or by an auxiliary verb. For example, in the phrases *wanted to leave* and *will play tomorrow,* the words *leave* and *play* are infinitives.

infinity (ĭn-fĭn′ĭ-tē) *n., pl.* **infinities 1.** A space, period of time, or quantity that is without a limit. **2.** The quality or condition of being infinite. **3.** A quantity that is greater than any other quantity, however large.

infirm (ĭn-fûrm′) *adj.* Weak in body, as from sickness; feeble. —**in·firm′ly** *adv.*

infirmary (ĭn-fûr′mə-rē) *n., pl.* **infirmaries** A place for the care of sick or injured people, especially a small hospital or dispensary in a large institution.

infirmity (ĭn-fûr′mĭ-tē) *n., pl.* **infirmities 1.** The condition of being infirm; weakness; frailty: *The doctor hesitated to perform surgery because of the patient's infirmity.* **2.** A sickness; an illness.

inflame (ĭn-flām′) *v.* **inflamed, inflaming, inflames** ❖ *tr.v.* **1.** To cause redness, swelling, and soreness in (a body part). **2.** To stir up anger or other strong emotion in (someone); excite: *The speech inflamed the crowd.*

inflamed (ĭn-flāmd′) *adj.* **1.** Swollen and sore: *an inflamed toe.* **2.** Excited; stirred up: *an inflamed audience.*

inflammable (ĭn-flăm′ə-bəl) *adj.* **1.** Tending to catch fire easily and burn rapidly; flammable: *Gasoline is very inflammable.* **2.** Quickly or easily aroused to strong emotion: *an inflammable boss.*

inflammation (ĭn′flə-mā′shən) *n.* **1.** The reaction of the immune system to an infection or injury in a body part, marked by pain, redness, swelling, and heat that result from increased blood flow and the leakage of fluid into the tissues. Inflammation is important for helping to heal damaged tissue, but it is also associated with chronic diseases such as rheumatoid arthritis. **2.** The act or condition of being inflamed.

inflammatory (ĭn-flăm′ə-tôr′ē) *adj.* **1.** Tending to arouse strong emotion: *the speaker's inflammatory language.* **2.** Characterized by or causing inflammation: *Arthritis is an inflammatory disease.*

inflatable (ĭn-flā′tə-bəl) *adj.* Capable of being inflated: *an inflatable rubber boat.* ❖ *n.* A large helium or hot-air balloon constructed so as to resemble a figure or object when inflated.

inflate (ĭn-flāt′) *v.* **inflated, inflating, inflates** —*tr.* **1.** To cause to expand with air or gas: *Did you inflate the tires on your bicycle?* **2.** To enlarge or raise abnormally or im-

properly: *The flattering attention inflated the athlete's ego.* —*intr.* To become inflated: *The balloon inflated quickly.* —**in·flat′er, in·fla′tor** *n.*

inflation (ĭn-flā′shən) *n.* **1.** The act or process of inflating something: *The inflation of the giant balloon took an hour.* **2.** A continuing rise in the price of goods and services in an economy.

inflationary (ĭn-flā′shə-nĕr′ē) *adj.* Relating or contributing to inflation: *inflationary policies.*

inflect (ĭn-flĕkt′) *tr.v.* **inflected, inflecting, inflects 1.** To vary the tone or pitch of (the voice), especially in speaking. **2.** To change the form of (a word) to show number, tense, person, comparison, or other grammatical function. For example, *book* is inflected to *books* in the plural. **3.** To bend; curve: *a prism inflects light rays.*

inflection (ĭn-flĕk′shən) *n.* **1.** A change in the tone or pitch of the voice, especially in speech: *Questions usually end with a rising inflection.* **2a.** The process that changes the form of a word to indicate number, tense, person, comparison, or other grammatical function. For example, the comparative *quicker* is formed from *quick* by inflection. **b.** A word formed by this process; an inflected form. For example, *drives, drove,* and *driven* are all inflections of the word *drive.* **c.** A suffix used in this process. **3.** The act of inflecting or the condition of being inflected. **4.** A bend or curve: *an inflection at an angle of 45°.* —**in·flec′tion·al** *adj.*

inflexible (ĭn-flĕk′sə-bəl) *adj.* **1.** Not flexible; rigid. **2.** Not subject to change or modification: *an inflexible rule.* **3.** Refusing to change; unyielding: *They are inflexible in their demand for better service.* —**in·flex′i·bil′i·ty** *n.* —**in·flex′i·bly** *adv.*

inflict (ĭn-flĭkt′) *tr.v.* **inflicted, inflicting, inflicts 1.** To cause (something injurious or harmful) to be endured or suffered, as to a person, group, or area: *claws that inflicted a deep wound; a storm that inflicted widespread damage.* **2.** To force someone to undergo or experience (something unwanted): *The players grew weary of the stern lectures that the coach inflicted on them.* **3.** To give or deliver (a blow).

infliction (ĭn-flĭk′shən) *n.* **1.** The act or process of inflicting: *the infliction of punishment.* **2.** Something, such as punishment, that is inflicted.

inflorescence (ĭn′flə-rĕs′əns) *n.* A cluster of flowers arranged in a characteristic way on a stem.

inflow (ĭn′flō′) *n.* **1.** The act or process of flowing in or into: *The inflow of requests has increased.* **2.** Something that flows in or into: *a lake fed by an inflow from the mountains.*

influence (ĭn′floo-əns) *n.* **1.** A power that brings about changes or has an effect, especially without any apparent use of force: *Public opinion is an influence on politicians.* **2.** Power to sway or affect that results from wealth or high position in society: *He got the job because of his aunt's influence.* **3.** A person or thing that brings about change without the use of force: *Travel has had a broadening influence on you.* ❖ *tr.v.* **influenced, influencing, influences** To have an effect on; change: *Computers have influenced the way people live.* —SEE NOTE AT **fluent.**

influential (ĭn′floo-ĕn′shəl) *adj.* Having or exercising influence: *an influential newspaper.* —**in′flu·en′tial·ly** *adv.*

influenza (ĭn′floo-ĕn′zə) *n.* **1.** A contagious viral disease in humans, characterized by fever, coughing, headache, and muscular pain. **2.** Any of various viral infections of birds or other animals, generally characterized by fever and respiratory involvement.

influx (ĭn′flŭks′) *n.* A flowing in: *an influx of tourists to the park.* —SEE NOTE AT **fluent.**

info (ĭn′fō) *n. Informal* Information.

inform (ĭn-fôrm′) *v.* **informed, informing, informs** —*tr.* **1.** To give information to; tell; notify: *The notice informed us that the meeting was canceled.* **2.** To acquaint (oneself) with knowledge of a subject: *I watch the news to inform myself about current events.* —*intr.* To give secret or damaging information: *The gang was captured after one of its members informed on the others.*

informal (ĭn-fôr′məl) *adj.* **1.** Not following or requiring fixed ceremonies or rules; unofficial: *an informal agreement made with a handshake.* **2.** Suitable for everyday use or for casual occasions: *informal dress.* **3.** Not suitable for formal writing but frequently used in conversation and ordinary writing. For example, the use of *kid* to mean "a child" is informal. —**in·for′mal·ly** *adv.*

informality (ĭn′fôr-măl′ĭ-tē) *n., pl.* **informalities 1.** The state or quality of being informal: *the informality of a picnic.* **2.** An informal act; informal behavior.

informant (ĭn-fôr′mənt) *n.* A person who provides information to another.

information (ĭn′fər-mā′shən) *n.* **1.** Knowledge or facts learned, especially about a certain event or subject: *The newspaper provides information on the day's events.* **2.** The act of informing or the condition of being informed: *This brochure is for your information.* **3.** Data that a computer transmits, processes, or stores. **4.** Nerve impulses or the perceptions and signals they convey: *information sent from the brain to the fingers.*

informative (ĭn-fôr′mə-tĭv) *adj.* Providing information; instructive: *an informative TV series on dinosaurs.*

informed (ĭn-fôrmd′) *adj.* Provided with information; knowledgeable: *an informed reporter.*

informer (ĭn-fôr′mər) *n.* A person who notifies authorities of secret and often illegal activities.

infra– A prefix that means below or beneath: *infrasonic.*

infraction (ĭn-frăk′shən) *n.* A breach or breaking of a law or rule; a violation.

infrangible (ĭn-frăn′jə-bəl) *adj.* **1.** Difficult or impossible to break or separate into parts. **2.** Inviolable: *infrangible human rights.* —**in·fran′gi·bil′i·ty** *n.* —**in·fran′gi·bly** *adv.*

infrared (ĭn′frə-rĕd′) *adj.* Relating to the invisible part of the electromagnetic spectrum with wavelengths longer than those of visible red light but shorter than those of microwaves: *infrared light.*

infrasonic (ĭn′frə-sŏn′ĭk) *adj.* Generating or using sound waves that are too low in frequency to be heard by human ears.

infrastructure (ĭn′frə-strŭk′chər) *n.* An underlying base or foundation for something, especially the basic facilities necessary for a community to function, including roads, bridges, water pipes, and power lines.

infrequent (ĭn-frē′kwənt) *adj.* Not occurring often; occasional or rare: *an infrequent visitor.* —**in·fre′quen·cy** *n.* —**in·fre′quent·ly** *adv.*

infringe (ĭn-frĭnj′) *tr.v.* **infringed, infringing, infringes** To violate or interfere with (a law, right, or obligation); fail to respect: *Censorship infringes the right to free speech.* ♦ **infringe on** or **infringe upon** To intrude or encroach upon; trespass on: *Reading someone else's diary infringes on that person's privacy.* —**in·fring′er** *n.* —**in·fringe′ment** *n.*

infuriate (ĭn-fyoͮor′ē-āt′) *tr.v.* **infuriated, infuriating, infu-riates** To make furious; enrage: *I was infuriated by their taunts.* —**in·fu′ri·a′tion** *n.*

infuse (ĭn-fyooz′) *tr.v.* **infused, infusing, infuses 1.** To fill; inspire: *Winning the game infused us with the hope that we might win the championship.* **2.** To put into or introduce; instill: *The executive infused new vigor into the company.* **3.** To steep or soak without boiling in order to extract a substance: *Tea is made by infusing tea leaves in hot water.* —SEE NOTE AT **transfusion.**

infusion (ĭn-fyoo′zhən) *n.* **1.** The act or process of infusing. **2.** Something infused or introduced: *With an infusion of money the business recovered.* **3.** A liquid product obtained by infusing: *drank an infusion of medicinal herbs.*

–ing¹ A suffix that forms: **1.** The present participle of verbs: *living.* **2.** Adjectives resembling present participles but not formed from verbs: *swashbuckling.*

–ing² A suffix that means: **1.** An action, process, or art: *dancing; thinking.* **2.** An instance of an action, process, or art: *a meeting.* **3.** The result of an action or process: *a painting.* **4.** Something used in or connected with an action or process: *roofing.*

ingenious (ĭn-jēn′yəs) *adj.* **1.** Clever at devising or making; inventive; creative: *an ingenious storyteller.* **2.** Planned, made, or done with originality and imagination: *The telephone is an ingenious device.* —**in·gen′ious·ly** *adv.* —**in·gen′ious·ness** *n.*

ingénue (ăn′zhə-noo′) *n.* **1.** A naive, innocent girl or young woman. **2.** An actress playing the role of an ingénue.

ingenuity (ĭn′jə-noo′ĭ-tē) *n., pl.* **ingenuities** Inventive skill or imagination; cleverness.

ingenuous (ĭn-jĕn′yoo-əs) *adj.* **1.** Frank and open; candid: *They were being quite ingenuous in telling us the whole story.* **2.** Lacking in cunning or guile: *The young child had an ingenuous smile.* —**in·gen′u·ous·ly** *adv.* —**in·gen′u·ous·ness** *n.*

ingest (ĭn-jĕst′) *tr.v.* **ingested, ingesting, ingests** To take in or absorb, especially as food or drink: *Do not ingest any water before your surgery.* —**in·ges′tion** *n.*

inglenook (ĭng′gəl-nook′) *n.* A nook or corner beside an open fireplace.

inglorious (ĭn-glôr′ē-əs) *adj.* Shameful; dishonorable: *An inglorious incident of cowardice clouded the soldier's career.*

ingot (ĭng′gət) *n.* A mass of metal shaped in the form of a bar or block for convenient storage or transportation.

ingrain (ĭn-grān′) *tr.v.* **ingrained, ingraining, ingrains** To fix or impress deeply, as in the mind: *The coach ingrained a sense of fairness into the players.*

ingrained (ĭn-grānd′) *adj.* Firmly established; deep-seated: *an ingrained habit.*

ingrate (ĭn′grāt′) *n.* An ungrateful person.

ingratiate (ĭn-grā′shē-āt′) *tr.v.* **ingratiated, ingratiating, ingratiates** To gain favor for (oneself) from another; make (oneself) agreeable to another: *He tried to ingratiate himself with his new boss by working long hours.*

ingratiating (ĭn-grā′shē-ā′tĭng) *adj.* **1.** Agreeable; pleasing: *an ingratiating smile.* **2.** Intended to win someone's liking or approval: *an ingratiating remark.* —**in·gra′ti·at′ing·ly** *adv.*

ingratitude (ĭn-grăt′ĭ-tood′) *n.* Lack of gratitude; ungratefulness.

ingredient (ĭn-grē′dē-ənt) *n.* An element in a mixture or compound: *The main ingredient of bread is flour. Sand is an ingredient of concrete.*

ingress (ĭn′grĕs′) *n.* **1.** A means or place of going in; an entrance. **2.** The right or permission to enter: *Only employees of the company have ingress to its building.* **3.** The act of going in or entering.

ingrown (ĭn′grōn′) *adj.* Grown abnormally into the skin or flesh: *an ingrown toenail.*

inhabit (ĭn-hăb′ĭt) *tr.v.* **inhabited, inhabiting, inhabits** To live in; have as a dwelling place: *Dinosaurs inhabited the earth millions of years ago.*

inhabitable (ĭn-hăb′ĭ-tə-bəl) *adj.* Suitable for living in: *an inhabitable land.*

inhabitant (ĭn-hăb′ĭ-tənt) *n.* A permanent resident of a particular place.

inhalant (ĭn-hā′lənt) *n.* **1.** A substance inhaled for medicinal purposes in vapor or aerosol form. **2.** A substance inhaled as an intoxicant, usually in the form of a vapor.

inhalation (ĭn′hə-lā′shən) *n.* The act or an instance of inhaling.

inhalator (ĭn′hə-lā′tər) *n.* A device used to inhale a medicine.

inhale (ĭn-hāl′) *v.* **inhaled, inhaling, inhales** —*tr.* **1.** To draw (air or a fragrance, for example) into the lungs by breathing: *I inhaled the fresh sea air.* **2.** *Informal* To consume rapidly or eagerly; devour: *We inhaled the pizza.* —*intr.* **1.** To breathe in: *inhale deeply.* **2.** To draw smoke into the lungs.

inhaler (ĭn-hā′lər) *n.* A device used to inhale a medicine.

inharmonious (ĭn′här-mō′nē-əs) *adj.* **1.** Not in harmony; discordant: *inharmonious music.* **2.** Not in accord or agreement: *inharmonious relations between countries.* —**in′har·mo′ni·ous·ly** *adv.*

inhere (ĭn-hîr′) *intr.v.* **inhered, inhering, inheres** To be inherent or innate. —**in·her′ence** (ĭn-hîr′əns), **in·her′en·cy** *n.*

inherent (ĭn-hîr′ənt *or* ĭn-hĕr′ənt) *adj.* Being part of the basic nature of a person or thing; essential; intrinsic: *The student's inherent curiosity led to an interest in science.* —**in·her′ent·ly** *adv.*

inherit (ĭn-hĕr′ĭt) *v.* **inherited, inheriting, inherits** —*tr.* **1.** To receive (property or a title) from a person who has died, usually through a will. **2.** To receive or take over from someone else: *Upon taking office, the mayor inherited many serious problems.* **3.** To acquire (characteristics) by genetic transmission from a parent or ancestor: *I inherited my father's hair color. These puppies have inherited the best traits of the breed.* —*intr.* To receive an inheritance. —**in·her′i·tor** *n.*

inheritance (ĭn-hĕr′ĭ-təns) *n.* **1.** The act of inheriting: *They gained their wealth by inheritance.* **2.** Something that is inherited or is to be inherited at a person's death. **3.** Something regarded as a heritage: *The concept of democracy is an inheritance from the ancient Greeks.* **4.** The process by which characteristics are acquired by genetic transmission from one's parents or ancestors.

inhibit (ĭn-hĭb′ĭt) *tr.v.* **inhibited, inhibiting, inhibits** To restrain or hold back; prevent: *Shyness inhibited the new student from talking freely in class.*

inhibition (ĭn′hə-bĭsh′ən *or* ĭn′ə-bĭsh′ən) *n.* **1.** The act of inhibiting or the condition of being inhibited. **2.** A feeling or state of mind that restrains a person from doing something: *My inhibition prevented me from asking a question of the famous writer.*

inhospitable (ĭn-hŏs′pĭ-tə-bəl *or* ĭn′hŏ-spĭt′ə-bəl) *adj.*

1. Showing no hospitality to others; unfriendly. **2.** Not providing shelter or food; barren: *the inhospitable Arctic winter.* —**in·hos′pi·ta·bly** *adv.*

inhuman (ĭn-hyoō′mən) *adj.* **1.** Lacking kindness or compassion; cruel. **2.** Not suited for human needs: *The moon is an inhuman environment.* **3.** Not of ordinary human form; monstrous. —**in·hu′man·ly** *adv.*

inhumane (ĭn′hyoō-mān′) *adj.* Lacking pity or compassion: *The law punishes inhumane treatment of animals.* —**in·hu·mane′ly** *adv.*

inhumanity (ĭn′hyoō-măn′ĭ-tē) *n., pl.* **inhumanities 1.** Lack of pity or compassion: *the basic inhumanity of war.* **2.** An inhuman or cruel act.

inimical (ĭ-nĭm′ĭ-kəl) *adj.* **1.** Harmful or injurious; adverse: *habits inimical to good health.* **2.** Unfriendly; hostile: *The countries have long been inimical neighbors.* —**in·im′i·cal·ly** *adv.*

inimitable (ĭ-nĭm′ĭ-tə-bəl) *adj.* Impossible to imitate; unique: *a singer's inimitable style.* —**in·im′i·ta·bil′i·ty** *n.* —**in·im′i·ta·bly** *adv.*

iniquitous (ĭ-nĭk′wĭ-təs) *adj.* Unjust; wicked. —**in·iq′ui·tous·ly** *adv.*

iniquity (ĭ-nĭk′wĭ-tē) *n., pl.* **iniquities 1.** Extreme injustice; wickedness: *The iniquity of the crime aroused great public anger.* **2.** An immoral act; a sin.

initial (ĭ-nĭsh′əl) *adj.* Relating to or occurring at the beginning; first: *the initial phase of a project.* ❖ *n.* **1.** The first letter of a word or name. **2.** A large, often decorated letter, as at the beginning of a chapter. ❖ *tr.v.* **initialed, initialing, initials** also **initialled, initialling, initials** To mark or sign with initials. —**in·i′tial·ly** *adv.*

initialize (ĭ-nĭsh′ə-līz′) *tr.v.* **initialized, initializing, initializes 1.** To prepare (a computer or printer) for use. **2.** To format (a computer disk or other storage medium).

initiate (ĭ-nĭsh′ē-āt′) *tr.v.* **initiated, initiating, initiates 1.** To cause (something) to begin; start: *The diplomat tried to initiate negotiations.* See Synonyms at **begin. 2.** To introduce (a person) to a new subject, interest, skill, or activity: *My music teacher initiated me into the world of opera.* **3.** To admit into a group, often with a special ceremony: *Several new members were initiated into the club.* ❖ *n.* (ĭ-nĭsh′ē-ĭt) A person who is being or has been initiated. —**in·i′ti·a′tor** *n.*

initiation (ĭ-nĭsh′ē-ā′shən) *n.* **1.** The act or process of initiating. **2.** Admission into a club, society, or organization. **3.** A ceremony or ritual with which a new member is initiated.

initiative (ĭ-nĭsh′ə-tĭv) *n.* **1.** The ability to undertake a task or to put a plan of action into effect without getting prior help or direction from others: *Starting one's own business requires much initiative.* **2.** The first step or action, especially when taken before others can; the lead over others: *Seizing the initiative, I applied for the job before it was advertised.* **3.** A proposed law or legal resolution included on a ballot during an election as a result of a petition signed by a certain number of citizens. ♦ **on (one's) own initiative** Without prompting or direction from others; on one's own.

inject (ĭn-jĕkt′) *tr.v.* **injected, injecting, injects 1a.** To force or drive (a liquid or gas) into something: *a mechanism that injects fuel into a cylinder of an engine.* **b.** To introduce (a fluid or medicine) into a body part, especially by a hypodermic syringe. **2.** To introduce; insert: *By mentioning cost, I injected some realism into our planning.* —**in·jec′tor** *n.*

WORD BUILDING The word root *ject-* in English words comes ultimately from the past participle *iactus* of the Latin verb *iacere*, "to throw, shoot." **Inject** thus literally means "to throw or shoot in" (using the prefix *in-²*, "in, into"). The root also appears in **abject**, literally "thrown away" (*ab-*, "away, away from"); **dejected** is literally "shot down," as we would say informally (*de-*, "down"); **reject** means "to throw back" (*re-*, "back, backward"); and **adjective** comes ultimately from *adiectus*, "thrown to or at, placed near" (*ad-*, "at, to, toward"). Thus, an adjective is a word "placed near" a noun to modify it.

injection (ĭn-jĕk′shən) *n.* **1.** The act of injecting. **2.** Something that is injected, especially a dose of a liquid medicine injected into the body.

injudicious (ĭn′jōō-dĭsh′əs) *adj.* Showing a lack of judgment; unwise: *an injudicious decision.* —**in′ju·di′cious·ly** *adv.* —**in′ju·di′cious·ness** *n.*

injunction (ĭn-jŭngk′shən) *n.* **1.** An order or command: *She ignored her doctor's injunction to get more exercise.* **2.** A court order prohibiting or requiring a specific course of action: *The judge issued an injunction stopping the strike and requiring further negotiations.*

injure (ĭn′jər) *tr.v.* **injured, injuring, injures** **1.** To cause physical harm to; hurt: *I injured my arm when I fell off my bicycle.* **2.** To harm or impair: *The false accusation injured his reputation.*

injurious (ĭn-jōōr′ē-əs) *adj.* Causing injury, damage, or wrong; harmful: *Sunburn is injurious to the skin.* —**in·ju′ri·ous·ly** *adv.* —**in·ju′ri·ous·ness** *n.*

injury (ĭn′jə-rē) *n., pl.* **injuries** Damage or harm done to a person or thing: *I escaped the fall with no serious injuries. The scandal caused lasting injury to the senator's reputation.*

injury time *n.* Stoppage time.

injustice (ĭn-jŭs′tĭs) *n.* **1.** Lack of justice; unfairness: *Tyranny always leads to injustice.* **2.** A specific unjust act; a wrong: *Jailing the protesters was a terrible injustice.*

ink (ĭngk) *n.* **1.** A colored or black liquid used especially for writing or printing. **2.** A dark liquid ejected for protection by squids, octopuses, and similar marine animals. **3.** *Informal* Coverage in the print media; publicity: *Her campaign rallies generated a lot of ink.* **4.** *Informal* A tattoo or tattoos. ❖ *tr.v.* **inked, inking, inks** **1.** To cover with ink; spread ink on: *The rubber stamp must be inked often.* **2.** *Informal* To tattoo.

inkblot (ĭngk′blŏt′) *n.* A blot made of spilled ink.

inkhorn (ĭngk′hôrn′) *n.* A small container made of horn or a similar material, formerly used to hold ink.

inkjet printer (ĭngk′jĕt′) *n.* A printer that directs streams of electrically charged ink onto a page.

inkling (ĭng′klĭng) *n.* A slight indication or hint; a vague idea: *You haven't an inkling of how much it costs to install solar heating.*

inkstand (ĭngk′stănd′) *n.* **1.** A tray or rack for pens and bottles of ink. **2.** An inkwell.

inkwell (ĭngk′wĕl′) *n.* A small container or reservoir for ink.

inky (ĭng′kē) *adj.* **inkier, inkiest** **1.** Stained or smeared with ink: *inky fingers.* **2.** Like ink; dark; murky: *inky shadows.* —**ink′i·ness** *n.*

inlaid (ĭn′lād′) *v.* Past tense and past participle of **inlay.** ❖ *adj.* **1.** Set smoothly into a surface to form a pattern or decoration: *inlaid decorative tile in a bathroom wall.* **2.** Decorated with a pattern set into the surface: *a table with an inlaid top of wood.*

inland (ĭn′lənd) *adj.* Relating to or located in the interior of a country or region: *The Great Lakes are inland waterways.* ❖ *adv.* In, toward, or into the interior of a country or region: *You must travel inland to find the source of a river.* ❖ *n.* (ĭn′lănd′ *or* ĭn′lənd) The interior of a country or region.

in-law (ĭn′lô′) *n.* A relative by marriage.

inlay (ĭn′lā′ *or* ĭn-lā′) *tr.v.* **inlaid** (ĭn′lād′), **inlaying, inlays** **1.** To set (pieces of contrasting material) into a surface to form a design: *inlay strips of gold on a silver bracelet.* **2.** To decorate by setting in such designs: *The jewelry box was inlaid with mother-of-pearl.* ❖ *n.* **1.** Contrasting material set into a surface in pieces to form a design. **2.** An inlaid decoration or design: *a table top with a star-shaped inlay of ivory and gold.* **3.** A filling of gold or other solid material, fitted and cemented into a tooth cavity.

inlet (ĭn′lĕt′ *or* ĭn′lĭt′) *n.* **1.** A stream or bay leading inland. **2.** A narrow passage of water, as between two islands. **3.** An opening providing a means of entrance.

inline skate (ĭn′līn′) *n.* A roller skate whose wheels are arranged in a straight line.

inmate (ĭn′māt′) *n.* A person confined to an institution, such as a prison or hospital.

inmost (ĭn′mōst′) *adj.* Farthest within; innermost.

inn (ĭn) *n.* **1.** A hotel that serves food and drink to travelers. **2.** A tavern or restaurant.

innards (ĭn′ərdz) *pl.n. Informal* **1.** The internal organs of the body, especially of the abdomen. **2.** The inner parts, as of a machine.

innate (ĭ-nāt′ *or* ĭn′āt′) *adj.* **1.** Possessed at birth; inborn: *innate intelligence.* **2.** Existing as a basic or essential characteristic; inherent: *Mountain climbing has certain innate dangers.* —**in·nate′ly** *adv.* —**in·nate′ness** *n.*

inner (ĭn′ər) *adj.* **1.** Located farther inside: *The inner core of the earth lies under the crust and mantle.* **2.** Relating to the spirit or mind: *Sitting beside the brook, he felt an inner peace.* **3.** More exclusive, private, or important: *the inner circles of government.*

inner city *n.* The older central part of a city, especially when run-down and impoverished.

inner ear *n.* The innermost part of the ear, consisting of the cochlea, vestibule, and semicircular canals. The inner ear contains the essential organs of hearing and of balance.

innermost (ĭn′ər-mōst′) *adj.* **1.** Located farthest within: *the innermost room in the palace.* **2.** Most private or intimate: *innermost feelings.*

inner tube *n.* A hollow rubber ring that can be inserted inside the casing of a tire and inflated.

inning (ĭn′ĭng) *n.* One of the nine divisions of a baseball game during which each team has a turn at bat.

innkeeper (ĭn′kē′pər) *n.* A person who owns or manages an inn.

innocence (ĭn′ə-səns) *n.* The condition, quality, or fact of being innocent, especially freedom from guilt.

innocent (ĭn′ə-sənt) *adj.* **1.** Free of evil or wrongdoing; not guilty of a crime or sin: *The jury found the defendant innocent of the crime.* **2.** Unaware of evil or wrongdoing; naive: *We do not remain innocent children for long.* **3.** Not intended to cause harm: *an innocent joke.* ❖ *n.* **1.** A person, especially a child, who is free of evil or sin. **2.** A simple inexperienced person who has no intention of deceiving others. —**in′no·cent·ly** *adv.*

innocuous (ĭ-nŏk′yōō-əs) *adj.* Harmless; innocent: *an innocuous remark.* —**in·noc′u·ous·ly** *adv.*

innovate (ĭn′ə-vāt′) *v.* **innovated, innovating, innovates**

—tr. To begin or introduce for the first time: *innovate a new design for microchips. —intr.* To begin or introduce something new. **—in′no·va′tor** *n.*

innovation (ĭn′ə-vā′shən) *n.* **1.** The act of innovating: *The Industrial Revolution was a time of great innovation.* **2.** Something newly introduced: *Laptops were a major innovation in computer design.*

innovative (ĭn′ə-vā′tĭv) *adj.* Tending to innovate or characterized by innovation: *an innovative architect; an innovative product.*

innuendo (ĭn′yoō-ĕn′dō) *n., pl.* **innuendoes** An indirect hint or suggestion, usually intended to hurt the good name or standing of someone; an insinuation: *The star athlete claimed that the news reports were full of lies and innuendoes.*

innumerable (ĭ-noō′mər-ə-bəl) *adj.* Too numerous to be counted: *innumerable difficulties.* **—in·nu′mer·a·ble·ness** *n.* **—in·nu′mer·a·bly** *adv.*

inoculate (ĭ-nŏk′yə-lāt′) *tr.v.* **inoculated, inoculating, inoculates 1.** To inject (a person or animal) with a vaccine or serum, to protect against disease. **2.** To introduce microorganisms into (something, especially a culture): *inculated the broth with bacteria.*

inoculation (ĭ-nŏk′yə-lā′shən) *n.* **1.** The act of inoculating. **2.** An injection, as of a vaccine, given to make the body resistant to a disease.

inoffensive (ĭn′ə-fĕn′sĭv) *adj.* Giving no offense; harmless: *an inoffensive joke.* **—in′of·fen′sive·ly** *adv.* **—in′of·fen′sive·ness** *n.*

inoperable (ĭn-ŏp′ər-ə-bəl *or* ĭn-ŏp′rə-bəl) *adj.* **1.** Not suitable for surgery: *an inoperable tumor.* **2.** Not functioning; inoperative.

inoperative (ĭn-ŏp′ər-ə-tĭv *or* ĭn-ŏp′rə-tĭv) *adj.* **1.** Not working or functioning: *The computer is inoperative at this time.* **2.** No longer in force: *The governor declared her latest policy inoperative.*

inopportune (ĭn-ŏp′ər-toōn′) *adj.* Coming at the wrong time; inappropriate: *a phone call at a most inopportune moment.*

inordinate (ĭn-ôr′dn-ĭt) *adj.* Exceeding reasonable limits; immoderate; excessive: *The speech lasted an inordinate amount of time.* **—in·or′di·nate·ly** *adv.*

inorganic (ĭn′ôr-găn′ĭk) *adj.* **1.** Not involving living organisms or the products of their life processes: *Granite is inorganic in origin.* **2.** Relating to compounds that are not organic. Inorganic compounds usually do not contain carbon and are not derived from living organisms. **—in′or·gan′i·cal·ly** *adv.*

inpatient (ĭn′pā′shənt) *n.* A patient who stays overnight in a hospital or clinic for treatment. ❖ *adj.* Relating to inpatients or their care: *an inpatient psychiatric facility.*

input (ĭn′poŏt′) *n.* **1.** Something that is contributed or put into a project or process: *creative input from a design consultant; a new business that will require a large input of money.* **2.** The power supplied to an electronic circuit or device. **3.** The data or programs put into a computer. ❖ *tr.v.* **inputted** or **input, inputting, inputs** To enter (data or a program) into a computer.

input device *n.* A device, such as a keyboard or a mouse, used to enter information into a computer.

inquest (ĭn′kwĕst′) *n.* **1.** A legal investigation into the cause of a death, especially one made before a jury or an official. **2.** An investigation.

inquire (ĭn-kwīr′) *v.* **inquired, inquiring, inquires** *—intr.* **1.** To seek information by asking a question: *If you can't find your size, inquire at the sales desk.* See Synonyms at **ask. 2.** To make a search or study; investigate: *The police inquired into the missing person's whereabouts. —tr.* To ask, especially politely or formally: *Our host inquired why we were leaving so soon.* ◆ **inquire after** To ask about the health or condition of (someone). **—in·quir′er** *n.* **—in·quir′ing·ly** *adv.*

inquiry (ĭn′kwə-rē *or* ĭn-kwīr′ē) *n., pl.* **inquiries 1.** The act of inquiring: *engaged in scientific inquiry.* **2.** A request for information; a question: *many inquiries about the new mail rates.* **3.** A detailed examination of a matter; an investigation: *an inquiry into why water bills are so high.*

inquisition (ĭn′kwĭ-zĭsh′ən) *n.* **1.** An investigation that violates the privacy or rights of individuals. **2.** A thorough harsh questioning: *the reporters' inquisition of the coach during the press conference.* **3. Inquisition** A former tribunal of the Roman Catholic Church established to seek out and punish people considered guilty of heresy.

inquisitive (ĭn-kwĭz′ĭ-tĭv) *adj.* **1.** Eager for learning or knowledge; curious: *an inquisitive mind.* **2.** Prying into the affairs of others; unduly curious. **—in·quis′i·tive·ly** *adv.* **—in·quis′i·tive·ness** *n.*

inquisitor (ĭn-kwĭz′ĭ-tər) *n.* A person who conducts an inquisition. **—in·quis′i·to′ri·al** (ĭn-kwĭz′ĭ-tôr′ē-əl) *adj.*

inroad (ĭn′rōd′) *n.* An advance at another's expense; an encroachment: *Foreign companies have made inroads into American markets.*

inrush (ĭn′rŭsh′) *n.* A sudden rushing in; an influx: *an inrush of commuter traffic to the city.*

insane (ĭn-sān′) *adj.* **1.** Having a serious mental disorder, especially one that distorts the perception of reality. This term is no longer used in medical diagnosis. **2.** Characteristic of or intended for people with such disorders: *an insane asylum.* **3.** Mentally unfit to be held legally responsible for one's actions or to be able to understand the proceedings at one's trial. **4.** Mentally or emotionally agitated or distressed: *That noisy neighbor has been driving us insane.* **5.** Very foolish; not sensible: *an insane stunt.* **—in·sane′ly** *adv.*

insanitary (ĭn-săn′ĭ-tĕr′ē) *adj.* Not sanitary; unclean: *insanitary bandages.*

insanity (ĭn-săn′ĭ-tē) *n., pl.* **insanities 1.** A state of serious mental illness, especially one in which the perception of reality is distorted. This term is no longer used in medical diagnosis. **2.** The condition of having been judged to be legally insane. **3.** Extreme foolishness; utter folly: *Trying to do three jobs at once is sheer insanity.*

insatiable (ĭn-sā′shə-bəl *or* ĭn-sā′shē-ə-bəl) *adj.* Impossible to satisfy; never satisfied: *an insatiable appetite.* **—in·sa′tia·bly** *adv.*

inscribe (ĭn-skrīb′) *tr.v.* **inscribed, inscribing, inscribes 1a.** To write, print, carve, or engrave (words, letters, or a design) on a surface: *Inscribe the winners' names on a plaque.* **b.** To mark or engrave (a surface) with words, letters, or design: *inscribe a plaque with the names of the winners.* **2.** To sign one's name or write a brief message in or on (a book or picture given as a gift). **3.** To impress deeply on the mind: *Our last day of school is inscribed on my memory.* **4.** To enter in a list; sign up. **5.** To draw (a geometric figure) within another so that the inner figure touches the outer figure at as many points as possible. **—in·scrib′er** *n.*

inscription (ĭn-skrĭp′shən) *n.* **1.** The act or an example of inscribing: *The monument has a space for the inscription of the names of the flood victims.* **2.** Something inscribed: *a wall covered with ancient Egyptian inscriptions.* **3.** A short signed message in a book or on a picture given as a gift.

inscrutable (ĭn-skrōō′tə-bəl) *adj.* Difficult or impossible to understand or make out; mysterious: *an inscrutable smile; an inscrutable coded message.* —**in·scru′ta·bil′i·ty,** **in·scru′ta·ble·ness** *n.* —**in·scru′ta·bly** *adv.*

inseam (ĭn′sēm′) *n.* **1.** The inside seam of a pant leg. **2.** The length or measurement of such a seam.

insect (ĭn′sĕkt′) *n.* Any of a large group of arthropods that in the adult stage have six legs, a body with three main divisions, and usually one or two pairs of wings. Flies, bees, grasshoppers, butterflies, and beetles are insects. —SEE NOTE AT **segment.**

insecticide (ĭn-sĕk′tĭ-sīd′) *n.* A chemical substance used to kill insects.

insectivore (ĭn-sĕk′tə-vôr′) *n.* **1.** Any of a group of small mammals, such as the shrews, moles, and hedgehogs, that feed chiefly on insects and other small invertebrates. **2.** An animal or plant that feeds mainly on insects.

insectivorous (ĭn′sĕk-tĭv′ər-əs) *adj.* Feeding on insects.

insecure (ĭn′sĭ-kyŏor′) *adj.* **1.** Not sure or certain; doubtful: *an insecure future.* **2.** Not secure or safe; not fully protected: *an insecure post on the frontier; an insecure transaction on the Internet.* **3.** Not firm or sure; shaky: *an insecure hold on the dog's leash.* **4.** Lacking self-confidence: *an insecure person.* —**in′se·cure′ly** *adv.* —**in′se·cu′ri·ty** (ĭn′sĭ-kyŏor′ĭ-tē) *n.*

inseminate (ĭn-sĕm′ə-nāt′) *tr.v.* **inseminated, inseminating, inseminates** To introduce semen into the reproductive tract of (a female). —**in·sem′i·na′tion** *n.*

insensate (ĭn-sĕn′sāt′ or ĭn-sĕn′sĭt) *adj.* **1.** Lacking sensation or awareness; inanimate: *rocks, trees, and other insensate objects.* **2.** Unconscious: *The insensate patient was in a deep coma.* **3.** Insensitive; unfeeling: *The insensate official was not interested in my complaints.* **4.** Lacking sense; foolish. —**in·sen′sate′ly** *adv.*

insensible (ĭn-sĕn′sə-bəl) *adj.* **1.** Not noticeable; imperceptible: *an insensible change in the weather.* **2.** Lacking the ability to feel sensation; numb: *insensible to cold.* **3.** Not mindful; unaware: *insensible to good advice.* **4.** Emotionally cold; indifferent: *He is insensible to other people's sorrow.* **5.** Unconscious: *The victim lay insensible on the sidewalk.* —**in·sen′si·bil′i·ty** *n.* —**in·sen′si·bly** *adv.*

insensitive (ĭn-sĕn′sĭ-tĭv) *adj.* **1.** Not physically sensitive; numb: *An injection made the tooth insensitive.* **2.** Lacking in sensitivity for others; cold; unfeeling. **3.** Unresponsive: *We must never be insensitive to the needs of our customers.* —**in·sen′si·tive·ly** *adv.* —**in·sen′si·tiv′i·ty** *n.*

inseparable (ĭn-sĕp′ər-ə-bəl or ĭn-sĕp′rə-bəl) *adj.* Impossible to separate: *inseparable friends.* —**in·sep′a·ra·bil′i·ty, in·sep′a·ra·ble·ness** *n.* —**in·sep′a·ra·bly** *adv.*

insert (ĭn-sûrt′) *tr.v.* **inserted, inserting, inserts** To put or set into, between, or among: *insert a key in a lock; insert pictures between chapters in the book.* ❖ *n.* (ĭn′sûrt′) Something inserted or meant to be inserted, as into a manuscript: *An advertising insert fell out of the magazine.*

insertion (ĭn-sûr′shən) *n.* **1.** The act of inserting: *the insertion of a cork into a bottle.* **2.** Something inserted: *Please add this insertion to my report.*

inset (ĭn′sĕt′ or ĭn-sĕt′) *tr.v.* **inset, insetting, insets** To set in; insert. ❖ *n.* (ĭn′sĕt′) Something set in, as a small map

or illustration set within a larger one, or a piece of material set into a dress.

inshore (ĭn′shôr′) *adv. & adj.* **1.** Close to a shore. **2.** Toward or coming toward shore: *an inshore wind.*

inside (ĭn-sīd′ or ĭn′sīd′) *n.* **1.** An inner part, side, or surface: *the inside of a house; articles on the inside of a magazine.* **2. insides** *Informal* **a.** The inner organs, especially those of the abdomen; entrails. **b.** The inner workings: *the insides of a TV set.* ❖ *adj.* **1.** Inner; interior: *the inside pocket of a jacket.* **2.** Relating to, coming from, or known by those within a group: *inside information; a theft that was definitely an inside job.* **3.** In baseball, passing on the side of home plate nearer the batter: *The first pitch was a fast ball, high and inside.* ❖ *adv.* Into or in the interior; within: *go inside; staying inside.* ❖ *prep.* Into or in the interior of: *inside the package; go inside the house.* ◆ **inside out 1.** With the inner surface turned out; reversed: *wearing his socks inside out.* **2.** *Informal* Thoroughly: *A taxi driver must know the city inside out.*

inside of *prep.* Within: *inside of an hour.*

insider (ĭn-sī′dər) *n.* **1.** An accepted member of a group. **2.** A person who has special knowledge or access to private information.

insidious (ĭn-sĭd′ē-əs) *adj.* **1.** Working or spreading harmfully in a subtle or hidden manner: *insidious rumors; an insidious disease.* **2.** Intended to entrap; treacherous: *an insidious plot.* —**in·sid′i·ous·ly** *adv.*

insight (ĭn′sīt′) *n.* **1.** The capacity to perceive the true nature of something, especially by intuition: *Einstein's insight into the workings of the universe.* **2.** A perception of the true nature of something: *The critic had a brilliant insight about the meaning of the movie.*

insightful (ĭn-sīt′fəl or ĭn′sīt′fəl) *adj.* Showing or having insight; perceptive: *an insightful analysis of the painting.*

insignia (ĭn-sĭg′nē-ə) *n., pl.* **insignia** or **insignias** A badge of office, rank, membership, or nationality; an emblem.

insignificant (ĭn′sĭg-nĭf′ĭ-kənt) *adj.* **1.** Of no importance; trivial: *an insignificant detail.* **2.** Small in size, power, or value: *an insignificant contribution; an insignificant job.* **3.** Having little or no meaning: *insignificant doodles on a notepad.* —**in′sig·nif′i·cance** *n.* —**in′sig·nif′i·cant·ly** *adv.*

insincere (ĭn′sĭn-sîr′) *adj.* Not sincere; hypocritical: *an insincere apology.* —**in′sin·cere′ly** *adv.* —**in′sin·cer′i·ty** (ĭn′sĭn-sĕr′ĭ-tē) *n.*

insinuate (ĭn-sĭn′yōō-āt′) *tr.v.* **insinuated, insinuating, insinuates** **1.** To introduce or suggest in a sly or indirect way: *Are you insinuating that I'm not good enough for the team?* **2.** To introduce or insert (oneself) by artful means: *The stranger insinuated himself into the wedding reception.*

insinuation (ĭn-sĭn′yōō-ā′shən) *n.* An indirect hint or suggestion: *an insinuation of wrongdoing.*

insipid (ĭn-sĭp′ĭd) *adj.* **1.** Lacking flavor; bland: *an insipid watery soup.* **2.** Lacking qualities that excite or interest; dull: *an insipid group of people.* —**in·sip′id·ly** *adv.*

insist (ĭn-sĭst′) *v.* **insisted, insisting, insists** —*intr.* To be firm in a course or demand; take a strong stand: *I insist on paying my share of the expenses.* —*tr.* To assert or demand vehemently and persistently: *We insist that you stay for dinner.*

insistent (ĭn-sĭs′tənt) *adj.* **1.** Firm or persistent in a course or demand: *The doctor was insistent that the water be boiled before use.* **2.** Demanding attention or a response: *my alarm clock's insistent ring.* —**in·sis′tence** *n.* —**in·sis′tent·ly** *adv.*

insofar as (ĭn′sō-fär′) *conj.* To the extent that: *Insofar as I am able, I will carry out your orders.*

insole (ĭn′sōl′) *n.* **1.** The inner sole of a shoe or boot. **2.** An extra strip of material put inside a shoe for comfort or protection.

insolent (ĭn′sə-lənt) *adj.* Disrespectful and rude; impudent: *an insolent reply.* —**in′so·lence** *n.* —**in′so·lent·ly** *adv.*

insoluble (ĭn-sŏl′yə-bəl) *adj.* **1.** Not capable of being dissolved: *an insoluble salt.* **2.** Difficult or impossible to solve or explain: *an insoluble riddle.* —**in·sol′u·bil′i·ty** *n.* —**in·sol′u·bly** *adv.*

insolvent (ĭn-sŏl′vənt) *adj.* Unable to pay one's debts; bankrupt: *an insolvent business.* —**in·sol′ven·cy** *n.*

insomnia (ĭn-sŏm′nē-ə) *n.* Persistent inability to sleep; sleeplessness.

insouciant (ĭn-sōō′sē-ənt) *adj.* Marked by blithe lack of concern; carefree. —**in·sou′ci·ant·ly** *adv.*

inspect (ĭn-spĕkt′) *tr.v.* **inspected, inspecting, inspects 1.** To examine carefully and critically, especially for flaws: *We inspect all of our products to ensure they are of the highest quality.* **2.** To examine or review formally; evaluate officially: *An officer inspects the troops every Saturday.* —SEE NOTE AT **spectator.**

inspection (ĭn-spĕk′shən) *n.* **1.** The act of inspecting: *Inspection of the wiring will take two days.* **2.** An official examination or review: *Demerits will be given to anyone who is late for inspection.*

inspector (ĭn-spĕk′tər) *n.* **1.** A person who is appointed or employed to inspect something: *Government inspectors try to ensure food safety.* **2.** A police officer ranking next below a superintendent.

inspiration (ĭn′spə-rā′shən) *n.* **1.** The excitement of the mind, emotions, or imagination, as in creating something or solving a problem: *Some writers get inspiration for a story from reading the newspaper.* **2.** A person or thing that excites the mind or the emotions: *The brilliant scientist was an inspiration to younger colleagues.* **3.** Something, such as an original idea, that is inspired: *Your suggestion to open a store in town was an inspiration.* —**in′spi·ra′tion·al** *adj.*

inspire (ĭn-spīr′) *v.* **inspired, inspiring, inspires 1.** To fill with great emotion: *a singing performance that inspired the entire audience.* **2.** To stimulate to creativity or action: *The story about that great discovery inspired us to look for fossils.* **3.** To cause (a feeling or attitude) in another or others; influence: *The candidate inspired confidence in the voters.* **4.** To be the cause or source of: *The book inspired a movie.* —**in·spir′er** *n.*

inspired (ĭn-spīrd′) *adj.* Resulting from creative inspiration; extremely well-made or well-done: *an inspired performance.*

inspiring (ĭn-spīr′ĭng) *adj.* Causing one to feel creative, uplifted, or motivated; stimulating: *an inspiring story of courage.*

instability (ĭn′stə-bĭl′ĭ-tē) *n., pl.* **instabilities** Lack of stability; unsteadiness: *The building was evacuated because of the instability of the roof.*

install (ĭn-stôl′) *tr.v.* **installed, installing, installs 1.** To connect or set in position and prepare for use: *The company installed the new phones yesterday.* **2.** To place in an office, rank, or position, usually with ceremony: *The new mayor was installed soon after election.* **3.** To settle; place:

The mice installed themselves behind the baseboard.

installation (ĭn′stə-lā′shən) *n.* **1.** The act of installing: *the installation of telephones.* **2.** A system of machinery or other apparatus set up for use: *A computer system is a complicated installation.* **3.** A military base.

installment[1] (ĭn-stôl′mənt) *n.* **1.** One of a series of payments in settlement of a debt: *We paid $1,600 for our TV set in four installments of $400 each.* **2.** A portion of something issued or presented at intervals: *The final installment of the trilogy didn't disappoint its audience.*

installment[2] (ĭn-stôl′mənt) *n.* The act of installing; installation: *the installment of new plumbing.*

instance (ĭn′stəns) *n.* A case or example: *This is another instance of her great leadership.* ◆ **for instance** As an example; for example.

instant (ĭn′stənt) *n.* **1.** A period of time almost too brief to detect; a moment. **2.** A precise point in time: *Please call the instant they arrive.* ❖ *adj.* **1.** Immediate: *an instant success.* **2.** Urgent: *an instant need.* **3.** Prepared by a manufacturer for quick preparation by the consumer: *instant cocoa.*

instantaneous (ĭn′stən-tā′nē-əs) *adj.* Happening without delay; immediate: *an instantaneous reaction.* —**in′stan·ta′ne·ous·ly** *adv.*

instantiate (ĭn-stăn′shē-āt′) *tr.v.* **instantiated, instantiating, instantiates** To represent (an abstract concept) by a concrete or tangible example: *an incident that instantiates the difficulty of reporting in a war zone.* —**in·stan′ti·a′tion** *n.* —**in·stan′tia·tive** (ĭn-stăn′shə-tĭv) *adj.*

instantly (ĭn′stənt-lē) *adv.* At once; immediately: *The frog was instantly transformed into a prince.*

instant message *n.* An electronic message transmitted by instant messaging.

instant messaging *n.* The transmission of an electronic message over a computer network using software that immediately displays the message in a window on the screen when it arrives.

instead (ĭn-stĕd′) *adv.* In place of something previously mentioned; as a substitute or alternative: *They didn't have cider, so I got apple juice instead.*

instead of *prep.* In place of; rather than: *They walked home instead of taking the bus.*

instep (ĭn′stĕp′) *n.* **1.** The arched middle part of the human foot between the toes and the ankle. **2.** The part of a shoe or stocking covering this part of the foot.

instigate (ĭn′stĭ-gāt′) *tr.v.* **instigated, instigating, instigates 1.** To bring about or initiate: *an incident that instigated an uprising.* **2.** To urge or provoke (someone) to do something. —**in′sti·ga′tion** *n.* —**in′sti·ga′tor** *n.*

instill (ĭn-stĭl′) *tr.v.* **instilled, instilling, instills** To introduce little by little; implant gradually: *Regular practice instilled a sense of confidence in the players.*

instinct (ĭn′stĭngkt′) *n.* **1.** An inborn pattern of behavior that is characteristic of a given species: *the salmon's instinct to swim upstream to spawn.* **2.** A natural talent or ability: *an instinct for politics.*

instinctive (ĭn-stĭngk′tĭv) *adj.* Relating to or arising from instinct: *Building nests is instinctive behavior in most birds.* —**in·stinc′tive·ly** *adv.*

institute (ĭn′stĭ-tōōt′) *tr.v.* **instituted, instituting, institutes** To establish, organize, and set in operation; initiate: *The government instituted a new trade policy.* See Synonyms at **establish.** ❖ *n.* **1.** An organization established to promote a cause: *a research institute.* **2.** An educational institution: *an art institute.* **3.** The building or buildings of such an institution.

institution (ĭn'stĭ-tōō'shən) *n.* **1.** The act or process of instituting: *the institution of new rules for student conduct.* **2.** A custom, practice, or pattern of behavior that is important in the cultural life of a society: *the institution of marriage.* **3a.** An organization or foundation, especially one dedicated to public service: *an educational institution.* **b.** The building or buildings housing such an organization. **c.** A place for the care of people who are destitute, disabled, or mentally ill. —**in·sti·tu'tion·al** *adj.*

institutionalize (ĭn'stĭ-tōō'shə-nə-līz') *tr.v.* **institutionalized, institutionalizing, institutionalizes 1.** To place (a person) in the care of an institution. **2.** To make part of a structured system: *rules that were intended to institutionalize nondiscriminatory practices throughout the corporation.*

instruct (ĭn-strŭkt') *tr.v.* **instructed, instructing, instructs 1.** To give knowledge or skill to; teach: *Our guide instructed us in the basics of rock-climbing.* See Synonyms at **teach. 2.** To give orders to; direct: *The coach instructed us to run around the track.*

instruction (ĭn-strŭk'shən) *n.* **1.** Something that is taught; a lesson: *instructions in modern and classical music.* **2.** The act of teaching or instructing; education. **3.** A sequence of code that instructs a computer to perform a particular operation. **4. instructions** Directions; orders: *The model airplane came with clear instructions.* —**in·struc'tion·al** *adj.*

instructive (ĭn-strŭk'tĭv) *adj.* Providing knowledge or information: *an instructive example; an instructive experience.* —**in·struc'tive·ly** *adv.*

instructor (ĭn-strŭk'tər) *n.* **1.** A person who instructs; a teacher. **2.** A college or university teacher ranking below an assistant professor.

instrument (ĭn'strə-mənt) *n.* **1.** An implement used to do work, especially one used by a physician, dentist, or scientist: *surgical instruments.* **2.** A device used for playing or producing music: *the instruments of an orchestra.* **3.** A device for recording or measuring, as in a control system: *A fuel gauge and a compass are important instruments in an aircraft.* **4.** A means by which something is done: *The law to protect jobs was an important instrument of the governor's policy.* **5.** A legal document, such as a deed or will.

instrumental (ĭn'strə-mĕn'tl) *adj.* **1.** Serving as the means; useful; helpful: *Her fund-raising skill was instrumental in getting the bike path built.* **2.** Performed on or written for musical instruments: *instrumental music.* —**in'stru·men'tal·ly** *adv.*

instrumentalist (ĭn'strə-mĕn'tl-ĭst) *n.* A person who plays a musical instrument.

instrumentality (ĭn'strə-mĕn-tăl'ĭ-tē) *n., pl.* **instrumentalities 1.** The quality or condition of being instrumental; usefulness. **2.** A means; a help to achieve an end.

instrumentation (ĭn'strə-mĕn-tā'shən) *n.* **1.** The arrangement or orchestration of music for instruments. **2.** The application or use of instruments.

insubordinate (ĭn'sə-bôr'dn-ĭt) *adj.* Not submissive to authority: *punished for being insubordinate to a superior.* —**in'sub·or'di·nate·ly** *adv.* —**in'sub·or'di·na'tion** (ĭn'-sə-bôr'dn-ā'shən) *n.*

insubstantial (ĭn'səb-stăn'shəl) *adj.* **1.** Not firm or solid; weak or flimsy: *a shed made of insubstantial materials.* **2.** Lacking substance or reality; imaginary: *not facts, but insubstantial visions.* **3.** Not substantial in size or amount: *an insubstantial salary.* —**in'sub·stan'ti·al'i·ty** (ĭn'səb-stăn'shē-ăl'ĭ-tē) *n.* —**in'sub·stan'tial·ly** *adv.*

insufferable (ĭn-sŭf'ər-ə-bəl *or* ĭn-sŭf'rə-bəl) *adj.* Difficult or impossible to endure; intolerable: *insufferable rudeness.* —**in·suf'fer·a·bly** *adv.*

insufficiency (ĭn'sə-fĭsh'ən-sē) *n., pl.* **insufficiencies** A lack or deficiency: *An insufficiency of funds made it impossible to build a new pool.*

insufficient (ĭn'sə-fĭsh'ənt) *adj.* Not enough; inadequate: *insufficient rainfall for a good harvest.* —**in'suf·fi'cient·ly** *adv.*

insular (ĭn'sə-lər *or* ĭns'yə-lər) *adj.* **1.** Relating to or forming an island: *England is an insular nation.* **2.** Living or located on an island: *insular people.* **3.** Alone; isolated: *an insular life.* —**in'su·lar'i·ty** (ĭn'sə-lăr'ĭ-tē *or* ĭns'yə-lär'ĭ-tē) *n.*

insulate (ĭn'sə-lāt') *tr.v.* **insulated, insulating, insulates 1.** To cover or surround with a material that prevents the passage of heat, electricity, or sound into or out of: *We insulated our attic to keep out the cold.* **2.** To detach; isolate: *The mountain valley is insulated from outside influences.*

insulation (ĭn'sə-lā'shən) *n.* **1a.** The act of insulating: *Insulation of the windows will keep the cold air out.* **b.** The condition of being insulated: *kept warm by insulation.* **2.** Material that is used for insulating: *There is a layer of fiberglass insulation in the attic.*

insulator (ĭn'sə-lā'tər) *n.* A substance or device that insulates, especially a nonconductor of electricity, heat, or sound.

insulin (ĭn'sə-lĭn) *n.* **1.** A hormone that is produced in the pancreas and acts to regulate the amount of sugar in the blood. **2.** A drug containing this hormone, obtained from the pancreas of animals or produced synthetically and used in treating diabetes.

insult (ĭn-sŭlt') *tr.v.* **insulted, insulting, insults** To treat with insensitivity or contempt; offend: *She insulted me by saying hello to everyone but me.* ❖ *n.* (ĭn'sŭlt') An offensive action or remark. —**in·sult'ing·ly** *adv.*

insuperable (ĭn-sōō'pər-ə-bəl) *adj.* Impossible to overcome; insurmountable: *insuperable odds.* —**in·su'per·a·bly** *adv.*

insupportable (ĭn'sə-pôr'tə-bəl) *adj.* Unbearable; intolerable: *insupportable pain.*

insurance (ĭn-shōōr'əns) *n.* **1.** The act or business of guaranteeing to pay for another's future losses or debts, as in the case of damage, theft, illness, or death. Insurance typically involves transferring the risk of a specified loss to another party in exchange for regular payments of an agreed sum of money. **2a.** A contract making such guarantees to a person or group in return for regular payments. **b.** The total amount to be paid to the party insured: *bought $500,000 of life insurance.* **c.** A periodic amount paid for such coverage; a premium: *Our health insurance went up this year.* **3.** A protective measure: *biking helmets that provide insurance against a head injury.*

insure (ĭn-shōōr') *tr.v.* **insured, insuring, insures 1a.** To provide or arrange insurance for: *companies that insure homeowners.* **b.** To acquire or have insurance for: *insured her car for theft.* **2.** To make sure or certain; guarantee; ensure: *Proper diet helps to insure good health.* —**in·sur'er** *n.* —SEE NOTE AT **assure.**

insured (ĭn-shōōrd') *n., pl.* **insured** or **insureds** A person or thing covered by an insurance policy.

insurgence (ĭn-sûr'jəns) *n.* An uprising; a rebellion.

insurgent (ĭn-sûr'jənt) *adj.* Rising in revolt: *The insurgent forces overthrew the government.* ❖ *n.* A person who revolts against authority; a rebel.

insurmountable (ĭn′sər-moun′tə-bəl) *adj.* Impossible to overcome; insuperable: *an insurmountable obstacle.*

insurrection (ĭn′sə-rĕk′shən) *n.* An uprising against an established authority or government; a rebellion. —**in′-sur·rec′tion·ist** *n.*

intact (ĭn-tăkt′) *adj.* Not weakened, injured, damaged, or separated; whole: *The contents were intact in spite of the damage to the box.*

intake (ĭn′tāk′) *n.* **1.** An opening through which a liquid or gas enters a container or pipe: *an intake clogged with dirt.* **2a.** The act of taking in: *an efficient air intake.* **b.** Something, or the amount of something, taken in: *an adequate intake of food.*

intangible (ĭn-tăn′jə-bəl) *adj.* **1.** Incapable of being touched; lacking physical substance: *Inner satisfaction is one of the intangible rewards of community service.* **2.** Incapable of being defined; vague; elusive: *an intangible change of attitude.* ❖ *n.* Something intangible: *intangibles such as goodwill and dedication.* —**in·tan′gi·bly** *adv.*

integer (ĭn′tĭ-jər) *n.* A positive or negative whole number or zero.

integral (ĭn′tĭ-grəl *or* ĭn-tĕg′rəl) *adj.* **1.** Necessary to form a whole or make something complete: *Rafters are an integral part of a roof.* **2.** Having everything essential; entire. **3.** (ĭn′tĭ-grəl) Involving or expressed as an integer or integers. —**in′te·gral·ly** *adv.*

integrate (ĭn′tĭ-grāt′) *v.* **integrated, integrating, integrates** —*tr.* **1.** To make into a whole by bringing all parts together; unify: *Our school integrated math and computer courses last fall.* **2.** To open to people of all races or ethnic groups without restriction; desegregate. —*intr.* To become integrated.

integrated (ĭn′tĭ-grā′tĭd) *adj.* **1.** Having people of all races; desegregated: *an integrated neighborhood.* **2.** Having all parts combined into a whole; united: *an integrated system.*

integrated circuit *n.* An electronic circuit whose components, such as transistors and resistors, are etched or deposited on a single slice of semiconductor material to produce a chip.

integration (ĭn′tĭ-grā′shən) *n.* **1.** The act or process of integrating. **2.** The bringing of people of different racial or ethnic groups into equal association; desegregation. —**in′te·gra′tion·ist** *n.*

integrity (ĭn-tĕg′rĭ-tē) *n.* **1.** Moral uprightness; honesty: *A judge must be a person of integrity.* **2.** Completeness; unity: *The country maintained its integrity by defending its borders.*

integument (ĭn-tĕg′yŏō-mənt) *n.* A natural outer covering of an animal or plant, as skin, a seed coat, or a shell.

intellect (ĭn′tl-ĕkt′) *n.* **1.** The power of the mind to think, reason, and learn. **2.** Great intelligence or mental ability: *We admire people of intellect.* **3.** A person of great intellectual ability: *a gathering of scientific intellects.*

intellectual (ĭn′tl-ĕk′chōō-əl) *adj.* **1.** Engaging the intellect: *an intellectual discussion.* **2.** Having or showing intelligence: *an intellectual person.* ❖ *n.* A person of intelligence, especially a person who is informed and interested in many things. —**in′tel·lec′tu·al·ly** *adv.*

intelligence (ĭn-tĕl′ə-jəns) *n.* **1.** The ability to gain, understand, and use knowledge: *a person of average intelligence.* **2.** Information or news, especially secret information about an enemy. **3.** An agency or office employed in gathering secret information.

intelligence quotient *n.* A number seen as a measure of a person's intelligence. The number is usually derived from a person's score on an intelligence test compared to the scores of others who have taken the same test, with the average score set at 100.

intelligence test *n.* A test used to measure intelligence or mental development.

intelligent (ĭn-tĕl′ə-jənt) *adj.* **1.** Having intelligence, especially of a high degree: *an intelligent history student.* **2.** Showing intelligence; wise or thoughtful: *an intelligent decision.* —**in·tel′li·gent·ly** *adv.*
✦ **SYNONYMS intelligent, bright, brilliant, quick-witted, smart** *adj.*

intelligentsia (ĭn-tĕl′ə-jĕnt′sē-ə) *n.* The most educated group of people in a society.

intelligible (ĭn-tĕl′ĭ-jə-bəl) *adj.* Capable of being understood; comprehensible: *We need someone to write intelligible instructions on using this computer program.* —**in·tel′li·gi·bly** *adv.*

intemperance (ĭn-tĕm′pər-əns *or* ĭn-tĕm′prəns) *n.* Lack of self-control, as in giving in to a craving for food or not controlling one's temper.

intemperate (ĭn-tĕm′pər-ĭt *or* ĭn-tĕm′prĭt) *adj.* Not temperate or moderate; excessive. —**in·tem′per·ate·ly** *adv.*

intend (ĭn-tĕnd′) *tr.v.* **intended, intending, intends** **1.** To have as a purpose; have in mind; plan: *We intend to get an early start.* **2.** To design for a specific purpose or use: *This saw is intended to cut metal.*

intended (ĭn-tĕn′dĭd) *adj.* Planned; intentional: *an intended result.* ❖ *n. Informal* A person who is engaged to be married; a fiancé or fiancée: *My sister and her intended came along.*

intense (ĭn-tĕns′) *adj.* **intenser, intensest** **1.** Existing in an extreme degree; very strong: *an intense blue; intense heat.* **2.** Having or showing strong feeling or great seriousness: *an intense look; an intense music teacher.* —**in·tense′ly** *adv.*

intensifier (ĭn-tĕn′sə-fī′ər) *n.* In grammar, a word, phrase, prefix, or suffix that gives force or emphasis. For example, in the sentences *We are very pleased* and *That student is extremely intelligent,* the adverbs *very* and *extremely* are intensifiers.

intensify (ĭn-tĕn′sə-fī′) *tr. & intr.v.* **intensified, intensifying, intensifies** To make or become intense or more intense: *The police intensified their investigation.* *Our review sessions intensified as exams drew near.* —**in·ten′-si·fi·ca′tion** (ĭn-tĕn′sə-fĭ-kā′shən) *n.*

intensity (ĭn-tĕn′sĭ-tē) *n., pl.* **intensities** **1.** Extreme force, strength, or concentration: *Our team played with emotional intensity.* **2.** The strength of a color: *The two colors vary in intensity.* **3.** The amount of strength of electricity, heat, light, or sound per unit of area, volume, or mass.

intensive (ĭn-tĕn′sĭv) *adj.* **1.** Marked by intensity; deep; concentrated: *intensive study.* **2.** In grammar, giving emphasis: *an intensive adverb.* ❖ *n.* An intensifier. —**in·ten′sive·ly** *adv.*

intensive care *n.* Health care, especially in a hospital, in which a severely ill or injured person is closely watched at all times.

intent (ĭn-tĕnt′) *n.* A purpose or aim; an intention: *It was never my intent to start an argument.* ❖ *adj.* **1.** Showing concentration; intense: *an intent expression while studying.* **2.** Firmly fixed on some purpose; determined: *We are intent on securing a new trade agreement.* ✦ **for all intents and purposes** *or* **to all intents and purposes** In every practical sense; practically. —in·tent′ly *adv.* —in·tent′ness *n.*

intention (ĭn-tĕn′shən) *n.* **1.** A plan or purpose in doing something. **2. intentions** Purposes or motives in mind: *with the best of intentions.*

intentional (ĭn-tĕn′shə-nəl) *adj.* Done deliberately; meant; intended: *an intentional slight.* —in·ten′tion·al·ly *adv.*

inter (ĭn-tûr′) *tr.v.* **interred, interring, inters** To place in a grave; bury.

inter– A prefix that means: **1.** Between; among: *international.* **2.** Mutually; together: *interact.*

WORD BUILDING The prefix **inter–** comes from the Latin prefix *inter-*, from the preposition *inter,* meaning "between, among." Thus the word *intercede,* in which *inter-* combines with the Latin verb *cēdere,* "to go," means "to go between." Similarly, *interject,* which comes from Latin *iacere,* "to throw," means literally "to throw something between or among others." And *intervene,* coming from Latin *venīre,* "to come," means "to come between people or things." In English, *inter-* is still producing new words, such as *interfaith, intertwine,* and *intercellular.*

---

interact (ĭn′tər-ăkt′) *intr.v.* **interacted, interacting, interacts** To act on or affect each other: *The mechanic's adjustments made the gears interact more smoothly.* —in′ter·ac′tion *n.*

interactive (ĭn′tər-ăk′tĭv) *adj.* **1.** Relating to a computer program that responds to user activity: *interactive computer games.* **2.** Relating to a form of television entertainment in which the viewer participates directly.

interbreed (ĭn′tər-brēd′) *v.* **interbred** (ĭn′tər-brĕd′), **interbreeding, interbreeds** —*intr.* **1.** To breed with an individual of another breed, variety, or species: *Dogs and wolves sometimes interbreed.* **2.** To breed with another individual of the same species, especially as part of a larger group: *found that bullfrogs from different ponds were interbreeding.* —*tr.* To cause (an organism or group of organisms) to breed with one of a different variety or species: *interbreed two varieties of cattle.*

intercede (ĭn′tər-sēd′) *intr.v.* **interceded, interceding, intercedes** **1.** To plead on another's behalf; seek some favor for another: *Two of my professors interceded to get my scholarship reinstated.* **2.** To act as a mediator in a dispute: *The government can appoint people to intercede in certain labor disputes.*

intercellular (ĭn′tər-sĕl′yə-lər) *adj.* Located or occurring between or among cells: *intercellular fluid; intercellular communication.*

intercept (ĭn′tər-sĕpt′) *tr.v.* **intercepted, intercepting, intercepts** **1.** To stop or interrupt the intended course or progress of: *intercept a messenger.* **2.** In sports, to gain possession of (an opponent's pass), as in football or basketball. **3.** To mark off (a space) between two points or lines. ❖ *n.* (ĭn′tər-sĕpt′) In a Cartesian coordinate system, the point or coordinate at which a line, curve, or surface intersects a coordinate axis. For example, if a curve intersects the x-axis at (4,0), then 4 is the curve's x-intercept.

interception (ĭn′tər-sĕp′shən) *n.* **1.** The act or an instance of intercepting: *The interception of an enemy message provided important information.* **2.** In sports, a pass that is intercepted, especially in football.

interceptor also **intercepter** (ĭn′tər-sĕp′tər) *n.* **1.** A person or thing that intercepts. **2.** A fast-climbing, highly maneuverable fighter plane designed to intercept enemy aircraft.

intercession (ĭn′tər-sĕsh′ən) *n.* **1.** The act of interceding. **2.** An earnest request made in favor of another. —in′ter·ces′sor *n.*

interchange (ĭn′tər-chānj′) *v.* **interchanged, interchanging, interchanges** —*tr.* **1.** To switch each of (two things) into the place of the other: *If you interchange the first and last letters of the word "pal," it becomes "lap."* **2.** To give and receive mutually; exchange: *A vigorous discussion is the best way to interchange ideas.* —*intr.* To change places with each other. ❖ *n.* (ĭn′tər-chānj′) **1.** The act of interchanging: *Trade is the interchange of commodities.* **2.** A highway intersection that allows traffic to flow freely from one road to another without crossing another line of traffic.

interchangeable (ĭn′tər-chān′jə-bəl) *adj.* Capable of being switched or interchanged: *These two cars have interchangeable parts.* —in′ter·change′a·bly *adv.*

intercollegiate (ĭn′tər-kə-lē′jĭt *or* ĭn′tər-kə-lē′jē-ĭt) *adj.* Involving two or more colleges or universities: *an intercollegiate tournament.*

intercom (ĭn′tər-kŏm′) *n.* An electronic communication system, as between rooms of a building or areas of a ship.

intercommunicate (ĭn′tər-kə-myōō′nĭ-kāt′) *intr.v.* **intercommunicated, intercommunicating, intercommunicates** To communicate with each other. —in′ter·com·mu′ni·ca′tion *n.*

interconnect (ĭn′tər-kə-nĕkt′) *intr. & tr.v.* **interconnected, interconnecting, interconnects** To connect or be connected with each other. —in′ter·con·nec′tion *n.*

intercontinental (ĭn′tər-kŏn′tə-nĕn′tl) *adj.* **1.** Involving or extending between two or more continents: *intercontinental weather patterns.* **2.** Having the capability of traveling from one continent to another: *an intercontinental airline.*

intercourse (ĭn′tər-kôrs′) *n.* **1.** Sexual intercourse. **2.** Dealings or communication between people or groups: *cafés as places for social intercourse.*

interdenominational (ĭn′tər-də-nŏm′ə-nā′shə-nəl) *adj.* Involving different religious denominations: *an interdenominational service.*

interdependent (ĭn′tər-dĭ-pĕn′dənt) *adj.* Dependent on one another; mutually dependent. —in′ter·de·pen′dence *n.* —in′ter·de·pen′dent·ly *adv.*

interdict (ĭn′tər-dĭkt′) *tr.v.* **interdicted, interdicting, interdicts** **1.** To prohibit (an action or thing) or forbid (someone) to do something, especially by order of a legal body or church. **2.** To halt the activities or entry of; block: *were successful in interdicting the smuggled goods.* ❖ *n.* (ĭn′tər-dĭkt′) **1.** An authoritative prohibition, especially by court order. **2.** In the Roman Catholic Church, a censure that bars a person, group, or district from participation in most sacraments. —in′ter·dic′tion *n.*

interest (ĭn′trĭst *or* ĭn′tər-ĭst) *n.* **1a.** A feeling of curiosity or concern about something: *An exciting story will arouse the reader's interest.* **b.** The quality of arousing such a feeling: *a tedious speech that lacked interest for me.* **c.** A subject that arouses such a feeling: *Music, science fiction, and computer games are among my interests.* **2.** often **interests** Advantage; benefit: *The company's decision to burn coal is not in the public interest.* *She kept her own interests in mind.* **3a.** A right, claim, or legal share in something: *an interest in a business.* **b.** Something in which such a right, claim, or share is held: *American interests in China.* **c.** A group of people holding such a right, claim, or share. **4.** A charge for borrowing money, usually a percentage of the amount borrowed: *a bank with an interest rate of five percent.* **5.** An excess or bonus beyond what is expected or due: *Our host paid back the compliment with interest.* ❖ *tr.v.* **interested, interesting, interests 1.** To arouse the curiosity or hold the attention of: *Modern sculpture interests me a lot.* **2.** To cause to become involved or concerned: *The salesperson tried to interest us in the options on the car.* ◆ **in the interest of** or **in the interests of** To the advantage of; for the sake of: *I agreed to switch chores in the interest of peace.*

interested (ĭn′trĭ-stĭd *or* ĭn′tə-rĕs′tĭd) *adj.* **1.** Having or showing interest, fascination, or concern: *Good teaching usually produces interested students.* **2.** Having a right, claim, or share: *The interested parties met to settle the dispute.* —**in′ter·est·ed·ly** *adv.*

interest group *n.* A group of people working to support a particular cause, such as an item of legislation.

interesting (ĭn′trĭ-stĭng *or* ĭn′tə-rĕs′tĭng) *adj.* Arousing or holding interest or attention. —**in′ter·est·ing·ly** *adv.*

✦ **SYNONYMS interesting, engaging, fascinating, intriguing** *adj.*

interface (ĭn′tər-fās′) *n.* **1.** A surface forming a common boundary between any two regions, bodies, or phases. **2.** A point at which two systems or groups interact: *the interface between religion and politics.* **3a.** A system of interaction or communication between a computer and another entity such as a printer, a network, or a human user. **b.** The layout or design of the interactive elements of a computer program, a website, or an electronic device. ❖ *intr.v.* (ĭn′tər-fās′) **interfaced, interfacing, interfaces** To work together or communicate, especially with a computer or other electronic device.

interfaith (ĭn′tər-fāth′) *adj.* Relating to or involving people of different religious faiths: *attended an interfaith gathering.*

interfere (ĭn′tər-fîr′) *intr.v.* **interfered, interfering, interferes 1.** To get in the way as an obstacle or hindrance: *The rain interfered with our plans to go on a picnic.* **2.** To intrude in the affairs of others; meddle.

interference (ĭn′tər-fîr′əns) *n.* **1.** The act or an instance of interfering: *Human interference has upset the balance in the environment.* **2.** In sports, the obstruction of an opposing player in a manner prohibited by the rules. **3.** In football, the legal blocking of defensive players to make way for a ball carrier. **4.** The combining of two or more waves of the same frequency, resulting in a new wave or, if the waves match up with each other, the cancellation of both waves. The amplitude of any new wave may be larger or smaller than the amplitude of the combining waves, depending on the differences in their peaks and troughs. **5.** In electronics: **a.** The distortion or interruption of one broadcast signal by others. **b.** The distorted part of a broadcast signal; static.

interferon (ĭn′tər-fîr′ŏn′) *n.* Any of a group of proteins that are produced by animal cells in response to infection by a virus and that prevent replication of the virus. Synthetic interferons are used in the treatment of certain diseases.

interim (ĭn′tər-ĭm) *n.* An interval of time between two events, periods, or processes: *During the interim between expeditions, the explorer wrote a book of memoirs.* ❖ *adj.*

Relating to or during an interim; temporary: *After an interim job as a cook, he returned to college.*

interior (ĭn-tîr′ē-ər) *adj.* **1.** Relating to or located in the inside; inner: *The interior surfaces of the pipe are corroded.* **2.** Located away from a coast or border; inland: *Interior Australia is sparsely populated.* ❖ *n.* **1.** The inner part of something; the inside: *the interior of a house.* **2.** The inland part of a country or geographical area: *The interior of Alaska is very mountainous.* **3.** The affairs within a country; domestic affairs.

interior angle *n.* **1.** Any of the four angles formed inside two straight lines intersected by a third straight line. **2.** An angle formed by two adjacent sides of a polygon and included within the polygon.

interior decorator *n.* A person who specializes in the decoration and furnishing of the interiors of homes, offices, or other buildings.

interj. An abbreviation of interjection.

interject (ĭn′tər-jĕkt′) *tr.v.* **interjected, interjecting, interjects 1.** To say suddenly, often interrupting the remarks of another: *"I disagree," she interjected.* **2.** To put in between or among other things; insert: *The speaker paused in the talk to interject a personal remark.*

interjection (ĭn′tər-jĕk′shən) *n.* **1.** A sudden phrase or remark that is interjected; an exclamation. **2a.** The part of speech that expresses emotion and can stand alone. **b.** A word belonging to this part of speech. *Ouch!* and *Hurrah!* are interjections. —**in′ter·jec′tion·al** *adj.*

interlace (ĭn′tər-lās′) *tr. & intr.v.* **interlaced, interlacing, interlaces** To weave, lace, or twine together: *A weaver interlaces threads in order to make cloth.*

interlard (ĭn′tər-lärd′) *tr.v.* **interlarded, interlarding, interlards** To mix something different into; intersperse: *To illustrate the point, the writer interlarded the report with many examples.*

interlock (ĭn′tər-lŏk′) *tr. & intr.v.* **interlocked, interlocking, interlocks** To unite firmly or join tightly, as by hooking: *The dancers form a circle and interlock hands.*

interloper (ĭn′tər-lō′pər) *n.* A person who intrudes or interferes in the affairs of others; a meddler.

interlude (ĭn′tər-lōōd′) *n.* **1.** An intervening episode or period of time: *There was a brief interlude of sunshine on this mostly cloudy day.* **2.** A short entertainment between the acts of a play. **3.** A short piece of music that occurs between parts of a longer composition.

intermarry (ĭn′tər-măr′ē) *intr.v.* **intermarried, intermarrying, intermarries 1.** To marry someone of another religion, nationality, or ethnic group. **2.** To be bound together by marriage, as families, religious groups, or ethnic groups, for example. **3.** To marry someone who is a member of one's own family, clan, or tribe. —**in′ter·mar′riage** (ĭn′tər-măr′ĭj) *n.*

intermediary (ĭn′tər-mē′dē-ĕr′ē) *adj.* **1.** Acting as a mediator: *A labor negotiator plays an intermediary role between management and striking workers.* **2.** Existing or occurring between; intermediate: *A tadpole is an intermediary stage in the development of a frog.* ❖ *n., pl.* **intermediaries** A person or group acting as a mediator between opposing parties to bring about an agreement.

intermediate (ĭn′tər-mē′dē-ĭt) *adj.* Being or occurring between; in the middle: *Middle school is intermediate between high school and elementary school.* ❖ *n.* Something intermediate.

interment (ĭn-tûr′mənt) *n.* The act of interring; burial.

intermezzo (ĭn′tər-mĕt′sō *or* ĭn′tər-mĕd′zō) *n., pl.* **inter-**

mezzos or **intermezzi** (ĭn′tər-mĕt′sē or ĭn′tər-mĕd′zē) **1.** A short piece of music played between sections of a long musical work. **2.** A brief entertainment between two acts of a play.

interminable (ĭn-tûr′mə-nə-bəl) *adj.* Having or seeming to have no end; endless: *fell asleep during the second act of the interminable play.* —**in·ter′mi·na·bly** *adv.*

intermingle (ĭn′tər-mĭng′gəl) *tr. & intr.v.* **intermingled, intermingling, intermingles** To mix or become mixed together: *A party presents a good chance to intermingle with others.*

intermission (ĭn′tər-mĭsh′ən) *n.* An interval between periods of activity; a pause: *The orchestra took a short intermission during the concert.* See Synonyms at **pause.**

intermittent (ĭn′tər-mĭt′nt) *adj.* Stopping and starting at intervals; not continuous: *The foghorn sounded intermittent blasts at intervals of 15 seconds.* —**in′ter·mit′tent·ly** *adv.*

intermix (ĭn′tər-mĭks′) *tr. & intr.v.* **intermixed, intermixing, intermixes** To mix or become mixed together: *Oil and water do not intermix.*

intern (ĭn′tûrn′) *n.* An advanced student or recent graduate undergoing practical training, especially a recent medical school graduate who is undergoing supervised training in a hospital or clinic. ❖ *v.* **interned, interning, interns** —*intr.* To train or serve as an intern. —*tr.* (*also* ĭn-tûrn′) To detain or confine within a country or place, especially in wartime: *intern an enemy ship.* —**in·tern′-ment** *n.*

internal (ĭn-tûr′nəl) *adj.* **1.** Located within the limits or surface of something; inner; interior: *the internal workings of a clock.* **2.** Located or acting inside the body: *pills and other internal medicines.* **3.** Relating to domestic affairs within a country or organization: *Environmental issues are no longer internal political matters but require global attention.* —**in·ter′nal·ly** *adv.*

internal-combustion engine (ĭn-tûr′nəl-kəm-bŭs′chən) *n.* An engine whose fuel is burned inside the engine itself rather than in an outside furnace or burner. A gasoline or diesel engine is an internal-combustion engine; a steam engine is not.

internalize (ĭn-tûr′nə-līz′) *tr.v.* **internalized, internalizing, internalizes** To take in and make an integral part of one's attitudes or beliefs: *had internalized the cultural values of the Poles after a year of living in Warsaw.* —**in·ter′-nal·i·za′tion** (ĭn-tûr′nə-lĭ-zā′shən) *n.*

internal medicine *n.* The branch of medicine that deals with the diagnosis and nonsurgical treatment of diseases in adults.

international (ĭn′tər-năsh′ə-nəl) *adj.* Relating to or involving two or more nations: *The United Nations is an international organization.* —**in′ter·na′tion·al·ly** *adv.*

International Date Line *n.* An imaginary line through the Pacific Ocean roughly along the 180th meridian, agreed upon as the place where each new calendar day begins. The calendar day to the east of the line is one day earlier than to the west.

internationalism (ĭn′tər-năsh′ə-nə-lĭz′əm) *n.* A policy or principle of cooperation among nations for mutual benefit.

internationalize (ĭn′tər-năsh′ə-nə-līz′) *tr.v.* **internationalized, internationalizing, internationalizes** To put under international control; make international: *a peace treaty that internationalized the fishing grounds.*

International System *n.* A system of units that are used as international standards especially in science for measuring length, time, electric current, temperature, light intensity, and mass. For example, in the International System (abbreviated SI), the unit of length is the meter and the unit of time is the second. See table at **measurement.**

internecine (ĭn′tər-nĕs′ēn′ or ĭn′tər-nĕs′īn) *adj.* **1.** Destructive or fatal to both sides: *A long internecine war impoverished both groups in the region.* **2.** Relating to struggle within a nation, organization, or group: *The delegates engaged in an internecine struggle for leadership of the party.*

internee (ĭn′tûr-nē′) *n.* A person who is interned or confined, especially during a war.

Internet also **internet** (ĭn′tər-nĕt′) *n.* A publicly accessible system of networks that connects computers around the world and that transmits and receives data using a common software protocol called TCP/IP (Transmission Control Protocol/Internet Protocol).

internist (ĭn-tûr′nĭst) *n.* A physician who specializes in internal medicine.

internship (ĭn′tûrn-shĭp′) *n.* A period of service as an intern.

interphase (ĭn′tər-fāz′) *n.* The stage of a cell between two occurrences of cell division.

interplanetary (ĭn′tər-plăn′ĭ-tĕr′ē) *adj.* Located or occurring between planets; in the region of the planets: *interplanetary flight.*

interplay (ĭn′tər-plā′) *n.* Mutual action or influence; interaction: *The interplay between the two main characters provided most of the humor in the movie.*

interpolate (ĭn-tûr′pə-lāt′) *tr.v.* **interpolated, interpolating, interpolates** **1.** In mathematics, to estimate (an unknown value, as of a logarithm or trigonometric function) between two known values. **2.** To change (a text) by inserting new material: *This manuscript has been so interpolated it is hard to recognize the original.* **3.** To insert or add (new material) to a text. —**in·ter′-po·la′tion** *n.*

interpose (ĭn′tər-pōz′) *v.* **interposed, interposing, interposes** —*tr.* **1.** To put between parts; insert: *Winter ice interposes a barrier between the harbor and the islands.* **2.** To interject (a remark or question) into a conversation. —*intr.* **1.** To come between things. **2.** To come between parties in a dispute; intervene: *The coach interposed in the argument between the players.* —**in′ter·po·si′tion** (ĭn′-tər-pə-zĭsh′ən) *n.*

interpret (ĭn-tûr′prĭt) *v.* **interpreted, interpreting, interprets** —*tr.* **1.** To explain the meaning of: *The critic interprets the poem in an essay.* **2.** To understand in one's own way; construe: *We interpreted his smile to be an agreement.* **3.** To present the meaning of, especially through artistic performance: *an actor interpreting a role.* **4.** To translate (something). —*intr.* To serve as an interpreter, especially for speakers of a foreign language.

interpretation (ĭn-tûr′prĭ-tā′shən) *n.* **1.** The act or process of interpreting: *the interpretation of statistical data.* **2.** An explanation of the meaning of something, especially of a work of art: *an unusual interpretation of* Romeo and Juliet. **3.** A performer's unique version of a work of art, such as a song or dance.

interpreter (ĭn-tûr′prĭ-tər) *n.* **1.** A person who translates from one language to another, especially while a conversation or speech is taking place. **2.** A person who interprets or explains something.

interpretive (ĭn-tûr′prĭ-tĭv) also **interpretative** (ĭn-tûr′-prĭ-tā′tĭv) *adj.* Relating to or marked by interpretation; explanatory: *an interpretive comment.*

interracial (ĭn′tər-rā′shəl) *adj.* Relating to or involving people of different races: *an interracial marriage.*

interregnum (ĭn′tər-rĕg′nəm) *n., pl.* **interregnums** or **interregna** (ĭn′tər-rĕg′nə) The period between the end of one ruler's reign and the beginning of the next ruler's reign.

interrelate (ĭn′tər-rĭ-lāt′) *tr. & intr.v.* **interrelated, interrelating, interrelates** To place in or come into mutual relationship. —**in′ter·re·la′tion** *n.* —**in′ter·re·la′tion·ship′** *n.*

interrelated (ĭn′tər-rĭ-lā′tĭd) *adj.* Related to each other; affecting one another: *interrelated conditions of starvation and disease.*

interrogate (ĭn-tĕr′ə-gāt′) *tr.v.* **interrogated, interrogating, interrogates** To question formally and closely: *The police interrogated witnesses of the accident.* —**in·ter′ro·ga′tion** *n.* —**in·ter′ro·ga′tor** *n.*

interrogative (ĭn′tə-rŏg′ə-tĭv) *adj.* **1.** Asking a question or having the nature of a question: *an interrogative sentence.* **2.** Used in asking a question: When, why, *and* where *are interrogative words.* ❖ *n.* **1.** A word or form used in asking a question. For example, in the questions *Where did you go?* and *Whom did you see?* the words *where* and *whom* are interrogatives. **2.** A sentence or expression that asks a question.

interrogatory (ĭn′tə-rŏg′ə-tôr′ē) *adj.* Interrogative.

interrupt (ĭn′tə-rŭpt′) *v.* **interrupted, interrupting, interrupts** —*tr.* **1.** To stop (someone engaged in an activity) by saying or doing something: *I was about to finish the joke when my friend interrupted me.* **2.** To cause a sudden or abrupt break in; break the continuity of: *Rain interrupted the baseball game for an hour.* —*intr.* To cause an activity to stop by saying or doing something: *Please don't interrupt when I'm talking.* —**in′ter·rup′tion** *n.*

interscholastic (ĭn′tər-skə-lăs′tĭk) *adj.* Existing or conducted between or among schools: *an interscholastic tournament.*

intersect (ĭn′tər-sĕkt′) *v.* **intersected, intersecting, intersects** —*tr.* To cut across or through; divide: *A fence intersects the pasture.* —*intr.* To cut across each other; overlap: *The road intersects with the highway north of town.* —SEE NOTE AT **segment.**

intersection (ĭn′tər-sĕk′shən *or* ĭn′tər-sĕk′shən) *n.* **1.** The act or result of intersecting. **2.** A place where two or more things intersect, especially a place where two or more roads cross. **3.** In geometry, the point where one line, surface, or solid crosses another: *The intersection of two planes determines a straight line.* **4.** In mathematics, the set that contains only those elements shared by two or more sets.

intersexual (ĭn′tər-sĕk′shoo-əl) *adj.* **1.** Existing or occurring between the sexes: *intersexual competition.* **2.** Having reproductive organs or secondary sexual characteristics that are not typical of either males or females. ❖ *n.* An intersexual person. —**in′ter·sex′u·al′i·ty** (ĭn′tər-sĕk′shoo-ăl′ĭ-tē) *n.*

intersperse (ĭn′tər-spûrs′) *tr.v.* **interspersed, interspersing, intersperses 1.** To scatter or insert here and there among other things: *The florist interspersed greens among the flowers.* **2.** To vary by distributing things here and there: *The fashion magazine is interspersed with advertisements.*

interstate (ĭn′tər-stāt′) *adj.* Involving, existing between, or connecting two or more states: *laws concerning interstate commerce.* ❖ *n.* One of a national system of expressways connecting major population centers in the United States.

interstellar (ĭn′tər-stĕl′ər) *adj.* Between or among the stars: *interstellar gases.*

interstitial (ĭn′tər-stĭsh′əl) *adj.* Relating to or situated in the small, narrow spaces between tissues or parts of an organ: *interstitial cells; interstitial fluid.* —**in′ter·sti′tial·ly** *adv.*

intertidal (ĭn′tər-tīd′l) *adj.* Relating to or being the region between the highest point that the sea reaches at high tide and the lowest point it reaches at low tide: *the intertidal zone.*

intertwine (ĭn′tər-twīn′) *tr. & intr.v.* **intertwined, intertwining, intertwines** To join or become joined by twining together: *She intertwined the strands into a braid. The dancers' arms intertwined.*

interval (ĭn′tər-vəl) *n.* **1.** A space between objects, points, or units, especially when making uniform amounts of separation: *We set up hurdles at intervals of 15 yards around the track.* **2.** An amount of time between events, especially of uniform duration separating events in a series: *We ran laps at 30-second intervals.* **3.** In mathematics and statistics, the set of all numbers between two given numbers. **4.** The difference, usually expressed in the number of steps, between two musical pitches.

intervene (ĭn′tər-vēn′) *intr.v.* **intervened, intervening, intervenes 1a.** To come between so as to hinder or change a course of events: *The coach intervened to settle the dispute.* **b.** To interfere, usually with force, in the affairs of another nation. **2.** To come or lie between two things: *The road goes nearly to the shore, but a farm intervenes.* **3.** To come between two events: *A period of calm intervened between stormy sessions of the legislature.*

WORD BUILDING The word root *ven–* in English words comes from the Latin verb *venīre,* "to come." The word **intervene** means literally "to come between, as between two people fighting" (using the prefix *inter–,* "between"). The word **convene** means "to come together, as for a meeting or a **convention**" (*com–, con–,* "together, with"). *Venīre* has a past participle *ventum,* which provides the word **event,** literally an "outcome" (*ē–,* a form of *ex–,* "out, out of").

intervention (ĭn′tər-vĕn′shən) *n.* **1.** The act or process of intervening: *The governor's intervention saved the park from development. Congress debated military intervention.* **2.** Steps taken to prevent or correct a social, educational, or developmental problem: *early intervention for toddlers diagnosed with autism.*

interview (ĭn′tər-vyoo′) *n.* **1.** A face-to-face meeting for a specified purpose: *an interview for a job.* **2a.** A conversation, such as one between a reporter and another person, for the purpose of obtaining information. **b.** An account or broadcast of such information. ❖ *tr.v.* **interviewed, interviewing, interviews** To have an interview with: *The committee interviewed candidates for the job.* —**in′ter·view′er** *n.*

interweave (ĭn′tər-wēv′) *v.* **interwove** (ĭn′tər-wōv′), **interwoven** (ĭn′tər-wō′vən), **interweaving, interweaves** —*tr.* **1.** To weave together: *Cloth is made by interweaving* threads. **2.** To blend; intermix: *The author skillfully interweaves two plots in a single story.* —*intr.* To intertwine.

intestate (ĭn-tĕs′tāt′ *or* ĭn-tĕs′tĭt) *adj.* Having made no legal will: *a person who died intestate.*

intestinal (ĭn-tĕs′tə-nəl) *adj.* Relating to or involving the intestines: *an intestinal parasite.* —**in·tes′ti·nal·ly** *adv.*

intestine (ĭn-tĕs′tĭn) *n.* The part of the digestive tract extending from the stomach to the anus, consisting of the large intestine and small intestine.

intimacy (ĭn′tə-mə-sē) *n., pl.* **intimacies** **1.** The condition of being intimate, especially personal closeness. **2.** An instance of being intimate.

intimate¹ (ĭn′tə-mĭt) *adj.* **1.** Marked by close personal association or familiarity: *intimate friends.* **2.** Very personal; private: *an intimate letter.* **3.** Detailed or thorough: *Cab drivers have an intimate knowledge of the city's streets.* **4.** Relating to or involved in a sexual relationship. ❖ *n.* A close friend or confidant. —**in′ti·mate·ly** *adv.*

intimate² (ĭn′tə-māt′) *tr.v.* **intimated, intimating, intimates** To state or express indirectly; imply: *He intimated that the award would go to someone in our class.* —**in′ti·ma′tion** *n.*

intimidate (ĭn-tĭm′ĭ-dāt′) *tr.v.* **intimidated, intimidating, intimidates** To fill with fear; frighten or discourage: *The rough water intimidated us in our light canoe.* —**in·tim′i·da′tion** *n.* —**in·tim′i·da′tor** *n.*

into (ĭn′tōō) *prep.* **1.** To the inside of: *going into the house.* **2.** So as to be in or within: *enter into an agreement.* **3.** To the action or occupation of: *go into banking.* **4.** To the condition or form of: *break into pieces.* **5.** To a time or place in the course of: *It's getting well into the week.* **6.** Toward; in the direction of: *looking into the distance.* **7.** Against: *run into a tree.* **8.** *Informal* Interested in or involved with: *They are into health foods.* **9.** As a divisor of: *5 into 30 is 6.*

intolerable (ĭn-tŏl′ər-ə-bəl) *adj.* Impossible to tolerate; unbearable: *We found the noise in the sawmill intolerable.* —**in·tol′er·a·bly** *adv.*

intolerance (ĭn-tŏl′ər-əns) *n.* The quality or condition of being intolerant.

intolerant (ĭn-tŏl′ər-ənt) *adj.* **1.** Unwilling to tolerate opinions or beliefs that differ from one's own. **2.** Unable to endure or tolerate physically: *Allergies can make a person intolerant of certain foods.*

intonation (ĭn′tə-nā′shən) *n.* **1.** The way in which the speaking voice rises or falls in pitch in order to convey meaning. **2.** An intoned utterance. **3.** The manner in which musical tones are sung or played, especially with regard to accuracy of pitch.

intone (ĭn-tōn′) *tr. & intr.v.* **intoned, intoning, intones** To recite in a singing or chanting voice: *The choir intoned prayers at several points during the church service.*

intoxicant (ĭn-tŏk′sĭ-kənt) *n.* Something that intoxicates, especially an alcoholic drink.

intoxicate (ĭn-tŏk′sĭ-kāt′) *tr.v.* **intoxicated, intoxicating, intoxicates** **1.** To cause (a person) to lose control of physical or mental powers by means of alcohol or a drug. **2.** To fill with great excitement or enthusiasm; exhilarate: *The grandeur of the mountains intoxicated the tourists.*

intoxicated (ĭn-tŏk′sĭ-kātĭd) *adj.* **1.** Drunk; stupefied: *an intoxicated driver.* **2.** Very excited; overjoyed.

intoxication (ĭn-tŏk′sĭ-kā′shən) *n.* **1.** The condition of being intoxicated, especially drunkenness. **2.** Great excitement or enthusiasm.

intr. An abbreviation of intransitive.

intra– A prefix that means inside of or within: *intravenous.*

intractable (ĭn-trăk′tə-bəl) *adj.* **1.** Difficult to manage, deal with, or change: *an intractable conflict; intractable pain.* **2.** Difficult to persuade or keep under control: *an intractable opponent.* —**in·trac′ta·bly** *adv.*

intramural (ĭn′trə-myŏŏr′əl) *adj.* Involving members of the same school or institution: *our school's intramural athletic program.*

intranet (ĭn′trə-nĕt′) *n.* A privately maintained computer network that can be accessed only by authorized people.

intransigent (ĭn-trăn′zə-jənt) *adj.* Refusing to compromise; stubborn. —**in·tran′si·gence** *n.* —**in·tran′si·gent·ly** *adv.*

intransitive (ĭn-trăn′zĭ-tĭv) *adj.* Relating to a verb that does not require a direct object to complete its meaning. In the sentence *The bell rang loudly,* the verb *rang* is intransitive. —**in·tran′si·tive·ly** *adv.* —SEE NOTE AT **verb.**

intravenous (ĭn′trə-vē′nəs) *adj.* Within or into a vein: *an intravenous injection of serum.* —**in′tra·ve′nous·ly** *adv.*

intrepid (ĭn-trĕp′ĭd) *adj.* Brave; bold; fearless: *Early explorers of Antarctica were intrepid and resourceful.* —**in′tre·pid′i·ty** (ĭn′trə-pĭd′ĭ-tē) *n.* —**in·trep′id·ly** *adv.*

intricacy (ĭn′trĭ-kə-sē) *n., pl.* **intricacies** **1.** The quality or condition of being intricate; complexity: *The intricacy of a maze makes it hard to follow.* **2.** Something intricate; a complication: *The intricacies of human anatomy require years of study.*

intricate (ĭn′trĭ-kĭt) *adj.* Having a complex structure or pattern; elaborate: *the intricate arrangement of gears in a clock.* —**in′tri·cate·ly** *adv.*

intrigue (ĭn′trēg′ *or* ĭn-trēg′) *n.* **1.** Plotting or scheming that is done secretly: *a royal court that was full of intrigue.* **2.** A secret plot or scheme: *the intrigues of foreign spies.* ❖ *v.* (ĭn-trēg′) **intrigued, intriguing, intrigues** —*intr.* To plot or scheme secretly: *The political rivals intrigued against one another.* —*tr.* To excite the interest and curiosity of; fascinate: *The mystery of hibernation has long intrigued biologists.*

intriguing (ĭn-trē′gĭng) *adj.* Exciting the interest or curiosity; fascinating. See Synonyms at **interesting.**

intrinsic (ĭn-trĭn′zĭk *or* ĭn-trĭn′sĭk) *adj.* Relating to the basic nature of a thing; essential; inherent: *He recommended the adventure movie on its intrinsic merits, not on its special effects.* —**in·trin′si·cal·ly** *adv.*

intro (ĭn′trō′) *n., pl.* **intros** *Informal* An introduction.

intro– A prefix that means inward: *introvert.*

introduce (ĭn′trə-dōōs′) *tr.v.* **introduced, introducing, introduces** **1.** To present (someone) by name to another in order to establish an acquaintance: *Please introduce me to your old friend.* **2.** To bring into use or practice: *That company has introduced several new products.* **3.** To provide (someone) with a first experience of something: *My father introduced me to fishing.* **4.** To present for consideration: *introduce legislation in Congress.* **5.** To talk or write about (something) in advance: *The professor introduced the movie with a short lecture.* **6.** To bring in and establish in a new place or environment: *European starlings were introduced into North America in the late 1800s.* **7.** To put in; insert or inject: *introduce a new character into a story.* —**in′tro·duc′er** *n.*

introduction (ĭn′trə-dŭk′shən) *n.* **1.** The act or process of introducing: *The introduction of printing made books cheaper and more widely available.* **2.** Something introduced or brought into use: *Like many European intro-*

ductions, *the starling has established itself widely in North America.* **3.** The first part of a book, speech, or musical composition. **4.** A first book in a course of study: *This book is an introduction to physics.*

introductory (ĭn′trə-dŭk′tə-rē) *adj.* Serving to introduce a subject or person: *a few introductory remarks by the speaker.*

introspection (ĭn′trə-spĕk′shən) *n.* The examination of one's own thoughts and feelings. —SEE NOTE AT **spectator.**

introspective (ĭn′trə-spĕk′tĭv) *adj.* Given to examining one's own thoughts and feelings: *an introspective philosopher.* —**in′tro·spec′tive·ly** *adv.*

introvert (ĭn′trə-vûrt′) *n.* A person who is not very sociable or outgoing and who tends to be preoccupied with his or her own thoughts and feelings. —**in′tro·vert·ed** *adj.*

intrude (ĭn-trood′) *v.* **intruded, intruding, intrudes** —*intr.* **1.** To break or come in without being wanted or asked: *The new neighbors were always intruding on her quiet afternoons.* **2.** To violate or advance wrongly into the scope or extent of something: *The lawsuit claims that the government intruded on their right to privacy.* —*tr.* **1.** To put or force in without invitation: *They intruded their opinions into our conversation.* **2.** To cause (molten rock) to be forced into existing rock. —**in·trud′er** *n.*

intrusion (ĭn-troo′zhən) *n.* **1.** The act of intruding: *Your barging into my room is an intrusion on my privacy.* **2.** The forcing of molten rock into an existing rock formation. **3.** The rock mass produced by this process.

intrusive (ĭn-troo′sĭv) *adj.* **1.** Intruding or tending to intrude: *a rude intrusive question.* **2.** Relating to or being igneous rock that is forced while molten into cracks or between other layers of rock. —**in·tru′sive·ly** *adv.*

intuit (ĭn-too′ĭt) *tr.v.* **intuited, intuiting, intuits** To know or understand by intuition.

intuition (ĭn′too-ĭsh′ən) *n.* **1.** The power of knowing or understanding something without reasoning or proof: *My intuition tells me that the experiment will work if we try it again.* **2.** Knowledge gained immediately without reasoning or proof; an insight.

intuitive (ĭn-too′ĭ-tĭv) *adj.* **1.** Based on intuition: *an intuitive understanding of musical harmony.* **2.** Having or showing intuition: *an intuitive mind.* —**in·tu′i·tive·ly** *adv.*

Inuit (ĭn′yoo-ĭt) *n., pl.* **Inuit** or **Inuits 1.** *(used with a plural verb)* The members of the Eskimo peoples inhabiting the Arctic from northwest Alaska eastward to eastern Greenland, particularly those inhabiting Canada. **2.** Any or all of the languages of the Inuit. —**In′u·it** *adj.*

inundate (ĭn′ŭn-dāt′) *tr.v.* **inundated, inundating, inundates 1.** To cover with water; flood: *The storm tide inundated the waterfront.* **2.** To overwhelm as if with a flood: *The store was inundated with shoppers during the holiday sale.* —**in′un·da′tion** *n.*

inure (ĭn-yoor′) *tr.v.* **inured, inuring, inures** To make used to; accustom: *Severe winters inured the pioneers to cold.*

invade (ĭn-vād′) *v.* **invaded, invading, invades** —*tr.* **1.** To enter (a place) by force in order to attack or conquer: *The Romans invaded Britain.* **2.** To enter (a cell or tissue), usually multiplying or spreading: *Viruses invaded the cells; bacteria have invaded the lungs.* **3.** To enter (a place) and occupy it in large numbers, often destructively; overrun: *Skiers invaded the mountain town. A South American weed is invading waterways in Florida.* **4.** To

intrude on; violate: *invade someone's privacy.* —*intr.* To make an invasion. —**in·vad′er** *n.*

invalid[1] (ĭn-văl′ĭd) *adj.* Not valid or proper; without force, foundation, or authority: *Unless a contract is signed, it is invalid.* —**in·val′id·ly** *adv.*

invalid[2] (ĭn′və-lĭd) *n.* A person who is unable to function independently because of severe disease or injury.

WORD HISTORY Invalid[1] comes from Latin *invalidus,* meaning "weak, not strong." The meaning of **invalid**[2] was influenced by English *invalid*[1] and French *invalide,* meaning "sickly."

---

invalidate (ĭn-văl′ĭ-dāt′) *tr.v.* **invalidated, invalidating, invalidates** To make invalid or worthless; nullify: *The lack of a signature invalidated the check.* —**in·val′i·da′tion** *n.*

invaluable (ĭn-văl′yoo-ə-bəl) *adj.* Of a value greater than can be measured; priceless: *invaluable art treasures.* —**in·val′u·a·bly** *adv.*

invariable (ĭn-vâr′ē-ə-bəl) *adj.* Not changing or varying; constant: *the invariable return of spring.* —**in·var′i·a·bil′i·ty** *n.* —**in·var′i·a·bly** *adv.*

invariance (ĭn-vâr′ē-əns) *n.* **1.** The condition or quality of being unchanging: *invariance in the speed of light.* **2.** The property of being mathematically invariant.

invariant (ĭn-vâr′ē-ənt) *adj.* **1.** Not varying; constant. **2.** Unaffected by a designated mathematical operation, such as a transformation of coordinates. ❖ *n.* An invariant quantity, function, configuration, or system.

invasion (ĭn-vā′zhən) *n.* **1.** The act of invading, especially the entry of an armed force in order to conquer another country. **2.** An intrusion or violation: *The loud music from next door is an invasion of our privacy.*

invasive (ĭn-vā′sĭv) *adj.* **1.** Tending to invade, especially tending to invade healthy cells or tissues: *an invasive tumor.* **2.** Involving entry into a part of the body, as by surgical incision: *invasive techniques for curing a heart defect.* **3.** Tending to intrude: *was annoyed by his invasive questions.* **4.** Tending to spread widely in a habitat or ecosystem: *invasive grasses.*

invective (ĭn-vĕk′tĭv) *n.* Harsh words used to attack; abusive language.

inveigh (ĭn-vā′) *intr.v.* **inveighed, inveighing, inveighs** To protest by speaking out violently and bitterly: *The tenants inveighed against higher rents.*

inveigle (ĭn-vā′gəl *or* ĭn-vē′gəl) *tr.v.* **inveigled, inveigling, inveigles 1.** To win over by flattery or artful talk: *The saleswoman inveigled me into buying a ring.* **2.** To obtain by flattery or artful talk: *He inveigled free passes from the ticket seller.* —**in·vei′gler** *n.*

invent (ĭn-vĕnt′) *tr.v.* **invented, inventing, invents 1.** To produce or create (something new) by using the imagination: *Thomas Edison invented the light bulb.* **2.** To make up; devise in the mind: *They invented an excuse for having to leave earlier than usual.*

invention (ĭn-vĕn′shən) *n.* **1.** Something invented, as a new device or process: *The computer is a revolutionary modern invention.* **2.** The act of inventing: *The invention of movable type made books widely available.* **3.** The power or ability to invent: *Only a mystery writer of great invention could create so complicated a plot.* **4.** Something that is made up, especially a falsehood. —**in·ven′tor** *n.*

inventive (ĭn-vĕn′tĭv) *adj.* **1.** Skillful at inventing; creative: *An inventive writer is able to keep the reader's attention.* **2.** Relating to or characterized by invention. —**in·ven′tive·ly** *adv.*

inventor (ĭn-věn′tər) *n.* A person who invents new ideas, things, or methods.

inventory (ĭn′vən-tôr′ē) *n., pl.* **inventories 1.** A detailed list of goods or possessions, especially a survey of all goods and materials in stock. **2.** The process of making such a survey or list. **3.** The supply of goods on hand; stock: *The store's inventory is getting low.* ❖ *tr.v.* **inventoried, inventorying, inventories** To make a detailed list of: *Before reordering, the store inventoried its stock.*

inverse (ĭn-vûrs′ *or* ĭn′vûrs′) *adj.* Opposite or reversed, as in character or order: *CBA is ABC in inverse order.* ❖ *n.* (ĭn′vûrs′ *or* ĭn-vûrs′) **1.** Something exactly opposite in order or character. **2.** One of a pair of elements in a set whose result under the operation of the set is the identity element. For example, the inverse of 5 under multiplication is ⅕, since $5 \times ⅕ = 1$. The inverse of 5 under addition is -5, since $5 + -5 = 0$. —**in·verse′ly** *adv.*

inversion (ĭn-vûr′zhən *or* ĭn-vûr′shən) *n.* **1.** The act of inverting or the condition of being inverted. **2.** Something inverted.

invert (ĭn-vûrt′) *tr.v.* **inverted, inverting, inverts 1.** To turn upside down: *invert an hourglass.* **2.** To reverse the order, position, or condition of: *A mirror inverts the placement of things in its reflection.*

invertebrate (ĭn-vûr′tə-brĭt *or* ĭn-vûr′tə-brāt′) *adj.* **1.** Having no backbone: *invertebrate animals.* **2.** Relating to invertebrates: *invertebrate fossils; invertebrate anatomy.* ❖ *n.* An animal, such as an insect or octopus, that has no backbone.

invest (ĭn-věst′) *v.* **invested, investing, invests** — *tr.* **1.** To put (money) into something, such as property, stocks, or a business, in order to earn interest or make a profit: *Many people invest their savings in mutual funds.* **2.** To devote or spend for future advantage or benefit: *The candidates invested much time and energy in the election campaign.* **3.** To entrust with a right or power: *The Constitution invests Congress with the power to make laws.* **4.** To put in office with a formal ceremony: *The president is invested with an inauguration.* **5.** To provide with a certain quality: *The writer invested the novel with many historical details.* — *intr.* To make an investment: *The bank invested heavily in real estate.*

investigate (ĭn-věs′tĭ-gāt′) *v.* **investigated, investigating, investigates** — *tr.* To look into or search carefully for facts, knowledge, or information: *The police investigate crimes to determine who commits them.* — *intr.* To make an investigation.

investigation (ĭn-věs′tĭ-gā′shən) *n.* A careful examination or search in order to discover facts or gain information.

investigator (ĭn-věs′tĭ-gā′tər) *n.* A person who investigates, especially a detective.

investiture (ĭn-věs′tĭ-chŏŏr′ *or* ĭn-věs′tĭ-chər) *n.* The act or formal ceremony putting a person in a high office or position of authority.

investment (ĭn-věst′mənt) *n.* **1.** The act of investing money for profit or advantage: *The company made an investment in new equipment.* **2.** A sum of money invested: *interest earned on an investment.* **3.** Something in which money is invested: *Land is a good investment.* **4.** A commitment, as of time or effort: *She's made a large investment in training for the marathon.*

investor (ĭn-věs′tər) *n.* A person or group that invests money for profit.

inveterate (ĭn-vět′ər-ĭt) *adj.* **1.** Fixed in a habit or practice; habitual: *An inveterate reader needs no incentive to pick up a good book.* **2.** Firmly established for a long time; deep-rooted: *Inveterate prejudice is resistant to change or reform.*

invidious (ĭn-vĭd′ē-əs) *adj.* **1.** Likely to produce anger, ill will, or resentment: *She was given the invidious task of identifying the person who had made the error.* **2.** Offensive and unfair: *The article makes invidious comparisons between immigrants and native-born people.* —**in·vid′i·ous·ly** *adv.*

invigorate (ĭn-vĭg′ə-rāt′) *tr.v.* **invigorated, invigorating, invigorates** To fill with energy, strength, or vigor: *The cool autumn air invigorated us.* —**in·vig′or·a′tion** *n.*

invincible (ĭn-vĭn′sə-bəl) *adj.* Incapable of being defeated or overcome: *an invincible army; invincible courage.* —**in·vin′ci·bil′i·ty** *n.* —**in·vin′ci·bly** *adv.*

inviolable (ĭn-vī′ə-lə-bəl) *adj.* **1.** Regarded as sacred and not to be violated: *an inviolable promise.* **2.** Incapable of being assaulted or trespassed: *an inviolable castle.* —**in·vi′o·la·bly** *adv.*

inviolate (ĭn-vī′ə-lĭt) *adj.* Not violated or broken; intact: *Personal integrity requires inviolate honesty in dealing with others.*

invisible (ĭn-vĭz′ə-bəl) *adj.* Impossible to see; not visible: *Air is colorless and invisible.* —**in·vis′i·bil′i·ty** *n.* —**in·vis′i·bly** *adv.*

invitation (ĭn′vĭ-tā′shən) *n.* **1.** A spoken or written request for a person to come somewhere or do something: *an invitation to a party.* **2.** The act of inviting.

invitational (ĭn′vĭ-tā′shə-nəl) *adj.* Restricted to people who have been invited to participate: *an invitational golf tournament.*

invite (ĭn-vīt′) *tr.v.* **invited, inviting, invites 1.** To ask (a person or persons) politely to come somewhere or do something: *invite guests to a party.* **2.** To ask; request: *The author invited questions from the audience.* **3.** To tend to bring on; provoke: *Exercising too much invites injury.* **4.** To tempt, lure, or attract: *After days of rain, the bright sun invited us outside.*

invitee (ĭn′vī-tē′) *n.* A person who is invited: *The invitees placed their wedding gifts on the table at the reception.*

inviting (ĭn-vī′tĭng) *adj.* Attractive; tempting: *A swimming pool looks inviting on a hot day.* —**in·vit′ing·ly** *adv.*

in vitro (ĭn vē′trō) *adv. & adj.* In an artificial environment, such as a test tube, outside a living organism: *grow tissue in vitro.*

in vitro fertilization *n.* The production of an embryo or embryos by combining egg and sperm cells together outside the body.

in vivo (vē′vō) *adv. & adj.* Inside a living organism: *test a new drug in vivo.*

invocation (ĭn′və-kā′shən) *n.* **1.** The act or an instance of invoking, especially an appeal for help from a higher power: *ancient peoples' invocation of their gods for a bountiful harvest.* **2.** A prayer or appeal used in invoking help or protection, as at the opening of a religious service. **3.** A set of words spoken as a magic charm to bring forth a spirit.

invoice (ĭn′vois′) *n.* A detailed list of goods shipped or services rendered, with an account of all costs and charges. ❖ *tr.v.* **invoiced, invoicing, invoices** To make an invoice of; bill: *The company invoiced the shipment.*

invoke (ĭn-vōk′) *tr.v.* **invoked, invoking, invokes 1.** To call on for help or protection: *Viking mariners invoked their gods before long voyages at sea.* **2.** To ask or call for earnestly: *The defendant invoked the mercy of the court.* **3.** To use or apply: *In defending their right to protest, the lawyer invoked the Constitution.* **4.** To call up (a spirit) with magic words or spells. **5.** To activate or start (a computer program, for example).

involuntary (ĭn-vŏl′ən-tĕr′ē) *adj.* **1.** Not subject to conscious control; automatic: *Sneezing is involuntary.* **2.** Not done willingly or on purpose; unintentional or accidental: *an involuntary gesture; an involuntary mishap.* —**in·vol′un·tar′i·ly** *adv.*

involve (ĭn-vŏlv′) *tr.v.* **involved, involving, involves 1.** To have as a necessary feature or outcome; include or entail: *His new job involves a lot of travel.* **2.** To draw in; mix up; embroil: *By asking my opinion, he involved me in their argument.* **3.** To spread to: *The fire involved the house next door.* **4.** To hold the interest of; absorb: *The children were completely involved in their game.* —**in·volve′ment** *n.*

involved (ĭn-vŏlvd′) *adj.* Complicated; complex; intricate: *a long involved sentence.*

invulnerable (ĭn-vŭl′nər-ə-bəl) *adj.* Impossible to attack, damage, or hurt: *an invulnerable fort; an invulnerable argument.* —**in·vul′ner·a·bil′i·ty** *n.* —**in·vul′ner·a·bly** *adv.*

inward (ĭn′wərd) *adj.* **1.** Directed toward the inside: *an inward rush of water into the submarine's holding tanks.* **2.** Located on the inside; inner: *the inward surface of the fuel tank.* **3.** Relating to or existing in the thoughts or mind: *inward feelings.* ❖ *adv.* also **inwards** (ĭn′wərdz) **1.** Toward the inside or center: *The door swung inward.* **2.** Toward one's own mind or self: *His thoughts turned inward.*

inward dive *n.* A dive in which the diver, standing on the end of the board with the back to the water, leaps up and rotates forward.

inwardly (ĭn′wərd-lē) *adv.* **1.** On or in the inside; internally. **2.** To oneself; privately: *chuckling inwardly.*

IOC An abbreviation of International Olympic Committee.

iodide (ī′ə-dīd′) *n.* A chemical compound of iodine with another element or radical.

iodine (ī′ə-dīn′ *or* ī′ə-dĭn) *n.* **1.** *Symbol* **I** A shiny, purple-black nonmetallic element that is corrosive and poisonous. Small amounts of iodine are essential for proper thyroid function. Iodine compounds are used in antiseptics and dyes. Atomic number 53. See **Periodic Table. 2.** A liquid antiseptic preparation containing iodine, used to treat wounds.

iodize (ī′ə-dīz′) *tr.v.* **iodized, iodizing, iodizes** To treat or combine with iodine or an iodide: *iodize table salt.*

ion (ī′ŏn′ *or* ī′ən) *n.* An atom or a group of atoms that has an electric charge. Positive ions are formed by the loss of electrons; negative ions are formed by the gain of electrons.

–ion A suffix that means: **1.** Action or process: *completion.* **2.** Result of an action or process: *indentation.* **3.** State or condition: *elation.*

ionic (ī-ŏn′ĭk) *adj.* Containing ions.

Ionic *adj.* **1.** Relating to an order of ancient Greek and Roman architecture characterized by columns with two decorative scrolls at the top. **2.** Relating to the ancient Greek region of Ionia in present-day Turkey or to the Ionians.

ionize (ī′ə-nīz′) *v.* **ionized, ionizing, ionizes** —*tr.* To produce ions in: *Lightning ionizes the air it moves through.* —*intr.* To break apart or change into ions: *Acids, bases,*

and salts ionize when they are dissolved in a solution. —**i′-on·i·za′tion** (ī′ə-nĭ-zā′shən) *n.*

ionosphere (ī-ŏn′ə-sfîr′) *n.* A region of the earth's atmosphere extending from about 43 miles (70 kilometers) to more than 250 miles (400 kilometers) above the earth. It is composed of layers of ionized gases that enable radio signals to be transmitted over long distances.

iota (ī-ō′tə) *n.* **1.** The ninth letter of the Greek alphabet, written I, ι. In English it is represented as *I, i.* **2.** A very small amount; a bit: *There is not an iota of truth in that gossip.*

IOU (ī′ō-yōō′) *n.* A written promise to pay a debt, bearing the letters IOU, which stand for "I owe you," followed by the amount owed.

Iowa (ī′ə-wə) *n., pl.* **Iowa** *or* **Iowas 1.** A member of a Native American people formerly living in Iowa and Minnesota, with present-day populations in Nebraska, Kansas, and Oklahoma. **2.** The Siouan language of the Iowa.

ipecac (ĭp′ĭ-kăk′) *n.* A medicine prepared from the root of a South American shrub, used chiefly to induce vomiting.

ipso facto (ĭp′sō făk′tō) *adv.* By the fact itself; by that very fact: *An alien, ipso facto, has no right to a US passport.*

IQ An abbreviation of intelligence quotient.

ir– Variant of **in–**.

Iranian (ĭ-rä′nē-ən *or* ī-rä′nē-ən) *adj.* **1.** Relating to Iran or its people, languages, or cultures. **2.** Relating to a branch of the Indo-European language family that includes Persian, Kurdish, Pashto, and other languages of Iran, Afghanistan, and western Pakistan. ❖ *n.* **1.** A native or inhabitant of Iran. **2.** The Iranian branch of Indo-European.

Iraqi (ĭ-răk′ē *or* ī-rä′kē *or* ī-răk′ē) *n., pl.* **Iraqis 1.** A native or inhabitant of Iraq. **2.** The modern dialect of Arabic spoken in Iraq. ❖ *adj.* Relating to Iraq, its people, language, or culture.

Iraq War *n.* A war in Iraq that began in 2003 with an attack by a group of forces led by the United States and that resulted in the overthrow of Saddam Hussein's regime. US combat troops were withdrawn in 2010.

irascible (ĭ-răs′ə-bəl *or* ī-răs′ə-bəl) *adj.* Easily angered; highly irritable: *The long trip made the children very irascible.* —**i·ras′ci·bly** *adv.*

irate (ī-rāt′ *or* ī′rāt′) *adj.* Angry; enraged: *A group of irate citizens turned out to protest the tax increase.* —**i·rate′-ly** *adv.*

ire (īr) *n.* Anger; wrath. —**ire′ful** *adj.*

iridescence (ĭr′ĭ-dĕs′əns) *n.* The quality or state of being iridescent.

iridescent (ĭr′ĭ-dĕs′ənt) *adj.* Showing a display of lustrous colors: *iridescent soap bubbles.* —**ir′i·des′cent·ly** *adv.*

iridium (ĭ-rĭd′ē-əm) *n. Symbol* **Ir** A yellowish, very hard and brittle metallic element that is used to make hard alloys of platinum for jewelry and electrical contacts. Atomic number 77. See **Periodic Table.**

iris (ī′rĭs) *n., pl.* **irises** *or* **irides** (ī′rĭ-dēz′ *or* ĭr′ĭ-dēz′) **1.** The colored part around the pupil of the eye, located between the cornea and the lens. The iris regulates the amount of light entering the eye. **2.** Any of numerous widely cultivated plants having long sword-shaped leaves and showy flowers of various colors.

Irish (ī′rĭsh) *adj.* Relating to Ireland or its people, language, or culture. ❖ *n.* **1.** (*used with a plural verb*) The people of Ireland. **2.** Irish Gaelic.

Irish Gaelic *n.* The Celtic language of Ireland.

Irishman (ī′rĭsh-mən) *n.* A man who is a native or inhabitant of Ireland.

Irish setter *n.* A dog of a breed developed in Ireland for bird hunting, having a silky reddish coat.

Irish stew *n.* A stew of meat and vegetables.

Irish terrier *n.* A dog of a breed developed in Ireland, having a wiry reddish-brown coat.

Irishwoman (ī′rĭsh-wōŏm′ən) *n.* A woman who is a native or inhabitant of Ireland.

irk (ûrk) *tr.v.* **irked, irking, irks** To annoy, bother, or irritate: *Nothing irks a busy person so much as to be kept waiting.*

irksome (ûrk′səm) *adj.* Tiresome; tedious; annoying: *irksome paperwork.* —**irk′some·ly** *adv.*

iron (ī′ərn) *n.* **1.** *Symbol* **Fe** A silvery-white, hard, brittle metallic element that can be magnetized and is used to make steel. Iron occurs in hemoglobin in red blood cells. Atomic number 26. See **Periodic Table. 2a.** A metal appliance with a handle and flat bottom, used when heated to press wrinkles from cloth. **b.** An implement made of iron or a similar metal: *a branding iron; a curling iron.* **3. irons** Shackles; fetters: *a prisoner restrained by handcuffs and leg irons.* **4.** Any of a series of golf clubs with a bladelike metal head. **5.** Great strength, firmness, or hardness: *a grip of iron; a will of iron.* ❖ *adj.* **1.** Made of or containing iron: *an iron gate.* **2.** Very hard, strong, or determined: *an iron will.* ❖ *v.* **ironed, ironing, irons** —*tr.* To press or smooth with a heated iron: *iron a shirt.* —*intr.* To press clothes with a heated iron: *She watched television while she was ironing.* ◆ **iron out** To settle through discussion or compromise; work out.

Iron Age *n.* The period of human culture following the Bronze Age in Asia, Europe, and Africa, marked by the introduction of iron tools and weapons. In Europe it began around 800 BC.

ironclad (ī′ərn-klăd′) *adj.* **1.** Covered with iron plates for protection: *an ironclad ship.* **2.** Not easily broken or changed; fixed: *an ironclad rule.* ❖ *n.* A warship of the 1800s with protective metal plates.

Iron Curtain *n.* The military and political barrier separating the Soviet Union and the countries under its influence from the western European nations during the Cold War.

iron fist *n.* Strict, tyrannical control: *a dictator who ruled with an iron fist.*

ironic (ī-rŏn′ĭk) *adj.* Containing or expressing irony: *an ironic comment.* —**i·ron′i·cal·ly** *adv.*

ironing board (ī′ər-nĭng) *n.* A padded board, usually on collapsible legs, for ironing clothing.

iron lung *n.* A metal tank enclosing the entire body except the head and providing artificial respiration through changes in internal air pressure when normal breathing is impaired.

ironwood (ī′ərn-wŏŏd′) *n.* **1.** Any of numerous trees having very hard wood. **2.** The wood of such a tree.

ironwork (ī′ərn-wûrk′) *n.* Work in iron, such as gratings and rails.

ironworker (ī′ərn-wûr′kər) *n.* **1.** A person who makes iron or iron articles. **2.** A construction worker who builds steel structures.

ironworks (ī′ərn-wûrks′) *pl.n.* (*used with a singular or plural verb*) A place where iron is made or articles made of iron are produced.

irony (ī′rə-nē *or* ī′ər-nē) *n., pl.* **ironies 1.** The use of words to express something different to and often opposite from what they mean literally. Referring to a mess as "a pretty sight" is an example of irony. **2.** A conflict between what might be expected and what actually occurs: *We noted the irony that the boy who always complained about the cold weather became a famous skier.*

Iroquoian (ĭr′ə-kwoi′ən) *n.* **1.** A family of Native American languages spoken in Canada and the eastern United States. **2.** A member of an Iroquoian-speaking people. —**Ir′o·quoi′an** *adj.*

Iroquois (ĭr′ə-kwoi′) *n., pl.* **Iroquois** (ĭr′ə-kwoi′ *or* ĭr′ə-kwoiz′) **1.** A member of a Native American confederacy inhabiting New York State and originally including the Cayuga, Mohawk, Oneida, Onondaga, and Seneca peoples. In 1722, the Tuscaroras joined the Iroquois confederacy. **2.** Any or all of the languages of the Iroquois. —**Ir′o·quois′** *adj.*

irradiate (ĭ-rā′dē-āt′) *tr.v.* **irradiated, irradiating, irradiates 1.** To expose to or treat with radiation: *irradiating food to kill bacteria.* **2.** To shed light on; illuminate: *The morning sun irradiated the room.* —**ir·ra′di·a′tion** *n.*

irrational (ĭ-răsh′ə-nəl) *adj.* **1.** Not capable of reasoning or thinking clearly. **2.** Not based on or guided by reason; unreasonable; illogical: *an irrational fear of heights.* **3.** Relating to an irrational number. —**ir·ra′tion·al·ly** *adv.*

irrationality (ĭ-răsh′ə-năl′ĭ-tē) *n., pl.* **irrationalities 1.** The condition or quality of being irrational. **2.** Something irrational or absurd.

irrational number *n.* A real number that cannot be written as an integer or as a fraction whose numerator and denominator are both integers; $\sqrt{2}$ and pi (symbolized by π) are irrational numbers.

irreclaimable (ĭr′ĭ-klā′mə-bəl) *adj.* Impossible to reclaim: *irreclaimable land.* —**ir′re·claim′a·bly** *adv.*

irreconcilable (ĭ-rĕk′ən-sī′lə-bəl *or* ĭ-rĕk′ən-sī′lə-bəl) *adj.* Impossible to reconcile: *irreconcilable enemies; irreconcilable differences of opinion.*

irrecoverable (ĭr′ĭ-kŭv′ər-ə-bəl) *adj.* Impossible to recover: *irrecoverable losses.* —**ir′re·cov′er·a·bly** *adv.*

irredeemable (ĭr′ĭ-dē′mə-bəl) *adj.* **1.** Not capable of being brought back or paid off: *an irredeemable coupon.* **2.** Impossible to remedy or reform: *an irredeemable loss; an irredeemable sinner.* **3.** Not convertible into coin: *irredeemable Confederate dollar bills.* —**ir′re·deem′a·bly** *adv.*

irreducible (ĭr′ĭ-dōō′sə-bəl) *adj.* Impossible to reduce to a smaller or simpler amount or form: *¾ is an irreducible fraction.* —**ir′re·duc′i·bly** *adv.*

irrefutable (ĭ-rĕf′yə-tə-bəl *or* ĭr′ĭ-fyōō′tə-bəl) *adj.* Impossible to refute or disprove: *irrefutable facts.* —**ir·ref′u·ta·bly** *adv.*

irregardless (ĭr′ĭ-gärd′lĭs) *adv.* *Nonstandard* Regardless.

USAGE The word **irregardless** is considered unacceptable by many people because it has both a negative prefix (*ir–*) and a negative suffix (*–less*). It is therefore not considered to be a logical word. The word *regardless*, however, is acceptable: *Regardless of what you say, I still like that song.* For more information, see Note at **nonstandard.**

irregular (ĭ-rĕg′yə-lər) *adj.* **1.** Not done according to rule, accepted order, or general practice: *a highly irregular proceeding.* **2.** Uneven in occurrence or rate: *an irregular heartbeat.* **3.** Not straight, uniform, or balanced: *an irregular coastline.* **4.** In grammar, not following the usual pattern of inflected forms. For example, *do* is an irregular verb, with the irregular principal parts *did* and *done.* **5.** Not up to standard because of flaws or imperfections: *an*

irregular piece of cloth. —ir·reg′u·lar·ly *adv.*
irregularity (ĭ-rĕg′yə-lăr′ĭ-tē) *n., pl.* **irregularities 1.** The quality or condition of being irregular. **2.** Something irregular: *irregularities in the earth's surface.*
irrelevant (ĭ-rĕl′ə-vənt) *adj.* Having no relation to the matter at hand; beside the point: *an irrelevant question.* —ir·rel′e·vance *n.* —ir·rel′e·vant·ly *adv.*
irreligious (ĭr′ĭ-lĭj′əs) *adj.* **1.** Indifferent to religion. **2.** Contrary or hostile to religion. —ir′re·li′gious·ly *adv.*
irremediable (ĭr′ĭ-mē′dē-ə-bəl) *adj.* Impossible to remedy, correct, cure, or repair: *an irremediable blunder.* —ir′re·me′di·a·bly *adv.*
irreparable (ĭ-rĕp′ər-ə-bəl) *adj.* Impossible to repair, remedy, or set right: *The statue has suffered irreparable damage.* —ir·rep′a·ra·bly *adv.*
irreplaceable (ĭr′ĭ-plā′sə-bəl) *adj.* Impossible to replace: *irreplaceable natural resources such as coal and oil.*
irrepressible (ĭr′ĭ-prĕs′ə-bəl) *adj.* Impossible to hold back, control, or restrain: *irrepressible laughter.* —ir′·re·press′i·bly *adv.*
irreproachable (ĭr′ĭ-prō′chə-bəl) *adj.* Perfect or blameless; faultless: *irreproachable behavior.* —ir′re·proach′·a·bly *adv.*
irresistible (ĭr′ĭ-zĭs′tə-bəl) *adj.* Too great or overpowering to be resisted; impossible to resist: *an irresistible impulse.* —ir′re·sist′i·bil′i·ty *n.* —ir′re·sist′i·bly *adv.*
irresolute (ĭ-rĕz′ə-loot′) *adj.* Unsure of how to act; undecided; indecisive: *The irresolute editor was always asking for advice from his colleagues.* —ir·res′o·lute′ly *adv.* —ir·res′o·lute′ness, ir·res′o·lu′tion *n.*
irrespective of (ĭr′ĭ-spĕk′tĭv) *prep.* Without consideration of; regardless of.
irresponsibility (ĭr′ĭ-spŏn′sə-bĭl′ĭ-tē) *n.* Lack of responsibility or concern for consequences.
irresponsible (ĭr′ĭ-spŏn′sə-bəl) *adj.* **1.** Showing a lack of responsibility: *Much of our pollution comes from irresponsible manufacturing processes.* **2.** Lacking a sense of responsibility; unreliable or untrustworthy: *an irresponsible driver.* **3.** Not accountable or responsible to a higher authority: *favored representative democracy over irresponsible forms of government such as a dictatorship or monarchy.* —ir′re·spon′si·bly *adv.*
irretrievable (ĭr′ĭ-trē′və-bəl) *adj.* Difficult or impossible to retrieve or recover: *After the computer's hard disk crashed, all files were irretrievable.* —ir′re·triev′a·bly *adv.*
irreverence (ĭ-rĕv′ər-əns) *n.* **1.** Lack of reverence or respect. **2.** A disrespectful act or remark.
irreverent (ĭ-rĕv′ər-ənt) *adj.* Having or showing a lack of reverence or respect; disrespectful: *an irreverent attitude toward the ceremony.* —ir·rev′er·ent·ly *adv.*
irreversible (ĭr′ĭ-vûr′sə-bəl) *adj.* Impossible to reverse: *rolling on an irreversible downhill path.* —ir′re·vers′i·bly *adv.*
irrevocable (ĭ-rĕv′ə-kə-bəl) *adj.* Not capable of being changed or undone: *an irrevocable judgment.* —ir·rev′·o·ca·bly *adv.*
irrigate (ĭr′ĭ-gāt′) *tr.v.* **irrigated, irrigating, irrigates 1.** To supply with water by means of pipes, sprinklers, ditches, or streams: *Ancient Egyptians used water from the Nile to irrigate barren land.* **2.** To wash out (a wound or opening) with water or a medicated solution: *The dentist irrigated the infected area around the tooth.* —ir′ri·ga′tion *n.*

irritability (ĭr′ĭ-tə-bĭl′ĭ-tē) *n.* The quality or condition of being irritable.
irritable (ĭr′ĭ-tə-bəl) *adj.* **1.** Easily annoyed or angered: *Lack of sleep will make anyone irritable.* **2.** Very sensitive: *irritable skin around a scrape.* —ir′ri·ta·bly *adv.*
irritant (ĭr′ĭ-tənt) *n.* Something that irritates: *They found the city air full of irritants such as dust, soot, and smoke.* ❖ *adj.* Causing irritation.
irritate (ĭr′ĭ-tāt′) *tr.v.* **irritated, irritating, irritates 1.** To make angry or impatient; annoy: *The reporter's repeated questions on the same subject irritated the speaker.* **2.** To make sore or inflamed: *The smoke irritated the firefighter's eyes.* —ir′ri·ta′ting·ly *adv.* —ir′ri·ta′tor *n.*
irritation (ĭr′ĭ-tā′shən) *n.* The act of irritating or the state of being irritated: *His irritation was apparent in his scowl. Dust can cause irritation of the eyes.*
irrupt (ĭ-rŭpt′) *intr.v.* **irrupted, irrupting, irrupts 1.** To break or burst in: *The soldiers irrupted into the building.* **2.** To increase rapidly in number, especially beyond the normal range. Used of animals: *snowy owls that irrupted southward.* —ir·rup′tion *n.*
IRS An abbreviation of Internal Revenue Service.
is (ĭz) *v.* Third person singular present tense of **be**.
Is. An abbreviation of: **1.** island. **2.** islands.
Isaiah (ī-zā′ə) *n.* A book of the Bible containing the prophecies of the prophet Isaiah, offering an ethical critique of society and a vision of a perfected world.
ischium (ĭs′kē-əm) *n., pl.* **ischia** (ĭs′kē-ə) The lowest of the three large bones forming either side of the pelvis.
-ise Variant of **-ize**.
Iseult (ĭ-soolt′) also **Isolde** (ĭ-sōl′də) *n.* In Arthurian legend, an Irish princess who married a British king and fell in love with his knight Tristan.
-ish A suffix that means: **1.** Relating to: *Finnish.* **2.** Having the character of; like: *sheepish; childish.* **3.** Approximately; somewhat: *greenish.* **4.** Tending toward; interested in: *selfish.*
Ishtar (ĭsh′tär′) *n.* The chief Babylonian and Assyrian goddess, associated with love, fertility, and war.
isinglass (ī′zən-glăs′ *or* ī′zĭng-glăs′) *n.* **1.** A transparent, almost pure gelatin obtained from the swim bladders of sturgeon and certain other fishes and used in making glue. **2.** Mica in thin transparent sheets.
Isis (ī′sĭs) *n.* In Egyptian mythology, a goddess of fertility and magic who was the sister and wife of Osiris.
Islam (ĭs-läm′ *or* ĭz-läm′ *or* ĭz′läm′ *or* ĭz-läm′) *n.* **1.** A monotheistic religion founded by the Arab prophet Muhammad (570?–632). Islam is marked by the doctrine of absolute submission to God and by reverence for Muhammad as the chief and last prophet of God. **2a.** The people or nations that practice Islam; the Muslim world. **b.** The civilization based on Islam. —Is·lam′ic *adj.*
Islamic calendar *n.* The lunar calendar used by Muslims reckoned from the year of the Hegira in AD 622.
island (ī′lənd) *n.* **1.** A body of land, especially one smaller than a continent, entirely surrounded by water: *Iceland is an island in the Atlantic Ocean.* **2.** Something resembling an island by being separated or different in character from what surrounds it: *The library is an island of quiet in the teeming city.*

WORD HISTORY Although the words **island** and **isle** look similar, they are not historically related. *Isle* comes from the Old French word *isle*, which comes from the Latin word *insula*, meaning "island." The Latin word also shows up in our word *peninsula*, which in both Latin and

English means "almost an island" (*paene* in Latin means "almost"). As for *island,* it was originally spelled *iland* or *ilond* in Middle English, and it only acquired an *s* in the 1500s when people confused it with the French word *isle.*

islander (ī′lən-dər) *n.* A person who lives on an island.

isle (īl) *n.* An island, especially a small one. —SEE NOTE AT **island.**

islet (ī′lĭt) *n.* A very small island.

islets of Langerhans (ī′lĭts əv läng′ər-häns′) *pl.n.* Irregular clusters of endocrine cells in the pancreas that secrete insulin.

ism (ĭz′əm) *n. Informal* A distinctive doctrine, system or theory: *capitalism, communism, and other competing isms.*

–ism A suffix that means: **1.** Action, practice, or process: *criticism.* **2.** State or condition: *optimism.* **3.** Characteristic behavior or quality: *heroism.* **4.** A distinctive or characteristic trait, as of a language or people: *Briticism.* **5.** A doctrine, theory, or system: *pacifism.*

WORD BUILDING The suffix **–ism** is a noun suffix. That is, when added to words or word roots, it forms nouns. It comes from the Greek noun suffix *–ismos* and means roughly "the act, state, or theory of." Nouns that end in *–ism* often have related verbs that end in *–ize* (*criticism/criticize*), related personal nouns that end in *–ist* (*optimism/optimist*), and related adjectives that end in *–istic* (*optimistic*). For more information, see Note at **–ize.**

isn't (ĭz′ənt) Contraction of *is not.*

isobar (ī′sə-bär′) *n.* A line on a weather map connecting places having the same barometric pressure. Isobars show the distribution of atmospheric pressure at a given time, and are used in forecasting the weather.

isolate (ī′sə-lāt′) *tr.v.* **isolated, isolating, isolates 1.** To separate from others; set apart: *We isolated the new kitten from our other pets for a few days.* **2.** To place in quarantine.

isolated (ī′sə-lā′tĭd) *adj.* Separated from others; solitary: *an isolated cabin deep in the woods.*

isolation (ī′sə-lā′shən) *n.* **1.** The condition of being isolated: *living in isolation on a remote island.* **2.** The act of isolating: *the isolation of patients with tuberculosis.*

isolationism (ī′sə-lā′shə-nĭz′əm) *n.* The policy or principle that a nation should avoid political and economic relationships with other countries. —**i′so·la′tion·ist** *n. & adj.*

Isolde (ĭ-sōl′də *or* ĭ-zōl′də) *n.* Variant of **Iseult.**

isoleucine (ī′sə-lōō′sēn′) *n.* An essential amino acid that is found in plant and animal protein. Isoleucine has the same chemical composition as leucine, but the atoms are arranged differently.

isomer (ī′sə-mər) *n.* One of two or more compounds that have the same chemical formula but differ in the way their atoms are arranged or connected, often leading to different properties.

isometric (ī′sə-mĕt′rĭk) *adj.* Involving contraction of a muscle under constant tension without change in length: *isometric exercises.*

isopod (ī′sə-pŏd′) *n.* Any of numerous small crustaceans of a group that includes the woodlice, characterized by a flattened segmented body with seven pairs of legs.

isosceles triangle (ī-sŏs′ə-lēz′) *n.* A triangle having two sides of equal length.

isotherm (ī′sə-thûrm′) *n.* A line on a weather map connecting places having the same average temperature.

isotope (ī′sə-tōp′) *n.* One of two or more forms of an element that have the same chemical properties and the same atomic number but different atomic weights and slightly different physical properties because of different numbers of neutrons in their atomic nuclei. —**i′so·top′ic** (ī′sə-tŏp′ĭk) *adj.*

Israel (ĭz′rē-əl) *n.* **1.** In the Bible, the name given to the Hebrew patriarch Jacob by the angel with whom he wrestled. **2.** The Jewish people, regarded in the Bible as the chosen people of God.

Israeli (ĭz-rā′lē) *adj.* Relating to modern Israel or its people. ❖ *n., pl.* **Israelis** A native or inhabitant of modern Israel.

Israelite (ĭz′rē-ə-līt′) *adj.* Relating to the ancient kingdom of Israel or to its people. ❖ *n.* **1.** A native or inhabitant of ancient Israel. **2.** A descendant of Jacob; a Jew.

issuance (ĭsh′ōō-əns) *n.* The act of issuing: *the issuance of driver's licenses.*

issue (ĭsh′ōō) *n.* **1.** A subject being discussed or disputed; a question under debate: *the issue of reforming campaign laws.* **2a.** A complaint or objection: *Many students have issues with the plan to increase tuition.* **b.** A problem or difficulty: *a movie star who had to deal with some issues before continuing his career.* **3.** The act of distributing or putting out; release: *the government's issue of new postage stamps.* **4.** A newspaper or magazine published at a given time: *the June issue of the news magazine.* **5a.** The act of flowing or giving out: *the issue of water from the spring.* **b.** A place of outflow; an outlet: *a lake with no issue to the sea.* **6.** An outcome or result: *The policy was the issue of extensive debate.* **7.** Offspring; children: *died without issue.* ❖ *v.* **issued, issuing, issues** —*intr.* **1.** To come out; flow out: *Water issued from the broken pipe.* **2.** To proceed from a source; emerge or result: *ideas that issued from the discussion.* —*tr.* **1.** To give out; distribute: *issue uniforms to members of the team.* **2.** To put in circulation; publish: *The Postal Service issues stamps.* **3.** To cause to flow out: *a chimney that was issuing smoke.* ❖ **at issue** In question; in dispute: *Your conduct is not at issue here.* **take issue** To take an opposing point of view; disagree. —**is′su·er** *n.*

–ist A suffix that means: **1.** A person who performs an action: *lobbyist.* **2.** A person who produces, makes, operates, plays, or is connected with a specified thing: *novelist.* **3.** A person who specializes in a specified art, science, or skill: *biologist.* **4.** A person who believes in a certain doctrine or system: *socialist.* **5.** A person characterized as having a particular trait: *romanticist.*

isthmus (ĭs′məs) *n., pl.* **isthmuses** or **isthmi** (ĭs′mī′) A narrow strip of land with water on both sides, connecting two larger masses of land.

it (ĭt) *pron.* **1.** The thing, being, or action last mentioned or thought to be understood: *I polished the table until it shone. They played with the puppy until it got tired. Whatever you choose, give it your best. I couldn't find out who it was on the telephone.* **2.** Used as the subject of an impersonal verb: *It is snowing.* **3.** Used as the subject of a clause that introduces a phrase or clause that presents the idea of the sentence: *It is important to get enough exercise.* **4.** Used to designate a player in a game, such as tag, who attempts to find or catch the other players.

Italian (ĭ-tăl′yən) *adj.* Relating to Italy or its people, language, or culture. ❖ *n.* **1.** A native or inhabitant of Italy. **2.** The Romance language of Italy and a part of Switzerland.

italic (ĭ-tăl′ĭk *or* ī-tăl′ĭk) *adj.* Being a style of printing type with the letters slanting to the right, used chiefly to set off a word or passage within a text of roman print: *This is italic print.* ❖ *n.* often **italics** Italic print or typeface: *The example sentences in this dictionary are printed in italics.*

italicize (ĭ-tăl′ĭ-sīz′ *or* ī-tăl′ĭ-sīz′) *tr.v.* **italicized, italicizing, italicizes** To print in italic type: *italicize the title of a book.*

itch (ĭch) *n.* **1.** An irritated feeling in the skin that causes a desire to scratch. **2.** Any of various skin diseases that cause a desire to scratch. **3.** A restless craving or desire: *Every summer I get an itch to go to the beach.* ❖ *v.* **itched, itching, itches** —*intr.* **1.** To feel, have, or cause an itch: *I itch all over from mosquito bites.* **2.** To have a restless craving or desire: *I'm just itching to try out my new camera.* —*tr.* To cause to have an itch: *This wool shirt itches my back.*

itchy (ĭch′ē) *adj.* **itchier, itchiest 1.** Having or causing an itch: *an itchy bug bite.* **2.** Restless; jumpy: *I get itchy if I have to sit for a long period of time.* —**itch′i·ness** *n.*

–ite A suffix that means: **1.** A native or resident of: *Brooklynite.* **2.** Descendant of: *Israelite.* **3.** Rock; mineral: *graphite.*

item (ī′təm) *n.* **1.** A single thing or unit: *I bought a shirt and several other items of clothing. You must show a receipt for each item purchased.* **2.** A piece of news or information: *an interesting item in the newspaper.*

itemize (ī′tə-mīz′) *tr.v.* **itemized, itemizing, itemizes** To place or include on a list of items: *itemizing all charges on the bill.*

iterate (ĭt′ə-rāt′) *tr.v.* **iterated, iterating, iterates** To say or do again; repeat. —**it′er·a′tion** *n.*

itinerant (ī-tĭn′ər-ənt *or* ī-tĭn′ər-ənt) *adj.* Traveling from place to place: *At harvest time many farmers employ itinerant workers.* ❖ *n.* A person who travels from place to place.

itinerary (ī-tĭn′ə-rĕr′ē *or* ī-tĭn′ə-rĕr′ē) *n., pl.* **itineraries 1.** A schedule of places to be visited in the course of a journey: *The tourists' itinerary includes stops in Denver and Salt Lake City.* **2.** An account or record of a journey. **3.** A traveler's guidebook.

–itis A suffix that means an inflammation or inflammatory disease of: *bronchitis.*

it'll (ĭt′l) Contraction of *it will.*

its (ĭts) *adj.* The possessive form of **it.** Belonging to the thing just mentioned: *How does the picture look? We just changed its frame.*

USAGE The word **its** is the possessive form of the pronoun *it* and is never written with an apostrophe: *I like the park because of its big trees.* The contraction **it's** (for *it is* or *it has*) is always written with an apostrophe: *It's a long way from my house to the park. It's been a long time since we've been to the park.*

it's (ĭts) Contraction of *it is* or *it has.* —SEE NOTE AT **its.**

itself (ĭt-sĕlf′) *pron.* **1.** That one that is the same as it: **a.** Used as the direct object or indirect object of a verb or as the object of a preposition to show that the action of the verb refers back to the subject: *The cat scratched itself. Congress voted itself a pay raise. The robot moves by itself.* **b.** Used to give emphasis: *The trouble is in the motor itself.* **2.** Its normal or healthy condition or state: *The dog has not been itself since the hot weather began.*

–ity A suffix that means a quality or condition: *authenticity.* —SEE NOTE AT **–ty.**

–ive A suffix that means tending toward or performing a specified action: *disruptive.*

I've (īv) Contraction of *I have.*

IVF An abbreviation of in vitro fertilization.

ivied (ī′vēd) *adj.* Overgrown or covered with ivy: *ivied brick walls.*

ivory (ī′və-rē *or* īv′rē) *n., pl.* **ivories 1.** The hard, smooth, yellowish-white substance forming the tusks of elephants and the tusks or teeth of certain other animals. It was formerly used for making piano keys and decorative objects. **2.** A yellowish white. **3. ivories** *Slang* **a.** The keys of a piano. **b.** The teeth: *He smiled and flashed his ivories.* ❖ *adj.* **1.** Made of or resembling ivory: *ivory chess pieces.* **2.** Yellowish-white.

ivy (ī′vē) *n., pl.* **ivies** Any of several climbing or trailing plants having evergreen leaves.

–ize *or* **–ise** A suffix that means: **1.** To cause to be or become: *dramatize.* **2.** To become; become like: *materialize; crystallize.* **3.** To treat like: *idolize.* **4.** To subject to or with: *satirize; anesthetize.* **5.** To perform, engage in, or produce: *fraternize.*

WORD BUILDING The suffix **–ize**, which comes from the Greek verb suffix *–izein*, is used in English to turn nouns and adjectives into verbs. The oldest words in *–ize* exist alongside related words ending in *–ism* or *–ist*, such as *baptize/baptism/Baptist.* But for hundreds of years now, verbs in *–ize* have been coined from almost any source: *legalize, modernize, popularize* from adjectives, and *authorize, computerize, hospitalize* from nouns. These newer verbs form nouns in *–ization* and *–izer* rather than *–ism* and *–ist: legalization, hospitalization; authorizer, popularizer.* For more information, see Note at **–ism.**

Jj

j or **J** (jā) *n., pl.* **j's** or **J's** or **Js** The tenth letter of the English alphabet.

jab (jăb) *v.* **jabbed, jabbing, jabs** —*tr.* **1.** To poke or thrust abruptly: *She jabbed the fork into the meat.* **2.** To stab or pierce: *He jabbed the meat with his fork.* **3.** To punch with short quick blows: *The boxer jabbed his opponent.* —*intr.* **1.** To make an abrupt poking or thrusting motion: *He jabbed at the air with his fingers while talking.* **2.** To deliver a quick punch: *She jabbed at the punching bag.* ❖ *n.* **1.** A quick blow or stab: *He gave me a jab in the ribs with his elbow.* **2.** In boxing, a short, straight punch.

jabber (jăb′ər) *intr.v.* **jabbered, jabbering, jabbers** To talk rapidly and in a senseless manner; chatter: *They jabbered on about their neighbors.* ❖ *n.* Rapid or babbling talk.

jabot (zhă-bō′ *or* jăb′ō) *n.* A series of frills or ruffles down the front of a shirt, blouse, or dress.

jacaranda (jăk′ə-răn′də) *n.* Any of several tropical American trees or shrubs having feathery leaves and clusters of pale purple flowers.

jack (jăk) *n.* **1.** A person who works in a specified manual trade: *a lumberjack; a steeplejack.* **2.** A usually portable device used to raise heavy objects by means of force applied to a lever, screw, or hydraulic press. **3.** A socket into which a plug is inserted in order to make an electrical connection: *a telephone jack.* **4.** A playing card bearing the figure of a young man and ranking below a queen. **5a.** **jacks** *(used with a singular or plural verb)* A game in which each player in turn bounces and catches a small ball while picking up small six-pointed metal pieces with the same hand. **b.** One of the six-pointed pieces used in this game. **6.** A male donkey. **7.** A small flag flown on a ship, usually to show nationality. ❖ *tr.v.* **jacked, jacking, jacks** **1.** To hoist by means of a jack: *The mechanic jacked the rear of the car to fix the tire.* **2.** To raise (something) to a higher level, as in cost: *The landlord jacked rents, causing much concern among tenants.*

jackal (jăk′əl) *n.* Any of several wild dogs of Africa, Asia, and southeast Europe that eat a variety of foods including plants, insects, rodents, and the flesh of dead animals.

jackanapes (jăk′ə-nāps′) *n.* A vain or disrespectful person.

jackass (jăk′ăs′) *n.* **1.** A male donkey. **2.** A foolish or stupid person.

jackboot (jăk′bōōt′) *n.* **1.** A sturdy military boot extending above the knee. **2.** A person who uses bullying tactics, especially to force compliance.

jackdaw (jăk′dô′) *n.* A bird of Eurasia and northern Africa that is related to and resembles the crows and has black and gray feathers.

jacket (jăk′ĭt) *n.* **1.** A short coat usually extending to the hips. **2.** An outer covering or casing, as of a book.

Jack Frost *n.* Frost or cold weather personified as an old man.

jackhammer (jăk′hăm′ər) *n.* A drill that is powered by compressed air, used especially to drill rock or break up concrete.

jack-in-the-box (jăk′ĭn-*th*ə-bŏks′) *n., pl.* **jack-in-the-boxes** or **jacks-in-the-box** A toy consisting of a box from which a clownlike puppet springs when the lid is opened.

jack-in-the-pulpit (jăk′ĭn-*th*ə-pōōl′pĭt *or* jăk′ĭn-*th*ə-pŭl′pĭt) *n., pl.* **jack-in-the-pulpits** A North American plant having a hood-shaped sheath arching over an upright stalk covered with very small greenish flowers.

jackknife (jăk′nīf′) *n.* **1.** A large pocketknife with blades that can be folded back into the handle. **2.** A forward dive in which the diver bends in midair, touching the feet while keeping the legs straight, and then straightens out before entering the water hands first. ❖ *intr.v.* **jackknifed, jackknifing, jackknifes** To fold or bend like a jackknife: *The trailer truck jackknifed on the icy road.*

jacklight (jăk′līt′) *n.* A light that is used as a lure in night hunting or fishing. ❖ *intr.v.* **jacklighted, jacklighting, jacklights** To hunt or fish with a jacklight.

jack-of-all-trades (jăk′əv-ôl′trādz′) *n., pl.* **jacks-of-all-trades** A person who can do many different kinds of work.

jack-o′-lantern (jăk′ə-lăn′tərn) *n., pl.* **jack-o′-lanterns** A lantern made from a hollowed-out pumpkin with a carved face, used at Halloween.

jackpot (jăk′pŏt′) *n.* **1.** The collection of bets that grows larger with each stage of a poker game. **2.** The largest prize or award in various games or contests.

jackrabbit or **jack rabbit** (jăk′răb′ĭt) *n.* Any of several hares of western North America having long ears and long, powerful hind legs.

jackstraw (jăk′strô′) *n.* **1.** **jackstraws** *(used with a singular verb)* A children's game played with straws or thin sticks thrown in a pile from which the players try in turn to remove single sticks without disturbing the others. **2.** One of the straws or sticks used in this game.

jade (jād) *n.* **1.** A hard mineral that is pale green or white and either carved or used as a gemstone. **2.** A light bluish-green. —**jade** *adj.*

jaded (jā′dĭd) *adj.* **1.** Tired or worn out: *a jaded look.* **2.** Dulled by having had too much of something: *a jaded appetite.* **3.** Cynically callous or unsympathetic: *a jaded attitude.* —**jad′ed·ly** *adv.* —**jad′ed·ness** *n.*

jag (jăg) *n.* A sharp projecting point. ❖ *tr.v.* **jagged, jagging, jags** To cut or tear unevenly; notch.

jagged (jăg′ĭd) *adj.* Having notches or indentations; irregular: *jagged edges of broken glass; a jagged coastline.* —**jag′ged·ly** *adv.*

jaguar (jăg′wär′) *n.* A large wild cat that resembles a leopard and has a coat of light-brown fur spotted with black marks. Jaguars are found from Mexico south to Argentina.

jai alai (hī′ lī′ *or* hī′ ə-lī′ *or* hī′ ə-lī′) *n.* A game similar to handball, played on a walled court, in which the players use a long basket strapped to the wrist to catch and throw the ball.

jail (jāl) *n.* A place for lawfully confining people, especially those who are awaiting trial for a crime and have not been released on bail or for those who are serving short sentences after being convicted of a misdemeanor. ❖ *tr.v.* **jailed, jailing, jails** To detain in jail.

jailer also **jailor** (jā′lər) *n.* A person in charge of a jail.

jalapeño (hä′lə-pān′yō) *n., pl.* **jalapeños** A green or red chili pepper that is very pungent.

jalopy (jə-lŏp′ē) *n., pl.* **jalopies** *Informal* An old automobile that is in bad condition.

jalousie (jăl′ə-sē) *n.* A blind or shutter having horizontal slats that can be tilted to admit or keep out air or light.

jam¹ (jăm) *v.* **jammed, jamming, jams** —*tr.* **1.** To drive or wedge into a tight space: *jam a cork into a bottle.* **2.** To fill (something) to excess: *Holiday shoppers jammed the store.* **3.** To cause to become unworkable because a part is stuck: *Grass jammed the mower.* **4.** To crush or bruise: *jam one's finger in the door.* **5.** To activate or apply (a brake) suddenly: *My bike skidded when I jammed on the brakes.* **6.** To make (electronic signals) difficult or impossible to receive by broadcasting an interfering signal. —*intr.* **1.** To become wedged or stuck in a tight space: *The coin jammed in the slot.* **2.** To stop working because a part is stuck: *The copier jammed again.* **3.** To force one's way into a limited space: *Everyone jammed into the elevator.* **4.** To participate in a jam session. ❖ *n.* **1.** A crush or congestion of people or things in a limited space, making it difficult or impossible to move: *a traffic jam; a log jam.* **2.** *Informal* A difficult situation: *We're really in a jam.*

jam² (jăm) *n.* A preserve made from whole fruit boiled to a pulp with sugar.

jamb (jăm) *n.* One of the vertical posts or pieces that form sides of a door or window.

jambalaya (jŭm′bə-lī′ə) *n.* A Creole dish consisting of rice that has been cooked with shrimp, oysters, ham, or chicken and seasoned with spices and herbs.

jamboree (jăm′bə-rē′) *n.* **1.** A noisy party or celebration. **2.** A large assembly of Boy Scouts or Girl Scouts.

James (jāmz) *n.* A book of the New Testament, traditionally attributed to James the Just, written in the form of a letter exhorting Christians to act morally.

jam session *n.* An informal gathering of musicians to play improvised or unrehearsed music.

Jane Doe (jān) *n.* **1.** A made-up name used in legal proceedings to refer to an unknown or unidentified woman or girl. **2.** An average or ordinary woman.

jangle (jăng′gəl) *v.* **jangled, jangling, jangles** —*intr.* To make a harsh metallic sound: *The coins jangled in my pocket.* —*tr.* **1.** To cause to make a harsh metallic sound: *I jangled my keys.* **2.** To have an irritating effect on: *The racket from the street jangled my nerves.* ❖ *n.* A harsh metallic sound.

janitor (jăn′ĭ-tər) *n.* A person whose job is to clean and take care of a building.

January (jăn′yōō-ĕr′ē) *n., pl.* **Januaries** The first month of the year in the Gregorian calendar, having 31 days.

Janus (jā′nəs) *n.* In Roman mythology, the god that protects doorways and city gates, shown with two faces looking in opposite directions.

Japanese (jăp′ə-nēz′ *or* jăp′ə-nēs′) *adj.* Relating to Japan or its people, language, or culture. ❖ *n., pl.* **Japanese 1.** A native or inhabitant of Japan. **2.** The language of Japan.

Japanese beetle *n.* A green and brown beetle native to eastern Asia that is a common plant pest in North America.

jar¹ (jär) *n.* **1.** A cylindrical container of glass or earthenware with a wide mouth and usually no handles. **2.** The amount that a jar can hold: *We ate a jar of peanut butter in two weeks.*

jar² (jär) *v.* **jarred, jarring, jars** —*intr.* **1.** To cause shaking or vibrations: *The ride over the old road was jarring.* **2.** To have an irritating effect: *The loud music jars on my nerves.* **3.** To be out of harmony; clash or conflict: *The statements of the opposing candidates frequently jarred.* —*tr.* **1.** To bump or cause to shake; rock: *His heavy steps jarred the floor.* **2.** To unsettle or shock: *The defeat jarred everyone on the team.* ❖ *n.* A jolt or shock.

WORD HISTORY Jar¹ comes from Middle English *jarre,* meaning "a liquid measure," which came (by way of Old French and Latin) from Arabic *jarra,* meaning "to draw, pull." **Jar²** may be imitative in origin.

jargon (jär′gən) *n.* **1.** The specialized language of a trade, profession, or class, especially when viewed as difficult to understand by outsiders: *medical jargon.* **2.** Nonsensical or meaningless talk; gibberish.

jasmine (jăz′mĭn) also **jessamine** (jĕs′ə-mĭn) *n.* Any of several vines or shrubs having fragrant, usually yellow or white flowers.

Jason (jā′sən) *n.* In Greek mythology, the leader of the Argonauts in quest of the Golden Fleece.

jasper (jăs′pər) *n.* A red, brown, or yellow variety of opaque quartz.

jaundice (jôn′dĭs *or* jän′dĭs) *n.* An abnormal yellow coloration of the tissues of the body, resulting from the accumulation of pigments that are normally excreted in bile. Jaundice can be caused by several conditions, such as liver disease.

jaundiced (jôn′dĭst *or* jän′dĭst) *adj.* **1.** Affected with jaundice. **2.** Showing or feeling bitterness or negativity: *a jaundiced viewpoint.*

jaunt (jônt *or* jänt) *n.* A short trip or excursion; an outing. ❖ *intr.v.* **jaunted, jaunting, jaunts** To make a short trip or excursion.

jaunty (jôn′tē *or* jän′tē) *adj.* **jauntier, jauntiest 1.** Having or expressing a carefree self-confident air: *a jaunty grin; a hat worn at a jaunty angle.* **2.** Lively; sprightly: *music with jaunty rhythms.* —**jaun′ti·ly** *adv.* —**jaun′ti·ness** *n.*

java (jä′və *or* jăv′ə) *n. Informal* Brewed coffee.

Java man (jä′və *or* jăv′ə) *n.* Pithecanthropus.

Javanese (jăv′ə-nēz′ *or* jăv′ə-nēs′) *adj.* Relating to the Indonesian island of Java or to its people, language, or culture. ❖ *n., pl.* **Javanese 1.** A native or inhabitant of Java. **2.** The language spoken by the main ethnic group of Java.

javelin (jăv′lĭn *or* jăv′ə-lĭn) *n.* **1.** A light spear that is thrown for distance in an athletic contest. **2.** A light spear thrown with the hand and used as a weapon.

jaw (jô) *n.* **1.** Either of two structures of bone or cartilage that in most vertebrates form the framework of the mouth, help to open and close it, and hold the teeth. **2.** often **jaws** The parts of the body that form the walls of the mouth and serve to open and close it: *His jaws ached after his braces were tightened.* **3.** Any of various structures of invertebrate animals, such as the pincers of spiders or mites, that function similarly to the jaws of vertebrates. **4. jaws** Something resembling or conceived as a pair of jaws: *the jaws of a large wrench; into the jaws of defeat.* ❖ *intr.v.* **jawed, jawing, jaws** *Slang* To talk in a gossipy manner; chatter. —**jaw′less** *adj.*

jawbone (jô′bōn′) *n.* One of the bones in which the teeth are set, especially the lower jaw.

jawless fish (jô′lĭs) *n.* Any of various long thin fishes that lack a jaw and paired fins. Lampreys and hagfishes are jawless fishes.

jay (jā) *n.* Any of various birds that have a loud harsh call, are usually brightly colored, and often have a crest, such as the blue jay of North America.

jaywalk (jā′wôk′) *intr.v.* **jaywalked, jaywalking, jaywalks** To cross a street in violation of the traffic rules, especially by crossing in the middle of a block or when the light is red. —**jay′walk′er** *n.*

jazz (jăz) *n.* **1.** A style of music native to the United States that has strong and often complex rhythms and melodies that are made up by musicians as variations of a main melody. **2.** *Slang* Empty talk; nonsense. ◆ **jazz up** *Slang* To make more lively or engaging: *Try to jazz up your writing a bit.*

jazzy (jăz′ē) *adj.* **jazzier, jazziest 1.** Resembling jazz. **2.** *Slang* Showy; flashy: *a jazzy car.*

JD An abbreviation of: **1.** Juris Doctor (Doctor of Law). **2.** juvenile delinquent.

jealous (jĕl′əs) *adj.* **1.** Resenting another's success or advantages; envious: *jealous of the success of others.* **2.** Fearful of losing affection or position to another. **3.** Concerning or caused by feelings of envy or the fear of losing position or affection: *jealous thoughts.* **4.** Careful or watchful in guarding something: *We are jealous of our good name.* —**jeal′ous·ly** *adv.*

jealousy (jĕl′ə-sē) *n., pl.* **jealousies** A jealous attitude or feeling.

jean (jēn) *n.* **1.** A strong twilled cotton, used in making uniforms and work clothes. **2.** **jeans** Pants made of jean or denim.

jeep (jēp) *n.* A small rugged motor vehicle with four-wheel drive, used by the US Army during and after World War II.

jeer (jîr) *v.* **jeered, jeering, jeers** —*intr.* To speak or shout in a mocking or scoffing way. —*tr.* To speak to or shout at in a mocking or scoffing way; taunt: *Hecklers jeered the speaker during the lecture.* ◆ *n.* A mocking or scoffing remark or shout.

Jehovah (jĭ-hō′və) *n.* God, especially in older translations of the Old Testament.

Jehovah's Witness (jĭ-hō′vəz) *n.* A member of a religious group preaching the imminent end of the world and opposed to war and to the authority of the government in matters of conscience.

jejune (jə-jōōn′) *adj.* Not interesting; dull: *another jejune political speech full of empty promises.*

jejunum (jə-jōō′nəm) *n., pl.* **jejuna** (jə-jōō′nə) The part of the small intestine between the duodenum and the ileum.

jell (jĕl) *intr.v.* **jelled, jelling, jells 1.** To become firm or thicken; congeal: *The gravy jelled as it cooled.* **2.** To take shape; crystallize: *Plans for the weekend haven't jelled yet.*

jellied (jĕl′ēd) *adj.* **1.** Caused to become jelly or have the consistency of jelly: *a jellied sauce.* **2.** Coated or spread with jelly: *a slice of jellied toast.*

jelly (jĕl′ē) *n., pl.* **jellies 1.** A soft clear food with a springy consistency that is made by boiling fruit juice or other liquid with pectin or gelatin. **2.** A substance resembling this: *petroleum jelly.* **3.** A jellyfish. ◆ *intr.v.* **jellied, jellying, jellies** To become thickened; turn into jelly.

jellybean (jĕl′ē-bēn′) *n.* A small chewy candy, shaped

somewhat like a bean, with a hard sugar coating.

jellyfish (jĕl′ē-fĭsh′) *n.* Any of numerous chiefly marine invertebrate animals having a soft, often umbrella-shaped body with stinging tentacles.

jennet (jĕn′ĭt) *n.* **1.** A female donkey. **2.** A small Spanish horse used for riding.

jenny (jĕn′ē) *n., pl.* **jennies 1.** The female of certain animals, especially the donkey. **2.** A spinning jenny.

jeopardize (jĕp′ər-dīz′) *tr.v.* **jeopardized, jeopardizing, jeopardizes** To put at risk of loss or injury; endanger: *Not getting enough sleep can jeopardize one's health.*

jeopardy (jĕp′ər-dē) *n., pl.* **jeopardies** Risk of loss or injury; danger or peril: *The active volcano put the nearby city in jeopardy.*

jerboa (jər-bō′ə) *n.* Any of various small rodents of Asia and northern Africa having a long tufted tail and long hind legs used for leaping.

jeremiad (jĕr′ə-mī′əd) *n.* A literary work or speech expressing a bitter lament or a righteous prophecy of doom.

Jeremiah (jĕr′ə-mī′ə) *n.* A book of the Bible in which the prophet Jeremiah denounces the sins of the Israelites and prophesies the destruction of Jerusalem.

jerk[1] (jûrk) *v.* **jerked, jerking, jerks** —*tr.* To move (something) with a quick pull, push, or twist: *I jerked my foot out of the cold water.* —*intr.* To move in sudden uneven motions: *The train jerked as we left the station.* ◆ *n.* **1.** A sudden abrupt motion, such as a yank or twist. **2.** A sudden and uncontrolled contraction of a muscle. **3.** *Slang* A stupid or foolish person. **4.** A lift in weightlifting in which the weight is heaved above the head from shoulder height with a sudden motion.

jerk[2] (jûrk) *tr.v.* **jerked, jerking, jerks** To cut (meat) into strips and dry in the sun or cure with smoke.

jerkin (jûr′kĭn) *n.* A close-fitting, hip-length jacket having no sleeves and no collar, worn over a doublet by men, especially in the 1500s.

jerky[1] (jûr′kē) *adj.* **jerkier, jerkiest 1.** Making sudden starts and stops: *jerky movements.* **2.** *Slang* Silly; foolish. —**jerk′i·ly** *adv.* —**jerk′i·ness** *n.*

jerky[2] (jûr′kē) *n.* Meat, such as beef, that has been cut into strips and dried in the sun or cured with smoke.

jerry-build (jĕr′ē-bĭld′) *tr.v.* **jerry-built** (jĕr′ē-bĭlt′), **jerry-building, jerry-builds** To build hastily, cheaply, and poorly.

jersey (jûr′zē) *n., pl.* **jerseys 1.** A soft knitted fabric of polyester, cotton, or other material, used for clothing. **2.** A garment made of this or a similar fabric. **3.** A shirt worn by an athlete, often displaying the name of the player, team, or sponsor. **4.** often **Jersey** Any of a breed of light brown cattle developed on the island of Jersey and raised for milk.

Jerusalem artichoke (jə-rōō′zə-ləm) *n.* **1.** A North American sunflower having edible tubers. **2.** The tuber of this plant.

jessamine (jĕs′ə-mĭn) *n.* Variant of **jasmine.**

jest (jĕst) *n.* **1.** A playful mood or manner: *Their teasing was only done in jest.* **2.** A playful act or remark. ◆ *intr.v.* **jested, jesting, jests** To act or speak playfully.

jester (jĕs′tər) *n.* A person who jests, especially a person employed to entertain by joking at a medieval court.

Jesuit (jĕzh′ōō-ĭt *or* jĕz′ōō-ĭt) *n.* A member of the Society of Jesus, a Roman Catholic religious order for men.

jet[1] (jĕt) *n.* **1.** A dense black form of coal that can be polished to a bright shine and used to make beads and other ornaments. **2.** A deep black.

jet² (jĕt) *n.* **1.** A high velocity stream of liquid or gas forced through a small opening or nozzle under pressure: *A jet of water shot out of the hose.* **2.** An outlet or nozzle through which a stream is forced: *a gas jet.* **3a.** An aircraft or other vehicle propelled by a jet engine. **b.** A jet engine. ❖ *v.* **jetted, jetting, jets** —*intr.* **1.** To travel by jet plane: *jetted from New York City to Seattle.* **2.** To move very quickly. —*tr.* To propel outward or squirt as under pressure.

WORD HISTORY Jet¹ comes from Middle English *get*, which comes from Greek *gagátēs* (meaning "a dense black form of coal"), which was named after the ancient town of *Gagas* in what is now southern Turkey where this mineral was found. **Jet²** comes from Old French *jeter* (meaning "to spout forth"), which comes from Latin *iactāre*, meaning "to throw."

jeté (zhə-tā′) *n.* A jump in dance from one foot to the other.

jet engine *n.* An engine that develops its thrust from a jet of exhaust gases produced by burned fuel.

jet lag *n.* The temporary disruption of body rhythms, such as sleeping and waking, that results from high-speed air travel through several time zones.

jet-propelled (jĕt′prə-pĕld′) *adj.* Propelled by one or more jet engines: *a jet-propelled airplane.*

jet propulsion *n.* **1.** The driving of an aircraft by the powerful thrust developed when a jet of gas is forced out of a jet engine. **2.** Propulsion by means of any fluid that is forced out in a stream in the opposite direction.

jetsam (jĕt′səm) *n.* Cargo and other things thrown overboard to lighten a ship in distress.

jet stream *n.* **1.** A strong wind, often reaching very high speeds, that blows from a westerly direction at altitudes of 10 to 15 miles (16 to 24 kilometers). **2.** A rapidly moving stream of liquid or gas as from a jet engine.

jettison (jĕt′ĭ-sən *or* jĕt′ĭ-zən) *tr.v.* **jettisoned, jettisoning, jettisons** **1.** To cast (something) overboard, especially as a means of lightening a ship or aircraft in distress. **2.** *Informal* To discard (something) as unwanted or burdensome: *jettisoned the marketing plan.*

jetty (jĕt′ē) *n., pl.* **jetties** **1.** A structure, as of stone, earth, and timbers, projecting into a body of water to affect the current or tide or to protect a harbor or shoreline. **2.** A wharf.

Jew (jōō) *n.* **1.** A person who is an adherent of Judaism. **2.** A member of the widely dispersed people originally descended from the ancient Hebrews and sharing an ethnic heritage based on Judaism.

jewel (jōō′əl) *n.* **1.** A precious stone; a gem. **2.** A costly ornament, such as a ring or necklace, made of precious metal set with gems. **3.** A small gem or crystal used as a bearing in a watch. **4.** A person or thing that is greatly admired or valued: *The only grandchild is the jewel of the family.* ❖ *tr.v.* **jeweled, jeweling, jewels** or **jewelled, jewelling, jewels** To adorn with jewels.

jeweler (jōō′ə-lər) *n.* A person who makes, repairs, or sells jewelry.

jewelry (jōō′əl-rē) *n.* Ornaments, such as bracelets or rings, made of precious metals and gems or of inexpensive or imitation materials.

Jewish (jōō′ĭsh) *adj.* Relating to the Jews or their culture or religion. —**Jew′ish·ness** *n.*

Jewry (jōō′rē) *n.* The Jewish people.

Jew's harp also **jew's harp** (jōōz) *n.* A small musical instrument consisting of a U-shaped frame that is held between the teeth and an attached blade of flexible metal that is plucked to produce twanging tones.

jib (jĭb) *n.* A triangular sail set forward of the mast and stretching to the bow or bowsprit.

jibe¹ (jĭb) *v.* **jibed, jibing, jibes** —*intr.* To shift a sail from one side of a boat or ship to the other when sailing before the wind. —*tr.* To cause (a sail) to shift from one side of a boat or ship to the other when sailing before the wind. ❖ *n.* The act of jibing.

jibe² (jĭb) *intr.v.* **jibed, jibing, jibes** To be in accord; agree: *The account of the other witness doesn't jibe with yours.*

WORD HISTORY Jibe¹ comes from obsolete Dutch *gijben*, meaning "to shift a sail." The origin of **jibe²** is unknown.

jibe³ (jĭb) *n. & n.* Variant of **gibe.**

jicama (hē′kə-mə *or* hĭk′ə-mə) *n.* A crisp, sweet root vegetable used raw in salads or cooked in stews.

jiffy (jĭf′ē) *n., pl.* **jiffies** *Informal* A moment; an instant: *I'll have this fixed in a jiffy.*

jig (jĭg) *n.* **1a.** Any of various lively dances in triple time. **b.** Music written for such a dance. **2.** Any of various devices used to guide a tool or hold work as it is put into a machine, such as a saw or drill. **3.** A metal fishing lure with one or more hooks, designed to bob up and down to attract fish. ❖ *intr.v.* **jigged, jigging, jigs** **1.** To dance a jig. **2.** To move up and down or to and fro in a quick, jerky way.

jigger (jĭg′ər) *n.* A small cup holding 1½ ounces (44 milliliters) of liquor.

jiggle (jĭg′əl) *tr. & intr.v.* **jiggled, jiggling, jiggles** To shake or cause to shake up and down or back and forth with short quick jerks: *By jiggling the wire we got the light to work. The plane jiggled slightly as it landed on the ground.* ❖ *n.* A jiggling motion.

jigsaw (jĭg′sô′) *n.* A saw with a narrow blade that moves up and down, used for cutting curves.

jigsaw puzzle *n.* A puzzle consisting of irregularly shaped pieces of wood or cardboard that form a picture when fitted together.

jihad (jĭ-häd′) *n.* **1.** In Islam, an individual's striving for spiritual perfection. **2.** A Muslim holy war or political struggle to defend the faith against unbelievers.

jilbab (jĭl-bäb′) *n.* A loose, long-sleeved, full-length outer garment worn by Muslim women.

jilt (jĭlt) *tr.v.* **jilted, jilting, jilts** To drop or cast aside (a lover or sweetheart) suddenly or without care.

Jim Crow or **jim crow** (jĭm) *n.* The practice of segregating and openly discriminating against black people, especially in the American South from the late 1800s until the mid-1900s.

jimmy (jĭm′ē) *n., pl.* **jimmies** A short crowbar with curved ends. ❖ *tr.v.* **jimmied, jimmying, jimmies** To pry (something) open with or as with a jimmy: *jimmy a door.*

jimsonweed (jĭm′sən-wēd′) *n.* A tall, coarse, poisonous plant having large, trumpet-shaped white or purplish flowers and prickly seed capsules.

jingle (jĭng′gəl) *intr. & tr.v.* **jingled, jingling, jingles** To make or cause to make a tinkling or ringing metallic sound: *Coins jingled in the fare box as the passengers boarded the bus.* ❖ *n.* **1.** A tinkling or ringing sound made by small metal objects striking together: *the jingle of sleigh bells.* **2.** A catchy rhyme or verse often used in advertising slogans.

jingoism (jĭng′gō-ĭz′əm) *n.* Extreme nationalism characterized by hostility to foreign countries.

jinni (jĭn′ē or jĭ-nē′) *n., pl.* **jinn** (jĭn) In the Koran and Muslim tradition, a spirit able to appear in either human or animal form and exercising supernatural influence over people.

jinriksha (jĭn-rĭk′shô′) *n.* A small two-wheeled carriage drawn by one or two people.

jinx (jĭngks) *n.* **1.** A person or thing that is believed to bring bad luck; a hex. **2.** A condition or period of bad luck that appears to have been caused by a specific person or thing. ❖ *tr.v.* **jinxed, jinxing, jinxes** To bring bad luck to.

jitney (jĭt′nē) *n., pl.* **jitneys** A small vehicle, especially a bus or van, that carries passengers for a low fare: *A jitney runs from the apartment buildings to the shopping center.*

jitterbug (jĭt′ər-bŭg′) *n.* A vigorous energetic dance performed to fast jazz or swing music, popular in the 1940s. ❖ *intr.v.* **jitterbugged, jitterbugging, jitterbugs** To perform this dance.

jitters (jĭt′ərz) *pl.n.* A fit of nervousness: *The exam gave me a case of the jitters.*

jittery (jĭt′ə-rē) *adj.* **jitterier, jitteriest** Having or feeling nervous unease.

jiujitsu (joō-jĭt′soō) *n.* Variant of **jujitsu.**

jive (jīv) *n.* **1.** *Slang* Nonsensical or deceptive talk. **2.** Jazz or swing music. **3.** The jargon used by jazz musicians and fans.

job (jŏb) *n.* **1.** A position at which an activity is regularly done for pay: *Her job is doing research at a laboratory.* **2.** A task that must be done; a duty: *My job is to fix lunch; your job is to wash the dishes.* See Synonyms at **task. 3.** Something resulting from or produced by work: *You did a fine job on the report.* **4.** An operation done to improve one's appearance, or the result of such an operation: *a nose job.* ◆ **on the job** At work: *Do not surf the Internet while on the job.*

Job (jŏb) *n.* A book of the Bible in which God allows Satan to afflict Job, a prosperous and pious man, as a test of his faith.

jobber (jŏb′ər) *n.* **1.** A person who buys merchandise from manufacturers and sells it to retailers at a profit. **2.** A person who works by the job or by the contract.

jobless (jŏb′lĭs) *adj.* **1.** Having no job; unemployed. **2.** Relating to those who are without jobs: *jobless benefits.* ❖ *n.* (*used with a plural verb*) Unemployed people considered as a group. —**job′less·ness** *n.*

Jocasta (jō-kăs′tə) *n.* In Greek mythology, a queen of Thebes who unknowingly married her son, Oedipus.

jock (jŏk) *n.* **1.** An athlete, especially in a school setting. **2.** An athletic supporter.

jockey (jŏk′ē) *n., pl.* **jockeys** A person who rides horses in races, especially as a profession. ❖ *v.* **jockeyed, jockeying, jockeys** —*tr.* **1.** To direct or maneuver by cleverness or skill: *She jockeyed the car into a tight parking space.* To ride (a horse) in a race. —*intr.* **1.** To ride a horse as a jockey. **2.** To maneuver for a certain position or advantage: *jockeyed for a promotion.*

jockstrap (jŏk′străp′) *n.* An athletic supporter.

jocose (jō-kōs′) *adj.* Given to joking; merry. —**jo·cose′ly** *adv.* —**jo·cos′i·ty** (jō-kŏs′ĭ-tē) *n.*

jocular (jŏk′yə-lər) *adj.* **1.** Given to joking. **2.** Meant as a joke; humorous: *a jocular remark.* —**joc′u·lar′i·ty** (jŏk′-yə-lăr′ĭ-tē) *n.* —**joc′u·lar·ly** *adv.*

jocund (jŏk′ənd or jō′kənd) *adj.* Having a cheerful disposition or quality; merry; lighthearted. —**joc′und·ly** *adv.*

jodhpurs (jŏd′pərz) *pl.n.* Pants that fit loosely above the

knees and tightly from the knees to the ankles, worn for horseback riding.

Joel (jō′əl) *n.* A book of the Bible in which the prophet Joel describes a plague of locusts and warns of a coming day of judgment by God.

joey (jō′ē) *n., pl.* **joeys** A young marsupial, especially a baby kangaroo.

jog (jŏg) *v.* **jogged, jogging, jogs** —*tr.* **1.** To move by shoving, bumping, or jerking; jar: *The old horse trotted along jogging me up and down.* **2.** To stir or shake up; rouse: *Let's see if I can jog your memory.* —*intr.* **1.** To run at a steady slow trot, especially for exercise. **2.** To go or travel at a slow pace: *The old car jogged along until it reached the hill.* ❖ *n.* **1.** A slight push; a nudge. **2.** A slow steady pace. **3.** A bumping or jolting motion. —**jog′ger** *n.*

joggle (jŏg′əl) *tr. & intr.v.* **joggled, joggling, joggles** To shake a little; nudge. ❖ *n.* A shake or nudge.

John (jŏn) *n.* **1.** The fourth Gospel of the New Testament, traditionally thought to have been written by Jesus's apostle John. **2.** Any of three books of the New Testament written in the form of letters, traditionally thought to have been written by Jesus's apostle John.

John Bull *n.* A personification of England or the English people.

John Doe *n.* **1.** A made-up name used in legal proceedings to refer to an unknown or unidentified man or boy. **2.** An average or ordinary man.

John Hancock *n. Informal* A person's signature.

johnnycake (jŏn′ē-kāk′) *n.* Thin flat cornmeal bread, often baked on a griddle.

join (join) *v.* **joined, joining, joins** —*tr.* **1.** To put or bring together; link; connect: *The George Washington Bridge joins New York and New Jersey. The children joined hands.* **2.** To put or bring into close association: *The two families were joined by marriage.* **3.** To meet and merge with; be united with: *The Missouri River joins the Mississippi near St. Louis.* **4.** To become a member of: *join the photography club.* **5.** To enter into the company of: *Can you join us for lunch?* —*intr.* **1.** To come together: *The roads join just before the bridge.* **2.** To act together; join forces: *The two groups joined together to oppose the new law.* **3.** To become a member of a group. **4.** To take part; participate. ❖ *n.* A joint; a junction.

✦ **SYNONYMS join, combine, connect, link, unite** *v.*

joiner (joi′nər) *n.* **1.** A skilled carpenter who makes woodwork, such as cabinets and doors, for houses and other buildings. **2.** *Informal* A person inclined to join many groups or organizations.

joint (joint) *n.* **1.** A place where two or more things are joined together: *a joint in a pipe.* **2.** A point at which movable body parts are connected or come together in an animal: *a knee joint; the joints in a spider's leg.* **3.** The way in which two parts are joined or the place at which two parts are held together: *A flexible joint allows the table leg to move.* **4.** The place on the stem of a plant, especially a grass, from which a leaf grows. **5.** A large cut of meat for roasting. **6.** *Slang* **a.** A cheap or disreputable gathering place. **b.** A building or dwelling. **7.** *Slang* A marijuana cigarette. ❖ *adj.* **1.** Undertaken or shared by two or more people or parties: *a joint effort; a joint bank account.* **2.** Sharing with another or others: *joint owners.* **3.** Involving both houses of a legislature: *a joint session of Congress.* ❖ *tr.v.* **jointed, jointing, joints 1.** To connect with a joint or joints: *The plumber jointed the new pipes.* **2.** To cut (meat) apart at the joints. ◆ **out of joint 1.** Not in place at the joint; dislocated. **2.** *Informal* Out of order or unsatisfactory: *Her whole world was out of joint.*

Joint Chiefs of Staff *n.* The principal military advisory group to the president of the United States, composed of the chiefs of the Army, Navy, and Air Force and the commandant of the Marine Corps.

jointly (joint′lē) *adv.* Together; in common: *The business is owned jointly by three partners.*

joist (joist) *n.* Any of the parallel horizontal beams that support a floor or ceiling.

jojoba (hə-hō′bə) *n.* An evergreen shrub of the southwest United States and northern Mexico having seeds that yield an oil used in cosmetics and as a lubricant.

joke (jōk) *n.* **1.** Something said or done to cause laughter, especially an amusing story with a punchline. **2.** A mischievous trick; a prank. **3.** A person or thing that is an object of amusement or laughter. ❖ *intr.v.* **joked, joking, jokes** To tell or play jokes.

joker (jō′kər) *n.* **1.** A person who tells or plays jokes. **2.** A playing card bearing the figure of a jester, used as the highest card or as any card the holder desires.

jokester (jōk′stər) *n.* A person who tells or plays jokes.

jollity (jŏl′ĭ-tē) *n., pl.* **jollities** Merriment or revelry.

jolly (jŏl′ē) *adj.* **jollier, jolliest 1.** Full of fun and good spirits. **2.** Showing or causing happiness or mirth; cheerful. ❖ *adv. Chiefly British* Very: *That's a jolly good idea!*

Jolly Roger *n.* A black flag bearing a white skull and crossbones, formerly used on pirate ships.

jolt (jōlt) *v.* **jolted, jolting, jolts** —*tr.* **1.** To move or dislodge with a sudden force: *The bicycle jolted me off the seat as it bumped over some rocks.* **2.** To make suddenly active or effective: *My remark jolted her memory.* **3.** To disturb suddenly and severely: *He was jolted by the betrayal of his best friend.* —*intr.* To move in a bumpy or jerky fashion: *The bus jolted to a stop as the driver jammed on the brakes.* ❖ *n.* **1.** A sudden jerk or bump. **2.** A sudden shock or surprise: *The news of their arrival came as quite a jolt.*

Jonah (jō′nə) *n.* A book of the Bible in which Jonah, a prophet sent by God to rebuke the Assyrians, tries to shirk his duty but repents after he is swallowed by a huge fish and later disgorged unharmed.

jonquil (jŏng′kwəl *or* jŏn′kwəl) *n.* A kind of daffodil with long narrow leaves and flowers with a short cup-shaped central part.

josh (jŏsh) *v.* **joshed, joshing, joshes** —*tr.* To tease in a lighthearted playful way: *She joshed her brother about his strange new haircut.* —*intr.* To make or exchange jokes.

Joshua (jŏsh′ōō-ə) *n.* A book of the Bible that relates the Israelites' conquest of Canaan, a country in the ancient Middle East.

jostle (jŏs′əl) *tr.v.* **jostled, jostling, jostles** To push and come into rough contact with while moving; bump: *The students jostled each other on the crowded dance floor.* ❖ *n.* A rough shove or push. —**jos′tler** *n.*

jot (jŏt) *n.* The smallest bit; an iota: *They didn't care one jot.* ❖ *tr.v.* **jotted, jotting, jots** To write down briefly and hastily: *She jotted some notes. He jotted down my address.*

joule (jōōl *or* joul) *n.* A unit used to measure energy, equal to the work done when a force of 1 newton acts over a distance of 1 meter.

jounce (jouns) *intr. & tr.v.* **jounced, jouncing, jounces** To move or cause to move with bumps and jolts. ❖ *n.* A rough jolting movement.

journal (jûr′nəl) *n.* **1.** A daily record of events, experiences, proceedings, or business transactions; a diary or log. **2.** A periodical containing articles on a particular subject: *a medical journal.* **3.** The part of an axle or a machine shaft that is supported by a bearing.

journalism (jûr′nə-lĭz′əm) *n.* The collecting, writing, editing, and presenting of news or news articles.

journalist (jûr′nə-lĭst) *n.* A person employed in journalism, especially a reporter or editor.

journalistic (jûr′nə-lĭs′tĭk) *adj.* Relating to or characteristic of journalism or journalists.

journey (jûr′nē) *n., pl.* **journeys 1.** A trip, especially one over a great distance: *a long journey across Europe and Asia.* **2.** The distance traveled on a journey or the time required for such a trip: *a thousand-mile journey; a three-day journey.* **3.** A process that is compared to traveling, such as a series of experiences: *her journey from teenager to adult.* ❖ *intr.v.* **journeyed, journeying, journeys** To travel; make a trip: *We journeyed throughout India.*

journeyman (jûr′nē-mən) *n.* **1.** A person who has completed an apprenticeship and works for another person. **2.** A competent but undistinguished worker.

joust (joust *or* jŭst) *n.* A combat between two armored knights on horseback armed with lances. ❖ *intr.v.* **jousted, jousting, jousts** To take part in a joust.

Jove (jōv) *n.* In Roman mythology, Jupiter.

jovial (jō′vē-əl) *adj.* Full of fun and good cheer; jolly: *a jovial host.* —**jo′vi·al′i·ty** (jō′vē-ăl′ĭ-tē) *n.* —**jo′vi·al·ly** *adv.*

jowl[1] (joul) *n.* **1.** The jaw, especially the lower jaw. **2.** The cheek, especially of a hog.

jowl[2] (joul) *n.* Loosely hanging flesh on or near the lower jaw.

WORD HISTORY Jowl[1] comes from Middle English *chavel, jaule,* which comes from Old English *ceafl.* **Jowl**[2] comes from Middle English *cholle.* The meanings of both forms of *jowl* have remained the same during their development, and both words were influenced by Middle English *jaue* ("jaw") or *jol* ("head").

---

joy (joi) *n.* **1.** A feeling of great happiness or delight. **2.** A source or cause of joy: *Some books are a joy to read.*

joyful (joi′fəl) *adj.* Feeling, causing, or showing joy: *a joyful celebration; a joyful shout.* See Synonyms at **glad.** —**joy′ful·ly** *adv.* —**joy′ful·ness** *n.*

joyless (joi′lĭs) *adj.* Without cheer or joy; dismal.

joyous (joi′əs) *adj.* Full of joy; joyful: *a joyous occasion.* —**joy′ous·ly** *adv.* —**joy′ous·ness** *n.*

joy ride *n. Slang* A fast and reckless automobile ride, often in a stolen car.

joystick (joi′stĭk′) *n.* **1.** A stick or handle used to control an aircraft. **2.** A manual control used to control onscreen graphics, especially in a video game.

jr. *or* **Jr.** An abbreviation of junior.

jubilant (jōō′bə-lənt) *adj.* Full of joyful exultation; rejoicing: *A jubilant crowd celebrated their team's victory.* —**ju′bi·lant·ly** *adv.*

jubilation (jōō′bə-lā′shən) *n.* Great rejoicing: *The good news was greeted with jubilation.*

jubilee (jōō′bə-lē′ *or* jōō′bə-lē′) *n.* **1.** A special anniversary, especially a 50th anniversary, or the celebration of it. **2.** A season or occasion of joyful celebration.

Judaic (jōō-dā′ĭk) *adj.* Relating to or characteristic of Jews or Judaism: *Judaic traditions.*

Judaism (jōō′dē-ĭz′əm *or* jōō′dā-ĭz′əm *or* jōō-dā′ĭz′əm) *n.* **1.** The religion of the Jewish people, based on belief in one God and on the teachings set forth especially in the Hebrew Scriptures and the Talmud. **2.** The cultural, religious, and social practices and beliefs of the Jews.

Judas (jōō′dəs) *n.* A person who betrays others under the appearance of friendship.

Jude (jōōd) *n.* A book of the New Testament written in the form of a letter in which Saint Jude denounces false preachers.

judge (jŭj) *v.* **judged, judging, judges** — *tr.* **1.** To form an opinion about or an evaluation of (something) after careful consideration: *The critic judged the play to be compelling drama.* **2.** To hear and decide (a case) in a court of law. **3.** To determine the winners of (a contest or issue): *The teachers judged the school spelling bee.* — *intr.* **1.** To form an opinion or evaluation. **2.** To act or decide as a judge. ❖ *n.* **1.** A person who gives an opinion about the value, quality, or outcome of something: *a good judge of character; a poor judge of painting.* **2.** A public official who hears and decides cases in a court of law. **3.** A person who decides the outcome of a dispute or the winner of a contest or competition. **4. Judges** *(used with a singular verb)* A book of the Bible containing a history of the Israelites after the death of Joshua. — **judg′er** *n.*

judgeship (jŭj′shĭp′) *n.* The position of responsibilities of a judge or the period during which a judge is in office.

judgment also **judgement** (jŭj′mənt) *n.* **1.** The ability to make distinctions and form opinions or evaluations: *Saving money shows good judgment.* **2.** An opinion or estimate made after careful consideration: *We await the judgment of the referee.* **3.** A decision reached in a court of law: *The high court handed down their judgment.*

judgmental (jŭj-mĕn′tl) *adj.* **1.** Relating to or dependent on judgment: *a judgmental error.* **2.** Inclined to make judgments, especially moral or personal ones: *a marriage counselor who tries not to be judgmental.* — **judg·men′tal·ly** *adv.*

Judgment Day *n.* In Judeo-Christian and Muslim traditions, the day at the end of the world when God judges the moral worth of individual humans or the whole human race.

judicial (jōō-dĭsh′əl) *adj.* **1.** Relating to courts of law or the administration of justice: *the judicial branch of government.* **2.** Relating to or appropriate to the office of a judge: *judicial robes.* **3.** Decreed by a court: *a judicial decision.* — **ju·di′cial·ly** *adv.*

judiciary (jōō-dĭsh′ē-ĕr′ē or jōō-dĭsh′ə-rē) *n., pl.* **judiciaries 1.** The judicial branch of government. **2.** A system of courts of law and judges. **3.** The judges of these courts.

judicious (jōō-dĭsh′əs) *adj.* Having or showing wise and sound judgment; prudent: *Conservation involves the judicious use of resources.* — **ju·di′cious·ly** *adv.* — **ju·di′cious·ness** *n.*

judo (jōō′dō) *n.* A sport and method of physical training similar to wresting. Judo was developed in Japan in the late 1800s and was adapted from jujitsu.

jug (jŭg) *n.* **1.** A tall, often rounded vessel with a narrow mouth, a handle, and usually a stopper or cap. **2.** The amount that a jug can hold: *We drank a jug of cider.* **3.** A small pitcher.

juggernaut (jŭg′ər-nôt′) *n.* A force that is overwhelming or unstoppable.

juggle (jŭg′əl) *v.* **juggled, juggling, juggles** — *tr.* **1.** To keep (two or more objects) in the air at one time by alternately tossing and catching them. **2.** To have difficulty holding or balancing: *The tourist was juggling luggage and cameras.* **3.** To change or rearrange so as to mislead or cheat: *juggled the figures in the account books.* — *intr.* **1.** To perform as a juggler. **2.** To use trickery to deceive.

juggler (jŭg′lər) *n.* **1.** An entertainer who juggles balls or other objects. **2.** A person who uses tricks to mislead or cheat.

jugular (jŭg′yə-lər) *adj.* Relating to or located in the neck or throat. ❖ *n.* A jugular vein.

jugular vein *n.* Any of several large veins in the neck that carry blood from the head into other veins that empty into the heart.

juice (jōōs) *n.* **1.** A liquid naturally contained in plant or animal tissue, especially in plant parts such as fruits, stems, or roots. **2.** A beverage made from such a liquid, often with other ingredients added. **3.** A fluid secreted within the body: *digestive juices.* **4.** *Slang* Electric current.

juicer (jōō′sər) *n.* An appliance used to extract juice from fruits and vegetables.

juicy (jōō′sē) *adj.* **juicier, juiciest 1.** Full of juice: *juicy berries.* **2.** Arousing interest or excitement: *He told me a juicy piece of gossip.* **3.** Rewarding or gratifying: *She was given a juicy part in the play.* — **juic′i·ly** *adv.* — **juic′i·ness** *n.*

jujitsu also **jiujitsu** (jōō-jĭt′sōō) *n.* An art of weaponless self-defense developed in Japan that uses techniques that exploit an opponent's weight and strength to one's own advantage.

jukebox (jōōk′bŏks′) *n.* A money-operated machine that plays music, usually equipped with pushbuttons for the selection of particular recordings.

julep (jōō′lĭp) *n.* A mint julep.

Julian calendar (jōōl′yən) *n.* The solar calendar introduced by the Roman dictator Julius Caesar in 46 BC having a year of 365 days and a leap year of 366 days every fourth year. It has been replaced by the Gregorian calendar.

julienne (jōō′lē-ĕn′) *n.* A clear soup or broth containing vegetables cut into long thin strips. ❖ *adj.* Cut into long thin strips: *julienne potatoes.*

July (jōō-lī′) *n.* The seventh month of the year in the Gregorian calendar, having 31 days.

jumble (jŭm′bəl) *tr.v.* **jumbled, jumbling, jumbles** To mix in a confused way; throw together carelessly: *The shirts were all jumbled together in a heap on the floor.* ❖ *n.* **1.** A confused or disordered mass: *a jumble of socks in a drawer.* **2.** A disordered state; a muddle.

jumbo (jŭm′bō) *n., pl.* **jumbos** An unusually large person, animal, or thing. ❖ *adj.* Very large: *jumbo shrimp; a jumbo jet.*

jump (jŭmp) *v.* **jumped, jumping, jumps** — *intr.* **1.** To rise upward or over a distance in a single quick motion or series of such motions: *The children jumped on the trampoline. The fish are jumping.* **2.** To move suddenly and in one motion: *jump out of bed.* **3.** To move quickly or involuntarily, as in fear or surprise: *I jumped at the sudden noise.* **4.** To enter eagerly into an activity: *She jumped into the race for mayor.* **5.** To form an opinion or judgment hastily: *Let's not jump to conclusions.* **6.** To rise or increase suddenly: *Prices jumped over the past month.* **7.** To pass from one part to another further on; skip: *We jumped ahead to the middle chapters.* — *tr.* **1.** To leap over or across: *jumped the stream.* **2.** To leap onto: *jump a bus.* **3.** *Slang* To spring upon in or as if in attack: *The robbers jumped the unsuspecting tourists in the park.* **4.** To cause to leap: *jump a horse over a fence.* **5.** To skip; move ahead: *jump a space in typing.* **6.** To leave (a course or track): *Two subway cars jumped the tracks.* ❖ *n.* **1.** A leap or spring: *The cat made a graceful jump from the floor to the shelf.* **2.** The distance covered by a leap: *a jump of 16 feet.* **3.** Any of several track-and-field events in which contestants jump. **4.** An abrupt rise: *a jump in temperature.* **5.** A sudden involuntary movement; a jerk or start: *gave a jump in surprise.* ◆ **jump the gun** To start doing something too soon. **jump the shark** To undergo a sustained decline in quality or popularity. **jump through hoops** To make extraordinary efforts, especially in following an established procedure.

jump ball *n.* In basketball, a method of starting play or determining which team should have the ball, in which an official tosses the ball up between two opposing players who jump and try to tap it to a teammate.

jumper[1] (jŭm′pər) *n.* **1.** A person, animal, or thing that jumps: *That horse is a good jumper.* **2.** A short length of wire or other electrical conductor used to make a temporary electrical connection.

jumper[2] (jŭm′pər) *n.* **1.** A sleeveless dress worn over a blouse or sweater. **2.** A loose smock or jacket worn over other clothes to protect them. **3.** *Chiefly British* A pullover sweater.

WORD HISTORY Jumper[1] is derived from *jump.* **Jumper**[2] is probably from an older English word, also spelled *jump* but meaning "short coat," that ultimately comes from Arabic *jubba,* meaning "long garment with wide open sleeves."

jumping bean (jŭm′pĭng) *n.* A seed of certain Mexican plants that contains a moth larva whose movements cause the seed to jerk or roll.

jumping jack *n.* **1.** A toy figure with jointed limbs that can be made to dance by pulling an attached string. **2.** An exercise that is performed by jumping to a position with the legs spread wide and the hands touching overhead and then returning to a position with the feet together and the arms at the sides.

jump rope *n.* **1.** A rope held at each end and twirled so that one can jump over it as it touches the ground. **2.** The game or activity played with a jump rope.

jump shot *n.* A basketball shot made by a player at the highest point of a jump.

jump-start (jŭmp′stärt′) *tr.v.* **jump-started, jump-starting, jump-starts** To start (the engine of a motor vehicle) by using a cable connected to the battery of another vehicle or by engaging the clutch when the vehicle is rolling downhill or being pushed. ❖ *n.* The act of jump-starting a motor vehicle.

jump suit *n.* **1.** A parachutist's uniform. **2.** also **jumpsuit** (jŭmp′sōōt′) A one-piece garment that consists of a shirt and attached pants.

jumpy (jŭm′pē) *adj.* **jumpier, jumpiest 1.** Moving in jumps; jerky. **2.** Easily upset or excited; nervous. —**jump′i·ness** *n.*

junco (jŭng′kō) *n., pl.* **juncos** or **juncoes** Any of various North American songbirds having a gray or brown body with white outer tail feathers.

junction (jŭngk′shən) *n.* **1.** The act of joining or the condition of being joined: *The junction of the Missouri and Mississippi Rivers takes place at St. Louis.* **2.** The place at which two things join or meet: *There is a motel at the junction of the two highways.*

juncture (jŭngk′chər) *n.* **1.** The act of joining or the condition of being joined. **2.** The point, line, or seam at which two things join; a joint: *Many small animals live along the juncture between meadow and woodland.* **3.** A point in time, especially a crisis or turning point: *At this juncture, a new government was formed.*

June (jōōn) *n.* The sixth month of the year in the Gregorian calendar, having 30 days.

June beetle *n.* The June bug.

June bug *n.* Any of various large brown beetles having adults that emerge in the spring and larvae that feed on roots and can damage crops.

Juneteenth (jōōn-tēnth′) *n.* June 19, an African-American holiday commemorating the date in 1865 when many slaves in Texas learned they had been freed by the Emancipation Proclamation issued earlier on January 1, 1863.

jungle (jŭng′gəl) *n.* **1.** An area of land having a dense growth of tropical plants. **2.** A confused or tangled mass, often the scene of intense competition or violence: *He felt totally out of place in the corporate jungle.*

jungle gym *n.* A structure of crisscrossing poles and bars on which children can play and climb.

junior (jōōn′yər) *adj.* **1.** Used to distinguish a son from his father when both have the same name. **2.** Intended for or including youthful people: *the junior skating championship.* **3.** Lower in rank or shorter in length of service: *a junior partner in a law firm; the junior senator from Texas.* **4.** Relating to or for the third year of a four-year high school or college: *the junior class.* ❖ *n.* **1.** A person who is younger than another: *I am my aunt's junior by twenty-five years.* **2.** A person of lower rank or shorter service. **3.** A student in the third year at a four-year high school or college.

junior college *n.* An educational institution offering a two-year course that is generally the equivalent of the first two years of a four-year undergraduate course.

junior high school *n.* A school attended between elementary and high school that includes the seventh, eighth, and sometimes ninth grades.

junior varsity *n.* A high-school or college sports team that competes on the level below varsity.

juniper (jōō′nə-pər) *n.* Any of various evergreen trees or shrubs having needlelike or scalelike leaves and small bluish-gray cones that resemble berries.

junk[1] (jŭngk) *n.* **1.** Material of any kind that is old, worn-out, and fit to be discarded or recycled, such as scrap metal, rags, or paper; trash. **2.** *Informal* Something cheap or shoddy: *That cheap toaster is nothing but junk.* ❖ *tr.v.* **junked, junking, junks** To discard as worn-out or useless: *He junked the old toaster after it stopped working.*

junk[2] (jŭngk) *n.* A Chinese flatbottom sailing vessel with a high stern and battened sails.

WORD HISTORY Junk[1] comes from Middle English *jonk,* meaning "an old cable or rope." **Junk**[2] comes from Javanese *djong,* meaning "seagoing ship."

junket (jŭng′kĭt) *n.* **1.** A trip made by a government official at public expense. **2.** A dessert made from flavored milk and rennet.

junk food *n.* Food that is high in calories but low in nutritional value.

junkie (jŭng′kē) *n. Slang* **1.** A person addicted to narcotics. **2.** A person who has an unflagging interest in something; a devotee: *a video game junkie.*

junk mail *n.* Unrequested mail, such as advertisements and catalogs, sent to large numbers of people.

junkyard (jŭngk′yärd′) *n.* A yard or other open area used to store junk, such as scrap metal or car parts.

Juno (jōō′nō) *n.* In Roman mythology, the chief goddess and the wife and sister of Jupiter, worshipped as the goddess of women, marriage, childbirth, and the moon, and as the protector of the state. She was identified with the Greek Hera.

junta (hŏŏn′tə *or* jŭn′tə) *n.* **1.** A group of military leaders who jointly govern a nation after seizing power. **2.** A council or small legislative body in government, especially in Central or South America.

Jupiter (jōō′pĭ-tər) *n.* **1.** In Roman mythology, the chief god, the patron of the Roman state, and the husband and brother of Juno. He is identified with the Greek Zeus. **2.** The fifth planet from the sun and the largest in the solar system, with a diameter about 11 times that of Earth. It turns on its axis faster than any other planet.

Jurassic (jōō-răs′ĭk) *n.* The second and middle period of the Mesozoic Era, from about 200 to 146 million years ago. During the Jurassic, dinosaurs were the dominant form of land life and the earliest birds appeared. —**Ju·ras′sic** *adj.*

jurisdiction (jōōr′ĭs-dĭk′shən) *n.* **1.** The right of a court to hear a particular case, based on the scope of its authority: *A justice of the peace has jurisdiction in a town or village.* **2.** Authority or control; power: *Schools come under the jurisdiction of the state education department.* **3.** The range or extent of authority or control: *Cases of treason are beyond the jurisdiction of local courts.* **4.** A geographic area under a specified authority or control.

jurisprudence (jōōr′ĭs-prōōd′ns) *n.* **1.** The science or philosophy of law. **2.** A division, type, or particular body of law: *federal jurisprudence; bankruptcy jurisprudence.*

jurist (jōōr′ĭst) *n.* A person who is skilled in the law, especially a judge, lawyer, or legal scholar.

juror (jōōr′ər *or* jōōr′ôr′) *n.* A member of a jury.

jury (jōōr′ē) *n., pl.* **juries 1.** A body of people selected to decide a verdict in a legal case, based on the evidence presented: *the right to trial by jury.* **2.** A group of people chosen to judge contestants or award prizes, as in a competition.

jury-rig (jōōr′ē-rĭg′) *tr.v.* **jury-rigged, jury-rigging, jury-rigs** To rig or assemble for temporary emergency use; improvise.

just (jŭst) *adj.* **1.** Honorable and fair: *a just ruler of the people.* **2.** Morally right; righteous: *a just cause.* **3.** Properly due or deserved; merited: *just punishment.* **4.** Based on fact or good reason; well-founded: *a just appraisal of his work.* **5.** Valid according to the law; lawful: *a jury's just decision.* ❖ *adv.* (jəst *or* jĭst; jŭst *when stressed*) **1.** Exactly: *Everything went just as we had predicted.* **2.** Only a moment ago: *We've just run out of milk.* **3.** By a small amount; barely: *just made the bus; just after 6:00.* **4.** Only; merely: *It was just a dream.* **5.** Perhaps; possibly: *I just may go.* ◆ **just about** Almost; very nearly: *We are just about finished.* —**just′ly** *adv.* —**just′ness** *n.*

justice (jŭs′tĭs) *n.* **1.** The quality of being just or fair: *A sense of justice forced the reporter to investigate both sides of the story.* **2.** Moral rightness in action or attitude; righteousness: *We argued for the justice of our cause.* **3.** Fair treatment in accordance with honor or the law: *We only seek justice for the accused.* **4.** The carrying out of the law or the way in which the law is carried out: *the administration of justice through local and county courts.* **5.** A judge or a justice of the peace: *a local justice; a justice of the Supreme Court.* **6.** Good reason; sound basis: *The customer was angry, and with justice.* ◆ **do justice to** To treat adequately or fairly: *I cannot do justice to her accomplishments in this brief report.*

justice of the peace *n.* A judge, especially one who is associated with a town or county, who has authority to try minor offenses, perform marriages, and authorize arrests.

justifiable (jŭs′tə-fī′ə-bəl *or* jŭs′tə-fī′ə-bəl) *adj.* Having sufficient grounds for justification; possible to justify: *The high price of the table is justifiable when one considers the fine workmanship.* —**jus′ti·fi′a·bly** *adv.*

justification (jŭs′tə-fĭ-kā′shən) *n.* **1.** The act of justifying or the condition of being justified. **2.** Something that justifies; a good reason.

justify (jŭs′tə-fī′) *tr.v.* **justified, justifying, justifies 1.** To show or prove to be right, just, or valid: *His fine performance justified the director's decision of casting him in the play.* **2.** To declare innocent; clear of blame: *The jury decided that the evidence justified the defendant's actions.* **3.** To format (a paragraph, for example) so that the lines of text begin and end evenly at a straight margin.

jut (jŭt) *intr.v.* **jutted, jutting, juts** To extend sharply outward or upward; project: *The branches of that huge tree jut over the street.*

jute (jōōt) *n.* **1.** A strong fiber used to make rope, twine, and coarse cloth such as burlap. **2.** Either of two Asian plants that yield such fiber.

Jute *n.* A member of a Germanic people who invaded Great Britain in the fifth and sixth centuries AD and settled there with the Angles and Saxons, eventually forming the Anglo-Saxon peoples.

juvenile (jōō′və-nīl′ *or* jōō′və-nəl) *adj.* **1.** Not fully grown or developed; young: *a juvenile coyote.* **2.** Relating to or for children or young people: *the juvenile section of the library.* **3.** Immature; childish: *juvenile behavior.* See Synonyms at **young.** ❖ *n.* A young person or animal.

juvenile delinquency *n.* Antisocial or criminal behavior by children or adolescents.

juvenile delinquent *n.* A child or adolescent guilty of antisocial or juvenile behavior.

juxtapose (jŭk′stə-pōz′) *tr.v.* **juxtaposed, juxtaposing, juxtaposes** To place side by side, especially for comparison or contrast: *We juxtaposed the two photographs of the house to see how it had changed.* —**jux′ta·po·si′tion** (jŭk′stə-pə-zĭsh′ən) *n.*

JV An abbreviation of junior varsity.

Kk

k¹ or **K** (kā) *n., pl.* **k's** or **K's** or **Ks** The 11th letter of the English alphabet.

k² An abbreviation of karat.

K An abbreviation of: **1.** kelvin. **2.** kilobyte. **3.** kindergarten. **4.** strikeout.

Kaaba (kä′bə) *n.* A Muslim shrine at Mecca, Saudi Arabia. Muslims throughout the world turn in the direction of this shrine when praying.

kabbalah or **kabbala** or **kabala** or **cabala** (kăb′ə-lə *or* kə-bä′lə) *n.* often **Kabbalah** A form of Jewish mystical theology based on esoteric interpretations of the Hebrew Scriptures. —**kab′ba·lism** *n.* —**kab′ba·list** *n.* —**kab′ba·list′ic** *adj.*

kabob (kə-bŏb′) *n.* A variant of **kebab**.

Kabuki (kə-boo′kē) *n.* A type of popular Japanese drama, evolved from the older No theater. In Kabuki, elaborately costumed performers use stylized movements, dances, and songs to enact tragedies and comedies.

Kaddish (kä′dĭsh) *n.* A Jewish prayer recited in Hebrew at daily services and by mourners after the death of a close relative.

kaffiyeh (kə-fē′ə) *n.* Variant of **keffiyeh**.

kaftan (kăf′tăn′ *or* kăf-tăn′) *n.* Variant of **caftan**.

Kaiser (kī′zər) *n.* Any of the emperors of the Holy Roman Empire (AD 962–1806), of Austria (1804–1918), or of Germany (1871–1918).

kaiser roll *n.* A large roll with a hard crust, often used for sandwiches.

kalamata olive also **calamata olive** (kä′lə-mä′tə *or* kăl′-ə-mä′tə) *n.* A variety of olive that has a fruity flavor and a meaty texture.

kale (kāl) *n.* A plant having large, dark-green, usually wrinkled leaves that are eaten as a vegetable.

kaleidoscope (kə-lī′də-skōp′) *n.* **1.** A tube in which mirrors reflect light from bits of loose colored glass contained at one end, causing them to appear as changing symmetrical designs when viewed from the other end as the tube is rotated. **2.** A series of changing phases or events: *American politics is a kaleidoscope of ideas.* —**ka·lei′do·scop′ic** (kə-lī′də-skŏp′ĭk) *adj.* —**ka·lei′do·scop′i·cal·ly** *adv.*

kalimba (kə-lĭm′bə) *n.* An mbira.

kameez (kə-mēz′) *n.* A long loose tunic, typically extending to or below the knees and slit to the waist at the sides, worn chiefly by women in southern Asia.

kamikaze (kä′mĭ-kä′zē) *n.* A Japanese pilot in World War II trained to make a suicidal crash attack, especially upon a ship.

kangaroo (kăng′gə-roo′) *n., pl.* **kangaroo** or **kangaroos** Any of various Australian marsupials having short forelegs, long hind legs used for leaping, and a long strong tail. The female kangaroo carries the newborn in a pouch on the outside of her body.

kangaroo court *n.* A court that is not authorized or legal, especially one that is hastily assembled with the sole purpose of condemning a prisoner.

kangaroo rat *n.* Any of various small long-tailed rodents found in dry regions of western North America, having long hind legs used for leaping.

kaolin (kā′ə-lĭn) *n.* A fine clay used in making ceramics.

kapok (kā′pŏk′) *n.* A silky fiber from the seedpods of a large tropical tree, used as a stuffing for pillows, mattresses, and life preservers.

kappa (kăp′ə) *n.* The tenth letter of the Greek alphabet, written K, κ. In English it is represented as *K, k.*

kaput (kə-poot′) *adj. Informal* Incapacitated or destroyed.

karaoke (kăr′ē-ō′kē) *n.* A music entertainment system that plays previously recorded musical accompaniment to songs that a person sings live.

karat also **carat** (kăr′ət) *n.* A unit of measure used to indicate the proportion of pure gold contained in an alloy. For example, since 24 karats is pure gold, a bracelet of 12-karat gold contains 12 parts gold and 12 parts alloy.

karate (kə-rä′tē) *n.* An art of self-defense developed in Japan, in which sharp blows and kicks are delivered to sensitive points on the body of an opponent.

karma (kär′mə) *n.* **1.** In Hinduism and Buddhism, the total effect of a person's actions and conduct, believed to determine that person's destiny in this life or in a future reincarnation. **2.** Fate; destiny. —**kar′mic** *adj.*

kata (kä′tä) *n., pl.* **kata** or **katas** A system of basic body positioning and movement exercises, as in karate or judo.

katydid (kā′tē-dĭd′) *n.* Any of various usually green insects that have long antennae and are closely related to the grasshoppers. The males make shrill sounds by rubbing their front wings together.

kayak (kī′ăk′) *n.* **1.** An Inuit or Yupik boat consisting of a light wooden frame covered with watertight skins, with only a small opening for the paddler. **2.** A lightweight sports canoe of a similar design. ❖ *intr.v.* **kayaked, kayaking, kayaks** To travel or race in a kayak.

kayo (kā-ō′ *or* kā′ō′) *n., pl.* **kayos** A knockout in boxing. ❖ *tr.v.* **kayoed, kayoing, kayos** To knock (someone) out in boxing.

Kazakh (kä′zăk′ *or* kə-zäk′) *adj.* Relating to Kazakhstan or its people, language, or culture. ❖ *n., pl.* **Kazakhs** or **Kazakh 1.** A native or inhabitant of Kazakhstan. **2.** The Turkic language of the Kazakhs.

kazoo (kə-zoo′) *n., pl.* **kazoos** A toy musical instrument with a membrane in the mouthpiece that vibrates and produces a buzzing sound when the player hums into it.

Kb An abbreviation of kilobit.

KB An abbreviation of kilobyte.

KBO An abbreviation of Kuiper belt object.

kc An abbreviation of kilocycle.

kea (kē′ə) *n.* A brownish-green New Zealand parrot that has a powerful curved beak and eats plants, insects, and carrion.

kebab or **kebob** also **kabob** (kə-bŏb′) *n.* Shish kebab.

keel (kēl) *n.* **1.** A strong beam, as of wood or metal, that runs along the center line of a vessel from one end to the other. The frame of the entire vessel is built up from the keel. **2.** A ridge extending down from the bottom of the hull of a boat or ship that improves directional control and is often weighted for added stability. ◆ **keel over** To collapse or fall down: *I almost keeled over with surprise.*

keelboat (kēl′bōt′) *n.* A riverboat with a keel but without sails, used for carrying freight.

keelhaul (kēl′hôl′) *tr.v.* **keelhauled, keelhauling, keelhauls 1.** To drag (a person) under the keel of a ship as punishment. **2.** To scold or criticize harshly.

keen¹ (kēn) *adj.* **keener, keenest 1.** Having a sharp edge or point: *A keen knife slit the heavy canvas.* **2.** Having highly attuned senses; very sensitive: *the keen eyes of the owl.* **3.** Characterized by intellectual quickness; sharp; bright: *a keen observer of politics.* **4.** Intense or bracing: *a keen wind.* **5.** Eager; enthusiastic: *He's really keen on hunting for fossils.* —**keen′ly** *adv.* —**keen′ness** *n.*

keen² (kēn) *intr.v.* **keened, keening, keens** To cry or wail in sorrow for the dead. ❖ *n.* A crying or wailing in sorrow for the dead.

WORD HISTORY Keen¹ comes from Middle English *kene*, which comes from Old English *cēne*, both meaning "brave." **Keen²** comes from Irish Gaelic *caonim*, meaning "I lament."

---

keep (kēp) *v.* **kept** (kĕpt), **keeping, keeps** —*tr.* **1.** To retain in one's possession; continue to have: *She kept the vase even though it was broken.* **2.** To hold for future use; save: *I kept some food for you.* **3.** To put in a customary place; store: *Where do you keep your bike?* **4.** To cause to continue in a certain position or condition: *Keep the boat headed for that island.* **5.** To continue or maintain (an activity, for example): *keep watch.* **6.** To take care of; provide for or manage: *keep house; keep a large family.* **7.** To raise: *We keep ducks and geese.* **8.** To make regular entries in: *keep a record; keep a diary.* **9.** To celebrate or observe: *keeping the Sabbath.* **10.** To habitually do something, such as work, during (a certain time period): *kept office hours on Tuesdays.* **11.** To be faithful to; fulfill: *keep a promise.* **12.** To prevent or restrain: *We kept the kite from hitting the tree.* **13.** To refrain from telling: *keep a secret.* **14.** To detain or delay: *The student was kept after school.* —*intr.* **1.** To remain in a state or condition: *keep warm; keep in touch.* **2.** To continue or persist: *He kept on talking.* **3.** To restrain oneself: *I could not keep from laughing.* **4.** To stay fresh or unspoiled: *Fish doesn't keep well.* ❖ *n.* **1.** The things needed to live: *There are many ways to earn one's keep.* **2.** The stronghold of a castle or fort. **3.** Care; charge: *The child was in my keep for the day.* ◆ **for keeps** Permanently: *The ring is yours for keeps.* **keep an eye on** To watch over attentively; mind: *Please keep an eye on the cookies and make sure they don't burn.* **keep down 1.** To prevent from growing, accomplishing, or succeeding: *They kept the rebellion down.* **2.** To hold under control or at a reduced level: *Please keep your voice down.* **3.** To refrain from vomiting: *I felt sick, but I managed to keep my food down.* **keep (one's) eyes open** or **keep (one's) eyes peeled** To be on the lookout: *Keep your eyes peeled for fireflies.* **keep to (oneself) 1.** To avoid other people; remain alone. **2.** To refrain from telling others: *We could not keep such good news to ourselves.* **keep up 1.** To maintain in good condi-

tion: *keep up the gardens.* **2.** To continue at the same level or pace: *The wind kept up all night.* **3.** To match others in success or lifestyle: *Our company must keep up with the competition.* **4.** To remain adequately informed: *keeping up with the latest styles.*

◆ **SYNONYMS keep, reserve, retain, withhold** *v.*

keeper (kē′pər) *n.* **1.** A person who watches over or guards something; an attendant or guard. **2.** A person who takes care of or manages something: *the keeper of a small shop.* **3.** *Informal* Something that is worth keeping, especially a fish that is large enough to be legally caught.

keeping (kē′pĭng) *n.* **1.** Care; custody: *documents in the keeping of my lawyer.* See Synonyms at **care. 2.** Agreement; conformity: *wearing formal clothes in keeping with the important occasion.*

keepsake (kēp′sāk′) *n.* An object that someone keeps in memory of the person who gave it or the place it came from; a memento.

keffiyeh or **kaffiyeh** (kə-fē′ə) *n.* A square of cloth, often embroidered, traditionally worn as a headdress by Arab men, either by winding it around the head or by folding it into a triangle, draping it over the head, and securing it with an agal.

keg (kĕg) *n.* **1.** A small barrel with a capacity of about 30 gallons (114 liters). **2.** A keg and its contents: *a keg of mackerel in brine.*

kelp (kĕlp) *n.* Any of various brown or green seaweeds of ocean waters that can grow very long and are often found in large clusters.

Kelt (kĕlt) *n.* Variant of **Celt.**

Keltic (kĕl′tĭk) *n. & adj.* Variant of **Celtic.**

kelvin (kĕl′vĭn) *n.* A unit of absolute temperature having the same value as one Celsius degree. It is used in the Kelvin scale. See table at **measurement.**

Kelvin scale *n.* A temperature scale beginning at absolute zero (−273.15°C), in which each degree is equal to one kelvin. On the Kelvin scale, water freezes at 273.15 degrees and boils at 373.15 degrees.

ken (kĕn) *n.* **1.** Range of understanding; comprehension: *Many forces of nature are beyond our ken.* **2.** Range of vision: *The powerful telescope brought many unobserved stars within our ken.* ❖ *intr.v.* **kenned** or **kent** (kĕnt), **kenning, kens** *Scots* To have an understanding of something.

kennel (kĕn′əl) *n.* **1.** A shelter for a dog or dogs. **2.** An establishment for the breeding, training, or boarding of dogs. ❖ *tr.v.* **kenneled, kenneling, kennels** or **kennelled, kennelling, kennels** To place or keep in or as if in a kennel.

kent (kĕnt) *v. Scots* A past tense and past participle of **ken.**

kente (kĕn′tā) *n.* **1.** A brightly patterned, hand-woven ceremonial cloth of the Ashanti. **2.** A durable machine-woven fabric similar to this fabric.

kepi (kā′pē or kĕp′ē) *n., pl.* **kepis** A French military cap with a flat round top and a visor.

kept (kĕpt) *v.* Past tense and past participle of **keep.**

keratin (kĕr′ə-tĭn) *n.* A tough fibrous protein that is found in the outer layer of skin of vertebrate animals and is the main component of hair, nails, horns, claws, and feathers. —SEE NOTE AT **triceratops.**

kerchief (kûr′chĭf or kûr′chēf′) *n., pl.* **kerchiefs** also **kerchieves** (kûr′chĭvz or kûr′chēvz) **1.** A square scarf worn over the head or around the neck. **2.** A handkerchief.

kernel (kûr′nəl) *n.* **1.** A grain or seed, especially of a cereal plant such as corn or wheat. **2.** The often edible seed inside the shell of a nut. **3.** The most important or essential part; the core: *the kernel of truth in a witty saying.*

kerosene (kĕr′ə-sēn′ *or* kăr′ə-sēn′) *n.* A thin light-colored oil that is obtained from petroleum and used chiefly as a fuel for heating and cooking and in lamps.

kestrel (kĕs′trəl) *n.* Any of various small falcons that have reddish-brown feathers and that hover for long periods of time when hunting.

ketch (kĕch) *n.* A two-masted fore-and-aft-rigged sailing vessel with a large sail on the mainmast and a shorter mast placed aft.

ketchup (kĕch′əp *or* kăch′əp) also **catsup** (kăt′səp *or* kăch′əp *or* kĕch′əp) *n.* A thick spicy sauce, usually made with tomatoes, used as a seasoning.

kettle (kĕt′l) *n.* **1.** A metal pot, usually with a lid, for boiling liquids or for cooking. **2.** A teakettle.

kettledrum (kĕt′l-drŭm′) *n.* A large drum having a bowl-shaped body of brass or copper and a parchment head that can be tuned by adjusting its tension.

key¹ (kē) *n., pl.* **keys 1.** A small piece of metal with notches or grooves that is inserted into a lock to open or close it. **2.** A device that functions like a key: *a key for opening cans; a clock key.* **3.** A keycard. **4.** Something that contributes to an accomplishment or achievement: *Your hard work has been the key to our success.* **5.** Something that solves a problem or explains a mystery: *evidence that became the key to solving the crime.* **6.** A set of answers to a test. **7.** An explanatory table, such as that explaining colors and symbols on a map. **8.** Any of the buttons or levers moved by the fingers in operating a machine or playing a musical instrument: *piano keys; the shift key on a computer keyboard.* **9.** A scale or group of musical tones related to a primary tone: *a piece written in the key of D.* **10.** The pitch of a voice or other sound. **11.** A general tone or level of intensity: *The candidate spoke in a relaxed and lower key to friends and supporters.* **12.** An area at each end of a basketball court between the baseline and the foul line and including the circle around the foul line. ❖ *adj.* Of crucial importance; significant: *key decisions.* ❖ *tr.v.* **keyed, keying, keys 1.** To adapt to special conditions; adjust: *Farming methods are keyed to the local weather conditions.* **2.** To enter (data) into a computer by means of a keyboard. **3.** To tune (a musical instrument) to a particular note: *Key the guitar to E flat.* **4.** To lock with a key. ◆ **key on** To pay close attention to; focus on: *We keyed on playing good defense.* **key up** To make nervous; excite: *I was too keyed up about my trip to eat.*

key² (kē) *n., pl.* **keys** A low-lying island or reef along a coast, especially in the Gulf of Mexico.

WORD HISTORY Key¹ comes from Old English *cæg,* meaning "piece of metal for opening or closing a lock." **Key²** comes from Spanish *cayo,* meaning "shoal, reef."

keyboard (kē′bôrd′) *n.* **1.** A panel of buttons used for typing and performing other functions on a computer or typewriter. **2.** A row of levers that are pressed with the fingers to produce or alter the sound of a musical instrument, such as a piano or organ. ❖ *tr.v.* **keyboarded, keyboarding, keyboards** To enter (text or data) into a computer by using a keyboard. —**key′board′er** *n.*

keycard (kē′kärd′) *n.* A usually plastic card, typically bearing a magnetic strip or containing an electronic chip, used to operate a lock or other mechanism.

key fob *n.* A small, portable electronic device that remotely unlocks, activates, or deactivates a piece of equip-

ment, such as a car, motorized door, or alarm.

keyhole (kē′hōl′) *n.* The opening in a lock into which a key fits.

keylogger (kē′lô′gər) *n.* A software program or hardware device that records or transmits a computer user's keystrokes. A keylogger is usually installed without the user's knowledge.

keynote (kē′nōt′) *n.* **1.** The principal tone of a musical scale or key; the tonic. **2.** The basic idea or theme, as of a speech, book, or political campaign.

keynote address *n.* An opening address, as at a political convention, that outlines the issues to be considered.

keypad (kē′păd′) *n.* A panel of buttons or keys arranged in a grid, used to input data into a cell phone, calculator, or other electronic device.

keypunch (kē′pŭnch′) *n.* A keyboard machine formerly used to punch holes in cards for data-processing systems.

key signature *n.* The group of sharps or flats placed to the right of the clef on a staff to show the musical key of a piece.

keystone (kē′stōn′) *n.* **1.** The central wedge-shaped stone of an arch that locks the other stones together. **2.** The essential element that supports a whole: *The keystone of their business was their downtown store.*

keystroke (kē′strōk′) *n.* A stroke of a key, as on a computer keyboard.

keyword (kē′wûrd′) *n.* A word used to find information about that word or to find other words: *keywords at the top of a dictionary column; entered a keyword in the search engine.*

kg An abbreviation of kilogram.

KGB (kā′jē-bē′) *n.* The intelligence and internal security agency of the former Soviet Union.

khaki (kăk′ē *or* kä′kē) *n.* **1.** A yellowish brown. **2.** A strong, heavy, khaki-colored cloth. **3. khakis a.** Pants made of this cloth. **b.** A uniform made of this cloth. —**khak′i** *adj.*

khan (kän *or* kăn) *n.* **1.** A ruler, official, or important person in India and some countries of central Asia. **2.** A medieval ruler of a Mongol, Tartar, or Turkish tribe.

khipu or **quipu** (kē′pōō) *n., pl.* **khipu** or **quipu** also **khipus** or **quipus** A record-keeping device of the Inca Empire consisting of a series of variously colored strings attached to a base rope and knotted so as to encode information, used especially for accounting purposes.

Khmer (kmâr) *n., pl.* **Khmer** or **Khmers 1.** A member of a people of Cambodia. **2.** The official language of Cambodia.

kibble (kĭb′əl) *tr.v.* **kibbled, kibbling, kibbles** To crush or grind (grain, for example) coarsely. ❖ *n.* A meal ground by this process and used in the form of pellets especially for pet food.

kibbutz (kĭ-bōōts′ *or* kĭ-bŏŏts′) *n., pl.* **kibbutzim** (kĭb′-ōōt-sēm′ *or* kĭb′ŏŏt-sēm′) A collective farm or settlement in modern Israel.

kibitz (kĭb′ĭts) *intr.v.* **kibitzed, kibitzing, kibitzes** *Informal* **1.** To chat; converse. **2.** To look on and offer unwanted advice. —**kib′itz·er** *n.*

kick (kĭk) *v.* **kicked, kicking, kicks** —*intr.* **1.** To extend the leg away from the body; strike out with the foot or feet. **2.** In sports, to score, gain ground, or begin play by kicking a ball. **3.** To propel the body in swimming by moving the legs. **4.** To recoil when fired: *The rifle kicked after he pulled the trigger.* —*tr.* **1.** To strike with the foot: *The mule kicked the stable door.* **2.** To propel or produce by striking with the foot: *a herd of cattle that kicked up swirls of dust.*

3. To spring back against suddenly: *The rifle kicked her shoulder when she fired it.* **4.** In sports, to score (a goal or point) by kicking a ball. **5.** *Slang* To free oneself of; overcome: *kicking a bad habit.* ❖ *n.* **1.** A blow with the foot: *The cow gave the bucket a kick.* **2a.** The action of kicking a ball, as in a football kickoff or punt. **b.** A kicked ball: *Block that kick!* **c.** The distance covered by a kicked ball. **3.** Any of various moves in dance in which the leg is extended from the body. **4.** The recoil of a cannon or firearm. **5.** *Slang* A feeling of pleasure; a thrill: *They will get a kick out of this greeting card.* ◆ **kick around** *Informal* **1.** To treat badly; abuse. **2.** To move from place to place. **3.** To think about or discuss: *Several new ideas were kicked around at the meeting.* **kick back 1.** To recoil unexpectedly and violently: *The rifle kicked back and bruised my shoulder.* **2.** *Informal* To take it easy; relax: *kicked back at home and watched TV.* **kick in** *Informal* To contribute (one's share) to a common fund: *kick in a few dollars for the office party.* **kick off 1.** *Informal* To begin; start: *kicked off the day with a big breakfast.* **2.** In football, to begin or resume play with a kickoff. **kick out** *Slang* To throw out; dismiss: *was kicked out of the library for repeated talking.* **kick the bucket** *Slang* To die. **kick up** *Informal* To stir up (trouble): *Our cats kick up a fuss until they are fed.* —**kick′er** *n.*

Kickapoo (kĭk′ə-pōō′) *n., pl.* **Kickapoo** or **Kickapoos 1.** A member of a Native American people formerly living in Wisconsin and Illinois and now living in Kansas, Oklahoma, and Mexico. **2.** The Algonquian language of the Kickapoo.

kickback (kĭk′băk′) *n.* **1.** A sharp reaction or recoil. **2.** *Slang* A part of a payment returned by agreement to the payer, especially in the form of a bribe.

kickball (kĭk′bôl′) *n.* A game having rules similar to baseball but played with a large ball that is rolled and kicked instead of being pitched and batted.

kickboard (kĭk′bôrd′) *n.* A board that floats, held on to by a swimmer so that the legs can move freely in the water while the upper part of the body remains afloat.

kickboxing (kĭk′bŏk′sĭng) *n.* A martial art in which competitors wear boxing gloves and throw punches as in boxing and kick with their bare feet as in karate. —**kick′box·er** *n.*

kickoff (kĭk′ôf′) *n.* **1.** In football, soccer, or rugby, a kick of a stationary ball that begins play. **2.** *Informal* A beginning: *The concert was the kickoff for the orchestra's new season.*

kickstand (kĭk′stănd′) *n.* A metal bar that can be pushed down to hold a bicycle or motorcycle upright when it is not being ridden.

kid (kĭd) *n.* **1a.** A young goat. **b.** Leather made from the skin of a young goat; kidskin. **2.** *Informal* A child or young person. ❖ *adj.* **1.** Made of kid: *kid gloves.* **2.** *Informal* Younger than oneself: *my kid brother.* ❖ *v.* **kidded, kidding, kids** —*tr.* **1.** To make fun of; tease: *They kidded me about my mismatched socks.* **2.** To deceive, especially for fun; fool: *Are you kidding me or have you really won the lottery?* —*intr.* To engage in teasing or good-humored fooling. —**kid′der** *n.*

kidnap (kĭd′năp′) *tr.v.* **kidnapped, kidnapping, kidnaps** or **kidnaped, kidnaping, kidnaps** To abduct or confine (a person) illegally by force or threat of force. —**kid′nap′per, kid′nap′er** *n.*

kidney (kĭd′nē) *n., pl.* **kidneys 1.** Either of a pair of organs that are located in the rear of the abdominal cavity of vertebrate animals. They regulate the amount of water in the body and filter wastes from the blood. **2.** The kidney of certain animals, eaten as food.

kidney bean *n.* A type of bean having large, reddish seeds shaped somewhat like a kidney.

kidskin (kĭd′skĭn′) *n.* Soft leather made from the skin of a young goat.

kielbasa (kĭl-bä′sə) *n.* A spicy smoked Polish sausage.

kill¹ (kĭl) *v.* **killed, killing, kills** —*tr.* **1.** To cause the death of; deprive of life. **2.** To put an end to; destroy: *The rainy weekend killed our plans for a picnic.* **3.** To cause severe pain to; hurt intensely: *These narrow boots are killing my feet.* **4.** To pass (time) in idle activity: *kill an hour looking at magazines.* **5.** To thwart passage of; veto: *kill a congressional bill.* **6.** To cause to stop working: *kill a motor.* **7.** To delete or remove: *kill several paragraphs of a news story.* **8.** In ice hockey, to prevent a team on a power play from scoring during (a penalty). —*intr.* **1.** To cause death. **2.** To make such a strong impression as to overcome: *always dresses to kill when going to dinner parties.* ❖ *n.* **1.** An act of killing. **2.** An animal that has just been killed, especially in hunting. ◆ **kill off** To destroy totally or on a large scale: *Continued destruction of marshes could kill off several species of fish.*

kill² (kĭl) *n.* A creek.

WORD HISTORY Kill¹ comes from Middle English *killen,* meaning "to cause death, kill." **Kill²** comes from Dutch *kil,* meaning "creek."

---

killdeer (kĭl′dîr′) *n., pl.* **killdeer** or **killdeers** A North American wading bird having two black bands across the breast and a shrill call that sounds like its name.

killer (kĭl′ər) *n.* **1.** A person, animal, or thing that kills. **2.** *Slang* Something that is extremely difficult to deal with or withstand: *That test was a killer!* ❖ *adj.* **1.** Causing death and destruction: *a killer tornado.* **2.** *Slang* Having a big or effective impact; formidable: *a killer smile; made killer profits.*

killer T cell *n.* Any of various T cells that recognize and kill cancer cells and cells that have been infected with a virus.

killer whale *n.* An orca.

killing (kĭl′ĭng) *n.* **1.** The act or action of causing death. **2.** A sudden large profit: *make a killing in the stock market.*

killjoy (kĭl′joi′) *n.* A person who spoils the fun of others.

kiln (kĭln or kĭl) *n.* Any of various ovens used for hardening, burning, or drying things such as grain or clay, especially an oven used for firing pottery, porcelain, or brick.

kilo (kē′lō) *n., pl.* **kilos** A kilogram.

kilo– A prefix that means: **1.** One thousand (10^3): *kilowatt.* **2.** 1,024 (2^{10}): *kilobyte.*

kilobit (kĭl′ə-bĭt′) *n.* One thousand bits, used as a unit to measure the rate of the transmission of computer data.

kilobyte (kĭl′ə-bīt′) *n.* A unit of computer memory equal to 1,024 (2^{10}) bytes.

kilocalorie (kĭl′ə-kăl′ə-rē) *n.* The quantity of heat needed to raise the temperature of one kilogram of water one degree Celsius.

kilocycle (kĭl′ə-sī′kəl) *n.* A kilohertz.

kilogram (kĭl′ə-grăm′) *n.* The basic unit of mass or weight in the metric system, equal to 1,000 grams (about 2.2 pounds). See table at **measurement.**

kilohertz (kĭl′ə-hûrts′) *n.* A unit of frequency equal to 1,000 cycles per second, used to express the frequency of radio waves.

kiloliter (kĭl′ə-lē′tər) *n.* A metric unit of volume equal to 1,000 liters.

kilometer (kĭ-lŏm′ĭ-tər *or* kĭl′ə-mē′tər) *n.* A unit of length equal to 1,000 meters (0.62 mile). See table at **measurement.**

kiloton (kĭl′ə-tŭn′) *n.* **1.** A unit of weight or capacity equal to 1,000 metric tons. **2.** A unit of explosive force equal to the force with which 1,000 metric tons of TNT explode.

kilowatt (kĭl′ə-wŏt′) *n.* A unit of power, especially electric power, equal to 1,000 watts.

kilowatt-hour (kĭl′ə-wŏt-our′) *n.* A unit of energy, especially electrical energy, equivalent to one kilowatt acting for a period of one hour.

kilt (kĭlt) *n.* **1.** A knee-length pleated skirt, usually of a tartan wool, worn by men in the Scottish Highlands. **2.** A similar skirt worn by women, girls, and boys.

kilter (kĭl′tər) *n.* Good condition; proper form: *programs designed to bring the economy back into kilter.*

kimchi (kĭm′chē) *n., pl.* **kimchis** A spicy Korean dish made of salted, fermented vegetables.

kimono (kə-mō′nō) *n., pl.* **kimonos** A long loose robe with wide sleeves and a sash, traditionally worn in Japan especially for formal occasions.

kin (kĭn) *n.* (*used with a plural verb*) **1.** A person's relatives; family: *visited my aunt and her kin.* **2.** A group of related organisms or species: *whales and their kin.* ❖ *adj.* Related; kindred: *We found out that the Wilsons are kin to us.* —SEE NOTE AT **king.**

kinara (kē-när′ə) *n.* A holder for one black, three red, and three green candles, used in celebrating Kwanzaa.

kind¹ (kīnd) *adj.* **kinder, kindest 1.** Having a friendly, generous, or warm-hearted nature: *It was kind of you to offer to babysit.* **2.** Showing understanding for others: *kind words.*

kind² (kīnd) *n.* A particular sort or type: *What kind of toothpaste do you use?* ◆ **in kind 1.** With produce or goods rather than with money: *paying in kind.* **2.** In the same manner or with an equivalent: *return a polite remark in kind.* **kind of** *Informal* Rather; somewhat: *I'm kind of hungry.*

WORD HISTORY Kind¹ comes from the Old English adjective *gecynde,* meaning "natural, kind." **Kind²** comes from the Old English noun *gecynd,* meaning "race, offspring, kind."

kindergarten (kĭn′dər-gär′tn) *n.* A class for children from four to six years of age that prepares them for elementary school.

kindhearted (kīnd′här′tĭd) *adj.* Kind, sympathetic, or generous. —**kind′heart′ed·ly** *adv.* —**kind′heart′ed·ness** *n.*

kindle (kĭn′dl) *v.* **kindled, kindling, kindles** —*tr.* **1.** To build and start (a fire). **2.** To arouse; excite: *That year of studying in Italy kindled my interest in art.* —*intr.* **1.** To catch fire: *The paper kindled on the third match.* **2.** To become inflamed or stirred up: *Passion kindled in their hearts.* —**kin′dler** *n.*

kindling (kĭnd′lĭng) *n.* Sticks and other small pieces of material used to start a fire.

kindly (kĭnd′lē) *adj.* **kindlier, kindliest 1.** Considerate and helpful; kind: *a kindly and warm-hearted friend; kindly advice.* **2.** Agreeable; pleasant: *a kindly breeze.* ❖ *adv.* **1.** Out of kindness: *She kindly offered to help.* **2.** In a kind way; cordially; warmly: *greeted them kindly.* **3.** As a matter of courtesy; please: *Kindly read the notice aloud.* —**kind′li·ness** *n.*

kindness (kīnd′nĭs) *n.* **1.** The quality or state of being

kind; generosity. **2.** A kind act or kind treatment; a favor: *We are grateful for your many kindnesses.*

kindred (kĭn′drĭd) *n.* **1.** A group of related people, such as a clan. **2.** (*used with a plural verb*) A person's family or relatives. ❖ *adj.* Having a similar origin or nature: *kindred feelings.*

kinematics (kĭn′ə-măt′ĭks) *n.* (*used with a singular verb*) The branch of physics that deals with the characteristics of motion, without reference to mass or the causes of motion.

kinetic (kə-nĕt′ĭk *or* kī-nĕt′ĭk) *adj.* Relating to or produced by motion.

kinetic energy *n.* The energy possessed by a body because it is in motion.

kinetics (kə-nĕt′ĭks *or* kī-nĕt′ĭks) *n.* (*used with a singular verb*) The branch of physics that deals with forces and motion; dynamics.

kinfolk (kĭn′fōk′) *also* **kinsfolk** (kĭnz′fōk′) *or* **kinfolks** (kĭn′fōks′) *pl.n.* A person's relatives; kindred.

king (kĭng) *n.* **1.** A man who rules a nation, usually inheriting his position for life. **2.** A person who is the most outstanding or important in a particular group or category: *That reporter is king of sportswriters.* **3.** Something that is regarded as the most powerful or important: *In the South, cotton was once king.* **4.** The most important piece in chess, able to move one square in any direction. **5.** In checkers, a piece that has reached the opponent's side of the board and is able to move both backward and forward. **6.** A playing card bearing the figure of a king and ranking next above a queen. **7. Kings** Either of two biblical books, I Kings and II Kings, that tell the history of the kings of Israel and Judah.

WORD HISTORY Our Modern English noun **king** comes from the Old English noun *cyning.* The word root *cyn*– is related to the modern word **kin,** as in "kinfolk, relatives." The suffix –*ing* originally meant "son of, descended from." Thus the family names Browning and Whiting mean "son of Brown" and "descendant of White," and *cyning* meant literally "son of the people," which can be understood as "(royal) descendant of the nation."

kingbird (kĭng′bûrd′) *n.* Any of various insect-eating songbirds of the Americas that defend their territories by chasing away other birds.

kingbolt (kĭng′bōlt′) *n.* A vertical bolt that connects the front axle to the body of a wagon or other vehicle and acts as a pivot when the vehicle turns.

king crab *n.* Any of several large crabs found along the coastal waters of Alaska, Japan, and Siberia, valued for their meat.

kingdom (kĭng′dəm) *n.* **1.** A country or other political unit that is ruled by a king or queen. **2.** An area, province, or realm: *the kingdom of the imagination.* **3.** A broad classification into which organisms are grouped, ranking above a phylum and, in some systems, below a domain. One common system of classification divides life into five kingdoms: prokaryotes (bacteria and archaea), protists, fungi, plants, and animals.

kingfisher (kĭng′fĭsh′ər) *n.* Any of various colorful birds that feed on fish and have a long bill and a crest on the head.

King James Bible *n.* An English translation of the Bible from Hebrew and Greek published in 1611 at the direction of James I for the Church of England; the Authorized Version.

kingly (kĭng′lē) *adj.* **kinglier, kingliest** Relating to or fit for a king; regal; royal. —**king′li·ness** *n.* —**king′ly** *adv.*

kingpin (kĭng′pĭn′) *n.* **1.** A headpin. **2.** The most important person or part in an organization, industry, or system. **3.** A kingbolt.

kingship (kĭng′shĭp′) *n.* **1.** The position or power of a king. **2.** The area ruled by a king; a kingdom. **3.** The period during which a king rules; a reign.

king-size (kĭng′sīz′) or **king-sized** (kĭng′sīzd′) *adj.* **1.** Larger or longer than the usual or standard size: *king-size muffins.* **2.** Large in intensity: *a king-sized headache.*

king snake *n.* Any of various nonvenomous snakes of the Americas, having a black or brown body with white, yellow, or reddish markings. King snakes are constrictors and eat small animals and other snakes.

kink (kĭngk) *n.* **1.** A tight curl or twist, as in a hair, wire, or rope. **2.** A painful cramp or stiffness in a muscle, especially of the neck or back; a crick. **3.** A flaw or difficulty, as in a plan: *Technicians finally got the kinks out of the new computer program.* ❖ *intr. & tr.v.* **kinked, kinking, kinks** To form or cause to form a kink; curl or twist sharply: *When the hose kinks, water can't flow through it.*

kinkajou (kĭng′kə-jōō′) *n.* A furry tree-dwelling mammal of tropical America having a long tail that can curl around objects.

kinky (kĭng′kē) *adj.* **kinkier, kinkiest 1.** Full of kinks; tightly curled or twisted: *kinky wire; kinky hair.* **2.** Having or appealing to unconventional tastes. —**kink′i·ness** *n.*

kinsfolk (kĭnz′fōk′) *pl.n.* Variant of **kinfolk**.

kinship (kĭn′shĭp′) *n.* **1.** The condition of being related by blood, marriage, or adoption; family relationship. **2.** A connection or similarity between people or things.

kinsman (kĭnz′mən) *n.* A male relative.

kinswoman (kĭnz′wŏŏm′ən) *n.* A female relative.

kiosk (kē′ŏsk′ or kē-ŏsk′) *n.* **1.** A small structure, usually opened in front, that is used as a newsstand, as a place for selling goods, or as a place to conduct transactions, as at a bank. **2.** A cylindrical structure on which advertisements are posted.

Kiowa (kī′ə-wô′ or kī′ə-wä′ or kī′ə-wā′) *n., pl.* **Kiowa** or **Kiowas 1.** A member of a Native American people of the south-central United States. **2.** The language of the Kiowa.

kipper (kĭp′ər) *n.* A herring or salmon that has been split, salted, and smoked. ❖ *tr.v.* **kippered, kippering, kippers** To prepare (fish) by splitting, salting, and smoking.

kirk (kûrk) *n. Scots* A church.

Kirghiz (kîr-gēz′) *adj. & n.* Variant of **Kyrgyz**.

kismet (kĭz′mĕt′) *n.* Fate; fortune.

kiss (kĭs) *v.* **kissed, kissing, kisses** —*tr.* **1.** To touch with the lips as a sign of affection, greeting, or reverence. **2.** To touch lightly or gently: *Rain kissed the flowers.* **3.** To strike lightly; brush against: *I barely kissed her car with my bumper.* —*intr.* To engage in mutual touching or caressing with the lips. ❖ *n.* **1.** A touch with the lips as a token of affection, greeting, or reverence. **2.** A slight or gentle touch. **3.** A small piece of candy, especially of chocolate.

kisser (kĭs′ər) *n.* **1.** A person who kisses. **2.** *Slang* The mouth or face.

kit¹ (kĭt) *n.* **1a.** A set of articles or tools for a certain purpose: *a first-aid kit; a sewing kit.* **b.** A bag or other container for carrying such a set. **2.** A set of parts or materials to be assembled: *a model airplane kit.*

kit² (kĭt) *n.* A kitten or one of the young of certain other fur-bearing mammals, such as a fox or rabbit.

WORD HISTORY Kit¹ comes from Middle English *kitte,* meaning "wooden tub." **Kit²** is short for *kitten.*

kitchen (kĭch′ən) *n.* A room or area where food is prepared or cooked.

kitchenette (kĭch′ə-nĕt′) *n.* A small kitchen.

kitchen police *n.* **1.** Enlisted military personnel assigned to work in a kitchen. **2.** Military duty helping the cooks in a kitchen.

kite (kīt) *n.* **1.** A light frame, as of wood, covered with paper or similar material and designed to be flown in the wind at the end of a long string. **2.** Any of various graceful birds of prey having long pointed wings and often a forked tail.

kiteboard (kīt′bôrd′) *n.* Any of the boards, usually equipped with bindings for the feet, used in kiteboarding. ❖ *intr.v.* **kiteboarded, kiteboarding, kiteboards** To engage in kiteboarding. —**kite′board·er** *n.*

kiteboarding (kīt′bôr′dĭng) *n.* Any of several sports, such as kitesurfing and snowkiting, in which a person, often wearing a harness, is pulled by holding a control bar that is attached to a power kite.

kitesurfing (kīt′bôr′dĭng) *n.* **1.** A form of kiteboarding in which a person is pulled by a power kite across water while riding a kiteboard or wakeboard. **2.** A similar sport, such as snowkiting. —**kite′surf′** *v.* —**kite′surf′er** *n.*

kith and kin (kĭth′ ən kĭn′) *pl.n.* Friends and relatives.

kitsch (kĭch) *n.* Pieces of art or other objects that appeal to popular or uncultivated taste, as in being garish or overly sentimental. —**kitsch′i·fy′** *v.* —**kitsch′y** *adj.*

kitten (kĭt′n) *n.* A young cat.

kitty¹ (kĭt′ē) *n., pl.* **kitties** A collection of money funded by more than one person, such as the players in a card game.

kitty² (kĭt′ē) *n., pl.* **kitties** A kitten or cat.

kitty-cornered (kĭt′ē-kôr′nərd) *adj. & adv.* Variant of **cater-cornered**.

kiwi (kē′wē) *n., pl.* **kiwis 1.** Any of several flightless birds of New Zealand having a long slender bill, a rounded body, and brownish feathers. **2.** A kiwifruit.

kiwifruit (kē′wē-frōōt′) *n.* **1.** A fuzzy brown fruit with sweet green pulp. **2.** The woody vine that bears this fruit, native to China and widely grown in New Zealand.

KKK An abbreviation of Ku Klux Klan.

Klan (klăn) *n.* The Ku Klux Klan.

Kleenex (klē′nĕks′) A trademark used for a soft facial tissue.

kleptomania (klĕp′tə-mā′nē-ə or klĕp′tə-mān′yə) *n.* An uncontrollable urge to steal, especially when there is no personal need or desire for the things stolen. —**klep′-to·ma′ni·ac′** (klĕp′tə-mā′nē-ăk′) *n.*

klezmer (klĕz′mər) *n.* The traditional music of the Jews of eastern Europe, played by small traveling bands.

klieg light (klēg) *n.* A powerful lamp used especially when making movies to light a scene.

klutz (klŭts) *n. Slang* A clumsy or stupid person.

km An abbreviation of kilometer.

knack (năk) *n.* **1.** A special talent or skill: *The mechanic has a knack for fixing cars.* **2.** A tendency or pattern of behavior: *has a knack for saying the wrong thing.*

knackwurst or **knockwurst** (nŏk′wûrst′ or nŏk′wŏŏrst′) *n.* A short, thick, highly seasoned sausage.

knapsack (năp′săk′) *n.* A bag made of sturdy material and having shoulder straps for carrying articles such as camping supplies on the back.

knave (nāv) *n.* **1.** A dishonest crafty man: *The knave got the advantage by trickery.* **2.** A male servant: *a kitchen knave.* **3.** A man of humble birth or position. **4.** A jack in a deck of playing cards. **—knav′ish** *adj.* **—knav′ish·ly** *adv.* —SEE NOTE AT **knit.**

knavery (nā′və-rē) *n.* Dishonest or crafty dealing.

knead (nēd) *tr.v.* **kneaded, kneading, kneads 1.** To mix and work (a substance) into a pliable mass, as by folding, stretching, and pressing: *The cook kneaded the pizza dough.* **2.** To squeeze, press, or roll with the hands, as in massaging: *The coach kneaded the runner's sore leg muscles.* **3.** To make or shape by or as if by kneading. **—knead′er** *n.*

knee (nē) *n.* **1a.** The joint at which the human thigh and lower leg come together. **b.** The region around this joint. **2.** A corresponding joint in the leg of another animal. **3.** Something that resembles a knee, as a point where something bends sharply. **4.** The part of a pair of pants that covers the knee. ❖ *tr.v.* **kneed, kneeing, knees** To push or strike with the knee: *The waiter kneed the kitchen door open.* —SEE NOTE AT **knit.**

knee breeches *pl.n.* Trousers extending to or just below the knee.

kneecap (nē′kăp′) *n.* The patella.

knee-deep (nē′dēp′) *adj.* **1.** Reaching as high as the knees: *The prairie grass was knee-deep.* **2.** Submerged to the knees: *The hikers were knee-deep in swampy water.* **3.** Deeply occupied or engaged: *I'm knee-deep in work.*

knee-high (nē′hī′) *adj.* Reaching as high as the knee: *knee-high boots.* ❖ *n.* (nē′hī′) A sock or stocking that extends to just below the knee.

knee-jerk (nē′jûrk′) *adj.* *Slang* **1.** Easily predictable; automatic: *a knee-jerk response to criticism.* **2.** Reacting spontaneously in the expected manner: *a knee-jerk cynic.*

kneel (nēl) *intr.v.* **knelt** (nēlt) or **kneeled, kneeling, kneels** To rest or fall on one or both knees: *The tailor knelt to mark the pants for hemming.*

kneeler (nē′lər) *n.* **1.** A person who kneels, as when praying. **2.** Something, such as a stool, cushion, or board, on which to kneel.

kneepad (nē′păd′) *n.* A protective covering for the knee.

knell (nĕl) *intr.v.* **knelled, knelling, knells** To ring slowly and solemnly: *The church bells knelled all day.* ❖ *n.* **1.** The sound of a bell rung slowly and solemnly, as for a funeral. **2.** A signal of disaster, death, or destruction: *Construction of a new highway sounded the knell of the farm.*

knelt (nĕlt) *v.* A past tense and a past participle of **kneel.**

Knesset (knĕs′ĕt′) *n.* The parliament of Israel.

knew (nōō) *v.* Past tense of **know.**

knickerbockers (nĭk′ər-bŏk′ərz) *pl.n.* Loose pants that are gathered in a band just below the knees.

knickers (nĭk′ərz) *pl.n.* **1.** Long bloomers formerly worn as underwear by women and girls. **2.** Loose pants that are gathered in with a band just below the knees.

knickknack also **nicknack** (nĭk′năk′) *n.* A small ornamental article; a trinket.

knife (nīf) *n., pl.* **knives** (nīvz) **1.** A tool made of a sharp blade with a handle, used for cutting, carving, or spreading. **2.** A cutting edge or blade of a tool or machine. ❖ *v.* **knifed, knifing, knifes** —*tr.* **1.** To stab with a knife. **2.** *Informal* To betray by underhand means. —*intr.* To cut or slash a way through something: *The shark's fin knifed through the water.*

knight (nīt) *n.* **1.** In the Middle Ages, a man who served a king or lord as a mounted soldier in return for the right to hold and profit from land, especially such a man raised to an order of chivalry after training as a page and squire. **2.** A man given a rank of honor by a sovereign for personal merit or service to the country. **3.** A chess piece shaped like the head of a horse that can be moved two squares horizontally and one vertically or two squares vertically and one horizontally. ❖ *tr.v.* **knighted, knighting, knights** To make (a person) a knight. **—knight′ly** *adj. & adv.* —SEE NOTE AT **knit.**

knight-errant (nīt′ĕr′ənt) *n., pl.* **knights-errant** In medieval times, a knight who traveled in search of adventure.

knighthood (nīt′hŏŏd′) *n.* **1.** The rank or dignity of a knight. **2.** The behavior or qualities suitable for a knight; chivalry. **3.** Knights considered as a group.

knish (kə-nĭsh′) *n.* A piece of dough stuffed with potato, meat, or cheese and baked or fried.

knit (nĭt) *v.* **knit** or **knitted, knitting, knits** —*tr.* **1.** To make (a fabric or garment) by forming yarn or thread into interlocked loops either by hand with special needles or by machine: *I knit a sweater.* **2.** To join closely; unite securely: *Shared interests knitted the group together.* **3.** To draw together in wrinkles; furrow: *knit one's brows in thought.* —*intr.* **1.** To make a fabric or garment by knitting: *I would like to learn to knit.* **2.** To grow together or become joined, as a fractured bone. **3.** To come together in wrinkles or furrows, as the brows. ❖ *n.* A fabric or garment made by knitting: *a cotton knit.* **—knit′ter** *n.*

WORD HISTORY The *k* at the beginning of the word **knit** is one of those mysterious "silent letters" that make no sense and that we just have to memorize when learning to spell. Once upon a time, though, most of these "silent letters" did make sense because they weren't silent. Over 500 years ago, *knit* (and similar words like **knave, knee,** and **knight**) were pronounced with a consonant cluster (kn) at the beginning. As time passed, a (k) sound at the beginning of a word was lost in pronunciation if it was followed by an (n) sound.

knitting (nĭt′ĭng) *n.* **1.** The act or process of making knitted fabric or garments: *Knitting is a useful skill.* **2.** Fabric or a garment that has been knitted or is being knitted: *I brought along my knitting.*

knitting needle *n.* A long, thin, pointed rod used in pairs or sets to knit yarn into cloth.

knitwear (nĭt′wâr′) *n.* Knitted garments.

knives (nīvz) *n.* Plural of **knife.**

knob (nŏb) *n.* **1.** A rounded lump or mass: *a brass knob on top of a bedpost.* **2.** A rounded handle or dial: *the knob that controls the stereo's volume.* **—knob′by** *adj.*

knock (nŏk) *v.* **knocked, knocking, knocks** —*tr.* **1.** To strike with a hard blow or hit: *knocked the ball out of the park.* **2.** To affect in a specified way by striking hard: *I accidentally knocked the glass of water over.* **3.** To cause to strike: *I knocked my head on the low doorway.* **4.** To produce by hitting or striking: *knocked a hole in the wall.* **5.** *Slang* To criticize; find fault with: *The critic knocked the actor's performance.* —*intr.* **1.** To strike a blow or series of blows causing a noise: *The neighbor knocked on our door.* **2.** To collide with something: *In the dark, I knocked into the table.* **3.** To make a pounding or clanking noise: *The old car's engine knocks whenever we drive up a hill.* ❖ *n.* **1.** A sharp blow or hit: *The doctor gave me a knock on the knee.* **2.** The sound of a blow on a hard surface; a rap. **3.**

A pounding or clanking noise, as of an engine in need of repairs. ◆ **knock down** To break up or take apart: *We knocked down the tent and packed it in the car.* **knock off** *Informal* **1.** To cease; stop: *knock off work; knock off piano practice.* **2.** To complete, accomplish, or dispose of hastily or easily; finish: *I knocked off several letters this afternoon.* **3.** To eliminate; deduct: *Using the coupon knocked five dollars off our bill.* **knock out 1.** To make unconscious, as by a blow with the fist. **2.** To make useless or prevent from working: *The storm knocked out power in our neighborhood.* **3.** *Informal* To exhaust completely: *That long math exam really knocked me out.*

knockabout (nŏk′ə-bout′) *adj.* **1.** Rough and boisterous. **2.** Suitable for rough use. ❖ *n.* A small sailing boat with a mainsail and a jib.

knockdown (nŏk′doun′) *n.* The act or an instance of knocking down. ❖ *adj.* **1.** Powerful and overwhelming: *a knockdown punch.* **2.** Designed to be put together and taken apart quickly and easily: *knockdown furniture.*

knocker (nŏk′ər) *n.* A metal ring, knob, or hammer hinged to a door for use in knocking.

knock-knee (nŏk′nē′) *n.* A deformity of the legs in which the knees are abnormally close together and the ankles are spread apart. —**knock′-kneed′** *adj.*

knockoff (nŏk′ôf′) *n. Informal* An unauthorized copy or imitation, as of designer clothing.

knockout (nŏk′out′) *n.* **1.** A victory in boxing in which the loser is unable to rise from the canvas within a specified period of time. **2.** A blow that renders a person unconscious or gains such a victory. **3.** *Slang* A strikingly attractive person or thing.

knockwurst (nŏk′wûrst′ *or* nŏk′wŏorst′) *n.* Variant of **knackwurst.**

knoll (nōl) *n.* A small rounded hill.

knot (nŏt) *n.* **1.** A tangle of interlacing thread, cord, hair, or similar material. **2.** A fastening made by tying material such as string, rope, or cord in a certain way: *a square knot.* **3.** A decorative bow of ribbon, fabric, or braid. **4.** A tight cluster of people or things: *a knot of spectators at the theater's entrance.* **5.** A difficult problem. **6.** A feeling of tightness in the body: *a knot in my stomach.* **7a.** A round swelling on a tree trunk where a branch grows out. **b.** The hard dark spot in a board where such a branch grew. **8.** A unit of speed equal to one nautical mile per hour, about 1.15 statute miles (1.85 kilometers) per hour, used especially by ships and aircraft. ❖ *tr.v.* **knotted, knotting, knots 1.** To tie or fasten in or with a knot: *We knotted the rope around the post.* **2.** To entangle in knots: *My hair got knotted by the wind.*

knothole (nŏt′hōl′) *n.* A hole in a piece of lumber where a knot has dropped out or been removed.

knotty (nŏt′ē) *adj.* **knottier, knottiest 1.** Tied or snarled in knots: *knotty string.* **2.** Having many knots or knobs: *knotty lumber.* **3.** Difficult to understand or solve: *a knotty algebra problem.*

know (nō) *v.* **knew** (nōō), **known** (nōn), **knowing, knows** —*tr.* **1.** To believe correctly and with good reason: *He knows that two plus two equals four.* **2.** To have a correct idea about: *She knows the answer to the question.* **3.** To regard as true; be sure of: *I know that the play will be a success.* **4.** To have skill in or a practical grasp of: *I know how to make lasagna.* **5.** To be acquainted or familiar with: *I know my neighbors well.* **6.** To recognize: *I know the tune, but I can't remember the words.* **7.** To have fixed in memory: *The actors must know their lines well.* **8.** To be

able to distinguish: *Does that little child know right from left?* —*intr.* **1.** To possess knowledge or understanding: *My sister knows about the history of photography.* **2.** To be aware: *I knew about their plans for the weekend.* ◆ **in the know** *Informal* In possession of special or secret information: *My job at the town hall put me in the know about local politics.* —**know′a·ble** *adj.* —**know′er** *n.*

know-how (nō′hou′) *n.* Practical knowledge; skill: *Building a house requires lots of know-how.*

knowing (nō′ing) *adj.* **1.** Having knowledge or awareness: *a knowing hiker, wise in the ways of the woods.* **2.** Showing shrewdness or resourcefulness. **3.** Suggestive of inside or secret information: *a knowing glance.* —**know′ing·ly** *adv.*

know-it-all (nō′ĭt-ôl′) *n. Informal* A person who claims or pretends to know everything.

knowledge (nŏl′ĭj) *n.* **1.** Awareness or understanding gained through experience or study: *He has a thorough knowledge of carpentry.* **2.** The fact or state of knowing: *Knowledge of the company's bad sales record made investors cautious.*

knowledgeable (nŏl′ĭ-jə-bəl) *adj.* Having or showing knowledge or intelligence; well informed: *a candidate who is knowledgeable about foreign policy.*

known (nōn) *v.* Past participle of **know.** ❖ *adj.* Proved or generally recognized: *a singer of known talent.*

knuckle (nŭk′əl) *n.* **1.** A joint of a finger, especially one of the joints connecting a finger to the hand. **2.** The rounded mass formed by the bones in a joint of the finger: *I scraped my knuckles on the sidewalk.* **3.** A cut of meat from a leg joint: *pig's knuckles.* ❖ *tr.v.* **knuckled, knuckling, knuckles** To rub, press, or hit with the knuckles. ◆ **knuckle down** To apply oneself earnestly to a task: *We knuckled down and studied for the test.* **knuckle under** To yield to pressure; give in: *I knuckled under and agreed to go to the store.*

knuckle ball *n.* In baseball, a slow pitch that has no spin and veers erratically, thrown by gripping the ball with the nails or knuckles near the tips of the index and middle fingers, and often the third finger.

knucklehead (nŭk′əl-hĕd′) *n. Informal* A stupid person; a blockhead.

KO (kā′ō′) *Slang tr.v.* **KO'd, KO'ing, KO's** To knock out, as in boxing. ❖ *n.* (kā-ō′ *or* kā′ō′) A knockout, as in boxing.

koala (kō-ä′lə) *n.* An Australian marsupial that has dense grayish fur, large ears, and sharp claws. Koalas live in eucalyptus trees and feed chiefly on their leaves. The female koala carries her young in a pouch.

kohlrabi (kōl-rä′bē *or* kōl-răb′ē) *n., pl.* **kohlrabies** A plant related to the cabbage, having a thick rounded stem that resembles a turnip and is eaten as a vegetable.

kola (kō′lə) *n.* Variant of **cola²**.

Komodo dragon (kə-mō′dō) *n.* A large monitor lizard of Indonesia measuring up to 10 feet (3 meters) long.

kook (kōōk) *n. Informal* A crazy or eccentric person.

kookaburra (kōōk′ə-bûr′ə) *n.* A large kingfisher of southern and eastern Australia, having a call that sounds like wild laughter.

kooky (kōō′kē) *adj.* **kookier, kookiest** *Slang* Strange or crazy: *a kooky idea.* —**kook′i·ness** *n.*

kopek (kō′pĕk) *n.* A Russian coin equal to ¹/₁₀₀ of a ruble.

Koran or **Qur'an** (kə-rän′ *or* kə-răn′) *n.* The sacred book of Islam, believed by Muslims to contain the word of Allah as revealed to the prophet Muhammad.

Korean (kə-rē′ən) *adj.* Relating to Korea or its people, language, or culture. ❖ *n.* **1.** A native or inhabitant of Korea. **2.** The language of the Koreans.

Korean War *n.* A war fought between North Korea, aided by China, and South Korea, aided by United Nations forces consisting mainly of US troops, lasting from 1950 to 1953.

kosher (kō′shər) *adj.* **1.** Conforming to or prepared in accordance with Jewish dietary laws. **2.** *Slang* Proper; correct: *Is it kosher to wear jeans in the office?* ❖ *tr.v.* **koshered, koshering, koshers** To make proper or ritually pure. ◆ **keep kosher** To observe Jewish dietary laws.

koto (kō′tō) *n., pl.* **kotos** A Japanese musical instrument having usually 13 silk strings stretched over a long, hollow, wooden body and played by plucking.

kowtow (kou-tou′ *or* kou′tou′) *intr.v.* **kowtowed, kowtowing, kowtows** **1.** To kneel and touch the forehead to the ground in expression of deep respect, worship, or submission. **2.** To show exaggerated respect or obedience; fawn: *kowtowed to the boss hoping to win favor.* ❖ *n.* The act of kneeling and touching the forehead to the ground.

KP *n.* **1.** The assignment of working in a kitchen for one of the armed services. **2.** The soldiers or other military personnel who have such an assignment.

kph An abbreviation of kilometers per hour.

kraal (krôl *or* kräl) *n.* **1.** A village of southern Africa, usually surrounded by a fence or stockade. **2.** A pen for sheep or cattle in southern Africa.

Kremlin (krĕm′lĭn) *n.* **1.** The citadel of Moscow, housing the major offices of the government. **2.** The government of Russia and formerly of the Soviet Union.

krill (krĭl) *n., pl.* **krill** Small shrimplike crustaceans that are the principal food of certain whales and are also eaten by seals, fishes, and other marine animals.

Krishna (krĭsh′nə) *n.* A Hindu god worshiped as an incarnation of the god Vishnu.

Kriss Kringle (krĭs′ krĭng′gəl) *n.* Santa Claus.

krona (krō′nə) *n.* **1.** *pl.* **kronur** (krō′nər) The basic monetary unit of Iceland. **2.** *pl.* **kronor** (krō′nôr′ *or* krō′nər) The basic monetary unit of Sweden.

krone (krō′nə) *n., pl.* **kroner** (krō′nər) The basic monetary unit of Norway and Denmark.

krypton (krĭp′tŏn′) *n.* *Symbol* **Kr** A colorless, chemically inert gaseous element used chiefly in fluorescent lamps and photographic flash lamps. Atomic number 36. See **Periodic Table.**

kudos (kōō′dōz′ *or* kōō′dōs′ *or* kōō′dōs′) *n.* Praise, fame, or renown for exceptional achievement: *The diplomat received kudos for settling the dispute.*

USAGE The word **kudos** looks like a plural noun, but historically it is a singular noun: *Kudos is* (not *are*) *due her for her fine work.* Nowadays, *kudos* is often treated as a plural: *She received many kudos for her work.* Because of this plural use, a singular form *kudo*, meaning "a compliment," has arisen. This change follows the pattern whereby the words *pea* and *cherry* were shortened from nouns ending with an (s) sound (English *pease* and French *cerise*) that were mistakenly thought to be plu-

ral. The singular *kudo* is usually viewed as incorrect in formal contexts.

kudu (kōō′dōō) *n.* Either of two large African antelopes having a brownish or grayish coat with white vertical stripes. The male has long horns twisted in a spiral.

kudzu (kŭd′zōō) *n.* An Asian vine that has clusters of purple flowers and is a common weed in the southeast United States.

kufi (kōō′fē) *n., pl.* **kufis** **1.** Any of various styles of brimless hats and caps traditionally worn by Muslim men, especially a crocheted or knit skullcap. **2.** A brimless cylindrical hat traditionally worn by men in western Africa.

kugel (kōō′gəl) *n.* A baked pudding of noodles or potatoes, eggs, and seasonings, traditionally eaten by Jews on the Sabbath.

Kuiper belt (kī′pər) *n.* A disk-shaped region in the outer solar system, lying beyond the orbit of Neptune and containing thousands of small, icy celestial objects. Some of these objects enter the inner solar system as comets.

Kuiper belt object *n.* Any of the small icy bodies orbiting the sun in the Kuiper belt, generally having a diameter less than Pluto's. Pluto is a Kuiper belt object.

Ku Klux Klan (kōō′ klŭks klăn′) *n.* **1.** A secret society founded in the southern United States after the Civil War to restore the domination of whites over blacks through the use of terrorism. **2.** A secret organization founded in Georgia in 1915 for a similar purpose and modeled on the earlier society.

kumquat (kŭm′kwŏt′) *n.* **1.** A small thin-skinned fruit somewhat like an orange but having sweet edible skin and sour pulp. **2.** Any of several trees or shrubs that bear such fruit.

kung fu (kŭng′ fōō′) *n.* Any of various Chinese martial arts using sharp blows and kicks.

Kurd (kûrd *or* kōōrd) *n.* A member of a group of peoples speaking Iranian languages and living primarily in an extensive plateau region of southeast Turkey, northeast Iraq, and northwest Iran.

Kurdish (kûr′dĭsh *or* kōōr′dĭsh) *adj.* Relating to the Kurds or their language or culture. ❖ *n.* The language of the Kurds.

kurta (kûr′tə) *n.* A loose long-sleeved shirt, often extending to the knees, worn primarily in southern Asia.

kvetch (kvĕch) *Slang intr.v.* **kvetched, kvetching, kvetches** *Informal* To complain persistently and whiningly. ❖ *n.* **1.** A chronic, whining complainer. **2.** A nagging complaint.

kW An abbreviation of kilowatt.

Kwanzaa also **Kwanza** (kwän′zə) *n.* An African-American cultural festival, celebrated from December 26 to January 1.

kwashiorkor (kwä′shē-ôr′kôr′) *n.* A severe form of malnutrition, usually of children, caused by a lack of protein in the diet and characterized by protrusion of the abdomen and discoloration of the skin and hair.

kWh or **kW-hr** An abbreviation of kilowatt-hour.

Kyrgyz or **Kirghiz** (kîr-gēz′) *adj.* Relating to Kyrgyzstan or its people, language, or culture. ❖ *n., pl.* **Kyrgyz** or **Kyrgyzes** or **Kirghiz** or **Kirghizes** **1.** A native or inhabitant of Kyrgyzstan. **2.** The language of the Kyrgyz.

Ll

l¹ or **L** (ĕl) *n., pl.* **l's** or **L's** or **Ls** The 12th letter of the English alphabet.

WORD HISTORY Have you ever noticed that we pronounce the **l** in *hold* and *help*, but not in *half* and *talk*? Where did the *l* go? Over a period of about 200 years, from about 1500 to 1700, the sound represented by the letter *l* disappeared in the pronunciation of many words such as *should, would, calf, half, talk, walk, balm, calm,* and *palm.* But it didn't disappear completely because of people's awareness of spelling. That's why you may occasionally hear this silent *l* pronounced in certain words such as *almond, alms, balm, calm,* and *palm.*

---

l² An abbreviation of: **1.** length. **2.** liter.

L¹ also **l** The symbol for the Roman numeral 50.

L² An abbreviation of: **1.** large. **2.** left. **3.** low

L. An abbreviation of: **1.** lake. **2.** Latin.

la (lä) *n.* In music, the sixth tone of a major scale.

lab (lăb) *n.* A laboratory.

Lab or **lab** (lăb) *n.* A Labrador retriever.

label (lā′bəl) *n.* **1.** An item, such as a small piece of paper or cloth attached to an article, that is used to identify a thing or person, or to provide other appropriate information: *the label on a can of peaches; the address label on a package.* **2.** A descriptive word or phrase: *the political labels* liberal *and* conservative. ❖ *tr.v.* **labeled, labeling, labels** or **labelled, labelling, labels 1.** To attach a label to: *label a package for mailing.* **2.** To identify or designate with a label; describe or classify: *The government labeled the writers dissidents.*

labia (lā′bē-ə) *n.* Plural of **labium.**

labial (lā′bē-əl) *adj.* **1.** Relating to the lips or the labia. **2.** Formed by closing or partly closing the lips, as the sounds *b, m,* or *w.* ❖ *n.* A labial consonant.

labile (lā′bĭl′) *adj.* **1.** Open to change; readily changeable or unstable: *labile chemical compounds; tissues with labile cell populations.* **2.** Fluctuating widely: *labile hypertension; labile emotions.* **3.** Decomposing readily: *the labile component of organic matter.* —**la·bil′i·ty** (lā-bĭl′ĭ-tē) *n.*

labium (lā′bē-əm) *n., pl.* **labia** (lā′bē-ə) **1.** Any of four folds of tissue of the female external genitals. **2.** Any of several liplike structures of certain plants or animals.

labor (lā′bər) *n.* **1.** Physical or mental effort; work: *the labor involved in digging a ditch.* **2.** A specific task or piece of work: *the twelve labors of Hercules.* **3.** Work for wages. **4a.** Workers considered as a group: *negotiations between labor and management.* **b.** Labor unions considered as a group. **5.** The process by which a mammal gives birth, beginning with contractions of the uterus and ending with the delivery of the fetus or infant and the placenta. ❖ *intr.v.* **labored, laboring, labors 1.** To work; toil: *Many workers labored in the fields picking lettuce.* **2.** To move slowly and with difficulty; struggle: *The long freight train labored over the mountain pass.* **3.** To suffer from a burden or disadvantage: *They are laboring under the*

misconception that others will cooperate. —**la′bor·er** *n.*

laboratory (lăb′rə-tôr′ē) *n., pl.* **laboratories 1.** A room or building equipped for scientific research or experiments. **2.** A place where medical drugs or chemicals are manufactured.

Labor Day *n.* The first Monday in September, celebrated as a holiday in honor of working people.

labored (lā′bərd) *adj.* Showing obvious effort; forced; strained: *labored breathing.*

labor-intensive (lā′bər-ĭn-tĕn′sĭv) *adj.* Requiring a large amount of labor or work, especially in comparison to the amount of money or materials that are needed: *An archaeological dig is a labor-intensive undertaking.*

laborious (lə-bôr′ē-əs) *adj.* **1.** Demanding great effort; difficult: *a laborious task.* **2.** Hard-working; industrious: *Restoring artworks requires skilled and laborious workers.* —**la·bo′ri·ous·ly** *adv.* —**la·bo′ri·ous·ness** *n.*

laborsaving (lā′bər-sā′vĭng) *adj.* Designed to save or reduce human labor: *A dishwasher is a laborsaving device.*

labor union *n.* An organization of workers formed to protect and further their mutual interests by bargaining as a group with their employers over wages, working conditions, and benefits.

labour (lā′bər) *n. & v.* Chiefly British Variant of **labor.**

Labrador retriever *n.* A dog of a breed developed in Canada, having a short yellow, black, or brown coat and often used to retrieve game.

laburnum (lə-bûr′nəm) *n.* Any of several poisonous trees or shrubs that are planted for their drooping clusters of yellow flowers.

labyrinth (lăb′ə-rĭnth′) *n.* **1.** A complex structure of connected passages through which it is difficult to find one's way; a maze. **2. Labyrinth** In Greek mythology, the maze built by Daedalus in Crete to confine the Minotaur. **3.** Something complicated or confusing in design or construction. **4.** The system of tubes and spaces that make up the inner ear of many vertebrate animals.

labyrinthine (lăb′ə-rĭn′thĭn *or* lăb′ə-rĭn′thēn′) *adj.* Relating to or resembling a labyrinth.

lac (lăk) *n.* A resinous substance secreted by a tropical Asian scale insect and used in making shellac.

lace (lās) *n.* **1.** A delicate fabric of fine threads woven in an open weblike pattern with fancy designs. **2.** A cord or string drawn through eyelets or around hooks to pull and tie opposite edges together, as of a shoe. ❖ *tr.v.* **laced, lacing, laces 1.** To draw together and tie the laces of: *laced her skates tightly before the game.* **2.** To weave in and out; interlace: *laced his fingers together; lace a vine onto a trellis.* **3.** To add a substance, especially alcohol or a poison, to: *laced the punch with rum.*

lacerate (lăs′ə-rāt′) *tr.v.* **lacerated, lacerating, lacerates** To rip or tear, especially in an injury: *He fell off the bicycle and lacerated his arm.*

laceration (lăs′ə-rā′shən) *n.* A jagged wound or cut.

lacewing (lās′wĭng′) *n.* Any of various insects that have two pairs of delicate wings and long antennae. Lacewing larvae feed on aphids and other garden pests.

lachrymose also **lacrimose** (lăk′rə-mōs′) *adj.* **1.** Weeping or inclined to weep; tearful. **2.** Causing or tending to cause tears. —**lach′ry·mos′i·ty, lac′ri·mos′i·ty** (lăk′-rə-mŏs′ĭ-tē) *n.*

lack (lăk) *n.* **1.** Shortage or absence: *Lack of water leads to dehydration.* **2.** A particular shortage or absence: *The lack of instructions made it hard to assemble the bookcase.* ❖ *v.* **lacked, lacking, lacks** —*tr.* To be without: *Some streets lack trees altogether.* —*intr.* To be wanting or deficient: *A diet of nothing but rice is lacking in protein.*

lackadaisical (lăk′ə-dā′zĭ-kəl) *adj.* Lacking spirit or interest; listless. —**lack′a·dai′si·cal·ly** *adv.*

lackey (lăk′ē) *n., pl.* **lackeys 1.** A male servant in uniform; a footman. **2.** A follower who behaves like a servant; a flunky.

lackluster (lăk′lŭs′tər) *adj.* Lacking in excellence or distinction; mediocre; dull: *a lackluster piano solo.*

laconic (lə-kŏn′ĭk) *adj.* Using few words; terse; concise: *a laconic reply.* —**la·con′i·cal·ly** *adv.*

lacquer (lăk′ər) *n.* Any of various materials similar to varnish that are applied to a surface and leave a glossy finish when dry. ❖ *tr.v.* **lacquered, lacquering, lacquers** To coat with lacquer.

lacrimal (lăk′rə-məl) *adj.* Relating to or producing tears: *the lacrimal glands.*

lacrosse (lə-krôs′) *n.* A game played on a field by two teams of ten players each, in which players use a long stick with a webbed pouch on one end to carry and pass a ball, the object being to propel the ball into the opposing team's goal.

lactase (lăk′tās′) *n.* An enzyme that breaks lactose down into simpler sugars. It is found in some yeasts and in the digestive juices of young mammals and many adult humans.

lactate (lăk′tāt′) *intr.v.* **lactated, lactating, lactates** To secrete milk.

lactation (lăk-tā′shən) *n.* **1.** The production and secretion of milk by the mammary glands. **2.** The period during which the mammary glands secrete milk: *vitamins needed during lactation.*

lactic (lăk′tĭk) *adj.* Relating to or derived from milk.

lactic acid *n.* An organic acid that is produced by the bacteria that cause milk to sour or fruit to ferment and is used as a flavoring and preservative for foods. It is also produced by muscle tissue during exercise.

lactose (lăk′tōs′) *n.* A white crystalline sugar that is found in milk and has the formula $C_{12}H_{22}O_{11}$. It is used in infant foods, bakery products, and various sweets.

lacuna (lə-kyōō′nə *or* lə-kōō′nə) *n., pl.* **lacunae** (lə-kyōō′nē *or* lə-kōō′nē) *or* **lacunas 1.** An empty space or missing part; a gap: *The committee found a lacuna in the zoning regulations.* **2.** A space or cavity in bone or tissue.

lacustrine (lə-kŭs′trĭn) *adj.* **1.** Relating to lakes: *marine and lacustrine sediments.* **2.** Living or growing in or along the edges of lakes: *lacustrine salmon.*

lacy (lā′sē) *adj.* **lacier, laciest** Relating to or resembling lace: *a lacy shawl; a lacy covering of moss and lichens.*

lad (lăd) *n.* A boy or young man.

ladder (lăd′ər) *n.* **1.** A usually portable device for climbing up or down, consisting of two long side pieces joined by equally spaced rungs or steps. **2.** A means of moving higher or lower: *He used his accomplishments as a ladder to success.* **3.** A series of levels or stages: *She's high on the corporate ladder.*

laddie (lăd′ē) *n.* A boy or young man; a lad.

lade (lād) *v.* **laded, laden** (lād′n) *or* **laded, lading, lades** —*tr.* To load or burden. —*intr.* To take on a load.

laden (lād′n) *adj.* **1.** Weighed down with a load; heavy: *a ship laden with goods from China.* **2.** Oppressed; burdened: *a company laden with debts.*

lading (lā′dĭng) *n.* **1.** The act of loading. **2.** Cargo; freight: *a bill of lading.*

ladle (lād′l) *n.* A long-handled spoon with a deep bowl used for serving liquids. ❖ *tr.v.* **ladled, ladling, ladles** To lift out and pour with a ladle.

lady (lā′dē) *n., pl.* **ladies 1.** A woman of high social standing. **2.** A woman with good manners or polite behavior. **3.** A woman, especially when spoken of in a polite way: *the lady who lives next door.* **4.** A woman who is the head of a household. **5. ladies** Used as a form of address for a group of women: *Good evening, ladies and gentlemen.* **6. Lady** *Chiefly British* A general feminine title of nobility or other high rank.

ladybird (lā′dē-bûrd′) *n.* A ladybug.

ladybug (lā′dē-bŭg′) *n.* Any of numerous small beetles, often reddish with black spots, that feed mostly on other insects, including aphids and other pests.

lady in waiting *n., pl.* **ladies in waiting** A woman appointed to attend a queen or princess in a royal court.

ladylike (lā′dē-līk′) *adj.* Characteristic of or appropriate for a lady.

ladyship also **Ladyship** (lā′dē-shĭp′) *n.* Used as a title and form of address for a woman holding the rank of lady.

lady's slipper (lā′dēz) *n.* Any of various orchids of northern regions having flowers with a large petal that resembles a slipper or shoe.

lag (lăg) *intr.v.* **lagged, lagging, lags 1.** To fail to keep up; straggle: *Several runners began to lag behind the main group in the race.* **2.** To weaken or diminish; slacken: *Our enthusiasm for the hike lagged as the sky clouded over.* ❖ *n.* **1.** The act or condition of lagging: *The cold weather caused a lag in interest in the field trip.* **2.** The extent or degree of lagging; a gap: *A huge lag separated the first and second place finishers in the race.* —**lag′ger** *n.*

lager (lä′gər) *n.* A type of beer of German origin that is fermented for a relatively long time at a low temperature.

laggard (lăg′ərd) *n.* A person who lags behind; a straggler. ❖ *adj.* Lagging behind; slow: *a laggard runner.*

lagoon (lə-gōōn′) *n.* A shallow body of water separated from the sea by sandbars or reefs.

laid (lād) *v.* Past tense and past participle of **lay**[1].

laid-back (lād′băk′) *adj. Informal* Casual or relaxed in atmosphere or character; easy-going.

lain (lān) *v.* Past participle of **lie**[1].

lair (lâr) *n.* The den or dwelling place of a wild animal.

laird (lârd) *n. Scots* The owner of a landed estate; a lord.

laissez faire (lĕs′ā fâr′) *n.* An economic doctrine that opposes government regulation of commerce and industry beyond the minimum necessary for free enterprise to operate.

laity (lā′ĭ-tē) *n.* The laypeople of a religious group as distinguished from the clergy.

lake (lāk) *n.* A large inland body of fresh water or salt water.

lake dwelling *n.* A dwelling, especially a prehistoric dwelling, that rests on piles over a shallow lake. —**lake dweller** *n.*

lake trout *n.* A large North American trout that has dark coloring with pale spots and lives in lakes.

Lakota (lə-kō′tə) *n., pl.* **Lakota** or **Lakotas 1.** A member of the largest group of the Sioux peoples, living in the western Great Plains. **2.** The Siouan language of the Lakota.

lama (lä′mə) *n.* A Tibetan Buddhist monk, especially one having religious authority in a monastery.

lamb (lăm) *n.* **1.** A young sheep. **2.** The meat of a young sheep. **3.** A sweet mild-mannered person. ❖ *intr.v.* **lambed, lambing, lambs** To give birth to a lamb or lambs.

lambaste (lăm-bāst′) *tr.v.* **lambasted, lambasting, lambastes** *Informal* **1.** To thrash; beat. **2.** To scold; berate: *The two candidates lambasted each other in the debate.*

lambda (lăm′də) *n.* The eleventh letter of the Greek alphabet, written Λ, λ. In English it is represented as *L, l.*

lambent (lăm′bənt) *adj.* **1.** Flickering gently over a surface: *lambent moonlight reflected on the surface of the lake.* **2.** Glowing softly; luminous: *lambent eyes.* **3.** Showing effortless brilliance or lightness: *a lambent mind.*

lambskin (lăm′skĭn′) *n.* **1.** The hide of a lamb, especially with its wool still on it. **2.** Leather made from the dressed hide of a lamb. **3.** Parchment made from such hide.

lame (lām) *adj.* **lamer, lamest 1.** Unable to walk easily or at all; disabled: *A leg injury made me lame.* **2.** Painful or stiff: *My back is lame after all that heavy lifting.* **3.** Weak and ineffectual; unsatisfactory: *Forgetfulness is a lame excuse for missing our meeting.* ❖ *tr.v.* **lamed, laming, lames** To make lame; disable. —**lame′ly** *adv.* —**lame′ness** *n.*

lamé (lă-mā′) *n.* A fabric in which flat metal threads, often of gold or silver, are woven with threads of fiber such as silk.

lame duck *n.* **1.** A public officeholder who has not been reelected and is filling out a term of office before the inauguration of a successor. **2.** An ineffective person; a weakling.

lament (lə-mĕnt′) *v.* **lamented, lamenting, laments** —*tr.* **1.** To express grief for or about; mourn: *lament the death of a loved one.* **2.** To regret deeply; deplore: *lament the state of the city.* —*intr.* To express or show grief; mourn. ❖ *n.* **1.** An expression of grief: *giving way to tears and laments.* **2.** A sorrowful song or poem.

lamentable (lə-mĕn′tə-bəl or lăm′ən-tə-bəl) *adj.* Deserving of lament or regret: *a lamentable mistake.* —**la·men′ta·bly** *adv.*

lamentation (lăm′ən-tā′shən) *n.* **1.** The act of lamenting. **2. Lamentations** *(used with a singular verb)* A book of the Bible traditionally considered to be written by Jeremiah, in which the fall of Jerusalem is lamented.

lamina (lăm′ə-nə) *n., pl.* **laminae** (lăm′ə-nē′) or **laminas 1.** A thin plate, scale, or layer. **2.** The flat wide part of a leaf; a blade.

laminate (lăm′ə-nāt′) *tr.v.* **laminated, laminating, laminates 1.** To cover with a thin sheet of material, as for preservation. **2.** To make (plywood, glass, or plastics) by joining several layers. **3.** To beat or press into a thin plate or sheet. **4.** To split into thin layers. ❖ *n.* *(also* lăm′ə-nĭt) Something, such as plywood, made by joining layers together. —**lam′i·na′tor** *n.*

lamination (lăm′ə-nā′shən) *n.* **1.** The act or process of laminating or the state of being laminated. **2.** A thin layer.

lamp (lămp) *n.* **1.** A device that uses oil, gas, or electricity to give off light and often heat: *a fluorescent lamp; a heat lamp.* **2.** An apparatus or piece of furniture used as a stand or holder for such a device.

lampblack (lămp′blăk′) *n.* A gray or black soot that col-

lects when substances containing carbon, such as oil or gas, burn incompletely. Lampblack is used as a pigment and in explosives and fertilizers.

lamplight (lămp′līt′) *n.* The light shed by a lamp.

lamplighter (lămp′lī′tər) *n.* A person formerly employed to light gas-burning street lights.

lampoon (lăm-pōōn′) *n.* A piece of writing that uses satire to make fun of a person, group, idea, or institution. ❖ *tr.v.* **lampooned, lampooning, lampoons** To make fun of with a lampoon: *The comedy lampooned the manners of the upper class.*

lamppost (lămp′pōst′) *n.* A post supporting a street lamp.

lamprey (lăm′prē) *n., pl.* **lampreys** Any of various fishes having a long thin body and a jawless sucking mouth. Lampreys attach to other fish and feed on their body fluids.

lampshade (lămp′shād′) *n.* A shade placed over a lamp to soften its direct light.

lance (lăns) *n.* **1.** A long wooden spear with a sharp metal head, used as a weapon, especially by knights or soldiers on horseback. **2.** An implement used for spearing fish. ❖ *tr.v.* **lanced, lancing, lances 1.** To pierce with a lance. **2.** To make a surgical incision in: *lanced the swelling.*

lance corporal *n.* An enlisted person in the US Marine Corps ranking above private first class and below corporal.

lancelet (lăns′lĭt) *n.* Any of various small fishlike marine animals that have a long thin body with a stiff rodlike strip of cells along the back but no skull or backbone. Lancelets are usually found buried in sand.

Lancelot (lăn′sə-lŏt′) *n.* In Arthurian legend, a knight of the Round Table whose love for Guinevere caused him to go to war with King Arthur.

lancer (lăn′sər) *n.* A soldier on horseback equipped with a lance.

lancet (lăn′sĭt) *n.* A surgical knife with a short, pointed, double-edged blade.

land (lănd) *n.* **1.** The part of the earth's surface not covered by water; ground: *Only one third of the earth's surface is land.* **2.** A particular part of the earth, especially a region or country. **3.** An area of ground that is publicly or privately owned, especially when not developed; landed property: *buy land in Hawaii.* **4.** Soil; earth: *Farmers plow the land.* ❖ *v.* **landed, landing, lands** —*tr.* **1.** To bring to and unload on land: *land cargo.* **2.** To set (a vehicle) down on the ground or another surface: *land a plane.* **3.** *Informal* To cause to arrive in a place or condition: *Their protest landed them in court.* **4.** To catch and pull in (a fish). **5.** *Informal* To get, secure, or win: *landed a good job.* **6.** *Informal* To deliver (a blow). —*intr.* **1.** To come to shore: *The boat landed in heavy surf.* **2.** To go or put ashore; disembark: *We landed on the dock.* **3.** To descend and settle on the ground or another surface: *The seaplane landed on the lake.* **4.** *Informal* To arrive in a place or certain condition: *Her proposal landed on my desk.*

landau (lăn′dô′ or lăn′dou′) *n.* **1.** A four-wheeled carriage with two passenger seats facing each other and a top that can be lowered. **2.** An automobile with a top similar to that of this carriage.

land bridge *n.* An isthmus.

landed (lăn′dĭd) *adj.* **1.** Owning land: *the landed gentry.* **2.** Consisting of land in the form of property: *a landed estate.*

landfall (lănd′fôl′) *n.* **1.** The act or an instance of sight-ing or reaching land after a voyage or flight. **2.** The land sighted or reached after a voyage or flight. **3.** The reaching of land by a storm or a part of a storm.

landfill (lănd**′**fĭl**′**) *n.* **1.** A tract of land in which trash is buried between layers of dirt. **2.** A method of disposing of trash using such tracts of land.

landform (lănd**′**fôrm**′**) *n.* A feature of the earth's surface, such as a plateau, valley, or mountain.

land grant *n.* A grant of public land made by a government for a railroad, state college, or other public use.

landholder (lănd**′**hōl**′**dər) *n.* A person who owns land. **—land′hold′ing** *adj. & n.*

landing (lăn**′**dĭng) *n.* **1.** The act or process of coming to land or of coming to rest, as after a voyage or flight: *the landing of a spacecraft on the moon.* **2.** A wharf or pier: *an old boat landing.* **3.** A platform or area at the top or bottom of a set of stairs.

landing field *n.* An area of level land used by aircraft for landings and takeoffs.

landing gear *n.* The structure attached to the underside of an aircraft or a spacecraft that supports it on land or in water.

landing strip *n.* An aircraft runway without airport facilities.

landlady (lănd**′**lā**′**dē) *n.* **1.** A woman who owns land or buildings rented to tenants. **2.** A woman who runs an inn or a boarding house.

landless (lănd**′**lĭs) *adj.* Owning or having no land.

landlocked (lănd**′**lŏkt**′**) *adj.* **1.** Entirely or almost entirely surrounded by land: *Switzerland is a landlocked country.* **2.** Living only in inland waters: *landlocked salmon.*

landlord (lănd**′**lôrd**′**) *n.* **1.** A person, especially a man, who owns land or buildings rented to tenants. **2.** A man who runs an inn or a boarding house.

landlubber (lănd**′**lŭb**′**ər) *n.* A person unfamiliar with sailing or with life aboard a ship or boat.

landmark (lănd**′**märk**′**) *n.* **1.** A familiar or easily recognized feature of a landscape. **2.** A fixed object that marks a boundary, as a stone or metal post. **3.** An event that is important in history: *The discovery of penicillin was a landmark in the treatment of certain diseases.* **4.** A building or place preserved for its special historical importance or interest.

landmass (lănd**′**măs**′**) *n.* A large area of land, such as a continent, that is wholly or mostly surrounded by water: *the landmass of Eurasia.*

land mine *n.* A small bomb or similar device buried in the ground and set to explode when stepped on or run over by a vehicle.

landowner (lănd**′**ō**′**nər) *n.* A person who owns land. **—land′own′ing** *adj.*

land plant *n.* Any of a large group of plants that live on land, including the vascular plants and the mosses, liverworts, and hornworts.

landscape (lănd**′**skăp**′**) *n.* **1.** An expanse of scenery that can be seen from one place. **2.** A painting or picture showing such an expanse of scenery. ❖ *v.* **landscaped, landscaping, landscapes** —*tr.* To change or improve the appearance of (a piece of land) by moving soil and planting trees, shrubs, or flowers. —*intr.* To change or improve grounds as a profession.

landslide (lănd**′**slīd**′**) *n.* **1a.** The downward sliding of a relatively dry mass of earth and rock: *The earthquake*

caused several landslides. **b.** The mass of soil and rock that moves in this way: *cleared the landslide with heavy equipment.* **2.** A very large majority of votes resulting in victory for a candidate or political party.

landward (lănd**′**wərd) *adv. & adj.* To or toward land: *drifted landward; the landward side of the boat.*

lane (lān) *n.* **1.** A narrow path or road, often bordered by hedges, trees, fences, or walls: *a country lane; a lane between old houses.* **2.** A set course or way used by ships or aircraft: *the shipping lanes of the Atlantic.* **3.** A strip marked off on a street or highway to accommodate one line of traffic: *a highway with four lanes.* **4.** A similar strip marked off or divided from others for contestants in a race. **5.** A bowling alley. **6.** In basketball, the rectangular area marked on a court from the end line to the foul line.

language (lăng**′**gwĭj) *n.* **1a.** Communication of thoughts and feelings through a system of arbitrary signals, such as voice sounds, gestures, or written symbols. **b.** Such a system including its rules for combining its components, such as words: *Over a thousand languages are spoken in Africa.* **2.** A system of signs, symbols, rules, or gestures used to convey information: *a computer language.* **3.** The special words and expressions used by members of a group or profession: *medical language.* **4.** A particular way or style of speaking or writing: *formal language.* **5.** Words or wording, as of a legal document: *the language of a contract.*

language arts *pl.n.* Courses that develop the use of language skills, especially reading, spelling, and written composition.

languid (lăng**′**gwĭd) *adj.* **1.** Lacking speed or force: *a languid wave of the hand.* **2.** Lacking spirit or energy; listless: *a languid mood.* **—lan′guid·ly** *adv.*

languish (lăng**′**gwĭsh) *intr.v.* **languished, languishing, languishes** **1.** To lose strength or vigor; grow weak: *During a long drought crops languish from lack of rain.* **2.** To suffer from miserable or depressing conditions: *languishing in prison.* **3.** To remain unattended or be neglected: *legislation that languished in committee.* **4.** To become listless and depressed; pine: *languishing for his lover.*

languor (lăng**′**gər *or* lăng**′**ər) *n.* **1.** Lack of energy; tiredness; listlessness. **2.** A dreamy, lazy mood or quality: *the languor of a summer afternoon.* **3.** Extreme stillness or quiet. **—lan′guor·ous** *adj.*

La Niña (lä nēn**′**yä) *n.* A periodic cooling of the ocean surface off the western coast of South America that affects Pacific and other weather patterns.

lank (lăngk) *adj.* **lanker, lankest** **1.** Long and lean; slender: *the athlete's lank body.* **2.** Long, straight, and limp: *lank hair.* **—lank′ly** *adv.*

lanky (lăng**′**kē) *adj.* **lankier, lankiest** Tall, thin, and gawky. **—lank′i·ness** *n.*

lanolin (lăn**′**ə-lĭn) *n.* A yellowish-white fatty substance obtained from wool and used in soaps, cosmetics, and ointments.

lantern (lăn**′**tərn) *n.* **1.** A case or container that protects a light from the weather, usually designed to be carried. **2.** A room at the top of a lighthouse where the light is located. **3.** A structure built on top of a roof or dome as decoration or to let in light and air.

lanthanide (lăn**′**thə-nīd**′**) *n.* Any of a series of naturally occurring metallic elements with atomic numbers ranging from 57 to 71. See **Periodic Table.**

lanthanum (lăn**′**thə-nəm) *n. Symbol* **La** A soft, silvery metallic element that is used in making glass for lenses and lights for movie and television studios. Atomic number 57. See **Periodic Table.**

lanyard (lăn**ʹ**yərd) *n.* **1.** A short rope used to secure rigging on a ship. **2.** A cord worn around the neck for carrying a knife, key, or whistle. **3.** A cord with a hook at one end, used to fire a cannon.

Lao (lou) *n., pl.* **Lao** or **Laos** (louz) **1.** A member of a traditionally Buddhist people inhabiting the area of the Mekong River in Laos and Thailand. **2.** The Tai language of the Lao. ❖ *adj.* Relating to the Lao or their language or culture.

Laotian (lā-ōʹshən *or* louʹshən) *adj.* **1.** Relating to Laos or its people, language, or culture. **2.** Relating to the Lao people. ❖ *n.* **1a.** A native or inhabitant of Laos. **b.** A person of Laotian ancestry. **2.** A Lao.

lap¹ (lăp) *n.* **1.** The flat place formed by the front part of the legs above the knees of a person who is sitting: *The puppy curled up in my lap.* **2.** The part of a person's clothing that covers the lap: *the lap of a skirt.* **3.** An area of responsibility, interest, or control: *The opportunity just dropped in my lap.*

lap² (lăp) *v.* **lapped, lapping, laps** —*tr.* **1.** To fold, wrap, or wind over or around: *Lap the pie dough over the edge of the pan.* **2.** To extend partly over (something else); overlap: *The shingles lap one another to make the roof watertight.* —*intr.* **1.** To fold or wind around something. **2.** To extend over something else; overlap: *Shingles lap in straight rows.* ❖ *n.* **1a.** A part folded or extending over something else; an overlapping part: *the front lap of a jacket.* **b.** The amount that a part extends over something else: *The curtains have a lap of three inches.* **2a.** One complete length or circuit, as of a pool or track: *a race of four laps.* **b.** A part or stage, as of a journey: *The first lap of our trip across the country was from New York to Ohio.*

lap³ (lăp) *v.* **lapped, lapping, laps** —*tr.* **1.** To take up and swallow (a liquid) by using the tongue: *The kitten lapped up the milk.* **2.** To wash or splash with a light slapping sound: *The sea lapped the shore gently.* —*intr.* To wash or splash against something with a light slapping sound: *Waves lapped against the dock.* ❖ *n.* The act or sound of lapping: *listened to the lap of the waves.*

WORD HISTORY Lap¹ is from Middle English *lappe,* which is from Old English *læppa,* both meaning "a garment part that is loose enough to be grabbed, folded, or lifted." **Lap**² is from Middle English *lappen,* meaning "to wrap, enfold." **Lap**³ is from Middle English *lapen,* which comes from Old English *lapian,* both meaning "to drink with the tongue."

---

lap dog *n.* **1.** A pet dog that is small enough to be held in the lap. **2.** *Informal* A person who is eager to do what another asks, especially as a way to maintain a position of privilege or favor.

lapel (lə-pĕlʹ) *n.* One of the two flaps that extend down from the collar of a coat or jacket and fold back against the chest.

lapidary (lăpʹĭ-dĕrʹē) *n., pl.* **lapidaries** A person who cuts, polishes, or engraves gems. ❖ *adj.* **1.** Relating to gemstones or the art of working with them. **2.** Marked by conciseness, precise, or refined expression: *a writer with a lapidary style.*

lapis lazuli (lăpʹĭs lăzʹə-lē *or* lăzʹyə-lē) *n.* **1.** A typically opaque, deep-blue rock that is used as a gemstone. **2.** A deep blue.

Lapp (lăp) *n. Often Offensive* A Sami.

lap robe *n.* A blanket or fur piece for covering the lap, legs, and feet.

lapse (lăps) *intr.v.* **lapsed, lapsing, lapses** **1.** To fall to a lower or worse condition: *lapse into bad habits.* **2.** To pass gradually or smoothly; slip: *He lapsed into unconsciousness.* **3.** To be no longer valid or active; end or expire: *I let my membership in the club lapse.* ❖ *n.* **1.** A slip or failure, especially a minor one: *a lapse of memory.* **2.** A fall into a lower or worse condition: *a lapse into bad habits.* **3.** A period of time; an interval: *a lapse of three months between trips.* **4.** The ending of an agreement, right, privilege, or custom through neglect, disuse, or the passage of time: *the lapse of a lease.*

laptop (lăpʹtŏpʹ) *n.* A portable computer small enough to use on one's lap.

larboard (lärʹbərd) *n.* The port side of a ship or boat. ❖ *adj.* On the port side.

larcenous (lärʹsə-nəs) *adj.* **1.** Relating to or involving larceny: *Auto theft is a larcenous crime.* **2.** Guilty of larceny.

larceny (lärʹsə-nē) *n., pl.* **larcenies** The crime of taking another's property without right or permission; theft.

larch (lärch) *n.* **1.** Any of various cone-bearing trees having clusters of needlelike leaves that are shed every year. **2.** The hard strong wood of such a tree.

lard (lärd) *n.* A solid or semisolid white substance made from pig fat and used in cooking. ❖ *tr.v.* **larded, larding, lards** **1.** To cover or coat with lard or a similar fat. **2.** To insert strips of fat or bacon in (meat) before cooking. **3.** To enrich with additions; embellish: *She larded her lecture with jokes.*

larder (lärʹdər) *n.* **1.** A room or cupboard where food is stored. **2.** A supply of food.

large (lärj) *adj.* **larger, largest** **1.** Greater than average in size, amount, or number; big: *The blue whale is the largest mammal. He paid a large amount for that sports car.* **2.** Important; significant: *The scientists announced a large discovery of fossils.* ◆ **at large 1.** Not in confinement or captivity; at liberty: *The thief has not been found yet and is still at large.* **2.** As a whole; in general: *The economy at large is doing well.* **3.** Representing a nation, state, or district as a whole: *a councilor-at-large.* —**largeʹness** *n.*

◆ **SYNONYMS large, big, enormous, great, huge** *adj.*

large-hearted (lärjʹhärʹtĭd) *adj.* Having a generous or sympathetic nature.

large intestine *n.* The wide lower section of the intestine that extends from the end of the small intestine to the anus. It absorbs water and eliminates the waste matter that is left after food is digested.

largely (lärjʹlē) *adv.* For the most part; mainly: *The hills are largely covered with trees.*

large-scale (lärjʹskālʹ) *adj.* **1.** Large in scope or effect; extensive: *large-scale farming of huge acreages.* **2.** Drawn or made larger in size than average, especially to show detail: *a large-scale map.*

largess also **largesse** (lär-zhĕsʹ *or* lär-jĕsʹ) *n.* **1.** Generosity in giving gifts. **2.** Money or gifts given.

largo (lärʹgō) *adv. & adj.* In music, in a very slow tempo.

lariat (lărʹē-ət) *n.* A lasso.

lark¹ (lärk) *n.* **1.** Any of various songbirds found mostly in Eurasia and Africa and having a melodious song, especially the skylark. **2.** Any of several similar but unrelated birds, such as the meadowlark.

lark² (lärk) *n.* Something done just for fun or adventure: *We went to the zoo on a lark.* ❖ *intr.v.* **larked, larking, larks** To engage in fun or pranks.

WORD HISTORY Lark¹ comes from Old English *lāwerce*, referring to the same kind of bird as in Modern English. **Lark²** may be short for *skylark*, meaning "to frolic," or from an obsolete word spelled *lake*, meaning "play."

larkspur (lärk′spûr′) *n.* The delphinium.

larva (lär′və) *n., pl.* **larvae** (lär′vē) or **larvas 1.** The immature wormlike form of certain insects, from the time it hatches from the egg until it changes into the adult form. A caterpillar is the larva of a butterfly or moth. **2.** The immature stage of certain other animals, usually differing greatly in form from the parent. A tadpole is the larva of a frog or toad. —**lar′val** *adj.*

laryngeal (lə-rĭn′jē-əl *or* lăr′ən-jē′əl) *adj.* Relating to, affecting, or near the larynx.

laryngitis (lăr′ĭn-jī′tĭs) *n.* Inflammation of the larynx, causing hoarseness and sometimes temporary loss of the voice.

larynx (lăr′ĭngks) *n., pl.* **larynges** (lə-rĭn′jēz) or **larynxes** The upper part of the windpipe, containing the vocal cords.

lasagna (lə-zän′yə) *n.* **1.** Pasta in flat, very wide strips. **2.** A dish made by baking this pasta with layers of sauce and fillings such as cheese or meat.

lascivious (lə-sĭv′ē-əs) *adj.* **1.** Feeling or showing lust; lewd. **2.** Tending to excite lust. —**las·civ′i·ous·ly** *adv.*

laser (lā′zər) *n.* **1.** A device that emits a very narrow and intense beam of light or other radiation of a single wavelength either continuously or in pulses. Light from lasers can be used to cut hard substances, remove diseased tissue, or transmit communications signals. **2.** The beam of light produced by one of these devices.

laser disc *n.* An optical disc.

laser printer *n.* A printer that uses a laser to produce an image on a rotating drum before transferring the image to paper.

lash¹ (lăsh) *n.* **1.** A stroke or blow given with a whip or other flexible object. **2.** The flexible part of a whip. **3.** An eyelash. ❖ *v.* **lashed, lashing, lashes** —*tr.* **1.** To strike with a whip or other flexible object. **2.** To strike with force or violence: *The storm lashed the shore with high winds.* **3.** To move or wave rapidly: *The alligator lashed its tail in the water.* **4.** To attack or criticize with harsh language: *Newspaper editorials lashed the government for incompetence.* —*intr.* **1.** To move rapidly or violently; dash: *The waves lashed against the shore.* **2.** To strike with a whip or other flexible object: *The mule's tail lashed at the flies.* **3.** To make a harsh verbal or written attack: *The president lashed out against critics of the government.*

lash² (lăsh) *tr.v.* **lashed, lashing, lashes** To fasten or secure, as with a rope or cord: *lashed the cargo in place.*

WORD HISTORY Lash¹ probably comes from Middle English *lashen*, meaning "to deal a blow," which may be of imitative origin. **Lash²** comes from Middle English *lasen, lashen*, which comes from Old French *lachier*, both meaning "to lace."

Lasik (lā′sĭk) *n.* Eye surgery in which the cornea is reshaped using a laser, performed to correct certain refractive disorders, such as myopia.

lass (lăs) *n.* A girl or young woman.

lassie (lăs′ē) *n.* A lass.

lassitude (lăs′ĭ-tōōd′) *n.* A state or feeling of weariness, diminished energy, or listlessness.

lasso (lăs′ō *or* lă-sōō′) *n., pl.* **lassos** or **lassoes** A long rope with an adjustable loop at one end, used especially to catch horses and cattle. ❖ *tr.v.* **lassoed, lassoing, lassos** or **lassoes** To catch with a lasso: *lasso a runaway calf.*

last¹ (lăst) *adj.* **1.** Being, coming, or placed after all others; final: *the last day of the school year.* **2.** Being the only one left: *my last dime.* **3.** Most recent; just passed: *last week.* **4.** Most unlikely; least expected: *The last thing you would expect is snow during the summer.* **5.** The latest possible: *We waited until the last second to get on the plane.* ❖ *adv.* **1.** After all others; at the end: *The recipe says to add the flour last.* **2.** Most recently; latest: *I last saw them when I was a child.* ❖ *n.* **1.** A person or thing that is last: *I've read every chapter but the last.* **2.** The end: *They held out until the last.* ◆ **at last** After a long time; finally: *At last we fell asleep.* —**last′ly** *adv.*

last² (lăst) *v.* **lasted, lasting, lasts** —*intr.* **1.** To continue; go on: *The song lasted three minutes.* **2.** To remain in good condition; endure: *Appliances don't last like they used to.* **3.** To be enough: *The food supply should last for a long time.* —*tr.* To supply adequately; be enough for: *One loaf of bread can't last us a week.*

last³ (lăst) *n.* A block shaped like a human foot and used in making and repairing shoes.

WORD HISTORY Last¹ comes from Old English *latost, lætest*, meaning "latest." **Last²** comes from Middle English *lasten*, which comes from Old English *læstan*, both meaning "to continue, go on." **Last³** comes from Old English *læste* (meaning "block shaped like a foot"), which comes from Old English *læst*, meaning "sole of the foot."

last-ditch (lăst′dĭch′) *adj.* Done or made as a final recourse, especially to prevent a crisis or disaster: *a last-ditch effort to avert a strike.*

lasting (lăs′tĭng) *adj.* Continuing or remaining for a long time; enduring: *a lasting peace between nations.* —**last′ing·ly** *adv.*

Last Judgment *n.* In Christianity and certain other religious traditions, the final judgment by God of all humankind.

last minute *n.* The moment just before it is too late: *We made our preparations at the last minute before the wedding.* —**last′-min′ute** *adj.*

last rites *pl.n.* Religious rites performed for a person in danger of dying or in connection with burial.

last straw *n.* The last in a series of annoyances or disappointments that finally leads to loss of patience, trust, or hope.

Last Supper *n.* In the New Testament, the last meal of Jesus with the Apostles on the night before his crucifixion.

last word *n.* **1.** The final statement, as in a verbal argument. **2.** The power or authority to make a final decision. **3.** A convincing or authoritative statement or treatment: *This report is the last word on nutrition.* **4.** *Informal* The newest or most up-to-date style or development; the latest thing: *The model is the last word in racing bikes.*

lat. An abbreviation of latitude.

latch (lăch) *n.* A fastener for a door, gate, or window, usually consisting of a movable bar that fits into a notch or slot. ❖ *tr. & intr.v.* **latched, latching, latches** To close or be closed with a latch: *Latch the door. Does the door latch securely?* ◆ **latch on to** or **latch onto** To get hold of; obtain.

latchkey (lăch′kē′) *n.* A key for unfastening a latch or lock, especially one on a door.

late (lāt) *adj.* **later, latest 1.** Coming or happening after the expected, usual, or proper time; tardy: *I am late for my appointment.* **2.** Coming toward the end or more advanced part of a time period or series of events: *It was late in the meeting when we discussed that issue.* **3.** Of a time just past; recent: *a late model car; the late recession.* **4.** Having recently died: *The senator's late husband was a surgeon.* ❖ *adv.* **later, latest 1.** After the usual, expected, or proper time: *The train arrived late.* **2.** At the end or at an advanced stage: *Our team scored the winning run late in the game.* **3.** Recently: *as late as last week.* ◆ **of late** Recently; lately: *The trains have been running on a new schedule of late.* —**late′ness** *n.*

latecomer (lāt′kŭm′ər) *n.* A person or thing that arrives later than others or has arrived recently: *Latecomers to the show may have difficulty finding seats.*

lateen (lə-tēn′ *or* lă-tēn′) *adj.* Being, relating to, or rigged with a triangular sail hung on a long pole attached at an angle to the top of a short mast.

Late Latin *n.* Latin from the third to the seventh century AD.

lately (lāt′lē) *adv.* Not long ago; recently: *The weather has been cold lately.*

latent (lāt′nt) *adj.* Present but not evident or active; hidden: *Many of a child's latent talents only emerge in adulthood.* —**la′ten·cy** *n.*

later (lā′tər) *adj.* Comparative of **late.** More recent: *The later plays of Shakespeare.* ❖ *adv.* Comparative of **late.** At a later time or period: *That job can be done later.* ❖ *interj. Informal* Used to express goodbye.

lateral (lăt′ər-əl) *adj.* Relating to, situated on, directed toward, or coming from the side: *Lateral growth on a plant branches out from the stem. A lateral pass in football is to the side of the field.* ❖ *n.* In football, a usually underhand pass that is thrown sideways or somewhat backward from the passer. ❖ *v.* **lateraled, lateraling, laterals** *also* **lateralled, lateralling, laterals** —*intr.* In football, to throw a lateral. —*tr.* In football, to throw (the ball) in a lateral. —**lat′er·al·ly** *adv.*

lateral line *n.* A series of sensory pores along the head and sides of fishes and some amphibians by which water currents, vibrations, and pressure changes are detected.

latest (lā′tĭst) *adj.* Superlative of **late.** Most recent: *the latest popular songs.* ◆ **at the latest** No later than: *I'll visit them next week at the latest.*

latex (lā′tĕks′) *n.* **1.** The milky or colorless sap of certain plants, such as the rubber tree and milkweeds, that hardens when exposed to air. **2.** A material made of such sap from rubber trees, used to manufacture thin elastic products such as balloons, disposable gloves, and medical devices; natural latex. Some people are allergic to this substance. **3.** A synthetic material made from petroleum, used in paints, adhesives, and other products; synthetic latex.

lath (lăth) *n., pl.* **laths** (lă*th*z *or* lăths) **1.** A thin narrow strip of wood or metal used as a supporting structure for plaster, shingles, slates, or tiles. **2.** A quantity of laths or work made using laths. ❖ *tr.v.* **lathed, lathing, laths** To cover or line with laths.

lathe (lā*th*) *n.* A machine for shaping a piece of material, such as wood, by spinning the material rapidly about its axis while pressing a fixed cutting or scraping tool against it.

lather (lă*th*′ər) *n.* **1.** Foam formed when soap and water mix. **2.** Froth formed by heavy sweating, especially on a

horse. **3.** *Informal* A condition of anxious agitation: *The students were in a lather over the proposed restrictions.* ❖ *v.* **lathered, lathering, lathers** —*tr.* To cover with lather. —*intr.* To produce or form lather: *The race caused the horse to lather heavily.*

Latin (lăt′n) *n.* **1a.** The language of the ancient Romans, later widely used in science, law, and diplomacy and in the liturgy of the Roman Catholic Church. **b.** The classical form of this language, used from about 200 BC to about 200 AD. **2a.** A member of a Latin people, especially a native or inhabitant of Latin America. **b.** A Latino or Latina. ❖ *adj.* **1.** Relating to the Latin language. **2a.** Relating to the peoples or countries of Latin America. **b.** Relating to Latinos or their culture. **3.** Relating to the languages that developed from Latin, such as French, Italian, and Spanish.

Latina (lə-tē′nə *or* lä-tē′nə) *n.* A Latino woman or girl.

Latin alphabet *n.* The alphabet of the ancient Romans, adapted from the Etruscan and Greek alphabets and consisting of 23 letters that form the basis of many modern alphabets, including those of western Europe.

Latin American *n.* **1.** A native or inhabitant of Latin America. **2.** A person of Latin-American ancestry. —**Lat′in-A·mer′i·can** *adj.*

Latino (lə-tē′nō *or* lä-tē′nō) *n., pl.* **Latinos 1.** A Latin American. **2.** A person of Latin-American ancestry, especially one living in the United States.

latitude (lăt′ĭ-tōōd′) *n.* **1.** Distance north or south of the equator measured in degrees. A degree of latitude is about 69 statute miles or 60 nautical miles. **2.** A region of the earth indicated by its approximate latitude: *Some of the coldest temperatures on earth occur in the polar latitudes.* **3.** Freedom from confining regulations or restrictions: *The attorney general gave his staff wide latitude in investigating this case.* —**lat′i·tu′di·nal** *adj.*

latke (lät′kə) *n.* A pancake made of grated potato.

latrine (lə-trēn′) *n.* A communal toilet of the type often used in camps or military barracks.

latte (lä′tä) *n.* A caffe latte.

latter (lăt′ər) *adj.* **1.** Being the second of two that are mentioned: *Apples and oranges are both tasty but I prefer the latter fruit.* **2.** Closer to the end: *November comes in the latter part of the year.* —**lat′ter·ly** *adv.*

Latter-day Saint (lăt′ər-dā′) *n.* A Mormon.

lattice (lăt′ĭs) *n.* **1.** An open framework made of strips of wood, metal, or a similar material that cross at regular intervals. **2.** A screen, window, or grate made of such framework. ❖ *tr.v.* **latticed, latticing, lattices 1.** To form into a lattice: *We latticed strips of cane to make the chair seat.* **2.** To furnish with a lattice. —**lat′ticed** *adj.*

latticework (lăt′ĭs-wûrk′) *n.* **1.** A lattice or structure resembling a lattice. **2.** An open, crisscross pattern or weave.

Latvian (lăt′vē-ən) *adj.* Relating to Latvia or its people, language, or culture. ❖ *n.* **1.** A native or inhabitant of Latvia. **2.** The Baltic language of Latvia.

laud (lôd) *tr.v.* **lauded, lauding, lauds** To praise highly: *My boss lauded my work on the project.*

laudable (lô′də-bəl) *adj.* Deserving praise; praiseworthy. —**laud′a·bly** *adv.*

laudanum (lôd′n-əm) *n.* An alcohol solution of opium, formerly used as a painkiller.

laudatory (lô′də-tôr′ē) *adj.* Expressing praise: *laudatory remarks.*

laugh (lăf) *v.* **laughed, laughing, laughs** —*intr.* To make sounds and facial movements to express certain emotions, especially happiness, amusement, scorn, or nervousness. —*tr.* To affect or influence by laughter: *We laughed our worries away.* ❖ *n.* **1.** The act or sound of laughing: *a good-natured laugh.* **2.** often **laughs** Fun; amusement: *dressed up like clowns just for laughs.* ◆ **laugh at 1.** To be amused by: *I could only laugh at how wrong I had been.* **2.** To make fun of; mock: *The umpire told them to stop laughing at the pitcher.* **laugh off** To consider or treat as ridiculously or laughably trivial: *The politician laughed off her opponent's allegation.*

laughable (lăf'ə-bəl) *adj.* Causing or deserving of laughter; amusing or ridiculous. —**laugh'a·bly** *adv.*

laughing gas (lăf'ĭng) *n.* Nitrous oxide.

laughingstock (lăf'ĭng-stŏk') *n.* A person or thing that is made fun of; an object of ridicule.

laughter (lăf'tər) *n.* The act or sound of laughing.

launch¹ (lônch *or* länch) *v.* **launched, launching, launches** —*tr.* **1.** To throw or propel with force; hurl: *launch a spear.* **2.** To cause (a self-propelled vehicle or projectile) to go into motion: *launch a rocket.* **3.** To put (a boat or ship) into the water; set afloat. **4.** To set going or start into action: *The institute launched a new research program.* See Synonyms at **begin.** —*intr.* **1.** To set out; make a start: *He launched forth on a new career.* **2.** To enter energetically into something; plunge: *She launched into a review of the new movie.* ❖ *n.* The act of launching something, such as a rocket or spacecraft. —**launch'·er** *n.*

launch² (lônch *or* länch) *n.* **1.** A large boat carried by a ship. **2.** A large, open motorboat.

WORD HISTORY Launch¹ is from Middle English *launchen* (meaning "to pierce, thrust"), which comes from Latin *lanceāre,* meaning "to wield a lance." **Launch²** is probably an alteration of Malay *lancha* and was probably influenced by *launch¹.*

launch pad or **launching pad** (lôn'chĭng *or* län'chĭng) *n.* The platform or base from which a rocket or space vehicle is launched.

launder (lôn'dər *or* län'dər) *tr.v.* **laundered, laundering, launders 1.** To wash or wash and iron (clothes, for example). **2.** To make (illegally obtained money) appear lawfully obtained or legitimate, especially by transferring it from one legitimate account or business to another.

laundromat (lôn'drə-măt' *or* län'drə-măt') *n.* A self-service laundry where customers wash and dry clothes in coin-operated machines.

laundry (lôn'drē *or* län'drē) *n., pl.* **laundries 1.** Clothes and linens that have just been or will be washed: *Sort the laundry by color.* **2.** A place or business establishment where clothes and linens are washed and ironed.

laureate (lôr'ē-ĭt) *n.* A person who has been honored for achievements, especially in the arts or sciences. **2.** A poet laureate.

laurel (lôr'əl) *n.* **1a.** A small shrub or tree native to the Mediterranean region, having glossy, aromatic, evergreen leaves. **b.** Any of various related shrubs or trees, such as the mountain laurel. **2.** A wreath of laurel given as a mark of honor. **3.** often **laurels** Honors and glory won for great achievement: *The soldier won laurels for her bravery.*

lava (lä'və *or* lăv'ə) *n.* **1.** Molten rock that flows from a

volcano or from a crack in the earth. **2.** The rock formed when this substance cools and hardens.

lavatory (lăv'ə-tôr'ē) *n., pl.* **lavatories 1.** A room with a sink for washing and often a toilet; a bathroom. **2.** A sink or washbowl, especially one with running water and a drain. **3.** A flush toilet.

lave (lāv) *tr. & intr.v.* **laved, laving, laves** To wash or bathe.

lavender (lăv'ən-dər) *n.* **1a.** Any of various plants having small, fragrant purplish flowers that yield an oil used in perfumes, cosmetics, and soaps. **b.** The fragrant dried flowers or leaves of these plants. **2.** A pale or light purple. —**lav'en·der** *adj.*

lavish (lăv'ĭsh) *adj.* **1.** Given or provided very plentifully: *a party with lavish refreshments.* **2.** Very generous or free in giving: *Be lavish with praise.* ❖ *tr.v.* **lavished, lavishing, lavishes** To give or bestow in abundance: *lavished affection on their grandchildren.* —**lav'ish·ly** *adv.*

law (lô) *n.* **1.** A rule that requires or forbids certain conduct or activities, established by custom or by an authority, such as a legislature. **2.** A set or system of such rules: *Corporate law governs business.* **3.** The condition of social order created by obedience to such rules: *a breakdown of law and order.* **4.** The study of such rules: *a professor of law.* **5.** The profession of a lawyer: *practice the law.* **6.** The system of courts administering the laws of a community: *We are all equal before the law.* **7.** A person or agency responsible for enforcing the law: *a fugitive pursued by the law.* **8.** A statement or ruling that must be obeyed: *The king's word was law.* **9. Law** The body of principles held to express the will of God, especially as revealed in the Bible: *Mosaic Law.* **10.** A generally accepted rule, principle, or practice: *the laws of good health.* **11.** A statement describing how particular phenomena always behave when specific conditions exist: *the law of gravity.*

law-abiding (lô'ə-bī'dĭng) *adj.* Obeying the law: *law-abiding citizens.*

lawbreaker (lô'brā'kər) *n.* A person or organization that breaks the law.

lawful (lô'fəl) *adj.* **1.** Allowed by law: *lawful acts.* **2.** Established or recognized by the law: *a lawful heir.* **3.** Law-abiding: *lawful citizens.* —**law'ful·ly** *adv.* —**law'ful·ness** *n.*

lawgiver (lô'gĭv'ər) *n.* A person who establishes a set or system of laws for a people.

lawless (lô'lĭs) *adj.* **1.** Not governed by law: *the lawless frontier.* **2.** Disregarding or violating the law: *a lawless mob.* —**law'less·ly** *adv.* —**law'less·ness** *n.*

lawmaker (lô'mā'kər) *n.* A person who takes part in writing or passing laws; a legislator. —**law'mak'ing** *n.*

lawn¹ (lôn) *n.* A piece of ground planted with grass that is usually mowed regularly, as near a house or in a park.

lawn² (lôn) *n.* A very fine thin fabric of cotton or linen.

WORD HISTORY Lawn¹ comes from Middle English *launde* (meaning "glade"), which comes from Old French *launde,* meaning "pasture, wooded area." **Lawn²** comes from Middle English *laun* (meaning "fine linen"), which is named after *Laon,* a city of northern France.

lawn bowling *n.* A game played on a level lawn in which players roll wooden balls as close as possible to a smaller target ball.

lawn mower also **lawnmower** (lôn'mō'ər) *n.* A machine that has rotating blades for cutting grass.

lawn tennis *n.* Tennis, especially as played on a grass court.

lawrencium (lô-rĕn′sē-əm) *n. Symbol* **Lr** A radioactive element that has been artificially produced by scientists. The half-life of its longest-lived isotope is about four hours. Atomic number 103. See **Periodic Table.**

lawsuit (lô′sōōt′) *n.* A suit or case brought before a court of law for settlement.

lawyer (loi′yər) *n.* A person who is trained and qualified to give legal advice to clients and represent them in a court of law; an attorney.

lax (lăks) *adj.* **laxer, laxest 1.** Not careful or strict; negligent: *lax about paying bills.* **2.** Not firm; loose; slack: *a lax cable.* —**lax′ly** *adv.* —**lax′ness** *n.*

laxative (lăk′sə-tĭv) *n.* A medicine or food that stimulates bowel movements. ❖ *adj.* Stimulating bowel movements.

laxity (lăk′sĭ-tē) *n.* The quality or condition of being lax.

lay¹ (lā) *v.* **laid** (lād), **laying, lays** —*tr.* **1a.** To place or put, especially on a flat surface or in a horizontal position: *I laid the baby in the crib.* **b.** To put or place in a certain condition: *They laid themselves open for trouble.* **2.** To put or set in place: *lay tiles for flooring.* **3.** To produce (an egg or eggs). **4.** To cause to settle, subside, or become calm: *The rain laid the dust.* **5.** To assign; charge: *They lay the blame on us.* **6.** To put in order; prepare: *lay the table for dinner.* **7.** To spread over a surface: *lay paint on a canvas.* **8.** To impose as a burden or punishment: *lay a fine on an offender.* **9.** To place or give (importance, for example): *lay emphasis.* **10.** To present for consideration: *lay a case before the court.* **11.** To place (a bet); wager. —*intr.* To produce an egg or eggs: *The hens stopped laying suddenly.* ❖ *n.* The way or arrangement in which something is situated or organized: *the lay of the land.* ◆ **lay aside 1.** To give up; abandon. **2.** To save for future use. **lay away 1.** To save for future use. **2.** To reserve (merchandise) until wanted or paid for. **lay by** To save for future use. **lay down 1.** To give up and surrender: *laid down their arms.* **2.** To specify: *lay down rules by which to live.* **lay in** To store for future use: *lay in supplies for a blizzard.* **lay into** *Slang* **1.** To scold harshly. **2.** To beat up physically. **lay off 1.** To dismiss or suspend from a job. **2.** *Slang* To stop doing something; quit. **lay out 1.** To arrange according to plan: *laying out the streets of a new housing development.* **2.** To spend (money). **lay over** To make a stopover in the course of a journey. **lay up 1.** To store for future needs. **2.** *Informal* To keep in bed or out of action with an illness or injury. **lay waste to** To ravage: *Rebel troops laid waste to the town.*

USAGE The verbs **lay** and **lie** are frequently confused. *Lay* means "to put, place, or prepare" and normally takes an object. Its past tense is *laid: He always lays his glasses down carefully. I laid* (not *lay*) *the newspaper on the table and left the room. Lie* means "to recline or be situated" and does not take an object. Its past tense is *lay: She sometimes lies on the sofa after lunch. When I lay down, I fell asleep. She was lying* (not *laying*) *on the sofa.*

lay² (lā) *adj.* **1.** Relating to or involving people who are not members of the clergy: *a lay missionary.* **2.** Not of or belonging to a particular profession: *a lay observer on the scientific expedition.*

lay³ (lā) *n.* A poem or song that tells a story; a ballad.

WORD HISTORY Lay¹ comes from Middle English *leien,* which comes from Old English *lecgan,* both meaning "to put, place." **Lay²** comes from a Middle English word *lai* (meaning "belonging to the common people, not to the priesthood"), which comes from Greek *lāos,* meaning "the people." **Lay³** comes from a different Middle English word also spelled *lai,* which comes from Old French *lai,* both meaning "narrative poem."

lay⁴ (lā) *v.* Past tense of **lie¹.**

layaway (lā′ə-wā′) *n.* A payment plan in which a seller agrees to hold a piece of merchandise for a customer who has left a deposit until the full price is paid.

layer (lā′ər) *n.* **1.** A single thickness of material lying between others or covering a surface: *a cake with three layers.* **2.** A depth or level: *a novel with many layers of meaning.* **3.** A person who lays something: *a carpet layer.* **4.** A hen kept for laying eggs. ❖ *tr. & intr.v.* **layered, layering, layers** To form, arrange, or split into layers. —**lay′er·ing** *n.*

layette (lā-ĕt′) *n.* A set of clothing, bedding, and other supplies for a newborn child.

layman (lā′mən) *n.* **1.** A person who is not a cleric. **2.** A person who does not have the specialized knowledge or training of a member of a profession.

layoff (lā′ôf′) *n.* **1.** A dismissal or suspension of one or more employees, especially because there is no longer enough available work or because the company is being restructured. **2.** A period of temporary inactivity.

layout (lā′out′) *n.* A planned arrangement of parts or areas: *the layout of a factory.*

layover (lā′ō′vər) *n.* A short stop or break in a journey.

layperson (lā′pûr′sən) *n.* **1.** A person who is not a cleric. **2.** A person who does not have the specialized knowledge or training of a member of a profession.

lay-up (lā′ŭp′) *n.* In basketball, a usually one-handed, banked shot made close to the basket after driving in.

laywoman (lā′wŏom′ən) *n.* **1.** A woman who is not a cleric. **2.** A woman who does not have the specialized knowledge or training of a member of a profession.

laze (lāz) *intr.v.* **lazed, lazing, lazes** To relax lazily; loaf: *lazed around all day in the sun.*

lazy (lā′zē) *adj.* **lazier, laziest 1.** Not willing to work or be energetic: *a lazy person.* **2.** Causing idleness or a lack of energy: *lazy summer afternoons.* **3.** Slow-moving: *lazy clouds floating overhead.* —**la′zi·ly** *adv.* —**la′zi·ness** *n.*

lazy Susan *n.* A revolving tray for condiments or food.

lb. An abbreviation of pound.

lcd An abbreviation of least common denominator.

LCD An abbreviation of liquid-crystal display.

lcm An abbreviation of least common multiple.

lea (lē or lā) *n.* A stretch of grassy ground; a meadow.

leach (lēch) *tr.v.* **leached, leaching, leaches 1.** To dissolve out (soluble materials) by passing a liquid through ashes, rock, or other matter: *Heavy rains leached minerals from the soil.* **2.** To pass a liquid through (a substance), dissolving the soluble materials in it: *Heavy rains leached the soil of minerals.*

lead¹ (lēd) *v.* **led** (lĕd), **leading, leads** —*tr.* **1.** To show the way to, as by going along or ahead; conduct: *The guide will lead us to the top of the mountain.* See Synonyms at **guide. 2.** To guide, as by the hand or an attached rope: *I led the pony out of the barn.* **3.** To serve as a route for: *The trail led us to a cabin.* **4.** To serve as a channel or passage for: *This pipe leads the water away from the house.* **5.** To cause to think or act in a certain way: *His remarks led me to conclude that he was a musician.* **6.** To be the head of; direct: *He led the group in a song.* **7.** To go at the head of; be first in: *She's still leading the race.* **8.** To live; experience: *A pilot often leads an exciting life.* —*intr.* **1.** To be first; be ahead: *Only one runner is now leading in the race.* **2.** To act as a guide: *The scouts led as the army followed.* **3.** To be or form a way, route, or passage: *The trail leads to a little stream.* **4.** To make the first play in a game or contest. **5.** To guide a partner in a dance. ❖ *n.* **1.** The front, foremost, or winning position: *Our team took the lead in the game.* **2.** The amount by which one is ahead: *a five-point lead.* **3.** A guiding indication; a clue or hint: *leads that helped solve the crime.* **4.** An example or preceding event: *They followed the committee's lead and voted against the amendment.* **5.** The main role, as in a play or movie. **6.** The opening paragraph of a news story. ◆ **lead off** To begin; start. **lead on** To draw into unwise action or mistaken opinion; deceive: *They led the investors on with false promises of oil discoveries.* **lead to** To tend toward or result in: *The discovery of oil led to the development of a city here.* **lead up to** To result in by a series of steps: *These events led up to a change in management of the company.*

lead² (lĕd) *n.* **1.** *Symbol* **Pb** A soft, heavy, bluish-gray metallic element that is easily shaped, very durable, and resistant to corrosion. It is used in making radiation shielding, solder, and containers for corrosive substances. Atomic number 82. See **Periodic Table. 2.** A piece of lead or other metal attached to a length of line, used in measuring depths. **3.** A material, often made mostly of graphite, used as the writing substance in pencils. **4.** Bullets from or for firearms; shot. ❖ *tr.v.* **leaded, leading, leads 1.** To treat with lead or a lead compound: *leaded paint.* **2.** To cover, join, or weight with lead.

WORD HISTORY Lead¹ comes from Middle English *leden*, which comes from Old English *lǣdan*, both meaning "to guide, direct." **Lead²** comes from Middle English *led*, which comes from Old English *lēad*, both referring to the same metal as in Modern English.

leaden (lĕd′n) *adj.* **1.** Made of lead: *a leaden fishing weight.* **2.** Dull dark gray: *leaden skies.* **3.** Heavy or sluggish: *leaden feet worn out from a long hike.* **4.** Gloomy; depressed: *leaden spirits.*

leader (lē′dər) *n.* **1.** A person who leads, guides, or has power over others. **2.** One who is ahead of others, as in a race. **3.** A short length of fishing line between the main line and the hook.

leadership (lē′dər-shĭp′) *n.* **1.** The position or office of a leader. **2.** The guidance or command of a leader or leaders: *Under the leadership of skillful diplomats, the peace conference was a success.* **3.** Ability to lead: *The mayor showed strong leadership during the crisis.* **4.** A group of leaders: *the leadership of the labor union.*

leading (lē′dĭng) *adj.* **1.** Having the first or front position: *the leading swimmer in the race.* **2.** Most important; main; principal: *the leading industrial countries.*

leadoff (lĕd′ôf′) *n.* **1.** An opening play or move. **2.** A person or thing that leads off. —**lead′off′** *adj.*

leaf (lēf) *n., pl.* **leaves** (lēvz) **1.** A flat, usually green structure that is attached to the stem of a plant and that functions mainly to make food for the plant through the process of photosynthesis. **2.** A sheet of paper in a book. **3a.** A very thin sheet of metal. **b.** Such sheets considered as a group: *gold leaf.* **4.** A movable or removable part of a table top. ❖ *intr.v.* **leafed, leafing, leafs 1.** To produce or put forth leaves: *Most trees leafed out early this spring.* **2.** To turn through pages: *leaf through a book.*

leaflet (lē′flĭt) *n.* **1.** One of the separate segments of a compound leaf, as of a clover. **2.** A booklet or small pamphlet.

leafstalk (lēf′stôk′) *n.* The stalk by which a leaf is attached to a stem.

leafy (lē′fē) *adj.* **leafier, leafiest 1.** Covered with or having many leaves: *leafy branches.* **2.** Consisting of leaves: *kale and other leafy vegetables.*

league¹ (lēg) *n.* **1.** An association or alliance of nations, organizations, or people working to help one another. **2.** An association of sports teams or clubs that compete chiefly with each other. **3.** A level of competition: *The ski jump was out of his league.* ❖ *intr.v.* **leagued, leaguing, leagues** To form an association or alliance. ◆ **in league** Joined or working together.

league² (lēg) *n.* A unit of distance, approximately equal to three miles (4.8 kilometers).

WORD HISTORY League¹ is an alteration of Middle English *liege*, which is from Medieval Latin *liga* (both meaning "agreement"), which is from Latin *ligāre*, meaning "to bind." **League²** is from Middle English *lege* which is from Latin *leuga*, both referring to a measure of distance.

leaguer (lē′gər) *n.* A person who belongs to a league.

leak (lēk) *v.* **leaked, leaking, leaks** —*intr.* **1.** To allow something to escape, enter, or pass through an opening or openings: *The roof leaks in a heavy rain.* **2.** To escape or pass through an opening or break: *Water leaked from the rusty pail.* **3.** To become known through a break in secrecy: *The news leaked out.* —*tr.* **1.** To let (something) escape or pass through a hole or opening: *The roof leaks water.* **2.** To disclose (secret information) without permission: *Someone leaked the jury's verdict before it was announced in court.* ❖ *n.* **1.** A hole, crack, or similar opening through which something can escape or pass: *I fixed the leak in the roof.* **2.** A disclosure of secret information.

leakage (lē′kĭj) *n.* **1.** The process, act, or an instance of leaking. **2a.** Something that escapes or enters by leaking. **b.** An amount lost as the result of leaking.

leaky (lē′kē) *adj.* **leakier, leakiest** Having or allowing a leak or leaks: *a leaky valve.* —**leak′i·ness** *n.*

lean¹ (lēn) *v.* **leaned, leaning, leans** —*intr.* **1.** To slant from an upright position: *The tree leaned in the high wind.* **2.** To rest one's weight on or against for support: *I leaned against the wall to rest.* **3.** To rely for assistance or support; depend: *Friends lean on each other for encouragement.* **4.** To have a tendency or preference: *I lean toward the challenger in this election.* —*tr.* To set or place in a slanting or supported position: *I leaned the ladder against the tree. Lean your head a bit to the right.* ❖ *n.* A slant or inclination: *The lean of the ladder makes it look as if it will fall.*

lean² (lēn) *adj.* **leaner, leanest 1.** Not fat or fleshy; thin: *a lean meat.* See Synonyms at **skinny. 2.** Containing little or no fat: *lean meat.* **3.** Not productive, plentiful, or satisfying: *The long drought brought a lean harvest.* ❖ *n.* Meat with little or no fat. —**lean′ness** *n.*

WORD HISTORY Lean¹ comes from Middle English *lenen*, which comes from Old English *hleonian*, both meaning "to rest on or against for support." **Lean²** comes from Middle English *lene*, which comes from Old English *hlǣne*, both meaning "slender, skinny."

leaning (lē′nĭng) *n.* An inclination, tendency, or preference.

leant (lĕnt) *v. Chiefly British* A past tense and a past participle of **lean¹**.

lean-to (lēn′tōō′) *n., pl.* **lean-tos 1.** A shed with a sloping roof, built against a wall or the side of a building. **2.** A simple shelter, often having a roof that slopes in one direction and an open side.

leap (lēp) *v.* **leaped** or **leapt** (lēpt or lĕpt), **leaping, leaps** —*intr.* **1.** To jump or bound upward; spring: *The toad leaped from my hand.* **2.** To move suddenly from one state or subject to another: *A solution leaped into mind.* —*tr.* **1.** To jump or spring over: *The deer leap our garden fence.* **2.** To cause to jump: *leap a horse over a fence.* ❖ *n.* **1.** The act of leaping; a spring or jump. **2.** The distance covered in a jump: *a leap of ten feet.*

leapfrog (lēp′frŏg′) *n.* A game in which one player bends over while the next in line jumps over him or her. ❖ *v.* **leapfrogged, leapfrogging, leapfrogs** —*tr.* To leap over in a game of leap frog. —*intr.* To move quickly to a more advanced position or state, especially when skipping an intermediate level.

leap year *n.* A year in which there are 366 days, the extra day being February 29. A year is a leap year if its number can be divided exactly by four, except years at the end of a century, which must be exactly divisible by 400.

learn (lûrn) *v.* **learned** also **learnt** (lûrnt), **learning, learns** —*tr.* **1.** To gain knowledge of or skill in (something) through study or experience: *I learned how to ski last winter.* **2.** To find out: *We learned who won the election from the newspaper.* **3.** To memorize: *Learn the tune and then add the words.* —*intr.* To gain knowledge or skill: *I learned of their plans by letter.*

learned (lûr′nĭd) *adj.* **1.** Having or showing deep knowledge; scholarly: *a learned professor.* **2.** Meant for scholars: *a learned journal.* —**learn′ed·ly** *adv.*

learning (lûr′nĭng) *n.* **1.** Instruction; education: *Learning was a lot easier once the noise stopped.* **2.** Thorough knowledge or skill gained by study: *Fortunately I have teachers of great learning.*

learning disability *n.* Any of various disorders of attention, memory, or reasoning that interfere with the ability to learn academic skills, such as reading or math.

lease (lēs) *n.* **1.** A written agreement granting use of property for a certain time in exchange for rent. **2.** The period of time specified in such an agreement. ❖ *tr.v.* **leased, leasing, leases 1.** To grant the use of (property) by lease: *The landlord leased the house to new tenants.* **2.** To acquire or hold (property) by lease: *We leased the house from the landlord.*

leash (lēsh) *n.* **1.** A cord, chain, or strap attached to a collar or harness and used to hold or lead a dog or other animal. **2.** A strap or cord used to keep something close to its user or in a designated location. ❖ *tr.v.* **leashed, leashing, leashes** To restrain with or as if with a leash.

least (lēst) *adj.* A superlative of **little.** Smallest in degree, size, or importance: *I made the least number of mistakes of anyone in my group.* ❖ *adv.* Superlative of **little.** To the smallest degree: *I like vanilla ice cream least.* ❖ *n.* The smallest thing or amount: *The least you could do would be to apologize.* ◆ **at least 1.** According to the lowest estimate; not less than: *I go running at least three days a week.* **2.** In any event; anyway: *You might at least call before you come over.* **in the least** At all: *I'm not in the least concerned.*

least common denominator *n.* The least common multiple of the denominators of a set of fractions.

least common multiple *n.* The smallest number that is a common multiple of two other numbers; for example, 12

is the least common multiple of 3 and 4.

leastwise (lēst′wīz′) *adv. Informal* In any event; at least.

leather (lĕth′ər) *n.* Material made from the cleaned and tanned hide of an animal.

leatherette (lĕth′ə-rĕt′) *n.* Imitation leather.

leathern (lĕth′ərn) *adj.* Made of or resembling leather.

leathery (lĕth′ə-rē) *adj.* Resembling leather: *leathery hands.*

leave¹ (lēv) *v.* **left** (lĕft), **leaving, leaves** —*tr.* **1.** To go out of or go away from: *She just left the room. He left town on Thursday.* **2.** To end one's association with; withdraw from: *He left our band and started another.* **3.** To go without taking; forget: *I left my umbrella on the train.* **4.** To allow to remain unused: *I left some milk in the glass.* **5.** To allow to remain in a certain condition or place: *I left the light on all night.* **6.** To give to another to do or use; entrust: *Leave the job to me.* **7.** To give by will; bequeath: *His uncle left him a piece of land.* **8.** To have as a remainder after subtraction: *12 minus 5 leaves 7.* —*intr.* To go away; depart: *We left after lunch.* ◆ **leave alone** or **let alone** To refrain from disturbing or interfering: *Leave the puzzle alone.* **leave off** To stop; cease: *Let's start the story where we left off.* **leave out** To omit: *Don't leave out the pepper from the recipe.*

leave² (lēv) *n.* **1.** Permission; consent: *My parents gave me leave to stay up late.* **2.** Official permission to be absent from work or duty; leave of absence. **3.** The length of such an absence.

WORD HISTORY Leave¹ comes from Middle English *leven,* which comes from Old English *lǣfan,* meaning "to stop, depart." **Leave**² comes from Middle English *leve,* which comes from Old English *lēafe,* meaning "permission, authority."

leaven (lĕv′ən) *n.* **1.** A substance, such as yeast, used to cause dough or batter to rise. **2.** An influence or element that serves to lighten or enliven the whole: *The leaven of good humor made it a friendly debate.* ❖ *tr.v.* **leavened, leavening, leavens 1.** To cause (dough or batter) to rise, as by adding yeast. **2.** To spread through so as to change or enliven.

leavening (lĕv′ə-nĭng) *n.* Something that leavens; leaven.

leave of absence *n., pl.* **leaves of absence 1.** Official permission to be absent from work or duty, as that granted to military or corporate personnel. **2.** The period of time granted by such permission.

leaves (lēvz) *n.* Plural of **leaf.**

leave-taking (lēv′tā′kĭng) *n.* An exchange of goodbyes; a farewell.

leavings (lē′vĭngz) *pl.n.* Scraps left over; remains: *The turkey leavings were fed to the dog.*

Lebanese (lĕb′ə-nēz′ *or* lĕb′ə-nēs′) *adj.* Relating to Lebanon or its people or culture. ❖ *n., pl.* **Lebanese** A native or inhabitant of Lebanon.

lecher (lĕch′ər) *n.* A man who engages in lechery.

lecherous (lĕch′ər-əs) *adj.* Given to, characterized by, or inciting lechery. —**lech′er·ous·ly** *adv.*

lechery (lĕch′ə-rē) *n.* Excessive interest in or indulgence in sexual activity.

lecithin (lĕs′ə-thĭn) *n.* Any of various fatty substances containing phosphorus, present in the cell membranes of plant and animal cells. Lecithin is extracted from seeds and used commercially in foods, cosmetics, paints, and plastics.

lectern (lĕk′tərn) *n.* **1.** A desk with a slanted top for holding books from which to read scriptures during a church service. **2.** A stand that serves as a support for the notes or books of a speaker.

lecture (lĕk′chər) *n.* **1.** A prepared talk providing information about a given subject, delivered before an audience or a class. **2.** A serious lengthy warning or scolding: *The judge gave the reckless driver a lecture in court.* ❖ *v.* **lectured, lecturing, lectures** — *intr.* To deliver a lecture or lectures: *lecturing on history at the university.* — *tr.* **1.** To give a lecture to (an audience or class). **2.** To scold or warn at length. —**lec′tur·er** *n.*

led (lĕd) *v.* Past tense and past participle of **lead**[1].

LED (ĕl′ē-dē′ *or* lĕd) *n.* A semiconductor diode that produces light when an electric current is applied to it. LEDs are used in light bulbs and digital displays. LED is short for *light-emitting diode*.

Leda (lē′də) *n.* In Greek mythology, the mother of Helen and Pollux by Zeus in the form of a swan, and of Castor and Clytemnestra by her own husband.

lede (lēd) *n.* The first sentence or introductory portion of a news story.

ledge (lĕj) *n.* **1.** A narrow shelf projecting from a wall: *a window ledge.* **2.** A cut or projection with a flat horizontal surface on the side of a cliff or rock wall.

ledger (lĕj′ər) *n.* An account book in which sums of money received and paid out by a business are recorded.

lee (lē) *n.* The side away from the wind; the sheltered side: *sailing along the lee of the island.* ❖ *adj.* Sheltered or away from the wind: *the lee side of a ship.*

leech (lēch) *n.* **1.** Any of various segmented worms that suck blood from other animals, including humans, and are usually found in freshwater habitats. **2.** A person who constantly attempts to gain from someone else; a parasite.

leek (lēk) *n.* A vegetable related to the onion, having a narrow white bulb and long dark-green leaves.

leer (lîr) *n.* A sly, lustful, or cunning look. ❖ *intr.v.* **leered, leering, leers** To look with a leer.

leery (lîr′ē) *adj.* **leerier, leeriest** Suspicious; wary: *was leery of the stranger's request.* —**leer′i·ly** *adv.*

lees (lēz) *pl.n.* Sediment that settles during fermentation, especially in wine; dregs.

leeward (lē′wərd *or* lōō′ərd) *adv. & adj.* On or toward the side to which the wind is blowing: *the leeward side of the boat.* ❖ *n.* The lee side: *a whale to leeward of us.*

leeway (lē′wā′) *n.* **1.** Extra space, time, or resources allowing freedom or safety: *We left plenty of leeway to reach the airport during rush hour.* **2.** The drift of a ship or plane to leeward of its course.

left[1] (lĕft) *adj.* **1a.** Belonging to or located on the side of the body to the west when one is facing north: *writes with her left hand.* **b.** Relating to, directed toward, or located on the left side: *the left arm of the chair.* **2.** often **Left** Belonging to the political left; leftist. ❖ *n.* **1a.** The direction or position on the left side: *The sun set on my left as I drove north.* **b.** The left side. **c.** A turn in the direction of the left hand or side. **2.** often **Left** The people and groups who advocate liberal or radical ways to change society, especially in politics, in an attempt to achieve equality or improve the life of the working classes. **3.** A punch or blow delivered with the left hand. ❖ *adv.* On or to the left.

left[2] (lĕft) *v.* Past tense and past participle of **leave**[1].

left field *n.* **1.** In baseball, the section of the outfield that

is to the left, looking from home plate. **2.** The position played by the left fielder.

left fielder *n.* In baseball, the player who defends left field.

left-hand (lĕft′hănd′) *adj.* **1.** Relating to or located on the left: *the upper left-hand corner.* **2.** Relating to, designed for, or done with the left hand.

left-handed (lĕft′hăn′dĭd) *adj.* **1a.** Using the left hand, as for writing or throwing, more skillfully or easily than the right hand. **b.** In sports, swinging from left to right: *a left-handed golfer.* **2a.** Done with the left hand. **b.** Designed for use by the left hand: *left-handed scissors.* **3.** Turning or moving from right to left: *a left-handed screw.* **4.** Insincere or doubtful: *a left-handed compliment.* ❖ *adv.* **1.** With the left hand. **2.** From the left to the right: *She is the only player who bats left-handed on her team.* —**left′-hand′ed·ly** *adv.* —**left′-hand′ed·ness** *n.*

left-hander (lĕft′hăn′dər) *n.* A person who is left-handed.

leftist (lĕf′tĭst) *n.* A person who advocates or sympathizes with the ideas of the political left, especially a socialist or communist. —**left′ist** *adj.*

leftover (lĕft′ō′vər) *adj.* Remaining unused or uneaten: *leftover fabric; leftover rice.*

leftovers (lĕft′ō′vərs) *pl.n.* Remaining food kept after a meal for future consumption: *had leftovers for dinner.*

left wing also **Left Wing** *n.* The liberal or radical faction of a group. —**left′-wing′** *adj.* —**left′wing′er** *n.*

lefty (lĕf′tē) *n., pl.* **lefties** *Informal* A person who is left-handed.

leg (lĕg) *n.* **1.** A limb of a human or other animal that is used for support or for moving from place to place. **2.** The part of a garment, especially of a pair of pants, that covers the leg. **3.** A supporting part resembling a leg in shape or function: *a table leg.* **4.** Either of the sides of a right triangle that is not the hypotenuse. **5.** A stage of a journey or course: *the first leg of the trip.* ◆ **leg it** To walk or run. **on (one's) last legs** At the end of one's strength or resources; ready to collapse, fail, or die.

legacy (lĕg′ə-sē) *n., pl.* **legacies 1.** An inheritance consisting of money or property. **2.** Something passed on to those who come later in time; a heritage: *a legacy of religious freedom.*

legal (lē′gəl) *adj.* **1.** Relating to the law: *legal knowledge.* **2.** Established or permitted by law: *legal activities.* **3.** Relating to or characteristic of lawyers or their profession: *legal fees.* **4.** Acceptable or allowable under official rules: *the legal moves in chess.* —**le′gal·ly** *adv.*

legal age *n.* The age at which a person assumes the legal rights and responsibilities of an adult.

legality (lē-găl′ĭ-tē) *n., pl.* **legalities 1.** The state of being legal; lawfulness. **2.** Something required by law.

legalize (lē′gə-līz′) *tr.v.* **legalized, legalizing, legalizes** To make legal. —**le′gal·i·za′tion** (lē′gə-lĭ-zā′shən) *n.*

legal tender *n.* Money that must by law be accepted in payment of a debt.

legate (lĕg′ĭt) *n.* An official envoy or ambassador, especially one representing the pope.

legatee (lĕg′ə-tē′) *n.* The inheritor of a legacy.

legation (lĭ-gā′shən) *n.* **1.** A group of diplomatic representatives in a foreign country ranking below an embassy. **2.** The building occupied by such a group.

legato (lĭ-gä′tō) *adv. & adj.* In a musical style in which notes are connected smoothly without any noticeable break between them.

legend (lĕj′ənd) *n.* **1a.** A story handed down from earlier times, often believed to be historically true. **b.** A group of such stories. **2.** A person or thing that is famous enough to inspire legends: *He's a legend in his own time.* **3.** An inscription on a coin, a banner, or another object. **4.** An explanatory caption under a map, chart, or illustration.

legendary (lĕj′ən-dĕr′ē) *adj.* **1.** Relating to or based on a legend: *legendary heroes.* **2.** Talked about or celebrated in a legend or legends: *The fox's cunning is legendary.* **3.** Very well-known; famous.

legerdemain (lĕj′ər-də-mān′) *n.* **1.** Skill in performing tricks with the hands, especially by a magician or juggler; sleight of hand. **2.** A display of trickery.

legged (lĕg′ĭd *or* lĕgd) *adj.* Having a certain kind or number of legs: *four-legged animals.*

legging (lĕg′ĭng) *n.* **1.** A leg covering worn especially by soldiers and workers, often made of cloth or leather and usually extending from the waist or knee to the ankle. **2.** Tight-fitting knit pants, usually worn by women and children.

leggy (lĕg′ē) *adj.* **leggier, leggiest 1.** Having long legs: *a tall, leggy boy.* **2.** Having long, often leafless stems: *leggy petunias.*

Leghorn (lĕg′hôrn′ *or* lĕg′ərn) *n.* Any of a breed of white chickens that produce a large number of white eggs.

legible (lĕj′ə-bəl) *adj.* Capable of being read: *clear, legible handwriting.* —**leg′i·bil′i·ty** *n.* —**leg′i·bly** *adv.*

legion (lē′jən) *n.* **1.** The major unit of the ancient Roman army, consisting of at least 3,000 foot soldiers and 100 cavalry troops. **2.** A large military unit. **3.** A large group or number of people or things; a multitude: *Legions of insects settled on the fields.* **4.** often **Legion** A national organization of people who once served in the armed forces.

legionary (lē′jə-nĕr′ē) *adj.* Relating to or belonging to a legion. ❖ *n., pl.* **legionaries** A soldier of a legion.

legionnaire (lē′jə-nâr′) *n.* A member of a legion.

legislate (lĕj′ĭ-slāt′) *v.* **legislated, legislating, legislates** —*tr.* To create or bring about by making laws: *legislate reforms in the housing code.* —*intr.* To make or pass laws.

legislation (lĕj′ĭ-slā′shən) *n.* **1.** The act or process of making laws: *Our Constitution gives Congress the authority of legislation.* **2.** A proposed or enacted law or group of laws: *legislation being discussed in Congress.*

legislative (lĕj′ĭ-slā′tĭv) *adj.* **1.** Relating to the making of laws: *legislative powers.* **2.** Relating to a legislature: *legislative decree.* **3.** Having power to make laws: *the legislative branch of government.*

legislator (lĕj′ĭ-slā′tər) *n.* A member of a government body that makes laws: *Senators and representatives are legislators.*

legislature (lĕj′ĭ-slā′chər) *n.* A body of people empowered to make and change the laws of a nation or state.

legitimacy (lə-jĭt′ə-mə-sē) *n.* The quality or fact of being legitimate.

legitimate (lə-jĭt′ə-mĭt) *adj.* **1.** In accordance with the law; lawful: *the legitimate owner of the property.* **2.** Supported by logic or common sense; reasonable: *Some problems have more than one legitimate solution.* **3.** Authentic; genuine; real: *We have a legitimate complaint.* **4.** *Often Offensive* Born of legally married parents: *a legitimate child.* —**le·git′i·mate·ly** *adv.*

legitimize (lə-jĭt′ə-mīz′) *tr.v.* **legitimized, legitimizing, legitimizes** To make legitimate.

legume (lĕg′yōom′ *or* lə-gyōom′) *n.* **1.** Any of a group of related plants having seedpods that split along two sides. Beans, peas, clover, and alfalfa are all legumes. **2.** The pod or seed of such a plant, used as food.

leguminous (lə-gyōo′mə-nəs) *adj.* Relating to legumes.

leg warmer *n.* A knitted covering for the leg, resembling a sock without a foot.

lei (lā *or* lā′ē) *n., pl.* **leis** A garland of flowers worn around the neck as an ornament.

leisure (lē′zhər *or* lĕzh′ər) *n.* Freedom from work or time-consuming tasks: *Vacation is customarily a time of leisure and relaxation.* ◆ **at (one's) leisure** When one has free time; at one's convenience: *Respond to this letter at your leisure.*

leisurely (lē′zhər-lē *or* lĕzh′ər-lē) *adj.* Characterized by leisure; unhurried: *a leisurely lunch.* ❖ *adv.* In an unhurried manner; slowly: *strolled leisurely toward town.* —**lei′sure·li·ness** *n.*

leitmotif *also* **leitmotiv** (līt′mō-tēf′) *n.* **1.** A melodic passage or phrase associated with a specific character, situation, or element, as in an opera. **2.** A dominant and recurring theme: *Lace is the leitmotif of this fall's fashions.*

lemming (lĕm′ĭng) *n.* Any of various small stout rodents that live in northern regions and are noted for their mass migrations.

lemon (lĕm′ən) *n.* **1a.** An oval yellow citrus fruit having sour juicy pulp. **b.** The spiny evergreen tree that bears such fruit. **2.** *Informal* Something that is unsatisfactory or defective: *That car is a lemon; it breaks down all the time.* —**lem′on·y** *adj.*

lemonade (lĕm′ə-nād′) *n.* A drink made of lemon juice, water, and sugar.

lemur (lē′mər) *n.* Any of various small primates of the island of Madagascar that have large eyes, soft fur, and a long tail. Lemurs live in trees and are active chiefly at night.

Lenape (lĕn′ə-pē) *n., pl.* **Lenape** or **Lenapes** A Delaware Indian.

lend (lĕnd) *v.* **lent** (lĕnt), **lending, lends** —*tr.* **1.** To give or allow the use of (something) with the understanding that it is to be returned: *Will you lend me your car to go to the movies?* **2.** To provide (money) temporarily on condition that the amount borrowed be returned, usually with an interest fee. **3.** To contribute; impart: *The painting lent a feeling of warmth to the room.* **4.** To make available for another's use: *The neighbors lent their help after the storm.* —*intr.* To make a loan. ◆ **lend a hand** To be of assistance. **lend itself to** To be suitable for: *This novel lends itself to several interpretations.* —**lend′er** *n.* —SEE NOTE AT **borrow.**

length (lĕngkth *or* lĕngth) *n.* **1.** The measured distance of a thing from end to end along its greatest dimension: *the length of a boat.* **2.** The extent of something: *traveled the length of the Nile River.* **3.** The amount of time something takes; duration: *the length of the meeting.* **4.** The state, quality, or fact of being long: *The length of the journey wore us out.* **5.** The measure of something used as a unit to estimate distances: *two arm's lengths.* **6.** A piece of something, often of a standard size: *a length of wire.* **7.** often **lengths** The extent or degree to which a goal is pursued: *went to great lengths to prove his point.* ◆ **at length 1.** After some time; eventually: *At length we arrived at the dock.* **2.** In detail; fully: *spoke at length about her travels.*

lengthen (lĕngk′thən *or* lĕng′thən) *tr. & intr.v.* **lengthened, lengthening, lengthens** To make or become longer: *lengthen pants legs; shadows that lengthen near sunset.*

lengthwise (lĕngkth′wīz′ *or* lĕngth′wīz′) *adv.* Along the direction of the length: *fold a sheet of paper lengthwise.*

❖ *adj.* In the direction of the length: *lengthwise folds in the paper.*

lengthy (lĕngk′thē *or* lĕng′thē) *adj.* **lengthier, lengthiest** Long, especially too long: *a lengthy explanation.* —**length′i·ly** *adv.* —**length′i·ness** *n.*

lenient (lē′nē-ənt *or* lēn′yənt) *adj.* Inclined to forgive; merciful; generous: *a lenient judge.* —**le′ni·ence, le′ni·en·cy** *n.*

Lenni Lenape (lĕn′ē lĕn′ə-pē) *n.* A Delaware Indian.

lens (lĕnz) *n., pl.* **lenses 1a.** A piece of glass or plastic shaped so that light rays passing through it converge or diverge to form an image. **b.** A combination of two or more such pieces, sometimes with other optical devices such as prisms, used to form an image as in a camera or telescope; a compound lens. **c.** A thin piece of glass or plastic, as on a pair of sunglasses, that transmits light without refraction. **2.** A transparent, curved structure in the eye that is located behind the iris and focuses light rays entering through the pupil to form an image on the retina. Vertebrate animals and cephalopods, such as squids and octopuses, have eyes with lenses.

lent (lĕnt) *v.* Past tense and past participle of **lend**.

Lent *n.* A 40-day period of fasting and penitence observed by many Christians, usually from Ash Wednesday until Easter, not counting Sundays. —**Lent′en** *adj.*

lentil (lĕn′təl) *n.* **1.** The round flat seed of a pod-bearing plant related to the beans and peas, eaten as a vegetable. **2.** The plant that bears such seeds.

Leo (lē′ō) *n.* **1.** A constellation in the Northern Hemisphere near Cancer, traditionally pictured as a lion. **2.** The fifth sign of the zodiac in astrology.

leonine (lē′ə-nīn′) *adj.* Relating to or characteristic of a lion: *a leonine roar.*

leopard (lĕp′ərd) *n.* A large meat-eating wild cat of Africa and Asia, having either light-brown fur with black spots or black fur.

leotard (lē′ə-tärd′) *n.* A tight-fitting one-piece garment, sometimes with sleeves, worn especially by dancers and acrobats.

leper (lĕp′ər) *n.* A person who has leprosy.

lepidopteran (lĕp′ĭ-dŏp′tər-ən) *n.* A butterfly or moth. —**lep′i·dop′ter·an** *adj.*

leprechaun (lĕp′rī-kŏn′) *n.* In Irish folklore, an elflike creature who can reveal hidden treasure if caught.

leprosy (lĕp′rə-sē) *n.* A mildly contagious disease caused by a bacterium that damages nerves, skin, and other organs. If untreated, leprosy eventually destroys the affected body tissues. —**lep′rous** (lĕp′rəs) *adj.*

lesbian (lĕz′bē-ən) *n.* A woman whose sexual orientation is toward women. ❖ *adj.* Relating to or being a lesbian. —SEE NOTE AT **gay**.

lesion (lē′zhən) *n.* An abnormal structure in a bodily organ or tissue, such as a wound, sore, or tumor, caused usually by injury or disease.

less (lĕs) *adj.* A comparative of **little**. **1.** Smaller in amount, quantity, or degree; not so much: *less time to spare; less food to eat.* **2.** Lower in importance or rank: *No less a person than the president gave the order.* ❖ *adv.* Comparative of **little**. To a smaller extent, degree, or quantity: *The game was less enjoyable than I had hoped.* ❖ *prep.* Minus; without: *Five less three is two.* ❖ *n.* A smaller amount or quantity: *The house sold for less than we thought.* ◆ **less than** Not at all: *a less than satisfactory answer.* **much less**

or **still less** Especially not: *I'm not blaming anyone, much less you.* —SEE NOTE AT **few**.

–less A suffix that means: **1.** Without or lacking: *motherless; nameless.* **2.** Not acting in a certain way: *relentless.* **3.** Not acted on in a certain way: *dauntless.*

WORD BUILDING The suffix **–less** comes from the Old English suffix *–lēas,* from the word *lēas,* meaning "without." In Old English and Middle English, *–less* was often used to convey the negative or opposite of words ending in *–ful,* as in *careful/careless* and *fearful/fearless.* But *–less* was also used to coin words that had no counterpart ending in *–ful: headless, loveless, motherless.* Although *–less* normally forms adjectives by attaching to nouns, sometimes it attaches to verbs, as in *tireless,* "without tiring."

lessee (lĕ-sē′) *n.* A tenant holding a lease.

lessen (lĕs′ən) *tr. & intr.v.* **lessened, lessening, lessens** To make or become less: *a drug to lessen the pain; pain that lessened immediately.* See Synonyms at **decrease**.

lesser (lĕs′ər) *adj.* A comparative of **little**. **1.** Smaller in amount, value, or importance: *a lesser evil; lesser gods.* **2.** Of a smaller size than other similar forms: *the lesser anteater.* ❖ *adv.* A comparative of **little**. Less. Used before a participle: *works by lesser-known authors.* ❖ *n.* A person or thing that is lower in importance, rank, size, or degree: *the lesser of two evils.*

lesson (lĕs′ən) *n.* **1.** Something to be learned, especially an assignment or exercise in which something is studied or taught: *an Spanish textbook divided into 40 lessons.* **2.** A period of time devoted to teaching or learning a certain subject: *three piano lessons a week.* **3.** An experience or example from which one can learn: *The accident taught her a lesson about driving more carefully.* **4.** A reading from the Bible given as part of a religious service.

lessor (lĕs′ôr′ *or* lĕ-sôr′) *n.* A person who rents property to another by lease.

lest (lĕst) *conj.* **1.** For fear that: *tiptoed lest the guard should hear her.* **2.** So that something or someone will not or would not: *double-knotted his shoelaces lest they come untied.*

let¹ (lĕt) *v.* **let, letting, lets** —*tr.* **1a.** To grant permission to: *The crowd let the speaker continue without interruption.* **b.** To allow something to happen: *Let your hot cocoa cool a bit.* **2.** To cause to: *Let me know what happened.* **3.** Used as an auxiliary verb to express a request, command, or warning: *Let's finish the job!* **4.** Used as an auxiliary verb to express a proposal or assumption: *Let x equal 3.* **5.** To permit to move in a specified way: *Let the cat out.* **6.** To permit to escape; release: *Who let the air out of the balloon?* **7.** To rent or lease: *They let rooms to students.* —*intr.* To become rented or leased. ◆ **let down 1.** To cause to come down gradually; lower: *The crane let down the piano.* **2.** To fail to meet the expectations of; disappoint: *Don't let me down.* **let off 1.** To excuse from work or duty: *They let me off so I could go home early.* **2.** To release with little or no punishment: *They were let off with a warning.* **let on 1.** To allow to be known; admit: *Don't let on that I'm going too.* **2.** To pretend: *They let on that they had been to Europe.* **let out 1.** To come to a close; end: *School lets out next week.* **2.** To make known; reveal: *Who let that information out?* **3.** To increase the size of (a garment, for example). **let up** To slow down, diminish, or stop: *The rain finally let up.*

let² (lĕt) *n.* A stroke in tennis or other net games that must be repeated, especially a serve that has touched the net before falling into the proper part of the court.

WORD HISTORY Let[1] comes from Middle English *leten*, which comes from Old English *lǣtan*, both meaning "to allow." **Let**[2] comes from Middle English *lette* (meaning "obstacle"), which comes from Old English *lettan*, meaning "to hinder."

–let A suffix that means: **1.** A small one: *booklet*. **2.** Something worn on: *armlet*.

letdown (lĕt′doun′) *n.* **1.** A decrease or slowing down, as in energy or effort. **2.** A disappointment: *Losing that game was a real letdown.*

lethal (lē′thəl) *adj.* Causing or capable of causing death: *a lethal disease; a lethal weapon.* —**le′thal·ly** *adv.*

lethargic (lə-thär′jĭk) *adj.* Relating to, causing, or characterized by lethargy: *spend a lethargic afternoon lying on the beach.* —**le·thar′gi·cal·ly** *adv.*

lethargy (lĕth′ər-jē) *n., pl.* **lethargies 1a.** Lack of energy or vigor; sluggishness. **b.** Lack of interest or enthusiasm; apathy. **2.** An abnormal state of drowsiness, as caused by disease or drugs.

Leto (lē′tō) *n.* In Greek mythology, a goddess who was the mother of Apollo and Artemis by Zeus.

let's (lĕts) Contraction of *let us.*

Lett (lĕt) *n.* A member of a Baltic people that make up the main population of Latvia.

letter (lĕt′ər) *n.* **1.** A symbol or character that is part of an alphabet, is used in the writing of a word, and usually indicates a speech sound. **2.** A written or printed message addressed to a person: *She wrote a letter to her lawyer.* **3.** often **letters** A document giving the person who bears it certain rights or privileges: *letters of protection from the king.* **4. letters** *(used with a singular verb)* Literature: *English letters.* **5.** The exact or literal meaning: *the letter of the law.* **6.** An emblem in the shape of the initial of a school, awarded for achievement in athletics. ❖ *v.* **lettered, lettering, letters** —*tr.* To mark or write with letters: *lettered our name on the mailbox.* —*intr.* To earn a school letter, as for outstanding athletic achievement: *She lettered in three collegiate sports.* ◆ **to the letter** To the last detail; exactly: *We followed the instructions to the letter.* —**let′ter·er** *n.*

letter carrier *n.* A mail carrier.

letterhead (lĕt′ər-hĕd′) *n.* **1.** A printed heading at the top of a sheet of letter paper, usually consisting of the name and address of the sender. **2.** Letter paper with such a heading.

lettering (lĕt′ər-ĭng) *n.* **1.** The act of forming letters. The letters formed, drawn, or painted, as on a sign.

letter-perfect (lĕt′ər-pûr′fĭkt) *adj.* Perfect in every detail.

Lettish (lĕt′ĭsh) *adj.* Relating to the Letts or their language or culture. ❖ *n.* The Latvian language.

lettuce (lĕt′əs) *n.* Any of various forms of a plant cultivated for its large green or reddish leaves, used in salad.

letup (lĕt′ŭp′) *n.* **1.** A reduction in pace, force, or intensity. **2.** A pause or stop: *no letup in the storm.*

leucine (loō′sēn′) *n.* An essential amino acid that is found in plant and animal protein.

leukemia (loō-kē′mē-ə) *n.* Any of several cancers of the blood characterized by the uncontrolled growth in the number of white blood cells.

leukocyte also **leucocyte** (loō′kə-sīt′) *n.* A white blood cell.

levee (lĕv′ē) *n.* **1.** A bank of earth or other material built up along a river to keep it from flooding. **2.** A landing place on a river.

level (lĕv′əl) *n.* **1.** Relative position or rank on a scale: *Science gets more complex at the college level.* **2.** Position along a vertical axis; height or depth: *The divers descended to a level of 60 feet.* **3.** A story or floor of a building. **4.** A flat stretch of land. **5.** An instrument for determining whether a surface is horizontal or vertical, used especially by carpenters and masons. ❖ *adj.* **1.** Having a flat even surface: *level farmland.* **2.** Horizontal: *Is the picture on this wall level?* **3.** Steady; uniform: *a level tone of voice.* **4.** Being at the same height, rank, or position; even: *The two tabletops are level with each other.* **5.** Reasonable and careful; sensible: *a level head.* ❖ *v.* **leveled, leveling, levels** or **levelled, levelling, levels** —*tr.* **1.** To make smooth, flat, or horizontal: *level ground for a new building.* **2.** To cut, tear, or knock down to the ground: *A tornado leveled several buildings.* **3.** To place on the same level; equalize: *level differences between schools.* **4.** To aim carefully: *level a rifle at the target.* —*intr. Informal* To be frank and open: *Let's level with each other.* ◆ **(one's) level best** The best one can do. **on the level** *Informal* Without deception; honest. —**lev′el·er, lev′el·ler** *n.* —**lev′el·ly** *adv.* —**lev′el·ness** *n.*

levelheaded (lĕv′əl-hĕd′ĭd) *adj.* Having common sense and good judgment; sensible. —**lev′el·head′ed·ness** *n.*

lever (lĕv′ər *or* lē′vər) *n.* **1.** A simple machine consisting of a rigid bar that pivots on a fixed point and can be used to transmit force, as in raising or moving a weight at one end by pushing down on the other. **2.** A projecting handle used to control, adjust, or operate a device or machine: *a gear shift lever.*

leverage (lĕv′ər-ĭj *or* lē′vər-ĭj) *n.* **1.** The action or mechanical advantage of a lever. **2.** An advantage in position or in power to act effectively: *Great wealth gives a person leverage in many business situations.* **3.** The use of borrowed funds, often for a risky investment. ❖ *tr.v.* **leveraged, leveraging, leverages** To provide (a company, for instance) with leverage.

leviathan (lə-vī′ə-thən) *n.* **1.** A huge sea creature mentioned in the Bible. **2.** Something of enormous size or bulk.

levitate (lĕv′ĭ-tāt′) *intr. & tr.v.* **levitated, levitating, levitates** To rise or cause to rise into the air and float, especially through supposed supernatural means.

Levite (lē′vīt′) *n.* In the Bible, a member of the tribe of Levi but not descended from Aaron and, if male, chosen to assist the Temple priests.

Leviticus (lə-vĭt′ĭ-kəs) *n.* A book of the Bible that contains Hebrew ceremonial rituals and laws governing the priests and Levites.

levity (lĕv′ĭ-tē) *n., pl.* **levities** A light humorous manner or attitude; frivolity.

levy (lĕv′ē) *tr.v.* **levied, levying, levies 1.** To impose or collect: *levy a sales tax; levy tariffs.* **2.** To draft into military service. **3.** To declare and carry on (war). ❖ *n., pl.* **levies 1.** The act of levying. **2.** Money collected as a tax, tariff, or other fee. **3.** A body of troops drafted into military service.

lewd (loōd) *adj.* **lewder, lewdest 1.** Lustful. **2.** Obscene; indecent. —**lewd′ly** *adv.* —**lewd′ness** *n.*

lexicographer (lĕk′sĭ-kŏg′rə-phər) *n.* A person who writes, edits, or compiles a dictionary.

lexicography (lĕk′sĭ-kŏg′rə-fē) *n.* The process or work of writing, editing, or compiling dictionaries.

lexicon (lĕk′sĭ-kŏn′) *n.* **1.** A dictionary, especially one giving translations of words from an ancient language.

2. A stock of terms used in a particular subject or profession or by a particular person; a vocabulary.

Leyden jar (līd′n) *n.* An early device for storing electric charge that consists of a jar covered inside and out with metal foil and a metal rod that touches the inner foil and passes out of the jar through an insulated stopper. The rod is used to conduct electric charge into the jar.

LF An abbreviation of left field.

LGBT An abbreviation of lesbian, gay, bisexual, transgender.

liability (lī′ə-bĭl′ĭ-tē) *n., pl.* **liabilities 1.** The state of being liable. **2.** Something for which one is liable; an obligation, responsibility, or debt: *My insurance company limits my liability to $1,000 if my car is damaged.* **3.** Something that holds one back; a disadvantage.

liable (lī′ə-bəl) *adj.* **1.** Legally obligated or responsible: *The drivers argued about who was liable to pay for fixing the cars.* **2.** Subject; susceptible; prone: *Delicate glass is liable to breakage.* **3.** Likely: *liable to make mistakes.*

liaison (lē′ā-zŏn′ *or* lē-ā′zŏn′) *n.* **1.** A means of communication between different groups or units of an organization, especially in the military. **2.** A person who maintains communication: *I work as the company's liaison with the people who sell our line of products.*

liana (lē-ä′nə *or* lē-ăn′ə) *n.* A climbing tropical vine having woody stems.

liar (lī′ər) *n.* A person who tells lies.

libation (lī-bā′shən) *n.* **1a.** The pouring of a liquid offering as a religious ritual. **b.** The liquid so poured. **2.** *Informal* **a.** A beverage, especially an intoxicating beverage. **b.** The act of drinking an intoxicating beverage. —**li·ba′tion·ar·y** (lī-bā′shə-nĕr′ē) *adj.*

libel (lī′bəl) *n.* **1.** A false or misleading publication or broadcast that damages a person's reputation. **2.** The act of presenting such material to the public: *charged the writer with libel.* ❖ *tr.v.* **libeled, libeling, libels** *or* **libelled, libelling, libels** To write or publish a false or damaging statement about (a person). —**li′bel·er** *n.*

libelous *also* **libellous** (lī′bə-ləs) *adj.* Involving or being a libel: *a libelous story in the newspaper.*

liberal (lĭb′ər-əl *or* lĭb′rəl) *adj.* **1.** Tending to give generously: *a liberal contributor to the charity.* **2.** Generous in amount; ample: *a liberal helping of food.* **3.** Not strict or literal; approximate: *The movie is a liberal adaptation of the story.* **4.** Relating to the liberal arts. **5.** Open to new ideas and tolerant of the ideas and behavior of others; broad-minded: *a person with liberal attitudes.* **6.** *often* **Liberal** Relating to a political party that believes in the natural goodness of humans and favors civil liberties, democratic reform, and social progress. ❖ *n.* **1.** A person who is liberal. **2.** *often* **Liberal** A member of a liberal party. —**lib′er·al·ly** *adv.* —**lib′er·al·ness** *n.*

liberal arts *pl.n.* College studies such as languages, history, philosophy, and science that provide general knowledge and the ability to think analytically, rather than practical or professional skills.

liberalism (lĭb′ər-ə-lĭz′əm *or* lĭb′rə-lĭz′əm) *n.* **1.** Liberal political views and policies. **2.** Generosity; liberality: *a donor known for her liberalism in support of the arts.*

liberality (lĭb′ə-răl′ĭ-tē) *n., pl.* **liberalities 1.** The quality or state of being liberal or generous. **2.** An instance of being liberal.

liberalize (lĭb′ər-ə-līz′ *or* lĭb′rə-līz′) *tr. & intr.v.* **liberal-** ized, liberalizing, liberalizes To make or become more liberal: *liberalized some of the regulations.* —**lib′er·al·i·za′tion** (lĭb′ər-ə-lī-zā′shən *or* lĭb′rə-lī-zā′shən) *n.*

liberate (lĭb′ə-rāt′) *tr.v.* **liberated, liberating, liberates 1.** To set free, as from confinement or control: *The Emancipation Proclamation liberated many slaves.* **2.** To set free as a result of chemical combination: *liberate a gas.* —**lib′er·a′tion** *n.* —**lib′er·a′tor** *n.*

libertarian (lĭb′ər-târ′ē-ən) *n.* **1.** One who advocates maximizing individual rights and minimizing the role of the state. **2.** One who believes in free will. —**lib′er·tar′i·an** *adj.* —**lib′er·tar′i·an·ism** *n.*

libertine (lĭb′ər-tēn′) *n.* A person who lives an irresponsible immoral life; a rake. ❖ *adj.* Morally unrestrained: *a libertine existence.*

liberty (lĭb′ər-tē) *n., pl.* **liberties 1.** Freedom from imprisonment, slavery, or forced labor. **2a.** Freedom from oppressive restriction or control by a government or other power. **b.** A right to engage in certain actions without interference by a government or other power: *the liberties protected by the Bill of Rights.* **3.** The right or power to act as one chooses: *Freelance writers have great liberty in setting their work schedules.* **4.** *often* **liberties** An action that is unwarranted or improper: *He takes liberties with history to make his argument sound better.* **5.** A period during which a sailor is permitted to go ashore. ◆ **at liberty** Not in confinement or under constraint; free: *Am I at liberty to speak openly?*

libido (lĭ-bē′dō) *n., pl.* **libidos** Sexual desire. —**li·bid′i·nal** (lĭ-bĭd′n-əl) *adj.* —**li·bid′i·nal·ly** *adv.*

Libra (lē′brə) *n.* **1.** A constellation in the Southern Hemisphere near Scorpius, traditionally pictured as a balance. **2.** The seventh sign of the zodiac in astrology.

librarian (lī-brâr′ē-ən) *n.* A person who is specially trained to work in a library.

library (lī′brĕr′ē) *n., pl.* **libraries 1.** A place where books, magazines, recordings, and other materials are kept in an organized arrangement so they can be easily found for reading and borrowing. **2.** A collection of books or other items containing information. **3.** A room in a private home for such a collection.

librettist (lĭ-brĕt′ĭst) *n.* The author of a libretto.

libretto (lĭ-brĕt′ō) *n., pl.* **librettos** *or* **libretti** (lĭ-brĕt′ē) The text of a dramatic musical work, such as an opera.

lice (līs) *n.* Plural of **louse** (sense 1).

license (lī′səns) *n.* **1a.** Official or legal permission to do or own a specified thing: *The group has license to run a daycare center.* **b.** A document, card, plate, or tag issued as proof that such permission has been granted: *The doctor's license is hung on the wall.* **2.** Freedom of action: *I took the license to stop by without calling beforehand.* ❖ *tr.v.* **licensed, licensing, licenses** To grant a license to or for: *The doctor was not licensed to practice medicine in this state.*

licensed practical nurse (lī′sənst) *n.* A nurse who has completed a practical nursing program and is licensed by a state to provide routine patient care under the direction of a registered nurse or physician.

license plate *n.* A rectangular, usually metal plate having numbers or letters or both, used to identify a vehicle that is officially registered with the government.

licentious (lī-sĕn′shəs) *adj.* Lacking moral restraint; immoral. —**li·cen′tious·ly** *adv.* —**li·cen′tious·ness** *n.*

lichee (lē′chē) *n.* Variant of **lychee.**

lichen (lī′kən) *n.* An organism that consists of a fungus and an alga growing in close association with each other.

Lichens often live on rocks and tree bark and can also be found in extremely cold environments.

lick (lĭk) *tr.v.* **licked, licking, licks 1a.** To pass the tongue over: *The dog licks her pups.* **b.** To lap up: *The cat licked cream from a dish.* **2.** To move or flicker like a tongue: *Flames lick the burning logs.* **3.** *Slang* To punish with a beating; thrash. **4.** *Slang* To defeat soundly: *We licked the other team.* ❖ *n.* **1.** A movement of the tongue over something: *a kitten's wet lick.* **2.** A small quantity; bit: *We couldn't find a lick of evidence.* **3.** A salt lick. **4.** A blow or hard stroke. ◆ **lick (one's) wounds** To recover from a defeat.

licorice (lĭk′ər-ĭs *or* lĭk′ər-ĭsh) *n.* **1a.** A plant having a sweet strong-tasting root used as a flavoring. **b.** The root of this plant. **2a.** A candy made from or flavored with the licorice root. **b.** A chewy candy made from sugar, corn syrup, and flavorings, often manufactured in long flexible tubes.

lid (lĭd) *n.* **1.** A removable cover or top for a hollow container: *the lid for a jar; the lid of a box.* **2.** An eyelid.

lie¹ (lī) *intr.v.* **lay** (lā), **lain** (lān), **lying** (lī′ĭng), **lies 1.** To place oneself in a flat or resting position: *The cow lay down in the pasture.* **2.** To be in a flat or resting position: *I lay in the hammock all afternoon.* **3.** To be or rest on a surface: *Forks and spoons lay on the table.* **4.** To be located: *Many tiny islands lie off the coast.* **5.** To remain in a certain condition or position: *We let the land lie unused.* **6.** To consist of or have as a basis: *The answer lay in further research.* **7.** To extend: *Our land lies between the river and the trees.* **8.** To be buried: *Here lie my grandparents.* ❖ *n.* The manner or position in which something lies, as the surface or slope of a piece of land. ◆ **lie low 1.** To keep oneself or one's plans hidden. **2.** To wait until it is the right moment to act.

lie² (lī) *n.* An untrue statement made in order to deceive someone; a falsehood. ❖ *intr.v.* **lied, lying** (lī′ĭng), **lies 1.** To tell a lie or lies: *The suspect lied to the police.* **2.** To create an illusion or a false impression: *Even photographs can lie.*

WORD HISTORY Lie¹ comes from Middle English *lien*, which comes from Old English *licgan*, both meaning "to place or be placed in a flat, resting position." **Lie²** comes from Middle English *lie*, which comes from Old English *lyge*, both meaning "untrue statement."

lie detector *n.* An instrument that records changes in bodily conditions, such as blood pressure and pulse rate, that usually occur when a person is not telling the truth.

lief (lēf) *adv.* **liefer, liefest** *Archaic* Readily; willingly: *I would as lief go now as later.* ❖ *adj.* **liefer, liefest 1.** Beloved; dear. **2.** Ready or willing.

liege (lēj) *n.* **1.** A lord to whom subjects owed allegiance and services in feudal times. **2.** A person owing allegiance and services to such a lord; a vassal. ❖ *adj.* Relating to the relationship between lord and vassal: *my liege lord.*

liegeman (lēj′mən) *n.* **1.** A feudal vassal or subject. **2.** A loyal supporter, follower, or subject.

lien (lēn *or* lē′ən) *n.* A legal claim on the property of a person as payment for a debt.

lieu (lōō) *n. Archaic* Place; stead. ◆ **in lieu of** In place of; instead of: *received a check in lieu of cash.*

lieutenancy (lōō-tĕn′ən-sē) *n.* The duty, authority, or rank of a lieutenant.

lieutenant (lōō-tĕn′ənt) *n.* **1a.** A first lieutenant. **b.** A second lieutenant. **2.** An officer in the Navy ranking above

an ensign and below a lieutenant commander. **3.** An officer in a police or fire department ranking next below a captain. **4.** A chief assistant; a deputy.

lieutenant colonel *n.* An officer in the US Army, Air Force, or Marine Corps, ranking above a major and below a colonel.

lieutenant commander *n.* An officer in the US Navy or Coast Guard ranking above a lieutenant and below a commander.

lieutenant general *n.* An officer in the US Army, Air Force, or Marine Corps, ranking above a major general and below a general.

lieutenant governor *n.* **1.** An elected official ranking just below the governor of a US state. **2.** The nonelected chief of government of a Canadian province.

lieutenant junior grade *n., pl.* **lieutenants junior grade** A lower-ranking lieutenant in the US Navy or Coast Guard, ranking just above an ensign.

life (līf) *n., pl.* **lives** (līvz) **1.** The property or quality that distinguishes living organisms from dead organisms and nonliving matter. Living organisms have the ability to grow, reproduce, and respond to their environment. **2.** The fact of being alive: *risk one's life.* **3.** The period of time between birth and death; a lifetime: *a long and interesting life.* **4.** The time during which something exists and works: *the life of a car.* **5.** Living organisms considered as a group: *plant life; marine life.* **6.** A living person: *Dozens of lives were lost in the flood.* **7.** A way of living: *the outdoor life; city life.* **8.** Liveliness; spirit: *a puppy, curious and full of life.* **9.** An account of a person's life; a biography. ◆ **bring to life 1.** To cause to regain life or consciousness. **2.** To make lively or lifelike: *A good actor brings a character to life.* **come to life** To become lively; grow excited: *She always comes to life when talking about her granddaughter.* **for life** Till the end of one's life: *They were friends for life.* **take (someone's) life** To commit murder.

lifeblood (līf′blŭd′) *n.* **1.** Blood regarded as necessary for life. **2.** An essential or vital part: *The conductor is the lifeblood of the orchestra.*

lifeboat (līf′bōt′) *n.* A strong boat carried on a ship or kept along the shore, used if the ship has to be abandoned or for rescue service.

life buoy *n.* A ring made of cork or other buoyant material for keeping a person afloat.

life cycle *n.* The series of changes through which a living organism passes, from its beginning as a fertilized egg to its mature state in which offspring can be produced.

life expectancy *n.* The length of time a person is expected to live, as determined by statistical studies.

life form *n.* A kind of organism: *marine life forms.*

lifeguard (līf′gärd′) *n.* An expert swimmer trained and employed to watch over other swimmers, as at a beach or swimming pool.

life insurance *n.* Insurance on a person's life, paid for by regular premiums and guaranteeing a certain sum of money to a specified person, such as a spouse or child, on the death of the holder.

life jacket *n.* A life preserver in the form of a jacket or vest.

lifeless (līf′lĭs) *adj.* **1.** Having no life; dead or inanimate. **2.** Not supporting life; having no living organisms: *a lifeless planet.* **3.** Lacking spirit or vitality; dull: *a lifeless party.* **—life′less·ly** *adv.* **—life′less·ness** *n.*

lifelike (līf′līk′) *adj.* Accurately representing real life: *a lifelike statue.*

lifeline (līf′līn′) *n.* **1.** An anchored line thrown as a support to someone falling or drowning. **2.** A line used to raise and lower deep-sea divers. **3.** A means or route for transporting vital supplies.

lifelong (līf′lông′) *adj.* Lasting over a lifetime: *a lifelong friend; a lifelong ambition.*

life preserver *n.* A device, such as a vest filled with a buoyant material, designed to keep a person afloat in the water.

life raft *n.* A usually inflatable raft used by people who have been forced into water by an emergency, such as a shipwreck or airplane crash.

lifesaver (līf′sā′vər) *n.* **1.** A lifeguard or other person who saves the lives of others. **2.** A person or thing that provides help in a crisis or emergency: *Their call to the fire department was a lifesaver.* **3.** A life preserver shaped like a ring.

lifesaving (līf′sā′vĭng) *n.* The skills and methods used in saving lives, especially in keeping people from drowning.

life science *n.* Any of the sciences, such as botany, zoology, microbiology, or ecology, that deal mainly with living organisms.

life-size (līf′sīz′) also **life-sized** (līf′sīzd′) *adj.* Being of the same size as the person or object represented: *a life-size statue of a person.*

lifespan or **life span** (līf′spăn′) *n.* The average or longest period of time that an organism or an object can be expected to survive or last: *exercise to increase your lifespan; the lifespan of a bridge.*

lifestyle (līf′stīl′) *n.* The way of life or style of living of a person or group, including diet, tastes, work, and interests.

life support *n.* The methods or equipment needed to keep someone alive who might otherwise die, either from disease or from environmental conditions that are not capable of sustaining life. —**life′-sup·port′** (līf′sə-pôrt′) *adj.*

lifetime (līf′tīm′) *n.* The period of time that a person lives or a thing exists or works properly: *the average lifetime of a person; the lifetime of our car.* ❖ *adj.* Continuing for all one's life; lifelong: *a lifetime friend.*

lifework (līf′wûrk′) *n.* The chief or entire work of a person's lifetime.

lift (līft) *v.* **lifted, lifting, lifts** —*tr.* **1.** To raise to a higher position; elevate: *lifted her eyes; lift the suitcase from the floor.* **2.** To transport by air: *The helicopter lifted supplies to the town.* **3.** To raise or improve in condition, status, or estimation: *The news lifted everybody's spirits.* **4.** To end; stop; suspend: *lift a siege.* **5.** *Informal* To steal; pilfer: *The robber lifted a priceless painting.* **6.** To copy from something already published; plagiarize: *The reporter lifted the paragraph from a book.* —*intr.* **1.** To be raised: *These windows lift easily.* **2.** To disappear by or as if by rising: *The heavy fog finally lifted.* ❖ *n.* **1.** The act of lifting or being lifted: *Give me a lift into the saddle.* **2.** A short ride in a vehicle: *Can I have a lift to the store?* **3.** The extent or height something is raised. **4.** An elevation of the spirit: *The victory gave the team a lift.* **5.** An amount or weight lifted; a load. **6.** *Chiefly British* An elevator. **7.** An upward force acting on an object, as on an airplane wing during takeoff. ◆ **lift off** To begin flight: *The rocket lifted off at dawn.*

liftoff (līft′ôf′) *n.* The takeoff of a rocket from its launch pad.

ligament (lĭg′ə-mənt) *n.* A sheet or band of tough fibrous tissue that connects two bones or holds an organ of the body in place.

ligature (lĭg′ə-choŏr′ *or* lĭg′ə-chər) *n.* **1.** Something used for tying or binding, such as a thread used in surgery to tie off a bleeding vein or artery. **2.** In printing, two or three letters joined to form a single character, as œ. **3.** A curved line connecting a series of notes on a musical score to indicate that they are to be played or sung smoothly.

light (līt) *n.* **1.** A form of radiant energy that can be perceived by the human eye. It is made up of electromagnetic waves that travel at a speed of about 186,282 miles (299,792 kilometers) per second. **2.** Radiant energy that cannot be perceived by the human eye, such as infrared light and ultraviolet light. **3.** Illumination; brightness: *The fireworks produced bursts of light.* **4.** A source of light, such as the sun or a lamp: *a light in the window.* **5.** Daylight: *This room gets a lot of light because it has a south window.* **6.** A source of fire, such as a match: *Do you have a light?* **7.** Understanding through knowledge and information: *Their research shed new light on what caused the extinction of the dinosaurs.* **8.** Public attention; general knowledge: *Reports brought to light the need for improvements in fire protection.* **9.** A famous or outstanding person: *one of the leading lights of the theater.* **10.** A way of looking at or considering a certain matter: *This puts the problem in a different light.* **11.** A light shade or color: *the lights and darks in the painting.* **12. lights** Pieces of laundry that are not dark in color. ❖ *v.* **lighted** or **lit** (līt), **lighting, lights** —*tr.* **1.** To set burning; ignite: *light a fire.* **2.** To cause to give out light; turn on: *light a lamp.* **3.** To provide, cover, or fill with light: *Let's light the room with candles.* **4.** To make lively or bright: *A smile lighted the child's face.* **5.** To guide or direct by means of a light: *A flashlight was enough to light our way along the path.* —*intr.* **1.** To start to burn; become ignited: *The oven won't light for some reason.* **2.** To become light or bright: *The neon sign lighted up after dark.* **3.** To come to rest; land; perch: *The bird lit on the feeder.* **4.** To get down, as from a mount or vehicle; alight: *Several passengers lighted from the rear of the plane.* ❖ *adj.* **lighter, lightest 1.** Having light; not dark or shadowy: *a nice light room to work in.* **2.** Bright; not dark: *light gray; light hair.* **3.** Having little weight; not heavy: *a light suitcase; a light jacket.* **4.** Having little force or impact: *a light breeze; a light blow.* **5.** Low in intensity or amount: *a light rain; a light lunch.* **6.** Not harsh or severe: *The judge gave the convict a light sentence.* **7.** Indistinct; faint: *The light print was hard to read.* **8.** Not serious or profound: *light comedy.* **9.** Carrying little weight or equipment: *light cavalry.* **10.** Free from care or worry: *a light heart.* **11.** Moving easily and quickly; nimble: *a dancer with a light step.* **12.** Requiring little effort or exertion: *light household chores.* **13.** Somewhat unsteady or faint; dizzy: *feel light in the head.* **14.** Containing a relatively small amount of a potentially harmful ingredient, such as sugar, fat, or alcohol: *light cola; light beer.* **15.** Easily awakened or disturbed: *a light sleeper.* ❖ *adv.* **lighter, lightest** Lightly, especially with little baggage: *We always travel light.* ◆ **in light of** Taking into consideration: *In light of the report, let's try a different approach to the problem.* **light into** *Informal* To attack verbally or physically; assail.

light bulb *n.* A device consisting of a gas-filled glass tube or bulb that emits light when an electric current is supplied to it.

lighten (līt′n) *v.* **lightened, lightening, lightens** —*tr.* **1.** To make lighter in color or brighter: *He lightened the blue paint by mixing in some white.* **2.** To make less heavy; reduce the weight of: *She lightened her pack by taking out some books.* **3.** To make less troublesome or oppressive: *hire an assistant to lighten the load of work.* **4.** To gladden or cheer: *a song to lighten everyone's heart.* —*intr.* **1.** To become lighter in color or brighter: *The clouds thinned and the sky lightened quickly.* **2.** To become less in weight: *My bag of supplies lightened as I began passing out the equipment.* **3.** To become less troublesome or oppressive: *Our work lightened after the new assistant was hired.* **4.** To become less worried or more cheerful: *Her mood lightened after she talked with her friend.*

lighter (līt′ər) *n.* A person or device that lights or ignites something: *a lamp lighter; a cigarette lighter.*

lightface (līt′fās′) *n.* A typeface that has thin light lines. This definition is in lightface.

light-footed (līt′foŏt′id) *adj.* Moving with light and graceful steps; nimble.

lightheaded (līt′hĕd′id) *adj.* Faint or dizzy: *felt lightheaded from running.* —**light′head′ed·ly** *adv.* —**light′head′ed·ness** *n.*

lighthearted (līt′här′tid) *adj.* Carefree and cheerful: *a lighthearted attitude.* See Synonyms at **glad.** —**light′heart′ed·ly** *adv.* —**light′heart′ed·ness** *n.*

lighthouse (līt′hous′) *n.* A tower with a powerful light at the top, used to mark the entrance to a harbor or to warn ships away from dangerous waters.

lighting (lī′tĭng) *n.* **1.** Light supplied, as for a room or an area; illumination: *right lighting for reading.* **2.** The arrangement or equipment that provides light: *installed outdoor lighting.*

lightly (līt′lē) *adv.* **1.** With little pressure or force: *Tread lightly on the floor to avoid waking the baby.* **2.** To a small amount or degree: *The streets were lightly covered with snow.* **3a.** In a carefree manner; cheerfully: *took the setback lightly.* **b.** Without proper care or consideration: *treated his illness lightly.* **4.** With agility; nimbly: *The deer leaped lightly over the fence.*

light meter *n.* A device that measures the intensity of light, used especially in photography.

lightness (līt′nĭs) *n.* **1.** The quality or condition of being lighted; brightness: *The artist liked the lightness of her studio, which had large windows facing east.* **2.** Paleness of color: *the lightness of the paint used in the nursery.* **3.** The property or quality of having little weight or force: *the lightness of straw.* **4.** Ease or quickness of movement; agility: *lightness of step.* **5.** Freedom from worry or trouble: *lightness of heart.* **6.** Lack of appropriate seriousness: *treated the tragedy with lightness.*

lightning (līt′nĭng) *n.* A flash of light in the sky caused by an electrical discharge between clouds or between a cloud and the earth's surface. The flash heats the air and usually causes thunder.

lightning bug *n.* A firefly.

lightning rod *n.* A metal rod placed high on a building to prevent damage from lightning by conducting electricity along a wire to the ground.

lightship (līt′shĭp′) *n.* A ship with powerful lights and other warning signals, anchored in dangerous waters to alert and guide other vessels.

lightweight (līt′wāt′) *n.* **1.** A person or thing that weighs relatively little. **2a.** A boxer weighing more than 126 and not more than 135 pounds (about 57–61 kilograms). **b.**

A contestant in some other sports in a similar weight class. **3.** *Informal* A person of little ability, importance, or influence. ❖ *adj.* Not heavy; weighing relatively little: *a lightweight jacket.*

light year *n.* The distance that light travels in one year, about 5.88 trillion miles (9.46 trillion kilometers).

lignite (lĭg′nīt′) *n.* A soft brownish-black form of coal in which the condition of the plant matter is between peat and bituminous coal; brown coal.

likable also **likeable** (lī′kə-bəl) *adj.* Easy to like; having a pleasing personality: *a political candidate who is friendly and likable.*

like¹ (līk) *v.* **liked, liking, likes** —*tr.* **1.** To be fond of: *We are old friends and like each other.* **2.** To find pleasant; enjoy: *They liked the place and decided to stay.* **3.** To feel about; regard: *How did you like the play?* **4.** To want to have: *Would you like some gravy?* —*intr.* To have a desire or preference: *If you like, we can go home now.* ❖ *n.* Something that is liked; a preference: *my likes and dislikes.*

like² (līk) *prep.* **1.** Resembling; similar to: *You look like your mother.* **2.** In the same way as: *Don't act like a clown.* **3.** In the typical manner of: *It's not like him to give up easily.* **4.** Such as: *I draw things like buildings and street scenes.* **5.** As if it is likely to be: *It looks like a good year for farmers.* **6.** Inclined to; desirous of: *I felt like going home.* ❖ *adj.* **1.** Having the same or almost the same characteristics; similar: *We made this and like repairs to the car.* **2.** Equivalent: *The company will donate a like amount to the charity.* ❖ *adv.* As if: *We worked like crazy to get the job done on time.* ❖ *n.* **1.** Something equal or similar to something else: *Owls eat mice, chipmunks, and the like.* **2.** Nearly; approximately: *a price more like fifty dollars.* ❖ *conj.* **1.** In the same way that: *To dance like she does takes lots of practice.* **2.** As if: *It looks like we'll finish on time.*

USAGE *Sales rose like we expected them to. I ran like my life depended on it.* In sentences such as these, *like* acts as a conjunction meaning "as" or "as if." Though this use of *like* dates back many centuries and is very common, it is often frowned on in formal writing and is easily avoided by replacing *like* with *as* or *as if: Sales of new models rose as we expected them to. I ran as if my life depended on it. Like* is acceptable as a conjunction when used with verbs such as *feel, look,* and *seem: It looks like we are in for a rough winter.*

WORD HISTORY Like¹ comes from Old English *līcian,* meaning "to please." **Like²** comes from Old English *gelīc,* meaning "similar."

–like A suffix that means similar to or characteristic of: *childlike; lifelike.*

likeable (lī′kə-bəl) *adj.* Variant of **likable.**

likelihood (līk′lē-hoŏd′) *n.* The chance of a thing happening; probability: *The likelihood of snow is very remote in July.*

likely (līk′lē) *adj.* **likelier, likeliest. 1.** Having or showing a tendency or probability: *It is likely to rain at any moment.* **2.** Seeming to be true; credible: *a likely excuse for being late.* **3.** Appropriate or suitable: *She seems a likely choice for the job.* **4.** Showing promise of success; promising: *a likely way of proceeding.* ❖ *adv.* Probably: *Most likely the barn will need some repairs.*

liken (lī′kən) *tr.v.* **likened, likening, likens** To describe as resembling something else; compare: *He likened his youth to a summer day.*

likeness (līk′nǐs) *n.* **1.** Similarity or resemblance: *an amazing likeness between brothers.* **2.** A copy or picture of a person or thing: *The portrait is a perfect likeness of you.* **3.** Appearance; form: *At once the prince took on the likeness of a frog.*

likewise (līk′wīz′) *adv.* **1.** Similarly; in like manner: *Once he saw her open her package, he did likewise.* **2.** Moreover; besides: *The Sahara Desert is hot and likewise dry.*

liking (lī′kǐng) *n.* A feeling of fondness or affection; a preference: *a special liking for apples.*

lilac (lī′lək *or* lī′lŏk *or* lī′lăk) *n.* **1.** A shrub that bears clusters of fragrant purplish or white flowers. **2.** A pale purple.

Lilliputian *also* **lilliputian** (lĭl′ə-pyōō′shən) *n.* A very small person or being. ❖ *adj.* **1.** Very small; diminutive. **2.** Trivial; petty.

lilt (lĭlt) *n.* **1.** A cheerful lively manner of speaking. **2.** A light happy tune or song. ❖ *tr. & intr.v.* **lilted, lilting, lilts** To sing, play, or speak in a lively rhythmic manner: *the bird lilted its song.*

lily (lĭl′ē) *n., pl.* **lilies 1.** Any of various plants that grow from bulbs and have showy flowers shaped like trumpets. **2.** Any of various similar or related plants, such as a water lily. **3.** The flower of any of these plants.

lily of the valley *n., pl.* **lilies of the valley** A plant having a slender one-sided cluster of fragrant, bell-shaped white flowers.

lily pad *n.* One of the large, flat floating leaves of a water lily.

lima bean (lī′mə) *n.* **1.** The light-green kidney-shaped seed of a tropical American plant, eaten as a vegetable. **2.** The plant that bears such seeds.

limb (lĭm) *n.* **1.** A leg, arm, wing, or other paired appendage of an animal body, usually used for grasping or moving. **2.** One of the larger branches of a tree.

limber (lĭm′bər) *adj.* Bending or moving easily; flexible: *limber muscles; a limber athlete.* ❖ *tr. & intr.v.* **limbered, limbering, limbers** To exercise so as to make or become limber: *She stretched to limber up her muscles. He limbered up before the important game.* —**lim′ber·ness** *n.*

limbo¹ (lĭm′bō) *n., pl.* **limbos 1.** often **Limbo** In Roman Catholic belief, the abode of just or innocent souls, such as unbaptized people, kept from heaven but not condemned to Purgatory or Hell. **2.** A place or condition of neglect or oblivion: *Construction for the new pool was kept in limbo until new funds were found.*

limbo² (lĭm′bō) *n., pl.* **limbos** A West Indian dance in which dancers bend over backward to pass under a horizontal pole.

WORD HISTORY Limbo¹ is from Middle English *limbo* (referring to the same theological concept as in Modern English), which is from Latin *limbus* meaning "border." **Limbo²** is probably of African origin.

Limburger (lĭm′bûr′gər) *n.* A soft white cheese with a very strong odor.

lime¹ (līm) *n.* **1.** An oval green citrus fruit having sour juicy pulp. **2.** Any of several trees that bear such fruit.

lime² (līm) *n.* A European linden.

lime³ (līm) *n.* Calcium oxide. ❖ *tr.v.* **limed, liming, limes** To treat with lime; apply lime to. —**lim′y** *adj.*

WORD HISTORY Lime¹ comes from French *lime*, which comes from Spanish *lima*, which comes from Arabic

līma, which comes from Persian *līmū*, which all mean "lemon" or various related citrus fruits. **Lime²** comes from Old English *lind*, referring to the same kind of tree as in Modern English. **Lime³** comes from Old English *līm,* meaning "birdlime."

limelight (līm′līt′) *n.* **1.** The center of public attention: *The president is always in the limelight.* **2.** An early type of light used in the theater, in which lime was heated to produce light.

limerick (lĭm′ər-ĭk) *n.* A humorous five-line poem that follows the rhyme scheme *aabba.*

limestone (līm′stōn′) *n.* A form of sedimentary rock that consists mainly of calcium carbonate, used as a building material and in making lime and cement.

limewater (līm′wô′tər) *n.* A solution of calcium hydroxide and water, used in calamine lotion and sometimes as an antacid.

liminal (lĭm′ə-nəl) *adj.* Intermediate between two states, conditions, or regions; transitional or indeterminate: *frontiers and other liminal places.* —**lim′i·nal′i·ty** (lĭm′ə-năl′ĭ-tē) *n.* —**lim′i·nal·ly** *adv.*

limit (lĭm′ĭt) *n.* **1.** A point or line beyond which something ends or cannot go: *the 12-mile fishing limit.* **2. limits** The boundary surrounding a certain area: *within the city limits.* **3.** The greatest amount of something allowed: *a speed limit.* ❖ *tr.v.* **limited, limiting, limits** To place a limit on; confine: *Try to limit your talk to ten minutes.*

limitation (lĭm′ĭ-tā′shən) *n.* **1.** Something that limits; a restriction: *Poor ice conditions put limitations on how fast the bobsled could go.* **2.** The act of limiting or the state of being limited.

limited (lĭm′ĭ-tĭd) *adj.* **1.** Confined within certain limits; restricted: *a small house with limited space.* **2.** Not accomplishing the greatest achievements or possessing the best talent: *a popular but limited actor.* **3.** Traveling fast and making few stops: *a limited train.* ❖ *n.* A limited train or bus.

limitless (lĭm′ĭt-lĭs) *adj.* Having no limit or boundary; unrestricted or infinite: *limitless space in the sky.*

limn (lĭm) *tr.v.* **limned, limning** (lĭm′nĭng)**, limns 1.** To draw or paint. **2.** To describe.

limnology (lĭm-nŏl′ə-jē) *n.* The study of the physics, chemistry, geology, and biology of lakes and other inland waters. —**lim′no·log′i·cal** (lĭm-nə-lŏj′ĭ-kəl) *adj.* —**lim′no·log′i·cal·ly** *adv.* —**lim·nol′o·gist** *n.*

limousine (lĭm′ə-zēn′ *or* lĭm′ə-zēn′) *n.* **1.** A large, luxurious vehicle driven by a chauffeur. **2.** A van or small bus used to carry passengers especially to airports and hotels.

limp (lĭmp) *intr.v.* **limped, limping, limps 1.** To walk lamely: *After my knee injury, I limped for several days.* **2.** To move or proceed haltingly or with difficulty: *The damaged ship limped back to port.* ❖ *n.* A lame or irregular way of walking. ❖ *adj.* **limper, limpest 1.** Lacking stiffness: *a limp wet towel.* **2.** Not vigorous or strong; weak: *a limp handshake.* —**limp′ly** *adv.* —**limp′ness** *n.*

limpet (lĭm′pĭt) *n.* Any of numerous small saltwater mollusks that have a cone-shaped shell and cling to rocks.

limpid (lĭm′pĭd) *adj.* Perfectly clear; transparent: *limpid water.*

linchpin (lĭnch′pĭn′) *n.* **1.** An iron pin inserted in the end of an axle to prevent a wheel from slipping off. **2.** Something that keeps different parts together and functioning: *The linchpin of the candidate's campaign was his proposal for improving the economy.*

linden (lĭn′dən) *n.* Any of various trees having heart-shaped leaves and clusters of fragrant yellowish flowers, often planted for shade.

line¹ (līn) *n.* **1.** A geometric figure formed by a point moving in a fixed direction and in the reverse direction. A line has infinite length but no width. **2a.** A thin continuous mark, as one made on paper by a pen or pencil. **b.** Something resembling such a mark: *a brow furrowed with deep lines.* **3.** A border or boundary: *the county line; the line between courage and rashness.* **4.** A group of people or things arranged in a row: *a line of customers at the counter.* **5.** often **lines** Outline, contour, or styling: *the lines of a new car.* **6a.** A row of words printed or written across a page or column. **b.** A brief letter: *I'll drop you a line.* **7a.** A single verse of poetry. **b.** A unit of continuous text spoken by an actor. **8.** A cable, rope, cord, or wire: *a fishing line.* **9.** A course or direction: *the line of flight of migrating birds.* **10.** A general method or way of doing something: *Let's continue our present line in teaching safety at school.* **11.** A series of people or things following one another in time: *the line of French kings.* **12.** Ancestry or lineage: *Her family line goes back to China.* **13a.** A system of transportation: *a bus line.* **b.** A branch of a transportation system: *all lines go through Detroit.* **c.** A railroad track. **14a.** A wire or system of wires connecting telephone or telegraph stations. **b.** A telephone connection: *Their line is busy.* **15.** A pipe, channel, or wire used to carry water, gas, or electricity from one point to another. **16.** A range of merchandise having several styles and sizes: *a line of fashionable dresses.* **17.** A person's trade or occupation: *What is your line of work?* **18.** The range of a person's ability or interests: *That sort of work is out of my line.* **19.** A connected series of musical notes: *a melodic line.* **20.** In football, the players stationed at the line of scrimmage as a play begins. **21.** The battle area or combat troops closest to the enemy: *The wounded were taken behind the lines.* **22.** *Informal* False or exaggerated talk intended to impress or deceive a listener: *Disgraced politicians often try to feed voters a line about reforming themselves.* ❖ *v.* **lined, lining, lines** —*tr.* **1.** To mark or cover with lines: *line paper.* **2.** To form a line along: *Thousands of people lined the sidewalks.* **3.** To place in a line or row: *Line the children up by the door.* **4.** In baseball, to hit (a ball) hard in a straight line. —*intr.* In baseball, to hit a line drive: *The batter lined out to the shortstop.* ◆ **all along the line 1.** In every place. **2.** At every stage or moment: *Building the house has been difficult all along the line.* **in line for** Next in order for: *She's in line for a promotion.* **line up 1.** To arrange in or form a line. **2.** To organize and make ready: *We lined up support for a class in scuba diving.* **out of line 1.** Uncalled for; improper: *That remark was out of line.* **2.** Unruly and out of control.

line² (līn) *tr.v.* **lined, lining, lines 1.** To cover the inside surface of with a layer of material: *The tailor lined the coat with satin.* **2.** To serve as a lining for or in: *Tissue paper lined the box.* **3.** To fill plentifully: *The store shelves were lined with toys.* ◆ **line (one's) pockets** To make a profit, especially by illegitimate means.

WORD HISTORY Line¹ comes from Middle English *line,* which comes from both Old English *līne* and Old French *ligne* (all referring to the same geometric figure as in Modern English), which come from Latin *līnum,* meaning "thread, flax, linen cloth." **Line²** comes from Middle English *linen,* meaning "to line a garment with cloth," which comes from Middle English *line,* which comes

from Old English *līn,* which comes from Latin *līnum,* all meaning "thread, flax, linen cloth."

lineage (līn′ē-ĭj) *n.* **1.** Direct descent from a particular ancestor; ancestry. **2.** All of the descendants of a particular ancestor.

lineal (līn′ē-əl) *adj.* **1.** Being in the direct line of descent: *Without children, the couple had no lineal descendants.* **2.** Linear. —**lin′e·al·ly** *adv.*

lineament (līn′ē-ə-mənt) *n.* A distinctive outline or feature, especially of a face.

linear (līn′ē-ər) *adj.* **1.** Relating to or resembling a line, especially a straight line: *linear distance.* **2.** Consisting of or using lines: *a linear design.* **3.** Relating to length: *The meter is a unit of linear measurement.* **4.** Following a sequential or chronological order: *a linear narrative.* —**lin′e·ar′i·ty** (līn′ē-âr′ĭ-tē) *n.* —**lin′e·ar·ly** *adv.*

linear accelerator *n.* A device that accelerates charged subatomic particles, such as protons and electrons, in a straight line by means of alternating negative and positive impulses from electric fields. Linear accelerators are used to bring about high-speed particle collisions in order to study subatomic structures.

linear equation *n.* An algebraic equation, such as $y = 2x + 7$, in which each term is either a constant or a single variable multiplied by a constant. The graph of a linear equation with two variables is a straight line.

linear measure *n.* **1.** Measurement of length. **2.** A system of units, such as miles, feet, and inches, used for measuring length.

linebacker (līn′băk′ər) *n.* In football, a player stationed just behind a team's defensive line.

line drive *n.* A baseball hit sharply so that it flies low and fast in a nearly straight line.

line-item veto (līn′ī′təm) *n.* The right or power of a government executive to reject any of the individual provisions that make up a legislative bill.

lineman (līn′mən) *n.* **1.** A person who installs or repairs telephone, telegraph, or electric power lines. **2.** A person who inspects and repairs railroad tracks. **3.** In football, a player positioned on the line of scrimmage at the snap of the ball.

linen (līn′ən) *n.* **1a.** Thread spun from fibers of the flax plant. **b.** Cloth woven from this thread. **2.** also **linens** Articles or garments, such as sheets, tablecloths, or shirts, made of linen or a similar material, such as cotton.

line of force *n., pl.* **lines of force** An imaginary line in a field of electric or magnetic force that indicates the direction in which the force is acting.

line of scrimmage *n., pl.* **lines of scrimmage** In football, either of two imaginary lines that run parallel to the goal line at either end of the ball as it rests before being snapped. Each team lines up at its own line of scrimmage for a new play.

liner¹ (lī′nər) *n.* **1.** A person or thing that draws lines. **2.** A commercial ship or airplane carrying passengers on a regular route. **3.** In baseball, a line drive.

liner² (lī′nər) *n.* **1.** A person who makes or puts in linings. **2.** Something used as a lining. **3.** A jacket for a phonograph record.

line segment *n.* The part of a line lying between two given points on the line.

linesman (līnz′mən) *n.* **1a.** In football, an official who marks the downs and the position of the ball and watches for violations from the sidelines. **b.** In soccer and similar field games, an official who indicates when the ball has gone out of bounds. **c.** In tennis and other court games, an official whose chief duty is to call shots that fall out of bounds. **d.** In ice hockey, an official whose chief duty is to call offsides and icing. **2.** A person who installs or repairs telephone, telegraph, or electric power lines.

line spectrum *n.* A spectrum produced by a luminous gas or vapor and consisting of a series of distinct, fairly narrow lines characteristically produced by the atoms of that gas or vapor.

lineup (līn′ŭp′) *n.* **1a.** The members of a team chosen to start a game. **b.** A list of such players. **2.** A group of people lined up, as for purposes of identification: *a lineup of possible suspects in the crime.* **3.** A group of people, organizations, or things enlisted for a specific purpose.

–ling[1] A suffix that means: **1.** A person connected with: *earthling.* **2.** A person or thing having a specified quality: *hireling.* **3.** A person or thing that is small, young, or inferior: *duckling.*

–ling[2] A suffix that means in a specified way or condition: *darkling.*

linger (lĭng′gər) *intr.v.* **lingered, lingering, lingers 1.** To stay in a place or be slow in leaving it: *The children lingered in the toy shop until closing.* See Synonyms at **stay**[1]. **2.** To continue or persist: *The taste of cherries lingered in my mouth.* **3.** To consider or do something in an unhurried or leisurely fashion: *We lingered at the restaurant.*

lingerie (län′zhə-rā′) *n.* Women's underwear.

lingo (lĭng′gō) *n., pl.* **lingoes** Language that is difficult to understand, as the jargon of a special group: *Doctors have a lingo all their own.*

lingua franca (lĭng′gwə frăng′kə) *n.* A language widely used for communication between people who normally speak different languages.

lingual (lĭng′gwəl) *adj.* **1.** Relating to the tongue. **2.** Produced by the tongue, as the sound of the letter *l* is.

linguine also **linguini** (lĭng-gwē′nē) *n.* Pasta in long, flat, thin strands.

linguist (lĭng′gwĭst) *n.* **1.** A person who speaks several languages fluently. **2.** A specialist in linguistics.

linguistic (lĭng-gwĭs′tĭk) *adj.* Relating to language or linguistics. **—lin·guis′ti·cal·ly** *adv.*

linguistics (lĭng-gwĭs′tĭks) *n. (used with a singular verb)* The study of the nature and structure of language.

liniment (lĭn′ə-mənt) *n.* A liquid medicine rubbed on the skin to soothe pain or relieve stiffness, as from bruises or sore muscles.

lining (lī′nĭng) *n.* **1.** An inner covering or coating: *the stomach lining; the lining in a jacket.* **2.** Material used as such a covering or coating.

link (lĭngk) *n.* **1a.** One of the rings or loops forming a chain. **b.** One of a series of connected units: *a sausage link.* **2.** Something that joins or connects: *a new rail link between the city and the airport.* **3.** An association or relationship: *The governor denied that he had links to organized crime.* **4.** A graphical item or segment of text in a webpage or other electronic document that, when clicked, causes another webpage or section of the same webpage to be displayed: *That newspaper's homepage includes links to numerous government resources.* ❖ *v.* **linked, linking, links —***tr.* **1.** To connect or join with or as if with a link: *The telephone links the far corners of the globe.* See Synonyms at **join**. **2a.** To make or have a link to (another webpage or electronic document): *The*

blog links important news stories from across the web. **b.** To make a link in (a webpage or electronic document): *The professor linked the class website to an online map.* **—***intr.* **1.** To become connected with or as if with a link: *The two expeditions plan to link up by radio.* **2a.** To make or have a link to a webpage or electronic document: *The article linked to photos of the damage.* **b.** To follow a link in a webpage or electronic document: *With a click of the mouse, I linked to the museum's website.*

linkage (lĭng′kĭj) *n.* **1.** The act or process of linking. **2.** The state or condition of being linked. **3.** A system or arrangement of machine parts, such as rods, springs, or pivots, used to transmit power or motion.

linking verb (lĭng′kĭng) *n.* A verb that connects the subject of a sentence with a predicate that describes or refers to the subject; a copula. For example, the verbs *are* and *seem* are linking verbs in the sentences *Those trees are pines* and *You seem sleepy.*

links (lĭngks) *pl.n.* A golf course.

linnet (lĭn′ĭt) *n.* A small brownish finch of Eurasia and Africa.

linoleum (lĭ-nō′lē-əm) *n.* A sturdy washable material made in sheets by pressing a mixture of hot linseed oil, rosin, powdered cork, and coloring onto a cloth backing, used especially for covering floors.

linseed (lĭn′sēd′) *n.* The seed of the flax plant, especially when used as the source of linseed oil; flaxseed.

linseed oil *n.* A yellow oil extracted from flax seeds that thickens and hardens when exposed to air and is used in paints, varnishes, printing inks, and linoleum.

linsey-woolsey (lĭn′zē-wŏŏl′zē) *n., pl.* **linsey-woolseys** A coarse fabric of cotton or linen woven with wool.

lint (lĭnt) *n.* **1.** Clinging bits of fiber and fluff from a material. **2.** Downy material scraped from linen cloth and used to dress wounds.

lintel (lĭn′tl) *n.* The horizontal beam that forms the top of a door or window frame and supports the structure above it.

lion (lī′ən) *n.* **1.** A large wild cat of Africa and India, having a tawny coat and a heavy mane around the neck and shoulders in the male. **2.** A cougar. **3.** A powerful or influential person. ◆ **lion's share** The greatest or best part: *One candidate got the lion's share of the media attention.*

lioness (lī′ə-nĭs) *n.* A female lion.

lionhearted (lī′ən-här′tĭd) *adj.* Extraordinarily courageous.

lionize (lī′ə-nīz′) *tr.v.* **lionized, lionizing, lionizes** To treat as a celebrity: *The public lionized the popular author.*

lip (lĭp) *n.* **1.** Either of the two fleshy muscular folds of tissue that together surround the mouth. **2.** A structure or part that encircles or bounds an opening. **3.** The tip of a pouring spout, as on a pitcher. **4.** Either of the two parts into which the corolla or calyx of certain plants is divided: *the lips of a snapdragon blossom.* **5.** *Slang* Disrespectful talk: *Don't give me any of your lip!*

lipase (lĭp′ās′ or lī′pās′) *n.* An enzyme that promotes the breakdown of fats into glycerol and fatty acids.

lipid (lĭp′ĭd) *n.* Any of a large group of organic compounds, including fats, oils, waxes, and sterols, that are oily to the touch and insoluble in water. They are a source of stored energy and are a component of cell membranes.

liposuction (lĭp′ō-sŭk′shən or lī′pō-sŭk′shən) *n.* A cosmetic surgical procedure in which excess fatty tissue is removed from a specific area of the body, such as the thighs or abdomen, by means of suction.

lip-read (lĭp′rēd′) *intr.v.* **lip-read** (lĭp′rĕd′), **lip-reading, lip-reads** To interpret utterances by lip reading.

lip reading *n.* The skill of understanding unheard speech by interpreting movements of the lips and face of the speaker.

lip service *n.* Agreement or respect expressed in words but without sincerity or the intention of doing anything.

lipstick (lĭp′stĭk′) *n.* A stick of waxy coloring matter applied to the lips and enclosed in a small case.

liquefaction (lĭk′wə-făk′shən) *n.* **1.** The act or process of liquefying. **2.** The condition of being liquefied.

liquefy (lĭk′wə-fī′) *tr. & intr.v.* **liquefied, liquefying, liquefies** To make or become liquid: *Butter liquefies at low heat.* —**liq′ue·fi′a·ble** *adj.* —**liq′ue·fi′er** *n.*

liqueur (lĭ-kûr′) *n.* A sweet syrupy alcoholic beverage usually served after dinner.

liquid (lĭk′wĭd) *n.* **1.** A substance that is neither a solid nor a gas, with molecules that move freely within the container in which it is put. The volume of a liquid usually remains unchanged or changes only slightly under pressure. **2.** A substance that people drink for nourishment or refreshment: *It's hot today, so be sure to drink plenty of liquids.* ❖ *adj.* **1.** Being a liquid: *a liquid rocket fuel.* **2.** Clear and shining like water. **3.** Flowing without abrupt breaks: *a cascade of liquid piano notes.* **4.** Existing as or readily converted into cash: *liquid assets such as savings bonds.*

liquidate (lĭk′wĭ-dāt′) *tr.v.* **liquidated, liquidating, liquidates** **1.** To pay off or settle: *liquidate one's debts.* **2.** To close down (a business firm) by settling its accounts and dividing up any remaining assets. **3.** To eliminate, especially by killing. —**liq′ui·da′tion** *n.*

liquid-crystal display (lĭk′wĭd-krĭs′təl) *n.* A thin display screen that is made of an array of cells containing a liquid whose molecules align to block or transmit light in response to an electric current.

liquidity (lĭ-kwĭd′ĭ-tē) *n.* **1.** The quality or condition of being liquid. **2.** The quality of being readily convertible to cash.

liquid measure *n.* A system of units for measuring the volume of liquids, as in pints, gallons, or liters.

liquid oxygen *n.* A very cold transparent liquid formed when oxygen is put under great pressure and cooled. It is used as a rocket fuel and in explosives.

liquor (lĭk′ər) *n.* An alcoholic beverage, such as whiskey or gin, made by distillation rather than by fermentation.

lira (lîr′ə) *n., pl.* **lire** (lîr′ā) or **liras** **1.** The former basic monetary unit of Italy. **2.** The basic monetary unit of Turkey.

lisle (līl) *n.* A fine, smooth, tightly twisted cotton thread or a fabric knitted from it, often used to make underwear, socks, and gloves.

lisp (lĭsp) *n.* A speech defect in which sounds represented by *s* and *z* are pronounced *th* as in *thin* and *then.* ❖ *intr. & tr.v.* **lisped, lisping, lisps** To speak or say with a lisp.

lissome also **lissom** (lĭs′əm) *adj.* Moving or bending easily; lithe. —**lis′some·ly** *adv.*

list¹ (lĭst) *n.* A series of names, words, or other items written or printed one after the other: *a guest list; a shopping list.* ❖ *tr.v.* **listed, listing, lists** To make a list of; include in a list: *The hotel's guests are listed in the register.*

list² (lĭst) *n.* A tilt to one side, as of a ship: *a ship's sudden list to starboard.* ❖ *intr. & tr.v.* **listed, listing, lists** To lean or cause to lean to one side, as a ship; heel: *The ship listed heavily in the sudden gust of wind.*

list³ (lĭst) *intr. & tr.v.* **listed, listing, lists** *Archaic* To listen to; hear.

WORD HISTORY List¹ comes from French and Old French *liste*, which comes from Old Italian *lista* (all meaning "series of items") and is of Germanic origin. The origin of **list²** is unknown. **List³** comes from Middle English *listen*, meaning "to listen."

listen (lĭs′ən) *intr.v.* **listened, listening, listens** **1.** To make an effort to hear something: *I listened to music on the radio.* **2.** To pay attention; heed: *No one listened to my advice.* ◆ **listen in** **1.** To listen to a conversation between others; eavesdrop. **2.** To tune in and listen to a broadcast. —**lis′ten·er** *n.*

listing (lĭs′tĭng) *n.* **1.** An entry in a list or directory: *a telephone listing.* **2.** A list: *a listing of dentists.*

listless (lĭst′lĭs) *adj.* Lacking energy or enthusiasm; lethargic: *The long days indoors left us feeling dull and listless.* —**list′less·ly** *adv.* —**list′less·ness** *n.*

list price *n.* A basic price published in a price list, often reduced by a dealer.

lit (lĭt) *v.* A past tense and a past participle of **light.**

lit. An abbreviation of: **1.** liter. **2.** literature.

litany (lĭt′n-ē) *n., pl.* **litanies** **1.** A Christian liturgical prayer consisting of phrases recited by a leader alternating with responses by the congregation. **2.** A repetitive recital, series, or list: *Each negotiator recited a familiar litany of grievances and demands.*

litchi (lē′chē) *n.* Variant of **lychee.**

liter (lē′tər) *n.* A metric unit of volume equal to 1,000 cubic centimeters, or about 1.06 liquid quarts. See table at **measurement.**

literacy (lĭt′ər-ə-sē) *n.* **1.** The ability to read or write. **2.** Understanding or knowledge of a particular field: *computer literacy.*

literal (lĭt′ər-əl) *adj.* **1.** Following the usual or exact meaning of a word or group of words: *The literal interpretation of a poem is often too narrow.* **2.** Corresponding word for word with the original: *a literal translation.* **3.** Not exaggerated; factual: *a literal account of events.*

literally (lĭt′ər-ə-lē) *adv.* **1.** In a literal manner: *Translated literally, "carte blanche" means "blank card."* **2.** Really; actually: *Literally millions of lives were saved by the vaccine.*

literary (lĭt′ə-rĕr′ē) *adj.* **1.** Relating to literature: *a literary critic.* **2.** Relating to writers or the profession of writing.

literate (lĭt′ər-ĭt) *adj.* **1.** Able to read and write. **2.** Familiar with literature; literary. **3.** Having knowledge in a particular field: *literate in architecture.* ❖ *n.* A person who can read and write.

literature (lĭt′ər-ə-chŏŏr′ or lĭt′ər-ə-chər) *n.* **1.** A body of writing in prose or verse, especially writing having recognized artistic value: *has read much American literature of the 1900s.* **2.** The art or occupation of a literary writer. **3.** The study of literature. **4.** A body of writing on a given subject: *medical literature.* **5.** Printed material: *election campaign literature.*

lithe (līth) *adj.* **lither, lithest** **1.** Easily bent; supple: *lithe birch branches.* **2.** Marked by effortless grace: *a lithe dancer.* —**lithe′ly** *adv.*

lithium (lĭth′ē-əm) *n. Symbol* **Li** A soft, silvery metallic element that is highly reactive and occurs in small quantities in some minerals. Lithium is the lightest of all metals and is used in batteries, alloys, ceramics, and glass for large telescopes. Atomic number 3. See **Periodic Table.**

lithograph (lĭth′ə-grăf′) *n.* A print produced by lithography. ❖ *tr.v.* **lithographed, lithographing, lithographs** To produce by lithography. —**li·thog′ra·pher** (lĭ-thŏg′rə-fər) *n.* —**lith′o·graph′ic** *adj.*

lithography (lĭ-thŏg′rə-fē) *n.* A printing process in which an image is drawn on a flat printing surface such as a metal plate and treated to hold ink. The other areas of the surface are treated to repel ink.

lithosphere (lĭth′ə-sfîr′) *n.* The outer part of the earth, consisting of the crust and upper mantle. It is approximately 62 miles (100 kilometers) thick.

Lithuanian (lĭth′ōō-ā′nē-ən) *adj.* Relating to Lithuania, its people, language, or culture. ❖ *n.* **1.** A native or inhabitant of Lithuania. **2.** The Baltic language of the Lithuanians.

litigant (lĭt′ĭ-gənt) *n.* A person or group that is prosecuting or defending a lawsuit or legal action.

litigate (lĭt′ĭ-gāt′) *intr.v.* **litigated, litigating, litigates** To prosecute or defend (a lawsuit or legal action).

litigation (lĭt′ĭ-gā′shən) *n.* **1.** The process of carrying on a lawsuit: *prolonged litigation over a contested will.* **2.** A lawsuit.

litmus (lĭt′məs) *n.* A bluish powder, obtained from certain lichens, that changes to red with increasing acidity and to deeper blue with increasing alkalinity.

litmus paper *n.* Paper that has been treated with litmus, used to distinguish acid and alkaline solutions.

litmus test *n.* **1.** A test for chemical acidity or alkalinity using litmus paper. **2.** A test that uses a single issue for a decision: *using the candidates' stand on taxes as a litmus test.*

litre (lē′tər) *n.* Chiefly British Variant of **liter.**

litter (lĭt′ər) *n.* **1.** Carelessly scattered scraps of paper or other waste material. **2.** The group of offspring born to a mammal at a single time. **3a.** Material, such as straw or hay, spread for animals to sleep on. **b.** Loose material, especially clay, spread to absorb the urine and feces of an animal. **4.** A stretcher used to carry a sick or wounded person. **5.** A couch mounted on a framework covered with curtains and used to carry a person from place to place. **6.** Fallen leaves and other decaying organic matter that make up the top layer of a forest floor. ❖ *v.* **littered, littering, litters** —*tr.* **1.** To make untidy by discarding garbage carelessly: *The crowds of revelers littered the street with trash.* **2.** To give birth to (a litter). —*intr.* **1.** To scatter bits of trash. **2.** To give birth to a litter.

litterbug (lĭt′ər-bŭg′) *n.* Informal A person who litters public areas with trash.

little (lĭt′l) *adj.* **littler** or **less** (lĕs) also **lesser** (lĕs′ər), **littlest** or **least** (lēst) **1.** Small in size, quantity, or degree: *a little book; little money.* **2.** Short in duration; brief: *We have little time left.* **3.** Younger or youngest. Used especially of a sibling: *her little brother.* **4.** Unimportant; trivial: *a little problem.* ❖ *adv.* **less** also **least 1.** Not much: *He slept very little that night.* **2.** Not at all: *Little did he realize that he had sent his text message to the wrong person.* ❖ *n.* **1.** A small amount: *I received only a little of what they owed me.* **2.** A short distance or time: *waited a little.* ◆ **a little** Somewhat; a bit: *She feels a little better now.* **little by little** By small degrees; gradually.

✦ **SYNONYMS little, miniature, small, tiny** *adj.*

Little Dipper *n.* A group of seven stars in the constellation Ursa Minor that forms the outline of a dipper.

Little League *n.* An organization of baseball and softball teams for children.

littoral (lĭt′ər-əl) *adj.* On or relating to a shore, especially a seashore: *a littoral property.* ❖ *n.* **1.** A coastal region; a shore. **2.** The region or zone between the limits of high and low tides.

liturgical (lĭ-tûr′jĭ-kəl) *adj.* Relating to or used in liturgy.

liturgy (lĭt′ər-jē) *n., pl.* **liturgies 1.** An established form or set of forms for public religious worship. **2.** often **Liturgy** In Christianity, the public celebration of the Eucharist.

livable also **liveable** (lĭv′ə-bəl) *adj.* **1.** Suitable for living in: *a very livable house.* **2.** Bearable; endurable: *a life of hardship that was barely livable.*

live[1] (lĭv) *v.* **lived, living, lives** —*intr.* **1.** To be alive; exist: *Birch trees live only in cold climates.* **2.** To continue to remain alive: *My grandmother lived to be 85.* **3.** To support oneself; subsist: *It takes hard work to live off the land.* **4.** To reside or dwell: *They live in an apartment.* **5.** To conduct one's life in a certain manner: *live happily.* —*tr.* To spend or pass (one's life): *I have lived my whole life in this town.* ◆ **live down** To overcome or reduce the shame of (a misdeed, for example) over a period of time. **live up to 1.** To live or act in accordance with: *I try to live up to my ideals.* **2.** To prove equal to: *The new car did not live up to our expectations.* **3.** To carry out; fulfill: *She lived up to her part of the bargain.* **live with** To put up with; resign oneself to: *We'll just have to live with the situation.*

live[2] (līv) *adj.* **1.** Alive; living: *live animals in the circus.* **2.** Glowing; burning: *live coals.* **3.** Active and energetic: *a live and forceful personality.* **4.** Carrying electric current: *a live circuit.* **5.** Not yet exploded, but capable of being fired: *live ammunition.* **6.** Of current interest or importance: *a live issue.* **7.** Broadcast while actually being performed: *a live television program.* **8.** Containing living bacteria or active viruses, sometimes in a weakened form: *a live polio vaccine.* ❖ *adv.* At, during, or from the time of actual occurrence or performance: *The concert was broadcast live on television.*

WORD HISTORY Live[1] comes from Middle English *liven,* which comes from Old English *libban, lifian,* meaning "to be alive." **Live**[2] is short for *alive.*

livelihood (līv′lē-hood′) *n.* The means of supporting life; a way of earning a living: *She earns her livelihood by designing posters.*

livelong (līv′lông′) *adj.* Whole; entire: *all the livelong day.*

lively (līv′lē) *adj.* **livelier, liveliest 1.** Full of life, energy, or activity: *a lively baby.* **2.** Full of spirit; exciting: *a lively discussion.* **3.** Tending to bounce or rebound strongly: *a lively soccer ball.* ❖ *adv.* **livelier, liveliest** In a lively manner: *The whirling dancers stepped lively about the floor.* —**live′li·ness** *n.*

liven (lī′vən) *tr. & intr.v.* **livened, livening, livens** To make or become lively: *Music livens up a party. The party livened up as more guests arrived.*

live oak (līv) *n.* Any of various evergreen oak trees of the southern and western United States and Mexico.

liver[1] (lĭv′ər) *n.* **1.** A large organ located in the abdomen of vertebrate animals. The liver secretes bile and acts in the formation of blood proteins, the breakdown of toxins, the metabolism of fats, and the storage of carbohydrates. **2.** A similar organ of invertebrate animals. **3.** The liver of certain animals, used as food.

liver[2] (lĭv′ər) *n.* A person who lives in a specified manner: *city livers.*

livermorium (lĭv′ər-môr′ē-əm) *n.* Symbol **Lv** A radioactive element that has been artificially produced by scientists. The half-life of its most stable isotope is about 53 milliseconds. Atomic number 116. See **Periodic Table.**

liverwort (lĭv′ər-wûrt′ or lĭv′ər-wôrt′) n. Any of numerous small plants that are related to the mosses and do not bear flowers. Liverworts are leafy or flat and usually grow in damp areas.

liverwurst (lĭv′ər-wûrst′ or lĭv′ər-woŏrst′) n. A type of sausage containing mostly ground liver.

livery (lĭv′ə-rē or lĭv′rē) n., pl. **liveries 1.** A uniform worn by servants: a chauffeur dressed in livery. **2.** The distinctive clothing worn by members of a specific group. **3.** The stabling and care of horses for a fee. **4.** A livery stable.

livery stable n. A stable that boards horses and keeps horses and carriages for hire.

lives (līvz) n. Plural of **life.**

livestock (līv′stŏk′) n. Domestic animals that are raised for home use or for profit, especially on a farm. Cattle, horses, sheep, and pigs are livestock.

live wire n. **1.** A wire that is charged with an electric current. **2.** Slang An exciting, energetic, or imaginative person.

livid (lĭv′ĭd) adj. **1.** Discolored, as from a bruise; black-and-blue. **2.** Pale or ashen, as from shock. **3.** Extremely angry; furious. —**liv′id·ly** adv.

living (lĭv′ĭng) adj. **1.** Having life; alive: famous living persons. **2.** Currently existing or in use: a living language. **3.** Relating to the routine conduct of life: the difficult living conditions of the arctic winter. **4.** Enough to live on: a living wage. **5.** True to life: a portrait that is the living image of my parents. ❖ n. **1.** The condition of being alive: the high cost of living. **2.** A manner or style of life: We prefer simple living. **3.** A means of maintaining life; livelihood: They make their living by fishing.

living room n. A room in a household for leisure activities and entertaining guests.

living will n. A document in which a person specifies what medical treatments, if any, are to be used to prolong life in a situation where that person cannot directly communicate his or her intentions.

lizard (lĭz′ərd) n. Any of numerous reptiles having a scaly, often slender body, a tapering tail, and usually four legs. Iguanas and chameleons are lizards.

llama (lä′mə) n. A South American mammal related to the camel, raised for its warm wool and used for carrying loads.

llano (lä′nō or yä′nō) n., pl. **llanos** A broad, grassy, almost treeless plain, as in South America and the south-central United States.

lo (lō) interj. An expression used to attract attention.

load (lōd) n. **1.** The weight or force supported by a structure or some part of it. **2a.** Something that is carried, as by a vehicle, person, or animal: a load of firewood. **b.** The quantity or amount carried: a wagon with a full load of hay. **3.** The amount of work required of or done by a person or machine: has a heavy teaching load this semester. **4.** The amount of material that can be inserted into a device or machine at one time: two loads of laundry. **5.** A single charge of ammunition for a gun. **6.** Something that oppresses or burdens: That's a load off my mind. **7.** The mechanical resistance that a machine must overcome. **8.** The power output of a generator or power plant. **9.** often **loads** Informal A large number or amount: There were loads of people at the parade. ❖ v. **loaded, loading, loads** —tr. **1.** To put (something) into or onto a structure or vehicle: load grain onto a train. **2.** To put something into

or onto (a structure or vehicle): load a ship. **3.** To provide or fill nearly to overflowing: Our hosts loaded the table with food. **4.** To weigh down; burden: loaded the students with homework. **5a.** To put (something necessary) into a device: load paper into a printer; load cartridges into a rifle. **b.** To put something necessary into (a device): load a flashlight with new batteries. **c.** To put (a computer program or data) into a computer's memory. —intr. **1.** To receive a load: The ship loaded in port. **2.** To put ammunition into a firearm. **3.** To be transferred into a computer's memory. ◆ **get a load of** Slang To look at or listen to (something considered ridiculous or impressive): Hey, get a load of this goofy picture! —**load′er** n.

loaded (lō′dĭd) adj. **1.** Carrying a load. **2.** Having ammunition in place: a loaded weapon. **3.** Having a hidden or underlying implication: a loaded question. **4.** Slang Very wealthy.

loadstar (lōd′stär′) n. Variant of **lodestar.**

loadstone (lōd′stōn′) n. Variant of **lodestone.**

loaf[1] (lōf) n., pl. **loaves** (lōvz) **1.** A shaped mass of bread baked in one piece. **2.** A shaped mass of food: a meatloaf.

loaf[2] (lōf) intr.v. **loafed, loafing, loafs** To spend time lazily or aimlessly; idle: We loafed all morning accomplishing little.

WORD HISTORY Loaf[1] comes from Middle English lof, which comes from Old English hlāf, both meaning "a shaped mass of baked bread." **Loaf**[2] is probably a back-formation from loafer.

loafer (lō′fər) n. A person who spends time lazily or idly; an idler.

Loafer A trademark for a slip-on leather shoe resembling a moccasin but with a flat, low heel.

loam (lōm) n. Soil composed of sand, clay, silt, and decayed plant matter. —**loam′y** adj.

loan (lōn) n. **1.** The act of lending: the loan of a raincoat to a friend. **2a.** Something lent for temporary use: The lamp is a loan from my neighbor. **b.** A sum of money that is lent, usually with an interest fee: took out a loan to buy a car; repaid the loan over five years. ❖ tr.v. **loaned, loaning, loans** To lend: Libraries loan books to the public. —SEE NOTE AT **borrow.**

loanword (lōn′wûrd′) n. A word that has been borrowed from a foreign language; for example, encore, haiku, and sombrero are loanwords in English.

loath (lōth or lōth) adj. Not willing; reluctant; averse: They were loath to accept the offer of help from their rivals.

loathe (lōth) tr.v. **loathed, loathing, loathes** To dislike greatly; detest: I loathe cleaning the bathroom.

loathing (lō′thĭng) n. Extreme dislike; abhorrence.

loathsome (lōth′səm or lōth′səm) adj. Detestable; abhorrent. —**loath′some·ly** adv. —**loath′some·ness** n.

loaves (lōvz) n. Plural of **loaf**[1].

lob (lŏb) tr.v. **lobbed, lobbing, lobs** To hit, throw, or propel (a ball) in a high arc. ❖ n. A ball that is lobbed.

lobby (lŏb′ē) n., pl. **lobbies 1.** An entrance hall or a waiting room at or near the entrance to a building such as a hotel or theater. **2.** A group of people who try to influence lawmakers in favor of a cause. ❖ v. **lobbied, lobbying, lobbies** —intr. To try to influence lawmakers for or against a cause: Industry groups often lobby against antipollution laws. —tr. To seek to influence (lawmakers) in their voting: lobbied Congress to approve the bill.

lobbyist (lŏb′ē·ĭst) n. A person who tries to influence lawmakers for or against a cause.

lobe (lōb) *n.* A rounded part or projection, especially of a leaf or organ of the body, such as the lungs.

lobed (lōbd) *adj.* Having a lobe or lobes: *a lobed leaf.*

lobelia (lō-bēl′lē-ə *or* lō-bēl′yə) *n.* Any of numerous plants having clusters of blue, red, or purplish flowers.

lobotomy (lə-bŏt′ə-mē) *n., pl.* **lobotomies** Surgical incision into the frontal lobe of the brain to sever one or more nerve tracts, a technique formerly used to treat certain mental disorders but now rarely performed.

lobster (lŏb′stər) *n.* Any of various marine animals related to the crabs and shrimps, having a long hard-shelled body with five pairs of legs, the first pair of which are claws. ❖ *intr.v.* **lobstered, lobstering, lobsters** To catch or try to catch lobsters.

lobster pot *n.* A cage used for catching lobsters.

local (lō′kəl) *adj.* **1.** Relating to or characteristic of a particular area or place: *local governments; a local storm.* **2.** Making all stops on a route; not express: *a local train.* **3.** Affecting only one part of the body: *a local infection.* ❖ *n.* **1.** A person who lives in a certain region or neighborhood: *The locals are concerned about the town's growth.* **2.** A local branch of an organization, especially of a labor union. **3.** A train or bus that makes all stops along its route. —**lo′cal·ly** *adv.*

locale (lō-kăl′) *n.* A place, especially with reference to a particular event or circumstance: *The locale in many of Dickens's stories is London.*

localism (lō′kə-lĭz′əm) *n.* A local custom, habit, or expression.

locality (lō-kăl′ĭ-tē) *n., pl.* **localities** A certain neighborhood, place, or region.

localize (lō′kə-līz′) *tr. & intr.v.* **localized, localizing, localizes** To confine or become restricted to a particular area: *The pain localized in my abdomen.*

locate (lō′kāt′ *or* lō-kāt′) *v.* **located, locating, locates** —*tr.* **1.** To determine or show the position of: *locate Austria on a map.* **2.** To find by searching, inquiring, or examining: *locate information.* **3.** To place or situate: *We located the vegetables in a sunny corner of the garden.* —*intr.* To go and live somewhere; settle: *The family located in Iowa.*

location (lō-kā′shən) *n.* **1.** A place where something is or could be located; a site: *The view makes this a good location for a house.* **2.** The act or process of locating: *the location of water by drilling.* **3.** A site away from a movie studio where filming occurs: *shot on location in Spain.*

loch (lŏk *or* lŏкн) *n. Scots* **1.** A lake. **2.** An arm of the sea partly surrounded by land.

loci (lō′sī′) *n.* Plural of **locus.**

lock¹ (lŏk) *n.* **1.** A device used to fasten and secure something, such as a door or lid of a box, operated by a key, combination, or card. **2.** A section of a waterway, closed off with gates, in which a ship can be raised or lowered by pumping water in or out. **3.** A mechanism in a firearm for exploding the charge. **4.** One of several wrestling holds. **5.** A secure hold; control: *The popular candidate had a lock on the election.* ❖ *v.* **locked, locking, locks** —*tr.* **1.** To fasten or secure with a lock or locks: *lock the door.* **2.** To confine by means of a lock: *The keepers locked the animals in their cages.* **3.** To fix in place so that movement is impossible: *The ship was locked in the ice.* **4.** To join or link firmly; intertwine: *The two friends locked arms and walked off.* —*intr.* **1.** To become tightly held, fastened, or secured: *The door locks automatically.* **2.** To become

joined or intertwined: *The railroad cars locked as they came together.*

lock² (lŏk) *n.* **1.** A strand or curl of hair. **2.** **locks** The hair of the head: *the baby's red locks.* **3.** A small tuft of wool or cotton.

WORD HISTORY Lock¹ comes from Old English *loc,* meaning "bolt, bar." **Lock²** comes from a different Old English word spelled *loc,* meaning "a length of hair, a tress."

locker (lŏk′ər) *n.* **1.** A compartment, as in a gymnasium, that can be locked to keep clothes or valuables safe. **2.** A refrigerated cabinet or room for storing frozen foods. **3.** A flat trunk used for storage.

locket (lŏk′ĭt) *n.* A small ornamental metal case for a picture, a lock of hair, or another keepsake, usually worn on a chain around the neck.

lockjaw (lŏk′jô′) *n.* Tetanus.

lockout (lŏk′out′) *n.* The act of closing a workplace during a labor dispute in order to force employees to meet the employer's terms.

locksmith (lŏk′smĭth′) *n.* A person who makes or repairs locks.

locomotion (lō′kə-mō′shən) *n.* The act or power of moving from place to place.

locomotive (lō′kə-mō′tĭv) *n.* An engine that moves on its own power and is used to pull or push railroad cars. ❖ *adj.* **1.** Able to move independently from place to place. **2.** Relating to locomotion.

locoweed (lō′kō-wēd′) *n.* Any of several plants of western North America that cause severe illness when eaten by cattle, sheep, and other grazing animals.

locus (lō′kəs) *n., pl.* **loci** (lō′sī′) **1.** A locality; a place. **2.** A curve, a surface, or another figure that contains all and only the points that satisfy a given mathematical condition.

locust (lō′kəst) *n.* **1.** Any of various grasshoppers that travel in large swarms and can do great damage to crops. **2.** Any of certain cicadas. **3.** Any of several trees having feathery leaves, drooping clusters of fragrant flowers, and long pods.

locution (lō-kyōō′shən) *n.* **1.** A particular word, phrase, or expression. **2.** A manner or style of speaking; phraseology.

lode (lōd) *n.* **1.** A deposit or vein of a metal-bearing ore: *The miner found a rich lode of silver.* **2.** A rich source or supply: *a lode of important documents in the archives.*

lodestar also **loadstar** (lōd′stär′) *n.* A star, such as Polaris, used as point of navigational reference.

lodestone also **loadstone** (lōd′stōn′) *n.* A piece of magnetite that acts like a magnet.

lodge (lŏj) *n.* **1.** A cottage or cabin, especially a temporary house used during a vacation or for recreational activity: *a fishing lodge.* **2.** Any of various Native American dwellings, such as a wigwam or hogan. **3.** An inn. **4.** The den of certain animals, such as beavers. **5.** A branch or meeting place of a fraternal organization or secret society. ❖ *v.* **lodged, lodging, lodges** —*tr.* **1.** To provide with a place to stay temporarily: *We can lodge many guests in our home.* **2.** To rent a room to: *We lodge local students at reasonable rates.* **3.** To fix or implant: *The surveyors lodged stakes in the ground at the corners of the property.* **4.** To present (a charge or complaint) to an appropriate official or office; register: *The angry tenant lodged a complaint with the housing agency.* —*intr.* **1.** To live in a place temporarily:

We lodged in an old hotel. **2.** To live in a rented room or rooms: *He is lodging above a restaurant this year.* **3.** To be or become fixed or implanted: *The blade of the saw lodged in the wood.*

lodger (lŏj′ər) *n.* A person who rents a room or rooms in another person's house.

lodging (lŏj′ĭng) *n.* **1.** A temporary place to live or stay: *The vacationers sought lodging for the weekend.* **2. lodgings** A rented room or rooms.

lodgment also **lodgement** (lŏj′mənt) *n.* **1.** The act of lodging or the state of being lodged. **2.** Something lodged or deposited.

loess (lō′əs *or* lĕs *or* lŭs) *n.* A yellow to gray fine-grained silt or clay, thought to be deposited as dust blown by the wind.

loft (lôft) *n.* **1.** A large, open, upper floor in a commercial building or warehouse. **2.** Such a floor used as an apartment or artist's studio. **3.** An open space under a roof; an attic or garret. **4.** A gallery or balcony, as in a church: *a choir loft.* **5.** A hayloft. ❖ *tr.v.* **lofted, lofting, lofts** To send (a ball) in a high arc.

lofty (lôf′tē) *adj.* **loftier, loftiest 1.** Of great height; towering: *lofty mountains.* **2.** Elevated in character or spirit; exalted; noble: *lofty thoughts; lofty principles.* **3.** Arrogant; haughty: *Lofty treatment of others does not win friends.* —**loft′i·ly** *adv.* —**loft′i·ness** *n.*

log[1] (lôg) *n.* **1.** A long thick segment of a tree, used for building, firewood, or lumber. **2.** A device trailed from a ship to determine its speed through the water. **3a.** An official record of speed, progress, and important events, kept on a ship or aircraft. **b.** A journal or record. ❖ *v.* **logged, logging, logs** —*tr.* **1.** To cut down the trees on (a section of land). **2.** To cut (trees) into logs. **3.** To enter (something) in a logbook. **4.** To travel (a certain distance or at a certain speed): *We logged 800 miles in our two-day journey.* —*intr.* To cut down, trim, and haul timber. ❖ **log in** or **log on** To enter into a computer the information required to begin a session. **log out** or **log off** To enter into a computer the command to end a session.

log[2] (lôg) *n.* A logarithm.

WORD HISTORY Log[1] comes from Middle English *logge,* meaning "segment of tree." **Log**[2] is short for *logarithm.*

loganberry (lō′gən-bĕr′ē) *n.* **1.** The edible dark-red fruit of a prickly plant related to the blackberry and the raspberry. **2.** The plant that bears such fruit.

logarithm (lô′gə-rĭth′əm) *n.* The power to which a base, usually 10, must be raised to produce a given number. For example, if the base is 10, then 2 is the logarithm of 100 because 100 is 10^2. —**log′a·rith′mic** (lô′gə-rĭth′mĭk) *adj.*

logbook (lôg′bŏŏk′) *n.* The official record book of a ship or aircraft.

logger (lô′gər) *n.* **1.** A person who logs; a lumberjack. **2.** A tractor, crane, or other machine used for hauling or loading logs.

loggerhead (lô′gər-hĕd′) *n.* A large sea turtle that has a large head and powerful jaws and feeds chiefly on invertebrate animals such as mollusks and jellyfish. ❖ **at loggerheads** In disagreement; at odds: *The legislators were at loggerheads over the budget.*

loggia (lŏj′ē-ə) *n.* A gallery or arcade along the front or side of a building that is open on at least one side.

logging (lô′gĭng) *n.* The work of cutting down trees, sawing them into logs, and moving the logs to a mill.

logic (lŏj′ĭk) *n.* **1.** The study of the principles of reasoning; the science of reasoning and of proof. **2.** Sound thinking; clear reasoning: *Their logic is undeniable when it comes to this issue.* **3.** A particular method of reasoning; a way of thinking: *By my logic, the car's starter is faulty, not the battery.*

logical (lŏj′ĭ-kəl) *adj.* **1.** Using or agreeing with the principles of logic: *a logical consequence.* **2.** Reasonably expected: *A small apartment is a logical choice for a single person.* **3.** Reasoning or capable of reasoning clearly and rationally: *a logical mind.* —**log′i·cal·ly** *adv.*

logician (lō-jĭsh′ən) *n.* A person who practices or is skilled in logic.

logistic (lō-jĭs′tĭk) also **logistical** (lō-jĭs′tĭ-kəl) *adj.* Relating to logistics.

logistics (lō-jĭs′tĭks *or* lə-jĭs′tĭks) *n. (used with a singular or plural verb)* **1.** The planning and carrying out of a military operation. Logistics includes the transportation, housing, and supplying of troops. **2.** The management of the details of an operation or process.

logjam (lôg′jăm′) *n.* **1.** An immovable mass of floating logs crowded together. **2.** A deadlock, as in negotiations; an impasse.

logo (lō′gō′) *n., pl.* **logos** A symbol or design that identifies a brand.

logrolling (lôg′rō′lĭng) *n.* **1.** A sport in which two people stand on a floating log, spinning it with their feet until one falls. **2.** The exchange of political favors among lawmakers who agree to vote for each other's legislation.

logy (lō′gē) *adj.* **logier, logiest** Sluggish; lethargic: *felt logy after eating the turkey.*

–logy A suffix that means: **1.** Oral or written expression: *phraseology.* **2.** Science, theory, or study: *sociology.*

loin (loin) *n.* **1a.** The part of the body of a person or four-legged animal on each side of the spine between the ribs and hipbones. **b.** A cut of meat taken from this part of an animal. **2. loins a.** The region of the hips, groin, and lower abdomen. **b.** The reproductive organs.

loincloth (loin′klôth′) *n.* A strip of cloth worn around the hips and groin.

loiter (loi′tər) *intr.v.* **loitered, loitering, loiters 1.** To stand about idly; linger: *I loitered about the station, waiting for the bus.* **2.** To go slowly, stopping often: *The shoppers loitered on their way past the store.* —**loi′ter·er** *n.*

loll (lŏl) *v.* **lolled, lolling, lolls** —*intr.* **1.** To move, stand, sit, or rest in a lazy way: *The bathers lolled about the side of the pool.* **2.** To hang or let hang loosely or droop: *The limp flag lolled from the pole.* —*tr.* To allow to hang or droop: *The calf lolled its tongue on the hot day.*

lollipop also **lollypop** (lŏl′ē-pŏp′) *n.* A piece of hard candy on the end of a stick.

lo mein (lō′ mān′) *n.* A Chinese dish of wheat noodles that are boiled then seasoned and stir-fried.

lone (lōn) *adj.* **1.** Alone; solitary: *a lone traveler on the deserted road.* **2.** Being the only one of its kind; sole: *the lone hiker to reach the summit.* **3.** Standing by itself; remote: *a lone tree on the hillside.*

lonely (lōn′lē) *adj.* **lonelier, loneliest 1.** Sad at being alone: *feeling lonely with no friends.* See Synonyms at **alone. 2.** Without others of a similar kind; solitary: *Hers was a lonely voice of protest in a culture of complacency.* **3.** Not used or visited by people; remote: *a lonely road.* —**lone′li·ness** *n.*

loner (lō′nər) *n.* One who avoids the company of other people.

lonesome (lōn′səm) *adj.* **1.** Sad at being alone. See Synonyms at **alone. 2.** Producing a feeling of loneliness: *a lonesome voyage.* **3.** Not used or visited by people; remote: *a lonesome mountain trail.*

long¹ (lông) *adj.* **longer, longest 1.** Measuring a large amount from end to end; having great distance: *The Mississippi is a long river.* **2.** Having great duration: *The candidate gave a long speech.* **3.** Of a certain extent or duration: *The movie was two hours long.* **4.** Made up of many items: *a long shopping list.* **5a.** Extending beyond average or standard length: *a long chess game.* **b.** Extending or landing beyond a given boundary, limit, or goal: *Her serve was long.* **6.** Having an abundance of: *long on kindness.* **7.** Relating to the vowel sounds in words such as *mate, meet, mite, mote, moot,* and *mute.* ❖ *adv.* **longer, longest 1.** During or for a large amount of time: *Stay as long as you like.* **2.** For or throughout a specific period: *all night long.* **3.** Beyond a given boundary, limit, or goal: *Her serve went long.* **4.** At a very distant time: *That was long before you were born.* ❖ *n.* A long time: *It won't be long before we leave.* ◆ **long ago** At a time or during a period well before the present: *I read that book long ago.* **no longer** Not now as formerly: *no longer in business.*

long² (lông) *intr.v.* **longed, longing, longs** To have a strong desire; wish very much: *The students longed for summer vacation.*

WORD HISTORY Long¹ comes from Old English *lang,* meaning "measuring a long amount from end to end." **Long²** comes from Old English *langian,* meaning "to wish; yearn."

long. An abbreviation of longitude.

longboat (lông′bōt′) *n.* The longest boat carried by a sailing ship.

longbow (lông′bō′) *n.* A large bow for shooting arrows, used during the Middle Ages.

long-distance (lông′dĭs′təns) *adj.* Covering or carried over a great distance: *a long-distance race.*

long division *n.* The process of dividing one number by another in which each step of the division is written out, especially when the divisor is a large number.

longevity (lŏn-jĕv′ĭ-tē) *n., pl.* **longevities** Long life.

longhand (lông′hănd′) *n.* Ordinary handwriting in which the words are fully written out.

longhorn (lông′hôrn′) *n.* Any of various cattle having long horns, especially a breed that originated in the region that is now Texas.

longhouse or **long house** (lông′hous′) *n.* A long dwelling, especially of certain Native American, Polynesian, and Indonesian peoples, designed to house numerous families under the same roof.

longing (lông′ĭng) *n.* A deep yearning; a strong desire: *a longing for success.* **—long′ing·ly** *adv.*

longitude (lŏn′jĭ-tōod′) *n.* Distance east or west on the earth's surface, measured in degrees from a certain meridian, usually the Prime Meridian in Greenwich, England.

longitudinal (lŏn′jĭ-tōod′n-əl) *adj.* **1.** Involving length or longitude. **2.** Placed or running lengthwise: *longitudinal stripes running the length of the garter snake.* **—lon′gi·tu′di·nal·ly** *adv.*

long johns *pl.n. Informal* Warm underwear covering the legs down to the ankles.

long jump *n.* A jump for distance rather than height in an athletic contest.

long-lived (lông′līvd′ *or* lông′lĭvd′) *adj.* Having a long life; existing for a long time: *a long-lived partnership.*

long-playing record (lông′plā′ĭng) *n.* A phonograph record that turns at 33⅓ revolutions per minute and usually provides about 25 minutes of sound on each side.

long-range (lông′rānj′) *adj.* **1.** Involving a lengthy period; not immediate: *long-range plans.* **2.** Designed for covering great distances: *long-range transport planes.*

longshoreman (lông′shôr′mən) *n.* A dock worker who loads and unloads ships.

long shot *n.* **1.** An entry, as in a horse race, with only a slight chance of winning. **2.** Something that is risky but rewarding if successful. ◆ **by a long shot** To any extent; at all. Usually used in negative sentences: *That's not going to happen by a long shot.*

long-standing or **longstanding** (lông′stăn′dĭng) *adj.* Of long duration: *a long-standing business partnership.*

long-suffering (lông′sŭf′ər-ĭng) *adj.* Patiently enduring pain or difficulty.

long-term (lông′tûrm′) *adj.* Involving a long period of time: *a long-term investment.*

long ton *n.* A ton weighing 2,240 pounds (1,016 kilograms). See table at **measurement.**

long-winded (lông′wĭn′dĭd) *adj.* Writing or talking at great length; tiresome. **—long′-wind′ed·ly** *adv.*

loo (lōo) *n., pl.* **loos** *Chiefly British* A toilet.

look (lŏok) *v.* **looked, looking, looks** *—intr.* **1.** To use the eyes to see; perceive by sight: *I looked at the clock.* **2.** To turn one's gaze or attention: *Everyone looked toward the camera. You must look carefully at all of the facts.* **3.** To appear; seem: *These bananas look ripe.* **4.** To search: *I looked all over for my keys.* **5.** To face in a certain direction: *The house looks on the sea. —tr.* **1.** To turn one's eyes upon: *The judge looked her in the eye.* **2.** To show by one's appearance: *He looks his age.* ❖ *n.* **1.** The action of looking; a gaze or glance: *a quick look at the map.* **2.** An expression or appearance: *The gathering clouds have a threatening look.* **3. looks** Personal appearance: *The children have their parents' good looks.* ◆ **look after** To take care of: *Someone must look after the baby.* **look a gift horse in the mouth** To be critical or suspicious of something that has been received for free. **look alive** or **look sharp** *Informal* To act or respond quickly. **look down on** To regard with contempt or scorn. **look for** To search for; seek: *a bird looking for food.* **look forward to** To think of (a future event) with pleasure and excitement. **look into** To inquire into; investigate: *The detective looked into the matter of the missing money.* **look on** or **look upon** To regard; consider: *We look on them as allies.* **look out** To be watchful or careful; take care: *Look out for that speeding car!* **look over** To examine, often hastily: *The police looked over the scene and determined it was safe to move forward.* **look up 1.** To search for and find, as in a reference book. **2.** To visit: *look up an old friend.* **3.** To become better; improve: *Things are at last looking up.* **look up to** To admire: *The players look up to their coach.* **—look′er** *n.*

looking glass (lŏok′ĭng) *n.* A mirror.

lookout (lŏok′out′) *n.* **1.** The act of looking or watching: *keeping a sharp lookout.* **2.** A high place with a wide view for keeping watch. **3.** A person assigned to watch for something: *The captain sent a lookout up the mast.*

loom¹ (lōom) *intr.v.* **loomed, looming, looms 1.** To come into view, often with a threatening appearance: *Storm* *clouds loomed over the mountains.* **2.** To seem close at hand; be about to happen: *The examination loomed before the students.*

loom² (lōom) *n.* A machine or frame on which threads or yarns are woven to make cloth.

WORD HISTORY Loom¹ may be of Scandinavian origin. **Loom²** comes from Old English *gelōma,* meaning "tool."

loon¹ (lōon) *n.* Any of several large diving birds having a dark speckled back, a pointed bill, webbed feet, and a cry that resembles a laugh.

loon² (lōon) *n. Informal* A foolish or crazy person.

WORD HISTORY Loon¹ may come from Old Norse *lōmr,* meaning "diver." **Loon²** probably comes from *loon¹* and is influenced by *lunatic.*

loony (lōo′nē) *Informal adj.* **loonier, looniest 1.** Very foolish or silly: *How did you come up with that loony idea?* **2.** Crazy; mad: *He thinks he makes sense, but we think he's loony.* ❖ *n., pl.* **loonies** A foolish or crazy person.

loop (lōop) *n.* **1.** A length of rope, thread, or wire that crosses over itself, making an opening. **2.** A circular path or oval pattern that closes or nearly closes on itself: *The car followed a loop around the town.* **3.** A fastening or ornament made from a bent or crossed piece of cloth, cord, or other material: *a belt loop.* **4.** A closed electric circuit. **5.** A series of instructions in a computer program that are repeated a specified number of times or until a certain result has been achieved. **6.** A maneuver in which an aircraft flies a circular path in a vertical plane. ❖ *v.* **looped, looping, loops** —*tr.* **1.** To make into a loop or loops: *loop string and tie the ends.* **2.** To fasten or join with a loop or loops: *looped together the pieces of string.* **3.** To encircle with a loop: *loop the pole with this rope.* **4.** To fly (an aircraft) in a loop or loops. —*intr.* **1.** To form a loop: *yarn that loops easily for knitting.* **2.** To move or fly in a loop. ◆ **in the loop** Part of a group that is kept informed about something. **out of the loop** Not part of a group that is kept informed about something.

loophole (lōop′hōl′) *n.* **1.** A way of avoiding or escaping a cost or legal burden that would otherwise apply. Loopholes often involve an omission or an unclear provision in a law or contract: *A loophole in the law allowed the corporation to avoid paying the new tax.* **2.** A small hole or slit in a wall for looking or shooting through.

loose (lōos) *adj.* **looser, loosest 1.** Not tightly fastened or secured: *a loose shoelace; loose bricks.* **2.** Free from confinement, bonds, or fetters: *The stallion was loose on the prairie.* **3.** Not tight-fitting or tightly fitted: *a loose robe.* **4.** Not tightly stretched; slack: *the loose skin of a cow's neck.* **5.** Not tightly packed; not compact: *loose gravel.* **6.** Not bound or gathered together: *loose notebook pages.* **7.** Lacking moral restraint: *loose conduct.* **8.** Not strict or exact: *a loose translation.* ❖ *adv.* In a loose manner or condition. ❖ *tr.v.* **loosed, loosing, looses 1.** To set free; release: *We loosed our dog from its leash.* **2.** To make less tight, firm, or compact. **3.** To untie, undo, or unwrap: *We loosed the ribbon from the package.* **4.** To discharge (a missile): *loose an arrow.* —**loose′ly** *adv.* —**loose′ness** *n.*

loosen (lōo′sən) *v.* **loosened, loosening, loosens** —*tr.* **1.** To make looser or less tight: *loosened his tie; loosened her grip on the rope.* **2.** To make less strict or rigid; relax: *The school loosened its student dress code.* —*intr.* To become loose or looser: *The knot loosened easily.* —**loos′en·er** *n.*

loot (lōot) *n.* **1.** Valuable things pillaged in time of war;

spoils. **2.** Stolen goods or money. **3.** *Slang* Money. ❖ *v.* **looted, looting, loots** —*tr.* To take things from (a place) by force or without right; plunder: *Rioters looted the downtown stores.* —*intr.* To take goods by force or through lawless behavior. —**loot′er** *n.*

lop¹ (lŏp) *tr.v.* **lopped, lopping, lops 1.** To cut (a part) from; remove: *lopped dead branches from the tree.* **2.** To cut off a part or parts from; trim: *lopped the shrub.*

lop² (lŏp) *intr.v.* **lopped, lopping, lops** To hang loosely; droop: *The puppy's ears lopped.*

lope (lōp) *intr.v.* **loped, loping, lopes** To run or ride with a long easy gait: *The horse loped along the trail.* ❖ *n.* A long easy gait.

lop-eared (lŏp′îrd′) *adj.* Having bent or drooping ears: *a lop-eared rabbit.*

lopsided (lŏp′sī′dĭd) *adj.* **1.** Heavier or larger on one side than on the other. **2.** Leaning or sagging to one side: *a lopsided stack of books.* **3.** Characterized by a large margin of victory. —**lop′sid′ed·ly** *adv.* —**lop′sid′ed·ness** *n.*

loquacious (lō-kwā′shəs) *adj.* Very talkative; talking a great deal or too much. —**lo·qua′cious·ly** *adv.*

lord (lôrd) *n.* **1.** In feudal times, a man of high rank, as a king or the owner of a manor. **2. Lord** *Chiefly British* A general masculine title of nobility or other high rank. **3. Lord** God. **4.** A man with great authority or power: *a press lord who owns many newspapers.* ◆ **lord it over** To behave in a domineering manner toward: *The older students lorded it over the newcomers.*

lordly (lôrd′lē) *adj.* **lordlier, lordliest 1.** Characteristic of a lord: *a lordly estate; a lordly deed.* **2.** Arrogant; haughty: *a lordly and superior manner.* —**lord′li·ness** *n.*

lordship (lôrd′shĭp′) *n.* **1.** often **Lordship** Used as a title and form of address for a man holding the rank of lord: *your Lordship.* **2.** The rank or domain of a lord.

Lord's Prayer (lôrdz prâr) *n.* In Christianity, the prayer taught by Jesus to his disciples. In English it begins with the words *Our Father.*

lore (lôr) *n.* The accumulated facts, traditions, or beliefs about something, especially when passed from generation to generation by oral tradition: *sailing lore.*

lorry (lôr′ē) *n., pl.* **lorries** *Chiefly British* A motor truck.

lose (lōoz) *v.* **lost** (lôst), **losing, loses** —*tr.* **1.** To be unable to find; mislay: *I lost my gloves yesterday.* **2.** To be deprived of (something one has had): *We lost our peach trees during the storm. She lost her husband in the accident.* **3.** To be unable to keep control or the allegiance of: *We lost their support. Don't lose your temper.* **4.** To fail to win: *They lost the game.* **5.** To fail to use; waste: *lose a chance by hesitating.* **6.** To stray or wander from: *lose one's way.* **7.** To fail to see, hear, understand, or follow: *lose the airplane in the clouds; lose track of what was said.* **8.** To outrun or escape capture by: *The swift deer was able to lose the pursuing wolves.* **9.** To cause (someone) to be deprived of; cost: *That blunder lost him the job.* **10.** To destroy. Usually used in the passive: *All my belongings were lost in the fire.* —*intr.* **1.** To suffer loss or destruction: *Many investors lost heavily in the recession.* **2.** To be defeated: *Their team lost in overtime.* ◆ **lose it** *Slang* To lose control mentally or emotionally: *I completely lost it when I heard the bad news.* **lose out** To be unsuccessful. **lose out on** To fail to win or get; miss: *He lost out on the opportunity because he did not say he was interested.* **lose time 1.** To operate too slowly. Said of a timepiece. **2.** To delay forward progress: *We'll lost a lot of time stuck in traffic.*

loser (lōo′zər) *n.* **1a.** One that fails to win: *the losers of* *the game.* **b.** A person who takes loss in a specified way: *a graceful loser; a poor loser.* **2a.** A person who is unable to be successful on a sustained basis: *considers her son's friends to be a bunch of losers.* **b.** One that loses opportunities or advantages: *The losers in the latest round of budget cuts included retirees and pensioners.* **c.** One that is bad in quality: *That book is a real loser.*

losing (lōō′zĭng) *adj.* **1.** Failing to win: *the losing team.* **2.** Relating to one that fails to win: *a losing season.* ❖ *n.* **1.** The act of one who loses; loss. **2.** often **losings** Something lost, such as money.

loss (lôs) *n.* **1a.** The act or an instance of losing: *a loss of memory; the loss of a game.* **b.** The state of being deprived of a person or thing: *Her loss was made easier by her cheerful outlook.* **2.** A person or thing that is lost: *Because of the accident, our car was a complete loss.* **3.** The suffering or damage caused by losing a person or thing: *The doctor's retirement is a great loss to the community.* **4. losses** Soldiers killed or wounded; casualties. ◆ **at a loss 1.** Below cost: *They sold the cherry crop at a loss.* **2.** Perplexed; puzzled: *I am at a loss to explain his behavior.*

lost (lôst) *v.* Past tense and past participle of **lose.** ❖ *adj.* **1.** Unable to find the way: *a lost tourist.* **2a.** No longer in one's possession, care, or control: *a lost fortune; a lost opportunity.* **b.** No longer known or practiced: *a lost art.* **c.** Beyond reach, communication, or influence: *lost to the world.* **3.** Not won or unlikely to be won; unsuccessful: *a lost cause.* **4.** Confused; bewildered: *At first we were lost in the advanced class.* **5.** Beyond recovery or redemption; destroyed: *lost honor; a lost soul.* **6.** Completely involved or preoccupied: *lost in thought.*

lot (lŏt) *n.* **1. a lot** or **lots** *Informal* A large amount or number: *I have a lot of work to do. We made lots of new friends.* **2.** A number of people or things considered as a group: *We packed this lot of fruit for shipment.* **3.** A piece of land: *the empty lot behind the house.* **4.** A movie studio. **5.** One of a set of objects, such as bits of paper or straw, used to determine something by chance: *They drew lots to see who would go first.* **6.** The use of lots to determine something: *We decided who would go first by lot.* **7.** The decision made in this manner. **8.** Fortune in life; luck: *It is the lot of many to struggle for a living.*

USAGE When *a lot* is the grammatical subject of a clause and is followed by a prepositional phrase beginning with *of,* it can take either a singular or a plural verb, depending on whether the object of the preposition is singular or plural: *A lot of my apartment is carpeted. A lot of people live in Los Angeles.* You will sometimes see the phrase *a lot* as in *a lot of money* spelled as one word, *alot.* This is not an acceptable spelling.

lotion (lō′shən) *n.* A liquid or cream applied to the skin to heal, soften, cleanse, or soothe.

lottery (lŏt′ə-rē) *n., pl.* **lotteries** A contest in which tickets are sold, the winning ticket or tickets being determined in a random drawing.

lotus (lō′təs) *n.* **1.** Any of various water plants with large floating leaves and fragrant flowers, especially an Asian species with pink flowers and a North American species with yellow flowers. **2.** In Greek mythology, a fruit that causes a dreamy idle state in those who eat it.

loud (loud) *adj.* **louder, loudest 1.** Characterized by high volume and intensity of sound: *loud music.* **2.** Producing

loud sounds: *a loud trumpet.* **3.** Clamorous or insistent: *made loud denunciations.* **4.** Too bright; gaudy; flashy: *a loud garish suit.* ❖ *adv.* **louder, loudest** In a loud manner: *Speak louder, please.* —**loud′ly** *adv.* —**loud′ness** *n.*

loudmouth (loud′mouth′) *n. Informal* A person given to loud or unpleasant talk.

loudspeaker (loud′spē′kər) *n.* A device that changes an electric signal into sound, especially one that is part of a public-address or stereophonic system.

Louisiana French *n.* French as spoken by the descendants of the French settlers of Louisiana.

lounge (lounj) *intr.v.* **lounged, lounging, lounges 1.** To move or act in a lazy or relaxed way: *lounge in a comfortable chair.* **2.** To pass time idly: *I lounged around the house on my day off.* ❖ *n.* **1a.** A waiting room or bar in a hotel or airport terminal. **b.** An informal room for relaxing or gathering: *the new student lounge.* **2.** A long couch or sofa.

lour (lour) *v. & n.* Variant of **lower**[1].

louse (lous) *n.* **1.** *pl.* **lice** (līs) Any of numerous small wingless insects that live as parasites on the bodies of many birds and mammals, including humans. **2.** *pl.* **louses** *Slang* A mean or contemptible person.

lousy (lou′zē) *adj.* **lousier, lousiest 1.** Low in quality; inferior: *a lousy restaurant.* **2.** Mean or contemptible: *What a lousy thing to do!* **3.** Sick or unwell: *I feel lousy.* **4.** Covered or overrun with lice. —**lous′i·ly** *adv.*

lout (lout) *n.* An awkward, often boorish person; an oaf.

louver (lōō′vər) *n.* **1.** An opening, as in a door, fitted with horizontal slats set at a slant so as to admit light and air and often to keep out rain. **2.** One of the slats used in such an opening. —**lou′vered** *adj.*

lovable also **loveable** (lŭv′ə-bəl) *adj.* Having qualities that attract affection; endearing: *a lovable kitten.* —**lov′-a·ble·ness** *n.* —**lov′a·bly** *adv.*

love (lŭv) *n.* **1.** A feeling of affection, concern, or devotion toward a person. **2a.** A strong liking for something: *a love of reading.* **b.** Something that is very much liked: *Gardening is her great love.* **3.** A beloved person: *He met his love when he was on vacation.* **4.** A score of zero in tennis. ❖ *tr.v.* **loved, loving, loves 1.** To feel love or strong affection for: *We love our parents.* **2.** To like enthusiastically; delight in: *The audience loved the performance.* ◆ **in love** Feeling love and devotion toward someone.

lovebird (lŭv′bûrd′) *n.* Any of various small parrots that are often kept as pets and seem to show great fondness between mates.

loveless (lŭv′lĭs) *adj.* **1.** Showing or feeling no love: *a loveless tone in his voice.* **2.** Receiving no love; unloved.

lovelorn (lŭv′lôrn′) *adj.* Deprived of love or one's lover.

lovely (lŭv′lē) *adj.* **lovelier, loveliest 1.** Having attractive qualities of character or appearance; beautiful or endearing: *a lovely person; a lovely house.* **2.** Pleasing or enjoyable; delightful: *We spent a lovely weekend at the lake.* —**love′li·ness** *n.*

lover (lŭv′ər) *n.* **1.** A person who loves another person, especially one who is involved in a romantic relationship with another. **2.** A person who is fond of or devoted to something: *a lover of jazz.*

love seat or **loveseat** (lŭv′sēt′) *n.* A small sofa that seats two people.

lovesick (lŭv′sĭk′) *adj.* Unable to act normally as a result of feeling love.

loving (lŭv′ĭng) *adj.* Feeling or showing love; affectionate. —**lov′ing·ly** *adv.*

low¹ (lō) *adj.* **lower, lowest 1.** Being a relatively small distance above a certain level, as above sea level or the surface of the earth: *a low wall.* **2.** Situated below the surrounding surfaces: *water standing in low spots.* **3.** Near to the ground or horizon: *low branches; low clouds.* **4.** Near or nearer to from a reference point: *took a low position next to the goal.* **5.** Of less than usual depth; shallow: *The river is low.* **6a.** Less than usual or expected in degree, intensity, or amount: *a low temperature; a low cost; a low level of understanding.* **b.** Inferior in rank, position, or status: *a low grade of oil.* **7.** Not very advanced in development or complexity: *the lowest forms of life.* **8.** Below the middle range of musical pitch: *the low tones of a tuba.* **9.** Not loud; soft: *Speak in a low voice.* **10.** Being at or near the worst or least desirable point: *Her career reached a low point at that company.* **11.** Inadequate in amount; almost gone: *Our supplies are low.* **12.** Immoral or contemptible; base: *a low trick.* **13.** Lacking liveliness or good spirits; discouraged or dejected: *feeling low.* **14.** Lacking strength or vigor; weak: *a patient in low condition.* **15.** Not favorable; disapproving: *She has a low opinion of his work.* **16.** Relating to a gear setting, as in a car transmission, that produces a lower vehicle speed than normal as compared with engine speed. **17.** Situated near the equator: *the low latitudes.* ❖ *adv.* **lower, lowest 1.** In or to a low position, level, or degree: *The plane flew low over the canyon.* **2.** Softly; quietly: *speak low.* ❖ *n.* **1.** A low position, level, or degree: *The price of peanuts fell to a new low.* **2.** A region of atmospheric pressure that is below normal. **3.** Low gear: *She put the car in low when driving down the steep road.* —**low′ness** *n.*

low² (lō) *n.* A deep sound made by cattle; a moo. ❖ *intr.v.* **lowed, lowing, lows** To make such a sound; moo.

WORD HISTORY Low¹ comes from Middle English *loue,* which comes from Old Norse *lāgr,* both meaning "short, not high." **Low²** comes from Old English *hlōwan,* meaning "to moo."

lowboy (lō′boi′) *n.* A low chest of drawers with a top that can be used as a table.

lowbrow (lō′brou′) *adj.* Having tastes and preferences that are not sophisticated. —**low′brow′** *n.*

low-cal (lō′kăl′) *adj.* Having fewer calories than what is typical: *low-cal food.*

low-down or **lowdown** (lō′doun′) *adj.* Despicable; contemptible: *a low-down way of gaining success.* ❖ *n.* Correct information or details: *the low-down on the scandal.*

lower¹ (lou′ər or lour) also **lour** (lour) *intr.v.* **lowered, lowering, lowers** also **loured, louring, lours 1.** To look angry or sullen; scowl. **2.** To appear dark or stormy, as the sky or weather: *The sky lowered as the hurricane approached.* ❖ *n.* A sullen or angry look.

lower² (lō′ər) *adj.* Comparative of **low¹. 1.** Below another in rank, position, or authority: *the lower court.* **2.** Situated below a similar or comparable thing: *a lower shelf.* **3.** Relating to or being an older division of the geologic period named. ❖ *v.* **lowered, lowering, lowers** —*tr.* **1.** To let, bring, or move something down: *lower the flag; lower one's head.* **2.** To reduce, as in height, amount, degree, or quality: *The company lowered its prices.* **3.** To reduce in strength or intensity: *Lower your voice.* **4.** To reduce in standing or respect: *I wouldn't lower myself to do that.* —*intr.* **1.** To move down: *The helicopter lowered over the roof.* **2.** To become less: *The temperature lowered at dusk.*

WORD HISTORY Lower¹ comes from Middle English *louren,* meaning "to scowl." **Lower²** is derived from *low¹.*

lowercase (lō′ər-kās′) *adj.* Relating to a letter that is smaller than and often having a different shape from its capital letter, such as *v* or *i,* as contrasted with *V* and *I.* ❖ *n.* Lowercase letters.

lower house (lō′ər) *n.* The branch of a bicameral legislature, such as the US House of Representatives, that is larger and more representative of the population.

lowermost (lō′ər-mōst′) *adj.* Lowest.

lowest common denominator (lō′ĭst) *n.* A least common denominator.

lowest common multiple *n.* Least common multiple.

low frequency *n.* A radio-wave frequency in the range between 30 kilohertz and 300 kilohertz.

Low German *n.* **1.** The German dialects spoken in northern Germany. **2.** A group of Germanic languages, including Dutch and Flemish, spoken in Belgium and the Netherlands.

low-key (lō′kē′) also **low-keyed** (lō′kēd′) *adj.* **1.** Having low intensity; restrained, as in style or quality; subdued. **2.** Having or producing uniformly dark tones with few areas of contrast, as in a photograph or film.

lowland (lō′lənd) *n.* An area of land that is low in relation to the surrounding country. ❖ *adj.* Relating to or characteristic of a lowland.

lowlander (lō′lən-dər) *n.* A native or inhabitant of a lowland.

lowly (lō′lē) *adj.* **lowlier, lowliest 1.** Low in rank or position: *a person of lowly birth.* **2.** Meek or humble in manner: *a lowly person.* ❖ *adv.* In a meek and humble manner. —**low′li·ness** *n.*

low-pitched (lō′pĭcht′) *adj.* **1.** Low in tone: *a low-pitched voice.* **2.** Having little slope: *a low-pitched roof.*

low-pressure (lō′prĕsh′ər) *adj.* **1.** Having or using less than the usual pressure: *a low-pressure tire.* **2.** Having a relatively low barometric pressure.

low profile *n.* Behavior or activity carried out so as not to attract attention.

low-spirited (lō′spĭr′ĭ-tĭd) *adj.* Being in low spirits; depressed; sad.

low-tech (lō′tĕk′) *adj.* Relating to low technology.

low technology *n.* Technology that does not involve highly advanced scientific methods or newly developed and specialized devices. —**low′-tech·nol′o·gy** *adj.*

low tide *n.* **1.** The tide as it reaches its lowest point. **2.** The time at which this occurs.

lox (lŏks) *n., pl.* **lox** or **loxes** Salmon that has been cured in brine and is often smoked.

loyal (loi′əl) *adj.* **1.** Faithful to a person, idea, custom, or duty: *a loyal worker.* **2.** Faithful to a country or government: *a loyal citizen.* —**loy′al·ly** *adv.*

loyalist (loi′ə-lĭst) *n.* A person who remains loyal to the established government, political party, or ruler, especially during a civil war or revolution.

loyalty (loi′əl-tē) *n., pl.* **loyalties 1.** The condition of being loyal; faithful and loyal conduct. **2.** often **loyalties** A feeling or attitude of devoted attachment and affection: *My loyalties lie with my family.*

lozenge (lŏz′ĭnj) *n.* **1.** A flat diamond-shaped figure. **2.** A small candy, especially one containing medicine for soothing a sore throat.

LP (ĕl′pē′) *n.* A long-playing phonograph record.

LPN An abbreviation of licensed practical nurse.

LSD (ĕl′ĕs-dē′) *n.* A synthetic chemical compound that is a powerful hallucinogenic drug. LSD is short for *lysergic acid diethylamide.*

LT or **Lt.** An abbreviation of lieutenant.

Ltd. or **ltd.** An abbreviation of limited.

luau (lōō-ou′ *or* lōō′ou′) *n.* An elaborate Hawaiian feast with traditional foods and entertainment. —SEE NOTE AT **ukulele.**

lubber (lŭb′ər) *n.* **1.** A clumsy person. **2.** An inexperienced sailor; a landlubber.

lubricant (lōō′brĭ-kənt) *n.* A slippery substance, such as oil, grease, or graphite, used to coat the surfaces of objects that move against each other, to reduce friction and wear.

lubricate (lōō′brĭ-kāt′) *v.* **lubricated, lubricating, lubricates** —*tr.* **1.** To apply a lubricant to or to make slippery: *lubricate a bike chain.* **2.** To make easier: *Concessions by both sides helped to lubricate the agreement.* —*intr.* To act as a lubricant. —**lu′bri·ca′tion** *n.* —**lu′bri·ca′tor** *n.*

lucent (lōō′sənt) *adj.* **1.** Giving off light; luminous; bright. **2.** Translucent; clear; lucid.

lucid (lōō′sĭd) *adj.* **1.** Easily understood; clear: *a lucid explanation.* **2.** Thinking or expressing oneself clearly, especially between periods of confusion: *The feverish patient was lucid now and then.* **3.** Transparent: *lucid waters.* —**lu·cid′i·ty, lu′cid·ness** *n.* —**lu′cid·ly** *adv.*

Lucifer (lōō′sə-fər) *n.* In Christian tradition, an angelic being who was cast from heaven as punishment for his rebellious pride. Lucifer is traditionally identified with Satan.

luck (lŭk) *n.* **1.** The chance happening of good or bad events; fate; fortune: *Luck favored our team with a winning season.* **2.** Good fortune; success: *beginner's luck.* ♦ **in luck** Enjoying success; fortunate. **out of luck** Lacking good fortune. **press (one's) luck** or **push (one's) luck** To risk one's good fortune, often by acting with too much confidence.

luckily (lŭk′ə-lē) *adv.* With or by favorable chance; fortunately.

luckless (lŭk′lĭs) *adj.* Having no luck; unlucky.

lucky (lŭk′ē) *adj.* **luckier, luckiest 1.** Marked by or having good luck; fortunate: *a lucky day; a lucky person.* **2.** Seeming to cause good luck: *a lucky penny.* —**luck′i·ness** *n.*

lucrative (lōō′krə-tĭv) *adj.* Producing wealth; profitable: *a lucrative investment.* —**lu′cra·tive·ly** *adv.*

lucre (lōō′kər) *n.* Money or profits.

Luddite (lŭd′īt) *n.* **1.** Any of a group of British workers who between 1811 and 1816 rioted and destroyed labor-saving textile machinery in the belief that such machinery would diminish employment. **2.** A person who opposes technical or technological change. —**Lud′dism** *n.*

ludicrous (lōō′dĭ-krəs) *adj.* Laughable because of obvious absurdity; ridiculous. —**lu′di·crous·ly** *adv.*

luff (lŭf) *n.* **1.** The act of sailing toward the wind. **2.** The forward edge of a fore-and-aft sail. ♦ *intr.v.* **luffed, luffing, luffs** To steer a sailing vessel toward the wind.

lug[1] (lŭg) *n.* **1.** A projecting part, as on a machine, used to support something: *take the nuts off the lugs to remove the tire.* **2.** A projecting part of a larger piece that helps to provide traction, as on the sole of a boot. **3.** *Slang* A clumsy fool; a blockhead.

lug[2] (lŭg) *tr.v.* **lugged, lugging, lugs** To drag or haul with great difficulty: *lug boxes up to the attic.*

WORD HISTORY Lug[1] comes from Middle English *lugge* (meaning "earflap") and is of Scandinavian origin. **Lug**[2] comes from Middle English *luggen* (meaning "to drag") and is likewise of Scandinavian origin.

luggage (lŭg′ĭj) *n.* The bags, suitcases, boxes, or trunks for carrying belongings on a trip; baggage.

lugsail (lŭg′səl) *n.* A four-sided sail that hangs on a yard slanting across the mast.

lugubrious (lōō-gōō′brē-əs) *adj.* Sad or mournful; sorrowful: *the lugubrious cry of wolves.* —**lu·gu′bri·ous·ly** *adv.* —**lu·gu′bri·ous·ness** *n.*

Luke (lōōk) *n.* The third Gospel of the New Testament, traditionally thought to have been written by Luke, a companion of the Apostle Paul.

lukewarm (lōōk′wôrm′) *adj.* **1.** Neither hot nor cold; mildly warm: *lukewarm water.* **2.** Lacking in enthusiasm; indifferent: *a lukewarm greeting.* —**luke′warm′ly** *adv.*

lull (lŭl) *v.* **lulled, lulling, lulls** —*tr.* To cause to sleep or rest; calm; soothe: *a song to lull a baby to sleep.* —*intr.* To become calm: *The high winds finally lulled.* ♦ *n.* A temporary lessening of activity or noise; a calm interval: *a lull in the storm; a lull in sales.*

lullaby (lŭl′ə-bī′) *n., pl.* **lullabies** A soothing song meant to lull a child to sleep.

lumbago (lŭm-bā′gō) *n.* A pain that affects the muscles and tendons of the lower back and hips.

lumbar (lŭm′bər *or* lŭm′bär′) *adj.* Relating to, near, or situated in the part of the back and sides between the lowest ribs and the pelvis.

Lumbee (lŭm′bē) *n., pl.* **Lumbee** or **Lumbees** A member of a Native American people of southeast North Carolina.

lumber[1] (lŭm′bər) *n.* Timber sawed into boards and planks. ♦ *intr.v.* **lumbered, lumbering, lumbers** To cut down and prepare lumber.

lumber[2] (lŭm′bər) *intr.v.* **lumbered, lumbering, lumbers** To walk or move in a clumsy or noisy manner: *The truck lumbered down the bumpy road.*

WORD HISTORY The noun **lumber**[1] may come from the verb **lumber**[2], which comes from Middle English *lomeren,* which means "to move clumsily" and may be of Scandinavian origin.

lumberjack (lŭm′bər-jăk′) *n.* A person whose work is to chop down trees and transport timber to a sawmill.

lumberyard (lŭm′bər-yärd′) *n.* A business that sells lumber and other building materials from a yard.

lumen (lōō′mən) *n., pl.* **lumens** or **lumina** (lōō′mə-nə) **1.** The open space within a tubular organ, such as a blood vessel or an intestine. **2.** A unit used to measure the amount of light passing through a given area per second. One lumen is equal to the amount of light that passes through a given area (shaped like a cone) that is illuminated by a light with a brightness of one candela.

luminary (lōō′mə-nĕr′ē) *n., pl.* **luminaries 1.** A celestial object that gives off light, particularly the sun or moon. **2.** A famous person, especially one noted for high achievement: *a luminary of stage and screen.*

luminescence (lōō′mə-nĕs′əns) *n.* The production of light accompanied by little heat and at a temperature below that of incandescent bodies. Fluorescence and phosphorescence are examples of luminescence that can be produced by biochemical or chemical processes. —**lu′mi·nes′cent** *adj.*

luminosity (lōō′mə-nŏs′ĭ-tē) *n., pl.* **luminosities 1.** The condition or property of being luminous. **2.** Something luminous.

luminous (loō′mə-nəs) *adj.* **1.** Giving off its own light; shining: *the luminous firefly.* **2.** Full of light; bright: *a full luminous moon.* **3.** Easily understood; clear: *simple luminous prose.* —**lu′mi·nous·ly** *adv.*

lummox (lŭm′əks) *n. Informal* A clumsy or stupid person.

lump¹ (lŭmp) *n.* **1.** An irregularly shaped mass or piece: *a lump of rock.* **2.** A small cube of sugar. **3.** A swelling or bump: *A lump rose on my finger where I was stung.* ❖ *adj.* **1.** Formed into a lump or lumps: *lump sugar.* **2.** Not divided into parts; whole: *We want the entire payment in one lump sum.* ❖ *v.* **lumped, lumping, lumps** —*tr.* To put or consider together as a single group: *I lumped my sheets and clothes together and washed them in one load.* —*intr.* To form into a lump or lumps: *The sauce lumped because we didn't stir it.*

lump² (lŭmp) *tr.v.* **lumped, lumping, lumps** *Informal* To endure or put up with something: *You can like my cooking or lump it.*

lumpectomy (lŭm-pĕk′tə-mē) *n., pl.* **lumpectomies** Surgical removal of a tumor from the breast, along with a small amount of surrounding tissue.

lumpy (lŭm′pē) *adj.* **lumpier, lumpiest** Full of or covered with lumps: *lumpy gravy.* —**lump′i·ness** *n.*

lunacy (loō′nə-sē) *n., pl.* **lunacies** **1.** Mental derangement. **2.** Foolish or reckless conduct.

lunar (loō′nər) *adj.* **1.** Relating to the moon: *lunar phases; a lunar crater.* **2.** Measured by the revolution of the moon around Earth: *a lunar calendar.*

lunar month *n.* An interval of about 29½ days between one new moon and the next, during which the moon makes one revolution around Earth relative to the sun.

lunar year *n.* A period of 12 lunar months, about 354⅓ days.

lunatic (loō′nə-tĭk) *n.* **1.** A mentally deranged person. **2.** A very foolish person. ❖ *adj.* **1.** Mentally deranged; mad. **2.** Relating to or for the mentally ill: *a lunatic asylum.* **3.** Wildly or recklessly foolish: *a lunatic idea.*

lunch (lŭnch) *n.* **1.** A meal eaten between breakfast and dinner, usually at midday. **2.** The food for this meal. ❖ *intr.v.* **lunched, lunching, lunches** To eat lunch.

luncheon (lŭn′chən) *n.* Lunch, often a formal lunch.

luncheonette (lŭn′chə-nĕt′) *n.* A restaurant that serves light meals such as breakfast or lunch.

lunchmeat (lŭnch′mēt′) *n.* Processed meat, often molded into a loaf and sliced for use in sandwiches or salads.

lunchroom (lŭnch′roōm′ *or* lŭnch′roōm′) *n.* The cafeteria or room in a building, such as a school, where light meals are served and eaten.

lung (lŭng) *n.* **1.** Either of two spongy organs that occupy the chest cavity of air-breathing vertebrates and provide oxygen to the blood while removing carbon dioxide. **2.** A similar organ found in some invertebrate animals.

lunge (lŭnj) *n.* **1.** A sudden thrust or pass, as with a sword. **2.** A sudden forward movement: *The fielder made a lunge for the ball.* ❖ *intr.v.* **lunged, lunging, lunges** To make a sudden forward movement: *The cat lunged at the bird.* —**lung′er** *n.*

lungfish (lŭng′fĭsh′) *n.* Any of several freshwater fishes of Africa, Australia, and South America, having gills as well as a lunglike organ that enables them to breathe air and survive out of water, especially during drought conditions.

lupine also **lupin** (loō′pən) *n.* Any of numerous plants having compound leaves and long spikes of variously colored flowers.

lupus (loō′pəs) *n.* A chronic inflammatory autoimmune disorder characterized by fatigue, fever, skin lesions, joint pain or arthritis, and anemia, and often affecting the kidneys, spleen, and various other organs.

lurch¹ (lûrch) *intr.v.* **lurched, lurching, lurches 1a.** To make an abrupt sudden movement: *The train lurched and moved away from the platform.* **b.** To move suddenly and unsteadily; stagger: *He lurched forward under the heavy load of his backpack.* **2.** To roll or pitch suddenly: *The ship lurched as the wave hit the bow.* ❖ *n.* **1.** A staggering or tottering movement. **2.** A sudden rolling or pitching: *The train gave a lurch and started out of the station.*

lurch² (lûrch) *n.* A condition of having lost a cribbage game by a wide margin. ◆ **in the lurch** In a difficult or embarrassing position.

lure (loōr) *n.* **1.** A strong attraction, charm, or enticement: *the lure of fame.* **2.** A decoy used in catching animals, especially an artificial bait used to attract and catch fish. ❖ *tr.v.* **lured, luring, lures** To attract or tempt, especially with a bait: *We lured the cat inside with a dish of food.*

lurid (loōr′ĭd) *adj.* **1.** Causing shock or horror: *a lurid description of a train crash.* **2.** Bright and intense in color; vivid: *The lurid flames of a distant fire lit up the night sky.* —**lu′rid·ly** *adv.* —**lu′rid·ness** *n.*

lurk (lûrk) *intr.v.* **lurked, lurking, lurks 1.** To wait out of view: *The cat lurked in the grass, waiting for the mouse to approach.* **2.** To move about secretly; sneak. **3.** To exist without being seen or suspected: *Danger lurked around every corner.* —**lurk′er** *n.*

luscious (lŭsh′əs) *adj.* **1.** Having a delicious taste or smell: *a luscious peach.* **2.** Appealing to the senses or the mind: *a luscious singing voice.* —**lus′cious·ly** *adv.*

lush¹ (lŭsh) *adj.* **lusher, lushest 1.** Having or covered in thick plentiful plant growth: *a lush green lawn.* **2.** Juicy and tender: *lush pears.* **3.** Luxurious; abundant and rich: *the lush decor of a royal palace.* —**lush′ly** *adv.* —**lush′ness** *n.*

lush² (lŭsh) *n. Slang* A drunkard.

lust (lŭst) *n.* **1.** Intense sexual desire. **2.** An overwhelming desire or craving: *a lust for power.* ❖ *intr.v.* **lusted, lusting, lusts** To have an intense or overwhelming desire: *The pirates lusted after riches.*

luster (lŭs′tər) *n.* **1.** Soft reflected light; sheen; gloss: *the luster of pearls.* **2.** Radiance of light; brightness: *the luster of the warming sun.* **3.** Glory; splendor: *Her newest discoveries add luster to her name.* **4.** The shiny metallic surface that is found on pottery and china.

lustful (lŭst′fəl) *adj.* Full of lust; lewd. —**lust′ful·ly** *adv.* —**lust′ful·ness** *n.*

lustre (lŭs′tər) *n. & v. Chiefly British* Variant of **luster.**

lustrous (lŭs′trəs) *adj.* **1.** Having luster; shining; gleaming: *a silk cloth with a lustrous sheen.* **2.** Well-known or distinguished; illustrious: *lustrous achievements.* —**lus′trous·ly** *adv.* —**lus′trous·ness** *n.*

lusty (lŭs′tē) *adj.* **lustier, lustiest** Full of strength and vitality; robust. —**lust′i·ly** *adv.* —**lust′i·ness** *n.*

lute (loōt) *n.* A stringed instrument having a body shaped like a pear sliced lengthwise and a fingerboard that has frets. It is played by plucking.

lutetium (loō-tē′shē-əm) *n. Symbol* **Lu** A silvery-white metallic element used in nuclear technology. Atomic number 71. See **Periodic Table.**

Lutheran (loō′thər-ən) *adj.* Relating to the German theologian and reformer Martin Luther (1483–1546) or the Protestant denomination founded on his teachings. ❖ *n.* A member of the Lutheran Church.

luthier (lōō′tē-ər) *n.* A person who makes or repairs stringed instruments, such as violins.

luxuriant (lŭg-zhŏŏr′ē-ənt *or* lŭk-shŏŏr′ē-ənt) *adj.* **1.** Growing abundantly; lush: *luxuriant vegetation.* **2.** Abundantly productive: *luxuriant fields.* **3.** Highly ornamented: *a luxuriant dining room.* —**lux·u′ri·ance** *n.* —**lux·u′ri·ant·ly** *adv.*

luxuriate (lŭg-zhŏŏr′ē-āt′ *or* lŭk-shŏŏr′ē-āt′) *intr.v.* **luxuriated, luxuriating, luxuriates 1.** To indulge oneself in luxury: *We luxuriated by taking a room in the expensive hotel.* **2.** To take great pleasure or delight: *luxuriate in the warm sunshine.*

luxurious (lŭg-zhŏŏr′ē-əs *or* lŭk-shŏŏr′ē-əs) *adj.* **1.** Fond of luxury: *a luxurious taste for expensive clothes.* **2.** Providing great pleasure or comfort, especially at great cost: *luxurious bedsheets that are made of silk.* —**lux·u′ri·ous·ly** *adv.* —**lux·u′ri·ous·ness** *n.*

luxury (lŭg′zhə-rē *or* lŭk′shə-rē) *n., pl.* **luxuries 1.** Something that is not essential but gives pleasure or comfort: *Eating in a good restaurant is a luxury I can't afford these days.* **2.** A way of living that brings comfort; use of the best or most costly things: *live in luxury.* ❖ *adj.* Providing luxury: *a luxury car.*

–ly¹ A suffix that means: **1.** Having the characteristics of; like: *sisterly.* **2.** Recurring at a specified interval of time: *hourly.*

–ly² A suffix that means: **1.** In a specified manner: *gradually.* **2.** At a specified interval: *weekly.*

lyceum (lī-sē′əm) *n.* **1.** A hall in which lectures and concerts are presented. **2.** An organization that sponsors educational programs and entertainment.

lychee also **litchi** or **lichee** (lē′chē) *n., pl.* **lychees** or **litchis 1.** A sweet edible fruit of a tree native to China, having leathery red skin with white pulp and a large seed. **2.** The tree that bears such fruit.

lye (lī) *n.* **1.** A strong alkaline solution made by allowing water to wash through wood ashes, used in making soap and in cleaning. **2.** Sodium hydroxide.

lying¹ (lī′ĭng) *v.* Present participle of **lie¹**.

lying² (lī′ĭng) *v.* Present participle of **lie²**. ❖ *adj.* Given to or marked by falsehood: *a lying witness.*

Lyme disease (līm) *n.* A disease caused by bacteria and usually characterized by skin rash, chills, fever, and fatigue often lasting for several weeks. It is transmitted by deer ticks.

lymph (līmf) *n.* The clear fluid that flows through the vessels of the lymphatic system. Lymph carries waste from tissues and transports white blood cells.

lymphatic (lĭm-făt′ĭk) *adj.* Relating to or carrying lymph.

lymphatic system *n.* A network of vessels, tissues, and organs in vertebrate animals that regulates fluid balance by draining excess fluid from the tissues and returning it to the blood and that also produces and carries cells that help the body fight disease. In humans the lymphatic system includes the bone marrow, thymus, spleen, and lymph nodes.

lymph node *n.* Any of the small, bean-shaped masses of tissue found along the vessels of the lymphatic system. Lymph nodes filter foreign substances from the blood and may become swollen during infection.

lymphocyte (līm′fə-sīt′) *n.* Any of various white blood cells that are formed in the lymphatic system and function as part of the body's immune system. Lymphocytes include B cells and T cells.

lymphoid (līm′foid′) *adj.* Relating to lymph, lymphocytes, or the lymphatic system.

lymphoma (līm-fō′mə) *n., pl.* **lymphomata** (līm-fō′mə-tə) or **lymphomas 1.** Any of various cancers of the lymphocytes. **2.** Any of various usually malignant tumors that arise in the lymph nodes or in other lymphoid tissue.

lynch (līnch) *tr.v.* **lynched, lynching, lynches** To execute (a person), especially by hanging, without due process of law. —**lynch′er** *n.*

lynx (līngks) *n., pl.* **lynx** or **lynxes** Any of several wild cats having thick soft fur, tufted ears, and a short tail.

lyonnaise (lī′ə-nāz′ *or* lē′ə-nĕz′) *adj.* Cooked with onion: *lyonnaise potatoes.*

Lyra (lī′rə) *n.* A constellation in the Northern Hemisphere traditionally pictured as a lyre.

lyre (līr) *n.* A stringed instrument related to the harp that has two curved arms connected at the upper end by a crossbar. It is used to accompany a singer or reciter of poetry, as was commonly done in ancient Greece.

lyrebird (līr′bûrd′) *n.* An Australian bird, the male of which has a long tail that is shaped like a lyre when spread.

lyric (līr′ĭk) *adj.* **1.** Relating to poetry that expresses personal feelings and thoughts. **2.** Relating to musical drama, especially opera. ❖ *n.* **1.** A lyric poem. **2.** often **lyrics** The words of a song.

lyrical (līr′ĭ-kəl) *adj.* **1.** Expressing deep personal feelings or thoughts: *a lyrical description of her youth.* **2.** Lyric.

lyricism (līr′ĭ-sīz′əm) *n.* The quality of being lyric; lyric expression.

lyricist (līr′ĭ-sĭst) *n.* A writer of song lyrics or of lyric poetry.

lysine (lī′sēn′) *n.* An essential amino acid that is formed by the reaction of certain proteins with water.

lysis (lī′sĭs) *n., pl.* **lyses** (lī′sēz′) The destruction of a cell, as by a virus.

lysosome (lī′sə-sōm′) *n.* A structure in animal cells that contains enzymes that break down cellular waste materials and food particles or other materials from outside the cell.

lytic (lĭt′ĭk) *adj.* Relating to lysis.

Mm

m[1] or **M** (ĕm) *n., pl.* **m's** or **M's** or **Ms** The 13th letter of the English alphabet.

m[2] An abbreviation of: **1.** mass. **2.** meter (measurement). **3.** minute.

M[1] also **m** The symbol for the Roman numeral 1,000.

M[2] An abbreviation of: **1.** male. **2.** medium. **3.** Monsieur **4.** month.

M. An abbreviation of master.

ma (mä *or* mô) *n. Informal* Mother.

MA An abbreviation of Master of Arts.

ma'am (măm) *n.* Madam.

macabre (mə-kä′brə *or* mə-käb′) *adj.* Suggesting the horror of death or injury; gruesome: *a macabre play set during a plague.*

macadam (mə-kăd′əm) *n.* Pavement made of layers of small stones packed together, now usually bound with asphalt or tar.

macadamia nut (măk′ə-dā′mē-ə) *n.* The round, hard-shelled nut or the edible white kernel of either of two evergreen trees native to Australia and widely cultivated in Hawaii.

macadamize (mə-kăd′ə-mīz′) *tr.v.* **macadamized, macadamizing, macadamizes** To build or pave (a road) with macadam.

macaque (mə-kăk′ *or* mə-käk′) *n.* Any of several monkeys of Asia and northern Africa having short tails.

macaroni (măk′ə-rō′nē) *n.* Pasta in any of various hollow shapes, especially short curved tubes.

macaroon (măk′ə-rōōn′) *n.* A chewy cookie made with sugar, egg whites, and ground almonds or coconut.

macaw (mə-kô′) *n.* Any of various large, often brightly colored parrots with a long tail and strong beak, found in Mexico and Central and South America.

mace[1] (mās) *n.* **1.** A heavy club with a spiked metal head, used as a weapon in medieval times. **2.** A ceremonial staff carried or displayed as a symbol of authority.

mace[2] (mās) *n.* A spice made from the bright red covering of the seed of the nutmeg.

WORD HISTORY Mace[1] comes from Middle English *mace*, which comes from Old French *masse*, both meaning "heavy club." **Mace**[2] comes from Middle English *macis*, referring to the same spice as in Modern English.

Mace A trademark for an aerosol spray that causes irritation to the eyes, skin, and respiratory tract, used to repel an attacker.

Macedonian (măs′ĭ-dō′nē-ən) *adj.* Relating to ancient or modern Macedonia or its peoples, languages, or cultures. ❖ *n.* **1.** A native or inhabitant of ancient or modern Macedonia. **2.** The language of ancient Macedonia. **3.** The Slavic language of modern Macedonia.

macerate (măs′ə-rāt′) *v.* **macerated, macerating, macerates** — *tr.* **1.** To make soft by soaking in a liquid: *Macerate strawberries in sweetened water before serving them.* **2.** To

cause (the body) to become thin. — *intr.* To become soft by soaking.

Mach also **mach** (mäk) *n.* Mach number.

machete (mə-shĕt′ē *or* mə-chĕt′ē) *n.* A large heavy knife with a broad blade, used as a weapon and as a tool for clearing paths and cutting sugar cane.

Machiavellian (măk′ē-ə-vĕl′ē-ən) *adj.* **1.** Relating to the ideas of the Italian political theorist Niccolò Machiavelli (1469–1527), whose book *The Prince* describes the achievement and maintenance of power by a ruler who is indifferent to moral concerns. **2.** Showing or being deceptive or underhanded; crafty; cunning: *accused the politician of using Machiavellian methods to gain supporters.* ❖ *n.* A person who follows Machiavelli's political principles or who uses cunning and deceit to achieve or maintain power.

machination (măk′ə-nā′shən *or* măsh′ə-nā′shən) *n.* A cunning scheme or plot to do something harmful.

machine (mə-shēn′) *n.* **1.** A device of fixed and moving parts for performing tasks: *a washing machine.* **2.** A simple device that applies force or changes its direction. The gear, inclined plane, lever, and screw are all simple machines. **3.** A person who acts or performs a task mechanically without thinking. **4.** An organized group of people that controls the policies and activities of a political party in an area: *the key members of the local political machine.* **5.** A computer: *The librarian can't check out books right now because the machine is down.* **6.** An answering machine. ❖ *tr.v.* **machined, machining, machines** To cut, shape, or finish by machine: *The workers machine metal at the factory.*

machine gun *n.* A gun that fires rapidly and repeatedly when the trigger is pressed.

machine-gun (mə-shēn′gŭn′) *tr.v.* **machine-gunned, machine-gunning, machine-guns** To fire at with a machine gun.

machinery (mə-shē′nə-rē *or* mə-shēn′rē) *n., pl.* **machineries 1.** Machines or machine parts considered as a group: *The factory is full of machinery.* **2.** The working parts of a particular machine: *The machinery of an automobile engine includes pistons and gears.* **3.** A system of people or things that operate together to keep something going: *the complex machinery of modern society.*

machine shop *n.* A workshop where machines or machine parts are made, finished, or repaired.

machine tool *n.* A power-driven tool used to cut or shape metal.

machinist (mə-shē′nĭst) *n.* **1.** A person skilled in the use of machine tools to work metal. **2.** A person who makes, operates, or repairs machines.

machismo (mä-chēz′mō) *n.* An exaggerated sense of manliness that places great value on strength, courage, and aggressiveness.

Mach number also **mach number** (mäk) *n.* The ratio of the speed of an object to the speed of sound in a particular surrounding medium. For example, an aircraft flying through air at twice the speed of sound has a Mach number of 2.

macho (mä′chō) *adj.* Characterized by or showing machismo: *The cowboy has a macho image.* ❖ *n., pl.* **machos 1.** Machismo. **2.** A person characterized by machismo.

macintosh (măk′ĭn-tŏsh′) *n.* Variant of **mackintosh.**

mackerel (măk′ər-əl *or* măk′rəl) *n., pl.* **mackerel** or **mackerels** Any of several silvery fishes, especially one of the northern Atlantic Ocean that has dark markings on the back and is used as food.

mackerel sky *n.* A sky covered with a series of small, puff-like clouds resembling the scales of a mackerel.

mackinaw (măk′ə-nô′) *n.* A short coat of heavy, usually plaid woolen material.

Mackinaw blanket *n.* A thick woolen blanket in solid colors or stripes, formerly used in northern and western North America.

mackintosh also **macintosh** (măk′ĭn-tŏsh′) *n. Chiefly British* A raincoat.

macramé (măk′rə-mā′) *n.* Coarse lacework made by weaving and knotting threads or cords into a pattern.

macro– A prefix that means large: *macrophage.* —SEE NOTE AT **micro–.**

macrobiotics (măk′rō-bī-ŏt′ĭks) *n. (used with a singular verb)* A theory or practice of promoting well-being and longevity, principally by means of a diet consisting of unprocessed foods such as whole grains, vegetables, and beans. —**mac′ro·bi·ot′ic** *adj.*

macrocosm (măk′rə-kŏz′əm) *n.* The entire world; the universe.

macron (mā′krŏn′ *or* măk′rŏn′) *n.* **1.** A mark (‾) placed over a vowel to show that it has a long sound, as in (ā), the vowel sound in *make.* **2.** A similar mark used to indicate that a syllable is stressed in a foot of verse.

macrophage (măk′rə-fāj′) *n.* Any of the large cells of the immune system that engulf and destroy pathogens that enter the body.

mad (măd) *adj.* **madder, maddest 1.** Very irritated; angry: *The unfair accusation made me mad.* **2a.** Having a serious mental disorder, especially one that distorts the perception of reality. **b.** Characteristic of such illness: *mad laughter.* **3.** Mentally or emotionally agitated or distressed: *He's been going mad with jealousy.* **4.** Very foolish or unwise: *a mad idea.* **5.** Feeling or showing strong liking or enthusiasm: *He is mad about skiing.* **6.** Wildly excited or confused; frantic: *a mad scramble for the bus.* **7.** Affected by rabies; rabid: *a mad dog.* ◆ **like mad** *Informal* **1.** With great energy; rapidly: *ran like mad.* **2.** To a great extent: *It's snowing like mad.* —**mad′ly** *adv.*

madam (măd′əm) *n.* Used as a polite form of address for a woman: *Right this way, madam.*

Madame (mə-dăm′ *or* măd′əm) *n., pl.* **Mesdames** (mā-däm′ *or* mā-dăm′) Used as a courtesy title before the name of a woman, especially a married woman, in a French-speaking area: *Madame Cartier.*

madcap (măd′kăp′) *adj.* Not sensible; rash; impulsive: *a madcap idea.*

mad cow disease *n.* A fatal disease of cattle in which the tissues of the brain deteriorate and take on a spongy appearance, resulting in abnormal behaviors and loss of muscle control. A form of the disease can be transmitted

to humans through the eating of infected meat.

madden (măd′n) *v.* **maddened, maddening, maddens** —*tr.* To make mad: *Heat and the flies maddened the horse.* —*intr.* To become mad.

maddening (măd′n-ĭng) *adj.* Causing great anger; infuriating: *a maddening racket outside my window.* —**mad′den·ing·ly** *adv.*

madder (măd′ər) *n.* **1.** A Eurasian plant having small yellow flowers and a fleshy red root that is the source of dye. **2.** A red dye made from the root of this plant.

made (mād) *v.* Past tense and past participle of **make.** ❖ *adj.* **1.** Constructed, shaped, or formed: *a carefully made piece.* **2.** Assured of success: *a made man.* ◆ **made for** Perfectly suited for: *Those two are made for each other.*

madeleine (măd′ə-lĕn′) *n.* A small rich cake, baked in a mold that is shaped like a shell.

Mademoiselle (măd′ə-mə-zĕl′ *or* măd-mwä-zĕl′) *n., pl.* **Mademoiselles** (măd′ə-mə-zĕlz′ *or* măd-mwä-zĕlz′) or **Mesdemoiselles** (măd′mwä-zĕl′) Used as a courtesy title before the name of a girl or an unmarried woman in a French-speaking area: *Mademoiselle Leblanc.*

made-to-order (măd′tōō-ôr′dər) *adj.* Made in accordance with particular instructions or requirements; custom-made: *a made-to-order suit.*

made-up (măd′ŭp′) *adj.* **1.** Not real; imaginary; invented: *made-up stories.* **2.** Covered with cosmetics or makeup: *the clown's made-up face.*

madhouse (măd′hous′) *n.* **1.** *Offensive* A hospital or asylum for people with mental disorders. **2.** *Informal* A place of great confusion or disorder.

madman (măd′măn′ *or* măd′mən) *n.* A man who is or appears to be mentally ill.

madness (măd′nĭs) *n.* **1.** The condition of being mentally deranged. **2.** Great folly: *It was sheer madness to attempt the drive during a blizzard.* **3.** Enthusiasm; excitement: *the madness of Mardi Gras.*

Madonna (mə-dŏn′ə) *n.* The Virgin Mary, especially as depicted in religious art.

madras (măd′rəs *or* mə-drăs′ *or* mə-dräs′) *n.* A lightweight cotton cloth, usually having a plaid, striped, or checked pattern.

madrigal (măd′rĭ-gəl) *n.* **1.** A musical composition written for two or more unaccompanied voices. **2.** A short poem about love that can be set to music.

madwoman (măd′wŏŏm′ən) *n.* A woman who is or appears to be mentally ill.

maelstrom (māl′strəm) *n.* **1.** A large and violent whirlpool. **2.** A violent or turbulent situation: *the maelstrom of war.*

maestro (mīs′trō) *n., pl.* **maestros** or **maestri** (mīs′trē) A master in an art, especially a conductor, composer, or music teacher.

Mafia (mä′fē-ə) *n.* **1.** A secret criminal organization that originated in the Italian island of Sicily, employs violence against people who do not cooperate with it, and operates especially in Italy and the United States. **2.** Any of various similar criminal organizations, especially when dominated by members of a single nationality.

magazine (măg′ə-zēn′ *or* măg′ə-zēn′) *n.* **1.** A publication, often issued weekly or monthly, that contains written matter, such as articles or stories, and usually pictures and advertising. **2.** A building or room in a fort or on a warship where ammunition is stored. **3.** In some firearms, a container in which cartridges are held until they pass into the chamber for firing.

Magellanic Clouds (măj′ə-lăn′ĭk) *pl.n.* Two small galaxies that are the galaxies closest to the Milky Way.

magenta (mə-jĕn′tə) *n.* A bright purplish-red.

maggot (măg′ət) *n.* The legless, soft-bodied, wormlike larva of any of various flies, usually found in decaying matter.

magi (mā′jī′) *n.* Plural of **magus**.

magic (măj′ĭk) *n.* **1.** The art that claims to use supernatural powers to control natural events, effects, or forces through charms, spells, or rituals. **2.** The art or skill of using sleight of hand and other tricks to produce entertaining and baffling effects. **3.** A mysterious quality that seems to enchant; a special charm: *the magic of the woods in the fall.* ❖ *adj.* Relating to magic and its practice: *a magic trick; a magic wand.*

magical (măj′ĭ-kəl) *adj.* **1.** Relating to or produced by magic: *the magical appearance of a rabbit from a hat.* **2.** Enchanting; charming: *a magical performance of the play.* —**mag′i·cal·ly** *adv.*

magician (mə-jĭsh′ən) *n.* **1.** A person who uses magic; a sorcerer; a wizard. **2.** An entertainer who performs tricks of magic.

magic lantern *n.* An early kind of slide projector.

magisterial (măj′ĭ-stîr′ē-əl) *adj.* **1.** Relating to a magistrate or a magistrate's official functions: *magisterial duties.* **2.** Having or showing authority; authoritative: *a magisterial account of the American Revolution.* **3.** Domineering; overbearing; dogmatic: *The director's magisterial attitude offended the actors.* —**mag′is·te′ri·al·ly** *adv.*

magistracy (măj′ĭs-trə-sē) *n., pl.* **magistracies 1.** The position, duties, or term of office of a magistrate. **2.** A body of magistrates.

magistrate (măj′ĭ-strāt′ *or* măj′ĭ-strĭt) *n.* **1.** A civil official with the authority to administer the law. **2.** A judge, such as a justice of the peace, who has limited authority.

magma (măg′mə) *n.* The molten rock material under the earth's crust that forms igneous rock when it has cooled.

Magna Carta or **Magna Charta** (măg′nə kär′tə) *n.* A document of English political and civil liberties issued by King John in 1215. The Magna Carta guaranteed certain liberties to the people of England and limited the king's power.

magna cum laude (măg′nə kōōm lou′də) *adv.* With high honors. Used to show that someone has achieved academic distinction: *graduate magna cum laude.*

magnanimity (măg′nə-nĭm′ĭ-tē) *n., pl.* **magnanimities** The quality of being magnanimous; nobility.

magnanimous (măg-năn′ə-məs) *adj.* Moral and dignified, especially in showing kindness or forgiveness; generous and unselfish: *a magnanimous person.* —**mag·nan′i·mous·ly** *adv.*

magnate (măg′nāt′ *or* măg′nĭt) *n.* A powerful and influential person, especially in business: *a real estate magnate.*

magnesia (măg-nē′zhə *or* măg-nē′shə) *n.* Magnesium oxide.

magnesium (măg-nē′zē-əm *or* măg-nē′zhəm) *n. Symbol* **Mg** A lightweight, moderately hard, silvery metallic element that burns with an intense white flame and is an essential component of chlorophyll. Atomic number 12. See **Periodic Table**.

magnesium oxide *n.* A white powdery compound, MgO, used in making electrical insulation, cosmetics, antacids, and pharmaceuticals.

magnet (măg′nĭt) *n.* **1.** A stone, piece of metal, or other solid that has the property, either natural or induced, of attracting iron or steel. **2.** An electromagnet. **3.** A person, place, object, or situation that exerts a powerful attraction: *Our garden is a magnet for rabbits.*

magnetic (măg-nĕt′ĭk) *adj.* **1.** Relating to magnetism or magnets. **2.** Having the properties of a magnet; showing magnetism. **3.** Producing, caused by, or operating by magnetism: *a magnetic compass; a magnetic recording.* **4.** Relating to the magnetic properties of the earth: *The earth's magnetic north pole is in a different place from the geographic North Pole.* **5.** Having the power to attract or charm: *a popular performer with a magnetic personality.* —**mag·net′i·cal·ly** *adv.*

magnetic disk *n.* A memory device, such as a hard disk, that is covered with a magnetic coating. Data is encoded on the disk by magnetizing extremely small iron particles that are scattered throughout the coating.

magnetic field *n.* A condition found in the region around a magnet or an electric current, characterized by the existence of a detectable magnetic force at every point in the region and by the existence of magnetic poles.

magnetic flux *n.* A measure of the strength of the magnetic field around a magnet or an electric current. It is based on the total number of magnetic lines of force that pass through a specific area.

magnetic needle *n.* A narrow thin piece of magnetized steel for use in a compass. It points toward the earth's magnetic poles.

magnetic north *n.* The direction in which the earth's north magnetic pole lies, to which the magnetic needle of a compass points. In most places, magnetic north differs from the true or geographic north.

magnetic pole *n.* **1.** Either of two regions of a magnet where the magnetic field is strongest. **2.** Either of two variable points on the earth's surface toward which a compass needle points. The magnetic poles differ from the geographic poles. The north magnetic pole is in the Arctic, and the south magnetic pole is in Antarctica.

magnetic resonance imaging *n.* A technique that uses a magnetic field and radio waves to produce images of structures inside the body.

magnetic tape *n.* A plastic tape coated with tiny magnetic particles for use in recording sounds or pictures.

magnetism (măg′nĭ-tĭz′əm) *n.* **1.** The force produced by a magnetic field. **2.** The properties or effects of magnets: *Magnetism causes a compass needle to point north.* **3.** An unusual power to attract or influence: *The popular leader had a great deal of personal magnetism.*

magnetite (măg′nĭ-tīt′) *n.* A mineral composed of iron oxide that is strongly attracted by a magnet and is an important iron ore.

magnetize (măg′nĭ-tīz′) *tr.v.* **magnetized, magnetizing, magnetizes** To make (an object) magnetic: *You can magnetize a nail by wrapping it in a wire that will carry an electric current.* —**mag′net·i·za′tion** (măg′nĭ-tĭ-zā′shən) *n.* —**mag′net·iz′er** *n.*

magneto (măg-nē′tō) *n., pl.* **magnetos** A device that produces alternating current and is used to fire spark plugs in some internal-combustion engines.

magnetron (măg′nĭ-trŏn′) *n.* A type of electron tube that produces microwave radiation by applying magnetic and electric fields to a stream of electrons that a heated filament emits. Magnetrons are used in radar and in microwave ovens.

magnet school *n.* A public school designed to attract students from a wide geographic area by offering specialized educational programs, often in a specific area, such as science, the humanities, or art.

magnification (măg′nə-fĭ-kā′shən) *n.* The act, process, or degree of magnifying.

magnificence (măg-nĭf′ĭ-səns) *n.* Richness or splendor of surroundings; grand or imposing beauty: *the magnificence of the Grand Canyon.*

magnificent (măg-nĭf′ĭ-sənt) *adj.* **1.** Splendid in appearance; grand; remarkable: *a magnificent cathedral.* See Synonyms at **grand. 2.** Outstanding of its kind; excellent: *a magnificent place for sailing.* —**mag·nif′i·cent·ly** *adv.*

magnify (măg′nə-fī′) *v.* **magnified, magnifying, magnifies** —*tr.* **1.** To make (an object) appear larger than it really is: *A microscope magnifies the cell so that you can study it.* **2.** To cause to appear greater or seem more important; exaggerate: *The wind magnifies the effect of the cold.* —*intr.* To make or be capable of making an object appear larger than it really is. —**mag′ni·fi′er** *n.*

magnifying glass (măg′nə-fī′ĭng) *n.* A lens or combination of lenses that makes objects appear larger than they really are.

magnitude (măg′nĭ-tōōd′) *n.* **1.** Greatness, as of position, size, or significance: *finally understood the magnitude of the problem.* **2.** A measure of the total amount of energy released by an earthquake, as indicated on the Richter scale. **3.** The relative brightness of a star or other celestial object as measured on a numerical scale in which lower numbers mean greater brightness.

magnolia (măg-nōl′yə) *n.* **1.** Any of numerous trees or shrubs having large white, pink, or yellow flowers that are often fragrant. **2.** The flower of such a tree or shrub.

magnum opus (măg′nəm ō′pəs) *n.* **1.** A great work, especially a literary or artistic masterpiece. **2.** The greatest single work of an artist, writer, or composer.

magpie (măg′pī′) *n.* **1.** Any of various usually black and white birds that have a long tail and a loud, harsh call. **2.** A person who chatters.

maguey (mə-gā′ *or* măg′wā) *n., pl.* **magueys 1.** Any of various agaves of Mexico that are harvested for their sap and for their large stiff leaves, which yield a fiber used for making rope or twine. **2.** The fiber of such a plant.

magus (mā′gəs) *n., pl.* **magi** (mā′jī′) **1.** A member of the Zoroastrian priestly caste of the Medes and Persians. **2. Magus** In the New Testament, one of the wise men from the East who traveled to Bethlehem to pay homage to the infant Jesus. **3.** A sorcerer; a magician. —**ma′gi·an** (mā′jē-ən) *adj.*

Magyar (măg′yär′ *or* mä′dyär′) *n.* **1.** A member of the main ethnic group of Hungary. **2.** The language of the Magyars; Hungarian. —**Mag′yar** *adj.*

maharaja or **maharajah** (mä′hə-rä′jə *or* mä′hə-rä′zhə) *n.* A king or prince in India ranking above a raja.

maharani or **maharanee** (mä′hə-rä′nē) *n., pl.* **maharanis** or **maharanees 1.** The wife of a maharaja. **2.** A princess in India ranking above a rani.

mahatma (mə-hät′mə *or* mə-hăt′mə) *n.* **1.** In Hinduism, a person revered for great knowledge and love of humanity. **2. Mahatma** Used especially in Hinduism as a title of respect for a holy person.

Mahican (mə-hē′kən) also **Mohican** (mō-hē′kən *or* mə-hē′kən) *n., pl.* **Mahican** or **Mahicans** also **Mohican** or **Mohicans 1.** A member of a Native American people, for-

merly living in eastern New York, with populations now living in Oklahoma and Wisconsin. **2.** The Algonquian language of the Mahican.

mahjong also **mahjongg** (mä′zhŏng′) *n.* A game of Chinese origin usually played by four people using tiles bearing various designs. Each player tries to win by forming certain combinations by drawing and discarding tiles.

mahogany (mə-hŏg′ə-nē) *n., pl.* **mahoganies 1a.** Any of various tropical American trees having hard reddish-brown wood. **b.** The wood of such a tree or a similar tree, used in making furniture and musical instruments. **2.** A reddish brown.

mahout (mə-hout′) *n.* The keeper and driver of an elephant.

maid (mād) *n.* **1.** A housemaid or chambermaid. **2.** A woman servant. **3.** *Archaic* An unmarried girl or woman.

maiden (mād′n) *n. Archaic* An unmarried girl or woman. ❖ *adj.* **1.** Relating to or suited to a maiden: *youthful maiden beauty.* **2.** Unmarried. Used of a girl or woman: *a maiden aunt.* **3.** First or earliest: *a ship's maiden voyage.*

maidenhair fern (mād′n-hâr′) *n.* Any of various ferns having thin dark stalks and delicate feathery fronds.

maidenhood (mād′n-hŏŏd′) *n.* The quality or condition of being a maiden.

maiden name *n.* The surname that a girl is given at birth and that some women change when they marry.

maid in waiting *n., pl.* **maids in waiting** An unmarried woman who attends a queen or princess.

maid of honor *n., pl.* **maids of honor 1.** An unmarried woman who is the bride's chief attendant at a wedding. **2.** An unmarried noblewoman who attends a queen or princess.

maidservant (mād′sûr′vənt) *n.* A woman servant.

mail[1] (māl) *n.* **1a.** Letters, postcards, packages, and printed matter sent through a postal system. **b.** Such materials for a specified person or organization: *What came in the mail today?* **2.** often **mails** A system by which letters and other postal materials are transported. **3.** Mail or messages sent electronically; email. ❖ *tr.v.* **mailed, mailing, mails** To send by mail.

mail[2] (māl) *n.* Flexible armor made of connected metal rings, loops of chain, or overlapping scales, worn to protect the body in battle.

WORD HISTORY Mail[1] comes from Middle English *male,* meaning "bag." **Mail**[2] comes from Middle English *maille,* which comes from Old French *maile* (both having the same meaning as the Modern English word), which comes from Latin *macula,* meaning "blemish, mesh."

mailbag (māl′băg′) *n.* A large canvas sack that is used for carrying mail.

mailbox (māl′bŏks′) *n.* **1.** A public box for depositing outgoing mail. **2.** A private box where incoming mail is delivered. **3.** A computer file or set of files for collecting and storing email.

mail carrier *n.* A person who delivers mail or collects it from mailboxes.

mailing (mā′lĭng) *n.* Something sent by mail: *The senator sent out a mailing that explained her voting record.*

mailman (māl′măn′ *or* māl′mən) *n.* A man who carries and delivers mail.

mail order *n.* An order for goods to be shipped through the mail.

mailroom (māl′rōōm′ *or* māl′rŏŏm′) *n.* A room where all of the mail that is sent to or from a company is handled.

mailwoman (māl′wŏŏm′ən) *n.* A woman who carries and delivers mail.

maim (mām) *tr.v.* **maimed, maiming, maims** To disable, usually by causing the loss of the use of a limb: *Accidents maim many people each year.*

main (mān) *adj.* Most important; principal; chief: *Look for the main idea in each paragraph. The main reason I want to travel to Italy is to see the museums.* ❖ *n.* **1.** A large pipe, duct, conduit, or conductor used to carry water, oil, gas, or electricity. **2.** The open sea. ◆ **in the main** For the most part; on the whole: *Your ideas are, in the main, useful.*

main clause *n.* The independent clause in a complex sentence. For example, in the sentence *When we reached the summit, we admired the view,* the clause *we admired the view* is the main clause.

main drag *n. Slang* The principal street of a city or town.

mainframe (mān′frām′) *n.* A powerful computer, often serving many terminals and usually used by large, complex organizations.

mainland (mān′lănd′ *or* mān′lənd) *n.* The principal land mass of a country, territory, or continent as opposed to its islands or peninsulas: *took a ferry across the strait to the mainland.*

mainly (mān′lē) *adv.* For the most part; chiefly: *The houses in this region are constructed mainly of stone.*

mainmast (mān′məst *or* mān′măst′) *n.* The principal mast of a sailing ship.

mainsail (mān′səl *or* mān′sāl′) *n.* The largest sail set on the mainmast of a sailing ship.

mainspring (mān′sprĭng′) *n.* **1.** The spring that drives a mechanism, especially a clock or watch. **2.** The most important cause or force: *A desire for justice was the mainspring of the reform movement.*

mainstay (mān′stā′) *n.* **1.** A main support: *Agriculture is a mainstay of the economy.* **2.** A strong rope or cable that holds in place the mainmast of a sailing vessel.

mainstream (mān′strēm′) *n.* The prevailing attitudes, values, and practices of a society or group: *Their ideas are outside the mainstream.* ❖ *tr.v.* **mainstreamed, mainstreaming, mainstreams** To integrate (a student with special needs) into regular school classes.

maintain (mān-tān′) *tr.v.* **maintained, maintaining, maintains 1.** To keep up; carry on; continue: *The train maintains its speed on hills. She maintained good relations with her former employer.* **2.** To keep in an existing state or condition: *maintained my composure during the ordeal.* **3.** To keep in good repair: *maintain public roads.* **4.** To provide for the upkeep of; bear the expenses of: *maintain a large family.* **5.** To defend against criticism or attack: *The politician maintained his stance against new taxes.* **6.** To declare as true; affirm: *maintain one's innocence.*

maintenance (mān′tə-nəns) *n.* **1.** The act of maintaining or the condition of being maintained: *maintenance of calm during the emergency; maintenance of the traditions by the family.* **2.** The work involved in maintaining; care; upkeep: *maintenance of an old building.* **3.** Means of support or livelihood: *Wages provide maintenance.*

maintop (mān′tŏp′) *n.* A platform on the mainmast of a ship.

main verb *n.* The verb in a verb phrase that expresses the action, state, or relation and is not an auxiliary verb. In the sentence *The bird has flown,* the main verb is *flown.*

main yard *n.* The yard or pole on which the mainsail of a sailing ship is extended.

maitre d' (mā′trə dē′ *or* mā′tər dē′) *n., pl.* **maitre d's**

(mā′trə dēz′ *or* mā′tər dēz′) *Informal* A headwaiter.

maize (māz) *n.* The corn plant or its edible kernels.

Maj. or **MAJ** An abbreviation of major (military rank).

majestic (mə-jĕs′tĭk) *adj.* Impressive or beautiful in a dignified or inspiring way. See Synonyms at **grand.** —**ma·jes′ti·cal** *adj.* —**ma·jes′ti·cal·ly** *adv.*

majesty (măj′ĭ-stē) *n., pl.* **majesties 1.** The greatness and dignity of a sovereign: *The royal couple arrived at the palace in all their majesty.* **2.** Supreme authority or power: *the majesty of the law.* **3. Majesty** Used as a title for a sovereign, such as a king or queen: *Your Majesty.* **4.** A quality of stateliness, splendor, or grandeur: *the majesty of the Rocky Mountains.*

Maj. Gen. or **MajGen** An abbreviation of major general.

major (mā′jər) *adj.* **1.** Greater than others in importance or rank: *a major American novelist.* **2.** Great in scope or effect: *a major improvement.* **3a.** Relating to or based on a major scale: *a major chord.* **b.** Relating to a musical tone that is a half step greater than a minor interval. ❖ *n.* **1.** An officer in the US Army, Air Force, or Marine Corps ranking above a captain and below a lieutenant colonel. **2.** In schools and colleges, a field of study chosen as a specialty: *My major is French.* **3.** A major scale, key, or interval: *the key of D major.* **4. majors** The major leagues of a sport, especially baseball. ❖ *intr.v.* **majored, majoring, majors** To study or specialize in a particular subject: *I am majoring in Spanish.*

major-domo (mā′jər-dō′mō) *n., pl.* **major-domos** The head steward or butler in the household of a sovereign or great noble.

majorette (mā′jə-rĕt′) *n.* **1.** A female dancer who twirls a baton, usually in a group and sometimes with a marching band. **2.** A drum majorette.

major general *n.* An officer in the US Army, Air Force, or Marine Corps ranking above a brigadier general and below a lieutenant general.

majority (mə-jôr′ĭ-tē) *n., pl.* **majorities 1.** The greater number or part of something; a number more than half of a total: *The majority of the class did well on the test.* **2.** The amount by which a greater number of votes exceeds the remaining number of votes: *The candidate won by a majority of 5,000 votes.* **3.** A political party or group that has the greater number of members or supporters: *The party is a majority in the city.* **4.** The status of having reached the age of legal responsibility, usually 18 or 21.

USAGE When **majority** refers to a particular number of votes, it takes a singular verb: *Her majority was five votes.* When it refers to a group of people or things that are in the majority, it may take either a singular or plural verb, depending on whether the group is considered as a whole or as a set of people considered individually. So we say *The majority elects the candidate it wants,* since the election is accomplished by the group as a whole, but we say *The majority of the voters live in the city,* since living in the city is something that each voter does individually.

major league *n.* **1.** Either of the two principal groups of professional baseball teams in the United States. **2.** A league of principal importance in other professional sports.

major-league (mā′jər-lēg′) *adj.* **1.** Relating to a major league: *a major-league player.* **2.** *Informal* Prominent or important: *a major-league decision.* **3.** *Informal* Extreme: *You are a major-league pain in the neck.*

major-leaguer (mā′jər-lē′gər) *n.* A member of a major-league sports team.

majorly (mā′jər-lē) *adv. Slang* To a great or an intense degree; extremely: *a lecture that was majorly boring.*

Major Prophets *n.* The biblical Books of Isaiah, Jeremiah, and Ezekiel.

major scale *n.* A musical scale in which the third and fourth tones and the seventh and eighth tones are separated by half steps and all other tones are separated by whole steps.

make (māk) *v.* **made** (mād), **making, makes** —*tr.* **1.** To cause to exist or happen; bring about; create: *The students made noise in the hall.* **2a.** To bring into existence by shaping, changing, or putting together material: *make a dress; make a wall of stones.* **b.** To draw up; establish; enact: *make rules.* **3.** To change from one form or function into another: *made clay into bricks.* **4.** To cause to be or become: *The invitation made us happy.* **5a.** To cause to act in a specified way: *The pepper made me sneeze.* **b.** To force; compel: *His allergies made him stay home.* **6.** To prepare; fix: *make breakfast.* **7.** To carry out, perform, or engage in: *make a phone call; make war.* **8.** To reach in time: *We just made the bus.* **9.** To acquire the rank of or a place on: *made lieutenant; made the baseball team.* **10.** To gain or acquire: *make money; make friends.* **11.** To be suited for: *This area would make a good soccer field.* **12.** To develop into: *She will make a fine doctor.* **13.** To arrange or agree to: *make a date.* **14a.** To formulate or arrive at one's mind: *make plans; make a decision.* **b.** To determine the meaning of: *What do you make of their proposal?* **15.** To form or amount to; constitute: *Two wrongs don't make a right.* **16.** To cover (a distance): *made 200 miles before sunset.* **17.** To assure the success of: *The scenery makes the movie.* —*intr.* **1.** To cause something to be in a specified manner: *The actors made ready for the play.* **2.** To go or move, as in a certain direction: *The ship made for harbor.* ❖ *n.* **1.** A style or manner in which something is made: *disliked the make of the coat.* **2.** A specific line of manufactured goods; a brand: *Three makes of small trucks are available.* **3.** The origin of a product's manufacturing: *a bicycle of French make.* ◆ **make a face** To distort the features of the face: *She made a face when she saw the moldy bread.* **make away with** To carry off; steal. **make believe** To pretend. **make do** To manage; get along. **make ends meet** To make enough money to pay one's expenses. **make for** To help promote; further: *The steady breeze made for excellent sailing.* **make fun of** To mock; ridicule. **make good 1.** To carry out successfully: *He made good his escape.* **2.** To fulfill: *I will make good my promise.* **3.** To make compensation for; make up for: *He made good the loss.* **4.** To succeed: *She made good as an artist.* **make it** *Informal* To be successful. **make light of** To treat as unimportant: *He made light of his promotion.* **make love 1.** To engage in amorous caressing. **2.** To engage in sexual intercourse. **make much of** To treat as of great importance. **make off** To depart in haste; run away: *She made off before I could thank her.* **make off with** To snatch or steal: *A thief made off with the jewelry.* **make out 1.** To see or identify, especially with difficulty: *Can you make out that sign?* **2.** To understand: *I can't make out what she means in the letter.* **3.** To write out or fill out: *make out a tax form.* **4.** *Informal* To represent as being: *You make me out to be a liar.* **5.** To get along in a given way; fare: *How are you making out with the dance lessons?* **6.** *Informal* To kiss and caress. **make over 1.** To redo; renovate. **2.** To change or

transfer the ownership of, usually by a legal document: *She made the property over to her son.* **make sense 1.** To be understandable: *The explanation made no sense.* **2.** To be practical or advisable: *It makes sense to go now.* **make something of** To start a fight or quarrel over. **make the best of** To accept (a bad situation) in as good a light as possible. **make the most of** To use to the greatest advantage. **make up 1.** To put together; construct or compose: *We made up a model of the new building.* **2.** To constitute; form: *A basketball team is made up of five players.* **3.** To apply cosmetics. **4.** To devise as a fiction or falsehood; invent: *make up a story.* **5.** To compensate for: *We made up the lost time by taking a short cut.* **6.** To resolve a quarrel: *They talked over the their differences and made up.* **7.** To take (an examination or course) again or at a later time. **make up (one's) mind** To come to a definite decision or opinion. —**mak′a·ble, make′a·ble** *adj.*

make-believe (māk′bĭ-lēv′) *n.* Playful imagining or acting as if one were another person or in an invented place: *Fairies exist in the land of make-believe.* ❖ *adj.* Imaginary; fictional.

maker (mā′kər) *n.* **1.** A person or thing that makes. **2. Maker** God: *prayed to their Maker.*

makeshift (māk′shĭft′) *adj.* Serving as a temporary substitute: *a makeshift table.* ❖ *n.* Something used or assembled as a temporary substitute: *I didn't have a chair, so I used the crate as a makeshift.*

makeup or **make-up** (māk′ŭp′) *n.* **1.** The way in which something is put together or arranged; construction: *What is the makeup of the police department?* **2.** The qualities or temperament that make up a personality; disposition: *It's just not in my makeup to complain.* **3.** Cosmetics applied especially to the face. **4.** A special examination given to a student who has missed or failed a previous one.

mal– A prefix that means bad or wrongly: *malpractice; malformed.*

Malachi (măl′ə-kī′) *n.* A book of the Bible in which the prophet Malachi warns the Jews to follow God's laws.

malachite (măl′ə-kīt′) *n.* A light green to dark green copper carbonate mineral. It is used as a source of copper and in making ornamental objects, jewelry, and stonework.

maladjusted (măl′ə-jŭs′tĭd) *adj.* Poorly adjusted to the demands or stresses of daily living.

maladjustment (măl′ə-jŭst′mənt) *n.* Inability to adjust to one's environment or one's circumstances.

maladroit (măl′ə-droit′) *adj.* Lacking skill; awkward or inept. —**mal′a·droit′ly** *adv.*

malady (măl′ə-dē) *n., pl.* **maladies 1.** A disease, disorder, or ailment. **2.** An unwholesome condition.

Malagasy (măl′ə-găs′ē) *n., pl.* **Malagasy** or **Malagasies 1.** A native or inhabitant of Madagascar. **2.** The Austronesian language of the Malagasy. ❖ *adj.* Relating to Madagascar, the Malagasy, or their language or culture.

malaise (mă-lāz′) *n.* A general feeling of discomfort or unease.

malamute also **malemute** (măl′ə-myōōt′) *n.* A large dog of a breed developed in the North American Arctic as a sled dog, having erect ears, a bushy tail, and a thick coat.

malapropism (măl′ə-prŏp-ĭz′əm) *n.* **1.** Ludicrous misuse of a word, especially by confusion with one of similar sound. **2.** An example of such misuse. —**mal′a·prop′i·an** (măl′ə-prŏp′ē-ən) *adj.*

malaria (mə-lâr′ē-ə) *n.* An infectious disease of tropical areas that is characterized by repeated episodes of chills, fever, and sweating. It is caused by a parasite that multiplies inside red blood cells and is transmitted by the bite of an infected mosquito. —**ma·lar′i·al** *adj.*

malarkey (mə-lär′kē) *n. Slang* Exaggerated or foolish talk, usually intended to deceive.

Malay (mə-lā′ *or* mā′lā′) *adj.* **1.** Relating to Malaysia or to the archipelago including eastern Malaysia, Indonesia, and the Philippines. **2.** Relating to a people inhabiting Malaysia and some adjacent regions. ❖ *n.* **1.** A member of this people. **2.** The language of this people. —**Ma·lay′an** (mə-lā′ən) *adj. & n.*

Malayalam (măl′ə-yä′ləm) *n.* A language spoken on the southwest coast of India.

malcontent (măl′kən-tĕnt′) *adj.* Dissatisfied with existing conditions. ❖ *n.* A dissatisfied or rebellious person.

male (māl) *adj.* **1a.** Relating to or characteristic of the sex that can fertilize egg cells and father offspring. **b.** Relating to or being a reproductive organ that produces male gametes: *male flower parts.* **c.** Relating to or being the gamete that is smaller and more motile than the other corresponding gamete: *male reproductive cells.* **2.** Composed of men or boys: *a male choir.* **3.** Designed to be inserted into a socket or opening: *a male plug.* ❖ *n.* **1.** A male organism. **2.** A man or boy. —**male′ness** *n.*

malediction (măl′ĭ-dĭk′shən) *n.* **1.** A curse: *a witch's malediction.* **2.** Slander.

malefactor (măl′ə-făk′tər) *n.* **1.** A person who has committed a crime; a criminal. **2.** An evildoer.

maleficent (mə-lĕf′ĭ-sənt) *adj.* Having a harmful influence or effect.

malevolence (mə-lĕv′ə-ləns) *n.* The wish for harm or evil to come to others; ill will; malice.

malevolent (mə-lĕv′ə-lənt) *adj.* Wishing harm to others; malicious. —**ma·lev′o·lent·ly** *adv.*

malfeasance (măl-fē′zəns) *n.* Wrongdoing or misconduct, especially by a public official: *An official who accepts a bribe is guilty of malfeasance.*

malformation (măl′fôr-mā′shən) *n.* **1.** The condition of being malformed; deformity. **2.** A body part that is malformed; a deformity.

malformed (măl-fôrmd′) *adj.* Having an imperfect or abnormal form: *blight that causes malformed ears of corn.*

malfunction (măl-fŭngk′shən) *intr.v.* **malfunctioned, malfunctioning, malfunctions** To fail to function properly. ❖ *n.* A failure to function well: *a malfunction in the computer.*

malice (măl′ĭs) *n.* **1.** The desire to harm others or to see others suffer; ill will; spite. **2.** The intent to commit an unlawful act without justification or excuse.

malicious (mə-lĭsh′əs) *adj.* Having, showing, or motivated by malice; deliberately harmful; spiteful: *told malicious lies.* —**ma·li′cious·ly** *adv.* —**ma·li′cious·ness** *n.*

malign (mə-līn′) *tr.v.* **maligned, maligning, maligns** To make evil, harmful, and often false statements about: *malign a person's reputation; maligned the other candidates in his speech.* ❖ *adj.* **1.** Evil in nature; injurious: *Poverty can be a malign influence.* **2.** Intending or threatening harm or ill will: *a malign look.*

malignancy (mə-lĭg′nən-sē) *n., pl.* **malignancies 1.** The quality or condition of being malignant. **2.** A malignant tumor or condition.

malignant (mə-lĭg′nənt) *adj.* **1a.** Threatening to life or health; deadly: *a malignant disease.* **b.** Tending to grow and spread throughout the body: *a malignant tumor.*

2. Having or showing ill will; malicious: *malignant thoughts.* —**ma·lig′nant·ly** *adv.*

malignity (mə-lĭg′nĭ-tē) *n., pl.* **malignities 1.** Intense ill will or hatred; malice. **2.** An act or feeling of great malice.

malinger (mə-lĭng′gər) *intr.v.* **malingered, malingering, malingers** To pretend to be ill or injured in order to avoid work or duty. —**ma·lin′ger·er** *n.*

mall (môl) *n.* **1.** A large shopping center containing different kinds of stores and businesses. **2.** A street lined with shops and closed to vehicles. **3.** A shady public walk or promenade.

mallard (măl′ərd) *n., pl.* **mallard** or **mallards** A wild duck, the male of which has a glossy green head and a white ring around the neck.

malleable (măl′ē-ə-bəl) *adj.* **1.** Capable of being shaped or formed, as by pressure or hammering: *copper and other malleable metals.* **2.** Easily controlled or influenced: *a boss who wanted a malleable workforce.* **3.** Able to adjust to changing circumstances; adaptable. —**mal′le·a·bil′i·ty** *n.*

mallet (măl′ĭt) *n.* **1a.** A hammer with a wooden head and a short handle, used to drive a chisel or wedge. **b.** A similar tool with a rubber, leather, or plastic head, used to strike a surface without damaging it. **2.** A long-handled hammer used to strike the ball in the games of croquet and polo.

malleus (măl′ē-əs) *n., pl.* **mallei** (măl′ē-ī′) The largest and outermost of the three small bones in the middle ear; the hammer.

mallow (măl′ō) *n.* Any of various plants having showy flowers that are pink, purple, or white and have five petals.

malnourished (măl-nûr′ĭsht) *adj.* Suffering from malnutrition: *food shipments for the malnourished refugees.*

malnutrition (măl′nōō-trĭsh′ən) *n.* Nutrition that is inadequate for the body's needs. Malnutrition can be caused by a poor diet or by the inability to digest food properly.

malocclusion (măl′ə-klōō′zhən) *n.* A condition in which the upper and lower teeth do not meet properly when the jaw is closed; a faulty bite.

malodorous (măl-ō′dər-əs) *adj.* Having a bad odor: *a malodorous swamp.* —**mal·o′dor·ous·ly** *adv.*

malpractice (măl-prăk′tĭs) *n.* Improper or substandard performance in providing professional services: *a doctor who had been sued by several patients for malpractice.*

malt (môlt) *n.* **1.** Barley or other grain that has been soaked in water and allowed to sprout and then dried. It is used chiefly in brewing and distilling. **2.** Malted milk. ❖ *tr.v.* **malted, malting, malts 1.** To make (grain) into malt. **2.** To mix or prepare with malt.

malted milk (môl′tĭd) *n.* A drink made of milk mixed with a powder of dried milk, malted barley, and wheat flour, often with the addition of ice cream and flavoring.

Maltese (môl-tēz′ *or* môl-tēs′) *adj.* Relating to Malta or its people, language, or culture. ❖ *n., pl.* **Maltese 1.** A native or inhabitant of Malta. **2.** The Semitic language of the Maltese. **3.** A dog of a toy breed having a long silky white coat.

Maltese cross *n.* A cross having the form of four arrowheads placed with their points toward the center of a circle.

maltose (môl′tōs′ *or* môl′tōz′) *n.* A sugar made by the action of various enzymes on starch. It is formed in the body during digestion.

maltreat (măl-trēt′) *tr.v.* **maltreated, maltreating, mal-**

treats To treat cruelly or roughly. —**mal·treat′ment** *n.*

malware (măl′wâr′) *n.* Computer software that is designed to do harm by interfering with normal computer functions or by sending personal data about the user to unauthorized parties over the Internet.

mama or **mamma** (mä′mə *or* mə-mä′) *n. Informal* Mother.

mambo (mäm′bō) *n., pl.* **mambos 1.** A Latin-American dance resembling the rumba. **2.** The music for this dance. ❖ *intr.v.* **mamboed, mamboing, mambos** To perform this dance.

mammal (măm′əl) *n.* Any of various warm-blooded animals that have a backbone, hair or fur, and, in the females, mammary glands that produce milk for feeding their young. Cats, dogs, bats, elephants, whales, humans, and kangaroos are all mammals. —**mam·ma′li·an** (mă-mā′lē-ən) *adj. & n.*

mammary gland (măm′ə-rē) *n.* One of the milk-producing glands in a female mammal, consisting of a system of ducts that convey the milk to an external nipple or teat.

mammogram (măm′ə-grăm′) *n.* **1.** An x-ray image of the human breast. **2.** The procedure performed to produce such an image.

Mammon (măm′ən) *n.* **1.** In the New Testament, riches and avarice personified as a false god. **2.** often **mammon** Riches regarded as an evil influence.

mammoth (măm′əth) *n.* Any of various extinct elephants that were often very large and had long, upwardly curving tusks and thick hair. Mammoths lived throughout the Northern Hemisphere during the Ice Age. ❖ *adj.* Huge; gigantic: *a mammoth skyscraper.*

man (măn) *n., pl.* **men** (měn) **1.** An adult male human. **2.** A human without regard to sex or age; a person. **3.** A human or an adult human male belong to a specific occupation, group, nationality, or other category: *a milkman; a congressman; an Irishman.* **4.** Humans considered as a group; humanity: *man's quest for peace.* **5.** A male human endowed with qualities, such as strength, considered characteristic of manhood. **6.** A husband or male lover. **7.** A male servant, employee, or worker: *ten men on the job.* **8.** Any of the pieces used in board games, such as chess or checkers. ❖ *tr.v.* **manned, manning, mans 1.** To take one's place or post at; get ready to work or operate: *Man the oars.* **2.** To supply with men: *The captain manned the ship with a new crew of sailors.* ❖ *interj.* An expression used to show intense feeling: *Man! What fun!* ◆ **to a man** Without exception: *They supported the new labor contract to a man.*

USAGE The use of **man** to mean "a human; a man or woman" has a long history in English. Many people feel that it is unfair to women to use a word that is mainly thought of as male to represent women. Therefore, many job titles in which *man* occurs are being replaced by neutral terms. For example, *firefighter* is often used instead of *fireman, Member of Congress* instead of *Congressman,* and *chair* or *chairperson* instead of *chairman.* In addition, compounds formed with *woman,* as in *businesswoman, policewoman,* and *chairwoman,* are now used as parallel terms to the compounds formed with *man.*

manacle (măn′ə-kəl) *n.* often **manacles 1.** Handcuffs. **2.** Something that restricts freedom or restrains. ❖ *tr.v.*

manacled, manacling, manacles 1. To put manacles on: *The police officer manacled the thief.* **2.** To restrain; hamper: *manacled by my tiny office.*

manage (măn′ĭj) *v.* **managed, managing, manages** —*tr.* **1.** To exert control over; be in charge of; direct: *manage a restaurant; manages a staff of 20.* **2.** To direct or control the use of; handle or operate: *manage a bulldozer.* **3.** To succeed in doing or accomplishing; contrive or arrange: *Despite the bitter cold, I managed to stay warm.* —*intr.* **1.** To direct or conduct business affairs: *The book offers advice to executives on how to manage effectively.* **2.** To carry on; get along: *I don't know how we managed without your help.*

manageable (măn′ĭ-jə-bəl) *adj.* Capable of being managed or controlled: *a manageable problem.* —**man′age·a·bil′i·ty** *n.*

management (măn′ĭj-mənt) *n.* **1.** The act, manner, or practice of managing: *hotel management.* **2.** The people who manage a business or organization: *I work for the management.*

manager (măn′ĭ-jər) *n.* **1.** A person who manages a business or another enterprise. **2.** A person who is in charge of the business affairs of an entertainer. **3.** A person who is in charge of the training and performance of an athlete or team.

managerial (măn′ĭ-jîr′ē-əl) *adj.* Relating to or characteristic of a manager or management: *managerial skills.*

man-at-arms (măn′ət-ärmz′) *n., pl.* **men-at-arms** (měn′ət-ärmz′) A soldier, especially a heavily armed mounted soldier in the Middle Ages.

manatee (măn′ə-tē′) *n.* Any of various large plant-eating water mammals that have flippers shaped like paddles and are found in warm coastal waters of the Atlantic Ocean.

Manchu (măn′chōō *or* măn-chōō′) *n., pl.* **Manchu** or **Manchus 1.** A member of a people native to Manchuria who ruled China from 1644 to 1912. **2.** The language of the Manchu. ❖ *adj.* Relating to the Manchu or their language or culture.

mandala (mŭn′də-lə) *n.* Any of various complex geometric designs used in Hinduism and Buddhism as aids to meditation.

Mandan (măn′dăn′) *n., pl.* **Mandan** or **Mandans 1.** A member of a Native American people living in North Dakota. **2.** The Siouan language of the Mandan.

mandarin (măn′də-rĭn) *n.* **1.** A high public official in the Chinese Empire. **2.** A high government official or a person having great influence. **3.** A mandarin orange.

Mandarin *n.* **1.** Any of a group of related dialects of Chinese spoken mainly in the north and west of China. **2.** The official language of China, based on the Mandarin dialect spoken in and around Beijing.

mandarin orange *n.* A small sweet orange having loose skin and segments that separate easily.

mandate (măn′dāt′) *n.* **1.** The support or approval of the voters, expressed in the results of an election of their representatives. **2.** An official and authoritative command, order, or instruction, especially one issued by a higher court to a lower court. **3a.** A commission from the League of Nations giving a member nation control over the government of a territory. **b.** A territory under such control. ❖ *tr.v.* **mandated, mandating, mandates 1.** To put (a territory) under a mandate. **2.** To make mandatory; require: *The law mandates desegregation in all schools.*

mandatory (măn′də-tôr′ē) *adj.* Required; obligatory: *A* *college degree is mandatory for most teaching jobs.*

mandible (măn′də-bəl) *n.* **1.** The lower jaw of a vertebrate animal. **2.** The upper or lower part of a bird's beak. **3.** An organ in the mouth of many invertebrate animals used for seizing and biting food, especially either of a pair of such organs in an insect or other arthropod.

mandolin (măn′də-lĭn′ *or* măn′dl-ĭn) *n.* A musical instrument having a pear-shaped body and a neck with frets over which pairs of strings are stretched and played with a pick.

mandrake (măn′drāk′) *n.* A low-growing European plant having a forked root thought to resemble the human body. The root was once believed to have magical powers and was used in medicines.

mandrill (măn′drəl) *n.* A large monkey of west-central Africa having an olive-brown body with a brightly colored rump and face that are especially pronounced in the male.

mane (mān) *n.* **1.** A growth of long hair on the neck of certain mammals, such as a horse or a male lion. **2.** A long thick growth of hair on a person's head.

maneuver (mə-nōō′vər) *n.* **1.** A movement or combination of movements involving skill and dexterity: *a gymnastics maneuver.* **2.** A controlled change in movement or direction of a vehicle or vessel, especially an aircraft. **3a.** A planned movement of troops or warships: *By a series of brilliant maneuvers, the general outwitted the enemy.* **b.** often **maneuvers** A large-scale military exercise in which battle movements are practiced. ❖ *v.* **maneuvered, maneuvering, maneuvers** —*intr.* **1.** To make controlled changes in movement or direction: *The ship had to maneuver very carefully to avoid the icebergs.* **2.** To change tactics or approach; plan skillfully: *Our lawyer maneuvered in order to get the trial postponed.* **3.** To carry out a military maneuver. —*tr.* **1.** To direct skillfully by changes in course or in position: *They taught me how to maneuver a car on an icy road.* **2.** To manage or direct, especially by trickery: *She maneuvered her opponent into taking a position that lost him the election.* **3.** To cause (troops or warships) to carry out a military maneuver. —**ma·neu′ver·a·bil′i·ty** *n.* —**ma·neu′ver·a·ble** *adj.*

manful (măn′fəl) *adj.* Having or showing characteristics traditionally associated with masculinity, such as courage or reserve. —**man′ful·ly** *adv.*

manga (mäng′gə) *n.* A style of comic strip or comic book originally developed in Japan, characterized by stylized, colorful art.

manganese (măng′gə-nēz′) *n. Symbol* **Mn** A grayish, brittle metallic element found in several minerals and used to increase the hardness and strength of steel and other important alloys. Atomic number 25. See **Periodic Table.**

mange (mānj) *n.* A skin disease of dogs and other mammals, caused by mites and characterized by itching and loss of hair.

manger (mān′jər) *n.* A trough or open box in which feed for horses or cattle is placed.

mangle¹ (măng′gəl) *tr.v.* **mangled, mangling, mangles** **1.** To disfigure by crushing, hacking, or tearing: *The accident completely mangled our car.* **2.** To ruin; spoil: *The orchestra completely mangled the music.*

mangle² (măng′gəl) *n.* A machine that presses fabrics by running them between heated rollers. ❖ *tr.v.* **mangled, mangling, mangles** To smooth or press with a mangle: *mangle sheets.*

WORD HISTORY Mangle¹ comes from Middle English *manglen* (meaning "to mutilate"), which comes from Old French *mangoner,* meaning "to cut to bits." **Mangle²** comes from Dutch *mangel,* referring to the same kind of machine as in English.

mango (măng′gō) *n., pl.* **mangoes** or **mangos 1.** A tropical fruit having a smooth rind and sweet, juicy, yellow-orange flesh. **2.** The tree that bears such fruit.

mangrove (măng′grōv′ *or* măng′grōv′) *n.* Any of various tropical trees or shrubs that can live in salt water and often form dense thickets along seacoasts. Mangroves have roots that grow from the stem and provide support.

mangy (mān′jē) *adj.* **mangier, mangiest 1.** Having or appearing to have mange: *a mangy stray dog.* **2.** Having many bare spots; shabby: *a mangy old coat.* —**man′gi·ness** *n.*

manhandle (măn′hăn′dl) *tr.v.* **manhandled, manhandling, manhandles** To handle in a rough manner: *The porters manhandled the suitcases.*

manhole (măn′hōl′) *n.* A hole in a street, with a removable cover, that allows a person to reach underground sewers, pipes, or other structures for repair or inspection.

manhood (măn′hŏŏd′) *n.* **1.** The state of being an adult male person: *He has reached manhood.* **2.** The group of qualities, such as courage and strength, thought of as appropriate to a man. **3.** Men in general: *the manhood of the country.*

man-hour (măn′our′) *n.* A unit of labor equal to one person working for one hour, used to express industrial production and costs.

mania (mā′nē-ə *or* mān′yə) *n.* **1.** An intense enthusiasm or desire: *He has a mania for horror movies.* **2.** A manifestation of bipolar disorder in which a person becomes excessively active and has rapidly changing ideas.

maniac (mā′nē-ăk′) *n.* **1.** A mentally deranged person. **2.** A person who acts in a wildly irresponsible way: *Look at that maniac zooming through the red light!* **3.** A person who has extreme enthusiasm for something: *She's a soccer maniac.* —**ma′ni·ac′, ma·ni′a·cal** (mə-nī′ə-kəl) *adj.*

manic (măn′ĭk) *adj.* **1.** Full of or characterized by frenetic activity or wild excitement: *the manic pace of modern life in the city.* **2.** Relating to or affected by mania.

manic-depressive disorder (măn′ĭk-dĭ-prĕs′ĭv) *n.* Bipolar disorder.

Manichaeism (măn′ĭ-kē′ĭz′əm) also **Manichaeanism** (măn′ĭ-kē′ə-nĭz′əm) *n.* **1.** The dualistic religious philosophy of the Persian prophet Mani, combining elements of Zoroastrian, Christian, and Gnostic thought. **2.** A dualistic philosophy dividing the world between good and evil principles or regarding matter as intrinsically evil and mind as intrinsically good. —**Man·i·chae·an** (măn′-ĭ-kē′ən) *n. & adj.*

manicotti (măn′ĭ-kŏt′ē) *n.* **1.** Pasta in large-sized tubes. **2.** A dish consisting of such tubes stuffed with meat or cheese, usually served hot with a tomato sauce.

manicure (măn′ĭ-kyŏŏr′) *n.* A cosmetic treatment for the fingernails, including shaping and polishing. ❖ *tr.v.* **manicured, manicuring, manicures** To trim, clean, and polish (the fingernails).

manicurist (măn′ĭ-kyŏŏr′ĭst) *n.* A person who gives manicures.

manifest (măn′ə-fĕst′) *adj.* Clear and apparent; obvious: *It is strange that such a manifest hoax has fooled so many* *people.* ❖ *tr.v.* **manifested, manifesting, manifests** To reveal; show; display: *Her fidgeting manifested a desire to leave.* ❖ *n.* A list of cargo or passengers: *The ship's manifest was incomplete.* —**man′i·fest·ly** *adv.*

manifestation (măn′ə-fĕ-stā′shən) *n.* **1.** The act of showing, demonstrating, or proving: *a manifestation of bravery.* **2.** Something that reveals; a sign or indication: *Rust on the pipes was a manifestation of tiny leaks.*

Manifest Destiny *n.* The belief during the 1800s that the United States was both destined and morally obligated to expand throughout North America.

manifesto (măn′ə-fĕs′tō) *n., pl.* **manifestoes** or **manifestos** A public declaration of principles and aims, especially of a political nature.

manifold (măn′ə-fōld′) *adj.* **1.** Of many kinds; varied: *This work involves manifold tasks.* **2.** Having many parts, forms, or aspects: *A knowledge of many subjects demonstrates manifold intelligence.* ❖ *n.* A pipe or tube that has several openings for making multiple connections: *The exhaust manifold of an engine connects to each cylinder.*

manila or **manilla** (mə-nĭl′ə) *n.* Manila paper. ❖ *adj.* Made of Manila paper.

Manila paper *n.* A strong paper or thin cardboard with a smooth finish, usually brown or yellow in color. Manila paper was originally made from Manila hemp, a plant resembling the banana that is native to the Philippines.

manioc (măn′ē-ŏk′) *n.* Cassava.

manipulate (mə-nĭp′yə-lāt′) *tr.v.* **manipulated, manipulating, manipulates 1.** To arrange, operate, or control by the hands or by mechanical means: *The pilot manipulated the airplane's controls.* **2.** To influence or manage in a clever or devious way: *He manipulated public opinion in his favor.* —**ma·nip′u·la′tive** *adj.* —**ma·nip′u·la′tor** *n.*

manipulation (mə-nĭp′yə-lā′shən) *n.* **1.** The act of manipulating. **2.** Clever or devious management: *the manipulation of public opinion through advertising.*

manitou (măn′ĭ-tōō′) *n., pl.* **manitous** In Algonquian religious belief, a supernatural power that exists throughout the world and is possessed by both spirits and humans.

mankind (măn′kīnd′) *n.* **1.** The human race; humankind. **2.** Men, as opposed to women, considered as a group.

manly (măn′lē) *adj.* **manlier, manliest 1.** Relating to or characteristic of men, especially when considered traditionally masculine: *manly courage.* **2.** Having well-developed or toned muscles: *a manly physique.* —**man′li·ness** *n.*

manmade or **man-made** (măn′mād′) *adj.* Made by humans rather than occurring in nature; synthetic: *man-made fibers; a man-made lake.*

manna (măn′ə) *n.* **1.** In the Bible, the food miraculously provided for the Israelites in the wilderness after their flight from Egypt. **2.** Something of value that a person receives unexpectedly: *viewed the bonus as manna from heaven.*

manned (mănd) *adj.* Occupied, operated, or performed by a person: *manned spacecraft.*

mannequin (măn′ĭ-kĭn) *n.* A life-size model of the human body, used mainly for fitting or displaying clothes.

manner (măn′ər) *n.* **1.** The way in which something is done or happens: *We always work in a careful manner.* See Synonyms at **method. 2.** A way of acting; behavior: *The new boss has a gruff manner.* **3. manners** Socially proper behavior; etiquette: *Did no one ever teach him*

manners? **4.** Kind; sort: *We had all manner of incidents on our long trip.* ◆ **in a manner of speaking** In a way; so to speak.

mannered (măn′ərd) *adj.* **1.** Having manners of a specific kind: *ill-mannered people.* **2.** Artificial or affected: *quaint and mannered speech.*

mannerism (măn′ə-rĭz′əm) *n.* A distinctive personal trait; a quirk: *She has a mannerism of scratching her chin when thinking.*

mannerly (măn′ər-lē) *adj.* Having good manners; polite. ❖ *adv.* With good manners; politely.

mannish (măn′ĭsh) *adj.* **1.** Relating to men; masculine. **2.** Resembling or suggestive of a man rather than a woman: *a mannish way of walking.* —**man′nish·ly** *adv.*

mano (mä′nō) *n., pl.* **manos** A handheld stone or roller for grinding corn or other grains on a metate.

manoeuvre (mə-nōō′vər) *n. & v. Chiefly British* Variant of **maneuver.**

man-of-war (măn′ə-wôr′) *n., pl.* **men-of-war** (mĕn′ə-wôr′) A warship, especially a sailing ship.

manometer (mă-nŏm′ĭ-tər) *n.* An instrument that measures the pressure of liquids and gases.

manor (măn′ər) *n.* **1.** An estate including its lands. **2.** The main house on an estate. **3.** The estate of a feudal lord.

manorial (mə-nôr′ē-əl) *adj.* Relating to or like a manor: *a manorial estate.*

manpower (măn′pou′ər) *n.* **1.** The power supplied by human physical effort: *Lifting that piano requires a lot of manpower.* **2.** The people working or available for work, especially on a particular task: *Most of their manpower is now devoted to developing new products.*

mansard roof (măn′särd′) *n.* A roof having two slopes on all four sides, with the lower slope much steeper than the upper.

manse (măns) *n.* **1.** A house lived in by a Christian minister. **2.** A large stately residence; a mansion.

manservant (măn′sûr′vənt) *n., pl.* **menservants** (mĕn′-sûr′vənts) A male servant.

mansion (măn′shən) *n.* A large stately house.

manslaughter (măn′slô′tər) *n.* The unlawful killing of a person without having murderous intent or under extenuating circumstances.

manta (măn′tə) *n.* A very large ray found in warm seas worldwide, having a long thin tail and two hornlike fins on the front of the head.

manta ray *n.* The manta.

mantel also **mantle** (măn′tl) *n.* **1.** An ornamental facing around a fireplace. **2.** A mantelpiece.

mantelpiece (măn′tl-pēs′) *n.* The shelf over a fireplace.

mantilla (măn-tē′yə or măn-tĭl′ə) *n.* A scarf, usually of lace, traditionally worn over the head and shoulders by women in Spain and Latin America.

mantis (măn′tĭs) *n., pl.* **mantises** or **mantes** (măn′tēz) Any of various large, mostly tropical insects having powerful front legs used for preying on other insects.

mantissa (măn-tĭs′ə) *n.* The fractional part of a logarithm to the base ten. In the logarithm 2.749, the mantissa is .749.

mantle (măn′tl) *n.* **1.** A loose sleeveless coat worn over outer garments; a cloak. **2.** Something that covers or conceals: *a soft mantle of snow.* **3.** The layer of the earth between the crust and the core. **4.** A sheath of threads that is used in gas lights and lanterns and gives a brilliant light when heated by a flame. **5.** The layer of soft tissue that covers the body of a mollusk, such as a clam or an oyster, and secretes the material that forms the shell. **6.** Variant of **mantel.** ❖ *tr.v.* **mantled, mantling, mantles** To cover with or as if with a cloak: *Night mantled the earth.*

mantra (măn**′**trə) *n.* **1.** In Hinduism, a sacred word or phrase repeated when praying or meditating. **2.** A commonly repeated word or phrase: *The politician's mantra was "Better education for all."*

manual (măn**′**yōō-əl) *adj.* **1.** Relating to the hands: *manual dexterity.* **2.** Used by or operated with the hands: *manual controls.* **3.** Employing human rather than mechanical energy: *manual labor.* ❖ *n.* A small book of instructions; a handbook. —**man′u·al·ly** *adv.*

manual alphabet *n.* An alphabet used for communication by hearing-impaired people in which finger positions represent letters.

manufacture (măn′yə-făk**′**chər) *tr.v.* **manufactured, manufacturing, manufactures 1.** To make or process (a product), especially with the use of machines: *a factory that manufactures cars.* **2.** To make or process (a raw material) into a finished product: *manufacture cotton to make fabric.* **3.** To make up; concoct: *manufactured a flimsy excuse.* ❖ *n.* The act or process of manufacturing products.

manufacturer (măn′yə-făk**′**chər-ər) *n.* A person or company that manufactures something, especially the owner or operator of a factory.

manumit (măn′yə-mĭt**′**) *tr.v.* **manumitted, manumitting, manumits** To free from slavery or bondage; emancipate. —**man′u·mis′sion** (măn′yə-mĭsh**′**ən) *n.* —**man′u·mit′ter** *n.*

manure (mə-nŏŏr**′**) *n.* Animal dung, especially the dung of cattle, used as fertilizer.

manuscript (măn**′**yə-skrĭpt′) *n.* **1a.** A handwritten book, poem, or other document. **b.** A collection of such handwritten documents bound together. **2.** The form of a book, paper, or article as it is submitted for publication in print: *send a manuscript to a publisher.* **3.** Handwriting as opposed to printing.

Manx (măngks) *adj.* Relating to the Isle of Man, an island between Great Britain and Ireland, or to its people, language, or culture. ❖ *n., pl.* **Manx 1.** *(used with a plural verb)* The natives or inhabitants of the Isle of Man. **2.** The extinct Celtic language of the Isle of Man. **3.** A domestic cat of a tailless breed that originated on the Isle of Man.

many (měn**′**ē) *adj.* **more** (môr), **most** (mōst) **1.** Consisting of or amounting to a large number; numerous: *There are many students in the introductory psychology class.* **2.** Being one of a large number: *Many a brave person has refused to go down these rapids.* ❖ *n. (used with a plural verb)* **1.** The majority of the people: *the will of the many.* **2.** A large number of people or things: *A good many of us were at the party.* ❖ *pron. (used with a plural verb)* A large number of people or things: *Many were invited but few came.* ◆ **as many** The same number of: *moved three times in as many years.*

many-sided (měn′ē-sī**′**dĭd) *adj.* **1.** Having many sides: *a many-sided polygon.* **2.** Having many aspects, talents, or interests.

Maoism (mou**′**ĭz′əm) *n.* The beliefs and practices of Mao Zedong (1893–1976), the Chinese Communist leader who served as the first head of state of the People's Republic of China (1949–1959). —**Mao′ist** *adj. & n.*

Maori (mou**′**rē) *n., pl.* **Maori** or **Maoris 1.** A member of a Polynesian people of New Zealand. **2.** The language of the Maori. ❖ *adj.* Relating to the Maori or their language or culture.

map (măp) *n.* **1.** A drawing or chart of a region of the earth, often showing political divisions such as countries and physical features such as mountains and rivers. **2.** A drawing or chart of the moon, a planet, the stars, or other features of the sky. **3.** A visual display of the arrangement of genes on a chromosome: *a genetic map of a fruit fly.* **4.** A visual representation of the arrangement of the parts of something complex, such as the pages on a website. ❖ *tr.v.* **mapped, mapping, maps 1.** To make a map of; represent on a map. **2.** To plan in detail: *Let's map out our schedule.* **3.** To locate (a gene) on a chromosome in relation to other known genes. ◆ **put on the map** To make well-known or famous: *The new racetrack put the rural town on the map.*

maple (mā**′**pəl) *n.* **1.** Any of various trees or shrubs having broad leaves with deep notches and paired, winged seeds. **2.** The hard wood of a maple, often used in making furniture. **3.** The flavor of the concentrated sap of the sugar maple.

maple sugar *n.* A sugar made by boiling down maple syrup.

maple syrup *n.* **1.** A sweet syrup made from the sap of the sugar maple. **2.** Syrup made from various sugars and flavored with maple syrup or artificial maple flavoring.

mapmaker (măp**′**mā′kər) *n.* A person who makes maps; a cartographer.

maquiladora (mä-kē′lä-dō**′**rä) *n.* An assembly plant in Mexico, especially one along the border between the United States and Mexico, to which foreign materials and parts are shipped and from which the finished product is returned to the original market.

mar (mär) *tr.v.* **marred, marring, mars 1.** To deface or damage: *marred the top of the table with a knife.* **2.** To spoil; ruin: *Rain marred their day at the beach.*

marabou (măr**′**ə-bōō′) *n.* A large African stork that scavenges for carrion and has a naked head and neck, black wings, and soft white down on the underside.

maraca (mə-rä**′**kə) *n.* A Latin-American percussion instrument consisting of a hollow gourd rattle containing pebbles or dried beans. Maracas are often played in pairs.

maraschino cherry (măr′ə-skē**′**nō or măr′ə-shē**′**nō) *n.* A cherry preserved in a sweet red syrup, used especially in desserts and cocktails.

Marathi (mə-rä**′**tē) *n.* The principal Indic language of west-central India.

marathon (măr**′**ə-thŏn′) *n.* **1.** A cross-country footrace of 26 miles, 385 yards (42.195 kilometers). **2.** A long-distance race other than a footrace: *a swimming marathon.* **3.** A contest of endurance: *a dance marathon.*

maraud (mə-rôd**′**) *v.* **marauded, marauding, marauds** —*intr.* To roam and raid in search of plunder. —*tr.* To raid or pillage for plunder. —**ma·raud′er** *n.*

marble (mär**′**bəl) *n.* **1.** A hard rock made from the action of heat and pressure on limestone or dolomite. Some kinds of marble have irregularly colored marks due to impurities. Marble can be polished to a smooth luster and is used in buildings and statues. **2a.** A little ball made of a hard substance such as glass. **b.** **marbles** *(used with a singular verb)* A children's game played with such balls. ❖ *tr.v.* **marbled, marbling, marbles** To color and streak (paper, for example) in imitation of marble. ❖ *adj.* Made of or resembling marble: *a marble floor.*

march¹ (märch) *v.* **marched, marching, marches** —*intr.* **1.** To walk steadily and rhythmically forward in step with others: *The band marched down the street during the pa-*

rade. **2.** To walk in a purposeful or determined manner; stride: *I marched up to the podium and read my speech.* **3.** To advance with a steady movement: *Time marches on.* **4.** To participate in an organized walk, as for a public cause. —*tr.* To cause to march: *The duck marched its ducklings to the edge of the lake.* ❖ *n.* **1.** The act of marching: *the army's rapid march to the fort.* **2.** A long tiring journey by foot: *a march of ten miles.* **3.** The distance covered by marching: *We were still a march of six hours from camp.* **4.** Forward movement; progress: *the dramatic march of modern science.* **5.** A musical composition in regularly accented meter that is appropriate to accompany marching. **6.** An organized walk or procession by a group of people for a specific cause or issue.

march² (märch) *n.* A border region; a frontier.

WORD HISTORY March¹ comes from Middle English *marchen,* which comes from Old French *marchier* (meaning "to walk steadily and rhythmically") and is of Germanic origin. **March²** comes from Middle English *march,* which comes from Old French *marche* (meaning "border region") and is of Germanic origin.

March *n.* The third month of the year in the Gregorian calendar, having 31 days.

marchioness (mär′shə-nĭs *or* mär′shə-nĕs′) *n.* **1.** The wife or widow of a marquis. **2.** A noblewoman ranking above a countess and below a duchess.

Mardi Gras (mär′dē grä′) *n.* The day before Ash Wednesday, celebrated as a holiday in many places with carnivals and parades.

mare¹ (mâr) *n.* An adult female horse, zebra, donkey, or other related animal.

mare² (mä′rā) *n., pl.* **maria** (mä′rē-ə) Any of the large dark areas on the moon, Mars, or other planets.

WORD HISTORY Mare¹ comes from Middle English *mere,* meaning "horse." **Mare²** comes from Latin *mare,* meaning "sea."

margarine (mär′jər-ĭn) *n.* A substitute for butter made from vegetable oils and other ingredients.

margarita (mär′gə-rē′tə) *n.* A cocktail made with tequila, an orange-flavored liqueur, and lemon or lime juice, often served with salt encrusted on the rim of the glass.

margin (mär′jĭn) *n.* **1.** An edge or border: *the margins of the forest.* See Synonyms at **border. 2.** The blank space that surrounds the written or printed area on a page. **3.** An extra amount allowed beyond what is needed: *You should allow a ten-minute margin for delays in getting to school.* **4.** A measure, quantity, or degree of difference: *We won the election by a large margin.* **5.** The difference between the cost and the selling price of something: *wanted to improve the product's margin of profitability.*

marginal (mär′jə-nəl) *adj.* **1.** Written or printed in the margin: *There were marginal notes through the whole book.* **2.** Relating to, in, or on the border or edge: *the northern states marginal to Canada.* **3.** Barely acceptable: *marginal writing ability.* **4.** Making a very small profit: *a marginal business.* —**mar′gin·al·ly** *adv.*

marginalize (mär′jə-nə-līz′) *tr.v.* **marginalized, marginalizing, marginalizes** To confine to a lower or outer limit, as in society: *policies that marginalized homeless people.*

maria (mä′rē-ə) *n.* Plural of **mare².**

marigold (mâr′ĭ-gōld′) *n.* Any of various plants of the

Americas that have showy orange, yellow, or reddish flowers and are often planted in gardens.

marijuana (mär′ə-wä′nə) *n.* **1.** The dried leaves or flowers of the hemp plant, which contain an illegal intoxicating drug. Certain states allow the medical use of marijuana for the treatment of nausea, loss of appetite, and other symptoms of diseases such as cancer and AIDS. **2.** The hemp plant.

marimba (mə-rĭm′bə) *n.* A musical instrument somewhat like a large xylophone, having tuned wooden bars that are struck with wooden mallets.

marina (mə-rē′nə) *n.* A boat basin that has docks, moorings, supplies, and repair facilities for small boats.

marinade (mär′ə-nād′) *n.* A mixture of oil, vinegar or wine, and spices, used for soaking meat, poultry, fish, or vegetables before cooking. ❖ *tr.v.* (mär′ə-nād′) **marinaded, marinading, marinades** To marinate.

marinara (mär′ə-när′ə) *adj.* Being or served with a sauce made of tomatoes, onions, garlic, and herbs: *spaghetti marinara.* ❖ *n.* Marinara sauce.

marinate (mär′ə-nāt′) *tr.v.* **marinated, marinating, marinates** To soak (meat or fish, for example) in a marinade.

marine (mə-rēn′) *adj.* **1.** Relating to the sea: *marine biology.* **2.** Living or found in the sea: *marine life.* **3.** Relating to shipping or navigation: *a marine chart.* ❖ *n.* **1.** A soldier serving on a ship or at a naval base. **2. Marine** A member of the US Marine Corps.

Marine Corps *n.* A branch of the US armed forces whose troops are specially trained for amphibious landings and combat.

mariner (mär′ə-nər) *n.* A person who navigates or helps to navigate a ship.

marionette (mär′ē-ə-nĕt′) *n.* A puppet controlled from above by strings or wires attached to its limbs.

marital (mär′ĭ-tl) *adj.* Relating to marriage: *marital vows.* —**mar′i·tal·ly** *adv.*

maritime (mär′ĭ-tīm′) *adj.* **1.** Located on or near the sea: *a maritime fishing village.* **2.** Relating to shipping or navigation: *maritime law.*

marjoram (mär′jər-əm) *n.* A perennial plant related to mint, having aromatic leaves that are used as a seasoning.

mark¹ (märk) *n.* **1.** A visible trace or impression, such as a line or spot, left on a surface. **2.** A written or printed symbol used for punctuation. **3.** An indication of some quality or condition: *Taking responsibility for your own mistakes is a mark of maturity.* **4.** A lasting impression: *The Crusades left their mark on Western civilization.* **5.** Something that is aimed at; a target: *The arrow found its mark.* **6.** A label, seal, or inscription placed on an article: *The manufacturer's mark can be found on every product.* **7.** A recognized standard of quality: *Your latest work is not up to the mark.* **8.** A letter or number used to indicate the quality of a person's work: *excellent marks in arithmetic.* **9a.** The place from which racers begin and sometimes end their contest. **b.** A point reached or gained in a race: *The swimmers just passed the halfway mark.* ❖ *v.* **marked, marking, marks** —*tr.* **1.** To make a mark on: *Someone had marked the important pages of the book.* **2.** To form, make, or write by a mark: *marked a square on the sidewalk.* **3.** To give evidence of; reveal: *The cool winds mark the beginning of fall.* **4.** To be a feature of; distinguish; characterize: *Her painting is marked by an unusual use of color.* **5.** To give attention to; notice: *Mark my words: they are asking for trouble.* **6.** To take note of in writing; write down: *marked the appointment on my calendar.* **7.** To determine the quality of (something) according to a grade or mark: *The teacher is marking the tests now.* **8.** To guard (an opponent), as in soccer. —*intr.* **1.** To make a visible impression: *The pen marks under water.* **2.** To give grades for school work: *I've never had a teacher that marks easily.* ◆ **mark down** To mark for sale at a lower price. **mark time 1.** To indicate or signal the rhythm or pace of a piece of music. **2.** To move the feet in a marching step without advancing. **3.** To suspend progress for the time being; wait: *The work crew marked time while the architects changed the plans.* **4.** To perform the actions of a job or task without really accomplishing anything. **mark up 1.** To cover with marks. **2.** To mark for sale at a higher price.

mark² (märk) *n.* A deutsche mark.

Mark (märk) *n.* The second Gospel of the New Testament, traditionally thought to have been written by Mark, a disciple of Jesus's apostle Peter.

markdown (märk′doun′) *n.* **1.** A reduction in price. **2.** The amount by which a price is reduced.

marked (märkt) *adj.* **1.** Having a mark or marks: *Pedestrians use the marked crosswalk.* **2.** Clearly defined and evident; noticeable: *a marked difference in price.* **3.** Singled out or distinguished, as for a dire fate: *a marked man.*

markedly (mär′kĭd-lē) *adv.* In a manner that is noticeable and obvious: *Prices have gone up markedly since last year.*

marker (mär′kər) *n.* **1.** An implement, especially a pen with a felt tip, used for marking or writing: *We used markers to make posters for the science fair.* **2.** Something that marks a place, as a bookmark or tombstone. **3.** A person who marks, especially a person who gives academic grades.

market (mär′kĭt) *n.* **1a.** A public gathering for buying and selling goods: *The farmer took cheese to market.* **b.** A place where goods are offered for sale: *We walked by the market before going home.* **2.** A store that sells a particular type of merchandise: *a fish market.* **3.** A system of exchange in which prices are determined by people competing to buy and sell things: *She works in the bond market.* **4.** The business of buying and selling a particular product: *the international coffee market.* **5a.** A region or country where goods may be sold: *We produce computers for foreign markets.* **b.** A particular type or group of buyers: *The college market includes people 16 to 22 years old.* **6.** A desire to buy; demand: *There is always a market for our bicycles.* ❖ *tr.v.* **marketed, marketing, markets 1.** To sell or offer for sale: *The co-op marketed vegetables from local farmers.* **2.** To try to make (a product or service) appealing to particular groups of consumers; promote by marketing. ◆ **in the market** Interested in buying: *We are in the market for a new car.* **on the market 1.** Available for buying: *There are several good brands of skis on the market.* **2.** Up for sale: *He put the family business on the market.* —**mar′ket·er** *n.*

marketable (mär′kĭ-tə-bəl) *adj.* **1.** Fit for sale, as in a market: *marketable produce.* **2.** In demand by buyers or employers: *marketable goods; marketable skills.* —**mar′-ket·a·bil′i·ty** *n.*

marketing (mär′kĭ-tĭng) *n.* The business activity of identifying particular groups of consumers and making a product or service appealing to them, usually including advertising, branding, and pricing.

marketplace (mär′kĭt-plās′) *n.* **1.** A public square or other place in which a market is set up. **2.** The general process of buying and selling; business activities.

marking (mär′kĭng) *n.* A mark or marks: *markings left*

along the trail. **2.** A mark or pattern of marks on an organism: *a snake with dark markings on the head.*

marksman (märks′mən) *n.* A man skilled at shooting at a target.

marksmanship (märks′mən-shĭp′) *n.* Skill at shooting a gun or another weapon.

markswoman (märks′wŏŏm′ən) *n.* A woman skilled at shooting at a target.

markup (märk′ŭp′) *n.* **1.** An increase in the price of an item for sale. **2.** An amount added to the cost of an item to figure its selling price. **3.** The collection of tags that describe the format of an electronic document.

markup language *n.* A coding system, such as HTML, used to structure and link electronic text files.

marl (märl) *n.* A kind of rock or a loose soil mixture that contains clay, carbonate of lime, and shells, used as fertilizer.

marlin (mär′lĭn) *n.* Any of several large ocean fishes that have a long spearlike upper jaw and are often caught for sport.

marline (mär′lĭn) *n.* A light rope made of two loosely twisted strands, used to finish off the ends of larger ropes to keep them from unraveling.

marlinespike (mär′lĭn-spīk′) *n.* A pointed metal tool used to separate strands of rope or wire in splicing.

marmalade (mär′mə-lād′) *n.* A jam made by boiling the pulp and rind of fruits.

marmoset (mär′mə-sĕt′ *or* mär′mə-zĕt′) *n.* Any of various very small Central and South American monkeys that have a long tail and feed on sap and gum from trees.

marmot (mär′mət) *n.* Any of various burrowing rodents having short legs, short ears, and a bushy tail, such as the woodchuck.

maroon¹ (mə-rōōn′) *tr.v.* **marooned, marooning, maroons 1.** To put (a person) ashore on a deserted island. **2.** To leave alone and helpless: *I was marooned with a cold while everyone else went skating.*

maroon² (mə-rōōn′) *n.* A dark reddish brown to dark purplish red.

WORD HISTORY Maroon¹ comes from Spanish *cimarrón,* meaning "wild, runaway." **Maroon²** comes from French *marron,* which comes from Italian *marrone,* both meaning "chestnut."

marquee (mär-kē′) *n.* A structure that projects over the entrance to a building, such as a theater or hotel, and often bears a signboard.

marquess also **marquis** (mär′kwĭs) *n.* A British nobleman ranking below a duke and above an earl or count.

marquetry (mär′kĭ-trē) *n., pl.* **marquetries** Material, such as wood or ivory, inlaid piece by piece into a wood surface in an intricate design and veneered to another surface, especially of furniture, for decoration.

marquis (mär-kē′) *n., pl.* **marquis** (mär-kēz′) **1.** A nobleman ranking below a duke and above an earl or count, used especially outside of Great Britain. **2.** (mär′kwĭs) *pl.* **marquises** (mär′kwĭ-sĭz) Variant of **marquess.**

marquise (mär-kēz′) *n.* A marchioness.

marriage (mär′ĭj) *n.* **1.** The legal union of a man and woman as husband and wife, and in some jurisdictions, between two people of the same sex. **2.** The state or relationship of two adults who are married: *Theirs is a very happy marriage.* **3.** A close union: *Poetry is a marriage of beautiful sound and intense meaning.*

marriageable (mär′ĭ-jə-bəl) *adj.* Suitable for marriage.

married (măr′ēd) *adj.* **1.** Having a spouse: *a married woman; a married man.* **2.** Joined by marriage: *a married couple.* **3.** Relating to marriage: *married life.*

marrow (măr′ō) *n.* **1.** Bone marrow. **2.** The essential, innermost, or most important part; the pith: *the marrow of an argument.*

marry[1] (măr′ē) *v.* **married, marrying, marries** —*tr.* **1.** To join in marriage: *They have been married for 25 years.* **2.** To take as a spouse: *She married him two years ago.* **3.** To perform a marriage ceremony for: *The rabbi married the couple.* **4.** To give in marriage. —*intr.* To enter into marriage; wed: *They married in June.*

marry[2] (măr′ē) *interj.* Archaic An expression used to show surprise or emphasis.

WORD HISTORY Marry[1] comes from Middle English *marien,* which comes from Old French *marier,* which in turn comes from Latin *maritāre,* all three forms meaning "to marry." **Marry**[2] comes from Middle English *Marie,* referring to Mary, the mother of Jesus.

Mars (märz) *n.* **1.** In Roman mythology, the god of war, identified with the Greek Ares. **2.** The fourth planet from the sun, with a diameter about half that of Earth. Because its axis is tilted Mars has seasons, but they are twice as long as those on Earth.

marsh (märsh) *n.* An area of low-lying wet land that usually has few trees and other woody plants growing in it.

marshal (mär′shəl) *n.* **1a.** In some countries, a military officer of the highest rank. **b.** A field marshal. **2.** In the United States: **a.** A federal or city officer who carries out court orders and performs duties similar to those of a sheriff. **b.** The head of a police or fire department. **3.** A person in charge of a ceremony or parade. ❖ *tr.v.* **marshaled, marshaling, marshals** also **marshalled, marshalling, marshals** To place in proper or methodical order; organize: *The research team marshaled facts to defend its theory.*

marsh gas *n.* Methane that occurs naturally in swamps.

marshland (märsh′lănd′) *n.* A marshy tract of land.

marshmallow (märsh′mĕl′ō *or* märsh′măl′ō) *n.* **1.** A soft white candy with a spongy texture. **2.** also **marsh mallow** A plant found in marshes of Europe and North America, having pink flowers and a spongy root formerly used in making marshmallow candies.

marsh marigold *n.* Any of several plants that grow in wet places and have bright-yellow flowers resembling those of the buttercup.

marshy (mär′shē) *adj.* **marshier, marshiest** Relating to or resembling a marsh. —**marsh′i·ness** *n.*

marsupial (mär-soo′pē-əl) *n.* Any of various mammals whose young continue to develop after birth in a pouch on the outside of the female's body. Kangaroos, opossums, and wombats are marsupials. ❖ *adj.* Relating to or being a marsupial.

mart (märt) *n.* A trading center, market, or store: *a fruit and vegetable mart.*

marten (mär′tn) *n., pl.* **marten** or **martens** **1.** Any of several mammals related to the weasel and the mink, having thick soft brown fur. **2.** The fur of such a mammal.

martial (mär′shəl) *adj.* **1.** Relating to or suitable for war: *martial music.* **2.** Relating to the armed forces or the military profession: *martial training.*

martial art *n.* Any of several Asian arts of combat or self-

defense, including karate and judo, that are usually practiced as a sport.

martial law *n.* Temporary military rule of a civilian population, as in an emergency or during a war.

Martian (mär′shən) *adj.* Relating to the planet Mars. ❖ *n.* A being that supposedly lives on the planet Mars.

martin (mär′tn) *n.* Any of several swallows, especially one that has glossy blue-black feathers and a forked tail.

martinet (mär′tn-ĕt′) *n.* A person who believes in and demands strict obedience to rules.

martini (mär-tē′nē) *n., pl.* **martinis** A cocktail made of gin or vodka and dry vermouth.

Martin Luther King Day *n.* The third Monday in January, observed in the United States in honor of the birthday of Martin Luther King, Jr.

martyr (mär′tər) *n.* **1.** A person who chooses to suffer death or torture rather than give up religious principles. **2.** A person who suffers much or makes great sacrifices to further a belief, cause, or principle. **3.** A person who endures great suffering. ❖ *tr.v.* **martyred, martyring, martyrs** **1.** To make a martyr of. **2.** To cause to suffer; torture or torment.

martyrdom (mär′tər-dəm) *n.* **1.** The condition of being a martyr. **2.** The suffering of death by a martyr. **3.** Extreme suffering.

marvel (mär′vəl) *n.* A person or thing that causes surprise, astonishment, or wonder: *recalled the days when radio was considered a marvel of technology.* See Synonyms at **wonder.** ❖ *intr.v.* **marveled, marveling, marvels** also **marvelled, marvelling, marvels** To be filled with surprise, astonishment, or wonder: *We marveled at the gymnast's strength and grace.*

marvelous also **marvellous** (mär′və-ləs) *adj.* **1.** Causing wonder or astonishment: *a marvelous cure for the disease.* **2.** Excellent; notably superior: *a marvelous collection of rare books.* —**mar′vel·ous·ly** *adv.*

Marxism (märk′sĭz′əm) *n.* The political, economic, and social theories of the German philosopher Karl Marx (1818–1883), which claim that struggle between the classes plays a central role in the development of societies, and which predict that all societies will eventually develop from capitalism through socialism to communism. —**Marx′ist** *adj. & n.*

marzipan (mär′zə-păn′) *n.* A very sweet confection flavored with ground almonds. It is molded into decorative shapes and often colored to look like fruit.

masa (mä′sə) *n.* Dough made of dried corn that has been soaked in limewater, then rinsed and ground. Masa is used to make tortillas and tamales.

Masai (mä-sī′ *or* mä′sī) *n., pl.* **Masai** or **Masais** **1.** A member of a chiefly pastoral people of Kenya and parts of Tanzania. **2.** The Nilotic language of this people. —**Ma·sai′** *adj.*

masala (mä-sä′lä) *n.* Any of various mixtures of spices that are used in southern Asian cuisine.

masc. An abbreviation of masculine.

mascara (mă-skăr′ə) *n.* A cosmetic used to darken the eyelashes.

mascarpone (mäs′kär-pō′nĕ *or* mäs′kär-pōn′) *n.* A fresh soft Italian cheese with a high butterfat content, made from light cream.

mascot (măs′kŏt′ *or* măs′kət) *n.* An animal, person, or object believed to bring good luck or used as the symbol of a sports team or other organization.

masculine (măs′kyə-lĭn) *adj.* **1.** Relating to men or boys.

2. Marked by or possessing qualities traditionally attributed to a man: *a masculine hair style.* **3.** In grammar, relating to or belonging to the gender of nouns that refer to males or to things classified as male: *In French the word for "boat" is masculine.*

masculinity (măs′kyə-lĭn′ĭ-tē) *n.* The quality or condition of being masculine.

maser (mā′zər) *n.* **1.** Any of several devices that amplify or generate microwaves. Masers are similar to lasers but emit microwaves instead of light. **2.** A natural object or region of space that acts like a maser, as a region where stars are formed.

mash (măsh) *n.* **1.** A mixture of crushed grain and water that ferments and is used in making beer, ale, and whiskey. **2.** A mixture of crushed grain and water fed to livestock and fowl. **3.** A soft pulpy mixture. ❖ *tr.v.* **mashed, mashing, mashes 1.** To convert (grain) into mash. **2.** To convert into a soft pulpy mixture: *mash potatoes.* **3.** To crush; smash: *I mashed the walnut with a hammer.* ◆ **mash up** To combine (two or more audio or video recordings) to produce a composite recording. —**mash′er** *n.*

mashed potatoes (măsht) *pl.n.* Potatoes that are boiled and mashed, often with milk and butter.

mask (măsk) *n.* **1.** A covering, often having openings for the eyes, worn over part or all of the face as a disguise: *a Halloween mask.* **2.** A protective covering for the face: *a welder's mask.* **3.** A covering for the mouth and nose: *a dust mask.* **4.** A usually rubber frame that forms a watertight seal around the eyes and nose and holds a transparent piece of plastic or glass, allowing the wearer to see underwater. **5.** A representation of a face, often made of plaster or clay. **6.** Something that disguises or conceals: *His smile was a mask to cover his true feelings.* **7.** An area of contrasting color on the face and usually across the eyes of an animal. ❖ *tr.v.* **masked, masking, masks 1.** To cover with a mask: *The robbers masked their faces.* **2.** To cover in order to conceal, protect, or disguise: *She masked the baseboard with tape before painting the wall.*

masked (măskt) *adj.* **1.** Wearing or marked with a mask: *a masked bandit; a masked monkey.* **2.** Disguised; hidden: *masked disappointment.*

masking tape (măs′kĭng) *n.* A tape with adhesive on one side used for various purposes, such as to cover a surface that is not to be painted.

masochism (măs′ə-kĭz′əm) *n.* The tendency to derive pleasure from being subjected to pain or mistreatment. —**mas′o·chist** *n.*

mason (mā′sən) *n.* **1.** A person who builds or works with stone or brick. **2. Mason** A Freemason.

Masonic (mə-sŏn′ĭk) *adj.* Relating to Freemasons or Freemasonry.

Mason jar *n.* A glass jar with a wide mouth and an airtight metal lid, used for canning and preserving food.

masonry (mā′sən-rē) *n., pl.* **masonries 1.** The trade or skill of a mason. **2.** Work done by a mason; stonework or brickwork. **3. Masonry** Freemasonry.

masque (măsk) *n.* **1.** A dramatic entertainment performed by masked players and popular in European courts in the 1500s and 1600s. **2.** A masquerade dance or party.

masquerade (măs′kə-rād′) *n.* **1a.** A dance or party at which masks and fancy costumes are worn. **b.** A costume worn at such a dance or party. **2.** A disguise or false pretense. ❖ *intr.v.* **masqueraded, masquerading, masquerades 1.** To wear a mask or disguise, as at a masquerade.

2. To have a deceptive appearance; disguise oneself: *The undercover police officer masqueraded as a taxi driver.* —**mas′quer·ad′er** *n.*

mass (măs) *n.* **1.** A unified body of matter with no specific shape: *a mass of clay.* **2.** A large amount or number that is not specified: *A mass of people entered the stadium.* **3.** The major part; the majority: *The mass of voters supported the winning candidate.* **4.** The physical bulk or size of a solid body: *the huge mass of the ocean liner.* **5.** A measure of the amount of matter contained in a physical body. Mass is independent of gravity and therefore is different from weight. **6. masses** The ordinary people, as distinguished from the political or social elite. ❖ *tr. & intr.v.* **massed, massing, masses** To gather into or assemble in a mass: *The army massed its troops at the country's borders. The people massed downtown to watch the parade.* ❖ *adj.* **1.** Relating to, involving, or attended by large numbers of people: *a mass demonstration.* **2.** Done on a large scale: *mass production.*

Mass also **mass** *n.* **1.** The public celebration of the Eucharist in the Roman Catholic Church and some Protestant churches. **2.** A musical composition written for certain parts of the Mass.

Massachusett also **Massachuset** (măs′ə-chōō′sĭt *or* măs′-ə-chōō′zĭt) *n., pl.* **Massachusett** or **Massachusetts** also **Massachuset** or **Massachusets 1.** A member of a Native American people formerly living along the eastern coast of Massachusetts. **2.** Their extinct Algonquian language.

massacre (măs′ə-kər) *n.* **1.** An act of cruelly killing a large number of people. **2.** The slaughter of a large number of animals. ❖ *tr.v.* **massacred** (măs′ə-kərd), **massacring** (măs′ə-krĭng *or* măs′ə-kər-ĭng), **massacres** To kill cruelly in large numbers; slaughter.

massage (mə-säzh′ *or* mə-säj′) *n.* The rubbing or kneading of muscles and joints of the body to improve blood circulation and relax muscles. ❖ *tr.v.* **massaged, massaging, massages 1.** To give a massage to. **2.** To manipulate (data, for example): *The pollsters massaged the numbers to favor their candidate.*

mass-energy equivalence (măs′ĕn′ər-jē) *n.* The principle that mass and energy can be converted into each other and that a particular quantity of mass is equivalent to a particular quantity of energy. The principle can be stated mathematically as $E = mc^2$, where E is the energy in ergs, m is the mass in grams, and c is the speed of light in centimeters per second.

masseur (mă-sûr′ *or* mə-sûr′) *n.* A man who gives massages professionally.

masseuse (mă-sœz′) *n.* A woman who gives massages professionally.

massive (măs′ĭv) *adj.* **1.** Bulky, heavy, and solid: *a massive dining room table; a massive building.* **2.** Large in comparison with the usual amount: *a massive dose of penicillin.* **3.** Large or impressive in scope, intensity, degree, or scale: *a massive migration of birds.* —**mas′sive·ly** *adv.*

mass media *pl.n.* The various media of public communication by which information is conveyed to a large audience, such as television, radio, films, newspapers, and blogs.

mass noun *n.* A noun that refers to something that cannot be counted and thus does not take a plural form or appear with an article such as *a* or *an*. *Furniture, honesty,* and *wildlife* are mass nouns.

mass number *n.* The total of the neutrons and protons present in an atomic nucleus.

mass-produce (măs′prə-do͞os′) *tr.v.* **mass-produced, mass-producing, mass-produces** To produce in large quantities, especially on an assembly line: *mass-produce cars.*

mass production *n.* The act or process of producing large quantities of a product, as on an assembly line.

mass transit *n.* The public transportation system of a city and the area around it. Buses, subways, and trains are forms of mass transit.

mast (măst) *n.* **1.** A tall upright pole that supports the sails and rigging of a ship or boat. **2.** A tall vertical structure, such as an antenna for radio transmission.

mastectomy (mă-stĕk′tə-mē) *n., pl.* **mastectomies** Surgical removal of all or part of a breast, usually performed as a treatment for cancer.

master (măs′tər) *n.* **1.** A person who directs, rules, or controls others; a ruler: *Caesar was the master of the Roman Empire.* **2a.** The owner or keeper of an animal. **b.** The owner of a slave. **3.** A person in control of something: *the master of a banana plantation.* **4.** The captain of a merchant ship. **5.** An artisan who employs others, especially a person who trains apprentices. **6.** A male teacher, schoolmaster, or tutor, especially in a private school. **7.** A person of great learning, skill, or ability; an expert: *a master in metalwork.* **8. Master** A person who has received a master's degree. **9. Master** Used as a title before the name of a boy not considered old enough to be addressed as Mister. ❖ *adj.* **1.** Relating to or characteristic of a master. **2.** Principal; chief: *a master bedroom.* **3.** Highly skilled; expert: *a master carpenter.* **4.** Being a part of a mechanism that controls all other parts: *a master switch.* **5.** Being the original from which copies are made: *a master recording.* ❖ *tr.v.* **mastered, mastering, masters 1.** To become the master of; bring under control: *master one's emotions.* **2.** To become skilled in the use of: *master a foreign language.*

masterful (măs′tər-fəl) *adj.* **1.** Acting like a master; domineering. **2.** Expert; skillful: *a masterful performance of the concerto.* —**mas′ter·ful·ly** *adv.* —**mas′ter·ful·ness** *n.*

masterly (măs′tər-lē) *adj.* Knowledgeable and skillful like a master: *a masterly debate.* ❖ *adv.* With the skill of a master. —**mas′ter·li·ness** *n.*

mastermind (măs′tər-mīnd′) *n.* A person who plans or directs something. ❖ *tr.v.* **masterminded, masterminding, masterminds** To plan or direct (something): *mastermind the team's turnaround.*

master of ceremonies *n., pl.* **masters of ceremonies** A person who acts as the host at a formal gathering and introduces the speakers and entertainers.

masterpiece (măs′tər-pēs′) *n.* **1.** An outstanding work; something done with skill or brilliance: *The bridge was a masterpiece of engineering.* **2.** The greatest work of an artist or craftsperson: *This figure is the sculptor's masterpiece.*

master's degree (măs′tərz) *n.* A degree awarded by a college or university to a student who has completed at least one year of study beyond the bachelor's degree in a program. It ranks below a doctorate.

master sergeant *n.* **1.** A noncommissioned officer in the US Army and Marine Corps below sergeant major. **2.** A high-ranking noncommissioned officer in the US Air Force.

masterwork (măs′tər-wûrk′) *n.* A masterpiece.

mastery (măs′tə-rē) *n., pl.* **masteries 1.** Complete control or domination. **2.** Possession of great skill, knowledge, or technique: *the musician's great mastery of the piano.*

masthead (măst′hĕd′) *n.* **1.** The top of a ship's mast. **2.** The listing in a newspaper, a magazine, or another publication of its owners, staff, and information about its operation.

masticate (măs′tĭ-kāt′) *tr.v.* **masticated, masticating, masticates** To chew (food). —**mas′ti·ca′tion** *n.*

mastiff (măs′tĭf) *n.* A dog of a large powerful breed developed as a guard dog, having a short coat, large head, and square jaws.

mastodon (măs′tə-dŏn′) *n.* Any of several extinct mammals that resembled elephants and had long curved tusks. Mastodons disappeared from North America about 10,000 years ago.

mastoid (măs′toid′) *n.* The bone in the lower part of the skull behind the ear.

masturbate (măs′tər-bāt′) *intr.v.* **masturbated, masturbating, masturbates** To perform an act of masturbation.

masturbation (măs′tər-bā′shən) *n.* The act of stimulating the genitals, usually manually, to produce sexual pleasure.

mat¹ (măt) *n.* **1.** A flat piece of coarse material, often made of woven straw, hemp, or rushes, used as a floor covering or for wiping one's shoes. **2.** A small piece of material put under a dish, vase, or other object to protect or decorate the top of a table. **3.** A thick pad or mattress used on the floor for tumbling, wrestling, or acrobatics. **4.** A dense or tangled mass: *a mat of hair.* ❖ *v.* **matted, matting, mats** —*tr.* **1.** To tangle into a thick compact mass: *mat fibers together to make felt.* **2.** To cover with a mat or matting: *They matted the floor of the hut.* —*intr.* To become tangled into a thick compact mass: *The cat's fur matted without brushing.*

mat² (măt) *n.* **1.** A piece of cardboard or other material placed around a picture as a frame or border between the picture and its frame. **2.** Variant of **matte.** ❖ *tr.v.* **matted, matting, mats** To put a mat around (a picture). ❖ *adj.* Variant of **matte.**

WORD HISTORY Mat¹ comes from Old English *matte,* which comes from Late Latin *matta,* both meaning "piece of material placed on the floor." **Mat²** comes from French *mat,* meaning "dull."

matador (măt′ə-dôr′) *n.* The person who fights and kills the bull in a bullfight.

match¹ (măch) *n.* **1a.** A person or thing exactly like another: *Find the match for this fabric.* **b.** A person or thing that is similar to or goes well with another: *This tie is a good match for your shirt.* **2.** A person or thing with equal or near equal capabilities: *The runners were a good match and ran a very close race.* **3.** A sports contest: *a wrestling match.* **4a.** A marriage or an arrangement of marriage. **b.** A person viewed as a possible partner in marriage. ❖ *v.* **matched, matching, matches** —*tr.* **1.** To be alike; correspond exactly to: *This sock doesn't match that one.* **2.** To resemble or harmonize with; be suitable for: *Your shirt matches your slacks.* **3.** To fit together: *Match the edges of the seam and sew them together.* **4.** To find or provide a match for: *We could not match the color of the old paint on the door.* **5a.** To provide with an opponent or competitor: *The competition matched two relative newcomers against each other.* **b.** To place in competition: *They matched wits.* **6.** To join or give in marriage. —*intr.* **1.** To be alike or equal: *Finally your socks match.* **2.** To harmonize with another: *This tie and this shirt match.*

match² (măch) *n.* **1.** A narrow piece of material, usually wood or cardboard, that is coated at one end with a substance that catches fire easily when scratched against a surface that is rough or that has been treated with chemicals. **2.** An easily ignited cord or wick, formerly used to fire cannons and muskets or matchlock guns.

WORD HISTORY Match¹ comes from Middle English *macche,* which comes from Old English *gemæcca,* both meaning "companion, mate." **Match²** comes from Middle English *mecche,* meaning "lamp wick."

matchbook (măch′bŏŏk′) *n.* A small cardboard folder containing safety matches and a surface for striking them.

matchbox (măch′bŏks′) *n.* A box for matches that usually has a surface for striking them.

matchless (măch′lĭs) *adj.* Having no rival or equal: *his matchless ability to play the guitar.*

matchlock (măch′lŏk′) *n.* A musket in which the powder charge is ignited by a wick or match.

matchmaker (măch′mā′kər) *n.* **1.** A person who arranges or tries to arrange marriages for others. **2.** A person who arranges athletic competitions, especially in professional boxing.

matchstick (măch′stĭk′) *n.* A short slender piece of wood from which a match is made.

matchup (măch′ŭp′) *n.* The pairing of two people or things, as for sports competition or for comparison: *The finals featured a matchup of two former champions.*

mate¹ (māt) *n.* **1.** One of a matched pair: *Where is the mate to this sock?* **2.** A spouse or romantic partner. **3.** The male or female of a pair of animals that are breeding. **4.** A close associate; a partner: *We need more help from our mates to finish the job.* **5a.** An officer on a merchant ship ranking below the master. **b.** An officer of the US Navy ranking below and assisting a warrant officer. ❖ *v.* **mated, mating, mates** —*tr.* **1.** To join closely; pair. **2.** To unite in marriage. **3.** To bring (a male and a female animal) together for breeding. —*intr.* To pair; breed: *Many animals mate in the spring.*

mate² (māt) *n.* In chess, a checkmate. ❖ *tr. & intr.v.* **mated, mating, mates** To checkmate or achieve a checkmate.

mate³ (mä′tā) *also* **maté** (mä-tĕ′) *n.* **1.** A drink resembling tea, made from the dried leaves of an evergreen South American shrub related to holly. **2.** The shrub that bears such leaves.

WORD HISTORY Mate¹ comes from Middle English *mate,* which comes from Middle Low German *gemate,* both meaning "companion." **Mate²** comes from Middle English *mat,* meaning "checkmate," which comes from Arabic *māt,* meaning "he has died." **Mate³** comes from Quechua *mati,* meaning "calabash container."

material (mə-tîr′ē-əl) *n.* **1.** The substance or substances from which something is or can be made: *Hemp is often used as material for ropes.* **2.** Cloth or fabric: *a length of silk material.* **3.** Something, such as an idea or information, that is used or developed to make something else: *historical material for a novel.* **4. materials** Tools or apparatus needed to perform a certain task: *building materials.* ❖ *adj.* **1.** Relating to or composed of matter: *not a ghost, but a material being.* **2.** Relating to or affecting physical well-being: *material comforts.* **3.** Relating to or

concerned with the physical as opposed to the spiritual or intellectual: *I did it not for material gain but for personal satisfaction.* **4.** Important; relevant: *Is your remark material to this discussion?*

materialism (mə-tîr′ē-ə-lĭz′əm) *n.* **1.** The philosophical doctrine that physical matter is the only reality and that everything, including the mind, thoughts, and feelings, can be explained in terms of matter. **2.** The tendency to be concerned with money and possessions rather than with spiritual or intellectual things. —**ma·te′ri·al·ist** *n.* —**ma·te′ri·al·is′tic** *adj.* —**ma·te′ri·al·is′ti·cal·ly** *adv.*

materialize (mə-tîr′ē-ə-līz′) *intr.v.* **materialized, materializing, materializes** **1.** To come into existence; become real: *Support for the project never materialized.* **2.** To appear, especially suddenly: *The mountains in the distance materialized as the fog lifted.*

materially (mə-tîr′ē-ə-lē) *adv.* **1.** With regard to material well-being; physically: *He is doing well materially, but he isn't very happy.* **2.** To a significant extent or degree; considerably: *The additional data did not materially affect our conclusions.*

materiel *or* **matériel** (mə-tîr′ē-ĕl′) *n.* Equipment, apparatus, and supplies, especially those used by a military force.

maternal (mə-tûr′nəl) *adj.* **1.** Relating to or characteristic of a mother or motherhood: *maternal health.* **2.** Inherited from one's mother: *a maternal trait.* **3.** Related through one's mother: *maternal aunts and uncles.* —**ma·ter′nal·ly** *adv.*

maternity (mə-tûr′nĭ-tē) *n., pl.* **maternities** **1.** The state of being a mother. **2.** The feelings or characteristics that are part of being a mother; motherliness. ❖ *adj.* Relating to or effective during pregnancy, childbirth, or the first months of motherhood: *a maternity dress; maternity care.*

math (măth) *n.* Mathematics.

mathematical (măth′ə-măt′ĭ-kəl) *adj.* **1.** Relating to mathematics. **2.** Precise; exact: *mathematical correctness.* —**math′e·mat′i·cal·ly** *adv.*

mathematician (măth′ə-mə-tĭsh′ən) *n.* A person who is skilled in or who specializes in mathematics.

mathematics (măth′ə-măt′ĭks) *n. (used with a singular verb)* The study of the measurement, properties, and relationships of quantities and sets, using numbers and symbols. Arithmetic, algebra, and geometry are branches of mathematics.

matinee *or* **matinée** (măt′n-ā′) *n.* An entertainment, such as a movie or a dramatic performance, presented in the afternoon.

matriarch (mā′trē-ärk′) *n.* **1.** A woman who is a mother and head of a family, clan, or tribe. **2.** A respected older woman.

matriarchy (mā′trē-är′kē) *n., pl.* **matriarchies** A social system in which the mother is the head of the family and women have authority over men and children. —**ma′tri·ar′chal** (mā′trē-är′kəl) *adj.*

matrices (mā′trĭ-sēz′ *or* măt′rĭ-sēz′) *n.* A plural of **matrix.**

matricide (măt′rĭ-sīd′) *n.* **1.** The act of killing one's mother. **2.** Someone who kills his or her mother. —**mat′ri·cid′al** *adj.*

matriculate (mə-trĭk′yə-lāt′) *tr. & intr.v.* **matriculated, matriculating, matriculates** To enroll or allow to enroll in a college or university. —**ma·tric′u·la′tion** *n.*

matrimony (măt′rə-mō′nē) *n., pl.* **matrimonies** The act or condition of being married; marriage. —**mat′ri·mo′-ni·al** *adj.*

matrix (mā′trĭks) *n., pl.* **matrices** (mā′trĭ-sēz′ *or* măt′-rĭ-sēz′) or **matrixes 1.** A situation or substance within which something is contained, originates, or develops. The mineral grains of a rock in which fossils are embedded are a matrix. **2.** A regular arrangement of things, such as words or mathematical symbols, in columns and rows.

matron (mā′trən) *n.* **1.** A married woman or widow, especially a mother who is dignified and has an established social position. **2.** A woman who acts as a supervisor or guard in a school, hospital, or prison, or other public institution. —**ma′tron·ly** *adv. & adj.*

matron of honor *n., pl.* **matrons of honor** A married woman who serves as chief attendant of the bride at a wedding.

matte also **mat** (măt) *n.* A dull finish on something, as of paint or paper. ❖ *adj.* Having a dull finish.

matted (măt′ĭd) *adj.* **1.** Formed into a mass; tangled: *matted underbrush.* **2.** Covered with mats or matting: *a matted floor.*

matter (măt′ər) *n.* **1a.** Something that occupies space, has mass, and can exist ordinarily as a solid, liquid, or gas. **b.** A specific type of substance: *organic matter.* **2.** The substance or content of something: *The matter of the book was very interesting.* See Synonyms at **subject. 3.** A subject of concern, feeling, or action: *For me, this exam is a serious matter.* **4.** Trouble; difficulty: *What's the matter with them?* **5.** A certain quantity, amount, or extent: *The highway construction lasted a matter of years.* **6.** Something written or printed or to be written or printed: *reading matter.* ❖ *intr.v.* **mattered, mattering, matters** To be of importance: *Our success mattered a great deal to us.* ◆ **as a matter of fact** In fact; actually. **no matter** Regardless of: *No matter where you go, I'll be thinking of you.*

matter of course *n.* Something that is expected; a natural or logical result.

matter-of-fact (măt′ər-əv-făkt′) *adj.* **1.** Adhering strictly to the facts; literal: *a matter-of-fact description of the party.* **2.** Showing no emotion: *a matter-of-fact tone of voice.* —**mat′ter-of-fact′ly** *adv.*

Matthew (măth′yoō) *n.* The first Gospel of the New Testament, traditionally thought to have been written by Jesus's apostle Matthew.

matting (măt′ĭng) *n.* **1.** A coarse fabric of woven straw, hemp, or rushes, used especially for making mats or covering floors. **2.** Material formed into a mat: *a matting of leaves on the forest floor.*

mattock (măt′ək) *n.* A digging tool with a flat blade, used for cutting roots or breaking up soil.

mattress (măt′rĭs) *n.* A pad of heavy cloth filled with soft material or a group of springs, used on or as a bed.

maturation (măch′ə-rā′shən) *n.* The process of maturing or ripening.

mature (mə-tyoōr′ *or* mə-choōr′) *adj.* **maturer, maturest 1.** Having reached full growth or development: *a mature dragonfly.* **2.** Having the mental, emotional, or physical qualities associated with an adult: *a child who seems very mature.* **3.** Suitable or intended for adults: *a film with mature subject matter.* **4.** Worked out fully in the mind: *a mature plan of action.* **5.** Having reached the limit of its time; due: *a mature savings bond.* ❖ *v.* **matured, maturing, matures** —*tr.* To bring to full development: *Work-*

ing in the hospital has matured him. —*intr.* **1.** To reach full growth or development: *The peaches matured on the tree.* **2.** To become due: *This bond matures in seven years.* —**ma·ture′ly** *adv.*

maturity (mə-tyoōr′ĭ-tē *or* mə-toōr′ĭ-tē *or* mə-choōr′ĭ-tē) *n., pl.* **maturities 1.** The condition of being mature; full growth or development: *Tomatoes reach maturity in late summer.* **2.** The time at which payment of a loan or bond becomes due.

matzo or **matzoh** (măt′sə) *n., pl.* **matzos** or **matzohs** (măt′-səz) or **matzot** or **matzoth** (mät-sôt′) A brittle flat piece of unleavened bread, eaten especially during Passover.

maudlin (môd′lĭn) *adj.* Overly or foolishly sentimental.

maul (môl) *n.* A heavy hammer or mallet, used to drive stakes, piles, or wedges. ❖ *tr.v.* **mauled, mauling, mauls 1.** To injure or damage by beating: *The bear cub mauled the salmon before eating it.* **2.** To handle roughly: *The package was mauled in the mail.*

maunder (môn′dər *or* män′dər) *intr.v.* **maundered, maundering, maunders 1.** To talk in a rambling or confused way. **2.** To wander about in an aimless or confused way.

mausoleum (mô′zə-lē′əm) *n.* A stately building housing a tomb or tombs.

mauve (mōv) *n.* A light rosy or grayish purple.

maven (mā′vən) *n.* A person who has special knowledge or experience; an expert.

maverick (măv′ər-ĭk *or* măv′rĭk) *n.* **1.** A person who refuses to go along with the policies or views of a group. **2.** An unbranded calf or colt, traditionally belonging to the first person to brand it.

maw (mô) *n.* The mouth, throat, gullet, or stomach of an animal.

mawkish (mô′kĭsh) *adj.* Excessively and foolishly sentimental: *a mawkish poem about romantic love.* —**mawk′-ish·ly** *adv.* —**mawk′ish·ness** *n.*

max (măks) *Slang n.* The maximum: *The car can seat five adults, but that's the max.* ❖ *adj.* Maximal. ❖ *adv.* Maximally: *We'll pay $250 max.* ❖ *intr.v.* **maxed, maxing, maxes 1.** To reach one's limit, as of endurance or capability: *The weightlifter maxed out at 180 kilograms.* **2.** To reach a point from which no additional growth, improvement, or benefit is possible: *The salary for this position maxes at $65,000.*

max. An abbreviation of maximum.

maxilla (măk-sĭl′ə) *n., pl.* **maxillae** (măk-sĭl′ē) or **maxillas 1.** The upper jawbone in mammals or a similar bone in other vertebrates. **2.** Either of a pair of appendages behind the mandibles in insects, spiders, crabs, and other arthropods.

maxillary (măk′sə-lĕr′ē) *adj.* Relating to a maxilla. ❖ *n., pl.* **maxillaries** A maxilla bone.

maxim (măk′sĭm) *n.* A brief statement of a basic principle or rule of behavior; a proverb.

maximize (măk′sə-mīz′) *tr.v.* **maximized, maximizing, maximizes** To make as great or large as possible: *Working hard will maximize your opportunities.*

maximum (măk′sə-məm) *n., pl.* **maximums** or **maxima** (măk′sə-mə) **1.** The greatest known or greatest possible number, measure, quantity, or degree: *The temperature reached a maximum of only 10 degrees today.* **2.** An upper limit permitted by law or other authority: *The maximum speed limit on this road is 55 miles per hour.* ❖ *adj.* Having or being the greatest number, measure, quantity, or degree that is possible: *The train has a maximum speed of 120 miles per hour.*

may (mā) *aux.v.* Past tense **might** (mīt) **1.** To be allowed or permitted to: *May I go outside?* **2.** Used to indicate likelihood or possibility: *It may rain today.* **3.** Used to express a desire or wish: *May your days be filled with laughter.* **4.** Used to express purpose or result in clauses starting with *so that: I tell you this so that you may understand.*

May *n.* The fifth month of the year in the Gregorian calendar, having 31 days.

Maya (mä′yə) *n., pl.* **Maya** or **Mayas 1.** A member of an American Indian people of southeast Mexico, Guatemala, and Belize whose civilization reached its height around AD 300–900. **2.** Any of the languages spoken by the Maya.

Mayan (mä′yən) *n.* **1.** A Maya. **2.** A family of Indian languages spoken in Central America, especially by the Maya. ❖ *adj.* Relating to the Maya or their languages or culture.

maybe (mā′bē) *adv.* Possibly; perhaps: *Maybe we can go swimming tomorrow.* ❖ *n.* **1.** An uncertainty: *There are too many maybes with the current plans to formalize a schedule.* **2.** An uncertain reply: *I invited a dozen people; ten people are definitely coming, but two are maybes.*

mayday (mā′dā′) *interj.* An expression used internationally as a call for help, especially for planes or ships in trouble.

May Day *n.* May 1, celebrated in some countries as a spring holiday, and in others in honor of workers.

mayflower (mā′flou′ər) *n.* Any of various plants that bloom in spring.

mayfly (mā′flī′) *n.* Any of various delicate insects having transparent wings and long filaments extending from the end of the body. Adult mayflies live for only a few days and do not feed.

mayhem (mā′hĕm′ *or* mā′əm) *n.* **1.** In law, the willful maiming or injuring of a person. **2.** A state of confusion or destructive disorder.

mayn't (mā′ənt *or* mānt) Contraction of *may not.*

mayonnaise (mā′ə-nāz′ *or* mā′ə-nāz′) *n.* A thick dressing made of beaten raw egg yolk, oil, lemon juice or vinegar, and seasonings.

mayor (mā′ər *or* mâr) *n.* The chief government official of a city or town. **—may′or·al** *adj.*

mayoralty (mā′ər-əl-tē *or* mâr′əl-tē) *n., pl.* **mayoralties 1.** The position of a mayor. **2.** The term of office of a mayor.

Maypole also **maypole** (mā′pōl′) *n.* A pole decorated with streamers, ribbons, and flowers, around which people dance on May Day.

maze (māz) *n.* **1.** A complicated and often confusing network of pathways. **2.** A muddle or tangle: *a maze of contradictions.*

mazel tov (mä′zəl tôf′ *or* mä′zəl tôv′) *interj.* Used to express congratulations or best wishes.

mazurka (mə-zûr′kə *or* mə-zŏŏr′kə) *n.* **1.** A Polish dance that resembles the polka. **2.** Music written for this dance.

Mb An abbreviation of megabit.

MB An abbreviation of megabyte.

mbira (ĕm-bir′ə) *n.* A musical instrument consisting of a hollow gourd or wooden resonator and a number of usually metal strips that vibrate when plucked.

Mbps An abbreviation of megabits per second.

MC (ĕm′sē′) *n.* A master of ceremonies.

MD An abbreviation of: **1.** Medicinae Doctor (Doctor of Medicine). **2.** muscular dystrophy.

me (mē) *pron.* The objective form of I[1]. **1.** Used as the direct object of a verb: *He helped me.* **2.** Used as the indirect

object of a verb: *She sent me a letter.* **3.** Used as the object of a preposition: *They brought the books to me.*

USAGE The correct pronoun to use in sentences like *John and* _____ *are going home* is the nominative form, such as *I, he, she,* or *they,* not the objective form, such as *me, him, her,* or *them.* Therefore you say *John and I are going home,* not *Me and John are going home.*

mea culpa (mā′ə kŏŏl′pə *or* mē′ə kŏŏl′pə) *n.* An acknowledgment of a personal error or fault: *The authors issued a mea culpa after their plagiarism was revealed.* ❖ *interj.* An expression used to indicate guilt for a personal error or fault.

WORD HISTORY Mea culpa is from the Latin phrase *meā culpā,* meaning "through my fault."

mead[1] (mēd) *n.* An alcoholic beverage made of fermented honey and water.

mead[2] (mēd) *n. Archaic* A meadow.

WORD HISTORY Mead[1] comes from Old English *meodu,* meaning "alcoholic beverage made from fermented honey." **Mead**[2] comes from Old English *mǣd,* meaning "meadow."

meadow (mĕd′ō) *n.* A tract of land that is covered in grasses, especially one used as a pasture or for hay.

meadowlark (mĕd′ō-lärk′) *n.* Any of several songbirds of the Americas that have a brownish back and a yellow breast with a black V-shaped marking.

meager also **meagre** (mē′gər) *adj.* **1.** Lacking in quantity or richness; scanty: *a meager dinner.* **2.** Having little flesh; thin: *a meager face.* **—mea′ger·ly** *adv.*

meal[1] (mēl) *n.* A substance, especially grain, that has been ground.

meal[2] (mēl) *n.* **1.** The food served and eaten in one sitting. **2.** The customary time for eating food: *Don't eat between meals.*

WORD HISTORY Meal[1] comes from Middle English *mele,* which comes from Old English *melu,* both meaning "ground cereal grains." **Meal**[2] comes from Middle English *mel,* which comes from Old English *mǣl,* both meaning "the time for eating food."

mealtime (mēl′tīm′) *n.* The usual time for eating a meal.

mealy (mē′lē) *adj.* **mealier, mealiest 1.** Like meal; dry and granular: *a soft, mealy apple.* **2.** Made of or containing meal: *mealy chicken feed.* **3.** Covered with meal: *slipped on the mealy floor.* **4.** Lacking color; pale: *a mealy complexion.* **—meal′i·ness** *n.*

mealy-mouthed (mē′lē-mou*th*d′ *or* mē′lē-mouth′) *adj.* Unwilling to say directly or simply what one thinks is right or true.

mean[1] (mēn) *v.* **meant** (mĕnt), **meaning, means —** *tr.* **1.** To be used to convey; have the sense of; signify: *The Spanish word "frijol" means "bean."* **2.** To intend to convey or indicate: *What did you mean by that statement?* **3.** To have as a purpose or intention: *They mean no harm.* **4.** To design or intend for a certain purpose or end: *This building was meant for grain storage.* **5.** To be likely to result in; be attended by: *Dark clouds often mean a storm.* **6.** To bring about or have as a consequence: *Friction means heat.* **7.** To be of a specified importance; matter: *Your friendship means a great deal to me.* *—intr.* To have intentions of a certain kind: *She means well, despite her mistakes.* ◆ **mean business** *Informal* To be in earnest.

mean² (mēn) *adj.* **meaner, meanest 1.** Lacking kindness and goodwill: *The librarian was not being mean in asking you to be quiet.* **2.** Cruel; spiteful: *a mean remark made in anger.* **3.** Miserly; stingy. **4.** Low, as in quality, rank, or value; inferior: *rose from mean origins to fame and success.* **5.** *Slang* Hard to cope with; difficult: *She throws a mean curve ball.* **6.** Excellent: *He plays a mean game of chess.*

mean³ (mēn) *n.* **1.** Something that is midway between two extremes. **2.** A number or quantity that has a value that is intermediate between other numbers or quantities, especially an arithmetic mean or average. **3.** Either the second or third term of a proportion of four terms. In the proportion ⅔ = ⁴⁄₆, the means are 3 and 4. **4. means a.** Something, such as a method or course of action, by which an act or end is achieved: *a practical means of using the sun's energy to generate electricity.* **b.** Money, property, or other wealth: *a person of means.* ❖ *adj.* **1.** Occupying a middle or intermediate position between two extremes: *mean test scores.* **2.** Middling; average. ◆ **by all means** Without fail; certainly. **by any means** In any way possible; to any extent: *We must fix this problem by any means.* **by means of** With the use of; owing to: *They crossed the river by means of a raft.* **by no means** In no sense; certainly not: *By no means should you go sailing in rough weather.*

USAGE When **means** has the meaning of "financial resources," it takes a plural verb: *Her means are more than adequate for her to live there.* When *means* has the sense of "a way to an end," the word is singular when it refers to a particular method: *The best means of traveling there is by plane.* Means is plural when it refers to a group of methods: *What are the most effective means for doing this project?*

WORD HISTORY Mean¹ comes from Old English *mǣnan*, meaning "to tell of." **Mean²** comes from Old English *gemǣne*, meaning "common." **Mean³** comes from Middle English *mene*, which comes from Latin *mediāus*, both meaning "middle."

meander (mē-ăn′dər) *intr.v.* **meandered, meandering, meanders 1.** To follow a winding and turning course: *The river meanders through the valley.* **2.** To wander aimlessly and idly: *We meandered through the fields and woods.* See Synonyms at **wander.**

meaning (mē′nĭng) *n.* **1.** Something that is meant or signified, especially by language: *The word "head" has several meanings.* **2.** Something that one wishes to communicate: *The writer's meaning was easy to understand.* **3.** A goal or purpose: *What is the meaning of all this?* ❖ *adj.* Full of meaning; expressive: *a meaning smile.* —**mean′ing·ly** *adv.*

meaningful (mē′nĭng-fəl) *adj.* Full of meaning; significant: *a meaningful discussion.* —**mean′ing·ful·ly** *adv.*

meaningless (mē′nĭng-lĭs) *adj.* Having no meaning or significance: *a meaningless phrase.* —**mean′ing·less·ly** *adv.*

meanness (mēn′nĭs) *n.* **1.** The condition of being inferior or lacking in quality, character, or value. **2.** Selfishness; stinginess: *a miser's meanness.* **3.** A spiteful act.

mean sea level *n.* The average level of the ocean's surface, used as the standard for determining land elevations and ocean depths. Mean sea level is determined by measuring tide levels every hour for an extended time period and finding their arithmetical mean.

meant (mĕnt) *v.* Past tense and past participle of **mean¹.**

meantime (mēn′tīm′) *n.* The time between one occurrence and another: *In the meantime, keep practicing your music.* ❖ *adv.* Meanwhile.

meanwhile (mēn′wīl′) *n.* Meantime. ❖ *adv.* **1.** During or in the time between two events: *Meanwhile, she continued to improve her swimming stroke.* **2.** At the same time: *I'll put the food on the plates, and meanwhile, you set the table.*

measles (mē′zəlz) *n.* *(used with a singular or plural verb)* **1.** A highly contagious viral disease with symptoms that include coughing, fever, and red spots on the skin. **2.** Any of several milder diseases that have symptoms similar to measles, especially German measles.

measly (mēz′lē) *adj.* **measlier, measliest 1.** *Slang* Contemptibly small; meager: *A measly dollar is all they gave me.* **2.** Having measles.

measurable (mĕzh′ər-ə-bəl) *adj.* Possible to be measured: *The speed of light is very fast, but it is nonetheless measurable.* —**meas′ur·a·bly** *adv.*

measure (mĕzh′ər) *n.* **1.** The size or amount of something as determined by comparison with a standard: *What are the measures of that window?* **2.** A unit of measure specified by a scale, as an inch or pint. **3.** A system of such standards and units, as the metric system. **4.** Something, such as a container or ruler, used for measuring. **5.** The extent or degree of something: *There is a large measure of planning involved in putting on a play.* **6.** A standard of evaluation or basis for comparison: *A book's sales shouldn't be the only measure of its success.* **7.** Limit; bounds: *His generosity knows no measure.* **8.** often **measures** An action taken for a specified purpose or end: *It took drastic measures to clean up the harbor.* **9.** A legislative bill or act; a law. **10.** Poetic meter. **11.** The music between two bars on a staff. ❖ *v.* **measured, measuring, measures** —*tr.* **1.** To find the size, amount, capacity, or degree of: *Measure this board for me.* **2.** To serve as a measure of: *The foot measures length.* **3.** To mark off or dole out by measuring: *measure off a yard of fabric.* **4.** To estimate by comparison or evaluation; appraise: *measure the importance of a problem.* **5.** To choose with care; weigh: *I measured my words before answering the question.* —*intr.* **1.** To have a measurement: *The paper measures 8 by 12 inches.* **2.** To take measurements: *Always measure accurately.* ◆ **for good measure** In addition to the required amount. **measure up** To have the necessary qualifications: *The baseball player didn't measure up and was sent to the minors.* **measure up to** To be the equal of; fulfill or meet: *Did the concert measure up to your expectations?*

measured (mĕzh′ərd) *adj.* **1.** Found out by measuring: *the measured distance of almost a mile.* **2.** Regular in rhythm and number: *a measured beat.* **3.** Careful; deliberate: *measured and precise words.* —**meas′ured·ly** *adv.*

measureless (mĕzh′ər-lĭs) *adj.* Too great to be measured; immeasurable: *Infinity is measureless.*

measurement (mĕzh′ər-mənt) *n.* **1.** The act or process of measuring: *The experiment begins with measurement of the solution's acidity.* **2.** The dimension, quantity, or capacity found by measuring and expressed in units: *The tailor took my measurements.* See table on page 595.

measuring worm (mĕzh′ə-rĭng) *n.* An inchworm.

meat (mēt) *n.* **1.** The flesh of an animal eaten as food, especially beef, pork, or lamb, as distinguished from fish or poultry. **2.** The edible part of a nut or fruit: *chop nut meats.* **3.** The essential part of something; the gist: *the meat of the story.* **4.** *Archaic* Food: *meat and drink.*

Measurement

INTERNATIONAL SYSTEM

The International System (abbreviated SI, for Système International, the French name for the system) is an expanded and modified version of the metric system made up of seven base units from which all others in the system are derived. Larger or smaller multiples of any base unit are formed by adding a prefix to the unit and multiplying it by the appropriate factor. For example, to get a kilometer (multiplying factor $= 10^3$), you would multiply one meter by 1,000. Similarly, to get a centimeter (multiplying factor $= 10^{-2}$), you would multiply one meter by 0.01.

BASE UNITS

Unit	Quantity	Symbol
meter	length	m
kilogram	mass	kg
second	time	s
ampere	electric current	A
kelvin	temperature	K
mole	amount of matter	mol
candela	luminous intensity	cd

PREFIXES

Prefix	Symbol	Multiplying Factor	Prefix	Symbol	Multiplying Factor
tera-	T	$10^{12} = 1,000,000,000,000$	deci-	d	$10^{-1} = 0.1$
giga-	G	$10^9 = 1,000,000,000$	centi-	c	$10^{-2} = 0.01$
mega-	M	$10^6 = 1,000,000$	milli-	m	$10^{-3} = 0.001$
kilo-	k	$10^3 = 1,000$	micro-	m	$10^{-6} = 0.000,001$
hecto-	h	$10^2 = 100$	nano-	n	$10^{-9} = 0.000,000,001$
deca-	da	$10^1 = 10$	pico-	p	$10^{-12} = 0.000,000,000,001$

US CUSTOMARY SYSTEM

Unlike the International System of Units, the United States Customary System grew more out of customs and habits than as a planned system. For this reason it is not based on a carefully devised decimal system, but on commonly known distances and quantities. For example, the unit foot is based on the average length of a human foot, and the unit gallon is based on the quantity held by a container commonly used for holding wine.

LENGTH

Unit	Relation to Other US Customary Units
inch	½ foot
foot	12 inches or ⅓ yard
yard	36 inches or 3 feet
rod	16½ feet or 5¼ yards
furlong	220 yards or ⅛ mile
mile	5,280 feet or 1,760 yards

LIQUID VOLUME OR CAPACITY

Unit	Relation to Other US Customary
ounce	1/16 pint
gill	4 ounces
pint	16 ounces
quart	2 pints or ¼ gallon
gallon	128 ounces or 8 pints

WEIGHT

Units	Relation to Other US Customary Units
grain	1/7000 pound
dram	1/16 ounce
ounce	16 drams
pound	16 ounces
ton (short)	2,000 pounds
ton (long)	2,240 pounds

CONVERSION BETWEEN METRIC AND US CUSTOMARY SYSTEMS

The metric system is very similar to the International System, but it contains more than just the base units. For example, it includes multiples of base units, such as centimeters, deci-grams, and milliseconds. It also includes a unit of volume, the liter, defined as a thousand cubic centimeters.

FROM US CUSTOMARY TO METRIC

When you know	multiply by	to find
inches	25.4	millimeters
	2.54	centimeters
feet	30.48	centimeters
yards	0.91	meters
miles	1.61	kilometers
fluid ounces	29.57	milliliters
pints	0.47	liters
quarts	0.95	liters
gallons	3.79	liters
ounces	28.35	grams
pounds	0.45	kilograms

FROM METRIC TO US CUSTOMARY

When you know	multiply by	to find
millimeters	0.04	inches
centimeters	0.39	inches
meters	3.28	feet
	1.09	yards
kilometers	0.62	miles
milliliters	0.03	fluid ounces
liters	1.06	quarts
	0.26	gallons
	2.11	pints
grams	0.035	ounces
kilograms	2.20	pounds

TEMPERATURE CONVERSION BETWEEN CELSIUS AND FAHRENHEIT

$°C = (°F - 32) \div 1.8°$

Condition	Fahrenheit	Celsius
Boiling point of water	212°	100°
Normal body temperature	98.6°	37°

$°F = (°C \times 1.8) + 32$

Condition	Fahrenheit	Celsius
Freezing point of water	32°	0°
Lowest temperature Gabriel Fahrenheit could obtain mixing salt and ice	0°	−17.8°

meatball (mĕt′bôl′) *n.* A small ball of ground meat combined with various ingredients or seasonings and cooked.

meatloaf (mēt′lōf′) *n.* A baked loaf of ground meat and other ingredients.

meaty (mē′tē) *adj.* **meatier, meatiest 1.** Full of meat; fleshy: *a large meaty turkey.* **2.** Relating to or like meat: *a meaty odor.* **3.** Rich in substance; significant: *a meaty book.* —**meat′i·ness** *n.*

mecca (mĕk′ə) *n.* A place regarded as a center of activity or interest: *The scientist's lab was a mecca for young chemists.*

mechanic (mĭ-kăn′ĭk) *n.* A worker skilled in making, using, or repairing machines and tools. —**me·chan′ic** *adj.*

mechanical (mĭ-kăn′ĭ-kəl) *adj.* **1.** Relating to or involving machines or tools: *mechanical difficulties with the power saw.* **2.** Operated, produced, or performed by machine. **3.** Performed as if by a machine; showing no variety; dull: *routine mechanical tasks.* **4.** Relating to the science of mechanics. —**me·chan′i·cal·ly** *adv.*

mechanical drawing *n.* **1.** A drawing, as of tools or machines, done with rulers, compasses, and similar instruments. **2.** The technique or art of making such drawings; drafting.

mechanical engineering *n.* The branch of engineering that specializes in the design, production, and uses of machines.

mechanics (mĭ-kăn′ĭks) *n.* **1.** *(used with a singular verb)* The branch of physics that studies the action of forces on solids, liquids, and gases at rest or in motion. **2.** *(used with a singular or plural verb)* The development, production, and use of machines or mechanical structures. **3.** *(used with a plural verb)* The technical aspects of something, such as an activity or a sport: *the mechanics of swimming.*

mechanism (mĕk′ə-nĭz′əm) *n.* **1a.** A machine or mechanical device: *An egg beater is a useful mechanism.* **b.** The working parts of a machine: *an old clock's simple mechanism.* **2.** A system of parts that interact: *the mechanism of the solar system.* **3.** A process or means by which something is done or is brought into being: *A constitution is a mechanism for establishing a democratic government.*

mechanistic (mĕk′ə-nĭs′tĭk) *adj.* **1.** Relating to mechanics as a branch of physics. **2.** Relating to the philosophy that all natural events can be explained by material causes and physical principles.

mechanize (mĕk′ə-nīz′) *tr.v.* **mechanized, mechanizing, mechanizes** To equip with machinery: *mechanize a bakery.* —**mech′a·ni·za′tion** (mĕk′ə-nĭ-zā′shən) *n.*

med (mĕd) *adj. Informal* Medical: *med school; med students.* ❖ *n.* often **meds** *Slang* A medication or dose of medication.

med. An abbreviation of: **1.** medicine. **2.** medium.

medal (mĕd′l) *n.* A flat piece of metal with a special design, given as an award.

medalist (mĕd′l-ĭst) *n.* **1.** A person who has received a medal. **2.** A person who designs, makes, or collects medals.

medallion (mĭ-dăl′yən) *n.* **1.** A large medal. **2.** A round or oval ornament or design resembling a large medal. **3.** A circular portion of food, especially a cut of meat without any bones: *medallions of veal.*

meddle (mĕd′l) *intr.v.* **meddled, meddling, meddles 1.** To interfere in other people's business. **2.** To handle something carelessly or ignorantly; tamper: *Don't meddle with my cell phone!* —**med′dler** *n.*

meddlesome (mĕd′l-səm) *adj.* Inclined to interfere in other people's business.

Mede (mēd) *n.* A native or inhabitant of Media, a country in ancient Iran.

Medea (mĭ-dē′ə) *n.* In Greek mythology, a princess and sorceress who helps Jason obtain the Golden Fleece.

medevac (mĕd′ĭ-văk′) *n.* **1.** Transport of sick or wounded people, especially by helicopter, to a place where they can receive medical care; medical evacuation. **2.** A helicopter or other aircraft used for such transport. ❖ *tr.v.* **medevaced, medevacing, medevacs** To transport (a sick or wounded person) to a place where medical care is available, especially by helicopter.

media (mē′dē-ə) *n.* A plural of **medium.**

mediaeval (mē′dē-ē′vəl *or* mĕd′ē-ē′vəl *or* mĭ-dē′vəl) *adj.* Variant of **medieval.**

medial (mē′dē-əl) *adj.* **1.** Relating to or occurring in the middle: *the medial position.* **2.** Average; ordinary. **3.** In mathematics, relating to a mean or average. —**me′di·al·ly** *adv.*

median (mē′dē-ən) *adj.* **1.** Located in the middle: *a median barrier.* **2.** Relating to or constituting the middle value in a set of numbers: *median score.* ❖ *n.* **1.** Something that lies halfway between two extremes; a medium. **2.** The dividing area, either paved or landscaped, between opposing lanes of traffic on some highways. **3.** In mathematics, the middle number of a sequence having an odd number of values or the average of the two middle values if the sequence has an even number of values. For example, in the sequence 3, 4, 5, 6, 7, the median is 5; in the sequence 4, 8, 12, 16, the median is 10. **4.** In geometry: **a.** A line joining a vertex of a triangle to the midpoint of the opposite side. **b.** A line that joins the midpoints of the sides of a trapezoid that are not parallel.

mediate (mē′dē-āt′) *v.* **mediated, mediating, mediates** —*tr.* **1.** To settle (differences) by working with all sides: *mediate a dispute.* **2.** To bring about (an agreement) by working with all sides: *A negotiator mediated the new contract between the company and its workers.* —*intr.* To help the opposing sides in a dispute come to an agreement: *mediated between the warring factions.* —**me′di·a′tion** *n.*

mediator (mē′dē-ā′tər) *n.* A person or agency that mediates in a dispute.

medic (mĕd′ĭk) *n.* **1.** A person in a medical corps of the armed services. **2.** A physician or surgeon. **3.** A medical student or intern.

Medicaid (mĕd′ĭ-kād′) *n.* A program in the United States, jointly funded by the federal government and the states, that pays hospitals and physicians for providing medical care to people whose incomes are below a certain level.

medical (mĕd′ĭ-kəl) *adj.* Relating to the study or practice of medicine: *a medical problem; medical school.* —**med′i·cal·ly** *adv.*

Medicare (mĕd′ĭ-kâr′) *n.* A program in the United States, funded by the federal government, that pays hospitals and physicians for medical care provided to people over 65 years old.

medicate (mĕd′ĭ-kāt′) *tr.v.* **medicated, medicating, medicates 1.** To treat (a person, injury, or part of the body) with medicine. **2.** To put medicine on or in: *medicate a bandage.*

medication (mĕd′ĭ-kā′shən) *n.* **1.** A substance that helps to cure a disease, heal an injury, or relieve pain; a medicine. **2.** The act or process of medicating.

medicinal (mĭ-dĭs′ə-nəl) *adj.* **1.** Relating to or having the properties of medicine: *medicinal plants.* **2.** Having an unappealing, bitter flavor. **—me·dic′i·nal·ly** *adv.*

medicine (mĕd′ĭ-sĭn) *n.* **1.** The scientific study of diseases and disorders of the body and the methods of diagnosing, treating, and preventing them. **2.** The practice of this science as a profession. **3.** A drug or other substance used to treat a disease or injury. **4a.** A group of practices or beliefs, especially among Native Americans, believed to control nature, influence spiritual beings, or prevent or cure disease. **b.** Something, such as a ceremony or a sacred object, believed to have such abilities.

medicine ball *n.* A large heavy stuffed ball used for conditioning exercises.

medicine man *n.* A male shaman, especially among Native American peoples.

medicine woman *n.* A female shaman, especially among Native American peoples.

medieval also **mediaeval** (mē′dē-ē′vəl *or* mĕd′ē-ē′vəl *or* mĭ-dē′vəl) *adj.* **1.** also **Medieval a.** Relating to or characteristic of the Middle Ages. **b.** Relating to a historical period roughly coinciding with the European Middle Ages and characterized by feudal or aristocratic social structures, as in Japan or China. **2.** *Informal* Old-fashioned or lacking insight: *medieval ideas about social reform.*

Medieval Latin *n.* Latin as used from about 700 to 1500.

mediocre (mē′dē-ō′kər) *adj.* Neither good nor bad; ordinary; undistinguished: *a mediocre actor.*

mediocrity (mē′dē-ŏk′rĭ-tē) *n., pl.* **mediocrities 1.** The fact or condition of being mediocre. **2.** An ordinary undistinguished quality or performance.

meditate (mĕd′ĭ-tāt′) *v.* **meditated, meditating, meditates** *—intr.* **1.** To train, calm, or empty the mind, often by achieving an altered state, as by focusing on a single object. **2.** To think deeply and quietly; reflect: *The counselor meditated on the problem before coming to a decision.* *—tr.* **1.** To reflect on; contemplate. **2.** To consider at length; plan: *meditated a change of jobs.* **—med′i·ta′tor** *n.*

meditation (mĕd′ĭ-tā′shən) *n.* **1.** The process of meditating; contemplation: *The poet stared out the window, lost in meditation.* **2.** Deep reflection on spiritual or religious matters.

meditative (mĕd′ĭ-tā′tĭv) *adj.* Devoted to or characterized by meditation. **—med′i·ta′tive·ly** *adv.*

medium (mē′dē-əm) *n., pl.* **media** (mē′dē-ə) *or* **mediums 1.** A position, choice, or course of action midway between extremes: *a happy medium between hot and cold weather.* **2a.** The substance or surrounding environment in which an animal, plant, or other organism normally lives and thrives: *Some plants can grow in a salty medium.* **b.** The environment or surroundings in which a person thrives: *She's in her medium when she's on the stage.* **c.** An artificial substance in which bacteria or other microorganisms are grown for scientific purposes. **3.** A substance through which something is transmitted: *Air is one of the media through which sound can travel.* **4.** An agency by which something is accomplished, transported, or transferred: *Money is a medium of exchange.* **5.** One of the techniques, materials, or means of expression available to an artist: *That artist uses the medium of lithography.* **6.** *pl.* **media a.** A means for communicating to large

numbers of people: *television, radio, and other media.* **b.** Any of various kinds of devices for storing digital data. **7. media** *(used with a singular or plural verb)* The group of journalists and others whose work involves communicating information: *The governor provided a statement to the media.* **8.** *pl.* **mediums** A person who claims to be able to communicate with the spirits of the dead. **❖** *adj.* Occurring midway between extremes; intermediate: *of medium height.*

medium frequency *n.* A radio-wave frequency lying in the range between 300 and 3,000 kilohertz.

medley (mĕd′lē) *n., pl.* **medleys 1.** A mixture or variety: *a medley of events in the program.* **2.** A musical arrangement that uses a series of melodies from different sources.

medulla (mĭ-dŭl′ə *or* mĭ-do͞o′lə) *n., pl.* **medullas** or **medullae** (mĭ-dŭl′ē *or* mĭ-do͞o′lē) **1.** The inner core of certain structures of vertebrate animals, as the marrow of bone. **2.** The medulla oblongata.

medulla oblongata (ŏb′lông-gä′tə) *n., pl.* **medulla oblongatas** or **medullae oblongatae** (ŏb′lông-gä′tē) A mass of nerve tissue located at the top of the spinal cord and at the base of the brain. It controls breathing, blood pressure, heart rate, and certain other involuntary functions.

medusa (mĭ-do͞o′sə) *n., pl.* **medusas** or **medusae** (mĭ-do͞o′sē) The dome-shaped structure of jellyfish and certain other related animals, having a mouth underneath surrounded by tentacles.

Medusa (mĭ-do͞o′sə) *n.* In Greek mythology, the Gorgon who was killed by Perseus.

meek (mēk) *adj.* **meeker, meekest 1.** Showing patience and humility; gentle. **2.** Easily imposed upon; submissive: *Meek customers often fail to demand prompt service.* **—meek′ly** *adv.* **—meek′ness** *n.*

meerkat (mîr′kăt′) *n.* A small burrowing mammal of southern Africa, having brownish-gray fur and a long tail, which it uses for balance when it stands on its hind legs.

meerschaum (mîr′shəm *or* mîr′shôm′) *n.* **1.** A soft clay-like material that is usually white and is used as a building stone and for making tobacco pipes. **2.** A tobacco pipe with a meerschaum bowl.

meet[1] (mēt) *v.* **met** (mĕt), **meeting, meets** *—tr.* **1.** To come upon by chance or arrangement: *I was surprised to meet my old teacher in the park. I am supposed to meet my friends at the restaurant.* **2.** To get to know (another person) initially, especially by being introduced: *Have you met my sister?* **3.** To come together in conflict or opposition: *Our team will meet theirs in the playoffs.* **4.** To be present at the arrival of: *She is on her way to meet the train.* **5.** To come into contact with; join: *The stream meets the river at the rapids.* **6.** To come to the notice of: *There is more here than meets the eye.* **7.** To deal or cope with effectively: *We have met every problem and continued our progress.* **8.** To satisfy (a requirement, for example); fulfill: *You meet all the conditions for getting the loan.* **9.** To pay; settle: *Is there enough money to meet our expenses?* *—intr.* **1.** To come together; come face to face: *We'll meet tonight at the ice rink.* **2.** To become acquainted with one another for the first time: *My parents met on the ferry.* **3.** To come into contact; be joined: *The boards meet at the corner.* **4.** To come together as opponents: *The two teams met again last night.* **5.** To come together in a group; assemble: *The committee meets tonight.* **❖** *n.* A meeting or contest: *a track meet.* **◆ meet (one's) Maker** To die. **meet**

with **1.** To experience or undergo: *The explorers met with great difficulty when crossing the mountains.* **2.** To receive: *Our plan met with their approval.*

meet² (mēt) *Archaic adj.* Fitting; proper. —**meet′ly** *adv.*

WORD HISTORY Meet¹ comes from Old English *mētan*, meaning "to encounter, come across." **Meet²** comes from Old English *gemǣte*, meaning "suitable, proper."

meeting (mē′tĭng) *n.* **1.** A coming together; an encounter: *a chance meeting of friends.* **2.** A gathering or assembly of people, usually for a business, social, or religious purpose. **3.** A point where two or more things come together; a junction: *the meeting of two railroad lines.* ◆ **meeting of the minds** Agreement; concord.

meetinghouse (mē′tĭng-hous′) *n.* A building used for public meetings and especially for Quaker religious services.

meg (mĕg) *n. Informal* A megabyte.

mega– A prefix that means: **1.** One million (10⁶): *mega-hertz; megabit.* **2.** 1,048,576 (2²⁰): *megabyte.* **3.** Large: *megalith.* **4.** Surpassing other examples of its kind; extraordinary: *megahit.*

megabit (mĕg′ə-bĭt′) *n.* One million bits, used as a unit to measure the rate of the transmission of computer data.

megabyte (mĕg′ə-bīt′) *n.* A unit of computer memory equal to 1,024 kilobytes (2²⁰ bytes).

megacycle (mĕg′ə-sī′kəl) *n.* One megahertz.

megahertz (mĕg′ə-hûrts′) *n., pl.* **megahertz** A unit of frequency equal to one million cycles per second, used to express the frequency of radio waves.

megahit (mĕg′ə-hĭt′) *n.* A product or event, such as a movie or concert, that is exceedingly successful.

megalith (mĕg′ə-lĭth′) *n.* A very large stone used in the building of prehistoric monuments.

megalomania (mĕg′ə-lō-mā′nē-ə *or* mĕg′ə-lō-mān′yə) *n.* An obsession with making oneself powerful or getting what one wants, especially on a grand scale. —**meg′-a·lo·ma′ni·ac′** *n.*

megalopolis (mĕg′ə-lŏp′ə-lĭs) *n.* A large urban region containing several large cities that border each other.

megaphone (mĕg′ə-fōn′) *n.* A large funnel-shaped horn, used to direct and amplify the voice.

megapixel (mĕg′ə-pĭk′səl) *n.* One million pixels.

megaton (mĕg′ə-tŭn′) *n.* A unit of explosive force equal to that of one million metric tons of TNT.

megawatt (mĕg′ə-wŏt′) *n.* A unit of electrical power equal to one million watts.

meiosis (mī-ō′sĭs) *n., pl.* **meioses** (mī-ō′sēz′) A form of cell division in which the number of chromosomes is reduced to half the original number, resulting in the production of reproductive cells such as gametes in animals and spores in plants and fungi.

meitnerium (mīt-nûr′ē-əm) *n. Symbol* **Mt** A radioactive element that has been artificially produced by scientists. The half-life of its longest-lived isotope is seven-tenths of a second. Atomic number 109. See **Periodic Table.**

melancholia (mĕl′ən-kō′lē-ə) *n.* Extreme, persistent sadness or depression.

melancholic (mĕl′ən-kŏl′ĭk) *adj.* **1.** Sad and gloomy; melancholy. **2.** Relating to or suffering from melancholia. —SEE NOTE AT **humor.**

melancholy (mĕl′ən-kŏl′ē) *n.* Sadness or depression of the spirits. ◆ *adj.* **1.** Sad; gloomy. See Synonyms at **sad.**

2. Inspiring sadness; depressing: *the melancholy notes of a funeral dirge.*

Melanesian (mĕl′ə-nē′zhən) *adj.* Relating to Melanesia or its peoples, languages, or cultures. ❖ *n.* **1.** A member of any of the peoples of Melanesia. **2.** The group of languages spoken in Melanesia.

mélange also **melange** (mā-länzh′) *n.* A mixture.

melanin (mĕl′ə-nĭn) *n.* A dark pigment found in most animals. In humans it occurs in the skin, hair, and eyes.

melanoma (mĕl′ə-nō′mə) *n.* A dark-colored, usually malignant tumor that most often arises in the skin.

Melba toast (mĕl′bə) *n.* Crisp, thinly sliced toast.

meld¹ (mĕld) *intr. & tr.v.* **melded, melding, melds** To merge or cause to merge; unite; blend. ❖ *n.* A blend or a merger: *This restaurant features a meld of French and Indian cuisines.*

meld² (mĕld) *v.* **melded, melding, melds** —*tr.* In certain card games, to declare or show (a card or combination of cards) as a means of adding points to a score. —*intr.* To meld a card or combination of cards. ❖ *n.* A combination of cards to be presented for a score.

WORD HISTORY Meld¹ may have been coined by blending *melt* and *weld*. **Meld²** probably comes from German *melden*, meaning "to announce."

melee (mā′lā′ *or* mā-lā′) *n.* A confused fight among a number of people.

mellifluous (mə-lĭf′lōō-əs) *adj.* Having a pleasant and soothing sound: *a mellifluous voice.* —**mel·lif′lu·ous·ly** *adv.*

mellophone (mĕl′ə-fōn′) *n.* A brass musical instrument, similar to the French horn, often used in military or marching bands.

mellow (mĕl′ō) *adj.* **mellower, mellowest 1a.** Soft, sweet, or juicy; fully ripened: *a mellow peach.* **b.** Rich and full in flavor; properly aged: *mellow wine.* **2.** Rich and soft in quality: *the mellow colors of autumn.* **3.** Having or showing gentleness, wisdom, and tolerance; mature. **4.** Relaxed and unhurried; easygoing: *a mellow conversation.* ❖ *tr. & intr.v.* **mellowed, mellowing, mellows** To make or become mellow: *Time often mellows youthful intolerance. Wine mellows over a period of years.* —**mel′low·ly** *adv.*

melodic (mə-lŏd′ĭk) *adj.* Relating to or containing melody. —**me·lod′i·cal·ly** *adv.*

melodious (mə-lō′dē-əs) *adj.* Containing pleasant sounds; pleasant to listen to: *a melodious voice.* —**me·lo′-di·ous·ly** *adv.*

melodrama (mĕl′ə-drä′mə *or* mĕl′ə-drăm′ə) *n.* **1.** A drama characterized by exaggerated emotions, conflicts between characters, and often a happy ending. **2.** This kind of drama: *Melodrama is common on daytime TV.* **3.** Behavior or occurrences full of exaggerated emotions.

melodramatic (mĕl′ə-drə-măt′ĭk) *adj.* **1.** Relating to or characteristic of melodrama: *a melodramatic ending.* **2.** Exaggerated in emotion or sentiment: *a melodramatic speech.* —**mel′o·dra·mat′i·cal·ly** *adv.*

melody (mĕl′ə-dē) *n., pl.* **melodies 1a.** A succession of rhythmically arranged musical tones that forms a complete unit, often repeated several times in a song or other composition. **b.** The main part in a musical composition that has harmony. **2.** A pleasing arrangement of sounds: *The melody of a robin singing.*

melon (mĕl′ən) *n.* **1.** Any of several large fruits, such as a cantaloupe or watermelon, that grow on a vine and have a hard rind and juicy edible flesh. **2.** Any of the vines that bear such fruit.

melt (mĕlt) *v.* **melted, melting, melts** —*intr.* **1.** To be changed from a solid to a liquid state, especially by heating: *The ice melted in the sun.* **2.** To be taken up into a solution; dissolve: *Sugar melts in water.* **3.** To disappear gradually: *The crowd melted away after the rally.* **4.** To pass or merge into something else: *The blue melted into the green in the painting.* **5.** To become gentle in feeling: *Their hearts melted at the sight of the baby.* —*tr.* **1.** To change (a solid) to a liquid, especially by heating. **2.** To dissolve (a substance) in a solution: *The perfume consists of strong-smelling oils that are melted in alcohol.* **3.** To make gentler or milder; soften: *a look to melt the hardest heart.* ❖ *n.* A sandwich with melted cheese over the main ingredient, sometimes without the top slice of bread: *a tuna melt.* —**melt′er** *n.*

meltdown (mĕlt′doun′) *n.* **1.** The overheating of the core of a nuclear reactor, resulting in melting of the core and escape of radiation. **2.** *Informal* An emotional breakdown.

melting point (mĕl′tĭng) *n.* The temperature at which a given solid becomes a liquid. The melting point of ice is 0°C.

melting pot *n.* **1.** A container in which a substance is melted; a crucible. **2.** A place where people of different cultures or races form a single culture.

member (mĕm′bər) *n.* **1.** A part or organ of a plant, animal, or human body, especially a leg, arm, wing, or branch. **2.** A person or thing that belongs to a group: *a member of the cat family; a member of the United Nations.* **3.** A quantity that belongs to a mathematical set; an element of a set.

membership (mĕm′bər-shĭp′) *n.* **1.** The condition or state of being a member. **2.** The total number of members in a group: *The membership voted in a new club president.*

membrane (mĕm′brān′) *n.* **1.** A thin flexible layer of tissue that covers, lines, separates, or connects parts of a living organism. **2.** A layer that surrounds a cell or organelle, typically consisting of molecules of lipids and proteins. **3.** A thin sheet or layer of natural or artificial material.

membranous (mĕm′brə-nəs) *adj.* Relating to, made of, or similar to a membrane.

meme (mēm) *n.* A unit of cultural information, such as a cultural practice or idea, that is transmitted verbally or by repeated action from one mind to another.

memento (mə-mĕn′tō) *n., pl.* **mementos** or **mementoes** A reminder of the past; a keepsake: *These shells are mementos of our trip to the beach.*

memento mori (mə-mĕn′tō môr′ē) *n., pl.* **memento mori** A reminder of death or mortality, especially a death's-head.

memo (mĕm′ō) *n., pl.* **memos** A memorandum.

memoir (mĕm′wär′ or mĕm′wôr′) *n.* **1.** An account of the personal experiences of an author: *a memoir of childhood on a farm.* **2.** often **memoirs** An account of a person's own life; an autobiography: *wrote her memoirs when she turned 80.* **3.** A biography.

memorabilia (mĕm′ər-ə-bĭl′ē-ə or mĕm′ər-ə-bĭl′yə) *pl.n.* Things from the past that are worth remembering or keeping.

memorable (mĕm′ər-ə-bəl) *adj.* Worth being remembered or noted: *Memorable events are sometimes pictured on stamps.* —**mem′o·ra·bly** *adv.*

memorandum (mĕm′ə-răn′dəm) *n., pl.* **memorandums** or **memoranda** (mĕm′ə-răn′də) **1.** A short note written

as a reminder. **2.** A written record or communication, as in a business office. **3.** A short written statement outlining the terms of a legal or business agreement.

memorial (mə-môr′ē-əl) *n.* **1.** Something, such as a monument or holiday, established to serve as a remembrance of a person or event. **2.** A written statement of facts or a petition addressed to a government or legislature. ❖ *adj.* Serving as a remembrance of a person or event; commemorative: *memorial services; a memorial plaque.*

Memorial Day *n.* The last Monday in May, observed in the United States in honor of those members of the armed forces killed in war. Before 1971, it had been observed on May 30.

memorialize (mə-môr′ē-ə-līz′) *tr.v.* **memorialized, memorializing, memorializes** **1.** To honor with a memorial; commemorate. **2.** To present a memorial to; petition.

memorize (mĕm′ə-rīz′) *tr.v.* **memorized, memorizing, memorizes** To commit to memory; learn by heart. —**mem′o·ri·za′tion** (mĕm′ə-rĭ-zā′shən) *n.* —**mem′o·riz′er** *n.*

memory (mĕm′ə-rē) *n., pl.* **memories** **1.** The power or ability of remembering past experiences: *Thanks to a good memory, I could recall the details of what happened.* **2.** The part of the mind where knowledge is stored: *I committed the poem to memory.* **3.** Something remembered: *a pleasant memory of summer vacation.* **4.** The fact of being remembered; remembrance: *a ceremony in memory of our forebears.* **5.** The period of time covered by the ability of a group of people to remember: *the heaviest gale in living memory.* **6a.** A unit of a computer in which data is stored for later use. **b.** A computer's capacity for storing information: *How much memory does this computer have?*

men (mĕn) *n.* Plural of **man.**

USAGE When *man* and *men* are used in compounds, such as *fireman, firemen, salesman,* and *salesmen,* both *-man* and *-men* are usually pronounced (mən).

menace (mĕn′ĭs) *n.* **1.** A threat or danger: *a reef that is a menace to passing ships.* **2.** A troublesome or annoying person. ❖ *tr.v.* **menaced, menacing, menaces** To threaten; endanger: *The erupting volcano menaced the nearby town.*

menagerie (mə-năj′ə-rē or mə-năzh′ə-rē) *n.* **1.** A collection of wild animals kept in cages or pens on exhibition. **2.** A place where such animals are kept.

menarche (mə-när′kē) *n.* The time at which menstruation begins, usually occurring between ages 9 and 15. —**men·nar′che·al** *adj.*

men-at-arms (mĕn′ət-ärmz′) *n.* Plural of **man-at-arms.**

mend (mĕnd) *v.* **mended, mending, mends** —*tr.* **1.** To make repairs to; fix: *mend a jacket.* **2.** To reform or correct: *The judge always warns criminals to mend their ways.* —*intr.* **1.** To improve in health: *The patient is mending well.* **2.** To heal: *Her ankle mended slowly.* ❖ *n.* The act of mending. ◆ **on the mend** Improving, especially in health. —**mend′er** *n.*

mendacious (mĕn-dā′shəs) *adj.* **1.** Lying; untruthful: *a mendacious person.* **2.** False; untrue: *a mendacious explanation.* —**men·da′cious·ly** *adv.*

mendacity (mĕn-dăs′ĭ-tē) *n., pl.* **mendacities** **1.** The condition of being mendacious; untruthfulness. **2.** A lie: *The witness's testimony is a complete mendacity.*

mendelevium (mĕn′də-lē′vē-əm) *n. Symbol* **Md** A radioactive metallic element that has been artificially produced by scientists. Atomic number 101. See **Periodic Table.**

mendicant (mĕn′dĭ-kənt) *adj.* Depending on alms for a living: *a mendicant order of friars.* ❖ *n.* A beggar. —**men′di·can·cy** *n.*

Menelaus (mĕn′ə-lā′əs) *n.* In Greek mythology, a Spartan king who fights in the Trojan War for the return of his wife, Helen.

menfolk (mĕn′fōk′) or **menfolks** (mĕn′fōks′) *pl.n.* **1.** Men considered as a group. **2.** The members of a community or family who are men.

menhaden (mĕn-hād′n) *n., pl.* **menhaden** or **menhadens** Any of several fishes of western Atlantic waters, used chiefly as bait and as a source of fish oil and fertilizer.

menial (mē′nē-əl or mēn′yəl) *adj.* **1.** Relating to work or a job regarded as servile; lowly: *They let me run errands and perform other menial tasks for them.* **2.** Relating to or appropriate for a servant. ❖ *n.* A servant who performs the simplest or most unpleasant tasks. —**me′ni·al·ly** *adv.*

meningitis (mĕn′ĭn-jī′tĭs) *n.* Inflammation of the membranes that enclose the brain and spinal cord, usually resulting from a bacterial or viral infection.

meninx (mē′nĭngks) *n., pl.* **meninges** (mə-nĭn′jēz) Any of the three membranes enclosing the brain and spinal cord.

meniscus (mə-nĭs′kəs) *n., pl.* **menisci** (mə-nĭs′ī or mə-nĭs′kī) or **meniscuses** **1.** A crescent or crescent-shaped body, as the piece of cartilage at the knee joint. **2.** A lens that is concave on one side and convex on the other. **3.** The curved upper surface of a column of liquid. The surface is concave if the liquid adheres to the container walls and convex if it does not.

Mennonite (mĕn′ə-nīt′) *n.* A member of an Anabaptist church noted for its simplicity of living and pacifism.

men-of-war (mĕn′ə-wôr′) *n.* Plural of **man-of-war.**

Menominee (mə-nŏm′ə-nē) *n., pl.* **Menominee** or **Menominees** **1.** A member of a Native American people living in northeast Wisconsin. **2.** The Algonquian language of the Menominee.

menopause (mĕn′ə-pôz′) *n.* **1.** The time at which menstruation ceases, occurring usually between 45 and 55 years of age. **2.** The period during which such cessation occurs.

menorah (mə-nôr′ə) *n.* A candelabrum used in Jewish religious ceremonies, especially one with nine branches used in the celebration of Hanukkah.

mensch (mĕnsh) *n., pl.* **mensches** or **menschen** (mĕn′shən) *Informal* A person of integrity and honor.

menservants (mĕn′sûr′vənts) *n.* Plural of **manservant.**

menses (mĕn′sēz) *pl.n. (used with a singular or plural verb)* Menstruation.

menstrual (mĕn′strōō-əl) *adj.* Relating to or involving menstruation.

menstrual period *n.* A single monthly occurrence of menstruation.

menstruate (mĕn′strōō-āt′) *intr.v.* **menstruated, menstruating, menstruates** To undergo menstruation.

menstruation (mĕn′strōō-ā′shən) *n.* The monthly flow of blood from the uterus that begins at puberty in women and that results from the shedding of the lining of the uterus when fertilization of an egg does not take place. Certain other primates also undergo menstruation.

mensuration (mĕn′sə-rā′shən or mĕn′shə-rā′shən) *n.*

1. The act, process, or technique of measuring. **2.** The branch of mathematics that deals with finding measurements, such as lengths, areas, and volumes.

–ment A suffix that means: **1.** Act, action, or process: *statement; government.* **2.** State of being acted upon: *amazement; involvement.* **3.** Result of an action or a process: *advancement.* **4.** Means, instrument, or agent of an action or a process: *inducement.*

WORD BUILDING The suffix **–ment** forms nouns, chiefly by attaching to verbs. It can have several meanings, the most common being "an act or an instance of doing something" or "the state of being acted upon." Thus an *entertainment* can be "an act of entertaining" and *amazement* is "the state of being amazed." The suffix *–ment* can be traced back to the Latin noun suffix *–mentum.* Although its use in English dates back to the 1300s, it wasn't until the 1500s and 1600s that a great number of words were coined with *–ment.*

mental (mĕn′tl) *adj.* **1.** Relating to the mind: *mental capacity.* **2.** Occurring in or done by the mind: *a mental image; mental arithmetic.* **3.** *Often Offensive* Intended for the care of the mentally ill: *a mental hospital.* —**men′tal·ly** *adv.*

mental disorder *n.* Any of various disorders or diseases, such as schizophrenia or bipolar disorder, characterized by patterns of thought and behavior that cause significant distress or disability.

mental health *n.* **1a.** A state of emotional and psychological well-being: *Rest is important for your mental health.* **b.** A person's overall emotional and psychological condition: *Her mental health was poor after she lost her job.* **2.** A field made up of various professions, such as psychiatry and social work, that deals with the promotion of psychological well-being.

mental illness *n.* A mental disorder.

mentality (mĕn-tăl′ĭ-tē) *n., pl.* **mentalities** **1.** An outlook or characteristic way of thinking: *a cautious mentality.* **2.** Mental ability or capacity; intelligence: *a studious group of scholars of high mentality.*

mental retardation *n. Often Offensive* Impaired mental development due to disease, injury, or genetic defect.

menthol (mĕn′thôl′) *n.* A white crystalline compound obtained from peppermint oil and used in perfumes, as a flavoring, and as a mild anesthetic.

mention (mĕn′shən) *tr.v.* **mentioned, mentioning, mentions** To speak or write about briefly; refer to: *I mentioned your idea during the conversation.* ❖ *n.* The act of referring to something briefly or casually: *He made no mention of the incident in his report.* ◆ **not to mention** In addition to; as well as: *He was depressed, not to mention worried, about losing his cell phone.*

mentor (mĕn′tôr′ or mĕn′tər) *n.* **1.** A wise and trusted advisor. **2. Mentor** In Greek mythology, Odysseus's trusted counselor.

menu (mĕn′yōō) *n.* **1.** A list of foods and drinks available or served, as at a restaurant. **2.** The foods served or available at a meal. **3.** A list of available options, especially as displayed on a screen: *used the mouse to select "paste" from the menu.*

meow (mē-ou′) *n.* The cry of a cat. ❖ *intr.v.* **meowed, meowing, meows** To make the crying sound of a cat.

Mephistopheles (mĕf′ĭ-stŏf′ə-lēz′) *n.* The devil in the Faust legend to whom Faust sells his soul.

Mercalli scale (mər-kä′lē) *n.* A scale of earthquake intensity based on observed effects and ranging from I (detectable only with instruments) to XII (causing almost total destruction).

mercantile (mûr′kən-těl′ *or* mûr′kən-tīl′) *adj.* **1.** Relating to merchants or trade: *mercantile law.* **2.** Relating to mercantilism.

mercantilism (mûr′kən-tē-lĭz′əm) *n.* The economic system that prevailed in Europe in the 1500s and 1600s and stressed government regulation of the economy, profit from foreign trade, the founding of colonies and trade monopolies, and the storing of wealth in the form of gold and silver. —**mer′can·til·ist** *n.*

Mercator projection (mər-kā′tər) *n.* A map projection made with parallel straight lines instead of curved lines for latitude and longitude. In a Mercator projection, the areas near the poles appear disproportionately large, because the lines of longitude on the globe decrease in distance from each other as they approach the poles.

mercenary (mûr′sə-něr′ē) *adj.* **1.** Working only out of a desire for money. **2.** Hired for service in a foreign army. ❖ *n., pl.* **mercenaries** A soldier who is hired to serve in a foreign army.

mercerize (mûr′sə-rīz′) *tr.v.* **mercerized, mercerizing, mercerizes** To treat (cotton thread) with sodium hydroxide, so as to shrink the fibers, add luster, and make it dye more easily.

merchandise (mûr′chən-dīz′ *or* mûr′chən-dīs′) *n.* Things that may be bought or sold; commercial goods. ❖ *v.* (mûr′chən-diz′) **merchandised, merchandising, merchandises** —*tr.* **1.** To buy and sell (goods). **2.** To promote the sale of, as through advertising. —*intr.* To buy and sell goods; trade commercially. —**mer′chan·dis′er** *n.*

merchant (mûr′chənt) *n.* **1.** A person who buys and sells goods for profit. **2.** A person who runs a retail business; a shopkeeper. ❖ *adj.* **1.** Relating to trade or commerce; commercial: *a merchant establishment.* **2.** Relating to the merchant marine: *a merchant sailor.*

merchantman (mûr′chənt-mən) *n.* A ship used in commerce.

merchant marine *n.* **1.** A nation's commercial or trading ships considered as a group. **2.** The personnel who serve on such ships.

merciful (mûr′sĭ-fəl) *adj.* Having, showing, or feeling mercy; compassionate. —**mer′ci·ful·ly** *adv.*

merciless (mûr′sĭ-lĭs) *adj.* Having or showing no mercy; cruel: *a merciless tyrant.* —**mer′ci·less·ly** *adv.*

mercurial (mər-kyŏor′ē-əl) *adj.* **1.** Clever, shrewd, or quick. **2.** Changeable; fickle: *a mercurial disposition.* **3.** Containing or caused by the action of the element mercury. —**mer·cu′ri·al·ly** *adv.*

mercuric (mər-kyŏor′ĭk) *adj.* Relating to or containing mercury with a valence of 2.

mercuric chloride *n.* A poisonous white compound used as an antiseptic, in insecticides and batteries, and in photography.

mercuric sulfide *n.* A poisonous black or red compound formed by the reaction of mercury and sulfur and used as a pigment.

mercury (mûr′kyə-rē) *n.* **1.** *Symbol* **Hg** A silvery-white, poisonous metallic element that is a liquid at room temperature and is used in thermometers, barometers, and pesticides. Atomic number 80. See **Periodic Table. 2.** Temperature: *The mercury only rose to 25°F today.*

Mercury *n.* **1.** In Roman mythology, the messenger of the gods and patron of travelers, thieves, and commerce,

identified with the Greek Hermes. **2.** The planet nearest the sun and the smallest in the solar system, with a diameter about two fifths that of Earth. It orbits the sun once every 88 days, the shortest time for any planet.

mercy (mûr′sē) *n., pl.* **mercies 1.** Kindness or compassion toward another person: *The victorious army showed great mercy toward the vanquished foe.* **2.** A tendency to be kind and forgiving. **3.** Something for which to be thankful; a blessing: *It's a mercy no one was hurt.* ◆ **at the mercy of** Without any protection against; helpless before: *Drifting in the boat, they were at the mercy of the weather.*

mercy killing *n.* Euthanasia.

mere (mîr) *adj.* Superlative **merest** Being nothing more than what is specified: *The king at that time was a mere child.*

merely (mîr′lē) *adv.* Only; simply: *The fact that they arrived at the party at the same time was merely a coincidence.*

merengue (mə-rěng′gā) *n.* **1.** A dance in 2/4 time that originated in the Dominican Republic and Haiti having a quick tempo and characterized by a sliding step. **2.** The music for this dance.

meretricious (měr′ĭ-trĭsh′əs) *adj.* **1.** Attracting attention in a vulgar way. **2.** Plausible but actually false or insincere: *meretricious arguments.* **3.** Relating to prostitutes or prostitution. —**mer′e·tri′cious·ly** *adv.* —**mer′e·tri′cious·ness** *n.*

merganser (mər-găn′sər) *n.* Any of various fish-eating diving ducks having a long narrow hooked bill and usually a crested head.

merge (mûrj) *v.* **merged, merging, merges** —*tr.* To bring together so as to become one; unite: *The new management merged the two companies.* —*intr.* To come together to form one; blend together: *The two streams merge below town.*

merger (mûr′jər) *n.* The action of merging, especially the union of two or more corporations or organizations.

meridian (mə-rĭd′ē-ən) *n.* **1a.** An imaginary great circle passing through any place on the earth's surface and through the North and South Poles. **b.** Either half of such a circle from pole to pole. All the places on the same meridian have the same longitude. **2.** A similar semicircle that joins the poles of a celestial object or the poles of the celestial sphere. **3.** The highest point; the zenith: *High office is the meridian of a career in politics.*

meringue (mə-răng′) *n.* **1.** A mixture of stiffly beaten egg whites and sugar, often used as a topping for cakes or pies. **2.** A small pastry shell made of meringue.

merino (mə-rē′nō) *n., pl.* **merinos 1.** Any of a breed of sheep originally from Spain, having fine soft wool. **2.** Cloth or yarn made from this wool or any fine wool.

meristem (měr′ĭ-stěm′) *n.* The undifferentiated plant tissue from which new cells are formed, as that at the tip of a stem or root. —**mer′i·ste·mat′ic** (měr′ĭ-stə-măt′ĭk) *adj.* —**mer′i·ste·mat′i·cal·ly** *adv.*

merit (měr′ĭt) *n.* **1.** Superior worth; excellence: *a painting of great merit.* **2.** Something deserving of praise or reward: *the merits of a good education.* **3. merits** The actual facts of a matter, whether good or bad: *They discussed the merits of the different proposals.* ❖ *tr.v.* **merited, meriting, merits** To be worthy of; deserve: *Good deeds merit praise.*

meritocracy (měr′ĭ-tŏk′rə-sē) *n., pl.* **meritocracies** A social system in which promotions and pay are based on individual ability or achievement.

meritorious (měr′ĭ-tôr′ē-əs) *adj.* Having merit; deserving praise. —**mer′i·to′ri·ous·ly** *adv.*

Merlin (mûr′lĭn) *n.* In Arthurian legend, a magician who served as the royal counselor to King Arthur.

mermaid (mûr′mād′) *n.* An imaginary sea creature with the head and upper body of a woman and the tail of a fish.

merman (mûr′măn′ *or* mûr′mən) *n.* An imaginary sea creature with the head and upper body of a man and the tail of a fish.

merriment (mĕr′ĭ-mənt) *n.* Enjoyable fun and amusement.

merry (mĕr′ē) *adj.* **merrier, merriest 1.** Full of cheerfulness, liveliness, and good feelings: *a merry and festive crowd.* **2.** Characterized by fun and liveliness; festive: *a merry celebration.* **—mer′ri·ly** *adv.*

merry-go-round (mĕr′ē-gō-round′) *n.* A revolving circular platform having seats, usually in the form of horses, on which people ride for amusement.

merrymaking (mĕr′ē-mā′kĭng) *n.* **1.** Participation in festive activities. **2.** A festive party or celebration. **—mer′-ry·mak′er** *n.*

mesa (mā′sə) *n.* A high land area with a flat top and steep sides, larger than a butte and smaller than a plateau, common in the southwest United States.

mescaline (mĕs′kə-lēn′ *or* mĕs′kə-lĭn) *n.* A hallucinogenic drug derived from certain cactuses.

mesclun (mĕs′klən) *n.* A mixture of young, leafy greens used as salad.

Mesdames (mā-däm′ *or* mā-dăm′) *n.* Plural of **Madame.**

Mesdemoiselles (mād′mwä-zĕl′) *n.* A plural of **Mademoiselle.**

mesh (mĕsh) *n.* **1a.** Any of the open spaces in a net, sieve, or wire screen: *The meshes of this fishing net are one inch square.* **b.** often **meshes** The cords, threads, or wires forming a net or screen: *the fine wire meshes of the screen.* **2.** A net or network: *a fine mesh of interlacing wires.* **3.** A fabric with an open network of interlacing threads. **4.** **meshes** An entanglement; a trap: *caught in the meshes of their own bad decisions.* **5.** The engagement of two sets of gear teeth. ❖ *v.* **meshed, meshing, meshes** —*tr.* **1.** To catch in or as if in a net. **2.** To cause (gear teeth) to become engaged. —*intr.* To become engaged or interlocked: *The teeth of the gears failed to mesh.*

meshwork (mĕsh′wûrk′) *n.* Meshed material: *Macramé is an art form involving meshwork.*

mesic (mĕz′ĭk *or* mē′zĭk) *adj.* Relating to, characterized by, or adapted to a moderately moist habitat: *mesic grasslands; mesic species.*

mesmerize (mĕz′mə-rīz′) *tr.v.* **mesmerized, mesmerizing, mesmerizes 1.** To fascinate or enthrall: *The performance mesmerized the audience.* **2.** To hypnotize.

mesoderm (mĕz′ə-dûrm′ *or* mĕs′ə-dûrm′) *n.* The middle of the three layers of cells found in the early embryo of most animals, developing into muscles, bones, cartilage, blood vessels, and the organs of the reproductive system and the urinary tract.

Mesolithic (mĕz′ə-lĭth′ĭk *or* mĕs′ə-lĭth′ĭk) *adj.* Relating to the middle period of human culture in the Stone Age, between the Paleolithic and Neolithic Periods, beginning around 15,000 to 11,500 years ago in western Asia and southern Europe. The Mesolithic Period is characterized by the appearance of small-bladed stone tools and weapons and by the beginnings of settled communities. ❖ *n.* The Mesolithic Period.

mesosphere (mĕz′ə-sfîr′ *or* mĕs′ə-sfîr′) *n.* A layer of the atmosphere, between the stratosphere and the thermosphere, that extends from about 31 to about 50 miles (50 to 80 kilometers) above the earth's surface.

Mesozoic (mĕz′ə-zō′ĭk *or* mĕs′ə-zō′ĭk) *n.* The era of geologic time from about 251 to 66 million years ago. The Mesozoic Era was characterized by the development of flowering plants and by the appearance and extinction of dinosaurs. **—Mes′o·zo′ic** *adj.*

mesquite (mĕ-skēt′) *n.* Any of several thorny shrubs or small trees found in hot, dry regions of the Americas, having edible pods that are often used as forage for livestock.

mess (mĕs) *n.* **1a.** An untidy or dirty condition: *The kitchen is in a mess.* **b.** A person or thing that is in such a condition: *The house is a mess.* **2.** A disorderly mass or collection of things: *Who left the mess on the kitchen table?* **3.** A confusing or troublesome situation; a muddle: *We're in a mess because we ran out of paper.* **4.** A portion or quantity of food: *caught and cooked a mess of fish.* **5a.** A meal served to a group of people, especially a military group: *The soldiers lined up for morning mess.* **b.** A group, especially a military group, that takes its meals together. **c.** A room or hall where such a group takes meals. ❖ *v.* **messed, messing, messes** —*tr.* To make untidy or disorderly: *We took off our muddy boots so as not to mess the rug.* —*intr.* **1.** To use or handle something carelessly: *Who messed with the computer?* **2.** To take a meal: *The officers messed with their units.* ◆ **mess around** *Informal* To pass time aimlessly. **mess up 1.** To botch or ruin: *Losing my notes messed up my chances of doing well on the examination.* **2.** To make a mistake: *I messed up and overcooked the fish.*

message (mĕs′ĭj) *n.* **1.** A usually short communication sent from one person or group to another: *I found the message you left at my desk. She sent me a quick message by email.* **2.** An official statement delivered to a group: *a presidential message to Congress.* **3.** A basic theme, lesson, or moral: *a movie with a message for all of us.* ❖ *tr.v.* **messaged, messaging, messages** To send a message to: *As soon as I turned on my computer, my friends started messaging me.*

Messeigneurs (mā-sĕ-nyœr′) *n.* Plural of **Monseigneur.**

messenger (mĕs′ən-jər) *n.* **1.** A person who carries messages or runs errands. **2.** Something that indicates what is about to happen; a forerunner. ❖ *tr.v.* **messengered, messengering, messengers** To send by messenger: *We messengered the documents to our lawyer.*

messenger RNA *n.* A form of RNA that carries genetic information from the DNA in the nucleus of a cell to the ribosomes in the cytoplasm, specifying the particular protein to be synthesized.

Messiah (mĭ-sī′ə) *n.* **1.** The expected savior and king of the Jews, foretold by the prophets of the Hebrew Scriptures. **2.** In Christianity, another name for Jesus. **3.** **messiah** A leader who is regarded as a savior or liberator of a people.

messianic also **Messianic** (mĕs′ē-ăn′ĭk) *adj.* **1.** Relating to a messiah. **2.** Characterized by the belief that a particular cause or movement will triumph or save the world: *messianic nationalism.*

Messieurs (mā-syœ′ *or* mĕs′ərz) *n.* Plural of **Monsieur.**

mess kit *n.* A compact kit containing cooking and eating utensils, used by soldiers and campers.

Messrs.[1] (mĕs′ərz) *n.* Plural of **Mr.**

Messrs.[2] An abbreviation of Messieurs.

messy (mĕs′ē) *adj.* **messier, messiest 1.** In a mess; untidy: *a messy house.* **2.** Causing a mess: *the messy work of car repair.* **3.** Given to making messes; not neat or organized: *a messy roommate.* **4.** Difficult or unpleasant; complicated: *a messy situation.* —**mess′i·ly** *adv.* —**mess′i·ness** *n.*

mestiza (mĕs-tē′zə) *n.* A woman having European and Native American ancestors.

mestizo (mĕs-tē′zō) *n., pl.* **mestizos** or **mestizoes** A person having European and Native American ancestors.

met (mĕt) *v.* Past tense and past participle of **meet**[1].

metabolic (mĕt′ə-bŏl′ĭk) *adj.* Relating to or resulting from metabolism. —**met′a·bol′i·cal·ly** *adv.*

metabolism (mĭ-tăb′ə-lĭz′əm) *n.* **1.** The chemical processes taking place in a cell or organism that are needed to sustain life. In metabolism, some substances are broken down to yield the energy used for biological activities such as cell growth and repair, while other substances are synthesized from simple molecules. **2.** The processing of a specific substance in a cell or organism: *carbohydrate metabolism.*

metabolize (mĭ-tăb′ə-līz′) *v.* **metabolized, metabolizing, metabolizes** —*tr.* To subject (a substance) to metabolism: *Humans cannot metabolize cellulose.* —*intr.* To undergo metabolism: *Simple sugars metabolize quickly.*

metacarpal (mĕt′ə-kär′pəl) *adj.* Relating to the metacarpus. ❖ *n.* Any of the bones of the metacarpus.

metacarpus (mĕt′ə-kär′pəs) *n., pl.* **metacarpi** (mĕt′ə-kär′pī) **1.** The part of the human hand that includes the five bones between the wrist and the fingers. **2.** The corresponding part of the forefoot of a four-legged animal.

metal (mĕt′l) *n.* **1.** Any of a large group of elements, including iron, gold, copper, lead, and magnesium, that tend to lose electrons (becoming positive ions) and that conduct heat and electricity well. Metals usually have a shiny surface and can be hammered into thin sheets or drawn into wires. **2.** An alloy, such as steel or bronze, made of two or more metals.

metalanguage (mĕt′ə-lăng′gwĭj) *n.* A language or vocabulary used to describe or analyze another language.

metallic (mĭ-tăl′ĭk) *adj.* **1.** Relating to or having the qualities of a metal: *a metallic gleam.* **2.** Containing metal: *a metallic chemical compound.*

metalloid (mĕt′l-oid′) *n.* **1.** A nonmetallic element, such as arsenic, having properties of both a metal and a nonmetal. **2.** A nonmetallic element, such as carbon, that can form alloys with metals. ❖ *adj.* Relating to or having the property of a metalloid.

metallurgist (mĕt′l-ûr′jĭst) *n.* A person who specializes in metallurgy.

metallurgy (mĕt′l-ûr′jē) *n.* The science and technology of extracting metals from their ores, refining them for use, and creating alloys and useful objects from metals. —**met′al·lur′gi·cal** (mĕt′l-ûr′jə-kəl) *adj.*

metalwork (mĕt′l-wûrk′) *n.* Articles, especially decorative objects, made of metal.

metalworking (mĕt′l-wûr′kĭng) *n.* The act or process of making or shaping things out of metal.

metamorphic (mĕt′ə-môr′fĭk) *adj.* **1.** Changed by metamorphism: *metamorphic rock.* **2.** Relating to or characterized by metamorphosis: *metamorphic development of a moth.*

metamorphism (mĕt′ə-môr′fĭz′əm) *n.* The process by which rocks are changed in composition, texture, or internal structure by great heat or pressure.

metamorphose (mĕt′ə-môr′fōz′ *or* mĕt′ə-môr′fōs′)

v. **metamorphosed, metamorphosing, metamorphoses** —*intr.* **1.** To undergo metamorphism or metamorphosis: *Limestone metamorphoses into marble. The tadpoles will metamorphose into frogs.* **2.** To change completely in form or appearance; transform: *In the book, the teenager metamorphoses into a werewolf.* —*tr.* To cause to undergo metamorphism or metamorphosis.

metamorphosis (mĕt′ə-môr′fə-sĭs) *n., pl.* **metamorphoses** (mĕt′ə-môr′fə-sēz′) **1.** A marked or complete change in appearance, character, or form. **2.** Change in the form and habits of an animal during natural development after the embryonic stage. Metamorphosis occurs when caterpillars become butterflies and when tadpoles become frogs.

metaphase (mĕt′ə-fāz′) *n.* The stage in mitosis and meiosis during which the chromosomes group together toward the center of the cell and line up before separating.

metaphor (mĕt′ə-fôr′) *n.* **1.** A figure of speech in which a word or phrase that is ordinarily associated with one thing is applied to something else, thus making a comparison between the two. For example, when Shakespeare wrote, "All the world's a stage," he was using metaphor. **2.** Something that is meant to be viewed as a representation of something else; a symbol: *Her play is meant to be a metaphor for corporate greed.*

metaphorical (mĕt′ə-fôr′ĭ-kəl) or **metaphoric** (mĕt′ə-fôr′ĭk) *adj.* Relating to or using metaphors: *used a metaphorical expression to describe the experience.* —**met′a·phor′i·cal·ly** *adv.*

metaphysical (mĕt′ə-fĭz′ĭ-kəl) *adj.* **1.** Relating to metaphysics. **2.** Hard to understand; highly abstract. —**met′a·phys′i·cal·ly** *adv.*

metaphysician (mĕt′ə-fĭ-zĭsh′ən) *n.* A person who specializes or is skilled in metaphysics.

metaphysics (mĕt′ə-fĭz′ĭks) *n. (used with a singular verb)* The branch of philosophy that deals with the ultimate nature of things.

metastasis (mĭ-tăs′tə-sĭs) *n., pl.* **metastases** (mĭ-tăs′tə-sēz′) **1.** The spread of disease-causing cells, especially cancerous cells, from one location in the body to other locations. **2.** A secondary cancerous growth formed by the spread of cancerous cells from a primary growth located elsewhere in the body.

metastasize (mə-tăs′tə-sīz′) *intr.v.* **metastasized, metastasizing, metastasizes** To spread from one part of the body to another.

metatag (mĕt′ə-tăg′) *n.* A tag in a markup language that contains descriptive information about a webpage and does not appear when the webpage is displayed in a browser.

metatarsal (mĕt′ə-tär′səl) *adj.* Relating to the metatarsus. ❖ *n.* Any of the bones of the metatarsus.

metatarsus (mĕt′ə-tär′səs) *n., pl.* **metatarsi** (mĕt′ə-tär′sī) **1.** The part of the human foot that forms the instep and includes the five bones between the ankle and the toes. **2.** The corresponding part of the foot of a bird or the hind foot of a four-legged animal.

metate (mĭ-tä′tē *or* mĕ-tä′tĕ) *n.* A stone block with a shallow concave surface, used with a mano for grinding corn or other grains.

mete (mēt) *tr.v.* **meted, meting, metes** To distribute by or as if by measuring portions; allot: *The judge meted out a punishment to fit the crime.*

meteor (mē′tē-ər *or* mē′tē-ôr′) *n.* A bright trail or streak in the night sky, formed when a meteoroid enters the atmosphere and is so heated by friction with air molecules that it glows.

meteoric (mē′tē-ôr′ĭk) *adj.* **1.** Relating to or produced by meteors: *a meteoric flash.* **2.** Relating to the atmosphere: *Clouds are meteoric phenomena.* **3.** Like a meteor in speed, brilliance, or briefness: *the book's meteoric surge in popularity.*

meteorite (mē′tē-ə-rīt′) *n.* A meteoroid that has fallen to the earth's surface from outer space without completely burning up.

meteoroid (mē′tē-ə-roid′) *n.* A solid body that travels through space and is smaller than an asteroid and at least as large as a speck of dust.

meteorologist (mē′tē-ə-rŏl′ə-jĭst) *n.* **1.** A person who specializes in meteorology. **2.** A person who reports and forecasts weather conditions.

meteorology (mē′tē-ə-rŏl′ə-jē) *n.* The science that deals with the atmosphere and atmospheric conditions or phenomena, especially weather and weather conditions. —**me′te·or·o·log′i·cal** (mē′tē-ər-ə-lŏj′ĭ-kəl) *adj.* —**me′te·or·o·log′i·cal·ly** *adv.*

meter¹ (mē′tər) *n.* **1.** The arrangement of accented and unaccented syllables in a line of poetry; poetic rhythm. **2.** The pattern of beats in a measure of music; musical rhythm.

meter² (mē′tər) *n.* The basic unit of length in the metric system, equal to 39.37 inches. It was redefined in 1983 as the distance traveled by light in a vacuum in 1/299,792,458 of a second. See table at **measurement.**

meter³ (mē′tər) *n.* **1.** A device used to measure and record speed, temperature, or distance, or to indicate the amount of something used, as gas or electricity. **2.** A parking meter. ❖ *tr.v.* **metered, metering, meters** To measure with a meter: *metered the flow of water.*

WORD HISTORY All three forms of **meter** ultimately come from Greek *metron,* meaning "measure." **Meter¹** entered Modern English from Middle English *meter* (which comes from Old French *metre,* which comes from Latin *metrum*), **meter²** from French *mètre,* and **meter³** from the suffix *–meter.*

–meter A suffix that means measuring device: *speedometer.*

meter-kilogram-second (mē′tər-kĭl′ə-grăm-sĕk′ənd) *adj.* Relating to a system of measurement in which the meter, the kilogram, and the second are the basic units of length, mass, and time.

meth (mĕth) *n. Slang* Methamphetamine.

methadone (mĕth′ə-dōn′) *n.* A strong synthetic narcotic drug that is less addictive than morphine or heroin. It is used as a substitute for these drugs in programs for treating addiction.

methamphetamine (mĕth′ăm-fĕt′ə-mēn′) *n.* A derivative of amphetamine that is used in crystalline form as a central nervous system stimulant, both medically and illicitly.

methane (mĕth′ān′) *n.* A colorless, odorless, flammable gas that is the simplest of the hydrocarbons and has the formula CH_4. It is the major constituent of natural gas and forms by the decomposition of plant or other organic compounds, as in marshes and coal mines.

methanol (mĕth′ə-nôl′ *or* mĕth′ə-nōl′) *n.* A colorless, flammable, and poisonous liquid compound having the

formula CH_3OH. It is used as an antifreeze, a fuel, and a solvent.

methicillin (mĕth′ĭ-sĭl′ĭn) *n.* An antibiotic used to treat infections caused by staphylococcus bacteria that are resistant to penicillin. It is no longer in wide use.

methinks (mĭ-thĭngks′) *intr.v.* Past tense **methought** (mĭ-thôt′) *Archaic* It seems to me.

WORD HISTORY Most people nowadays regard **methinks** as a weird way of saying "I think." Actually, in Shakespeare's day, 400 years ago, it meant "it seems to me." There were originally two separate verbs spelled *think,* one meaning "to use the mind" and the other meaning "to seem." The second one could be used in phrases like *it thinks me* or (in reverse order) *me thinks it, me thinks,* meaning "it seems to me." Since *methinks* could introduce thoughts in a similar manner to *I think,* it was easily reinterpreted as an old-fashioned equivalent of *I think.*

methionine (mə-thī′ə-nēn′) *n.* An essential amino acid that is found in various proteins.

method (mĕth′əd) *n.* **1.** A regular or orderly way of doing something: *Boiling is one method of cooking rice.* **2.** Orderly arrangement of parts or steps in order to accomplish a goal: *Lack of method in solving problems wastes time.*

✦ **SYNONYMS** method, manner, routine, system *n.*

methodical (mə-thŏd′ĭ-kəl) *also* **methodic** (mə-thŏd′ĭk) *adj.* **1.** Arranged or done in regular order; systematic: *a methodical inspection.* **2.** Characterized by orderly habits or behavior: *a methodical researcher.* —**me·thod′i·cal·ly** *adv.* —**me·thod′i·cal·ness** *n.*

Methodism (mĕth′ə-dĭz′əm) *n.* The beliefs and worship of the Methodists.

Methodist (mĕth′ə-dĭst) *n.* A member of a Protestant church founded in England in the 1700s on the teachings of John and Charles Wesley.

methought (mĭ-thôt′) *v. Archaic* Past tense of **methinks.**

methyl (mĕth′əl) *adj.* Relating to or being the simplest hydrocarbon unit, CH_3, that is derived from methane and occurs in many important chemical compounds.

methyl alcohol *n.* Methanol.

meticulous (mĭ-tĭk′yə-ləs) *adj.* Showing or acting with extreme concern for details. —**me·tic′u·lous·ly** *adv.*

metonymy (mə-tŏn′ə-mē) *n., pl.* **metonymies** A figure of speech in which one word or phrase is substituted for another with which it is closely associated, as in the use of *Washington* for *the United States government* or of *the sword* for *military power.* —**met′o·nym′ic** (mĕt′ə-nĭm′ĭk), **met′o·nym′i·cal** *adj.* —**met′o·nym′i·cal·ly** *adv.*

metre (mē′tər) *n. Chiefly British* **1.** Variant of **meter¹. 2.** Variant of **meter².**

metric¹ (mĕt′rĭk) *adj.* Relating to the metric system.

metric² (mĕt′rĭk) *n.* A standard of measurement, especially one that evaluates a complex process or system.

WORD HISTORY **Metric¹** comes from French *métrique,* meaning "relating to the meter or the metric system." **Metric²** comes from Latin *metricus,* meaning "relating to measurement."

metrical (mĕt′rĭ-kəl) *adj.* **1.** Relating to or composed in poetic meter. **2.** Relating to measurement. —**met′ri·cal·ly** *adv.*

metrication (mĕt′rĭ-kā′shən) *n.* Conversion to the metric system of weights and measures.

metric system *n.* A decimal system of weights and measures based on the meter as its unit of length, the kilogram as its unit of mass, and the second as its unit of time.

metric ton *n.* A unit of mass or weight equal to 1,000 kilograms (2,205 pounds).

metro¹ (mĕt′rō) *n., pl.* **metros** A subway system.

metro² (mĕt′rō) *Informal adj.* Metropolitan: *metro Los Angeles.*

WORD HISTORY Both forms of **metro** are closely related to *metropolitan*; however, **metro¹** (spelled *métro* in French) comes not from the English word *metropolitan* but from the French phrase *chemin de fer métropolitain,* meaning "metropolitan railway."

metronome (mĕt′rə-nōm′) *n.* A device that makes a series of regularly repeated clicks at adjustable intervals. It is used to provide a steady beat for practicing music.

metropolis (mĭ-trŏp′ə-lĭs) *n.* **1.** A major city, especially the largest or most important city of a country, state, or region. **2.** A city regarded as at the center of a specific activity: *a great cultural metropolis.*

metropolitan (mĕt′rə-pŏl′ĭ-tən) *adj.* Relating to or characteristic of a major city: *metropolitan bus routes.* ❖ *n.* **1.** A person from a major city. **2.** A bishop who presides over a church province.

–metry A suffix that means process or science of measurement: *photometry.*

mettle (mĕt′l) *n.* The ability to meet a challenge or persevere under demanding circumstances; determination: *Adversity never fails to test someone's mettle.*

mettlesome (mĕt′l-səm) *adj.* Full of mettle; spirited.

MeV or **mev** An abbreviation of million electron volts.

mew (myōō) *intr.v.* **mewed, mewing, mews** To make the high-pitched cry of a cat. ❖ *n.* The crying sound of a cat.

mewl (myōōl) *intr.v.* **mewled, mewling, mewls** To cry softly, as a baby does; whimper.

mews (myōōz) *pl.n. (used with a singular or plural verb)* **1.** A group of buildings originally containing stables and often converted into apartments. **2.** A street or alley on which such buildings stand.

Mexican (mĕk′sĭ-kən) *adj.* Relating to Mexico or its people, languages, or cultures. ❖ *n.* A native or inhabitant of Mexico.

Mexican American *n.* A US citizen or resident of Mexican ancestry. —**Mex′i·can-A·mer′i·can** *adj.*

Mexican War *n.* A war (1846–1848) between the United States and Mexico that resulted in Mexico's giving up lands that now make up all or most of California, Arizona, New Mexico, Nevada, Utah, and Colorado.

mezuzah also **mezuza** (mə-zōōz′ə or mə-zōō-zä′) *n., pl.* **mezuzahs** also **mezuzas** (mə-zōōz′əz) or **mezuzot** (mə-zōō-zôt′) A small piece of parchment inscribed with biblical passages, rolled up in a container, and attached by many Jewish families to their door frames as a sign of faith.

mezzanine (mĕz′ə-nēn′ or mĕz′ə-nēn′) *n.* **1.** A partial story between two main stories of a building. **2.** The lowest balcony in a theater or the first few rows of the balcony.

mezzo forte (mĕt′sō fôr′tā′) *adv. & adj.* In music, moderately loud.

mezzo piano (pē-ä′nō) *adv. & adj.* In music, moderately soft.

mezzo-soprano (mĕt′sō-sə-prăn′ō or mĕt′sō-sə-prä′nō) *n., pl.* **mezzo-sopranos** **1.** A woman's singing voice of medium range, lower than a soprano and higher than

a contralto. **2.** A woman having such a voice. **3.** A part written in the range of this voice.

mg An abbreviation of milligram.

mgmt. An abbreviation of management.

mgr. An abbreviation of manager.

Mgr. An abbreviation of: **1.** Monseigneur. **2.** Monsignor.

MHz An abbreviation of megahertz.

mi (mē) *n.* In music, the third tone of a major scale.

mi. or **mi** An abbreviation of mile.

Miami (mī-ăm′ē or mī-ăm′ə) *n., pl.* **Miami** or **Miamis** **1.** A member of a Native American people originally living in Wisconsin and now living in Indiana and Oklahoma. **2.** The variety of Illinois spoken by the Miami.

miasma (mī-ăz′mə or mē-ăz′mə) *n.* **1.** A harmful atmosphere or influence. **2.** A bad-smelling vapor arising from rotting organic matter and formerly thought to cause disease. **3.** A thick vaporous atmosphere or emanation: *wreathed in a miasma of cigarette smoke.* —**mi·as′mal** *adj.*

mic (mīk) *n. Informal* A microphone.

mica (mī′kə) *n.* A member of a group of aluminum silicate minerals that can be split easily into thin, partly transparent sheets. Mica is highly resistant to heat and is used in electric fuses and other electrical equipment.

Micah (mī′kə) *n.* A book of the Bible in which the prophet Micah predicts the destruction of Jerusalem and the coming of the Messiah.

mice (mīs) *n.* Plural of **mouse.**

Michael (mī′kəl) *n.* The guardian archangel of the Jews in the Hebrew Scriptures. In Christian tradition, Michael was the leader of the angels in the war against Satan.

Michaelmas (mĭk′əl-məs) *n.* September 29, on which a Christian feast in honor of the archangel Michael is observed.

Micmac (mĭk′măk′) *n., pl.* **Micmac** or **Micmacs** Variant of **Mi'kmaq.**

micra (mī′krə) *n.* A plural of **micron.**

micro– or **micr–** A prefix that means: **1.** Small or smaller: *microcircuit.* **2.** Requiring or involving magnification or enlargement: *microscope.* **3.** One millionth: *microsecond.*

WORD BUILDING The basic meaning of the prefix **micro–** is "small." It comes from Greek *mīkros,* meaning "small." In English *micro–* has been chiefly used since the 1800s to form scientific words. It is the counterpart for the prefix *macro–* ("large") in pairs such as *microcosm/ macrocosm.*

microbe (mī′krōb′) *n.* A microorganism, especially a bacterium that causes disease. —**mi·cro′bi·al** (mī-krō′-bē-al) *adj.*

microbiologist (mī′krō-bī-ŏl′ə-jĭst) *n.* A scientist who specializes in microbiology.

microbiology (mī′krō-bī-ŏl′ə-jē) *n.* The branch of biology that deals with microorganisms. —**mi′cro·bi′o·log′i·cal** (mī′krō-bī′ə-lŏj′ĭ-kəl) *adj.*

microchip (mī′crə-chĭp′) *n.* An integrated circuit.

microcircuit (mī′krō-sûr′kĭt) *n.* An electric circuit made of miniaturized components.

microcosm (mī′krə-kŏz′əm) *n.* Something regarded as a miniature representation of something else: *The problems of the family are the nation's problems in microcosm.*

microcredit (mī′krō-krĕd′ĭt) *n.* The business or policy of making microloans to impoverished entrepreneurs.

microfiber (mī′krō-fī′bər) *n.* A very thin synthetic fiber that can be woven or knit into cloth that looks and feels like natural-fiber cloth but is more water-repellent and easier to care for.

microfilm (mī′krə-fĭlm′) *n.* **1.** A film on which written or printed material can be reproduced in greatly reduced size. **2.** A reproduction made on microfilm. ❖ *tr.v.* **microfilmed, microfilming, microfilms** To reproduce on microfilm.

microloan (mī′krō-lōn′) *n.* A very small, often short-term loan made to an impoverished entrepreneur, as in an underdeveloped country.

micromanage (mī′krō-măn′ĭj) *tr.v.* **micromanaged, micromanaging, micromanages** To manage (employees or projects), in such detail that it is meddlesome or irritating.

micrometeorite (mī′krō-mē′tē-ə-rīt′) *n.* A tiny particle of meteorite dust.

micrometer[1] (mī-krŏm′ĭ-tər) *n.* A device for measuring very small distances, angles, or objects, especially one based on the rotation of a finely threaded screw.

micrometer[2] (mī′krō-mē′tər) *n.* A unit of length equal to one millionth (10^{-6}) of a meter; a micron.

micron (mī′krŏn′) *n., pl.* **microns** or **micra** (mī′krə) A unit of length equal to one millionth (10^{-6}) of a meter.

Micronesian (mī′krə-nē′zhən) *adj.* Relating to Micronesia or its peoples, languages, or cultures. ❖ *n.* **1.** A member of any of the peoples inhabiting Micronesia. **2.** A group of languages spoken in Micronesia.

micronutrient (mī′krō-no͞o′trē-ənt) *n.* A substance, such as a vitamin or mineral, that is essential in very small amounts for the proper growth and metabolism of a living organism.

microorganism (mī′krō-ôr′gə-nĭz′əm) *n.* A microscopically small organism or virus. Bacteria, protozoans, and many fungi are microorganisms.

microphone (mī′krə-fōn′) *n.* A device that converts sound waves into an electric current, usually fed into an amplifier, a recorder, or broadcast transmitter.

microprocessor (mī′krō-prŏs′ĕs-ər) *n.* An integrated circuit that contains the entire central processing unit of a computer on a single chip.

microscope (mī′krə-skōp′) *n.* **1.** An optical instrument consisting of a lens or combination of lenses for magnifying objects that are invisible or indistinct to the unaided eye. **2.** An instrument, such as an electron microscope, that uses electrons or other means to produce magnified images.

microscopic (mī′krə-skŏp′ĭk) *adj.* **1.** Too small to be seen by the eye alone but large enough to be seen through a microscope: *microscopic cells.* **2.** Relating to or done with a microscope: *microscopic study of a specimen.* **3.** Done with great attention to detail: *a microscopic analysis of the city's budget.* —**mi′cro·scop′i·cal·ly** *adv.*

microscopy (mī-krŏs′kə-pē) *n., pl.* **microscopies 1.** The study or use of microscopes. **2.** Investigation using a microscope.

microsecond (mī′krō-sĕk′ənd) *n.* A unit of time equal to one millionth (10^{-6}) of a second.

microwave (mī′krō-wāv′) *adj.* Relating to electromagnetic radiation having wavelengths longer than those of infrared light but shorter than those of radio waves. Microwave radiation has wavelengths between 1 meter and 1 millimeter. ❖ *n.* **1.** A wave of microwave radiation. **2.** A microwave oven. ❖ *tr.v.* **microwaved, microwaving,**

microwaves To cook or heat (food) in a microwave oven.

microwave oven *n.* An oven in which microwaves are used to heat and cook food.

mid[1] (mĭd) *adj.* Middle; central.

mid[2] (mĭd) *prep.* Amid: *mid smoke and flame.*

mid– A prefix that means middle: *midsummer.*

WORD BUILDING The prefix **mid–**, which means "middle," is mostly added to nouns that refer to a time (*midmorning, midsummer, midyear*) or place (*midbrain, midstream, midtown*). When *mid–* is attached to a word beginning with a capital letter, it is always necessary to use a hyphen: *mid-November, Mid-Atlantic States.* The prefix *mid–* can be traced back to the Old English adjective *midd*, meaning "middle."

midair (mĭd′âr′) *n.* A point or region in the air: *a trapeze suspended in midair.* ❖ *adj.* Occurring in midair: *a midair collision.*

Midas (mī′dəs) *n.* In Greek mythology, a king who is given the power of turning all that he touches to gold.

midbrain (mĭd′brān′) *n.* The part of the brain that lies between the forebrain and the hindbrain. Its functions include control of reflex actions and eye movements.

midday (mĭd′dā′) *n.* The middle of the day; noon.

midden (mĭd′n) *n.* **1.** A mound or deposit containing shells, animal bones, and other refuse that indicates the site of a human settlement. **2.** A mound of discarded plant debris and other material created by an animal such as a pack rat or a squirrel.

middle (mĭd′l) *adj.* **1.** Equally distant from extremes; central: *the middle seats of the row.* **2.** Being halfway or intermediate in a sequence or series: *the middle child of three in the family.* **3.** often **Middle** Being a stage in the development of a thing, form, or period that is between earlier and later stages: *the Middle Kingdom of ancient Egypt.* ❖ *n.* **1.** An area or point equally distant from extremes; a center: *the middle of the room.* **2.** Something between a beginning and an end; an intermediate part: *A story has a beginning, a middle, and an end.* **3.** The middle part of the human body; the waist.

middle age *n.* The time of human life between youth and old age, usually reckoned as the years between 40 and 60.

middle-aged (mĭd′l-ājd′) *adj.* Relating to middle age.

Middle Ages *pl.n.* The period in European history between ancient times and the Renaissance, often dated from AD 476 to 1453.

middle C *n.* The musical tone represented by a note on the first ledger line above the bass clef.

middle class *n.* The people of a society who occupy a social and economic position between the working classes and the wealthy. The middle class usually includes professionals and highly skilled workers.

Middle Dutch *n.* The Dutch language from the middle of the 1100s through the 1400s.

middle ear *n.* The space between the eardrum and the inner ear. In humans and other mammals it contains three small bones that carry sound vibrations from the eardrum to the inner ear.

Middle English *n.* The English language from about 1100 to 1500, between Old English and Modern English.

Middle French *n.* The French language from around the middle of the 1300s to around the end of 1500s.

Middle Low German *n.* Low German from the middle of the 1200s through the 1400s.

middleman (mĭd′l-măn′) *n.* **1.** A trader who buys goods from producers and sells to retailers or consumers. **2.** An intermediary or a go-between.

middle school *n.* A school at a level between elementary and high school, typically including grades five or six through eight. —**mid′dle-school′** *adj.*

middleweight (mĭd′l-wāt′) *n.* **1.** A boxer weighing more than 147 and not more than 160 pounds (about 66–72 kilograms). **2.** A contestant in other sports in a similar weight class.

middling (mĭd′lĭng *or* mĭd′lĭn) *adj.* Of medium size, position, or quality; average: *a middling performance on the test.*

midfield (mĭd′fēld′) *n.* In sports, the section of a playing field midway between goals.

midfielder (mĭd′fēl′dər) *n.* A player in certain sports, such as soccer and lacrosse, positioned behind the forward line and playing both offense and defense.

midge (mĭj) *n.* Any of various very small flies, some of which form large swarms near ponds and lakes.

midget (mĭj′ĭt) *n.* **1.** *Offensive* A very small person of normal proportions. **2.** A small or miniature version of something.

midland (mĭd′lənd) *n.* The middle or interior part of a country or region.

midmost (mĭd′mōst′) *adj.* Situated in the exact middle or nearest the middle.

midnight (mĭd′nīt′) *n.* The middle of the night, specifically 12:00 at night.

midnight sun *n.* The sun as seen at midnight during the summer within the Arctic and Antarctic Circles.

midpoint (mĭd′point′) *n.* A point halfway between limits or endpoints.

midrib (mĭd′rĭb′) *n.* The central vein of a leaf.

midriff (mĭd′rĭf) *n.* The middle part of the human body that extends from just below the chest to the waist.

midsection (mĭd′sĕk′shən) *n.* A middle section, especially the midriff of the human body.

midship (mĭd′shĭp′) *adj.* Relating to or located in the middle of a ship.

midshipman (mĭd′shĭp′mən *or* mĭd-shĭp′mən) *n.* A student training to be an officer at a naval academy.

midships (mĭd′shĭps′) *adv.* Amidships.

midst (mĭdst *or* mĭtst) *n.* **1.** The middle position or part; the center: *a tree in the midst of the garden.* **2.** The condition of being surrounded by something: *trouble in the midst of good fortune.* **3.** A position near or among others: *a stranger in our midst.* ❖ *prep.* Among; amid.

midstream (mĭd′strēm′) *n.* **1.** The middle of a stream. **2.** The middle of a course of action or period of time: *We changed plans in midstream.*

midsummer (mĭd′sŭm′ər) *n.* **1.** The middle of the summer. **2.** The summer solstice, occurring on or about June 21 in the Northern Hemisphere. ❖ *adj.* Relating to or occurring during the middle of summer.

midterm (mĭd′tûrm′) *n.* **1.** The middle of a school term or a political term of office. **2.** An examination given at the middle of a school term. —**mid′term′** *adj.*

midtown (mĭd′toun′) *n.* The central part of a town or city.

midway (mĭd′wā′) *n.* The area of a fair, carnival, or circus where sideshows and other amusements are located. ❖ *adv.* In the middle of a distance or period of time.

midweek (mĭd′wēk′) *n.* The middle of the week.

midwife (mĭd′wīf′) *n., pl.* **midwives** (mĭd′wīvz′) A person, usually a woman, who is trained to assist women in childbirth. —**mid·wife′ry** (mĭd-wīf′ə-rē *or* mĭd′wīf′rē) —SEE NOTE AT **with.**

midwinter (mĭd′wĭn′tər) *n.* **1.** The middle of the winter. **2.** The winter solstice, occurring on or about December 22 in the Northern Hemisphere. ❖ *adj.* Relating to or occurring in the middle of the winter.

midyear (mĭd′yîr′) *adj.* Relating to or occurring in the middle of a year: *midyear reviews.*

mien (mēn) *n.* A person's manner of behavior or appearance; bearing: *the mien of a dignified professor.*

miff (mĭf) *tr.v.* **miffed, miffing, miffs** To offend or annoy: *I was miffed by their failure to do the job properly.*

might¹ (mīt) *n.* **1.** Great power or force: *the might of a great army.* **2.** Physical strength: *pushed with all my might.* See Synonyms at **strength.**

might² (mīt) *aux.v.* Past tense of **may. 1.** Used to indicate possibility or probability: *We might go to the beach tomorrow.* **2.** Used to express permission: *She asked if she might stay out late.*

WORD HISTORY Might¹ comes from Old English *meaht, miht* meaning "power." **Might²** ultimately comes from conjugated forms of the Old English verb *magan,* meaning "to be able."

mighty (mī′tē) *adj.* **mightier, mightiest 1.** Having or showing great power, strength, or skill: *a mighty hunter.* **2.** Great in size, scope, or intensity: *a mighty stone fortress.* ❖ *adv. Informal* Very; extremely: *They've been gone a mighty long time.* —**might′i·ly** *adv.* —**might′i·ness** *n.*

migraine (mī′grān′) *n.* A very severe headache, often accompanied by nausea, that usually affects only one side of the head and tends to recur.

migrant (mī′grənt) *n.* **1.** A person or animal that migrates. **2.** A farm worker who travels from one area to another in search of work. ❖ *adj.* Migratory; migrating.

migrate (mī′grāt′) *intr.v.* **migrated, migrating, migrates 1.** To move from one country or region and settle in another. **2.** To move regularly to a different region, especially at a particular time of the year: *Many monarch butterflies migrate from Canada to Mexico in the fall.*

migration (mī-grā′shən) *n.* The act or an instance of migrating.

migratory (mī′grə-tôr′ē) *adj.* Traveling from one place to another; migrating regularly: *migratory birds.* **2.** Relating to migration: *long migratory flights.*

mikado (mĭ-kä′dō) *n., pl.* **mikados** An emperor of Japan.

mike (mīk) *Informal n.* A microphone. ❖ *tr.v.* **miked, miking, mikes** To supply with or transmit through a microphone: *The assistant miked the singers before they went onstage.*

Mi'kmaq *or* **Micmac** (mĭk′măk′) *n., pl.* **Mi'kmaq** *or* **Mi'kmaqs** *or* **Micmac** *or* **Micmacs 1.** A member of a Native American people living in northeast Maine and southeast Canada. **2.** The Algonquian language of the Mi'kmaq.

mil (mĭl) *n.* A unit of length equal to one thousandth (10^{-3}) of an inch (0.025 millimeter), used chiefly to measure the diameter of wires.

milady (mĭ-lā′dē) *n.* Used as a form of address for an English noblewoman.

milch (mĭlch) *adj.* Giving milk: *a milch cow.*

mild (mīld) *adj.* **milder, mildest 1.** Gentle or kind in disposition, manner, or behavior: *a mild grandparent.* **2.** Moderate in type, degree, effect, or force: *a mild reprimand; a mild soap.* **3a.** Not extreme, as in temperature: *a mild climate.* **b.** Warm and full of sunshine: *a mild day.* —**mild′ly** *adv.* —**mild′ness** *n.*

mildew (mĭl′dōō′) *n.* **1.** Any of various fungi or water molds that form a white or grayish coating on surfaces, such as plant leaves, cloth, or leather, especially under damp warm conditions. **2.** The coating formed by such a fungus or water mold. ❖ *v.* **mildewed, mildewing, mildews** —*intr.* To become covered or spotted with mildew: *The leather coat mildewed in the damp closet.* —*tr.* To cause to become covered or spotted with mildew.

mile (mīl) *n.* **1.** A unit of length equal to 5,280 feet or 1,760 yards (about 1,609 meters); a statute mile. See table at **measurement. 2.** A nautical mile.

mileage (mī′lĭj) *n.* **1.** Length or distance in miles: *The mileage between the two cities is considerable.* **2a.** Total miles covered or traveled over a given time: *We haven't put much mileage on the car in the last month.* **b.** The amount of service, use, or wear measured by miles used or traveled: *a tire that gives long mileage.* **3.** The distance a motor vehicle travels on a given amount of fuel: *a mileage of 32 miles per gallon.* **4.** An allowance of a given amount for traveling expenses at a certain rate per mile: *The company pays a mileage of 45 cents per mile when I use my car for business travel.*

milepost (mīl′pōst′) *n.* A post along a highway that indicates the distance in miles to a certain place.

milestone (mīl′stōn′) *n.* **1.** A stone marker set up on a roadside to indicate the distance in miles from a given point. **2.** An important event; a turning point: *The Bill of Rights was a milestone in the history of human rights.*

milieu (mĭl-yōō′ *or* mē-lyœ′) *n., pl.* **milieus** *or* **milieux** (mē-lyœ′) An environment or a setting: *People often feel most comfortable in their own milieu.*

militant (mĭl′ĭ-tənt) *adj.* **1.** Fighting or making war: *militant bands of insurgents.* **2.** Aggressive or combative, especially in the service of a cause: *Militant strikers blocked the entrances to the business.* ❖ *n.* A militant person. —**mil′i·tan·cy** *n.* —**mil′i·tant·ly** *adv.*

militarism (mĭl′ĭ-tə-rĭz′əm) *n.* **1.** Glorification of military spirit or ideals. **2.** A policy in which maintaining strong armed forces is of chief importance to a country or an organization. —**mil′i·ta·ris′tic** *adj.*

militarist (mĭl′ĭ-tər-ĭst) *n.* A person who supports militarism.

militarize (mĭl′ĭ-tə-rīz′) *tr.v.* **militarized, militarizing, militarizes 1.** To equip or train for war. **2.** To fill with militarism. —**mil′i·ta·ri·za′tion** (mĭl′ĭ-tər-ĭ-zā′shən) *n.*

military (mĭl′ĭ-tĕr′ē) *adj.* **1.** Relating to or characteristic of the army, navy, or other branches of the armed forces: *a military base; military uniforms.* **2.** Relating to war: *military history.* ❖ *n., pl.* **military** *also* **militaries** The army, navy, or other branches of the armed forces of a country: *funding for the military; a takeover by the military.* —**mil′i·tar′i·ly** (mĭl′ĭ-târ′ə-lē) *adv.*

militate (mĭl′ĭ-tāt′) *intr.v.* **militated, militating, militates** To have force or influence; bring about an effect or change: *Carelessness militates against doing a good job.*

militia (mə-lĭsh′ə) *n.* **1.** An army composed of citizens rather than professional soldiers. **2.** A military force that is not part of a regular army and is subject to call for service in an emergency.

militiaman (mə-lĭsh′ə-mən) *n.* A man who is a member of a militia.

milk (mĭlk) *n.* **1a.** A white liquid produced by the mammary glands of female mammals for feeding their young.

b. The milk of certain mammals, especially cows, used as food by humans. **2.** A liquid resembling milk: *coconut milk.* ❖ *v.* **milked, milking, milks** —*tr.* **1a.** To squeeze milk from the teats or udder of (a cow, goat, or other mammal). **b.** To draw out or extract a liquid from: *milked the snake of its venom.* **2.** *Informal* To obtain money or benefits from, in order to achieve personal gain: *milk the treasury of its funds.* **3.** *Informal* **a.** To draw out or extract something from: *milked the witness for information.* **b.** To obtain the greatest possible advantage from (a situation). —*intr.* To draw milk from a cow, goat, or other animal.

milker (mĭl′kər) *n.* **1.** A person or machine that milks animals. **2.** An animal kept to give milk, as a cow or goat.

milkmaid (mĭlk′mād′) *n.* A girl or woman who milks cows.

milkman (mĭlk′măn′) *n.* A man who sells or delivers milk.

milk of magnesia *n.* A milky white suspension of magnesium hydroxide in water used as an antacid and a laxative.

milkshake (mĭlk′shāk′) *n.* A beverage that is made of milk, flavoring, and usually ice cream and is blended or shaken until foamy.

milk snake *n.* Any of various king snakes often having red, black, and yellow or white bands.

milksop (mĭlk′sŏp′) *n.* A person who lacks courage; a weakling.

milk sugar *n.* Lactose.

milk tooth *n.* Any of the temporary teeth that first grow in the mouth of a young mammal.

milkweed (mĭlk′wēd′) *n.* Any of numerous plants having small flowers in clusters, milky juice, and pods that split open to release seeds with downy tufts.

milky (mĭl′kē) *adj.* **milkier, milkiest 1.** Resembling milk, especially in color. **2.** Consisting of or yielding milk. —**milk′i·ness** *n.*

Milky Way *n.* The galaxy containing the solar system, visible as a broad band of faint light in the night sky.

mill¹ (mĭl) *n.* **1.** A building equipped with machines for grinding grain into flour or meal. **2.** A device or machine that grinds grain. **3.** A device or machine for grinding, crushing, or pressing: *a cider mill.* **4.** A building or group of buildings equipped with machinery for processing a material of some kind: *a steel mill.* **5.** A business or institution that produces something in great numbers and without regard for standards of quality: *a diploma mill; a puppy mill.* ❖ *v.* **milled, milling, mills** —*tr.* **1.** To grind or crush into powder or fine grains: *mill wheat.* **2.** To process or produce (steel, paper, or another product) in a mill. **3.** To put ridges or grooves on the edge of (a coin). —*intr.* To move around in a confused or disorderly manner: *During the fire drill the students milled about the playground.*

mill² (mĭl) *n.* A unit of money equal to one thousandth of a US dollar, or one tenth of a cent.

WORD HISTORY Mill¹ comes from Old English *mylen,* which comes from Late Latin *molīna* (both meaning "building where grain is ground"), which comes from Latin *molere,* meaning "to grind." **Mill²** comes from Latin *mīllēsimus,* meaning "thousandth."

milldam (mĭl′dăm′) *n.* A dam built across a stream to raise the water level and provide water power to turn a mill wheel.

millenarian (mĭl′ə-nâr′ē-ən) *adj.* **1.** Relating to a thousand, especially to a thousand years. **2.** Relating to or believing in the Christian doctrine of the millennium or in a coming age of joy, peace, and plenty. ❖ *n.* A person who believes in the Christian doctrine of the millennium or in a coming age of joy, peace, and plenty. —**mil′le·nar′i·an·ism** *n.*

millennium (mə-lĕn′ē-əm) *n., pl.* **millennia** (mə-lĕn′-ē-ə) or **millenniums 1.** A span of one thousand years. **2.** In Christianity, the prophecied thousand-year reign of Jesus on the earth after his Second Coming. **3.** A coming period of joy, plenty, and peace. —**mil·len′ni·al** *adj.*

miller (mĭl′ər) *n.* **1.** A person who owns or operates a mill for grinding grain. **2.** Any of various moths whose wings and body have a powdery appearance.

millet (mĭl′ĭt) *n.* **1.** The small seeds of any of several cereal grasses, widely used for food, livestock feed, and birdseed. **2.** The plant that bears such seeds, often used as hay.

milli– A prefix that means one thousandth: *millimeter.*

millibar (mĭl′ə-bär′) *n.* A unit of atmospheric pressure equal to one thousandth (10⁻³) of a bar. Standard atmospheric pressure at sea level is about 1,013 millibars.

milligram (mĭl′ĭ-grăm′) *n.* A unit of mass or weight equal to one thousandth (10⁻³) of a gram.

milliliter (mĭl′ə-lē′tər) *n.* A metric unit of volume equal to one thousandth (10⁻³) of a liter. See table at **measurement.**

millimeter (mĭl′ə-mē′tər) *n.* A unit of length equal to one thousandth (10⁻³) of a meter. See table at **measurement.**

milliner (mĭl′ə-nər) *n.* A person who makes, trims, designs, or sells women's hats.

millinery (mĭl′ə-nĕr′ē) *n., pl.* **millineries 1.** Women's hats, including trimmings for hats. **2.** The business of making, designing, or selling women's hats.

milling (mĭl′ĭng) *n.* **1.** The act or process of grinding, especially of grinding grain into flour or meal. **2.** The act or process of cutting ridges on the edges of coins. **3.** The ridges cut on the edges of coins.

million (mĭl′yən) *n., pl.* **million** or **millions 1.** The number, written as 10⁶ or 1 followed by six zeros, that is equal to 1,000 × 1,000. **2.** An indefinitely large number: *There are millions of things to do in a big city.*

millionaire (mĭl′yə-nâr′) *n.* A person whose wealth amounts to at least a million dollars, pounds, or similar units in another currency.

millionth (mĭl′yənth) *n.* **1.** The ordinal number matching the number 1,000,000 in a series. **2.** One of a million equal parts. —**mil′lionth** *adv. & adj.*

millipede or **millepede** (mĭl′ə-pēd′) *n.* Any of various small invertebrate animals having a cylindrical body composed of many narrow segments, most of which have two pairs of legs.

millisecond (mĭl′ĭ-sĕk′ənd) *n.* A unit of time equal to one thousandth (10⁻³) of a second.

millpond (mĭl′pŏnd′) *n.* A pond formed by a milldam, used to supply water to run a mill.

millrace (mĭl′rās′) *n.* **1.** The fast-moving stream of water that drives a mill wheel. **2.** The channel for the water that drives a mill wheel.

millstone (mĭl′stōn′) *n.* **1.** One of a pair of large cylindrical stones used to grind grain. **2.** An obstacle to success.

mill wheel *n.* A wheel, usually turned by moving water, that supplies the power for a mill.

milord (mĭ-lôrd′) *n.* Used to address an English nobleman or gentleman.

milquetoast (mĭlk′tōst′) *n.* A person who is meek or timid.

milt (mĭlt) *n.* The sperm cells of male fishes, together with the milky liquid containing them.

mime (mīm) *n.* **1.** Acting by means of gestures and movements without speech; pantomime. **2.** An actor in pantomime. ❖ *v.* **mimed, miming, mimes** —*tr.* To act out (something) with gestures and body movements. —*intr.* To act as a mimic. —**mim′er** *n.*

mimeograph (mĭm′ē-ə-grăf′) *n.* **1.** A machine that makes copies of material that is written, drawn, or typed on a stencil. **2.** A copy made by such a machine. ❖ *v.* **mimeographed, mimeographing, mimeographs** To copy with a mimeograph.

mimesis (mĭ-mē′sĭs) *n.* The imitation or representation of aspects of the physical world, especially human actions, in literature and art.

mimic (mĭm′ĭk) *tr.v.* **mimicked, mimicking, mimics 1.** To copy or imitate closely, as in speech, expression, or gesture, often so as to ridicule: *That bird can mimic its owner. The boy mimicked his father's laugh.* See Synonyms at **imitate. 2.** To simulate or reproduce: *trying to mimic conditions on the surface of the moon.* **3.** To resemble by biological mimicry: *an insect mimicking a twig.* ❖ *n.* **1.** A person who imitates, especially a performer or comedian skilled in pantomime. **2.** A copy or imitation.

mimicry (mĭm′ĭ-krē) *n., pl.* **mimicries 1.** The art or practice of mimicking. **2.** The resemblance of one organism to another or to an object in its surroundings, especially for concealment or protection.

mimosa (mĭ-mō′sə *or* mĭ-mō′zə) *n.* **1.** Any of various tropical trees or shrubs having feathery leaves and clusters of small yellow, pink, or white flowers. **2.** A drink of champagne and orange juice.

min. An abbreviation of: **1.** minimum. **2.** minor. **3.** minute.

minaret (mĭn′ə-rĕt′) *n.* A tall slender tower on a mosque from which a muezzin summons the people to prayer.

minatory (mĭn′ə-tôr′ē) also **minatorial** (mĭn′ə-tôr′ē-əl) *adj.* Of a menacing or threatening nature. —**min′a·to′ri·ly** *adv.*

mince (mĭns) *v.* **minced, mincing, minces** —*tr.* **1.** To cut or chop into very small pieces. **2.** To change or make (words) less distressing, especially for the sake of politeness: *The doctor minced no words in describing the patient's condition.* —*intr.* **1.** To walk in an affected way or with very short steps. **2.** To speak in an affected way. ❖ *n.* Mincemeat.

mincemeat (mĭns′mēt′) *n.* A mixture of finely chopped fruit, spices, suet, and sometimes meat, used especially as a pie filling.

mind (mīnd) *n.* **1.** The part or faculty of a person by which one feels, perceives, thinks, remembers, desires, and imagines: *Use your mind to solve the problem.* **2.** A person of great intellect or intelligence: *Isaac Newton was one of the great minds of science.* **3.** Focus of thought and attention: *Sometimes it's hard to keep your mind on your work.* **4.** Remembrance; memory: *Keep our invitation in mind.* **5.** Opinion or sentiment; attitude or point of view: *It's not too late to change your mind.* **6.** Desire or inclination: *I have a mind to take up karate.* **7.** A healthy mental condition; sanity: *lose one's mind.* ❖ *v.* **minded, minding, minds** —*tr.* **1.** To pay attention to: *Mind what I'm saying.* **2.** To obey: *The children were told to mind the babysitter.* **3.** To be careful about: *Mind how you swing the hammer.* **4.** To take care of; look after: *stayed home to mind the baby.* **5.** To object to or dislike: *I don't mind mopping the floor.* —*intr.* **1.** To be troubled or concerned: *I don't mind* *if you borrow the car.* **2.** To behave obediently: *I hope the children mind while we're in the car.* **3.** To take notice; pay attention: *You'll slip on the ice if you don't mind.* ◆ **bring to mind** or **call to mind** To cause (something) to be remembered or thought of: *a meal that brought to mind her childhood in the country.* **of one mind** In agreement: *We're of one mind about the proposed tunnel.*

mind-boggling (mīnd′bŏg′lĭng) *adj. Informal* Overwhelming; perplexing: *was faced with a mind-boggling problem.*

minded (mīn′dĭd) *adj.* **1.** Disposed; inclined: *Come over for a visit if you are so minded.* **2.** Having a specific kind of mind: *a strong-minded person.*

mindful (mīnd′fəl) *adj.* Attentive; heedful: *always mindful of the importance of reading.* —**mind′ful·ly** *adv.* —**mind′ful·ness** *n.*

mindless (mīnd′lĭs) *adj.* **1.** Lacking intelligence; foolish. **2.** Having no purpose or meaning: *a mindless act.* —**mind′less·ly** *adv.*

mind reading *n.* The supposed ability to know or discern another's thoughts through extrasensory means of communication; telepathy. —**mind reader** *n.*

mindset or **mind-set** (mīnd′sĕt′) *n.* A particular attitude or disposition regarding a situation: *Thanks to his positive mindset, he was able to overcome the setback.*

mind's eye (mīndz) *n.* The ability of forming mental images of something that is not real or present; the imagination.

mine¹ (mīn) *n.* **1a.** A hole or passage dug in the earth to extract metals, coal, salt, or other minerals: *a gold mine.* **b.** An excavation made on the surface of the ground in which the topmost layer of earth is removed and ore and minerals are extracted from that layer. **2.** An abundant supply or source: *The Internet is a mine of information.* **3.** A tunnel dug under enemy positions or fortifications to cause them to collapse, to lay explosives, or to gain an entrance. **4.** An explosive device that can be buried in the ground or concealed in a body of water: *a land mine.* ❖ *v.* **mined, mining, mines** —*tr.* **1a.** To extract (ores or minerals) from the earth: *mined copper.* **b.** To dig or tunnel in (the earth) for this purpose. **2.** To place explosive mines in or under: *mine a harbor.* **3.** To analyze in detail in order to make use of: *The company mined the data collected by its website to determine what kinds of people were buying its products.* —*intr.* **1.** To dig in the earth to extract ore or minerals: *The company is mining for diamonds.* **2.** To work in a mine. **3.** To tunnel in the earth, especially under enemy fortifications.

mine² (mīn) *pron.* (*used with a singular or plural verb*) The one or ones belonging to me: *Your car is different from mine.* ❖ *adj.* A possessive form of I¹. *Archaic* Used instead of *my* before a vowel or the letter *h: mine eyes; mine honor.*

minefield (mīn′fēld′) *n.* **1.** An area in which explosive mines have been placed. **2.** A situation that has many potential hazards or dangers.

miner (mī′nər) *n.* A person who works in a mine, especially to extract ores or minerals from the earth.

mineral (mĭn′ər-əl) *n.* **1.** An inorganic solid substance found in nature that has a uniform chemical composition, a regular crystalline form, and a characteristic hardness and color. **2.** A substance, such as gold, iron ore, or stone, that is obtained by mining or quarrying.

3. A substance that is neither animal nor vegetable. **4.** An inorganic element, such as calcium, iron, potassium, sodium, or zinc, that is essential to the nutrition of living organisms. ❖ *adj.* **1.** Relating to, resembling, or containing a mineral or minerals. **2.** Not animal or vegetable; inorganic.

mineralogy (mĭn′ə-rŏl′ə-jē or mĭn′ə-răl′ə-jē) *n.* The scientific study of minerals. —**min′er·a·log′i·cal** (mĭn′-ər-ə-lŏj′ĭ-kəl) *adj.* —**min′er·a·log′ical·ly** *adv.* —**min′er·al′o·gist** *n.*

mineral oil *n.* A colorless, odorless, tasteless oil distilled from petroleum and used in medicine as a laxative.

Minerva (mĭ-nûr′və) *n.* In Roman mythology, the goddess of wisdom and the arts, identified with the Greek Athena.

mineshaft (mīn′shăft′) *n.* A vertical or sloping passageway dug in the earth for finding or mining ore.

minestrone (mĭn′ĭ-strō′nē) *n.* A soup containing vegetables, pasta, and herbs in a meat or vegetable broth.

minesweeper (mīn′swēp′ər) *n.* A ship equipped for finding and destroying or removing explosive underwater mines.

mingle (mĭng′gəl) *v.* **mingled, mingling, mingles** —*tr.* To mix or combine; unite: *The poem mingled passion and wit.* —*intr.* **1.** To become mixed or united. **2.** To associate or join with others: *The guests mingled freely at the party.*

mini (mĭn′ē) *n., pl.* **minis** Something smaller or shorter than others of its kind. —**min′i** *adj.*

mini– A prefix that means small: *minibike.*

miniature (mĭn′ē-ə-chər or mĭn′ə-chər) *n.* **1.** A copy or reproduction on a small scale: *The architects made a miniature of the proposed building.* **2.** A very small painting or portrait. **3.** A dog of a small breed or of a variety smaller than the standard variety of its breed. ❖ *adj.* Greatly reduced in size or scale. See Synonyms at **little**.

miniaturize (mĭn′ē-ə-chə-rīz′ or mĭn′ə-chə-rīz′) *tr.v.* **miniaturized, miniaturizing, miniaturizes** To plan or make on a very small scale.

minibike (mĭn′ē-bīk′) *n.* A small motorcycle.

minimal (mĭn′ə-məl) *adj.* **1.** Smallest in amount or degree; least possible: *outlined the minimal qualifications for the job.* **2.** Small in amount or degree: *prescribed a drug with minimal side effects.* —**min′i·mal·ly** *adv.*

minimalism (mĭn′ə-mə-lĭz′əm) *n.* **1.** A school of abstract painting and sculpture that emphasizes extreme simplification of form, as by the use of basic shapes and monochromatic palettes of primary colors, objectivity, and anonymity of style. **2.** Use of the fewest and barest essentials or elements, as in the arts, literature, or design. **3.** *Music* A style of music marked by extreme simplification of rhythms, patterns, and harmonies, prolonged chordal or melodic repetitions, and often a trancelike effect.

minimize (mĭn′ə-mīz′) *tr.v.* **minimized, minimizing, minimizes** **1.** To reduce to the smallest possible amount or degree: *In winter, we try to minimize the amount of heat that escapes our house.* **2.** To represent as having little importance, value, or size; depreciate. —**min′i·mi·za′tion** (mĭn′ə-mĭ-zā′shən) *n.* —**min′i·miz′er** *n.*

minimum (mĭn′ə-məm) *n., pl.* **minimums** or **minima** (mĭn′ə-mə) **1.** The smallest amount or degree possible: *We need a minimum of an hour to make dinner.* **2.** The lowest amount or degree reached or recorded: *The temperature's minimum yesterday was 45°.* ❖ *adj.* Representing the least possible or the lowest amount or degree.

minimum wage *n.* The lowest wage, set by law or contract, that an employer may pay an employee for a specified job.

mining (mī′nǐng) *n.* **1.** The work, process, or business of extracting coal, minerals, or ore from the earth. **2.** The process of placing explosive mines.

minion (mǐn′yən) *n.* **1.** A person who follows or serves another in a slavish or servile manner. **2.** A person who is much loved or admired; a favorite.

miniskirt (mǐn′ē-skûrt′) *n.* A short skirt with a hemline that falls several inches above the knee.

minister (mǐn′ĭ-stər) *n.* **1.** A person who is authorized to perform religious functions in a Christian church. **2.** A person in charge of a government department: *the minister of finance.* **3.** A diplomat ranking below an ambassador, who represents his or her government in a foreign country. ❖ *intr.v.* **ministered, ministering, ministers** To attend to another's needs; give aid or comfort: *The nurses ministered to the sick.* —**min′is·te′ri·al** (mǐn′ĭ-stîr′ē-əl) *adj.* —**min′is·te′ri·al·ly** *adv.*

ministration (mǐn′ĭ-strā′shən) *n.* **1.** The act or process of serving or aiding. **2.** The act of performing the duties of a minister or cleric.

ministry (mǐn′ĭ-strē) *n., pl.* **ministries 1.** The position and duties of a Christian minister or cleric. **2.** The Christian clergy considered as a group. **3.** A department of government under the charge of a minister. **4.** Governmental ministers in general. **5.** The act of serving or aiding.

minivan (mǐn′ē-văn′) *n.* A van designed primarily for carrying passengers, often having rear seats that can be removed for loading cargo.

mink (mǐngk) *n., pl.* **mink** or **minks 1.** Either of two meat-eating mammals of North America or Europe that live around water and have a pointed snout, short legs, and thick soft brown fur. **2.** The fur of the American mink, often used to make or trim clothing.

minnow (mǐn′ō) *n., pl.* **minnow** or **minnows** Any of various small freshwater fishes often used as bait.

Minoan (mǐ-nō′ən) *adj.* Relating to the Bronze Age culture that flourished in Crete from about 3000 to 1100 BC. ❖ *n.* A native or inhabitant of ancient Crete.

minor (mī′nər) *adj.* **1.** Lesser or smaller in degree, size, or extent: *a minor change.* **2.** Lesser in importance or rank: *a minor role in the play.* **3.** Lesser in seriousness or danger: *a minor injury.* **4.** Not yet a legal adult: *minor children.* **5a.** Relating to or based on a minor scale: *a minor key.* **b.** Relating to a musical tone that is smaller by a half step than a major interval: *a minor third.* ❖ *n.* **1.** A person who is not yet the legal age of an adult. **2.** A secondary area of academic specialization: *graduated from college with a major in physics and a minor in philosophy.* **3.** A minor key, scale, or interval. **4. minors** The minor leagues of a sport, especially baseball. ❖ *intr.v.* **minored, minoring, minors** To pursue academic studies in a minor: *She chose to minor in chemistry.*

minority (mə-nôr′ĭ-tē *or* mī-nôr′ĭ-tē) *n., pl.* **minorities 1.** The smaller in number of two groups forming a whole. **2a.** A racial, religious, political, national, or other group thought to be different from the larger group of which it is part. **b.** A group having little power or representation relative to other groups in a society. **c.** A member of one of these groups: *Several minorities were appointed to the committee for energy conservation.* **3.** The state or period of being younger than the age for legal adulthood.

minor league *n.* In sports, a professional league that ranks below a major league.

Minor Prophets *n.* The biblical Books of Hosea, Joel, Amos, Obadiah, Jonah, Micah, Nahum, Habakkuk, Zephaniah, Haggai, Zechariah, and Malachi.

minor scale *n.* Any of a set of musical scales having a half step instead of a whole step between the second and third tones, and sometimes one or two half steps at higher intervals.

Minos (mī′nəs) *n.* In Greek mythology, a king of Crete who became a judge in the underworld after his death.

Minotaur (mǐn′ə-tôr′ *or* mī′nə-tôr′) *n.* In Greek mythology, a monster, half bull and half human, kept in the Labyrinth in Crete until Theseus killed him.

minstrel (mǐn′strəl) *n.* **1.** A medieval musician who traveled from place to place, singing and reciting poetry. **2.** A performer in a minstrel show.

minstrel show *n.* A comic variety show of the 1800s and early 1900s, usually featuring white performers who wore black makeup on their faces.

mint¹ (mǐnt) *n.* **1.** A place where the coins of a country are made by authority of the government. **2.** A large amount, especially of money: *That painting is worth a mint.* ❖ *tr.v.* **minted, minting, mints 1.** To produce (money) by stamping metal; coin. **2.** To invent; make up: *The scientist minted a name for the newly discovered chemical.* ❖ *adj.* In original condition; undamaged: *an antique car in mint condition.*

mint² (mǐnt) *n.* **1.** Any of various plants, such as the spearmint and peppermint, having aromatic leaves that yield an oil used as a flavoring. **2.** A candy with natural or artificial mint flavor.

WORD HISTORY Mint¹ comes from Old English *mynet* which comes from Latin *monēta*, both meaning "coinage, money." **Mint²** comes from Old English *minte*, which comes from Latin *menta*, both referring to the same kinds of plants as in Modern English.

mintage (mǐn′tĭj) *n.* **1.** The act or process of minting coins. **2.** Coins manufactured in a mint. **3.** The fee paid to a mint by a government for which coins have been made. **4.** The impression stamped on a coin.

mint julep *n.* A drink made of bourbon, sugar, and mint leaves.

minuend (mǐn′yōō-ĕnd′) *n.* A number from which another is to be subtracted; for example, in the expression 100 − 23 = 77, the minuend is 100.

minuet (mǐn′yōō-ĕt′) *n.* **1.** A slow stately dance in 3/4 time that originated in France in the 1600s. **2.** Music for or in the rhythm of this dance.

minus (mī′nəs) *prep.* **1.** Reduced by the subtraction of; decreased by: *Seven minus four equals three.* **2.** *Informal* Without; lacking: *We arrived at the theater minus our tickets.* ❖ *adj.* **1.** Less than zero; negative: *a minus value.* **2.** Slightly lower or less than: *a grade of A minus.* ❖ *n.* **1.** The minus sign. **2.** A negative number or quantity: *That value should be a minus, not a plus.* **3.** A disadvantage or drawback: *The lack of a pool at the hotel was a minus.*

minuscule (mǐn′ə-skyōōl′ *or* mī-nŭs′kyōōl′) *adj.* Very small; tiny.

minus sign *n.* The symbol −, as in 4 − 2 = 2, that is used to indicate subtraction or a negative quantity.

minute¹ (mǐn′ĭt) *n.* **1.** A unit of time equal to ¹⁄₆₀ of an hour or 60 seconds. **2.** A unit of angular measurement that is equal to ¹⁄₆₀ of a degree or 60 seconds. **3.** A short interval of time; a moment: *Wait a minute.* **4.** A specific point in time: *leaving this very minute.* **5. minutes** An official record of the events or discussion at a meeting of an organization.

minute² (mī-nōōt′ *or* mĭ-nōōt′) *adj.* **1.** Exceptionally small; tiny: *a minute organism.* **2.** Not worth noticing; insignificant: *a minute problem.* **3.** Marked by close examination or careful study of small details: *a minute inspection.* —**mi·nute′ly** *adv.*

WORD HISTORY Minute¹ comes from Middle English *minute,* which comes from Medieval Latin *pars minūta prīma,* meaning "primary small part." **Minute²** comes from a different Middle English word spelled *minute,* which comes from Latin *minūtus,* meaning "diminished, tiny."

---

minuteman (mĭn′ĭt-măn′) *n.* A member of the American militia pledged to be ready to answer a call to fight on a minute's notice just before and during the Revolutionary War in the United States.

minx (mĭngks) *n.* A girl or young woman who is considered bold or flirtatious.

Miocene (mī′ə-sēn′) *n.* The fourth epoch of the Tertiary Period, from about 23 to 5.3 million years ago. During the Miocene, grasses and grazing mammals spread. —**Mi′o·cene′** *adj.*

miracle (mĭr′ə-kəl) *n.* **1.** An event believed to be an act of God or of a supernatural power because it appears impossible to explain by the laws of nature. **2.** A person, thing, or event that causes great admiration, awe, or wonder: *surgical miracles.* See Synonyms at **wonder.**

miracle play *n.* A Christian religious drama of the Middle Ages that portrays miraculous events from the lives of saints and martyrs.

miraculous (mĭ-răk′yə-ləs) *adj.* **1.** Having the nature of a miracle: *a miraculous event.* **2.** Having the power to work miracles: *a miraculous drug.* —**mi·rac′u·lous·ly** *adv.*

mirage (mĭ-räzh′) *n.* An optical illusion in which nonexistent bodies of water and upside-down reflections of distant objects are seen. It is caused by distortions that occur as light passes between layers of air that are at different temperatures.

mire (mīr) *n.* **1.** An area of wet muddy ground; a bog. **2.** Deep slimy soil or mud. ❖ *v.* **mired, miring, mires** —*tr.* To cause to sink or become stuck in mire. —*intr.* To sink or become stuck in mire.

mirror (mĭr′ər) *n.* **1.** A surface that is able to reflect light, often used to form an image of an object placed in front of it. **2.** Something that reflects or gives a true picture of something else: *The city's progress is a mirror of the nation's progress.* ❖ *tr.v.* **mirrored, mirroring, mirrors** To reflect in or as if in a mirror: *The lake mirrored the clouds.*

mirror image *n.* An image that is the exact likeness of another one, but is reversed like an image in a mirror.

mirth (mûrth) *n.* Gladness and merriment, especially when expressed with laughter.

mirthful (mûrth′fəl) *adj.* Full of gladness and merriment. —**mirth′ful·ly** *adv.*

mirthless (mûrth′lĭs) *adj.* Showing no merriment. —**mirth′less·ly** *adv.*

miry (mīr′ē) *adj.* **mirier, miriest 1.** Full of or resembling mire; swampy. **2.** Smeared with mud; muddy.

mis– A prefix that means: **1.** Error or wrongness: *misspell.* **2.** Badness or impropriety: *misbehave.* **3.** Failure or lack of: *misfire; mistrust.*

WORD BUILDING The basic meaning of the prefix **mis–** is "bad; badly; wrong; wrongly." Thus *misfortune* means "bad fortune" and *misbehave* means "to behave badly." Likewise, a *misdeed* is "a wrong deed" and *misdo* means "to do wrongly." *Mis–* mostly forms compounds by attaching to verbs: *mishear, misremember. Mis–* also frequently forms compounds by attaching to nouns that come from verbs: *miscalculation, mismanagement, mispronunciation.*

---

misadventure (mĭs′əd-vĕn′chər) *n.* An example of misfortune; a mishap.

misanthrope (mĭs′ən-thrōp′) *n.* A person who hates or distrusts humankind.

misanthropic (mĭs′ən-thrŏp′ĭk) *adj.* Relating to or characteristic of a misanthrope. —**mis′an·throp′i·cal·ly** *adv.*

misanthropy (mĭs-ăn′thrə-pē) *n.* Hatred or distrust of humankind.

misapply (mĭs′ə-plī′) *tr.v.* **misapplied, misapplying, misapplies** To use or apply wrongly: *The word "horns" is often misapplied to include antlers.* —**mis·ap′pli·ca′tion** (mĭs-ăp′lĭ-kā′shən) *n.*

misapprehend (mĭs-ăp′rĭ-hĕnd′) *tr.v.* **misapprehended, misapprehending, misapprehends** To fail to understand correctly; misunderstand: *misapprehend an order.* —**mis·ap′pre·hen′sion** (mĭs-ăp′rĭ-hĕn′shən) *n.*

misappropriate (mĭs′ə-prō′prē-āt′) *tr.v.* **misappropriated, misappropriating, misappropriates** To take dishonestly for one's own use; embezzle: *misappropriate government funds.* —**mis′ap·pro′pri·a′tion** *n.*

misbegotten (mĭs′bĭ-gŏt′n) *adj.* **1.** *Offensive* Born to parents who are not married to each other. **2.** Not lawfully obtained: *misbegotten wealth.*

misbehave (mĭs′bĭ-hāv′) *v.* **misbehaved, misbehaving, misbehaves** —*intr.* To behave badly. —*tr.* To behave or conduct (oneself) badly or inappropriately. —**mis′-be·hav′ior** (mĭs′bĭ-hāv′yər) *n.*

misc. An abbreviation of miscellaneous.

miscalculate (mĭs-kăl′kyə-lāt′) *tr. & intr. v.* **miscalculated, miscalculating, miscalculates** To calculate or estimate incorrectly. —**mis·cal′cu·la′tion** *n.*

miscarriage (mĭs′kăr′ĭj *or* mĭs-kăr′ĭj) *n.* **1.** The ending of a pregnancy when an embryo or fetus is expelled from the uterus before it is developed enough to survive. **2.** A failure to achieve the proper or desired result: *a miscarriage of justice.*

miscarry (mĭs′kăr′ē *or* mĭs-kăr′ē) *intr.v.* **miscarried, miscarrying, miscarries 1.** To have a miscarriage. **2.** To fail; go wrong: *The plan miscarried.*

miscast (mĭs-kăst′) *tr.v.* **miscast, miscasting, miscasts 1.** To cast (a performer) in an unsuitable role: *The young actor was miscast in a role that required considerable experience.* **2.** To cast (a role, play, or film) in an unsuitable way: *The musical was miscast with actors who couldn't sing.*

miscegenation (mĭ-sĕj′ə-nā′shən *or* mĭs′ĭ-jə-nā′shən) *n.* Marriage or sexual relations between two people of different races, especially in historical contexts as a violation of the law.

miscellaneous (mĭs′ə-lā′nē-əs) *adj.* **1.** Made up of a variety of different elements or ingredients: *a miscellaneous assortment of books.* **2.** Concerned with a variety of different subjects or aspects: *a website that provides miscellaneous information.*

miscellany (mĭs′ə-lā′nē) *n., pl.* **miscellanies** A collection of various items, parts, or ingredients.

mischance (mĭs-chănsʹ) *n.* An unfortunate occurrence caused by chance or luck: *If by some mischance I am late, please wait for me.*

mischief (mĭsʹchĭf) *n.* **1a.** Annoying or improper behavior. **b.** Damage, injury, or trouble resulting from such behavior. **2.** A tendency to play pranks or cause trouble.

mischievous (mĭsʹchə-vəs) *adj.* **1.** Causing mischief; naughty: *a mischievous child.* **2.** Showing a tendency to play pranks or tease: *a mischievous look on one's face.* **3.** Causing injury or damage: *a mischievous act.* —**misʹchie·vous·ly** *adv.* —**misʹchie·vous·ness** *n.*

miscible (mĭsʹə-bəl) *adj.* Capable of being mixed in all proportions: *Water and alcohol are miscible.*

miscommunication (mĭsʹkə-myōō′nĭ-kāʹshən) *n.* **1.** Lack of clear or adequate communication. **2.** An unclear or inadequate communication.

misconceive (mĭsʹkən-sēvʹ) *tr.v.* **misconceived, misconceiving, misconceives** To interpret incorrectly; misunderstand.

misconception (mĭsʹkən-sĕpʹshən) *n.* A mistaken idea; a delusion.

misconduct (mĭs-kŏnʹdŭkt) *n.* Improper conduct or behavior.

misconstrue (mĭsʹkən-strōōʹ) *tr.v.* **misconstrued, misconstruing, misconstrues** To mistake the meaning of; misinterpret: *misconstrue someone's words.*

miscopy (mĭs-kŏpʹē) *tr.v.* **miscopied, miscopying, miscopies** To copy (something) inaccurately: *miscopied her cell phone number.*

miscount (mĭs-kountʹ) *v.* **miscounted, miscounting, miscounts** —*tr.* To count (something) incorrectly. —*intr.* To make an incorrect count. ❖ *n.* (mĭsʹkount′) An inaccurate count.

miscreant (mĭsʹkrē-ənt) *n.* A person who behaves badly, usually by breaking rules of conduct or the law.

misdeal (mĭs-dēlʹ) *tr. & intr.v.* **misdealt** (mĭs-dĕltʹ), **misdealing, misdeals** To deal (playing cards) incorrectly. —**misʹdealʹ** *n.*

misdeed (mĭs-dēdʹ) *n.* A wrong or illegal act.

misdemeanor (mĭsʹdĭ-mēʹnər) *n.* A crime, such as petty theft, that is less serious than a felony and is punished less severely.

misdirect (mĭsʹdĭ-rĕktʹ *or* mĭsʹdī-rĕktʹ) *tr.v.* **misdirected, misdirecting, misdirects 1.** To give incorrect or inaccurate instructions to: *misdirect a tourist.* **2.** To put a wrong address on (a piece of mail): *misdirect a letter.* **3.** To aim (a punch or projectile, for example) badly. —**misʹdi·recʹtion** *n.*

misdo (mĭs-dōōʹ) *tr.v.* **misdid** (mĭs-dĭdʹ), **misdone** (mĭs-dŭnʹ), **misdoing, misdoes** (mĭs-dŭzʹ) To do wrongly or poorly; botch. —**mis·doʹing** *n.*

miser (mīʹzər) *n.* A stingy person, especially one who lives poorly in order to hoard money.

miserable (mĭzʹər-ə-bəl *or* mĭzʹrə-bəl) *adj.* **1.** Very unhappy or uncomfortable: *I was miserable all night with a headache and high fever.* **2.** Causing discomfort or unhappiness: *miserable weather.* **3.** Wretchedly poor or inadequate: *a miserable shack.* —**misʹer·a·bly** *adv.*

miserly (mīʹzər-lē) *adj.* Relating to or characteristic of a miser; stingy. —**miʹser·li·ness** *n.*

misery (mĭzʹə-rē) *n., pl.* **miseries 1.** Miserable conditions of life; dire poverty. **2.** Mental or emotional suffering or distress.

misfire (mĭs-fīrʹ) *intr.v.* **misfired, misfiring, misfires 1.** To fail to fire or go off: *The gun misfired.* **2.** To fail to achieve the desired result; go awry: *Their plan misfired.* —**misʹfireʹ** *n.*

misfit (mĭsʹfĭtʹ) *n.* A person who has adjusted poorly to his or her situation in life or does not get along well with others.

misfortune (mĭs-fôrʹchən) *n.* **1.** Bad luck or fortune. **2.** An occurrence that is unfortunate or that causes great distress: *The hurricane was a great misfortune for the fishing industry.*

misgiving (mĭs-gĭvʹĭng) *n.* **1.** A feeling of doubt or concern: *We had misgivings about using our savings to buy a new car.* **2.** Doubt or concern: *We left the meeting full of misgiving.*

misgovern (mĭs-gŭvʹərn) *tr.v.* **misgoverned, misgoverning, misgoverns** To govern or rule badly. —**mis·govʹern·ment** *n.*

misguide (mĭs-gīdʹ) *tr.v.* **misguided, misguiding, misguides** To give wrong or misleading directions to; lead astray. —**mis·guidʹance** *n.*

misguided (mĭs-gīʹdĭd) *adj.* Acting or done out of mistaken or unrealistic opinions or beliefs: *misguided efforts.* —**mis·guidʹed·ly** *adv.*

mishandle (mĭs-hănʹdl) *tr.v.* **mishandled, mishandling, mishandles 1.** To handle roughly: *mishandle a parcel in the mail.* **2.** To manage badly: *mishandle money.*

mishap (mĭsʹhăp′ *or* mĭs-hăpʹ) *n.* **1.** Bad luck. **2.** An unfortunate accident: *The trip was completed without mishap.*

mishmash (mĭshʹmăsh′) *n.* A random mixture of unrelated things; a hodgepodge.

misinform (mĭsʹĭn-fôrmʹ) *tr.v.* **misinformed, misinforming, misinforms** To give wrong or inaccurate information to. —**mis·inʹfor·maʹtion** (mĭs-ĭnʹfər-māʹshən) *n.*

misinterpret (mĭsʹĭn-tûrʹprĭt) *tr.v.* **misinterpreted, misinterpreting, misinterprets** To interpret or explain incorrectly: *misinterpret someone's remarks.* —**misʹin·terʹpre·taʹtion** *n.*

misjudge (mĭs-jŭjʹ) *v.* **misjudged, misjudging, misjudges** —*tr.* To judge incorrectly: *misjudge a person.* —*intr.* To be wrong in judging something. —**mis·judgʹment** *n.*

mislay (mĭs-lāʹ) *tr.v.* **mislaid** (mĭs-lādʹ), **mislaying, mislays 1.** To lay or put down in a place one cannot remember. **2.** To place or put down incorrectly: *They mislaid the carpet.*

mislead (mĭs-lēdʹ) *tr.v.* **misled** (mĭs-lĕdʹ), **misleading, misleads 1.** To lead or guide in the wrong direction: *The sign at the traffic circle completely misled us.* **2.** To lead into error of thought or wrongdoing, especially by intentional deception.

misleading (mĭs-lēʹdĭng) *adj.* Tending to mislead: *misleading information.*

mismanage (mĭs-mănʹĭj) *tr.v.* **mismanaged, mismanaging, mismanages** To manage badly or ineptly. —**mis·manʹage·ment** *n.*

mismatch (mĭs-măchʹ) *tr.v.* **mismatched, mismatching, mismatches** To match in an unsuitable way: *The two teams are mismatched.* ❖ *n.* (mĭsʹmăch′ *or* mĭs-măchʹ) An unsuitable match.

misnomer (mĭs-nōʹmər) *n.* **1.** An error in naming a person or place. **2.** A name or designation wrongly or unsuitably applied: *To call a whale "a fish" is to use a misnomer.*

miso (mēʹsō) *n., pl.* **misos** A thick fermented paste made of cooked soybeans, salt, and often rice or barley, and used especially in making soups and sauces.

misogynist (mĭ-sŏjʹə-nĭst) *n.* A person who hates or mistrusts women.

misogyny (mĭ-sŏj′ə-nē) *n.* Hatred or mistrust of women.
misplace (mĭs-plās′) *tr.v.* **misplaced, misplacing, misplaces 1.** To put in a wrong place. **2.** To mislay; lose: *misplace one's keys.* **3.** To place (trust, for example) in an improper or unworthy person or idea: *I fear that your confidence in me is misplaced.*
misplaced modifier (mĭs′plāst′) *n.* A modifying clause or phrase that is placed in a sentence in a way that creates ambiguity or misunderstanding. For example, in *Streaking through the sky, we watched the rocket reenter the atmosphere,* the phrase *Streaking through the sky* is misplaced because it might be taken as modifying the subject *we.*
misplay (mĭs-plā′ *or* mĭs′plā′) *n.* A mistaken play in a game or sport. ❖ *tr.v.* (mĭs-plā′) **misplayed, misplaying, misplays** To make a misplay of.
misprint (mĭs-prĭnt′) *tr.v.* **misprinted, misprinting, misprints** To print incorrectly. ❖ *n.* (mĭs′prĭnt′ *or* mĭs-prĭnt′) An error in printing.
misprision (mĭs-prĭzh′ən) *n.* **1.** Neglect in performing the duties of public office. **2.** The criminal offense of concealing, or neglecting to report or prevent, a felony or act of treason one had knowledge of but did not participate in: *misprision of a felony.* **3.** Misunderstanding or misinterpretation: *misprision of the author's meaning.*
mispronounce (mĭs′prə-nouns′) *tr.v.* **mispronounced, mispronouncing, mispronounces** To pronounce incorrectly.
misquote (mĭs-kwōt′) *tr.v.* **misquoted, misquoting, misquotes** To quote incorrectly. —**mis′quo·ta′tion** *n.*
misread (mĭs-rēd′) *tr.v.* **misread** (mĭs-rĕd′), **misreading, misreads 1.** To read incorrectly: *misread a sign.* **2.** To draw the wrong conclusion from; misinterpret: *I misread your nod to mean "yes."*
misrepresent (mĭs-rĕp′rĭ-zĕnt′) *tr.v.* **misrepresented, misrepresenting, misrepresents** To represent in a false or misleading manner: *The newspaper misrepresented the mayor's statements.* —**mis·rep′re·sen·ta′tion** *n.*
misrule (mĭs-rōōl′) *n.* Incompetent or unjust rule. ❖ *tr.v.* **misruled, misruling, misrules** To rule incompetently or unjustly.
miss¹ (mĭs) *v.* **missed, missing, misses** —*tr.* **1.** To fail to hit, catch, or make contact with: *The receiver missed the pass. The ball missed the basket.* **2.** To be too late for or fail to meet: *I missed the 7:15 bus.* **3.** To fail to see or notice: *We missed the television special last night.* **4.** To fail to attend or be present for: *She has never missed a day of school.* **5.** To fail to accomplish: *He just missed winning the race.* **6.** To fail to understand or grasp: *You're missing my point.* **7.** To fail to answer correctly; get wrong: *I missed two questions on the test.* **8.** To let slip by; fail to benefit from: *We missed our chance to see our favorite actor.* **9.** To feel or regret the absence or loss of: *I miss my hometown.* **10.** To notice the absence or loss of: *After we left the theater, I missed my coat.* **11.** To avoid or escape: *If you go that way, you'll miss most of the traffic.* **12.** To lack: *The book is missing a few pages.* —*intr.* **1.** To fail to hit or make contact with something: *The ball flew toward the corner of the goal but missed.* **2.** To be unsuccessful; fail: *This is a sure-fire plan; it can't miss.* ❖ *n.* A failure to hit, succeed, or find. ◆ **miss out on** To lose a chance for: *Don't miss out on this great opportunity.* **miss the boat** *Informal* To fail to take advantage of an opportunity. **miss the mark 1.** To set

a goal and fail to fulfill it. **2.** To fail to be correct or exact.
miss² (mĭs) *n.* **1. Miss** A title of courtesy used before the last name or full name of an unmarried woman or girl. **2.** Used as a form of polite address for a young woman or girl: *I beg your pardon, miss.* **3.** An unmarried woman or girl. **4. misses** A range of clothing sizes for girls and women.

WORD HISTORY Miss¹ comes from Middle English *missen,* which comes from Old English *missan,* meaning "to fail to make contact" or "to lack." **Miss²** is short for *mistress.*

missal (mĭs′əl) *n.* A book containing all the prayers and responses necessary for celebrating the Roman Catholic Mass throughout the year.
misshape (mĭs-shāp′) *tr.v.* **misshaped, misshaped** or **misshapen** (mĭs-shā′pən), **misshaping, misshapes** To shape badly; deform.
missile (mĭs′əl *or* mĭs′īl′) *n.* **1.** An object or weapon that is thrown, fired, dropped, or otherwise launched at a target. **2.** A guided missile. **3.** A ballistic missile.
missing (mĭs′ĭng) *adj.* **1.** Lost: *missing persons.* **2.** Not present; absent: *Who is missing from class today?* **3.** Lacking; wanting: *This book has 12 missing pages.*
mission (mĭsh′ən) *n.* **1.** An assignment that a person or group of people is sent to carry out; a task: *a rescue mission.* **2.** A combat operation, especially a flight into a combat zone by military aircraft. **3.** Something that a person assumes to be the main task of his or her life: *My mission in life is to become a teacher.* **4.** A permanent diplomatic office in a foreign country. **5.** A body of people sent to a foreign land, especially by a Christian organization to spread its religion or provide educational, medical, or other assistance. **6.** An establishment of missionaries in some territory or foreign country: *Los Angeles started as a small Spanish mission.*
missionary (mĭsh′ə-nĕr′ē) *n., pl.* **missionaries** A person sent by a religious organization to make converts or do charitable work in a territory or foreign country.
Mississippian (mĭs′ĭ-sĭp′ē-ən) *n.* The earlier of two subdivisions of the Carboniferous Period, from about 359 to 318 million years ago. During the Mississippian, shallow seas spread over many former land areas. —**Mis′sis·sip′pi·an** *adj.*
missive (mĭs′ĭv) *n.* A letter or message.
Missouri (mĭ-zōōr′ē) *n., pl.* **Missouri** or **Missouris 1.** A member of a Native American people formerly living in Missouri, with a present-day population in Oklahoma. **2.** The Siouan language of the Missouri.
misspeak (mĭs-spēk′) *tr. & intr.v.* **misspoke** (mĭs-spōk′), **misspoken** (mĭs-spō′kən), **misspeaking, misspeaks** To pronounce or speak incorrectly: *misspeak one's lines.*
misspell (mĭs-spĕl′) *tr.v.* **misspelled** or **misspelt** (mĭs-spĕlt′), **misspelling, misspells** To spell incorrectly.
misspend (mĭs-spĕnd′) *tr.v.* **misspent** (mĭs-spĕnt′), **misspending, misspends** To spend improperly, foolishly, or wastefully; squander.
misstate (mĭs-stāt′) *tr.v.* **misstated, misstating, misstates** To state wrongly or falsely. —**mis·state′ment** *n.*
misstep (mĭs-stĕp′) *n.* **1.** A misplaced or awkward step. **2.** A mistake in action or conduct.
mist (mĭst) *n.* **1.** A mass of tiny droplets of water in the air, close to or touching the earth. **2.** Water vapor that condenses on and clouds a surface: *mist on a windowpane.* **3.** A mass of tiny drops of a liquid, such as perfume, sprayed

into the air. **4.** Something that dims or obscures; a haze. ❖ *v.* **misted, misting, mists** —*intr.* **1.** To be or become obscured or blurred by mist. **2.** To rain in a fine shower: *It began to mist at 4:00.* —*tr.* To conceal or cloud with or as if with mist.

mistake (mĭ-stāk′) *n.* An error or fault resulting from poor judgment, ignorance, or carelessness. ❖ *tr.v.* **mistook** (mĭ-stŏŏk′), **mistaken** (mĭ-stā′kən), **mistaking, mistakes 1.** To understand incorrectly; misinterpret: *mistook politeness as friendliness.* **2.** To recognize or identify incorrectly: *mistook satin for silk.*

mistaken (mĭ-stā′kən) *adj.* Wrong; in error: *If I am not mistaken, you were last here a year ago.* —**mis·tak′en·ly** *adv.*

Mister (mĭs′tər) *n.* **1.** Used as a courtesy title before the last name or full name of a man. **2. mister** *Informal* Used as a form of polite address for a man: *Do you need directions to town, mister?*

mistletoe (mĭs′əl-tō′) *n.* **1.** Any of several plants that grow as semiparasites on trees and that have leathery evergreen leaves and white berries. **2.** A sprig of certain of these plants, often used as a Christmas decoration.

mistook (mĭ-stŏŏk′) *v.* Past tense of **mistake.**

mistreat (mĭs-trēt′) *tr.v.* **mistreated, mistreating, mistreats** To treat roughly or wrongly. —**mis·treat′ment** *n.*

mistress (mĭs′trĭs) *n.* **1.** A woman who has a continuing romantic relationship with a man, usually a man married to someone else. **2.** A woman in a position of authority, control, or ownership, as the head of a household. **3a.** A woman who owns or keeps an animal. **b.** A woman who owns a slave. **4.** A nation or country that has dominance over others. **5. Mistress** Used formerly as a courtesy title and form of address for a woman.

mistrial (mĭs′trī′əl *or* mĭs-trī′əl) *n.* A trial declared invalid because of a serious procedural error or because the jurors are unable to agree on a verdict.

mistrust (mĭs-trŭst′) *n.* Lack of trust or confidence: *I viewed the advice on the website with mistrust.* ❖ *tr.v.* **mistrusted, mistrusting, mistrusts 1.** To have no trust in; regard with suspicion: *mistrust strangers.* **2.** To doubt the truth or sincerity of: *I mistrust everything he says.* —**mis·trust′ful** *adj.* —**mis·trust′ful·ly** *adv.*

misty (mĭs′tē) *adj.* **mistier, mistiest 1.** Consisting of, filled with, or covered by mist. **2.** Obscured by or as by mist; vague: *misty recollections.* **3.** Full of emotion; sentimental. —**mist′i·ly** *adv.* —**mist′i·ness** *n.*

misunderstand (mĭs′ŭn-dər-stănd′) *tr.v.* **misunderstood** (mĭs′ŭn-dər-stŏŏd′), **misunderstanding, misunderstands** To understand incorrectly or imperfectly.

misunderstanding (mĭs′ŭn-dər-stăn′dĭng) *n.* **1.** A failure to understand. **2.** A quarrel or disagreement.

misuse (mĭs-yōōz′) *tr.v.* **misused, misusing, misuses 1.** To use wrongly or incorrectly: *misuse a word in a sentence.* **2.** To make improper use of; abuse: *Let's not misuse our natural resources.* ❖ *n.* (mĭs-yōōs′) Wrong or improper use: *the misuse of language.*

mite[1] (mīt) *n.* Any of numerous very small animals that are related to ticks and spiders. Mites often live as parasites on plants or on other animals.

mite[2] (mīt) *n.* **1.** A small amount of money, especially one given as a contribution. **2.** A coin of very small value. **3.** A very small creature or object. ◆ **a mite** *Informal* To a small degree; somewhat: *That remark was a mite unfair.*

WORD HISTORY Mite[1] comes from Old English *mīte,* meaning "moth, worm, louse." **Mite**[2] comes from Middle

English *mite,* which comes from Middle Dutch and Middle Low German *mīte,* meaning "a coin of small value."

miter (mī′tər) *n.* **1.** A tall pointed hat worn by a Christian bishop as a mark of office. **2a.** A miter joint. **b.** The edge of a piece of material that has been beveled in order to make a miter joint. ❖ *tr.v.* **mitered, mitering, miters** To join with a miter joint.

miter box *n.* A device for guiding a handsaw, consisting of two upright sides joined at the bottom and having narrow slots for the saw.

miter joint *n.* A joint made by fitting together two beveled surfaces to form a right angle.

mitigate (mĭt′ĭ-gāt′) *tr.v.* **mitigated, mitigating, mitigates 1.** To make less severe or intense; moderate: *The judge mitigated the sentence.* **2.** To make alterations to (land) to make it less polluted. —**mit′i·ga′tion** *n.*

mitochondrion (mī′tə-kŏn′drē-ən) *n., pl.* **mitochondria** (mī′tə-kŏn′drē-ə) Any of certain microscopic structures found in the cytoplasm of all living cells except bacteria and archaea, containing enzymes that act in converting food to usable energy.

mitosis (mī-tō′sĭs) *n., pl.* **mitoses** (mī-tō′sēz) A form of cell division in which the nucleus of a cell divides, producing two new nuclei, each having the same genetic material as the original cell.

mitt (mĭt) *n.* **1.** A glove that extends over the hand but only partially covers the fingers. **2.** A large padded leather glove worn to protect the hand when catching a baseball. **3.** A mitten. **4.** *Slang* A hand or fist: *Keep your mitts off the paintings.*

mitten (mĭt′n) *n.* A covering for the hand, with a separate section for the thumb and one wide section for all four fingers.

mix (mĭks) *v.* **mixed, mixing, mixes** —*tr.* **1.** To combine or blend into a single mass, as by pouring, stirring, or shaking: *mix flour, water, and eggs to form dough.* **2.** To make or create by combining different ingredients: *mix cement.* **3.** To add (an ingredient or element) to something else: *mix the egg into the batter.* **4.** To combine or join: *mix joy with sorrow.* **5.** To bring into social contact: *The new league mixes boys with girls on the teams.* **6.** To combine (two or more audio tracks or channels) to produce a single audio recording. —*intr.* To become or be capable of being mixed or blended together: *Stir until the eggs mix with the flour. Oil does not mix with water.* ❖ *n.* **1.** A combination of diverse elements: *The downtown has a good mix of stores and restaurants.* **2.** A mixture, especially of ingredients packaged and sold commercially: *a brownie mix.* **3.** A recording made by combining and adjusting two or more audio tracks or channels. **4.** An animal, especially a cat or dog, resulting from the mating of two different breeds. ◆ **mix up 1.** To confuse; confound: *Your directions only mixed us up even more.* **2.** To involve, concern, or implicate: *He was mixed up in a fraudulent scheme.*

mixed (mĭkst) *adj.* **1.** Blended together into one mass: *mixed baby formula.* **2.** Composed of various elements: *a mixed reaction from the critics.* **3.** Relating to or made up of different kinds of people, as of different races or social classes: *people of mixed backgrounds.*

mixed bag *n.* A collection of dissimilar things; an assortment.

mixed martial art *n.* Any of various sports that combine techniques from different martial arts, allowing punches, throws, holds, and often kicks.

mixed metaphor *n.* A succession of metaphors whose literal meanings form a contradictory or illogical combination, thus producing an absurd effect; for example, *Lying down on the job left me out on a limb* is a mixed metaphor.

mixed number *n.* A number, such as 7⅜, consisting of a whole number and a fraction.

mixer (mĭk′sər) *n.* **1.** A device that mixes or blends ingredients, especially by mechanical action: *a cement mixer.* **2.** A device used to mix two or more audio tracks or channels. **3.** An informal party where people can get to know each other.

mixture (mĭks′chər) *n.* **1.** Something made up of different ingredients, things, or kinds: *The day was a mixture of sun and clouds.* **2.** Something made up of two or more substances that are not chemically combined with each other and are capable of being separated. **3.** The act or process of mixing: *an alloy made from the mixture of two metals.*

mix-up also **mixup** (mĭks′ŭp′) *n.* A state of confusion or a misunderstanding: *a mix-up over the starting time of the game.*

mizzen (mĭz′ən) *n.* **1.** A fore-and-aft sail set on the mizzenmast. **2.** A mizzenmast.

mizzenmast or **mizenmast** (mĭz′ən-məst or mĭz′ən-măst′) *n.* The mast aft of a mainmast on a ship having three or more masts.

mks An abbreviation of meter-kilogram second.

mL or **ml** An abbreviation of milliliter.

MLB An abbreviation of Major League Baseball.

Mlle An abbreviation of Mademoiselle.

Mlles An abbreviation of Mesdemoiselles.

mm An abbreviation of millimeter.

Mme An abbreviation of Madame.

Mmes An abbreviation of Mesdames.

mnemonic (nĭ-mŏn′ĭk) *adj.* Relating to or assisting the memory. ❖ *n.* Something, such as a formula or rhyme, that helps one to remember something; for example, *i before e except after c* is a mnemonic.

mo. An abbreviation of month.

moa (mō′ə) *n.* Any of various large extinct birds of New Zealand that resembled an ostrich.

moan (mōn) *n.* **1.** A low, drawn-out, mournful sound, usually of sorrow or pain. **2.** A similar sound: *the moan of the wind.* ❖ *v.* **moaned, moaning, moans** —*intr.* **1.** To utter a moan or moans. **2.** To make a sound resembling a moan: *The wind moaned in the chimney.* **3.** To complain, lament, or grieve: *They moaned about the lost opportunity.* —*tr.* To utter with a moan or moans: *"We can't seem to win a game," moaned the coach.*

moat (mōt) *n.* A wide deep ditch, usually filled with water, especially one surrounding a medieval town or fortress.

mob (mŏb) *n.* **1.** A large disorderly crowd. **2.** The mass of common people. **3.** often **Mob** A criminal organization, especially the Mafia operating in the United States. ❖ *tr.v.* **mobbed, mobbing, mobs** **1.** To crowd around and jostle or annoy, especially in anger or enthusiasm: *Autograph seekers mobbed the stars.* **2.** To crowd into or jam (a place): *Visitors mobbed the museum.*

mobile (mō′bəl or mō′bīl′ or mō′bēl′) *adj.* **1.** Capable of moving or being moved from place to place: *a mobile hospital; a mobile organism.* **2.** Relating to wireless communication devices, such as cell phones. **3.** Capable of moving or changing easily: *mobile features.* **4.** Fluid or

flowing freely: *Mercury is a mobile metal.* **5.** Allowing relatively easy movement from one social class to another: *a mobile society.* ❖ *n.* **1.** (mō′bēl′) A type of sculpture consisting of parts that move, especially in response to air currents. **2.** A mobile phone. —**mo·bil′i·ty** (mō-bĭl′ĭ-tē) *n.*

mobile home *n.* A house trailer that is used as a permanent house and is usually hooked up to utilities.

mobile phone *n.* A cell phone.

mobilize (mō′bə-līz′) *v.* **mobilized, mobilizing, mobilizes** —*tr.* **1.** To assemble or prepare for war: *mobilize troops.* **2.** To assemble or coordinate for a particular purpose or action: *mobilize public opinion to support the campaign.* —*intr.* To become prepared for war or other coordinated action. —**mo′bi·li·za′tion** (mō′bə-lĭ-zā′shən) *n.*

Möbius strip (mō′bē-əs or mœ′bē-əs) *n.* A continuous one-sided surface that can be formed by rotating one end of a rectangular strip of paper 180° and attaching it to the other end.

mobster (mŏb′stər) *n. Informal* A member of a criminal gang.

moccasin (mŏk′ə-sĭn) *n.* **1.** A soft leather slipper traditionally worn by certain Native American peoples. **2.** A shoe resembling a moccasin. **3.** The water moccasin.

moccasin flower *n.* A lady's slipper orchid.

mocha (mō′kə) *n.* **1.** A rich Arabian coffee. **2.** A coffee beverage flavored with milk, sugar, and cocoa. **3.** A flavoring made of coffee mixed with chocolate.

mock (mŏk) *v.* **mocked, mocking, mocks** —*tr.* **1.** To make fun of, often by imitating or depicting in an insulting way; ridicule. **2.** To treat with scorn or contempt; deride. —*intr.* To express contempt; scoff. ❖ *adj.* Simulated; false; sham: *a mock battle.* ❖ *n.* The act of mocking; mockery: *made mock of his silly behavior.* —**mock′er** *n.*

mockery (mŏk′ə-rē) *n., pl.* **mockeries** **1.** Ridicule; derision. **2.** An object of ridicule. **3.** A false, offensive, or ridiculous imitation of something: *The trial was a mockery of justice.*

mockingbird (mŏk′ĭng-bûrd′) *n.* Any of several birds of the Americas that often imitate the songs of other birds.

mock orange *n.* Any of various shrubs having fragrant white flowers resembling orange blossoms.

mockup also **mock-up** (mŏk′ŭp′) *n.* A full-sized model, as of an airplane or building, used for demonstration, study, or testing.

mod (mŏd) *adj.* Stylishly up-to-date, especially in a modern unconventional way.

modal (mōd′l) *adj.* **1.** Relating to or characteristic of a mode. **2.** Relating to or expressing grammatical mood. ❖ *n.* A modal auxiliary.

modal auxiliary *n.* An auxiliary verb, such as *can, could, may, might, must, shall, should, will,* or *would,* that is used to express mood or tense as well as possibility, obligation, or intention.

mode (mōd) *n.* **1.** A way, manner, or style of doing: *a mode of living; a mode of travel.* **2.** The current fashion or style in dress: *a hat in the latest mode.* **3.** A given condition of functioning; a status or operation: *The spacecraft was in its recovery mode.* **4.** Any of the musical scales produced by starting, in turn, on each of the tones of a major scale and proceeding through an octave. Modes were commonly used in medieval church music. **5.** The value that occurs most frequently in a data set or series. For example, in the series 125, 140, 172, 164, 140, and 110, the mode is 140.

model (mŏd′l) *n.* **1.** A small-scale reproduction or representation of something: *a model of a ship.* **2.** A style or design of something: *This car is last year's model.* **3.** A person or thing serving as an ideal example of something: *The farm is a model of efficient management.* **4.** A person hired to wear clothes in order to show them off, as in fashion shows or advertisements. **5.** A person hired to pose for an artist or photographer. **6.** In science, a description or concept of a system or set of observable events that accounts for all its known properties in a reasonable way. ❖ *v.* **modeled, modeling, models** also **modelled, modelling, models** —*tr.* **1.** To make or construct a model of: *The library was modeled after the Library of Congress in Washington, DC.* **2a.** To make (something) by shaping a plastic substance: *modeled a statue from clay.* **b.** To form (a substance) into a shape: *modeled the clay into a statue.* **3.** To display (clothing, for example) to show others how it looks: *She modeled her new dress.* —*intr.* **1.** To serve or work as a model. **2.** To make a model. ❖ *adj.* **1.** Being, serving, or used as a model: *a model home.* **2.** Serving as a standard of excellence; worthy of imitation: *a model child.* —**mod′el·er** *n.*

modeling (mŏd′l-ĭng) *n.* **1.** The act or art of constructing a model out of a pliable material. **2.** The act or profession of being a model.

modem (mō′dəm) *n.* A device that transmits and receives data using a modulated carrier wave. Modems are used to establish network and Internet connections.

moderate (mŏd′ər-ĭt) *adj.* **1.** Kept within reasonable limits; not excessive or extreme: *moderate prices.* **2.** Medium or average in amount or quality: *a moderate income.* **3.** Not severe; mild; temperate: *a moderate climate.* **4.** Opposed to radical or extreme views or measures, especially in politics or religion. ❖ *n.* A person who holds moderate views or opinions, especially in politics or religion. ❖ *v.* (mŏd′ə-rāt′) **moderated, moderating, moderates** —*tr.* **1.** To make less extreme: *moderate one's demands.* **2.** To preside over (a meeting or panel discussion). —*intr.* **1.** To become less extreme. **2.** To act as a moderator. —**mod′er·ate·ly** *adv.*

moderation (mŏd′ə-rā′shən) *n.* **1.** The act of making more moderate: *moderation of one's demands.* **2.** The avoidance of extremes: *an advocate of political moderation.*

moderato (mŏd′ə-rä′tō) *adv. & adj.* In music, in moderate tempo.

moderator (mŏd′ə-rā′tər) *n.* **1.** The person who presides over a meeting or panel discussion. **2.** A substance, such as graphite or water, placed in a nuclear reactor to slow neutrons down to speeds at which they are likely to cause additional nuclear fission.

modern (mŏd′ərn) *adj.* **1.** Relating to the present or the recent past: *modern history; Modern English.* **2.** Relating to a recently developed style, technique, or technology: *modern methods of farming.* **3.** Experimental; avant-garde. ❖ *n.* **1.** A person who lives in modern times. **2.** A person with modern ideas, tastes, or beliefs.

Modern English *n.* English since about 1500.

modernism (mŏd′ər-nĭz′əm) *n.* **1.** Modern thought, character, or practice. **2.** often **Modernism** The use of innovative forms that characterizes many styles in the art and literature of the 1900s. —**mod′ern·ist** *n.*

modernity (mŏ-dûr′nĭ-tē or mŏ-dûr′nĭ-tē) *n., pl.* **modernities** The quality of being modern.

modernize (mŏd′ər-nīz′) *v.* **modernized, modernizing,**

modernizes —*tr.* To make modern in appearance, style, or character; update: *modernize a kitchen.* —*intr.* To become modern; accept or adopt modern ways. —**mod′ern·i·za′tion** (mŏd′ər-nĭ-zā′shən) *n.*

modest (mŏd′ĭst) *adj.* **1.** Having or showing a moderate estimation of one's own talents, abilities, or accomplishments. **2.** Retiring or reserved in manner; shy: *a quiet modest demeanor.* **3.** Not elaborate or showy; unpretentious: *a modest house.* **4.** Moderate in size or amount; not large: *a modest salary.* —**mod′est·ly** *adv.*

modesty (mŏd′ĭ-stē) *n.* **1.** The state or quality of being modest. **2.** Reserve in behavior, dress, or speech. **3.** Lack of pretentiousness; simplicity.

modicum (mŏd′ĭ-kəm) *n.* A small amount: *a subject in which I have only a modicum of interest.*

modification (mŏd′ə-fĭ-kā′shən) *n.* **1.** The action or process of modifying: *The theory is still subject to some modification.* **2.** A result of modifying; a change or adaptation: *The design was approved with certain modifications.* **3.** A small alteration, adjustment, or limitation.

modifier (mŏd′ə-fī′ər) *n.* A word, phrase, or clause that grammatically modifies another word or phrase. Adjectives and adverbs are modifiers.

modify (mŏd′ə-fī′) *v.* **modified, modifying, modifies** —*tr.* **1.** To change in form or character; alter: *modify the terms of a deal.* **2.** In grammar, to add further detail about the meaning of (a word or phrase, for example). —*intr.* To be or become modified; change.

modish (mō′dĭsh) *adj.* Stylish; fashionable. —**mod′ish·ly** *adv.* —**mod′ish·ness** *n.*

modulate (mŏj′ə-lāt′) *v.* **modulated, modulating, modulates** —*tr.* **1.** To change or vary the pitch, intensity, or tone of (one's voice or a musical instrument, for example). **2.** To vary the amplitude, frequency, or some other characteristic of (electromagnetic waves) in a way that makes them correspond to a signal or information that is to be transmitted. —*intr.* To pass from one musical key or tonality to another by means of a melodic or chord progression.

modulation (mŏj′ə-lā′shən) *n.* **1.** The act or process of modulating. **2.** The state of being modulated. **3.** The process by which a characteristic of electromagnetic waves, such as amplitude or frequency, is changed to make the waves correspond to a signal or information that is to be transmitted. **4.** In music, a passing or transition from one key or tonality to another.

modulator (mŏj′ə-lā′tər) *n.* A device that modulates an electromagnetic wave.

module (mŏj′ool) *n.* **1.** A standard element that is used over and over again in forming a building or structure. **2.** A self-contained unit of electronic components and circuitry that is installed as a unit. **3.** A self-contained unit of a spacecraft that is used for a particular job or set of jobs: *a lunar module.* **4.** A unit of education or instruction in which a single topic is studied for a given period of time. —**mod′u·lar** (mŏj′ə-lər) *adj.*

modus operandi (mō′dəs ŏp′ə-răn′dē or mō′dəs ŏp′ə-răn′dī′) *n., pl.* **modi operandi** (mō′dē or mō′dī) **1.** A method of operating or functioning. **2.** A person's manner of working.

mogul¹ (mō′gəl) *n.* A small hard mound or bump on a ski slope.

mogul² (mō′gəl or mō-gŭl′) *n.* **1.** A very rich or powerful person; a magnate. **2.** **Mogul** Variant of **Mughal.**

WORD HISTORY Mogul[1] is probably of Scandinavian origin. **Mogul**[2] is from Urdu *mugal, mugul,* meaning "Mughal."

mohair (mō′hâr′) *n.* **1.** The long silky hair of the Angora goat. **2.** Fabric or yarn made from this hair.

Mohave also **Mojave** (mō-hä′vē) *n., pl.* **Mohave** or **Mohaves** also **Mojave** or **Mojaves** **1.** A member of a Native American people living in southeast California and western Arizona. **2.** The Yuman language of the Mohave.

Mohawk (mō′hôk′) *n., pl.* **Mohawk** or **Mohawks** **1.** A member of a Native American people living in upstate New York and southern Ontario. **2.** The Iroquoian language of the Mohawk.

Mohegan (mō-hē′gən) *n., pl.* **Mohegan** or **Mohegans** **1.** A member of a Native American people formerly living in Connecticut, with present-day populations in Connecticut and Wisconsin. **2.** The Algonquian language of the Mohegan.

Mohican (mō-hē′kən *or* mə-hē′kən) *n.* Variant of **Mahican.**

Mohs scale (mōz) *n.* A scale used to measure the relative hardness of a mineral by its resistance to scratching by ten standard minerals ranging from talc, the softest, to diamond, the hardest.

moiety (moi′ĭ-tē) *n., pl.* **moieties** **1.** A half. **2.** A part, portion, or share.

moiré (mwä-rā′ *or* mô-rā′) *adj.* Having a wavy or rippled surface pattern. ❖ *n.* **1.** A wavy or rippled pattern pressed on cloth by engraved rollers. **2.** Cloth, especially silk, that has a watery rippled look.

moist (moist) *adj.* **moister, moistest** **1.** Slightly wet; damp: *a moist sponge.* See Synonyms at **wet. 2.** Humid or rainy: *the moist gulf air; a moist climate.* **3.** Juicy or succulent; not dried out: *Basting keeps the turkey moist in the oven.* —**moist′ness** *n.*

moisten (moi′sən) *tr. & intr.v.* **moistened, moistening, moistens** To make or become moist.

moisture (mois′chər) *n.* Wetness, especially that caused by water present in the air as vapor or spread thinly over a surface or surfaces.

moisturizer (mois′chə-rī′zər) *n.* A cosmetic lotion or cream applied to the skin to counter dryness.

Mojave (mō-hä′vē) *n.* Variant of **Mohave.**

mojo (mō′jō′) *n., pl.* **mojos** or **mojoes** **1.** A saying or item believed to have magical powers; a spell or charm. **2.** An ability or quality that causes one to excel or have good luck: *a pitcher who lost his mojo when he entered the major leagues.*

molar[1] (mō′lər) *n.* **1.** Relating to or designating the molarity of a solution. **2.** Relating to one mole of a substance.

molar[2] (mō′lər) *n.* Any of the teeth located toward the back of the jaws, having broad crowns for grinding food. Humans have 12 molars.

molarity (mō-lăr′ĭ-tē) *n., pl.* **molarities** The concentration of a solution expressed in moles of solute per liter of solution.

molasses (mə-lăs′ĭz) *n.* A thick brown syrup produced in refining sugar.

mold[1] (mōld) *n.* **1.** A hollow container of a particular shape, used for shaping a liquid or plastic substance: *pour the batter into a mold.* **2.** Something made or shaped from a mold. **3.** General shape; form: *the round mold of*

a face. **4.** Distinctive character, kind, or type: *men and women of serious mold.* ❖ *tr.v.* **molded, molding, molds** **1.** To shape in a mold. **2.** To determine the general character of; shape in a particular way: *mold clay; mold a student's mind.* —**mold′a·ble** *adj.* —**mold′er** *n.*

mold[2] (mōld) *n.* **1.** Any of various fungi that often form a fuzzy coating on the surface of food and other organic matter. **2.** The coating formed by such a fungus.

WORD HISTORY Mold[1] comes from Middle English *molde* (meaning "pattern, model"), which is from Latin *modulus,* which is the diminutive of Latin *modus,* meaning "measure." **Mold**[2] comes from Middle English *moulde,* which is probably from the past participle of Middle English *moulen,* meaning "to grow moldy."

molder (mōl′dər) *v.* **moldered, moldering, molders** —*intr.* To turn gradually to dust; crumble: *The ancient ruins are beginning to molder away.* —*tr.* To cause to crumble.

molding (mōl′dĭng) *n.* **1.** The act or process of molding. **2.** Something that is molded. **3.** An ornamental strip used to decorate a surface.

moldy (mōl′dē) *adj.* **moldier, moldiest** **1.** Covered with or containing mold: *moldy bread.* **2.** Damp and musty: *a dark moldy cupboard.* —**mold′i·ness** *n.*

mole[1] (mōl) *n.* A small, usually dark growth on the skin.

mole[2] (mōl) *n.* **1.** Any of various small burrowing mammals having strong claws, tiny eyes, a narrow snout, and short silky fur. **2.** A spy within an organization, especially a double agent.

mole[3] (mōl) *n.* In the International System, a unit that represents the amount of molecules, ions, or other elementary units in a substance, equal to the number of atoms in 0.012 kilogram of carbon-12. (That number is 6.0221×10^{23}, or Avogadro's number.) A mole of a chemical has a mass in grams numerically equal to its molecular weight. For example, carbon dioxide, CO_2, has a molecular weight of 44; therefore, one mole of it weighs 44 grams. See table at **measurement.**

WORD HISTORY Mole[1] comes from Middle English *mol,* which comes from Old English *māl,* both meaning "spot, blemish." **Mole**[2] comes from Middle English *molle,* referring to the same kind of animal as in Modern English. **Mole**[3] comes from German *Mol* (referring to the same unit as in English), which is short for German *Molekül,* meaning "molecule."

molecular (mə-lĕk′yə-lər) *adj.* Relating to, caused by, or consisting of molecules. —**mo·lec′u·lar·ly** *adv.*

molecular weight *n.* The sum of the atomic weights of the atoms contained in a molecule.

molecule (mŏl′ĭ-kyōōl′) *n.* **1.** A group of two or more atoms linked together by sharing electrons in a covalent bond. **2.** A small particle; a tiny bit.

molehill (mōl′hĭl′) *n.* A small mound of earth dug up by a burrowing mole.

moleskin (mōl′skĭn′) *n.* **1.** The short, soft, silky fur of a mole. **2.** A sturdy cotton cloth with a thick fine nap on one side.

molest (mə-lĕst′) *tr.v.* **molested, molesting, molests** **1.** To annoy, bother, or disturb: *Few animals dare molest a badger.* **2.** To subject to unwanted or improper sexual activity. —**mo·lest′er** *n.* —**mo′les·ta′tion** (mō′lĕ-stā′shən) *n.*

mollify (mŏl′ə-fī′) *tr.v.* **mollified, mollifying, mollifies** **1.** To lessen the anger of; placate: *a new film designed to mollify critics.* **2.** To make less intense; soften or soothe: *The* *tender words mollified the child's distress.* —**mol′li·fi·ca′- tion** (mŏl′ə-fĭ-kā′shən) *n.*

mollusk also **mollusc** (mŏl′əsk) *n.* Any of numerous soft-bodied invertebrate animals, such as snails, clams, and oysters, usually living in water and having a hard outer shell. Some mollusks, such as octopuses, squids, and slugs, have no outer shell.

Moloch (mō′lŏk′ *or* mŏl′ək) *n.* **1.** In the Bible, a god of some non-Hebrew peoples to whom children were sacrificed. **2.** Something that requires severe sacrifice.

Molotov cocktail (mŏl′ə-tôf′) *n.* A makeshift bomb made usually of a glass bottle filled with flammable liquid and provided with a rag wick that is lighted just before being hurled.

molt (mōlt) *v.* **molted, molting, molts** —*intr.* To shed an outer covering, such as skin or feathers, for replacement by a new growth: *Some snakes molt in spring.* —*tr.* To shed (an outer covering): *molt feathers.* ❖ *n.* The act or process of molting.

molten (mōl′tən) *adj.* Made liquid by heat; melted: *molten metal.*

molybdenum (mə-lĭb′də-nəm) *n. Symbol* **Mo** A hard, silvery-white metallic element that is used to toughen and harden steel and is an essential trace element in plant metabolism. Atomic number 42. See **Periodic Table.**

mom (mŏm) *n. Informal* Mother.

mom-and-pop (mŏm′ən-pŏp′) *adj.* Relating to or being a small business that is run by the owners: *a mom-and-pop grocery store.*

moment (mō′mənt) *n.* **1.** A very brief interval of time; an instant: *I'll be ready in a moment.* **2.** A certain important point in time: *the happiest moment of my life.* **3.** The present time: *I am busy at the moment.* **4.** Great significance or importance: *We were proud to witness an event of such moment.*

momenta (mō-mĕn′tə) *n.* A plural of **momentum.**

momentarily (mō′mən-târ′ə-lē) *adv.* **1.** For an instant or a moment: *I was momentarily at a loss for words.* **2.** At any moment; very soon: *The doctor will see you momentarily.*

momentary (mō′mən-tĕr′ē) *adj.* Lasting only an instant or moment: *a momentary glance.*

momentous (mō-mĕn′təs) *adj.* Of the utmost importance or significance: *a momentous occasion.*

momentum (mō-mĕn′təm) *n., pl.* **momenta** (mō-mĕn′tə) or **momentums 1.** A measure of the motion of a moving body, equal to the body's mass multiplied by its velocity. **2.** Force or speed of motion; impetus: *The sled gained momentum as it raced down the hill.*

mommy (mŏm′ē) *n., pl.* **mommies** *Informal* Mother.

monarch (mŏn′ərk *or* mŏn′ärk′) *n.* **1.** A ruler or sovereign, such as a king or queen, who reigns over a state, usually for life and by hereditary right. **2.** A monarch butterfly. —**mo·nar′chic** (mə-när′kĭk) *adj.* —**mo·nar′- chi·cal** *adj.*

monarch butterfly *n.* A large orange-and-black American butterfly noted for its long-distance migrations.

monarchism (mŏn′ər-kĭz′əm *or* mŏn′är′kĭz′əm) *n.* Belief in or support of government by a monarch.

monarchist (mŏn′ər-kĭst *or* mŏn′är′kĭst) *n.* A person who believes in or supports monarchy.

monarchy (mŏn′ər-kē *or* mŏn′är′kē) *n., pl.* **monarchies 1.** Government by a monarch. **2.** A country ruled by a monarch.

monastery (mŏn′ə-stĕr′ē) *n., pl.* **monasteries 1.** A community of monks. **2.** The building or buildings occupied by monks. —**mon′as·te′ri·al** (mŏn′ə-stîr′ē-əl *or* mŏn′- ə-stĕr′ē-əl) *adj.*

monastic (mə-năs′tĭk) *adj.* **1.** Relating to or characteristic of a monastery. **2.** Resembling life in a monastery. ❖ *n.* A monk.

monaural (mŏn-ôr′əl) *adj.* **1.** Relating to sound reception with only one ear. **2.** Using a single channel to transmit or reproduce sound; monophonic.

Monday (mŭn′dē *or* mŭn′dā′) *n.* The day of the week that comes after Sunday and before Tuesday. In many countries and according to international standards, Monday is considered the first day of the week. —**Mon′days** *adv.*

monetary (mŏn′ĭ-tĕr′ē) *adj.* **1.** Relating to money: *the monetary value of a painting.* **2.** Relating to a nation's currency or coinage: *a monetary system.* —**mon′e·tar′i·ly** *adv.*

monetize (mŏn′ĭ-tīz′ *or* mŭn′ĭ-tīz′) *tr.v.* **monetized, monetizing, monetizes 1.** To convert (an asset) into cash, as by selling the asset or using it as security for a loan. **2.** To convert into a source of income: *monetized website visitors by selling advertising space.* **3.** To purchase (government debt) in the open market using central bank funds, leading to an expansion of the money supply. **4.** To establish (a metal) as a currency, especially by minting coins. **5.** To convert (an economy) from a system based on barter to one based on the exchange of money. —**mon′- e·ti·za′tion** (mŏn′ĭ-tĭ-zā′shən *or* mŭn′ĭ-tĭ-zā′shən) *n.*

money (mŭn′ē) *n., pl.* **moneys** *or* **monies 1.** Something, such as gold or an officially issued coin or paper note, that is legally declared to have a fixed value and to be exchangeable for all goods and services. **2.** The official coins and paper notes issued by a government and used to buy or pay for things; currency. **3.** Wealth; property and assets: *a family with plenty of money.* **4.** *often* **moneys, monies** Sums of money collected or stored; funds: *state tax moneys; monies set aside for research.* **5.** An amount of money sufficient for some purpose: *They lacked the money for a vacation.* **6.** Monetary profit or loss: *won big money on the lottery.*

moneybag (mŭn′ē-băg′) *n.* **1.** A bag for holding money. **2. moneybags** *(used with a singular verb) Slang* A rich and greedy person.

moneyed (mŭn′ēd) *adj.* **1.** Having much money; wealthy: *the large moneyed corporations.* **2.** Representing or arising from money or wealth: *the power of moneyed interests in Washington, DC.*

moneylender (mŭn′ē-lĕn′dər) *n.* A person whose business is lending money for a fee.

money order *n.* An order authorizing the payment of a specified amount of money to the bearer. Money orders can usually be bought or cashed at a bank or post office.

monger (mŭng′gər *or* mŏng′gər) *n.* **1.** A dealer in a specific product or commodity: *an ironmonger.* **2.** A person who promotes something undesirable or discreditable: *a scandalmonger.*

Mongol (mŏng′gəl *or* mŏng′gōl′) *adj.* Relating to Mongolia or its people, language, or culture. ❖ *n.* **1.** A member of any of the traditionally nomadic peoples of Mongolia. **2.** The language of these peoples; Mongolian.

Mongolian (mŏng-gō′lē-ən *or* mŏng-gōl′yən) *n.* **1.** A native or inhabitant of Mongolia. **2.** Any of the languages of Mongolia, related to Turkish. ❖ *adj.* Relating to Mongolia, the Mongols, or their language or culture.

mongoose (mŏng′gōōs′ *or* mŏn′gōōs′) *n., pl.* **mongooses** Any of various mammals of Asia, southern Europe, and Africa that resemble weasels and are noted for their ability to kill venomous snakes.

mongrel (mŏng′grəl) *n.* A dog that is the result of crossing different breeds or that is of an unknown breed.

monies (mŭn′ēz) *n.* A plural of **money.**

monitor (mŏn′ĭ-tər) *n.* **1.** A person who gives warnings, corrective advice, or instruction. **2.** A student who assists a teacher in routine duties such as taking attendance. **3.** A usually electronic device used to record, regulate, or control a process or activity: *a radiation monitor.* **4.** A video display or speaker used in a production studio to check audio or video quality: *The sound engineer detected a hiss on the monitor.* **5.** A device that accepts video signals from a computer and displays information on a screen. **6.** A monitor lizard. ❖ *v.* **monitored, monitoring, monitors** —*tr.* **1.** To keep watch over; supervise: *monitor an election.* **2.** To keep track of systematically: *monitor a patient's heartbeat.* **3.** To check the quality or content of (an electronic audio or a visual signal) by means of a receiver. —*intr.* To act as a monitor.

monitor lizard *n.* Any of various meat-eating, often large lizards of tropical Africa, Asia, and Australia, having a forked tongue and a long neck.

monitory (mŏn′ĭ-tôr′ē) *adj.* Giving a warning or rebuke: *a monitory glance.*

monk (mŭngk) *n.* A member of a group of men living in a monastery and bound by vows to the rules and practices of a religious order.

monkey (mŭng′kē) *n., pl.* **monkeys 1.** Any of various primates having long tails and hands and feet that are used for grasping. Monkeys include the baboons, macaques, and marmosets. **2.** A playful or mischievous person. ❖ *intr.v.* **monkeyed, monkeying, monkeys** *Informal* **1.** To behave in a silly or mischievous way: *Don't monkey around during the ceremony.* **2.** To tamper or meddle with something: *Who was monkeying with my computer?*

monkey bars *pl.n.* A jungle gym.

monkey wrench *n.* **1.** A hand tool with adjustable jaws for turning nuts and bolts of various sizes. **2.** Something that disrupts: *Bad weather threw a monkey wrench into our plans.*

monkish (mŭng′kĭsh) *adj.* Relating to or characteristic of monks.

mono (mŏn′ō) *n. Informal* Infectious mononucleosis.

mono– or **mon–** A prefix that means: **1.** One; only; single: *monogamy.* **2.** Containing a single atom, radical, or group: *monoxide.*

monochromatic (mŏn′ə-krō-măt′ĭk) *adj.* **1.** Having a single color: *a monochromatic beige rug.* **2.** Consisting of a single wavelength of light or other radiation: *monochromatic x-rays.*

monochrome (mŏn′ə-krōm′) *n.* **1.** The state of being in a single color. **2.** An image, such as a painting or photograph, that is rendered in black and white or in shades of a single color.

monocle (mŏn′ə-kəl) *n.* An eyeglass, typically having a cord attached, worn in front of one eye.

monocot (mŏn′ə-kŏt) *n.* A monocotyledon.

monocotyledon (mŏn′ə-kŏt′l-ēd′n) *n.* A flowering plant having a single cotyledon and usually other characteristics such as leaf veins that are parallel, flower parts in multiples of three, and a lack of woody growth. Tulips, onions, grasses, and palms are monocotyledons. —**mon′o·cot′y·le′don·ous** *adj.*

monocular (mə-nŏk′yə-lər) *adj.* **1.** Relating to or having a single eye. **2.** Designed for use with only one eye: *a monocular microscope.*

monoecious (mə-nē′shəs) *adj.* Having separate male flowers or cones and female flowers or cones on the same plant. Oaks, pines, and corn plants are monoecious.

monogamy (mə-nŏg′ə-mē) *n.* **1.** The custom or condition of being married to only one person at a time. **2.** The custom or condition of having only one sexual partner at a time. **3.** The condition of having only one mate during a breeding season or during the breeding life of a pair: *monogamy in birds.* —**mo·nog′a·mous** (mə-nŏg′ə-məs) *adj.*

monogram (mŏn′ə-grăm′) *n.* A design made up of one or more letters, usually the initials of a name. ❖ *tr.v.* **monogrammed, monogramming, monograms** also **monogramed, monograming, monograms** To mark with a monogram: *She monogrammed the sheets and towels.*

monograph (mŏn′ə-grăf′) *n.* A scholarly book or article on a specific and usually limited subject.

monolith (mŏn′ə-lĭth′) *n.* **1.** A large single block of stone. **2.** A memorial, monument, or other structure made from a single block of stone.

monolithic (mŏn′ə-lĭth′ĭk) *adj.* **1.** Consisting of a monolith: *a monolithic column.* **2.** Like a monolith in being massive, uniform, or unvarying: *a monolithic business empire.*

monologue (mŏn′ə-lôg′) *n.* **1.** A long speech delivered by an actor on the stage or a character in a story or poem. **2.** A series of jokes and stories told by a comedian while alone on the stage. **3.** A long speech made by one person in a group: *He talked so much that our conversation turned into a monologue.*

monomania (mŏn′ə-mā′nē-ə *or* mŏn′ə-mān′yə) *n.* An intense preoccupation with one subject or idea. —**mon′o·ma′ni·ac′** (mŏn′ə-mā′nē-ăk′) *n.*

monomial (mō-nō′mē-əl) *n.* An algebraic expression consisting of a single term.

mononucleosis (mŏn′ō-nōō′klē-ō′sĭs) *n.* Infectious mononucleosis.

monophonic (mŏn′ə-fŏn′ĭk) *adj.* **1.** Having a single melodic line or part. **2.** Using a single channel to record, store, or reproduce sound: *a monophonic recording.*

monoplane (mŏn′ə-plān′) *n.* An airplane having a single pair of wings.

monopolist (mə-nŏp′ə-lĭst) *n.* A business leader who owns or promotes monopolies.

monopolistic (mə-nŏp′ə-lĭs′tĭk) *adj.* **1.** Maintaining a monopoly. **2.** Relating to or characteristic of a monopoly or a monopolist.

monopolize (mə-nŏp′ə-līz′) *tr.v.* **monopolized, monopolizing, monopolizes 1.** To gain a monopoly over. **2.** To get or have sole control over: *Don't monopolize the conversation.* —**mo·nop′o·li·za′tion** (mə-nŏp′ə-lĭ-zā′shən) *n.* —**mo·nop′o·liz′er** *n.*

monopoly (mə-nŏp′ə-lē) *n., pl.* **monopolies 1a.** Complete control by one group of the means of producing or selling a product or service: *The early railroads had a near monopoly on freight and passenger transportation.* **b.** A company having such complete control: *laws to limit the power of monopolies.* **c.** A product, service, or commercial activity completely controlled by one group. **2.** The right given by a government to a person to have exclusive control of the sale and manufacture of commercial goods. **3.** Sole possession or control of something: *The US monopoly on the atomic bomb did not last long.*

monorail (mŏn′ə-rāl′) *n.* **1.** A single rail serving as a track for trains that travel on it or hang from it. **2.** A railway system using a track with such a rail.

monosodium glutamate (mŏn′ə-sō′dē-əm glōō′tə-māt′) *n.* A white crystalline compound used to enhance flavor in food.

monosyllabic (mŏn′ə-sĭ-lăb′ĭk) *adj.* **1.** Having only one syllable: *a monosyllabic word.* **2.** Consisting of or characterized by monosyllables: *monosyllabic speech.*

monosyllable (mŏn′ə-sĭl′ə-bəl) *n.* A word, such as *hat* or *hate,* having one syllable.

monotheism (mŏn′ə-thē-ĭz′əm) *n.* The belief that there is only one God. —**mon′o·the′ist** *n.* —**mon′o·the·is′-tic** *adj.*

monotone (mŏn′ə-tōn′) *n.* **1.** A succession of sounds or words uttered in a single tone of voice: *read the list of names in a monotone.* **2a.** A single tone repeated with different words or time values, as in chanting. **b.** A chant sung on a single tone. **3.** A tiresome repetition, as in sound, color, or style.

monotonous (mə-nŏt′n-əs) *adj.* **1.** Uttered or sounded in one repeated tone; unvarying in pitch: *delivered the speech in a monotonous voice.* **2.** Never varied or enlivened; repetitiously dull: *a monotonous lecture; a monotonous diet.* —**mo·not′o·nous·ly** *adv.*

monotony (mə-nŏt′n-ē) *n., pl.* **monotonies** Tiresome sameness or repetition.

monotreme (mŏn′ə-trēm′) *n.* Any of various egg-laying mammals of a group that includes only the platypus and the echidnas.

monounsaturated (mŏn′ō-ŭn-săch′ə-rā′tĭd) *adj.* Relating to an organic compound, especially an oil or fatty acid, in which there is only one double or triple bond per molecule.

monoxide (mə-nŏk′sīd′) *n.* An oxide in which each molecule contains a single atom of oxygen.

Monseigneur (môn-sĕ-nyœr′) *n., pl.* **Messeigneurs** (mā-sĕ-nyœr′) Used as a title of honor or respect in French-speaking areas for princes or highly ranked clergy.

Monsieur (mə-syœ′) *n., pl.* **Messieurs** (mā-syœ′ or mĕs′-ərz) Used as a courtesy title before the name of a man in a French-speaking area: *Monsieur Fournier.*

monsoon (mŏn-sōōn′) *n.* **1.** A system of winds that influences the climate of a large area and that changes direction with the seasons, especially the wind system that produces the wet and dry seasons in southern Asia. **2.** The season during which this wind blows from the southwest, usually accompanied by heavy rains.

monster (mŏn′stər) *n.* **1.** A dangerous or frightening creature, especially an imaginary or legendary one: *ancient stories about a monster that lives in the lake; dressed up as a monster for Halloween.* **2.** *Informal* Something that is extremely large: *a monster of a shark.* ❖ *adj. Informal* Extremely large; gigantic: *a monster wave; a song that was a monster hit.*

monstrosity (mŏn-strŏs′ĭ-tē) *n., pl.* **monstrosities 1.** A person or thing that is monstrous. **2.** The quality or condition of being monstrous.

monstrous (mŏn′strəs) *adj.* **1.** Having a frightful or hideous appearance: *a deep-sea creature with monstrous teeth.* **2.** Huge; enormous: *a monstrous iceberg.* **3.** Extremely immoral or cruel; inhuman: *a monstrous dictator.* **4.** Relating to or resembling a legendary monster: *the Cyclops and other monstrous creatures of Greek mythology.* —**mon′strous·ly** *adv.* —**mon′strous·ness** *n.*

montage (mŏn-täzh′) *n.* **1a.** A picture made from many other pictures or designs placed next to or on top of one another. **b.** The art or process of making such a picture. **2a.** A rapid succession of different shots in a movie. **b.** The use of such a succession as a technique of making movies.

montane (mŏn-tān′ *or* mŏn′tān′) *adj.* Relating to or characteristic of mountain areas: *animals adapted to montane forests.*

Monterey jack (mŏn′tə-rā′) *n.* A mild cheese with a high moisture content.

month (mŭnth) *n.* **1.** One of the 12 calendar divisions of the year, especially according to the Gregorian calendar, lasting about 30 days. **2.** A period extending from a date in one calendar month to the corresponding date in the following month. **3.** A lunar month.

monthly (mŭnth′lē) *adj.* **1.** Occurring, appearing, or payable every month: *a monthly meeting; monthly bills.* **2.** Continuing or lasting for a month: *average monthly rainfall.* ❖ *adv.* Every month: *a magazine published monthly.* ❖ *n., pl.* **monthlies** A periodical publication appearing once each month.

monument (mŏn′yə-mənt) *n.* **1.** A structure, such as a tower, statue, or building, erected to honor a person, group, or event. **2.** A tombstone. **3.** Something admired for its historical importance: *The Alamo is a monument of American history.* **4.** An outstanding or enduring work: *The book is a monument of scholarship.*

monumental (mŏn′yə-mĕn′tl) *adj.* **1.** Relating to, like, or serving as a monument: *a monumental arch.* **2.** Impressively large, sturdy, and enduring: *a monumental dam.* **3.** Of outstanding significance: *Einstein's monumental discoveries in physics.* **4.** Astounding: *monumental talent.* —**mon′u·men′tal·ly** *adv.*

moo (mōō) *intr.v.* **mooed, mooing, moos** To emit the deep bellowing sound made by a cow; low. ❖ *n., pl.* **moos** The lowing of a cow or a similar sound.

mooch (mōōch) *v.* **mooched, mooching, mooches** *Slang* —*tr.* To get or try to get by begging: *always mooching food from me.* See Synonyms at **cadge.** —*intr.* To get or try to get something for free: *lived by mooching off friends.* —**mooch′er** *n.*

mood[1] (mōōd) *n.* **1.** A state of mind or feeling: *I was in a good mood after the party.* **2.** An impression on the feelings or spirits of a person: *The painting has a somber mood.* **3.** Inclination; disposition: *I'm in no mood to argue.*

mood[2] (mōōd) *n.* A set of verb forms that tells how certain the speaker is of the action expressed. In English, the indicative mood is used to make factual statements, the imperative mood to give commands, and the subjunctive mood to suggest doubt or unlikelihood.

WORD HISTORY Mood[1] comes from Old English *mōd,* meaning "disposition." **Mood**[2] is an alteration of *mode.*

moody (mōō′dē) *adj.* **moodier, moodiest 1.** Apt to change moods often, especially having spells of anger or gloom. **2.** Gloomy; morose; glum: *his moody silence.* —**mood′i·ly** *adv.* —**mood′i·ness** *n.*

moon (mōōn) *n.* **1.** often **Moon** The natural satellite of Earth, visible by reflected sunlight and traveling around Earth in a slightly elliptical orbit at an average distance of about 238,900 miles (384,400 kilometers). Its average diameter is 2,160 miles (3,475 kilometers) and its mass about 1/80 that of Earth. **2.** A natural satellite of a planet other than Earth: *the moons of Jupiter.* **3.** Earth's moon as seen at a particular time in its cycle of phases: *a half moon.* **4.** A month, especially a lunar month. **5.** A disk, ball, or crescent resembling the moon. ❖ *v.* **mooned, mooning, moons** —*intr.* **1.** To pass time idly or aimlessly: *just mooning about.* **2.** *Slang* To expose one's buttocks as a prank or disrespectful gesture. —*tr. Slang* To expose one's buttocks (to others) as a prank or disrespectful gesture.

moonbeam (mōōn′bēm′) *n.* A ray of moonlight.

mooncalf (mōōn′kǎf′) *n.* A foolish person.

moonlight (mōōn′līt′) *n.* The light that is reflected from the surface of the moon. ❖ *intr.v.* **moonlighted, moonlighting, moonlights** *Informal* To work at a second job, often at night, in addition to one's regular job. —**moon′light′er** *n.*

moonlit (mōōn′lĭt′) *adj.* Lighted by the moon: *a moonlit pond.*

moonscape (mōōn′skāp′) *n.* A view or picture of the surface of the moon.

moonshine (mōōn′shīn′) *n.* **1.** Moonlight. **2.** *Informal* Foolish talk or thinking; nonsense. **3.** Whiskey that is distilled illegally. ❖ *intr.v.* **moonshined, moonshining, moonshines** To distill and sell liquor illegally.

moonstone (mōōn′stōn′) *n.* Any of several pearly translucent forms of feldspar that are valued as gemstones.

moonstruck (mōōn′strŭk′) *adj.* **1.** Dazed with romantic love; infatuated. **2.** Mentally deranged; crazed.

moony (mōō′nē) *adj.* **moonier, mooniest 1.** Relating to or suggestive of the moon or moonlight: *a moony luster.* **2.** Given to dreamy moods; absent-minded.

moor[1] (mŏŏr) *v.* **moored, mooring, moors** —*tr.* To secure (a vessel or aircraft, for example) by means of cables, lines, or anchors. —*intr.* **1.** To secure a vessel or aircraft with lines or anchors: *We moored out in the bay.* **2.** To be secured with lines or anchors: *The sloop moored alongside the wharf.*

moor[2] (mŏŏr) *n.* A broad stretch of open land, often with boggy areas and patches of low shrubs.

WORD HISTORY Moor[1] comes from Middle English *moren,* meaning "to take root, fasten to." **Moor**[2] comes from Middle English *mor,* which comes from Old English *mōr,* which both refer to the same kind of land as in Modern English.

Moor (mŏŏr) *n.* **1.** A member of a traditionally Muslim people now living in northwest Africa. **2.** One of the Muslims who invaded Spain in the 8th century and established a civilization that lasted until the late 15th century.

mooring (mŏŏr′ĭng) *n.* **1.** The act or an instance of securing a vessel or aircraft. **2.** A place at which a vessel or aircraft may be secured. **3.** often **moorings** Equipment, such as anchors, chains, or lines, for securing a vessel or aircraft: *In the storm the boat pulled free from its moorings.*

Moorish (mŏŏr′ĭsh) *adj.* Relating to the Moors or their culture.

moose (mōōs) *n., pl.* **moose** A large deer of northern regions, having a large head, high shoulders, and broad antlers in the male.

moot (mōōt) *adj.* **1.** Of no practical importance; irrelevant: *Now that he's dead, the question of whether to punish him is moot.* **2.** Open to debate; arguable: *a discussion of a moot and difficult point.*

mop (mŏp) *n.* **1.** An implement for washing, dusting, or drying floors, consisting of a sponge or a bundle of yarn or rags attached to a long handle. **2.** A loosely tangled bunch or mass: *a mop of hair.* ❖ *tr.v.* **mopped, mopping, mops** To wash or wipe with or as if with a mop: *mopped the hallway; mopped her forehead with a towel.* ◆ **mop up 1.** To clear (an area) of remaining enemy troops after a victory. **2.** *Informal* To finish a nearly completed task.

mope (mōp) *intr.v.* **moped, moping, mopes 1.** To be gloomy or quietly resentful; sulk. **2.** To move or pass time aimlessly; dawdle: *moped around the house all day.* ❖ *n.* **1.** A person who often has gloomy moods. **2. mopes** Low spirits.

moped (mō′pĕd′) *n.* A lightweight motorized bicycle that can be pedaled.

moppet (mŏp′ĭt) *n.* A young child.

moraine (mə-rān′) *n.* A mass of boulders, stones, and other material that has been carried and deposited by a glacier.

moral (môr′əl) *adj.* **1.** Relating to the judgment of right or wrong of human action and character: *moral principles.* **2.** Teaching or showing good, correct, or honorable behavior: *a moral lesson.* **3.** Being or acting in accord with standards of what is good, just, or honorable: *a moral person; a moral way of living.* **4.** Arising from the inner sense of right and wrong: *She felt she had a moral duty to help.* **5.** Psychological rather than physical or concrete: *a moral victory; gave me some moral support.* ❖ *n.* **1.** The lesson or principle taught by a fable, story, or event. **2. morals** Rules of good or correct conduct.

morale (mə-rǎl′) *n.* The state of a person's or group's spirits, as shown in confidence, cheerfulness, and willingness to work toward a goal: *The pep talk boosted our morale, and we went on to win the game.*

moralist (môr′ə-lĭst) *n.* **1.** A person who is concerned with moral principles and questions. **2.** A person who follows a system of moral principles. **3.** A person who is unduly concerned with the morals of others.

moralistic (môr′ə-lĭs′tĭk) *adj.* **1.** Concerned with morality. **2.** Marked by a narrow-minded morality. —**mor′al·is′ti·cal·ly** *adv.*

morality (mə-rǎl′ĭ-tē) *n., pl.* **moralities 1.** The quality of being in conformity with standards of good, right, or honorable behavior: *the questionable morality of his actions.* **2.** A set of ideas about what is right and wrong in human conduct and relationships: *religious morality.*

moralize (môr′ə-līz′) *v.* **moralized, moralizing, moralizes** —*intr.* To think about or express moral judgments. —*tr.* To interpret or explain the moral meaning of; draw a moral from.

morally (môr′ə-lē) *adv.* **1.** According to moral principles: *Is it morally right to tell a lie to keep from hurting someone's feelings?* **2.** According to accepted rules of conduct; virtuously: *live one's life morally.* **3.** According to strong conviction or likelihood: *I am morally certain that she's wrong.*

morass (mə-rǎs′ or mô-rǎs′) *n.* **1.** An area of low soggy ground; a bog or marsh. **2.** A condition or situation that is overwhelming or confusing: *We are floundering in a morass of details.*

moratorium (môr′ə-tôr′ē-əm) *n., pl.* **moratoriums** or **moratoria** (môr′ə-tôr′ē-ə) **1.** A stopping of some activity for the time being; a temporary ban or pause: *a moratorium on whaling.* **2.** A period of delay granted before a debt must be paid.

Moravian (mə-rā′vē-ən) *n.* A native or inhabitant of Moravia, a region of the eastern Czech Republic. —**Mo·ra′vi·an** *adj.*

moray (môr′ā *or* mə-rā′) *n.* Any of numerous eels that have sharp teeth, are often brightly colored, and are found mostly in tropical seas.

morbid (môr′bĭd) *adj.* **1.** Relating to, caused by, or having to do with disease: *morbid changes in body tissues.* **2.** Preoccupied with death, decay, or other unwholesome matters; gruesome: *a morbid imagination.* —**mor′bid·ly** *adv.* —**mor′bid·ness** *n.*

morbidity (môr-bĭd′ĭ-tē) *n., pl.* **morbidities 1.** The condition of being morbid. **2.** The rate of occurrence of a disease.

mordant (môr′dnt) *adj.* Bitter; sarcastic: *expressed resentment in mordant remarks.* —**mor′dan·cy** *n.* —**mor′-dant·ly** *adv.*

more (môr) *adj.* Comparative of **many, much. 1a.** Greater in number: *More people came to the show tonight than ever before.* **b.** Greater in size, amount, extent, or degree: *He does more work than anybody else.* **2.** Additional; extra: *I need more time to finish making dinner.* ❖ *n.* A greater or additional quantity, number, degree, or amount: *More of our textbooks have arrived in the store.* ❖ *pron. (used with a plural verb)* A greater number of people or things: *I thought I had found all the empty bottles, but there were more in the basement.* ❖ *adv.* Comparative of **much. 1a.** To or in a greater extent or degree: *After seeing the movie again, we liked it even more.* **b.** Used to form the comparative of many adjectives and adverbs: *more difficult; more intelligently.* **2.** In addition; again: *I telephoned twice more, but got no answer.* ◆ **more and more** To a steadily increasing extent or degree: *got more and more annoyed at the noise.* **more or less 1.** About; approximately: *The trip takes six hours, more or less.* **2.** To an undetermined degree: *We were more or less in agreement.*

morel (mə-rĕl′ *or* mô-rĕl′) *n.* Any of various edible mushrooms having a cap with irregular pits and ridges.

moreover (môr-ō′vər *or* môr′ō′vər) *adv.* Beyond what has been said; besides: *We are, moreover, delighted to report that progress has been made.*

mores (môr′āz′ *or* môr′ēz) *pl.n.* **1.** The accepted customs and rules of behavior of a particular social group. **2.** Attitudes about proper behavior; moral conventions: *the manners and mores of suburban life.*

Morgan le Fay (lə fā′) *n.* In the legend of King Arthur, the sorceress who is Arthur's sister and enemy.

morgue (môrg) *n.* A place where the bodies of people found dead are kept until identified or claimed.

moribund (môr′ə-bŭnd′) *adj.* **1.** At the point of death; about to die. **2.** At the point of dying out or becoming obsolete: *a moribund tradition.*

Mormon (môr′mən) *n.* **1.** A member of the Mormon Church. **2.** In the Mormon Church, an ancient prophet believed to have composed a sacred history of the Americas, which was translated and published by Joseph Smith as the Book of Mormon in 1830. ❖ *adj.* Relating to the Mormons or their church. —**Mor′mon·ism** *n.*

Mormon Church *n.* A Christian church founded by Joseph Smith in 1830, having doctrines based chiefly on the Bible and the Book of Mormon. The church's headquarters have been in Salt Lake City, Utah, since 1847.

morn (môrn) *n.* The morning.

morning (môr′nĭng) *n.* **1.** The early part of the day, from midnight to noon or from sunrise to noon. **2.** The time

of sunrise; dawn. **3.** The first or early part; the beginning: *the morning of a new nation.*

morning-after pill (môr′nĭng-ăf′tər) *n.* Any of various oral drugs that can be taken up to five days after sexual intercourse in order to prevent pregnancy.

morning glory *n.* Any of numerous twining vines having showy trumpet-shaped flowers that generally open in the morning and fade by evening.

morning sickness *n.* Nausea and vomiting upon rising in the morning, especially during early pregnancy.

morning star *n.* A planet, especially Venus, that shines brightly in the eastern sky before sunrise.

Moro (môr′ō) *n., pl.* **Moro** or **Moros** A member of any of the mostly Muslim Malay peoples of the southern Philippines.

morocco (mə-rŏk′ō) *n., pl.* **moroccos** A soft fine leather of goatskin, made originally in Morocco and used chiefly for binding books.

moron (môr′ŏn′) *n.* A person who is considered stupid or foolish. —**mo·ron′ic** (mə-rŏn′ĭk *or* mô-rŏn′ĭk) *adj.*

morose (mə-rōs′ *or* mô-rōs′) *adj.* Ill-humored; gloomy. —**mo·rose′ly** *adv.* —**mo·rose′ness** *n.*

morph (môrf) *v.* **morphed, morphing, morphs** —*tr.* To transform (an image) by computer: *morphed the villain into a snake.* —*intr.* To be transformed: *a small computer glitch that morphed into a huge problem.*

morpheme (môr′fēm′) *n.* A unit of language that has meaning and that cannot be divided into smaller meaningful parts. For example, *fire* is a morpheme; the plural suffix *-s* in *fires* is also a morpheme.

Morpheus (môr′fē-əs) *n.* In Greek mythology, the god of dreams.

morphine (môr′fēn′) *n.* An addictive narcotic drug extracted from opium and used in medicine as an anesthetic and sedative.

morphology (môr-fŏl′ə-jē) *n., pl.* **morphologies 1.** The branch of biology that deals with the form and structure of living organisms. **2.** The form and structure of an organism. **3.** In linguistics, the study of the structure and form of words, including inflections and derivations. —**mor′pho·log′i·cal, mor′pho·log′ic** *adj.*

morrow (môr′ō) *n.* **1.** The following day; the next day: *They set out on the morrow.* **2.** *Archaic* The morning.

Morse code *n.* Either of two codes used for sending messages in which letters of the alphabet and numbers are represented by combinations of short and long sounds or beams of light, known as dots and dashes.

morsel (môr′səl) *n.* **1.** A small piece of food: *ate just a few morsels.* **2.** A small amount; a piece: *a morsel of gossip.*

mortal (môr′tl) *adj.* **1.** Subject to death: *All humans are mortal.* **2.** Causing or accompanying death: *a mortal wound.* **3.** Breaking a basic religious moral law and therefore seen as bringing eternal damnation: *a mortal sin.* **4.** Fought to the death: *mortal battles.* **5.** Unrelenting; deadly: *a mortal enemy.* **6.** Extreme or severe: *in mortal fear.* ❖ *n.* A human. —**mor′tal·ly** *adv.*

mortality (môr-tăl′ĭ-tē) *n., pl.* **mortalities 1.** The condition of being subject to death. **2.** Death, especially of large numbers: *a war accompanied by widespread civilian mortality.* **3.** The proportion of a given group of people that dies in a given period of time; death rate.

mortar (môr′tər) *n.* **1.** A bowl used to hold substances while they are crushed or ground with a pestle. **2.** A machine in which substances are ground or crushed. **3.** A building material made of sand, water, lime, and often cement, used to hold together bricks, stones, or building blocks. **4.** A muzzle-loading cannon used to fire shells in a high arc. ❖ *tr.v.* **mortared, mortaring, mortars 1.** To plaster or join with mortar. **2.** To bombard with mortar shells.

mortarboard (môr′tər-bôrd′) *n.* **1.** A square board with a handle, used for holding and carrying mortar. **2.** An academic cap with a flat square top and a tassel, worn upon graduation, for example.

mortgage (môr′gĭj) *n.* **1.** A loan for the purchase of real property, such as a house, with the property itself serving as the security for the lender: *took out a mortgage from the bank to buy their new home.* **2.** A written agreement specifying the terms of such a loan. **3.** The money that the borrower owes to the holder of a mortgage: *a family that couldn't afford their mortgage.* ❖ *tr.v.* **mortgaged, mortgaging, mortgages 1.** To pledge (property) as security for the payment of a debt. **2.** To put in jeopardy for some immediate benefit; risk: *He mortgaged his future by borrowing lots of money.*

mortgagee (môr′gĭ-jē′) *n.* The holder of a mortgage, usually a bank or other lender.

mortgagor (môr′gĭ-jôr′ *or* môr′gĭ-jər) also **mortgager** (môr′gĭ-jər) *n.* A person who mortgages his or her property.

mortice (môr′tĭs) *n. & v.* Variant of **mortise.**

mortician (môr-tĭsh′ən) *n.* A funeral director; an undertaker.

mortification (môr′tə-fĭ-kā′shən) *n.* **1.** Humiliation; embarrassment. **2.** The act or practice of mortifying one's body or desires. **3.** Death or decay of a part of a living body; gangrene.

mortify (môr′tə-fī′) *v.* **mortified, mortifying, mortifies** —*tr.* **1.** To cause to feel shame or embarrassment; humiliate: *I was mortified by my cousin's rudeness at the ceremony.* **2.** To discipline (one's body or physical desires) through self-denial or self-punishment, especially for religious reasons. —*intr.* To become gangrenous. —**mor′ti·fi′er** *n.*

mortise also **mortice** (môr′tĭs) *n.* A rectangular hole in a piece of wood or other material, prepared to receive a tenon of another piece, so as to form a joint. ❖ *tr.v.* **mortised, mortising, mortises** also **morticed, morticing, mortices 1.** To cut a mortise in. **2.** To join (two pieces) by means of a mortise and tenon.

mortuary (môr′chōō-ĕr′ē) *n., pl.* **mortuaries** A place where dead bodies are prepared or kept before burial or cremation.

mos. An abbreviation of months.

mosaic (mō-zā′ĭk) *n.* **1.** A picture or design made on a surface by fitting and cementing together small colored pieces, as of tile, glass, or stone. **2.** The art or process of making such pictures or designs. **3.** Something that resembles a mosaic: *a mosaic of impressions.* **4.** A viral disease of certain plants, such as tobacco or tomatoes, that causes the leaves to become spotted or wrinkled. **5.** An organism or a part having adjacent cells or tissues of different genetic types.

Mosaic (mō-zā′ĭk) *adj.* Relating to the Hebrew prophet Moses or to the laws said to have been written by him.

mosey (mō′zē) *intr.v.* **moseyed, moseying, moseys** *Informal* **1.** To move slowly or leisurely; stroll. **2.** To get going; leave.

mosh (mŏsh) *intr.v.* **moshed, moshing, moshes** To knock against others intentionally while dancing at a rock concert.

Moslem (mŏz′ləm *or* mŏs′ləm) *n.* Variant of **Muslim.**

mosque (mŏsk) *n.* A building used as a place of Muslim worship.

mosquito (mə-skē′tō) *n., pl.* **mosquitoes** or **mosquitos** Any of numerous winged insects whose females bite and suck blood from humans and other animals. Some kinds transmit diseases such as malaria and yellow fever.

WORD HISTORY How is a **mosquito** like a **musket**? Both words come from the Latin noun *musca,* "a fly" (the insect). The Latin word became *mosca* in Spanish. By adding the diminutive ending *–ito* to *mosca,* Spanish formed the word *mosquito,* meaning "little fly," which became the term for the bothersome insect we all love to hate. Latin *musca* became *mosca* in Italian also. Italian formed a diminutive noun *moschetto* (literally "little fly"), meaning "the bolt or dart fired from a catapult." Later, Italian used that word to mean "a small gun that fires lead balls" (that is, a *musket*). French borrowed this word, changing the spelling to *mousquet,* and this was borrowed into English as *musket.*

moss (môs) *n.* **1.** Any of various small nonvascular plants that bear spores in a capsule and often form a dense growth on damp ground, rocks, or tree trunks. **2.** Any of several similar but unrelated plants, such as Spanish moss.

mossy (mô′sē) *adj.* **mossier, mossiest** Covered with or resembling moss.

most (mōst) *adj.* Superlative of **many, much. 1a.** Greatest in number: *Who won the most votes?* **b.** Largest in amount, size, or degree: *the most money.* **2.** In the greatest number of instances: *Most fish have fins.* ❖ *n.* The greatest amount or degree: *She has the most to gain.* ❖ *pron.* (used with a singular or plural verb) The greatest part or number: *Most of the apples have been picked.* ❖ *adv.* Superlative of **more, much. 1.** In the highest degree, quantity, or extent. Used with many adjectives and adverbs to form the superlative: *most honest; most impatiently.* **2.** Very: *a most impressive piece of work.* **3.** *Informal* Almost; just about: *Most everybody's here already.* ◆ **at most** or **at the most** At the maximum: *The professor spoke for ten minutes at most. We ran for two miles at the most.*

–most A suffix that means most: *innermost.*

mostly (mōst′lē) *adv.* **1.** For the most part; mainly: *The strawberry plants are mostly thriving.* **2.** Generally; usually: *We mostly try to get to bed before midnight.*

mote (mōt) *n.* A speck, especially of dust: *Motes drifted in the sunlight near the window.*

motel (mō-tĕl′) *n.* A hotel for motorists, usually with rooms that open directly on a parking area.

motet (mō-tĕt′) *n.* A polyphonic composition based on a sacred text and usually sung without accompaniment.

moth (môth) *n., pl.* **moths** (mô*th*z *or* môths) Any of numerous insects that are closely related to the butterflies but usually fly at night and have a stouter body and feathery or slender antennae.

mothball (môth′bôl′) *n.* **1.** A marble-sized ball of naphthalene, stored with clothing to repel clothes moths. **2. mothballs** A condition of long-term storage with protection against the weather: *After decades of use, the ocean liner was put into mothballs.* ❖ *tr.v.* **mothballed, mothballing, mothballs** To put into protective storage: *The* *experimental airplane was mothballed after its funding was canceled.*

moth-eaten (môth′ēt′n) *adj.* **1.** Eaten away by the larvae of clothes moths: *a moth-eaten bedspread.* **2.** Old and overused: *a moth-eaten saying.*

mother (mŭth′ər) *n.* **1.** A female parent or guardian of a child. **2.** A female parent of an animal. **3.** A mother superior. **4.** A woman who creates, starts, or founds something: *Susan B. Anthony was one of the mothers of the women's suffrage movement.* **5.** A source or cause: *Necessity is the mother of invention.* ❖ *adj.* **1.** Being the source or origin: *the mother church.* **2.** Native: *one's mother country.* ❖ *tr.v.* **mothered, mothering, mothers** **1.** To give birth to: *She mothered two children.* **2.** To watch over or nourish: *The teacher mothered her students.*

motherboard (mŭth′ər-bôrd′) *n.* The main circuit board of a computer, usually containing the central processing unit, the main system memory, and other essential components.

Mother Goose *n.* The imaginary author of *Mother Goose's Tales,* a collection of English nursery rhymes published in the 1700s.

motherhood (mŭth′ər-hŏod′) *n.* The condition of being a mother.

mother-in-law (mŭth′ər-ĭn-lô′) *n., pl.* **mothers-in-law** The mother of one's wife or husband.

motherland (mŭth′ər-lănd′) *n.* **1.** A person's native land; the country of one's birth. **2.** The land of one's ancestors.

motherless (mŭth′ər-ləs′) *adj.* Having no living or known mother.

mother lode *n.* **1.** The main vein of ore in a region: *After digging for weeks, the miners finally hit the mother lode.* **2.** An abundant or rich source.

motherly (mŭth′ər-lē) *adj.* Relating to, like, or appropriate to a mother: *motherly affection.* —**moth′er·li·ness** *n.*

Mother Nature *n.* The personification of nature as a powerful woman: *We're hoping that Mother Nature doesn't ruin our plans for an outdoor wedding.*

mother-of-pearl (mŭth′ər-əv-pûrl′) *n.* The hard, smooth, pearly layer on the inside of certain oyster shells and other seashells, used to make buttons and jewelry.

Mother's Day (mŭth′ərz) *n.* The second Sunday in May, celebrated as a holiday in honor of mothers.

mother superior *n., pl.* **mothers superior** or **mother superiors** A woman in charge of a religious community of women.

mother tongue *n.* **1.** One's native language. **2.** A language from which another language develops.

mother wit *n.* Natural good judgment that does not come from schooling; common sense.

motif (mō-tēf′) *n.* **1.** An idea or symbol that recurs in a literary or artistic work. **2.** A short passage or theme that is repeated and varied in a musical composition. **3.** A repeated figure or design in architecture or decoration: *a necktie with a floral motif.*

motile (mōt′l or mō′tīl′) *adj.* Moving or able to move by itself; capable of spontaneous movement. —**mo·til′i·ty** (mō-tĭl′ĭ-tē) *n.*

motion (mō′shən) *n.* **1a.** The process of moving; change of position. **b.** An act of moving; a movement: *the darting motions of dragonflies.* **2.** The ability to move: *The motion in his arm returned after physical therapy.* **3.** Operation; activity: *put the engine in motion.* **4.** A formal application or request: *No state by its own mere motion can get out of the Union.* **5.** A proposal put to a vote in a group

following parliamentary procedure: *I moved to adjourn the meeting, and the motion passed by voice vote.* ❖ *v.* **motioned, motioning, motions** —*tr.* To direct by a wave of the hand or another gesture; to signal: *The driver stopped and motioned us to cross.* —*intr.* To make a gesture expressing one's wishes: *motioned for us to enter the room.*
◆ **go through the motions** To do something in a way that shows lack of purpose or interest.

motionless (mō′shən-lĭs) *adj.* Not moving. —**mo′tion·less·ly** *adv.*

motion picture *n.* **1.** A movie. **2. motion pictures** The movie industry.

motion sickness *n.* Nausea and dizziness caused by motion, as from traveling in a car or ship.

motivate (mō′tə-vāt′) *tr.v.* **motivated, motivating, motivates** To provide with an incentive; move to action: *Time was running out, which motivated us to play even harder.*

motivation (mō′tə-vā′shən) *n.* **1.** The process of providing motives: *studied the motivation of people who run for public office.* **2.** The condition of being motivated, especially to perform well: *These students have a high level of motivation.* **3.** A motive or set of motives; an incentive.

motive (mō′tĭv) *n.* An emotion, need, or purpose that causes a person to act in a certain way: *Our motive in writing the book was to make people aware of the issue.* ❖ *adj.* Causing or able to cause motion: *motive power supplied by a jet engine.*

motley (mŏt′lē) *adj.* **1.** Made up of an odd assortment of different types: *a motley team with players of all different abilities.* **2.** Made up of many different colors: *the motley suit of a clown.* ❖ *n., pl.* **motleys** A costume of many colors worn by a clown or jester.

motor (mō′tər) *n.* **1.** A device that changes electric energy into mechanical energy. **2.** A device that produces mechanical energy from a fuel; an engine. **3.** Something, such as a machine or engine, that produces or imparts motion: *the motor of a clock.* ❖ *adj.* **1.** Propelled by an engine or motor: *a motor yacht.* **2.** Causing or producing motion: *motor power.* **3.** Relating to or intended for an engine or motor: *motor oil.* **4.** Carrying impulses from the central nervous system to the muscles: *motor nerves.* **5.** Relating to or involving muscles and their movement: *a motor reflex.* ❖ *intr.v.* **motored, motoring, motors** To drive or travel in a motor vehicle.

motorbike (mō′tər-bīk′) *n.* **1.** A lightweight motorcycle. **2.** A pedal bicycle that has an attached motor.

motorboat (mō′tər-bōt′) *n.* A boat powered by an internal-combustion engine.

motorcade (mō′tər-kād′) *n.* A procession of motor vehicles.

motorcar (mō′tər-kär′) *n.* An automobile.

motorcycle (mō′tər-sī′kəl) *n.* A vehicle with two wheels, similar to a bicycle but larger and heavier, propelled by an internal-combustion engine. ❖ *intr.v.* **motorcycled, motorcycling, motorcycles** To ride a motorcycle. —**mo′tor·cy′clist** *n.*

motor home *n.* A large motor vehicle with facilities for cooking and sleeping, used as living quarters for recreational travel.

motorist (mō′tər-ĭst) *n.* A person who drives or rides in an automobile.

motorize (mō′tə-rīz′) *tr.v.* **motorized, motorizing, motorizes** **1.** To equip with a motor or motors. **2.** To supply with motor-driven vehicles.

motor scooter *n.* A small, low-powered motor vehicle similar to a motorcycle but with smaller wheels, a chair-like seat, and a floorboard for the feet to rest on.

motor vehicle *n.* A self-propelled vehicle that travels on wheels but does not run on rails.

mottle (mŏt′l) *tr.v.* **mottled, mottling, mottles** To cover (a surface) with spots or streaks of different colors: *Her arms were lightly mottled with freckles.*

mottled (mŏt′ld) *adj.* Spotted or streaked with different colors: *a bird with mottled plumage.*

motto (mŏt′ō) *n., pl.* **mottoes** or **mottos 1.** A phrase or statement expressing a principle, goal, or ideal: *"Don't tread on me" was the motto on the flag of the Continental Navy during the American Revolution.* **2.** A brief expression of a guiding principle; a slogan: *His motto has always been "He who hesitates is lost."*

mound (mound) *n.* **1.** A pile of earth or rocks heaped up, as for protection or concealment: *the mound marking a woodchuck's hole; a burial mound.* **2.** A naturally formed area of high ground, as a small hill. **3.** A pile or mass of something: *mounds of mashed potatoes.* See Synonyms at **heap. 4.** The raised pitcher's area in the middle of a baseball diamond.

mount¹ (mount) *v.* **mounted, mounting, mounts** —*tr.* **1.** To climb; ascend: *mounted the stairs.* **2a.** To get up on: *mount a bicycle.* **b.** To provide with a riding horse. **3.** To plan and start to carry out: *mounted a campaign for literacy.* **4.** To provide (a theatrical performance) with scenery and costumes; stage. **5a.** To set in a raised position: *mounted the weathervane on the roof.* **b.** To set (guns) in position for firing. **c.** To fix securely to a support: *mount an engine in a car.* **d.** To place in a secure position for display or study: *mount a specimen on a microscope slide.* **6.** To post (a guard): *mount sentries around the encampment.* —*intr.* **1.** To go upward; rise: *We watched the airplane mount into the sky.* **2.** To get up on something, such as a horse. **3.** To increase; grow higher: *Expenses are mounting quickly.* ❖ *n.* **1.** A horse or another animal for riding. **2.** A frame or structure for holding or supporting something: *the mounts of a telescope.*

mount² (mount) *n.* A mountain.

WORD HISTORY Mount¹ comes from Middle English *mounten,* which comes from Old French *monter* (both meaning "to climb up, ascend"), which comes from Latin *mōns,* meaning "mountain, hill." **Mount²** comes from Middle English *mount,* which comes from Old English *munt,* which comes from Latin *mōns,* all meaning "mountain, hill."

mountain (moun′tən) *n.* **1.** A raised portion of the earth's surface, generally massive and rising to a great height, having more or less steep sides. **2.** A large heap or quantity: *a mountain of paperwork.* ◆ **make a mountain out of a molehill** To give too much weight or importance to a minor problem.

mountain bike *n.* A bicycle with wide tires and horizontal handlebars, often used for cycling on unpaved trails or rugged areas. —**mountain biking** *n.*

mountaineer (moun′tə-nîr′) *n.* **1.** A person who lives in a mountainous area. **2.** A person who climbs mountains for sport. ❖ *intr.v.* **mountaineered, mountaineering, mountaineers** To climb mountains for sport.

mountain goat *n.* A mammal of the northern Rocky

Mountains that resembles a goat and has short black horns and thick white hair.

mountain laurel *n.* A shrub of eastern North America having poisonous evergreen leaves and clusters of pink or white flowers.

mountain lion *n.* A cougar.

mountainous (moun′tə-nəs) *adj.* **1.** Having many mountains: *a mountainous region.* **2.** Huge; massive: *mountainous snowdrifts.*

mountain range *n.* A row or group of connected mountains.

mountainside (moun′tən-sīd′) *n.* The side of a mountain.

Mountain Standard Time *n.* Standard time in the seventh time zone west of Greenwich, England, used in the west-central United States, for example.

mountaintop (moun′tən-tŏp′) *n.* The top of a mountain.

mountebank (moun′tə-băngk′) *n.* **1.** A seller of quack medicines who attracts customers with stories or tricks. **2.** A swindler; a charlatan.

Mountie also **Mounty** (moun′tē) *n., pl.* **Mounties** *Informal* A member of the Royal Canadian Mounted Police.

mounting (moun′tĭng) *n.* A supporting structure or frame; a mount: *a mounting for a gem.*

mourn (môrn) *v.* **mourned, mourning, mourns** —*intr.* To feel or express sorrow, especially for a person's death; grieve. —*tr.* **1.** To grieve over (a person who has died). **2.** To feel or express regret about: *mourning his lost opportunities.* —**mourn′er** *n.*

mournful (môrn′fəl) *adj.* **1.** Feeling or showing grief. **2.** Causing or suggesting grief: *the mournful wail of a foghorn.* —**mourn′ful·ly** *adv.* —**mourn′ful·ness** *n.*

mourning (môr′nĭng) *n.* **1.** The expression of grief and respect for a beloved person who has died: *The flag was flown at half-mast as a sign of mourning.* **2.** The condition of a person showing grief over a death or loss: *in mourning for her sister.* **3.** Traditional signs of grief for the dead, such as black clothes. **4.** The period during which a death is mourned.

mourning dove *n.* A grayish-brown dove of North and Central America, having a long tail and a mournful call.

mouse (mous) *n., pl.* **mice** (mīs) **1.** Any of numerous small rodents usually having a pointed snout, rounded ears, and a long narrow tail. Some kinds live in or near human dwellings. **2.** A timid person. **3.** *pl.* **mice** or **mouses** (mous′ĭz) An input device that is moved along a flat surface to control the movement of a cursor on a computer screen. ❖ *intr.v.* (mouz) **moused, mousing, mouses** To hunt for mice.

mousepad (mous′păd′) *n.* A flat pad that provides a surface for using a computer mouse.

mouser (mou′zər *or* mou′sər) *n.* An animal, especially a cat, that catches mice.

mousetrap (mous′trăp′) *n.* A trap for catching mice.

mousse (mōōs) *n.* **1.** A chilled dessert made from whipped cream or beaten egg whites, gelatin, and flavoring. **2.** A molded dish made from meat, fish, or shellfish and whipped cream. **3.** A styling foam for hair.

moustache (mŭs′tăsh′ *or* mə-stăsh′) *n.* Variant of **mustache.**

mousy also **mousey** (mou′sē *or* mou′zē) *adj.* **mousier, mousiest 1.** Resembling a mouse, especially in color: *mousy brown hair.* **2.** Timid and shy: *a mousy person.*

mouth (mouth) *n., pl.* **mouths** (mouthz) **1a.** The opening of the body through which an animal takes in food. **b.** The group of organs or structures associated with this opening, such as the teeth, lips, and tongue. **c.** The opening to a cavity or canal in an organ or organism. **2.** Excessive or impudent talk: *Watch your mouth.* **3.** A natural opening, such as the opening of a cave or canyon or the part of a river that empties into a larger body of water. **4.** An opening into a container or enclosure: *the mouth of a bottle.* ❖ *tr.v.* (mou**th**) **mouthed, mouthing, mouths 1.** To speak or pronounce: *mouthed phrases of encouragement.* **2.** To form (words) soundlessly: *waved and mouthed "goodbye."* **3.** To hold or move around in the mouth: *The baby was mouthing her spoon.* ◆ **down in the mouth** or **down at the mouth** Discouraged; sad. **mouth off** *Slang* To speak impudently; talk back.

mouthful (mouth′fŏŏl′) *n.* **1.** An amount taken into the mouth at one time: *We enjoyed every mouthful of the dessert.* **2.** An important or intelligent remark: *You just said a mouthful.* **3.** A word or phrase that is long and hard to pronounce.

mouth organ *n.* **1.** A harmonica. **2.** A panpipe.

mouthpart (mouth′pärt′) *n.* Any of the parts of the mouth of an insect or a similar animal, especially a part adapted to a specific way of feeding.

mouthpiece (mouth′pēs′) *n.* **1.** The part of a device that is in or near the mouth when the device is in use: *the mouthpiece of a telephone.* **2.** A protective piece of rubber worn over the teeth, as by a football player. **3.** *Informal* A person who expresses the viewpoint of another person or of a group.

mouth-to-mouth resuscitation (mouth′tə-mouth′) *n.* A method of providing air to a person who has stopped breathing, in which the rescuer presses his or her mouth to the mouth of the victim and blows air into the victim's lungs at regular intervals.

mouthwash (mouth′wŏsh′) *n.* A flavored, usually antiseptic liquid used to cleanse the mouth and freshen the breath.

movable also **moveable** (mŏŏ′və-bəl) *adj.* **1.** Possible to move: *a movable rock.* **2.** Changing its date from year to year: *a movable holiday such as Thanksgiving.* ❖ *n.* often **movables** Furniture or other personal possessions that can be moved.

move (mŏŏv) *v.* **moved, moving, moves** —*intr.* **1.** To change in position from one place or point to another: *The speaker moved to the middle of the stage.* **2.** To follow a specified course: *The earth moves around the sun.* **3.** To change one's place of residence or business: *Our family moved here last year.* **4.** To advance; progress: *Work on the house was moving slowly.* **5.** To make a formal request or proposal: *move for a court adjournment.* **6.** To be active in a particular social setting: *She moves in the highest diplomatic circles.* **7.** To take action: *If we don't move quickly, there won't be any woods left.* —*tr.* **1.** To change the place or position of: *Let's move the desk against the wall.* **2.** To cause to go from one place to another: *The police moved the crowd away from the stadium gates.* **3.** To change (a piece) to another position on a board, as in chess. **4.** To persuade or motivate: *What moved her to switch schools?* **5.** To arouse the emotions of: *That song moved me the first time I heard it.* **6.** To propose or request in a formal way, as at a meeting: *I move that we adjourn.* **7.** To empty (the bowels). ❖ *n.* **1.** The act of moving: *He made a move to open the door.* **2.** A calculated action to achieve an end: *The opponents, in a surprise move, changed their game plan.* **3a.** An act of changing the position of a piece in a board game. **b.** A player's turn to move a piece, as in

checkers: *It's your move.* ◆ **get a move on** *Informal* To get started; get going. **move in** To begin to occupy a residence or place of business. **move on** To shift one's attention or emotions to other matters, often as part of recovering from a setback or difficulty: *After he didn't make the team, he moved on and tried a different sport.* **on the move 1.** Moving about from one place to another: *The taxi driver was on the move all day.* **2.** Making progress; advancing: *This area of research is really on the move.*

moveable (mŏŏ′və-bəl) *adj.* & *n.* Variant of **movable.**

movement (mŏŏv′mənt) *n.* **1.** The act or an instance of moving: *We watched the steady movement of a boat along the horizon. She snatched the ball in one quick movement.* **2.** A change in the location of military troops, ships, or aircraft. **3.** The activities of a group of people toward a specific goal: *the civil rights movement.* **4.** A tendency or trend: *a movement toward smaller cars.* **5.** A mass migration: *the westward movement of the pioneers.* **6a.** An emptying of the bowels. **b.** The waste matter removed by this action. **7.** One of the large, often separate sections of a musical composition, such as a symphony, often contrasting in tempo, rhythm, or mood with surrounding material. **8.** A mechanical device or system that produces or transmits motion: *the movement of a watch.*

mover (mŏŏ′vər) *n.* **1.** A person or thing that moves: *The railroad became a prime mover of people and products in all directions.* **2.** A person or company that is hired to move furniture and other belongings from one place to another: *The movers hoisted the piano up to the third floor.*

movie (mŏŏ′vē) *n.* **1a.** A sequence of film or video images displayed on a screen in rapid succession, creating the illusion that what is in the pictures moves as in real life. **b.** A story told in such pictures: *a movie about alien space invaders.* **2.** A showing of a movie: *He laughed during the movie. She went to the movies last night.* **3. movies** The industry that makes movies.

moving (mŏŏ′vĭng) *adj.* **1.** Changing or capable of changing position: *the moving parts of an engine.* **2.** Relating to or involving the transfer of furniture from one location to another: *a moving van.* **3.** Involving a motor vehicle in motion: *got a ticket for a moving violation.* **4.** Affecting the emotions: *a moving love story.* —**mov′ing·ly** *adv.*

moving picture *n.* A movie.

mow¹ (mou) *n.* **1.** A pile of hay or grain, especially one stored in a barn. **2.** The part of a barn where such a pile is stored.

mow² (mō) *v.* **mowed, mowed** or **mown** (mōn), **mowing, mows** —*tr.* **1.** To cut down (grass or grain) with a scythe or a machine such as a lawn mower: *Mow the grass before it gets too high.* **2.** To cut the grass or grain from: *mow the lawn; mow a field.* —*intr.* To cut down grass or other growth. ◆ **mow down** To destroy in great numbers as if cutting down, as in battle.

WORD HISTORY Mow¹ comes from Middle English *moue,* which comes from Old English *mūga,* both meaning "a pile of hay." **Mow²** comes from Middle English *mouen,* which comes from Old English *māwan,* both meaning "to cut grass or crops."

mower (mō′ər) *n.* **1.** A person who mows: *The mowers went out early to the fields.* **2.** A machine that mows: *a lawn mower.*

moxie (mŏk′sē) *n. Slang* **1.** The ability to face difficulty with spirit and courage. **2.** Aggressive energy; initiative. **3.** Skill; know-how.

mozzarella (mŏt'sə-rĕl'ə) *n.* A soft white Italian cheese that is often eaten melted, as on pizza.

MP An abbreviation of: **1.** member of Parliament. **2.** military police. **3.** mounted police.

MP3 (ĕm'pē-thrē') *n.* A computer file of a song, music, or other audio information stored in a digital format for transmission over the Internet.

mpg An abbreviation of miles per gallon.

mph An abbreviation of miles per hour.

Mr. (mĭs'tər) *n., pl.* **Messrs.** (mĕs'ərz) Mister. Used as a courtesy title before the surname or full name of a man.

MRI (ĕm'är'ī') *n.* **1.** An image produced by magnetic resonance imaging. **2.** The process of making such an image, especially of part of the body: *She went in for an MRI of her back.*

mRNA An abbreviation of messenger RNA.

Mrs. (mĭs'ĭz) *n., pl.* **Mmes.** (mā-dăm' *or* mā-dăm') Used as a courtesy title before the last name or full name of a married, widowed, or divorced woman.

MRSA (mŭr'sə) *n.* An antibiotic-resistant strain of a common bacterium. MRSA can cause severe infections of the skin and other parts of the body.

WORD HISTORY The abbreviation **MRSA** is short for "methicillin-resistant *Staphylococcus aureus.*" *Methicillin* is an antibiotic, and *Staphylococcus aureus* is the scientific name of this bacterium.

ms An abbreviation of millisecond.

MS An abbreviation of: **1.** Master of Science. **2.** multiple sclerosis.

Ms. also **Ms** (mĭz) *n., pl.* **Mses.** also **Mses** also **Mss.** also **Mss** (mĭz'ĭz) Used as a courtesy title before the last name or full name of a woman or girl.

Msgr. An abbreviation of Monseigneur.

MST An abbreviation of Mountain Standard Time.

Mt. An abbreviation of: **1.** mount. **2.** mountain.

mu (myōō *or* mōō) *n.* The 12th letter of the Greek alphabet, written M, μ. In English it is represented as *M, m.*

much (mŭch) *adj.* **more** (môr), **most** (mōst) Great in quantity, degree, or extent: *much talk and little action.* ❖ *n.* **1.** A large quantity or amount: *Did you get much done?* **2.** Something remarkable or important: *In spite of all our work, the experiment did not amount to much.* ❖ *adv.* **more, most 1.** To a large extent; greatly: *We are much impressed with the results of our research.* **2.** Just about; almost: *much the same.* ◆ **as much** The same: *I found his jokes offensive, and I said as much to him.*

much as *conj.* Even though; however much: *Much as I love skating, I'd rather go to the movies.*

much less *conj.* And certainly not: *I'd hate to fail a test, much less an entire class.*

mucilage (myōō'sə-lĭj) *n.* **1.** A clear brown adhesive made from the natural gum of plants. **2.** Any of various sticky gelatinous secretions produced by certain plants, algae, and bacteria.

muck (mŭk) *n.* **1.** A moist sticky mixture, as of mud and filth. **2.** Moist animal dung; manure. **3.** Dark soil containing rotting vegetable matter.

muckrake (mŭk'rāk') *intr.v.* **muckraked, muckraking, muckrakes** To search for and expose corruption in public affairs. —**muck'rak'er** *n.*

mucous (myōō'kəs) *adj.* **1.** Relating to or like mucus. **2.** Producing or secreting mucus.

mucous membrane *n.* Any of the membranes lining the passages of the body that open onto the outside, such as those of the digestive tract and the respiratory system. Glands and cells in the mucous membranes secrete mucus, which lubricates the membranes.

mucus (myōō'kəs) *n.* The sticky, slippery liquid secreted by the cells and glands of the mucous membranes. Mucus lubricates and protects the mucous membranes.

mud (mŭd) *n.* **1.** Wet, sticky, soft earth. **2.** Slanderous charges: *sling mud at a political opponent.*

muddle (mŭd'l) *v.* **muddled, muddling, muddles** —*tr.* **1.** To confuse; befuddle: *Being sleepy can muddle your thinking.* **2.** To make a mess of; bungle: *muddle a task.* —*intr.* To act in a confused or aimless way: *I want to do well in school this year, not just muddle along.* ❖ *n.* A jumble; a mess: *The project turned into a big muddle.* ◆ **muddle through** To keep going in a disorganized way until reaching an acceptable outcome: *The actor muddled through the rest of the scene after forgetting his lines.*

muddy (mŭd'ē) *adj.* **muddier, muddiest 1.** Covered or soiled with mud: *a muddy field; muddy shoes.* **2.** Cloudy or dull with or as if with mud: *a muddy creek; muddy coffee.* **3.** Confused; vague: *muddy thinking.* ❖ *tr.v.* **muddied, muddying, muddies 1.** To make soiled with mud: *He muddied his boots crossing the yard.* **2.** To make cloudy or dull with or as if with mud: *soil erosion muddies the rivers.* **3.** To confuse: *remarks that only muddied the issue.* —**mud'di·ly** *adv.* —**mud'di·ness** *n.*

mudpuppy also **mud puppy** (mŭd'pŭp'ē) *n., pl.* **mudpuppies** also **mud puppies** Any of several North American salamanders of lakes, ponds, and streams, having prominent clusters of dark red external gills.

mudslinging (mŭd'slĭng'ĭng) *n.* The practice of making malicious charges against an opponent, especially in a political campaign. —**mud'sling'er** *n.*

Muenster or **Munster** (mŭn'stər) *n.* A semisoft, creamy cheese with a mild flavor.

muesli (myōōz'lē) *n.* A mixture of rolled oats, nuts, and dried fruit, often used as a breakfast cereal.

muezzin (myōō-ĕz'ĭn *or* mōō-ĕz'ĭn) *n.* A crier who calls Muslims to prayer five times a day.

muff¹ (mŭf) *tr.v.* **muffed, muffing, muffs 1.** To perform or handle clumsily; bungle: *She played the first song well, but muffed the second. I muffed my chance for the job.* **2.** To fail to make (a catch), as in baseball.

muff² (mŭf) *n.* A tubelike cover of fur or cloth with open ends into which the hands are put for warmth.

WORD HISTORY The origin of **muff¹** is unknown. **Muff²** comes from Dutch *mof,* meaning "tubelike cover of fur" which comes from Old French *moufle,* which comes from Medieval Latin *muffula,* both meaning "mitten."

muffin (mŭf'ĭn) *n.* **1.** A small, usually sweetened quick bread baked in a cup-shaped container. **2.** An English muffin.

muffle (mŭf'əl) *tr.v.* **muffled, muffling, muffles 1.** To wrap up in order to keep warm, conceal, or protect: *I muffled myself in a thick shawl.* **2a.** To make less loud or less distinct; deaden: *Heavy snow muffled the sound of the traffic.* **b.** To wrap up or pad in order to deaden the sound of: *muffle a drum.*

muffler (mŭf'lər) *n.* **1.** A scarf worn around the neck for warmth. **2.** A device that deadens noise, especially one used on an automobile engine.